The World Book Atlas

The World Book

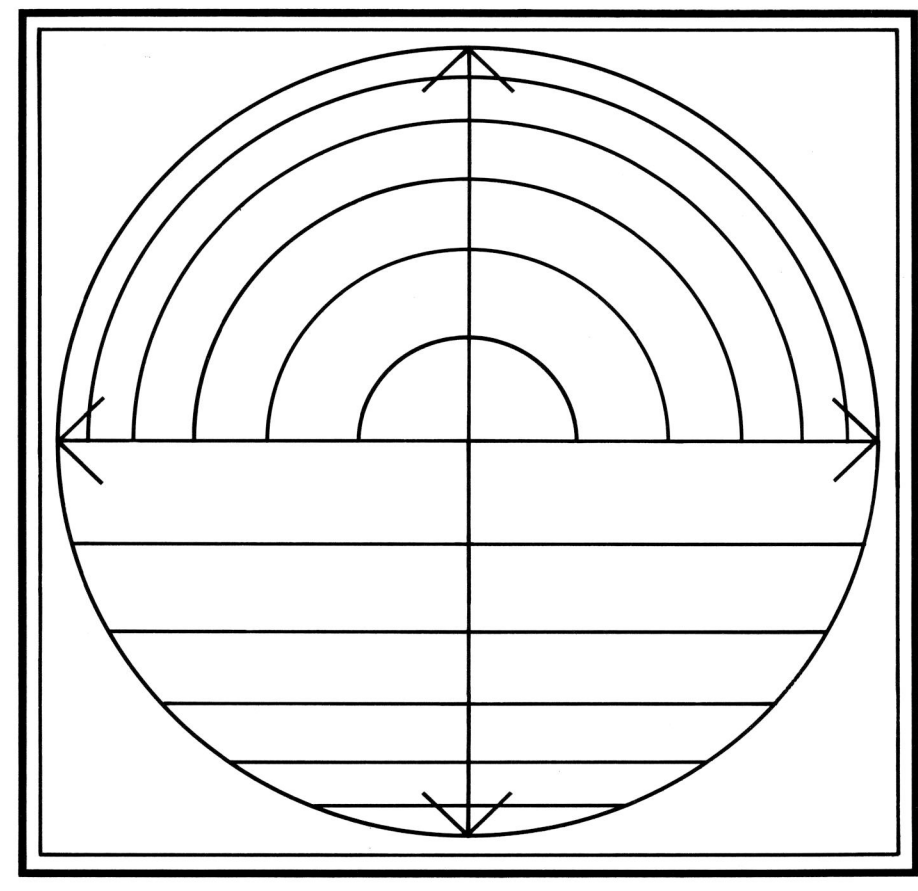

Atlas

World Book, Inc.
a Scott Fetzer company
Chicago London Sydney Toronto

Staff

World Book Staff

Publisher emeritus   *William H. Nault*

President   *John E. Frere*

Editorial

Vice president, editor in chief
Dick Dell

Managing editor
Maureen Mostyn Liebenson

Associate editor
Sharon Nowakowski

Staff editor
Melissa Raskovich

Permissions editor
Janet T. Peterson

Art

Executive director
Roberta Dimmer

Art director
Wilma Stevens

Senior photographs editor
Sandra Dyrlund

Designer
Chestnut House

Product production

Vice president, production and technology
Daniel N. Bach

Director, manufacturing/ pre-press
Sandra Van den Broucke

Manufacturing manager
Barbara Podczerwinski

Senior production manager
Randi Park

The World Book Atlas
©1996, 1995, 1994, 1992, 1986 World Book, Inc. All rights reserved. This volume may not be reproduced in whole or in part in any form without prior written permission from the publisher.

World Book, Inc.
525 W. Monroe
Chicago, IL 60661

United States and Canada Map Section from
Atlas of the United States
Copyright ©, Rand McNally & Company
and
Cosmopolitan World Atlas
Copyright ©, Rand McNally & Company

Thematic Maps on pages 68-91, and some illustrative material on pages 8-96 from
Goode's World Atlas
Copyright ©, Rand McNally & Company

Maps of the World and Index, and some illustrative material on pages 8-96 from
The Great Geographical Atlas
Copyright ©, Istituto Geografico
De Agostini, S.p.A., Novara, Italy

ISBN 0-7166-2698-5
Library of Congress Catalog Card Number 95-62473

Printed in the United States of America
17 18 19 20 99 98 97 96

Maps of the World credits

Cartographic and geographic director
Giuseppe Motta

Geographic research
G. Baselli
M. Colombo

Terrain illustration
S. Andenna
E. Ferrari

Cartographic production
F. Tosi
G. Capitini
A. Carnero

Coordination
S. Binda
L. Pasquali
G. Zanetta

Consultants

Lawrence C. Bliss, B.S., M.S., Ph.D.
Professor and Chairman
Department of Botany
University of Washington

Kempton E. Webb, A.B., M.A., Ph.D.
Professor and Chairperson
Department of Geography
and Anthropology
William Paterson College of New Jersey

James S. Sweitzer, B.S., M.S., Ph.D.
Astonomer
Chicago, Illinois

Rand McNally & Company Staff

Product director
Russell L. Voisin

Managing editor
Jon M. Leverenz

Geographic research
V. Patrick Healy

Research coordinator
Susan K. Hudson

Cartographic production
Ronald F. Peters

Acknowledgments

Illustration credits read from top to bottom and from left to right on each page. Illustrations that extend over two pages are credited to the left-hand page.

8, NASA. 9, John Shaw, Bruce Coleman Ltd.; © Marty Snyderman; Phil Degginger from E. R. Degginger. 10, *Artwork* © Mitchell Beazley Pub. Ltd. 1973 as *The Good Earth*. 11, © John Eastcott/Yva Momatiuk, Woodfin Camp, Inc.; © Marty Snyderman; © Jeff Foott, Bruce Coleman Ltd. 12, © Leo Touchet, Woodfin Camp, Inc.; Henry Ausloss, World Wildlife Fund from Bruce Coleman Ltd. 13, WORLD BOOK *diagrams;* Terraphotographics/BPS; Carlos Elmer, Shostal; Robert Glaze; © Loren McIntyre. 14, *Artwork* Brian Delf. 15, Ronald Thompson/Frank W. Lane, Bruce Coleman Ltd.; © Jim Brandenburg, Woodfin Camp, Inc.; Charlie Ott, Bruce Coleman Ltd. 16, © David Muench; WORLD BOOK *artwork*. 17, © Dwight Kuhn; *Artwork* © Mitchell Beazley Pub. Ltd. 1973 as *The Good Earth*. 18, Norman Tomalin, Bruce Coleman Ltd. 19, © David Muench; © Jeff Foott. 20, *Animals* Coral Mula; *trees* Donald Myall. 21, E. R. Degginger; Mike Price, Bruce Coleman Ltd. 22, Hutchison Library; *Artwork* Bob Bampton/The Garden Studio. 23, G. R. Plage, Bruce Coleman Ltd. 24, © Jodi Cobb, Woodfin Camp, Inc.; *Artwork,* Jim Robins. 26, © Dwight R. Kuhn; © J. Alsop, Bruce Coleman Inc.; © Dwight R. Kuhn. 27, E. R. Degginger; *Artwork,* Donald Myall. 28, W. E. Ruth, Bruce Coleman Inc. 29, Phil Degginger from E. R. Degginger; © Jim Brandenburg, Woodfin Camp, Inc.; *Wolf* Jean Hellmer for WORLD BOOK; *other animals* Coral Mula. 30, WORLD BOOK *artwork;* © B. and C. Alexander. 31, TSW/Chicago Ltd.; U.S. Naval Photographic Center; *Artwork* Jim Robins.

32, © Loren McIntyre, Woodfin Camp, Inc. 33, Hutchison Library; Photri; Shostal. 34, © Odyssey Productions. 35, Robert Glaze; © Odyssey Productions. 36, Cameramann International Ltd. 37, © Enrique Shore, Woodfin Camp, Inc.; © Steve Vidler, The Stock House Ltd.; Pedro Luis Roata, Shostal. 38, © Wenzel Fischer, FPG. 39, Eric Carle, Shostal; © Alon Reininger, Woodfin Camp, Inc. 40, © Marc F. Bernheim, Woodfin Camp, Inc. 41, © Robert Azzi, Woodfin Camp, Inc.; © D. and J. Heaton, The Stock House Ltd.; © Malcolm Holmes, The Stock House Ltd. 42, © Robert Azzi, Woodfin Camp, Inc. 43, Masood Quereshi, Bruce Coleman Ltd.; S. Trevor/D. B., Bruce Coleman Inc.; © Carl Frank, Photo Researchers. 44, Fritz Prenzel, Bruce Coleman Ltd. 45, © Odyssey Productions; Shostal; © Robin Smith, The Stock House Ltd. 46, Cameramann International, Ltd. 47, Cameramann International, Ltd.; © N. Devore III, Bruce Coleman Inc. 48, TASS from Sovfoto. 49, Chris Bonington, Bruce Coleman Ltd.; David Falconer, © David R. Frazier Photolibrary. 50, NASA. 51, © Harold Sund; E. R. Degginger. 52, WORLD BOOK *diagram.* 53, WORLD BOOK *diagrams;* © David F. Malin, Anglo-Australian Telescope Board. 54, NASA. 55, WORLD BOOK *diagrams.* 56, WORLD BOOK *diagram.* 57, WORLD BOOK *diagram;* John S. Shelton. 58-59, *Artwork* © Mitchell Beazley Pub. Ltd. 1973 as *The Good Earth*. 59, © George Hall, Woodfin Camp, Inc. 60, Gene Ahrens; *Artwork* © Mitchell Beazley Pub. Ltd. 1973 as *The Good Earth*. 61, © Odyssey Productions; John S. Shelton. 62-63, *Map* Librairie Hachette; *Artwork* © Mitchell Beazley Pub. Ltd. 1973 as *The Good Earth*. 64, Nicholas Devore III, Bruce Coleman Inc.; E. R. Degginger. 65, Smithsonian Collection from E. R. Degginger;

WORLD BOOK *photo;* Smithsonian Collection from E. R. Degginger; Smithsonian Collection from E. R. Degginger; © Lee Boltin. 66, © Craig Aurness, West Light. 67, *Map* from *Goode's World Atlas;* G. R. Roberts. 73, NASA. 75, Jeff Foott; © Thomas Nebbia, Woodfin Camp, Inc. 77, E. R. Degginger; N. G. Blake, Bruce Coleman Ltd. 79, © Mike Yamashita, Woodfin Camp, Inc.; © Craig Aurness, Woodfin Camp, Inc.; © Tsang Yan-sau, The Stock House Ltd. 81, © Mike Yamashita, Woodfin Camp, Inc.; © William Strode, Woodfin Camp, Inc.; © Lincoln Potter, The Stock House Ltd. 82, © David J. Cross from Peter Arnold. 84, E. R. Degginger. 85, E. R. Degginger. 86, E. R. Degginger. 87, Standard Oil Company of California. 88, The Gas Council. 91, © Loren McIntyre, Woodfin Camp, Inc.; © Thomas Hopker, Woodfin Camp, Inc. 92, NASA. 93, © Scala, Art Resource; Hunting Surveys Ltd. 94, British Museum; Harvard Semitic Museum, Cambridge Mass.; British Library. 95, Michael Holford, Science Museum, London; *Diagrams* Creative Cartography Ltd.; NASA. 96, Map Istituto Geografico De Agostini; WORLD BOOK *diagram*.

Locator maps on pages 20, 22, 25, 27, 28, 31, 34, 36, 38, 40, 42, 44, 46, 48 were created exclusively for *The World Book Atlas*.

Structure and Contents

Structure of The World Book Atlas

The World Book Atlas is arranged according to the structure that follows.

Contents of The World Book Atlas

Looking at Earth's

The earth in space

Mount McKinley, the highest summit in North America

Dolphins at play in the Atlantic Ocean

Gently rolling lowland of New Jersey, U.S.

Features

EARTH POSSESSES a vast ocean of water, flowing rivers, bright lakes, great forests, green plains, towering mountains, windswept deserts, and snowy polar caps. This combination of features makes earth unique among all the planets and moons in the solar system.

The Ocean

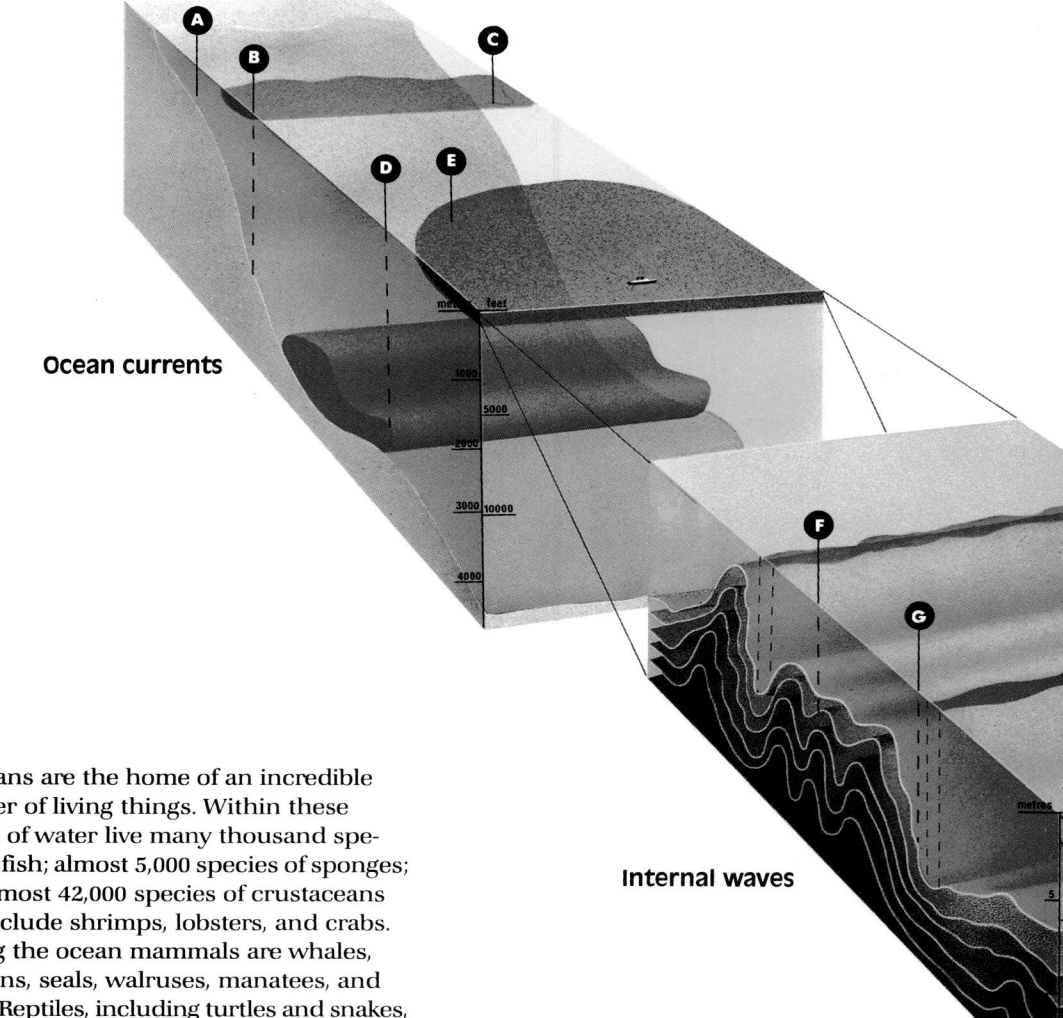

Ocean currents

Internal waves

More than 70 per cent of the world's surface is covered by oceans. Oceans have been given different names, such as Atlantic and Pacific, but they are actually all one large interconnected body of water, swept by winds that create waves, and moved by tides caused by the tug of the moon.

Oceans, often known as seas, are deep as well as vast. The bottoms of some seas lie more than 6 miles (10 kilometers) below their surfaces. Great mountains can rise from their floors and stick out above the water as islands.

Oceans are very important parts of the earth. The action of the sun's heat pouring down on an ocean turns enormous amounts of its surface into water vapor. This vapor rises into the air, cools, and forms clouds, which are carried by wind. When clouds are cooled even more, much of the water vapor forming them turns back into water and falls as rain or snow. This moisture creates the fresh water of rivers and lakes. It also provides the ground water that helps plants to grow, and thus animal life to exist.

Ocean water moves constantly in streams called currents. Currents are caused by a combination of the wind, the sun's heat, the salinity of the water, and the earth's rotation. The temperature of a current affects the temperature of the air above it. Therefore, warm currents bring warm air and water to some places, and cool currents bring cool air and water to other places. Without the help of the Equatorial Current, the Gulf Stream, and other currents, the air around the planet would be hotter both day and night near the equator and cooler both day and night at high latitudes.

Ocean water is salty. There is enough salt in the sea to cover every bit of dry land with a layer of salt 150 feet (45 meters) high. Actually, much of this salt originally came from the land. For countless millions of years, rivers that were supplied by rainfall runoff moved down mountainsides and across rolling lands. These rivers washed millions of tons of minerals out of the channels through which they flowed. The minerals, mainly various kinds of salts, were carried along by the rivers. Eventually, the rivers flowed into the ocean and released their cargoes of mud and salt. This accumulation of salt in its water keeps the ocean salty. Only pure water evaporates from its surface when water vapor forms.

Oceans are the home of an incredible number of living things. Within these bodies of water live many thousand species of fish; almost 5,000 species of sponges; and almost 42,000 species of crustaceans that include shrimps, lobsters, and crabs. Among the ocean mammals are whales, dolphins, seals, walruses, manatees, and otters. Reptiles, including turtles and snakes, and thousands of species of worms also live in the sea. Oceans do differ from one another in their species of plants and animals. That is because the seas vary in terms of climate.

All these animals, together with ocean plants, are members of complex ecological systems. The ocean food chain begins with microscopic plantlike organisms. These organisms, called phytoplankton, drift in masses near the sunlit surfaces and give the water a greenish tint. Like green plants, they use sunlight to manufacture food for themselves. As a by-product of this process, the phytoplankton produce tiny amounts of oxygen. This oxygen is used by sea animals and plants. It also helps replenish the oxygen in the earth's air.

Floating among the phytoplankton are trillions of microscopic animals called zooplankton. These creatures cannot make their own food. Instead they feed on phytoplankton. Zooplankton themselves are eaten by small fish and crustaceans, which are eaten by bigger fish and other creatures. They, in turn, are food for still larger animals, such as 60-foot-long sperm whales. But without the tiny phytoplankton, the earth's oceans could not support this complex food chain.

A continental shelf is the land around a continent that slopes deeply underwater (A). Farther offshore, the continental slope (B) plunges to the ocean bottom. Ocean characteristics vary greatly. Below the warm Gulf Stream (C) off the United States east coast moves a cold current (D). Near its source, the Gulf Stream borders the Sargasso Sea (E), a region of slow ocean currents surrounded by a boundary of fast-moving currents. Waves beneath the ocean surface (F) are caused by differences in salt content, density, and temperature. These internal waves move up and down like surface waves (G). Sometimes a dark band (H) on the surface marks an internal wave. The internal wave motion (I) shows how deep water is held back while surface waves lunge forward. A beach's breakpoint and foreshore determine where waves break. For example, a breakpoint at position (J) and foreshore at position (K) would cause waves to break at position (L). When the moon is full or new, incoming tides are at their highest and outgoing tides at their lowest. These tides are called spring tides. In the diagram, (M-M) shows the spring tidal range. At the quarters of the moon, tides are neither high nor low. Such tides are called neap tides. The neap tidal range is shown at (N-N). Location (O) shows the average tide level. Strong ocean waves wear away shoreline rocks, producing sand. Sand can be dry (P) or permanently wet (Q). Surface sand often has ripple marks (R) created when water recedes after each wave.

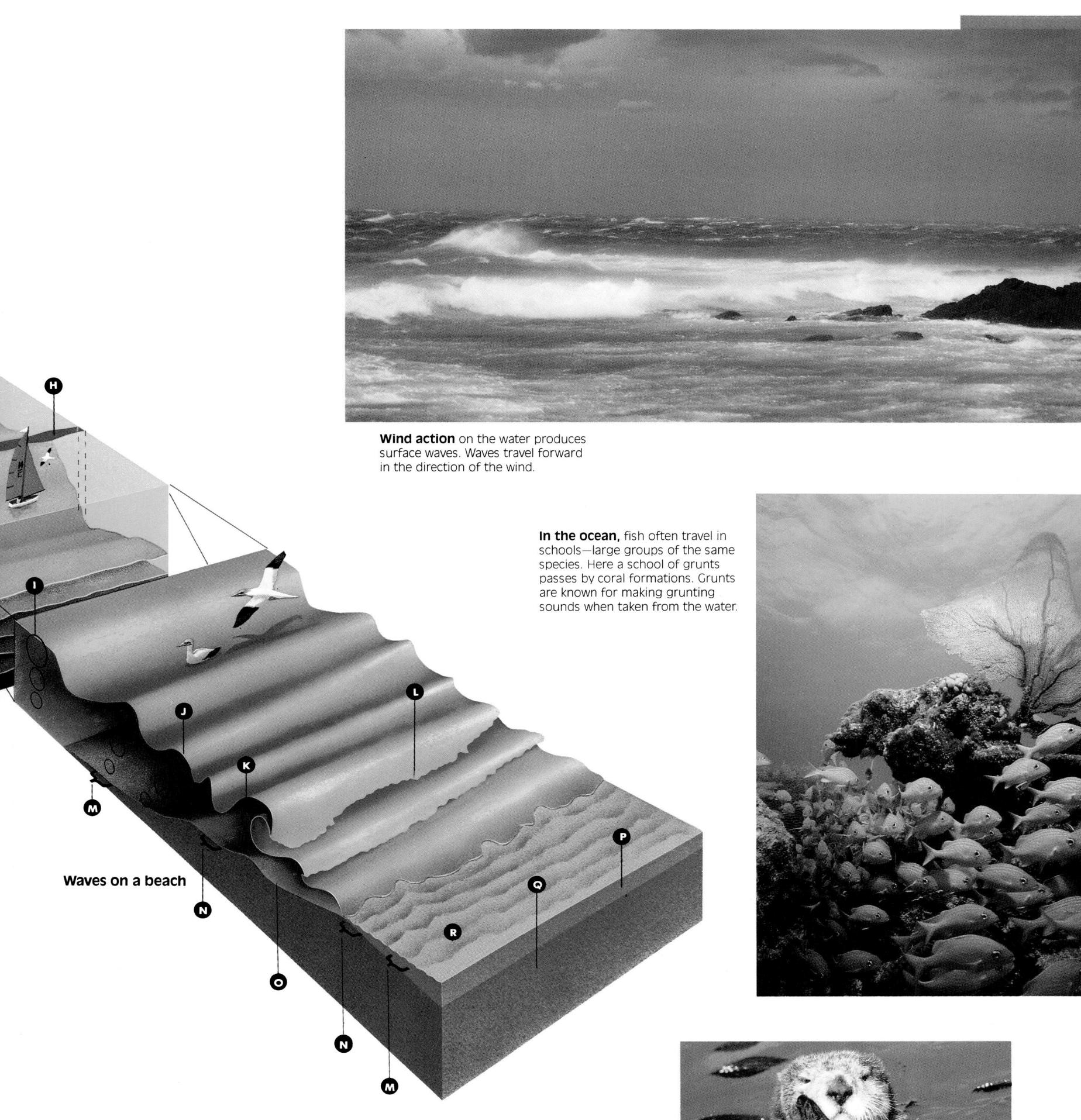

Wind action on the water produces surface waves. Waves travel forward in the direction of the wind.

In the ocean, fish often travel in schools—large groups of the same species. Here a school of grunts passes by coral formations. Grunts are known for making grunting sounds when taken from the water.

Waves on a beach

The sea otter swims, often on its back, in the North Pacific Ocean and near the shores of western North America and Siberia. This brown, furry animal floats in masses of seaweed called kelp.

Mountains

Mount Saint Elias, Alaska, is one of the highest peaks in North America. It stands in the Saint Elias Mountains, a rugged series of the highest coastal mountains in the world.

About one-fifth of the earth's land surface is made up of mountains. Mountains are composed of rock formations that rise 2,000 feet (610 meters) or more above the surrounding land. There are also mountains underwater. Those rock formations, called submarine mountains, form islands or are part of the ocean floor.

On land, mountains may be rocky and barren, or they may be green with vegetation. They may have high pointed peaks and narrow ridges. Their sides, or slopes, are long, broad, or slanting. Often mountains are cut by deep, wide indentations called canyons or valleys. Due to the decrease in temperature as elevation increases, mountainsides are made up of several different environments.

Mountains are formed over enormous amounts of time by movements of the earth's rocky crust. In some places, sideways shifts of the crust make huge wavelike wrinkles or folds. These movements result in fold mountains such as the Jura Mountains of Europe and the Appalachian Mountains of eastern North America. In other places, the crust is broken into gigantic blocks that are pushed upward along a fracture line called a fault to form fault-block mountains. The Sierra Nevada of California is an example of fault-block mountains. Dome mountains such as the Harlech Dome in Wales are created when molten rock called magma is forced upward under the surface rock to form a blister-like swelling. The volcanic mountains of Washington and Oregon were created by volcanic activity.

The top of a very high mountain is generally covered with ice and snow. But a little farther down the slope, melted snow can

An ibex climbs a rocky slope in the Italian Alps. The thinness of the forest shows that the animal is nearing the timber line.

provide moisture for lichens, mosses, and low-growing flowering plants that flourish where soil develops. This region is called the alpine zone. A number of species of insects, particularly springtails and bristle-tails, thrive in this region. Brightly colored butterflies flit among the flowers. The American Rocky Mountain goat and the European ibex live here too. Small animals such as conies, chipmunks, and mountain ground hogs also make their homes near a mountain's top.

The animals of the high mountain regions are especially fitted for their environment. Many have enlarged hearts and lungs, and their blood contains extra oxygen-bearing red corpuscles. These features help the animals survive in a mountaintop's thin air. When winter comes, most of the smaller creatures take shelter in burrows and live on seeds and hay stored during summer. Larger animals and even some birds simply move a short way down the mountainside. There the temperature is not as cold and food is still available.

A little below the alpine region is the timber line. This is the highest point at which a tree can survive without freezing. The tallest trees in this region are often bush-size dwarf willows, birches, aspens, spruces, firs, and pines. Each winter they are mostly covered by snow, which actually protects them from the terrible freezing wind of the mountaintop. These trees may, however, have some shoots that reach above the snow. At lower levels of mountains, the same kinds of trees can reach full size and form forests. Birds, squirrels, deer, and bears are at home in openings in these wooded areas.

The lower the elevation, the higher the temperature. If a mountain is in a place that gets plenty of rainfall, there will generally be a forest growing on its lower slopes. But if the mountain is in a dry region, its lower slopes will be covered with grassy meadow or maybe even desert. The animals that live here are not true "mountain animals." The same kinds of creatures may be found in other environments that feature similar conditions.

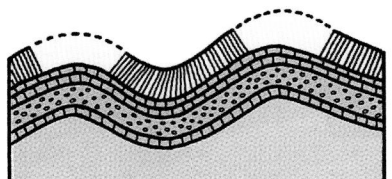

Fold mountains include the European Alps, *right*. The valleys and ridges that are characteristic of fold mountains are shown in the diagram above.

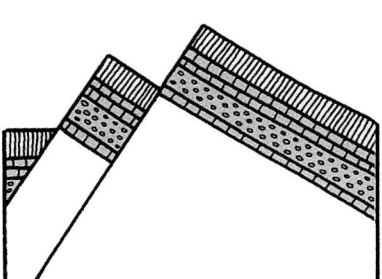

Fault-block mountains are found in the desert land near Las Vegas, Nevada, *right*. The diagram above shows the layers of cleanly broken sedimentary rock that are characteristic of fault-block mountains.

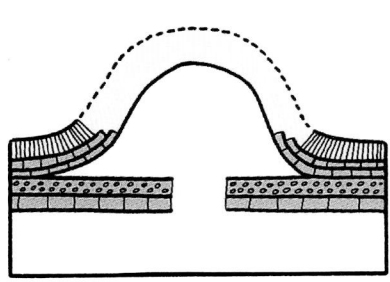

Dome mountains, such as Harlech Dome in Wales, *right,* are formed when the earth's crust rises into domes. The diagram above indicates that a dome's softer rock is eventually eroded.

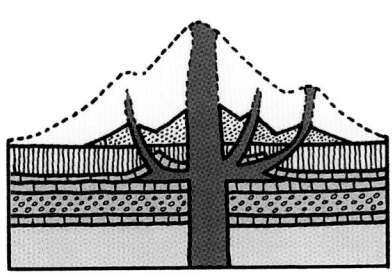

Volcanic mountains are the remains of volcanoes. The diagram above shows the pipeline vents through which lava moves inside a volcano. The material piles up and results in volcanic mountains such as the Cascade Mountains of Washington and Oregon, *right*.

Rivers and Streams

Rivers and streams are bodies of water that flow through land in long passages called channels. As they flow, always downhill, they are fed by other waters that enrich them and increase their size. Eventually they flow into another body of water, such as a larger river, a lake, or the ocean.

A river or stream channel is formed by the wearing away, or friction, of flowing water. The bottom of a channel is called the bed, and the sides are known as the banks. The channel of a small stream can be a few feet wide and less than a mile long. The channel of a large river, however, can be miles wide and extend for thousands of miles.

A river often begins high on a mountain. It can start as trickles of water from melting snow, as a spring bubbling out of rocks, or as a stream flowing from a mountain lake. As the water flows along, it is fed by streams and smaller rivers. It becomes deeper and wider, and its size is increased further by rainfall.

A river or stream is a habitat for plant and animal life. The character of that life depends upon the temperature, depth, and speed of the water. A swift-moving, shallow mountain stream is bare of most plant life. The exception is the jellylike algae that coat the rocky bottom. Black fly larvae use their tiny hooks to anchor themselves to the stream's rocks. These creatures have their food—microscopic plants and ani-

mals—delivered to them by the swift-flowing water. The larvae, in turn, are a source of nourishment for different species of birds such as dippers, or water ouzels, of western North America. These birds spend much of their time wading in swift streams and feeding on the insect life present.

A larger, slow-moving river that is far from its mountain beginnings is a very different environment. Unlike a swift-flowing stream that sweeps its floor clean, the bed of a slow-moving river is filled with mud and silt. These materials form soil for plant life. "Forests" of algae or eelgrass often cover a sluggish river's bottom. Cattails and bulrushes grow thickly along the banks. Water lilies and similar plants float on the surface. Fish such as pike and bass lurk among the bottom greenery and dart out to snap up frogs and smaller fishes. Muskrats use cattails and other plants both as food and to line the insides of riverbank burrows. Frogs attach their eggs to plants and rocks. Insects rely on the river plants as resting places.

Many kinds of insects lurk and burrow in the mud below the water. They are food for fish such as carp. Many kinds of predatory swimming insects, including dragonfly nymphs and diving beetles, often

thrive in surface waters where light is more plentiful. Small fish, frogs, otters, and birds such as kingfishers are also among the creatures that make these waters their regular hunting place. And in parts of Africa, warm, slow rivers are the natural habitat of hippopotamuses.

The place where a river empties into the sea is called the mouth. A low plain made up of clay, gravel, sand, and other sediments at a river's mouth is known as a delta, and a deep, broad mouth is called an estuary. In an estuary there is a mingling of fresh water and salt water. This mixing creates a new and different kind of environment for life. The most common kind of estuary animal is the oyster. Hundreds of thousands of oysters may cover an estuary's bottom. Shrimps, crabs, and fish such as flounder are typical dwellers of this environment. Sea plants such as turtle grass and sea lettuce can also thrive in the quiet shallow, salty environment where a river and the ocean meet.

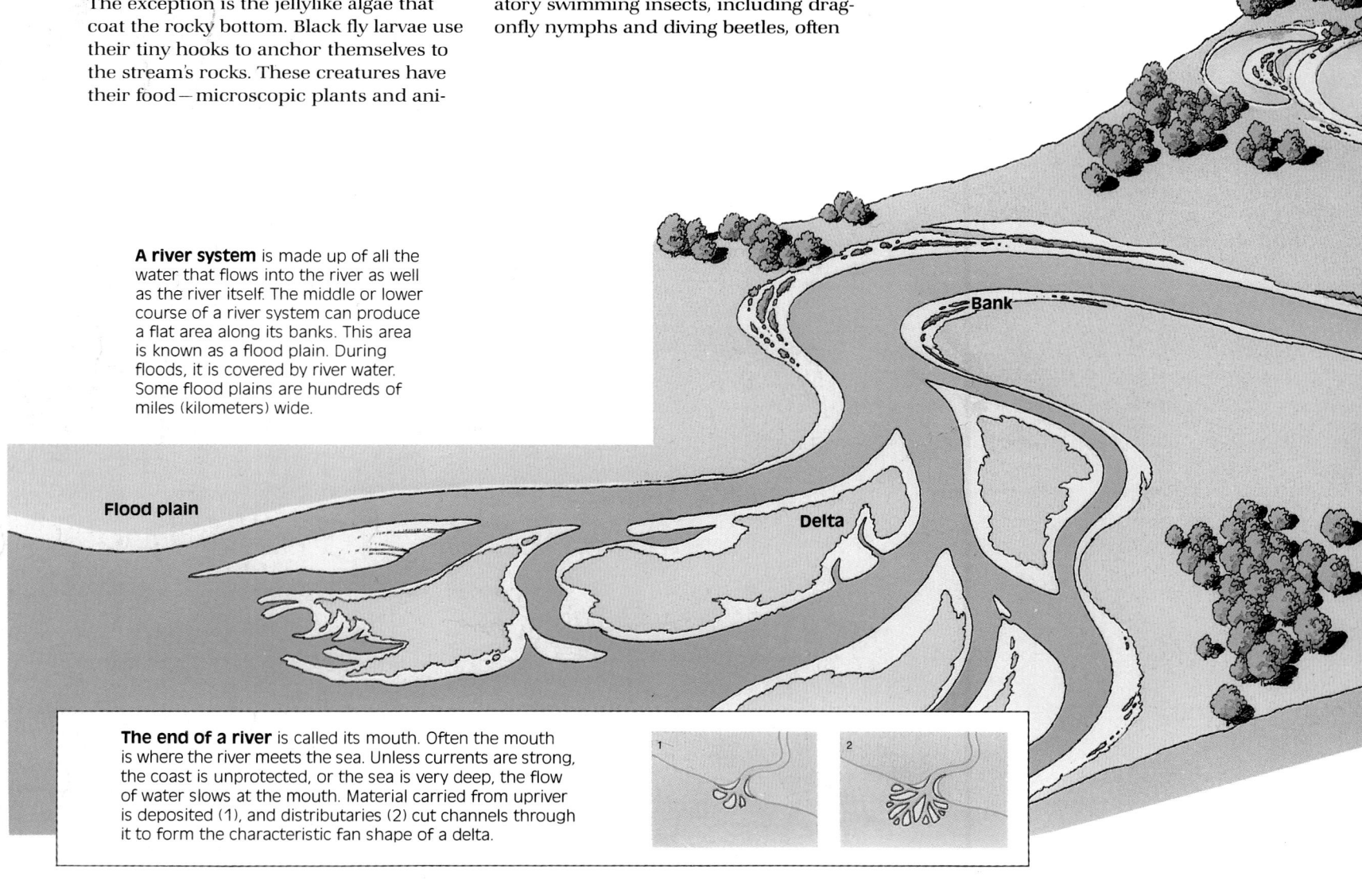

A river system is made up of all the water that flows into the river as well as the river itself. The middle or lower course of a river system can produce a flat area along its banks. This area is known as a flood plain. During floods, it is covered by river water. Some flood plains are hundreds of miles (kilometers) wide.

Bank

Flood plain

Delta

The end of a river is called its mouth. Often the mouth is where the river meets the sea. Unless currents are strong, the coast is unprotected, or the sea is very deep, the flow of water slows at the mouth. Material carried from upriver is deposited (1), and distributaries (2) cut channels through it to form the characteristic fan shape of a delta.

The flow of water in most rivers is fastest in the upper courses. Salmon have to fight to reach their upstream spawning grounds.

A river's slope tends to flatten near the mouth, and the water slows down. Painted turtles are at home in this environment.

Oxbow lake

The muddy Klamath River enters the clean, blue water of the Pacific Ocean north of Redwood National Park in northern California.

Lakes and Ponds

Lakes and ponds are bodies of standing water that are surrounded by land.

Lakes, which are larger than ponds, may be formed in many ways. Some lakes are made by stranded blocks of ice and blocked rivers that result when glaciers melt. Others are formed by the slow accumulation of rain water in volcanic craters. Still others are caused by the gradual filling in of sinkholes with ground water. Sinkholes are depressions in the earth caused by the collapse of underground rock.

Lakes can be fed in many ways. Some lakes are fed by rivers and mountain streams. Others are supplied by underground springs or streams, as well as ground water replenishment. Some lakes have inlets but no outlets. The excess waters of these kinds of lakes do not drain away. Instead, they slowly evaporate.

The presence of a large lake can affect weather conditions for the land around it. In summer, a lake will not get as warm as the surrounding land. Cool winds blowing off the water will help hold down the temperature. In winter, a lake will not cool off as fast as the land does. This will help keep the nearby land warmer, at least until the lake freezes. Then the lake acts the same way as a cold land surface.

Crater Lake is located in an inactive volcano in the Cascade Mountains of Oregon. It is the deepest lake in the United States, measuring 1,932 feet (589 meters).

Lake waters are divided into distinct layers, which are determined by the amount of penetrating sunlight. Each descending layer receives less sunlight than the one above it, unless the water is very clear. Therefore, the deeper a layer is, the colder and darker its waters.

The different layers of a lake are inhabited by distinct communities of animal and plant life. These communities depend on one another for food. For example, microscopic plants that drift in a lake's upper waters are eaten by microscopic animals. Both the tiny plants and the tiny animals are called plankton. Plankton is eaten by fish that live near a lake's surface.

Many kinds of insects live in the upper water of a lake. Whirligig beetles swim in this region. Their divided eyes look both above and below the water. Backswimmers, another type of insect, reside just at the surface, and they swim faceup. Water striders actually walk *upon* the water, which for them is like solid ground. All these insects feed on other insects that fall or alight upon the quiet surface water.

Many of a lake's plants and animals live near the shore, in what is called the littoral zone. Here snails and worms creep on plant stems, and predatory fish lurk among bulrushes and other water plants. In the shallows near the shore, water birds often hunt and use bits of plants as nesting material.

Few of the littoral zone animals or water animals are found on the lake bottom.

There is also little if any plant life there. The main inhabitants include snails and shrimplike crustaceans. These creatures eat the remains of dead plants and animals that drift down from the upper regions of the lake.

A pond is basically a miniature lake that is shallow enough for sunlight to reach the bottom and enable plants to grow there. Many ponds are formed naturally, but a great many are made by people. Most of the same creatures that are found in lakes are also found in ponds. Such creatures include fish, frogs, and water insects. In many cases, eggs and larvae of these animals are brought from one lake or pond to another by water birds. The birds carry the transported material on their feet or in their feathers. The wind is another transporter. It carries plant seeds from one water home to another. The seeds of water plants can also float to new locations.

Many ponds and small, shallow lakes are temporary features. Over time, the build-up of material on the water's floor and the spread of vegetation will fill in a small pond. Eventually it will become a marsh or swamp. Over many hundreds or many thousands of years, climate change, sediment accumulation, and vegetation growth will turn even a large, shallow lake into a wetland.

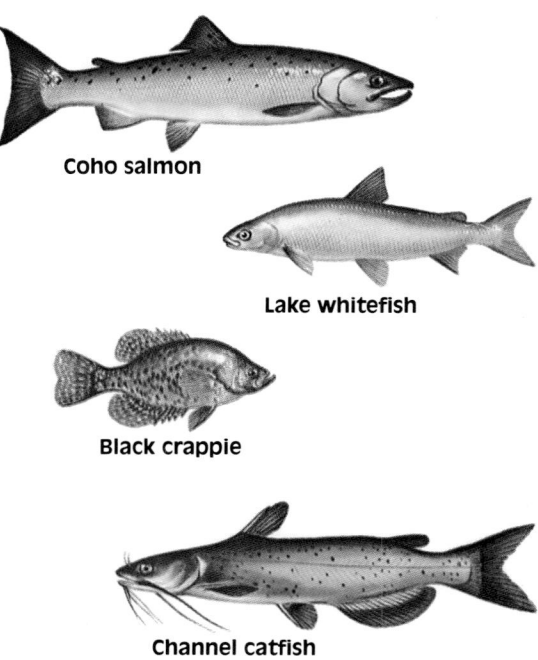

Many species of fish are found in lakes. If a lake freezes over in winter, the fish that live there can swim down to warmer water near the bottom until spring.

Coho salmon

Lake whitefish

Black crappie

Channel catfish

Eutrophication is a process that destroys the delicate balance of water life. This dying pond is naturally eutrophic, but there are other ponds that are killed by pollution.

Pond animal and plant life

In a pond, the primary food producers are microscopic plants that use sunlight to make food for primary consumers, such as tadpoles. A fish (secondary consumer) may eat the tadpole. Decomposers complete the food chain by cleaning up the waste and producing chemicals that primary producers use to make food.

The pond environment

The pond environment

1	Common frog (male, x 0.5)
2	Starwort (x 0.5)
3	Water crowfoot (x 0.25)
4	Aplecta hypnorum (x 2)
5	Wandering snail (x 0.75)
6	Keeled ramshorn snail (x 0.5)
7	Curled pondweed (x 0.25)
8	Bithynia (x 1)
9	Ramshorn snail (x 0.3)
10	Water lily root (x 0.25)
11	Great pond snail (x 0.8)

Near the surface

12	Pond skater (x 0.5)
13	Whirligig beetle (x 0.25)
14	Water boatman (x 1)
15	Nonbiting midge (x 5)
16	Mosquito pupa (x 5)
17	Dragonfly (male, x 0.65)
18	China-marks moth (x 0.75)
19	Mayfly (female, x 0.2)

Middle depths

20	Water flea (Daphnia, x 2.5)
21	Smooth newt (male, x 0.5)
22	Cyclops (typical of species, x 8)
23	Flagellate (x 650)
24	Great diving beetle (male, x 1)
25	Hydra (x 4)
26	Stickleback (male, x 0.5)
27	Common frog tadpole (x 1.5)
28	Flagellate (Euglena, x 180)
29	Water mite (x 5)

The bottom

30	Caddis-fly larva in case
31	Chaetonotus (x 150)
32	Horny-orb shell (x 1)
33	Tubifex worms (x 0.2)
34	Midge larva (x 3.5)
35	Pond sponge (x 0.2)
36	Leech (Helobdella sp., x 4)
37	Water hog-louse (x 2.5)
38	Flatworm (x 2)

Near the surface

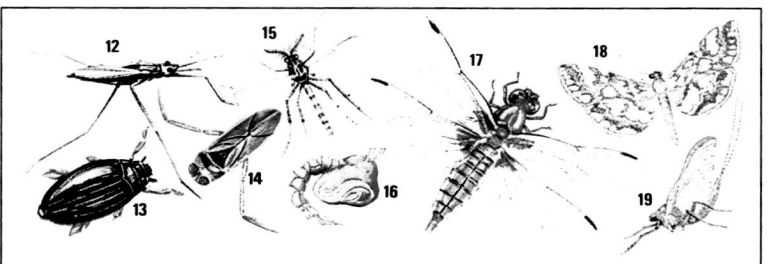

Middle depths

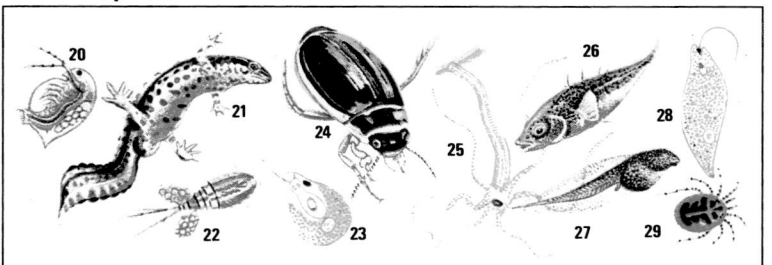

The bottom

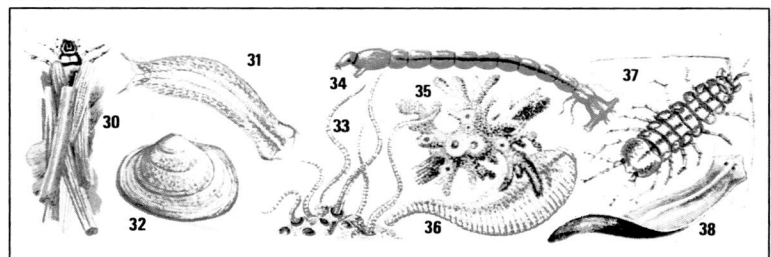

Swamps, Marshes, and Bogs

Okefenokee Swamp, in southeastern Georgia and northeastern Florida, is the home of many animals, including deer, bears, wildcats, otters, raccoons, opossums, and alligators. About two-thirds of the swamp is a government wildlife preserve.

Swamps, marshes, and bogs are known as the earth's wetlands. A wetland is a land area where the water level remains near or above the surface of the ground for most of the year.

Swamps, the first type of wetland, are areas of muddy, watery land covered by trees and bushes. The major kinds of swamps are deepwater, shallow-water, and mangrove.

Deepwater swamps are near large, slow-flowing rivers that flood regularly. These floods spread water over adjoining land. Bald cypress and black gum trees, which thrive in muddy soil, grow easily in such areas. The thick foliage of these trees blocks out much of the sunlight. Thus, only certain kinds of plants can grow on the muddy ground.

Shallow-water swamps are usually found in areas where soil stays moist or water-covered for only part of the year. Bushes and trees such as willows, oaks, and maples, flourish there. Water lilies and similar plants cover the surface of the standing water in springtime.

Unlike the other deepwater and shallow-water swamps that have fresh water, mangrove swamps have salt water. These swamps lie along tropical seacoasts and are named for the mangrove shrubs that grow there.

Swamp water swarms with insects, frogs, and fish. These creatures are food for long-legged birds such as herons and egrets. The birds wade in the water and use their beaks to spear prey. In the tropics and subtropics, swamps are home to alligators, crocodiles, turtles, and snakes. Such animals prefer the combination of hot weather and watery conditions.

Many animals are equally at home in swamps and in inland marshes. Marshes, the second kind of wetland, are flat, treeless areas covered with water. There are, however, animals such as American red-winged blackbirds and muskrats that prefer marshes. Blackbirds nest among the cattails, bulrushes, and other water plants that grow thickly in this environment. Those same plants are food for muskrats and also nesting places for many kinds of waterfowl. Like muskrats, these birds are prey for mink, which live on marshland edges.

An inland marsh is also a major source of food for animals that do not actually inhabit it. Raccoons visit marshes to hunt fish and crayfish in the shallow water. Raccoons also dig up nests of turtle eggs and search for the egg-filled nests of ducks and

other waterfowl. Deer also visit marshes. There, they browse on water lilies, marsh marigolds, grasses, and grasslike plants called sedges.

In addition to inland marshes, there are also saltwater marshes. These form where river deltas empty into the sea. Fish, crabs, oysters, and mussels flourish in salt marshes where salt grasses are abundant. Diving birds such as ospreys are salt marsh dwellers, and gulls are frequent visitors.

Bogs, the third type of wetland, are wet, spongy areas. They are filled with mosses and large amounts of partly decayed plant matter called peat. These environments are usually found in the colder, northern parts of the world. Bogs generally evolve from deep lakes that have become filled with dead, compacted plant material. Sphagnum moss and sedges form a thick mat on the surface of the water. There, wild cranberries, other berry bushes, and a few dwarf trees may grow. Other species of plants that thrive in and around bogs are carnivorous plants such as the sundew, pitcher plant, and Venus's-flytrap. Aside from insects and frogs, few animals live permanently in this type of wetland. But many animals, among them moose and bear, visit bogs in search of food.

In addition to supporting plant and animal communities, wetlands are ecologically valuable in other ways. They can store large amounts of water for long periods of time. And because they hold back water, they help prevent floods.

Bogs, with their acidic soil and water, favor the growth of mosses—especially sphagnum moss, which absorbs water like a sponge.

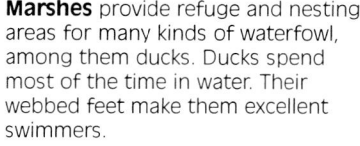

Marshes provide refuge and nesting areas for many kinds of waterfowl, among them ducks. Ducks spend most of the time in water. Their webbed feet make them excellent swimmers.

Tropical Forests

A broad band around the middle of the earth receives the planet's greatest amount of sunlight. This zone, known as the tropics, generally features year-round summer conditions. Humidity and temperatures are constantly high. Days are long and sunny, and many tropical regions are frequently rainy. In this climate, huge forests flourish. They are called tropical rain forests, and they almost always lie near the equator. These forests cover the tropical portions of Africa, Asia, Australia, Central and South America, and the Pacific islands.

Unlike a midlatitude forest, a tropical rain forest has few seasonal temperature changes. Because of the unending summer conditions, most trees in a tropical forest stay green all year. Such trees gradually lose old leaves as they grow new ones. However, there are some deciduous trees in tropical forests that shed all their leaves briefly during the dry season.

Generally all the trees in a tropical rain forest have tall, straight trunks with branches only at the very top. The tops of the trees are called the crowns, and they merge to form a covering of leaves high in the air. This covering is known as the upper canopy. Its thickness blocks most of the sunlight from reaching the forest floor. Because the floor is so dim, few plants can grow there. Mushrooms and other fungi that need little light flourish in this environment.

Orchids, wild pineapples, other flowering plants, and ferns grow high up on the trunks of tropical trees. These plants begin as seeds that are carried by the wind. The seeds lodge within crevices in the tree bark, and are warmed by sunlight. For water, the seeds soak up moisture from the air and rain that runs down the tree trunks.

Forest vines are rooted in the ground. Often they wind up tree trunks and other vines until they reach the treetops. There they can spread out among the leafy branches of the upper canopy. Extremely tall trees called emergents thrust through the upper canopy's vines and branches. Many kinds of insects and insect-eating birds live in the emergents. Large, predatory birds live there too. Such birds include harpy eagles, which prey on the monkeys that live below in the upper canopy.

Monkeys and many other creatures are attracted by the upper canopy's abundance of fruit and nuts. Fruit-eating birds, such as toucans, and leaf-eating mammals, such as sloths, also thrive in the crowns of tall trees. Hummingbirds and brilliantly colored butterflies flutter between the canopy's leaves and flowers. Tree frogs and lizards creep through the upper canopy branches, hunting insects. Snakes lurk among the leaves to capture these creatures. Other residents of the upper canopy include gliding animals such as large bats called flying foxes and flying dragons, a type of lizard.

Not all trees are tall enough to reach the upper canopy. Some full-grown trees can thrive at lower levels in the forest because they do not require an abundance of light. The crowns of these trees form one or two lower canopies that are generally quite sturdy. The lower canopies are inhabited by larger forest animals such as apes and leopards. These animals live both in trees and on the forest floor.

In many parts of a tropical rain forest, tree trunks are spread far apart and few plants grow on the ground. But in places where abundant sunlight is able to reach the ground, there is a thick, tangled growth of bushes and low plants. Such areas are called jungles, and they grow frequently in former clearings and along the banks of wide rivers in the tropical regions of the world.

Equator

Tropical Forests

Upper canopy

Abundant fruits and nuts at this level, from 100 to 150 feet (30 to 45 meters) high, provide food for monkeys, birds, leaf-eating mammals, snakes, tree frogs, and lizards. Well adapted to treetop life, they seldom touch the ground.

Royal python

Tree shrew

Sacred langur

Lower canopy

The crowns of shorter trees support larger creatures that also spend time on the ground. Plants such as orchids and mosses are abundant in the lower canopy, or understory, which rises from 16 to 100 feet (5 to 30 meters) from the forest floor.

Leopard

Orangutan

Pouched tree frog

Shrub layer

Woody shrubs at this layer rarely reach higher than 16 feet (5 meters). The plants spring up to fill the space available between larger, taller trees.

Four-striped squirrel

Oriental civet

Tree pangolin

Forest floor

The ground layer of the forest is dark. It receives less than 1 per cent of sunlight. Only ferns and other shade-loving plants can survive here. Animals that live here must be able to tolerate high humidity, so insects abound. Many ground-layer mammals have compact bodies that help them move through dense undergrowth.

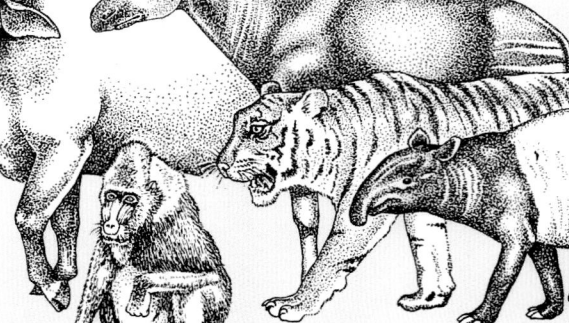

Okapi

Forest buffalo

Indian tiger

Malayan tapir

Congo forest mouse

Short-eared elephant shrew

Orange-rumped agouti

Mandrill

Emergent layer

The tallest trees in a tropical forest form the emergent layer, up to 200 feet (61 meters) high. Animal life at this level is mostly birds and insects.

Demidoff's bushbaby

Flying fox

Gray parrot

Flying squirrel

Gold Coast turaco

Chameleon

Chimpanzee

Orchids, which thrive in humid conditions, abound in tropical forests. They range in size from small flowers to huge vines as long as 100 feet (30 meters).

In the dim light near the edge of a Sumatra rain forest, the forest floor is relatively free of plant life.

Layers of the forest

Living conditions at different heights determine what creatures inhabit different layers of the forest. The topmost layers are so high up that only birds and insects are found there. To survive in the dense canopy and middle layer, animals must be streamlined and adapted for climbing. In the high humidity and gloom of the ground layer, insects and fungi break down rotting fruit and leaves from above. These decomposers enrich the soil that feeds the forest.

Deserts

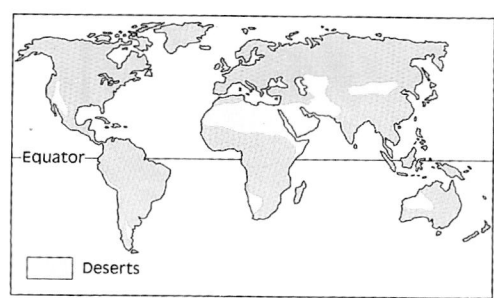

Deserts

About one-seventh of the earth's land is covered by deserts. In general, deserts are any areas that have little rainfall, dry soil, and a limited amount of very special kinds of plants. But there is no "typical" desert. Some, such as parts of the Sahara, consist mainly of lifeless, rocky surfaces and smaller areas of shifting piles of sand called dunes. Others are limited to rocky, dry areas full of plant and animal life. Those deserts, located in the subtropics, remain searingly hot throughout the year. But others such as the Great Basin and the Gobi Desert are bitterly cold in winter and very hot in summer.

Often a desert will gradually merge with a fertile grassland. But unlike the neighboring grasses, desert plants must cope with a minimal supply of water. Some of these plants have long roots that probe far underground to find water. Others have shallow, widespread roots that absorb the tiniest amounts of dew and rain that soak down from the surface. The leaves of these plants are small, and they often fall off during the dry season.

Many types of desert vegetation flourish only when there is a little rain. After a rainfall, previously inactive seeds quickly germinate and grow into plants. These plants—known as annuals—flower, form more seeds, then die. The new seeds lie dormant until it rains again. The next rainfall, however, may be years away.

Desert plants vary in form from the prickly pear cactus to giant cacti. Many shrub and low tree species also grow in deserts. Such desert plants enable wildlife to live among them. They do this by providing animals with food and moisture. Some desert plants also provide animals with shelter. For example, North American Gila woodpeckers drill holes in giant cacti. In these hollows, the birds raise their families. When they leave, the holes are taken over by other kinds of birds or by lizards, rats, or mice.

Extreme heat can kill an animal. That is why desert creatures must be able to keep their bodies from becoming too hot. There are various ways animals can control their body temperatures. Small creatures, among them insects, snakes, and tiny mammals, hide from the heat. They dig down into the sand and stay there. Or they keep cool in underground burrows or dark crevices in the rocks. Some creatures pant to cool themselves. Others escape the heat by going into a kind of hibernation for days or weeks. During this time, their bodies stay cool. Some desert animals have special body features that help them lose heat. The big ears of a desert fox or jack rabbit are examples of these features. Blood carries body heat up into the thin skin of these animals' ears. From the ears, heat radiates into the dry, hot air of the desert. Thus the body temperature of the animals is lowered.

In addition to surviving the heat, desert animals must be adapted for an environment that has very little water. Desert larks of the Sahara, for example, can thrive for weeks without a drink. Camels and little furry dassies of South Africa can often live without drinking for months. These birds and mammals get moisture from the food they eat. They are also able to store this moisture in their bodies for a long time. There are also desert creatures, among them the kangaroo rat, that never need to drink. Their food gives them all the moisture they require.

Some desert dwellers, however, must find water each day. One such animal is the red kangaroo of the Australian Desert. This large mammal is known for grazing in the dry grasslands that border the desert. Each day, in search of water, the kangaroo must travel from the grasslands to one of the few watering holes in the almost waterless environment of the desert.

Long-nosed bat

Different deserts are home to different species of plants and animals. All desert creatures and vegetation, however, share the need to obtain and conserve water.

Scattered throughout the world's largest desert, the Sahara, are fertile areas known as oases. The water for Saharan oases comes mainly from springs or underground streams.

Agave

Esparto grass

Monument Valley, Utah, gets bitterly cold in winter. Red sandstone formations rise 1,000 feet (300 meters) from the desert floor.

Elf owl

Great horned owl

Gila monster

Roadrunner

Fennec fox

Desert hedgehog

Saguaro cactus

Desert tortoise

Kangaroo rat

Fat sand rat

Welwitschia

Addax antelope

Dorcas gazelle

Grasslands

Between humid forests and arid deserts lie the earth's sun-filled grasslands. These areas, which may be flat or hilly, are literally seas of grasses.

The three types of grasslands are steppes, prairies, and savannas. A grassland is classified into one of these three types according to the average height of the grass that grows there. Plant height depends upon the amount of rainfall received.

Steppes, which are the driest grassland, are covered mainly by short grasses. Most plants in a steppe do not grow over 1 foot (30 centimeters) high. Steppes cover large areas of the interior of North America and Europe, and also extend into central Asia.

Prairies, which receive moderate rainfall, are blanketed chiefly by tall grasses. In moist prairies, grass may grow 6 feet (1.8 meters) high or even taller. The North American prairie reaches from central Texas to southern Saskatchewan. Saskatchewan, Alberta, and Manitoba are called Canada's "Prairie Provinces." Other prairies include the Pampa of Argentina.

Savannas are grasslands with widely scattered trees and shrubs. Most savannas are in the tropics, but some are in temperate regions. This type of grassland covers more than two-fifths of Africa and large parts of Australia, South America, and India.

One of the main types of grassland animals is the grazer, or grass-eater. The larger grazers are generally animals that live in herds, such as the American bison and antelope and the African gnu and zebra. In many places, however, wild grazers have been replaced by domesticated grazers such as sheep and cattle. The herds of grass-eaters roam across a grassland, eating as they go. The area they move across looks like a mowed lawn for a time, but the grass quickly grows again unless it is the dry season.

Actually, there are many more small grazers than big ones. Small grazers include many kinds of grasshoppers, ants, aphids, leaf hoppers, and other insects. Just as large predators prey on large grazers, small predators such as birds and mice prey on small grazers.

Many kinds of flowering plants such as sunflowers, prairie clover, and cornflowers grow in grasslands. They produce seeds and leaves that are eaten by the region's wildlife, which includes jack rabbits and colonies of prairie dogs. There are many predators of these seed- and leaf-eaters. All grasslands contain snakes, which hunt for prey among the grass stems. But in addition to being the hunter, snakes are also the hunted. The sky over a grassland is the natural range for hawks and other birds of prey that will swoop down to seize snakes, as well as rabbits.

In tropical savannas, the temperature stays hot all year, so life goes on unchanged, except for alternating rainy and dry seasons. But the steppes and prairies have warm summers and cool to cold winters. In most of these regions the grassland life is curtailed by cold weather. The ground freezes and the grass stops growing. Much of the insect life dies or burrows underground. The insect-eating birds migrate to other regions. Most of the smaller animals hibernate or remain in burrows through the cold season, living on stored food. But with the coming of spring and the thawing of the ground, the grasslands quickly return to life.

Much of the world's grasslands have been turned into farmland where wheat and corn, which are actually grasses, are grown. Even in man-made grasslands, however, much of the same life which may be found in a natural grassland exists. Insects, birds, small mammals, and other creatures thrive among the cultivated grasses.

American buffalo, or bison, live in herds and graze on the grasses and small plants found on American prairies.

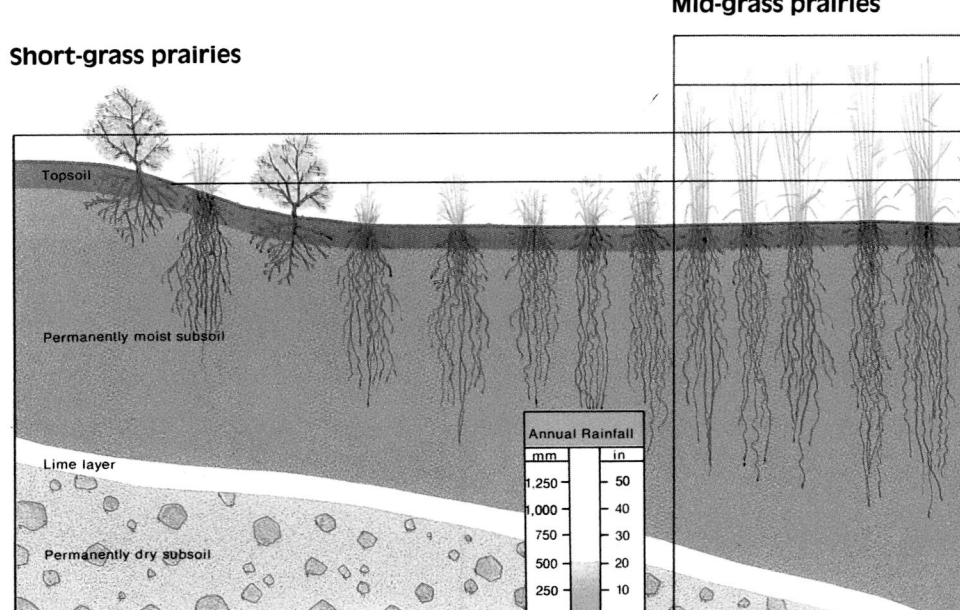

Short-grass prairies

Mid-grass prairies

Topsoil

Permanently moist subsoil

Lime layer

Permanently dry subsoil

Annual Rainfall	
mm	in
1,250	50
1,000	40
750	30
500	20
250	10

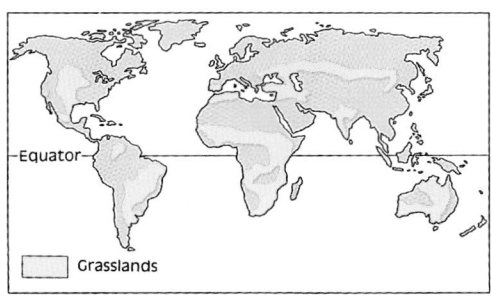

Equator

Grasslands

Grassland creatures solve the problem of survival by adapting to the environment in various ways. Many, such as small burrowing animals and certain invertebrates, seek protection underground. The marsupial mole lives almost entirely underground, while the prairie dog surfaces to eat. Snakes, of course, are well adapted for the pursuit of burrowing creatures. Small carnivores like the pampas cat often surprise their victims. Certain grassland predators rely on speed for catching prey—as do some of the creatures they hunt in the race for survival. The sharp-eyed hawk rides thermal winds in search of food, while the meadowlark adapts to a mostly treeless environment by singing to declare its territory. Camouflage protects many insects.

Red-tailed hawk

Western meadowlark

Burrowing owl

Rainfall determines what grasses grow where on the North American prairies. In general, the drier the climate, the shorter the grasses. In regions where annual rainfall is no more than 20 inches (500 millimeters), only short grass—with short root systems—can survive in the relatively narrow layer of permanently moist subsoil. As the depth of the subsoil increases, it can support the longer root systems of mid-grass and tall-grass prairies. Tall bluestem and Indian grass predominate in the regions where annual rainfall measures 40 inches (1,000 millimeters). The North American prairie includes most of Oklahoma, Kansas, Nebraska, Iowa, Illinois, South Dakota, and North Dakota, and parts of neighboring states and provinces. Alberta, Saskatchewan, and Manitoba are the "Prairie Provinces" of Canada.

Saiga

American bison

European hare

Guanaco

Springhaas

Tall-grass prairies

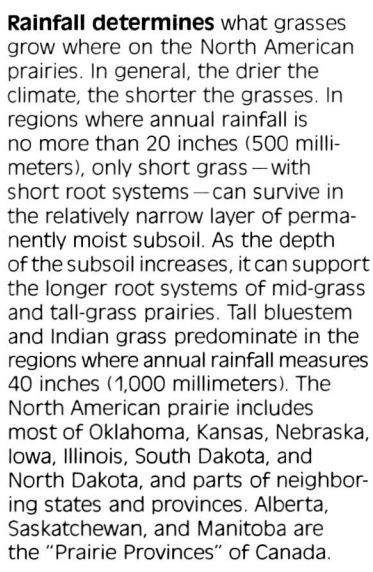

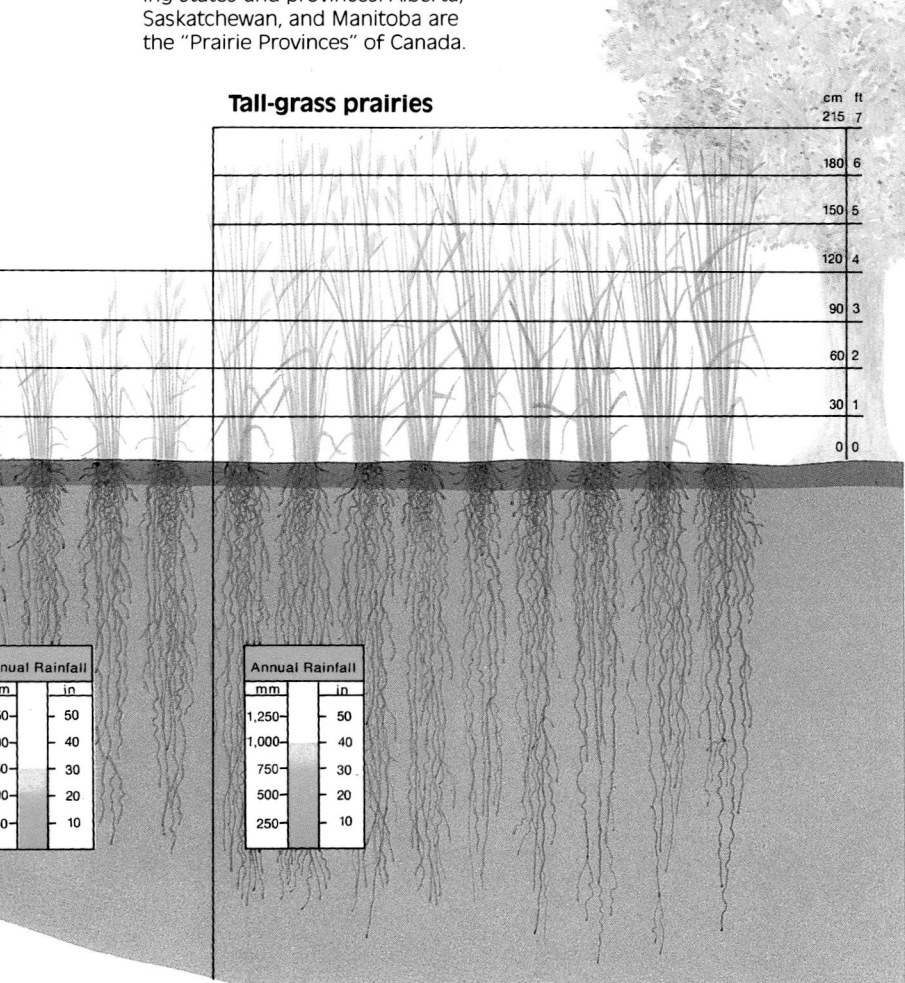

cm	ft
215	7
180	6
150	5
120	4
90	3
60	2
30	1
0	0

Annual Rainfall	
mm	in
1,250	50
1,000	40
750	30
500	20
250	10

Annual Rainfall	
mm	in
1,250	50
1,000	40
750	30
500	20
250	10

Marbled polecat

Pampas cat

Gopher snake

Marsupial mole

Prairie dog

European souslik

Viscacha

Lubber grasshopper

Praying mantis

Tumble bug

Midlatitude Forests

The earth's midlatitude regions lie between the polar circles and the tropics. Here, the seasonal climate ranges from warm summers to cold winters and, in some places, offers distinct dry and rainy seasons.

Deciduous trees, those with broad leaves that are shed annually, grow best in midlatitude regions where it is warm and moist at least four to five months a year. They are the main trees of most midlatitude forests, but many kinds of needle-leaved or broad-leaved evergreens also thrive in such a climate.

Midlatitude forests once covered eastern North America, western Europe, and eastern Asia. Changes in climate, together with activities such as forestry and farming, have reduced these forests to small areas.

Ground water generally freezes in midlatitude regions during winter. Thus, deciduous trees cannot draw up water into their leaves, and the leaves cannot tolerate freezing. This is why trees shed their leaves in autumn and stand bare during winter. However, evergreens can hold water in their needles throughout wintertime. This is how they can remain green all year.

In spring, when the ground begins to thaw, small flowers of the forest floor are first to bloom. Buds soon appear on trees and bushes and burst into pastel-colored flowers and tiny, pale-green leaves. Hibernating creatures stir. Birds return from the warm lands where they spent the winter. Insect and spider eggs, produced in autumn, now hatch by the millions.

Summer days are long and filled with sunshine and frequent rain. During this season, the tree leaves grow and become dark green with the substance called chlorophyll. Leaves are a tree's foodmakers. Using sunlight for power, their chlorophyll turns water absorbed by the roots and carbon dioxide from the air into sugars.

To get at this food in the leaves, leaf-eating insects, such as aphids, grasshoppers, and caterpillars, swarm among the upper branches of the trees. Many predatory insects and spiders live there too, preying on the leaf-eaters. And such a plentiful supply of insects and spiders attracts a variety of insect-eating birds.

The tops of the taller deciduous trees form the roof, or canopy, of the forest. The canopy is the home of insects, spiders, songbirds, squirrels, and nocturnal flying squirrels. Beneath the canopy is a second "layer" of trees called the understory. Some young trees in this layer must grow into the sunlight or they will die. Others are low-growing trees that do not need as much sunlight.

Beneath the understory is a layer of shrubs. These shrubs produce berries and seeds that are a source of food for mice and chipmunks. Under the bushes, upon the forest floor, are low-growing flowering plants, ferns, and mosses, which do not need much sunlight to make their food. Mushrooms also grow there. They need little sunlight, for they take their food from the rotting, decaying things on which they grow. Grouse, woodcocks, and pheasants feed on this vegetation. Deer also browse on the forest floor, and insects swarm there and are hunted by mice, frogs, and toads. They in turn are preyed upon by snakes, foxes, and raccoons.

In late summer, deciduous trees begin to prepare for winter. A layer of corklike substance grows where each leaf stem is attached to the branch. No more water can reach the leaves. Their green color fades, and their true color, generally yellow or orange, is seen. After chlorophyll breaks down, red or purple pigments form in a dying leaf.

With no water, the leaves die, turn brown, and wither. Autumn wind and rains tear them loose to swirl to the ground. There, they become food for mushrooms, other fungi, and tiny animals. These will help turn the leaves into the soil of the forest floor. The seasonal cycle is now complete, and winter is approaching.

Seasonal climate is an important feature of midlatitude forests. Deciduous trees, which lose their leaves each autumn, flourish in such an environment.

Mushrooms get their nourishment from dead matter, such as decaying bark.

A paper wasp makes its nest from chewed-up wood.

A flying squirrel can spread its legs and glide through the air from tree to tree.

Midlatitude forests provide food and shelter for many animals and for a variety of plants.

Equator

Midlatitude Forests

Hazel mouse

Acorn woodpecker

American black bear

European woodcock

Stag beetle

Bluebell

Hepatica

Subarctic Cold Lands

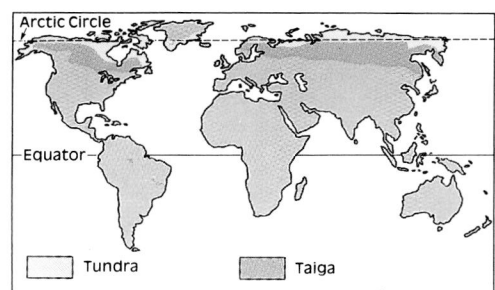

Tundra   Taiga

The transitional area between tundra and taiga is marked by shrubs, grasses, and the shoots of deciduous trees.

The dry, treeless, subarctic cold lands that lie near the Arctic Ocean are called arctic tundras. They include the northern parts of North America, Europe, and Asia. For three to four months a year, the sky over arctic tundras is dark both day and night. Beneath the darkened sky, snow blankets the frozen ground.

Change occurs on the tundra in spring, when the northern part of the earth is tilted toward the sun. This causes the tundra sky to lighten. Sunlight melts the snow and thaws the land's upper layer of soil, which is about one-foot (30 centimeters) deep. Below this layer is the perpetually frozen ground known as permafrost.

Plants that have been dormant through the months of darkness abruptly burst into bloom in springtime. These plants are tough, low-growing, and ground-hugging. They include mosses, lichens, grasses, and small flowering plants such as bilberries and bearberries. The very cold winters with strong winds prevent plants from growing higher than the depth of the protective snow. Therefore, no full-size trees can survive on the tundra. Some willow shrubs, however, grow 3 to 10 feet (91 to 305 centimeters) high on slopes and valleys where winter snows are deep.

In spring and summer, the many flowering plants of the tundra turn the region into a sea of color. Arctic foxes, ermines, and snowy owls prey on the little mouselike lemming and arctic hare that search the tundra for tender leaves. Birds such as the willow ptarmigan nest and raise their young among the flowers. Mosquitoes, midges, and black flies are everywhere. Polar bears may leave the icepack and come on land to find food. Caribou, reindeer, and musk oxen browse on plants and are hunted by packs of wolves.

When earth tilts away from the sun, winter returns suddenly. In late August or early September, the ground freezes and snow begins to fall. Most birds and animals migrate southward during winter, but some live year-round on the tundra. Lemmings spend the winter in nests of leaves and feed on the green shoots of flowering plants and mosses. In winter, herds of shaggy musk oxen use their broad hoofs to search for grasses buried beneath the snow in patches.

The tundra regions spread southward for hundreds of miles until they reach regions that are slightly warmer. There, where the ground thaws more in summer, short trees grow far apart from one anoth-

er. A little farther south, taller trees grow closer and closer together until they form vast, thick stretches of forest. This is the northern boreal forest, or taiga. It covers much of Canada and the northern parts of the Scandinavian countries and Russia.

The trees of the taiga are mainly needle-leaf evergreens, such as the white spruce. A few species of hardy deciduous trees, among them birches, are also present. Mosses, lichens, and very few flowering plants cover the forest floor.

Throughout winter, trees in the taiga stand heaped with snow. Elk, caribou, reindeer, and moose graze through the forests. As they go, they eat shrubs, grasses, and shoots of deciduous trees. Snowshoe hare, squirrels, and ptarmigan are abundant and preyed on by lynxes, martins, and wolves. Bears spend their winters in the taiga in long periods of sleep or in complete hibernation.

In spring, the snow melts, soaking into the ground. This provides the taiga with a new supply of water for all the trees. Mosquitoes and horseflies swarm. Birds arrive. Hibernating animals become active. Like the tundra, the taiga teems with life through the short, warm summer.

Flowers, mosses, and lichens carpet the tundra when springtime relieves the long months of darkness. To survive, they must reproduce before the first snows come in September.

With the spring thaws, bears emerge from their winter hibernation to forage along the banks of the McNeil River in Alaska.

Musk ox

Brant goose

Raven

Seasonal changes have tremendous effect on the animals of subarctic cold lands. Rock ptarmigans and arctic hares turn white in winter for warmth and camouflage. In spring, brant geese and 30 other species of birds migrate to the Arctic. Capercaillies move southward from the taiga each summer.

Wolf

Snowy owl

Capercaillie

Arctic hare

Brown lemming

Rock ptarmigan

Polar Caps

The polar caps are regions of permanent ice and snow located at earth's North and South Poles. These regions are the parts of the planet that receive the least sunlight. During four months of winter, no sunlight touches either pole. In summer, much of the continuous light that does reach the poles is reflected into space by the glare of snow.

The two polar caps are very different from one another. The North Pole lies on a frozen sea, the Arctic Ocean. The South Pole sits upon the continent of Antarctica, which is covered by a layer of ice and snow at least a mile (1.6 kilometers) deep. The ice at the North Pole is frozen salty seawater, but the ice covering Antarctica is frozen fresh water — the largest concentration of fresh water in the world.

These frozen regions are deserts for plants. Animal life, however, does exist in the seas at both polar caps. Many kinds of fish, including the 8- to 14-foot (2.4- to 4.2-meter) long polar shark, live beneath the ice in the Arctic Ocean waters. Seals and walruses are also at home in the sea, and it is there that they find their food. Seals eat mainly fish, while walruses dive to the ocean floor to scoop up clams and other shellfish. Even in the coldest waters, these large mammals are kept warm by their extremely thick skin and layer of blubber. Of course, seals and walruses are air breathers. Thus, they must find or make openings in the ice so they can put their noses above water and breathe.

At the north polar cap, polar bears roam over the ice hunting for seals and other animals. These bears are excellent swimmers, and their thick, dense fur keeps them warm in freezing water. The fur's white color helps the animals blend in against their environment. Thus camouflaged, a bear can wait on ice near a seal's breathing hole and seize an unsuspecting victim when it comes up for air.

Several kinds of whales also make the Arctic Ocean their home. Such whales include the beluga, or white whale, and the narwhal. The narwhal is a small whale that has a maximum length of 18 feet (5.4 meters). Male narwhals have long, spiral tusks that jut from the mammals' upper jaw. The much larger bowhead whale is also an inhabitant of the Arctic Ocean.

The sea around Antarctica is the summer home of several species of whales that feed on small, shrimplike creatures called krill. These include blue, fin, humpback, and right whales. Southern bottlenose and southern fourtooth whales, which feed on squid and fish, are also Antarctic residents. Killer whales swim year-round in the cold Antarctic waters, preying on penguins, seals, and smaller whales in addition to fish and squid. A number of seal species, including krill-eating Antarctic fur seals and crabeater seals, aggressive leopard seals, and massive southern elephant seals, nest on the Antarctic coastline or on nearby islands.

The main creature found on land at the southern pole cap is the penguin, a flightless bird that walks with a clumsy waddle. One species of penguin, the emperor penguin, lays eggs and rears its young on the snow-covered slopes of Antarctica during winter. The birds' feathers and layers of fat keep them warm. To keep their eggs warm, the male birds hold them on their feet and cover them with their bellies.

Although they are at home on land for several months of the year, penguins are primarily sea creatures. Emperor penguins are superb swimmers that live on fish, and the birds spend months at a time in cold, polar waters.

A mother polar bear usually has twin cubs. Most cubs stay with their mother for about two years.

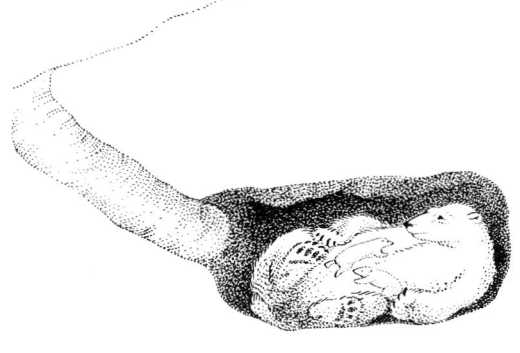

Polar bears live in underground shelters called dens during the colder months. Bears usually dig their dens in deep snowbanks.

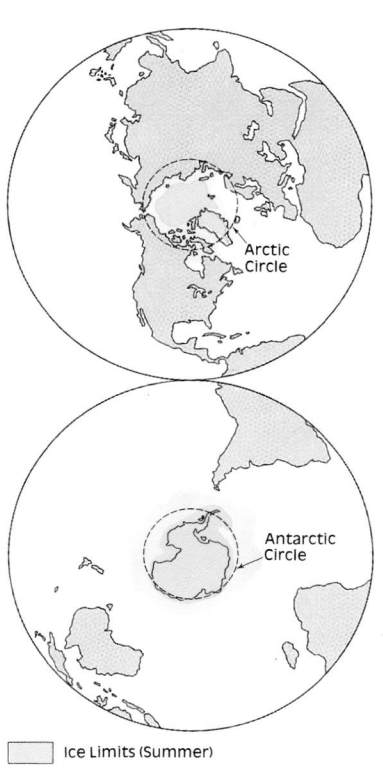

Arctic Circle

Antarctic Circle

▢ Ice Limits (Summer)
▢ Ice Limits (Winter)

Penguins have adapted to Antarctic conditions with short, dense feathers, thick layers of fat, webbed feet, and wings that serve as flippers.

The Antarctic landscape is made up of mountains, glaciers, and dry valleys, like those shown at the left. A dry valley is an ice-free rocky area carved out by a glacier that has retreated. Wind sweeps away most of the snow that falls in dry valleys.

Blue whales and crabeater seals eat millions of tons of krill, the Antarctic's chief food source. Leopard seals and killer whales prey on penguins.

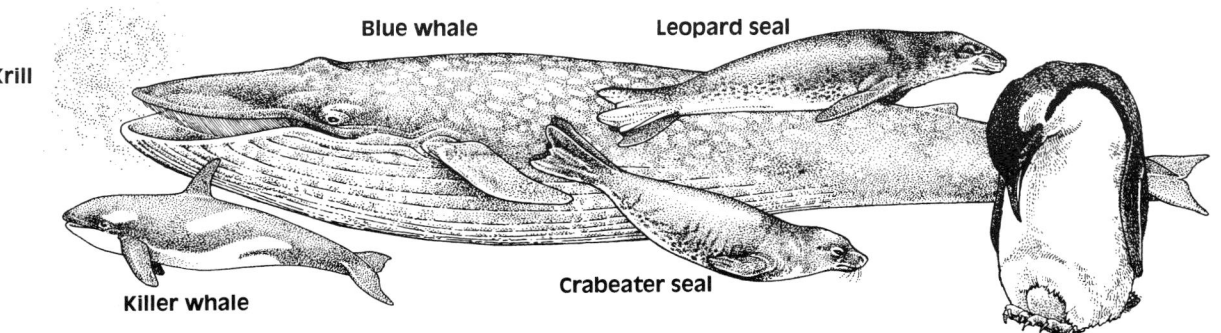

Krill

Blue whale

Leopard seal

Killer whale

Crabeater seal

Emperor penguin

Looking at Earth's

Highlands in Peru

Rockefeller Center Plaza in New York City, New York, U.S.

Rice fields in the Yangtze Valley, China

Supermarket in Luanda, Angola

People and Their Lands

BILLIONS OF PEOPLE live on earth. They live on all the planet's land, from frozen polar caps to tropical regions. Their ways of life range from simple cultures to complex societies. People are the most adaptable of earth's creatures.

North America

The continent of North America extends from islands in the frozen Arctic Ocean southward to the tropical country of Panama, the connecting link to South America. North America includes Greenland, Canada, the United States, Mexico, Guatemala, Honduras, Nicaragua, Costa Rica, Panama, El Salvador, Belize, and the islands of the West Indies. These places are home to people who speak many different languages and have vastly different ways of life.

Greenland, the world's largest island, has been the home of Inuit people, or Eskimos, for about 5,000 years. Eric the Red, a Norse chieftain, discovered Greenland about A.D. 982. In 1721, Norwegians established a mission and trading center on the island. Today, Greenland is a province of Denmark, and Greenlanders are mostly a mixture of Danish and Inuit. They speak an Inuit language called Greenlandic, but many also speak Danish.

American Indians and Inuit were living in what is now Canada when the first European settlers arrived from France in the 1600's. For a time, Canada was a colony of France, but Great Britain gained control of most of it in 1763. Thousands of English, Scottish, and Irish colonists then began to arrive. In the late 1800's and in the 1900's, especially after World War II, people from other parts of Europe came to Canada.

Those people were chiefly from Germany, Italy, and Hungary. Today, about forty per cent of all Canadians are of British or Irish descent. About a fourth have French ancestry, and another fourth are from other parts of Europe. There are also still about 350,000 American Indians and 25,000 Inuit in Canada. The language most widely spoken in the world's second-largest country is English. French, however, is spoken by most people in the province of Quebec.

The United States has been called a "melting pot" because its people are a mixture from all over the world. The first permanent European settlement in what is now the United States was founded by Spaniards in 1565. In the 1600's and 1700's, many people from England, as well as some from the Netherlands, Sweden, and France, founded colonies on the east coast. Some of these people brought with them black slaves from Africa. During the 1600's, 1700's, and 1800's, many people from all parts of Europe migrated to the new land, but since most of the first colonists had been British, English became the main language. In the 1800's, many Chinese men were brought to help work on the railroads, and eventually they sent for their families. During the 1900's, immigrants from Japan, India, Pakistan, and other parts of Asia came to the United States. Also in the 1900's, people from Mexico and Latin America immigrated to the United States. And the country is

still the home of about 1,400,000 American Indians.

Mexico, Guatemala, Honduras, Nicaragua, Costa Rica, Panama, and El Salvador were all colonized in the 1500's and 1600's by people from Spain. The colonists intermarried with the American Indians who were already living there. Thus, the people of these countries are nearly all a mixture of Spanish and American Indian. There are also, however, some black people whose ancestors were from Africa.

The languages of all these countries settled by Spain is Spanish, but many people, especially in the small towns, still speak American Indian languages. English is the official language of Belize, another country that has a racially mixed population. About half the people have full or partial black African ancestry, about two-fifths have American Indian ancestry, and most of the rest of the people are of European, East Indian, Chinese, or Lebanese descent.

In the 1500's and 1600's, most of the West Indies islands were colonized by people from Spain, England, France, and the Netherlands. Most of the people now on many other islands are descendants of black Africans originally brought there as slaves. Others are descendants of European colonists. Depending on who were the original colonists of an island, the main spoken language is Spanish, English, or French.

A jungle village in Mexico's Chiapas Highlands climbs steeply up the mountainside. The area has great blocklike mountains cut by broad, deep valleys.

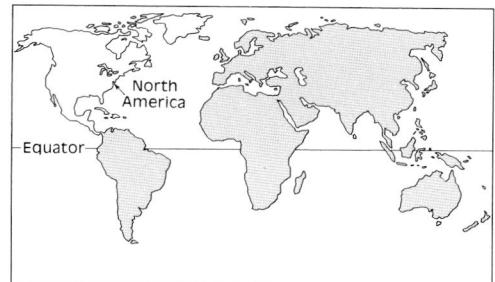

Schoolchildren in Chicago, Illinois, reflect the city's rich ethnic variety.

The city of Quebec is the capital of the province of Quebec, Canada. Street signs on Rue Champlain in the old section of the city are in French, the language of most of Quebec's residents.

South America

The continent of South America extends from a northernmost corner of land in the warm Caribbean Sea southward to a cold, tiny island only some 600 miles from the tip of snow-covered Antarctica. Between those points lie the continent's 12 independent countries. In order of size, those countries are: Brazil, Argentina, Peru, Colombia, Bolivia, Venezuela, Chile, Paraguay, Ecuador, Guyana, Uruguay, and Suriname. South America also includes French Guiana, an overseas department (administrative district) of France, and the Falkland Islands, a British dependency.

The equator runs through the northern part of South America, and more than three-fourths of the continent is in the tropics. A huge tropical rain forest covers more than one-third of the land mass, and the world's longest mountain range above sea level, the Andes, spans the entire west coast.

South America was inhabited by millions of American Indians for about 15,000 years before the first European explorers arrived. Some of the ancient peoples were quite primitive, but others achieved a fairly high degree of civilization. For example, the Inca established a great empire.

In the 1500's and 1600's, South America was explored and colonized by Europeans, chiefly from Spain and Portugal. For 300 years, the parts of South America that are now the nations of Argentina, Bolivia, Chile, Colombia, Ecuador, Paraguay, Peru, Uruguay, and Venezuela, were Spanish colonies. Many people in these countries today are descendants of Spanish colonists, and a great many are descended from Spaniards and American Indians who intermarried. The main language in these countries is Spanish. But there are still many American Indians, especially in Bolivia, Ecuador, and Peru, who speak their ancient languages. Peru, in fact, has two official languages. One is Spanish, and the other is Quechua, the country's chief Indian tongue.

Brazil covers almost half the continent. The country was settled by colonists from Portugal, and the main language of Brazil today is Portuguese. About half of South America's people live in Brazil. It is one of the world's largest nations in population. Many Brazilians are descended from Portuguese colonists and other Europeans. Many others are descendants of Europeans and American Indians, or of Europeans and black African slaves. Still others are Asians, chiefly Japanese.

The small country of Suriname was ruled by the Netherlands during most of the period from 1667 until 1975, when it gained independence. Today Suriname is officially a Dutch-speaking country. Its population is made up of people of a great many backgrounds. Many of these people are Hindustanis, descendants of people from India. Others are of mixed European and black African ancestry. The population also includes blacks, Chinese, and Indonesians. A few American Indian tribes still live in the rain forests that cover much of the nation.

The country of Guyana was a British colony from 1831 to 1966, and its official language is English. But more than half of Guyana's population is made up of East Indians whose ancestors were brought from India to work on plantations. The rest of the country's people are blacks, American Indians, Europeans, and Chinese. Many of these people speak their own language, as well as English.

French Guiana became an overseas department of France in 1946. French is the district's official language. Most of the people's ancestors were black African, European, or both.

The Falkland Islands are a dependency of the United Kingdom, but the islands are also claimed by Argentina. Most of the islanders, however, are British people, and the main language is English.

A farmer inspects his sugar cane field in Brazil, one of the most populated nations in the world.

Buenos Aires, Argentina, is the nation's capital and largest city, as well as its chief port and leading industrial center.

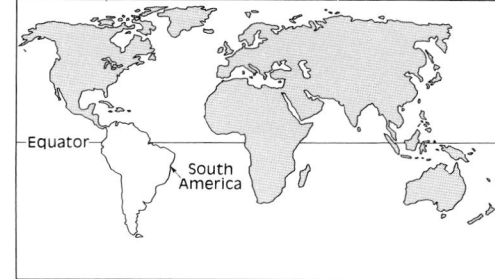

Markets like this one in the Peruvian highlands are a main source of both income and recreation for farmers. Conversation is exchanged along with goods and money.

Argentina's gauchos are typically people of mixed Amerindian and European ancestry. Gauchos chiefly work as ranch hands on estates or large ranches known as estancias.

Europe

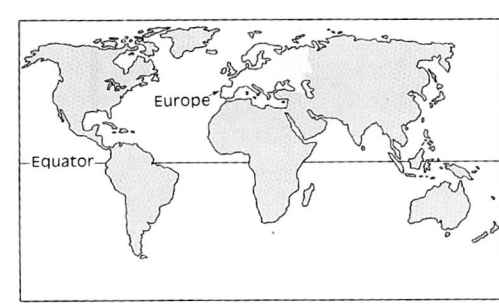

The land mass known as the continent of Europe is actually a huge peninsula—a piece of land nearly surrounded by water—that extends westward from the continent of Asia. Geographers say that Europe begins at the Ural Mountains and reaches into the Atlantic Ocean. There it includes the British Isles, Iceland, and a large number of small islands. From north to south, Europe extends from the Arctic Ocean to the Mediterranean Sea. In terms of area, Europe is smaller than any other continent except Australia. In terms of population, it is packed with more people than any other continent except Asia.

In the late 1990's, Europe consisted of 47 countries; 42 of these lay entirely within Europe and 5 lay partially in Europe and partially in Asia. The countries of Europe range in size from the world's biggest country, Russia, to the world's smallest one, Vatican City. Vatican City, which is the administrative center of the Roman Catholic Church, consists of only 0.17 of a square mile (0.44 square kilometer).

Europe is often called the birthplace of Western civilization. Most of the major scientific, philosophical, and political ideas affecting the Western world were developed by Europeans.

The majority of the people living in Europe today are descended from primitive tribes that lived there thousands of years ago. The members of these tribes and their descendants did not always remain in the same areas. Throughout the centuries of European history, various groups of people have moved around and settled in different countries. As a result, many European countries are inhabited by several ethnic groups—people who share a common ancestry, language, religion, and way of life. For example, there are the Flemings and the Walloons in Belgium. The members of the various ethnic groups within a country may all think of themselves as citizens of the same country. Still, they are likely to associate mainly with the people of their own ethnic group and to marry members of that same group.

About 50 different languages are spoken in Europe. Often, people in various parts of a country speak a dialect of that country's language. Every dialect has its own pronunciation and sentence structure and may even have its own vocabulary. The same language, then, may be spoken differently in different parts of a country. There are more than 100 different dialects among the languages of Europe.

In many European countries, more than one language is spoken. Ireland, for example, has two official languages—English and Gaelic. Everyone in Ireland speaks English, and about 30 per cent of the Irish people can speak Gaelic too. Gaelic is a form of the language spoken by the ancient Celts, from whom many of the Irish are descended. Switzerland has three official languages and four national languages. The official languages are German, French, and Italian. The national languages are the three official languages plus Romansh. Romansh, which is similar to Latin, is spoken by only about 1 per cent of the Swiss population.

Throughout Europe, many people can speak a second language, usually the language of the foreign country nearest to them. In the western part of Europe, a great number of people also speak English.

Europeans are generally light-skinned, and many are light-haired. However, in recent years, people of other racial groups from other continents have moved to Europe, chiefly to find jobs. Those people are now Europeans. Just as the Americas may be viewed as "melting pots," so has Europe become a place where people of various national and cultural backgrounds live together.

Vienna, Austria's capital and largest city, is a leading European cultural center. The many historic buildings and sidewalk cafes of Vienna's old "Inner City" add to its beauty and charm.

Crowds gather for the pope's weekly audience in the Square of Saint Peter in Vatican City. Vatican City is the world's smallest independent state. It lies entirely within the city of Rome, Italy.

Agriculture employs many Romanians. Although the nation's larger farms are modern, many smaller ones rely on old-fashioned farm equipment.

Asia

The largest continent, Asia, includes almost one-third of all the earth's land. The northernmost part of the continent, which is the tip of Siberia in Russia, lies in the bitter cold of the Arctic Circle. The southernmost part, the islands of Indonesia, lies in the simmering tropics near the equator. From west to east, Asia stretches across the earth from Africa and Europe to the Pacific Ocean. Examples of every known kind of plant-and-animal habitat, from tundra to tropical rain forest, can be found in Asia.

In the late 1990's, there were 49 independent countries in Asia; seven of these lay partially in Asia and partially in either Europe or Oceania. In addition, other political units were located in Asia, including the Portuguese territory, Macao.

Asia's smallest country is the Maldives, a group of islands in the Indian Ocean, with a population of about 234,000. The most populated is gigantic China, with a population of more than 1 billion. A variety of races and many different ethnic groups inhabit Asia. They make up about 60 per cent of all the world's people.

Few people live in large areas of Asia because those areas are either too cold, too hot, too mountainous, or too dry. The result is that Asians are jammed tightly into the places where the climate and the physical features of the land are more agreeable.

Most of these people live in valleys, near rivers, or on the seacoast.

Different groups of Asians often differ greatly from each other in appearance. Most of the people in Southwest Asian countries such as Saudi Arabia and Turkey resemble Europeans. Some Asians, however, have darker skin and hair. People of southern India have dark skin and straight hair. Inhabitants of the Indonesian part of New Guinea and other islands of Southeast Asia have brown or yellow skin and curly hair. The people of most of East Asia, those who live in countries such as China and Japan, have yellowish to brownish skin and dark straight hair.

Numerous languages and dialects are spoken throughout Asia. Often, many different languages are spoken within the same country. In India alone, there are 16 major languages and more than 1,000 minor languages and dialects. Thus, the people of one village may not speak the same language as the people of the neighboring village. These language differences often cause serious problems in matters of education and commerce.

Ways of life, too, are often very different in various parts of Asia. In Southwest Asia, about half of the people are farmers. Most of them live, dress, and work in much the same way as their ancestors have always done. On the other hand, about 77 per cent of the people of Japan live and work in or near cities that resemble those of Western countries. Many of these urban dwellers work in tall office buildings and ride modern elevated and subway trains. But in Central Asian Mongolia, Sinkiang, and Tibet, life is simpler. Most people live by herding sheep, goats, cattle, horses, camels, or yaks on the vast dry plains. The few inhabitants of New Guinea also live uncomplicated lives in tiny primitive villages that lie within tropical rain forests. Most New Guineans supply all their own needs. Some live in isolated mountain valleys and never have contact with the outside world.

Asia has played an important part in human history. It was the ancient people of Southeast Asia who developed the world's first civilization some 5,500 years ago. Asia was also the site of a number of significant inventions, such as movable type and gunpowder. And it was in Asia that all the major religions of the world began—Christianity, Judaism, Islam, Buddhism, Hinduism, Shinto, and Taoism.

Raising livestock has long been the chief economic activity in Mongolia, though few Mongolians still follow the traditional nomadic way of life.

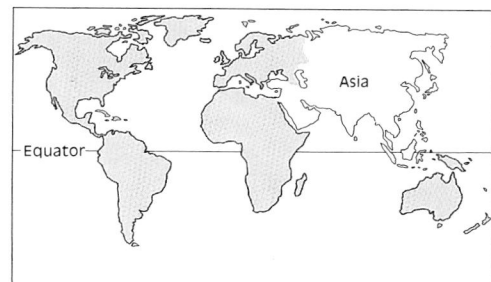

At floating markets in Bangkok, baskets of produce and other goods are exchanged from boat to boat.

At a used-car market in Saudi Arabia, a hawker sporting both Arab and Western dress uses a modern bullhorn to attract customers.

The Ganges River in India is sacred to Hindus. Each year, thousands of pilgrims climb down stairways called ghats to bathe in the river's waters.

Africa

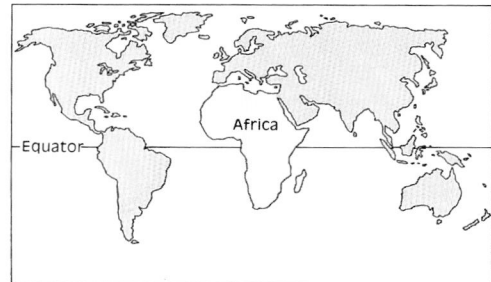

Africa, the second largest continent, occupies about one-fifth of the earth's land. The continent is an immense plateau, a region of striking contrasts. Less than one-fifth of the land is covered by great forests, most of them tropical rain forests. Although much of the continent is grassland, the world's largest desert, the Sahara, lies across 3½ million square miles (9 million square kilometers) of the northern region. The world's longest river, the Nile, flows through Africa's northeastern section.

The equator passes through almost the exact middle of the continent. Thus, about 90 per cent of Africa is in the tropic zones. The parts of the continent that lie at low elevations are hot all year long. Rain falls year-round in the Congo Basin and in some of the coastal areas, where the rain forests are located. But most of Africa has long, dry seasons with only one or two spells of heavy rainfall.

Many different kinds of people inhabit Africa. In northern Africa, mainly in Algeria and Morocco, live a group of people called Berbers. Most Berbers are light-skinned, dark-haired people. Their ancestors can be traced back thousands of years in Africa. Also living in this region are Arabs whose ancestors came from the Arabian Peninsula more than 1,300 years ago. Another group, people of European descent whose ancestors settled in Africa in the 1600's, live along the Mediterranean coast.

Black Africans make up about 70 per cent of all the African people. They are dark-skinned and have black, curly hair. Most of the people of the Sahara are black Africans.

Black African people also inhabit much of the land south of the Sahara. Their ancestors lived in the north many thousands of years ago, when the Sahara was a fertile grassland. Many began moving southward when the Sahara started to become a desert.

A group of small people called Pygmies dwell in the rain forests of central Africa. Pygmies have reddish-brown skin and tightly curled brown hair. They live primarily in small bands of fewer than 50 members. Each Pygmy band has its own territory in the forest. These people look on the forest as the giver of life, because it provides them with food, clothing, protection, and shelter.

In southwest Africa live two groups of people who have yellowish-brown skin and black, tightly coiled hair. These people, known as San (or Bushmen) and Khoikhoi,

The Nile River is the world's longest river. It flows northward from Burundi, through Sudan, Ethiopia, and Egypt to the Mediterranean Sea.

Nairobi, the capital of Kenya, is the most important commercial center in eastern Africa. The central area of the city has many modern buildings and tree-lined streets.

are members of the African Khoisan culture. Some of these Africans gather wild plant food and hunt animals. Others work on rural reserves, cattle ranches, or farms.

The major groups living in the far south are descendants of Europeans who came to Africa during the last four hundred years and of East Indians who came during the last century. The African island of Madagascar is home to many people whose ancestors came there from Indonesia about 2,000 years ago.

All these people make up hundreds of different ethnic groups, each with its own language or dialect. There are more than 800 different languages and many dialects in Africa. The fact that European nations had at one time established colonies throughout Africa is reflected in the official languages of a number of Africa's 53 nations. French, English, or Portuguese serves as the official language in many African nations. While a large number of educated citizens can speak their country's official language, most people speak mainly the language or dialect of their own ethnic group.

In Africa, as in Asia, a great many people still live in rural areas in exactly the same way that their ancestors lived for hundreds of years. However, some Africans lead very modern lives in large cities that are similar in many ways to ones in North America and Europe. Most urban dwellers have a higher standard of living than rural people. Better schools and medical facilities, as well as other attractions, lead more and more rural people to move into the cities.

Berber women perform a ceremonial dance in Morocco. About 20 million Berbers live in northwest Africa and the Sahara.

A San hunter in the Kalahari Desert of Botswana, Africa, drinks water that has been stored in an ostrich egg container.

Australia and New Zealand

Australia, the smallest continent, lies entirely in the Southern Hemisphere between the Indian and the South Pacific oceans. The northern third of Australia is in the tropics and stays hot all year long. The other two-thirds have warm summers and mild winters. About one-third of the total land area of the continent is covered by desert.

All of Australia is a single nation, the Commonwealth of Australia, which is composed of six states. It is an independent nation with its own government, but it is a member of the Commonwealth of Nations. Australia regards the British monarch as its head of state.

Two groups of people make up most of Australia's population of about 17,000,000. Nearly all are European immigrants or descendants of European immigrants — mainly British — who came to Australia during the last 200 years. Some are more recent arrivals, having immigrated during the last 40 years. These people are all white-skinned, and many are fair-haired and have light-colored eyes. All speak English.

About 1 per cent of the Australian population is made up of a group of people known as Aborigines. Aborigines are descendants of a people who came to Australia at least 40,000 years ago, probably from somewhere in Southeast Asia. While all Aborigines are dark-skinned, some have dark brown hair and others have light brown or blond hair.

At one time, there were 300,000 Aborigines, separated into hundreds of tribes. Each of those tribes had its own language. Today, there are some 206,000 Australians who are classed as Aborigines. Most of them, however, are actually a mixture of Aborigine and European as a result of intermarriage among their ancestors. Aborigines now generally speak English, although many can also speak their ancient language.

Although these two groups make up most of Australia's population, several other groups are represented. Since the 1970's, an increasing number of immigrants from New Zealand and Southeast Asia have settled in Australia. There are also a small number of people from Canada and the United States.

Most Australians of European descent live in the southeastern quarter of the continent. They have settled largely in cities along the coast, where it is cooler and there is more rainfall. Some live along the extreme southwest coast. The way of life of these people is much like that of people in the United States and Canada. Although some Aborigines have moved into the cities, most live in the forested lands of central and northern Australia.

About 1,000 miles (1,600 kilometers) southeast of Australia in the Southwest Pacific Ocean lie two large islands and several dozen small ones. This cluster of islands forms the nation of New Zealand. Located far south of the equator, New Zealand has a mild climate with a good deal of rainfall. Much of the land is green and fertile, with numerous lakes, rivers, and snow-capped mountains.

Like Australia, New Zealand is a member of the Commonwealth of Nations and regards the British monarch as its head of state. Also like Australia, New Zealand's population, which is over 3 million, is made up primarily of two groups of people. Most of them are descendants of the British who settled in New Zealand during the 1800's. The other group, the Maoris, are descendants of a people who came to New Zealand about 1,000 years ago from some other South Pacific islands. Maoris, who belong to the Polynesian race, have light brown skin, dark hair, and dark eyes.

New Zealanders live much as people do in Great Britain. Their language is, of course, English. Many Maoris, however, can also speak the language of their ancestors.

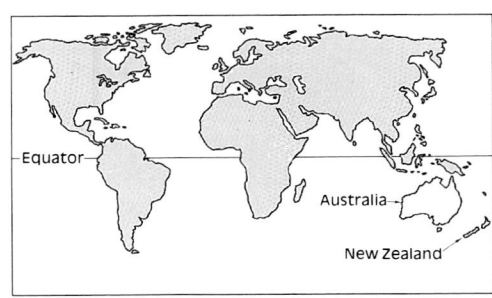

The Opera House in Sydney, Australia, has facilities for opera, concerts, and theater. The building, which is internationally known, was completed in 1973.

A sheep farmer in New Zealand uses a minibike to round up his herd. Lamb and wool are among the nation's chief exports.

The ancestors of these Aboriginal stockmen were the first people to live in Australia. Most Aborigines today live in the rural areas of the continent.

New Zealanders love outdoor sports and activities in all kinds of weather. Skiing is becoming increasingly popular.

Pacific Islands

A vast portion of the Pacific Ocean is dotted with many thousands of big and little islands. This region of ocean and islands is known as the Pacific Islands, or Oceania. Not all islands in the Pacific Ocean, however, are a part of Oceania. For example, islands near the mainland of Asia are considered part of Asia, and islands near North and South America are grouped with those continents.

Geographers divide the Pacific Islands into three parts. Scattered across the central Pacific are thousands of islands that make up the portion called Polynesia, meaning "many islands." Polynesia includes Hawaii, New Zealand, and Midway Island. North and east of Australia lie groups of islands that form what is called Melanesia, meaning "black islands." Fiji, the Solomon Islands, and New Caledonia are Melanesian islands. Between Melanesia and Japan lie islands that form Micronesia, meaning "small islands." Some of the Micronesian islands are Guam, Wake Island, and the Caroline Islands.

All these islands fall into one of two types. High Islands, such as the main islands of Hawaii, are hilly and mountainous and often have volcanoes. Low Islands such as the Marshall Islands are formed of coral reefs that are generally just above sea level. Most of Oceania lies in the tropics. There-

fore, the weather on the islands is quite warm year-round. Although the area, in general, gets plenty of rainfall, some islands may receive little rain.

Generally, a different kind of people lives in each part of the Pacific Islands. In Melanesia, the people are rather short, with dark skin and coarse, curly black hair. They resemble the black people of Africa. Scientists believe that the ancestors of the Melanesians came from somewhere in Asia many thousands of years ago.

The people of Micronesia are a little taller than the Melanesians and have lighter skin. Most also have coarse, curly, or wavy black hair. Their ancestors, too, probably came from Asia, but at a later time than the ancestors of the Melanesians.

Polynesians are taller than both other groups. All have light brown skin, but some have wavy hair and others have straight hair. Their ancestors probably came from Melanesia or Micronesia.

There have been other influences on the people of the Pacific Islands. For example, many people from other lands have settled on the Polynesian islands in the past. Thus, many Polynesians have Asian and European ancestors. A large number of people living on Fiji are descended from East Indians who came there to work about 100 years ago. And people of European and Asian descent live on many of the other Pacific Islands.

The Melanesians, Micronesians, and Polynesians all have similar ways of life. There are, however, some differences in language, law, dress, and religion. Many hundreds of languages are spoken throughout Oceania. The people of Melanesia, particularly, speak a number of different languages. English is spoken on a great many of the islands that were once colonies of Great Britain or that are now governed by Great Britain or the United States. French is spoken on a number of islands that are governed by France.

Many of the islands of Oceania are independent and have their own governments. Hawaii, American Samoa, Guam, Midway Island, and Wake Island, however, belong to the United States. Pitcairn Island comes under the authority of Great Britain. France, Chile, and New Zealand all govern islands. And a part of New Guinea is governed by Indonesia.

Of all the Pacific Islands, only Hawaii and New Zealand have large, modern cities and towns. Most Pacific Islanders live in small villages and make their livings by farming or fishing, much as their ancestors have done for hundreds of years.

At a kava ceremony in Leone, American Samoa, a woman prepares a beverage called kava, which the participants will drink as they give thanks for their blessings. Such traditional ceremonies play a major role in Polynesian village life.

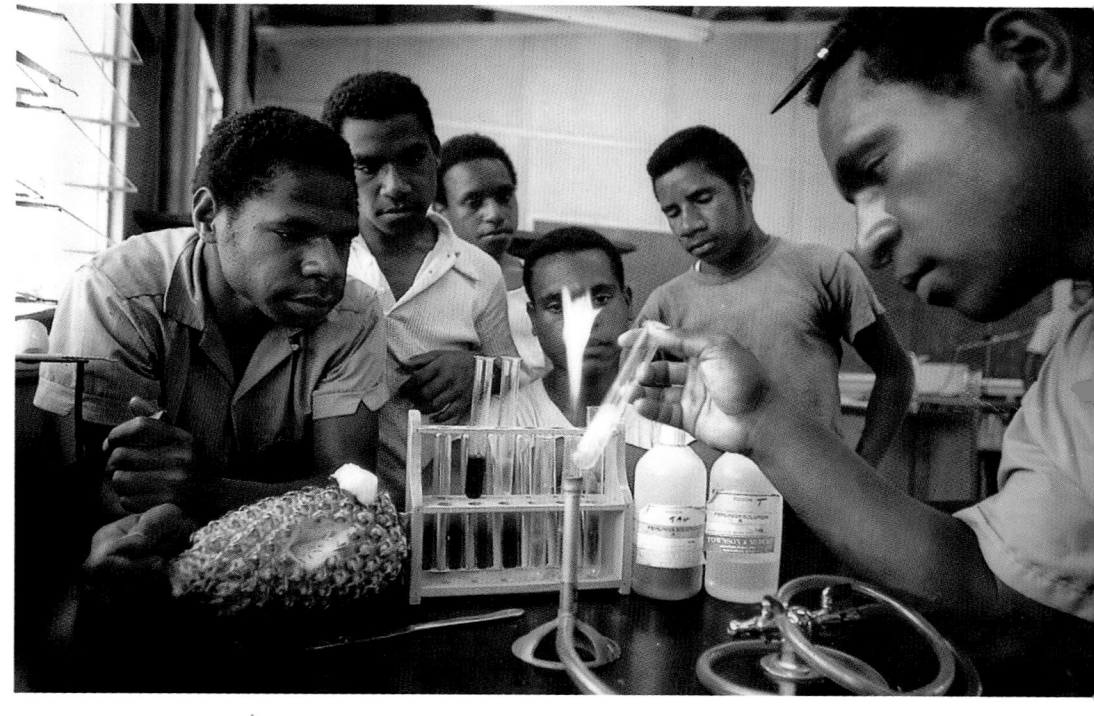

Off the Caroline Islands in Micronesia, some fishermen still travel in hand-hewn sailing canoes.

Melanesian students study pineapple extract in their school laboratory.

Polar Regions

The earth's north polar region, the Arctic, does not seem a likely place for people to live. Nevertheless, large numbers of people do live in the parts of North America, Europe, and Asia that lie within the Arctic Circle.

Large supplies of oil, uranium, titanium, and other valuable minerals have been found in the Arctic. This has caused the settlement of some areas by communities of scientists, technicians, miners, and oil field workers. Modern technology enables these settlements to survive in the Arctic's hostile environment.

Most Arctic residents, however, live simpler lives. Many follow the traditions of their ancestors.

In North America, about 117,000 of the people known as Inuit, or Eskimos, live in the northern parts of Greenland, Canada, and Alaska. Inuit are stocky people with short arms and legs. They resemble the Mongoloid people of Asia, and scientists believe they came to North America about 10,000 years ago via a land connection that once existed between Alaska and northeastern Asia. Inuit throughout the Arctic speak essentially the same language.

For thousands of years, Inuit followed a traditional way of life that had been developed to meet the demands of living in the Arctic. They lived mainly on the meat of seals and caribou, which they hunted with harpoons. During the short Arctic summer, they stayed in tents of sealskin or caribou skin, and they fished for arctic trout called char. In winter, the Inuit made temporary dome-shaped houses of snow. They traveled by means of dog sleds and boats made of wood, bone, and skins. Today, that way of life is largely gone. Most Inuit now hunt with rifles, travel by snowmobile and motorboat, and live in heated houses in settlements.

About 1,500 Inuit also live in Siberia, the northern part of Asian Russia. Several tribes of people who greatly resemble Amerindians of the Pacific Northwest live in northeastern Siberia. These tribes — the Kamchadals, the Koryaks, and the Chukchi — live by hunting and fishing. They number about 20,000 people. Tribes of Mongoloid people — the Yakuts, Tungus, and Samoyeds — reside in north-central Siberia and live mainly by raising reindeer. There are nearly 420,000 of these people.

The European part of the Arctic lies across the northern parts of Russia, Finland, Norway, and Sweden. In the Arctic part of European Russia live some 250,000 people called Zyrians. These people, who are related to modern Finlanders, hunt, fish, and herd reindeer for a living.

The Arctic part of Norway, Sweden, and Finland, together with a bit of Russia, has long been known as Lapland, the home of people called Lapps. Lapps are short and muscular, with slightly yellowish skin and straight black hair. Scientists think the Lapps may have come to Lapland from central Asia many thousands of years ago.

There are nearly 45,000 Lapps. Some are nomadic. They raise herds of reindeer that they follow from place to place as the animals search for edible vegetation. Other Lapps live near the sea and make their living mainly by fishing. Still others hunt, fish, and raise reindeer. All Lapps speak a language that is much like Finnish, but it is spoken with different dialects in different parts of Lapland.

People have never settled in the earth's south polar region, the Antarctic, as they have in the Arctic. People do live in Antarctica today, but they are mainly scientists studying the continent for various reasons. These people are really only visitors, however. They live in temporary housing, and their supplies are delivered by ship or by airplane.

Murmansk is Russia's chief port on the Arctic Ocean and the world's largest city north of the Arctic Circle.

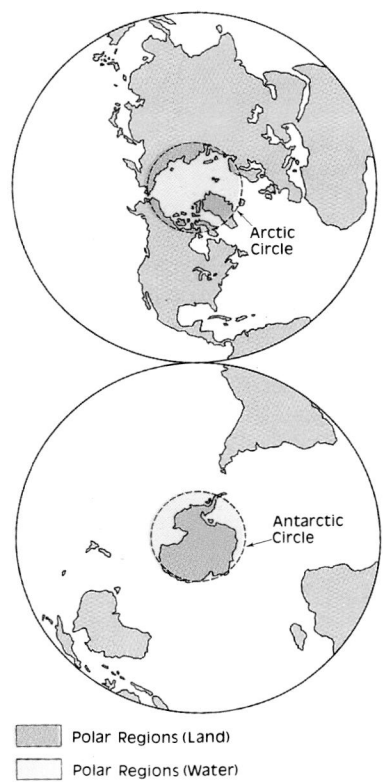

Polar Regions (Land)
Polar Regions (Water)

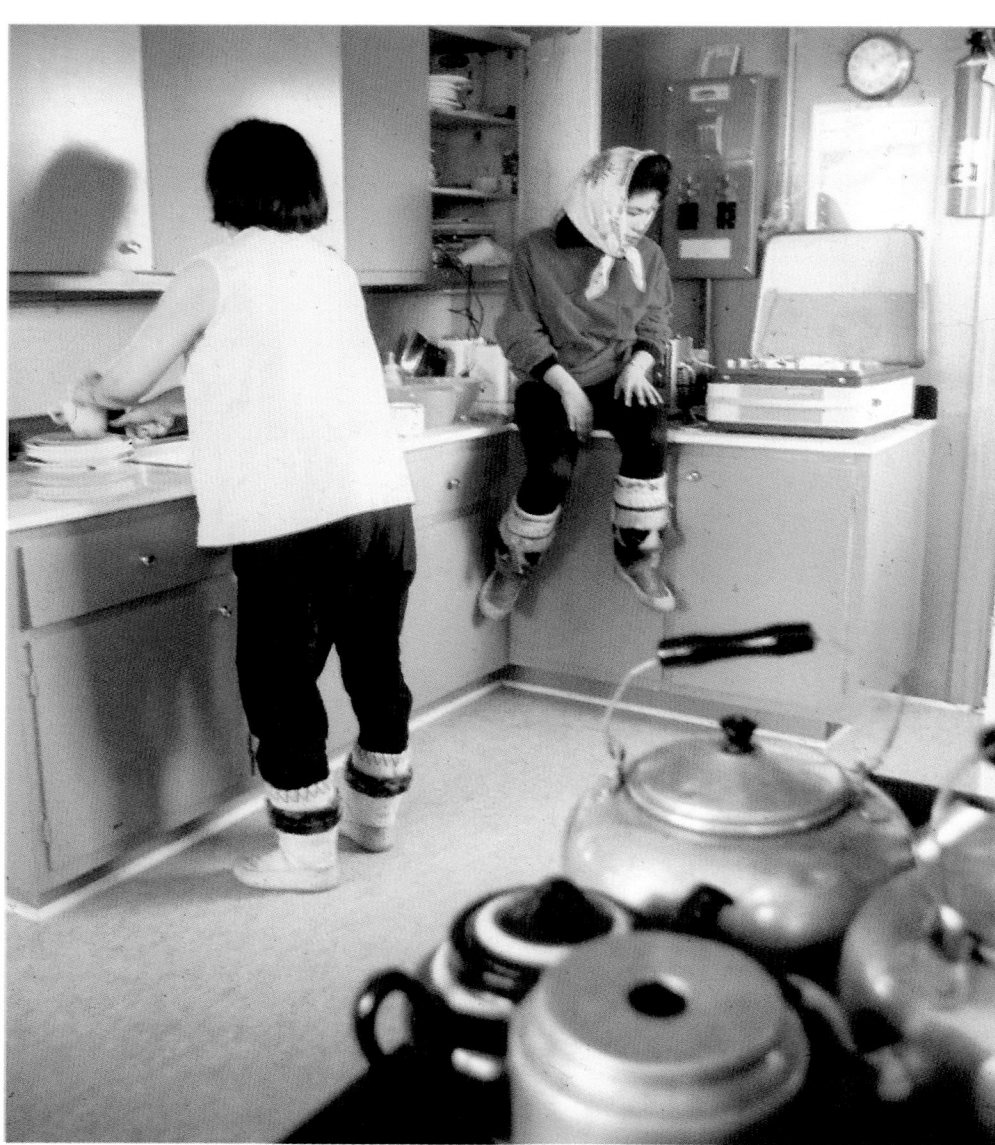

Most Inuit today live in wooden or prefabricated housing, instead of in tents or houses made of snow or sod.

Some Lapps support themselves by raising reindeer, which they sell for meat. These Lapps, mostly young men known as Mountain Lapps, live north in the summer and move south with their herds in winter.

Looking at Earth

Earthrise over the moon

Glaciers in southeastern Alaska, U.S.

Kilauea in southeastern Hawaii, U.S.

As a Planet

Eₐᵣₜₕ ...

EARTH IS ONE of the four rocky inner planets of the solar system. It is a ball of molten stone and metal enclosed by a shell of rock. The features of this active planet are in constant change from the action of volcanoes, earthquakes, water, and wind.

Earth in the Solar System

The planet Earth is a huge ball covered with water, rock, and soil. It travels in an orbit — an oval-shaped path — around a star, the sun. The sun, in turn, moves in an orbit around the center of a vast system of stars called a galaxy.

There are at least 100 billion galaxies scattered throughout the observable universe. Each consists of from less than a billion to a trillion or more stars. The galaxy in which Earth and the sun are located is known as the Milky Way.

The Milky Way is a spiral-shaped galaxy of hundreds of billions of stars. All these stars are at incredible distances from one another. The nearest star to the sun and to Earth is approximately 25 million million miles (40 million million kilometers) away.

All stars within a galaxy revolve around the center of the galaxy. The stars that are

The solar system, *below,* contains nine planets and their satellites, plus numerous comets, meteorites, and interplanetary dust. The planets orbit the sun, a rather ordinary star lying about 30,000 light years from the center of the Milky Way.

farthest from the center naturally take longer to make the journey. Both the sun and Earth are located far from the center of the Milky Way. It would take the sun and Earth about 250 million years to make one complete revolution around the center.

Earth is only one of a number of objects that orbit the sun. There are eight other major planets and their moons. There are also some very small minor planets, called asteroids. In addition, various-sized chunks of rock called meteoroids orbit the sun. And there are comets and clouds of dust and gas. All these things, together with the sun, make up what is known as the solar system.

The nine known planets of the solar system orbit the sun at various distances. In order of distance from the sun, these planets are Mercury, Venus, Earth, Mars, Jupiter, Saturn, Uranus, Neptune, and Pluto. Although Pluto is normally the outermost planet, it crossed inside Neptune's orbit in 1979 and will remain there until 1999.

Mercury, Venus, Earth, and Mars are essentially balls of rock and metal. Jupiter,

Saturn, Uranus, and Neptune, called the giant planets, are made up chiefly of gases that are compressed into fluids and contain little iron and rock. Pluto's composition is still unknown. Scientists, however, believe Pluto is like a ball of ice, similar to the satellites of the giant planets.

Earth, the third planet from the sun, circles it at an average distance of 93 million miles (150 million kilometers). The closest planet to Earth is Venus, the second planet from the sun. Venus approaches to within 25.7 million miles (approximately 40 million kilometers) of Earth during its orbit.

But the closest to Earth of all solar-system bodies is its own moon. The moon's mean distance from Earth is only about 238,857 miles (384,403 kilometers). The moon is held in orbit around Earth by the pull of the planet's gravity. Earth's moon is a barren, airless ball of rock. It is about one-fourth the size of Earth. The moon's surface has mountains, valleys, and plains. It is pitted with billions of craters, caused by

Distances from the sun (Figures in millions)

Sun	Mercury	Venus	Earth	Mars	Jupiter
	36 miles	67.2 miles	93 miles	141.6 miles	483.6 miles
	57.9 kilometers	109 kilometers	150 kilometers	228 kilometers	777 kilometers

Mercury is the planet closest to the sun. It also moves around the sun faster than any other planet — once every 88 Earth days. Like Venus, Mercury does not have a moon.

Venus is almost the same size and mass as Earth. But its atmosphere is mostly carbon dioxide, and its temperature is too high to allow life to exist.

Earth, like Pluto, has only one moon. The gravitational pull of Earth keeps the moon in its orbit. Without this pull from Earth, the moon would fly off into space.

Mars has surface conditions that are closer to Earth's than any other planet's. In spite of experiments conducted by space probes, scientists have not been able to determine whether life exists on Mars.

Jupiter, the largest planet, has the fastest spin in the solar system. It rotates once every 9 hours 55 minutes. The rapid spin flattens the planet at the poles. Jupiter has 16 known satellites.

the impact of pieces of rock that have smashed into its surface.

Earth's moon shines because sunlight reflects off its surface. The amount of light-reflecting surface visible from Earth varies when the moon is in different positions as it moves around the planet. These differences account for the phases of the moon, such as first quarter and full moon.

An eclipse of the moon occurs when Earth is directly between the sun and the full moon, casting its shadow on the moon's surface. An eclipse of the sun occurs when the moon passes directly between the sun and Earth, blocking off the sun's light and casting a shadow on Earth.

The spiral galaxy, *above,* like the Milky Way, resembles an enormous pinwheel. However, because of Earth's position in the Milky Way, its pinwheel shape cannot be seen from Earth. Instead, the galaxy appears as a broad, hazy band of starlight stretching across the sky.

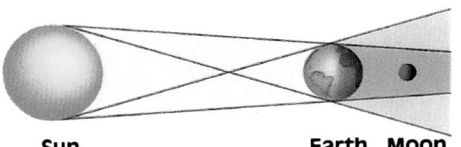

Sun   Earth   Moon

A lunar eclipse takes place when Earth passes between the sun and moon.

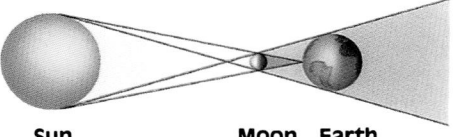

Sun   Moon   Earth

A solar eclipse occurs when the moon passes between the sun and Earth.

Saturn	Uranus	Neptune	Pluto
888.2 miles	1,786.4 miles	2,798.8 miles	3,666.2 miles
1,424 kilometers	2,869 kilometers	4,495 kilometers	5,890 kilometers

Neptune, like Pluto, cannot be seen without a telescope. Neptune has eight moons. One of them, Triton, is the only large satellite in the solar system that travels from east to west.

Saturn, the second largest planet, is circled by seven major rings. Jupiter, Neptune, and Uranus are the only other planets known to have rings, but theirs are much fainter than Saturn's.

Uranus is believed to be basically featureless and surrounded by clouds. Little is known about the planet's surface.

Pluto, which has a moon more than one-third its size, is the most distant planet from the sun. At some point in its oval-shaped orbit, Pluto enters Neptune's orbit and stays there for about 20 years. This event occurs every 248 years.

Earth's Atmosphere and Motion

Like the moon, Earth also glows with reflected sunlight. Seen from space, the planet appears to be a large, dark blue and brown ball covered with wispy white patches. The brown areas are Earth's continents, and the vast blue expanses are its oceans. Of all the planets in the solar system, only Earth has water in liquid form. Oceans, which contain most of Earth's water, cover about 70 per cent of the planet's surface. The white patches are the clouds that drift in Earth's atmosphere.

Earth's atmosphere is the layer of gases that surrounds the planet. The atmosphere of Earth is a mixture of 78 per cent nitrogen, 21 per cent oxygen, and small amounts of several other gases. The atmosphere extends 1,000 miles (1,600 kilometers) from the planet's surface. Earth's atmosphere is thickest within the first 50 miles (80 kilometers) of the planet, and it becomes progressively thinner thereafter.

Venus and Mars also have an atmosphere. The atmosphere of Venus is a thick mixture of mainly carbon dioxide and other gases. It is filled with clouds formed largely of droplets of sulfuric acid and sulfur. The atmosphere of Mars is a thin mixture of carbon dioxide and other gases.

Earth is fifth in size among all the planets and the largest of the rocky inner planets. The Earth's diameter, or distance from one side to the other through its center, is about 7,900 miles (12,713 kilometers) measured from North Pole to South Pole. Earth's circumference, or distance around the planet, is about 24,901.5 miles (40,075.16 kilometers) measured at the equator.

Venus is only slightly smaller than Earth. Mars is about half the size of Earth, and Mercury is about two-fifths as big. However, the diameter of Jupiter—the solar system's largest planet—is more than 11 times the length of Earth's.

Earth rotates on its axis, an imaginary line through the center of the planet from the North Pole to the South Pole. This

Earth is the only planet in the solar system that has enough oxygen surrounding it and enough water on its surface to support life as it is known today. About 70 per cent of Earth's surface is water; the rest is land. All Earth's animals and plants live on or close to the planet's surface.

rotation causes day and night on Earth. As the planet rotates, half of it faces the sun. There it is daytime. The other half faces away from the sun into the blackness of space, and on that half it is nighttime. The planet makes one complete rotation every 23 hours 56 minutes 4.09 seconds. This is the length of Earth's day.

As Earth rotates, it also moves in an orbit around the sun. Earth moves through space at an average speed of 66,600 miles (107,200 kilometers) an hour. One orbit, or revolution around the sun, takes 365 days 6 hours 9 minutes 9.54 seconds. This is the length of Earth's year.

Earth's axis is tilted, rather than straight up and down. This tilt and Earth's orbit around the sun cause the seasons. During part of the orbit, the northern half of the planet is tilted toward the sun. In this position, the northern half receives more light and heat than the southern half. This is summer for the northern portion of the planet and winter for the southern portion, which is tilted away from the sun. During another part of the orbit, the southern half of the planet is tilted toward the sun, and seasons are reversed.

Rotation

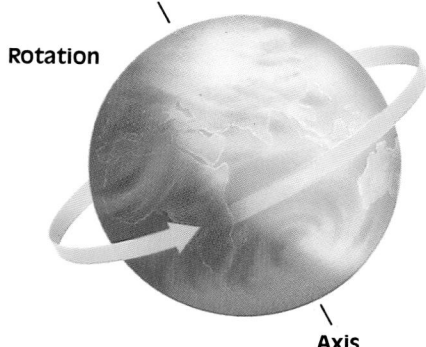

Axis

Earth spins eastward around its axis once every 23 hours 56 minutes and 4.09 seconds. Earth circles the sun once every 365 days 6 hours 9 minutes and 9.54 seconds.

Revolution

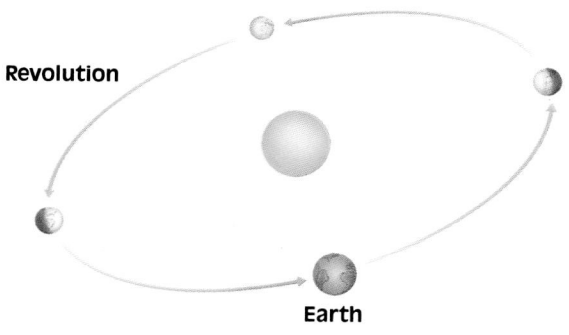

Earth

Altitude

Divisions of the Atmosphere

600 mi. (960 km)

550 mi. (890 km)

500 mi. (800 km)

450 mi. (720 km)

400 mi. (640 km)

350 mi. (560 km)

300 mi. (480 km)

250 mi. (400 km)

200 mi. (320 km)

150 mi. (240 km)

100 mi. (160 km)

50 mi. (80 km)

0 mi./km

Earth's atmosphere consists of four layers, the troposphere, the stratosphere, the mesosphere, and the thermosphere. The diagram on the right shows a detailed enlargement of the first three layers and the lower 70 miles (112 kilometers) of the thermosphere. More than 75 per cent of Earth's air and almost all its weather occurs in the troposphere. The stratosphere contains the ozone layer, which absorbs harmful rays from the sun. Meteor trails can be seen in the mesosphere. Auroral displays, or northern and southern lights, occur in the lower thermosphere.

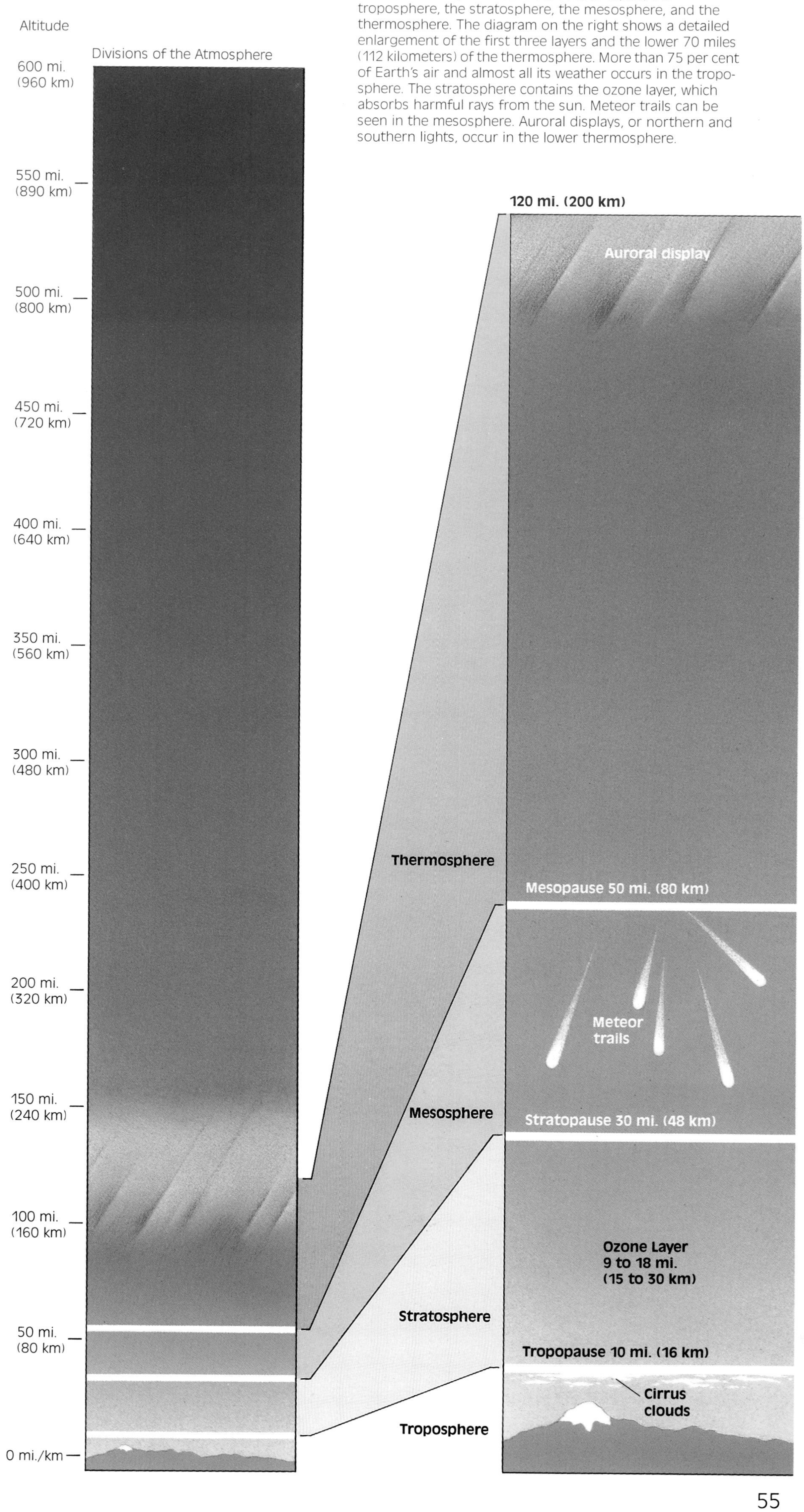

120 mi. (200 km)

Auroral display

Thermosphere

Mesopause 50 mi. (80 km)

Meteor trails

Mesosphere

Stratopause 30 mi. (48 km)

Ozone Layer 9 to 18 mi. (15 to 30 km)

Stratosphere

Tropopause 10 mi. (16 km)

Cirrus clouds

Troposphere

Earth's Structure

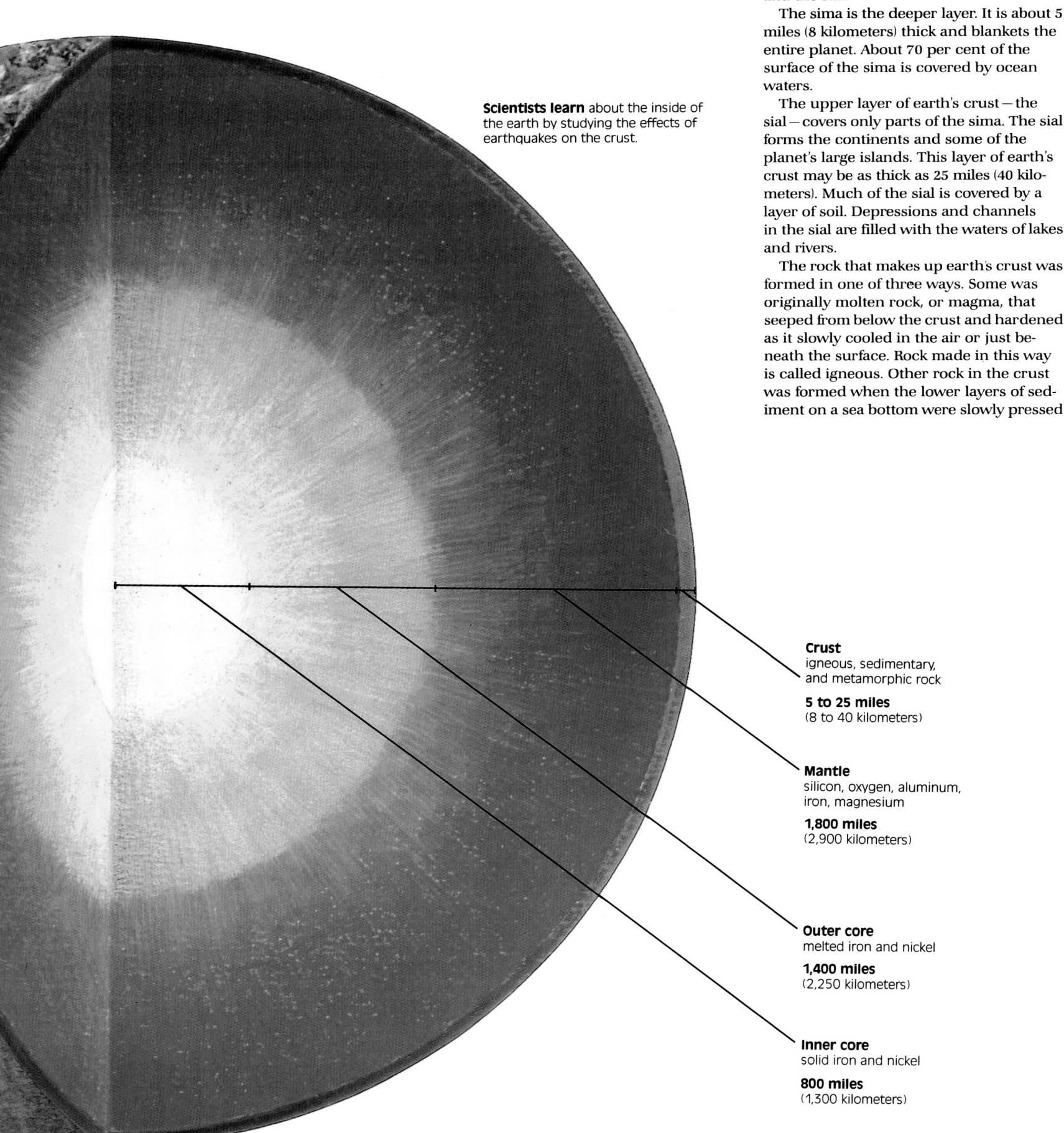

Scientists learn about the inside of the earth by studying the effects of earthquakes on the crust.

The earth is covered by a thin shell of cold, hard rock. This shell is called the crust. It is made up of two layers, the sima and the sial.

The sima is the deeper layer. It is about 5 miles (8 kilometers) thick and blankets the entire planet. About 70 per cent of the surface of the sima is covered by ocean waters.

The upper layer of earth's crust—the sial—covers only parts of the sima. The sial forms the continents and some of the planet's large islands. This layer of earth's crust may be as thick as 25 miles (40 kilometers). Much of the sial is covered by a layer of soil. Depressions and channels in the sial are filled with the waters of lakes and rivers.

The rock that makes up earth's crust was formed in one of three ways. Some was originally molten rock, or magma, that seeped from below the crust and hardened as it slowly cooled in the air or just beneath the surface. Rock made in this way is called igneous. Other rock in the crust was formed when the lower layers of sediment on a sea bottom were slowly pressed

Crust
igneous, sedimentary, and metamorphic rock

5 to 25 miles
(8 to 40 kilometers)

Mantle
silicon, oxygen, aluminum, iron, magnesium

1,800 miles
(2,900 kilometers)

Outer core
melted iron and nickel

1,400 miles
(2,250 kilometers)

Inner core
solid iron and nickel

800 miles
(1,300 kilometers)

together by the tremendous weight of sediment and water from above. This pressure formed the sediment into the kind of rock called sedimentary. Still other rock was formed when igneous and sedimentary rocks were changed by tremendous heat and pressure deep within earth's crust. Later, this rock was pushed to the surface. Such rock is called metamorphic.

Although much of the rock in earth's crust was formed long ago, the process of rock formation continues. Igneous rock is still formed by the cooling of magma. Sedimentary rock is still formed in shallow seas. Metamorphic rock is still pushed up from the lower layer of earth's crust.

Beneath the crust lies a layer of rock called the mantle. This layer extends to a depth of 1,800 miles (2,900 kilometers) thick. The temperatures of rock within the earth get progressively higher toward the center of the planet. The deepest part of the mantle reaches a temperature of 4000° F. (2200° C).

Beneath the mantle is the earth's outer core, which scientists believe is made of melted iron and nickel 1,400 miles (2,250 kilometers) thick. In the outer core, temperatures range from about 4000° F. (2200° C) at the upper level to about 9000° F. (5000° C) at the deepest level. Earth's magnetic field is generated by electricity in the outer core. It is the magnetic field that allows compasses to function.

At the very center of earth lies the inner core. Some scientists believe that this layer is a solid ball of iron and nickel about 800 miles (1,300 kilometers) thick. The temperature of the inner core is about 9000° F. (5000° C). Although the metal of the inner core is hot enough to be melted, the atoms of the metal are pressed together so tightly by gravity that melting is impossible.

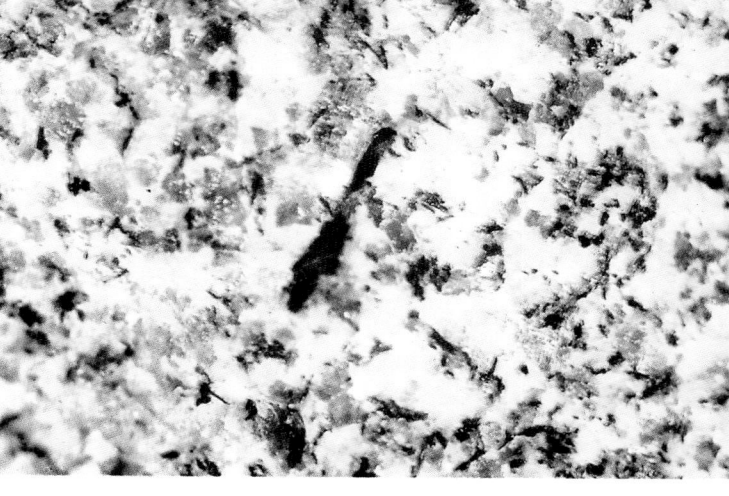

Igneous rocks are formed when melted rock deep inside the crust cools and hardens.

Metamorphic rocks are formed when igneous and sedimentary rocks are chemically and physically changed by heat and pressure.

Sedimentary rocks are developed from material worn away from the land. These rocks may contain fossils—shells, bones, and other remains of living things.

The earth's crust has two layers — the sial, made up of granitelike rocks, and the sima, similar to hardened lava. The moho is the boundary between the crust and the mantle.

Earthquakes and Volcanoes

The earth's crust is continually changing. Most of the time, this change is so gradual that only the most sophisticated scientific equipment can detect it. But sometimes tremendous forces inside the earth unleash their power in sudden events that cause dramatic changes in the earth's surface. These events include volcanic eruptions and earthquakes.

An earthquake is the sometimes violent shaking of the earth's surface that happens as a result of the movement of the materials in the crust and mantle beneath it. The strongest earthquakes can tumble buildings, change the course of rivers, or shift parts of the ocean floor and send giant tidal waves charging across the sea. A volcano is an opening in the earth's surface where red-hot molten rock, called magma, escapes from deep inside the earth. Volcanic eruptions can create mountains and islands and cover hundreds of square miles (kilometers) with flowing lava or ash.

Most earthquakes and volcanoes occur at the boundaries between giant sections of the earth's outermost layer, called plates. These plates are in constant motion in relation to one another. They slowly glide over a zone of partially melted rock in the earth's mantle at a rate of ½ to 4 inches (1.3 to 10 centimeters) a year. Most earthquakes and volcanoes occur as a result of this movement.

Earthquakes occur along faults, which are breaks in the earth's crust. The rock that makes up the earth's crust is cold and rigid. As a result, it does not glide along smoothly as does the hot rock at deeper levels. The movement of the plates past each other combined with the resistance of the rock on each side of the fault create a build-up of stress at the fault. Eventually, the stress exceeds the rock's strength. Each side of the fault snaps to a new position to "catch up" with the plate it is attached to, and an earthquake occurs.

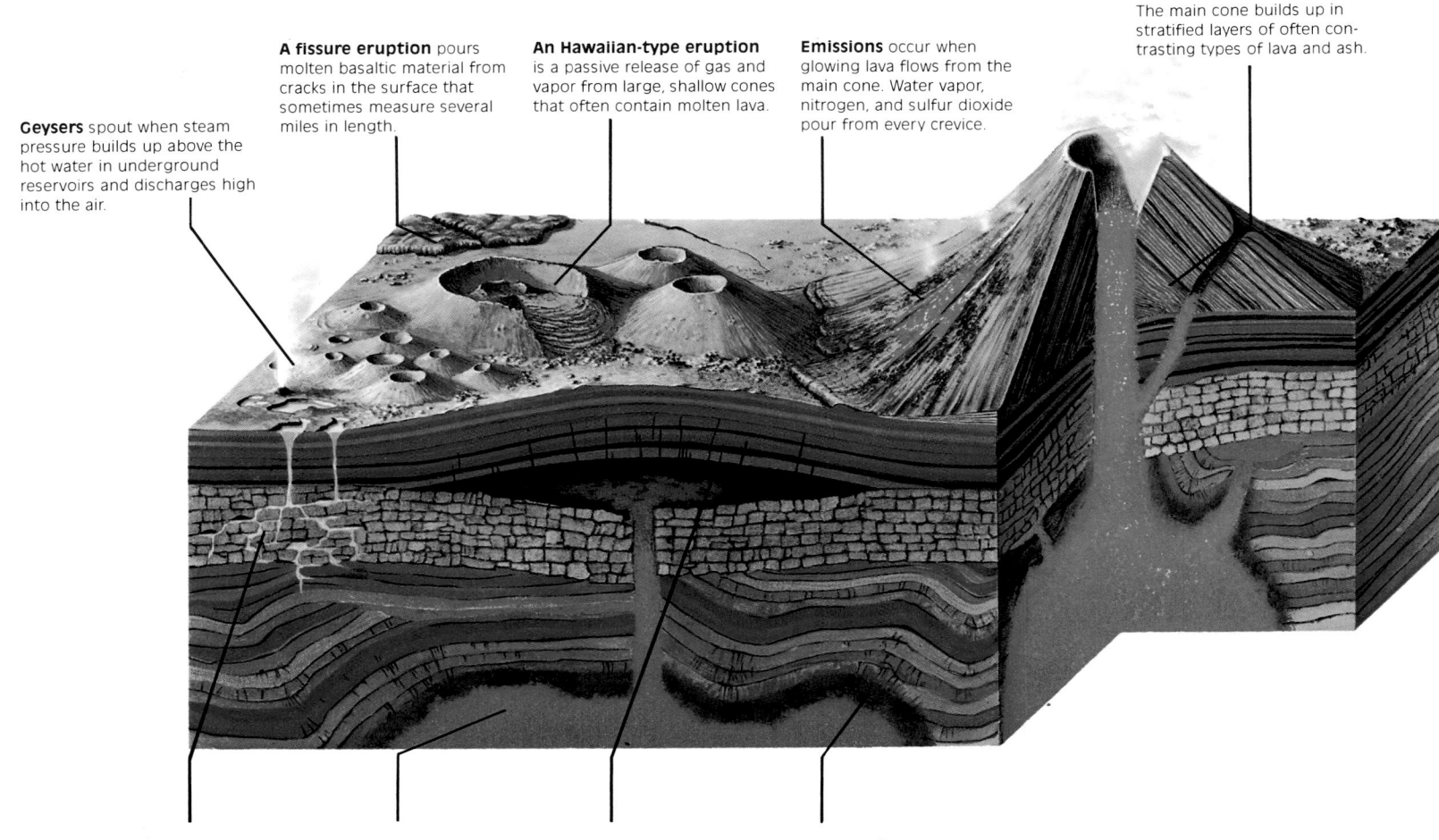

Geysers spout when steam pressure builds up above the hot water in underground reservoirs and discharges high into the air.

A fissure eruption pours molten basaltic material from cracks in the surface that sometimes measure several miles in length.

An Hawaiian-type eruption is a passive release of gas and vapor from large, shallow cones that often contain molten lava.

Emissions occur when glowing lava flows from the main cone. Water vapor, nitrogen, and sulfur dioxide pour from every crevice.

Layering is the product of millions of years of eruptions. The main cone builds up in stratified layers of often contrasting types of lava and ash.

Underground water, heated under pressure to beyond the normal boiling point, rushes out whenever pressure is relieved.

A magma chamber contains intensely hot magma under high pressure. Every volcano has one.

Laccolith forms a huge lens of cooled rock above the hot magma chamber.

Metamorphic rock forms near the magma chamber when heat and intense pressure create chemical and physical changes in sedimentary and igneous strata.

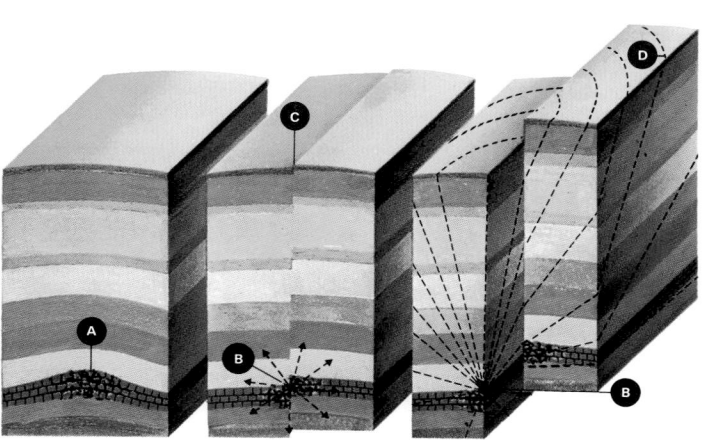

How earthquakes happen.
Stresses build over many years until the breaking strength of some part of the rock along a fault line or other line of potential movement is exceeded (**A**). Shock waves move out in all directions (**B**). The epicenter (**C**) is on the surface directly above the break. The most damage is done by the earthquake when the shock waves reach the surface (**D**).

The San Andreas Fault, a major break in the earth's crust, extends more than 750 miles (1,210 kilometers) through California and produces a major quake every few hundred years.

The snapping of the rock causes vibrations called seismic waves to move out in all directions. The waves move like ripples in a pond after a stone is dropped into it. It is these waves that cause the damage to the earth's surface and to objects on it.

Earthquakes may occur at the surface of the earth or at depths of up to 400 miles (640 kilometers) below the surface. The point of an earthquake's origin is called its focus. The quake's epicenter is the place on the surface of the earth directly above the focus.

Many volcanoes form where the edge of one plate overlaps another and pushes it down into the mantle. There, portions of the plate melt to form magma and large amounts of gas. The mixture rises toward the surface and eventually collects in a magma chamber just beneath the earth's surface. The pressure of the surrounding rock forces the mixture in the magma chamber up through the surface of the earth, creating an opening called a central vent. Magma that has penetrated the earth's surface is called lava.

Lava builds up around the central vent. As the lava cools, it forms a cone-shaped volcanic mountain. Volcanic mountains can be either low and broad or tall and pointed.

Some volcanoes also form when the edges of two plates move apart from each other, allowing magma from the mantle to seep up between them. Most of this type of volcanic activity occurs on the ocean floor. The tops of some of these volcanoes become islands, such as Iceland.

A few volcanoes have developed near the center of plates far from the edges. Scientists think this happens when huge magma columns, called plumes, push up into the crust. The Hawaiian Islands were formed by this type of volcanic action, which continues today at Kilauea, a famous volcano on the island of Hawaii.

Seismographic stations throughout the Pacific watch for earthquake shocks and oceanic tidal waves that sometimes follow. Here concentric rings show the time necessary for a tidal wave to travel from the point above the earthquake's center in Hawaii.

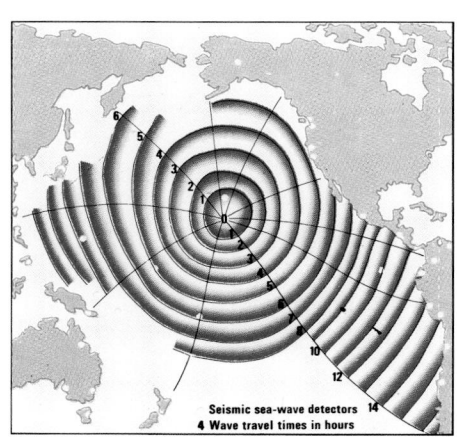

Earth's Changing Surface

The earth's surface is constantly undergoing changes. Some changes are rapid, such as those caused by landslides, earthquakes, and volcanic eruptions. But other changes are slow and steady. Mountains are worn flat. Deep canyons are carved. Fertile lands lose their rich soil. Coastlines change shape.

One of the chief causes of the slow and steady changes in earth's surface is erosion, or the breaking down and movement of the planet's rock and soil by natural forces. A major factor in erosion is water, both in its liquid and in its solid form — ice.

Erosion begins with weathering, a process in which various environmental factors break down soil and rock and release them from earth's surface. Ice is a primary factor in weathering. Ice forms when water trapped inside the cracks of rocks freezes. As water becomes ice, it expands and can break the rock into fragments. Melting snow and rain that beats down on weathered rocks washes away billions of dust-sized particles. These bits of rock are carried into streams and rivers. As rivers move along, they tear more tiny bits of rock out of the channels through which they flow. After many thousands or millions of years, the action of flowing water can form a deep canyon or flatten a mountain.

Coastlines and lake shores are also altered by the force of water. Waves crashing against cliffs break away loose pieces of rock. The constant beating of the waves causes a crushing and grinding that breaks boulders into pebbles and pebbles into sand. In some places, the shoreline is slowly pushed back, and the sea takes its place. In other places, waves combine with wind, another major factor in erosion, to increase the land by moving sand from one location to another. This process helps build up beaches.

Wind can carry particles of earth great distances. If there are no trees or grasses to protect the land, wind may pick up tons of dry, dusty soil. This can rob farmland of rich soil. In time, the area may become almost a desert.

Wind that carries sand or sandy soil can also cause erosion in rocky places. A steady stream of wind-blown sand striking against stone can rub off or sandblast tiny particles and carry them away. Rocks that have been eroded in this way are common in many deserts.

The effects of water erosion can be as spectacular as the gooseneck canyons cut by the San Juan River in Utah.

Wind erosion: (1) parabolic blowout, **(2)** parabolic hairpin, **(3)** longitudinal ridge.

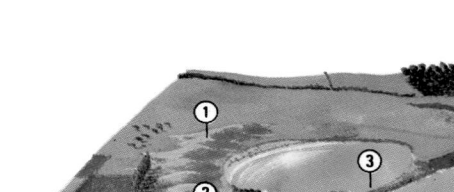

Sea erosion: (1) dunes, **(2)** deposition, **(3)** spit, **(4)** arch, **(5)** stack, **(6)** raised beach, **(7)** caves.

River erosion: (A) youthful stage, **(B)** mature stage, **(C)** old age stage, **(1)** pothole, **(2)** oxbow, **(3)** meander.

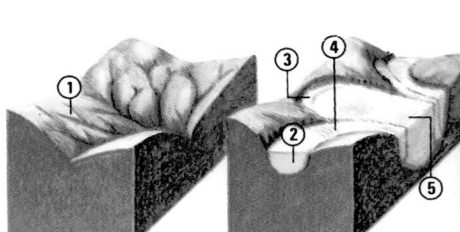

Glacial erosion: (1) preglacial rock, **(2)** valley, **(3)** bergschrund, **(4)** crevasses, **(5)** longitudinal moraine, **(6)** valley-floor moraines, **(7)** peaks and **(8)** valley carved by tributary, **(9)** terminal moraine.

Ice, in the form of glaciers, has been responsible for enormous changes on earth's surface in the past. Glaciers are huge rivers of ice that move at very slow rates and flow over anything in their paths. Some glaciers are still at work. They form when deep snow turns to ice on mountaintops. The ice, which can move slowly downward, may widen an old valley or gouge out a new one. It can also pick up and carry tons of soil or rock and deposit them hundreds of miles (kilometers) away. When a glacier melts, it can fill a depression with fresh water, thus creating a new lake. If the Antarctic icecap, which is a glacier, would melt, it could drastically raise the level of ocean waters. This would cause floods that could change the coastlines of continents.

The Australian rock formation, *above,* shows the sculptural effects of wind carrying sand and other debris.

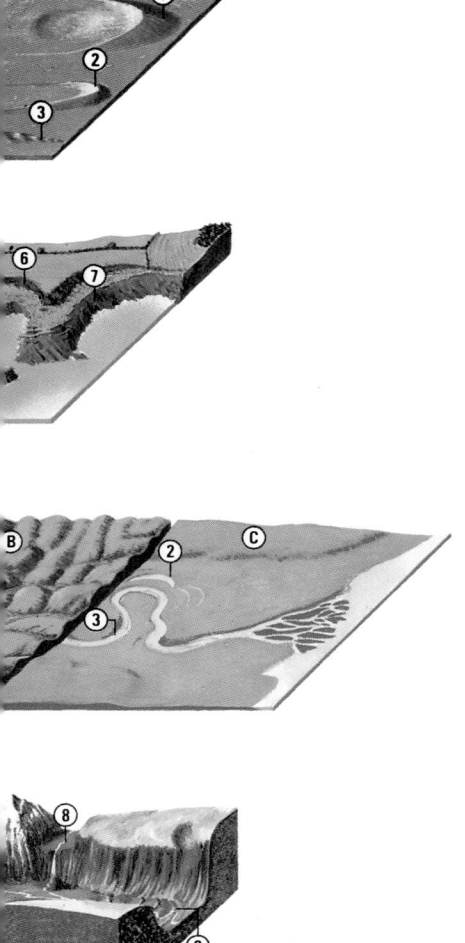

Glaciated valleys and terraces such as those in Ortnevik, Norway, are typically formed over thousands of years.

Beneath the Ocean

If all earth's ocean water would suddenly vanish, the planet would present a new landscape. There would be vast plains, slopes, deep valleys, and ranges of towering mountains never seen before. These features now lie beneath the water, forming the sea bottom.

Along the coasts of the continents, from the edges of the shores, the muddy or rocky ocean bottom slopes gently out beneath the water. This submerged land is known as the continental shelves. They are coated by thick layers of sediment that were carried to the coasts by rivers.

From the edges of the continental shelves, the ocean bottom slants downward more sharply, forming what are called the continental slopes. Deep canyons cut through the slopes in some places. Far below the surface of the water, the continental slopes merge with the abyss, or deep ocean bottom. The depth of the abyss ranges from 10,000 feet (3,040 meters) to 18,000 feet (5,486 meters). The abyssal plains are broad, almost completely flat areas that make up 30 per cent of earth's total surface. Most of the plains are covered with thick sediment.

A range of towering submarine mountains, known as the Mid-Atlantic Ridge, stretches north to south along the middle of the Atlantic Ocean bottom for 10,000 miles (16,000 kilometers). The peaks of a number of mountains in this range stick up above the water. They create islands in the Atlantic Ocean, such as the Azores

All submarine landscapes follow the same general pattern, although details vary from ocean to ocean. The layout includes a volcanic ridge, which may break the surface in places, broad abyssal plains with occasional deep trenches, and continents bordered by shallow slopes and shelves.

A Volcano in midocean ridge
B Deep oceanic trench
C Continental shelf
D Abyssal plain
E Midocean ridge
F Guyots
G Oceanic islands
X1 Upper granitic crust and sediments
X2 Lower granitic crust
Y Basaltic crust
S Sediment
Z Mantle

Features of the ocean floor

Aleutian Basin	B	8	Canada Plain	A	8	East Pacific Rise	E	9
Aleutian Trench	B	8	Canary Basin	C	2	Eltanin		
Angola Basin	D	3	Challenger			Fracture Zone	E	9
Arabian Basin	D	5	Fracture Zone	E	9	Emperor Seamounts	C	7
Argentine Basin	E	2	Clarion			Falkland Trough	E	2
Atlantic-Indian			Fracture Zone	C	9	Grand Banks	B	2
Basin	F	4	Clipperton			Hawaiian Ridge	C	8
Atlantic-Indian			Fracture Zone	D	9	Japan Trench	C	7
Ridge	F	4	Diamantina			Kerguelen		
Baffin Basin	A	1	Fracture Zone	E	6	Plateau	F	5
Bermuda Rise	C	1	Dogger Bank	B	3	Kermadec Trench	E	8

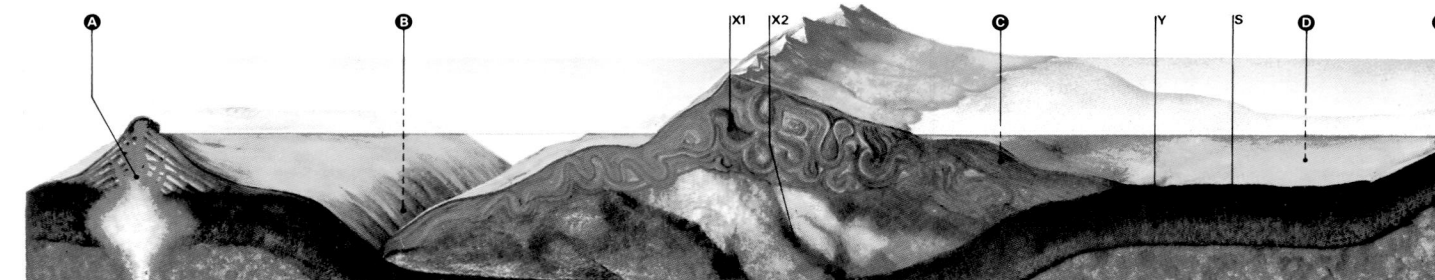

The ocean floor consists of narrow valleys, broad plains, and huge mountain ranges. Major undersea landforms are shown on the map, *below.* The map index indicates their locations.

and Ascension. A continuation of the Mid-Atlantic Ridge circles the southern tip of Africa and extends beneath the Indian Ocean. Underwater mountains also extend between Australia and Antarctica, as well as beneath the Pacific Ocean to Mexico.

The deepest parts of the ocean bottom are long, narrow trenches, or valleys. These trenches are filled with sediment that is often hundreds of feet (meters) thick. The earth's deepest trench is the Mariana Trench. It is 43 miles (68.8 kilometers) wide and 1,580 miles (2,550 kilometers) long. Its bottom is 36,198 feet (11,033 meters) below the surface of the Pacific Ocean.

Many of earth's resources, such as minerals, oil, and gas, are found beneath the ocean waters. The continental shelves are particularly rich in oil. In fact, about 20 per cent of the world's oil supply comes from offshore drilling in modern or ancient river deltas. Rocks containing manganese, a mineral that is important in the production of steel, are scattered all over the ocean floor. There are large deposits of metals, among them nickel and cobalt, on some parts of the sea floor. It seems likely that additional deposits of minerals and other useful substances will be discovered beneath the sea.

Stages of a coral island are shown here from left to right. First, a volcanic peak on a submarine ridge starts to sink beneath the sea. Next, coral grows, forming a shallow saltwater lagoon. When the original island disappears, the coral continues its upward growth and fills in the lagoon. Eventually the coral atoll sinks beneath the surface. The submerged island is called a guyot.

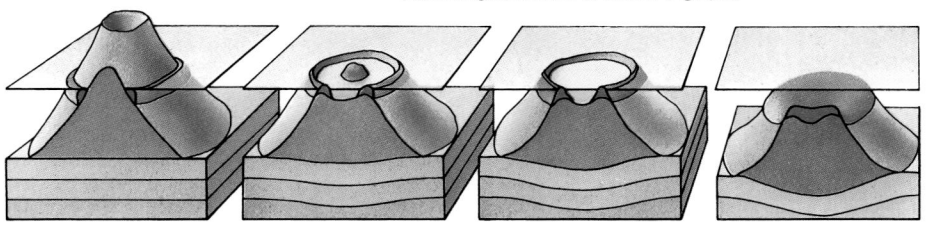

Earth's Minerals

All the rock on earth is formed of materials known as minerals. These substances are inorganic, which means they are made of matter that was never living. Some minerals such as gold are one single chemical element. Others are mixtures of elements. For example, hematite, also known as iron ore, consists of iron and oxygen.

The word "mineral" means something that is mined, or dug out of the earth. Nearly all minerals are formed inside the earth and can be removed only by mining. However, not all substances that are mined are minerals. Coal and oil are mined from the earth, but these substances are not minerals because they were formed from the remains of living things.

Atoms are incredibly tiny basic units of matter. In minerals, atoms are always arranged in repeated, three-dimensional patterns of flat surfaces and angles. These patterns of square or triangular shapes are called crystals. Its crystalline pattern determines one of the chief characteristics of a mineral—hardness. For example, a crystalline pattern formed of loosely packed atoms is softer than one formed of tightly packed atoms. Thus, some minerals, among them talc, are soft enough to be scratched by a fingernail. Other minerals, however, such as diamonds are extremely hard.

In addition to hardness, three other main characteristics of a mineral are its luster, cleavage, and color. The luster of a mineral may be shiny like metal, or it may be nonmetallic. A mineral's cleavage is the way it splits into pieces that have flat surfaces. The color of a mineral can result from its chemical composition or from chemical impurities in its crystals.

Minerals form in different ways. Many are brought into earth's crust in the hot, molten rock that seeps up from the mantle. The atoms of the various elements and compounds that make up the hot liquid are far apart and moving rapidly. As the liquid cools, the atoms slow down and come together, settling into crystalline patterns and forming minerals.

Some minerals form when hot gases erupt from volcanoes and vents in the earth's crust. The hot gases carry steam and particles of dust into the air. The gases cool suddenly when they reach the surface, and the atoms of certain elements join to form crystals that fall to the ground.

Still other minerals form by the slow evaporation of water in which the minerals are dissolved. As some of the water evaporates, the atoms of mineral elements move together in the remaining waters. Finally the atoms form into their crystalline shape.

There are about 3,000 different minerals. Many are highly useful to people, and some are essential. Minerals are used in food preparation, art, manufacturing, building, agriculture, and medicine. Many countries make their coins out of the metal minerals silver and nickel. Gold is a highly valued mineral used as international currency. Other minerals form valuable gemstones such as emeralds, rubies, and sapphires.

Copper, one of the world's most useful minerals, is used in products ranging from wiring for homes and machinery to pots and pans. Copper is mined throughout the world, often in large open-pit mines like the one shown here.

Salt crystals are almost perfect cubes. The source of all salt, even underground deposits, is brine, or salty water.

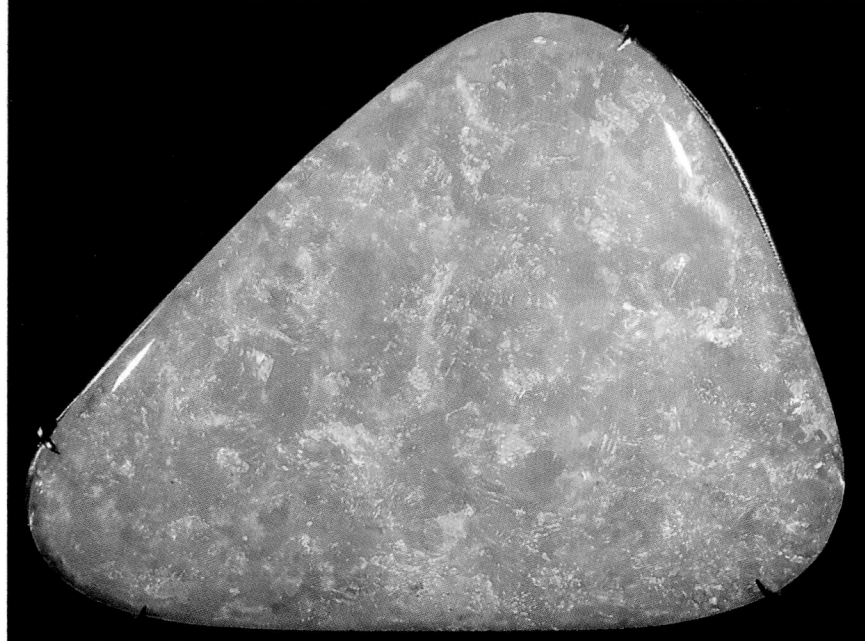

Opal is a gem made of silica that contains water. The water in an opal breaks the light that strikes it into brilliant internal colors.

An azure-blue color is characteristic of azurite, a copper mineral chiefly used as jewelry.

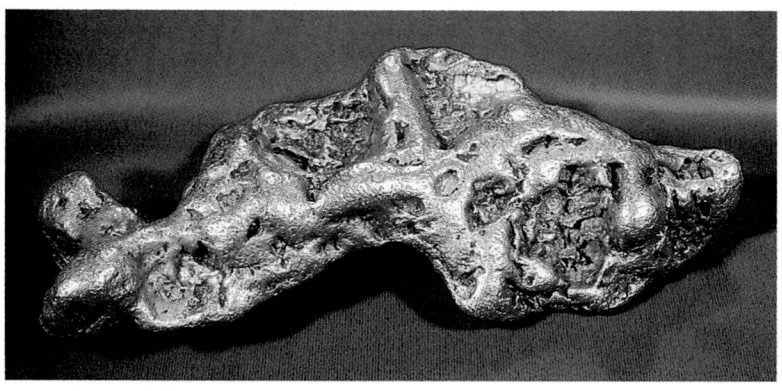

The metallic luster of gold does not tarnish. Gold, one of the first known metals, is prized for its beauty and scarcity.

Mica cleaves along specific planes — that is, it splits in one direction and forms thin sheets.

The hardest mineral is the diamond. It has a hardness of 10 on a hardness scale developed by Friedrich Mohs in 1822. A fingernail has a hardness of about 2 on the scale.

Natural vegetation in
New Mexico, U.S.

World map made in Italy in the mid-1500's

Egyptian painting from the 2000's B.C. that appears to show the mapping of a field

Understanding Maps

To UNDERSTAND the meanings of the lines, words, symbols, and colors on a map is to understand the distribution and arrangement of part or all of the earth's features.

The History of Maps

It is likely that some forms of maps were made as long ago as prehistoric times. There are archaeologists who believe that certain markings in cave paintings and other marks scratched onto bone tablets could have shown game routes and hunting trails.

The earliest map in existence that clearly shows features of land is a Babylonian clay tablet. It dates back to about 2500 B.C. In 1300 B.C., the Egyptians were also making maps of their surrounding area. It was not until the time of the Greek philosophers and geographers that people began to think about the nature of the earth as a whole. It was the Greeks who first projected the idea that the earth was round. It was they who developed a system of parallels and meridians and a method of projecting them.

The greatest geographer and mapmaker of the ancient world was Claudius Ptolemy, who lived in Alexandria, Egypt, about A.D. 150. Ptolemy wrote the eight-volume *Geographia*. This work includes Ptolemy's map of the world, as well as instructions for making maps.

The earliest surviving globe was made in 1623 by Jesuit missionaries. The long legend on the globe contains one of the earliest known references to the force of gravity.

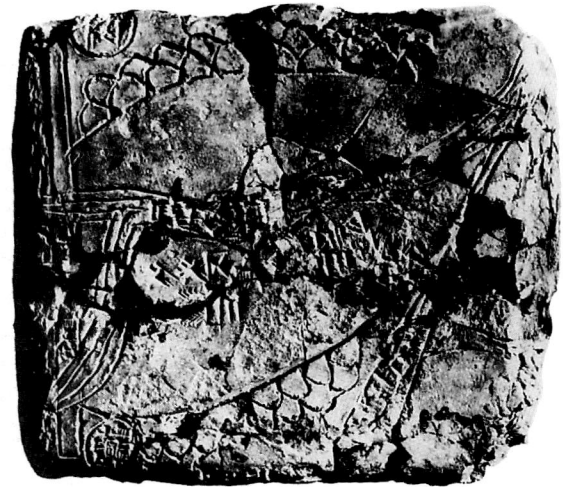

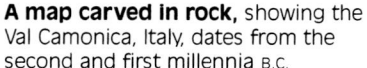

The oldest known map, made about 2500 B.C., is on a clay tablet found in Iraq that seems to show a valley estate.

A map carved in rock, showing the Val Camonica, Italy, dates from the second and first millennia B.C.

Ptolemy made one error that had far-reaching effects. He showed Europe and Asia as taking up half the globe and being much closer to each other than they actually are. Ptolemy's influence was so strong that about 1,700 years later, Columbus thought he had to sail only about 2,400 nautical miles (4,400 kilometers) to reach Asia from Spain. The actual distance is about 11,000 nautical miles (20,400 kilometers). Instead of reaching Cathay and India as he planned to do, Columbus discovered America.

The Middle Ages saw little progress in mapmaking. However, toward the end of that period, about the year 1300, the portolan chart came into being. Drawn on sheepskin, portolan charts were much in demand by people involved in trade and shipping. Ships' pilots and captains from cities such as Genoa, Pisa, Venice, and Barcelona contributed information about sailing routes, ports, and anchorages.

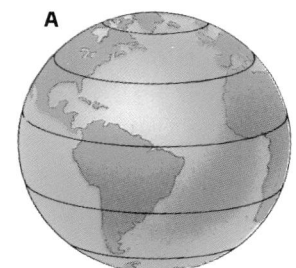
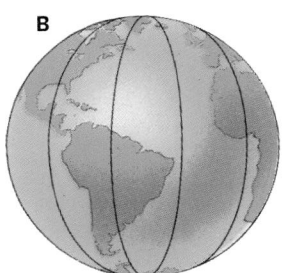
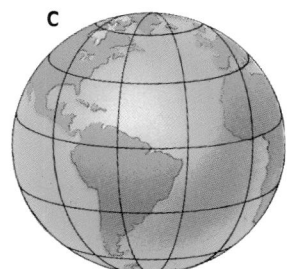

Lines of latitude (A) **and longitude** (B) are measured in degrees and enable every place on earth to be located by coordinates (C). The astrolabe, *left,* helped navigators in the Middle Ages establish latitude, or distance north and south from the equator, which has a latitude of 0 degrees. Longitude measures east-west distance from the prime meridian that passes through Greenwich, a borough of London, England. The longitude of the prime meridian is 0 degrees.

LandSat 1, a satellite, took the 46 infrared pictures that form this photomosaic of Italy.

Another thing that occurred in the Middle Ages also interested people in world maps and increased the sales of such maps. Marco Polo's travels to China gave people a desire to know the world. This desire probably helped lead to the great age of discovery and exploration.

The discoveries of explorers such as Columbus, da Gama, Vespucci, and Magellan changed the world maps during the 1400's and 1500's. The most important mapmaker of the period was Mercator of Flanders. He produced both globes and maps. Mercator also developed a map projection that was of great aid to sailors.

Mapmaking became more accurate and more scientific beginning in the 1700's. The use of new instruments such as the telescope and the chronometer—an instrument used in determining longitude at sea—made much more information available to mapmakers.

Great progress in mapping took place in the 1900's. Road maps for car travel first became widely used about 1910. Air travel, another form of transportation that developed in the early 1900's, required entirely different kinds of maps. Ever since World War I, aerial photography has played the major role in mapping. In 1940, after the U.S. Air Force reported that less than 10 per cent of the world was mapped sufficiently for the use of pilots, a major program was developed to map great areas of the world.

Much of the equipment still in use today had been developed by World War II. Since then, computers, satellites, and automation have made mapping even easier and more accurate.

How to Read Maps

Map language is a kind of code made up of elements such as scale, symbols, color, and grids. Understanding those elements allows the reader to break the map code.

Scale refers to the measurement on a map that represents a certain portion of the earth. A map scale may be shown as a representative fraction, in written form, or graphically.

As a representative fraction, a map scale might be written *1:3,300,000*. This means that one unit on the map represents 3,300,000 of the same units on the earth's surface (1 inch = 3,300,000 inches; 1 centimeter = 3,300,000 centimeters). In written form, the same proportion would be *1 inch = about 52 miles* or *1 centimeter = 33 kilometers.*

A graphic scale, also called a bar scale, is represented by a straight line on which distances have been marked off. Each mark represents a certain number of miles or kilometers.

Symbols allow mapmakers, or cartographers, to include a great deal of information clearly and concisely. Some symbols represent natural features of the land, such as mountains and lakes. Others represent cultural features such as cities and roads. Usually, a map contains a legend, which is a key that lists and explains the symbols used.

Color helps the map reader interpret what is shown. Mapmakers generally use blue for water, green for vegetation, and black or red for roads and place names.

Grid lines called meridians and parallels are used to mark longitude and latitude. Meridians are north-south lines drawn from pole to pole. Parallels are east-west lines drawn around a globe.

Learning to read maps is a skill. Like all skills, it requires practice. The ability to interpret a map will help the reader understand the earth, its features, and its people.

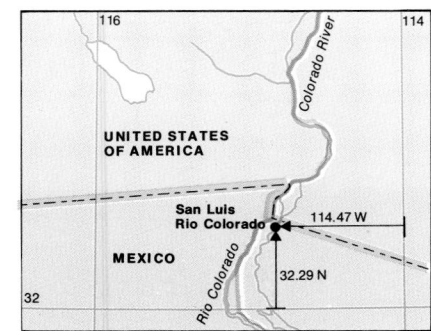

Any location can be expressed in terms of its latitude and longitude, the straight blue lines on the diagram above. San Luis on the Rio Colorado in Mexico is 32 degrees, 29 minutes (sixtieths of a degree) north of the equator and 114 degrees, 47 minutes west of Greenwich.

Maps often attempt to show what the surface of the earth looks like. For example, shading suggests that mountains rise above the land's surface. Detailed information about cities, boundaries, and roads can also appear on a map. The locations of various points of interest can be indicated as well.

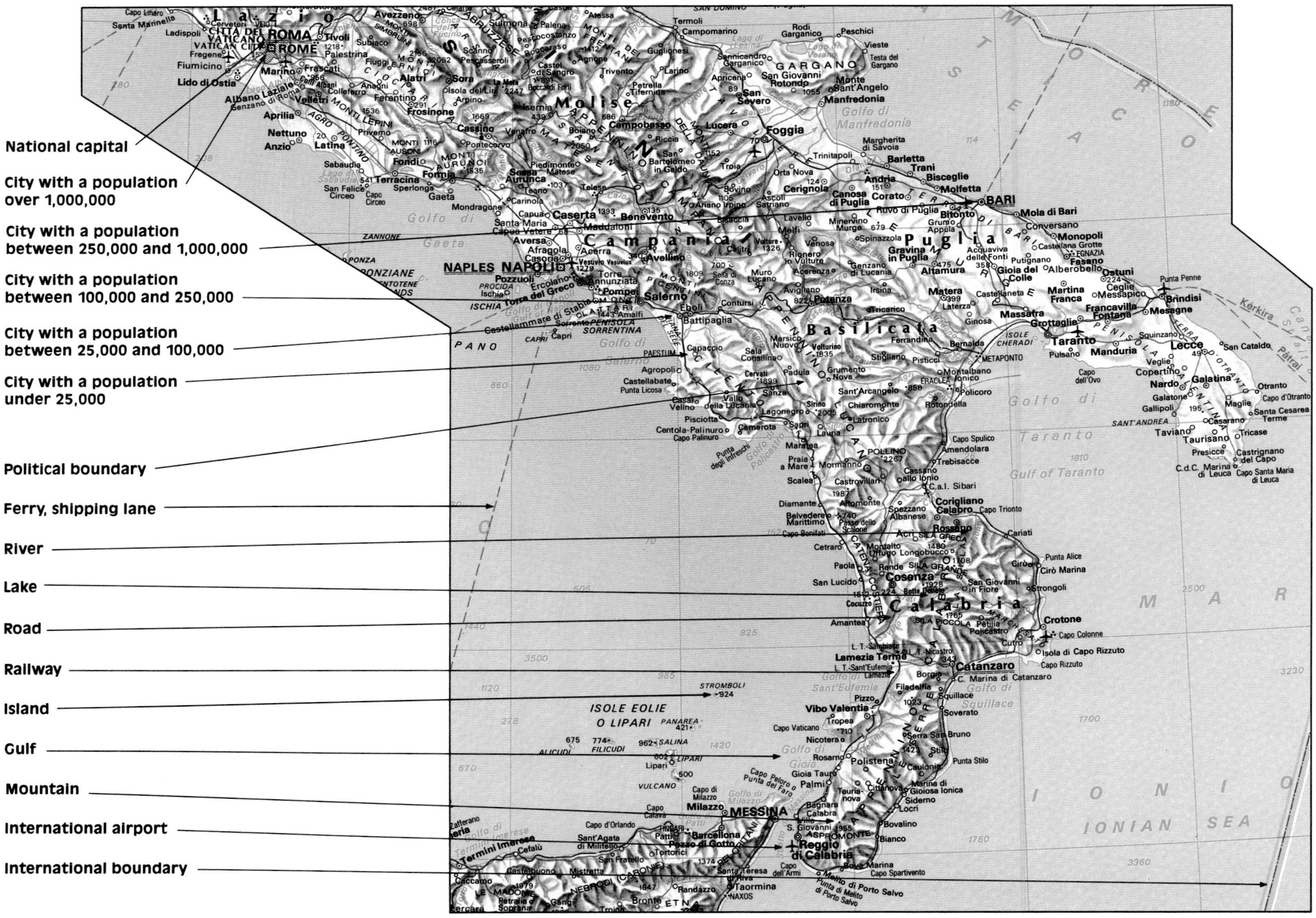

National capital

City with a population over 1,000,000

City with a population between 250,000 and 1,000,000

City with a population between 100,000 and 250,000

City with a population between 25,000 and 100,000

City with a population under 25,000

Political boundary

Ferry, shipping lane

River

Lake

Road

Railway

Island

Gulf

Mountain

International airport

International boundary

Maps of the World

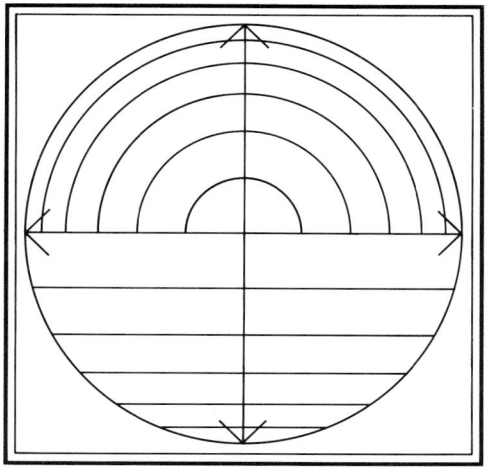

LEGEND

Hydrographic and Topographic Features
Symboles hydrographiques et morphologiques
Gewässer- und Geländeformen
Idrografia, Morfologia
Hidrografía y morfología

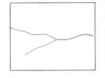 **River, Stream**
Cours d'eau permanent
Ständig wasserführender Fluß
Corso d'acqua perenne
Corriente de agua de régimen permanente

 Lake
Lac d'eau douce
Süßwassersee
Lago d'acqua dolce
Lago de agua dulce

 Rocks
Ecueils, Roches
Klippen, Felsriffe
Scogli, Rocce
Escollos, Rocas

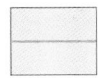 **Summer Limit of Pack-Ice**
Limite du pack en été
Packeisgrenze im Sommer
Limite estivo del pack ghiacciato
Limite estival de banco de hielo

 Intermittent Stream
Cours d'eau intermittent
Zeitweilig wasserführender Fluß
Corso d'acqua periodico
Corriente de agua intermitente

 Intermittent Lake
Lac d'eau douce temporaire
Zeitweiliger Süßwassersee
Lago d'acqua dolce periodico
Lago de agua dulce intermitente

 Reef, Atoll
Barrière, Atoll
Riff, Atoll
Barriera, Atollo
Barrera de arrecifes

 **Winter Limit of Pack-Ice**
Limite du pack en hiver
Packeisgrenze im Winter
Limite invernale del pack ghiacciato
Límite invernal de banco de hielo

 Disappearing Stream
Perte de cours d'eau
Versickernder Fluß
Corso d'acqua che si inabissa
Corriente de agua que desaparece

 **Salt Lake**
Lac d'eau salée
Salzsee
Lago d'acqua salata
Lago de agua salada

 **Mangrove**
Mangrove
Mangrove
Mangrovie
Manglar

 **Limit of Icebergs**
Limite des glaces flottantes
Treibeisgrenze
Limite dei ghiacci alla deriva
Límite de hielo a la deriva

 Undefined or Fluctuating River Course
Cours d'eau incertain
Fluß mit veränderlichem Lauf
Fiume dal corso incerto
Corriente de agua incerta

 Intermittent Salt Lake
Lac d'eau salée temporaire
Zeitweiliger Salzsee
Lago d'acqua salata periodico
Lago de agua salada intermitente

Continental Ice-cap
Glacier continental
Inlandeis. Gletscher
Ghiacciaio continentale
Glaciar continental

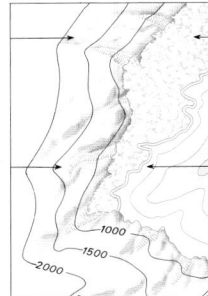 **Ice Shelf**
Banquise
Schelfeis oder Eisschelf
Banchisa polare (Ice-shelf)
Banquisa

 Waterfall, Rapids, Cataract
Chute, Rapide, Cataracte
Wasserfall, Stromschnelle, Katarakt
Cascada, Rapida, Cateratta
Cascada, Rapido, Catarata

 Dry Lake Bed
Lac asséché
Trockener Seeboden
Alveo di lago asciutto
Lecho de lago seco

Glacial Tongue
Langue glaciaire
Gletscherzunge
Lingua di ghiaccio
Lengua de glaciar

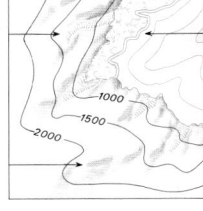 **Limit of Ice Shelf**
Limite de la banquise
Schelfeisgrenze
Limite della banchisa
Límite de la banquisa

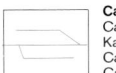 **Canal**
Canal
Kanal
Canale
Canal

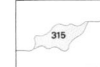 **Lake Surface Elevation**
Cote du lac au-dessus du niveau de la mer
Höhe des Seespiegels
Altitudine del lago
Elevación de lago sobre el nivel del mar

Rocky Areas (Antarctica)
Région de roches (Antarctique)
Eisfreie Gebiete, Gebirge (Antarktika)
Aree rocciose (Antartide)
Area rocosa (Antártida)

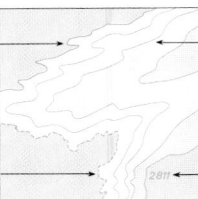 **Contour Lines in Continental Ice**
Courbes de niveau dans les régions glaciaires
Höhenlinien auf vergletschertem Gebiet
Curve altimetriche nelle aree ghiacciate
Curvas de nivel en aréas heladas

 Navigable Canal
Canal navigable
Schiffbarer Kanal
Canale navigabile
Canal navegable

 Lake Depth
Profondeur du lac
Seetiefe
Profondità del lago
Profundidad del lago

Defined Shoreline
Trait de côte définie
Küsten- oder Uferlinie
Linea di costa definita
Línea de costa definida

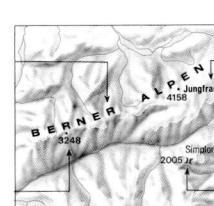 **Bathymetric Contour**
Courbe bathymétrique
Tiefenlinie
Curva batimetrica
Curva batimétrica

 Swamp
Marais
Sumpf
Palude d'acqua dolce
Pantano

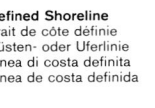 **Sand Area**
Région de sable, Désert
Sandgebiet, Sandwüste
Area sabbiosa, Deserto
Zona arenosa, desierto

Undefined or Fluctuating Shoreline
Trait de côte indéfinie
Unbestimmte oder veränderliche Uferlinie
Linea di costa indefinita
Línea de costa indefinida

Depth of Water
Valeur de sonde
Tiefenzahl
Quota batimetrica
Cota batimétrica

Salt Marsh
Marais d'eau salée
Salzsumpf
Palude d'acqua salata
Pantano de agua salada

 Sandbank, Sandbar
Banc de sable
Sandbank
Bassofondo sabbioso
Banco submarino de arena

Mountain Range
Chaîne de montagnes
Bergkette
Catena di monti
Cadena montañosa

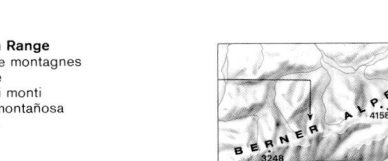 **Mountain**
Mont
Berg, Bergmassiv
Monte
Monte

Salt Pan
Marais salant
Salzpfanne
Salina
Salina

 Port Facilities
Installations portuaires
Hafenanlagen
Impianti portuali
Instalaciones portuarias

Elevation
Cote, Altitude
Höhenzahl
Quota altimetrica
Cota altimétrica

Mountain Pass, Gap
Passage, Col, Port
Paß, Joch, Sattel
Passo, Colle, Valico
Paso, Collado, Puerto de montaña

Key to Elevation and Depth Tints
Hypsométrie, Bathymétrie
Höhenstufen, Tiefenstufen
Altimetria, Batimetria
Altimetría, Batimetría

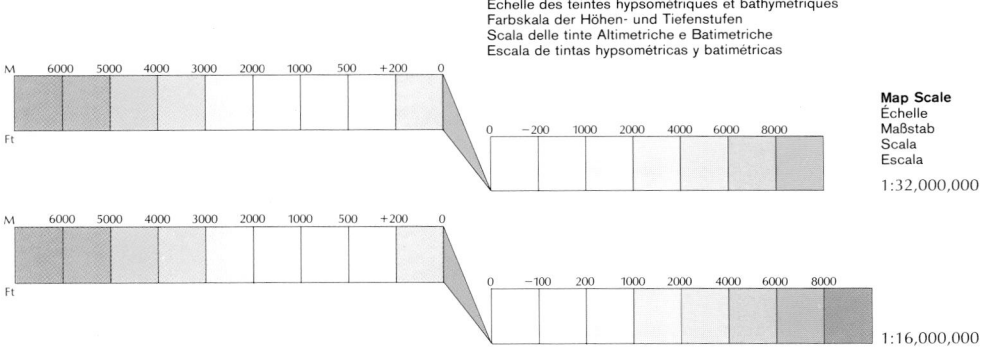

Scales in Metric and English Measures
Échelle des teintes hypsométriques et bathymétriques
Farbskala der Höhen- und Tiefenstufen
Scala delle tinte Altimetriche e Batimetriche
Escala de tintas hipsométricas y batimétricas

M 6000 5000 4000 3000 2000 1000 500 +200 0
Ft
0 −200 1000 2000 4000 6000 8000

Map Scale
Échelle
Maßstab
Scala
Escala

1:32,000,000

M 6000 5000 4000 3000 2000 1000 500 +200 0
Ft
0 −100 200 1000 2000 4000 6000 8000

1:16,000,000

Land Elevation Below Sea Level
Dépression et cote au-dessous du niveau de la mer
Senke mit Tiefenzahl unter dem Meeresspiegel
Depressione e quota sotto il livello del mare
Depresión y elevación bajo el nivel del mar

−155

Map Projections
Projections cartographiques
Kartennetzentwürfe
Proiezioni cartografiche
Proyecciones cartográficas

The projections appearing in this atlas have been plotted by computer

Les réseaux des projections ont été obtenus par élaboration automatique à partir de formules mathématiques

Die Kartennetze aller im Atlas vorkommenden Abbildungen wurden mit Hilfe der Datenverarbeitung (EDV) völlig neu errechnet

I disegni delle proiezioni presenti in quest'opera sono stati realizzati interamente ex-novo con l'uso del computer e del plotter a partire dalle formule matematiche

El reticulado de las proyecciones (redes geográficas) incluidas en esta obra han sido obtenidas por proceso automático a partir de las fórmulas matemáticas

The meanings of the symbols on the Legend pages are in English, French, German, Italian, and Spanish languages to permit the interpretation of the maps by a broad readership.

Boundaries, Capitals
Frontières, Soulignements — Confini, Sottolineature
Grenzen, Unterstreichungen — Límites, Subrayados

International Boundary
Frontière internationale
Staatsgrenze
Confine di Stato
Límite de Nación

Second-order Political Boundary
Frontière d'État fédéré, Région
Bundesstaats-, Regionsgrenze
Confine di Stato federato, Regione
Límite de Estado federado, Región

International Boundary (Continent Maps)
Frontière internationale (Continents)
Staatsgrenze (Erdteilkarten)
Confine di Stato (Carte dei Continenti)
Límite de Nación (Continentes)

Third-order Political Boundary
Frontière de Province, Comté, Bezirk
Provinz-, Grafschafts-, Bezirksgrenze
Confine di Provincia, Contea, Bezirk
Límite de Provincia, Condado, Bezirk

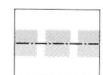
Undefined International Boundary
Frontière internationale indéfinie
Nicht genau festgelegte Staatsgrenze
Confine di Stato indefinito
Límite de Nación indefinido

Administrative District Boundary
Frontière de Circonscription
Kreisgrenze
Confine di Circondario
Límite de Circunscripción administrativa

International Ocean Floor Boundary Defined by Treaty or Bilateral Agreement
Frontière d'état en mer définie par traités et conventions bilatéraux
Durch Verträge festgelegte Staatsgrenze im Meeresgebiet
Confine di Stato nel mare definito da trattati e convenzioni bilaterali
Límite de Nación en el Mar definido por los tratados bilaterales

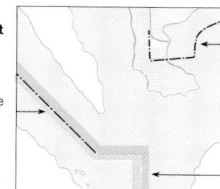

International Ocean Floor Boundary
Frontière d'état en mer
Staatsgrenze im Meeresgebiet
Confine di Stato nel mare
Límite de Nación en el mar

Undefined Ocean Floor Boundary
Frontière indéfinie d'état tracée en mer
Unbstimmte Staatsgrenze im Meeresgebiet
Confine di Stato indefinito nel mare
Límite indefinido de Nación en el mar

ROMA
National Capital
Capitale d'État
Hauptstadt eines unabhängigen Staates
Capitale di Stato
Capital de Nación

Kristiansand
Third-order Capital
Capitale de Province, Comté, Bezirk
Provinz-, Grafschafts-, Bezirkshauptstadt
Capoluogo di Provincia, Contea, Bezirk
Capital de Provincia, Condado, Bezirk

LYON
Dependency or Second-order Capital
Capitale d'État fédéré, Région
Bundesstaats-, Regionshauptstadt
Capitale di Stato federato, Regione
Capital de Estado federado, Región

Anadyr
Administrative District Capital
Capitale de Circonscription
Kreishauptstadt
Capoluogo di Circondario
Capital de Circunscripción administrativa

Other Symbols
Symboles divers — Simboli vari
Sonstige Zeichen — Signos varios

International Airport
Aéroport international
Internationaler Flughafen
Aeroporto internazionale
Aeropuerto internacional

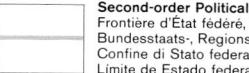 *(SANTAS CREUS)*
Church, Monastery, Abbey
Monastère, Eglise, Abbaye
Kloster, Kirche, Abtei
Monastero, Chiesa, Abbazia
Monasterio, Iglesia, Abadía

Lighthouse
Phare
Leuchtturm
Faro
Faro

(DAMPIERRE)
Castle
Château
Burg, Schloß
Castello
Castillo

 (BUI DAM)
Dam
Barrage
Staudamm, Staumauer
Diga artificiale, Sbarramento
Presa

(PAESTUM)
Ruin, Archeological Site
Ruine, Centre archéologique
Ruine, Archäologisches Zentrum
Rovina, Zona archeologica
Ruina, Zona arqueológica

 (L-GREENWICH / V-IJmuiden)
Section of a City
Faubourg
Stadt- oder Ortsteil
Sobborgo urbano
Suburbio

(MOLENS VAN KINDERDIJK)
Monument, Historic Site, etc.
Monument
Denkmal
Monumento
Monumento

 (Bidon V)
Uninhabited Locality, Hamlet
Ville inhabitée, Ferme, Hameau
Unbewohnte Stadt, Gehöft, Weiler
Città disabitata, Fattoria, Nucleo di case
Ciudad despoblada, Granja, Casar

(HADRIAN'S WALL)
Wall
Muraille
Wall, Mauer
Vallo, Muraglia
Muralla

(Bi'r Nāhid)
Periodically Inhabited Oasis
Oasis habitées périodiquement
Zeitweilig bewohnte Oase
Oasi periodicamente abitate
Oasis periodicamente habitados

(GIANT'S CAUSEWAY)
Point of Interest
Curiosité
Sehenswürdigkeit
Curiosità
Curiosidad

(Casey (Australia))
Scientific Station
Base géophysique
Geophysikalische Beobachtungsstation
Base geofisica
Base geofísica

(CUEVAS DE ARTÁ)
Cave
Grotte, Caverne
Höhle
Grotta, Caverna
Cueva, Gruta

Populated Places
Population — Popolazione
Bevölkerung — Población

Continent Maps
Cartes des Continents — Carte dei Continenti
Erdteilkarten — Mapas de Continentes
○ < 25 000
⊙ 25 000-100 000
◉ 100 000-250 000
◉ 250 000-1 000 000
▣ > 1 000 000

Regional Maps
Cartes à plus grande échelle — Carte di sviluppo
Karten größeren Maßstabs — Mapas a gran escala
○ < 10 000
○ 10 000-25 000
⊙ 25 000-100 000
◉ 100 000-250 000
◉ 250 000-1 000 000
▣ > 1 000 000

Symbols represent population of inhabited localities
Les symboles représentent le nombre d'habitants des localités
Die Signaturen entsprechen der Einwohnerzahl des Ortes
I simboli sono relativi al valore demografico dei centri abitati
Los simbolos son proporcionales a la población del lugar

Town area symbol represents the shape of the urban area
Le petit plan de la ville reproduit la configuration de l'aire urbaine
Die Plansignatur stellt die Gestalt des Stadtgebietes dar
La piantina della città rappresenta la configurazione dell'area urbana
El pequeño plano de la ciudad representa la forma del area urbana

Transportation
Communications — Comunicazioni
Verkehrsnetz — Comunicaciones

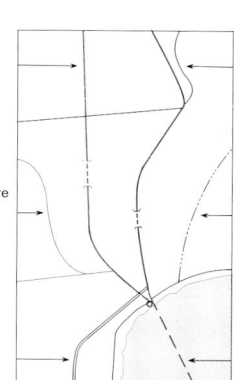

Primary Railway
Chemin de fer principal
Hauptbahn
Ferrovia principale
Ferrocarril principal

Road
Route de grande communication, Autres Routes
Fernverkehrsstraße, andere Straßen
Strada principale, Altre Strade
Carretera principal, Otras Carreteras

Secondary Railway
Chemin de fer secondaire
Sonstige Bahn
Ferrovia secondaria
Ferrocarril secundario

Trail, Caravan Route
Piste, Voie caravanière
Wüstenpiste, Karawanenweg
Pista nel deserto, Carovaniera
Pista en el desierto, Vía de Carabanas

Motorway, Expressway
Autoroute
Autobahn
Autostrada
Autopista

Ferry, Shipping Lane
Bac, Ligne maritime
Fähre, Schiffahrtslinie
Traghetto, Linea di navigazione
Transbordador (Ferry), Línea de navegación

Type Styles
Caractères utilisés pour la toponymie — Caratteri usati per la toponomastica
Zur Namenschreibung verwendete Schriftarten — Caracteres utilizados para la toponimia

ITALY
Hessen RIBE
Political Units
Etat, Dépendance, Division administrative
Staat, abhängiges Gebiet, Verwaltungsgliederung
Stato, Dipendenza, Divisione amministrativa
Nación, Dependencia, Division administrativa

Ankaratra — Monte Bianco
Tsiafajavona — Ngorongoro Crater
Nevado del Tolima — Kings Peak

Small Mountain Range, Mountain, Peak
Petit massif, Mont, Cime
Bergmassiv, Berg, Gipfel
Piccolo gruppo montuoso, Monte, Vetta
Macizo pequeño, Monte, Cima

LABRADOR SEA
Gulf of Alaska — Hudson Bay
Estrecho de Magallanes

Sea, Gulf, Bay, Strait
Mer, Golfe, Baie, Détroit
Meer, Golf, Bucht, Meeresstraße
Mare, Golfo, Baia, Stretto
Mar, Golfo, Bahía, Estrecho

SAXONY
THRACE SUSSEX
Historical or Cultural Region
Région historique ou culturelle
Historische oder Kulturlandschaft
Regione storico - culturale
Región histórica y cultural

Cabo de São Vicente — Land's End
Mizen Head — Point Conception
Col de la Perche — Passo della Cisa

Cape, Point, Pass
Cap, Pointe, Passe
Kap, Landspitze, Paß
Capo, Punta, Passo
Cabo, Punta, Paso

West Mariana Basin
Galapagos Fracture Zone
Mid-Atlantic Ridge

Undersea Features
Formes du relief sous-marin
Formen des Meeresbodens
Forme del rilievo sottomarino
Formas del relieve submarino

PATAGONIA
BASSIN DE RENNES
PENÍNSULA DE YUCATÁN
Physical Region (plain, peninsula)
Région physique (plaine, péninsule)
Landschaft (Ebene, Halbinsel)
Regione fisica (pianura, penisola)
Región natural (llanura, península)

MAHÉ ALDABRA ISLANDS
CORSE CHANNEL ISLANDS
SULU ARCHIPELAGO

Island, Archipelago
Ile, Archipel
Insel, Archipel
Isola, Arcipelago
Isla, Archipiélago

Tarfaya
Tombouctou
Agadir
Nouakchott
BRAZZAVILLE
CASABLANCA

Size of type indicates relative importance of inhabited localities
La dimension des caractères indique l'importance d'une localité
Die Schriftgröße entspricht der Gesamtbedeutung des Ortes
La grandezza del carattere è proporzionale all'importanza della località
La dimensión de los caracteres de imprenta indica la importancia de la localidad

PYRENEES
CUMBRIAN MOUNTAINS
SIERRA DE GÁDOR LA SILA
Mountain Range
Chaîne de montagnes
Bergkette, Gebirge
Catena di monti
Cadena montañosa

Thames Po Victoria Falls
Lotagipi Swamp Göta kanal
Lago Maggiore

River, Waterfall, Cataract, Canal, Lake
Fleuve, Chute d'eau, Cataracte, Canal, Lac
Fluß, Wasserfall, Katarakt, Kanal, See
Fiume, Cascata, Cateratta, Canale, Lago
Río, Cascada, Catarata, Canal, Lago

INDEX MAPS

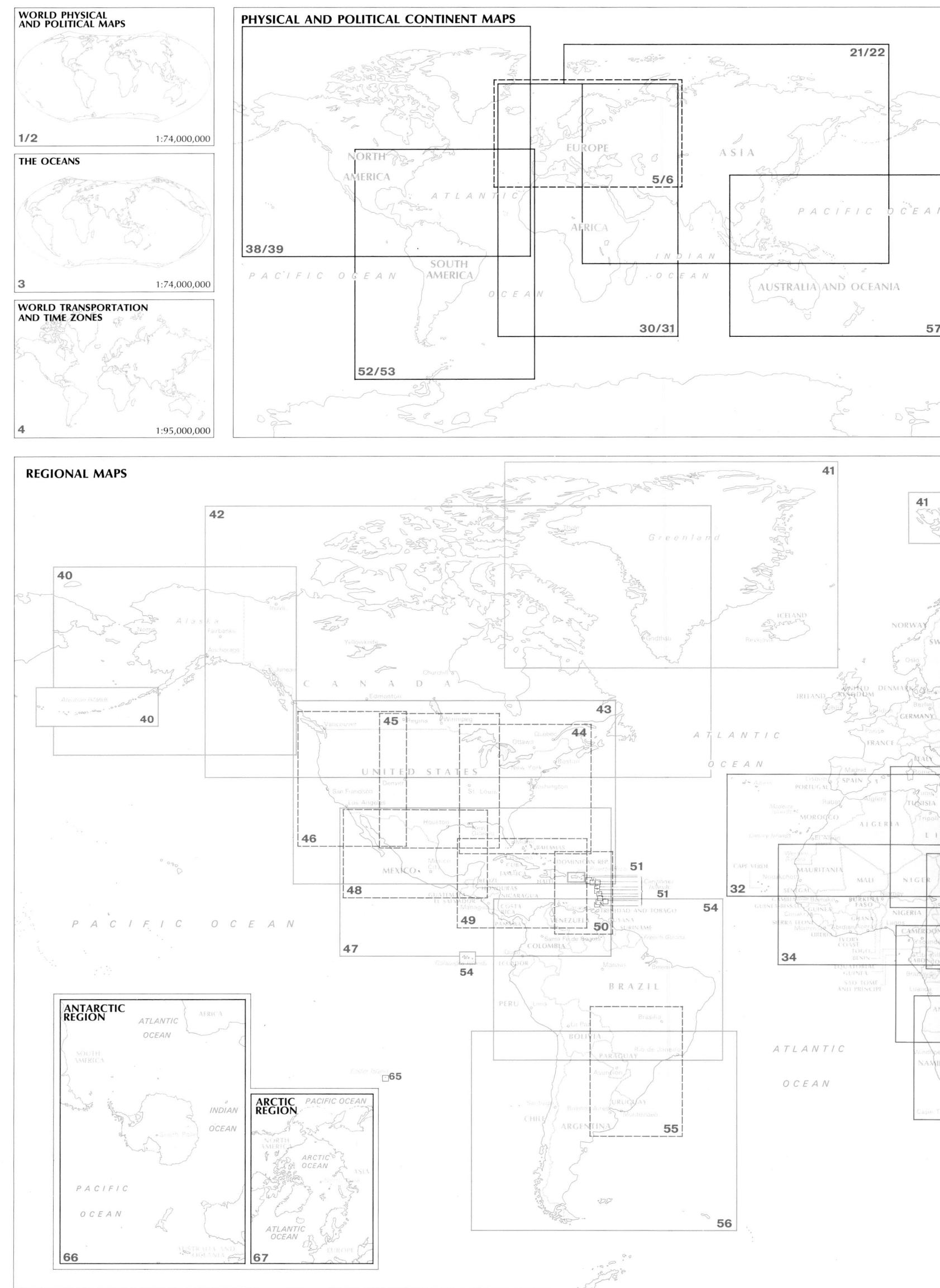

WORLD PHYSICAL AND POLITICAL MAPS

1/2   1:74,000,000

THE OCEANS

3   1:74,000,000

WORLD TRANSPORTATION AND TIME ZONES

4   1:95,000,000

PHYSICAL AND POLITICAL CONTINENT MAPS

21/22

NORTH AMERICA

EUROPE

ASIA

5/6

38/39

AFRICA

PACIFIC OCEAN

ATLANTIC OCEAN

SOUTH AMERICA

INDIAN OCEAN

AUSTRALIA AND OCEANIA

30/31

52/53

57

REGIONAL MAPS

41

42

41

40

Greenland

40

ICELAND

NORWAY

CANADA

43

ATLANTIC OCEAN

45

44

UNITED STATES

46

MEXICO

48

51

32

49

50

54

47

54

BRAZIL

34

65

ANTARCTIC REGION

55

56

66

ARCTIC REGION

67

REGIONAL MAPS OF EUROPE

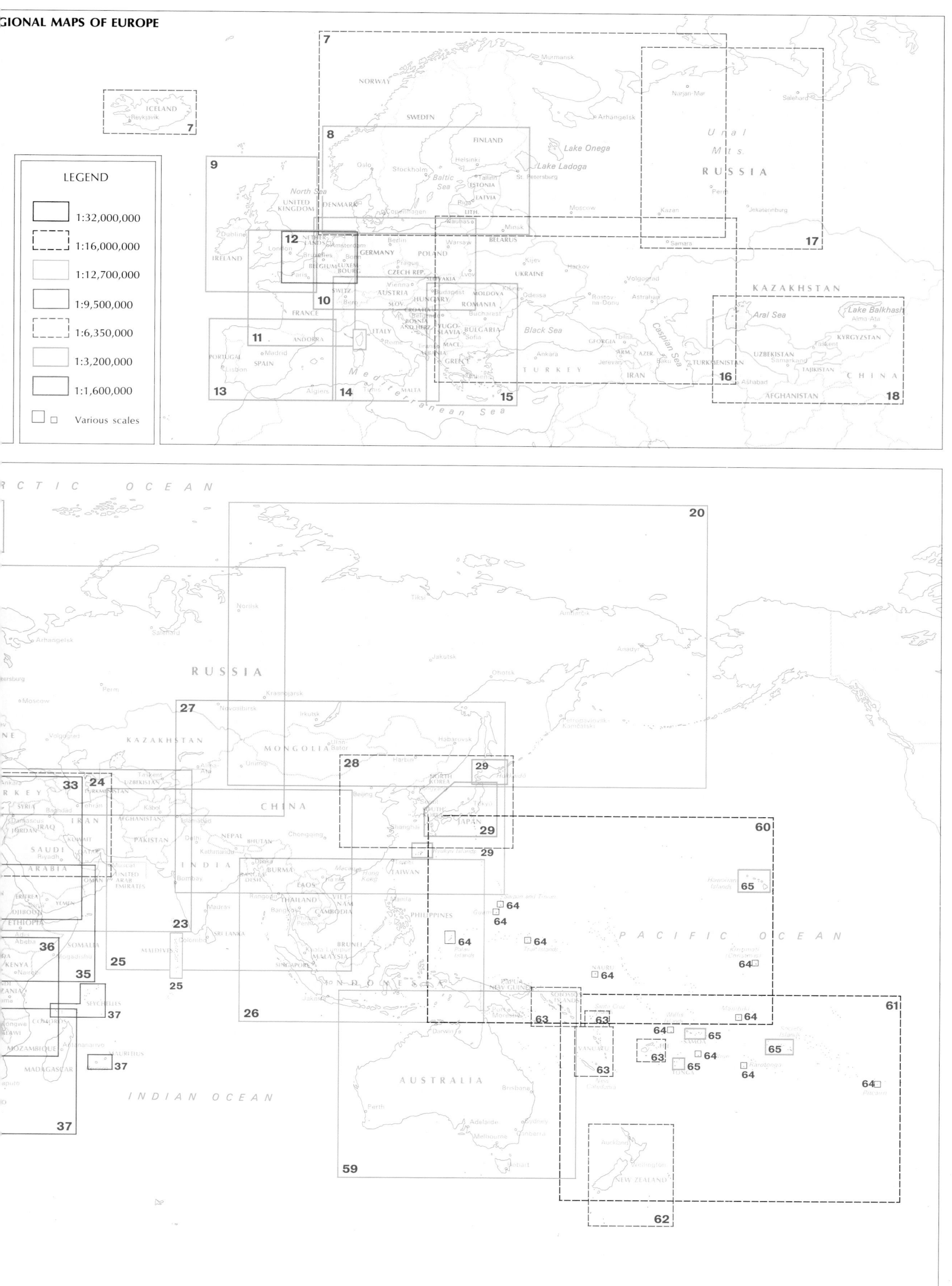

LEGEND

	1:32,000,000
	1:16,000,000
	1:12,700,000
	1:9,500,000
	1:6,350,000
	1:3,200,000
	1:1,600,000
□	Various scales

Map 1 **WORLD, PHYSICAL**

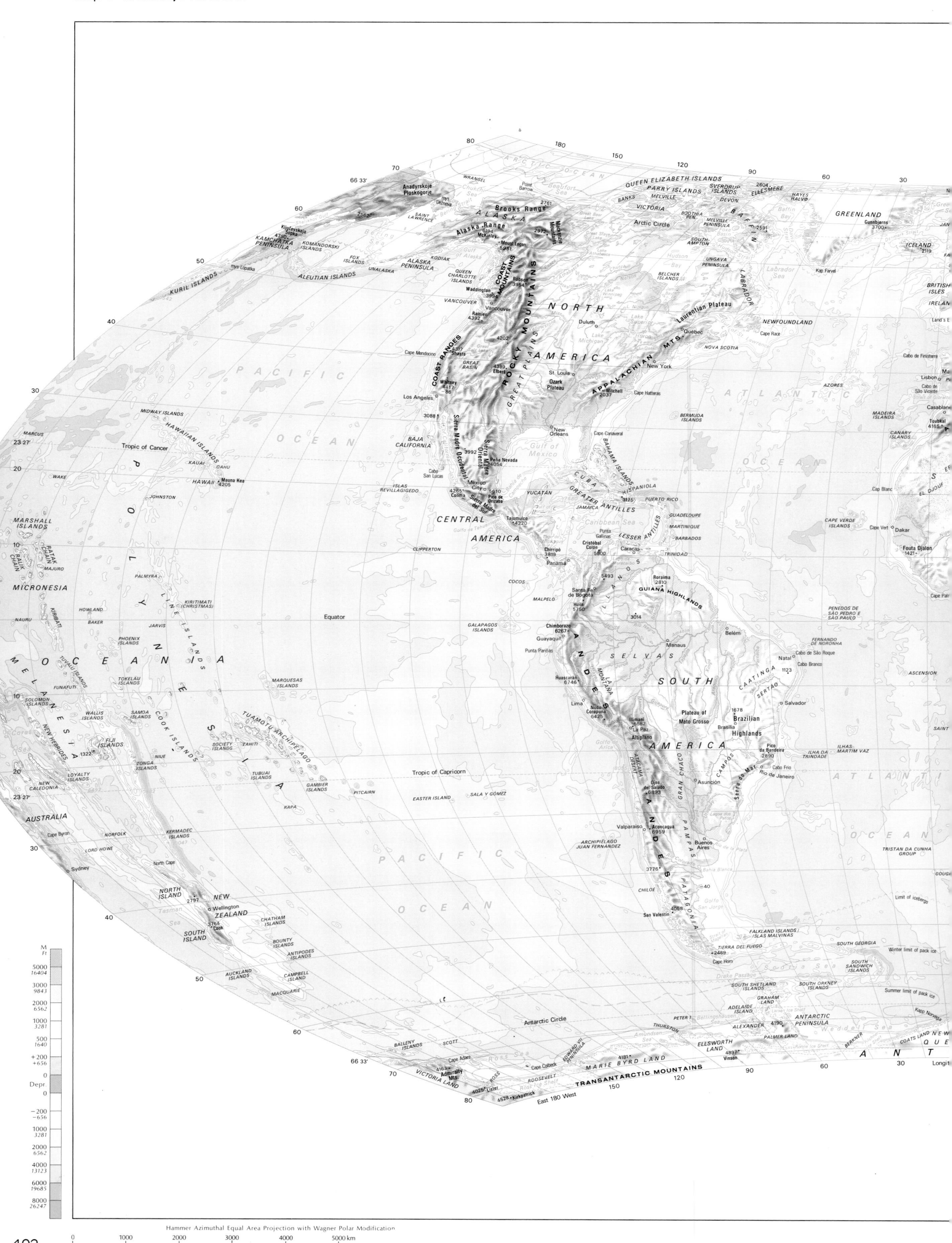

Hammer Azimuthal Equal Area Projection with Wagner Polar Modification

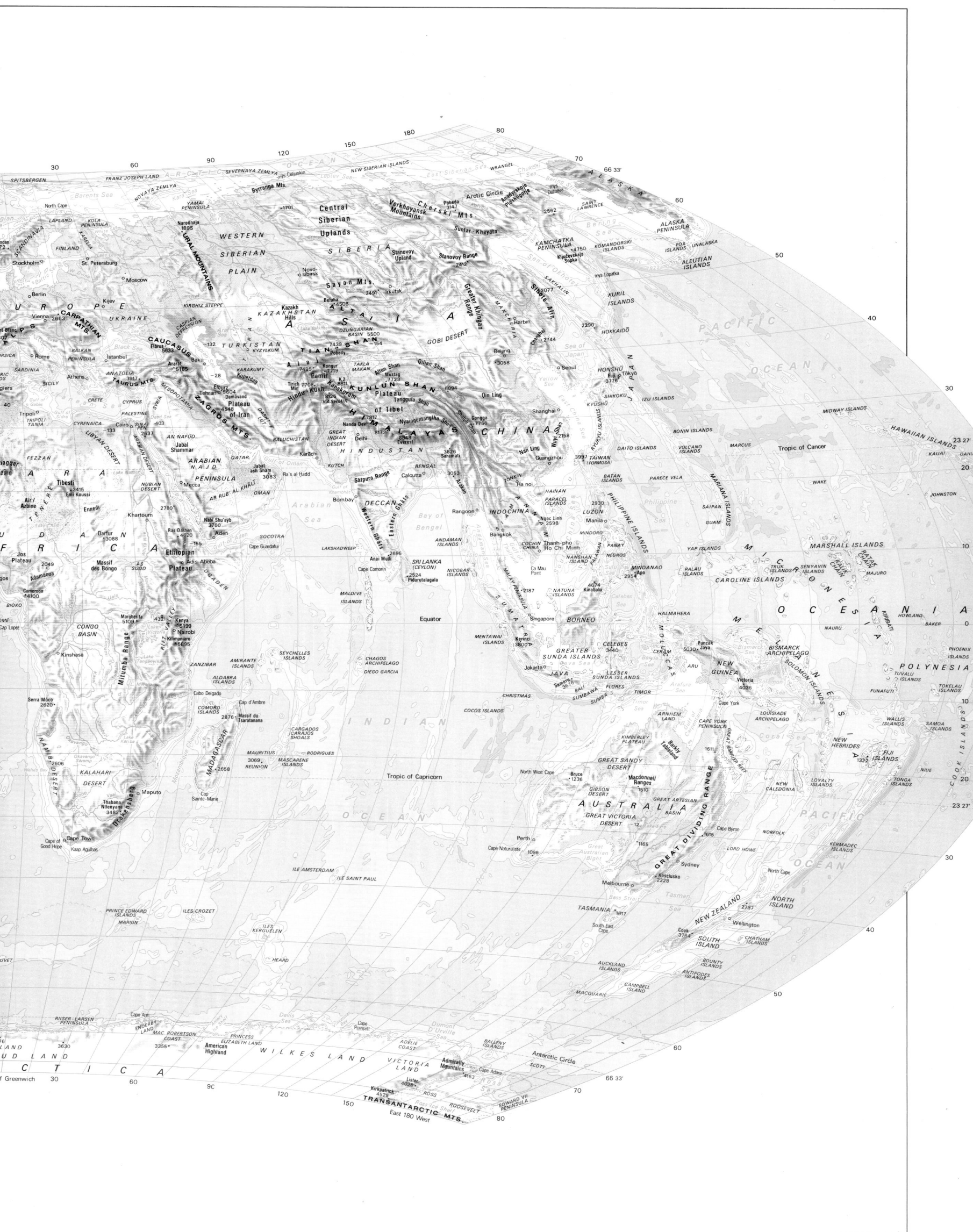

Map 2 **WORLD, POLITICAL**

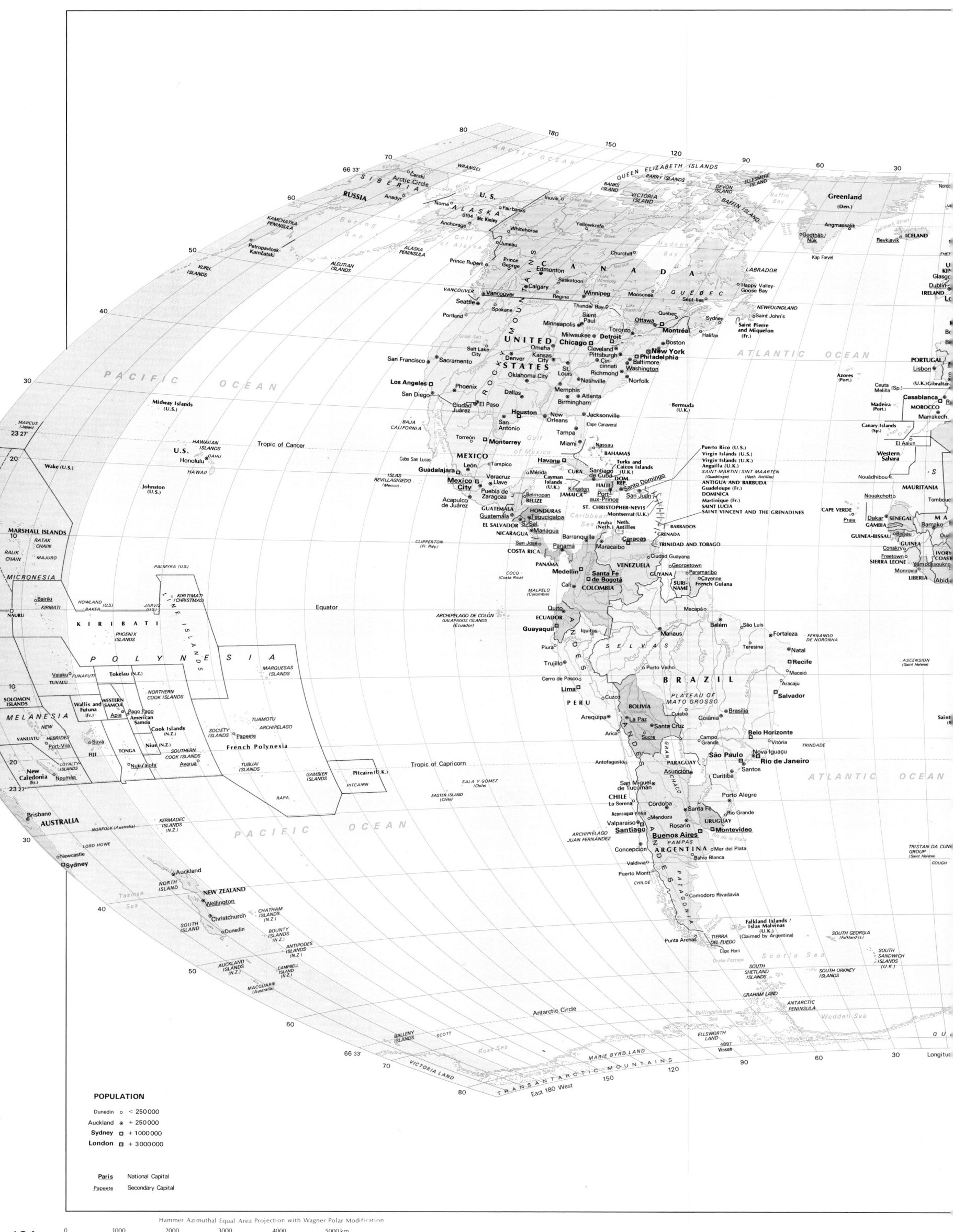

POPULATION

Dunedin   ○   < 250 000
Auckland   ⊙   + 250 000
Sydney   □   + 1 000 000
London   ⬛   + 3 000 000

Paris   National Capital
Papeete   Secondary Capital

Hammer Azimuthal Equal Area Projection with Wagner Polar Modification

0   1000   2000   3000   4000   5000 km
0   1000   2000   3000 miles

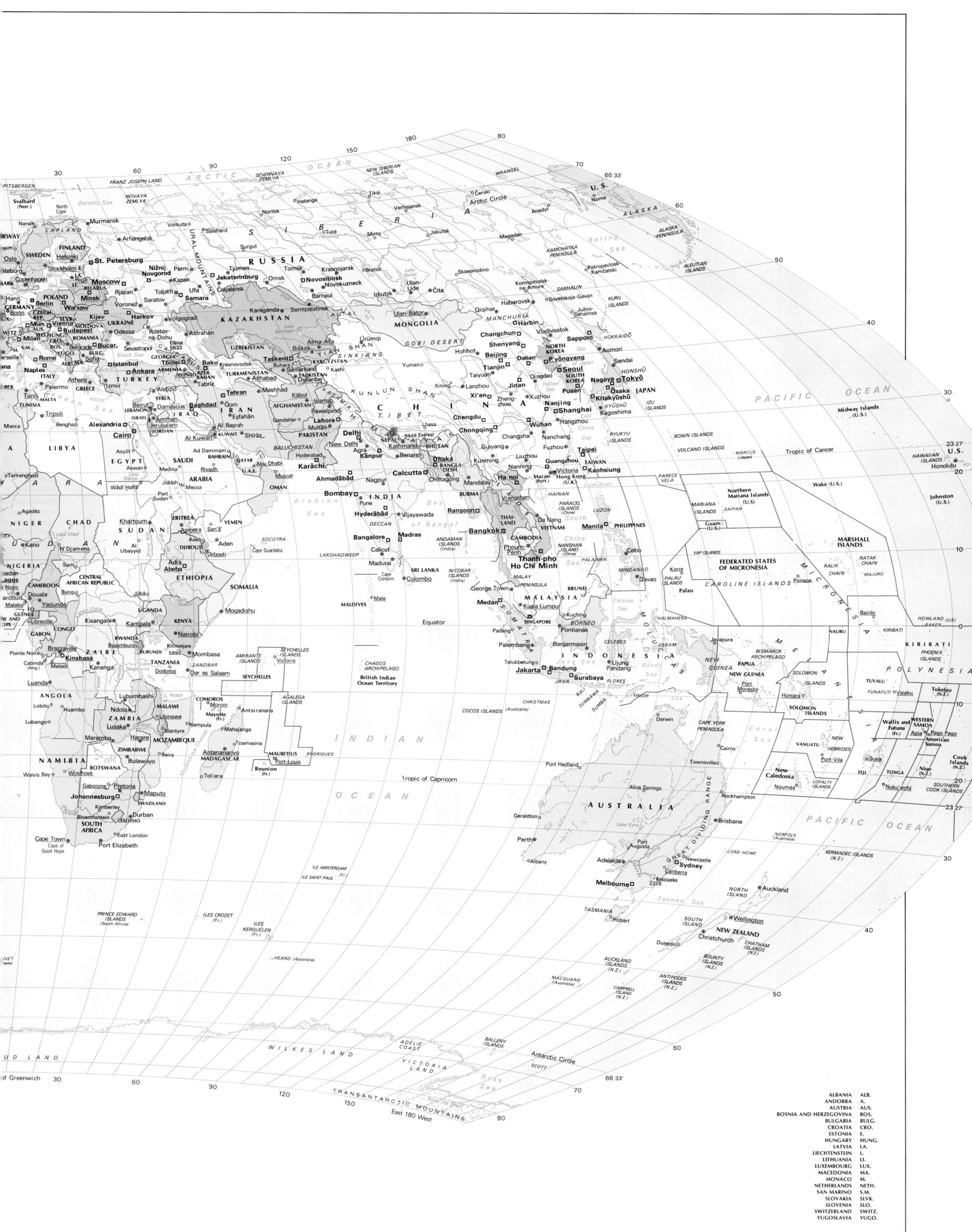

ALBANIA ALB.
ANDORRA A.
AUSTRIA AUS.
BOSNIA AND HERZEGOVINA BOS.
BULGARIA BULG.
CROATIA CRO.
ESTONIA E.
HUNGARY HUNG.
LATVIA LA.
LIECHTENSTEIN LI.
LITHUANIA LIT.
LUXEMBOURG LUX.
MACEDONIA MA.
MONACO M.
NETHERLANDS NETH.
SAN MARINO S.M.
SLOVAKIA SLVK.
SLOVENIA SLO.
SWITZERLAND SWITZ.
YUGOSLAVIA YUGO.

▲-510000-280 -8- 7-10 ®

Map 3 **THE OCEANS**

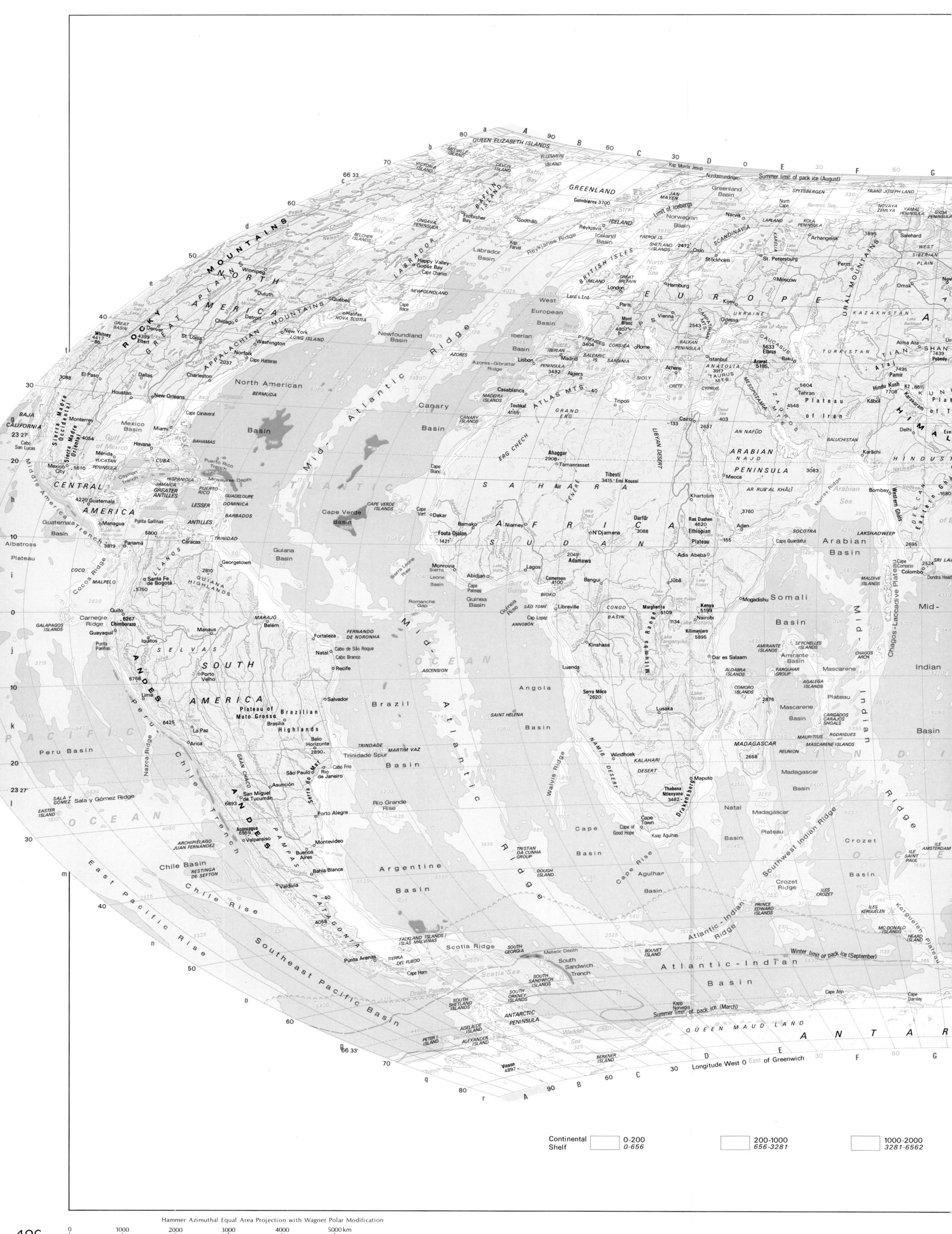

Continental Shelf		0-200 *0-656*		200-1000 *656-3281*		1000-2000 *3281-6562*

Hammer Azimuthal Equal Area Projection with Wagner Polar Modification

0   1000   2000   3000   4000   5000 km
0   1000   2000   3000 miles

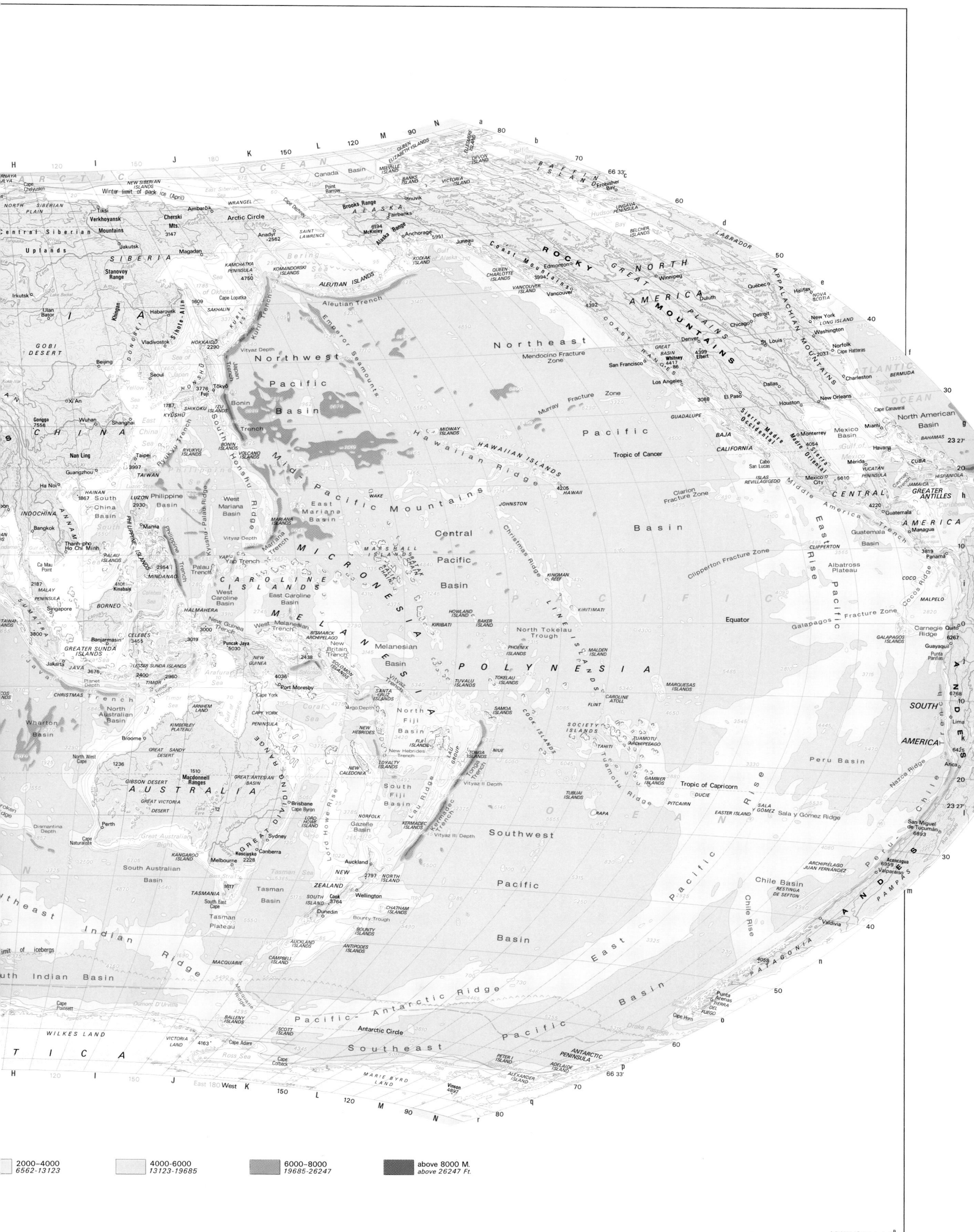

2000–4000	4000–6000	6000–8000	above 8000 M.
6562-13123	13123-19685	19685-26247	above 26247 Ft.

Map 4 **WORLD TRANSPORTATION AND TIME ZONES**

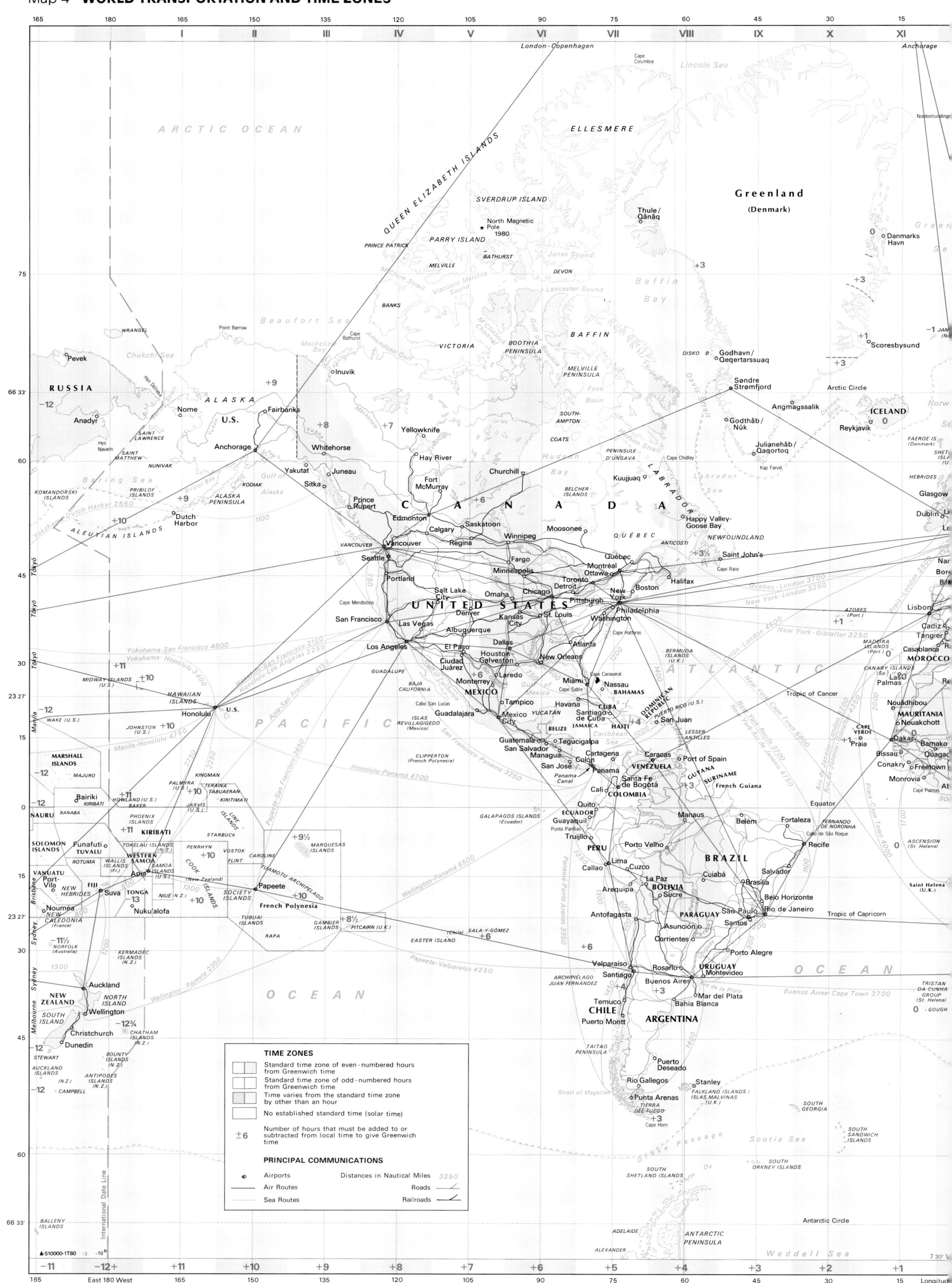

TIME ZONES

	Standard time zone of even-numbered hours from Greenwich time
	Standard time zone of odd-numbered hours from Greenwich time
	Time varies from the standard time zone by other than an hour
	No established standard time (solar time)
±6	Number of hours that must be added to or subtracted from local time to give Greenwich time

PRINCIPAL COMMUNICATIONS

Airports	Distances in Nautical Miles 3250
Air Routes	Roads
Sea Routes	Railroads

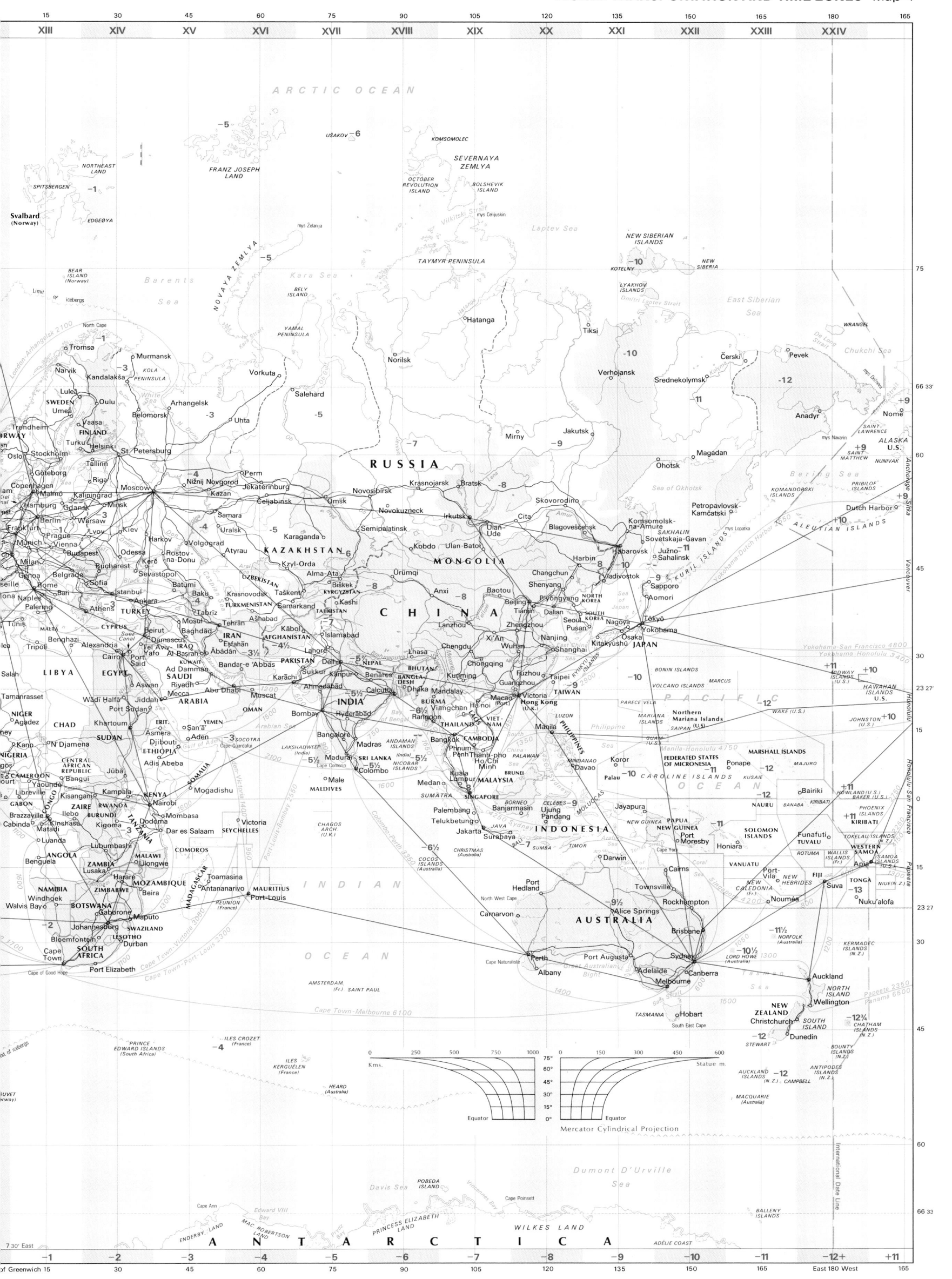

Mercator Cylindrical Projection

Map 5 **EUROPE, PHYSICAL**

Lambert Azimuthal Equal Area Projection

0   200   400   600   800   1000 km
0   250   500 miles

Longitude East 0 of Greenwich

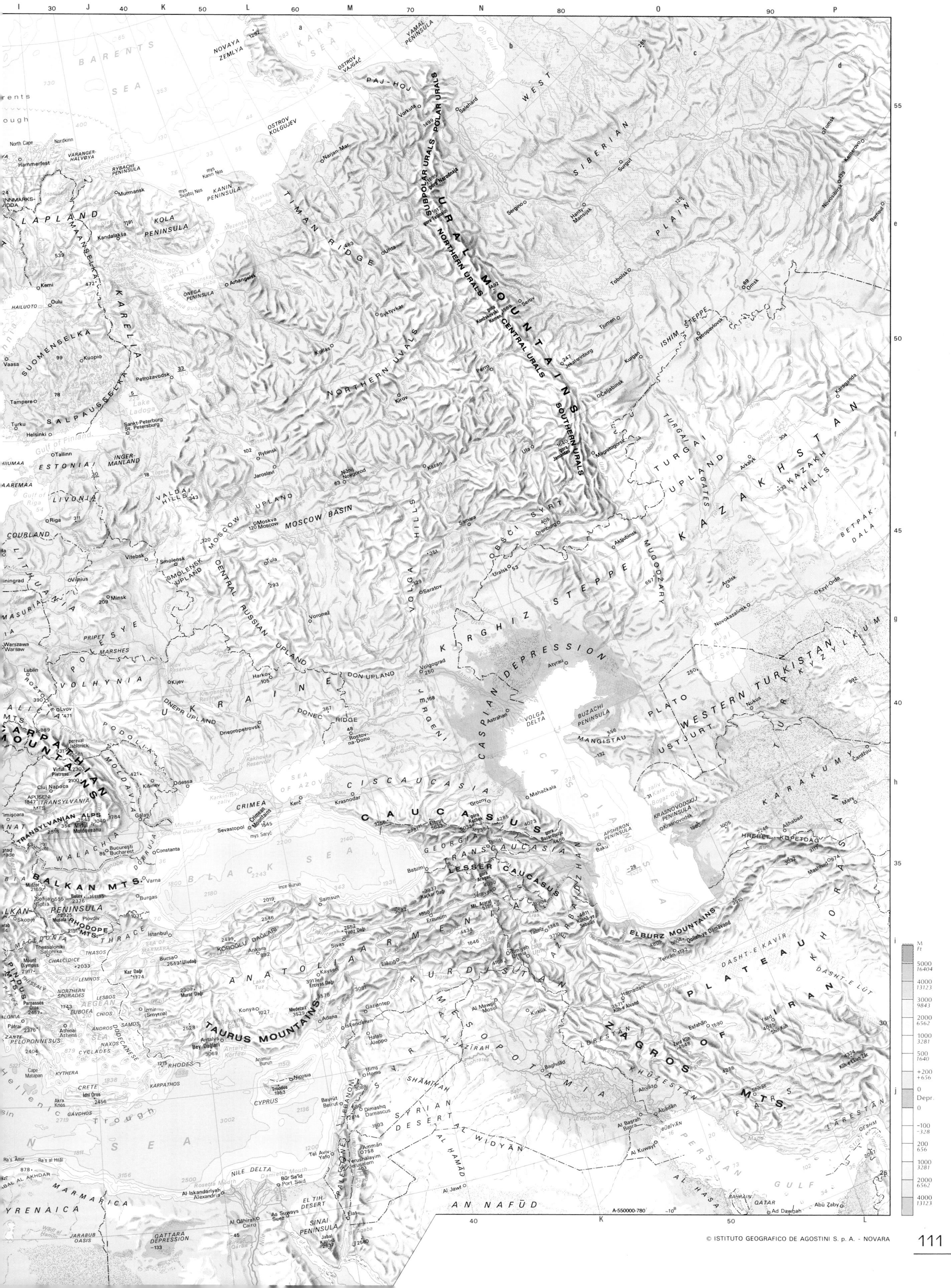

BARENTS SEA

NOVAYA ZEMLYA

KARA SEA

OSTROV VAJGAČ

YAMAL PENINSULA

PAJ-HOJ

POLAR URALS

SUBPOLAR URALS

NORTHERN URALS

WEST SIBERIAN PLAIN

OSTROV KOLGUJEV

KANIN PENINSULA

TIMAN RIDGE

U R A L   M O U N T A I N S

CENTRAL URALS

SOUTHERN URALS

North Cape
Nordkinn
Hammerfest
VARANGER-HALVØYA
RYBACHI PENINSULA
Murmansk
KOLA PENINSULA
WHITE SEA
ONEGA PENINSULA
Arhangelsk

LAPLAND
KARELIA
Kandalakša
Kemi
Oulu
Naryan-Mar
Vorkuta
Salehard
Sergino
Hanty-Mansijsk
Surgut

SUOMENSELKÄ
Vaasa
Kuopio
Tampere
Turku
Helsinki
SALPAUSSELKÄ
Petrozavodsk
Lake Ladoga

HIIUMAA
ESTONIA
INGERMANLAND
Sankt-Peterburg
St. Petersburg
Syktyvkar
NORTHERN URALS
Tobolsk
ISHIM STEPPE
Tjumen
Petropavlovsk
Omsk

AAREMAA
Gulf of Riga
Riga
LIVONIA
COURLAND
VALDAI HILLS
MOSCOW UPLAND
Jaroslavl
Rybinsk
N. Novgorod
Kazan
Perm
Jekaterinburg
Čeljabinsk
TURGAI UPLAND
TURGAI GATES
K A Z A K H S T A N
KAZAKH HILLS

LITHUANIA
Kaliningrad
Vilnius
Minsk
MASURIA
Warszawa
Warsaw
PRIPET MARSHES
POLESYE
VOLHYNIA
Lublin
MOSCOW BASIN
Moskva Moscow
Smolensk
SMOLENSK UPLAND
CENTRAL RUSSIAN UPLAND
Tula
Voronez
DON UPLAND
Saratov
VOLGA HILLS
Samara
OBŠČIJ SYRT
Orenburg
Uralsk
BETPAK DALA
Aralsk
MUGODŽARY
Novokazalinsk
Kyzyl-Orda

CARPATHIAN MOUNTAINS
Lvov
PODOLIA
MOLDAVIA
U K R A I N E
DNEPR UPLAND
Kijev
Harkov
Dnepropetrovsk
DONEC RIDGE
Rostov-na-Donu
K I R G H I Z   S T E P P E
C A S P I A N   D E P R E S S I O N
Volgograd
ERGENI
Atyrau
Astrahan
VOLGA DELTA
BUZACHI PENINSULA
MANGISTAU
P L A T O   U S T J U R T
W E S T E R N   T U R K I S T A N
KYZYLKUM

TRANSYLVANIAN ALPS
Nirul Moldoveanu
Cluj Napoca
TRANSYLVANIA
APUSENI MTS
Bucureşti
Bucharest
WALACHIA
DOBRUJA
Galaţi
Constanţa
CRIMEA
Sevastopol
Kerc
SEA OF AZOV
Krasnodar
CISCAUCASIA
C A U C A S U S
Groznyj
Mahačkala
APSHERON PENINSULA
Baku
KRASNOVODSKIJ PENINSULA
Krasnovodsk
K A R A K U M Y
Mary
HREBET KOPETDAG
Aşhabad

BALKAN MTS.
Varna
Burgas
B L A C K   S E A
GEORGIA
TRANSCAUCASIA
LESSER CAUCASUS
Batumi
A R M E N I A
Mt. Ararat
Erzurum
ELBURZ MOUNTAINS
Tehran

Sofija
Sofia
Skopje
RHODOPE MTS.
THRACE
PENINSULA
MACEDONIA
Plovdiv
istanbul
SEA OF MARMARA
KÖROĞLU DAĞLARI
Ankara
Sivas
Erzincan
KURDISTAN
Tabriz
AZERBAIJAN
DASHT-E KAVIR
Hamadan
Qom
P L A T E A U   O F   I R A N

Thessaloniki
Salonika
Mount Olympus
NORTHERN SPORADES
EUBOEA
LEMNOS
LESBOS
CHIOS
A N A T O L I A
İzmir (Smyrna)
Konya
Kayseri
Ercyas Dağı
Erciyas Dağı
Murat Dağı
Elazığ
Gaziantep
Adana
M E S O P O T A M I A
Mosul
Kirkuk
Esfahan
Shiraz
Z A G R O S   M T S.
LORESTAN
KHUZESTAN
Ahvaz

PINDUS
PELOPONNESUS
CYCLADES
NAXOS
SAMOS
DODECANESE
Athinai
Athens
T A U R U S   M O U N T A I N S
Antalya
Bey Dağları
CYPRUS
Nicosia
Troodos
Halab
Aleppo
SHĀMĪYAH
SYRIAN DESERT
Ḥimş
Ḥomş
Dimashq
Damascus
Baghdad
Al Başrah
Basra
BŪBĪYĀN
BAHRAIN
QATAR
Abū Ẓaby

CRETE
KARPATHOS
RHODES
MARMARICA
CYRENAICA
NILE DELTA
Al Iskandarīyah
Alexandria
Al Qāhirah
Cairo
Port Said
Bür Saīd
SINAI PENINSULA
Elat
Bayrūt
Beirut
LEBANON
Tel Aviv
Yafo
Yerushalayim
Jerusalem
Ammān
AL WIDYĀN
AN NAFŪD
Al Jawf
AL HASA
Ad Dawhah

EL TIH DESERT
GATTARA DEPRESSION
JARABUB OASIS
G U L F
AL ḤAMĀD

M / Ft	
5000	16404
4000	13123
3000	9843
2000	6562
1000	3281
500	1640
+200	+656
0	Depr
0	
-100	-328
200	656
1000	3281
2000	6562
4000	13123

A-550000-780

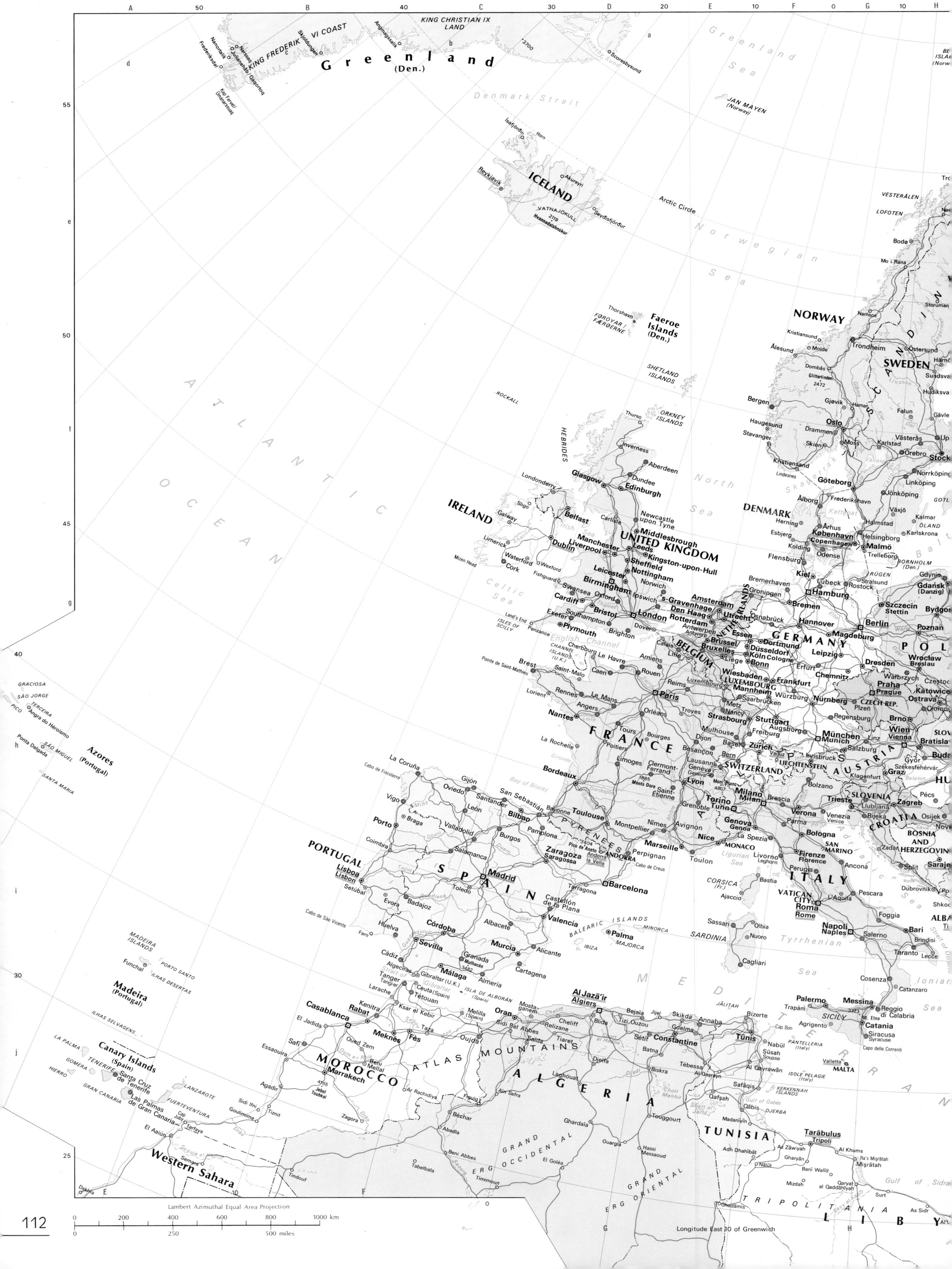

Map 6 **EUROPE, POLITICAL**

Lambert Azimuthal Equal Area Projection

Longitude East 0 of Greenwich

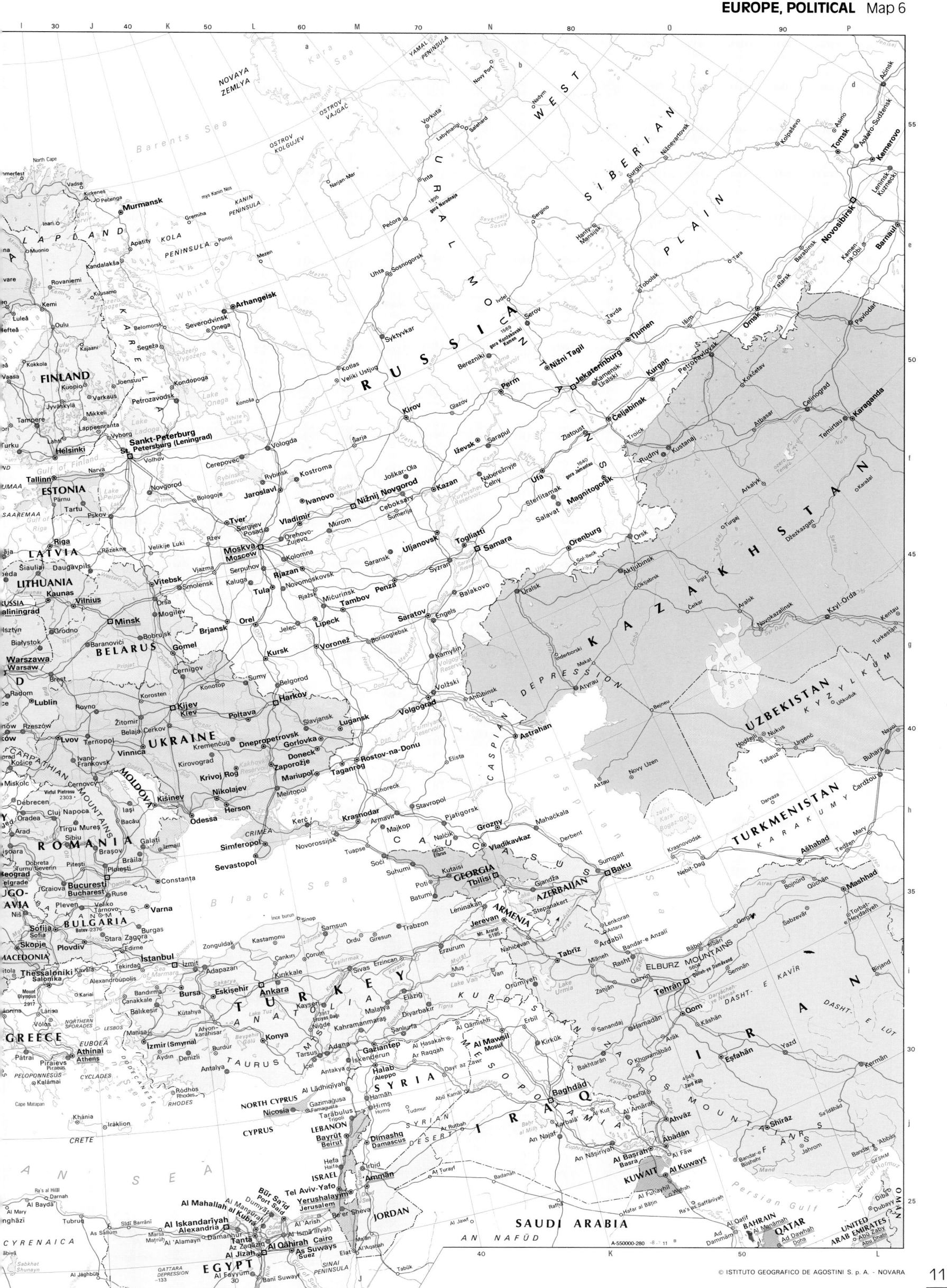

Map 7 **NORTHERN EUROPE**

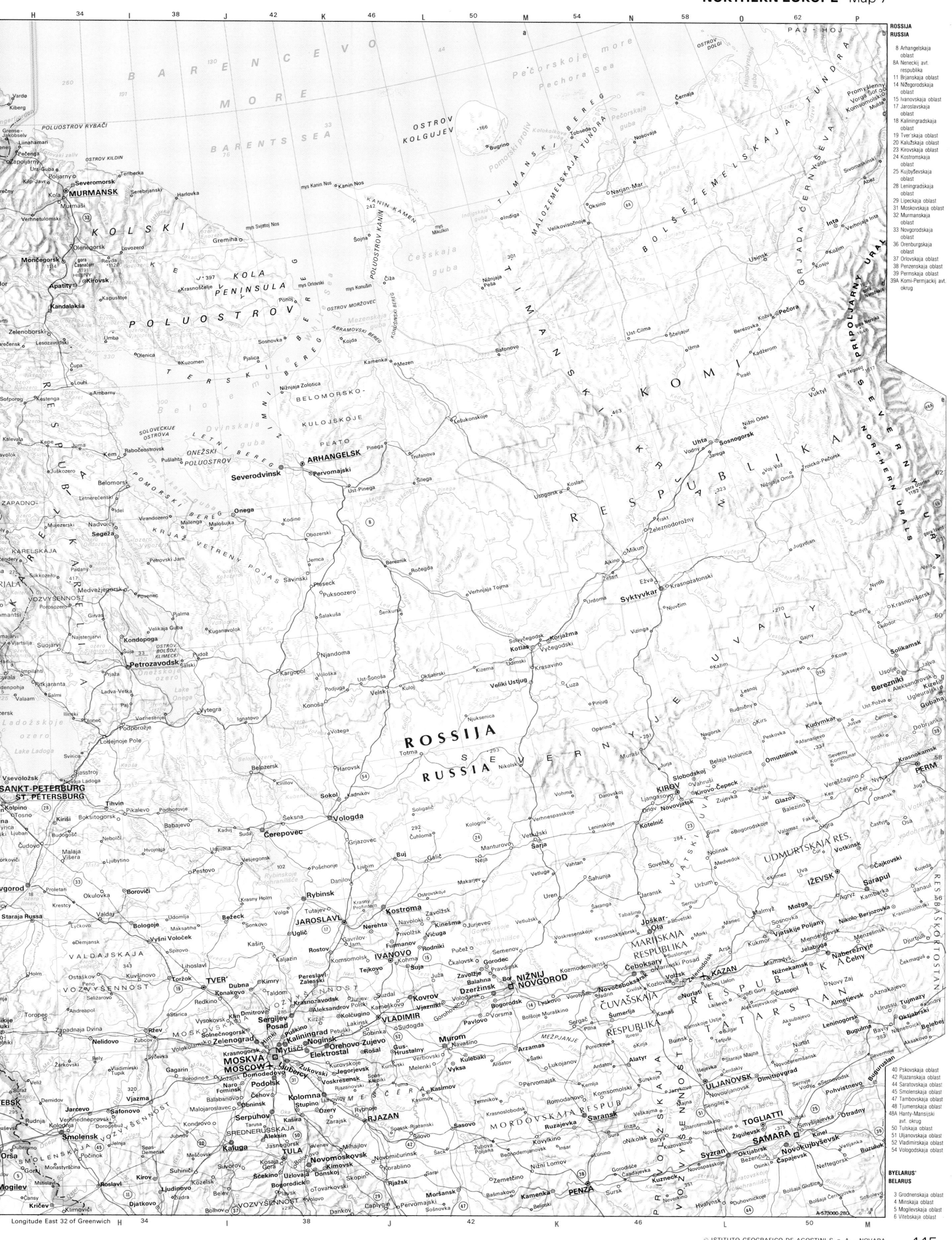

© ISTITUTO GEOGRAFICO DE AGOSTINI S. p. A. - NOVARA

Map 8 **BALTIC REGION**

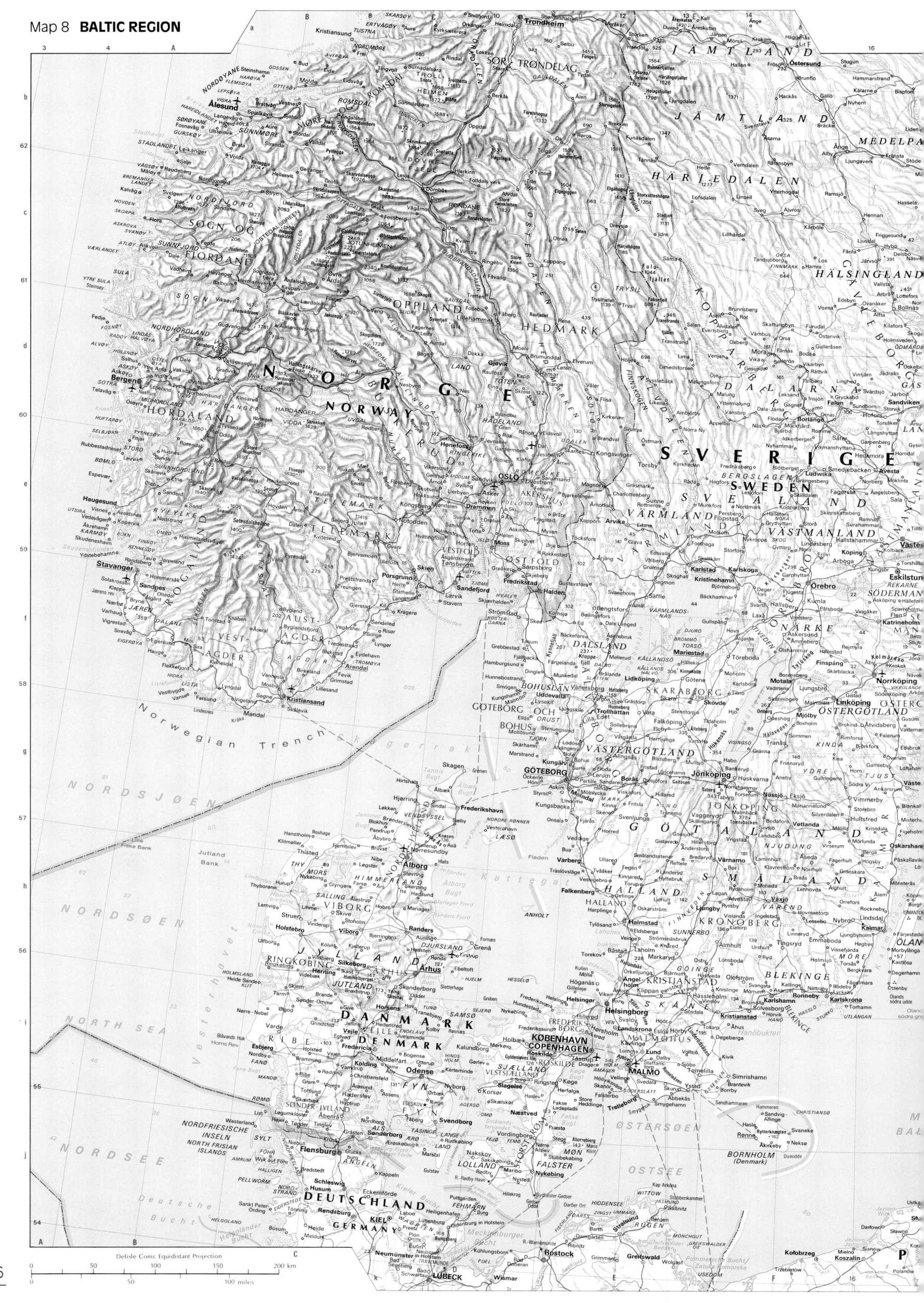

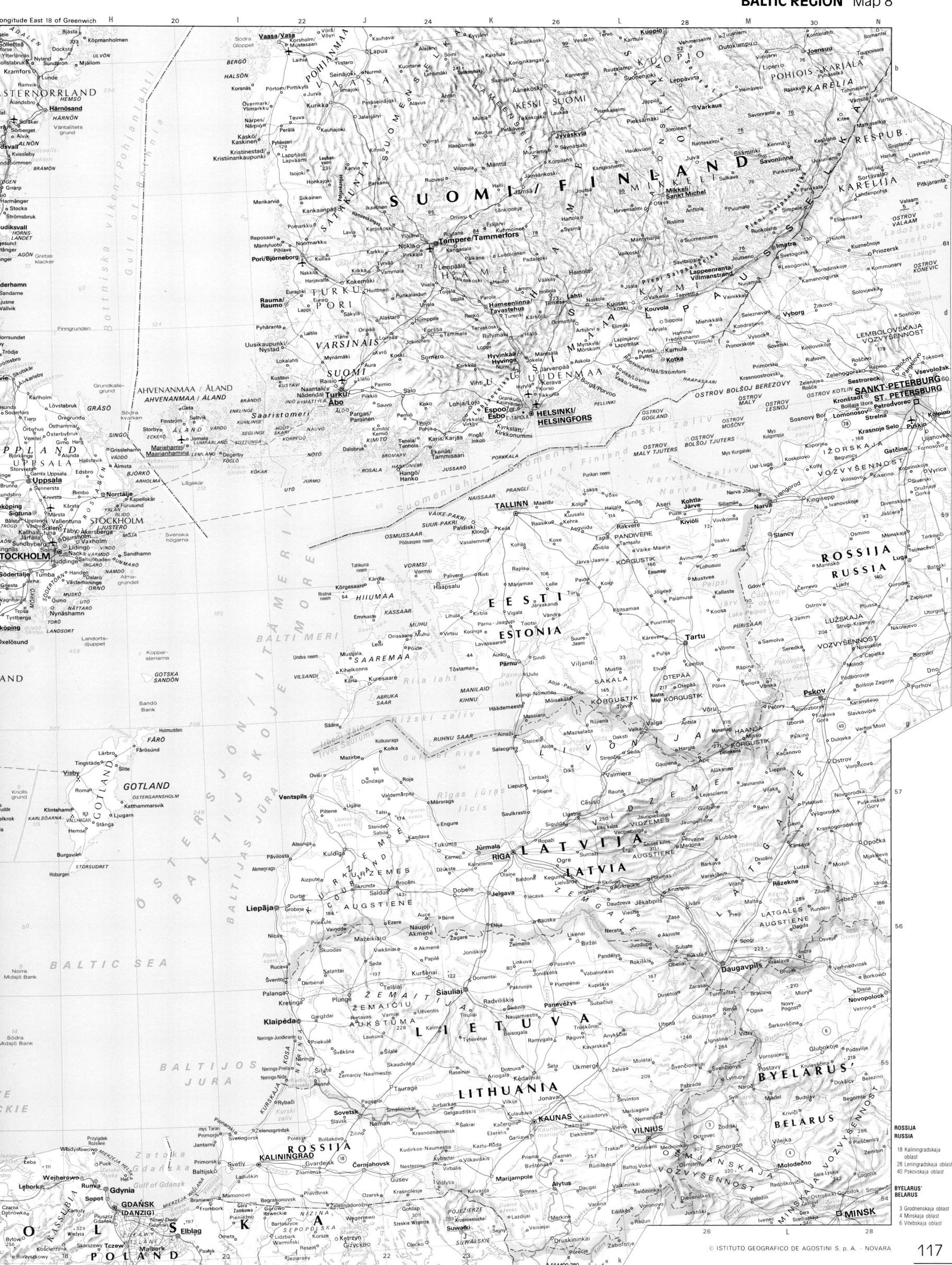

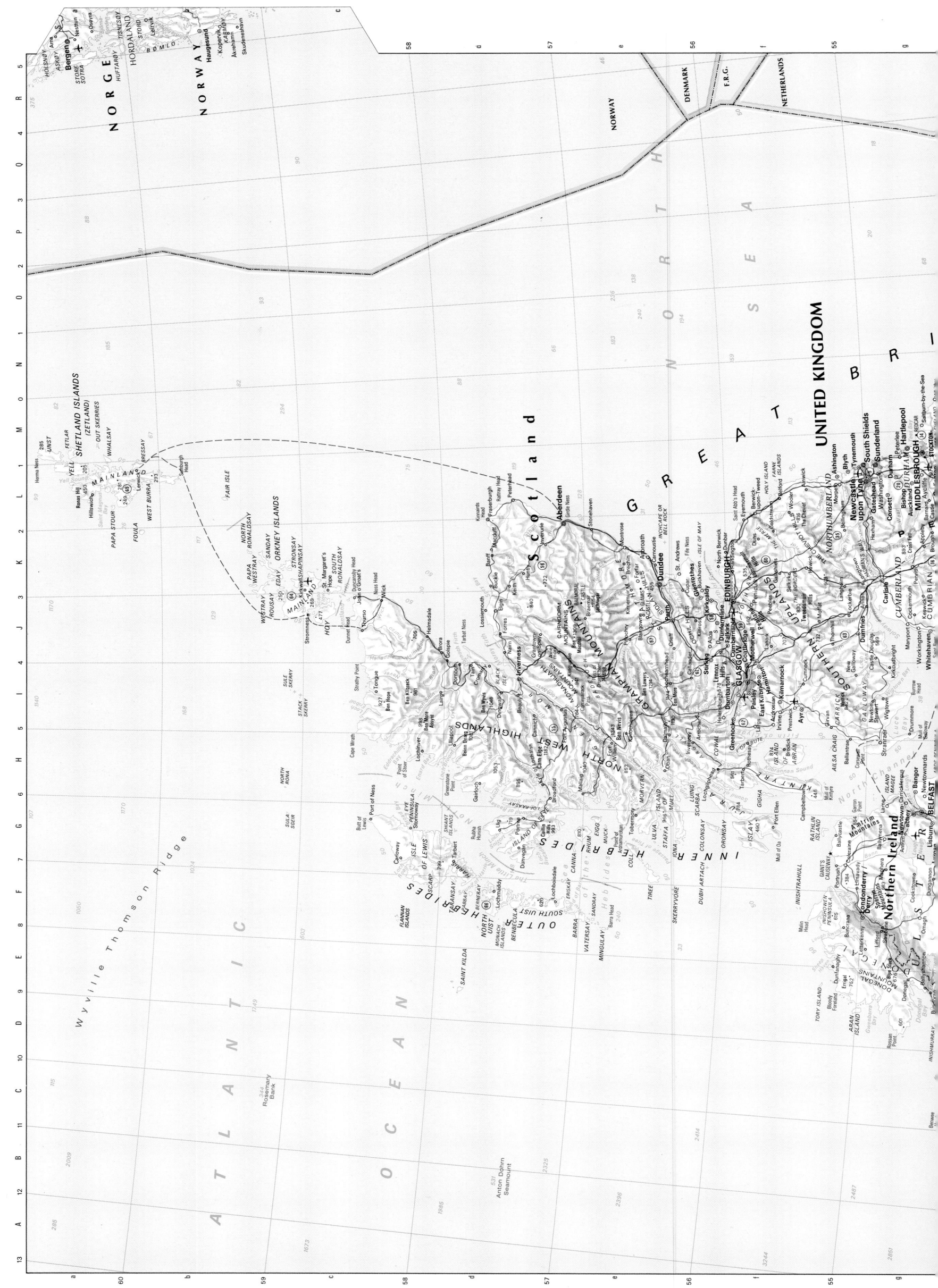

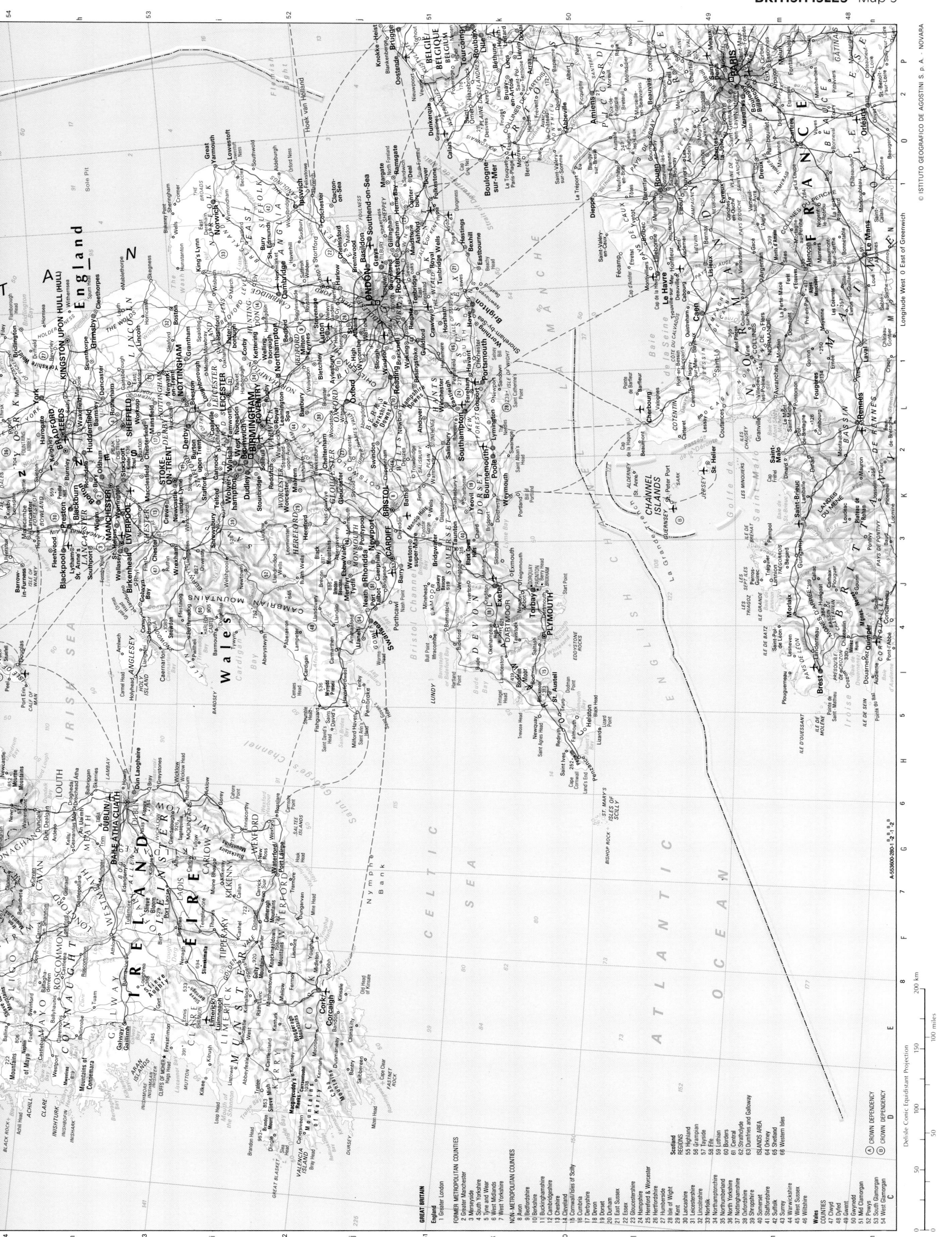

Longitude West 0 East of Greenwich

Delisle Conic Equidistant Projection

Map 10 **CENTRAL EUROPE**

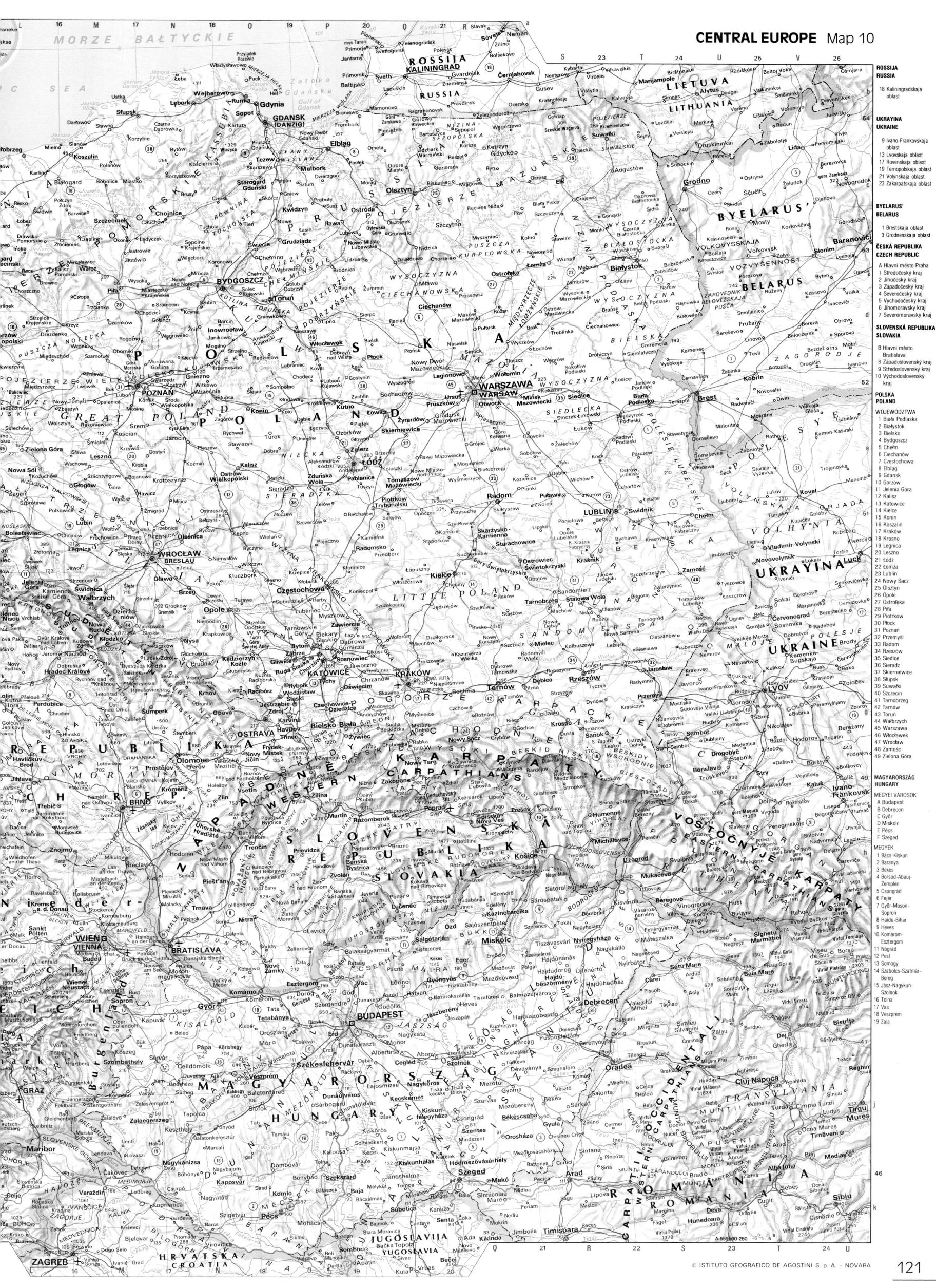

© ISTITUTO GEOGRAFICO DE AGOSTINI S.p.A - NOVARA

Map 11 **FRANCE AND BENELUX**

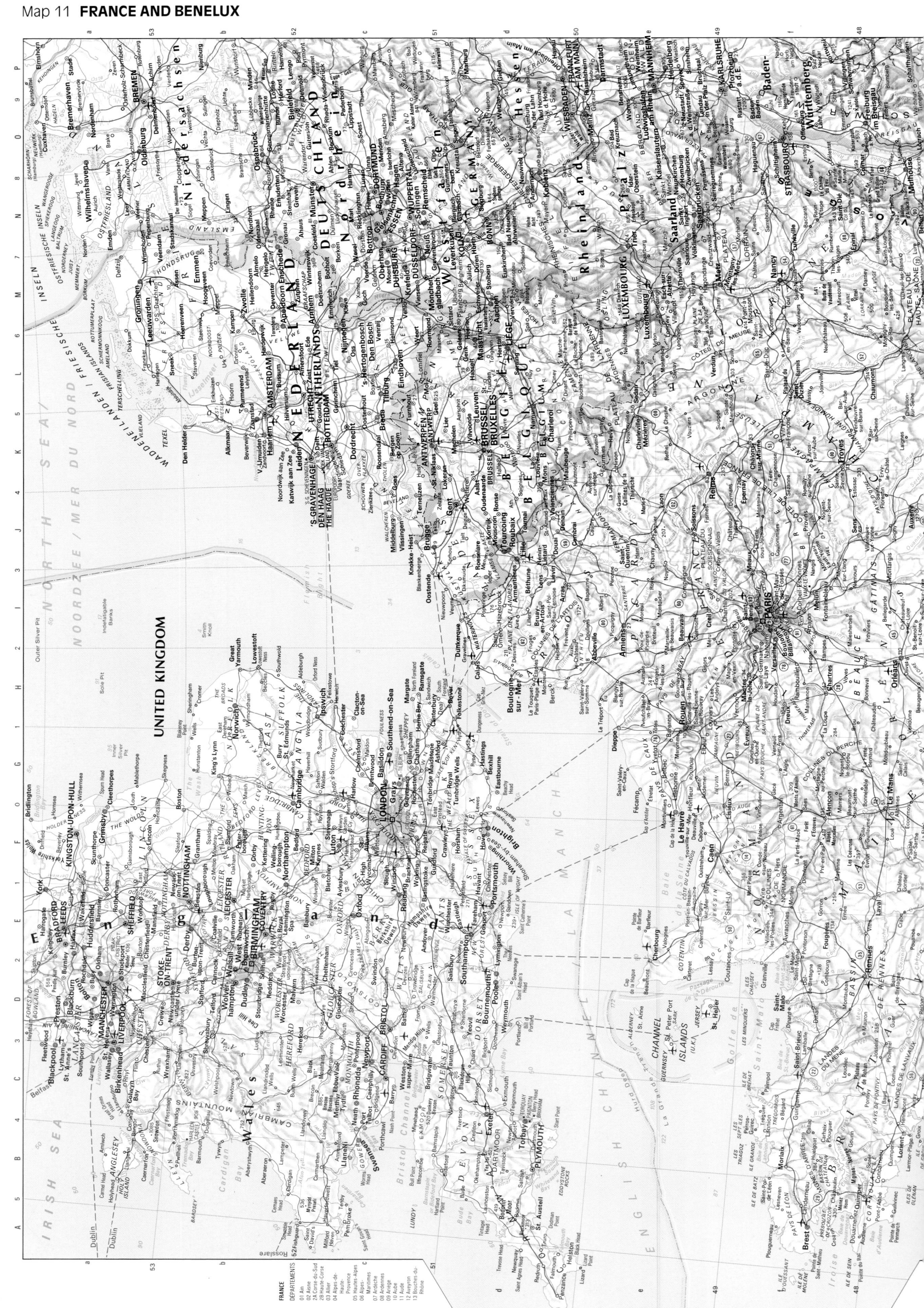

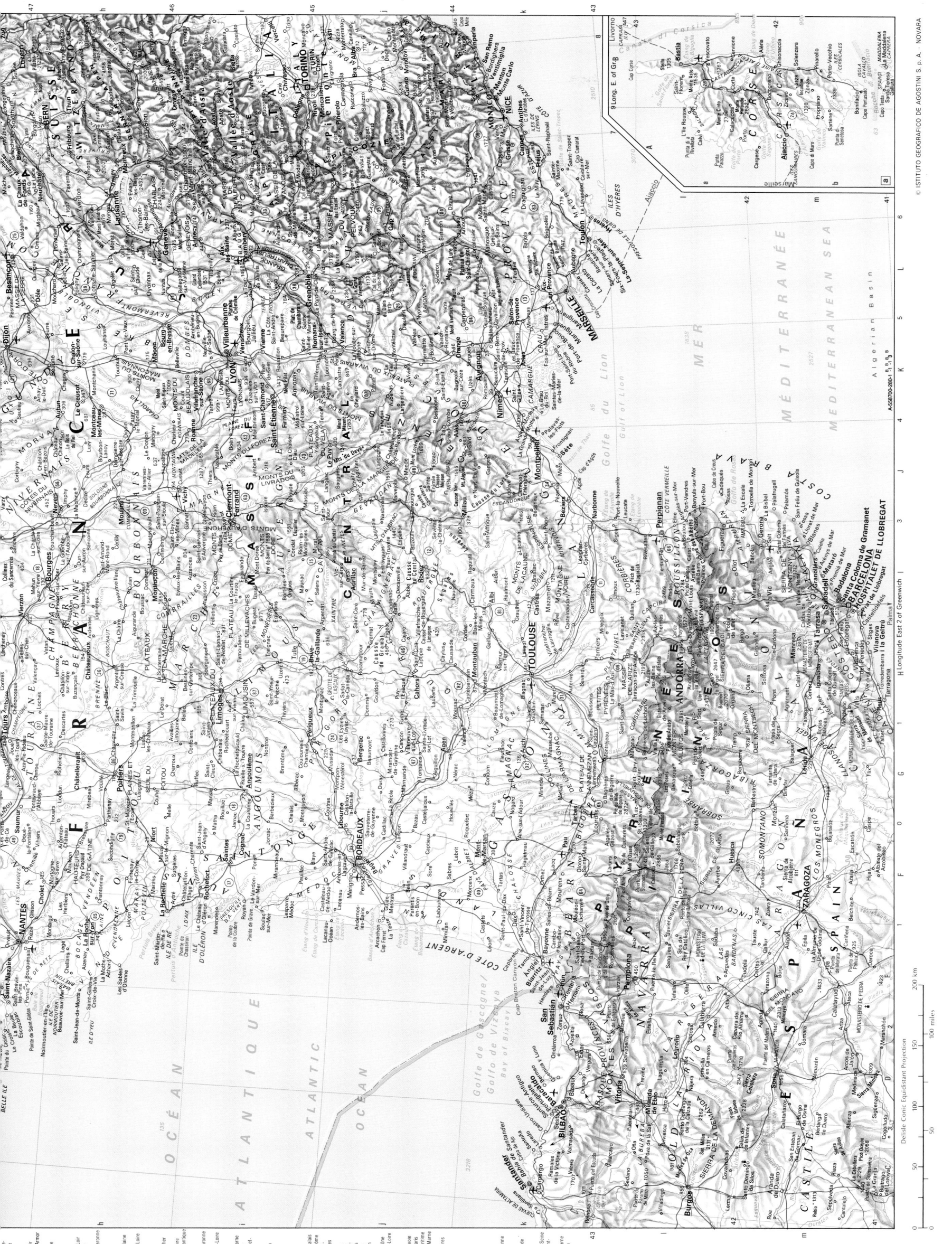

Map 12 **BELGIUM, NETHERLANDS AND LUXEMBOURG**

UNITED KINGDOM

England

NOTTINGHAMSHIRE LINCOLNSHIRE LEICESTERSHIRE RUTLAND NORTHAMPTONSHIRE CAMBRIDGESHIRE NORFOLK EAST ANGLIA SUFFOLK THE SANDLINGS BEDFORDSHIRE BUCKINGHAMSHIRE HERTFORDSHIRE ESSEX OXFORDSHIRE BERKSHIRE HAMPSHIRE SURREY WEST SUSSEX EAST SUSSEX KENT NORTH DOWNS SOUTH DOWNS THE WEALD ROMNEY MARSH ISLE OF WIGHT NEW FOREST

GREATER LONDON **LONDON**

NED
NET

NORTH SEA / NOORDZEE /
MER DU NORD 'S-GRAVEN

Flemish Bight

ZEELAND WALCHEREN NOORD-BEVELAND ZU BEVELAND

Brugge Oostende WEST- VLAANDEREN GENT GHENT OOST **Lille** Roubaix Tourcoing HAINAUT B E

FRANCE

NORD PAS-DE-CALAIS ARTOIS PICARDIE PICARDY SOMME OISE AISNE EURE SEINE-MARITIME PAYS DE CAUX CALVADOS MANCHE ORNE EURE-ET-LOIR YVELINES SEINE-ET-MARNE VAL D'OISE

PARIS Versailles Boulogne-Billancourt Meaux Compiègne Soissons **Amiens** **Arras** **Abbeville** **Boulogne-sur-Mer** **Calais** Dunkerque **Rouen** Le Havre Caen Bayeux **Évreux** Dreux Beauvais Creil Chantilly Senlis

ENGLISH CHANNEL / LA MANCHE

Strait of Dover / Pas de Calais

Baie de la Seine
Bay of the Seine

CÔTE DU CALVADOS BESSIN NORMANDIE

Delisle Conic Equidistant Projection

0   25   50   75   100 km
0   25   50 miles

Map 12

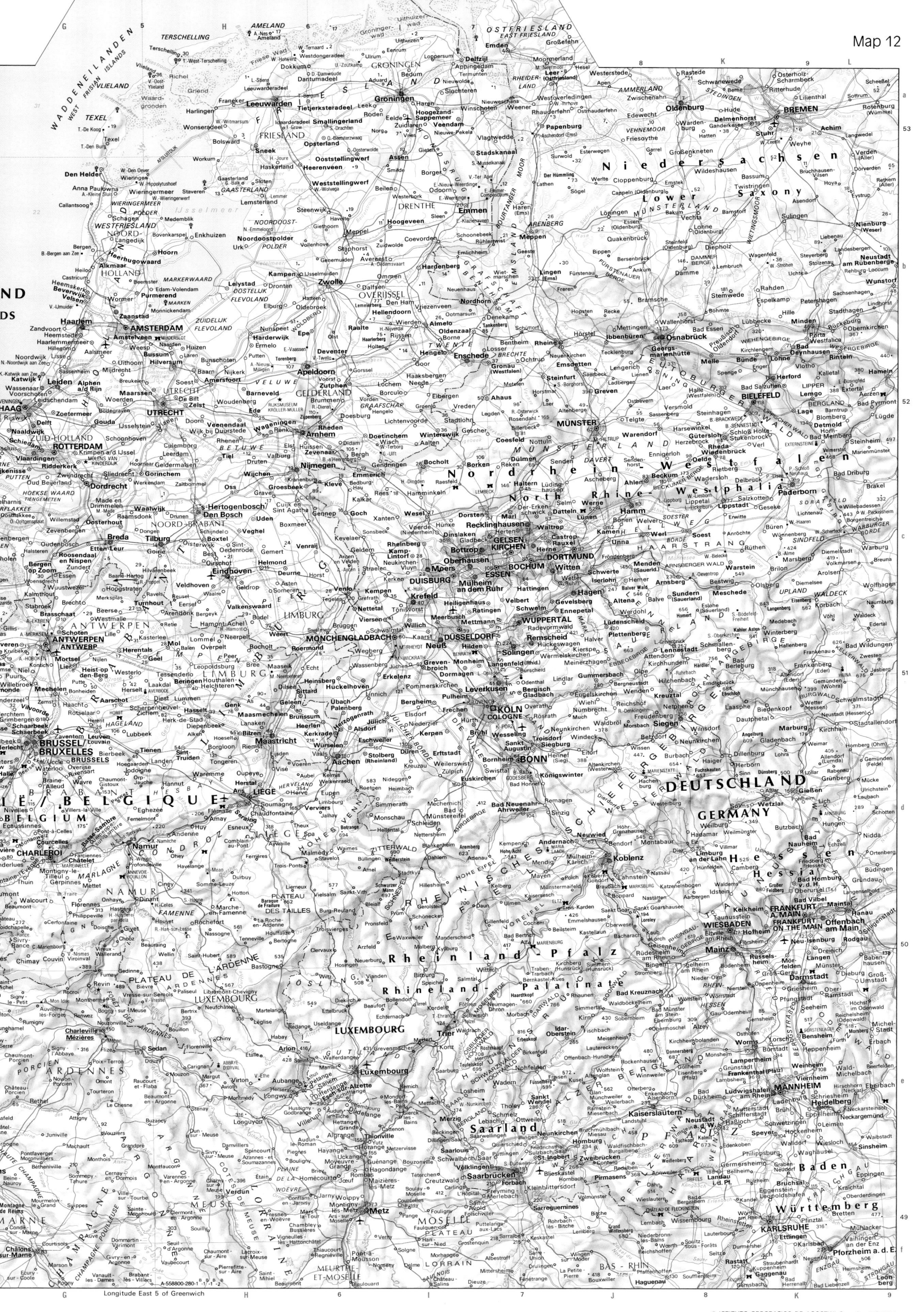

Map 13 **SPAIN AND PORTUGAL**

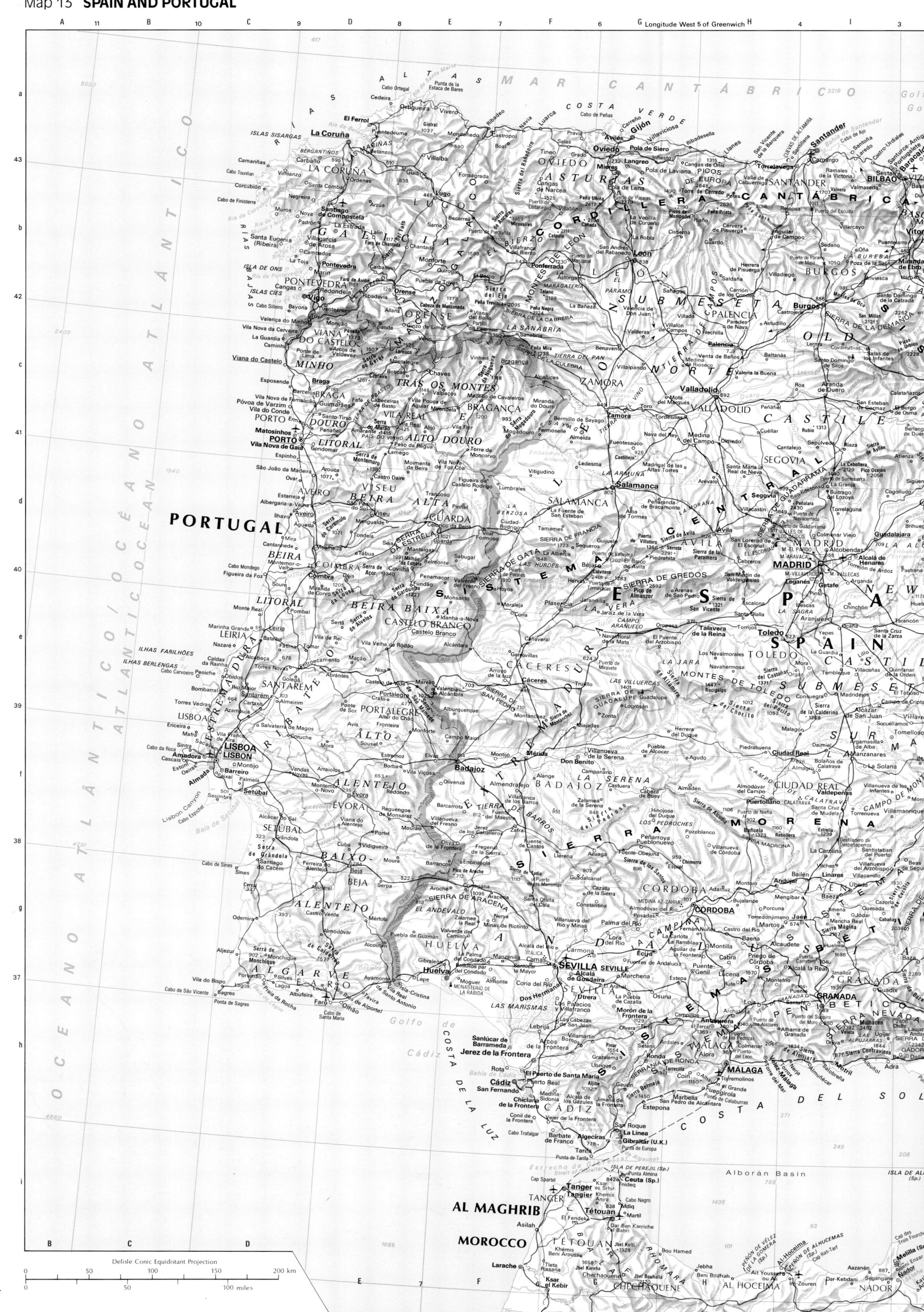

Delisle Conic Equidistant Projection

Map 14   ITALY, AUSTRIA AND SWITZERLAND

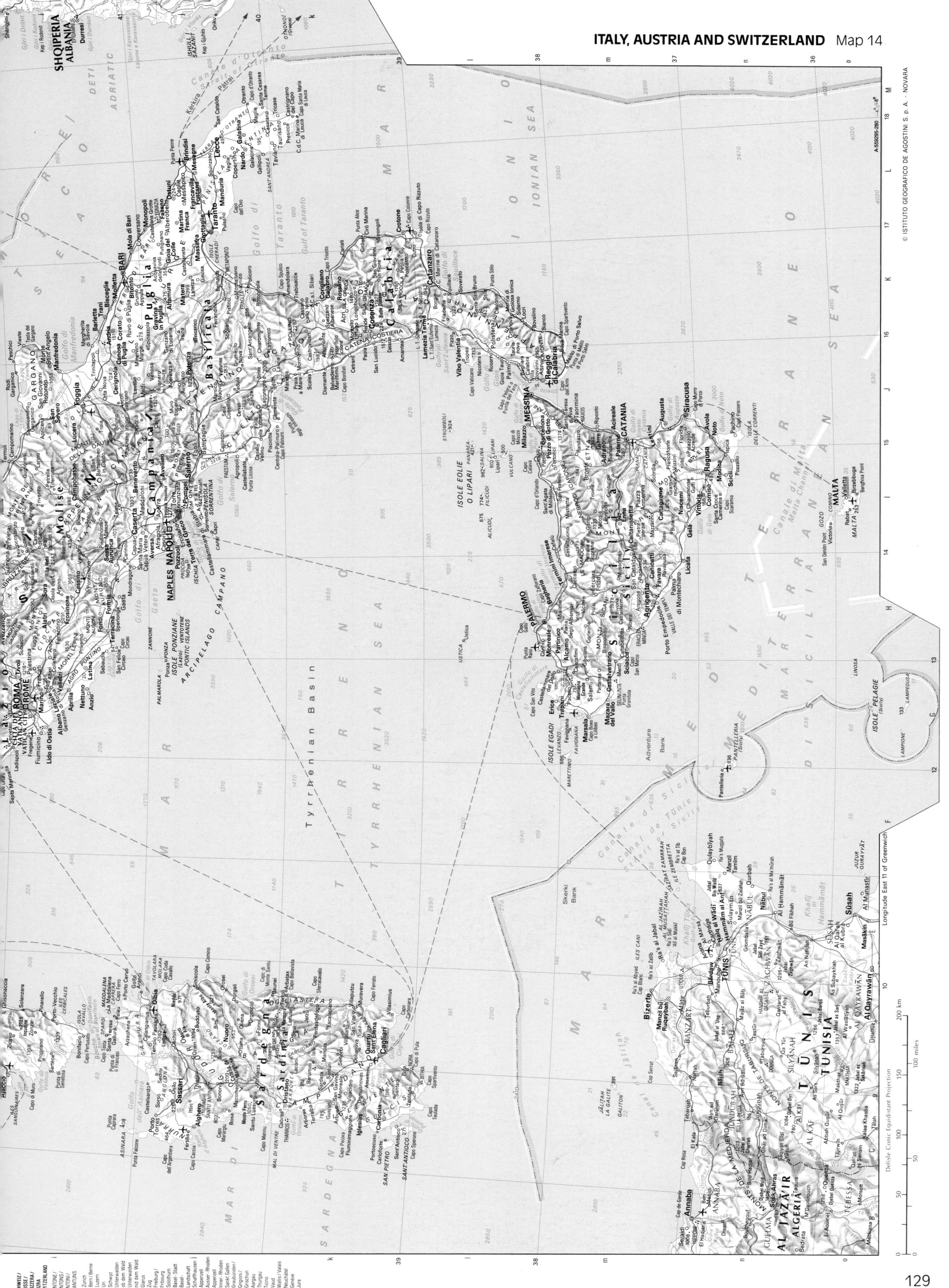

Map 15 **SOUTHEASTERN EUROPE**

Map 15

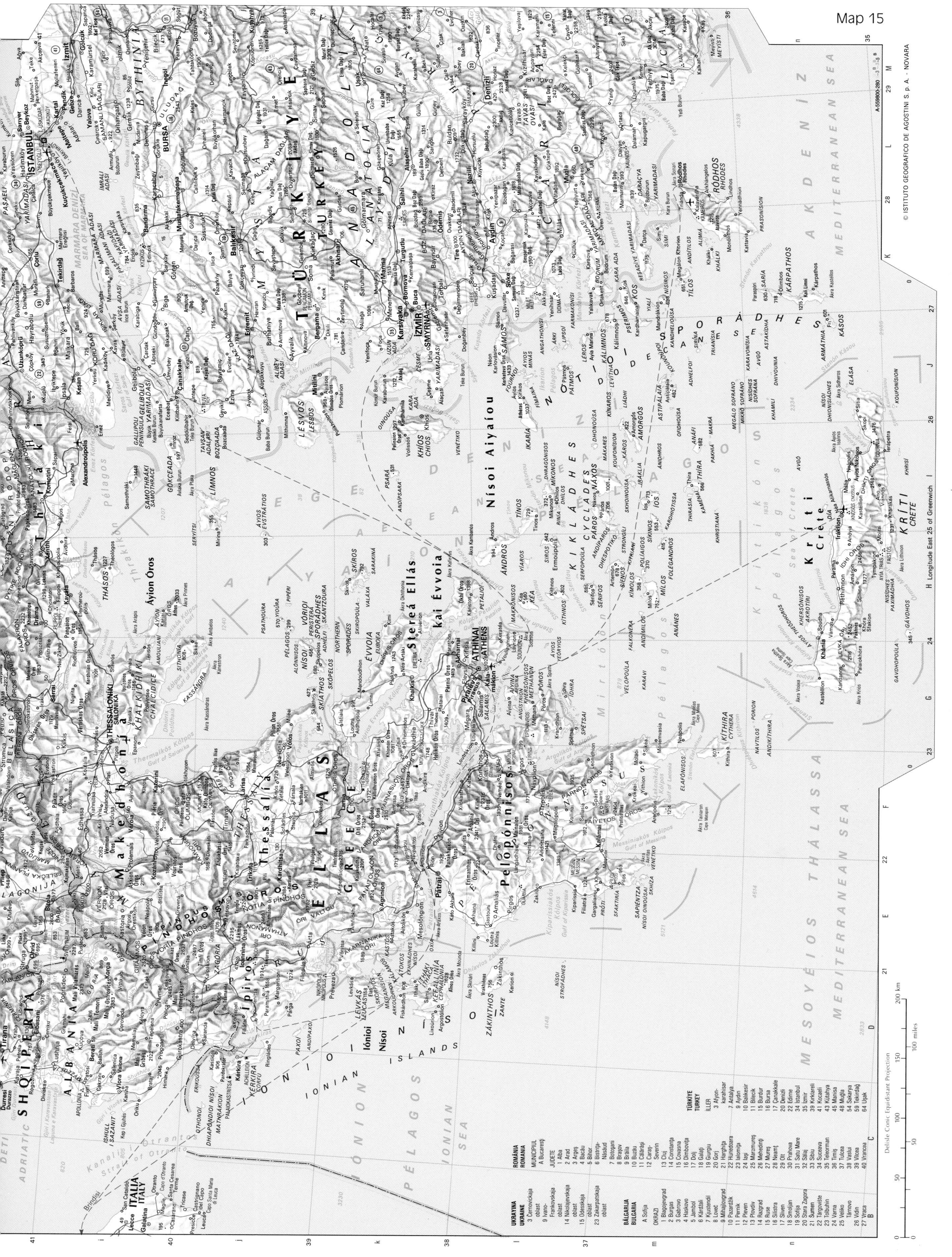

Map 16 **BLACK AND CASPIAN SEAS REGION**

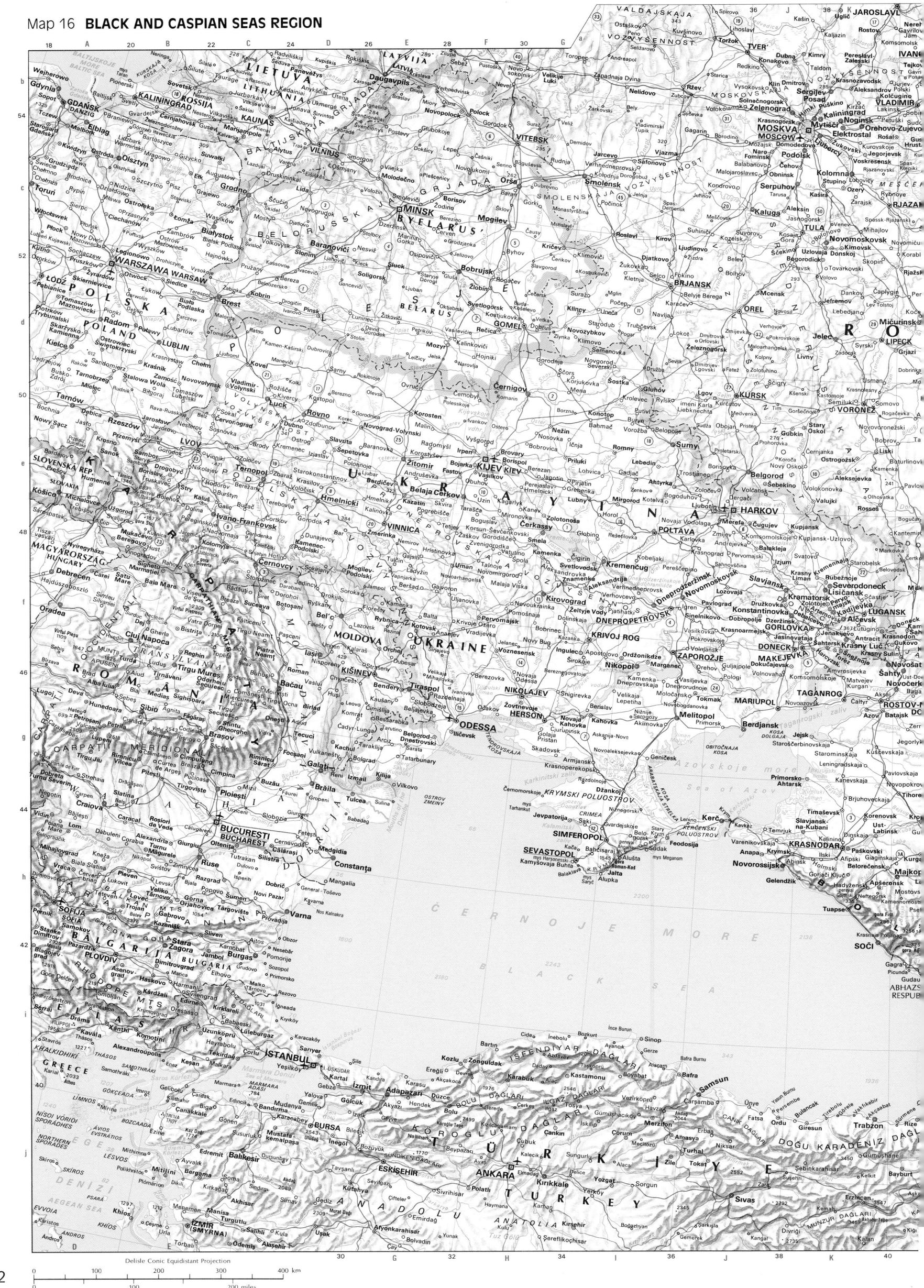

Delisle Conic Equidistant Projection

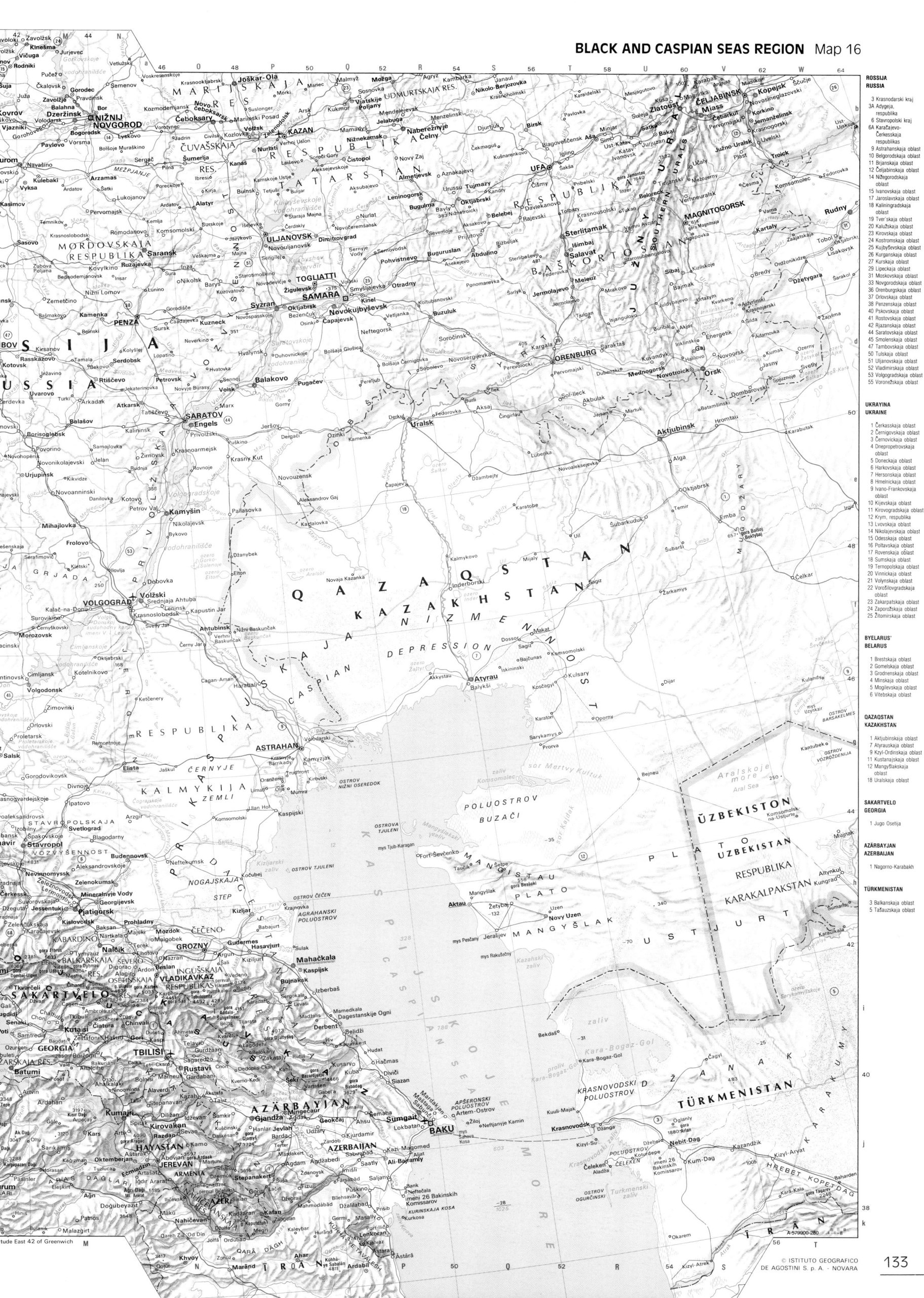

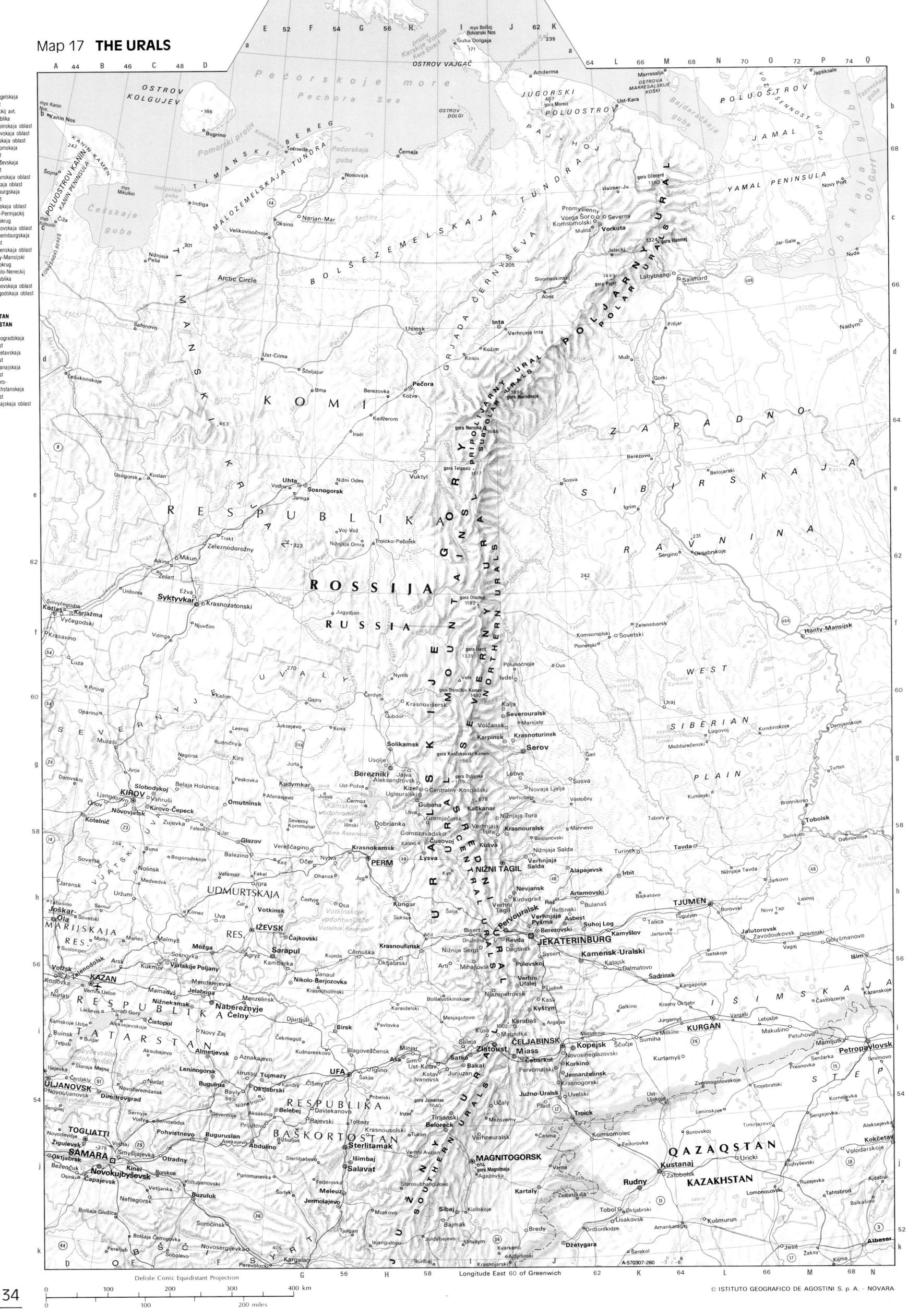

Map 17 **THE URALS**

ROSSIJA
RUSSIA

8 Arhangelskaja oblast
8A Neneckij avt. republika
12 Čeljabinskaja oblast
14 Gorkovskaja oblast
23 Kirovskaja oblast
24 Kostromskaja oblast
25 Kujbiševskaja oblast
26 Kurganskaja oblast
35 Omskaja oblast
36 Orenburgskaja oblast
39 Permskaja oblast
39A Komi-Permjackij avt. okrug
44 Saratovskaja oblast
46 Jekaterinburgskaja oblast
48 Tjumenskaja oblast
48A Hanty-Mansijskij avt. okrug
48B Jamalo-Neneckij respublika
51 Uljanovskaja oblast
54 Vologodskaja oblast

QAZAQSTAN
KAZAKHSTAN

3 Celinogradskaja oblast
10 Kokčetavskaja oblast
11 Kustanajskaja oblast
15 Severo-Kazahstanskaja oblast
17 Turgajskaja oblast

Delisle Conic Equidistant Projection

0 100 200 300 400 km
0 100 200 miles

Longitude East 60 of Greenwich

A-570307-280

© ISTITUTO GEOGRAFICO DE AGOSTINI S. p. A. - NOVARA

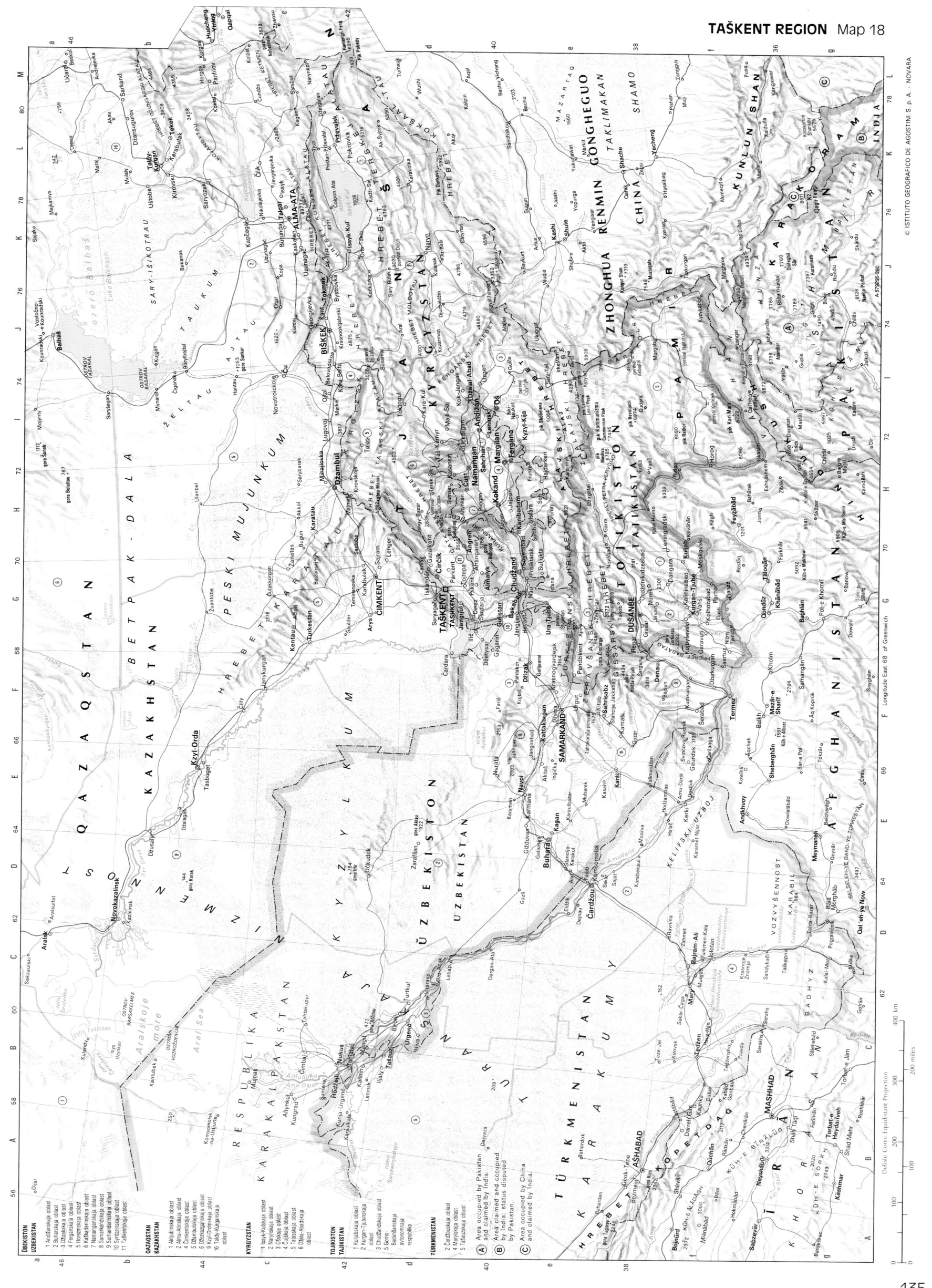

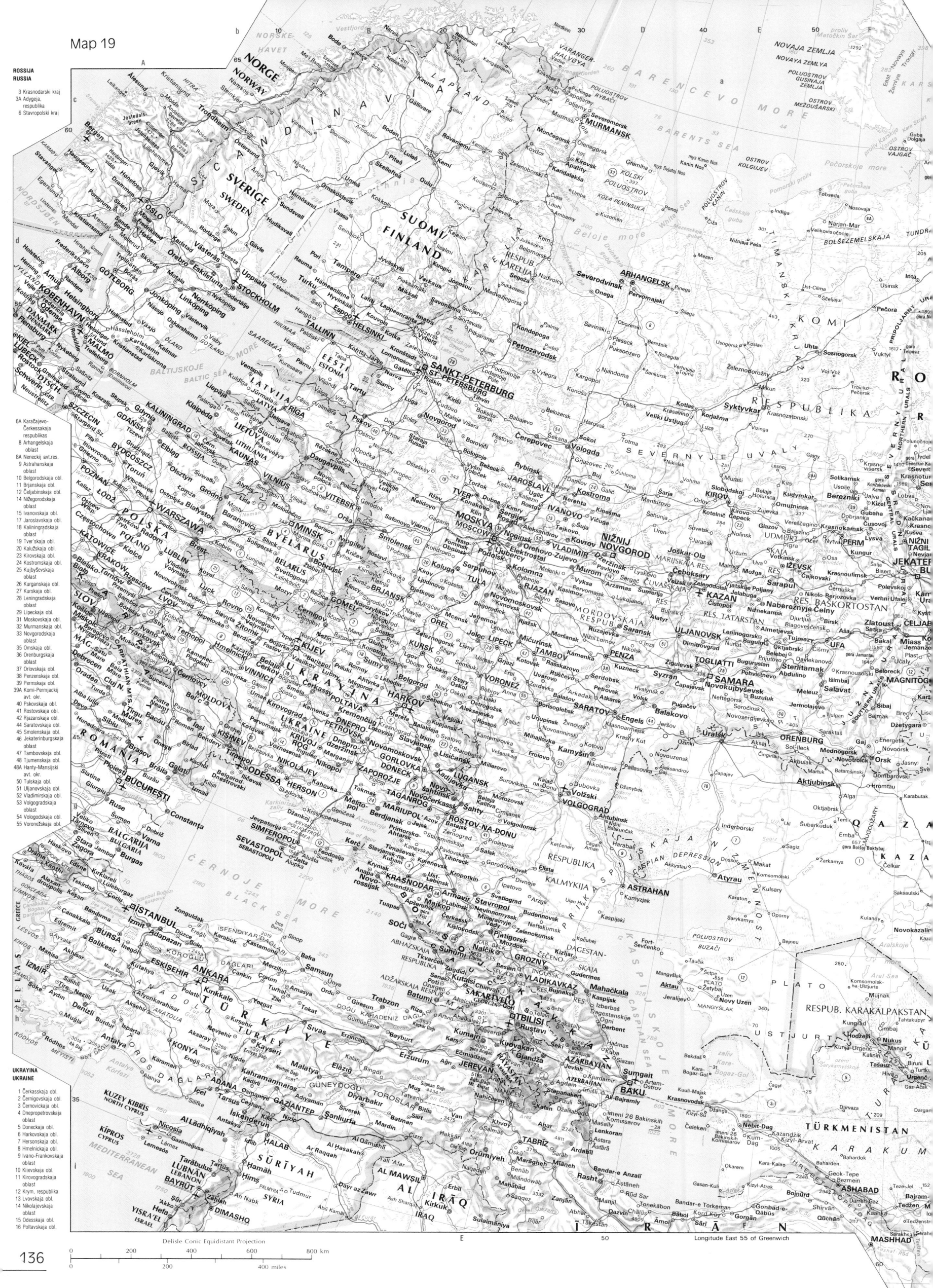

Map 19

ROSSIJA
RUSSIA

3 Krasnodarski kraj
3A Adygeja,
   respublika
6 Stavropolski kraj

6A Karačajevo-
   Čerkasskaja
   respublikas
8 Arhangelskaja
   oblast
8A Neneckij avt.res.
9 Astrahanskaja
   oblast
10 Belgorodskaja obl.
11 Brjanskaja obl.
12 Čeljabinskaja obl.
14 Nižegorodskaja
   oblast
15 Ivanovskaja obl.
17 Jaroslavskaja obl.
18 Kaliningradskaja
   oblast
19 Tver´skaja obl.
21 Kalužskaja obl.
23 Kirovskaja obl.
24 Kostromskaja obl.
25 Kujbyševskaja
   oblast
26 Kurganskaja obl.
27 Kurskaja obl.
28 Leningradskaja
   oblast
31 Lipeckaja obl.
33 Moskovskaja obl.
34 Murmanskaja obl.
35 Novgorodskaja
   oblast
35 Omskaja obl.
36 Orenburgskaja
   oblast
37 Orlovskaja obl.
38 Penzenskaja obl.
39 Permskaja obl.
39A Komi-Permjackij
   avt. okr.
40 Orlovskaja obl.
41 Rostovskaja obl.
42 Rjazanskaja obl.
44 Saratovskaja obl.
45 Smolenskaja obl.
46 Jekaterinburgskaja
   oblast
47 Tambovskaja obl.
48 Tjumenskaja obl.
48A Hanty-Mansijski
   avt. okr.
50 Tulskaja obl.
51 Uljanovskaja obl.
52 Vladimirskaja obl.
53 Volgogradskaja
   oblast
54 Vologodskaja obl.
55 Voronežskaja obl.

UKRAYINA
UKRAINE

1 Čerkasskaja obl.
2 Černigovskaja obl.
3 Černovickaja obl.
4 Dnepropetrovskaja
   oblast
5 Doneckaja obl.
6 Harkovskaja obl.
7 Hersonskaja obl.
8 Hmelnickaja obl.
9 Ivano-Frankovskaja
   oblast
10 Kievskaja obl.
11 Kirovogradskaja
   oblast
12 Krym, respublika
13 Lvovskaja obl.
14 Nikolajevskaja
   oblast
15 Odesskaja obl.
16 Poltavskaja obl.

Delisle Conic Equidistant Projection

Longitude East 55 of Greenwich

0   200   400   600   800 km
0   200   400 miles

The Commonwealth of Independent States (CIS) was created by republics of the former Soviet Union.

UKRAYINA
UKRAINE
17 Rovenskaja obl.
18 Sumskaja obl.
19 Ternopolskaja obl.
20 Vinnickaja obl.
21 Volynskaja obl.
22 Vorošilovgradskaja obl.
23 Zakarpatskaja obl.
24 Zaporožskaja obl.
25 Žitomirskaja obl.

BYELARUS'
BELARUS
1 Brestskaja obl.
2 Gomelskaja obl.
3 Grodnenskaja obl.
4 Minskaja obl.
5 Mogilevskaja obl.
6 Vitebskaja obl.

ÜZBEKISTON
UZBEKISTAN
1 Andižanskaja obl.
2 Buharskaja obl.
3 Džizakskaja obl.
4 Ferganskaja obl.
5 Horezmskaja obl.
6 Kašdadarinskaja oblast
7 Namanganskaja oblast
8 Samarkandskaja oblast
9 Surhandarinskaja oblast
10 Syrdarinskaja obl.
11 Taškentskaja obl.

QAZAQSTAN
KAZAKHSTAN
1 Aktjubinskaja obl.
2 Alma-Atinskaja oblast
3 Celinogradskaja oblast
4 Čimkentskaja obl.
5 Džambulskaja obl.
6 Džezkazganskaja oblast
7 Atyrauskaja obl.
8 Karagandinskaja oblast
9 Kzyl-Ordinskaja oblast
10 Kokčetavskaja obl.
11 Kustanajskaja obl.
12 Mangyšlakskaja obl.
13 Pavlodarskaja obl.
14 Semipalatinskaja obl.
15 Severo-Kazahstanskaja obl.
16 Taldy-Kurganskaja obl.
17 Turgajskaja obl.
18 Uralskaja obl.
19 Vostočno-Kazahstanskaja obl.

SAKARTVELO
GEORGIA
1 Jugo Osetija

AZÄRBAYJAN
AZERBAIJAN
1 Nagorno-Karabah

KYRGYZSTAN
1 Issyk-Kulskaja oblast
2 Narynskaja obl.
3 Ošskaja obl.
4 Gujskaja oblast
5 Talasskaja obl.
6 Džalal-Abadskaja oblast

TOJIKISTON
TAJIKISTAN
1 Kuljabskaja obl.
2 Kurgan-Tjubinskaja oblast
3 Chudžandskaja oblast
5 Gorno-Badahšanskaja avt. respublika

TÜRKMENISTAN
2 Čardžouskaja obl.
3 Balkanskaja oblast
4 Maryjskaja obl.
5 Tašauzskaja obl.

137

© ISTITUTO GEOGRAFICO DE AGOSTINI S.p.A. - NOVARA

Map 20

Delisle Conic Equidistant Projection

0   200   400   600   800 km

0   200   400 miles

ZHONGHUA RENMIN GONGHEGUO CHI

The Commonwealth of
Independent States (CIS)
was created by republics
of the former Soviet Union.

ARCTIC OCEAN

NY LEDOVITY OKEAN

NEW SIBERIAN ISLANDS
NOVOSIBIRSKIJE
OSTROVA ANŽU
ANJOU ISLANDS
OSTROVA DE-LONGA
DE LONG ISLANDS

OSTROV WRANGEL

ČUKOTSKOJE MORE
CHUKCHI SEA

CHUKCHI PENINSULA
ČUKOTSKIJ POLUOSTROV

VOSTOČNO-SIBIRSKOJE MORE
EAST SIBERIAN SEA

ANADYRSKOGORJE
PLOSKOGORJE

KOLYMSKAJA NIZMENNOST

KORJAKSKOJE NAGORJE

BERING SEA
BERINGOVO MORE

V E R H O J A N S K I J   H R E B E T

HREBET ČERSKOGO

JANO-INDIGIRSKAJA NIZMENNOST

Jakutsk

POLUOSTROV KAMČATKA
KAMCHATKA PENINSULA

SREDINNYJ HREBET

Magadan

Petropavlovsk-Kamčatski

HREBET DŽUGDŽUR
DŽUGDŽUR RANGE

OHOTSKOJE MORE
SEA OF OKHOTSK

STANOVOY RANGE

ALDANSKOJE NAGORJE
ALDAN PLATEAU

Komsomolsk-na-Amure

OSTROV SAHALIN
SAKHALIN

Nikolajevsk-na-Amure

Blagoveščensk

HABAROVSK

Birobidžan

KURILSKIJE OSTROVA
KURIL ISLANDS

KOMANDORSKIJE OSTROVA
KOMANDORSKI ISLANDS

Južno-Sahalinsk
Korsakov

HARBIN

MUDANJIANG

VLADIVOSTOK

CHANGCHUN

JILIN

QIQIHAR

MANCHURIA

HOKKAIDO

SAPPORO

ASAHIKAWA

Kushiro

HAKODATE

NIPPON
JAPAN

SEA OF JAPAN
JAPONSKOJE MORE

PACIFIC OCEAN
TIHI OKEAN

Aleutian Trench

Obruchev Rise

Kuril Basin

HONSHŪ

Ostrov Kunašir, ostrov Šikotan, ostrov
Iturup and Malaja Kurilskaja Grjada,
occupied since 1945,
are claimed by Japan pending a final
peace treaty.

Longitude East 150 of Greenwich

© ISTITUTO GEOGRAFICO DE AGOSTINI S. p A. · NOVARA

**ROSSIJA
RUSSIA**

1 Altajski kraj
1A Gornyj Altaj, respublika
2 Habarovski kraj
2A Evrejskaja avt. respublika
4 Krasnojarski kraj
4A Hakasija, respublika
5 Primorski kraj
7 Amurskaja oblast
8A Neneckij avt. respublika
13 Čitinskaja oblast
16 Irkutskaja oblast
16A Ust-Ordynski Burjatski avt. okrug
21 Kamčatskaja oblast
21A Korjakski avt. okrug
22 Kemerovskaja oblast
30 Magadanskaja oblast
30A Čukotski avt. okrug
34 Novosibirskaja oblast
35 Omskaja oblast
43 Sahalinskaja oblast
48 Tjumenskaja oblast
48A Hanty-Mansijski avt. okrug
48B Jamalo-Neneckij respublika
49 Tomskaja oblast

**QAZAQSTAN
KAZAKHSTAN**

13 Pavlodarskaja oblast
14 Semipalatinskaja oblast
19 Vostočno-Kazahstanskaja oblast

A-579395-280

139

Map 21 **ASIA, PHYSICAL**

Lambert Azimuthal Equal Area Projection

Longitude East 80 of Greenwich

Map 22 **ASIA, POLITICAL**

PACIFIC OCEAN

LEUTIAN ISLANDS

Bering Sea

Sea of Okhotsk

KURIL ISLANDS

KAMCHATKA PENINSULA

ALASKA (U.S.)

BROOKS RANGE

ALASKA RANGE

Gulf of Alaska

Anchorage

Fairbanks

Beaufort Sea

Chukchi Sea

CHUKCHA PENINSULA

East Siberian Sea

WRANGEL

NEW SIBERIAN ISLANDS

CHERSKI MOUNTAINS

VERKHOYANSK MOUNTAINS

STANOVOY RANGE

GREATER KHINGAN RANGE

ARCTIC OCEAN

North Pole

CANADA

BAFFIN

VICTORIA

BANKS

DEVON

ELLESMERE

QUEEN ELIZABETH ISLANDS

RASMUSSEN LAND

Greenland (Den.)

LAPTEV SEA

TAYMYR PENINSULA

SEVERNAYA ZEMLYA

CENTRAL SIBERIAN UPLANDS

RUSSIA

WEST SIBERIAN PLAIN

MONGOLIA

GOBI DESERT

SAYAN MOUNTAINS

ALTAY MOUNTAINS

Irkutsk

Ulan-Bator

Novosibirsk

Omsk

Tomsk

Krasnoyarsk

Kara Sea

NOVAYA ZEMLYA

FRANZ JOSEPH LAND

SPITSBERGEN

Svalbard (Norway)

Longyearbyen

Barents Sea

Greenland Sea

Norwegian Sea

ICELAND

Reykjavik

FAEROE ISLANDS (Den.)

SHETLAND ISLANDS (U.K.)

KAZAKHSTAN

UZBEKISTAN

TURKMENISTAN

Tashkent

Samarkand

Ashabad

Aral Sea

Murmansk

KOLA PENINSULA

Arhangelsk

FINLAND

Helsinki

Sankt-Peterburg

Moskva (Moscow)

NORWAY

SWEDEN

Oslo

Stockholm

Trondheim

Bergen

Göteborg

Caspian Sea

Baku

Tbilisi

Yerevan

GEORGIA

CAUCASUS

ESTONIA

Tallinn

LATVIA

Riga

LITHUANIA

Vilnius

BELARUS

Minsk

UKRAINE

Kijev

Odessa

Black Sea

TURKEY

Ankara

Istanbul

IRAQ

SYRIA

LEBANON

ISRAEL

CYPRUS

N. CYPRUS

EGYPT

Mediterranean Sea

CRETE

GREECE

Athina

BULGARIA

Sofija

ROMANIA

Bucuresti

HUNGARY

Budapest

AUSTRIA

SLOVAKIA

Bratislava

CZECH

Praha

POLAND

Warszawa

Kraków

GERMANY

Berlin

Hamburg

München

Frankfurt

DENMARK

København

UNITED KINGDOM

London

Edinburgh

Glasgow

Belfast

Dublin

IRELAND

Bristol

Plymouth

Manchester

Liverpool

Birm.

North Sea

HEBRIDES

Aberdeen

English Channel

BELGIUM

Bruxelles

Paris

FRANCE

Lyon

Marseille

Bordeaux

Nantes

Brest

Le Havre

SWITZ.

Milano

Torino

Genova

Firenze

Roma

Napoli

Bari

ITALY

CORSICA

SARDINIA

Adriatic Sea

CROATIA

Sarajevo

Beograd

ALBANIA

Skopje

ATLANTIC OCEAN

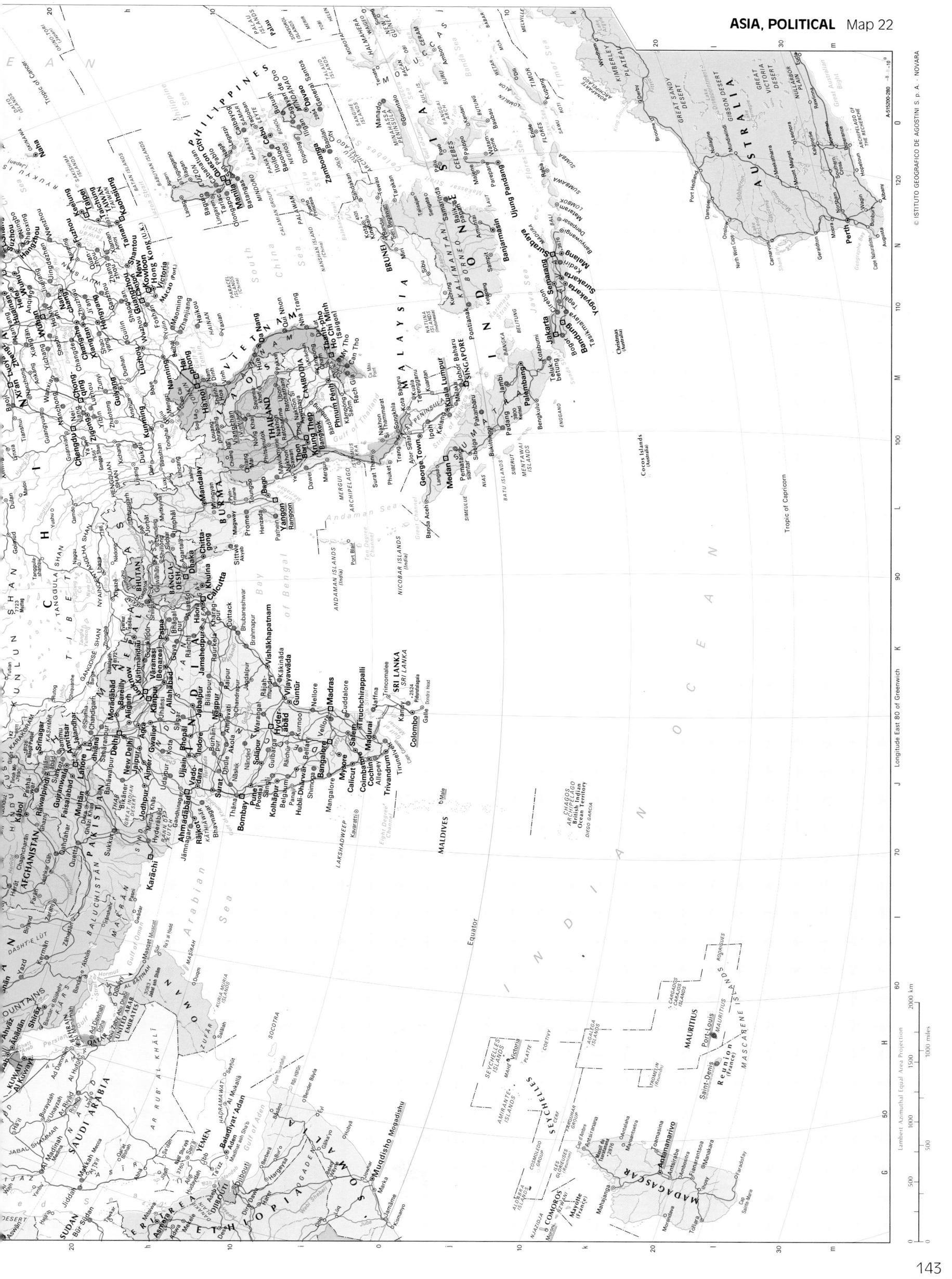

© ISTITUTO GEOGRAFICO DE AGOSTINI S. p. A. - NOVARA

143

Map 23 **SOUTHWESTERN ASIA**

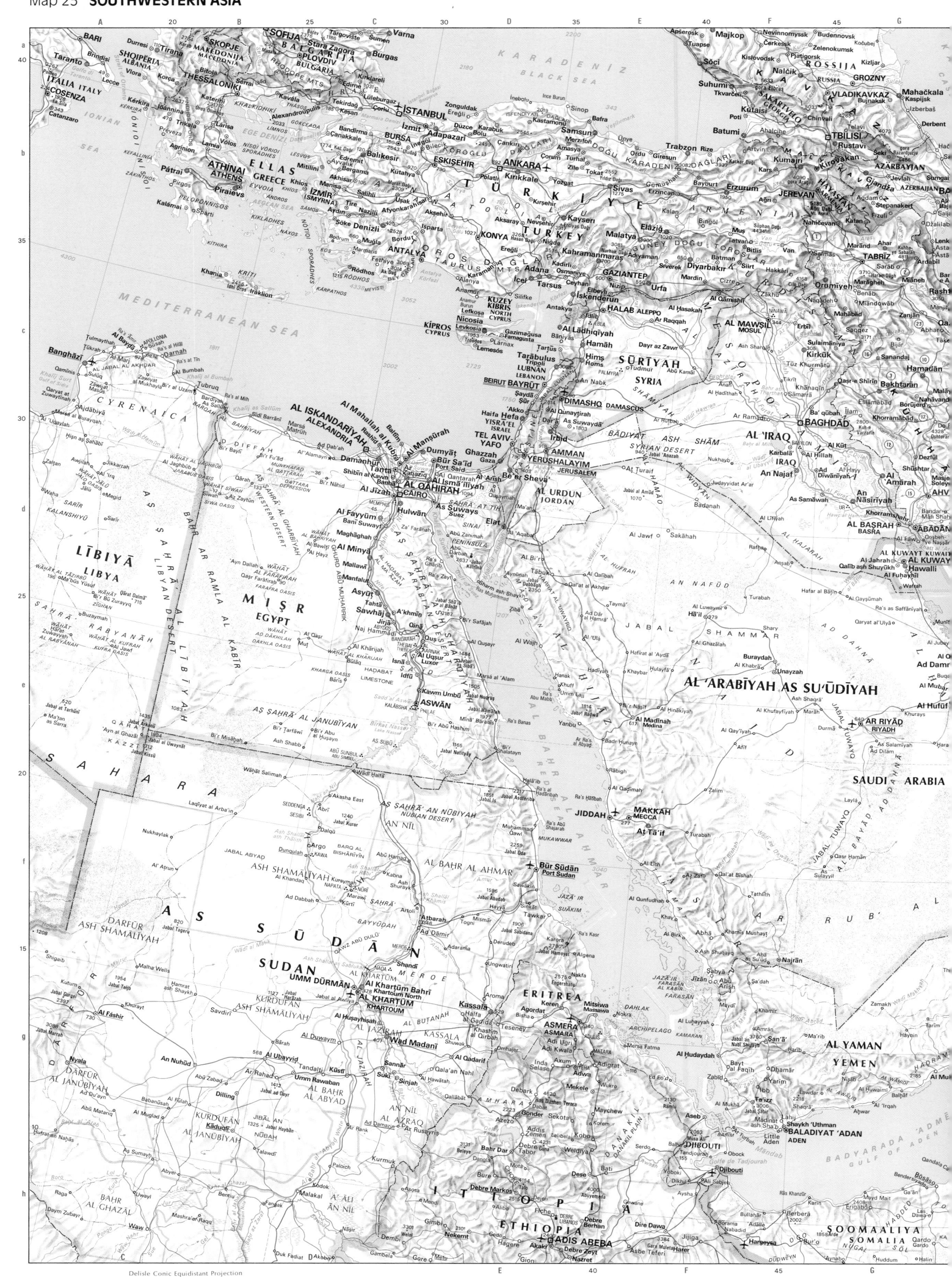

Delisle Conic Equidistant Projection

0   200   400   600   800 km

0   200   400 miles

AFGHANISTAN

VELĀYAT

1 Badakhshān
2 Bādghīsāt
3 Baghlān
4 Balkh
5 Bāmiān
6 Farāh
7 Fāryāb
8 Ghaznī
9 Ghowr
10 Helmand
11 Herāt
12 Jowzjān
13 Kābol
14 Kāpīsā
15 Konarha
16 Laghmān
17 Lowgar
18 Nangarhār
19 Nīmrūz
20 Orūzgān
21 Paktiā
22 Parvān
23 Qandahār
24 Qondūz
25 Samangān
26 Takhār
27 Vardak
28 Zābol

ĪRĀN

OSTĀN

1 Āzarbāījān-e Gharbī
2 Āzarbāījān-e Sharqī
3 Bakhtarān
4 Boyer Ahmadī-e Kohkīlūyeh
5 Būshehr
6 Chahār Mahāl-e Bakhtiārī
7 Esfahān
8 Fārs
9 Gīlān
10 Hamadān
11 Hormozgān
12 Īlām
13 Kermān
14 Khorāsān
15 Khūzestān
16 Kordestān
17 Lorestān
18 Markazī
19 Māzandarān
20 Semnān
21 Sīstāne-e Balūchestān
22 Yazd
23 Zanjān

Ⓐ Area occupied by Pakistan and claimed by India.
Ⓑ Area claimed and occupied by India; status disputed by Pakistan.
Ⓒ Area occupied by China and claimed by India.

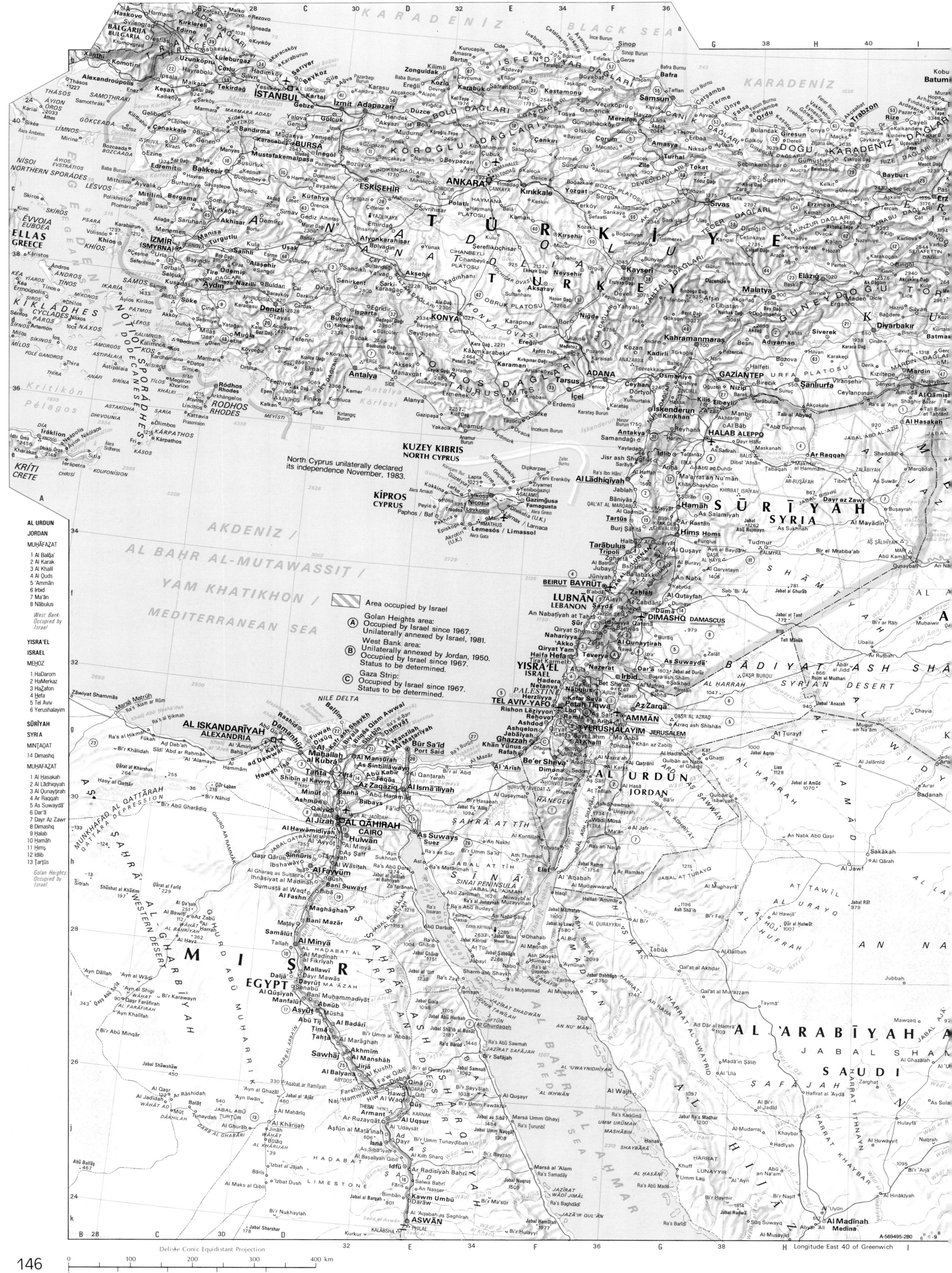

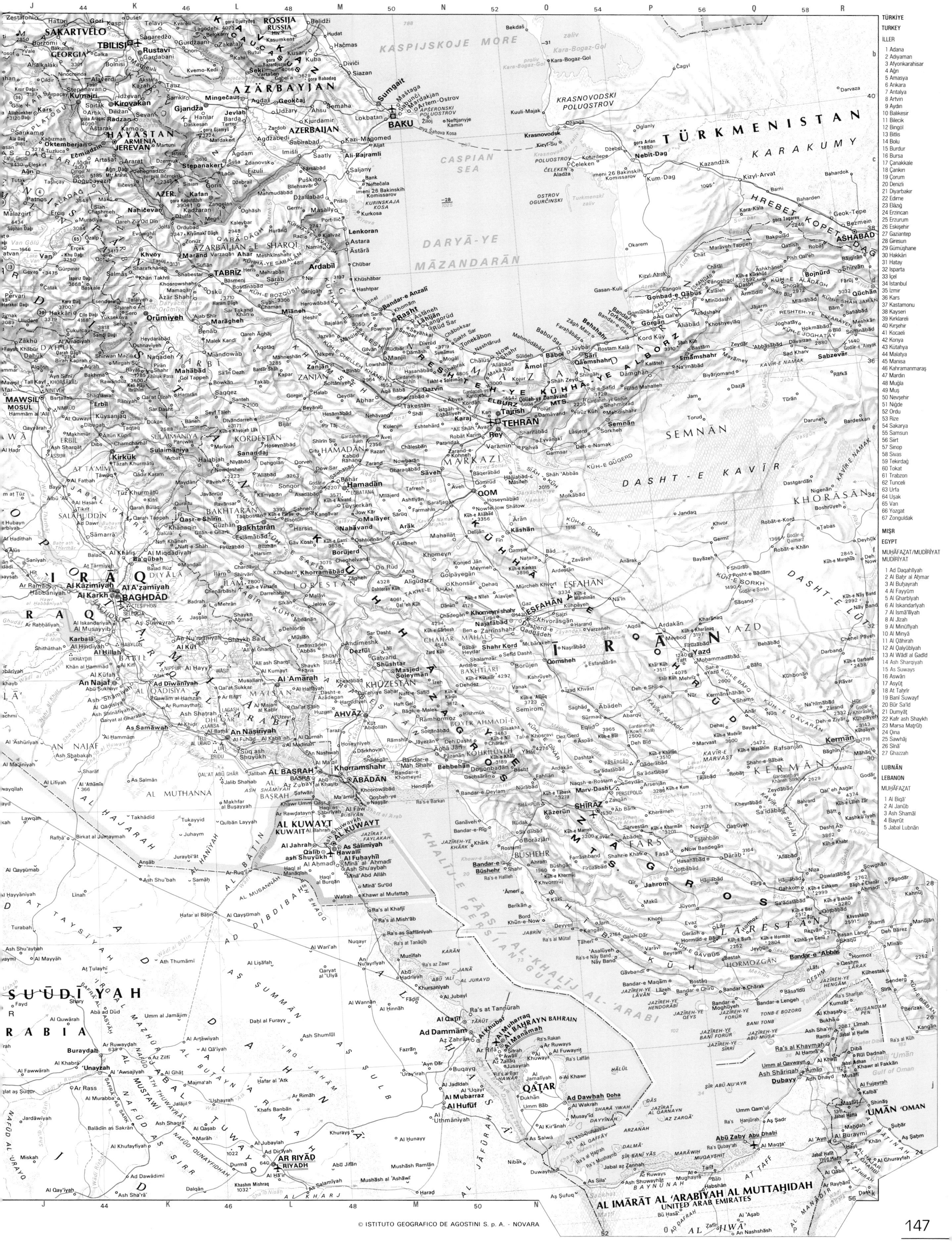

TÜRKIYE
TURKEY
İLLER

1 Adana
2 Adıyaman
3 Afyonkarahisar
4 Ağrı
5 Amasya
6 Ankara
7 Antalya
8 Artvin
9 Aydın
10 Balıkesir
11 Bilecik
12 Bingöl
13 Bitlis
14 Bolu
15 Burdur
16 Bursa
17 Çanakkale
18 Çankırı
19 Çorum
20 Denizli
21 Diyarbakır
22 Edirne
23 Elazığ
24 Erzincan
25 Erzurum
26 Eskişehir
27 Gaziantep
28 Giresun
29 Gümüşhane
30 Hakkari
31 Hatay
32 Isparta
33 İçel
34 Istanbul
35 İzmir
36 Kars
37 Kastamonu
38 Kayseri
39 Kırklareli
40 Kırşehir
41 Kocaeli
42 Konya
43 Kütahya
44 Malatya
45 Manisa
46 Kahramanmaraş
47 Mardin
48 Muğla
49 Muş
50 Nevşehir
51 Niğde
52 Ordu
53 Rize
54 Sakarya
55 Samsun
56 Siirt
57 Sinop
58 Sivas
59 Tekirdağ
60 Tokat
61 Trabzon
62 Tunceli
63 Urfa
64 Uşak
65 Van
66 Yozgat
67 Zonguldak

MISR
EGYPT
MUHĀFAZĀT/MUDĪRĪYAT
MUDIRIYAT

1 Ad Daqahlīyah
2 Al Bahr al Aḥmar
3 Al Buḥayrah
4 Al Fayyūm
5 Al Gharbīyah
6 Al Iskandarīyah
7 Al Ismā'īlīyah
8 Al Jīzah
9 Al Minūfīyah
10 Al Minyā
11 Al Qāhirah
12 Al Qalyūbīyah
13 Al Wādī al Gadīd
14 As Sharqīyah
15 As Suways
16 Aswān
17 Asyūṭ
18 At Taḥrīr
19 Banī Suwayf
20 Būr Sa'īd
21 Dumyāṭ
22 Kafr ash Shaykh
23 Marsa Maṭrūḥ
24 Qinā
25 Sawhāj
26 Sīnā'
27 Ghazzah

LUBNĀN
LEBANON
MUHĀFAZĀT

1 Al Biqā'
2 Al Janūb
3 Ash Shamāli
4 Bayrūt
5 Jabal Lubnān

© ISTITUTO GEOGRAFICO DE AGOSTINI S.p.A. - NOVARA

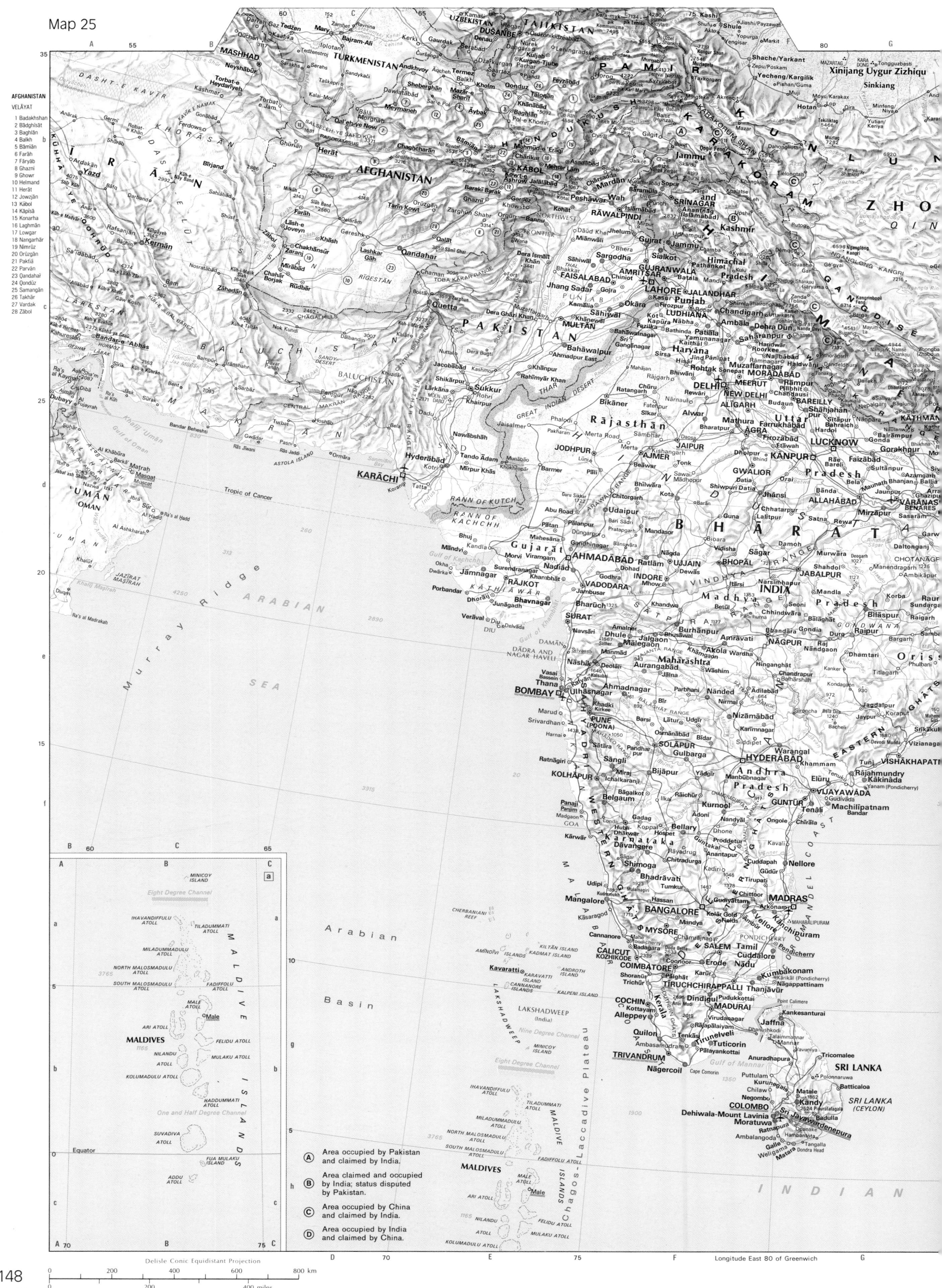

Map 25

AFGHANISTAN
VELĀYAT

1 Badakhshān
2 Bādghīsāt
3 Baghlān
4 Balkh
5 Bāmīān
6 Farāh
7 Fāryāb
8 Ghaznī
9 Ghowr
10 Helmand
11 Herāt
12 Jowzjān
13 Kābol
14 Kāpīsā
15 Konarhā
16 Laghmān
17 Lowgar
18 Nangarhār
19 Nīmrūz
20 Orūzgān
21 Paktiā
22 Parvān
23 Qandahār
24 Qondūz
25 Samangān
26 Takhār
27 Vardak
28 Zābol

Area occupied by Pakistan and claimed by India.

Area claimed and occupied by India; status disputed by Pakistan.

Area occupied by China and claimed by India.

Area occupied by India and claimed by China.

Delisle Conic Equidistant Projection

Longitude East 80 of Greenwich

0   200   400   600   800 km
0   200   400 miles

Map 26 **SOUTHEAST ASIA**

Mercator Cylindrical Projection

Longitude East 110 of Greenwich

Tropic of Cancer

KEELUNG
Taoyuan
TAIPEI
Hsinchu
Hirara
NIPPON JAPAN
TAICHUNG
Changhua
Nantou Hualien
Yunlin
TAIWAN
CHIAYI
TAINAN Taitung
Hsinying
KAOHSIUNG Pingtung
Fangliao

Zhangping
Longyan
Quanzhou
Xiamen Amoy
Zhangzhou
Yunxiao
Jieyang
Chaoyang
SHANTOU
Hui'an

DONGSHA QUNDAO

Luzon Strait

ITBAYAT
Basco BATAN ISLANDS
BATAN
SABTANG

PHILIPPINE

SEA

West

Mariana

Philippine Basin

Basin

OKINO-TORI-SHIMA
PARECE VELA (Japan)

PACIFIC

OCEAN

CALAYAN
DALUPIRI FUGA CAMIGUIN
BABUYAN ISLANDS
Mayraira Point
Bangui Aparri
Laoag Escarpada Point
San Vicente
Banguid Tuguegarao
Vigan Ilagan
San Fernando
Baguio
Dagupan
LUZON

LUBANG ISLANDS
MANILA
QUEZON CITY
PILIPINAS
PHILIPPINES

FEDERATED STATES

OF MICRONESIA

MINDORO

PANAY
Iloilo
Bacolod
CEBU
NEGROS
Dumaguete

SAMAR
Calbayog
Catbalogan
Tacloban
LEYTE

ULITHI ATOLL

45

FAIS

YAP ISLANDS
Colonia

NGULU ATOLL

Dipolog
Cagayan de Oro
Iligan
Marawi
ZAMBOANGA
Basilan City
Isabela
Jolo

Butuan

MINDANAO
DAVAO
General Santos

SULU SEA

SULU ARCHIPELAGO

KAYANGEL ISLANDS

BABELTHUAP
Koror
PALAU ISLANDS
ANGAUR PELELIU

CAROLINE ISLANDS

Palau

Belau

SOROL ATOLL

Sabah
Tawau

PULAU MIANGAS (Indonesia)

SARANGANI ISLANDS

KEPULAUAN NANUSA

PULO ANNA

MERIR

SONSOROL ISLANDS

West

Caroline

Basin

KALIMANTAN
TIMUR
Tarakan

Celebes Basin

CELEBES SEA
LAUT SULAWESI

KEPULAUAN TALAUD
TALAUD ISLANDS

PULAU KARAKELONG

TOBI

HELEN REEF

Samarinda

Manado
Tondano
SULAWESI UTARA

HALMAHERA
Ternate
Tidore

Equator

Jayapura

INDONESIA

Balikpapan

KALIMANTAN

Palu

SULAWESI TENGAH
CELEBES

Poso

SERAM CERAM
Ambon

PEGUNUNGAN VAN REES

IRIAN JAYA

PAPUA
NEW GUINEA

Makale
Palopo
Majene
Parepare
SULAWESI SELATAN
SULAWESI TENGGARA
Watampone

PULAU BURU

MALUKU

NEW GUINEA

UJUNG PANDANG (MAKASAR)

Baubau

BANDA SEA

PULAU IRIAN

PULAU DOLAK

MERAUKE

PULAU SUMBAWA
Mataram
PULAU LOMBOK

PULAU FLORES

LAUT FLORES

SAWU SEA

TIMOR TIMUR
TIMOR

Kupang

FLORES SEA

ARAFURA SEA

LAUT ARAFURA

NUSA TENGGARA TIMUR

LAUT TIMOR
TIMOR SEA

Torres Strait

MULGRAVE ISLAND

Darwin
AUSTRALIA

151

Map 27 **CHINA AND MONGOLIA**

Delisle Conic Equidistant Projection

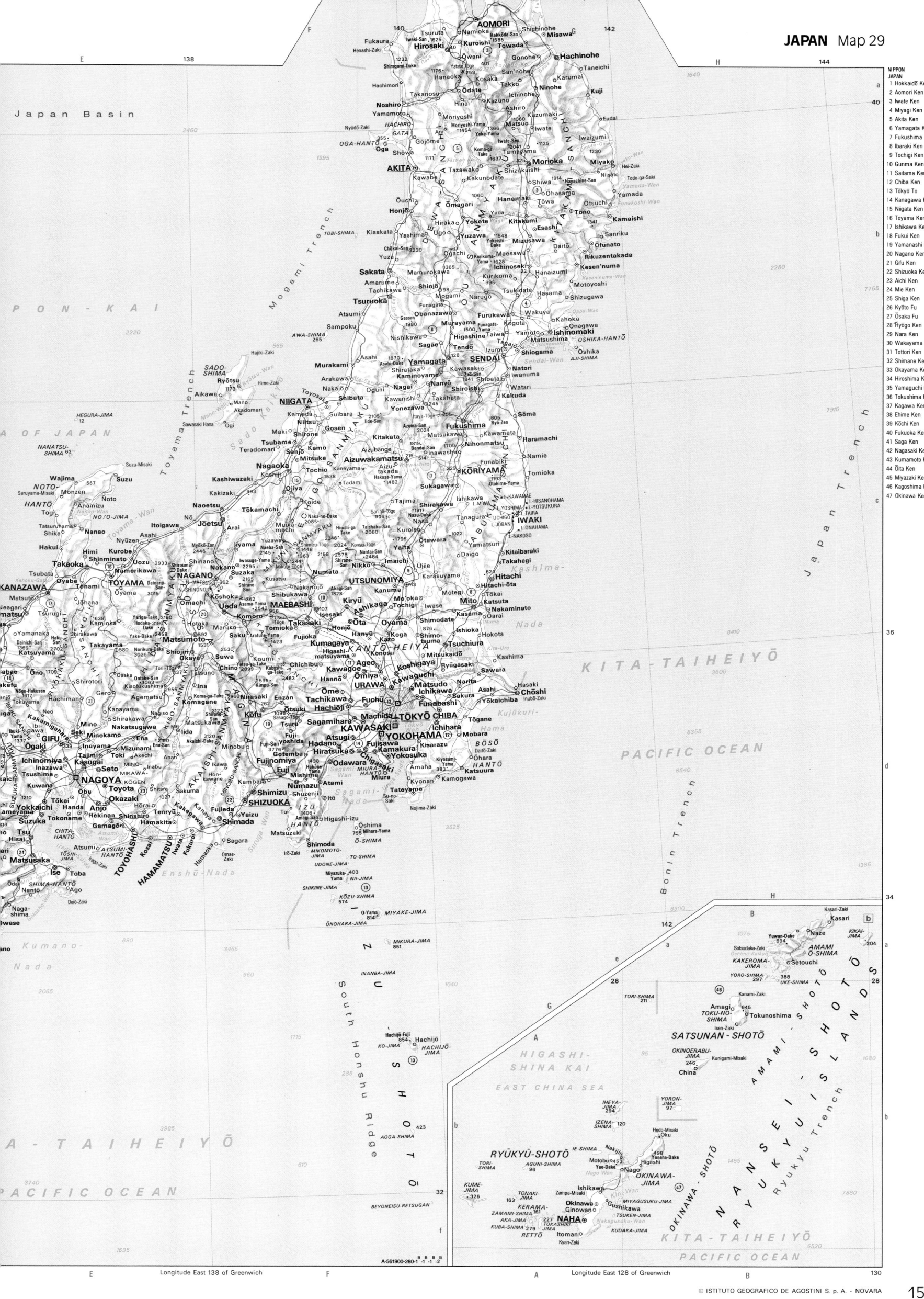

NIPPON
JAPAN
1 Hokkaidō Ken
2 Aomori Ken
3 Iwate Ken
4 Miyagi Ken
5 Akita Ken
6 Yamagata Ken
7 Fukushima Ken
8 Ibaraki Ken
9 Tochigi Ken
10 Gunma Ken
11 Saitama Ken
12 Chiba Ken
13 Tōkyō To
14 Kanagawa Ken
15 Niigata Ken
16 Toyama Ken
17 Ishikawa Ken
18 Fukui Ken
19 Yamanashi Ken
20 Nagano Ken
21 Gifu Ken
22 Shizuoka Ken
23 Aichi Ken
24 Mie Ken
25 Shiga Ken
26 Kyōto Fu
27 Ōsaka Fu
28 Hyōgo Ken
29 Nara Ken
30 Wakayama Ken
31 Tottori Ken
32 Shimane Ken
33 Okayama Ken
34 Hiroshima Ken
35 Yamaguchi Ken
36 Tokushima Ken
37 Kagawa Ken
38 Ehime Ken
39 Kōchi Ken
40 Fukuoka Ken
41 Saga Ken
42 Nagasaki Ken
43 Kumamoto Ken
44 Ōita Ken
45 Miyazaki Ken
46 Kagoshima Ken
47 Okinawa Ken

Map 30 **AFRICA, PHYSICAL**

Map 30

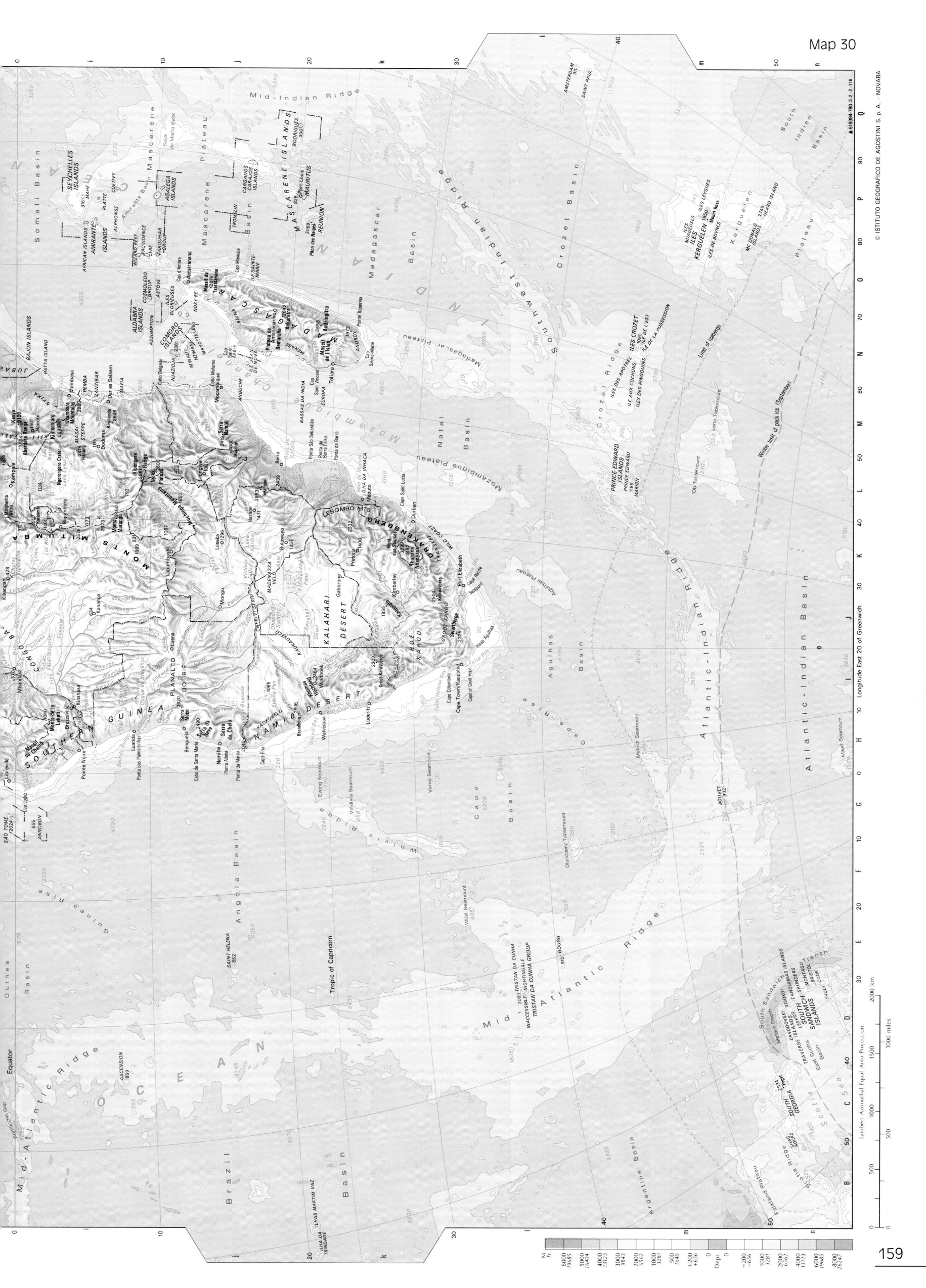

© ISTITUTO GEOGRAFICO DE AGOSTINI S. p. A. - NOVARA

159

Map 31 **AFRICA, POLITICAL**

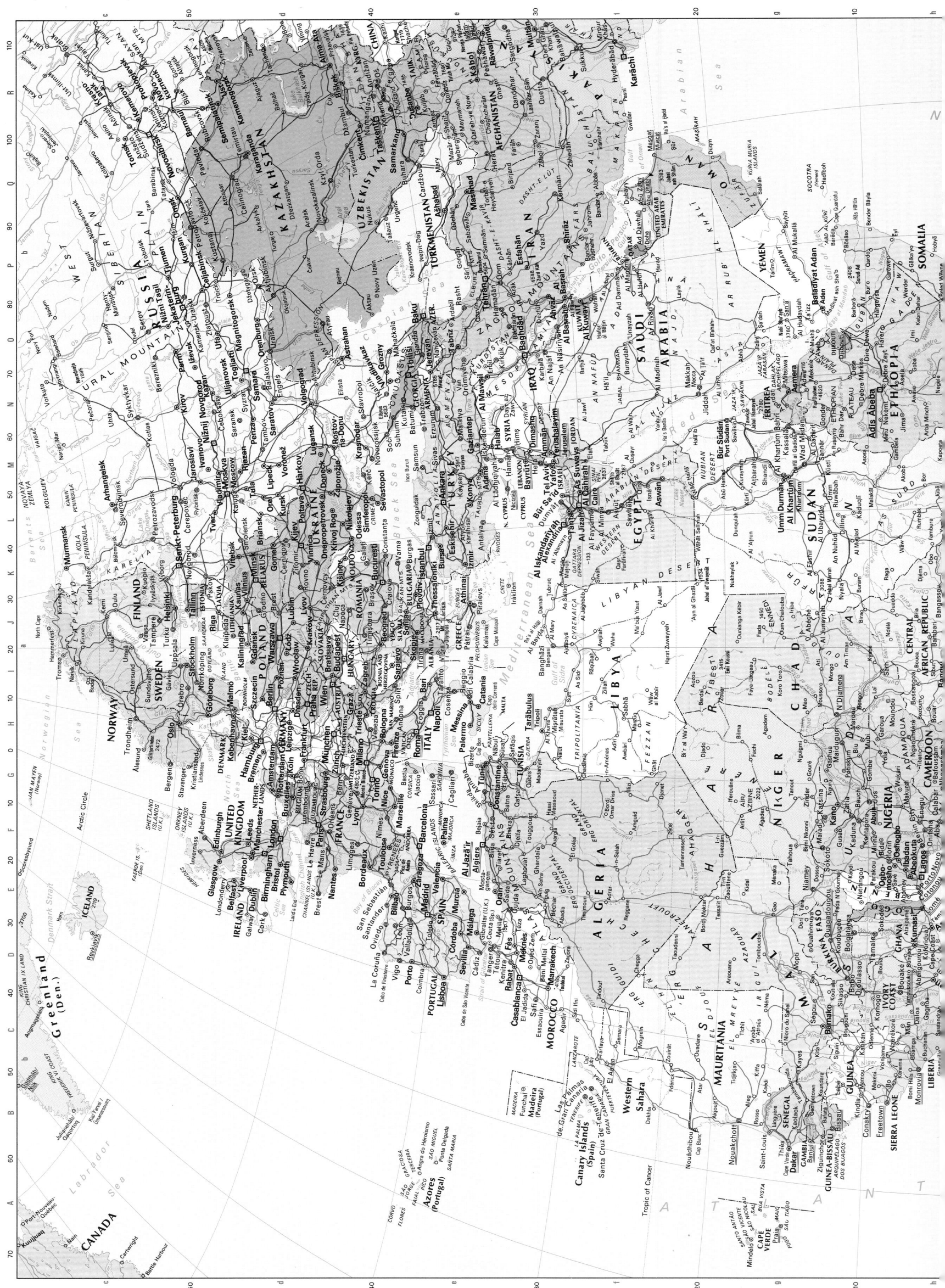

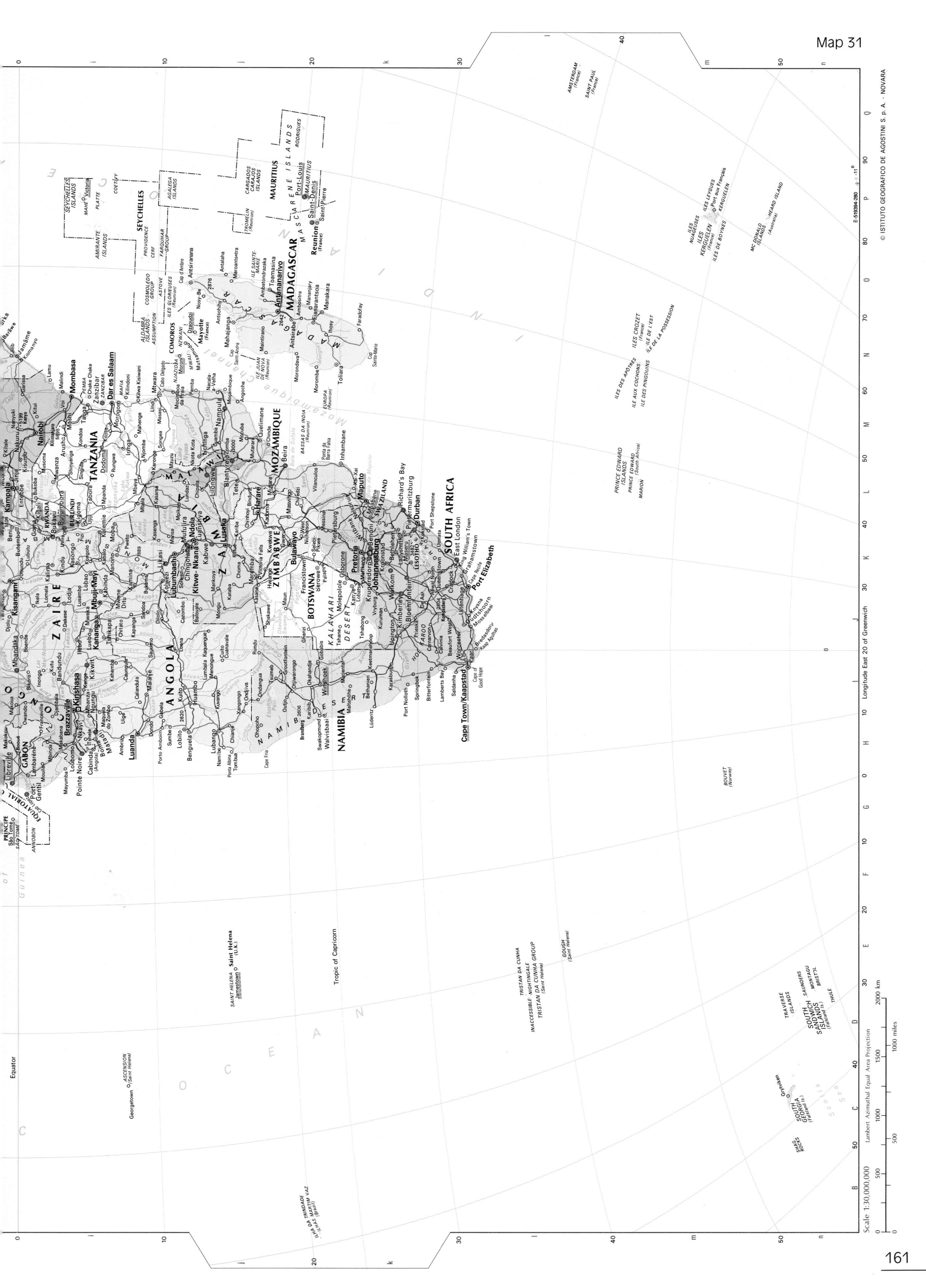

Map 31

© ISTITUTO GEOGRAFICO DE AGOSTINI S. p. A. - NOVARA

Scale 1:30,000,000   Lambert Azimuthal Equal Area Projection

Longitude East 20 of Greenwich

Tropic of Capricorn

Equator

Map 32

AL JAZĀ'IR
ALGERIA
WILĀYATE
1 Adrar
2 Al Jazā'ir
3 Annaba
4 Batna
5 Béchar
6 Bejaia
7 Biskra
8 Blida
9 Bouira
10 Cheliff
11 Constantine
12 Djelfa
13 Guelma
14 Jijel
15 Laghouat
16 Mascara
17 Médéa
18 Mostaganem
19 M'Sila
20 Oran
21 Ouargla
22 Oum el Bouaghi
23 Saïda
24 Setif
25 Sidi Bel Abbes
26 Skikda
27 Tamanrasset
28 Tébessa
29 Tiaret
30 Tizi Ouzou
31 Tlemcen

AL MAGHRIB
MOROCCO
PRÉFECTURES
A Casablanca
B Rabat-Salé

PROVINCES
1 Agadir
2 Al Hoceima
3 Ar Rachidiya
4 Azilal
5 Beni Mellal
6 Boulemane
7 Chechaouene
8 El Jadida
9 El Kelaa des Srarhna
10 Essaouira
11 Fès
12 Figuig
13 Kenitra
14 Khemisset
15 Khenifra
16 Khouribga
17 Marrakech
18 Meknès
19 Nador
20 Ouarzazate
21 Oujda
22 Safi
23 Settat
24 Tanger
25 Tan Tan
26 Taounate
27 Tata
28 Taza
29 Tétouan
30 Tiznit

TŪNIS
TUNISIA
WILĀYATE
1 Al Kāf
2 Al Mahdīyah
3 Al Munastir
4 Al Qaşrayn
5 Al Qayrawān
6 Bājah
7 Bizerte
8 Jundūbah
9 Madanīyin
10 Nābul
11 Qābis
12 Qafşah
13 Qamūdah
14 Şafāqis
15 Silyānah
16 Sūsah
17 Tūnis
18 Zaghwān

OCEANO ATLÂNTICO/

Iberian Basin

ARQUIPÉLAGO DOS AÇORES
AZORES
CORVO
941 Santa Cruz
FLORES
HORTA
FAIAL
1021 Velas
Horta 2320
PICO 1066
Lajes do Pico
Açores
(Portugal)
Azores
ANGRA DO HEROÍSMO
Santa Cruz
411 GRACIOSA
SÃO JORGE
1023 TERCEIRA
Angra do Heróismo
2900
SÃO MIGUEL
1105
Ponta Delgada
Vila Franca do Campo
PONTA DELGADA
FORMIGAS
SANTA MARIA
590 Vila do Porto

Azores-Gibraltar Ridge

Josephine Seamount
175
Gettysburg Seamount
35

Ampère Seamount
55

Seewarte Seamounts

Seine Seamount
170

Great Meteor Tablemount
−275

PORTO SANTO
Porto Moniz
MADEIRA 1861
Funchal
ILHAS DESERTAS
ARQUIPÉLAGO DA MADEIRA
MADEIRA ISLANDS
Madeira
(Portugal)

AL BAHR AL MUHĪT/

Dacia Seamount
85

ILHAS SELVAGENS

Islas Canarias
Canary Islands
(Spain)
Santa Cruz de Tenerife
ALEGRANZA
GRACIOSA
675 LANZAROTE
Arrecife
Los Llanos de Aridane
Santa Cruz de la Palma
LA PALMA 2423
TENERIFE
Puerto de la Cruz
SANTA CRUZ DE TENERIFE
3715
GOMERA 1481
San Sebastián de la Gomera
Valverde
HIERRO
1949
LOBOS
FUERTEVENTURA
LAS PALMAS
Gáldar 807
Las Palmas de Gran Canaria
GRAN CANARIA
ISLAS CANARIAS
CANARY ISLANDS

Canary Basin

OCÉAN ATLANTIQUE

Echo Seamount
260

Tropic of Cancer

ATLANTIC OCEAN

Cape Verde Terrace

SANTO ANTÃO
1979 Ribeira Grande
Porto Novo
Mindelo 774 SÃO VICENTE
BARLAVENTO
SANTA LUZIA 330
BRANCO Ribeira Brava
RAZO SÃO NICOLAU
406 Pedra Lume
BOA VISTA SAL
Sal-Rei 387
Curral-Velho
ILHAS DO CABO VERDE
CAPE VERDE ISLANDS
CAPE VERDE
Tarrafal
MAIO
436 Maio
ILHÉUS SECOS FOGO
Nova Sintra 2829
BRAVA 1423
São Filipe
Praia SÃO TIAGO
SOTAVENTO

AL MAGHRIB
MOROCCO

A CASA
Azemm
El Jadid
Oualidia
Ras Beddouza
Safi
Talmest
Essaouira
Cap Sim Jebel Amsittene
Tamri
Cap Rhir
Agadir
Inezgane
Tafraout
SIDI Ifni
Goulimime
Tan Tan Plage
Tan Tan
Tarfaya
El Aaiún
Edchera
Hausa Echdeiria
Semara
Bu Craa
Bir Lehlu
Western
A Sahara

SAGUIA EL-HAMRA
ZEMMOUR
Oued ben Till
TIRIS ZEMMOUR

Taguersimet
Bir Enzarán
Dakhla
Punta Durnford
El Aargub
Bahía de Río de Oro
1145

RIO DE ORO

Cabo Barbas
Hasi Ausert
Fderick
Zouirát
Kédia d'Idjil
Agüenit
Tourine
Touâjil
Bir Gandús
Boû Lanouar
Tichla Zug
Char
Choum
Nouâdhibou
Güerao
Ras Nouâdhibou
Cap Blanc
NOUADHIBOU
ILE TIDRA
Atar
Chinguetti
732
INCHIRI
Akjoujt
Cap Timiris
Nouamrhar
Bennichab
Boû Rjeimat
Tiouilit

MŪRĪTĀNIYĀ
MAURITANIA

TAGANT
HODH

Nouakchott
Bella
DISTRICT DE NOUAKCHOTT
Idini
TRARZA
Nimjad
Boutilimit
Moudjéria
Tiguent
Mederdra
Rkiz
Aleg
BRAKNA
Keur Massène
Rosso
Podor
Richard-Toll
Dagana
Saint-Louis
Kébémer
Louga
Darou Khoudos
Linguère
Ranérou
Tivaouane
Mékhé
Dahra
Thiès
Mbacké
DAKAR
Rufisque
Diourbel
Mbour
Fatick
Joal-Fadiout
Kaolack
Kaffrine
SÉNÉGAL
Kébémer

Lambert Azimuthal Equal Area Projection

A Western Sahara is occupied by Morocco.

A-589791-280-1

0   200   400   600 km
0   200 miles

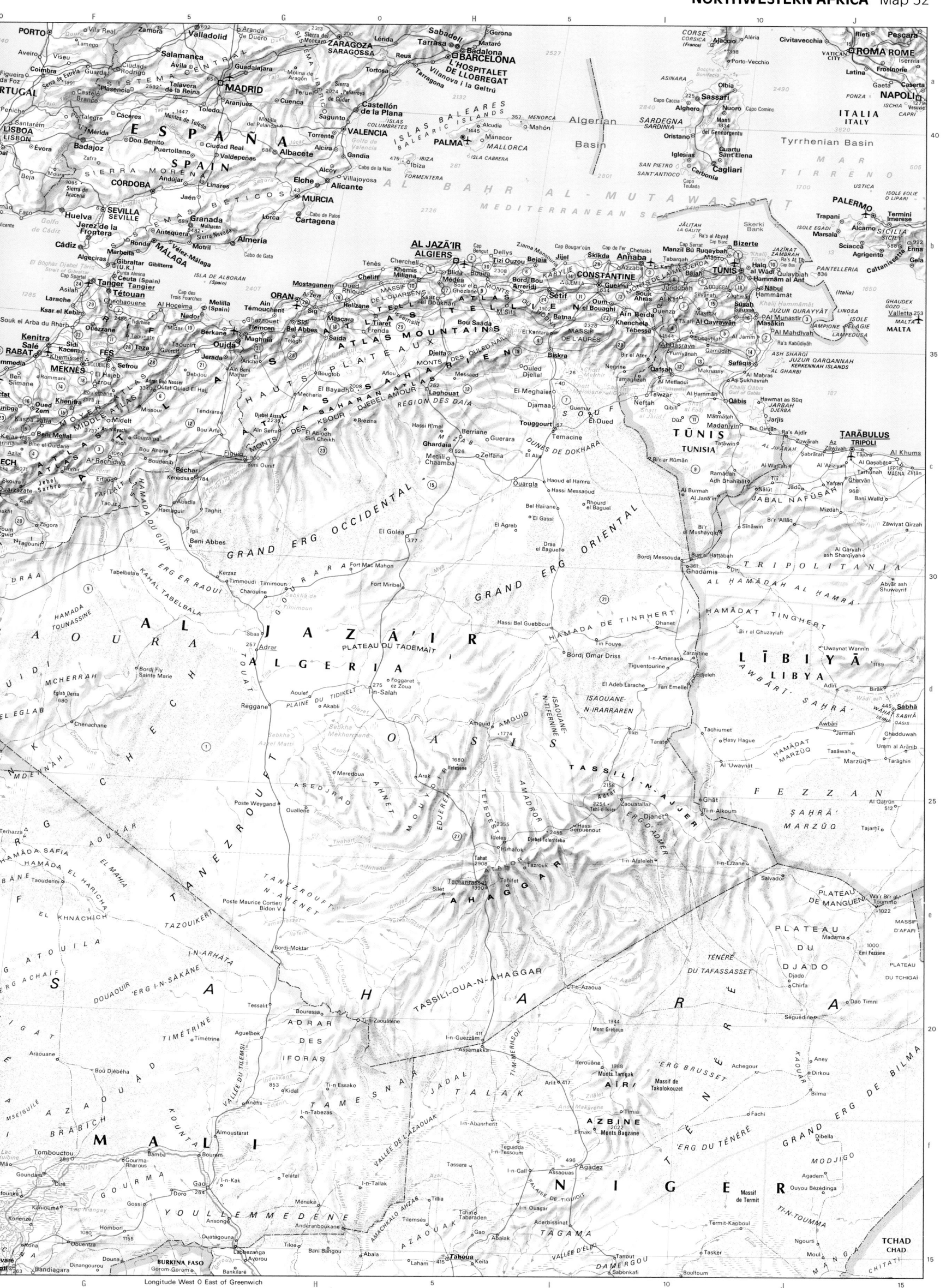

Map 33 **NORTHEASTERN AFRICA**

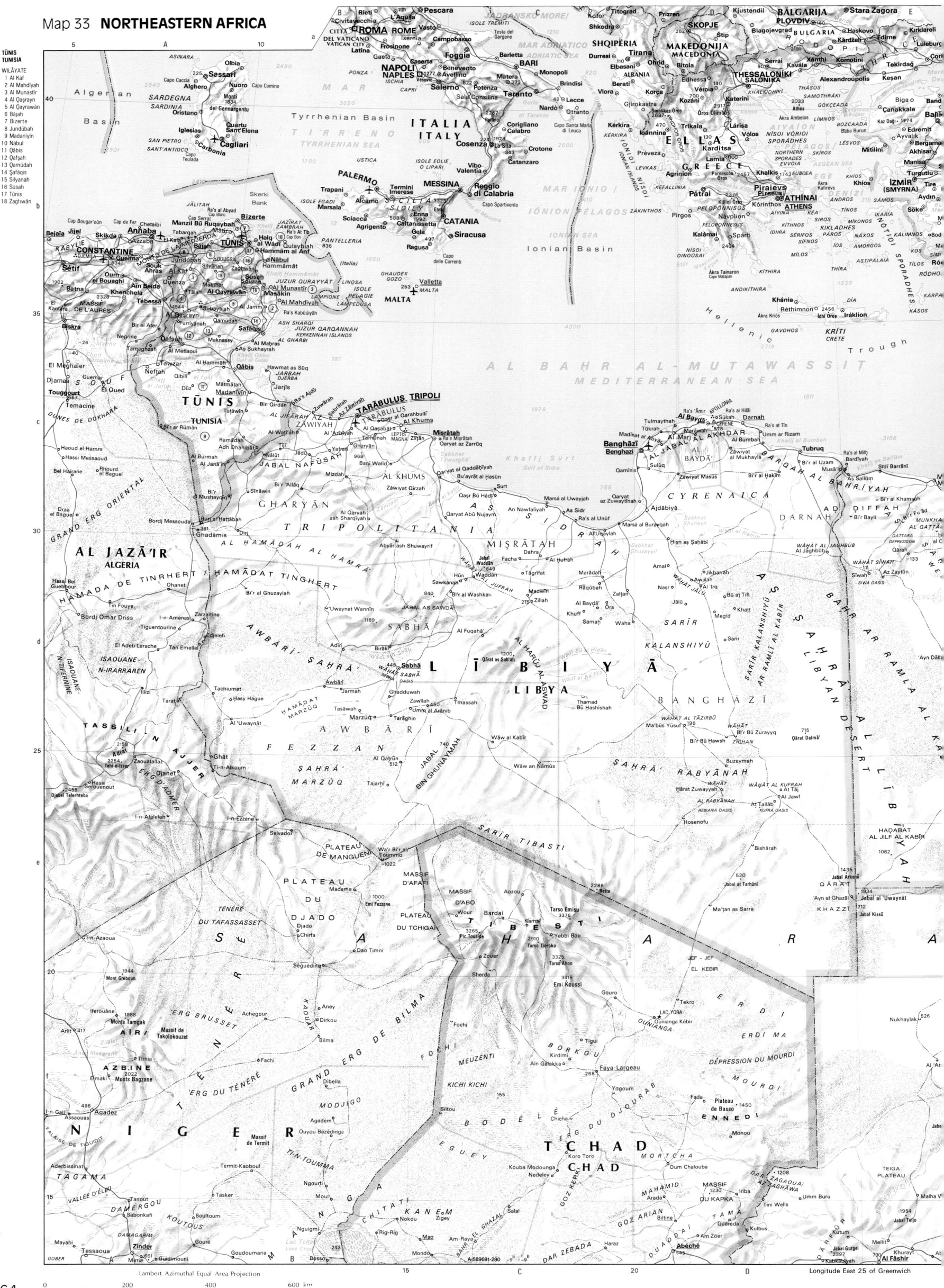

TÛNIS
TUNISIA
WILÂYATE
1 Al Kâf
2 Al Mahdiyah
3 Al Munastîr
4 Al Qasrayn
5 Al Qayrawân
6 Bâjah
7 Bizerte
8 Jundûbah
9 Madaniyin
10 Nâbul
11 Qâbis
12 Qafsah
13 Qamûdah
14 Safâqis
15 Silyânah
16 Sûsah
17 Tûnis
18 Zaghwân

Lambert Azimuthal Equal Area Projection

Longitude East 25 of Greenwich

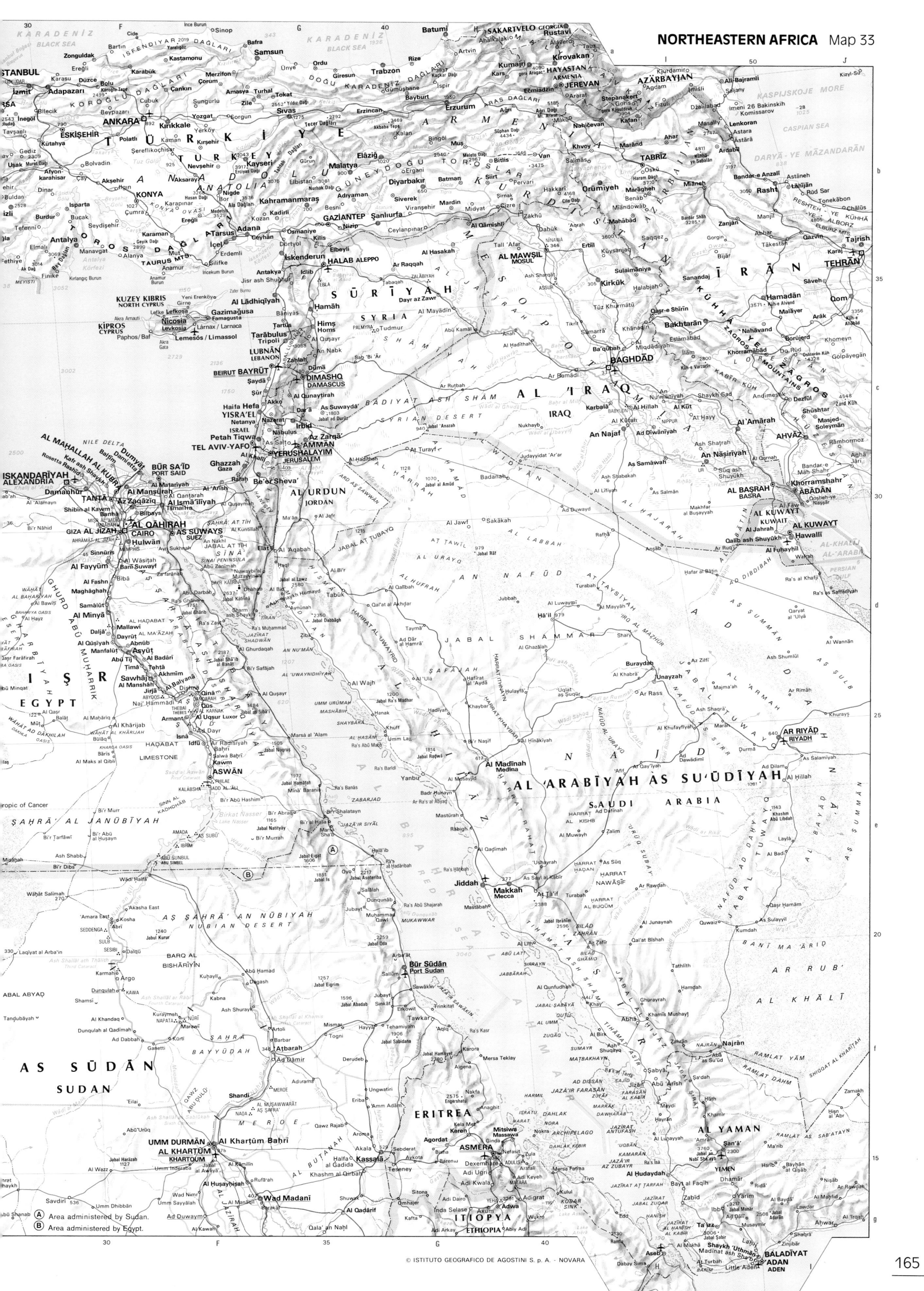

Ⓐ Area administered by Sudan.
Ⓑ Area administered by Egypt.

© ISTITUTO GEOGRAFICO DE AGOSTINI S.p.A. - NOVARA

Map 34 **WEST-CENTRAL AFRICA**

LIBERIA
COUNTIES
1 Bong
2 Cape Mount
3 Grand Bassa
4 Grand Gedeh
5 Lofa
6 Maryland
7 Montserrado
8 Nimba
9 Sinoe

CÔTE D'IVOIRE
IVORY COAST
DÉPARTEMENTS
1 Abengourou
2 Abidjan
3 Aboisso
4 Adzopé
5 Agboville
6 Biankouma
7 Bondoukou
8 Bongouanou
9 Bouaflé
10 Bouaké
11 Bouna
12 Boundiali
13 Dabakala
14 Daloa
15 Danané
16 Dimbokro
17 Divo
18 Ferkessédougou
19 Gagnoa
20 Guiglo
21 Issia
22 Katiola
23 Korhogo
24 Lakota
25 Man
26 Mankono
27 Odienne
28 Oumé
29 Sassandra
30 Séguéla
31 Soubré
32 Tengrela
33 Touba
34 Zuenoula

BURKINA FASO
DÉPARTEMENTS
1 Centre
2 Centre-Est
3 Centre-Nord
4 Centre-Ouest
5 Est
6 Hauts-Bassins
7 Komoé
8 Nord
9 Sahel
10 Sud-Ouest
11 Volta Noire

TOGO
RÉGIONS
1 Centre
2 Kara
3 Maritime
4 Plateaux
5 Savanes

BÉNIN
PROVINCES
1 Atakora
2 Atlantique
3 Borgou
4 Mono
5 Oueme
6 Zou

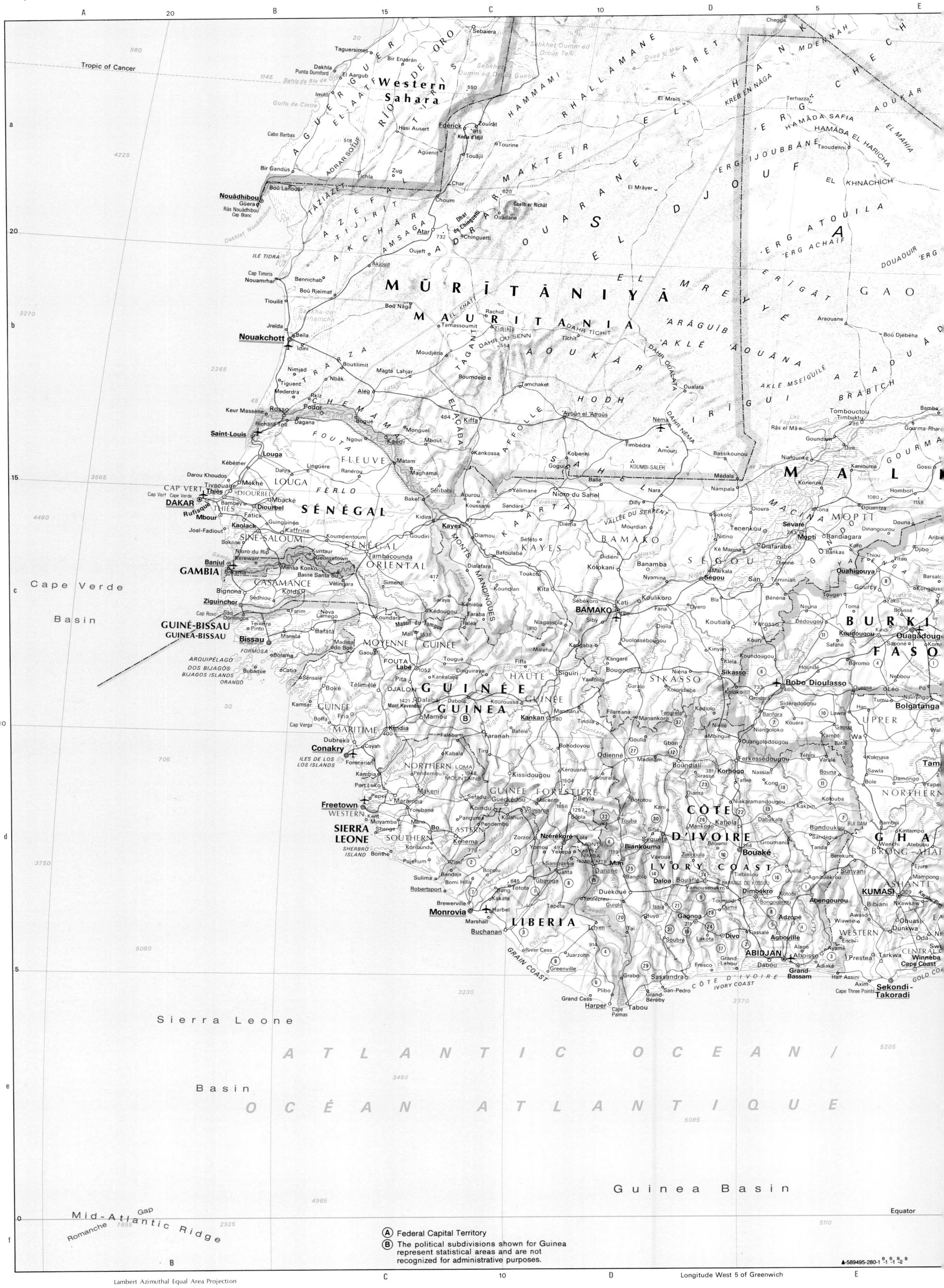

Western
Sahara

MŪRĪTĀNIYĀ
MAURITANIA

Nouâdhibou

Nouakchott

SÉNÉGAL

DAKAR

Saint-Louis

GAMBIA

GUINÉ-BISSAU
GUINEA-BISSAU
Bissau

MALI

BAMAKO

GUINÉE
GUINEA

Conakry

SIERRA
LEONE
Freetown

CÔTE
D'IVOIRE
IVORY COAST

LIBERIA

Monrovia

BURKINA
FASO

GHANA

KUMASI

ABIDJAN

Cape Verde
Basin

A T L A N T I C   O C E A N /

Sierra Leone
Basin

O C É A N   A T L A N T I Q U E

Guinea Basin

Mid-Atlantic Ridge

Equator

Ⓐ Federal Capital Territory
Ⓑ The political subdivisions shown for Guinea
represent statistical areas and are not
recognized for administrative purposes.

Lambert Azimuthal Equal Area Projection

0   200   400   600 km
0   200 miles

Longitude West 5 of Greenwich

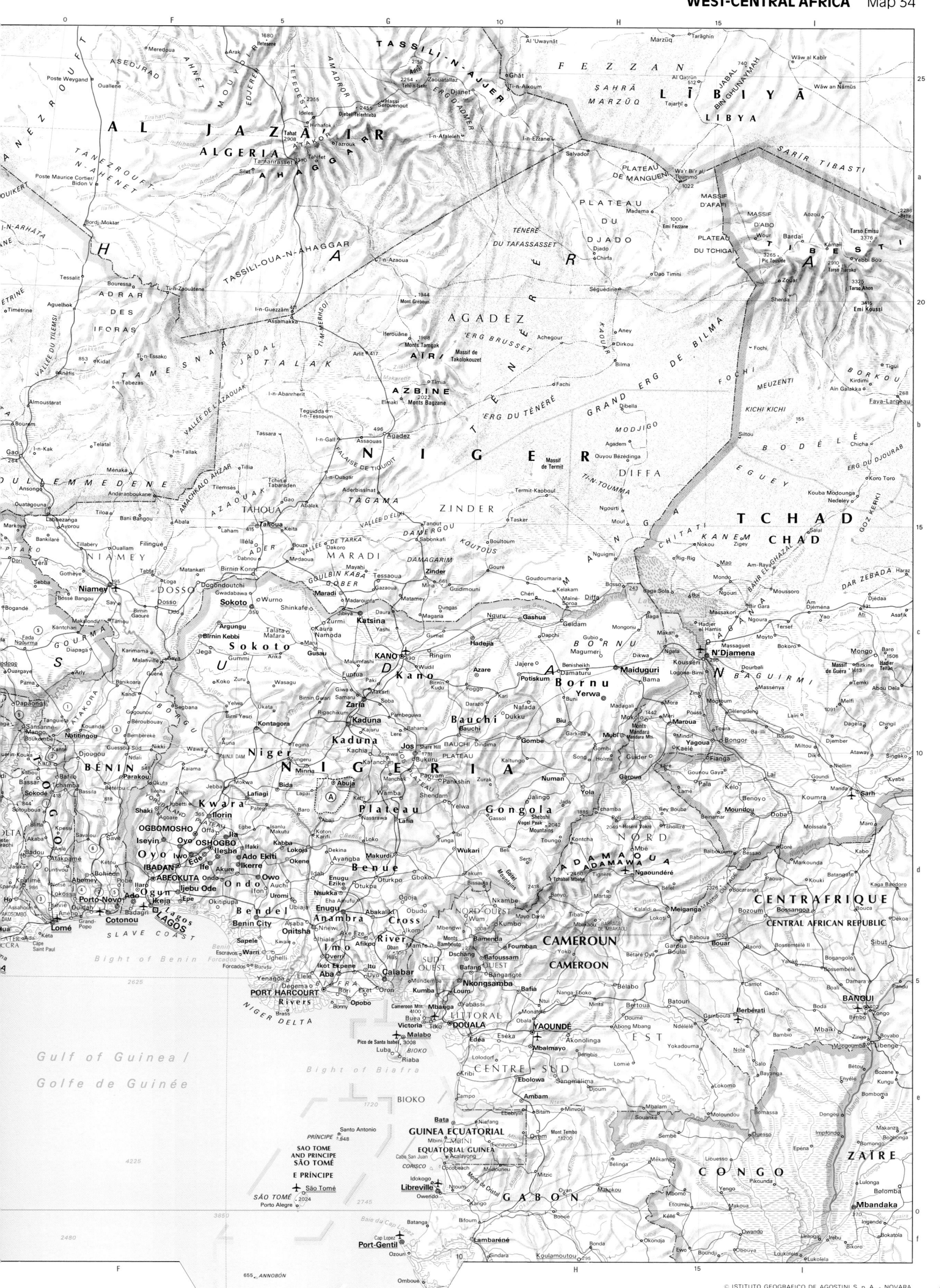

Map 35 **EAST-CENTRAL AFRICA**

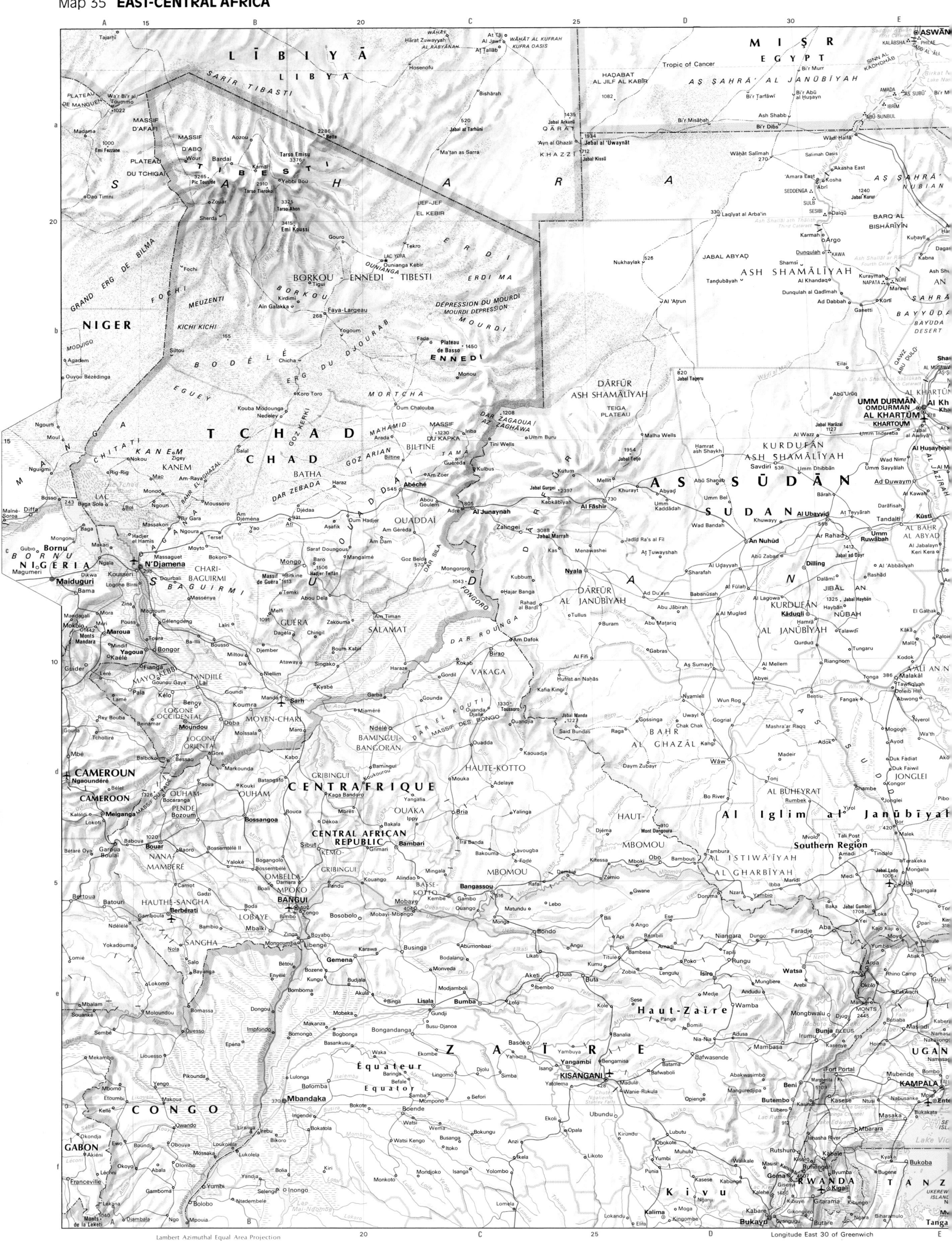

Lambert Azimuthal Equal Area Projection

Longitude East 30 of Greenwich

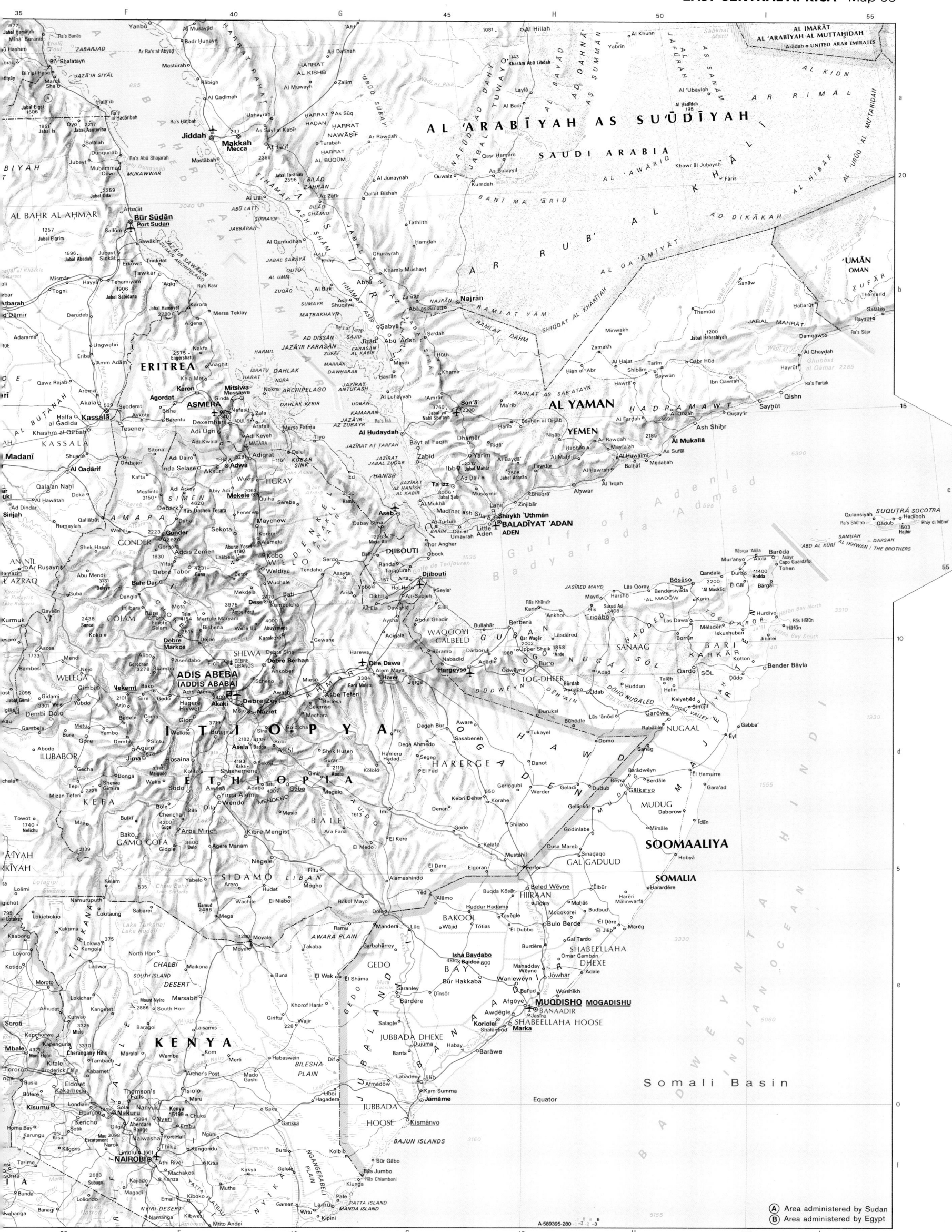

Map 36 **EQUATORIAL AFRICA**

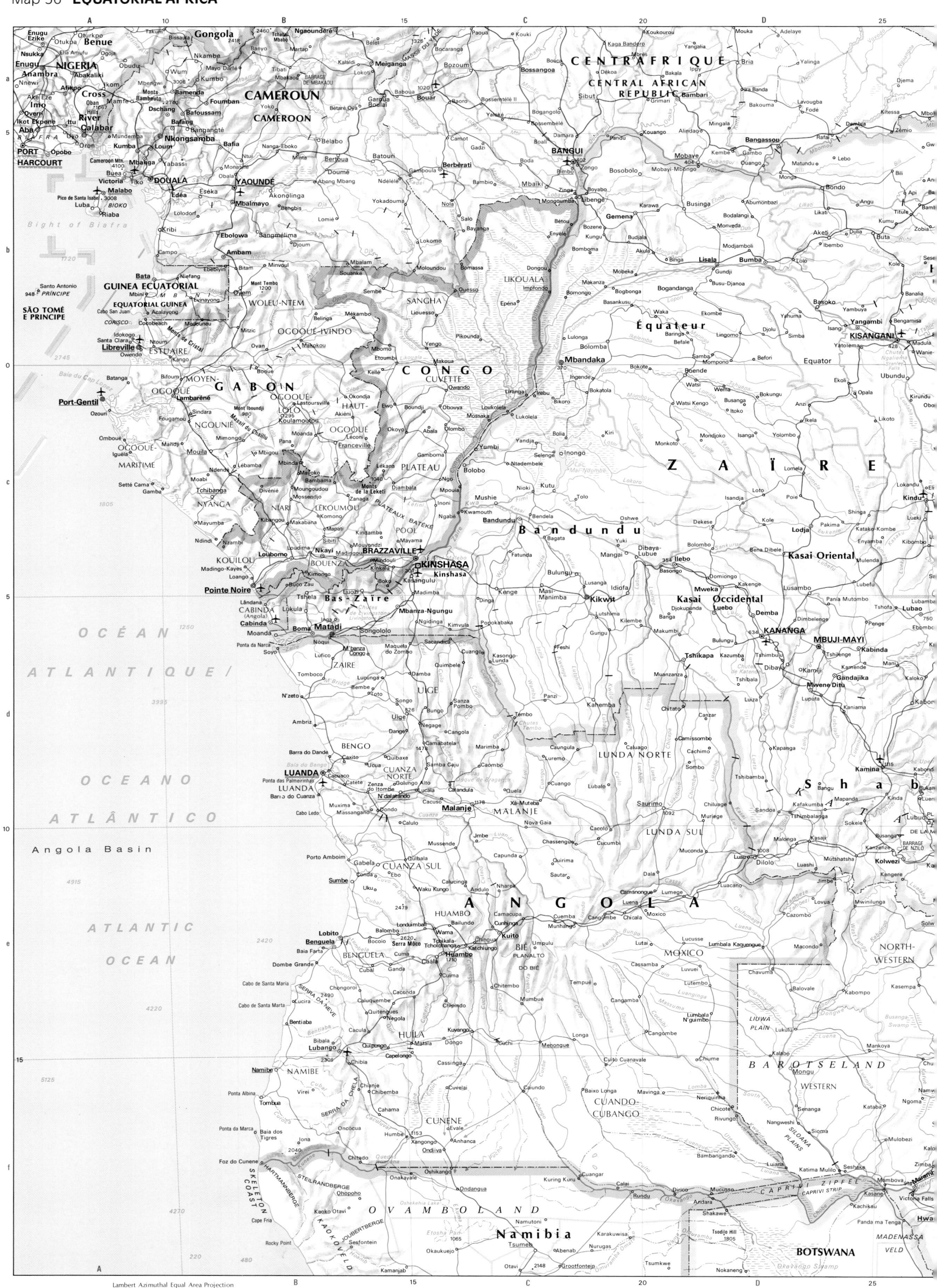

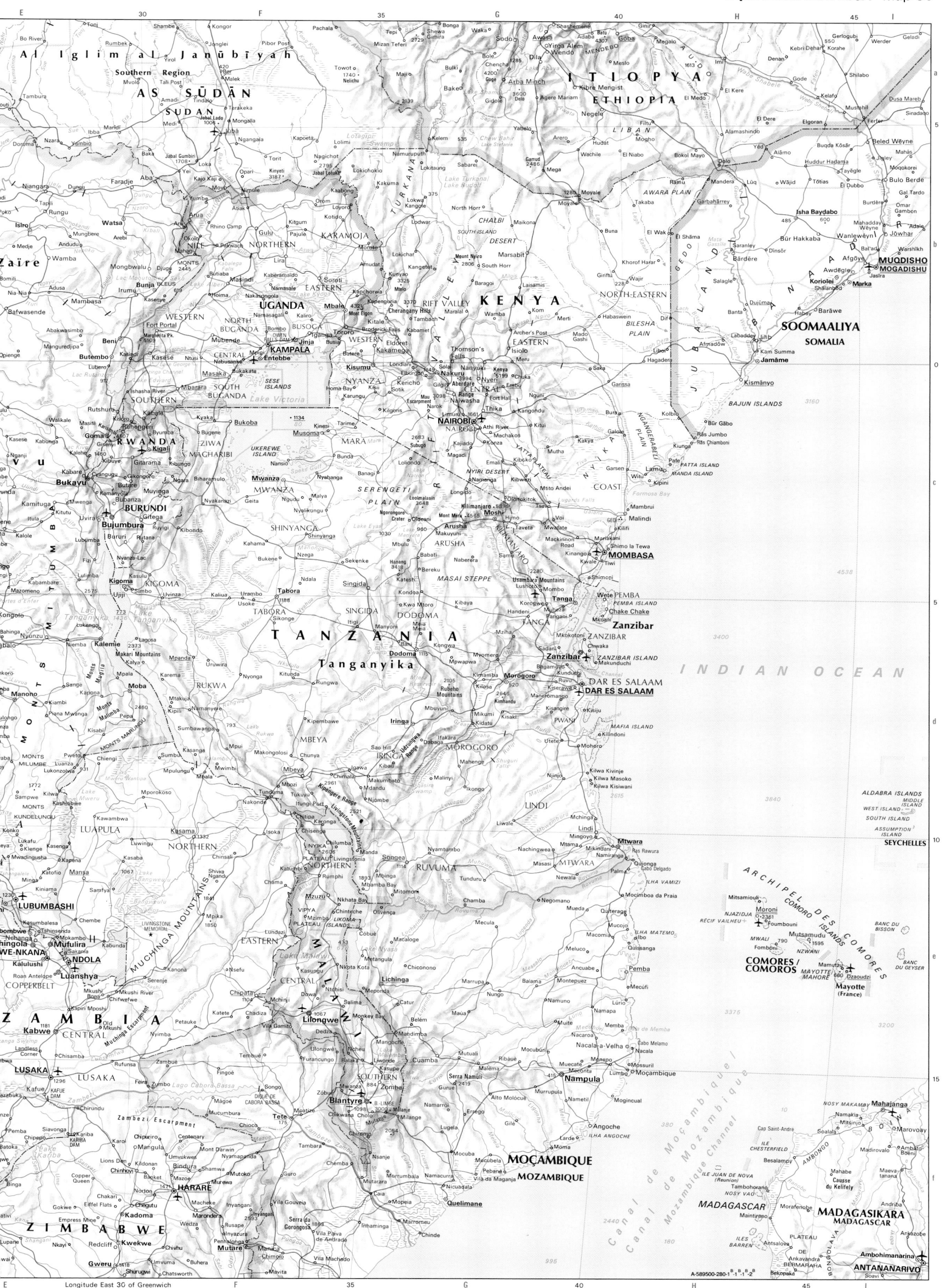

Map 37 **SOUTHERN AFRICA**

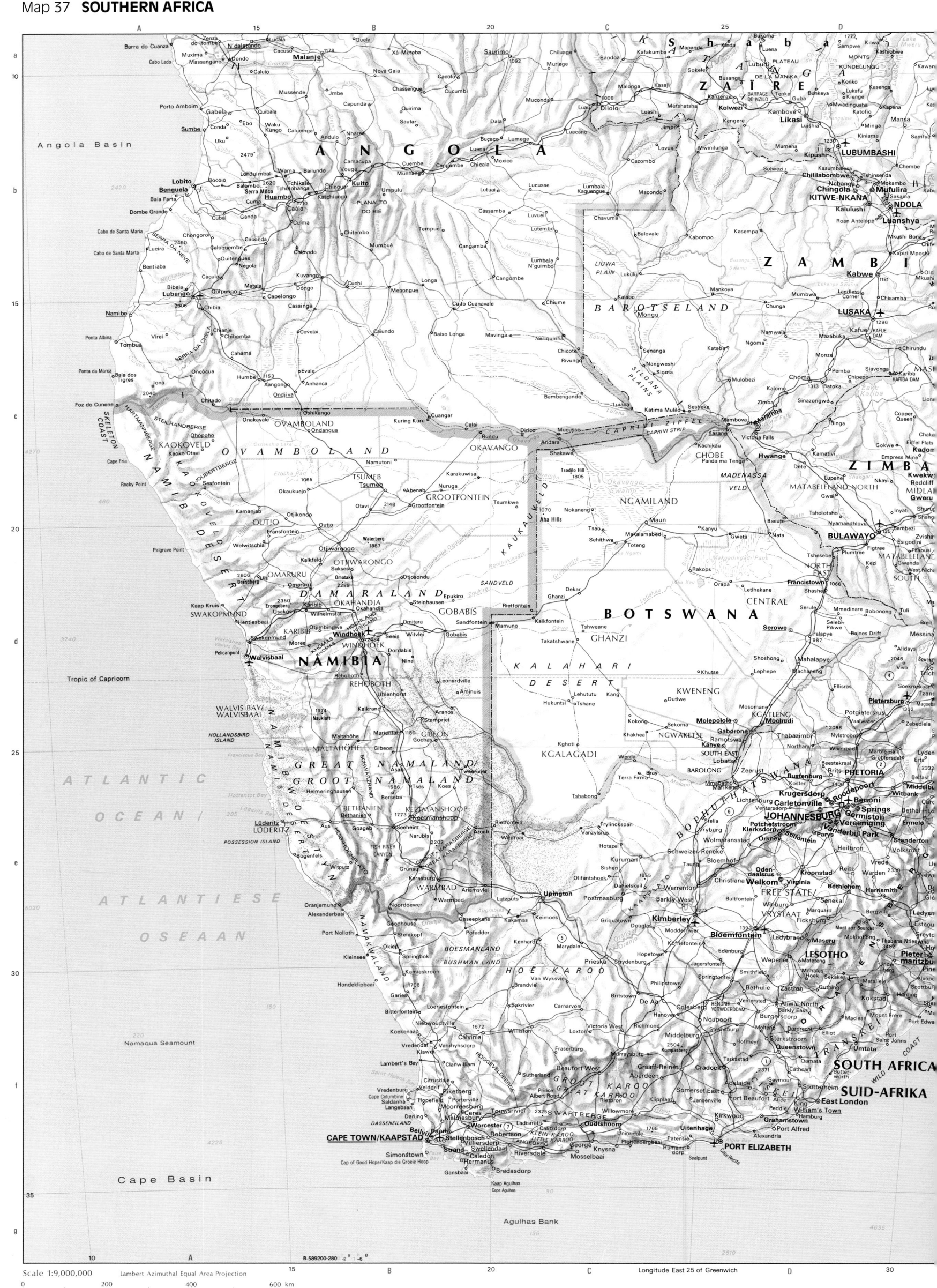

Scale 1:9,000,000   Lambert Azimuthal Equal Area Projection

Longitude East 25 of Greenwich

0   200   400   600 km

0   200 miles

SOUTH AFRICA
SUID-AFRIKA
PROVINCES
1 Eastern Cape
2 Gauteng
3 Mpumalanga
4 Northern
5 Northern Cape
6 North-West
7 Western Cape

SEYCHELLES
ALDABRA ISLANDS
WEST ISLAND MIDDLE ISLAND
SOUTH ISLAND ALDABRA
ASSUMPTION GROUP COSMOLEDO
ISLAND GROUP
ASTOVE
ISLAND

ILES GLORIEUSES
(Reunion)

BANC DU BISSON

BANC DU GEYSER

**COMORES /
COMOROS**

**MOÇAMBIQUE
MOZAMBIQUE**

MADAGASCAR

MADAGASIKARA

MADAGASCAR

OCEANO ÍNDICO / OCÉAN INDIEN /

INDIAN OCEAN / INDIESE OSEAAN

Natal Basin

Mozambique Plateau

Madagascar Plateau

Amirante Basin

MAURITIUS
MAURITIUS
Port-Louis
Beau-Bassin **Curepipe**
Mahébourg
Saint-Denis
Saint-Paul Pas des Neiges
Saint-Pierre 3069
RÉUNION Saint-Joseph
Réunion
(France)
ILES MASCAREIGNES/
MASCARENE ISLANDS

ALDABRA ISLANDS
WEST ISLAND MIDDLE ISLAND
SOUTH ISLAND ALDABRA
ASSUMPTION GROUP COSMOLEDO
ISLAND GROUP
ASTOVE
ISLAND
WIZARD REEF
SAINT PIERRE PROVIDENCE
ISLAND ISLAND
CERF ISLAND
FARQUHAR
GROUP
NORTH ISLAND
SOUTH ISLAND
GOELETTE ISLAND
AGALEGA ISLANDS
(Mauritius)

SEYCHELLES
BIRD ISLAND DENIS ISLAND
SEYCHELLES ISLANDS
PRASLIN ISLAND LA DIGUE ISLAND
SILHOUETTE ISLAND
MAHÉ ISLAND Victoria
AFRICAN ISLANDS
REMIRE REEF
BENJAMEN D'ARROS ISLAND
ISLAND FOUQUET ISLAND
POIVRE ISLANDS ILE DES ROCHES
ETOILE CAY PLATTE ISLAND
BOUDEUSE CAY MAHIE LOUISE
ILE DES NOEUF ISLAND
AMIRANTE ISLANDS
ALPHONSE ISLAND
BUDUTIER ISLAND COETIVY ISLAND
SAINT FRANÇOIS
ISLAND

INDIAN OCEAN

Longitude East 50 of Greenwich

Map 38 **NORTH AMERICA, PHYSICAL**

Map 39 **NORTH AMERICA, POLITICAL**

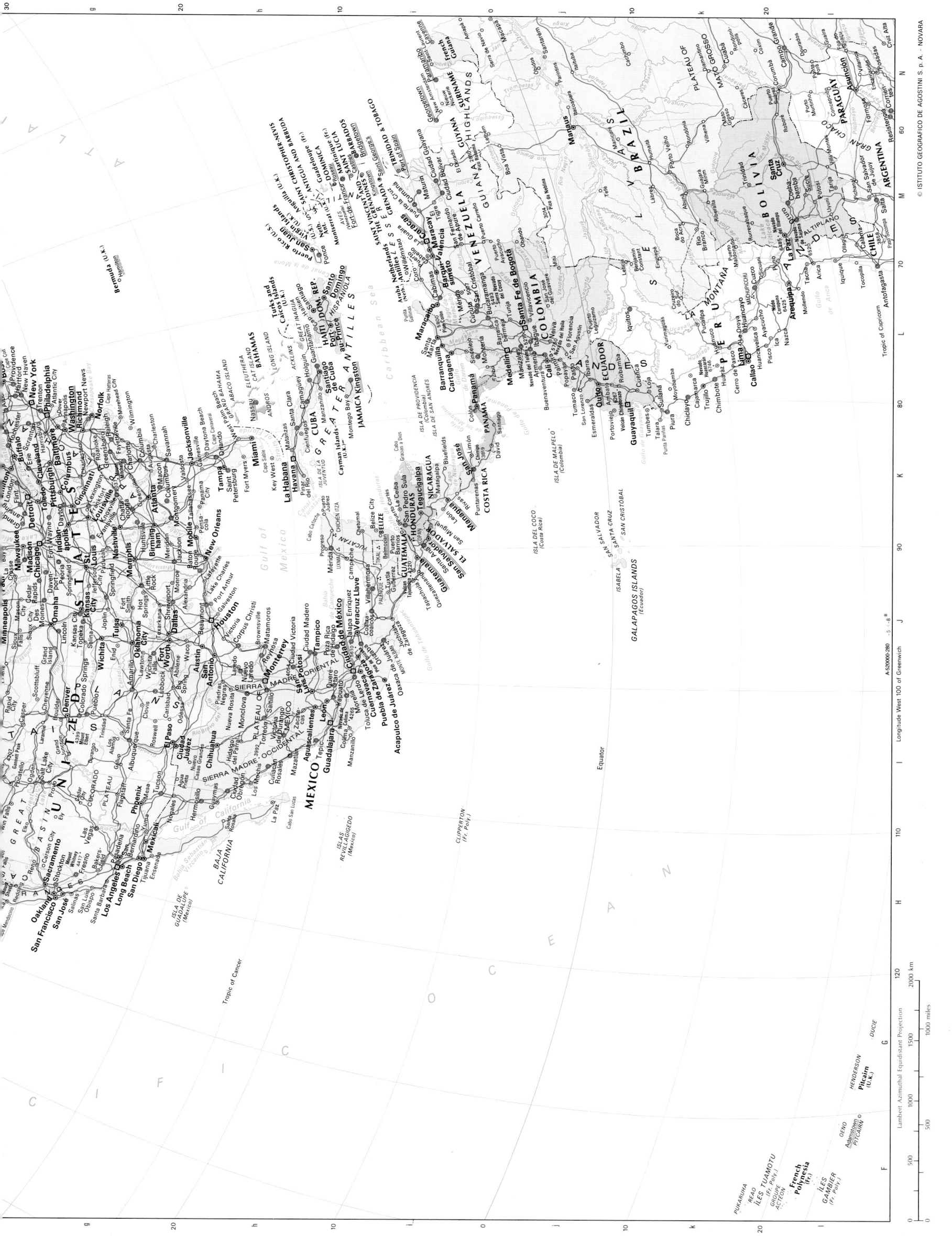

Lambert Azimuthal Equidistant Projection

A-520000-280

Longitude West 100 of Greenwich

Map 40 **ALASKA**

Lambert Azimuthal Equal Area Projection

0   200   400   600   800 km

0   200   400 miles

Longitude West 145 of Greenwich

© ISTITUTO GEOGRAFICO DE AGOSTINI S. p. A. - NOVARA

A-520502-280-1 -1 -1 -2

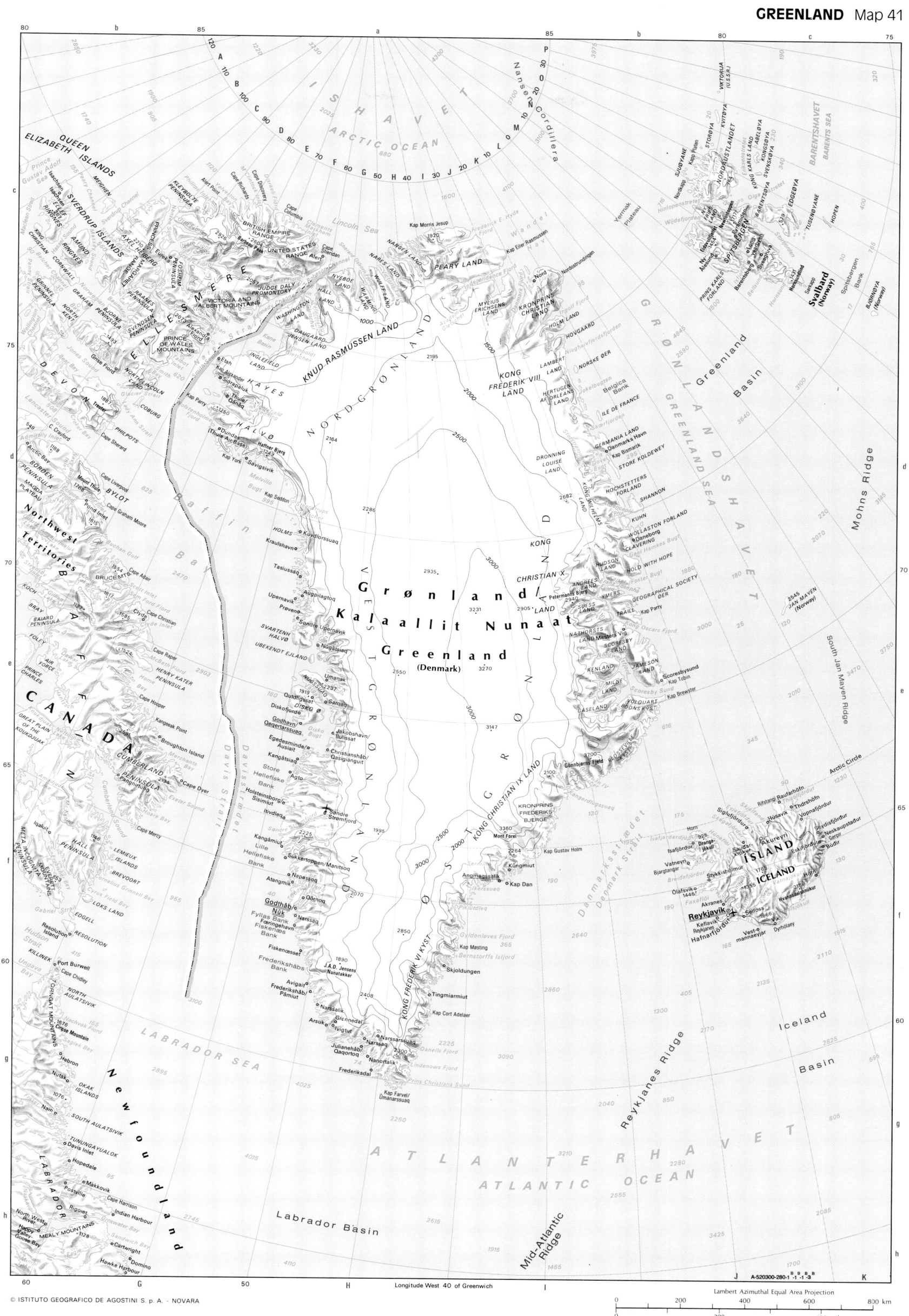

© ISTITUTO GEOGRAFICO DE AGOSTINI S. p. A. - NOVARA

Lambert Azimuthal Equal Area Projection

Map 42 **CANADA**

Lambert Azimuthal Equal Area Projection

Longitude West 100 of Greenwich

Map 43 **UNITED STATES**

Lambert Azimuthal Equidistant Projection

Longitude West 100 of Greenwich

| 0 | 200 | 400 | 600 | 800 km |

| 0 | 200 | 400 miles |

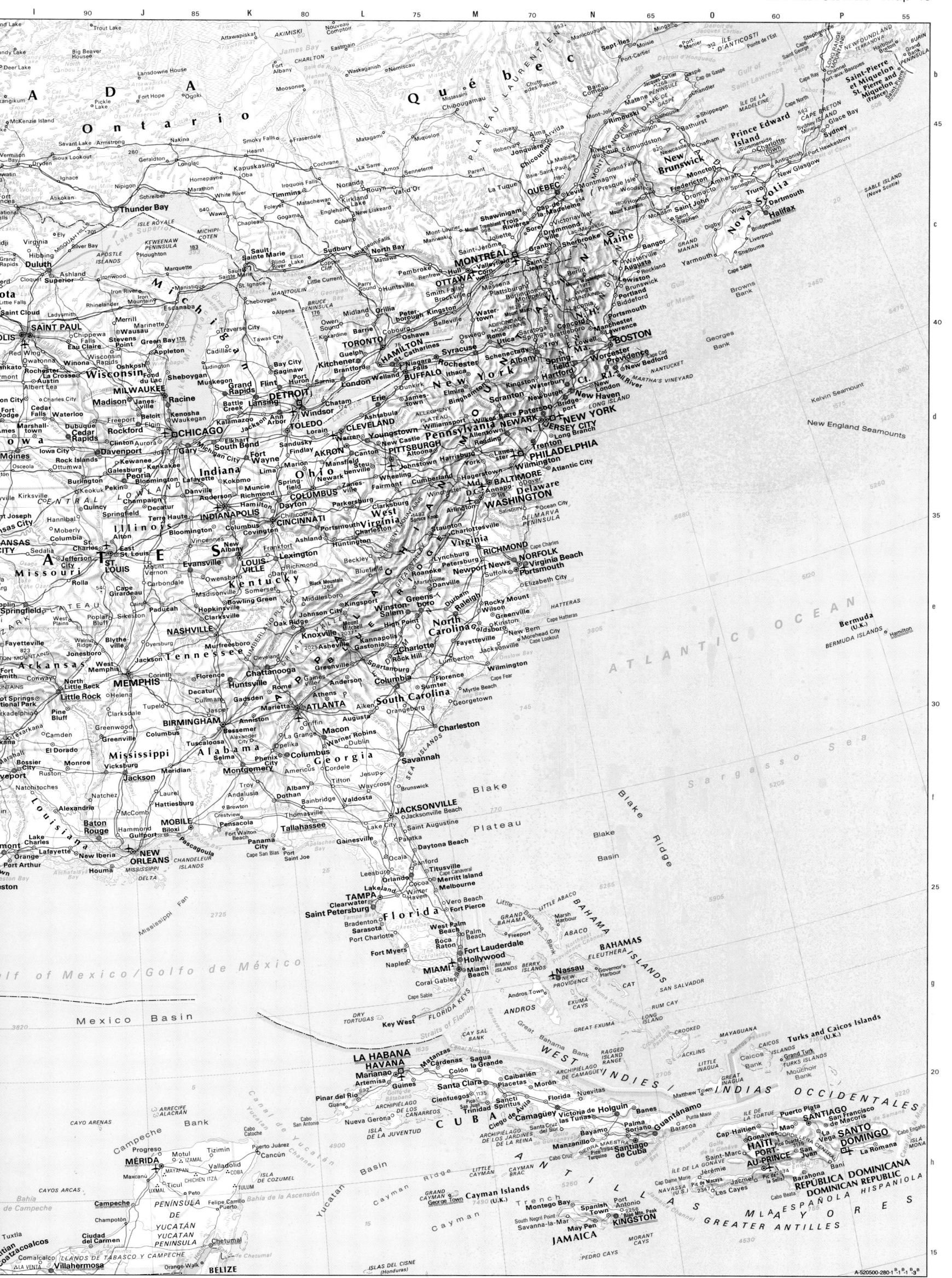

Map 44

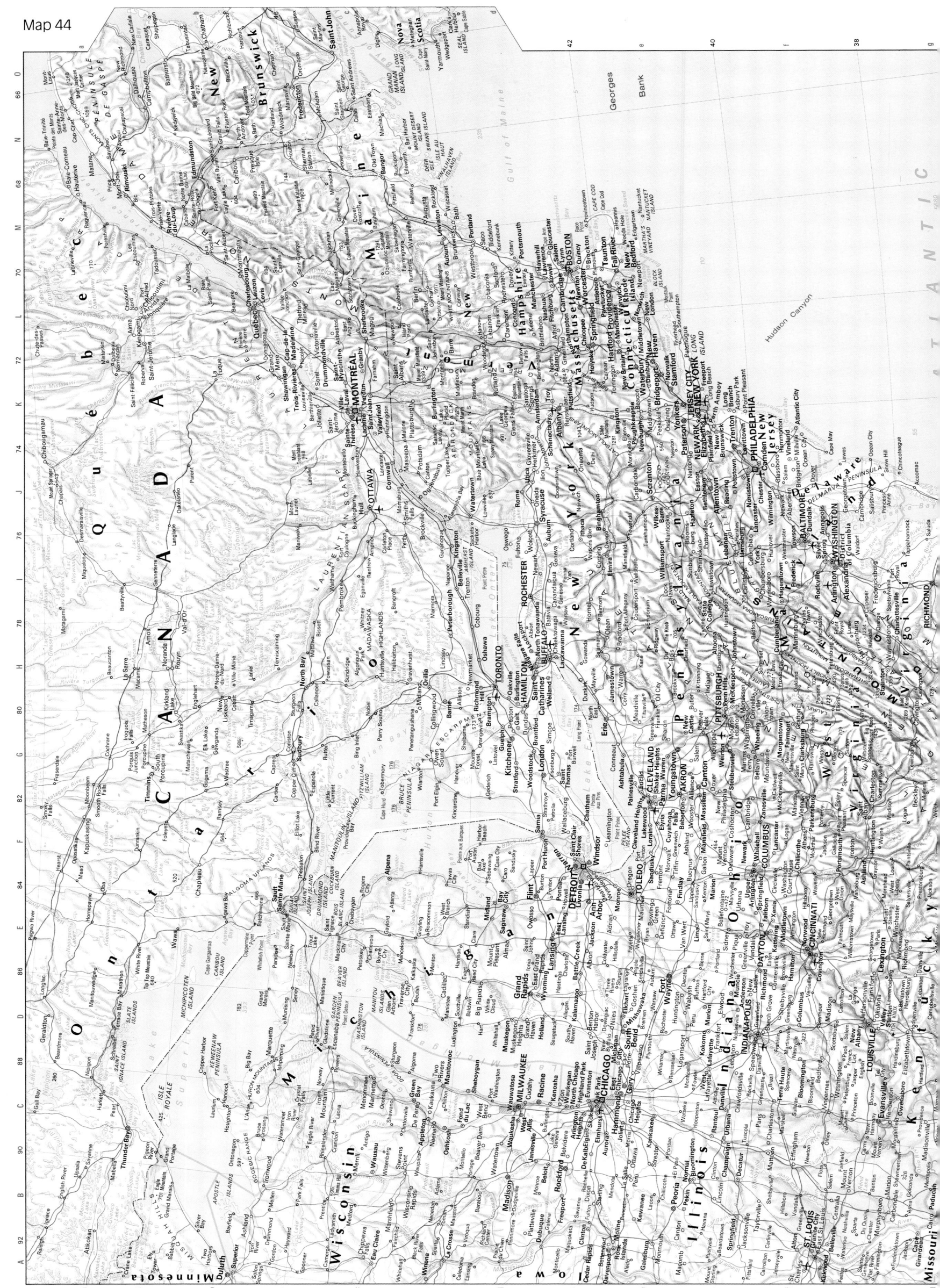

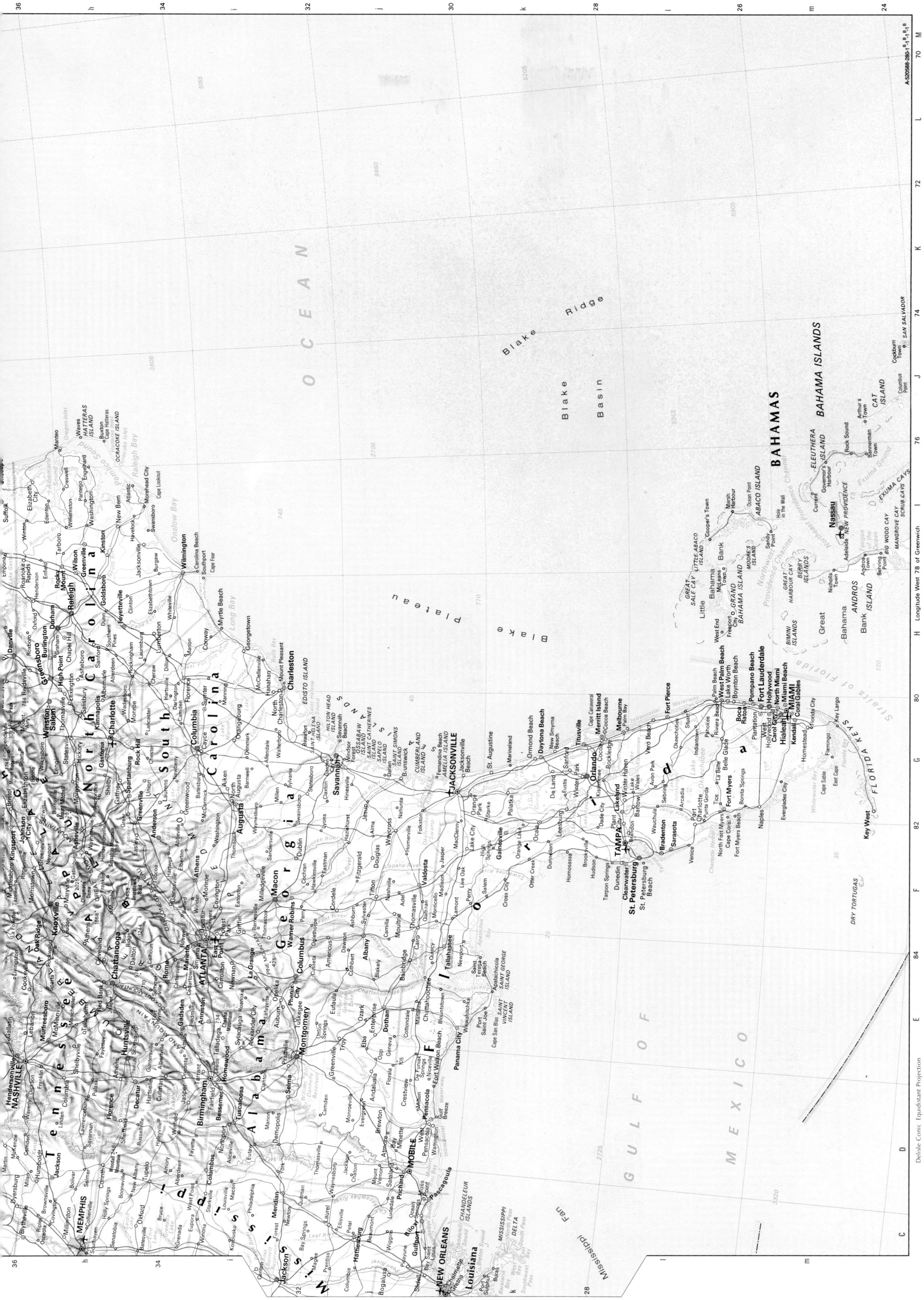
O C E A N
Blake Ridge
Blake Basin
Blake plateau
BAHAMAS
BAHAMA ISLANDS
GULF OF MEXICO
Straits of Florida
FLORIDA KEYS
Tennessee
North Carolina
South Carolina
Georgia
Alabama
Mississippi
Florida
Louisiana
Mississippi Fan
NASHVILLE
MEMPHIS
ATLANTA
JACKSONVILLE
TAMPA
MIAMI
NEW ORLEANS
MOBILE
Charlotte
Raleigh
Columbia
Montgomery
Tallahassee
Orlando
Savannah
Charleston
Birmingham
Chattanooga
Knoxville
Nassau
Key West
Longitude West 78 of Greenwich
Delisle Conic Equidistant Projection
200 miles
400 km

Map 45

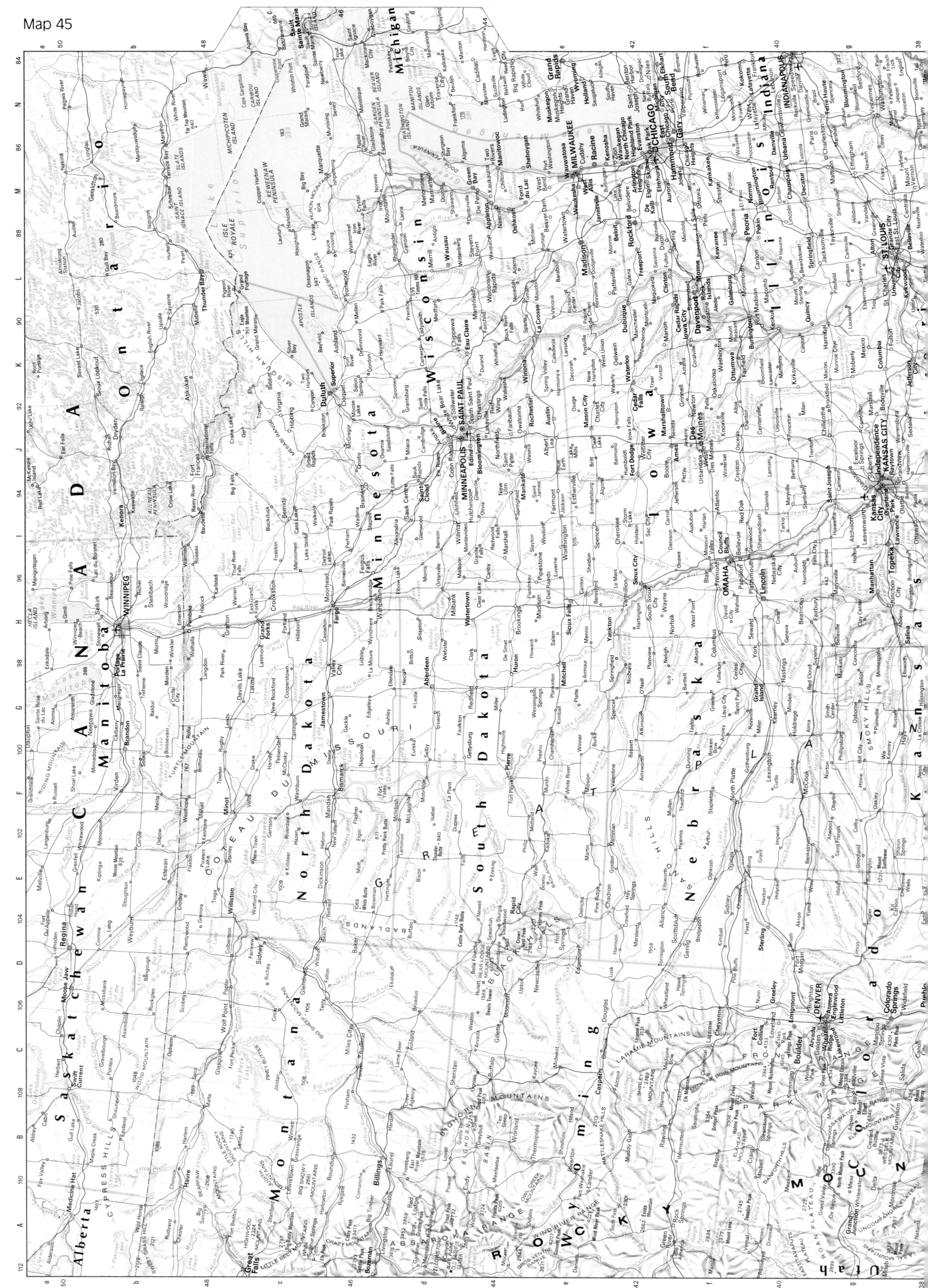

Map 46 **WESTERN UNITED STATES**

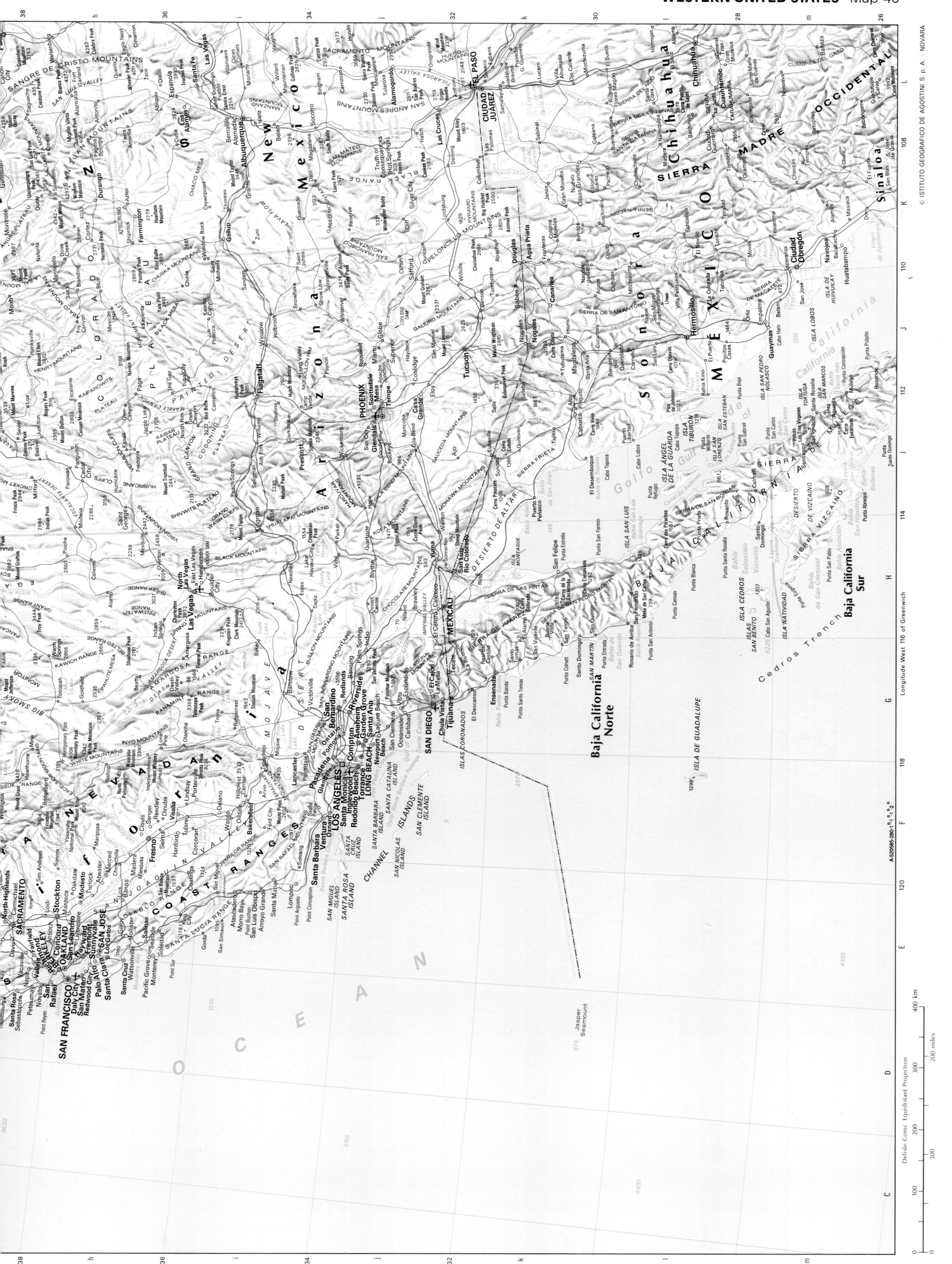

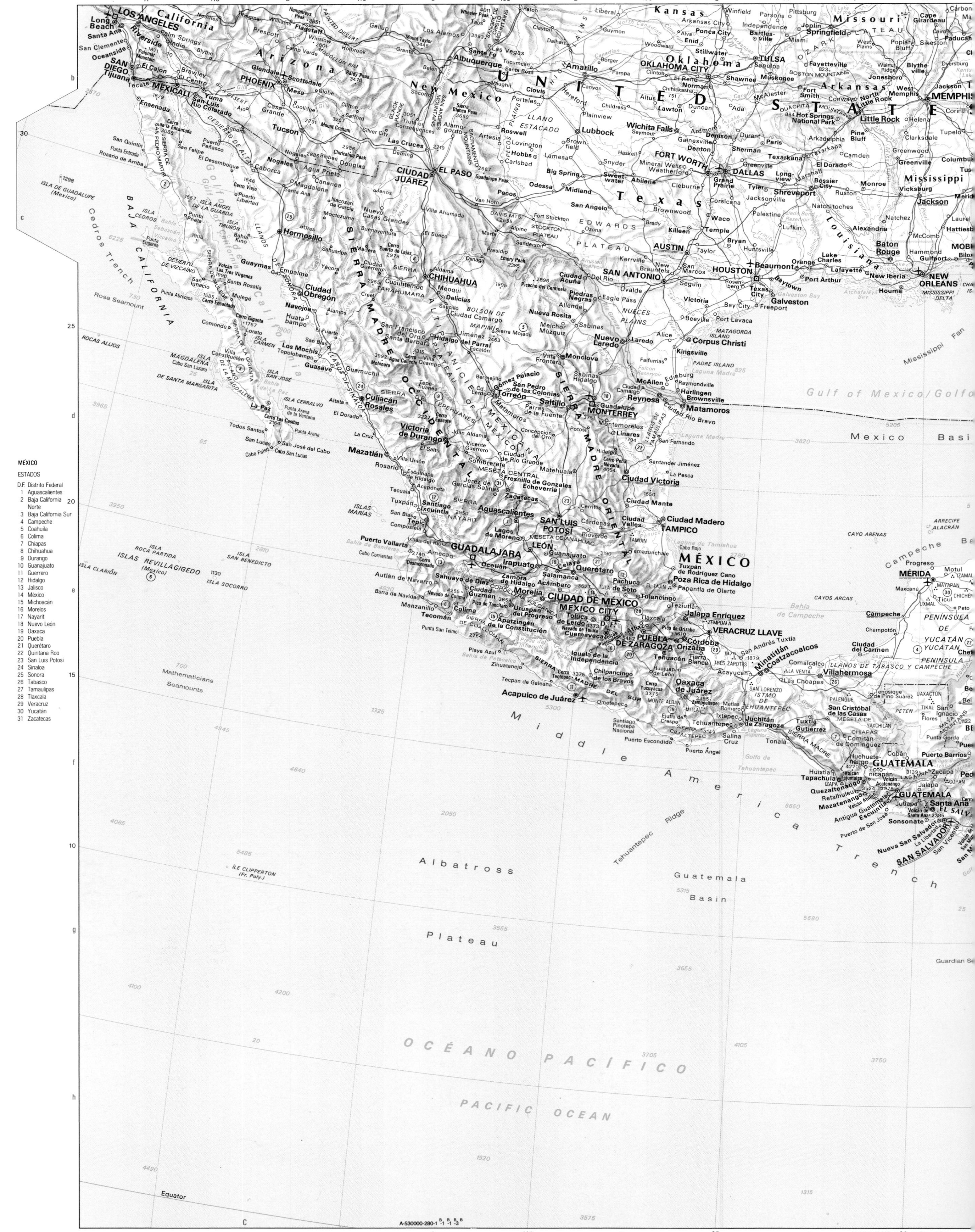

Map 47 **MIDDLE AMERICA**

MÉXICO

ESTADOS

D.F. Distrito Federal
1 Aguascalientes
2 Baja California Norte
3 Baja California Sur
4 Campeche
5 Coahuila
6 Colima
7 Chiapas
8 Chihuahua
9 Durango
10 Guanajuato
11 Guerrero
12 Hidalgo
13 Jalisco
14 México
15 Michoacán
16 Morelos
17 Nayarit
18 Nuevo León
19 Oaxaca
20 Puebla
21 Querétaro
22 Quintana Roo
23 San Luis Potosí
24 Sinaloa
25 Sonora
26 Tabasco
27 Tamaulipas
28 Tlaxcala
29 Veracruz
30 Yucatán
31 Zacatecas

Lambert Azimuthal Equal Area Projection

A-530000-280-1 -1 -1 -3

0   200   400   600   800 km
0   200   400 miles

Longitude West 90 of Greenwich

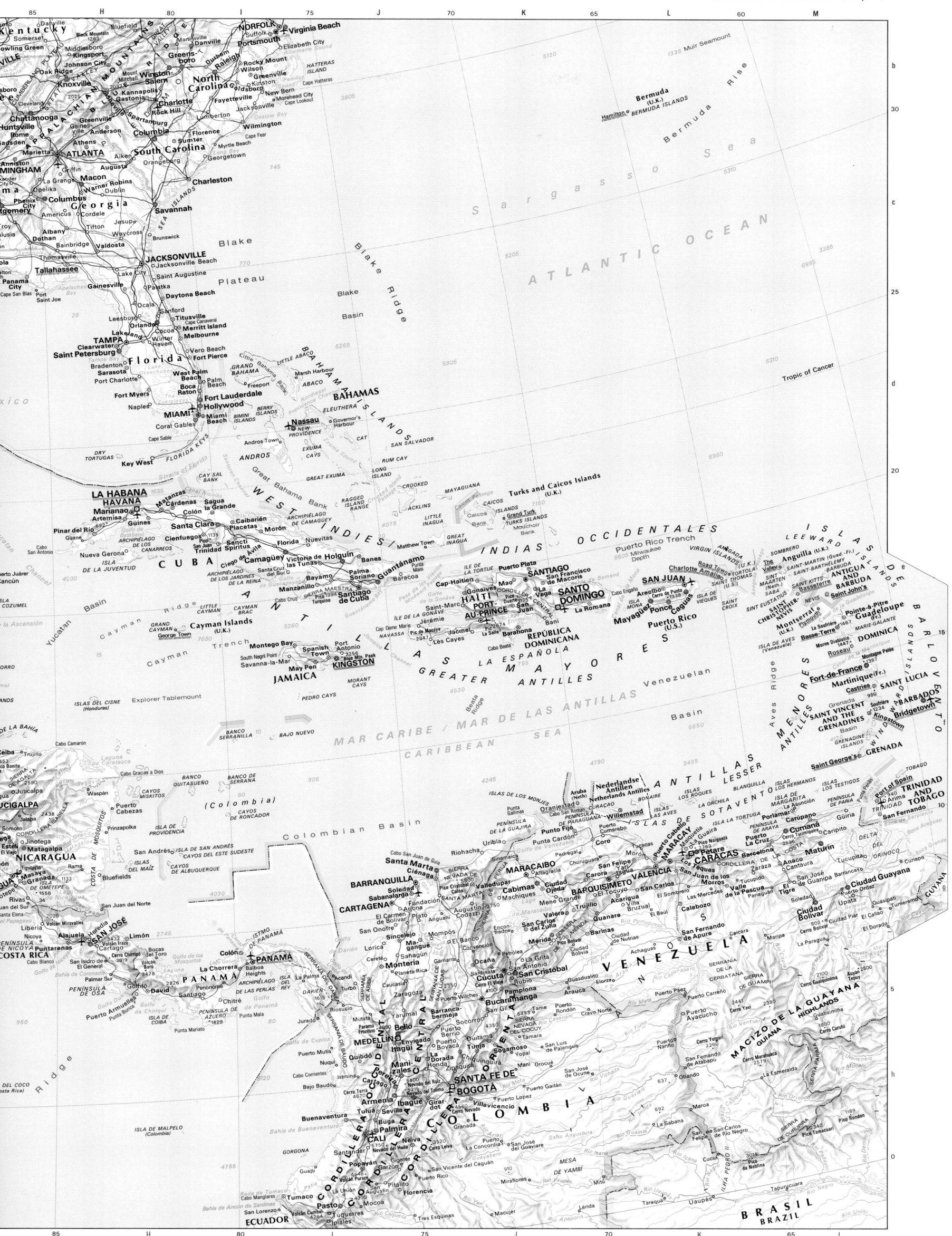

SAN DIEGO
Tijuana
ISLA CORONADO
El Descanso
Ensenada
Punta Banda
Punta Santo Tomás
Santo Tomás
Punta Colnett
Punta San Antonio
Rosario de Arriba
Punta Baja

Baja California

Punta Canoas
Punta Blanca
Punta Prieta

ISLAS SAN BENITO
ISLA CEDROS
ISLA NATIVIDAD
Punta Eugenia
ROCAS ALIJOS

Baja California Sur

ISLA MAGDALENA
Cabo San Lazaro
Puerto Magdalena
ISLA DE SANTA MARGARITA

Tropic of Cancer

Cabo San Lucas
San Lucas

OCÉANO PACÍFICO

ISLAS REVILLAGIGEDO
(Mexico)
ISLA CLARIÓN
ISLA SOCORRO
ISLA ROCA PARTIDA
ISLA SAN BENEDICTO

PACIFIC OCEAN

Mathematicians
Seamount

El Cajón
Chula Vista
El Centro
Tecate
MEXICALI
Río Colorado
Rito
DESIERTO DE ALTAR
Sonora
Hermosillo
Guaymas
Ciudad Obregón
Navojoa
Huatabampo

Arizona
Tucson
Nogales
Douglas
Agua Prieta

New Mexico
Las Cruces
CIUDAD JUÁREZ
EL PASO

UNITED

Chihuahua
Chihuahua
Cuauhtémoc

Coahu

Culiacán Rosales
Durango
Victoria de Durango
Mazatlán

ALTIPLANICIE MEXICANA

Torreón
Gómez Palacio

PLATEAU OF MEXI

Zacatecas

Aguascalie
AGUASCALIE

Tepic
Nayarit

GUADALAJARA

Jalisco

Colima
Colima

Micho

Delisle Conic Equidistant Projection

0   100   200   300   400 km
0   100   200 miles

G Longitude West 104 of Greenwich   H

MÉXICO

GOLFO DE MÉXICO
GULF OF MEXICO

Mexico Basin

UNITED STATES

Texas
Louisiana
Mississippi
Alabama
Florida

FORT WORTH
DALLAS
AUSTIN
SAN ANTONIO
HOUSTON
Galveston
Corpus Christi
Laredo
Nuevo Laredo
MONTERREY
Shreveport
Baton Rouge
NEW ORLEANS
MOBILE
Pensacola

Nuevo León
Tamaulipas
Ciudad Victoria
Ciudad Madero
TAMPICO
San Luis Potosí
Querétaro
Hidalgo
CIUDAD DE MÉXICO
MÉXICO CITY
México D.F.
CUERNAVACA
Morelos
Puebla
PUEBLA DE ZARAGOZA
Tlaxcala
Jalapa Enríquez
Veracruz
VERACRUZ LLAVE
Córdoba
Orizaba
Guerrero
CHILPANCINGO
de los Bravos
ACAPULCO DE JUÁREZ
Oaxaca
de Juárez
Oaxaca
Tuxtla Gutiérrez
Chiapas
Tabasco
Coatzacoalcos
Minatitlán
Villahermosa
San Cristóbal de las Casas

Campeche
Yucatán
MÉRIDA
Progreso
Quintana Roo
PENÍNSULA DE YUCATÁN
Campeche
Chetumal
Ciudad del Carmen

Bahía de Campeche

ISTMO DE TEHUANTEPEC

GUATEMALA
GUATEMALA
Quezaltenango
Tapachula

BELIZE
Belize City
Belmopan

HONDURAS
San Pedro Sula
Puerto Cortés

SIERRA MADRE ORIENTAL
SIERRA MADRE OCCIDENTAL
SIERRA MADRE DEL SUR
EASTERN SIERRA MADRE

LLANOS DE TABASCO Y CAMPECHE

Laguna Madre

Campeche Bank

Map 49 **CENTRAL AMERICA AND WESTERN CARIBBEAN**

A 92 B 90 C 88 D 86 E 84 F G H

UNITED STATES
Florida

Naples
Fort Lauderdale
Hollywood
North Miami
Miami Beach
MIAMI
Coral Gables

G O L F O   D E   M É X I C O

G U L F   O F   M E X I C O

CUBA

LA HABANA
HAVANA
Marianao
Matanzas
Cárdenas

C U B A

MÉXICO

Yucatán

MÉRIDA

Campeche

Quintana Roo

P E N Í N S U L A

Chetumal

Tabasco

Chiapas

GUATEMALA

GUATEMALA

BELIZE

Belize City

Belmopan

Cayman Islands
(U.K.)

George Town
GRAND CAYMAN

LITTLE CAYMAN
CAYMAN BRAC

C a y m a n   T r e n c h

HONDURAS

TEGUCIGALPA

San Pedro Sula

La Ceiba

ISLAS DE LA BAHÍA

EL SALVADOR

SAN SALVADOR

Santa Ana
San Miguel

NICARAGUA

MANAGUA
Masaya
Granada

León

COSTA RICA

SAN JOSÉ
Cartago

Limón

PANAMÁ

PANAMÁ
Colón
La Chorrera

David

O C É A N O   P A C Í F I C O

PACIFIC   OCEAN

M i d d l e   A m e r i c a   T r e n c h

PENÍNSULA
DE NICOYA

SAN ANDRÉS
Y PROVIDENCIA
(Colombia)

M A R

Delisle Conic Equidistant Projection

0   100   200   300   400 km

0   100   200 miles

A-533800-280-1 -1 -1 -1

B 86 C 84 F 82 G 80 H

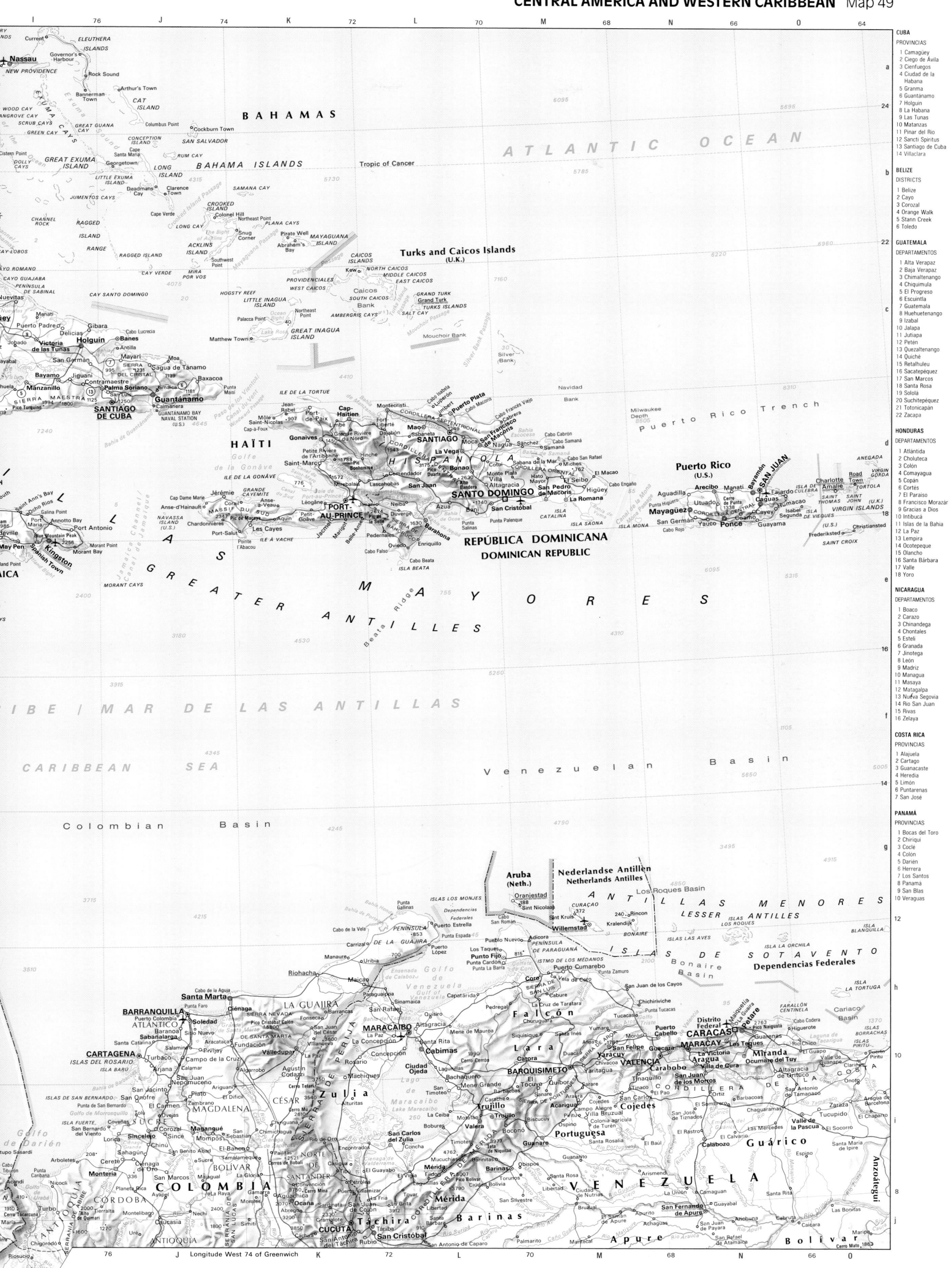

Map 50 **EASTERN CARIBBEAN**

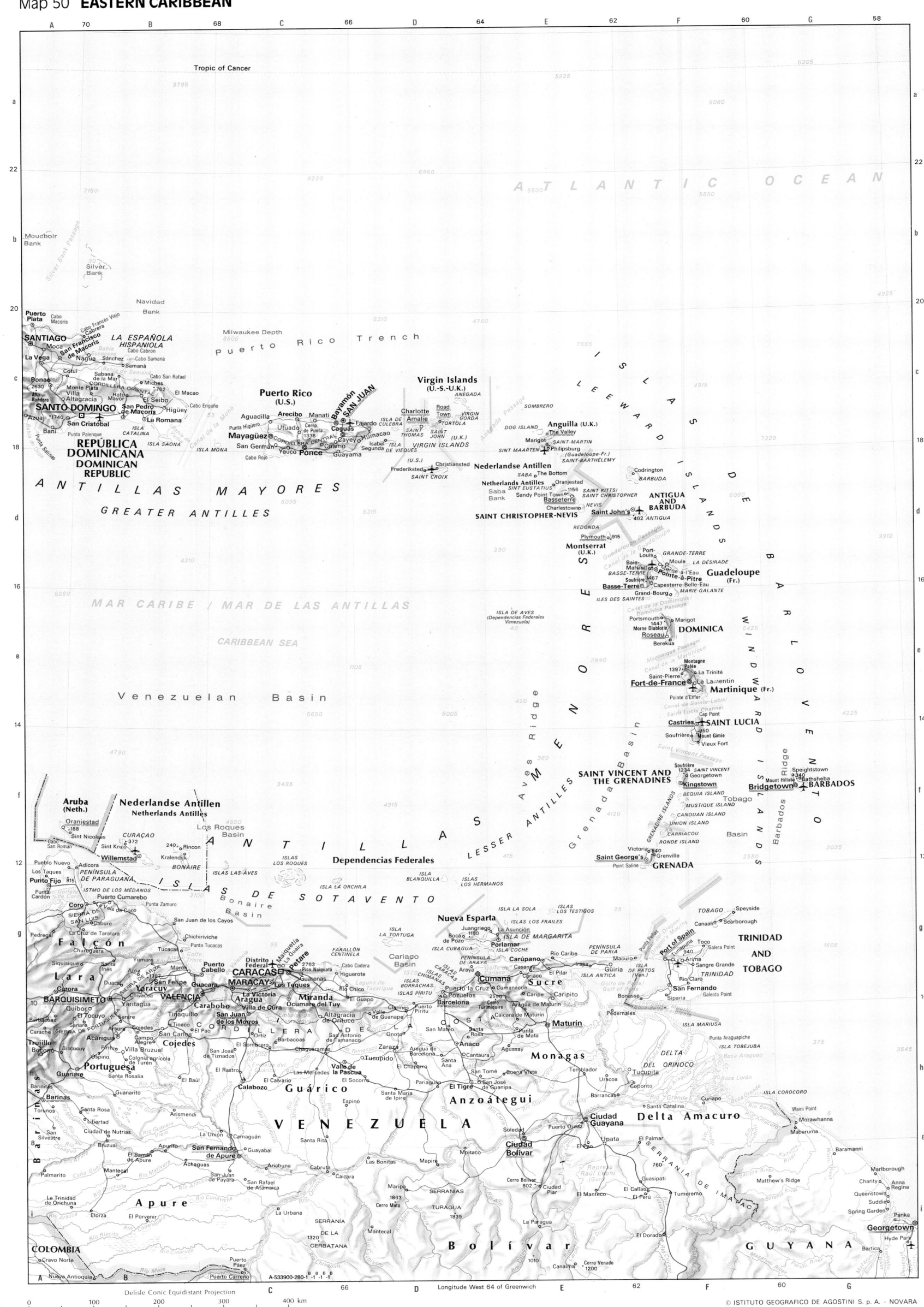

Tropic of Cancer

A T L A N T I C   O C E A N

Mouchoir Bank

Silver Bank

Navidad Bank

Puerto Rico Trench

Virgin Islands (U.S.-U.K.)
ANEGADA

Puerto Plata
SANTIAGO
Moca
La Vega
Bonao
Monte Plata
SANTO DOMINGO
San Cristóbal
Baní

Puerto Rico (U.S.)
Aguadilla
Arecibo
Manati
SAN JUAN
Caguas
Mayagüez
San Germán
Yauco Ponce
Guayama

Charlotte Amalie
SAINT THOMAS
Road Town
VIRGIN GORDA
TORTOLA
SAINT JOHN (U.K.)
VIRGIN ISLANDS (U.S.)
Christiansted
Frederiksted
SAINT CROIX

Anguilla (U.K.)
The Valley
Marigot SAINT-MARTIN
Philipsburg
SINT MAARTEN
SAINT-BARTHÉLEMY

Nederlandse Antillen
Netherlands Antilles
SABA The Bottom
Oranjestad
SINT EUSTATIUS
Saba Bank
Sandy Point Town
Basseterre
Charlestown
SAINT CHRISTOPHER-NEVIS
NEVIS Saint John's
Codrington
BARBUDA
ANTIGUA AND BARBUDA
ANTIGUA

REDONDA
Plymouth 915
Montserrat (U.K.)
Port-Louis
Baie GRANDE-TERRE
Mahault Moule LA DÉSIRADE
Soufrière Pointe-à-Pitre
BASSE-TERRE 1467
Basse-Terre Capesterre-Belle-Eau
Grand-Bourg
Guadeloupe (Fr.)
MARIE-GALANTE
ÎLES DES SAINTES

REPÚBLICA DOMINICANA
DOMINICAN REPUBLIC

LA ESPAÑOLA
HISPANIOLA

A N T I L L A S   M A Y O R E S
G R E A T E R   A N T I L L E S

M A R   C A R I B E / M A R   D E   L A S   A N T I L L A S
CARIBBEAN SEA

ISLA DE AVES
(Dependencias Federales Venezuela)

Portsmouth Marigot
Morne Diablotin
Roseau **DOMINICA**
Berekua

Montagne Pelée
1397 La Trinité
Saint-Pierre
Fort-de-France Le Lamentin
Martinique (Fr.)
Pointe d'Enfer

Cap Point
Castries **SAINT LUCIA**
950
Soufrière Mount Gimie
Vieux Fort

Venezuelan Basin

Soufrière **SAINT VINCENT**
1234
Georgetown
SAINT VINCENT AND THE GRENADINES
Mount Hillaby
Kingstown
BEQUIA ISLAND
Speightstown
Bridgetown **BARBADOS**
Bathsheba
MUSTIQUE ISLAND
CANOUAN ISLAND
UNION ISLAND
Tobago
CARRIACOU
RONDE ISLAND
Victoria
Saint George's Grenville
Point Saline **GRENADA**

Aves Ridge

Grenada Basin

Aruba (Neth.)
Oranjestad
188

Nederlandse Antillen
Netherlands Antilles

Los Roques Basin

A N T I L L A S

CURAÇAO 372
Willemstad
Kralendijk
BONAIRE
240 Rincon
Bonaire Basin

ISLAS LAS-AVES

ISLAS LOS ROQUES
Dependencias Federales

ISLA LA ORCHILA

ISLA LA BLANQUILLA
ISLAS LOS HERMANOS

ISLAS DE SOTAVENTO

TOBAGO Speyside
Scarborough
Canaan
TRINIDAD AND TOBAGO

ISLA LA SOLA
ISLAS LOS TESTIGOS

Nueva Esparta
Juangriego
Boca de Pozo La Asunción
Porlamar
ISLA DE MARGARITA
ISLA CUBAGUA
ISLA COCHE

Pueblo Nuevo
Adicora
Punto Fijo
Coro
PENÍNSULA DE PARAGUANÁ

Puerto Cumarebo
Punta Zamuro
San Juan de los Cayos
Chichiriviche
Tucacas

Maiquetía
La Guaira
CARACAS
Petare
Los Teques
Guarenas

Higuerote
Río Chico
PENÍNSULA DE ARAYA
Cumaná
Barcelona
Carúpano
Güiria
Sucre
PENÍNSULA DE PARIA
ISLA DE PATOS (Ven.)
Port of Spain
Arima
Sangre Grande
TRINIDAD
San Fernando
Galeota Point

Falcón

Barquisimeto
VALENCIA
MARACAY
CARACAS

V E N E Z U E L A

Monagas
Maturin

Anzoátegui
El Tigre
Anaco
San Tomé
Pariaguán
Soledad
Ciudad Guayana
Upata
Ciudad Bolívar

DELTA DEL ORINOCO
Delta Amacuro
Tucupita

Guárico
Calabozo
Valle de la Pascua
Zaraza

Bolívar
El Dorado
Tumeremo
El Callao

Apure
San Fernando de Apure

COLOMBIA

G U Y A N A
Georgetown

© ISTITUTO GEOGRAFICO DE AGOSTINI S. p. A. - NOVARA

Delisle Conic Equidistant Projection

Longitude West 64 of Greenwich

0 100 200 300 400 km
0 100 200 miles

A-533900-280-1 -1 -1 -1

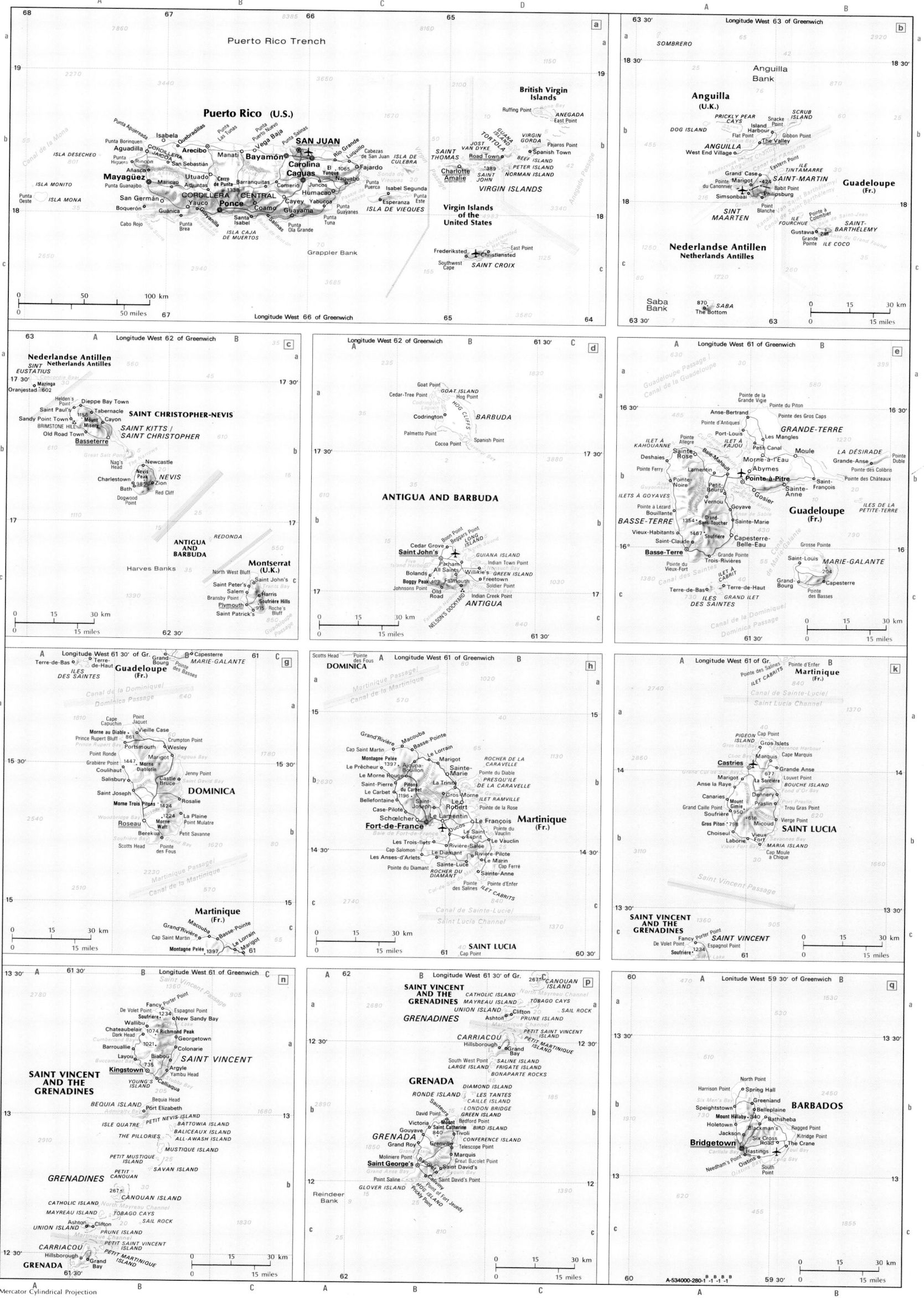

Mercator Cylindrical Projection

© ISTITUTO GEOGRAFICO DE AGOSTINI S. p. A. - NOVARA

Map 52

SOUTH AMERICA, PHYSICAL

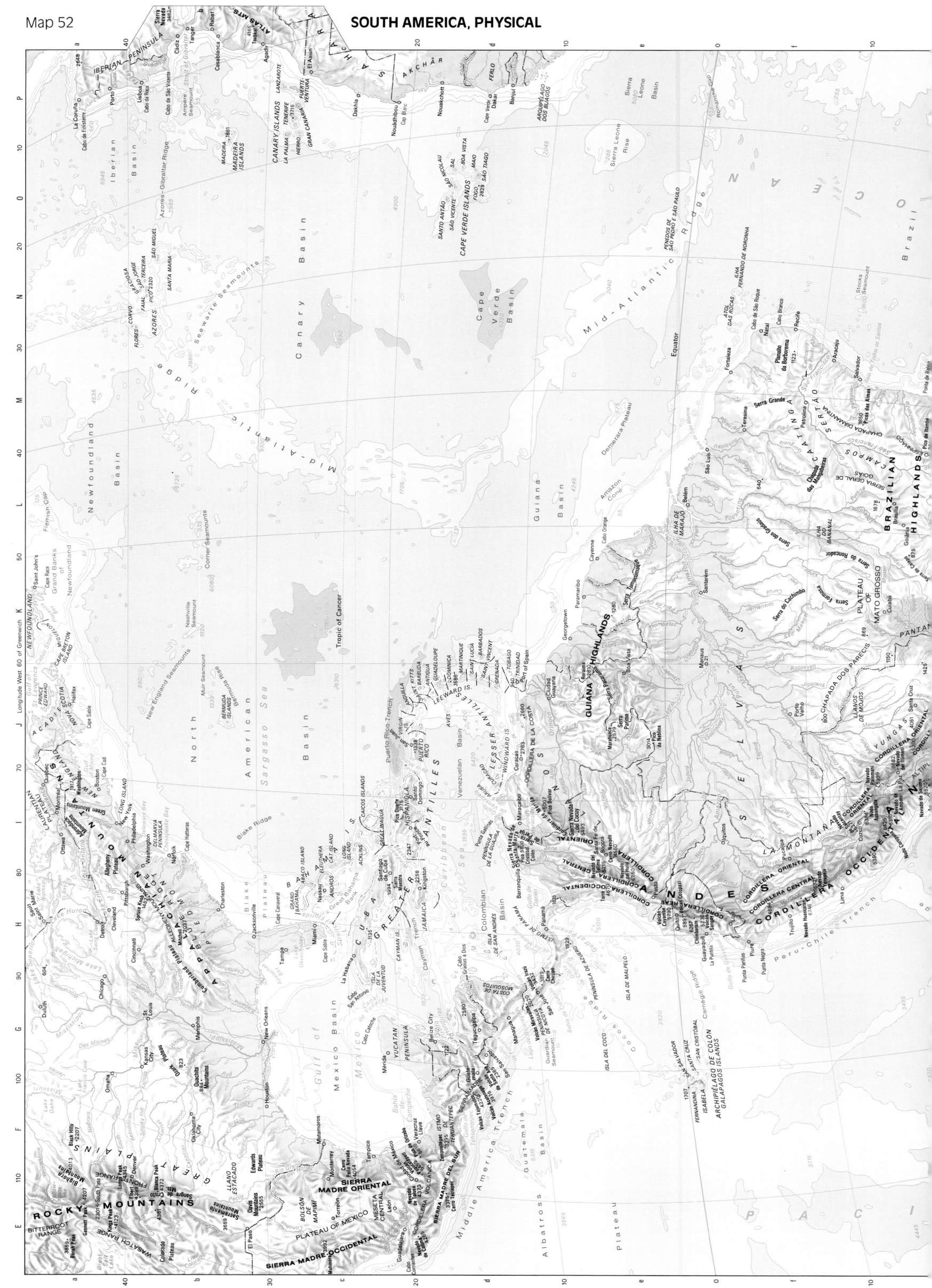

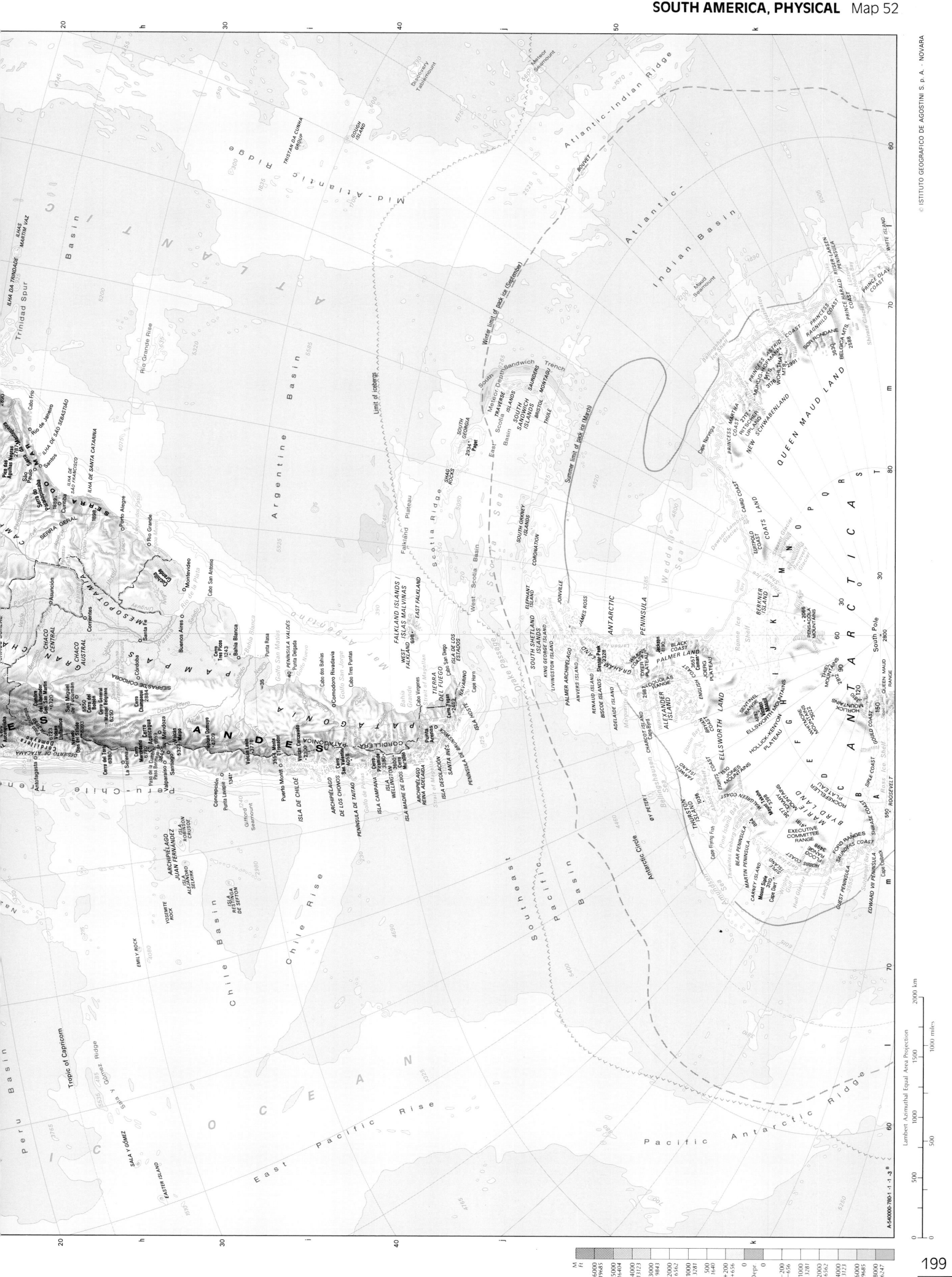

© ISTITUTO GEOGRAFICO DE AGOSTINI S. p. A. - NOVARA

Lambert Azimuthal Equal Area Projection

A-540000-780-1 -1 -1 -3 B

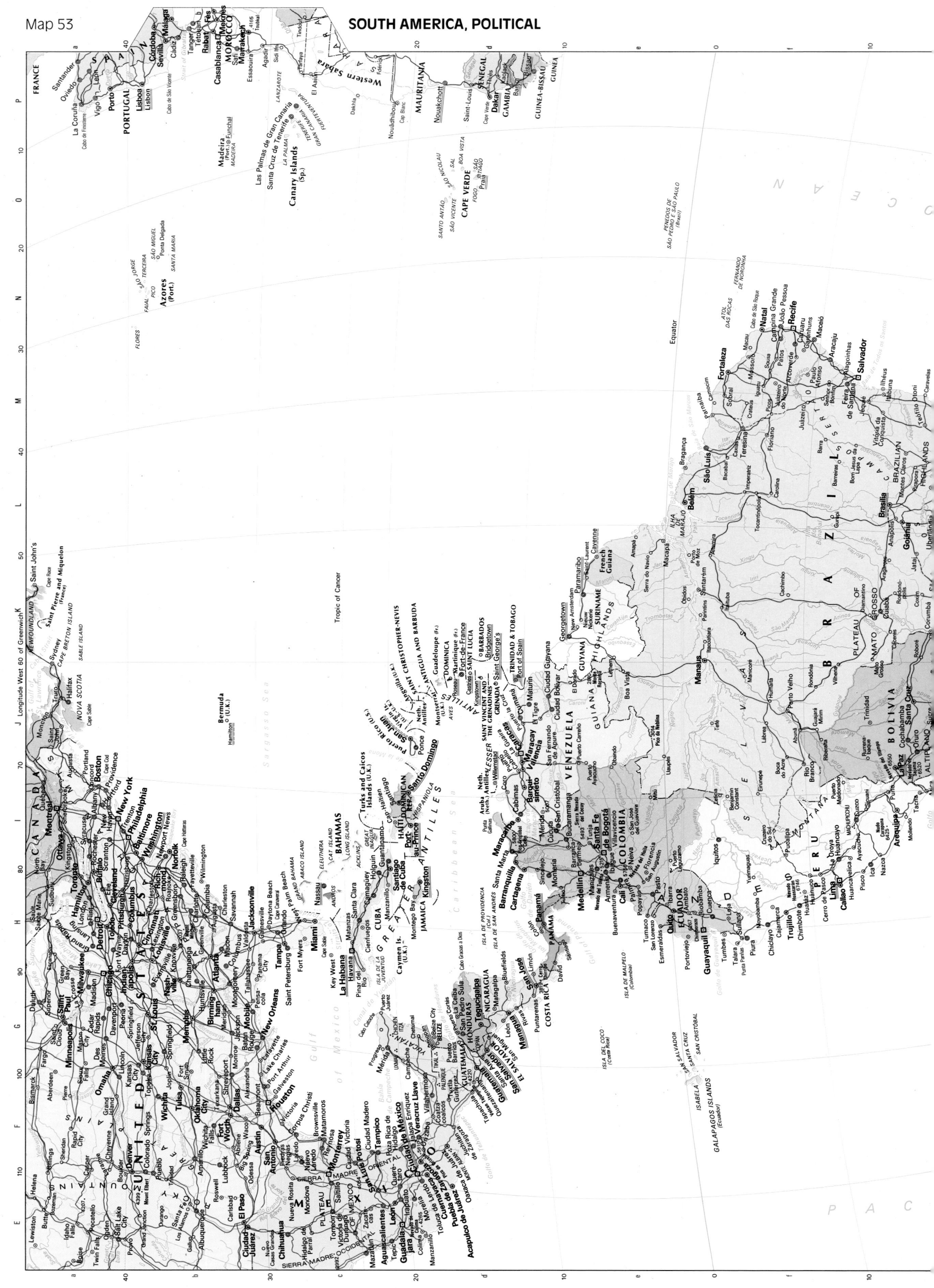

Map 53

SOUTH AMERICA, POLITICAL

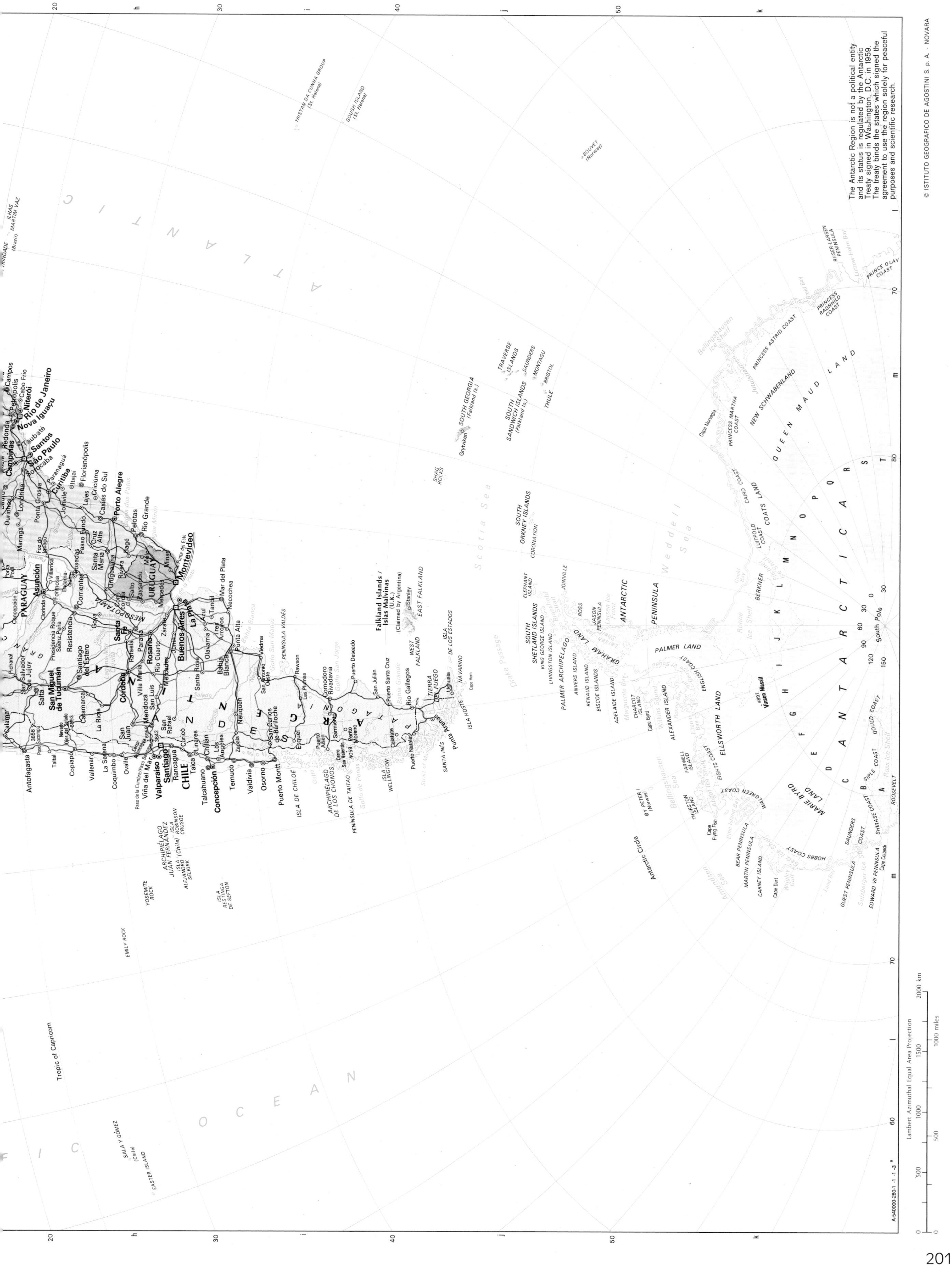

The Antarctic Region is not a political entity and its status is regulated by the Antarctic Treaty signed in Washington, D.C. in 1959. The treaty binds the states which signed the agreement to use the region solely for peaceful purposes and scientific research.

A T L A N T I C

ILHAS MARTIM VAZ (Brazil)

TRISTAN DA CUNHA GROUP (St. Helena)

GOUGH ISLAND (St. Helena)

BOUVET (Norway)

Campos
Cabo Frio
Rio de Janeiro
Niterói
Campinas
Santos
São Paulo
Sorocaba
Curitiba
Joinville
Florianópolis
Criciúma
Porto Alegre
Rio Grande
Caxias do Sul
Pelotas
Santa Maria
Bagé
Uruguaiana
PARAGUAY
Asunción
URUGUAY
Montevideo
Punta del Este
Corrientes
Resistencia
Santa Fe
Paraná
Rosario
Córdoba
Santiago del Estero
San Miguel de Tucumán
Salta
Catamarca
La Rioja
Mendoza
San Juan
San Luis
San Rafael
Buenos Aires
La Plata
Mar del Plata
Necochea
Bahía Blanca
Villa María
Río Cuarto
Santa Rosa
Neuquén
PENÍNSULA VALDÉS
Viedma
Rawson
Trelew
Puerto Madryn
Comodoro Rivadavia
Puerto Deseado
Puerto San Julián
Río Gallegos
Punta Arenas
TIERRA DEL FUEGO
Cape Horn

CHILE
Antofagasta
Taltal
Copiapó
Vallenar
La Serena
Coquimbo
Ovalle
Valparaíso
Viña del Mar
Santiago
Rancagua
San Fernando
Curicó
Talca
Chillán
Concepción
Talcahuano
Temuco
Valdivia
Osorno
Puerto Montt
ISLA DE CHILOÉ
ARCHIPIÉLAGO DE LOS CHONOS
PENÍNSULA DE TAITAO
Golfo de Penas
ARCHIPIÉLAGO JUAN FERNÁNDEZ (Chile)
ISLA ROBINSON CRUSOE
ALEJANDRO SELKIRK

SALA Y GÓMEZ (Chile)
EASTER ISLAND

Tropic of Capricorn

P A C I F I C   O C E A N

Falkland Islands / Islas Malvinas (U.K.) (Claimed by Argentina)
WEST FALKLAND
EAST FALKLAND
Stanley
ISLA DE LOS ESTADOS

SOUTH GEORGIA (Falkland Is.)
Grytviken

SHAG ROCKS

SOUTH SANDWICH ISLANDS (Falkland Is.)
TRAVERSE ISLANDS
SAUNDERS
MONTAGU
BRISTOL
THULE

Scotia Sea

SOUTH ORKNEY ISLANDS
CORONATION

SOUTH SHETLAND ISLANDS
ELEPHANT ISLAND
KING GEORGE ISLAND
LIVINGSTON ISLAND

Drake Passage

Weddell Sea

PALMER ARCHIPELAGO
ANVERS ISLAND
RENAUD ISLAND
BISCOE ISLANDS
ADELAIDE ISLAND
CHARCOT ISLAND
ALEXANDER ISLAND
PETER I ØY (Norway)

ANTARCTIC PENINSULA
GRAHAM LAND
PALMER LAND
ELLSWORTH LAND

A N T A R C T I C A

QUEEN MAUD LAND
NEW SCHWABENLAND
COATS LAND
BERKNER
CAIRD COAST
LUITPOLD COAST
ENGLISH COAST

South Pole

MARIE BYRD LAND
Vinson Massif

Bellingshausen Sea
Amundsen Sea
Ross Ice Shelf

Antarctic Circle

Lambert Azimuthal Equal Area Projection

0   500   1000   1500   2000 km
0   500   1000 miles

201

Map 54 **NORTHERN SOUTH AMERICA**

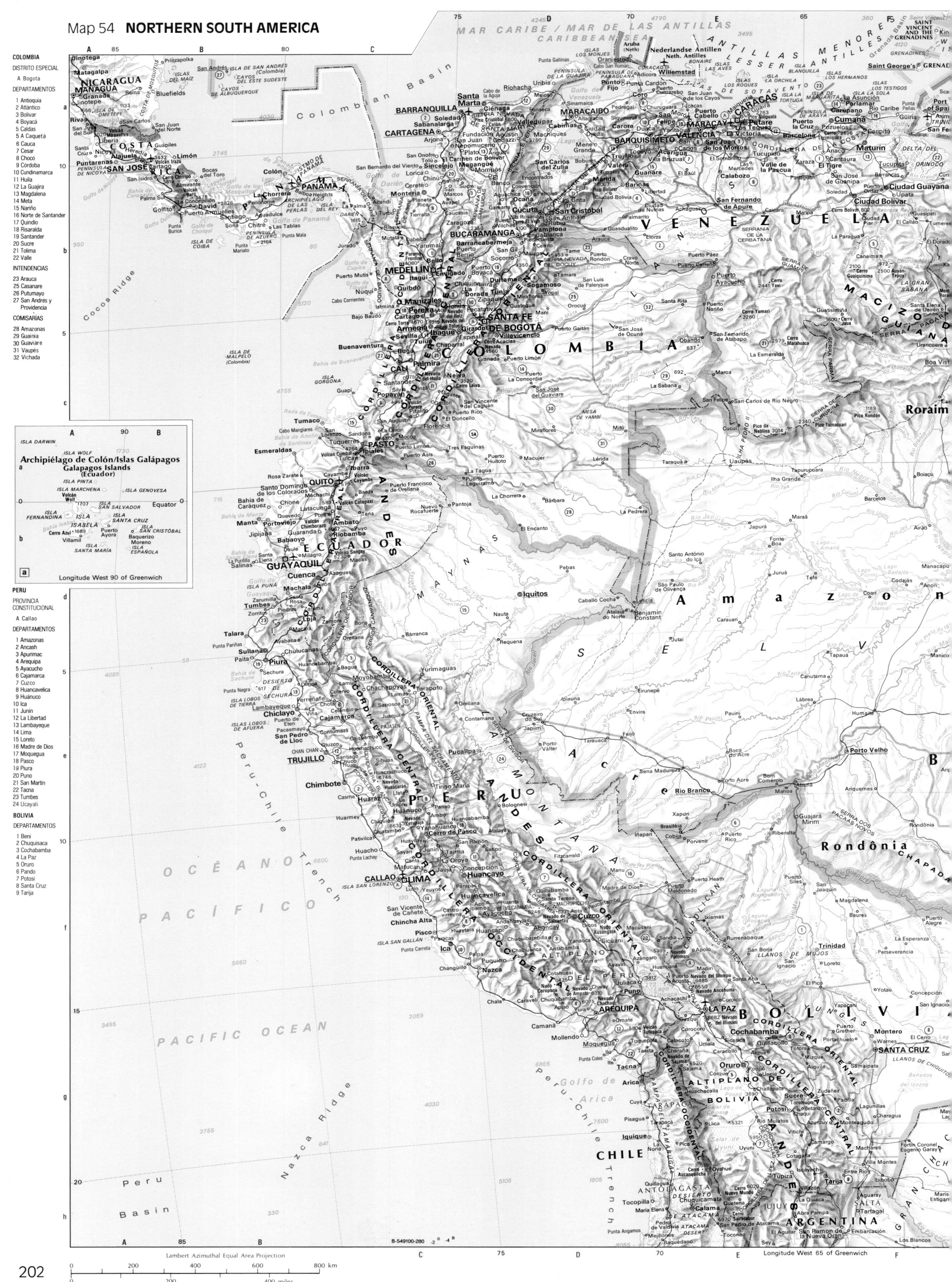

BARBADOS
Bridgetown

GUYANA
Georgetown
New Amsterdam
Linden

SURINAME
Paramaribo

Guyane
Française
French
Guiana
Cayenne

Amapá
Macapá

OCEANO ATLÂNTICO

Guiana Basin

Mid-Atlantic Ridge

ATLANTIC OCEAN

Equator

BELÉM

P a r á

Santarém

B R A Z I L

Maranhão

São Luís
Teresina
FORTALEZA

C e a r á

Rio Grande
do Norte
NATAL
João Pessoa
Olinda
RECIFE

Pernambuco

Piauí

Paulo Afonso

Alagoas
Maceió

Sergipe
Aracaju

SALVADOR

B a h i a

Tocantins

G o i á s

Mato Grosso

PLANALTO DO
MATO GROSSO

PLATEAU OF
MATO GROSSO

Cuiabá

BRASÍLIA Distrito
Federal

GOIÂNIA

Ilhéus

M i n a s

PLANALTO
DO BRASIL
BRAZILIAN
HIGHLANDS

Mato
Grosso
do Sul

Campo Grande

G e r a i s

BELO
HORIZONTE

Governador
Valadares

Espírito
Santo

Vitória

PARAGUAY

P a r a n á

S ã o
P a u l o

CAMPINAS

SÃO PAULO
SANTOS

Campos

RIO DE JANEIRO
Niterói

Tropic of Capricorn

OCEANO ATLÂNTICO

ATLANTIC OCEAN

Trinidade Spur

Map 55 **EAST-CENTRAL SOUTH AMERICA**

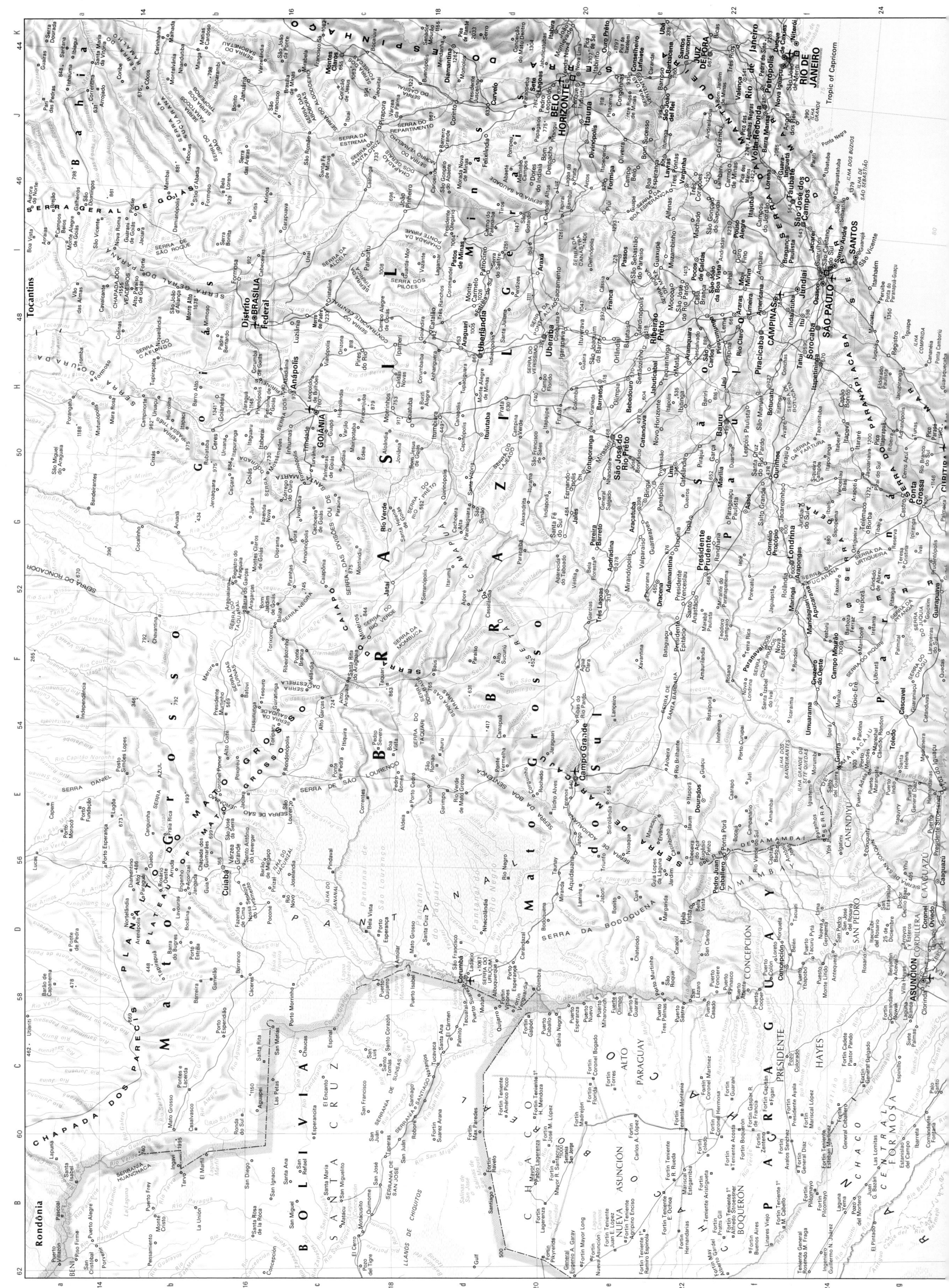

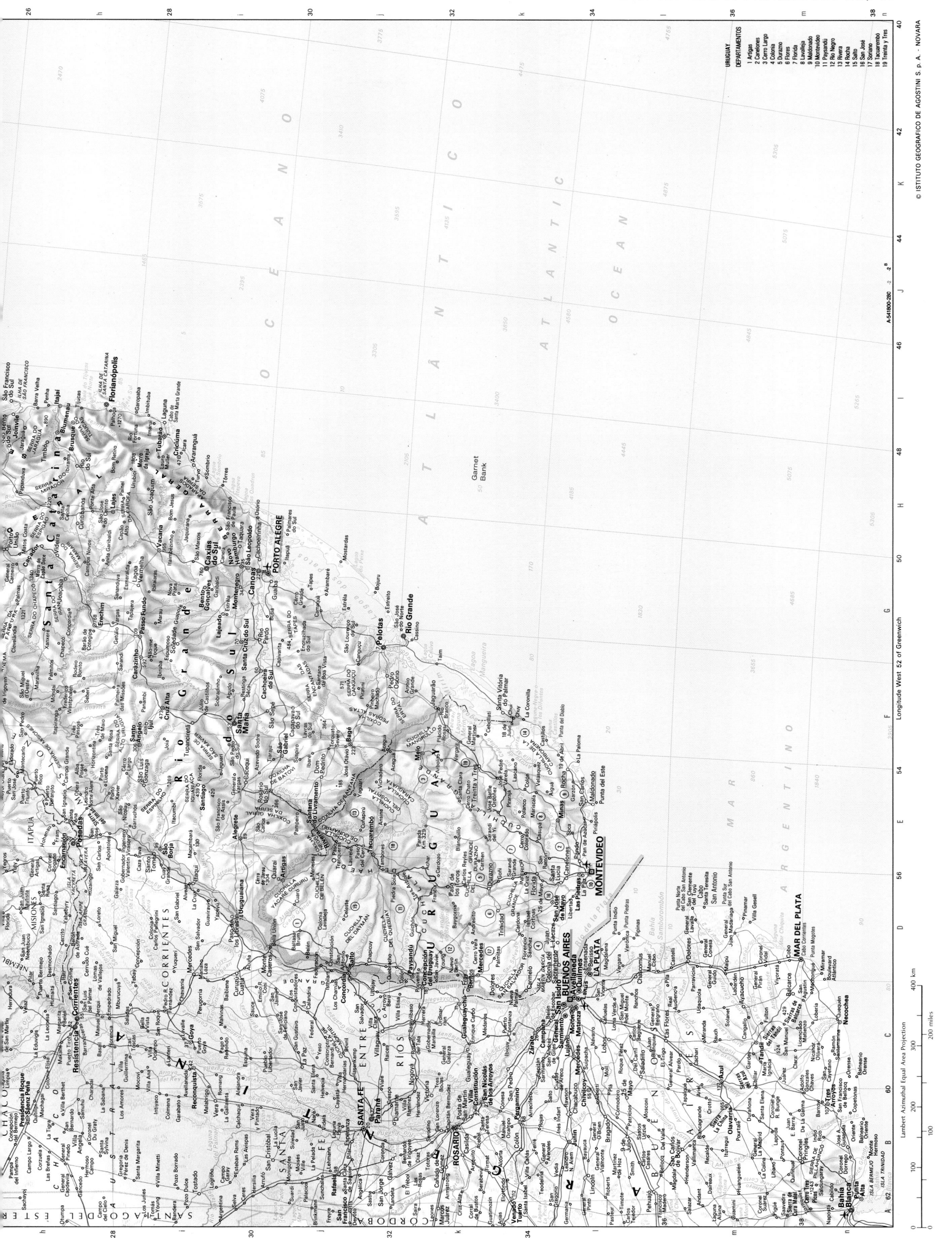

URUGUAY
DEPARTAMENTOS

1 Artigas
2 Canelones
3 Cerro Largo
4 Colonia
5 Durazno
6 Flores
7 Florida
8 Lavalleja
9 Maldonado
10 Montevideo
11 Paysandú
12 Río Negro
13 Rivera
14 Rocha
15 Salto
16 San José
17 Soriano
18 Tacuarembó
19 Treinta y Tres

Lambert Azimuthal Equal Area Projection

Longitude West 52 of Greenwich

0   100   200   300   400 km
0   100   200 miles

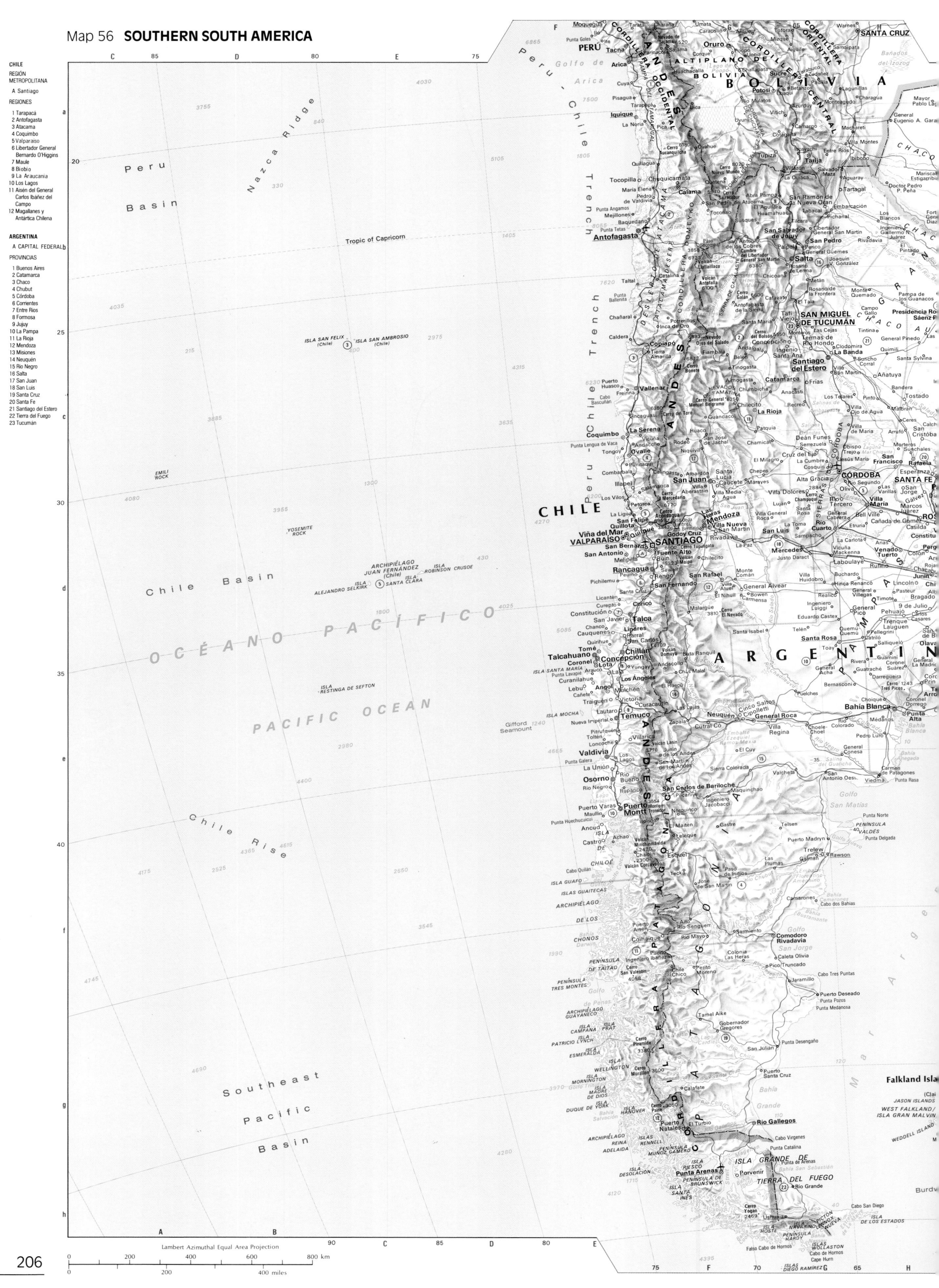

Map 56 **SOUTHERN SOUTH AMERICA**

CHILE

REGIÓN
METROPOLITANA

A Santiago

REGIONES

1 Tarapacá
2 Antofagasta
3 Atacama
4 Coquimbo
5 Valparaíso
6 Libertador General
Bernardo O'Higgins
7 Maule
8 Biobío
9 La Araucanía
10 Los Lagos
11 Aisén del General
Carlos Ibáñez del
Campo
12 Magallanes y
Antártica Chilena

ARGENTINA

A CAPITAL FEDERAL

PROVINCIAS

1 Buenos Aires
2 Catamarca
3 Chaco
4 Chubut
5 Córdoba
6 Corrientes
7 Entre Ríos
8 Formosa
9 Jujuy
10 La Pampa
11 La Rioja
12 Mendoza
13 Misiones
14 Neuquén
15 Río Negro
16 Salta
17 San Juan
18 San Luis
19 Santa Cruz
20 Santa Fe
21 Santiago del Estero
22 Tierra del Fuego
23 Tucumán

Lambert Azimuthal Equal Area Projection

Map 57 **AUSTRALIA AND OCEANIA, PHYSICAL**

Lambert Azimuthal Equal Area Projection

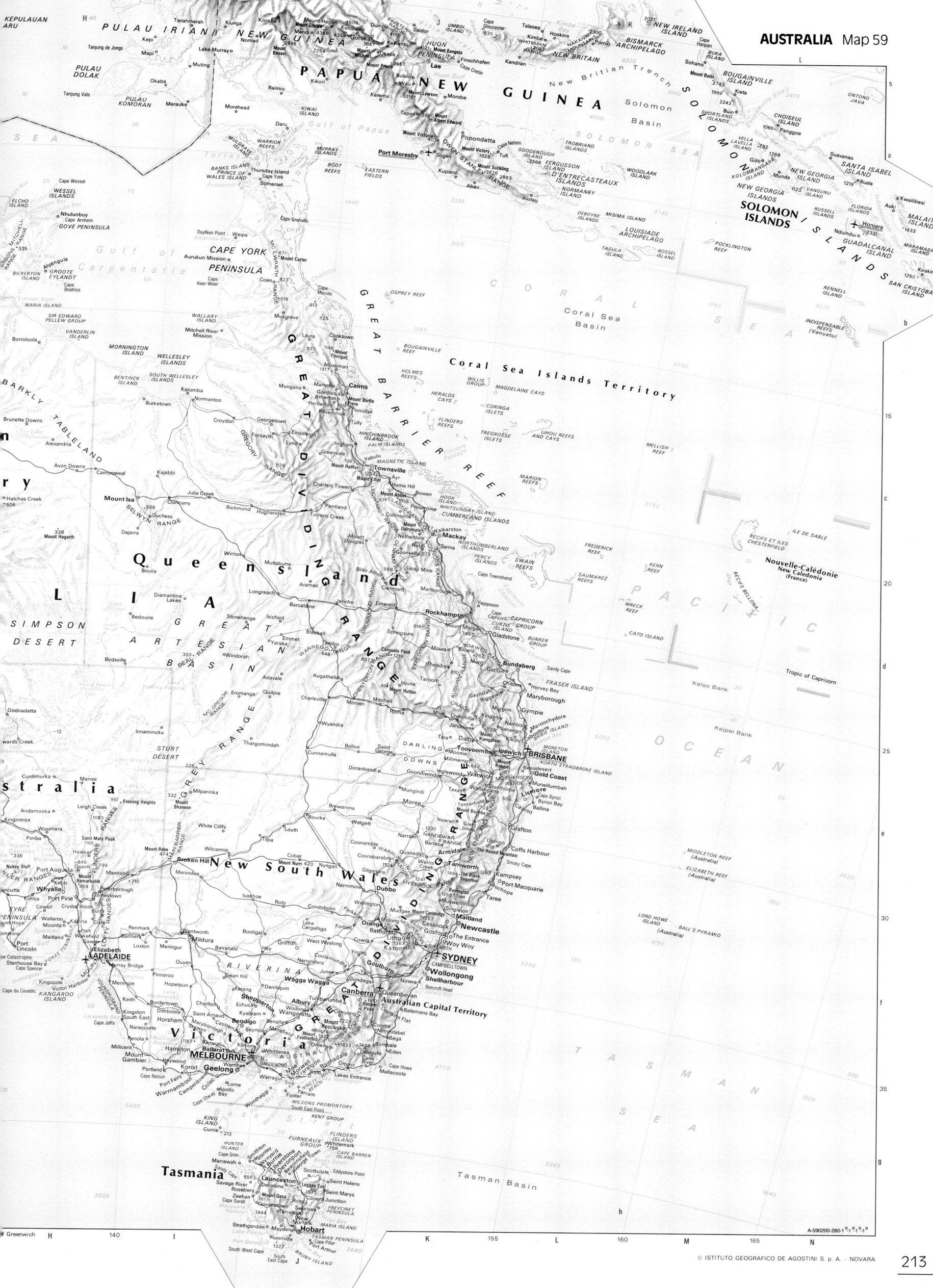

PULAU IRIAN

NEW GUINEA

PAPUA NEW GUINEA

Gulf of Papua

Port Moresby

CAPE YORK PENINSULA

Gulf of Carpentaria

SIMPSON DESERT

Queensland

GREAT ARTESIAN BASIN

STURT DESERT

Broken Hill

New South Wales

ADELAIDE

Wagga Wagga

Canberra

Australian Capital Territory

Victoria

MELBOURNE

Geelong

Tasmania

Launceston

Hobart

BISMARCK ARCHIPELAGO

NEW IRELAND ISLAND

NEW BRITAIN

BOUGAINVILLE ISLAND

Solomon Sea Basin

SOLOMON SEA

SOLOMON ISLANDS

Coral Sea Basin

Coral Sea Islands Territory

CORAL SEA

GREAT BARRIER REEF

Cairns

Townsville

Mackay

Rockhampton

Gladstone

Bundaberg

FRASER ISLAND

Tropic of Capricorn

Nouvelle-Calédonie New Caledonia (France)

PACIFIC OCEAN

BRISBANE

Gold Coast

Toowoomba

Newcastle

SYDNEY

Wollongong

LORD HOWE ISLAND (Australia)

BALL'S PYRAMID (Australia)

TASMAN SEA

Tasman Basin

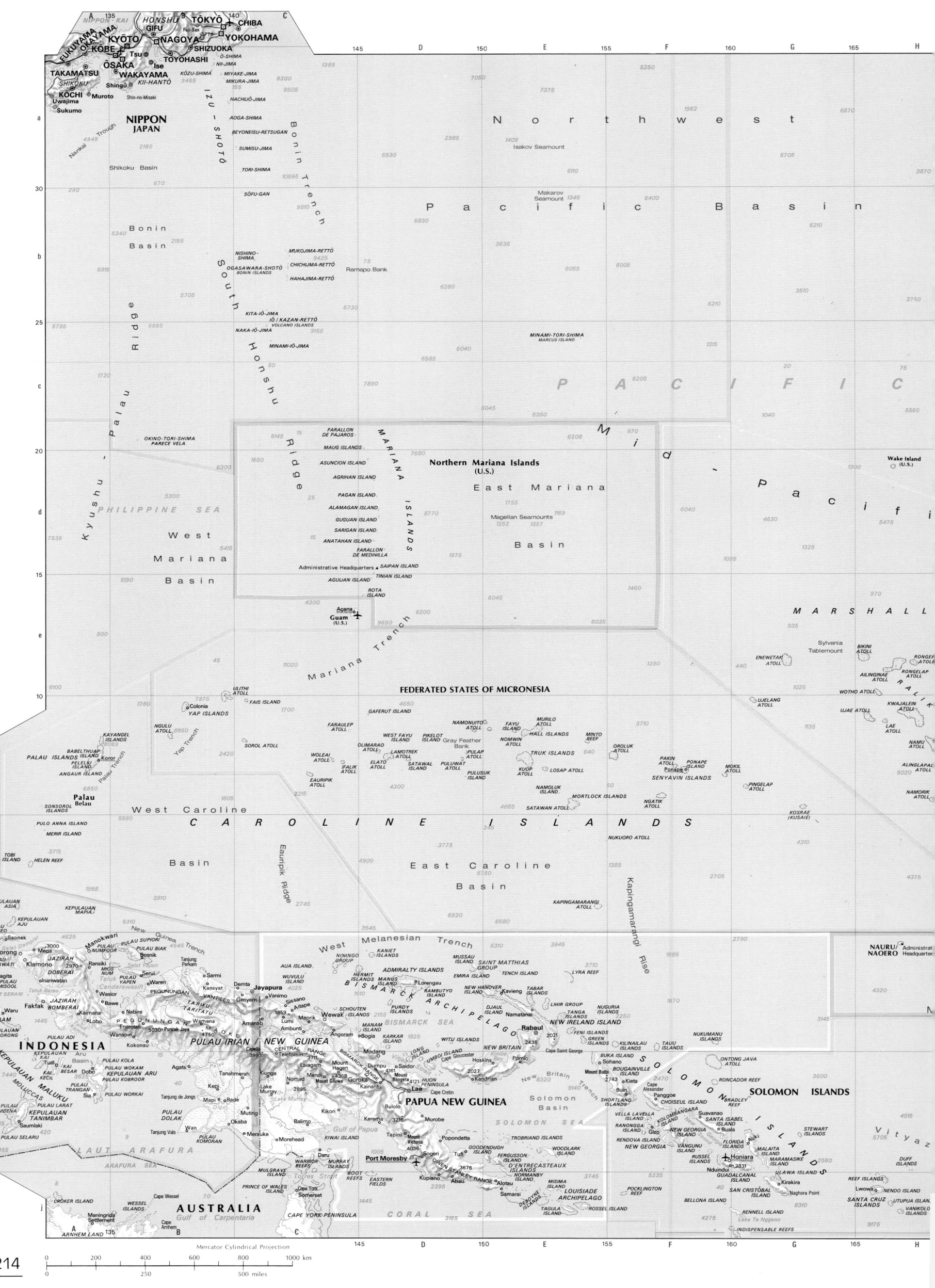

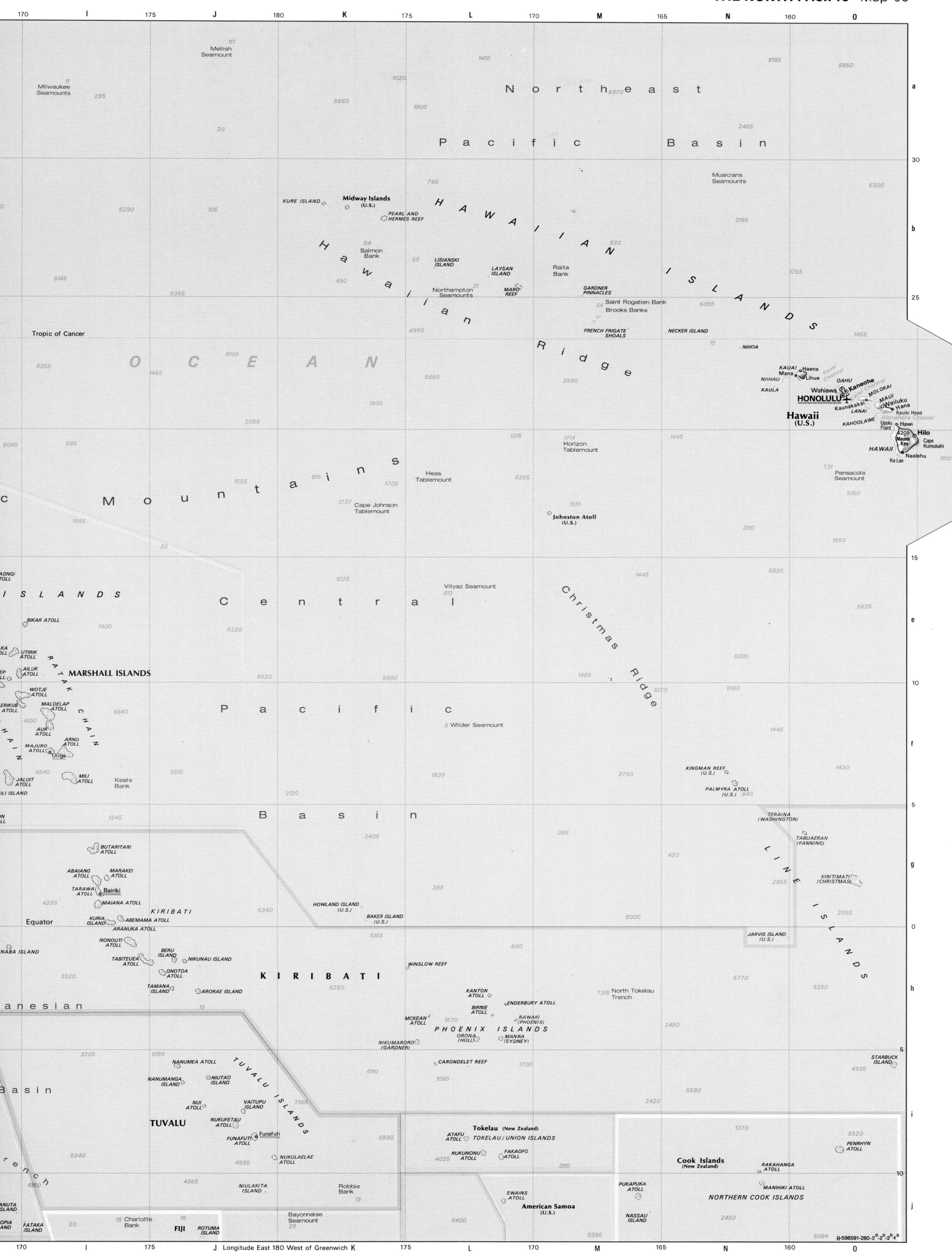

Mellish
Seamount
117

Milwaukee
Seamounts
11
295
20

Northeast

Pacific   Basin

6970

6185

5850

1410
1020
795
1900
5560
6290
105

Musicians
Seamounts
6300

KURE ISLAND   Midway Islands
(U.S.)

PEARL AND
HERMES REEF

2195

2485

Salmon
Bank
54

54

Salmon
Bank
830

LISIANSKI
ISLAND
55

LAYSAN
ISLAND

Raita
Bank

1755

6145
6355
490

Northampton
Seamounts
31

MARO
REEF

GARDNER
PINNACLES

Saint Rogatien Bank
54
Brooks Banks
5055

OCEAN

6365
1465

6100

5560

2580

FRENCH FRIGATE
SHOALS

NECKER ISLAND
15

1465

KAUAI
Mana
Haena
Lihue

NIHOA

Kauai
Channel

Kauai
Channel

NIIHAU

KAULA

OAHU
Wahiawa   Kaneohe
HONOLULU
Kaunakakai   MOLOKAI
MAUI
LANAI   Wailuku
Kauiki Head
Hana

1900

2085

1315

Horizon
Tablemount

1714

1445

Hawaii
(U.S.)

6045
585

KAHOOLAWE
Alenuihaha Channel
Upolu
Point
Hawi
Hilo
Cape
Kumukahi

4205
Mauna
Kea
HAWAII
Mauna
Loa
Ka Lae
Naalehu
731

1810

Pensacola
Seamount
1050

Mountains

1555
815

Hess
Tablemount

5265

1510

1950

1737   Cape Johnson
Tablemount

Johnston Atoll
(U.S.)

3110

1705

1950

1955

30

6125

Vityaz Seamount
813

1445

5835

AONGI
ATOLL

Central

Christmas

Ridge

5625

ISLANDS

BIKAR ATOLL

1400

6220

5000

AKA
OLL

UTIRIK
ATOLL

MARSHALL ISLANDS

6520

5890

1485

1070

1090

REP
LL
LL

AILUK
ATOLL

WOTJE
ATOLL

Pacific

1445

ERIKUB
ATOLL

MALOELAP
ATOLL

4840

AUR
ATOLL

4100

Wilder Seamount
5

MAJURO
ATOLL   ARNO
ATOLL

4540
Uliga

JALUIT
ATOLL

MILI
ATOLL

Keats
Bank

3510

1830

3750

KINGMAN REEF
(U.S.)

1430

CILI ISLAND

2120

PALMYRA ATOLL
(U.S.) 840

Basin

TERAINA
(WASHINGTON)

ON
LL

1245

2405

365

420

TABUAERAN
(FANNING)

BUTARITARI
ATOLL

2855

ABAIANG
ATOLL   MARAKEI
ATOLL

TARAWA
ATOLL   Bairiki

385

KIRITIMATI
(CHRISTMAS)

2055

KURIA
ISLAND   ABEMAMA ATOLL

KIRIBATI

5340

HOWLAND ISLAND
(U.S.)

6000

MAIANA ATOLL

4295

ARANUKA ATOLL

BAKER ISLAND
(U.S.)

NABA ISLAND

NONOUTI
ATOLL

1065

JARVIS ISLAND
(U.S.)

TABITEUEA
ATOLL

BERU
ISLAND   NIKUNAU ISLAND

WINSLOW REEF

640

ONOTOA
ATOLL

3520

KIRIBATI

5770

5260

TAMANA
ISLAND   ARORAE ISLAND

6250

KANTON
ATOLL

ENDERBURY ATOLL

North Tokelau
Trench
7315

2480

MCKEAN
ISLAND
1570

BIRNIE
ATOLL

RAWAKI
(PHOENIX)

anesian

15

NIKUMARORO
(GARDNER)

PHOENIX   ISLANDS

ORONA
(HULL)

MANRA
(SYDNEY)

CARONDELET REEF

1700

STARBUCK
ISLAND

Basin

3705
5190

NANUMEA ATOLL

6110

1095

4935

TUVALU

NANUMANGA
ISLAND   NIUTAO
ISLAND

5580

NUI
ATOLL   VAITUPU
ISLAND

7130

2420

NUKUFETAU
ATOLL

TUVALU

FUNAFUTI
ATOLL   Funafuti

5590

Tokelau (New Zealand)

1370

5520

ATAFU
ATOLL   TOKELAU / UNION ISLANDS

PENRHYN
ATOLL

5340

NUKULAELAE
ATOLL

NUKUNONU
ATOLL   FAKAOFO
ATOLL

4025

3110

Cook Islands
(New Zealand)

RAKAHANGA
ATOLL

4935

4965

NIULAKITA
ISLAND

Robbie
Bank
13

SWAINS
ATOLL

PUKAPUKA
ATOLL

MANIHIKI ATOLL

ANUTA
ISLAND

18 Charlotte
Bank
15

Bayonnaise
Seamount
29

American Samoa
(U.S.)

NASSAU
ISLAND

NORTHERN COOK ISLANDS

2450

KOPIA

FATAKA
ISLAND

20

FIJI

ROTUMA
ISLAND

5400

5395

5084

B-598591-280-2ᴮ-2ᴮ-2ᴮ4ᴮ

RATAK   CHAIN

HAWAIIAN   ISLANDS

Hawaiian   Ridge

Line   Islands

Tuvalu   Islands

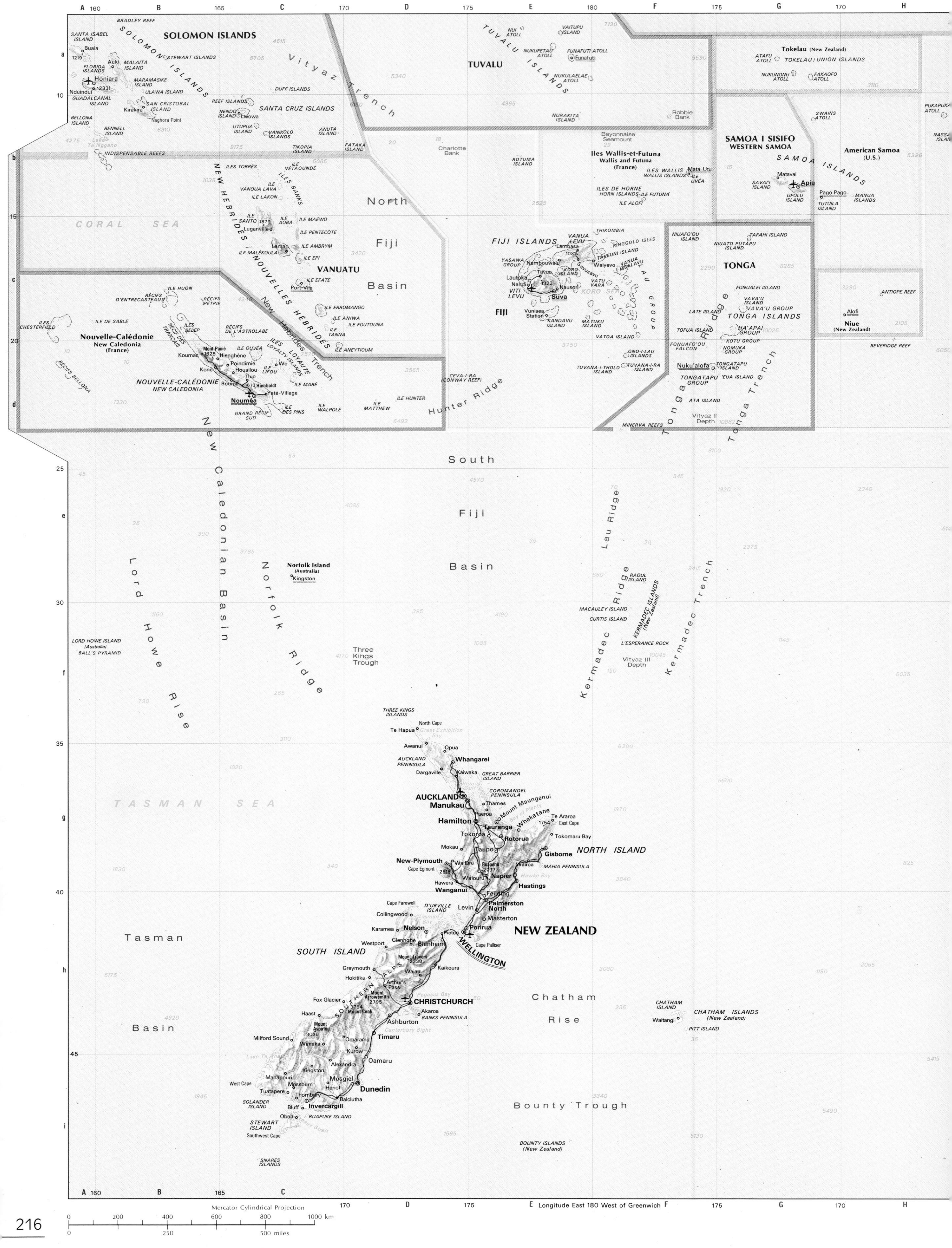

Map 61 **THE SOUTH PACIFIC**

SOLOMON ISLANDS

BRADLEY REEF
SANTA ISABEL ISLAND
Buala
1219
FLORIDA ISLANDS
Auki MALAITA ISLAND
MARAMASIKE ISLAND
Honiara
2331
Nduindui
GUADALCANAL ISLAND
Kirakira SAN CRISTOBAL ISLAND
ULAWA ISLAND
Naghora Point
BELLONA ISLAND
RENNELL ISLAND
8310
Lake Te Nggano
4275
STEWART ISLANDS
DUFF ISLANDS
REEF ISLANDS
NENDO ISLAND
UTUPUA ISLAND
VANIKOLO ISLANDS
SANTA CRUZ ISLANDS
Lwowa
ANUTA ISLAND
TIKOPIA ISLAND
FATAKA ISLAND
4515
5705
5340
4965

Vityaz Trench

INDISPENSABLE REEFS
9175
20
650

TUVALU
NUI ATOLL
NUKUFETAU ATOLL
VAITUPU ISLAND
FUNAFUTI ATOLL
Funafuti
NUKULAELAE ATOLL
NURAKITA ISLAND
Robbie Bank
7130
6590
13

TUVALU ISLANDS

Tokelau (New Zealand)
ATAFU ATOLL
TOKELAU / UNION ISLANDS
NUKUNONU ATOLL
FAKAOFO ATOLL
SWAINS ISLAND
NASSAU
PUKAPUKA ATOLL
3110
5396

ILES TORRÉS
ILE VANUA LAVA
ILE LAKON
ILES BANKS
ILE VÉTAOUNDÉ
1035
5085

North
Fiji
Basin

Charlotte Bank
20
4965
ROTUMA ISLAND

Bayonnaise Seamount
THIKOMBIA
VANUA LEVU
RINGGOLD ISLES

SAMOA I SISIFO
WESTERN SAMOA
Matavai
SAVAI'I ISLAND
Apia
UPOLU ISLAND

American Samoa (U.S.)
Pago Pago
TUTUILA ISLAND
MANUA ISLANDS

SAMOA ISLANDS

CORAL SEA
15

VANUATU
ILE SANTO 1879
Luganville
ILF MALÉKOULA
ILE AOBA
ILE MAÉWO
ILE PENTECÔTE
ILE AMBRYM
Lamap
ILE EPI
ILE EFATÉ
Port-Vila
ILE ERROMANGO
ILE ANIWA
ILE TANNA
ILE FOUTOUNA
ILE ANEYTIOUM
3420
2525
42·B
5085

NEW HEBRIDES / NOUVELLES HÉBRIDES
NEW HEBRIDES TRENCH

Iles Wallis-et-Futuna
Wallis and Futuna (France)
ILES DE HORNE
HORN ISLANDS – ILE FUTUNA
ILE ALOFI
ILES WALLIS
WALLIS ISLANDS – ILE UVÉA
Mata-Utu

FIJI ISLANDS
Lambasa
TAVEUNI ISLAND
VANUA MBALAVU
Nambouwalu
YASAWA GROUP
Lautoka
KORO ISLAND
Tavua
VITI LEVU
Nandi
1322
Nausori
Suva
FIJI
KORO SEA
Vunisea Station
KANDAVU ISLAND
VATOA ISLAND
1031¼
MATUKU ISLAND
ONO-I-LAU ISLANDS
TUVANA-I-THOLO ISLAND
TUVANA-I-RA ISLAND
CEVA-I-RA (CONWAY REEF)
3750

LAU GROUP
Lau Ridge

TONGA
NIUAFO'OU ISLAND
NIUATO PUTAPU ISLAND
TAFAHI ISLAND
FONUALEI ISLAND
LATE ISLAND
VAVA'U GROUP
VAVA'U
HA'APAI GROUP
TOFUA ISLAND
KOTU GROUP
NOMUKA GROUP
FONUAFO'OU FALCON
Nuku'alofa
TONGATAPU GROUP
'EUA ISLAND
Tongatapu Island
ATA ISLAND
MINERVA REEFS
Tyaz II Depth 10882
2290
8285
10025
3290

Niue (New Zealand)
Alofi
ANTIOPE REEF
BEVERIDGE REEF
2105
6050

Nouvelle-Calédonie
New Caledonia (France)
ILE HUON
RÉCIFS D'ENTRECASTEAUX
ILE BELEP
Koumac
Mont Panié 1628
Hienghène
Poindimié
Houailou
Kone
Thio
Bourail 1618
Humboldt
Yaté-Village
Nouméa
NOUVELLE-CALÉDONIE
NEW CALEDONIA
ILE OUVÉA
WÉ
ILE LIFOU
ILE MARÉ
ILES LOYAUTÉ
LOYALTY ISLANDS
ILE DES PINS
GRAND RÉCIF SUD
ILE WALPOLE
ILE MATTHEW
ILE HUNTER
1230
3565
6492
Hunter Ridge

ILES CHESTERFIELD
ILE DE SABLE
RÉCIFS DE L'ASTROLABE
RÉCIFS PÉTRIE
RÉCIFS DES FRANÇAIS
RÉCIFS BELLONA

South
Fiji
Basin

25
45
4570
4085
3785
390
65
8100
345
4190
2375
2340
1320

New Caledonian Basin
Norfolk Ridge
Lord Howe Rise

Norfolk Island (Australia)
Kingston

Lau Ridge
RAOUL ISLAND
MACAULEY ISLAND
CURTIS ISLAND
L'ESPERANCE ROCK
Vityaz III Depth 10045
KERMADEC ISLANDS (New Zealand)
860
9415
6035

Kermadec Ridge
Kermadec Trench

LORD HOWE ISLAND (Australia)
BALL'S PYRAMID
1150
730

THREE KINGS ISLANDS
Three Kings Trough
2110
4700
265
395
1089

TASMAN SEA
1020
1830

THREE KINGS ISLANDS
Te Hapua
North Cape
Great Exhibition Bay
Awanui
Opua
Whangarei
AUCKLAND PENINSULA
Dargaville
Kaiwaka
GREAT BARRIER ISLAND
COROMANDEL PENINSULA
AUCKLAND
Manukau
Thames
Paeroa
Mount Maunganui
Hamilton
Tauranga
Tokoroa
Rotorua
Te Araroa
East Cape
1754
Tokomaru Bay
Mokau
Taupo
New-Plymouth
Waitara
Inglewood
Wairoa
Gisborne
MAHIA PENINSULA
Cape Egmont 2518
NORTH ISLAND
Waiouru 2797
Hawera
Napier
Hastings
Hawke Bay
Wanganui
Feilding
Palmerston North
Levin
NEW ZEALAND
Cape Farewell
D'URVILLE ISLAND
Masterton
Collingwood
Tasman Bay
Porirua
Karamea
Nelson
Picton
WELLINGTON
Westport
Glenhope
Blenheim
Cape Palliser
SOUTH ISLAND
Mount Travers 2338
Kaikoura
Greymouth
Hokitika
SOUTHERN ALPS
Arthur's Pass
Waiau
3080
Fox Glacier
Mount Arrowsmith 2795
Mount Cook 3764
CHRISTCHURCH
Akaroa
BANKS PENINSULA
Haast
Mount Aspiring 3036
Ashburton
Canterbury Bight
Milford Sound
Timaru
Wanaka
Omarama
Kurow
Chatham Rise
CHATHAM ISLAND
CHATHAM ISLANDS (New Zealand)
Waitangi
PITT ISLAND
West Cape
Manapouri
Mossburn
Alexandra
Mosgiel
Oamaru
Dunedin
Kingston
Heriot
Tuatapere
Thornbury
Balclutha
Invercargill
SOLANDER ISLAND
Bluff
Oban
RUAPUKE ISLAND
STEWART ISLAND
Southwest Cape
SNARES ISLANDS
Bounty Trough
BOUNTY ISLANDS (New Zealand)

Tasman Basin
5175
4920
3036
1945
1595
5130
5490
5416
235
35

Mercator Cylindrical Projection

0 200 400 600 800 1000 km
0 250 500 miles

Longitude East 180 West of Greenwich

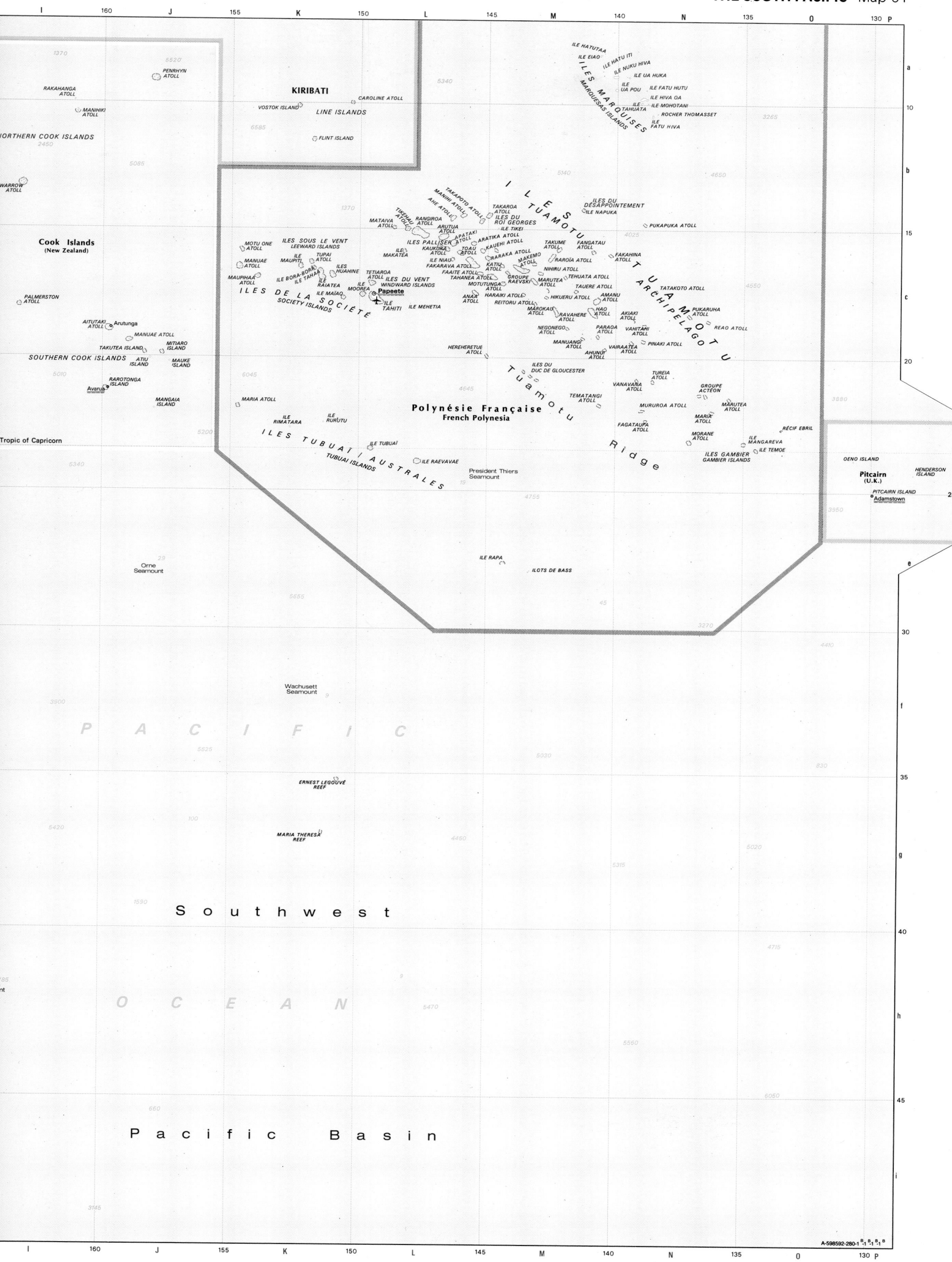

1370
5520
a

RAKAHANGA
ATOLL
PENRHYN
ATOLL

KIRIBATI
5340
ILE HATUTAA
ILE EIAO
ILE HATU ITI
ILE NUKU HIVA
ILE UA HUKA
ILE UA POU · ILE FATU HUTU

MANIHIKI
ATOLL
VOSTOK ISLAND
CAROLINE ATOLL
LINE ISLANDS
ILE HIVA OA
ILE TAHUATA
ILE MOHOTANI
ROCHER THOMASSET
10
3265

NORTHERN COOK ISLANDS
2450
6585
FLINT ISLAND
ILE
FATU HIVA

5085
5140
4680
b

WARROW
ATOLL
1370
ILES DU
DESAPPOINTEMENT
ILE NAPUKA

TAKAPOTO ATOLL
MANIHI ATOLL
TAKAROA
ATOLL
ILES DU
ROI GEORGES
PUKAPUKA ATOLL

Cook Islands
(New Zealand)
MATAIVA
ATOLL
TIKEHAU
ATOLL
RANGIROA
ATOLL
AHE ATOLL
ARUTUA
ATOLL
ILE TIKEI
4025
15

MOTU ONE
ATOLL
ILES SOUS LE VENT
LEEWARD ISLANDS
ILES PALLISER
MAKATEA
APATAKI
ATOLL
ARATIKA ATOLL
KAUEHI ATOLL
TAKUME
ATOLL
FANGATAU
ATOLL

MANUAE
ATOLL
ILE
MAUPITI
TUPAI
ATOLL
KAUKURA
ATOLL
TOAU
ATOLL
RARAKA ATOLL
MAKEMO
ATOLL
RAROIA ATOLL
FAKAHINA
ATOLL

MAUPIHAA
ATOLL
ILE BORA-BORA
ILE TAHAA
ILES
HUAHINE
TETIAROA
ATOLL
ILE NIAU
FAKARAVA ATOLL
KATIU
ATOLL
NIHIRU ATOLL
TEHUATA ATOLL

PALMERSTON
ATOLL
ILE RAIATEA
ILE
MOOREA
ILES DU VENT
WINDWARD ISLANDS
FAAITE ATOLL
TAHANEA ATOLL
GROUPE
RAEVSKI
MARUTEA
ATOLL
TATAKOTO ATOLL
4550

ILES DE LA SOCIÉTÉ
ILE MAIAO
Papeete
MOTUTUNGA
ATOLL
TAUERE ATOLL

SOCIETY ISLANDS
ILE
TAHITI
ANAA
ATOLL
HARAIKI ATOLL
HIKUERU ATOLL
AMANU
ATOLL
PUKARUHA
ATOLL

AITUTAKI
ATOLL
Arutunga
ILE MEHETIA
REITORU ATOLL
MAROKAU
ATOLL
HAO
ATOLL
AKIAKI
ATOLL
REAO ATOLL

MANUAE ATOLL
RAVAHERE
ATOLL
PARAOA
ATOLL
VAHITAHI
ATOLL
c

TAKUTEA ISLAND
MITIARO
ISLAND
NEGONEGO
ATOLL
PINAKI ATOLL

SOUTHERN COOK ISLANDS
ATIU
ISLAND
MAUKE
ISLAND
HEREHERETUE
ATOLL
MANUANGI
ATOLL
VAIRAATEA
ATOLL

5010
6045
4645
AHUNUI
ATOLL
20

RAROTONGA
ISLAND
ILES DU
DUC DE GLOUCESTER
TUREIA
ATOLL

Avarua
MANGAIA
ISLAND
MARIA ATOLL
VANAVANA
ATOLL
GROUPE
ACTÉON

Polynésie Française
French Polynesia
TEMATANGI
ATOLL
MURUROA ATOLL
MARUTEA
ATOLL

ILE
RIMATARA
ILE
RURUTU
MARIA
ATOLL
RÉCIF EBRIL
3880

Tropic of Capricorn
FAGATAUPA
ATOLL
MORANE
ATOLL
ILE MANGAREVA

5340
5200
ILE TUBUAI
ILES DE LA SOCIÉTÉ
ILES GAMBIER
GAMBIER ISLANDS
ILE TEMOE
d

ILES TUBUAI / AUSTRALES
President Thiers
Seamount
OENO ISLAND

TUBUAI ISLANDS
ILE RAEVAVAE
19
Pitcairn
(U.K.)
HENDERSON
ISLAND

5340
4755
PITCAIRN ISLAND
Adamstown
25

3950

ILE RAPA
e

Orne
Seamount
29
ILOTS DE BASS

5685
45
3270
30

4410

Wachusett
Seamount
9

3900
5020
830
f

5825
5030
35

ERNEST LEGOUVÉ
REEF

5420
100
g

MARIA THERESA
REEF
4450
5020

1590
5315

S o u t h w e s t
40

O   C   E   A   N
5470
4715
h

785
5550

P a c i f i c   B a s i n
6060
45

660
i

3145

A-598592-280-1

Map 62 **NEW ZEALAND**

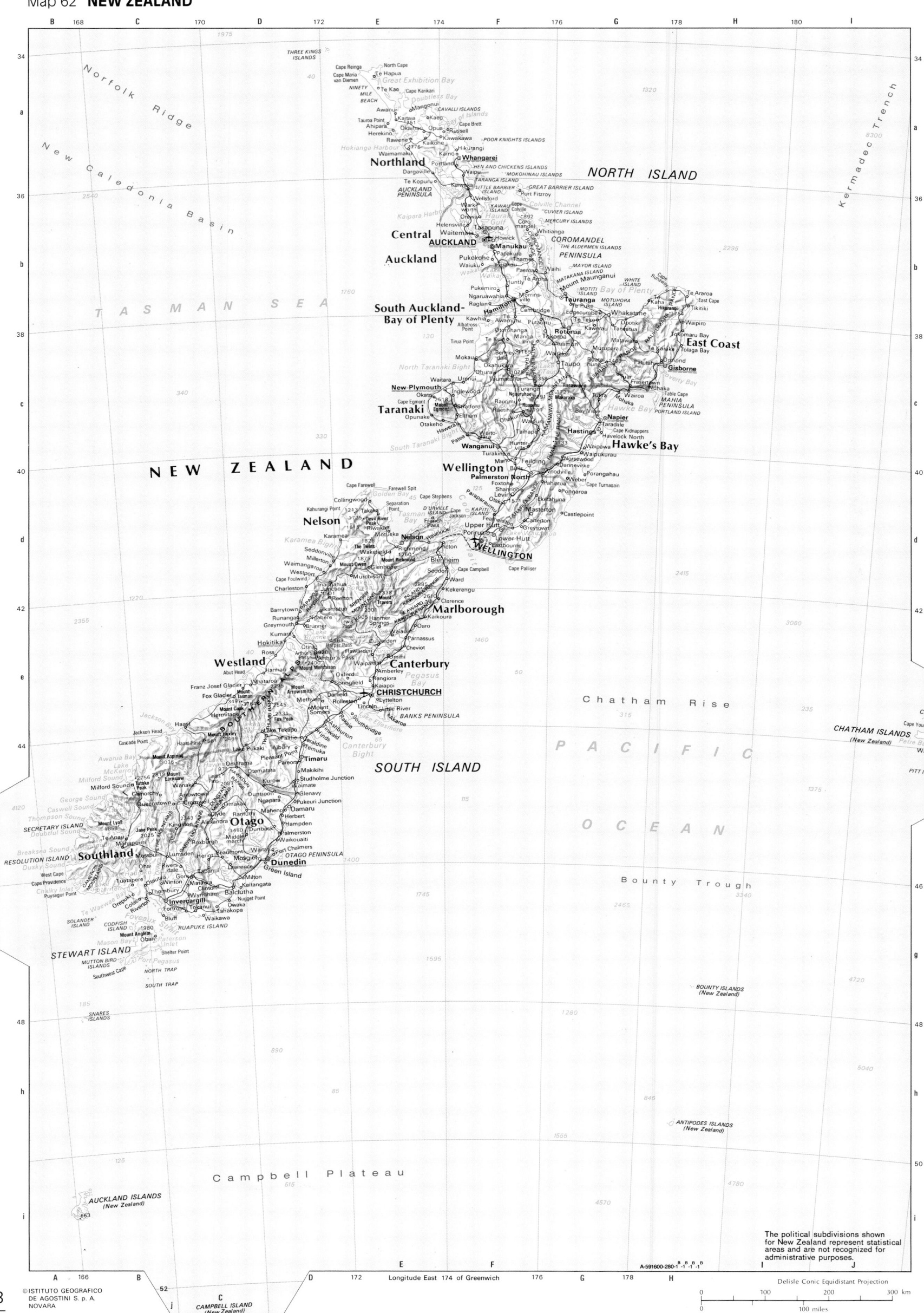

NORTH ISLAND

Norfolk Ridge

New Caledonia Basin

TASMAN SEA

Northland

Central Auckland

AUCKLAND

Auckland

South Auckland–Bay of Plenty

COROMANDEL PENINSULA

Bay of Plenty

East Coast

Gisborne

NEW ZEALAND

Taranaki

New Plymouth

Hawke's Bay

Napier

Hastings

Wanganui

Wellington

Palmerston North

WELLINGTON

Nelson

Marlborough

Westland

Canterbury

CHRISTCHURCH

SOUTH ISLAND

Chatham Rise

CHATHAM ISLANDS
(New Zealand)

PACIFIC OCEAN

Timaru

Otago

Southland

Dunedin

Bounty Trough

Invercargill

STEWART ISLAND

BOUNTY ISLANDS
(New Zealand)

SNARES ISLANDS

ANTIPODES ISLANDS
(New Zealand)

AUCKLAND ISLANDS
(New Zealand)

Campbell Plateau

The political subdivisions shown
for New Zealand represent statistical
areas and are not recognized for
administrative purposes.

CAMPBELL ISLAND
(New Zealand)

Longitude East 174 of Greenwich

Delisle Conic Equidistant Projection

0   100   200   300 km

0   100 miles

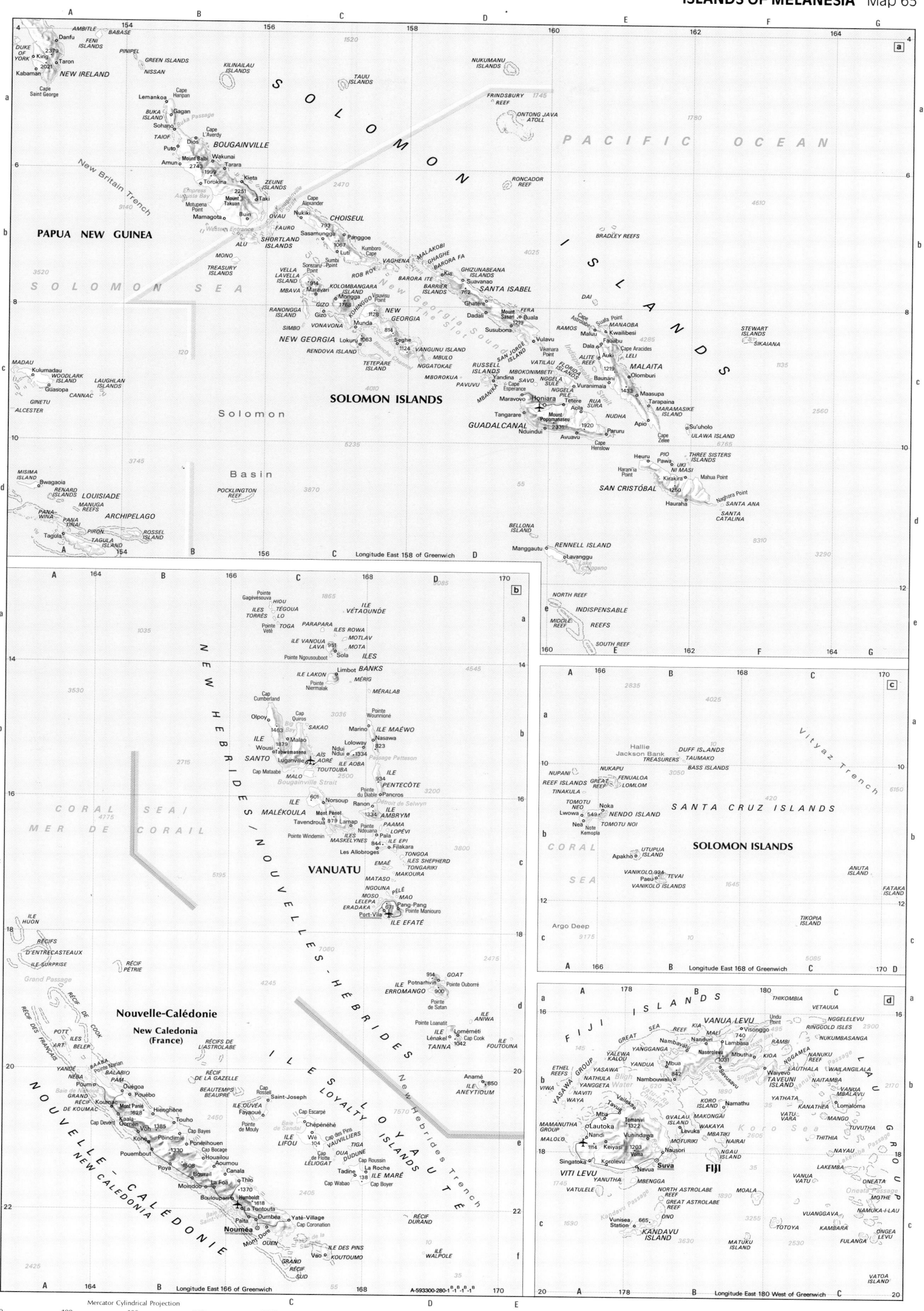

Mercator Cylindrical Projection

0   100   200   300   400 km

0   100   200 miles

A-593300-280-1⁻¹ · ¹ · ¹ · ¹ · ¹

© ISTITUTO GEOGRAFICO DE AGOSTINI S. p. A. - NOVARA

Map 64 **ISLANDS OF MICRONESIA-POLYNESIA**

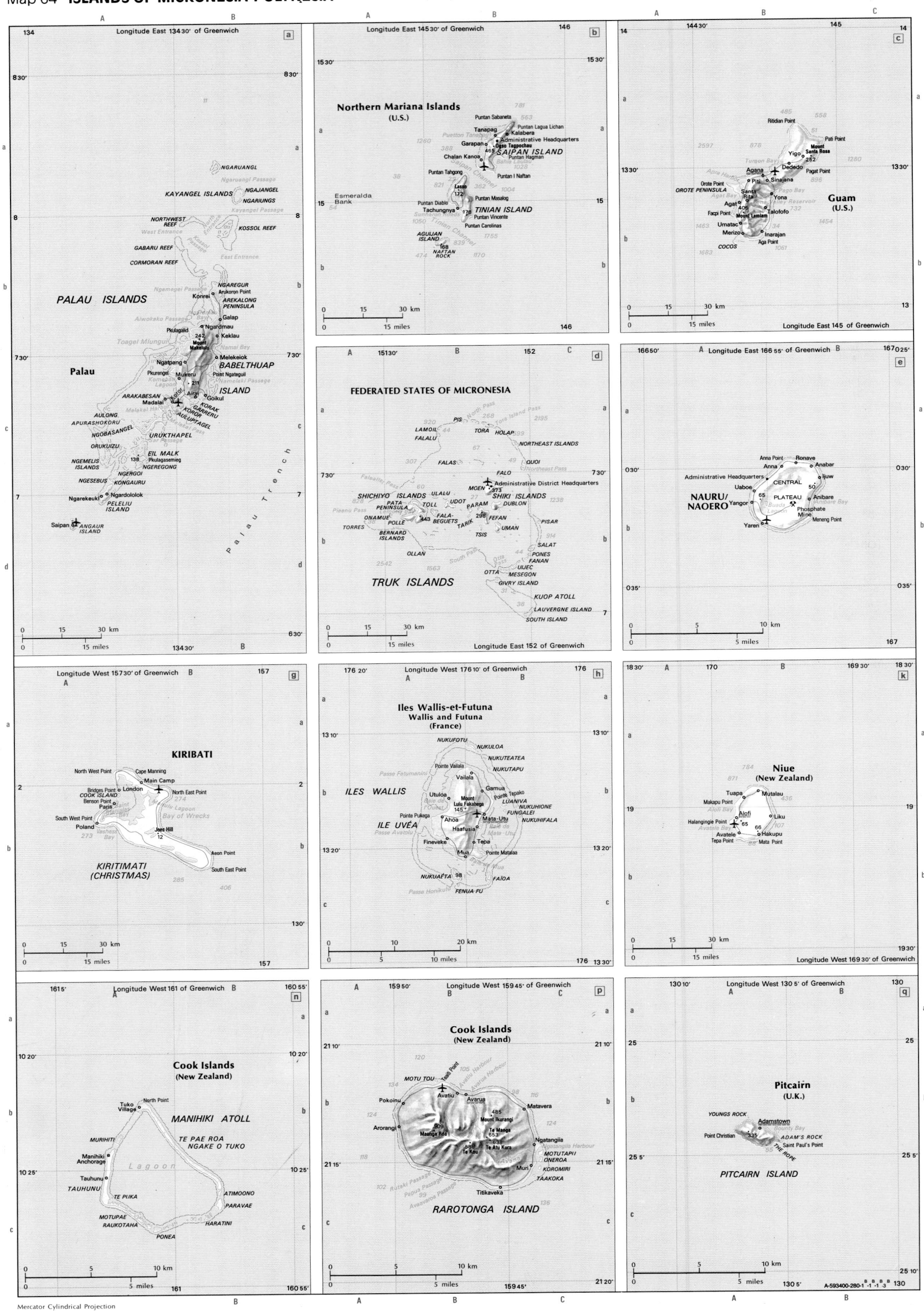

Mercator Cylindrical Projection

© ISTITUTO GEOGRAFICO DE AGOSTINI S. p. A. - NOVARA

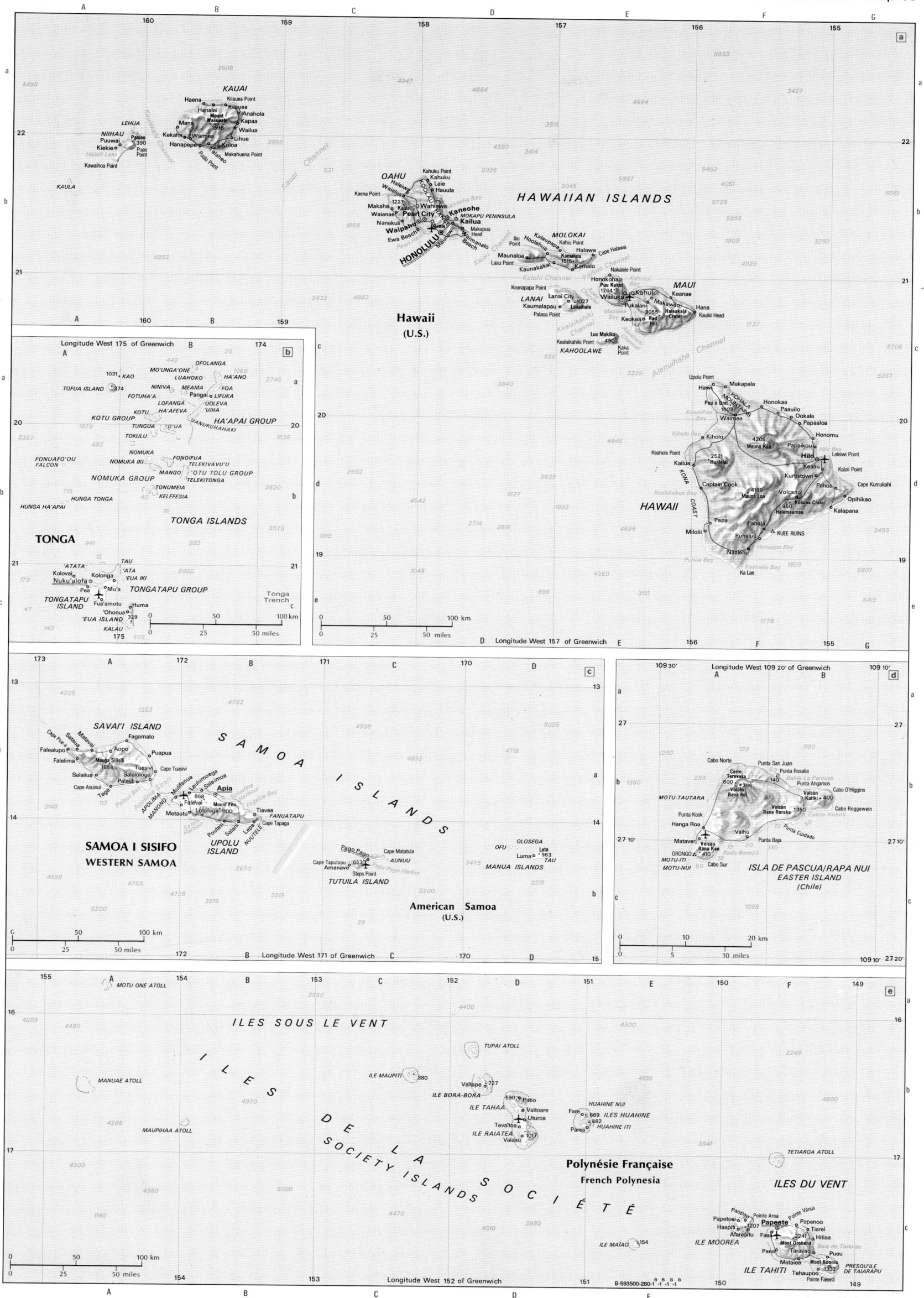

HAWAIIAN ISLANDS

KAUAI

Haena
Kilauea Point
Hanalei
Kilauea
Anahola
Mana
Mount Waialeale 1598
Kapaa
Wailua
Kekaha
Waimea
Lihue
Hanapepe
Koloa
Puolo
Kalaheo
Makahuena Point

NIIHAU
LEHUA
Puuwai
Pahiau 390
Kiekie
Pueo Point

KAULA
Kawaihoa Point

OAHU
Kahuku Point
Kahuku
Laie
Hauula
Kaena Point
Wahiawa
Waialua
Waianae
Pearl City
Kaneohe
MOKAPU PENINSULA
Makaha
Kailua
Nanakuli
Waipahu
Makapuu Head
Ewa Beach
Waimanalo
HONOLULU
Waikiki

MOLOKAI
Ilio Point
Kalaupapa
Kahiu Point
Hoolehua
Halawa
Cape Halawa
Maunaloa
Kamakou 1515
Kaunakakai
Kamalo
Laau Point
Nakalele Point

LANAI
Keanapapa Point
Kaumalapau
Lanai City
Palaoa Point

MAUI
Honokohau
Pau Kukui
Honokahua
Kahului
Wailuku
Keanae
Keanae
Makawao
Hana
Puukalani
Haleakala Crater 3055
Kauiki Head
Pukalane
Keokea
Red Hill
Kealaikahiki Point
Lua Makika 450
Kaka Point

KAHOOLAWE

HAWAII

Upolu Point
Makapala
Hawi
KOHALA
Honokaa
Paauilo
Pau a Pili 1603
Honokaa
Ookala
Waimea
Papaaloa
Kiholo
Mauna Kea 4205
Papaikou
Keahole Point
2521 Hualalai
Hilo
Kailua
4169 Mauna Loa
Keaau
Captain Cook
Kurtistown
Kaloli Point
Cape Kumukahi
3680 Mauna Loa
Volcano
Opihikao
Papa
Kilauea Crater
Pahoa
Halemaumau
Kalapana
Milolii
Pahala
Punaluu
KIILEE RUINS
Naalehu
Ka Lae

Hawaii (U.S.)

Longitude West 175 of Greenwich

TONGA ISLANDS

OFOLANGA
MO'UNGA'ONE
LUAHOKO
HA'ANO
KAO
NINIVA
MEAMA
FOA
TOFUA ISLAND 374
FOTUHA'A
LOFANGA
LIFUKA
HA'AFEVA
UOLEVA
UIHA
KOTU GROUP
KOTU
TUNGUA
TO'UA
VANUKUHAHAKI
HA'APAI GROUP
TOKULU
NOMUKA
FONUAFO'OU
FALCON
NOMUKA IKI
FONOIFUA
TELEKIVAVU'U
MANGO
'OTU TOLU GROUP
TELEKITONGA
NOMUKA GROUP
TONUMEIA
HUNGA TONGA
KELEFESIA
HUNGA HA'APAI

TONGA

TONGA ISLANDS

'ATATA
TAU
'ATA
Koloval
Kolonga
'EUA IKI
Nuku'alofa
Mu'a
Pea
TONGATAPU GROUP
Fua'amotu
Huma
TONGATAPU ISLAND
'Ohonua
'EUA ISLAND 329
KALAU

Tonga Trench

Longitude West 157 of Greenwich

SAMOA ISLANDS

SAVAI'I ISLAND
Cape Puava
Sataua
Matavai
Fagamalo
Falealupo
Aopo
Puapua
Falelima
Mauga Silisili 1858
Tuasivi
Cape Tuasivi
Cape Asuisui
Salailua
Saleologa
Palauli
Taga

MANONO
APOLIMA
Leulumoega
Apia
Mulifanua
868
Faleolo
Mount Fito 1100
Lotofaga
UPOLU ISLAND
Metautu
Saleaula
Poutasi
Safata
Lepa
Tiavea
Sasina
FANUATAPU
NUUTELE

**SAMOA I SISIFO
WESTERN SAMOA**

Pago Pago
Cape Matatula
OFU
OLOSEGA
Cape Taputapu
Aunuu
Lata 963
Amanave
Steps Point
Lumaa
TAU
TUTUILA ISLAND
Pago Pago Harbor
MANUA ISLANDS

American Samoa (U.S.)

Longitude West 109 20' of Greenwich

Cabo Norte
Punta San Juan
Cerro Terevaka 600
Punta Rosalia
Rano Aroi
Punta Angamos
MOTU-TAUTARA
Volcán Katiki 400
Cabo O'Higgins
Punta Kook
Volcán Rana Roraku
Hanga Roa
Vaihu
Punta Cuidado
Mataveri
Volcán Rana Kao 410
ORONGO
MOTU-ITI
Rada Benepu
MOTU-NUI
Cabo Sur
Cabo Roggeween

**ISLA DE PASCUA/RAPA NUI
EASTER ISLAND
(Chile)**

Longitude West 171 of Greenwich

ILES SOUS LE VENT

MOTU ONE ATOLL

TUPAI ATOLL

MANUAE ATOLL

ILE MAUPITI 380

Vaitape 727
ILE BORA-BORA
MAUPIHAA ATOLL
ILE TAHAA
590 Patio
Vaitoare
HUAHINE NUI
Fare 669
ILES HUAHINE
Uturoa 662
Tevaitoa
HUAHINE ITI
ILE RAIATEA
Parea
Vaiaau 1017

**ILES DE LA SOCIÉTÉ
SOCIETY ISLANDS**

TETIAROA ATOLL

**Polynésie Française
French Polynesia**

ILES DU VENT

ILE MAIAO 154

Paopao
Pointe Aroa
Pointe Vénus
Papetoai
Papeete
Papenoo
Haapiti
Afareaitu
Tiarei
Mont Orohena 2241
Hitiaa
ILE MOOREA
Faaa
Taravao
Pueu
Mataiea
Mont Rooniu 1332
Tehaupoo
PRESQU'ILE
DE TAIARAPU
ILE TAHITI
Pointe Faaea

Longitude West 152 of Greenwich

B-593500-280-1 -1 -1 -1
Mercator Cylindrical Projection
© ISTITUTO GEOGRAFICO DE AGOSTINI S. p. A. - NOVARA

Map 66 **ANTARCTIC REGION, PHYSICAL**

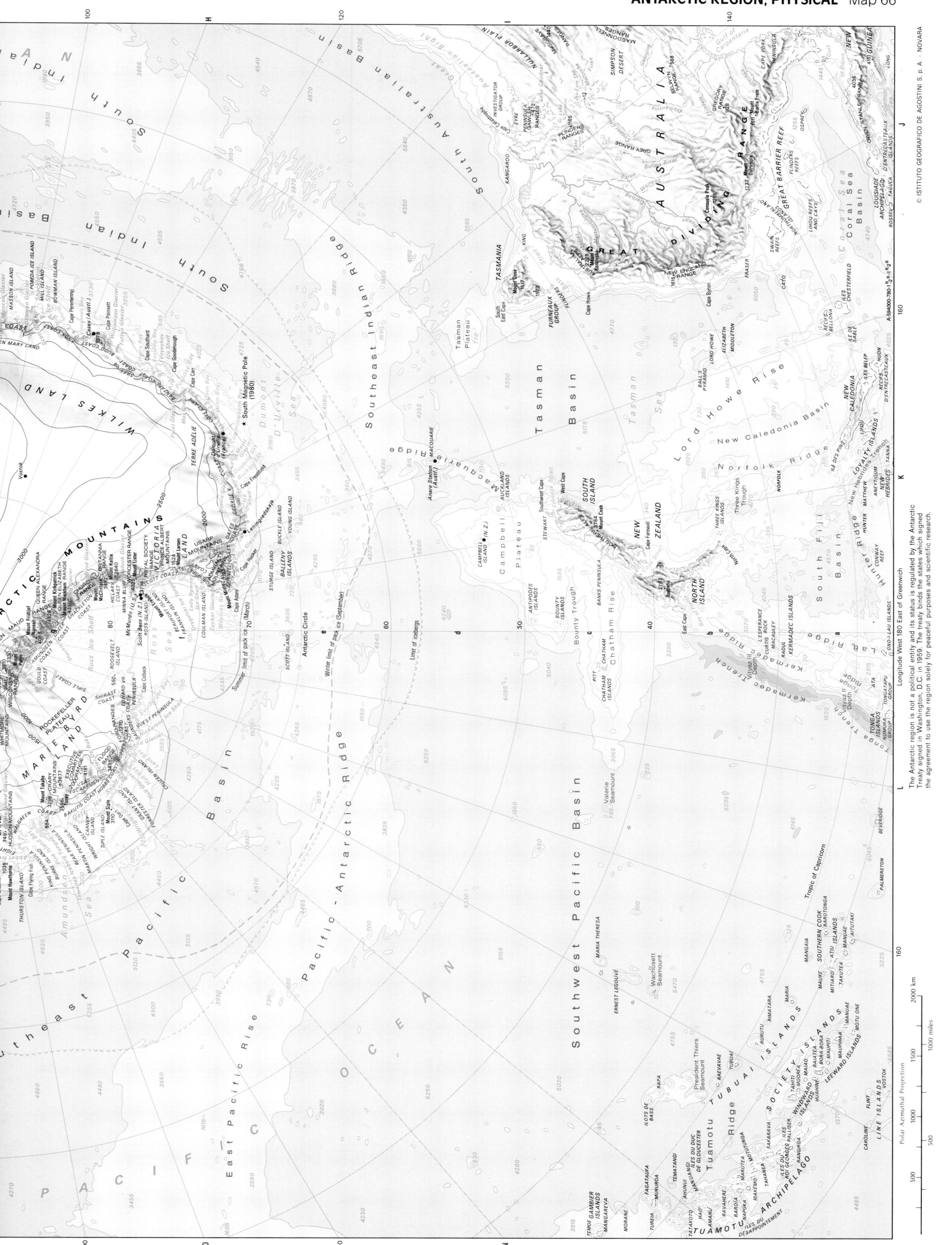

Longitude West 180 East of Greenwich

Polar Azimuthal Projection

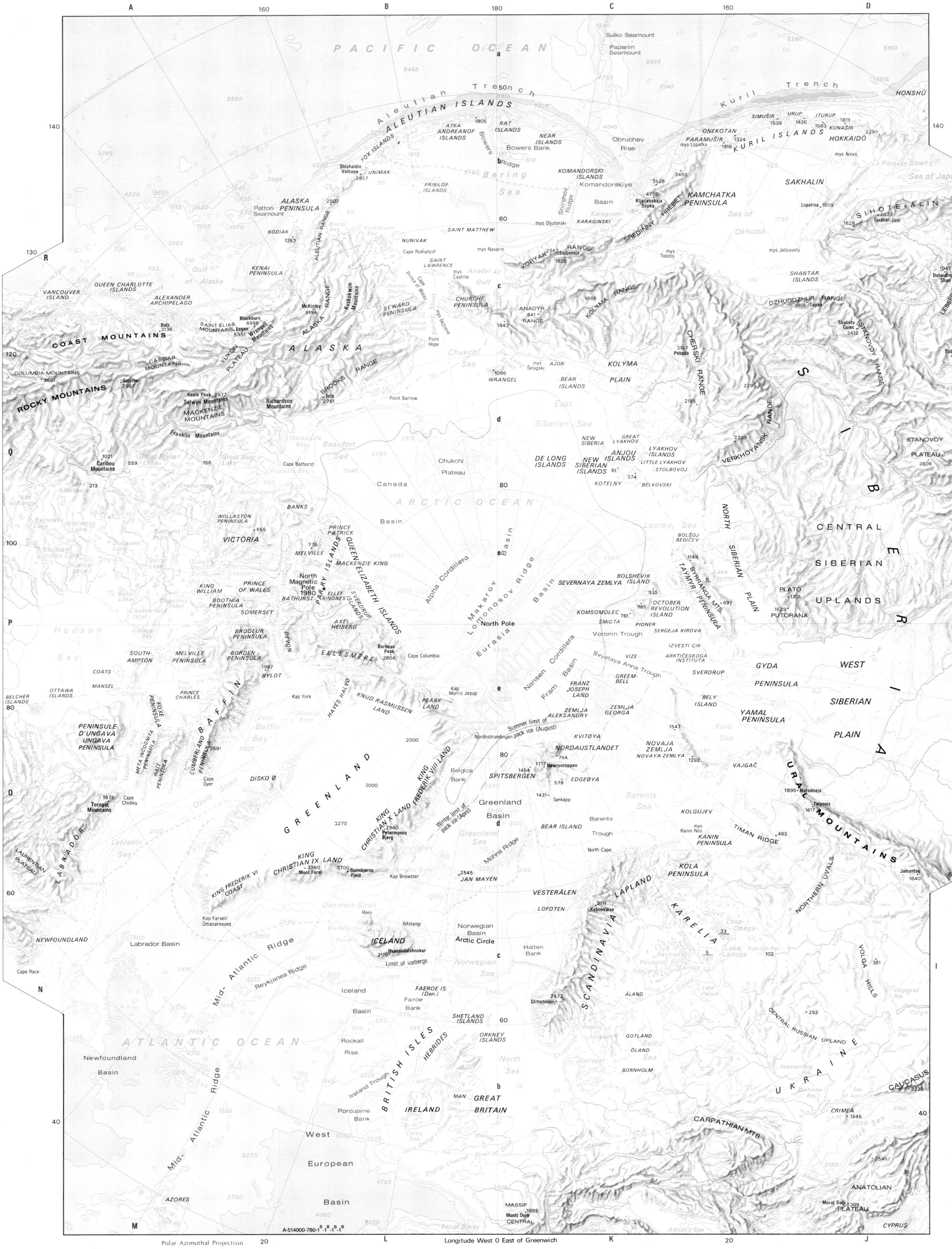

Map 67 **ARCTIC REGION, PHYSICAL**

Maps of the United States and Canada

MAP LEGEND

CULTURAL FEATURES

Political Boundaries

International

Secondary (State or Province)

County

Populated Places

Cities, towns, and villages

 Symbol size represents population of the place

Chicago
Gary
Racine
Glenview
Edgewood

Type size represents relative importance of the place

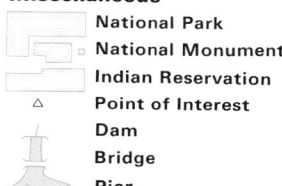 **Major Urban Areas**
Area of continuous commercial, industrial, and residential development in and around a major city

○ Community within a city

✪ Capital of major political unit

✪ Capital of state or province

○ County Seat

▲ Military Installation

Transportation

Major Highway

Railroad

Tunnel

Miscellaneous

National Park

National Monument

Indian Reservation

△ Point of Interest

Dam

Bridge

Pier

LAND FEATURES

Mountain Ranges

Mountain Peak

Point of Elevation in Feet above Sea Level → + 11,278

Pass

Escarpment, Bluffs, Cliffs

Lava Flows

Plains, Flatlands

WATER FEATURES

Coastlines and Shorelines

Indefinite or Unsurveyed Coastlines and Shorelines

Lakes and Reservoirs

Canals

Rivers and Streams

Falls and Rapids

Intermittent or Unsurveyed Rivers and Streams

Swamps and Marshes

Directional Flow Arrow

Rocks, Shoals and Reefs

TYPE STYLES USED TO NAME FEATURES

Note: Size of type varies according to importance and available space. Letters for names of major features are spread across the extent of the feature.

CANADA	Country, State, or Province	*U I N T A* *DESERT*	Major Terrain Features
Naval *Air Station*	Military Installation	MT. MORIAH	Individual Mountain
CROCKETT	County	MESA VERDE SAN XAVIER	National Park or Monument, Indian Res.

NUNIVAK Island or Coastal Feature

Ocean *Lake* *River* *Canal* Hydrographic Features

Longitude West of Greenwich

Lambert Conformal Conic Projection

ALABAMA

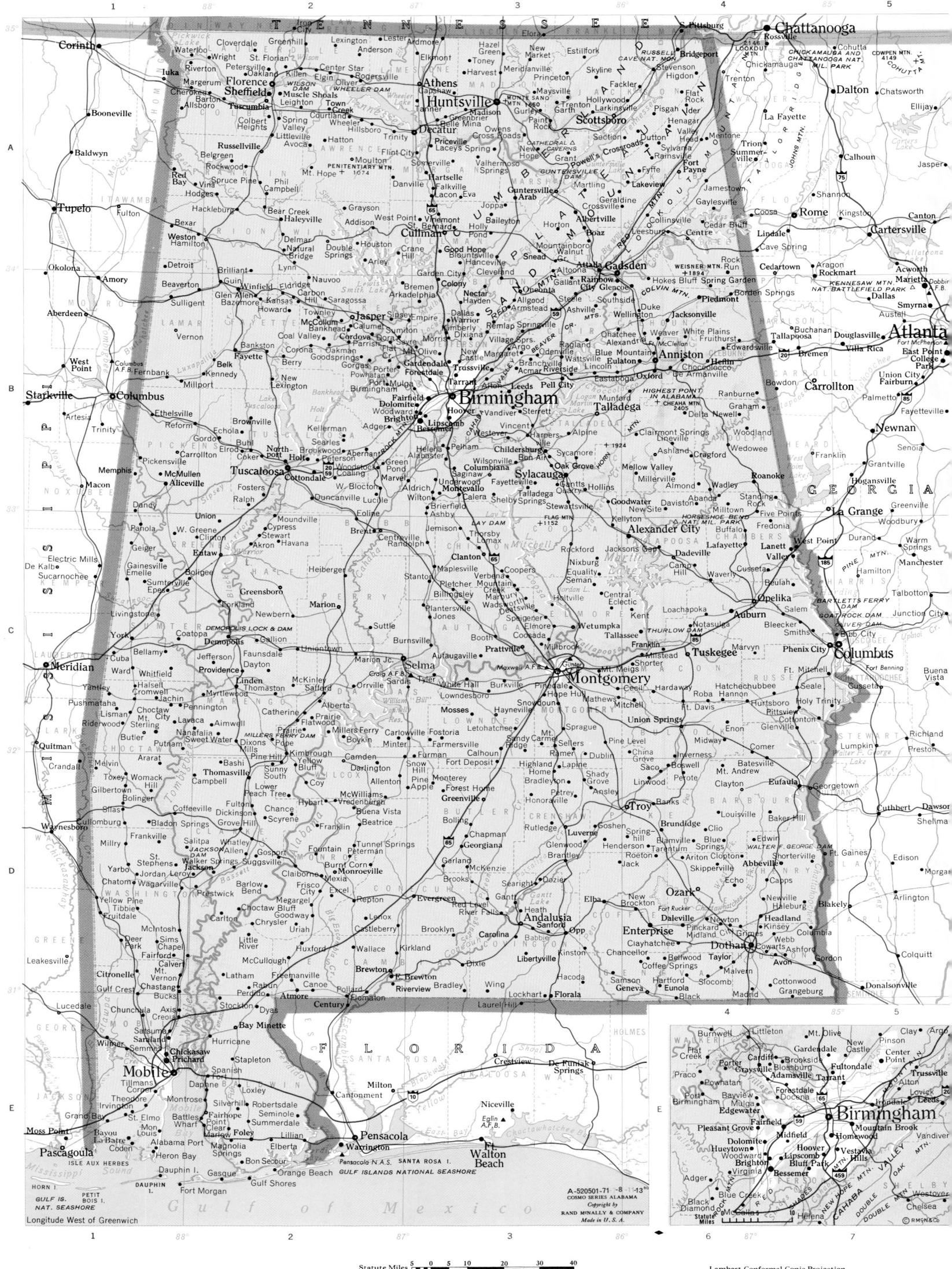

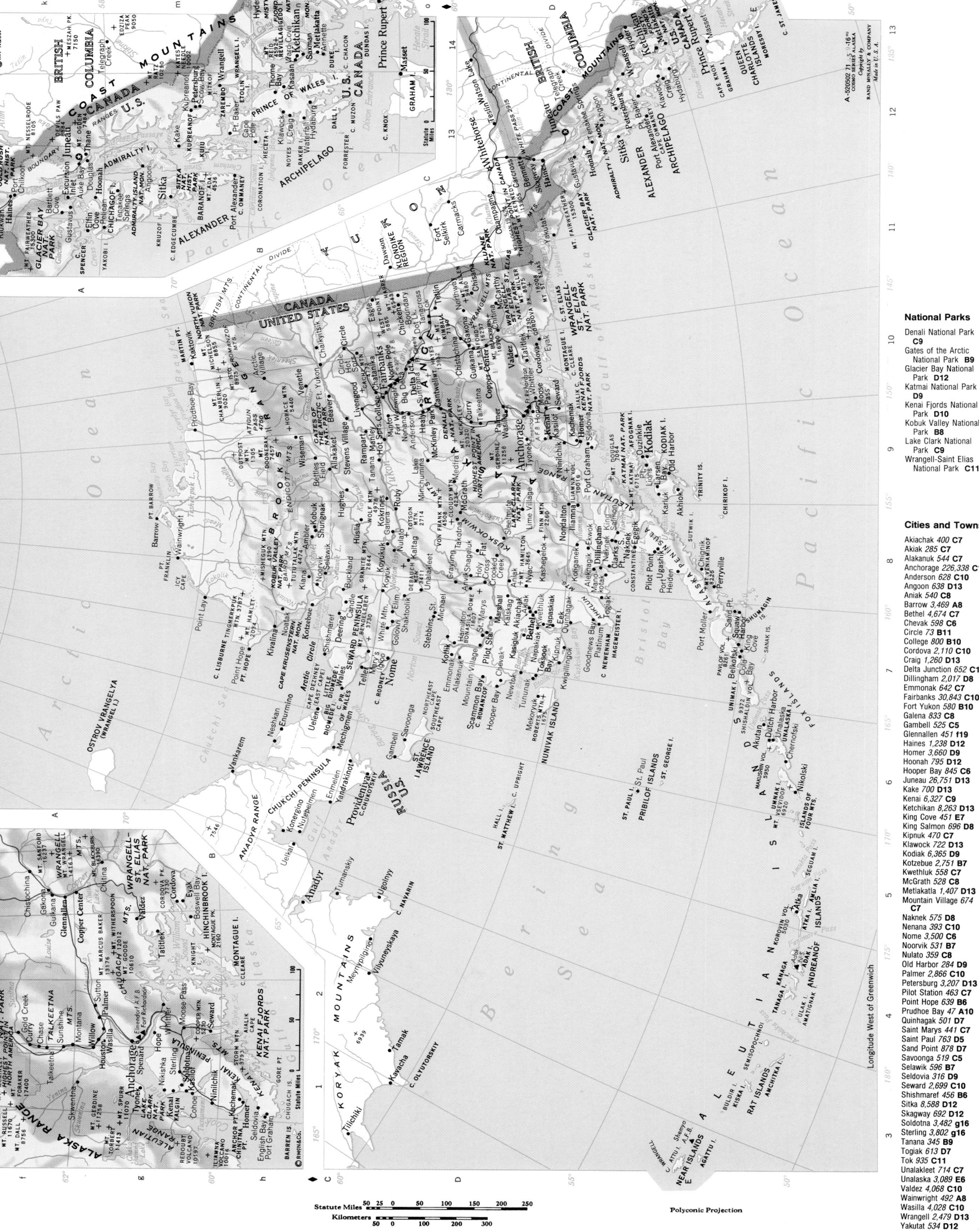

National Parks

Denali National Park **C9**
Gates of the Arctic
National Park **B9**
Glacier Bay National
Park **D12**
Katmai National Park **D9**
Kenai Fjords National
Park **D10**
Kobuk Valley National
Park **B8**
Lake Clark National
Park **C9**
Wrangell-Saint Elias
National Park **C11**

Cities and Towns

Akiachak *400* **C7**
Akiak *285* **C7**
Alakanuk *544* **C7**
Anchorage *226,338* **C10**
Anderson *628* **D13**
Angoon *638* **D13**
Aniak *540* **C8**
Barrow *3,469* **A8**
Bethel *4,674* **C7**
Chevak *598* **C6**
Circle *73* **B11**
College *800* **B10**
Cordova *2,110* **C10**
Craig *1,260* **D13**
Delta Junction *652* **C10**
Dillingham *2,017* **D8**
Emmonak *642* **C7**
Fairbanks *30,843* **C10**
Fort Yukon *580* **B10**
Galena *833* **C8**
Gambell *525* **C5**
Glennallen *451* **f19**
Haines *1,238* **D12**
Homer *3,660* **D9**
Hoonah *795* **D12**
Hooper Bay *845* **C6**
Juneau *26,751* **D13**
Kake *700* **D13**
Kenai *6,327* **C9**
Ketchikan *8,263* **D13**
King Cove *451* **E7**
King Salmon *696* **D8**
Kipnuk *470* **C7**
Klawock *722* **D13**
Kodiak *6,365* **D9**
Kotzebue *2,751* **B7**
Kwethluk *558* **C7**
McGrath *528* **C8**
Metlakatla *1,407* **D13**
Mountain Village *674*
C7
Naknek *575* **D8**
Nenana *393* **C10**
Nome *3,500* **C6**
Noorvik *531* **B7**
Nulato *359* **C8**
Old Harbor *284* **D9**
Palmer *2,866* **C10**
Petersburg *3,207* **D13**
Pilot Station *463* **C7**
Point Hope *639* **B6**
Prudhoe Bay *47* **A10**
Quinhagak *501* **D7**
Saint Marys *441* **C7**
Saint Paul *763* **D5**
Sand Point *878* **D7**
Savoonga *519* **C5**
Selawik *596* **B7**
Seldovia *316* **D9**
Seward *2,699* **C10**
Shishmaref *456* **B6**
Sitka *8,588* **D12**
Skagway *692* **D12**
Soldotna *3,482* **g16**
Sterling *3,802* **g16**
Tanana *345* **B9**
Togiak *613* **D7**
Tok *935* **C11**
Unalakleet *714* **C7**
Unalaska *3,089* **E6**
Valdez *4,068* **C10**
Wainwright *492* **A8**
Wasilla *4,028* **C10**
Wrangell *2,479* **D13**
Yakutat *534* **D12**

229

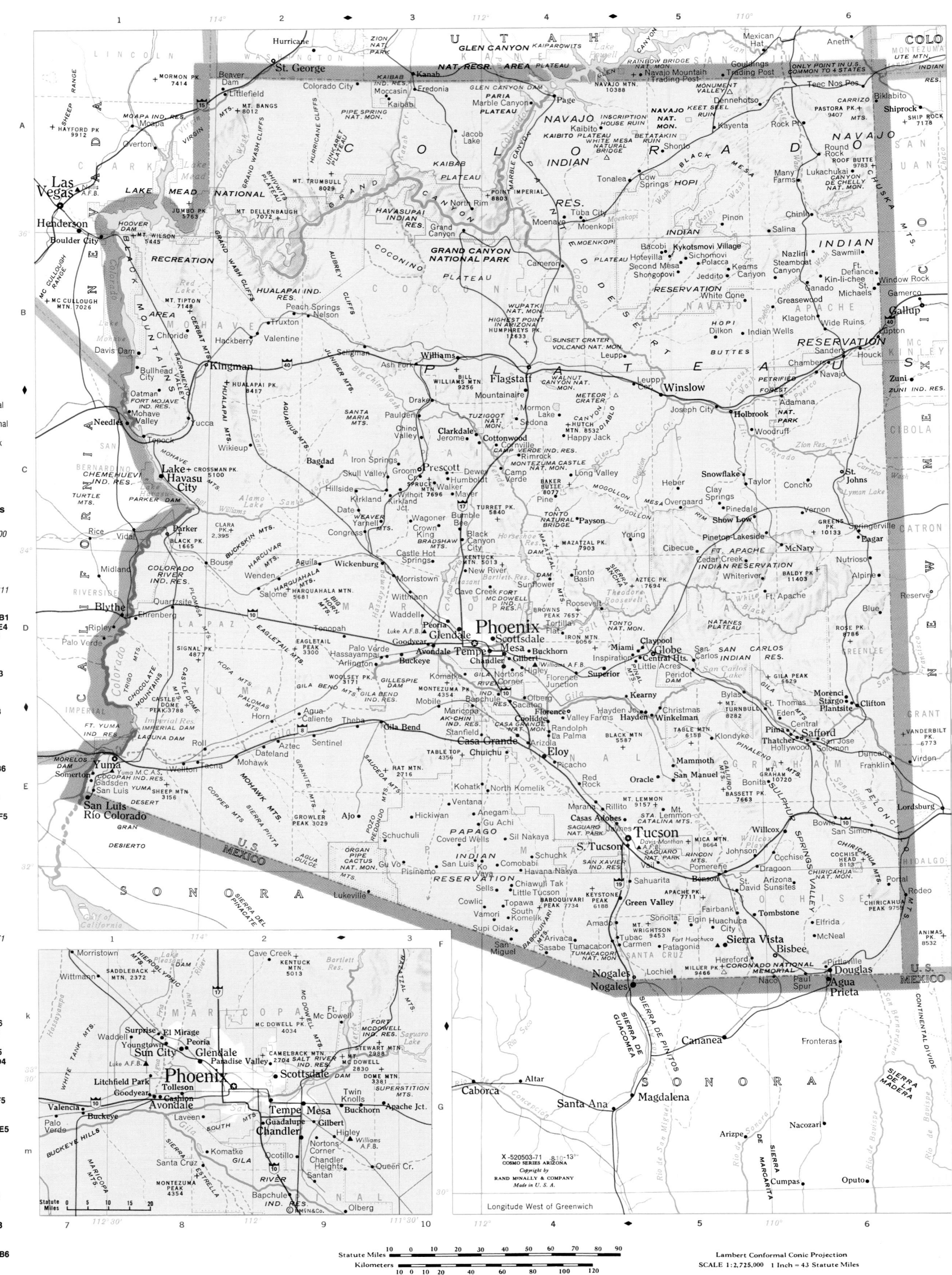

National Parks

Grand Canyon National
Park **B3**
Petrified Forest National
Park **B6**
Saguaro National Park
E4

Cities and Towns

Ajo *2,919* **E3**
Apache Junction *18,100*
m9
Avondale *16,169* **D3**
Bagdad *1,858* **C2**
Benson *3,824* **F5**
Bisbee *6,288* **F6**
Black Canyon City *1,811*
C3
Blythe **D1**
Buckeye *5,038* **D3**
Bullhead City *21,951* **B1**
Casa Grande *19,082* **E4**
Casas Adobes *12,155*
E5
Chandler *90,533* **D4**
Chinle *5,059* **A6**
Chino Valley *4,837* **C3**
Claypool *1,942* **D5**
Clifton *2,840* **D6**
Coolidge *6,927* **E4**
Cottonwood *5,918* **C3**
Douglas *12,822* **F6**
Eagar *4,025* **C6**
Eloy *7,211* **E4**
Flagstaff *45,857* **B4**
Florence *7,510* **E4**
Fort Defiance *4,489* **B6**
Gila Bend *1,747* **E3**
Gilbert *29,188* **D4**
Glendale *148,134* **D3**
Globe *6,062* **D5**
Green Valley *13,231* **F5**
Holbrook *4,686* **C5**
Kayenta *4,372* **A5**
Kearny *2,262* **D5**
Kingman *12,722* **B1**
Lake Havasu City
24,363 **C1**
Mammoth *1,845* **E5**
Mesa *288,091* **D4**
Miami *2,018* **D5**
Nogales *19,489* **F5**
Oracle *3,043* **E5**
Page *6,598* **A4**
Paradise Valley *11,671*
k9
Parker *2,897* **C1**
Payson *8,377* **C4**
Peoria *50,618* **D3**
Phoenix *983,403* **D3**
Prescott *26,455* **C3**
Sacaton *1,452* **D4**
Safford *7,359* **E6**
Saint Johns *3,294* **C6**
San Carlos *2,918* **D5**
San Luis *4,212* **E1**
San Manuel *4,009* **E5**
Scottsdale *130,069* **D4**
Sedona *7,720* **C4**
Sells *2,750* **F4**
Show Low *5,019* **C5**
Sierra Vista *32,983* **F5**
Snowflake *3,679* **C5**
Somerton *5,282* **E1**
South Tucson *5,093* **E5**
Sun City *38,126* **k8**
Superior *3,468* **D4**
Surprise *7,122* **k8**
Taylor *2,418* **C5**
Tempe *141,865* **D4**
Thatcher *3,763* **E6**
Tombstone *1,220* **F5**
Tuba City *7,323* **A4**
Tucson *405,390* **E5**
Willcox *3,122* **E6**
Williams *2,532* **B3**
Window Rock *3,306* **B6**
Winslow *8,190* **C5**
Yuma *54,923* **E1**

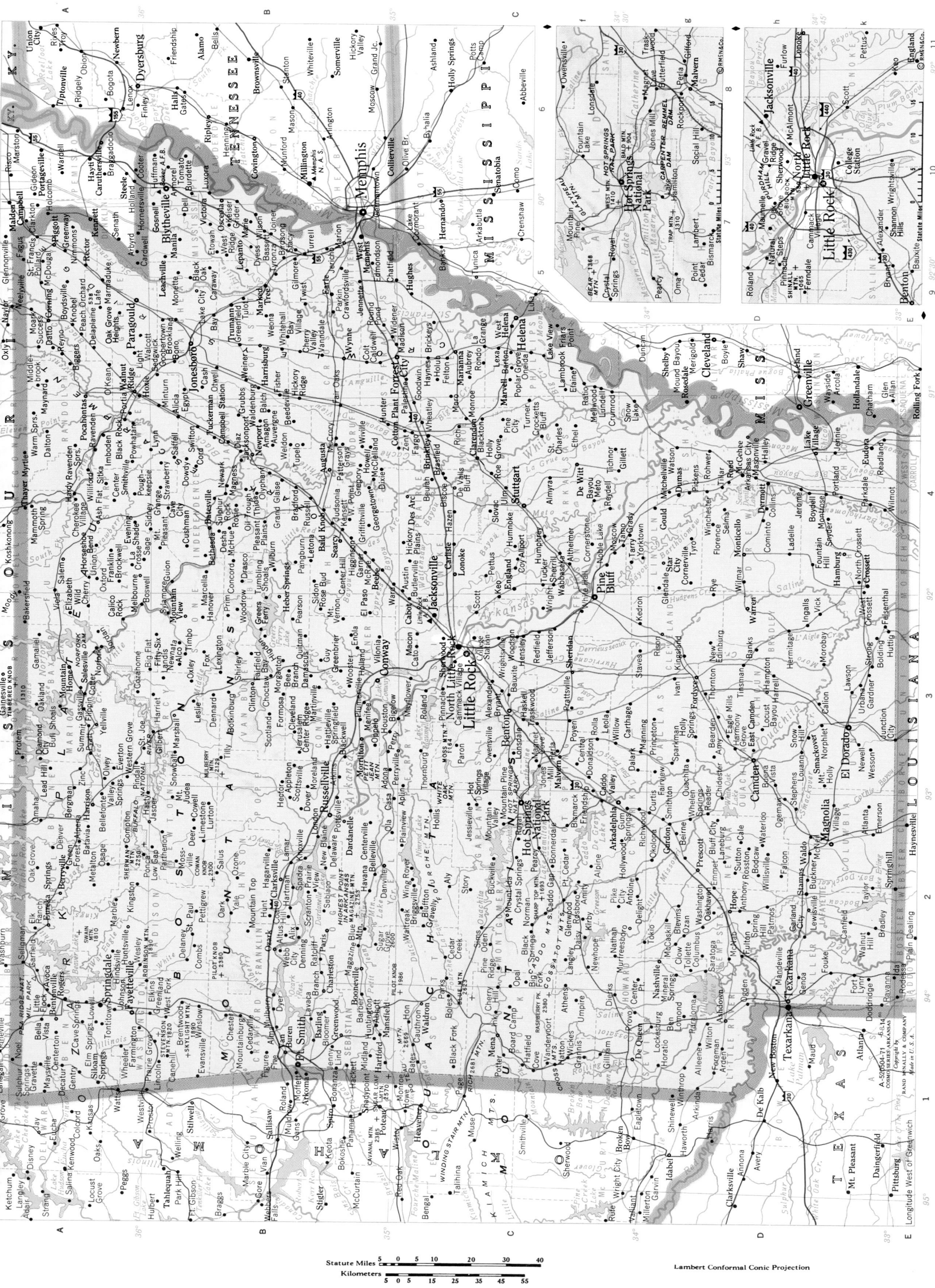

National Parks

Hot Springs National
Park **C2**

Cities and Towns

Arkadelphia 10,014 **C2**
Ashdown 5,150 **D1**
Barling 4,078 **B1**
Batesville 9,187 **B4**
Beebe 4,455 **B4**
Benton 18,177 **C3**
Bentonville 11,257 **A1**
Berryville 3,212 **A2**
Blytheville 22,906 **B6**
Booneville 3,804 **B2**
Brinkley 4,234 **C4**
Cabot 8,319 **C3**
Camden 14,380 **D3**
Clarksville 5,833 **B2**
Conway 26,481 **B3**
Corning 3,323 **A5**
Crossett 6,282 **D4**
Dardanelle 3,722 **B2**
De Queen 4,633 **C1**
Dermott 4,715 **D4**
De Witt 3,553 **C4**
Dumas 5,520 **D4**
El Dorado 23,146 **D3**
Eudora 3,155 **D4**
Eureka Springs 1,900
  A2
Fayetteville 42,099 **A1**
Fordyce 4,729 **D3**
Forrest City 13,364 **B5**
Fort Smith 72,798 **B1**
Harrison 9,922 **A2**
Heber Springs 5,628 **B3**
Helena 7,491 **C5**
Hope 9,643 **D2**
Hot Springs National
  Park 32,462 **C2**
Jacksonville 29,101 **C3**
Jonesboro 46,535 **B5**
Little Rock 175,795 **C3**
Lonoke 4,022 **C4**
Magnolia 11,151 **D2**
Malvern 9,256 **C3**
Marianna 5,910 **C5**
McGehee 4,997 **D4**
Mena 5,475 **C1**
Monticello 8,116 **D4**
Morrilton 6,551 **B3**
Mountain Home 9,027
  A3
Mountain View 2,439
  B3
Nashville 4,639 **D2**
Newport 7,459 **B4**
North Little Rock 61,741
  C3
Osceola 8,930 **B6**
Ozark 3,330 **B2**
Paragould 18,540 **A5**
Paris 3,674 **B2**
Piggott 3,777 **A5**
Pine Bluff 57,140 **C4**
Pocahontas 6,151 **A5**
Prescott 3,673 **D2**
Rogers 24,692 **A1**
Russellville 21,260 **B2**
Searcy 15,180 **B4**
Sherwood 18,893 **C3**
Siloam Springs 8,151
  A1
Springdale 29,941 **A1**
Stuttgart 10,420 **C4**
Texarkana 22,631 **D1**
Tontitown 460 **A1**
Trumann 6,304 **B5**
Van Buren 14,979 **B1**
Walnut Ridge 4,388 **A5**
Warren 6,455 **D3**
West Helena 9,695 **C5**
West Memphis 28,259
  B5
Wynne 8,187 **B5**

231

CALIFORNIA

National Parks

Channel Islands
National Park **F4**
Death Valley National
Park **D5**
Joshua Tree National
Park **F6**
Kings Canyon National
Park **D4**
Lassen Volcanic
National Park **B3**
Redwood National Park
B2
Sequoia National Park
D4
Yosemite National Park
D4

Cities and Towns

Anaheim *266,406* **F5**
Antioch *62,195* **h9**
Bakersfield *174,820* **E4**
Berkeley *102,724* **D2**
Beverly Hills *31,971*
m12
Burbank *93,643* **E4**
Calexico *18,633* **F6**
Chico *40,079* **C3**
Chula Vista *135,163* **F5**
Concord *111,348* **h8**
Costa Mesa *96,357* **n13**
Davis *46,209* **C3**
East Los Angeles
126,379 **m12**
El Cajon *88,693* **F5**
El Centro *31,384* **F6**
Escondido *108,635* **F5**
Eureka *27,025* **B1**
Fairfield *77,211* **C2**
Fremont *173,339* **D2**
Fresno *354,202* **D4**
Fullerton *114,144* **n13**
Garden Grove *143,050*
n13
Glendale *180,038* **m12**
Hayward *111,498* **h8**
Huntington Beach
181,519 **F4**
Indio *36,793* **F5**
Lancaster *97,291* **E4**
Lompoc *37,649* **E3**
Long Beach *429,433* **F4**
Los Angeles *3,485,398*
E4
Marysville *12,324* **C3**
Menlo Park *28,040* **k8**
Merced *56,216* **D3**
Modesto *164,730* **D3**
Monterey *31,954* **D3**
Napa *61,842* **C2**
Newport Beach *66,643*
n13
Oakland *372,242* **D2**
Oceanside *128,398* **F5**
Ontario *133,179* **E5**
Oxnard *142,216* **E4**
Palm Springs *40,181*
F5
Palo Alto *55,900* **D2**
Pasadena *131,591* **E4**
Pomona *131,723* **E5**
Redding *66,462* **B2**
Redwood City *66,072*
D2
Richmond *87,425* **D2**
Riverside *226,505* **F5**
Sacramento *369,365* **C3**
Salinas *108,777* **D3**
San Bernardino *164,164*
E5
San Clemente *41,100*
F5
San Diego *1,110,549* **F5**
San Francisco *723,959*
D2
San Jose *782,248* **D3**
San Juan Capistrano
26,183 **F5**
San Luis Obispo *41,958*
E3
Santa Ana *293,742* **F5**
Santa Barbara *85,571*
E4
Santa Cruz *49,040* **D2**
Santa Maria *61,284* **E3**
Santa Monica *86,905*
m12
Santa Rosa *113,313* **C2**
South Lake Tahoe
21,586 **C4**
Stockton *210,943* **D3**
Sunnyvale *117,229* **k8**
Torrance *133,107* **n12**
Tulare *33,249* **D4**
Turlock *42,198* **D3**
Vallejo *109,199* **C2**
Ventura (San
Buenaventura) *92,575*
E4
Visalia *75,636* **D4**
Yuba City *27,437* **C3**

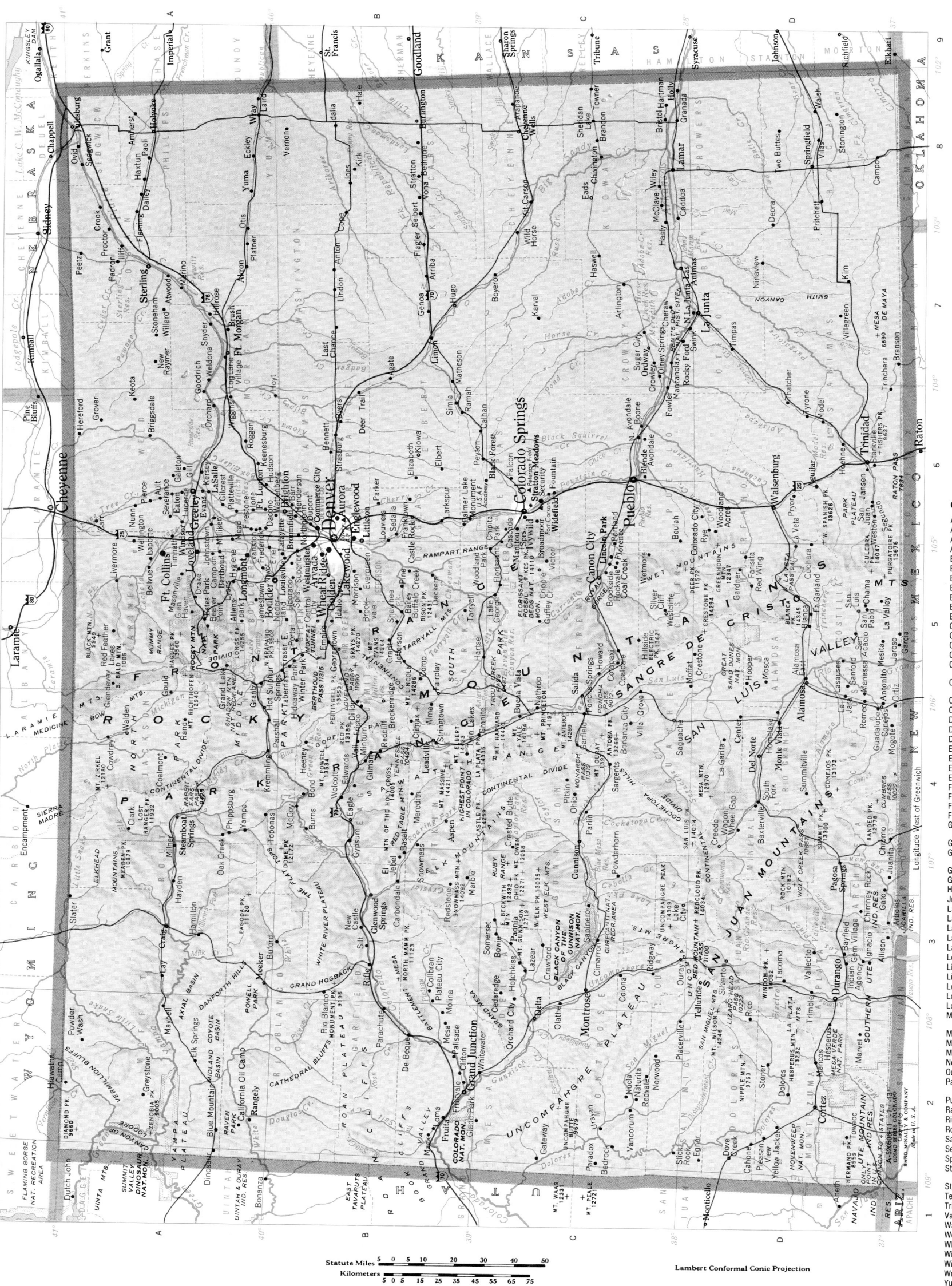

National Parks

Mesa Verde National
Park **D2**
Rocky Mountain
National Park **A5**

Cities and Towns

Alamosa 7,579 **D5**
Arvada 89,235 **B5**
Aspen 5,049 **B4**
Aurora 222,103 **B6**
Black Forest 8,143 **C6**
Boulder 83,312 **A5**
Breckenridge 1,285 **B4**
Brighton 14,203 **B6**
Broomfield 24,638 **B5**
Brush 4,165 **A7**
Burlington 2,941 **B8**
Canon City 12,687 **C5**
Castle Rock 8,708 **B6**
Central City 335 **B5**
Clifton 12,671 **B2**
Colorado Springs
281,140 **C6**
Commerce City 16,466
B6
Cortez 7,284 **D2**
Craig 8,091 **A3**
Delta 3,789 **C2**
Denver 467,610 **B6**
Durango 12,430 **D3**
Englewood 29,387 **B6**
Estes Park 3,184 **A5**
Evans 5,877 **A6**
Evergreen 7,582 **B5**
Fort Collins 87,758 **A5**
Fort Lupton 5,159 **A6**
Fort Morgan 9,068 **A7**
Fountain 9,984 **C6**
Glenwood Springs 6,561
B3
Golden 13,116 **B5**
Grand Junction 29,034
B2
Greeley 60,536 **A6**
Gunnison 4,636 **C4**
Holyoke 1,931 **A8**
Julesburg 1,295 **A8**
Lafayette 14,548 **B5**
La Junta 7,637 **D7**
Lakewood 126,481 **B5**
Lamar 8,343 **C8**
Las Animas 2,481 **C7**
Leadville 2,629 **B4**
Limon 1,831 **B7**
Littleton 33,685 **B6**
Longmont 51,555 **A5**
Louisville 12,361 **B5**
Loveland 37,352 **A5**
Manitou Springs 4,535
C6
Meeker 2,098 **A3**
Monte Vista 4,324 **D4**
Montrose 8,854 **C3**
Northglenn 27,195 **B5**
Ouray 644 **C3**
Pagosa Springs 1,207
D3
Pueblo 98,640 **C6**
Rangely 2,278 **A2**
Rifle 4,636 **B3**
Rocky Ford 4,162 **C7**
Salida 4,737 **C5**
Security 6,660 **C6**
Springfield 1,475 **D8**
Steamboat Springs
6,695 **A4**
Sterling 10,362 **A7**
Telluride 1,309 **D3**
Trinidad 8,580 **D6**
Vail 3,659 **B4**
Walsenburg 3,300 **D6**
Westminster 74,625 **B5**
Wheat Ridge 29,419 **B5**
Widefield 12,112 **C6**
Windsor 5,062 **A6**
Wray 1,998 **A8**
Yuma 2,719 **A8**

Statute Miles

Kilometers

Lambert Conformal Conic Projection

CONNECTICUT

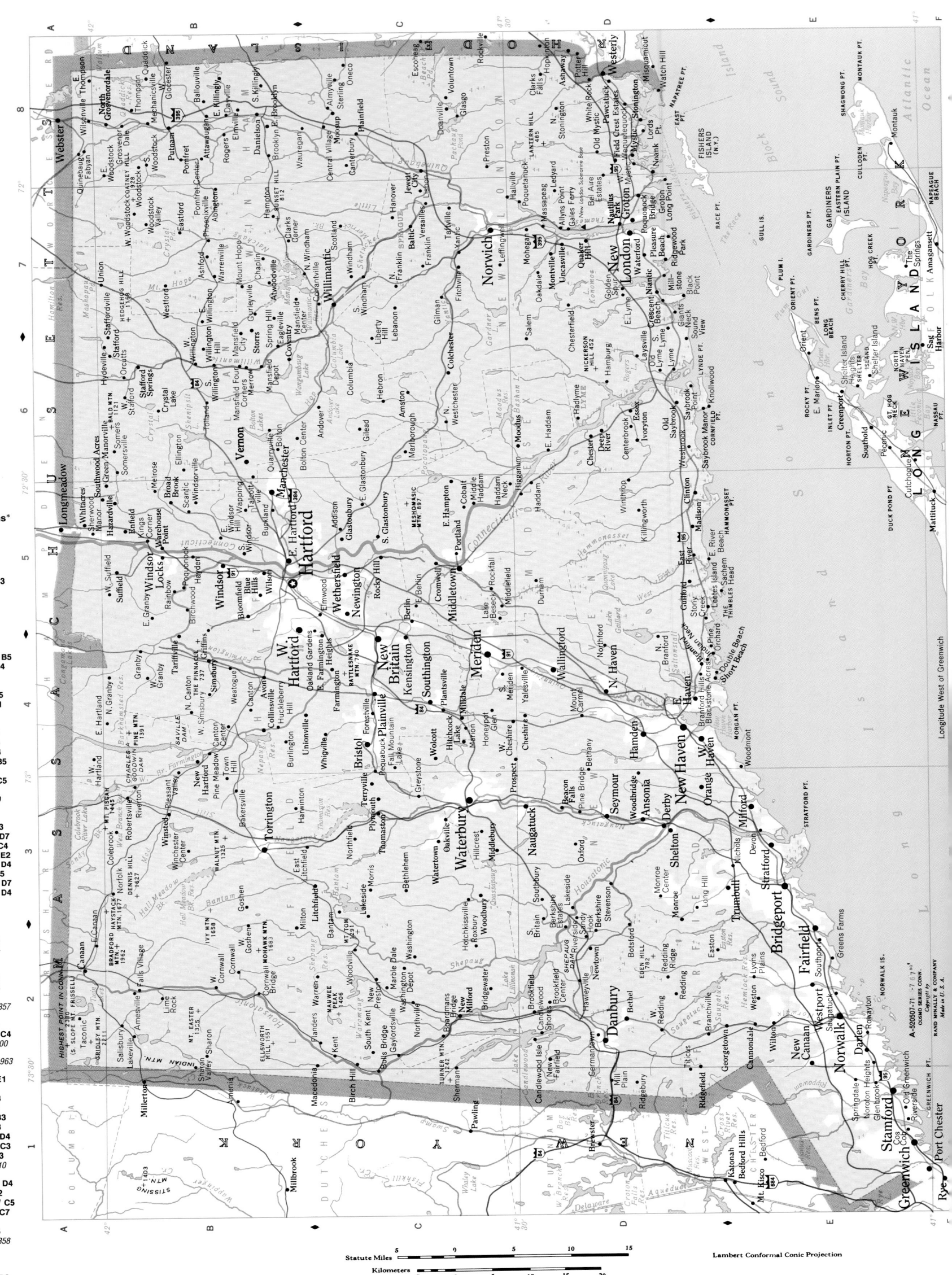

Cities and Towns*

Ansonia 18,403 **D3**
Bethel 8,835 **D2**
Bloomfield 7,120 **B5**
Blue Hills 3,206 **B5**
Branford 5,688 **D4**
Bridgeport 141,686 **E3**
Bristol 60,640 **C4**
Cheshire 5,759 **D4**
Clinton 3,439 **D5**
Cromwell 1,100 **C5**
Danbury 65,585 **D2**
Darien 18,130 **E2**
Derby 12,199 **D3**
East Hartford 50,452 **B5**
East Haven 26,144 **D4**
Enfield 8,458 **B5**
Fairfield 53,418 **E2**
Glastonbury 7,082 **C5**
Greenwich 58,441 **E1**
Groton 9,837 **D7**
Hamden 52,434 **D4**
Hartford 139,739 **B5**
Hazardville 5,179 **B5**
Kensington 8,306 **C4**
Manchester 51,618 **B5**
Meriden 59,479 **C4**
Middletown 42,762 **C5**
Milford 48,168 **E3**
Monroe Center 7,900 **D3**
Mystic 2,618 **D8**
Naugatuck 30,625 **D3**
Nautilus Park 6,500 **D7**
New Britain 75,491 **C4**
New Canaan 17,864 **E2**
New Haven 130,474 **D4**
Newington 29,208 **C5**
New London 28,540 **D7**
North Haven 22,249 **D4**
Norwalk 78,331 **E2**
Norwich 37,391 **C7**
Oakville 8,741 **C3**
Orange 12,830 **D3**
Plainville 17,392 **C4**
Plantsville 7,050 **C4**
Portland 5,645 **C5**
Putnam 6,835 **B8**
Ridgefield 6,363 **D2**
Seymour 14,288 **D3**
Shelton 35,418 **D3**
Sherwood Manor 6,357 **A5**
Simsbury 5,577 **B4**
Southington 38,518 **C4**
South Windsor 10,800 **B5**
Southwood Acres 8,963 **A5**
Stamford 108,056 **E1**
Storrs 12,198 **B7**
Stratford 49,389 **E3**
Terryville 5,426 **C3**
Torrington 33,687 **B3**
Trumbull 32,000 **E3**
Wallingford 17,827 **D4**
Waterbury 108,961 **C3**
Watertown 5,920 **C3**
West Hartford 60,110 **B4**
West Haven 54,021 **D4**
Westport 24,407 **E2**
Wethersfield 25,651 **C5**
Willimantic 14,746 **C7**
Wilton 7,200 **E2**
Windsor 27,817 **B5**
Windsor Locks 12,358 **B5**
Winsted 8,254 **B3**
Wolcott 6,070 **C4**
Woodbridge 7,924 **D3**

*Populations are for localities, not incorporated towns.

Statute Miles

Kilometers

Lambert Conformal Conic Projection

A-50507-71 -7 [ ] mi²
COSMO SERIES CONN.
RAND M$NALLY & COMPANY
Made in U.S.A.

234

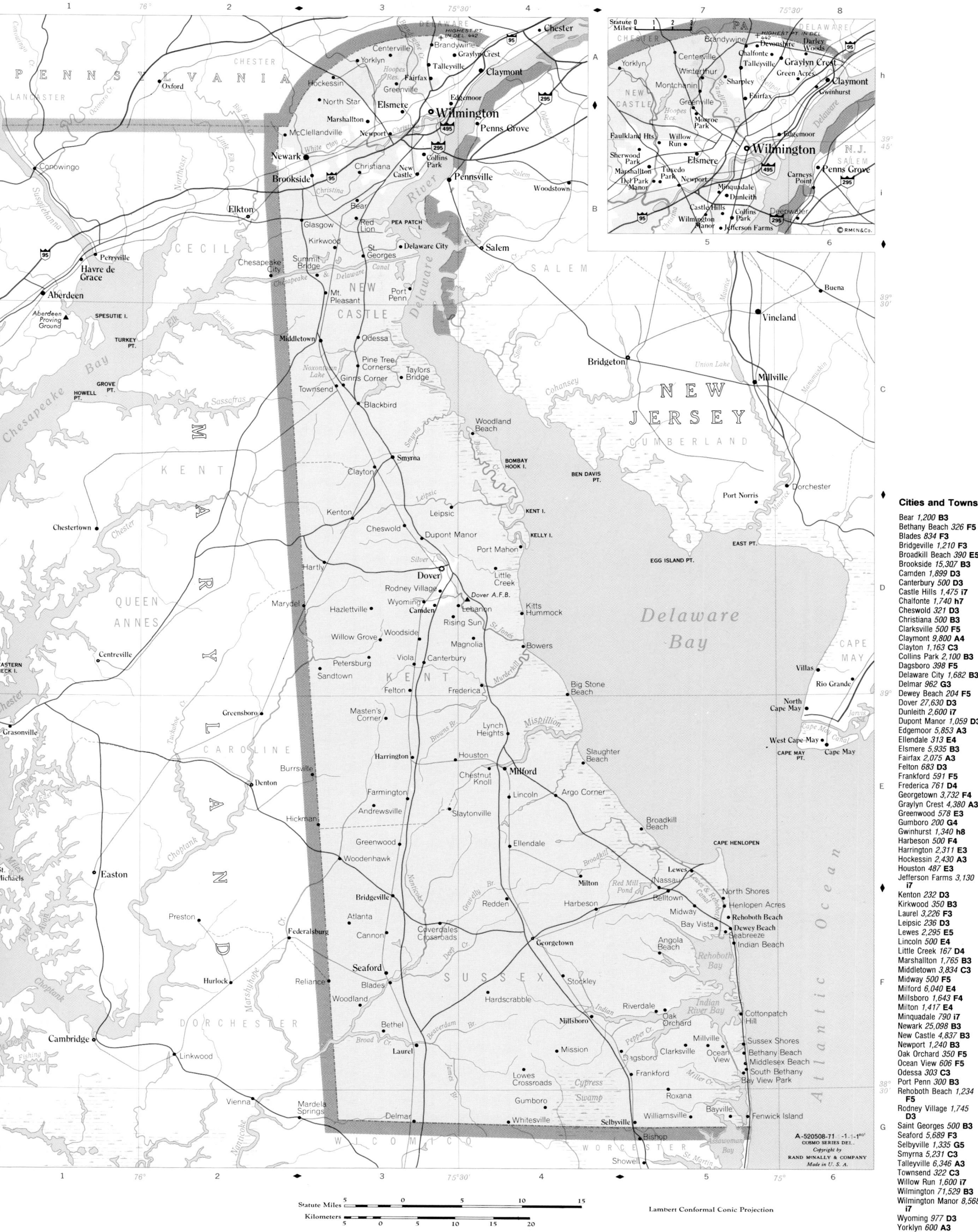

Cities and Towns

Bear 1,200 **B3**
Bethany Beach 326 **F5**
Blades 834 **F3**
Bridgeville 1,210 **F3**
Broadkill Beach 390 **E5**
Brookside 15,307 **B3**
Camden 1,899 **D3**
Canterbury 500 **D3**
Castle Hills 1,475 **i7**
Chalfonte 1,740 **h7**
Cheswold 321 **D3**
Christiana 500 **B3**
Clarksville 500 **F5**
Claymont 9,800 **A4**
Clayton 1,163 **C3**
Collins Park 2,100 **B3**
Dagsboro 398 **F5**
Delaware City 1,682 **B3**
Delmar 962 **G3**
Dewey Beach 204 **F5**
Dover 27,630 **D3**
Dunleith 2,600 **i7**
Dupont Manor 1,059 **D3**
Edgemoor 5,853 **A3**
Ellendale 313 **E4**
Elsmere 5,935 **B3**
Fairfax 2,075 **A3**
Felton 683 **D3**
Frankford 591 **F5**
Frederica 761 **D4**
Georgetown 3,732 **F4**
Graylyn Crest 4,380 **A3**
Greenwood 578 **E3**
Gumboro 200 **G4**
Gwinhurst 1,340 **h8**
Harbeson 500 **F4**
Harrington 2,311 **E3**
Hockessin 2,430 **A3**
Houston 487 **E3**
Jefferson Farms 3,130 **i7**
Kenton 232 **D3**
Kirkwood 350 **B3**
Laurel 3,226 **F3**
Leipsic 236 **D3**
Lewes 2,295 **E5**
Lincoln 500 **E4**
Little Creek 167 **D4**
Marshallton 1,765 **B3**
Middletown 3,834 **C3**
Midway 500 **F5**
Milford 6,040 **E4**
Millsboro 1,643 **F4**
Milton 1,417 **E4**
Minquadale 790 **i7**
Newark 25,098 **B3**
New Castle 4,837 **B3**
Newport 1,240 **B3**
Oak Orchard 350 **F5**
Ocean View 606 **F5**
Odessa 303 **C3**
Port Penn 300 **B3**
Rehoboth Beach 1,234 **F5**
Rodney Village 1,745 **D3**
Saint Georges 500 **B3**
Seaford 5,689 **F3**
Selbyville 1,335 **G5**
Smyrna 5,231 **C3**
Talleyville 6,346 **A3**
Townsend 322 **C3**
Willow Run 1,600 **i7**
Wilmington 71,529 **B3**
Wilmington Manor 8,568 **i7**
Wyoming 977 **D3**
Yorklyn 600 **A3**

FLORIDA

National Parks

Biscayne National Park **G6**

Dry Tortugas National Park **H4**

Everglades National Park **G5**

Cities and Towns

Bartow 14,716 **E5**
Belle Glade 16,177 **F6**
Boca Raton 61,492 **F6**
Boynton Beach 46,194 **F6**
Bradenton 43,779 **E4**
Brandon 57,985 **E4**
Cape Canaveral 8,014 **D6**
Cape Coral 74,991 **F5**
Carol City 53,331 **s13**
Clearwater 98,784 **E4**
Cocoa 17,722 **D6**
Coral Gables 40,091 **G6**
Daytona Beach 61,921 **C5**
Deerfield Beach 46,325 **F6**
De Land 16,491 **C5**
Delray Beach 47,181 **F6**
Dunedin 34,012 **D4**
Fort Lauderdale 149,377 **F6**
Fort Myers 45,206 **F5**
Fort Pierce 36,830 **E6**
Fort Walton Beach 21,471 **u15**
Gainesville 84,770 **C4**
Hallandale 30,996 **G6**
Hialeah 188,004 **G6**
Hollywood 121,697 **F6**
Homestead 26,866 **G6**
Immokalee 14,120 **F5**
Jacksonville 672,971 **B5**
Kendall 87,271 **s13**
Key Largo 11,336 **G6**
Key West 24,832 **H5**
Kissimmee 30,050 **D5**
Lake City 10,005 **B4**
Lakeland 70,576 **D5**
Lake Worth 28,564 **F6**
Largo 65,674 **E4**
Leesburg 14,903 **D5**
Marathon 8,857 **H5**
Margate 42,985 **F6**
Melbourne 59,646 **D6**
Merritt Island 32,886 **D6**
Miami 358,548 **G6**
Miami Beach 92,639 **G6**
Miramar 40,663 **s13**
Naples 19,505 **F5**
New Smyrna Beach 16,543 **C6**
North Miami 49,998 **G6**
North Miami Beach 35,359 **s13**
Ocala 42,045 **C4**
Orlando 164,693 **D5**
Panama City 34,378 **u16**
Pembroke Pines 65,452 **r13**
Pensacola 58,165 **u14**
Pinellas Park 43,426 **E4**
Plantation 66,692 **r13**
Plant City 22,754 **D4**
Pompano Beach 72,411 **F6**
Port Charlotte 41,535 **F5**
Riviera Beach 27,639 **F6**
Saint Augustine 11,692 **C5**
Saint Petersburg 238,629 **E4**
Sanford 32,387 **D5**
Sarasota 50,961 **E4**
Sebring 8,900 **E5**
Tallahassee 124,773 **B2**
Tampa 280,015 **E4**
Tarpon Springs 17,906 **D4**
Titusville 39,394 **D6**
Venice 16,922 **E4**
Vero Beach 17,350 **E6**
West Palm Beach 67,643 **F6**
West Pensacola 22,107 **u14**
Winter Haven 24,725 **D5**

Lambert Conformal Conic Projection
SCALE 1:2,425,000   1 Inch = 38 Statute Miles

Statute Miles 5 0 5 10   20   30   40   50

Kilometers 5 0 5 15 25 35 45 55 65

Same Scale as Main Map

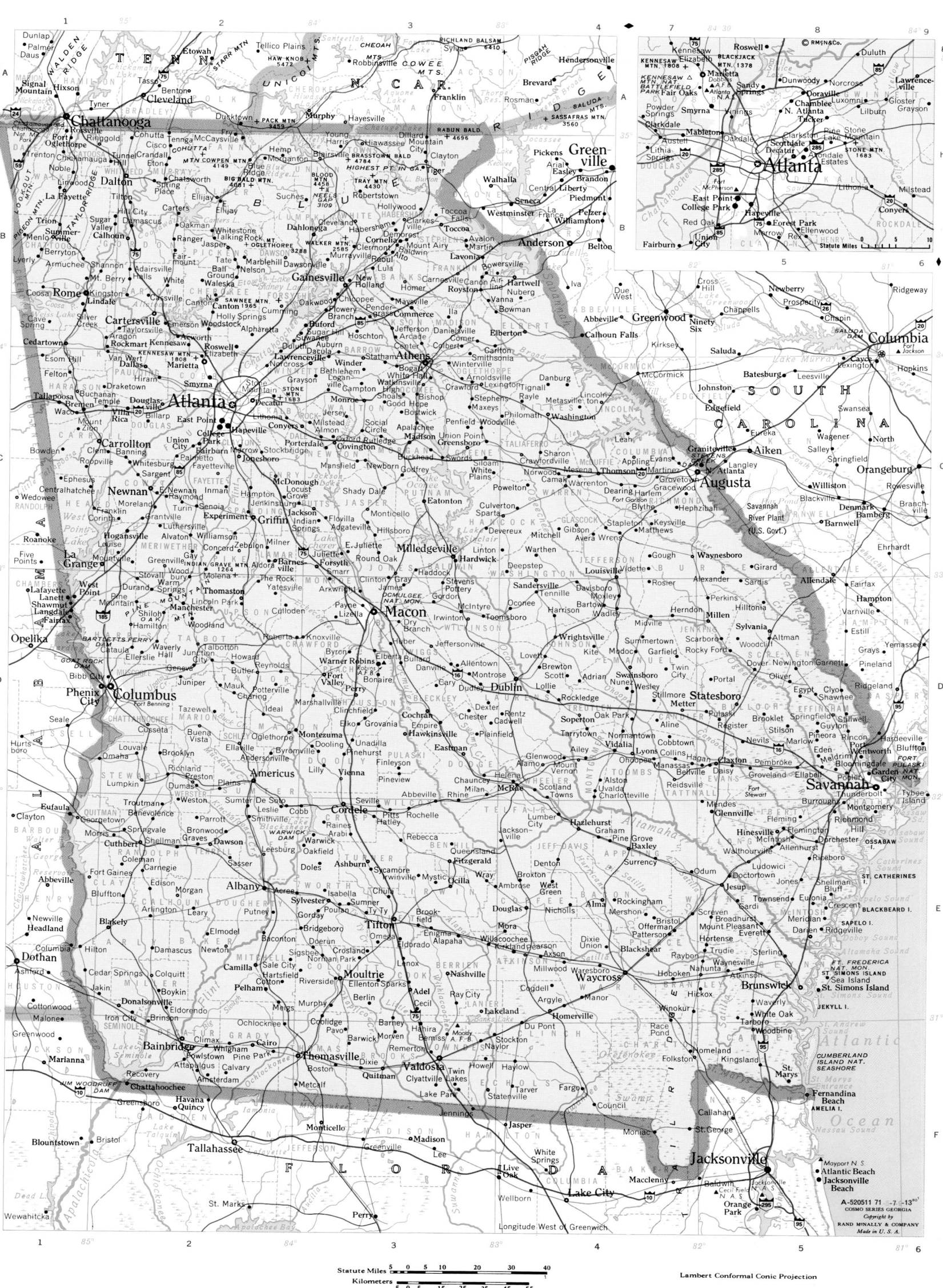

237

HAWAII

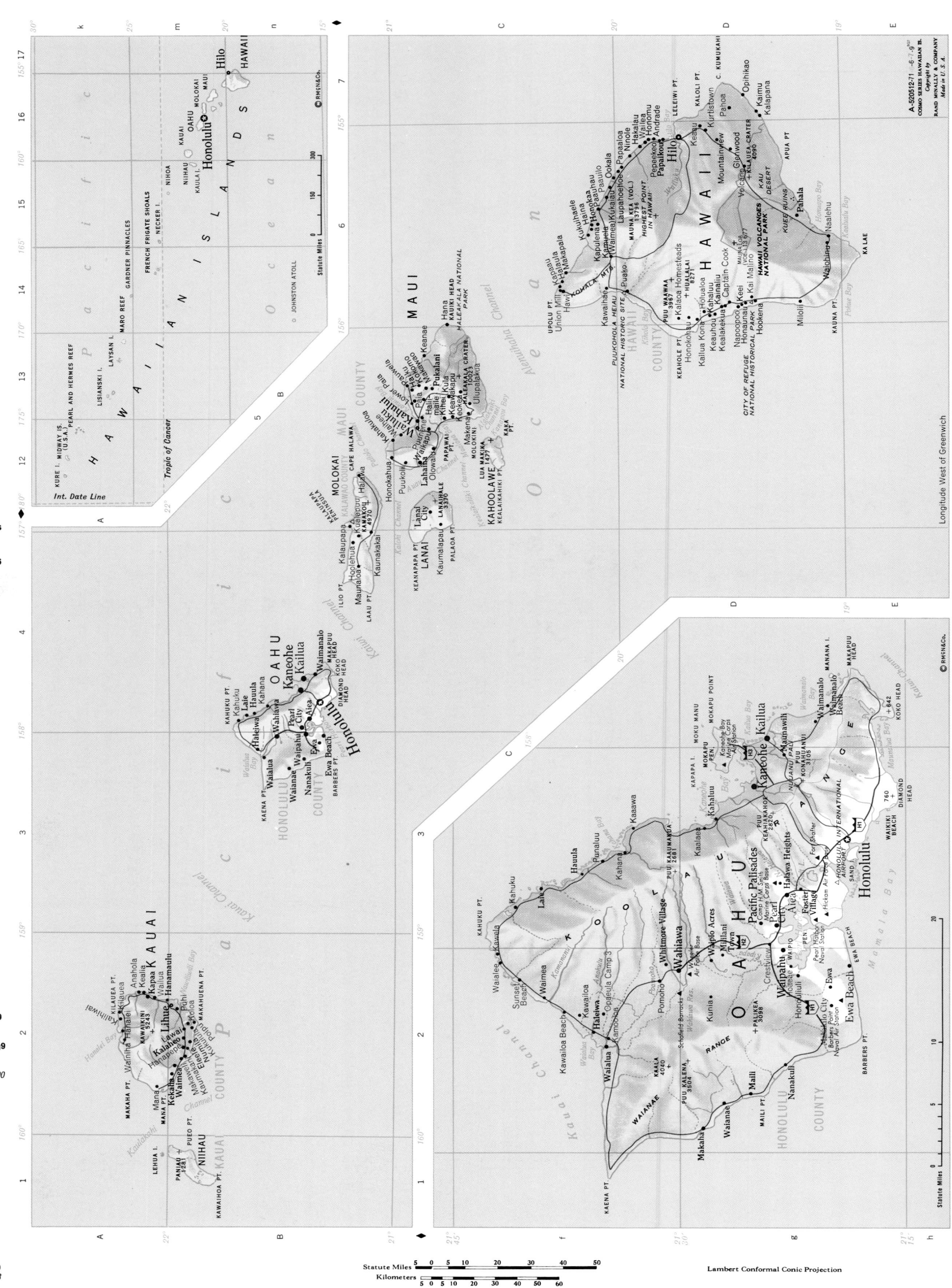

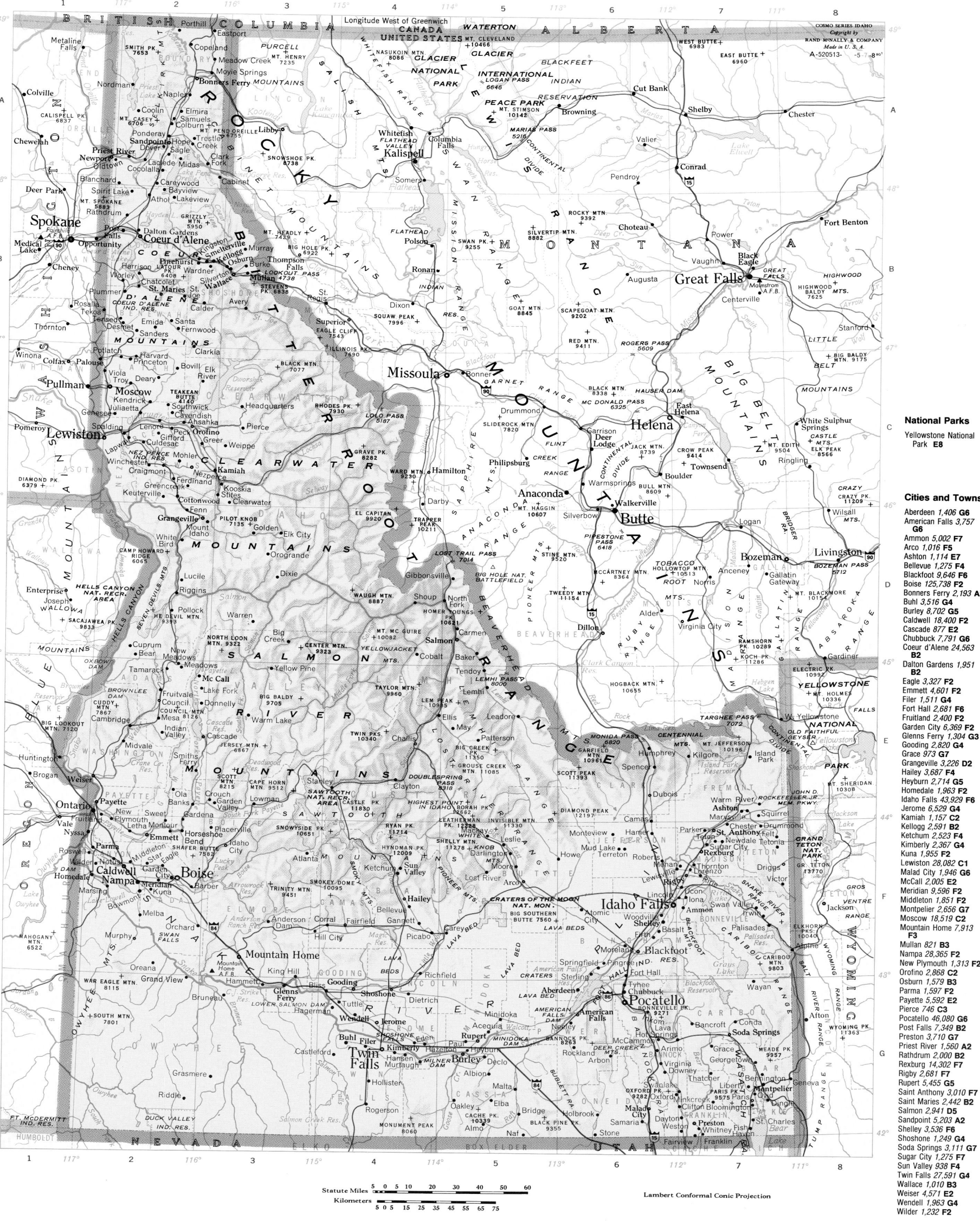

National Parks

Yellowstone National
Park **E8**

Cities and Towns

Aberdeen *1,406* **G6**
American Falls *3,757*
G6
Ammon *5,002* **F7**
Arco *1,016* **F5**
Ashton *1,114* **E7**
Bellevue *1,275* **F4**
Blackfoot *9,646* **F6**
Boise *125,738* **F2**
Bonners Ferry *2,193* **A2**
Buhl *3,516* **G4**
Burley *8,702* **G5**
Caldwell *18,400* **F2**
Cascade *877* **E2**
Chubbuck *7,791* **G6**
Coeur d'Alene *24,563*
B2
Dalton Gardens *1,951*
B2
Eagle *3,327* **F2**
Emmett *4,601* **F2**
Filer *1,511* **G4**
Fort Hall *2,681* **F6**
Fruitland *2,400* **F2**
Garden City *6,369* **F2**
Glenns Ferry *1,304* **G3**
Gooding *2,820* **G4**
Grace *973* **G7**
Grangeville *3,226* **D2**
Hailey *3,687* **F4**
Heyburn *2,714* **G5**
Homedale *1,963* **F2**
Idaho Falls *43,929* **F6**
Jerome *6,529* **G4**
Kamiah *1,157* **C2**
Kellogg *2,591* **B2**
Ketchum *2,523* **F4**
Kimberly *2,367* **G4**
Kuna *1,955* **F2**
Lewiston *28,082* **C1**
Malad City *1,946* **G6**
McCall *2,005* **E2**
Meridian *9,596* **F2**
Middleton *1,851* **F2**
Montpelier *2,656* **G7**
Moscow *18,519* **C2**
Mountain Home *7,913*
F3
Mullan *821* **B3**
Nampa *28,365* **F2**
New Plymouth *1,313* **F2**
Orofino *2,868* **C2**
Osburn *1,579* **B3**
Parma *1,597* **F2**
Payette *5,592* **E2**
Pierce *746* **C3**
Pocatello *46,080* **G6**
Post Falls *7,349* **B2**
Preston *3,710* **G7**
Priest River *1,560* **A2**
Rathdrum *2,000* **B2**
Rexburg *14,302* **F7**
Rigby *2,681* **F7**
Rupert *5,455* **G5**
Saint Anthony *3,010* **F7**
Saint Maries *2,442* **C2**
Salmon *2,941* **D5**
Sandpoint *5,203* **A2**
Shelley *3,536* **F6**
Shoshone *1,249* **G4**
Soda Springs *3,111* **G7**
Sugar City *1,275* **F7**
Sun Valley *938* **F4**
Twin Falls *27,591* **G4**
Wallace *1,010* **B3**
Weiser *4,571* **E2**
Wendell *1,963* **G4**
Wilder *1,232* **F2**

ILLINOIS

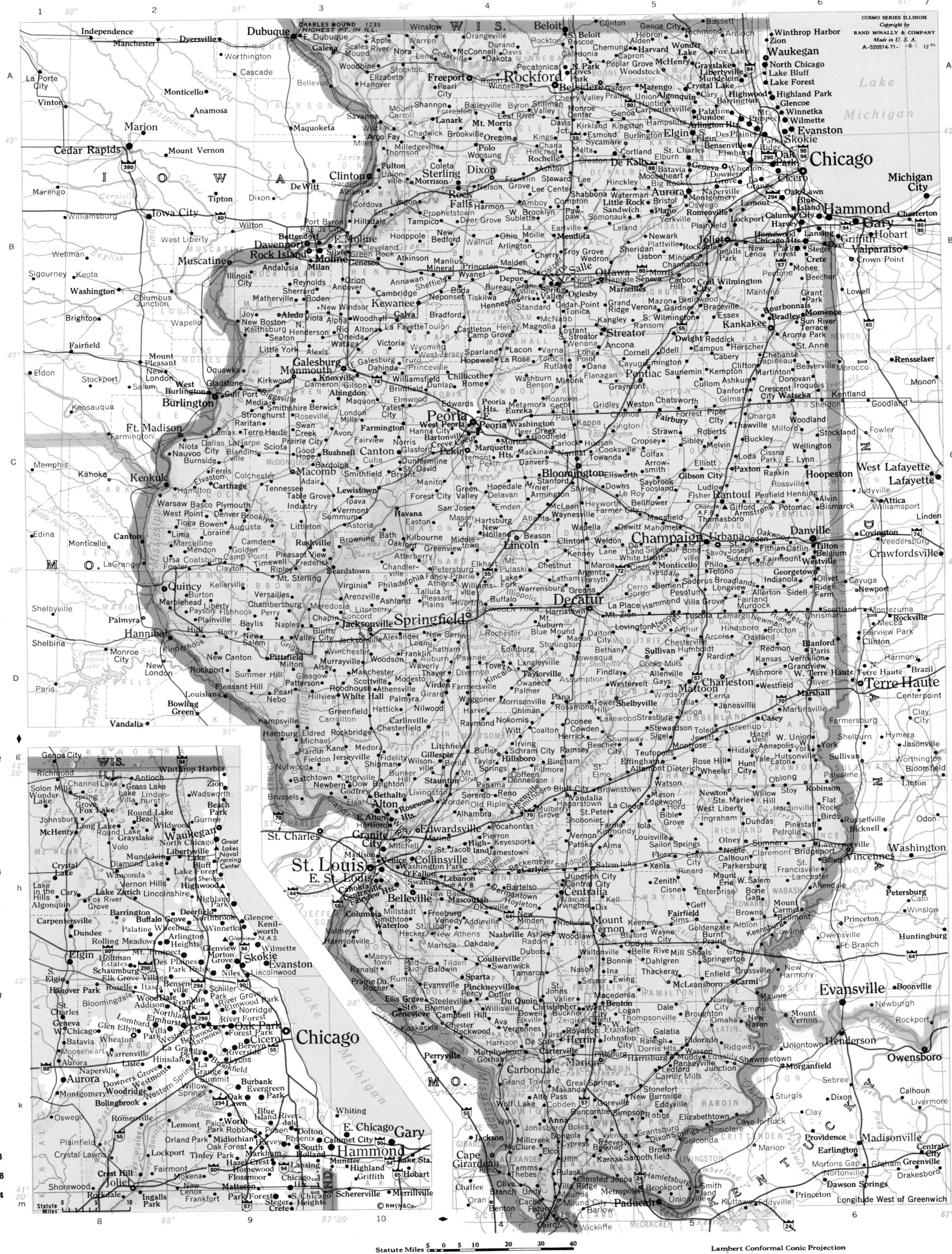

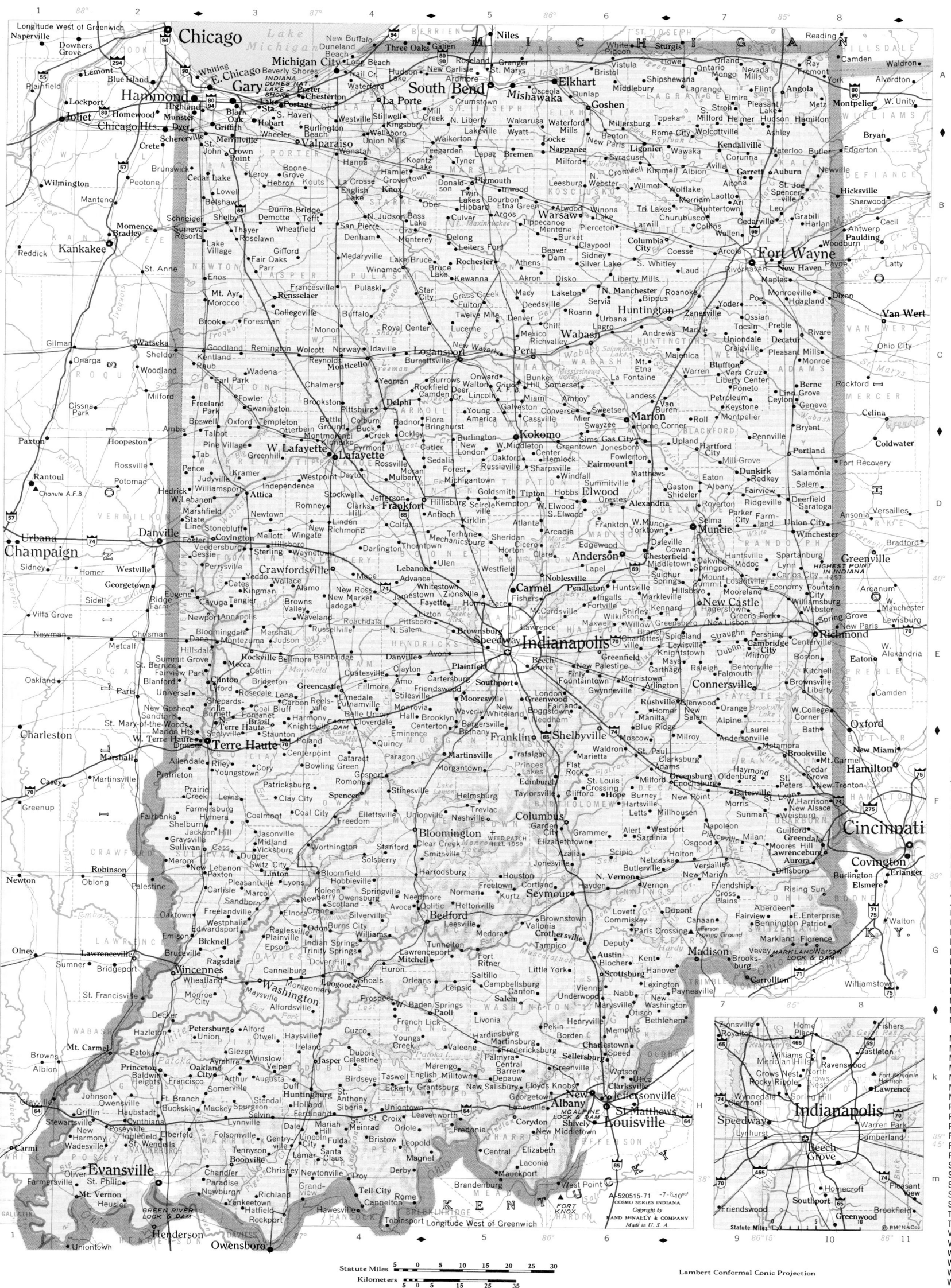

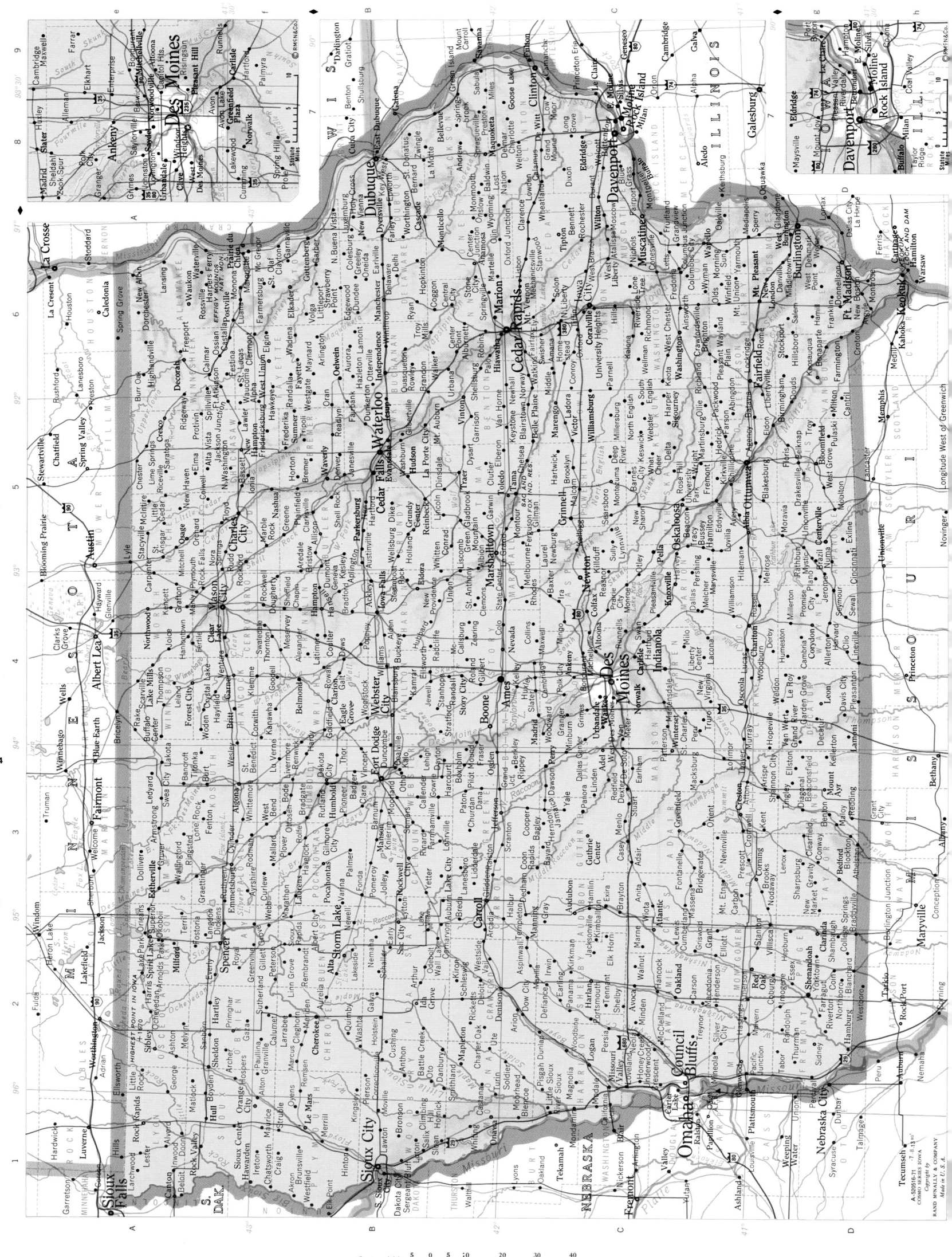

Cities and Towns

Algona *6,015* **A3**
Amana *540* **C6**
Ames *47,198* **B4**
Anamosa *5,100* **B6**
Ankeny *18,482* **C4**
Atlantic *7,432* **C2**
Bettendorf *28,132* **C7**
Boone *12,392* **B4**
Burlington *27,208* **D6**
Carroll *9,579* **B3**
Cedar Falls *34,298* **B5**
Cedar Rapids *108,751*
  C6
Centerville *5,936* **D5**
Chariton *4,616* **C4**
Charles City *7,878* **A5**
Cherokee *6,026* **B2**
Clarinda *5,104* **D2**
Clinton *29,201* **C7**
Council Bluffs *54,315*
  C2
Creston *7,911* **C3**
Davenport *95,333* **C7**
Decorah *8,063* **A6**
Denison *6,604* **B2**
Des Moines *193,187* **C4**
De Witt *4,514* **C7**
Dubuque *57,546* **B7**
Emmetsburg *3,940* **A3**
Estherville *6,720* **A3**
Fairfield *9,768* **C6**
Fort Dodge *25,894* **B3**
Fort Madison *11,618*
  D6
Glenwood *4,571* **C2**
Grinnell *8,902* **C5**
Guttenberg *2,257* **B6**
Hampton *4,133* **B4**
Harlan *5,148* **C2**
Humboldt *4,438* **B3**
Independence *5,972* **B6**
Indianola *11,340* **C4**
Iowa City *59,738* **C6**
Iowa Falls *5,424* **B4**
Jefferson *4,292* **B3**
Keokuk *12,451* **D6**
Knoxville *8,232* **C4**
Le Mars *8,454* **B1**
Manchester *5,137* **B6**
Maquoketa *6,111* **B7**
Marion *20,403* **B6**
Marshalltown *25,178*
  B5
Mason City *29,040* **A4**
Mount Pleasant *8,027*
  D6
Muscatine *22,881* **C6**
Newton *14,789* **C4**
Oelwein *6,493* **B6**
Orange City *4,940* **B1**
Oskaloosa *10,632* **C5**
Ottumwa *24,488* **C5**
Pella *9,270* **C5**
Perry *6,652* **C3**
Red Oak *6,264* **D2**
Sheldon *4,937* **A2**
Shenandoah *5,572* **D2**
Sioux Center *5,074* **A1**
Sioux City *80,505* **B1**
Spencer *11,066* **A2**
Storm Lake *8,769* **B2**
Urbandale *23,500* **C4**
Vinton *5,103* **B5**
Washington *7,074* **C6**
Waterloo *66,467* **B5**
Waverly *8,539* **B5**
Webster City *7,894* **B4**
West Branch *1,908* **C6**
West Des Moines
  31,702 **C4**

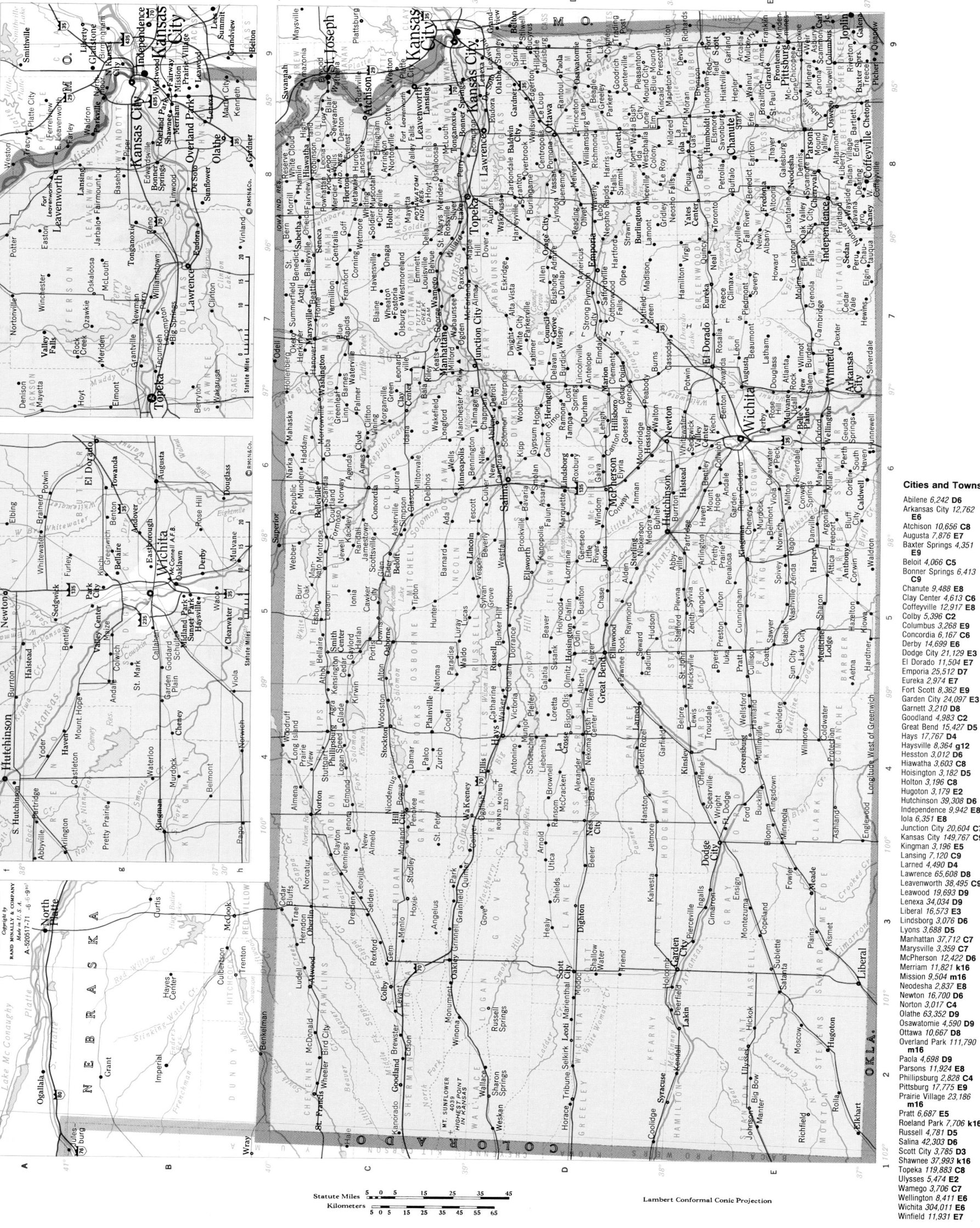

KANSAS

Cities and Towns

Abilene 6,242 **D6**
Arkansas City 12,762 **E6**
Atchison 10,656 **C8**
Augusta 7,876 **E7**
Baxter Springs 4,351 **E9**
Beloit 4,066 **C5**
Bonner Springs 6,413 **C9**
Chanute 9,488 **E8**
Clay Center 4,613 **C6**
Coffeyville 12,917 **E8**
Colby 5,396 **C2**
Columbus 3,268 **E9**
Concordia 6,167 **C6**
Derby 14,699 **E6**
Dodge City 21,129 **E3**
El Dorado 11,504 **E7**
Emporia 25,512 **D7**
Eureka 2,974 **E7**
Fort Scott 8,362 **E9**
Garden City 24,097 **E3**
Garnett 3,210 **D8**
Goodland 4,983 **C2**
Great Bend 15,427 **D5**
Hays 17,767 **D4**
Haysville 8,364 **g12**
Hesston 3,012 **D6**
Hiawatha 3,603 **C8**
Hoisington 3,182 **D5**
Holton 3,196 **C8**
Hugoton 3,179 **E2**
Hutchinson 39,308 **D6**
Independence 9,942 **E8**
Iola 6,351 **E8**
Junction City 20,604 **C7**
Kansas City 149,767 **C9**
Kingman 3,196 **E5**
Lansing 7,120 **C9**
Larned 4,490 **D4**
Lawrence 65,608 **D8**
Leavenworth 38,495 **C9**
Leawood 19,693 **D9**
Lenexa 34,034 **D9**
Liberal 16,573 **E3**
Lindsborg 3,076 **D6**
Lyons 3,688 **D5**
Manhattan 37,712 **C7**
Marysville 3,359 **C7**
McPherson 12,422 **D6**
Merriam 11,821 **k16**
Mission 9,504 **m16**
Neodesha 2,837 **E8**
Newton 16,700 **D6**
Norton 3,017 **C4**
Olathe 63,352 **D9**
Osawatomie 4,590 **D9**
Ottawa 10,667 **D8**
Overland Park 111,790 **m16**
Paola 4,698 **D9**
Parsons 11,924 **E8**
Phillipsburg 2,828 **C4**
Pittsburg 17,775 **E9**
Prairie Village 23,186 **m16**
Pratt 6,687 **E5**
Roeland Park 7,706 **k16**
Russell 4,781 **D5**
Salina 42,303 **D6**
Scott City 3,785 **D3**
Shawnee 37,993 **k16**
Topeka 119,883 **C8**
Ulysses 5,474 **E2**
Wamego 3,706 **C7**
Wellington 8,411 **E6**
Wichita 304,011 **E6**
Winfield 11,931 **E7**

Statute Miles 5 0 5 15 25 35 45
Kilometers 5 0 5 15 25 35 45 55 65

Lambert Conformal Conic Projection

243

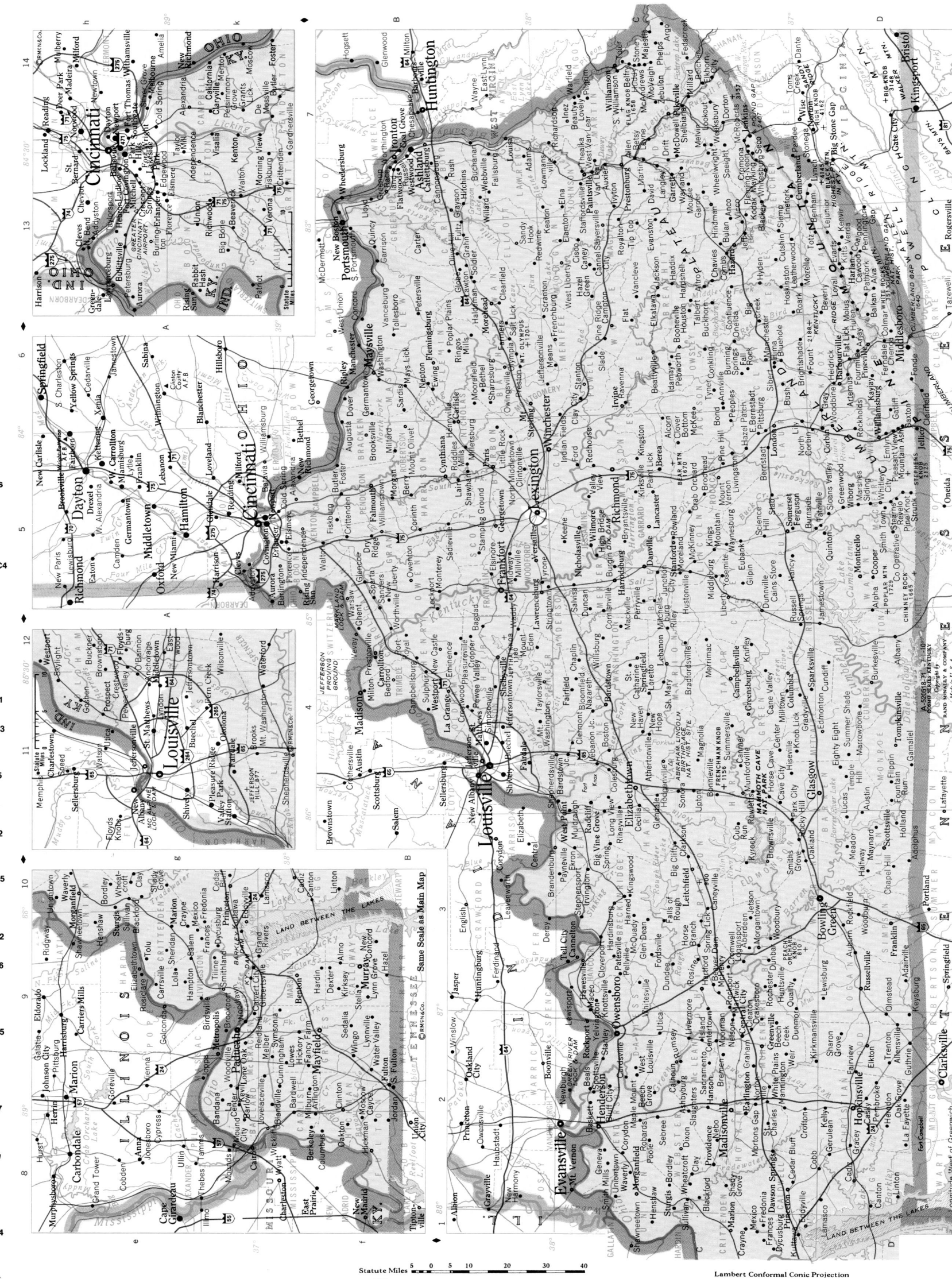

Statute Miles 5 0 5 10 20 30 40
Kilometers 5 0 5 10 20 30 40 60

Lambert Conformal Conic Projection

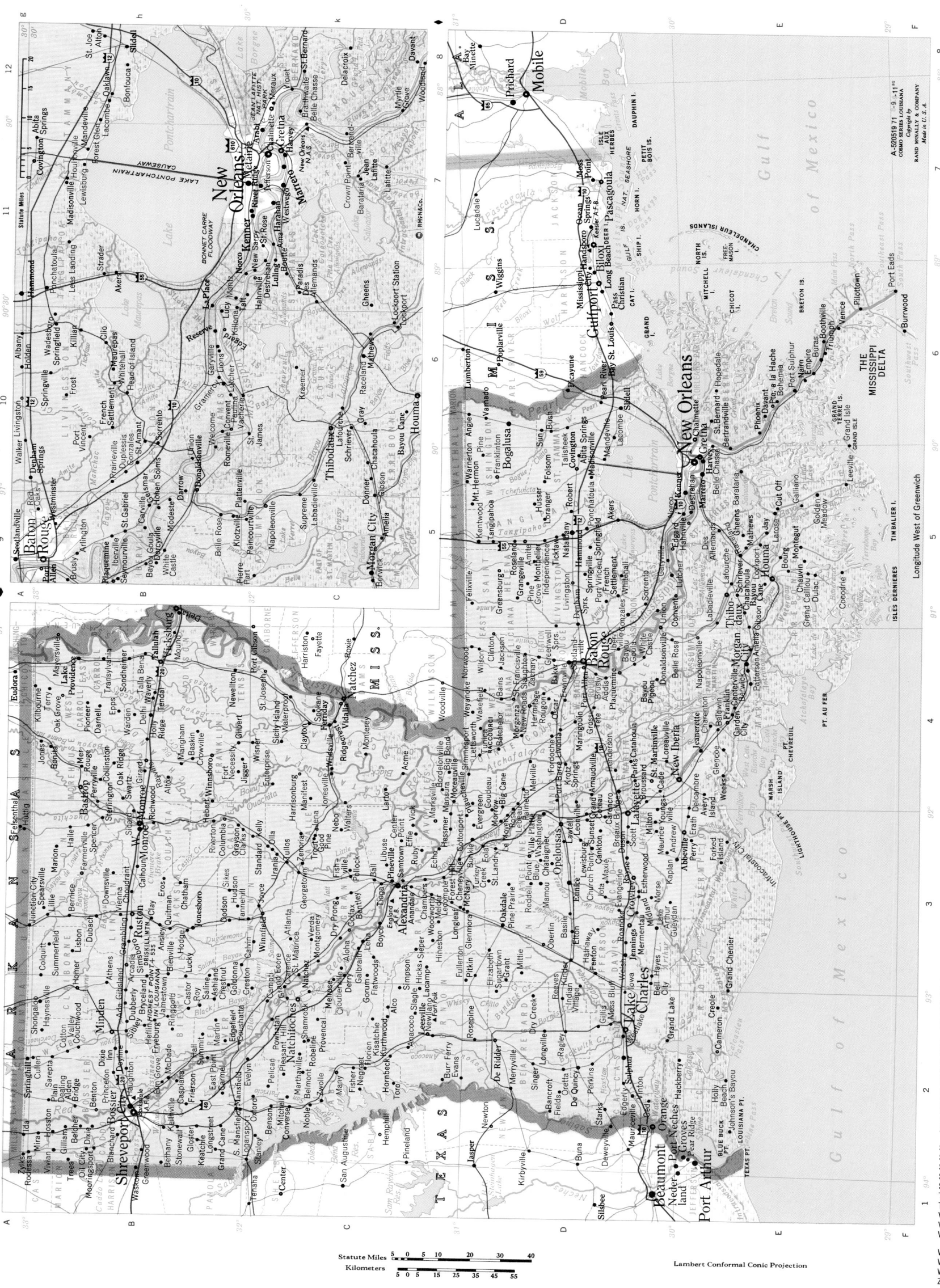

Statute Miles
Kilometers

Lambert Conformal Conic Projection

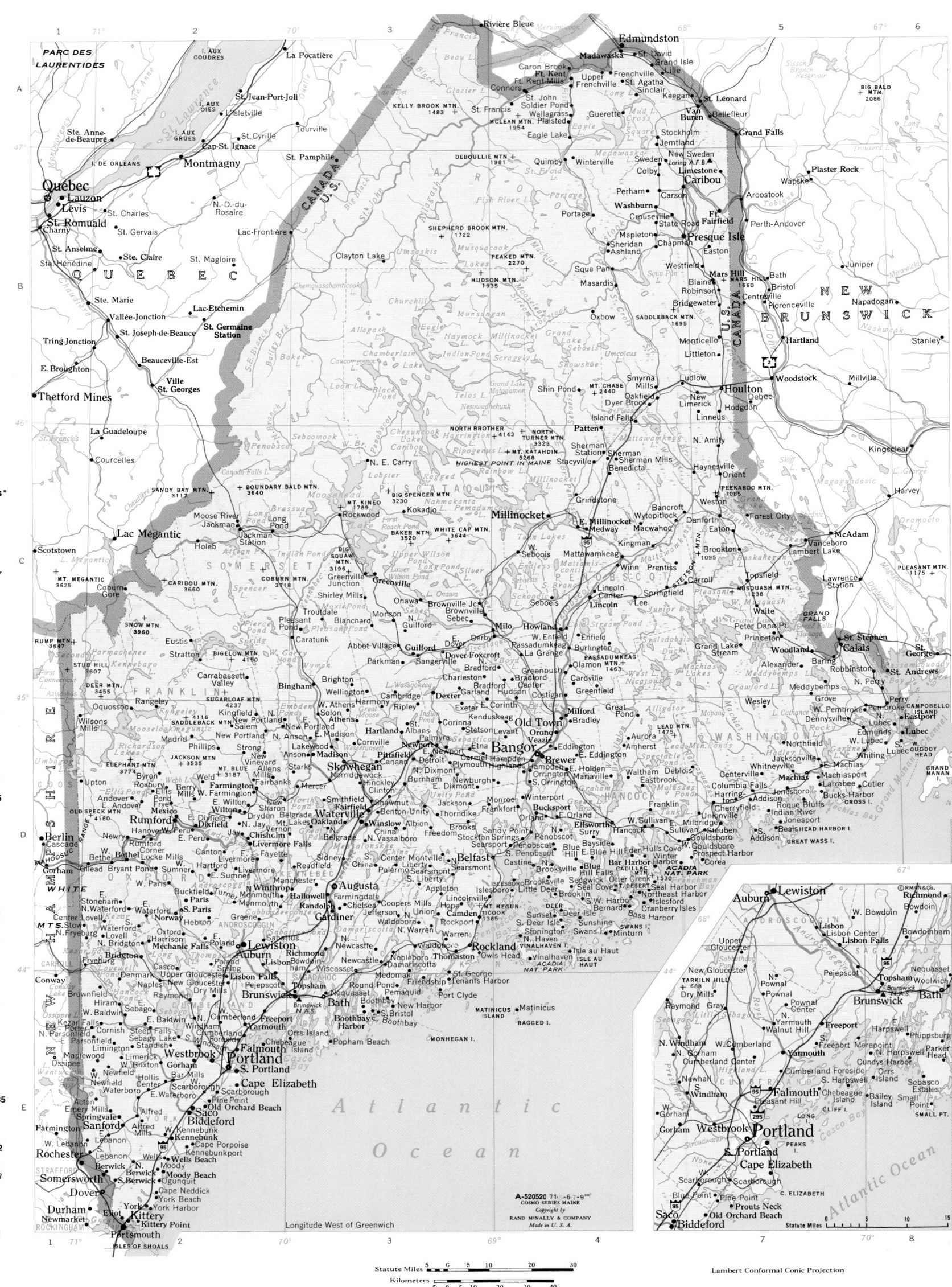

National Parks

Acadia National Park
D4

Cities and Towns*

Auburn 24,309 **D2**
Augusta 21,325 **D3**
Bangor 33,181 **D4**
Bar Harbor 2,768 **D4**
Bath 9,799 **E3**
Belfast 6,355 **D3**
Biddeford 20,710 **E2**
Boothbay Harbor 1,267
   E3
Brewer 9,021 **D4**
Brunswick 14,683 **E3**
Bucksport 2,989 **D4**
Calais 3,563 **C5**
Camden 4,022 **D3**
Cape Elizabeth 8,854
   E2
Caribou 9,415 **B5**
Cumberland Center
   1,890 **g7**
Dexter 2,650 **C3**
Dover-Foxcroft 3,077
   C3
East Millinocket 2,075
   C4
Eastport 1,965 **D6**
Eliot 150 **E2**
Ellsworth 5,975 **D4**
Fairfield 2,794 **D3**
Falmouth 7,610 **E2**
Farmingdale 2,070 **D3**
Farmington 4,197 **D2**
Fort Fairfield 1,729 **B5**
Fort Kent 2,123 **A4**
Freeport 1,829 **E2**
Gardiner 6,746 **D3**
Gorham 3,618 **E2**
Hallowell 2,534 **D3**
Hampden 3,895 **D4**
Houlton 5,627 **B5**
Kennebunk 4,206 **E2**
Kittery 5,151 **E2**
Lewiston 39,757 **D2**
Lincoln 3,399 **C4**
Lisbon Falls 4,674 **E2**
Livermore Falls 1,935
   D2
Madawaska 3,653 **A4**
Madison 2,956 **D3**
Mechanic Falls 2,388
   D2
Mexico 2,302 **D2**
Millinocket 6,922 **C4**
Milo 2,129 **C4**
North Windham 4,077
   E2
Norway 3,023 **D2**
Oakland 3,510 **D3**
Old Orchard Beach
   7,789 **E2**
Old Town 8,317 **D4**
Orono 9,989 **D4**
Pittsfield 3,222 **D3**
Portland 64,358 **E2**
Presque Isle 10,550 **B5**
Rockland 7,972 **D3**
Rumford 5,419 **D2**
Saco 15,181 **E2**
Sanford 10,296 **E2**
Scarborough 2,586 **E2**
Skowhegan 6,990 **D3**
South Paris 2,320 **D2**
South Portland 23,163
   E2
Thomaston 2,445 **D3**
Topsham 6,147 **E3**
Van Buren 2,759 **A5**
Waterville 17,173 **D3**
Westbrook 16,121 **E2**
Wilton 2,453 **D2**
Winslow 5,436 **D3**
Winthrop 2,819 **D3**
Yarmouth 3,338 **E2**
York 3,130 **E2**
York Harbor 2,555 **E2**

*Populations are for localities, not incorporated towns.

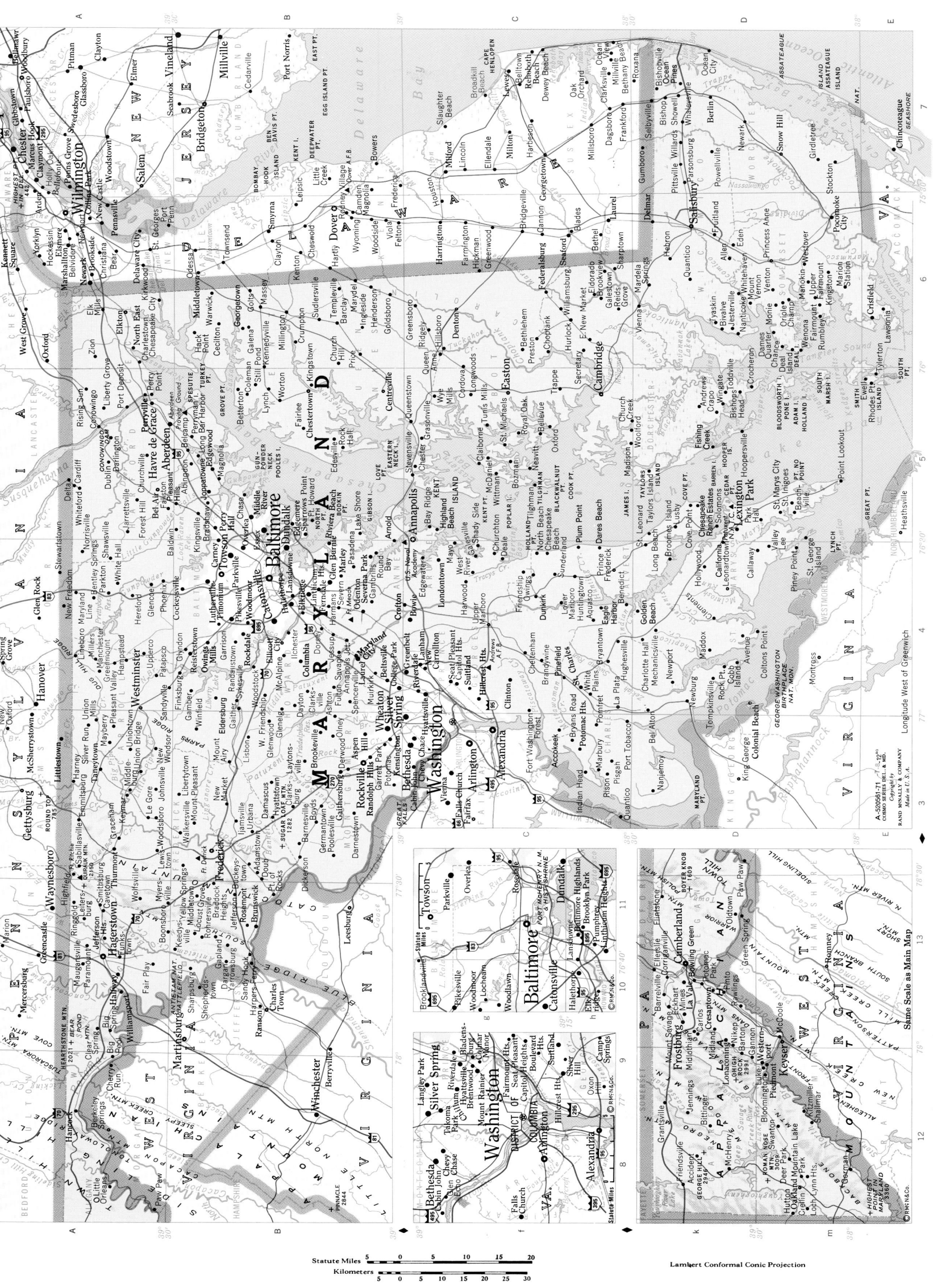

Cities and Towns

Aberdeen *13,087* **A5**
Annapolis *33,187* **C5**
Baltimore *736,014* **B4**
Bel Air *8,860* **A5**
Beltsville *14,476* **B4**
Bethesda *62,936* **C3**
Bladensburg *8,064* **f9**
Bowie *37,589* **B4**
Brentwood *3,005* **f9**
Brunswick *5,117* **B2**
Cambridge *11,514* **C5**
Catonsville *35,233* **B4**
Chevy Chase *8,559* **C3**
Chillum *31,309* **f9**
Clinton *19,987* **C4**
Cockeysville *18,668* **B4**
College Park *21,927* **C4**
Columbia *75,883* **B4**
Crofton *12,781* **B4**
Cumberland *23,706* **k13**
Dundalk *65,800* **B4**
Easton *9,372* **C5**
Edgewood *23,903* **B5**
Elkton *9,073* **A6**
Essex *40,872* **B5**
Frederick *40,148* **B3**
Frostburg *8,075* **k13**
Gaithersburg *39,542* **B3**
Germantown *41,145* **B3**
Glen Burnie *37,305* **B4**
Greenbelt *21,096* **C4**
Hagerstown *35,445* **A2**
Halethorpe *19,750* **B4**
Halfway *8,873* **A2**
Havre de Grace *8,952*
A5
Hillcrest Heights *17,136*
C4
Hyattsville *13,864* **C4**
Joppatowne *11,084* **B5**
Langley Park *17,474* **f9**
Lansdowne *9,430* **B4**
Laurel *19,438* **B4**
Lexington Park *9,943*
D5
Lutherville-Timonium
16,442 **B4**
Middle River *24,616* **B5**
Oakland *2,078* **m12**
Ocean City *5,146* **D7**
Olney *23,019* **B3**
Overlea *12,137* **B4**
Owings Mills *9,474* **B4**
Oxon Hill *3,730* **f9**
Parkville *31,617* **B4**
Perry Hall *22,723* **B5**
Pikesville *24,815* **B4**
Pocomoke City *3,922*
D6
Potomac *45,634* **B3**
Randallstown *26,277*
B4
Reisterstown *19,314* **B4**
Rockville *44,835* **B3**
Rosedale *18,703* **g11**
Salisbury *20,592* **D6**
Severn *24,499* **B4**
Severna Park *25,879*
B4
Sharpsburg *659* **B2**
Silver Spring *76,046* **C3**
Snow Hill *2,217* **D7**
Suitland *35,400* **C4**
Takoma Park *16,700* **f8**
Towson *49,445* **B4**
Westminster *13,068* **A4**
Wheaton *58,300* **B3**
White Plains *3,560* **C4**
Woodlawn *5,329* **g10**

District of Columbia

Washington *606,900* **C3**

MASSACHUSETTS

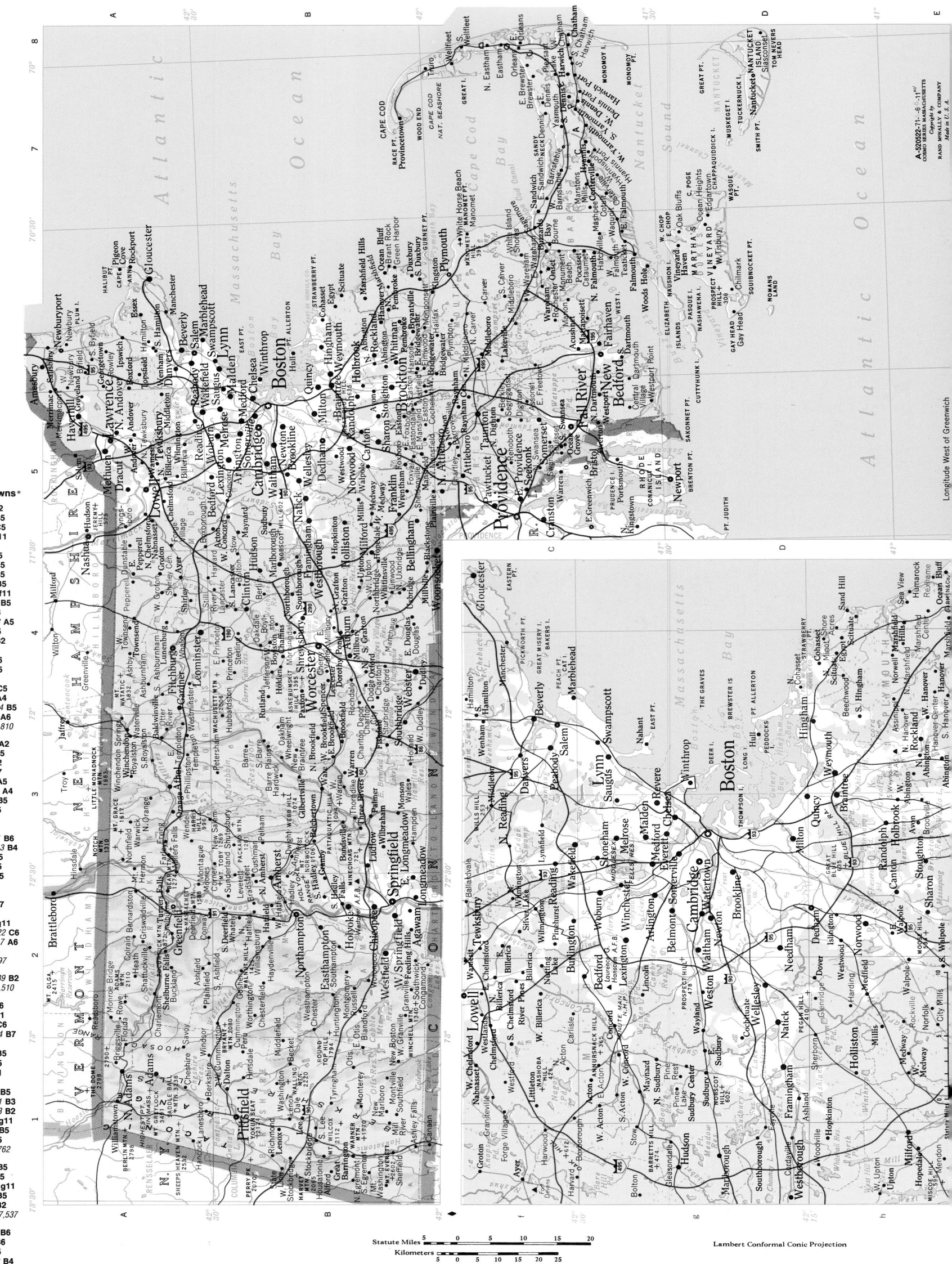

Cities and Towns*

Amherst 17,824 **B2**
Arlington 44,630 **B5**
Attleboro 38,383 **C5**
Belmont 24,720 **g11**
Beverly 38,195 **A6**
Boston 574,283 **B5**
Braintree 33,836 **B5**
Brockton 92,788 **B5**
Brookline 54,718 **B5**
Burlington 23,302 **f11**
Cambridge 95,802 **B5**
Chatham 1,922 **C8**
Chelmsford 32,383 **A5**
Chelsea 28,710 **B5**
Chicopee 56,632 **B2**
Concord 4,680 **B5**
Danvers 24,174 **A6**
Dedham 23,782 **B5**
Dracut 25,594 **A5**
Fall River 92,703 **C5**
Fitchburg 41,194 **A4**
Framingham 64,994 **B5**
Gloucester 28,716 **A6**
Great Barrington 2,810 **B1**
Greenfield 14,016 **A2**
Haverhill 51,418 **A5**
Holyoke 43,704 **B2**
Hyannis 14,120 **C7**
Lawrence 70,207 **A5**
Leominster 38,145 **A4**
Lexington 28,974 **B5**
Lowell 103,439 **A5**
Lynn 81,245 **B6**
Malden 53,884 **B5**
Marblehead 19,971 **B6**
Marlborough 31,813 **B4**
Medford 57,407 **B5**
Melrose 28,150 **B5**
Methuen 39,990 **A5**
Milford 23,339 **B4**
Milton 25,725 **B5**
Nantucket 3,069 **D7**
Natick 30,100 **B5**
Needham 27,557 **g11**
New Bedford 99,922 **C6**
Newburyport 16,317 **A6**
Newton 82,585 **B5**
North Adams 16,797 **A1**
Northampton 29,289 **B2**
North Attleboro 30,510 **C5**
Peabody 47,039 **A6**
Pittsfield 48,622 **B1**
Plymouth 16,178 **C6**
Provincetown 3,374 **B7**
Quincy 84,985 **B5**
Randolph 30,093 **B5**
Reading 22,539 **A5**
Revere 42,786 **g11**
Salem 38,091 **A6**
Somerville 76,210 **B5**
Southbridge 13,631 **B3**
Springfield 156,983 **B2**
Stoneham 22,203 **g11**
Stoughton 26,777 **B5**
Taunton 49,832 **C5**
Vineyard Haven 1,762 **D6**
Wakefield 24,825 **B5**
Waltham 57,878 **B5**
Watertown 33,284 **g11**
Wellesley 26,615 **B5**
Westfield 38,372 **B2**
West Springfield 27,537 **B2**
Weymouth 54,063 **B6**
Winthrop 18,127 **B6**
Woburn 35,943 **B5**
Worcester 169,759 **B4**

*Populations are for localities, not incorporated towns.

Statute Miles
Kilometers

Lambert Conformal Conic Projection

A-520522-71--6-1-81°
COSMO SERIES — MASSACHUSETTS
Copyright by
RAND M^{c}NALLY & COMPANY
Made in U. S. A.

248

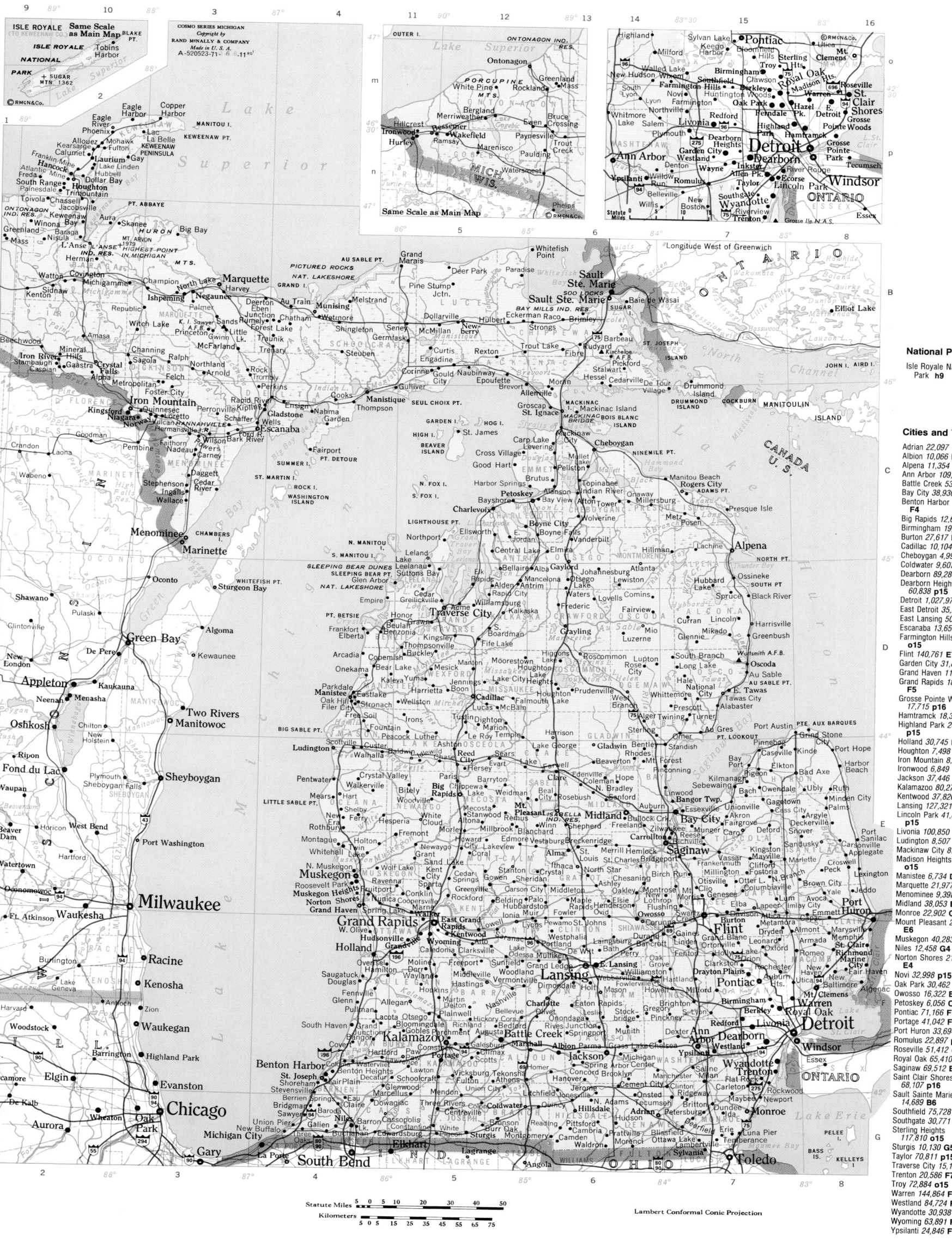

National Parks

Isle Royale National Park **h9**

Cities and Towns

Adrian 22,097 **G6**
Albion 10,066 **F6**
Alpena 11,354 **C7**
Ann Arbor 109,592 **F7**
Battle Creek 53,540 **F5**
Bay City 38,936 **E7**
Benton Harbor 12,818 **F4**
Big Rapids 12,603 **E5**
Birmingham 19,997 **F7**
Burton 27,617 **E7**
Cadillac 10,104 **D5**
Cheboygan 4,999 **C6**
Coldwater 9,607 **G5**
Dearborn 89,286 **F7**
Dearborn Heights 60,838 **p15**
Detroit 1,027,974 **F7**
East Detroit 35,283 **p16**
East Lansing 50,677 **F6**
Escanaba 13,659 **C3**
Farmington Hills 74,652 **o15**
Flint 140,761 **E7**
Garden City 31,846 **p15**
Grand Haven 11,951 **F4**
Grand Rapids 189,126 **F5**
Grosse Pointe Woods 17,715 **p16**
Hamtramck 18,372 **p15**
Highland Park 20,121 **p15**
Holland 30,745 **A2**
Houghton 7,498 **A2**
Iron Mountain 8,525 **C2**
Ironwood 7,849 **n11**
Jackson 37,446 **F6**
Kalamazoo 80,277 **F5**
Kentwood 37,826 **F5**
Lansing 127,321 **F6**
Lincoln Park 41,832 **p15**
Livonia 100,850 **F7**
Ludington 8,507 **E4**
Mackinaw City 875 **C6**
Madison Heights 32,196 **o15**
Manistee 6,734 **D4**
Marquette 21,977 **B3**
Menominee 9,398 **C3**
Midland 38,053 **E6**
Monroe 22,902 **G7**
Mount Pleasant 23,285 **E6**
Muskegon 40,283 **E4**
Niles 12,458 **G4**
Norton Shores 21,755 **E4**
Novi 32,998 **p15**
Oak Park 30,462 **p15**
Owosso 16,322 **E6**
Petoskey 6,056 **C6**
Pontiac 71,166 **F7**
Portage 41,042 **F5**
Port Huron 33,694 **F7**
Romulus 22,897 **p15**
Roseville 51,412 **o16**
Royal Oak 65,410 **F7**
Saginaw 69,512 **E7**
Saint Clair Shores 68,107 **p16**
Sault Sainte Marie 14,689 **B6**
Southfield 75,728 **o15**
Southgate 30,771 **p15**
Sterling Heights 117,810 **o15**
Sturgis 10,130 **G5**
Taylor 70,811 **p15**
Traverse City 15,155 **D5**
Trenton 20,586 **F7**
Troy 72,884 **o15**
Warren 144,864 **F7**
Westland 84,724 **F7**
Wyandotte 30,938 **F7**
Wyoming 63,891 **F5**
Ypsilanti 24,846 **F7**

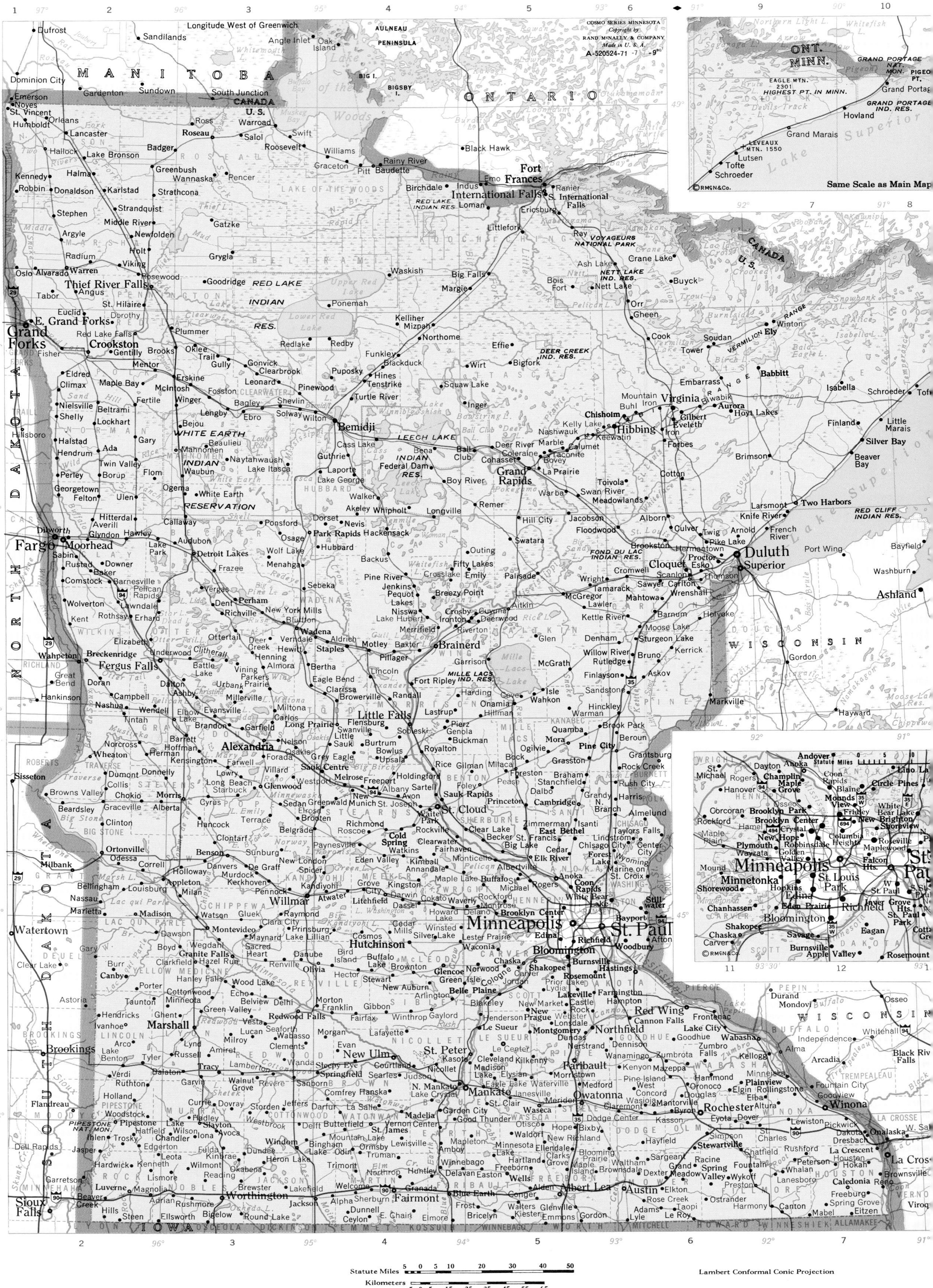

COSMO SERIES MINNESOTA
Copyright by
RAND McNALLY & COMPANY
Made in U. S. A.
A-520524-71 -7 -9²⁰

National Parks

Voyageurs National
Park **B5**

Cities and Towns

Albert Lea *18,310* **G5**
Alexandria *7,838* **E3**
Anoka *17,192* **E5**
Apple Valley *34,598*
  n12
Austin *21,907* **G6**
Bemidji *11,245* **C4**
Blaine *38,975* **m12**
Bloomington *86,335* **F5**
Brainerd *12,353* **D4**
Brooklyn Center *28,887*
  E5
Brooklyn Park *56,381*
  m12
Burnsville *51,288* **F5**
Chisholm *5,290* **C6**
Cloquet *10,885* **D6**
Columbia Heights
  18,910 **m12**
Coon Rapids *52,978* **E5**
Cottage Grove *22,935*
  n13
Crookston *8,119* **C2**
Crystal *23,788* **m12**
Detroit Lakes *6,635* **D3**
Duluth *85,493* **D6**
Eagan *47,409* **n12**
East Bethel *8,050* **E5**
East Grand Forks *8,658*
  C2
Eden Prairie *39,311* **n12**
Edina *46,070* **F5**
Ely *3,968* **C7**
Fairmont *11,265* **G4**
Faribault *17,085* **F5**
Fergus Falls *12,362* **D2**
Fridley *28,335* **m12**
Golden Valley *20,971*
  n12
Grand Marais *1,171* **k9**
Grand Rapids *7,976* **C5**
Hibbing *18,046* **C6**
Hutchinson *11,523* **F4**
International Falls *8,325*
  B5
Inver Grove Heights
  22,477 **n12**
Lakeville *24,854* **F5**
Litchfield *6,041* **E4**
Little Falls *7,232* **E4**
Mankato *31,477* **F5**
Maple Grove *38,736*
  m12
Maplewood *30,954* **n12**
Marshall *12,023* **F3**
Minneapolis *368,383* **F5**
Minnetonka *48,370* **n12**
Montevideo *5,499* **F3**
Moorhead *32,295* **D2**
Morris *5,613* **E3**
New Brighton *22,207*
  m12
New Hope *21,853* **m12**
New Ulm *13,132* **F4**
Northfield *14,684* **F5**
Owatonna *19,386* **F5**
Pipestone *4,554* **G2**
Plymouth *50,889* **m12**
Red Wing *15,134* **F6**
Redwood Falls *4,859*
  F3
Richfield *35,710* **F5**
Rochester *70,745* **F6**
Roseville *33,485* **m12**
Saint Cloud *48,812* **E4**
Saint Louis Park *43,787*
  n12
Saint Paul *272,235* **F5**
Saint Peter *9,421* **F5**
Shoreview *24,587* **m12**
South Saint Paul *20,197*
  n12
Thief River Falls *8,010*
  B2
Virginia *9,410* **C6**
Waseca *8,385* **F5**
West Saint Paul *19,248*
  n12
White Bear Lake *24,704*
  E5
Willmar *17,531* **E3**
Winona *25,399* **F7**
Worthington *9,977* **G3**

Statute Miles 5 0 5 10   20   30   40   50
Kilometers 5 0 5 15 25 35 45 55 65

Lambert Conformal Conic Projection

Same Scale as Main Map

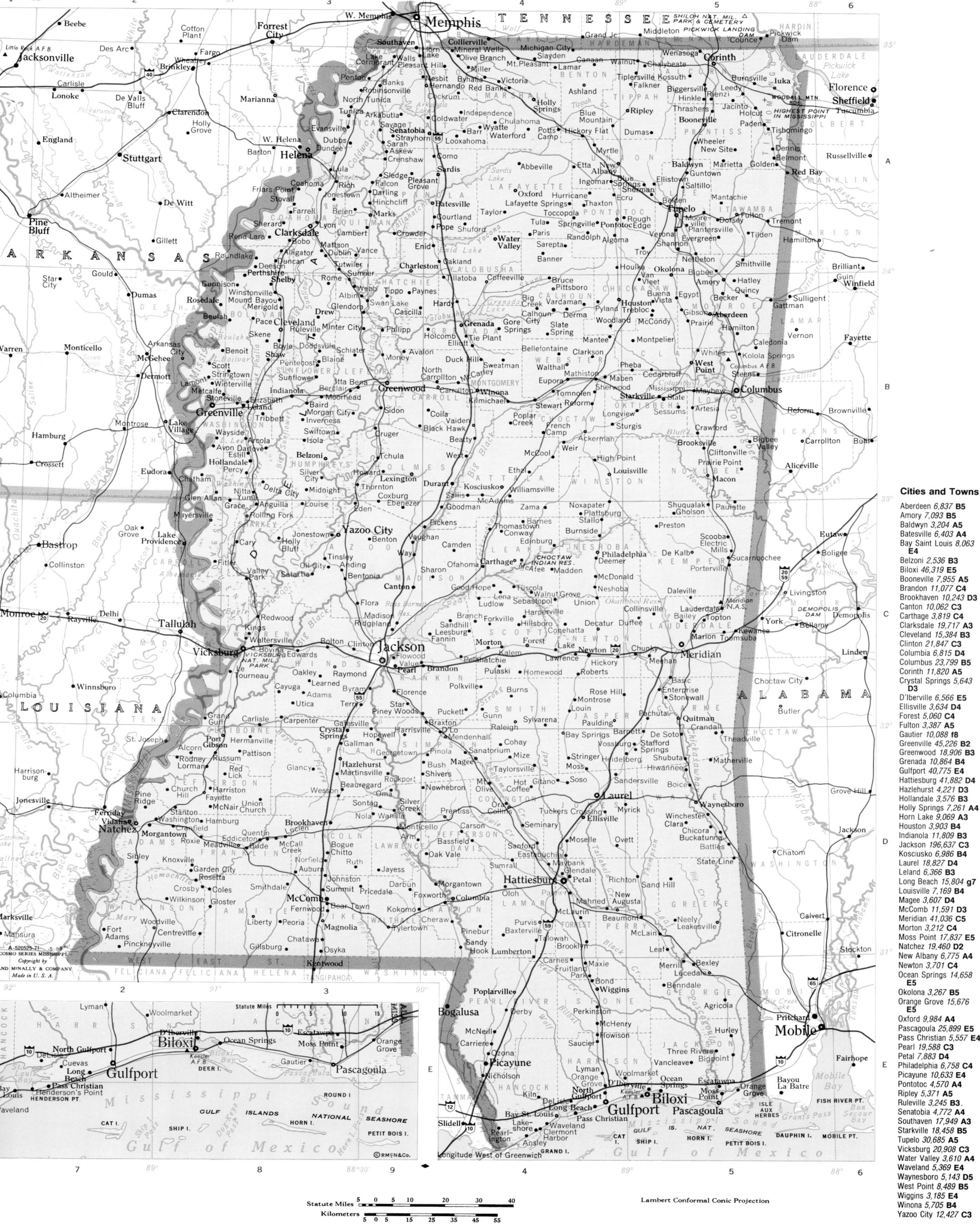

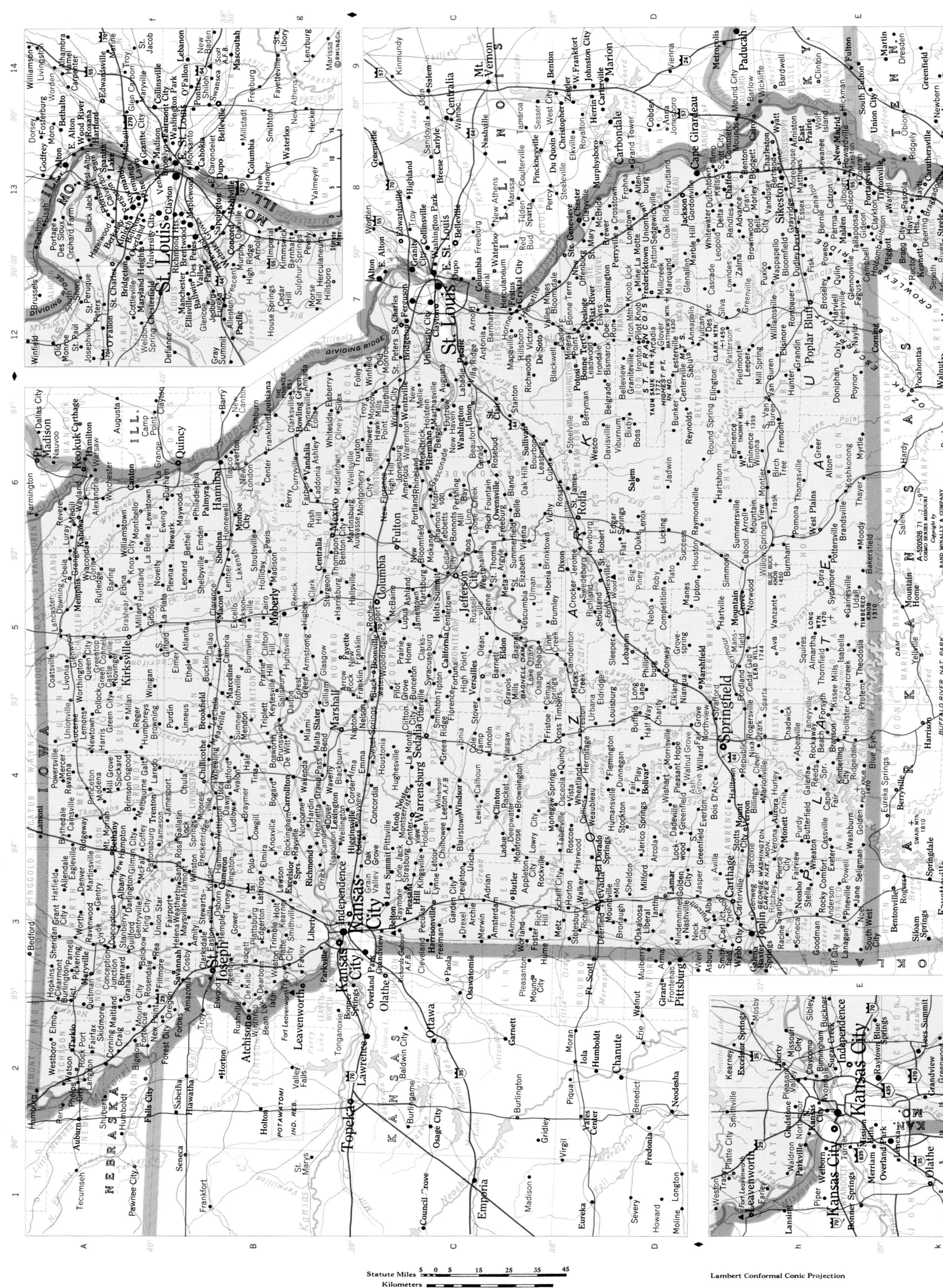

Cities and Towns

Arnold 18,828 **C7**
Aurora 6,459 **E4**
Ballwin 21,816 **f12**
Belton 18,150 **C3**
Berkeley 12,450 **f13**
Blue Springs 40,153 **h11**
Bolivar 6,845 **D4**
Boonville 7,095 **C5**
Branson 3,706 **E4**
Bridgeton 17,779 **C7**
Cape Girardeau 34,438 **D8**
Carthage 10,747 **D3**
Caruthersville 7,389 **E8**
Charleston 5,085 **E8**
Chillicothe 8,804 **B4**
Clayton 13,874 **f13**
Clinton 8,703 **C4**
Columbia 69,101 **C5**
Concord 19,859 **g13**
De Soto 5,993 **C7**
Dexter 7,559 **E8**
Eureka 4,683 **f12**
Excelsior Springs 10,354 **B3**
Farmington 11,598 **D7**
Ferguson 22,286 **C7**
Festus 8,105 **C7**
Florissant 51,206 **f13**
Fulton 10,033 **C6**
Gladstone 26,243 **h10**
Grandview 24,967 **C3**
Hannibal 18,004 **B6**
Independence 112,301 **B3**
Jackson 9,256 **D8**
Jefferson City 35,481 **C5**
Jennings 15,905 **f13**
Joplin 40,961 **D3**
Kansas City 435,146 **B3**
Kennett 10,941 **E7**
Kirksville 17,152 **A5**
Kirkwood 27,291 **f13**
Lebanon 9,983 **D5**
Lees Summit 46,418 **C3**
Liberty 20,459 **B3**
Malden 5,123 **E8**
Marshall 12,711 **B4**
Maryville 10,663 **A3**
Mehlville 27,557 **f13**
Mexico 11,290 **B6**
Moberly 12,839 **B5**
Monett 6,529 **E4**
Neosho 9,254 **E3**
Nevada 8,597 **D3**
Overland 17,987 **f13**
Perryville 6,933 **D8**
Poplar Bluff 16,996 **E7**
Raytown 30,601 **h11**
Richmond Heights 10,448 **f13**
Rolla 14,090 **D6**
Saint Charles 54,555 **C7**
Sainte Genevieve 4,411 **D7**
Saint Joseph 71,852 **B3**
Saint Louis 396,685 **C7**
Saint Peters 45,779 **C7**
Sappington 10,917 **f13**
Sedalia 19,800 **C4**
Sikeston 17,641 **E8**
Spanish Lake 20,322 **f13**
Springfield 140,494 **D4**
Sullivan 5,661 **C6**
Trenton 6,129 **A4**
University City 40,087 **C7**
Warrensburg 15,244 **C4**
Washington 10,704 **C6**
Webster Groves 22,987 **f13**
West Plains 8,913 **E6**

Statute Miles 5 0 5   15   25   35   45
Kilometers 5 0 5   15   25   35   45   55   65

Lambert Conformal Conic Projection

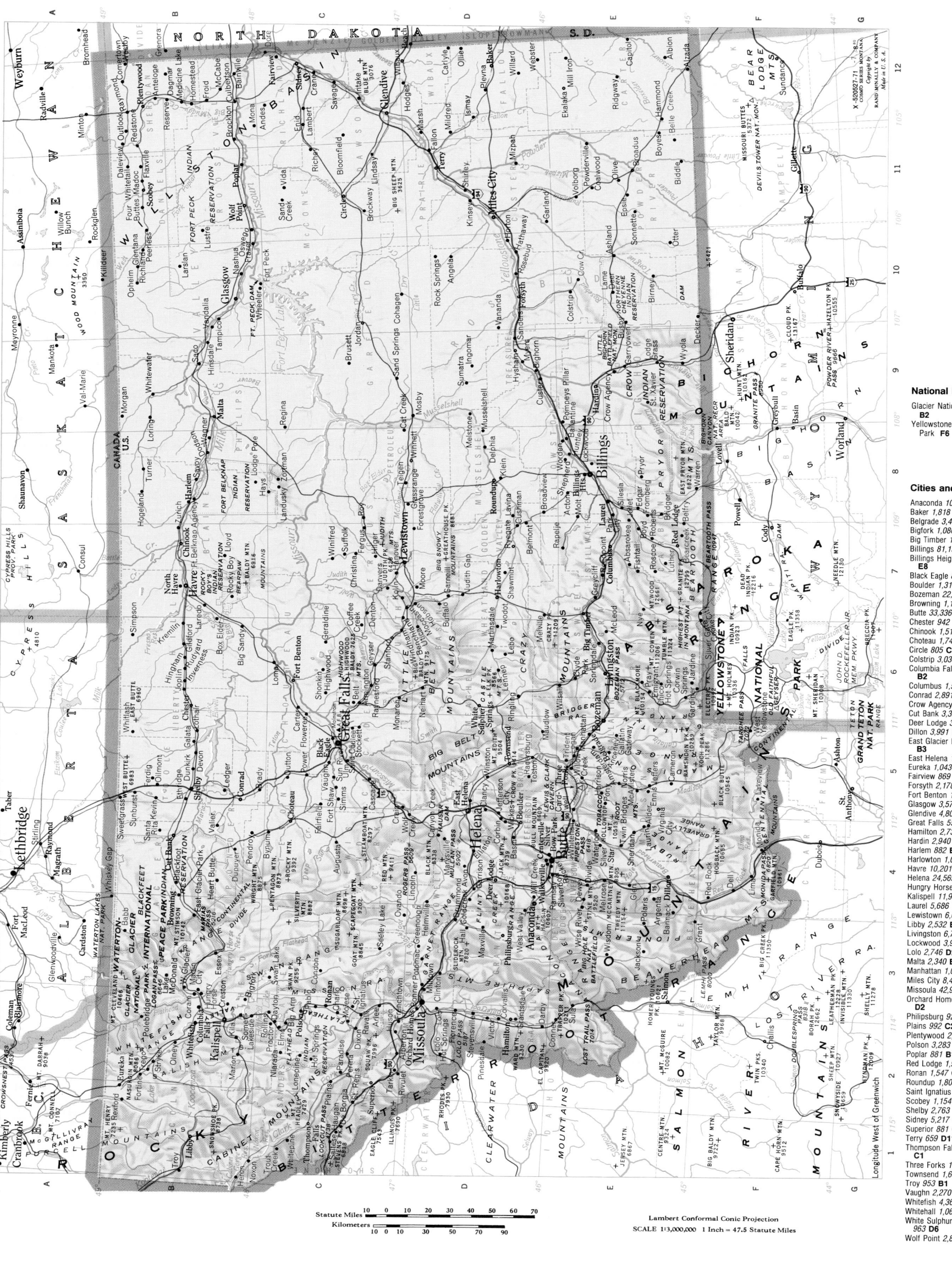

National Parks

Glacier National Park **B2**

Yellowstone National Park **F6**

Cities and Towns

Anaconda *10,278* **D4**
Baker *1,818* **D12**
Belgrade *3,411* **E5**
Bigfork *1,080* **B2**
Big Timber *1,557* **E7**
Billings *81,151* **E8**
Billings Heights *8,480* **E8**
Black Eagle *850* **C5**
Boulder *1,316* **D4**
Bozeman *22,660* **E5**
Browning *1,170* **B3**
Butte *33,336* **E4**
Chester *942* **B6**
Chinook *1,512* **B7**
Choteau *1,741* **C4**
Circle *805* **C11**
Colstrip *3,035* **E10**
Columbia Falls *2,942* **B2**
Columbus *1,573* **E7**
Conrad *2,891* **B5**
Crow Agency *1,446* **E9**
Cut Bank *3,329* **B4**
Deer Lodge *3,378* **D4**
Dillon *3,991* **E4**
East Glacier Park *326* **B3**
East Helena *1,538* **D5**
Eureka *1,043* **B1**
Fairview *869* **C12**
Forsyth *2,178* **D10**
Fort Benton *1,660* **C6**
Glasgow *3,572* **B10**
Glendive *4,802* **C12**
Great Falls *55,097* **C5**
Hamilton *2,737* **D2**
Hardin *2,940* **E9**
Harlem *882* **B8**
Harlowton *1,049* **D7**
Havre *10,201* **B7**
Helena *24,569* **D4**
Hungry Horse *940* **B2**
Kalispell *11,917* **B2**
Laurel *5,686* **E8**
Lewistown *6,051* **C7**
Libby *2,532* **B1**
Livingston *6,701* **E6**
Lockwood *3,967* **E8**
Lolo *2,746* **D2**
Malta *2,340* **B9**
Manhattan *1,034* **E5**
Miles City *8,461* **D11**
Missoula *42,918* **D2**
Orchard Homes *10,317* **D2**
Philipsburg *925* **D3**
Plains *992* **C2**
Plentywood *2,136* **B12**
Polson *3,283* **C2**
Poplar *881* **B11**
Red Lodge *1,958* **E7**
Ronan *1,547* **C2**
Roundup *1,808* **D8**
Saint Ignatius *778* **C2**
Scobey *1,154* **B11**
Shelby *2,763* **B5**
Sidney *5,217* **C12**
Superior *881* **C2**
Terry *659* **D11**
Thompson Falls *1,319* **C1**
Three Forks *1,203* **E5**
Townsend *1,635* **D5**
Troy *953* **B1**
Vaughn *2,270* **C5**
Whitefish *4,368* **B2**
Whitehall *1,067* **E4**
White Sulphur Springs *963* **D6**
Wolf Point *2,880* **B11**

NEBRASKA

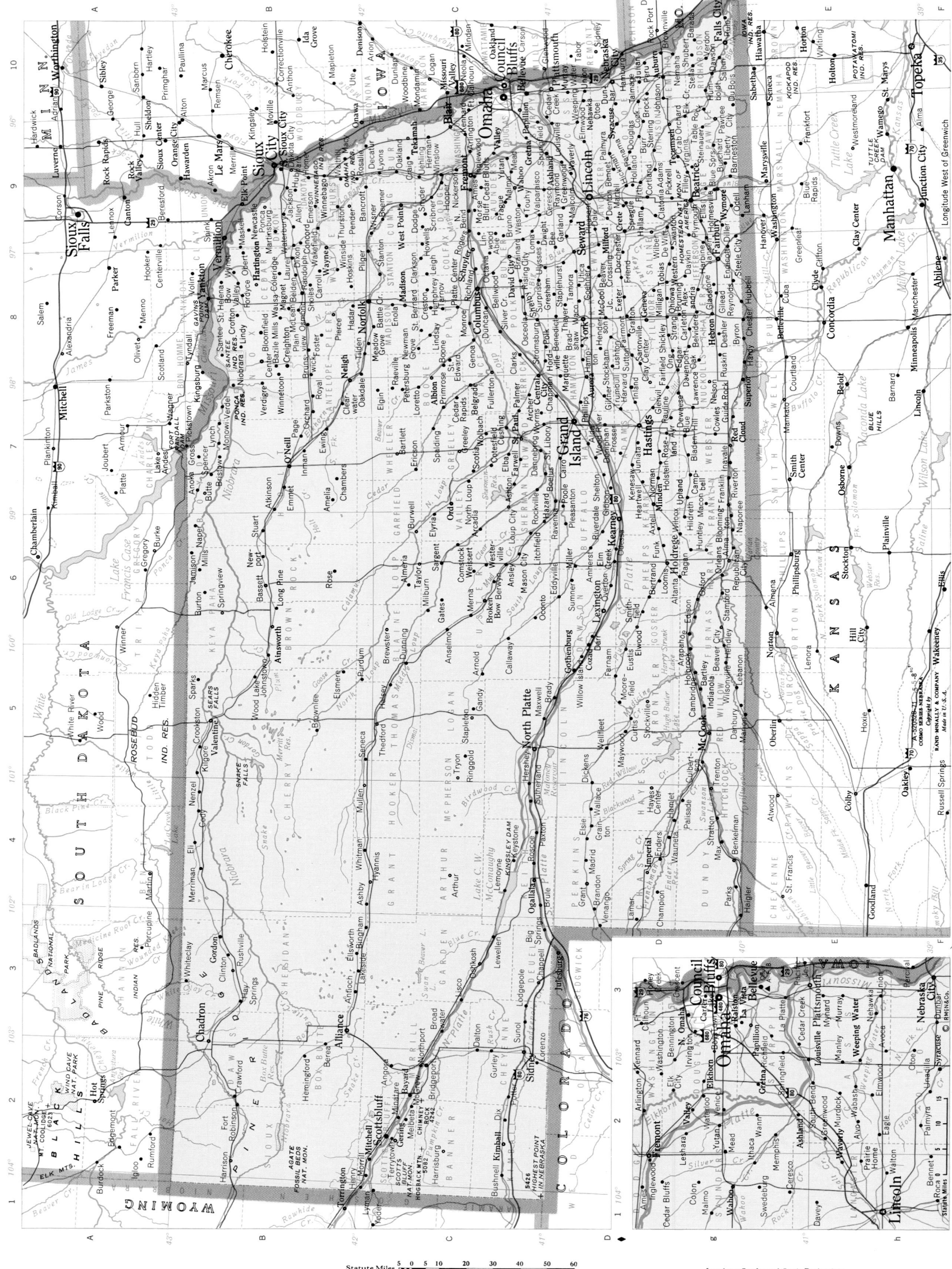

Statute Miles

Kilometers

Lambert Conformal Conic Projection

254

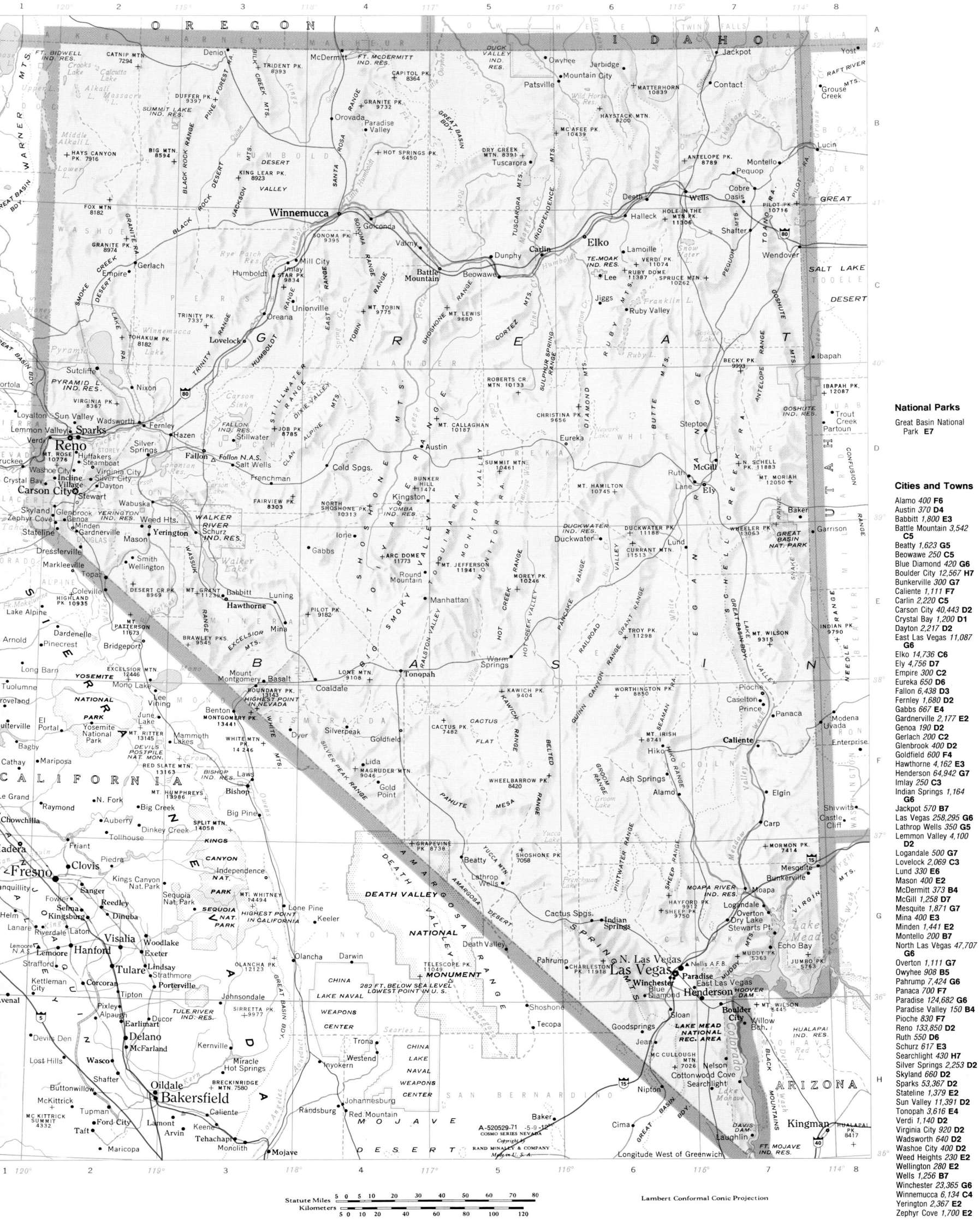

NEW HAMPSHIRE

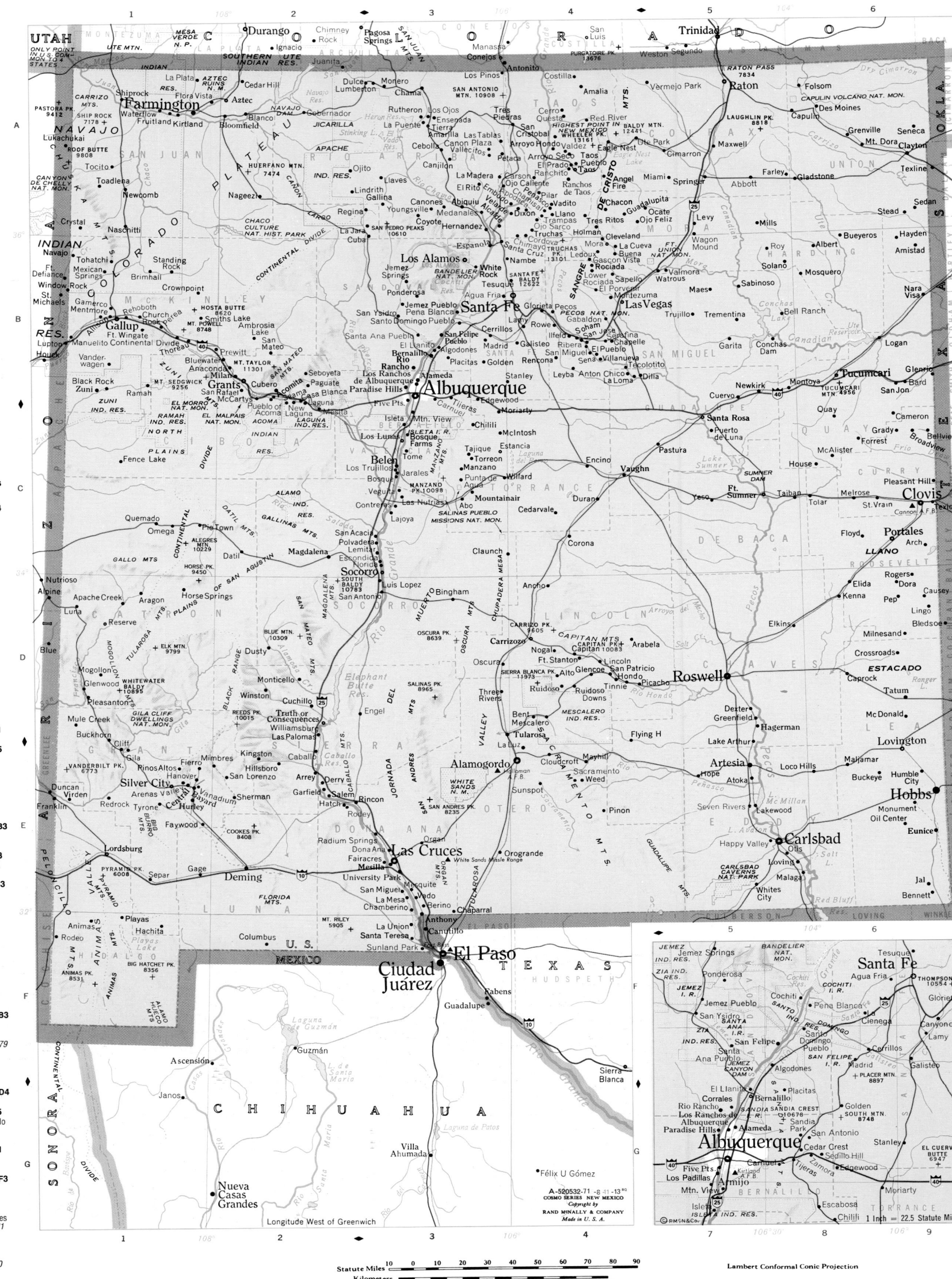

Statute Miles 5 0 5 10 20 30 40
Kilometers 5 0 5 15 25 35 45 55

Lambert Conformal Conic Projection

Cities and Towns

Albany *101,082* C7
Amherst *45,600* C2
Amityville *9,286* E7
Amsterdam *20,714* C6
Auburn *31,258* C4
Batavia *16,310* C2
Binghamton *53,008* C5
Brentwood *45,218* E7
Brighton *34,455* B3
Buffalo *328,123* C2
Centereach *26,720* n15
Central Islip *26,028* n15
Cheektowaga *84,387* C2
Cooperstown *2,180* C6
Corning *11,938* C3
Cortland *19,801* C4
Deer Park *28,840* n15
Dunkirk *13,989* C1
Elmira *33,724* C4
Elmont *28,612* k13
Freeport *39,894* n15
Fulton *12,929* B4
Geneseo *7,187* C3
Geneva *14,143* C4
Glens Falls *15,023* B7
Gloversville *16,656* B6
Greece *15,632* B3
Hempstead *49,453* n15
Hicksville *40,174* E7
Hornell *9,877* C3
Hudson *8,034* C7
Hyde Park *2,550* D7
Irondequoit *52,322* B3
Ithaca *29,541* C4
Jamestown *34,681* C1
Kingston *23,095* D6
Lackawanna *20,585* C2
Lake Placid *2,485* A7
Levittown *53,286* E7
Lockport *24,426* B2
Long Beach *33,510* E7
Massena *11,719* f10
Middletown *24,160* D6
Mount Vernon *67,153*
 h13
Newburgh *26,454* D6
New City *33,673* D6
New Rochelle *67,265*
 E7
New York *7,322,554* E7
Niagara Falls *61,840* B1
North Tonawanda
 34,989 B2
Ogdensburg *13,521* f9
Olean *16,946* C2
Oneonta *13,954* C5
Ossining *22,582* D7
Oswego *19,195* B4
Palmyra *3,566* B3
Plattsburgh *21,255* f11
Port Chester *24,728* E7
Poughkeepsie *28,844*
 D7
Rochester *231,636* B3
Rome *44,350* B5
Rotterdam *21,228* C6
Saratoga Springs
 25,001 B7
Schenectady *65,566* C7
Syracuse *163,860* B4
Ticonderoga *2,770* B7
Troy *54,269* C7
Utica *68,637* B5
Valley Stream *33,946*
 n15
Watertown *29,429* B5
West Point *8,024* D7
West Seneca *47,866* C2
White Plains *48,718* D7
Yonkers *188,082* E7

259

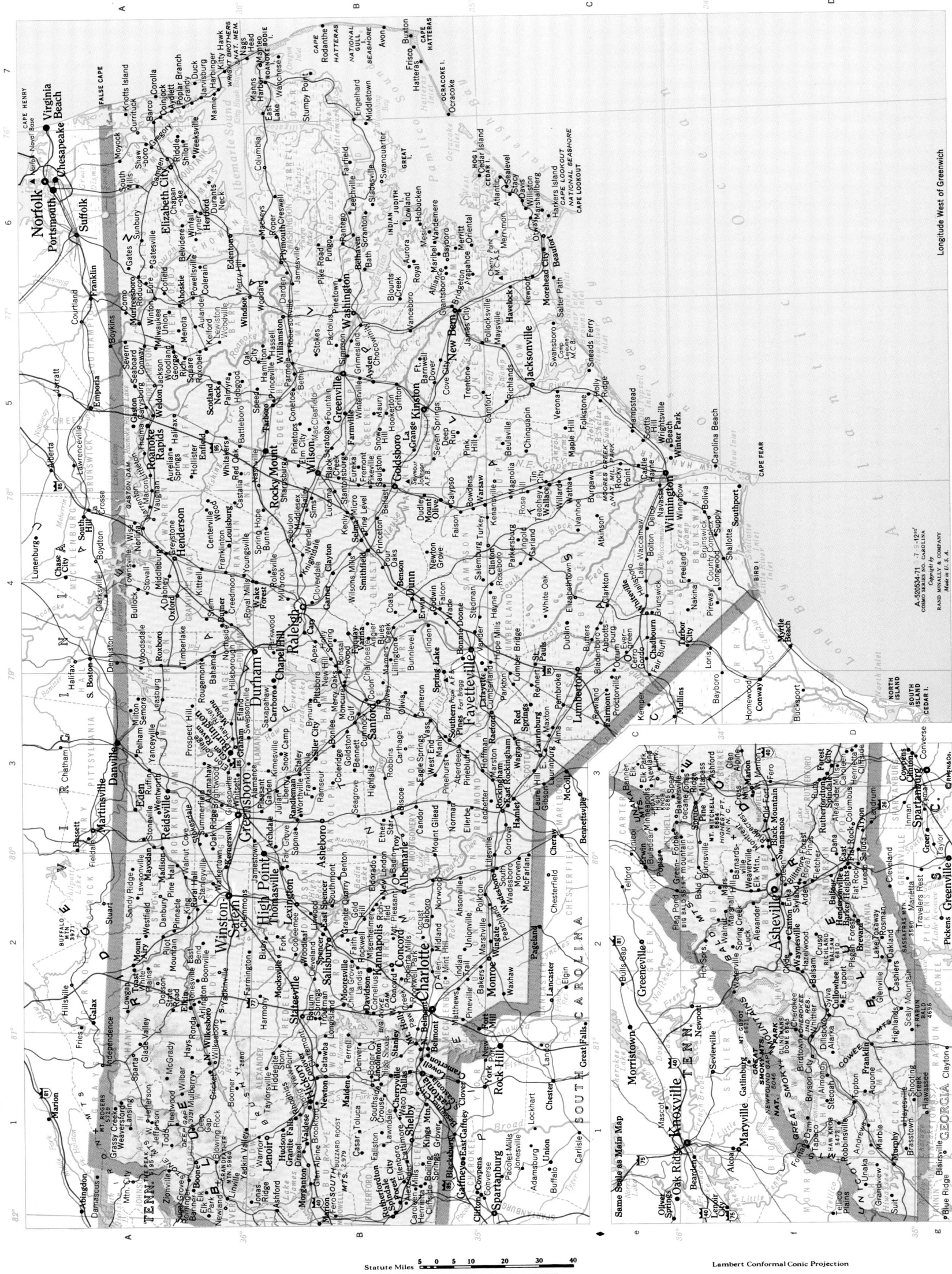

Statute Miles
Kilometers

Lambert Conformal Conic Projection

National Parks

Theodore Roosevelt
National Park (South
Unit) C2
Theodore Roosevelt
National Park (North
Unit) B2

Cities and Towns

Ashley 1,052 C6
Beach 1,205 C1
Belcourt 2,458 A6
Belfield 887 C2
Beulah 3,363 B4
Bismarck 49,256 C5
Bottineau 2,598 A5
Bowman 1,741 C2
Cando 1,564 A6
Carrington 2,267 B6
Casselton 1,601 C8
Cavalier 1,508 A8
Center 826 B4
Cooperstown 1,247 B7
Crosby 1,312 A2
Devils Lake 7,782 A7
Dickinson 16,097 C3
Drayton 961 A8
Edgeley 680 C7
Elgin 765 C4
Ellendale 1,798 C7
Enderlin 997 C8
Fargo 74,111 C9
Garrison 1,530 B4
Glen Ullin 927 C4
Grafton 4,840 A8
Grand Forks 49,425 B8
Hankinson 1,038 C9
Harvey 2,263 B6
Hazen 2,818 B4
Hebron 888 C3
Hettinger 1,574 D3
Hillsboro 1,488 B8
Jamestown 15,571 C6
Kenmare 1,214 A3
Lakota 898 A7
La Moure 970 C7
Langdon 2,241 A7
Larimore 1,464 B8
Lidgerwood 799 C8
Linton 1,410 C5
Lisbon 2,177 C8
Mandan 15,177 C5
Mayville 2,092 B8
Minot 34,544 A4
Mohall 931 A4
Mott 1,019 C3
Napoleon 930 C6
New Rockford 1,604 B6
New Salem 909 C4
New Town 1,388 B3
Northwood 1,166 B8
Oakes 1,775 C7
Park River 1,725 A8
Parshall 943 B3
Rolla 1,286 A6
Rugby 2,909 A6
Stanley 1,371 A3
Steele 762 C6
Surrey 856 A4
Tioga 1,278 A3
Towner 669 A5
Turtle Lake 681 B5
Underwood 976 B4
Valley City 7,163 C8
Velva 968 A5
Wahpeton 8,751 C9
Walhalla 1,131 A8
Washburn 1,506 B5
Watford City 1,784 B2
West Fargo 12,287 C9
Williston 13,131 A2
Wilton 728 B5
Wishek 1,171 C6

OHIO

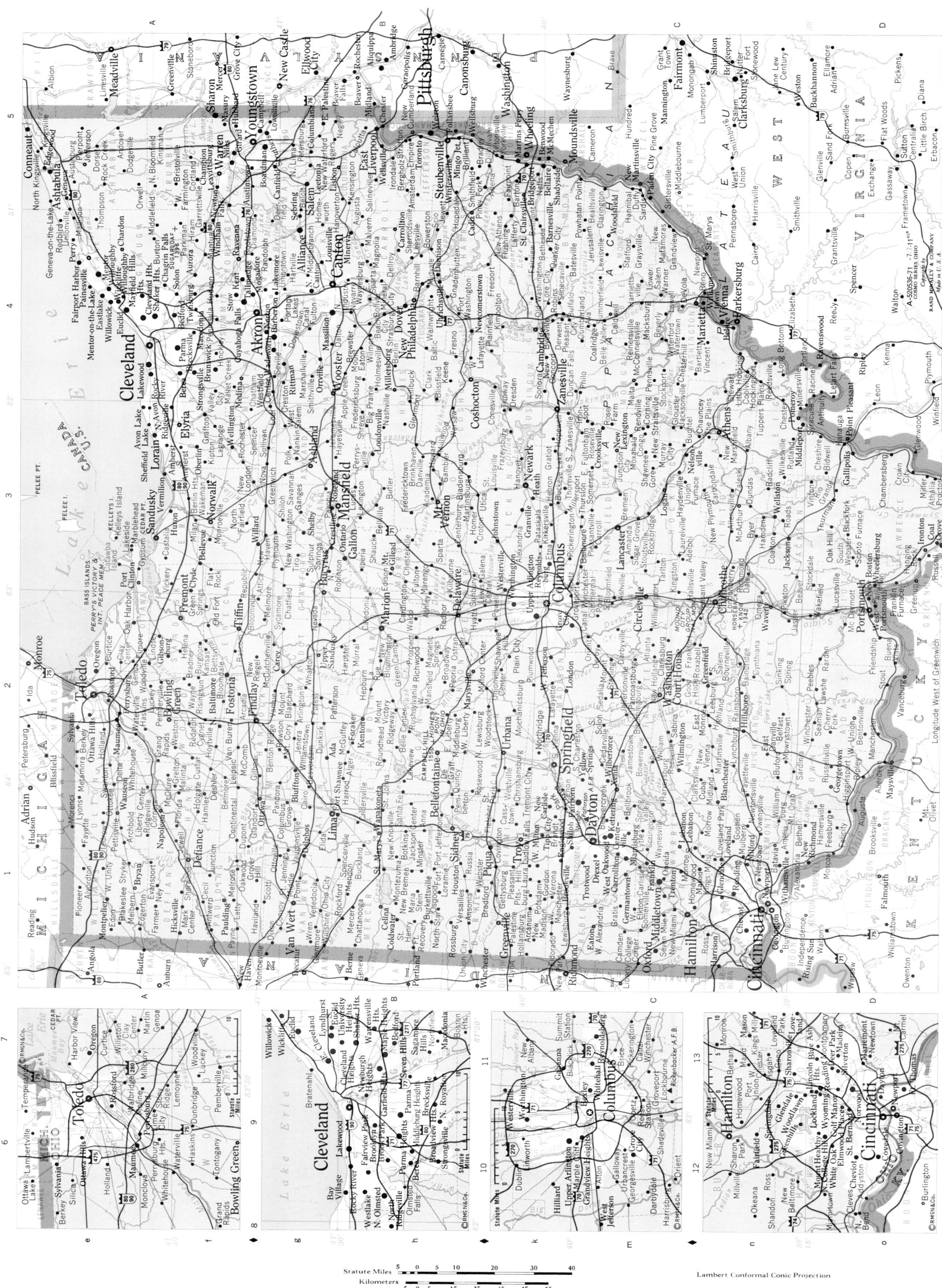

Statute Miles

Kilometers

Lambert Conformal Conic Projection

Statute Miles 5 0   5   10   20   30   40
Kilometers 5 0 5 15   25   35   45   55

Lambert Conformal Conic Projection

OREGON

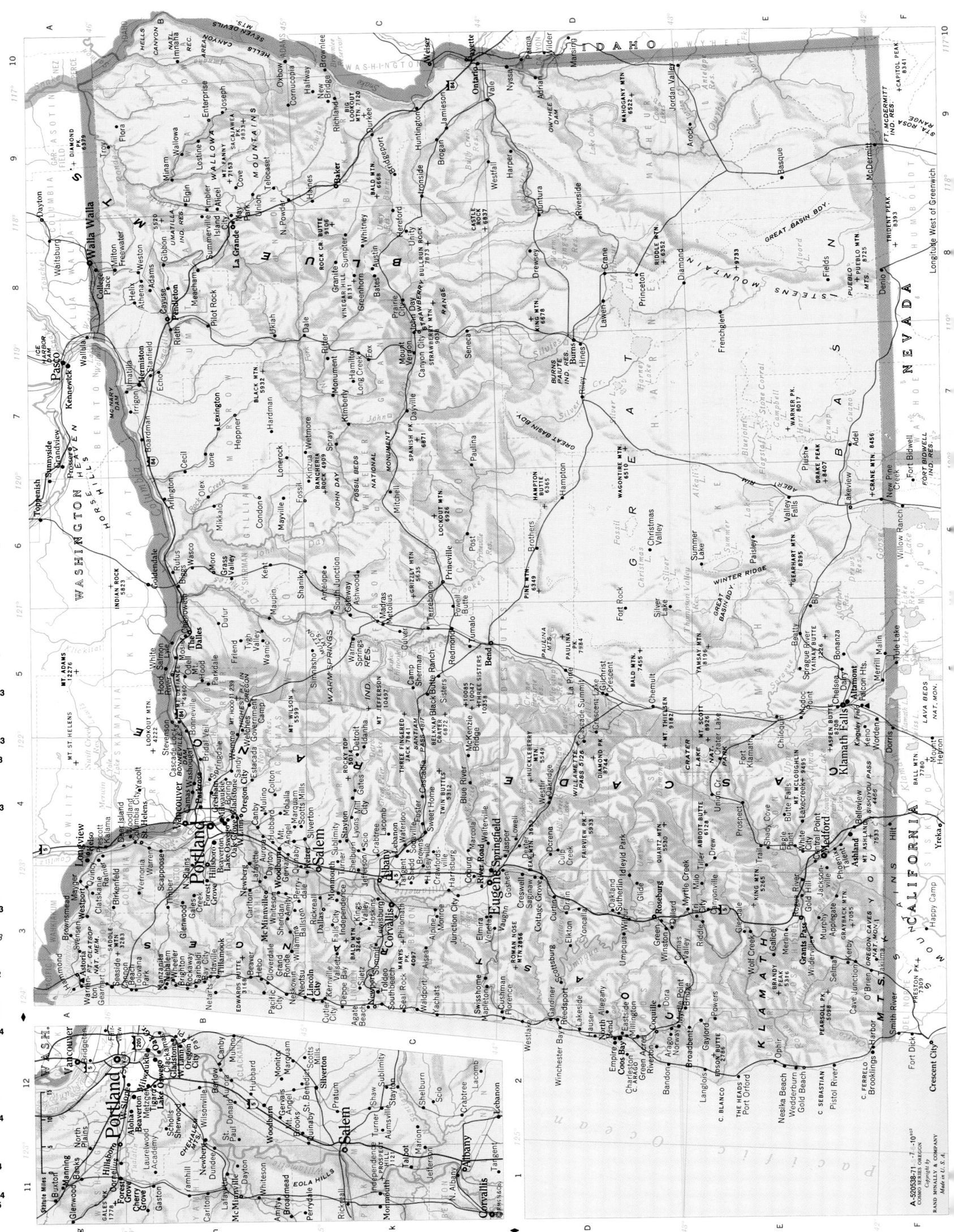

Lambert Conformal Conic Projection
SCALE 1:2,329,000 1 Inch = 37 Statute Miles

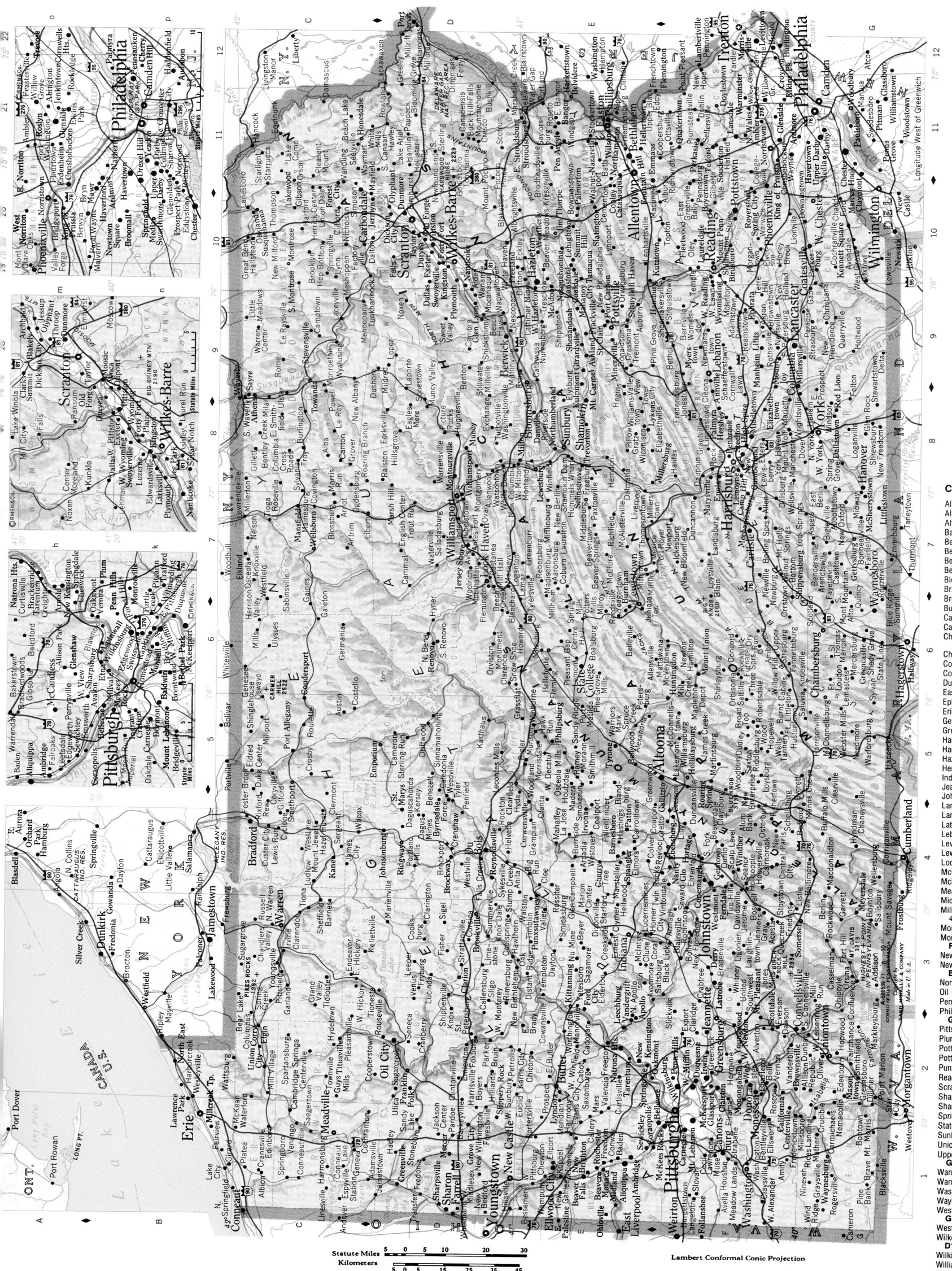

Statute Miles 5 0 5 10 20 30
Kilometers 5 0 5 15 25 35 45

Lambert Conformal Conic Projection

265

RHODE ISLAND

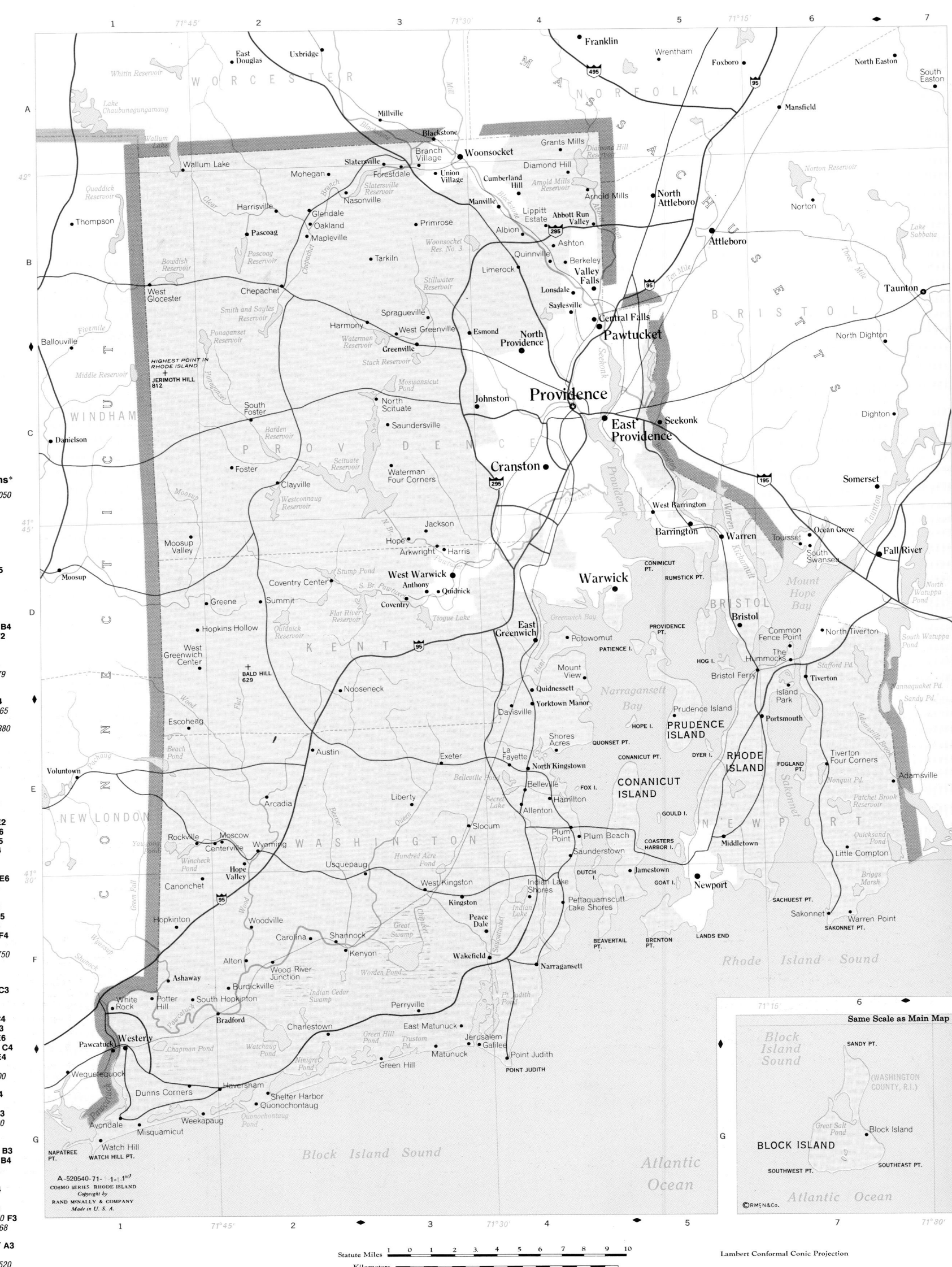

*Populations are for localities, not incorporated towns.

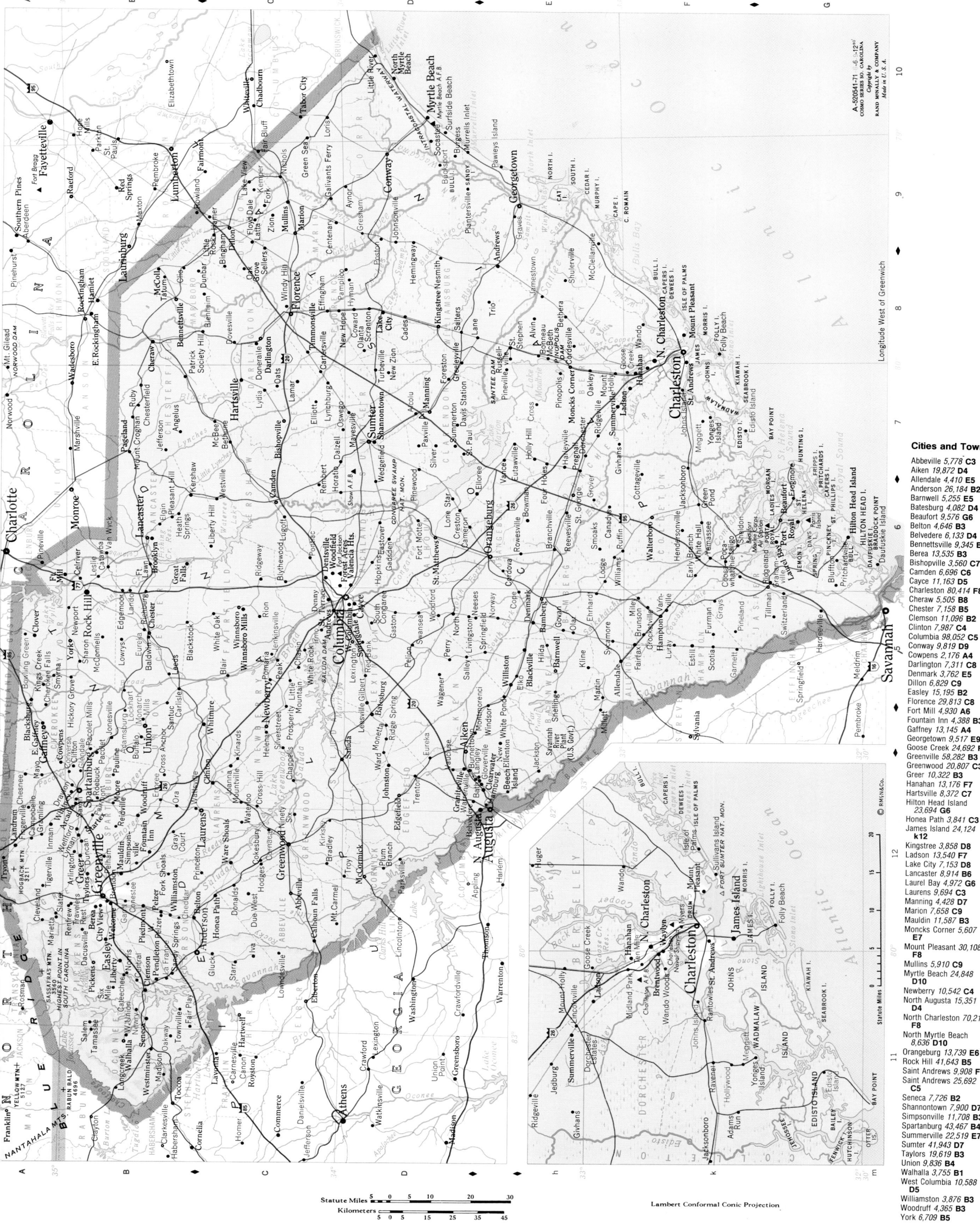

A-500541-71 :6 .-12nd
COSMO SERIES SO. CAROLINA
Myrtle Beach A.F.B.
Copyright by
RAND McNALLY & COMPANY
Made in U. S. A.

Cities and Towns

Abbeville 5,778 **C3**
Aiken 19,872 **D4**
Allendale 4,410 **E5**
Anderson 26,184 **B2**
Barnwell 5,255 **E5**
Batesburg 4,082 **D4**
Beaufort 9,576 **G6**
Belton 4,646 **B3**
Belvedere 6,133 **D4**
Bennettsville 9,345 **B8**
Berea 13,535 **B3**
Bishopville 3,560 **C7**
Camden 6,696 **C6**
Cayce 11,163 **D5**
Charleston 80,414 **F8**
Cheraw 5,505 **B8**
Chester 7,158 **B5**
Clemson 11,096 **B2**
Clinton 7,987 **C4**
Columbia 98,052 **C5**
Conway 9,819 **D9**
Cowpens 2,176 **A4**
Darlington 7,311 **C8**
Denmark 3,762 **E5**
Dillon 6,829 **C9**
Easley 15,195 **B2**
Florence 29,813 **C8**
Fort Mill 4,930 **A6**
Fountain Inn 4,388 **B3**
Gaffney 13,145 **A4**
Georgetown 9,517 **E9**
Goose Creek 24,692 **F7**
Greenville 58,282 **B3**
Greenwood 20,807 **C3**
Greer 10,322 **B3**
Hanahan 13,176 **F7**
Hartsville 8,372 **C7**
Hilton Head Island
23,694 **G6**
Honea Path 3,841 **C3**
James Island 24,124
k12
Kingstree 3,858 **D8**
Ladson 13,540 **F7**
Lake City 7,153 **D8**
Lancaster 8,914 **B6**
Laurel Bay 4,972 **G6**
Laurens 9,694 **C3**
Manning 4,428 **D7**
Marion 7,658 **C9**
Mauldin 11,587 **B3**
Moncks Corner 5,607
E7
Mount Pleasant 30,108
F8
Mullins 5,910 **C9**
Myrtle Beach 24,848
D10
Newberry 10,542 **C4**
North Augusta 15,351
D4
North Charleston 70,218
F8
North Myrtle Beach
8,636 **D10**
Orangeburg 13,739 **E6**
Rock Hill 41,643 **B5**
Saint Andrews 9,908 **F7**
Saint Andrews 25,692
C5
Seneca 7,726 **B2**
Shannontown 7,900 **D7**
Simpsonville 11,708 **B3**
Spartanburg 43,467 **B4**
Summerville 22,519 **E7**
Sumter 41,943 **D7**
Taylors 19,619 **B3**
Union 9,836 **B4**
Walhalla 3,755 **B1**
West Columbia 10,588
D5
Williamston 3,876 **B3**
Woodruff 4,365 **B3**
York 6,709 **B5**

Statute Miles 5 0 5 10 20 30
Kilometers 5 0 5 15 25 35 45

Lambert Conformal Conic Projection

© RM&Co.

SOUTH DAKOTA

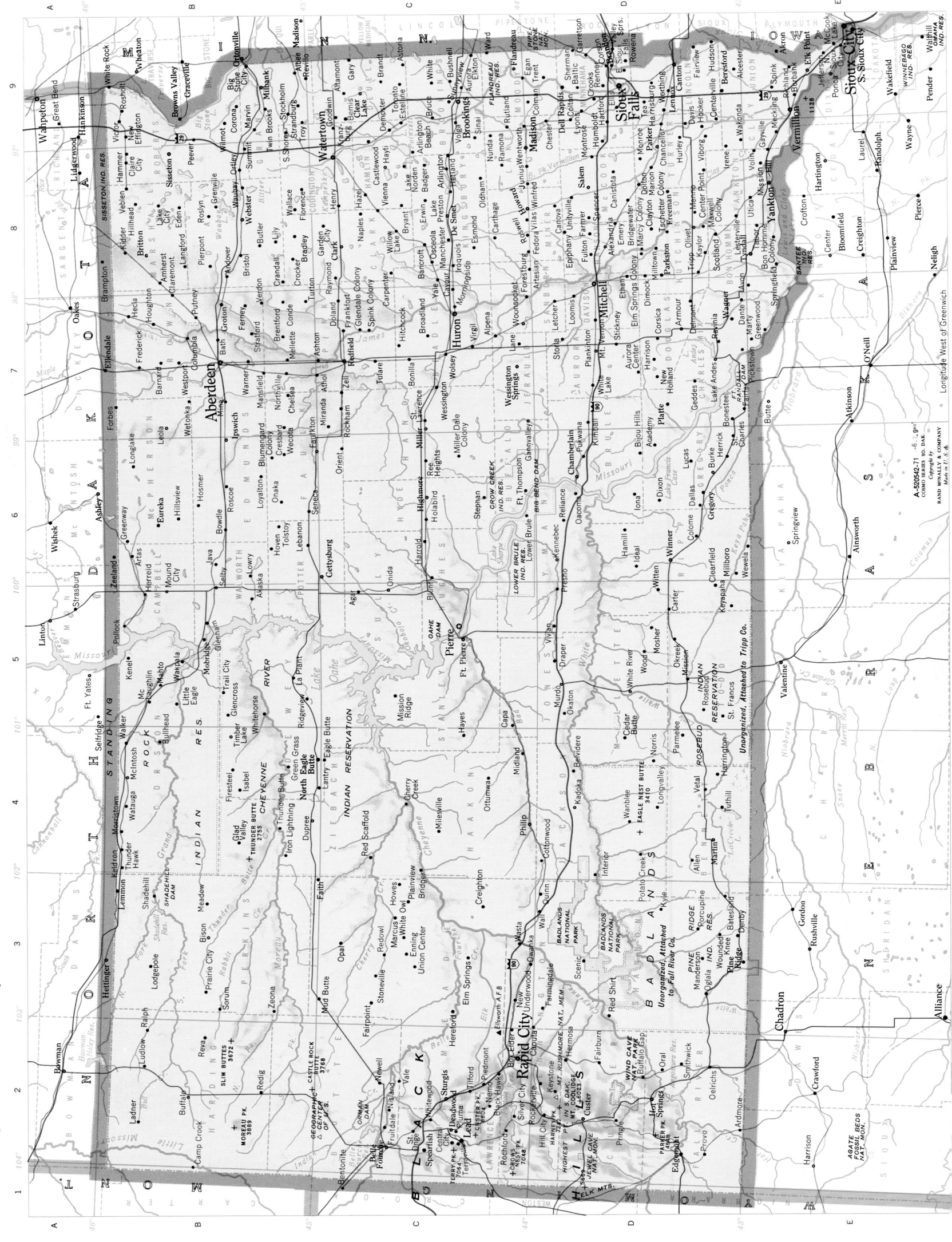

Statute Miles   5 0 5 10   20   30   40   50   60
Kilometers   5 0 5 15   25   35   45   55   65   75

Lambert Conformal Conic Projection

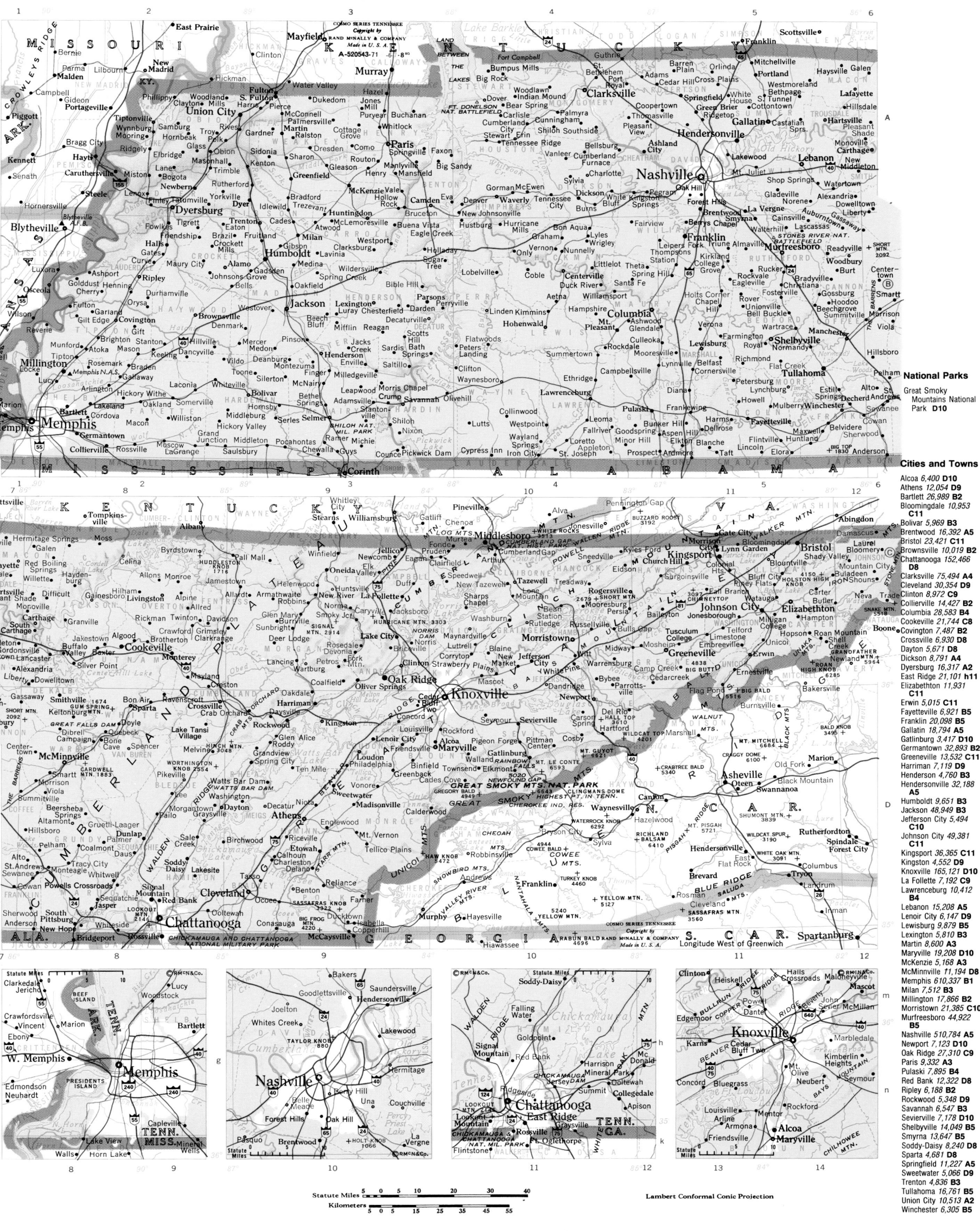

National Parks

Great Smoky
  Mountains National
  Park **D10**

Cities and Towns

Alcoa 6,400 **D10**
Athens 12,054 **D9**
Bartlett 26,989 **B2**
Bloomingdale 10,953
  C11
Bolivar 5,969 **B3**
Brentwood 16,392 **A5**
Bristol 23,421 **C11**
Brownsville 10,019 **B2**
Chattanooga 152,466
  D8
Clarksville 75,494 **A4**
Cleveland 30,354 **D9**
Clinton 8,972 **C9**
Collierville 14,427 **B2**
Columbia 28,583 **B4**
Cookeville 21,744 **C8**
Covington 7,487 **B2**
Crossville 6,930 **D8**
Dayton 5,671 **D8**
Dickson 8,791 **A4**
Dyersburg 16,317 **A2**
East Ridge 21,101 **h11**
Elizabethton 11,931
  C11
Erwin 5,015 **C11**
Fayetteville 6,921 **B5**
Franklin 20,098 **B5**
Gallatin 18,794 **A5**
Gatlinburg 3,417 **D10**
Germantown 32,893 **B2**
Greeneville 13,532 **C11**
Harriman 7,119 **D9**
Henderson 4,760 **B3**
Hendersonville 32,188
  A5
Humboldt 9,651 **B3**
Jackson 48,949 **B3**
Jefferson City 5,494
  C10
Johnson City 49,381
  C11
Kingsport 36,365 **C11**
Kingston 4,552 **D9**
Knoxville 165,121 **D10**
La Follette 7,192 **C9**
Lawrenceburg 10,412
  B4
Lebanon 15,208 **A5**
Lenoir City 6,147 **D9**
Lewisburg 9,879 **B5**
Lexington 5,810 **B3**
Martin 8,600 **A3**
Maryville 19,208 **D10**
McKenzie 5,168 **A3**
McMinnville 11,194 **D8**
Memphis 610,337 **B1**
Milan 7,512 **B3**
Millington 17,866 **B2**
Morristown 21,385 **C10**
Murfreesboro 44,922
  B5
Nashville 510,784 **A5**
Newport 7,123 **D10**
Oak Ridge 27,310 **C9**
Paris 9,332 **A3**
Pulaski 7,895 **B4**
Red Bank 12,322 **D8**
Ripley 6,188 **B2**
Rockwood 5,348 **D9**
Savannah 6,547 **B3**
Sevierville 7,178 **D9**
Shelbyville 14,049 **B5**
Smyrna 13,647 **B5**
Soddy-Daisy 8,240 **D8**
Sparta 4,681 **D8**
Springfield 11,227 **A5**
Sweetwater 5,066 **D9**
Trenton 4,836 **B3**
Tullahoma 16,761 **B5**
Union City 10,513 **A2**
Winchester 6,305 **B5**

National Parks

Big Bend National Park
  E1
Guadalupe Mountains
  National Park o12

Cities and Towns

Abilene 106,654 C3
Alice 19,788 F3
Amarillo 157,615 B2
Arlington 261,721 n9
Austin 465,622 D4
Bay City 18,170 E5
Baytown 63,850 E5
Beaumont 114,323 D5
Big Spring 23,093 C2
Borger 15,675 B2
Brownsville 98,962 G4
Brownwood 18,387 D3
Bryan 55,002 D4
Cleburne 22,205 C4
College Station 52,456
  D4
Conroe 27,610 D5
Copperas Cove 24,079
  D4
Corpus Christi 257,453
  F4
Corsicana 22,911 C4
Dallas 1,006,877 C4
Del Rio 30,705 E2
Denison 21,505 C4
Denton 66,270 C4
Eagle Pass 20,651 E2
Edinburg 29,885 F3
El Paso 515,342 o11
Fort Worth 447,619 C4
Galveston 59,070 E5
Garland 180,650 n10
Grand Prairie 99,616
  n10
Greenville 23,071 C4
Harlingen 48,735 F4
Hereford 14,745 B1
Houston 1,630,553 E5
Huntsville 27,925 D5
Irving 155,037 n10
Kerrville 17,384 D3
Killeen 63,535 D4
Kingsville 25,276 F4
Lake Lake 22,776
  E5
Laredo 122,899 F3
Longview 70,311 C5
Lubbock 186,206 C2
Lufkin 30,206 D5
Marshall 23,682 C5
McAllen 84,021 F3
Mesquite 101,484 n10
Midland 89,443 D1
Mineral Wells 14,870
  C3
Nacogdoches 30,872
  D5
New Braunfels 27,334
  E3
Odessa 89,699 D1
Orange 19,381 D6
Palestine 18,042 D5
Pampa 19,959 B2
Paris 24,699 C5
Pasadena 119,363 r14
Pecos 12,069 D1
Plainview 21,700 B2
Port Arthur 58,724 E6
Richardson 74,840 n10
San Angelo 84,474 D2
San Antonio 935,933
  E3
San Benito 20,125 F4
San Marcos 28,743 E4
Sherman 31,601 C4
Temple 46,109 D4
Texarkana 31,656 C5
Texas City 40,822 E5
Tyler 75,450 C5
Uvalde 14,729 E3
Victoria 55,076 E4
Waco 103,590 D4
Waxahachie 18,168 C4
Wichita Falls 96,259 C3

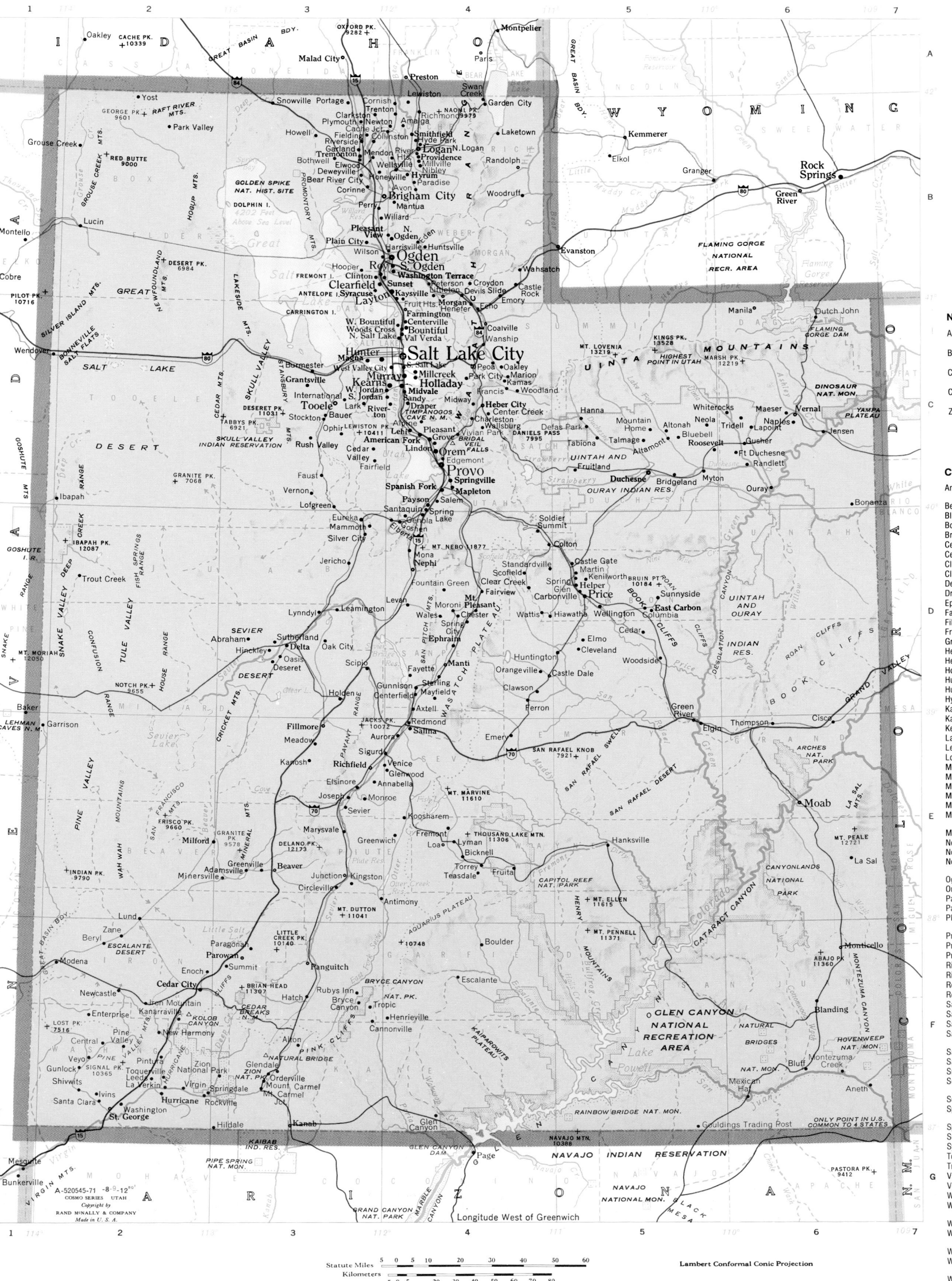

Arches National Park **E6**
Bryce Canyon National Park **F3**
Canyonlands National Park **E6**
Capitol Reef National Park **E4**
Zion National Park **F3**

Cities and Towns

American Fork *15,696* **C4**
Beaver *1,998* **E3**
Blanding *3,162* **F6**
Bountiful *36,659* **C4**
Brigham City *15,644* **B3**
Cedar City *13,443* **F2**
Centerville *11,500* **C4**
Clearfield *21,435* **B3**
Clinton *7,945* **B3**
Delta *2,998* **D3**
Draper *7,257* **C4**
Ephraim *3,363* **D4**
Farmington *9,028* **C4**
Fillmore *1,956* **E3**
Fruit Heights *3,900* **B4**
Grantsville *4,500* **C3**
Heber City *4,782* **C4**
Helper *2,148* **D5**
Holladay *26,200* **C4**
Huntington *1,875* **D5**
Hurricane *3,915* **F2**
Hyrum *4,829* **B4**
Kanab *3,289* **F3**
Kaysville *13,961* **B4**
Kearns *28,374* **C4**
Layton *41,784* **B4**
Lehi *8,475* **C4**
Logan *32,762* **B4**
Magna *17,829* **C3**
Manti *2,268* **D4**
Midvale *11,886* **C4**
Moab *3,971* **E6**
Monticello *1,806* **F6**
Mount Pleasant *2,092* **D4**
Murray *31,282* **C4**
Nephi *3,515* **D4**
North Ogden *11,668* **B4**
North Salt Lake *6,474* **C4**
Ogden *63,909* **B4**
Orem *67,561* **C4**
Panguitch *1,444* **F3**
Payson *9,510* **C4**
Pleasant Grove *13,476* **C4**
Price *8,712* **D5**
Providence *3,344* **B4**
Provo *86,835* **C4**
Richfield *5,593* **E3**
Riverton *11,261* **C4**
Roosevelt *3,915* **C5**
Roy *24,603* **B3**
Saint George *28,502* **F2**
Salem *2,284* **C4**
Salina *1,943* **E4**
Salt Lake City *159,936* **C4**
Sandy *75,058* **C4**
Santaquin *2,386* **D4**
Smithfield *5,566* **B4**
South Jordan *12,220* **C3**
South Ogden *12,105* **B4**
Spanish Fork *11,272* **C4**
Springville *13,950* **C4**
Sunset *5,128* **B4**
Syracuse *4,658* **B3**
Tooele *13,887* **C3**
Tremonton *4,264* **B3**
Val Verda *3,712* **C4**
Vernal *6,644* **C6**
Washington *4,198* **F2**
Washington Terrace *8,189* **B4**
Wendover *1,127* **C1**
West Bountiful *4,477* **C4**
West Jordan *42,892* **C4**
West Valley City *86,976* **C4**
Woods Cross *5,384* **C4**

VERMONT

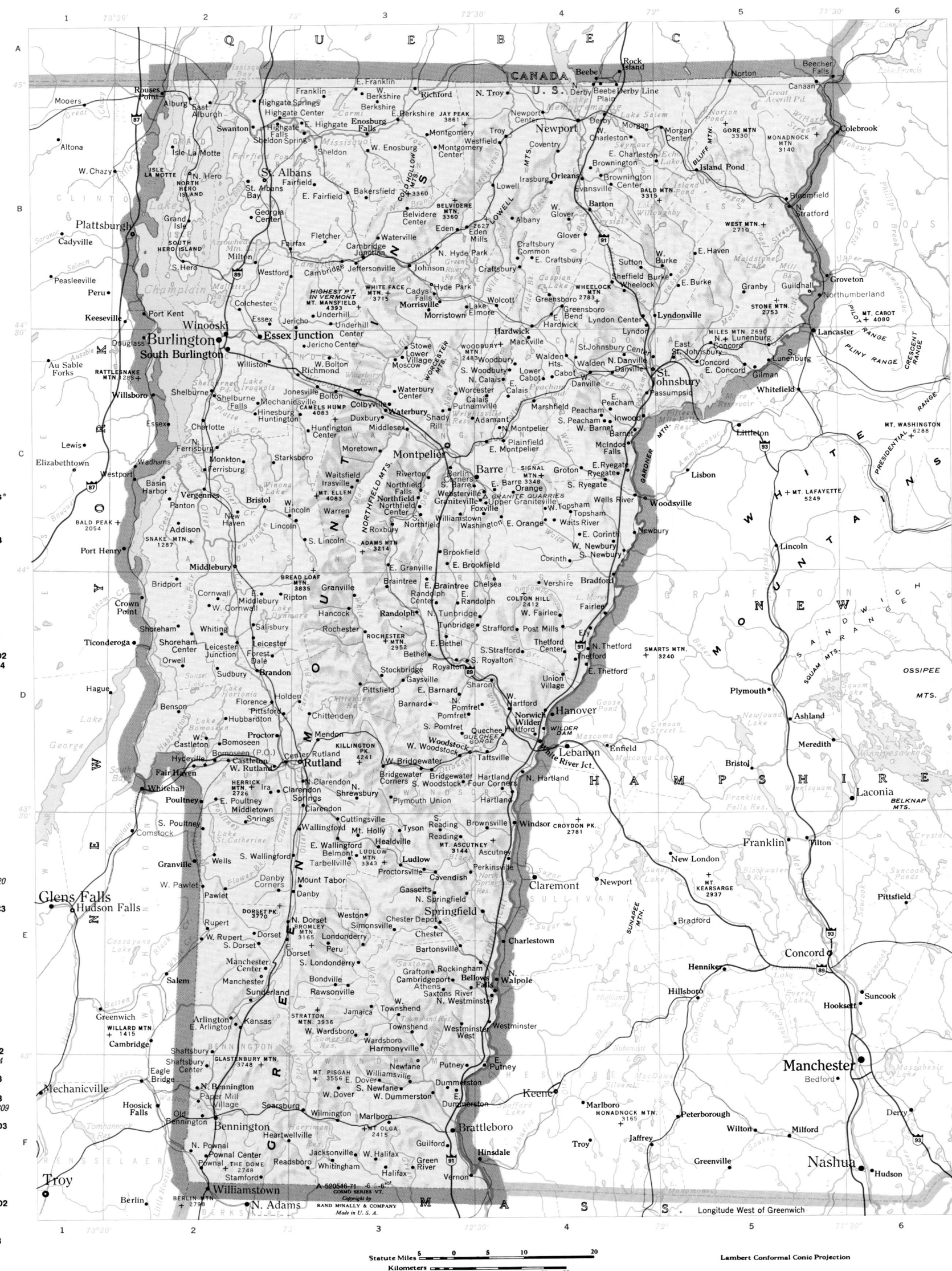

*Populations are for localities, not incorporated towns.

272

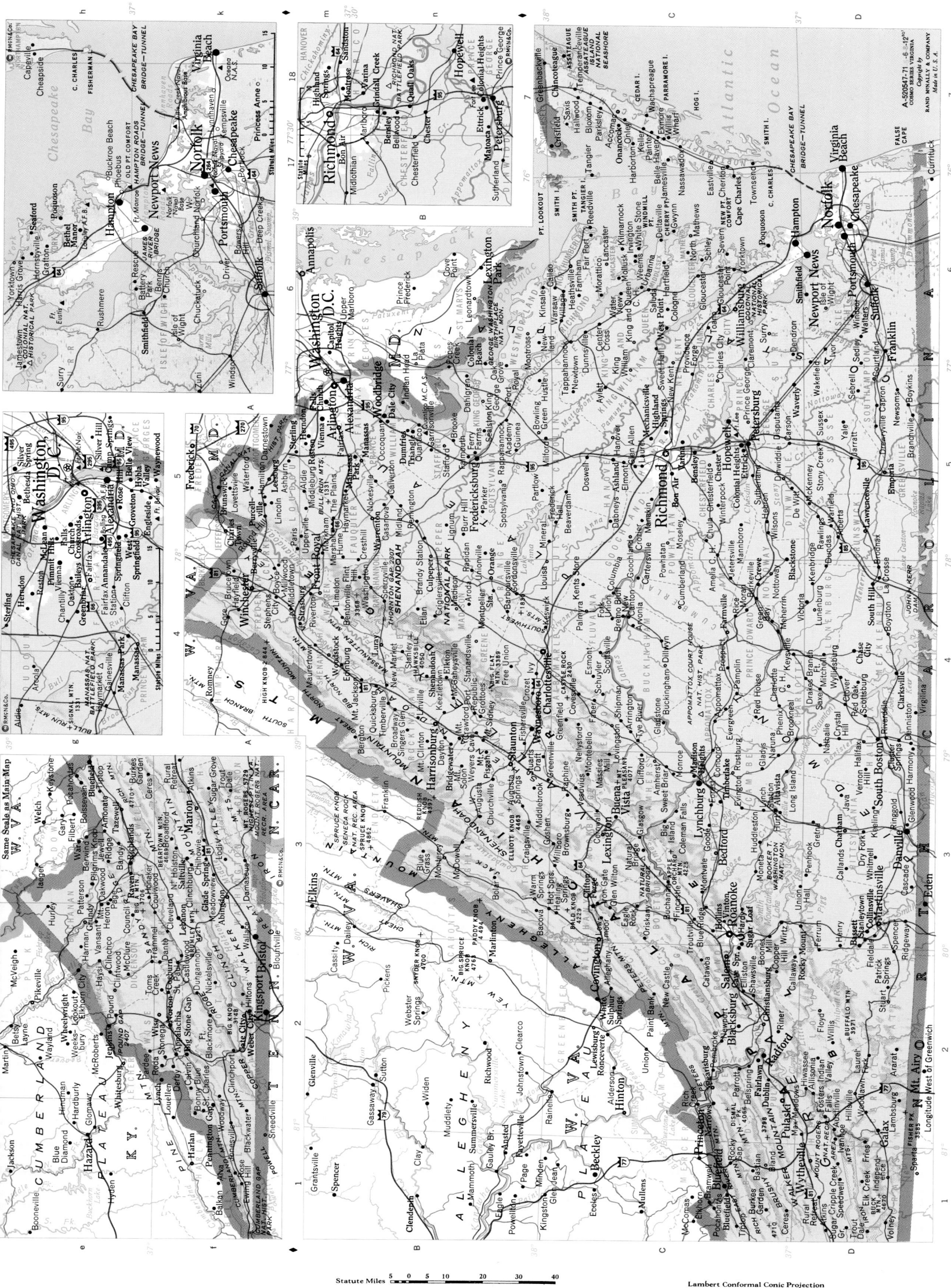

National Parks

Shenandoah National
Park **B4**

Cities and Towns

Alexandria 111,183 **B5**
Annandale 50,975 **g12**
Appomattox 1,707 **C4**
Arlington 170,936 **B5**
Bedford 6,073 **C3**
Big Stone Gap 4,748 **f9**
Blacksburg 34,590 **C2**
Bluefield 5,363 **C1**
Bon Air 16,413 **C5**
Bristol 18,426 **f9**
Buena Vista 6,406 **C3**
Charlottesville 40,341
  B4
Chesapeake 151,976 **D6**
Chester 14,896 **C5**
Chincoteague 3,572 **C7**
Christiansburg 15,004
  C2
Clifton Forge 4,679 **C3**
Collinsville 7,280 **D3**
Colonial Heights 16,064
  C5
Covington 6,991 **C3**
Culpeper 6,621 **B5**
Dale City 47,170 **B5**
Danville 53,056 **D3**
Emporia 5,306 **D5**
Engleside 27,485 **g12**
Fairfax 19,622 **B5**
Farmville 6,046 **C4**
Franklin 7,864 **D6**
Fredericksburg 19,027
  B5
Front Royal 11,880 **B4**
Galax 6,670 **D2**
Hampton 133,793 **D6**
Harrisonburg 30,707 **B4**
Herndon 16,139 **B5**
Highland Springs 13,823
  C5
Hollins 13,305 **C3**
Hopewell 23,101 **C5**
Leesburg 16,202 **A5**
Lexington 6,959 **C3**
Lynchburg 66,049 **C3**
Manassas 27,957 **B5**
Manassas Park 6,734
  B5
Marion 6,630 **f10**
Martinsville 16,162 **D3**
McLean 38,168 **g12**
Mechanicsville 22,027
  C5
Newport News 170,045
  D6
Norfolk 261,229 **D6**
Norton 4,247 **f9**
Petersburg 38,386 **C5**
Poquoson 11,005 **C6**
Portsmouth 103,907 **D6**
Pulaski 9,985 **C2**
Radford 15,940 **C2**
Reston 48,556 **B5**
Richlands 4,456 **e10**
Richmond 203,056 **C5**
Roanoke 96,397 **C3**
Salem 23,756 **C2**
Shenandoah 2,213 **B4**
South Boston 6,997 **D4**
Springfield 23,706 **g12**
Staunton 24,461 **B3**
Sterling 20,512 **A5**
Suffolk 52,141 **D6**
Tazewell 4,176 **e10**
Vienna 14,852 **B5**
Vinton 7,665 **C3**
Virginia Beach 393,069
  D7
Waynesboro 18,549 **B4**
West Springfield 28,126
  g12
Williamsburg 11,530 **C6**
Winchester 21,947 **A4**
Woodbridge 26,401 **B5**
Wytheville 8,038 **D1**
Yorktown 270 **C6**

Statute Miles
Kilometers

Lambert Conformal Conic Projection

WASHINGTON

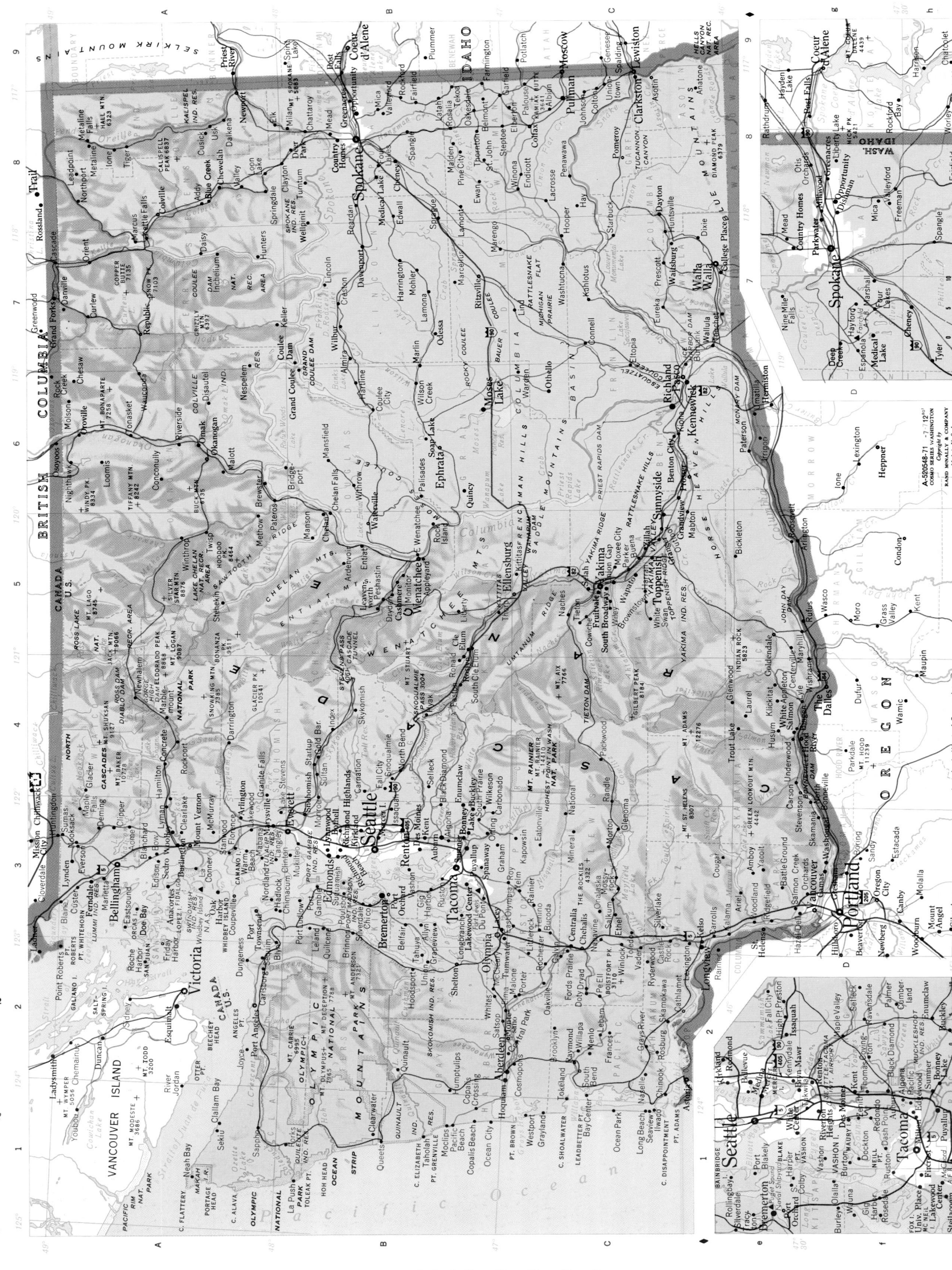

Statute Miles 5 0 5 10   20   30   40   50
Kilometers 5 0 5 15 25 35 45 55 65

Lambert Conformal Conic Projection

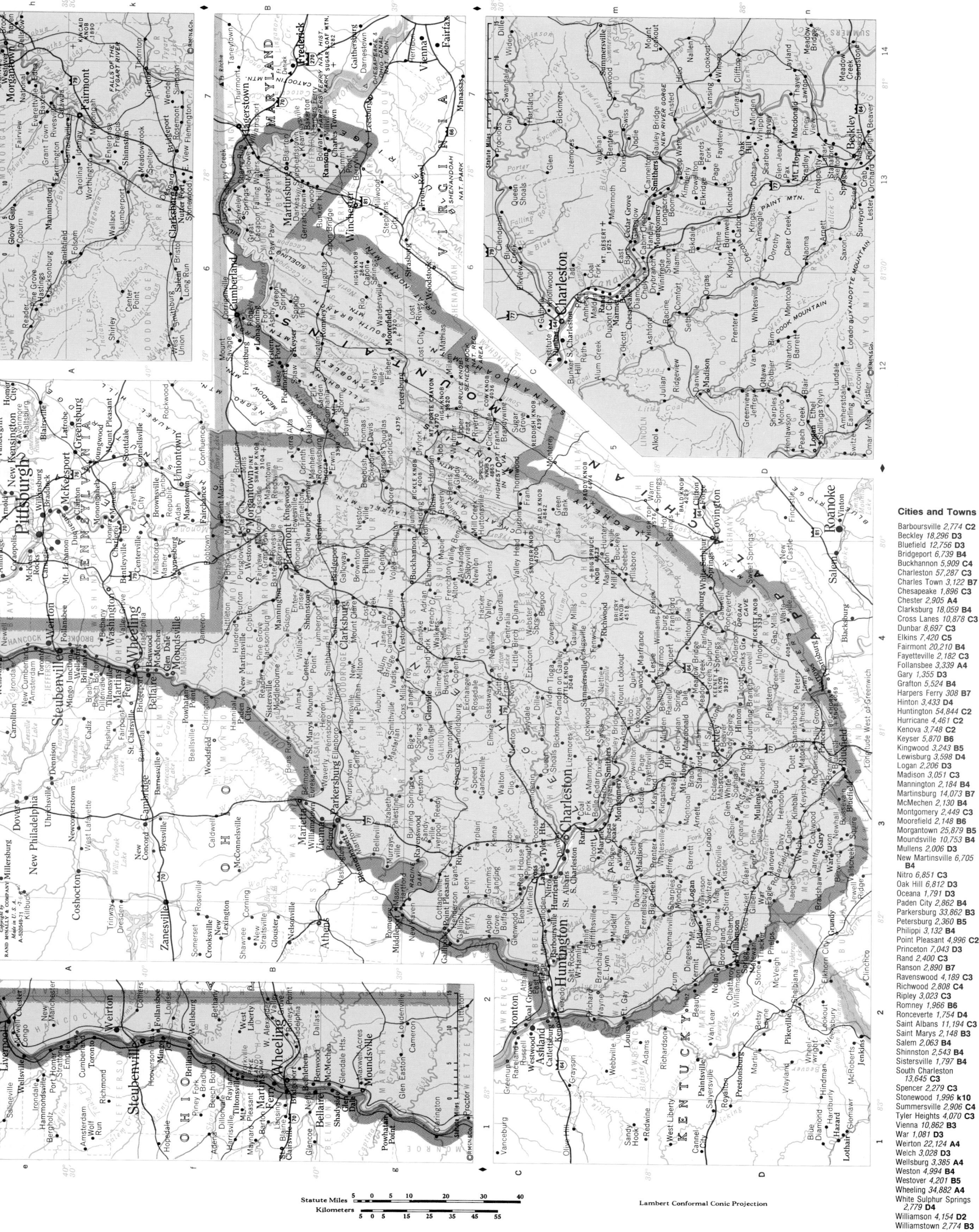

Cities and Towns

Barboursville 2,774 **C2**
Beckley 18,296 **D3**
Bluefield 12,756 **D3**
Bridgeport 6,739 **B4**
Buckhannon 5,909 **C4**
Charleston 57,287 **C3**
Charles Town 3,122 **B7**
Chesapeake 1,896 **C3**
Chester 2,905 **A4**
Clarksburg 18,059 **B4**
Cross Lanes 10,878 **C3**
Dunbar 8,697 **C3**
Elkins 7,420 **C5**
Fairmont 20,210 **B4**
Fayetteville 2,182 **C3**
Follansbee 3,339 **A4**
Gary 1,355 **D3**
Grafton 5,524 **B4**
Harpers Ferry 308 **B7**
Hinton 3,433 **D4**
Huntington 54,844 **C2**
Hurricane 4,461 **C2**
Kenova 3,748 **C2**
Keyser 5,870 **B6**
Kingwood 3,243 **B5**
Lewisburg 3,598 **D4**
Logan 2,206 **D3**
Madison 3,051 **C3**
Mannington 2,184 **B4**
Martinsburg 14,073 **B7**
McMechen 2,130 **B4**
Montgomery 2,449 **C3**
Moorefield 2,148 **B6**
Morgantown 25,879 **B5**
Moundsville 10,753 **B4**
Mullens 2,006 **D3**
New Martinsville 6,705 **B4**
Nitro 6,851 **C3**
Oak Hill 6,812 **D3**
Oceana 1,791 **D3**
Paden City 2,862 **B4**
Parkersburg 33,862 **B3**
Petersburg 2,360 **B5**
Philippi 3,132 **B4**
Point Pleasant 4,996 **C2**
Princeton 7,043 **D3**
Rand 2,400 **C3**
Ranson 2,890 **B7**
Ravenswood 4,189 **C3**
Richwood 2,808 **C4**
Ripley 3,023 **C3**
Romney 1,966 **B6**
Ronceverte 1,754 **D4**
Saint Albans 11,194 **C3**
Saint Marys 2,148 **B3**
Salem 2,063 **B4**
Shinnston 2,543 **B4**
Sistersville 1,797 **B4**
South Charleston 13,645 **C3**
Spencer 2,279 **C3**
Stonewood 1,996 **k10**
Summersville 2,906 **C4**
Tyler Heights 4,070 **C3**
Vienna 10,862 **B3**
War 1,081 **D3**
Weirton 22,124 **A4**
Welch 3,028 **D3**
Wellsburg 3,385 **A4**
Weston 4,994 **B4**
Westover 4,201 **B5**
Wheeling 34,882 **A4**
White Sulphur Springs 2,779 **D4**
Williamson 4,154 **D2**
Williamstown 2,774 **B3**

Statute Miles
Kilometers

Lambert Conformal Conic Projection

275

Longitude West of Greenwich

APOSTLE ISLANDS NAT. LAKESHORE

Lake Superior

Cities and Towns

Antigo 8,276 **C4**
Appleton 65,695 **D5**
Ashland 8,695 **B3**
Baraboo 9,203 **E4**
Beaver Dam 14,196 **E5**
Beloit 35,573 **F4**
Brookfield 35,184 **m11**
Burlington 8,855 **F5**
Chippewa Falls 12,727 **D2**
Cudahy 18,659 **F6**
De Pere 16,569 **D5**
Eau Claire 56,856 **D2**
Fond du Lac 37,757 **E5**
Fort Atkinson 10,227 **F5**
Franklin 21,855 **n11**
Green Bay 96,466 **D6**
Greendale 15,128 **F6**
Greenfield 33,403 **n11**
Hayward 1,897 **B2**
Hudson 6,378 **D1**
Janesville 52,133 **F4**
Kaukauna 11,982 **D5**
Kenosha 80,352 **F6**
La Crosse 51,003 **E2**
Lake Geneva 5,979 **F5**
Madison 191,262 **E4**
Manitowoc 32,520 **D6**
Marinette 11,843 **C6**
Marshfield 19,291 **D3**
Menasha 14,711 **D5**
Menomonee Falls 26,840 **E5**
Menomonie 13,547 **D2**
Mequon 18,885 **E6**
Merrill 9,860 **C4**
Milwaukee 628,088 **E6**
Monroe 10,241 **F4**
Muskego 16,813 **F5**
Neenah 23,219 **D5**
New Berlin 33,592 **n11**
New London 6,658 **D5**
Oak Creek 19,513 **n12**
Oconomowoc 10,993 **E5**
Oconto 4,474 **D6**
Oshkosh 55,006 **D5**
Park Falls 3,104 **C3**
Platteville 9,708 **F3**
Portage 8,640 **E4**
Port Washington 9,338 **E6**
Prairie du Chien 5,659 **F2**
Racine 84,298 **F6**
Reedsburg 5,834 **E3**
Rhinelander 7,427 **C4**
Rice Lake 7,998 **C2**
River Falls 10,610 **D1**
Shawano 7,598 **D5**
Sheboygan 49,676 **E6**
South Milwaukee 20,958 **F6**
Stevens Point 23,006 **D4**
Stoughton 8,786 **F4**
Sturgeon Bay 9,176 **D6**
Sun Prairie 15,333 **E4**
Superior 27,134 **B1**
Tomah 7,570 **E3**
Two Rivers 13,030 **D6**
Watertown 19,142 **E5**
Waukesha 56,958 **F5**
Waupun 8,207 **E5**
Wausau 37,060 **D4**
Wauwatosa 49,366 **m12**
West Allis 63,221 **m11**
West Bend 23,916 **E5**
Whitefish Bay 14,272 **m12**
Whitewater 12,636 **F5**
Wisconsin Dells 2,393 **E4**
Wisconsin Rapids 18,245 **D4**

Statute Miles   5 0 5 10   20   30   40
Kilometers   5 0 5 15 25 35 45 55

Lambert Conformal Conic Projection

A-520550-71
COSMO SERIES WISCONSIN
Copyright by
RAND M\=NALLY & COMPANY
Made in U.S.A.

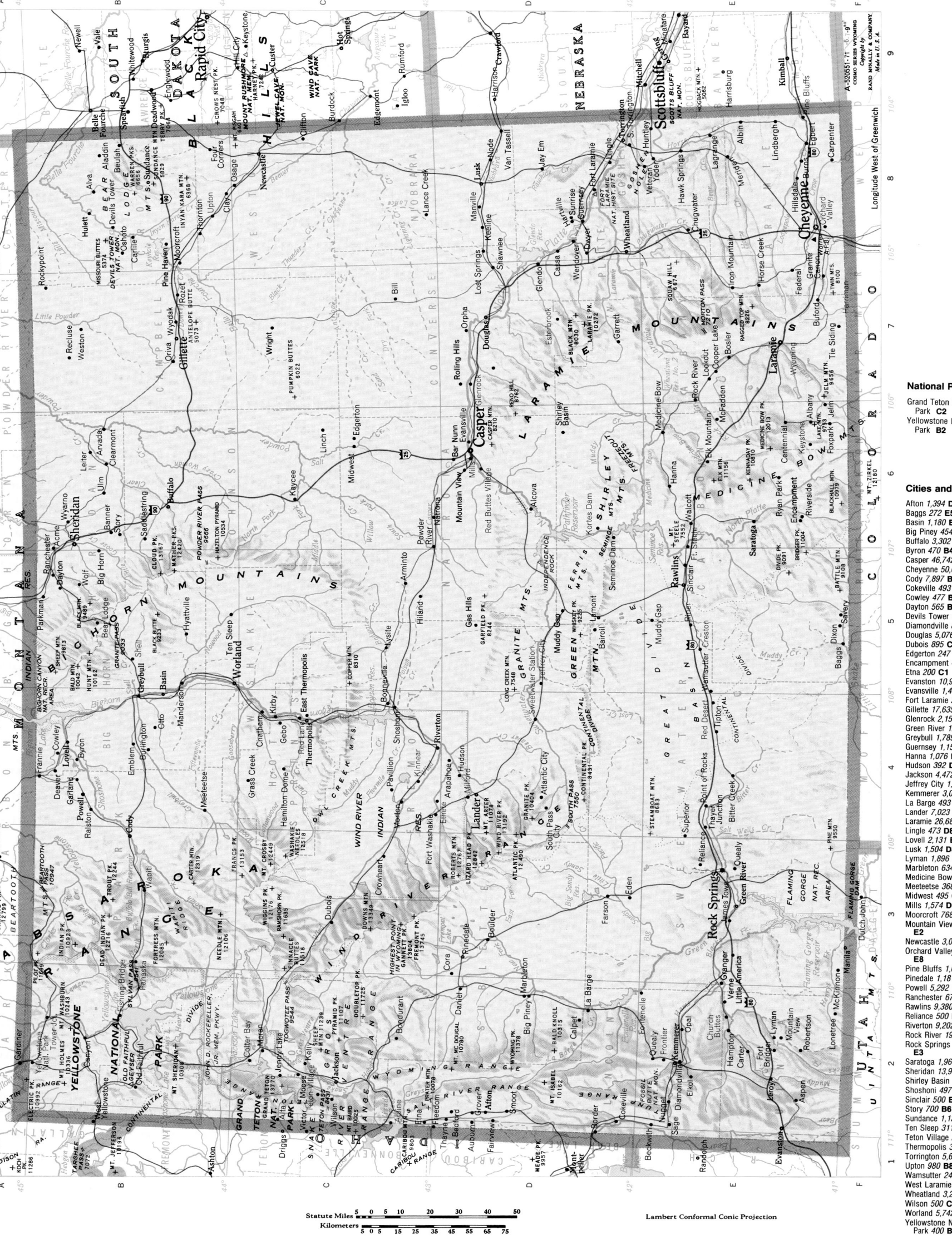

A-520551-71 -6 ,-9"
COSMO SERIES WYOMING
Copyright by
RAND McNALLY & COMPANY
Made in U. S. A.

Longitude West of Greenwich

National Parks

Grand Teton National
Park **C2**
Yellowstone National
Park **B2**

Cities and Towns

Afton *1,394* **D2**
Baggs *272* **E5**
Basin *1,180* **B4**
Big Piney *454* **D2**
Buffalo *3,302* **B6**
Byron *470* **B4**
Casper *46,742* **D6**
Cheyenne *50,008* **E8**
Cody *7,897* **B3**
Cokeville *493* **D2**
Cowley *477* **B4**
Dayton *565* **B5**
Devils Tower *40* **B8**
Diamondville *864* **E2**
Douglas *5,076* **D7**
Dubois *895* **C3**
Edgerton *247* **C6**
Encampment *490* **E6**
Etna *200* **C1**
Evanston *10,903* **E2**
Evansville *1,403* **D6**
Fort Laramie *243* **D8**
Gillette *17,635* **B7**
Glenrock *2,153* **D7**
Green River *12,711* **E3**
Greybull *1,789* **B4**
Guernsey *1,155* **D8**
Hanna *1,076* **E6**
Hudson *392* **D4**
Jackson *4,472* **C2**
Jeffrey City *1,882* **D5**
Kemmerer *3,020* **E2**
La Barge *493* **D2**
Lander *7,023* **D4**
Laramie *26,687* **E7**
Lingle *473* **D8**
Lovell *2,131* **B4**
Lusk *1,504* **D8**
Lyman *1,896* **E2**
Marbleton *634* **D2**
Medicine Bow *389* **E6**
Meeteetse *368* **B4**
Midwest *495* **C6**
Mills *1,574* **D6**
Moorcroft *768* **B8**
Mountain View *1,189*
E2
Newcastle *3,003* **C8**
Orchard Valley *3,321*
E8
Pine Bluffs *1,054* **E8**
Pinedale *1,181* **D3**
Powell *5,292* **B4**
Ranchester *676* **B5**
Rawlins *9,380* **E5**
Reliance *500* **E3**
Riverton *9,202* **C4**
Rock River *190* **E7**
Rock Springs *19,050*
E3
Saratoga *1,969* **E6**
Sheridan *13,900* **B6**
Shirley Basin *100* **D6**
Shoshoni *497* **C4**
Sinclair *500* **E5**
Story *700* **B6**
Sundance *1,139* **B8**
Ten Sleep *311* **B5**
Teton Village *250* **C2**
Thermopolis *3,247* **C4**
Torrington *5,651* **D8**
Upton *980* **B8**
Wamsutter *240* **E5**
West Laramie *2,000* **E7**
Wheatland *3,271* **D8**
Wilson *500* **C2**
Worland *5,742* **B5**
Yellowstone National
Park *400* **B2**

Statute Miles
Kilometers

Lambert Conformal Conic Projection

277

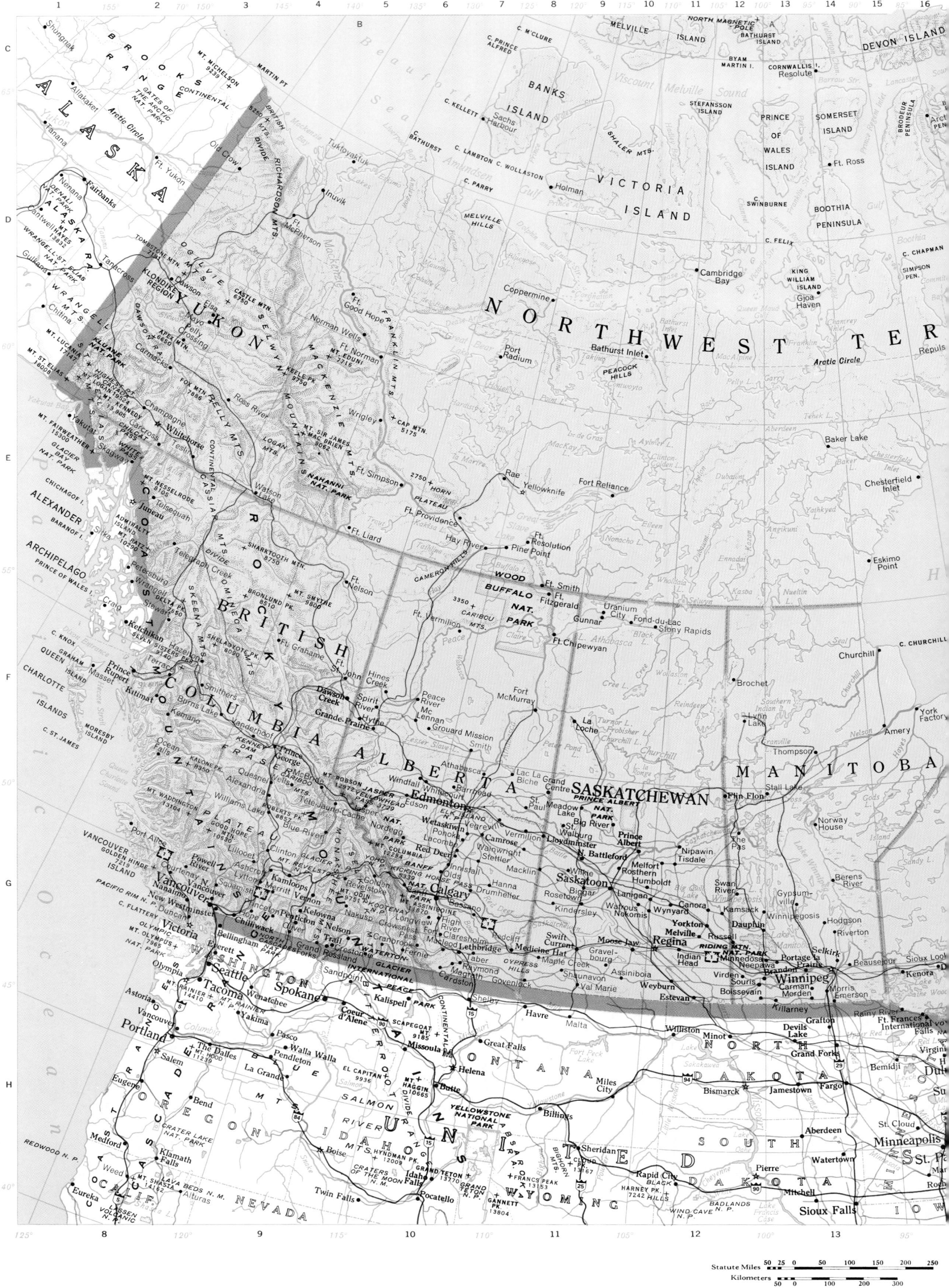

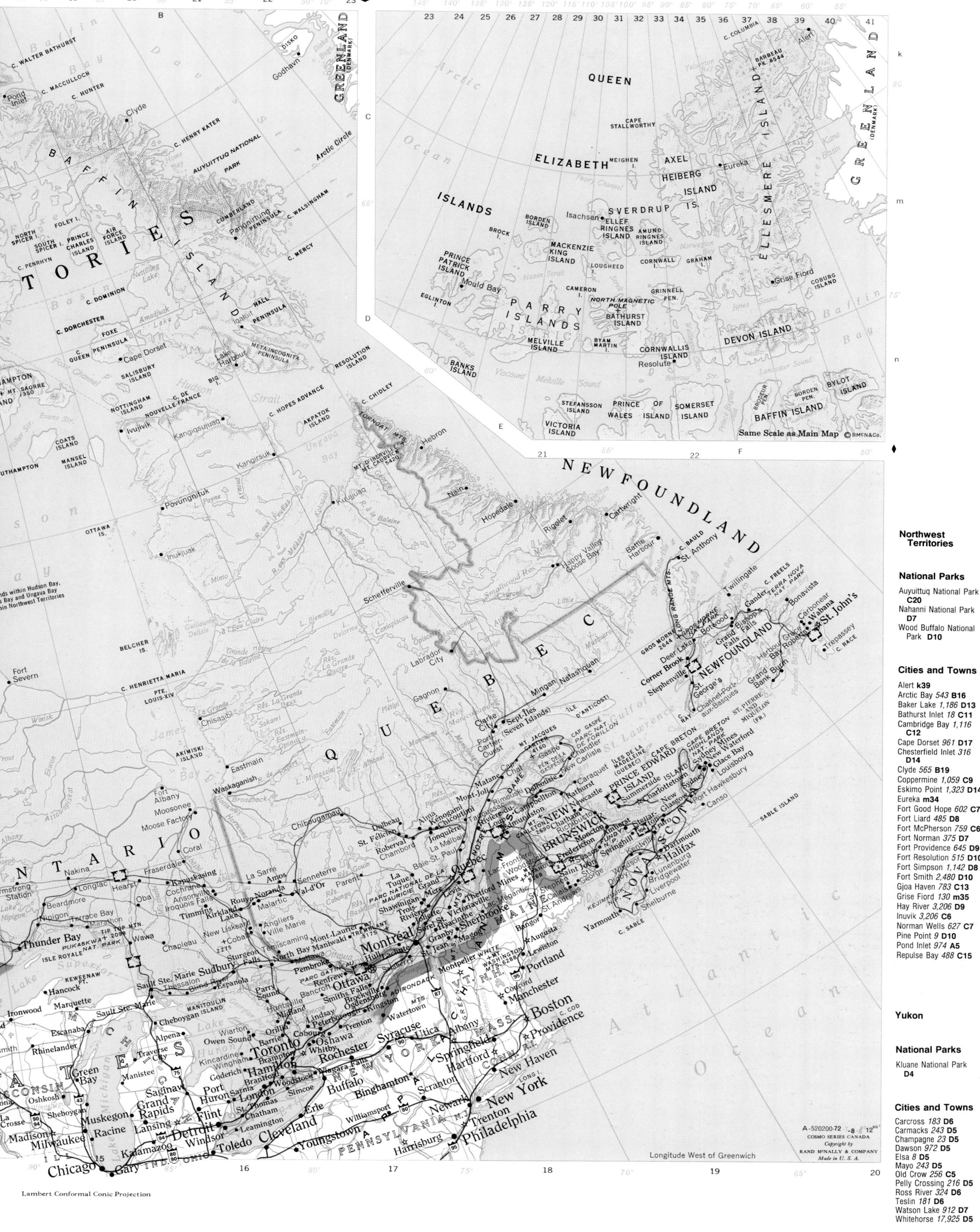

Northwest Territories

National Parks

Auyuittuq National Park **C20**
Nahanni National Park **D7**
Wood Buffalo National Park **D10**

Cities and Towns

Alert **k39**
Arctic Bay *543* **B16**
Baker Lake *1,186* **D13**
Bathurst Inlet *18* **C11**
Cambridge Bay *1,116* **C12**
Cape Dorset *961* **D17**
Chesterfield Inlet *316* **D14**
Clyde *565* **B19**
Coppermine *1,059* **C9**
Eskimo Point *1,323* **D14**
Eureka **m34**
Fort Good Hope *602* **C7**
Fort Liard *485* **D8**
Fort McPherson *759* **C6**
Fort Norman *375* **D7**
Fort Providence *645* **D9**
Fort Resolution *515* **D10**
Fort Simpson *1,142* **D8**
Fort Smith *2,480* **D10**
Gjoa Haven *783* **C13**
Grise Fiord *130* **m35**
Hay River *3,206* **D9**
Inuvik *3,206* **C6**
Norman Wells *627* **C7**
Pine Point *9* **D10**
Pond Inlet *974* **A5**
Repulse Bay *488* **C15**

Yukon

National Parks

Kluane National Park **D4**

Cities and Towns

Carcross *183* **D6**
Carmacks *243* **D5**
Champagne *23* **D5**
Dawson *972* **D5**
Elsa *8* **D5**
Mayo *243* **D5**
Old Crow *256* **C5**
Pelly Crossing *216* **D5**
Ross River *324* **D6**
Teslin *181* **D6**
Watson Lake *912* **D7**
Whitehorse *17,925* **D5**

Lambert Conformal Conic Projection

A-520200-72   8   12
COSMO SERIES CANADA
Copyright by
RAND McNALLY & COMPANY
Made in U.S.A.

Longitude West of Greenwich

National Parks

Banff National Park
D2
Elk Island National
Park **C4**
Jasper National Park
C1
Waterton Lakes
National Park **E3**

Cities and Towns

Airdrie *12,456* **D3**
Athabasca *1,965* **B4**
Banff *5,688* **D3**
Barrhead *4,160* **B3**
Bonnyville *5,132* **B5**
Bow Island *1,484* **E5**
Brooks *9,433* **D5**
Calgary *710,677* **D3**
Camrose *13,420* **C4**
Canmore *5,681* **D3**
Cardston *3,480* **E4**
Claresholm *3,297* **D4**
Coaldale *5,310* **E4**
Cochrane *5,265* **D3**
Cold Lake *3,878* **B5**
Coronation *1,184* **C5**
Crowsnest Pass *6,679*
E3
Devon *4,082* **C4**
Didsbury *3,355* **D3**
Drayton Valley *5,983*
C3
Drumheller *6,277* **D4**
Edmonton *616,741* **C4**
Edson *7,323* **C2**
Fairview *3,023* **A1**
Fort Chipewyan *537* **f8**
Fort Macleod *3,112* **E4**
Fort McMurray *34,706*
A5
Fort Saskatchewan
12,078 **C4**
Gibbons *2,639* **C4**
Grand Centre *3,877* **B5**
Grande Cache *3,842* **C1**
Grande Prairie *28,271*
B1
Grimshaw *2,812* **A2**
Hanna *2,996* **D5**
High Prairie *2,932* **B2**
High River *6,269* **D4**
Hinton *9,046* **C2**
Innisfail *5,700* **C4**
Jasper **C1**
Lac La Biche *2,549* **B5**
La Crete *902* **f7**
Lake Louise *500* **D2**
Leduc *13,970* **C4**
Lethbridge *60,974* **E4**
Lloydminster *17,283* **C5**
Magrath *1,743* **E4**
Medicine Hat *43,625* **D5**
Morinville *6,104* **C4**
Nordegg **C2**
Okotoks *6,720* **D4**
Olds *5,542* **D3**
Peace River *6,717* **A2**
Pincher Creek *3,660* **E4**
Ponoka *5,861* **C4**
Raymond *3,130* **E4**
Redcliff *3,768* **D5**
Red Deer *58,134* **C4**
Rocky Mountain House
5,461 **C3**
Saint Albert *42,146* **C4**
Saint Paul *4,881* **B5**
Slave Lake *5,607* **B3**
Smith *258* **B3**
Spruce Grove *12,884*
C4
Stettler *4,947* **C4**
Stony Plain *7,226* **C3**
Strathmore *4,185* **D4**
Swan Hills *2,348* **B3**
Sylvan Lake *4,197* **C3**
Taber *6,660* **E4**
Valleyview *1,980* **B2**
Vegreville *5,138* **C4**
Vermilion *3,891* **C5**
Vulcan *1,466* **D4**
Wainwright *4,732* **C5**
Westlock *4,719* **B4**
Wetaskiwin *10,634* **C4**
Whitecourt *6,938* **B3**

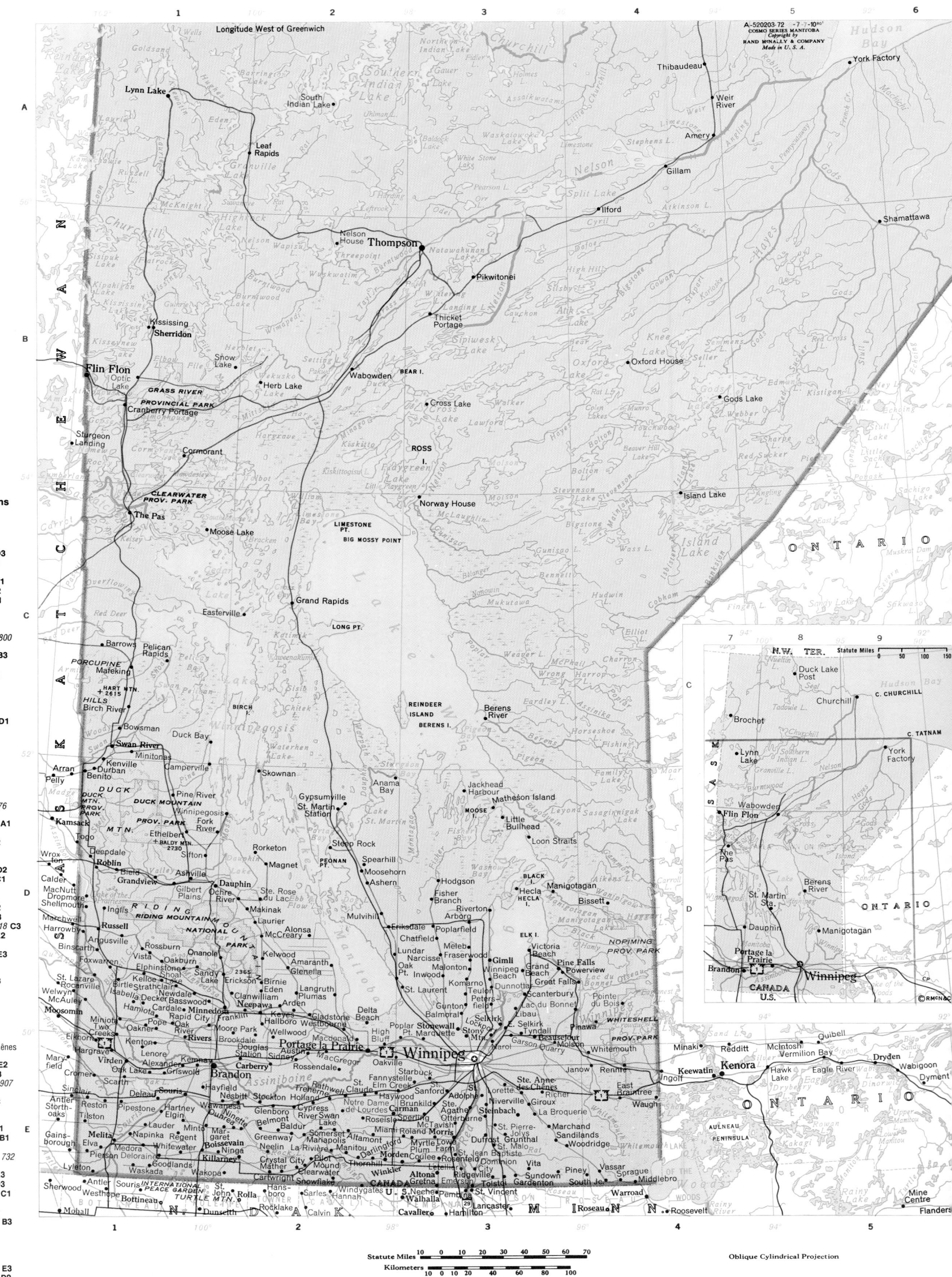

National Parks

Riding Mountain
National Park **D1**

Cities and Towns

Altona *3,060* **E3**
Arborg *1,039* **D3**
Ashern *692* **D2**
Beausejour *2,633* **D3**
Birch River *419* **C1**
Birtle *802* **D1**
Boissevain *1,484* **E1**
Brandon *38,567* **E2**
Camperville *579* **D1**
Carberry *1,481* **E2**
Carman *2,567* **E2**
Churchill *1,143* **f9**
Cranberry Portage *800*
  B1
Cross Lake *1,292* **B3**
Dauphin *8,453* **D1**
Deloraine *1,045* **E1**
Duck Bay *427* **C1**
Easterville **C2**
Emerson *721* **E3**
Flin Flon *7,449* **B1**
Gilbert Plains *741* **D1**
Gillam *1,893* **A4**
Gimli *1,579* **D3**
Gladstone *928* **D2**
Glenboro *674* **E2**
Grandview *870* **D1**
Grunthal *733* **E3**
Hamiota *823* **D1**
Killarney *2,163* **E2**
Lac du Bonnet *1,076*
  D3
Leaf Rapids *1,613* **A1**
Lorette *1,474* **E3**
MacGregor *852* **E2**
Manitou *811* **E2**
Melita *1,134* **E1**
Minnedosa *2,526* **D2**
Moose Lake *420* **C1**
Morden *5,273* **E2**
Morris *1,616* **E3**
Neepawa *3,258* **D2**
Niverville *1,514* **E3**
Norway House *2,818* **C3**
Pilot Mound *747* **E2**
Pine Falls *794* **D3**
Plum Coulee *676* **E3**
Portage la Prairie
  13,186 **E2**
Powerview *736* **D3**
Reston *620* **E1**
Rivers *1,076* **D1**
Roblin *1,838* **D1**
Rossburn *609* **D1**
Russell *1,616* **D1**
Saint Adolphe **E3**
Sainte Anne-des-Chênes
  1,477 **E3**
Saint Claude *613* **E2**
Saint Malo *846* **E3**
Saint Pierre-Jolys *907*
  E3
Sainte Rose du Lac
  1,008 **D2**
Selkirk *9,815* **D3**
Shoal Lake *784* **D1**
Snow Lake *1,598* **B1**
Souris *1,662* **E1**
South Indian Lake *732*
  A2
Steinbach *8,213* **E3**
Stonewall *2,997* **D3**
Swan River *3,917* **C1**
Teulon *1,016* **D3**
The Pas *6,166* **C1**
Thompson *14,977* **B3**
Treherne *661* **E2**
Virden *2,894* **E1**
Wabowden **B2**
Winkler *6,397* **E3**
Winnipeg *616,790* **E3**
Winnipegosis *771* **D2**

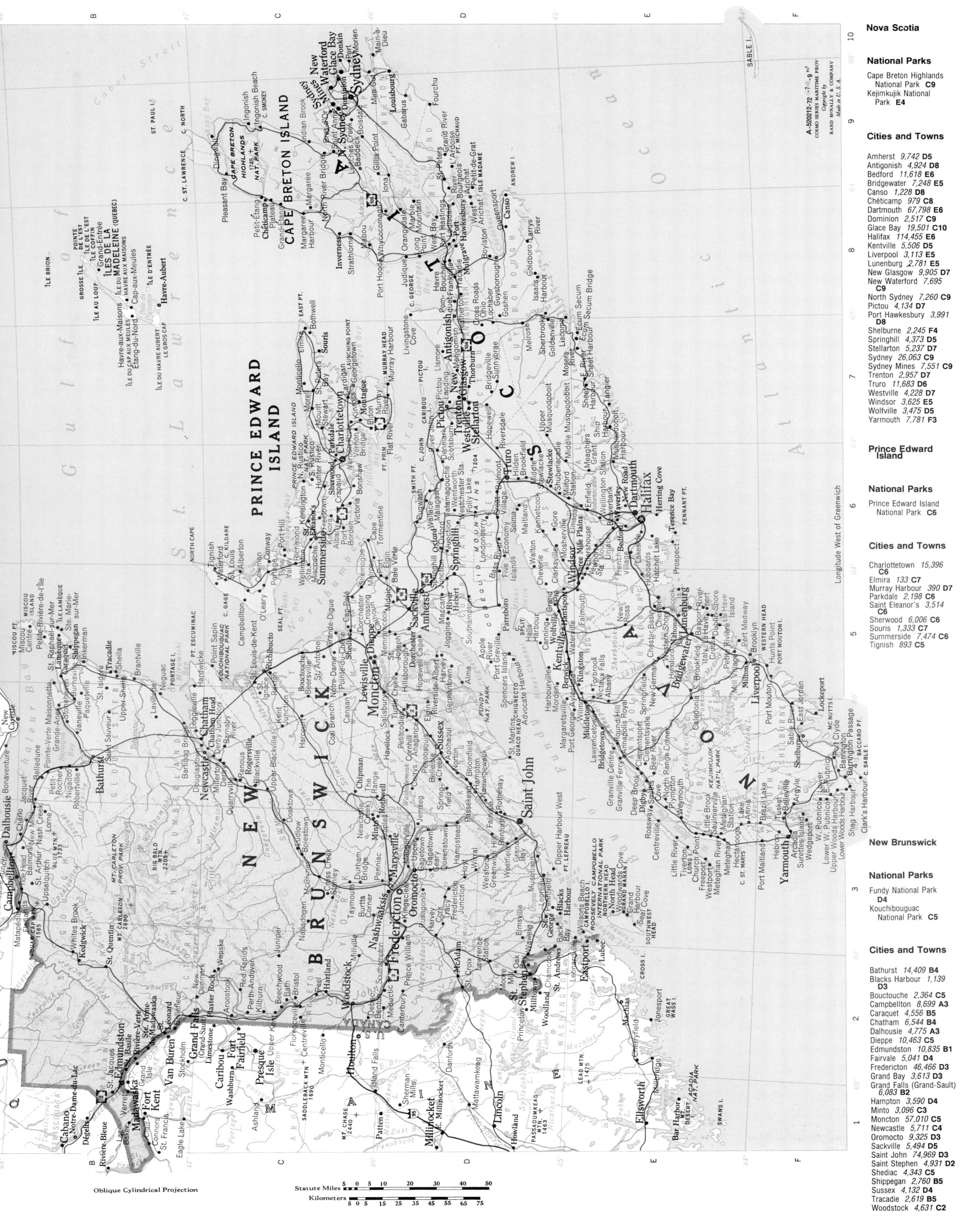

Nova Scotia

National Parks

Cape Breton Highlands
  National Park **C9**
Kejimkujik National
  Park **E4**

Cities and Towns

Amherst *9,742* **D5**
Antigonish *4,924* **D8**
Bedford *11,618* **E6**
Bridgewater *7,248* **E5**
Canso *1,228* **D8**
Chéticamp *979* **C8**
Dartmouth *67,798* **E6**
Dominion *2,517* **C9**
Glace Bay *19,501* **C10**
Halifax *114,455* **E6**
Kentville *5,506* **D5**
Liverpool *3,113* **E5**
Lunenburg *2,781* **E5**
New Glasgow *9,905* **D7**
New Waterford *7,695*
  C9
North Sydney *7,260* **C9**
Pictou *4,134* **D7**
Port Hawkesbury *3,991*
  D8
Shelburne *2,245* **F4**
Springhill *4,373* **D5**
Stellarton *5,237* **D7**
Sydney *26,063* **C9**
Sydney Mines *7,551* **C9**
Trenton *2,957* **D7**
Truro *11,683* **D6**
Westville *4,228* **D7**
Windsor *3,625* **E5**
Wolfville *3,475* **D5**
Yarmouth *7,781* **F3**

**Prince Edward
Island**

National Parks

Prince Edward Island
  National Park **C6**

Cities and Towns

Charlottetown *15,396*
  C6
Elmira *133* **C7**
Murray Harbour *390* **D7**
Parkdale *2,198* **C6**
Saint Eleanor's *3,514*
  C6
Sherwood *6,006* **C6**
Souris *1,333* **C7**
Summerside *7,474* **C6**
Tignish *893* **C5**

New Brunswick

National Parks

Fundy National Park **D4**
Kouchibouguac
  National Park **C5**

Cities and Towns

Bathurst *14,409* **B4**
Blacks Harbour *1,139*
  D3
Bouctouche *2,364* **C5**
Campbellton *8,699* **A3**
Caraquet *4,556* **B5**
Chatham *6,544* **B4**
Dalhousie *4,775* **A3**
Dieppe *10,463* **C5**
Edmundston *10,835* **B1**
Fairvale *5,041* **D4**
Fredericton *46,466* **D3**
Grand Bay *3,613* **D3**
Grand Falls (Grand-Sault)
  6,083 **B2**
Hampton *3,590* **D4**
Minto *3,096* **C3**
Moncton *57,010* **C5**
Newcastle *5,711* **C4**
Oromocto *9,325* **D3**
Sackville *5,494* **D5**
Saint John *74,969* **D3**
Saint Stephen *4,931* **D2**
Shediac *4,343* **C5**
Shippegan *2,760* **B5**
Sussex *4,132* **D4**
Tracadie *2,619* **B5**
Woodstock *4,631* **C2**

NEWFOUNDLAND

National Parks

Gros Morne National
Park **D3**
Terra Nova National
Park **D4**

Cities and Towns

Badger 1,073 **D3**
Baie Verte 1,913 **D3**
Bay Bulls 1,065 **E5**
Bay Roberts 5,474 **E5**
Bishop's Falls 4,232 **D4**
Bonavista 4,597 **D5**
Botwood 3,663 **D4**
Buchans 1,164 **D3**
Burgeo 611 **E3**
Burin 2,940 **E4**
Carbonear 5,259 **E5**
Cartwright 611 **B3**
Catalina 1,205 **D5**
Channel-Port-aux-
Basques 5,644 **E2**
Clarenville 3,071 **D4**
Corner Brook 22,410 **D3**
Deer Lake 4,327 **D3**
Dunville 1,688 **E5**
Durrell 1,002 **D4**
Fogo 1,030 **D4**
Fortune 2,177 **E4**
Gambo 2,496 **D4**
Gander 10,339 **D4**
Glenwood 984 **D4**
Glovertown 2,276 **D4**
Grand Bank 3,528 **E4**
Grand Falls [-Windsor]
14,693 **D4**
Happy Valley-Goose Bay
8,610 **B1**
Harbour Breton 2,418
E4
Harbour Grace 3,419 **E5**
Hare Bay 1,387 **D4**
Isle-aux-Morts 1,146 **E2**
Joe Batt's Arm [-Barr'd
Islands-Shoal Bay]
1,164 **D4**
Labrador City 9,061 **h8**
La Scie 1,412 **D4**
Lewisporte 3,848 **D4**
Marystown 6,739 **E4**
Milltown [-Head of Bay
d'Espoir] 1,161 **E4**
Mount Pearl 23,689 **E5**
Musgrave Harbour 1,528
D5
Nain 1,069 **g9**
Norris Arm 1,089 **D4**
Norris Point 927 **D3**
Pasadena 3,428 **D3**
Placentia 1,954 **E5**
Pouch Cove 1,976 **E5**
Ramea 1,224 **E3**
Red Bay 288 **C3**
Rigolet 334 **A2**
Robert's Arm 994 **D4**
Rocky Harbour 1,138
D3
Roddickton 1,153 **C3**
Saint Alban's 1,586 **E4**
Saint Anthony 3,164 **C4**
Saint George's 1,678
D2
Saint John's 95,770 **E5**
Saint Lawrence 1,743
E4
Spaniard's Bay 2,198
E5
Springdale 3,545 **D3**
Stephenville 7,621 **D2**
Stephenville Crossing
2,172 **D2**
Summerford 1,157 **D4**
Torbay 4,707 **E5**
Trepassey 1,198 **E5**
Twillingate 1,397 **D4**
Upper Island Cove
2,038 **E5**
Victoria 1,831 **E5**
Wabana (Bell Island)
3,608 **E5**
Wabush 2,331 **h8**
Wesleyville 1,126 **D5**
Windsor (part of Grand
Falls-Windsor) **D4**

National Parks

Bruce Peninsula
  National Park **B3**
Georgian Bay Islands
  National Park **C4**
Point Pelee National
  Park **F2**
Pukaskwa National Park
  o18
St. Lawrence Islands
  National Park **C9**

Cities and Towns

Ajax 57,350 **D6**
Barrie 62,728 **C5**
Belleville 37,243 **C7**
Brampton 234,445 **D5**
Brantford 81,997 **D4**
Brockville 21,582 **C9**
Burlington 129,575 **D5**
Cambridge 92,772 **D4**
Chatham 43,557 **E2**
Cobourg 15,079 **D6**
Cornwall 47,137 **B10**
Dryden 6,505 **o16**
Dundas 21,868 **D5**
East York 102,696 **D5**
Etobicoke 309,993 **D5**
Fergus 7,940 **D4**
Fort Erie 26,006 **E6**
Gloucester 101,677 **h12**
Guelph 87,976 **D4**
Haileybury 4,962 **p20**
Hamilton 318,499 **D5**
Hawkesbury 9,706 **B10**
Kapuskasing 10,344
  o19
Kenora 9,782 **o16**
Kingston 56,597 **C8**
Kirkland Lake 10,440
  o19
Kitchener 168,282 **D4**
Leamington 14,182 **E2**
Lindsay 16,696 **C6**
London 303,165 **E3**
Markham 153,811 **D5**
Midland 13,865 **C5**
Milton 32,075 **D5**
Mississauga 463,388
  D5
Moosonee **o19**
Nanticoke 22,727 **E4**
Nepean 107,627 **h12**
Newcastle 49,479 **D6**
Newmarket 45,474 **C5**
Niagara Falls 75,399 **D5**
North Bay 55,405 **A5**
North York 562,564 **D5**
Oakville 114,670 **D5**
Orillia 25,925 **C5**
Oshawa 129,344 **D6**
Ottawa 313,987 **B9**
Owen Sound 21,674 **C4**
Pembroke 13,997 **B7**
Petawawa 5,793 **B7**
Peterborough 68,371 **C6**
Pickering 68,631 **D5**
Port Colborne 18,766
  E5
Richmond Hill 80,142
  D5
Saint Catharines
  129,300 **D5**
Sarnia 74,376 **E2**
Sault Sainte Marie
  81,476 **p18**
Scarborough 524,598
  m15
Sioux Lookout 3,311
  o17
Smiths Falls 9,396 **C8**
Stratford 27,666 **D3**
Sturgeon Falls 5,837 **A5**
Sudbury 92,884 **A4**
Tecumseh 10,495 **E2**
Thunder Bay 113,946
  o17
Timmins 47,461 **o19**
Toronto 635,395 **D5**

Trenton 16,908 **C7**
Vanier 18,150 **h12**
Vaughan 111,359 **D5**
Waterloo 71,181 **D4**
Welland 47,914 **E5**
Whitby 61,281 **D6**
Windsor 191,435 **E1**
Woodstock 30,075 **D4**
York 140,525 **D5**

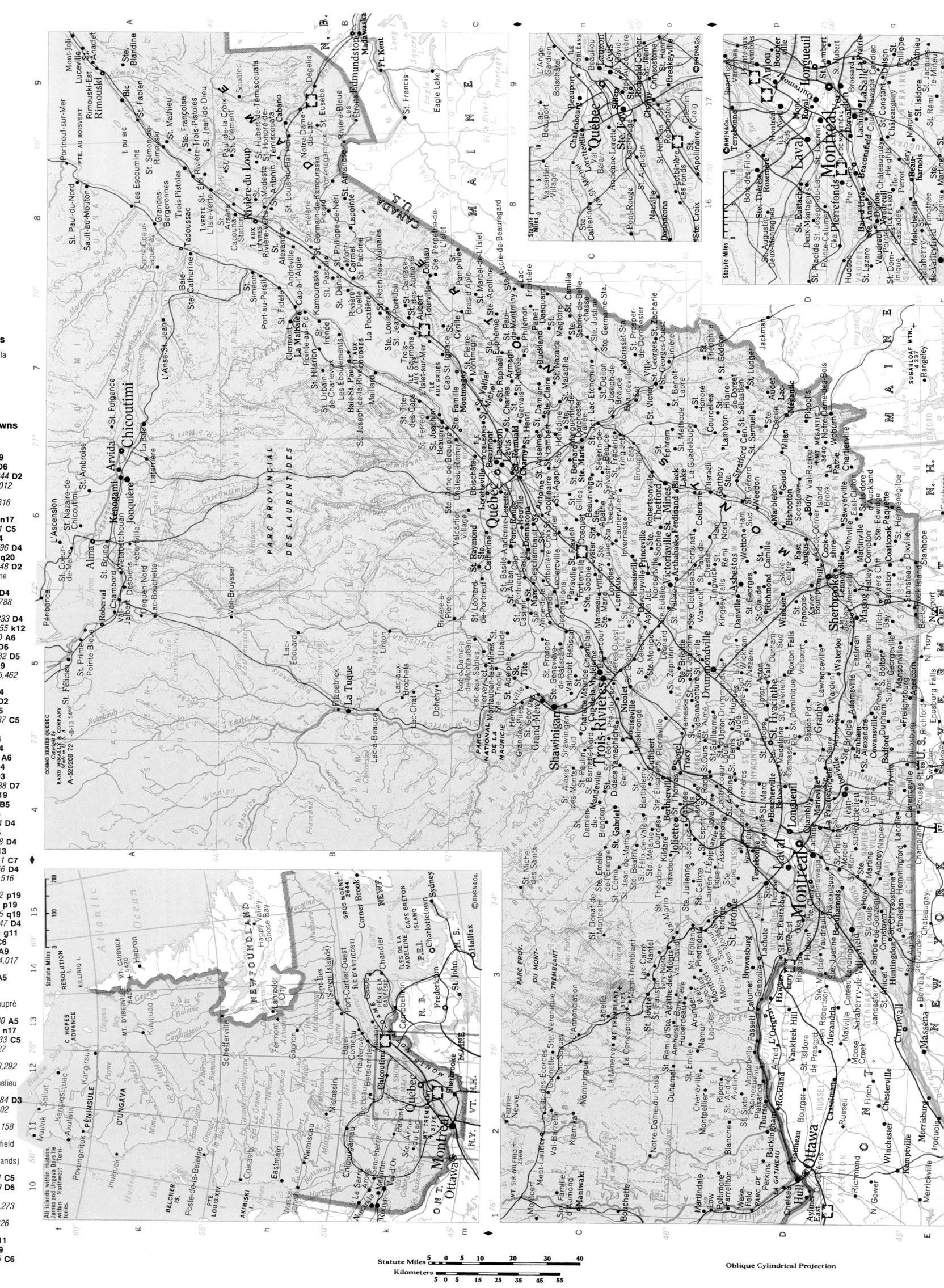

National Parks

Parc Nacional de la
  Mauricie **C4**

Cities and Towns

Alma *25,910* **A6**
Anjou *37,210* **p19**
Asbestos *6,487* **D6**
Aylmer East *32,244* **D2**
Baie-Comeau *26,012*
  k13
Beaconsfield *19,616*
  q19
Beauport *69,158* **n17**
Bécancour *10,911* **C5**
Beloil *18,516* **D4**
Boucherville *33,796* **D4**
Brossard *64,793* **q20**
Buckingham *10,548* **D2**
Cap-de-la-Madeleine
  33,716 **C5**
Chambly *15,893* **D4**
Charlesbourg *70,788*
  n17
Châteauguay *39,833* **D4**
Chibougamau *8,855* **k12**
Chicoutimi *62,670* **A6**
Coaticook *6,637* **D6**
Cowansville *11,982* **D5**
Dorval *17,249* **q19**
Drummondville *35,462*
  D5
Gaspé *16,402* **k14**
Gatineau *92,284* **D2**
Granby *42,804* **D5**
Grand-Mère *14,287* **C5**
Hull *60,707* **D2**
Iberville *9,352* **D4**
Joliette *17,396* **C4**
Jonquière *57,933* **A6**
Lachine *35,266* **D4**
Lachute *11,730* **D3**
Lac-Mégantic *5,838* **D7**
LaSalle *73,804* **q19**
La Tuque *10,003* **B5**
Laval *314,398* **D4**
Longueuil *129,874* **D4**
Magog *14,034* **D5**
Mascouche *25,828* **D4**
Matane *12,756* **k13**
Montmagny *11,861* **C7**
Montréal *1,017,666* **D4**
Montréal-Nord *85,516*
  p19
Mont-Royal *18,212* **p19**
Outremont *22,935* **p19**
Pierrefonds *48,735* **q19**
Pointe-Claire *27,647* **D4**
Poste-de-la-Baleine **g11**
Québec *167,517* **C6**
Rimouski *30,873* **A9**
Rivière-du-Loup *14,017*
  B8
Roberval *11,628* **A5**
Rouyn [-Noranda]
  26,448 **k11**
Sainte-Anne-de-Beaupré
  3,146 **B7**
Saint-Félicien *9,340* **A5**
Sainte-Foy *71,133* **n17**
Saint-Georges *3,933* **C5**
Saint-Hubert *74,027*
  q20
Saint-Hyacinthe *39,292*
  D5
Saint-Jean-sur-Richelieu
  37,607 **D4**
Saint-Jérôme *23,384* **D3**
Saint-Laurent *72,402*
  p19
Sainte-Thérèse *24,158*
  D4
Salaberry-de-Valleyfield
  27,598 **D3**
Sept-Îles (Seven Islands)
  24,848 **h13**
Shawinigan *19,931* **C5**
Sherbrooke *76,429* **D6**
Sorel *18,786* **C4**
Thetford Mines *17,273*
  C6
Trois-Rivières *49,426*
  C5
Val-d'Or *23,842* **k11**
Verdun *61,307* **q19**
Victoriaville *21,495* **C6**
Ville Saint-Georges
  19,583 **C7**

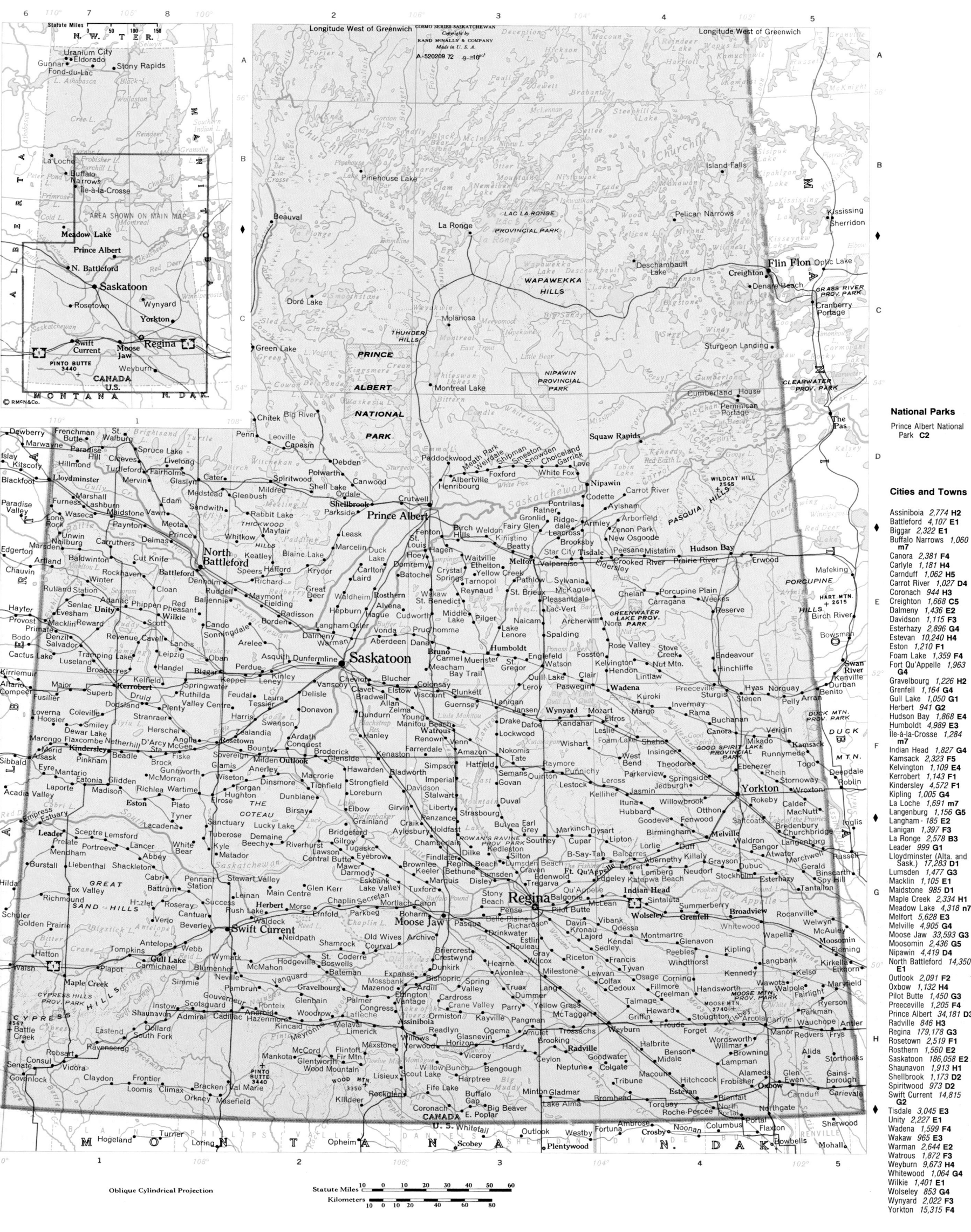

Cities and Towns

Assiniboia *2,774* **H2**
Battleford *4,107* **E1**
Biggar *2,322* **E1**
Buffalo Narrows *1,060*
  m7
Canora *2,381* **F4**
Carlyle *1,181* **H4**
Carnduff *1,062* **H5**
Carrot River *1,027* **D4**
Coronach *944* **H3**
Creighton *1,668* **C5**
Dalmeny *1,436* **E2**
Davidson *1,115* **F3**
Esterhazy *2,896* **G4**
Estevan *10,240* **H4**
Eston *1,210* **F1**
Foam Lake *1,359* **F4**
Fort Qu'Appelle *1,963*
  G4
Gravelbourg *1,226* **H2**
Grenfell *1,164* **G4**
Gull Lake *1,050* **G1**
Herbert *941* **G2**
Hudson Bay *1,868* **E4**
Humboldt *4,989* **E3**
Île-à-la-Crosse *1,284*
  m7
Indian Head *1,827* **G4**
Kamsack *2,323* **F5**
Kelvington *1,109* **E4**
Kerrobert *1,143* **F1**
Kindersley *4,572* **F1**
Kipling *1,005* **G4**
La Loche *1,691* **m7**
Langenburg *1,156* **G5**
Langham *185* **E2**
Lanigan *1,397* **F3**
La Ronge *2,436* **B3**
Leader *999* **G1**
Lloydminster (Alta. and
  Sask.) *17,283* **D1**
Lumsden *1,477* **G3**
Macklin *1,105* **E1**
Maidstone *985* **D1**
Maple Creek *2,334* **H1**
Meadow Lake *4,318* **m7**
Melfort *5,628* **E3**
Melville *4,905* **G4**
Moose Jaw *33,593* **G3**
Moosomin *2,436* **G5**
Nipawin *4,419* **D4**
North Battleford *14,350*
  E1
Outlook *2,091* **F2**
Oxbow *1,132* **H4**
Pilot Butte *1,450* **G3**
Preeceville *1,205* **F4**
Prince Albert *34,181* **D3**
Radville *846* **H3**
Regina *179,178* **G3**
Rosetown *2,519* **F1**
Rosthern *985* **E2**
Saskatoon *186,058* **E2**
Shaunavon *1,913* **H1**
Shellbrook *1,173* **D2**
Spiritwood *973* **D2**
Swift Current *14,815*
  G2
Tisdale *3,045* **E3**
Unity *2,227* **E1**
Wadena *1,599* **E3**
Wakaw *965* **E3**
Warman *2,644* **E2**
Watrous *1,872* **F3**
Weyburn *9,673* **H4**
Whitewood *1,064* **G4**
Wilkie *1,401* **E1**
Wolseley *853* **G4**
Wynyard *2,022* **F3**
Yorkton *15,315* **F4**

The United States and Canada / Facts in Brief

The table below provides a brief description of the United States and Canada. The chief products list includes the top products for each state, province, or territory in three major areas of production. The summary entry for each country indicates the national capital and the country's major products in agriculture, manufacturing, and mining.

The United States

CHIEF PRODUCTS

State	Entered Union	Capital	Agriculture	Manufacturing	Mining
Alabama	December 14, 1819, 22nd state	Montgomery	Broilers, beef cattle, soybeans	Paper prod., chemicals, textiles	Coal, natural gas, petroleum
Alaska	January 3, 1959, 49th state	Juneau	Milk, eggs, beef cattle, greenhouse and nursery prod.	Food, petroleum prod., paper prod.	Petroleum, natural gas, gold
Arizona	February 14, 1912, 48th state	Phoenix	Beef cattle, cotton, milk, lettuce	Elec. equip., trans. equip., elec. and nonelec. machinery	Copper, molybdenum, coal
Arkansas	June 15, 1836, 25th state	Little Rock	Broilers, soybeans, rice	Food, elec. equip., metal prod., paper prod.	Natural gas, petroleum, bromine
California	September 9, 1850, 31st state	Sacramento	Milk, beef cattle, cotton, grapes	Elec. equip., trans. equip., food	Petroleum, natural gas, boron
Colorado	August 1, 1876, 38th state	Denver	Beef cattle, wheat, corn	Instruments, food, trans. equip.	Petroleum, coal, natural gas
Connecticut	January 9, 1788, 5th state	Hartford	Eggs, milk, greenhouse and nursery prod.	Trans. equip., nonelec. machinery, metal prod.	Stone, sand and gravel
Delaware	December 7, 1787, 1st state	Dover	Broilers, soybeans, corn	Chemicals, food, trans. equip.	Magnesium compounds, sand and gravel
Florida	March 3, 1845, 27th state	Tallahassee	Oranges, sugar cane, beef cattle, greenhouse and nursery prod.	Elec. equip., food, printed materials, trans. equip.	Phosphate rock, petroleum, stone
Georgia	January 2, 1788, 4th state	Atlanta	Broilers, peanuts, peaches	Trans. equip., textiles, food, paper products	Clays, stone, sand and gravel
Hawaii	August 21, 1959, 50th state	Honolulu	Sugar cane, pineapples, flowers	Food, printed materials, refined petroleum	Stone, sand and gravel
Idaho	July 3, 1890, 43rd state	Boise	Potatoes, wheat, beef cattle	Food, lumber and wood prod., machinery	Silver, phosphate rock, gold
Illinois	December 3, 1818, 21st state	Springfield	Corn, soybeans, hogs	Nonelec. machinery, food, elec. equip., chemicals	Coal, petroleum, stone
Indiana	December 11, 1816, 19th state	Indianapolis	Corn, soybeans, tomatoes	Metals, trans. equip., elec. equip., chemicals	Coal, petroleum, stone
Iowa	December 28, 1846, 29th state	Des Moines	Corn, soybeans, hogs, beef cattle	Food, nonelec. machinery, elec. equip.	Stone, gypsum, sand and gravel
Kansas	January 29, 1861, 34th state	Topeka	Beef cattle, wheat, grain sorghum	Trans. equip., food, printed materials	Petroleum, natural gas, coal
Kentucky	June 1, 1792, 15th state	Frankfort	Tobacco, horses, beef cattle, milk	Trans. equip., chemicals, elec. equip., nonelec. machinery	Coal, natural gas, petroleum
Louisiana	April 30, 1812, 18th state	Baton Rouge	Soybeans, cotton, beef cattle	Chemicals, petroleum and coal prod., food	Natural gas, petroleum
Maine	March 15, 1820, 23rd state	Augusta	Milk, eggs, potatoes	Paper prod., wood prod., elec. equip.	Sand and gravel, stone
Maryland	April 28, 1788, 7th state	Annapolis	Broilers, milk, greenhouse and nursery prod.	Elec. equip., food, chemicals	Stone, coal, sand and gravel
Massachusetts	February 6, 1788, 6th state	Boston	Greenhouse and nursery prod., cranberries, milk	Elec. and nonelec. machinery, elec. equip., instruments, printed materials	Sand and gravel, stone
Michigan	January 26, 1837, 26th state	Lansing	Milk, beef cattle, corn, cherries	Trans. equip., elec. and nonelec. machinery, metal prod.	Natural gas, iron ore, petroleum
Minnesota	May 11, 1858, 32nd state	St. Paul	Milk, corn, soybeans, beef cattle	Elec. and nonelec. machinery, food	Iron ore, stone, clay
Mississippi	December 10, 1817, 20th state	Jackson	Broilers, cotton, soybeans	Trans. equip., elec. equip., food, clothing	Petroleum, natural gas
Missouri	August 10, 1821, 24th state	Jefferson City	Soybeans, beef cattle, hogs	Trans. equip., food, chemicals	Lead, stone, coal
Montana	November 8, 1889, 41st state	Helena	Beef cattle, wheat, hay, barley	Lumber and wood prod., food, printed materials	Coal, petroleum, copper, gold
Nebraska	March 1, 1867, 37th state	Lincoln	Beef cattle, corn, hogs, soybeans	Food, nonelec. machinery, elec. and electronic equip.	Petroleum, sand and gravel
Nevada	October 31, 1864, 36th state	Carson City	Beef cattle, milk, hay	Elec. machinery, printed materials, food	Gold, silver, diatomite
New Hampshire	June 21, 1788, 9th state	Concord	Milk, hay, beef cattle	Elec. and electronic equip., nonelec. machinery, plastic prod.	Sand and gravel, stone
New Jersey	December 18, 1787, 3rd state	Trenton	Greenhouse and nursery products, milk, tomatoes	Chemicals, food, elec. equip., printed materials	Stone, sand and gravel
New Mexico	January 6, 1912, 47th state	Santa Fe	Beef cattle, milk, chili peppers	Elec. equip., petroleum prod., food	Natural gas, petroleum, coal, potash
New York	July 26, 1788, 11th state	Albany	Milk, beef cattle, apples	Printed materials, instruments, elec. equip.	Stone, salt, sand and gravel
North Carolina	November 21, 1789, 12th state	Raleigh	Broilers, tobacco, hogs	Textiles, tobacco prod., chemicals	Stone, phosphate rock, sand and gravel
North Dakota	November 2, 1889, 39th state	Bismarck	Wheat, beef cattle, sunflower seeds	Food, nonelec. machinery, petroleum prod.	Petroleum, coal, natural gas
Ohio	March 1, 1803, 17th state	Columbus	Corn, soybeans, milk, hogs	Trans. equip., metal prod., nonelec. machinery	Coal, natural gas, stone
Oklahoma	November 16, 1907, 46th state	Oklahoma City	Beef cattle, wheat, hay	Trans. equip., elec. and nonelec. machinery, elec. equip.	Petroleum, natural gas, coal
Oregon	February 14, 1859, 33rd state	Salem	Timber, beef cattle, wheat	Lumber and wood prod., food, paper prod.	Sand and gravel, stone, pumice
Pennsylvania	December 12, 1787, 2nd state	Harrisburg	Milk, beef cattle, mushrooms	Food, chemicals, elec. and nonelec. machinery	Coal, stone, natural gas
Rhode Island	May 29, 1790, 13th state	Providence	Greenhouse and nursery prod., milk	Jewelry and silverware, metal prod., elec. equip.	Stone, sand and gravel
South Carolina	May 23, 1788, 8th state	Columbia	Tobacco, beef cattle, soybeans	Textiles, chemicals, paper prod.	Stone, clays
South Dakota	November 2, 1889, 40th state	Pierre	Beef cattle, hogs, corn	Food, nonelec. machinery	Gold, petroleum
Tennessee	June 1, 1796, 16th state	Nashville	Beef cattle, milk, soybeans	Chemicals, food, nonelec. machinery	Coal, stone, zinc
Texas	December 29, 1845, 28th state	Austin	Beef cattle, cotton, milk	Chemicals, food, elec. equip., petroleum prod.	Petroleum, natural gas, stone, magnesium
Utah	January 4, 1896, 45th state	Salt Lake City	Beef cattle, milk, hay	Elec. and nonelec. machinery, trans. equip., food	Petroleum, coal, uranium
Vermont	March 4, 1791, 14th state	Montpelier	Milk, beef cattle, maple syrup	Elec. equip., metal prod., printed materials, paper prod.	Stone, sand and gravel
Virginia	June 25, 1788, 10th state	Richmond	Beef cattle, tobacco, milk	Chemicals, tobacco prod., food	Coal, stone
Washington	November 11, 1889, 42nd state	Olympia	Timber, wheat, hops, apples	Trans. equip., food, paper and wood prod.	Coal, gold, magnesium
West Virginia	June 20, 1863, 35th state	Charleston	Beef cattle, milk, apples	Chemicals; metals; stone, clay, glass prod.	Coal, natural gas, petroleum
Wisconsin	May 29, 1848, 30th state	Madison	Milk, beef cattle, hogs	Nonelec. machinery, food, paper prod.	Stone, sand and gravel
Wyoming	July 10, 1890, 44th state	Cheyenne	Beef cattle, sheep, sugar beets	Chemicals, petroleum prod., nonelec. machinery	Petroleum, coal, natural gas
UNITED STATES	. . .	Washington, D.C.	Beef cattle, milk, corn	Trans. equip., food, chemicals	Petroleum, natural gas, coal

Canada

CHIEF PRODUCTS

Province/Territory	Entered Dominion	Capital	Agriculture	Manufacturing	Mining
Alberta	September 1, 1905, with Saskatchewan, 8th and 9th provinces	Edmonton	Beef cattle, wheat, canola	Chemicals, food, refined petroleum	Petroleum, natural gas, coal
British Columbia	July 20, 1871, 6th province	Victoria	Milk, apples, beef cattle	Wood prod., paper prod., food	Coal, copper, natural gas
Manitoba	July 15, 1870, 5th province	Winnipeg	Wheat, beef cattle, barley	Food, trans. equip., printed materials	Nickel, copper, zinc
New Brunswick	July 1, 1867, one of four original provinces	Fredericton	Milk, potatoes, beef cattle	Paper prod., food, wood prod.	Zinc, lead, potash
Newfoundland	March 31, 1949, 10th province	St. John's	Chickens, eggs, milk	Food, paper prod.	Iron ore, zinc, gold
Northwest Territories	——	Yellowknife	——	Food, petroleum prod., wood prod.	Zinc, gold, petroleum
Nova Scotia	July 1, 1867, one of four original provinces	Halifax	Milk, beef cattle, chickens	Food, paper prod., tires	Coal, gypsum, tin
Ontario	July 1, 1867, one of four original provinces	Toronto	Beef cattle, milk, hogs	Trans. equip., chemicals, food	Nickel, gold, copper
Prince Edward Island	July 1, 1873, 7th province	Charlottetown	Potatoes, milk, beef cattle	Food, printed materials, wood prod.	——
Québec	July 1, 1867, one of four original provinces	Québec	Milk, hogs, corn	Paper prod., food, trans. equip.	Gold, iron ore, titanium
Saskatchewan	September 1, 1905, with Alberta, 8th and 9th provinces	Regina	Wheat, beef cattle, canola	Food, printed materials, elec. equip.	Petroleum, potash, uranium
Yukon Territory	——	Whitehorse	——	Lumber and wood prod., printed materials, food	Zinc, gold, lead
CANADA	. . .	Ottawa	Beef cattle, wheat, milk	Trans. equip., food, chemicals	Petroleum, natural gas, nickel, uranium

Abbreviations: elec. = electric; equip. = equipment; nonelec. = nonelectric; prod. = products; trans. equip. = transportation equipment

Geographical Information and Maps of the World Index

World Nations and Other Political Units

This table gives the area, population, population density, form of government, capital, and location of all the world's independent nations and other important political units.

Names of independent nations appear in **boldface type.** Continents are preceded by daggers.

Area figures include inland water.

The populations are either recent census figures (C) or estimates (E) from *The World Book Encyclopedia*. An asterisk (*) following a population indicates that the figure is a 1995 or earlier estimate based on figures from official government and United Nations sources.

Map plate numbers refer to the Maps of the World section of the atlas.

Political unit	Local name	Area sq. miles	km²	Population	Date	Population density per sq. mile	km²	Form of govt./ Political status	Capital	Continent	Map plate
Afghanistan	Afghanistan	251,773	652,090	18,828,000	1995E	75	29	Transitional	Kabul	Asia	23
†Africa	—	11,681,000	30,253,000	717,000,000	1995E	61	24	—	—	Africa	30–31
Alabama, U.S.	Alabama	51,718	133,950	4,062,608	1990C	79	30	State (U.S.)	Montgomery	North America	44
Alaska, U.S.	Alaska	587,878	1,522,596	551,947	1990C	0.9	0.4	State (U.S.)	Juneau	North America	40
Albania	Shqipëri	11,100	28,748	3,390,000	1995E	305	118	Republic	Tiranë	Europe	15
Alberta, Can.	Alberta	255,287	661,190	2,545,553	1991C	10	4	Province (Canada)	Edmonton	North America	42
Algeria	Al Jaza'ir	919,595	2,381,741	28,581,000	1995E	31	12	Republic; under military control	Algiers	Africa	32
American Samoa	American Samoa	77	199	48,000	*	623	241	U.S. Territory	Pago Pago	Oceania	65
Andaman and Nicobar Islands, India	Andaman and Nicobar	3,185	8,249	322,000	*	101	39	Territory of India	Port Blair	Asia	25
Andorra	Valls d'Andorra (Valleys of Andorra)	175	453	59,000	1995E	337	130	Principality; joint Spanish and French rule	Andorra	Europe	13
Angola	Angola	481,354	1,246,700	11,072,000	1995E	23	9	Republic	Luanda	Africa	36
Anguilla	Anguilla	37	96	7,000	*	189	73	British Dependency	The Valley	North America	51
Anhui, China	Anhwei	54,016	139,900	56,180,813	1990C	1,040	402	Province (China)	Hefei (Ho-fei)	Asia	28
†Antarctica	—	5,400,000	14,000,000	(1)	—	—	—	—	—	Antarctica	66
Antigua and Barbuda	Antigua and Barbuda	171	442	69,000	1995E	480	186	Constitutional Monarchy	St. John's	North America	51
Arabian Peninsula (2)	—	1,160,000	3,004,000	32,755,000	*	28	12	—	—	Asia	23
Argentina	Argentina	1,073,519	2,780,400	34,883,000	1995E	32	13	Republic	Buenos Aires	South America	56
Arizona, U.S.	Arizona	114,007	295,276	3,677,985	1990C	32	12	State (U.S.)	Phoenix	North America	46
Arkansas, U.S.	Arkansas	53,183	137,742	2,362,239	1990C	44	17	State (U.S.)	Little Rock	North America	45
Armenia	Hayastan	11,506	29,800	3,730,000	1995E	324	125	Republic	Yerevan	Asia	16
Aruba	Aruba	75	193	68,897	1991C	919	357	Self-governing	Oranjestad	North America	49
Ascension	Ascension	34	88	1,500	1984E	44	17	Belongs to United Kingdom, under administration of St. Helena	Georgetown	Africa	30–31
†Asia	—	16,992,000	44,008,000	3,506,000,000	1995E	206	80	—	—	Asia	21–22
†**Australia**	Commonwealth of Australia	2,978,147	7,713,364	17,820,000	1995E	6	2	Constitutional Monarchy	Canberra	Australia	59
Australian Capital Territory (Canberra)	Australian Capital Territory	930	2,400	278,894	1991C	300	116	Territory (Australia)	Canberra	Australia	59
Austria	Österreich	32,376	83,853	7,861,000	1995E	243	94	Federal Republic	Vienna (Wien)	Europe	14
Azerbaijan	Azerbaijan	33,436	86,599	7,447,000	1995E	223	86	Republic	Baku	Asia/Europe	16
Azores	Açores	868	2,247	240,520	*	277	107	Part of Portugal's territory	Ponta Delgada	Europe	32
Bahamas	Bahamas	5,358	13,878	277,000	1995E	52	20	Constitutional Monarchy	Nassau	North America	47
Bahrain	Al Bahrayn	262	678	578,000	1995E	2,206	853	Emirate	Manama	Asia	24
Balearic Islands, Spain	Islas Baleares	1,936	5,014	709,138	1991C	366	141	Province of Spain	Palma	Europe	13
Bangladesh	Bangladesh	55,598	143,998	118,786,000	1995E	2,137	825	Republic	Dhaka	Asia	25
Barbados	Barbados	166	430	261,000	1995E	1,572	607	Constitutional Monarchy	Bridgetown	North America	51
Beijing (Peking), China	Beijing	6,873	17,800	10,819,407	1990C	1,574	608	Special Municipal District of China	—	Asia	28
Belarus	Belarus	80,155	207,600	10,310,000	1995E	129	50	Republic	Minsk	Europe	16
Belgium	Belgique (French), België (Flemish)	11,783	30,519	10,031,000	1995E	851	329	Constitutional Monarchy	Brussels	Europe	12
Belize	Belize	8,867	22,965	205,000	1995E	24	9	Constitutional Monarchy	Belmopan	North America	49
Benin	Bénin	43,484	112,622	5,399,000	1995E	124	48	Republic	Porto-Novo and Cotonou	Africa	34
Bermuda	Bermuda	21	54	58,000	*	2,762	1,074	British Dependency	Hamilton	North America	47
Bhutan	Druk	18,147	47,000	1,729,000	1995E	95	37	Monarchy	Thimphu	Asia	25
Bioko, Equat. Gui.	Bioko	785	2,034	57,190	1983C	73	28	Territory of Equatorial Guinea	Malabo	Africa	34
Bolivia	Bolivia	424,165	1,098,581	8,074,000	1995E	19	7	Republic	Sucre (official); La Paz (actual)	South America	54
Borneo (3)	—	288,151	746,308	12,000,000	*	42	16	—	—	Asia	26
Bosnia—Hercegovina	Bosna i Hercegovina	19,741	51,129	4,454,000	1995E	226	87	Republic	Sarajevo	Europe	14
Botswana	Botswana	224,607	581,730	1,433,000	1995E	6	2	Republic	Gaborone	Africa	37
Brazil	Brasil	3,286,488	8,511,965	161,382,000	1995E	49	19	Federal Republic	Brasília	South America	54–56
British Columbia, Can.	British Columbia	365,900	947,800	3,282,061	1991C	9	3	Province (Canada)	Victoria	North America	42
British Honduras, *see* Belize	—	—	—	—	—	—	—	—	—	—	—
British Indian Ocean Territory	British Indian Ocean Territory	30	78	2,000	1987E	67	26	British Dependency	—	Asia	22
British Solomon Islands, *see* Solomon Islands	—	—	—	—	—	—	—	—	—	—	—
Brunei	Brunei	2,226	5,765	288,000	1995E	129	50	Monarchy	Bandar Seri Begawan	Asia	26
Bulgaria	Balgarija	42,823	110,912	8,887,000	1995E	208	80	Republic	Sofia	Europe	15
Burkina Faso	Burkina Faso	105,869	274,200	10,352,000	1995E	99	38	Military Rule	Ouagadougou	Africa	34
Burma	Burma	261,228	676,578	46,548,000	1995E	178	69	Military Rule	Rangoon	Asia	25
Burundi	Burundi	10,747	27,834	6,343,000	1995E	590	228	Single-party Rule	Bujumbura	Africa	36
California, U.S.	California	158,648	410,896	29,839,250	1990C	188	73	State (U.S.)	Sacramento	North America	46
Cambodia	Kâmpŭchéa	69,898	181,035	9,447,000	1995E	135	52	Transitional	Phnom-Penh	Asia	26
Cameroon	Cameroun	183,569	475,442	13,275,000	1995E	72	28	Republic	Yaoundé	Africa	34
Canada	Canada	3,849,674	9,970,610	28,537,000	1995E	7	3	Constitutional Monarchy	Ottawa	North America	42

Political unit	Local name	Area sq. miles	Area km²	Population	Date	Pop. density per sq. mile	Pop. density per km²	Form of govt./ Political status	Capital	Continent	Map plate
Canary Islands	Islas Canarias	2,796	7,242	1,444,626	1981C	517	199	Part of Spain (2 provinces)	Santa Cruz de Tenerife; Las Palmas de Gran Canaria	Africa	32
Cape Verde	Cabo Verde	1,557	4,033	419,000	1995E	269	104	Republic	Praia	Africa	32
Cayman Islands	Cayman Islands	100	259	30,000	*	300	116	British Dependency	Georgetown	North America	49
Celebes (Indonesia)	Sulawesi	73,057	189,216	12,507,700	1989E	171	66	Part of Indonesia	—	Asia	26
Central African Republic	Centrafrique	240,535	622,984	3,429,000	1995E	14	6	Military Rule	Bangui	Africa	35
Central America	—	202,000	523,000	33,000,000	1995E	163	63	—	—	North America	49
Ceylon, see Sri Lanka	—	—	—	—	—	—	—	—	—	—	—
Chad	Tchad	495,755	1,284,000	6,361,000	1995E	13	5	Republic	N'Djamena	Africa	35
Channel Islands	Channel Islands	75	195	142,949	1991C	1,907	733	British Crown Dependencies	St. Peter Port; St. Helier	Europe	9
Chile	Chile	292,258	756,945	14,237,000	1995E	49	19	Republic	Santiago	South America	56
China	Zhonghua Renmin Gongheguo	3,696,032	9,572,678	1,238,319,000	1995E	335	129	Communist Dictatorship	Beijing (Peking)	Asia	27
Christmas Island (Austl.)	Christmas Island	52	135	2,500	*	48	19	External Territory (Australia)	Flying Fish Cove	Asia	26
Cocos (Keeling) Islands (Austl.)	Cocos (Keeling) Islands	5	13	647	1991C	129	50	External Territory (Australia)	—	Asia	22
Colombia	Colombia	439,737	1,138,914	35,101,000	1995E	80	31	Republic	Bogotá	South America	54
Colorado, U.S.	Colorado	104,100	269,618	3,307,912	1990C	32	12	State (U.S.)	Denver	North America	45
Commonwealth of Independent States	—	8,533,206	22,100,900	288,562,000	1995E	34	13	Association of 12 former Soviet republics	—	—	—
Commonwealth of Nations	—	14,353,000	37,173,000	1,670,000,000	*	116	45	Association of 51 independent countries & 26 political units	—	—	—
Comoros	Comores	863	2,235	653,000	1995E	757	292	Republic	Moroni	Africa	37
Congo	Congo	132,047	342,000	2,590,000	1995E	20	8	Republic	Brazzaville	Africa	36
Connecticut, U.S.	Connecticut	5,006	12,966	3,295,669	1990C	658	254	State (U.S.)	Hartford	North America	44
Cook Islands	Cook Islands	91	236	18,000	1993E	198	76	Self-governing Dependency of New Zealand	Avarua	Oceania	61
Corsica	Corse	3,352	8,681	250,400	1990C	75	29	Part of France (2 departments)	Ajaccio	Europe	11
Costa Rica	Costa Rica	19,730	51,100	3,424,000	1995E	174	67	Republic	San José	North America	49
Croatia	Hrvatska	21,829	56,538	4,803,000	1995E	220	85	Republic	Zagreb	Europe	14
Cuba	Cuba	42,804	110,861	11,091,000	1995E	259	100	Socialist State and a Republic (Dictatorship)	Havana (La Habana)	North America	49
Curaçao	Curaçao	171	443	150,000	*	877	339	Largest Island of the Netherlands Antilles	Willemstad	North America	49
Cyprus	Kypros (Greek), Kibris (Turkish)	3,572	9,251	736,000	1995E	206	80	Republic	Nicosia	Asia	24
Czech Republic	Česká Republika	30,450	78,864	10,407,000	1995E	342	132	Republic	Prague (Praha)	Europe	10
Dahomey, see Benin	—	—	—	—	—	—	—	—	—	—	—
Delaware, U.S.	Delaware	2,026	5,246	668,696	1990C	330	127	State (U.S.)	Dover	North America	44
Denmark	Danmark	16,662	43,077	5,192,000	1995E	312	121	Constitutional Monarchy	Copenhagen (København)	Europe	8
District of Columbia (D.C.) [Washington, D.C., U.S.]	District of Columbia	68	177	606,900	1990C	8,925	3,429	U.S. Federal District	Washington, D.C.	North America	44
Djibouti	Djibouti	8,958	23,200	317,000	1995E	35	14	Republic	Djibouti (city)	Africa	35
Dominica	Dominica	290	751	75,000	1995E	259	100	Republic	Roseau	North America	51
Dominican Republic	República Dominicana	18,816	48,734	7,915,000	1995E	421	162	Republic	Santo Domingo	North America	49
Dutch Guiana, see Suriname	—	—	—	—	—	—	—	—	—	—	—
Ecuador	Ecuador	109,484	283,561	11,822,000	1995E	108	42	Republic	Quito	South America	54
Egypt	Miṣr	386,662	1,001,449	58,519,000	1995E	151	58	Republic	Cairo (Al Qahirah)	Africa/Asia	33
Ellice Islands, see Tuvalu	—	—	—	—	—	—	—	—	—	—	—
El Salvador	El Salvador	8,124	21,041	5,768,000	1995E	710	274	Republic	San Salvador	North America	49
England	England	50,378	130,478	48,367,000	1995E	960	371	Constitutional Monarchy	London	Europe	9
Equatorial Guinea	Guinea Ecuatorial	10,831	28,051	400,000	1995E	37	14	Military Rule	Malabo on Bioko	Africa	36
Eritrea	Eritrea	45,405	117,598	3,651,000	1995E	80	31	Transitional	Asmara	Africa	
Estonia	Eesti	17,413	45,100	1,571,000	1995E	90	35	Republic	Tallinn	Europe	8
Ethiopia	Itiopya	426,373	1,104,302	53,711,000	1995E	126	49	Transitional	Addis Ababa	Africa	35
Eurasia	—	21,025,000	54,453,000	4,215,000,000	*	Europe: 176 Asia: 206	Europe: 68 Asia: 80	—	—	Europe and Asia	
†Europe	—	4,033,000	10,445,000	709,000,000	1995E	176	68	—	—	Europe	5–6
Faeroe Islands	Føroyar (Faeroese) Færøerne (Danish)	540	1,399	42,000	*	78	30	Self-governing Community of Denmark	Tórshavn	Europe	6
Falkland Islands (Islas Malvinas—Argentina)	Falkland Islands	4,699	12,170	2,000	*	0.4	0.2	British Dependency [claimed by Argentina]	Stanley	South America	56
Federated States of Micronesia, see Micronesia, Federated States of	—	—	—	—	—	—	—	—	—	—	—
Fiji	Fiji	7,056	18,274	787,000	1995E	112	43	Constitutional Monarchy	Suva	Oceania	63
Finland	Suomi (Finnish) Finland (Swedish)	130,559	338,145	5,046,000	1995E	39	15	Republic	Helsinki (Helsingfors)	Europe	7
Florida, U.S.	Florida	58,681	151,982	13,003,362	1990C	222	86	State (U.S.)	Tallahassee	North America	44
France	France	212,935	551,500	57,769,000	1995E	271	105	Republic	Paris	Europe	11
French Guiana	Guyane Française	35,135	91,000	73,000	*	2	1	Overseas Department (France)	Cayenne	South America	54
French Polynesia	Polynésie Française	1,544	4,000	220,000	*	131	51	Overseas Territory (France)	Papeete	Oceania	61
French West Indies	Guadaloupe and Martinique	1,083	2,806	657,000	*	607	234	2 Overseas Departments of France	Basse-Terre; Fort de France	North America	50
Fujian (Fukien), China	Fujian	47,529	123,100	30,048,224	1990C	632	244	Province (China)	Fuzhou (Fu-chóu)	Asia	27

Political unit	Local name	Area sq. miles	km²	Population	Date	Population density per sq. mile	km²	Form of govt./ Political status	Capital	Continent	Map plate
Gabon	Gabon	103,347	267,667	1,367,000	1995E	13	5	Republic	Libreville	Africa	36
Galapagos Islands, Ecuador	Archipiélago de Colón	3,029	7,844	9,700	1990E	3	1	Province of Ecuador (Galapagos Islands)	Baquerizo Moreno	South America	54
Gambia	Gambia	4,361	11,295	980,000	1995E	225	87	Republic	Banjul	Africa	34
Gansu (Kansu), China	Gansu	141,500	366,500	22,371,141	1990C	158	61	Province (China)	Lanzhou (Lan-chou)	Asia	27
Gaza Strip	R'tzuat Aza	146	378	710,000	*	4,863	1,878	Transitional	Gaza	Asia	24
Georgia, U.S.	Georgia	58,930	152,627	6,508,419	1990C	110	43	State (U.S.)	Atlanta	North America	44
Georgia	Sakartveto	26,911	69,700	5,473,000	1995E	203	79	Transitional	Tbilisi	Asia/Europe	16
Germany	Deutschland	137,358	355,754	81,264,000	1995E	592	228	Federal Republic	Berlin, Bonn	Europe	10
Ghana	Ghana	92,098	238,533	17,453,000	1995E	190	73	Republic	Accra	Africa	34
Gibraltar	Gibraltar	2.3	6.0	28,051	*	12,196	4,675	British Dependency	Gibraltar	Europe	13
Gilbert Islands	Gilbert Islands	105	272	67,187	1990C	640	247	Part of Kiribati	—	Oceania	—
Golan Heights	Ramat ha-Golan	454	1,176	28,500	1993E	63	24	Occupied by Israel; formerly part of Syria	—	Asia	24
Great Britain, see The United Kingdom of Great Britain and Northern Ireland	—	—	—	—	—	—	—	—	—	—	—
Greece	Ellas	50,962	131,990	10,322,000	1995E	203	78	Republic	Athens (Athinai)	Europe	15
Greenland	Grønland (Danish) Kalaallit Nunaat (Eskimo)	840,004	2,175,600	58,000	1995E	0.07	0.03	Province of Denmark	Godthåb	North America	41
Grenada	Grenada	133	344	92,000	1995E	692	267	Parliamentary	St. George's	North America	51
Guadeloupe	Guadeloupe	687	1,780	345,000	1991E	502	194	Overseas Department (France)	Basse-Terre	North America	51
Guam	Guam	209	541	133,000	1993E	636	246	Territory of the United States	Agana	Oceania	64
Guangdong (Kwangtung), China	Guangdong	76,240	197,400	62,829,236	1990C	824	318	Province (China)	Guangzhou (Canton)	Asia	27
Guangxi (Kwangsi), China	Guangxi	85,100	220,400	42,245,765	1990C	496	192	Autonomous Region, China	Nanning (Nan-ning)	Asia	27
Guatemala	Guatemala	42,042	108,889	10,621,000	1995E	253	98	Republic	Guatemala City	North America	49
Guernsey	Guernsey	24	62	58,867	1991C	2,453	949	British Crown Dependency	St. Peter Port	Europe	9
Guinea	Guinée	94,926	245,857	67,000,000	1995E	71	27	Transitional	Conakry	Africa	34
Guinea-Bissau	Guiné-Bissau	13,948	36,125	1,073,000	1995E	77	30	Military Republic	Bissau	Africa	34
Guizhou (Kweichow), China	Guizhou	67,180	174,000	32,391,066	1990C	482	186	Province (China)	Guiyang (Kuei-yang)	Asia	27
Guyana	Guyana	83,000	214,969	834,000	1995E	10	4	Republic	Georgetown	South America	54
Haiti	Haïti	10,714	27,750	7,180,000	1995E	671	259	Military Rule	Port-au-Prince	North America	49
Hawaii, U.S.	Hawaii	6,459	16,729	1,115,274	1990C	173	67	State (U.S.)	Honolulu	Oceania	60
Hebei (Hopeh), China	Hebei	78,260	202,700	61,082,439	1990C	781	301	Province (China)	Shijiazhuang (Shih-chiachuang)	Asia	28
Heilongjiang (Heilungkiang), China	Heilongjiang	179,000	463,600	35,214,873	1990C	197	76	Province (China)	Harbin (Harbin)	Asia	27
Henan (Honan), China	Henan	64,480	167,000	85,509,535	1990C	1,326	512	Province (China)	Zheng-zhou (Cheng-chou)	Asia	27
Hispaniola	La Isla Española	29,530	76,484	15,095,000	*	511	197	Haiti; Dominican Republic	Port-au-Prince; Santo Domingo	North America	49
Holland, see Netherlands	—	—	—	—	—	—	—	—	—	—	—
Honduras	Honduras	43,277	112,088	5,968,000	1995E	138	53	Republic	Tegucigalpa	North America	49
Hong Kong	Hong Kong	400	1,045	5,724,000	1995E	14,310	5,478	British Dependency	Victoria	Asia	27
Hubei (Hupeh), China	Hubei	72,394	187,500	53,969,210	1990C	745	288	Province (China)	Wuhan (Wu-han)	Asia	27
Hunan, China	Hunan	81,275	210,500	60,659,754	1990C	746	288	Province (China)	Changsha (C'hang-sha)	Asia	27
Hungary	Magyarország	35,920	93,032	10,542,000	1995E	293	113	Republic	Budapest	Europe	10
Iceland	Ìsland	39,769	103,000	268,000	1995E	7	3	Republic	Reykjavík	Europe	7
Idaho, U.S.	Idaho	83,574	216,456	1,011,986	1990C	12	5	State (U.S.)	Boise	North America	46
Illinois, U.S.	Illinois	53,343	145,928	11,466,682	1990C	204	79	State (U.S.)	Springfield	North America	45
India	Bharat	1,269,346	3,287,590	931,044,000	1995E	733	283	Federal Republic	New Delhi	Asia	25
Indiana, U.S.	Indiana	36,185	93,720	5,564,228	1990C	154	59	State (U.S.)	Indianapolis	North America	44
Indonesia	Indonesia	741,101	1,919,443	201,477,000	1995E	272	105	Republic	Jakarta	Asia	26
Inner Mongolia, China	Nei Mongol	454,600	1,177,500	21,456,798	1990C	47	18	Autonomous Region (China)	Hohhot (Hu-ho-hao-t'e)	Asia	27
Iowa, U.S.	Iowa	56,276	145,754	2,787,424	1990C	50	19	State (U.S.)	Des Moines	North America	45
Iran	Īrān	636,296	1,648,000	66,720,000	1995E	105	40	Islamic Republic	Teheran	Asia	23
Iraq	Al'Irāq	169,235	438,317	21,224,000	1995E	125	48	Republic	Baghdad	Asia	24
Ireland	Éire	27,137	70,284	3,469,000	1995E	128	49	Republic	Dublin	Europe	9
Israel	Yisra'el	8,019	20,770	5,884,000	1995E	734	283	Republic	Jerusalem	Asia	24
Italy	Italia	116,320	301,268	57,910,000	1995E	498	192	Republic	Rome (Roma)	Europe	14
Ivory Coast	Côte d'Ivoire	124,504	322,463	14,401,000	1995E	116	45	Republic	Abidjan	Africa	34
Jamaica	Jamaica	4,243	10,990	2,547,000	1995E	600	232	Constitutional Monarchy	Kingston	North America	49
Jammu and Kashmir	Jammu and Kashmīr	85,806	222,237	9,920,000	*	115	45	In dispute (India and Pakistan)	Srinagar and Jammu	Asia	25
Japan	Nippon	145,870	377,801	125,879,000	1995E	863	333	Constitutional Monarchy	Tokyo	Asia	29
Java (incl. Madura)	Jawa	51,038	132,187	107,581,306	1990C	2,108	814	Part of Indonesia	—	Asia	26
Jersey	Jersey	45	117	84,082	1991C	1,868	719	British Crown Dependency	St. Helier	Europe	9
Jiangsu (Kiangsu), China	Jiangsu	39,460	102,200	67,056,519	1990C	1,699	656	Province (China)	Nanjing (Nan-ching)	Asia	28
Jiangxi (Kiangsi), China	Jiangxi	63,630	164,800	37,710,281	1990C	593	229	Province (China)	Nanchang (Nan-ch'ang)	Asia	27
Jilin (Kirin), China	Jilin	72,200	187,000	24,658,721	1990C	342	132	Province (China)	Changchun (Ch'ang-ch'un)	Asia	27
Jordan	Al Urdun	35,475	91,880	4,013,000	1995E	113	44	Constitutional Monarchy	Amman	Asia	24

I-4

Political unit	Local name	Area sq. miles	km²	Population	Date	Population density per sq. mile	km²	Form of govt./ Political status	Capital	Continent	Map plate
Kampuchea, see Cambodia	—	—	—	—	—	—	—				
Kansas, U.S.	Kansas	82,282	213,110	2,485,600	1990C	30	12	State (U.S.)	Topeka	North America	45
Kazakhstan	Kazakhstan	1,049,156	2,717,300	17,436,000	1995E	17	6	Republic	Alma-Ata	Asia/Europe	19
Kentucky, U.S.	Kentucky	40,411	104,665	3,698,969	1990C	92	35	State (U.S.)	Frankfort	North America	44
Kenya	Kenya	224,081	580,367	27,885,000	1995E	124	48	Republic	Nairobi	Africa	36
Kerguelen Island	Iles Kerguèlen	2,577	6,674	(1)	—	—	—	Part of French Southern and Antarctic Territories	—	Antarctica	30–31
Kiribati	Kiribati	280	726	79,000	1995E	282	109	Republic	Tarawa	Oceania	60
Korea, see North Korea; South Korea	—	—	—	—	—	—	—				
Kuwait	Al Kuwayt	6,880	17,818	1,804,000	1995E	262	101	Emirate	Kuwait	Asia	24
Kyrgyzstan	Kyrgyzstan	76,641	198,499	4,693,000	1995E	61	24	Republic	Biškek	Asia	18
Labrador (Can.)	Labrador	113,641	294,330	30,379	1991C	0.3	0.1	Part of Newfoundland Province (Canada)	—	North America	42
Laos	Laos	91,429	236,800	4,882,000	1995E	53	21	Socialist Republic (Communist)	Vientiane	Asia	26
Latin America	—	8,000,000	21,000,000	481,000,000	1995E	59	23	—	—	North America, South America	52–53
Latvia	Latvija	24,749	64,100	2,650,000	1995E	107	41	Republic	Riga	Europe	8
Lebanon	Lubnăn	4,015	10,400	3,028,000	1995E	754	291	Republic	Beirut	Asia	24
Lesotho	Lesotho	11,720	30,355	1,997,000	1995E	169	65	Military Rule	Maseru	Africa	37
Liaoning (Liaoning), China	Liaoning	58,300	151,000	39,459,697	1990C	677	261	Province (China)	Shenyang (Shen-yang)	Asia	28
Liberia	Liberia	43,000	111,369	3,039,000	1995E	71	27	Transitional	Monrovia	Africa	34
Libya	Lībiyă	679,362	1,759,540	5,407,000	1995E	8	3	Socialist Republic/ Military Rule	Tripoli	Africa	33
Liechtenstein	Liechtenstein	62	160	28,000	1995E	452	175	Constitutional Monarchy	Vaduz	Europe	14
Lithuania	Lietuva	25,174	65,200	3,771,000	1995E	150	58	Republic	Vilnius	Europe	8
Louisiana, U.S.	Louisiana	47,720	123,593	4,238,216	1990C	89	34	State (U.S.)	Baton Rouge	North America	45
Luxembourg	Luxembourg	998	2,586	386,000	1995E	387	149	Constitutional Monarchy	Luxembourg	Europe	12
Macao	Macau	6.5	16	436,000	*	67,077	27,250	Portuguese Territory	Macao	Asia	27
Macedonia	Makedonija	9,928	25,713	2,117,000	1995E	213	82	Republic	Skopje	Europe	15
Macias Nguema Biyogo, see Bioko	—	—	—	—	—	—	—				
Madagascar	Madagasikara	226,658	587,041	14,155,000	1995E	62	24	Republic	Antananarivo	Africa	37
Madeira Islands	Arquipélago da Madeira	307	794	271,000	*	882	341	District of Portugal	Funchal	Africa	32
Maine, U.S.	Maine	33,128	85,801	1,233,223	1990C	37	14	State (U.S.)	Augusta	North America	44
Malagasy Republic, see Madagascar	—	—	—	—	—	—	—			—	
Malawi	Malawi	45,747	118,484	11,304,000	1995E	247	95	Republic	Lilongwe	Africa	36
Malaya	Malaya	50,806	131,588	16,100,200	*	262	101	Part of Malaysia	—	Asia	26
Malaysia	Malaysia	127,317	329,749	20,125,000	1995E	158	61	Constitutional Monarchy	Kuala Lumpur	Asia	26
Maldives	Maldives	115	298	248,000	1995E	2,157	832	Republic	Male	Asia	34
Mali	Mali	478,841	1,240,192	10,797,000	1995E	23	9	Republic	Bamako	Africa	34
Malta	Malta	122	316	367,000	1995E	3,008	1,161	Republic	Valletta	Europe	14
Man, Isle of	Isle of Man	227	588	65,000	*	286	111	British Crown Dependency	Douglas	Europe	9
Manitoba, Can.	Manitoba	250,947	649,950	1,091,942	1991C	4	2	Province (Canada)	Winnipeg	North America	42
Marshall Islands	Marshall Islands	70	181	43,000	1995E	614	238	Republic in free association with U.S.	Majaro	Oceania	60
Martinique	Martinique	425	1,102	382,200	*	847	347	Overseas Department (France)	Fort-de-France	North America	51
Maryland, U.S.	Maryland	10,455	27,077	4,798,622	1990C	459	177	State (U.S.)	Annapolis	North America	44
Massachusetts, U.S.	Massachusetts	8,262	21,398	6,029,051	1990C	899	282	State (U.S.)	Boston	North America	44
Mauritania	Mūrĭtănĭyă	397,956	1,030,700	2,335,000	1995E	6	2	Republic	Nouakchott	Africa	32
Mauritius	Mauritius	788	2,040	1,130,000	1995E	1,434	541	Constitutional Monarchy	Port Louis	Africa	37
Mayotte	Mayotte	144	374	54,000	*	375	144	French possession— claimed by Comoros	Dzaoudzi	Africa	37
Mexico	México	756,066	1,958,201	93,670,000	1995E	124	48	Republic	Mexico City	North America	48
Michigan, U.S.	Michigan	58,513	151,548	9,328,784	1990C	159	62	State (U.S.)	Lansing	North America	44
Micronesia, Federated States of	Federated States of Micronesia	271	702	122,000	1995E	465	179	Republic in free association with U.S.	Kolonia	Oceania	60
Midway Island	Midway Island	2	5	450	*	225	90	U.S. Possession	—	Oceania	60
Minnesota, U.S.	Minnesota	84,397	218,587	4,387,029	1990C	52	20	State (U.S.)	St. Paul	North America	45
Mississippi, U.S.	Mississippi	47,695	123,530	2,586,443	1990C	54	21	State (U.S.)	Jackson	North America	45
Missouri, U.S.	Missouri	69,709	180,546	5,137,804	1990C	74	28	State (U.S.)	Jefferson City	North America	45
Moldova	Moldova	13,012	33,701	4,350,000	1995E	334	129	Republic	Kišinev	Europe	16
Monaco	Monaco	.75	1.95	30,000	1995E	40,000	15,384	Principality	Monaco	Europe	11
Mongolia	Mongol Ard Uls	604,829	1,566,500	2,498,000	1995E	4	2	Republic	Ulan Bator	Asia	27
Montana, U.S.	Montana	147,047	380,849	803,655	1990C	5	2	State (U.S.)	Helena	North America	46
Montserrat	Montserrat	39	102	13,000	1995E	333	127	British Dependency	Plymouth	North America	51
Morocco	Al Maghrib	172,414	446,550	28,260,000	1995E	164	63	Constitutional Monarchy	Rabat	Africa	32
Mozambique	Moçambique	309,496	801,590	16,359,000	1995E	53	20	Transitional	Maputo	Africa	37
Muscat and Oman, see Oman	—	—	—	—	—	—	—				—
Namibia	Namibia	318,261	824,292	1,688,000	1995E	5	2	Republic	Windhoek	Africa	37
Nationalist China, see Taiwan	—	—	—	—	—	—	—			—	
Nauru	Nauru (English) Naoero (Nauruan)	8	21	11,000	1995E	1,375	524	Republic	—	Oceania	64
Nebraska, U.S.	Nebraska	77,359	200,358	1,584,617	1990C	20	8	State (U.S.)	Lincoln	North America	45
Nepal	Nepal	54,362	140,797	22,124,000	1995E	407	157	Constitutional Monarchy	Kathmandu	Asia	25
Netherlands	Nederland	16,163	41,863	14,499,000	1995E	1,183	457	Constitutional Monarchy	Amsterdam	Europe	12
Netherlands Antilles	Nederlandse Antillen	308	798	185,000	*	597	231	Self-governing; part of Kingdom of the Netherlands	Willemstad	North America	50
Nevada, U.S.	Nevada	110,567	286,367	1,206,152	1990C	11	4	State (U.S.)	Carson City	North America	46
New Brunswick, Can.	New Brunswick	28,355	73,440	723,900	1991C	26	10	Province (Canada)	Fredericton	North America	42
New Caledonia	Nouvelle-Calédonie	7,366	19,079	165,000	*	22	9	Overseas Territory (France)	Nouméa	Oceania	63

Political unit	Local name	Area sq. miles	km²	Population	Date	Population density per sq. mile	km²	Form of govt./ Political status	Capital	Continent	Map plate
Newfoundland, Can.	Newfoundland	156,649	405,720	568,474	1991C	4	2	Province (Canada)	St. John's	North America	42
Newfoundland (island of), (Can.)	Newfoundland	43,008	111,390	538,099	1991C	13	5	Part of Newfoundland Province, Canada	—	North America	42
New Guinea (5)	Pulau Irian	316,000	818,000	5,900,000	1995E	19	7	—	—	Oceania	60
New Hampshire, U.S.	New Hampshire	9,283	24,044	1,113,915	1990C	120	46	State (U.S.)	Concord	North America	44
New Hebrides Islands, see Vanuatu	—	—	—	—	—	—	—	—	—	—	—
New Jersey, U.S.	New Jersey	7,790	20,175	7,748,634	1990C	995	384	State (U.S.)	Trenton	North America	44
New Mexico, U.S.	New Mexico	121,599	314,939	1,521,779	1990C	13	5	State (U.S.)	Santa Fe	North America	45
New South Wales, Austl.	New South Wales	309,500	801,600	5,731,926	1991C	19	7	State (Australia)	Sydney	Australia	59
New York, U.S.	New York	49,112	127,200	18,044,505	1990C	367	142	State (U.S.)	Albany	North America	44
New Zealand	New Zealand	103,883	269,057	3,552,000	1995E	34	13	Constitutional Monarchy	Wellington	Oceania	62
Nicaragua	Nicaragua	50,193	130,000	4,433,000	1995E	88	34	Republic	Managua	North America	49
Niger	Niger	489,191	1,267,000	9,102,000	1995E	19	7	Military Republic	Niamey	Africa	34
Nigeria	Nigeria	356,669	923,768	105,134,000	1995E	295	114	Transitional	Lagos and Abuja	Africa	34
Ningxia (Ningsia), China	Ningxia	25,640	66,400	4,655,451	1990C	182	70	Autonomous Region (China)	Yinchuan	Asia	27
Niue Island	Niue	100	259	2,239	1991C	22	9	Self-governing area associated with New Zealand	—	Oceania	64
Norfolk Island (Austl.)	Norfolk Island	14	36	1,800	1991C	129	50	External Territory (Australia)	—	Australia	61
†North America	—	9,348,000	24,211,000	453,000,000	1995E	48	19	—	—	North America	38–39
North Borneo, see Sabah	—	—	—	—	—	—	—	—	—	—	—
North Carolina, U.S.	North Carolina	52,672	136,421	6,657,630	1990C	126	49	State (U.S.)	Raleigh	North America	44
North Dakota, U.S.	North Dakota	70,704	183,123	641,364	1990C	9	4	State (U.S.)	Bismarck	North America	45
North Korea	Choson-minjujuui-inmin-konghwaguk	46,540 (4)	120,538 (4)	23,922,000	1995E	514	198	Republic (Communist rule)	Pyongyang	Asia	28
Northern Ireland	Northern Ireland	5,461	14,144	1,610,000	1995E	295	114	Constitutional Monarchy	Belfast	Europe	9
Northern Mariana Islands	Northern Mariana Islands	184	477	43,000	1990C	234	90	U.S. Commonwealth	Saipan	Oceania	60
Northern Territory, Austl.	Northern Territory	519,800	1,346,200	175,253	1991C	0.3	0.1	Territory (Australia)	Darwin	Australia	59
Northwest Territories, Can.	Northwest Territories	1,332,910	3,426,320	57,649	1991C	0.04	0.02	Territory (Canada)	Yellowknife	North America	42
Norway	Norge	149,405	386,958	4,357,000	1995E	29	11	Constitutional Monarchy	Oslo	Europe	7
Nova Scotia, Can.	Nova Scotia	21,423	55,490	899,942	1991C	42	16	Province (Canada)	Halifax	North America	42
Oceania, see Pacific Islands	—	—	—	—	—	—	—	—	—	—	—
Ohio, U.S.	Ohio	41,328	107,040	10,887,325	1990C	263	102	State (U.S.)	Columbus	North America	44
Oklahoma, U.S.	Oklahoma	69,903	181,048	3,157,604	1990C	45	17	State (U.S.)	Oklahoma City	North America	45
Oman	'Umān	82,030	212,457	1,822,000	1995E	22	9	Sultanate	Muscat (Masqat)	Asia	23
Ontario, Can.	Ontario	412,581	1,068,580	10,084,885	1991C	24	9	Province (Canada)	Toronto	North America	42
Oregon, U.S.	Oregon	97,052	351,365	2,853,733	1990C	29	11	State (U.S.)	Salem	North America	46
Orkney Islands	Orkney Islands	377	976	19,351	*	51	20	Part of Scotland	Kirkwall	Europe	9
Pacific Islands	—	488,297	1,264,450	13,000,000	1995E	27	10	—	—	Oceania	57–58
Pakistan	Pākistān	307,374	796,095	134,974,000	1995E	439	170	Republic	Islamabad	Asia	25
Palau	Belau	192	497	17,000	1995E	96	37	Republic in free association with U.S.	Koror	Oceania	60
Panama	Panamá	30,193	78,200	2,659,000	1995E	88	34	Republic	Panama City	North America	49
Papua New Guinea	Papua New Guinea	178,704	462,840	4,344,000	1995E	24	9	Constitutional Monarchy	Port Moresby	Oceania	60
Paraguay	Paraguay	157,048	406,752	4,465,000	1995E	28	11	Republic	Asunción	South America	56
Pennsylvania, U.S.	Pennsylvania	45,310	117,351	11,924,710	1990C	263	102	State (U.S.)	Harrisburg	North America	44
Persia, see Iran	—	—	—	—	—	—	—	—	—	—	—
Peru	Peru	496,225	1,285,216	23,854,000	1995E	48	19	Presidential Dictatorship	Lima	South America	54
Philippines	Pilipinas	115,831	300,000	67,078,000	1995E	579	224	Republic	Manila	Asia	26
Pitcairn Island	Pitcairn	2	5	60	*	30	12	Part of British Dependency: Pitcairn Islands Group	Adamstown	Oceania	61
Poland	Polska	120,725	312,677	38,736,000	1995E	321	124	Republic	Warsaw (Warszawa)	Europe	10
Portugal	Portugal	34,340	88,941	9,884,000	1995E	288	111	Republic	Lisbon (Lisboa)	Europe	13
Portuguese Guinea, see Guinea-Bissau	—	—	—	—	—	—	—	—	—	—	—
Prince Edward Island, Can.	Prince Edward Island	2,185	5,660	129,765	1991C	59	23	Province (Canada)	Charlottetown	North America	42
Puerto Rico	Puerto Rico	3,515	9,103	3,522,037	1990C	1,004	387	Commonwealth (U.S. Protection)	San Juan	North America	51
Qatar	Qaṭar	4,247	11,000	490,000	1995E	115	45	Emirate	Doha (Ad Dawhah)	Asia	24
Qinghai (Tsinghai), China	Qinghai	278,400	721,000	.4,456,946	1990C	16	6	Province(China)	Xining (Hsi-ning)	Asia	27
Quebec, Can.	Québec	594,860	1,540,680	6,895,963	1991C	12	4	Province (Canada)	Quebec (Quebec City)	North America	42
Queensland, Austl.	Queensland	666,900	1,727,200	2,978,617	1991C	5	2	State (Australia)	Brisbane	Australia	59
Reunion	Réunion	970	2,512	597,828	1990C	616	238	Overseas Department (France)	Saint-Denis	Africa	37
Rhode Island, U.S.	Rhode Island	1,213	3,142	1,005,984	1990C	829	320	State (U.S.)	Providence	North America	44
Rhodesia, see Zimbabwe	—	—	—	—	—	—	—	—	—	—	—
Rodrigues	Rodrigues	42	109	34,536	*	822	317	Part of Mauritius	—	Africa	30–31
Romania (Rumania)	România	91,700	237,500	23,505,000	1995E	256	99	Republic	Bucharest (Bucureşti)	Europe	15
Russia	Rossija	6,592,849	17,075,399	149,740,000	1995E	23	9	Transitional	Moscow	Europe/Asia	19–20
Rwanda	Rwanda	10,169	26,338	8,000,000	1995E	787	304	Republic	Kigali	Africa	36
Sabah, Malaysia	Sabah	28,460	73,711	1,736,902	1990C	61	24	State of Malaysia	Kota Kinabalu	Asia	26
Saint Christopher and Nevis	St. Christopher-Nevis	101	261	44,400	*	440	170	Constitutional Monarchy	Basseterre	North America	51
St. Helena	St. Helena	47	122	5,700	*	121	48	British Dependency	Jamestown	Africa	31

Political unit	Local name	Area sq. miles	Area km²	Population	Date	Population density per sq. mile	Population density per km²	Form of govt./ Political status	Capital	Continent	Map plate
Saint Lucia	Saint Lucia	240	622	144,000	1995E	600	232	Constitutional Monarchy	Castries	North America	51
Saint-Pierre and Miquelon	St.-Pierre et Miquelon	93	242	6,000	*	65	25	Territorial Collectivity (France)	St.-Pierre	North America	42
Saint Vincent and the Grenadines	St. Vincent	150	388	112,000	1995E	747	289	Constitutional Monarchy	Kingstown	North America	50
Samoa, *see* American Samoa; Western Samoa	—	—	—	—	—	—	—	—	—	—	—
San Marino	San Marino	24	61	23,000	1995E	958	377	Republic	San Marino	Europe	14
São Tomé and Príncipe	São Tomé e Príncipe	372	964	133,000	1995E	358	138	Republic	São Tomé	Africa	34
Sarawak, Malaysia	Sarawak	48,050	124,450	1,648,217	1990C	34	13	State of Malaysia	Kuching	Asia	26
Sardinia	Sardegna	9,301	24,090	1,648,248	1991C	177	68	Region of Italy	Cagliari	Europe	14
Saskatchewan, Can.	Saskatchewan	251,866	652,330	988,928	1991C	4	2	Province (Canada)	Regina	North America	42
Saudi Arabia	Al 'Arabīyah as Sa'ūdīyah	830,000	2,149,690	17,608,000	1995E	21	8	Monarchy	Riyadh (Ar Riyad)	Asia	23
Scandinavia	Denmark, Norway, Sweden	339,769	879,999	18,322,000	*	54	21	—		Europe	7
Scotland	Scotland	30,420	78,789	5,056,000	1995E	166	64	Constitutional Monarchy	Edinburgh	Europe	9
Senegal	Sénégal	75,955	196,722	8,387,000	1995E	110	43	Republic	Dakar	Africa	34
Senegambia	Senegambia	80,316	208,017	8,566,000	*	107	41	Confederation	—	Africa	34
Seychelles	Seychelles	176	455	74,000	1995E	421	163	Republic	Victoria	Africa	37
Shaanxi (Shensi), China	Shaanxi	75,599	195,800	32,882,403	1990C	435	168	Province (China)	Xi'an (Sian)	Asia	27
Shandong (Shantung), China	Shandong	59,189	153,300	84,392,827	1990C	1,426	551	Province (China)	Jinan (Tsinan)	Asia	28
Shanghai, China	Shanghai	2,240	5,800	13,341,896	1990C	5,956	2,300	Special Municipality (China)	—	Asia	28
Shanxi (Shansi), China	Shanxi	60,657	157,100	28,759,014	1990C	474	183	Province (China)	Taiyaun (Tai-yaun)	Asia	27
Shetland Islands	Shetland Islands	552	1,430	23,500	1995E	43	16	Region of Scotland; part of Great Britain	Lerwick	Europe	9
Siam, *see* Thailand	—	—	—	—	—	—	—	—	—	—	—
Sichuan (Szechwan), China	Sichuan	219,700	569,000	107,218,173	1990C	488	188	Province (China)	Chengdu (Ch'eng-tu)	Asia	27
Sicily	Sicilia	9,926	25,708	4,966,386	1991C	500	193	Region of Italy	Palermo	Europe	14
Sierra Leone	Sierra Leone	27,699	71,740	4,740,000	1995E	171	66	Republic	Freetown	Africa	34
Singapore	Singapore (English) Singapura (Malay)	239	618	2,853,000	1995E	11,937	4,617	Republic	Singapore	Asia	26
Slovakia	Slovensko	18,933	49,035	5,353,000	1995E	283	109	Republic	Bratislava	Europe	—
Slovenia	Slovenija	7,836	20,296	2,012,000	1995E	257	99	Republic	Ljubljana	Europe	14
Solomon Islands	Solomon Islands	10,639	27,566	378,000	1995E	36	14	Constitutional Monarchy	Honiara	Oceania	63
Somalia	Soomaaliya	246,201	637,657	7,233,000	1995E	29	11	Transitional	Mogadishu	Africa	35
South Africa	South Africa (English) Suid-Afrika (Afrikaans)	471,445	1,221,037	42,741,000	1995E	91	35	Republic	Cape Town, Pretoria, Bloemfontein	Africa	37
†South America	—	6,885,000	17,832,000	318,000,000	1995E	46	18	—		South America	52–53
South Australia, Austl.	South Australia	380,070	984,377	1,400,655	1995E	4	1	State (Australia)	Adelaide	Australia	59
South Carolina, U.S.	South Carolina	31,117	80,593	3,505,707	1990C	113	43	State (U.S.)	Columbia	North America	44
South Dakota, U.S.	South Dakota	77,122	199,744	699,999	1990C	9	4	State (U.S.)	Pierre	North America	45
South Georgia (3)	South Georgia	1,580	4,092	(1)	—	—	—	Dependency of Falkland Islands (U.K.)	—	South America	56
South Korea	Taehan-Minguk	38,230 (4)	99,016 (4)	45,182,000	1995E	1,182	456	Republic	Seoul	Asia	28
South West Africa, *see* Namibia	—	—	—	—	—	—	—	—	—	—	—
Spain	España	194,885	504,750	39,276,000	1995E	202	78	Parliamentary Monarchy	Madrid	Europe	13
Spanish North Africa (6) (Sp.)	Plazas de Soberanía en el Norte de África	12	32	124,000	*	10,333	3,875	Five Possessions (no central government)	—	Africa	13
Spanish Sahara, *see* Western Sahara	—	—	—	—	—	—	—	—	—	—	—
Sri Lanka	Sri Lanka	25,332	65,610	18,346,000	1995E	724	280	Republic	Colombo	Asia	25
Sudan	As Sūdān	967,500	2,505,813	28,960,000	1995E	30	12	Republic	Khartoum	Africa	35
Sumatra	Sumatera	182,860	473,606	36,882,000	1995E	153	59	Part of Indonesia	—	Asia	26
Suriname	Suríname	63,037	163,265	463,000	1989C	7	3	Republic	Paramaribo	South America	54
Swaziland	Swaziland	6,704	17,364	859,000	1995E	128	49	Monarchy	Mbabane and Lobamba	Africa	37
Sweden	Sverige	173,732	449,964	8,773,000	1995E	50	19	Constitutional Monarchy	Stockholm	Europe	7
Switzerland	Schweiz (German) Suisse (French) Svizzera (Italian)	15,943	41,293	6,955,000	1995E	436	168	Federal Republic	Bern	Europe	14
Syria	Sūrīyah	71,498	185,180	14,775,000	1995E	207	52	Republic	Damascus	Asia	24
Taiwan	Taiwan	13,892	35,980	21,512,000	1995E	1,549	598	Republic	Taipei	Asia	27
Tajikistan	Tajikistan	55,251	143,099	6,005,000	1995E	109	42	Republic	Dušanbe	Asia	18
Tanzania	Tanzania	364,900	945,087	30,742,000	1995E	84	33	Single-party Republic	Dar es Salaam	Africa	36
Tasmania, Austl.	Tasmania	26,200	67,800	453,000	1995E	17	7	State (Australia)	Hobart	Australia	59
Tennessee, U.S.	Tennessee	42,146	109,158	4,896,641	1990C	116	45	State (U.S.)	Nashville	North America	44
Texas, U.S.	Texas	266,874	691,201	17,059,805	1990C	64	25	State (U.S.)	Austin	North America	45
Thailand	Muang Thai	198,115	513,115	58,265,000	1995E	294	114	Constitutional Monarchy	Bangkok	Asia	26
Tianjin (Tientsin), China	Tianjin	4,250	11,000	8,758,402	1990C	2,061	796	Special Municipality (China)	—	Asia	28
Tibet, China	Xizang	471,662	1,221,600	2,196,010	1990C	5	2	Autonomous Region (China)	Lhasa	Asia	27
Togo	Togo	21,925	56,785	4,138,000	1995E	189	73	Transitional	Lomé	Africa	34
Tokelau (N.Z.)	Tokelau	4	10	2,000	*	500	200	Territory of New Zealand	—	Oceania	61
Tonga	Tonga	288	747	99,000	1995E	344	133	Constitutional Monarchy	Nukualofa	Oceania	61
Trinidad and Tobago	Trinidad and Tobago	1,981	5,130	1,305,000	1995E	659	254	Republic	Port-of-Spain	North America	50
Tristan da Cunha	Tristan da Cunha	40	104	300	*	7.5	2.9	Dependency of St. Helena (U.K.)	Edinburgh	Africa	30–31
Trucial States, *see* United Arab Emirates	—	—	—	—	—	—	—	—	—	—	—
Tunisia	Tūnis	63,170	163,610	8,933,000	1995E	141	55	Republic	Tunis	Africa	32
Turkey	Türkiye	300,948	779,452	62,032,000	1995E	206	80	Republic	Ankara	Asia/Europe	24
Turkmenistan	Turkmenistan	188,456	488,099	4,156,000	1995E	22	9	Republic	Ašhabad	Asia	19
Turks and Caicos Islands	Turks and Caicos Islands	166	430	13,000	1995E	78	30	British Dependency	Grand Turk	North America	49
Tuvalu	Tuvalu	10	26	13,000	1995E	1,300	500	Constitutional Monarchy	Funafuti	Oceania	60

Political unit	Local name	Area sq. miles	km²	Population	Date	Population density per sq. mile	km²	Form of govt./ Political status	Capital	Continent	Map plate
Uganda	Uganda	91,074	235,880	18,764,000	1995E	206	80	Republic	Kampala	Africa	36
Ukraine	Ukraine	233,090	603,700	52,393,000	1995E	225	87	Republic	Kijev	Europe	16
United Arab Emirates	Al Imārāt al 'Arabīyah al Muttaḥidah	32,278	83,600	1,785,000	1995E	55	21	Federation	Abu Dhabi	Asia	23
United Arab Republic, *see* Egypt	—	—	—	—	—	—	—	—	—	—	—
United Kingdom of Great Britain and Northern Ireland	United Kingdom	94,277	244,177	57,988,000	1995E	615	237	Constitutional Monarchy	London	Europe	9
United States	United States	3,615,292	9,363,563	262,648,000	1995E	73	28	Republic	Washington, D.C.	North America	43
Upper Volta, *see* Burkina Faso	—	—	—	—	—	—	—	—	—	—	—
Uruguay	Uruguay	68,500	177,414	3,186,000	1995E	47	18	Republic	Montevideo	South America	55
Utah, U.S.	Utah	84,905	219,902	1,727,784	1990C	20	8	State (U.S.)	Salt Lake City	North America	46
Uzbekistan	Uzbekistan	172,742	447,400	22,829,000	1995E	132	51	Republic	Tǎskent	Asia	19
Vanuatu	Vanuatu	4,706	12,189	169,000	1995E	36	14	Republic	Port-Vila	Oceania	63
Vatican City	Città del Vaticano	0.17	0.44	1,000	1995E	5,882	2,273	Independent State	—	Europe	14
Venezuela	Venezuela	352,145	912,050	20,108,000	1995E	57	22	Federal Republic	Caracas	South America	54
Vermont, U.S.	Vermont	9,615	24,903	564,964	1990C	59	23	State (U.S.)	Montpelier	North America	44
Victoria, Austl.	Victoria	87,900	227,600	4,243,719	1991C	48	19	State (Australia)	Melbourne	Australia	59
Vietnam	Viet-nam Dan-chu Cong-hoa	128,066	331,689	73,811,000	1995E	576	223	Communist Dictatorship	Hanoi	Asia	26
Virgin Islands (U.S.)	Virgin Islands	132	342	101,809	1990C	771	298	Self-governing Territory of U.S.	Charlotte Amalie	North America	51
Virgin Islands, British	British Virgin Islands	59	153	16,553	1991C	281	108	British Dependency	Road Town	North America	51
Virginia, U.S.	Virginia	40,598	105,149	6,216,568	1990C	153	59	State (U.S.)	Richmond	North America	44
Wake Island	Wake Island	3	8	300	*	100	38	Unincorporated Possession (U.S.)	—	Oceania	60
Wales	Wales	8,019	20,766	2,955,000	1995E	369	142	Constitutional Monarchy	Cardiff	Europe	9
Wallis and Futuna Islands	Iles Wallis-et-Futuna	106	275	12,000	*	113	44	Overseas Territory (France)	Mata-Utu	Oceania	61
Washington, U.S.	Washington	68,126	176,446	4,887,941	1990C	72	28	State (U.S.)	Olympia	North America	46
West Bank	Yehuda v'Shomron (Judea and Samaria)	2,263	5,860	1,500,000	1995E	663	256	Transitional	—	Asia	24
West Indies	West Indies (English) Indias Occidentales (Spanish)	91,000	235,000	36,000,000	1995E	396	153	—	—	North America	47
West Virginia, U.S.	West Virginia	24,231	62,759	1,801,625	1990C	74	29	State (U.S.)	Charleston	North America	44
Western Australia, Austl.	Western Australia	975,100	2,525,500	1,586,393	1991C	2	1	State (Australia)	Perth	Australia	59
Western Sahara	—	102,700	266,000	220,000	*	2	1	Claimed by Morocco	—	Africa	32
Western Samoa	Samoa i Sisifo	1,093	2,831	170,000	1995E	156	60	Parliamentary	Apia	Oceania	65
Wisconsin, U.S.	Wisconsin	56,145	145,414	4,906,745	1990C	87	34	State (U.S.)	Madison	North America	45
Wyoming, U.S.	Wyoming	97,818	253,349	455,975	1990C	5	2	State (U.S.)	Cheyenne	North America	46
Xinjiang (Sinkiang), China	Xinjiang	635,833	1,646,800	15,155,778	1990C	24	9	Autonomous Region (China)	Ūrümqi (Urumchi)	Asia	27
Yemen	Al Yaman	203,850	527,968	13,897,000	1995E	68	26	Republic	Sana	Asia	23
Yugoslavia	Jugoslavija	39,449	102,173	9,898,000	1995E	251	97	Republic	Belgrade	Europe	14–15
Yukon Territory, Can.	Yukon Territory	186,661	483,450	27,797	1991C	0.15	0.06	Territory (Canada)	Whitehorse	North America	42
Yunnan, China	Yunnan	168,420	436,200	36,972,610	1990C	220	85	Province (China)	Kunming (K'un-ming)	Asia	27
Zaire	Zaïre	905,568	2,345,409	43,814,000	1995E	48	19	Presidential Regime	Kinshasa	Africa	36
Zambia	Zambia	290,587	752,618	9,381,000	1995E	32	12	Republic	Lusaka	Africa	36
Zanzibar	Zanzibar	640	1,658	1,254,250	*	1,230	475	Part of Tanzania	Zanzibar	Africa	36
Zhejiang (Chekiang), China	Zhejiang	39,305	101,800	41,445,930	1990C	1,054	407	Province (China)	Hangzhou (Hang-chou)	Asia	27
Zimbabwe	Zimbabwe	150,873	390,759	11,536,000	1995E	76	30	Republic; Parliamentary	Harare	Africa	37
World	—	57,807,000	149,719,000	5,734,000,000	1995E	99	38	—	—	—	1–2

C = Census; E = Estimate from *The World Book Encyclopedia*

† Continent

* Populations are 1995 and earlier estimates based on figures from official government and United Nations sources.

— none, or not applicable

(1) No permanent population.

(2) Comprises Bahrain, Kuwait, Oman, Qatar, Saudi Arabia, United Arab Emirates, and Yemen

(3) Comprises Kalimantin (part of Indonesia), Sabah and Sarawak (states of Malaysia), and Brunei

(4) The 487 sq. mi. or 1,262 km² of the demilitarized zone are not included in either North Korea or South Korea.

(5) Comprises Papua New Guinea and Irian Jaya (part of Indonesia)

(6) Comprises Ceuta, Melilla, and several small islands

World Geographical Tables

Earth: Land and Water

	Total area		Area of land			Area of water		
	sq. miles	sq. kilometers	sq. miles	sq. kilometers	per cent	sq. miles	sq. kilometers	per cent
Earth	196,800,000	509,700,000	57,300,000	148,400,000	29%	139,500,000	361,300,000	71%

Continents

Name	Area sq. miles/sq. kilometers	1995 population estimate	Population per sq. mile/sq. kilometer	Highest elevation place/feet/meters	Lowest elevation place/feet/meters (below sea level)	Highest recorded temperature place/°F/°C	Lowest recorded temperature place/°F/°C
Africa	11,681,000/30,253,000	717,000,000	61/24	Kilimanjaro, Tanzania 19,340/5,895	Lake Assal, Djibouti −509/−155	Al Aziziyah, Libya 136°F/58°C	Ifrane, Morocco −11°F/−24°C
Antarctica	5,400,000/14,000,000	(no permanent population)	—	Vinson Massif 16,864/5,140	sea level	Esperanza 58°F/14°C	Vostok Station −127°F/−88°C
Asia	16,992,000/44,009,000	3,506,000,000	206/80	Mount Everest, Nepal-Tibet 29,028/8,848	Dead Sea, Israel-Jordan −1,310/−399	Tirat Zevi, Israel 129°F/54°C	Verkhoyansk, Russia −93°F/−69°C
Australia	2,978,147/7,713,364	17,820,000	6/2	Mount Kosciusko 7,310/2,228	Lake Eyre −52/−16	Cloncurry 128°F/53°C	Charlotte Pass −80°F/−22°C
Europe	4,033,000/10,445,000	709,000,000	176/68	Mount Elbrus 18,481/5,633	Caspian Sea, Kazakhstan-Russia −92/−28	Seville, Spain 122°F/50°C	Ust-Ščugor, Russia −67°F/−55°C
North America	9,348,000/24,211,000	453,000,000	48/19	Mount McKinley, U.S. 20,320/6,194	Death Valley, U.S. −282/−86	Death Valley, U.S. 134°F/57°C	Northice, Greenland −87°F/−66°C
South America	6,885,000/17,883,000	318,000,000	46/18	Mount Aconcagua, Argentina 22,831/6,959	Valdés Peninsula, Argentina −131/−40	Rivadavia, Argentina 120°F/49°C	Sarmiento, Argentina −27°F/−33°C

Historical Population of the World

Area	1650	1750	1800	1850	1900	1914	1920	1939	1950	1982	1995E
Europe	*100,000,000*	*140,000,000*	*190,000,000*	265,000,000	400,000,000	470,000,000	453,000,000	526,000,000	530,000,000	666,000,000	709,000,000
Asia	*335,000,000*	*476,000,000*	*593,000,000*	754,000,000	932,000,000	1,006,000,000	1,000,000,000	1,247,000,000	1,418,000,000	2,725,000,000	3,506,000,000
Africa	*100,000,000*	*95,000,000*	*90,000,000*	*95,000,000*	118,000,000	130,000,000	140,000,000	170,000,000	199,000,000	490,000,000	717,000,000
North America	*5,000,000*	*5,000,000*	13,000,000	39,000,000	106,000,000	141,000,000	147,000,000	186,000,000	219,000,000	490,000,000	453,000,000
South America	*8,000,000*	*7,000,000*	12,000,000	20,000,000	38,000,000	55,000,000	61,000,000	90,000,000	219,000,000	379,000,000	453,000,000
Oceania, incl. Australia	*2,000,000*	*2,000,000*	*2,000,000*	*2,000,000*	6,000,000	8,000,000	9,000,000	11,000,000	13,000,000	248,000,000	318,000,000
World	*500,000,000*	*725,000,000*	*900,000,000*	1,175,000,000	1,600,000,000	1,810,000,000	1,810,000,000	2,230,000,000	2,490,000,000	23,000,000	31,000,000
										4,531,000,000	5,734,000,000

Figures are rounded to the nearest million.   Figures in italics represent very rough estimates.

Largest Countries: Population

	Name	Population 1995 estimate	1997 estimate
1.	China	1,238,319,000	1,217,861,000
2.	India	931,044,000	984,053,000
3.	United States	262,648,000	261,786,000
4.	Indonesia	201,477,000	200,067,000
5.	Brazil	161,382,000	170,643,000
6.	Russia	149,740,000	155,474,000
7.	Pakistan	134,974,000	149,494,000
8.	Japan	125,879,000	127,433,000
9.	Bangladesh	118,786,000	139,184,000
10.	Nigeria	105,134,000	143,614,000
11.	Mexico	93,670,000	95,794,000
12.	Germany	81,264,000	76,663,000
13.	Vietnam	73,811,000	74,798,000
14.	Philippines	67,078,000	72,804,000
15.	Iran	66,720,000	68,269,000
16.	Turkey	62,032,000	63,260,000
17.	Thailand	58,519,000	61,189,000
18.	Egypt	58,265,000	62,864,000
19.	United Kingdom	57,988,000	58,571,000
20.	Italy	57,910,000	57,706,000
21.	France	57,769,000	57,589,000
22.	Ethiopia	53,711,000	56,348,000
23.	Ukraine	52,393,000	54,541,000
24.	Burma	46,548,000	48,145,000
25.	South Korea	45,182,000	46,679,000
26.	Zaire	43,814,000	44,915,000
27.	South Africa	42,741,000	47,334,000
28.	Spain	39,276,000	40,357,000
29.	Poland	38,736,000	39,760,000
30.	Colombia	35,101,000	36,123,000
31.	Argentina	34,883,000	35,036,000
32.	Tanzania	30,742,000	35,371,000
33.	Sudan	28,960,000	30,811,000
34.	Algeria	28,581,000	30,802,000
35.	Canada	28,537,000	27,938,000
36.	Morocco	28,260,000	29,457,000
37.	Kenya	27,885,000	33,329,000
38.	North Korea	23,922,000	26,554,000
39.	Peru	23,854,000	26,205,000
40.	Romania	23,505,000	24,026,000
41.	Uzbekistan	22,829,000	20,998,000
42.	Nepal	22,124,000	22,500,000
43.	Taiwan	21,512,000	22,182,000
44.	Venezuela	20,108,000	23,174,000
45.	Uganda	18,764,000	23,603,000

Smallest Countries: Population

	Name	Population 1995 estimate	1997 estimate
1.	Vatican City	1,000	1,000
2.	Tuvalu	11,000	10,000
3.	Nauru	13,000	10,000
4.	Paláu	17,000	18,000
5.	San Marino	23,000	24,000
6.	Liechtenstein	28,000	29,000
7.	Monaco	30,000	31,000
8.	Saint Christopher and Nevis	44,000	52,000
9.	Andorra	59,000	62,000
10.	Antigua and Barbuda	69,000	83,000
11.	Seychelles	74,000	73,000
12.	Dominica	75,000	94,000
13.	Kiribati	79,000	78,000
14.	Grenada	92,000	113,000
15.	Tonga	99,000	103,000
16.	Saint Vincent and the Grenadines	112,000	121,000
17.	São Tomé and Príncipe	133,000	153,000
18.	Saint Lucia	144,000	183,000
19.	Vanuatu	169,000	178,000
20.	Western Samoa	170,000	179,000
21.	Belize	205,000	209,000
22.	Maldives	248,000	281,000
23.	Iceland	261,000	268,000
24.	Barbados	268,000	277,000
25.	Bahamas	277,000	285,000
26.	Brunei	288,000	368,000
27.	Malta	367,000	363,000
28.	Solomon Islands	378,000	415,000
29.	Luxembourg	386,000	368,000
30.	Equatorial Guinea	400,000	522,000
31.	Cape Verde	419,000	472,000
32.	Suriname	463,000	448,000
33.	Qatar	490,000	529,000
34.	Djibouti	511,000	503,000
35.	Bahrain	578,000	632,000
36.	Comoros	653,000	645,000
37.	Cyprus	736,000	746,000

Largest Countries: Area

	Name	Area sq. miles	km²
1.	Russia	6,592,850	17,075,400
2.	Canada	3,849,674	9,970,610
3.	China	3,696,032	9,572,678
4.	United States	3,615,292	9,363,353
5.	Brazil	3,286,502	8,511,999
6.	Australia	2,978,147	7,713,364
7.	India	1,269,346	3,287,590
8.	Argentina	1,073,519	2,780,400
9.	Kazakhstan	1,049,156	2,717,300
10.	Sudan	967,500	2,505,813
11.	Algeria	919,595	2,381,741
12.	Zaire	905,568	2,345,409
13.	Saudi Arabia	830,000	2,149,690
14.	Mexico	756,066	1,958,205
15.	Indonesia	741,101	1,919,443
16.	Libya	679,362	1,759,540
17.	Iran	636,296	1,648,000
18.	Mongolia	604,829	1,566,300
19.	Peru	496,225	1,285,216
20.	Chad	495,755	1,284,000
21.	Niger	489,191	1,267,000
22.	Angola	481,354	1,246,700
23.	Mali	478,841	1,240,192
24.	South Africa	471,445	1,221,037
25.	Colombia	439,737	1,138,914
26.	Ethiopia	426,373	1,104,302
27.	Bolivia	424,165	1,098,581
28.	Mauritania	397,956	1,030,700
29.	Egypt	386,662	1,001,449
30.	Tanzania	364,900	945,087
31.	Nigeria	356,669	923,768
32.	Venezuela	352,145	912,050
33.	Namibia	318,261	824,292
34.	Mozambique	309,496	801,590
35.	Pakistan	307,374	796,095
36.	Turkey	300,948	779,452
37.	Chile	292,258	756,945
38.	Zambia	290,586	752,614
39.	Burma	261,228	676,578
40.	Afghanistan	251,773	652,090
41.	Somalia	246,201	637,657
42.	Central African Republic	240,535	622,984
43.	Ukraine	233,090	603,700
44.	Madagascar	226,658	587,041
45.	Botswana	224,607	581,730

Smallest Countries: Area

	Name	Area sq. miles	km²
1.	Vatican City	0.17	0.44
2.	Monaco	0.75	1.95
3.	Nauru	8	21
4.	Tuvalu	10	26
5.	San Marino	24	61
6.	Liechtenstein	62	160
7.	Saint Christopher and Nevis	101	261
8.	Maldives	115	298
9.	Malta	122	316
10.	Grenada	133	344
11.	Saint Vincent and the Grenadines	150	388
12.	Barbados	166	430
13.	Antigua and Barbuda	171	442
14.	Andorra	175	453
15.	Seychelles	176	455
16.	Palau	177	459
17.	Singapore	239	618
18.	Saint Lucia	240	622
19.	Bahrain	262	678
20.	Kiribati	280	726
21.	Tonga	288	747
22.	Dominica	290	751
23.	São Tomé and Príncipe	372	964
24.	Mauritius	788	2,040
25.	Comoros	863	2,235
26.	Luxembourg	998	2,586
27.	Western Samoa	1,093	2,831
28.	Cape Verde	1,557	4,033
29.	Trinidad and Tobago	1,981	5,130
30.	Brunei	2,226	5,765
31.	Cyprus	3,572	9,251
32.	Lebanon	4,015	10,400
33.	Jamaica	4,243	10,990
34.	Qatar	4,247	11,000
35.	Gambia	4,361	11,295
36.	Vanuatu	4,706	12,189
37.	Bahamas	5,358	13,878
38.	Swaziland	6,704	17,363
39.	Kuwait	6,880	17,818
40.	Fiji	7,056	18,274
41.	Israel	8,019	20,770
42.	El Salvador	8,124	21,041
43.	Belize	8,867	22,965
44.	Djibouti	8,958	23,200
45.	Rwanda	10,169	26,338

Highest Population Densities

	Country	Population density per sq. mile	km²
1.	Monaco	40,000	15,384
2.	Singapore	11,937	4,617
3.	Vatican City	5,882	2,273
4.	Malta	3,008	1,161
5.	Bahrain	2,206	853
6.	Maldives	2,157	832
7.	Bangladesh	2,137	825
8.	Barbados	1,572	607
9.	Taiwan	1,549	598
10.	Mauritius	1,434	541
11.	Nauru	1,375	524
12.	Tuvalu	1,300	500
13.	Netherlands	1,183	456
14.	South Korea	1,182	456
15.	San Marino	958	377
16.	Japan	863	333
17.	Belgium	851	329
18.	Rwanda	787	304
19.	Comoros	757	292
20.	Lebanon	754	291
21.	St. Vincent and the Grenadines	747	289
22.	India	733	283
23.	Sri Lanka	724	280
24.	El Salvador	710	274
25.	Grenada	692	267
26.	Haiti	671	259
27.	Trinidad and Tobago	659	254
28.	Saint Lucia	600	232

Lowest Population Densities

	Country	Population density per sq. mile	km²
1.	Mongolia	4	2
2.	Namibia	5	2
3.	Australia	6	2
4.	Botswana	6	2
5.	Mauritania	6	2
6.	Canada	7	3
7.	Iceland	7	3
8.	Suriname	7	3
9.	Libya	8	3
10.	Guyana	10	4
11.	Gabon	13	5
12.	Chad	13	5
13.	Central African Republic	14	6
14.	Kazakhstan	17	6
15.	Niger	19	7
16.	Bolivia	19	7
17.	Congo	20	8
18.	Saudi Arabia	21	8
19.	Oman	22	9
20.	Turkmenistan	22	9
21.	Angola	23	9
22.	Mali	23	9
23.	Russia	23	9
24.	Belize	24	9
25.	Papua New Guinea	24	9
26.	Norway	29	11
27.	Sudan	30	12
28.	Algeria	31	12

Principal Rivers

Name	Location	Length miles	km
Nile	Africa	4,145	6,671
Amazon	South America	4,000	6,437
Yangtze (Yangtze Kiang; Chang Jiang)	China	3,915	6,300
Huang He	China	2,903	4,672
Congo	Africa	2,900	4,667
Amur	Russia	2,744	4,416
Lena	Russia	2,734	4,400
Mekong	Asia (Indochinese Peninsula)	2,600	4,180
Niger	Africa	2,600	4,180
Yenisey	Russia	2,543	4,093
Missouri	United States	2,540	4,090
Paraná	South America	2,485	3,999
Mississippi	United States	2,340	3,766
Murray-Darling	Australia	2,310	3,718
Ob	Russia	2,268	3,650
Volga	Russia	2,193	3,530
Purús	Peru-Brazil	2,100	3,380
Madeira	Brazil	2,000	3,200
São Francisco	Brazil	1,988	3,199
Yukon	Canada-United States	1,979	3,185
Rio Grande	United States-Mexico	1,885	3,034
Indus	Tibet-Pakistan	1,800	2,897
Danube	Europe	1,777	2,860
Darling	Australia	1,702	2,739
Euphrates	Asia	1,700	2,736
Zambezi	Africa	1,700	2,736
Brahmaputra	Asia	1,680	2,704
Murray	Australia	1,609	2,589
Paraguay	South America	1,584	2,549
Ural	Russia-Kazakhstan	1,570	2,527
Amu Darya (Oxus)	Asia	1,560	2,511
Ganges	India-Bangladesh	1,540	2,478
Salween (Salwin)	Burma-Tibet	1,500	2,414
Arkansas	United States	1,459	2,348
Colorado	United States-Mexico	1,450	2,334
Dnepr (Dnieper)	Europe	1,400	2,200
Orinoco	Venezuela-Colombia	1,284	2,066
Irrawaddy (Irawadi)	Burma	1,250	2,010
Saskatchewan	Canada	1,205	1,939
Mackenzie	Canada	1,071	1,724

Principal Mountains

Name	Height above sea level In feet	In meters	Location
Aconcagua	22,831	6,959	Andes in Argentina
Annapurna	26,504	8,078	Himalaya in Nepal
Ararat	17,011	5,185	Eastern Plateau in Turkey
Chimborazo	20,561	6,267	Andes in Ecuador
Cotopaxi	19,347	5,897	Andes in Ecuador
Ixtacihuatl	17,343	5,286	Plateau of Mexico
Jungfrau	13,642	4,158	Alps in Switzerland
Kilimanjaro	19,340	5,895	Isolated peak in Tanzania
Lassen Peak	10,457	3,187	Cascade in California
Matterhorn	14,692	4,478	Alps on Switzerland-Italy border
Mauna Kea	13,796	4,205	Island of Hawaii
Mauna Loa	13,677	4,169	Island of Hawaii
Mont Blanc	15,771	4,807	Alps on France-Italy-Switzerland border
Mount Cook	12,349	3,764	Southern Alps in New Zealand
Mount Elbrus	18,481	5,633	Caucasus in Russia
Mount Etna	11,122	3,390	Island of Sicily
Mount Everest	29,028	8,848	Himalaya on Nepal-Tibet border
Mount Fuji	12,388	3,776	Island of Honshu in Japan
Mount Godwin Austen, or K2, or Dapsang	28,250*	8,611*	Karakoram, or Mustagh, in Kashmir
Mount Hood	11,239	3,426	Cascade in Oregon
Mount Kanchenjunga, or Kinchinjunga	28,208	8,598	Himalaya on Nepal-India border
Mount Kenya	17,058	5,199	Central Kenya
Mount Kosciusko	7,310	2,228	Australian Alps
Mount Logan	19,524	5,951	St. Elias in Canada
Mount Makalu	27,824	8,481	Himalaya on Nepal-Tibet border
Mount McKinley	20,320	6,194	Alaska Range in Alaska
Mount Rainier	14,410	4,392	Cascade in Washington
Mount Saint Helens	8,364	2,549	Cascade in Washington
Mount Shasta	14,162	4,317	Cascade in California
Mount Whitney	14,491	4,418	Sierra Nevada in California
Olympus	9,570	2,917	Greece
Orizaba, or Citlaltépetl	18,701	5,700	Plateau of Mexico
Pikes Peak	14,110	4,301	Front Range in Colorado
Popocatepetl	17,887	5,452	Plateau of Mexico
Vesuvius	4,190	1,277	Italy

*Traditional measurement.

Major Lakes

Name	Location	Area sq. miles	km²	Depth feet	meters
Caspian Sea	Europe-Asia	143,630	372,000	3,363	1,025
Lake Superior	United States-Canada	31,700	82,103	1,333	406
Lake Victoria	Africa	26,828	69,484	270	82
Aral Sea	Uzbekistan-Kazakhstan	25,660	66,459	223	68
Lake Huron	United States-Canada	23,050	59,699	750	229
Lake Michigan	United States	22,300	57,757	923	281
Lake Tanganyika	Africa	12,700	32,893	4,708	1,435
Great Bear Lake	Canada	12,275	31,792	1,350	411
Lake Baikal	Russia	12,162	31,499	5,315	1,620
Lake Nyasa	Africa	11,100	28,749	2,300	701
Great Slave Lake	Canada	10,980	28,438	2,015	614
Lake Erie	United States-Canada	9,910	25,667	210	64
Lake Winnipeg	Canada	9,398	24,341	70	21
Lake Ontario	United States-Canada	7,550	19,554	802	244
Lake Ladoga	Russia	6,835	17,703	738	225
Lake Balkhash	Kazakhstan	6,670	17,275	85	26
Lake Chad	Africa	6,300	16,300	22	7
Lake Onega	Russia	3,820	9,894	393	120
Lake Eyre	Australia	3,700	9,583	52	16
				feet below sea level	meters below sea level
Lake Titicaca	Peru-Bolivia	3,200	8,300	900	270
Lake Athabasca	Canada	3,120	8,081	407	124
Lake Nicaragua	Nicaragua	3,060	7,925	141	43
Lake Turkana (Lake Rudolf)	Kenya-Ethiopia	2,473	6,405	200	61
Reindeer Lake	Canada	2,444	6,330	720	219
Lake Torrens	Australia	2,230	5,776	shallow body of water	
Lake Vänern	Sweden	2,156	5,584	328	100
Lake Winnipegosis	Canada	2,013	5,214	38	12

Oceans, Seas, and Gulfs

Name	Area sq. miles	km²	Greatest depth feet	meters
Pacific Ocean	63,800,000	165,200,000	36,198	11,033
Atlantic Ocean	31,530,000	81,662,000	28,374	8,648
Indian Ocean	28,356,300	73,441,700	25,344	7,725
Arctic Ocean	3,662,000	9,485,100	17,880	5,450
Arabian Sea	1,492,000	3,863,000	19,029	5,800
South China Sea	1,300,000	3,370,000	18,241	5,560
Bering Sea	1,140,000	2,952,900	13,422	4,091
Caribbean Sea	1,105,000	2,877,000	24,720	7,535
Mediterranean Sea	969,100	2,510,000	16,302	5,093
Bay of Bengal	839,000	2,172,000	17,251	5,258
Gulf of Mexico	700,000	1,800,000	12,700	3,871
Norwegian Sea	597,000	1,547,000	13,189	4,020
Okhotsk, Sea of	589,800	1,527,600	11,063	3,372
Greenland Sea	465,000	1,205,000	15,899	4,846
Hudson Bay	316,500	819,731	850	259

Principal Islands

Name	Area sq. miles	km²	Highest point name	feet	meters
Greenland	840,004	2,175,600	Mount Gunnbjørn	12,139	3,700
New Guinea	311,737	807,396	Puncak Jaya	16,503	5,030
Borneo	288,151	746,308	Mount Kinabalu	13,455	4,101
Madagascar	226,658	587,041	Maromokotro	9,436	2,876
Baffin Island	195,927	507,449	(unnamed)	7,045	2,147
Sumatra (Sumatera)	182,860	473,606	Kerinci	12,484	3,805
Honshu	87,805	227,414	Mount Fuji	12,388	3,776
Great Britain	84,550	218,980	Ben Nevis	4,406	1,343
Victoria Island (N.W.T., Can.)	83,896	217,290	(unnamed)	2,150	655
Ellesmere Island	75,767	196,236	Barbeau Peak	8,584	2,616
Celebes (Sulawesi)	73,057	189,216	Rantekombola	11,335	3,455
South Island (New Zealand)	58,965	152,719	Mount Cook	12,349	3,764
Java (Djawa)	51,038	132,187	Semeru	12,060	3,676
North Island (New Zealand)	44,244	114,592	Mount Ruapehu	9,175	2,797
(island of) Newfoundland	43,008	111,390	Lewis Hills	2,672	814
Cuba	42,804	110,861	Pico Turquino	6,542	1,994
Luzon (Philippines)	40,420	104,688	Mount Pulog	9,606	2,928
Iceland	39,800	103,000	Hvannadalsh-núkur	6,952	2,119
Mindanao (Philippines)	36,537	94,630	Mount Apo	9,692	2,954
Ireland	32,588	84,404	Carrauntoohill	3,414	1,041
Hokkaido	30,144	78,073	Asahi Mountain	7,513	2,290
Hispaniola	29,418	76,192	Duarte Peak	10,417	3,175
Sakhalin (Russia)	29,100	75,369	Lopatina	5,279	1,609
Tasmania	26,200	67,800	Mount Ossa	5,305	1,617
Sri Lanka	25,333	65,610	Pidurutalagala	8,281	2,524
Novaya Zemlya (northern island)	20,000	52,000	(unnamed)	5,075	1,574
Tierra del Fuego	19,280	49,935	Yogan	8,100	2,469
Kyushu	14,114	36,554	Kuju Mountain	5,866	1,788

Waterfalls

Name	Country	River	Height feet	meters
Angel	Venezuela	Churún	3,212	979
Yosemite	United States	Yosemite Creek	2,425	739
Tugela	South Africa	Tugela	2,014	614
Sutherland	New Zealand	Milford Sound	1,904	580
Gavarnie	France	Gave de Pau	1,385	422
Krimml	Austria	Krimml	1,312	400
Takakkaw	Canada	Yoho	1,200	366
Staubbach	Switzerland	Staubbach	984	300
Jog	India	—	830	253
Kaieteur	Guyana	Potaro	741	226

Drainage Basins

Name	Continent	Area sq. miles	km²
Amazon River	South America	2,700,000	7,000,000
Congo River	Africa	1,400,000	3,630,000
Mississippi River	North America	1,247,300	3,230,490
Ob River	Asia	1,125,200	2,914,250
Lena River	Asia	1,000,000	2,600,000
Yenisey River	Asia (Siberia)	1,000,000	2,600,000
Amur River	Asia	770,000	1,990,000
Yangtze River (Yangtze Kiang; Chang Jiang)	Asia	706,000	1,829,000
Mackenzie River system	North America	682,000	1,766,000
Niger River	Africa	580,000	1,500,000
Volga River	Europe	525,000	1,360,000
Saint Lawrence River	North America	498,500	1,291,100

Populations of Major Cities

The largest and most important of the world's major cities are listed in the following table. Also included are some smaller cities because of their regional significance.

Local official names have primarily been used throughout the table. When a commonly used conventional name exists, it has been featured. An alternate name follows in parentheses. A former name is identified in *italics*.

The population of each city has been dated, and is identified as either an official estimate (E) or a census figure (C).

City	Country	City population	Metropolitan area population	Date
Aachen	Germany	241,861	—	1990E
Abidjan	Ivory Coast	1,850,000	—	1982E
Acapulco (Acapulco de Juárez)	Mexico	515,374	—	1990C
Accra	Ghana	964,879	1,420,065	1984C
Addis Ababa	Ethiopia	1,412,577	—	1984C
Adelaide	Australia	1,023,617	—	1991C
Aden	Yemen	318,000	—	1984E
Agra	India	955,694	—	1991C
Ahmadabad	India	2,954,526	3,297,655	1991C
Al Basrah (Basra)	Iraq	678,000	—	1991E
Aleppo	Syria	961,000	—	1980E
Alexandria (Al Iskandariyah)	Egypt	2,917,327	—	1986C
Algiers (Alger)	Algeria	1,721,607	—	1983E
Allahabad	India	806,486	858,213	1991C
Alma-Ata	Kazakhstan	1,147,000	—	1991C
Amman	Jordan	900,000	—	1988E
Amritsar	India	709,456	—	1991C
Amsterdam	Netherlands	687,397	945,062	1983E
Ankara	Turkey	2,559,500	—	1990C
Anshan (An-shan)	China	1,390,000	—	1990E
Antananarivo	Madagascar	662,585	—	1985E
Antwerp (Antwerpen, Anvers)	Belgium	462,880	—	1994E
Asansol	India	763,854	—	1991C
Asmara	Eritrea	358,100	—	1990E
Asunción	Paraguay	457,210	655,000	1982C
Athens (Athinai)	Greece	748,110	3,096,775	1991C
Atlanta	(Georgia) U.S.	394,017	2,833,511	1990C
Auckland	New Zealand	855,571	—	1991C
Augsburg	Germany	250,197	—	1990C
Austin	(Texas) U.S.	465,622	781,572	1990C
Baghdad	Iraq	5,908,000	—	1991E
Baku	Azerbaijan	1,084,000	1,661,000	1984E
Baltimore	(Maryland) U.S.	736,014	2,382,172	1990C
Bamako	Mali	646,000	—	1990E
Bandung	Indonesia	1,401,108	—	1989E
Bangalore	India	3,302,296	4,086,548	1991C
Bangkok (Krung Thep)	Thailand	5,876,000	—	1990C
Barcelona	Spain	1,625,542	—	1991C
Barranquilla	Colombia	899,781	950,000	1985C
Basel	Switzerland	178,428	406,391	1990C
Beijing (Peking)	China	7,362,425	10,819,407	1990C
Beirut	Lebanon	1,500,000	—	1988E
Belém	Brazil	1,203,151	1,418,061	1990C
Belfast	Northern Ireland	301,600	—	1985E
Belgrade (Beograd)	Yugoslavia	1,168,454	—	1991C
Belo Horizonte	Brazil	2,145,908	3,615,234	1990C
Berlin	Germany	3,433,695	—	1990C
Bern (Berne)	Switzerland	136,338	332,494	1990C
Bhopal	India	1,063,662	—	1991C
Bielefeld	Germany	319,037	—	1990C
Bilbao	Spain	367,710	—	1991C
Birmingham	England (U.K.)	934,900	2,500,400	1991C
Birmingham	(Alabama) U.S.	265,968	907,810	1990C
Biškek (Pišpek)	Kyrgyzstan	641,400	—	1991E
Bologna	Italy	404,378	—	1991C
Bombay	India	9,925,891	—	1991C
Bonn	Germany	292,234	—	1990E
Bordeaux	France	213,274	685,456	1990C
Boston	(Massachusetts) U.S.	574,283	2,870,669	1990C
Brasília	Brazil	1,803,478	—	1990C
Bratislava	Slovakia	409,100	—	1993E
Brazzaville	Congo	596,200	—	1985E
Bremen	Germany	551,219	—	1990E
Bremerhaven	Germany	130,446	—	1990E
Brisbane	Australia	1,334,746	—	1991C
Bristol	England (U.K.)	370,300	—	1991C
Brussels (Brussel, Bruxelles)	Belgium	134,856	—	1994C
Bucharest (Bucuresti)	Romania	1,961,189	2,227,568	1983E
Budapest	Hungary	1,995,696	—	1994E
Buenos Aires	Argentina	2,965,403	10,934,727	1991C
Buffalo	(New York) U.S.	328,123	968,532	1990C
Bulawayo	Zimbabwe	600,000	—	1990E
Bursa	Turkey	834,600	—	1990C
Cairo (Al Qahirah)	Egypt	6,052,836	8,500,000	1986C
Calcutta	India	4,399,819	10,916,272	1991C
Cali	Colombia	1,350,565	—	1985C
Canberra	Australia	278,894	—	1990C
Cape Town	South Africa	854,616	1,869,144	1991C
Caracas	Venezuela	1,824,892	2,784,042	1988E
Cardiff	Wales (U.K.)	272,000	—	1991C
Casablanca	Morocco	2,139,204	—	1982C
Catania	Italy	333,075	—	1991C
Cebu	Philippines	627,124	—	1990E
Changchun (Ch'ang-ch'un)	China	2,110,000	—	1990E
Changsha (Ch'ang-sha)	China	1,330,000	—	1990E
Charleroi	Belgium	206,898	—	1994E
Chelyabinsk	Russia	1,148,000	—	1990E
Chengdu (Ch'eng-tu)	China	2,810,000	—	1990E
Chicago	(Illinois) U.S.	2,783,726	6,069,974	1990C
Chittagong	Bangladesh	1,566,070	—	1991C
Chongqing (Chungking, Ch'ung-ch'ing)	China	2,980,000	—	1990E
Cincinnati	(Ohio) U.S.	364,040	1,452,645	1990C
Cleveland	(Ohio) U.S.	505,616	1,831,122	1990C
Cochin	India	1,139,543	—	1991C
Coimbatore	India	1,135,549	—	1991C
Cologne (Köln)	Germany	953,551	—	1990E
Colombo	Sri Lanka	683,000	—	1986E
Columbus	(Ohio) U.S.	632,910	1,377,419	1990C
Copenhagen (København)	Denmark	464,566	1,339,395	1992E
Córdoba	Argentina	1,148,305	1,179,372	1991C
Coventry	England (U.K.)	292,600	—	1991C
Curitiba	Brazil	1,398,599	1,966,426	1990E
Dakar	Senegal	1,571,614	—	1988C
Dalian (Dairen)	China	2,400,000	—	1990E
Dallas	(Texas) U.S.	1,006,877	2,533,362	1990C
Damascus	Syria	1,200,000	—	1980E
Dar es Salaam	Tanzania	1,360,850	—	1988C
Dayton	(Ohio) U.S.	182,044	951,270	1990C
Delhi	India	7,206,704	8,375,188	1991C
Denver	(Colorado) U.S.	467,610	1,622,980	1990C
Detroit	(Michigan) U.S.	1,027,974	4,382,299	1990C
Dhaka (Dacca)	Bangladesh	3,637,892	—	1991C
Dnepropetrovsk	Ukraine	1,187,000	—	1991C
Donetsk (Stalino)	Ukraine	1,117,000	—	1990E
Dortmund	Germany	599,055	—	1990E
Douala	Cameroon	1,029,731	—	1990E
Dresden	Germany	490,571	—	1987C
Dublin	Ireland	502,749	983,683	1986C
Duisburg	Germany	535,447	—	1990E
Durban	South Africa	715,669	1,106,971	1994E
Düsseldorf	Germany	575,794	—	1990E
Edinburgh	Scotland (U.K.)	421,213	—	1991C
Edmonton	(Alberta) Canada	616,741	839,924	1991C
El Paso	(Texas) U.S.	515,342	591,610	1990C
Essen	Germany	626,973	—	1990C
Florence (Firenze)	Italy	403,294	—	1991C
Fortaleza	Brazil	1,824,911	2,119,774	1990C
Frankfurt am Main	Germany	644,865	—	1990E
Freetown	Sierra Leone	469,776	—	1985C
Fukuoka	Japan	1,237,062	—	1990C
Fushun (Fu-shun)	China	1,350,000	—	1990E
Gdańsk (German: Danzig)	Poland	466,500	—	1991C
Geneva (Genève, Genf)	Switzerland	171,042	424,028	1990C
Genoa (Genova)	Italy	678,771	—	1991C
Ghent (Gent)	Belgium	228,450	—	1994C
Giza (Al Jizah)	Egypt	1,870,508	—	1986C
Glasgow	Scotland (U.K.)	654,542	—	1991C
Göteborg (Gothenburg)	Sweden	437,313	—	1993C
Graz	Austria	237,810	—	1991C
Guadalajara	Mexico	1,650,205	2,846,720	1990C
Guangzhou (Canton)	China	3,580,000	—	1990E
Guatemala City	Guatemala	754,243	—	1981C
Guayaquil	Ecuador	1,764,170	—	1990E
Guiyang (Kuei-yang)	China	1,530,000	—	1990E
The Hague ('s Gravenhage)	Netherlands	445,279	695,217	1994E
Hai Phong	Vietnam	1,448,000	—	1989C
Haifa	Israel	246,500	—	1993E
Hamburg	Germany	1,652,363	—	1990E
Hangzhou (Hang-chou)	China	1,340,000	—	1990E
Hannover (Hanover)	Germany	513,010	—	1990C
Hanoi	Vietnam	3,057,000	—	1989C
Harare (Salisbury)	Zimbabwe	656,100	—	1982C
Harbin	China	2,830,000	—	1990E
Hartford	(Connecticut) U.S.	139,739	767,841	1990C
Havana (La Habana)	Cuba	1,924,886	—	1981C
Helsinki (Helsingfors)	Finland	508,588	888,871	1993E
Hiroshima	Japan	1,085,705	—	1990C
Ho Chi Minh City (Saigon)	Vietnam	3,934,000	—	1989C
Honolulu	(Hawaii) U.S.	365,272	836,231	1990C
Houston	(Texas) U.S.	1,630,553	3,301,937	1990C
Hyderabad	India	3,145,939	4,280,261	1991C
Hyderabad	Pakistan	751,529	—	1981C
Ibadan	Nigeria	1,060,000	—	1991C
Inchon	South Korea	1,387,491	—	1985C
Indianapolis	(Indiana) U.S.	741,952	1,249,822	1990C
Innsbruck	Austria	118,112	—	1991C
Irkutsk	Russia	635,000	—	1990E
Istanbul	Turkey	6,620,600	—	1990C
Izmir (Smyrna)	Turkey	1,757,100	—	1990C
Jacksonville	(Florida) U.S.	672,971	906,727	1990C
Jaipur	India	1,514,425	—	1981C
Jakarta	Indonesia	6,761,886	—	1898C
Jekaterinburg (Sverdlovsk)	Russia	1,372,000	—	1990E
Jerusalem	Israel	424,400	—	1983E
Jidda (Jeddah, Juddah)	Saudi Arabia	1,210,000	—	1986E
Jinan (Tsinan)	China	2,320,000	—	1990E
Johannesburg	South Africa	712,507	1,907,229	1991C
Juárez (Ciudad Juárez)	Mexico	789,522	—	1990C
Kabul	Afghanistan	1,036,407	—	1982E
Kananga	Zaire	460,091	—	1984E
Kano	Nigeria	487,100	—	1991C
Kanpur	India	1,879,420	2,111,284	1991C
Kansas City	(Missouri) U.S.	435,146	1,566,280	1992E
Kaohsiung	Taiwan	1,396,425	—	1992E
Karachi	Pakistan	5,208,170	—	1981C
Karaganda	Kazakhstan	596,000	—	1993E
Kathmandu	Nepal	419,073	—	1991C
Katowice	Poland	366,900	—	1991C
Kawasaki	Japan	1,173,603	—	1990C
Kazan	Russia	1,103,000	—	1990E
Khabarovsk	Russia	608,000	—	1990E
Kharkov	Ukraine	1,618,000	—	1990E
Khartoum	Sudan	476,218	817,364	1983C
Kiel	Germany	245,567	—	1990C
Kijev (Kiev)	Ukraine	2,616,000	—	1990E
Kingston	Jamaica	104,041	524,638	1982C
Kinshasa	Zaire	2,222,981	—	1984E
Kišinev	Moldova	676,000	—	1991C
Kitakyushu	Japan	1,026,455	—	1990C
Kobe	Japan	1,477,410	—	1990C
Kowloon	Hong Kong	799,123	—	1981C
Kraków	Poland	751,300	—	1991E
Krasnoyarsk	Russia	922,000	—	1990E
Kuala Lumpur	Malaysia	937,875	—	1980C
Kunming (K'un-ming)	China	1,520,000	—	1990E
Kuwait	Kuwait	44,335	—	1985C
Kwangju	South Korea	906,129	—	1985C
Kyoto	Japan	1,461,103	—	1990C

City	Country	City population	Metropolitan area population	Date
Lagos	Nigeria	1,097,000	—	1991C
Lahore	Pakistan	2,952,689	—	1981C
Lanzhou (Lan-chou)	China	1,510,000	—	1990E
La Paz	Bolivia	976,800	—	1989E
Leeds	England (U.K.)	674,400	1,984,700	1991C
Leipzig	Germany	511,079	—	1991E
León	Mexico	758,279	—	1990C
Liège	Belgium	195,389	—	1994E
Lille	France	178,301	950,265	1990C
Lima	Peru	6,313,000	—	1988E
Linz	Austria	203,044	—	1991C
Lisbon (Lisboa)	Portugal	663,315	2,052,910	1994E
Liverpool	England (U.K.)	448,300	1,376,800	1991C
Łódź	Poland	844,900	—	1991E
London	England (U.K.)	6,378,600	—	1991C
Los Angeles	(California) U.S.	3,485,398	8,863,164	1990C
Louisville	(Kentucky) U.S.	269,063	952,662	1990C
Luanda	Angola	1,200,000	—	1988E
Lubumbashi	Zaire	596,297	—	1984E
Lucknow	India	1,642,134	—	1991C
Ludhiana	India	1,012,062	—	1991C
Lusaka	Zambia	818,994	—	1987E
Lvov	Ukraine	798,000	—	1990E
Lyalipur	Pakistan	1,104,209	—	1981C
Lyon	France	422,444	1,262,223	1990C
Madras	India	3,841,396	5,361,468	1991C
Madrid	Spain	2,909,792	—	1991C
Madurai	India	1,093,702	—	1991C
Managua	Nicaragua	677,680	—	1980E
Manchester	England (U.K.)	397,400	2,445,200	1991C
Mandalay	Burma	472,512	—	1979E
Manila	Philippines	1,876,195	6,720,050	1990E
Mannheim	Germany	310,411	—	1990E
Maputo (Lourenço Marques)	Mozambique	1,006,765	1,551,457	1987E
Mariupol (Zhdanov)	Ukraine	520,000	—	1990E
Maracaibo	Venezuela	1,151,933	—	1988E
Marseille	France	807,726	1,087,372	1990E
Mecca (Makkah)	Saudi Arabia	463,000	—	1986E
Medan	Indonesia	1,715,670	—	1989E
Medellín	Colombia	1,468,089	—	1985C
Melbourne	Australia	3,022,157	—	1991C
Memphis	(Tennessee) U.S.	610,337	981,747	1990C
Mexico City	Mexico	8,235,744	15,047,685	1990C
Miami	(Florida) U.S.	358,548	1,937,094	1990C
Milan (Milano)	Italy	1,369,231	—	1991C
Milwaukee	(Wisconsin) U.S.	628,088	1,432,149	1990C
Minneapolis	(Minnesota) U.S.	368,383	2,464,124	1990C
Minsk	Belarus	1,613,000	—	1991C
Mombasa	Kenya	442,369	—	1985E
Monrovia	Liberia	421,058	—	1984E
Monterrey	Mexico	1,069,238	2,521,697	1990C
Montevideo	Uruguay	1,247,920	—	1985C
Montreal	(Quebec) Canada	1,017,666	3,127,242	1991C
Moscow	Russia	8,801,000	8,967,000	1990E
Multan	Pakistan	736,925	—	1981C
Munich (München)	Germany	1,229,026	—	1990E
Mysore	India	652,246	—	1991C
Nagoya	Japan	2,154,793	—	1990C
Nagpur	India	1,661,409	—	1991C
Nairobi	Kenya	1,162,189	—	1985E
Nanjing (Nan-ching) (Nanking)	China	2,500,000	—	1990E
Nantes	France	252,029	492,255	1990C
Naples (Napoli)	Italy	1,067,365	—	1991C
Nashville	(Tennessee) U.S.	510,784	985,026	1990C
New Delhi	India	301,297	—	1991C
New Kowloon (Linked with Kowloon)	Hong Kong	1,651,064	—	1981C
New Orleans	(Louisiana) U.S.	496,938	1,238,816	1990C
Newcastle upon Tyne (Newcastle)	England (U.K.)	263,000	—	1991C
New York City	(New York) U.S.	7,322,564	8,546,846	1990C
Niamey	Niger	360,000	—	1981E
Niznij Novgorod (Gorki)	Russia	1,443,000	—	1990E
Norfolk	(Virginia) U.S.	261,229	1,396,107	1990C
Nottingham	England (U.K.)	279,400	—	1985E
Novokuznetsk	Russia	601,000	—	1990E
Novosibirsk	Russia	1,443,000	—	1990E
Nuremberg (Nürnberg)	Germany	493,692	—	1990E
Odessa	Ukraine	1,106,000	—	1990E
Okayama	Japan	593,730	—	1990C
Oklahoma City	(Oklahoma) U.S.	444,719	958,839	1990C
Omaha	(Nebraska) U.S.	335,795	618,262	1990C
Omsk	Russia	1,159,000	—	1990E
Orlando	(Florida) U.S.	164,693	1,072,748	1990C
Osaka	Japan	2,623,801	—	1990C
Oslo	Norway	457,818	—	1990E
Ostrava	Czech Republic	331,448	—	1990E
Ottawa	(Ontario) Canada	313,987	920,857	1991C
Palermo	Italy	698,556	—	1991C
Panama City	Panama	389,172	794,300	1980C
Paris	France	2,175,200	9,060,257	1990C
Patna	India	1,098,572	—	1991C
Perm	Russia	1,094,000	—	1990E
Perth	Australia	1,143,265	—	1991C
Philadelphia	(Pennsylvania) U.S.	1,585,577	4,856,881	1990C
Phnom Penh	Cambodia	700,000	—	1985E
Phoenix	(Arizona) U.S.	983,403	2,122,101	1990C
Pittsburgh	(Pennsylvania) U.S.	369,879	2,056,705	1990C
Port-au-Prince	Haiti	738,342	—	1984E
Portland	(Oregon) U.S.	437,319	1,239,842	1990C
Porto (Oporto)	Portugal	302,467	1,672,360	1994E
Pôrto Alegre	Brazil	1,386,828	2,906,472	1990E
Portsmouth	England (U.K.)	174,700	—	1991E
Poznań	Poland	589,700	—	1991E
Prague (Praha)	Czech Republic	1,215,656	—	1990E
Pretoria	South Africa	525,583	1,025,790	1991C
Providence	(Rhode Island) U.S.	160,728	654,854	1990C
Puebla (Puebla de Zaragoza)	Mexico	1,007,170	—	1990C
Pune	India	2,485,014	—	1991C
Pusan	South Korea	3,516,807	—	1985C
Pyongyang	North Korea	2,639,448	—	1984E
Qingdao (Tsingtao)	China	2,060,000	—	1990E
Quebec (Québec)	(Quebec) Canada	167,517	645,550	1991C
Quezon City	Philippines	1,587,140	—	1990C
Quito	Ecuador	1,281,849	—	1990E
Rabat	Morocco	518,616	—	1982C
Rangoon	Burma	2,458,712	3,973,782	1983C
Rawalpindi	Pakistan	794,843	—	1981C
Recife	Brazil	1,375,404	2,814,795	1990C
Richmond	(Virginia) U.S.	203,056	865,640	1990C
Riga	Latvia	885,625	—	1992C
Rio de Janeiro	Brazil	6,042,411	11,205,567	1990C
Riyadh (Ar Riyad)	Saudi Arabia	1,380,000	—	1986E
Rochester	(New York) U.S.	231,636	1,002,410	1990C
Rome (Roma)	Italy	2,775,250	—	1991C
Rosario	Argentina	894,645	1,079,359	1991C
Rostov-on-Don	Russia	1,025,000	—	1990C
Rotterdam	Netherlands	598,521	1,074,387	1994E
Saarbrücken	Germany	191,694	—	1990E
Sacramento	(California) U.S.	369,365	1,481,102	1990C
Saint Louis	(Missouri) U.S.	396,685	2,444,099	1990C
Saint Paul	(Minnesota) U.S.	272,235	—	1990C
Saint Petersburg	(Florida) U.S.	238,629	—	1990C
St. Petersburg (Sankt Peterburg; Leningrad)	Russia	4,468,000	—	1990E
Sakai	Japan	807,765	—	1990C
Salonika (Thessaloniki)	Greece	396,807	739,998	1991C
Salt Lake City	(Utah) U.S.	159,936	1,072,227	1990C
Salvador (Bahia)	Brazil	2,050,133	2,424,878	1990C
Samara (Kujbysev)	Russia	1,258,000	—	1990E
Samarkand	Uzbekistan	370,000	—	1990C
Sana	Yemen	472,185	—	1986E
San Antonio	(Texas) U.S.	935,933	1,302,099	1990C
San Bernardino	(California) U.S.	164,164	—	1990C
San Diego	(California) U.S.	1,110,549	2,498,016	1990C
San Francisco	(California) U.S.	723,959	1,603,678	1990C
San José	Costa Rica	241,464	560,000	1984C
San Juan	Puerto Rico	437,745	1,086,376	1991C
San Justo	Argentina	18,257	—	1991C
San Salvador	El Salvador	452,614	—	1984E
Santa Fe de Bogotá (Bogotá)	Colombia	3,982,941	—	1985C
Santiago	Chile	4,385,481	—	1990E
Santo Domingo	Dominican Rep.	1,313,172	—	1981C
Santos	Brazil	486,810	—	1990C
São Paulo	Brazil	11,128,848	17,128,848	1990C
Saragossa (Zaragoza)	Spain	586,219	—	1991C
Saratov	Russia	909,000	—	1990E
Seattle	(Washington) U.S.	516,259	1,972,961	1990C
Semarang	Indonesia	1,112,175	—	1989E
Sendai	Japan	918,398	—	1990C
Seoul	South Korea	9,645,932	—	1985C
Seville (Sevilla)	Spain	659,126	—	1991C
Shanghai	China	8,214,436	13,341,896	1990C
Sheffield	England (U.K.)	500,500	1,249,300	1991C
Shenyang (Shen-yang)	China	4,540,000	—	1990E
Shijiazhuang (Shih-chia-chuang)	China	1,320,000	—	1990E
Singapore	Singapore	2,874,000	—	1993E
Sofia	Bulgaria	1,128,859	1,208,200	1987E
Southampton	England (U.K.)	194,400	—	1991C
Stockholm	Sweden	692,954	—	1993E
Stuttgart	Germany	579,988	—	1990E
Suez (As Suways)	Egypt	326,820	—	1986C
Surabaya	Indonesia	2,159,170	—	1989E
Surat	India	1,517,076	—	1991C
Sydney	Australia	3,538,970	—	1991C
Taegu	South Korea	2,030,672	—	1985C
Taichung	Taiwan	774,197	—	1992E
Tainan	Taiwan	689,541	—	1992E
Taipei	Taiwan	2,637,100	—	1987E
Taiyuan (T'ai-yuan)	China	1,960,000	—	1990E
Tallinn	Estonia	478,496	497,183	1991E
Tampa	(Florida) U.S.	280,015	2,067,959	1990C
Taškent	Uzbekistan	2,094,000	—	1990E
Tbilisi (Tiflis)	Georgia	1,268,000	—	1990E
Tegucigalpa	Honduras	624,542	—	1988C
Teheran (Tehran)	Iran	6,042,584	—	1986C
Tel Aviv-Yafo	Israel	357,400	—	1993E
Tianjin (Tientsin)	China	5,855,068	8,785,402	1990C
Tiranë (Tirana)	Albania	260,000	—	1983E
Tokyo	Japan	8,163,573	11,927,457	1990C
Toledo	(Ohio) U.S.	332,943	614,128	1990C
Toronto	(Ontario) Canada	635,395	3,893,046	1991C
Tripoli (Tarabulus)	Libya	990,697	—	1984C
Tucson	(Arizona) U.S.	405,390	666,880	1990C
Tula	Russia	543,000	—	1990E
Tulsa	(Oklahoma) U.S.	367,302	708,954	1990C
Tunis	Tunisia	596,654	—	1984C
Turin (Torino)	Italy	962,507	—	1991C
Ufa	Russia	1,094,000	—	1990E
Ujung Pandang	Indonesia	806,129	—	1989E
Ulan Bator (Urga)	Mongolia	515,000	—	1989C
Vadodara	India	1,115,265	—	1991C
Valencia	Spain	752,909	—	1991C
Valparaíso	Chile	276,756	—	1990E
Vancouver	(British Columbia) Canada	471,844	1,602,502	1991C
Varanasi	India	1,026,467	—	1991C
Venice (Venezia)	Italy	309,422	—	1991C
Victoria	Hong Kong	1,183,621	—	1981C
Vienna (Wien)	Austria	1,539,848	—	1991C
Vilnius	Lithuania	591,066	—	1991C
Vladivostok	Russia	643,000	—	1990E
Volgograd (Stalingrad)	Russia	1,005,000	—	1990E
Voronezh	Russia	895,000	—	1990E
Warsaw (Warszawa)	Poland	1,653,300	—	1991E
Washington, D.C.	U.S.	606,900	3,923,574	1980C
Wellington	New Zealand	324,600	—	1991C
Wiesbaden	Germany	260,301	—	1990E
Winnipeg	(Manitoba) Canada	616,790	652,354	1991C
Wrocław (Breslau)	Poland	643,600	—	1991E
Wuhan (Wu-han)	China	3,750,000	—	1990E
Wuppertal	Germany	383,660	—	1990E
Xi'an (Sian)	China	2,760,000	—	1990E
Xuzhou (Suchow)	China	779,289	—	1982E
Yaoundé	Cameroon	653,670	—	1986E
Yerevan	Armenia	1,254,000	—	1990E
Yokohama	Japan	3,220,331	—	1990C
Zagreb	Croatia	953,607	—	1991C
Zaporozhye	Ukraine	891,000	—	1990E
Zhengzhou (Cheng-chou)	China	1,710,000	—	1990E
Zurich (Zürich)	Switzerland	365,043	940,180	1990C

C = Census
E = Official Estimate

Sources

The maps in the Atlas have been compiled from diverse source materials, which are cited in the following lists. The citations are organized by continent and region or country. Within each regional or country group, atlases are listed alphabetically by title and then followed by maps, which are listed according to scale, from the smallest to the largest. Other sources, listed alphabetically by title, follow the map listings.

GENERAL SOURCES

Atlante dei confini sottomarini, *A. Giuffrè Editore, Milano 1979*
Atlante Internazionale del Touring Club Italiano, *TCI, Milano 1977*
Atlas Mira, *G.U.G.K. Moskva 1967*
Atlas Okeanov-Atlantičeski i Indijski Okeany, *Ministerstvo Oborony SSSR-Vojenno-Morskoj Flot, Moskva 1977*
Atlas Okeanov-Tihi Okean, *Ministerstvo Oborony SSSR-Vojenno-Morskoj Flot, Moska 1974*
Atlas of the World, *National Geographic Society (N.G.S.), Washington 1981*
Atlas zur Ozeanographie, *Bibliographisches Institut, Mannheim 1971*
Bertelsmann Atlas International, *C. Bertelsmann Verlag GmbH, München 1963*
Grande Atlante degli Oceani, *Instituto Geografico De Agostini (I.G.D.A.), Novara 1978*
Meyers Neuer Geographischer Handatlas, *Bibliographisches Institut, Mannheim 1966*
The New International Atlas, *Rand McNally & Company, Chicago 1980*
The Odyssey World Atlas, *Western Publishing Company Inc., New York 1966*
The Times Atlas of the World, *John Bartholomew & Son Ltd, Edinburgh 1980*
The World Book Atlas, *World Book Encyclopedia Inc, 1979*
The World Shipping Scene, *Weststadt-Verlag, München 1963*
Weltatlas Erdöl und Erdgas, *George Westermann Verlag, Braunschweig 1976*
Pacific Ocean Floor 1:36,432,000, *N.G.S., Washington 1969*
Atlantic Ocean Floor 1:30,580,000, *N.G.S., Washington 1973*
Indian Ocean 1:25,720,000, *N.G.S. Washington 1967*
Deutsche Meereskarte 1:25,000,000, *Kartographisches Institut Meyer*
Carte générale du Monde 1:10,000,000, *Institut Géographique National (I.G.N.), Paris*
Artic Ocean Floor 1:9,757,000, *N.G.S., Washington 1971*
Carte du Monde 1:5,000,000, *I.G.N., Paris*
Karta Mira 1:2,500,000, *G.U.G.K., Moskva*
Carte Internationale du Monde 1:1,000,000, *Geographical Survey Institute*
Carte Aéronautique du Monde 1:1,000,000, *I.G.N., Paris*
Calendario Atlante, *I.G.D.A., Novara 1982*
Cartactual, *Cartographia, Budapest*
Demographic Yearbook, *United Nations, New York, 1978*
Duden Wörterbuch Geographischer Namen, *Bibliographisches Institut, Mannheim 1966*
Gazetteers (Various), *U.S. Board on Geographical Names, Washington*
Meyers Enzyklopädisches Lexikon, *Bibliographisches Institut, Mannheim 1972–81*
Schtag nach!-Die Staaten der Erde, *Bibliographisches Institut, Mannheim 1977*
Statistical Yearbook, *United Nations, New York, 1978*
Statistik des Auslandes-Länderkurzberichte, *Statistisches Bundesamt, Wiesbaden*
The Columbia Lippincott Gazetteer of the World, *Columbia University Press, New York 1961*
The Europa Year Book 1981, *Europa Publication Ltd., London*
The Statesman's Yearbook 1981–82, *The Macmillan Press Ltd., London*
Webster's New Geographical Dictionary, *G & C Merriam Co, Springfield 1972*

EUROPE

ALBANIA
Shqiperia-Hartë Fizike 1:500,000, *MMS "Hamid Shijaku", Tirana 1970*
Shqiperia Politiko Administrative 1:500,000, *MMS "Hamid Shijaku", Tirana 1969*
Gjeografia e Shqiperise per shkollat e mesme, *Shtëpia Botuese e Librit Shkollor, Tirana 1970*

AUSTRIA
Neuer Schulatlas, *Freytag-Berndt und Artaria KG, Wien 1971*
Generalkarte Österreich 1:200,000, *Mairs Geographischer Verlag, Stuttgart 1974*
Gemeindeverzeichnis von Österreich, *Österreichischen Statistischen Zentralamt, Wien 1970*
Geographisches Namenbuch Österreichs, *Verlag der Österreichischen Akademie der Wissenschaften, Wien 1975*
Statistisches Handbuch für die Republik Österreich, *Österreichischen Statistischen Zentralamt, Wien 1978*

BELGIUM
Atlas de Belgique-Atlas van België, *Comité National de Géographie, Bruxelles 1974*
België, Luxemburg, Belgien 1:350,000, *Pneu. Michelin, Bruxelles 1976*
Belgique, Grand-Duché de Luxembourg, *Pneu. Michelin, Paris 1978*
Lista Alphabetique des Communes-fusion de 1963 à 1977, *Institut National de Statistique, Bruxelles*
Statistique Demographiques 1980, *Institut National de Statistique, Bruxelles*

BULGARIA
Atlas Narodna Republika Bulgarija, *Glavno Upravlenie po Geodezija i Kartografija, Sofija 1973*
Bulgaria 1:1,000,000, *PPWK, Warszawa 1977*
Statističeski Godišnik na Narodna Republika Bălgarija 1973, *Ministerstvo na Informacijata i Săobšenijata, Sofija*

CZECHOSLOVAKIA
Atlas ČSSR, *Kartografie, Praha 1972*
Školní Zeměpisný Atlas Čescoslovenské Socialistické Republiky, *Kartografické* Nakladatelství, Praha 1970
Auto Atlas Č.S.S.R., *Kartografie, Praha 1971*
Č.S.S.R.-Fyzická Mapa 1:500,000, *Ústřední Správa Geodezie a Kartografie, Praha 1963*
Statistická Ročenka Č.S.S.R., *Federální Statistický Úřad, Praha 1980*

DENMARK
Haases Atlas, *P. Haase & Søns Forlag, København 1972*
Opgivne og Tilplantede Landbrugsarealer i Jylland, *Det Kongelige Danske Geografiske Selskab, København 1976*
Danmark 1:300,000, *Geodætisk Institut, København 1972*
Statistisk Årbog Danmark 1980, *Danmarks Statistik, København*

FINLAND
Oppikoulun Kartasto, *Werner Söderström Osakeyhtiö, Porvoo 1972*
Suomi-Finland 1:1,000,000, *Naanmittaushallituksen Kivipaino, Helsinki 1972*
Finland-Suomi 1:1,000,000, *Kümmerly & Frey, Bern 1981*
Suomen Tilastollinen Vuosikirja 1975, *Tilastokeskus, Helsinki*

FRANCE
Atlas Général Larousse, *Librairie Larousse, Paris 1976*
Atlas Général Bordas, *Bordas, Paris 1972*
Atlas Géographique Alpha, *I.G.D.A., Novara 1972*
Atlas Moderne Larousse, *Librairie Larousse-I.G.D.A., Paris 1976*
Carte Administrative de la France 1:1,400,000, *I.G.N., Paris 1977*
Carte de la France 1:1,000,000, *I.G.N., Paris 1971*
France: Routes-Autoroutes 1:1,000,000, *I.G.N., Paris 1978*
Carte Touristique 1:250,000, *I.G.N., Paris 1978*
France 1:200,000, *Pneu. Michelin, Paris*
Carte Touristique 1:100,000, *I.G.N., Paris*
Michelin 1977-France, *Pneu. Michelin, Paris*
Population de la France-Recensement 1975, *Institut National de la Statistique et des Études Économiques, Paris*

GERMAN DEMOCRATIC REPUBLIC
Haack Weltatlas, *V.E.B. Hermann Haack Geographisch-Kartographische Anstalt, Gotha-Leipzig 1972*
Weltatlas-Die Staaten der Erde und ihre Wirtschaft, *V.E.B. Hermann Haack Geographisch-Kartographische Anstalt, Gotha-Leipzig 1972*
Autokarte der D.D.R. 1:600,000, *V.E.B. Landkartenverlag, Berlin 1972*
Statistisches Jahrbuch der Deutschen Demokratischen Republik 1981, *Staatsverlag der D.D.R., Berlin*

GERMANY, FEDERAL REPUBLIC OF
Diercke Weltatlas, *Westermann Verlag, Braunschweig 1977*
Der Grosse Shell Atlas, *Mairs Geographischer Verlag, Stuttgart 1981–82*
Der Neue Weltatlas, *I.G.D.A., Novara 1977*
Deutschland-Strassenkarte 1:1,000,000, *Kümmerly & Frey, Bern 1981*
Bundesrepublik Deutschland-Übersichtskarte 1:500,000, *Institut für Angewandte Geodäsie, Frankfurt 1978*
Topographische Übersichtskarte 1:200,000, *Institut für Angewandte Geodäsie, Frankfurt*
Bevölkerung der Gemeinden, *Statistisches Bundesamt, Wiesbaden 1979*
Statistisches Jahrbuch für die B.R.D. 1980, *Statistisches Bundesamt, Wiesbaden*

GREECE
Greece-Autokarte 1:1,000,000, *Kümmerly & Frey, Bern*
Greece-Autokarte 1:650,000, *Freytag & Berndt, Wien*
Genikos Chartis tis Hellados 1:400,000, *Geografiki Hypiresia Stratoy, Athínai*
Etniki Statistiki Hypiresia tis Hellados 1:200,000, *E.S.Y.E., Athínai*
Statistiki Epetiris tis Hellados 1979, *E.S.Y.E., Athínai*

HUNGARY
Földrajzi Atlas a Középiskolák Számára, *Kartográfiai Vallalat, Budapest 1980*
A Magyar Népköztársaság 1:400,000, *Kartográfiai Vallalat, Budapest 1974*
Magyarorszag Domborzata és Vizei 1:350,000, *Kartogràfiai Vallalat, Budapest 1961*
Megye Terképe, *Cartographia, Budapest 1979–80*
A Magyar Népköztársaság Helységnévtára 1973, *Statisztikai Kiadó Vállalat, Budapest*
Statistical Pocket Book of Hungary 1980, *Statistical Publishing House, Budapest*

ICELAND
Landabréfabok, *Ríkisutgáfa Námsbóka, Reykjavik 1970*
Iceland-Road Guide, *Örn & Örlygur H.F., Reykjavik 1975*

IRELAND
Irish Student's Atlas, *Educational Company of Ireland, Dublin-Cork 1971*
Ireland 1:575,000, *Ordnance Survey Office, Dublin 1979*
Ireland 1:250,000, *Ordnance Survey Office, Dublin 1962*
Census of Population of Ireland 1979, *The Stationery Office, Dublin*

ITALY
Atlante Metodico, *I.G.D.A., Novara 1981*
Atlante Stradale d'Italia 1:200,000, *Touring Club Italiano, Milano*
Carta d'Italia 1:1,250,000, *Instituto Geografico Militare, Firenze 1972*
Carte batimetriche, *Istituto Idrografico della Marina, Genova*
Carta Generale d'Italia 1:500,000, *Touring Club Italiano, Milano 1979*
Carta Generale d'Italia 1:200,000, *I.G.M., Firenze*
Enciclopedia Italiana, *Istituto della Enciclopedia Italiana G. Treccani, Roma*
Il Mare, *I.G.D.A., Novara*
La Montagna, *I.G.D.A., Novara*
XI Censimento Generale della Popolazione 24 ottobre 1971, *Istituto Centrale di Statistica, Roma*
XII Censimento Generale della Popolazione 25 ottobre 1981, *Istituto Centrale di Statistica, Roma*

LUXEMBOURG
Grand-Duché de Luxembourg 1:100,000, *I.G.N., Paris 1970*
Annuaire Statistique-Luxembourg 1981–82, *Service Central de la Statistique et des Études Économiques, Paris*

NETHERLANDS
Atlas van Nederland, *Staatsdrukkerij-en Uitgeverijbedrijf,'s-Gravenhage*
De Grote Vara Gezinsatlas, *Vara Omroepvereniging, Hilversum 1975*
Der Kleine Bosatlas, *Wolter-Noordhoff, Groningen 1974*
Pays-Bas/Nederland 1:400,000, *Pneu. Michelin, Paris 1981*
Gegevens per Gemeente Betreffende de Loop der Bevolking in het Jaar 1980, *Centraal Bureau voor der Statistik, Amsterdam*

NORWAY
Atlas-Større Utgave for Gymnaset, *J. W. Cappelens Forlag A.S., Oslo 1969*
Bilkart Bok Road Atlas, *J. W. Cappelens Forlag A.S., Oslo 1967*
Norge-Bit-Og Turistkart 1:400,000, *J. W. Cappelens Forlag A.S., Oslo 1965*
Folketallet i Kommunene 1972–73, *Statistik Sentralbyraå, Oslo*
Statistisk Årbok 1981, *Statistik Sentralbyrå, Oslo*

POLAND
Atlas Geograficzny, *PPWK, Warszawa 1979*
Narodowy Atlas Polski, *Polska Akademia Nauk, Warszawa 1978*
Polska Kontynenty Świat, *P.P.W.K., Warszawa 1977*
Powszechny Atlas Świat, *P.P.W.K. Warszawa 1981*
Polska Rzeczpospolito. Ludowa-Mapa Administracyjna 1:500,000, *P.P.W.K., Warszawa 1980*
Rocznik Statystyczny 1978, *Glówny Urzad Statystyczny, Warszawa*

PORTUGAL
Portugal 1:1,500,000, *Pneu. Michelin, Paris 1981*
Mapa do Estado das Estradas de Portugal 1:550,000, *Automovel Club de Portugal, Lisboa 1979*
Carto. Corográfica de Portugal 1:400,000, *Instituto Geografico e Cadastral, Lisboa 1968*
Anuário Estatístico-Portugal 1974, *Instituto Nacional de Estatística, Lisboa*

ROMANIA
Atlas Geografic General, *Editura Didactica si Pedagogica, Bucureşti 1974*
Atlasul Republicii Socialiste România, *Institutul de Geologie si Geofizica, Bucureşti*
Rumanien-Bulgarien 1:1,000,000, *Freytag-Berndt und Artaria K.G., Wien*
Anuarul Statistic al Republicii Socialiste România 1980, *Direcţia Centrala de Statistică, Bucureşti*

SPAIN
Atlas Bachillerato Universal y de España, *Aguilar, Madrid 1968*
Atlas Básico Universal, *I.G.D.A. Teide, Novara 1969*
Gran Atlas Aguilar, *Aguilar, Madrid 1969*
Peninsula Iberica, Baleares y Canarias 1:1,000,000, *Instituto Geografico y Catastral, Madrid 1966*
Mapa Militar de España 1:800,000, *Servicio Geografico del Ejercito, Madrid 1971*
España 1:500,000, *Firestone Hispania, Madrid*
España-Mapa Oficial de Carreteras 1:400,000 *Ministerio de Obras Publica, Madrid*
España-Anuario Estadistico 1979, *Instituto Nacional de Estadistica, Madrid*

SWEDEN
Atlas Över Välden, *Generalstabens Litografiska Anstalt, Stockholm 1972*
Atlas Över Välden, *Natur Miljö Befolkning, Stockholm 1974*
Kak Bil Atlas, *Generalstabens Litografiska Anstalt, Stockholm 1973*
Sverige-Bilkarta 1:625,000, *A.B. Kartlitografen, Stockholm 1972*
Statistisk Årsbok 1980, *Statistiska Centralbyrån, Stockholm*

SWITZERLAND
Atlas der Schweiz, *Verlag des Bundesamtes fur Landestopographie, Wabern-Bern*
Schweizerischer Mittelschulatlas, *Konferenz der Kantonalen Erziehungsdirektoren, Zürich 1976*
Switzerland 1:300,000, *Kümmerly & Frey, Bern 1979*
Carte Nazionale de la Suisse 1:200,000, *Service Topographique Federale, Wabern-Bern*

U.S.S.R.
Atlas Avtomobilnyh Dorog, *G.U.G.K., Moskva 1976*
Atlas Obrazovanie i Razvitie Sojuza S.S.R., *G.U.G.K., Moskva 1972*
Malyi Atlas S.S.S.R., *G.U.G.K., Moskva 1973*
SSSR 1:8,000,000, *G.U.G.K., Moskva 1980*
SSSR 1:4,000,000, *G.U.G.K., Moskva 1972*
Latvijskaja SSR 1:600,000, *G.U.G.K., Moskva 1967*
Litovskaja SSR 1:600,000, *G.U.G.K., Moskva 1969*
S.S.S.R. Administrativno-Territorialnoje Delenie Sojuznyh Respublik, *Prezidium Verhovnogo Soveta Sojuza Sovetskih Socialističeskih Respublik Moskva 1971*

UNITED KINGDOM
Philips' Modern School Economic Atlas, *George Philip & Son Ltd, London 1981*
Roads Atlas of Great Britain and Ireland, *George Philip & Son Ltd, London 1971*
The Atlas of Britain and Northern Ireland, *Clarendon Press, Oxford 1963*
Route Planning Map 1:625,000, *Ordnance Survey, Southampton 1973*
Cartes 1:400,000, *Michelin Tyre Co. Ltd., London 1981*

YUGOSLAVIA
Atlas, *Izrađenou u Oour Kartografiji Tlos "Učila", Zagreb 1980*
Jugoslavija-Auto Atlas, *Jugoslavenski Leksikografski Zavod, Zagreb 1972*
Školki Atlas, *Izrađenou u Oour Kartografiji Tlos "Učila", Zagreb 1975*
Jugoslavija 1:1,000,000, *Grafički Zavod Hrvatske, Zagreb 1980*
Statistički Godišnjak Jugoslavije 1975, *Savezni Zavod za Statistiku, Beograd*

ASIA

ARABIAN PENINSULA
The Oxford Map of Saudi Arabia 1:2,600,000, *GEO-projects, Beirut 1981*
Arabian Peninsula 1:2,000,000, *United States Geological Survey, Washington 1963*
Arabische Republik Jemen 1:1,000,000, *Deutsch-Jemenitische Gesellschaft e V, Schwaig 1976*
The United Arab Emirates 1:750,000, *GEO-projects, Beirut 1981*

MIDDLE EAST
Atlas of Iran, *"Sahab" Geographic & Drafting Institute, Tehrán 1971*
Modern Büyük Atlas, *Arkin Kitabevi-I.G.D.A., Istanbul 1981*
The New Israel Atlas-Zev Vilnay, *Israel Universities Press, Yerushalaym 1968*
Iran 1:2,500,000, *Imperial Government of Iran, Tehrān 1968*
Guide Map of Iran 1:2,250,000, *Gita Shenassi Co. Ltd, Tehrān*
Guide Map of Iraq 1:2,000,000, *"Sahab" Geographic & Drafting Institute, Tehrān 1971*
Türkiye 1:2,000,000, *Ravenstein Verlag GmbH, Frankfurt 1975*
Iran 1:1,500,000, *Imperial Government of Iran, Tehrān 1968*
Iraq Tourist Map 1:1,500,000, *Summer Resorts and Tourism Service, Baghdād 1967*
The Oxford Map of Syria 1:1,000,000, *GEO-projects, Beirut 1980*
Turkey-Road Map 1:1,000,000, *Kümmerly & Frey, Bern 1980*
Türkei und Naher Osten 1:800,000, *Reis und Verkehrsverlag, Berlin-Stuttgart 1977*
Israel und Angrenzende Länder-Strassenkarte 1:750,000, *Kümmerly & Frey, Bern 1981*
The Oxford Map of Jordan 1:730,000, *GEO-projects, Beirut 1979*
Map of Israel 1:500,000, *Survey of Israel, Yerushalaym 1979*
The Oxford Map of Kuwait 1:500,000, *GEO-projects, Beirut 1980*
The Oxford Map of Qatar 1:270,000, *GEO-projects, Beirut 1980*
Israel Map of the Cease-Fire Lines 1:250,000, *Survey of Israel, Yerushalaym 1973*
Qatar-Visitor's Map 1:250,000, *Ministry of Information, Doha 1979*
Carte Générale du Liban 1:200,000, *Ministère de la Défense Nationale, Beirut 1967*
Qatar 1:200,000, *Hunting Surveys Ltd., Borchamwood 1975*
Bahrain Islands 1:63,360, *Public Works Department, Al Manāmah 1968*
The Oxford Map of Bahrain 1:57,750, *GEO-projects, Beirut 1980*
Bahrain—A Map for Visitors 1:50,000, *Ministry of Information, Al Manāmah 1976*
Annual Abstract of Statistics 1978, *Central Statistical Organization, Baghdād*
Genel Nüfus Sayımı 12 ekim 1980, *Başbakanlik Devlet İstatistik Enstitüsü, Ankara*
Kuwait—Annual Statistical Abstract, *Central Statistical Office-Ministry of Planning, Al Kuwayt 1976*
List of Localities—Geographical Information and Population 1948–1961–1972–1975, *Central Bureau of Statistics, Yerushalaym*
Recueil de Statistiques Libanaises No. 8-1972, *Direction Centrale de la Statistique, Bayrūt*
Republic of Cyprus—Statistical Abstract 1973, *The Statistics and Research Department, Levkosia*
Statistical Abstract—Syrian Arab Republic 1973, *Central Bureau of Statistics, Dimashq*
Statistical Abstract of Israel 1979, *Central Bureau of Statistics, Yerushalaym*
The Hashemite Kingdom of Jordan, Statistical Yearbook 1976, *Department of Statistics, Ammān*
Türkiye İstatistik Yıllığı 1975, *Başbakanlik Devlet İstatistik Enstitüsü, Ankara*

SOUTH ASIA
National Atlas of India, *National Atlas & Thematic Mapping Organization, Calcutta*
Oxford School Atlas for Pakistan, *Oxford University Press—Pakistan Branch, Karachi 1973*
Tourist Atlas of India, *National Atlas Organization, Calcutta*
Physical Map of India 1:4,500,000, *Survey of India, Calcutta 1974*
Political Map of India 1:4,500,000, *Survey of India, Calcutta 1972*
Railway Map of India 1:3,500,000, *Government of India, Calcutta 1971*
Pākistān 1:3,168,000, *Survey of Pākistān, Rāwalpindi 1966*
Bangladesh 1:2,800,000, *Survey of Bangladesh, Dacca 1979*
Burma 1:2,000,000, *Army Map Service, Washington 1963*
Physical and Political Map of Afghanistan 1:1,500,000, *Afghan Cartographic Institute, Kabul 1968*
Ceylon Physical 1:1,000,000, *Survey Department, Colombo 1973*
New Map of Afghanistan 1:1,000,000, *"Sahab" Geographic & Drafting Institute, Tehrān*
Pākistān 1:1,000,000, *Survey of Pākistān, Rāwalpindi 1968*
Motor Map of Ceylon 1:506,880, *Survey Department, Colombo 1973*
Nepal 1:506,880, *Ministry of Defence, London 1967*
Nepal 1:408,000, *Kümmerly & Frey, Bern 1980*
Bangladesh Population Census Report 1974, *Statistics Division-Ministry of Planning, Dacca*
Geomedical Monograph Series—Afghanistan, *Springer-Verlag, Berlin 1968*
Pakistan Statistical Yearbook 1978, *Statistics Division, Karachi*
Statistical Pocket Book of the Democratic Socialist Republic of Sri Lanka 1979, *Department of Census and Statistics, Colombo*

SOUTHEAST ASIA
Atlas Indonesia, *Yayasan Dwidjendra, Denpasar-Jakarta 1977*
Atlas of Thailand, *Royal Thai Survey Department, Bangkok 1974*
Secondary Atlas for Malaysia and Singapore, *Niugini Press Pty. Ltd., Port Moresby 1975*
Secondary School Atlas for Malaysia, *McGraw-Hill Far Eastern Publishers Ltd., Singapore 1970*
Hành Chính Viet Nam 1:2,500,000, *Hô Chí Minh 1976*
Maluku dan Irian Jaya 1:2,250,000, *Pembina, Jakarta 1975–76*
Bàu-dô Viet Nam 1:2,000,000, *Saigon 1972*
Laos Administratif 1:2,000,000, *Service Géographique National du Laos, Vientiane 1968*
Malaysia 1:2,000,000, *Jabatanarah Pemetaan Negara, 1976*
Map of Thailand and Bangkok 1:2,000,000, *The Shell Company of Thailand Ltd., Bangkok*
Vietnam 1:2,000,000, *G.U.G.K., Moskva 1972*
Kalimantan 1:1,500,000, *Pembina, Jakarta 1975–76*
Philippines 1:1,500,000, *Philippine Coast and Geodetic Survey, Manila 1968*
Cambodia & South Vietnam—Southeast Asia 1:1,250,000, *Army Map Service, Washington 1966*
Carte Générale du Laos, *Service Géographique National du Laos, Vientiane 1968*
Sumatera 1:790,000, *Pembina, Jakarta 1975–76*
Malaysia Barat—West Malaysia 1:760,000, *Jabatanarah Pemetaan Negara, 1968*
Jawa Barat & D.K.I. Jakarta 1:500,000, *Pembina, Jakarta 1974–75*
Jawa Tengah & D.I. Yogyakarta 1:500,000, *Pembina, Jakarta 1974–75*
Jawa Timur 1:500,000, *Pembina, Jakarta 1974–75*

Sabah 1:500,000, *Jabatanarah Pemetaan Negara, 1976*
Nusa Tenggara Barat & Nusa Tenggara Timur 1:330,000, *Pembina, Jakarta 1975*
Jawa Madura 1:225,000, *Pembina, Jakarta 1975–76*
Sulawesi 1:220,000, *Pembina, Jakarta 1975–76*
Gulongan Masharakat-Banchi Pendudok dan Perumahan Malaysia 1970, *Jabatan Perangkaan, Kuala Lumpur*
Sensus Penduluk 1971, *Biro Pusat Statistik, Jakarta*
Statistical Summary of Thailand 1978, *Statistical Reports Division, Bangkok*
Statistik Indonesia 1974–75, *Biro Pusat Statistik, Jakarta*

CHINA, MONGOLIA
Zhonghua Renmin Gongheguo Fen Sheng Dituji, *Ditu Chubanshe, Beijing 1977*
Zhonghua Renmin Gongheguo Ditu 1:6,000,000, *Ditu Chubanshe, Beijing 1980*
China 1:5,500,000, *Cartographia, Budapest 1967*
Zhonghua Renmin Gongheguo Ditu 1:4,000,000, *Ditu Chubanshe, Beijing 1980*
Mongolskaja Narodnaja Respublika 1:3,000,000, *G.U.G.K., Moskva 1972*
Taiwan/Formosa 1:500,000, *Army Map Service, Washington 1964*
China's Changing Map, *Methuen & Co., London 1972*

JAPAN, KOREA
Japan—The Pocket Atlas, *Heibonsha Ltd., Tōkyō 1970*
The National Atlas of Japan, *Geographical Survey Institute, Tōkyō 1977*
Teikoku's Complete Atlas of Japan, *Teikoku Shoin Company Ltd., Tōkyō 1977*
Tourist Map of Japan 1:5,300,000, *Japan National Tourist Organisation, Tōkyō 1974*
Republic of Korea 1:1,000,000, *Chungang Map & Chart Service, Sŏul 1973*
Northern Korea—Road Map of Korea, *Republic of Korea Army Map Service, Sŏul 1971*
Southern Korea 1:700,000, *Republic of Korea Army Map Service, Sŏul 1977*

AFRICA
The Atlas of Africa, *Editions Jeune Afrique, Paris 1973*
Africa 1:14,000,000, *N.G.S., Washington 1980*
Africa 1:9,000,000, *V.E.B. Hermann Haack, Gotha-Leipzig 1977*
Afrique/Africa 1:4,000,000, *Pneu. Michelin, Paris-London*
Africa 1:2,000,000, *Army Map Service, Washington*

NORTH WEST AFRICA
Atlas International de l'Ouest Africain 1:2,500,000, *Organisation de l'Unité Africaine, Dakar 1971*
Mauritanie 1:2,500,000, *I.G.N., Paris 1978*
Algérie-Tunisie 1:1,000,000, *Pneu. Michelin, Paris 1975*
Maroc 1:1,000,000, *Pneu. Michelin, Paris 1975*
Generalkarte Gran Canaria-Tenerife 1:150,000, *Mairs Geographischer Verlag, Stuttgart 1979*
Annuaire Statistique du Maroc, *Direction de la Statistique, Rabat 1976*
Code Géographique National—Code des Communes, *Secretariat d'État au Plan, Alger 1975*
Recensement Général de la Population et des Logements 1975, *Institut National de la Statistique, Tūnis*

NORTH EAST AFRICA
Egypte 1:750,000, *Kummerly & Frey, Bern 1977*
Population Census 1973, *Census and Statistical Department, Tarābulus*

WEST AFRICA
Atlas de Côte d'Ivoire, *Institut de Géographie Tropicale-Université d'Abidjan, Abidjan 1971*
Atlas de Haute-Volta, *Centre Voltaïque de la Recherche Scientifique, Ouagadougou 1969*
Atlas du Cameroun, *Institut de Recherches Scientifiques du Cameroun, Yaoundé*
Atlas for the United Republic of Cameroon, *Collins-Longman, Glasgow 1977*
Ghana Junior Atlas, *E. A. Boateng-Thomas Nelson and Sons Ltd., London 1965*
Liberia in Maps, *Stefan von Gnielinski, Hamburg 1972*
Oxford Atlas for Nigeria, *Oxford University Press, London-Ibadan 1971*
School Atlas for Sierra Leone, *Collins-Longman, Glasgow 1975*
République du Mali 1:2,500,000, *I.G.N., Paris 1971*
Ghana-Administrative 1:2,000,000, *Survey of Ghana, Accra 1968*
Road Map of Nigeria 1:585,000, *Federal Surveys, Lagos 1969*
République Unie du Cameroun 1:1,000,000, *I.G.N., Paris 1972*
République de Haute-Volta-Carte Routière 1:1,000,000, *I.G.N., Paris 1968*
Philips' School Room Map of Ghana 1:1,000,000, *George Philip & Son Ltd., London 1963*
Sénégal 1:1,000,000, *I.G.N., Paris 1974*
Sénégal-Carte Administrative 1:1,000,000, *I.G.N., Paris 1966*
Physical Map of Nigeria 1:1,000,000, *Federal Surveys, Lagos 1965*
République du Côte d'Ivoire 1:1,000,000, *I.G.N., Paris 1970*
Côte d'Ivoire 1:800,000, *Pneu. Michelin, Paris 1978*
Mapa da Guiné 1:650,000, *J. R. Silva, Lisboa 1969*
République du Dahomey-Carte Routière et Touristique 1:500,000, *I.G.N., Paris 1968*
Road Map of Ghana 1:500,000, *Survey of Ghana, Accra 1970*
The Gambia Road Map 1:500,000, *Survey Department The Gambia, Banjul 1973*
Nigeria-Digest of Statistics 1973, *Federal Office of Statistics, Lagos*

EAST AND CENTRAL AFRICA
Atlas Pratique du Tchad, *Institut Tchadien pour les Sciences Humaines, Paris 1972*
Sudan Roads 1:4,000,000, *Sudan Survey Department, Khartoum 1976*
Äthiopie/Ethiopia 1:4,000,000, *Medizinische Länderkunde/Geomedical Monograph Series, Berlin 1972*
Carte de l'Afrique Centrale 1:2,500,000, *I.G.N., Paris 1968*
Highway Map of Ethiopia 1:2,000,000, *Imperial Ethiopian Government, Addis Ababa 1961*
République du Tchad-Carte Routière 1:1,500,000, *I.G.N., Paris 1968*
République Centrafricaine-Carte Routière 1:1,500,000, *I.G.N., Paris 1969*
Territoire Française des Afars et des Issas 1:400,000, *Office Developpement du Tourisme, Djibouti 1970*
Ethiopia-Statistical Abstract 1976, *Central Statistical Office, Addis Ababa*

EQUATORIAL AFRICA
Atlas du Congo, *Office de la Recherche Scientifique et Techique Outre-Mer, Brazzaville 1969*
Atlas for Malawi, *Collins-Longman, Glasgow 1969*
Atlas of Uganda, *Department of Lands and Surveys, Kampala 1967*
Malawi in Maps, *University of London Press Ltd., London 1972*
Tanzania in Maps, *University of London Press, Ltd., London 1975*
The First Kenya Atlas, *George Philip & Son Ltd., London 1973*
Carte de l'Afrique Centrale 1:2,500,000, *I.G.N., Paris 1968*
Carta Rodoviária de Angola 1:2,000,000, *Lello S.A.R.L., Luanda 1974*
Republic of Zambia 1:1,500,000, *Surveyor General, Ministry of Lands and Natural Resources, Lusaka 1972*
Tanzania 1:1,250,000, *Shell & B.P. Tanzania Ltd., Dar es Salaam 1973*
Malawi 1:1,000,000, *Malawi Government, Blantyre 1971*
Road Map of Kenya 1:1,000,000, *George Philip & Son Ltd., London 1972*
République Populaire du Congo 1:1,000,000, *I.G.N., Paris 1973*
Gabon 1:1,000,000, *I.G.N., Paris 1975*
Statistical Abstract 1979, *Central Bureau of Statistics, Nairobi*

SOUTHERN AFRICA
Large Print Atlas for Southern Africa, *George Philip & Son Ltd., London 1976*
Atlas de Madagascar, *Association des Géographes de Madagascar, Antananarivo 1971*
Atlas for Mauritius, *Macmillan Education Ltd., London 1971*
Ontwikkelingsatlas-Development Atlas, *Republic of South Africa-Department of Planning, Pretoria 1966*
Botswana Road Map and Climate Chart 1:6,000,000, *Department of Surveys and Lands, Gaborone 1980*
Madagascar et Comores 1:4,000,000, *I.G.N., Paris 1970*
Suidelike Afrika/Southern Africa 1:2,500,000, *The Government Printer, Pretoria 1973*
Roads of Zimbabwe 1:2,100,000, *Shell Zimbabwe Ltd., Salisbury, 1980*
Carta de Moçambique 1:2,000,000, *Ministerio do Ultramar, Lisboa 1971*
Mapa Rodoviário de Maçambique 1:2,000,000, *J.A.E.M. 1972*
The Black Homelands of South Africa 1:1,900,000, *Perskor Boeke Tekenkantoor, Johannesburg*
Road Map of Zimbabwe 1:1,800,000, *A.A. of Zimbabwe, Salisbury 1980*
Zimbabwe-Mobil 1:1,470,000, *M.O. Collins Ltd., Salisbury 1976*
Rhodesia Relief 1:1,000,000, *Surveyor General, Salisbury 1973*
Lafatsche La Botsvana/Republic of Botswana 1:1,000,000, *Department of Surveys and Lands, Gaborone 1970*
Suid Afrika/South Africa 1:500,000, *The Government Printer, Pretoria*
Lesotho, 1:250,000, *Government Overseas Surveys, Maseru 1969*

Île Maurice-Carte Touristique 1:100,000, *I.G.N., Paris 1978*
La Réunion-Carte Touristique 1:100,000, *I.G.N., Paris 1978*
Annual Statistical Bulletin 1973, *The Bureau of Statistics, Maseru*
Bi-Annual Digest of Statistics 1976, *Central Statistical Office, Port Louis*
Population Census 1970, *Department of Statistics, Pretoria*
Population de Madagascar au Ier Janvier 1972, *Direction Général du Gouvernement, Antananarivo*
South Africa 1980–81-Official Yearbook, *Chris van Rensburg Publications Ltd., Johannesburg*

NORTH AMERICA
CANADA
Atlas Larousse Canadien, *Les Editions Françaises Inc., Québec - Montréal 1971*
Oxford Regional Economic Atlas - United States & Canada, *Clarendon Press, Oxford 1967*
Road Atlas United States - Canada - Mexico, *Rand McNally & Co., Chicago 1981*
The National Atlas of Canada, *Department of Energy, Mines and Resources, Ottawa 1972*
Northwest Territories - Yukon Territory 1:4,000,000, *Department of Energy, Mines and Resources, Ottawa 1974*
Quebec and Newfoundland 1:3,700,000, *N.G.S., Washington 1980*
British Columbia, Alberta and the Yukon Territory 1:3,500,000, *N.G.S., Washington 1978*
Ontario 1:3,000,000, *N.G.S., Washington 1980*
Saskatchewan and Manitoba 1:2,600,000, *N.G.S., Washington 1979*
Canada Year Book 1978-79, *Minister of Industry, Trade and Commerce, Ottawa*

UNITED STATES
Oxford Regional Economic Atlas - United States & Canada, *Clarendon Press, Oxford 1967*
Road Atlas United States - Canada - Mexico, *Rand McNally & Co., Chicago 1981*
Transportation Map of the United States, *U.S. Department of Transportation, Washington 1976*
National Energy Transportation System 7,500,000, *U.S. Geological Survey, Reston, Virginia 1977*
Close-up: Alaska 1:3,295,000, *N.G.S., Washington 1975*
Close-up: The Southwest 1:2,124,000, *N.G.S., Washington 1977*
Close-up: The Northwest 1:2,000,000, *N.G.S., Washington 1973*
Close-up: The Southeast 1:1,780,000, *N.G.S., Washington 1975*
Close-up: California and Nevada 1:1,700,000, *N.G.S., Washington 1978*
Close-up: Florida 1:1,331,000, *N.G.S., Washington 1973*
Close-up: Illinois, Indiana, Ohio and Kentucky 1:1,267,000, *N.G.S., Washington 1977*
Close-up: The Northeast 1:1,215,000, *N.G.S., Washington 1978*
Close-up: The Mid-Atlantic States 1:886,000, *N.G.S., Washington 1973*
Topographic Maps 1:500,000, *U.S. Geological Survey, Washington*
Topographic Maps 1:250,000, *U.S. Geological Survey, Washington*
Togographic Maps 1:24,000, *U.S. Geological Survey, Washington*
Census of Population and Housing 1980, *Bureau of the Census, Washington*

MEXICO
Atlas of Mexico, *Bureau of Business Research, University of Texas, Austin 1975*
Road Atlas United States - Canada - Mexico, *Rand McNally & Co., Chicago 1981*
Mapas de los Estados-Serie Patria, *Libreria Patria S.A., México*
Carta Geografica de México 1:2,500,000, *Asociación Nacional Automovilística, Ciudad de México 1976*
Archeological Map of Middle America 1:2,250,000, *N.G.S., Washington 1968*

CENTRAL AMERICA AND THE CARIBBEAN
Atlas for Barbados, Windwards and Leewards, *Macmillan Education Ltd., London 1974*
Atlas for Guyana & Trinidad & Tobago, *Macmillan Education Ltd, London 1973*
Atlas for the Eastern Caribbean, *Collins-Longman, London 1977*
Atlas Nacional de Cuba, *Academia de Ciencias de Cuba, La Habana 1970*
Atlas of the Commonwealth of the Bahamas, *Kingston Publishers Ltd.-Ministry of Education, Kingston-Nassau 1976*
Jamaica in Maps, *University of London Press Ltd., London 1974*
West Indies and Central Amerika 1:4,500,000, *N.G.S., Washington 1981*
Mapa General-República de Honduras 1:1,000,000, *Instituto Geográfico Nacional, Tegucigalpa 1980*
Mapa Oficial de la República de Panamá 1:1,000,000, *Instituto Geográfico Nacional, Panamá 1979*
Mapa Preliminar de la República de Guatemala 1:1,000,000, *Instituto Geográfico Nacional, Guatemala 1976*
República de Nicaragua 1:1,000,000, *Instituto Geográfico Nacional, Managua 1975*
Belize 1:800,000, *Directorate of Overseas Surveys, London 1974*
Mapa de la República Dominicana 1:600,000, *Instituto Geográfico Universitario, Santo Domingo 1979*
Costa Rica - Mapa Fisico-Politico 1:500,000, *Instituto Geográfico de Costa Rica, San José 1974*
El Salvador 1:500,000, *Ministerio de Obras Públicas, San Salvador 1978*
Mapa Hipsométrico de la República de Guatemala 1:500,000, *Instituto Geográfico Nacional, Guatemala 1979*
Jamaica 1:280,000, *Fairey Surveys Ltd., Maidenhead 1974*
Mapa de Carreteras Estatales de Puerto Rico 1:250,000, *Autoridad de Carreteras Estatales, San Juan 1972*
Nicaragua-Costa Rica 1:250,000, *Instituto Geográfico Nacional, Managua 1972*
Puerto Rico e Islas Limitrofes 1:240,000, *U.S. Geological Survey, Washington 1970*
Turks & Caicos Islands 1:200,000, *Directorate of Overseas Surveys, London 1971*
Cayman Islands 1:150,000, *Directorate of Overseas Surveys, London 1972*
Trinidad 1:150,000, *Director of Surveys-Ministry of Defense, London 1970*
Guadeloupe-Carte Touristique 1:100,000, *I.G.N., Paris 1978*
Martinique-Carte Touristique 1:100,000, *I.G.N., Paris 1977*
Lesser Antilles-Antigua 1:50,000, *Directorate of Overseas Surveys, London 1973*
Tourist Map of Tobago 1:50,000, *Lands & Surveys Department, Port of Spain 1969*
Dominica 1:25,000, *Directorate of Overseas Surveys, London 1978*
Lesser Antilles-Barbuda 1:25,000, *Directorate of Overseas Surveys, London 1970*
Annuario Estadístico de Costa Rica 1977, *Dirección General de Estadística, San José*
Annuario Estadístico de Cuba 1973, *Dirección Central de Estadística, La Habana*
Caribbean Year Book 1978-80, *Caribook Ltd., Toronto*
Fact Sheets on the Commonwealth-Antigua, *British Information Services, London 1974*
Fact Sheets on the Commonwealth-Belize, *British Information Services, London 1976*
Guatemala-III Censo de Habitación 26 de marzo de 1973, *Dirección General de Estadística, Guatemala*
Honduras-Annuario Estadístico 1978, *Dirección General de Estadística, Censos, Tegucigalpa*
Nicaragua-Annuario Estadístico 1975, *Oficina Ejecutiva de Encuestas y Censos, Managua*
Statistical Yearbook for Latin America, *United Nations, New York 1976*
Zentralamerika-Karten zur Bevölkerungs und Wirtschaftsstruktur 1975, *H. Nuhn, P. Krieg & W. Schlick, Hamburg*

SOUTH AMERICA
NORTHERN SOUTH AMERICA
Atlas Basico de Colombia, *Instituto Geográfico Agustin Codazzi, Bogotá 1970*
Atlas de Colombia, *Instituto Geográfico Agustin Codazzi, Bogotá 1979*
Atlas de Venezuela, *Ministerio de Obras Públicas, Caracas 1970*
Atlas for Guyana, Trinidad & Tobago, *Macmillan Education Ltd., London 1973*
Atlas Histórico Geográfico y de Paisajes Peruanos, *Instituto Nacional de Planificación, Lima 1970*
Atlas Nacional do Brasil, *Instituto Brasileiro de Geografia*
Atlas Universal y del Peru, *Thomas Nelson & Sons Ltd., Sunbury on Thames 1968*
Brasil-Didáctico, Rodoviário, Turístico 1:5,000,000, *Gr. Editôra e Publicidade Ltda., Rio de Janeiro*
Mapa de la República de Bolivia 1:4,000,000, *Instituto Geográfico Militar, La Paz 1974*
Mapa Politico del Perú 1:2,400,000, *Editorial "Navarrete", Lima 1975*
Mapa de Carreteras del Perú 1:2,200,000, *Instituto Geográfico Militar, Lima 1979*
Mapa Fisico-Politico 1:2,000,000, *Instituto Geográfico Militar, Lima 1970*
Mapa Fisico de la República de Venezuela 1:2,000,000, *Ministerio de Obras Públicas, Bogotá 1975*
Brasil-Mapa Rodoviário 1:2,000,000, *Ministério dos Transportes, 1971*

Carte de la Guyane Française 1:1,500,000, *I.G.N., Paris 1973*
República de Colombia 1:1,500,000, *Ministerio de Hacienda y Credito Público, Bogotá 1979*
Ecuador 1:1,000,000, *Instituto Geográfico Militar, Quito 1971*
Kaart van Suriname 1:1,000,000, *C. Kersten & Co. N.V., Paramaribo*
Mapa de Bolivia 1:1,000,000, *Instituto Geográfico Militar, La Paz 1973*
Mapa Vial 1:1,000,000, *Ministerio de Obras Públicas, Caracas 1970*
República del Perú-Mapa Fisico-Politico, 1:1,000,000, *Instituto Geográfico Militar, Lima 1978*
Carte de la Guyane Française 1:500,000, *I.G.N., Paris 1976*
Suriname 1:500,000, *Uitgave Centraal Bureau Luchtkartering, 1969*
Guyana 1:500,000, *Ordnance Survey, Georgetown 1972*
Annuário Estatístico do Brasil 1978, *Fundacão Instituto Brasileiro de Geografia e Estatística, Rio de Janeiro*
Boletín Mensual de Estadística-agosto 1977, *D.A.N.E., Bogotá*
Dicionário Geográfico Brasileiro, *Editora Globo, Pôrto Alegre 1972*
Discover Bolivia, *Los Amigos del Libro, La Paz 1972*
Venezuela-Annuário Estadístico 1976, *Oficina Central de Estadística e Informatica, Caracas*

SOUTHERN SOUTH AMERICA
Atlas de la República Argentina, *Instituto Geográfico Militar, Buenos Aires 1972*
Atlas de la República Argentina, *Instituto Geográfico Militar, Santiago 1976*
Atlas de la República de Chile, *Instituto Geográfico Militar, Santiago 1970*
Atlas Escolar de Chile, *Instituto Geográfico Militar, Santiago 1978*
Atlas Universal y de la República Argentina, *Aguilar Argentina S.A. de Ediciones, Buenos Aires 1972*
Mapa de la República Argentina 1:5,000,000, *Instituto Geográfico Militar, Buenos Aires 1973*
Paraguay 1:1,000,000, *Instituto Geográfico Militar, Asunción 1974*
República Oriental del Uruguay 1:500,000, *Servicio Geográfico Militar, Montevideo 1961*
Uruguay-Moyennes et Petites Villes 1972, *Institut des Hautes Etudes de l'Amerique Latine, Paris*

AUSTRALIA AND OCEANIA
Atlas of Australian Resources, *Division of National Mapping, Canberra 1980*
New Zealand-Mobil Travel Map, *Mobil Oil New Zealand Ltd., Wellington 1973*
New Zealand Atlas, *A.R. Shearer Government Printer, Wellington 1976*
The Jacaranda Atlas, *Jacaranda Press Pty. Ltd., 1971*
The Jacaranda Atlas For New Zealand, *Jacaranda Press Pty. Ltd., 1971*
Australia-Geographic Map 1:2,500,000, *Minister for National Development, Canberra 1967*
Territory of Papua and New Guinea 1:2,500,000, *Division of National Mapping, Canberra 1970*
Carte de l'Oceanie Française 1:2,000,000, *I.G.N., Paris 1971*
Îles Tuamotu-Îles Marquises 1:2,000,000, *I.G.N., Paris 1969*
New Zealand-Map Guide 1:1,900,000, *New Zealand Tourist and Publicity Department, Wellington 1978*
Mobil New Zealand Road Map, *Mobil Oil New Zealand Ltd., Wellington 1973*
Fiji Islands-World Aeronautical Chart 1:1,000,000, *Ordnance Survey, Southampton 1970*
Close-up: Hawaii 1:675,000, *N.G.S., Washington 1978*
Archipel des Nouvelles-Hébrides 1:500,000, *I.G.N., Paris 1976*
New Zealand 1:500,000, *Department of Lands and Survey, Wellington 1976*
Nouvelle Calédonie 1:500,000, *I.G.N., Paris 1978*
Palau Islands 1:165,000, *Defense Mapping Agency Hydrographic Center, Washington 1973*
General Map of Tokelau Islands 1:100,000, *Department of Lands & Survey, Wellington 1969*
Tahiti-Carte Touristique 1:100,000, *I.G.N., Paris 1977*
Christmas Islands - Gilbert and Ellice Islands Colony 1:50,000, *Directorate of Overseas Survey, London 1970*
Tuvalu, *Government of Tuvalu 1979*
Annual Statistical Abstract-Fiji 1970-71, *Bureau of Statistics, Suva*
Australia - Population and Dwellings in Local Government Areas and Urban Centres 1976, *Australian Bureau of Statistics, Canberra*
Fact Sheet - Pitcairn Islands Group, *British Information Services, London 1974*
Fact Sheet - The Gilbert Islands, *British Information Services, London 1977*
Fact Sheet - The New Hebrides, *British Information Services, London 1976*
Fact Sheet - The Solomon Islands, *British Information Services, London 1976*
Fact Sheet - Tuvalu, *British Information Services, London 1977*
New Zealand Pocket Digest of Statistics 1979, *Department of Statistics, Wellington*
New Zealand Official Yearbook 1978, *Department of Statistics, Wellington*

POLAR REGIONS
Antarctica 1:11,250,000, *U.S. Naval Oceanographic Office, Washington 1965*
Antarctica 1:10,000,000, *American Geographical Society, New York 1970*
Antarctica 1:10,000,000, *Division of National Mapping, Canberra 1979*
Antarctica 1:5,000,000, *American Geographical Society, New York 1970*
Map of the Artic Region 1:5,000,000, *American Geographical Society, New York 1975*

Transliteration Systems

Toponymy: Criteria Used for the Writing of Names on the Maps

The language of geography is a language which defines geographic features in universally recognized terms. In creating this language, toponymy experts and cartographers have confronted complex problems in finding terms which are universally acceptable. So that the reader can fully understand the maps in this atlas, here is a brief explanation of how the toponyms (place-names for geographic features) have been written, particularly those relating to regions or countries where the Roman alphabet is not used. Among these are the Slavic-speaking nations such as Russia, Yugoslavia and Bulgaria; and China and Japan, which use ideographic characters. Of the European countries, Greece has its own alphabet, which is totally different from the Roman alphabet. Many of the Islamic countries use Arabic, with variations derived from local dialects.

There are two basic systems for Romanizing writing. The first is by phonetic transcription, using combinations of different alphabetical signs for each language when the phonetic sound in other languages should be maintained. For example, the Italian sound ''sc'' (which must be followed by an ''e'' or ''i'' to remain soft) in French is ''ch,'' in English is ''sh,'' and in German is ''sch.''

The second system is transliteration, in which the words, letters or characters of one language are represented or spelled in the letters or characters of another language.

Chinese, Japanese and Arabic Languages

Various Asian and African countries use non-Roman forms in their writing. For example, the Chinese and Japanese languages use ideographic characters instead of an alphabet, and these ideographic characters are transformed into the Roman alphabet through phonetic transcription. Until recently, one of the methods used for transforming Chinese was the Wade-Giles system, named for its English authors. Used in this atlas is the Pinyin system, which was approved by the Chinese government in 1958 and has been incorporated into the official maps of the People's Republic of China. The Pinyin system also has been adopted by the United States Board on Geographic Names and is used in official United Nations documents. The Pinyin names, however, often are accompanied by the Wade-Giles form, as the latter was widely known.

In Japan, ideographic characters are used, although the Roman alphabet is used in many Japanese scientific works. Japan uses two principal systems for standardizing names. They are the Kunreisiki, used by the government in official publications, and the Hepburn method. Adopted for this atlas is the Hepburn method, the system used in international English-language publications and by the United States Board on Geographic Names.

Romanization of the Arabic alphabet, which is used in many Islamic countries, is by transliteration. Since English and French are still used as international languages in many Arab countries, the name forms proposed by the major English and French sources have been taken into consideration. Generally, the systems proposed by the United States Board on Geographic Names and the Permanent Committee on Geographical Countries have been used for most Asian countries and Arab-speaking countries.

Greek, Russian and Other Slavic Languages

Practically all written languages in Europe use the Roman alphabet. The differences in phonetics and grammar are shown by the use of diacritical marks and by groupings of consonants, vocals and syllables which give meaning to the various tones in the language. According to a centuries-old tradition, each written language maintains its formal characters, using the translated form rather than the phonetic transcription when a geographical term must be given in another language. This system, therefore, makes it more a translation than a transliteration.

In the Aegean area, Greek and the Greek alphabet are particularly significant because of historical links to the beginning of European civilization. The 1962 United States Board on Geographic Names and the Permanent Committee on Geographical Names systems, based on modern Greek pronunciation, have been used in transcribing toponyms from official sources for these maps. (The table that follows has an example indicating essential norms for Romanizing the modern Greek alphabet.)

A different situation arises in countries using the Cyrillic alphabet. Six principal Slavic languages using this alphabet are Russian, Byelorussian, Ukrainian, Bulgarian, Serbian, and Macedonian. The Cyrillic alphabet also is used by some non-Slavic people of the former Soviet Union. The nomenclature of these regions has been transliterated in accordance with the system proposed by the International Organization for Standardization, taking into consideration sounds and letters and uses of the diacritical marks normal in Slavic languages. The International Organization for Standardization method is accepted and used in bibliographical works and international documents. (The table which follows gives the relationship between the letters of the Cyrillic and Roman alphabets for the above six languages.)

Special Cases: Conventional Forms and Multilinguals

Cartographic nomenclature generally derives from the official nomenclature of the sovereign and nonsovereign countries, although a number of cases need explanation.

In numerous situations, English conventional forms are used along with the local or conventional name in referring to a geographical entity used outside the official English language area. For example, Vienna, Prague, Copenhagen and Moscow are English forms for Wien, Praha, København and Moskva, respectively. There are cases, however, where the conventional or historical form commonly used in English cartography has been applied with the same meaning. Thus, Peking and Nanking are the English conventional forms for Beijing and Nanjing, while Tsinan, Tientsin and Mukden are the former conventional spellings or names for Jinan, Tianjin and Shenyang, respectively. Other examples are Saigon, the former name for Ho Chi Minh, Vietnam; and Bangkok, the name for Krung Thep, which is used in Thailand.

The lack of reliable data for countries, especially ex-colonies without a firm national cartographic tradition, has made it necessary to utilize mapping skills of former colonial nations such as France, the United Kingdom and Belgium. A lack of data has led to the adoption of French and British forms in many areas, as these two languages are widely used for official purposes.

Another special case is that of the multilingual areas. Many countries and areas officially recognize two or more written and spoken languages; therefore, all of the principal written forms appear on the maps. This is true, for example, of Belgium where the official languages are French and Dutch (e.g. Bruxelles/Brussel) and of Italian regions such as Valle d'Aosta and Alto Adige, where French, German and Italian are used (e.g. Aosta/Aoste) (Bolzano/Bozen).

In preparing this atlas, each of these special cases has been taken into full consideration within the limits of the scale, space and readability of the maps.

Transliteration of the Cyrillic Alphabet
(International System—ISO)

Cyrillic Letter	Roman Letter		Cyrillic Letter	Roman Letter	
А а	a		О о	o	
Б б	b		П п	p	
В в	v		Р р	r	
Г г	g		С с	s	
Д д	d		Т т	t	
Е е	e	initially, after a vowel or after the mute sign ''Ъ'', becomes ''je''	У у	u	
			Ф ф	f	
			Х х	h	
Ё ё	ё		Ц ц	c	
Ж ж	ž		Ч ч	č	
З з	z		Ш ш	š	
И и	i		Щ щ	šč	
Й й	j	not written if preceded by ''И'' or ''Ы''	Ъ ъ	—	not written
			Ы ы	y	
К к	k		Ь ь	—	not written
Л л	l		Э э	e	
М м	m		Ю ю	ju	
Н н	n		Я я	ja	

Transcription of Modern Greek
(U.S. B. G. N./P.C.G.N.)

Greek Letter (or combination)	Roman Letter (or combination)		Greek Letter (or combination)	Roman Letter (or combination)	
Α α	a		μπ	b	beginning a word
αι	ai			mb	within a word
αυ	av		Ν ν	n	
Β β	v		ντ	d	beginning a word
Γ γ	g			nd	within a word
γγ	ng		Ξ ξ	x	
γκ	g	beginning a word	Ο ο	o	
	ng	within a word	οι	oi	
			ου	ou	
Δ δ	d		Π π	p	
Ε ε	e		Ρ ρ	r	
ει	i		Σ σ	s	
ευ	ev		ς	s	ending a word
Ζ ζ	z		Τ τ	t	
Η η	i		τζ	tz	
ηυ	iv		Υ υ	i	
Θ θ	th		υι	i	
Ι ι	i		Φ φ	f	
Κ κ	k		Χ χ	kh	
Λ λ	l		Ψ ψ	ps	
Μ μ	m		Ω ω	o	

Geographical Glossary

The "Geographical Glossary" lists the principal geographical terms used on the maps. All of these terms, including abbreviations, prefixes and suffixes, appear in the cartographic table as they appear on the maps. Terms are listed in accordance with the English alphabet, without consideration of diacritical marks on letters or of particular groups of letters.

Prefixes and suffixes relating to principal names or forming part of geographical toponyms are followed or preceded by a dash and the language to which they refer: e.g. Chi-/*Dan.* (Chi, a Danish prefix, means large); -bor/*Slvk.* (-bor, a Slovakian suffix, means city). Suffixes can also appear as words in themselves. In this case, the suffix and primary word are coupled together: e.g. Berg, -berg (Berg, which means mountain, can be used alone or as part of another word, such as Hapsberg).

Certain terms are followed or preceded by their abbreviation used on the maps. Both instances are listed: e.g. Fjord, Fj. and Fj., Fjord.

All geographical terms are identified by the language or languages to which each belongs. The language or languages in italics follows the term: e.g. Abbey/*Eng.*; -bad/*Nor., Dut., Swed., Germ.* Each term is translated into a corresponding English term or terms.

Below is a table identifying the abbreviations of various language names used on the maps. Note that certain abbreviations represent a group of languages, instead of one language: e.g. Ural. is the abbreviation for Uralic, a group word for Udmurt, Komi, and Nenets.

Alt. = Altaic (Turkmen, Tatar, Bashkir, Kazakh, Karalpak, Nogai, Kirghiz, Uzbek, Uigur, Altaic, Yakut, Khakass)

Ban. = Bantu (KiSwahili, ChiLuba, Lingala, KiKongo)

Cauc. = Caucasian (Chechen, Ingush, Kalmuck, Georgian)

Iran. = Iranian (Baluchi, Tagus)

Mel. = Melanesian (Fijian, New Caledonian, Micronesian, Nauruan)

Mong. = Mongolian (Buryat, Khalka Mongol)

Poly. = Polynesian (Maori, Samoan, Tongan, Tahitian, Hawaiian)

Sah. = Saharan (Kanuri, Tubu)

Som. = Somalian (Somali, Galla)

Sud. = Sudanese (Peul, Ehoué, Mossi, Yoruba, Ibo)

Ural. = Uralic (Udmurt, Komi, Nenets).

Because of their technical application to geography, some geographical terms may not fully correspond with the meaning given for them in some dictionaries.

Abbreviations of Language Names

Abbreviations in English	English
Afr.	Afrikaans
A.I.	American Indian
Alb.	Albanian
Alt.	Altaic
Amh.	Amharic
Ar.	Arabic
Arm.	Armenian
Az.	Azerbaidzhani
Ban.	Bantu
Bas.	Basque
Beng.	Bengali
Ber.	Berber
Br.	Breton
Bulg.	Bulgarian
Burm.	Burmese
Cat.	Catalan
Cauc.	Caucasian
Chin.	Chinese
Cz.	Czech
Dan.	Danish
Dut.	Dutch
Eng.	English
Esk.	Eskimo
Est.	Estonian
Far.	Faroese
Finn.	Finnish
Fle.	Flemish
Fr.	French
Gae.	Gaelic
Georg.	Georgian
Germ.	German
Gr.	Greek
Hebr.	Hebrew
Hin.	Hindi
Hung.	Hungarian
Icel.	Icelandic
Indon.	Indonesian
Ir.	Irish
Iran.	Iranian
It.	Italian
Jap.	Japanese
Khm.	Khmer
Kor.	Korean
K.S.	Khoi-San
Laot.	Laotian
Lapp.	Lappish
Latv.	Latvian
Lith.	Lithuanian
Mal.	Malay
Malag.	Malagasy
Mel.	Melanesian
Mong.	Mongolian
Nep.	Nepalese
Nor.	Norwegian
Pash.	Pashto
Pers.	Persian
Pol.	Polish
Poly.	Polynesian
Port.	Portuguese
Prov.	Provençal
Rmsh.	Romansh
Rom.	Romanian
Rus.	Russian
Sah.	Saharan
S.C.	Serbo-Croatian
Sin.	Sinhalese
Slvk.	Slovak
Slvn.	Slovene
Som.	Somalian
Sp.	Spanish
Sud.	Sudanese
Swa.	Swahili
Swed.	Swedish
Tam.	Tamil
Thai	Thai
Tib.	Tibetan
Tur.	Turkish
Ural.	Uralic
Urdu	Urdu
Viet.	Vietnamese
Wall.	Walloon
Wel.	Welsh

Glossary of Geographical Terms

Local Form	English
A	
A- / *Ban.*	people
A' / *Icel.*	river
Å / *Dan.; Nor.; Swed.*	stream
a., an / *Germ.*	on
Aa / *Germ.*	stream
Aache / *Germ.*	stream
Aaiún / *Ar.*	springs
Aan / *Dut.; Fle.*	on
Āb / *Pers.*	stream
Ābād / *Pers.*	city, town
Abad, -abad / *Pers.*	city, town
Ābār / *Ar.*	spring
Abbadia / *It.*	abbey
Abbaye / *Fr.*	abbey
Abbazia / *It.*	abbey
Abbi / *Amh.*	great
Abd / *Ar.*	servant
Abeba / *Amh.*	flower
Aber / *Br.; Wel.*	estuary
Abhang / *Germ.*	slope
Abū / *Ar.*	father, master
Abyad / *Ar.*	white
Abyaḍ / *Ar.*	white
Abyār / *Ar.*	well
Abyss / *Eng.*	ocean depth, deep
Ach / *Germ.*	stream
Achaïf / *Ar.*	dunes
Ache / *Germ.*	stream
Achter / *Afr.; Dut.; Fle.*	back
Acqua / *It.*	water
Açu / *A.I.*	great
Açude / *Port.*	reservoir, dam
Ada / *Tur.*	island
Adalar / *Tur.*	archipelago
Adasr / *Tur.*	island
Addis / *Amh.*	new
Adi / *Amh.*	village
Adrar / *Ber.*	mount, mountains
Aéroport / *Fr.*	airport
Aeroporto / *It.; Port.*	airport
Aeropuerto / *Sp.*	airport
Af / *Som.*	mouth, gorge
Afsluitdijk / *Dut.*	dam
Agadir / *Ber.*	castle
Ağiz / *Tur.*	mouth
Agro / *Sp.; It.*	plain
Agua / *Sp.*	water
Aguja / *Sp.*	needle
Agulha / *Port.*	needle, promontory
Ahal / *Georg.*	new
Aḥmar / *Ar.*	red
Ahrāmāt / *Ar.*	pyramids
Ahzar / *Ber.*	wadi
Aigialós / *Gr.*	coast
Aigue / *Prov.*	water
Aiguille / *Fr.*	needle
Ain / *Ar.*	spring
Aït / *Ar.; Ber.*	sons
Aivi, -aivi / *Lapp.*	mountain
Ak / *Tur.*	white
'Aklé / *Ar.*	dunes
Akmeņs / *Latv.*	stone
Ákra / *Gr.*	point
Akti / *Gr.*	coast
Ala / *Malag.*	forest
Ala / *Finn.*	low, lower
Alan / *Tur.*	field
Alb / *Rom.*	white
Albo / *Sp.*	white
Albufera / *Sp.*	lagoon
Alcalá / *Sp.*	castle
Alcázar / *Sp.*	castle
Aldea / *Sp.*	village
Alföld / *Hung.*	lowland
Ali / *Amh.*	mountain
Alia / *Poly.*	stream
Alin / *Mong.*	range
Alm / *Germ.*	mountain pasture
Alor / *Mal.*	river
Alp / *Germ.*	mountain pasture
Alpe / *Germ.; Fr.; It.*	mountain pasture
Alps / *Eng.*	mountains
Alsó / *Hung.*	low, lower
Alt / *Germ.*	old
Altin / *Tur.*	lower
Altiplano / *Sp.*	plateau
Alto / *Sp.; It.; Port.*	high
Altopiano / *It.*	plateau
Älv / *Swed.*	river
Am / *Kor.*	mountain, peak
Amane / *Ber.*	water
Amba / *Amh.*	mountain
Ambato / *Malag.*	rock
An / *Gae.*	of
An, a. / *Germ.*	on
Ana / *Poly.*	grotto
Anatolikós / *Gr.*	eastern
Äng / *Swed.*	meadow
Angra / *Port.*	bay, anchorage
Ani- / *Malag.*	center
Áno / *Gr.*	upper
Ānou / *Ber.*	well
Anse / *Fr.*	inlet
Ant- / *Malag.*	center
Ao / *Chin.; Khm.; Thai*	gulf
'Âouâna / *Ar.*	well
Apă / *Rom.*	water
'Aqabat / *Ar.*	pass
Aqueduc / *Fr.*	aqueduct
Ar / *Mong.*	north
Ar / *Sin.; Tam.*	river
'Arâguib / *Ar.*	hills
Arba / *Amh.*	mount
Arbore / *Rom.*	tree
Archipiélago / *Sp.*	archipelago
Arcipelago / *It.*	archipelago
Arḍ / *Ar.*	region
Ard- / *Gae.*	high
Areg / *Ar.*	dune
Areia / *Port.*	beach
Arena / *Sp.*	beach
Argent / *Fr.*	silver
Arhipelag / *Rus.*	archipelago
Arkhaíos / *Gr.*	old, antique
Arm / *Eng.; Germ.*	branch
Arquipélago / *Port.*	archipelago
Arr., Arroyo / *Sp.*	stream
Arrecife / *Sp.*	reef
Arroio / *Port.*	stream
Art / *Tur.*	pass, watershed
Aru / *Sin.; Tam.*	river
Ås / *Dan.; Nor.; Swed.*	hills
Asfar / *Ar.*	yellow
Asif / *Ber.*	river
Asky / *Alt.*	lower
Áspros / *Gr.*	white
Assa / *Ber.*	wadi
Atalaya / *Sp.*	frontier
Áth / *Gae.*	ford
Átha / *Gae.*	ford
Atol / *Port.*	atoll
Au / *Germ.*	meadow
Aue / *Germ.*	irrigated field
Aust / *Nor.*	east
Austur / *Icel.*	east
Ava / *Poly.*	canal
Aven / *Fr.*	doline, sink
Awa / *Poly.*	bay
Áyios / *Gr.*	saint
'Ayn / *Ar.*	spring, well
'Ayoún / *Ar.*	springs, wells
'Ayoûn / *Ar.*	spring
Aza / *Ber.*	wadi
Azraq / *Ar.*	light blue
Azul / *Port.; Sp.*	light blue
Azur / *Fr.*	light blue
B	
B., Bay / *Eng.*	bay
b., bei / *Germ.*	by
B., Bucht / *Germ.*	bay
Ba / *Sud.*	river
Ba- / *Ban.*	people
Ba / *Mel.*	hill, mountain
Baai / *Afr.*	bay
Bab / *Ar.*	gate
Bac / *Viet.*	north
Bach / *Germ.*	brook, torrent
Bacino / *It.*	reservoir
Back / *Eng.*	ridge
Back / *Swed.*	brook
Bäck / *Swed.*	brook
Backe / *Swed.*	hill
Bad, -bad / *Dan.; Germ.; Nor.; Swed.*	thermal springs
Baden, -baden / *Germ.*	thermal springs
Bādiyat / *Ar.*	desert
Badwêynta / *Som.*	ocean
Badyarada / *Som.*	gulf
Baeg / *Kor.*	white
Bæk / *Dan.*	brook
Bælt / *Dan.*	strait
Bagni / *It.*	thermal springs
Baharu / *Mal.*	new
Bahia / *Port.*	bay
Bahía / *Sp.*	bay
Bahir / *Ar.*	river, lake, sea
Bahnhof / *Germ.*	railway station
Bahr / *Ar.*	wadi
Baḥr / *Ar.*	river, lake, sea
Baḥrat / *Ar.*	lake
Bahri / *Ar.*	north, northern
Baḥrī / *Ar.*	north
Bahrīyah / *Ar.*	northern
Bai / *Chin.*	white
Băi / *Rom.*	thermal springs
Baia / *Port.*	bay
Baie / *Fr.*	bay
Baigne / *Fr.*	seaside resort
Baile / *Gae.*	city, town
Bain / *Fr.*	thermal springs
Bains / *Fr.*	thermal springs
Baixo / *Port.*	low, lower
Bajan / *Mong.*	rich
Bajo / *Sp.*	low
Bajrak / *Alb.*	tribe
Bakhtīyārī / *Pers.*	western
Bakki / *Icel.*	hill
Bālā / *Pers.*	high
Bald / *Eng.*	peak
Balka / *Rus.*	gorge
Balkan / *Bulg.; Tur.*	mountain range
Ballin / *Gae.*	mouth
Ballon / *Fr.*	dome
Bally / *Gae.*	city, town
Balta / *Rom.*	marsh
Báltos / *Gr.*	marsh
Ban / *Laot.*	village
Bana / *Jap.*	promontory
Baña / *Slvk.*	mine
Bañados / *Sp.*	marsh
Banc / *Fr.*	bank
Banco / *It.; Sp.*	bank
Band / *Pers.*	dam, mountain range
Bandao / *Chin.*	peninsula
Bandar / *Ar.; Mal.; Pers.*	port, market
Bang / *Indon.; Mal.*	stream
Bangou / *Sud.*	well
Banhado / *Port.*	marsh
Bani / *Ar.*	sons
Banja / *Bulg.; S.C.; Slvn.*	thermal springs
Banjaran / *Mal.*	mountain range
Banka / *Rus.*	sandbank
Banke / *Dan.*	bank
Baño / *Sp.*	thermal springs
Banský / *Cz.*	upper
Bánya / *Hung.*	mine
Bar / *Gae.*	peak
Bar / *Eng.*	sandbar

Geographical Glossary

Local Form	English
Bar / Hin.	great
Bāra / Hin.	great
Bara / S.C.	pond
Barā / Urdu	great
Barajı / Tur.	dam
Barat / Indon.; Mal.	west, western
Barkas / Lith.	castle, city, town
Barlovento / Sp.	windward
Barq / Ar.	hill
Barra / Port.; Sp.	bar, bank
Barrage / Fr.	dam
Barragem / Port.	reservoir
Barranca / Sp.	gorge
Barranco / Port.; Sp.	gorge
Barre / Fr.	bar
Barun / Mong.	western
Bas / Fr.	low
-bas / Rus.	reservoir
Bassa / Port.	flat
Bassejn / Rus.	reservoir
Bassin / Fr.	basin
Bassure / Fr.	flat
Bassurelle / Fr.	flat
Bašta / S.C.	garden
Bataille / Fr.	battle
Batalha / Port.	battle
Batang / Indon.; Mal.	river
Batha / Sah.	stream
Baţin / Ar.	depression
Bāţlāq / Pers.	marsh
Batu / Mal.	rock
Bayan / Mong.	rich
Bayır / Tur.	mountain, slope
Bayou / Fr.	branch, stream
Bayt / Ar.	house
Bazar / Pers.	market
Be / Malag.	great
Beau / Fr.	beautiful
Becken / Germ.	basin
Bed / Eng.	river bed
Beek / Dut.	creek
Be'er / Hebr.	spring
Bei / Chin.	north
Bei, b. / Germ.	by
Beida / Ar.	white
Beinn / Gae.	mount
Bel / Ar.	son
Bel / Bulg.	white
Bel / Tur.	pass
Beled / Ar.	village
Belen / Tur.	mount
Belet / Ar.	village
Beli / S.C.; Slvn.	white
Beli / Tur.	pass
Bellah / Sah.	well
Belogorje / Rus.	mountains
Belt / Dan.; Germ.	strait
Bely / Rus.	white
Bělý / Cz.	white
Ben / Ar.	son
Ben / Gae.	mount
Bender / Pers.	port, market
Bendi / Tur.	dam
Beni / Ar.	son
Beo / S.C.	white
Bereg / Rus.	bank
Berg, -berg / Afr.; Dut.; Fle.; Germ.; Nor.; Swed.	mount
Berge / Afr.	mountain
Bergen / Dut.; Fle.	dunes
Bergland / Germ.	upland
Bermejo / Sp.	red
Besar / Mal.	great
Betsu / Jap.	river
Betta / Tam.	mountain
Bhani / Hin.	community
Bharu / Mal.	new
Bheag / Gae.	little
Bīābān / Pers.	desert
Biały / Pol.	white
Bianco / It.	white
Bien / Viet.	lake
Bight / Eng.	bay
Bijeli / S.C.	white
Bill / Eng.	promontory
Bilo / S.C.	range
Bílý / Cz.	white
Binnen / Dut.; Fle.; Germ.	inner
Biqā' / Ar.	valley
Bir / Ar.	well
Bi'r / Ar.	well
Birkat / Ar.	pond
Bistrica / Bulg.; S.C.; Slvn.	stream
Bjarg / Icel.	rock
Bjerg / Dan.	mount
Bjeshkët / Alb.	mountain pasture
Blaauw / Afr.	blue
Blanc / Fr.	white
Blanco / Sp.	white
Blau / Germ.	blue
Bleu / Fr.	blue
Bluff / Eng.	cliff
Bo- / Ban.	people
Bo / Chin.	white
Bo / Swed.	habitation
Boca / Sp.	gap, mouth
Bôca / Port.	gap, mouth
Bocage / Fr.	forest
Bocca / It.	gap, pass
Bocchetta / It.	gap, pass
Bodden / Germ.	bay, lagoon
Boden / Germ.	soil
Bœng / Khm.	lake, marsh
Bog / Eng.	marsh
Bogaz / Alt.; Az.; Tur.	strait
Boğazi / Tur.	strait
Bogdo / Mong.	high
Bogen / Nor.	bay
Bois / Fr.	forest
Boka / S.C.	channel
Boloto / Rus.	marsh
Bolšoj / Rus.	great
Bolsón / Sp.	basin
Bom / Port.	good
Bong / Kor.	peak
Bongo / Malag.	upland
Bor / Cz.; Rus.	coniferous forest
Bór / Pol.	forest
-bor / Slvn.	city, town
Bóras / Gr.	north
Börde / Germ.	fertile plain
Bordj / Ar.	fort
Bóreios / Gr.	northern
Borg, -borg / Dan.; Nor.; Swed.	castle
Borgo / It.	village
Born / Germ.	spring
Bory / Pol.	forest
Bosch / Dut.; Fle.	forest
Bosco / It.	wood
Bosque / Sp.	forest
Bosse / Fr.	hill
Botn / Nor.	bay
Bou / Ar.	father, master
Bouche / Fr.	mouth
Boula / Sud.	well
Bourg / Fr.	city, town
Bourne, - bourne / Eng.	frontier
Boven / Afr.	upper
Boz / Tur.	grey
Bozorg / Pers.	great
Brána / Cz.	gate
Braña / Sp.	mountain pasture
Branche / Fr.	branch
Branco / Port.	white
Braţul / Rom.	branch
Bravo / Sp.	wild
Brazo / Sp.	branch
Brdo / Cz.; S.C.	hill
Bre / Nor.	glacier
Bredning / Dan.	bay
Breg / Alb.; Bulg.; S.C.	hill, coast
Brjag / Bulg.	bank
Bro / Dan.; Nor.; Swed.	bridge
Brod / Bulg.; Cz.; Rus.; S.C.; Slvk.; Slvn.	ford
Bród / Pol.	ford
Bron / Afr.	spring
Bronn / Germ.	spring
Bru / Nor.	bridge
Bruch / Germ.	peat-bog
Bruchzone / Germ.	fracture zone
Bruck, -bruck / Germ.	bridge
Brücke / Germ.	bridge
Brug / Dut.; Fle.	bridge
Brugge / Dut.; Fle.	bridge
Bruk / Nor.	factory
Brunn / Swed.	spring
-brunn / Germ.	spring
Brunnen / Germ.	spring
Brygg / Swed.	bridge
Brzeg / Pol.	coast
Bū / Ar.	father, master
Bucht, B. / Germ.	bay
Bugt / Dan.	bay
Buḩayrat / Ar.	lake, lagoon
Bühel / Germ.	hill
Bühl / Germ.	hill
Buhta / Rus.	bay
Bukit / Mal.	mountain, peak
Bukt / Nor.; Swed.	bay
Buku / Indon.	hill, mountain
Bulag / Mong.; Tur.	spring
Bulak / Mong.; Tur.	spring
Būlāq / Tur.	spring
Bult / Afr.	hill
Bulu / Indon.	mountain
Bur / Som.	mount
Būr / Ar.	port
Burg, - burg / Afr.; Ar.; Dut.; Eng.; Germ.	castle
Burgh / Eng.	city, town
Burgo / Sp.	village
Burha / Hin.	old
Buri / Thai	city, town
Burj / Ar.	village
Burn / Eng.	stream
Burnu / Tur.	promontory
Burqat / Ar.	mount, marsh
Burun / Tur.	cape
Busen / Germ.	bay
Busu / Ban.	land
Būtat / Ar.	lake, pond
Butte / Eng.; Fr.	flat-topped hill
Büyük / Tur.	great
By / Eng.	near
By, -by / Dan.; Nor.; Swed.	city, town
Bystrica / Cz.; Slvk.	stream
Bystrzyca / Pol.	stream

C

Local Form	English
C., Cap / Cat.; Fr.; Rom.	cape
C., Cape / Eng.	cape
C., Colle / It.	pass
Caatinga / A.I.	forest
Cabeça / Port.	peak
Cabeço / Port.	peak
Cabeza / Sp.	peak
Cabezo / Sp.	peak, mountain
Cabo / Port.; Sp.	cape
Cachoeira / Port.	waterfall, rapids
Cachopo / Port.	reef
Cadena / Sp.	range
Caer / Wel.	castle
Cagan / Cauc.; Mong.	white
Cairn / Gae.	hill
Čaj / Az.; Tur.	river
Cajdam / Mong.	salt marsh
Caka / Chin.	lake
Cala / Sp.; It.	inlet
Calar / Sp.	plateau
Caldas / Sp.; Port.	thermal springs
Caleta / Sp.	inlet
Camp / Cat.; Fr.; Eng.	field
Campagna / It.	plain
Campagne / Fr.	plain
Campo / Sp.; It.; Port.	field
Cañada / Sp.	gorge, ravine
Canale / It.	canal, channel
Caño / Sp.	branch
Cañón / Sp.	gorge
Canyon / Eng.	gorge
Cao / Viet.	mountain
Cap, C. / Cat.; Fr.; Rom.	cape
Car / Gae.	castle
Càrn / Gae.	peak
Carrera / Sp.	road
Carrick / Gae.	rock
Casale / It.	hamlet
Cascada / Sp.	waterfall
Cascata / It.	waterfall
Castel / It.	castle
Castell / Cat.	castle
Castello / It.	castle
Castelo / Port.	castle
Castillo / Sp.	castle
Castro / Sp.; It.	village
Catarata / Sp.	cataract
Catena / It.	mountain range
Catinga / Port.	degraded forest
Cauce / Sp.	river bed
Causse / Fr.	highland
Cava / It.	stone quarry
Çay / Tur.	river
Cay / Eng.	islet, island
Caye / Fr.	island
Cayo / Sp.	islet, island
Ceann / Gae.	promontory
Centralny / Rus.	middle
Čeren / Alb.	black
Černi / Bulg.	black
Černý / Cz.	black
Čërny / Rus.	black
Cerrillo / Sp.	hill
Cerrito / Sp.	hill
Cerro / Sp.; Port.	hill, mountain
Cêrro / Port.	hill, mountain
Červen / Bulg.	red
Červony / Rus.	red
Cetate / Rom.	city, town
Chaco / Sp.	scrubland
Chāh / Pers.	well
Chaīf / Ar.	dunes
Chaîne / Fr.	mountain range
Champ / Fr.	field
Chang / Chin.	highland
Chapada / Port.	highland
Chapadão / Port.	highland
Château / Fr.	castle
Châtel / Fr.	castle
Chāy / Tur.	river
Chedo / Kor.	archipelago
Chenal / Fr.	canal
Cheng / Chin.	city, town, wall
Cheon / Kor.	city, river
Chergui / Ar.	eastern
Cherry, -cherry / Hin.; Tam.	city, town
Chew / Amh.	salt mine, salt
Chhâk / Khm.	bay
Chhotla / Hin.	little
Chi- / Ban.	great
Chi / Chin.	marsh, lake
Chi / Kor.	lake, pond
Chi- / Swa.	land
Chiang / Thai	city, town
Chico / Sp.	little
Chine / Eng.	ridge
Ch'on / Kor.	station
Ch'ŏn / Kor.	river
Chŏsuji / Kor.	reservoir
Chott / Ar.	salt marsh
Chu / Chin.; Viet.	mountain, hill
Chuŏr phnum / Khm.	mountain range
Chute / Fr.	waterfall
Chutes / Fr.	waterfalls
Cidade / Port.	city, town
Ciems / Latv.	village
Čierny / Slvk.	black
Cime / Fr.	peak
Cîmp / Rom.	field
Cîmpie / Rom.	plain
Cinco / Sp.; Port.	five
Citeli / Georg.	red
Città / It.	city, town
Ciudad / Sp.	city, town
Ckali / Georg.	water
Ckaro / Georg.	spring
Co / Chin.	lake
Col / Cat.; Fr.	pass
Colina / Port.; Sp.	hill
Coll / Cat.	hill
Collado / Sp.	pass
Colle, C. / It.	pass
Collina / It.	hill
Colline / Fr.	hill
Colonia / Sp.; It.	colony
Coma / Sp.	hill country
Comb / Eng.	basin
Comba / Sp.	basin
Combe / Fr.	basin
Comté / Fr.	county, shire
Con / Viet.	island
Conca / It.	depression
Condado / Sp.	county, shire
Cone / Eng.	volcanic cone
Cône / Fr.	volcanic cone
Contraforte / Port.	front range
Cordal / Sp.	crest
Cordilheira / Port.	mountain range
Cordillera / Sp.	mountain range
Coring / Chin.	lake
Corixa / A.I.	stream
Corno / It.	peak
Cornone / It.	peak
Corrente / It.; Port.	stream
Corriente / Sp.	stream
Costa / Sp.; It.; Port.	coast
Côte / Fr.	coast
Coteau / Fr.	height, slope
Coxilha / Port.	ridge
Craig / Gae.	rock
Cratère / Fr.	crater
Cresta / Sp.; It.	crest
Crêt / Fr.	crest
Crête / Fr.	crest
Crkva / S.C.	church
Crni / S.C.; Slvn.	black
Crven / S.C.	red
Csatorna / Hung.	canal
Cuchilla / Sp.	ridge
Cuenca / Sp.	basin
Cuesta / Sp.	escarpment
Cueva / Sp.	cave
Čuka / Bulg.; S.C.	peak
Çukur / Tur.	well
Cu Lao / Viet.	island
Cumbre / Sp.	peak
Cun / Chin.	village
Cura / A.I.	stone
Curr / Alb.	rock
Cy., City / Eng.	city, town
Czarny / Pol.	black

D

Local Form	English
Da / Chin.	great
Da / Viet.	mountain, peak
Daal / Dut.; Fle.	valley
Daba / Mong.	pass
Daba / Som.	hill
Daban / Chin.; Mong.	pass
Dae / Kor.	great
Dağ / Tur.	mountain
Dağ., Daği / Tur.	mountain
Dāgh / Pers.; Tur.	mountain
Dağı, Dağ. / Tur.	mountain
Dağları / Tur.	mountain range
Dahar / Ar.	hill
Dahr / Ar.	plateau, escarpment
Dai / Chin.; Jap.	great
Daiet / Ar.	marsh
Dak / Viet.	stream
Dake / Jap.	mountain
Dakhla / Ar.	depression
Dakhlet / Ar.	depression, bay
Dal, -dal / Afr.; Dan.; Dut.; Fle.; Nor.; Swed.	valley
Dala / Alt.	steppe, plain
Dalaj / Mong.	lake, sea
Dalan / Mong.	wall
Dallol / Sud.	valley, torrent
Dalur / Icel.	valley
Damm / Germ.	dam
Dan / Kor.	point

Local Form	English
Danau / Indon.	lake
Danda / Nep.	mountains
Dao / Chin.	island, peninsula
Dao / Viet.	island
Dar / Ar.	house, region
Dar / Swa.	port
Dara / Tur.	torrent, valley
Darb / Ar.	track
Darja / Alt.	river, sea
Darya, Daryā / Pers.	river, sea
Daryācheh / Pers.	lake, sea
Daš / Alt.; Az.	rock
Dasht / Pers.	desert, plain
Dawḩat / Ar.	bay
Dayr / Ar.	convent
De / Sp.; Fr.	of
Deal / Rom.	hill
Dearg / Gae.	red
Debre / Amh.	hill, monastery
Dega / Som.	stone
Deh / Pers.	village
Dēḩ / Som.	stream
Deich / Germ.	dike
Dél / Hung.	south
Delft / Dut.; Fle.	deep
Delger / Mong.	wide, market
-den / Eng.	city, town
Deniz / Tur.	sea
Denizi / Tur.	sea
Dent / Fr.	peak
Deo / Laot.; Viet.	pass
Dépression / Fr.	depression
Depressione / It.	depression
Der / Som.	high
Dera / Hin.; Urdu	temple
Derbent / Tur.	gorge, pass
Dere / Tur.	river, valley
Désert / Fr.	desert
Desfiladero / Sp.	pass
Desh / Hin.	land, country
Desierto / Sp.	desert
Det / Alb.	sea
Détroit / Fr.	strait
Deux / Fr.	two
Dezh / Pers.	castle
Dhar / Ar.	heights, hills
Dhār / Hin.; Urdu	mountain
Dhitikós / Gr.	western
Dien / Khm.; Viet.	rice-field
Diep / Dut.; Fle.	deep, strait
Dijk, -dijk / Dut.; Fle.	dam
Ding / Chin.	mountain, peak
Dique / Sp.	dam
Di Sopra / It.	upper
Di Sotto / It.	lower
Distrito / Sp.; Port.	district
Diu / Hin.	island
Diz / Pers.	castle
Djebel / Ar.	mountain
Dji / Ban.	water
Djup / Swed.	deep
Do / Kor.	Island
Do / S.C.	valley
Dō / Jap.	island, administrative division
Dōho / Som.	valley
Doi / Thai	mountain, peak
Dol / Bulg.; Cz.; Rus.; S.C.	valley
Doł / Pol.	valley
Dolen / Bulg.	low
Dolgi / Rus.	long
Dolina / Bulg.; Cz.; Pol.; Rus.; S.C.; Slvn.	valley
Dolni / Bulg.	low
Dolni / Pol.	lower
Dolny / Pol.	lower
Domb / Hung.	hill
Dôme / Fr.	dome
Dong / Chin.; Viet.	east
Dong / Kor.	city, town
Dong / Thai	mountain
Dong / Viet.	marsh, plain
Donji / S.C.	low, lower
Dorf, -dorf / Germ.	village
Doroga / Rus.	road
Dorp, -dorp / Afr.; Dut.; Fle.	village
Dos / Rom.	ridge
Dos / Sp.	two
Douarn / Br.	land
Dougou / Sud.	settlement
Doukou / Sud.	settlement
Down / Eng.	hill
Drâa / Ar.	dunes, hills
Dracht / Germ.	sandbank
Draw / Eng.	ravine, valley
Drif / Afr.	ford
Drift / Afr.	ford
Droichead / Gae.	bridge
Droûs / Ar.	crest
Dry / Pash.	river
Dubh / Gae.	black
Dugi / S.C.	long
Dugu / Sud.	settlement
Dun / Gae.	castle
Duna / Sp.; It.	dune
Düne / Germ.	dune

Local Form	English
Dungar / Hin.	mountain
Düngar / Hin.	mountain
Duong / Viet.	stream
Durchbruch / Germ.	gorge
Durg / Hin.	castle
-durga / Hin.	castle
Duży / Pol.	great
Dvor / Cz.	court
Dvorec / Rus.	castle
Dvůr / Cz.	castle
Dwór / Pol.	court
Džebel / Bulg.	mountain
Dzong / Tib.	fort, monastery

E

Local Form	English
Ea / Thai	river
Eau / Fr.	water
Ebe / Ban.	forest
Ebene / Germ.	plain
Eck / Germ.	point
Éclusa / Sp.	lock
Écluse / Fr.	lock
Écueil / Fr.	cliff
Edeien / Ber.	sand desert
Edjérir / Ber.	wadi
Egg / Germ.; Nor.	crest, point
Eglab / Ar.	hills
Ehi / Sah.	mountain
Eid / Nor.	isthmus
Eiland / Afr.	island
Eisen / Germ.	iron
Eisenerz / Germ.	iron ore
El / Amh.	well
Elv, -elv / Nor.	river
Embalse / Sp.	reservoir
Embouchure / Fr.	mouth
Emi / Sah.	mountain
En / Fr.	in
Ende / Germ.	end
Enneri / Sah.	stream
Ennis / Gae.	island
Enseada / Port.	Bay, inlet
Ensenada / Sp.	bay, inlet
Ér / Hung.	stream
Erdö / Hung.	forest
Erg / Ar.	sand desert
Erz / Germ.	ore
Espigão / Port.	plateau
Éstān / Pers.	land
Este / Sp.	east
Estero / Sp.	estuary, marsh
Estrecho / Sp.	strait
Estreito / Port.	strait
Estuaire / Fr.	estuary
Estuário / Port.	estuary
Estuario / Sp.; It.	estuary
Észak / Hung.	north
Étang / Fr.	pond
Ewaso / Ban.	river
Ey / Icel.	island
Eyja / Icel.	island
Eyjar / Icel.	islands
Eylandt / Dut.	island
Ezeras / Lith.	lake
Ezers / Latv.	lake

F

Local Form	English
Fa / Mel.	stream
Falaise / Fr.	cliff
Fall, -fall / Germ.; Eng.; Swed.	waterfall
Falls / Eng.	waterfall
Falu / Hung.	village
-falva / Hung.	village
Fan / Sah.	village
Faraglione / It.	cliff
Farallón / Sp.	cliff
Faro / Sp.; It.	lighthouse
Farvand / Dan.	strait
Fehér / Hung.	white
Fehn / Germ.	peat fen, peat-bog
Fekete / Hung.	black
Feld / Dan.; Germ.	field
Fell / Eng.	upland moor
Fell / Icel.	mountain
Fels / Germ.	rock
Fen / Eng.	marsh, peat-bog
Feng / Chin.	mountain, peak
Feste / Germ.	fort
Festung / Germ.	fort
Fier / Rom.	iron
Firn / Germ.	snow-field
Firth / Eng.	estuary, fjord
Fiume / It.	river
Fjäll / Swed.	mountain
Fjärd / Swed.	fjord
Fjell / Nor.	mountain
Fjöll / Icel.	mountain
Fjord, Fj. / Dan.; Nor.; Swed.	fjord
Fjörður / Icel.	fjord, bay
Fleuve / Fr.	river

Local Form	English
Fließ / Germ.	torrent
Fljót / Icel.	river
Flói / Icel.	bay, gulf
Floresta / Sp.; Port.	forest
Flow / Eng.	strait
Flughafen / Germ.	airport
Fluß / Germ.	river
Fo / Mel.	stream
Foa / Mel.	stream
Foa / Poly.	cove
Foce / It.	mouth
Föld / Hung.	plain
Fonn / Nor.	glacier
Fontaine / Fr.	fountain
Fonte / It.; Port.	spring
Fontein / Afr.; Dut.	spring
Foort / Afr.; Dut.	ford
Forca / It.	pass
Forcella / It.	defile
Ford / Rus.	fjord
Förde / Germ.	fjord, gulf
Foreland / Eng.	promontory
Foresta / It.	forest
Forêt / Fr.	forest
Fors / Swed.	rapids, waterfall
Forst / Germ.; Dut.	forest
Forte / It.; Port.	fort
Fortin / Sp.	fort
Fosa / Sp.	trench
Foss / Icel.; Nor.	rapids, waterfall
Fossé / Fr.	trench
Foum / Ar.	pass
Fourche / Fr.	pass
Foz / Sp.; Port.	mouth
Frei / Germ.	free
Fronteira / Port.	frontier
Frontera / Sp.	frontier
Frontón / Sp.	promontory
Fuente / Sp.	spring
Fuerte / Sp.	fort
Fuji / Jap.	mountain
Fūlat / Ar.	marsh
Furt / Germ.	ford
Fushë / Alb.	plain

G

Local Form	English
G., Gora / Bulg.; Rus.; S.C.	mountain, hill
G., Gunung / Indon.	mountain
Ga / Jap.	bay
Ga / Mel.	mountain, peak
Gabel / Germ.	pass
Gaissa / Lapp.	mountain
Gala / Sin.; Tam.	mountain
Gam / Hin.; Urdu	village
Gamle / Nor.; Swed.	old
Gana / Sud.	little
Gang / Germ.	passage
Gang / Chin.	port, bay
Gang / Kor.	stream, bay
Gang / Tib.	glacier
Ganga / Hin.	river
Ganj / Hin.; Urdu	market
-gaon / Hin.	city, town
Gaoyuan / Chin.	plateau
Gap / Kor.	point
Gar / Hin.	house
Gara / Bulg.	station
Gara / Ar.	hills, range
Gară / Rom.	station
Garaet / Ar.	marsh, intermittent lake
Garam / Beng.; Hin.; Urdu	village
-gard / Pol.	city, town
Gård, -gård / Dan.; Nor.; Swed.	farmhouse
Gardaneh / Pers.	pass
Gare / Fr.	railway station
Garet / Ar.	hill
Garh, -garh / Hin.; Urdu	castle
Garhi / Hin.; Nep.; Urdu	fort
Garten / Germ.	garden
Gat / Dan.; Fle.; Dut.	strait
Gata / Jap.	bay, lake
Gau, -gau / Germ.	district
Gäu, -gäu / Germ.	district
Gavan / Rus.	port
Gave / Bas.	torrent
Gawa / Jap.	river
Geb., Gebirge / Germ.	mountain range
Gebergte / Afr.; Dut.	mountain range
Gebirge, Geb. / Germ.	mountain range
Geç, Geçit / Tur.	pass
Geçidi / Tur.	pass
Geçit, Geç. / Tur.	pass
Geysir / Icel.	geyser
Ghar / Hin.; Urdu	house
Ghar / Pash.	mountain, mountain range
Gharbīyah / Ar.	western
Ghat / Hin.; Nep.; Urdu	pass
Ghubbat / Ar.	bay
Ghurd / Ar.	dune
Gi / Kor.	peninsula
Giang / Viet.	stream
Giri / Hin.; Urdu	mountain, hill

Local Form	English
Girlo / Rus.	branch
Gjebel / Ar.	mountain
Gji / Alb.	bay
Glace / Fr.	ice
Glaciar / Sp.	glacier
Glacier / Eng.; Fr.	glacier
Glen / Gae.	valley
Gletscher / Germ.	glacier
Gobi / Mong.	desert
Godār / Pers.	ford
Gok / Kor.	river
Gök / Tur.	blue
Gol / Cauc.; Mong.	river
Göl / Tur.	lake
Gola / It.	gorge
Gold / Germ.; Eng.	gold
Golet / S.C.	mountain
Golf / Germ.	gulf
Golfe / Fr.	gulf
Golfete / Sp.	inlet
Golfo / Sp.; It.; Port.	gulf
Goljam / Bulg.	great
Gölü / Tur.	lake
Gong / Tib.	high
Gonggar / Tib.	mountain
Gongo / Ban.	mountain
Góra / Pol.	mountain
Gora, G. / Bulg.; Rus.; S.C.	mountain, hill
Gorica / S.C.; Slvn.	hill
Gorje / S.C.	mountain range
Gorlo / Rus.	gorge
Gorm / Gae.	blue
Gorni / Bulg.; S.C.; Slvn.	upper
Gornji / S.C.; Slvn.	upper
Górny / Pol.	high
Gorod / Rus.	city, town
Gorodok / Rus.	village
Gorski / Bulg.	upper
Gory / Rus.	mountains
-gou / Chin.	river
Goulbi / Sud.	river, lake
Goulbin / Sud.	wadi
Goulet / Fr.	gap
Gour / Ar.	hills, range
Gourou / Sud.	wadi
Goz / Sah.	dune
Graafschap / Dut.	county, shire
Graben / Germ.	ditch, canal
Gracht / Dut.	canal
Grad, -grad / Bulg.; Rus.; S.C.; Slvn.	city, town, castle
Gradac / S.C.	castle
Gradec / Bulg.	village
Gradec / Slvn.	castle
Græn / Icel.	green
Gran / Sp.; It.	great
Grande / Sp.; It.; Port.	great
Grao / Cat.; Sp.	gap
Grat / Germ.	crest
Grève / Fr.	beach
Grind / Germ.	peak
Grjada / Rus.	range
Gród, -gród / Pol.	castle, city, town
Grön / Icel.	green
Grond / Afr.	soil
Gronden / Dut.; Fle.	flat
Groot / Afr.; Dut.; Fle.	great
Groß / Germ.	great
Grotta / It.	grotto
Grotte / Fr.; Germ.	grotto
Grube / Germ.	mine
Grün / Germ.	green
Grunn / Nor.	ground
Gruppe / Germ.	mountain system
Gruppo / It.	mountain system
Gua / Mal.	cave
Guaçu / A.I.	great
Guan / Chin.	pass
Guazú / A.I.	great
Guba / Rus.	bay
Guchi / Jap.	strait
Guelb / Ar.	hill, mountain
Guelta / Ar.	well
Guic / Br.	village
Güney / Tur.	south, southern
Gunong / Mal.	mountain
Guntô / Jap.	archipelago
Gunung, G. / Indon.	mountain
Guo / Chin.	state, land
Gur / Rom.	mountain
Guri / Jap.	cliff
Gurud / Ar.	hills, dunes
Gyár / Hung.	factory

H

Local Form	English
Haag / Dut.; Fle.	hedge
-håb / Dan.	port
Haḑabat / Ar.	highland
Hadd / Ar.	point
Hadjer / Ar.	hill, mountain
Hae / Kor.	bay, sea
Haehyeop / Kor.	strait

Local Form	English
Haf / Icel.	sea
Ḥafar / Ar.	well
Hafen / Germ.	port
Haff / Germ.	lagoon
Hafir / Ar.	spring, ditch
Hafnar / Icel.	port
Hāfün / Som.	bay
Hage / Dan.	point
Hage / Dut.; Fle.	hedge
Hågna / Swed.	peak
Hai / Chin.	sea, lake, bay
Hain / Germ.	forest
Haixia / Chin.	strait
Ḥajar / Ar.	hill, mountain
Hajar / Ar.	hill country
Halbinsel / Germ.	peninsula
Halma / Hung.	hill
Halom / Hung.	hill
Halq / Ar.	gap
Hals / Nor.	peninsula
Halvø / Dan.	peninsula
Halvøy / Nor.	peninsula
Hama / Jap.	beach
Hamāda / Ar.	rocky desert
Ḥamādah / Ar.	plateau
Ḥamādat / Ar.	plateau
Hammam / Ar.	thermal springs
Ḥammām / Ar.	well
Hamn / Nor.; Swed.	port
Hamrā' / Ar.	red
Hāmün / Jap.	salt lake
Hana / Jap.	cape
Hana / Poly.	bay
Hane / Tur.	house
Hang / Kor.	port
Hank / Ar.	escarpment, plateau
Hantō / Jap.	peninsula
Har / Hebr.	mountain
Hara / Mong.	black
Harar / Swa.	well
Ḥarrah / Ar.	lava field
Ḥarrat / Ar.	lava field
Hasi / Ar.	well
Ḥasi / Ar.	well
Hassi / Ar.	well
Ḥasy / Ar.	well
Haug / Nor.	hill
Haupt- / Germ.	principal
Haure / Lapp.	lake
Haus / Germ.	house
Hausen / Germ.	village
Haut / Fr.	high
Hauteur / Fr.	hill
Hauts Plateaux / Fr.	highlands
Hauz / Pers.	reservoir
Hav / Dan.; Nor.; Swed.	sea, gulf
Haven / Eng.; Fle.; Dut.	port
Havn / Dan.; Nor.	port
Havre / Fr.	port
Hawr / Ar.	lake, marsh
Ház / Hung.	house
-háza / Hung.	house
Hazm / Ar.	height, mountain range
He / Chin.	river
Head / Eng.	headland
Hed / Dan.; Swed.	heath
Hegy / Hung.	mountain
Hegység / Hung.	mountain
Hei / Nor.	heath
Heide / Germ.	heath
Heijde / Dut.; Fle.	heath
Heilig / Germ.	saint
Heim, -heim / Germ.; Nor.	house
Heiya / Jap.	plain
-hely / Hung.	locality
Hem / Swed.	home
Hen / Br.	old
Higashi / Jap.	east, eastern
Hima / Hin.	ice
Himal / Nep.	peak
Hisar / Tur.	castle
Ho / Chin.	reservoir, river
Ho / Kor.	river, reservoir
Hō / Jap.	mountain
Hoch / Germ.	high, upper
Hochland / Germ.	highland
Hochplato / Afr.	highland
Hodna / Ar.	highland
Hoek / Dut.; Fle.	cape
Hof / Dut.; Germ.	court
Höfn / Icel.	port
Høg / Nor.	peak
Hög / Swed.	mountain
Hogna / Nor.	peak
Höhe / Germ.	peak
Høj / Dan.	hill
Hoj / Ural.	mountain range
Hok / Jap.	north
Hoku / Jap.	north, northern
Holm / Dan.; Nor.; Swed.	island
Holz / Germ.	forest
Hon / Viet.	island, point
Hong / Chin.; Viet.	red
Hono / Poly.	bay, anchorage
Hoog / Afr.; Dut.; Fle.	high
Hook / Eng.	point
Hoorn / Afr.; Dut.; Fle.	cape, point
Hora / Cz.; Slvk.	point
Horn / Eng.; Germ.; Icel.; Nor.; Swed.	point
Horni / Cz.	high
Horný / Slvk.	upper
Horst / Germ.	mountain
Horvot / Hebr.	ruins
Hory / Cz.; Slvk.	mountain range
Hout / Dut.; Fle.	forest
Hovd, -hovd / Dan.; Nor.	cape
Ḥowz / Pers.	basin
Hrad / Cz.; Slvk.	castle, city, town
Hradiště / Cz.	citadel
Hřeben / Cz.	crest
Hrebet / Rus.	mountain range
Hu / Rmsh.	lake
Huang / Chin.	yellow
Hude / Germ.	pasture
Huerta / Sp.	market garden
Hügel / Germ.	hill
Hügelland / Germ.	hill country
Huis, -huis / Afr.; Dut.; Fle.	house
Huisie / Afr.	house
Huizen, -huizen / Dut.	houses
Huk / Afr.; Dan.; Swed.	cape
Hum / S.C.	hill
Hurst / Eng.	grove
Hus / Dut.; Nor.; Swed.	house
Huta / Pol.; Slvk.	hut
Hütte / Germ.	hut
Hver / Icel.	crater
Hvit / Icel.	white
Hvost / Rus.	spit

I

Local Form	English
I., Island / Eng.	island
Ierós / Gr.	holy
Igarapé / A.I.	river
Ighazer / Ber.	torrent
Ighil / Ber.	hill
Iguidi / Ber.	dunes
Ih / Mong.	great
Ike / Jap.	pond
Ile / Fr.	island
Ilha / Port.	island
Iller / Tur.	administrative division
Ilot / Fr.	islet
Imi / Ar.	spring
I-n / Ber.	well
Inch / Gae.	island
Inder / Dan.; Nor.	inner
Indre / Nor.	inner
Inferiore / It.	lower
Inish / Gae.	island
Insel / Germ.	island
Insulă / Rom.	island
Inver / Gae.	mouth
Irhazèr / Ber.	wadi
Irmak / Tur.	river
'Irq / Ar.	dunes
Is / Nor.	glacier
Ís / Icel.	ice
Isblink / Dan.	glacier
Ishi / Jap.	rock
Iske / Alt.	old
Isla / Sp.	island
Iso / Finn.	great
Iso / Jap.	cliff
Isola / It.	island
Isthmós / Gr.	isthmus
Istmo / Sp.; It.	isthmus
Ita / A.I.	stone
Itä / Finn.	east
Itivdleq / Esk.	isthmus
Iwa / Jap.	rock, cliff
Iztočni / Bulg.	eastern
Izvor / Bulg.; Rom.; S.C.; Slvn.	spring

J

Local Form	English
J., Jazīrat / Ar.	island
J., Jiang / Chin.	river
Jabal / Ar.	mountain
Jaha / Ural.	river
Jam / Ural.	lake, river
Jama / Rus.	cave
Jan / Alt.	great
Janga / Tur.	north
Jangi / Alt.; Iran.	new
Janūbiyah / Ar.	southern
Jar / Rus.	bank
Järv / Est.	lake
Järve / Finn.	lake
Järvi / Finn.	lake
Jasirēd / Som.	island
Jaun / Latv.	new
Jaur / Lapp.	lake
Jaure / Lapp.	lake
Javr / Lapp.	lake
Javrre / Lapp.	lake
Jazā'ir / Ar.	islands
Jazīrat, J. / Ar.	island
Jazovir / Bulg.	reservoir
Jbel / Ar.	mountain
Jebel / Ar.	mountain
Jedid / Ar.	new
Jedo / Kor.	archipelago
Jezero / S.C.; Slvn.	lake
Jezioro / Pol.	lake
Jhil / Hin.; Urdu	lake
Jian / Chin.	mountain
Jiang, J. / Chin.	river
Jiao / Chin.	cape, cliff
Jibāl / Ar.	mountain
Jih / Cz.	south
Jima / Jap.	island
Jin / Kor.	cove
Jing / Chin.	spring
Jisr / Ar.	bridge
Joch / Germ.	pass
Jōgi / Est.	river
Jøkel / Nor.	glacier
Joki / Finn.	river
Jokka / Lapp.	river
Jökull / Icel.	glacier
Jord, -jord / Nor.	earth
Ju / Ural.	river
Judeţ / Rom.	district
Jugan / Ural.	river
Jura / Lith.	sea
Jūra / Latv.	sea
Jūras Līcis / Latv.	bay
Jūrmala / Latv.	beach
Jurt / Cauc.	village
Južni / Bulg.; S.C.; Slvn.	southern
Južny / Rus.	southern
Juzur / Ar.	islands

K

Local Form	English
Ka / Poly.	lake
Kaap / Afr.	cape
Kabīr / Ar.	great
Kae / Kor.	inlet
Kāf / Ar.	peak, mountain
Kafr / Ar.	village
Kaga / Ban.	hills, mountain range
Kahal / Ar.	plateau, escarpment
Kai / Jap.	sea
Kaikyō / Jap.	strait
Kaise / Lapp.	mountain
Kal / Pers.	stream
Kala / Az.; Kor.	fort
Kala / Finn.	river
Kala / Hin.	black
Kala / Tur.	castle
Kalaa / Ar.	castle
Kalaki / Georg.	city, town
Kale / Tur.	castle
Kali / Hin.	black
Kali / Indon.; Mal.	bay, river
Kallio / Finn.	rock
Kaln / Latv.	mountain
Kalós / Gr.	beautiful, good
Kamen / Bulg.; Rus.; S.C.; Slvn.	mountain, peak
Kámen / Cz.	rock
Kameň / Slvk.	rock
Kami / Jap.	upper
Kamień / Pol.	rock
Kamm / Germ.	crest
Kamp / Germ.	field
Kâmpóng / Khm.	village
Kámpos / Gr.	field
Kampung / Indon.; Mal.	village
Kan., Kanal / Alb.; Dan.; Germ.; Nor.; Rus.; S.C.; Slvn.; Swed.; Tur.	canal, channel
Kanaal / Dut.; Fle.	canal
Kanał / Pol.	canal
Kanal, Kan. / Alb.; Dan.; Germ.; Nor.; Rus.; S.C.; Slvn.; Swed.; Tur.	canal, channel
Kand, -kand / Pers.; Tur.	city, town
Kang / Chin.; Kor.	bay, river
Kangas / Fle.	heath
Kange / Esk.	east
Kangri / Tib.	snow-capped mountain
Kantara / Ar.	bridge
Kaōh / Khm.	island
Kap / Dan.; Germ.	cape
Kapija / S.C.	gate, gorge
Kapp / Nor.	cape
Kar / Tib.	white
Kar / Ural.	city, town
Kara / Tur.	black
Karang / Indon.; Mal.	sandbank, cliff
Kari / Finn.	cliff
Kariba / Ban.	gorge
Kariet / Ar.	village
Karki / Finn.	peninsula
Kastel / Germ.	castle
Kástron / Gr.	fort, city, town
Káto / Gr.	lower
Kaupstadur / Icel.	city, town
Kaupunki / Finn.	city, town
Kavīr / Pers.	salt desert
Kawa / Jap.	river
Kawm / Ar.	hill
Kebir / Ar.	great
Kedi / Georg.	mountain range
Kédia / Ar.	mountain, plateau
Kedim / Ar.	old
Kef / Ar.	mountain
Kefála / Gr.	mountain, peak
Kefar / Hebr.	village
Kei / Jap.	river
Kelet / Hung.	east
Ken / Gae.	cape
Kent / Alt.; Iran.; Tur.	city, town
Kenya / Swa.	fog
Kep / Alb.	cape
Kep., Kepulauan / Mal.	archipelago
Kepulauan, Kep. / Mal.	archipelago
Kereszt / Hung.	cross
Kerk / Dut.; Fle.	church
Keski / Finn.	middle
Kette / Germ.	mountain range
Keur / Sud.	village
Key / Eng.	coral island
Kha / Tib.	valley
Khal / Hin.	canal
Khalīj / Ar.	gulf
Khand / Hin.	district
Khao / Thai	hill, mountain
Kharābeh / Pers.	ruins
Khashm / Ar.	promontory
Khatt / Ar.	wadi
Khawr / Ar.	mouth, bay
Khazzān / Ar.	dam
Khemis / Ar.	fifth
Khersónisos / Gr.	peninsula
Khirbat / Ar.	ruins
Khlong / Thai	stream, mouth
Khokhok / Thai	isthmus
Khor / Ar.	mouth, bay
Khóra / Gr.	land
Khorion / Gr.	village
Khowr / Pers.	bay
Khrısós / Gr.	gold
Ki- / Ban.	little
Kibali / Sud.	river
Kil / Gae.	church
Kilde / Dan.	spring
Kilima / Swa.	mountain
Kill / Gae.	strait
Kilwa / Ban.	lake
Kin / Gae.	cape
Kinn / Nor.	cape, point
Kirche / Germ.	church
Kirk / Eng.	church
Kis / Hung.	little
Kisiwa / Swa.	island
Kita / Jap.	north, northern
Kızıl / Tur.	red
Klein / Afr.; Dut.; Germ.	little
Kliff / Germ.	cliff
Klint / Dan.	reef
Klip / Afr.; Dut.	rock, cliff
Klit / Dan.	dune
Kloof / Afr.; Dut.	gorge
Kloster / Dan.; Germ.; Nor.; Swed.	convent
Knob / Eng.	mountain
Knock / Gae.	mountain, hill
Ko / Jap.	bay, lake, little
Ko / Sud.	stream
Ko / Thai	island, point
Købing / Dan.	town
Kogel / Germ.	dome
Kōgen / Jap.	plateau
Koh / Hin.; Pers.	mountain, mountain range
Kol / Alt.	river, valley
Kol / Alt.; Tur.	lake
Koll / Nor.	peak
Kólpos / Gr.	gulf
Kong / Dan.; Nor.; Swed.	king
Kong / Indon.; Mal.	mountain
Kong / Viet.	mountain, hill
Konge / Ban.	river
König / Germ.	king
Koog / Germ.	polder
Kop / Afr.	hill
Kopec / Cz.; Slvk.	hill
Kopf / Germ.	peak
Köping / Swed.	town
Köprü / Tur.	bridge
Körfezi / Tur.	gulf
Korfi / Gr.	rock
Koro / Mel.	mountain, island
Koro / Sud.	old
Koru / Tur.	forest
Kosa / Rus.	spit
Koška / Rus.	cliff
Koski / Finn.	rapids
Kosui / Jap.	lake
Kot / Urdu	castle
Kota / Mal.	city, town
Kotal / Pash.; Pers.	pass
Kotar / S.C.	cultivated area
Kotlina / Pol.	basin

Local Form	English
Kotlovina / *Rus.*	basin, plain
Kou / *Chin.*	mouth, pass
Kourou / *Sud.*	well
Kowr / *Pers.*	river
Kowtal / *Pers.*	pass
Koy / *Tur.*	bay
Köy / *Tur.*	village
Kraal / *Afr.*	village
Kraina / *Pol.*	land
Kraj / *Rus.; S.C.*	land
Kraj / *Rus.*	administrative division
Krajina / *S.C.*	land
Krak / *Ar.*	hill, castle
Krans / *Afr.*	mountain
Kras / *S.C.; Slvn.*	karst landscape
Krasny / *Rus.*	red
Kreb / *Ar.*	hills, mountain range
Kriaž / *Ar.*	mountain range
Krš / *S.C.*	karst area, limestone area
Krung / *Thai*	city, town
Ksar / *Ar.*	castle
Ksour / *Ar.*	fortified village
Ku- / *Ban.*	river branch
Kuala / *Mal.*	river, mouth
Kubra / *Ar.*	bridge
Küçük / *Tur.*	little
Kuduk / *Tur.*	spring
Kūh / *Pers.*	mountain
Kūhhā / *Pers.*	mountain range
Kul / *Alt.; Iran.; Tur.*	lake
Kulam, -kulam / *Hin.; Tam.*	pond
Kulle / *Swed.*	hill
Kulm / *Germ.*	peak
Kultuk / *Rus.*	bay
Kum / *Tur.*	dunes, sand desert
Kuppe / *Germ.*	dome, seamount
Kurayb / *Ar.*	hill
Kurgan / *Alt.*	hill
Kurgan / *Tur.*	fort
Kuro / *Jap.*	black
Kurort / *Bulg.; Germ.; Rus.*	spa
Kust / *Dut.; Fle.*	coast
Kust- / *Swed.*	coast
Küste / *Germ.*	coast
Kút / *Hung.*	spring
Kuyu / *Tur.*	spring
Kvemo / *Georg.*	low, lower
Kwa / *Ban.*	village
Kylä / *Finn.*	village
Kyle / *Gae.*	strait, channel
Kyō / *Jap.*	strait
Kyrka / *Swed.*	church
Kyst / *Dan.; Nor.*	coast
Kyun / *Burm.*	island
Kyūryō / *Jap.*	hills, mountains
Kyzyl / *Tur.*	red
Kzyl / *Tur.*	red

L

Local Form	English
L., Lake, Lago / *Eng.; It.; Port.; Sp.*	lake
La / *Tib.*	pass
Laagte / *Afr.*	stream, valley
Labuan / *Indon.; Mal.*	bay, port
Lac / *Fr.*	lake
Lach / *Som.*	stream, wadi
Lacul / *Rom.*	lake
Lae / *Poly.*	cape, point
Laem / *Thai*	bay, port
Låg / *Nor.; Swed.*	low, lower
Lag / *Swed.*	stream, wadi
Läge / *Swed.*	beach
Lagh / *Som.*	stream, wadi
Lago, L. / *It.; Port.; Sp.*	lake
Lagoa / *Port.*	lagoon
Laguna / *Alb.; It.; Rus.; Sp.*	lagoon, lake
Lagune / *Fr.*	lagoon
Laht / *Est.*	bay
Lahti / *Finn.*	bay, gulf
Laks / *Finn.*	bay
Lalla / *Ar.*	saint
Lampi / *Finn.*	pond
Lande / *Fr.*	heath
Lang / *Afr.; Dut.; Germ.*	long
Lang / *Viet.*	village
Lao / *Chin.*	old
Lapa / *Poly.*	mountain range, peak
Largo / *Port.; Sp.*	basin
Las / *Pol.*	forest
Las, Lās / *Som.*	well
Laut / *Mal.*	sea
Law / *Gae.*	hill, mountain
Lázně / *Cz.*	thermal springs
Lednik / *Rus.*	glacier
Leite / *Germ.*	coast
Lekh / *Nep.*	mountain range
Les / *Bulg.; Cz.; Rus.; Slvk.*	forest
Leso / *Rus.*	forested
Levante / *It.; Sp.*	eastern
Levkós / *Gr.*	white
Levy / *Rus.*	left
Lha / *Tib.*	temple
Lhari / *Hin.; Nep.*	mountain
Lho / *Tib.*	south
Lido / *It.*	sandbar
Liedao / *Chin.*	archipelago
Liehtao / *Chin.*	archipelago
Liels / *Latv.*	great
Lilla / *Swed.*	little
Lille / *Dan.; Nor.*	little
Liman / *Alb.; Rus.; Tur.*	lagoon, bay
Liman / *Tur.*	bay, port
Limin / *Gr.*	port
Limni / *Gr.*	lake
Ling / *Chin.*	mountain range, peak
Linna / *Finn.*	castle
Liqen / *Alb.*	lake
Lithos / *Gr.*	stone
Litoral / *Port.; Sp.*	littoral
Litorale / *It.*	littoral
Llan / *Wel.*	church
Llano / *Sp.*	plain
Llanura / *Sp.*	plain
Lo- / *Ban.*	river
Loch / *Gae.*	lake, inlet
Loch / *Germ.*	grotto
Loka / *Slvn.*	forest
Loma / *Sp.*	hill
Long / *Indon.*	stream
Loo / *Dut.; Fle.*	clearing
Lough / *Gae.*	lake
Loutrá / *Gr.*	thermal springs
Ložbina / *Rus.*	depression
Lu- / *Ban.*	river
Lua / *Ban.*	river
Lua / *Mel.*	island, reef
Lua / *Poly.*	crater
Luang / *Thai*	yellow
Luch / *Germ.*	peat-bog
Lücke / *Germ.*	pass
Lug / *Rus.*	meadow
Luka / *S.C.; Slvn.*	port
Lule / *Lapp.*	east, eastern
Lum / *Alb.*	river
Lund / *Dan.; Swed.*	forest
Lung / *Rom.*	long
Lung / *Tib.*	valley
Luoto / *Finn.*	shoal
Lurg / *Pers.*	salt flat
Lut / *Pers.*	desert

M

Local Form	English
M., Monte / *It.; Port.; Sp.*	mountain
Ma / *Ar.*	water
Ma- / *Ban.*	people
Maa / *Est.; Finn.*	island, land
Ma'arrat / *Ar.*	height
Machi / *Jap.*	district
Macizo / *Sp.*	massif
Madhya / *Hin.*	central
Madīnah / *Ar.*	city, town
Madīq / *Ar.*	strait
Mado / *Swa.*	well
Madu / *Tam.*	pond
Mae / *Thai*	stream
Mae nam / *Thai*	stream, mouth
Magh / *Gae.*	plain
Mägi / *Est.*	mountain
Măgura / *Rom.*	height
Mahā / *Hin.*	great
Mahal / *Hin.; Urdu*	palace
Mai / *Amh.; Ban.*	stream
Majdan / *S.C.*	quarry
Mäki / *Finn.*	mountain, hill
Makrós / *Gr.*	long
Mala / *Hin.; Tam.*	mountain
Malai / *Hin.; Tam.*	mountain
Malal / *A.I.*	fence
Malhão / *Port.*	dome
Mali / *Alb.*	mountain
Mali / *S.C.; Slvn.*	little
Malki / *Bulg.*	little
Malla / *Tam.*	mountain
Maly / *Rus.*	little
Malý / *Cz.; Slvk.*	little
Mały / *Pol.*	little
Man / *Kor.*	bay
Manastir / *Bulg.; S.C.*	monastery
Manche / *Fr.*	channel
Mar / *It.; Port.; Sp.*	sea
Mar / *Tib.*	red
Mar / *Ural.*	city, town
Marais / *Fr.*	marsh
Marché / *Fr.*	market
Mare / *Fr.*	pond
Mare / *It.; Rom.*	sea
Mare / *Rom.*	great
Marea / *Rom.*	sea
Marécage / *Fr.*	marsh
Marios / *Lith.*	reservoir
Marisma / *Sp.*	marsh
Mark / *Dan.; Nor.; Swed.*	land
Markt / *Germ.*	market
Marsa / *Ar.*	anchorage, bay
Marsch / *Germ.*	marsh
Maru / *Jap.*	mountain
Mas / *Prov.*	farmhouse
Maṣabb / *Ar.*	mouth
Mashra' / *Ar.*	landing, pier
Masivul / *Rom.*	massif
Massiv / *Germ.; Rus.*	massif
Mata / *Poly.*	point
Mata / *Port.; Sp.*	forest
Mata / *Som.*	waterfall
Mato / *Port.; Sp.*	forest
Matsu / *Jap.*	point
Mauna / *Poly.*	mountain
Mávros / *Gr.*	black
Mayo / *Sud.*	river
Maza / *Lith.*	little
Mazar / *Pers.; Tur.*	sanctuary
Mazs / *Latv.*	little
Me / *Khm.*	river
Me / *Mel.*	hill, mountain
Me / *Thai*	great
Medina / *Ar.*	city, town
Medjez / *Ar.*	ford
Meer / *Dut.; Fle.*	lake
Meer / *Germ.*	lake, sea
Megálos / *Gr.*	great
Mégas / *Gr.*	great
Megye / *Hung.*	district
Mélas / *Gr.*	black
Melkosopočnik / *Rus.*	hill country
Mellan / *Swed.*	central
Men / *Chin.*	gate, channel
Ménez / *Br.*	mountain
Menzel / *Ar.*	bivouac
Meos / *Indon.*	island
Mer / *Fr.*	sea
Mercato / *It.*	market
Merdja / *Ar.*	lagoon, marsh
Meri / *Est.; Finn.*	sea
Meridional / *Rom.; Sp.*	southern
Merín / *A.I.*	little
Merja / *Ar.*	lagoon, marsh
Mers / *Ar.*	port
Mersa / *Ar.*	port
Mesa / *Sp.*	mesa, tableland
Meseta / *Sp.*	plateau
Mésos / *Gr.*	central
Mesto / *Bulg.; S.C.; Slvk.; Slvn.*	city, town
Město / *Cz.*	city, town
Mestre / *Port.*	principal
Meydan / *Tur.*	square
Meẕad / *Hebr.*	castle
Mező / *Hung.*	field
Mgne., Montagne / *Fr.*	mountain
Mgnes., Montagnes / *Fr.*	mountains
Miao / *Chin.*	temple
Miasto / *Pol.*	city, town
Mic / *Rom.*	little
Middel / *Afr.; Dut.; Fle.*	middle
Midi / *Fr.*	noon, south
Między / *Pol.*	central
Miedzyrzecze / *Pol.*	interfluve
Mierzeja / *Pol.*	sand spit
Mifraz / *Hebr.*	bay, gulf
Miftah / *Ar.*	gorge
Mikrós / *Gr.*	little
Mina / *Port.; Sp.*	mine
Mīnā' / *Ar.*	port
Minami / *Jap.*	south, southern
Minamoto / *Jap.*	spring
Minato / *Jap.*	port
Mine / *Jap.*	peak
Mirim / *A.I.*	little
Misaki / *Jap.*	cape
Mittel- / *Germ.*	middle
Mo / *Chin.*	sand desert
Mo / *Nor.; Swed.*	heath
Moana / *Poly.*	lake
Mogila / *Bulg.; Rus.*	hill
Moku / *Poly.*	island
Mølle / *Dan.*	mill
Monasterio / *Sp.*	monastery
Mond / *Afr.; Dut.; Fle.*	mouth
Mong / *Burm.; Thai; Viet.*	city, town
Moni / *Gr.*	monastery
Mont / *Cat.; Fr.*	mountain
Montagna / *It.*	mountain
Montagne, Mgne. / *Fr.*	mountain
Montagnes, Mgnes. / *Fr.*	mountains
Montaña / *Sp.*	mountain
Monte, M. / *It.; Port.; Sp.*	mountain
Monts, Mts. / *Fr.*	mountains
Moos / *Germ.*	moor
Mór / *Gae.*	great
More / *Bulg.; Rus.; S.C.*	sea
More / *Gae.*	great
Mori / *Jap.*	mountain, forest
Morne / *Fr.*	mountain
Moron / *Mong.*	river
Morro / *Port.; Germ.*	hill, peak
Morrón / *Sp.*	mountain
Morze / *Pol.*	sea
Most / *Bulg.; Cz.; Pol.; Rus.; S.C.; Slvn.*	bridge
Moto / *Jap.*	spring
Motte / *Fr.*	hill
Motu / *Mel.; Poly.*	island, rock
Moutier / *Fr.*	monastery
Movilă / *Rom.*	hill
Moyen / *Fr.*	central
Mta / *Georg.*	mountain
Mts., Monts, Mountains / *Eng.; Fr.*	mountains
Muang / *Laot.; Thai*	city, town, land
Muara / *Indon.; Mal.*	mouth
Muela / *Sp.*	mountain
Mühle / *Germ.*	mill
Mui / *Mel.*	point
Mui / *Viet.*	point, cape
Muiden / *Dut.; Fle.*	mouth
Muir / *Gae.*	sea
Mukh / *Hin.*	mouth
Mull / *Gae.*	promontory
Münde / *Germ.*	mouth
Mündung / *Germ.*	mouth
Municipiul / *Rom.*	commune
Munkhafaḑ / *Ar.*	depression
Münster / *Germ.*	monastery
Munte / *Rom.*	mountain
Muntelé / *Rom.*	mountain
Munţii / *Rom.*	mountain range
Muren / *Mong.*	river
Mushāsh / *Ar.*	spring
Muz / *Tur.*	ice
Muztagh / *Tur.*	snow-capped mountain
Mwambo / *Ban.*	rock, cliff
Myit / *Burm.*	stream
Mynydd / *Wel.*	mountain
Myo / *Burm.*	city, town
Mýri / *Icel.*	marsh
Mys / *Rus.*	cape

N

Local Form	English
Na / *Cz.; Pol.; Rus.; S.C.; Slvn.*	on
Nab / *Ar.*	spring
Nad / *Cz.; Pol.; Rus.*	on
Nada / *Jap.*	bay, sea
Nadi, -nadi / *Hin.; Urdu*	river
Næs / *Dan.*	point
Nafūd / *Ar.*	dunes
Nag / *Tib.*	black
Nagar, -nagar / *Hin.; Tib.*	city, town
Nagaram / *Hin.; Tam.*	city, town
Nagorje / *Rus.*	plateau, mountains
Nagy / *Hung.*	great
Nahr / *Ar.*	river
Naikai / *Jap.*	sea
Naka / *Jap.*	central
Nakhon / *Thai*	city, town
Nam / *Burm.; Laot.; Thai*	river
Nam / *Kor.*	south
Namakzar / *Pers.*	salt desert
Nan / *Chin.*	south
Narrows / *Eng.*	strait
Narssaq / *Esk.*	plain, valley
Näs / *Swed.*	cape
Nationalpark / *Swed.; Germ.*	national park
Nau / *Lith.*	new
Nauja / *Lith.*	new
Navolok / *Rus.*	cape, promontory
Ne / *Jap.*	cliff
Neder / *Flę.; Dut.*	low
Neem / *Est.*	cape
Negro / *Port.; Sp.*	black
Negru / *Rom.*	black
Nehir / *Tur.*	river
Nei / *Chin.*	inner
Nene, -nene / *Ban.*	great
Néos / *Gr.*	new
Nero / *It.*	black
Nes / *Icel.; Nor.*	cape
Ness / *Gae.*	promontory
Neu / *Germ.*	new
Neuf / *Fr.*	new
Nevado / *Sp.*	snow-capped mountain
Nez / *Fr.*	cape
Ngok / *Viet.*	mountain, peak
Ngolo / *Ber.*	great
Ni / *Kor.*	village
Niecka / *Pol.*	basin
Niemi / *Finn.*	peninsula
Nieuw / *Fle.; Dut.*	new
Nij / *Dut.*	new
Nīl / *Hin.*	blue
Nishi / *Jap.*	west
Niski / *Pol.*	lower
Nisko / *S.C.*	low
Nisoi / *Gr.*	islands
Nísos / *Gr.*	island
Nizina / *Pol.*	lowland
Nižina / *Cz.*	depression
Nízký / *Cz.*	low, lower

Geographical Glossary

Local Form	English
Nizmennost / Rus.	lowland, depression
Nižni / Rus.	low, lower
Nižný / Slvk.	low, lower
No / Mel.	stream
Nock / Gae.	ridge
Noir / Fr.	black
Non / Thai	hill
Nong / Thai	lake, marsh
Noord / Afr.; Fle.; Dut.	north
Noordoost / Afr.; Fle.; Dut.	northeast
Nor / Arm.	new
Nord / Fr.; It.; Germ.	north
Nördlich / Germ.	northern
Nørdre / Dan.; Nor.	northern
Norra / Swed.	northern
Nørre / Dan.	northern
Norte / Sp.	north
Nos / Bulg.; Rus.; S.C.; Slvn.	cape
Nosy / Malag.	island
Nótios / Gr.	southern
Nou / Rom.	new
Novi / Bulg.; S.C.; Slvn.	new
Novo / Port.	new
Novy / Rus.	new
Nový / Cz.; Slvk.	new
Now / Pers.	new
Nowy / Pol.	new
Nudo / Sp.	mountain
Nuevo / Sp.	new
Nui / Viet.	mountain
Numa / Jap.	marsh, lake
Nummi / Finn.	heath
Nunatak / Esk.	peak
Nuovo / It.	new
Nur / Chin.	lake
Nusa / Mal.	island
Nut, -nut / Nor.	peak
Nuwara / Sin.; Tam.	city, town
Nuwe / Afr.	new
Nyanza / Ban.	water, river, lake
Nyasa / Ban.	lake
Nyeong / Kor.	pass
Nyika / Ban.	upland
Nyŏng / Kor.	mount, pass
Nyugat / Hung.	west

O

Local Form	English
Ō / Jap.	great
Ó / Hung.	old
Ö / Swed.	island
Ø, -ø / Dan.; Nor.	island
Öar / Swed.	islands
Ober / Germ.	upper
Oblast / Rus.	province
Obo / Mong.	mountain, hill
Occidental / Fr.; Rom.; Sp.	western
Océan / Fr.	ocean
Océano / Sp.	ocean
Oceano / It.; Port.	ocean
Ocnă / Rom.	salt mine
Odde / Dan.; Nor.	promontory
Oeste / Port.; Sp.	west
Oever / Fle.; Dut.	bank
Oewer / Afr.	bank
Oie / Germ.	islet
Ojos / Sp.	spring
Oka / Jap.	coast
Oke / Sud.	height
Okean / Rus.	ocean
Oki / Jap.	bay
Okrug / Rus.	district
Ola / Alt.	city, town
Omuramba / K.S.	stream
Onder / Afr.	under
Oni / Malag.	river
Oos / Afr.	east
Oost / Fle.; Dut.	east
Oostelijk / Dut.	eastern
Opatija / Slvn.	abbey
Or / Fr.	gold
Oraş / Rom.	city, town
Óri / Gr.	mountains
Oriental / Fr.; Port.; Rom.; Sp.	eastern
Orientale / It.	eastern
Orilla / Sp.	bank
Órmos / Gr.	bay
Óros / Gr.	mountain
Ország / Hung.	land
Ort / Germ.	cape
Orta / Tur.	central
Orto / Alt.	central
Oseaan / Afr.	ocean
Ōshima / Jap.	large island
Ost / Dan.; Germ.	east
Öst / Swed.	east
Ostän, -ostän / Pers.	province
Øster / Dan.; Nor.	east, eastern
Öster / Swed.	east, eastern
Östlich / Germ.	eastern
Ostrog / Rus.	castle
Ostrov / Rus.	island
Ostrovul / Rom.	island
Ostrów / Pol.	island
Ostrvo / S.C.	island
Otok / S.C.; Slvn.	island
Otrog / Rus.	front range (mountains)
Oua / Mel.	stream
Ouar / Ar.	rocky desert
Oud / Fle.; Dut.	old
Oued / Ar.	wadi
Ouest / Fr.	west
Ouled / Ar.	son
Oum / Ar.	mother
Ouro / Port.	gold
Outu / Poly.	cape
Ova / Ban.	people
Ova / Tur.	plain
Ovasi / Tur.	plain
Øver / Nor.	over
Över / Swed.	over
Övre / Swed.	over
Øy / Dan.; Nor.	island
oz., Ozero / Rus.	lake
Ozek / Alt.	hollow
Ozera / Rus.	lakes
Ozero, oz. / Rus.	lake

P

Local Form	English
P., Pulau / Mal.; Indon.	island
Pää / Finn.	principal
Pad / Rus.	valley
Padang / Indon.	plain
Padiş / Rom.	upland
Padół / Pol.	valley
Pădure / Rom.	forest
Pahorek / Cz.	hill
Pahorkatina / Cz.	plateau, hills
País / Port.; Sp.	land, country
Pak / Thai	mouth
Pala / It.	peak
Palaiós / Gr.	old
Palanka / S.C.	village
Pali / Poly.	cliff
-palli / Hin.	village
Pampa / Sp.	plain, prairie
Panda / Swa.	junction
Panev / Cz.	basin
Pantanal / Sp.	swamp
Pantano / Sp.	swamp, lake
Pao / Mel.	hill
Pará / A.I.	river
Paramera / Sp.	desert highland
Páramo / Sp.	moor
Paraná / A.I.	river
Parbat / Hin.; Urdu	mountain
Parc / Fr.	park
Parco / It.	park
Parco Nazionale / It.	national park
Pardo / Port.	grey
Parque / Sp.	park
Parque Nacional / Sp.; Port.	national park
Pas / Fr.; Rom.	pass, strait
Pasaje / Sp.	passage
Pasir / Mal.	sand, beach
Paso / Sp.	pass
Passágem / Port.	passage
Passe / Fr.	pass
Passo / It.; Port.	pass
Pasul / Rom.	pass
Patak / Hung.	stream
Patam, -patam / Hin.	city, town
Patnā / Hin.	city, town
Patnam, -patnam / Hin.	city, town
Pattinam, -pattinam / Hin.	city, town
Pays / Fr.	land, country
Pazar / Tur.	market
Pea / Est.	cape
Pech / Cat.	hill
Pedhiás / Gr.	plain
Pedra / Port.	rock, mountain
Peg., Pegunungan / Mal.; Indon.	mountain range
Pegunungan, Peg. / Mal.; Indon.	mountain range
Pélagos / Gr.	sea
Pele / Poly.	peak, hill
Pen / Br.	principal
Pen / Br.; Gae.	cape, mountain
Peña / Sp.	peak
Pendi / Chin.	basin
Pendiente / Sp.	slope
Penha / Port.	peak
Península / Port.; Sp.	peninsula
Péninsule / Fr.	peninsula
Penisola / It.	peninsula
Peñon / Sp.	rock, island
Pente / Fr.	slope
Perekop / Rus.	channel
Pereval / Rus.	pass
Perevoz / Rus.	ford
Pertuis / Fr.	strait
Peščara / S.C.	sandy soil
Peski / Rus.	sand desert

Local Form	English
Petit / Fr.	little
Pétra / Gr.	rock
Phanom / Thai; Khm.	mountain range, mountain
Phau / Laot.	mountain
Phnum / Khm.	hill, mountain
Phu / Viet.	mountain, hill
Phum / Thai	forest
Phumĭ / Khm.	village
Pi / Chin.	cape
Piana, Pianura / It.	plain
Piano / It.	plain
Piatră / Rom.	stone
Pic / Cat.; Fr.	peak
Picacho / Sp.	peak
Piccolo / It.	little
Pico / Port.; Sp.	peak
Piedra / Sp.	rock, cliff
Pietra / It.	stone
Pieve / It.	parish
Pik / Rus.	peak
Pils / Latv.	city, town
Pinar / Sp.	pine forest
Pingyuan / Chin.	plain
Pioda / It.	crest
Pirgos / Gr.	tower, peak
Pīsh / Pers.	anterior, before
Pitkä / Finn.	great
Piton / Fr.	mountain, peak
Piz / Rmsh.	peak
Pizzo / It.	peak
Pjasăci / Bulg.	beach
Plaat / Fle.; Dut.	sandbank
Plage / Fr.	beach
Plaine / Fr.	plain
Plan / Fr.	plain
Planalto / Port.	plateau
Planina / Bulg.	mountain
Plano / Sp.	plain
Plas / Dut.; Fle.	lake, marsh
Plato / Bulg.; Rus.	plateau
Platosu / Tur.	plateau
Platte / Germ.	plain, plateau
Plav / S.C.	blue
Plavnja / Rus.	marsh
Playa / Sp.	beach
Ploskogorje / Rus.	plateau
Plou / Br.	church
Po / Kor.	port
Po / Chin.	lake, white
P'o / Kor.	bay, lake
Poa / Mel.	hill
Poarta / Rom.	pass
Poartă / Rom.	gate
Pobla / Cat.	village
Pobrzeże / Pol.	littoral, coast
Poço / Port.	well
Poço / Port.	point
Pod / Cz.; Pol.; Rus.; S.C.; Slvn.	bridge
Podkamenny / Rus.	stony
Poggio / It.	hill
Pohja / Finn.	north, northern
Pohjois- / Finn.	north
Pojezierze / Pol.	lake region
Pol / Pers.	bridge
Pol, -pol / Rus.	city, town
Pola / Port.; Sp.	village
Polder / Fle.; Dut.	reclaimed land
Pole / Pol.	field
Pólis / Gr.	city, town
Poljana / Bulg.; Rus.; S.C.; Slvn.	field, terrace
Poljarny / Rus.	polar
Polje / S.C.; Slvn.	valley, field, basin
Poluostrov / Rus.	peninsula
Pomorije / Bulg.	littoral
Pomorze / Pol.	littoral
Ponente / It.	western
Pont / Cat.; Fr.	bridge
Ponta / Port.	point
Ponte / It.; Port.	bridge
Póntos / Gr.	sea
Poort / Afr.; Fle.; Dut.	pass
Pore, -pore / Hin.; Urdu	city, town
Porog / Rus.	rapids
Porte / Fr.	gate
Portile / Rom.	gorge
Portillo / Sp.	pass
Portiţa / Rom.	small gate
Porto / It.	port
Pôrto / Port.	port
Posht / Pers.	back, posterior
Potjo / Indon.	peak
Potok / Bulg.; Cz.; Pol.; Rus.; S.C.; Slvn.	stream
Póvoa / Port.	village
Pozo / Sp.	well
Pozzo / It.	well
Pradesh / Hin.	region, state
Prado / Sp.	meadow
Praia / Port.	beach
Prato / It.	meadow
Pré / Fr.	meadow
Prealpi / It.	prealps
Presa / Sp.	reservoir
Presqu'île / Fr.	peninsula
Prêto / Port.	black

Local Form	English
Priehradní nádrž / Cz.	reservoir
Pripoljarny / Rus.	subpolar
Pristan / Rus.	port
Prohod / Bulg.	pass
Proliv / Rus.	strait
Promontoire / Fr.	promontory
Průchod / Cz.	pass
Przedgorze / Pol.	front range (mountains)
Przełęcz / Pol.	pass
Przemysł / Pol.	industry
Przylądek / Pol.	cape
Pua / Mel.	hill
Puebla / Sp.	village
Puente / Sp.	bridge
Puerto / Sp.	port, pass
Puig / Cat.	peak
Puits / Fr.	well
Pul / Pash.	bridge
Pulau, P. / Mal.; Indon.	island
Pulau Pulau / Mal.	islands
Pulo / Mal.; Indon.	island
Puna / A.I.	upland
Puncak / Indon.	mountain
Punjung / Mal.; Indon.	mountain
Punt / Afr.	point
Punta / It.; Sp.	point
Pur, -pur / Hin.; Urdu	city, town
-pura / Hin.; Urdu	city, town
Pura / Indon.	city, town, temple
Puri, -puri / Hin.; Urdu	city, town
Pus / Alb.	spring
Pušća / Rus.	forest
Pustynja / Rus.	desert
Puszcza / Pol.	heath
Puszta / Hung.	lowland
Put / Afr.	well
Put / Rus.; S.C.	road
Putra, -putra / Hin.	son
Puu / Poly.	mountain, volcano
Puy / Fr.	peak
Pwell / Wel.	pond
Pyeong / Kor.	plain
Pyhä / Finn.	saint

Q

Local Form	English
Qagan / Mong.	white
Qala / Pash.	fortified town
Qal'at / Ar.	castle
Qalb / Ar.	hill
Qalīb / Ar.	spring
Qalīq / Ar.	spring
Qanāt / Ar.	canal
Qantara / Ar.	bridge
Qaqortoq / Esk.	white
Qar / Som.	mountain
Qara / Pers.	black
Qarah / Tur.	black
Qārat / Ar.	height, mountain
Qāret / Ar.	village, hill
Qaryah / Ar.	village
Qaryat / Ar.	village
Qaşr / Ar.	castle
Qawz / Ar.	dunes
Qeqertarssuaq / Esk.	peninsula
Qezel / Tur.	red
Qi / Chin.	river
Qing / Chin.	blue, green
Qiryat / Hebr.	city, town
Qolleh / Pers.	mountain, peak
Qu / Chin.	river, canal
Quan dao / Viet.	islands
Quebracho / Sp.	stream
Quebrada / Sp.	gorge, stream
Quedas / Port.	waterfalls
Qulbān / Ar.	well
Qundao / Chin.	archipelago
Qūr / Ar.	height, hill
Qytet / Alb.	city, town
Qyteti / Alb.	city, town

R

Local Form	English
R., Rio, River / Eng.; Sp.	river
Rada / It.; Sp.	anchorage
Rade / Fr.	anchorage
Rags / Latv.	cape
Rahad / Ar.	lake, pond
Rajon / Rus.	district
Rak / Fle.; Dut.	strait
Rakai / Poly.	reef
Ramla / Ar.	sand
Rancho / Port.; Sp.	farm, ranch
Rand / Afr.; Germ.	escarpment
Range / Eng.	mountain range
Rann / Urdu	marsh
Rano / Malag.	water
Ranta / Finn.	bank, beach
Rapide / Fr.	rapids
Ras / Amh.	peak
Rās / Ar.	point, cape

Local Form	English
Ras, Rás / Ar.	promontory, peak
Rāsiga / Som.	promontory
Rass / Ar.	promontory, peak
Rassa / Lapp.	mountain
Ráth / Gae.	castle
Raunina / Bulg.; Rus.	plain
Raz / Fr.	strait
Razliv / Rus.	flood plain
Récif / Fr.	reef
Recife / Port.	reef
Reede / Germ.; Dut.; Slvn.	anchorage
Reek / Afr.; Gae.	mountain range
Reg / Pash.	dunes
Région / Fr.	region
Rei / Port.	king
Reka / Bulg.; Rus.; S.C.; Slvn.	river
Řeka / Cz.	river
Réma / Gr.	torrent
Renne / Dan.; Nor.	deep
Reprêsa / Port.	dam, reservoir
Represa / Sp.	dam, reservoir
República / Port.; Sp.	republic
République / Fr.	republic
Rés., Réservoir / Fr.	reservoir
Res., Reservoir / Eng.	reservoir
Réservoir, Rés. / Fr.	reservoir
Reshteh / Pers.	mountain range
Respublika / Rus.	republic
Restinga / Port.	cliff, sandbank
Retsugan / Jap.	reef
Rettō / Jap.	archipelago
Rev / Dan.; Nor.; Swed.	reef
Rey / Sp.	king
Rì / Tib.	mountain
Ria / Sp.	estuary
Riacho / Port.	stream
Rialto / It.	plateau
Rialto / It.	rise
Riba / Port.	bank
Ribeira / Port.	river
Ribeirão / Port.	stream
Ribeiro / Port.	stream
Ribera / Sp.	coast
Ribnik / Slvn.	pond
Rid / Bulg.	mountain range
Rif / Icel.	cliff
Riff / Germ.	reef
Rīg / Pash.	dunes
Rijeka / S.C.	river
Rimāl / Ar.	sand desert
Rincón / Sp.	peninsula between two rivers
Ring / Tib.	long
Rinne / Germ.	trench
Rio / Port.	river
Rio, R. / Sp.	river
Riu / Rom.	river
Riva / It.	bank
Rive / Fr.	bank
Rivera / Sp.	brook, stream
Rivier, -rivier / Afr.; Dut.; Fle.	river
Riviera / It.	coast
Rivière / Fr.	river
Roads / Eng.	anchorage
Roc / Fr.	rock
Roca / Port.; Sp.	rock
Rocca / It.	castle
Roche / Fr.	rock
Rocher / Fr.	rock
Rock / Eng.	rock
Rod / Pash.	river
Rode / Germ.	tilled soil
Rodnik / Rus.	spring
Rog / Rus.; S.C.; Slvn.	peak
Roi / Fr.	king
Rojo / Sp.	red
Roque / Sp.	rock
Rot / Germ.	red
Roto / Poly.	lake
Rouge / Fr.	red
Równina / Pol.	plain
Rt / S.C.; Slvn.	cape
Ru / Tib.	mountain
Ruck / Germ.	ridge
Rücken / Germ.	ridge
Rud / Pers.	river
Ruda / Cz.; Slvk.	mine
Ruda / Pol.	ore
Rūdbār / Pers.	river
Rudha / Gae.	point
Rudnik / Rus.; S.C.; Slvn.	mine
Rug / Fle.; Dut.	ridge
Ruggen / Afr.	ridge
Ruina / Sp.	ruins
Ruine / Fr.; Dut.; Germ.	ruins
Rujm / Ar.	hill
Run / Eng.	stream

S

Local Form	English
S., See / Germ.	lake, sea
Saar / Est.	island
Saari / Finn.	island
Sabbia / It.	sand
Sabkhat / Ar.	salt flat, salt marsh
Sable / Fr.; Eng.	beach
Sacca / It.	anchorage
Saco / Port.	bay
Sad / Cz.; Slvk.	park
Sad / Pers.	wall
Sadd / Ar.; Pers.	cataract, dam
Safid / Pash.; Urdu; Hin.	white
Şafrā' / Ar.	desert
Sāgar / Hin.	reservoir
Saguia / Ar.	irrigation canal
Sahara / Ar.	desert
Sahel / Ar.	plain, coast
Sahr / Iran.	city, town
Şaḥrā' / Ar.	desert
Said / Ar.	sweet
Saj / Alt.	stream, valley
Saki / Jap.	point
Sala / Latv.; Lith.	island
Saladillo / Sp.	salt desert
Salar / Sp.	salt lake
Sale / Ural.	village
Salina / It.; Sp.	salt flat, salt marsh
Saline / Dut.; Fr.; Germ.	salt flat, salt marsh
Salmi / Finn.	strait
Salseleh-ye Kūh / Pers.	mountain range
Salto / Port.; Sp.	waterfall, rapids
Salz / Germ.	salt
Samudera / Indon.	ocean
Samudra / Hin.	lake
Samut / Thai	sea
San / Jap.; Kor.	mountain
San / It.; Sp.	saint
Sanchi / Jap.	mountain range
Sand / Dan.; Eng.; Nor.; Swed.; Germ.	beach
Šand / Mong.	spring
Sandur / Icel.	sand
Sank / Pers.	rock
Sankt, St. / Germ.; Swed.	saint
Sanmaeg / Kor.	mountain range
Sanmyaku / Jap.	mountain range
Sansanné / Sud.	campsite
Santo / It.; Port.; Sp.	saint
Santuario / It.	sanctuary
São / Port.	saint
Sar / Pers.	cape; peak
Šar / Rus.; Tur.	strait
Saraf / Ar.	well
Sari / Finn.	island
Sari / Tur.	yellow
Sarīr / Ar.	rocky desert
Sary / Tur.	yellow
Sasso / It.	stone
Sat / Rom.	village
Sattel / Germ.	pass
Saurum / Latv.	strait
Schleuse / Germ.	lock
Schloß / Germ.	castle
Schlucht / Germ.	gorge
Schnee / Germ.	snow
Schwarz / Germ.	black
Scoglio / It.	cliff
Se / Jap.	bank, shoal
Sebkha / Ar.	salt flat
Sebkhet / Ar.	salt flat
Sed / Ar.	dam
Seda / Ural.	mountain
See, S. / Germ.	lake, sea
Sefra / Ar.	yellow
Segara / Indon.	lagoon
Şehir / Tur.	city, town
Seki / Jap.	dam
Selat / Mal.; Indon.	strait
Selatan / Indon.	southern
Selkä / Finn.	ridge, lake
Sella / It.	pass
Selo / Bulg.; Rus.; S.C.; Slvn.	village
Selsela Kohe / Pers.	mountain range
Selva / It.; Sp.	forest
Semenanjung / Mal	peninsula
Sen / Jap.	mountain
Seong / Kor.	castle
Sep / Alt.	canal
Serir / Ar.	rocky desert
Serra / Cat.; Port.	mountain range
Serra / It.	mountain
Serrania / Sp.	mountain range
Sertão / Port.	steppe
Seto / Jap.	strait
Sett., Settentrionale / It.	northern
Settentrionale, Sett. / It.	northern
Seuil / Fr.	sill
Sev / Arm.	black
Sever / Rus.	north
Severny / Rus.	northern
Sfint / Rom.	saint
Sfîntu / Rom.	saint
Sgeir / Gae.	cliff
Sha'b / Ar.	cliff
Shahr / Pers.; Hin.	city, town
Sha'īb / Ar.	stream
Shallāl / Ar.	cataract

Local Form	English
Shām / Ar.	north; northern
Shamo / Chin.	sand desert
Shan / Chin.	mountain, mountain range
Shan / Gae.	old
Shand / Mong.	spring
Shankou / Chin.	pass
Shaqq / Ar.	wadi
Sharm / Ar.	bay
Sharqī / Ar.	east, eastern
Sharqīyah / Ar.	eastern
Shatt / Ar.	river, salt lake
Shatt / Tur.	stream
Shën / Alb.	saint
Sheng / Chin.	province
Shi / Chin.	city, town
Shibīn / Ar.	village
Shih / Chin.	rock
Shima / Jap.	island
Shimo / Jap.	lower
Shin / Jap.	new
Shō / Jap.	island
Shotō / Jap.	archipelago
Shū / Jap.	administrative division
Shui / Chin.	river
Shuiku / Chin.	reservoir
Shur / Pers.	salt
Sidhiros / Gr.	iron
Sidi / Ar.	master
Sieben / Germ.	seven
Sierra / Sp.	mountain range
Sikt / Ural.	village
Sillon / Fr.	furrow
Šine / Mong.	new
Sink / Eng.	depression
Sinn / Ar.	point
Sint / Dut.; Fle.	saint
Sirt / Tur.	mountain range
Sirtlar / Tur.	mountain range
Sistema / It.; Sp.	mountain system
Sīyāh / Pers.	black
Sje / Nor.	lake
Sjö / Swed.	lake, sea
Skag / Icel.	peninsula
Skala / Bulg.; Rus.	rock
Skála / Slvk.	rock
Skar / Nor.	pass
Skär / Swed.	cliff
Skeir / Gae.	cliff
Skerry / Gae.	cliff
Skog / Nor.; Swed.	forest
Skóg / Icel.	forest
Skov / Dan.; Nor.	forest
Slatina / S.C.; Slvn.	mineral water
Slätt / Swed.	plain
Slieve / Gae.	mountain
Slot / Dut.; Fle.	castle
Slott / Nor.; Swed.	castle
Slough / Eng.	creek, pond, marsh
Sluis / Dut.; Fle.	sluice
Små / Swed.	little
Sne / Nor.	snow
Sneeuw / Afr.; Dut.	snow
Snežny / Rus.	snowy
Snø / Nor.	snow
So / Kor.	little
Sø / Dan.; Nor.	lake; sea
So / Ural.	passage
Söder / Swed.	south
Södra / Swed.	southern
Solončak / Rus.	salt flat
Sommet / Fr.	peak
Son / Viet.	mountain
Sønder / Dan.; Nor.	southern
Søndre / Dan.	southern
Sone / Jap.	bank
Song / Viet.	river
Sopka / Rus.	volcano
Sopočnik / Rus.	mountain system
Soprana / It.	upper
Šor, Sor / Alt.	salt marsh
Sos / Sp.	upon
Sotavento / Sp.	leeward
Sotoviento / Sp.	leeward
Sottana / It.	lower
Souk / Ar.	market
Souq / Ar.	market
Sour / Ar.	rampart
Source / Eng.; Fr.	spring
Souto / Port.	forest
Spitze / Germ.	peak
Spruit / Afr.	current
Sreden / Bulg.	central
Sredni / Rus.	central
Średni / Pol.	central
Srednji / S.C.; Slvn.	central
St., Saint, Sankt / Eng.; Fr.; Germ.; Swed.	saint
Stadhur / Icel.	city, town
Stadt, -stadt / Germ.	city, town
Stag / Eng.	city, town
Stagno / It.	pond
-stan / Hin.; Pers.; Urdu	land
Star / Bulg.	old
Stari / S.C.; Slvn.	old

Local Form	English
Stary / Pol.; Rus.	old
Starý / Cz.; Slvk.	old
Stat / Afr.; Dan.; Fle.; Nor.; Dut.; Swed.	city, town
Stathmós / Gr.	railway station
Stausee / Germ.	reservoir
Stavrós / Gr.	cross
Sted / Dan.; Nor.	place
Stedt / Germ.	place
Stein, -stein / Nor.; Germ.	stone
Sten / Nor.; Swed.	stone
Stena / S.C.; Slvn.	rock
Stěna / Cz.	mountain range
Stenón / Gr.	strait, pass
Step / Rus.	steppe
-sthān / Hin.; Pers.; Urdu	land
Stift / Germ.	foundation
Štit / Cz.; Slvk.	peak
Stock / Germ.	massif
Stok / Pol.	slope
Stor / Dan.; Nor.; Swed.	great
Store / Dan.	great
Stræde / Dan.	strait
Strana / Rus.	land
Strand / Germ.; Nor.; Swed.; Afr.; Dan.	beach
Straße / Germ.	street, road
Strath / Gae.	valley
Straum / Nor.; Swed.	stream
Střední / Cz.	central
Stredný / Slvk.	central
Strelka / Rus.	spit
Stret / Nor.	strait
Stretto / It.	strait
Strom / Germ.	stream
Strøm / Nor.	stream
Ström / Swed.	stream
Stroom / Dut.	stream
Su / Jap.	sandbank
Su / Tur.	river
Suando / Finn.	pond
Suid / Afr.	south
Suidō / Jap.	strait
Sul / Port.	south
Sund / Dan.; Nor.; Swed.; Germ.	strait
Sungai / Mal.	river
Sunn / Afr.	south
Süq / Ar.	market
Sur / Fr.	on
Sur / Sp.	south
Surkh / Pers.	red
Suu / Finn.	mouth, river mouth
Suur / Cat.	great
Svart / Nor.; Swed.	black
Sveti / S.C.; Slvn.	saint
Swa / Ban.	great
Swart / Afr.	black
Świety / Pol.	saint
Syrt / Alt.	ridge
Szállás / Hung.	village
Szczyt / Pol.	peak
Szeg / Hung.	bend
Székes / Hung.	residence
Szent / Hung.	saint
Sziget / Hung.	river island

T

Local Form	English
Tadi / Ban.	rock, cliff
Tae / Kor.	great
Tafua / Poly.	mountain
Tag / Alt.; Tur.	mountain
Tahta / Ar.	lower
Tahti / Ar.	lower
Tai / Chin.; Jap.	great
Taipale / Finn.	isthmus
Tajga / Rus.	forest
Take / Jap.	mountain
Tal / Germ.	valley
Tala / Mong.	plain, steppe
Tala / Ber.	spring
Tall / Ar.	hill
Talsperre / Germ.	dam
Tam / Viet.	stream
Tamgout / Ber.	peak
Tan / Chin.; Kor.	sandbank
Tana / Malag.	city, town
Tanana / Malag.	city, town
Tandjung / Mal.	cape, point
Tanezrouft / Ber.	desert
Tang / Tib.	upland
Tangeh / Pers.	strait
Tanjong / Mal.	cape, point
Tanjung, Tg. / Indon.	cape, point
Tanout / Ber.	well
Tao / Chin.	island
Taourirt / Ber.	peak
Targ / Pol.	market
Tărg / Bulg.	market
Tarn / Eng.	glacial lake
Tarso / Sah.	crater
Taš / Alt.	stone

Geographical Glossary

Local Form	English
Tassili / *Ber.*	upland
Tau / *Tur.*	mountain
Taung / *Burm.*	mountain
Ţawîl / *Ar.*	hill
Tégi / *Sah.*	hill
Teguidda / *Ber.*	well
Tehi / *Ber.*	pass, mountain
Teich / *Germ.*	pond
Tell / *Tur.*	hill
Telok / *Mal.*	bay, port
Teluk / *Mal.*	bay, port
Tempio / *It.*	temple
Ténéré / *Ber.*	rocky desert
Tengah / *Indon.; Mal.*	central
Tepe / *Tur.*	hill
Tepesi / *Tur.*	hill
Termas / *Sp.*	thermal springs
Terme / *It.*	thermal springs
Terra / *It.; Dut.*	land, earth
Terrazzo / *It.*	guyot, tablemount
Terre / *Fr.*	land, earth
Teso / *Cat.*	hill
Téssa / *Ber.*	wadi, depression
Testa / *It.*	point
Tête / *Fr.*	peak
Tetri / *Georg.*	white
Teu / *Poly.*	reef
Teze / *Alt.*	new
Tg., Tanjung / *Indon.*	cape, point
Thaba / *Ban.*	mountain
Thabana / *Ban.*	mountain
Thal / *Germ.*	valley
Thálassa / *Gr.*	sea
Thale / *Thai*	lagoon
Thamad / *Ar.*	well
Theós / *Gr.*	god
Thermes / *Fr.*	thermal springs
Thog / *Tib.*	high, upper
Tian / *Chin.*	field
Tiefe / *Germ.*	deep
Tierra / *Sp.*	land, earth
Timur / *Indon.; Mal.*	eastern
Tind / *Nor.*	mountain
Tinto / *Sp.*	black
Tirg / *Rom.*	market
Tis / *Amh.*	new
Tizgui / *Ber.*	forest
Tizi / *Ber.*	pass
Tjåkko / *Lapp.*	mountain
Tjärn / *Swed.*	tarn, glacial lake
Tji / *Mal.*	stream
To / *Kor.*	island
To / *Mel.*	stream
Tô / *Jap.*	island
Tó / *Hung.*	lake
To / *Ural.*	lake
Tobe / *Tur.*	hill
Tofua / *Poly.*	mountain
Tog / *Som.*	valley
Tōge / *Jap.*	pass
Tokoj / *Alt.*	forest
Tônle / *Khm.*	stream, lake
Tope / *Dut.*	peak
Toplice / *S.C.; Slvn.*	thermal springs
Topp / *Nor.*	peak
Tor / *Gae.*	rock
Tor / *Germ.*	gate
Torbat / *Pers.*	tomb
Törl / *Germ.*	pass
Torp / *Swed.*	hut
Torre / *Cat.; It.; Sp.; Port.*	tower
Torrente / *It.; Sp.*	torrent, stream
Tossa / *Cat.*	mountain, peak
Tota / *Sin.*	port
Tour / *Fr.*	tower
Traforo / *It.*	tunnel
Träsk / *Swed.*	lake
Trg / *S.C.*	market
Trog / *Germ.*	trough, trench
Trois / *Fr.*	three
Trung / *Viet.*	central
Tse / *Tib.*	peak, point
Tsi / *Chin.*	pond
Tskali / *Georg.*	river
Tsu / *Jap.*	bay
Tulúl / *Ar.*	hills
Tûnel / *Pers.*	tunnel
Tunturi / *Lapp.*	mountain, tundra
Tur'ah / *Ar.*	irrigation canal
Turm / *Germ.*	tower
Turn / *Rom.*	tower
Turó / *Cat.*	dome
Tuz / *Tur.*	salt
Týn / *Cz.*	fortress

U

Local Form	English
U., Unter-, Upon / *Eng.; Germ.*	under, lower
Uaimh / *Gae.*	cave
Uchi / *Jap.*	bay
Udde / *Swed.*	cape
Údolní nádrž / *Cz.*	reservoir
Uebi / *Som.*	river
Új- / *Hung.*	new
Ujście / *Pol.*	mouth
Ujung / *Indon.*	point, cape
Ul / *Chin.; Mong.*	mountain, mountain range
Ula / *Mong.*	mountain range
Ulan / *Mong.*	red
Uls / *Mong.*	state
Umi / *Jap.*	bay
Umm / *Ar.*	mother, spring
Umne / *Mong.*	south
Under / *Mong.*	mountain, peak
Ungur / *Alt.*	cave
Unter-, U. / *Germ.*	under, lower
Upar / *Hin.*	river
'Uqlat / *Ar.*	well
Ûr / *Tam.*	city, town
Ura / *Jap.*	bay, coast
Ura / *Alt.*	depression
Urd / *Mong.*	south
Uru / *Tam.*	city, town
Ušće / *S.C.*	mouth
Uske / *Alt.*	upper
Ust / *Rus.*	mouth
Ústi / *Cz.*	mouth
Ustup / *Rus.*	terrace
Utan / *Indon.; Mal.*	forest
Utara / *Indon.*	north, northern
Uusi / *Finn.*	new
Uval / *Rus.*	height
Úval / *Cz.*	mountain
'Uwaynät / *Ar.*	well
Uzboj / *Alt.*	river bed
Uzun / *Tur.*	long
Užürekis / *Lith.*	gulf

V

Local Form	English
Va / *Alb.*	ford
Va / *Ural.*	water, river
Vaara / *Finn.*	mountain
Väärti / *Finn.*	bay
Vad / *Rom.*	ford
Vær / *Nor.*	port
Våg / *Nor.*	bay
Vähä / *Finn.*	little
Väike / *Est.*	little
Väin / *Est.*	strait
Val / *Fr.; It.*	valley
Val / *Rom.; Rus.*	wall
Valico / *It.*	pass
Vall / *Cat.*	valley
Vall / *Swed.*	pasture
Valle / *It.; Sp.*	valley
Vallée / *Fr.*	valley
Vallei / *Afr.*	valley
Vallo / *It.*	wall
Valta / *Finn.*	cape
Váltos / *Gr.*	marsh
Valul / *Rom.*	wall
Vann / *Dan.; Nor.*	water, lake
Vanua / *Mel.*	land
Vár / *Hung.*	fort
Vara / *Finn.*	mountain
Varoš / *S.C.*	city, town
Város / *Hung.*	city, town
Varre / *Lapp.*	mountain
Vary / *Cz.*	spring
Vas / *S.C.; Slvn.*	village
Vásár / *Hung.*	market
Väst / *Swed.*	west
Väster / *Swed.*	western
Vatn / *Icel.; Nor.*	lake
Vatten / *Swed.*	water, lake
Vatu / *Mel.; Poly.*	island, reef
Vdhr., Vodohranilišče / *Rus.*	reservoir
Vechiu / *Rom.*	old
Vecs / *Latv.*	old
Veen / *Dut.; Fle.*	moor
Vega / *Sp.*	irrigated crops
Veld / *Afr.; Dut.; Fle.*	field
Veli / *S.C.; Slvn.*	great
Velik / *Bulg.*	great
Veliki / *Rus.; S.C.; Slvn.*	great
Veliký / *Cz.*	great
Velký / *Cz.*	great
Vel'ky / *Slvk.*	great
Vella / *Cat.*	old
Ver / *Ural.*	forest
Verde / *It.; Sp.*	green
Verh / *Rus.*	peak
Verhni / *Rus.*	upper
Verk / *Swed.*	factory
Vermelho / *Port.*	red
Vert / *Fr.*	green
Ves / *Cz.*	village
Vesi / *Finn.*	water, lake
Vest / *Dan.; Nor.*	west
Vester / *Dan.; Nor.*	western
Vestur / *Icel.*	west
Vetta / *It.*	summit
Viaduc / *Fr.*	viaduct
Vidda / *Nor.*	upland
Vidde / *Nor.*	upland
Viejo / *Sp.*	old
Vier / *Germ.*	four
Viertel / *Germ.*	quarter
Vieux / *Fr.*	old
Vig / *Dan.*	bay
Vik / *Icel., Nor.; Swed.*	gulf, bay
Vila / *Port.*	city, town
Villa / *Sp.*	city, town
Ville, -ville / *Eng.; Fr.*	city, town
Vinh / *Viet.*	bay
Virful / *Rom.*	peak, mountain
Virta / *Finn.*	river
Višni / *Rus.*	high
Visok / *S.C.*	high
Viz / *Hung.*	water
Viztároló / *Hung.*	reservoir
Vlakte / *Dut.; Fle.*	plain
Vlei / *Afr.*	pond
Vliet / *Dut.; Fle.*	river
Vloer / *Afr.*	depression
Voda / *Bulg.; Cz.; Rus.; S.C.; Slvn.*	water
Vodny put / *Rus.*	stream, canal
Vodohranilišče, vdhr. / *Rus.*	reservoir
Vodopad / *Rus.*	waterfall
Volcan / *Fr.*	volcano
Volcán / *Sp.*	volcano
Voll / *Nor.*	meadow
Vórios / *Gr.*	northern
Vorota / *Rus.*	gate
Vorrás / *Gr.*	north
Vostočny / *Rus.*	eastern
Vostok / *Rus.*	east
Vötn / *Icel.*	lake, water
Vož / *Ural.*	mouth
Vozvyšennost / *Rus.*	upland
Vpadina / *Rus.*	depression
Vrah / *Bulg.*	peak
Vrata / *Bulg.; S.C.; Slvn.*	pass
Vrch / *Cz.; Slvk.*	mountain
Vrch / *S.C.; Slvn.*	peak
Vrchni- / *Cz.*	upper
Vrchovina / *Cz.*	upland
Vulcan / *Rom.; Rus.*	volcano
Vulcano / *It.*	volcano
Vulkan / *Germ.; Rus.*	volcano
Vuopio / *Lapp.*	bend
Vuori / *Finn.*	rock
Východný / *Cz.*	eastern
Vyšný / *Slvk.*	upper
Vysoki / *Rus.*	high
Vysoky / *Cz.; Slvk.*	high
Vyšši / *Cz.*	high

W

Local Form	English
W., Wâdî / *Ar.*	wadi
Wa / *Ban.*	people
Wabe / *Amh.*	stream
Wad / *Ar.*	wadi
Wad / *Dut.*	tidal flat
Wâdî, W. / *Ar.*	wadi
Wâḩät / *Ar.*	oasis
Wai / *Mel.; Poly.*	stream
Wal / *Afr.*	wall
Wala / *Hin.*	mountain range
Wald / *Germ*	forest
Wan / *Burm.*	village
Wan / *Chin.; Jap.*	bay
Wand / *Germ.*	bluff
War / *Som.*	pond
Wâr / *Ar.*	desert
-waram / *Hin.; Tam.*	village
Wasser / *Germ.*	water
Wat / *Pol.*	wall
Wat / *Thai*	church
Waterval / *Afr.; Dut.*	waterfall
Watt / *Germ.*	tidal flat
Wâw / *Ar.*	oasis
Weald / *Eng.*	wooded country
Webi / *Som.*	stream
Weg / *Germ.*	way, road
Wei / *Chin.*	cape, point
Weide / *Germ.*	pasture
Weiler / *Germ.*	village
Weiß / *Germ.*	white
Weon / *Kor.*	field
Wer / *Som.*	pond
Werder / *Germ.*	river island
Werk / *Germ.*	factory
Wes / *Afr.*	west
Westlich / *Germ.*	western
Westr- / *Sca.*	western
Wêyn / *Som.*	great
Wêyne / *Som.*	great
Wick / *Eng.*	village
Wiek / *Germ.*	bay
Wielki / *Pol.*	great
Wieś / *Pol.*	village
Wijk / *Dut.; Fle.*	quarter, district
-willer / *Germ.*	village
Woda / *Pol.*	water
Woestyn / *Afr.*	desert
Wold / *Dut.; Fle.; Eng.*	forest
Wörth / *Germ.*	river island
Woud / *Dut.; Fle.*	forest
Wschodni / *Pol.*	eastern
Wysoczyzna / *Pol.*	upland
Wysoki / *Pol.*	upper
Wyspa / *Pol.*	island
Wyżyna / *Pol.*	highland
Wzgórze / *Pol.*	hill

X

Local Form	English
Xi / *Chin.*	west
Xia / *Chin.*	gorge, strait
Xian / *Chin.*	county, shire
Xiang / *Chin.*	village
Xiao / *Chin.*	little
Xin / *Chin.*	new
Xu / *Chin.*	island

Y

Local Form	English
Yam / *Hebr.*	lake, sea
Yama / *Jap.*	mountain
Yan / *Chin.*	mountain
Yang / *Chin.*	strait, ocean
Yani / *Tur.*	new
Yar / *Tur.*	gorge
Yarimada / *Tur.*	peninsula
Yazı / *Tur.*	plain
Yegge / *Sah.*	well
Yeni / *Tur.*	new
Yeon / *Kor.*	sea
Yeong / *Kor.*	mountain
Yeşil / *Tur.*	green
Ylä / *Finn.*	upper
Yli- / *Finn.*	upper
Yō / *Jap.*	ocean
Yobe / *Sud.*	great
Yŏm / *Kor.*	island
Yoma / *Burm.*	mountain range
Yŏn / *Kor.*	lake, pond
Yŏng / *Kor.*	mountain, peak
Ytter / *Nor.; Swed.*	outer
Yttre / *Swed.*	outer
Yu / *Chin.*	old
Yu / *Chin.*	island
Yu / *Jap.*	thermal spring
Yüan / *Chin.*	spring, river
Yunhe / *Chin.*	canal

Z

Local Form	English
Zāb / *Ar.*	river
Zachodni / *Pol.*	western
Zaki / *Jap.*	cape
Zalew / *Pol.*	gulf
Zaliv / *Bulg.; Rus.; S.C.; Slvn.*	gulf
Zaljev / *Slvn.*	bay
Zámek / *Cz.*	castle
Zan / *Jap.*	mountain
Zand / *Dut.; Fle.*	sand
Zandt / *Dut.; Fle.*	sand
Zangbo / *Chin.*	river
Zapad / *Rus.*	west
Zapaden / *Bulg.*	western
Zapadni / *S.C.; Slvn.*	western
Západni / *Cz.*	western
Zapadny / *Rus.*	western
Zapovednik / *Rus.*	reserve
Zatoka / *Pol.*	gulf
Zavod / *Rus.*	roadstead
Zäwiyat / *Ar.*	monastery
Zdrój / *Pol.*	thermal springs
Ze / *Jap.*	islet
Zee / *Dut.; Fle.*	sea
Zelёny / *Rus.*	green
Žem / *Lith.*	land, country
Země / *Cz.; Slvk.*	land, country
Zemlja / *Rus.*	land
Zen / *Jap.*	mountain
Zhan / *Chin.*	mountain
Zhen / *Chin.*	market
Zhong / *Chin.*	central
Zhou / *Chin.*	quarter, district
Zhuang / *Chin.*	village
Ziemia / *Pol.*	land
Zigos / *Gr.*	pass
Zipfel / *Germ.*	tip, point
Ziwa / *Swa.*	marsh
Zizhiqu / *Chin.*	autonomous region
Zlato / *Bulg.*	gold
Zuid / *Dut.; Fle.*	south
Zuidelijk / *Dut.*	southern
Żuława / *Dut.*	marsh
Zun / *Mong.*	east
Zwart / *Dut.*	black
Zwei / *Germ.*	two

Maps of the World Index

of the toponyms (place-names) which appear on the maps are listed in
e Maps of the World Index. Each entry includes the following: Place-name
d, where applicable, other forms by which it is written or known; a symbol,
ere applicable, indicating what kind of feature it is; the page on which the
ap appears; and the map-reference letters and geographical coordinates
dicating its location on the map.

oponyms

ch toponym, or place-name, is written in full, with accents and diacritical
arks. Since many countries have more than one official language, many of
ese forms are included on the maps. For example, many Belgian
ace-names are listed as follows: Bruxelles/Brussel; Antwerpen/Anvers, and
e versa, Brussel/Bruxelles; Anvers/Antwerpen. In Italy, certain regions
ve a special status—they are largely autonomous and officially bilingual.
 a result, Index listings appears as follows: Aosta/Aoste; Alto Adige/Sud
ol, and vice versa. One name, however, may be the only name on the
ap.
In China, the written forms of commonly used regional languages have
en taken into account. These forms are enclosed in parenthesis following
e official name: e.g. Xiangshan (Dancheng). However, when the regional is
ed first, it is linked to the official name with an→: e.g. Dancheng→Xiangshan.
e same style is used for former or historical name forms: e.g.
odesia→Zimbabwe and Zimbabwe (Rhodesia).
Place-names for major features (countries, major cities, and large physical
atures), where applicable, include the English conventional form identified
 (EN) and linked in the local name or names with an = sign: e.g.
lia=Italy (EN), and vice versa, Italy (EN)=Italia. Former English names
 linked in the Index to the conventional form by an→.

ymbols

e last component with the place-name is a symbol, where applicable,
ecifying the broad category of the feature named. A table preceding the
dex lists all of the symbols used and their meanings; this information also
pears as a footnote on each page of the Index. Place names without
mbols are cities and towns.

lphabetization

ace-names are listed in English alphabetical order—26 letters, from A to
—because of its international usage. Names including two or more words
 listed alphabetically according to the first letter of the word: e.g. De
uyter is listed under D; Le Havre is listed under L. Names with the prefix
 are listed as if spelled Mac. The generic portion of a name (lake, sierra,
ountain, etc.) is placed after the name: e.g. Lake Erie is listed as Erie,
ke; Sierra Morena is listed as Morena, Sierra. In Spanish, "ch" and "ll"
oups and the letter "n" are included respectively under C, L, and N,
thout any distinction.
The same place-name sometimes is listed in the Index several times. It
ay because of the various translations of a name, or it may be that several
aces have the same name.

Various translations of a name appear as follows:

Danube (EN) = Dunav   Danube (EN) = Donau
Danube (EN) = Dunărea   Danube (EN) = Dunaj

Several places with the same name appear as follows; however, only in
these cases is the location—abbreviated and enclosed in brackets—included.
A table of these abbreviations precedes the Index.

Abbeville [U.S.]   Aberdeen [Scot.-U.K.]
Abbeville [Fr.]   Aberdeen [N.C.-U.S.]
Aberdeen [S. Afr.]

Page References

Page references to two-page maps always refer to the left-hand page. If a
page contains several maps or insets, a lowercase letter identifies the
specific map or inset.

Although a place-name may appear on one or more maps, it is indexed to
only one map. Most places are indexed to the regional maps. However, if a
place-name appears on either the physical or political continental maps, it is
indexed to one of the two types of map. For example, a river or mountain
would be indexed to a physical continental map; a city or state would be
indexed to a political continental map.

Map-Reference Letters and Geographical Coordinates

The next elements in the Index listing are the map-reference letters and the
geographical coordinates, respectively, locating the place on the map.

Map-reference letters consist of a capital and a lowercase letter. Capital
letters are across the top and bottom of the maps; lowercase letters are
down the sides. The map-reference letters assigned to each place-name
refer to the location of the name within the area formed by grid lines
connecting the geographical coordinates on either sides of the letters.

Geographical coordinates are the latitude (N for North, S for South) and
longitude (E for East, W for West) expressed in degrees and minutes and
based on the prime meridian, Greenwich.

Map-reference letters and coordinates for extensive geographical features,
such as mountain ranges and countries, are given for the approximate
central point of the area. Those for waterways, such as canals and rivers,
are given for the mouth of the river, the point where it enters another river or
where the feature reaches the map margin. On this page are sample maps
showing points to which features are indexed according to map-reference
letters and coordinates.

On most maps there is not enough space to place all the names of
administrative subdivisions. In these cases the location of the place is shown
on the map by a circled letter or number and the place-name and circled
letter or number are listed in the map margin. The map-reference numbers
and coordinates for these places refer to the location of the circled letter or
number on the map.

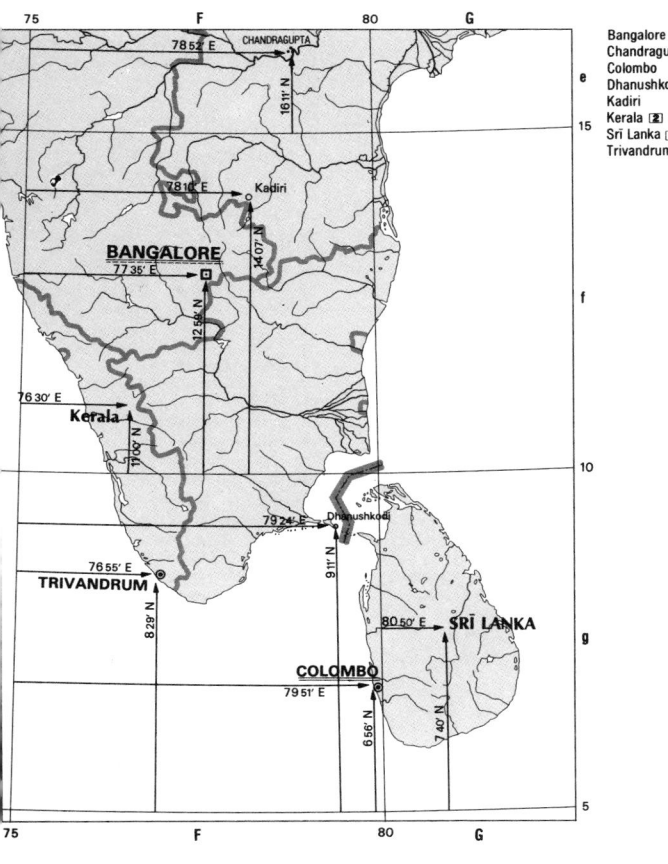

Bangalore	148	Ff	12°59'N 77°35'E
Chandragupta ▣	148	Fe	16°11'N 78°52'E
Colombo	148	Fg	6°56'N 79°51'E
Dhanushkodi	148	Fg	9°11'N 79°24'E
Kadiri	148	Ff	14°07'N 78°10'E
Kerala ②	148	Ff	11°00'N 76°30'E
Sri Lanka ①	148	Gg	7°40'N 80°50'E
Trivandrum	148	Fg	8°29'N 76°55'E

Alaska ▣	174	Dc	65°00'N 153°00'W
Alaska, Gulf of- ◪	174	Ed	58°00'N 146°00'W
Alexander Archipelago ▣	174	Fd	56°30'N 134°00'W
Barrow, Point- ▣	174	Db	71°23'N 156°30'W
Bering Strait ▣	174	Cc	65°30'N 169°00'W
Coast Mountains ▣	174	Gd	55°00'N 129°00'W
Kodiak ▣	174	Dd	57°30'N 153°30'W
Yukon ▣	174	Cc	62°33'N 163°59'W

List of Abbreviations

Afg. Afghanistan
Afr. Africa
Agl. Anguilla
Ak.-U.S. Alaska, U.S.
Al.-U.S. Alabama, U.S.
Alb. Albania
Alg. Algeria
Alta.-Can. Alberta, Canada
Am. Sam. American Samoa
And. Andorra
Ang. Angola
Ant. Antarctica
Ar.-U.S. Arkansas, U.S.
Arg. Argentina
Arm. Armenia
Asia Asia
Atg. Antigua and Barbuda
Aus. Austria
Austl. Australia
Az.-U.S. Arizona, U.S.
Azer. Azerbaijan
Azr. Azores
Bah. Bahamas
Bar. Barbados
B.A.T. British Antarctic Territory
B.C.-Can. British Columbia, Canada
Bel. Belgium
Bela. Belarus
Ben. Benin
Ber. Bermuda
Bhr. Bahrain
Bhu. Bhutan
Blz. Belize
Bnd. Burundi
Bngl. Bangladesh
Bol. Bolivia
Bos. Bosnia and Herzegovina
Bots. Botswana
Braz. Brazil
Bru. Brunei
Bul. Bulgaria
Bur. Burma
Burkina Burkina Faso
B.V.I. British Virgin Islands
Ca.-U.S. California, U.S.
Cam. Cameroon
C. Amer. Central America
Can. Canada
Can. Is. Canary Islands
C.A.R. Central African Republic
Cay. Is Cayman Islands
Chad Chad
Chan. Is. Channel Islands
Chile Chile
China China
Co.-U.S. Colorado, U.S.
Cocos Is. Cocos Islands
Col. Colombia
Con. Congo
Cook Cook Islands
Cor. Sea Is. Coral Sea Islands
C.R. Costa Rica
Cro. Croatia
Ct.-U.S. Connecticut, U.S.
Cuba Cuba

C.V. Cape Verde
Cyp. Cyprus
Czech. Czech Republic
D.C.-U.S. District of Columbia, U.S.
De.-U.S. Delaware, U.S.
Den. Denmark
Dji. Djibouti
Dom. Dominica
Dom. Rep. Dominican Republic
Ec. Ecuador
Eg. Egypt
El Sal. El Salvador
Eng.-U.K. England, U.K.
Eq. Gui. Equatorial Guinea
Est. Estonia
Eth. Ethiopia
Eur. Europe
Falk. Is. Falkland Islands
Far. Is. Faeroe Islands
Fiji Fiji
Fin. Finland
Fl.-U.S. Florida, U.S.
Fr. France
Fr. Gui. French Guiana
Fr. Poly. French Polynesia
F.S.M. Federated States of Micronesia
Ga.-U.S. Georgia, U.S.
Gabon Gabon
Gam. Gambia
Geor. Georgia
Ger. Germany
Ghana Ghana
Gib. Gibraltar
Grc. Greece
Gren. Grenada
Grld. Greenland
Guad. Guadeloupe
Guam Guam
Guat. Guatemala
Gui. Guinea
Gui. Bis. Guinea Bissau
Guy. Guyana
Haiti Haiti
Hi.-U.S. Hawaii, U.S.
H.K. Hong Kong
Hond. Honduras
Hun. Hungary
Ia.-U.S. Iowa, U.S.
I.C. Ivory Coast
Ice. Iceland
Id.-U.S. Idaho, U.S.
Il.-U.S. Illinois, U.S.
In.-U.S. Indiana, U.S.
India India
Indon. Indonesia
I. of M. Isle of Man
Iran Iran
Iraq Iraq
Ire. Ireland
Isr. Israel
It. Italy
Jam. Jamaica
Jap. Japan
Jor. Jordan
Kam. Cambodia
Kaz. Kazakhstan
Kenya Kenya

Ker. Is. Kermadec Islands
Kir. Kiribati
Ks.-U.S. Kansas, U.S.
Kuw. Kuwait
Ky.-U.S. Kentucky, U.S.
Kyrg. Kyrgyzstan
La.-U.S. Louisiana, U.S.
Laos Laos
Lat. Latvia
Lbr. Liberia
Leb. Lebanon
Les. Lesotho
Lib. Libya
Liech. Liechtenstein
Lith. Lithuania
Lux. Luxembourg
Ma.-U.S. Massachusetts, U.S.
Mac. Macao
Mace. Macedonia
Mad. Madagascar
Mala. Malaysia
Mald. Maldives
Mali Mali
Malta Malta
Man.-Can. Manitoba, Canada
Mar. Is. Marshall Islands
Mart. Martinique
Maur. Mauritius
May. Mayotte
Mco. Monaco
Md.-U.S. Maryland, U.S.
Me.-U.S. Maine, U.S.
Mex. Mexico
Mi.-U.S. Michigan, U.S.
Mid. Is. Midway Islands
Mn.-U.S. Minnesota, U.S.
Mo.-U.S. Missouri, U.S.
Mol. Moldova
Mong. Mongolia
Mont. Montserrat
Mor. Morocco
Moz. Mozambique
Ms.-U.S. Mississippi, U.S.
Mt.-U.S. Montana, U.S.
Mtna. Mauritania
Mwi. Malawi
Nam. Namibia
N. Amer. North America
Nauru Nauru
N.B.-Can. New Brunswick, Canada
Nb.-U.S. Nebraska, U.S.
N.C.-U.S. North Carolina, U.S.
N. Cal. New Caledonia
N.D.-U.S. North Dakota, U.S.
Nep. Nepal
Neth. Netherlands
Neth. Ant. Netherlands Antilles
Newf.-Can. Newfoundland, Canada
N.H.-U.S. New Hampshire, U.S.
Nic. Nicaragua
Nig. Nigeria
Niger Niger

N. Ire.-U.K. Northern Ireland, U.K.
N.J.-U.S. New Jersey, U.S.
N. Kor. North Korea
N.M.-U.S. New Mexico, U.S.
N. M. Is. Northern Mariana Islands
Nor. Norway
Nor. I. Norfolk Island
N.S.-Canada Nova Scotia, Canada
Nv.-U.S. Nevada, U.S.
N.W.T.-Can. Northwest Territories, Canada
N.Y.-U.S. New York, U.S.
N.Z. New Zealand
Ocn. Oceania
Oh.-U.S. Ohio, U.S.
Ok.-U.S. Oklahoma, U.S.
Oman Oman
Ont.-Ont. Ontario, Canada
Or.-U.S. Oregon, U.S.
Pa.-U.S. Pennsylvania, U.S.
Pak. Pakistan
Pal. Palau
Pan. Panama
Pap. N. Gui. Papua New Guinea
Par. Paraguay
Pas. Pascua
P.E.I.-Can. Prince Edward Island, Canada
Peru Peru
Phil. Philippines
Pit. Pitcairn
Pol. Poland
Port. Portugal
P.R. Puerto Rico
Qatar Qatar
Que.-Can. Quebec, Canada
Reu. Reunion
R.I.-U.S. Rhode Island, U.S.
Rom. Romania
Russia Russia
Rwn. Rwanda
S. Afr. South Africa
S. Amer. South America
Sao T.P. Sao Tome and Principe
Sask.-Can. Saskatchewan, Canada
Sau. Ar. Saudi Arabia
S.C.-U.S. South Carolina, U.S.
Scot.-U.K. Scotland, U.K.
S.D.-U.S. South Dakota, U.S.
Sen. Senegal
Sey. Seychelles
Sing. Singapore
S. Kor. South Korea
S.L. Sierra Leone
S. Lan. Sri Lanka
Slo. Slovenia
Slvk. Slovakia
S.M. San Marino
S.N.A. Spanish North Africa
Sol. Is. Solomon Islands
Som. Somalia
Sp. Spain

St. C.N. Saint Christopher-Nevis
St. Hel. Saint Helena
St. Luc. Saint Lucia
St. P.M. Saint Pierre and Miquelon
St. Vin. Saint Vincent and the Grenadines
Sud. Sudan
Sur. Suriname
Sval. Svalbard
Swe. Sweden
Switz. Switzerland
Syr. Syria
Tai. Taiwan
Taj. Tajikstan
Tan. Tanzania
T.C. Is. Turks and Caicos Islands
Thai. Thailand
Tn.-U.S. Tennessee, U.S.
Togo Togo
Ton. Tonga
Trin. Trinidad and Tobago
T.T.P.I. Trust Territory of the Pacific Islands
Tun. Tunisia
Tur. Turkey
Turk. Turkmenistan
Tuv. Tuvalu
Tx.-U.S. Texas, U.S.
U.A.E. United Arab Emirates
Ug. Uganda
U.K. United Kingdom
Ukr. Ukraine
Ur. Uruguay
U.S. United States
Ut.-U.S. Utah, U.S.
Uzb. Uzbekistan
Va.-U.S. Virginia, U.S.
Van. Vanuatu
V.C. Vatican City
Ven. Venezuela
Viet. Vietnam
V.I.U.S. Virgin Islands of the U.S.
Vt.-U.S. Vermont, U.S.
Wa.-U.S. Washington, U.S.
Wake Wake Island
Wales-U.K. Wales, U.K.
W.F. Wallis and Futuna
Wi.-U.S. Wisconsin, U.S.
W. Sah. Western Sahara
W. Sam. Western Samoa
W.V.-U.S. West Virginia, U.S.
Wy.-U.S. Wyoming, U.S.
Yem. Yemen
Yugo. Yugoslavia
Yuk.-Can. Yukon, Canada
Zaire Zaire
Zam. Zambia
Zimb. Zimbabwe

List of Symbols

Plains and Associated Features
Plain, Basin, Lowland
Delta
Salt Flat

Valleys and Depressions
Valley, Gorge, Ravine, Canyon
Cave, Crater, Quarry
Karst Features
Depression
Polder, Reclaimed Marsh

Vegetational Features
Desert, Dunes
Forest, Woods
Heath, Steppe, Tundra, Moor
Oasis

Political/Administrative Units
1 Independent Nation
2 State, Canton, Region
3 Province, Department, County, Territory, District
4 Municipality
5 Colony, Dependency, Administered Territory

Geographical Regions
Continent
Physical Region
Historical or Cultural Region

Mountain Features
Mount, Mountain, Peak
Volcano
Hill
Mountains, Mountain Range
Hills, Escarpment
Plateau, Highland, Upland
Pass, Gap

Coastal Features
Cape, Point
Coast, Beach
Cliff
Peninsula, Promontory
Isthmus
Sandbank, Tombolo, Sandbar

Islands Rocks, Reefs
Island
Atoll
Rock, Reef
Islands, Archipelago
Rocks, Reefs
Coral Reef

Hydrographic Features
Well, Spring
Geyser, Fumarole
River, Stream, Brook
Waterfall, Rapids, Cataract
River Mouth, Estuary
Lake
Salt Lake
Intermittent Lake, Dry Lake Bed
Reservoir, Artificial Lake
Swamp, Marsh, Pond
Irrigation Canal, Navigable Canal, Ditch, Aqueduct

Ice Features
Glacier, Snowfield
Ice Shelf, Pack Ice

Marine Features
Ocean
Sea
Gulf, Bay
Strait, Fjord, Sea Channel
Lagoon, Anchorage

Submarine Features
Bank, Shoal
Seamount
Rise, Plateau, Tablemount
Seamount Chain, Ridge
Platform, Shelf
Basin, Depression
Escarpment, Slope, Sea Scarp
Fracture
Trench, Abyss, Valley, Canyon

Other Features
National Park, Nature Reserve
Scenic Area, Point of Interest
Recreation Site, Sports Arena
Cave, Cavern
Historic Site, Memorial, Mausoleum, Museum
Ruins
Wall, Walls, Tower, Castle, Fortress
Church, Abbey, Cathedral, Sanctuary
Temple, Synagogue, Mosque
Research or Scientific Station
Railway station
Airport, Heliport
Port, Dock
Military installation
Lighthouse
Mine
Tunnel
Dam, Bridge

A

Å 114 Cc 67.53N 12.59 E
Aa [Eur.] 124 Ic 51.50N 6.25 E
Aa [Fr.] 122 Ic 51.01N 2.06 E
Aa [Fr.] 124 Dd 50.44N 2.18 E
Aa [Ger.] 124 Kb 52.07N 8.41 E
Aa [Ger.] 124 Jb 52.15N 7.18 E
Aa [Neth.] 124 Hc 51.42N 5.20 E
Aachen 120 Cf 50.46N 6.06 E
Aalen 120 Gh 48.50N 10.06 E
A'âlî an Nîl 168 Ed 9.15N 33.00 E
Aalsmeer 124 Gb 52.15N 4.45 E
Aalst/Alost 122 Kd 50.56N 4.02 E
Aalten 124 Ic 51.55N 6.35 E
Aalter 124 Fc 51.05N 3.27 E
Äänekoski 114 Fe 62.36N 25.44 E
Aa of Weerijs 124 Gc 51.35N 4.46 E
Aar 124 Kd 50.23N 8.00 E
Aarau 128 Cc 47.25N 8.02 E
Aarbergen 124 Kd 50.13N 8.03 E
Aare 128 Cc 47.37N 8.13 E
Aargau 128 Cc 47.30N 8.10 E
Aarlen/Arlon 122 Le 49.41N 5.49 E
Aarschot 122 Kd 50.59N 4.50 E
Aat/Ath 122 Jd 50.38N 3.47 E
Aazanèn 126 Ii 35.06N 3.02W
Āb 146 Md 36.00N 48.05 E
Aba [Nig.] 160 Hh 5.07N 7.22 E
Aba [Zaire] 160 Kh 3.52N 30.14 E
Aba/Ngawa 152 He 32.55N 101.45 E
Abā ad Dūd 146 Ki 27.02N 44.04 E
Abā as Su'ūd 144 Ff 17.28N 44.06 E
Abacaxis, Rio- 202 Gd 3.54S 58.50W
Abaco Island 174 Lg 26.25N 77.10W
Abacou, Pointe l'- 194 Kd 18.03N 73.47W
Abadab, Jabal- 168 Fb 18.53N 35.59 E
Ābādān 142 Gf 30.10N 48.50 E
Ābādeh [Iran] 144 Hc 31.10N 52.37 E
Ābādeh [Iran] 146 Oh 29.08N 52.52 E
Abadiânia 204 Hc 16.06S 48.48W
Abadla 160 Ge 31.01N 2.43W
Abaeté 204 Jd 19.09S 45.27W
Abaeté, Rio- 204 Jd 18.02S 45.12W
Abaetetuba 202 Id 1.42S 48.54W
Abagnar Qi (Xilin Hot) 142 Ne 43.58N 116.08 E
Abag Qi (Xin Hot) 152 Jc 44.01N 114.59 E
Abai 204 Eh 26.01S 55.57W
Abaiang Atoll 208 Id 1.51N 172.58 E
Abaj 136 Hf 49.38N 72.50 E
Abaji 166 Gd 8.28N 6.57 E
Abajo Mountains 188 Kh 37.50N 109.25W
Abakaliki 166 Gd 6.20N 8.03 E
Abakan 142 Ld 53.43N 91.26 E
Abakan 138 Ef 53.43N 91.30 E
Abakwasimbo 170 Eb 0.36N 28.43 E
Abala [Con.] 170 Cc 1.21S 15.30 E
Abala [Niger] 166 Fc 14.56N 3.26 E
Abalak 166 Gb 15.27N 6.17 E
Aban 138 Ee 56.40N 96.10 E
Abancay 202 Df 13.35S 72.55W
Abancourt 124 De 49.42N 1.46 E
Abanga 170 Bb 0.13N 10.28 E
Abano Terme 128 Fe 45.21N 11.47 E
Ābār al Jidd 146 Hf 32.50N 39.50 E
Abarqū 144 Hc 31.08N 53.17 E
Abarqu, Kavīr-e- 146 Og 31.00N 53.50 E
Abashiri 152 Pc 44.01N 144.17 E
Abashiri-Gawa 156a Db 43.56N 144.09 E
Abashiri-Ko 156a Da 44.00N 144.10 E
Abashiri-Wan 156a Da 44.00N 144.35 E
Abasolo 192 Je 24.04N 98.22W
Abatski 136 Hd 56.18N 70.28 E
Abau 214 Dj 10.11S 148.42 E
Abava 114 Eh 57.06N 21.54 E
Abay=Blue Nile (EN) 158 Kg 15.38N 32.31 E
Abaya, Lake- 158 Kh 6.20N 37.55 E
Abaza 138 Ef 52.39N 90.06 E
Abbadia San Salvatore 128 Fh 42.53N 11.41 E
Abbah Quşūr 128 Co 35.57N 8.50 E
Āb Bārīk 146 Oh 29.45N 52.37 E
'Abbāsābād 146 Qd 36.20N 56.25 E
Abbekås 116 Ei 55.24N 13.36 E
Abberton Reservoir 124 Cc 51.50N 0.55 E
Abbeville [Fr.] 122 Hd 50.06N 1.50 E
Abbeville [La.-U.S.] 186 Jl 29.58N 92.08W
Abbeville [S.C.-U.S.] 184 Fh 34.10N 82.23W
Abbey 188 Ka 50.43N 108.45W
Abbeyfeale/Mainistir na Féile 118 Di 52.24N 9.18W
Abbiategrasso 128 Ce 45.24N 8.54 E
Abbot, Mount- 212 Jd 20.03S 147.45 E
Abbot Ice Shelf 222 Pf 72.45S 96.00W
'Abd Al 'Azīz, Jabal- 146 Id 36.25N 40.20 E
'Abd al Kūrī 140 Hh 12.12N 52.13 E
Ābdānān 146 Lf 32.57N 47.26 E
Abdul Ghadir 168 Gc 10.42N 42.59 E
Abdulino 136 Fe 53.42N 53.38 E
Abe, Lake- 168 Gc 11.10N 41.45 E
Abéché 160 Jg 13.49N 20.49 E
Abeek 124 Hc 51.15N 6.00 E
Abe-Gawa 156 Fd 34.55N 138.22 E
Abeløya 179 Pc 79.00N 30.15 E
Abelvær 114 Cd 64.44N 11.11 E
Abemama Atoll 208 Id 0.21N 173.51 E
Abenab 172 Bc 19.12S 18.06 E
Abengourou 160 Gh 6.44N 3.29W
Abengourou 166 Ed 6.35N 3.25W
Åbenrå 114 Bi 55.02N 9.26 E
Åbenrå Fjord 116 Ci 55.05N 9.35 E
Abeokuta 160 Hh 7.09N 3.21 E
Aberaeron 118 Ii 52.15N 4.15W
Aberdare Range 158 Ki 0.25S 36.38 E
Aberdeen [Id.-U.S.] 188 Ie 42.57N 112.50W
Aberdeen [Md.-U.S.] 184 If 39.30N 76.14W
Aberdeen [Ms.-U.S.] 186 Lj 33.49N 88.33W
Aberdeen [N.C.-U.S.] 184 Hh 35.08N 79.26W
Aberdeen [S.Afr.] 172 Cf 32.29S 24.03 E
Aberdeen [Scot.-U.K.] 112 Fd 57.10N 2.04W
Aberdeen [S.D.-U.S.] 176 Je 45.28N 98.29W
Aberdeen [Wa.-U.S.] 182 Cb 46.59N 123.50W
Aberdeen Lake 180 Hd 64.28N 99.00W
Abergavenny 118 Kj 51.50N 3.00W
Aberystwyth 118 Ii 52.25N 4.05W
Abetone 128 Ef 44.08N 10.40 E
Abez 136 Gb 66.32N 61.46 E
Abhā 142 Gh 18.13N 42.30 E
Abhainn an Chláir/Clare 118 Dh 53.20N 9.03W
Abhainn an Lagáin/Lagan 118 Hg 54.37N 5.53W
Abhainn na Bandan/Bandon 118 Ej 51.40N 8.30W
Abhainn na Deirge/Derg 118 Fg 54.40N 7.25W
Abhar 144 Gb 36.09N 49.13 E
Abhar 146 Md 36.02N 49.45 E
Abhazskaja respublika 136 Eg 43.00N 41.10 E
Abibe, Serrania de- 202 Cb 8.00N 76.30W
Abidjan 160 Gh 5.19N 4.02W
Abidjan 166 Ed 5.30N 4.30W
Abilene [Ks.-U.S.] 186 Hg 38.55N 97.13W
Abilene [Tx.-U.S.] 176 Jf 32.27N 99.44W
Abingdon 118 Lj 51.41N 1.17W
Abinsk 132 Kg 44.52N 38.10 E
Abiquiu 186 Ch 36.12N 106.19W
Abiquiu Reservoir 186 Ch 36.18N 106.32W
Abisko 114 Eb 68.20N 18.51 E
Abitibi 180 Jf 51.04N 80.55W
Abitibi, Lake- 174 Le 48.42N 79.45W
Abiy Adi 168 Fc 13.37N 39.01 E
Abiyata, Lake- 168 Fd 7.38N 38.36 E
Abja-Paluoja 116 Kf 58.02N 25.14 E
Abnūb 164 Fd 27.16N 31.09 E
Åbo/Turku 112 Ic 60.27N 22.17 E
Abo, Massif d'- 168 Ba 21.41N 16.08 E
Abóboras, Serra das- 204 Jc 16.12S 44.35W
Abodo 168 Ed 7.50N 34.25 E
Aboisso 166 Ed 5.28N 3.12W
Aboisso 166 Ed 5.28N 3.02W
Abomey 160 Hh 7.11N 1.59 E
Abong Mbang 166 He 3.59N 13.11 E
Abony 120 Pi 47.11N 20.00 E
Aborigen, pik- 138 Jd 62.05N 149.10 E
Aborlan 150 Ge 9.26N 118.33 E
Aborrebierg 116 Ej 54.59N 12.32 E
Abou Deïa 168 Bc 11.27N 19.17 E
Abou Goulem 168 Cc 13.37N 21.38 E
Abovjan 132 Ni 40.14N 44.37 E
Abraham's Bay 194 Kb 22.21N 72.55W
Abramovski bereg 114 Kc 66.25N 43.05 E
Abrántes 126 De 39.28N 8.12W
Abra Pampa 206 Gb 22.43S 65.42W
Abrego 194 Ki 8.04N 73.14W
Abreojos, Punta- 190 Bc 26.42N 113.35W
Abrets, Les- 122 Li 45.32N 5.35 E
'Abrī 168 Ea 20.48N 30.20 E
Abrolhos, Arquipélago dos- 202 Kg 18.00S 38.40W
Abrud 130 Gc 46.16N 23.04 E
Abruka, ostrov- / Abruka saar 116 Jf 58.08N 22.25 E
Abruka saar / Abruka, ostrov- 116 Jf 58.08N 22.25 E
Abruzzi 128 Hh 42.20N 13.45 E
Absaroka Range 182 Fc 44.45N 109.50W
Abtenau 128 Hc 47.33N 13.21 E
Abū ad Duhūr 146 Ge 35.44N 37.02 E
Abū 'Alī 146 Mi 27.20N 49.33 E
Abū al Khaşīb 146 Lg 30.27N 47.59 E
Abū an Na'am 146 Hj 25.14N 38.49 E
Abū 'Arīsh 144 Ff 16.58N 42.50 E
Abū Ballāş 164 Ee 24.26N 27.39 E
Abū Daghmah 146 Hd 36.25N 38.15 E
Abū Darbah 164 Fd 28.29N 33.20 E
Abū Dhabi (EN)=Abū Zaby 142 Hg 24.28N 54.22 E
Abū Ḩad, Wādī- 146 Ei 27.46N 33.30 E
Abū Ḩadrīyah 146 Mi 27.20N 48.58 E
Abū Ḩamad 160 Kg 19.32N 33.19 E
Abū Ḩammād 146 Dg 30.32N 31.40 E
Abū Ḩarbah, Jabal- 146 Ei 27.17N 33.13 E
Abū Ḩashā'ifah, Khalīj- 146 Bg 31.16N 27.25 E
Abuja 160 Hh 9.10N 7.11 E
Abu Jābirah 168 Dc 11.04N 26.51 E
Abū Jifān 146 Lj 24.31N 47.43 E
Abū Kabīr 146 Dg 30.44N 31.40 E
Abū Kamāl 144 Fc 34.27N 40.55 E
Abukuma-Gawa 156 Gb 38.06N 140.52 E
Abukuma-Sanchi 156 Gc 37.20N 140.45 E
Abū Latt 164 Hf 19.58N 40.08 E
Abū Libdah, Khashm- 164 Ie 22.58N 46.13 E
Abū Madd, Ra's- 144 Ee 24.50N 37.12 E
Abū Maţāriq 168 Dc 10.58N 26.17 E
Abu Mendi 168 Fc 11.47N 35.42 E
Abumonbazi 170 Db 3.42N 22.10 E
Abū Muḩarrik, Ghurd- 164 Ed 27.00N 30.00 E
Abū Mūsa' 144 Hd 25.10N 55.00 E
Abū Musā, Jazīreh-ye- 144 Id 25.52N 55.03 E
Abunā 200 Jf 9.42S 65.23W
Abunā, Rio- 198 Jf 9.41S 65.23W
Abune Yosef 168 Fc 12.09N 39.12 E
Abū Qīr 146 Dg 31.19N 30.04 E
Abū Qīr, Khalīj- 146 Dg 31.20N 30.15 E
Abū Qumayyis, Ra's- 146 Nj 24.34N 51.30 E
Abu Road 148 Ed 24.29N 72.47 E
Abū Sawmah, Ra's- 146 Ei 26.51N 33.59 E
Abū Shanab 168 Dc 13.57N 27.47 E
Abu Simbel (EN) = Abū Sunbul 164 Fe 22.22N 31.38 E
Abū Şukhayr 146 Kg 31.52N 44.27 E
Abū Sunbul = Abu Simbel (EN) 164 Fe 22.22N 31.38 E
Abuta 154 Pc 42.31N 140.46 E
Abut Head 218 De 43.06S 170.15 E
Abū Tīj 164 Fd 27.02N 31.19 E
Abū Ţurţūr, Jabal- 146 Cj 25.20N 30.00 E
Abū'Urūq 168 Eb 15.54N 30.27 E
Abuyemeda 168 Fc 10.38N 39.43 E
Abū Zabad 168 Dc 12.21N 29.15 E
Abū Zaby=Abu Dhabi (EN) 142 Hg 24.28N 54.22 E
Abū Zanīmah 164 Fd 29.03N 33.06 E
Abwong 168 Ed 9.07N 32.12 E
Åby 116 Gf 58.40N 16.11 E
Abyad 168 Dc 13.46N 26.28 E
Abyaḑ, Al Baḩr al-=White Nile (EN) 168 Ec 12.40N 32.30 E
Abyaḑ, Al Baḩr al-=White Nile (EN) 158 Kg 15.38N 32.31 E
Abyaḑ, Ar Ra's al- 144 Ee 23.32N 38.32 E
Abyaḑ, Jabal- 168 Db 18.55N 28.40 E
Abyaḑ, Ra's al-=Blanc, Cape- (EN) 158 He 37.20N 9.50 E
Abyār Alī 146 Hj 24.25N 39.33 E
Abyār ash Shuwayrif 164 Bd 29.59N 14.16 E
Åbybro 114 Bh 57.09N 9.45 E
Abydos 164 Fd 26.11N 31.55 E
Abyei 168 Dd 9.36N 28.26 E
Ābyek 146 Nd 36.02N 50.31 E
Abymes 197e Ab 16.16N 61.31W
Acacías 202 Dc 3.59N 73.47W
Academy Gletscher 179 Ib 81.45N 33.35W
Acadie 174 Me 46.00N 65.00W
Acaill/Achill 118 Dh 54.00N 10.00W
Acajutla 194 Cg 13.36N 89.50W
Acalayong 166 Ge 1.05N 9.40 E
Acámbaro 190 Dd 20.02N 100.44W
Acandí 202 Cb 8.31N 77.17W
Acaponeta 190 Cd 22.30N 105.22W
Acaponeta, Rio- 192 Gf 22.20N 105.37W
Acapulco de Juárez 176 Jh 16.51N 99.55W
Acará 202 Id 1.57S 48.11W
Acarai, Serra- 202 Gc 1.50N 57.40W
Acaraú 202 Jd 2.53S 40.07W
Acaray, Rio- 204 Eg 25.29S 54.42W
Acari, Rio- [Braz.] 202 Ge 5.18S 59.42W
Acari, Rio- [Braz.] 204 Jb 16.00S 45.03W
Acarigua 202 Eb 9.33N 69.12W
Acatenango, Volcán- 174 Jh 14.30N 91.40W
Acatlán de Osorio 192 Jh 18.12N 98.03W
Acayucan 190 Fe 17.57N 94.55W
Accéglio 128 Af 44.28N 7.00 E
Aččitau, gora- 135 Cc 42.07N 60.31 E
Accomac 184 Jg 37.43N 75.40W
Accra 160 Gh 5.33N 0.13W
Acebal 204 Bk 33.14S 60.50W
Acebuches 192 Hc 28.15N 102.43W
Aceguá [Braz.] 204 Ej 31.52S 54.09W
Aceguá [Ur.] 204 Ej 31.52S 54.12W
Aceh 150 Cf 4.10N 96.50 E
Acerenza 128 Jj 40.48N 15.56 E
Acerra 128 Ij 40.57N 14.22 E
Achacachi 202 Eg 16.03S 68.43W
Achaguas 202 Eb 7.46N 68.14W
Achaïf, 'Erg- 166 Ea 20.49N 4.34W
Achao 206 Ff 42.28S 73.30W
Achar 204 Dk 32.25S 56.10W
Achegour 166 Hb 19.03N 11.53 E
Acheng 152 Mb 45.32N 126.56 E
Acheux-en-Amiénois 124 Ed 50.04N 2.32 E
Achiet-le-Grand 124 Ed 50.08N 2.47 E
Achill/Acaill 118 Dh 54.00N 10.00W
Achilleion 130 Cj 39.34N 19.55 E
Achill Head/Ceann Acla 118 Ch 53.59N 10.13W
Achim 120 Fc 53.02N 9.01 E
Achim 168 Bb 15.53N 19.31 E
Achterwasser 120 Jb 54.00N 13.57 E
Acı Gölü 146 Cd 37.50N 29.54 E
Ačinsk 142 Ld 56.17N 90.30 E
Acıpayam 146 Cd 37.25N 29.22 E
Acireale 128 Jm 37.37N 15.10 E
Acīş 130 Fb 47.32N 22.47 E
Ačisaj 135 Gc 43.33N 68.53 E
Ačit 134 Hh 56.48N 57.54 E
Ačit-Nur 152 Fb 49.30N 90.30 E
Acklins 174 Lg 22.25N 74.00W
Acklins, The Bight of- 194 Jb 22.30N 74.15W
Acle 124 Db 52.38N 1.33 E
Acobamba 202 Df 12.48S 74.34W
Acolin 122 Jh 46.49N 3.23 E
Aconcagua, Cerro- 198 Ji 32.39S 70.00W
Açor, Serra de- 126 Ed 40.13N 7.48W
Açores=Azores (EN) 160 Ee 38.30N 28.00W
Açores, Arquipélago dos-=Azores (EN) 158 Ee 38.30N 28.00W
Acorizal 204 Db 15.12S 56.22W
Acoyapa 194 Eh 11.58N 85.10W
Acquapendente 128 Fh 42.44N 11.52 E
Acquasanta Terme 128 Hh 42.46N 13.24 E
Acquasparta 128 Gh 42.41N 12.33 E
Acquaviva delle Fonti 128 Kj 40.54N 16.50 E
Acqui Terme 128 Cf 44.41N 8.28 E
Acraman, Lake- 212 Hf 32.05S 135.25 E
Acre 202 Ee 9.00S 70.00W
Acre, Rio- 198 Jf 8.45S 67.22W
Acri 128 Kk 39.29N 16.23 E
A Cruña / La Coruña 112 Fg 43.22N 8.23W
Actéon, Groupe- 208 Ng 21.20S 136.30W
Actopan 192 Jg 20.16N 98.56W
Açu 202 Ke 5.34S 36.54W
Acuña 204 Di 29.55S 57.58W
Ada [Ghana] 166 Fd 5.47N 0.38 E
Ada [Ok.-U.S.] 182 He 34.46N 96.41W
Ada [Yugo.] 130 Dd 45.48N 20.08 E
Adaba 168 Fd 7.03N 39.31 E
'Adad 168 Hd 8.23N 46.48 E
'Adādle 168 Gd 9.45N 44.41 E
Adair, Bahía- 192 Cb 31.30N 113.50W
Adair, Cape - 180 Kb 71.31N 71.24W
Adaja 126 Hc 41.32N 4.52W
Adak 178a Cb 51.45N 176.40W
Adalar 130 Mi 40.52N 29.07 E
'Adale 168 He 2.46N 46.20 E
Ådalen 116 Ga 63.20N 17.30 E
Adalselv 116 Dd 60.04N 10.11 E
Adam, Mount- 206 Hh 51.34S 60.04W
Adamantina 204 Ge 21.42S 51.04W
Adamaoua=Adamawa (EN) 158 Ih 7.00N 15.00 E
Adamawa (EN)= Adamaoua 158 Ih 7.00N 15.00 E
Adamello 128 Ed 46.09N 10.30 E
Adamovka 132 Ud 51.32N 59.59 E
Adams 186 Le 43.58N 89.49W
Adams, Mount- 182 Cb 46.12N 121.28W
Adams Lake 188 Fa 51.13N 119.33W
Adams River 180 Ff 50.54N 119.33W
Adam's Rock 220q Ab 25.04S 130.05W
Adamstown 210 Ng 25.04S 130.05W
Adamuz 126 Hf 38.02N 4.31W
Adana 142 Ff 37.01N 35.18 E
Adapazarı 146 Db 40.46N 30.24 E
Adarama 168 Eb 17.05N 34.54 E
Adarān, Jabal- 164 Ig 13.46N 45.08 E
Adare, Cape- 222 Kf 71.17S 170.14 E
Adavale 212 Ie 25.55S 144.36 E
Adda [It.] 110 Gf 45.08N 9.53 E
Adda [Sud.] 168 Cd 9.51N 24.50 E
Aḑ Ḑab'ah 164 Ec 31.02N 28.26 E
Ad Dabbah 168 Eb 18.03N 30.57 E
Ad Dafinah 164 He 23.18N 41.58 E
Aḑ Ḑafrah 146 Ok 23.25N 53.25 E
Ad Dahnā' 140 Gg 24.30N 48.10 E
Addala-Šuhgelmeer, gora- 132 Oh 42.20N 46.15 E
Aḑ Ḑālī' 164 Hg 13.42N 44.44 E
Ad Damazin 164 Ec 11.49N 34.23 E
Ad Dāmir 168 Eb 17.35N 33.58 E
Ad Dammām 142 Hg 26.26N 50.07 E
Ad Dār al Ḩamrā' 144 Ed 27.19N 37.44 E
Ad Dawādimī 146 Kj 24.28N 44.18 E
Ad Dawḩah=Doha (EN) 142 Hg 25.17N 51.32 E
Ad Dawr 146 Je 34.27N 43.47 E
Ad Dayr 164 Fd 25.20N 32.35 E
Ad Dibdibah 146 Lh 28.00N 46.30 E
Aḑ Ḑiffah 164 Ec 30.30N 25.30 E
Ad Dikākah 168 Ib 19.25N 51.30 E
Ad Dilam 144 Ge 23.59N 47.10 E
Ad Dindar 168 Ec 13.20N 34.05 E
Ad Dir'īyah 146 Lj 24.48N 46.32 E
Addis Ababa (EN) = Adis Abeba 160 Kh 9.01N 38.46 E
Ad Dissān 164 Hf 16.56N 41.41 E
Addis Zemen 168 Fc 12.05N 37.44 E
Ad Dīwānīya 144 Fc 31.59N 44.56 E
Addu Atoll 140 Jj 0.25S 73.10 E
Ad Du'ayn 168 Dc 11.26N 26.09 E
Ad Duwayd 146 Jg 30.13N 42.18 E
Ad Duwaym 168 Ec 14.00N 32.19 E
Adel [Ga.-U.S.] 184 Fj 31.18N 83.25W
Adel [Or.-U.S.] 188 Fe 42.11N 119.54W
Adelaide [Austl.] 210 Eh 34.56S 138.36 E
Adelaide [Bah.] 184 Im 25.00N 77.31W
Adelaide [S.Afr.] 172 Df 32.42S 26.20 E
Adelaide Island 222 Qe 67.15S 68.30W
Adelaide Peninsula 180 Hc 68.05N 97.50W
Adelaide River 210 Ef 13.15S 131.06 E
Adelaye 168 Cd 7.07N 22.49 E
Adelboden 128 Bd 46.30N 7.33 E
Adèle Island 212 Ec 15.30S 123.10 E
Adélie, Terre- 222 Ie 67.00S 139.00 E
Ademuz 126 Kd 40.04N 1.17W
Aden (EN) = Baladīyat 'Adan 142 Gh 12.46N 45.01 E
Aden, Gulf of- 158 Lg 12.00N 48.00 E
Aden, Gulf of- (EN) = 'Admēd, Badyarada- 158 Lg 12.00N 48.00 E
Adenau 124 Id 50.23N 6.56 E
Ader 158 Hg 14.10N 5.05 E
Aderbissinat 166 Gb 15.37N 7.52 E
Adhan, Jabal- 146 Qj 25.27N 56.13 E
Adh Dhahībāt 162 Jc 32.01N 10.42 E
Adh Dhayd 146 Pj 25.17N 55.53 E
Adhélfi 130 Gj 39.08N 23.59 E
Adhelfoi 130 Jm 36.25N 26.37 E
'Adhrīyāt, Jibāl- al- 146 Gg 30.25N 36.48 E
Adi, Pulau- 150 Jg 4.18S 133.26 E
Adiaké 166 Ed 5.16N 3.17W
Adi Arkay 168 Fc 13.31N 38.00 E
Adicora 202 Ea 11.57N 69.48W
Adi Dairo 168 Fc 14.21N 38.12 E
Adigala 168 Gc 10.24N 42.18 E
Adige/Etsch 110 Hf 45.10N 12.20 E
Adigrat 168 Fc 14.16N 39.28 E
Adi Keyeh 168 Fc 14.48N 39.23 E
Adi Kwala 168 Fc 14.37N 38.51 E
Ādīlābād 148 Fe 19.40N 78.32 E
Adīrī 160 If 27.30N 13.16 E
Adirondack Mountains 174 Le 44.00N 74.00W
Adis Abeba = Addis Ababa (EN) 160 Kh 9.01N 38.46 E
Adis Alem 168 Fd 9.03N 38.24 E
Adi Ugri 168 Fc 14.53N 38.49 E
Adiyaman 144 Eb 37.46N 38.17 E
Adjud 130 Kc 46.06N 27.10 E
Adjuntas 197a Bb 18.09N 66.43W
'Admēd, Badyarada- = Aden, Gulf of- (EN) 158 Lg 12.00N 48.00 E
Admer, Erg d'- 162 Ie 24.12N 9.10 E
Admiralty 178 Me 57.50N 134.30W
Admiralty Bay 197n Ba 13.00N 61.16W
Admiralty Gulf 212 Fb 14.20S 125.50 E
Admiralty Inlet 180 Ib 72.30N 86.00W
Admiralty Islands 208 Fe 2.10S 147.00 E
Admiralty Mountains 222 Kf 71.45S 168.30 E
Admont 128 Ic 47.34N 14.27 E
Ado 166 Fd 6.36N 2.56 E
Ado Ekiti 166 Gd 7.38N 5.13 E
Adok 168 Ed 8.11N 30.19 E
Adolfo Gonzales Chaves 204 Bn 38.02S 60.06W
Adolfo López Mateos, Presa- 192 Fe 25.05N 107.20W
Adonara, Pulau- 150 Hh 8.20S 123.10 E
Ādoni 148 Fe 15.38N 77.17 E
Adour 122 Ek 43.32N 1.32W
Adra 126 Ih 36.44N 3.01W
Adrano 128 Im 37.40N 14.50 E
Adrar 160 Gf 27.54N 0.17W
Adrar 158 Hf 25.12N 8.10 E
Adrar 158 Ff 20.30N 13.30W
Adrar [Alg.] 162 Gd 27.00N 1.00W
Adrar [Mtna.] 162 Fe 21.00N 11.00W
Adré 168 Cc 13.28N 22.12 E
Adria 128 Ge 45.03N 12.03 E
Adrian 184 Ee 41.54N 84.02W
Adrianópolis 204 Hg 24.41S 48.50W
Adriatic, Deti-=Adriatic Sea (EN) 110 Hg 43.00N 16.00 E
Adriatico, Mar-=Adriatic Sea (EN) 110 Hg 43.00N 16.00 E
Adriatic Sea (EN)=Adriatic, Deti- 110 Hg 43.00N 16.00 E
Adriatic Sea (EN)= Adriatico, Mar- 110 Hg 43.00N 16.00 E
Adriatic Sea (EN)= Jadransko More 110 Hg 43.00N 16.00 E
Aduard 124 Ia 53.15N 6.25 E
Adula 128 Dd 46.30N 9.05 E
Adulis 168 Fb 15.15N 39.37 E
Adur 124 Bd 50.49N 0.16W
Adusa 170 Eb 1.23N 28.01 E
Adventure Bank (EN) 128 Gm 37.20N 12.10 E
Adwa 160 Kg 14.10N 38.55 E
Adyča 140 Pc 68.13N 135.03 E
Adygalah 138 Jd 62.57N 146.25 E
Adygeja, respublika 136 Eg 44.30N 40.05 E
Adžarskaja respublika 136 Eg 41.40N 42.10 E
Adzopé 166 Ed 6.06N 3.52W
Adzopé 166 Ed 6.15N 3.45W
Adzva 134 Ic 66.36N 59.28 E
Aegean Sea (EN)=Aiyaion Pélagos 110 Ih 39.00N 25.00 E
Aegean Sea (EN)=Ege Denizi 110 Ih 39.00N 25.00 E
Aegina (EN) = Aiyina 130 Gl 37.40N 23.30 E
Aegviidu 116 Ke 59.17N 25.37 E
Aeon Point 220g Bb 1.46N 157.11W
Aerfort na Sionainne/Shannon 118 Ei 52.42N 8.57W
Ærø 116 Dj 54.55N 10.20 E
Ærøskøbing 116 Dj 54.53N 10.25 E
Aerzen 124 Lb 52.02N 9.16 E
Afafi, Massif d'- 166 Ha 22.15N 15.00 E
'Afak 146 Kf 32.04N 45.15 E
Afanasjevo 114 Mg 58.54N 53.16 E
Afareaitu 221e Fc 17.33S 149.47W
Afars and Issas (EN) → Djibouti 160 Lg 11.30N 43.00 E
Aff 122 Dg 47.43N 2.07W
Affollé 158 Fg 16.55N 10.25W
Affrica, Scoglio d'- 128 Eh 42.20N 10.05 E
Afghānistān 142 If 33.00N 65.00 E
Afgōye 168 He 2.09N 45.07 E
'Afif 144 Fe 23.55N 42.56 E
Afikpo 166 Gd 5.53N 7.55 E
Afipski 132 Kg 44.52N 38.50 E
Aflou 162 Hc 34.07N 2.06 E
Afmadōw 168 Ge 0.29N 42.06 E
Afognak 178 Ie 58.15N 152.30W
Afonso Cláudio 202 Jh 20.05S 41.08W
Afon Teifi 118 Ii 52.06N 4.43W
Afon Tywi 118 Ij 51.40N 4.15W
Afragola 128 Ij 40.55N 14.18 E
Afrēra, Lake- 168 Gc 13.20N 41.03 E
Africa (EN) 106 Eh 10.00N 22.00 E
African Islands 158 Mi 4.53S 53.24 E
Afşin 146 Gc 38.36N 36.55 E
Afsluitdijk 122 La 53.00N 5.15 E
Afton 188 Je 42.44N 110.56W
Afuá 202 Hd 0.10S 50.23W
'Afula 146 Ff 32.36N 35.17 E
Afyonkarahisar 142 Ff 38.45N 30.40 E
Agadem 160 Ig 16.50N 13.17 E
Agadez 160 Hg 16.58N 7.59 E
Agadez 166 Hb 19.45N 10.15 E
Agadez, Irhazer Oua-n- 166 Gb 17.28N 6.26 E
Agadir 160 Ge 30.25N 9.37W
Agadir 162 Fc 30.00N 9.00W
Agadyr 136 Hf 48.17N 72.53 E
Agalega Islands 158 Mj 10.24S 56.30 E
Agalta, Sierra de- 190 Ge 15.00N 85.53W
Agan 136 Hc 61.23N 74.35 E
Agana 210 Fc 13.28N 144.45 E
Agano-Gawa 154 Of 37.57N 139.07 E
Aga Point 220c Bb 13.14N 144.43 E
Agapovka 134 Ij 53.18N 59.10 E
Agaro 168 Fd 7.53N 36.36 E
Agartala 142 Lg 23.49N 91.16 E
Agassiz Pool 186 Ib 48.20N 95.58W
Agat 220c Bb 13.23N 144.39 E
Agat Bay 220c Bb 13.24N 144.39 E
Agats 210 Ee 5.33S 138.08 E
Agattu 178a Ab 52.25N 173.35 E
Agawa Bay 184 Eb 47.22N 84.33W
Agawa Bay 184 Eb 47.20N 84.42W
Agboville 166 Ed 5.56N 4.13W
Agboville 166 Ed 6.00N 4.15W
Agdam 136 Eh 39.58N 46.57 E
Agdaš 132 Oi 40.38N 47.29 E
Agde 122 Jk 43.19N 3.28 E
Agde, Cap d'- 122 Jk 43.16N 3.30 E
Agder 116 Cf 58.25N 8.15 E
Agdz 162 Fc 30.27N 7.56W
Agdžabedi 132 Oi 40.03N 47.28 E
Agematsu 156 Ed 35.47N 137.41 E
Agen 122 Gj 44.12N 0.38 E
Ageo 156 Fd 35.58N 139.35 E
Agepsta, gora- 132 Lh 43.32N 40.30 E
Ager 128 Hb 48.05N 13.51 E
Agere Mariam 168 Fd 5.39N 38.15 E

Age-Alb

Agersø 116 Di 55.10N 11.10 E
Agger 124 Jd 50.48N 7.11 E
Āghā Jārī 144 Gc 30.42N 49.50 E
Aghireşu 130 Gc 46.53N 23.15 E
Agiabampo, Estero de- 192 Ed 26.15N 109.15W
Ağın 146 Hc 38.57N 38.43 E
Aginskoje 138 Gf 51.03N 114.33 E
Agnew 212 Ee 28.01S 120.30 E
Agnibilékrou 166 Ed 7.08N 3.12W
Agnita 130 Hd 45.58N 24.37 E
Agno 128 Fe 45.32N 11.21 E
Agnone 128 Ii 41.48N 14.22 E
Ago 154 Ed 34.19N 136.50 E
Agoare 166 Fd 8.30N 3.25 E
Agogna 128 Ce 45.04N 8.54 E
Agön 116 Gc 61.35N 17.25 E
Agordat 160 Kg 15.32N 37.53 E
Ágordo 128 Gd 46.17N 12.02 E
Agout 122 Hk 43.47N 1.41 E
Āgra 142 Jg 27.11N 78.01 E
Agrahanski poluostrov 132 Oh 43.45N 47.35 E
Agramunt 126 Nc 41.47N 1.06 E
Agreda 126 Kc 41.51N 1.56W
Ağrı 144 Fb 39.44N 43.03 E
Agri 128 Kj 40.13N 16.44 E
Ağrıčaj 132 Oi 41.17N 46.43 E
Ağrı Dağı = Ararat, Mount- (EN) 140 Gf 39.40N 44.24 E
Agrigento 112 Hh 37.19N 13.34 E
Agrihan Island 208 Fc 18.46N 145.40 E
Agrij 130 Gb 47.15N 23.16 E
Agrínion 130 Ek 38.38N 21.25 E
Agropoli 128 Ij 40.21N 14.59 E
Agro Pontino 128 Gi 41.25N 12.55 E
Agryz 114 Mh 56.31N 53.01 E
Agto 179 Ge 67.37N 53.49W
Agua Brava, Laguna- 192 Gf 22.10N 105.32W
Agua Caliente, Cerro- 190 Cc 26.27N 106.12W
Aguachica 202 Db 8.18N 73.38W
Agua Clara 204 Fe 20.27S 52.52W
Aguada de Pasajeros 194 Gb 22.23N 80.51W
Aguadilla 194 Nd 18.26N 67.09W
Aguadulce 194 Gi 8.15N 80.33W
Agua Fria River 188 Ij 33.23N 112.21W
Agua Limpa, Rio- 204 Gb 14.58S 51.20W
Aguán, Río- 194 Ef 15.57N 85.44W
Aguanaval, Río- 192 Hf 25.28N 102.53W
Aguapeí 204 Cc 16.12S 59.43W
Aguapeí, Rio- 204 Cb 15.53S 58.25W
Aguapeí, Rio- 206 Jb 21.03S 51.47W
Aguapey, Río- 206 Di 29.07S 56.36W
Agua Prieta 176 If 31.18N 109.34W
Aguaray 206 Hb 22.16S 63.44W
Aguaray-Guazú, Río- [Par.] 204 Dg 24.05S 56.40W
Aguaray-Guazú, Río- [Par.] 204 Dg 24.47S 57.19W
Aguasay 196 Eh 9.25N 63.44W
Aguascalientes 176 Ig 21.53N 102.18W
Aguascalientes 190 Dd 22.00N 102.30W
Aguasvivas 126 Lc 41.20N 0.25W
Agua Verde, Rio- 204 Da 13.42S 56.43W
Agua Vermelha, Represa- 206 Ja 19.53S 50.17W
Agudo [Braz.] 204 Fi 29.38S 53.15W
Agudo [Sp.] 126 Hf 38.59N 4.52W
Águeda 126 Dd 40.34N 8.27W
Agueda 126 Fc 41.02N 6.56W
Aguelhok 166 Fb 19.28N 0.51 E
Agüenit 162 Ee 22.11N 13.08W
Aguerguer 158 Ff 23.09N 16.01W
Aguijan Island 208 Fc 14.51N 145.34 E
Aguilar de Campoo 126 Hb 42.48N 4.16W
Aguilar de la Frontera 126 Hg 37.31N 4.39W
Águilas 126 Kg 37.24N 1.35W
Aguililla 192 Hh 18.44N 102.44W
Aguirre, Rio- 196 Fh 8.28N 61.02W
Aguja, Cabo de la- 202 Da 11.21N 73.59W
Agujereada, Punta- 197a Ab 18.31N 67.08W
Agul 138 Ee 55.40N 95.45 E
Agulhas, Cape-(EN)= Agulhas, Kaap- 158 Jl 34.50S 20.00 E
Agulhas, Kaap-=Agulhas, Cape-(EN) 158 Jl 34.50S 20.00 E
Agulhas Basin (EN) 106 En 47.00S 20.00 E
Agulhas Negras, Pico das- 198 Lh 22.23S 44.38W
Agulhas Plateau (EN) 158 Jm 40.00S 26.00 E
Agung, Gunung- 150 Gh 8.21S 115.30 E
Aguni-Shima 152 Mf 26.35N 127.15 E
Ağva 146 Cb 41.05N 29.50 E
Ahaggar 158 Hf 23.10N 5.50 E
Ahaggar, Tassili-oua-n- 158 Hf 20.30N 5.00 E
Aha Hills 172 Cc 19.45S 21.10 E
Ahalcihe 136 Eg 41.38N 42.59 E
Ahalkalaki 136 Eg 41.25N 43.29 E
Ahangaran 135 Gd 40.57N 69.37 E
Ahar 144 Gb 38.28N 47.04 E
Ahat 130 Mk 38.39N 29.47 E
Ahaus 120 Cd 52.04N 7.00 E
Ahe Atoll 208 Mf 14.30S 146.18W
Ahenet, Tanezrouft-n- 162 He 22.00N 1.00 E
Ahini 138 Ff 53.18N 105.01 E
Ahipara 218 Ea 35.10S 173.09 E
Ahja jõgi 116 Lf 58.19N 27.15 E
Ahlat 146 Jc 38.45N 42.29 E
Ahlen 120 De 51.45N 7.55 E
Ahmadābād 142 Jg 23.02N 72.37 E
Aḥmadī 146 Qi 27.56N 56.42 E
Ahmadnagar 148 Ee 19.05N 74.44 E
Ahmadpur East 148 Ec 29.09N 71.16 E
Ahmar 158 Lh 9.23N 41.13 E
Aḥmar, Al Baḥr al-=Red Sea (EN) 158 Kf 25.00N 38.00 E
Ahmeta 132 Nh 42.02N 45.11 E
Ahmetli 130 Kk 38.31N 27.57 E
Ahnet 162 He 24.35N 3.15 E
Ahoa 220h Ab 13.17S 176.12W
Ahome 192 Ee 25.55N 109.11W
Ahon, Tarso- 168 Ba 20.23N 18.18 E
Ahr 120 Df 50.33N 7.17 E
Ahram 146 Nh 28.52N 51.16 E
Ahrāmāt al Jīzah 164 Fd 29.55N 31.05 E
Ahrensburg 120 Gc 53.41N 10.15 E
Ahrgebirge 124 Id 50.31N 6.54 E
Ahse 124 Jc 51.42N 7.51 E
Ahsu 132 Pi 40.35N 48.26 E
Ähtäri 114 Ee 62.02N 21.20 E
Ähtärinjärvi 116 Kb 62.40N 24.05 E
Ähtävänjoki 114 Fe 63.38N 22.48 E
Ahtopol 130 Kg 42.06N 27.57 E
Ahtuba 110 Kf 46.42N 48.00 E
Ahtubinsk 112 Kf 48.14N 46.14 E
Ahtyrka 136 De 50.19N 34.55 E
Ahuacapán 194 Cg 13.55N 89.51W
Ahuazotepec 192 Jg 20.03N 98.09W
Ahunui Atoll 208 Mf 19.35S 140.28W
Åhus 114 Di 55.55N 14.17 E
Ahváz 142 Gf 31.19N 48.42 E
Ahvenanmaa/Åland 114 Ef 60.15N 20.00 E
Ahvenanmaa/Åland 110 Hc 60.15N 20.00 E
Ahvenanmeri 116 Hd 60.00N 19.30 E
Ahwar 144 Gg 13.31N 46.42 E
Aibag Gol 154 Ad 41.42N 110.24 E
Aibetsu 156a Cb 43.55N 142.33 E
Aichach 120 Hh 48.28N 11.08 E
Aichi Ken 154 Ng 35.00N 137.07 E
Aiea 221a Db 21.23N 157.56W
Aigle 128 Ad 46.20N 6.59 E
Aigle, L'- 122 Gf 48.45N 0.38 E
Aigoual, Mont- 122 Jj 44.07N 3.35 E
Aiguá 204 El 34.12S 54.45W
Aigues 122 Kj 44.07N 4.43 E
Aigues-Mortes 122 Kk 43.34N 4.11 E
Aiguilles 122 Mj 44.47N 6.52 E
Aiguillon 122 Gj 44.18N 0.21 E
Aigurande 122 Hh 46.26N 1.50 E
Ai He 154 Hd 40.13N 124.30 E
Aihui (Heihe) 142 Od 50.13N 127.26 E
Aikawa 156 Fb 38.02N 138.14 E
Aiken 182 Ke 33.34N 81.44W
Ailao Shan 152 Hg 23.15N 102.20 E
Ailette 124 Fe 49.35N 3.10 E
Ailinginae Atoll 208 Hc 11.08N 166.24 E
Aillte an Mhothair/Moher, Cliffs of- 118 Di 52.58N 9.27W
Ailly-le-Haut-Clocher 124 Dd 50.05N 1.59 E
Ailly-sur-Noye 124 Ee 49.45N 2.22 E
Ailsa Craig 118 Hf 55.16N 5.07W
Ailuk Atoll 208 Hc 10.20N 169.56 E
Aim 138 Ie 58.48N 134.12 E
Aimogasta 206 Gc 28.33S 66.49W
Aimorés 202 Jg 19.30S 41.04W
Ain 122 Lh 46.10N 5.20 E
Ain 122 Li 45.48N 5.10 E
Ainaži/Ajnaži 114 Fh 57.52N 24.25 E
Aïn Beïda 162 Ib 35.48N 7.24 E
Aïn Beni Mathar 162 Gc 34.01N 2.01W
Aïn Bessem 126 Ph 36.18N 3.40 E
Aïn Boucif 126 Pi 35.53N 3.09 E
Aïn Defla 126 Nh 36.16N 1.58 E
Aïn el Berd 126 Li 35.21N 0.31W
Aïn el Hammam 126 Qh 36.34N 4.19 E
Aïn el Turck 126 Li 35.44N 0.46W
Aïn Galakka 168 Bb 18.05N 18.31 E
Ainos Óros 130 Dk 38.07N 20.40 E
Aïn Oulmene 126 Ri 35.55N 5.18 E
Aïn Oussera 126 Oi 35.27N 2.54 E
Aïn Sefra 160 Ge 32.45N 0.35W
Ainsworth 186 Ge 42.33N 99.52W
Aïn Taghrout 126 Rh 36.08N 5.05 E
Aïn Tedeles 126 Mh 36.00N 0.18 E
Aïn Témouchent 162 Gb 35.18N 1.08W
Aïn Tolba 126 Ki 35.15N 1.15W
Aioi 156 Dd 34.49N 134.28 E
Aiquile 202 Eg 18.10S 65.10W
Aïr/Azbine 158 Hg 18.00N 8.30 E
Airabu, Pulau- 150 Ef 2.46N 106.14 E
Airai 220a Bc 7.21N 134.34 E
Airaines 124 De 49.58N 1.57 E
Airão 202 Fd 1.56S 61.22W
Airbangis 150 Cf 0.12N 99.23 E
Airdrie 188 Ha 51.18N 114.02W
Aire 122 Id 50.38N 2.24 E
Aire [Eng.-U.K.] 118 Mh 53.44N 0.54W
Aire [Fr.] 122 Ke 49.19N 4.49 E
Aire, Canal d'- 122 Id 50.38N 2.25 E
Aire, Isla del- 126 Qe 39.47N 4.16 E
Aire-sur-l'Adour 122 Fk 43.42N 0.16W
Air Force 180 Kc 67.55N 74.05W
Airolo 128 Cd 46.33N 8.35 E
Aïs 219b Cb 15.26S 167.15 E
Aisch 120 Hg 49.46N 11.01 E
Aisén del General Carlos Ibáñez del Campo 206 Fg 46.00S 73.00W
Aishihik 180 Dd 61.34N 137.30W
Ai-Shima 156 Bd 34.30N 131.18 E
Aisne 124 Je 49.30N 3.30 E
Aisne 122 Ie 49.26N 2.50 E
Aisne à la Marne, Canal de l'- 122 Je 49.24N 3.55 E
Aïssa, Djebel- 162 Gc 32.51N 0.30W
Aitana, Pico- 126 Lf 38.39N 0.16W
Aitape 214 Ch 3.08S 142.21 E
Aitolikón 130 Ek 38.26N 21.21 E
Aitutaki Atoll 208 Lf 18.52S 159.45W
Ait Youssef ou Ali 126 Ii 35.09N 3.55W
Aiud 130 Gc 46.18N 23.43 E
Aiviekste/Ajviekste 114 Fh 56.36N 25.44 E
Aiwokako Passage 220a Bb 7.39N 134.33 E
Aix, Ile d'- 122 Eh 46.01N 1.10W
Aix-en-Provence 122 Lk 43.32N 5.26 E
Aixe-sur-Vienne 122 Hi 45.48N 1.08 E
Aix-les-Bains 122 Li 45.42N 5.55 E
Aiyaion Pélagos=Aegean Sea (EN) 110 Ih 39.00N 25.00 E
Aiyina 130 Gl 37.45N 23.26 E
Aiyina = Aegina (EN) 130 Gl 37.40N 23.30 E
Aiyinion 130 Fi 40.30N 22.33 E
Aiyion 130 Fk 38.15N 22.05 E
Aizawl 148 Id 23.44N 92.43 E
Aizenay 122 Eh 46.44N 1.37W
Aizpute/Ajzpute 114 Eh 56.45N 21.39 E
Aizubange 156 Fc 37.34N 139.49 E
Aizutakada 156 Fc 37.29N 139.48 E
Aizuwakamatsu 154 Of 37.30N 139.56 E
Ajā', Jabal- 146 Ii 27.30N 41.30 E
'Ajab Shīr 146 Kd 37.28N 45.54 E
Ajaccio 112 Gg 41.55N 8.44 E
Ajaccio, Golfe d'- 122a Ab 41.50N 8.41 E
Ajaguz 142 Ke 47.58N 80.27 E
Ajakli 138 Eb 70.13N 95.55 E
Ajan [Russia] 138 Fe 59.38N 106.45 E
Ajan [Russia] 138 Ie 56.27N 138.10 E
Ajanka 138 Ld 63.40N 167.30 E
Ajanta Range 148 Fd 20.30N 76.00 E
Ajat 134 Kj 52.54N 62.50 E
Ajax Peak 188 Id 45.20N 113.40W
Ajdābiyā 160 Je 30.46N 20.14 E
Ajdabul 136 Ge 52.42N 69.01 E
Ajdar 132 Ke 48.42N 39.13 E
Ajdar, Solončak- 135 Fd 40.50N 66.50 E
Ajdovščina 128 He 45.53N 13.53 E
Ajdyrlinski 134 Ij 52.03N 59.50 E
Ajhal 138 Gc 66.00N 111.32 E
Ajigasawa 154 Pd 40.47N 140.12 E
Aji-Shima 156 Gb 38.15N 141.30 E
Ajjer, Tassili-n- 158 Hf 25.30N 9.00 E
Ajka 120 Ni 47.06N 17.34 E
Ajke, ozero- 132 Vd 50.55N 61.35 E
Ajkino 134 De 62.15N 49.56 E
'Ajlūn 146 Ff 32.20N 35.45 E
'Ajmah, Jabal al- 146 Fh 29.12N 34.02 E
'Ajmān 144 Id 25.25N 55.27 E
Ajmer 142 Jg 26.27N 74.38 E
Ajnaži/Ainaži 114 Fh 57.52N 24.25 E
Ajni 135 Ge 39.23N 68.36 E
Ajo 182 Ee 32.22N 112.52W
Ajo, Cabo de- 126 Ia 43.31N 3.35W
Ajon, ostrov- 140 Sc 69.50N 168.40 E
Ajoupa-Bouillon 197h Ab 14.50N 61.08W
Ajsary 136 He 53.05N 71.00 E
Ajtos 130 Kg 42.42N 27.15 E
Aju, Kepulauan- 150 Jf 0.28N 131.03 E
'Ajūz, Jabal al- 146 Dj 25.49N 30.43 E
Ajviekste 114 Fh 56.36N 25.44 E
Ajzkraukle (Stučka) 114 Fh 56.36N 25.17 E
Ajzpute/Aizpute 114 Eh 56.45N 21.39 E
Akaba 166 Fd 7.57N 1.03 E
Akabira 154 Qc 43.30N 142.04 E
Akabli 162 Hd 26.42N 1.22 E
Akademika Obručeva, hrebet- 138 Ef 51.30N 96.45 E
Akadomari 156 Fc 37.54N 138.24 E
Aka-Gawa 156 Fb 38.54N 139.50 E
Akagi-San 156 Fc 36.33N 139.11 E
Akaishi-Dake 156 Fd 35.27N 138.09 E
Akaishi-Sanmyaku 156 Fd 35.25N 138.10 E
Akajaure 114 Dc 67.42N 17.30 E
Aka-Jima 156b Ab 26.14N 127.17 E
Akaki 168 Fd 8.51N 38.48 E
Akala 168 Fb 15.38N 36.12 E
Akan 156a Db 43.08N 144.07 E
Akan-Gawa 156a Db 43.00N 144.16 E
Akar 146 Dc 38.38N 31.06 E
Akarnaniká Óri 130 Dk 38.45N 21.00 E
Akaroa 216 Dh 43.48S 172.59 E
Akasaki 156 Cd 35.31N 133.38 E
'Akasha East 168 Ea 21.05N 30.43 E
Akashi 154 Mg 34.38N 134.59 E
Akbaba Tepe 146 Hc 39.32N 39.33 E
Akbajtal, pereval- 136 Hh 38.31N 73.41 E
Akbou 126 Qh 36.28N 4.32 E
Akbulak 136 Fe 51.03N 55.37 E
Akbura 135 Hd 40.34N 72.45 E
Akçaabat 146 Hb 40.59N 39.34 E
Akçadağ 146 Gc 38.21N 37.59 E
Akçakale 146 Hd 36.41N 38.56 E
Akçakara Dağı 146 Ic 38.40N 40.52 E
Akçakoca 146 Db 41.05N 31.09 E
Akçaova [Tur.] 130 Mh 41.03N 29.57 E
Akçaova [Tur.] 130 Ll 37.30N 28.02 E
Akčatau 136 Hf 47.59N 74.02 E
Akçay 130 Mm 36.36N 29.45 E
Akçay 130 Ll 37.50N 28.15 E
Akchâr 158 Ff 20.20N 14.28W
Akdağ [Tur.] 146 Gd 37.53N 37.56 E
Ak Dağ [Tur.] 146 Ib 40.35N 41.46 E
Akdağ [Tur.] 146 Fb 40.57N 35.55 E
Akdağ [Tur.] 146 Cc 39.15N 29.49 E
Akdağ [Tur.] 130 Mk 38.18N 29.58 E
Akdağ [Tur.] 130 Ll 37.42N 28.56 E
Akdağ [Tur.] 130 Jk 38.33N 26.30 E
Ak Dağ [Tur.] 144 Cb 36.32N 29.34 E
Ak Dağlar 146 Gc 39.30N 36.00 E
Ak Dağları 146 Ic 38.40N 40.12 E
Akdağmadeni 146 Fc 39.40N 35.54 E
Akdeniz=Mediterranean Sea (EN) 110 Hh 35.00N 20.00 E
Ak-Dovurak 138 Ef 51.10N 90.40 E
Akechi 156 Ed 35.18N 137.22 E
Ake Eze 166 Gd 5.55N 7.40 E
Akelamo 150 If 1.29N 128.39 E
Akera 132 Oj 39.09N 46.48 E
Åkersberga 116 He 59.29N 18.18 E
Akershus 114 Cf 60.00N 11.10 E
Aketi 160 Jh 2.44N 23.46 E
Akharnai 130 Gk 38.05N 23.44 E
Akhḑar, Al Jabal al- 158 Je 32.30N 21.30 E
Akhḑar, Al Jabal al- 140 Hg 23.15N 57.00 E
Akhḑar, Wādī al- 146 Gh 28.35N 36.35 E
Akhelóös 130 Ej 38.18N 21.10 E
Akhisar 144 Cb 38.55N 27.51 E
Akhmīm 164 Fd 26.34N 31.44 E
Akhtarīn 146 Gd 36.31N 37.20 E
Aki 156 Ce 33.30N 133.53 E
Akiaki Atoll 216 Nc 18.30S 139.12W
Akiéni 170 Bc 1.11S 13.53 E
Akimiski 174 Kd 53.00N 81.20W
Akimovka 132 If 46.42N 35.09 E
Aki-Nada 156 Cd 34.05N 132.40 E
Åkirkeby 116 Fi 55.04N 14.56 E
Akita 142 Qf 39.43N 140.07 E
Akita Ken 154 Pe 39.45N 140.20 E
Akjar 132 Ud 51.50N 58.14 E
Akjoujt 160 Fg 19.44N 14.22W
Akka 162 Fd 29.25N 8.15W
Akkanburluk 134 Mj 52.46N 66.35 E
Akko 144 Ec 32.55N 35.05 E
Akkol 135 Hc 43.25N 70.47 E
Akköy 146 Bd 37.29N 27.15 E
Akkystau 136 Ff 47.17N 51.03 E
Aklavik 180 Dc 68.14N 135.02W
Aklé 'Aouâna 162 Ff 18.09N 5.40W
Aklé Mseiguilé 166 Eb 16.20N 4.45W
Akmené/Akmene 116 Jh 56.14N 22.43 E
Akmenrags/Akmeņrags 116 Ih 56.54N 20.55 E
Akmeņrags/Akmenrags 116 Ih 56.54N 20.55 E
Akmeqit 152 Cd 37.05N 76.55 E
Akniste 116 Kh 56.10N 25.54 E
Akō 156 Dd 34.45N 134.23 E
Akobo 160 Kh 7.47N 33.01 E
Akobo 168 Ed 7.48N 33.03 E
Akola 142 Jg 20.44N 77.00 E
Akonolinga 166 He 3.46N 12.15 E
Akosombo Dam 166 Fd 6.16N 0.03 E
Akpatok 180 Kd 60.24N 68.05W
Akqi 152 Cc 40.50N 78.01 E
Ákra Ámbelos 130 Gj 39.56N 23.56 E
Ákra Kambanós 130 Hl 37.59N 24.45 E
Akranes 114a Ab 64.19N 22.06W
Ákra Spathí 130 Gl 37.27N 23.31 E
Åkrehamn 114 Ag 59.16N 5.11 E
Akrítas, Ákra- = Akritas, Cape- (EN) 130 Em 36.43N 21.53 E
Akritas Cape- (EN) = Akrítas, Ákra- 130 Em 36.43N 21.53 E
Akron [Co.-U.S.] 186 Ef 40.10N 103.13W
Akron [Oh.-U.S.] 182 Kc 41.04N 81.31W
Akrotiri 146 Ee 34.36N 32.57 E
Akša 138 Gf 50.17N 113.17 E
Aksaj 132 Oh 43.32N 46.55 E
Aksaj [Kaz.] 136 Fe 51.13N 53.01 E
Aksaj [Russia] 132 Kf 47.15N 39.52 E
Aksakal 130 Li 40.09N 28.07 E
Aksakovo 134 Gi 54.02N 54.09 E
Aksaray 144 Db 38.23N 34.03 E
Aksay 152 Fd 39.28N 94.15 E
Aksayqin Hu 152 Cd 35.12N 79.50 E
Akşehir 144 Db 38.21N 31.25 E
Akşehir Gölü 146 Dc 38.30N 31.28 E
Akseki 146 Dd 37.02N 31.48 E
Aksenovo-Zilovskoje 138 Gf 53.00N 117.35 E
'Aks-e Rostam 146 Ph 28.23N 54.52 E
Aksoran, gora- 136 Hf 48.25N 75.30 E
Akstafa 132 Ni 41.06N 45.28 E
Akstafa 132 Ni 41.13N 45.27 E
Aksu [China] 142 Ke 41.09N 80.15 E
Aksu [Kaz.] 136 Hf 46.20N 78.15 E
Aksu [Kaz.] 136 He 52.28N 71.59 E
Aksu [Kaz.] 135 Lb 45.34N 79.30 E
Aksu [Tur.] 130 Ll 37.56N 28.56 E
Aksu [Tur.] 146 Dd 36.51N 30.54 E
Aksuat 136 If 47.48N 82.50 E
Aksubajevo 114 Mi 54.52N 50.50 E
Aksu He 140 Ke 40.28N 80.52 E
Aksum 168 Fc 14.07N 38.44 E
Ak-Šyjrak 135 Ld 41.49N 78.44 E
Aktag 152 Dd 36.45N 84.40 E
Aktaš [Russia] 138 Df 50.18N 87.44 E
Aktaš [Uzb.] 136 Gh 39.55N 65.53 E
Aktau [Kaz.] 136 He 50.16N 73.07 E
Aktau (Ševčenko) [Kaz.] 142 He 43.35N 51.05 E
Aktau, gora- 136 Gg 41.45N 64.30 E
Aktjubinsk 112 Le 50.17N 57.10 E
Aktjubinskaja oblast 136 Ff 48.00N 58.00 E
Ak-Tjuz 135 Kc 42.50N 76.07 E
Akto 152 Cd 39.05N 76.02 E
Aktogaj 136 Hf 47.01N 79.40 E
Akula 170 Db 2.22N 20.11 E
Akun 178a Eb 54.12N 165.35W
Akune 154 Kh 32.01N 130.11 E
Akure 166 Gd 7.15N 5.12 E
Akureyri 112 Eb 65.40N 18.06W
Akuseki-Jima 154 Jj 29.28N 129.33 E
Akutan 178a Eb 54.08N 165.46W
Akutan 178a Eb 54.10N 165.55W
Akyab→Sittwe 142 Lg 20.09N 92.54 E
Akyazı 146 Db 40.41N 30.37 E
Akžajkyn, ozero- 135 Fb 44.55N 67.45 E
Akžal 136 If 49.13N 81.30 E
Ål 116 Cd 60.38N 8.34 E
Alà, Monti di- 128 Dj 40.35N 9.16 E
Alabama 182 Je 32.50N 87.30W
Alabama 174 Kf 31.08N 87.57W
Al'Abbāsīyah 168 Ec 12.10N 31.18 E
Alaca 146 Fb 40.10N 34.51 E
Alaçam 146 Fb 41.37N 35.37 E
Alaçam Dağları 130 Lj 39.20N 28.32 E
Alacant / Alicante 112 Fh 38.21N 0.29W
Alacant / Alicante 126 Lf 38.30N 0.30W
Alacant, Golf d' / Alicante, Golfo de- 126 Lf 38.20N 0.15W
Alaçati 130 Jk 38.16N 26.23 E
Aladağ 146 Jc 43.35N 39.20 E
Ala Dağ [Tur.] 146 Jb 40.10N 42.49 E
Ala Dağ [Tur.] 146 Ed 37.58N 32.04 E
Alādāgh, Kūh-e- 146 Qd 37.13N 57.30 E
Ala Dağları 146 Fd 37.55N 35.13 E
Aladža 132 Rj 39.21N 53.12 E
Aladža Manastir 130 Lf 43.17N 28.01 E
Alagir 132 Nh 43.01N 44.12 E
Alagna Valsesia 128 Be 45.51N 7.56 E
Alagnon 122 Ji 45.27N 3.19 E
Alagoas 202 Ke 9.30S 36.30W
Alagoas 202 Ke 9.00S 36.00W
Alagoinhas 200 Mg 12.07S 38.26W
Alagón 126 Kc 41.46N 1.07W
Alagón 126 Fe 39.44N 6.53W
Ala Gou 152 Ec 42.42N 89.12 E
Alahanpanjang 150 Dg 1.05S 100.47 E
Alahärmä 114 Fe 63.14N 22.51 E
Al Aḥmadī 146 Mh 29.05N 48.04 E
Alaid, vulkan- 138 Kf 50.50N 155.33 E
Alaior / Alayor 126 Qe 39.56N 4.08 E
Alajärvi 114 Fe 63.00N 23.49 E
Alajku 136 Hg 40.18N 74.29 E
Alajski hrebet 140 Jf 39.45N 72.30 E
Alajuela 190 Hf 10.01N 84.13W
Alajuela 194 Eh 10.30N 84.30W
Alajuela, Lago- 194 Hi 9.05N 79.24W
Alakol, ozero- 140 Ke 46.05N 81.50 E
Alakurtti 114 Hc 66.59N 30.20 E
Alalakeiki Channel 221a Ec 20.35N 156.30W
Al 'Alamayn 160 Je 30.49N 28.57 E
Alalau, Rio- 202 Fd 0.30S 61.10W
Al Amādīyah 146 Jd 37.06N 43.29 E
Alamagan Island 208 Fc 17.36N 145.50 E
Al 'Amārah 144 Gc 31.50N 47.09 E
'Alam ar Rūm, Ra's- 146 Bg 31.22N 27.21 E
Alāmarvdasht 146 Oi 27.52N 52.34 E
Alamashindo 168 Ge 4.51N 42.04 E
Alamata 168 Fc 12.25N 39.37 E
Alameda 186 Ci 35.11N 106.37W
Alaminos 150 Gc 16.10N 119.59 E
Al 'Āmirīyah 146 Cg 31.01N 29.48 E
Alamito Creek 186 Dl 29.31N 104.17W
Alamitos, Sierra de los- 192 Hd 26.20N 102.15W
Alamo 188 Hh 37.22N 115.10W
'Alāmo 168 Ge 4.23N 43.09 E
Alamogordo 182 Fe 32.54N 105.57W
Álamos 190 Cc 27.01N 108.56W
Álamos, Sierra- 192 Gc 28.25N 105.00W
Alamosa 182 Fd 37.28N 105.52W
Al Anbār 146 If 34.00N 42.00 E
Åland/Ahvenanmaa 114 Ef 60.15N 20.00 E
Åland/Ahvenanmaa 110 Hc 60.15N 20.00 E
Ålandsbro 116 Gb 62.40N 17.50 E
Ålandshav 116 Hd 60.00N 19.30 E
Alange 126 Ff 38.47N 6.15W
Alanje 194 Fi 8.24N 82.33W
Alanya 144 Db 36.33N 32.01 E
Alaotra, Lac- 172 Hc 17.30S 48.30 E
Alapaha River 184 Fj 30.28N 83.06W
Alapajevsk 136 Gd 57.52N 61.42 E
Alaplı 146 Db 41.08N 31.25 E
Al 'Aqabah=Aqaba (EN) 146 Dd 29.31N 35.00 E
Al 'Aqabah aş Şaghīrah 146 Ej 24.14N 32.53 E
Al 'Arabīyah As-Su'ūdīyah= Saudi Arabia (EN) 142 Gg 25.00N 45.00 E
Alarcón, Embalse de- 126 Je 39.45N 2.20W
Al 'Arīsh 164 Fc 31.08N 33.48 E
Al 'Armah 146 Lj 25.30N 46.30 E
Al Arţāwīyah 146 Ki 26.30N 45.20 E
Alas, Selat- 150 Gh 8.40S 116.40 E
Al 'Āşab 146 Pk 23.20N 54.10 E
Alaşehir 146 Cc 38.21N 28.32 E
Al Ashkharah 144 Ie 21.47N 59.30 E
Al 'Āshūrīyah 146 Jg 31.02N 43.05 E
Alaska 178 Ic 65.00N 153.00W
Alaska 174 Dc 65.00N 153.00W
Alaska, Gulf of- 174 Ed 58.00N 146.00W
Alaska Peninsula 174 Dd 57.00N 158.00W
Alaska Range 174 Ec 62.30N 150.00W
Alassio 128 Cf 44.00N 8.10 E
Alastaro 116 Jd 60.57N 22.51 E
Alat 135 De 39.26N 63.48 E
Alataw Shan 152 Cb 45.00N 80.00 E
Alataw Shankou= Dzungarian Gate (EN) 140 Ke 45.25N 82.25 E
Al 'Athāmīn 146 Jg 30.35N 43.40 E
Alatri 128 Hi 41.43N 13.21 E
Al 'Aţrun 160 Jg 18.11N 26.36 E
Alatyr 136 Ee 54.50N 46.36 E
Alatyr 114 Li 54.52N 46.36 E
Álava 126 Jb 42.50N 2.45W
Alava, Cape- 188 Cb 48.10N 124.43W
Alaverdi 136 Eg 41.07N 44.37 E
Alavījeh 146 Nf 33.03N 51.05 E
Alavo/Alavus 114 Fe 62.35N 23.37 E
Alavus/Alavo 114 Fe 62.35N 23.37 E
Al 'Awāliq 144 Gg 14.15N 46.30 E
Al 'Awāriq 168 Ha 20.25N 48.40 E
Al 'Awsajīyah 146 Ki 26.04N 44.08 E
'Ālayh 146 Ff 33.48N 35.36 E
Al 'Ayn [Oman] 144 Ie 24.15N 55.45 E
Al 'Ayn [Sau.Ar.] 146 Hj 25.04N 38.06 E
Alayor / Alaior 126 Qe 39.56N 4.08 E
Al 'Ayyōţ 146 Dh 29.37N 31.15 E
Al A'zamīyah 146 Kf 33.23N 44.22 E
Alazani 132 Oi 41.03N 46.40 E
Alazeja 138 Kb 70.55N 153.40 E
Al'Azīzīyah 164 Bc 32.32N 13.01 E
Alazores, Puerto de los- 126 Hg 37.05N 4.15W
Alb [Ger.] 124 Ke 49.04N 8.20 E
Alb [Ger.] 120 El 47.35N 8.08 E
Alba 128 Cf 44.42N 8.02 E
Alba 130 Gc 46.08N 23.30 E
Alba Adriatica 128 Hh 42.50N 13.56 E
Al Bāb 146 Gd 36.22N 37.31 E
Albac 130 Fc 46.27N 22.58 E
Albacete 112 Fh 38.59N 1.51W
Albacete 126 Kf 38.50N 2.00W
Al Badārī 164 Fd 26.59N 31.25 E
Alba de Tormes 126 Gd 40.49N 5.31W
Al Bādi 146 Ie 35.56N 41.32 E
Al Badi 164 Ie 22.02N 46.34 E
Ålbæk 116 Dg 57.36N 10.25 E

Index Symbols

- Independent Nation
- State, Region
- District, County
- Municipality
- Colony, Dependency
- Continent
- Physical Region
- Historical or Cultural Region
- Mount, Mountain
- Volcano
- Hill
- Mountains, Mountain Range
- Hills, Escarpment
- Plateau, Upland
- Pass, Gap
- Plain, Lowland
- Delta
- Salt Flat
- Valley, Canyon
- Crater, Cave
- Karst Features
- Depression
- Polder
- Desert, Dunes
- Forest, Woods
- Heath, Steppe
- Oasis
- Cape, Point
- Coast, Beach
- Cliff
- Peninsula
- Isthmus
- Sandbank
- Island
- Atoll
- Rock, Reef
- Islands, Archipelago
- Rocks, Reefs
- Coral Reef
- Well, Spring
- Geyser
- River, Stream
- Waterfall, Rapids
- River Mouth, Estuary
- Lake
- Salt Lake
- Intermittent Lake
- Reservoir
- Swamp, Pond
- Canal
- Glacier
- Ice Shelf, Pack Ice
- Ocean
- Sea
- Gulf, Bay
- Strait, Fjord
- Lagoon
- Bank
- Seamount
- Tablemount
- Ridge
- Shelf
- Basin
- Escarpment, Sea Scarp
- Fracture
- Trench, Abyss
- National Park, Reserve
- Point of Interest
- Recreation Site
- Cave, Cavern
- Historic Site
- Ruins
- Wall, Walls
- Church, Abbey
- Temple
- Scientific Station
- Railway station
- Airport
- Port
- Military installation
- Lighthouse
- Mine
- Tunnel
- Dam, Bridge

Alb-Alm

Ålbæk Bugt	116	Dg	57.35N	10.30 E
Al Bahrah	146	Lh	29.40N	47.52 E
Al Baḥr al Aḥmar [3]	168	Fb	19.50N	35.30 E
Al Baḥrayn	140	Hg	26.00N	50.30 E
Al Baḥrayn=Bahrain (EN) [1]	142	Hg	26.00N	50.29 E
Albaida	126	Lf	38.51N	0.31W
Alba Iulia	130	Gc	46.04N	23.35 E
Albalate del Arzobispo	126	Lc	41.07N	0.31W
Al Balqā' [3]	146	Ff	31.50N	35.40 E
Al Balyanā	164	Fd	26.14N	32.00 E
Alban	122	Ik	43.54N	2.28 E
Albanel, Lac-	180	Kf	51.05N	73.05W
Albani, Colli-	128	Gi	41.45N	12.45 E
Albania (EN)=Shqiperia [1]	112	Hg	41.00N	20.00 E
Albano, Lago-	128	Gi	41.45N	12.40 E
Albano Laziale	128	Gi	41.44N	12.39 E
Albany	174	Kd	52.17N	81.31W
Albany [Austl.]	210	Ch	35.02S	117.53 E
Albany [Ga.-U.S.]	182	Ke	31.35N	84.10W
Albany [Ky.-U.S.]	184	Eg	36.42N	85.08W
Albany [N.Y.-U.S.]	176	Le	42.39N	73.45W
Albany [Or.-U.S.]	182	Cc	44.38N	123.06W
Alba Posse	204	Eh	27.33S	54.42W
Albardón	206	Gd	31.26S	68.32W
Albarracin	126	Kd	40.25N	1.26W
Albarracin, Sierra de-	126	Kd	40.30N	1.30W
Al Başalīyah Qiblī	146	Ej	25.06N	32.47 E
Al Başrah [3]	146	Lg	30.30N	47.27 E
Al Başrah=Basra (EN)	142	Gf	30.30N	47.47 E
Al Baṭḥā'	146	Kg	31.07N	45.54 E
Al Bātin	146	Lh	29.00N	46.35 E
Al Bāṭinah	140	Hg	23.45N	57.20 E
Albatross Bank (EN)	178	Ie	56.10N	152.20W
Albatross Bay	212	Ib	12.45S	141.43 E
Albatross Plateau (EN)	106	Mi	10.00N	103.00W
Albatross Point	218	Fc	38.07S	174.40 E
Al Batrūn	146	Fe	34.15N	35.39 E
Al Bawīṭī	164	Ed	28.21N	28.52 E
Al Bayāḍ	140	Gg	22.00N	47.00 E
Al Bayḍā'	160	Je	32.46N	21.43 E
Al Bayḍā' [3]	164	Dc	32.00N	21.30 E
Al Bayḍā' [Lib.]	164	Cd	28.21N	18.58 E
Al Bayḍā' [Yem.]	164	Ig	13.58N	45.35 E
Albegna	128	Fh	42.30N	11.11 E
Albemarle	184	Gh	35.21N	80.12W
Albemarle Sound	182	Ld	36.03N	76.12W
Albenga	128	Cf	44.03N	8.13 E
Alberche	126	He	39.58N	4.46W
Alberdi	206	Ic	26.10S	58.09W
Albères, Chaîne des-	122	Il	42.28N	2.56 E
Albères, Montes-/Les Alberes	122	Il	42.28N	2.56 E
Albergaria-a-Velha	126	Dd	40.42N	8.29W
Alberic / Alberique	126	Le	39.07N	0.31W
Alberique / Alberic	126	Le	39.07N	0.31W
Alberobello	128	Lj	40.47N	17.16 E
Albert	122	Id	50.00N	2.39 E
Albert, Canal-/Albert Kanaal =Albert Canal (EN)	122	Lc	51.10N	5.10 E
Albert, Lake- [Afr.]	158	Kh	1.40N	31.00 E
Albert, Lake- [Or.-U.S.]	188	Ee	42.38N	120.13W
Albert, Lake- (EN)=Mobuto Sese Seko, Lac-	158	Kh	1.40N	31.00 E
Alberta [2]	180	Gf	55.00N	115.00W
Albert Canal (EN)=Albert, Canal-/Albert Kanaal	122	Lc	51.10N	5.10 E
Albert Canal (EN)=Albert Kanaal/Albert, Canal-	122	Lc	51.10N	5.10 E
Albert Edward, Mount-	212	Ja	8.23S	147.27 E
Albert Edward Bay	180	Hc	69.35N	103.10W
Alberti	206	He	35.02S	60.16W
Albertirsa	120	Pi	47.15N	19.37 E
Albert Kanaal/Albert, Canal- =Albert Canal (EN)	122	Lc	51.10N	5.10 E
Albert Lea	182	Ic	43.39N	93.22W
Albert Nile	158	Kh	3.36N	32.02 E
Albertville [Al.-U.S.]	184	Dh	34.16N	86.12W
Albertville [Fr.]	122	Mi	45.41N	6.23 E
Albestroff	124	If	48.56N	6.51 E
Albi	122	Ik	43.56N	2.09 E
Albia	186	Jf	41.02N	92.48W
Al Bid'	146	Fh	28.28N	35.01 E
Albina	202	Hb	5.30N	54.03W
Albina, Ponta-	158	Ij	15.51S	11.44 E
Albino	128	De	45.46N	9.47 E
Albion [Mi.-U.S.]	184	Ed	42.15N	84.45W
Albion [Nb.-U.S.]	186	Hf	41.42N	98.00W
Albion [N.Y.-U.S.]	184	Hd	43.15N	78.12W
Al Biqa' [3]	146	Ge	34.00N	36.00 E
Al Biqa'	146	Ge	34.10N	36.10 E
Al Bi'r	144	Ed	28.51N	36.15 E
Al Bi'r al Jadīd	146	Hi	26.01N	38.29 E
Al Birk	144	Ff	18.13N	41.33 E
Albis	128	Cc	47.20N	8.30 E
Albo, Monte-	128	Dj	40.32N	9.35 E
Albocácer / Albocàsser	126	Md	40.21N	0.02 E
Albocàsser / Albocácer	126	Md	40.21N	0.02 E
Alborán, Isla de-	110	Fh	35.58N	3.02W
Alboran Basin (EN)	126	Ii	36.00N	4.00W
Ålborg	112	Gd	57.03N	9.56 E
Ålborg Bugt	114	Ch	56.45N	10.30 E
Alborz, Reshteh-ye Kūhhā-ye-=Elburz Mountains (EN)	140	Hf	36.00N	53.00 E
Albox	126	Jg	37.23N	2.08W
Albret, Pays d'-	122	Fj	44.10N	0.20W
Albū 'Alī	146	Je	34.49N	43.35 E
Albufeira	126	Dg	37.05N	8.15W
Albū Gharz, Sabkhat-	146	Ie	34.45N	41.15 E
Al Buheyrat [3]	168	Dd	7.00N	29.30 E
Al Bumbah	164	Dc	32.13N	23.00 E
Albuñol	126	Ih	36.47N	3.12W
Albuquerque [Braz.]	204	Dd	19.23S	57.26W
Albuquerque [N.M.-U.S.]	176	If	35.05N	106.40W
Albuquerque, Cayos de-	190	Hf	12.10N	81.50W
Al Burayj	146	Ge	34.15N	36.46 E
Al Burmah	162	Ic	31.45N	9.02 E
Alburquerque	126	Ee	39.13N	7.00W
Albury [Austl.]	210	Fh	36.05S	146.55 E
Albury [N.Z.]	218	Df	44.14S	170.53 E
Al Buṭanah	158	Kg	15.00N	35.00 E
Al Buṭayn	146	Kj	25.52N	45.50 E
Alby	116	Fb	62.30N	15.28 E
Alcácer do Sal	126	Df	38.22N	8.30W
Alcáçovas	126	Df	38.25N	8.13W
Alcalá de Chivert / Alcalà de Xivert	126	Md	40.18N	0.14 E
Alcalá de Guadaira	126	Gg	37.20N	5.50W
Alcalá de Henares	126	Id	40.29N	3.22W
Alcalá del Júcar	126	Ke	39.12N	1.26W
Alcalá de los Gazules	126	Gh	36.28N	5.44W
Alcalá del Río	126	Gg	37.31N	5.59W
Alcalà de Xivert / Alcalá de Chivert	126	Md	40.18N	0.14 E
Alcalá la Real	126	Ig	37.28N	3.56W
Alcamo	128	Gm	37.59N	12.58 E
Alcanadre	126	Mc	41.37N	0.12 E
Alcanices	126	Fc	41.42N	6.21W
Alcañiz	126	Lc	41.03N	0.08W
Alcantara	128	Jm	37.49N	15.16 E
Alcântara [Braz.]	202	Jd	2.24S	44.24W
Alcántara [Sp.]	126	Fe	39.43N	6.53W
Alcántara, Embalse de-	126	Fe	39.45N	6.48W
Alcantarilla	126	Kg	37.58N	1.13W
Alcaraz	126	Jf	38.40N	2.29W
Alcaraz, Sierra de-	126	Jf	38.35N	2.25W
Alcaudete	126	Hg	37.36N	4.05W
Alcázar de San Juan	126	Ie	39.24N	3.12W
Alcester	219a	Ac	9.33S	152.25 E
Alčevsk (Kommunarsk)	132	Ke	48.27N	38.52 E
Alcira/Alzira	126	Le	39.09N	0.26W
Alcobaça [Braz.]	202	Kg	17.30S	39.13W
Alcobaça [Port.]	126	De	39.33N	8.59W
Alcobendas	126	Id	40.32N	3.38W
Alcoi/Alcoy	126	Lf	38.42N	0.28W
Alcolea del Pinar	126	Jc	41.02N	2.28W
Alcorta	204	Bk	33.32S	61.07W
Alcoutim	126	Eg	37.28N	7.28W
Alcova	188	Le	42.37N	106.36W
Alcoy/Alcoi	126	Lf	38.42N	0.28W
Alcubierre, Sierra de-	126	Lc	41.44N	0.29W
Alcudia / Alcúdia de Mallorca	126	Pe	39.52N	3.07 E
Alcudia, Bahia de-/Alcúdia, Badia d'-	126	Pe	39.48N	3.13 E
Alcudia, Sierra de-	126	Hf	38.35N	4.35W
Alcúdia de Mallorca / Alcudia	126	Pe	39.52N	3.07 E
Aldabra Group	172b	Ab	9.25S	46.22 E
Aldabra Islands	158	Li	9.25S	46.22 E
Aldama [Mex.]	190	Cc	28.51N	105.54W
Aldama [Mex.]	192	Jf	22.55N	98.04W
Aldan	142	Od	58.37N	125.24 E
Aldan	142	Oc	63.28N	129.35 E
Aldan Plateau (EN) = Aldanskoje nagorje	140	Od	57.30N	127.30 E
Aldanskoje nagorje = Aldan Plateau (EN)	140	Od	57.30N	127.30 E
Aldarhan	152	Gb	47.42N	96.36 E
Alde	124	Db	52.10N	1.32 E
Aldeburgh	118	Oi	52.09N	1.35 E
Aldeia	204	Ed	18.12S	55.10W
Aldeia, Serra da-	204	Ic	17.00S	46.50W
Alderney	118	Kl	49.43N	2.12W
Aldershot	124	Bc	51.15N	0.46W
Alderson	188	Ja	50.18N	111.26W
Aledo	186	Kf	41.12N	90.45W
Aleg	160	Fg	17.03N	13.53W
Alegranza	162	Ed	29.23N	13.30W
Alegre	202	Jh	20.46S	41.32W
Alegre, Rio-	204	Cb	15.14S	59.58W
Alegrete	206	Ic	29.46S	55.46W
Alej	136	Df	52.50N	83.35 E
Alejandra	204	Ci	29.54S	59.50W
Alejandro Selkirk, Isla-	198	Hi	33.45S	80.46W
Alejsk	138	Df	52.28N	82.45 E
Aleksandrija	132	He	48.40N	33.07 E
Aleksandrov	136	Dd	56.25N	38.42 E
Aleksandrov Gaj	136	Ee	50.08N	48.32 E
Aleksandrovka	132	He	48.59N	32.13 E
Aleksandrovsk	134	Hg	59.10N	57.35 E
Aleksandrovskoje	132	Mg	44.39N	43.00 E
Aleksandrovsk-Sahalinsk	142	Qd	50.54N	142.10 E
Aleksandrów Kujawski	120	Od	52.52N	18.42 E
Aleksandrów Łódzki	120	Pe	51.49N	19.19 E
Aleksandry, zemlja-	140	Ga	80.45N	46.00 E
Aleksejevka [Kaz.]	136	If	48.26N	85.40 E
Aleksejevka [Kaz.]	136	He	51.58N	70.59 E
Aleksejevka [Kaz.]	134	Nj	53.31N	69.28 E
Aleksejevka [Russia]	136	De	50.39N	38.42 E
Aleksejevsk	138	Fe	57.50N	108.23 E
Aleksejevskoje	132	Mi	55.19N	50.03 E
Aleksin	132	Jb	54.31N	37.07 E
Aleksinac	130	Ef	43.32N	21.43 E
Alem [Arg.]	206	Ic	27.31S	55.15W
Ålem [Swe.]	114	Dh	56.57N	16.23 E
Alem Maya	168	Gd	9.27N	41.58 E
Ålen	116	Db	62.51N	11.17 E
Alençon	122	Gf	48.26N	0.05 E
Alenquer	202	Hd	1.56S	54.46W
Alenuihaha Channel	214	Oc	20.26N	156.00W
Alépé	166	Ed	5.30N	3.39W
Aleppo (EN)=Ḥalab	142	Ff	36.12N	37.10 E
Aléria	122a	Ba	42.06N	9.31 E
Aléria, Plaine d'-	122a	Ba	42.05N	9.30 E
Alert	176	Ma	82.30N	62.00W
Alert Bay	188	Ba	50.35N	126.55W
Alès	122	Kj	44.08N	4.05 E
Aleşd	130	Fb	47.04N	22.25 E
Alessandria	128	Cf	44.54N	8.37 E
Ålestrup	116	Ch	56.42N	9.30 E
Ålesund	112	Gc	62.28N	6.09 E
Aleutian Basin (EN)	174	Ad	57.00N	177.00 E
Aleutian Islands	174	Bd	52.00N	176.00W
Aleutian Range	174	Dd	59.00N	155.00W
Aleutian Trench (EN)	106	Je	51.00N	179.00 E
Alexander, Cape-	214	Fi	6.35S	156.30 E
Alexander, Kap-	179	Ec	78.10N	72.45W
Alexander Archipelago	174	Fd	56.30N	134.00W
Alexanderbaai	172	Be	28.40S	16.30 E
Alexander City	182	Je	32.56N	85.57W
Alexander Island	222	Qe	71.00S	70.00W
Alexandra	216	Ci	45.15S	169.24 E
Alexandra Fiord	180	Ka	79.17N	75.00W
Alexandretta (EN)=İskenderun	142	Ff	36.37N	36.07 E
Alexandretta, Gulf of- (EN) =İskenderun Körfezi	144	Eb	36.30N	35.40 E
Alexándria	130	Fi	40.38N	22.27 E
Alexandria	172	Df	33.39S	26.24 E
Alexandria [Austl.]	212	Hc	19.05S	136.40 E
Alexandria [La.-U.S.]	176	Jf	31.18N	92.27W
Alexandria [Mn.-U.S.]	182	Hb	45.53N	95.22W
Alexandria [Rom.]	130	If	43.59N	25.20 E
Alexandria [Va.-U.S.]	184	If	38.49N	77.06W
Alexandria (EN)=Al Iskandarīyah [Eg.]	160	Je	31.12N	29.54 E
Alexandria Bay	184	Jc	44.20N	75.55W
Alexandrina, Lake-	212	Hg	35.25S	139.10 E
Alexandrita	202	Hg	19.42S	50.27W
Alexandroúpolis	112	Ig	40.51N	25.52 E
'Aleyak, Godār-e-	146	Qd	36.30N	57.45 E
Alf	120	Df	50.03N	7.07 E
Alfabia, Sierra de-	126	Oe	39.45N	2.48 E
Alfambra	126	Kd	40.21N	1.07W
Al Fardah	168	Hc	14.51N	48.26 E
Alfaro	126	Kb	42.11N	1.45W
Al Fāshir	160	Jg	13.38N	25.21 E
Al Fashn	164	Fd	28.49N	30.54 E
Alfatar	130	Kf	43.57N	27.17 E
Al Fathah	146	Je	35.04N	43.34 E
Al Fāw	144	Gd	29.58N	48.29 E
Al Fawwārah	146	Ji	26.03N	43.05 E
Al Fayyūm	160	Kf	29.19N	30.58 E
Alfbach	124	Jd	50.03N	7.08 E
Alfeld	120	Fe	51.59N	9.50 E
Alfenas	204	Ie	21.26S	45.57W
Al Fifi	168	Dc	10.03N	25.01 E
Alfiós	130	El	37.37N	21.27 E
Alföld	110	If	47.15N	20.25 E
Alfonsine	128	Gf	44.30N	12.03 E
Alford	124	Ca	53.15N	0.11 E
Ålfotbreen	116	Ac	61.45N	5.40 E
Alfreton	124	Aa	53.06N	1.23W
Alfta	114	Df	61.21N	16.05 E
Al Fuḥayḥīl	144	Gd	29.05N	48.08 E
Al Fuhūd	146	Lg	30.58N	46.43 E
Al Fujayrah	144	Id	25.06N	56.21 E
Al Fūlah	168	Dc	11.48N	28.24 E
Al Fuqahā'	164	Cd	27.50N	16.21 E
Al Furāt=Euphrates (EN)	140	Gf	30.00N	47.25 E
Al Fuwayriṭ	146	Ni	26.02N	51.22 E
Alga	136	Ff	49.55N	57.20 E
Algador	126	Ie	39.55N	3.53W
Algarås	116	Ff	58.48N	14.14 E
Ålgård	116	Af	58.46N	5.51 E
Algarrobo	194	Jh	10.12N	74.04W
Algarve	110	Fh	37.10N	8.15W
Algarve	126	Dg	37.10N	8.15W
Algeciras	112	Fh	36.08N	5.30W
Algeciras, Bahia de-	126	Gh	36.09N	5.25W
Algena	168	Fb	17.20N	38.34 E
Algeria (EN)=Al Jazā'ir [1]	160	Hf	28.00N	3.00 E
Algerian Basin (EN)	110	Gh	39.00N	5.00 E
Al Gharaq as Sulṭānī	146	Dh	29.08N	30.42 E
Al Gharbī	162	Jc	34.40N	11.13 E
Al Ghāṭ	146	Ki	26.00N	45.03 E
Al Ghaydah	144	Hf	16.12N	52.15 E
Al Ghazālah	144	Fd	26.47N	41.23 E
Alghero	128	Cj	40.33N	8.19 E
Alghero, Rada d'-	128	Cj	40.35N	8.20 E
Alghult	116	Fg	57.01N	15.34 E
Al Ghurāb	146	Dj	25.20N	30.20 E
Al Ghurayfah	146	Qk	23.59N	56.29 E
Al Ghurdaqah	164	Fd	27.14N	33.50 E
Algiers (EN)=Al Jazā'ir	160	He	36.47N	3.03 E
Algiers (EN)=Al Jazā'ir [3]	162	Hb	36.35N	3.00 E
Algoa Bay	158	Jl	33.50S	25.50 E
Algodoeiro, Serra do-	204	Jc	16.30S	44.45W
Algoma	186	Md	44.36N	87.27W
Algoma Uplands	184	Fb	47.00N	83.35W
Algona	186	Ie	43.04N	94.14W
Algonquin Park	184	Hc	45.27N	78.26W
Algrange	124	Ie	49.21N	6.03 E
Al Ḥabakah	146	Jh	29.51N	42.16 E
Al Ḥadd	144	Ie	22.29N	59.58 E
Al Ḥadīdah	168	Ia	21.31N	50.28 E
Al Ḥadīthah	146	Gg	31.28N	37.08 E
Al Ḥadīthah	146	Fc	34.07N	42.23 E
Al Ḥaḍr	146	Je	35.35N	42.44 E
Al Haffah	146	Ge	35.35N	36.02 E
Al Ḥā'ir	146	Lj	24.23N	46.50 E
Al Hajar	168	Hb	16.08N	47.50 E
Al Ḥajarah	144	Fc	30.25N	44.30 E
Al Halfāyah	146	Lg	31.49N	47.26 E
Alhama	126	Kb	42.11N	1.45W
Al Ḥamād	140	Ff	32.00N	39.30 E
Alhama de Granada	126	Ih	37.00N	3.59W
Alhama de Murcia	126	Kg	37.51N	1.25W
Alhamilla, Sierra-	126	Jh	36.58N	2.20W
Al Ḥammāh	162	Ic	33.54N	9.48 E
Al Ḥammām [Eg.]	146	Cg	30.50N	29.23 E
Al Ḥammām [Iraq]	146	Kg	31.08N	44.04 E
Al Ḥamrā	146	Pj	25.42N	55.47 E
Al Hanīyah	146	Kh	29.10N	45.50 E
Al Ḥarrah	146	Ch	28.20N	29.07 E
Al Ḥarrah	146	Hg	31.00N	38.40 E
Al Ḥarrah	146	Gf	32.30N	37.45 E
Al Harūj al Aswad	158	If	27.00N	17.10 E
Al Ḥasā	146	Fg	30.49N	35.59 E
Al Hasā'	140	Gg	26.35N	48.10 E
Al Ḥasakah	144	Fb	36.29N	40.45 E
Al Ḥasan	146	Je	34.39N	43.43 E
Al Ḥasānī	146	Gj	24.58N	37.05 E
Alhaurin el Grande	126	Hh	36.38N	4.41W
Al Ḥawāmidīyah	146	Dh	29.54N	31.15 E
Al Ḥawātah	168	Ec	13.25N	34.38 E
Al Ḥawjā'	146	Hh	28.59N	38.34 E
Al Ḥawrah	168	Hc	13.49N	47.35 E
Al Hayy	144	Gc	32.10N	46.03 E
Al Ḥayyānīyah	146	Jh	28.42N	42.18 E
Al Ḥayz	164	Ed	28.02N	28.39 E
Al Hibāk	144	He	20.20N	53.10 E
Al Ḥijāz	140	Fg	24.30N	38.30 E
Al Ḥijāz	144	Ee	24.30N	38.30 E
Al Ḥillah [Iraq]	144	Fc	32.29N	44.25 E
Al Ḥillah [Sau.Ar.]	164	Ie	23.50N	46.51 E
Al Ḥināḳīyah	144	Fe	24.51N	40.31 E
Al Hindiyah	146	Kf	32.32N	44.13 E
Al Ḥinnāh	146	Mi	26.56N	48.45 E
Al Hirmil	146	Ge	34.23N	36.23 E
Al Hoceima	162	Gb	35.15N	3.55W
Al Hoceima [3]	162	Gb	35.00N	4.15W
Alhucemas, Peñón de-	126	Ii	35.13N	3.53W
Al Ḥudaydah	142	Gh	14.48N	42.57 E
Al Ḥufrah	164	Cd	29.30N	17.55 E
Al Hufrah	144	Ed	28.49N	38.15 E
Al Hufūf	142	Gg	25.22N	49.34 E
Al Hūj	146	Hh	29.00N	38.25 E
Al Ḥunayy	146	Mj	24.48N	48.45 E
Al Ḥuşayḥişah	168	Ec	14.44N	33.18 E
Al Ḥuwaimī	144	Fg	13.58N	47.40 E
Al Ḥuwayyiṭ	146	Ij	25.36N	40.23 E
'Ali, Sadd al-	164	Fe	23.54N	32.52 E
Aliābād	146	Pd	36.56N	54.50 E
'Alīābād [Iran]	146	Nd	36.37N	51.33 E
'Alīābād [Iran]	146	Le	35.04N	46.58 E
'Alīābād [Iran]	144	Id	28.37N	55.51 E
'Alīābād, Kūh-e-	144	Hc	34.13N	50.46 E
Aliaga	126	Ld	40.40N	0.42W
Aliağa	146	Bc	38.48N	26.59 E
Aliákmon	130	Fi	40.30N	22.40 E
'Alī al Gharbī	146	Lf	32.27N	46.41 E
'Alī ash Sharqī	146	Lf	32.07N	46.44 E
Ali-Bajramly	136	Eh	39.55N	48.57 E
Alibej, ozero-	130	Nd	45.50N	30.00 E
Alibey Adası	130	Jj	39.20N	26.38 E
Alibo	168	Fd	9.53N	37.05 E
Alibori	166	Fc	11.56N	3.17 E
Alibunar	130	Dd	45.04N	20.58 E
Alicante / Alacant	112	Fh	38.21N	0.29W
Alicante / Alacant [3]	126	Lf	38.30N	0.30W
Alicante, Golfo de- / Alacant, Golf d'-	126	Lf	38.20N	0.15W
Alice [S.Afr.]	172	Df	32.47S	26.50 E
Alice [Tx.-U.S.]	182	Hf	27.45N	98.04W
Alice, Punta-	128	Lk	39.12N	17.09 E
Alice Springs	210	Eg	23.42S	133.53 E
Aliceville	184	Ci	33.08N	88.09W
Alicudi	128	Il	38.30N	14.20 E
Aligarh	142	Jg	28.02N	78.17 E
Al Iglim al Janūbīyah = Southern Region (EN) [2]	168	Dd	6.00N	30.00 E
Aligūdarz	146	Mf	33.24N	49.41 E
Alihe→Oroqen Zizhiqi	152	La	50.35N	123.42 E
Alijó	126	Ec	41.16N	7.28W
Alijos, Rocas-	190	Ad	24.57N	115.44W
'Al Ijūq, Kūh-e-	146	Ng	31.30N	51.45 E
Al Ikhwān	146	Fi	26.19N	34.52 E
Al Ikhwan	140	Hh	12.08N	53.10 E
Alima	158	Ii	1.36S	16.36 E
Al Imārāt al 'Arabīyah al Muttaḥidah = United Arab Emirates (EN) [1]	142	Hg	24.00N	54.00 E
Alimiá	130	Km	36.16N	27.43 E
Alindao	168	Cd	5.02N	21.13 E
Alinglapalap Atoll	208	Hd	7.08N	168.16 E
Alingsås	114	Ch	57.56N	12.31 E
Aliquippa	184	Ge	40.38N	80.16W
Al 'Irāq = Iraq (EN) [1]	142	Gf	33.00N	44.00 E
Al'Irq	164	Dd	29.01N	21.31 E
Al 'Irqah	144	Gg	13.40N	47.18 E
Ali-Sabjeh	168	Gc	11.08N	42.43 E
'Alī Shāh 'Avaz	146	Ne	35.39N	51.04 E
Al Iskandarīyah [Eg.] = Alexandria (EN)	160	Je	31.12N	29.54 E
Al Iskandarīyah [Iraq]	146	Kf	32.53N	44.21 E
Aliskerovo	138	Lc	67.52N	167.40 E
Al Ismā'īlīyah=Ismailia (EN)	164	Fc	30.35N	32.16 E
Al Istiwā'īyah al Gharbīyah [3]	168	Dd	5.20N	28.30 E
Al Istiwā'īyah al Sharkīyah [3]	168	Ed	5.20N	33.50 E
Alistráti	130	Gh	41.04N	23.58 E
Alitak, Cape-	178	Ie	56.51N	154.21W
Alite Reef	219a	Ec	8.53S	160.38 E
Alitus/Alytus	136	Ce	54.25N	24.08 E
Alivérion	130	Hk	38.25N	24.02 E
Aliwal North	160	Jl	30.44S	26.40 E
Al Jabalayn	168	Ec	12.36N	32.48 E
Al Jadīdah [Eg.]	146	Cj	25.34N	28.51 E
Al Jadīdah [Sau.Ar.]	146	Mj	25.39N	49.32 E
Al Jafr	146	Gg	30.18N	36.13 E
Al Jāfūrah	146	Nj	25.00N	50.15 E
Al Jāfūrah	146	Nj	23.25N	50.17 E
Al Jaghbūb	160	Jf	29.45N	24.31 E
Al Jahrah	144	Gc	29.20N	47.40 E
Al Jalāmīd	146	Ig	31.17N	40.06 E
Al Jamalīyah	146	Nj	25.37N	51.05 E
Al Jamm	162	Jb	35.18N	10.43 E
Al Janā'in	162	Jc	31.44N	10.09 E
Al Janūb [3]	146	Ff	33.20N	35.30 E
Aljat	132	Pj	39.58N	49.27 E
Al Jawf [Lib.]	160	Jf	24.12N	23.18 E
Al Jawf [Sau.Ar.]	142	Fg	29.50N	39.52 E
Al Jazā'ir=Algeria (EN) [1]	160	Hf	28.00N	3.00 E
Al Jazā'ir=Algiers (EN)	160	He	36.47N	3.03 E
Al Jazā'ir=Algiers (EN) [3]	162	Hb	36.35N	3.00 E
Al Jazā'ir-El Harrach	126	Ph	36.43N	3.08 E
Al Jazīrah [3]	168	Ec	14.40N	33.30 E
Al Jazīrah [Asia]	140	Gf	35.10N	42.00 E
Al Jazīrah [Sud.]	158	Kg	14.25N	33.00 E
Aljezur	126	Dg	37.19N	8.48W
Aljibe	126	Gh	36.31N	5.37W
Al Jifārah	158	Ie	32.30N	11.45 E
Al Jiwā'	144	He	23.00N	54.00 E
Al Jīzah=Giza (EN)	160	Ke	30.01N	31.13 E
Al Jubayl	144	Gd	27.01N	49.40 E
Al Jubaylah	146	Lj	24.54N	46.27 E
Al Junaynah [Sau.Ar.]	164	He	20.17N	42.48 E
Al Junaynah [Sud.]	160	Jg	13.27N	22.27 E
Al Juraid	146	Mi	27.11N	49.52 E
Aljustrel	126	Dg	37.52N	8.10W
Al Kaba'ish	146	Lg	30.58N	47.00 E
Al Kāf	162	Ib	36.11N	8.43 E
Al Kāf [3]	162	Ib	36.00N	9.00 E
Alkali Lake	188	Ff	41.42N	119.50W
Al Kāmilīn	168	Eb	15.05N	33.11 E
Al Karak	146	Fg	31.11N	35.42 E
Al Karak [3]	146	Fg	31.11N	35.42 E
Al Karkh	146	Kf	33.20N	44.20 E
Al Karnak	164	Fd	25.43N	32.39 E
Al Kawah	168	Ec	13.44N	32.30 E
Al Kāẓimīyah	146	Kf	33.22N	44.20 E
Alken	124	Hd	50.52N	5.18 E
Al Khabrā'	144	Fd	26.04N	43.33 E
Al Khābūra	144	Ie	23.50N	57.18 E
Al-Khalīj al- 'Arabi=Persian Gulf (EN)	140	Hg	27.00N	51.00 E
Al Khalīl	146	Fg	31.32N	35.06 E
Al Khalīl [3]	146	Fg	31.30N	35.05 E
Al Khālis	146	Kf	33.51N	44.32 E
Al Khandaq	168	Eb	18.36N	30.34 E
Al Khārijah	160	Kf	25.26N	30.33 E
Al Kharj	146	Lj	24.10N	47.30 E
Al Kharṭūm = Khartoum (EN) [3]	168	Eb	15.50N	33.00 E
Al Kharṭūm = Khartoum (EN)	160	Kg	15.36N	32.32 E
Al Kharṭūm Bahrī = Khartoum North (EN)	160	Kg	15.38N	32.33 E
Al Khaşab	146	Qi	26.12N	56.15 E
Al Khaṭṭ	146	Qk	25.37N	56.01 E
Al Khawr	144	Hd	25.40N	51.30 E
Al Khidr	146	Kg	31.12N	45.33 E
Al Khubar	144	Hd	26.17N	50.12 E
Al Khufayfīyah	144	Fe	24.55N	44.42 E
Al Khums	160	Ie	32.39N	14.16 E
Al Khums [3]	164	Bc	31.20N	14.10 E
Al Khunn	168	Ha	23.18N	49.15 E
Al Khuwayr	146	Ni	26.04N	51.05 E
Al Kidn	168	Ia	22.30N	54.00 E
Al Kifl	146	Kf	32.14N	44.22 E
Al Kilḥ Sharq	146	Ej	25.03N	32.52 E
Alkionidhon, Kólpos-	130	Fk	38.05N	23.00 E
Al Kir'ānah	146	Nj	25.00N	51.03 E
Alkmaar	122	Kb	52.37N	4.44 E
Al Kūfah	146	Kf	32.02N	44.24 E
Al Kumayt	146	Lf	32.02N	46.52 E
Al Kuntillah	164	Fc	30.00N	34.41 E
Al Kushḥ	146	Ei	26.14N	32.05 E
Al Kut	144	Gc	32.30N	45.49 E
Al Kuwayt = Kuwait (EN)	142	Gg	29.20N	47.59 E
Al Kuwayt=Kuwait (EN) [1]	142	Gg	29.30N	47.45 E
Al Labbah	144	Fd	29.20N	41.30 E
Al Lādhiqīyah=Latakia (EN)	142	Ff	35.31N	35.07 E
Allagash River	184	Mb	47.05N	69.20W
Al Lagowa	168	Dc	11.24N	29.08 E
Allahābād	142	Kg	25.27N	81.51 E
Allah-Jun	138	Id	61.08N	137.59 E
Allah-Jun	138	Id	60.27N	134.57 E
Allahüekber Dağı	146	Jb	40.35N	42.32 E
Allakaket	178	Ic	66.34N	152.41W
Allanmyo	148	Je	19.22N	95.13 E
'Allāqī, Wadī al-	164	Fe	23.07N	32.47 E
Allariz	126	Eb	42.11N	7.48W
All-Awash Island	197n	Bb	12.55N	61.10W
Alldays	172	Dd	22.41S	29.06 E
Ålleberg	116	Ef	58.08N	13.36 E
Allegan	184	Ed	42.32N	85.51W
Allegheny Mountains	174	Lf	38.30N	80.00W
Allegheny Plateau	174	Le	41.30N	78.00W
Allegheny Reservoir	184	He	42.00N	78.56W
Allegheny River	182	Lc	40.27N	80.00W
Allègre, Pointe-	197e	Ab	16.22N	61.45W
Allen	150	Hd	12.30N	124.17 E
Allen, Bog of-	118	Gh	53.20N	7.00W
Allen, Lough-/Loch Aillionn	118	Eg	54.08N	8.08W
Allendale	184	Gi	33.01N	81.19W
Allende	190	Dc	28.20N	100.51W
Allendorf (Eder)	124	Kc	51.02N	8.40 E
Allendorf (Lumda)	124	Kd	50.41N	8.50 E
Allentown	182	Lc	40.37N	75.30W
Alleppey	142	Ji	9.29N	76.19 E
Aller	120	Fd	52.57N	9.11 E
Allevard	122	Mi	45.24N	6.04 E
Allgäu	120	Gi	47.35N	10.10 E
Allgäuer Alpen	120	Gi	47.20N	10.25 E
Alliance [Nb.-U.S.]	182	Gc	42.06N	102.52W
Alliance [Oh.-U.S.]	184	Ge	40.56N	81.06W
Allier [3]	122	Ih	46.30N	3.00 E
Allier	110	Gf	46.57N	3.05 E
Al Lifīyah	144	Fc	30.35N	43.09 E
Al Lişāfah	146	Li	27.37N	46.52 E
Alliston	184	Hc	44.09N	79.52W
Al Līth	144	Fe	20.09N	40.16 E
Alloa	118	Je	56.07N	3.49W
Allonnes	122	Gg	47.58N	0.09 E
Allos	122	Mj	44.14N	6.38 E
All Saints	197d	Bb	17.03N	61.48W
Al Luḥayyah	144	Ff	15.43N	42.42 E
Al Luwaymī	144	Fd	27.54N	42.22 E
Alm	128	Hb	48.05N	13.55 E
Alma [Ga.-U.S.]	184	Fj	31.33N	82.28W
Alma [Mi.-U.S.]	184	Ed	43.23N	84.39W
Alma [Nb.-U.S.]	186	Gf	40.06N	99.22W

Alma [Que.-Can.] 180 Kg 48.32N 71.40W
Al Ma'ānīyah 146 Jg 30.44N 43.00 E
Alma-Ata 142 Je 43.15N 76.57 E
Alma-Atinskaja oblast [3] 136 Hg 44.00N 77.00 E
Almada 126 Cf 38.41N 9.09W
Almadén 126 Hf 38.46N 4.50W
Al Madīnah [Iraq] 146 Lg 30.57N 47.16 E
Al Madīnah [Sau.Ar.] = Medina (EN) 142 Fg 24.28N 39.36 E
Al Madīnah al Fikrīyah 146 Di 27.56N 30.49 E
'Al Madōw 168 Hc 10.59N 48.42 E
Al Mafraq 146 Gf 32.21N 36.12 E
Al Maghrib=Morocco (EN) [1] 160 Ge 32.00N 5.50W
Almagro 126 If 38.53N 3.43W
Almagrundet 116 He 59.06N 19.00 E
Al Maḥallah al Kubrá 164 Fc 30.58N 31.10 E
Al Maḥāriq 164 Fd 25.37N 30.39 E
Al Mahdīyah 162 Jb 35.30N 11.04 E
Al Mahdīyah [3] 162 Jb 35.35N 11.00 E
Al Maḥfid 164 Ig 14.03N 46.55 E
Al Mahrah 144 Hf 16.56N 52.15 E
Al Maḥras 162 Jc 34.32N 10.30 E
Al Majarr al Kabīr 146 Lg 31.34N 47.10 E
Almajului, Munţii- 130 Fe 44.43N 22.12 E
Al Maks al Qiblī 164 Fe 24.35N 30.38 E
Almalyk 136 Gg 40.49N 69.38 E
Al Manādir 146 Pk 23.10N 55.10 E
Al Manāmah=Manama (EN) 142 Hg 26.13N 50.35 E
Al Manāqil 168 Ec 14.15N 32.59 E
Almanor, Lake- 188 Ef 40.15N 121.08W
Almansa 126 Kf 38.52N 1.05W
Almansa, Puerto de- 126 Lf 38.49N 0.58W
Al Manshāh 164 Fd 26.28N 31.48 E
Almansor 126 Df 38.56N 8.54W
Al Manṣūrah 164 Fc 31.03N 31.23 E
Al Manzilah 146 Dg 31.09N 31.56 E
Almanzora / Guadalmanzor 126 Kg 37.14N 1.46W
Al Ma'qil 146 Lg 30.33N 47.48 E
Al Maqnah 146 Fh 28.24N 34.45 E
Al Maqṭa' 146 Pj 24.25N 54.29 E
Almar 126 Gd 40.54N 5.29W
Al Marāghah 146 Di 26.42N 31.36 E
Al Marsá 128 En 36.53N 10.20 E
Al Marj 160 Je 32.30N 20.54 E
Almaş 130 Gb 47.14N 23.19 E
Almas, Picos das- 198 Lg 13.33S 41.56W
Almas, Rio das- 202 If 14.35S 49.02W
'Al Maskād 168 Hc 11.18N 49.41 E
Almassora / Almazora 126 Le 39.57N 0.03W
Al Maṭarīyah 164 Fc 31.11N 32.02 E
Al Mawṣil=Mosul (EN) 142 Gf 36.20N 43.08 E
Al Mayādīn 146 Ie 35.01N 40.27 E
Al Mayyāh 146 Ji 27.51N 42.47 E
Almazán 126 Jc 41.29N 2.32W
Al Mazār 146 Eg 31.23N 33.23 E
Almazny 138 Gd 62.19N 114.04 E
Almazora / Almassora 126 Le 39.57N 0.03W
Al Mazra'ah 146 Fg 31.16N 35.31 E
Alme, Brilon- 124 Kc 51.27N 8.37 E
Almeida 126 Fc 41.16N 6.04W
Almeirim [Braz.] 202 Hd 1.32S 52.34W
Almeirim [Port.] 126 De 39.12N 8.38W
Al Mellem 168 Dd 9.49N 28.45 E
Almelo 122 Mb 52.21N 6.39 E
Almenara, Sierra de la- 126 Kg 37.35N 1.31W
Almendra, Embalse de- 126 Fc 41.13N 6.10W
Almendralejo 126 Ff 38.41N 6.24W
Almería 112 Fh 36.50N 2.27W
Almería [3] 126 Jg 37.10N 2.20W
Almería, Golfo de- 126 Jh 36.46N 2.30W
Almetjevsk 136 Fe 54.54N 52.20 E
Al Metlaoui 162 Ic 34.20N 8.24 E
Älmhult 114 Dh 56.33N 14.08 E
Almijara, Sierra de- 126 Ih 36.55N 3.55W
Almina, Punta- 126 Gi 35.54N 5.17W
Al Minyā [Eg.] 146 Dh 29.45N 31.18 E
Al Minyā [Eg.] 160 Kf 28.06N 30.45 E
Al Miqdādīyah 146 Kf 33.59N 44.56 E
Almirante 194 Fi 9.18N 82.24W
Almirante Brown 222 Qe 64.53S 62.53W
Almirós 130 Fj 39.11N 22.46 E
Almiroú, Órmos- 130 Hn 35.23N 24.20 E
Almodôvar 126 Dg 37.31N 8.04W
Almodóvar del Campo 126 Hf 38.43N 4.10W
Almodóvar del Río 126 Gg 37.48N 5.01W
Almonte 126 Fg 37.15N 6.31W
Almonte 126 Fe 39.42N 6.28W
Almoustarat 166 Fb 17.22N 0.07 E
Älmsta 116 He 59.58N 18.48 E
Al Mubarraz 144 Gd 25.25N 49.35 E
Al Mudarraj 146 Hj 25.41N 38.40 E
Al Mudawwarah 146 Fh 29.19N 35.59 E
Al Mudhari, Rujm- 146 Hf 32.45N 39.08 E
Al Mughayrā' [Sau.Ar.] 146 Gh 29.17N 37.41 E
Al Mughayrā' [U.A.E.] 146 Oj 24.05N 53.32 E
Al Muglad 160 Jg 11.02N 27.44 E
Al Muḥarraq 146 Ni 26.16N 50.37 E
Al Mukallā 142 Gh 14.32N 49.08 E
Al Mukhā 144 Fg 13.19N 43.15 E
Al Munastīr 162 Jb 35.47N 10.50 E
Al Munastīr [3] 162 Jb 35.40N 10.50 E
Almuñécar 126 Ih 36.43N 3.41W
Al Murabba' 146 Kj 25.43N 44.18 E
Almus 146 Gb 40.23N 36.55 E
Al Musannāh 146 Lh 29.02N 47.12 E
Al Muşawwarāt aş Şafra' 168 Eb 16.25N 33.22 E
Al Musayjid 146 Hj 24.05N 39.06 E
Al Musayyib 146 Kf 32.47N 44.18 E
Al Mustawī 146 Kj 25.55N 44.40 E
Al Muthanna [3] 146 Kg 30.50N 45.20 E
Al Muwayh 164 He 22.45N 41.35 E
Al Muwaylih 146 Fi 27.41N 35.28 E
Alnön 116 Gb 62.25N 17.25 E
Alnwick 118 Lf 55.25N 1.42W
Ålö 116 Jd 60.20N 22.15 E
Aloândia 204 Hc 17.43S 49.29W
Alofi 210 Kf 19.03S 169.56W
Alofi, Ile- 208 Jf 14.19S 178.02W
Alofi Bay 220k Bb 19.01S 169.56W
Aloja 114 Fh 57.44N 24.59 E
Along 148 Ic 28.10N 94.46 E
Alónnisos 130 Gj 39.13N 23.55 E
Alonsa 186 Ga 50.47N 99.00W
Alonso, Rio- 204 Gg 24.05S 51.35W
Alor, Kepulauan- 150 Hh 8.15S 124.30 E
Alor, Pulau- 140 Oj 8.15S 124.45 E
Alora 126 Hh 36.48N 4.42W
Alor Setar 142 Mi 6.07N 100.22 E
Alost/Aalst 122 Kd 50.56N 4.02 E
Alotau 214 Ej 10.31S 150.43 E
Aloysius, Mount- 212 Fe 26.00S 128.34 E
Alpen = Alps (EN) 110 Gf 46.25N 10.00 E
Alpena 182 Kb 45.04N 83.26W
Alpera 126 Kf 38.58N 1.13W
Alpes=Alps (EN) 110 Gf 46.25N 10.00 E
Alpes Cottiennes 128 Af 44.45N 7.00 E
Alpes-de-Haute-Provence [3] 122 Mj 44.10N 6.10 E
Alpes Grées/Alpi Graie 128 Be 45.30N 7.10 E
Alpes Mancelles 122 Ff 48.25N 0.10W
Alpes-Maritimes [3] 122 Nk 44.00N 7.10 E
Alpes Maritimes 128 Bf 44.15N 7.10 E
Alpes Pennines/Alpi Pennine 128 Bd 46.05N 7.50 E
Alpes Valaisannes 128 Bd 46.10N 7.30 E
Alpha Cordillera (EN) 224 Re 85.30N 125.00W
Alphen aan de Rijn 124 Gb 52.08N 4.42 E
Alphonse Island 158 Mi 7.00S 52.45 E
Alpi=Alps (EN) 110 Gf 46.25N 10.00 E
Alpi Apuane 128 Ef 44.05N 10.20 E
Alpi Aurine 120 Hi 47.00N 11.55 E
Alpi Carniche 128 Gd 46.40N 13.00 E
Alpi Cozie 128 Af 44.45N 7.00 E
Alpi Graie/Alpes Grées 128 Be 45.30N 7.10 E
Alpi Lepontine 128 Cd 46.25N 8.40 E
Alpi Liguri 128 Cf 44.10N 8.05 E
Alpi Marittime 128 Bf 44.15N 7.10 E
Alpine [Az.-U.S.] 188 Kj 33.51N 109.09W
Alpine [Tx.-U.S.] 182 Ge 30.22N 103.40W
Alpine [Wy.-U.S.] 188 Je 43.15N 110.59W
Alpi Orobie 128 Dd 46.00N 10.00 E
Alpi Pennine/Alpes Pennines 128 Bd 46.05N 7.50 E
Alpi Retiche=Rhaetian Alps (EN) 128 Dd 46.30N 10.00 E
Alpi Venoste 120 Gj 46.45N 10.55 E
Alprech, Cap d'- 124 Dd 50.42N 1.34 E
Alps (EN) = Alpen 110 Gf 46.25N 10.00 E
Alps (EN)=Alpes 110 Gf 46.25N 10.00 E
Alps (EN)=Alpi 110 Gf 46.25N 10.00 E
Al Qa 'āmiyāt 168 Hb 18.50N 48.30 E
Al Qābil 146 Pk 23.56N 55.49 E
Al Qaḍārif 160 Kg 14.02N 35.24 E
Al Qaḍīmah 144 Fe 22.21N 39.09 E
Al Qādisīya 146 Kg 31.42N 44.28 E
Al Qādisīya [3] 146 Kg 31.50N 45.00 E
Al Qadmūs 146 Ge 35.05N 36.10 E
Al Qaffāy 146 Nj 24.35N 51.44 E
Al Qāhirah=Cairo (EN) 160 Ke 30.03N 31.15 E
Al Qāhirah-Imbabah 164 Fc 30.05N 31.13 E
Al Qāhirah-Mişr al Jadīdah 164 Fc 30.06N 31.20 E
Al Qā'iyah 146 Ki 26.27N 45.35 E
Al Qal'ah al Kubrá 128 Eo 35.52N 10.32 E
Al Qalībah 144 Ed 28.24N 37.42 E
Al Qāmishlī 144 Fb 37.02N 41.14 E
Al Qanṭarah 164 Fc 30.52N 32.19 E
Al Qārah 146 Ih 29.52N 40.15 E
Al Qaryah ash Sharqīyah 164 Bc 30.24N 13.36 E
Al Qaryatayn 146 Ge 34.14N 37.14 E
Al Qaşab 146 Kj 25.18N 45.30 E
Al Qaşabāt 164 Bc 32.35N 14.03 E
Al Qa'şah 146 Ch 28.25N 28.56 E
Al Qaşr 164 Ed 25.42N 28.53 E
Al Qaşrayn 162 Ib 35.11N 8.48 E
Al Qaşrayn [3] 162 Ib 35.15N 9.00 E
Al Qaţīf 146 Mi 26.33N 50.00 E
Al Qaţrānī 146 Gg 31.15N 36.03 E
Al Qaţrūn 164 Be 24.56N 14.38 E
Al Qay'īyah 144 Fe 24.18N 43.30 E
Al Qayrawān 162 Jb 35.41N 10.07 E
Al Qayrawān [3] 162 Ib 35.30N 10.00 E
Al Qayşūmah [Sau.Ar.] 144 Gd 28.16N 46.03 E
Al Qayşūmah [Sau.Ar.] 146 Jh 29.11N 42.58 E
Alqōsh 146 Jd 36.44N 43.06 E
Al Qubayyāt 146 Ge 34.34N 36.17 E
Al Quds [3] 146 Fg 31.45N 35.20 E
Al Qunayţirah 144 Ec 33.07N 35.49 E
Al Qunfudhah 144 Ff 19.08N 41.05 E
Al Qurayyah 146 Gh 28.45N 36.12 E
Al Qurnah 146 Lg 31.00N 47.26 E
Al Quşaymah 164 Fc 30.40N 34.22 E
Al Quşayr [Eg.] 160 Kf 26.06N 34.17 E
Al Quşayr [Syr.] 146 Ge 34.31N 36.35 E
Al Qūşīyah 164 Fd 27.26N 30.49 E
Al Quşūr 128 Co 35.54N 8.53 E
Al Quţayfah 146 Gf 33.44N 36.36 E
Al Quwārah 146 Ji 26.47N 43.28 E
Al Quwayr 146 Jd 36.03N 43.30 E
Al Quzah 168 Hb 15.06N 49.08 E
Als 116 Ci 55.00N 9.55 E
Alsace 122 Nf 48.30N 7.30 E
Alsace, Ballon d'- 122 Mg 47.50N 6.51 E
Alsasua / Altsasu 126 Jb 42.54N 2.10W
Alsdorf 124 Id 50.53N 6.10 E
Alsea River 188 Cd 44.26N 124.05W
Alsenz 124 Je 49.59N 7.51 E
Alsfeld 120 Ff 50.45N 9.16 E
Alsina, Laguna- 204 Am 36.52S 62.07W
Alsten 114 Cd 65.57N 12.36 E
Alsterån 116 Gh 56.55N 16.26 E
Alsunga 116 Ig 57.02N 21.28 E
Alta 114 Fb 69.58N 23.14 E
Altaelva 114 Fb 69.58N 23.23 E
Altafjorden 114 Fa 70.12N 23.06 E
Altagracia 202 Da 10.07N 71.14W
Alta Gracia 206 Hd 31.40S 64.26W
Altagracia de Orituco 196 Ch 9.52N 66.23W
Altai (EN) = Altay Shan 140 Le 46.30N 93.00 E
Altaj 142 Le 46.20N 96.17 E
Altaj 140 Kd 51.30N 90.00 E
Altajski 138 Df 51.58N 85.30 E
Altajski kraj [3] 138 Df 52.00N 82.30 E
Altamaha River 182 Ke 31.19N 81.17W
Altamira 200 Kf 3.12S 52.12W
Altamira, Cuevas de- 126 Ha 43.23N 4.05W
Altamira, Sierra de- 126 Ge 39.35N 5.10W
Altamirano 192 Mi 16.53N 92.09W
Altamont 188 Ee 42.12N 121.44W
Altamura 128 Kj 40.49N 16.33 E
Altamura, Isla de- 192 Ee 25.00N 108.10W
Altan Bulag 152 Jc 44.19N 113.28 E
Altan-Emel → Xin Barag Youqi 152 Kb 48.41N 116.47 E
Altan Xiret → Ejin Horo Qi 152 Id 39.31N 109.45 E
Altar 192 Db 30.43N 111.44W
Altar, Desierto de- 174 Hf 31.50N 114.15W
Altar, Rio- 192 Db 30.39N 111.55W
Altar de los Sacrificios 194 Be 16.28N 90.32W
Altata 190 Cd 24.38N 107.55W
Alta Verapaz [3] 194 Bf 15.40N 90.00W
Altavista 184 Hg 37.07N 79.18W
Altay 142 Ke 47.52N 88.07 E
Altay Shan = Altai (EN) 140 Le 46.30N 93.00 E
Altdorf 128 Cd 46.53N 8.40 E
Altea 126 Lf 38.36N 0.03W
Altena 120 De 51.18N 7.40 E
Altenberge 124 Jb 52.03N 7.28 E
Altenburg 120 If 50.59N 12.27 E
Altenglan 124 Je 49.33N 7.28 E
Altenkirchen (Westerwald) 124 Jd 50.42N 7.39 E
Alter do Chão 126 Ee 39.12N 7.40W
Altevatnet 114 Eb 68.32N 19.30 E
Altındağ, Ankara- 146 Ec 39.56N 32.52 E
Altinoluk 130 Jj 39.34N 26.44 E
Altınova 130 Jj 39.13N 26.47 E
Altıntaş 146 Dc 39.04N 30.07 E
Altınyayla 130 Mm 36.59N 29.33 E
Altkirch 122 Ng 47.37N 7.15 E
Altmark 120 Hd 52.40N 11.20 E
Altmühl 120 Hh 48.55N 11.52 E
Alto, Morro- 204 Ib 13.46S 46.50W
Alto, Pico- 202 Kd 4.20S 39.00W
Alto Alentejo 126 Ef 38.50N 7.40W
Alto Araguaia 202 Hg 17.19S 53.12W
Alto Coité 204 Eb 15.47S 54.20W
Alto Garças 204 Fc 16.56S 53.32W
Alto Longá 202 Je 5.15S 42.12W
Alto Molócuè 172 Fc 15.38S 37.42 E
Altomonte 128 Kk 39.42N 16.08 E
Alton [Eng.-U.K.] 124 Bc 51.08N 0.59W
Alton [Il.-U.S.] 182 Id 38.54N 90.10W
Altona, Hamburg- 120 Fc 53.33N 9.57 E
Altoona 182 Lc 40.32N 78.23W
Alto Paraguai 202 Gf 14.30S 56.31W
Alto Paraguay [3] 206 Ce 21.00S 59.00W
Alto Paraíso de Goiás 204 Ib 14.12S 47.38W
Alto Paraná [3] 204 Eg 25.00S 54.50W
Alto Parnaíba 202 Ie 9.06S 45.57W
Alto Purús, Rio- 202 De 9.34S 70.36W
Alto Rio Senguerr 206 Fg 45.02S 70.50W
Altos 202 Jd 5.03S 42.28W
Alto Sucuriú 204 Fd 19.19S 52.47W
Altötting 120 Ih 48.14N 12.41 E
Alto Uruguai, Serra do- 204 Fh 27.35S 53.40W
Altsasu / Alsasua 126 Jb 42.54N 2.10W
Altun Ha 194 Ce 17.50N 88.20W
Āltūn Kūprī 146 Ke 35.45N 44.09 E
Altun Shan 140 Kf 38.00N 88.00 E
Alturas 182 Cc 41.29N 120.32W
Alturitas 196 Ki 9.45N 72.25W
Altus 182 He 34.38N 99.20W
Altynkan 136 Hd 41.03N 70.43 E
Altynkul 135 Bc 43.07N 58.55 E
Alu 219a Bb 7.05S 155.47 E
Al 'Ubaylah 168 Ia 21.59N 50.57 E
Al Ubayyiḍ 160 Kg 13.11N 30.13 E
Alucra 146 Hb 40.20N 38.46 E
Al 'Udaysāt 146 Ej 25.35N 32.29 E
Al Uḍayyah 168 Dc 12.03N 28.17 E
Alūksne/Aluksne 114 Gh 57.26N 27.01 E
Aluksne/Alūksne 114 Gh 57.26N 27.01 E
Aluksne ozero 116 Lg 57.22N 27.10 E
Aluksne ozero / Alūksnes ezers 116 Lg 57.22N 27.10 E
Alūksnes ezers / Aluksne ozero 116 Lg 57.22N 27.10 E
'Alūla 168 Ic 11.58N 50.48 E
Al 'Ulá 144 Ed 26.37N 37.52 E
Al Umm 164 Hf 18.18N 40.45 E
Alunda 116 Hd 60.04N 18.05 E
Alupka 136 Dg 44.24N 34.03 E
Al'Uqaylah 164 Cc 30.16N 19.12 E
Al 'Uqaylāt 146 Ii 26.43N 41.43 E
Al 'Uqayr 146 Nj 25.39N 50.13 E
Al Uqşur=Luxor (EN) 164 Fd 25.41N 32.39 E
Al Urayq 146 Hh 29.00N 39.10 E
Al Urdun=Jordan (EN) [1] 144 Ff 31.00N 36.00 E
Al 'Urūq al Mu'tariḍah 168 Ia 21.00N 54.00 E
Ālūs 146 Ie 34.02N 42.26 E
Alušta 136 Dg 44.42N 34.20 E
Al 'Uthmānīyah 146 Mj 25.15N 49.22 E
Al'Uwaynāt 164 Bd 25.48N 10.33 E
Al 'Uwaynidhīyah 146 Gi 26.38N 36.05 E
Al 'Uwayqīlah 146 Jg 30.21N 42.14 E
Al 'Uyūn 146 Hj 24.33N 39.35 E
Al Uzaym 146 Ke 34.02N 44.20 E
Al 'Uzayr 146 Lg 31.19N 47.25 E
Alva 182 Hd 36.48N 98.40W
Alva 126 Dd 40.18N 8.15W
Alvand, Kūh-e- 146 Me 34.41N 48.28 E
Ålvängen 116 Eg 57.56N 12.09 E
Alvaro Obregón, Presa- 192 Ed 28.00N 109.45W
Alvdal 114 Ce 62.07N 10.39 E
Älvdalen 114 Df 61.14N 14.02 E
Älvdalen 116 Ed 60.30N 13.00 E
Alvear 204 Di 29.06S 56.33W
Alvelos, Serra de- 126 De 39.55N 8.01W
Alvesta 114 Dh 56.54N 14.33 E
Ålvik [Nor.] 114 Bf 60.26N 6.26 E
Alvik [Swe.] 116 Gb 62.25N 17.24 E
Alvin 186 Il 29.25N 95.15W
Älvkarleby 114 Df 60.34N 17.27 E
Alvord Valley 188 Fe 42.45N 118.25W
Alvøy 116 Ad 60.35N 4.50 E
Älvros 116 Fb 62.03N 14.39 E
Älvsborg [2] 114 Cg 58.00N 12.30 E
Älvsbyn 114 Ed 65.40N 21.00 E
Al Wāḥidī 144 Gg 14.20N 47.50 E
Al Wajh 142 Fg 26.14N 36.28 E
Al Wakrah 146 Nj 25.10N 51.36 E
Al Wannān 146 Mi 26.55N 48.24 E
Alwar 148 Fc 27.34N 76.36 E
Al Wari'ah 146 Li 27.50N 47.29 E
Al Wāsiṭah 164 Fd 29.20N 31.12 E
Al Waslātīyah 128 Do 35.51N 9.35 E
Al Waṭī'ah 164 Bc 32.28N 11.46 E
Al Wazz 168 Eb 15.01N 30.10 E
Al Widyān 140 Gf 31.10N 40.45 E
Alxa Youqi (Ehen Hudag) 152 Hd 39.12N 101.40 E
Alxa Zuoqi (Bayan Hot) 152 Id 38.50N 105.32 E
Al Yaman = Yemen (EN) 142 Gh 15.00N 44.00 E
Al Yaman ad Dimuqrāṭīyah → Yemen (EN) 142 Gh 15.00N 44.00 E
Alyangula 212 Hb 13.50S 136.25 E
Alygdžer 138 Ef 53.38N 98.16 E
Alymka 134 Ng 59.01N 68.40 E
Alytus/Alitus 136 Ce 54.25N 24.08 E
Alz 120 Ih 48.10N 12.48 E
Alzamaj 138 Ee 55.33N 98.39 E
Alzey 120 Eg 49.45N 8.07 E
Alzira/Alcira 126 Le 39.09N 0.26W
Amachkalo Ahzar 166 Fb 15.30N 3.20 E
Amacuro, Rio- 202 Fb 8.32N 60.28W
Amada 164 Fe 22.45N 32.10 E
Amadeus, Lake- 208 Eg 24.50S 130.45 E
Amadi [Sud.] 168 Ed 5.31N 30.20 E
Amadi [Zaire] 170 Eb 3.35N 26.47 E
Amadjuak Lake 180 Kd 64.55N 71.00W
Amadora 126 Cf 38.45N 9.14W
Amadror 162 Ie 24.50N 6.25 E
Amadror 162 Id 26.00N 5.21W
Amagasaki 156 Dd 34.42N 135.25 E
Amager 116 Ei 55.35N 12.35 E
Amagi [Jap.] 156b Bb 27.47N 128.52 E
Amagi [Jap.] 156 Be 33.26N 130.39 E
Amagi-San 156 Fd 34.51N 139.00 E
Amaha 156 Fd 35.13N 139.51 E
Amahai 150 Ig 3.20S 128.55 E
Amain, Monts d'- 122 Gf 48.39N 0.20 E
Amajac, Rio- 192 Jg 21.15N 98.46W
Amakusa-Nada 154 Jh 32.25N 129.40 E
Amakusa-Shotō 154 Kh 32.22N 130.12 E
Amal [Lib.] 164 Dd 29.25N 21.10 E
Åmål [Swe.] 114 Cg 59.03N 12.42 E
Amalfi 128 Ij 40.38N 14.36 E
Amaliás 130 El 37.48N 21.21 E
Amalner 148 Fd 21.03N 75.04 E
Amambai 202 Gh 23.05S 55.13W
Amambai, Rio- 204 Ff 23.22S 53.56W
Amambai, Serra de- 204 Ef 23.10S 55.30W
Amambay [3] 204 Df 23.00S 56.00W
Amami Islands (EN) = Amami-Shotō 140 Og 28.16N 129.21 E
Amami-Ō-Shima 152 Mf 28.15N 129.20 E
Amami-Shotō = Amami Islands (EN) 140 Og 28.16N 129.21 E
Åmån 116 Fc 61.12N 14.45 E
Amana 186 Kf 41.45N 91.51W
Amanā, Lago- 202 Fd 2.35S 64.40W
Amana, Rio- 196 Eh 9.45N 62.39W
Amanab 214 Ch 3.38S 141.16 E
Amanave 221c Cb 14.19S 170.49W
Amandola 128 Hh 42.59N 13.21 E
Amangeldy 136 Ge 50.10N 65.13 E
Amankaragaj 134 Lj 52.27N 64.08 E
Amantea 128 Kk 39.07N 16.08 E
Amanu Atoll 208 Mf 17.48S 140.46W
Amanzimtoti 172 Ef 30.05S 30.53 E
Amapá 200 Ke 2.03N 50.48W
Amapá 202 Hc 1.30N 52.00W
Amapala 194 Dg 13.17N 87.40W
Amara 130 Ke 44.37N 27.19 E
Amara 158 Kg 11.30N 37.45 E
Amaradia 130 Ge 44.22N 23.43 E
Amara East 168 Ea 20.48N 30.23 E
Amarante [Braz.] 202 Je 6.14S 42.50W
Amarante [Port.] 126 Dc 41.16N 8.05W
Amaranth 186 Ga 50.36N 98.43W
Amargosa 188 Gh 36.18N 116.25W
Amargosa Desert 188 Gh 36.40N 116.30W
Amargosa Range 188 Gh 36.30N 116.45W
Amargosa River 188 Gh 36.13N 116.48W
Amarillo 176 If 35.13N 101.49W
Amárion 130 Hn 35.14N 24.39 E
Amarume 156 Fb 38.50N 139.54 E
Amasra 146 Eb 41.45N 32.34 E
Amasya 144 Ea 40.39N 35.51 E
Amathus 146 Ee 34.42N 33.08 E
Amatique, Bahía de- 194 Cf 15.55N 88.45W
Amatlán de Cañas 192 Gg 20.52N 104.27W
Amatrice 128 Hh 42.38N 13.17 E
Amaurilandia 204 Ff 22.10S 52.38W
Amay 124 Hd 50.33N 5.19 E
Amazar 138 Hf 53.54N 120.57 E
Amazon (EN)=Amazonas, Rio- (Solimões) 198 Lf 0.10S 49.00W
Amazon (EN) = Solimoes → Amazonas, Rio- 198 Lf 0.10S 49.00W
Amazon, Mouths of the- (EN) 198 Le 0.10S 49.00W
Amazonas [Braz.] [2] 202 Fd 5.00S 63.00W
Amazonas [Col.] [3] 202 Dd 1.00N 72.00W
Amazonas [Peru] [3] 202 Ce 5.00S 77.00W
Amazonas [Ven.] [3] 202 Ec 3.30N 66.00W
Amazonas, Rio- (Solimões) = Amazon (EN) 198 Lf 0.10S 49.00W
Amazon Cone (EN) 198 Le 4.30N 52.00W
Amba Ferit 168 Fc 10.55N 38.55 E
Ambāla 148 Fb 30.21N 76.50 E
Ambalangoda 148 Gg 6.14N 80.03 E
Ambalavao 172 Hd 21.50S 46.57 E
Ambam 166 He 2.23N 11.17 E
Ambanja 172 Hb 13.39S 48.27 E
Ambarčik 142 Sc 69.39N 162.20 E
Ambarès-et-Lagrave 122 Fj 44.55N 0.29W
Ambargasta, Salinas de- 206 Hc 29.20S 64.30W
Ambarny 136 Db 65.54N 33.41 E
Ambasamudram 148 Fg 8.42N 77.28 E
Ambato 200 If 1.15S 78.37W
Ambato-Boéni 172 Hc 16.28S 46.40 E
Ambatofinandrahana 172 Hd 20.33S 46.47 E
Ambatolampy 172 Hc 19.23S 47.25 E
Ambatondrazaka 160 Lj 17.48S 48.26 E
Ambatosoratra 172 Hc 17.36S 48.32 E
Ambelau, Pulau- 150 Ig 3.51S 127.12 E
Amberg 120 Hg 49.27N 11.52 E
Ambergris Cay 194 Dd 18.03N 87.56W
Ambergris Cays 194 Lc 21.18N 71.37W
Ambérieu-en-Bugey 122 Li 45.57N 5.21 E
Amberley [Eng.-U.K.] 124 Bd 50.55N 0.32W
Amberley [N.Z.] 218 Ee 43.09S 172.45 E
Ambert 122 Ji 45.33N 3.45 E
Ambikāpur 148 Gd 23.07N 83.12 E
Ambila 172 Hd 21.58S 47.59 E
Ambilobe 172 Hb 13.11S 49.03 E
Ambitle 219a Aa 4.05S 153.40 E
Ambjörby 116 Ed 60.30N 13.10 E
Ambla 116 Ke 59.10N 25.44 E
Amblève 122 Ld 50.28N 5.36 E
Amblève/Amel 124 Id 50.21N 6.09 E
Ambo 202 Cf 10.07S 76.10W
Amboasary Sud 172 He 25.01S 46.23 E
Ambodifototra 172 Hc 16.58S 49.52 E
Ambohimahasoa 172 Hd 21.08S 47.12 E
Ambohimanarina 172 Hc 18.49S 47.26 E
Ambohitralanana 172 Ic 15.15S 50.28 E
Amboise 122 Gg 47.25N 0.59 E
Ambon 210 De 3.43S 128.12 E
Ambon, Pulau- 150 Ig 3.40S 128.10 E
Ambongo 172 Gc 16.50S 45.00 E
Amboseli, Lake- 170 Gc 2.37S 37.08 E
Ambositra 160 Lk 20.30S 47.14 E
Ambovombe 172 He 25.09S 46.06 E
Ambre, Cap d'-=Ambre, Cape d'-(EN) 158 Lj 11.57S 49.17 E
Ambre, Cape d'-(EN)= Ambre, Cap d'- 158 Lj 11.57S 49.17 E
Ambre, Montagne d'- 172 Hb 12.30S 49.10 E
Ambriz 160 Ii 7.50S 13.08 E
Ambrolauri 132 Mh 42.31N 43.05 E
Ambrym, Ile- 208 Hf 16.15S 168.07 E
Ambunti 214 Ch 4.14S 142.50 E
Āmbūr 148 Ff 12.47N 78.42 E
Amchitka 178a Bb 51.30N 179.00 E
Amchitka Pass 178a Cb 51.30N 179.30W
Am Dafok 168 Cc 10.28N 23.17 E
Am Dam 168 Cc 12.46N 20.29 E
Amded 162 He 22.10N 3.15 E
Amderma 136 Gb 69.45N 61.39 E
Am Djéména 168 Bc 13.06N 17.19 E
Amdo 152 Fe 32.29N 91.47 E
Ameca 190 Dd 20.33N 104.02W
Ameca, Rio- 192 Gg 20.41N 105.18W
Amel/Amblève 124 Id 50.21N 6.09 E
Ameland 124 Ha 53.26N 5.48 E
Ameland- 122 La 53.25N 5.45 E
Ameland- Nes 124 Ha 53.26N 5.48 E
Amelia Island 184 Gj 30.37N 81.27W
Amélie-les-Bains-Palalda 122 Il 42.28N 2.40 E
Amendolara 128 Kk 39.57N 16.35 E
'Āmerī 146 Nh 28.30N 51.05 E
Americana 204 If 22.45S 47.20W
American Falls 188 Ie 42.47N 112.51W
American Falls Reservoir 188 Ie 43.00N 113.00W
American Fork 188 Jf 40.23N 111.48W
American Highland 222 Ff 72.30S 78.00 E
American Samoa [5] 210 Kf 14.50S 170.00W
Americus 182 Ke 32.04N 84.14W
Amersfoort 122 Lb 52.09N 5.24 E
Amery Ice Shelf 222 Fe 69.30S 72.00 E
Ames 182 Ic 42.02N 93.37W
Ametlla de Mar 126 Md 40.54N 0.48 E
Amfilokhia 130 Ek 38.52N 21.10 E
Amfissa 130 Fk 38.32N 22.23 E
Amfreville-la-Campagne 124 Ce 49.13N 0.57 E
Amga 138 Id 60.52N 131.50 E
Amga 140 Pc 62.40N 134.59 E
Amgalang → Xin Barag Zuoqi 152 Kb 48.13N 118.14 E
Am Géréda 168 Cc 12.52N 21.10 E
Amgu 154 Nb 45.51N 137.41 E
Amguema 138 Nc 68.03N 177.55W
Amguid 160 Hf 26.26N 5.22 E
Amguid 162 Id 26.30N 5.36 E
Amgun 140 Pd 52.56N 139.40 E
Amherst 180 Lg 45.49N 64.14W
Amherst, Mount- 212 Fc 18.11S 126.59 E
Amherst Island 184 Ic 44.12N 76.42W
Amiata, Monte- 128 Fh 42.53N 11.37 E
Amiens 112 Gf 49.54N 2.18 E
Āmij, Wādī- 146 If 33.48N 41.46 E
Amik Gölü 146 Gd 36.22N 36.17 E
Amili 148 Jc 28.26N 95.52 E
Amīndīvi Islands 148 Ef 11.23N 72.23 E
Aminuis 172 Bd 23.43S 19.21 E
'Āmir, Ra's- 158 Je 32.57N 21.43 E

Index Symbols

[1] Independent Nation
[2] State, Region
[3] District, County
[4] Municipality
[5] Colony, Dependency
Continent
Physical Region
Historical or Cultural Region
Mount, Mountain
Volcano
Hill
Mountains, Mountain Range
Hills, Escarpment
Plateau, Upland
Pass, Gap
Plain, Lowland
Delta
Salt Flat
Valley, Canyon
Crater, Cave
Karst Features
Depression
Polder
Desert, Dunes
Forest, Woods
Heath, Steppe
Oasis
Cape, Point
Coast, Beach
Cliff
Peninsula
Isthmus
Sandbank
Island
Atoll
Rock, Reef
Islands, Archipelago
Rocks, Reefs
Coral Reef
Well, Spring
Geyser
River, Stream
Waterfall, Rapids
River Mouth, Estuary
Lake
Salt Lake
Intermittent Lake
Reservoir
Swamp, Pond
Canal
Glacier
Ice Shelf, Pack Ice
Ocean
Sea
Gulf, Bay
Strait, Fjord
Lagoon
Bank
Seamount
Tablemount
Ridge
Shelf
Basin
Escarpment, Sea Scarp
Fracture
Trench, Abyss
National Park, Reserve
Point of Interest
Recreation Site
Cave, Cavern
Historic Site
Ruins
Wall, Walls
Church, Abbey
Temple
Scientific Station
Railway station
Airport
Port
Military installation
Lighthouse
Mine
Tunnel
Dam, Bridge

Amirante Basin (EN) 158 Mi 7.00S 55.00 E
Amirante Islands 158 Mi 6.00S 53.10 E
Amirante Trench (EN) 172b Bb 6.00S 52.30 E
Amisk Lake 180 Hf 54.35N 102.15W
Amistad, Presa de la- 186 Fl 28.34N 101.15W
Amistad Reservoir 182 Gf 28.34N 101.15W
Amite 186 Kk 30.44N 90.30W
Amlekhganj 148 Gc 27.17N 84.59 E
Amlia 178a Db 52.06N 173.30W
Amlwch 118 Ih 53.25N 4.20W
'Amm Adām 168 Fb 16.22N 36.09 E
'Ammān 142 Ff 31.57N 35.56 E
'Ammān [3] 146 Gg 31.57N 35.56 E
Ammanford 118 Jj 51.48N 3.59W
Ammarnäs 114 Dd 65.58N 16.12 E
Åmmeberg 116 Ff 58.52N 15.00 E
Ammer 120 Hi 47.57N 11.08 E
Ammerån 116 Ga 63.09N 16.13 E
Ammerland 120 Dc 53.15N 8.00 E
Ammersee 120 Hi 48.00N 11.08 E
Ammi-Moussa 126 Ni 35.52N 1.07 E
Ammokhostos → Famagusta (EN) 144 Dc 35.07N 33.57 E
Amnja 134 Me 63.45N 67.07 E
Amnok-kang 152 Ld 39.55N 124.20 E
Āmol 144 Hb 36.23N 52.20 E
Amolar 204 Dd 18.01S 57.30W
Amorgós 130 Im 36.50N 25.53 E
Amorgós 130 Im 36.50N 25.59 E
Amorinópolis 204 Gc 16.36S 51.08W
Amory 186 Lj 33.59N 88.29W
Amos 180 Jg 48.34N 78.07W
Åmot [Nor.] 114 Bg 59.54N 9.54 E
Åmot [Nor.] 116 Be 59.35N 8.00 E
Åmotfors 116 Ee 59.46N 12.22 E
Amoucha 126 Rh 36.23N 5.25 E
Amouliani 130 Gi 40.20N 23.55 E
Amour, Djebel- 162 Hc 33.45N 1.45 E
Amourj 162 Ff 16.10N 7.35W
Amoy (EN) = Xiamen 142 Ng 24.32N 118.06 E
Ampanihy 172 Gd 24.40S 44.45 E
Amparafaravola 172 Hc 17.36S 48.12 E
Amparo 204 If 22.42S 46.47W
Ampato, Nevado de- 198 Ig 15.50S 71.52W
Amper 120 Hh 48.10N 11.50 E
Ampère Seamount (EN) 110 Eh 35.05N 12.13W
Amphitrite Point 188 Cb 48.56N 125.35W
Amposta 126 Md 40.43N 0.35 E
Ampthill 124 Bb 52.02N 0.29W
Ampurdán / Empordà 126 Ob 42.12N 2.45 E
Ampurias / Empúries 126 Pb 42.10N 3.05 E
Amqui 184 Na 48.28N 67.26W
'Amrān 144 Ff 15.41N 43.55 E
Amrāvati 142 Jg 20.56N 77.45 E
Am-Raya 168 Bc 14.05N 16.30 E
Amritsar 142 Jf 31.35N 74.53 E
Amrum 120 Eb 54.40N 8.20 E
Amsaga 162 Ee 20.07N 14.10W
Amsittene, Jebel- 162 Fc 31.11N 9.40W
Amstel 124 Gb 52.22N 4.56 E
Amstelveen 124 Gb 52.18N 4.53 E
Amsterdam 158 Ol 37.57S 77.40 E
Amsterdam [Neth.] 112 Ge 52.22N 4.54 E
Amsterdam [N.Y.-U.S.] 184 Jd 42.56N 74.12W
Amsterdam-Rijnkanaal 124 Hc 51.57N 5.25 E
Amstetten 128 Ib 48.07N 14.52 E
Am Timan 160 Jg 11.02N 20.17 E
Amūd, Jabal al- 144 Ec 30.59N 39.20 E
Āmūdā 146 Id 37.05N 40.54 E
Amu-Darja 135 Ef 37.57N 65.15 E
Amudarja ⇒ Amu Darya (EN) 140 He 43.40N 59.01 E
Āmū Daryā = Amu Darya (EN) 140 He 43.40N 59.01 E
Amu Darya (EN) = Amudarja 140 He 43.40N 59.01 E
Amu Darya (EN) = Āmū Daryā 140 He 43.40N 59.01 E
Amudat 170 Fb 1.58N 34.56 E
Amukta Pass 178a Db 52.25N 172.00W
Amun 219a Ba 5.57S 154.45 E
Amund Ringnes 180 Ha 78.15N 97.00W
Amundsen Bay 222 Ee 66.55S 50.00 E
Amundsen Coast 222 Mg 85.30S 159.00W
Amundsen Glacier 222 Mg 85.35S 159.00W
Amundsen Gulf 174 Gb 71.00N 124.00W
Amundsen-Scott Station 222 Bg 90.00S 0.00
Amundsen Sea (EN) 222 Of 72.30S 112.00W
Amungen 116 Fc 61.10N 15.40 E
Amuntai 142 Nj 2.26S 115.15 E
Amur 140 Qd 52.56N 141.10 E
'Amūr, Wādī- 168 Eb 18.56N 33.34 E
Amurang 150 Hf 1.11N 124.35 E
Amursk 138 If 50.16N 136.55 E
Amurskaja oblast [3] 138 Hf 54.00N 128.00 E
Amurzet 138 Ig 47.41N 131.07 E
Amvrakia, Gulf of- (EN) = Amvrakikós Kólpos 130 Dk 39.00N 21.00 E
Amvrakikós Kólpos = Amvrakia, Gulf of- (EN) 130 Dk 39.00N 21.00 E
Amvrosijevka 132 Kf 47.44N 38.31 E
Am Zoer 168 Cc 14.13N 21.23 E
Anaa Atoll 216 Lc 17.25S 145.30W
Anabar 220e Ba 0.29S 166.57 E
Anabar 140 Nb 73.08N 113.36 E
Anabarskoje ploskogorje 140 Mc 70.00N 108.00 E
An Abhainn Dubh/Blackwater 118 Gh 53.39N 6.43W
An Abhainn Mhór/Blackwater [Ire.] 118 Fj 51.51N 7.50W
An Abhainn Mhór/Blackwater [N.Ire.-U.K.] 118 Gg 54.30N 6.35W
Anabuki 156 Dd 34.02N 134.11 E
Anacasti 206 Gc 28.49S 65.30W
Anaco 202 Fb 9.27N 64.28W
Anaconda 182 Eb 46.08N 112.57W
Anacortes 188 Db 48.30N 122.37W
Anadarko 186 Gi 35.04N 98.15W
Anadolu = Anatolia (EN) 140 Ff 39.00N 35.00 E
Anadyr 142 Tc 64.45N 177.29 E
Anadyr 140 Tc 64.55N 176.05 E
Anadyr Gulf (EN) = Anadyrski zaliv 140 Uc 64.00N 179.00W
Anadyr Range (EN) = Anadyrskoje ploskogorje 140 Tc 67.00N 174.00 E
Anadyrski liman 138 Md 64.30N 178.00 E
Anadyrski zaliv = Anadyr Gulf (EN) 140 Uc 64.00N 179.00W
Anadyrskoje ploskogorje = Anadyr Range (EN) 140 Tc 67.00N 174.00 E
Anáfi 130 Im 36.22N 25.47 E
Anaghit 168 Fb 16.20N 38.39 E
Anagni 128 Hi 41.44N 13.09 E
'Ānah 144 Fc 34.28N 41.56 E
Anaheim 188 Gj 33.51N 117.57W
Anahola 221a Ba 22.09N 159.19W
Anáhuac 192 Id 27.14N 100.09W
Anáhuac, Meseta de- 190 Dd 21.30N 101.00W
An Aird/Ards Peninsula 118 Hg 54.30N 5.30W
Anaj Mudi 140 Jh 10.10N 77.04 E
Anaktuvuk Pass 178 Ic 68.10N 151.50W
Analalava 172 Hb 14.38S 47.45 E
Analavelona 172 Gd 22.37S 44.10 E
Ana María, Golfo de- 194 Hc 21.25N 78.40W
Anambas, Kepulauan- = Anambas Islands (EN) 140 Mi 3.00N 106.00 E
Anambas Islands (EN) = Anambas, Kepulauan- 140 Mi 3.00N 106.00 E
Anambra [2] 166 Gd 6.30N 7.30 E
Anamé 219b De 20.08S 169.49 E
Anamizu 154 Nf 37.14N 136.54 E
Anamur 144 Db 36.06N 32.50 E
Anamur Burun 144 Db 36.03N 32.48 E
Anan [Jap.] 156 Ed 35.19N 137.48 E
Anan [Jap.] 154 Mh 33.55N 134.39 E
Anane, Djebel- 126 Mi 35.12N 0.47 E
Anánes 130 Hm 36.31N 24.08 E
Ananjev 132 Ff 47.43N 29.59 E
Anankwin 148 Je 15.41N 97.59 E
Anantapur 148 Ff 14.41N 77.36 E
Anantnāg (Islāmābād) 148 Fb 33.44N 75.09 E
Anapa 136 Dg 44.53N 37.19 E
Anapo 128 Jm 37.03N 15.16 E
Anápolis 200 Lg 16.20S 48.58W
Anapu, Rio- 202 Hd 2.15S 51.30W
Anār 144 Ic 30.53N 55.18 E
Anārak 144 Hc 33.20N 53.42 E
Anare Station 222 Jd 54.30S 158.55 E
Anaro, Río- 194 Lj 7.48N 70.12W
Añasco 197a Ab 18.17N 67.10W
Anatahan Island 208 Fc 16.22N 145.40 E
Anatolia (EN) = Anadolu 140 Ff 39.00N 35.00 E
Anatolikí Rodhópi 130 Ih 41.44N 25.31 E
Añatuya 206 Hc 28.28S 62.50W
Anauá, Rio- 202 Fc 0.58N 61.21W
Anazah, Jabal- 146 Hf 32.12N 39.18 E
Anazarba 146 Fd 37.15N 35.45 E
An Baile Meánach/Ballymena 118 Gg 54.52N 6.17W
An Bhanna/Bann 118 Gf 55.10N 6.46W
An Bhearú/Barrow 118 Gi 52.10N 7.00W
An Bhinn Bhuí/Benwee Head 118 Dg 54.21N 9.48W
An Bhograch/Boggeragh Mountains 118 Ei 52.05N 9.00W
Àn Bhóinn/Boyne 118 Gh 53.43N 6.15W
An Bhrosnach/Brosna 118 Fh 53.13N 7.58W
An Blascaod Mór/Great Blasket 118 Ci 52.05N 10.32W
Anbyŏn 154 Ie 39.02N 127.32 E
An Cabhán / Cavan 118 Fg 54.00N 7.21W
An Cabhán/Cavan [2] 118 Fh 53.55N 7.30W
An Caisleán Nua/Newcastle 118 Hg 54.12N 5.54W
An Caisleán Nua/Newcastle West 118 Di 52.27N 9.03W
An Caisleán Riabhach/Castlerea 118 Eh 53.46N 8.29W
An Caoláire Rua/Killary Harbour 118 Dh 53.38N 9.55W
Ancares, Sierra de- 126 Fb 42.46N 6.54W
Ancash [3] 202 Ce 9.30S 77.45W
Ancenis 122 Eg 47.22N 1.10W
An Chathair/Caher 118 Fi 52.22N 7.55W
An Cheacha/Caha Mountains 118 Dj 51.45N 9.45W
Anchorage 176 Ec 61.13N 149.53W
An Chorr Chríochach/Cookstown 118 Gg 54.39N 6.45W
Anci (Langfang) 152 Kd 39.29N 116.40 E
An Clár/Clare [2] 118 Ei 52.50N 9.00W
An Cóbh/Cóbh 118 Ej 51.51N 8.17W
Ancohuma, Nevado- 202 Eg 15.51S 68.36W
Ancona 112 Hg 43.38N 13.30 E
Ancón de Sardinas, Bahía de- 202 Cc 1.30N 79.50W
Ancre 122 Ie 49.54N 2.28 E
Ancuabe 172 Fb 12.58S 39.51 E
Ancud 206 Ff 41.52S 73.50W
Ancud, Golfo de- 206 Ff 42.05S 73.00W
Anda 152 Mb 46.24N 125.20 E
Anda (Sartu) 154 Ha 46.35N 125.00 E
Andacollo [Arg.] 206 Fe 37.11S 70.41W
Andacollo [Chile] 206 Fd 30.14S 71.06W
Andahuaylas 202 Df 13.39S 73.23W
An Daingean/Dingle 118 Ci 52.08N 10.15W
Andalgalá 206 Gc 27.36S 66.19W
Åndalsnes 114 Be 62.34N 7.42 E
Andalucía = Andalusia (EN) [2] 126 Hg 37.30N 4.30W
Andalucía = Andalusia (EN) 110 Fh 37.30N 4.30W
Andalusia 182 Je 31.19N 86.29W
Andalusia (EN) = Andalucía [2] 126 Hg 37.30N 4.30W
Andalusia (EN) = Andalucía 110 Fh 37.30N 4.30W
Andaman and Nicobar [3] 148 If 12.30N 92.45 E
Andaman Basin (EN) 140 Lh 10.00N 94.00 E
Andaman Islands 140 Lh 12.30N 92.43 E
Andaman Sea (EN) 140 Lh 10.00N 95.00 E
Andamooka 212 Hf 30.27S 137.12 E
'Andān, Wādī- 144 Ie 21.05N 58.23 E
Andant 204 Am 36.34S 62.07W
Andapa 172 Hb 14.38S 49.33 E
Andara 172 Cc 18.03S 21.27 E
Andelle 124 De 49.19N 1.14 E
Andelys, Les- 122 He 49.15N 1.25 E
Andenes 114 Db 69.19N 16.08 E
Andenne 124 Hd 50.29N 5.06 E
Andenne-Namêche 124 Hd 50.28N 5.00 E
Andéranboukane 166 Fb 15.26N 3.02 E
Anderlecht 124 Gd 50.50N 4.18 E
Anderlues 124 Gd 50.24N 4.16 E
Andermatt 128 Cd 46.38N 8.37 E
Andernach 120 Df 50.26N 7.24 E
Andernos-les-Bains 122 Ej 44.44N 1.06W
Anderson 180 Ec 69.42N 129.01W
Anderson [Ca.-U.S.] 188 Df 40.27N 122.18W
Anderson [In.-U.S.] 182 Jc 40.10N 85.41W
Anderson [S.C.-U.S.] 182 Ke 34.30N 82.39W
Anderstorp 116 Eg 57.17N 13.38 E
Andes (EN) = Andes, Cordillera de los- 198 Jh 20.00S 67.00W
Andes, Cordillera de los- = Andes (EN) 198 Jh 20.00S 67.00W
Andevoranto 172 Hc 18.56S 49.06 E
Andfjorden 114 Db 69.10N 16.20 E
Andhra Pradesh [3] 148 Fe 16.00N 79.00 E
Andía, Sierra de- / Andia, Sierra de- 126 Kb 42.45N 2.00W
Andia, Sierra de- / Andía, Sierra de- 126 Kb 42.45N 2.00W
Andikhásia Ōri 130 Ej 39.47N 21.55 E
Andikíra 130 Fk 38.23N 22.38 E
Andikíthira = Andikithira (EN) 130 Gn 35.52N 23.18 E
Andikithira (EN) = Andikíthira 130 Gn 35.52N 23.18 E
Andikithíron, Stenón- 130 Gn 35.45N 23.25 E
Andilamena 172 Hc 17.01S 48.32 E
Andilanatoby 172 Hc 17.56S 48.14 E
Andīmeshk 146 Mf 32.27N 48.21 E
Andímilos 130 Hm 36.47N 24.14 E
Andíparos 130 Il 37.00N 25.03 E
Andípaxoi 130 Dj 39.08N 20.14 E
Andípsara 130 Ik 38.33N 25.24 E
Andir He 152 Dd 38.00N 83.36 E
Andırın 146 Gd 37.34N 36.20 E
Andirlangar 152 Dd 37.36N 83.50 E
Andírrion 130 Ek 38.20N 21.46 E
Andítilos 130 Km 36.22N 27.28 E
Andižan 142 Je 40.45N 72.22 E
Andižanskaja oblast [3] 136 Hg 40.45N 72.20 E
Andkhvoy 144 Kb 36.56N 65.08 E
Andŏng 152 Md 36.36N 128.44 E
Andorra (Valls d'Andorra) [1] 112 Gg 42.30N 1.30 E
Andorra la Vella 112 Gg 42.31N 1.31 E
Andover 118 Lj 51.13N 1.28W
Andøya 114 Db 69.08N 15.54 E
Andradas 204 If 22.05S 46.35W
Andradina 206 Jb 20.54S 51.23W
Andraitx / Andratx 126 Oe 39.35N 2.25 E
Andratx / Andraitx 126 Oe 39.35N 2.25 E
Andreanof Islands 174 Bd 52.00N 176.00W
Andreapol 114 Hh 56.39N 32.16 E
Andrées Land 179 Jd 73.20N 26.30W
Andrejevka [Kaz.] 136 If 45.47N 80.35 E
Andrejevka [Ukr.] 132 Je 49.32N 36.40 E
Andrejevo-Ivanovka 130 Nb 47.31N 30.21 E
Andrejevsk 138 Ge 58.10N 114.15 E
Andrelândia 204 Je 21.44S 44.18W
Andresito 204 Dk 33.08S 57.09W
Andrespol 120 Pe 51.43N 19.40 E
Andrews 186 Ej 32.19N 102.33W
Andria 128 Ki 41.13N 16.17 E
Andriamena 172 Hc 17.28S 47.29 E
Andriba 172 Hc 17.36S 46.53 E
Andrijevica 130 Cg 42.44N 19.48 E
Andringitra 158 Lk 22.20S 46.55 E
Andrítsaina 130 El 37.29N 21.54 E
Androka 172 Gd 24.59S 44.04 E
Androna, Plateau de l'- 172 Hc 15.30S 48.20 E
Andropov → Rybinsk 112 Jd 58.03N 38.52 E
Ándros 130 Hl 37.50N 24.56 E
Andros 110 Ih 37.50N 24.50 E
Androscoggin River 184 Md 43.55N 69.55W
Andros Island 174 Lg 24.25N 78.00W
Andros Town 190 Id 24.43N 77.47W
Androth Island 148 Ef 10.50N 73.41 E
Androy 158 Lk 25.00S 45.40 E
Andruševka 132 Fe 49.59N 29.01 E
Andrychów 120 Pg 49.52N 19.21 E
Andselv 114 Eb 69.04N 18.30 E
Andudu 170 Eb 2.29N 28.41 E
Andújar 126 Hf 38.03N 4.04W
Andulo 170 Ce 11.28S 16.43 E
Andu Tan 150 Fe 7.35N 114.15 E
Anduze 122 Jj 44.03N 3.59 E
An Ea agail/Errigal 118 Ef 55.02N 8.07W
Aneby 116 Fg 57.50N 14.48 E
Anéfis 166 Fb 18.03N 0.36 E
Anegada 190 Le 18.45N 64.20W
Anegada, Bahía- 206 Hf 40.15S 62.15W
Anegada Passage 190 Le 18.30N 63.40W
Aného 166 Fd 6.14N 1.36 E
An Éirne/Erne 118 Eg 54.30N 8.15W
An Eithne/Inny 118 Fh 53.35N 7.50W
An Eoghanach/Annalee 118 Fg 54.02N 7.25W
Anet 124 Df 48.51N 1.26 E
Aneto, Pico de- 110 Gg 42.38N 0.40 E
Aney 166 Hb 19.24N 12.56 E
Aneytioum, Ile- 208 Hg 20.12S 169.49 E
An Feabhal / Foyle 118 Ff 55.04N 7.15W
An Fhéil/Feale 118 Di 52.28N 9.40W
An Fheoir/Nore 118 Gi 52.25N 6.58W
Angamos, Punta- [Chile] 206 Fb 23.01S 70.32W
Angamos, Punta- [Pas.] 221d Bb 27.04S 109.17W
Angara 140 Ld 58.06N 93.00 E
Angarsk 142 Md 52.34N 103.54 E
Angarski, pereval- 132 Ig 44.47N 34.25 E
Angarski krjaž 138 Fe 57.30N 103.00 E
Angathonísi 130 Jl 37.28N 27.00 E
Angaur Island 208 Ed 6.54N 134.09 E
Änge [Swe.] 116 Fa 63.27N 14.03 E
Ånge [Swe.] 114 De 62.31N 15.37 E
An Gearrán/Garron Point 118 Hf 55.05N 5.58W
Ángel, Cerro- 192 Hf 22.49N 102.34W
Angelburg 124 Kd 50.47N 8.25 E
Ángel de la Guarda, Isla- 190 Bc 29.20N 113.25W
Angeles 150 Hc 15.09N 120.35 E
Ángeles, Sierra de los- 192 Jf 23.10N 99.20W
Ángel Falls (EN) = Angel, Salto-/Churún Merú 198 Je 5.57N 62.30W
Ángel Falls (EN) = Churún Merú/Angel, Salto- 198 Je 5.57N 62.30W
Ängelholm 114 Ch 56.15N 12.51 E
Angélica 204 Bj 31.33S 61.33W
Angeln 120 Fb 54.40N 9.45 E
Angel Salto-/Churún Merú = Ángel Falls (EN) 198 Je 5.57N 62.30W
Ängelsberg 116 Ge 59.58N 16.02 E
Anger 168 Fd 9.40N 36.06 E
Angereb 168 Fc 13.44N 36.28 E
Ångermanälven 110 Hc 62.48N 17.56 E
Angermünde 120 Jc 53.02N 14.00 E
Angers 112 Ff 47.28N 0.33W
Angikuni Lake 180 Hd 62.10N 99.55W
Angístrion 130 Gl 37.40N 23.20 E
Angkor 148 Kf 13.26N 103.52 E
Anglem, Mount- 218 Bg 46.44S 167.54 E
Anglès 126 Oc 41.57N 2.39 E
Anglesey 110 Fe 53.18N 4.20W
Anglet 122 Ek 43.29N 1.32W
Angleton 186 Il 29.10N 95.26W
Anglin 122 Gh 46.42N 0.52 E
Anglona 128 Cj 40.45N 8.45 E
Anglo-Normandes, Iles- (F) = Channel Islands [5] 118 Kl 49.20N 2.20W
Angmagssalik 224 Mc 65.45N 37.30W
Ango 170 Eb 4.02N 25.52 E
Angoche 160 Kj 16.12S 39.54 E
Angoche, Ilha- 158 Kj 16.20S 39.51 E
Angol 206 Fe 37.48S 72.43W
Angola 184 Ee 41.38N 85.00W
Angola [1] 160 Ij 12.30S 18.30 E
Angola Basin (EN) 106 Ek 15.00S 3.00 E
Angoram 214 Ch 4.04S 144.04 E
Angostura 192 Ee 25.22N 108.11W
Angostura, Presa de la- 192 Mi 16.30N 92.30W
Angostura, Salto- 202 Dc 2.43N 70.57W
Angostura Reservoir 186 Ee 43.18N 103.27W
Angoulême 122 Gi 45.39N 0.09 E
Angoumois 122 Gi 45.30N 0.00
Angra do Héroísmo 160 Ee 38.39N 27.13W
Angra do Heroísmo [3] 162 Bb 38.42N 27.15W
Angra dos Reis 204 Jf 23.00S 44.18W
Angren 136 Hg 41.03N 70.10 E
Angu 170 Db 3.33N 24.28 E
Anguang 154 Gb 45.36N 123.48 E
Anguilla [5] 176 Mh 18.15N 63.05W
Anguilla 174 Mh 18.15N 63.05W
Anguilla, Canal de l'- = Anguilla Channel (EN) 197b Ab 18.09N 63.04W
Anguilla Bank (EN) 197b Ab 18.30N 63.03W
Anguilla Cays 194 Hb 23.31N 78.33W
Anguilla Channel 197b Ab 18.09N 63.04W
Anguilla Channel (EN) = Anguilla, Canal de l'- 197b Ab 18.09N 63.04W
Anguli Nur 154 Cd 41.23N 114.30 E
Anguo 154 Ce 38.25N 115.20 E
Anhanca 170 Cf 16.47S 15.33 E
Anhanguera 204 Hd 18.21S 48.17W
An Hoa 148 Le 15.46N 108.03 E
Anholt 114 Ch 56.40N 11.35 E
Anhua (Dongping) 152 Jf 28.27N 111.15 E
Anhui Sheng (An-hui Sheng) = Anhwei (EN) [2] 152 Ke 32.00N 117.00 E
An-hui Sheng → Anhui Sheng = Anhwei (EN) [2] 152 Ke 32.00N 117.00 E
Anhwei (EN) = Anhui Sheng (An-hui Sheng) [2] 152 Ke 32.00N 117.00 E
Anhwei (EN) = An-hui Sheng → Anhui Sheng [2] 152 Ke 32.00N 117.00 E
Ani 156 Gb 39.59N 140.25 E
Aniak 178 Hd 61.34N 159.30W
An Iarmhí/Westmeath [2] 118 Fh 53.30N 7.30W
Anibare 220e Bb 0.32S 166.57 E
Anibare Bay 220e Bb 0.32S 166.57 E
Aniche 124 Fd 50.20N 3.15 E
Ánidhros 130 Im 36.37N 25.41 E
Anié 166 Fd 7.45N 1.12 E
Anie, Pic d'- 122 Fl 42.57N 0.43W
Aniene 128 Gi 41.56N 12.30 E
Anijangying → Luanping 154 Dd 40.55N 117.19 E
Anikščjaj/Anykščiai 114 Fi 55.31N 25.08 E
Animas Peak 186 Bk 31.35N 108.47W
Anina 130 Ed 45.05N 21.51 E
Anita Garibaldi 204 Gh 27.37S 51.05W
Anittepe 130 Kh 41.21N 27.42 E
Aniva 138 Jg 46.41N 142.35 E
Aniva, mys- 138 Jg 46.00N 143.25 E
Aniva, zaliv- 138 Jg 46.20N 142.40 E
Anivorano Avaratra 172 Hb 12.43S 49.12 E
Anivorano Nord 172 Hb 12.43S 49.12 E
Aniwa, Ile- 208 Hf 19.16S 169.35 E
Anizy-le-Château 124 Fe 49.30N 3.27 E
Anjala 114 Gf 60.41N 26.50 E
Anji 154 Ei 30.39N 119.41 E
Anjiang → Qianyang 152 Jf 27.19N 110.13 E
Anjō 156 Ed 34.57N 137.05 E
Anjou 122 Fg 47.20N 0.30W
Anjou, Val d'- 122 Fg 47.25N 0.15W
Anjouan/Nzwani 158 Lj 12.15S 44.25 E
Anjou Islands (EN) = Anžu, ostrova- 140 Qb 75.30N 143.00 E
Anjozorobe 172 Hc 18.24S 47.52 E
Anju 152 Md 39.37N 125.40 E
Anjuj 138 Ig 49.20N 136.20 E
Anjujski hrebet 138 Lc 67.20N 166.00 E
Anka 166 Gc 12.07N 5.55 E
Ankang (Xing'an) 142 Mf 32.37N 109.03 E
Ankara 142 Ff 39.56N 32.52 E
Ankara-Altındağ 146 Ec 39.56N 32.52 E
Ankara-Çankaya 146 Ec 39.56N 32.52 E
Ankaratra 158 Lj 19.25S 47.12 E
Ankara-Yenimahalle 146 Ec 39.56N 32.52 E
Ankarsrum 114 Dh 57.42N 16.19 E
Ankavandra 172 Hc 18.45S 45.18 E
Ankazoabo 172 Gd 22.16S 44.30 E
Ankazobe 172 Hc 18.17S 47.05 E
Ankeny 186 Jf 41.44N 93.36W
'Ankhor 168 Hc 10.47N 46.18 E
Anklam 120 Jc 53.52N 13.42 E
Ankober 168 Fd 9.40N 39.44 E
Ankoro 170 Ed 6.45S 26.57 E
Ankum 124 Jb 52.33N 7.53 E
An Laoi/Lee 118 Ej 51.55N 8.30W
Anlong 152 If 25.02N 105.30 E
An Longfort / Longford 118 Fh 53.44N 7.47W
An Longfort/Longford [2] 118 Fh 53.40N 7.40W
An Lorgain/Lurgan 118 Gg 54.28N 6.20W
Anlu 152 Je 31.12N 113.46 E
An Mhí/Meath [2] 118 Gh 53.35N 6.40W
An Mhuaidh/Moy 118 Dg 54.12N 9.08W
An Mhuir Cheilteach = Celtic Sea (EN) 110 Fe 51.00N 7.00W
An Muileann gCearr/Mullingar 118 Fh 53.32N 7.20W
An Muirthead/Mullet Peninsula 118 Cg 54.15N 10.04W
Ånn 116 Ea 63.19N 12.33 E
Ånn 114 Ce 63.15N 12.35 E
Ann, Cape- [Ant.] 222 Ee 66.10S 51.22 E
Ann, Cape- [Ma.-U.S.] 184 Ld 42.39N 70.38W
Anna [Il.-U.S.] 186 Lh 37.28N 89.15W
Anna [Nauru] 220e Ba 0.29S 166.56 E
Anna [Russia] 136 Ee 51.29N 40.26 E
Annaba 160 He 36.54N 7.46 E
Annaba [3] 162 Ib 35.35N 8.00 E
An Nabaṭiyah at Taḥtā 146 Gf 33.23N 35.29 E
Annaberg-Buchholz 120 If 50.34N 13.00 E
An Nabī Şāliḩ 146 Eh 28.38N 33.59 E
An Nabk 144 Ec 34.01N 36.44 E
An Nabk Abū Qaşr 146 Hg 30.21N 38.34 E
An Nafīḑah 128 En 36.08N 10.23 E
An Nafūd 140 Gg 28.30N 41.00 E
An Nāḩiyah 146 Ie 34.26N 41.33 E
An Najaf 142 Gf 31.59N 44.20 E
An Najaf [3] 146 Kg 31.20N 44.07 E
An Nakhl 164 Fd 29.55N 33.45 E
Annalee/An Eoghanach 118 Fg 54.02N 7.25W
Annam (EN) = Trung Phan 140 Mh 15.00N 108.00 E
Annamitique, Chaîne- 148 Le 17.00N 106.00 E
Annan 118 Jg 55.00N 3.16W
Annan 118 Jg 54.59N 3.16W
Anna Paulowna 124 Gb 52.52N 4.52 E
Anna Paulowna-Kleine Sluis 124 Gb 52.52N 4.52 E
Anna Point 220e Ba 0.29S 166.56 E
Annapolis 176 Lf 38.59N 76.30W
Annapolis Royal 184 Oc 44.45N 65.31W
Annapurna 140 Kg 28.34N 83.50 E
Ann Arbor 182 Kc 42.18N 83.45W
Anna Regina 196 Gi 7.16N 58.30W
An Nás/Naas 118 Gh 53.13N 6.39W
An Nashshāsh 146 Pk 23.05N 54.02 E
An Nashwah 146 Lg 30.49N 47.36 E
An Nāşirīyah 144 Gc 31.02N 46.16 E
An Nasser 146 Ej 24.36N 32.58 E
An Nawfalīyah 164 Cc 30.47N 17.50 E
Annecy 122 Mi 45.54N 6.07 E
Annecy, Lac d'- 122 Mi 45.51N 6.11 E
Annemasse 122 Mh 46.12N 6.15 E
Annevoie-Rouillon 124 Gd 50.21N 4.50 E
An Nīl [3] 168 Ea 20.10N 33.00 E
An Nīl al Azraq [3] 168 Ec 12.20N 34.15 E
Anning 152 Hg 24.58N 102.29 E
Anniston 182 Je 33.40N 85.50W
Annobón 158 Hi 1.32S 5.38 E
Annonay 122 Ki 45.14N 4.40 E
Annotto Bay 194 Id 18.16N 76.46W
An Nu'ayrīyah 146 Mi 27.28N 48.27 E
An Nuhūd 160 Jg 12.42N 28.26 E
An Nu' Mān 146 Fi 27.06N 35.46 E
An Nu'mānīyah 146 Kf 32.32N 45.25 E
Annweiler am Trifels 124 Je 49.12N 7.58 E
Anoia/Noya 126 Nc 41.28N 1.56 E
Anoka 186 Jd 45.11N 93.23W
An Omaigh/Omagh 118 Fg 54.36N 7.18W
Anori 202 Fd 3.47S 61.38W
Anosyennes, Chaînes- 172 Hd 24.20S 47.00 E
Áno Viánnos 130 In 35.03N 25.25 E
Anóyia 130 Hn 35.15N 24.54 E
Anping [China] 154 Ce 38.13N 115.32 E
Anping [China] 154 Gd 41.10N 123.25 E
An Pointe/Warrenpoint 118 Gg 54.06N 6.15W
Anpu 152 Ig 21.30N 110.00 E
Anpu Gang 152 Ig 21.25N 109.40 E
Anqing 142 Nf 30.32N 116.59 E
Anqiu 154 Ef 36.25N 119.12 E
An Ráth/Ráth Luirc 118 Ei 52.21N 8.41W
An Ribhéar/Kenmare River 118 Dj 51.50N 9.50W
Anröchte 124 Kc 51.34N 8.20 E
Ans 124 Hd 50.39N 5.32 E
Anşāb 144 Fd 29.11N 44.43 E

Ansauvillers 124 Ee 49.34N 2.24 E
Ansbach 120 Gg 49.18N 10.35 E
An Sciobairín/Skibbereen 118 Dj 51.33N 9.15W
An Seancheann/Kinsale, Old Head of- 118 Ej 51.36N 8.32W
Anse-à-Veau 194 Kd 18.30N 73.19W
Anse-Bertrand 197e Ab 16.29N 61.31W
Anse-d'Hainault 194 Jd 18.30N 74.27W
Anse la Raye 197k Ab 13.57N 61.03W
Anshan 142 Oe 41.08N 122.59 E
Anshun 142 Mg 26.15N 105.58 E
Ansina 206 Id 31.54S 55.28W
Ansley 186 Gf 41.18N 99.23W
Anson Bay 212 Gb 13.20S 130.05 E
Ansongo 166 Fb 15.40N 0.31 E
An Srath Bán/Strabane 118 Fg 54.49N 7.27W
Anta 202 Df 13.29S 72.09W
Antabamba 202 Df 14.19S 72.55W
Antakya=Antioch (EN) 144 Eb 36.14N 36.07 E
Antalaha 160 Mj 14.55S 50.15 E
Antalya 142 Ff 36.53N 30.42 E
Antalya, Gulf of- (EN)= Antalya Körfezi 144 Db 36.30N 31.00 E
Antalya Körfezi=Antalya, Gulf of- (EN) 144 Db 36.30N 31.00 E
An Tan 148 Le 15.26N 108.39 E
Antananarivo 160 Lj 18.55S 47.30 E
Antananarivo [3] 172 Hc 19.00S 46.40 E
Antanimora 172 Hd 24.48S 45.39 E
An tAonach/Nenagh 118 Ei 52.52N 8.12W
Antarctica (EN) 106 Gr 90.00S 0.00
Antarctic Peninsula (EN) 222 Qe 69.30S 65.00W
Antas, Cachoeira das- 204 Ha 13.06S 48.09W
Antas, Rio das- 204 Gi 29.04S 51.21W
An Teampall Mór/Templemore 118 Fi 52.48N 7.50W
Antela, Laguna de- 126 Eb 42.07N 7.41W
Antelao 128 Gd 46.27N 12.16 E
Antelope Creek 188 Me 43.29N 105.23W
Anten 116 Ef 58.03N 12.30 E
Antequera [Par.] 204 Dg 24.08S 57.07W
Antequera [Sp.] 126 Hg 37.01N 4.33W
Anthony 186 Cj 32.00N 106.34W
Anti-Atlas 158 Ge 30.00N 8.30W
Antibes 122 Nk 43.35N 7.07 E
Antibes, Cap d'- 122 Nk 43.32N 7.07 E
Antica, Isla- 196 Eg 10.24N 62.43W
Anticosti, Ile d'- 174 Me 49.30N 63.00W
Antifer, Cap d'- 122 Ge 49.41N 0.10 E
Antigo 186 Ld 45.09N 89.09W
Antigonish 180 Lg 45.37N 61.58W
Antigua 174 Mh 17.03N 61.48W
Antigua and Barbuda [1] 176 Mh 17.03N 61.48W
Antigua Guatemala 190 Ff 14.34N 90.44W
Antiguo Cauce del Rio Bermejo 206 Hc 25.39S 60.11W
Antiguo Morelos 192 Jf 22.30N 99.05W
Antilla 194 Jc 20.50N 75.45W
Antillas, Mar de las-/Caribe, Mar-=Caribbean Sea (EN) 174 Lh 15.00N 73.00W
Antillas Mayores = Greater Antilles (EN) 174 Lh 20.00N 74.00W
Antillas Menores = Lesser Antilles (EN) 174 Mh 15.00N 61.00W
Antilles, Mer des-/Caraïbe, Mer-=Caribbean Sea (EN) 174 Lh 15.00N 73.00W
An tInbhear Mór/Arklow 118 Gi 52.48N 6.09W
Antioch 188 Eg 38.00N 121.49W
Antioch (EN)=Antakya 144 Eb 36.14N 36.07 E
Antioche, Pertuis d'- 122 Eh 46.05N 1.20W
Antiope Reef 208 Kf 18.18S 168.40W
Antioquia [3] 202 Cb 7.00N 75.30W
Antipajëta 138 Cc 69.09N 77.00 E
Antipodes Islands 208 Ii 49.40S 178.50 E
Antiques, Pointe d'- 197e Ab 16.26N 61.33W
an t-Iúr/Newry 118 Gg 54.11N 6.20W
Antler River 186 Fb 49.08N 101.00W
Antlers 186 Ii 34.14N 95.37W
Antofagasta 200 Ih 23.39S 70.24W
Antofagasta [2] 206 Gb 23.30S 69.00W
Antofagasta de la Sierra 206 Gc 26.04S 67.25W
Antofalla, Salar de- 206 Gc 25.44S 67.45W
Antofalla, Volcán- 206 Gc 25.34S 67.55W
Antoing 124 Fd 50.34N 3.27 E
Antón 194 Gi 8.24N 80.16W
Anton Dohrn Seamount (EN) 118 Cd 57.30N 11.00W
Antongil, Baie d'- 158 Lj 15.45S 49.50 E
Antonina 206 Kc 25.27S 48.43W
Antônio João 206 Ef 23.15S 55.31W
Antonito 186 Dh 37.05N 106.00W
Antón Lizardo, Punta de- 192 Lh 19.03N 95.58W
Antony 124 Ef 48.45N 2.18 E
Antpol 120 Ud 52.12N 24.53 E
Antracit 132 Ke 48.06N 39.06 E
Antreff 124 Ld 50.52N 9.15 E
Antrim/Aontroim 118 Gg 54.43N 6.13W
Antrim Mountains 118 Gf 55.00N 6.10W
Antrodoco 128 Hh 42.25N 13.05 E
Antsakabary 172 Hc 15.03S 48.56 E
Antsalova 172 Gc 18.42S 44.33 E
An tSionainn/Shannon 110 Fe 52.36N 9.41W
Antsirabe 160 Lj 19.51S 47.01 E
Antsiranana 160 Lj 12.17S 49.17 E
Antsiranana [3] 172 Hb 13.40S 49.15 E
An tSiúir/Suir 118 Gi 52.15N 7.00W
Antsla 114 Gh 57.52N 26.33 E
An tSláine/Slaney 118 Gi 52.21N 6.30W
Antsohihy 160 Lj 14.52S 47.58 E
An tSuca/Suck 118 Eh 53.16N 8.03W
Anttola 116 Lc 61.35N 27.39 E
Antu (Songjiang) 154 Jc 42.33N 128.20 E
Antufash, Jazīrat- 164 Hf 15.42N 42.25 E
An Tulach/Tullow 118 Gi 52.48N 6.44W
An Tulach Mhór/Tullamore 118 Fh 53.16N 7.30W
Antwerp (EN)=Antwerpen/Anvers 112 Ge 50.38N 5.34 E
Antwerp (EN)=Anvers/Antwerpen 112 Ge 50.38N 5.34 E
Antwerpen [3] 124 Gc 51.10N 4.30 E
Antwerpen/Anvers= Antwerp (EN) 112 Ge 50.38N 5.34 E
Antwerpen-Ekeren 122 Kc 51.17N 4.25 E
Antwerpen-Hoboken 124 Gc 51.10N 4.21 E
Antwerpen-Merksem 124 Gc 51.15N 4.27 E
Antykan 138 If 54.55N 135.13 E
An Uaimh (Navan) 118 Gh 53.39N 6.41W
Anuradhapura 148 Gg 8.21N 80.23 E
Anuta Island 208 Hf 11.38S 169.50 E
Anvers/Antwerpen= Antwerp (EN) 112 Ge 50.38N 5.34 E
Anvers Island 222 Oe 64.33S 63.35W
Anvik 178 Gd 62.40N 160.12W
Anxi 142 Le 40.30N 96.00 E
Anxiang 152 Jf 29.26N 112.11 E
Anxin 154 Ce 38.55N 115.56 E
Anxious Bay 212 Gf 33.25S 134.35 E
Anyang (Zhangde) 142 Nf 36.01N 114.25 E
A'nyêmaqen Shan 140 Lf 34.30N 100.00 E
Anyi 154 Cj 28.50N 115.31 E
Anykščiai/Anikščjaj 114 Fi 55.31N 25.08 E
Anza 128 Ce 46.00N 8.17 E
Anze 154 Bf 36.09N 112.14 E
Anzegem 124 Fd 50.50N 3.28 E
Anžero-Sudžensk 142 Kd 56.07N 86.00 E
Anzi 170 Dc 0.52S 23.24 E
Anzio 128 Gi 41.27N 12.37 E
Anzoátegui [2] 202 Fb 9.00N 64.30W
Anzob, pereval- 135 Ge 39.07N 68.53 E
Anžu, ostrova- = Anjou Islands (EN) 140 Qb 75.30N 143.00 E
Aoba, Ile- 216 Cc 15.25S 167.50 E
Ao Ban Don 148 Jg 9.20N 99.25 E
Aoga-Shima 152 Oe 32.30N 139.50 E
Aohan Qi (Xinhui) 154 Ec 42.18N 119.53 E
Aoiz 126 Kb 42.47N 1.22W
Aoji 154 Kc 42.31N 130.24 E
Aola 219a Ec 9.32S 160.29 E
Aomen/Macau=Macao (EN) 152 Jg 22.12N 113.33 E
Aomen/Macau=Macao (EN) [5] 142 Ng 22.10N 113.33 E
Aomori 142 Qe 40.49N 140.45 E
Aomori Ken [2] 154 Pd 40.40N 140.40 E
Aono-Yama 156 Bd 34.27N 131.48 E
Aontroim/Antrim 118 Gg 54.43N 6.13W
Aopo 221c Aa 13.29S 172.30W
Aôral, Phnum- 148 Kf 12.02N 104.10 E
Aoré 219b Cb 15.35S 167.10 E
Aosta / Aoste 128 Be 45.44N 7.20 E
Aoste / Aosta 128 Be 45.44N 7.20 E
Aouk, Bahr- 158 Ih 8.51N 18.53 E
Aoukalé 168 Cd 9.10N 20.30 E
Aoukâr [Afr.] 162 Ge 24.00N 2.30W
Aoukâr [Mtna.] 158 Gg 17.30N 9.30W
Aoulef 162 Hd 26.58N 1.05 E
Aoumou 219b Be 21.24S 165.49 E
Aourou 166 Cc 14.28N 11.34W
Aoya 156 Cd 35.32N 133.59 E
Aozou 160 If 21.49N 17.25 E
Apa, Rio- 206 Ib 22.06S 58.00W
Apača 138 Kf 52.50N 157.10 E
Apache 188 Kk 31.44N 109.07W
Apache Junction 188 Jj 33.26N 111.32W
Apahida 130 Gc 46.49N 23.45 E
Apakho 219c Bb 11.25S 166.32 E
Apalachee Bay 174 Kg 29.30N 84.00W
Apalachicola 184 Ek 29.44N 84.59W
Apalachicola River 184 Ek 29.44N 84.59W
Apan 192 Jh 19.43N 98.25W
Apaporis, Rio- 198 Jf 1.23S 69.25W
Aparecida do Taboado 202 Hg 20.05S 51.05W
Aparri 142 Oh 18.22N 121.39 E
Apataki Atoll 208 Mf 15.26S 146.20W
Apatin 130 Bd 45.40N 18.59 E
Apatity 112 Jb 67.34N 33.18 E
Apatzingán de la Constitucion 190 De 19.05N 102.21W
Apaxtla de Castrejón 192 Jh 18.09N 99.52W
Ape 114 Gh 57.32N 26.42 E
Apeldoorn 122 Lb 52.13N 5.58 E
Apeldoorn-Nieuw Milligen 124 Hb 52.14N 5.45 E
Apen 124 Ja 53.13N 7.48 E
Apennines (EN) = Appennini 110 Hg 43.00N 13.00 E
Apere, Rio- 202 Ef 13.44S 65.18W
Aphrodisias 146 Cd 37.45N 28.40 E
Api 170 Eb 3.40N 25.26 E
Api 140 Kf 30.00N 80.57 E
Apia 210 Jf 13.50S 171.44W
Apiacás, Serra dos- 202 Gf 10.15S 57.15W
Apio 219 Ec 9.39S 161.23 E
Apipé Grande, Isla- 204 Di 27.30S 56.54W
Apizaco 192 Jh 19.25N 98.09W
Aplao 202 Dg 16.05S 72.31W
Apo, Mount- 140 Oi 6.59N 125.16 E
Apodi 202 Ke 5.39S 37.48W
Apolda 120 He 51.01N 11.30 E
Apolima 221c Aa 13.49S 172.07W
Apolima Strait 221c Aa 13.50S 172.10W
Apollo Bay 212 Ig 38.45S 143.40 E
Apollonia [Alb.] 130 Ci 40.43N 19.27 E
Apollonia [Lib.] 164 Dc 32.54N 21.58 E
Apolo 202 Ef 14.43S 68.31W
Apón, Rio- 194 Kh 9.50N 72.23W
Apopka, Lake- 184 Gk 28.37N 81.38W
Aporé 204 Fd 18.58S 52.01W
Aporé, Rio- 198 Kg 19.27S 50.57W
Apostle Islands 182 Ib 46.50N 90.30W
Apóstoles 206 Ic 27.55S 55.46W
Apostolovo 132 Hf 47.39N 33.43 E
Apoteri 202 Gc 4.02N 58.34W
Apôtres, Iles des- 222 Ec 45.40S 50.20 E
Appalachia 184 Fg 36.54N 82.48W
Appalachian Mountains 174 Lc 41.00N 77.00W
Äppelbo 116 Ed 60.30N 14.00 E
Appennini = Apennines (EN) 110 Hg 43.00N 13.00 E
Appennino Abruzzese 128 Hh 42.00N 13.55 E
Appennino Calabro 128 Kl 39.00N 16.30 E
Appennino Campano 128 Ii 40.50N 14.45 E
Appennino Ligure 128 Cf 44.30N 9.00 E
Appennino Lucano 128 Jj 40.30N 16.00 E
Appennino Tosco-Emiliano 128 Fg 44.00N 1 830 E
Appennino Umbro-Marchigiano 128 Gg 43.20N 12.55 E
Appenzell 128 Dc 47.20N 9.25 E
Appenzell Ausser-Rhoden [2] 128 Dc 47.20N 9.20 E
Appenzell Inner-Rhoden [2] 128 Dc 47.15N 9.25 E
Appingedam 124 Ia 53.19N 6.52 E
Appleby 118 Kg 54.36N 2.29W
Appleton 182 Jc 44.16N 88.25W
Appomattox 184 Hg 37.21N 78.51W
Apra Harbor 220c Bb 13.27N 144.38 E
Apricena 128 Ji 41.47N 15.27 E
Aprilia 128 Gi 41.36N 12.39 E
Apšeronsk 136 Dg 44.27N 39.44 E
Apšeronskij poluostrov = Apsheron Peninsula (EN) 110 Lg 41.00N 50.50 E
Apsheron Peninsula (EN) = Apšeronskij poluostrov 110 Lg 41.00N 50.50 E
Apt 122 Lk 43.53N 5.24 E
Apucarana 206 Jb 23.33S 51.29W
Apucarana, Serra da- 204 Gf 23.50S 51.20W
Apuka 138 Ld 60.23N 169.45 E
Apuka 138 Ld 60.25N 169.35 E
Apulia (EN) = Puglia [2] 128 Ki 41.15N 16.15 E
Apurashokoru 220a Ac 7.17N 134.18 E
Apure [2] 202 Eb 7.10N 68.50W
Apure, Rio- 198 Je 7.37N 66.25W
Apurimac [3] 202 Df 14.00S 73.00W
Apurimac, Rio- 198 Ig 12.17S 73.56W
Apurito 196 Bi 7.56N 68.27W
Apuseni, Munţii-=Apuseni Mountains (EN) 110 If 46.30N 22.30 E
Apuseni Mountains (EN)= Apuseni, Munţii- 110 If 46.30N 22.30 E
Āq 146 Kc 38.59N 45.27 E
Āqā 146 Me 35.00N 47.00 E
Aqaba (EN)=Al 'Aqabah 144 Dd 29.31N 35.00 E
Aqaba, Gulf of- (EN)= 'Aqabah, Khalīj al- 158 Kf 29.00N 34.40 E
Āqā Bāba 146 Md 36.20N 49.46 E
'Aqabah, Khalīj al-=Aqaba, Gulf of- (EN) 158 Kf 29.00N 34.40 E
Āqcheh 144 Kb 36.56N 66.11 E
'Aqdā 146 Of 32.26N 53.37 E
'Aqīq 168 Fb 18.14N 38.12 E
Aqitag 152 Fc 41.49N 90.38 E
Āqotāq 146 Ld 37.10N 47.05 E
Āq Qal'eh 146 Pd 37.01N 54.30 E
Aqqikkol Hu 152 Ed 37.00N 88.20 E
'Aqrah 146 Jd 36.45N 43.54 E
Aqrin, Jabal- 146 Hg 31.32N 38.18 E
Āq Sū 146 Ke 34.35N 44.31 E
Aquidabã, Rio- 204 De 20.58S 57.50W
Aquidabán, Rio- 204 Df 23.11S 57.32W
Aquidauana 202 Gh 20.28S 55.48W
Aquidauana, Rio- 202 Gg 19.44S 56.50W
Aquidauana, Serra de- 204 Ee 20.50S 55.30W
Aquiles Serdán 192 Gc 28.36N 105.53W
Aquin 194 Kd 18.16N 73.24W
Aquitaine, Bassin d'-= Aquitaine Basin (EN) 110 Fg 44.00N 0.10W
Aquitaine Basin (EN) = Aquitaine, Bassin d'- 110 Fg 44.00N 0.10W
Ara 126 Mb 42.25N 0.09 E
'Arab, Baḩr al- 158 Jh 9.02N 29.28 E
'Arab, Khalīj al- 164 Ec 30.55N 29.05 E
'Arab, Shaţţ al- 140 Gf 30.28N 47.59 E
'Arabah, Wādī- 146 Eh 29.07N 32.39 E
'Arabah, Wādī al- 146 Fg 30.58N 32.24 E
Arabatskaja Strelka, kosa- 132 Ig 45.40N 35.05 E
'Arabestān 146 Mg 30.30N 50.00 E
Arabian Basin (EN) 106 Gh 11.30N 65.00 E
Arabian Desert (EN) = Sharqīyah, Aş Şaḩrā' ash- 158 Kf 28.00N 32.00 E
Arabian Peninsula (EN) 140 Gg 25.00N 45.00 E
Arabian Sea (EN) 140 Ih 15.00N 65.00 E
Araç 146 Eb 41.15N 33.21 E
Aracá, Rio- 202 Fd 0.25S 62.55W
Aracaju 200 Mg 10.55S 37.04W
Aracataca 194 Jh 10.35N 74.13W
Aracati 202 Kd 4.34S 37.46W
Araçatuba 200 Kh 21.12S 50.25W
Aracena 126 Fg 37.53N 6.33W
Aracena, Sierra de- 126 Fg 37.56N 6.50W
Aracides, Cape- 219a Ec 8.39S 161.01 E
Aracruz 202 Jg 19.49S 40.16W
Araçuai 202 Jg 16.52S 42.04W
Arad 112 If 46.11N 21.19 E
'Arad 146 Fg 31.15N 35.13 E
Arad [2] 130 Ec 46.11N 21.25 E
Arada 168 Cb 15.01N 20.40 E
'Arādah 168 Ia 22.59N 53.26 E
Arafali 168 Fb 15.04N 39.45 E
Ara Fana 168 Gd 6.01N 41.11 E
Arafune-Yama 156 Fc 36.12N 138.38 E
Arafura, Laut-=Arafura Sea (EN) 208 Ee 9.00S 133.00 E
Arafura Sea (EN) = Arafura, Laut- 208 Ee 9.00S 133.00 E
Aragac, gora- 110 Kg 40.31N 44.10 E
Aragarças 200 Kg 15.55S 52.15W
Aragón [2] 126 Lc 41.00N 1.00W
Aragón 110 Fg 41.00N 1.00W
Aragón 126 Kb 42.13N 1.44W
Aragona 128 Hm 37.24N 13.37 E
Aragua [2] 202 Eb 10.00N 67.10W
Araguacema 202 Ie 8.50S 49.34W
Aragua de Barcelona 196 Dh 9.28N 64.49W
Aragua de Maturin 196 Eh 9.58N 63.29W
Araguaia, Rio- 198 Lf 5.21S 48.41W
Araguaiana 204 Gb 16.49S 53.05W
Araguaia ou Javaes, Braço Menor do- 202 He 9.50S 50.12W
Araguaina 202 Ie 7.12S 48.12W
Araguao, Boca- 202 Fb 9.17N 60.48W
Araguao, Caño- 196 Fh 9.15N 60.50W
Araguapiche, Punta- 196 Fh 9.29N 60.56W
Araguari 202 Ig 18.38S 48.11W
Araguari, Rio- [Braz.] 198 Le 1.15N 49.55W
Araguari, Rio- [Braz.] 204 Hd 18.21S 48.40W
Araguatins 202 Ie 5.38S 48.07W
'Arâguîb 162 Ff 18.50N 7.45W
Aragvi 132 Ni 41.50N 44.43 E
Arai 154 Of 37.09N 138.06 E
Árainn/Inishmore 118 Dh 53.07N 9.45W
Árainn Mhór/Aran Island 118 Ef 55.00N 8.30W
Araioses 202 Jd 2.53S 41.55W
Arāk 142 Gf 34.05N 49.41 E
Arak 162 Hd 25.18N 3.45 E
Arakabesan 220a Ac 7.21N 134.27 E
Arakan [2] 148 Ie 19.00N 94.15 E
Arakan Yoma 140 Lh 19.00N 94.40 E
Arakawa 156 Fb 38.09N 139.25 E
Ara-Kawa [Jap.] 156 Fb 38.09N 139.23 E
Ara-Kawa [Jap.] 156 Fc 37.11N 138.15 E
Árakhthos 130 Ej 39.01N 21.03 E
Araks 140 Gf 39.56N 48.20 E
Aral [China] 152 Dc 40.38N 81.24 E
Aral [Kirg.-U.S.S.R.] 136 Hg 41.48N 74.25 E
Aral Sea (EN) = Aralskoje more 140 He 45.00N 60.00 E
Aralsk 142 Ie 46.48N 61.40 E
Aralskoje more = Aral Sea (EN) 140 He 45.00N 60.00 E
Aralsor, ozero- 132 Pe 49.05N 48.15 E
Aralsulfat 136 Gf 46.50N 61.59 E
Aramac 212 Jd 22.59S 145.14 E
Arambaré 204 Gj 30.55S 51.29W
Ārān 146 Ne 34.03N 51.30 E
Ara Naoimh/Aran Islands 118 Dh 53.07N 9.43W
Aranda de Duero 126 Ic 41.41N 3.41W
Arandelovac 130 De 44.18N 20.35 E
Arandilla 126 Ic 41.40N 3.41W
Aran Island/Árainn Mhór 118 Ef 55.00N 8.30W
Aran Islands/Ara Naoimh 118 Dh 53.07N 9.43W
Aranjuez 126 Id 40.02N 3.36W
Aranos 172 Bd 24.09S 19.09 E
Arañuelo, Campo- 126 Ge 39.55N 5.30W
Aranuka Atoll 208 Id 0.11N 173.36 E
Arao 156 Be 32.59N 130.27 E
Araouane 160 Gg 18.53N 3.35W
Arapahoe 186 Gf 40.18N 99.54W
Arapey Grande, Rio- 204 Dj 30.55S 57.49W
Arapiraca 202 Ke 9.45S 36.39W
Arápis, Ákra- 130 Hi 40.27N 24.00 E
Arapkir 146 Hc 39.03N 38.30 E
Arapoim, Rio- 204 Kb 15.45S 43.39W
Arapongas 206 Jb 23.23S 51.27W
Arapoti 204 Hg 24.08S 49.50W
'Ar'ar 146 Ig 30.59N 41.02 E
'Ar'ar, Wādī 146 Jg 31.23N 42.26 E
Araranguá 206 Kc 28.56S 49.29W
Araraquara 200 Lh 21.47S 48.10W
Araras 204 If 22.22S 47.23W
Araras, Açude- 202 Jd 4.30S 40.30W
Araras, Serra das- 204 Fd 18.45S 53.30W
Ararat [Arm.] 136 Eh 39.50N 44.43 E
Ararat [Austl.] 212 Ig 37.17S 142.56 E
Ararat, Mount- (EN) = Ağrı Dağı 140 Gf 39.40N 44.24 E
Arari 202 Jd 3.28S 44.47W
Arari, Lago- 202 Id 0.37S 49.07W
Aras 140 Gf 39.56N 48.20 E
Aras Dağları 146 Jc 40.00N 43.00 E
Aratika Atoll 208 Mf 15.32S 145.32W
Aratürük/Yiwu 152 Fc 43.15N 94.35 E
Arauca 202 Db 7.03N 70.47W
Arauca [3] 202 Db 6.30N 71.00W
Arauca, Rio- 198 Je 7.24N 66.35W
Arauco 206 Fe 37.15S 73.19W
Araure 196 Bh 9.38N 69.15W
Aravaca, Madrid- 126 Id 40.27N 3.47W
Aravis, Chaîne des- 122 Mi 45.53N 6.28 E
Arawalli Range 140 Jg 25.00N 73.30 E
Araxá 202 Ig 19.35S 46.55W
Áraxos, Ákra- 130 Ek 38.10N 21.23 E
Araya 196 Dg 10.34N 64.15W
Araya, Peninsula de- 202 Fa 10.35N 64.00W
Arba 126 Kc 41.52N 1.18W
Arba'āt 168 Fb 19.50N 37.03 E
Arba'īn, Darb al- 146 Di 26.40N 30.50 E
Arbaj-Here 152 Hb 46.15N 102.48 E
Arba Minch 160 Kh 5.59N 37.38 E
'Arbat 146 Ke 35.25N 45.35 E
Arbatax 128 Dk 39.56N 9.42 E
Arboga 114 Dg 59.24N 15.50 E
Arbogaån 116 Ge 59.26N 16.04 E
Arbois 122 Lh 46.54N 5.46 E
Arboletes 194 Ii 8.52N 76.25W
Arbolito 204 Ek 32.39S 54.15W
Arbon 128 Dc 47.30N 9.25 E
Arbore 130 Ib 47.44N 25.56 E
Arborea 128 Ck 39.46N 8.35 E
Arborea 128 Ck 39.50N 8.50 E
Arborg 186 Ha 50.55N 97.15W
Arbrå 114 Dc 61.29N 16.23 E
Arbresle, L'- 122 Ki 45.50N 4.37 E
Arbroath 118 Ke 56.34N 2.35W
Arbus 128 Ck 39.32N 8.36 E
Arc [Fr.] 122 Mi 45.34N 6.12 E
Arc [Fr.] 122 Lk 43.31N 5.07 E
Arcachon 122 Ej 44.39N 1.10W
Arcachon, Bassin d'- 122 Ej 44.42N 1.09W
Arcadia [Fl.-U.S.] 184 Gl 27.14N 81.52W
Arcadia [La.-U.S.] 186 Jj 32.33N 92.55W
Arcagly-Ajat 134 Jj 53.00N 61.50 E
Arcas, Cayos- 190 Fd 20.12N 91.58W
Arcata 188 Cf 40.52N 124.05W
Arcelia 192 Ih 18.17N 100.16W
Arcen, Arcen en Velden- 124 Ic 51.28N 6.11 E
Arcen en Velden 124 Ic 51.28N 6.11 E
Arcen en Velden - Arcen 124 Ic 51.28N 6.11 E
Arcevia 128 Gg 43.30N 12.56 E
Archangel (EN)= Arhangelsk 112 Kc 64.34N 40.32 E
Archaringa Creek 212 He 28.15S 135.15 E
Archer River 212 Ib 13.28S 141.41 E
Archer's Post 170 Gb 0.39N 37.41 E
Archidona 126 Hg 37.05N 4.23W
Arcidosso 128 Fh 42.52N 11.33 E
Arcipelago Campano 110 Hg 40.30N 13.20 E
Arcis-sur-Aube 122 Kf 48.32N 4.08 E
Arciz 132 Fg 45.59N 29.27 E
Arco [Id.-U.S.] 188 Ie 43.38N 113.18W
Arco [It.] 128 Ee 45.55N 10.53 E
Arconce 122 Kh 46.27N 4.00 E
Arcos 204 Je 20.17S 45.32W
Arcos de Jalón 126 Jc 41.13N 2.16W
Arcos de la Frontera 126 Gh 36.45N 5.48W
Arcos de Valdevez 126 Dc 41.51N 8.25W
Arcoverde 200 Mf 8.25S 37.04W
Arctic Bay 176 Kb 73.02N 85.11W
Arctic Ocean 224 Be 85.00N 170.00 E
Arctic Ocean (EN)= Ishavet 224 Be 85.00N 170.00 E
Arctic Ocean (EN) = Severny Ledovity okean 224 Be 85.00N 170.00 E
Arctic Red River 180 Ec 67.22N 133.30W
Arctic Red River 180 Ec 67.27N 133.45W
Arctic Village 178 Jc 68.08N 145.19W
Arda [Eur.] 130 Jh 41.39N 26.29 E
Arda [It.] 128 Ee 45.02N 10.02 E
Ardabīl 142 Gf 38.15N 48.18 E
Ardahan 146 Jb 41.07N 42.41 E
Ardakāh 144 Hc 32.19N 53.59 E
Ardakān 146 Og 30.16N 52.01 E
Ardal 146 Ng 31.59N 50.39 E
Ardales 126 Hh 36.52N 4.51W
Ardalsfjorden 116 Bc 61.15N 7.30 E
Årdalstangen 114 Bf 61.14N 7.43 E
Ardanuç 146 Jb 41.08N 42.03 E
Ardatov [Russia] 114 Ki 55.17N 43.12 E
Ardatov [Russia] 114 Li 54.53N 46.13 E
'Arde 168 Hd 9.58N 46.04 E
Ardèche [3] 122 Kj 44.40N 4.20 E
Ardèche 122 Kj 44.16N 4.39 E
Ardee/Béal Átha Fhirdhia 118 Gh 53.52N 6.33W
Ardencaple Fjord 179 Jd 75.15N 20.10W
Ardenne, Plateau de l'-/ Ardennen, Plateau van de- = Ardennes (EN) 110 Ge 50.10N 5.45 E
Ardennen, Plateau van de- / Ardenne, Plateau de l'- = Ardennes (EN) 110 Ge 50.10N 5.45 E
Ardennes [3] 122 Ke 49.40N 4.40 E
Ardennes (EN) = Ardenne, Plateau de l'-/Ardennen, Plateau van de- 110 Ge 50.10N 5.45 E
Ardennes (EN) = Ardennen, Plateau van de- / Ardenne, Plateau de l'- 110 Ge 50.10N 5.45 E
Ardennes, Canal des- 122 Ke 49.26N 4.02 E
Ardennes, Forêt des- 124 Ge 49.48N 4.50 E
Ardentes 122 Hh 46.45N 1.50 E
Ardeşen 146 Ib 41.12N 41.00 E
Ardestān 146 Of 33.22N 52.23 E
Árdhas 130 Jh 41.39N 26.29 E
Ardila 126 Ef 38.12N 7.28W
Ard Mhacha/Armagh 118 Gg 54.21N 6.39W
Ardmore 182 He 34.10N 97.08W
Ardnamurchan, Point of- 118 Ge 56.45N 6.30W
Ardon 132 Nh 43.07N 44.13 E
Ardooie 124 Fd 50.59N 3.12 E
Ardre 124 Fe 49.18N 3.40 E
Ardres 124 Dd 50.51N 1.59 E
Ardrossan 118 If 55.40N 4.55W
Ards Peninsula/An Aird 118 Hg 54.30N 5.30W
Ardud 130 Fb 47.38N 22.53 E
Arebi 170 Eb 2.50N 29.38 E
Arecibo 190 Ke 18.28N 66.43W
Arėgala/Ariogala 116 Ji 55.13N 23.30 E
Areia, Ribeirão da- 204 Jc 16.07S 45.52W
Areia Branca 202 Kd 4.57S 37.08W
Arekalong Peninsula 220a Bb 7.40N 134.38 E
Aremberg 124 Id 50.25N 6.49 E
Arena 150 He 9.14N 120.46 E
Arena, Point- 182 Cd 38.57N 123.44W
Arena, Punta- 190 Cd 23.30N 109.30W
Arena de la Ventana, Punta- 190 Cd 24.04N 109.52W
Arenápolis 202 Gf 14.26S 56.49W
Arenas, Cayo- 190 Fd 22.08N 91.24W
Arenas, Punta de- 206 Gh 53.09S 68.13W
Arenas de San Pedro 126 Gd 40.12N 5.05W
Arenberg 124 Jb 52.42N 7.20 E
Arendal 114 Bg 58.27N 8.48 E
Arendonk 124 Hc 51.19N 5.05 E
Arenys de Mar/Arénys de Mar 126 Oc 41.35N 2.33 E
Arénys de Mar/Arenys de Mar 126 Oc 41.35N 2.33 E
Areópolis 130 Fm 36.40N 22.23 E
Areq, Sebkha Bougg 126 Ji 35.10N 2.45W
Arequipa 200 Ig 16.24S 71.33W
Arequipa [3] 202 Dg 16.00S 72.30W
Arequito 204 Bk 33.09S 61.28W
Arero 168 Fe 4.44N 38.50 E

Index Symbols

[1] Independent Nation
[2] State, Region
[3] District, County
[4] Municipality
[5] Colony, Dependency
Continent
Physical Region
Historical or Cultural Region
Mount, Mountain
Volcano
Hill
Mountains, Mountain Range
Hills, Escarpment
Plateau, Upland
Pass, Gap
Plain, Lowland
Delta
Salt Flat
Valley, Canyon
Crater, Cave
Karst Features
Depression
Polder
Desert, Dunes
Forest, Woods
Heath, Steppe
Oasis
Cape, Point
Coast, Beach
Cliff
Peninsula
Isthmus
Sandbank
Island
Atoll
Rock, Reef
Islands, Archipelago
Rocks, Reefs
Coral Reef
Well, Spring
Geyser
River, Stream
Waterfall, Rapids
River Mouth, Estuary
Lake
Salt Lake
Intermittent Lake
Reservoir
Swamp, Pond
Canal
Glacier
Ice Shelf, Pack Ice
Ocean
Sea
Gulf, Bay
Strait, Fjord
Lagoon
Bank
Seamount
Tablemount
Ridge
Shelf
Basin
Escarpment, Sea Scarp
Fracture
Trench, Abyss
National Park, Reserve
Point of Interest
Recreation Site
Cave, Cavern
Historic Site
Ruins
Wall, Walls
Church, Abbey
Temple
Scientific Station
Railway station
Airport
Port
Military installation
Lighthouse
Mine
Tunnel
Dam, Bridge

Ares, Mola d'- / Ares, Muela de-	126	Ld	40.28N	0.07W
Ares, Muela de- / Ares, Mola d'-	126	Ld	40.28N	0.07W
Åreskutan	114	Ce	63.24N	13.06 E
Åreskutan	114	Ce	63.26N	13.06 E
Arévalo	126	Hc	41.04N	4.43W
Arezzo	128	Fg	43.25N	11.53 E
Arga	126	Kb	42.18N	1.47W
Argajas	134	Ji	55.31N	60.55 E
Argamasilla de Alba	126	Ie	39.07N	3.06W
Argan	152	Ec	40.09N	88.22 E
Arganda	126	Id	40.18N	3.26W
Arga-Sala	138	Gc	68.37N	112.05 E
Argelès-Gazost	122	Fk	43.01N	0.06W
Argelès-sur-Mer	122	Jl	42.33N	3.01 E
Argens	122	Mk	43.24N	6.44 E
Argent, Côte d'-	122	Ej	44.00N	1.30W
Argenta	128	Ff	44.37N	11.50 E
Argentan	122	Ff	48.45N	0.01W
Argentario, Monte-	128	Fh	42.24N	11.09 E
Argentat	122	Hi	45.06N	1.56 E
Argentera	128	Bf	44.10N	7.18 E
Argenteuil	122	If	48.57N	2.15 E
Argentiera, Capo dell'-	128	Cj	40.44N	8.08 E
Argentière-la-Bessée, L'-	122	Mj	44.47N	6.33 E
Argentina	204	Ai	29.33S	62.17W
Argentina [1]	200	Ji	34.00S	64.00W
Argentine Basin (EN)	106	Cn	45.00S	45.00W
Argentino, Lago-	198	Ik	50.13S	72.25W
Argentino, Mar-	198	Kj	46.00S	59.40W
Argenton	122	Fg	47.05N	0.13W
Argenton-Château	122	Fh	46.59N	0.27W
Argenton-sur-Creuse	122	Hh	46.35N	1.31 E
Argeş [2]	130	Hd	45.00N	24.50 E
Argeş	130	Je	44.04N	26.37 E
Arghandāb	144	Jc	31.27N	64.23 E
Argo	168	Eb	19.31N	30.25 E
Argolikós Kólpos = Argolis, Gulf of- (EN)	130	Fl	37.20N	22.55 E
Argolis, Gulf of- (EN) = Argolikós Kólpos	130	Fl	37.20N	22.55 E
Argonne	122	Ke	49.30N	5.00 E
Argonne	124	He	49.30N	5.00 E
Árgos	130	Fl	37.38N	22.44 E
Árgos Orestikón	130	Ei	40.30N	21.16 E
Argostólion	130	Dk	38.11N	20.29 E
Arguedas	126	Kb	42.10N	1.36W
Argueil-Fry	124	De	49.37N	1.31 E
Arguello, Point-	188	Ei	34.35N	120.39W
Arguenon	122	Df	48.35N	2.13W
Argun	132	Nh	43.16N	45.52 E
Argun	140	Od	53.20N	121.28 E
Argungu	166	Fc	12.45N	4.31 E
Argyle	197n	Ba	13.10N	61.10W
Argyle, Lake-	208	Df	16.15S	128.40 E
Argyll	118	Ie	56.20N	5.00W
Arhangelsk = Archangel (EN)	112	Kc	64.34N	40.32 E
Arhangelskaja oblast [3]	136	Ec	63.30N	43.00 E
Arhara	138	Ig	49.30N	130.09 E
Arhavi	146	Ib	41.22N	41.16 E
Arholma	116	He	59.50N	19.05 E
Ar Horqin Qi (Tianshan)	152	Lc	43.55N	120.05 E
Århus	112	Hd	56.09N	10.13 E
Århus [2]	116	Dh	56.10N	10.15 E
Århus Bugt	116	Dh	56.10N	10.20 E
Arhust	152	Ib	47.42N	107.50 E
Ariadnoje	138	Ig	45.08N	134.25 E
Ariake-Kai	154	Kh	32.55N	130.27 E
Ariamsvlei	172	Be	28.08S	19.50 E
Ariano Irpino	128	Ji	41.09N	15.05 E
Ariari, Rio-	202	Dc	2.35N	72.47W
Arias	206	Hd	33.38S	62.25W
Ari Atoll	148a	Bb	3.30N	72.45 E
Aribinda	166	Ec	14.14N	0.52W
Arica	200	Ig	18.29S	70.20W
Arica, Golfo de-	198	Ig	18.30S	70.30W
Arichuna	196	Ci	7.42N	67.08W
Arid, Cape-	212	Ef	34.00S	123.09 E
Arida	154	Mg	34.05N	135.07 E
Arida-Gawa	156	Dd	34.05N	135.06 E
Aridhaia	130	Fi	40.59N	22.04 E
Ariège [3]	122	Hk	43.00N	1.30 E
Ariège	122	Hk	43.31N	1.25 E
Ariel	204	Cm	36.32S	59.54W
Arieş	130	Gc	46.26N	23.59 E
Ariguaní	202	Db	9.50N	74.01W
Ariguani, Rio-	194	Ki	9.35N	73.46W
Arīḩā [Jor.]	146	Fg	31.52N	35.27 E
Arīḩā [Syr.]	146	Ge	35.48N	36.36 E
Arikaree River	186	Ff	40.01N	101.56W
Arikawa	156	Ae	32.59N	129.07 E
Arilje	130	Df	43.45N	20.06 E
Arima	202	Fa	10.38N	61.17W
Arinos	204	Ib	15.55S	46.04W
Arinos, Rio-	198	Kg	10.25S	58.20W
Arinos Novo, Rio-	204	Db	14.14S	56.01W
Ariogala/Arëgala	116	Ji	55.13N	23.30 E
Aripuanã	202	Fe	9.10S	60.38W
Aripuanã, Rio-	198	Jf	5.07S	60.24W
Ariquemes	202	Fe	9.56S	63.04W
Arisa	168	Gc	11.11N	41.38 E
'Arish, Wādī al-	146	Eg	31.09N	33.49 E
Arismendi	194	Mi	8.29N	68.22W
Arita	156	Ae	33.11N	129.52 E
Aritzo	128	Dk	39.57N	9.12 E
Arixang/Wenquan	152	Dc	44.59N	81.04 E
Ariza	126	Jc	41.19N	2.03W
Arizaro, Salar de-	206	Gb	24.42S	67.45W
Arize, Massif de l'-	122	Hl	42.50N	1.30 E
Arizona [2]	182	Ee	34.00N	112.00W
Arizpe	192	Db	30.20N	110.10W
Årjäng	114	Cg	59.23N	12.08 E
Arjeplog	114	Dc	66.03N	17.54 E
Arjo	168	Fd	8.45N	36.30 E
Arjona	202	Ca	10.15N	75.21W
Arkadak	136	Ee	51.58N	43.28 E
Arkadelphia	182	Ie	34.07N	93.04W
Arkalyk	142	Id	50.13N	66.50 E
Arkansas [2]	182	Id	34.50N	93.40W
Arkansas	174	Jf	33.48N	91.04W
Arkansas City	182	Hd	37.04N	97.02W
Arkanū, Jabal-	164	De	22.15N	24.45 E
Arkatag	140	Kf	36.45N	89.10 E
Arkhángelos	130	Lm	36.12N	28.08 E
Árki	130	Jl	37.22N	26.45 E
Arklow/An tInbhear Mór	118	Gi	52.48N	6.09W
Arkona, Kap-	120	Jb	54.41N	13.26 E
Arkonam	148	Ff	13.06N	79.40 E
Arkösund	116	Gf	58.30N	16.56 E
Arkoúdhion	130	Dk	38.33N	20.43 E
Arktičeskoga Instituta, ostrova- = Arkticheski Institut Islands (EN)	138	Da	75.20N	81.50 E
Arkticheski Institut Islands (EN) = Arktičeskoga Instituta, ostrova-	138	Da	75.20N	81.50 E
Arlan, gora-	132	Sj	39.43N	54.40 E
Arlanza	126	Hb	42.06N	4.09W
Arlanzón	126	Ib	42.03N	4.17W
Arlberg	128	Ec	47.08N	10.12 E
Arles	122	Kk	43.40N	4.38 E
Arlington [Or.-U.S.]	188	Ed	45.46N	120.13W
Arlington [Tx.-U.S.]	186	Hj	32.44N	97.07W
Arlington [Va.-U.S.]	182	Ld	38.52N	77.05W
Arlington Heights	186	Me	42.05N	87.59W
Arlit	160	Hg	19.00N	7.38 E
Arlon/Aarlen	122	Le	49.41N	5.49 E
Arlöv	116	Ei	55.39N	13.05 E
Arly	166	Fc	11.35N	1.28 E
Armagh/Ard Mhacha	118	Gg	54.21N	6.39W
Armagnac	122	Gk	43.45N	0.10 E
Armagnac, Collines de l'-	122	Gk	43.30N	0.30 E
Armah, Wādī-	144	Hf	18.12N	51.02 E
Arman	138	Ke	59.43N	150.12 E
Armançon	122	Jg	47.57N	3.30 E
Armandale, Perth-	212	Df	32.09S	116.00 E
Armant	164	Fd	25.37N	32.32 E
Armáthia	130	Jn	35.26N	26.52 E
Armavir	112	Kf	45.00N	41.08 E
Armenia	200	Ie	4.31N	75.41W
Armenia (EN) = Ermenistan	140	Gf	39.10N	43.00 E
Armenia (EN) = Ermenistan	144	Fb	39.10N	43.00 E
Armenia (EN) = Hayastan	136	Eg	40.00N	45.00 E
Armentiéres	122	Id	50.41N	2.53 E
Armería	192	Gh	18.56N	103.58W
Armi, Capo dell'-	128	Jm	37.57N	15.41 E
Armidale	210	Gh	30.31S	151.39 E
Armisvesi	116	Lb	62.30N	26.35 E
Armjansk	132	Hf	46.05N	33.41 E
Armjanskaja Sovetskaja Socialističeskaja Respublika → Hayastan	136	Eg	40.00N	45.00 E
Armjanskaja SSR/Haikakan Sovetaken Socialistakan Respublika → Hayastan	136	Eg	40.00N	45.00 E
Armjanskaja SSR → Hayastan	136	Eg	40.00N	45.00 E
Armoricain, Massif- = Armorican Massif (EN)	110	Ff	48.00N	3.00W
Armorican Massif (EN) = Armoricain, Massif-	110	Ff	48.00N	3.00W
Armour	186	Ge	43.19N	98.21W
Arm River	188	Ma	50.46N	105.00W
Armstrong [Arg.]	204	Bk	32.47S	61.36W
Armstrong [B.C.-Can.]	188	Fa	50.27N	119.12W
Armstrong [Ont.-Can.]	180	If	50.18N	89.02W
Ārmūdiū	146	Qd	37.15N	56.05 E
Armutçuk Dağ	130	Ki	40.05N	27.23 E
Armutlu	130	Li	40.31N	28.50 E
Armutova	130	Jj	39.23N	26.50 E
Arnaia	130	Gi	40.29N	23.36 E
Arnaud	180	Kd	60.00N	69.55W
Arnautis, Akra-	146	Ee	35.06N	32.17 E
Arnay-le-Duc	122	Kg	47.08N	4.29 E
Arnedo	126	Jb	42.13N	2.06W
Årnes	114	Cf	60.09N	11.28 E
Arnhem	122	Lc	51.59N	5.55 E
Arnhem, Cape-	208	Ef	12.21S	136.21 E
Arnhem Bay	212	Hb	12.20S	136.10 E
Arnhem Land	208	Ef	13.10S	134.30 E
Arno	110	Hg	43.41N	10.17 E
Arno Atoll	208	Id	7.05N	171.41 E
Arnold	124	Aa	53.00N	1.08W
Arnon	122	Ig	47.13N	2.01 E
Arnøy	114	Ea	70.08N	20.36 E
Arnprior	184	Ic	45.26N	76.21W
Arnsberg	120	Ee	51.23N	8.05 E
Arnsberger Wald	124	Kc	51.26N	8.10 E
Arnsberg-Oeventrop	124	Kc	51.24N	8.08 E
Arnsburg	124	Kd	50.29N	8.48 E
Arnstadt	120	Gf	50.50N	10.57 E
Aro, Río-	196	Di	8.01N	64.11W
Aroa	196	Bg	10.26N	68.54W
Aroa, Pointe-	221e	Fc	17.28S	149.46W
Aroa, Río-	196	Bg	10.41N	68.18W
Aroa, Sierra de-	196	Bg	10.15N	68.55W
Aroab	172	Be	26.47S	19.40 E
Aroánia Óri	130	Fl	37.57N	22.13 E
Aroche	126	Fg	37.57N	6.57W
Aroche, Pico de-	126	Ff	38.01N	6.56W
Aroeira	204	Ee	21.41S	54.25W
Arolsen	120	Ff	51.22N	9.01 E
Aroma	168	Fb	15.49N	36.08 E
Aron	122	Jh	46.50N	3.27 E
Arona	128	Ce	45.46N	8.34 E
Aroostook River	184	Nb	46.48N	67.45W
Arorae Island	208	Ie	2.38S	176.49 E
Arorangi	220p	Bb	21.13S	159.49W
Aros, Río-	192	Ec	29.30N	109.15W
Arosa	128	Dd	46.47N	9.40 E
Arosa, Ría de- / Arousa, Ría de-	126	Db	42.28N	8.57W
Aros Papigochic, Río-	192	Ec	29.09N	108.35W
Årøsund	116	Ci	55.15N	9.43 E
Arouca	126	Dd	40.56N	8.15W
Arousa, Ría de- / Arosa, Ría de-	126	Db	42.28N	8.57W
Arpaçay	146	Jb	40.45N	43.25 E
Arpajon	122	If	48.35N	2.15 E
Arpino	128	Hi	41.39N	13.36 E
Arquata Scrivia	128	Cf	44.41N	8.53 E
Arque	202	Eg	17.48S	66.23W
Arques-la-Bataille	124	De	49.53N	1.08 E
Ar Rachidiya	162	Gc	31.55N	4.40W
Ar Rachidiya [3]	162	Gc	31.00N	4.00W
Ar Radīsīyah Baḩrī	164	Fe	24.57N	32.53 E
Arrah	148	Gc	25.34N	84.40 E
Ar Rahad	158	Kg	14.28N	33.31 E
Ar Raḩḩālīyah	146	Jf	32.44N	43.23 E
Arraias	202	If	12.56S	46.57W
Arraias, Rio- [Braz.]	204	Ia	12.28S	47.18W
Arraias, Rio- [Braz.]	202	Hf	11.10S	53.35W
Arraiolos	126	Ef	38.43N	7.59W
Ar Ramādī	144	Fc	33.25N	43.17 E
Ar Ramlah	146	Fh	29.32N	35.57 E
Ar Ramlī al Kabīr	164	Dd	26.30N	22.10 E
Arran, Island of-	118	Hf	55.35N	5.15W
Ar Rank	168	Ec	11.45N	32.48 E
Ar Raqqah	144	Eb	35.56N	39.01 E
Arras	122	Id	50.17N	2.47 E
Ar Rāshidah	146	Cj	25.35N	28.56 E
Ar Rass	146	Jj	25.52N	43.28 E
Ar Rastān	146	Ge	34.55N	36.44 E
Arrats	122	Gj	44.06N	0.52 E
Ar Rawḑah	164	He	21.16N	42.50 E
Ar Rawḑah	164	Ig	14.28N	47.17 E
Ar Rawḑatayn	146	Lh	29.53N	47.44 E
Ar Rayḩānī	146	Pk	23.37N	55.58 E
Arrecife	162	Ed	28.57N	13.32W
Arrecife Alacrán	190	Gd	22.24N	89.42W
Arrecifes	206	Hd	34.03S	60.07W
Arrecifes, Rio-	204	Ck	33.46S	59.31W
Arrée, Monts d'-	122	Cf	48.26N	3.55W
Arresø	116	Ei	55.55N	82.05 E
Arriaga	192	Mi	16.14N	93.54W
Ar Rifā	144	Hd	26.07N	50.03 E
Ar Rifā'ī	146	Lg	31.43N	46.07 E
Ar Rıhāb	146	Kg	30.52N	45.30 E
Ar Rimāh	146	Lj	25.34N	47.09 E
Ar Rimāl	140	Hg	22.00N	52.50 E
Ar Riyāḑ = Riyadh (EN)	142	Gg	24.38N	46.43 E
Arrochar	118	Ie	56.12N	4.45W
Arroio Grande	204	Fk	32.14S	53.05W
Arrojado	204	Ja	13.29S	44.37W
Arrojado, Rio-	204	Ja	13.24S	44.20W
Arromanches-les-Bains	124	Be	49.20N	0.37W
Arros	122	Gk	43.40N	0.02 E
Arroscia	128	Cg	44.03N	8.11 E
Arroux	122	Jh	46.29N	3.58 E
Arrow, Lough-/Loch Arabhach	118	Eg	54.05N	8.20W
Arrowsmith, Mount-	216	Dh	43.21S	170.59 E
Arrowtown	218	Cf	44.56S	168.50 E
Arroyo Barú	204	Cj	31.52S	58.26W
Arroyo de la Luz	126	Fe	39.29N	6.35W
Arroyo Grande	188	Ei	35.07N	120.34W
Arroyos y Esteros	204	Dg	25.04S	57.06W
Ar Rub'al Khālī	140	Hg	21.00N	51.00 E
Arruda	204	Db	15.02S	56.07W
Arrufó	206	Hd	30.15S	61.45W
Ar Rumaythah	146	Kg	31.32N	45.12 E
Ar Ruq'ī	146	Lh	29.01N	46.33 E
Ar Rusāfah	146	He	35.02N	36.17 E
Ar Ruşayriş	160	Kg	11.51N	34.23 E
Ar Ruţbah	144	Fc	33.02N	40.17 E
Ar Ruwayḑah	146	Ki	26.23N	44.14 E
Ar Ruways [Qatar]	144	Hd	26.08N	51.13 E
Ar Ruways [U.A.E.]	144	He	24.08N	52.45 E
Ar Ruzayqāt	146	Ej	25.35N	32.28 E
Års	116	Ch	56.48N	9.32 E
Arsenjān	146	Oh	29.56N	53.18 E
Arsenjev	138	Ih	44.12N	133.20 E
Arsi [3]	168	Fd	7.10N	40.00 E
Arsk	114	Lh	56.07N	49.52 E
Årskogen	116	Gb	62.05N	17.20 E
Arslanköy	146	Fd	37.01N	34.17 E
Ars-sur-Moselle	124	Ie	49.05N	6.04 E
Arsuk	179	Hf	61.11N	48.30W
Årsunda	116	Gd	60.32N	16.44 E
Art	219b	Ad	19.43S	163.39 E
Arta	168	Gc	11.31N	42.50 E
Árta	130	Dj	39.09N	20.59 E
Artá / Artà	126	Pe	39.42N	3.21 E
Artà / Artá	126	Pe	39.42N	3.21 E
Artà, Coves d'- / Artá, Cuevas de-	126	Pe	39.40N	3.24W
Artá, Cuevas de- / Artà, Coves d'-	126	Pe	39.40N	3.24W
Artašat	132	Nj	39.59N	44.33 E
Arteaga	192	Hh	18.28N	102.25W
Artem	138	Ih	43.23N	132.10 E
Artemisa	190	Hd	22.49N	82.46W
Artemón	130	Hm	36.57N	24.43 E
Artem-Ostrov	136	Fg	40.28N	50.18 E
Artemovsk [Russia]	138	Ef	54.23N	93.30 E
Artemovsk [Ukr.]	132	Ke	48.33N	38.03 E
Artemovski	134	Jh	57.25N	61.58 E
Artesa de Segre	126	Nc	41.54N	1.03 E
Artesia	182	Ge	32.51N	104.24W
Arthur	186	Ff	41.35N	101.31W
Arthur Creek	212	Hd	23.00S	136.58 E
Arthur River	212	Ih	41.00S	144.55 E
Arthur's Pass	216	Dh	42.57S	171.34 E
Arthur's Pass	218	De	42.54S	171.34 E
Arthur's Town	194	Ja	24.38N	75.32W
Arti	134	Ih	56.26N	58.32 E
Artibonite, Rivière de l'-	194	Kd	19.15N	72.47W
Artigas	206	Id	30.42S	56.28W
Artigas [3]	204	Dj	30.35S	57.00W
Artijarvi/Artsjö	116	Ld	60.45N	26.05 E
Artik	132	Mi	40.36N	43.58 E
Artillery Lake	180	Gd	63.08N	107.45W
Artois	122	Id	50.10N	2.30 E
Artois, Collines de l'-	122	Id	50.30N	2.15 E
Artoli	168	Eb	18.19N	33.54 E
Artrutx, Cap d'- / Dartuch, Cabo-	126	Pe	39.56N	3.48 E
Artsjö/Artijarvi	116	Ld	60.45N	26.05 E
Artux	152	Cd	39.40N	76.10 E
Artvin	144	Fa	41.11N	41.49 E
Artyk	138	Jd	64.12N	145.15 E
Aru	170	Fb	2.52N	30.51 E
Aru, Kepulauan- = Aru Islands (EN)	208	Ee	6.00S	134.30 E
Arua	160	Kh	3.01N	30.55 E
Aruanã	204	Gb	14.54S	51.05W
Aruba [5]	200	Jd	12.30N	70.00W
Aruba	198	Jd	12.30N	70.00W
Aru Bassin (EN)	150	Jg	5.00S	134.00 E
Aru Islands (EN) = Aru, Kepulauan-	208	Ee	6.00S	134.30 E
Arukoron Point	220a	Bb	7.43N	134.38 E
Arun	118	Mk	50.48N	0.33W
Arunāchal Pradesh [3]	148	Ic	27.50N	94.50 E
Arundel	124	Bd	50.51N	0.33W
Arun He	152	Lb	47.36N	124.06 E
Arun Qi	152	Lb	48.09N	123.29 E
Arus, Tanjung-	150	Hf	1.24N	125.06 E
Arusha	160	Ki	3.22S	36.41 E
Arusha [3]	170	Gc	3.30S	36.00 E
Arutua Atoll	216	Lc	15.18S	146.44W
Arutunga	216	Jc	18.52S	159.46W
Aruwimi	158	Jh	1.13N	23.36 E
Arvada [Co.-U.S.]	186	Dg	39.50N	105.05W
Arvada [Wy.-U.S.]	188	Ld	44.40N	106.03W
Arve	122	Mh	46.12N	6.08 E
Arvert, Presqu'île d'-	122	Ei	45.45N	1.05W
Arvida	180	Kg	48.26N	71.11W
Arvidsjaur	114	Ed	65.35N	19.10 E
Arvika	114	Cg	59.39N	12.36 E
Årviksand	114	Ea	70.12N	20.32 E
Arvin	188	Fi	35.12N	118.50W
Arxan	152	Lb	47.11N	119.58 E
Aryānah	128	En	36.52N	10.11 E
Arys	136	Gg	42.26N	68.48 E
Arys	135	Gc	42.48N	68.15 E
Arys, ozero-	135	Fb	45.50N	66.20 E
Arz	122	Dg	47.39N	2.06W
Arzachena	128	Di	41.05N	9.23 E
Arzamas	136	Ed	55.23N	43.50 E
Arzanah	146	Oj	24.47N	52.34 E
Aržano	128	Kg	43.35N	16.59 E
Arzew	162	Gb	35.51N	0.19W
Arzew, Golfe d'-	126	Li	35.50N	0.10W
Arzew, Salines d'-	126	Li	35.42N	0.18W
Arzfeld	124	Id	50.05N	6.16 E
Arzgir	136	Ef	45.22N	44.13 E
Arzúa	126	Db	42.56N	8.09W
Aš	120	If	50.13N	12.12 E
Ås	116	De	59.40N	10.48 E
As	124	Hc	51.01N	5.35 E
Aša	136	Fd	55.02N	57.18 E
Aså	116	Dg	57.09N	10.25 E
Asab	172	Be	25.29S	17.59 E
Asaba	166	Gd	6.11N	6.45 E
Asad, Buḩayrat al-	146	He	35.57N	38.10 E
Asadābād [Afg.]	144	Lc	34.52N	71.09 E
Asadābād [Iran]	146	Me	34.47N	48.07 E
Asafik	168	Bc	13.10N	19.26 E
Asahi [Jap.]	156	Gd	35.43N	140.35 E
Asahi [Jap.]	156a	Ca	44.08N	142.35 E
Asahi [Jap.]	156	Fb	38.15N	139.30 E
Asahi [Jap.]	156	Ec	36.57N	137.34 E
Asahi-Dake	156	Fb	38.16N	139.55 E
Asahi-Gawa	156	Cd	34.36N	133.58 E
Asahikawa	142	Qe	43.46N	142.22 E
Asaka-Drainage	156	Gc	37.30N	140.15 E
Asale, Lake-	168	Gc	14.00N	40.20 E
'Asalūyeh	146	Oi	27.28N	52.37 E
Asama-Yama	154	Of	36.27N	138.30 E
Asan-Man	154	If	36.56N	126.51 E
Asansol	142	Kg	23.41N	86.59 E
Asarna	114	De	62.39N	14.21 E
Asarum	116	Fh	56.12N	14.50 E
'Asäyr = Guardafui, Cape- (EN)	158	Mg	11.49N	51.15 E
Asayta	168	Gc	11.33N	41.27 E
Asbest	134	Jh	57.01N	61.31 E
Asbestos	184	Lc	45.46N	71.57W
Asbe Teferi	168	Gd	9.05N	40.51 E
Asbury Park	184	Je	40.14N	74.01W
Ascension	158	Fi	7.57S	14.22W
Ascensión, Bahía de la-	190	Ge	19.40N	87.30W
Ascensión, Laguna de la-	192	Fb	31.05N	107.55W
Aschaffenburg	120	Fg	49.59N	9.09 E
Ascheberg	124	Jc	51.47N	7.37 E
Aschendorf (Ems), Papenburg-	124	Ja	53.04N	7.22 E
Aschersleben	120	He	51.45N	11.28 E
Aščikol, ozero-	135	Fb	45.05N	67.20 E
Aščiozek	132	Pe	49.12N	48.06 E
Ascoli Piceno	128	Hh	42.51N	13.34 E
Ascoli Satriano	128	Ji	41.12N	15.34 E
Ascot	124	Bc	51.24N	0.40W
Aseb	160	Lg	13.00N	42.44 E
Åseda	114	Dh	57.10N	15.20 E
Asedjrad	158	Hf	24.42N	1.40 E
Asekejevo	132	Rc	53.36N	52.51 E
As Ela	168	Gc	11.06N	42.06 E
Asela	160	Kh	7.58N	39.08 E
Åsele	114	Dd	64.10N	17.20 E
Åsen [Nor.]	114	Ce	63.36N	11.03 E
Åsen [Swe.]	114	Cf	61.17N	13.50 E
Asendabo	168	Fd	9.47N	37.36 E
Asendorf	124	Kb	52.46N	9.00 E
Asenovgrad	130	Hg	42.01N	24.52 E
Åsensbruk	116	Ef	58.48N	12.25 E
Åseral	116	Bf	58.37N	7.25 E
Aseri/Azeri	114	Gg	59.29N	26.51 E
Asfeld	124	Ge	49.28N	4.07 E
Aşfūn al Maţā'inah	146	Ej	25.23N	32.32 E
Åsgårdstrand	116	De	59.21N	10.28 E
Ašhabad	142	Hf	37.57N	58.23 E
Ashanti [3]	166	Ed	6.45N	1.30W
Ashburn	184	Fj	31.43N	83.39W
Ashburton	216	Dh	43.54S	171.45 E
Ashburton River	208	Cg	21.40S	114.56 E
Ashdod	146	Fg	31.49N	34.39 E
Ashdown	186	Ij	33.41N	94.08W
Asheboro	184	Hh	35.42N	79.49W
Asheroft	188	Ea	50.43N	121.17W
Asheville	182	Kd	35.34N	82.33W
Ashford	118	Nj	51.09N	0.53 E
Ashford Airport	124	Cc	51.10N	0.59 E
Ash Fork	188	Ii	35.13N	112.29W
Ashibetsu	154	Qc	43.31N	142.11 E
Ashikaga	156	Fc	36.21N	139.27 E
Ashington	118	Lf	55.11N	1.34W
Ashiro	156	Ga	40.06N	141.01 E
Ashiya	156	Be	33.53N	130.40 E
Ashizuri-Misaki	154	Lh	32.44N	133.01 E
Ashkal, Qar'at al-	128	Dm	37.10N	9.40 E
Āshkhāneh	146	Qd	37.28N	57.00 E
Ashland [Ks.-U.S.]	186	Gh	37.11N	99.46W
Ashland [Ky.-U.S.]	182	Kd	38.28N	82.38W
Ashland [Mt.-U.S.]	188	Ld	45.35N	106.16W
Ashland [Oh.-U.S.]	184	Fe	40.52N	82.19W
Ashland [Or.-U.S.]	182	Cc	42.12N	122.42W
Ashland [Wi.-U.S.]	182	Ib	46.35N	90.53W
Ashland, Mount-	188	De	42.05N	122.43W
Ashley	186	Gc	46.02N	99.22W
Ashmore Islands	208	Df	12.15S	123.05 E
Ashmūn	146	Dg	30.18N	30.58 E
Ashoro	156a	Cb	43.14N	143.31 E
Ashqelon	146	Fg	31.40N	34.35 E
Ash Shabakah	146	Jg	30.49N	43.39 E
Ash Shabb	164	Ee	22.19N	29.46 E
Ash Shā'ib	146	Gh	28.59N	37.07 E
Ash Shallāl	158	Kf	24.03N	32.53 E
Ash Sha'm	144	Id	26.02N	56.05 E
Ash Shamāl [3]	146	Fe	34.30N	36.00 E
Ash Shamālīyah [3]	168	Db	18.40N	30.00 E
Ash 'Shāmīyah	146	Kg	31.57N	44.36 E
Ash Shāmīyah	146	Lg	30.15N	46.55 E
Ash Shaqq	146	Lh	28.20N	47.30 E
Ash Shaqrā'	144	Gd	25.15N	45.15 E
Ash Sha'rā'	146	Kj	24.16N	44.11 E
Ash Shariqah	144	Id	25.22N	55.23 E
Ash Sharqāţ	144	Fb	35.27N	43.16 E
Ash Sharqī	146	Ge	34.00N	36.30 E
Ash Sharqī	162	Jc	34.45N	11.15 E
Ash Sharqīyah	144	Ie	22.15N	58.30 E
Ash Shatrah	146	Lg	31.25N	46.10 E
Ash Shawbak	146	Fg	30.32N	35.34 E
Ash Shaykh Ḩumayd	146	Fh	28.07N	34.34 E
Ash Shifā	146	Fh	28.30N	35.30 E
Ash Shiḩr	144	Gg	14.44N	49.35 E
Ash Shināfīyah	146	Kg	31.35N	44.39 E
Ash Shu'aybah [Kuw.]	146	Mh	29.03N	48.08 E
Ash Shu'aybah [Sau.Ar.]	146	Ji	27.53N	42.43 E
Ash Shu'bah	146	Kh	28.54N	44.44 E
Ash Shumlūl	146	Li	26.31N	47.20 E
Ash Shuqayq	144	Ff	17.44N	42.01 E
Ash Shurayk	168	Eb	18.48N	33.34 E
Ash Shuwayhāt	146	Oj	24.05N	52.28 E
Ash Shuwaykh	146	Lh	29.21N	47.55 E
Ashtabula	182	Kc	41.53N	80.47W
Ashtabula, Lake-	186	Hc	47.11N	97.58W
Ashtīyān	146	Me	34.30N	49.55 E
Ashton [Id.-U.S.]	188	Jd	44.04N	111.27W
Ashton [St.Vin.]	197n	Bb	12.36N	61.27W
Ashuanipi	180	Kf	52.55N	66.00W
Ashuanipi Lake	180	Kf	52.45N	66.10W
'Āşī, Nahr al- = Orontes (EN)	144	Eb	36.02N	35.58 E
Asia (EN)	106	Ge	40.00N	85.00 E
Asia, Kepulauan-	150	Jf	1.03N	131.18 E
Asiago	128	Fe	45.52N	11.30 E
Asiago, Altopiano di-	128	Fe	45.54N	11.30 E
Asilah	162	Fb	35.28N	6.02W
Asinara	110	Gg	41.04N	8.15 E
Asinara, Golfo dell'-	128	Cj	41.00N	8.35 E
Asino	138	De	56.58N	86.09 E
'Asīr	140	Gh	19.00N	42.00 E
'Asīr	144	Ff	19.00N	42.00 E
Aškadar	134	Hi	53.37N	56.01 E
Aşkale	146	Ic	39.55N	40.42 E
Askanija-Nova	132	Hf	46.27N	33.52 E
Asker	116	De	59.50N	10.26 E
Askersund	114	Dg	58.53N	14.54 E
Askī Al Mawşil	146	Jd	36.34N	42.42 E
Askim [Nor.]	116	De	59.35N	11.10 E
Askim [Swe.]	116	Dg	57.38N	11.56 E
Áskion Óros	130	Ei	40.22N	21.34 E
Askiz	138	Ef	53.08N	90.32 E
Askja	110	Eb	65.03N	16.48W
Askola	116	Kd	60.32N	25.36 E
Äsköping	116	Ge	59.09N	16.04 E
Askøy	116	Ad	60.24N	5.11 E
Askøy	116	Ad	60.30N	5.05 E
Askrova	116	Ac	61.30N	4.55 E
Askvoll	114	Af	61.21N	5.04 E
Asl	146	Eh	29.30N	32.43 E
Aslanapa	130	Mj	39.13N	29.52 E
Asmara (EN) = Asmera	160	Kg	15.19N	38.57 E
Asmera = Asmara (EN)	160	Kg	15.19N	38.57 E
Åsnen	116	Fh	56.40N	14.40 E
Asni	162	Fc	31.15N	7.59W
Asnières-sur-Seine	124	Ef	48.55N	2.17 E
Aso	156	Be	32.58N	131.02 E
Aso	128	Hg	43.06N	13.51 E
Asola	128	Ee	45.13N	10.24 E
Asosa	160	Kg	10.02N	34.32 E

Aso-Axi

Aso-San 156 Be 32.53N 131.06 E
Asoteriba, Jabal- 168 Fa 21.51N 36.30 E
Asouf Mellene 162 Hd 25.40N 2.08 E
Asō-Wan 156 Ad 34.20N 129.15 E
Āspās 146 Og 30.40N 52.24 E
Aspe 126 Lf 38.21N 0.46W
Aspen 182 Fd 39.11N 106.49W
Aspermont 186 Fj 33.08N 100.14W
Aspiring, Mount- 216 Ch 44.23S 168.44 E
Aspromonte 128 Jl 38.10N 16.00 E
Assa 162 Fd 28.37N 9.25W
Aş Şadr 144 He 24.40N 54.41 E
Aş Şaff 146 Dh 29.34N 31.17 E
Aş Şāfī 146 Fg 31.02N 35.28 E
As Safirah 146 Gd 36.04N 37.22 E
Aş Şaḩm 146 Qj 24.10N 56.53 E
Assahoun 166 Fd 6.27N 0.55 E
Aş Şa'īd 158 Kf 26.00N 32.00 E
Assal, Lac- 168 Gc 11.40N 42.22 E
As Salamīyah [Sau.Ar.] 144 Ge 24.12N 47.23 E
As Salamīyah [Syr.] 146 Ge 35.01N 37.03 E
Aş Şāliḩīyah 146 Ie 34.44N 40.45 E
As Sālimīyah 146 Mh 29.20N 48.04 E
As Sallūm 160 Je 31.34N 25.09 E
As Salmān 146 Kg 30.26N 44.30 E
As Salt 146 Ff 32.03N 35.44 E
As Salwá 144 He 24.45N 50.49 E
Assam [3] 148 Ic 26.00N 93.00 E
Assam 140 Lg 26.50N 94.00 E
Assamakka 166 Gb 19.21N 5.38 E
As Samawah 144 Gc 31.18N 45.17 E
As Sanām 168 Ia 22.00N 51.10 E
Assaouas 166 Gb 16.52N 7.27 E
As Sars 128 Dn 36.05N 9.01 E
As Sayl al Kabīr 164 He 21.38N 40.25 E
Asse 124 Gd 50.56N 4.12 E
Asse 122 Lk 43.53N 5.53 E
Assebroek, Brugge- 124 Fc 51.12N 3.16 E
Assekkâraï 166 Fb 15.50N 2.52 E
Assemini 128 Dk 39.17N 9.01 E
Assen 122 Ma 53.00N 6.34 E
Assenede 124 Fc 51.14N 3.45 E
Assens 116 Ci 55.16N 9.55 E
As Sībā'īyah 146 Ej 25.11N 32.41 E
As Sidr 160 Ie 30.39N 18.22 E
As Sidrah = Sirte Desert (EN) 158 Ie 30.30N 17.30 E
As Sila' 144 He 24.02N 51.46 E
As Sinbillāwayn 146 Dg 30.53N 31.27 E
Assiniboia 180 Gg 49.38N 105.59W
Assiniboine 174 Je 49.53N 97.08W
Assiniboine, Mount- 174 Hd 50.52N 115.39W
Assis 206 Jb 22.40S 50.25W
Assisi 128 Gg 43.04N 12.37 E
Aßlar 124 Kd 50.36N 8.28 E
Assos 130 Jj 39.31N 26.20 E
As Subaykhah 128 Eo 35.56N 10.01 E
As Subū' 164 Fe 22.45N 32.34 E
As Sūdān = Sudan (EN) [1] 160 Jg 15.00N 30.00 E
As Sudd 158 Kh 8.00N 31.00 E
As Sufāl 168 Hc 14.06N 48.43 E
Aş Şufuq 146 Nk 23.52N 51.45 E
Aş Şukhayrah 162 Jc 34.17N 10.06 E
As Sukhnah 146 He 34.52N 38.52 E
As Sulaymī 146 Ii 26.17N 41.21 E
As Sulayyil 144 Ge 20.27N 45.34 E
Aş Şulb 146 Mj 25.42N 48.25 E
Aş Sumayḩ 168 Dd 9.49N 27.39 E
Aş Şummān 146 Li 27.00N 47.00 E
Aş Şummān 164 Ie 23.00N 48.00 E
Assumption Island 158 Li 9.45S 46.30 E
As Sūq 164 He 21.54N 42.03 E
Assur 146 Je 35.25N 43.16 E
Aş Şuwār 146 Ie 35.30N 40.39 E
As Suwaydā' 144 Ec 32.42N 36.34 E
Aş Şuwayrah 146 Kf 32.55N 44.47 E
As Suways = Suez (EN) 160 Kf 29.58N 32.33 E
Astakidha 130 Jn 35.53N 26.50 E
Astakós 130 Ek 38.32N 21.05 E
Āstāneh [Iran] 146 Md 37.17N 49.59 E
Āstāneh [Iran] 146 Mf 33.53N 49.22 E
Āstārā 144 Gb 38.26N 48.52 E
Astara 112 Kh 38.28N 48.52 E
Aštarak 132 Ni 40.16N 44.18 E
Asten 124 Hc 51.24N 5.45 E
Asti 128 Cf 44.54N 8.12 E
Astico 128 Fe 45.37N 11.37 E
Astipálaia 130 Jm 36.33N 26.21 E
Astipálaia 130 Jm 36.35N 26.20 E
Asto, Monte- 122a Ba 42.30N 9.15 E
Astola Island 148 Cc 25.07N 63.51 E
Astorga 126 Fb 42.27N 6.03W
Astoria 182 Cb 46.11N 123.50W
Åstorp 116 Eh 56.08N 12.57 E
Astove Island 158 Lj 10.06S 47.45 E
Astrahan 112 Kf 46.21N 48.03 E
Astrahanskaja oblast [3] 136 Ef 47.10N 47.30 E
Astrolabe, Cape- 219a Ec 8.20S 160.34 E
Astrolabe, Récifs de l'- 208 Hf 19.49S 165.35 E
Astudillo 126 Hb 42.12N 4.18W
Asturias [2] 126 Ga 43.20N 6.00W
Asuisui, Cape- 221c Aa 13.47S 172.29W
Asunción 200 Kh 25.16S 57.40W
Asunción, Bahía- 192 Bd 27.05N 114.10W
Asunción, Cerro de la- 192 Je 24.15N 99.56W
Asuncion Island 208 Fc 19.40N 145.24 E
Asunción Mita 194 Cf 14.20N 89.43W
Asunción Nochixtlán 192 Ki 17.28N 97.14W
Åsunden 116 Eg 57.44N 13.22 E
Åsunden 116 Fg 58.00N 15.50 E
Aswa 170 Fb 3.43N 31.55 E
Aswān 160 Kf 24.05N 32.53 E
Aswān, Sadd al- = Aswān High Dam (EN) 164 Fe 24.01N 32.52 E
Aswān High Dam (EN) = Aswān, Sadd al- 164 Fe 24.01N 32.52 E
Asyūţ 160 Kf 27.11N 31.11 E
Asyūţī, Wādī al- 146 Di 27.10N 31.16 E
Aszód 120 Pi 47.39N 19.30 E
'Ata 221b Bc 21.03S 174.59W
Atacama [2] 206 Gc 27.30S 70.00W
Atacama, Desierto de- = Atacama Desert (EN) 198 Jh 22.30S 69.15W
Atacama, Salar de- 198 Jh 23.30S 68.15W
Atacama Desert (EN) = Atacama, Desierto de- 198 Jh 22.30S 69.15W
Atafu Atoll 208 Je 8.33S 172.30W
Atagaj 138 Ee 55.06N 99.25 E
Ata Island 208 Jg 21.03S 175.00W
Atakor 158 Hf 23.13N 5.40 E
Atakora [3] 166 Fc 10.00N 1.35 E
Atakora 166 Fc 10.45N 1.30 E
Atakpamé 160 Hh 7.32N 1.08 E
Atalaia do Norte 202 Dd 4.20S 70.12W
Atalándi 130 Fk 38.39N 23.00 E
Atalaya 202 Df 10.44S 73.45W
Atalayasa / sa Talaiassa 126 Nf 38.55N 1.15 E
Atambua 150 Hh 9.07S 124.54 E
Atami 156 Fd 35.05N 139.02 E
Atangmik 179 Gf 64.53N 52.00W
Aţâr 160 Ff 20.30N 13.03W
Atas-Bogdo-Ula 152 Gc 43.20N 96.30 E
Atascadero 188 Ei 35.29N 120.41W
Atasu 136 Hf 48.42N 71.38 E
'Atata 221b Ac 21.03S 175.15W
Atatürk Barajı 146 Hd 37.30N 38.30 E
Atauro, Pulau 150 Ih 8.13S 125.35 E
Atáviros 130 Km 36.12N 27.52 E
Ataway 168 Bd 9.59N 18.38 E
Atbara 168 Eb 17.40N 33.56 E
'Aţbarah 160 Kg 17.42N 33.59 E
'Aţbarah 158 Kg 17.40N 33.56 E
Atbasar 142 Id 51.48N 68.20 E
At-Baši 136 Hg 41.08N 75.51 E
Atça 130 Ll 37.53N 28.13 E
Atchafalaya Bay 182 If 29.25N 91.20W
Atchison 182 Hd 39.34N 95.07W
Atebubu 166 Ed 7.45N 0.59W
Ateca 126 Kc 41.20N 1.47W
Aterno 128 Hh 42.11N 13.51 E
Atessa 128 Ih 42.04N 14.27 E
Ath/Aat 122 Jd 50.38N 3.47 E
Athabasca 180 Gf 54.43N 113.17W
Athabasca 174 Hd 58.40N 110.50W
Athabasca, Lake- 174 Id 59.07N 110.00W
Athamánon, Óri- 130 Ej 39.27N 21.08 E
Athamánon Óri 130 Ej 39.27N 21.08 E
Athens [Al.-U.S.] 184 Dh 34.48N 86.58W
Athens [Ga.-U.S.] 182 Ke 33.57N 83.23W
Athens [Oh.-U.S.] 184 Ff 39.20N 82.06W
Athens [Tn.-U.S.] 184 Eh 35.28N 84.35W
Athens [Tx.-U.S.] 186 Ij 32.12N 95.51W
Athens (EN) = Athínai [Grc.] 112 Ih 37.59N 23.44 E
Athéras 130 Jl 37.38N 26.15 E
Atherton 212 Jc 17.16S 145.29 E
Athi 170 Gc 2.59S 38.31 E
Athies-sous-Laon 124 Fe 49.34N 3.41 E
Athínai [Grc.] = Athens (EN) 112 Ih 37.59N 23.44 E
Athi River 170 Gc 1.27S 36.59 E
Athis-de-l'Orne 124 Bf 48.49N 0.30W
Athlone/Baile Átha Luain 118 Fh 53.25N 7.56W
Athol 184 Kd 42.36N 72.14W
Áthos 130 Hi 40.10N 24.20 E
Athos, Mount- (EN) = Áyion Óros [2] 130 Hi 40.15N 24.15 E
Ath Thamad 146 Fh 29.41N 34.18 E
Ath Thumāmī 146 Ki 27.42N 44.59 E
Athus, Aubange- 124 He 49.34N 5.50 E
Athy 118 Gi 53.00N 7.00W
Ati 160 Ig 13.13N 18.20 E
Atiak 170 Fb 3.16N 32.07 E
Atiamuri 218 Gc 38.23S 176.02 E
Atibaia, Rio- 204 If 22.42S 47.17W
Atienza 126 Jc 41.12N 2.52W
Atikokan 180 Ig 48.45N 91.37W
Atikonak Lake 180 Lf 52.40N 64.35W
Atimoono 220n Bc 10.26S 160.58W
Atitlán, Lago de- 194 Bf 14.42N 91.12W
Atitlán, Volcán- 190 Ff 14.35N 91.11W
Atiu Island 208 Lg 20.02S 158.07W
'Atk, Wādī al- 146 Li 26.03N 46.30 E
Atka 174 Bd 52.15N 174.30W
Atka [Ak.-U.S.] 178a Db 52.12N 174.12W
Atka [Russia] 138 Kd 60.49N 151.58 E
Atka Iceport 222 Bf 70.35S 7.45W
Atkarsk 136 Ee 51.52N 44.59 E
Atkasook 178 Hb 70.28N 157.24W
Atkinson 186 Ge 42.32N 98.59W
Atlacomulco de Fabela 192 Jh 19.48N 99.53W
Atlanta [Ga.-U.S.] 176 Kf 33.45N 84.23W
Atlanta [Mi.-U.S.] 184 Ec 45.00N 84.09W
Atlanta [Tx.-U.S.] 186 Ij 33.07N 94.10W
Atlanterhavet = Atlantic Ocean (EN) 106 Di 2.00N 25.00W
Atlantic [Ia.-U.S.] 186 If 41.24N 95.01W
Atlantic [N.C.-U.S.] 184 Ih 34.54N 76.20W
Atlantic City 176 Lf 39.27N 74.35W
Atlantic Coastal Plain (EN) 174 Lf 34.00N 79.00W
Atlantic-Indian Basin (EN) 222 Ce 60.00S 15.00 E
Atlantic-Indian Ridge (EN) 106 Eo 52.00S 25.00 E
Atlántico [3] 202 Da 10.40N 75.00W
Atlântico, Oceano- = Atlantic Ocean (EN) 106 Di 2.00N 25.00W
Atlántico, Océano- = Atlantic Ocean (EN) 106 Di 2.00N 25.00W
Atlantic Ocean 106 Di 2.00N 25.00W
Atlantic Ocean (EN) = Atlanterhavet 106 Di 2.00N 25.00W
Atlantic Ocean (EN) = Atlántico, Océano- 106 Di 2.00N 25.00W
Atlantic Ocean (EN) = Atlântico, Oceano- 106 Di 2.00N 25.00W
Atlantic Ocean (EN) = Atlantiese Oseaan 106 Di 2.00N 25.00W
Atlantic Ocean (EN) = Atlantique, Océan- 106 Di 2.00N 25.00W
Atlantic Ocean (EN) = Atlantshaf 106 Di 2.00N 25.00W
Atlantic Ocean (EN) = Muhīt, Al Baḩr al- 106 Di 2.00N 25.00W
Atlántida [3] 194 Df 15.30N 87.00W
Atlantiese Oseaan = Atlantic Ocean (EN) 106 Di 2.00N 25.00W
Atlantique [3] 166 Fd 6.35N 2.15 E
Atlantique, Océan- = Atlantic Ocean (EN) 106 Di 2.00N 25.00W
Atlantshaf = Atlantic Ocean (EN) 106 Di 2.00N 25.00W
Atlas = Atlas Mountains (EN) 158 Ge 32.00N 2.00W
Atlas Mountains (EN) = Atlas 158 Ge 32.00N 2.00W
Atlasova, ostrov- 138 Kf 50.50N 155.25 E
Atlasovo 138 Jg 46.00N 142.09 E
Atlas Saharien = Saharan Atlas (EN) 158 He 34.00N 2.00 E
Atlas Tellien = Tell Atlas (EN) 158 He 36.00N 2.00 E
Atlin 180 Ee 59.35N 133.42W
Atlin Lake 180 Ee 59.35N 133.43W
Atlixco 190 Ee 18.54N 98.26W
Atløy 116 Ac 61.20N 4.55 E
Atmore 184 Dj 31.02N 87.29W
Atna 116 Dc 61.44N 10.49 E
Atna Peak 180 Ef 53.57N 128.04W
Atō 156 Bd 34.24N 131.43 E
Atoka 186 Hi 34.23N 96.08W
Átokos 130 Dk 38.29N 20.49 E
Atotonilco el Alto 192 Hg 20.33N 102.31W
Atoui, Khatt- 162 De 20.04N 15.58W
Atouila, 'Erg- 158 Gf 21.15N 3.20W
Atoyac, Río- 192 Ki 16.30N 97.31W
Atoyac de Álvarez 192 Ii 17.12N 100.26W
Atrak 140 Hf 37.23N 53.57 E
Ätran 114 Ch 56.53N 12.30 E
Atrato, Río- 198 Ie 8.17N 76.58W
Atrek 140 Hf 37.23N 53.57 E
Atri 128 Hh 42.35N 13.59 E
Atsugi 156 Fd 35.26N 139.20 E
Atsukeshi 154 Rc 43.02N 144.51 E
Atsukeshi-Wan 156a Db 43.00N 144.45 E
Atsumi [Jap.] 154 Oe 38.37N 139.35 E
Atsumi [Jap.] 156 Ed 34.37N 137.05 E
Atsumi-Hantō 156 Ed 34.40N 137.15 E
Atsumi-Wan 156 Ed 34.45N 137.15 E
Atsuta 156a Bb 43.24N 141.25 E
Aţ Ţaff 144 He 23.55N 54.25 E
Aţ Ţafīlah 146 Fg 30.50N 35.36 E
Aţ Ţā'if 142 Gg 21.16N 40.25 E
At Tāj 164 De 24.13N 23.18 E
Attalla 184 Dh 34.01N 86.05W
Aţ Ţallāb 164 De 24.01N 23.10 E
At Ta'mīm [3] 146 Ke 36.00N 44.00 E
Attapu 148 Lf 14.48N 106.50 E
Aţ Ţārmīyah 146 Kf 33.40N 44.24 E
Attawapiskat 176 Kd 52.55N 82.26W
Attawapiskat 174 Kd 52.57N 82.18W
Attawapiskat Lake 180 If 52.15N 87.50W
Aţ Ţawīl 146 Hh 29.20N 39.35 E
At Taysīyah 146 Jh 28.00N 44.00 E
Aţ Ţayyārah 168 Ec 13.12N 30.47 E
Attendorn 124 Jc 51.07N 7.54 E
Attersee (Kammersee) 128 Hc 47.55N 13.33 E
Attert 124 Ie 49.49N 6.05 E
Attica 184 De 40.17N 87.15W
Attichy 124 Fe 49.25N 3.03 E
Attigny 124 Ge 49.29N 4.35 E
At Tīh Desert (EN) = Tīh, Şaḩrā' at- 164 Fc 30.05N 34.00 E
Attikamagen Lake 180 Ke 55.00N 66.30W
Attleboro 184 Le 41.56N 71.17W
Attleborough 124 Db 52.31N 1.01 E
Attre 124 Fd 50.37N 3.50 E
Attu 178a Ab 52.56N 173.15 E
Attu 178a Ab 52.55N 173.00 E
Aţ Ţulayhī 146 Ki 27.33N 44.08 E
Aţ Ţūr 146 Eh 28.14N 33.37 E
Aţ Ţurayf 144 Ec 31.44N 38.33 E
At Turbah 144 Fg 12.40N 43.30 E
Aţ Ţuwayshah 168 Dc 12.21N 26.32 E
Åtvidaberg 114 Dg 58.12N 16.00 E
Atwater 188 Eh 37.21N 120.36W
Atwood 186 Fg 39.45N 101.03W
Atyrau (Gurjev) 112 Lf 47.07N 51.56 E
Atyrauskaja oblast 136 Ff 47.30N 52.00 E
Auasbila 194 Ef 14.52N 84.40W
Auatu 168 Gd 7.17N 41.03 E
Auau Channel 221a Ec 20.51N 156.45W
Aubagne 122 Lk 43.17N 5.34 E
Aubange 124 He 49.35N 5.48 E
Aubange-Athus 124 He 49.34N 5.50 E
Aube [3] 122 Kf 48.15N 4.05 E
Aube 122 Jf 48.34N 3.43 E
Aubel 124 Hd 50.42N 5.51 E
Aubenas 122 Kj 44.37N 4.23 E
Aubenton 124 Ge 49.50N 4.12 E
Aubetin 124 Ff 48.49N 3.01 E
Aubigny-en-Artois 124 Ed 50.21N 2.35 E
Aubigny-sur-Nère 122 Ig 47.29N 2.26 E
Aubin 122 Ij 44.32N 2.15 E
Aubrac, Monts d'- 122 Ij 44.38N 3.00 E
Aubry, Lake - 180 Ec 67.25N 126.30W
Auburn [Al.-U.S.] 184 Ei 32.36N 85.29W
Auburn [Ca.-U.S.] 188 Eg 38.54N 121.04W
Auburn [In.-U.S.] 184 Ee 41.22N 85.04W
Auburn [Me.-U.S.] 184 Lc 44.06N 70.14W
Auburn [Nb.-U.S.] 186 If 40.23N 95.51W
Auburn [N.Y.-U.S.] 184 Id 42.57N 76.34W
Auburn [Wa.-U.S.] 188 Dc 47.18N 122.13W
Auburn Range 212 Ke 25.10S 150.30 E
Aubusson 122 Ii 45.57N 2.10 E
Aucanquilcha, Cerro- 198 Jh 21.14S 68.28W
Auce 116 Jh 56.28N 22.50 E
Auch 122 Gk 43.39N 0.35 E
Auchel 124 Ed 50.30N 2.28 E
Auchi 166 Gd 7.04N 6.16 E
Auckland 210 Ih 36.52S 174.45 E
Auckland Islands 208 Hi 50.35S 166.00 E
Auckland Peninsula 216 Dg 36.15S 174.00 E
Aude [3] 122 Ik 43.05N 2.30 E
Aude 122 Jk 43.13N 3.14 E
Auden 186 Ma 50.13N 87.47W
Audenarde/Oudenaarde 122 Jd 50.51N 3.36 E
Audierne 122 Bf 48.01N 4.32W
Audierne, Baie d'- 122 Bg 47.57N 4.28W
Audincourt 122 Mg 47.29N 6.50 E
Audo 168 Gd 6.09N 41.53 E
Audresselles 124 Dd 50.49N 1.35 E
Audru 116 Kf 58.20N 24.19 E
Audruicq 124 Ed 50.53N 2.05 E
Audubon 186 If 41.43N 94.55W
Audun-le-Roman 124 He 49.22N 5.53 E
Audun-le-Tiche 124 He 49.28N 5.57 E
Aue 120 If 50.35N 12.42 E
Aue [Ger.] 120 Fd 52.33N 9.05 E
Aue [Ger.] 124 Lb 52.27N 9.28 E
Aue [Ger.] 124 Kb 52.16N 8.59 E
Auerbach 120 If 50.31N 12.24 E
Auezov 136 If 49.40N 81.40 E
Auffay 124 De 49.43N 1.06 E
Augathella 210 Fg 25.48S 146.35 E
Auge, Pays d'- 122 Ge 49.05N 0.10 E
Augpilagtoq 179 Gd 72.45N 55.35W
Augrabies Falls 158 Jk 28.35S 20.23 E
Augsburg 112 Hf 48.22N 10.53 E
Augusta [Ar.-U.S.] 186 Ki 35.17N 91.22W
Augusta [Austl.] 210 Ch 34.10S 115.10 E
Augusta [Ga.-U.S.] 176 Kf 33.29N 81.57W
Augusta [It.] 128 Jm 37.13N 15.13 E
Augusta [Ks.-U.S.] 186 Hh 37.41N 96.58W
Augusta [Me.-U.S.] 176 Me 44.19N 69.47W
Augusta [Mt.-U.S.] 188 Ic 47.30N 112.24W
Augusta, Golfo di- 128 Jm 37.10N 15.15 E
Augustin Codazzi 202 Da 10.02N 73.15W
Augustów 120 Sc 53.51N 22.59 E
Augustowski, Kanał- 120 Tc 53.54N 23.26 E
Augustus, Mount- 208 Cg 24.20S 116.50 E
Auki 210 He 8.45S 160.42 E
Auld, Lake- 212 Ed 22.30S 123.45 E
Aulla 128 Df 44.12N 9.58 E
Aulne 122 Bf 48.17N 4.16W
Aulneau Peninsula 186 Ib 49.23N 94.29W
Aulnoye-Aymeries 124 Fd 50.12N 3.50 E
Aulong 220a Ac 7.17N 134.17 E
Ault 124 Dd 50.06N 1.27 E
Auluptagel 220a Ac 7.19N 134.29 E
Aulus-les-Bains 122 Hl 42.48N 1.20 E
Aumale 122 He 49.46N 1.45 E
Auna 166 Fc 10.11N 4.43 E
Aunay-sur-Odon 124 Be 49.01N 0.38W
Auneuil 124 Ee 49.22N 2.00 E
Auning 114 Ch 56.26N 10.23 E
Aunis 122 Fh 46.10N 1.00W
Aunuu 221c Cb 14.17S 170.33W
Auob 158 Jk 26.27S 20.38 E
Aura 116 Jd 60.36N 22.34 E
Aurangābād 148 Fe 19.53N 75.20 E
Aurari Bay 212 Gb 11.40S 133.40 E
Aur Atoll 208 Id 8.16N 171.06 E
Auray 122 Dg 47.40N 2.59W
Aurdal 114 Bf 60.56N 9.24 E
Aure 122 Ee 49.20N 1.07W
Aure [Nor.] 114 Be 63.13N 8.32 E
Aure [Nor.] 116 Bb 62.24N 6.36 E
Aurejärvi 116 Jb 62.05N 23.25 E
Aurès, Massif de l'- 158 He 35.14N 6.10 E
Aurich 120 Dc 53.28N 7.29 E
Aurillac 122 Ij 44.55N 2.27 E
Aurlandsfjorden 116 Bc 61.05N 7.05 E
Aurlandsvangen 114 Bf 60.54N 7.11 E
Auron 122 Ig 47.06N 2.24 E
Aurora [Co.-U.S.] 182 Gd 39.44N 104.52W
Aurora [Il.-U.S.] 182 Jc 42.46N 88.19W
Aurora [Mo.-U.S.] 186 Jh 36.58N 93.43W
Aurora [Phil.] 150 He 7.57N 123.36 E
Aurora do Norte 204 Ia 12.38S 46.23W
Aursjøen 116 Cb 62.20N 8.40 E
Aursunden 116 Db 62.40N 11.40 E
Aurukun Mission 212 Ib 13.19S 141.45 E
Aurunci, Monti- 128 Hi 41.20N 13.40 E
Aus 172 Be 26.40S 16.15 E
Au Sable River 184 Fc 44.25N 83.20W
Ausangate, Nudo- 198 Ig 13.47S 71.13W
Ausiait/Egedesminde 224 Nc 68.50N 52.45W
Ausoni, Monti- 128 Hi 41.25N 13.20 E
Aust-Agder [2] 114 Bg 58.50N 8.00 E
Austfonna 179 Oc 79.55N 25.00 E
Austin [Mn.-U.S.] 182 Ic 43.40N 92.59W
Austin [Nv.-U.S.] 182 Dd 39.30N 117.04W
Austin [Tx.-U.S.] 176 Jf 30.16N 97.45W
Austin, Lake- 212 De 27.40S 118.00 E
Austral, Chaco- 198 Jh 25.00S 61.00W
Australes, Iles- → Tubuaï, Iles- 208 Lg 23.00S 150.00W
Australia [1] 210 Eg 25.00S 135.00 E
Australia 106 Il 25.00S 135.00 E
Australian Alps 208 Fh 37.00S 148.00 E
Australian Capital Territory [3] 212 Jg 35.30S 149.00 E
Australia Occidentale (I) = Western Australia [2] 212 Ed 25.00S 122.00 E
Austria (EN) = Österreich [1] 112 Hf 47.30N 14.00 E
Austvågøy 114 Db 68.20N 14.36 E
Autazes 202 Gd 3.35S 59.08W
Autheuil-Authouillet 124 De 49.06N 1.17 E
Authie 122 Hd 50.21N 1.38 E
Autlán de Navarro 190 De 19.46N 104.22W
Autun 122 Kh 46.57N 4.18 E
Auve 124 Ge 49.02N 4.42 E
Auvergne 122 Ii 45.20N 3.00 E
Auvergne, Monts d'- 122 Ii 45.30N 2.45 E
Auvézère 122 Gi 45.12N 0.50 E
Auvillers-lès-Forges-Mon Idée 124 Ge 49.52N 4.21 E
Auxerre 122 Jg 47.48N 3.34 E
Auxi-le-Château 122 Id 50.14N 2.07 E
Auxois 122 Kg 47.20N 4.30 E
Auxonne 122 Lg 47.12N 5.23 E
Auyán-Tepuy 202 Fb 5.55N 62.32W
Auzances 122 Ih 46.01N 2.30 E
Auzoue 122 Gj 44.03N 0.15 E
Avaavaroa Passage 220p Bc 21.16S 159.47W
Availles-Limouzine 122 Gh 46.07N 0.39 E
Avala 130 De 44.42N 20.31 E
Avaldsnes 116 Ae 59.21N 5.16 E
Avallon 122 Jg 47.29N 3.54 E
Avalon Peninsula 180 Mg 47.30N 53.30W
Avana 220p Cb 21.14S 159.41W
Avaré 204 Hf 23.05S 48.55W
Avarua 210 Lg 21.12S 159.46W
Avarua Harbour 220p Bb 21.11S 159.46W
Avatele 220k Bb 19.06S 169.55W
Avatele Bay 220k Bb 19.05S 169.56W
Avatiu 220p Bb 21.12S 159.47W
Avatiu Harbour 220p Bb 21.11S 159.47W
Avatolu, Passe- 220h Ab 13.19S 176.14W
Ávdhira 130 Hi 40.59N 24.57 E
Ave 126 Dc 41.20N 8.45W
Aveh 146 Ne 34.47N 50.25 E
Aveh, Gardaneh-ye- 146 Me 35.32N 49.09 E
Aveiro [2] 126 Dd 40.45N 8.30W
Aveiro [Braz.] 202 Gd 3.15S 55.10W
Aveiro [Port.] 126 Dd 40.38N 8.39W
Āvej 146 Me 35.34N 49.13 E
Avelgem 124 Fd 50.46N 3.26 E
Avellaneda [Arg.] 206 Ic 29.07S 59.40W
Avellaneda [Arg.] 206 Id 34.39S 58.23W
Avellino 128 Ij 40.54N 14.47 E
Aven Armand 122 Jj 44.15N 3.22 E
Averbode 124 Gc 51.02N 4.59 E
Avereest 124 Ib 52.37N 6.27 E
Avereest-Dedemsvaart 124 Ib 52.37N 6.27 E
Averøya 114 Be 63.00N 7.35 E
Aversa 128 Ij 40.58N 14.12 E
Aves, Isla- 174 Mh 15.42N 63.38W
Avesnes-le-Compte 124 Ed 50.17N 2.32 E
Avesnes-les-Aubert 124 Fd 50.12N 3.23 E
Avesnes-sur-Helpe 122 Jd 50.07N 3.56 E
Aves Ridge (EN) 190 Lf 14.00N 63.30W
Avesta 114 Df 60.09N 16.12 E
Aveyron [3] 122 Ij 44.15N 2.30 E
Aveyron 122 Hj 44.05N 1.16 E
Avezzano 128 Hh 42.02N 13.25 E
Avgan 130 Mk 38.25N 29.24 E
Avgó [Grc.] 130 In 35.36N 25.34 E
Avgó [Grc.] 130 Jn 35.55N 26.30 E
Aviemore 118 Jd 57.12N 3.50W
Avigait 179 Gf 62.15N 50.00W
Avigliano 128 Jj 40.44N 15.43 E
Avignon 112 Gg 43.57N 4.49 E
Ávila 126 Hd 40.39N 4.42W
Ávila [3] 126 Hd 40.35N 5.00W
Ávila, Sierra de- 126 Gd 40.35N 5.08W
Avilés 126 Ga 43.33N 5.55W
Avinurme 116 Lf 58.55N 26.50 E
Avion 124 Ed 50.24N 2.50 E
Avioth 124 He 49.34N 5.24 E
Avis 126 Ee 39.03N 7.53W
Avisio 128 Fd 46.07N 11.05 E
Avize 124 Gf 48.58N 4.01 E
Avlaka Burun 130 Ii 40.07N 25.40 E
Avola [B.C.-Can.] 188 Fa 51.47N 119.19W
Avola [It.] 128 Jn 36.54N 15.08 E
Avon [3] 118 Kj 51.30N 2.30W
Avon [Eng.-U.K.] 118 Lk 50.43N 1.46W
Avon [Eng.-U.K.] 118 Kj 51.30N 2.43W
Avon [Eng.-U.K.] 118 Kj 51.59N 2.10W
Avon Downs 210 Eg 20.05S 137.30 E
Avon Park 184 Gl 27.36N 81.31W
Avon River 212 Df 31.40S 116.07 E
Avranches 122 Ef 48.41N 1.22W
Avre [Fr.] 122 Ie 49.53N 2.20 E
Avre [Fr.] 122 Hf 48.47N 1.22 E
Avrig 130 Hd 45.43N 24.23 E
Avron 122 Ki 45.15N 4.50 E
Avşa Adası 130 Ki 40.30N 27.30 E
Avuavu 219a Ec 9.50S 160.23 E
Awaji 154 Mg 34.35N 135.01 E
Awaji-Shima 154 Mg 34.25N 134.50 E
'Awālī 146 Ni 26.05N 50.33 E
Awanui 216 Dg 35.03S 173.15 E
Awara Plain 170 Hb 3.45N 41.07 E
Aware 168 Gd 8.14N 44.10 E
Awarua Bay 218 Cf 44.20S 168.05 E
Awasa 160 Kh 7.02N 38.29 E
Awash 168 Gd 8.59N 40.10 E
Awash 158 Lg 11.12N 41.40 E
Awa-Shima 154 Oe 38.27N 139.14 E
Awaso 166 Ed 6.14N 2.16W
Awat 152 Dc 40.38N 80.22 E
Awata 168 Fe 4.45N 39.26 E
Awatere 218 Fd 41.36S 174.10 E
Awbārī 160 If 26.35N 12.46 E
Awbārī [3] 164 Bd 26.35N 12.46 E
Awbārī' Şaḩrā' 158 If 27.30N 11.30 E
Awḑēgle 168 Ge 1.58N 44.51 E
Awe, Loch- 118 He 56.15N 5.15W
Awjilah 160 Jf 29.06N 21.17 E
Axel 124 Fc 51.16N 3.54 E
Axel Heiberg 174 Ja 80.30N 92.00W
Axim 166 Ee 4.52N 2.14W
Axiós 130 Fi 40.35N 22.50 E
Axixá 202 Jd 2.51S 44.04W

Index Symbols

- [1] Independent Nation
- [2] State, Region
- [3] District, County
- [4] Municipality
- [5] Colony, Dependency
- Continent
- Physical Region
- Historical or Cultural Region
- Mount, Mountain
- Volcano
- Hill
- Mountains, Mountain Range
- Hills, Escarpment
- Plateau, Upland
- Pass, Gap
- Plain, Lowland
- Delta
- Salt Flat
- Valley, Canyon
- Crater, Cave
- Karst Features
- Depression
- Polder
- Desert, Dunes
- Forest, Woods
- Heath, Steppe
- Oasis
- Cape, Point
- Coast, Beach
- Cliff
- Peninsula
- Isthmus
- Sandbank
- Island
- Atoll
- Rock, Reef
- Islands, Archipelago
- Rocks, Reefs
- Coral Reef
- Well, Spring
- Geyser
- River, Stream
- Waterfall, Rapids
- River Mouth, Estuary
- Lake
- Salt Lake
- Intermittent Lake
- Reservoir
- Swamp, Pond
- Canal
- Glacier
- Ice Shelf, Pack Ice
- Ocean
- Sea
- Gulf, Bay
- Strait, Fjord
- Lagoon
- Bank
- Seamount
- Tablemount
- Ridge
- Shelf
- Basin
- Escarpment, Sea Scarp
- Fracture
- Trench, Abyss
- National Park, Reserve
- Point of Interest
- Recreation Site
- Cave, Cavern
- Historic Site
- Ruins
- Wall, Walls
- Church, Abbey
- Temple
- Scientific Station
- Railway station
- Airport
- Port
- Military installation
- Lighthouse
- Mine
- Tunnel
- Dam, Bridge

Ax-les-Thermes	122	Hl	42.43N	1.50 E
Ayabaca	202	Cd	4.38 S	79.43W
Ayabe	154	Mg	35.18N	135.15 E
Ayachi, Ari n'- ▲	162	Gc	32.30N	4.50W
Ayacucho [3]	202	Df	14.00 S	74.00W
Ayacucho [Arg.]	206	Ie	37.09 S	58.29W
Ayacucho [Peru]	200	Ig	13.07 S	74.13W
Ayakkum Hu ≋	152	Ed	37.30N	89.20 E
Ayamé	166	Ed	5.37N	3.11W
Ayamonte	126	Eg	37.13N	7.24W
Ayancık	146	Fb	41.57N	34.36 E
Ayangba	166	Gd	7.31N	7.08 E
Ayapel	202	Cb	8.18N	75.08W
Ayas	146	Eb	40.01N	32.21 E
Ayaviri	202	Df	14.52 S	70.35W
Āybak	144	Kb	36.16N	68.01 E
Aybastı	146	Gb	40.41N	37.24 E
Aycliffe	118	Lg	54.36N	1.34W
'Aydim, Wādī- ≈	168	Ib	18.08N	53.08 E
Aydın	144	Cb	37.51N	27.51 E
Aydincik	146	Ed	36.08N	33.17 E
Aydın Dağları ⛰	146	Bc	38.00N	28.00 E
Aydingkol Hu ≋	152	Ec	42.40N	89.15 E
Aydinkent	146	Dd	37.06N	31.36 E
Aydos Dağı ▲	146	Fd	37.21N	34.22 E
Ayerbe	126	Lb	42.17N	0.41W
Ayer Hitam	150	Df	1.55N	103.11 E
Ayeyarwady	148	Ie	17.00N	95.00 E
Ayeyarwady = Irrawaddy (EN)	140	Lg	15.50N	95.06 E
Ayiá	130	Fj	39.43N	22.46 E
Ayia Marina	130	Jl	37.09N	26.52 E
Ayiásos	130	Jj	39.06N	26.22 E
Ayion Oros = Athos, Mount- (EN) [2]	130	Hi	40.15N	24.15 E
Áyios Evstrátios ◙	130	Ij	39.31N	25.00 E
Áyios Ioánnis, Ákra- ►	130	In	35.20N	25.46 E
Áyios Kírikos	130	Jl	37.35N	26.14 E
Áyios Minás ◙	130	Jl	37.36N	26.34 E
Áyios Nikólaos	130	In	35.11N	25.43 E
Áyios Theódhoros ◙	130	Gn	35.32N	23.56 E
Ayios Theodóros	146	Fe	35.20N	34.01 E
Áyios Yeóryios ◙	130	Gl	37.28N	23.56 E
Aykota	168	Fb	15.10N	37.03 E
Aylesbury	118	Mj	51.50N	0.50W
Ayllón, Sierra de- ⛰	126	Ic	41.15N	3.25W
Aylmer Lake ≋	180	Gd	64.05N	108.30W
Aylsham	124	Db	52.47N	1.15 E
Ayna	126	Jf	38.33N	2.05W
'Aynabo	168	Hd	8.57N	46.30 E
'Ayn ad Darāhim	128	Cn	36.47N	8.42 E
'Ayn al Baydā	146	Ge	34.32N	37.55 E
'Ayn al Ghazāl [Eg.]	146	Dj	25.46N	30.38 E
'Ayn al Ghazāl [Lib.]	160	Jf	21.50N	24.55 E
'Ayn al Shigi	146	Ci	27.01N	28.02 E
'Ayn al Wādī	146	Ci	27.23N	28.13 E
'Ayn Bū Sālim	128	Cn	36.37N	8.59 E
'Ayn Dāllah	164	Ed	27.19N	27.20 E
'Ayn Dār	146	Mj	25.58N	49.14 E
'Ayn Dīwār	146	Jd	37.17N	42.11 E
'Ayn Ilwān	146	Dj	25.44N	30.25 E
'Ayn Khalīfah	146	Bi	26.46N	27.47 E
'Ayn Sifnī	146	Jd	36.42N	43.21 E
'Ayn Sukhnah	164	Fd	29.30N	32.10 E
'Aynūnah	144	Ed	28.05N	35.08 E
Ayod	168	Ed	8.08N	31.24 E
Ayora	126	Ke	39.04N	1.03W
Ayorou	166	Fc	14.44N	0.55 E
'Ayoûn el 'Atroûs	160	Gg	16.38N	9.36W
Ayr ≈	118	If	55.29N	4.28W
Ayr [Austl.]	212	Jc	19.35 S	147.24 E
Ayr [Scot.-U.K.]	118	If	55.28N	4.38W
Ayre, Point of- ►	118	Ig	54.26N	4.22W
Ayrolle, Étang de l'- ▥	122	Jk	43.16N	3.30 E
Aysha	168	Gc	10.45N	42.35 E
Aytré	122	Eh	46.08N	1.06W
Ayutla	192	Gg	20.07N	104.22W
Ayutla de los Libres	192	Ji	16.54N	99.13W
Ayvacik	130	Jj	39.36N	26.24 E
Ayvacık	146	Gb	41.00N	36.45 E
Ayvalık	144	Cb	39.18N	26.41 E
Aywaille	124	Hd	50.28N	5.40 E
Āzādshahr	146	Pd	37.05N	55.08 E
Azahar, Costa del- / Tarongers, Costa dels- ⌓	126	Me	39.58N	0.01 E
Azaila	126	Lc	41.17N	0.29W
Azambuja	126	De	39.04N	8.52W
Azamgarh	148	Gc	26.04N	83.11 E
Azángaro	202	Df	14.55 S	70.13W
Azannes-et-Soumazannes	124	He	49.18N	5.28 E
Azaouâd = Azaouad (EN) ◢	158	Gg	19.00N	3.00W
Azaouad (EN) = Azaouâd ◢	158	Gg	19.00N	3.00W
Azaouak ◢	158	Hg	13.48N	3.36 E
Azaouak ≈	166	Fb	15.30N	3.18 E
Azaouak, Vallée de l'- ☒	158	Hg	17.30N	3.40 E
Azar ≈	166	Fb	16.02N	4.04 E
Āzarbāijān-e Gharbī [3]	144	Fb	37.00N	45.00 E
Āzarbāijān-e Sharqī [3]	144	Gb	37.00N	47.00 E
Azarbaijčan SSR → Azärbayjan	136	Eg	40.30N	47.30 E
Azärbayjan = Azerbaijan (EN)	136	Eg	40.30N	47.30 E
Azare	166	Hc	11.41N	10.12 E
Āzār Shahr	146	Kd	37.45N	45.59 E
Azay-le-Rideau	122	Gg	47.16N	0.28 E
A 'zāz	146	Gd	36.35N	37.03 E
Azazga	126	Qh	36.44N	4.22 E
Azbine/Aïr ⛰	158	Hg	18.00N	8.30 E
Azdaak, gora- ▲	132	Ni	40.13N	44.59 E
Azdavay	146	Eb	41.39N	33.18 E
Azefal ◢	158	Ff	21.00N	14.45W
Azeffoun	126	Qh	36.53N	4.25 E
Azemmour	162	Fc	33.17N	8.21W
Azerbaijan (EN) = Azärbayjan	136	Eg	40.30N	47.30 E
Azerbajdžanskaja Sovetskaja Socialističeskaja Respublika → Azärbayjan	136	Eg	40.30N	47.30 E
Azerbajdžanskaja SSR/ Azarbaijčan Sovet Socialistik Respublicasy → Azärbayjan	136	Eg	40.30N	47.30 E
Azerbajdžanskaja SSR → Azärbayjan	136	Eg	40.30N	47.30 E
Azeri/Aseri	114	Gg	59.29N	26.51 E
Azevedo Sodré	204	Ej	30.04 S	54.36W
Azezo	168	Fc	12.33N	37.25 E
Azilal	162	Fc	31.58N	6.35W
Azilal [3]	162	Fc	32.09N	6.05W
Aznā	146	Mf	33.56N	49.24 E
Aznakajevo	114	Mi	54.56N	53.04 E
Azogues	202	Cd	2.44 S	78.48W
Azores (EN) = Açores [5]	160	Ee	38.30N	28.00W
Azores (EN) = Açores, Arquipélago dos- ⁘	158	Ee	38.30N	28.00W
Azores-Gibraltar Ridge (EN) ◭	106	Df	37.00N	16.00W
Azoum, Bahr- ≈	158	Jg	10.53N	20.15 E
Azov	136	Df	47.05N	39.25 E
Azov, Sea of- (EN) = Azovskoje more ▤	110	Jf	46.00N	36.00 E
Azovskoje more = Azov, Sea of- (EN) ▤	110	Jf	46.00N	36.00 E
Azpeitia	126	Ja	43.11N	2.16W
Azrak, Bahr- ≈	168	Bc	10.50N	19.50 E
Azraq, Baḩr al- = Blue Nile (EN) ≈	158	Kg	15.38N	32.31 E
Azraq ash Shīshān	146	Gg	31.50N	36.49 E
Azrou	162	Fc	33.26N	5.13W
Aztec	186	Ch	36.49N	107.59W
Aztec Ruins ⛬	188	Kh	36.51N	108.10W
Azua	194	Ld	18.27N	70.44W
Azuaga	126	Gf	38.16N	5.41W
Azuar ≈	126	Ie	39.08N	3.36W
Azuero, Peninsula de- = Azuero Peninsula (EN) ▰	174	Ki	7.40N	80.30W
Azuero Peninsula (EN) = Azuero, Peninsula de- ▰	174	Ki	7.40N	80.30W
Azul	200	Ki	36.45 S	59.50W
Azul, Cerro- ▲	202a	Ab	0.54 S	91.21W
Azul, Cordillera- ⛰	202	Ce	8.30 S	76.00W
Azul, Río- ≈	192	Oi	17.54N	88.52W
Azul, Serra- ⛰	204	Eb	14.50 S	54.50W
Azul, Sierras del- ⛰	204	Cm	37.02 S	59.55W
Azūm ≈	168	Cc	10.53N	20.15 E
Azuma-San ▲	156	Gc	37.44N	140.08 E
Azur, Côte d'- ⌓	122	Nk	43.30N	7.00 E
Azurduy	202	Fg	19.59 S	64.29W
Azzaba	162	Ib	36.44N	7.06 E
Az Zāb al Kabīr ≈	144	Fb	36.00N	43.21 E
Az Zāb aş Şaghīr ≈	144	Fb	35.12N	43.25 E
Az Zabdānī	146	Gf	33.43N	36.05 E
Az Zabū	146	Ch	28.22N	28.56 E
Aẕ Ẕafīr	144	Ff	19.57N	41.30 E
Az Zaghāwa ☒	168	Cb	15.15N	23.14 E
Aẓ Ẓāhirah ☒	146	Qk	23.30N	56.15 E
Aẓ Ẓahrān	146	Ni	26.18N	50.05 E
Az Zallāq	146	Ni	26.03N	50.29 E
Az Zaqāzīq	164	Fc	30.35N	31.31 E
Az Zarqā'	146	Gf	32.05N	36.06 E
Az Zarqā' ◙	146	Oj	24.53N	53.04 E
Az Zāwiyah	164	Bc	32.45N	12.44 E
Az Zāwiyah [3]	164	Bc	32.40N	12.10 E
Az Zaytūn	164	Ed	29.09N	25.47 E
Azzel Matti, Sebkha- ≋	158	Hf	26.00N	0.55 E
Az Zilfī	146	Ki	26.18N	44.48 E
Az Zubayr	146	Lg	30.23N	47.43 E

B

Baa	150	Hi	10.43 S	123.03 E
Baaba ◙	219b	Ae	20.03 S	163.58 E
Ba'ādwēyn	168	Hd	7.12N	47.24 E
Bá an Daingin/Dingle Bay ◧	118	Ci	52.05N	10.15W
Baar ☒	120	Ei	48.00N	8.30 E
Baarle-Hertog	124	Gc	51.27N	4.56 E
Baarn	124	Hb	52.14N	5.17 E
Baas, Bassure de- ▦	124	Dd	50.30N	1.15 E
Bāb	146	Ok	23.55N	53.45 E
Baba ⛰	130	Ei	40.55N	21.10 E
Baba ≈	168	Bd	6.25N	17.07 E
Baba Burun [Tur.] ►	146	Bc	39.29N	26.04 E
Baba Burun [Tur.] ►	146	Db	41.18N	31.26 E
Babadağ	130	Ll	37.48N	28.52 E
Babadag	130	Le	44.54N	28.43 E
Babadag, gora- ▲	132	Pi	41.01N	48.29 E
Babaeski	146	Bb	41.26N	27.06 E
Bābā-Ḩeydar	146	Nf	32.20N	50.28 E
Babahoyo	202	Cd	1.50 S	79.30W
Babajevo	136	Dd	59.24N	35.55 E
Babajtag, gora- ▲	135	Hd	41.13N	70.16 E
Babajurt	132	Oh	43.35N	46.47 E
Bāb al Māndab = Bab el Mandeb (EN) ⇌	158	Lg	12.35N	43.25 E
Babanūsah	168	Dc	11.20N	27.48 E
Babao → Qilian	152	Hd	38.14N	100.15 E
Babar, Kepulauan- ⁘	150	Ih	7.50 S	129.45 E
Babar, Pulau- ◙	208	De	7.55 S	129.45 E
Babase ◙	219a	Aa	4.01 S	153.42 E
Babatag, hrebet- ⛰	135	Ge	38.00N	68.10 E
Babati	170	Gc	4.13 S	35.45 E
Babbitt	186	Kc	47.43N	91.57W
B'abdā	146	Ff	33.50N	35.32 E
Bab el Mandeb (EN) = Bāb al Māndab ⇌	158	Lg	12.35N	43.25 E
Babelthuap Island ◙	208	Ed	7.30N	134.36 E
Babenhausen [Ger.]	120	Gh	48.09N	10.15 E
Babenhausen [Ger.]	124	Ke	49.58N	8.57 E
Babeni	130	He	44.59N	24.15 E
Baberton	184	Ge	41.02N	81.38W
Bá Bheanntrai/Bantry Bay ◧	118	Dj	51.38N	9.48W
Babian Jiang [Asia] = Black River (EN) ≈	140	Mg	20.17N	106.34 E
Babil [3]	146	Kf	32.40N	44.50 E
Babine Lake ≋	180	Ef	54.45N	126.00W
Babino Polje	128	Lh	42.43N	17.33 E
Babit Point ►	197b	Ab	18.03N	63.02W
Babo	150	Jg	2.33 S	133.25 E
Bābol	144	Hb	36.34N	52.42 E
Babol Sar	146	Od	36.43N	52.39 E
Baboquivari Peak ▲	188	Jk	31.46N	111.35W
Babor, Djebel- ▲	126	Rh	36.32N	5.28 E
Baborigame	192	Fd	26.27N	107.16W
Baboua	168	Ad	5.48N	14.49 E
Babozero, ozero- ≋	114	Ic	66.30N	37.25 E
Babu → Hexian	152	Jg	24.28N	111.34 E
Babuna ⛰	130	Eh	41.30N	21.40 E
Babuyan	150	Gd	10.01N	118.58 E
Babuyan ◙	150	Hc	19.32N	121.57 E
Babuyan Channel ⇌	150	Hc	18.44N	121.40 E
Babuyan Islands ⁘	140	Oh	19.15N	121.40 E
Babylon ⛬	144	Fc	32.32N	44.25 E
Bač	130	Cd	45.23N	19.14 E
Bacabachi	192	Ed	26.55N	109.24W
Bacabal	200	Lf	4.14 S	44.47W
Ba-Cagan	152	Gb	45.40N	99.30 E
Bacajá, Rio- ≈	202	Hd	3.25 S	51.50W
Bacalar	192	Oh	18.43N	88.27W
Bacalar, Laguna de- ≋	192	Oh	18.43N	88.22W
Bacalar Chico, Boca- ⇌	194	Dd	18.12N	87.53W
Bacan, Kepulauan- ⁘	150	Ig	0.35 S	127.30 E
Bacan, Pulau- ◙	150	Ig	0.35 S	127.30 E
Bacău	112	If	46.34N	26.54 E
Bacău [2]	130	Jc	46.36N	27.00 E
Baccarat	122	Mf	48.27N	6.45 E
Bacchiglione ≈	128	Ge	45.11N	12.14 E
Baceşti	130	Kc	46.51N	27.14 E
Bachaquero	194	Li	9.56N	71.08W
Bacharach	124	Jd	50.04N	7.46 E
Bacheli	148	Ge	18.40N	81.15 E
Bachiniva	192	Fc	28.45N	107.15W
Bachu/Maralwexi	152	Cd	39.46N	78.15 E
Bačka ☒	130	Cd	45.50N	19.30 E
Bačka Palanka	130	Cd	45.15N	19.22 E
Bačka Topola	130	Cd	45.49N	19.39 E
Bäckefors	116	Ef	58.48N	12.10 E
Bäckhammar	116	Fe	59.10N	14.11 E
Backnang	120	Fh	48.57N	9.26 E
Bačkovski Manastir ✠	130	Hh	41.56N	24.51 E
Back River ≈	174	Jc	67.15N	95.15W
Bac Lieu	148	Lg	9.17N	105.43 E
Bac Ninh	148	Ld	21.11N	106.03 E
Bacolet	197p	Bb	12.02N	61.41W
Bacolod	142	Oh	10.40N	122.57 E
Bac-Phan = Tonkin (EN) ☒	140	Mg	22.00N	105.00 E
Bacqueville, Lac- ≋	180	Ke	58.00N	74.00W
Bacqueville-en Caux	124	Ce	49.47N	1.00 E
Bácsalmás	120	Pj	46.08N	19.20 E
Bács-Kiskun [2]	120	Pj	46.30N	19.25 E
Bacton	124	Db	52.51N	1.28 E
Bād	144	Hc	33.41N	52.01 E
Bada Dağı ▲	130	Mm	36.32N	29.10 E
Badagara	148	Ff	11.36N	75.35 E
Badagri	166	Fd	6.25N	2.53 E
Badain Jaran Shamo ◢	140	Me	40.20N	101.40 E
Badajós, Lago- ≋	202	Fd	3.15 S	62.45W
Badajoz	112	Fh	38.53N	6.58W
Badajoz [3]	126	Ff	38.40N	6.10W
Badakhshan [3]	144	Lb	36.45N	72.00 E
Badalona	126	Oc	41.27N	2.15 E
Badanah	144	Fc	30.59N	41.02 E
Badaohao	154	Fd	41.50N	121.59 E
Badas, Kepulauan- ⁘	150	Ef	0.35N	107.06 E
Bad Aussee	128	Hc	47.36N	13.47 E
Bad Axe	184	Fd	43.48N	83.00W
Bad Bergzabern	120	Dg	49.06N	8.00 E
Bad Berleburg	124	Kc	51.04N	8.24 E
Bad Bertrich	124	Jd	50.03N	7.02 E
Bad Bramstedt	120	Fc	53.55N	9.53 E
Bad Brückenau	120	Ff	50.18N	9.45 E
Badda ▲	168	Fd	7.55N	39.23 E
Baddo ≈	148	Cc	27.59N	64.21 E
Bad Doberan	120	Hb	54.06N	11.54 E
Bad Driburg	124	Lc	51.44N	9.01 E
Bad Düben	120	Ie	51.36N	12.35 E
Bad Dürkheim	124	Ke	49.28N	8.12 E
Bade	150	Kh	7.10 S	139.35 E
Bademli	130	Lk	38.04N	28.04 E
Baden [Aus.]	128	Kb	48.01N	16.14 E
Baden [Switz.]	128	Cc	47.28N	8.18 E
Baden-Baden	120	Eh	48.45N	8.15 E
Badenoch ☒	118	Je	56.50N	4.00W
Baden-Württemberg [2]	120	Eh	48.30N	9.00 E
Bad Essen	124	Kb	52.19N	8.20 E
Bad Freienwalde	120	Kd	52.47N	14.02 E
Badgastein	128	Hc	47.07N	13.08 E
Bādghīsat [3]	144	Jc	35.00N	63.45 E
Bad Gleichenberg	128	Jd	46.52N	15.54 E
Bad Godesberg, Bonn-	120	Df	50.41N	7.09 E
Bad Hall	128	Ib	48.02N	14.12 E
Bad Harzburg	120	Ge	51.53N	10.34 E
Bad Herrenalb	124	Kf	48.48N	8.25 E
Bad Hersfeld	120	Ff	50.52N	9.42 E
Bad Homburg von der Hoehe	120	Ef	50.13N	8.37 E
Bad Honnef	124	Jd	50.38N	7.12 E
Bá Dhún na nGall/Donegal Bay ◧	110	Fe	54.30N	8.30W
Badhyz ⛰	135	Cg	35.50N	62.00 E
Badiraguato	192	Fe	25.22N	107.31W
Bad Ischl	128	Hc	47.43N	13.37 E
Bad Kissingen	120	Gf	50.12N	10.05 E
Bad Kreuznach	120	Dg	49.50N	7.52 E
Badlands ⛰	182	Gb	46.45N	103.30W
Bad Langensalza	120	Ge	51.06N	10.39 E
Bad Lauterberg am Harz	120	Ge	51.38N	10.28 E
Bad Liebenwerda	120	Je	51.31N	13.24 E
Bad Liebenzell	124	Kf	48.46N	8.44 E
Bad Mergentheim	120	Fg	49.29N	9.46 E
Bad Mondorf/Mondorf-les-Bains	124	Ie	49.30N	6.17 E
Bad Münster am Stein-Ebernburg	124	Je	49.49N	7.51 E
Bad Münstereifel	124	Id	50.34N	6.45 E
Bad Nauheim	124	Kd	50.22N	8.45 E
Bad Neuenahr-Ahrweiler	120	Df	50.33N	7.08 E
Bad Neustadt an der Saale	120	Gf	50.20N	10.13 E
Bad Oeynhausen	124	Kb	52.12N	8.48 E
Bad Oldesloe	120	Gc	53.49N	10.23 E
Badou [China]	154	Df	36.27N	117.56 E
Badou [Togo]	166	Fd	7.35N	0.36 E
Bad Pyrmont	120	Fe	51.59N	9.15 E
Bad Ragaz	128	Dc	47.00N	9.30 E
Badrah	146	Kf	33.06N	45.58 E
Bad Reichenhall	120	Ii	47.44N	12.53 E
Badr Ḩunayn	144	Ee	23.44N	38.46 E
Bad River ≈	186	Fd	44.22N	100.22W
Bad Salzuflen	124	Kb	52.05N	8.46 E
Bad Salzungen	120	Gf	50.49N	10.14 E
Bad Schwartau	120	Gc	53.55N	10.42 E
Bad Segeberg	120	Gc	53.56N	10.19 E
Bad Tölz	120	Hi	47.46N	11.34 E
Badulla	148	Gg	6.59N	81.03 E
Bad Vilbel	124	Kd	50.11N	8.45 E
Bad Wildungen	120	Fe	51.07N	9.07 E
Bad Wimpfen	120	Fg	49.14N	9.08 E
Baena	126	Hg	37.37N	4.19W
Baeza [Ec.]	202	Cd	0.28 S	77.53W
Baeza [Sp.]	126	Ig	37.59N	3.28W
Baf/Paphos	146	Ee	34.50N	32.35 E
Bafa Gölü ≋	146	Bd	37.30N	27.25 E
Bafang	166	Hd	5.09N	10.11 E
Bafatà	160	Fg	12.10N	14.40W
Bafélé	166	Cc	10.09N	10.08W
Baffin ◙	174	Mc	68.00N	70.00W
Baffin Bay [N.Amer.] ◧	174	Mb	73.00N	65.00W
Baffin Bay [Tx.-U.S.] ◧	186	Hm	27.15N	97.30W
Bafia	166	He	4.45N	11.14 E
Bafilo	166	Fd	9.21N	1.16 E
Bafing [Afr.] ≈	158	Fg	13.49N	10.50W
Bafing [I.C.] ≈	166	Dd	7.52N	7.07W
Bafoulabé	166	Cc	13.48N	10.50W
Bafoussam	160	Ih	5.28N	10.25 E
Bāfq	144	Ic	31.35N	55.24 E
Bāfq, Kūh-e- ⛰	146	Pg	31.20N	55.10 E
Bafra	144	Ea	41.34N	35.56 E
Bāft	146	Qh	29.14N	56.38 E
Bafwaboli	170	Eb	0.39N	26.10 E
Bafwasende	170	Eb	1.05N	27.16 E
Baga	166	Hc	13.06N	13.50 E
Bagaces	194	Eh	10.31N	85.15W
Bagagem, Rio- ≈	204	Ha	13.58 S	48.21W
Bagajevski	132	Lf	47.19N	40.25 E
Bāgalkot	148	Fe	16.11N	75.42 E
Bagamoyo	170	Gd	6.26 S	38.54 E
Bagansiapi-Api	150	Df	2.09N	100.49 E
Bağarasi	130	Kl	37.42N	27.33 E
Baga Sola	168	Ac	13.32N	14.19 E
Bagata	170	Cc	3.44 S	17.57 E
Bagdad	192	Ke	25.57N	97.09W
Bagdarin	138	Gf	54.30N	113.36 E
Bagdati (Majakovski)	132	Mh	42.02N	42.47 E
Bağdere	146	Ic	38.10N	40.45 E
Bagé	200	Ki	31.20 S	54.06W
Bages et de Sigean, Étang de- ▥	122	Jk	43.05N	3.01 E
Baggs	188	Lf	41.02N	107.39W
Bágh Baile na Sgealg/ Ballinskelligs Bay ◧	118	Cj	51.50N	10.15W
Baghdād	142	Gf	33.21N	44.23 E
Baghdād [3]	146	Kf	33.18N	44.36 E
Baghdādī, Ra's- ►	146	Fj	24.40N	35.06 E
Bāgh-e Chenār ▲	146	Qh	28.11N	56.54 E
Bāgh-e-Malek	146	Mg	31.32N	49.55 E
Bagheria	128	Hl	38.05N	13.30 E
Bāghīn	144	Ic	30.12N	56.48 E
Baghlān	144	Kb	36.13N	68.46 E
Baghlān [3]	144	Kb	35.45N	69.00 E
Bāglung	148	Gc	28.16N	83.36 E
Bagn	116	Cd	60.49N	9.34 E
Bagnara Calabra	128	Jl	38.17N	15.48 E
Bagnères-de-Bigorre	122	Gk	43.04N	0.09 E
Bagnères-de-Luchon	122	Gl	42.47N	0.36 E
Bagni di Lucca	128	Ef	44.01N	10.35 E
Bagno di Romagna	128	Fg	43.50N	11.57 E
Bagnolo Mella	128	Ee	45.26N	10.10 E
Bagnols-sur-Cèze	122	Kj	44.10N	4.37 E
Bago	142	Lh	17.30N	96.30 E
Bagoé ≈	158	Gg	12.36N	6.34W
Bagolino	128	Ee	45.49N	10.28 E
Bagrationovsk	116	Ij	54.23N	20.40 E
Bagrax/Bohu	152	Ec	41.58N	86.29 E
Bagrax Hu/Bosten ≋	140	Ke	42.00N	87.00 E
Bagua	202	Ce	5.40 S	78.31W
Baguio	142	Oh	16.25N	120.36 E
Baguirmi ☒	158	Ig	11.40N	16.20 E
Bagzane, Monts- ⛰	158	Hg	17.43N	8.45 E
Bahama Islands ⁘	174	Lg	24.15N	76.00W
Bahamas [1]	176	Lg	24.15N	76.00W
Bahamas, Canal Viejo de- = Old Bahama Channel (EN) ⇌	194	Ib	22.30N	78.05W
Bahār	146	Me	34.54N	48.26 E
Baharampur	148	Hd	24.06N	88.15 E
Baharden	136	Fh	38.28N	57.28 E
Bahardok	136	Fh	38.51N	58.24 E
Bahariya Oasis (EN) = Baḩarīyah, Wāḩāt al- 🌴	164	Ed	28.15N	28.57 E
Bahaur	150	Fg	3.20N	114.00 E
Bahāwalnagar	148	Ec	29.59N	73.16 E
Bahāwalpur	142	Jg	29.24N	71.41 E
Bahçe	146	Gd	37.14N	36.34 E
Bahčisaraj	132	Hg	44.45N	33.51 E
Bahi	170	Gd	5.39 S	35.19 E
Bahia [2]	202	Jf	12.00 S	42.00W
Bahía, Islas de la- ⁘	190	Ge	16.20N	86.30W
Bahía Blanca	200	Ji	38.44 S	62.16W
Bahía de Caráquez	202	Bd	0.37 S	80.25W
Bahía Kino	190	Bc	28.50N	111.55W
Bahía Negra	206	Ib	20.15 S	58.12W
Bahías, Cabo dos- ►	198	Jj	44.55 S	65.32W
Bahīj	146	Cg	30.56N	29.35 E
Bahinga	170	Ed	5.57 S	27.06 E
Bahi Swamp ▥	170	Gd	6.05 S	35.10 E
Bahlui ≈	130	Kb	47.08N	27.44 E
Bahmač	136	De	51.11N	32.50 E
Bahoruco, Sierra de- ⛰	194	Ld	18.10N	71.25W
Bahraich	148	Gc	27.35N	81.36 E
Bahrain (EN) = Al Baḩrayn [1]	142	Hg	26.00N	50.29 E
Baḩr al Ghazāl [3]	168	Dd	8.15N	26.50 E
Baḩr ar Ramla al Kabīr ◢	164	Ed	27.00N	26.00 E
Baḩrayn, Khalij al- ◧	146	Nj	25.45N	50.40 E
Bahr Dar	160	Kg	11.36N	37.22 E
Bahta	138	Dd	62.20N	89.15 E
Bahuşi	130	Jc	46.43N	26.42 E
Baia	130	Le	44 43N	28.40 E
Baia de Aramă	130	Fe	45.00N	22.50 E
Baia de Fier	130	Gd	45.10N	23.46 E
Baía dos Tigres	170	Bf	16.35 S	11.43 E
Baia Farta	170	Be	12.37 S	13.26 E
Baia Mare	130	Gb	47.40N	23.35 E
Baião	202	Id	2.41 S	49.41W
Baia Sprie	130	Gb	47.40N	23.42 E
Baibiene	204	Ci	29.36 S	58.10W
Baïbokoum	168	Bd	7.45N	15.41 E
Baicheng	142	Oe	45.34N	122.49 E
Baicheng/Bay	152	Dc	41.46N	81.52 E
Băicoi	130	Id	45.02N	25.51 E
Băiculesti	130	Hd	45.04N	24.42 E
Baidoa (EN) = Isha Baydabo	160	Lh	3.04N	43.48 E
Baie-Comeau	176	Me	49.13N	68.10W
Baie-Mahault	196	Fd	16.16N	61.35W
Baie-Saint-Paul	180	Kg	47.27N	70.30W
Baie-Trinité	184	Na	49.24N	67.19W
Baie Verte	180	Lg	49.55N	56.11W
Baiguan → Shangyu	154	Fi	30.01N	120.53 E
Baihe	152	Je	32.46N	110.06 E
Bai He [China] ≈	154	Bh	32.10N	112.20 E
Bai He [China] ≈	154	Dd	40.43N	116.33 E
Baikal Lake (EN) = Bajkal, ozero- ≋	140	Md	53.00N	107.40 E
Baikal Range (EN) = Bajkalski hrebet ⛰	140	Md	55.00N	108.40 E
Baile an Chaistil/ Ballycastle	118	Gf	55.12N	6.15W
Baile an Róba/Ballinrobe	118	Dh	53.37N	9.13W
Baile Átha Cliath/Dublin	112	Fe	53.20N	6.15W
Baile Átha Cliath/Dublin [2]	118	Gh	53.20N	6.15W
Baile Átha Luain/Athlone	118	Fh	53.25N	7.56W
Baile Átha Troim/Trim	118	Gh	53.34N	6.47W
Băile Borşa	130	Hb	47.41N	24.43 E
Baile Brigín/Balbriggan	118	Gh	53.37N	6.11W
Băile Govora	130	Hd	45.05N	24.11 E
Baile Locha Riach/Loughrea	118	Eh	53.12N	8.34W
Baile Mhistéala/ Mitchelstown	118	Ei	52.16N	8.16W
Bailén	126	If	38.06N	3.46W
Baile na Mainistreach/ Newtownabbey	118	Hg	54.42N	5.54W
Baile Nua na hArda/ Newtownards	118	Hg	54.36N	5.41W
Băile Olăneşti	130	Hd	45.12N	24.14 E
Băileşti	130	Ge	44.01N	23.21 E
Bailleul	124	Ed	50.44N	2.44 E
Bailleul ▲	124	Ce	49.12N	0.26 E
Ba Illi	168	Bc	10.31N	16.29 E
Bailong Jiang ≈	152	Ie	32.42N	105.15 E
Bailundo	170	Ce	12.10 S	15.56 E
Baima	152	He	33.05N	100.29 E
Bain ≈	124	Ba	53.04N	0.12W
Bainbridge	182	Ke	30.54N	84.34W
Bain-de-Bretagne	122	Eg	47.50N	1.41W
Baines Drift	172	Dd	22.30 S	28.43 E
Baing	150	Hi	10.14 S	120.34 E
Baingoin	152	Ee	31.36N	89.48 E
Baiona / Bayona	126	Db	42.07N	8.51W
Baiquan	152	Mb	47.38N	126.04 E
Bā'ir	146	Gg	30.46N	36.41 E
Bā'ir, Wādī- ≈	146	Gg	31.12N	37.31 E
Baird	186	Gj	32.24N	99.24W
Baird Inlet ◧	178	Gd	60.45N	164.00W
Baird Mountains ⛰	178	Gc	67.35N	161.30W
Baird Peninsula ▰	180	Jc	69.00N	75.15W
Bairiki	210	Id	1.20N	173.01 E
Bairin Youqi (Daban)	152	Kc	43.30N	118.37 E
Bairin Zuoqi (Lindong)	152	Kc	43.59N	119.22 E
Bairnsdale	210	Fh	37.50 S	147.38 E
Bais	150	He	9.35N	123.07 E
Baïse ≈	122	Gj	44.17N	0.18 E
Baisha → Jiande	152	Kf	29.31N	119.17 E
Bai Shan ▲	152	Fc	40.53N	93.48 E
Baisogala/Bajsogala	116	Ji	55.35N	23.44 E
Baitou Shan ▲	140	Oe	42.00N	128.00 E
Baitoushan Tian Chi ≋	154	Jc	42.00N	128.03 E
Baixiang	154	Cf	37.29N	114.44 E
Baixo Alentejo ▣	126	Dg	37.55N	8.10W
Baixo Guandu	202	Jg	19.31 S	41.01W
Baixo Longa	170	Cf	15.42 S	18.38 E
Baiyanghe	152	Ec	43.12N	88.28 E
Baiyü	152	Ge	31.13N	98.51 E
Baja	120	Oj	46.11N	18.58 E
Baja, Punta- [Mex.] ►	192	Dc	28.25N	111.45W
Baja, Punta- [Pas.] ►	221d	Ab	27.10 S	109.22W
Baja California, Peninsula de- = Lower California (EN) ▰	174	Hg	28.00N	112.00W
Baja California	190	Ac	30.00N	115.00W
Baja California Sur	190	Bd	25.50N	111.50W
Bājah	162	Ib	36.44N	9.11 E
Bājah [3]	162	Ib	36.30N	9.30 E

Bajalān	146	Md	37.18N	48.47 E
Bajan	152	Jb	49.15N	111.58 E
Bajanaul	136	He	50.47N	75.42 E
Bajandaj	138	Ff	53.04N	105.30 E
Bajan-Delger	152	Jb	45.55N	112.15 E
Bajangol	138	Ff	50.40N	103.25 E
Bajan-Hongor	142	Me	46.20N	100.40 E
Bajan-Ula [Mong.]	152	Jb	49.07N	112.45 E
Bajan-Ula [Mong.]	152	Gb	47.05N	95.15 E
Bajan-Under	152	Gc	44.45N	98.45 E
Baja Verapaz [3]	194	Bf	15.05N	90.20W
Bajawa	150	Hh	8.47 S	120.59 E
Bajčunas	132	Rf	47.17N	53.03 E
Bajdarackaja guba	138	Bc	69.00N	67.30 E
Bajdarata	134	Nb	68.12N	68.18 E
Bajdrag Gol	152	Hb	45.10N	100.45 E
Bājgīrān	146	Rd	37.36N	58.24 E
Baj-Haak	138	Ef	51.07N	94.34 E
Bajiazi	154	Jc	42.41N	129.13 E
Bajina Bašta	130	Cf	43.58N	19.34 E
Bajkal	138	Ff	51.53N	104.47 E
Bajkal, ozero- = Baikal Lake (EN)	140	Md	53.00N	107.40 E
Bajkalovo	134	Kh	57.24N	63.40 E
Bajkalsk	138	Ff	51.30N	104.05 E
Bajkalski hrebet = Baikal Range (EN)	140	Md	55.00N	108.40 E
Bajkit	138	Ed	61.41N	96.25 E
Bajkonur	136	Gf	47.50N	66.07 E
Bajmak	136	Fe	52.36N	58.19 E
Bajmba, Mount-	212	Ke	29.20 S	152.05 E
Bajmok	130	Cd	45.58N	19.26 E
Bajo Baudó	202	Cc	4.58N	77.22W
Bajo Boquete	194	Fi	8.46N	82.26W
Bajo Nuevo	190	Ie	15.50N	78.40W
Bajram-Ali	136	Gh	37.39N	62.12 E
Bajram Curri	130	Dg	42.21N	20.04 E
Bajsogala/Baisogala	116	Ji	55.35N	23.44 E
Bajsun	135	Fe	38.14N	67.12 E
Bajun Islands	158	Li	0.50 S	42.15 E
Bajžansaj	135	Gc	43.13N	69.56 E
Baka	168	Ee	4.33N	30.05 E
Bakacak	130	Ki	40.12N	27.05 E
Bakadžicite	130	Jg	42.25N	26.43 E
Bakal	136	Fe	54.56N	58.48 E
Bakala	168	Cd	6.11N	20.22 E
Bakanas	136	Hg	44.48N	76.15 E
Bakar	128	Ie	45.18N	14.32 E
Bakčar	138	De	57.01N	82.10 E
Bake	150	Dg	3.03 S	100.16 E
Bakel	166	Cc	14.54N	12.27W
Baker [Ca.-U.S.]	188	Gi	35.15N	116.02W
Baker [La.-U.S.]	186	Kk	30.35N	91.10W
Baker [Mt.-U.S.]	182	Gb	46.22N	104.17W
Baker [Or.-U.S.]	182	Dc	44.47N	117.50W
Baker, Mount-	182	Cb	48.47N	121.49W
Baker Island	208	Jd	0.15N	176.27W
Baker Lake	176	Jc	64.10N	95.30W
Baker Lake	174	Jc	64.10N	95.30W
Bakersfield	176	Hf	35.23N	119.01W
Bâ Kêv	148	Lf	13.42N	107.12 E
Bakhma	146	Kd	36.38N	44.17 E
Bakhtarān	142	Gf	34.19N	47.04 E
Bakhtarān [3]	144	Gc	34.15N	47.20 E
Bakhtegān, Daryācheh-ye-	146	Ph	29.20N	54.05 E
Bakhūn, Kūh-e-	144	Id	27.56N	56.18 E
Bakir	146	Bc	38.55N	27.00 E
Bakırköy, İstanbul-	130	Li	40.59N	28.52 E
Bakkaflói	114a	Ca	66.10N	14.45W
Baklan	130	Ml	37.58N	29.36 E
Bako	168	Fd	7.19N	35.08 E
Bako [Eth.]	168	Fd	5.50N	36.37 E
Bako [Eth.]	168	Fd	9.05N	37.07 E
Bakony = Bakony Mountains (EN)	110	Hf	47.15N	17.50 E
Bakony Mountains (EN) = Bakony	110	Hf	47.15N	17.50 E
Bakool [3]	168	Ge	4.10N	43.50 E
Bakouma	168	Cd	5.42N	22.47 E
Bakoye	166	Cc	13.49N	10.50W
Bakpulād	146	Qc	38.10N	57.00 E
Baksan	132	Mh	43.40N	43.28 E
Baksan	132	Nh	43.42N	44.03 E
Baku	112	Kg	40.23N	49.51 E
Bakum	124	Kb	52.44N	8.11 E
Bakungan	150	Cf	2.56N	97.30 E
Bakuriani	132	Mi	41.43N	43.31 E
Bakutis Coast	222	Of	74.45 S	120.00W
Balâ	146	Ec	39.34N	33.08 E
Bala, Cerros de-	202	Ef	14.30 S	67.40W
Balabac	150	Ge	7.59N	117.04 E
Balabac	150	Ge	7.57N	117.01 E
Balabac, Selat- = Balabac Strait (EN)	140	Ni	7.40N	117.00 E
Balabac Strait (EN) = Balabac, Selat-	140	Ni	7.40N	117.00 E
Ba'labakk	146	Ge	34.00N	36.12 E
Balabalangan, Kepulauan-	150	Gg	2.20 S	117.25 E
Balaban Dağı	146	Hb	40.28N	39.15 E
Balabanovo	132	Jb	55.11N	36.40 E
Balabio	219b	Be	20.07 S	164.11 E
Balaci	130	He	44.21N	24.55 E
Balad	146	Ke	34.01N	44.01 E
Bal'ad	168	He	2.22N	45.24 E
Balādīn as Sakrān	146	Kj	25.12N	44.37 E
Baladīyat 'Adan = Aden (EN)	142	Gh	12.46N	45.01 E
Balad Rūz	146	Kf	33.42N	45.05 E
Balagannoje	138	Je	59.43N	149.15 E
Balagansk	138	Ff	53.58N	103.02 E
Bālāghāt	148	Gd	21.48N	80.11 E
Bālāghāt Range	148	Fe	18.45N	76.30 E
Balagna	122a	Aa	42.35N	8.50 E
Balaguer	126	Mc	41.47N	0.49 E
Balahna	114	Kh	56.31N	43.37 E
Balahta	138	Ee	55.24N	91.37 E
Balaka	170	Fe	14.59 S	34.57 E
Balaklava	132	Hg	44.31N	33.34 E
Balakleja	136	Df	49.27N	36.52 E
Balakovo	112	Ke	52.02N	47.45 E
Balama	172	Fb	13.16 S	38.36 E
Balambangam, Pulau-	150	Ge	7.17N	116.55 E
Bālā Morghāb	144	Jb	35.35N	63.20 E
Balan Dağı	130	Lm	36.52N	28.20 E
Balankanche	192	Og	20.45N	88.30W
Balasan	150	Hd	11.28N	123.05 E
Balasore → Bāleshwar	148	Hd	21.30N	86.56 E
Balašov	136	Ee	51.33N	43.10 E
Balassagyarmat	120	Ph	48.05N	19.18 E
Balāţ	164	Ed	25.33N	29.16 E
Balaton	110	Hf	46.50N	17.45 E
Balatonfüred	120	Nj	46.57N	17.53 E
Balatonkeresztúr	120	Nj	46.42N	17.23 E
Balaurin	150	Hh	8.15 S	123.43 E
Bălăuşeri	130	Hc	46.24N	24.41 E
Balayan	150	Hd	13.57N	120.44 E
Balazote	126	Jf	38.53N	2.08W
Balbi, Mount-	214	Ei	5.55 S	154.59 E
Balboa Heights	190	Ig	8.57N	79.33W
Balbriggan/Baile Brigín	118	Gh	53.37N	6.11W
Balcarce	206	Ie	37.50 S	58.15W
Balcarce, Sierras de-	204	Cm	37.50 S	58.40W
Bălceşti	130	Ge	44.37N	23.57 E
Balčik	130	Lf	43.25N	28.10 E
Balclutha	216	Ci	46.14 S	169.44 E
Bald Eagle Mountain	184	Ie	41.00N	77.45W
Bald Head	212	Dg	35.07 S	118.01 E
Bald Knob	186	Ki	35.19N	91.34W
Bald Knob	184	Hg	37.56N	79.51W
Baldo, Monte-	128	Ee	45.40N	10.50 E
Baldock	124	Bc	51.59N	0.11W
Baldone	116	Kh	56.41N	24.22 E
Baldur	186	Gb	49.23N	99.15W
Baldwin	184	Ed	43.54N	85.51W
Baldy Peak	182	Fe	33.55N	109.35W
Bale [3]	168	Gd	6.00N	41.00 E
Baleares / Balears [2]	126	Oe	39.30N	3.00 E
Balearic Islands (EN) = Baleares, Islas-/Balears, Illes-	110	Gh	39.30N	3.00 E
Balearic Islands (EN) = Balears, Illes-/Baleares, Islas-	110	Gh	39.30N	3.00 E
Balears / Baleares [2]	126	Oe	39.30N	3.00 E
Balears, Illes-/Baleares, Islas- = Balearic Islands (EN)	110	Gh	39.30N	3.00 E
Balease, Gunung-	150	Hg	2.24 S	120.33 E
Baleia, Ponta da-	198	Mg	17.40 S	36.07W
Baleine, Rivière à la-	180	Ke	58.15N	67.38W
Balej	138	Gf	51.35N	116.38 E
Balen	124	Hc	51.10N	5.09 E
Baler	150	Hc	15.46N	121.34 E
Bāleshwar	148	Hd	21.30N	86.56 E
Balezino	136	Fd	57.59N	53.02 E
Balfate	194	Df	15.48N	86.25W
Bălgarija = Bulgaria (EN) [1]	112	Ig	43.00N	25.00 E
Balgazyn	138	Ef	50.58N	95.12 E
Balguntay	152	Ec	42.45N	86.18 E
Balḩāf	144	Fg	13.58N	48.11 E
Balhārshāh	148	Fe	19.50N	79.22 E
Balhaš = Balkhash (EN)	142	Je	46.49N	74.59 E
Balhaš, ozero- = Balkhash, Lake- (EN)	140	Je	46.00N	74.00 E
Balho	168	Gc	12.00N	42.10 E
Balholm	114	Bf	61.12N	6.33 E
Bali [3]	150	Gh	8.30 S	115.00 E
Bali, Laut- = Bali Sea (EN)	140	Nj	7.45 S	115.30 E
Bali, Pulau-	140	Nj	8.20 S	115.00 E
Bali, Selat- = Bali Strait (EN)	150	Fh	8.18 S	114.25 E
Baliceaux Island	197n	Bb	12.57N	61.08W
Baliem	150	Kg	4.25 S	138.59 E
Balige	150	Cf	2.20N	99.04 E
Balikesir	144	Cb	39.39N	27.53 E
Balık Gölü	146	Jc	39.45N	43.36 E
Balīkh, Nahr-	146	He	35.53N	39.10 E
Balikpapan	142	Nj	1.17 S	116.50 E
Balimbing	150	Dh	5.55 S	104.34 E
Balimo	214	Ci	8.03 S	142.56 E
Balingen	120	Eh	48.17N	8.51 E
Balinqiao	154	Ec	43.16N	118.38 E
Balintang Channel	150	Hc	19.49N	121.40 E
Bali Sea (EN) = Bali, Laut-	140	Nj	7.45 S	115.30 E
Bali Strait (EN) = Bali, Selat-	150	Fh	8.18 S	114.25 E
Baliza	204	Fc	16.15 S	52.25W
Balk, Gaasterland-	124	Hb	52.54N	5.36 E
Balkan Mountains (EN) = Stara Planina	110	Ig	43.15N	25.00 E
Balkan Peninsula (EN)	110	Ig	41.30N	23.00 E
Balkanskaja oblast	136	Fh	39.50N	55.00 E
Balkašino	136	Ge	52.32N	68.46 E
Balkh	144	Kb	36.46N	66.54 E
Balkh [3]	144	Kb	36.30N	67.00 E
Balkhash (EN) = Balhaš	142	Je	46.49N	74.59 E
Balkhash, Lake- (EN) = Balhaš, ozero-	140	Je	46.00N	74.00 E
Balladonia	212	Ef	32.27 S	123.51 E
Ballagen	114	Db	68.20N	16.50 E
Ballaghaderreen/Bealach an Doirín	118	Eh	53.55N	8.35W
Ballantrae	118	If	55.06N	5.00W
Ballantyne Strait	180	Ga	77.30N	115.00W
Ballarat	210	Fh	37.34 S	143.52 E
Ballard, Lake-	212	Ee	29.25 S	120.55 E
Ballé	166	Db	15.20N	8.36W
Ballenas, Bahía-	192	Cd	26.45N	113.25W
Ballenas, Canal de-	192	Cc	29.10N	113.25W
Ballenero, Canal-	206	Fh	54.50 S	71.00W
Ballenita, Punta-	206	Fc	25.46 S	70.44W
Balleny Islands	222	Ke	66.35 S	162.50 E
Balleroy	124	Be	49.11N	0.50W
Balleza	192	Fd	26.57N	106.21W
Balli	130	Ki	40.50N	27.03 E
Ballia	148	Gc	25.45N	84.10 E
Ballina	212	Ke	28.52 S	153.33 E
Ballina/Béal an Átha	118	Dg	54.07N	9.09W
Ballinasloe/Béal Átha na Sluaighe	118	Eh	53.20N	8.13W
Ballinger	186	Gk	31.44N	99.57W
Ballinrobe/Baile an Róba	118	Dh	53.37N	9.13W
Ballinskelligs Bay/Bágh Baile na Sgealg	118	Cj	51.50N	10.15W
Ballshi	130	Ci	40.36N	19.44 E
Ball's Pyramid	208	Gh	31.45 S	159.15 E
Ballycastle/Baile an Chaistil	118	Gf	55.12N	6.15W
Ballyhaunis/Béal Átha hAmhnais	118	Eh	53.46N	8.46W
Ballymena/An Baile Meánach	118	Gg	54.52N	6.17W
Ballyshannon/Béal Átha Seanaidh	118	Eg	54.30N	8.11W
Balmaseda / Valmaseda	126	Ia	43.12N	3.12W
Balmazújváros	120	Ri	47.37N	21.21 E
Balmoral Castle	118	Jd	57.02N	3.15W
Balneario Orense	204	Cn	38.49 S	59.46W
Balneario Oriente	204	Bn	38.55 S	60.32W
Balombo	170	Be	12.21 S	14.43 E
Balonne River	208	Fg	28.47 S	147.56 E
Balota, Vîrful-	130	Gd	45.18N	23.53 E
Balovale	160	Jj	13.33 S	23.07 E
Balrāmpur	148	Gc	27.26N	82.11 E
Balranald	212	If	34.38 S	143.33 E
Balş	130	He	44.21N	24.06 E
Balsas [Braz.]	202	Ie	7.31 S	46.02W
Balsas [Mex.]	192	Jh	18.00N	99.47W
Balsas, Depresión del-	192	Ih	18.00N	100.10W
Balsas, Río- [Mex.]	174	Ih	17.55N	102.10W
Balsas, Río- [Pan.]	194	Ii	8.15N	77.59W
Balsas, Rio das- [Braz.]	202	Ie	9.58 S	47.52W
Balsas, Rio das- [Braz.]	202	Je	7.14 S	44.33W
Bålsta	116	Ge	59.35N	17.30 E
Balsthal	128	Bc	47.19N	7.42 E
Balta	132	Ff	47.57N	29.38 E
Baltanás	126	Hc	41.56N	4.15W
Baltasar Brum	206	Id	30.44 S	57.19W
Baltaţi	130	Kb	47.13N	27.09 E
Baltic Sea (EN) = Baltijas jūra	110	Hd	57.00N	19.00 E
Baltic Sea (EN) = Baltijos jura	110	Hd	57.00N	19.00 E
Baltic Sea (EN) = Baltijskoje more	110	Hd	57.00N	19.00 E
Baltic Sea (EN) = Balti meri	110	Hd	57.00N	19.00 E
Baltic Sea (EN) = Bałtyckie, Morze-	110	Hd	57.00N	19.00 E
Baltic Sea (EN) = Itämeri	110	Hd	57.00N	19.00 E
Baltic Sea (EN) = Östersjön	110	Hd	57.00N	19.00 E
Baltic Sea (EN) = Østersøen	110	Hd	57.00N	19.00 E
Baltic Sea (EN) = Ostsee	110	Hd	57.00N	19.00 E
Baltijas jūra = Baltic Sea (EN)	110	Hd	57.00N	19.00 E
Baltijos jura = Baltic Sea (EN)	110	Hd	57.00N	19.00 E
Baltijsk	136	Be	54.40N	19.58 E
Baltijskaja grjada	114	Fi	55.00N	25.00 E
Baltijskoje more = Baltic Sea (EN)	110	Hd	57.00N	19.00 E
Balţīm	164	Fc	31.33N	31.05 E
Balti meri = Baltic Sea (EN)	110	Hd	57.00N	19.00 E
Baltimore	176	Lf	39.17N	76.37W
Baltit (Hunza)	148	Ea	36.20N	74.40 E
Baltoj Voke	116	Kj	54.24N	25.16 E
Baltrum	120	Dc	53.44N	7.23 E
Bałtyckie, Morze- = Baltic Sea (EN)	110	Hd	57.00N	19.00 E
Baluarte, Río-	192	Ff	22.49N	106.02W
Baluchistān = Baluchistan (EN) [3]	148	Cc	28.00N	63.00 E
Baluchistān = Baluchistan (EN)	140	Ig	28.00N	63.00 E
Baluchistan (EN) = Baluchistān [3]	148	Cc	28.00N	63.00 E
Baluchistan (EN) = Baluchistān	140	Ig	28.00N	63.00 E
Balupe	116	Lh	56.54N	27.02 E
Balurghat	148	Hc	25.13N	88.46 E
Balvard	146	Qh	29.25N	56.06 E
Balve	124	Jc	51.20N	7.52 E
Balver Wald	124	Jc	51.21N	7.51 E
Balvi/Balvy	114	Gh	57.08N	27.20 E
Balvy/Balvi	114	Gh	57.08N	27.20 E
Balya	146	Bc	39.45N	27.35 E
Balygyčan	138	Kd	64.00N	154.10 E
Balykši	132	Qf	47.02N	51.55 E
Bām	146	Qd	36.58N	57.59 E
Bam	144	Id	29.06N	58.21 E
Bama	166	Hc	11.31N	13.41 E
Bamaji Lake	186	Ka	51.09N	91.25W
Bamako	160	Gg	12.38N	8.00W
Bamako [3]	166	Dc	13.00N	8.00W
Bamba	166	Eb	17.02N	1.24W
Bambama	170	Bc	2.32 S	13.33 E
Bambana, Río-	194	Fg	13.27N	83.50W
Bambangando	170	Df	16.59 S	20.57 E
Bambari	160	Jh	5.45N	20.40 E
Bamberg	120	Gg	49.42N	10.52 E
Bambesa	170	Eb	3.28N	25.43 E
Bambesi	168	Ed	9.45N	34.44 E
Bambey	166	Bc	14.42N	16.28W
Bambezi	172	Dc	19.57 S	28.55 E
Bambili	170	Eb	3.39N	26.07 E
Bambio	168	Be	3.54N	16.59 E
Bamboi	166	Ed	8.10N	2.02W
Bambouti	168	Dd	5.24N	27.12 E
Bambouto, Monts-	158	Ih	5.44N	10.04 E
Bambuí	204	Je	20.01 S	45.58W
Bam Co	152	Fe	31.15N	90.32 E
Bamenda	166	Hd	5.56N	10.10 E
Bāmīān	144	Kc	34.50N	67.50 E
Bāmīān [3]	144	Kc	34.45N	67.15 E
Bamiancheng	154	Gc	43.15N	124.00 E
Bamiantong → Muling	154	Kb	44.55N	130.32 E
Bamingui	168	Cd	7.34N	20.11 E
Bamingui	158	Ih	8.33N	19.05 E
Bamingui-Bangoran [3]	168	Cd	7.50N	20.15 E
Bampūr	144	Jd	27.12N	60.27 E
Bampūr	144	Id	27.18N	59.06 E
Banaadir [3]	168	He	2.00N	45.15 E
Banaadir	158	Lh	1.00N	44.00 E
Banaba Island	208	He	0.52 S	169.35 E
Banabuiú, Açude-	202	Ke	5.20 S	39.00W
Banagi	170	Fc	2.16 S	34.51 E
Banalia	170	Eb	1.33N	25.20 E
Banamba	166	Dc	13.32N	7.27W
Bananal, Ilha do- [Braz.]	198	Kg	11.30 S	50.15W
Bananal, Ilha do- [Braz.]	204	Dc	17.05 S	56.25W
Bananga	148	Ig	6.57N	93.54 E
Banarli	130	Kh	41.04N	27.20 E
Banās, Ra's-	158	Kf	23.54N	35.48 E
Banat	110	If	45.30N	21.00 E
Banat	130	Dd	45.30N	21.00 E
Banaz	146	Cc	38.46N	29.46 E
Banaz	146	Cc	38.12N	29.14 E
Banbar	152	Fe	30.48N	94.52 E
Banbridge/Droichead na Banna	118	Gg	54.21N	6.16W
Banbury	118	Li	52.04N	1.20W
Banco, Punta-	194	Fi	8.23N	83.09W
Bancroft	184	Ic	45.03N	77.51W
Bānda	148	Gc	25.29N	80.20 E
Banda, Kepulauan- = Banda Islands (EN)	150	Ig	4.35 S	129.55 E
Banda, Laut- = Banda Sea (EN)	208	De	5.00 S	128.00 E
Banda, Punta-	192	Ab	31.45N	116.45W
Banda Aceh	142	Li	5.34N	95.20 E
Bandai-San	156	Gc	37.38N	140.04 E
Banda Islands (EN) = Banda, Kepulauan-	150	Ig	4.35 S	129.55 E
Bandak	116	Ce	59.25N	8.15 E
Bandar → Machilipatnam	148	Ge	16.10N	81.08 E
Bandar Beheshtī	144	Jd	25.18N	60.37 E
Bandar-e 'Abbās	142	Hg	27.11N	56.17 E
Bandar-e Anzalī	144	Gb	37.28N	49.27 E
Bandar-e Būshehr	142	Hg	28.59N	50.50 E
Bandar-e Chārak	146	Pi	26.43N	54.16 E
Bandar-e Chīrū	146	Oi	26.43N	53.43 E
Bandar-e Deylam	144	Hg	30.05N	50.07 E
Bandar-e-Gaz	146	Od	36.47N	53.59 E
Bandar-e-Khomeynī	146	Mg	30.25N	49.08 E
Bandar-e Lengeh	144	Hd	26.33N	54.53 E
Bandar-e Māh Shahr	144	Gc	30.33N	49.12 E
Bandar-e Maqām	144	Hd	26.56N	53.29 E
Bandar-e Moghūyeh	146	Pi	26.35N	54.31 E
Bandar-e-Rīg	146	Nh	29.29N	50.38 E
Bandar-e Torkeman	144	Hb	36.56N	54.06 E
Bandar Seri Begawan	142	Ni	4.53N	114.56 E
Banda Sea (EN) = Banda, Laut-	208	De	5.00 S	128.00 E
Bande	126	Eb	42.02N	7.58W
Bandeira, Pico da-	198	Lh	20.26 S	41.47W
Bandeirantes	204	Ga	13.41 S	50.48W
Bandeirantes, Ilha dos-	204	Ff	23.22 S	53.50W
Bandera	206	Hc	28.54 S	62.16W
Bandera, Alto-	194	Ld	18.49N	70.37W
Banderas, Bahía de-	190	Cd	20.40N	105.25W
Bandiagara	166	Ec	14.20N	3.37W
Bandiat	122	Gi	45.46N	0.20 E
Bandırma	144	Ca	40.20N	27.58 E
Bandirma Körfezi	130	Ki	40.25N	28.00 E
Bandol	122	Lk	43.08N	5.45 E
Bandon	188	Ce	43.07N	124.25W
Bandon/Abhainn na Bandan	118	Ej	51.40N	8.30W
Bandon/Droichead na Bandan	118	Ej	51.45N	8.45W
Ban Don, Ao-	148	Jg	9.20N	99.25 E
Bandundu	160	Ii	3.18 S	17.20 E
Bandundu [2]	170	Cc	5.00 S	17.00 E
Bandung	142	Mj	6.54 S	107.36 E
Bāneh	146	Ke	35.59N	45.53 E
Banes	190	Id	20.58N	75.43W
Banff [Alta.-Can.]	180	Ff	51.10N	115.34W
Banff [Scot.-U.K.]	118	Kd	57.40N	2.31W
Banfora	166	Ec	10.38N	4.46W
Banga	170	Dd	5.57 S	20.28 E
Bangalore	142	Jh	12.59N	77.35 E
Bangangté	166	Hd	5.09N	10.31 E
Bangar	150	Gf	4.43N	115.04 E
Bangassou	160	Jh	4.44N	22.49 E
Bangeta, Mount-	214	Di	6.16 S	147.04 E
Banggai	150	Hg	1.34 S	123.30 E
Banggai, Kepulauan- = Banggai Archipelago (EN)	208	De	1.30 S	123.15 E
Banggai, Selat-	150	Hg	1.55 S	124.00 E
Banggai Archipelago (EN) = Banggai, Kepulauan-	208	De	1.30 S	123.15 E
Banggi, Pulau-	150	Ge	7.17N	117.12 E
Banghāzī = Benghazi (EN)	160	Je	32.07N	20.04 E
Banghāzī = Benghazi (EN) [3]	164	Dd	27.00N	20.30 E
Bangka, Pulau- [Indon.]	150	If	1.48N	125.09 E
Bangka, Pulau- [Indon.]	140	Mj	2.15 S	106.00 E
Bangka, Selat-	150	Eg	2.30 S	105.40 E
Bangka, Selat- = Bangka Strait (EN)	150	Eg	2.20 S	105.45 E
Bangkalan	150	Fh	7.02 S	112.44 E
Bangka Strait (EN) = Bangka, Selat-	150	Eg	2.20 S	105.45 E
Bangkinang	150	Df	0.21N	101.02 E
Bangko	150	Dg	2.05 S	102.17 E
Bangkok (EN) = Krung Thep	142	Mh	13.45N	100.31 E
Bangladesh [1]	142	Kg	24.00N	90.00 E
Bangli	150	Gh	8.27 S	115.21 E
Bangolo	166	Dd	7.01N	7.09W
Bangong Co	152	Ce	33.45N	79.15 E
Bangor [Me.-U.S.]	182	Nc	44.49N	68.47W
Bangor [Wales-U.K.]	118	Ih	53.13N	4.08W
Bangor/Beannchar	118	Hg	54.40N	5.40W
Bangoran	168	Bd	8.42N	19.06 E
Bangsund	114	Cd	64.24N	11.24 E
Bangu	170	Dd	9.05 S	23.44 E
Bangued	150	Hc	17.36N	120.37 E
Bangui [C.A.R.]	160	Ih	4.22N	18.35 E
Bangui [Phil.]	150	Hc	18.32N	120.46 E
Bangweulu, Lake-	158	Jj	11.05 S	29.45 E
Bangweulu Swamps	170	Fe	11.30 S	30.15 E
Banhā	164	Fc	30.28N	31.11 E
Ban Houayxay	148	Kd	20.18N	100.26 E
Baní	190	Je	18.17N	70.20W
Bani	158	Gg	14.30N	4.12W
Bani, Jbel-	158	Gf	28.30N	9.00W
Bani Bangou	166	Fb	15.03N	2.42 E
Banie	120	Kc	53.08N	14.38 E
Banifing	166	Dc	12.43N	6.25W
Banī Forūr, Jazīreh-ye-	146	Pi	26.07N	54.28 E
Banihal Pass	148	Fb	33.15N	75.09 E
Banija	128	Ke	45.10N	16.10 E
Banikoara	166	Fc	11.18N	2.26 E
Banī ma 'Āriḑ	164	Ie	20.42N	47.42 E
Banī Mazār	164	Fd	28.30N	30.48 E
Banī Muḩammadīyāt	146	Di	27.17N	31.05 E
Banī Suwayf	164	Fd	29.05N	31.05 E
Banī Tonb	146	Pi	26.12N	54.56 E
Banī Walīd	164	Bc	31.46N	13.59 E
Bāniyās	144	Ec	33.15N	35.41 E
Banja	130	Hg	42.33N	24.50 E
Banja Koviljača	130	Ce	44.30N	19.11 E
Banja Luka	128	Lf	44.46N	17.10 E
Banjarmarsin	142	Nj	3.20 S	114.35 E
Banjul	160	Fg	13.27N	16.35W
Bank	132	Pj	39.27N	49.14 E
Bankas	166	Ec	14.05N	3.31W
Bankeryd	116	Fg	57.51N	14.07 E
Banket	172	Ec	17.23 S	30.24 E
Bankhead Lake	184	Di	33.30N	87.15W
Bankilaré	166	Fc	14.35N	0.44 E
Bankja	130	Gg	42.42N	23.08 E
Ban Kongmi	148	Lf	14.31N	106.55 E
Banks [Can.]	174	Gb	73.15N	121.30W
Banks [Can.]	180	Ef	53.25N	130.10W
Banks, Iles- = Banks Islands (EN)	208	Hf	13.50 S	167.35 E
Banks Island	212	Ib	10.10 S	142.15 E
Banks Islands (EN) = Banks, Iles-	208	Hf	13.50 S	167.35 E
Banks Lake	188	Fc	47.45N	119.15W
Banks Peninsula	208	Ii	43.40 S	172.40 E
Banks Strait	212	Jh	40.40 S	148.10 E
Bann/An Bhanna	118	Gf	55.10N	6.46W
Ban Na San	148	Jg	8.53N	99.17 E
Bannerman Town	184	Im	24.09N	76.09W
Banning	188	Gj	33.56N	116.52W
Bannock Range	188	Ie	42.30N	112.20W
Bannu	148	Eb	32.59N	70.36 E
Bañolas / Banyoles	126	Ob	42.07N	2.46 E
Bánovce nad Bebravou	120	Oh	48.44N	18.15 E
Banqiao	152	Hf	25.28N	104.02 E
Banská Bystrica	120	Ph	48.44N	19.09 E
Banská Štiavnica	120	Oh	48.27N	18.55 E
Bansko	130	Gh	41.50N	23.29 E
Bānswāra	148	Ed	23.33N	74.27 E
Banta	168	Ge	1.13N	42.30 E
Bantenan, Tanjung-	150	Fh	8.47 S	114.33 E
Bantry/Beanntraí	118	Dj	51.41N	9.27W
Bantry Bay/Bá Bheanntraí	118	Dj	51.38N	9.48W
Bañuela	126	Hf	38.24N	4.11W
Banyak, Kepulauan- = Banyak Islands (EN)	150	Cf	2.10N	97.15 E
Banyak Islands (EN) = Banyak, Kepulauan-	150	Cf	2.10N	97.15 E
Banyo	166	Hd	6.45N	11.49 E
Banyoles / Bañolas	126	Ob	42.07N	2.46 E
Banyuls-sur-Mer	122	Jl	42.29N	3.08 E
Banyuwangi	142	Nj	8.12 S	114.21 E
Banzare Coast	222	Ie	67.00 S	126.00 E
Banzare Seamounts (EN)	222	Fd	58.50 S	77.44 E
Banzart, Buḩayrat-	128	Dm	37.11N	9.52 E
Bao'an	152	Jg	22.35N	114.10 E
Bao'an → Zhidan	152	Id	36.48N	108.46 E
Baochang → Taibus Qi	152	Kc	41.55N	115.22 E
Baode	152	Jd	38.59N	111.07 E
Baodi	154	De	39.43N	117.18 E
Baoding	142	Nf	38.47N	115.30 E
Baofeng	154	Bh	33.52N	113.04 E
Baoji	142	Mf	34.26N	107.12 E
Baokang	152	Je	31.49N	111.13 E
Baokang → Horqin Zuoyi Zhongqi	152	Lc	44.06N	123.19 E
Bao Loc	148	Lf	11.32N	107.48 E
Baoqing	152	Nb	46.20N	132.11 E
Baoro	168	Bd	5.40N	15.58 E
Baoshan	142	Lg	25.09N	99.12 E
Baotou	142	Me	40.38N	110.00 E
Baoulé [Afr.]	158	Gg	12.35N	6.34W
Baoulé [Mali]	158	Gg	13.33N	9.54W
Baoying	154	Eh	33.15N	119.18 E
Bapaume	122	Id	50.06N	2.51 E
Baqên (Dartang)	152	Fe	31.58N	94.00 E
Bāqerābād	146	Ne	34.56N	50.50 E
Ba'qūbah	144	Fc	33.45N	44.38 E
Baquedano	206	Gb	23.20 S	69.51W
Baquerizo Moreno	202a	Bb	0.54 S	89.37W
Bar	124	Ge	49.42N	4.50 E
Bar [Ukr.]	132	Ee	49.02N	27.40 E
Bar [Yugo]	130	Cg	42.05N	19.06 E

Index Symbols

[1] Independent Nation
[2] State, Region
[3] District, County
[4] Municipality
[5] Colony, Dependency
Continent
Physical Region
Historical or Cultural Region
Mount, Mountain
Volcano
Hill
Mountains, Mountain Range
Hills, Escarpment
Plateau, Upland
Pass, Gap
Plain, Lowland
Delta
Salt Flat
Valley, Canyon
Crater, Cave
Karst Features
Depression
Polder
Desert, Dunes
Forest, Woods
Heath, Steppe
Oasis
Cape, Point
Coast, Beach
Cliff
Peninsula
Isthmus
Sandbank
Island
Atoll
Rock, Reef
Islands, Archipelago
Rocks, Reefs
Coral Reef
Well, Spring
Geyser
River, Stream
Waterfall, Rapids
River Mouth, Estuary
Lake
Salt Lake
Intermittent Lake
Reservoir
Swamp, Pond
Canal
Glacier
Ice Shelf, Pack Ice
Ocean
Sea
Gulf, Bay
Strait, Fjord
Lagoon
Bank
Seamount
Tablemount
Ridge
Shelf
Basin
Escarpment, Sea Scarp
Fracture
Trench, Abyss
National Park, Reserve
Point of Interest
Recreation Site
Cave, Cavern
Historic Site
Ruins
Wall, Walls
Church, Abbey
Temple
Scientific Station
Railway station
Airport
Port
Military installation
Lighthouse
Mine
Tunnel
Dam, Bridge

Bar-Bay

Barabai 150 Gg 2.35S 115.23 E
Barabinsk 142 Jd 55.21N 78.21 E
Barabinskaja Step 138 Ce 55.00N 79.00 E
Baraboo 186 Le 43.28N 89.45W
Baracaldo 126 Ja 43.18N 2.59W
Baracoa 190 Jd 20.21N 74.30W
Bărăganului, Cîmpia- 130 Ke 44.55N 27.15 E
Baragoi 170 Gb 1.47N 36.47 E
Bārah 168 Ec 13.42N 30.22 E
Barahona 190 Je 18.12N 71.06W
Barak 146 Gd 36.51N 37.59 E
Baraka 168 Fb 18.13N 37.35 E
Barakah 168 Fb 18.13N 37.35 E
Barakāt 168 Ec 14.20N 33.36 E
Barakī Barak 144 Kc 33.58N 68.58 E
Baram 150 Ff 4.36N 113.58 E
Baram 150 Ff 4.36N 113.59 E
Baramanni 196 Gi 7.50N 59.13W
Barama River 196 Gi 7.40N 59.15W
Bārāmūla 148 Eb 34.12N 74.21 E
Baran 114 Hi 54.29N 30.19 E
Bārān 148 Fc 25.06N 76.31 E
Baraniha 138 Lc 68.31N 168.25 E
Baranja 128 Me 46.00N 18.30 E
Baranoa 194 Jh 10.49N 75.03W
Baranof 178 Le 57.00N 135.00W
Baranoviči 112 Ie 53.08N 26.02 E
Baranovka 132 Ed 50.18N 27.41 E
Baranya [2] 120 Oj 46.05N 18.15 E
Barão de Capanema 204 Da 13.19S 57.52W
Barão de Cotegipe 204 Fh 27.37S 52.23W
Barão de Grajaú 202 Je 6.45S 43.01W
Barão de Melgaço 202 Gg 16.13S 55.58W
Baraque de Fraiture 122 Ld 50.16N 5.45 E
Baratang 148 If 12.13N 92.45 E
Barataria Bay 186 Ll 29.22N 89.57W
Barat Daya, Kepulauan- 140 Oj 7.25S 128.00 E
Barāwe 160 Lh 1.09N 44.03 E
Barbacena 200 Lh 21.14S 43.46W
Barbacoas [Ven.] 194 Li 9.49N 70.03W
Barbacoas [Ven.] 196 Ch 9.29N 66.58W
Barbacoas, Bahia de- 194 Jh 10.10N 75.35W
Barbado, Rio- 204 Cb 15.12S 58.58W
Barbados [1] 176 Nh 13.10N 59.32W
Barbados 174 Nh 13.10N 59.32W
Barbados Ridge (EN) 176 Gf 12.45N 59.35W
Barbagia 128 Dj 40.10N 9.10 E
Barbar 168 Eb 18.01N 33.59 E
Bārbara 202 Dd 0.52S 72.30W
Barbaria, Cap de- / Berberia, Cabo- 126 Nf 38.38N 1.23 E
Barbaros 130 Ki 40.54N 27.27 E
Barbas, Cabo- 162 De 22.18N 16.41W
Barbastro 126 Mb 42.02N 0.08 E
Barbate de Franco 126 Gh 36.12N 5.55W
Barbeau Peak 174 La 81.54N 75.01W
Barbeton 172 Ee 25.48S 31.03 E
Barbezieux-Saint-Hilaire 122 Fi 45.28N 0.09W
Barbourville 184 Fg 36.52N 83.53W
Barboza Ferraz 204 Fg 24.04S 52.03W
Barbuda 174 Mh 17.38N 61.48W
Barcaldine 210 Fg 23.33S 145.17 E
Barcarrota 126 Ff 38.31N 6.51W
Barcău 130 Ec 46.59N 21.07 E
Barcellona Pozzo di Gotto 128 Jl 38.09N 15.13 E
Barcelona [3] 126 Nc 41.40N 2.00 E
Barcelona [Sp.] 112 Gg 41.23N 2.11 E
Barcelona [Ven.] 202 Fa 10.08N 64.42W
Barcelonnette 122 Mj 44.23N 6.39 E
Barcelos [Braz.] 202 Fd 0.58S 62.57W
Barcelos [Port.] 126 Dc 41.32N 8.37W
Barcin 120 Nd 52.52N 17.57 E
Barcoo River 212 Ie 25.30S 142.50 E
Barcs 120 Nk 45.58N 17.28 E
Barda 132 Oi 40.25N 47.05 E
Bardagé 168 Ba 22.06N 16.28 E
Bardaï 160 If 21.21N 16.59 E
Bardār Shāh 146 Ld 36.45N 47.15 E
Bārdaw 128 En 36.49N 10.08 E
Barddhamān 148 Hd 23.15N 87.51 E
Bardejov 120 Rg 49.18N 21.16 E
Bārdēre 160 Lh 2.20N 42.20 E
Bardeskan 146 Qe 35.12N 57.58 E
Bardīyah 164 Ed 31.46N 25.06 E
Bardonecchia 128 Ae 45.05N 6.42 E
Bardsey 118 Ii 52.45N 4.45W
Bardstown 184 Eg 37.49N 85.28W
Barēda 160 Mg 11.52N 51.03 E
Bareilly 142 Jg 28.25N 79.23 E
Barencevo more = Barents Sea (EN) 224 Jd 74.00N 36.00 E
Barentin 122 Ge 49.33N 0.57 E
Barentsburg 224 Kd 78.04N 14.14 E
Barentshavet = Barents Sea (EN) 224 Jd 74.00N 36.00 E
Barentsøya 179 Oc 78.27N 21.15 E
Barents Sea (EN) = Barencevo more 224 Jd 74.00N 36.00 E
Barents Sea (EN) = Barentshavet 224 Jd 74.00N 36.00 E
Barents Trough (EN) 110 Ia 73.00N 29.00 E
Barentu 168 Fb 15.06N 37.36 E
Barfleur 122 Ee 49.40N 1.15W
Barfleur, Pointe de- 122 Ee 49.42N 1.16W
Barga 142 Kf 30.48N 81.17 E
Bārgāl 168 Ic 11.18N 51.07 E
Bargarh 148 Gd 21.20N 83.37 E
Barguelonne 122 Gj 44.07N 0.50 E
Barguzin 138 Ff 53.27N 108.58 E
Barguzinski hrebet 138 Ff 54.30N 110.00 E
Bar Harbor 184 Mc 44.23N 68.13W
Barhi 148 Hd 24.18N 85.25 E
Bari 112 Hg 41.08N 16.51 E
Bari [3] 168 Hd 10.00N 50.00 E
Bari, Terra di- 128 Kj 41.05N 16.50 E
Ba Ria 148 Lf 10.30N 107.10 E
Barīdī, Ra's- 146 Gj 24.17N 37.31 E
Barika 126 Ri 35.22N 5.05 E
Barīm 164 Hg 12.39N 43.25 E
Barima, Rio- 196 Fh 8.35N 60.25W
Barima River 196 Fh 8.35N 60.25W
Barinas 202 Db 8.38N 70.12W
Barinas [2] 202 Eb 8.10N 70.00W
Baring, Cape- 180 Fb 70.01N 117.28W
Baringa 170 Db 0.45N 20.52 E
Barinitas 194 Li 8.45N 70.25W
Baripāda 148 Hd 21.56N 86.43 E
Bariri 204 Hf 22.04S 48.44W
Bariri, Reprêsa- 204 Hf 22.21S 48.39W
Barīs 164 Fe 24.40N 30.36 E
Bari Sādri 148 Ed 24.25N 74.28 E
Barisāl 148 Id 22.42N 90.22 E
Barisan, Pegunungan- = Barisan Mountains (EN) 140 Mj 3.00S 102.15 E
Barisan Mountains (EN) = Barisan, Pegunungan- 140 Mj 3.00S 102.15 E
Barito 140 Nj 3.32S 114.29 E
Barjols 122 Lk 43.33N 6.00 E
Barkā' 144 Ie 23.35N 57.55 E
Barkam 152 He 31.45N 102.32 E
Barkan, Ra's-e- 146 Mg 30.01N 49.35 E
Barkava 116 Lh 56.40N 26.45 E
Barkley, Lake- 182 Jd 36.40N 87.55W
Barkley Sound 188 Cb 48.53N 125.20W
Barkly East 172 Df 30.58S 27.33 E
Barkly Tableland 208 Ef 19.00S 138.00 E
Barkly West 172 Ce 28.05S 24.31 E
Barkol 152 Fc 43.35N 92.51 E
Barkol Hu 152 Fc 43.40N 92.39 E
Barlavento [3] 162 Cf 16.10N 24.40W
Bar-le-Duc 122 Lf 48.47N 5.10 E
Barlee, Lake- 208 Cg 29.10S 119.30 E
Barlee Range 212 Dd 23.35S 116.00 E
Barletta 128 Ki 41.19N 16.17 E
Barlinek 120 Lc 53.00N 15.12 E
Barlovento, Islas de- = Windward Islands (EN) 174 Mh 15.00N 61.00W
Barma 150 Jg 1.54S 133.00 E
Barmer 148 Ec 25.45N 71.23 E
Barmera 212 If 34.15S 140.28 E
Barmouth 118 Ii 52.43N 4.03W
Barnard Castle 118 Lg 54.33N 1.55W
Barnaul 142 Kd 53.22N 83.45 E
Barnes Ice Cap 180 Kc 70.00N 73.30W
Barnesville [Ga.-U.S.] 184 Ei 33.04N 84.09W
Barnesville [Mn.-U.S.] 186 Hc 46.39N 96.25W
Barnet, London- 124 Bc 51.39N 0.12W
Barneveld 124 Hb 52.08N 5.34 E
Barneville-Carteret 122 Ee 49.23N 1.47W
Barnim 120 Jd 52.40N 13.45 E
Barnsley 118 Lh 53.34N 1.28W
Barnstaple 118 Ij 51.05N 4.04W
Barnstaple (Bideford Bay) 118 Ij 51.05N 4.20W
Barnstorf 124 Kb 52.43N 8.30 E
Barntrup 124 Lc 51.59N 9.07 E
Barnwell 184 Gi 33.14N 81.21W
Baro 158 Kh 8.26N 33.14 E
Baro [Chad] 168 Bc 12.12N 18.58 E
Baro [Nig.] 166 Gd 8.36N 6.25 E
Baroghil Pass 148 Ea 36.54N 73.22 E
Baronnies 122 Lj 44.15N 5.30 E
Barora Fa 219a Db 7.30S 158.20 E
Barora Ite 219a Db 7.36S 158.24 E
Barotseland 170 Df 15.05S 24.00 E
Barqah = Cyrenaica (EN) 158 Je 31.00N 23.00 E
Barqah = Cyrenaica (EN) 164 Dc 31.00N 22.30 E
Barqah, Jabal al- 146 Ej 24.24N 32.34 E
Barqah al Bahrīyah = Marmarica (EN) 158 Je 31.40N 24.30 E
Barqū, Jabal- 128 Dn 36.04N 9.37 E
Barques, Pointe aux- 184 Fc 44.04N 82.58W
Barquisimeto 200 Jd 10.04N 69.19W
Barr 122 Nf 48.24N 7.27 E
Barr, Ra's al- 146 Nj 25.47N 50.34 E
Barra 200 Lg 11.05S 43.10W
Barra 118 Fd 57.00N 7.30W
Barra, Ponta da- 158 Kk 23.47S 35.32 E
Barra, Sound of- 118 Fd 57.10N 7.20W
Barraba 212 Kf 30.22S 150.36 E
Barra Bonita, Reprêsa- 204 Hf 22.38S 48.20W
Barra de Navidad 190 De 19.12N 104.41W
Barra do Bugres 202 Gg 15.05S 57.11W
Barra do Corda 202 Ie 5.30S 45.15W
Barra do Cuanza 170 Bd 9.18S 13.09 E
Barra do Dande 170 Bd 8.28S 13.22 E
Barra do Garças 202 Hg 15.53S 52.15W
Barra Falsa, Ponta da- 158 Kk 22.55S 35.37 E
Barra Head 118 Fe 56.46N 7.36W
Barra Mansa 202 Jh 22.32S 44.11W
Barrāmīyah, Wādī al- 146 Ej 25.00N 33.23 E
Barranca 202 Cd 4.50S 76.42W
Barrancabermeja 200 Ie 7.03N 73.52W
Barrancas [Col.] 194 Kh 10.57N 72.50W
Barrancas [Ven.] 202 Fb 8.42N 62.11W
Barrancas, Arroyo- 204 Cj 30.19S 59.25W
Barranco 204 Db 15.56S 57.41W
Barrancos 126 Ff 38.08N 6.59W
Barranqueras 206 Ic 27.29S 58.56W
Barranquilla 200 Id 10.59N 74.48W
Barranquitas 197a Bb 18.12N 66.23W
Barra Patuca 194 Ef 15.50N 84.17W
Barras 202 Jd 4.15S 42.18W
Barra Velha 204 Hh 26.39S 48.43W
Barre 184 Kc 44.12N 72.30W
Barreira 204 Db 15.24S 57.52W
Barreiras 200 Lg 12.08S 45.00W
Barreirinha 202 Gd 2.47S 57.03W
Barreirinhas 202 Jd 2.45S 42.50W
Barreiro 126 Cf 38.40N 9.04W
Barreiro, Rio- 204 Fb 15.43S 52.45W
Barreiro Grande 204 Jd 18.12S 45.10W
Barreiros 202 Ke 8.49S 35.12W
Barren 148 If 12.16N 93.51 E
Barren, Iles- 172 Gc 18.25S 43.40 E
Barren Islands 178 Ie 58.55N 152.15W
Barretos 206 Kb 20.33S 48.33W
Barrie 180 Jh 44.24N 79.40W
Barrier Bay 222 Ge 67.45S 81.10 E
Barrier Islands 219a Db 7.44S 158.32 E
Barrington Tops 212 Kf 32.00S 151.28 E
Barro Alto 204 Hb 15.04S 48.58W
Barrois, Plateaux du- 122 Kf 48.45N 5.00 E
Barros, Lagoa dos- 204 Gi 29.56S 50.23W
Barros, Tierra de- 126 Ff 38.40N 6.25W
Barroso 204 Ke 21.11S 43.58W
Barrouallie 197n Ba 13.14N 61.17W
Barrow [Ak.-U.S.] 176 Db 71.17N 156.47W
Barrow [Arg.] 204 Bn 38.18S 60.14W
Barrow/An Bhearú 118 Gi 52.10N 7.00W
Barrow, Point- 174 Db 71.23N 156.30W
Barrow Creek 210 Eg 21.33S 133.53 E
Barrow-in-Furness 118 Jg 54.07N 3.14W
Barrow Island 208 Cg 20.50S 115.25 E
Barrow Range 212 Fe 26.05S 127.30 E
Barrow Strait 174 Jb 74.21N 94.10W
Barru 150 Gg 4.25S 119.37 E
Barry 118 Jj 51.24N 3.18W
Barrytown 218 De 42.14S 171.20 E
Barsakelmes, ostrov- 135 Bb 45.40N 59.55 E
Barsalogo 166 Ec 13.25N 1.03W
Barsatas 136 Hf 48.13N 78.33 E
Baršć/Forst 120 Ke 51.44N 14.38 E
Bārsi 148 Fe 18.14N 75.42 E
Barsinghausen 120 Fd 52.18N 9.27 E
Barstow 182 De 34.54N 117.01W
Bar-sur-Aube 122 Kf 48.14N 4.43 E
Bar-sur-Seine 122 Kf 48.07N 4.22 E
Baršyn 136 Gf 49.45N 69.36 E
Barta/Bārta 116 Ih 56.57N 20.57 E
Bārta/Barta 116 Ih 56.57N 20.57 E
Bartallah 146 Jd 36.23N 43.25 E
Bartang 135 Hf 37.55N 71.33 E
Barth 120 Ib 54.22N 12.44 E
Bartholomew, Bayou- 186 Jj 32.43N 92.04W
Bartica 202 Gb 6.24N 58.37W
Bartın 146 Eb 41.38N 32.21 E
Bartle Frere, Mount- 212 Ff 17.23S 145.49 E
Bartlesville 182 Hd 36.45N 95.59W
Bartlett 186 Gf 41.53N 98.33W
Bartoszyce 120 Qb 54.16N 20.49 E
Bartow 184 Gl 27.54N 81.50W
Barú, Isla- 194 Jh 10.26N 75.35W
Barú, Volcán 190 Hg 8.48N 82.33W
Bārūd, Ra's- 146 Ei 26.47N 33.39 E
Barumini 128 Dk 39.42N 9.01 E
Barun-Bogdo-Ula 152 Hb 45.00N 100.20 E
Bāruni 146 Hc 25.29N 85.59 E
Barun-Šabartuj, gora- 138 Fg 49.43N 109.58 E
Barun-Urt 152 Jb 46.40N 113.12 E
Barwice 120 Mc 53.45N 16.22 E
Barwon River 208 Fg 30.00S 148.05 E
Barycz 120 Me 51.42N 16.15 E
Baryš 114 Lj 53.40N 47.08 E
Baryš 114 Li 54.35N 46.47 E
Bāsa'īdū 146 Pi 26.39N 55.17 E
Basail 204 Ch 27.52S 59.18W
Basankusu 170 Cb 1.14N 19.48 E
Basaral, ostrov- 135 Ib 45.25N 73.45 E
Basauri 126 Ja 43.13N 2.53W
Basavilbaso 204 Ck 32.22S 58.53W
Bas Champs 124 Dd 50.10N 1.41 E
Basco 150 Hb 20.27N 121.58 E
Bascuñán, Cabo- 206 Fc 28.51S 71.30W
Basel 112 Gf 47.30N 7.30 E
Basel-Landschaft [2] 128 Bc 47.30N 7.45 E
Basel-Stadt [2] 128 Bc 47.35N 7.40 E
Basentello 128 Kj 40.40N 16.23 E
Basento 128 Kj 40.20N 16.49 E
Başeu 130 Kb 47.44N 27.15 E
Basey 150 Id 11.17N 125.04 E
Bashi Channel (EN) = Bashi Haixia 152 Lg 22.00N 121.00 E
Bashi Haixia = Bashi Channel (EN) 152 Lg 22.00N 121.00 E
Bāsht 146 Ng 30.21N 51.09 E
Ba Shui 154 Ci 30.25N 115.02 E
Basilan 140 Oi 6.34N 122.03 E
Basilan City (Isabela) 142 Oi 6.42N 121.58 E
Basilan Strait 150 He 6.49N 122.05 E
Basildon 118 Nj 51.34N 0.25 E
Basilicata [2] 128 Kj 40.30N 16.30 E
Basingstoke 118 Lj 51.16N 1.05W
Basjanovski 134 Jg 58.19N 60.44 E
Başkale 146 Jc 38.02N 44.00 E
Baskatong, Réservoir- 180 Jg 46.47N 75.50W
Baškaus 138 Df 51.09N 87.43 E
Baskil 146 Hc 38.35N 38.40 E
Baškortostan respublika 136 Fe 55.00N 56.00 E
Baskunčak, ozero 132 Oe 48.10N 46.55 E
Bašmakovo 132 Mc 53.12N 43.03 E
Bāsmenj 146 Ld 37.59N 46.29 E
Basoko 170 Db 1.14N 23.36 E
Basongo 170 Dc 4.20S 20.24 E
Basque Provinces (EN) = Euzkadi / Vascongadas 126 Ja 43.00N 2.30W
Basque Provinces (EN) = Vascongadas / Euzkadi 126 Ja 43.00N 2.30W
Basra (EN) = Al Başrah 142 Gf 30.30N 47.47 E
Bas-Rhin [3] 122 Nf 48.35N 7.40 E
Bass, Ilots de- 208 Mg 27.55S 143.26W
Bassano 188 Ia 50.47N 112.28W
Bassano del Grappa 128 Fe 45.46N 11.44 E
Bassar 166 Fd 9.15N 0.47 E
Bassas da India 158 Lk 21.25S 39.42 E
Bassein → Pathein 142 Lh 16.47N 94.44 E
Bassein → Vasai 148 Ee 19.21N 72.48 E
Basse-Kotto [3] 168 Ce 5.00N 21.30 E
Basse-Pointe 197h Ab 14.52N 61.07W
Basses, Pointe des- 197e Bc 15.52N 61.17W
Basse-Sambre 124 Gd 50.27N 4.37 E
Basse Santa Su 166 Cc 13.19N 14.13W
Basse-Terre 190 Le 16.00N 61.44W
Basseterre 190 Le 17.18N 62.43W
Basse-Terre 196 Fd 16.10N 61.40W
Bassett 186 Ge 42.35N 99.32W
Bassigny 122 Lf 48.00N 5.30 E
Bassikounou 162 Ff 15.52N 5.58W
Bassila 166 Fd 9.01N 1.40 E
Bass Islands 219c Ba 9.58S 167.17 E
Basso, Plateau de- 168 Jg 17.20N 22.40 E
Bass Strait 208 Fh 39.20S 145.30 E
Bassum 124 Kb 52.51N 8.44 E
Basswood Lake 186 Kb 48.05N 91.35W
Båstad 114 Ch 56.26N 12.51 E
Bastak 146 Pi 27.14N 54.22 E
Bastām 146 Pd 36.29N 55.04 E
Bastenaken/Bastogne 122 Le 50.00N 5.43 E
Bastia [Fr.] 112 Gg 42.42N 9.27 E
Bastia [It.] 128 Gg 43.04N 12.33 E
Bastogne/Bastenaken 122 Le 50.00N 5.43 E
Bastrop 186 Kj 32.47N 91.55W
Basuo → Dongfang 152 Ih 19.14N 108.39 E
Basuto 172 Dc 19.52S 26.32 E
Bas-Zaïre [2] 170 Bd 5.30S 14.30 E
Bata 160 Hh 1.51N 9.45 E
Batabanó, Golfo de- 190 Hd 22.15N 82.30W
Batagaj 138 Ic 67.38N 134.38 E
Batagaj-Alyta 138 Ic 67.53N 130.31 E
Bataguaçu 202 Hh 21.42S 52.22W
Bataiporã 204 Ff 22.20S 53.17W
Batajnica 130 De 44.54N 20.17 E
Batajsk 136 Df 47.05N 39.46 E
Batak 130 Hh 41.57N 24.13 E
Bataklık Gölü 146 Ed 37.42N 33.07 E
Batala 148 Fb 31.48N 75.12 E
Batalha 126 De 39.39N 8.50W
Batama 170 Eb 0.56N 26.39 E
Batamaj 138 Hd 63.30N 129.25 E
Batamšinski 136 Fe 50.36N 58.17 E
Batan 150 Hb 20.30N 121.50 E
Batang [China] 152 Ge 30.02N 99.10 E
Batang [Indon.] 150 Eh 6.55S 109.42 E
Batanga 170 Ac 0.21S 9.18 E
Batangafo 168 Bd 7.18N 18.18 E
Batangas 142 Oh 13.45N 121.03 E
Batanghari 140 Mj 1.00S 104.20 E
Batanghari 150 Mj 1.00S 104.00 E
Batan Islands 140 Og 20.30N 121.50 E
Batanta, Pulau- 150 Jg 0.50S 130.40 E
Bátaszék 120 Oj 46.11N 18.44 E
Batatais 204 Ie 20.53S 47.37W
Batavia 184 Hd 43.00N 78.11W
Bat-Cengel 152 Hb 47.47N 101.58 E
Batchawana 184 Eb 46.58N 84.34W
Batchelor 212 Gb 13.04S 131.01 E
Bătdâmbâng 142 Mh 13.06N 103.12 E
Batecki 116 Nf 58.38N 30.31 E
Batéké, Plateaux- 170 Cc 3.30S 15.45 E
Batel, Esteros del- 204 Ci 28.30S 58.20W
Batemans Bay 212 Kg 35.43S 150.11 E
Batesburg 184 Gi 33.56N 81.33W
Batesville [Ar.-U.S.] 186 Ki 35.46N 91.39W
Batesville [Ms.-U.S.] 186 Li 34.18N 90.00W
Bath [Eng.-U.K.] 118 Kj 51.23N 2.22W
Bath [Me.-U.S.] 184 Md 43.55N 69.49W
Bath [N.B.-Can.] 184 Nb 46.32N 67.33W
Bath [St.C.N.] 197c Ab 17.08N 62.37W
Batha 168 Bc 14.00N 19.00 E
Bathinda 148 Fb 30.12N 74.57 E
Bá Thrá Lí/Tralee Bay 118 Di 52.15N 9.59W
Bathsheba 196 Gf 13.13N 59.31W
Bá Thuath Reanna/Liscannor Bay 118 Di 52.55N 9.25W
Bathurst 174 Ib 76.00N 100.30W
Bathurst [Austl.] 212 Jf 33.25S 149.35 E
Bathurst [N.B.-Can.] 176 Me 47.36N 65.39W
Bathurst, Cape- 174 Gb 70.35N 128.00W
Bathurst Inlet 176 Ic 66.50N 108.01W
Bathurst Inlet 174 Ic 68.10N 108.50W
Bathurst Island 208 Ef 11.35S 130.25 E
Bati 168 Gc 11.13N 40.01 E
Batié 166 Ed 9.53N 2.55W
Bāţin, Wādī al- 144 Gc 30.25N 47.35 E
Batman 144 Fb 37.52N 41.07 E
Batman 146 Id 37.45N 41.00 E
Batna 160 He 35.34N 6.11 E
Batna [3] 162 Ib 35.10N 6.00 E
Ba To 148 Lf 14.46N 108.44 E
Bato Bato 150 Ge 5.06N 119.50 E
Batoka 170 Ef 16.47S 27.15 E
Baton Rouge 176 Jf 30.23N 91.11W
Batopilas 192 Fd 27.01N 107.44W
Batouri 166 He 4.26N 14.22 E
Batovi 204 Fb 15.53S 53.24W
Batovi, Coxilha de- 204 Ej 30.33S 54.27W
Båtsfjord 114 Ga 70.38N 29.44 E
Bat-Sumber 152 Ib 48.25N 106.42 E
Batticaloa 148 Gg 7.43N 81.42 E
Batti Maly 148 Ig 8.50N 92.51 E
Battipaglia 128 Ij 40.37N 14.58 E
Battle 124 Cd 50.55N 0.30 E
Battle 180 Gf 52.42N 108.15W
Battle Creek 182 Jc 42.19N 85.11W
Battle Creek 188 Kb 48.36N 109.11W
Battle Harbour 176 Nd 52.17N 55.35W
Battle Mountain 182 Dc 40.38N 116.56W
Battonya 120 Rj 46.17N 21.01 E
Battowia Island 197n Bb 12.58N 61.09W
Batu 168 Fd 6.59N 39.37 E
Batu, Kepulauan- = Batu Islands (EN) 140 Lj 0.18S 98.28 E
Batuasa 150 Jg 3.32S 130.08 E
Batuata, Pulau- 150 Hh 6.12S 122.42 E
Batudaka, Pulau- 150 Hg 0.28S 121.48 E
Batui 150 Hg 1.17S 122.33 E
Batu Islands (EN) = Batu, Kepulauan- 140 Lj 0.18S 98.28 E
Batumi 112 Kg 41.38N 41.38 E
Batu Pahat 150 Df 1.51N 102.56 E
Baturaja 150 Dg 4.08S 104.10 E
Baturino 138 De 57.45N 85.12 E
Baturité 202 Kd 4.20S 38.53W
Batz, Ile de- 122 Bf 48.45N 4.01W
Bau 150 Ff 1.25N 110.09 E
Baubau 142 Oj 5.28S 122.38 E
Baucau 150 Ih 8.27S 126.27 E
Bauchi 160 Hg 10.19N 9.50 E
Bauchi [2] 166 Hc 10.40N 10.00 E
Bauchi Plateau 166 Gc 10.00N 9.30 E
Baud 122 Cg 47.52N 3.01W
Baudette 186 Ib 48.43N 94.36W
Baudo, Serrania de- 202 Cb 6.00N 77.05W
Baudour, Saint-Ghislain- 124 Fd 50.29N 3.49 E
Baugé 122 Fg 47.33N 0.06W
Bauges 122 Mi 45.38N 6.10 E
Baúl, Cerro- 192 Ii 17.38N 100.19W
Baula 150 Hg 4.09S 121.41 E
Bauld, Cape- 174 Nd 51.38N 55.25W
Baule-Escoublac, La- 122 Dg 47.17N 2.24W
Bauman Fiord 180 Ia 77.45N 86.00W
Baume-les-Dames 122 Mg 47.21N 6.22 E
Baunach 120 Gg 49.59N 10.51 E
Baunani 219a Ec 9.08S 160.51 E
Baunei 128 Dj 40.02N 9.40 E
Baures 202 Ff 13.35S 63.35W
Bauru 200 Lh 22.19S 49.04W
Baús 204 Fd 18.19S 53.10W
Baús, Serra dos- 204 Fd 18.20S 53.25W
Bauska 114 Fh 56.24N 24.13 E
Bautzen/Budyšin 120 Ke 51.11N 14.26 E
Baux-de-Provence, Les- 122 Kk 43.45N 4.48 E
Bavaria (EN) = Bayern [2] 120 Hg 49.00N 11.30 E
Bavaria (EN) = Bayern 110 Hf 49.00N 11.30 E
Bavarian Forest (EN) = Bayerischer Wald 120 Ig 49.00N 12.55 E
Bavay 124 Fd 50.18N 3.47 E
Båven 116 Ge 59.00N 16.55 E
Bavispe 192 Eb 30.24N 108.50W
Bavispe, Rio de- 192 Ec 29.15N 109.11W
Bavly 114 Mi 54.26N 53.18 E
Bawah, Pulau- 150 Ef 2.31N 106.03 E
Bawal, Pulau- 150 Fg 2.44S 110.06 E
Bawe 210 Ee 2.59S 134.43 E
Bawean, Pulau- 150 Fh 5.46S 112.40 E
Bawku 166 Ec 11.03N 0.15W
Baxian 152 Kd 39.03N 116.24 E
Baxoi 152 Ge 30.07N 96.56 E
Bay [3] 168 Ge 2.50N 43.30 E
Bay/Baicheng 152 Dc 41.46N 81.52 E
Bayamo 190 Id 20.23N 76.39W
Bayamón 194 Nd 18.24N 66.09W
Bayan 154 Ia 46.05N 127.24 E
Bayanbulak 152 Dc 43.05N 84.05 E
Bayanga 168 Be 2.53N 16.19 E
Bayan Gol 152 Gd 37.18N 96.50 E
Bayan Gol → Dengkou 142 Me 40.25N 106.59 E
Bayan Har Shan 140 Lf 34.20N 97.00 E
Bayan Har Shankou 152 Ge 34.06N 97.38 E
Bayan Hot → Alxa Zuoqi 152 Id 38.50N 105.32 E
Bayan Hure → Chen Barag Qi 152 Kb 49.21N 119.25 E
Bayan Huxu → Horqin Youyi Zhongqi 152 Lb 45.04N 121.27 E
Bayano, Lago de- 194 Hi 9.00N 78.30W
Bayan Obo 152 Ic 41.50N 109.58 E
Bayan Qagan 154 Ga 46.11N 123.59 E
Bayan Qagan → Qahar Youyi Houqi 154 Bd 41.28N 113.10 E
Bayan Ul Hot → Xi Ujimqin Qi 152 Kc 44.31N 117.33 E
Bayas 192 Gf 23.32N 104.50W
Bayat 146 Fb 40.39N 34.15 E
Bayauca 204 Bl 34.51S 61.18W
Bayawan 150 He 9.20N 123.00 E
Bayāz 146 Pg 30.42N 55.28 E
Bayāzeh 146 Pf 30.42N 55.28 E
Baybay 150 Hd 10.41N 124.48 E
Bayburt 144 Fa 40.16N 40.15 E
Bay City [Mi.-U.S.] 182 Kc 43.36N 83.53W
Bay City [Tx.-U.S.] 182 Hf 29.09N 95.39W
Bayerische Alpen 120 Hi 47.30N 11.30 E
Bayerischer Wald = Bavarian Forest (EN) 120 Ig 49.00N 12.55 E
Bayern = Bavaria (EN) [2] 120 Hg 49.00N 11.30 E
Bayern = Bavaria (EN) 110 Hf 49.00N 11.30 E
Bayes, Cap- 219b Be 20.57S 165.25 E
Bayeux 122 Fe 49.16N 0.42W
Bayfield 186 Kc 46.49N 90.49W
Bay Fiord 180 Ia 79.00N 84.00W
Baygorria 204 Dk 32.52S 56.44W
Baygorria, Lago Artificial de- 204 Dk 33.05S 57.00W
Bayḩān al Qişāb 164 Ig 14.48N 45.44 E
Bayındır 146 Bc 38.13N 27.40 E
Bayjı 146 Je 34.56N 43.29 E
Bay Minette 184 Dj 30.53N 87.47W
Baynūnah 146 Ok 23.50N 52.50 E
Bayombong 150 Hc 16.29N 121.09 E
Bayona / Baiona 126 Db 42.07N 8.51W
Bayonnaise Seamount (EN) 208 Jf 12.00S 179.30W
Bayonne 112 Fg 43.29N 1.29W
Bayou Bodcau Lake 186 Jj 32.58N 93.30W
Bayou D'Arbonne Lake 186 Jj 32.45N 92.27W
Bayramiç 130 Jj 39.48N 26.37 E
Bayreuth 120 Hg 49.57N 11.35 E
Bayrūt [3] 146 Ff 33.56N 35.30 E
Bayrūt = Beirut (EN) 142 Ff 33.53N 35.30 E
Bay Saint Louis 186 Lk 30.19N 89.20W
Bay Springs 186 Lk 31.59N 89.17W
Bayt al Faqīh 164 Fj 14.31N 43.17 E
Baytik Shan 152 Fb 45.15N 90.50 E
Bayt Laḩm = Bethlehem (EN) 146 Fg 31.43N 35.12 E
Baytown 182 Ff 29.44N 94.58W
Bayuda Desert (EN) = Bayyūḑah, Şaḩrā'- 158 Kg 18.00N 33.00 E
Bayunglencir 150 Dg 2.03S 103.41 E
Bayview 188 Gc 48.00N 116.30W
Bay View 218 Gc 39.26S 176.52 E
Bayy al Kabīr 164 Cc 31.11N 15.53 E

Bayyūḍah, Ṣaḥrā'- = Bayuda Desert (EN) 158 Kg 18.00N 33.00 E
Baza 126 Jg 37.29N 2.46W
Baza, Sierra de- 126 Jg 37.15N 2.45W
Bazardjuzju, gora- 110 Kg 41.13N 47.51 E
Bazaruto, Ilha do- 172 Fd 21.40S 35.25 E
Bazas 122 Fj 44.26N 0.13W
Bazhong 152 Ie 31.54N 106.42 E
Bazoches-sur-Vesle 124 Fe 49.19N 3.37 E
Baztan / Baztán 126 Ka 43.09N 1.31 E
Baztán / Baztan 126 Ka 43.09N 1.31 E
Beach 182 Gb 46.55N 103.52W
Beachy Head 118 Nk 50.44N 0.16 E
Beacon 184 Ke 41.31N 73.59W
Beaconsfield [Austl.] 212 Jh 41.12S 146.48 E
Beaconsfield [Eng.-U.K.] 124 Bc 51.36N 0.38W
Beagle, Canal- 206 Gh 54.53S 68.10W
Beagle Gulf 212 Gb 12.00S 130.20 E
Bealach an Doirin/Ballaghaderreen 118 Eh 53.55N 8.35W
Béalanana 172 Hb 14.33S 48.44 E
Béal an Átha/Ballina 118 Dg 54.07N 9.09W
Béal an Bheara/Gweebarra Bay 118 Eg 54.52N 8.20W
Béal Átha Fhirdhia/Ardee 118 Gh 53.52N 6.33W
Béal Átha hAmhnais/Ballyhaunis 118 Eh 53.46N 8.46W
Béal Átha na Muice/Swinford 118 Eh 53.57N 8.57W
Béal Átha na Sluaighe/Ballinasloe 118 Eh 53.20N 8.13W
Béal Átha Seanaidh/Ballyshannon 118 Eg 54.30N 8.11W
Beale, Cape- 188 Cb 48.44N 125.20W
Béal Easa/Foxford 118 Dh 53.59N 9.07W
Béal Feirste/Belfast 112 Fe 54.35N 5.55W
Beal Range 212 Ie 25.30S 141.30 E
Béal Tairbirt/Belturbet 118 Fg 54.06N 7.26W
Beanna Boirche/Mourne Mountains 118 Gg 54.10N 6.04W
Beannchar/Bangor 118 Hg 54.40N 5.40W
Beanntrai/Bantry 118 Dj 51.41N 9.27W
Bear Bay 180 Ia 75.45N 86.30W
Beardmore 186 Mb 49.36N 87.57W
Beardstown 186 Kg 39.59N 90.26W
Bear Island (EN) = Bjørnøya 110 Ha 74.30N 19.00 E
Bear Islands (EN) = Medvezi, ostrova- 140 Sb 70.52N 161.26 E
Bear Lake 182 Ec 42.00N 111.20W
Bear Lodge Mountains 186 Dd 44.35N 104.15W
Béarn 122 Fk 43.20N 0.45W
Bearpaw Mountains 188 Kb 48.15N 109.30W
Bear Peninsula 222 Of 74.36S 110.50W
Bear River 188 If 41.30N 112.08W
Bearskin Lake 180 If 53.57N 90.59W
Beās 148 Eb 31.10N 74.59 E
Beas de Segura 126 Jf 38.15N 2.53W
Beata, Cabo- 190 Je 17.36N 71.25W
Beata, Isla- 194 Le 17.35N 71.31W
Beata Ridge (EN) 190 Je 16.00N 72.30W
Beatrice 182 Hc 40.16N 96.44W
Beatrice, Cape- 212 Hb 14.15S 137.00 E
Beatton 180 Fe 56.06N 120.22W
Beatton River 180 Fe 56.10N 120.25W
Beatty 182 Dd 36.54N 116.46W
Beattyville 184 Ia 48.52N 77.10W
Beatys Butte 188 Fe 42.23N 119.20W
Beau-Bassin 172a Bb 20.13S 57.27 E
Beaucaire 122 Kk 43.48N 4.38 E
Beaucamps-le-Vieux 124 De 49.50N 1.47 E
Beaucanton 184 Ha 49.05N 79.15W
Beauce 122 Hf 48.22N 1.50 E
Beaudesert 212 Ke 27.59S 153.00 E
Beaufort [Mala.] 150 Ge 5.20N 115.45 E
Beaufort [S.C.-U.S.] 184 Gi 32.26N 80.40W
Beaufort/Befort 124 Ie 49.50N 6.18 E
Beaufort, Massif de- 122 Mi 45.50N 6.40 E
Beaufort Island 222 Kf 76.57S 166.56 E
Beaufort Sea 224 Ad 73.00N 140.00W
Beaufort West 160 Jl 32.20S 22.33 E
Beaugency 122 Hg 47.47N 1.38 E
Beaujolais, Monts du- 122 Kh 46.00N 4.22 E
Beauly 118 Id 57.29N 4.29W
Beaumesnil 124 Ce 49.01N 0.43 E
Beaumetz-lès-Loges 124 Ed 50.14N 2.39 E
Beaumont [Bel.] 124 Gd 50.14N 4.14 E
Beaumont [Fr.] 122 Gj 44.46N 0.46 E
Beaumont [Fr.] 122 Ee 49.40N 1.51W
Beaumont [Fr.] 124 Hf 48.51N 5.47 E
Beaumont [Ms.-U.S.] 186 Lk 31.11N 88.55W
Beaumont [N.Z.] 218 Cf 45.49S 169.32 E
Beaumont [Tx.-U.S.] 176 Jf 30.05N 94.06W
Beaumont-de-Lomagne 122 Gk 43.53N 0.59 E
Beaumont-en-Argonne 124 He 49.32N 5.03 E
Beaumont-le-Roger 124 Ce 49.05N 0.47 E
Beaumont-sur-Oise 124 Ee 49.08N 2.17 E
Beaumont-sur-Sarthe 122 Gf 48.13N 0.08 E
Beaune 122 Kg 47.02N 4.50 E
Beaupré 184 Lb 47.03N 70.53W
Beauraing 124 Gd 50.07N 4.48 E
Beaurepaire 122 Li 45.20N 5.03 E
Beausejour 180 Hf 50.04N 96.33W
Beautemps Beaupré 219b Ce 20.25S 166.08 E
Beauvais 122 Ie 49.26N 2.05 E
Beauval 124 Ed 50.06N 2.20 E
Beauvoir-sur-Mer 122 Dh 46.55N 2.03W
Beaver [Ak.-U.S.] 178 Jc 66.22N 147.24W
Beaver [Ok.-U.S.] 186 Fh 36.48N 100.30W
Beaver [Ut.-U.S.] 182 Ed 38.17N 112.38W
Beaver Creek [Co.-U.S.] 186 Ef 40.20N 103.33W
Beaver Creek [U.S.] 186 Gf 40.04N 99.20W
Beaver Creek [U.S.] 186 Ec 47.20N 103.39W
Beaver Creek [U.S.] 186 Ee 43.25N 103.59W
Beaver Dam 186 Le 43.28N 88.50W
Beaver Falls 184 Ge 40.45N 80.21W
Beaverhead Mountains 188 Id 45.00N 113.20W
Beaver Island 184 Ec 45.40N 85.31W
Beaver Lake 186 Jh 36.20N 93.55W
Beaver River [U.S.] 186 Gh 36.10N 98.45W
Beaver River [Ut.-U.S.] 188 Ig 39.10N 112.57W
Beaverton 188 Dd 45.29N 122.48W
Beāwar 148 Ec 26.06N 74.19 E
Bebedouro 206 Kb 20.56S 48.28W
Becan 192 Oh 18.37N 89.35W
Becanchén 192 Oh 19.50N 89.22W
Beccles 118 Oi 52.28N 1.34 E
Bečej 130 Dd 45.37N 20.03 E
Beceni 130 Jd 45.23N 26.47 E
Becerreá 126 Eb 42.51N 7.10W
Becerro, Cayos- 194 Ff 15.57N 83.17W
Béchar 160 Ge 31.37N 2.13W
Béchar [3] 162 Gd 30.00N 2.00W
Becharof Lake 178 He 58.00N 156.30W
Bechet 130 Gf 43.46N 23.57 E
Bechevin Bay 178 Ge 55.00N 163.27W
Bechyně 120 Kg 49.18N 14.28 E
Beckingen 124 Ie 49.24N 6.42 E
Beckley 182 Kd 37.46N 81.12W
Beckum 120 Ee 51.45N 8.02 E
Beckumer Berge 124 Kc 51.43N 8.10 E
Beclean 130 Hb 47.11N 24.11 E
Bédarieux 122 Jk 43.37N 3.09 E
Bedburg-Hau 124 Ic 51.46N 6.11 E
Bedele 168 Fd 8.27N 36.22 E
Bedesa 168 Gd 8.53N 40.46 E
Bedford 118 Mi 52.10N 0.50W
Bedford [Eng.-U.K.] 118 Mi 52.08N 0.29W
Bedford [In.-U.S.] 184 Df 38.52N 86.29W
Bedford [Pa.-U.S.] 184 He 40.00N 78.31W
Bedford [Va.-U.S.] 184 Hg 37.20N 79.31W
Bedford Level 118 Ni 52.30N 0.05 E
Bedford Point 197b Bb 12.13N 61.36W
Bedfordshire [3] 118 Mi 52.05N 0.20W
Bednja 128 Kd 46.18N 16.45 E
Bednodemjanovsk 132 Mc 53.55N 43.12 E
Bedourie 212 Hd 24.21S 139.28 E
Bedum 124 Ia 53.18N 6.39 E
Beech Grove 184 Df 39.43N 86.03W
Beecroft Head 212 Kg 35.01S 150.50 E
Beef Island 197a Db 18.27N 64.31W
Beelitz 120 Id 52.14N 12.58 E
Beemster 124 Gb 52.34N 4.56 E
Beerfelden 124 Ke 49.34N 8.59 E
Beernem 124 Fc 51.09N 3.20 E
Beerse 124 Gc 51.19N 4.52 E
Beersel 124 Gd 50.46N 4.18 E
Beersheba (EN) = Be'er Sheva' 144 Dc 31.14N 34.47 E
Be'er Sheva' = Beersheba (EN) 144 Dc 31.14N 34.47 E
Beerze 124 Hc 51.36N 5.19 E
Beeskow 120 Kd 52.10N 14.14 E
Beestekraal 172 De 25.23S 27.38 E
Beeston 118 Li 52.56N 1.12W
Beethoven Peninsula 222 Qf 71.40S 73.45W
Beetsterzwaag, Opsterland- 124 Ia 53.03N 6.04 E
Beeville 182 Hf 28.24N 97.45W
Befale 170 Db 0.28N 20.58 E
Befandriana Avaratra 172 Hc 15.15S 48.32 E
Befandriana Nord 172 Hc 15.15S 48.32 E
Befandriana Sud 172 Gd 22.06S 43.54 E
Befori 170 Db 0.06N 22.17 E
Befort/Beaufort 124 Ie 49.50N 6.18 E
Bega 210 Fh 36.40S 149.50 E
Bega 130 Dd 45.13N 20.19 E
Bégard 122 Cf 48.38N 3.18W
Begejski kanal 130 Dd 45.27N 20.27 E
Beggars Point 197d Bb 17.10N 61.48W
Bègles 122 Fj 44.48N 0.32W
Begna 114 Bf 60.35N 10.00 E
Begoml 116 Mj 54.46N 28.14 E
Begunicy 116 Me 59.31N 29.30 E
Behābād 146 Pg 31.52N 55.57 E
Behbehān 144 Hc 30.35N 50.14 E
Behring Point 194 Ia 24.27N 77.43W
Behshahr 144 Hb 36.43N 53.34 E
Bei'an 142 Oe 48.16N 126.29 E
Beibu Wan = Tonkin, Gulf of- (EN) 140 Mh 20.00N 108.00 E
Beida He 152 Gc 40.18N 99.01 E
Beihai 142 Mg 21.31N 109.07 E
Bei Hulsan Hu 152 Gd 36.55N 95.55 E
Bei Jiang 152 Jg 23.02N 112.58 E
Beijing = Peking (EN) 142 Nf 39.55N 116.23 E
Beijing Shi (Pei-ching Shih) [4] 152 Kc 40.15N 116.30 E
Beila 162 Df 18.10N 15.53W
Beilen 124 Ib 52.52N 6.32 E
Beilerstroom 124 Ib 52.41N 6.12 E
Beiliutang He 154 Eg 34.12N 119.33 E
Beilstein 124 Jd 50.07N 7.15 E
Beilu He 152 Fe 34.34N 94.00 E
Beinamar 168 Bd 8.40N 15.23 E
Beine-Nauroy 124 Ge 49.15N 4.13 E
Beipiao 152 Lc 41.49N 120.45 E
Beira 160 Kj 19.50S 34.52 E
Beira Alta 126 Ed 40.40N 7.35W
Beira Baixa 126 Ee 39.55N 7.30W
Beira Litoral 126 Dd 40.15N 8.25W
Beiru He 154 Bh 33.40N 113.35 E
Beirut (EN) = Bayrūt 142 Ff 33.53N 35.30 E
Bei Shan 140 Le 41.30N 96.00 E
Beitstad 114 Cd 64.05N 11.22 E
Beiuş 130 Fc 46.40N 22.21 E
Beiwei Tan 152 Kg 21.10N 116.10 E
Beizhen [China] 152 Kd 37.24N 117.59 E
Beizhen [China] 154 Fd 41.36N 121.47 E
Beja 126 Ef 38.01N 7.52W
Beja [2] 126 Eg 37.58N 7.50W
Bejaïa 160 He 36.45N 5.05 E
Bejaïa [3] 162 Ib 36.40N 5.10 E
Bejaïa, Golfe de- 126 Rh 36.45N 5.20 E
Béjar 126 Gd 40.23N 5.46W
Beji 148 Dc 29.47N 67.58 E
Bejneu 136 Ff 45.15N 55.05 E
Bejsug 132 Kf 46.02N 38.35 E
Bejsugski liman 132 Kf 46.05N 38.25 E
Bekabad 136 Gg 40.13N 69.14 E
Bekasi 150 Eh 6.14S 106.59 E
Bekdaš 136 Fg 41.31N 52.40 E
Békés 120 Rj 46.46N 21.08 E
Békés [2] 120 Qj 46.45N 21.00 E
Békéscsaba 120 Rj 46.41N 21.06 E
Bekilli 130 Mk 38.14N 29.26 E
Bekily 172 Hd 24.12S 45.18 E
Bekkai 156a Db 43.25N 145.07 E
Bekoji 168 Fd 7.32N 39.15 E
Bekopaka 172 Gc 19.08S 44.45 E
Bekovo 132 Mc 52.29N 43.45 E
Bela [India] 148 Gc 25.56N 81.59 E
Bela [Pak.] 146 Dc 26.14N 66.19 E
Bélabo 166 He 4.52N 13.10 E
Bela Crkva 130 Ee 44.54N 21.26 E
Bela Dila 148 Ge 18.40N 80.55 E
Bela Floresta 204 Ge 20.36S 51.16W
Belaga 150 Ff 2.42N 113.47 E
Belaja [Russia] 110 Ld 56.00N 54.32 E
Belaja [Russia] 132 Kg 45.03N 39.25 E
Belaja [Russia] 138 Mc 65.30N 173.15 E
Belaja Cerkov 112 Jf 49.49N 30.07 E
Belaja Gora 138 Jc 68.30N 146.15 E
Belaja Holunica 136 Fd 58.53N 50.50 E
Belaja Kalitva 136 Ef 48.09N 40.49 E
Bela Krajina 128 Je 45.35N 15.15 E
Bela Lorena 204 Ib 15.13S 46.01W
Belang 150 Hf 0.57N 124.47 E
Bela Palanka 130 Ff 43.13N 22.19 E
Belarbi 126 Li 35.09N 0.27W
Belarus (EN) = Byelarus' 136 Ce 53.50N 28.00 E
Belasica 130 Fh 41.21N 22.50 E
Belau → Palau (EN) 210 Ed 7.30N 134.30 E
Bela Vista [Braz.] 204 Dc 17.37S 57.01W
Bela Vista [Braz.] 202 Gh 22.06S 56.31W
Bela Vista [Moz.] 172 Ee 26.20S 32.40 E
Belawan 150 Cf 3.47N 98.41 E
Běla Woda/Weißwasser 120 Ke 51.31N 14.38 E
Belayan 150 Gg 0.14S 116.36 E
Bel'c' 136 Cf 47.46N 27.55 E
Belchatow 120 Pe 51.22N 19.21 E
Belcher Channel 180 Ia 77.20N 94.30W
Belcher Islands 174 Ld 56.20N 79.30W
Belchite 126 Lc 41.18N 0.45W
Belczyna 120 Ne 51.25N 17.50 E
Belebej 136 Fe 54.10N 54.07 E
Belecke, Warstein- 124 Kc 51.29N 8.20 E
Beled 128 Ni 47.28N 17.06 E
Beled Wēyne 160 Lh 4.47N 45.12 E
Bélel 166 Hd 7.03N 14.26 E
Belém [Braz.] 200 Lf 1.27S 48.29W
Belem [Mex.] 192 Dd 27.45N 110.28W
Belém [Moz.] 172 Fb 14.08S 35.58 E
Belém de São Francisco 202 Ke 8.46S 38.58W
Belen 182 Fe 34.40N 106.46W
Belén [Arg.] 206 Gc 27.39S 67.02W
Belén [Nic.] 194 Eh 11.30N 85.53W
Belén [Par.] 204 Df 23.30S 57.06W
Belén [Ur.] 204 Dj 30.47S 57.47W
Belén, Cuchilla de- 204 Dj 30.55S 56.30W
Belén de Escobar 204 Cl 34.21S 58.47W
Belene 130 If 43.39N 25.07 E
Bélep, Iles- 208 Hf 19.45S 163.40 E
Beles 168 Fc 10.55N 35.10 E
Belev 132 Jc 53.50N 36.10 E
Beleye 168 Fc 11.24N 36.10 E
Belfast [Me.-U.S.] 184 Mc 44.27N 69.01W
Belfast [S.Afr.] 172 Ee 25.43S 30.03 E
Belfast/Béal Feirste 112 Fe 54.35N 5.55W
Belfast Lough/Loch Lao 118 Hg 54.40N 5.50W
Belfield 186 Ec 46.53N 103.12W
Belford 118 Lf 55.36N 1.49W
Belfort 122 Mg 47.45N 7.00 E
Belgaum 142 Jh 15.52N 74.30 E
Belgica Bank (EN) 224 Ld 78.28N 15.00W
Belgicafjella 222 Df 72.35S 31.10 E
België/Belgique = Belgium (EN) [1] 112 Ge 50.30N 4.30 E
Belgique/België = Belgium (EN) [1] 112 Ge 50.30N 4.30 E
Belgium (EN) = België/Belgique [1] 112 Ge 50.30N 4.30 E
Belgium (EN) = Belgique/België [1] 112 Ge 50.30N 4.30 E
Belgorod 112 Je 50.36N 36.35 E
Belgorod-Dnestrovski 136 Df 46.12N 30.17 E
Belgorodskaja oblast [3] 136 De 50.45N 37.30 E
Belgrade (EN) = Beograd 112 Ig 44.50N 20.30 E
Bel Hairane 162 Ic 31.17N 6.20 E
Beli 166 Hd 7.52N 10.58 E
Belice 128 Gm 37.35N 12.52 E
Beli Drim 130 Dg 42.05N 20.20 E
Belidži 132 Pi 41.53N 48.20 E
Beli Lom 130 If 43.41N 26.00 E
Beli Manastir 128 Me 45.46N 18.37 E
Belimbegovo 130 Eh 42.00N 21.35 E
Belin-Béliet 122 Fj 44.30N 0.47W
Belinga 170 Bb 1.04N 13.12 E
Belinski 132 Mc 52.58N 43.29 E
Belinyu 150 Eg 1.38S 105.46 E
Beliş 130 Gc 46.39N 23.02 E
Beli Timok 130 Ff 43.55N 22.18 E
Belitung, Pulau- 140 Mj 2.50S 107.55 E
Belize [3] 194 Ce 17.35N 88.35W
Belize (British Honduras) [1] 176 Kh 17.15N 88.45W
Belize City 176 Kh 17.30N 88.12W
Belize River 194 Ce 17.32N 88.14W
Beljajevka 132 Gf 46.29N 30.14 E
Beljanica 130 Ee 44.07N 21.43 E
Belka 116 Mg 57.40N 29.47 E
Belkovski, ostrov- 138 Ia 75.30N 136.00 E
Bellac 122 Hh 46.07N 1.03 E
Bella Coola 180 Ef 52.22N 126.46W
Bellagio 128 De 45.59N 9.15 E
Bellaire [Oh.-U.S.] 184 Ge 40.02N 80.46W
Bellaire [Tx.-U.S.] 186 Il 29.43N 95.28W
Bellaria-Igea Marina 128 Gf 44.09N 12.28 E
Bellary 142 Jh 15.09N 76.56 E
Bella Unión 204 Dj 30.15S 57.35W
Bella Vista [Arg.] 206 Ic 28.30S 59.03W
Bella Vista [Par.] 204 Df 22.08S 56.31W
Bellavista, Capo- 128 Dk 39.56N 9.43 E
Bell Bay 180 Jb 71.10N 84.55W
Belle-Anse 194 Kd 18.14N 72.04W
Belledonne 122 Mi 45.18N 6.08 E
Bellefontaine [Mart.] 197h Ab 14.40N 61.10W
Bellefontaine [Oh.-U.S.] 184 Fe 40.22N 83.45W
Belle Fourche 182 Gc 44.40N 103.51W
Belle Fourche River 186 Ed 44.26N 102.19W
Bellegarde 122 Ig 47.59N 2.26 E
Bellegarde-sur-Valserine 122 Lh 46.06N 5.49 E
Belle Glade 184 Gl 26.41N 80.40W
Belle Ile 110 Ff 47.19N 3.11W
Belle Isle 180 Lf 51.55N 55.20W
Belle Isle, Strait of- 174 Nd 51.35N 56.30W
Bellencombre 124 De 49.42N 1.14 E
Belleplaine 197q Ab 13.15N 59.34W
Belleville [Fr.] 122 Kh 46.06N 4.45 E
Belleville [Il.-U.S.] 186 Lg 38.31N 90.00W
Belleville [Ks.-U.S.] 186 Hg 39.49N 97.38W
Belleville [Ont.-Can.] 180 Jh 44.10N 77.23W
Bellevue [Nb.-U.S.] 186 If 41.09N 95.54W
Bellevue [Wa.-U.S.] 188 Dc 47.37N 122.12W
Belley 122 Li 45.46N 5.41 E
Bellheim 124 Ke 49.12N 8.17 E
Bellingham [Eng.-U.K.] 118 Kf 55.09N 2.16W
Bellingham [Wa.-U.S.] 176 Ge 48.46N 122.29W
Bellingsfors 116 Ef 58.59N 12.15 E
Bellingshausen 222 Re 62.12S 58.56W
Bellingshausen Ice Shelf 222 Ce 71.00S 89.00W
Bellingshausen Sea (EN) 222 Pf 71.00S 85.00W
Bellinzona 128 Dd 46.11N 9.02 E
Bello 202 Cb 6.19N 75.34W
Bellocq 204 Bl 35.55S 61.32W
Bellona, Récifs- 208 Gg 21.00S 159.00 E
Bellona Island 214 Fj 11.17S 159.47 E
Bellot Strait 180 Ib 72.00N 94.30W
Bellow Falls 184 Kd 43.08N 72.28W
Bell Peninsula 180 Jd 63.45N 81.30W
Bell River 180 Jg 49.49N 77.39W
Bell Rock → Inchcape 118 Ke 56.26N 2.24W
Bellsund 179 Nc 77.39N 14.15 E
Belluno 128 Gd 46.09N 12.13 E
Bellville 172 Bf 33.53S 18.36 E
Bell Ville 206 Hd 32.37S 62.42W
Belmond 186 Je 42.51N 93.37W
Belmont 184 Hd 42.14N 78.02W
Belmonte [Braz.] 202 Kg 15.51S 38.54W
Belmonte [Port.] 126 Ed 40.21N 7.21W
Belmonte [Sp.] 126 Je 39.34N 2.42W
Belmopan 176 Kh 17.15N 88.46W
Belo 172 Gd 20.44S 44.00 E
Beloeil 124 Fd 50.35N 3.43 E
Belogorsk [Russia] 142 Od 50.57N 128.25 E
Belogorsk [Russia] 138 De 55.02N 88.28 E
Belogorsk [Ukr.] 132 Ig 45.03N 34.33 E
Belogradčik 130 Ff 43.38N 22.41 E
Belogradčiški prohod 130 Ff 43.38N 22.28 E
Belo Horizonte 200 Lg 19.55S 43.56W
Beloit [Ks.-U.S.] 186 Gg 39.28N 98.06W
Beloit [Wi.-U.S.] 182 Jc 42.31N 89.02W
Belojarovo 138 Hf 51.35N 128.55 E
Belojarski 136 Gc 63.40N 66.45 E
Beloje more = White Sea (EN) 110 Kb 66.00N 44.00 E
Beloje ozero = White Lake (EN) 110 Jc 60.11N 37.35 E
Belokany 132 Oi 41.43N 46.28 E
Belomorsk 112 Jc 64.29N 34.43 E
Belomorsko-Baltijski kanal = White Sea-Baltic Canal (EN) 110 Jc 63.30N 34.48 E
Belomorsko-Kulojskoje plato 114 Jd 65.20N 41.50 E
Beloozersk 132 Dc 52.28N 25.13 E
Belopolje 136 De 51.09N 34.18 E
Belorečensk 132 Kg 44.43N 39.52 E
Beloreck 136 Fe 53.58N 58.24 E
Belorusskaja grjada 132 Ec 53.50N 27.00 E
Belorusskaja Sovetskaja Socialističeskaja Respublika → Belarus 136 Ce 53.50N 28.00 E
Belorusskaja SSR/Belaruskaja Sovetskaja Socialistyčnaja Respublika → Belarus 136 Ce 53.50N 28.00 E
Belorusskaja SSR → Belarus 136 Ce 53.50N 28.00 E
Belo-sur-Mer 172 Gd 20.44S 44.00 E
Belo-sur-Tsiribihina 172 Gc 19.39S 44.32 E
Belot, Lac- 180 Ec 66.50N 126.20W
Belo-Tsiribihina 172 Gc 19.39S 44.32 E
Beloveżskaja Pušča, zapovednik- 120 Ud 52.45N 24.15 E
Belovo 138 Df 54.25N 86.18 E
Belovodsk 132 Ke 49.10N 39.33 E
Belovodskoe 135 Jc 42.47N 74.13 E
Belozersk 136 Dd 60.03N 37.48 E
Belper 124 Aa 53.02N 1.28W
Belted Range 188 Gh 37.25N 116.10W
Belton [Mo.-U.S.] 186 Ig 38.49N 94.32W
Belton [Tx.-U.S.] 186 Hk 31.04N 97.28W
Belton Lake 186 Hk 31.08N 97.32W
Belturbet/Béal Tairbirt 118 Fg 54.06N 7.26W
Beluha, gora- 138 Df 49.48N 86.35 E
Belvedere Marittimo 128 Jk 39.37N 15.52 E
Belvidere 186 Le 42.15N 88.50W
Bely 114 Hi 55.50N 32.58 E
Bely, Island (EN) = Bely, ostrov- 140 Jb 73.10N 70.45 E
Bely, ostrov- = Bely, Island (EN) 140 Jb 73.10N 70.45 E
Belyando River 212 Jd 21.38S 146.50 E
Bely Čeremoš 130 Ia 48.06N 25.04 E
Bely Jar 138 De 58.26N 85.03 E
Belyje Berega 132 Ic 53.12N 34.42 E
Belz 132 Dd 50.23N 24.03 E
Bełżec 120 Tf 50.24N 23.26 E
Belzoni 186 Kj 33.11N 90.29W
Bełżyce 120 Se 51.11N 22.18 E
Bemaraha, Plateau de- 158 Lj 19.00S 45.15 E
Bembe 170 Bd 7.02S 14.18 E
Bembéréké 166 Fc 10.13N 2.40 E
Bembézar 126 Gg 37.45N 5.13W
Bembridge 124 Ad 50.41N 1.05W
Bemidji 182 Ib 47.29N 94.53W
Ben 146 Nf 32.32N 50.45 E
Benāb 144 Gb 37.18N 46.05 E
Benabarre / Benavarri 126 Mb 42.07N 0.29 E
Benaco → Garda, Lago di- 110 Hf 45.35N 10.35 E
Bena Dibele 170 Dc 4.07S 22.50 E
Benaize 122 Hh 46.34N 1.04 E
Benalla 212 Jg 36.33S 145.59 E
Benares → Vārānasi 142 Kg 25.20N 83.00 E
Benasc/Benasque 126 Mb 42.36N 0.32 E
Benasque/Benasc 126 Mb 42.36N 0.32 E
Benavarri / Benabarre 126 Mb 42.07N 0.29 E
Benavente 126 Gc 42.00N 5.41W
Benbecula 118 Fd 57.27N 7.20W
Bencheng → Luannan 154 Ee 39.30N 118.42 E
Ben-Chicao, Col de- 126 Oh 36.12N 2.51 E
Bend 182 Cc 44.03N 121.19W
Bendaja 166 Cd 7.10N 11.15W
Bendel [2] 166 Gd 6.00N 5.50 E
Bendela 170 Cc 3.18S 17.36 E
Bender Bäyla 160 Mh 9.30N 50.30 E
Bendersiyada 168 Hc 11.14N 48.57 E
Bendery 136 Cf 46.48N 29.22 E
Bendigo 210 Fh 36.46S 144.17 E
Bendorf 124 Jd 50.26N 7.34 E
Bēne/Bene 116 Jh 56.28N 23.01 E
Bene/Bēne 116 Jh 56.28N 23.01 E
Bénéna 166 Ec 13.06N 4.22W
Benepú, Rada- 221d Ac 27.10S 109.25W
Benešov 120 Kg 49.47N 14.40 E
Benevento 128 Ii 41.08N 14.45 E
Bengal 140 Kg 24.00N 90.00 E
Bengal, Bay of- (EN) 140 Kh 15.00N 90.00 E
Bengamisa 170 Eb 0.57N 25.10 E
Bengbis 166 He 3.27N 12.27 E
Bengbu 142 Nf 32.47N 117.23 E
Benghazi (EN) = Banghāzī 160 Je 32.07N 20.04 E
Benghazi (EN) = Banghāzī [3] 164 Dd 27.00N 20.30 E
Beng He 154 Eg 35.04N 118.22 E
Benghisa Point 128 Io 35.50N 14.35 E
Bengkalis 150 Df 1.28N 102.08 E
Bengkulu 142 Mj 3.48S 102.16 E
Bengkulu [3] 150 Dg 3.48S 102.16 E
Bengo [3] 170 Bd 8.30S 13.40 E
Bengo, Baia do- 158 Ii 8.43S 13.21 E
Bengough 188 Mb 49.24N 105.08W
Bengtsfors 114 Cg 59.02N 12.13 E
Benguela 160 Ij 12.35S 13.26 E
Benguela [3] 170 Be 12.00S 15.00 E
Benguerir 162 Fc 32.14N 7.57W
Benguérua, Ilha- 172 Fd 21.53S 35.26 E
Bengue Viejo 194 Ce 17.05N 89.08W
Bengut, Cap- 162 Hb 36.55N 3.54 E
Beni 160 Jh 0.30N 29.28 E
Beni [3] 202 Ef 14.00S 65.30W
Beni, Rio- 196 Jg 10.23S 65.24W
Beni Abbes 162 Gc 30.08N 2.10W
Beni Baufrah 126 Hi 35.05N 4.18W
Benicarló 126 Md 40.25N 0.26 E
Benicasim / Benicàssim 126 Md 40.03N 0.04 E
Benicàssim / Benicasim 126 Md 40.03N 0.04 E
Beni Chougran, Monts des- 126 Mi 35.30N 0.15 E
Benidorm 126 Lf 38.32N 0.08W
Beni Enzar 126 Ji 35.14N 2.57W
Beni Haoua 126 Nh 36.32N 1.34 E
Beni Mellal 160 Ge 32.20N 6.21W
Beni Mellal [3] 162 Fc 32.30N 6.30W
Benin 166 Gd 5.45N 5.04 E
Bénin (Dahomey) [1] 160 Hh 9.30N 2.15 E
Benin, Bight of- 158 Hh 5.30N 4.00 E
Benin City 160 Hh 6.20N 5.38 E
Beni Ounif 162 Gc 32.03N 1.15W
Benisa / Benissa 126 Mf 38.43N 0.03 E
Beni Saf 126 Ki 35.19N 1.23W
Benisheikh 166 Hc 11.48N 12.29 E
Benissa / Benisa 126 Mf 38.43N 0.03 E
Benito Juárez 192 Mi 17.50N 92.32W
Benito Juárez, Presa- 192 Li 16.27N 95.30W
Benjamen Island 172b Bb 5.27S 53.21 E
Benjamin 186 Gj 33.35N 99.48W
Benjamin Aceval 204 Dg 24.58S 57.34W
Benjamin Constant 200 If 4.22S 70.02W
Benjamin Hill 192 Db 30.10N 111.10W
Benkei-Misaki 156a Bb 42.50N 140.11 E
Benkelman 186 Ff 40.03N 101.32W
Benkovac 128 Jf 44.02N 15.37 E
Ben Mehidi 128 Bn 36.46N 7.54 E
Bennett, Lake- 212 Gd 23.50S 131.00 E
Bennetta, ostrov- 138 Ja 76.45N 149.00 E
Benneydale 218 Fc 38.31S 175.21 E
Bennichab 162 Df 19.26N 15.21W
Bennington 184 Kd 42.53N 73.12W
Benom 150 Df 3.50N 102.06 E
Benoni 160 Jk 26.19S 28.27 E
Bénoué = Benue (EN) 158 Hh 7.48N 6.46 E
Benoy 168 Bd 8.59N 16.19 E
Benrath 124 Ic 51.10N 6.52 E
Bensekrane 126 Ki 35.04N 1.13W
Bensheim 120 Eg 49.41N 8.37 E
Ben Slimane 162 Fc 33.37N 7.07W
Benson [Az.-U.S.] 188 Jk 31.58N 110.18W

Index Symbols

[1] Independent Nation
[2] State, Region
[3] District, County
[4] Municipality
[5] Colony, Dependency
Continent
Physical Region
Historical or Cultural Region
Mount, Mountain
Volcano
Hill
Mountains, Mountain Range
Hills, Escarpment
Plateau, Upland
Pass, Gap
Plain, Lowland
Delta
Salt Flat
Valley, Canyon
Crater, Cave
Karst Features
Depression
Polder
Desert, Dunes
Forest, Woods
Heath, Steppe
Oasis
Cape, Point
Coast, Beach
Cliff
Peninsula
Isthmus
Sandbank
Island
Atoll
Rock, Reef
Islands, Archipelago
Rocks, Reefs
Coral Reef
Well, Spring
Geyser
River, Stream
Waterfall, Rapids
River Mouth, Estuary
Lake
Salt Lake
Intermittent Lake
Reservoir
Swamp, Pond
Canal
Glacier
Ice Shelf, Pack Ice
Ocean
Sea
Gulf, Bay
Strait, Fjord
Lagoon
Bank
Seamount
Tablemount
Ridge
Shelf
Basin
Escarpment, Sea Scarp
Fracture
Trench, Abyss
National Park, Reserve
Point of Interest
Recreation Site
Cave, Cavern
Historic Site
Ruins
Wall, Walls
Church, Abbey
Temple
Scientific Station
Railway station
Airport
Port
Military installation
Lighthouse
Mine
Tunnel
Dam, Bridge

Benson [Mn.-U.S.] 186 Id 45.19N 95.36W
Benson Point 220g Ab 1.56N 157.30W
Bent 144 Id 26.17N 59.31 E
Benteng [Indon.] 150 Hg 0.24S 121.59 E
Benteng [Indon.] 150 Hh 6.08N 120.27 E
Bentheim 120 Dd 52.19N 7.10 E
Bentiaba 170 Be 14.15S 12.24 E
Bentiaba 170 Be 14.29S 12.50 E
Bentinck 148 Jf 11.45N 98.03 E
Bentinck Island 212 Hc 17.05S 139.30 E
Bentiu 168 Dd 9.14N 29.50 E
Bento Gonçalves 206 Jc 29.10S 51.31W
Bento Gomes, Rio- 204 Dc 16.40S 57.12W
Benton [Ar.-U.S.] 186 Ji 34.34N 92.35W
Benton [Il.-U.S.] 186 Lg 38.01N 88.55W
Bentong 150 Df 3.32N 101.55 E
Benton Harbor 184 Dd 42.07N 86.27W
Bentonville 186 Ih 36.22N 94.13W
Ben Tre 148 Lf 10.14N 106.23 E
Benue 166 Gd 7.15N 8.20 E
Benue 158 Hh 7.48N 6.46 E
Benue (EN)=Bénoué 158 Hh 7.48N 6.46 E
Benwee Head/An Bhinn Bhui 118 Dg 54.21N 9.48W
Benxi 142 Oe 41.16N 123.48 E
Bény-Bocage, Le- 124 Bf 48.56N 0.50W
Beo 150 If 4.15N 126.48 E
Beograd = Belgrade (EN) 112 Ig 44.50N 20.30 E
Beograd-Krnjača 130 De 44.52N 20.28 E
Beograd-Zemun 130 De 44.53N 20.25 E
Béoumi 166 Dd 7.40N 5.34W
Beppu 152 Ne 33.17N 131.30 E
Beppu-Wan 156 Be 33.20N 131.35 E
Bequia Head 197n Ba 13.03N 61.14W
Bequia Island 196 Ff 13.01N 61.13W
Berabevú 204 Bk 33.20S 61.52W
Beraketa 172 Hd 24.11S 45.42 E
Berati 130 Ci 40.42N 19.57 E
Beratus, Gunung- 150 Gg 1.02S 116.20 E
Berau, Teluk-=McCluer Gulf (EN) 150 Jg 2.30S 132.30 E
Berberä 160 Lg 10.25N 45.02 E
Berbérati 160 Ih 4.16N 15.47 E
Berberia, Cabo- / Barbaria, Cap de- 126 Nf 38.38N 1.23 E
Berbice River 202 Gb 6.17N 57.32W
Berca 132 Jd 45.17N 26.41 E
Berchères-sur-Vesgre 124 Df 48.51N 1.33 E
Berchtesgaden 120 Ii 47.38N 13.00 E
Berck 122 Hd 50.24N 1.36 E
Berck-Berck-Plage 124 Dd 50.24N 1.34 E
Berda 132 Jf 46.47N 36.52 E
Berdâle 168 Hd 7.04N 47.51 E
Berdičev 136 Cf 49.53N 28.36 E
Berdigestjah 138 Hd 62.03N 126.50 E
Berdjansk 136 Df 46.43N 36.48 E
Berdsk 138 Df 54.47N 83.05 E
Beregomet 130 Ia 48.10N 25.24 E
Beregovo 136 Cf 48.13N 22.41 E
Bereku 170 Gc 4.27S 35.44 E
Berekua 196 Fe 15.14N 61.19W
Berekum 166 Ed 7.27N 2.35W
Berens 180 Hf 52.21N 97.01W
Berens River 180 Hf 52.22N 97.02W
Beresford 186 He 43.05N 96.47W
Berestečko 120 Vf 50.16N 25.14 E
Berești 130 Kc 46.06N 27.53 E
Berettyó 130 Ec 46.59N 21.07 E
Berettyóújfalu 120 Ri 47.13N 21.33 E
Bereza 136 Ce 52.33N 24.58 E
Berezan 132 Gd 50.19N 31.31 E
Berežany 136 De 49.29N 25.00 E
Berezina [Bela.] 132 Dc 53.48N 25.59 E
Berezina [Eur.] 110 Je 52.33N 30.14 E
Berezino [Bela.] 132 Fc 53.51N 29.00 E
Berezino [Bela.] 116 Mj 54.55N 28.16 E
Berezino [Ukr.] 130 Mc 46.16N 29.11 E
Bereznegovatoje 132 Hf 47.20N 32.49 E
Bereznik 136 Ec 62.53N 42.42 E
Berezniki 112 Ld 59.24N 56.46 E
Berezno 132 Ed 51.01N 26.45 E
Berezovka [Bela.] 120 Vc 53.40N 25.37 E
Berezovka [Russia] 134 Hd 64.59N 56.29 E
Berezovka [Ukr.] 136 Df 47.12N 30.56 E
Berezovka Višerka 134 Hf 60.55N 56.50 E
Berezovo 136 Gc 63.58N 65.00 E
Berezovski [Russia] 138 De 55.39N 86.16 E
Berezovski [Russia] 134 Jh 56.55N 60.50 E
Berezovy 138 If 51.41N 135.52 E
Berga [Sp.] 126 Nb 42.06N 1.51 E
Berga [Swe.] 116 Gg 57.13N 16.02 E
Bergama 144 Cb 39.07N 27.10 E
Bergamo 128 De 45.41N 9.43 E
Bergantiños 126 Da 43.20N 8.45W
Bergara / Vergara 126 Ja 43.07N 2.25W
Bergby 114 Df 60.56N 17.02 E
Bergen [Ger.] 120 Jb 54.25N 13.26 E
Bergen [Neth.] 124 Gb 52.40N 4.42 E
Bergen [Nor.] 112 Gc 60.23N 5.20 E
Bergen/Mons 122 Jd 50.27N 3.56 E
Bergen aan Zee, Bergen- 124 Gb 52.40N 4.38 E
Bergen-Bergen aan Zee 124 Gb 52.40N 4.38 E
Bergen op Zoom 124 Kc 51.30N 4.17 E
Bergerac 122 Gj 44.51N 0.29 E
Bergeyk 124 Hc 51.19N 5.22 E
Bergh 124 Ic 51.53N 6.16 E
Bergheim 120 Cf 50.58N 6.39 E
Bergh- 's Heerenberg 124 Ic 51.53N 6.16 E
Bergisches Land 120 De 51.15N 7.10 E
Bergisch Gladbach 120 Df 50.59N 7.08 E
Bergkvara 116 Gh 56.23N 16.05 E
Bergneustadt 124 Jc 51.02N 7.39 E
Bergö 116 Ib 62.55N 21.10 E
Bergsjö 114 Df 61.59N 17.04 E
Bergslagen 116 Fd 60.05N 14.30 E
Bergstraße 124 Ke 49.40N 8.40 E
Bergues 124 Ed 50.58N 2.26 E
Bergum, Tietjerksteradeel- 124 Ha 53.12N 6.00 E
Bergviken 116 Gc 61.10N 16.45 E
Bergville 172 De 28.52S 29.18 E
Berh 152 Jb 47.45N 111.07 E
Berhala, Selat- 150 Dg 0.48S 104.25 E
Berici, Monti- 128 Fe 45.26N 11.31 E
Berīkān 146 Nh 28.17N 51.14 E
Berikulski 138 De 55.32N 88.08 E
Beringa, ostrov- = Bering Island (EN) 138 Lf 55.00N 166.10 E
Beringen 124 Hc 51.03N 5.13 E
Bering Glacier 178 Kd 60.15N 143.30W
Bering Island (EN) = Beringa, ostrov- 138 Lf 55.00N 166.10 E
Beringovo more = Bering Sea (EN) 174 Bd 60.00N 175.00W
Beringovski 142 Tc 63.07N 179.19 E
Bering proliv = Bering Strait (EN) 174 Cc 65.30N 169.00W
Bering Sea 174 Bd 60.00N 175.00W
Bering Sea (EN) = Beringovo more 174 Bd 60.00N 175.00W
Bering Strait 174 Cc 65.30N 169.00W
Bering Strait (EN) = Bering proliv 174 Cc 65.30N 169.00W
Berislav 132 Hf 46.51N 33.29 E
Berisso 204 Dl 34.52S 57.53W
Berit Dağı 146 Gc 38.01N 36.52 E
Berīzak 146 Qi 26.06N 57.15 E
Berja 126 Jh 36.51N 2.57W
Berkåk 114 Be 62.50N 10.00 E
Berkane 162 Gc 34.56N 2.20W
Berkel 120 Cd 52.09N 6.12 E
Berkeley 182 Cd 37.57N 122.18W
Berkhamsted 124 Bc 51.45N 0.33W
Berkner Island 222 Rf 79.30S 49.30W
Berkovica 130 Gf 43.14N 23.07 E
Berks 118 Lj 51.15N 1.20W
Berkshire 118 Lj 51.30N 1.10W
Berkshire Downs 118 Lj 51.35N 1.25W
Berkshire Hills 184 Kd 42.20N 73.10W
Berlaimont 124 Fd 50.12N 3.49 E
Berlanga de Duero 126 Jc 41.28N 2.51W
Berlengas, Ilhas- 126 Ce 39.25N 9.30W
Berlevåg 114 Ga 70.51N 29.06 E
Berlin [N.H.-U.S.] 182 Mc 44.29N 71.10W
Berlin [Germany] 112 He 52.31N 13.24 E
Berlin (Ost) = Berlin 112 He 52.31N 13.24 E
Berlin (West) = Berlin 112 He 52.31N 13.24 E
Berlin-Pankow 120 Jd 52.34N 13.24 E
Bermeja, Sierra- 126 Gh 36.30N 5.15W
Bermejillo 190 Dc 25.53N 103.37W
Bermejito, Río- 204 Bg 25.39S 60.11W
Bermejo, Isla- 204 An 39.01S 62.01W
Bermejo, Paso del- 198 Ii 32.50S 70.05W
Bermejo, Río- [Arg.] 198 Ji 31.52S 67.22W
Bermejo, Río- [S.Amer.] 198 Kh 26.52S 58.23W
Bermen, Lac- 180 Kf 53.35N 68.55W
Bermeo 126 Ja 43.26N 2.43W
Bermillo de Sayago 126 Fc 41.22N 6.06W
Bermuda 176 Mf 32.20N 64.45W
Bermuda Islands 174 Mf 32.20N 64.45W
Bermuda Rise (EN) 174 Mf 32.30N 65.00W
Bern/Berne 112 Gf 46.55N 7.30 E
Bern / Berne 128 Bd 46.55N 7.40 E
Bernalda 128 Kj 40.24N 16.41 E
Bernalillo 186 Ci 35.18N 106.33W
Bernard Islands 220d Bb 7.18N 151.32 E
Bernardo de Irigoyen 204 Bk 32.10S 61.09W
Bernardo de Irigoyen 206 Jc 26.15S 53.39W
Bernasconi 206 He 37.54S 63.43W
Bernau bei Berlin 120 Jd 52.40N 13.35 E
Bernaville 124 Ed 50.08N 2.10 E
Bernay 122 Ge 49.06N 0.36 E
Bernburg 120 He 51.48N 11.44 E
Berndorf 128 Kc 47.57N 16.06 E
Berne [Ger.] 124 Ka 53.11N 8.29 E
Berne [In.-U.S.] 184 Ee 40.39N 84.57W
Berne/Bern 112 Gf 46.55N 7.30 E
Berne / Bern 128 Bd 46.55N 7.40 E
Berner Alpen=Bernese Alps (EN) 128 Bd 46.25N 7.30 E
Berneray 118 Fd 57.43N 7.15W
Bernese Alps (EN)=Berner Alpen 128 Bd 46.25N 7.30 E
Bernesga 126 Gb 42.28N 5.31W
Bernesq 124 Be 49.16N 0.56W
Bernier Bay 180 Ib 71.08N 88.00W
Bernier Island 212 Cd 24.50S 113.10 E
Bernina 128 Dd 46.23N 9.54 E
Bernina 128 Ed 46.25N 10.01 E
Bernina, Piz- 128 Dd 46.23N 9.54 E
Berninapaß 128 Ed 46.25N 10.01 E
Bernissart 124 Fd 50.28N 3.38 E
Bernkastel-Kues 124 Jd 49.55N 7.04 E
Bernstorffs Isfjord 179 Hf 63.10N 40.45W
Berón de Astrada 204 Dh 27.33S 57.32W
Beroroha 172 Hd 21.39S 45.10 E
Béroubouay 166 Fc 10.32N 2.44 E
Beroun 120 Kg 49.58N 14.04 E
Berounka 120 Kg 50.00N 14.24 E
Berovo 130 Fh 41.43N 22.51 E
Berre, Étang de- 122 Lk 43.27N 5.08 E
Berriane 162 Hc 32.50N 3.46 E
Berrouaghia 126 Oh 36.08N 2.55 E
Berry 122 Hh 47.00N 2.00 E
Berry-au-Bac 124 Fe 49.24N 3.54 E
Berryessa, Lake- 188 Dg 38.37N 122.16W
Berry Head 118 Jk 50.24N 3.29W
Berry Islands 190 Ic 25.34N 77.45W
Berry River 188 Ja 50.50N 111.36W
Beršad 136 Cf 48.23N 29.33 E
Berseba 172 Be 26.01S 17.41 E
Bersenbrück 124 Jb 52.33N 7.56 E
Berthierville 184 Kb 46.05N 73.11W
Bertincourt 124 Ed 50.05N 2.59 E
Bertogne 124 Hd 50.05N 5.40 E
Bertolinia 202 Je 7.38S 43.57W
Bertoua 160 Ih 4.35N 13.41 E
Bertraghboy Bay 118 Dh 53.23N 9.50W
Bertrix 124 He 49.51N 5.15 E
Beru Island 208 Ie 1.20S 176.00 E
Berwick-upon-Tweed 118 Lf 55.46N 2.00W
Berwyn 118 Ji 52.53N 3.24W
Besalampy 172 Gc 16.44S 44.24 E
Besançon 112 Gf 47.15N 6.02 E
Besar, Gunung- 150 Gg 1.25S 115.39 E
Besbre 122 Jh 46.33N 3.44 E
Besed 132 Gc 52.38N 31.11 E
Besikama 150 Hh 9.36S 124.57 E
Beskid Mountains (EN) 110 Hf 49.40N 20.00 E
Beskid Niski 120 Rg 49.20N 21.30 E
Beskid Średni 120 Pg 49.45N 19.20 E
Beskid Wysoki 120 Pg 49.32N 20.00 E
Beskidy Wschodnie 120 Sg 49.20N 22.30 E
Beskidy Zachodnie 120 Pg 49.30N 19.30 E
Beskol 135 Ma 46.06N 81.01 E
Beslan 136 Eg 43.10N 44.35 E
Besna Kobila 130 Fg 42.32N 22.14 E
Besni 146 Gd 37.41N 37.52 E
Besparmak Dağ 130 Kl 37.30N 27.35 E
Bessao 168 Bd 7.53N 15.59 E
Bessarabia (EN)= Bessarabija 130 Lb 47.00N 28.30 E
Bessarabija=Bessarabia (EN) 130 Lb 47.00N 28.30 E
Bessarabka 132 Ff 46.20N 28.59 E
Bességes 122 Kj 44.17N 4.06 E
Bessemer 182 Je 33.25N 86.57W
Bessin 122 Fe 49.10N 1.00W
Bessines-sur-Gartempe 122 Hh 46.06N 1.22 E
Besšoki, gora- 132 Rh 43.57N 52.30 E
Best 124 Hc 51.30N 5.24 E
Bestjah [Russia] 138 Hc 66.00N 123.35 E
Bestjah [Russia] 138 Hd 61.17N 128.50 E
Bestobe 136 He 52.30N 73.05 E
Bestwig 124 Kc 51.22N 8.24 E
Betafo 172 Hc 19.49S 46.50 E
Betanzos [Bol.] 202 Eg 19.34S 65.27W
Betanzos [Sp.] 126 Da 43.17N 8.12W
Betanzos, Ría de- 126 Da 43.23N 8.15W
Bétaré Oya 166 Hd 5.36N 14.05 E
Bétérou 166 Fd 9.12N 2.16 E
Beteta 126 Jd 40.34N 2.04W
Bethal 172 De 26.27S 29.28 E
Bethanien 160 Ik 26.32S 17.11 E
Bethanien 172 Be 26.30S 17.00 E
Bethany [Mo.-U.S.] 186 If 40.16N 94.02W
Bethany [Ok.-U.S.] 186 Hi 35.31N 97.38W
Bethel 176 Cc 60.48N 161.46W
Bétheniville 124 Ge 49.18N 4.22 E
Bethlehem [Pa.-U.S.] 184 Je 40.36N 75.22W
Bethlehem [S.Afr.] 160 Jk 28.15S 28.15 E
Bethlehem (EN)=Bayt Laḥm 146 Fg 31.43N 35.12 E
Bethulie 172 Df 30.32S 25.59 E
Béthune 122 Id 50.32N 2.38 E
Béthune 122 He 49.53N 1.09 E
Béticas, Cordilleras- 110 Fh 37.35N 3.30W
Betioky 172 Gd 23.42S 44.22 E
Betong [Mala.] 150 Ff 1.26N 111.30 E
Betong [Thai.] 148 Kg 5.45N 101.05 E
Betor 168 Fc 11.37N 39.00 E
Bétou 170 Cb 3.03N 18.31 E
Betpak-Dala 140 Ie 46.00N 70.00 E
Betroka 172 Hd 23.15S 46.05 E
Bet She'an 146 Ff 32.30N 35.30 E
Betsiamites, Rivière- 180 Kg 48.56N 68.38W
Betsiboka 158 Lj 16.03S 46.36 E
Bette, Picco- 158 If 22.00N 19.12 E
Bettembourg/Bettemburg 124 Ie 49.31N 6.06 E
Bettemburg/Bettembourg 124 Ie 49.31N 6.06 E
Bettendorf 186 Kf 41.32N 90.30W
Bettles Field 178 Ic 66.53N 151.51W
Bettna 116 Gf 58.55N 16.38 E
Bettola 128 Df 44.47N 9.36 E
Betül 148 Fd 21.55N 77.54 E
Betuwe 124 Hc 51.55N 5.40 E
Betwa 148 Hc 25.55N 80.12 E
Betz 124 Ee 49.09N 2.57 E
Betzdorf 120 Df 50.47N 7.53 E
Beulah 184 Dc 44.38N 86.06W
Beult 124 Cc 51.13N 0.26 E
Beuvron 122 Hg 47.29N 1.15 E
Beuzeville 124 Ce 49.20N 0.21 E
Beveland 122 Jc 51.30N 3.40 E
Beveren 124 Gc 51.13N 4.15 E
Beveridge Reef 208 Kg 20.00S 168.00W
Beverley [Austl.] 212 Df 32.06S 116.56 E
Beverley [Eng.-U.K.] 118 Mh 53.51N 0.26W
Beverwijk 122 Kb 52.28N 4.40 E
Bewsher, Mount- 222 Ff 70.54S 65.28 E
Bexhill 118 Nk 50.50N 0.29 E
Bexley, London- 124 Cc 51.26N 0.09 E
Beyağaç 130 Ll 37.13N 28.57 E
Beyānlū 146 Ld 36.02N 47.53 E
Bey Dağı 146 Hc 38.15N 38.22 E
Bey Dağları 144 Db 36.40N 30.15 E
Beykoz 146 Cb 41.08N 29.05 E
Beyla 166 Dd 8.41N 8.38W
Beyoğlu, İstanbul- 130 Lh 41.02N 28.59 E
Beyoneisu-Retsugan 152 Oe 31.55N 139.55 E
Beypazari 146 Db 40.10N 31.55 E
Beyra 168 Hd 6.57N 47.19 E
Beyram 146 Oi 27.26N 53.31 E
Beyşehir 146 Dd 37.41N 31.43 E
Beyşehir Gölü 144 Db 37.41N 31.33 E
Bezaha 172 Gd 23.29S 44.30 E
Bežanickaja vozvyšennost 114 Gh 56.45N 29.30 E
Bežanicy 114 Gh 56.58N 29.57 E
Bezdan 130 Bd 45.51N 18.56 E
Bezdež 120 Vd 52.18N 25.20 E
Bezděz 120 Kf 50.32N 14.43 E
Bežeck 136 Dd 57.50N 36.41 E
Bezenčuk 114 Lj 53.01N 49.24 E
Bezerra, Rio- 204 Ia 13.16S 47.31W
Bezerros 202 Ke 8.14S 35.45W
Béziers 122 Jk 43.21N 3.15 E
Bezmein 136 Fh 38.05N 58.12 E
Bežta 136 Eg 42.08N 46.08 E
Bhadrak 148 Hd 21.04N 86.30 E
Bhadrāvati 148 Ff 13.52N 75.43 E
Bhāgalpur 142 Kg 25.15N 87.00 E
Bhaironghati 148 Fb 31.01N 78.53 E
Bhakkar 148 Eb 31.38N 71.04 E
Bhamo 148 Jd 24.16N 97.14 E
Bhandāra 148 Fd 21.10N 79.39 E
Bhanjan 148 Gc 25.47N 83.36 E
Bhārat Juktarashtra=India (EN) 142 Jh 20.00N 77.00 E
Bharatpur 148 Fc 27.13N 77.29 E
Bharūch 148 Ed 21.46N 72.54 E
Bhatinda → Bathinda 148 Eb 30.12N 74.57 E
Bhātpāra 148 Hd 22.52N 88.24 E
Bhavnagar 142 Jg 21.46N 72.09 E
Bhera 148 Eb 32.29N 72.55 E
Bheri 148 Gc 28.44N 81.16 E
Bhikhna-Thori 148 Gc 27.20N 84.38 E
Bhilwāra 148 Ec 25.21N 74.38 E
Bhīma 140 Jh 16.25N 77.17 E
Bhind 148 Fc 26.34N 78.48 E
Bhiwāni 148 Fc 28.47N 76.08 E
Bhopāl 142 Jg 23.16N 77.24 E
Bhubaneshwar 142 Kg 20.14N 85.50 E
Bhuj 148 Dd 23.16N 69.40 E
Bhusāwal 148 Fd 21.03N 75.46 E
Bhutan (Druk-Yul) 142 Lg 27.30N 90.30 E
Bia 166 Ed 5.21N 3.11W
Bia, Phou- 140 Mh 18.36N 103.01 E
Biá, Rio- 202 Ed 3.28S 67.23W
Bīābān, Kūh-e- 146 Qi 26.30N 57.25 E
Biabou 197n Ba 13.12N 61.09W
Biafra 158 Hh 5.00N 7.30 E
Biafra, Bight of- 158 Hh 3.20N 9.20 E
Biak 150 Kg 1.10S 136.06 E
Biak, Pulau- 208 Ee 1.00S 136.00 E
Biała Piska 120 Sc 53.37N 22.04 E
Biała Podlaska 120 Td 52.02N 23.06 E
Biała Podlaska 120 Td 52.00N 23.05 E
Białobrzegi 120 Qe 51.40N 20.57 E
Białogard 120 Lb 54.01N 16.00 E
Białostocka, Wysoczyzna- 120 Tc 53.23N 23.10 E
Białowieża 120 Td 52.41N 23.50 E
Białystok 112 Ie 53.09N 23.09 E
Białystok 120 Tc 53.10N 23.10 E
Biancavilla 128 Im 37.38N 14.52 E
Bianco 128 Kl 38.05N 16.09 E
Bianco, Monte- / Blanc, Mont- 110 Gf 45.50N 6.52 E
Biankouma 166 Dd 7.44N 7.37W
Biankouma 166 Dd 7.43N 7.40W
Bianzhuang → Cangshan 154 Eg 34.51N 118.03 E
Biaro, Pulau- 150 If 2.05N 125.20 E
Biarritz 122 Ek 43.29N 1.34W
Biasca 128 Cd 46.22N 8.57 E
Bibā 164 Fd 28.55N 30.59 E
Bibai 152 Pc 43.19N 141.52 E
Bibala 170 Be 14.50S 13.30 E
Biban, Chaine des- 126 Qh 36.12N 4.25 E
Bibbiena 128 Fg 43.42N 11.49 E
Biberach an der Riß 120 Fh 48.06N 9.48 E
Bibiani 166 Ed 6.28N 2.20W
Bic 184 Ma 48.22N 68.42W
Bicaj 130 Dh 41.59N 20.25 E
Bicas 204 Ke 21.43S 43.04W
Bicaz 130 Jc 46.55N 26.04 E
Bicaz, Pasul- 130 Ic 46.49N 25.52 E
Bičenekski, pereval- 132 Nj 39.33N 45.48 E
Bicester 118 Lj 51.54N 1.09W
Bichena 168 Fc 10.21N 38.14 E
Bickerton Island 212 Hb 13.45S 136.10 E
Bicske 120 Oi 47.29N 18.38 E
Bičura 138 Ff 50.36N 107.35 E
Bīd 146 Qd 36.33N 57.35 E
Bida 160 Hh 9.05N 6.01 E
Bīdar 148 Fe 17.54N 77.33 E
Bidasoa 126 Ka 43.22N 1.47W
Biddeford 182 Mc 43.30N 70.26W
Bideford 118 Ij 51.01N 4.13W
Bideford Bay → Barnstaple Bay 118 Ij 51.05N 4.20W
Bidon V/Poste Maurice Cortier 162 He 22.18N 1.05 E
Bié 170 Ce 13.00S 17.30 E
Bié, Planalto do- 158 Ij 13.30S 17.02 E
Biebrza 120 Sc 53.13N 22.28 E
Biecz 120 Rg 49.44N 21.14 E
Biedenkopf 120 Ef 50.55N 8.32 E
Biei 156a Cb 43.35N 142.28 E
Biel/Bienne 128 Bc 47.10N 7.15 E
Bielefeld 120 Ed 52.02N 8.32 E
Bielefeld-Brackwede 124 Kc 51.59N 8.31 E
Bielefeld-Sennestadt 124 Kc 51.57N 8.35 E
Biella 128 Ce 45.34N 8.03 E
Bielsk 120 Pd 52.40N 19.49 E
Bielska, Wysoczyzna- 120 Sd 52.35N 23.00 E
Bielsko 120 Og 49.50N 19.00 E
Bielsko-Biała 120 Pg 49.49N 19.02 E
Bielsk Podlaski 120 Td 52.47N 23.12 E
Bien Dong=South China Sea (EN) 140 Ni 10.00N 113.00 E
Bien Hoa 148 Lf 10.57N 106.49 E
Bienne 122 Lh 46.20N 5.38 E
Bienne/Biel 128 Bc 47.10N 7.15 E
Bienvenida 126 Jd 40.30N 2.30W
Bienville, Lac- 180 Ke 55.20N 72.40W
Bierbeek 124 Gd 50.50N 4.46 E
Bieszczady 120 Sg 49.10N 22.35 E
Bièvre 124 He 49.56N 5.01 E
Biferno 128 Ji 41.59N 15.02 E
Bifoum 170 Bc 0.20S 10.23 E
Bifuka 154 Qb 44.29N 142.21 E
Biga 146 Bb 40.13N 27.14 E
Bigadiç 146 Cc 39.23N 28.08 E
Big Bald Mountain 184 Nb 47.37N 66.38W
Big Baldy Mountain 188 Jc 46.58N 110.37W
Big Bay [Mi.-U.S.] 184 Db 46.49N 87.44W
Big Bay [Van.] 219b Cb 15.05S 166.54 E
Big Beaver House 180 If 52.58N 89.57W
Big Belt Mountains 188 Jc 46.40N 111.25W
Big Black River 186 Kj 32.00N 91.05W
Big Blue River 182 Hd 39.11N 96.32W
Big Creek Peak 188 Id 44.28N 113.32W
Big Dry Creek 188 Lc 47.30N 106.19W
Big Falls 186 Jb 48.11N 93.46W
Biggar 180 Gf 52.04N 108.00W
Biggenden 212 Ke 25.30S 152.00 E
Biggleswade 118 Mi 52.05N 0.17W
Big Hatchet Peak 186 Bk 31.37N 108.20W
Big Hole River 188 Id 45.34N 112.20W
Bighorn Basin 182 Fc 44.15N 108.10W
Bighorn Lake 188 Kd 45.08N 108.10W
Bighorn Mountains 174 Ie 44.00N 107.30W
Bighorn River 182 Fb 46.09N 107.28W
Bight, Head of- 212 Gf 31.30S 131.10 E
Big Island 180 Kd 62.43N 70.40W
Big Lake 186 Fk 31.12N 101.28W
Big Lake 184 Nc 45.10N 67.40W
Big Lost River 188 Ie 43.50N 112.44W
Big Muddy Creek 188 Mb 48.08N 104.36W
Big Muddy Lake 188 Mb 49.08N 104.54W
Bignona 166 Bc 12.49N 16.14W
Bigorre 122 Gk 43.06N 0.05 E
Big Porcupine Creek 188 Lc 46.17N 106.47W
Big Quill Lake 180 Hf 51.51N 104.18W
Big Rapids 184 Ed 43.42N 85.29W
Big River 180 Gf 53.50N 107.01W
Big River 180 Fb 72.50N 125.00W
Big Sand Lake 180 He 57.45N 99.45W
Big Sandy 188 Jb 48.11N 110.07W
Big Sandy Creek 186 Eg 38.06N 102.29W
Big Sandy River [Az.-U.S.] 188 Ii 34.19N 113.31W
Big Sandy River [Wy.-U.S.] 188 Kf 41.50N 109.48W
Big Sheep Mountains 188 Mc 47.03N 105.43W
Big Sioux River 182 Hc 42.30N 96.25W
Big Smoky Valley 182 Dd 38.30N 117.15W
Big Snowy Mountains 188 Kc 46.50N 109.30W
Big Spring 176 If 32.15N 101.28W
Big Spruce Knob 184 Gf 38.16N 80.12W
Big Stone Lake 186 Hd 45.25N 96.40W
Big Timber 188 Kd 45.50N 109.57W
Big Trout Lake 180 If 53.45N 90.00W
Biguglia, Étang de- 122a Ba 42.36N 9.29 E
Big Wood Cay 194 Ia 24.21N 77.44W
Big Wood River 188 He 42.52N 114.55W
Bihać 128 Jf 44.49N 15.52 E
Bihār 148 Hc 25.11N 85.31 E
Bihār 148 Hd 25.00N 86.00 E
Biharamulo 170 Fc 2.38S 31.20 E
Bihor 130 Fc 47.00N 22.00 E
Bihoro 152 Pc 43.49N 144.07 E
Bihorului, Munţii- 130 Fc 46.40N 22.45 E
Bija 140 Kd 52.25N 85.05 E
Bijagós, Arquipélago dos-= Bijagos Islands (EN) 158 Fg 11.15N 16.05W
Bijagos Islands (EN)= Bijagós, Arquipélago dos- 158 Fg 11.15N 16.05W
Bijapur 148 Fe 16.50N 75.42 E
Bijār 144 Gb 35.52N 47.36 E
Bijeljina 128 Nf 44.45N 19.13 E
Bijelo Polje 130 Cf 43.02N 19.45 E
Bijiang (Zhiziluo) 152 Gf 26.39N 99.00 E
Bijie 152 If 27.15N 105.16 E
Bijlikol, ozero- 135 Hc 43.05N 70.40 E
Bijou Creek 186 Ef 40.17N 103.52W
Bijoutier Island 172b Bb 7.04S 52.45 E
Bijsk 142 Kd 52.34N 85.15 E
Bikāner 142 Jg 28.01N 73.18 E
Bikar Atoll 208 Ic 12.15N 170.06 E
Bikeqi 154 Ad 40.45N 111.17 E
Bikin 138 Ig 46.51N 134.02 E
Bikin 138 Ig 46.43N 134.02 E
Bikini Atoll 208 Hc 11.35N 165.23 E
Bikoro 160 Ii 0.45S 18.07 E
Bilād Ghāmid 164 Hf 19.58N 41.38 E
Bilād Zahrān 164 He 20.15N 41.15 E
Bilāspur 142 Kg 22.03N 82.10 E
Bilate 168 Fd 6.34N 38.01 E
Bilauktaung Range 140 Lh 13.00N 99.00 E
Bilbao 112 Fg 43.15N 2.58W
Bilbays 164 Fc 30.25N 31.34 E
Bileća 128 Mh 42.53N 18.26 E
Bilecik 144 Ca 40.09N 29.59 E
Bilehsavār 146 Mc 39.28N 48.20 E
Bilé Karpaty=White Carpathians (EN) 120 Nh 48.55N 17.50 E
Bilesha Plain 170 Hb 0.35N 40.45 E
Biłgoraj 120 Sf 50.34N 22.43 E
Bili 170 Eb 4.09N 25.16 E
Bili 170 Db 4.50N 22.29 E
Bilibino 142 Sc 68.03N 166.20 E
Biliran 150 Hd 11.35N 124.28 E
Bilishti 130 Di 40.37N 20.59 E
Biliu He 154 Ge 39.30N 122.36 E
Bill Baileys Bank (EN) 118 Ca 60.40N 10.20W
Billerbeck 124 Jc 51.58N 7.18 E
Billericay 124 Cc 51.37N 0.35 E
Billingen 116 Ef 58.24N 13.45 E
Billings 176 Ie 45.47N 108.27W
Billings, Represa- 204 If 23.45S 46.40W
Billingshurst 124 Bc 51.01N 0.27W
Bill Williams River 188 Hi 34.17N 114.03W
Billy Chinook, Lake- 188 Ed 44.33N 121.20W
Bilma 160 Ig 18.41N 12.56 E

Bil-Bod

Index Symbols

Bodegraven	124	Gb	52.06N	4.44 E
Bodélé ⊠	158	Ig	16.30N	17.30 E
Boden	112	Ib	65.50N	21.42 E
Bodenheim	124	Ke	49.56N	8.18 E
Bodensee=Constance, Lake- (EN) ⊟	110	Gf	47.35N	9.25 E
Boderg, Lough- ⊟	118	Fh	53.52N	8.00W
Bodmin	118	Ik	50.29N	4.43W
Bodmin Moor ▲	118	Ik	50.35N	4.40W
Bodø	112	Hb	67.17N	14.23 E
Bodoquena	204	De	20.12S	56.48W
Bodoquena, Serra da- ▲	202	Gh	21.00S	56.50W
Bodrog ∿	120	Rh	48.07N	21.25 E
Bodrogköz ⊠	120	Rh	48.15N	21.45 E
Bodrum	144	Cb	37.02N	27.06 E
Bodrum Yarımadası ▬	130	Kl	37.05N	27.30 E
Bodva ∿	120	Qh	48.12N	20.47 E
Boën	122	Ji	45.44N	4.00 E
Boende	160	Ji	0.13S	20.52 E
Boeo, Capo- (Lilibeo, Capo-) ►	128	Gm	37.34N	12.41 E
Boerne	186	Gl	29.47N	98.44W
Boesmanland= Bushmanland (EN) ⊠	172	Be	29.30S	19.00 E
Boffa	166	Cc	10.10N	14.02W
Boga	130	Cg	42.24N	19.38 E
Bogale	148	Je	16.17N	95.24 E
Bogalusa	186	Lk	30.47N	89.52W
Bogandé	166	Ec	12.59N	0.08W
Bogangolo	168	Bd	5.34N	18.15 E
Bogatić	130	Ce	44.51N	19.29 E
Bogatynia	120	Kf	50.55N	14.59 E
Boğazkale	146	Fb	40.01N	34.35 E
Boğazlıyan	146	Fc	39.12N	35.15 E
Bogbonga	170	Cb	1.35N	19.25 E
Bogda Feng ▲	152	Ec	43.45N	88.32 E
Bogdan ▲	130	Hg	42.37N	24.28 E
Bogdanovka → Ninocminda	132	Mi	41.15N	43.36 E
Boqda Shan	140	Ke	43.35N	90.00 E
Bogen	114	Db	68.32N	17.00 E
Bogenfels	172	Be	27.23S	15.22 E
Bogense	116	Di	55.34N	10.06 E
Boggeragh Mountains/An Bhograch ▲	118	Ei	52.05N	9.00W
Boggy Peak ▲	197d	Bb	17.03N	61.51W
Boghar	126	Oi	35.55N	2.43 E
Boghni	126	Ph	36.32N	3.57 E
Bogia	214	Ch	4.16S	144.58 E
Bognor Regis	124	Bd	50.47N	0.39W
Bogny-sur-Meuse	124	Ge	49.54N	4.43 E
Bogoduhov	132	Id	50.12N	35.31 E
Bogomila	130	Eh	41.36N	21.28 E
Bogor	142	Mj	6.35S	106.47 E
Bogoridick	136	De	53.50N	38.08 E
Bogorodčany	120	Uh	48.45N	24.40 E
Bogorodsk	114	Kh	56.09N	43.32 E
Bogorodskoje [Russia]	114	Mh	57.51N	50.48 E
Bogorodskoje [Russia]	138	Jf	52.22N	140.30 E
Bogotá → Santa Fe de Bogotá	200	Ie	4.36N	74.05W
Bogotá [3]	202	Dc	4.20N	74.10W
Bogotol	138	De	56.17N	89.43 E
Bogøy	114	Dc	67.54N	15.11 E
Bogra	148	Hd	24.51N	89.22 E
Bogučany	138	Ee	58.23N	97.39 E
Bogučar	132	Le	49.57N	40.33 E
Bogué	162	Ef	16.36N	14.15W
Boguševsk	114	Hi	54.50N	30.13 E
Boguslav	136	Df	49.33N	30.54 E
Bo Hai=Chihli, Gulf of- (EN) ◧	140	Nf	38.30N	120.00 E
Bohai Haixia ▬	152	Ld	38.00N	121.30 E
Bohain-en-Vermandois	124	Fe	49.59N	3.27 E
Bohemia (EN)=Čechy ⊠	110	Hf	50.00N	14.30 E
Bohemia (EN)=Čechy ▣	120	Kf	50.00N	14.30 E
Bohemian Forest (EN)= Böhmerwald ▲	110	Hf	49.00N	13.30 E
Bohemian Forest (EN)= Šumava ▲	110	Hf	49.00N	13.30 E
Bohicon	166	Fd	7.12N	2.04 E
Bohmte	124	Kb	52.22N	8.19 E
Bohodoyou	166	Dd	9.46N	9.04W
Bohol ⊕	140	Oi	9.50N	124.10 E
Böhönye	120	Nj	46.24N	17.24 E
Bohor ▲	128	Jd	46.04N	15.26 E
Bohu/Bagrax	152	Ec	41.58N	86.29 E
Bohus	116	Eg	57.51N	12.01 E
Bohuslän ▣	116	Df	58.15N	11.50 E
Boiaçu	202	Fd	0.27S	61.46W
Boiano	128	Ii	41.29N	14.29 E
Boina ⊠	158	Lj	16.00S	46.30 E
Bois, Lac des - ⊟	180	Ec	66.50N	125.15W
Bois, Rio dos- [Braz.] ∿	204	Gd	18.35S	50.02W
Bois, Rio dos- [Braz.] ∿	204	Ha	13.55S	49.51W
Bois Blanc Island ⊕	184	Ec	45.45N	84.28W
Boischaut ⊠	122	Hh	46.40N	1.45 E
Boise	176	He	43.37N	116.13W
Boise City	186	Eh	36.44N	102.31W
Boise River ∿	188	Ge	43.49N	117.01W
Boissay	124	De	49.31N	1.21 E
Boissevain	180	Hg	49.14N	100.03W
Boizenburg	120	Gc	53.23N	10.43 E
Bojador, Cabo- ►	158	Ff	26.08N	14.30W
Bojana ∿	130	Ch	41.52N	19.22 E
Bojanowo	120	Me	51.42N	16.44 E
Bojarka	136	De	50.19N	30.20 E
Bojčinovci	130	Gf	43.28N	23.20 E
Bojnūrd	144	Ib	37.28N	57.19 E
Bojonegoro	150	Fh	7.09S	111.52 E
Bojuru	204	Gj	31.38S	51.26W
Bokatola	170	Cc	0.38S	18.46 E
Boké	166	Cc	10.56N	14.13W
Bokhara River ∿	212	Je	29.55S	146.42 E
Bokn ⊕	116	Ae	59.15N	5.25 E
Boknafjorden ▬	110	Gd	59.10N	5.35 E
Boko	170	Bc	4.47S	14.38 E
Bokol Mayo	168	Ge	4.31N	41.32 E
Bokoro	168	Bc	12.23N	17.03 E
Bokote	170	Dc	0.05S	20.08 E
Bokpyin	148	Jf	11.16N	98.46 E
Boksitogorsk	136	Dd	59.29N	33.52 E
Bokungu	170	Dc	0.41S	22.19 E
Bol [Chad]	168	Ac	13.30N	14.41 E
Bol [Cro.]	128	Kg	43.16N	16.40 E
Bola, Bahr- ∿	168	Bd	9.50N	18.59 E
Bolama	166	Bc	11.35N	15.28W
Bolands	197d	Bb	17.02N	61.53W
Bolaños, Río- ∿	192	Gg	21.14N	104.08W
Bolaños de Calatrava	126	If	38.54N	3.40W
Bolattau, gora- ▲	135	Ha	46.44N	71.54 E
Bolayir	130	Ji	40.31N	26.45 E
Bolbec	122	Ge	49.34N	0.29 E
Bolda ∿	132	Pg	45.58N	48.35 E
Bole [Eth.]	168	Fd	6.37N	37.22 E
Bole [Ghana]	166	Ed	9.02N	2.29W
Bole/Bortala	152	Dc	44.59N	81.57 E
Bolehov	132	Ce	49.03N	23.50 E
Bolesławiec	120	Le	51.16N	15.34 E
Bolgatanga	160	Gg	10.47N	0.51W
Bolgrad	132	Fg	45.40N	28.38 E
Bolhov	136	De	53.30N	36.01 E
Boli	152	Nb	45.46N	130.31 E
Bolia	170	Cc	1.36S	18.23 E
Boliden	114	Ed	64.52N	20.23 E
Bolinao, Cape- ►	150	Gc	16.22N	119.50 E
Bolintin Vale	130	Ie	44.27N	25.46 E
Bolívar [2]	202	Fb	6.20N	63.30W
Bolívar [3]	202	Db	9.00N	74.40W
Bolivar [Mo.-U.S.]	186	Jh	37.37N	93.25W
Bolivar [Tn.-U.S.]	184	Ch	35.15N	88.59W
Bolívar, Cerro- ▲	202	Fb	7.28N	63.25W
Bolivar, Pico- ▲	198	Ie	8.30N	71.02W
Bolivia [1]	200	Jg	17.00S	65.00W
Bolivia, Altiplano de- ▭	198	Jg	18.00S	68.00W
Boljevac	130	Ef	43.50N	21.58 E
Bollendorf	124	Ie	49.51N	6.22 E
Bollène	122	Kj	44.17N	4.45 E
Bollnäs	114	Df	61.21N	16.25 E
Bollon	212	Je	28.02S	147.28 E
Bollstabruk	116	Ga	63.00N	17.41 E
Bollullos par del Condado	126	Fg	37.20N	6.32W
Bolmen ⊟	114	Ch	56.55N	13.40 E
Bolnisi	132	Ni	41.28N	44.31 E
Bolobo	170	Cc	2.10S	16.14 E
Bolodek	138	If	53.43N	133.09 E
Bologna	112	Hg	44.29N	11.20 E
Bolognesi	202	Df	10.01S	74.05W
Bologoje	112	Jd	57.54N	34.02 E
Bolohovo	132	Jb	54.05N	37.52 E
Bolomba	170	Cb	0.29N	19.12 E
Bolombo	170	Dc	3.59S	21.22 E
Bolon	138	Ig	49.58N	136.04 E
Bolotnoje	138	De	55.41N	84.33 E
Bolovens, Plateau des- ▭	148	Le	15.20N	106.20 E
Bolšaja Balahnja ∿	138	Fb	73.37N	107.05 E
Bolšaja Berestovica	120	Uc	53.09N	24.02 E
Bolšaja Černigovka	114	Mj	52.08N	50.48 E
Bolšaja Glušica	114	Mj	52.24N	50.29 E
Bolšaja Ižora	116	Me	59.55N	29.40 E
Bolšaja Kinel ∿	114	Mj	53.14N	50.32 E
Bolšaja Koksaga ∿	114	Lh	56.07N	47.48 E
Bolšaja Kuonamka ∿	138	Gb	70.50N	113.20 E
Bolšaja Oju ∿	134	Jb	69.42N	60.42 E
Bolšaja Rogovaja ∿	134	Jc	66.30N	60.40 E
Bolšaja Synja ∿	134	Id	65.58N	58.01 E
Bolšaja Tap ∿	134	Lg	59.55N	65.42 E
Bolšaja Ussurka ∿	138	Ig	46.00N	133.30 E
Bolšaja Vladimirovka	136	He	50.53N	79.30 E
Bolšakovo	116	Ij	54.50N	21.36 E
Bolsena	128	Fh	42.39N	11.59 E
Bolsena, Lago di- ⊟	128	Fh	42.35N	11.55 E
Bolšerečje	136	Hd	56.06N	74.38 E
Bolšereck	138	Kf	52.22N	156.24 E
Bolšeustikinskoje	134	Ii	55.57N	58.20 E
Bolševik	138	Jd	62.40N	147.30 E
Bolševik, ostrov- = Bolshevik Island (EN) ⊕	140	Mb	78.40N	102.30 E
Bolšezemelskaja tundra ☷	136	Fb	67.30N	58.30 E
Bolshevik Island (EN) = Bolševik, ostrov- ⊕	140	Mb	78.40N	102.30 E
Bolšije Uki	136	Hd	56.57N	72.37 E
Bolšoj Anjuj ∿	138	Lc	68.30N	160.50 E
Bolšoj Begičev, ostrov- ⊕	138	Gb	74.20N	112.30 E
Bolšoj Berezovy, ostrov- ⊕	116	Md	60.15N	28.35 E
Bolšoj Boktybaj, gora- ▲	136	Ff	48.30N	58.20 E
Bolšoj Bolvanski Nos, mys- ►	134	Ia	70.27N	59.05 E
Bolšoj Čeremšan ∿	114	Li	54.12N	49.40 E
Bolšoje Muraškino	114	Ki	55.47N	44.46 E
Bolšoje Vlasjevo	138	Jf	53.25N	140.55 E
Bolšoje Zagorje	116	Mg	57.47N	28.58 E
Bolšoj Gašun ∿	132	Mf	47.22N	42.42 E
Bolšoj Ik ∿	134	Hj	51.47N	56.20 E
Bolšoj Irgiz ∿	136	Ee	52.01N	47.24 E
Bolšoj Jenisej ∿	138	Ef	51.40N	94.26 E
Bolšoj Jugan ∿	136	Hc	60.55N	73.40 E
Bolšoj Kamen	138	Ih	43.08N	132.28 E
Bolšoj Klimecki, ostrov- ⊕	114	Ie	62.00N	35.15 E
Bolšoj Kujalnik ∿	132	Gf	46.46N	30.38 E
Bolšoj Kumak ∿	132	Ud	51.22N	58.55 E
Bolšoj Ljahovski, ostrov- = Great Lyakhov (EN) ⊕	138	Jb	73.35N	142.00 E
Bolšoj Murta	138	Ee	56.55N	93.10 E
Bolšoj Nimnyr	138	He	58.08N	125.45 E
Bolšoj Pit ∿	138	Ee	59.02N	91.40 E
Bolšoj Tjuters, ostrov- ⊕	116	Le	59.50N	27.10 E
Bolšoj Uluj	138	Ee	56.45N	90.46 E
Bolšoj Uvat, ozero- ⊟	134	Oh	57.35N	70.30 E
Bolšoj Uzen ∿	110	Kf	48.50N	49.40 E
Bolsón, Cerro del- ▲	198	Jh	27.13S	66.06W
Bolšovcy	120	Ug	49.08N	24.47 E
Bolsward	124	Ha	53.04N	5.30 E
Boltaña	126	Mb	42.27N	0.04 E
Bolton	118	Kh	53.35N	2.26W
Bolu	144	Da	40.44N	31.37 E
Bolu Dağları ▲	146	Eb	41.05N	32.05 E
Bolungarvík	114a	Aa	66.09N	23.15W
Boluntay	152	Fd	36.29N	92.18 E
Bolva ∿	132	Ic	53.17N	34.20 E
Bolvadin	146	Dc	38.42N	31.04 E
Bolzano/Bozen	112	Hf	46.31N	11.22 E
Bom, Rio- ∿	204	Gf	23.56S	51.44W
Boma	160	Ii	5.51S	13.03 E
Bomassa	170	Cb	2.12N	16.12 E
Bombala	212	Jg	36.54S	149.14 E
Bombarral	126	Ce	39.16N	9.09W
Bombay	142	Jh	18.58N	72.50 E
Bomberai, Jazirah- ▬	150	Jg	3.00S	133.00 E
Bombo	170	Fb	0.35N	32.32 E
Bomboma	170	Cb	2.26N	18.57 E
Bom Comércio	202	Ee	9.45S	65.54W
Bom Conselho	202	Ke	9.10S	36.41W
Bom Despacho	202	Ig	19.43S	45.15W
Bomdila	148	Ic	27.16N	92.23 E
Bomi/Bowo	152	Ge	30.02N	95.39 E
Bomi Hills	160	Fh	6.52N	10.45W
Bomili	170	Eb	1.40N	27.01 E
Bom Jardim de Goiás	204	Fc	16.17S	52.07W
Bom Jardim de Minas	204	Je	21.57S	44.11W
Bom Jesus	204	Gi	28.42S	50.24W
Bom Jesus da Lapa	200	Lg	13.15S	43.25W
Bom Jesus de Goiás	204	Hd	18.12S	49.37W
Bømlafjorden ▬	116	Ae	59.40N	5.20 E
Bømlo ⊕	114	Ag	59.45N	5.10 E
Bomokandi ∿	170	Eb	3.30N	26.08 E
Bomongo	170	Cb	1.22N	18.21 E
Bom Retiro	204	Hh	27.48S	49.31W
Bom Sucesso	204	Je	21.02S	44.46W
Bomu ∿	158	Jh	4.08N	22.26 E
Bomu (EN)=Mbomou [3]	168	Cd	5.30N	23.30 E
Bomu (EN)=Mbomou ∿	158	Jh	4.08N	22.26 E
Bon, Cape- (EN) = Ţib Ra's aţ- ►	158	Ie	37.05N	11.03 E
Bona, Mount- ▲	178	Kd	61.20N	141.50W
Bonaire ⊕	202	Ea	12.10N	68.15W
Bonaire Basin (EN) ≋	196	Cg	11.25N	67.30W
Bonampak ∴	192	Ni	16.43N	91.05W
Bonanza	194	Ef	14.01N	84.35W
Bonanza Peak ▲	188	Eb	48.14N	120.52W
Bonao	194	Ld	18.56N	70.25W
Bonaparte, Mount- ▲	188	Fb	48.45N	119.08W
Bonaparte Archipelago ⊡	208	Df	14.20S	125.20 E
Bonaparte Lake ⊟	188	Ea	51.16N	120.35W
Bonaparte Rocks ⊞	197p	Cb	12.24N	61.30W
Bonasse	196	Fg	10.05N	61.52W
Bonavista	180	Mg	48.39N	53.07W
Bonavista Bay ◧	180	Mg	49.00N	53.20W
Bon-Cagan-Nur ⊟	152	Gb	45.35N	99.15 E
Bonda	170	Bc	0.49S	12.42 E
Bondeno	128	Ff	44.53N	11.25 E
Bondo	160	Jh	3.49N	23.40 E
Bondoukou	166	Ed	8.02N	2.48W
Bondoukou [3]	166	Ed	8.20N	2.55W
Bondowoso	150	Fh	7.55S	113.49 E
Bone, Gulf of- (EN)=Bone, Teluk- ◧	140	Oj	4.00S	120.40 E
Bone, Teluk-=Bone, Gulf of- (EN) ◧	140	Oj	4.00S	120.40 E
Bone Bay ◧	197a	Db	18.45N	64.22W
Bonelohe	150	Hh	5.48S	120.27 E
Bönen	124	Jc	51.36N	7.46 E
Bone Rate, Kepulauan- ⊡	150	Hh	7.00S	121.00 E
Bone Rate, Pulau- ⊕	150	Hh	7.22S	121.08 E
Bonete, Cerro- ▲	206	Gc	27.51S	68.47W
Bong	166	Cd	6.49N	10.19W
Bong [3]	166	Dd	7.00N	9.40W
Bonga	168	Fd	7.16N	36.14 E
Bongabong	150	Hd	12.45N	121.29 E
Bongandanga	170	Db	1.30N	21.03 E
Bongo, Massif des- ▲	158	Jh	8.40N	22.25 E
Bongolava ▲	172	Hc	18.35S	45.20 E
Bongor	160	Ig	10.17N	15.22 E
Bongouanou	166	Ed	6.39N	4.12W
Bongouanou [3]	166	Ed	6.43N	4.12W
Bong Son	148	Lf	14.26N	109.01 E
Bonham	186	Hj	33.35N	96.11W
Bonheiden	124	Gc	51.02N	4.32 E
Bonhomme, Pic- ▲	194	Kd	19.05N	72.15W
Bonifacio	122a	Bb	41.23N	9.09 E
Bonifacio, Bocche di- = Bonifacio, Strait of- (EN) ▬	110	Gg	41.18N	9.15 E
Bonifacio, Bouches de- = Bonifacio, Strait of- (EN) ▬	110	Gg	41.18N	9.15 E
Bonifacio, Strait of- (EN) = Bonifacio, Bocche di- ▬	110	Gg	41.18N	9.15 E
Bonifacio, Strait of- (EN) = Bonifacio, Bouches de- ▬	110	Gg	41.18N	9.15 E
Bonifati, Capo- ►	128	Jk	39.33N	15.52 E
Bonin Basin (EN) ≋	214	Bb	29.00N	137.00 E
Bonin Islands (EN)= Ogasawara-Shotō ⊡	140	Qg	27.00N	142.10 E
Bonin Trench (EN) ≋	106	If	30.00N	145.00 E
Bonita Springs	184	Gl	26.21N	81.47W
Bonito [Braz.]	204	De	21.08S	56.28W
Bonito [Braz.]	204	Jb	15.20S	44.46W
Bonito, Pico- ▲	190	Ge	15.38N	86.55W
Bonito, Rio- [Braz.] ∿	204	Hb	15.18S	49.36W
Bonito, Rio- [Braz.] ∿	204	Gc	16.31S	51.23W
Bonn	112	Ge	50.44N	7.06 E
Bonn-Bad Godesberg	120	Df	50.41N	7.09 E
Bonnebosq	124	Ce	49.12N	0.05 E
Bonnechère River ∿	184	Ic	45.31N	76.33W
Bonners Ferry	188	Gb	48.41N	116.18W
Bonnet, Lac du- ⊟	186	Ia	50.22N	95.55W
Bonnétable	122	Gf	48.11N	0.26 E
Bonnet Plume ∿	180	Ec	65.53N	134.58W
Bonneval	122	Hf	48.11N	1.24 E
Bonneville	122	Mh	46.05N	6.25 E
Bonneville Salt Flats ⊟	188	If	40.45N	113.50W
Bonnières-sur-Seine	124	De	49.02N	1.35 E
Bonningues-lès-Ardres	124	Ed	50.47N	2.01 E
Bonny	166	Ge	4.25N	7.10 E
Bono	128	Dj	40.25N	9.02 E
Bō-no-Misaki ►	156	Bf	31.15N	130.13 E
Bonorva	128	Cj	40.25N	8.46 E
Bontang	150	Gf	0.08N	117.30 E
Bonthain	150	Gh	5.32S	119.56 E
Bonthe	166	Cd	7.32N	12.30W
Bontoc	150	Hc	17.05N	120.58 E
Bonyhád	120	Oj	46.18N	18.32 E
Boo, Kepulauan- ⊡	150	Ig	1.12S	129.24 E
Boola	166	Dd	8.22N	8.43W
Booligal	212	If	33.52S	144.53 E
Boone [Ia.-U.S.]	186	Je	42.04N	93.53W
Boone [N.C.-U.S.]	184	Gg	36.13N	81.41W
Booneville [Ar.-U.S.]	186	Ji	35.08N	93.55W
Booneville [Ms.-U.S.]	186	Li	34.39N	88.34W
Boon Point ►	197d	Bb	17.10N	61.50W
Boonville [In.-U.S.]	184	Df	38.03N	87.16W
Boonville [Mo.-U.S.]	186	Jg	38.58N	92.44W
Boos	124	De	49.23N	1.12 E
Boothia, Gulf of- ◧	174	Jb	71.00N	91.00W
Boothia Peninsula ▬	174	Jb	70.30N	95.00W
Boot Reefs ⊞	214	Cj	10.00S	144.35 E
Booué	160	Ii	0.06S	11.56 E
Bophuthatswana ▣	172	De	26.00S	25.30 E
Bopolu	166	Cd	7.04N	10.29W
Boppard	124	Jd	50.14N	7.36 E
Boquerón	197a	Ab	18.03N	67.09W
Boquerón [3]	204	Bf	23.00S	61.00W
Boquilla, Presa de la- ⊟	192	Gd	27.30N	105.30W
Boquillas del Carmen	192	Hc	29.17N	102.53W
Bor [Czech.]	120	Ig	49.43N	12.47 E
Bor [Russia]	114	Kh	56.23N	44.07 E
Bor [Sud.]	160	Kh	6.12N	31.33 E
Bor [Swe.]	116	Fg	57.07N	14.10 E
Bor [Tur.]	146	Fd	37.54N	34.34 E
Bor [Yugo.]	130	Fe	44.06N	22.06 E
Bora-Bora, Ile- ⊕	208	Lf	16.30S	151.45W
Boraha, Nosy- ⊕	158	Lj	16.50S	49.55 E
Borah Peak ▲	174	He	44.08N	113.14W
Boraldaj ∿	135	Gc	42.30N	69.05 E
Bōramo	168	Gd	9.58N	43.07 E
Borås	114	Ch	57.43N	12.55 E
Borāzjān	146	Nh	29.16N	51.12 E
Borba [Braz.]	202	Gd	4.24S	59.35W
Borba [Port.]	126	Ef	38.48N	7.27W
Borborema, Planalto da- ▭	198	Mf	7.00S	37.00W
Borca	130	Ib	47.11N	25.46 E
Borcea	130	Ke	44.20N	27.45 E
Borcea, Braţul- ∿	130	Ke	44.40N	27.53 E
Borchgrevink Coast ⌒	222	Kf	73.00S	171.00 E
Borçka	146	Ib	41.22N	41.40 E
Borculo	124	Ib	52.07N	6.31 E
Borda da Mata, Serra- ▲	204	Ie	21.18S	47.06W
Bordeaux	112	Fg	44.50N	0.34W
Borden ⊕	180	Ga	78.30N	110.30W
Borden Peninsula ▬	174	Kb	73.00N	83.00W
Borders [3]	118	Kf	55.35N	3.00W
Bordertown	210	Fh	36.19S	140.47 E
Bordighera	128	Bg	43.46N	7.39 E
Bordj Bou Arreridj	162	Hb	36.04N	4.46 E
Bordj el Emir Abdelkader	126	Oi	35.52N	2.16 E
Bordj Fly Sainte Marie	162	Gd	27.18N	2.59W
Bordj Menaïel	126	Ph	36.44N	3.43 E
Bordj Messouda	162	Ic	30.12N	9.25 E
Bordj Moktar	160	Hf	21.20N	0.56 E
Bordj Omar Driss	160	Hf	28.09N	6.49 E
Bord Khūn-e Now	146	Nh	28.03N	51.28 E
Bordon Camp	124	Bc	51.07N	0.51W
Boreal, Chaco- ⊠	198	Kh	23.00S	60.00W
Boren ⊟	116	Ff	58.35N	15.10 E
Borensberg	116	Ff	58.34N	15.17 E
Borgå/Porvoo	114	Ff	60.24N	25.40 E
Borgarnes	114a	Bb	64.32N	21.55W
Børgefjell ▲	114	Cd	65.23N	13.50 E
Borgentreich	124	Lc	51.34N	9.15 E
Borger [Neth.]	124	Ib	52.55N	6.48 E
Borger [Tx.-U.S.]	182	Gd	35.39N	101.24W
Borgholm	114	Dh	56.53N	16.39 E
Borghorst, Steinfurt-	124	Jb	52.08N	7.25 E
Borgia	128	Kl	38.49N	16.30 E
Borgloon	124	Hd	50.48N	5.20 E
Borgomanero	128	Ce	45.42N	8.28 E
Borgorose	128	Hh	42.11N	13.15 E
Borgo San Dalmazzo	128	Bf	44.20N	7.30 E
Borgo San Lorenzo	128	Fg	43.57N	11.23 E
Borgosesia	128	Ce	45.43N	8.16 E
Borgou [3]	166	Fc	10.30N	2.50 E
Borgo Val di Taro	128	Df	44.29N	9.46 E
Borgo Valsugana	128	Fd	46.03N	11.27 E
Borgu ⊠	158	Hg	10.35N	3.40 E
Borgworm/Waremme	122	Ld	50.42N	5.15 E
Bori	166	Ge	4.42N	7.21 E
Borinquen, Punta- ►	197a	Ab	18.30N	67.10W
Borislav	136	Cf	49.18N	23.27 E
Borisoglebsk	112	Ke	51.23N	42.06 E
Borisov	136	Ce	54.15N	28.30 E
Borisovka	132	Jd	50.36N	36.06 E
Borispol	136	De	50.23N	30.59 E
Bo River	168	Dd	6.48N	27.55 E
Borja ▲	128	Lf	44.31N	17.44 E
Borja [Peru]	202	Cd	4.26S	77.33W
Borja [Sp.]	126	Kc	41.50N	1.32W
Borjas Blancas / les Borges Blanques	126	Mc	41.31N	0.52 E
Borken	120	Ce	51.51N	6.52 E
Borkou ⊠	158	Ig	18.15N	18.50 E
Borkou-Ennedi-Tibesti [3]	168	Bb	18.00N	19.00 E
Borkoviči	116	Mi	55.38N	28.23 E
Borkum ⊕	120	Cc	53.35N	6.41 E
Borlänge	114	Df	60.29N	15.25 E
Borlu	146	Cc	38.44N	28.27 E
Bormida ∿	128	Cf	44.56N	8.40 E
Bormio	128	Ed	46.28N	10.22 E
Born ⊠	122	Ej	44.30N	1.00W
Borna	120	Ie	51.07N	12.30 E
Borndiep ▬	124	Ha	53.25N	5.35 E
Borne	124	Ib	52.18N	6.45 E
Borneo/Kalimantan ⊕	140	Ni	1.00N	114.00 E
Bornheim	124	Id	50.46N	7.00 E
Bornholm [2]	116	Fi	55.10N	15.00 E
Bornholm ⊕	110	Hd	55.10N	15.00 E
Bornos	126	Gh	36.48N	5.44W
Bornova, İzmir-	146	Bc	38.27N	27.14 E
Bornu [2]	166	Hc	12.00N	12.40 E
Bornu ⊠	158	Ig	12.30N	13.00 E
Boro ∿	158	Jh	8.52N	26.11 E
Borodino [Russia]	114	Ii	55.32N	35.49 E
Borodino [Russia]	138	Ee	55.57N	95.03 E
Borodinskoje	116	Md	61.00N	29.29 E
Borogoncy	138	Id	62.39N	131.08 E
Borohoro Shan ▲	140	Ke	42.00N	85.00 E
Boromo	166	Ec	11.45N	2.56W
Borongan	150	Id	11.37N	125.26 E
Borotou	166	Dd	8.44N	7.30W
Borovan	130	Gf	43.26N	23.45 E
Borovec	130	Gg	42.16N	23.35 E
Boroviči	136	Dd	58.24N	33.56 E
Borovici	116	Mg	57.58N	29.47 E
Borovljanka	138	Df	52.38N	84.35 E
Borovo	128	Me	45.24N	18.59 E
Borovski	136	Gd	57.03N	65.44 E
Borovskoj	136	Ge	53.48N	64.17 E
Borrachas, Islas- ⊡	196	Dg	10.18N	64.44W
Borrān	168	Hc	10.11N	48.53 E
Borrby	116	Fi	55.27N	14.10 E
Borriana / Burriana	126	Le	39.53N	0.05W
Borroloola	210	Ef	16.04S	136.17 E
Borş	130	Eb	47.07N	21.49 E
Borşa	130	Hb	47.39N	24.40 E
•Borščovočny hrebet = Borshchovochny Range (EN) ▲	138	Gf	52.00N	118.30 E
Borsec	130	Ic	46.57N	25.34 E
Borshchovochny Range (EN) = Borščovočny hrebet ▲	138	Gf	52.00N	118.30 E
Borsod-Abaúj-Zemplén [2]	120	Qh	48.15N	21.00 E
Bortala/Bole	152	Dc	44.59N	81.57 E
Bortala He ∿	152	Dc	44.53N	82.45 E
Bort-les-Orgues	122	Ii	45.24N	2.30 E
Borūjen	146	Ng	31.59N	51.18 E
Borūjerd	144	Gc	33.54N	48.46 E
Borzja	142	Nd	50.24N	116.31 E
Borzna	132	Hd	51.15N	32.29 E
Boržomi	132	Mi	41.50N	43.25 E
Borzsöny ▲	120	Oi	47.55N	19.00 E
Borzyszkowy	120	Nb	54.03N	17.22 E
Bosa	128	Cj	40.18N	8.30 E
Bosanska Dubica	128	Ke	45.11N	16.48 E
Bosanska Gradiška	128	Le	45.09N	17.15 E
Bosanska Krupa	128	Kf	44.53N	16.10 E
Bosanski Brod	128	Me	45.08N	18.01 E
Bosanski Novi	128	Ke	45.03N	16.22 E
Bosanski Petrovac	128	Kf	44.34N	16.21 E
Bosanski Šamac	128	Me	45.04N	18.28 E
Bosansko Grahovo	128	Kf	44.11N	16.22 E
Bōsāso	160	Lg	11.13N	49.08 E
Bosavi, Mount- ▲	212	Ia	6.35S	142.50 E
Bosbeek ∿	124	Hc	51.06N	5.48 E
Bose	142	Mg	24.01N	106.32 E
Boshan	152	Kd	36.30N	117.50 E
Boshrūyeh	146	Qf	33.53N	57.26 E
Bosilegrad	130	Fg	42.30N	22.28 E
Bosingfeld, Extertal-	124	Lb	52.04N	9.07 E
Bosna ▲	130	Kg	42.11N	27.27 E
Bosna ∿	128	Me	45.04N	18.28 E
Bosna=Bosnia (EN) ⊠	110	Hg	44.00N	18.00 E
Bosna = Bosnia (EN) ▣	128	Lf	44.00N	18.00 E
Bosna i Hercegovina = Bosnia and Herzegovina (EN)	128	Lf	44.15N	17.50 E
Bosnia (EN) = Bosna	128	Lf	44.00N	18.00 E
Bosnia (EN) = Bosna	110	Hg	44.00N	18.00 E
Bosnia and Herzegovina (EN) = Bosna i Hercegovina	128	Lf	44.15N	17.50 E
Bosnik	150	Kg	1.10S	136.14 E
Bošnjakovo	138	Jg	49.41N	142.10 E
Bosobolo	170	Cb	4.11N	19.54 E
Bōsō-Hantō ▬	154	Pg	35.20N	140.10 E
Bosporus (EN) = Instanbul Boğazi ▬	110	Ig	41.00N	29.00 E
Bosque Bonito	192	Gb	30.42N	105.06W
Bossangoa	160	Ih	6.29N	17.27 E
Bossé Bangou	166	Fc	13.21N	1.18 E
Bossembélé	168	Bd	5.16N	17.39 E
Bossemtélé II	168	Bd	5.41N	16.38 E
Bossier City	182	Ie	32.31N	93.43W
Bosso	166	Hc	13.42N	13.19 E
Bosso, Dallol- ∿	158	Hg	12.25N	2.50 E
Bossut, Cape- ►	212	Ec	18.43S	121.38 E
Bostān	148	Db	30.26N	67.02 E
Bostānābād	146	Ld	37.50N	46.50 E
Bosten/Bagrax Hu ⊟	140	Ke	42.00N	87.00 E
Boston [Eng.-U.K.]	118	Mi	52.59N	0.01W
Boston [Ma.-U.S.]	176	Le	42.21N	71.04W
Boston Bar	188	Eb	49.52N	121.26W
Boston Deeps ≋	124	Ca	53.00N	0.15 E
Boston Mountains ▲	182	Id	35.50N	93.20W
Botan ∿	146	Id	37.44N	41.48 E
Botas, Ribeirão das- ∿	204	Fe	20.26S	53.43W
Botesdale	124	Db	52.20N	1.01 E
Botev ▲	110	Ig	42.43N	24.55 E
Botevgrad	130	Gg	42.54N	23.47 E
Bothnia, Gulf of- (EN)= Bottniska viken ◧	110	Hc	63.00N	20.00 E
Bothnia, Gulf of- (EN)= Pohjanlahti ◧	110	Hc	63.00N	20.00 E
Boticas	126	Ec	41.41N	7.40W
Botletle ∿	172	Cd	21.07S	24.42 E
Botlih	132	Oh	42.41N	46.13 E
Botna ∿	130	Mc	46.48N	29.30 E
Botoşani	130	Jb	47.45N	26.40 E
Botoşani [2]	130	Jb	47.40N	26.43 E
Botrange ▲	122	Md	50.30N	6.08 E
Botswana [1]	160	Jk	22.00S	24.00 E

Botte Donato 128 Kk 39.17N 16.27 E
Bottineau 182 Gb 48.50N 100.27W
Bottniska viken=Bothnia, Gulf of- (EN) 110 Hc 63.00N 20.00 E
Bottrop 120 Ce 51.31N 6.55 E
Botucatu 206 Kb 22.52S 48.26W
Botucatu, Serra de- 204 Hf 23.00S 48.20W
Botwood 180 Lg 49.08N 55.21W
Bouaflé 166 Dd 6.59N 5.45W
Bouaflé [3] 166 Dd 7.03N 5.48W
Bouaké 160 Gh 7.41N 5.02W
Bouaké [3] 166 Dd 7.45N 5.02W
Bou Anane 162 Gc 32.02N 3.03W
Bouar 160 Ih 5.57N 15.36 E
Bou Arfa 162 Gc 32.32N 1.57W
Boubin 120 Jh 48.58N 13.50 E
Bouca 160 Ih 6.30N 18.17 E
Bouchain 124 Fd 50.17N 3.19 E
Bouchegouf 128 Bn 36.28N 7.44 E
Bouche Island 197k Bb 13.57N 60.53W
Bouches-du-Rhône [3] 122 Kk 43.30N 5.00 E
Boudenib 162 Gc 31.57N 3.36W
Boudeuse Cay 172b Bb 6.05S 52.51 E
Boû Djébéha 166 Eb 18.33N 2.45W
Bouenza [3] 170 Bc 3.00S 13.00 E
Boufarik 126 Oh 36.36N 2.54 E
Bougaa 126 Rh 36.20N 5.05 E
Bougainville Island 208 Ge 6.00S 155.00 E
Bougainville Reef 212 Jc 15.30S 147.05 E
Bougainville Strait [Ocn.] 219a Cb 6.40S 156.10 E
Bougainville Strait [Van.] 219b Cb 15.50S 167.10 E
Bougouni 160 Gg 11.25N 7.28W
Bougtob 162 Hc 34.02N 0.05 E
Bouguenais 122 Eg 47.11N 1.37W
Bouguirat 126 Mi 35.45N 0.15 E
Bougzoul 126 Oi 35.42N 2.51 E
Bou Hadjar 128 Cn 36.30N 8.06 E
Bouhalla, Jbel- 126 Gi 35.06N 5.07W
Bou Hamed 126 Hi 35.19N 4.58W
Bouillante 197e Ab 16.08N 61.46W
Bouillon 122 Le 49.48N 5.04 E
Bouira 162 Hb 36.23N 3.54 E
Bouira [3] 162 Hb 36.15N 4.10 E
Bou Ismail 126 Oh 36.38N 2.41 E
Bou Izakarn 162 Fd 29.10N 9.44W
Bou Kadir 126 Nh 36.04N 1.07 E
Boukombé 166 Fc 10.11N 1.06 E
Boû Lanouâr 162 De 21.16N 16.30W
Boulay-Moselle 124 Ie 49.11N 6.30 E
Boulder [Co.-U.S.] 176 Ie 40.01N 105.17W
Boulder [Mt.-U.S.] 188 Ic 46.14N 112.07W
Boulder City 188 Hi 35.59N 114.50W
Boulemane 162 Gc 33.22N 4.45W
Boulemane [3] 162 Gc 33.02N 4.45W
Boulevard Atlántico 204 Dn 38.19S 57.59W
Boulia 212 Hd 22.54S 139.54 E
Bouligny 122 Le 49.17N 5.45 E
Boulogne 122 Eg 47.05N 1.40W
Boulogne-Billancourt 122 If 48.50N 2.15 E
Boulogne-sur-Mer 122 Hd 50.43N 1.37 E
Boulonnais 122 Hd 50.42N 1.40 E
Boulou, Le- 122 Il 42.31N 2.50 E
Bouloupari 219b Ce 21.52S 166.03 E
Boulsa 166 Ec 12.39N 0.34W
Boultoum 166 Hc 14.40N 10.18 E
Bou Maad, Djebel- 126 Oh 36.26N 2.08 E
Boumba 166 Ie 2.02N 15.12 E
Boumdeïd 162 Ef 17.26N 11.21W
Boum Kabir 168 Bc 10.11N 19.24 E
Boumort 126 Nb 42.14N 1.08 E
Bouna 160 Gh 9.16N 3.00W
Bouna [3] 166 Ed 9.15N 3.20W
Boû Nâga 162 Ef 19.00N 13.13W
Bou Nasser, Adrar- 162 Gc 33.35N 3.53W
Boundary Peak 188 Fh 37.51N 118.21W
Boundiali 166 Dd 9.31N 6.29W
Boundiali [3] 166 Dd 9.23N 6.32W
Boundji 170 Cc 1.03S 15.22 E
Boungou 168 Cd 6.45N 22.06 E
Bountiful 182 Ec 40.53N 111.53W
Bounty Bay 220q Ab 25.03S 130.05W
Bounty Islands 208 Ii 47.45S 179.05 E
Bounty Trough (EN) 106 Jn 46.00S 178.00 E
Bourail 216 Cd 21.34S 165.30 E
Bourbon-Lancy 122 Jh 46.37N 3.47 E
Bourbonnais 122 Ih 46.30N 3.00 E
Bourbonne-les-Bains 122 Lg 47.57N 5.45 E
Bourbourg 124 Ed 50.57N 2.12 E
Bourbre 122 Li 45.47N 5.11 E
Bourem 166 Eb 16.58N 0.21W
Bouressa 166 Fa 20.01N 2.18 E
Bourg-Achard 124 Ce 49.21N 0.49 E
Bourganeuf 122 Hi 45.57N 1.45 E
Bourgar'oûn, Cap- 162 Ib 37.06N 6.28 E
Bourg-de-Péage 122 Li 45.02N 5.03 E
Bourg-en-Bresse 122 Lh 46.12N 5.13 E
Bourges 112 Gf 47.05N 2.24 E
Bourget, Lac du- 122 Li 45.44N 5.52 E
Bourgneuf, Baie de- 122 Dg 47.05N 2.13W
Bourgogne 124 Ge 49.21N 4.04 E
Bourgogne=Burgundy (EN) 110 Gf 47.00N 4.30 E
Bourgogne=Burgundy (EN) 122 Kg 47.00N 4.30 E
Bourgogne, Canal de- 122 Jg 47.58N 3.30 E
Bourgogne, Porte de- 122 Mg 47.38N 6.52 E
Bourgoin-Jallieu 122 Li 45.35N 5.17 E
Bourgtheroulde-Infreville 124 Ce 49.18N 0.53 E
Bourguébus 124 Be 49.07N 0.18W
Boû Rjeïmât 162 Df 19.04N 15.08W
Bourke 210 Fh 30.05S 145.56 E
Bourne 124 Bb 52.46N 0.23W
Bournemouth 118 Lk 50.43N 1.54W
Bourtanger Moor 124 Jb 52.50N 7.06 E
Bourth 124 Cf 48.46N 0.49 E
Bou Saâda 162 Hb 35.12N 4.11 E
Bou Sellam 126 Qh 36.26N 4.34 E
Boussac 122 Ih 46.21N 2.13 E
Boussé 166 Ec 12.39N 1.53W
Boussens 122 Gk 43.11N 0.58 E
Bousso 168 Bc 10.29N 16.43 E
Bouthaleb, Djebel- 126 Ri 35.48N 5.12 E
Boutilimit 162 Ef 17.33N 14.42W
Bou Tlelis 126 Li 35.34N 0.54W
Boutonne 122 Fi 45.55N 0.49W
Bouvet Øy 222 Cd 54.26S 3.24 E
Bouxwiller 124 Jf 48.49N 7.29 E
Bouza 166 Gc 14.25N 6.02 E
Bouzanne 122 Hh 46.38N 1.28 E
Bouzghaïa 126 Nh 36.20N 1.15 E
Bouzonville 124 Ie 49.18N 6.32 E
Bovalino 128 Kl 38.09N 16.11 E
Bova Marina 128 Jm 37.56N 15.55 E
Bovec 128 Hd 46.20N 13.33 E
Bovenkarspel 124 Hb 52.42N 5.17 E
Boves 124 Ee 49.51N 2.23 E
Bovino 128 Jj 41.15N 15.20 E
Bovril 204 Cj 31.21S 59.26W
Bowa → Muli 152 Hf 27.55N 101.13 E
Bowen [Arg.] 206 Ge 35.02S 67.31W
Bowen [Austl.] 210 Fg 20.01S 148.15 E
Bowers Bank (EN) 178a Bb 54.00N 180.00
Bowers Ridge (EN) 178a Bb 54.30N 180.00
Bowie 186 Hj 33.34N 97.51W
Bowkān 146 Ld 36.31N 46.12 E
Bowland, Forest of- 118 Kh 54.00N 2.35W
Bowling Green [Ky.-U.S.] 182 Jd 37.00N 86.27W
Bowling Green [Oh.-U.S.] 184 Fe 41.22N 83.40W
Bowman 182 Gb 46.11N 103.24W
Bowman Bay 180 Kc 65.33N 73.40W
Bowman Island 222 He 65.17S 103.08 E
Bowman, Mount- 188 Ea 51.10N 121.55W
Bowo/Bomi 152 Ge 30.02N 95.39 E
Bowokan, Kepulauan- 150 Hg 2.05S 123.35 E
Bowral 212 Kf 34.28S 150.25 E
Bow River 188 Gg 49.56N 111.42W
Box Elder Creek 188 Kc 46.57N 108.04W
Boxelder Creek 188 Nd 45.59N 103.57W
Boxholm 114 Dg 58.12N 15.03 E
Boxian 152 Ke 33.46N 115.44 E
Boxing 152 Kd 37.07N 118.04 E
Boxmeer 124 Hc 51.39N 5.57 E
Boxtel 122 Lc 51.35N 5.20 E
Boyabat 146 Fb 41.28N 34.47 E
Boyabo 170 Cb 3.43N 18.46 E
Boyacá [3] 202 Db 5.30N 72.50W
Boyang 152 Kf 29.00N 116.41 E
Boyer, Cap- 219b De 21.37S 168.07 E
Boyer Ahmadī-e Kohkīlūyeh [3] 144 Hc 31.00N 50.30 E
Boyle/Mainistir na Búille 118 Eh 53.58N 8.18W
Boyne/An Bhóinn 118 Gh 53.43N 6.15W
Boyne City 184 Ec 45.13N 85.01W
Boynes, Iles de- 158 Nm 49.58S 69.59 E
Boynton Beach 184 Gl 26.32N 80.03W
Boysen Reservoir 188 Ke 43.19N 108.11W
Boz, Kūh-e- 146 Pi 27.46N 55.54 E
Bozburun 130 Lm 36.41N 28.04 E
Bozburun 130 Li 40.32N 28.46 E
Bozburun Dağı 146 Dd 37.18N 31.03 E
Bozcaada 146 Bc 39.50N 26.04 E
Bozcaada 146 Bc 39.49N 26.03 E
Bozdağ 130 Lk 38.20N 28.06 E
Boz Dağı [Tur.] 146 Cd 37.18N 29.12 E
Boz Dağı [Tur.] 146 Cc 38.19N 28.08 E
Boz Dağları 130 Kj 38.20N 27.45 E
Bozdoğan 130 Ll 37.40N 28.19 E
Bozeman 176 He 45.41N 111.02W
Bozen / Bolzano 112 Hf 46.31N 11.22 E
Bozene 170 Cb 2.56N 19.12 E
Bozhen 154 De 38.04N 116.34 E
Bozkol, zaliv- 135 Cb 45.20N 61.45 E
Bozkurt 146 Fb 41.57N 34.01 E
Bozok Platosu 146 Fc 39.05N 35.05 E
Bozouls 122 Ij 44.28N 2.43 E
Bozoum 160 Ih 6.19N 16.23 E
Bozova 146 Hd 37.22N 38.31 E
Bozovici 128 Fe 44.56N 22.00 E
Bozqūsh, Kūh-e- 146 Ld 37.45N 47.40 E
Bozüyük 146 Dc 39.54N 30.03 E
Bra 128 Bf 44.42N 7.51 E
Braås 116 Fg 57.04N 15.03 E
Braathen, Cape- 222 Pf 71.48S 96.05W
Brabant [3] 124 Gd 50.45N 4.30 E
Brabant [?] 122 Lc 51.10N 5.05 E
Brabant-les-Villers 124 Gf 48.51N 4.59 E
Brâbich 166 Eb 17.30N 3.00W
Brač 128 Kg 43.19N 16.40 E
Bracadale, Loch- 118 Gd 57.20N 6.35W
Bracciano 128 Gh 42.06N 12.40 E
Bracciano, Lago di- 128 Gh 42.05N 12.15 E
Bräcke 114 De 62.43N 15.27 E
Brackettville 186 Fl 29.19N 100.24W
Bračkí kanal 128 Kg 43.24N 16.40 E
Brackley 124 Ab 52.02N 1.09W
Bracknell 118 Mj 51.26N 0.46W
Brackwede, Bielefeld- 124 Kc 51.59N 8.31 E
Brad 130 Fc 46.08N 22.47 E
Bradano 128 Kj 40.23N 16.51 E
Bradenton 182 Kf 27.29N 82.34W
Bradford [Eng.-U.K.] 118 Lh 53.48N 1.45W
Bradford [Pa.-U.S.] 184 He 41.57N 78.39W
Bradley Reef 214 Gi 6.52S 160.48 E
Brady 182 He 31.08N 99.20W
Brady Mountains 186 Gk 31.20N 99.40W
Brædstrup 116 Ci 55.58N 9.37 E
Braemar 118 Jd 57.01N 3.24W
Braga 112 Fg 41.33N 8.26W
Braga [?] 126 Dc 41.35N 8.25W
Bragadiru 130 If 43.46N 25.31 E
Bragado 206 He 35.08S 60.30W
Bragança [2] 126 Fc 41.30N 6.45W
Bragança [Braz.] 200 Lf 1.03S 46.46W
Bragança [Port.] 126 Fc 41.49N 6.45W
Bragança Paulista 204 If 22.57S 46.34W
Brahestad/Raahe 114 Fd 64.41N 24.29 E
Brāhmanbāria 148 Id 23.59N 91.07 E
Brahmapur 142 Kh 19.19N 84.47 E
Brahmaputra 140 Lg 24.02N 90.59 E
Brăila 112 If 45.16N 27.59 E
Brăila [2] 130 Kd 45.13N 27.48 E
Brăilei, Balta- 130 Ke 45.00N 28.00 E
Braine 124 Fe 49.20N 3.32 E
Braine-l'Alleud/Eigenbrakel 124 Gd 50.41N 4.22 E
Brainerd 182 Ib 46.21N 94.12W
Braintree 124 Cc 51.53N 0.34 E
Braithwaite Point 212 Gb 11.58S 134.00 E
Brake (Unterweser) 120 Ec 53.20N 8.29 E
Brakel [Bel.] 124 Fd 50.47N 3.45 E
Brakel [Ger.] 124 Lc 51.43N 9.11 E
Brakna [3] 162 Ef 17.30N 13.30W
Brålanda 116 Ef 58.34N 12.22 E
Bralorne 188 Da 50.47N 122.49W
Bramming 116 Ci 55.28N 8.42 E
Brämön 116 Gb 62.10N 17.40 E
Brampton 184 Hd 43.41N 79.46W
Bramsche 120 Dd 52.24N 7.59 E
Bran, Pasul- 130 Id 45.26N 25.17 E
Branco 162 Cf 16.39N 24.41W
Branco, Cabo- 198 Mf 7.09S 34.47W
Branco, Rio- [Braz.] 198 Jf 1.24S 61.51W
Branco, Rio- [Braz.] 204 De 21.00S 57.48W
Branco ou Cabixi, Rio- 204 Ba 13.55S 60.10W
Brandberg 158 Ik 21.08S 14.35 E
Brandbu 114 Cf 60.26N 10.28 E
Brande 114 Bi 55.57N 9.07 E
Brandenburg 120 Id 52.25N 12.33 E
Brandenburg [?] 120 Jd 52.10N 13.30 E
Brändö 116 Id 60.25N 21.05 E
Brandon [Eng.-U.K.] 124 Cb 52.27N 0.37 E
Brandon [Fl.-U.S.] 184 Fl 27.56N 82.17W
Brandon [Man.-Can.] 176 Je 49.50N 99.57W
Brandon [Vt.-U.S.] 184 Kd 43.47N 73.05W
Brandon Head/Na Machairí 118 Ci 52.16N 10.15W
Brandon Mount/Cnoc Bréanainn 118 Ci 52.14N 10.15W
Brandval 116 Ed 60.19N 12.02 E
Brandvlei 172 Cf 30.25S 20.30 E
Brandýs nad Labem-Stará Boleslav 120 Kf 50.11N 14.40 E
Brănești 130 Je 44.27N 26.20 E
Braniewo 120 Pb 54.24N 19.50 E
Bransby Point 197c Bc 16.43N 62.14W
Bransfield Strait 222 Re 63.00S 59.00W
Brańsk 120 Sd 52.45N 22.51 E
Branson 186 Jh 36.39N 93.13W
Brantevik 116 Fi 55.31N 14.21 E
Brantford 180 Jh 43.08N 80.16W
Brantôme 122 Gi 45.22N 0.39 E
Bras d'Or Lake 180 Lg 45.50N 60.50W
Brasil=Brazil (EN) [1] 200 Kf 9.00S 53.00W
Brasil, Planalto do-=Brazilian Highlands (EN) 198 Lg 17.00S 45.00W
Brasiléia 202 Ef 11.00S 68.44W
Brasilia 200 Lg 15.47S 47.55W
Brasilia de Minas 204 Jc 16.12S 44.26W
Brasla 116 Kg 57.08N 24.50 E
Braslav 114 Gi 55.37N 27.05 E
Brașov 112 If 45.38N 25.35 E
Brașov [2] 130 Id 45.40N 25.10 E
Brass 166 Ge 4.19N 6.14 E
Brassac 122 Ik 43.38N 2.30 E
Brasschaat 124 Gc 51.17N 4.27 E
Brasstown Bald 184 Fh 34.52N 83.48W
Brastavățu 130 Hf 43.55N 24.24 E
Brataj 130 Ci 40.16N 19.40 E
Bratca 130 Fc 46.56N 22.37 E
Bråte 116 De 59.43N 11.27 E
Bratislava 112 Hf 48.09N 17.07 E
Bratsk 142 Md 56.05N 101.48 E
Bratskoje vodohranilišče=Bratsk Reservoir (EN) 138 Fe 56.30N 102.00 E
Bratsk Reservoir (EN)=Bratskoje vodohranilišče 138 Fe 56.30N 102.00 E
Brattleboro 182 Mc 42.51N 72.36W
Brattvåg 116 Bb 62.36N 6.27 E
Braubach 124 Jd 50.17N 7.40 E
Braunau am Inn 128 Hb 48.16N 13.02 E
Braunschweig 120 Gd 52.16N 10.32 E
Brava 158 Eg 14.52N 24.43W
Brava, Costa- 126 Pc 41.45N 3.04 E
Bråviken 116 Gf 58.40N 16.30 E
Bravo del Norte, Rio-=Grande, Rio- (EN) 174 Jg 25.57N 97.09W
Brawley 182 De 32.59N 115.34W
Bray 172 Ce 25.26S 23.38 E
Bray 180 Jc 69.20N 77.00W
Bray/Brè 118 Gh 53.12N 6.06W
Bray, Pays de- 122 He 49.46N 1.26 E
Bray-Dunes 124 Ec 51.05N 2.31 E
Braye 122 Gg 47.45N 0.42 E
Bray Head 118 Cj 51.53N 10.25W
Bray-sur-Somme 124 Ee 49.56N 2.43 E
Brazi 130 Je 44.52N 26.01 E
Brazil 184 Df 39.32N 87.08W
Brazil (EN)=Brasil [1] 200 Kf 9.00S 53.00W
Brazil Basin (EN) 106 Dk 15.00S 25.00W
Brazilian Highlands (EN)=Brasil, Planalto do- 198 Lg 17.00S 45.00W
Brazos 174 Jg 28.53N 95.23W
Brazos Santiago Pass 186 Hm 26.05N 97.16W
Brazzaville 160 Ii 4.16S 15.17 E
Brčko 128 Mf 44.52N 18.49 E
Brda 120 Oc 53.07N 18.08 E
Brdy 120 Jg 49.35N 13.50 E
Bré/Bray 118 Gh 53.12N 6.06W
Brea, Punta- 197a Bc 17.54N 66.55W
Breaden, Lake- 212 Fe 25.45S 125.40 E
Breaksea Sound 218 Bf 45.35S 166.40 E
Breaza [Rom.] 130 Id 45.11N 25.40 E
Breaza [Rom.] 130 Ib 47.37N 25.20 E
Breaza, Vîrful- 130 Hb 47.22N 24.02 E
Brebes 150 Eh 6.53S 109.03 E
Brêche 124 Ee 49.16N 2.30 E
Brechin 118 Ke 56.44N 2.40W
Brecht 124 Gc 51.21N 4.38 E
Brechte 124 Jb 52.15N 7.10 E
Breckenridge [Mn.-U.S.] 186 Hc 46.16N 96.35W
Breckenridge [Tx.-U.S.] 186 Gj 32.45N 98.54W
Breckland 118 Ni 52.30N 0.35 E
Břeclav 120 Mh 48.46N 16.54 E
Brecon 118 Jj 51.57N 3.24W
Brecon Beacons 118 Jj 51.53N 3.31W
Breda 122 Kc 51.35N 4.46 E
Bredaryd 116 Eg 57.10N 13.44 E
Bredasdorp 160 Jl 34.32S 20.02 E
Brede 124 Cd 50.55N 0.43 E
Bredene 124 Ec 51.14N 2.58 E
Bredstedt 120 Eb 54.37N 8.59 E
Bredy 136 Ge 52.26N 60.21 E
Bree 124 Hc 51.08N 5.36 E
Breg 120 Ei 47.57N 8.31 E
Bregalnica 130 Eh 41.36N 21.56 E
Bregenz 128 Dc 47.30N 9.46 E
Bréhat, Ile de- 122 Df 48.51N 3.00W
Breiðafjörður 110 Db 65.15N 23.15W
Breidvika 222 Df 70.15S 24.15 E
Breimsvatnet 116 Bc 61.40N 6.25 E
Breisach am Rhein 120 Dh 48.02N 7.35 E
Breisgau 120 Di 47.50N 7.42 E
Breisund 116 Ab 62.30N 6.00 E
Breit Bridge 172 Dd 22.12S 29.59 E
Breivikbotn 114 Fa 70.37N 22.29 E
Brejão 204 Ia 12.59S 46.28W
Brekken 114 Ce 62.39N 11.53 E
Brekstad 114 Be 63.41N 9.41 E
Bremangerlandet 114 Af 61.50N 5.00 E
Brembana, Val- 128 De 45.55N 9.40 E
Brembo 128 De 45.35N 9.32 E
Bremen [2] 120 Ec 53.05N 8.50 E
Bremen [Ger.] 112 Ge 53.05N 8.48 E
Bremen [In.-U.S.] 184 De 41.27N 86.09W
Bremerhaven 112 Ge 53.33N 8.35 E
Bremerton 182 Cb 47.34N 122.38W
Bremervörde 120 Fc 53.29N 9.08 E
Brendel 188 Kg 38.57N 109.50W
Brenham 186 Hk 30.10N 96.24W
Brenne 122 Hh 46.44N 1.14 E
Brennero, Passo del-=Brenner Pass (EN) 110 Hf 47.00N 11.30 E
Brennerpaß=Brenner Pass (EN) 110 Hf 47.00N 11.30 E
Brenner Pass (EN)=Brennero, Passo del- 110 Hf 47.00N 11.30 E
Brenner Pass (EN)=Brennerpaß 110 Hf 47.00N 11.30 E
Brenta 128 Ge 45.11N 12.18 E
Brentwood 118 Nj 51.38N 0.18 E
Brescia 112 Hf 45.33N 10.15 E
Breskens 124 Fc 51.24N 3.33 E
Breslau (EN)=Wrocław 112 He 51.06N 17.00 E
Bresle 122 Hd 50.04N 1.22 E
Bressanone / Brixen 128 Fd 46.43N 11.39 E
Bressay 118 La 60.08N 1.05W
Bresse 122 Lh 46.30N 5.15 E
Bressuire 122 Fh 46.51N 0.29W
Brest [Bela.] 112 Ie 52.06N 23.42 E
Brest [Fr.] 112 Ff 48.24N 4.29W
Brestova 128 Ie 45.08N 14.14 E
Brestskaja oblast [3] 136 Ce 52.20N 25.30 E
Bretagne=Brittany (EN) 110 Ff 48.00N 3.00W
Bretagne=Brittany (EN) 122 Df 48.00N 3.00W
Brețcu 130 Jc 46.03N 26.18 E
Breteuil [Fr.] 124 Cf 48.50N 0.55 E
Breteuil [Fr.] 122 Ie 49.38N 2.18 E
Breton, Marais- 122 Eh 46.56N 2.00W
Breton, Pertuis- 122 Eh 46.16N 1.22W
Breton Sound 186 Ll 29.30N 89.30W
Brett 124 Cc 51.58N 0.57 E
Brett, Cape- 218 Fa 35.10S 174.20 E
Bretten 124 Ke 49.03N 8.42 E
Bretteville-sur-Laize 124 Be 49.03N 0.20W
Breueh, Pulau- 150 Be 5.41N 95.05 E
Breuil-Cervinia 128 Be 45.56N 7.38 E
Breukelen 124 Db 52.10N 5.01 E
Breuna 124 Lc 51.25N 9.11 E
Breves 202 Hd 1.40S 50.29W
Brevik 114 Bg 59.04N 9.42 E
Brevoort 180 Ld 63.30N 64.20W
Brewarrina 212 Je 29.57S 146.52 E
Brewerville 166 Cd 6.25N 10.47W
Brewster 188 Fb 48.06N 119.47W
Brewster, Kap- 224 Md 70.10N 21.30W
Brewton 182 Je 31.07N 87.04W
Brezice 128 Je 45.54N 15.35 E
Brézina 162 Hc 33.05N 1.16 E
Březnice 120 Jg 49.33N 13.57 E
Breznik 130 Fg 42.44N 22.54 E
Brezno 120 Ph 48.49N 19.39 E
Brezoi 130 Hd 45.21N 24.15 E
Brezolles 124 Df 48.41N 1.04 E
Brezovo 130 Ig 42.21N 25.05 E
Bria 160 Jh 6.32N 21.59 E
Briance 122 Hi 45.47N 1.12 E
Briançon 122 Mj 44.54N 6.39 E
Brianza 128 De 45.45N 9.15 E
Briare, Canal de- 122 If 48.02N 2.43 E
Bribie Island 212 Ke 27.00S 153.05 E
Bričany 130 Ka 48.18N 27.04 E
Bride 118 Fi 52.05N 7.52W
Bridgend 118 Jj 51.31N 3.35W
Bridgeport [Ca.-U.S.] 188 Fg 38.10N 119.13W
Bridgeport [Ct.-U.S.] 182 Mc 41.11N 73.11W
Bridgeport [Nb.-U.S.] 186 Ef 41.40N 103.06W
Bridge River 188 Ea 50.45N 121.55W
Bridger Peak 188 Lf 41.12N 107.02W
Bridges Point 220g Bb 1.58N 157.28W
Bridgeton 184 Jf 39.26N 75.14W
Bridgetown [Austl.] 212 Df 33.57S 116.08 E
Bridgetown [Bar.] 176 Nh 13.06N 59.37W
Bridgewater 180 Lh 44.23N 64.31W
Bridgwater 118 Kj 51.08N 3.00W
Bridgwater Bay 118 Jj 51.16N 3.12W
Bridlington 118 Mg 54.05N 0.12W
Bridlington Bay 118 Mg 54.04N 0.08W
Bridport 118 Kk 50.44N 2.46W
Brie 122 Jf 48.40N 3.30 E
Brielle 124 Gc 51.54N 4.10 E
Brienzer See 128 Bd 46.45N 7.55 E
Briey 122 Le 49.15N 5.56 E
Brig 128 Bd 46.20N 8.00 E
Brigach 120 Ei 47.58N 8.30 E
Brigham City 182 Ec 41.31N 112.01W
Brighstone 124 Ad 50.38N 1.23W
Bright 212 Jg 36.44S 146.58 E
Brightlingsea 124 Dc 51.48N 1.02 E
Brighton [Co.-U.S.] 186 Dg 39.59N 104.49W
Brighton [Eng.-U.K.] 112 Fe 50.50N 0.10W
Brignoles 122 Mk 43.24N 6.04 E
Brihuega 126 Jd 40.45N 2.52W
Brijuni 128 Hf 44.55N 13.46 E
Brikama 166 Bc 13.16N 16.39W
Brilhante, Rio- 202 Hh 21.58S 54.18W
Brilon 124 Kc 51.24N 8.35 E
Brilon-Alme 124 Kc 51.27N 8.37 E
Brimstone Hill 197c Ab 17.21N 62.49W
Brindisi 112 Hg 40.38N 17.56 E
Brinkley 186 Ki 34.53N 91.12W
Brinkmann 204 Aj 30.52S 62.02W
Brionne 124 Ce 49.12N 0.43 E
Brioude 122 Ji 45.18N 3.24 E
Brisbane 210 Gg 27.28S 153.02 E
Brisighella 128 Ff 44.13N 11.46 E
Bristol 222 Ad 59.02S 26.31W
Bristol [Eng.-U.K.] 112 Fe 51.27N 2.35W
Bristol [Tn.-U.S.] 184 Fg 36.36N 82.11W
Bristol Bay 174 Dd 58.00N 159.00W
Bristol Channel 110 Fe 51.20N 4.00W
Bristol Lake 188 Hi 34.28N 115.41W
Bristow 186 Hi 35.50N 96.23W
Britannia Range 222 Jf 80.00S 158.00 E
British Columbia [2] 180 Fe 55.00N 125.00W
British Honduras → Belize [1] 176 Kh 17.15N 88.45W
British Indian Ocean Territory (EN) [5] 142 Jj 7.00S 72.00 E
British Isles 110 Fd 54.00N 4.00W
British Mountains 178 Kc 69.20N 140.20W
British Solomon Islands → Solomon Islands [1] 210 Ge 8.00S 159.00 E
British Virgin Islands [5] 176 Mh 18.20N 64.50W
Brits 172 De 25.40S 27.46 E
Britstown 172 Cf 30.37S 23.30 E
Britt 186 Je 43.06N 93.48W
Brittany (EN)=Bretagne 110 Ff 48.00N 3.00W
Brittany (EN)=Bretagne 122 Df 48.00N 3.00W
Britton 186 Hd 45.48N 97.45W
Brive-la-Gaillarde 122 Hi 45.09N 1.32 E
Briviesca 126 Ib 42.33N 3.19W
Brixen / Bressanone 128 Fd 46.43N 11.39 E
Brixham, Torbay- 118 Jk 50.24N 3.30W
Brjansk 112 Je 53.15N 34.22 E
Brjanskaja oblast [3] 136 De 52.50N 33.20 E
Brjuhoveckaja 132 Kg 45.46N 39.01 E
Brjukoviči 120 Tg 49.52N 24.00 E
Brno 112 Hf 49.12N 16.37 E
Broa, Ensenada de la- 194 Fb 22.35N 82.00W
Broadback 180 Jf 51.21N 78.53W
Broad Bay 118 Gc 58.15N 6.15W
Broadford 118 Hd 57.14N 5.54W
Broad Sound 212 Jd 22.10S 149.45 E
Broadstairs 124 Dc 51.22N 1.27 E
Broadus 182 Fb 45.27N 105.25W
Brocēni/Broceny 116 Jh 56.41N 22.30 E
Broceny/Brocēni 116 Jh 56.41N 22.30 E
Brochet 180 He 57.53N 101.40W
Brochu, Lac- 184 Ja 48.26N 74.15W
Brock 180 Ga 77.55N 114.30W
Brocken 120 Ge 51.48N 10.36 E
Brockman, Mount- 212 Dd 22.28S 117.18 E
Brockton 184 Ld 42.05N 71.01W
Brockville 180 Jh 44.35N 75.41W
Brod 130 Eh 41.31N 21.14 E
Brodarevo 130 Cf 43.14N 19.43 E
Broderick Falls 170 Fb 0.37N 34.46 E
Brodeur Peninsula 174 Kb 73.00N 88.00W
Brodick 118 Hf 55.35N 5.09W
Brodnica 120 Pc 53.16N 19.23 E
Brody 132 Dd 50.04N 25.12 E
Broglie 124 Ce 49.01N 0.32 E
Brok 120 Rd 52.43N 21.52 E
Brok 120 Rd 52.38N 21.55 E
Broken Arrow 186 Ih 36.03N 95.48W
Broken Bow 186 Gf 41.24N 99.38W
Broken Bow Lake 186 Ii 34.10N 94.40W
Broken Hill 210 Fh 31.57S 141.27 E
Broken Ridge (EN) 106 Hm 31.30S 95.00 E
Brokind 116 Ff 58.13N 15.40 E
Brokopondo 202 Hb 5.04N 55.00W
Bromary 116 Je 59.55N 23.00 E
Bromley, London- 124 Cc 51.25N 0.01 E
Bromölla 114 Dh 56.04N 14.28 E
Brønderslev 116 Cg 57.16N 9.58 E
Brong-Ahafo [3] 166 Ed 7.45N 1.30W
Bronnikovo 134 Ng 58.29N 68.27 E
Brønnøysund 114 Cd 65.28N 12.13 E
Bronte 128 Im 37.47N 14.50 E
Brooke's Point 150 Ge 8.47N 117.50 E
Brookfield 186 Jg 39.47N 93.04W
Brookhaven 186 Kk 31.35N 90.26W
Brookings [Or.-U.S.] 182 Cc 42.03N 124.17W
Brookings [S.D.-U.S.] 182 Hc 44.19N 96.48W
Brooks 180 Gf 50.35N 111.53W
Brooks Banks (EN) 214 Mc 24.05N 166.50W
Brooks Range 174 Dc 68.00N 154.00W
Brookston 186 Jc 46.50N 92.32W

Index Symbols

[1] Independent Nation
[2] State, Region
[3] District, County
[4] Municipality
[5] Colony, Dependency
Continent
Physical Region
Historical or Cultural Region
Mount, Mountain
Volcano
Hill
Mountains, Mountain Range
Hills, Escarpment
Plateau, Upland
Pass, Gap
Plain, Lowland
Delta
Salt Flat
Valley, Canyon
Crater, Cave
Karst Features
Depression
Polder
Desert, Dunes
Forest, Woods
Heath, Steppe
Oasis
Cape, Point
Coast, Beach
Cliff
Peninsula
Isthmus
Sandbank
Island
Atoll
Rock, Reef
Islands, Archipelago
Rocks, Reefs
Coral Reef
Well, Spring
Geyser
River, Stream
Waterfall, Rapids
River Mouth, Estuary
Lake
Salt Lake
Intermittent Lake
Reservoir
Swamp, Pond
Canal
Glacier
Ice Shelf, Pack Ice
Ocean
Sea
Gulf, Bay
Strait, Fjord
Lagoon
Bank
Seamount
Tablemount
Ridge
Shelf
Basin
Escarpment, Sea Scarp
Fracture
Trench, Abyss
National Park, Reserve
Point of Interest
Recreation Site
Cave, Cavern
Historic Site
Ruins
Wall, Walls
Church, Abbey
Temple
Scientific Station
Railway station
Airport
Port
Military installation
Lighthouse
Mine
Tunnel
Dam, Bridge

Brooksville 184 Fk 28.33N 82.23W
Brookton 212 Df 32.22S 117.01 E
Brookville [In.-U.S.] 184 Ef 39.25N 85.01W
Brookville [Pa.-U.S.] 184 He 41.10N 79.06W
Broom 118 Hd 57.45N 5.05W
Broom, Loch- 118 Hd 57.55N 5.15W
Broome 210 Df 17.58S 122.14 E
Brora 118 Jc 58.01N 3.51W
Brora 118 Jc 58.00N 3.50W
Brosna/An Bhrosnach 118 Fh 53.13N 7.58W
Broşteni 130 Ib 47.14N 25.42 E
Brou 122 Hf 48.13N 1.11 E
Brough 118 Kg 54.32N 2.19W
Broughton Island 176 Mc 67.35N 63.50W
Broussard 186 Kk 30.09N 91.58W
Brovary 132 Gd 50.32N 30.48 E
Brovst 116 Cg 57.06N 9.32 E
Brown Bank (EN)=Bruine Bank 124 Fb 52.35N 3.20 E
Brownfield 182 Ge 33.11N 102.16W
Browning 188 Ib 48.34N 113.01W
Browns Bank (EN) 180 Kh 42.40N 66.05W
Brownsville [Tn.-U.S.] 184 Ch 35.36N 89.15W
Brownsville [Tx.-U.S.] 176 Jg 25.54N 97.30W
Brownwood 182 He 31.43N 98.59W
Browse Island 212 Eb 14.05S 123.35 E
Bruay-en-Artois 122 Id 50.29N 2.33 E
Bruay-sur-l'Escaut 124 Fd 50.23N 3.32 E
Bruce 186 Lj 33.59N 89.21W
Bruce, Mount- 208 Cg 22.36S 118.08 E
Bruce Crossing 184 Cb 46.32N 89.10W
Bruce Peninsula 180 Jh 44.59N 81.20W
Bruce Rock 212 Df 31.53S 118.09 E
Bruche 122 Nf 48.34N 7.43 E
Bruchhausen-Vilsen 124 Lb 52.50N 9.01 E
Bruchmühlbach-Miesau 124 Je 49.23N 7.28 E
Bruchsal 120 Eg 49.08N 8.36 E
Bruck an der Leitha 128 Kb 48.01N 16.46 E
Bruck an der Mur 128 Jc 47.25N 15.17 E
Brue 118 Kj 51.13N 3.00W
Bruges/Brugge 122 Jc 51.13N 3.14 E
Brugg 128 Cc 47.29N 8.12 E
Brugge/Bruges 122 Jc 51.13N 3.14 E
Brugge-Assebroek 124 Fc 51.12N 3.16 E
Brüggen 124 Ic 51.15N 6.11 E
Brugge-Sint-Andries 124 Fc 51.12N 3.10 E
Brühl [Ger.] 124 Ke 49.24N 8.32 E
Brühl [Ger.] 124 Id 50.50N 6.54 E
Bruine Bank = Brown Bank (EN) 124 Fb 52.35N 3.20 E
Bruin Point 182 Ed 39.39N 110.22W
Brule River 184 Cc 45.57N 88.12W
Brumado 202 Jf 14.13S 41.40W
Brummen 124 Ib 52.06N 6.10 E
Brummo 116 Ef 58.50N 13.40 E
Brumunddal 114 Cf 60.53N 10.56 E
Bruna 128 Eh 42.45N 10.53 E
Brune 124 Fe 49.45N 3.47 E
Bruneau 188 He 42.53N 115.48W
Bruneau River 188 He 42.57N 115.58W
Bruneck / Brunico 128 Fd 46.48N 11.56 E
Brunehamel 124 Ge 49.46N 4.11 E
Brunei 142 Ni 4.30N 114.40 E
Brunei, Teluk- 140 Ni 5.05N 115.18 E
Brunette Downs 212 Hc 18.38S 135.57 E
Brunflo 116 Fa 63.05N 14.49 E
Brunico / Bruneck 128 Fd 46.48N 11.56 E
Brunna 116 Ge 59.52N 17.25 E
Brunner 218 De 42.26S 171.19 E
Brunner, Lake- 218 De 42.35S 171.25 E
Brunnsberg 116 Ec 61.17N 13.55 E
Brunsbüttel 120 Fc 53.54N 9.07 E
Brunssum 124 Hd 50.57N 5.57 E
Brunswick [Ga.-U.S.] 182 Ke 31.10N 81.29W
Brunswick [Me.-U.S.] 182 Nc 43.55N 69.58W
Brunswick, Peninsula- 198 Ik 53.30S 71.25W
Brunswick Lake 184 Fa 49.00N 83.23W
Bruntál 120 Ng 49.59N 17.28 E
Bruny Island 212 Jh 43.30S 147.05 E
Brus 130 Ef 43.23N 21.02 E
Brus, Laguna de- 194 Ef 15.50N 84.35W
Brush 182 Gc 40.15N 103.37W
Brus Laguna 194 Ef 15.47N 84.35W
Brusque 206 Kc 27.06S 48.56W
Brussel/Bruxelles=Brussels (EN) 112 Ge 50.50N 4.20 E
Brussels (EN)=Brussel/Bruxelles 112 Ge 50.50N 4.20 E
Brussels (EN)=Bruxelles/Brussel 112 Ge 50.50N 4.20 E
Brusset, 'Erg- 166 Hb 18.55N 10.30 E
Brusturi 130 Fb 47.09N 22.15 E
Brusy 120 Nc 53.53N 17.45 E
Bruxelles/Brussel=Brussels (EN) 112 Ge 50.50N 4.20 E
Bruzual 196 Bh 8.03N 69.19W
Bryan [Oh.-U.S.] 184 Ee 41.30N 84.34W
Bryan [Tx.-U.S.] 182 He 30.40N 96.22W
Bryan Coast 222 Pf 73.35S 84.00W
Bryne 114 Ag 58.44N 5.39 E
Brza Palanka 130 Fe 44.28N 22.27 E
Brzava kanal 130 Dd 45.16N 20.49 E
Brzeg 120 Nf 50.52N 17.27 E
Brzeg Dolny 120 Me 51.15N 16.40 E
Brzeziny 120 Pe 51.48N 19.46 E
Brzozów 120 Sg 49.42N 22.02 E
Bsharrī 146 Ge 34.15N 36.01 E
Bū 124 Df 48.48N 1.34 E
Bua 116 Eg 57.14N 12.07 E
Buada Lagoon 220e Ab 0.32S 166.54 E
Buala 210 Ge 8.10S 159.35 E
Bū al Ḩidān, Wādī- 164 Cd 27.25N 19.22 E
Buapinang 150 Hg 4.46S 121.34 E
Buatan 150 Df 0.44N 101.51 E
Bū aţ Ţifl 164 Dd 28.54N 22.30 E
Bua Yai 148 Ke 15.34N 102.24 E
Bu'ayrāt al Ḩasūn 164 Cc 31.24N 15.44 E
Bubanza 170 Ec 3.06S 29.23 E
Bubaque 166 Bc 11.17N 15.50W
Būbīyan 146 Mh 29.45N 48.15 E
Bubu 170 Gd 6.03S 35.19 E
Bubye 172 Ed 22.20S 31.07 E
Buca 130 Kk 38.22N 27.11 E
Bučač 132 De 49.04N 25.23 E
Bucacăča 138 Gf 52.59N 116.55 E
Bucak 146 Dd 37.28N 30.36 E
Bucaramanga 200 Ie 7.08N 73.09W
Bucas Grande 150 Ie 9.40N 125.58 E
Buccament Bay 197n Ba 13.12N 61.17W
Buccaneer Archipelago 212 Ec 16.17S 123.20 E
Bucecea 130 Jb 47.46N 26.26 E
Buchanan 160 Fh 5.53N 10.03W
Buchanan, Lake- [Austl.] 212 Jd 21.30S 145.50 E
Buchanan, Lake- [Tx.-U.S.] 186 Gk 30.48N 98.25W
Buchanan Bay 180 Ka 78.55N 75.00W
Buchan Gulf 180 Kb 71.48N 74.06W
Buchardo 206 Hd 34.43S 63.31W
Bucharest (EN)=Bucureşti 112 Ig 44.26N 26.06 E
Buchen 120 Fg 49.31N 9.20 E
Buchholz in der Nordheide 120 Fc 53.20N 9.52 E
Buchon, Point- 188 Ei 35.15N 120.54W
Buchs 128 Dc 47.10N 9.30 E
Buchy 124 De 49.35N 1.22 E
Bückeburg 124 Lb 52.16N 9.03 E
Buckeye 188 Ij 33.22N 112.35W
Buckhaven 118 Je 56.11N 3.03W
Buckie 118 Kd 57.40N 2.58W
Buckingham [Eng.-U.K.] 124 Bb 52.00N 0.59W
Buckingham [Que.-Can.] 184 Jc 45.35N 75.25W
Buckingham Bay 212 Hb 12.10S 135.46 E
Buckinghamshire 118 Mj 51.50N 0.55W
Buckland 178 Gc 66.16N 161.20W
Buckle Island 222 Ke 66.47S 163.14 E
Buckley Bay 222 Je 68.16S 148.12 E
Bucks 118 Mj 51.50N 0.55W
Bucksport 184 Mc 44.34N 68.48W
Buco Zau 170 Bc 4.50S 12.33 E
Bu Craa 162 Ed 26.17N 12.46W
Bucureşti 130 Je 44.30N 26.05 E
Bucureşti=Bucharest (EN) 112 Ig 44.26N 26.06 E
Bucy-lès-Pierrepont 124 Fe 49.39N 3.54 E
Bucyrus 184 Fe 40.47N 82.57W
Bud 114 Be 62.55N 6.55 E
Budacu, Vîrful- 130 Ib 47.07N 25.41 E
Buda-Koševelevo 132 Gc 52.43N 30.39 E
Budapest 112 Hf 47.30N 19.05 E
Budapest 120 Pi 47.30N 19.05 E
Búðardalur 114a Bb 65.07N 21.46W
Budaun 148 Fc 28.03N 79.07 E
Budbud 168 He 4.13N 46.31 E
Budd Coast 222 He 66.30S 113.00 E
Buddusò 128 Dj 40.35N 9.15 E
Bude [Eng.-U.K.] 118 Ik 50.50N 4.33W
Bude [Ms.-U.S.] 186 Kk 31.28N 90.51W
Bude Bay 118 Ik 50.50N 4.37W
Budel 124 Hc 51.16N 5.30 E
Budennovsk 136 Eg 44.45N 44.08 E
Budeşti 130 Je 44.14N 26.27 E
Budia 126 Jd 40.38N 2.45W
Büdingen 120 Ff 50.18N 9.07 E
Búdir 114a Cb 64.56N 14.01W
Budjala 170 Cb 2.39N 19.42 E
Budkowiczanka 120 Nf 50.52N 17.33 E
Budogošč 132 Hg 59.19N 32.29 E
Budrio 128 Ff 44.32N 11.32 E
Budslav 116 Lj 54.49N 27.32 E
Budva 130 Bg 42.17N 18.51 E
Budyšin/Bautzen 120 Ke 51.11N 14.26 E
Budžjak 130 Lc 46.15N 28.45 E
Buea 166 Ge 4.09N 9.14 E
Buëch 122 Lj 44.12N 5.57 E
Buenaventura [Col.] 200 Ie 3.53N 77.04W
Buenaventura [Mex.] 190 Cc 29.51N 107.29W
Buenaventura, Bahía de- 202 Cc 3.45N 77.15W
Buena Vista 192 Bb 31.10N 115.40W
Buenavista 192 Ef 23.39N 109.42W
Buena Vista [Co.-U.S.] 186 Cg 38.50N 106.08W
Buena Vista [Mex.] 192 Mi 16.05N 93.00W
Buena Vista [Ven.] 196 Eh 9.02N 63.49W
Buena Vista, Bahía de- 194 Hb 22.30N 79.08W
Buendía, Embalse de- 126 Jd 40.25N 2.43W
Buenópolis 204 Jc 17.54S 44.11W
Buenos Aires 206 Ie 36.00S 60.00W
Buenos Aires [Arg.] 200 Ki 34.36S 58.27W
Buenos Aires [C.R.] 194 Fi 10.04N 84.26W
Buenos Aires, Lago- 198 Ij 46.30S 72.00W
Buffalo 180 Fe 60.52N 115.03W
Buffalo [N.Y.-U.S.] 176 Le 42.54N 78.53W
Buffalo [Ok.-U.S.] 186 Gh 36.50N 99.38W
Buffalo [S.D.-U.S.] 182 Gb 45.35N 103.33W
Buffalo [Tx.-U.S.] 186 Hk 31.28N 96.04W
Buffalo [Wy.-U.S.] 182 Fc 44.21N 106.42W
Buffalo Bill Reservoir 188 Kd 44.29N 109.13W
Buffalo Lake 180 Fd 60.12N 115.25W
Buffalo Narrows 180 Ge 55.51N 108.30W
Buffalo Pound Lake 188 Ma 50.38N 105.20W
Buffels 172 Be 29.41S 17.04 E
Bū Fīshah 128 En 36.18N 10.28 E
Buford 184 Fh 34.07N 84.00W
Buftea 130 Ie 44.34N 25.57 E
Bug 110 Ie 52.31N 21.05 E
Buga 202 Cc 3.55N 76.18W
Bugarach, Pech de- 122 Il 42.52N 2.23 E
Bugeat 122 Hi 45.36N 1.56 E
Bugene 170 Fc 1.35S 31.08 E
Bugey 122 Li 45.48N 5.30 E
Bugojno 128 Lf 44.03N 17.27 E
Bugøynes 114 Gb 69.58N 29.39 E
Bugrino 136 Db 68.48N 49.09 E
Bugsuk 150 Ge 8.15N 117.18 E
Bugt 152 Lb 48.47N 121.55 E
Bugulma 136 Fe 54.33N 52.48 E
Bugun 135 Hc 43.22N 70.10 E
Bugun 136 Gc 42.56N 68.36 E
Bügür/Luntai 152 Dc 41.46N 84.10 E
Buguruslan 136 Fe 53.39N 52.30 E
Buhara 142 If 39.49N 64.25 E
Buharskaja oblast 136 Gg 41.20N 64.20 E
Bū Ḩaşā' 146 Ok 23.20N 53.20 E
Buhera 172 Ec 19.18S 31.29 E
Buh He 152 Gd 36.58N 99.48 E
Buhl 188 He 42.36N 114.46W
Bühl 120 Eh 48.42N 8.09 E
Bühödle 168 Hd 8.15N 46.20 E
Buhtarminskoje vodohranilišče 136 If 49.10N 84.00 E
Bui Dam 166 Ed 8.22N 2.10W
Builth Wells 118 Ji 52.09N 3.24W
Buin [Chile] 206 Fd 33.44S 70.44W
Buin [Pap.N.Gui.] 214 Fi 6.50S 155.44 E
Buinsk 136 Ee 54.59N 48.17 E
Buir Nur 152 Kb 47.48N 117.42 E
Buitrago del Lozoya 126 Id 41.00N 3.38W
Buj 136 Ed 58.29N 41.31 E
Buj 134 Gh 56.15N 54.12 E
Bujalance 126 Hg 37.54N 4.22W
Bujanovac 130 Eg 42.28N 21.47 E
Bujaraloz 126 Lc 41.30N 0.09W
Buje 128 He 45.24N 13.40 E
Bujnaksk 136 Eg 42.49N 47.07 E
Bujukly 138 Jg 49.33N 142.55 E
Bujumbura 160 Ji 3.23S 29.22 E
Bujunda 138 Kd 62.00N 153.30 E
Bük 120 Mi 47.23N 16.45 E
Buk 120 Md 52.22N 16.31 E
Buka Island 208 Ge 5.15S 154.35 E
Bukakata 170 Fc 0.18S 32.02 E
Bukama 160 Ji 9.12S 25.51 E
Buka Passage 219a Ba 5.25S 154.41 E
Bukavu 160 Ji 2.30S 28.52 E
Bukene 170 Fc 4.14S 32.53 E
Bukhā 146 Qi 26.10N 56.09 E
Bukit Besi 150 Df 4.46N 103.12 E
Bukit Mertajam 150 Ce 5.22N 100.28 E
Bukittinggi 142 Mj 0.19S 100.22 E
Bükk 120 Qh 48.05N 20.30 E
Bukoba 160 Ki 1.20S 31.49 E
Bukovina 130 Ia 48.00N 25.30 E
Bukowiec 120 Ld 52.23N 15.20 E
Bukuru 166 Gd 9.48N 8.52 E
Būl, Kūh-e- 144 Hc 30.48N 52.45 E
Bulajevo 136 He 54.53N 70.26 E
Bulan 150 Hd 12.40N 123.52 E
Bulanaš 134 Kh 57.16N 62.02 E
Bulancak 146 Hb 40.57N 38.14 E
Bulanık 146 Jc 39.05N 42.15 E
Būlāq 164 Fd 25.12N 30.32 E
Bulawayo 160 Jk 20.09S 28.34 E
Buldan 146 Cc 38.03N 28.51 E
Bulgan [Mong.] 152 Hc 44.05N 103.32 E
Bulgan [Mong.] 152 Hb 48.45N 103.34 E
Bulgan [Mong.] 152 Fb 46.05N 91.34 E
Bulgar (Kujbyšev) 114 Li 55.01N 49.06 E
Bulgaria (EN)=Bălgarija 112 Ig 43.00N 25.00 E
Buli 150 If 0.53N 128.18 E
Buli, Teluk- 150 If 0.45N 128.30 E
Buliluyan, Cape- 150 Ge 8.20N 117.11 E
Bulki 168 Fd 6.01N 36.36 E
Bullahār 168 Gc 10.23N 44.27 E
Bullange/Büllingen 124 Id 50.25N 6.16 E
Bullaque 126 Hf 38.59N 4.17W
Bulla Regia 128 Cn 36.33N 8.45 E
Bullas 126 Kf 38.03N 1.40W
Bulle 128 Bd 46.37N 7.04 E
Buller 218 Dd 41.44S 171.35 E
Bullfinch 212 Df 30.59S 119.06 E
Büllingen/Bullange 124 Id 50.25N 6.16 E
Bullion Mountains 188 Hi 34.25N 116.00W
Bulloo River 212 Ie 28.43S 142.30 E
Bull Point [Eng.-U.K.] 118 Ij 51.12N 4.10W
Bull Point [Falk.Is.] 206 Ih 52.19S 59.18W
Bulls 218 Fd 40.10S 175.23 E
Bulls Bay 184 Hi 32.59N 79.33W
Bull Shoals Lake 186 Jh 36.30N 92.50W
Bully Choop Mountain 188 Df 40.35N 122.45W
Bully-les-Mines 124 Ed 50.26N 2.43 E
Bulo Berde 168 He 3.52N 45.40 E
Bulolo 214 Di 7.12S 146.39 E
Bulqiza 130 Dh 41.30N 20.21 E
Bulter 186 Ig 38.16N 94.20W
Bultfontein 172 De 28.20S 26.05 E
Bulukumba 150 Hh 5.33S 120.11 E
Bulungu [Zaire] 170 Cc 4.33S 18.36 E
Bulungu [Zaire] 170 Dd 6.04S 21.54 E
Bumba 160 Jh 2.11N 22.28 E
Bumbah, Khalīj al- 164 Dc 32.25N 23.06 E
Buna 170 Gb 2.47N 39.31 E
Buna 130 Ch 41.52N 19.22 E
Bunbury 210 Ch 33.19S 115.38 E
Buncrana/Bun Crannċa 118 Ff 55.08N 7.27W
Bun Crannċa/Buncrana 118 Ff 55.08N 7.27W
Bunda 170 Fc 2.03S 33.52 E
Bundaberg 210 Gg 24.52S 152.21 E
Bünde 120 Ed 52.12N 8.35 E
Bundesrepublik Deutschland = Germany 112 Ge 51.00N 10.00 E
Bun Dobhráin/Bundoran 118 Eg 54.28N 8.17W
Bundoran/Bun Dobhráin 118 Eg 54.28N 8.17W
Bungay 124 Db 52.27N 1.27 E
Bungku 150 Hg 2.33S 121.58 E
Bungo 170 Cd 7.26S 15.24 E
Bungo Strait (EN)=Bungo-Suidō 154 Lh 32.40N 132.18 E
Bungo-Suidō=Bungo Strait (EN) 154 Lh 32.40N 132.18 E
Bungotakada 156 Be 33.33N 131.27 E
Bungsberg 120 Gb 54.12N 10.43 E
Buni 166 Hc 11.12N 12.02 E
Bunja 160 Kh 1.34N 30.15 E
Bunji 148 Ea 35.40N 74.36 E
Bunker 186 Kh 37.27N 91.13W
Bunker Group 212 Kd 23.50S 152.20 E
Bunkeya 170 Ee 10.24S 26.58 E
Bunkie 186 Jk 30.57N 92.11W
Bunnerfjällen 116 Ea 63.10N 12.34 E
Buñol 126 Le 39.25N 0.47W
Bunschoten 124 Hb 52.14N 5.24 E
Buntingford 124 Bc 51.57N 0.01W
Buntok 150 Fg 1.42S 114.48 E
Bünyan 146 Fc 38.51N 35.52 E
Bunyu, Pulau- 150 Gf 3.30N 117.50 E
Buon Me Thuot 148 Lf 12.40N 108.03 E
Buor-Haja, guba- 138 Ib 71.00N 131.00 E
Buotama 138 Hd 61.17N 128.55 E
Buqayq 144 Gd 25.56N 49.40 E
Buqda Kōsār 168 Ge 4.31N 44.49 E
Buqūm, Ḩarrat 164 He 20.54N 42.00 E
Bur 138 Hb 71.40N 123.40 E
Bura 170 Gc 1.06S 39.57 E
Buram 160 Jg 10.49N 25.10 E
Buran 136 If 48.04N 85.15 E
Burang 152 De 30.18N 81.08 E
Burāq 146 Gf 33.10N 36.29 E
Buras 186 Ll 29.21N 89.32W
Buraydah 142 Gg 26.20N 43.59 E
Burbach 124 Kd 50.43N 8.03 E
Būrdab 168 Hd 9.05N 46.30 E
Burdekin River 212 Jc 19.39S 147.30 E
Burdêre 168 He 3.30N 45.37 E
Burdur 144 Db 37.43N 30.17 E
Burdur Gölü 146 Dd 37.44N 30.12 E
Burdwood Bank (EN) 206 Ih 54.15S 59.00W
Bure 124 Db 52.38N 1.45 E
Bure [Eth.] 168 Fd 8.20N 35.08 E
Bure [Eth.] 168 Fc 10.43N 37.03 E
Bureå 114 Ed 64.37N 21.12 E
Bureinski hrebet = Bureya Range (EN) 140 Pd 50.40N 134.00 E
Bureja 138 Hg 49.43N 129.51 E
Bureja 140 Oe 49.25N 129.35 E
Büren 120 Ee 51.33N 8.34 E
Buren-Cogt 152 Jb 46.45N 111.30 E
Bureya Range (EN) = Bureinski hrebet 140 Pd 50.40N 134.00 E
Burfjord 114 Fb 69.56N 22.03 E
Būr Gābo 168 Gf 1.10S 41.50 E
Burgas 112 Ig 42.30N 27.28 E
Burgas 130 Kg 42.30N 27.20 E
Burgas, Gulf of- (EN)= Burgaski Zaliv 130 Kg 42.30N 27.33 E
Burgaski Zaliv=Burgas, Gulf of- (EN) 130 Kg 42.30N 27.33 E
Burg auf Fehmarn 120 Hb 54.26N 11.12 E
Burg auf Fehmarn-Puttgarden 120 Hb 54.30N 11.13 E
Burgaw 184 Ih 34.33N 77.56W
Burgaz Dağı 130 Mk 38.25N 29.46 E
Burg bei Magdeburg 120 Hd 52.16N 11.51 E
Burgdorf [Ger.] 120 Gd 52.27N 10.01 E
Burgdorf [Switz.] 128 Bc 47.04N 7.37 E
Burgenland 128 Kc 47.30N 16.25 E
Burgersdorp 172 Df 31.00S 26.20 E
Burgess Hill 124 Bd 50.58N 0.08W
Burgfjället 114 Dd 64.56N 15.03 E
Burghausen 120 Ih 48.10N 12.50 E
Burghūth, Sabkhat al- 146 Ie 34.58N 41.06 E
Burglengenfeld 120 Ig 49.12N 12.02 E
Burgos 126 Ib 42.20N 3.40W
Burgos [Mex.] 192 Je 24.57N 98.57W
Burgos [Sp.] 112 Fg 42.21N 3.42W
Burg-Reuland 124 Id 50.12N 6.09 E
Burgsvik 114 Eh 57.03N 18.16 E
Burgundy (EN)= Bourgogne 110 Gf 47.00N 4.30 E
Burgundy (EN)= Bourgogne 122 Kg 47.00N 4.30 E
Burgwald 124 Kd 50.57N 8.48 E
Būr Hakkaba 168 Ge 2.43N 44.10 E
Burhaniye 146 Bc 39.30N 26.58 E
Burhānpur 142 Jg 21.18N 76.14 E
Burias 150 Hd 12.57N 123.08 E
Buribaj 134 Ik 51.57N 58.11 E
Burica, Punta- 190 Hg 8.03N 82.53W
Burien 188 Dc 47.27N 122.21W
Burin Peninsula 180 Lg 47.00N 55.40W
Buriram 148 Kf 14.59N 103.08 E
Buriti, Rio- 204 Ca 12.50S 58.28W
Buriti Alegre 204 Hd 18.09S 49.03W
Buriti Bravo 202 Je 5.50S 43.50W
Buriti dos Lopes 202 Jd 3.10S 41.52W
Buritis 204 Ib 15.37S 46.26W
Burj al Ḩaţţābah 162 Ic 30.20N 9.30 E
Burjassot / Burjassot 126 Le 39.31N 0.25W
Burjassot/Burjasot 126 Le 39.31N 0.25W
Burjatija, respublika 138 Ff 53.00N 110.00 E
Burj Şāfītā 146 Ge 34.49N 36.07 E
Burkandja 138 Jd 63.27N 147.27 E
Burkburnett 186 Gi 34.06N 98.34W
Burke 186 Ge 43.11N 99.18W
Burke, Mount- 188 Ha 50.18N 114.30W
Burke Island 222 Of 73.08S 105.06W
Burke River 212 Hd 23.12S 139.33 E
Burkesville 184 Eg 36.48N 85.22W
Burketown 210 Ef 17.44S 139.22 E
Burkina Faso (Upper Volta) 160 Gg 13.00N 2.00W
Burley 182 Ec 42.32N 113.48W
Burli 132 Rd 51.28N 52.44 E
Burlingame 186 Ig 38.45N 95.50W
Burlington [Co.-U.S.] 182 Gd 39.18N 102.16W
Burlington [Ia.-U.S.] 186 Ic 40.49N 91.07W
Burlington [Ks.-U.S.] 186 Ig 38.12N 95.45W
Burlington [N.C.-U.S.] 184 Hg 36.06N 79.26W
Burlington [Ont.-Can.] 184 Hd 43.19N 79.43W
Burlington [Vt.-U.S.] 182 Mc 44.28N 73.14W
Burlington [Wi.-U.S.] 186 Le 42.41N 88.17W
Burma (Myanmar-Nainggan-Daw) 142 Lg 22.00N 98.00 E
Burnazului, Cîmpia- 130 Ie 44.10N 25.50 E
Burnett River 212 Kd 24.46S 152.25 E
Burney 188 Ef 40.53N 121.40W
Burnham Market 124 Cb 52.57N 0.44 E
Burnham-on-Crouch 124 Cc 51.37N 0.50 E
Burnie 212 Jh 41.04S 145.54 E
Burnley 118 Kh 53.48N 2.14W
Burns 182 Dc 43.35N 119.03W
Burnside 180 Gc 66.51N 108.04W
Burnside, Lake- 212 Ee 25.20S 123.10 E
Burns Lake 180 Ef 54.14N 125.46W
Burnsville 184 Fh 35.55N 82.18W
Burnt Lava Flow 188 Ef 41.35N 121.35W
Burnt River 184 Hc 44.35N 78.46W
Burntwood 180 He 56.08N 96.33W
Bur'o 160 Lh 9.30N 45.34 E
Burqin 152 Eb 47.43N 86.53 E
Burqin He 152 Eb 47.42N 86.50 E
Burra 212 Hf 33.40S 138.56 E
Burragorang Lake 212 Kf 34.00S 150.25 E
Burreli 130 Ch 41.37N 20.00 E
Burrendong Reservoir 212 Jf 32.40S 149.10 E
Burriana / Borriana 126 Le 39.53N 0.05W
Burro, Serranías del- 192 Ic 28.50N 101.35W
Burrow Head 118 Ig 54.41N 4.24W
Bursa 142 Ee 40.11N 29.04 E
Būr Sa'īd = Port Said (EN) 160 Ke 31.16N 32.18 E
Burscheid 124 Jc 51.06N 7.07 E
Bürstadt 124 Ke 49.38N 8.27 E
Burštyn 132 De 49.16N 24.37 E
Būr Sūdān=Port Sudan (EN) 160 Kg 19.37N 37.14 E
Burt Lake 184 Ec 45.27N 84.40W
Burtnieku, ozero- / Burtnieku ezers 116 Kg 57.35N 25.10 E
Burtnieku ezers / Burtnieku, ozero- 116 Kg 57.35N 25.10 E
Burton 184 Fd 43.02N 83.36W
Burton Latimer 124 Bb 52.21N 0.40W
Burton upon Trent 118 Li 52.49N 1.36W
Burträsk 114 Ed 64.31N 20.39 E
Buru, Pulau- 208 De 3.24S 126.40 E
Burullus, Buḩayrat al- 146 Dg 31.30N 30.50 E
Burultokay/Fuhai 152 Eb 47.06N 87.23 E
Burum Gana 166 Hc 13.00N 11.57 E
Burūn, Ra's- 146 Eg 31.14N 33.04 E
Burundaj 136 Hg 43.20N 76.49 E
Burundi 160 Ki 3.15S 30.00 E
Bururi 170 Ec 3.57S 29.37 E
Burutu 166 Gd 5.21N 5.31 E
Bury 118 Kh 53.36N 2.17W
Burylbajtal 135 Ib 44.56N 73.59 E
Buryn 132 Hd 51.13N 33.48 E
Bury Saint Edmunds 118 Ni 52.15N 0.43 E
Burzil Pass 148 Fb 34.54N 75.06 E
Busalla 128 Cf 44.34N 8.57 E
Busanga [Zaire] 170 Ee 10.12S 25.23 E
Busanga [Zaire] 170 Dc 0.51S 22.04 E
Busanga Swamp 170 Ee 14.10S 25.50 E
Buşayrah 146 Ie 35.09N 40.26 E
Būsh 146 Dh 29.09N 31.08 E
Būshehr 144 Hd 28.00N 52.00 E
Būshgān 146 Nh 28.48N 51.42 E
Bushimaie 158 Ji 6.02S 23.45 E
Bushmanland (EN)= Boesmanland 172 Be 29.30S 19.00 E
Busia 170 Fb 0.28N 34.06 E
Busigny 124 Fd 50.02N 3.28 E
Businga 170 Db 3.20N 20.53 E
Busira 158 Ii 0.15S 18.59 E
Busk 132 Dd 50.01N 24.37 E
Buskerud 114 Bf 60.30N 9.10 E
Busko-Zdrój 120 Qf 50.28N 20.44 E
Busoga 170 Fb 0.45N 33.30 E
Buşrá ash Shām 146 Gf 32.31N 36.29 E
Busselton 212 Df 33.39S 115.20 E
Bussum 122 Lb 52.16N 5.10 E
Bustamante, Bahía- 206 Gg 45.07S 66.27W
Buşteni 130 Id 45.24N 25.32 E
Busto Arsizio 128 Ce 45.37N 8.51 E
Buštyna 120 Th 48.03N 23.28 E
Busuanga 150 Hd 12.05N 120.05 E
Busu-Djanoa 170 Db 1.43N 21.23 E
Büsum 120 Eb 54.08N 8.51 E
Buta 160 Jh 2.48N 24.44 E
Butajira 168 Fd 8.08N 38.27 E
Buta Ranquil 206 Ge 37.03S 69.50W
Butare 170 Ec 2.36S 29.44 E
Butaritari Atoll 208 Id 3.03N 172.49 E
Bute, Island of- 118 Hf 55.50N 5.05W
Bute Inlet 188 Ca 50.37N 124.53W
Butembo 160 Jh 0.09N 29.17 E
Butera 128 Im 37.11N 14.11 E
Butere 170 Fb 0.13N 34.30 E
Butha Qi (Zalantum) 152 Lb 48.02N 122.42 E
Buthidaung 148 Id 20.52N 92.32 E
Butiá 206 Jd 30.07S 51.58W
Butiaba 170 Fb 1.49N 31.19 E
Butler 184 He 40.51N 79.55W
Butser Hill 124 Bd 50.57N 0.59W
Butte 176 He 46.00N 112.32W
Butterworth [Mala.] 150 Df 5.25N 100.24 E
Butterworth [S.Afr.] 172 Df 32.23S 28.04 E
Button Bay 180 Ie 58.45N 94.25W
Butuan 142 Oi 8.57N 125.33 E
Butung, Palau- 140 Oj 5.00S 122.55 E
Buturlinovka 132 Ld 50.48N 40.45 E
Butzbach 124 Kd 50.26N 8.41 E
Bützow 120 Hc 53.50N 11.59 E
Buxtehude 120 Fc 53.27N 9.42 E
Buxton [Eng.-U.K.] 118 Lh 53.15N 1.55W
Buxton [N.C.-U.S.] 184 Jh 35.16N 75.32W
Buyo 166 Dd 6.16N 7.03W
Büyükanafarta 130 Ji 40.17N 26.22 E
Büyükçekmece 130 Lh 41.01N 28.34 E
Büyükkarıştıran 130 Kh 41.18N 27.32 E
Büyük Kemikli Burun 130 Ji 40.18N 26.14 E
Büyük Mahya 130 Kh 41.47N 27.36 E

Büyük Menderes ≋ 144 Cb 37.57N 28.58 E
Büyükorhan 130 Lj 39.45N 28.55 E
Buyun Shan ▲ 152 Lc 40.06N 122.42 E
Buzači, poluostrov- ⊐ 110 Lf 45.00N 52.00 E
Buzan ≋ 132 Pf 46.18N 49.06 E
Buzançais 122 Hh 46.53N 1.25 E
Buzancy 124 Ge 49.25N 4.57 E
Buzău 130 Jd 45.09N 26.50 E
Buzău [2] 130 Jd 45.09N 26.50 E
Buzău ≋ 130 Kd 45.26N 27.44 E
Buzaymah 164 De 24.55N 22.02 E
Buzen 156 Be 33.37N 131.08 E
Buzet 128 He 45.24N 13.59 E
Būzhān 146 Le 34.09N 47.05 E
Búzi 172 Ec 19.51S 34.30 E
Búzi ≋ 172 Ec 19.52S 34.46 E
Buziaş 130 Ed 45.39N 21.36 E
Búzios, Ilha dos- ◆ 204 Jf 23.48S 45.08W
Bužora, gora- ▲ 120 Th 48.24N 23.15 E
Buzuluk 136 Fe 52.46N 52.17 E
Buzuluk [Russia] 132 Rc 52.47N 52.16 E
Buzuluk [Russia] 132 Md 50.13N 42.12 E
Buzzards Bay ◧ 184 Le 41.33N 70.47W
Bwagaoia 219a Ad 10.42S 152.50 E
Byälven ≋ 116 Ee 59.06N 12.54 E
Byam Martin ◆ 180 Ha 75.15N 104.15W
Byam Martin Channel ⇌ 180 Ha 76.00N 105.00W
Bychawa 120 Se 51.01N 22.32 E
Byczyna 120 Oe 51.07N 18.11 E
Bydgoszcz 112 He 53.08N 18.00 E
Bydgoszcz [2] 120 Nc 53.10N 18.00 E
Byelarus' = Belarus (EN) 136 Ce 53.50N 28.00 E
Bygdin 116 Cc 61.20N 8.35 E
Bygland 114 Bg 58.51N 7.51 E
Byglandsfjord 116 Bf 58.41N 7.48 E
Byglandsfjorden ≈ 116 Bf 58.50N 7.50 E
Byhov 136 De 53.31N 30.15 E
Byk ≋ 130 Mc 46.55N 29.25 E
Bykovec 130 Lb 47.12N 28.18 E
Bykovo 132 Ne 49.47N 45.25 E
Bykovski 138 Hb 71.56N 129.05 E
Bylot ◆ 174 Lb 73.13N 78.34W
Byrd, Cape- ► 222 Qe 69.38S 76.07W
Byrdbreen ❄ 222 Df 71.35S 26.00 E
Byrd Glacier ❄ 222 Jg 80.15S 160.20 E
Byron, Cape- ► 208 Gg 28.39S 153.38 E
Byron Bay 212 Ke 28.39S 153.37 E
Byron Bay ◧ 180 Gc 68.55N 108.25W
Byrranga, gory- = Byrranga Mountains (EN) ⛰ 140 Mb 75.00N 104.00 E
Byrranga Mountains (EN) = Byrranga, gory- ⛰ 140 Mb 75.00N 104.00 E
Bystraja ≋ 138 Kf 52.40N 156.10 E
Bystreyca ≋ 120 Se 51.40N 22.33 E
Bystřice ≋ 120 Lf 50.11N 15.30 E
Bystrovka 135 Jc 42.45N 75.43 E
Bystrzyca [Pol.] ≋ 120 Se 51.16N 22.45 E
Bystrzyca [Pol.] ≋ 120 Me 51.13N 16.54 E
Bystrzyca Kłodzka 120 Mf 50.19N 16.39 E
Bytantaj ≋ 138 Ic 68.40N 134.50 E
Bytča 120 Og 49.14N 18.35 E
Byten 120 Vd 52.49N 25.33 E
Bytom 120 Of 50.22N 18.54 E
Bytów 120 Nb 54.11N 17.30 E
Byumba 170 Fc 1.35S 30.04 E
Byxelkrok 114 Dh 57.20N 17.00 E
Bzura ≋ 120 Qd 52.23N 20.09 E
Bzyb ≋ 132 Lh 43.12N 40.15 E

C

Cà, Sông- ≋ 148 Le 18.40N 105.40 E
Caacupé 206 Ic 25.23S 57.09W
Čaadajevka 132 Nc 53.09N 45.56 E
Caaguazú 206 Ic 25.26S 56.02W
Caaguazú [3] 204 Eg 25.00S 55.45W
Caála 170 Ce 12.55S 15.35 E
Caapucú 204 Dh 26.13S 57.12W
Caarapó 204 Ef 22.38S 54.48W
Caatinga 202 Ig 17.10S 45.53W
Caatinga ⧗ 198 Lf 9.00S 42.00W
Caatinga, Rio- ≋ 204 Jc 17.10S 45.52W
Caazapá 206 Ic 26.09S 56.24W
Caazapá [3] 204 Dh 26.10S 56.00W
Cabaçal, Rio- ≋ 204 Db 16.00S 57.42W
Cabadbaran 150 Ie 9.10N 125.38 E
Cabaiguán 194 Hb 22.05N 79.30W
Caballeria, Cabo de- / Cavalleria, Cap de- ► 126 Qd 40.05N 4.05 E
Caballo Cocha 202 Dd 3.54S 70.32W
Caballo Reservoir ⊜ 186 Cj 32.58N 107.18W
Cabañas ▲ 126 Jg 37.40N 3.00W
Cabanatuan 142 Oh 15.29N 120.58 E
Cabano 184 Mb 47.41N 68.54W
Čabar 128 Ie 45.36N 14.39 E
Cabeceira do Apa 204 Ef 22.01S 55.46W
Cabeceiras 204 Ib 15.48S 46.59W
Cabeceiras de Basto 126 Ec 41.31N 7.59W
Cabeza, Arrecife- ✳ 192 Lh 19.04N 95.50W
Cabeza de Buey 126 Gf 38.43N 5.13W
Cabildo 204 Bn 38.29S 61.54W
Cabimas 200 Id 10.23N 71.28W
Cabinda 160 Ii 5.35S 12.13 E
Cabinda [3] 170 Bd 5.00S 12.30 E
Cabinet Mountains ⛰ 188 Hb 48.08N 115.46W
Cabixi, Rio- → Branco, Rio- ≋ 204 Ba 13.55S 60.10W
Cabo Bojador 162 Ed 26.08N 14.30W
Cabo Frio 200 Lh 22.53S 42.01W
Cabo Gracias a Dios 194 Ff 14.59N 83.10W
Cabonga, Réservoir- ⊜ 180 Jg 47.20N 76.35W
Caboolture 212 Ke 27.05S 152.50 E
Cabora Bassa, Dique de- ⟋ 172 Ec 15.34S 32.42 E
Cabora Bassa, Lago de- = Cabora Bassa, Lake- (EN) ≈ 158 Kj 15.40S 31.40 E
Cabora Bassa, Lake- (EN) = Cabora Bassa, Lago de- ≈ 158 Kj 15.40S 31.40 E
Caborca 190 Bb 30.37N 112.06W
Cabot Strait ⇌ 174 Ne 47.20N 59.30W
Cabourg 122 Fe 49.17N 0.08W
Cabo Verde = Cape Verde (EN) [1] 160 Eg 16.00N 24.00W
Cabo Verde, Ilhas do- = Cape Verde Islands (EN) ⁂ 158 Eg 16.00N 24.10W
Cabra 126 Hg 37.28N 4.27W
Cabral, Serra do- ⛰ 204 Jc 17.45S 44.22W
Cabras 128 Ck 39.56N 8.32 E
Cabras, Stagno di- ⩩ 128 Ck 39.55N 8.30 E
Cabreira ▲ 126 Dc 41.39N 8.04W
Cabrejas, Puerto de- ⩘ 126 Jd 40.08N 2.25W
Cabrera 194 Md 19.38N 69.54W
Cabrera, Illa- / Cabrera, Isla- ◆ 126 Oe 39.09N 2.56 E
Cabrera, Isla- / Cabrera, Illa- ◆ 126 Oe 39.09N 2.56 E
Cabrera, Sierra de- ⛰ 126 Fb 42.10N 6.25W
Cabri 188 Ka 50.37N 108.28W
Cabriel ≋ 126 Ke 39.14N 1.03W
Cabrit, Ilet à- ◆ 197e Ac 15.53N 61.36W
Cabrits, Ilet- ◆ 197h Bc 14.23N 60.52W
Cabrón, Cabo- ► 194 Md 19.22N 69.12W
Cabruta 196 Ci 7.38N 66.15W
Čabulja ⛰ 128 Lg 43.30N 17.35 E
Cabure 194 Mh 11.08N 69.38W
Cacacas, Islas- ⁂ 196 Dg 10.22N 64.26W
Caçador 206 Jc 26.47S 51.00W
Čačak 130 Df 43.54N 20.21 E
Caçapava dó Sul 206 Jd 30.30S 53.30W
Caccamo 128 Hm 37.56N 13.40 E
Caccia, Capo- ► 128 Cj 40.34N 8.09 E
Cacequi 204 Ei 29.53S 54.49W
Cáceres [3] 126 Ge 39.40N 6.00W
Cáceres [Braz.] 200 Kg 16.04S 57.41W
Cáceres [Sp.] 126 Fe 39.29N 6.22W
Cáceres, Laguna- ≈ 204 Dd 18.56S 57.48W
Cachari 206 Ie 36.24S 59.32W
Cache Peak ▲ 188 Ie 42.11N 113.40W
Cacheu ≋ 166 Bc 12.10N 16.21W
Cachimbo 200 Kf 9.08S 55.10W
Cachimbo, Serra do- ⛰ 198 Kf 8.30S 55.50W
Cachimo 170 Dd 8.20S 21.21 E
Cáchira 194 Kj 7.46N 73.03W
Cáchira, Río- ≋ 194 Kj 7.52N 73.40W
Cachoeira 202 Kf 12.36S 38.58W
Cachoeira Alta 204 Gd 18.48S 50.58W
Cachoeira de Goiás 204 Gc 16.44S 50.38W
Cachoeira do Arari 202 Id 1.01S 48.58W
Cachoeira do Sul 206 Jc 29.58S 52.54W
Cachoeira Dourada, Represa de- ⊜ 202 Ig 18.30S 49.00W
Cachoeirinha 204 Gi 29.57S 51.05W
Cachoeiro de Itapemirim 202 Jh 20.51S 41.06W
Cacinbinho 204 Ee 21.50S 55.43W
Căciulaţi 130 Je 44.38N 26.10 E
Cacolo 170 Ce 10.08S 19.18 E
Caconda 170 Ce 13.45S 15.05 E
Cacuaco 170 Bd 8.47S 13.21 E
Cacuchi ≋ 170 Ce 14.23S 16.59 E
Cacula 170 Be 14.29S 14.10 E
Caculé 202 Jf 14.30S 42.13W
Caculuvar ≋ 170 Bf 16.46S 14.56 E
Cacuso 170 Cd 9.26S 15.45 E
Čadan 138 Ef 51.17N 91.40 E
Cadaqués 126 Pb 42.17N 3.17 E
Čadca 120 Og 49.26N 18.48 E
Caddo Lake ≈ 186 Ij 32.42N 94.01W
Cadereyta Jiménez 192 Ie 25.36N 100.00W
Cadí, Serra de- / Cadí, Sierra del- ⛰ 126 Nb 42.17N 1.42 E
Cadí, Sierra del- / Cadí, Serra de- ⛰ 126 Nb 42.17N 1.42 E
Cadibarrawirracanna, Lake- ≈ 212 He 28.50S 135.25 E
Cadibona, Colle di- ⩘ 128 Cf 44.20N 8.22 E
Cadillac [Fr.] 122 Fj 44.38N 0.19W
Cadillac [Mi.-U.S.] 182 Jc 44.15N 85.24W
Cádiz 112 Fh 36.32N 6.18W
Cadiz 184 Dg 36.52N 87.50W
Cádiz [3] 126 Gh 36.30N 5.45W
Cadiz [Ca.-U.S.] 188 Hi 34.30N 115.30W
Cadiz [Phil.] 150 Hd 10.57N 123.18 E
Cádiz, Bahía de- ◧ 126 Fh 36.32N 6.16W
Cádiz, Golfo de- ◧ 110 Fh 36.50N 7.10W
Cadiz Lake ⩩ 188 Hi 34.18N 115.24W
Cadore ⧗ 128 Gd 46.30N 12.20 E
Cadwell 182 Dc 43.40N 116.41W
Čadyr-Lunga 132 Ff 46.04N 28.52 E
Caen 112 Ff 49.11N 0.21W
Caen, Campagne de- ⧗ 122 Fe 49.05N 0.20W
Caernarfon 118 Ih 53.08N 4.16W
Caernarfon Bay ◧ 118 Ih 53.05N 4.30W
Caerphilly 118 Jj 51.35N 3.14W
Caetité 202 Jf 14.04S 42.29W
Cafayate 206 Gc 26.05S 65.58W
Cafelândia [Braz.] 204 Fc 16.40S 53.25W
Cafelândia [Braz.] 204 He 21.49S 49.35W
Cafundó, Serra do- ⛰ 204 Hb 14.40S 48.23W
Čagan 136 He 50.30N 79.10 E
Cagan-Aman 136 Ef 47.32N 46.43 E
Cagan-Nur [Mong.] 152 Eb 49.40N 89.55 E
Cagan-Nur [Mong.] 152 Ia 50.25N 105.15 E
Cagan-Ula 152 Gb 49.35N 98.25 E
Cagatá, Arroyo- ≋ 204 Df 23.26S 56.36W
Cagayan ≋ 150 Hc 18.22N 121.37 E
Cagayan de Oro 142 Oi 8.29N 124.39 E
Cagayan Islands ⁂ 150 He 9.40N 121.16 E
Cagayan Sulu ◆ 150 Ge 7.01N 118.30 E
Čagda 138 Ie 58.42N 130.37 E
Cageri 132 Mh 42.39N 42.42 E
Çağiş 130 Lj 39.30N 28.01 E
Cagli 128 Gg 43.33N 12.39 E
Cagliari 112 Gh 39.13N 9.07 E
Cagliari, Golfo di- ◧ 128 Dk 39.10N 9.10 E
Cagliari, Stagno di- ⩩ 128 Dk 39.15N 9.05 E
Čaglinka ≋ 134 Nj 53.59N 69.47 E
Cagnes-sur-Mer 122 Nk 43.40N 7.09 E
Čagoda ≋ 114 Ig 59.12N 35.13 E
Čagodošča ≋ 114 Ig 58.58N 36.37 E
Caguas 190 Ke 18.14N 66.02W
Čagyl 136 Fg 40.43N 55.25 E
Cahama 170 Bf 16.16S 14.17 E
Caha Mountains/An Cheacha ▲ 118 Dj 51.45N 9.45W
Caher/An Chathair 118 Fi 52.22N 7.55W
Cahersiveen/Cathair Saidhbhín 118 Cj 51.57N 10.13W
Cahore Point/Rinn Chathóir 118 Gi 52.34N 6.11W
Cahors 122 Hj 44.26N 1.26 E
Caí, Rio- ≋ 204 Gi 29.56S 51.16W
Caia 172 Fc 17.49S 35.20 E
Caia ≋ 126 Ef 38.50N 7.05W
Caiabis, Serra dos- ⛰ 202 Gf 11.40S 56.30W
Caiapó, Rio- ≋ 204 Gb 15.49S 51.53W
Caiapó, Serra do- ⛰ 198 Kg 17.00S 52.00W
Caiapônia 204 Gc 16.57S 51.49W
Caibarién 190 Id 22.31N 79.28W
Caiçara 204 Gb 15.34S 50.12W
Caicara 202 Eb 7.37N 66.10W
Caicara de Maturín 196 Eh 9.49N 63.36W
Caicó 202 Ke 6.27S 37.06W
Caicos Bank (EN) ≡ 190 Jd 21.35N 71.55W
Caicos Islands ⁂ 174 Lg 21.45N 71.35W
Caicos Passage ⇌ 190 Jd 22.00N 72.30W
Caille Island ◆ 197p Bb 12.17N 61.35W
Caimanera 194 Jd 19.59N 75.09W
Caine, Río- ≋ 202 Eg 18.23S 65.21W
Cai Nuoc 148 Lg 8.56N 105.01 E
Caird Coast ⁓ 222 Af 76.00S 24.30W
Cairngorm Mountains ⛰ 118 Jd 57.06N 3.30W
Cairns 210 Ff 16.55S 145.46 E
Cairo [Ga.-U.S.] 184 Ej 30.53N 84.12W
Cairo [Il.-U.S.] 182 Jd 37.00N 89.11W
Cairo (EN) = Al Qāhirah 160 Ke 30.03N 31.15 E
Cairo Montenotte 128 Cf 44.24N 8.16 E
Caiseal/Cashel 118 Fi 52.31N 7.53W
Caisleán an Bharraigh/ Castlebar 118 Dh 53.52N 9.17W
Caister-on-Sea 124 Db 52.40N 1.45 E
Caiundo 170 Cf 15.42S 17.27 E
Caiúva, Lagoa- ◎ 204 Fk 32.24S 52.30W
Caiyuanzhen → Shengsi 154 Gi 30.42N 122,29 E
Caizi Hu ≈ 154 Di 30.48N 117.05 E
Čaja ≋ 138 De 58.17N 82.45 E
Cajabamba 202 Ce 7.58S 77.59W
Caja de Muertos, Isla- ◆ 197a Bc 17.53N 66.31W
Cajamarca 200 If 7.10S 78.31W
Cajamarca [3] 202 Ce 6.15S 78.50W
Cajapió 202 Jd 2.58S 44.48W
Cajarc 122 Hj 44.29N 1.51 E
Cajatambo 202 Cf 10.29S 77.02W
Čajkovski 136 Fd 56.47N 54.09 E
Çakırgöl Dağ ▲ 146 Hb 40.34N 39.42 E
Cakmak 146 Fd 37.37N 34.19 E
Cakmak Dağı ▲ 146 Jc 39.46N 42.12 E
Čakor ⩘ 130 Dg 42.40N 20.02 E
Čakovec 128 Kd 46.23N 16.26 E
Cakrani 130 Ci 40.36N 19.37 E
Çal 146 Cc 38.05N 29.24 E
Cal, Rio de la- ≋ 204 Cc 17.27S 58.15W
Calabar 160 Hh 4.57N 8.19 E
Calabozo 202 Eb 8.56N 67.26W
Calabozo, Ensenada de- ◧ 194 Lh 11.30N 71.45W
Calabria [2] 128 Kl 39.00N 16.30 E
Calaburras, Punta de- ► 126 Hh 36.30N 4.38W
Calacoto 202 Eg 17.18S 68.39W
Calacuccia 122a Ba 42.20N 9.01 E
Calaf 126 Nc 41.44N 1.31 E
Calafat 130 Ff 43.59N 22.56 E
Calafate 200 Ik 50.20S 72.16W
Cala Figuera, Cabo de- / Cala Figuera Cap de- ► 126 Oe 39.22N 2.46 E
Cala Figuera, Cap de- / Cala Figuera, Cabo de- ► 126 Oe 39.22N 2.46 E
Calagua Islands ⁂ 150 Hd 14.27N 122.55 E
Calahorra 126 Kb 42.18N 1.58W
Calai 170 Cf 17.50S 19.20 E
Calais [Fr.] 112 Ge 50.57N 1.50 E
Calais [Me.-U.S.] 184 Nc 45.11N 67.17W
Calais, Pas de- = Dover, Strait of- (EN) ⇌ 110 Ge 51.00N 1.30 E
Calakmul ⁘ 192 Oh 18.05N 89.55W
Calalaste, Sierra de- ⛰ 206 Gc 25.30S 67.30W
Calama 200 Jh 22.28S 68.56W
Calamar 194 Jh 10.14N 74.56W
Calamian Group ⁂ 140 Nh 12.00N 120.00 E
Calamocha 126 Kd 40.55N 1.18W
Călan 130 Fd 45.44N 22.59 E
Calanda 126 Ld 40.56N 0.14W
Calandula 160 Ii 9.06S 15.58 E
Calang 150 Cf 4.30N 95.40 E
Calangiánus 128 Dj 40.56N 9.11 E
Calapan 150 Hd 13.25N 121.10 E
Calar Alto ▲ 126 Jg 37.15N 2.25W
Călăraşi 130 Ke 44.12N 27.20 E
Călăraşi [2] 130 Je 44.15N 27.00 E
Cala Ratjada 126 Pe 39.42N 3.25 E
Calar del Mundo ⛰ 126 Jf 38.31N 2.28W
Calatafimi 128 Gm 37.55N 12.52 E
Calatañazor 126 Jc 41.42N 2.49W
Calatayud 126 Kc 41.21N 1.38W
Calatrava ⁘ 126 If 38.35N 3.48W
Calatrava, Campo de- ⧗ 126 Hf 38.50N 4.15W
Calavà, Capo- ► 128 Il 38.10N 14.55 E
Calavon ≋ 122 Kk 43.53N 5.25 E
Calayan ◆ 150 Hc 19.20N 121.27 E
Calbayog 142 Oh 12.04N 124.36 E
Calchaqui 206 Hc 29.54S 60.18W
Calçoene 202 Hc 2.30N 50.57W
Calcutta 142 Kg 22.32N 88.22 E
Caldaro / Kaltern 128 Fd 46.25N 11.14 E
Caldas [3] 202 Cb 5.15N 75.30W
Caldas da Rainha 126 Ce 39.24N 9.08W
Caldas Novas 204 Hc 17.45S 48.38W
Caldeirão, Serra de- ⛰ 126 Dg 37.19N 8.04W
Calder ≋ 118 Lh 53.44N 1.21W
Caldera 206 Fc 27.04S 70.50W
Calderina, Sierra de la- ⛰ 126 Ie 39.19N 3.48W
Caldes de Montbui 126 Oc 41.38N 2.10 E
Caldwell 184 Gf 39.44N 81.32W
Căleanu, Vîrful- ▲ 130 Fd 45.19N 22.32 E
Caledon 172 Bf 34.12S 19.23 E
Caledon ≋ 158 Jl 30.32S 26.05 E
Caledonia [Blz.] 194 Cd 18.14N 88.29W
Caledonia [Mn.-U.S.] 186 Ke 43.38N 91.29W
Caledonian Canal ═ 118 Id 57.20N 4.30W
Calella 126 Oc 41.37N 2.40 E
Caleta Olivia 206 Gg 46.26S 67.32W
Calexico 188 Hj 32.40N 115.30W
Çalgal Dağı ▲ 146 Hc 39.06N 38.05 E
Calgary 176 Hd 51.03N 114.05W
Calhoun 184 Eh 34.30N 84.57W
Cali 200 Ie 3.27N 76.31W
Calicut (Kozhikode) 142 Jh 11.19N 75.46 E
Caliente 182 Ed 37.37N 114.31W
California [2] 182 Dd 37.30N 119.30W
California, Golfo de- = California, Gulf of- (EN) ◧ 174 Hg 28.00N 112.00W
California, Gulf of- (EN) = California, Golfo de- ◧ 174 Hg 28.00N 112.00W
Căliman, Munţii- ⛰ 130 Ib 47.07N 25.03 E
Călimăneşti 130 Hd 45.14N 24.20 E
Calimere, Point- ► 148 Ff 10.18N 79.52 E
Calingasta 206 Gd 31.19S 69.25W
Calispell Peak ▲ 188 Gb 48.26N 117.30W
Calitri 128 Jj 40.54N 15.26 E
Calitzdorp 172 Cf 33.33S 21.42 E
Caliviny 197p Bb 12.01N 61.43W
Calixtlahuaca ⁘ 192 Jh 19.15N 99.45W
Calka 132 Ni 41.35N 44.05 E
Calkiní 192 Ng 20.22N 90.03W
Callabonna, Lake- ≈ 212 Ie 29.45S 140.05 E
Callac 122 Cf 48.24N 3.26W
Callaghan, Mount- ▲ 188 Gg 39.42N 116.57W
Callainn/Callan 118 Fi 52.33N 7.23W
Callan/Callainn 118 Fi 52.33N 7.23W
Callander [Ont.-Can.] 184 Hb 46.13N 79.23W
Callander [Scot.-U.K.] 118 Ie 56.15N 4.13W
Callantsoog 124 Gb 52.50N 4.41 E
Callao 200 Ig 12.02S 77.05W
Callao [3] 202 Cf 2.04S 77.09W
Calliaqua 197n Ba 13.08N 61.12W
Callosa de Ensarriá / Callosa d'eu Sarrià 126 Lf 38.39N 0.07W
Callosa de Segura 126 Lf 38.08N 0.52W
Callosa d'eu Sarrià / Callosa de Ensarriá 126 Lf 38.39N 0.07W
Calmalli 192 Cc 28.14N 113.33W
Călmăţui [Rom.] ≋ 130 Ke 44.50N 27.50 E
Călmăţui [Rom.] ≋ 130 If 43.46N 25.10 E
Calonne ≋ 124 Ce 49.17N 0.12 E
Calore ≋ 128 Ii 41.11N 14.28 E
Čalovo → Vel'ký Meder 120 Ni 47.52N 17.47 E
Calp / Calpe 126 Mf 38.39N 0.03 E
Calpe / Calp 126 Mf 38.39N 0.03 E
Caltabellotta 128 Hm 37.34N 13.13 E
Caltagirone 128 Im 37.14N 14.31 E
Caltanissetta 128 Im 37.29N 14.04 E
Caltilibük 130 Lj 39.57N 28.36 E
Čaltyr 132 Kf 47.17N 39.29 E
Caluago 170 Cd 8.21S 19.40 E
Calucinga 170 Ce 11.19S 16.13 E
Călugareni 130 Ie 44.11N 25.59 E
Calulo 170 Bd 9.59S 14.54 E
Caluquembe 170 Be 13.46S 14.41 E
Calvados [3] 122 Fe 49.10N 0.30W
Calvados, Côte du- ⁓ 122 Fe 49.22N 0.30W
Calvert Island ◆ 188 Ba 51.35N 128.00W
Calvert River ≋ 212 Hc 16.17S 137.44 E
Calvi 122a Aa 42.34N 8.45 E
Calvillo 192 Hg 21.51N 102.43W
Calvinia 160 Il 31.25S 19.45 E
Calvitero ▲ 126 Gd 40.20N 5.43W
Cam ≋ 118 Ni 52.21N 0.15 E
Camabatela 170 Cd 8.13S 15.23 E
Camacá 202 Kg 15.24S 39.30W
Camacupa 170 Ce 12.01S 17.22 E
Camaguán 196 Ch 8.06N 67.36W
Camagüey 176 Lg 21.23N 77.55W
Camagüey [3] 194 Ic 21.30N 78.10W
Camagüey, Archipiélago de- ⁂ 190 Id 22.18N 78.00W
Camaiore 128 Eg 43.56N 10.18 E
Camajuaní 194 Hb 22.28N 79.44W
Camamu 202 Kf 13.57S 39.07W
Camaná 202 Dg 16.37S 72.42W
Camanongue 170 De 11.27S 20.12 E
Camapuã 204 Ed 19.30S 54.05W
Camapuã, Sertão de- ⁖ 198 Kg 19.00S 51.30W
Camaquã 206 Jd 30.51S 51.49W
Camaquã, Rio- ≋ 204 Gj 31.17S 51.47W
Camarat, Cap- ► 122 Mk 43.12N 6.41 E
Camargo [Bol.] 202 Eh 20.39S 65.13W
Camargo [Sp.] 126 Ia 43.24N 3.54W
Camargos, Represa- ⊜ 204 Je 21.20S 44.30W
Camargue ⧗ 122 Kk 43.31N 4.34 E
Camariñas 126 Ca 43.07N 9.10W
Camarón, Cabo- ► 190 He 16.00N 85.04W
Camarones 206 Gf 44.48S 65.42W
Camarones, Bahía- ◧ 206 Gf 44.45S 65.34W
Camas [Sp.] 126 Fg 37.24N 6.02W
Camas [Wa.-U.S.] 188 Dd 45.35N 122.24W
Ca Mau 148 Lg 9.11N 105.08 E
Ca Mau, Mui = Ca Mau Point (EN) ► 140 Mi 8.38N 104.44 E
Ca Mau Point (EN) = Ca Mau, Mui- ► 140 Mi 8.38N 104.44 E
Cambados 126 Db 42.30N 8.48W
Camberg 124 Kd 50.18N 8.16 E
Camberley 124 Bc 51.21N 0.44W
Cambo ≋ 170 Cd 7.40S 17.17 E
Cambodia (EN) = Kampuchea 142 Mh 13.00N 105.00 E
Cambo-les-Bains 122 Ek 43.22N 1.24 E
Camboriú, Ponta- ► 204 Ig 25.10S 47.55W
Cambrai 122 Jd 50.10N 3.14 E
Cambremer 124 Ce 49.09N 0.03 E
Cambrésis ⧗ 124 Fd 50.15N 3.05 E
Cambrian Mountains ⛰ 110 Fe 52.35N 3.35W
Cambridge ▣ 118 Ni 52.25N 0.10 E
Cambridge [Eng.-U.K.] 118 Ni 52.12N 0.07 E
Cambridge [Id.-U.S.] 188 Gd 44.34N 116.41W
Cambridge [Ma.-U.S.] 184 Ld 42.22N 71.06W
Cambridge [Md.-U.S.] 184 If 38.34N 76.04W
Cambridge [Mn.-U.S.] 186 Jd 45.31N 93.14W
Cambridge [N.Z.] 218 Fb 37.53S 175.28 E
Cambridge [Oh.-U.S.] 184 Ge 40.02N 81.36W
Cambridge Airport ✈ 124 Cb 52.10N 0.08 E
Cambridge Bay 176 Ic 69.03N 105.05W
Cambridge Gulf ◧ 212 Fb 14.55S 128.15 E
Cambridgeshire [3] 118 Mi 52.25N 0.05W
Cambutal, Cerro- ▲ 194 Gj 7.16N 80.36W
Camden [Al.-U.S.] 184 Dj 32.00N 87.17W
Camden [Ar.-U.S.] 182 Ie 33.35N 92.50W
Camden [N.J.-U.S.] 184 Jf 39.57N 75.07W
Camden [S.C.-U.S.] 184 Gh 34.16N 80.36W
Camden [Tn.-U.S.] 184 Cg 36.04N 88.06W
Camden Bay ◧ 178 Kb 70.00N 145.00W
Camdenton 186 Jg 38.00N 92.45W
Camel ≋ 118 Ik 50.33N 4.55W
Çameli 146 Cd 37.05N 29.20 E
Camerino 128 Hg 43.08N 13.04 E
Cameron ◆ 180 Ha 76.15N 104.00W
Cameron [Az.-U.S.] 188 Ji 35.51N 111.25W
Cameron [La.-U.S.] 186 Jl 29.48N 93.19W
Cameron [Mo.-U.S.] 186 Ig 39.44N 94.14W
Cameron [Tx.-U.S.] 186 Hk 30.51N 96.59W
Cameron [Wi.-U.S.] 186 Kd 45.25N 91.44W
Cameron Hills ⌓ 180 Fe 60.00N 118.00W
Cameron Mountains ⛰ 218 Bf 46.00S 166.55 E
Cameroon (EN) = Cameroun [1] 160 Ih 6.00N 12.00 E
Cameroon Mountain ▲ 158 Hh 4.12N 9.11 E
Camerota 128 Jj 40.02N 15.22 E
Cameroun = Cameroon (EN) [1] 160 Ih 6.00N 12.00 E
Cametá 202 Id 2.15S 49.30W
Camiguin [Phil.] ◆ 150 He 9.11N 124.42 E
Camiguin [Phil.] ◆ 150 Hc 18.56N 121.55 E
Camiling 150 Hc 15.42N 120.24 E
Camilla 184 Ej 31.14N 84.12W
Caminha 126 Dc 41.52N 8.50W
Camissombo 170 Bd 8.10S 20.39 E
Camoapa 194 Eg 12.23N 85.31W
Camocim 200 Lf 2.54S 40.50W
Camonica, Val- ∨ 128 Ed 46.00N 10.20 E
Camooweal 212 Hc 19.55S 138.07 E
Camopi 202 Hc 3.13N 52.28W
Camorta ◆ 148 Ig 8.08N 93.30 E
Camotes Islands ◆ 150 Hd 11.00N 124.45 E
Campagne-lès-Hesdin 124 Dd 50.24N 1.52 E
Campana 204 Cl 34.10S 58.57W
Campana, Isla- ◆ 198 Ij 48.20S 75.15W
Campanario 126 Gf 38.52N 5.37W
Campanário 204 Ef 22.48S 55.03W
Campania [2] 128 Ii 41.00N 14.30 E
Campanquiz, Cerros- ⛰ 202 Cd 4.30S 77.40W
Campbell, Cape- ► 218 Fd 41.44S 174.16 E
Campbell Island ◆ 218 Ci 52.30S 169.10 E
Campbell Plateau (EN) ⊓ 208 Ij 51.00S 170.00 E
Campbell River 180 Ef 50.01N 125.15W
Campbellsville 184 Eg 37.21N 85.20W
Campbellton 180 Kg 48.00N 66.40W
Campbelltown, Sydney- 212 Kf 34.04S 150.49 E
Campbeltown 118 Hf 55.26N 5.36W
Campeche 176 Jh 19.51N 90.32W
Campeche [2] 190 Fe 19.00N 90.30W
Campeche, Bahía de- = Campeche, Gulf of- (EN) ◧ 174 Jg 20.00N 94.00W
Campeche, Gulf of- (EN) = Campeche, Bahía de- ◧ 174 Jg 20.00N 94.00W
Campeche Bank (EN) ≡ 190 Fd 22.00N 90.00W
Campechuela 194 Ic 20.14N 77.17W
Camperdown 212 Ig 38.14S 143.09 E
Campidano ▁ 128 Ck 39.30N 8.45 E
Campiglia Marittima 128 Eg 43.03N 10.37 E
Campillos 126 Hg 37.03N 4.51W
Campina Grande 200 Mf 7.13S 35.53W
Campinas 200 Lh 22.54S 47.05W
Campina Verde 204 Hd 19.31S 49.28W
Campine/Kempen ⧗ 122 Lc 51.10N 5.20 E
Campinorte 204 Hb 14.20S 49.08W
Campione d'Italia 128 Ce 45.59N 8.59 E
Campo 166 Ge 2.22N 9.49 E
Campo Alegre 196 Bh 9.15N 68.25W
Campo Alegre de Goiás 204 Ic 17.36S 47.46W
Campobasso 128 Ii 41.34N 14.39 E
Campo Belo 204 Je 20.53S 45.16W
Campo de Criptana 126 Ie 39.24N 3.07W
Campo de la Cruz 194 Jh 10.23N 74.52W
Campo del Cielo 204 Bh 27.53S 61.49W
Campo Florido 204 Hd 19.46S 48.34W
Campo Formoso 202 Jf 10.31S 40.20W
Campo Gallo 206 Hc 26.35S 62.51W
Campo Garay 204 Bi 29.41S 61.37W
Campo Grande [Arg.] 204 Eh 27.13S 54.58W
Campo Grande [Braz.] 200 Kh 20.27S 54.37W
Campo Largo [Arg.] 204 Bh 26.48S 60.50W
Campo Largo [Braz.] 204 Hg 25.26S 49.32W
Campo Maior [Braz.] 202 Jd 4.49S 42.10W
Campo Maior [Port.] 126 Ee 39.01N 7.04W
Campomarino 128 Ji 41.57N 15.02 E
Campo Mourão 206 Jb 24.03S 52.22W

Index Symbols

[1] Independent Nation
[2] State, Region
[3] District, County
[4] Municipality
[5] Colony, Dependency
■ Continent
⧗ Physical Region
▣ Historical or Cultural Region
▲ Mount, Mountain
🌋 Volcano
⌒ Hill
⛰ Mountains, Mountain Range
⌓ Hills, Escarpment
⏜ Plateau, Upland
⩘ Pass, Gap
▁ Plain, Lowland
Δ Delta
▤ Salt Flat
∨ Valley, Canyon
◉ Crater, Cave
⌬ Karst Features
⌄ Depression
⊟ Polder
∴ Desert, Dunes
♣ Forest, Woods
⁖ Heath, Steppe
✽ Oasis
► Cape, Point
⁓ Coast, Beach
◨ Cliff
⊐ Peninsula
⋈ Isthmus
⋯ Sandbank
◆ Island
○ Atoll
✳ Rock, Reef
⁂ Islands, Archipelago
⁑ Rocks, Reefs
✺ Coral Reef
⊙ Well, Spring
⊚ Geyser
≋ River, Stream
↡ Waterfall, Rapids
⊻ River Mouth, Estuary
≈ Lake
≊ Salt Lake
≂ Intermittent Lake
⊜ Reservoir
⩩ Swamp, Pond
═ Canal
❄ Glacier
❅ Ice Shelf, Pack Ice
🌊 Ocean
∿ Sea
◧ Gulf, Bay
⇌ Strait, Fjord
◎ Lagoon
≡ Bank
⩚ Seamount
⊓ Tablemount
⋀ Ridge
▬ Shelf
◡ Basin
⌇ Escarpment, Sea Scarp
ϟ Fracture
∪ Trench, Abyss
✿ National Park, Reserve
★ Point of Interest
⚑ Recreation Site
◠ Cave, Cavern
⌖ Historic Site
⁘ Ruins
▥ Wall, Walls
✝ Church, Abbey
⛩ Temple
⚗ Scientific Station
🚉 Railway station
✈ Airport
⚓ Port
⚔ Military installation
⛯ Lighthouse
⚒ Mine
∩ Tunnel
⟋ Dam, Bridge

Name	Page	Grid	Lat.	Long.
Campos	200	Lh	21.45S	41.18W
Campos [Braz.]	198	Kh	21.00S	51.00W
Campos [Braz.]	198	Lg	15.00S	44.30W
Campos, Laguna-	204	Be	20.50S	61.31W
Campos, Tierra de-	126	Hb	42.10N	4.50W
Campos Altos	204	Id	19.41S	46.10W
Campos Belos	204	Ia	13.03S	46.53W
Campos do Jordão	204	Jf	22.44S	45.35W
Campos Novos	204	Gh	27.24S	51.12W
Campos Sales	202	Je	7.04S	40.23W
Campo Tures / Sand in Taufers	128	Fd	46.55N	11.57 E
Camp Verde	182	Ee	34.34N	111.51W
Cam Ranh	148	Lf	11.54N	109.13 E
Camrose	180	Gf	53.01N	112.50W
Camseil	180	Fc	65.40N	118.07W
Camsell Portage	180	Ge	59.38N	109.42W
Çan	146	Bb	40.02N	27.03 E
Canaan [Ct.-U.S.]	184	Kd	42.02N	73.20W
Canaan [Trin.]	196	Fg	11.09N	60.49W
Canaan Mountain	188	Jh	37.45N	111.51W
Cana Brava, Ribeirão-	204	Ic	16.35S	46.34W
Cana Brava, Rio- [Braz.]	204	Ib	14.40S	47.07W
Cana Brava, Rio- [Braz.]	204	Ha	12.12S	48.40W
Cana Brava, Rio- [Braz.]	204	Ha	13.11S	48.11W
Canada	176	Jc	60.00N	95.00W
Cañada	126	Fb	42.50N	6.05W
Canada Basin (EN)	224	Ad	80.00N	145.00W
Cañada de Gómez	206	Hd	32.49S	61.24W
Canadian	186	Fi	35.55N	100.23W
Canadian River	174	Jf	35.27N	95.03W
Canaguá, Rio-	194	Mj	7.57N	69.36W
Canaima	202	Fb	6.07N	62.55W
Canakkale bogazı = Dardanelles (EN)	110	Ig	40.15N	26.25 E
Canala	219b	Be	21.32S	165.57 E
Canandaigua	184	Id	42.53N	77.19W
Cananea	190	Bb	30.57N	110.18W
Cananéia	204	Ig	25.01S	47.57W
Canapolis	204	Hd	18.44S	49.13W
Canarias, Islas-=Canary Islands (EN)	160	Ff	28.00N	15.30W
Canarias, Islas-=Canary Islands (EN)	158	Ff	28.00N	15.30W
Canaries	197k	Ab	13.55N	61.04W
Canaronero, Laguna-	192	Ff	23.00N	106.15W
Canarreos, Archipiélago de los-	190	Hd	21.50N	82.30W
Canary Basin (EN)	106	Dg	30.00N	25.00W
Canary Islands (EN)= Canarias, Islas-	160	Ff	28.00N	15.30W
Canary Islands (EN)= Canarias, Islas-	158	Ff	28.00N	15.30W
Cañas [C.R.]	194	Eh	10.25N	85.07W
Cañas [Pan.]	194	Gj	7.27N	80.16W
Canastra, Serra da-	204	Ie	20.00S	46.20W
Canatlán	192	Ge	24.31N	104.47W
Cañaveral	126	Fe	39.47N	6.23W
Canaveral, Cape-	174	Kg	28.30N	80.35W
Canavese	128	Be	45.20N	7.40 E
Canavieiras	202	Kg	15.39S	38.57W
Canazei	128	Fd	46.28N	11.46 E
Canberra	210	Fh	35.17S	149.08 E
Canby [Mn.-U.S.]	186	Hd	44.43N	96.16W
Canby [Or.-U.S.]	188	Dd	45.16N	122.42W
Cance	122	Ki	45.12N	4.48 E
Canche	122	Hd	50.31N	1.39 E
Cancon	122	Gj	44.32N	0.37 E
Cancún	190	Gd	21.05N	86.46W
Cancún, Isla-	192	Pg	21.05N	86.46W
Çandarli	130	Jk	38.56N	26.56 E
Çandarli Körfezi	130	Jk	38.52N	26.55 E
Candé	122	Eg	47.34N	1.02W
Candela	192	Id	26.50N	100.40W
Candelaria	192	Nh	18.18N	91.21W
Candelaria, Cerro-	192	Hf	23.25N	103.43W
Candelaria, Rio- [Bol.]	204	Cc	17.17S	58.39W
Candelaria, Rio- [Mex.]	192	Nh	18.38N	91.15W
Candelaro	128	Ji	41.34N	15.53 E
Cândido de Abreu	204	Gg	24.35S	51.20W
Cândido Mendes	202	Id	1.27S	45.43W
Candlemas Islands	222	Ad	57.03S	26.40W
Candói	204	Fg	25.43S	52.11W
Çandyr	132	Sj	38.13N	55.44 E
Canela	206	Jc	29.22S	50.50W
Canelli	128	Cf	44.43N	8.17 E
Canelones	204	Dl	34.32S	56.17W
Canelones	204	El	34.35S	56.00W
Canendiyu	204	Eg	24.20S	55.00W
Cañete [Chile]	206	Fe	37.48S	73.24W
Cañete [Sp.]	126	Kd	40.03N	1.39W
Cangallo	204	Cm	37.13S	58.42W
Cangamba	170	Ce	13.44S	19.53 E
Cangas	126	Db	42.16N	8.47W
Cangas de Narcea	126	Fa	43.11N	6.33W
Cangas de Onís	126	Ga	43.21N	5.07W
Cangola	170	Cd	7.58S	15.53 E
Cangombe	170	Ce	14.24S	19.59 E
Cangshan (Bianzhuang)	154	Eg	34.51N	118.03 E
Canguçu	204	Fj	31.24S	52.41W
Canguçu, Serra do-	204	Fj	31.20S	52.40W
Canguinha	204	Eb	14.42S	55.40W
Cangumbe	170	Ce	12.00S	19.09 E
Cangyuan	152	Gg	23.10N	99.15 E
Cangzhou	152	Kd	38.14N	116.58 E
Cani, Iles-	128	Em	37.21N	10.07 E
Caniapiscau	174	Md	57.40N	69.30W
Caniapiscau, Lac-	180	Kf	54.00N	70.10W
Canicatti	128	Hm	37.21N	13.51 E
Canigou	122	Il	42.31N	2.27 E
Canik Dağları	146	Gb	40.50N	37.10 E
Canim Lake	188	Ea	51.52N	120.45W
Canindé	202	Kd	4.22S	39.19W
Canindé, Rio-	202	Je	6.15S	42.52W
Cañitas de Felipe Pescador	192	Hf	23.36N	102.43W
Çankaya, Ankara-	146	Ec	39.56N	32.52 E
Çankırı	144	Da	40.36N	33.37 E
Canna	118	Gd	57.03N	6.33W
Cannac	219a	Ac	9.15S	153.29 E
Çannakale	144	Ca	40.09N	26.24 E
Cannanore	148	Ff	11.51N	75.22 E
Cannanore Islands	148	Ef	10.05N	72.10 E
Cannes	122	Nk	43.33N	7.01 E
Cannich	118	Id	57.20N	4.45W
Canning Basin	212	Ed	20.10S	123.00 E
Cannobio	128	Cd	46.04N	8.42 E
Cannock	118	Ki	52.42N	2.01W
Cannonball River	186	Fc	46.26N	100.38W
Cann River	212	Jg	37.34S	149.10 E
Caño, Isla del-	194	Fi	8.44N	83.53W
Canoas	206	Jc	29.56S	51.11W
Canoas, Punta-	192	Bc	29.25N	115.10W
Canoas, Rio-	206	Jc	27.36S	51.25W
Canoeiros	202	Ig	18.02S	45.31W
Canoinhas	204	Gh	26.10S	50.24W
Canoinhas, Rio-	204	Gh	26.07S	50.22W
Cañoles / Cànyoles	126	Le	39.02N	0.29W
Canon City	182	Fd	38.27N	105.14W
Canon Fiord	180	Ja	80.15N	83.00W
Canonnier, Pointe du-	197b	Ab	18.04N	63.10W
Canora	180	Hf	51.37N	102.26W
Canosa di Puglia	128	Ki	41.13N	16.04 E
Canouan Island	196	Ff	12.43N	61.20W
Canourgue, La-	122	Jj	44.25N	3.13 E
Canso, Strait of -	180	Lg	45.35N	61.23W
Canta	202	Cf	11.25S	76.38W
Cantabria	126	Ha	43.15N	4.00W
Cantabrian Mountains (EN) =Cantábrica, Cordillera-	110	Fg	43.00N	5.00W
Cantábrica, Cordillera-= Cantabrian Mountains (EN)	110	Fg	43.00N	5.00W
Cantábrico, Mar-	126	Ha	44.00N	4.00W
Cantal	122	Ii	45.05N	2.40 E
Cantal	110	Gf	45.10N	2.50 E
Cantalejo	126	Ic	41.15N	3.55W
Cantanhede	126	Dd	40.21N	8.36W
Cantaura	202	Fb	9.19N	64.21W
Cantavieja	126	Ld	40.32N	0.24W
Cantavir	130	Cd	45.55N	19.46 E
Canterbury	118	Oj	51.17N	1.05 E
Canterbury	218	De	43.30S	171.50 E
Canterbury Bight	208	Ii	44.10S	172.00 E
Can Tho	142	Mi	10.02N	105.47 E
Cantiles, Cayo-	194	Fc	21.36N	82.02W
Canto do Buriti	202	Je	8.07S	42.58W
Canton [Il.-U.S.]	186	Kf	40.33N	90.02W
Canton [Mo.-U.S.]	186	Kf	40.08N	91.32W
Canton [Ms.-U.S.]	186	Kj	32.37N	90.02W
Canton [N.Y.-U.S.]	184	Jc	44.37N	75.11W
Canton [Oh.-U.S.]	182	Kc	40.48N	81.23W
Canton [S.D.-U.S.]	186	He	43.18N	96.35W
Canton (EN)=Guangzhou	142	Ng	23.07N	113.18 E
Canton Atoll	208	Je	2.50S	171.41W
Cantù	128	De	45.44N	9.08 E
Cantwell	178	Jd	63.23N	148.57W
Cañuelas	204	Cl	35.03S	58.44W
Canumã, Rio-	198	Kf	3.55S	59.10W
Canutama	202	Fe	6.32S	64.20W
Canvey Island	124	Cc	51.31N	0.36 E
Çany	138	Ce	55.19N	76.56 E
Çany, ozero-	140	Jd	54.50N	77.30 E
Cany-Barville	124	Ce	49.47N	0.38 E
Cànyoles / Cañoles	126	Le	39.02N	0.29W
Canyon [Mn.-U.S.]	186	Jc	47.02N	92.29W
Canyon [Tx.-U.S.]	182	Ge	34.59N	101.55W
Canyon [Wy.-U.S.]	188	Jd	44.44N	110.30W
Canyon Lake	186	Gl	29.52N	98.16W
Canzar	170	Dd	7.36S	21.33 E
Cao Bang	148	Ld	22.40N	106.15 E
Caojiahe → Qichun	154	Ci	30.15N	115.26 E
Caojian	152	Gf	25.38N	99.07 E
Caombo	170	Cd	8.42S	16.33 E
Caorle	128	Ge	45.36N	12.53 E
Caoxian	154	Cg	34.49N	115.33 E
Caozhou → Heze	152	Kd	35.14N	115.28 E
Capaccio	128	Jj	40.25N	15.05 E
Čapajev	136	Fe	50.14N	51.08 E
Čapajevsk	136	Ee	53.01N	49.36 E
Capanaparo, Rio-	202	Eb	7.01N	67.07W
Capanema [Braz.]	204	Fg	25.40S	53.48W
Capanema [Braz.]	202	Id	1.12S	47.11W
Capanema, Serra do-	204	Fh	26.05S	53.16W
Capão Alto	204	Gh	27.56S	50.30W
Capão Bonito	204	Hf	24.01S	48.20W
Capão Doce, Morro do-	204	Gh	26.43S	51.25W
Caparo, Rio-	194	Lj	7.46N	70.23W
Capatárida	194	Lh	11.11N	70.37W
Capbreton	122	Ek	43.38N	1.26W
Cap Breton Canyon (EN)	122	Ek	43.40N	1.50W
Čapčama, pereval-	135	Hd	41.34N	70.50 E
Cap-Chat	184	Na	49.06N	66.42W
Capcir	122	Il	42.45N	2.10 E
Cap-de-la-Madeleine	180	Kg	46.22N	72.32W
Capdenac-Gare	122	Ij	44.34N	2.05 E
Cape Barren Island	212	Jh	40.25S	148.10 E
Cape Basin (EN)	106	Em	37.00S	7.00 E
Cape Breton Island	174	Me	46.00N	60.30W
Cape Charles	184	Jg	37.17N	76.00W
Cape Coast	160	Gh	5.06N	1.15W
Cape Cod Bay	184	Le	41.52N	70.22W
Cape Coral	184	Gl	26.33N	81.58W
Cape Dorset	176	Lc	64.14N	76.32W
Cape Dyer	176	Mc	66.30N	61.18W
Cape Fear River	184	Ii	33.53N	78.00W
Cape Girardeau	182	Jd	37.19N	89.32W
Cape Johnson Tablemount (EN)	208	Jc	17.08N	177.15W
Capel	124	Bc	51.08N	0.19W
Cape Lisburne	178	Fc	68.52N	166.05W
Capelka	116	Mf	58.02N	29.07 E
Capella	150	Lg	4.58S	141.06 E
Capelongo	170	Ce	14.54S	15.05 E
Capem	204	Ea	13.14S	55.14W
Cape May	184	Jf	38.56N	74.54W
Cape Mount	166	Cd	7.05N	10.50W
Cape Rise (EN)	106	En	42.00S	15.00 E
Cape Smith	180	Jd	60.44N	78.29W
Capesterre	197e	Bc	15.54N	61.13W
Capesterre-Belle-Eau	196	Fd	16.03N	61.34W
Cape Town / Kaapstad	160	Il	33.55S	18.22 E
Cape Verde (EN)=Cabo Verde	160	Eg	16.00N	24.00W
Cape Verde (EN)=Cap Vert	166	Bc	14.45N	17.20W
Cape Verde Basin (EN)	106	Ch	15.00N	30.00W
Cape Verde Islands (EN)= Cabo Verde, Ilhas do-	158	Eg	16.00N	24.10W
Cape Verde Terrace (EN)	162	Cf	18.00N	20.00W
Cape Yakataga	178	Kd	60.04N	142.26W
Cape York Peninsula	208	Ff	14.00S	142.30 E
Cap-Haïtien	176	Lh	19.45N	72.15W
Capiibary, Arroyo-	204	Dg	24.06S	56.26W
Capiibary, Rio-	204	Eg	25.30S	55.33W
Capim, Rio-	198	Lf	1.40S	47.47W
Capinópolis	204	Hd	18.41S	49.35W
Capira	194	Hi	8.45N	79.53W
Capital Federal	206	Id	34.36S	58.27W
Capitán Arturo Prat	222	Re	62.29S	59.39W
Capitán Bado	206	Ib	23.16S	55.32W
Capitán Bermúdez	204	Bk	32.49S	60.43W
Capitán Sarmiento	204	Cl	34.10S	59.48W
Capitão Noronha, Rio-	204	Ea	13.19S	54.36W
Capivara, Represa da-	204	Gf	22.40S	50.57W
Capivari, Rio-	204	Dd	19.16S	57.10W
Capivarita	204	Fj	30.18S	52.19W
Cap Lopez, Baie du-	170	Ac	0.40S	9.00 E
Čaplygin	132	Kc	53.17N	39.59 E
Cappelle, La-	122	Je	49.58N	3.55 E
Cappeln (Oldenburg)	124	Kb	52.49N	8.07 E
Cap Point	196	Fe	14.07N	60.57W
Capraia	128	Dg	43.05N	9.50 E
Caprara, Punta-	128	Ci	41.07N	8.19 E
Capreol	184	Gb	46.43N	80.56W
Caprera	128	Di	41.10N	9.30 E
Capri	128	Ij	40.33N	14.14 E
Capri	128	Ij	40.35N	14.15 E
Capricorn, Cape-	212	Kd	23.30S	151.15 E
Capricorn Channel	212	Kd	22.15S	151.30 E
Capricorn Group	208	Gg	23.30S	152.00 E
Caprivi Strip (EN) = Caprivizipfel	158	Jj	18.00S	23.00 E
Caprivizipfel = Caprivi Strip (EN)	158	Jj	18.00S	23.00 E
Captain Cook	221a	Fd	19.30N	155.55W
Captains Flat	212	Jg	35.35S	149.27 E
Captieux	122	Fj	44.17N	0.15W
Capua	128	Ii	41.06N	14.12 E
Capuchin, Cape-	197g	Ba	15.38N	61.28W
Capunda	170	Ce	10.41S	17.23 E
Cap Vert=Cape Verde (EN)	166	Bc	14.45N	17.20W
Caquetá	202	Dc	1.00N	74.00W
Çaquetá, Rio-	198	Jf	3.08S	64.46W
Çara	140	Oc	60.17N	120.40 E
Çara [Russia]	138	Ge	58.54N	118.12 E
Çara [Russia]	138	Ge	58.58N	118.17 E
Carabobo	202	Ea	10.10N	68.05W
Caracal	130	He	44.07N	24.21 E
Caracarai	202	Fc	1.50N	61.08W
Caracas	200	Jd	10.30N	66.56W
Caracas	202	Ea	10.15N	66.25W
Carache	194	Li	9.38N	70.14W
Caracol	204	De	21.59S	57.02W
Caracol, Rio-	204	Df	22.13S	57.03W
Caracollo	202	Eg	17.39S	67.10W
Caraguatá, Cuchilla-	204	Ek	32.05S	54.54W
Caraguatatuba	204	Jf	23.37S	45.25W
Caraïbe, Mer-/Antilles, Mer des-=Caribbean Sea (EN)	174	Lh	15.00N	73.00W
Carajas, Serra dos-	202	He	6.00S	51.20W
Caramoan Peninsula	150	Hd	13.48N	123.40 E
Caramulo, Serra do-	126	Dd	40.34N	8.11W
Caraná, Rio-	204	Ca	13.20S	59.17W
Carandai	204	Ke	20.57S	43.48W
Carandazal	204	Dd	19.50S	57.09W
Caransebeş	130	Fd	45.25N	22.13 E
Carapá, Rio-	204	Eg	24.30S	54.20W
Carapelle	128	Ji	41.30N	15.55 E
Caraquet	184	Ob	47.47N	64.57W
Caraş	130	Ee	44.49N	21.20 E
Caraş Severin	130	Ed	45.20N	22.00 E
Caratasca, Cayo-	194	Fe	16.02N	83.20W
Caratasca, Laguna de-	190	He	15.20N	83.50W
Caratinga	202	Jg	19.47S	42.08W
Carauari	202	Ed	4.52S	66.54W
Caraúbas	202	Kd	5.47S	37.34W
Caravaca	126	Kf	38.06N	1.51W
Caravelas	202	Kg	17.45S	39.15W
Caraveli	202	Dg	15.46S	73.22W
Caravelle, Presqu'île de la-	197h	Bb	14.45N	60.55W
Caravelle, Rocher de la-	197h	Bb	14.48N	60.53W
Caràzinho	206	Jc	28.18S	52.48W
Carazo	194	Dh	11.45N	86.15W
Carballino	126	Db	42.26N	8.04W
Carballo	126	Da	43.13N	8.41W
Carberry	186	Gb	49.52N	99.20W
Carbet, Pitons du-	197h	Ab	14.42N	61.07W
Carbon, Cap- [Alg.]	126	Li	35.54N	0.20W
Carbon, Cap- [Alg.]	126	Rh	36.47N	5.06 E
Carbonara, Capo-	128	Dk	39.06N	9.31 E
Carbondale [Il.-U.S.]	182	Jd	37.44N	89.13W
Carbondale [Pa.-U.S.]	184	Je	41.35N	75.31W
Carbonera, Cuchilla de la-	204	El	34.10S	54.00W
Carboneras	126	Kh	36.59N	1.54W
Carboneras, Cerro-	192	Ih	18.10N	101.10W
Carbones	126	Gg	37.36N	5.39W
Carbonia	128	Ck	39.10N	8.31 E
Carcans, Étang de-	122	Ei	45.06N	1.07W
Carcar	150	Hd	10.06N	123.38 E
Carcarañá, Rio-	204	Bk	32.27S	60.48W
Carcassonne	122	Ik	43.13N	2.21 E
Carcross	180	Ed	60.10N	134.42W
Çardak [Tur.]	130	Ji	40.22N	26.43 E
Çardak [Tur.]	146	Cd	37.48N	29.40 E
Čardara	136	Gg	41.15N	68.01 E
Čardarinskoje vodohranilišče	135	Gd	41.05N	68.15 E
Cárdenas [Cuba]	190	Hd	23.02N	81.12W
Cárdenas [Mex.]	192	Mi	17.59N	93.22W
Cárdenas [Mex.]	190	Ed	22.00N	99.40W
Cárdenas, Bahía de-	194	Gb	23.05N	81.10W
Cardener/Cardoner	126	Nc	41.41N	1.51 E
Cardiel, Lago-	206	Fg	48.55S	71.15W
Cardiff	112	Fe	51.30N	3.13W
Cardigan	118	Ii	52.06N	4.40W
Cardigan Bay	110	Fe	52.30N	4.20W
Cardona [Sp.]	126	Nc	41.55N	1.41 E
Cardona [Ur.]	204	Dk	33.54S	57.22W
Cardoner/Cardener	126	Nc	41.41N	1.51 E
Cardozo	204	Dk	32.38S	56.21W
Cardston	180	Gg	49.12N	113.18W
Čardžou	142	If	39.06N	63.34 E
Čardžouskaja oblast	136	Gh	39.00N	63.00 E
Carei	130	Fb	47.41N	22.28 E
Careiro	202	Gd	3.12S	59.45W
Carentan	122	Ee	49.18N	1.14W
Carey	188	Ie	43.20N	113.58W
Carey, Lake-	208	Dg	29.05S	122.15 E
Cargados Carajos Islands	158	Mj	16.35S	59.40 E
Cargèse	122a	Aa	42.08N	8.35 E
Carhaix-Plouguer	122	Cf	48.17N	3.35W
Cari	128	Hi	41.23N	13.50 E
Caria	130	Ll	37.30N	29.00 E
Cariacica	202	Jh	20.16S	40.25W
Cariaco	196	Eg	10.29N	63.33W
Cariaco, Golfo de-	196	Eg	10.30N	64.00W
Cariaco Basin (EN)	196	Dg	10.37N	65.10W
Cariati	128	Kk	39.30N	16.57 E
Caribana, Punta-	194	Ii	8.37N	76.52W
Caribbean Sea	174	Lh	15.00N	73.00W
Caribbean Sea (EN)= Antillas, Mar de las-/ Caribe, Mar-	174	Lh	15.00N	73.00W
Caribbean Sea (EN)= Antilles, Mer des-/Caraïbe, Mer-	174	Lh	15.00N	73.00W
Caribbean Sea (EN)= Caraïbe, Mer-/Antilles, Mer des-	174	Lh	15.00N	73.00W
Caribbean Sea (EN)= Caribe, Mar-/Antillas, Mar de las-	174	Lh	15.00N	73.00W
Caribe, Mar-/Antillas, Mar de las-=Caribbean Sea (EN)	174	Lh	15.00N	73.00W
Cariboo Mountains	180	Ff	53.00N	121.00W
Caribou	184	Mb	46.52N	68.01W
Caribou	180	Ie	59.20N	94.45W
Caribou Island	184	Eb	47.27N	85.52W
Caribou Lake	186	La	50.25N	89.00W
Caribou Mountains	174	Hd	59.12N	115.40W
Caribou Range	188	Je	43.05N	111.15W
Caričin Grad	130	Eg	42.57N	21.45 E
Carignan	122	Le	49.38N	5.10 E
Carignano	128	Bf	44.55N	7.40 E
Cariñena	126	Kc	41.20N	1.13W
Carinhanha	202	Jf	14.08S	43.47W
Carinhanha, Rio-	204	Kb	14.20S	43.47W
Carini	128	Hl	38.08N	13.11 E
Carinola	128	Hi	41.11N	13.58 E
Carinthia (EN) = Kärnten	128	Hd	46.45N	14.00 E
Carinthia (EN) = Kärnten	128	Hd	46.45N	14.00 E
Caripe	196	Eg	10.21N	63.29W
Caripito	202	Fa	10.08N	63.06W
Caris, Rio-	196	Eh	8.09N	63.46W
Carlet	126	Le	39.14N	0.31W
Carleton Place	184	Ic	45.07N	76.08W
Carletonville	172	De	26.23S	27.22 E
Carlin	188	Gf	40.43N	116.07W
Carling	124	Ie	49.10N	6.43 E
Carlingford Lough/Loch Cairlinn	118	Gg	54.05N	6.14W
Carlinville	186	Lg	39.17N	89.53W
Carlisle [Eng.-U.K.]	112	Fe	54.54N	2.55W
Carlisle [Pa.-U.S.]	184	Ie	40.12N	77.12W
Carlisle Bay	197q	Ab	13.05N	59.37W
Carloforte	128	Ck	39.08N	8.18 E
Carlos Beguerie	204	Cl	35.29S	59.06W
Carlos Casares	206	He	35.38S	61.21W
Carlos Chagas	202	Jg	17.43S	40.45W
Carlos Reyles	204	Dk	33.03S	56.29W
Carlos Tejedor	204	Al	35.23S	62.25W
Carlow/Ceatharlach	118	Gi	52.50N	6.55W
Carlow/Ceatharlach	118	Gi	52.50N	7.00W
Carloway	118	Gc	58.17N	6.47W
Carlsbad [Ca.-U.S.]	188	Gj	33.10N	117.21W
Carlsbad [N.M.-U.S.]	176	If	32.25N	104.14W
Carlyle	180	Hg	49.38N	102.16W
Carlyle Lake	186	Lg	38.40N	89.18W
Carmacks	180	Dd	62.05N	136.18W
Carmagnola	128	Bf	44.51N	7.43 E
Carmarthen	118	Ij	51.52N	4.19W
Carmarthen Bay	118	Ij	51.40N	4.30W
Carmaux	122	Ij	44.03N	2.09 E
Carmel Head	118	Ih	53.24N	4.34W
Carmelita	194	Be	17.21N	90.10W
Carmelo	206	Id	34.00S	58.17W
Carmen	204	Dk	33.15S	56.01W
Carmen, Isla-	192	Bc	25.57N	111.12W
Carmen, Isla del-	192	Nh	18.42N	91.40W
Carmen, Laguna del-	192	Mh	18.15N	93.50W
Carmen, Rio del-	192	Fb	30.42N	106.29W
Carmen, Sierra del-	192	Hc	29.00N	102.30W
Carmen de Patagones	206	Hf	40.48S	62.59W
Carmensa	206	Ge	35.08S	67.38W
Carmi	186	Lg	38.07N	88.10W
Carmichael	188	Eg	38.38N	121.19W
Carmo de Minas	204	Jf	22.07S	45.08W
Carmo do Paranaiba	204	Id	18.59S	46.21W
Carmona	126	Gg	37.28N	5.38W
Carnac	122	Cg	47.35N	3.05W
Carnamah	212	De	29.42S	115.53 E
Carnarvon [Austl.]	210	Cg	24.53S	113.40 E
Carnarvon [S.Afr.]	160	Jl	30.56S	22.08 E
Carnarvon Range	212	Ee	25.10S	121.00 E
Carnatic (EN)	140	Jh	10.30N	79.00 E
Carnegie, Lake-	208	Dg	26.10S	122.30 E
Carnegie Ridge (EN)	106	Nj	1.00S	85.00W
Carn Eige	118	Hd	57.30N	5.05W
Carney Island	222	Nf	73.57S	121.00W
Carnia	128	Gd	46.25N	13.00 E
Car Nicobar	148	Ig	9.10N	92.47 E
Carnot	168	Be	4.48N	16.03 E
Carnoustie	118	Ke	56.30N	2.44W
Carnsore Point/Ceann an Chairn	118	Gi	52.10N	6.22W
Carn Ui Néid/Mizen Head	110	Fe	51.27N	9.49W
Caro	184	Fd	43.29N	83.24W
Carol City	184	Gm	25.56N	80.16W
Carolina [Braz.]	200	Lf	7.20S	47.28W
Carolina [P.R.]	197a	Cb	18.24N	65.57W
Carolina [S.Afr.]	172	Ee	26.05S	30.06 E
Carolina Beach	184	Ih	34.02N	77.54W
Carolinas, Puntan-	220b	Bb	14.54N	145.38 E
Caroline Atoll	208	Le	9.58S	150.13W
Caroline Islands	208	Fd	8.00N	147.00 E
Carondelet Reef	208	Je	5.34S	173.51W
Caroni, Rio-	198	Je	8.21N	62.43W
Caronie→Nebrodi	128	Im	37.55N	14.35 E
Carora	202	Da	10.11N	70.05W
Carpathian Mountains (EN)	110	If	48.00N	24.00 E
Carpathian Mountains (EN) = Carpaţii Occidentali	130	Fc	46.30N	22.10 E
Carpathian Mountains (EN) =Carpaţii Orientali	130	Ib	47.30N	25.30 E
Carpaţii Meridionali= Transylvanian Alps (EN)	110	If	45.30N	24.15 E
Carpaţii Occidentali = Carpathian Mountains (EN)	130	Fc	46.30N	22.10 E
Carpaţii Orientali= Carpathian Mountains (EN)	130	Ib	47.30N	25.30 E
Carpen	130	Ge	44.20N	23.15 E
Carpentaria, Gulf of-	208	Ef	14.00S	139.00 E
Carpentras	122	Lj	44.03N	5.03 E
Carpi	128	Ef	44.47N	10.53 E
Carpina	202	Ke	7.51S	35.15W
Carr, Cape-	222	Ie	66.07S	130.51 E
Carraig Fhearghais/ Carrickfergus	118	Hg	54.43N	5.44W
Carraig na Siúire / Carrick on Suir	118	Fi	52.21N	7.25W
Carrara	128	Ef	44.05N	10.06 E
Carrauntoohil	110	Fe	5200N	9.45W
Carreiro, Rio-	204	Gi	29.07S	51.43W
Carreño	126	Ga	43.35N	5.46W
Carreta, Punta-	202	Cf	14.13S	76.18W
Carretero, Puerto-	126	Ig	37.28N	3.40W
Carriacou	196	Ff	12.30N	61.27W
Carrick	118	If	55.15N	4.40W
Carrickfergus/Carraig Fhearghais	118	Hg	54.43N	5.44W
Carrick on Shannon / Cora Droma Rúisc	118	Eh	53.57N	8.05W
Carrick on Suir / Carraig na Siúire	118	Fi	52.21N	7.25W
Carrington	182	Hb	47.27N	99.08W
Carrión	126	Hc	41.53N	4.32W
Carrión de los Condes	126	Hb	42.20N	4.36W
Carrizal	194	Kh	11.58N	72.12W
Carrizo Peak	186	Dj	33.20N	105.38W
Carrizos	192	Gc	29.58N	105.16W
Carrizo Springs	186	Gl	28.31N	99.52W
Carrizo Wash	188	Ki	34.36N	109.26W
Carrizozo	186	Dj	33.38N	105.53W
Carroll	186	Ie	42.04N	94.52W
Carroll Inlet	222	Qf	73.18S	78.30W
Carrollton [Ga.-U.S.]	184	Ei	33.35N	85.05W
Carrollton [Il.-U.S.]	186	Kg	39.18N	90.24W
Carrollton [Ky.-U.S.]	184	Ef	38.41N	85.11W
Carrollton [Mo.-U.S.]	186	Jg	39.22N	93.30W
Carron, Loch-	118	Hd	57.30N	5.40W
Carrot	180	Hf	53.50N	101.18W
Carrowmore Lough	118	Dg	54.12N	9.47W
Çarşamba	146	Gb	41.12N	36.44 E
Çarşamba	146	Ed	37.53N	32.37 E
Čaršanga	136	Gh	37.31N	66.03 E
Čarsk	136	If	49.35N	81.05 E
Carson	188	Ed	45.44N	121.49W
Carson City	176	Hf	39.10N	119.46W
Carson Lake	188	Fg	39.19N	118.43W
Carson Sink	188	Fg	39.45N	118.30W
Cartagena [Col.]	200	Id	10.25N	75.32W
Cartagena [Sp.]	112	Fh	37.36N	0.59W
Cartago	194	Fi	9.50N	83.45W
Cartago [Col.]	202	Cc	4.46N	75.56W
Cartago [C.R.]	190	Hg	9.52N	83.55W
Cartaxo	126	De	39.09N	8.47W
Carter, Mount-	212	Ib	13.05S	143.15 E
Cartersville	184	Eh	34.10N	85.05W
Carterton	218	Fd	41.01S	175.31 E
Carthage [Mo.-U.S.]	186	Ih	37.11N	94.19W
Carthage [Tx.-U.S.]	186	Ij	32.09N	94.20W
Cartier	184	Gb	46.42N	81.32W
Cartier Island	208	Df	12.30S	123.30 E
Cartwright	176	Nd	53.50N	56.45W
Caruaru	200	Mf	8.17S	35.58W

Carúpano 202 Fa 10.40N 63.14W
Carutapera 202 Id 1.13S 46.01W
Čarvak 135 Gd 41.38N 69.56 E
Carvin 124 Ed 50.29N 2.58 E
Carvoeiro, Cabo- 126 Ce 39.21N 9.24W
Čaryn 135 Lc 43.50N 79.12 E
Čaryš 138 Df 52.22N 83.45 E
Casablanca 160 Ge 33.36N 7.37W
Casablanca [2] 162 Fc 33.37N 7.35W
Casa Branca 204 Ie 21.46S 47.05W
Casa Grande 182 Ee 32.53N 111.45W
Casalbordino 128 Ih 42.09N 14.35 E
Casale Monferrato 128 Ce 45.08N 8.27 E
Casalmaggiore 128 Ef 44.59N 10.26 E
Casalvasco 204 Cb 15.19S 59.59W
Casal Velino 128 Jj 40.11N 15.06 E
Casamance [3] 166 Bc 12.50N 15.00W
Casamance 166 Bc 12.33N 16.46W
Casanare [3] 202 Db 5.20N 72.00W
Casanare, Rio- 202 Eb 6.02N 69.51W
Casanay 196 Eg 10.30N 63.25W
Casa Nova 202 Je 9.25S 41.08W
Casarano 128 Mj 40.00N 18.10 E
Casas Grandes, Rio- 192 Eb 30.22N 107.31W
Casas-Ibáñez 126 Ke 39.17N 1.28W
Casca, Rio da- 204 Eb 14.52S 55.52W
Cascade 188 Hd 44.31N 115.59W
Cascade Point 218 Cf 44.01S 168.22 E
Cascade Range 174 Ge 45.00N 121.30W
Cascais 126 Cf 38.42N 9.25W
Cascavel [Braz.] 202 Kd 4.07S 38.14W
Cascavel [Braz.] 206 Jb 24.57S 53.28W
Cascia 128 Hh 42.43N 13.01 E
Casciana Terme 128 Eg 43.32N 10.38 E
Cascina 128 Eg 43.41N 10.33 E
Casentino 128 Fg 43.40N 11.50 E
Case-Pilote 197h Ab 14.38N 61.08W
Caserta 128 Ii 41.04N 14.20 E
Casey 222 He 66.17S 110.32 E
Casey Bay 222 Ee 67.00S 48.00 E
Cashel/Caiseal 118 Fi 52.31N 7.53W
Casigua 194 Ki 8.46N 72.30W
Casilda 206 Hd 33.03S 61.10W
Casimcea 130 Le 44.24N 28.33 E
Casino 212 Ke 28.52S 153.03 E
Casiquiare, Brazo- 202 Ec 2.01N 67.07W
Čáslav 120 Lg 49.55N 15.25 E
Casma 202 Ce 9.28S 78.19W
Časnačorr, gora- 114 Hc 67.45N 33.29 E
Čašniki 114 Gi 54.52N 29.08 E
Casoli 128 Ih 42.07N 14.18 E
Casoria 128 Ij 40.54N 14.17 E
Caspe 126 Lc 41.14N 0.02W
Casper 176 Ie 42.51N 106.19W
Caspian Depression (EN) = Prikaspijskaja nizmennost 110 Lf 48.00N 52.00 E
Caspian Sea (EN) = Kaspijskoje more 110 Lg 42.00N 50.30 E
Caspian Sea (EN) = Māzandarān, Daryā-ye- 110 Lg 42.00N 50.30 E
Cassai 158 Ii 3.02S 16.57 E
Cassamba 170 De 13.04S 20.25 E
Cassange, Rio- 204 Dc 17.06S 57.23W
Cassano allo Ionio 128 Kk 39.47N 16.19 E
Cassano allo Ionio-Sibari 128 Kk 39.45N 16.27 E
Cass City 184 Fd 43.36N 83.10W
Cassel 124 Ed 50.47N 2.29 E
Casselton 186 Hc 46.54N 97.13W
Cássia 204 Ie 20.36S 46.56W
Cassiar 180 Ee 59.16N 129.40W
Cassiar Mountains 174 Gd 59.00N 129.00W
Cassilândia 202 Hg 19.09S 51.45W
Cassinga 170 Cf 15.06S 16.06 E
Cassino [Braz.] 204 Fk 32.11S 52.10W
Cassino [It.] 128 Hi 41.30N 13.49 E
Cassis 122 Lk 43.13N 5.32 E
Cass Lake 186 Ic 47.23N 94.36W
Cass River 184 Fd 43.23N 83.59W
Cassununga 204 Fc 16.03S 53.38W
Castagneto Carducci 128 Eg 43.10N 10.36 E
Castagniccia 122a Ba 42.25N 9.30 E
Castañar, Sierra del- 126 He 39.35N 4.10W
Castanhal 202 Id 1.18S 47.55W
Castaños 192 Id 26.47N 101.25W
Castelbuono 128 Im 37.56N 14.05 E
Castel di Sangro 128 Ii 41.47N 14.06 E
Castelfidardo 128 Hg 43.28N 13.33 E
Castelfranco Veneto 128 Fe 45.40N 11.55 E
Casteljaloux 122 Gj 44.19N 0.06 E
Castellabate 128 Ij 40.17N 14.57 E
Castellammare, Golfo di- 128 Gl 38.10N 12.55 E
Castellammare del Golfo 128 Gl 38.01N 12.53 E
Castellammare di Stabia 128 Ij 40.42N 14.29 E
Castellana Grotte 128 Lj 40.53N 17.10 E
Castellane 122 Mk 43.51N 6.31 E
Castellaneta 128 Kj 40.38N 16.56 E
Castelldefels 126 Nc 41.17N 1.58 E
Castelli [Arg.] 206 Hc 25.57S 60.37W
Castelli [Arg.] 204 Dm 36.06S 57.47W
Castelló de la Plana / Castellón [3] 126 Ld 40.10N 0.10W
Castelló de la Plana/ Castellón de la Plana 112 Fh 39.59N 0.02W
Castellón / Castelló de la Plana [3] 126 Ld 40.10N 0.10W
Castellón de la Plana/ Castelló de la Plana 112 Fh 39.59N 0.02W
Castellón de la Plana-El Grao 126 Me 39.58N 0.01 E
Castellote 126 Ld 40.48N 0.19W
Castelnaudary 122 Hk 43.19N 1.57 E
Castelnau-de-Médoc 122 Fi 45.02N 0.48W
Castelnovo ne' Monti 128 Ef 44.26N 10.24 E
Castelo Branco 126 Ee 39.49N 7.30W
Castelo Branco [2] 126 Ee 40.00N 7.30W
Castelo de Vide 126 Ee 39.25N 7.27W
Castelo do Piauí 202 Je 5.20S 41.33W
Castel San Giovanni 128 De 45.04N 9.26 E
Castelsardo 128 Cj 40.55N 8.43 E
Castelsarrasin 122 Hj 44.02N 1.06 E
Casteltermini 128 Hm 37.32N 13.39 E
Castelvetrano 128 Gm 37.41N 12.47 E
Castets 122 Ek 43.53N 1.09W
Castiglione del Lago 128 Gg 43.07N 12.03 E
Castiglione della Pescaia 128 Eh 42.46N 10.53 E
Castiglion Fiorentino 128 Fg 43.20N 11.55 E
Castilla-La Mancha [2] 126 Ie 39.30N 3.30W
Castilla la Nueva=New Castile (EN) 126 Id 40.00N 3.45W
Castilla la Vieja=Old Castile (EN) 126 Ic 41.30N 4.00W
Castilla-León [2] 126 Hc 41.30N 4.30W
Castillejo 126 Gc 41.14N 5.30W
Castillon-la-Bataille 122 Fj 44.51N 0.02W
Castillonnès 122 Gj 44.39N 0.36 E
Castillos 206 Jd 34.12S 53.50W
Castillos, Laguna de- 204 Fl 34.20S 53.54W
Castlebar/Caisleán an Bharraigh 118 Dh 53.52N 9.17W
Castle Bruce 197g Bb 15.26N 61.16W
Castle Dome Peak 188 Hj 33.05N 114.08W
Castle Douglas 118 Jg 54.57N 3.56W
Castlegar 180 Fg 49.19N 117.40W
Castleisland/Oileán Ciarrai 118 Di 52.14N 9.27W
Castlemaine 212 Ig 37.04S 144.13 E
Castle Peak 188 Hd 44.03N 114.32W
Castlepoint 218 Gd 40.55S 176.13 E
Castlepollard 118 Fh 53.41N 7.17W
Castlerea/An Caisleán Riabhach 118 Eh 53.46N 8.29W
Castlereagh Bay 212 Hb 12.10S 135.10 E
Castle Rock Butte 186 Ed 45.00N 103.27W
Castle Rock Lake 186 Le 43.56N 89.58W
Častoozerje 134 Mi 55.34N 67.53 E
Castor 188 Ja 52.13N 111.53W
Castres 122 Ik 43.36N 2.15 E
Castricum 124 Gb 52.33N 4.42 E
Castries 176 Mh 14.01N 61.00W
Castrignano del Capo 128 Mk 39.50N 18.20 E
Castrignano del Capo-Marina di Leuca 128 Mk 39.48N 18.21 E
Castro [Braz.] 206 Jb 24.47S 50.03W
Castro [Chile] 206 Ff 42.29S 73.46W
Castro Alves 202 Kf 12.45S 39.26W
Castrocaro Terme e Terra del Sole 128 Ff 44.10N 11.57 E
Castro Daire 126 Ed 40.54N 7.56W
Castro del Rio 126 Hg 37.41N 4.28W
Castrojeriz 126 Hb 42.17N 4.08W
Castropol 126 Ea 43.32N 7.02W
Castro-Rauxel 124 Jc 51.33N 7.19 E
Castro-Urdiales 126 Ia 43.23N 3.13W
Castro Verde 126 Dg 37.42N 8.05W
Castrovillari 128 Kk 39.49N 16.12 E
Castrovirreyna 202 Cf 13.16S 75.19W
Castuera 126 Gf 38.43N 5.33W
Častyje 134 Gh 57.19N 54.59 E
Casupá 204 El 34.09S 55.38W
Caswell Sound 218 Bf 45.00S 167.10 E
Çat 146 Ic 39.40N 41.02 E
Čata 120 Oi 47.58N 18.40 E
Catacamas 194 Ef 14.54N 85.56W
Catahoula Lake 186 Jk 31.30N 92.06W
Çatak 146 Jc 38.01N 43.07 E
Çatak 146 Jd 37.53N 42.39 E
Catalan Coastal Range (EN) = Costero Catalana, Cadena- / Mediterrani Català, Sistema- 110 Gg 41.35N 1.40 E
Catalan Coastal Range (EN) = Mediterrani Català, Sistema- / Costero Catalana, Cadena- 110 Gg 41.35N 1.40 E
Catalana, Cadena- 110 Gg 41.35N 1.40 E
Catalão 202 Ig 18.10S 47.57W
Çatal Balkan 130 Jg 42.46N 27.00 E
Çatalca 130 Lh 41.09N 28.27 E
Çatal Dağ 130 Lj 39.51N 28.20 E
Catalina 206 Gc 25.13S 69.43W
Catalina, Isla- 194 Md 18.21N 69.00W
Catalina, Punta- 206 Gh 52.32S 68.47W
Catalonia (EN)=Cataluña/ Catalunya [2] 126 Nc 42.00N 2.00 E
Catalonia (EN)=Cataluña/ Catalunya 110 Gg 42.00N 2.00 E
Catalonia (EN)=Catalunya/ Cataluña [2] 126 Nc 42.00N 2.00 E
Catalonia (EN)=Catalunya/ Cataluña 110 Gg 42.00N 2.00 E
Cataluña/Catalunya= Catalonia (EN) [2] 126 Nc 42.00N 2.00 E
Cataluña/Catalunya= Catalonia (EN) 110 Gg 42.00N 2.00 E
Catalunya/Cataluña= Catalonia (EN) [2] 126 Nc 42.00N 2.00 E
Catalunya/Cataluña= Catalonia (EN) 110 Gg 42.00N 2.00 E
Çatalzeytin 146 Fb 41.57N 34.13 E
Catamarca [2] 206 Gc 27.00S 67.00W
Catanduanes 140 Oh 13.45N 124.15 E
Catanduva 206 Kb 21.08S 48.58W
Catanduvas 204 Fg 25.12S 53.08W
Catania 112 Hh 37.30N 15.06 E
Catania, Golfo di- 128 Jm 37.25N 15.10 E
Catania, Piana di- 128 Im 37.25N 14.50 E
Catanzaro 112 Hh 38.54N 16.35 E
Catanzaro-Marina di Catanzaro 128 Kl 38.49N 16.36 E
Catarman 150 Hd 12.30N 124.38 E
Catastrophe, Cape- 208 Eh 35.00S 136.00 E
Catatumbo, Rio- 194 Li 9.21N 71.45W
Catbalogan 150 Hd 11.46N 124.53 E
Catemaco, Lago- 192 Lh 18.25N 95.05W
Catete 170 Bd 9.07S 13.41 E
Cathair na Mart/Westport 118 Dh 53.48N 9.32W
Cathair Saidhbhín/ Cahersiveen 118 Cj 51.57N 10.13W
Cathcart 172 Df 32.18S 27.09 E
Catherine, Mount- 188 Ig 39.05N 112.04W
Catholic Island 197n Bb 12.40N 61.24W
Catio 166 Bc 11.17N 15.15W
Cat Island 174 Lg 24.30N 75.30W
Čatkal 135 Hd 41.36N 70.05 E
Čatkalski hrebet 136 Hg 41.30N 70.50 E
Cat Lake 180 If 51.40N 91.52W
Catoche, Cabo- 174 Kg 21.36N 87.07W
Cato Island 208 Gg 23.15S 155.35 E
Catolé do Rocha 202 Ke 6.21S 37.45W
Catoute 126 Fb 42.45N 6.20W
Catria 128 Gg 43.28N 12.42 E
Catriló 206 He 36.26S 63.24W
Catrimani, Rio- 202 Fc 0.28N 61.44W
Catskill Mountains 184 Jd 42.10N 74.30W
Cattenom 124 Ie 49.25N 6.15 E
Cattolica 128 Gg 43.58N 12.44 E
Catu 202 Kf 12.21S 38.23W
Catuane 172 Ee 26.48S 32.14 E
Catumbela 170 Be 12.27S 13.29 E
Catur 172 Fb 13.45S 35.37 E
Catwick, Iles- 148 Lg 10.00N 109.00 E
Čatyrkël, ozero- 135 Jd 40.35N 75.20 E
Čatyrtaš 135 Kd 40.52N 76.23 E
Cauca [3] 202 Cc 2.30N 77.00W
Cauca, Rio- 198 Ie 8.54N 74.28W
Caucasia 202 Cb 7.59N 75.13W
Caucasus (EN)=Kavkaz, Bolšoj- 110 Kg 42.30N 45.00 E
Caucete 206 Gd 31.38S 68.16W
Caudebec-en-Caux 124 Ce 49.32N 0.44 E
Caudete 126 Lf 38.42N 0.59W
Caudry 122 Jd 50.08N 3.25 E
Caulonia 128 Kl 38.23N 16.24 E
Caumont-l'Eventé 124 Be 49.05N 0.48W
Caungula 160 Ii 8.26S 18.37 E
Čaunskaja guba 138 Lc 69.30N 170.00 E
Caupolicán 202 Ef 13.30S 68.30W
Cauquenes 206 Fe 35.58S 72.21W
Caura, Rio- 198 Je 7.38N 64.53W
Causapscal 184 Na 48.22N 67.14W
Caussade 122 Hj 44.10N 1.32 E
Causy 132 Gc 53.50N 30.59 E
Cauterets 122 Fl 42.53N 0.07W
Cauto, Rio- 194 Ic 20.33N 77.15W
Cauvery 140 Jh 11.09N 78.52 E
Caux, Pays de- 122 Ge 49.40N 0.40 E
Cávado 126 Dc 41.32N 8.48W
Cavaillon 122 Lk 43.50N 5.02 E
Cavalaire-sur-Mer 122 Mk 43.10N 6.32 E
Cavalcante 204 Ia 13.48S 47.30W
Cavalese 128 Fd 46.17N 11.27 E
Cavalleria, Cap de- / Caballería, Cabo de- 126 Qd 40.05N 4.05 E
Cavalli Islands 218 Ea 35.00S 173.55 E
Cavallo, Isola- 122a Bb 41.22N 9.16 E
Cavallo Pass 186 Hl 28.25N 96.26W
Cavally 158 Gh 4.22N 7.32W
Cavan/An Cabhán 118 Fg 54.00N 7.21W
Cavan/An Cabhán [2] 118 Fh 53.55N 7.30W
Cavarzere 128 Ge 45.08N 12.05 E
Çavdarhisar 130 Mj 39.12N 29.37 E
Çavdir 130 Ml 37.09N 29.42 E
Caviana, Ilha- 202 Hc 0.10N 50.05W
Cavili 150 He 9.17N 120.50 E
Cavour, Canale- 128 Be 45.11N 7.54 E
Cavtat 128 Mh 42.35N 18.13 E
Caxambu 204 Je 21.59S 44.56W
Caxias 200 Lf 4.50S 43.21W
Caxias do Sul 200 Kh 29.10S 51.11W
Caxito 170 Bd 8.34S 13.40 E
Çay 146 Dc 38.35N 31.02 E
Cayambe 202 Cc 0.05N 78.08W
Cayambe, Volcán- 198 Ie 0.02N 77.59W
Cayastá 204 Bj 31.12S 60.10W
Cayce 184 Gi 33.59N 81.04W
Çaycuma 146 Eb 41.25N 32.05 E
Çayeli 146 Ib 41.05N 40.44 E
Cayenne 200 Ke 4.56N 52.20W
Cayeux-sur-Mer 124 Dd 50.11N 1.29 E
Cayey 194 Nd 18.07N 66.10W
Çayirli 146 Ic 39.48N 40.01 E
Çaykara 146 Ib 40.45N 40.19 E
Caylus 122 Hj 44.14N 1.47 E
Cayman Brac 190 Ie 19.43N 79.49W
Cayman Islands [5] 176 Kh 19.30N 80.30W
Cayman Islands 174 Kh 19.30N 80.30W
Cayman Ridge (EN) 190 He 19.30N 80.30W
Cayman Trench (EN) 106 Bh 19.00N 80.00W
Cayo [3] 194 Ce 17.10N 88.50W
Cayon 197c Ab 17.21N 62.43W
Cayones, Cayos- 194 Fe 16.05N 83.12W
Cay Sal Bank 190 Hd 23.45N 80.00W
Cayuga Lake 184 Id 42.45N 76.45W
Cazalla de la Sierra 126 Gg 37.56N 5.45W
Caza Pava 204 Di 28.17S 56.07W
Cazaux et de Sanguinet, Étang de- 122 Ej 44.29N 1.10W
Cazombo 160 Jj 11.54S 22.53 E
Cazorla 126 Jg 37.55N 3.00W
Cazorla, Sierra de- 126 Jf 37.55N 2.55W
Cea 126 Gb 42.00N 5.36W
Ceahlău 130 Ib 47.03N 25.58 E
Ceanannas Mór/Kells 118 Gh 53.44N 6.53W
Ceanna Caillighe/Hags Head 118 Di 52.57N 9.28W
Ceann Acla/Achill Head 118 Ch 53.59N 10.13W
Ceann an Chairn/Carnsore Point 118 Gi 52.10N 6.22W
Ceann Chill Mhantáin/ Wicklow Head 118 Hi 52.58N 6.00W
Ceann Iorrais/Erris Head 110 Fe 54.19N 10.00W
Ceann Léime/Loop Head 118 Di 52.34N 9.56W
Ceann Ros Eoghain/Rossan Point 118 Eg 54.42N 8.48W
Ceann Sléibhe/Slea Head 118 Ci 52.06N 10.27W
Ceann Toirc/Kanturk 118 Ei 52.10N 8.55W
Ceará [2] 202 Kd 5.00S 39.30W
Ceará-Mirim 202 Ke 5.38S 35.26W
Ceatharlach/Carlow 118 Gi 52.50N 6.55W
Ceatharlach/Carlow [2] 118 Gi 52.50N 7.00W
Cébaco, Isla- 194 Gj 7.32N 81.09W
Ceballos 192 Gd 26.32N 104.09W
Čebarkul 134 Ji 54.58N 60.25 E
Čeboksary 112 Kd 56.09N 47.15 E
Cebollati 204 Fk 33.16S 53.47W
Cebollati, Rio- 204 Fk 33.09S 53.38W
Cebollera, La- 126 Ic 41.10N 3.32W
Cebollera, Sierra- 126 Jc 42.00N 2.40W
Ceboruco, Volcán- 192 Gg 21.09N 104.30W
Cebreros 126 Hd 40.27N 4.28W
Cebrikovo 130 Nb 47.09N 30.02 E
Cebu 142 Oh 10.18N 123.54 E
Cebu 140 Oh 10.20N 123.45 E
Cece 120 Oj 46.46N 18.39 E
Čečen, ostrov- 132 Og 44.00N 47.45 E
Čečeno respublika 136 Eg 43.15N 45.30 E
Cecen-Ula 152 Gb 48.45N 95.55 E
Cecerleg 142 Me 47.30N 101.27 E
Čečersk 132 Gc 52.56N 30.58 E
Čechy=Bohemia (EN) 110 Hf 50.00N 14.30 E
Čechy=Bohemia (EN) 120 Kf 50.00N 14.30 E
Cecina 128 Eg 43.19N 10.31 E
Cecina 128 Eg 43.18N 10.29 E
Čečuisk 138 Fe 58.07N 108.32 E
Cedar City 176 Hf 37.41N 113.04W
Cedar Creek 186 Fc 46.07N 101.18W
Cedar Creek Reservoir 186 Hj 32.20N 96.10W
Cedar Falls 182 Ic 42.32N 92.27W
Cedar Grove 197d Bb 17.10N 61.49W
Cedar Lake 180 Hf 53.25N 100.00W
Cedar Rapids 176 Je 41.59N 91.40W
Cedar River [Nb.-U.S.] 186 Hf 41.22N 97.57W
Cedar River [U.S.] 182 Ic 41.17N 91.20W
Cedartown 184 Eh 34.01N 85.15W
Cedar-Tree Point 197d Ba 17.42N 61.53W
Cedeira 126 Da 43.39N 8.03W
Cedral 192 If 23.48N 100.44W
Cedrino 128 Dj 40.23N 9.44 E
Cedro 202 Ke 6.36S 39.03W
Cedrón 126 Ie 39.48N 3.33W
Cedros, Isla-=Cedros Island (EN) 174 Hg 28.10N 115.15W
Cedros Island (EN)=Cedros, Isla- 174 Hg 28.10N 115.15W
Cedros Trench (EN) 190 Ac 27.45N 115.45W
Ceduna 212 Gf 32.07S 133.40 E
Cedynia 120 Kd 52.50N 14.14 E
Cefalù 128 Il 38.02N 14.01 E
Cega 126 Hc 41.33N 4.46W
Čegdomyn 142 Pd 51.07N 133.05 E
Čegem 132 Mh 43.36N 43.48 E
Cegléd 120 Pi 47.10N 19.48 E
Ceglie Messapico 128 Lj 40.39N 17.31 E
Cehegin 126 Kf 38.06N 1.48W
Čehotina 130 Bf 43.31N 18.45 E
Čehov [Russia] 114 Ii 55.11N 37.29 E
Čehov [Russia] 138 Jg 47.24N 142.05 E
Ceica 130 Fc 46.51N 22.11 E
Çekerek 146 Fb 40.04N 35.31 E
Çekerek 146 Fb 40.34N 35.46 E
Čekmaguš 134 Gi 55.10N 54.40 E
Celano 128 Hh 42.05N 13.33 E
Celaya 190 Dd 20.31N 100.37W
Čelbas 132 Kf 46.06N 38.59 E
Célé 122 Hj 44.28N 1.38 E
Celebes/Sulawesi 140 Oj 2.00S 121.10 E
Celebes Basin (EN) 150 Hf 4.00N 122.00 E
Celebes Sea (EN)= Sulawesi, Laut- 140 Oi 3.00N 122.00 E
Čeleken 136 Fh 39.27N 53.10 E
Čeleken, poluostrov- 132 Rj 39.25N 53.35 E
Celendin 202 Ce 6.52S 78.09W
Celerain, Punta- 192 Pg 20.16N 86.59W
Celeste 204 Dj 31.18S 57.04W
Celestún 192 Ng 20.52N 90.24W
Celinograd 142 Jd 51.10N 71.30 E
Celinogradskaja oblast [3] 136 Gh 51.00N 70.00 E
Čeljabinsk 142 Id 55.10N 61.24 E
Čeljabinskaja oblast [3] 136 Ge 54.00N 61.00 E
Celje 128 Jd 46.14N 15.16 E
Čeljuskin, mys- 140 Mb 77.45N 104.20 E
Celkar 136 Ff 47.50N 59.29 E
Celldömölk 120 Ni 47.15N 17.09 E
Celle 120 Gd 52.37N 10.05 E
Celles 124 Fd 50.43N 3.27 E
Celles, Houyet- 124 Hd 50.19N 5.01 E
Cellina 128 Gd 46.02N 12.47 E
Celone 128 Ji 41.36N 15.41 E
Celorico da Beira 126 Ed 40.38N 7.23W
Celtic Sea 110 Fe 51.00N 7.00W
Celtic Sea (EN)=An Mhuir Cheilteach 110 Fe 51.00N 7.00W
Cemaes Head 118 Ii 52.07N 4.44W
Čemal 138 Df 51.25N 86.05 E
Čemdalsk 138 Fe 59.45N 103.18 E
Cemernica 128 Lf 44.30N 17.15 E
Čemerno 130 Df 43.36N 20.26 E
Çemişkezek 146 Hc 39.04N 38.55 E
Cenajo, Embalse de- 126 Kf 38.20N 1.55W
Cenderawasih, Teluk- 150 Kg 2.25S 135.10 E
Cengel 152 Eb 48.56N 89.10 E
Çengel Geçidi 146 Kc 39.45N 44.02 E
Ceno 128 Ef 44.41N 10.05 E
Centenary 172 Ec 16.44S 31.07 E
Centennial 188 Lf 41.51N 106.07W
Centennial Lake 184 Ic 45.15N 77.00W
Centennial Mountains 188 Jd 44.35N 111.55W
Center 186 Ik 31.48N 94.11W
Center Hill Lake 184 Eg 36.00N 85.45W
Centerville 186 Jf 40.43N 92.52W
Centinela, Farallón- 196 Cg 10.49N 66.05W
Centinela, Picacho del- 190 Dc 29.07N 102.27W
Cento 128 Ff 44.43N 11.17 E
Centola-Palinuro 128 Jj 40.02N 15.17 E
Centrafrique=Central African Republic (EN) [1] 160 Jh 7.00N 21.00 E
Central [Bots.] [3] 172 Dd 21.30S 26.00 E
Central [Ghana] [3] 166 Ed 5.30N 1.00W
Central [Kenya] [3] 170 Gc 0.45S 37.00 E
Central [Mwi.] [3] 170 Fe 13.30S 34.00 E
Central [Par.] [3] 204 Dg 25.30S 57.30W
Central [Scot.-U.K.] [3] 118 Ie 56.15N 4.10W
Central [Ug.] [3] 170 Fb 0.10N 32.05 E
Central [Zam.] [3] 170 Ee 14.30S 29.00 E
Central, Chaco- 198 Kh 25.00S 59.45W
Central, Cordillera- [Col.] 198 Ie 5.00N 75.00W
Central, Cordillera- [Dom.Rep.] 190 Je 18.45N 70.30W
Central, Cordillera- [P.R.] 194 Nd 18.10N 66.35W
Central, Massif- 110 Gf 45.00N 3.10 E
Central, Meseta- 174 Ig 23.00N 103.00W
Central, Sistema- 110 Fg 40.30N 5.00W
Central African Republic (EN)=Centrafrique [1] 160 Jh 7.00N 21.00 E
Central America (EN) 106 Bh 20.00N 100.00W
Central Auckland [2] 218 Fb 36.45S 174.40 E
Central Brāhui Range 148 Dc 29.20N 66.55 E
Central City 186 Hf 41.07N 98.00W
Centralia [Il.-U.S.] 186 Lg 38.31N 89.08W
Centralia [Wa.-U.S.] 182 Cb 46.43N 122.58W
Central Makrān Range 148 Ig 26.40N 64.30 E
Centralno Tungusskoje plato 138 Fd 61.15N 102.00 E
Centralny-Kospašski 134 Hg 59.03N 57.50 E
Central Pacific Basin (EN) 106 Ki 5.00N 175.00W
Central Plains 174 Ke 40.20N 90.00W
Central Plateau 220e Bb 0.32S 166.56 E
Central Point 188 De 42.23N 122.57W
Central Range 208 Fe 5.00S 142.30 E
Central Russian Uplands (EN) = Srednerusskaja vozvyšennost 110 Je 52.00N 38.00 E
Central Siberian Uplands (EN) = Srednesibirskoje ploskogorje 140 Mc 65.00N 105.00 E
Central Urals (EN)=Srednij Ural 110 Ld 58.00N 59.00 E
Centre [Burkina] [3] 166 Ec 12.00N 1.00W
Centre [Togo] [3] 166 Fd 9.15N 1.00 E
Centre, Canal du- 122 Jh 46.28N 3.59 E
Centre-Est [3] 166 Ec 11.30N 0.20W
Centre-Nord [3] 166 Ec 13.20N 0.55W
Centre-Ouest [3] 166 Ec 12.00N 2.20W
Centre-Sud [3] 166 He 3.30N 11.50 E
Centro, Cayo- 192 Ph 18.35N 87.20W
Centuripe 128 Im 37.37N 14.44 E
Čepca 136 Fd 58.35N 50.05 E
Čepelare 130 Hh 41.44N 24.41 E
Cephalonia (EN)= Kefallinia 110 Ih 38.15N 20.35 E
Čepin 128 Me 45.32N 18.34 E
Ceplenița 130 Jb 47.23N 26.58 E
Cepu 150 Fh 7.09S 111.35 E
Cer 130 Ce 44.37N 19.28 E
Ceram Sea (EN)=Seram, Laut- 208 De 2.30S 128.00 E
Cerbatana, Serrania de la- 202 Eb 6.50N 66.15W
Cerbicale, Iles- 122a Bb 41.33N 9.22 E
Cercal 126 Dg 37.47N 8.42W
Čerchov 120 Rg 49.10N 21.05 E
Čerdakly 114 Li 54.23N 48.51 E
Čerdyn 134 Hf 60.25N 56.29 E
Cère 122 Hj 44.55N 1.49 E
Čereha 114 Gh 57.47N 28.22 E
Čeremhovo 142 Md 53.09N 103.05 E
Čerepanovo 136 Df 54.13N 83.32 E
Čerepovec 112 Jd 59.08N 37.54 E
Ceres [Arg.] 206 Hc 29.53S 61.57W
Ceres [Braz.] 202 Ig 15.17S 49.35W
Ceres [S.Afr.] 172 Bf 33.21S 19.18 E
Ceresio→Lugano, Lago di- 128 Cd 46.00N 9.00 E
Céret 122 Il 42.29N 2.45 E
Cereté 202 Cb 8.53N 75.47W
Cerf Island 158 Mi 9.31S 51.01 E
Cerfontaine 124 Gd 50.10N 4.25 E
Cergy 124 Ee 49.02N 2.04 E
Cerignola 128 Ji 41.16N 15.54 E
Čerikov 132 Gc 53.35N 31.25 E
Cérilly 122 Ih 46.37N 2.50 E
Čerkasskaja oblast [3] 136 Df 49.15N 31.15 E
Čerkassy 136 Df 49.26N 32.04 E
Çerkeş 146 Eb 40.50N 32.54 E
Čerkessk 136 Eg 44.14N 42.04 E
Čerkesskaja respublika 136 Eg 43.45N 41.45 E
Çerkezköy 130 Kh 41.17N 28.00 E
Čerlak 136 He 54.09N 74.58 E
Čerlakski 136 He 53.47N 74.31 E
Čermasan 134 Gi 55.10N 55.20 E
Cermei 130 Ec 46.33N 21.51 E
Çermenika 130 Dh 41.03N 20.20 E
Čermoz 134 Hg 58.47N 56.10 E
Cerna [Rom.] 130 Fe 45.53N 22.58 E
Cerna [Rom.] 130 Fd 44.42N 22.25 E
Cerna [Rom.] 130 Ge 44.37N 23.57 E
Černaja 134 Hb 68.35N 56.31 E
Černaja [Russia] 134 Hb 68.35N 56.30 E
Černaja [Ukr.] 130 Mb 47.39N 29.11 E
Černa Skala, prodod - 130 Fg 42.02N 22.47 E
Černatica 130 Hh 41.53N 24.33 E
Černavčicy 120 Td 52.11N 23.47 E
Cernavoda 130 Le 44.22N 28.01 E
Cernay 122 Ng 47.49N 7.10 E
Cernay-en-Dormois 124 Ge 49.13N 4.46 E
Černevo 116 Mf 58.35N 28.23 E
Černigov 112 Je 51.30N 31.18 E
Černigovskaja oblast [3] 136 De 51.20N 32.00 E
Černi Lom 130 If 43.33N 25.57 E

Index Symbols

[1] Independent Nation
[2] State, Region
[3] District, County
[4] Municipality
[5] Colony, Dependency
Continent
Physical Region
Historical or Cultural Region
Mount, Mountain
Volcano
Hill
Mountains, Mountain Range
Hills, Escarpment
Plateau, Upland
Pass, Gap
Plain, Lowland
Delta
Salt Flat
Valley, Canyon
Crater, Cave
Karst Features
Depression
Polder
Desert, Dunes
Forest, Woods
Heath, Steppe
Oasis
Cape, Point
Coast, Beach
Cliff
Peninsula
Isthmus
Sandbank
Island
Atoll
Rock, Reef
Islands, Archipelago
Rocks, Reefs
Coral Reef
Well, Spring
Geyser
River, Stream
Waterfall, Rapids
River Mouth, Estuary
Lake
Salt Lake
Intermittent Lake
Reservoir
Swamp, Pond
Canal
Glacier
Ice Shelf, Pack Ice
Ocean
Sea
Gulf, Bay
Strait, Fjord
Lagoon
Bank
Seamount
Tablemount
Ridge
Shelf
Basin
Escarpment, Sea Scarp
Fracture
Trench, Abyss
National Park, Reserve
Point of Interest
Recreation Site
Cave, Cavern
Historic Site
Ruins
Wall, Walls
Church, Abbey
Temple
Scientific Station
Railway station
Airport
Port
Military installation
Lighthouse
Mine
Tunnel
Dam, Bridge

Černjahovsk 136 Ce 54.38N 21.48 E
Černjanka 132 Jd 50.55N 37.49 E
Černobyl 136 De 51.17N 30.13 E
Černogorsk 138 Ef 53.45N 91.18 E
Černoje more = Black Sea (EN) 110 Jg 43.00N 35.00 E
Černo More=Black Sea (EN) 110 Jg 43.00N 35.00 E
Černomorskoje 132 Hg 45.31N 32.42 E
Černovcy 112 If 48.18N 25.56 E
Černovickaja oblast [3] 136 Cf 48.20N 26.10 E
Černuška 136 Fd 56.31N 56.03 E
Černy Jar 132 Oe 48.03N 46.05 E
Černyje Zemli 132 Nf 45.55N 46.00 E
Černyševa, grjada- 134 Ic 66.20N 59.45 E
Černyševa, zaliv- 135 Bh 45.50N 59.10 E
Černyševsk 138 Gf 52.35N 117.02 E
Černyševski 138 Gd 62.58N 112.15 E
Černyškovski 132 Me 48.27N 42.14 E
Cérou 122 Hj 44.08N 1.52 E
Cerralvo 192 Jd 26.06N 99.37W
Cerralvo, Isla- 190 Cd 24.15N 109.55W
Cerredo, Torre de- 126 Ha 43.13N 4.50W
Cerriku 130 Ch 41.02N 19.57 E
Cerrito [Col.] 202 Db 6.51N 72.42W
Cerrito [Par.] 204 Dh 27.19S 57.40W
Cerritos 190 Dd 22.26N 100.17W
Cêrro Azul 206 Kb 24.50S 49.15W
Cerro Azul 192 Kg 21.12N 97.44W
Cerro Chato 204 Ek 33.06S 55.08W
Cerro Colorado 204 Ek 33.52S 55.33W
Cerro de las Mesas 192 Kh 18.47N 96.05W
Cerro de Pasco 200 Ig 10.41S 76.16W
Cêrro Grande 204 Gj 30.36S 51.45W
Cerro Largo 206 Jc 28.09S 54.45W
Cerro Largo [3] 204 Ek 32.20S 54.20W
Cerrón, Cerro- 194 Lh 10.19N 70.39W
Cerro San Valentin 198 Ij 46.36S 73.20W
Cerros Colorados, Embalse- 206 Ge 38.35S 68.40W
Cerro Vera 204 Dk 33.11S 57.28W
Cerrudo Cué 204 Dh 27.34S 57.57W
Čerski 142 Sc 68.45N 161.45 E
Čerskogo, hrebet- [Russia] 138 Gf 52.00N 114.00 E
Čerskogo, hrebet- [Russia] = Cherski Mountains (EN) 140 Qc 65.00N 145.00 E
Certaldo 128 Fg 43.33N 11.02 E
Čertkovo 132 Le 49.20N 40.12 E
Cervaro 128 Ji 41.30N 15.52 E
Cervati 128 Jj 40.17N 15.29 E
Červen [Bul.] 130 Jf 43.37N 26.02 E
Červen [Bela.] 132 Fc 53.43N 28.29 E
Červen brjag 130 Hf 43.16N 24.06 E
Cervera 126 Nc 41.40N 1.17 E
Cervera del Rio Alhama 126 Kb 42.01N 1.57W
Cervera de Pisuerga 126 Hb 42.52N 4.30W
Cerveteri 128 Gh 42.00N 12.06 E
Cervia 128 Gf 44.15N 12.22 E
Cervin/Cervino 128 Be 45.58N 7.39 E
Cervino/Cervin 128 Be 45.58N 7.39 E
Cervione 122a Ba 42.20N 9.29 E
Červonoarmejsk 120 Vf 50.03N 25.18 E
Červonoarmejskoje 130 Ld 45.50N 28.38 E
Červonograd 136 Ce 50.24N 24.12 E
Cesano 128 Hg 43.45N 13.10 E
Cesar [3] 202 Db 9.50N 73.30W
Cesar, Rio- 194 Ki 9.00N 73.58W
Cesena 128 Gf 44.08N 12.15 E
Cesenatico 128 Gf 44.12N 12.24 E
Cēsis/Cesis 136 Cd 57.18N 25.18 E
Cesis/Cēsis 136 Cd 57.18N 25.18 E
Česká Lípa 120 Kf 50.42N 14.32 E
Česká Republika = Czech Republic (EN) 112 Hf 50.00N 13.00 E
Česká Třebová 120 Mg 49.54N 16.27 E
České Budějovice 120 Kh 48.58N 14.29 E
České středohoří 120 Jf 50.35N 14.00 E
České země [2] 120 Kg 49.45N 15.00 E
Českomoravská Vrchovina= Moravian Upland (EN) 110 Hf 49.20N 15.30 F
Český Krumlov 120 Kh 48.49N 14.19 E
Český Les=North Bohemian Forest (EN) 120 Ig 49.50N 12.30 E
Česma 134 Jj 53.50N 60.40 E
Česma 128 Ke 45.35N 16.29 E
Çeşme 146 Bc 38.18N 26.19 E
Çeşme Yarımadası 130 Jk 38.30N 26.30 E
Češskaja guba = Chesha Bay (EN) 110 Kb 67.20N 46.30 E
Cessnock 212 Kf 32.50S 151.21 E
Cestos 158 Gh 5.27N 9.35W
Cesvaine/Cesvajne 116 Lh 56.55N 26.20 E
Cesvajne/Cesvaine 116 Lh 56.55N 26.20 E
Cetate 130 Ge 44.06N 23.03 E
Cetina 128 Kg 43.27N 16.42 E
Cetinje 130 Bg 42.24N 18.55 E
Çetinkaya 146 Gc 39.15N 37.38 E
Cetraro 128 Jk 39.31N 15.56 E
Cetynia 120 Sd 52.33N 22.26 E
Ceuta [5] 160 Ge 35.53N 5.19W
Ceva-i-Ra (Conway Reef) 208 Ig 21.45S 174.35 E
Cevedale/Zufallspitze 128 Ed 46.27N 10.37 E
Cévennes 110 Gg 44.40N 4.00 E
Ceyhan 144 Eb 37.04N 35.47 E
Ceyhan 144 Eb 36.45N 35.42 E
Ceylanpınar 146 Id 36.51N 40.02 E
Ceylon → Sri Lanka [1] 142 Ki 7.40N 80.50 E
Cézallier 122 Ii 45.20N 3.00 E
Cèze 122 Kj 44.06N 4.42 E
Chaalis, Abbaye de- 124 Ee 49.10N 2.40 E
Cha-am 148 Jf 12.48N 99.58 E
Chabanais 122 Gi 45.52N 0.43 E
Chabjuwardoo Bay 212 Cd 22.55S 113.50 E
Chablais 122 Mh 46.20N 6.30 E
Chāboksar 146 Nd 36.58N 50.34 E
Chabówka 120 Pg 49.34N 19.58 E
Chacabuco 206 Hd 34.38S 60.29W
Chachani, Nevado- 202 Dg 16.12S 71.33W
Chachapoyas 202 Ce 6.13S 77.51W
Chachoengsao 148 Kf 13.41N 101.03 E
Chaco [2] 206 Hc 26.00S 60.30W
Chaco [3] 204 Bd 20.00S 60.30W
Chaco Mesa 186 Ci 35.50N 107.35W
Chaco River 186 Bh 36.46N 108.39W
Chad (EN)=Tchad [1] 160 Ig 15.00N 19.00 E
Chad, Lake- (EN) = Tchad, Lac- 158 Ig 13.20N 14.00 E
Chādegān 146 Nf 32.46N 50.38 E
Chadileuvú, Rio- 206 Ge 38.49S 64.57W
Chadiza 170 Fe 14.04S 32.26 E
Chadron 182 Gc 42.50N 103.02W
Chaeryŏng 154 He 38.24N 125.37 E
Chafarinas, Islas- 126 Ji 35.11N 2.26W
Chāgai Hills 140 Ig 29.30N 64.15 E
Chagang-Do [2] 154 Ie 40.50N 126.30 E
Chaghcharān 142 If 34.31N 65.15 E
Chagny 122 Kh 46.55N 4.45 E
Chagos Archipelago 140 Jj 6.00S 72.00 E
Chagos-Laccadive Plateau (EN) 106 Gi 3.00N 73.00 E
Chagu, Serra do- 204 Fg 25.10S 52.40W
Chaguaramas 196 Ch 9.20N 66.16W
Chahār Borjak 144 Jc 30.17N 62.03 E
Chahār Mahāl-e Bakhtīārī [3] 144 Hc 32.00N 50.00 E
Chahbounia 126 Oi 35.33N 2.36 E
Ch'aho 154 Jd 40.12N 128.38 E
Chai Badan 148 Ke 15.05N 101.04 E
Chaibāsa 148 Hd 22.34N 85.49 E
Chaigoubu → Huai'an 154 Cd 40.40N 114.25 E
Chai He 154 Gc 42.20N 123.51 E
Chaillu, Massif du- 158 Ii 2.32S 11.10 E
Chainat 148 Ke 15.10N 100.10 E
Chaise-Dieu, La- 122 Ji 45.19N 3.42 E
Chaitén 206 Ff 42.55S 72.43W
Chaiyaphum 148 Ke 16.09N 102.02 E
Chajul 194 Bf 15.30N 91.02W
Chakari 172 Dc 18.09S 29.52 E
Chak Chak 168 Dd 8.40N 26.54 E
Chake Chake 160 Ki 5.15S 39.46 E
Chakhānsūr 144 Jc 31.10N 62.04 E
Chala 202 Dg 15.52S 74.16W
Chalais 122 Gi 45.17N 0.02 E
Chalaltenango 194 Cf 14.03N 88.56W
Chalan Kanoa 220b Ba 15.08N 145.43 E
Chalbi Desert 158 Kh 3.00N 37.20 E
Chalchuapa 194 Cg 13.59N 89.41W
Chalcidice (EN)= Khalkidhiki 110 Ig 40.25N 23.25 E
Chālesbān 146 Ne 35.18N 50.03 E
Chaleur Bay 180 Kg 47.50N 65.30W
Chalhuanca 202 Df 14.17S 73.15W
Chaling 152 Jf 26.47N 113.32 E
Chalky Inlet 218 Bg 46.05S 166.30 E
Challans 122 Eh 46.51N 1.53W
Challapata 202 Eg 18.54S 66.47W
Challis 188 Hd 44.30N 114.14W
Chalmette 186 Ll 29.56N 89.58W
Châlons-sur-Marne 122 Kf 48.57N 4.22 E
Chalon-sur-Saône 122 Kh 46.47N 4.51 E
Chalosse 122 Fk 43.45N 0.30W
Chaltubo 132 Mh 42.19N 42.34 E
Chālūs 144 Hb 36.38N 51.26 E
Châlus 122 Gi 45.39N 0.59 E
Cham 120 Ig 49.13N 12.40 E
Chama 170 Fe 11.12S 33.10 E
Chama, Rio- 194 Li 9.03N 71.37W
Chama, Rio- 186 Ch 36.03N 106.05W
Chaman 148 Db 30.55N 66.27 E
Chaman Bīd 146 Qd 37.25N 56.38 E
Chamba [India] 148 Fb 32.34N 76.08 E
Chamba [Tan.] 170 Ge 11.35S 36.58 E
Chambal 140 Jg 26.29N 79.15 E
Chambaran, Plateau de- 122 Li 45.10N 5.20 E
Chambas 194 Hb 22.12N 78.55W
Chamberlain 186 Ge 43.49N 99.20W
Chamberlain Lake 184 Mb 46.17N 69.20W
Chamberlain River 212 Fc 15.35S 127.51 E
Chambersburg 184 If 39.57N 77.40W
Chambéry 122 Li 45.34N 5.56 E
Chambeshi 158 Jj 11.53S 29.48 E
Chambley-Bussières 124 He 49.03N 5.54 E
Chambly 124 Ee 49.10N 2.15 E
Chambois 124 Cf 48.48N 0.07 E
Chambon, Lac de- 122 Hh 46.25N 1.35 E
Chambord 122 Hg 47.37N 1.31 E
Chamchamal 146 Ke 35.32N 44.50 E
Chame, Punta- 194 Hi 8.39N 79.42W
Chamela 192 Gh 19.32N 105.05W
Chamela, Bahía- 192 Gh 19.30N 105.10W
Chamelecón, Río- 194 Df 15.51N 87.49W
Chamical 206 Gd 30.21S 66.19W
Chamiss Bay 188 Ba 50.07N 127.22W
Chamoli 148 Fb 30.24N 79.21 E
Chamonix-Mont-Blanc 122 Mi 45.55N 6.52 E
Chamouchouane, Rivière- 184 Ka 48.40N 72.20W
Champagne 110 Gf 49.00N 4.30 E
Champagne 122 Kf 49.00N 4.30 E
Champagne Berrichonne 122 Hh 47.00N 2.00 E
Champagne Humide 122 Kf 48.20N 4.30 E
Champagne Pouilleuse 122 Kf 48.40N 4.20 E
Champagnole 122 Lh 46.45N 5.55 E
Champaign 182 Jc 40.07N 88.14W
Champaqui, Cerro- 198 Ji 31.59S 64.56W
Champasak 148 Lf 14.53N 105.52 E
Champaubert 124 Ff 48.53N 3.47 E
Champdoré, Lac- 180 Ke 55.55N 65.45W
Champ du Feu, Le- 122 Nf 48.24N 7.15 E
Champeigne 122 Gg 47.15N 0.50 E
Champerico 194 Bf 14.18N 91.55W
Champlain, Lake- 182 Mc 44.45N 73.15W
Champlite 122 Lg 47.37N 5.31 E
Champotón 190 Fe 19.21N 90.43W
Champsaur 122 Mj 44.45N 6.10 E
Chāmrājnagar 148 Ff 11.55N 76.57 E
Chañaral 206 Fc 26.21S 70.37W
Chança 126 Eg 37.33N 7.31W
Chan Chan 202 Ce 8.07S 79.02W
Chanco 206 Fe 35.44S 72.32W
Chandalar 178 Jc 67.30N 148.30W
Chandalar 178 Jc 66.36N 145.48W
Chandausi 148 Fc 28.27N 78.46 E
Chandeleur Islands 182 Jf 29.48N 88.51W
Chandeleur Sound 186 Ll 29.55N 89.10W
Chandīgarh 142 Jf 30.44N 76.55 E
Chandler 180 Lg 48.21N 64.41W
Chandless, Rio- 202 Ee 9.08S 69.51W
Chāndpur 148 Id 23.13N 90.39 E
Chandragupta 148 Fe 16.11N 78.52 E
Chandrapur 142 Jh 19.57N 79.18 E
Chang, Ko- 148 Kf 12.00N 102.23 E
Changajn Nuruu = Khangai Mountains (EN) 140 Le 47.30N 100.00 E
Chang'an → Rong'an 152 If 25.16N 109.23 E
Changane 158 Kk 24.43S 33.32 E
Changbai 154 Jd 41.25N 128.11 E
Changbai Shan 140 Oe 42.00N 128.00 E
Changchun 142 Oe 43.51N 125.20 E
Changdao(Sihou) 154 Ff 37.56N 120.42 E
Changde 142 Ng 29.04N 111.42 E
Ch'angdo 154 Ie 38.30N 127.45 E
Changfeng (Shuijiahu) 154 Dh 32.29N 117.10 E
Changge 154 Bg 34.12N 113.45 E
Changhang 154 If 36.01N 126.42 E
Chang He 154 Ei 31.21N 118.21 E
Changhowŏn 154 If 37.07N 127.38 E
Changhua 152 Lg 24.05N 120.32 E
Changhŭng 154 Ig 34.40N 126.54 E
Changji 152 Ec 44.01N 87.16 E
Chang Jiang 154 Dj 28.59N 116.42 E
Changjiang (Shiliu) 152 Ih 19.20N 109.03 E
Chang Jiang (Yangtze Kiang) 140 Of 31.48N 121.10 E
Changjiang Kou 152 Le 31.24N 121.59 E
Changjin-gang 154 Id 40.30N 127.12 E
Changjin-ho 154 Id 40.30N 127.12 E
Changjin-ŭp 152 Mc 40.23N 127.15 E
Changli 154 Ee 39.43N 119.10 E
Changling 152 Lc 44.15N 123.58 E
Changlung 148 Fb 34.56N 77.29 E
Changping 154 Dd 40.14N 116.13 E
Changsha 142 Ng 28.12N 113.02 E
Changshan 154 Ej 28.55N 118.31 E
Changshan Qundao 154 Ge 39.10N 122.34 E
Changshu 154 Fi 31.38N 120.44 E
Changsŏng 154 Ig 35.19N 126.48 E
Changting 154 Jb 44.27N 128.50 E
Changtu 154 Hc 42.47N 124.08 E
Changuillo 202 Cf 14.40S 75.12W
Changuinola 194 Fi 9.26N 82.31W
Changwu 152 Id 35.17N 107.52 E
Changxing 154 Ei 31.01N 119.55 E
Changxing Dao 154 Fe 39.35N 121.42 E
Changyi 154 Ef 36.52N 119.25 E
Changyŏn 152 Md 38.15N 125.05 E
Changyuan 154 Cg 35.12N 114.40 E
Changzhi 152 Jd 36.07N 113.10 E
Changzhou 154 Ei 31.46N 119.56 E
Channel Islands [Chan.Is.] 110 Ff 49.20N 2.20W
Channel Islands [U.S.] 174 Hf 34.00N 120.00W
Channel Islands = Anglo-Normandes Iles- (F) [5] 118 Kl 49.20N 2.20W
Channel Port-aux-Basques 176 Ne 47.35N 59.11W
Channel Rock 194 Ib 23.00N 77.55W
Channing 186 Ei 35.41N 102.20W
Chantada 126 Eb 42.37N 7.46W
Chantengo, Laguna- 192 Ji 16.35N 99.10W
Chanthaburi 148 Kf 12.35N 102.06 E
Chantilly 122 Ie 49.12N 2.28 E
Chantonnay 122 Eh 46.41N 1.03W
Chantrey Inlet 174 Jc 67.48N 96.20W
Chanute 186 Ih 37.41N 95.27W
Chanza 126 Eg 37.33N 7.31W
Chao'an (Chaozhou) 152 Kg 23.41N 116.37 E
Chaobai Xinhe 154 De 39.07N 117.41 E
Chao He 154 Dd 40.36N 117.08 E
Chao Hu 154 Di 31.31N 117.33 E
Chao Phraya 140 Mh 13.32N 100.36 E
Chaor He 152 Lb 46.49N 123.45 E
Chaoxian 152 Ke 31.37N 117.49 E
Chaoyang [China] 152 Kg 23.17N 116.37 E
Chaoyang [China] 142 Oe 41.35N 120.26 E
Chaoyang → Huinan 154 Ic 42.41N 126.03 E
Chaoyang → Jiayin 152 Nb 48.52N 130.21 E
Chaoyangchuan 154 Jc 42.53N 129.23 E
Chaoyangcun 152 La 50.01N 124.22 E
Chaozhong 152 La 50.53N 121.23 E
Chaozhou → Chao'an 152 Kg 23.41N 116.37 E
Chapada dos Guimarães 202 Gg 15.26S 55.45W
Chapadinha 202 Jd 3.44S 43.21W
Chapais 184 Ja 49.47N 74.56W
Chapala 192 Hg 20.18N 103.12W
Chapala, Lago de- 174 Ig 20.15N 103.00W
Chaparral 202 Cc 3.43N 75.28W
Chapecó 206 Jc 27.06S 52.36W
Chapecó, Rio- 204 Fh 27.06S 53.01W
Chapecó, Serra do- 204 Gh 26.44S 51.54W
Chapel Hill 184 Hh 35.55N 79.04W
Chapicuy 204 Dj 31.40S 57.55W
Chapleau 180 Jg 47.50N 83.24W
Chaplin 188 La 50.28N 106.40W
Chaplin Lake 188 La 50.18N 106.35W
Chapman, Cape- 180 Ic 69.15N 89.27W
Chappell 186 Ef 41.06N 102.28W
Châpra 148 Gc 25.46N 84.45 E
Chapultepec 192 Hf 23.27N 103.04W
Chaqui 202 Eg 19.36S 65.32W
Char 162 Ee 21.31N 12.51W
Charadai 204 Ch 27.38S 59.54W
Charagua 202 Fg 19.48S 63.13W
Charām 146 Ng 30.45N 50.44 E
Charaña 202 Eg 17.36S 69.28W
Charcas 192 If 23.08N 101.07W
Charco de la Aguja 192 Gc 28.25N 104.01W
Charcot Island 222 Qe 69.45S 75.15W
Chard [Alta.-Can.] 180 Ge 55.48N 111.10W
Chard [Eng.-U.K.] 118 Kk 50.53N 2.58W
Chardāvol 146 Lf 33.45N 46.38 E
Chardonnières 194 Jd 18.16N 74.10W
Charente [3] 122 Gi 45.40N 0.05 E
Charente 122 Ei 45.57N 1.05W
Charente-Maritime [3] 122 Fi 45.30N 0.45W
Charentonne 124 Ce 49.07N 0.44 E
Chari 158 Ig 12.58N 14.31 E
Chari-Baguirmi [3] 168 Bc 12.00N 17.00 E
Chārīkār 144 Kb 35.01N 69.11 E
Charing 124 Cc 51.12N 0.48 E
Charité-sur-Loire, La- 122 Jg 47.11N 3.01 E
Chariton 186 Jf 41.00N 93.19W
Chariton River 186 Jg 39.19N 92.57W
Charity 202 Gb 7.24N 58.36W
Charleroi 122 Kd 50.25N 4.26 E
Charleroi-Jumet 122 Kd 50.27N 4.26 E
Charleroi-Marcinelle 124 Gd 50.25N 4.28 E
Charles 180 Kd 62.38N 74.15W
Charles, Cape- [Can.] 174 Nd 52.13N 55.40W
Charles, Cape- [Va.-U.S.] 182 Ld 37.08N 75.58W
Charles, Peak- 212 Ef 32.52S 121.11 E
Charlesbourg 184 Lb 46.52N 71.16W
Charles City 182 Ic 43.04N 92.40W
Charles de Gaulle, Aéroport- = Charles de Gaulle, Airport- (EN) 124 Ee 49.02N 2.35 E
Charles de Gaulle, Airport- (EN) = Charles de Gaulle, Aéroport- 124 Ee 49.02N 2.35 E
Charleston [Il.-U.S.] 186 Lg 39.30N 88.10W
Charleston [Mo.-U.S.] 186 Lh 36.55N 89.21W
Charleston [Ms.-U.S.] 186 Ki 34.01N 90.04W
Charleston [N.Z.] 218 Dd 41.54S 171.27 E
Charleston [S.C.-U.S.] 176 Lf 32.48N 79.57W
Charleston [W.V.-U.S.] 176 Kf 38.21N 81.38W
Charleston Peak 182 Dd 36.16N 115.42W
Charles Town 184 If 39.18N 77.52W
Charlestown 196 Ed 17.12N 62.35W
Charleval 124 De 49.22N 1.23 E
Charleville 210 Fg 26.24S 146.15 E
Charleville-Mézières 122 Ke 49.46N 4.43 E
Charleville Mézières-Mohon 124 Ge 49.46N 4.43 E
Charlevoix 184 Ec 45.19N 85.16W
Charlieu 122 Kh 46.09N 4.11 E
Charlotte [Mi.-U.S.] 184 Ed 42.36N 84.50W
Charlotte [N.C.-U.S.] 176 Kf 35.14N 80.50W
Charlotte Amalie 190 Le 18.21N 64.56W
Charlotte Bank (EN) 208 If 11.47S 173.13 E
Charlotte Harbor 184 Fl 26.45N 82.12W
Charlottenberg 116 Ee 59.53N 12.17 E
Charlottesville 182 Ld 38.02N 78.29W
Charlottetown 176 Me 46.14N 63.08W
Charlton 212 Ig 36.16S 143.21 E
Charlton 180 Jf 52.00N 79.26W
Charly 124 Ff 48.58N 3.17 E
Charmes 122 Mf 48.22N 6.17 E
Charnley River 212 Ec 16.20S 124.53 E
Charny-sur-Meuse 124 He 49.12N 5.22 E
Charollais 122 Kh 46.26N 4.16 E
Charouine 162 Gd 29.01N 0.16W
Charroux 122 Gh 46.09N 0.24 E
Chārsadda 148 Eb 34.09N 71.44 E
Charters Towers 210 Fg 20.05S 146.16 E
Chartres 122 Hf 48.27N 1.30 E
Charzykowskie, Jezioro- 120 Nc 53.47N 17.30 E
Chascomus 206 Ie 35.34S 58.01W
Chase 188 Fa 50.49N 119.41W
Chasŏng 154 Id 41.25N 126.35 E
Chassengue 170 Ce 10.26S 18.32 E
Chassezac 122 Kj 44.26N 4.19 E
Chassiron, Pointe de- 122 Eh 46.03N 1.24W
Chat 146 Pd 37.59N 55.16 E
Châtaigneraie 122 Ij 44.45N 2.20 E
Chātāl 146 Pd 37.40N 55.45 E
Château-Arnoux 122 Lj 44.06N 6.00 E
Chateaubelair 197n Ba 13.17N 61.15W
Châteaubriant 122 Eg 47.43N 1.23W
Château-Chinon 122 Jg 47.04N 3.56 E
Château-d'Oléron, Le- 122 Ei 45.54N 1.12W
Château-du-Loir 122 Gg 47.42N 0.25 E
Châteaudun 122 Hf 48.05N 1.20 E
Château-Gontier 122 Fg 47.50N 0.42W
Châteaulin 122 Bf 48.12N 4.05W
Châteaulin, Bassin de- 122 Cf 48.18N 3.50W
Châteaumeillant 122 Ih 46.34N 2.12 E
Châteauneuf-de-Randon 122 Jj 44.39N 3.40 E
Châteauneuf-sur-Cher 122 Ih 46.51N 2.19 E
Châteauneuf-sur-Loire 122 Ig 47.52N 2.14 E
Château-Porcien 124 Ge 49.32N 4.15 E
Châteaurenard 122 Kk 43.53N 4.51 E
Château-Renault 122 Gg 47.35N 0.54 E
Châteauroux 122 Hh 46.49N 1.42 E
Château-Salins 122 Mf 48.49N 6.30 E
Château-Thierry 122 Je 49.03N 3.24 E
Châteaux, Pointe des- 197e Bb 16.15N 61.11W
Châtelaillon-Plage 122 Eh 46.04N 1.05W
Châtelet 124 Gd 50.24N 4.31 E
Châtelguyon 122 Ji 45.55N 3.04 E
Châtellerault 122 Gh 46.48N 0.32 E
Chatelodo 204 De 21.19S 57.28W
Chatham [Eng.-U.K.] 118 Nj 51.23N 0.32 E
Chatham [N.B.-Can.] 180 Kg 47.02N 65.26W
Chatham [Ont.-Can.] 180 Jh 42.24N 82.11W
Chatham [Va.-U.S.] 184 Hg 36.49N 79.26W
Chatham Island 208 Ji 44.00S 176.30W
Chatham Islands 208 Ji 44.00S 176.30W
Chatham Rise (EN) 208 Ii 43.30S 180.00
Chatham Strait 178 Me 57.30N 134.45W
Châtillon-en-Bazois 122 Jg 47.03N 3.40 E
Châtillon-sur-Indre 122 Hh 46.59N 1.10 E
Châtillon-sur-Marne 124 Fe 49.06N 3.45 E
Châtillon-sur-Seine 122 Kg 47.51N 4.33 E
Chatom 184 Cj 31.28N 88.16W
Châtre, La- 122 Hh 46.35N 1.59 E
Chatsworth 172 Ec 19.38S 30.50 E
Chattahoochee 184 Ej 30.42N 84.51W
Chattahoochee 174 Kf 30.52N 84.57W
Chattanooga 176 Kf 35.03N 85.19W
Chatteris 124 Cb 52.27N 0.03 E
Chaucas 204 Cc 16.46S 58.44W
Chaudfontaine 124 Hd 50.35N 5.38 E
Chaudière, Rivière- 184 Lb 46.43N 71.17W
Chau Doc 148 Lf 10.42N 105.07 E
Chauk 148 Id 20.53N 94.49 E
Chaulnes 124 Ee 49.49N 2.48 E
Chaumont 122 Lf 48.07N 5.08 E
Chaumont-en-Vexin 124 De 49.16N 1.53 E
Chaumont-Gistoux 124 Gd 50.41N 4.44 E
Chaumont-Porcien 124 Ge 49.39N 4.15 E
Chaumont-sur-Aire 124 Hf 48.56N 5.15 E
Chaumont-sur-Loire 122 Hg 47.29N 1.11 E
Chauny 122 Je 49.37N 3.13 E
Chausey, Iles- 122 Ef 48.53N 1.50W
Chauvigny 122 Gh 46.34N 0.39 E
Chavantina 202 Hf 14.40S 52.21W
Chavarria 204 Ci 28.57S 58.35W
Chaves [Braz.] 202 Id 0.10S 49.55W
Chaves [Port.] 126 Ec 41.44N 7.28W
Chavigny, Lac- 180 Je 58.00N 75.05W
Chavuma 170 De 13.05S 22.42 E
Chayia 146 If 32.09N 40.58 E
Chazelles-sur-Lyon 122 Ki 45.38N 4.23 E
Chbar 148 Lf 12.46N 107.10 E
Cheaha Mountain 184 Ei 33.30N 85.47W
Cheat River 184 Hf 39.45N 79.55W
Cheb 120 If 50.04N 12.23 E
Cheboygan 182 Kb 45.39N 84.29W
Chech, 'Erg- 158 Gf 25.00N 3.00W
Chechaouene 162 Fb 35.10N 5.16W
Chechaouene [3] 162 Fb 35.00N 5.00W
Checheng 152 Lg 22.05N 120.42 E
Che-Chiang Sheng → Zhejiang Sheng [2] 152 Kf 29.00N 120.00 E
Chech'ŏn 154 Jf 37.08N 128.12 E
Chęciny 120 Qf 50.48N 20.28 E
Cheddar Gorge 118 Kj 51.13N 2.47W
Cheduba 148 Ie 18.48N 93.38 E
Chée 124 Gf 48.45N 4.39 E
Cheektowaga 184 Hd 42.57N 78.38W
Chefu 172 Ed 22.27S 32.45 E
Chegga 160 Gf 25.22N 5.49W
Cheghelvandī 146 Mf 33.42N 48.25 E
Chegutu 172 Ec 18.07S 30.08 E
Chehel Pāyeh 146 Qg 31.54N 57.14 E
Cheju 152 Me 33.31N 126.32 E
Cheju-Do [2] 154 Ih 33.25N 126.30 E
Cheju-Do 140 Of 33.25N 126.30 E
Cheju-Haehyŏp 154 Ih 33.40N 126.28 E
Chela, Serra da- 158 Ij 16.00S 13.10 E
Chelan 188 Ec 47.51N 120.01W
Chelan, Lake- 188 Eb 48.05N 120.30W
Chelforó, Arroyo- 204 Cm 36.55S 58.12W
Cheliff 162 Hb 36.10N 1.20 E
Cheliff [3] 162 Hb 36.10N 1.45 E
Cheliff 158 He 36.02N 0.08 E
Cheliff, Plaine du- 126 Mi 35.57N 0.45 E
Chellalat el Adhaouara 126 Pi 35.56N 3.25 E
Chelleh Khāneh, Kūh-e- 146 Md 36.52N 48.36 E
Chełm 120 Te 51.10N 23.28 E
Chełm [2] 120 Te 51.10N 23.30 E
Chelmer 124 Cc 51.44N 0.42 E
Chełmińskie, Pojezierze- 120 Oc 53.20N 19.00 E
Chełmno 120 Oc 53.22N 18.26 E
Chelmsford 118 Nj 51.44N 0.28 E
Chełmża 120 Oc 53.12N 18.37 E
Cheltenham 118 Kj 51.54N 2.04W
Chelva 126 Ke 39.45N 0.59W
Chemainus 188 Db 48.55N 123.43W
Chemâma 162 Ef 16.50N 14.00 E
Chemba 172 Ec 17.09S 34.53 E
Chembe 170 Ee 11.58S 28.45 E
Chemillé 122 Fg 47.13N 0.43W
Chemnitz = Karl-Marx-Stadt 112 He 50.50N 12.55 E
Chemult 188 Ee 43.13N 121.47W
Chenāb 140 Jg 29.13N 70.49 E
Chenachane 162 Gd 26.00N 4.15W
Chenachane 162 Gd 25.17N 3.10W
Chenārbāshi 146 Lf 33.20N 46.20 E
Chen Barag Qi (Bayan Hure) 152 Kb 49.21N 119.25 E
Chencha 168 Fd 6.17N 37.40 E
Chencoyi 192 Nh 19.48N 90.14W
Cheney 188 Gc 47.29N 117.34W
Cheney Reservoir 186 Hh 37.45N 97.50W
Cheng'an 154 Cf 36.27N 114.41 E
Chengde 142 Ne 41.00N 117.57 E
Chengdu 142 Mf 30.45N 104.04 E
Chengkou 152 Ie 31.54N 108.37 E
Chengmai 152 Ih 19.50N 109.59 E
Chengshan Jiao 152 Ld 37.24N 122.42 E
Chengxi Hu 154 Dh 32.22N 116.12 E
Chengzitan 152 Ld 39.31N 122.28 E
Chenisckali 132 Mh 42.06N 42.16 E
Chenjiagang 154 Eg 34.22N 119.48 E
Chenonceaux 122 Hg 47.20N 1.04 E
Chenxi 152 Jf 28.02N 110.15 E
Chenxian 152 Jf 25.49N 113.04 E
Chenying → Wannian 154 Dj 28.42N 117.04 E
Cheo Reo 148 Lf 13.24N 108.27 E
Chépénéhé 219b Ce 20.47S 167.09 E
Chepes 206 Gd 31.21S 66.36W
Chepo 194 Hi 9.10N 79.06W
Cher [3] 122 Ig 47.00N 2.30 E
Cher 110 Gf 47.21N 0.29 E

Cheradi, Isole- → Coradi, Isole- 128 Lj 40.27N 17.09 E
Cherangany Hills 170 Gb 1.15N 35.27 E
Cheraw 184 Hh 34.42N 79.53W
Cherbaniani Reef 148 Ef 12.18N 71.53 E
Cherbourg 112 Ff 49.39N 1.39W
Cherchell 162 Hb 36.36N 2.12 E
Chère 122 Eg 47.42N 1.50W
Chergui, Chott Ech- 158 He 34.21N 0.30 E
Chéri 166 Hc 13.26N 11.21 E
Cherlen → Kerulen 140 Ne 48.48N 117.00 E
Cherokee 186 Ie 42.45N 95.33W
Cherokees, Lake O' the- 186 Ih 36.39N 94.49W
Cherski Mountains (EN) = Čerskogo, hrebet- [Russia] 140 Qc 65.00N 145.00 E
Chertsey 124 Bc 51.23N 0.30W
Cherwell 118 Lj 51.44N 1.15W
Chesapeake 184 Ig 36.45N 76.15W
Chesapeake Bay 174 Lf 38.40N 76.25W
Chesapeake Bay Bridge-Tunnel 184 Ig 37.00N 76.02W
Chesha Bay (EN) = Češskaja guba 110 Kb 67.20N 46.30 E
Chesham 124 Bc 51.42N 0.36W
Cheshire [3] 118 Kh 53.15N 2.30W
Cheshire Plain 118 Kh 53.20N 2.40W
Cheshunt 124 Bc 51.42N 0.02W
Chesne, Le- 122 Ke 49.31N 4.46 E
Chester 118 Kh 53.10N 2.55W
Chester [Eng.-U.K.] 118 Kh 53.12N 2.54W
Chester [Il.-U.S.] 186 Lh 37.55N 89.49W
Chester [Mt.-U.S.] 188 Jb 48.31N 110.58W
Chester [Pa.-U.S.] 184 Jf 39.50N 75.23W
Chester [S.C.-U.S.] 184 Gh 34.40N 81.12W
Chesterfield 118 Lh 53.15N 1.25W
Chesterfield, Ile- 172 Gc 16.20S 43.58 E
Chesterfield, Récifs et Iles- = Chesterfield Reefs and Islands (EN) 208 Gf 20.00S 159.00 E
Chesterfield Inlet 176 Jc 63.21N 90.42W
Chesterfield Inlet 174 Jc 63.25N 90.45W
Chesterfield Reefs and Islands (EN) = Chesterfield, Récifs et Iles- 208 Gf 20.00S 159.00 E
Chesterton Range 212 Je 25.30S 147.30 E
Chestnut Ridge 184 He 40.10N 79.25W
Chesuncook Lake 184 Mb 46.00N 69.20W
Chetaibi 162 Ib 37.04N 7.23 E
Chetumal 176 Kh 18.35N 88.07W
Chetumal, Bahia de- 190 Ge 18.20N 88.05W
Cheviot 218 Ee 42.49S 173.16 E
Chew Bahir = Stefanie, Lake- (EN) 158 Kh 4.38N 36.50 E
Chewelah 188 Gb 48.17N 117.43W
Cheyenne [Ok.-U.S.] 186 Gi 35.37N 99.40W
Cheyenne [Wy.-U.S.] 176 Ie 41.08N 104.49W
Cheyenne River 182 Gc 44.40N 101.15W
Cheyenne Wells 186 Eg 38.51N 102.11W
Cheylard, Le- 122 Kj 44.54N 4.25 E
Cheyne Bay 212 Df 34.35S 118.50 E
Chhatarpur 148 Fd 24.54N 79.36 E
Chhindwāra 148 Fd 22.04N 78.56 E
Chi 148 Ke 15.11N 104.43 E
Chiamboni, Rās- 168 Gf 1.38S 41.36 E
Chiana, Val di- 128 Fg 43.15N 11.50 E
Chianciano Terme 128 Fg 43.02N 11.49 E
Chiange 160 Ij 15.45S 13.54 E
Chiang-hsi Sheng → Jiangxi Sheng [2] 152 Kf 28.00N 116.00 E
Chiang Mai 142 Lh 18.46N 98.58 E
Chiang Rai 142 Lh 19.54N 99.50 E
Chiang-su Sheng → Jiangsu Sheng = Kiangsu (EN) [2] 152 Ke 33.00N 120.00 E
Chiani 128 Gh 42.44N 12.07 E
Chianti 128 Fg 43.30N 11.25 E
Chiapa, Rio- 192 Mj 16.30N 93.10W
Chiapas [2] 190 Fe 16.30N 92.30W
Chiapas, Meseta de- 190 Fe 16.30N 92.00W
Chiaramonte Gulfi 128 Im 37.02N 14.42 E
Chiaravalle 128 Hg 43.36N 13.19 E
Chiaromonte 128 Kj 40.07N 16.13 E
Chiautla de Tapia 192 Jh 18.17N 98.36W
Chiavari 128 Df 44.19N 9.19 E
Chiavenna 128 Dd 46.19N 9.24 E
Chiayi 152 Lg 23.29N 120.27 E
Chiba 152 Pd 35.36N 140.07 E
Chiba Ken [2] 154 Pg 35.40N 140.20 E
Chibemba 170 Bf 15.45S 14.06 E
Chibia 170 Bf 15.11S 13.41 E
Chibougamau 176 Le 49.53N 74.21W
Chibougamau, Lac- 184 Ja 49.50N 74.15W
Chibougamau, Rivière- 184 Ja 49.50N 74.25W
Chiburi-Jima 154 Lf 36.00N 133.02 E
Chibuto 172 Ed 24.42S 33.33 E
Chicago 176 Ke 41.53N 87.38W
Chicago Heights 186 Mf 41.30N 87.38W
Chicala 170 Ce 11.59S 19.30 E
Chicapa 158 Ji 6.25S 20.48 E
Chic-Chocs, Monts- 184 Na 48.55N 66.45W
Chicha 168 Bb 16.52N 18.33 E
Chichagof 178 Le 57.30N 135.30W
Chichancanab, Laguna de- 192 Oh 19.54N 88.46W
Chichaoua 162 Fc 31.32N 8.46W
Chichas, Cordillera de- 202 Eh 20.30S 66.30W
Chicheng 152 Kc 40.55N 115.47 E
Chichén Itzá 176 Kg 20.40N 88.35W
Chichester 118 Mk 50.50N 0.48W
Chichester Range 212 Dd 22.20S 119.20 E
Chichibu 154 Og 35.59N 139.05 E
Chichigalpa 194 Dg 12.34N 87.02W
Chichijima-Rettō 214 Cb 27.06N 142.12 E
Chichilla de Monte Aragón 126 Kf 38.55N 1.43W
Chichiriviche 194 Mh 10.56N 68.16W
Chickasawhay River 186 Lk 31.00N 88.45W
Chickasha 182 Hd 35.02N 97.58W
Chicken 178 Kd 64.04N 141.56W
Chiclana de la Frontera 126 Fh 36.25N 6.08W
Chiclayo 200 If 6.46S 79.50W
Chico 182 Cd 39.44N 121.50W
Chico, Rio- [Arg.] 198 Jj 49.56S 68.32W
Chico, Rio- [Arg.] 198 Jj 43.48S 66.25W
Chicoana 206 Gc 25.06S 65.33W
Chicomo 172 Ed 24.31S 34.17 E
Chiconono 172 Fb 12.57S 35.45 E
Chicopee 184 Kd 42.10N 72.36W
Chicote 170 Df 16.01S 21.48 E
Chicoutimi 176 Le 48.26N 71.04W
Chicoutimi Nord 184 La 48.29N 71.02W
Chicualacuala 172 Ed 22.05S 31.42 E
Chidenguele 172 Ed 24.55S 34.10 E
Chidley, Cape- 174 Mc 60.25N 64.30W
Chiemsee 120 Ii 47.54N 12.29 E
Chiengi 170 Ed 8.39S 29.10 E
Chienti 128 Hg 43.18N 13.45 E
Chieri 128 Be 45.01N 7.49 E
Chiers 128 He 49.39N 5.00 E
Chiese 128 Ee 45.08N 10.25 E
Chieti 128 Ih 42.21N 14.10 E
Chièvres 124 Fd 50.35N 3.48 E
Chifeng/Ulanhad 152 Kc 42.16N 118.57 E
Chifumage 170 De 12.10S 22.30 E
Chifwefwe 170 Fe 13.35S 29.35 E
Chigasaki 156 Fd 35.19N 139.24 E
Chignik 178 He 56.18N 158.23W
Chigombe 172 Ed 23.26S 33.19 E
Chigorodó 194 Ij 7.41N 76.41W
Chigubo 172 Ed 22.50S 33.31 E
Chigu Co 152 Ff 28.40N 91.50 E
Chi He 154 Dh 32.51N 117.59 E
Chihli, Gulf of- (EN) = Bo Hai 140 Nf 38.30N 120.00 E
Chihuahua 176 Ig 28.38N 106.05W
Chihuahua [2] 190 Cc 28.30N 106.00W
Chii-san 154 Ig 35.20N 127.44 E
Chikaskia River 186 Hh 36.37N 97.15W
Chikugo 156 Be 33.13N 130.30 E
Chikugo-Gawa 156 Be 33.10N 130.21 E
Chikuma-Gawa 156 Fc 37.00N 138.35 E
Chikwana 170 Ff 16.03S 34.48 E
Chilapa de Álvarez 192 Ji 17.36N 99.10W
Chilās 148 Ea 35.26N 74.05 E
Chilaw 148 Fg 7.34N 79.47 E
Chilcotin 180 Ff 51.46N 122.22W
Childers 212 Ke 25.14S 152.17 E
Childress 182 Ge 34.25N 100.13W
Chile [1] 200 Ii 30.00S 71.00W
Chile Basin (EN) 106 Mm 33.00S 90.00W
Chile Chico 206 Fg 46.33S 71.44W
Chilecito [Arg.] 206 Gc 29.10S 67.30W
Chilecito [Arg.] 206 Gd 33.53S 69.03W
Chile Rise (EN) 106 Mm 40.00S 90.00W
Chili 168 Cb 16.44N 20.53 E
Chilia, Braţul- 130 Md 45.13N 29.43 E
Chililabombwe 170 Ee 12.22S 27.50 E
Chi-lin Sheng → Jilin Sheng = Kirin (EN) [2] 152 Mc 43.00N 126.00 E
Chilko Lake 188 Ca 51.20N 124.05W
Chilko River 188 Da 52.00N 123.40W
Chillán 200 Ii 36.36S 72.07W
Chillar 206 Ie 37.18S 59.59W
Chillicothe [Il.-U.S.] 186 Lf 40.55N 89.29W
Chillicothe [Mo.-U.S.] 186 Jg 39.48N 93.33W
Chillicothe [Oh.-U.S.] 182 Kd 38.20N 82.59W
Chilliwack 188 Eb 49.10N 121.57W
Chiloé, Isla de- 198 Ij 42.30S 73.55W
Chilón 192 Mi 17.14N 92.25W
Chiloquin 188 Ee 42.35N 121.52W
Chilpancingo de los Bravos 190 Ee 17.33N 99.30W
Chiltern Hills 118 Mj 51.42N 0.48W
Chilton 186 Ld 44.02N 88.10W
Chiluage 170 Dd 9.31S 21.46 E
Chilumba 170 Fe 10.27S 34.16 E
Chilwa, Lake- 170 Gf 15.12S 35.50 E
Chimala 170 Fd 8.51S 34.01 E
Chimaltenango 194 Bf 14.39N 90.49W
Chimaltenango [3] 194 Bf 14.40N 90.55W
Chimán 194 Hi 8.42N 78.37W
Chimanas, Islas- 196 Dg 10.17N 64.38W
Chimanimani 172 Ec 19.48S 32.50 E
Chimay 124 Gd 50.03N 4.19 E
Chimborazo, Volcán- 198 If 1.28S 78.48W
Chimbote 200 If 9.05S 78.36W
Chimichagua 194 Ki 9.16N 73.49W
Chimoio 172 Ec 19.00S 33.23 E
Chimorra 126 Hf 38.18N 4.53W
Chin [2] 148 Id 22.00N 93.30 E
China [Jap.] 156b Bb 27.20N 128.36 E
China [Mex.] 192 Je 25.42N 99.14W
China (EN) = Zhōngguó 140 Mg 35.00N 105.00 E
China (EN) = Zhonghua Renmin Gongheguo [1] 142 Mf 35.00N 105.00 E
Chinacates 192 Ge 25.00N 105.13W
China Lake 188 Gi 35.46N 117.39W
Chinandega 190 Gf 12.37N 87.09W
Chinandega [3] 194 Dg 12.45N 87.05W
Chinati Peak 186 Dl 29.57N 104.29W
Chincha Alta 202 Cf 13.27S 76.08W
Chinchaga 180 Fe 58.52N 118.19W
Chinchilla 212 Ke 26.45S 150.38 E
Chinchón 126 Id 40.08N 3.25W
Chinchorro, Banco- 190 Ge 18.35N 87.20W
Chincoteague 184 Jg 37.55N 75.23W
Chinde 160 Kj 18.34S 36.27 E
Chin-Do 154 Ig 34.25N 126.15 E
Chindu 152 Ge 33.30N 96.31 E
Chindwin 140 Lg 21.26N 95.15 E
Ch'ing-hai Sheng → Qinghai Sheng = Tsinghai (EN) [2] 152 Gd 36.00N 96.00 E
Chingil 168 Bc 10.33N 18.57 E
Chingola 160 Jj 12.32S 27.52 E
Chinguar 170 Ce 12.33S 16.22 E
Chinguetti 162 Ee 20.27N 12.21W
Chinguetti, Dahr de- 162 Ee 20.43N 12.20W
Chinhae 154 Jg 35.08N 128.40 E
Chinhoyi 160 Kj 17.22S 30.12 E
Chiniot 148 Eb 31.43N 72.59 E
Chinipas 192 Ed 27.23N 108.32W
Chinju 152 Md 35.11N 128.05 E
Chinko 158 Jh 4.50N 23.53 E
Chinle 188 Kh 36.09N 109.33W
Chinle Creek 188 Kh 37.12N 109.43W
Chinmen = Quemoy (EN) 152 Kg 24.25N 118.25 E
Chino 156 Fd 36.00N 138.09 E
Chinon 122 Gg 47.10N 0.15 E
Chinook 188 Kb 48.35N 109.14W
Chinquila 192 Pg 21.30N 87.25W
Chinsali 170 Fe 10.33S 32.04 E
Chinteche 170 Fe 11.50S 34.10 E
Chinú 202 Cb 9.06N 75.24W
Chinvali 136 Eg 42.13N 43.57 E
Chiny 124 He 49.44N 5.20 E
Chinyŏng 154 Jg 35.18N 128.44 E
Chioco 172 Ec 16.25S 32.50 E
Chioggia 128 Ge 45.13N 12.17 E
Chios (EN) = Khios 110 Ih 38.22N 26.00 E
Chipata 160 Kj 13.39S 32.40 E
Chipepo 170 Ef 16.49S 27.50 E
Chipindo 170 Ce 13.48S 15.48 E
Chiping 154 Df 36.35N 116.16 E
Chipinge 172 Ed 20.12S 32.38 E
Chipman 184 Ob 46.11N 65.53W
Chippenham 118 Kj 51.28N 2.07W
Chippewa, Lake- 186 Kd 45.56N 91.13W
Chippewa Falls 182 Ic 44.56N 91.24W
Chippewa River [Mn.-U.S.] 186 Id 44.56N 95.44W
Chippewa River [Wi.-U.S.] 186 Jd 44.25N 92.10W
Chipping Ongar 124 Cc 51.42N 0.15 E
Chiputneticook Lakes 184 Mc 45.45N 68.45W
Chiquián 202 Cf 10.09S 77.11W
Chiquimula 194 Cf 14.48N 89.33W
Chiquimula [3] 194 Cf 14.40N 89.25W
Chiquimulilla 194 Bf 14.05N 90.23W
Chiquinquirá 202 Db 5.37N 73.50W
Chiquitos, Llanos de- 202 Fg 18.00S 61.30W
Chīrāla 148 Ge 15.49N 80.21 E
Chiran 156 Bf 31.22N 130.27 E
Chiredzi 170 Fg 21.03S 31.45 E
Chirfa 166 Ha 20.57N 12.21 E
Chirgua, Rio- 196 Bh 8.30N 68.01W
Chiricahua Peak 182 Fe 31.52N 109.20W
Chiriguaná 194 Ki 9.22N 73.37W
Chirikof 178 He 55.50N 155.35W
Chiriqui [3] 194 Fi 8.30N 82.00W
Chiriquí, Golfo de- 174 Ki 8.00N 82.20W
Chiriquí, Laguna de- 190 Hg 9.03N 82.00W
Chiriquí Grande 194 Fi 8.57N 82.07W
Chirnogi 130 Je 44.07N 26.34 E
Chiromo 170 Gf 16.33S 35.08 E
Chirripó, Cerro- 174 Ki 9.29N 83.29W
Chirripó, Rio- [C.R.] 194 Fh 10.41N 83.41W
Chirripó, Rio- [C.R.] 194 Fh 10.03N 83.16W
Chirundu 170 Ef 15.59S 28.54 E
Chisamba 170 Ee 14.59S 28.23 E
Chisāpāni Garhi 148 Hc 27.34N 85.08 E
Chisasibi 176 Ld 53.50N 79.00W
Chisenga 170 Fd 9.56S 33.26 E
Chishui 152 If 28.30N 105.44 E
Chişineu Criş 130 Ec 46.32N 21.31 E
Chisone 128 Bf 44.49N 7.25 E
Chitado 170 Bf 17.18S 13.54 E
Chita-Hantō 156 Ed 34.50N 136.50 E
Chitati 168 Ac 14.40N 14.30 E
Chitato 160 Ji 7.22S 20.49 E
Chitembo 170 Ce 13.31S 16.45 E
Chitina 178 Kd 61.31N 144.27W
Chitina 178 Kd 61.30N 144.28W
Chitipa 170 Fd 9.43S 33.16 E
Chitorgarh 148 Ed 24.53N 74.38 E
Chitose 154 Pc 42.49N 141.39 E
Chitradurga 148 Ff 14.14N 76.24 E
Chitrāl 148 Ea 35.51N 71.47 E
Chitré 190 Hg 7.58N 80.26W
Chittagong 142 Lg 22.20N 91.50 E
Chittoor 148 Ff 13.12N 79.07 E
Chiumbe 158 Ji 6.59S 21.12 E
Chiume 170 Df 15.08S 21.12 E
Chiusi 128 Fg 43.01N 11.57 E
Chiusi, Lago di- 128 Fg 43.05N 12.00 E
Chiva 126 Le 39.28N 0.43W
Chivacoa 196 Bg 10.10N 68.54W
Chivapuri, Rio- 196 Ci 6.25N 66.23W
Chivasso 128 Be 45.11N 7.53 E
Chivay 202 Dg 15.38S 71.36W
Chivhu 172 Ec 19.01S 30.53 E
Chivilcoy 206 Hd 34.53S 60.01W
Chizou → Guichi 152 Ke 30.38N 117.30 E
Chizu 156 Dd 35.15N 134.14 E
Chŏām Khsant 148 Kf 14.13N 104.56 E
Choapa, Rio- 206 Dd 31.38S 71.34W
Chobe [3] 172 Cc 18.30S 25.00 E
Chobe 158 Jj 17.47S 25.10 E
Choc Bay 197k Ba 14.03N 60.59W
Choch'iwŏn 154 If 36.36N 127.18 E
Chocó [3] 202 Cb 6.00N 77.00W
Chocolate Mountains 188 Hj 33.25N 114.10W
Chodecz 120 Pd 52.24N 19.01 E
Chodov 120 If 50.15N 12.45 E
Chodzież 120 Md 52.59N 16.56 E
Choele-Choel 206 Ge 39.16S 65.41W
Choique 206 He 38.28S 62.43W
Choiseul 197k Ab 13.47N 61.03W
Choiseul Island 208 Ge 7.00S 157.00 E
Choix 192 Ed 26.43N 108.17W
Chojna 120 Kd 52.58N 14.28 E
Chojnice 120 Nc 53.42N 17.34 E
Chojnów 120 Le 51.17N 15.56 E
Chōkai-San 140 Qf 39.10N 140.02 E
Choke 158 Kg 10.45N 37.35 E
Chókué 172 Ed 24.27S 32.55 E
Cho La 152 Ge 31.52N 98.51 E
Cholet 122 Fg 47.04N 0.53W
Chŏlla-Namdo [2] 154 Ig 34.45N 127.00 E
Chŏlla-Pukto [2] 154 Ig 35.45N 127.15 E
Cholo 170 Gf 16.04S 35.08 E
Cholula 192 Jh 19.04N 98.18W
Choluteca 190 Gf 13.18N 87.12W
Choluteca [3] 194 Dg 13.20N 87.10W
Choluteca, Rio- 194 Dg 13.07N 87.19W
Choma 160 Jj 16.49S 26.59 E
Chomo/Yadong 152 Ef 27.38N 89.03 E
Chomo Lhari 152 Ef 27.50N 89.16 E
Chomutov 120 Jf 50.28N 13.25 E
Ch'ŏnan 152 Md 36.48N 127.09 E
Chon Buri 142 Kf 13.22N 100.59 E
Chone 202 Bd 0.42S 80.07W
Ch'ŏngch'ŏn-gang 154 He 39.35N 125.28 E
Ch'ŏngjin 142 Oe 41.46N 129.49 E
Ch'ŏngjin Si [2] 154 Jd 41.45N 129.45 E
Ch'ŏngju 152 Md 36.38N 127.30 E
Chŏngju 152 Md 39.51N 125.15 E
Chongli (Xiwanzi) 154 Cd 40.57N 115.12 E
Chongming 154 Fi 31.38N 121.24 E
Chongming Dao 154 Fi 31.36N 121.33 E
Chongoroi 170 Be 13.34S 13.55 E
Chongqing (Chungking) 142 Mg 29.34N 106.27 E
Ch'ŏngsan-Do 154 Ig 34.11N 126.54 E
Chŏngŭp 154 Ig 35.34N 126.51 E
Chongyang 154 Cj 29.32N 114.02 E
Chongzuo 152 Ig 22.29N 107.22 E
Chŏnju 152 Md 35.49N 127.09 E
Choni (Culukidze) 132 Mh 42.18N 42.25 E
Chonos, Archipiélago de los- 198 Ij 45.00S 74.00W
Chontaleña, Cordillera- 194 Eh 11.50N 85.00W
Chontales [3] 194 Eg 12.05N 85.10W
Chopim, Rio- 204 Fg 25.35S 53.05W
Chopinzinho 204 Fg 25.51S 52.30W
Chorito, Sierra del- 126 He 39.25N 4.25W
Choroszcz 120 Sc 53.09N 22.59 E
Chorreras, Cerro- 192 Fd 26.02N 106.21W
Ch'ŏrwŏn 152 Md 38.15N 127.13 E
Chorzele 120 Qc 53.16N 20.55 E
Chorzów 120 Of 50.19N 18.57 E
Ch'osan 154 Hd 40.45N 125.50 E
Chośebuz/Cottbus 120 Ke 51.46N 14.20 E
Chōshi 154 Pg 35.44N 140.50 E
Chos Malal 206 Fe 37.23S 70.16W
Chosŏn M.I.K. = North Korea (EN) [1] 142 Oe 40.00N 127.30 E
Chosŏn Minjujuŭi-Inmin-Konghwaguk [1] 142 Oe 40.00N 127.30 E
Choszczno 120 Lc 53.10N 15.26 E
Chota 202 Ce 6.33S 78.39W
Chotanāgpur Plateau 140 Kg 22.00N 86.00 E
Choteau 188 Ic 47.49N 112.11W
Chotla, Cerro de- 192 Ii 17.55N 101.31W
Choukchot, Djebel- 126 Qh 36.01N 4.11 E
Choum 162 Ee 21.18N 12.59W
Chovd → Kobdo 152 Fb 48.06N 92.11 E
Chövsgöl Nuur → Hubsugul Nur 140 Md 51.00N 100.30 E
Chowchilla 188 Eh 37.07N 120.16W
Chowra 148 Ig 8.27N 93.02 E
Chréa 126 Oh 36.25N 2.53 E
Chřiby 120 Ng 49.10N 17.20 E
Christchurch 210 Ii 43.32S 172.37 E
Christian, Cape- 180 Kb 70.32N 68.18W
Christian, Point- 220q Ab 25.04S 130.07W
Christiana 172 De 27.52S 25.08 E
Christian IV Gletscher 179 Ie 68.40N 30.20W
Christiansburg 184 Gg 37.07N 80.26W
Christiansfeld 116 Ci 55.21N 9.29 E
Christianshåb/Qasigiánguit 179 Ge 68.45N 51.30W
Christiansø 116 Fi 55.20N 15.10 E
Christian Sound 178 Me 55.56N 134.40W
Christiansted 196 Dd 17.45N 64.40W
Christiansted Harbor 197a Dc 17.46N 64.42W
Christie Bay 180 Gd 62.45N 110.15W
Christmas [5] 142 Mk 10.30S 105.40 E
Christmas → Kiritimati Atoll 208 Ld 1.52N 157.20W
Christmas Creek 212 Fc 18.53S 125.55 E
Christmas Creek 212 Fc 18.29S 125.23 E
Christmas Island 140 Mk 10.30S 105.40 E
Christmas Ridge (EN) 106 Ki 10.00N 165.00W
Chrudim 120 Lg 49.57N 15.47 E
Chrzanów 120 Pf 50.09N 19.24 E
Chrząstowa 120 Nc 53.35N 16.58 E
Chuansha 154 Fi 31.11N 121.42 E
Chūbar 146 Mc 38.11N 48.51 E
Chubut [2] 206 Gf 44.00S 69.00W
Chubut, Rio- 198 Jj 43.20S 65.03W
Chudžand (Leninabad) 142 Ie 40.17N 69.37 E
Chudžandskaja oblast 136 Gh 40.00N 69.10 E
Chugach Mountains 178 Jd 61.00N 145.00W
Chūgoku-Sanchi 140 Pf 35.15N 133.30 E
Chu He 154 Eh 32.15N 119.03 E
Chuhuichupa 192 Ec 29.38N 108.22W
Chui 204 Fk 33.41S 53.27W
Chuka 170 Gc 0.20S 37.39 E
Chukai 150 Df 4.15N 103.25 E
Chukchi Peninsula (EN) = Čukotski poluostrov 140 Uc 66.00N 175.00W
Chukchi Plateau (EN) 224 Bd 78.00N 165.00W
Chukchi Sea 224 Bd 69.00N 171.00W
Chukchi Sea (EN) = Čukotskoje more 224 Bd 69.00N 171.00W
Chula Vista 188 Gj 32.39N 117.05W
Chulitna 178 Jd 62.55N 149.39W
Chullo 126 Jg 37.10N 2.57W
Chulucanas 202 Be 5.06S 80.10W
Chumbicha 206 Gc 28.52S 66.14W
Chumphon 148 Jf 10.32N 99.13 E
Chumunjin 154 Jf 37.53N 128.49 E
Ch'unch'ŏn 152 Md 37.52N 127.44 E
Chunga 170 Ef 15.03S 26.00 E
Ch'ungch'ŏng-Namdo [2] 154 If 36.30N 127.00 E
Ch'ungch'ŏng-Pukto [2] 154 Jf 36.45N 128.00 E
Ch'ungju 152 Md 36.58N 127.56 E
Chungking → Chongqing 142 Mg 29.34N 106.27 E
Ch'ungmu 154 Jg 34.51N 128.26 E
Chunya 170 Fd 8.32S 33.25 E
Chuquibamba 202 Dg 15.50S 72.39W
Chuquibambilla 202 Df 14.07S 72.43W
Chuquicamata 206 Gb 22.19S 68.56W
Chuquisaca [3] 202 Fg 20.00S 64.20W
Chur/Cuera 128 Dd 46.50N 9.35 E
Churchill 176 Jd 58.46N 94.10W
Churchill [Can.] 174 Md 53.30N 60.10W
Churchill [Can.] 174 Jd 58.47N 94.12W
Churchill, Cape- 180 Ie 58.46N 93.12W
Churchill Falls 180 Lf 53.30N 64.10W
Churchill Lake 180 Ge 56.05N 108.15W
Churchill Peak 180 Ee 58.20N 125.02W
Churchill Range 222 Jg 81.30S 158.30 E
Chūru 148 Ec 28.18N 74.57 E
Churuguara 202 Ea 10.49N 69.32W
Churún Merú/Angel, Salto- = Ángel Falls (EN) 198 Je 5.57N 62.30W
Chuska Mountains 188 Kh 36.15N 108.50W
Chute-des-Passes 180 Kg 49.50N 71.00W
Chuxian 152 Ke 32.18N 118.15 E
Chuxiong 152 Hf 25.02N 101.32 E
Chuy 204 Fk 33.41S 53.27W
Chyncěšt' (Kotovsk) 132 Ff 46.49N 28.33 E
Ciamis 150 Eh 7.20S 108.21 E
Cianjur 150 Eh 6.49S 107.08 E
Ciarraí/Kerry [2] 118 Di 52.10N 9.30W
Ćiatura 132 Mh 42.17N 43.15 E
Cibuta, Cerro- 192 Db 31.02N 110.58W
Ćićarija 128 He 45.28N 13.54 E
Ćićevac 130 Ef 43.43N 21.27 E
Cicicleja 130 Nb 47.23N 30.50 E
Cicolano 128 Hh 42.15N 13.10 E
Cidacos 126 Kb 42.19N 1.55W
Cide 146 Eb 41.54N 33.00 E
Cidlina 120 Lf 50.09N 15.12 E
Ciechanów 120 Qd 52.53N 20.38 E
Ciechanów [2] 120 Qd 52.55N 20.40 E
Ciechanowiec 120 Sd 52.42N 22.31 E
Ciechanowska, Wysoczyzna- 120 Qc 53.10N 20.30 E
Ciego de Ávila 190 Id 21.51N 78.46W
Ciego de Ávila [3] 194 Hb 22.00N 78.40W
Ciénaga 202 Da 11.00N 74.14W
Ciénaga de Flores 192 Ie 25.57N 100.11W
Ciénaga de Oro 194 Ji 8.53N 75.38W
Cieneguita 192 Fd 27.57N 106.59W
Cienfuegos 176 Kg 22.09N 80.27W
Cienfuegos [3] 194 Gb 22.15N 80.30W
Cies, Islas- 126 Db 42.13N 8.54W
Cieszanów 120 Tf 50.16N 23.08 E
Cieza 126 Kf 38.14N 1.25W
Çifteler 146 Dc 39.22N 31.03 E
Cifuentes 126 Jd 40.47N 2.37W
Čiganak 136 Hf 45.05N 73.58 E
Čigirin 132 He 49.03N 32.42 E
Cigüela 126 Ie 39.08N 3.44W
Cihanbeyli 146 Ec 38.40N 32.56 E
Cihanbeyli Platosu 146 Ec 38.40N 32.45 E
Čihareši 132 Mh 42.47N 43.02 E
Cihuatlán 192 Gh 19.14N 104.35W
Čiily 136 Gg 44.13N 66.46 E
Cijara, Embalse de- 126 He 39.18N 4.52W
Cijulang 150 Eh 7.44S 108.27 E
Čik 130 Dd 45.42N 20.04 E
Čikoj 138 Ff 51.02N 106.39 E
Čikurački, vulkan- 138 Kf 50.15N 155.29 E
Cilacap 150 Eh 7.44S 109.00 E
Çıldır 146 Jb 41.08N 43.07 E
Çıldır Gölü 146 Jb 41.04N 43.15 E
Cilento 128 Jj 40.20N 15.20 E
Čilik 136 Hg 43.35N 78.12 E
Čilik 135 Lc 43.42N 78.14 E
Cill Airne/Killarney 118 Di 52.03N 9.30W
Cill Chainnigh/Kilkenny 118 Fi 52.39N 7.15W
Cill Chainnigh/Kilkenny [2] 118 Fi 52.40N 7.20W
Cill Chaoi/Kilkee 118 Di 52.41N 9.38W
Cill Dara/Kildare 118 Gh 53.10N 6.55W
Cill Dara/Kildare [2] 118 Gh 53.15N 6.45W
Cill Mhantáin/Wicklow 118 Gi 52.59N 6.03W
Cill Mhantáin/Wicklow [2] 118 Gi 53.00N 6.30W
Cill Mocheallóg/Kilmallock 118 Ei 52.25N 8.35W
Cill Rois/Kilrush 118 Di 52.39N 9.29W
Cilma 134 Fd 65.25N 52.05 E
Cilo Dağı 146 Kd 37.30N 44.00 E
Cimaltepec, Sierra- 190 Ee 16.00N 96.40W
Cimarron 186 Dh 36.31N 104.55W
Cimarron 174 Jf 36.10N 96.17W
Čimbaj 136 Fg 42.59N 59.47 E
Cimini, Monti- 128 Gh 42.24N 12.12 E
Čimišlija 132 Ff 46.32N 28.46 E
Čimkent 142 Ie 42.18N 69.36 E
Čimkentskaja oblast [3] 136 Gg 43.00N 68.40 E
Cimljansk 136 Ef 47.37N 42.04 E
Cimljanskoje vodohranilišče = Tsimlyansk Reservoir (EN) 110 Kf 48.00N 43.00 E
Cimone 110 Hg 44.12N 10.40 E
Cîmpeni 130 Gc 46.22N 23.03 E
Cîmpia Turzii 130 Gc 46.33N 23.53 E
Cîmpina 130 Id 45.08N 25.44 E
Cîmpulung 130 Id 45.16N 25.03 E
Cîmpulung Moldovenesc 130 Ib 47.32N 25.34 E
Čimtarga, gora- 135 Ge 39.14N 68.12 E
Cina, Tanjung- 150 Dh 5.55S 104.35 E
Çınar 146 Id 37.39N 40.06 E
Çınarcık 130 Mi 40.39N 29.06 E
Cinaruco, Rio- 196 Ci 6.41N 67.07W
Cina Selatan, Laut- = South China Sea (EN) 140 Ni 10.00N 113.00 E
Cinaz 135 Gd 40.56N 68.45 E
Cinca 126 Mc 41.26N 0.21 E
Cincar 128 Lg 43.54N 17.04 E
Cincinnati 176 Kf 39.06N 84.31W

Index Symbols

- [1] Independent Nation
- [2] State, Region
- [3] District, County
- [4] Municipality
- [5] Colony, Dependency
- Continent
- Physical Region
- Historical or Cultural Region
- Mount, Mountain
- Volcano
- Hill
- Mountains, Mountain Range
- Hills, Escarpment
- Plateau, Upland
- Pass, Gap
- Plain, Lowland
- Delta
- Salt Flat
- Valley, Canyon
- Crater, Cave
- Karst Features
- Depression
- Polder
- Desert, Dunes
- Forest, Woods
- Heath, Steppe
- Oasis
- Cape, Point
- Coast, Beach
- Cliff
- Peninsula
- Isthmus
- Sandbank
- Island
- Atoll
- Rock, Reef
- Islands, Archipelago
- Rocks, Reefs
- Coral Reef
- Well, Spring
- Geyser
- River, Stream
- Waterfall, Rapids
- River Mouth, Estuary
- Lake
- Salt Lake
- Intermittent Lake
- Reservoir
- Swamp, Pond
- Canal
- Glacier
- Ice Shelf, Pack Ice
- Ocean
- Sea
- Gulf, Bay
- Strait, Fjord
- Lagoon
- Bank
- Seamount
- Tablemount
- Ridge
- Shelf
- Basin
- Escarpment, Sea Scarp
- Fracture
- Trench, Abyss
- National Park, Reserve
- Point of Interest
- Recreation Site
- Cave, Cavern
- Historic Site
- Ruins
- Wall, Walls
- Church, Abbey
- Temple
- Scientific Station
- Railway station
- Airport
- Port
- Military installation
- Lighthouse
- Mine
- Tunnel
- Dam, Bridge

Cin-Com

Cinco Irmãos, Serra dos- 204 Ff 22.55S 52.50W
Cinco Saltos 206 Ge 38.49S 68.04W
Cindrelu, Vîrful- 130 Gd 45.35N 23.48 E
Çine 146 Cd 37.36N 28.04 E
Çine 130 Kl 37.46N 27.49 E
Ciney 122 Ld 50.18N 5.06 E
Cingirlau 136 Fe 51.07N 54.05 E
Cingoli 128 Hg 43.22N 13.13 E
Cintalapa de Figueroa 192 Mi 16.44N 93.43W
Cinto, Monte- 110 Gg 42.23N 8.56 E
Cintra, Golfo de- 162 De 23.00N 16.15W
Cinzas, Rio das- 204 Gf 22.56S 50.32W
Ciociaria 128 Hi 41.45N 13.15 E
Cionn Mhálanna/Malin Head 110 Fd 55.23N 7.24W
Cionn tSáile/Kinsale 118 Ej 51.42N 8.32W
Ciorani 130 Je 44.49N 26.25 E
Ciotat, La- 122 Lk 43.10N 5.36 E
Čiovo 128 Kg 43.30N 16.18 E
Cipa 138 Ge 55.20N 115.55 E
Cipikan 138 Gf 54.58N 113.21 E
Cipó 202 Kf 11.06S 38.31W
Cipolletti 206 Ge 38.56S 67.59W
Čiprovci 130 Ff 43.23N 22.53 E
Čir 132 Me 48.35N 42.55 E
Circeo, Capo- 128 Hi 41.14N 13.03 E
Čirčik 136 Gg 41.28N 69.35 E
Circle [Ak.-U.S.] 178 Kc 65.50N 144.04W
Circle [Mt.-U.S.] 188 Mc 47.25N 105.35W
Circleville 184 Ff 39.36N 82.57W
Cirebon 142 Mj 6.44S 108.34 E
Cirencester 118 Lj 51.44N 1.59W
Ciriè 128 Be 45.14N 7.36 E
Čirinda 138 Fc 67.30N 100.35 E
Čirip, vulkan- 138 Jg 45.20N 147.58 E
Čirka-Kem 114 Hd 64.45N 32.10 E
Cirò 128 Lk 39.23N 17.04 E
Cirò Marina 128 Lk 39.22N 17.08 E
Ciron 122 Fj 44.36N 0.18W
Čirpan 130 Ig 42.12N 25.20 E
Cirque Mountain 180 Le 58.55N 63.33W
Cisa, Passo della- 128 Df 44.28N 9.55 E
Ciscaucasia (EN) 110 Kf 45.00N 43.00 E
Cisco 186 Gj 32.23N 98.59W
Ciskei 172 Df 31.30S 26.40 E
Čišmy 136 Fe 54.35N 55.25 E
Cisnădie 130 Hd 45.43N 24.09 E
Cisne, Islas del- 190 He 17.22N 83.51W
Cistern Point 194 Ib 24.40N 77.45W
Cistierna 126 Gb 42.48N 5.07W
Čistoozernoje 138 Cf 54.43N 76.43 E
Čistopol 136 Fd 55.23N 50.39 E
Čita 142 Nd 52.03N 113.30 E
Çitak 130 Mk 38.08N 29.39 E
Čitinskaya oblast 138 Gf 52.30N 117.30 E
Citlaltépetl, Volcán - → Orizaba, Pico de- 174 Jh 19.01N 97.16W
Citrusdale 172 Bf 32.36S 19.00 E
Città del Vaticano = Vatican City (EN) [1] 112 Hg 41.54N 12.27 E
Città di Castello 128 Gg 43.27N 12.14 E
Cittanova 128 Kl 38.21N 16.05 E
Ciucaşu, Vîrful- 130 Id 45.31N 25.55 E
Ciucea 130 Fc 46.57N 22.49 E
Ciudad 192 Gf 23.44N 105.44W
Ciudad Acuña 190 Dc 29.18N 100.55W
Ciudad Altamirano 192 Ih 18.20N 100.40W
Ciudad Bolívar 200 Je 8.08N 63.33W
Ciudad Bolivia 202 Db 8.21N 70.34W
Ciudad Camargo [Mex.] 190 Cc 27.40N 105.10W
Ciudad Camargo [Mex.] 190 Ec 26.19N 98.50W
Ciudad Cuauhtémoc 192 Mj 15.37N 92.00W
Ciudad Darío 194 Dg 12.43N 86.08W
Ciudad de Areco 204 Cl 34.18S 59.46W
Ciudad de la Habana [3] 194 Fb 23.10N 82.10W
Ciudad del Carmen 190 Fe 18.38N 91.50W
Ciudad del Maíz 192 Jf 22.24N 99.36W
Ciudad de México = Mexico City (EN) 176 Jh 19.24N 99.09W
Ciudad de Nutrias 202 Eb 8.07N 69.19W
Ciudad de Río Grande 190 Dd 23.50N 103.02W
Ciudadela/Ciutadella 126 Pd 40.02N 3.50 E
Ciudad Guayana 200 Je 8.22N 62.40W
Ciudad Guerrero 190 Cc 28.33N 107.30W
Ciudad Guzmán 190 De 19.41N 103.29W
Ciudad Hidalgo [Mex.] 192 Ih 19.41N 100.34W
Ciudad Hidalgo [Mex.] 192 Mj 14.41N 92.09W
Ciudad Juárez 176 If 31.44N 106.29W
Ciudad Lerdo 190 Dc 25.32N 103.32W
Ciudad Madero 176 Jg 22.16N 97.50W
Ciudad Mante 190 Ed 22.44N 98.57W
Ciudad Mendoza 192 Kh 18.48N 97.11W
Ciudad Obregón 176 Ig 27.59N 109.56W
Ciudad Ojeda 202 Da 10.12N 71.19W
Ciudad Piar 202 Fb 7.27N 63.19W
Ciudad Real 126 If 38.59N 3.56W
Ciudad Real [3] 126 If 39.00N 4.00W
Ciudad Río Bravo 190 Ec 25.59N 98.06W
Ciudad-Rodrigo 126 Fd 40.36N 6.32W
Ciudad Valles 190 Ed 21.59N 99.01W
Ciudad Victoria 176 Jg 23.44N 99.08W
Ciutadella/Ciudadela 126 Pd 40.02N 3.50 E
Civa Burnu 146 Gb 41.22N 36.35 E
Cividale del Friuli 128 Hd 46.06N 13.25 E
Civilsk 114 Li 55.53N 47.29 E
Civita Castellana 128 Gh 42.17N 12.25 E
Civitanova Marche 128 Hg 43.18N 13.44 E
Civitavecchia 128 Fh 42.06N 11.48 E
Civitella del Tronto 128 Hh 42.46N 13.40 E
Çivril 146 Cc 38.56N 35.29 E
Cixerri 128 Ck 39.17N 8.59 E
Cixi (Hushan) 154 Fi 30.10N 121.14 E
Cixian 154 Cf 36.22N 114.22 E
Čiža 136 Eb 67.06N 44.19 E
Cizre 144 Fb 37.20N 42.12 E
Cjurupinsk 132 Hf 46.37N 32.43 E
Čkalovsk 114 Kh 56.47N 43.17 E
Clacton-on-Sea 118 Oj 51.48N 1.09 E
Clain 122 Gh 46.47N 0.33 E
Claire, Côte- 222 Ie 66.30S 133.00 E
Claire, Lake - 180 Ge 58.30N 112.00W
Clair Engle Lake 188 Df 40.52N 122.43W
Claise 122 Gh 46.56N 0.42 E
Clamecy 122 Jg 47.27N 3.31 E
Clan Alpine Mountains 188 Gg 39.40N 117.55W
Clanton 184 Di 32.50N 86.38W
Clanwilliam 172 Bf 32.11S 18.54 E
Claraz 204 Cm 37.54S 59.17W
Clár Chlainne Mhuiris/Claremorris 118 Eh 53.44N 9.00W
Clare [Austl.] 212 Hf 33.50S 138.36 E
Clare [Mi.-U.S.] 184 Ed 43.49N 84.46W
Clare/Abhainn an Chláir 118 Dh 53.20N 9.03W
Clare/An Clár [2] 118 Ei 52.50N 9.00W
Clare/Cliara 118 Dh 53.49N 10.00W
Claremont 184 Kd 43.23N 72.21W
Claremore 186 Ih 36.19N 95.36W
Claremorris/Clár Chlainne Mhuiris 118 Eh 53.44N 9.00W
Clarence 218 Ee 42.10S 173.56 E
Clarence 218 Ee 42.10S 173.57 E
Clarence, Cape - 180 Ib 73.55N 90.12W
Clarence Cannon Reservoir 186 Kg 39.31N 91.45W
Clarence Island 222 Re 61.12S 54.05W
Clarence River 212 Ke 29.25S 153.22 E
Clarence Strait [Ak.-U.S.] 178 Me 55.25N 132.00W
Clarence Strait [Austl.] 212 Gb 12.00S 131.00 E
Clarence Town 194 Jb 23.06N 74.59W
Clarendon 186 Fi 34.56N 100.53W
Clarenville 180 Mg 48.09N 53.58W
Claresholm 180 Gf 50.02N 113.35W
Clarinda 186 If 40.44N 95.02W
Clarines 196 Dh 9.56N 65.10W
Clarión, Isla- 190 Be 18.22N 114.44W
Clarion Fracture Zone (EN) 106 Lh 18.00N 130.00W
Clarion River 184 He 41.07N 79.41W
Clark 186 Hd 44.53N 97.44W
Clark, Lake- 178 Id 60.15N 154.15W
Clark, Mount - 180 Fd 64.25N 124.14W
Clarkdale 188 Ii 34.46N 112.03W
Clarke Range 212 Jd 20.50S 148.35 E
Clark Fork 174 He 48.09N 116.15W
Clark Hill Lake 184 Fi 33.50N 82.20W
Clark Mountain 188 Hi 35.32N 115.35W
Clarksburg 182 Kd 39.17N 80.21W
Clarksdale 182 Ie 34.12N 90.34W
Clarks Fork 188 Kd 45.39N 108.43W
Clark's Harbour 184 Od 43.26N 65.38W
Clarkston 188 Gc 46.30N 117.03W
Clarksville [Ar.-U.S.] 186 Ji 35.28N 93.28W
Clarksville [Tn.-U.S.] 182 Jd 36.32N 87.21W
Clarksville [Tx.-U.S.] 186 Ij 33.37N 95.03W
Claro, Rio- [Braz.] 202 Hg 15.28S 51.45W
Claro, Rio- [Braz.] 202 Hg 19.08S 50.40W
Clary 124 Fd 50.00N 3.24 E
Claude 186 Fi 35.07N 101.22W
Claustra / Klosters 128 Dd 46.52N 9.52 E
Clavering 179 Jd 74.20N 21.10W
Claxton 184 Gi 32.10N 81.55W
Clay Center 186 Hg 39.23N 96.08W
Clay Cross 124 Aa 53.09N 1.25W
Claye-Souilly 124 Ef 48.57N 2.42 E
Clayton 182 Gd 36.27N 103.11W
Clear, Cape- 118 Dj 51.26N 9.31W
Clear Boggy Creek 186 Ii 34.03N 95.47W
Clear Creek [Az.-U.S.] 188 Ji 34.59N 110.38W
Clear Creek [Wy.-U.S.] 188 Ld 44.53N 106.04W
Clearfield [Pa.-U.S.] 184 He 41.02N 78.27W
Clearfield [Ut.-U.S.] 188 If 41.07N 112.01W
Clear Fork Brazos 186 Gj 33.01N 98.40W
Clear Lake 182 Cd 39.02N 122.50W
Clear Lake [Ia.-U.S.] 186 Je 43.08N 93.23W
Clear Lake [S.D.-U.S.] 186 Hd 44.45N 96.41W
Clear Lake Reservoir 188 Ef 41.52N 121.08W
Clearwater 182 Kf 27.58N 82.48W
Clearwater 180 Ge 56.45N 111.22W
Clearwater Mountains 182 Db 46.00N 115.30W
Clearwater River [Alta.-Can.] 188 Ha 52.23N 114.50W
Clearwater River [U.S.] 188 Gc 46.25N 117.02W
Cleburne 186 Hj 32.21N 97.23W
Clécy 124 Bf 48.55N 0.29W
Clee Hills 118 Ki 52.25N 2.35W
Cleethorpes 118 Mh 53.34N 0.02W
Clères 124 De 49.36N 1.07 E
Clerf/Clervaux 124 Id 50.03N 6.02 E
Clermont [Austl.] 212 Jd 22.49S 147.39 E
Clermont [Fr.] 122 Ie 49.23N 2.24 E
Clermont-en-Argonne 124 He 49.06N 5.04 E
Clermont-Ferrand 112 Gf 45.47N 3.05 E
Clermont-l'Hérault 122 Jk 43.37N 3.26 E
Clervaux/Clerf 124 Id 50.03N 6.02 E
Clervé 124 Ie 49.57N 6.01 E
Cles 128 Fd 46.22N 11.02 E
Clevedon 118 Kj 51.27N 2.51W
Cleveland [3] 118 Mg 54.40N 1.00W
Cleveland 118 Lg 54.25N 1.05W
Cleveland [Ms.-U.S.] 186 Kj 33.45N 90.50W
Cleveland [Oh.-U.S.] 176 Ke 41.30N 81.41W
Cleveland [Tn.-U.S.] 182 Kd 35.10N 84.53W
Cleveland [Tx.-U.S.] 186 Ik 30.21N 95.05W
Cleveland, Mount- 182 Eb 48.56N 113.51W
Cleveland Heights 184 Ge 41.30N 81.34W
Clevelândia 204 Fh 26.24S 52.21W
Cleveland Mountain 188 Ic 46.37N 113.47W
Clew Bay/Cuan Mó 118 Dh 53.50N 9.50W
Cliara/Clare 118 Dh 53.49N 10.00W
Cliff 186 Bj 32.59N 108.36W
Clifton [Az.-U.S.] 182 Fe 33.03N 109.18W
Clifton [St.Vin.] 197n Bb 12.36N 61.26W
Clifton [Tx.-U.S.] 186 Hk 31.47N 97.35W
Clinch River 184 Eh 35.53N 84.29W
Cline, Mount- 188 Ga 52.10N 116.40W
Clines Corners 186 Di 35.01N 105.34W
Clingmans Dome 184 Fh 35.35N 83.30W
Clinton [Ar.-U.S.] 186 Ji 35.36N 92.28W
Clinton [B.C.-Can.] 180 Ff 51.05N 121.35W
Clinton [Ia.-U.S.] 182 Ic 41.51N 90.12W
Clinton [Il.-U.S.] 186 Lf 40.09N 88.57W
Clinton [Mo.-U.S.] 186 Jg 38.22N 93.46W
Clinton [Ms.-U.S.] 186 Kj 32.20N 90.20W
Clinton [N.C.-U.S.] 184 Hh 34.59N 78.20W
Clinton [N.Z.] 218 Cg 46.13S 169.23 E
Clinton [Ok.-U.S.] 182 Hd 35.31N 98.59W
Clinton-Colden Lake 180 Gd 63.55N 107.30W
Clintonville 186 Ld 44.37N 88.46W
Clipperton, Ile- 174 Ih 10.17N 109.13W
Clipperton Fracture Zone (EN) 106 Li 10.00N 115.00W
Clisson 122 Eg 47.05N 1.17W
Cloates, Point- 212 Cd 22.45S 113.40 E
Clochán an Aifir/Giant's Causeway 118 Gf 55.15N 6.35W
Clodomira 206 Hc 27.35S 64.08W
Cloich na Coillte/Clonakilty 118 Ej 51.37N 8.54W
Clonakilty/Cloich na Coillte 118 Ej 51.37N 8.54W
Cloncurry 210 Fg 20.42S 140.30 E
Clones/Cluain Eois 118 Fg 54.11N 7.14W
Clonmel/Cluain Meala 118 Fi 52.21N 7.42W
Cloppenburg 120 Ed 52.51N 8.02 E
Cloquet 182 Ib 46.43N 92.28W
Clorinda 200 Kh 25.20S 57.40W
Cloud Peak 182 Fc 44.25N 107.10W
Clouère 122 Gh 46.26N 0.17 E
Cloverdale 188 Dg 38.48N 123.01W
Clovis [Ca.-U.S.] 188 Fh 36.49N 119.42W
Clovis [N.M.-U.S.] 176 If 34.24N 103.12W
Cluain Meala/Clonmel 118 Fi 52.21N 7.42W
Cluan Eois/Clones 118 Fg 54.11N 7.14W
Cluj [2] 130 Gc 46.49N 23.35 E
Cluj Napoca 112 If 46.46N 23.36 E
Cluny 122 Kh 46.26N 4.39 E
Cluses 122 Mh 46.04N 6.36 E
Clusone 128 De 45.53N 9.57 E
Clutha 218 Cg 46.21S 169.48 E
Clwyd [3] 118 Jh 53.10N 3.15W
Clwyd 118 Jh 53.20N 3.30W
Clyde 118 If 55.56N 4.29W
Clyde [N.W.T.-Can.] 176 Mb 70.25N 68.30W
Clyde [N.Z.] 218 Cf 45.11S 169.19 E
Clyde, Firth of- 118 If 55.42N 5.00W
Clyde Inlet 180 Kb 70.20N 68.20W
Cna 110 Ke 54.32N 42.05 E
Cnoc Bréanainn/Brandon Mount 118 Ci 52.14N 10.15W
Cnoc Fola/Bloody Foreland 118 Ef 55.09N 8.17W
Cnoc Mhaoldonn/Knockmealdown Mountains 118 Fi 52.15N 8.00W
Cnori 132 Ni 41.35N 45.59 E
Cnossus (EN) = Knosós 130 In 35.18N 25.10 E
Côa 126 Ec 41.05N 7.06W
Coachella Canal 188 Hj 33.34N 116.00W
Coahuayana 192 Hh 18.44N 103.41W
Coahuila [2] 190 Dc 27.20N 102.00W
Coalcomán, Sierra de- 190 De 18.30N 102.55W
Coalcomán de Matamoros 192 Hh 18.47N 103.09W
Coaldale 188 Ib 49.43N 112.37W
Coalgate 186 Hi 34.32N 96.13W
Coalinga 188 Eh 36.09N 120.21W
Coalville 118 Li 52.44N 1.20W
Coamo 194 Nd 18.05N 66.22W
Coari 202 Fd 4.05S 63.08W
Coari, Lago de- 202 Fd 4.15S 63.25W
Coari, Rio- 198 Jf 4.30S 63.33W
Coast [3] 170 Gc 3.00S 39.30 E
Coast Mountains 174 Gd 55.00N 129.00W
Coast Plain (EN) = Kustvlakte 122 Ic 51.00N 2.30 E
Coast Plain (EN) = Maritime, Plaine- 122 Ic 51.00N 2.30 E
Coast Ranges 174 Ge 41.00N 123.30W
Coatbridge 118 If 55.52N 4.01W
Coatepec 192 Kh 19.27N 96.58W
Coatepel, Cerro- 192 Kh 18.25N 97.35W
Coatepeque 194 Bf 14.42N 91.52W
Coats 174 Kc 62.30N 83.00W
Coats Land (EN) 222 Af 77.00S 28.00W
Coatzacoalcos 176 Jh 18.09N 94.25W
Coatzacoalcos, Bahía- 192 Lh 18.10N 94.27W
Coatzacoalcos, Río- 192 Lh 18.09N 94.24W
Coba 190 Gd 20.36N 87.35W
Cobadin 130 Le 44.05N 28.13 E
Cobalt 180 Jg 47.24N 79.41W
Cobán 190 Fe 15.29N 90.19W
Cobar 212 Jf 31.30S 145.49 E
Cobb, Mount- 188 Dg 38.45N 122.40W
Cobb Seamount (EN) 174 Fe 46.46N 130.43W
Cóbh/An Cóbh 118 Ej 51.51N 8.17W
Cobija 202 Ef 11.02S 68.44W
Cobo 204 Dm 37.48S 57.38W
Cobourg 180 Jh 43.58N 78.10W
Cobourg Peninsula 212 Gb 11.20S 132.15 E
Cóbué 172 Eb 12.07S 34.52 E
Coburg 120 Gf 50.15N 10.58 E
Coburg 180 Ja 75.57N 79.00W
Coburn Mountain 184 Lc 45.28N 70.06W
Coca, Pizzo di- 128 Ed 46.04N 10.01 E
Cocalinho 204 Gb 14.22S 51.00W
Cocentaina 126 Lf 38.45N 0.26W
Cochabamba 200 Jg 17.24S 66.09W
Cochabamba [3] 202 Eg 17.30S 65.40W
Coche, Isla- 196 Eg 10.47N 63.56W
Cochem 120 Df 50.08N 7.09 E
Cochin 142 Ji 9.58N 76.14 E
Cochin China (EN) = Nam Phan 140 Mg 11.00N 107.00 E
Cochinos, Bahía de- = Pigs, Bay of- (EN) 194 Gb 22.07N 81.10W
Cochons, Ile aux- 222 Ec 46.05S 50.08 E
Cochran 184 Fi 32.23N 83.21W
Cochrane 180 He 57.55N 101.32W
Cochrane [Alta.-Can.] 188 Ha 51.11N 114.28W
Cochrane [Ont.-Can.] 176 Ke 49.04N 81.01W
Cockburn, Canal- 206 Fh 54.20S 71.30W
Cockburn, Mount- 212 Gd 22.46S 130.36 E
Cockburn Bank 118 El 49.40N 8.50W
Cockburn Island 184 Fc 45.55N 83.22W
Cockburn Town 194 Ja 24.02N 74.31W
Cockermouth 118 Jg 54.40N 3.21W
Coclé [3] 194 Gi 8.30N 80.15W
Coco, Cayo- 194 Hb 22.30N 78.28W
Coco, Ile- 197b Bc 17.52N 62.49W
Coco, Isla del- 174 Ki 5.32N 87.04W
Cocoa 182 Kf 28.21N 80.44W
Cocoa Beach 184 Gk 28.19N 80.36W
Cocoa Point 197d Ba 17.33N 61.46W
Cocobeach 170 Ab 0.59N 9.36 E
Coco Channel 148 If 14.00N 93.00 E
Coco Islands 148 If 14.05N 93.18 E
Coconino Plateau 188 Ii 35.50N 112.30W
Coco o Segovia, Río- 174 Kh 15.00N 83.08W
Cocorocuma, Cayos- 194 Ff 15.45N 83.00W
Côcos 204 Jb 14.10S 44.33W
Cocos 220c Bb 13.14N 144.39 E
Cocos Islands (Keeling Islands) [5] 142 Lk 12.10S 96.55 E
Cocos Islands (Keeling Islands) 140 Lk 12.10S 96.55 E
Cocos Ridge (EN) 106 Ni 5.30N 86.00W
Cocula 192 Hg 20.23N 103.50W
Cocuzzo 128 Kk 39.13N 16.08 E
Cod, Cape- 174 Le 41.42N 70.15W
Cod, Cape- 184 Me 41.50N 70.00W
Coda Cavallo, Capo- 128 Dj 40.51N 9.43 E
Codaeşti 130 Kc 46.52N 27.45 E
Codajás 202 Fd 3.50S 62.05W
Codera, Cabo- 196 Cg 10.35N 66.04W
Codfish Island 218 Bg 46.45S 167.40 E
Codigoro 128 Gf 44.49N 12.08 E
Codlea 130 Id 45.42N 25.27 E
Codó 202 Jd 4.29S 43.53W
Codogno 128 De 45.09N 9.42 E
Codrington 196 Fd 17.38N 61.50W
Codrington Lagoon 197d Ba 17.39N 61.51W
Codrului, Munţii- 130 Fc 46.35N 22.10 E
Cody 182 Fc 44.32N 109.05W
Coen 210 Ff 13.56S 143.12 E
Coesfeld 120 De 51.56N 7.09 E
Coetivy Island 158 Mi 7.08S 56.16 E
Coeur d'Alene 182 Db 47.41N 116.46W
Coevorden 122 Mb 52.40N 6.45 E
Coëvrons, Les- 122 Ff 48.12N 0.10W
Coffeyville 186 Ih 37.02N 95.37W
Coffs Harbour 210 Gh 30.18S 153.08 E
Cofre de Perote, Cerro- (Nauhcampatépetl) 192 Kh 19.29N 97.08W
Cofrentes 126 Ke 39.14N 1.04W
Coggeshall 124 Cc 51.52N 0.41 E
Coghinas 128 Cj 40.56N 8.48 E
Coghinas, Lago del- 128 Dj 40.45N 9.05 E
Coglians 128 Gd 46.37N 12.53 E
Cognac 122 Fi 45.42N 0.20W
Cogne 128 Be 45.37N 7.21 E
Cogolludo 126 Id 40.57N 3.05W
Čograjskoje vodohranilišče 132 Ng 45.30N 44.30 E
Coiba, Isla de- 190 Hg 7.27N 81.45W
Coig, Rio- (Coyle) 206 Gh 50.58S 69.11W
Coihaique 206 Fg 45.34S 72.04W
Coimbatore 142 Jh 11.00N 76.58 E
Coimbra [2] 126 Dd 40.12N 8.25W
Coimbra [Braz.] 204 Dd 19.55S 57.47W
Coimbra [Port.] 112 Fg 40.12N 8.25W
Coin 126 Hh 36.40N 4.45W
Coipasa, Salar de- 202 Eg 19.30S 68.10W
Čojbalsan 142 Ne 48.04N 114.30 E
Cojedes 196 Bh 9.37N 68.55W
Cojedes [2] 202 Eb 9.20N 68.20W
Cojedes, Río- 196 Bh 8.44N 68.15W
Cojutepeque 194 Cg 13.43N 88.56W
Čoka 130 Dd 45.56N 20.09 E
Cokeville 188 Je 42.05N 110.55W
Cokover River 212 Ed 20.40S 120.45 E
Čokurdah 138 Jb 70.38N 147.55 E
Colac [Austl.] 212 Ig 38.20S 143.35 E
Colac [N.Z.] 218 Bg 46.22S 167.53 E
Colatina 200 Lg 19.32S 40.37W
Colbeck, Cape- 222 Mf 77.06S 157.48W
Colbitz-Letzlinger Heide 120 Hd 52.27N 11.35 E
Colby 186 Fg 39.24N 101.03W
Colchester 118 Nj 51.54N 0.54 E
Cold Bay 178 Ge 55.11N 162.30W
Cold Lake 180 Gf 54.27N 110.10W
Coldstream 118 Kf 55.39N 2.15W
Coldwater [Ks.-U.S.] 186 Gh 37.16N 99.19W
Coldwater [Mi.-U.S.] 184 Ee 41.57N 85.00W
Colebrook 184 Lc 44.53N 71.30W
Coleman 186 Gk 31.50N 99.26W
Coleman River 212 Ic 15.06S 141.38 E
Coleraine/Cúil Raithin 118 Gf 55.08N 6.40W
Coleridge, Lake- 218 De 43.20S 171.30 E
Coles, Punta- 202 Dg 17.42S 71.23W
Colesberg 172 Df 30.45S 25.05 E
Colfax [La.-U.S.] 186 Jk 31.31N 92.42W
Colfax [Wa.-U.S.] 188 Gc 46.53N 117.22W
Colfontaine 124 Fd 50.25N 3.50 E
Colhué Huapi, Lago- 206 Gg 45.30S 68.48W
Colibaşi 130 He 44.56N 24.54 E
Colibris, Pointe des- 197e Bb 16.17N 61.06W
Colima 176 Ih 19.14N 103.43W
Colima [2] 190 De 19.10N 104.00W
Colima, Nevado de- 174 Ih 19.33N 103.38W
Colinas 204 Hb 14.12S 48.03W
Coll 118 Ge 56.40N 6.35W
Collado Bajo 126 Kd 40.14N 1.50W
Collarada 126 Lb 42.43N 0.29W
Colle di Val d'Elsa 128 Fg 43.25N 11.07 E
Colleferro 128 Gi 41.44N 12.59 E
College 178 Jd 64.51N 147.47W
College Place 188 Fc 46.03N 118.23W
College Station 186 Hk 30.37N 96.21W
Collegno 128 Be 45.05N 7.34 E
Collie 212 Df 33.21S 116.09 E
Collier Bay 212 Ec 16.10S 124.15 E
Collierville 184 Ch 35.03N 89.40W
Collingwood [N.Z.] 216 Dh 40.41S 172.41 E
Collingwood [Ont.-Can.] 184 Gc 44.29N 80.13W
Collinson Peninsula 180 Hb 70.00N 101.10W
Collinsville 212 Jd 20.34S 147.51 E
Collmberg 120 Je 51.15N 13.02 E
Colmar 122 Nf 48.05N 7.22 E
Colmena 204 Bi 28.45S 60.06W
Colmenar 126 Hh 36.54N 4.20W
Colmenar Viejo 126 Id 40.40N 3.46W
Colne 124 Cc 51.51N 0.59 E
Colne Point 124 Dc 51.46N 1.03 E
Colnett, Punta- 192 Ab 31.00N 116.20W
Cologne (EN) = Köln 112 Ge 50.56N 6.57 E
Colombia 204 He 20.10S 48.40W
Colombia [1] 200 Ie 4.00N 72.00W
Colombian Basin (EN) 174 Lh 13.00N 76.00W
Colombier, Pointe à- 197b Bc 17.55N 62.53W
Colombo 142 Ji 6.56N 79.51 E
Colón [Arg.] 206 Hd 33.53S 61.07W
Colón [Arg.] 206 Id 32.13S 58.08W
Colón [Cuba] 190 Hd 22.43N 80.54W
Colón [Hond.] [3] 194 Ef 15.20N 84.30W
Colón [Pan.] 176 Li 9.22N 79.54W
Colón [Pan.] [3] 194 Hi 9.30N 79.15W
Colón [Ur.] 204 Ek 33.53S 54.43W
Colón, Archipiélago de-/Galápagos, Islas- = Galapagos Islands (EN) 198 Gf 0.30S 90.30W
Colón, Montañas de- 194 Ef 14.55N 84.45W
Colona 212 Gf 31.38S 132.05 E
Colonarie 197n Ba 13.14N 61.08W
Colonarie 197n Ba 13.14N 61.08W
Colonel Hill 194 Jb 22.52N 74.15W
Colonia 214 Bf 9.31N 138.08 E
Colonia [2] 204 Dl 34.10S 57.30W
Colonia agricola de Turén 196 Bh 9.15N 69.05W
Colonia Carlos Pellegrini 204 Di 28.32S 57.10W
Colonia del Sacramento 206 Id 34.28S 57.51W
Colonia Elisa 204 Ch 26.56S 59.32W
Colonia Juárez 192 Eb 30.19N 108.05W
Colonia Las Heras 206 Gg 46.33S 68.57W
Colonia Lavalleja 206 Id 31.06S 57.01W
Colonial Heights 184 Ig 37.15N 77.25W
Colonia Morelos 192 Eb 30.50N 109.10W
Colonne, Capo- 128 Lk 39.02N 17.12 E
Colonsay 118 Ge 56.05N 6.10W
Colorado 194 Fh 10.46N 83.35W
Colorado [2] 182 Fd 39.30N 105.30W
Colorado, Cerro- 192 Bb 31.31N 115.31W
Colorado, Rio- [Arg.] 198 Ji 39.50S 62.08W
Colorado, Rio- [N.Amer.] 174 Hf 31.45N 114.40W
Colorado City 186 Fj 32.24N 100.52W
Colorado Plateau 174 Hf 36.30N 118.00W
Colorado River [N.Amer.] 174 Hf 31.45N 114.40W
Colorado River [U.S.] 174 Jg 28.36N 95.58W
Colorados, Archipiélago de los- 194 Eb 22.36N 84.20W
Colorado Springs 176 If 38.50N 104.49W
Colotlán 192 Hf 22.03N 103.16W
Colpon-Ata 135 Kc 42.39N 77.06 E
Coltishall 124 Db 52.44N 1.22 E
Colui 170 Cf 15.10S 16.40 E
Columbia 174 Ge 46.15N 124.05W
Columbia [Ky.-U.S.] 184 Eg 37.06N 85.18W
Columbia [Mo.-U.S.] 182 Id 38.57N 92.20W
Columbia [Ms.-U.S.] 186 Lk 31.15N 89.56W
Columbia [Pa.-U.S.] 184 Ie 40.02N 76.30W
Columbia [S.C.-U.S.] 176 Kf 34.00N 81.03W
Columbia [Tn.-U.S.] 184 Dh 35.37N 87.02W
Columbia, Cape- 174 La 83.08N 70.35W
Columbia, Mount- 174 Hd 57.00N 117.00W
Columbia Basin 182 Db 46.45N 119.05W
Columbia Falls 188 Hb 48.23N 114.11W
Columbia Mountains 174 Hd 52.00N 119.00W
Columbia Plateau 174 He 44.00N 117.30W
Columbia Seamount (EN) 202 Lh 20.40S 31.30W
Columbine, Cape- 158 Il 32.49S 17.51 E
Columbretes, Islas-/Columbrets, Els- 126 Me 39.52N 0.40 E
Columbrets, Els-/Columbretes, Islas- 126 Me 39.52N 0.40 E
Columbus [Ga.-U.S.] 176 Kf 32.29N 84.59W
Columbus [In.-U.S.] 182 Jd 39.13N 85.55W
Columbus [Ks.-U.S.] 186 Ih 37.10N 94.50W
Columbus [Ms.-U.S.] 182 Je 33.30N 88.25W
Columbus [Mt.-U.S.] 188 Kd 45.38N 109.15W
Columbus [Nb.-U.S.] 182 Hc 41.25N 97.22W
Columbus [N.M.-U.S.] 186 Ck 31.50N 107.38W
Columbus [Oh.-U.S.] 176 Kf 39.57N 83.00W
Columbus [Tx.-U.S.] 186 Hl 29.42N 96.33W
Columbus Point 194 Ja 24.08N 75.16W
Colville 174 Dc 70.25N 150.30W
Colville, Cape- 218 Fb 36.28S 175.21 E
Colville Channel 218 Fb 36.25S 175.30 E
Colville Lake 180 Ec 67.06N 126.00W
Colville Lake 180 Ec 67.10N 126.00W
Col Visentin 128 Gd 46.05N 12.20 E
Colwyn Bay 118 Jh 53.18N 3.43W
Coma 168 Fd 8.27N 36.55 E
Comacchio 128 Gf 44.42N 12.11 E
Comacchio, Valli di- 128 Gf 44.40N 12.05 E
Comai (Damxoi) 152 Ff 28.26N 91.32 E
Comala 192 Hh 19.19N 103.45W
Comalcalco 190 Fe 18.16N 93.13W
Coman, Mount- 222 Qf 73.49S 64.18W
Comanche [Mt.-U.S.] 188 Kc 46.02N 108.54W
Comanche [Tx.-U.S.] 186 Gk 31.54N 98.36W
Comandante Fontana 204 Cg 25.20S 59.41W

Comandău 130 Jd 45.46N 26.16 E
Comănești 130 Jc 46.25N 26.26 E
Comayagua 190 Gf 14.25N 87.37W
Comayagua ③ 194 Df 14.30N 87.40W
Combarbala 206 Fd 31.11S 71.02W
Combeaufontaine 122 Lg 47.43N 5.53 E
Combermere Bay ◧ 148 Ie 19.37N 93.34 E
Comblain-au-Pont 124 Hd 50.28N 5.35 E
Combles 124 Ed 50.01N 2.52 E
Combourg 122 Ef 48.25N 1.45W
Combraille ⌧ 122 Jh 46.30N 3.10 E
Combrailles ⌧ 122 Ih 46.15N 2.10 E
Comedero 192 Fe 24.37N 106.46W
Comendador 194 Ld 18.53N 71.42W
Comeragh Mountains/Na Comaraigh ⛰ 118 Fi 52.13N 7.35W
Comerío 197a Bb 18.13N 66.16W
Comilla 148 Id 23.27N 91.12 E
Comines 124 Fd 50.46N 3.01 E
Comines/Komen 124 Ed 50.46N 2.59 E
Comino ◆ 128 In 36.00N 14.20 E
Comino, Capo- ► 128 Dj 40.32N 9.49 E
Comiso 128 In 36.56N 14.36 E
Comitán de Domínguez 190 Fe 16.15N 92.08W
Commentry 122 Ih 46.17N 2.45 E
Commerce 186 Ij 33.15N 95.54W
Commercy 122 Lf 48.45N 5.35 E
Comminges ⌧ 122 Gk 43.15N 0.45 E
Committee Bay ◧ 174 Kc 68.30N 86.30W
Commonwealth Bay ◧ 222 Je 66.54S 142.40 E
Communism Peak (EN) = Kommunizma, pik- ▲ 140 Jf 38.57N 72.08 E
Como 128 De 45.47N 9.05 E
Como, Lago di- (Lario) ≋ 128 Dd 46.00N 9.15 E
Comodoro 204 Bl 35.19S 60.31W
Comodoro Rivadavia 200 Jj 45.50S 67.30W
Comondú 190 Bc 26.03N 111.46W
Comores/Comoros ① 160 Lj 12.10S 44.10 E
Comores, Archipel des- = Comoro Islands (EN) ⁘ 158 Lj 12.10S 44.15 E
Comorin, Cape- ► 140 Ji 8.04N 77.34 E
Comoro Islands (EN) = Comores, Archipel des- ⁘ 158 Lj 12.10S 44.15 E
Comoros/Comores ① 160 Lj 12.10S 44.10 E
Comox 188 Cb 49.40N 124.55W
Compiègne 122 Ie 49.25N 2.50 E
Compostela 190 Dd 21.14N 104.55W
Comprida, Ilha- ◆ 204 Ig 24.50S 47.42W
Compton 188 Fj 33.54N 118.13W
Comstock 186 Fl 29.41N 101.11W
Comtal, Causse du- ⏶ 122 Ij 44.26N 2.38 E
Cona 152 Ff 28.01N 91.57 E
Čona ⟍ 140 Mc 62.00N 110.00 E
Co Nag ≋ 152 Fe 32.00N 91.25 E
Conakry 160 Fh 9.31N 13.43W
Conara Junction 212 Jh 41.50S 147.26 E
Concarneau 122 Cg 47.52N 3.55W
Conceição da Barra 202 Kg 18.35S 39.45W
Conceição do Araguaia 202 Ie 8.15S 49.17W
Conceição do Mato Dentro 204 Kd 19.01S 43.25W
Concepción ③ 204 Df 23.00S 57.00W
Concepción [Arg.] 204 Di 28.23S 57.53W
Concepción [Arg.] 206 Gc 27.20S 65.35W
Concepción [Bol.] 202 Fg 16.15S 62.04W
Concepción [Chile] 200 Ii 36.50S 73.03W
Concepción [Par.] 200 Kh 23.25S 57.17W
Concepción [Peru] 202 Cf 11.55S 75.17W
Concepción [Ven.] 194 Lh 10.25N 71.41W
Concepción, Bahía- ◧ 192 Dd 26.40N 111.48W
Concepción, Laguna- ≋ 202 Fg 17.30S 61.25W
Concepción, Punta- ► 192 Dd 26.50N 111.50W
Concepción, Río- ⟍ 204 Ab 15.46S 62.10W
Concepción del Bermejo 204 Bh 26.36S 60.57W
Concepción del Oro 190 Dd 24.38N 101.25W
Concepción del Uruguay 206 Id 32.29S 58.14W
Conception, Point- ► 174 Gf 34.27N 120.27W
Conception Bay ◧ 180 Mg 48.00N 52.50W
Conception Island ◆ 194 Jb 23.52N 75.03W
Concha 194 Li 9.02N 71.45W
Conchas 204 Hf 23.01S 48.00W
Conchas Dam 186 Di 35.22N 104.11W
Conchas Lake ≋ 186 Di 35.25N 104.14W
Conches-en-Ouche 122 Gf 48.58N 0.56 E
Concho River ⟍ 186 Gk 31.32N 99.43W
Conchos, Río- [Mex.] ⟍ 174 Ig 25.35N 104.25W
Conchos, Río- [Mex.] ⟍ 192 Je 25.04N 98.32W
Concord [Ca.-U.S.] 188 Eh 37.59N 122.00W
Concord [N.H.-U.S.] 176 Le 43.12N 71.32W
Concordia [Arg.] 200 Ki 31.24S 58.02W
Concordia [Braz.] 204 Fh 27.14S 52.01W
Concordia [Ks.-U.S.] 186 Hg 39.34N 97.39W
Concordia [Mex.] 192 Ff 23.17N 106.04W
Concordia Baai ◧ 197c Aa 17.31N 62.58W
Con Cuong 148 Ke 19.02N 104.54 E
Conda 170 Be 11.06S 14.20 E
Condamine River ⟍ 212 Je 27.00S 149.50 E
Condat 122 Ii 45.22N 2.46 E
Conde 202 Kf 11.49S 37.37W
Condé-en-Brie 124 Fe 49.01N 3.33 E
Condega 194 Dg 13.21N 86.24W
Condé-sur-l'Escaut 124 Fd 50.27N 3.35 E
Condé-sur-Marne 124 Ge 49.03N 4.11 E
Condé-sur-Noireau 122 Ff 48.51N 0.33W
Condobolin 212 Jf 33.05S 147.09 E
Condom 122 Gk 43.58N 0.22 E
Condon 188 Ed 45.14N 120.11W
Cóndor, Cordillera del- ⛰ 202 Cd 4.20S 78.30W
Condroz/Condruzisch Plateau ⌧ 122 Kd 50.25N 5.00 E
Condruzisch Plateau/Condroz ⌧ 122 Kd 50.25N 5.00 E
Conecuh River ⟍ 184 Dj 30.58N 87.14W
Conegliano 128 Ge 45.53N 12.18 E
Conejera, Isla- / Conills, Illa des- ◆ 126 Oe 39.11N 2.57 E
Conejo 192 De 24.05N 111.00W
Conejo, Cerro- ▲ 192 Jg 21.24N 99.06W
Conero ▲ 128 Hg 43.33N 13.36 E
Conesa 204 Bk 33.36S 60.21W
Conference Island ◆ 197p Bb 12.09N 61.35W
Conflans-en-Jarnisy 124 He 49.10N 5.51 E
Conflans-Sainte-Honorine 124 Ef 48.59N 2.06 E
Confolens 122 Gh 46.01N 0.40 E
Confuso, Río- ⟍ 204 Dg 25.09S 57.34W
Conghua 152 Jg 23.31N 113.30 E
Congo ① 160 Ii 1.00S 15.00 E
Congo ⟍ 158 Ii 6.04S 12.24 E
Congo, Democratic Republic of the- → Zaïre ① 160 Ji 1.00S 25.00 E
Congo Basin (EN) ▭ 158 Ih 0.00 17.00 E
Congonhas 204 Ke 20.30S 43.52W
Conil de la Frontera 126 Fh 36.16N 6.05W
Conills, Illa des- / Conejera, Isla- ◆ 126 Oe 39.11N 2.57 E
Coniston 184 Gb 46.29N 80.51W
Conn, Lough-/Loch Con ≋ 118 Dg 54.04N 9.20W
Connacht/Connaught ▣ 118 Eh 53.30N 9.00W
Connaught/Connacht ▣ 118 Eh 53.30N 9.00W
Conneaut 184 Ge 41.58N 80.34W
Connecticut ② 182 Mc 41.45N 72.45W
Connecticut River ⟍ 182 Mc 41.17N 72.21W
Connell 188 Fc 46.40N 118.52W
Connellsville 184 He 40.02N 79.38W
Connemara, Mountains of- ⛰ 118 Dh 53.30N 9.45W
Connersville 184 Ef 39.39N 85.08W
Conn Lake ≋ 180 Kb 70.30N 73.30W
Connors Range ⛰ 212 Jd 21.40S 149.10 E
Conon ⟍ 118 Id 57.35N 4.30W
Conquista 204 Id 19.56S 47.33W
Conrad 188 Jb 48.10N 111.57W
Conroe 186 Ik 30.19N 95.27W
Conroe Lake ≋ 186 Ik 30.25N 95.37W
Conscripto Bernardi 204 Cj 31.03S 59.05W
Conselheiro Lafaiete 202 Jh 20.40S 43.48W
Conselice 128 Ff 44.31N 11.49 E
Consett 118 Lg 54.51N 1.49W
Consolación del Sur 194 Fb 22.30N 83.31W
Con Son ⁘ 148 Lg 8.43N 106.36 E
Constance, Lake- (EN) = Bodensee ≋ 110 Gf 47.35N 9.25 E
Constanța 112 Ig 44.11N 28.39 E
Constanța ② 130 Le 44.30N 28.30 E
Constantina 126 Gg 37.52N 5.37W
Constantine 160 He 36.22N 6.37 E
Constantine ③ 162 Ib 36.20N 6.35 E
Constantine, Cape- ► 178 He 58.25N 158.50W
Constitución [Chile] 206 Fe 35.20S 72.25W
Constitución [Ur.] 204 Dj 31.05S 57.50W
Consuegra 126 Ie 39.28N 3.36W
Consuelo Peak ▲ 208 Fg 24.58S 148.10 E
Contamana 202 De 7.15S 74.54W
Contas, Rio de- ⟍ 198 Mg 14.17S 39.01W
Contoy, Isla- ◆ 192 Pg 21.30N 86.48W
Contraforte Central, Serra do- ⛰ 204 Ic 17.15S 47.50W
Contramaestre 194 Ic 20.18N 76.15W
Contraviesa, Sierra- ⛰ 126 Ih 36.50N 3.10W
Contreras, Embalse de- ⊌ 126 Ke 39.32N 1.30W
Contreras, Islas- ⁘ 194 Gj 7.50N 81.47W
Contreras, Puerto de- ⩀ 126 Ke 39.32N 1.30W
Contres 122 Hg 47.25N 1.26 E
Contumazá 202 Ce 7.22S 78.49W
Contursi 128 Jj 40.39N 15.14 E
Contwig 124 Je 49.15N 7.26 E
Contwoyto Lake ≋ 180 Gc 65.40N 110.40W
Conty 124 Ee 49.44N 2.09 E
Convención 202 Db 8.28N 73.20W
Conversano 128 Lj 40.58N 17.07 E
Conway [Ar.-U.S.] 182 Id 35.05N 92.26W
Conway [N.H.-U.S.] 184 Ld 43.58N 71.07W
Conway [S.C.-U.S.] 184 Hi 33.51N 79.04W
Conway, Mount- ▲ 212 Gd 23.45S 133.25 E
Conway Reef → Ceva-i-Ra ❋ 208 Ig 21.45S 174.35 E
Conwy 118 Jh 53.17N 3.50W
Conwy ⟍ 118 Jh 53.17N 3.50W
Conyers 184 Fi 33.40N 84.00W
Conza, Sella di- 128 Jj 40.50N 15.18 E
Coober Pedy 210 Eg 29.01S 134.43 E
Cooch Behār → Koch Bihār 148 Hc 26.19N 89.26 E
Cook 212 Gf 30.37S 130.25 E
Cook ◆ 222 Ad 59.27S 27.10W
Cook, Bahía- ◧ 206 Fi 55.10S 70.10W
Cook, Cap- ► 219b Dd 19.32S 169.30 E
Cook, Cape- ► 188 Ba 50.08N 127.55W
Cook, Mount- ▲ 208 Hi 43.36S 170.09 E
Cook, Récif de- ❋ 219b Ad 19.25S 163.50 E
Cooke, Mount- ▲ 212 Df 32.25S 116.18 E
Cookes Peak ▲ 186 Cj 32.32N 107.44W
Cookeville 184 Eg 36.10N 85.31W
Cook Ice Shelf ⛆ 222 Je 68.40S 152.30 E
Cook Inlet ◧ 174 Dc 60.30N 152.00W
Cook Island ◆ 220g Bb 1.57N 157.28W
Cook Islands ⑤ 210 Lf 20.00S 158.00W
Cook Islands ⁘ 208 Lf 20.00S 158.00W
Cookstown/An Chorr Chríochach 118 Gg 54.39N 6.45W
Cook Strait ⇌ 208 Ii 41.20S 174.25 E
Cooktown 210 Ff 15.28S 145.15 E
Coolgardie 212 Ef 30.57S 121.10 E
Coolidge [Az.-U.S.] 182 Ee 32.59N 111.31W
Coolidge [Ks.-U.S.] 186 Fg 38.03N 101.59W
Coolidge Dam ◸ 188 Jj 33.12N 110.32W
Cooma 212 Jg 36.14S 149.08 E
Coonabarabran 212 Jf 31.16S 149.17 E
Coonamble 212 Jf 30.57S 148.23 E
Coonoor 148 Ff 11.21N 76.49 E
Coon Rapids 186 Jd 45.09N 93.18W
Cooper 186 Ij 33.23N 95.35W
Cooper, Mount- ▲ 188 Ga 50.13N 117.12W
Cooper Creek ⟍ 208 Eg 28.29S 137.46 E
Cooper's Town 184 Il 26.51N 77.31W
Cooperstown [N.D.-U.S.] 186 Gc 47.27N 98.07W
Cooperstown [N.Y.-U.S.] 184 Jd 42.43N 74.56W
Coosa River ⟍ 184 Di 32.30N 86.16W
Coos Bay 182 Cc 43.22N 124.13W
Coos Bay ◧ 188 Ce 43.23N 124.16W
Cootamundra 212 Jf 34.39S 148.02 E
Čop 132 Ce 48.26N 22.14 E
Copainalá 192 Mi 17.05N 93.12W
Copán 194 Cf 14.50N 89.12W
Copán ③ 194 Cf 14.50N 89.00W
Copán ⛬ 176 Kh 14.50N 89.09W
Copenhagen (EN) = København 112 Hi 55.40N 12.35 E
Copertino 128 Mj 40.16N 18.03 E
Copetonas 204 Bn 38.43N 60.27W
Copiapó 200 Ih 27.22S 70.20W
Copiapó, Río- ⟍ 206 Fc 27.19S 70.56W
Çöpköy 130 Jh 41.13N 26.49 E
Coporito 196 Fh 8.56N 62.00W
Coporolo ⟍ 170 Be 12.56S 13.00 E
Copparo 128 Ff 44.54N 11.49 E
Copper ⟍ 178 Kd 60.30N 144.50W
Copperbelt ③ 170 Ee 13.00S 28.00 E
Copper Center 178 Jd 61.58N 145.19W
Copper Cliff 180 Jg 46.28N 81.04W
Copper Harbor 184 Db 47.27N 87.53W
Coppermine 176 Hc 67.50N 115.05W
Coppermine ⟍ 174 Hc 67.49N 115.04W
Coppermine Point ► 184 Eb 46.59N 84.47W
Copper Queen 172 Dc 17.31S 29.20 E
Coqên (Maindong) 152 Ee 31.15N 85.13 E
Coquet ⟍ 118 Lf 55.22N 1.37W
Coquille 188 Ce 43.11N 124.11W
Coquimbo 200 Ih 29.58S 71.21W
Coquimbo ② 206 Fd 31.00S 71.00W
Corabia 130 Hf 43.47N 24.30 E
Coracão de Jesus 204 Jc 16.42S 44.22W
Coradi o Cheradi, Isole- ⁘ 128 Lj 40.27N 17.09 E
Cora Droma Rúisc / Carrick on Shannon 118 Eh 53.57N 8.05W
Corail 194 Kd 18.34N 73.53W
Corail, Mer de- = Coral Sea (EN) ▤ 208 Gf 20.00S 158.00 E
Coral, Cabeza de- ❋ 192 Ph 18.47N 87.19W
Coral Gables 182 Kf 25.45N 80.16W
Coral Harbour 176 Kc 64.08N 83.10W
Coral Sea ▤ 208 Gf 20.00S 158.00 E
Coral Sea (EN) = Corail, Mer de- ▤ 208 Gf 20.00S 158.00 E
Coral Sea Basin (EN) ⊍ 208 Gf 14.00S 152.00 E
Coral Sea Islands Territory ⑤ 212 Lc 18.00S 158.00 E
Coralville 186 Kf 41.40N 91.35W
Coralville Lake ⊌ 186 Kf 41.47N 91.48W
Corantijn River ⟍ 198 Ke 5.55N 57.05W
Corato 128 Ki 41.09N 16.25 E
Corbara, Lago di- ≋ 128 Gh 42.45N 12.15 E
Corbeil-Essones 122 If 48.36N 2.29 E
Corbie 124 Ee 49.55N 2.30 E
Corbières ⌧ 122 Il 42.55N 2.38 E
Corbigny 122 Jg 47.15N 3.40 E
Corby 118 Mi 52.29N 0.40W
Corcaigh/Cork 112 Fe 51.54N 8.28W
Corcaigh/Cork ② 118 Ej 52.00N 8.30W
Corcoran 188 Fh 36.06N 119.33W
Corcovado, Cerro- ▲ 192 Bb 30.40N 114.55W
Corcovado, Golfo- ◧ 198 Ij 43.30S 73.30W
Corcovado, Volcán- ⟁ 198 Ij 43.12S 72.48W
Corcubión 126 Cb 42.57N 9.11W
Corcubión, Ría de- ⋌ 126 Cb 42.54N 9.09W
Cordele 182 Ke 31.58N 83.47W
Cordes 122 Hj 44.04N 1.57 E
Cordevole ⟍ 128 Gd 46.05N 12.04 E
Cordilheiras, Serra das- ⛰ 202 Ie 7.30S 48.30W
Cordillera ③ 204 Dg 25.15S 57.00W
Cordillera Central [Phil.] ⛰ 150 Hc 17.20N 120.57 E
Cordillera Central [S.Amer.] ⛰ 198 If 8.00S 77.00W
Cordillera Occidental [S.Amer.] ⛰ 198 Ig 14.00S 74.00W
Cordillera Oriental [S.Amer.] ⛰ 198 If 7.00S 76.00W
Córdoba ② 206 Hd 32.00S 64.00W
Córdoba [Arg.] 200 Ji 31.25S 64.10W
Córdoba [Col.] ③ 202 Cb 8.20N 75.40W
Córdoba [Mex.] 190 Ee 18.53N 96.56W
Córdoba [Sp.] 112 Fh 37.53N 4.46W
Córdoba [Sp.] ③ 126 Hf 38.00N 4.50W
Córdoba, Sierras de- ⛰ 198 Ji 31.15S 64.00W
Cordova 176 Ec 60.33N 145.46W
Corfu (EN) = Kérkira ◆ 110 Hh 39.40N 19.45 E
Corfu, Strait of- (EN) = Kerkiras, Stenón- ⇌ 130 Dj 39.35N 20.05 E
Corguinho 204 Ed 19.53S 54.52W
Coria 126 Fe 39.59N 6.32W
Coria del Río 126 Fg 37.16N 6.03W
Coribe 204 Ja 13.50S 44.28W
Coricudgy, Mount- ▲ 212 Kf 32.50S 150.22 E
Corigliano Calabro 128 Kk 39.36N 16.31 E
Coringa Islets ⁘ 212 Jc 17.00S 150.00 E
Corinne 188 Ma 50.06N 104.32W
Corinth 182 Je 34.56N 88.31W
Corinth (EN) = Kórinthos ⛬ 130 Fl 37.55N 22.53 E
Corinth, Gulf of- (EN) = Korinthiakós Kólpos ◧ 110 Ih 38.12N 22.30 E
Corinth Canal (EN) = Korinthou, Dhiórix- ⇌ 130 Fl 37.57N 22.58 E
Corinto [Braz.] 202 Jg 18.21S 44.27W
Corinto [Nic.] 194 Dg 12.29N 87.10W
Corisco ◆ 166 Ge 0.55N 9.19 E
Cork/Corcaigh 112 Fe 51.54N 8.28W
Cork/Corcaigh ② 118 Ej 52.00N 8.30W
Cork Harbour ◧ 118 Ej 51.45N 8.15W
Corleone 128 Hm 37.49N 13.18 E
Çorlu 144 Ca 41.09N 27.48 E
Çorlu ⟍ 130 Kh 41.12N 27.28 E
Cormeilles 124 Ce 49.15N 0.23 E
Cormoran Reef ✱ 220a Bb 7.50N 134.32 E
Cornelio 192 Dc 29.55N 111.08W
Cornélio Procopio 206 Jb 23.08S 50.39W
Cornelius Grinnel Bay ◧ 180 Ld 63.20N 64.50W
Corner Brook 176 Ne 48.57N 57.57W
Corner Seamounts (EN) ⩘ 174 Nf 35.30N 51.30W
Cornia ⟍ 128 Eh 42.57N 10.33 E
Corning [Ar.-U.S.] 186 Kh 36.24N 90.35W
Corning [Ca.-U.S.] 188 Dg 39.56N 122.11W
Corning [N.Y.-U.S.] 184 Id 42.10N 77.04W
Corno Grande ▲ 128 Hh 42.28N 13.34 E
Cornouaille ⌧ 122 Cg 48.00N 4.00W
Cornwall 180 Kg 45.02N 74.44W
Cornwall ③ 118 Ik 50.30N 4.30W
Cornwall ⌧ 110 Fe 50.30N 4.40W
Cornwall ▣ 118 Hk 50.20N 5.05W
Cornwall ◆ 180 Ia 73.30N 95.00W
Cornwall, Cape- ► 118 Hk 50.08N 5.43W
Cornwallis ◆ 180 Ia 75.15N 95.00W
Coro 200 Jd 11.25N 69.41W
Coro, Golfete de- ◧ 194 Mh 11.34N 69.53W
Corocoro 202 Eg 17.12S 68.28W
Corocoro, Isla- ◆ 196 Fh 8.31N 60.05W
Corod 130 Kd 45.54N 27.37 E
Čoroh ⟍ 146 Ib 41.36N 41.35 E
Coroico 202 Eg 16.10S 67.44W
Coromandel [Braz.] 204 Id 18.28S 47.13W
Coromandel [N.Z.] 218 Fb 36.46S 175.30 E
Coromandel Coast ⌓ 140 Kh 14.00N 80.10 E
Coromandel Peninsula ▬ 216 Eg 36.50S 175.35 E
Coromandel Range ⛰ 218 Fb 37.00S 175.40 E
Coron 150 Hd 12.00N 120.12 E
Corona 186 Di 34.15N 105.36W
Corona Bank (EN) ⊥ 212 Db 12.20S 118.30 E
Coronado, Bahía de- ◧ 174 Ki 9.00N 83.50W
Coronado, Isla- ◆ 192 Aa 32.25N 117.15W
Coronados, Isla- ◆ 192 Dd 26.07N 111.17W
Coronation 188 Ja 52.05N 111.27W
Coronation ◆ 222 Re 60.37S 45.35W
Coronation, Cap- ► 219b Cf 22.15S 167.02 E
Coronation Gulf ◧ 174 Ic 68.25N 110.00W
Coronda 204 Bj 31.58S 60.55W
Coronda, Laguna- ≋ 204 Bk 32.06S 60.52W
Coronel 206 Fe 37.01S 73.08W
Coronel Bogado 206 Ic 27.11S 56.18W
Coronel Dorrego 206 He 38.42S 61.17W
Coronel du Graty 204 Bh 27.40S 60.56W
Coronel Fabriciano 202 Jg 19.31S 42.38W
Coronel Oviedo 206 Ic 25.25S 56.27W
Coronel Ponce 204 Eb 15.34S 55.01W
Coronel Pringles 206 He 37.58S 61.22W
Coronel Rodolfo Bunge 204 Bm 37.34S 60.08W
Coronel Suárez 206 He 37.28S 61.55W
Coronel Vidal 204 Dm 37.27S 57.43W
Coronel Vivida 204 Fg 25.58S 52.34W
Coropuna, Nudo- ▲ 198 Ig 15.30S 72.41W
Çorovoda 130 Di 40.30N 20.13 E
Corozal ③ 194 Cd 18.15N 88.17W
Corozal [Blz.] 194 Cd 18.24N 88.24W
Corozal [Col.] 194 Ji 9.18N 75.17W
Corpus Christi 176 Jg 27.48N 97.24W
Corpus Christi, Lake- ≋ 186 Hl 28.10N 97.53W
Corpus Christi Bay ◧ 186 Hm 27.48N 97.20W
Corque 202 Eg 18.21S 67.42W
Corral de Bustos 204 Ak 33.17S 62.12W
Correggio 128 Ef 44.46N 10.47 E
Córrego do Ouro 204 Gc 16.18S 50.32W
Corrente 202 If 10.27S 45.10W
Corrente, Rio- [Braz.] ⟍ 202 Hg 19.19S 50.50W
Corrente, Rio- [Braz.] ⟍ 204 Ka 13.08S 43.28W
Corrente, Rio- [Braz.] ⟍ 204 Ib 14.14S 46.58W
Correntes 204 Ec 17.37S 54.59W
Correntes, Rio- ⟍ 204 Ec 17.38S 55.08W
Correnti, Capo delle- ► 110 Hh 36.40N 15.05 E
Correnti, Isola delle- ◆ 128 Jn 36.38N 15.05 E
Correntina 202 Jf 13.20S 44.39W
Correntina, Rio- → Éguas, Rio das- ⟍ 204 Ja 13.26S 41.14W
Corrèze ③ 122 Hi 45.15N 1.50 E
Corrèze ⟍ 122 Hi 45.10N 1.28 E
Corrib, Lough-/Loch Coirib ≋ 118 Dh 53.05N 9.10W
Corrientes 200 Kh 27.30S 58.50W
Corrientes ② 206 Ic 29.00S 58.00W
Corrientes, Cabo- [Arg.] ► 204 Dn 38.01S 57.32W
Corrientes, Cabo- [Col.] ► 202 Cb 5.30N 77.34W
Corrientes, Cabo- [Cuba] ► 194 Ec 21.45N 84.31W
Corrientes, Cabo- [Mex.] ► 174 Ig 20.25N 105.42W
Corrientes, Ensenada de- ◧ 194 Ec 21.45N 84.31W
Corrientes, Río- [Arg.] ⟍ 204 Cj 30.21S 59.33W
Corrientes, Río- [Peru] ⟍ 202 Dd 3.43S 74.40W
Corrieyairack Pass ⩀ 118 Id 57.05N 4.40W
Corrigan 186 Ik 31.00N 94.50W
Corrigin 212 Df 32.21S 117.52 E
Corry 184 He 41.56N 79.39W
Corryong 212 Jg 36.12S 147.54 E
Corse = Corsica (EN) ◆ 110 Gg 42.00N 9.00 E
Corse, Cap- ► 110 Gg 43.00N 9.23 E
Corse-du-Sud ③ 122a Ab 41.50N 9.00 E
Corsewall Point ► 118 Hf 55.02N 5.05W
Corsica (EN) = Corse ◆ 110 Gg 42.00N 9.00 E
Corsica, Canale di- ⇌ 128 Dh 42.45N 9.45 E
Corsicana 182 He 32.06N 96.28W
Cort Adelaer, Kap- ► 179 Hf 61.45N 42.00W
Corte 122a Ba 42.18N 9.09 E
Cortegana 126 Fg 37.55N 6.49W
Cortes 126 Kc 41.55N 1.25W
Cortés ③ 194 Cf 15.30N 88.00W
Cortez 182 Fd 37.21N 108.35W
Cortina d'Ampezzo 128 Gd 46.32N 12.08 E
Čortkov 132 De 48.59N 25.50 E
Cortland 184 Id 42.36N 76.10W
Cortona 128 Fg 43.16N 11.59 E
Corubal ⟍ 166 Bc 11.57N 15.06W
Coruche 126 Df 38.57N 8.31W
Çoruh ⟍ 144 Fa 41.36N 41.35 E
Çorum 144 Da 40.33N 34.58 E
Çorum ⟍ 146 Fb 40.29N 35.36 E
Corumbá 200 Kg 19.01S 57.39W
Corumbá, Rio- ⟍ 202 Ig 18.19S 48.55W
Corumbá de Goiás 204 Hb 15.55S 48.48W
Corumbáiba 204 Hd 18.09S 48.34W
Corumo, Rio- ⟍ 196 Fi 6.49N 60.52W
Corvallis 182 Cc 44.34N 123.16W
Corvo ◆ 158 De 39.42N 31.06W
Corzuela 204 Bh 26.57S 60.58W
Cosalá 192 Fe 24.23N 106.41W
Cosamaloapan 192 Lh 18.22N 95.48W
Cosenza 112 Hh 39.18N 16.15 E
Coshocton 184 Ge 40.16N 81.53W
Cosigüina, Punta- ► 194 Dg 12.54N 87.41W
Cosmoledo Group ⁘ 158 Li 9.43S 47.35 E
Cosne-Cours-sur-Loire 122 Ig 47.24N 2.55 E
Cosquín 206 Hd 31.15S 64.29W
Cossato 128 Ce 45.34N 8.10 E
Costa, Cordillera de la- ⛰ 198 Je 9.50N 66.00W
Costa Rica ① 176 Ki 10.00N 84.00W
Costa Verde ⌧ 126 Ga 43.40N 5.40W
Costero Catalana, Cadena- / Mediterrani Català, Sistema- = Catalan Coastal Range (EN) ⛰ 110 Gg 41.35N 1.40 E
Costești 130 He 44.40N 24.53 E
Costiera, Catena- ⛰ 128 Kk 39.25N 16.10 E
Coswig 120 Je 51.08N 13.35 E
Cotabato 150 He 7.13N 124.15 E
Cotagaita 202 Eh 20.50S 65.41W
Cotahuasi 202 Dg 15.12S 72.56W
Côte-d'Ivoire = Ivory Coast (EN) ① 160 Gh 8.00N 5.00W
Côte-d'Or ③ 122 Kg 47.30N 4.50 E
Côte d'Or ⛰ 122 Kg 47.10N 4.50 E
Cotentin 110 Ff 49.30N 1.30W
Côtes-d'Armor 122 Df 48.25N 2.40W
Cotiella 126 Mb 42.31N 0.19 E
Cotmeana 130 He 44.58N 24.37 E
Cotmeana ⟍ 130 He 44.24N 24.45 E
Cotonou 160 Hh 6.21N 2.26 E
Cotopaxi, Volcán- ⟁ 198 If 0.40S 78.26W
Cotswold Hills ◭ 118 Kj 51.45N 2.10W
Cottage Grove 188 De 43.48N 123.03W
Cottenham 124 Cb 52.17N 0.08 E
Cottondale 184 Ej 30.48N 85.23W
Cottonwood Wash ⟍ 188 Ji 35.05N 110.22W
Cotuí 194 Ld 19.03N 70.09W
Cotulla 186 Gl 28.26N 99.14W
Coubre, Pointe de la- ► 122 Ei 45.42N 1.14W
Coucy-le-Château-Auffrique 124 Fe 49.31N 3.19 E
Coudekerque-Branche 124 Ec 51.02N 2.24 E
Coudersport 184 He 41.46N 78.01W
Couedic, Cape du- ► 212 Hg 36.10S 136.40 E
Couesnon ⟍ 122 Ef 48.37N 1.31W
Couhé 122 Gh 46.18N 0.11 E
Couilly-Pont-aux-Dames 124 Ef 48.53N 2.52 E
Coulee Dam 188 Fb 48.00N 118.59W
Coulihaut 197g Bb 15.30N 61.29W
Coulman Island ◆ 222 Kf 73.28S 169.45 E
Coulogne 124 Dd 50.55N 1.53 E
Coulommiers 122 Jf 48.49N 3.05 E
Coulonge, Rivière- ⟍ 184 Ic 45.51N 76.45W
Coulounieix-Chamiers 122 Gi 45.10N 0.42 E
Council 188 Gd 44.44N 116.26W
Council Bluffs 182 Hc 41.16N 95.52W
Courcelles 124 Gd 50.28N 4.22 E
Courcelles-Chaussy 124 Ie 49.07N 6.24 E
Courland (EN) = Kurzeme ⌧ 110 Id 56.50N 22.00 E
Courmayeur 128 Ae 45.47N 6.58 E
Couronne, La- 122 Gi 45.37N 0.06 E
Courseulles-sur-Mer 124 Be 49.20N 0.27W
Cours-la-Ville 122 Kh 46.06N 4.19 E
Courtenay 180 Fg 49.41N 125.00W
Courtine-le-Trucq, La- 122 Ii 45.42N 2.16 E
Courtisols 124 Gf 48.59N 4.31 E
Courtrai/Kortrijk 122 Jd 50.50N 3.16 E
Coushatta 186 Jj 32.00N 93.21W
Cousin ⟍ 122 Kh 46.58N 4.15 E
Coutances 122 Ee 49.03N 1.26W
Couto de Magalhães, Rio- ⟍ 204 Fa 13.37S 53.09W
Coutras 122 Fi 45.02N 0.08W
Couture, Lac - ≋ 180 Jd 60.05N 75.20W
Couvin 122 Kd 50.03N 4.20 E
Couvin-Mariembourg 124 Gd 50.06N 4.31 E
Covarrubias 126 Ib 42.04N 3.31W
Covasna 130 Jd 45.51N 26.11 E
Covasna ② 130 Id 46.00N 26.00 E
Coveñas 194 Ji 9.25N 75.42W
Coventry 118 Li 52.25N 1.30W
Covilhã 126 Ed 40.17N 7.30W
Covington [Ga.-U.S.] 184 Fi 33.37N 83.51W
Covington [Ky.-U.S.] 182 Kd 39.05N 84.30W
Covington [La.-U.S.] 186 Kk 30.29N 90.06W
Covington [Tn.-U.S.] 184 Ch 35.34N 89.39W
Covington [Va.-U.S.] 184 Hg 37.48N 79.59W
Covurlui ⟍ 130 Ld 45.46N 28.02 E
Cowal ⌧ 118 He 56.05N 5.10W
Cowan, Lake- ≋ 212 Ef 31.50S 121.50 E
Cowan Knob ▲ 186 Ji 35.52N 93.29W
Cowell 212 Hf 33.41S 136.55 E
Cowes 124 Ad 50.46N 1.18W
Cowichan Lake ≋ 188 Cb 48.54N 124.20W
Cowra 212 Jf 33.50S 148.41 E
Coxim 200 Kg 18.30S 54.45W
Coxim, Rio- ⟍ 204 Ed 18.34S 54.46W
Cox's Bāzār 148 Id 21.26N 91.59 E
Coyah 166 Cd 9.43N 13.23W
Coyame 192 Gc 29.28N 105.06W
Coyanosa Draw ⟍ 186 Ek 31.18N 103.06W
Coycoyan, Sierra de- ⛰ 192 Ji 17.30N 98.20W
Coyle, Río- → Coig, Río- ⟍ 206 Gh 50.58S 69.11W
Coyote, Río- ⟍ 192 Cb 30.48N 112.35W
Coyotitán 192 Ff 23.47N 106.35W
Coyuca, Laguna de- ≋ 192 Ii 16.57N 100.05W
Cozia, Pasul- ⩀ 130 Hd 45.15N 24.15 E
Cozumel 192 Pg 20.31N 86.55W
Cozumel, Isla de- ◆ 190 Gd 20.25N 86.55W

Index Symbols

- ① Independent Nation
- ② State, Region
- ③ District, County
- ④ Municipality
- ⑤ Colony, Dependency
- ■ Continent
- ⌧ Physical Region
- ▣ Historical or Cultural Region
- ▲ Mount, Mountain
- ⟁ Volcano
- ◮ Hill
- ⛰ Mountains, Mountain Range
- ◭ Hills, Escarpment
- ⏶ Plateau, Upland
- ⩀ Pass, Gap
- ▭ Plain, Lowland
- ◣ Delta
- ⊟ Salt Flat
- ⋎ Valley, Canyon
- ◒ Crater, Cave
- ✣ Karst Features
- ⌵ Depression
- ⊔ Polder
- ∴ Desert, Dunes
- ♣ Forest, Woods
- ⁂ Heath, Steppe
- ✳ Oasis
- ► Cape, Point
- ⌓ Coast, Beach
- ▐ Cliff
- ▬ Peninsula
- ⋈ Isthmus
- ⁚ Sandbank
- ◆ Island
- ◎ Atoll
- ✱ Rock, Reef
- ⁘ Islands, Archipelago
- ⊛ Rocks, Reefs
- ❋ Coral Reef
- ⊚ Well, Spring
- ⛲ Geyser
- ⟍ River, Stream
- ⫽ Waterfall, Rapids
- ⋌ River Mouth, Estuary
- ≋ Lake
- ≣ Salt Lake
- ◌ Intermittent Lake
- ⊌ Reservoir
- ⌸ Swamp, Pond
- ═ Canal
- ❄ Glacier
- ⛆ Ice Shelf, Pack Ice
- ≈ Ocean
- ▤ Sea
- ◧ Gulf, Bay
- ⇌ Strait, Fjord
- ⊖ Lagoon
- ⊥ Bank
- ⩘ Seamount
- ⊓ Tablemount
- ⋀ Ridge
- ⌒ Shelf
- ⊍ Basin
- ⌇ Escarpment, Sea Scarp
- ⚡ Fracture
- ⩡ Trench, Abyss
- ♠ National Park, Reserve
- ✦ Point of Interest
- ⚑ Recreation Site
- ◓ Cave, Cavern
- ⛫ Historic Site
- ⛬ Ruins
- ▥ Wall, Walls
- ✝ Church, Abbey
- ⛩ Temple
- ⊕ Scientific Station
- ⊞ Railway station
- ✈ Airport
- ⚓ Port
- ⊗ Military installation
- ⛯ Lighthouse
- ⚒ Mine
- ∩ Tunnel
- ◸ Dam, Bridge

Cradock	160	Jl	32.08S	25.36 E
Craig [Ak.-U.S.]	178	Me	55.29N	133.09W
Craig [Co.-U.S.]	182	Fc	40.31N	107.33W
Craigmont	188	Gc	46.15N	116.28W
Craigs Range ⛰	212	Ke	26.40S	151.30 E
Crailsheim	120	Gg	49.09N	10.05 E
Craiova	112	Ig	44.19N	23.48 E
Cranbrook [Austl.]	212	Df	34.18S	117.32 E
Cranbrook [B.C.-Can.]	180	Fg	49.31N	115.46W
Cranbrook [Eng.-U.K.]	124	Cc	51.05N	0.32 E
Crandon	186	Ld	45.34N	88.54W
Crane [Or.-U.S.]	188	Fe	43.25N	118.35W
Crane [Tx.-U.S.]	186	Ek	31.24N	102.21W
Crane Lake	186	Jb	48.16N	92.28W
Crane Lake ≈	188	Ka	50.06N	109.06W
Cranleigh	124	Bc	51.08N	0.29W
Craon	122	Fg	47.51N	0.57W
Craonne	124	Fe	49.26N	3.47 E
Crapaud, Puy- ▲	122	Fh	46.40N	0.40W
Crary Mountains ⛰	222	Of	76.48S	117.40W
Crasna ∿	130	Fa	48.09N	22.20 E
Crasna [Rom.]	130	Fb	47.10N	22.54 E
Crasna [Rom.]	130	Kc	46.31N	27.51 E
Crater Lake [Or.-U.S.] ≈	182	Cc	42.56N	122.06W
Crater Lake [St.Vin.] ≈	197n	Ba	13.19N	61.11W
Crateús	200	Lf	5.10S	40.40W
Crati ∿	128	Kk	39.43N	16.31 E
Crato [Braz.]	202	Ke	7.14S	39.23W
Crato [Port.]	126	Ee	39.17N	7.39W
Crau ▭	122	Kk	43.36N	4.50 E
Crauford, Cape - ▶	180	Jb	73.44N	84.51W
Cravo Norte	202	Db	6.17N	70.12W
Crawford	186	Ee	42.41N	103.25W
Crawfordsville	184	De	40.02N	86.54W
Crawley	118	Mj	51.07N	0.12W
Crazy Mountains ⛰	188	Jc	46.08N	110.20W
Crazy Peak ▲	182	Eb	46.01N	110.16W
Creciente, Isla- ✚	192	De	24.23N	111.37W
Crécy-en-Ponthieu	124	Dd	50.15N	1.53 E
Crécy-la-Chapelle	124	Ef	48.51N	2.55 E
Crécy-sur-Serre	124	Fe	49.42N	3.37 E
Crediton	118	Jk	50.47N	3.39W
Cree [Sask.-Can.] ∿	180	Ge	58.50N	105.40W
Cree [Scot.-U.K.] ∿	118	Ig	54.52N	4.20W
Creede	186	Ch	37.51N	106.56W
Creel	190	Cc	27.45N	107.38W
Cree Lake ≈	180	Ge	57.30N	106.30W
Creglingen	120	Gg	49.28N	10.02 E
Creil	122	Ie	49.16N	2.29 E
Crema	128	De	45.22N	9.41 E
Cremenea, Braţul- ∿	130	Ke	44.57N	27.54 E
Crémieu, Plateau de- ⌓	122	Li	45.40N	5.30 E
Cremona	128	Ee	45.07N	10.02 E
Crepaja	130	Dd	45.01N	20.39 E
Crepori, Rio- ∿	202	Ge	5.42S	57.08W
Crépy-en-Valois	122	Ie	49.14N	2.54 E
Cres	128	If	44.58N	14.24 E
Cres ✚	128	If	44.40N	14.25 E
Crescent	188	Ee	43.29N	121.41W
Crescent City	182	Cc	41.45N	124.12W
Crescent Lake ≈	184	Gk	29.28N	81.30W
Crespo	204	Bk	32.02S	60.19W
Crest	122	Lj	44.44N	5.02 E
Crested Butte	186	Cg	38.52N	106.59W
Creston [B.C.-Can.]	188	Gb	49.06N	116.31W
Creston [Ia.-U.S.]	182	Ic	41.04N	94.22W
Crestone Peak ▲	186	Dh	37.58N	105.36W
Crestview	182	Je	30.46N	86.34W
Creswell	184	Ih	35.52N	76.23W
Creswell Bay ◧	180	Ib	72.40N	93.30W
Creswell Creek ∿	212	Hc	18.10S	135.11 E
Crete	186	Hf	40.38N	96.58W
Crete (EN) = Kriti [2]	130	Hn	35.35N	25.00 E
Crete (EN) = Kriti ✚	110	Ih	35.15N	24.45 E
Crete, Sea of- (EN) = Kritikón Pélagos ≋	130	Hn	36.00N	25.00 E
Créteil	122	If	48.47N	2.28 E
Cretin, Cape- ▶	214	Di	6.40S	147.52 E
Creus, Cabo de-/Creus, Cap de- ▶	110	Gg	42.19N	3.19 E
Creus, Cap de-/Creus, Cabo de- ▶	110	Gg	42.19N	3.19 E
Creuse [3]	122	Hh	46.05N	2.00 E
Creuse ∿	122	Gh	47.00N	0.34 E
Creusot, Le-	122	Kh	46.48N	4.26 E
Creutzwald	122	Me	49.12N	6.41 E
Crèvecoeur-en-Auge	124	Ce	49.07N	0.01 E
Crèvecoeur-le-Grand	124	Ee	49.36N	2.05 E
Crevillent / Crevillente	126	Lf	38.15N	0.48W
Crevillente / Crevillent	126	Lf	38.15N	0.48W
Crewe	118	Kh	53.05N	2.27W
Crézancy	124	Fe	49.03N	3.30 E
Criciúma	200	Lh	28.40S	49.23W
Cricket Mountains ⛰	188	Ig	38.50N	113.00W
Crieff	118	Je	56.23N	3.52W
Criel-sur-Mer	124	Dd	50.01N	1.19 E
Criel-sur-Mer-Mesnil-Val	124	Dd	50.03N	1.20 E
Crikvenica	128	Ie	45.11N	14.42 E
Crillon	124	De	49.31N	1.56 E
Crimea (EN) = Krymski poluostrov ▶	110	Jf	45.00N	34.00 E
Crimean Mountains (EN) = Krymskije gory ⛰	110	Jg	44.45N	34.30 E
Crimmitschau	120	If	50.49N	12.23 E
Criquetot-l'Esneval	124	Ce	49.39N	0.16 E
Crissolo	128	Bf	44.42N	7.09 E
Cristal, Monts de- ⛰	170	Bb	0.30N	10.30 E
Cristal, Sierra del- ⛰	194	Jc	20.33N	75.31W
Cristalândia	202	If	10.36S	49.11W
Cristalina	202	Ig	16.45S	47.36W
Cristalino, Rio- ∿	202	Hf	12.40S	50.40W
Cristallo ▲	128	Gd	46.34N	12.12 E
Cristóbal Colón, Pico- ▲	198	Id	10.50N	73.45W
Cristuru Secuiesc	130	Ic	46.17N	25.02 E
Crişu Alb ∿	130	Ec	46.42N	21.16 E
Crişu Negru ∿	130	Ec	46.42N	21.16 E
Crişu Repede ∿	130	Dc	46.55N	20.59 E
Crixás	204	Hb	14.27S	49.58W
Crixás-Açu, Rio- ∿	202	Hf	13.19S	50.36W
Crixás Mirim, Rio- ∿	204	Ga	13.28S	50.36W
Crkvena Planina ▲	130	Fg	42.48N	22.22 E
Crna Gora ⛰	130	Eg	42.16N	21.35 E
Crna Gora ⧗	130	Ce	44.05N	19.50 E
Crna Gora = Montenegro (EN) [2]	130	Cg	42.30N	19.18 E
Crna Gora=Montenegro (EN) ▣	130	Cg	42.30N	19.18 E
Crna Reka ⧗	130	Ef	43.50N	21.55 E
Crna reka ∿	130	Eh	41.33N	21.59 E
Crni Drim ∿	130	Dg	42.05N	20.23 E
Crni Timok ∿	130	Ff	43.55N	22.18 E
Črni vrh ▲	128	Jd	46.29N	15.14 E
Crni vrh ▲	128	Kf	44.36N	16.30 E
Črnomelj	128	Je	45.34N	15.12 E
Croatia (EN) = Hrvatska	128	Jf	45.00N	15.30 E
Croatia (EN) = Hrvatska ⧗	110	Hf	45.00N	15.30 E
Croatia (EN) = Hrvatska ▣	128	Je	45.00N	15.30 E
Crocker, Banjaran- ⛰	150	Ge	5.40N	116.20 E
Crockett	186	Ik	31.19N	95.28W
Crocq	122	Ii	45.52N	2.22 E
Crocus Bay ◧	197b	Ab	18.13N	63.05W
Croisette, Cap- ▶	122	Lk	43.13N	5.20 E
Croisic, Le-	122	Dg	47.18N	2.30W
Croisic, Pointe du- ▶	122	Dg	47.17N	2.33W
Croisilles	124	Ed	50.12N	2.53 E
Croissy-sur-Celle	124	Ee	49.42N	2.11 E
Croix, Lac la- ≈	186	Jb	48.21N	92.05W
Croix-Haute, Col de la- ⌒	122	Lj	44.43N	5.40 E
Croker, Cape- ▶	212	Gb	10.58S	132.35 E
Croker Bay ◧	180	Jb	74.38N	83.15W
Croker Island ✚	212	Gb	11.10S	132.30 E
Cromarty	118	Id	57.40N	4.02W
Cromer	118	Oi	52.56N	1.18 E
Cromwell	218	Cf	45.03S	169.14 E
Crooked Island ✚	190	Jd	22.45N	74.13W
Crooked Island Passage ▬	190	Jd	22.55N	74.35W
Crooked River ∿	188	Ed	44.34N	121.16W
Crookston	182	Hb	47.47N	96.37W
Crosby [Mn.-U.S.]	186	Jc	46.28N	93.57W
Crosby [N.D.-U.S.]	186	Eb	48.55N	103.18W
Cross ∿	166	Ge	4.55N	8.15 E
Cross City	184	Fk	29.32N	83.07W
Crossett	186	Kj	33.08N	91.58W
Cross Fell ▲	118	Kg	54.42N	2.29W
Cross Lake ≈	180	Hf	54.47N	97.22W
Crossman Peak ▲	188	Hi	34.32N	114.07W
Cross River [2]	166	Gd	5.40N	8.10 E
Cross Sound ▬	178	Le	58.10N	136.30W
Crotone	128	Lk	39.05N	17.08 E
Crotto	204	Bm	36.35S	60.10W
Crouch ∿	124	Cc	51.37N	0.53 E
Crow Agency	188	Ld	45.36N	107.27W
Crowborough	124	Cc	51.03N	0.09 E
Crow Creek ∿	186	Df	40.23N	104.29W
Crowell	186	Gj	33.59N	99.43W
Crow Lake	186	Jb	49.12N	93.57W
Crowley	186	Jk	30.13N	92.22W
Crowley, Lake- ≈	188	Fh	37.37N	118.44W
Crowley Ridge ⛰	186	Ki	35.45N	90.45W
Crownpoint	186	Bi	35.42N	108.07W
Crown Prince Frederik ✚	180	Ic	70.05N	86.40W
Crowsnest Pass ⌒	180	Gg	49.00N	114.30W
Crows Nest Peak ▲	186	Ed	44.03N	103.58W
CroLdon	212	Ic	18.12S	142.14 E
Croydon, London-	118	Mj	51.23N	0.07W
Crozet, Iles- = Crozet Islands (EN) ⬡	222	Ec	46.30S	51.00 E
Crozet Basin (EN) ⌣	106	Gm	39.00S	60.00 E
Crozet Islands (EN) = Crozet, Iles- ⬡	222	Ec	46.30S	51.00 E
Crozet Ridge (EN) ⌢	106	Fn	45.00S	45.00 E
Crozon	122	Bf	48.15N	4.29W
Crozon, Presqu'île de- ▶	122	Bf	48.15N	4.25W
Crucero, Cerro- ▲	192	Gg	21.41N	104.25W
Cruces	194	Gb	22.21N	80.16W
Crump Lake ≈	188	Fe	42.17N	119.50W
Crumpton Point ▶	197g	Ba	15.35N	61.19W
Cruz, Cabo- ▶	190	Ie	19.51N	77.44W
Cruz Alta [Arg.]	204	Bk	33.01S	61.49W
Cruz Alta [Braz.]	200	Kh	28.39S	53.36W
Cruz del Eje	206	Hd	30.44S	64.48W
Cruzeiro do Oeste	206	Jb	23.46S	53.04W
Cruzeiro do Sul	200	If	7.38S	72.36W
Cruzen Island ✚	222	Mf	74.47S	140.42W
Cruz Grande	192	Ji	16.44N	99.08W
Crvanj ⛰	128	Mg	43.25N	18.11 E
Crvenka	130	Cd	45.39N	19.28 E
Crystal Brook	212	Hf	33.21S	138.13 E
Crystal City [Man.-Can.]	186	Gb	49.08N	98.57W
Crystal City [Tx.-U.S.]	186	Gl	28.41N	99.50W
Crystal Falls	184	Cb	46.06N	88.20W
Crystal Springs	186	Kk	31.59N	90.21W
Csákvár	120	Oi	47.24N	18.27 E
Cserhát ⛰	120	Pi	47.55N	19.30 E
Csongrád	120	Qj	46.42N	20.09 E
Csongrád [2]	120	Qj	46.25N	20.15 E
Csorna	120	Ni	47.37N	17.15 E
Csurgó	120	Nj	46.16N	17.06 E
Ctesiphon ⊡	146	Kf	33.05N	44.35 E
Ču	142	Je	43.33N	73.45 E
Ču ∿	140	Ie	45.00N	67.44 E
Cuajinicuilapa	192	Ji	16.28N	98.25W
Cuale ∿	170	Cd	7.40S	17.01 E
Cualiacán, Rio- ∿	192	Fe	24.31N	107.41W
Cuamba	160	Kj	14.49S	36.33 E
Cuan an Fhóid Duibh ◧	118	Dg	54.08N	10.00W
Cuan an Fhóid Duibh/Blacksod Bay ◧	118	Dg	54.08N	10.00W
Cuanavale ∿	170	Cf	15.07S	19.14 E
Cuan Bhaile Átha Cliath/Dublin Bay ◧	118	Gh	53.20N	6.06W
Cuan Chill Ala/Killala Bay ◧	118	Dg	54.15N	9.10W
Cuan Dhun Dealgan/Dundalk Bay ◧	118	Gh	53.57N	6.17W
Cuan Dhún Droma/Dundrum Bay ◧	118	Hg	54.13N	5.45W
Cuando ∿	158	Jj	18.27S	23.32 E
Cuando-Cubango [3]	170	Df	16.00S	20.30 E
Cuan Eochaille/Youghal Harbour ◧	118	Fj	51.52N	7.50W
Cuangar	170	Cf	17.36S	18.37 E
Cuango ∿	158	Ii	3.14S	17.22 E
Cuango [Ang.]	170	Cd	9.07S	18.05 E
Cuango [Ang.]	170	Cd	6.17S	16.41 E
Cuan Loch Garman/Wexford Harbour ◧	118	Gi	52.20N	6.25W
Cuan Mó/Clew Bay ◧	118	Dh	53.50N	9.50W
Cuan na Gaillimhe/Galway Bay ◧	110	Fe	53.10N	9.15W
Cuan na gCaorach/Sheep Haven ◧	118	Ff	55.10N	7.52W
Cuan Phort Láirge/Waterford Harbour ◧	118	Gi	52.10N	6.57W
Cuan Shligigh/Sligo Bay ◧	118	Eg	54.20N	8.40W
Cuanza ∿	158	Ii	9.19S	13.08 E
Cuanza Norte [3]	170	Bd	8.50S	14.30 E
Cuanza Sul [3]	170	Be	10.50S	14.50 E
Cuareim, Arroyo- ∿	204	Dj	30.12S	57.36W
Cuaró	204	Dj	30.37S	56.54W
Cuaró Grande, Arroyo- ∿	204	Dj	30.18S	57.12W
Cuarto, Rio- ∿	206	Hd	33.25S	63.02W
Cuatir ∿	170	Cf	17.01S	18.09 E
Cuatro Ciénegas de Carranza	192	Hd	26.59N	102.05W
Cuauhtémoc	190	Cc	28.25N	106.52W
Cuautitlán	192	Jh	19.40N	99.11W
Cuay Grande	204	Di	28.40S	56.17W
Cuba [1]	176	Lg	21.30N	80.00W
Cuba ✚	174	Lg	21.30N	80.00W
Cuba [Mo.-U.S.]	186	Kg	38.04N	91.24W
Cuba [N.M.-U.S.]	186	Ch	36.01N	107.04W
Cuba [Port.]	126	Ef	38.10N	7.53W
Cubabi, Cerro- ▲	192	Cb	31.42N	112.46W
Cubagua, Isla- ✚	196	Dg	10.49N	64.11W
Cubal	170	Be	13.03S	14.15 E
Cubal [Ang.] ∿	170	Be	11.19S	13.48 E
Cubal [Ang.] ∿	170	Bf	15.22S	12.39 E
Cubango ∿	158	Jj	18.53S	22.24 E
Çubuk	146	Eb	40.59N	32.05 E
Čubukulah, gora- ▲	138	Kc	66.23N	153.59 E
Cucalón, Sierra de- ⛰	126	Kd	40.59N	1.10W
Cuchi	170	Ce	14.40S	16.52 E
Cuchi ∿	158	Ij	15.28S	17.21 E
Cuchibi ∿	170	De	15.00S	20.45 E
Cuchilla Águila, Cerro- ▲	192	Ig	21.27N	101.03W
Cuchivero, Rio- ∿	196	Di	7.40N	65.57W
Cuchumatanes, Sierra de los- ⛰	194	Bf	15.35N	91.25W
Cuckfield	124	Bc	51.01N	0.08W
Cuckmere ∿	124	Cd	50.45N	0.09 E
Cucui	202	Ec	1.12N	66.50W
Cucumbi	170	Ce	10.17S	19.03 E
Cucurpe	192	Db	30.20N	110.43W
Cúcuta	200	Ie	7.54N	72.31W
Cudahy	186	Me	42.57N	87.52W
Cudalbi	130	Kd	45.47N	27.42 E
Cuddalore	142	Jh	11.45N	79.45 E
Cuddapah	148	Ff	14.28N	78.49 E
Čudovo	136	Dd	59.08N	31.41 E
Čudskoje ozero = Peipus, Lake- (EN) ≈	110	Id	58.45N	27.30 E
Cue	212	De	27.25S	117.54 E
Cuebe ∿	170	Cf	15.48S	17.30 E
Cuelei ∿	170	Cf	15.33S	17.21 E
Cuéllar	126	Hc	41.29N	4.19W
Cuemba	170	Ce	12.09S	18.07 E
Cuenca [3]	126	Ke	40.00N	2.00W
Cuenca [Ec.]	200	If	2.53S	78.59W
Cuenca [Sp.]	126	Jd	40.04N	2.08W
Cuenca, Serranía de- ⛰	110	Fg	40.10N	1.55W
Cuencamé de Ceniceros	192	He	24.53N	103.42W
Cuera/Chur	128	Dd	46.50N	9.35 E
Cuerda del Pozo, Embalse de la- ≈	126	Jc	41.51N	2.44W
Cuernavaca	176	Jh	18.55N	99.15W
Cuero	186	Hl	29.06N	97.18W
Cuevas del Almanzora	126	Kg	37.18N	1.53W
Cugir	130	Gd	45.50N	23.22 E
Cugo ∿	170	Cd	7.22S	17.06 E
Čugujev	132	Je	49.50N	36.41 E
Čugujevka	154	Mb	44.08N	133.53 E
Čuhloma	136	Ed	58.47N	42.41 E
Cuiabá	200	Kg	15.35S	56.05W
Cuiabá, Rio- ∿	198	Kg	17.05S	56.36W
Cuiabá Mirim, Rio- ∿	204	Ec	16.20S	55.55W
Cuidado, Punta- ▶	221d	Bb	27.08S	109.19W
Cuijk, Cuijk en Sint Agatha-	124	Hc	51.44N	5.52 E
Cuijk en Sint Agatha-Cuijk	124	Hc	51.44N	5.52 E
Cuilapa	194	Bf	14.17N	90.18W
Cuillin Hills ⛰	118	Gd	57.14N	6.15W
Cuilo [Afr.] ∿	158	Ii	3.22S	17.22 E
Cuilo [Ang.] ∿	170	Cd	5.52S	16.35 E
Cúil Raithin/Coleraine	118	Gf	55.08N	6.40W
Cuiluan	152	Mb	47.39N	128.34 E
Cuima	170	Ce	13.14S	15.38 E
Cuito ∿	158	Jj	18.01S	20.48 E
Cuito Cuanavale	160	Ij	15.13S	19.08 E
Cuitzeo, Lago de- ≈	192	Ih	19.55N	101.05W
Cuiuni, Rio- ∿	202	Fd	0.45S	63.07W
Cujmir	130	Fe	44.13N	22.56 E
Čujskaja oblast	136	Hg	42.30N	73.50 E
Čukotski avtonomnyj okrug [3]	138	Mc	66.00N	172.30 E
Čukotskij poluostrov = Chukchi Peninsula (EN) ▶	140	Uc	66.00N	175.00W
Čukotskoje more = Chukchi Sea (EN) ≋	224	Bd	69.00N	171.00W
Çukurca	146	Jd	37.15N	43.37 E
Çukurdağı	130	Ll	37.58N	28.44 E
Čulakkurgan	136	Gg	43.48N	69.12 E
Culan	122	Ih	46.33N	2.21 E
Cu Lao, Hon- ✚	148	Lf	10.30N	109.13 E
Culasi	150	Hd	11.26N	122.03 E
Culbertson	188	Mb	48.09N	104.31W
Culebra, Isla de- ✚	194	Od	18.19N	65.17W
Culebra, Sierra de la- ⛰	126	Fc	41.55N	6.20W
Culebra Peak ▲	186	Dh	37.06N	105.10W
Culemborg	124	Hc	51.57N	5.14 E
Culiacán Rosales	176	Ig	24.48N	107.24W
Culion	150	Hd	11.53N	120.01 E
Culion ✚	150	Gd	11.50N	119.55 E
Culiseu, Rio- ∿	202	Hf	12.14S	53.17W
Cullera	126	Le	39.10N	0.15W
Cullman	182	Je	34.11N	86.51W
Čulman	142	Od	56.52N	124.52 E
Culpeper	184	Hf	38.28N	78.01W
Culuene, Rio- ∿	198	Kg	12.56S	52.51W
Culver, Point- ▶	212	Ef	32.54S	124.43 E
Culverden	218	Ee	42.46S	172.51 E
Čulym	138	De	55.06N	80.58 E
Čulym ∿	140	Kd	57.40N	83.50 E
Čulyšman ∿	138	Df	51.20N	87.45 E
Cuma	170	Ce	12.52S	15.04 E
Cumaná	200	Jd	10.28N	64.10W
Cumanacoa	196	Eg	10.15N	63.55W
Cumaovası	130	Kk	38.15N	27.09 E
Cumbal, Volcán- ▲	202	Cc	0.57N	77.52W
Cumberland ▣	118	Kg	54.40N	2.50W
Cumberland ∿	174	Kf	37.09N	88.25W
Cumberland [B.C.-Can.]	188	Cb	49.37N	125.01W
Cumberland [Md.-U.S.]	182	Ld	39.39N	78.46W
Cumberland [Va.-U.S.]	184	Hg	37.31N	78.16W
Cumberland, Cap- ▶	219b	Cb	14.39S	166.37 E
Cumberland, Lake- ≈	184	Eg	36.57N	84.55W
Cumberland Bay ◧	197n	Ba	13.16N	61.17W
Cumberland Island ✚	184	Gj	30.51N	81.27W
Cumberland Islands ⬡	212	Jd	20.40S	149.10 E
Cumberland Lake ≈	180	Hf	54.00N	102.20W
Cumberland Peninsula ▶	174	Mc	66.50N	64.00W
Cumberland Plateau ⌓	174	Kf	36.00N	85.00W
Cumberland Sound ▬	174	Mc	65.10N	65.30W
Cumbernauld	118	Jf	55.58N	3.59W
Cumbria [3]	118	Kg	54.35N	2.45W
Cumbrian Mountains ⛰	118	Jg	54.30N	3.05W
Čumerna ▲	130	Ig	42.47N	25.58 E
Čumikan	138	If	54.42N	135.19 E
Cummins	212	Hf	34.16S	135.44 E
Cumnock	118	If	55.27N	4.16W
Cumpas	192	Eb	30.02N	109.48W
Çumra	146	Ed	37.34N	32.48 E
Čumyš ∿	138	Df	53.30N	83.10 E
Čuna ∿	140	Ld	57.42N	95.35 E
Cunagua	194	Hb	22.05N	78.20W
Cuñapirú	204	Ej	31.32S	55.35W
Cuñapirú, Arroyo- ∿	204	Ej	31.12S	55.31W
Cuñapirú, Cuchilla de- ⛰	204	Ej	31.12S	55.36W
Cunaviche, Rio- ∿	196	Ci	7.19N	67.11W
Cunderdin	212	Df	31.39S	117.15 E
Cundinamarca [3]	202	Db	5.00N	74.00W
Čundža	136	Hg	43.32N	79.28 E
Cunene [3]	170	Cf	16.30S	15.00 E
Cunene=Kunene (EN) ∿	158	Ij	17.20S	11.50 E
Cuneo	128	Bf	44.23N	7.32 E
Cunhinga	170	Ce	12.14S	16.48 E
Cunillera, Isla- / Sa Conillera, Illa- ✚	126	Nf	38.59N	1.12 E
Čunja ∿	140	Lc	61.30N	96.20 E
Cunnamulla	210	Fg	28.04S	145.41 E
Čunski [Russia]	138	Ee	57.23N	97.40 E
Čunski [Russia]	138	Ee	56.03N	99.48 E
Cuorgnè	128	Be	45.23N	7.39 E
Čupa	136	Db	66.17N	33.01 E
Cupar	118	Je	56.19N	3.01W
Cupica, Golfo de- ◧	202	Cb	6.35N	77.30W
Ćuprija	130	Ef	43.56N	21.22 E
Cúpula, Pico- ▲	192	De	24.47N	110.50W
Čur	114	Mh	57.11N	53.01 E
Curaçá	202	Ke	8.59S	39.54W
Curaçao ✚	198	Jd	12.11N	69.00W
Curacautín	206	Ff	38.26S	71.53W
Cura Malal, Sierra de- ⛰	204	Am	37.44S	62.16W
Curanilahue	206	Fe	37.28S	73.21W
Čurapča	138	Id	61.56N	132.18 E
Curaray, Rio- ∿	202	Dd	2.20S	74.05W
Curdimurka	210	Eg	29.30S	137.10 E
Curé	204	De	21.25S	56.25W
Cure ∿	122	Jg	47.40N	3.41 E
Curepipe	172a	Bb	20.19S	57.31 E
Curepto	206	Fe	35.05S	72.01W
Cureski prohod (Vitinja) ⌒	130	Gg	42.47N	23.45 E
Curiapo	202	Fb	8.33N	61.00W
Curicó	200	Ii	34.59S	71.14W
Curicuriari, Rio- ∿	202	Ed	0.14S	66.48W
Curitabanos	206	Jc	27.18S	50.36W
Curitiba	200	Lh	25.25S	49.15W
Curoca ∿	170	Bf	15.43S	11.55 E
Currais Novos	202	Ke	6.15S	36.31W
Curralinho	202	Id	1.48S	49.47W
Curral-Velho	162	Cf	15.59N	22.48W
Current	184	Im	25.27S	76.45W
Current River ∿	186	Kh	36.15N	90.57W
Currie	212	Ig	39.56S	143.52 E
Curtea de Argeş	130	Hd	45.08N	24.41 E
Curtici	130	Ec	46.21N	21.18 E
Curtis	186	Ff	40.38N	100.31W
Curtis Channel ▬	212	Kd	23.55S	152.05 E
Curtis Island [Austl.] ✚	212	Kd	23.40S	151.10 E
Curtis Island [Ker.Is.] ✚	208	Jh	30.35S	178.36W
Curuá, Rio- [Braz.] ∿	198	Kf	5.23S	54.22W
Curuá, Rio- [Braz.] ∿	204	Ga	13.26S	51.24W
Curuá, Rio- [Braz.] ∿	202	Gd	1.55S	55.07W
Curuçá	202	Id	0.43S	47.50W
Curuçá, Rio- ∿	202	Dd	4.27S	71.23W
Curuguaty	206	Ib	24.31S	55.42W
Curuguaty, Arroyo- ∿	204	Dg	24.06S	56.02W
Curup	150	Dg	3.28S	102.32 E
Curupira, Sierra de- ⛰	202	Fc	1.25N	64.30W
Cururupu	202	Jd	1.50S	44.52W
Curuzú Cuatiá	206	Ic	29.47S	58.03W
Curvelo	202	Jg	18.45S	44.25W
Cushing	186	Hi	35.59N	96.46W
Cushing, Mount - ▲	180	Ee	57.36N	126.51W
Cusio→Orta, Lago d'- ≈	128	Ce	45.50N	8.25 E
Čusovaja ∿	110	Ld	58.13N	56.30 E
Čusovoj	136	Fd	58.17N	57.50 E
Cusset	122	Jh	46.08N	3.28 E
Cusseta	184	Ei	32.18N	84.47W
Čust	135	Hd	41.00N	71.15 E
Custer	186	Ee	43.46N	103.36W
Cutato ∿	170	Ce	10.33S	16.48 E
Cut Bank	182	Eb	48.38N	112.20W
Cutervo	202	Ce	6.22S	78.51W
Cuthbert	184	Ej	31.46N	84.48W
Cutral Có	206	Ge	38.56S	69.14W
Cutro	128	Kk	39.02N	16.59 E
Cuttack	142	Kg	20.30N	85.50 E
Čuvašskaja respublika	136	Ed	55.30N	47.10 E
Cuvelai	170	Cf	15.40S	15.47 E
Cuvette [3]	170	Cc	0.10S	15.30 E
Cuvier Basin (EN) ⌣	212	Cd	22.00S	111.00 E
Cuvier Island ✚	218	Fb	36.25S	175.45 E
Cuvo ou Queve ∿	158	Ij	10.50S	13.47 E
Cuxhaven	120	Ec	53.53N	8.42 E
Cuya	206	Fa	19.07S	70.08W
Cuyahoga Falls	184	Ge	41.08N	81.55W
Cuyo Islands ⬡	150	Hd	11.04N	120.57 E
Cuyubini, Rio- ∿	196	Fh	8.20N	60.20W
Cuyuni, Rio- ∿	198	Ke	6.23N	58.41W
Cuyuni River ∿	198	Kf	6.23N	58.41W
Cuyutlán, Laguna- ≈	192	Gh	19.00N	104.10W
Cuzco	200	Ig	13.31S	71.59W
Cuzco [3]	202	Df	12.30S	72.30W
Cuzna ∿	126	Hf	38.04N	4.41W
Cvikov	120	Kf	50.48N	14.40 E
Čvrsnica ⛰	128	Lg	43.35N	17.35 E
Cyangugu	170	Ec	2.29S	28.54 E
Cybinka	120	Kd	52.12N	14.48 E
Cyclades (EN) = Kikládhes ⬡	110	Ih	37.00N	25.10 E
Čyjyrčyk, pereval- ⌒	135	Id	40.15N	73.20 E
Cypress Hills ⌓	174	Ie	49.40N	109.30W
Cypress Lake ≈	188	Kb	49.28N	109.29W
Cyprus (EN)=Kıbrıs/Kypros [1]	142	Ff	35.00N	33.00 E
Cyprus (EN)=Kıbrıs/Kypros ✚	140	Ff	35.00N	33.00 E
Cyprus (EN)=Kypros/Kıbrıs [1]	142	Ff	35.00N	33.00 E
Cyprus (EN)=Kypros/Kıbrıs ✚	140	Ff	35.00N	33.00 E
Cyrenaica (EN)=Barqah ⧗	158	Je	31.00N	23.00 E
Cyrenaica (EN)=Barqah ▣	164	Dc	31.00N	22.30 E
Cyrene ⊡	164	Dc	32.48N	21.59 E
Cyrus Field Bay ◧	180	Ld	62.50N	65.00W
Cysoing	124	Fd	50.34N	3.13 E
Cythera (EN)=Kithira	130	Fm	36.09N	23.00 E
Czaplinek	120	Mc	53.34N	16.14 E
Czarna [Pol.] ∿	120	Rf	50.30N	21.15 E
Czarna [Pol.] ∿	120	Pe	51.12N	19.53 E
Czarna Białostocka	120	Tc	53.18N	23.19 E
Czarna Dąbrówka	120	Nb	54.20N	17.32 E
Czarna Hańcza ∿	120	Tc	53.50N	23.47 E
Czarnków	120	Md	52.55N	16.34 E
Czchów	120	Qg	49.50N	20.39 E
Czechowice-Dziedzice	120	Og	49.54N	19.00 E
Czech Republic (EN) = Česká Republika	112	Hf	50.00N	13.00 E
Czeremcha	120	Td	52.32N	23.15 E
Czersk	120	Nc	53.48N	18.00 E
Częstochowa	112	He	50.49N	19.06 E
Częstochowa [2]	120	Pf	50.50N	19.05 E
Człopa	120	Mc	53.06N	16.08 E
Człuchów	120	Nc	53.41N	17.21 E

D

Đà, Sông- [Asia] = Black River (EN) ∿	140	Mg	20.17N	106.34 E
Da'an (Dalai)	152	Lb	45.35N	124.16 E
Dabaga	170	Gd	8.07S	35.55 E
Dabakala	166	Ed	8.22N	4.26W
Dabakala [3]	166	Ed	8.27N	4.28W
Daban→Bairin Youqi	152	Kc	43.30N	118.37 E
Dabas	120	Pi	47.11N	19.19 E
Daba Shan ⛰	140	Mf	32.15N	109.00 E
Dabat	168	Fc	12.58N	37.45 E
Dabay Sima	168	Gc	12.43N	42.17 E
Dabba/Daocheng	152	Hf	29.01N	100.26 E
Dabbāgh, Jabal- ▲	144	Ed	27.52N	35.45 E
Dabeiba	202	Cb	7.02N	76.16W
Dąbie	120	Od	52.06N	18.49 E
Dąbie, Jezioro- ≈	120	Kc	53.29N	14.40 E
Dabie Shan ⛰	140	Nf	31.15N	115.00 E
Dabl, Wādī- ∿	146	Gh	29.05N	36.14 E
Dabnou	166	Gc	14.09N	5.22 E
Dabola	166	Cc	10.45N	11.07W
Daborow	168	Hd	6.11N	48.22 E
Dabou	166	Ed	5.19N	4.23W
Dabqig→Uxin Qi	152	Id	38.27N	109.08 E
Dabrāš ⛰	130	Gh	41.40N	23.50 E
Dąbrowa Białostocka	120	Tc	53.40N	23.20 E
Dąbrowa Górnicza	120	Pf	50.20N	19.11 E
Dąbrowa Tarnowska	120	Qf	50.11N	21.00 E
Dabsan Hu ≈	152	Fd	36.58N	95.00 E
Dăbuleni	130	Hf	43.48N	24.05 E
Dabus ∿	168	Fc	10.38N	35.10 E
Dacata ∿	168	Gd	7.16N	42.15 E
Dacca → Dhaka	142	Lg	23.43N	90.25 E
Dachangzhen	154	Eh	32.13N	118.44 E
Dachau	120	Hh	48.16N	11.26 E
Dachen Dao ✚	154	Fj	28.29N	121.53 E
Dachstein ▲	128	Hc	47.30N	13.36 E
Dacia Seamount (EN) ⌢	110	Ei	31.10N	13.42W

Dac-Dea

Index Symbols

[1] Independent Nation	Historical or Cultural Region	Pass, Gap	Depression	Coast, Beach	Rock, Reef	Waterfall, Rapids	Canal	Lagoon	Escarpment, Sea Scarp	Historic Site	Airport
[2] State, Region	Mount, Mountain	Plain, Lowland	Polder	Cliff	Islands, Archipelago	River Mouth, Estuary	Glacier	Bank	Fracture	Ruins	Port
[3] District, County	Volcano	Delta	Desert, Dunes	Peninsula	Rocks, Reefs	Lake	Ice Shelf, Pack Ice	Seamount	Trench, Abyss	Wall, Walls	Military installation
[4] Municipality	Hill	Salt Flat	Forest, Woods	Isthmus	Coral Reef	Salt Lake	Ocean	Tablemount	National Park, Reserve	Church, Abbey	Lighthouse
[5] Colony, Dependency	Mountains, Mountain Range	Valley, Canyon	Heath, Steppe	Sandbank	Well, Spring	Intermittent Lake	Sea	Ridge	Point of Interest	Temple	Mine
[6] Continent	Hills, Escarpment	Crater, Cave	Oasis	Island	Geyser	Reservoir	Gulf, Bay	Shelf	Recreation Site	Scientific Station	Tunnel
[7] Physical Region	Plateau, Upland	Karst Features	Cape, Point	Atoll	River, Stream	Swamp, Pond	Strait, Fjord	Basin	Cave, Cavern	Railway station	Dam, Bridge

Death Valley	188	Gh	36.20N	116.50W
Death Valley	174	Hf	36.30N	117.00W
Deauville	122	Ge	49.22N	0.04 E
Debak	150	Ff	1.34N	111.25 E
Debalcevo	132	Ke	48.20N	38.29 E
Debao	152	Ig	23.17N	106.21 E
Debar	130	Dh	41.32N	20.32 E
Debark	168	Fc	13.08N	37.53 E
Debdou	162	Gc	33.59N	3.03W
Debed	132	Ni	41.22N	44.58 E
Deben	124	Db	52.01N	1.22 E
De Beque	186	Bg	39.20N	108.13W
Dębica	120	Rf	50.04N	21.24 E
De Bilt	124	Hb	52.06N	5.11 E
Debin	138	Kd	62.18N	150.47 E
Dęblin	120	Re	51.35N	21.50 E
Dębno	120	Kd	52.45N	14.40 E
Débo, Lac-	166	Eb	15.18N	4.09W
Deborah East, Lake-	212	Df	30.45S	119.10 E
Deborah West, Lake-	212	Df	30.45S	119.05 E
Deboyne Islands	208	Gf	10.43S	152.22 E
Debrc	130	Ce	44.37N	19.54 E
Debre Berhan	168	Fd	9.41N	39.33 E
Debrecen	112	If	47.32N	21.38 E
Debrecen (2)	120	Ri	47.31N	21.40 E
Debre Libanos	168	Fd	9.43N	38.52 E
Debre Markos	160	Kg	10.20N	37.44 E
Debre Sina	168	Fd	9.51N	39.46 E
Debre Tabor	168	Fc	11.51N	38.00 E
Debre Zeyt	160	Kh	8.47N	39.00 E
De-Buka, Glacier-	222	Nf	76.00S	131.00W
Decatur [Al.-U.S.]	182	Je	34.36N	86.59W
Decatur [Ga.-U.S.]	184	Ei	33.46N	84.18W
Decatur [Il.-U.S.]	182	Jd	39.51N	89.32W
Decatur [In.-U.S.]	184	Ee	40.50N	84.56W
Decatur [Tx.-U.S.]	186	Hj	33.14N	97.35W
Decazeville	122	Ij	44.33N	2.15 E
Deccan	140	Jh	14.00N	77.00 E
Decelles, Reservoir-	184	Hb	47.40N	78.08W
Deception Bay	212	Ia	7.07S	144.05 E
Dechang	152	Hf	27.22N	102.12 E
Děčín	120	Kf	50.47N	14.13 E
Decize	122	Jh	46.50N	3.28 E
Decorah	186	Ke	43.18N	91.48W
Deda	130	Hc	46.56N	24.54 E
Dededo	220c	Ba	13.31N	144.49 E
Dedemsvaart, Avereest-	124	Ib	52.37N	6.27 E
Dedopolis-Ckaro (Citeli-Ckaro)	132	Oi	41.28N	46.06 E
Dédougou	166	Ec	12.28N	3.28W
Dedoviči	114	Gh	57.33N	29.58 E
Dedza	170	Fe	14.22S	34.20 E
Dee [Eng.-U.K.]	118	Jh	53.19N	3.11W
Dee [Scot.-U.K.]	118	Jg	54.50N	4.03W
Dee [Scot.-U.K.]	118	Kd	57.08N	2.04W
Deep Creek Range	188	If	40.00N	113.57W
Deering	178	Gc	66.05N	162.43W
Deer Isle	184	Mc	44.13N	68.41W
Deer Lake [Newf.-Can.]	180	Lg	49.10N	57.25W
Deer Lake [Ont.-Can.]	180	If	52.40N	94.30W
Deer Lodge	188	Ic	46.25N	112.43W
Deer Park	188	Gc	47.57N	117.28W
Defiance	184	Ee	41.17N	84.21W
Defla	126	Qi	35.14N	4.26 E
De Funiak Springs	184	Dj	30.43N	86.07W
Dega Ahmedo	168	Gd	7.50N	42.53 E
Dêgê	152	Ge	31.52N	98.36 E
Degeberga	116	Fi	55.50N	14.05 E
Degeh Bur	168	Gd	8.13N	43.34 E
Degema	166	Ge	4.45N	6.46 E
Degerby	116	Id	60.02N	20.23 E
Degerfors	114	Dg	59.14N	14.26 E
Degerhamn	114	Dh	56.21N	16.24 E
Deggendorf	120	Ih	48.50N	12.58 E
Değirmendere	130	Kk	38.06N	27.09 E
De Gray Lake	186	Ji	34.15N	93.15W
De Grey River	212	Dd	20.12S	119.11 E
Degtarsk	134	Jh	56.42N	60.06 E
De Haan	124	Fc	51.16N	3.02 E
Dehaj	146	Pg	30.42N	54.53 E
Dehaq	146	Nf	32.55N	50.57 E
Deh Bārez	146	Qi	27.26N	57.12 E
Deh Bīd	146	Og	30.38N	53.13 E
Deh Dasht	146	Ng	30.47N	50.34 E
Dehdez	146	Ng	31.43N	50.17 E
Deh-e-Namak	146	Oe	35.25N	52.50 E
Deh-e Shīr	146	Og	31.29N	53.45 E
Deh-e Ziyār	146	Qg	30.40N	57.00 E
Dehgolān	146	Le	35.17N	47.25 E
Dehiwala-Mount Lavinia	148	Fg	6.50N	79.52 E
Dehlorān	146	Lf	32.41N	47.16 E
Deh Now	146	Qf	33.01N	57.41 E
Dehra Dūn	148	Fb	30.19N	78.02 E
Dehui	152	Mc	44.33N	125.38 E
Deinze	122	Jd	50.59N	3.32 E
Dej	130	Gb	47.09N	23.52 E
Deje	116	Ee	59.36N	13.28 E
Dejen	168	Fc	10.05N	38.11 E
Dejës, Mali i-	130	Dh	41.42N	20.10 E
Dejnau	136	Gh	39.18N	63.11 E
De Jongs, Tanjung-	150	Kh	6.56S	138.32 E
De Kalb	186	Lf	41.56N	88.45W
Dekar	172	Cd	21.30S	21.58 E
Dekese	160	Ji	3.27S	21.24 E
Dekina	166	Gd	7.42N	7.01 E
Dékoa	168	Bd	6.19N	19.04 E
De Koog, Texel-	124	Ga	53.07N	4.46 E
De La Garma	204	Bm	37.58S	60.25W
De Land	184	Gk	29.02N	81.18W
Delano	182	Dd	35.41N	119.15W
Delano Peak	182	Ed	38.22N	112.23W
Delārām	144	Jc	32.11N	63.25 E
Delarof Islands	178a	Cb	51.30N	178.45W
Delaware	184	Fe	40.18N	83.06W
Delaware (2)	182	Ld	39.10N	75.30W
Delaware	186	Ek	32.00N	104.00W
Delaware Bay	174	Lf	39.05N	75.15W
Delaware River	182	Ld	39.20N	75.25W
Delbrück	124	Kc	51.46N	8.34 E
Del Carril	204	Cl	35.31S	59.30W
Delčevo	130	Fh	41.58N	22.47 E
Del City	186	Hi	35.27N	97.27W
Delegate	212	Jg	37.03S	148.58 E
Delémont/Delsberg	128	Bc	47.22N	7.21 E
Delet/Teili	116	Id	60.15N	20.35 E
Delfinópolis	204	Ie	20.20S	46.51W
Delft	122	Kb	52.00N	4.21 E
Delfzijl	122	Ma	53.19N	6.56 E
Delgada, Punta-	198	Jj	42.46S	63.38W
Delgado, Cabo- = Delgado, Cape-(EN) (3)	172	Fb	12.30S	39.00 E
Delgado, Cabo- = Delgado, Cape-(EN)	158	Lj	10.40S	40.38 E
Delgado, Cape-(EN) = Delgado, Cabo- (3)	172	Fb	12.30S	39.00 E
Delgado, Cape-(EN) = Delgado, Cabo-	158	Lj	10.40S	40.38 E
Delger Muren	152	Hb	49.17N	100.40 E
Delhi [Co.-U.S.]	186	Eh	37.42N	103.58W
Delhi [India]	148	Jg	28.40N	77.13 E
Delhi [N.Y.-U.S.]	184	Jd	42.17N	74.57W
Deliblatska Peščara	130	Dd	45.00N	21.00 E
Delice	146	Fc	39.58N	34.02 E
Delicermak	146	Fb	40.28N	34.10 E
Delicias [Cuba]	194	Ic	21.11N	76.34W
Delicias [Mex.]	190	Cc	28.13N	105.28W
Delījān	146	Nf	33.59N	50.40 E
Delingha	152	Gd	37.26N	97.25 E
Dēliņkalns/Delinkalns, gora-	116	Lg	57.30N	27.02 E
Delinkalns, gora-/Dēliņkalns	116	Lg	57.30N	27.02 E
Delitzsch	120	Ie	51.32N	12.21 E
Deljatin	130	Ha	48.29N	24.45 E
Delle	122	Mg	47.30N	7.00 E
Dell Rapids	186	He	43.50N	96.43W
Dellys	162	Hb	36.55N	3.55 E
Delmarva Peninsula	174	Lf	38.50N	75.30W
Delme	124	If	48.53N	6.24 E
Delme	124	Ka	53.05N	8.40 E
Delmenhorst	120	Ec	53.03N	8.37 E
Delnice	128	Ie	45.24N	14.48 E
Delo	168	Fd	5.49N	37.57 E
De-Longa, ostrova- = De Long Islands (EN)	140	Rb	76.30N	153.00 E
De Long Islands (EN) = De-Longa, ostrova-	140	Rb	76.30N	153.00 E
De Long Mountains	178	Gc	68.20N	162.00W
De Long Strait (EN) = Longa, proliv-	140	Tb	70.20N	178.00 E
Deloraine	212	Jh	41.31S	146.39 E
Delorme, Lac-	180	Kf	54.35N	69.55W
Delphi (EN) = Dhelfoi	130	Fk	38.29N	22.30 E
Del Rio	182	Gf	29.22N	100.54W
Delsberg/Delémont	128	Bc	47.22N	7.21 E
Delsbo	114	Dc	61.48N	16.35 E
Delta [Co.-U.S.]	186	Fd	38.44N	108.04W
Delta [Ut.-U.S.]	182	Ed	39.21N	112.35W
Delta Amacuro (2)	202	Fb	8.30N	61.30W
Delta Junction	178	Jd	64.02N	145.41W
Delvāda	148	Ed	20.46N	71.02 E
Del Valle	204	Bl	35.54S	60.43W
Delvina	130	Dj	39.57N	20.06 E
Dēma	134	Gi	54.42N	55.58 E
Demanda, Sierra de la-	126	Ib	42.15N	3.05W
Demba	170	Dd	5.30S	22.16 E
Dembi	168	Fd	8.05N	36.28 E
Dembia	168	Cd	5.07N	24.25 E
Dembi Dolo	168	Ed	8.32N	34.49 E
Demer	122	Kd	50.58N	4.45 E
Demerara Plateau (EN)	198	Le	4.30N	44.00W
Demerara River	202	Gb	6.48N	58.10W
Demidov	132	Gb	55.15N	31.29 E
Demidovka	120	Vf	50.20N	25.27 E
Deming	182	Fe	32.16N	107.45W
Demini, Rio-	202	Fd	0.46S	62.56W
Demirci	146	Cc	39.03N	28.40 E
Demir Kapija	130	Fh	41.25N	22.15 E
Demirköy	130	Kh	41.49N	27.15 E
Demirtaş	130	Mi	40.16N	29.06 E
Demjanka	136	Gd	59.34N	69.20 E
Demjansk	114	Hh	57.38N	32.29 E
Demjanskoje	136	Gd	59.36N	69.18 E
Demmin	120	Jc	53.54N	13.02 E
Demopolis	184	Di	32.31N	87.50W
Dempo, Gunung-	140	Mj	4.02S	103.09 E
Demta	150	Lg	2.20S	140.08 E
Denain	122	Jd	50.20N	3.23 E
Denan	168	Gd	6.30N	43.30 E
Denau	136	Gh	38.18N	67.55 E
Den Bosch/'s-Hertogenbosch	122	Lc	51.41N	5.19 E
Den Burg, Texel-	124	Ga	53.03N	4.47 E
Den Chai	148	Ke	17.59N	100.04 E
Dendang	150	Eg	3.05S	107.54 E
Dender/Dendre	124	Kc	51.02N	4.06 E
Dendermonde/Termonde	124	Gc	51.02N	4.07 E
Dendre/Dender	124	Kc	51.02N	4.06 E
Dendtler Island	222	Pf	72.58S	89.57W
Denekamp	124	Jb	52.23N	7.00 E
Deneżkin Kamen, gora-	134	Fc	60.25N	59.31 E
Dengarh	148	Hd	23.50N	81.42 E
Dêngkagoin → Têwo	152	He	34.03N	103.21 E
Dengkou (Bayan Gol)	142	Me	40.25N	106.59 E
Dêngqên	152	Ge	31.29N	95.32 E
Dengzhou → Penglai	152	Ld	37.44N	120.45 E
Den Haag/'s-Gravenhage = The Hague (EN)	112	Ge	52.06N	4.18 E
Den Ham	124	Ib	52.28N	6.32 E
Denham → Shark Bay	212	Ce	25.55S	113.32 E
Denham, Mount-	194	Id	18.13N	77.32W
Denham Range	212	Jd	21.55S	147.45 E
Denham Sound	212	Ce	25.40S	113.15 E
Den Helder	122	Kb	52.54N	4.45 E
Denia / Denia	126	Mf	38.51N	0.07 E
Dénia / Denia	126	Mf	38.51N	0.07 E
Deniliquin	212	Ig	35.32S	144.58 E
Denio	188	Ff	41.59N	118.39W
Denis Island	172b	Ca	3.48S	55.40 E
Denison [Ia.-U.S.]	182	Hc	42.01N	95.20W
Denison [Tx.-U.S.]	182	He	33.45N	96.33W
Denison, Mount-	178	Ie	58.25N	154.27W
Denizli	144	Cb	37.46N	29.06 E
Denklingen, Reichshof-	124	Jd	50.55N	7.39 E
Denman Glacier	222	Ge	66.45S	99.25 E
Denmark [Austl.]	212	Df	34.57S	117.21 E
Denmark [S.C.-U.S.]	184	Gi	33.19N	81.09W
Denmark (EN) = Danmark (1)	112	Gd	56.00N	10.00 E
Denmark Strait (EN) = Danmarksstrædet	110	Dc	67.00N	25.00W
Dennery	197k	Bb	13.55N	60.54W
Den Oever, Wieringen-	124	Hb	52.56N	5.02 E
Denpasar	142	Nj	8.39S	115.13 E
Denton	182	He	33.13N	97.08W
D'Entrecasteaux, Point-	212	Df	34.50S	116.00 E
D'Entrecasteaux Islands	208	Ge	9.35S	150.40 E
D'Entrecasteaux Reefs (EN) = Entrecasteaux, Récifs d'-	208	Hf	18.20S	163.00 E
Denver	176	If	39.43N	105.01W
Deoghar	148	Hd	24.29N	86.42 E
Deolāli	148	Ee	19.54N	73.50 E
De Panne/La Panne	124	Ec	51.06N	2.35 E
Dependencias Federales (2)	202	Fa	11.45N	64.25W
De Pere	186	Ld	44.27N	88.04W
Deputatski	138	Ic	69.13N	139.55 E
Dêqên	152	Gf	28.32N	98.50 E
Deqing	152	Jg	23.14N	111.42 E
De Queen	186	Ii	34.02N	94.21W
De Quincy	186	Jk	30.27N	93.26W
Dequing	154	Fi	30.34N	120.05 E
Dera, Lach-	168	Ge	0.15N	42.17 E
Dera, Lagh-	158	Lh	0.15N	42.17 E
Dera Bugti	148	Dc	29.02N	69.09 E
Dera Ghāzi Khan	142	Jf	30.03N	70.38 E
Dera Ismāil Khan	148	Eb	31.50N	70.54 E
Derbent [Russia]	112	Kg	42.00N	48.18 E
Derbent [Turk.]	130	Lk	38.11N	28.33 E
Derby	118	Lh	53.05N	1.40W
Derby [Austl.]	210	Df	17.18S	123.38 E
Derby [Eng.-U.K.]	118	Li	52.55N	1.30W
Derby [Ks.-U.S.]	186	Hh	37.33N	97.16W
Derbyshire (3)	118	Lh	53.10N	1.35W
Đerdap	130	Fe	44.41N	22.10 E
Derecske	120	Ri	47.21N	21.34 E
Dereköy	130	Kh	41.56N	27.21 E
Dereli	146	Hb	40.45N	38.27 E
Derg/Abhainn na Deirge	118	Fg	54.40N	7.25W
Derg, Lough-/Loch Deirgeirt	118	Ei	53.00N	8.20W
Dergači [Russia]	132	Pd	51.13N	48.46 E
Dergači [Ukr.]	132	Jd	50.09N	36.09 E
Der Grabow	120	Ib	54.23N	12.50 E
De Ridder	186	Jk	30.51N	93.17W
Derik	146	Id	37.22N	40.17 E
Derkul	132	Qd	51.17N	51.15 E
Dermott	186	Kj	33.32N	91.26W
Dernieres, Isles-	186	Kl	29.02N	90.47W
Derong	152	Gf	28.44N	99.18 E
De Rose Hill	212	Ge	26.25S	133.15 E
Déroute, Passage de la-	122	Ee	49.12N	1.51W
Derry / Londonderry	112	Fd	55.00N	7.19W
Dersa, Eglab-	162	Gd	26.45N	4.26W
Dersca	130	Jb	47.59N	26.12 E
Dersingham	124	Cb	52.51N	0.30 E
Derudeb	168	Fb	17.32N	36.06 E
Derventa	128	Lf	44.59N	17.55 E
Derwent [Eng.-U.K.]	118	Mg	53.42N	0.40W
Derwent [Eng.-U.K.]	124	Ab	52.53N	1.17W
Derwent River	212	Jh	43.03S	147.22 E
Deržavinsk	136	Ge	51.03N	66.19 E
Desaguadero, Rio-	198	Ji	34.13S	66.47W
Désappointement, Iles du-	208	Mf	14.10S	141.20W
Des Arc	186	Ki	34.58N	91.30W
Desborough	124	Bb	52.26N	0.49W
Descalvado	204	Ie	21.54S	47.37W
Descartes	122	Gh	46.58N	0.45 E
Deschambault Lake	180	Hf	54.50N	103.30W
Deschutes River	182	Cb	45.38N	120.54W
Descoberto, Rio-	204	Hc	16.20S	48.19W
Dese	160	Kg	11.07N	39.38 E
Deseado, Rio-	198	Jj	47.45S	65.54W
Desecheo, Isla-	197a	Ab	18.25N	67.28W
Desengaño, Punta-	206	Gg	49.15S	67.37W
Desenzano del Garda	128	Ee	45.28N	10.32 E
Desertas, Ilhas-	162	Dc	32.30N	16.30W
Desert Center	188	Hj	33.42N	115.26W
Desert Peak	188	If	40.28N	112.38W
Deshaies	197e	Ab	16.18N	61.47W
Desiderio, Rio-	204	Ja	12.20S	44.50W
Desmaraisville	184	Ia	49.31N	76.10W
De Smet	186	Hd	44.23N	97.33W
Desmochado	204	Ch	27.07S	58.06W
Des Moines	174	Je	40.22N	91.26W
Des Moines [Ia.-U.S.]	176	Je	41.35N	93.37W
Des Moines [N.M.-U.S.]	186	Eh	36.46N	103.50W
Desmoronado, Cerro-	190	Dd	20.21N	105.01W
Desna	110	Je	50.33N	30.32 E
Desnățui	130	Ge	43.53N	23.35 E
Des Noeuf, Ile-	172b	Bb	6.14S	53.03 E
Desolación, Isla-	198	Ik	53.00S	74.10W
De Soto	186	Kg	38.08N	90.33W
Despeñaperros, Desfiladero de-	126	If	38.24N	3.30W
Des Roches, Ile-	172b	Bb	5.41S	53.41 E
Dessau	120	Ie	51.50N	12.15 E
Destruction Bay	180	Dd	61.20N	139.00W
Desvres	122	Hd	50.40N	1.50 E
Deta	130	Ed	45.24N	21.14 E
Dete	172	Dc	18.37S	26.51 E
Detmold	120	Ee	51.56N	8.53 E
Detour, Point-	184	Dc	45.36N	86.37W
Detroit [Mi.-U.S.]	176	Ke	42.20N	83.03W
Detroit [Or.-U.S.]	188	Dd	44.42N	122.10W
Detroit Lakes	186	Ic	46.49N	95.51W
Dettifoss	114a	Cb	65.49N	16.24W
Detva	120	Ph	48.34N	19.25 E
Deûle	124	Ed	50.44N	2.56 E
Deurdeur	126	Oh	36.14N	2.16 E
Deurne	124	Hc	51.28N	5.48 E
Deutsche Bucht	120	Db	54.30N	7.30 E
Deutsche Demokratische Republik = Germany	112	Ge	51.00N	10.00 E
Deutschlandsberg	128	Jd	46.49N	15.13 E
Deux-Bassins, Col des-	126	Ph	36.27N	3.18 E
Deux-Sevres (3)	122	Fh	46.30N	0.15W
Deva	130	Fd	45.53N	22.54 E
Dévaványa	120	Qi	47.02N	20.58 E
Deveci Dağları	146	Gb	40.05N	36.00 E
Devecser	120	Ni	47.06N	17.26 E
Develi	146	Fc	38.22N	35.06 E
Deventer	122	Mb	52.15N	6.10 E
Deverd, Cap-	219b	Be	20.46S	164.22 E
Deveron	118	Kd	57.40N	2.30W
Devès, Monts du-	122	Jj	44.57N	3.46 E
Devetak	128	Mg	43.58N	19.00 E
Devil River Peak	218	Ed	40.58S	172.39 E
Devil's Hole	118	Ne	56.38N	0.40 E
Devil's Island (EN) = Diable, Ile du-	202	Hb	5.17N	52.35W
Devils Lake	182	Hb	48.07N	98.59W
Devils Lake	186	Gb	48.01N	98.52W
Devils Paw	178	Me	58.44N	133.50W
Devils River	186	Fl	29.39N	100.58W
Devils Tower	188	Md	44.31N	104.57W
Devin	130	Hh	41.45N	24.24 E
Devizes	118	Lj	51.22N	1.59W
Devnja	130	Kf	43.13N	27.33 E
Devodi Munda	148	Ge	17.37N	82.57 E
De Volet Point	197n	Ba	13.22N	61.13W
Devolli	130	Di	40.30N	20.50 E
Devolli	130	Ci	40.49N	19.51 E
Dévoluy	122	Lj	44.39N	5.53 E
Devon (3)	118	Jk	50.50N	3.50W
Devon	118	Jk	50.50N	4.00W
Devon	174	Kb	75.00N	87.00W
Devon	124	Ba	53.04N	0.49W
Devonport	210	Fi	41.11S	146.21 E
Devoto	204	Aj	31.24S	62.19W
Devrek	146	Db	41.13N	31.57 E
Devrez	146	Ff	41.06N	34.25 E
Dewa	158	Lh	4.11N	42.06 E
Dewar Lakes	180	Kc	68.00N	73.00W
Dewās	148	Fd	22.58N	76.04 E
Dewa-Sanchi	156	Gb	39.30N	140.15 E
Dewey	186	Ih	36.48N	95.56W
De Witt	186	Ki	34.18N	91.20W
Dexemhare	168	Fb	15.04N	39.03 E
Dexing	154	Dj	28.55N	117.33 E
Dexter	186	Lh	36.48N	89.57W
Deyang	152	He	31.07N	104.25 E
Dey-Dey, Lake-	212	Ge	29.15S	131.05 E
Deyhūk	146	Qf	33.17N	57.30 E
Deyyer	144	Hd	27.50N	51.55 E
Dez	146	Mg	31.39N	48.52 E
Dezfūl	142	Gf	32.23N	48.24 E
Dez Gerd	146	Ng	30.45N	51.57 E
Dezhou	152	Kd	37.28N	116.18 E
Dežneva, mys-	140	Uc	66.06N	169.45W
Dháfni	130	Fl	37.46N	22.02 E
Dhahab	164	Fd	28.29N	34.32 E
Dhaka (Dacca)	142	Lg	23.43N	90.25 E
Dhamār	144	Fg	14.37N	44.23 E
Dhamtari	148	Gd	20.41N	81.34 E
Dhānbād	148	Hd	23.48N	86.27 E
Dhanghar	148	Gc	28.42N	80.36 E
Dhanushkodi	148	Fg	9.11N	79.24 E
Dhaulagiri	140	Kg	28.44N	83.25 E
Dhekeleia	146	Ee	35.03N	33.40 E
Dhelfoi = Delphi (EN)	130	Fk	38.29N	22.30 E
Dhelvinákion	130	Dj	39.56N	20.28 E
Dhenkanal	148	Hd	20.40N	85.36 E
Dheskáti	130	Ej	39.55N	21.49 E
Dhespotikó	130	Hm	36.58N	25.00 E
Dhiapóndioi Nisoi	130	Cj	39.50N	19.25 E
Dhībān	146	Fg	31.30N	35.47 E
Dhidhimótikhon	130	Jh	41.21N	26.30 E
Dhikti Óros	130	In	35.15N	25.30 E
Dhílos	130	Il	37.24N	25.16 E
Dhimitsána	130	Fl	37.36N	22.03 E
Dhionisiádhes, Nisoi-	130	Jn	35.21N	26.10 E
Dhiórix Potidhaia	130	Gi	40.10N	23.20 E
Dhī-Qār (3)	146	Lg	31.10N	46.10 E
Dhírfis Óros	130	Gk	38.38N	23.50 E
Dhísoron Óros	130	Fh	41.11N	22.57 E
Dhivouniá	130	Jn	35.50N	26.28 E
Dhodhekánisos = Dodecanese (EN)	130	Jm	36.20N	27.00 E
Dhodhóni = Dodona (EN)	130	Dj	39.33N	20.46 E
Dholpur	148	Fc	26.42N	77.54 E
Dhomokós	130	Fj	39.08N	22.18 E
Dhone	148	Fe	15.25N	77.53 E
Dhonousa	130	Il	37.10N	25.50 E
Dhoráji	148	Ed	21.44N	70.27 E
Dhoxáton	130	Hh	41.06N	24.14 E
Dhragónisos	130	Il	37.27N	25.29 E
Dhuburi	148	Hc	26.02N	89.58 E
Dhule	142	Jg	20.54N	74.47 E
Dhuliān	148	Hd	24.41N	87.58 E
Dia	130	In	35.27N	25.13 E
Diable, Ile du- = Devil's Island (EN)	202	Hb	5.17N	52.35W
Diable, Morne au-	197g	Ba	15.37N	61.27W
Diable, Pointe du- [Mart.]	197h	Bb	14.47N	60.54W
Diable, Pointe du- [Van.]	219b	Dc	16.01S	168.12 E
Diablo, Punta del-	204	Fl	34.22S	53.46W
Diablo, Puntan-	220b	Ba	15.00N	145.34 E
Diablo Range	188	Eh	36.45N	121.20W
Diafarabé	166	Ec	14.10N	5.00W
Dialafara	166	Cc	13.27N	11.23W
Diamant, Pointe du-	197h	Ac	14.27N	61.04W
Diamant, Rocher du-	197h	Ac	14.27N	61.03W
Diamante [Arg.]	206	Hd	32.04S	60.39W
Diamante [It.]	128	Jk	39.41N	15.49 E
Diamante, Punta del-	192	Ji	16.47N	99.52W
Diamantina	202	Jg	18.15S	43.36W
Diamantina, Chapada-	198	Lg	11.30S	41.10W
Diamantina, Rio-	204	Fc	16.42S	52.45W
Diamantina Depth (EN)	106	Hm	33.30S	102.00 E
Diamantina Lakes	212	Id	23.46S	141.09 E
Diamantina River	208	Eg	26.45S	139.10 E
Diamantina Trench (EN)	106	Hm	36.00S	104.00 E
Diamantino	200	Kg	14.25S	56.27W
Diamantino, Rio-	204	Fc	16.08S	52.28W
Diamond Harbour	148	Hd	22.12N	88.12 E
Diamond Island	197p	Bb	12.20N	61.35W
Diamond Jenness Peninsula	180	Fb	71.00N	117.00W
Diamond Peak [Nv.-U.S.]	188	Hg	39.40N	115.48W
Diamond Peak [Or.-U.S.]	188	De	43.33N	122.09W
Diamond Peak [U.S.]	188	Id	44.09N	113.05W
Diamond Peak [U.S.]	188	Gc	46.07N	117.32W
Diamou	166	Cc	14.05N	11.16W
Diana, Baie-	180	Kd	61.00N	70.00W
Dianbai	152	Jg	21.33N	110.58 E
Dianbu → Feidong	154	Di	31.53N	117.29 E
Diancang Shan	152	Hf	25.42N	100.02 E
Dian Chi	152	Hg	24.50N	102.45 E
Diane, Étang de-	122a	Ba	42.07N	9.32 E
Dianjiang	152	Ie	30.19N	107.25 E
Diano Marina	128	Cg	43.54N	8.05 E
Dianópolis	202	If	11.38S	46.50W
Dianra	166	Dd	8.45N	6.18W
Diapaga	166	Fc	12.04N	1.47 E
Diaz	204	Bk	32.22S	61.05W
Dibā	144	Id	25.39N	56.15 E
Dibā, Dawḩat-	146	Qk	25.38N	56.18 E
Dībagah	146	Je	35.52N	43.49 E
Dibang	148	Jc	27.50N	95.32 E
Dibaya	170	Dd	6.30S	22.57 E
Dibaya-Lubue	170	Cc	4.09S	19.52 E
Dibella	166	Hb	17.31N	12.59 E
Dibrugarh	142	Lg	27.29N	94.54 E
Dibs	146	Ke	35.40N	44.04 E
Dibsī Afnān	146	Ee	35.55N	38.16 E
Dickens	186	Fj	33.37N	100.50W
Dickinson	182	Gb	46.53N	102.47W
Dickins Seamount (EN)	178	Lf	54.30N	137.00W
Dickson	184	Dg	36.05N	87.23W
Dicle	146	Ic	38.22N	40.04 E
Dicle = Tigris (EN)	140	Gf	31.00N	47.25 E
Didam	124	Ic	51.56N	6.09 E
Didao	154	Kb	45.22N	130.48 E
Didcot	124	Ac	51.36N	1.15W
Didesa	168	Fd	9.30N	35.32 E
Didiéni	166	Dc	13.23N	8.05W
Didyma	130	Kl	37.21N	27.13 E
Die	122	Lj	44.45N	5.22 E
Dieburg	120	Eg	49.54N	8.51 E
Diecinueve de Abril	204	El	34.22S	54.04W
Dieciocho de Julio	204	Fk	33.41S	53.33W
Diefenbaker Lake	180	Gf	51.00N	107.00W
Diège	122	Ii	45.36N	2.16 E
Diego Garcia	140	Jj	6.20S	72.20 E
Diego Ramírez, Islas-	206	Hi	56.30S	68.44W
Diekirch	122	Me	49.53N	6.10 E
Die Lewitz	120	Hc	53.30N	11.30 E
Diéma	166	Dc	14.33N	9.11W
Diemel	120	Fe	51.39N	9.27 E
Diemelsee	124	Kc	51.19N	8.43 E
Diemelstadt	124	Lc	51.27N	9.01 E
Dien Bien Phu	148	Kd	21.23N	103.01 E
Diepenbeek	124	Hd	50.54N	5.24 E
Diepholz	120	Ed	52.36N	8.22 E
Dieppe	122	He	49.56N	1.05 E
Dieppe Bay Town	197c	Ab	17.25N	62.48W
Dierdorf	124	Jd	50.33N	7.40 E
Dieren, Rheden-	124	Ib	52.03N	6.08 E
Di'er Songhua Jiang	152	Lc	45.26N	124.39 E
Diest	124	Hd	50.59N	5.03 E
Dieulefit	122	Lj	44.31N	5.04 E
Dieulouard	124	If	48.51N	6.04 E
Dieuze	122	Mf	48.49N	6.43 E
Dievenišķes	116	Kj	54.10N	25.44 E
Die Ville	124	Id	50.40N	6.55 E
Diez	124	Kd	50.22N	8.01 E
Dif	170	Hb	0.59N	40.57 E
Diffa	166	Hc	13.19N	12.37 E
Diffa (2)	166	Hb	16.00N	13.30 E
Differdange/Differdingen	122	Le	49.32N	5.52 E
Differdingen/Differdange	122	Le	49.32N	5.52 E
Difuntos, Laguna de los- → Negra, Laguna-	204	Fl	34.03S	53.40W
Digby	180	Kh	44.40N	65.50W
Dighton	186	Fg	38.29N	100.28W
Digne	122	Mj	44.06N	6.14 E
Digoin	122	Jh	46.29N	3.59 E
Digora	132	Nh	43.07N	44.06 E
Digos	150	Ie	6.45N	125.20 E
Digranes	114a	Ca	66.02N	14.45W
Digul	150	Kh	7.05S	138.42 E
Dihāng	148	Jc	27.48N	95.30 E
Dijar	132	Tf	46.33N	56.05 E
Dijlah = Tigris (EN)	140	Gf	31.00N	47.25 E
Dijle	122	Kd	50.53N	4.42 E
Dijon	112	Gf	47.19N	5.01 E
Dik	168	Bd	9.58N	17.31 E
Dikanäs	114	Dd	65.14N	16.00 E
Dikhil	168	Gc	11.06N	42.22 E
Dikili	146	Bc	39.04N	26.53 E
Dikli	116	Kg	57.30N	25.00 E
Diksmuide/Dixmude	122	Ic	51.02N	2.52 E
Dikson	142	Kb	73.30N	80.35 E
Dikwa	166	Hc	12.02N	13.55 E

Dila 168 Fd 6.23N 38.19 E
Dilbeek 124 Gd 50.51N 4.16 E
Dili 142 Oj 8.33S 125.34 E
Di Linh 148 Lf 11.35N 108.04 E
Diližan 132 Ni 40.46N 44.55 E
Dilj 128 Me 45.16N 18.01 E
Dill 124 Kd 50.33N 8.29 E
Dillenburg 120 Ef 50.44N 8.17 E
Dillia 158 Ig 14.09N 12.50 E
Dilling 160 Jg 12.03N 29.39 E
Dillingen (Saar) 124 Ie 49.21N 6.44 E
Dillingham 176 Dd 59.02N 158.29W
Dillon [Mt.-U.S.] 182 Eb 45.13N 112.38W
Dillon [S.C.-U.S.] 184 Hh 34.25N 79.22W
Dilly 166 Dc 14.57N 7.43W
Dilolo 160 Jj 10.42S 22.20 E
Dilsen 124 Hc 51.02N 5.44 E
Dimashq=Damascus (EN) 142 Ff 33.30N 36.15 E
Dimbelenge 170 Dd 5.30S 23.53 E
Dimbokro 166 Ed 6.39N 4.42W
Dimbokro [3] 166 Ed 6.50N 4.45W
Dimboola 212 Ig 36.27S 142.02 E
Dîmboviţa [2] 130 Ie 44.55N 25.30 E
Dîmboviţa 130 Je 44.14N 26.27 E
Dimbovnic 130 Ie 44.20N 25.40 E
Dimitrovgrad [Bul.] 130 Ig 42.03N 25.36 E
Dimitrovgrad [Russia] 136 Ee 54.14N 49.42 E
Dimitrovrad [Yugo.] 130 Fg 43.01N 22.47 E
Dimmitt 186 Ei 34.33N 102.19W
Dimona 146 Fg 31.04N 35.02 E
Dimovo 130 Ff 43.44N 22.44 E
Dinagat 150 Id 10.12N 125.35 E
Dinājpur 148 Hc 25.38N 88.38 E
Dinan 122 Df 48.27N 2.02W
Dinangourou 166 Ec 14.27N 2.14W
Dinant 122 Kd 50.16N 4.55 E
Dinar 146 Dc 38.04N 30.10 E
Dinar, Kūh-e- 146 Ng 30.50N 51.35 E
Dinara 128 Kf 44.04N 16.23 E
Dinara=Dinaric Alps (EN) 110 Hg 43.50N 16.35 E
Dinard 122 Df 48.38N 2.04W
Dinaric Alps (EN)= Dinara 110 Hg 43.50N 16.35 E
Dindar, Nahr ad- 168 Ec 14.06N 33.40 E
Dinder 168 Ec 14.06N 33.40 E
Dindigul 148 Ff 10.21N 77.57 E
Dindima 166 Hc 10.14N 10.09 E
Dinga 170 Cd 5.19S 16.34 E
Dingbian 152 Id 37.35N 107.37 E
Dingden, Hamminkeln- 124 Ic 51.46N 6.37 E
Dinggyê 152 Ef 28.25N 87.45 E
Dinghai 152 Le 30.05N 122.07 E
Dingle 116 Df 58.32N 11.34 E
Dingle/An Daingean 118 Ci 52.08N 10.15W
Dingle Bay/Bá an Daingin 118 Ci 52.05N 10.15W
Dingolfing 120 Ih 48.38N 12.30 E
Dingshuzhen 154 Ei 31.16N 119.50 E
Dingtao 154 Cg 35.04N 115.35 E
Dinguiraye 166 Cc 11.18N 10.43W
Dingwall 118 Id 57.35N 4.26W
Dingxi 152 Hd 35.33N 104.32 E
Dingxian 152 Jd 39.29N 115.00 E
Dingxiang 154 Be 38.32N 112.59 E
Dingxing 152 Kd 39.11N 115.48 E
Dingyuan 154 Dh 32.32N 117.41 E
Dingzi Gang 154 Ff 36.33N 120.59 E
Dinh, Mui- 140 Mh 11.22N 109.01 E
Dinkel 124 Ib 52.30N 6.58 E
Dinosaur 186 Bf 40.15N 109.01W
Dinskaja 132 Kg 45.09N 39.12 E
Dinslaken 124 Ic 51.34N 6.44 E
Dinsôr 168 Ge 2.23N 42.58 E
Dintel 124 Gc 51.39N 4.24 E
Dinuba 188 Fh 36.36N 119.27W
Dinwiddie 188 Ig 37.05N 77.35W
Dioïla 166 Dc 12.28N 6.47W
Diois, Massif du- 122 Lj 44.35N 5.20 E
Diomede Islands 178 Fc 65.53N 169.00W
Dion 166 Dc 10.12N 8.39W
Diorama 204 Gc 16.21S 51.14W
Dios 219a Ba 5.33S 154.58 E
Diosig 130 Eb 47.18N 22.00 E
Dioura 166 Dc 14.51N 5.15W
Diourbel 166 Bc 14.40N 16.15W
Diourbel [3] 166 Bc 14.45N 16.10W
Dipkarpas 146 Fe 35.36N 34.23 E
Dipolog 142 Oi 8.35N 123.20 E
Dīr 148 Ea 35.12N 71.53 E
Dira, Djebel- 126 Ph 36.05N 3.38 E
Diré 166 Eb 16.15N 3.24W
Dire Dawa 160 Lh 9.35N 41.53 E
Diriamba 194 Dh 11.51N 86.14W
Dirico 170 Df 17.58S 20.45 E
Dirj 164 Bc 30.09N 10.26 E
Dirk Hartog Island 212 Ce 25.45S 113.00 E
Dirkou 166 Hb 19.01N 12.53 E
Dirranbandi 210 Fg 28.35S 148.14 E
Dirty Devil River 188 Jh 37.53N 110.24W
Disappointment, Cape- [B.A.T.] 206 Mh 54.53S 36.07W
Disappointment, Cape- [U.S.] 188 Cc 46.18N 124.03W
Disappointment, Lake- 208 Dg 23.30S 122.50 E
Discovery Tablemount (EN) 158 Hm 42.00S 0.10 E
Dishna 164 Fd 26.07N 32.28 E
Disko Bay (EN)=Disko Bugt 224 Nc 69.15N 52.30W
Disko Bugt=Disko Bay (EN) 224 Nc 69.15N 52.30W
Diskofjord 179 Ge 69.39N 53.45W
Disko Ø 224 Nc 69.50N 53.30W
Disna 114 Gi 55.33N 28.12 E
Disna 114 Gi 55.34N 28.12 E
Disnaj, ozero- / Dysnų ežeras 114 Gi 55.35N 26.32 E
Dispur 148 Ic 26.07N 91.48 E
Diss 124 Db 52.23N 1.07 E
District of Columbia, [2] 182 Ld 38.54N 77.01W
Distrito Federal [Braz.] [2] 202 Ig 15.45S 47.45W
Distrito Federal [Mex.] [2] 190 Ee 19.15N 99.10W
Disūq 146 Dg 31.08N 30.39 E
Dithmarschen 120 Fb 54.10N 9.15 E
Diträu 130 Ic 46.49N 25.31 E
Dittaino 128 Im 37.25N 15.00 E
Diu 148 Ed 20.42N 70.59 E
Dīvāndarreh 146 Le 35.55N 47.02 E
Divénié 170 Bc 2.41S 12.05 E
Divenskaja 116 Ne 59.09N 30.09 E
Dives [Fr.] 122 Fg 47.11N 0.05W
Dives [Fr.] 122 Fe 49.19N 0.05W
Dives-sur-Mer 124 Be 49.17N 0.06W
Diviaka 130 Ci 41.00N 19.32 E
Diviči 132 Pi 42.10N 49.01 E
Divin 120 Ue 51.57N 24.09 E
Divinópolis 200 Lh 20.09S 44.54W
Divion 124 Ed 50.28N 2.30 E
Divisões ou de Santa Marta, Serra das- 202 Hg 16.40S 50.50W
Divisor, Sierra de- 202 De 8.00S 73.50W
Divnogorsk 138 Ee 55.58N 92.32 E
Divnoje 136 Ef 45.53N 43.22 E
Divo 166 Dd 5.50N 5.22W
Divo [3] 166 Dd 5.57N 5.15W
Divoká Orlice 120 Mf 50.09N 16.06 E
Divor 126 Df 38.59N 8.29W
Divriği 146 Hc 39.23N 38.07 E
Dīvrūd 146 Nd 36.52N 49.34 E
Dixmude/Diksmuide 122 Ic 51.02N 2.52 E
Dixon [Il.-U.S.] 186 Lf 41.50N 89.29W
Dixon [N.M.-U.S.] 186 Dh 36.11N 105.53W
Dixon Entrance 174 Fd 54.25N 132.30W
Diyālá [3] 146 Kf 34.00N 45.00 E
Diyālá 140 Gf 33.14N 44.31 E
Diyarbakir 144 Fb 37.55N 40.14 E
Dizy 124 Fe 49.04N 3.58 E
Dizy-le-Gros 124 Ge 49.38N 4.01 E
Dja 158 Ih 2.02N 15.12 E
Djado 160 If 21.01N 12.18 E
Djado, Plateau du- 158 If 21.45N 12.50 E
Djakarta → Jakarta 142 Mj 6.10S 106.46 E
Djakovo 120 Th 48.03N 23.01 E
Djamaa 162 Ic 33.32N 6.00 E
Djambala 160 Ii 2.33S 14.45 E
Djanet 160 Hf 24.34N 9.29 E
Djaret 162 Hd 26.35N 1.38 E
Djatkovo 136 De 53.36N 34.20 E
Djatlovo 132 Dc 53.31N 25.24 E
Djaul Island 214 Eh 2.56S 150.55 E
Djebel Ţāriq, El Bōghāz-= Gibraltar, Strait of- (EN) 110 Fh 35.57N 5.36W
Djédaa 168 Bc 13.31N 18.34 E
Djedi 158 He 34.39N 5.55 E
Djedoug, Djebel- 126 Qi 35.53N 4.20 E
Djelfa 160 He 34.40N 3.15 E
Djelfa [3] 162 Hc 34.15N 3.30 E
Djéma 160 Jh 6.03N 25.19 E
Djember 168 Bc 10.25N 17.50 E
Djemila 162 Ib 36.19N 5.44 E
Djenane 126 Pi 35.43N 3.59 E
Djenné 166 Ec 13.55N 4.33W
Djerem 166 Hd 5.20N 13.24 E
Dji 168 Cd 6.47N 22.14 E
Djibo 166 Ec 14.06N 1.38W
Djibouti 160 Lg 11.35N 43.08 E
Djibouti (Afars and Issas) [1] 160 Lg 11.30N 43.00 E
Djokupunda 170 Dd 5.27S 20.58 E
Djolu 160 Jh 0.37N 22.21 E
Djoua 170 Bb 1.13N 13.12 E
Djougou 166 Fd 9.42N 1.40 E
Djoum 166 He 2.40N 12.40 E
Djourab, Erg du- 168 Bb 16.40N 18.50 E
Djugu 170 Fb 1.55N 30.30 E
Djultydag, gora- 132 Oi 41.58N 46.56 E
Djup 116 Bd 60.50N 8.00 E
Djúpi vogur 114a Cb 64.39N 14.17W
Djurbeldžin 135 Jd 41.10N 74.59 E
Djurdjura, Djebel- 126 Qh 36.27N 4.15 E
Djurmo 116 Fd 60.33N 15.10 E
Djurö 116 Ef 58.50N 13.30 E
Djursholm 116 He 59.24N 18.05 E
Djursland 116 Dh 56.20N 10.45 E
Djurtjuli 136 Fd 55.29N 54.55 E
Dmitrija Lapteva, proliv- = Dmitri Laptev Strait (EN) 140 Qb 73.00N 142.00 E
Dmitrijev-Lgovski 132 Ic 52.08N 35.05 E
Dmitri Laptev Strait (EN) = Dmitrija Lapteva, proliv- 140 Qb 73.00N 142.00 E
Dmitrov 114 Ih 56.26N 37.31 E
Dmitrovsk-Orlovski 132 Ic 52.31N 35.09 E
Dnepr 110 Jf 46.30N 32.18 E
Dneprodzeržinsk 136 Df 48.30N 34.37 E
Dneprodzeržinskoje vodohranilišče 132 Ie 48.45N 34.10 E
Dnepropetrovsk 112 Jf 48.27N 34.59 E
Dnepropetrovskaja oblast [3] 136 Df 48.15N 35.00 E
Dneprorudnoje 132 If 47.23N 35.01 E
Dneprovski liman 132 Gf 46.35N 31.55 E
Dneprovsko-Bugski kanal 132 Dc 52.03N 25.10 E
Dnepr Upland (EN) = Pridneprovskaja vozvyšennost 110 Jf 49.00N 32.00 E
Dnestr 110 Jf 46.18N 30.17 E
Dnestrovsk 130 Mc 46.39N 29.48 E
Dnestrovski liman 132 Gf 46.15N 30.15 E
Dno 136 Cd 57.49N 29.59 E
Doany 172 Hb 14.22S 49.30 E
Doba 168 Bd 8.39N 16.51 E
Dobbiaco / Toblach 128 Gd 46.44N 12.14 E
Dobele 114 Fh 56.39N 23.16 E
Döbeln 120 Je 51.07N 13.07 E
Doberai, Jazirah- 150 Jg 1.30S 132.30 E
Dobo 150 Jh 5.46S 134.13 E
Doboj 128 Mf 44.44N 18.05 E
Dobra 120 Oe 51.54N 18.37 E
Dobre Miasto 120 Qc 53.59N 20.25 E
Dobreta Turnu Severin 112 Ig 44.38N 22.40 E
Dobrič (Tolbuhin) 130 Kf 43.34N 27.50 E
Dobrinka 132 Lc 52.08N 40.29 E
Dobříš 120 Kg 49.47N 14.10 E
Dobrjanka 136 Fd 58.29N 56.29 E
Dobrodzień 120 Of 50.44N 18.27 E
Dobrogea = Dobruja (EN) 110 Ig 44.00N 28.00 E
Dobrogea=Dobruja (EN) 130 Ke 44.00N 28.00 E
Dobrogean, Masivul- 130 Le 44.50N 28.30 E
Dobromil 120 Sg 49.34N 22.49 E
Dobropolje 132 Je 48.28N 37.02 E
Dobroteşti 130 He 44.17N 24.53 E
Dobrotvor 120 Uf 50.10N 24.27 E
Dobrudžansko Plato 130 Kf 43.32N 27.50 E
Dobruja (EN) = Dobrogea 110 Ig 44.00N 28.00 E
Dobruja (EN)=Dobrogea 130 Ke 44.00N 28.00 E
Dobruš 132 Gc 52.26N 31.19 E
Dobruška 120 Mf 50.18N 16.10 E
Dobrzyń nad Wisłą 120 Pd 52.38N 19.20 E
Dobrzyńskie, Pojezierze- 120 Pc 53.00N 19.20 E
Dobšiná 120 Qh 48.49N 20.22 E
Doce, Rio- [Braz.] 204 Gd 18.28S 51.05W
Doce, Rio- [Braz.] 198 Mg 19.37S 39.49W
Doce Leguas, Cayos de las- 194 Hc 20.55N 79.05W
Doce Leguas, Laberinto de las- 194 Hc 20.39N 78.35W
Docker River 212 Fd 24.58S 129.03 E
Docksta 116 Ha 63.03N 18.20 E
Doctor Arroyo 192 If 23.40N 100.11W
Doctor Cecilio Báez 204 Dg 25.03S 56.19W
Doctor Pedro P. Peña 206 Hb 22.26S 62.22W
Doctor Petru Groza 130 Fc 46.37N 22.25 E
Doda 148 Fb 33.08N 75.34 E
Doda Betta 148 Ff 11.24N 76.44 E
Dodecanese (EN) = Dhodhekánisos 130 Jm 36.20N 27.00 E
Dodecanese (EN) = Nótioi Sporádhes 110 Ih 36.00N 27.00 E
Dodge City 182 Gd 37.45N 100.00W
Dodgeville 186 Ke 42.58N 90.08W
Dodman Point 118 Ik 50.13N 4.48W
Dodoma 160 Ki 6.11S 35.45 E
Dodoma [3] 170 Gd 6.00S 36.00 E
Dodona (EN) = Dhodhóni 130 Dj 39.33N 20.46 E
Dodurga 130 Mj 39.48N 29.55 E
Doesburg 124 Ib 52.01N 6.08 E
Doetinchem 122 Mc 51.58N 6.17 E
Dofa 150 Ig 1.47S 125.22 E
Dogai Coring 152 Ee 34.30N 89.10 E
Doğanbey 130 Jk 38.04N 26.53 E
Doğanşehir 146 Gc 38.06N 37.53 E
Dog Creek 188 Da 51.35N 122.15W
Dogger Bank 110 Ge 55.00N 3.00 E
Dog Island 196 Ec 18.15N 63.13W
Dog Lake [Man.-Can.] 186 Ga 51.02N 98.30W
Dog Lake [Ont.-Can.] 186 Lb 48.46N 89.32W
Dog Lake [Ont.-Can.] 184 Ea 48.18N 84.10W
Dogliani 128 Bf 44.32N 7.56 E
Dōgo 154 Lf 36.15N 133.17 E
Dogonbadān 144 Hc 30.21N 50.48 E
Dogondoutchi 166 Fc 13.38N 4.02 E
Dōgo-San 156 Cd 35.04N 133.14 E
Dog Rocks 194 Ha 24.05N 79.51W
Doğubayazıt 146 Kc 39.32N 44.08 E
Doğu Karadeniz Dağları 144 Ea 40.40N 40.00 E
Dogwood Point 197c Ab 17.06N 62.38W
Doha (EN)=Ad Dawḩah 142 Hg 25.17N 51.32 E
Dohad 148 Ed 22.50N 74.16 E
Dohāzāri 148 Id 22.10N 92.04 E
Doi Luang Chinag Dao 148 Je 19.23N 98.54 E
Doilungdêqên 152 Ff 29.47N 90.49 E
Doire Baltée/Dora Baltea 128 Ce 45.11N 8.03 E
Doische 124 Gd 50.08N 4.45 E
Dojransko jezero 130 Fh 41.13N 22.44 E
Doka 168 Fc 13.31N 35.46 E
Dokhara, Dunes de- 162 Ic 32.50N 6.00 E
Dokka 114 Cf 60.50N 10.05 E
Dokka 116 Dd 60.49N 10.05 E
Dokkum 122 La 53.19N 6.00 E
Dokšicy 114 Gi 54.56N 27.46 E
Doksy 120 Kf 50.34N 14.40 E
Dokučajevsk 132 Jf 47.43N 37.47 E
Dolak, Pulau- 208 Ee 7.50S 138.30 E
Dolbeau 180 Kg 48.52N 72.14W
Dol-de-Bretagne 122 Ef 48.33N 1.45W
Dôle 122 Lg 47.06N 5.30 E
Doleib Hill 168 Ed 9.22N 31.36 E
Dolenjsko 128 Je 45.50N 15.10 E
Dolgaja, kosa- 132 Jf 46.40N 37.45 E
Dolgellau 118 Ji 52.44N 3.53W
Dolgi, ostrov- 134 Ib 69.15N 59.05 E
Dolgi Most 138 Ee 56.45N 96.58 E
Dolianova 128 Dk 39.22N 9.10 E
Dolina 132 De 48.58N 24.01 E
Dolinsk 138 Jg 47.20N 142.50 E
Dolinskaja 136 Df 48.07N 32.44 E
Dolinskoje 130 Mb 47.33N 29.50 E
Dolj [2] 130 Ge 44.10N 23.40 E
Dollart 122 Na 53.17N 7.10 E
Dolly Cays 194 Ib 23.39N 77.22W
Dolni Dăbnik 130 Hf 43.24N 24.26 E
Dolní Dvořiště 120 Kh 48.39N 14.27 E
Dolnomoravský úval 120 Nh 49.00N 17.15 E
Dolnośląskie, Bory- 120 Le 51.25N 15.20 E
Dolný Kubín 120 Pg 49.12N 19.17 E
Dolo 160 Lh 4.11N 42.05 E
Dolomiten/Dolomiti = Dolomites (EN) 110 Hf 46.23N 11.51 E
Dolomites (EN) = Dolomiten/Dolomiti 110 Hf 46.23N 11.51 E
Dolomites (EN) = Dolomiti/ Dolomiten 110 Hf 46.23N 11.51 E
Dolomiti/Dolomiten = Dolomites (EN) 110 Hf 46.23N 11.51 E
Dolon, pereval- 135 Jd 41.48N 75.45 E
Dolonnur/Duolun 152 Kc 42.10N 116.30 E
Dolores [Arg.] 206 Ie 36.20S 57.40W
Dolores [Guat.] 194 Ce 16.31N 89.25W
Dolores [Ur.] 206 Id 33.33S 58.13W
Dolores Hidalgo 192 Ig 21.10N 100.56W
Dolores River 188 Kg 38.49N 109.17W
Dolphin, Cape- 206 Ih 51.15S 58.58W
Dolphin and Union Strait 180 Gc 69.00N 115.00W
Dom, Kūh-e- 146 Of 33.52N 53.00 E
Domačevo 120 Te 51.46N 23.37 E
Domaniç 146 Cc 39.48N 29.37 E
Domantaj/Domantaj 116 Ji 55.57N 23.19 E
Domantaj/Domantai 116 Ji 55.57N 23.19 E
Domart-en-Ponthieu 124 Ed 50.04N 2.07 E
Domaša, údolná nadrž- 120 Rg 49.05N 21.47 E
Domažlice 120 Ig 49.27N 12.56 E
Dombaj-Ulgen, gora- 132 Lh 43.14N 41.46 E
Dombarovski 136 Fe 50.47N 59.34 E
Dombås 112 Kc 62.05N 9.08 E
Dombe Grande 170 Be 12.56S 13.07 E
Dombes 122 Lh 46.00N 5.03 E
Dombóvár 120 Oj 46.23N 18.07 E
Dombrád 120 Rh 48.14N 21.56 E
Domburg 124 Fc 51.34N 3.30 E
Dôme, Monts- 122 Ii 45.45N 2.55 E
Dôme, Puy de- 122 Ii 45.47N 2.58 E
Domérat 122 Ih 46.21N 2.32 E
Domeyko, Cordillera- 198 Jh 24.30S 69.00W
Domfront 122 Ff 48.36N 0.39W
Domingo M. Irala 204 Eg 25.54S 54.43W
Domingos Martins 202 Jh 20.22S 40.40W
Dominica [1] 176 Mh 15.30N 61.20W
Dominica 174 Mh 15.30N 61.20W
Dominical 194 Fi 9.13N 83.51W
Dominicana, República-= Dominican Republic (EN) [1] 176 Lh 19.00N 70.40W
Dominican Republic (EN)= Dominicana, República- [1] 176 Lh 19.00N 70.40W
Dominica Passage 196 Fe 15.10N 61.15W
Dominica Passage (EN)= Dominique, Canal de la- 196 Fe 15.10N 61.15W
Dominion, Cape - 180 Kc 66.10N 74.30W
Dominique, Canal de la-= Dominica Passage (EN) 196 Fe 15.10N 61.15W
Domino 180 Lf 53.28N 55.46W
Domiongo 170 Dc 4.37S 21.15 E
Dommartin-Varimont 124 Gf 48.59N 4.46 E
Domme 122 Hj 44.48N 1.13 E
Dommel 122 Lc 51.40N 5.20 E
Domneşti 130 Hd 45.12N 24.50 E
Domo 168 Hd 7.57N 46.51 E
Domodedovo 114 Ii 55.27N 37.47 E
Domodossola 128 Cd 46.07N 8.17 E
Domont 124 Ee 49.02N 2.20 E
Dom Pedrito 206 Jd 30.59S 54.40W
Dom Pedro 202 Jd 5.00S 44.27W
Dompierre-sur-Besbre 122 Jh 46.31N 3.41 E
Dompu 150 Gh 8.32S 118.28 E
Domusnovas 128 Ck 39.19N 8.39 E
Domuyo, Volcán- 198 Ii 36.38S 70.26W
Don 192 Ed 26.26N 109.02W
Don [Eng.-U.K.] 118 Mh 53.39N 0.59W
Don [Fr.] 122 Eg 47.40N 1.56W
Don [Russia] 110 Jf 47.04N 39.18 E
Don [Scot.-U.K.] 118 Kd 57.10N 2.04W
Donaldsonville 186 Kk 30.06N 90.59W
Donau=Danube (EN) 110 If 45.20N 29.40 E
Donaueschingen 120 Ei 47.57N 8.30 E
Donaumoos 120 Hh 48.40N 11.15 E
Donauried 120 Gh 48.35N 10.40 E
Donauwörth 120 Gh 48.42N 10.48 E
Don Benito 126 Gf 38.57N 5.52W
Doncaster 118 Lh 53.32N 1.07W
Dondjušany 130 Ka 48.11N 27.31 E
Dondo [Ang.] 160 Ii 9.40S 14.26 E
Dondo [Moz.] 172 Ec 19.36S 34.44 E
Dondra Head 140 Ki 5.55N 80.35 E
Donec 110 Kf 47.40N 40.50 E
Doneck [Russia] 132 Ke 48.21N 39.59 E
Doneck [Ukr.] 112 Jf 48.00N 37.48 E
Doneckaja oblast [3] 136 Df 48.00N 37.45 E
Donecki krjaž = Donec Ridge (EN) 110 Jf 48.15N 38.45 E
Donec Ridge (EN) = Donecki krjaž 110 Jf 48.15N 38.45 E
Donegal/Dún na nGall 118 Eg 54.39N 8.06W
Donegal/Dún na nGall [2] 118 Fg 54.50N 8.00W
Donegal Bay/Bá Dhún na nGall 110 Fe 54.30N 8.30W
Donegal Mountains 118 Eg 54.50N 8.10W
Donga 166 Hd 8.19N 10.01 E
Dongara 212 Ce 29.15S 114.56 E
Dongbei Pingyuan 154 Gc 44.00N 124.00 E
Dongchuan (Tangdan) 152 Hf 26.07N 103.05 E
Dongcun → Lanxian 154 Ae 38.17N 111.38 E
Dong Dao 150 Fc 16.45N 113.00 E
Donge 124 Gc 51.41N 4.49 E
Dong'e (Tongcheng) 154 Df 36.19N 116.14 E
Dongen 124 Gc 51.37N 4.57 E
Donges 122 Dg 47.18N 2.04W
Dongfang (Basuo) 152 Ih 19.14N 108.39 E
Dongfanghong 154 Ls 46.15N 133.07 E
Dongfeng 154 Hc 42.41N 125.33 E
Donggala 150 Gg 0.40S 119.44 E
Donggou 152 Ld 39.55N 124.08 E
Dongguang 154 Df 37.54N 116.32 E
Dong Hai=East China Sea (EN) 140 Og 29.00N 125.00 E
Donghai Dao 152 Jg 21.00N 110.25 E
Dong He 152 Hc 42.12N 101.10 E
Dong Hoi 148 Le 17.29N 106.36 E
Dong Jang 140 Ng 23.02N 113.31 E
Dongkala 150 Hh 5.18S 122.03 E
Dongkan → Binhai 152 Ke 34.00N 119.52 E
Donglan 152 Ig 24.35N 107.22 E
Dongliao He 154 Gc 43.24N 123.42 E
Dongming 154 Cg 35.17N 115.04 E
Dongnan Qiuling 152 Jg 24.00N 113.00 E
Dongning 152 Nc 44.02N 131.06 E
Dongo 170 Ce 14.36S 15.43 E
Dongola (EN)=Dunqulah 160 Kg 19.10N 30.29 E
Dongou 170 Cb 2.02N 18.04 E
Dongoun→Haiyang 154 Ff 36.46N 121.09 E
Dongping 152 Kd 35.51N 116.15 E
Dongping → Anhua 152 Jf 28.27N 111.15 E
Dong Rak, Phanom-= Dangrek Range (EN) 140 Mh 14.25N 104.30 E
Dongsha Dao 152 Kg 20.45N 116.45 E
Dongsha Qundao 140 Ng 20.42N 116.43 E
Dongsheng 152 Id 39.48N 110.00 E
Dongtai 152 Le 32.47N 120.18 E
Dong Taijnar Hu 152 Fd 37.25N 94.00 E
Dongtin Hu 140 Ng 29.18N 112.45 E
Dong Ujimqin Qi (Uliastai) 152 Kc 45.31N 116.58 E
Dongwe 170 De 13.56S 23.53 E
Dongxiang 152 Kf 28.15N 116.38 E
Dongyang 154 Fj 29.16N 120.14 E
Dongying 152 Kd 37.30N 118.30 E
Dongzhi (Yaodu) 154 Di 30.06N 117.01 E
Donington 124 Bb 52.54N 0.12W
Doniphan 186 Kh 36.37N 90.50W
Donja Brela 128 Kg 43.23N 16.55 E
Donji Miholjac 128 Me 45.45N 18.10 E
Donji Vakuf 128 Lf 44.08N 17.24 E
Donjon, Le- 122 Jh 46.21N 3.48 E
Dønna 114 Cc 66.06N 12.35 E
Donnacona 184 Lb 46.40N 71.47W
Donner Pass 182 Cd 39.19N 120.20W
Donnersberg 124 Je 49.38N 7.55 E
Donner und Blitzen River 188 Fe 43.17N 118.49W
Donnybrook 212 Df 33.35S 115.49 E
Donostia / San Sebastián 112 Fg 43.19N 1.59W
Donskaja grjada = Don Upland (EN) 110 Kf 49.10N 42.00 E
Donskoj 132 Kb 54.01N 38.20 E
Don Upland (EN) = Donskaja grjada 110 Kf 49.10N 42.00 E
Donuzlav, ozero- 132 Hg 45.25N 33.10 E
Doolette Bay 222 Je 67.55S 147.00 E
Doon 118 If 55.26N 4.38W
Doonerak, Mount- 178 Ic 67.56N 150.37W
Doorn 124 Hb 52.02N 5.19 E
Doornik/Tournai 122 Jd 50.36N 3.23 E
Door Peninsula 186 Md 44.55N 87.20W
Do Qu 152 He 31.48N 102.09 E
Dora, Lake- 212 Ed 22.05S 122.56 E
Dora Baltea/Doire Baltée 128 Ce 45.11N 8.03 E
Dorada, Costa- / Daurada, Costa- 126 Nc 41.08N 1.10 E
Dora Riparia 128 Be 45.05N 7.44 E
Dorat, Le- 122 Hh 46.13N 1.05 E
Dorbiljin/Emin 152 Db 46.32N 83.39 E
Dorchester 118 Kk 50.43N 2.26W
Dorchester, Cape - 180 Jc 65.28N 77.30W
Dordabis 172 Bd 22.52S 17.38 E
Dordogne [3] 122 Gi 45.10N 0.50 E
Dordogne 110 Ff 45.02N 0.35W
Dordrecht [Neth.] 122 Kc 51.49N 4.40 E
Dordrecht [S.Afr.] 172 Df 31.20S 27.03 E
Dore 122 Ji 46.00N 3.28 E
Dore, Monts- 110 Gf 45.30N 2.45 E
Doré Lake 180 Gf 54.45N 107.20W
Dores do Indaiá 202 Ig 19.27S 45.36W
Dorgali 128 Dj 40.17N 9.35 E
Dori 160 Gg 14.02N 0.02W
Doring 158 Il 31.52S 18.39 E
Dorking 124 Bc 51.13N 0.20W
Dormagen 124 Ic 51.06N 6.50 E
Dormans 122 Je 49.04N 3.38 E
Dormidontovka 138 Ig 47.45N 134.58 E
Dornbirn 128 Dc 47.25N 9.44 E
Dornoch 118 Id 57.52N 4.02W
Dornoch Firth 118 Id 57.52N 4.02W
Doro 166 Eb 16.09N 0.51W
Dorog 120 Oi 47.43N 18.44 E
Dorogobuž 132 Hb 54.56N 33.15 E
Dorohoi 130 Jb 47.57N 26.24 E
Dorotea 114 Dd 64.16N 16.24 E
Dorre Island 212 Ce 25.10S 113.05 E
Dorrigo 212 Kf 30.20S 152.45 E
Dorset [3] 118 Kk 50.50N 2.10W
Dorset 118 Kk 50.55N 2.15W
Dorsten 120 Ce 51.40N 6.58 E
Dortmund 112 Ge 51.31N 7.27 E
Dortmund-Ems-Kanal 120 Dd 51.42N 7.27 E
Dörtyol 146 Gd 36.52N 36.12 E
Do Rūd 144 Gc 33.28N 49.04 E
Doruma 170 Eb 4.44N 27.42 E
Dörverden 124 Lb 52.51N 9.14 E
Doséo, Bahr- 168 Bd 9.01N 19.38 E
Dos Hermanas 126 Gg 37.17N 5.55W
Dos Lagunas 194 Ce 17.42N 89.36W
Dospat 130 Hh 41.39N 24.10 E
Dospat 130 Hh 41.23N 24.05 E
Dos Picachos, Cerro- 192 Bc 29.25N 114.10W
Dosse 120 Ic 53.13N 12.20 E
Dosso 160 Hg 13.03N 3.12 E
Dosso [2] 166 Fc 13.30N 3.30 E
Dossor 136 Ff 47.32N 53.01 E
Dostluk 135 Ef 37.45N 65.22 E
Dothan 182 Je 31.13N 85.24W
Dotnuva 116 Ji 55.18N 23.55 E
Douai 122 Jd 50.22N 3.04 E
Douala 160 Hh 4.03N 9.42 E
Douaouir 166 Ea 20.45N 2.30W
Douarnenez 122 Bf 48.06N 4.20W
Douarnenez, Baie de- 122 Bf 48.10N 4.25W
Double Mountain Fork Brazos 186 Gj 33.15N 100.00W
Doubrava 120 Lf 50.03N 15.20 E

Index Symbols

[1] Independent Nation
[2] State, Region
[3] District, County
[4] Municipality
[5] Colony, Dependency
Continent
Physical Region
Historical or Cultural Region
Mount, Mountain
Volcano
Hill
Mountains, Mountain Range
Hills, Escarpment
Plateau, Upland
Pass, Gap
Plain, Lowland
Delta
Salt Flat
Valley, Canyon
Crater, Cave
Karst Features
Depression
Polder
Desert, Dunes
Forest, Woods
Heath, Steppe
Oasis
Cape, Point
Coast, Beach
Cliff
Peninsula
Isthmus
Sandbank
Island
Atoll
Rock, Reef
Islands, Archipelago
Rocks, Reefs
Coral Reef
Well, Spring
Geyser
River, Stream
Waterfall, Rapids
River Mouth, Estuary
Lake
Salt Lake
Intermittent Lake
Reservoir
Swamp, Pond
Canal
Glacier
Ice Shelf, Pack Ice
Ocean
Sea
Gulf, Bay
Strait, Fjord
Lagoon
Bank
Seamount
Tablemount
Ridge
Shelf
Basin
Escarpment, Sea Scarp
Fracture
Trench, Abyss
National Park, Reserve
Point of Interest
Recreation Site
Cave, Cavern
Historic Site
Ruins
Wall, Walls
Church, Abbey
Temple
Scientific Station
Railway station
Airport
Port
Military installation
Lighthouse
Mine
Tunnel
Dam, Bridge

Doubs [3]	122	Mg	47.10N	6.25 E
Doubs	122	Lh	46.54N	5.02 E
Doubtful Sound	218	Bf	45.15S	166.50 E
Doubtless Bay	218	Ea	34.55S	173.25 E
Douchy-les-Mines	124	Fd	50.18N	3.23 E
Doudeville	124	Ce	49.43N	0.48 E
Doué-la-Fontaine	122	Fg	47.12N	0.17W
Douentza	166	Eb	15.03N	2.57W
Douera	126	Oh	36.40N	2.57 E
Dougga	162	Ib	36.24N	9.13 E
Douglas [Ak.-U.S.]	178	Me	58.16N	134.26W
Douglas [Az.-U.S.]	182	Fe	31.21N	109.33W
Douglas [Ga.-U.S.]	184	Fj	31.31N	82.51W
Douglas [I. of M.]	118	Ig	54.09N	4.28W
Douglas [S.Afr.]	172	Ce	29.04S	23.46 E
Douglas [Wy.-U.S.]	182	Fc	42.45N	105.24W
Douglas Lake	184	Fh	36.00N	83.22W
Douglas Range	222	Qf	70.00S	69.35W
Doullens	122	Id	50.09N	2.21 E
Doumé	166	He	4.14N	13.27 E
Douna	166	Ec	14.39N	1.43W
Doupovské hory	120	Jf	50.13N	13.08 E
Dour	124	Fd	50.24N	3.47 E
Dourada, Serra- [Braz.]	204	Gb	16.00S	50.05W
Dourada, Serra- [Braz.]	204	Ha	13.10S	48.45W
Dourados	200	Kh	22.13S	54.48W
Dourados, Rio- [Braz.]	204	Ee	21.58S	54.18W
Dourados, Rio- [Braz.]	204	Id	18.17S	47.36W
Dourbali	168	Bc	11.49N	15.52 E
Dourdan	122	If	48.32N	2.01 E
Douro	110	Fg	41.08N	8.40W
Douro Litoral	126	Dc	41.05N	8.20W
Doushi → Gong'an	152	Je	30.05N	112.12 E
Douve	122	Ee	49.19N	1.44W
Douvres-la-Delivrande	124	Be	49.17N	0.23W
Douze	122	Fk	43.54N	0.30W
Douzy	124	He	49.40N	5.03 E
Dove	118	Li	52.50N	1.35W
Dove Bugt	179	Jc	76.25N	21.00W
Dove Creek	186	Bh	37.46N	108.54W
Dover [De.-U.S.]	176	Lf	39.10N	75.32W
Dover [Eng.-U.K.]	112	Ge	51.08N	1.19 E
Dover [N.H.-U.S.]	184	Ld	43.12N	70.55W
Dover [Oh.-U.S.]	184	Ge	40.32N	81.30W
Dover, Strait of-	110	Ge	51.00N	1.30 E
Dover, Strait of- (EN) = Calais, Pas de-	110	Ge	51.00N	1.30 E
Dover Foxcroft	184	Mc	45.11N	69.13W
Dovey	118	Ji	52.34N	3.59W
Dovre	116	Cc	61.59N	9.15 E
Dovrefjell	110	Gc	62.10N	9.25 E
Dowa	170	Fe	13.39S	33.56 E
Dowagiac	184	De	41.59N	86.06W
Dowlatābād	146	Qh	28.20N	57.13 E
Downey	188	Ie	42.26N	112.07W
Downham Market	124	Cb	52.36N	0.22 E
Downieville	188	Eg	39.34N	120.50W
Downpatrick/Dún Pádraig	118	Hg	54.20N	5.43W
Dow Sar	146	Me	35.06N	48.02 E
Dōzen	156	Cc	36.05N	132.59 E
Dozois, Reservoir-	184	Ib	47.30N	77.00W
Dozulé	124	Be	49.14N	0.03W
Drâa	158	Ff	28.40N	11.07W
Drâa, Cap-	162	Ed	28.44N	11.05W
Drâa, Hamada du-	158	Gf	28.30N	7.30W
Draâ Ben Khedda	126	Ph	36.44N	3.57 E
Draa el Baguel	162	Ic	30.17N	6.25 E
Draa el Mizan	126	Ph	36.32N	3.50 E
Drac	122	Li	45.13N	5.41 E
Drac, Cuevas del-	126	Pe	39.32N	3.15 E
Dracena	204	Ge	21.32S	51.29W
Dragalina	130	Ke	44.26N	27.19 E
Dragan	114	Dd	64.00N	15.21 E
Drăgănești-Olt	130	He	44.09N	24.42 E
Drăgănești-Vlașca	130	Ie	44.06N	25.36 E
Drăgășani	130	He	44.39N	24.16 E
Dragobia	130	Cg	42.26N	19.59 E
Dragón, Bocas del-/Dragon's Mouths	202	Fa	10.45N	61.46W
Dragonera, Isla- / Sa Dragonera, Illa-	126	Oe	39.35N	2.19 E
Dragon's Mouths/Dragón, Bocas del-	202	Fa	10.45N	61.46W
Dragør	116	Ei	55.36N	12.41 E
Draguignan	122	Mk	43.32N	6.28 E
Drahanská vrchovina	120	Mg	49.30N	16.45 E
Drain	188	De	43.40N	123.19W
Drake	186	Fc	47.55N	100.23W
Drake, Paso- = Drake Passage (EN)	198	Jk	58.00S	70.00W
Drakensberg	158	Jk	29.00S	29.00 E
Drake Passage (EN) = Drake, Paso-	198	Jk	58.00S	70.00W
Dráma	130	Hh	41.09N	24.09 E
Drammen	112	Hd	59.44N	10.15 E
Dramselva	116	De	59.44N	10.14 E
Drangajökull	114a	Aa	66.09N	22.15W
Dranse	122	Mh	46.24N	6.30 E
Drau = Drava (EN)	110	Hf	45.33N	18.55 E
Drava	110	Hf	45.33N	18.55 E
Dráva = Drava (EN)	110	Hf	45.33N	18.55 E
Drava (EN) = Drau	110	Hf	45.33N	18.55 E
Drava (EN) = Dráva	110	Hf	45.33N	18.55 E
Dravograd	128	Jd	46.35N	15.01 E
Drawa	120	Ld	52.52N	15.59 E
Drawno	120	Lc	53.13N	15.45 E
Drawsko, Jezioro-	120	Mc	53.33N	16.10 E
Drawsko Pomorskie	120	Lc	53.32N	15.48 E
Drayton Valley	180	Gf	53.13N	115.00W
Drean	128	Bn	36.41N	7.45 E
Dreieich	124	Ke	50.01N	8.43 E
Drenovci	128	Mf	44.55N	18.55 E
Drenthe [3]	124	Ib	52.45N	6.30 E
Dresden	112	He	51.03N	13.45 E
Dreux	122	Hf	48.44N	1.22 E
Drevsjø	114	Cf	61.54N	12.02 E
Drezdenko	120	Ld	52.51N	15.50 E
Dricēni/Driceni	116	Lh	56.39N	27.11 E
Driceni/Dricēni	116	Lh	56.39N	27.11 E
Driffield	118	Mg	54.01N	0.26W
Driggs	188	Je	43.44N	111.14W
Drina	110	Hg	44.53N	19.21 E
Drincea	130	Fe	44.07N	22.59 E
Drin Gulf (EN) = Drinit, Gjiri i-	130	Ch	41.45N	19.28 E
Drini	110	Hg	41.45N	19.34 E
Drini i Zi	130	Dg	42.05N	20.23 E
Drinit, Gjiri i- = Drin Gulf (EN)	130	Ch	41.45N	19.28 E
Drinjača	128	Nf	44.17N	19.10 E
Drinosi	130	Di	40.17N	20.02 E
Drissa	114	Gi	55.47N	27.57 E
Drisvjaty, ozero- / Drūkšiu ežeras	116	Li	55.37N	26.45 E
Driva	116	Cb	62.40N	8.34 E
Drjanovo	130	Ig	42.58N	25.28 E
Drniš	128	Kg	43.52N	16.09 E
Drøbak	114	Cg	59.39N	10.39 E
Drocea, Virful-	130	Fc	46.12N	22.14 E
Drogheda/Droichead Átha	118	Gh	53.43N	6.21W
Drogičin	132	Dc	52.13N	25.10 E
Drogobyč	132	Ce	49.22N	23.33 E
Drohiczyn	120	Sd	52.24N	22.41 E
Droichead Átha/Drogheda	118	Gh	53.43N	6.21W
Droichead na Bandan/Bandon	118	Ej	51.45N	8.45W
Droichead na Banna/Banbridge	118	Gg	54.21N	6.16W
Drokija	132	Ee	48.01N	27.53 E
Drôme [3]	122	Lj	44.35N	5.10 E
Drôme	124	Be	49.19N	0.45W
Drömling	120	Hd	52.29N	11.04 E
Dronero	128	Bf	44.28N	7.22 E
Dronne	122	Fi	45.02N	0.09W
Dronning Fabiolafjella	222	Df	71.30S	35.40 E
Dronning Louise Land	179	Jc	76.45N	24.00W
Dronten	122	Lb	52.31N	5.42 E
Dropt	122	Fj	44.35N	0.06W
Drovjanoj	138	Cb	72.25N	72.45 E
Drowning River	186	Na	50.55N	84.35W
Druja	114	Gi	55.47N	27.29 E
Drūkšiu ežeras / Drisvjaty, ozero-	116	Li	55.37N	26.45 E
Druk-Yul → Bhutan [1]	142	Lg	27.30N	90.30 E
Drulingen	124	Jf	48.52N	7.11 E
Drumheller	180	Gf	51.28N	112.42W
Drummond [Mt.-U.S.]	188	Ic	46.40N	113.09W
Drummond [Wi.-U.S.]	186	Kc	46.20N	91.15W
Drummond Island	184	Fb	46.00N	83.40W
Drummond Range	212	Jd	23.30S	147.15 E
Drummondville	180	Kg	45.50N	72.20W
Drummore	118	Ig	54.42N	4.54W
Drumochter, Pass of-	118	Ie	56.50N	4.12W
Drunen	124	Hc	51.41N	5.10 E
Druskininkai/Druskininkaj	114	Fi	54.04N	24.06 E
Druskininkaj/Druskininkai	114	Fi	54.04N	24.06 E
Drut	132	Gc	53.04N	30.35 E
Druten	124	Hc	51.54N	5.38 E
Družba [Kaz.]	136	If	45.18N	82.29 E
Družba [Ukr.]	132	Hc	52.02N	33.59 E
Družkovka	132	Je	48.36N	37.33 E
Družnaja Gorka	116	Ne	59.11N	30.10 E
Družnino	134	Ih	56.48N	59.29 E
Družno, Jezioro-	120	Pb	54.08N	19.30 E
Drvar	128	Kf	44.22N	16.23 E
Drvenik	128	Lg	43.09N	17.15 E
Drweça	120	Oc	53.00N	18.42 E
Dryden	180	Ig	49.47N	92.50W
Dry Fork	188	Me	43.30N	105.24W
Drygalski Ice Tongue	222	Kf	75.24S	163.30 E
Drygalski Island	222	Ge	65.45S	92.30 E
Drysdale River	212	Fb	13.59S	126.51 E
Dry Tortugas	182	Kg	24.38N	82.55W
Drzewica	120	Qe	51.27N	20.28 E
Drzewiczka	120	Qe	51.33N	20.35 E
Dschang	166	Hd	5.27N	10.04 E
Dua	170	Db	3.20N	20.53 E
Duaca	202	Ea	10.18N	69.10W
Duancun → Wuxiang	154	Bf	36.50N	112.51 E
Duarte, Pico-	174	Lh	19.00N	71.00W
Duartina	204	Hf	22.24S	49.25W
Dubawnt	180	Hd	64.30N	100.06W
Dubawnt Lake	174	Ic	63.08N	101.30W
Dubay'ah, Ra's-	146	Pj	24.20N	54.09 E
Dubayy	142	Hg	25.18N	55.18 E
Dubbo	210	Fh	32.15S	148.36 E
Dübener Heide	120	Ie	51.40N	12.40 E
Dubenski	132	Td	51.29N	56.38 E
Dubesar'	132	Ff	47.17N	29.10 E
Dubh Artach	118	Ge	56.08N	6.39W
Dubica	128	Ke	45.13N	16.48 E
Dublin	186	Kj	32.32N	82.54W
Dublin/Baile Átha Cliath	112	Fe	53.20N	6.15W
Dublin/Baile Átha Cliath [2]	118	Gh	53.20N	6.15W
Dublin Bay/Cuan Bhaile Átha Cliath	118	Gh	53.20N	6.06W
Dubljany	120	Tg	49.26N	23.16 E
Dublon	220d	Bb	7.23N	151.53 E
Dubna	136	Dd	56.47N	37.10 E
Dubna	116	Lh	56.20N	26.31 E
Dubnica nad Váhom	120	Oh	48.58N	18.10 E
Dubno	136	Ce	50.29N	25.46 E
Du Bois	184	He	41.06N	78.46W
Dubois [Id.-U.S.]	188	Id	44.10N	112.14W
Dubois [Wy.-U.S.]	188	Ke	43.33N	109.38W
Dubovka	136	Ef	49.03N	44.50 E
Dubovoje	120	Th	48.08N	23.59 E
Dubreka	166	Cd	9.48N	13.31W
Dubrovica	132	Ed	51.34N	26.34 E
Dubrovnik	112	Hg	42.39N	18.07 E
Dubrovnoje	114	Hi	54.33N	30.41 E
Dubuque	136	Gd	57.58N	69.25 E
Dubysa	182	Ic	42.30N	90.41W
	116	Ji	55.02N	23.27 E
Duc de Gloucester, Iles du- = Duke of Gloucester, Islands (En)	208	Mg	20.38S	143.20W
Duchang	154	Dj	29.16N	116.11 E
Duchesne	188	Jf	40.10N	110.24W
Duchess	212	Hd	21.22S	139.52 E
Ducie Atoll	208	Og	24.40S	124.47W
Duck River	184	Dg	36.02N	87.52W
Duckwater Peak	188	Hg	38.58N	115.26W
Duclair	124	Ce	49.29N	0.53 E
Duc Lap	148	Lf	12.27N	107.38 E
Ducos	197h	Bb	14.34N	60.58W
Dudelange/Düdelingen	124	Ie	49.28N	6.06 E
Düdelingen/Dudelange	124	Ie	49.28N	6.06 E
Duderstadt	120	Ge	51.31N	10.16 E
Dudinka	142	Kc	69.25N	86.15 E
Dudley	118	Ki	52.30N	2.05W
Dūdo	168	Id	9.20N	50.14 E
Dudub	168	Hd	6.55N	46.42 E
Dudune	219b	Ce	21.21S	167.44 E
Dudweiler, Saarbrücken-	124	Je	49.17N	7.02 E
Düdwēyn	168	Gd	9.19N	44.53 E
Dudypta	138	Db	70.55N	89.50 E
Duékoué	166	Dd	6.45N	7.21W
Dueodde	116	Fj	54.59N	15.05 E
Duerna	126	Gb	42.19N	5.54W
Duero	110	Fg	41.08N	8.40W
Dufek Coast	222	Lg	84.30S	179.00W
Duffer Peak	188	Ff	41.40N	118.44W
Duff Islands	208	He	9.50S	167.10 E
Dugi Otok	128	Ig	44.00N	15.00 E
Dugo Selo	128	Ke	45.48N	16.15 E
Du Gué, Rivière-	180	Ke	57.20N	70.46W
Duhovnickoje	132	Pc	52.29N	48.15 E
Duijan Yan	152	He	31.01N	103.28 E
Duisburg	120	Ce	51.26N	6.45 E
Duitama	202	Db	5.50N	73.02W
Dujūma	168	Ge	1.14N	42.34 E
Dukagjini	130	Cg	42.18N	19.45 E
Dūkān	146	Ke	35.56N	44.58 E
Dūkān, Sad ad-	146	Kd	36.10N	44.56 E
Dukat	130	Fg	42.26N	22.21 E
Duke of Gloucester Islands (EN) = Duc de Gloucester, Iles du-	208	Mg	20.38S	143.20W
Duke of York	219a	Aa	4.10S	152.28 E
Duke of York Bay	180	Jc	65.25N	84.50W
Duk Fadiat	168	Ed	7.45N	31.25 E
Duk Faiwil	168	Ed	7.30N	31.29 E
Dukhān	144	Hd	25.25N	50.48 E
Dukielska, Przełęcz-	120	Rg	49.25N	21.42 E
Dukku	166	Hc	10.49N	10.46 E
Dukla	120	Rg	49.34N	21.41 E
Dukou	142	Mg	26.31N	101.44 E
Dūkštas/Dukštas	116	Li	55.32N	26.28 E
Dukštas/Dūkštas	116	Li	55.32N	26.28 E
Dulan (Qagan Us)	142	Lf	36.29N	98.29 E
Dulce, Bahía-	192	Ji	16.30N	98.50W
Dulce, Golfo-	190	Hg	8.36N	83.15W
Dulce, Rio-	198	Ji	30.31S	62.32W
Dulce Nombre de Culmi	194	Ef	15.09N	85.37W
Duldurga	138	Gf	50.38N	113.35 E
Dulgalah	140	Pc	67.30N	133.20 E
Dulia	170	Db	2.57N	24.08 E
Dülmen	120	De	51.50N	7.18 E
Dulovka	116	Mg	57.27N	28.29 E
Dulovo	130	Kf	43.49N	27.09 E
Duluth	176	Je	46.47N	92.06W
Dūmā	146	Gf	33.35N	36.24 E
Dumaguete	150	He	9.18N	123.18 E
Dumai	150	Df	1.41N	101.27 E
Dumaran	150	Gd	10.33N	119.51 E
Dumaresq River	212	Ke	28.40S	150.28 E
Dumas [Ar.-U.S.]	186	Kj	33.53N	91.29W
Dumas [Tx.-U.S.]	186	Fi	35.52N	101.58W
Dumayr	146	Gf	33.38N	36.40 E
Dumbarton	118	If	55.57N	4.35W
Dumbéa	219b	Cf	22.09S	166.27 E
Dumbrăveni [Rom.]	130	Kd	45.31N	27.09 E
Dumbrăveni [Rom.]	130	Hc	46.14N	24.34 E
Dumbrăveni [Rom.]	130	Jb	47.39N	26.25 E
Dumfries	118	Jf	55.04N	3.37W
Dumfries and Galloway [3]	118	Jf	55.10N	3.35W
Dumka	148	Hd	24.16N	87.15 E
Dumlupinar	130	Mk	38.52N	30.00 E
Dümmer	120	Ed	52.31N	8.19 E
Dumoine, Lac-	184	Ib	46.52N	77.52W
Dumoine, Rivière-	184	Ib	46.13N	77.50W
Dumont d'Urville	222	Je	66.40S	140.01 E
Dumont D'Urville Sea (EN)	222	Je	63.00S	140.00 E
Dumpu	210	Fe	5.52S	145.46 E
Dümrek	130	Lk	38.40N	28.24 E
Dumuhe	154	La	46.21N	133.33 E
Dumyāṭ = Damietta (EN)	160	Ke	31.25N	31.48 E
Dumyāṭ, Maṣabb-	146	Dg	31.27N	31.51 E
Duna = Danube (EN)	110	If	45.20N	29.40 E
Dunaföldvár	120	Oj	46.48N	18.56 E
Dunaharaszti	120	Pi	47.21N	19.05 E
Dunaj	138	Ih	42.57N	132.20 E
Dunaj = Danube (EN)	110	If	45.20N	29.40 E
Dunajec	120	Qf	50.15N	20.44 E
Dunajevcy	132	Ee	48.51N	26.44 E
Dunajská Streda	120	Ni	47.01N	17.38 E
Dunakeszi	120	Pi	47.38N	19.08 E
Dunántúl	120	Nj	47.00N	18.00 E
Dunărea = Danube (EN)	110	If	45.20N	29.40 E
Dunărea Veche	130	Ld	45.17N	28.02 E
Dunării, Delta- = Danube, Mouths of the- (EN)	110	If	45.30N	29.45 E
Duna-Tisza Köze	120	Pj	46.45N	19.30 E
Dunaújváros	120	Oj	46.58N	18.56 E
Dunav = Danube (EN)	110	If	45.20N	29.40 E
Dunavățu de Jos	130	Me	44.59N	29.13 E
Dunav-Tisa-Dunav kanal	128	Dd	45.10N	20.50 E
Dunback	218	Df	45.23S	170.38 E
Dunbar	118	Kf	56.00N	2.31W
Duncan [Az.-U.S.]	188	Kj	32.43N	109.06W
Duncan [B.C.-Can.]	188	Db	48.47N	123.42W
Duncan [Ok.-U.S.]	182	He	34.30N	97.57W
Duncan Passage	148	If	11.00N	92.00 E
Duncansby Head	110	Fd	58.39N	3.01W
Dundaga	116	Jg	57.31N	22.14 E
Dundalk	184	If	39.15N	76.31W
Dundalk/Dún Dealgan	118	Gg	54.01N	6.25W
Dundalk Bay/Cuan Dhun Dealgan	118	Gh	53.57N	6.17W
Dundas	184	Hd	43.16N	79.58W
Dundas (Thule Air Base)	179	Fc	76.30N	69.00W
Dundas, Lake-	212	Ef	32.35S	121.50 E
Dundas Peninsula	180	Gb	74.40N	113.00W
Dundas Strait	212	Gb	11.20S	131.35 E
Dún Dealgan/Dundalk	118	Gg	54.01N	6.25W
Dundee [S.Afr.]	172	Ee	28.12S	30.16 E
Dundee [Scot.-U.K.]	112	Fd	56.28N	3.00W
Dund Hot → Zhenglan Qi	154	Cc	42.14N	115.59 E
Dundrum Bay/Cuan Dhún Droma	118	Hg	54.13N	5.45W
Dunedin [Fl.-U.S.]	184	Fk	28.02N	82.47W
Dunedin [N.Z.]	210	Ii	45.53S	170.31 E
Dunfanaghy	118	Ff	55.11N	7.59W
Dunfermline	118	Je	56.04N	3.29W
Dungannon/Dún Geanainn	118	Gg	54.31N	6.46W
Dún Garbhán/Dungarvan	118	Fi	52.05N	7.37W
Dūngarpur	148	Ed	23.50N	73.43 E
Dungarvan/Dún Garbhán	118	Fi	52.05N	7.37W
Dungas	166	Gc	13.04N	9.20 E
Dungau	120	Ih	48.45N	12.30 E
Dún Geanainn/Dungannon	118	Gg	54.31N	6.46W
Dungeness	118	Nk	50.55N	0.58 E
Dungu	170	Eb	3.42N	28.40 E
Dungu	170	Eb	3.37N	28.34 E
Dunhua	152	Mc	43.22N	128.12 E
Dunhuang	152	Fc	40.10N	94.50 E
Dunkerque	122	Ic	51.03N	2.22 E
Dunkery Beacon	118	Jj	51.11N	3.35W
Dunkirk	182	Lc	42.29N	79.21W
Dunkwa	166	Ed	5.58N	1.47W
Dún Laoghaire	118	Gh	53.17N	6.08W
Dún Mánmhai/Dunmanway	118	Dj	51.43N	9.07W
Dunmanway/Dún Mánmhai	118	Dj	51.43N	9.07W
Dunn	184	Hh	35.19N	78.37W
Dún na nGall/Donegal	118	Eg	54.39N	8.06W
Dún na nGall/Donegal [2]	118	Fg	54.50N	8.00W
Dunnellon	184	Fk	29.03N	82.28W
Dunnet Head	118	Jc	58.39N	3.23W
Dunning	186	Ff	41.50N	100.06W
Dún Pádraig/Downpatrick	118	Hg	54.20N	5.43W
Dunqulah = Dongola (EN)	160	Kg	19.10N	30.29 E
Dunqulah al Qadīmah	168	Eb	18.13N	30.45 E
Dunqunāb	168	Fa	21.06N	37.05 E
Dunqunāb, Khalīj-	168	Fa	21.05N	37.08 E
Dunrankin	184	Fa	48.39N	83.04W
Duns	118	Kf	55.47N	2.20W
Dünsberg	124	Kd	50.39N	8.35 E
Dunsmuir	188	Df	41.13N	122.16W
Dunstable	124	Bc	51.53N	0.31W
Dunstan Mountains	218	Cf	44.55S	169.30 E
Dun-sur-Auron	122	Ih	46.53N	2.34 E
Dun-sur-Meuse	124	He	49.23N	5.11 E
Duntroon	218	Df	44.51S	170.41 E
Dunvegan	118	Gd	57.26N	6.35W
Duobukur	152	La	50.19N	124.57 E
Duolun/Dolonnur	152	Kc	42.10N	116.30 E
Dupree	186	Fd	45.03N	101.36W
Duqm	142	Hf	19.41N	57.32 E
Duque de Bragança, Quedas-	158	Ii	9.05S	16.10 E
Duque de Caxias	202	Jh	22.47S	43.18W
Duque de York, Isla-	206	Eh	50.40S	75.20W
Du Quoin	186	Lg	38.01N	89.14W
Durack Range	212	Fc	17.00S	128.00 E
Durack River	212	Fc	15.33S	127.52 E
Durağan	146	Fb	41.25N	35.04 E
Durance	110	Gg	43.55N	4.44 E
Durand	186	Kd	44.38N	91.58W
Durand, Récif-	219b	Df	22.02S	168.39 E
Durango [2]	190	Dd	24.50N	104.50W
Durango [Co.-U.S.]	176	If	37.16N	107.53W
Durango [Sp.]	126	Ja	43.10N	2.37W
Durañona	204	Bm	37.15S	60.31W
Durant	182	He	33.59N	96.23W
Duras	122	Gj	44.40N	0.11 E
Duratón	126	Hc	41.37N	4.07W
Durazno	206	Id	33.22S	56.31W
Durazno [2]	204	Dk	33.05S	56.05W
Durazno, Cuchilla Grande del-	204	Dk	33.15S	56.15W
Durazzo (EN) = Durresi	130	Ch	41.19N	19.26 E
Durban	160	Kk	29.55S	30.56 E
Durbe	116	Ih	56.39N	21.14 E
Durbet-Daba, pereval-	152	Eb	49.37N	89.25 E
Ḑurbo	168	Ic	11.30N	50.18 E
Durbuy	124	Hd	50.21N	5.28 E
Đurđevac	128	Ld	46.02N	17.04 E
Düren	120	Cf	50.48N	6.29 E
Durg	148	Gd	21.11N	81.17 E
Durgapur	148	Hd	23.30N	87.15 E
Durgen-Nur	152	Fb	47.40N	93.30 E
Durham [3]	118	Lg	54.45N	1.40W
Durham	118	Lg	54.45N	1.45W
Durham [Eng.-U.K.]	118	Lg	54.47N	1.34W
Durham [N.C.-U.S.]	182	Ld	35.59N	78.54W
Durkee	188	Gd	44.36N	117.28W
Durlas/Thurles	118	Fi	52.41N	7.49W
Ḑurmā	144	Ge	24.37N	46.08 E
Durmersheim	124	Kf	48.56N	8.16 E
Durmitor	110	Hg	43.09N	19.02 E
Durnford, Punta-	162	De	23.37N	16.00W
Durresi = Durazzo (EN)	130	Ch	41.19N	19.26 E
Durrësit, Gjiri-	130	Ch	41.16N	19.28 E
Dursey/Oiléan Baoi	118	Cj	51.36N	10.12W
Dursunbey	146	Cc	39.35N	28.38 E
Durtal	122	Fg	47.40N	0.15W
Duru → Wuchuan	152	If	28.28N	107.57 E
Duruksi	168	Hd	8.29N	45.38 E
Durusu Gölü	130	Lh	41.20N	28.38 E
Durūz, Jabal ad-	146	Gf	32.40N	36.44 E
D'Urville Island	216	Dh	40.50S	173.50 E
Dušak	135	Cf	37.15N	60.01 E
Dusa Mareb	168	Hd	5.31N	46.24 E
Dušanbe	142	If	38.35N	68.48 E
Dušeti	132	Nh	42.05N	44.42 E
Dusetos	116	Li	55.42N	26.02 E
Dushan	142	Mg	25.55N	107.36 E
Dushan Hu	154	Dg	35.06N	116.48 E
Dusios ežeras / Dusja, ozero-	116	Jj	54.15N	23.45 E
Dusja, ozero- / Dusios ežeras	116	Jj	54.15N	23.45 E
Dusky Sound	218	Bf	45.45S	166.30 E
Düsseldorf	112	Ge	51.13N	6.46 E
Dusti	135	Gf	37.22N	68.43 E
Dutch Harbor	178a	Eb	53.53N	166.32W
Dutlwe	172	Cd	23.58S	23.54 E
Dutton, Mount-	188	Ig	38.01N	112.13W
Duved	116	Ea	63.24N	12.52 E
Duvergé	194	Ld	18.22N	71.31W
Düvertepe	130	Lj	39.14N	28.27 E
Duvno	128	Lg	43.43N	17.14 E
Duwayhin	144	He	24.16N	51.20 E
Duwayhin, Khawr-	146	Nj	24.20N	51.25 E
Duyfken Point	212	Ib	12.35S	141.40 E
Duyun	152	If	26.20N	107.28 E
Düz	162	Ic	33.28N	9.01 E
Düzce	144	Da	40.50N	31.10 E
Dve Mogili	130	If	43.36N	25.52 E
Dvina Gulf (EN) = Dvinskaja guba	110	Jb	65.00N	39.45 E
Dvinskaja guba = Dvina Gulf (EN)	110	Jb	65.00N	39.45 E
Dvor	128	Ke	45.04N	16.23 E
Dvuh Cirkov, gora-	138	Lc	67.30N	168.20 E
Dvůr Králové nad Labem	120	Lf	50.26N	15.48 E
Dwārka	148	Dd	22.14N	68.58 E
Dworshak Reservoir	188	Hc	46.45N	116.00W
Dyer, Cape-	174	Mc	66.37N	61.18W
Dyero	166	Dc	12.50N	6.30W
Dyer Plateau	222	Qf	70.45S	65.30W
Dyersburg	182	Jd	36.03N	89.23W
Dyfed [3]	118	Ji	52.05N	4.00W
Dyhmau, gora-	132	Mh	43.05N	43.12 E
Dyje	120	Mh	48.37N	16.56 E
Dyjsko-Svratecký úval	120	Mh	48.56N	16.25 E
Dyle	124	Gd	50.57N	4.40 E
Dylewska Góra	120	Pc	53.34N	19.57 E
Dynów	120	Sg	49.49N	22.14 E
Dyr, Djebel-	128	Cn	36.13N	8.46 E
Dyrhólaey	110	Ec	63.24N	19.08W
Dysnų ežeras / Disnaj, ozero-	114	Gi	55.35N	26.32 E
Dytike Rodhópi	130	Hh	41.45N	24.05 E
Dzabhan	140	Le	48.54N	93.23 E
Džalagaš	136	Gf	45.05N	64.40 E
Džalal-Abad	135	Id	40.56N	73.05 E
Džalal-Abadskaja oblast	135	Hd	41.40N	71.50 E
Džalilabad	136	Eh	39.12N	48.31 E
Džalinda	138	Hf	53.31N	123.59 E
Džambejty	132	Rd	50.14N	52.38 E
Džambul [Kaz.]	136	Hf	47.17N	71.42 E
Džambul [Kaz.]	142	Je	42.54N	71.22 E
Džambulskaja oblast [3]	136	Hg	44.30N	72.30 E
Džamyn-Ud	152	Jb	43.50N	111.45 E
Džanak	132	Si	40.30N	55.35 E
Džanga	136	Fg	40.01N	53.10 E
Džankoj	136	Df	45.42N	34.22 E
Džansugurov	136	Hf	45.23N	79.29 E
Džanybek	136	Ef	49.24N	46.50 E
Dzaoudzi	160	Lj	12.47S	45.17 E
Džardžan	138	Hc	68.55N	124.05 E
Džargalant [Mong.]	152	Gb	47.20N	99.35 E
Džargalant [Mong.]	152	Ib	48.35N	105.50 E
Džarkurgan	136	Gh	37.29N	67.25 E
Džava	132	Mh	42.24N	43.53 E
Džebariki-Haja	138	Id	62.23N	135.50 E
Džebel [Bul]	130	Ih	41.30N	25.18 E
Džebel [Turk.]	132	Sj	39.37N	54.18 E
Džebrail	132	Oj	39.23N	47.01 E
Dzereg	152	Fb	47.08N	92.50 E
Džergalan	135	Lc	42.33N	79.02 E
Dzermuk	132	Nj	39.48N	45.39 E
Dzeržinsk [Bela.]	132	Ec	53.44N	27.08 E
Dzeržinsk [Russia]	136	Ed	56.16N	43.32 E
Dzeržinsk [Ukr.]	132	Je	48.22N	37.50 E
Dzeržinskaja, gora-	116	Lk	53.53N	27.10 E
Dzeržinskoje	138	Ee	56.49N	95.18 E
Džetygara	142	Id	52.11N	61.12 E
Džetysaj	135	Gd	40.49N	68.20 E
Džezkazgan [Kaz.]	142	Ie	47.47N	67.46 E
Džezkazgan [Kaz.]	136	Gf	47.53N	67.27 E
Džezkazganskaja oblast [3]	136	Gf	47.30N	70.00 E
Dzhugdzhur Range (EN) = Džugdžur, hrebet-	140	Pd	58.00N	136.00 E
Działdówka	120	Qd	52.58N	20.05 E
Działdowo	120	Qc	53.15N	20.10 E
Działoszyce	120	Qf	50.22N	20.21 E
Dzibalchén	192	Oh	19.31N	89.45W
Dzibilchaltún	192	Og	21.05N	89.36W
Dzierzgoń	120	Pc	53.56N	19.21 E
Dzierżoniów	120	Mf	50.44N	16.39 E
Džirgatal	135	He	39.13N	71.12 E
Džizak	136	Gg	40.07N	67.52 E
Džizakskaja oblast [3]	136	Gg	40.20N	67.40 E
Džugdžur, hrebet- = Dzhugdzhur Range (EN)	140	Pd	58.00N	136.00 E
Džūkste/Džukste	116	Jh	56.45N	23.10 E
Džukste/Džūkste	116	Jh	56.45N	23.10 E
Džulfa	132	Nj	38.59N	45.35 E
Džuma	135	Fe	39.44N	66.39 E
Dzun-Bajan	152	Jc	44.28N	110.03 E
Dzungarian Basin (EN) = Junggar Pendi	140	Ke	45.00N	88.00 E

Dzungarian Gate (EN) = Alatau Shankou 140 Ke 45.25N 82.25 E
Dzungarian Gate (EN) = Džungarskije vorota 140 Ke 45.25N 82.25 E
Džungarski Alatau, hrebet- 140 Ke 45.00N 81.00 E
Džungarskije vorota = Dzungarian Gate (EN) 140 Ke 45.25N 82.25 E
Dzun-Hara 152 Ib 48.40N 106.40 E
Dzun-Mod 152 Ib 47.50N 106.57 E
Džurak-Sal 132 Mf 47.18N 43.36 E
Džusaly 136 Gf 45.29N 64.05 E
Džvari 132 Mh 42.42N 42.02 E

E

Éadan Doire/Edenderry 118 Fh 53.21N 7.03W
Eads 186 Eg 38.29N 102.47W
Eagle 178 Kd 64.46N 141.16W
Eagle 180 Lf 53.35N 57.25W
Eagle Creek 188 La 52.22N 107.24W
Eagle Lake 184 Mb 47.02N 68.36W
Eagle Lake [Ca.-U.S.] 188 Ef 40.39N 120.44W
Eagle Lake [Me.-U.S.] 184 Mb 46.20N 69.20W
Eagle Lake [Ont.-Can.] 186 Jb 49.42N 93.13W
Eagle Mountain 186 Kc 47.54N 90.33W
Eagle Nest 186 Dh 36.35N 105.14W
Eagle Pass 182 Gf 28.43N 100.30W
Eagle Peak [Ca.-U.S.] 182 Cc 41.17N 120.12W
Eagle Peak [Tx.-U.S.] 186 Dk 30.56N 105.01W
Eagle River [Ak.-U.S.] 178 Jd 61.19N 149.34W
Eagle River [Wi.-U.S.] 186 Ld 45.55N 89.15W
Eagle Summit 178 Jc 65.30N 145.38W
Ealing, London- 124 Bc 51.30N 0.19W
Ear Falls 186 Ja 50.38N 93.13W
Earn 118 Je 56.25N 3.30W
Earn, Loch- 118 Ie 56.28N 4.10W
Earnslaw, Mount- 218 Cf 44.37S 168.25 E
Easley 184 Fh 34.50N 82.36W
East Alligator River 212 Gb 12.08S 132.42 E
East Anglia 118 Ni 52.25N 1.00 E
East Angus 184 Lc 45.29N 71.40W
East Bay [Can.] 180 Jd 64.05N 81.30W
East Bay [U.S.] 186 Ll 29.05N 89.15W
East Berlin = Berlin 112 He 52.31N 13.24 E
Eastbourne [Eng.-U.K.] 118 Nk 50.46N 0.17 E
Eastbourne [N.Z.] 218 Fd 41.17S 174.54 E
East Caicos 194 Lc 21.41N 71.30W
East Cape [Fl.-U.S.] 184 Gm 25.07N 81.05W
East Cape [N.Z.] 208 Ih 37.41S 178.33 E
East Caroline Basin (EN) 106 Ii 4.00N 146.45 E
East Chicago 184 De 41.38N 87.27W
East China Sea (EN) = Dong Hai 140 Og 29.00N 125.00 E
East China Sea (EN) = Higashi-Shina-Kai 140 Og 29.00N 125.00 E
East Coast [2] 218 Gc 38.20S 177.50 E
East Dereham 118 Ni 52.41N 0.56 E
Eastend 188 Kb 49.31N 108.48W
East Entrance 220a Bb 7.50N 134.40 E
Easter Island (EN) = Pascua, Isla de- / Rapa Nui 208 Qg 27.07S 109.22W
Easter Island (EN) = Rapa Nui / Pascua, Isla de- 208 Qg 27.07S 109.22W
Eastern [Ghana] [3] 166 Ed 6.30N 0.30W
Eastern [Kenya] [3] 170 Gb 0.05N 38.00 E
Eastern [S.L.] [3] 166 Cd 8.15N 11.00W
Eastern [Ug.] [3] 170 Fb 1.30N 33.50 E
Eastern [Zam.] [3] 170 Fe 13.00S 32.15 E
Eastern Fields 214 Dj 10.03S 145.22 E
Eastern Ghats 140 Jh 14.00N 78.50 E
Eastern Point 197b Ab 18.07N 63.01W
Eastern Sayans (EN) = Vostočny Sajan 140 Ld 53.00N 97.00 E
Eastern Siberia (EN) 140 Rc 65.00N 155.00 E
Eastern Sierra Madre (EN) = Madre Oriental, Sierra- 174 Jg 22.00N 99.30W
Eastern Turkistan (EN) 140 Jf 40.00N 80.00 E
East Falkland/Soledad, Isla- 198 Kk 51.45S 58.50W
East Fork 186 Ie 42.41N 94.12W
East Friesland (EN) = Ostfriesland 120 Dc 53.20N 7.40 E
East Frisian Islands (EN) = Ostfriesische Inseln 120 Dc 53.45N 7.25 E
East Grand Forks 186 Hc 47.56N 97.01W
East Grand Rapids 184 Ed 42.56N 85.35W
East Greenland (EN) = Østgrønland [2] 179 Id 72.00N 35.00W
East Grinstead 118 Mj 51.08N 0.01W
East Ilsley 124 Ac 51.32N 1.17W
East Kilbride 118 If 55.46N 4.10W
East Lansing 184 Ed 42.44N 84.29W
East Las Vegas 188 Hh 36.07N 115.01W
Eastleigh 118 Lk 50.58N 1.22W
East London 160 Jl 33.00S 27.55 E
East Lynn Lake 184 Ff 38.05N 82.20W
Eastmain 180 Jf 52.14N 78.31W
Eastmain 180 Jf 52.15N 78.34W
Eastman 184 Fi 32.12N 83.11W
East Mariana Basin (EN) 106 Jh 12.00N 153.00 E
East Midlands Airport 124 Ab 52.50N 1.20W
East Novaya Zemlya Trough (EN) 136 Fa 73.30N 61.00 E
Easton 184 Je 40.41N 75.13W
East Pacific Rise (EN) 106 Ml 20.00S 110.00W
East Point 184 Ei 33.40N 84.27W
East Point [B.V.I.] 197a Db 18.43N 64.16W
East Point [V.I.U.S.] 197a Db 17.46N 64.33W
Eastport 184 Nc 44.54N 67.00W
East Pryor Mountain 188 Kd 45.14N 108.30W
East Retford 118 Mh 53.19N 0.56W
East Road 124 Cd 51.00N 1.02 E
East Schelde (EN) = Oosterschelde 122 Jc 51.30N 4.00 E
East Scotia Basin (EN) 198 Mk 57.00S 35.00W
East Siberian Sea (EN) = Vostočno Sibirskoje more 224 Cd 74.00N 166.00 E
East St. Louis 182 Id 38.38N 90.05W
East Sussex [3] 118 Nk 50.55N 0.15 E
East Tavaputs Plateau 188 Kg 39.45N 109.30W
East Wear Bay 124 Dc 51.08N 1.18 E
Eaton 184 Ef 39.44N 84.37W
Eatonia 188 Ka 51.13N 109.23W
Eatonton 184 Fi 33.20N 83.23W
Eatonville 188 Dc 46.51N 122.17W
Eau Claire 182 Ic 44.49N 91.31W
Eau-Claire, Lac à l'- 180 Ke 56.20N 74.00W
Eauripik Atoll 208 Fd 6.42N 143.03 E
Eauripik Ridge (EN) 214 Cg 3.00N 142.00 E
Eauze 122 Gk 43.52N 0.06 E
Ébano 192 Jf 22.13N 98.24W
Ebbegebirge 120 De 51.10N 7.45 E
Ebbw Vale 118 Jj 51.47N 3.12W
Ebebiyin 166 He 2.09N 11.20 E
Ebeltoft 116 Dh 56.12N 10.41 E
Ebensburg 184 He 40.28N 78.44W
Ebensee 128 Hc 47.48N 13.46 E
Eberbach 120 Eg 49.28N 8.59 E
Eber Gölü 146 Dc 38.38N 31.12 E
Ebersbach 120 Ke 51.01N 14.35 E
Eberswalde 120 Jd 52.50N 13.50 E
Ebetsu 154 Pc 43.07N 141.34 E
Ebino 154 Kh 32.02N 130.47 E
Ebinur Hu 140 Ke 44.55N 82.55 E
Ebla 144 Eb 35.42N 36.50 E
Ebo 170 Ce 11.02S 14.40 E
Ebola 170 Db 3.20N 20.57 E
Eboli 128 Jj 40.36N 15.04 E
Ebolowa 160 Ih 2.54N 11.09 E
Ebombo 170 Ed 5.42S 26.07 E
Ebon Atoll 208 Hd 4.38N 168.43 E
Ebre/Ebro 110 Gg 40.43N 0.54 E
Ebre, Delta de l'-/Ebro, Delta del- = Ebro, Delta of the- (EN) 126 Md 40.43N 0.54 E
Ebril, Récif- 216 Od 22.40S 133.30W
Ebro/Ebre 110 Gg 40.43N 0.54 E
Ebro, Delta del-/Ebre, Delta de l'- = Ebro, Delta of the- (EN) 126 Md 40.43N 0.54 E
Ebro, Delta of the- (EN) = Ebre, Delta de l'-/Ebro, Delta del- 126 Md 40.43N 0.54 E
Ebro, Delta of the- (EN) = Ebro, Delta del-/Ebre, Delta de l'- 126 Md 40.43N 0.54 E
Ebro, Embalse del- 126 Ia 43.00N 3.58W
Ebschloh 120 Ef 50.58N 8.15 E
Ecaussines 124 Gd 50.34N 4.10 E
Ecbatana 146 Me 34.48N 48.30 E
Eceabat 130 Ji 40.11N 26.21 E
Echdeira 162 Ef 27.14N 10.27W
Echegarate, Puerto de- 126 Jb 42.57N 2.14W
Echeng [China] 152 Kd 30.16N 116.03 E
Echeng [China] 154 Ci 30.24N 114.52 E
Echez 122 Gk 43.28N 0.02 E
Echigo-Sanmyaku 156 Fc 37.30N 139.15 E
Echizen-Misaki 156 Dd 35.59N 135.57 E
Echo Bay 176 Hc 66.04N 118.00W
Echo Seamount (EN) 162 Dd 25.23N 19.25W
Echt 124 Hc 51.06N 5.52 E
Echternach 124 Ie 49.49N 6.25 E
Echuca 212 Ig 36.10S 144.45 E
Echzell 124 Kd 50.23N 8.52 E
Écija 126 Gg 37.32N 5.05W
Eckernförde 120 Fb 54.28N 9.50 E
Eckerö 114 Ef 60.15N 19.35 E
Eclipse Sound 180 Jb 72.40N 79.30W
Ečmiadzin 136 Eg 40.09N 44.18 E
Écommoy 122 Gg 47.50N 0.16 E
Ecos 124 De 49.10N 1.39 E
Ecouis 124 De 49.19N 1.26 E
Écouves, Forêt d'- 122 Gf 48.32N 0.04 E
Ecrins, Barre des- 122 Mj 44.55N 6.22 E
Ecuador [1] 200 If 2.00S 77.30W
Ecury-sur-Coole 124 Gf 48.54N 4.20 E
Ed [Eth.] 168 Gc 13.56N 41.40 E
Ed [Swe.] 114 Cg 58.54N 11.56 E
Edam-Volendam 124 Hb 52.30N 5.03 E
Edane 116 Ee 59.38N 12.49 E
Eday 118 Kb 59.11N 2.47W
Edchera 162 Ed 27.02N 13.04W
Eddrachillis Bay 118 Hc 58.19N 5.15W
Eddystone Point 212 Jh 41.00S 148.20 E
Eddystone Rocks 118 Ik 50.15N 4.10W
Eddyville 184 Cg 37.03N 88.04W
Ede [Neth.] 122 Lb 52.03N 5.40 E
Ede [Nig.] 166 Fd 7.44N 4.26 E
Edéa 160 Ih 3.48N 10.08 E
Edefors 114 Ec 66.13N 20.54 E
Edéia 204 Hc 17.18S 49.55W
Edelény 120 Qh 48.18N 20.44 E
Eden 118 Jg 54.57N 3.01W
Eden [Austl.] 212 Jg 37.04S 149.54 E
Eden [Tx.-U.S.] 186 Gk 31.13N 99.51W
Edenburg 172 De 29.45S 25.56 E
Edenderry/Éadan Doire 118 Fh 53.21N 7.03W
Edenkoben 124 Ke 49.17N 8.09 E
Edenton 184 Ig 36.04N 76.39W
Eder 120 Fe 51.13N 9.27 E
Edersee 124 Lc 51.11N 9.03 E
Edertal 124 Lc 51.09N 9.09 E
Edewecht 124 Ja 53.08N 7.59 E
Edgar Ranges 212 Ec 18.43S 123.25 E
Edgartown 184 Le 41.23N 70.31W
Edgecumbe 218 Gb 37.58S 176.50 E
Edgeley 186 Gc 46.22N 98.43W
Edgell 180 Ld 61.50N 65.00W
Edgemont 186 Ee 43.18N 103.50W
Edgeøya 224 Jd 77.45N 22.30 E
Édhessa 130 Fi 40.48N 22.03 E
Edina 186 Jd 44.55N 93.20W
Edinburg 182 Hf 26.18N 98.10W
Edinburgh 112 Fd 55.57N 3.13W
Edinburgh, Arrecife- 194 Ff 14.50N 82.39W
Edincik 146 Bb 40.20N 27.51 E
Edingen/Enghien 124 Gd 50.42N 4.02 E
Edirne 146 Bb 41.40N 26.34 E
Edisto Island 184 Gi 32.35N 80.10W
Edisto River 184 Gi 32.39N 80.24W
Edith, Mount- 188 Jc 46.26N 111.11W
Edith Ronne Land (EN) 222 Rg 81.40S 50.00W
Edjeleh 162 Id 27.42N 9.53 E
Edjereh 162 He 24.35N 4.30 E
Édjérir 166 Fb 18.06N 0.50 E
Edmond 186 Hi 35.39N 97.29W
Edmonds 188 Dc 47.48N 122.22W
Edmonton 176 Hd 53.33N 113.28W
Edmundston 180 Kg 47.22N 68.20W
Edna 186 Hl 28.42N 96.39W
Edremit 144 Cb 39.35N 27.01 E
Edremit, Gulf of- (EN) = Edremit Körfezi 146 Bc 39.30N 26.45 E
Edremit Körfezi = Edremit, Gulf of- (EN) 146 Bc 39.30N 26.45 E
Edsbro 114 Eg 59.54N 18.29 E
Edsbruk 116 Gf 58.02N 16.28 E
Edsbyn 116 Fc 61.23N 15.49 E
Edson 180 Ff 53.35N 116.26W
Edsvalla 116 Ee 59.26N 13.13 E
Eduardo Castex 206 He 35.54S 64.18W
Eduni, Mount- 180 Ed 64.08N 128.10W
Edward, Lake- 158 Ji 0.25S 29.30 E
Edward, Lake- (EN) = Rutanzige, Lac- 158 Ji 0.25S 29.30 E
Edwards Creek 212 He 28.21S 135.51 E
Edwards Plateau 174 If 31.20N 101.00W
Edward VIII Bay 222 Ee 66.50S 57.00 E
Edward VII Peninsula 222 Mf 77.40S 155.00W
Edzo 180 Fd 62.47N 116.08W
Eeklo 122 Jc 51.11N 3.34 E
Eelde 124 Ia 53.08N 6.33 E
Eel River 182 Cc 40.40N 124.20W
Eem 124 Hb 52.16N 5.20 E
Eems 124 Ja 53.19N 7.03 E
Eemskanaal 124 Ia 53.19N 6.57 E
Eenrum 124 Ia 53.23N 6.25 E
Eersel 124 Hc 51.22N 5.19 E
Eesti = Estonskaja SSR 136 Cd 59.00N 26.00 E
Eesti Nõukogude Socialistlik Vabarijk/Estonskaja SSR → Eesti 136 Cd 59.00N 26.00 E
Eesti NSV = Eesti (EN) 136 Cd 59.00N 26.00 E
Efaté, Ile- 208 Hf 17.40S 168.25 E
Eferding 128 Ib 48.19N 14.01 E
Efes = Ephesus (EN) 130 Kl 37.55N 27.20 E
Effingham 186 Lg 39.07N 88.33W
Eflâni 146 Eb 41.26N 32.57 E
Eforie 130 Le 44.01N 28.38 E
Ega 126 Kb 42.19N 1.55W
Egadi, Isole- = Egadi Islands (EN) 110 Hh 38.00N 12.15 E
Egadi Islands (EN) = Egadi, Isole- 110 Hh 38.00N 12.15 E
Egan Range 188 Hg 39.00N 115.00W
Eganville 184 Ic 47.33N 77.06W
Egbe 166 Gd 8.13N 5.31 E
Ege Denizi = Aegean Sea (EN) 110 Ih 39.00N 25.00 E
Egedesminde/Ausiait 224 Nc 68.50N 52.45W
Egegik 178 He 58.13N 157.22W
Egentliga Finland/Varsinais-Suomi 116 Jd 60.40N 22.30 E
Eger 120 Qi 47.54N 20.23 E
Eger 120 Kf 50.32N 14.08 E
Egersund 114 Ag 58.27N 6.00 E
Egerton, Mount- 212 Dd 24.45S 117.45 E
Egeskov 116 Di 55.10N 10.30 E
Eggegebirge 120 Ee 51.40N 8.55 E
Eggenfelden 120 Ih 48.24N 12.46 E
Eggenstein-Leopoldshafen 124 Ke 49.05N 8.23 E
Eggum 114 Cb 68.19N 13.42 E
Eghezée 124 Gd 50.36N 4.56 E
Egijn-Gol 152 Ha 49.24N 103.36 E
Égletons 122 Ii 45.24N 2.03 E
Eglinton 180 Fa 75.45N 118.50W
Egmont, Cape- 216 Dg 39.17S 173.45 E
Egmont, Mount- 218 Fc 39.18S 174.04 E
Egnazia 128 Lj 40.50N 17.25 E
Eğridir 146 Dd 37.52N 30.51 E
Eğridir Gölü 144 Db 38.02N 30.53 E
Eğrigöz Dağ 130 Mj 39.21N 29.07 E
Egtved 116 Ci 55.37N 9.18 E
Éguas ou Correntina, Rio das- 204 Ja 13.26S 44.14W
Eguey 158 Ig 16.10N 16.10 E
Egvekinot 142 Uc 66.19N 179.10W
Egypt (EN) = Mişr [1] 160 Jf 27.00N 30.00 E
Eha Amufu 166 Gd 6.40N 7.46 E
Ehen Hudag → Alxa Youqi 152 Hd 39.12N 101.40 E
Ehime Ken [2] 154 Lh 33.35N 132.40 E
Ehingen (Donau) 120 Fh 48.17N 9.44 E
Ehrang, Trier- 124 Ie 49.49N 6.41 E
Ehrwald 128 Ec 47.24N 10.55 E
Ei 156 Bf 31.13N 130.30 E
Eiao, Ile- 208 Me 8.00S 140.40W
Eibar 126 Ja 43.11N 2.28W
Eibergen 124 Ib 52.07N 6.40 E
Eichsfeld 120 Ge 51.25N 10.20 E
Eichstätt 120 Hh 48.53N 11.11 E
Eickelborn, Lippetal- 124 Kc 51.39N 8.13 E
Eide 116 Bb 62.55N 7.26 E
Eider 120 Eb 54.19N 8.58 E
Eiderstedt 120 Eb 54.22N 8.50 E
Eidet 114 Cd 64.27N 13.37 E
Eidfjord 114 Bf 60.28N 7.05 E
Eidfjorden 116 Bd 60.25N 6.45 E
Eidslandet 116 Ad 60.44N 5.45 E
Eidsvåg 114 Be 62.47N 8.03 E
Eidsvoll 114 Cf 60.19N 11.14 E
Eidsvollfjellet 179 Nc 79.00N 13.00 E
Eierlandse Gat 124 Ga 53.12N 4.52 E
Eifel 120 Cf 50.15N 6.45 E
Eiffel Flats 172 Dc 18.13S 29.48 E
Eigat, Jabal- 168 Fa 22.00N 35.01 E
Eigenbrakel/Braine-l'Alleud 124 Gd 50.41N 4.22 E
Eigerøya 116 Af 58.25N 5.55 E
Eigg 118 Ge 56.54N 6.10W
Eight Degree Channel 140 Ji 8.00N 73.00 E
Eights Coast 222 Pf 73.30S 96.00W
Eighty Mile Beach 212 Ec 19.45S 121.00 E
Eigrim, Jabal- 168 Fb 19.22N 35.18 E
Eijsden 124 Hd 50.46N 5.42 E
Eikeren 116 Ce 59.40N 10.00 E
Eikesdalsvatnet 116 Cb 62.35N 8.10 E
'Eilai 168 Eb 16.33N 30.54 E
Eildon, Lake- 212 Jg 37.10S 145.50 E
Eilenburg 120 Ie 51.28N 12.37 E
Eiler Rasmussen, Kap- 179 Kb 82.40N 20.00W
Eil Malk 220a Ac 7.09N 134.22 E
Eina 116 Dd 60.38N 10.36 E
Einasleigh 212 Ic 18.31S 144.05 E
Einasleigh River 212 Ic 17.30S 142.17 E
Einbeck 120 Fe 51.49N 9.52 E
Eindhoven 122 Lc 51.26N 5.28 E
Einsiedeln 128 Cc 47.08N 8.45 E
Éire/Ireland [1] 112 Fe 53.00N 8.00W
Eiriksjökull 114a Bb 64.46N 20.24W
Eirunepé 200 Jf 6.40S 69.52W
Eisack/Isarco 128 Fd 46.27N 11.18 E
Eisacktal/Isarco, Valle- 128 Fd 46.45N 11.35 E
Eisenach 120 Gf 50.59N 10.19 E
Eisenberg 120 Hf 50.58N 11.54 E
Eisenberg 124 Kc 51.15N 8.50 E
Eisenberg (Pfalz) 124 Ke 49.33N 8.06 E
Eisenerz 128 Ic 47.32N 14.53 E
Eisenerzer Alpen 128 Ic 47.30N 14.40 E
Eisenhüttenstadt 120 Kd 52.10N 14.42 E
Eisenstadt 128 Kc 47.51N 16.31 E
Eisenwurzen 128 Jc 47.56N 15.02 E
Eišiškes/Ejšiškes 114 Fi 54.14N 25.02 E
Eisleben 120 He 51.32N 11.33 E
Eitorf 124 Jd 50.46N 7.27 E
Eivissa/Ibiza = Iviza (EN) 110 Gh 39.00N 1.25 E
Eje, Sierra del- 126 Fb 42.20N 6.55W
Ejea de los Caballeros 126 Kb 42.08N 1.08W
Ejeda 172 Gd 24.19S 44.21 E
Ejido 202 Db 8.33N 71.14W
Ejido Insurgentes 192 De 25.12N 111.45W
Ejin Horo Qi (Altan Xiret) 152 Id 39.31N 109.45 E
Ejin Qi 142 Me 41.50N 100.50 E
Ejšiškes/Eišiškes 114 Fi 54.14N 25.02 E
Ejura 166 Ed 7.23N 1.22W
Ejutla de Crespo 190 Ee 16.34N 96.44W
Ekalaka 188 Md 45.53N 104.33W
Ekecek Dağı 146 Fc 38.39N 34.03 E
Ekenäs/Tammisaari 114 Fg 59.58N 23.26 E
Ekeren, Antwerpen- 122 Kc 51.17N 4.25 E
Eket 166 Ge 4.39N 7.56 E
Eketahuna 218 Fd 40.39S 175.44 E
Ekhinádhes Nisoi 130 Ek 38.25N 21.02 E
Ekiatapski hrebet 138 Mc 68.40N 177.50 E
Ekibastuz 136 He 51.42N 75.22 E
Ekimčan 138 If 53.07N 133.02 E
Ekoli 170 Dc 0.23S 24.16 E
Ekoln 116 Ge 59.45N 17.35 E
Ekombe 170 Db 1.16N 21.36 E
Ekonda 138 Fc 65.47N 105.17 E
Eksjö 114 Dh 57.40N 14.57 E
Ekuma 172 Bc 18.10S 15.47 E
Ekwan 180 Jf 53.12N 82.15W
El Aaiún 160 Ff 27.10N 13.12W
El Aargub 162 De 23.37N 15.52W
El Aatf 162 De 23.30N 15.30W
El Abadia 126 Nh 36.13N 1.40 E
El Abd 126 Mi 35.29N 0.42 E
El Abiodh Sidi Cheikh 162 Hc 32.53N 0.34 E
El 'Açâba [3] 162 Ef 16.30N 12.00W
El 'Açâba 162 Ef 16.49N 12.05W
El Adeb Larache 162 Id 27.22N 8.52 E
El Affroun 126 Oh 36.28N 2.37 E
Elafónisi Channel (EN) = Elafonisou, Stenon- 130 Fm 36.25N 23.00 E
Elafónisos 130 Fm 36.29N 22.58 E
Elafonisou Stenón- = Elafónisi Channel (EN) 130 Fm 36.25N 23.00 E
El Agreb 162 Ic 30.48N 5.30 E
El Aguilar 206 Gb 32.12S 65.42W
El Álamo 192 Ab 31.34N 116.02W
El Alia 162 Ic 32.42N 5.26 E
El Amria 126 Ki 35.32N 1.01W
Elan 130 Lc 46.06N 28.04 E
El Andévalo 126 Fg 37.40N 7.00W
El Aouinet 128 Bo 35.52N 7.54 E
El Arahal 126 Gg 37.16N 5.33W
El Aricha 162 Gc 34.13N 1.16W
Elása 130 Jn 35.17N 26.20 E
Elassón 130 Fj 39.54N 22.11 E
Elat 142 Fg 29.33N 34.57 E
Eláti 130 Dk 38.43N 20.39 E
Elato Atoll 208 Fd 7.28N 146.10 E
El Attaf 126 Nh 36.13N 1.40 E
Elâziğ 144 Eb 38.41N 39.14 E
El Azúcar, Presa de- 192 Jd 26.15N 99.00W
Elba 184 Dj 31.25N 86.04W
Elba 110 Hg 42.45N 10.15 E
Elban 138 If 50.05N 136.30 E
El Banco 202 Db 9.01N 73.58W
El Barco de Ávila 126 Gd 40.21N 5.31W
El Barco de Valdeorras 126 Fb 42.25N 6.59W
Elbasani 130 Dh 41.06N 20.05 E
El Baúl 202 Eb 8.57N 68.17W
El Bayadh 162 Hc 33.41N 1.01 E
Elbe 110 Ge 53.50N 9.00 E
Elbe (EN) = Labe 110 Gc 53.50N 9.00 E
Elbe-Lübeck-Kanal 120 Gc 53.50N 10.36 E
Elbert, Mount- 174 If 39.07N 106.27W
Elberton 184 Fh 34.07N 82.52W
Elbe-Seitenkanal 120 Gd 52.22N 10.34 E
Elbeuf 122 Ge 49.17N 1.00 E
Elbeyl 144 Eb 36.41N 37.26 E
El Bierzo 126 Fb 42.40N 6.50W
Elbistan 146 Gc 38.13N 37.12 E
Elbląg 112 He 54.10N 19.25 E
Elbląg [2] 120 Pb 54.10N 19.25 E
Elbląski, Kanał- 120 Pc 53.43N 19.53 E
El Bolsón 206 Ff 41.58S 71.31W
El Bonillo 126 Jf 38.57N 2.32W
Elbow 188 La 51.07N 106.35W
Elbow Cays 194 Gb 23.57N 80.29W
Elbow Lake 186 Id 46.00N 95.58W
Elbrus 110 Kg 43.21N 42.26 E
Elbsandsteingebirge 120 Kf 50.50N 14.12 E
'Ēlbūr 168 He 4.40N 46.40 E
Elburg 122 Lb 52.26N 5.50 E
El Burgo de Osma 126 Ic 41.35N 3.04W
Elburgon 170 Gc 0.18S 35.49 E
El Burro 192 Ic 29.16N 101.55W
Elburz Mountains (EN) = Alborz, Reshteh-ye Kūhhā-ye- 140 Hf 36.00N 53.00 E
El Cajon 182 De 32.48N 116.58W
El Callao 202 Fb 7.21N 61.49W
El Calvario 196 Ch 8.59N 67.00W
El Campo 186 Hl 29.12N 96.16W
El Canelo 192 Ie 24.19N 100.23W
El Cármen 204 Cd 18.49S 58.33W
El Carmen de Bolivar 202 Cb 9.43N 75.07W
El Casco 192 Ge 25.34N 104.35W
El Castillo 194 Eh 11.01N 84.24W
El Centro 182 De 32.48N 115.34W
El Cerro 202 Fg 17.31S 61.34W
El Chaparro 196 Dh 9.10N 65.01W
Elche / Elx 126 Lf 38.15N 0.42W
Elcho Island 212 Hb 11.55S 135.45 E
El Cuy 206 Ge 39.56S 68.20W
Elda 126 Lf 38.29N 0.47W
Ēldab 168 Hd 8.58N 46.38 E
Elde 120 Ic 53.17N 12.40 E
'Ēl Dēre 160 Lh 3.55N 47.10 E
El Dere 168 Gd 5.07N 43.12 E
El Descanso 192 Aa 32.12N 116.55W
El Desemboque 190 Bb 30.30N 112.59W
El Dificil 194 Ji 9.51N 74.14W
Eldikan 138 Id 60.38N 135.07 E
El Djouf 158 Gf 21.25N 6.40W
El Doncello 202 Cc 1.43N 75.17W
Eldorado 186 Fk 30.52N 100.36W
El Dorado 202 Cd 24.17N 107.31W
Eldorado 206 Jc 26.24S 54.38W
El Dorado [Ar.-U.S.] 182 Ie 33.13N 92.40W
El Dorado [Ks.-U.S.] 182 Hd 37.49N 96.52W
El Dorado [Ven.] 200 Je 6.44N 61.38W
Eldorado Paulista 204 Hg 24.32S 48.06W
El Dorado Springs 186 Ih 37.52N 94.01W
Eldoret 170 Gb 0.31N 35.17 E
Eldsberga 116 Eh 56.36N 12.59 E
'Ēl Dubbo 168 Ge 3.52N 44.45 E
Eldžik 135 De 39.25N 63.01 E
Elefantes, Rio dos- 172 Ed 24.03S 32.40 E
El Eglab 158 Gf 26.30N 5.00W
Elēja/Eleja 114 Fh 56.28N 23.41 E
Eleja/Elēja 114 Fh 56.28N 23.41 E
Elektrėnai/Elektrenaj 116 Kj 54.46N 24.47 E
Elektrenaj/Elektrėnai 116 Kj 54.46N 24.47 E
Elektrostal 136 Dd 55.48N 38.29 E
Elele 166 Gd 5.06N 6.49 E
Elena 130 Ig 42.56N 25.53 E
El Encanto [Bol.] 204 Cc 16.57S 59.24W
El Encanto [Col.] 202 Dd 1.37S 73.13W
Elephant Butte Reservoir 186 Cj 33.19N 107.10W
Elephant Island 222 Re 61.10S 55.14W
Elephant Mountain 186 Ek 30.02N 103.30W
Elesbão Veloso 202 Je 6.13S 42.08W
El Escorial 126 Hd 40.35N 4.10W
Eleşkirt 146 Jc 39.49N 42.40 E
El Estor 194 Cf 15.32N 89.21W
Eleuthera 174 Lg 25.15N 76.20W
Elevsis 130 Gk 38.02N 23.32 E
Elevtheroúpolis 130 Hi 40.55N 24.15 E
El Fendek 126 Gi 35.34N 5.35W
El Ferrol 126 Da 43.29N 8.14W
El Fud 168 Gd 7.15N 42.51 E
El Fuerte [Mex.] 192 Hf 23.50N 103.06W
El Fuerte [Mex.] 190 Cc 26.25N 108.39W
Elgåhogna 116 Eb 62.09N 12.04 E
'Ēl Gāl 168 Ic 11.23N 50.23 E
El Galhak 168 Ec 11.03N 32.42 E
El Gassi 162 Ic 30.55N 5.50 E
Elgen 138 Kd 62.45N 150.40 E
Elgepiggen 114 Ce 62.10N 11.22 E
El Ghomri 126 Mi 35.41N 0.12 E
Elgi 138 Jd 64.20N 142.05 E
Elgin [Il.-U.S.] 182 Jc 42.02N 88.17W
Elgin [N.D.-U.S.] 186 Fc 46.24N 101.51W
Elgin [Or.-U.S.] 188 Gd 45.34N 117.55W
Elgin [Scot.-U.K.] 118 Jd 57.39N 3.20W
Elginski 138 Jd 64.48N 141.50 E
Elgjaij 138 Gd 62.28N 117.37 E
El Goléa 160 Hf 30.34N 2.53 E
Elgon, Mont- 158 Kh 1.08N 34.33 E
Elgoran 168 Gd 5.04N 44.22 E
El Grao, Castellón de la Plana- 126 Me 39.58N 0.01 E
El Grao, Valencia- 126 Le 39.27N 0.20W
El Grao de Gandia, Gandia- 126 Lf 38.59N 0.09W
El Guapo 196 Dg 10.09N 65.58W
El Guayabo 194 Ki 8.37N 72.20W
El Hadjar 128 Bn 36.48N 7.45 E
El Hajeb 162 Fc 33.42N 5.22W
El Ham 126 Qi 35.42N 4.52 E
El Hammam 126 Li 35.50N 0.15W

Index Symbols

- [1] Independent Nation
- [2] State, Region
- [3] District, County
- [4] Municipality
- [5] Colony, Dependency
- Continent
- Physical Region
- Historical or Cultural Region
- Mount, Mountain
- Volcano
- Hill
- Mountains, Mountain Range
- Hills, Escarpment
- Plateau, Upland
- Pass, Gap
- Plain, Lowland
- Delta
- Salt Flat
- Valley, Canyon
- Crater, Cave
- Karst Features
- Depression
- Polder
- Desert, Dunes
- Forest, Woods
- Heath, Steppe
- Oasis
- Cape, Point
- Coast, Beach
- Cliff
- Peninsula
- Isthmus
- Sandbank
- Island
- Atoll
- Rock, Reef
- Islands, Archipelago
- Rocks, Reefs
- Coral Reef
- Well, Spring
- Geyser
- River, Stream
- Waterfall, Rapids
- River Mouth, Estuary
- Lake
- Salt Lake
- Intermittent Lake
- Reservoir
- Swamp, Pond
- Canal
- Glacier
- Ice Shelf, Pack Ice
- Ocean
- Sea
- Gulf, Bay
- Strait, Fjord
- Lagoon
- Bank
- Seamount
- Tablemount
- Ridge
- Shelf
- Basin
- Escarpment, Sea Scarp
- Fracture
- Trench, Abyss
- National Park, Reserve
- Point of Interest
- Recreation Site
- Cave, Cavern
- Historic Site
- Ruins
- Wall, Walls
- Church, Abbey
- Temple
- Scientific Station
- Railway station
- Airport
- Port
- Military installation
- Lighthouse
- Mine
- Tunnel
- Dam, Bridge

'Ēl Ḩamurre	168	Hd	7.11N	48.55 E
El Hank	158	Gf	24.00N	6.30W
El Harrach, Al Jazā'ir-	126	Ph	36.43N	3.08 E
Elhotovo	132	Nh	43.20N	44.13 E
Elhovo	130	Jg	42.10N	26.34 E
El Huecú	206	Fe	37.37S	70.36W
Elida	186	Ej	33.57N	103.39W
Éliki, Vallée d'-	166	Gc	14.45N	7.15 E
Elila	170	Ec	2.43S	25.53 E
Elila	158	Ji	2.45S	25.53 E
Elimäki	116	Ld	60.43N	26.28 E
Elin Pelin	130	Gg	42.40N	23.36 E
Elisejna	130	Gf	43.05N	23.29 E
Elisenvaara	116	Mc	61.19N	29.47 E
Elista	112	Kf	46.16N	44.14 E
Elizabeth [Austl.]	210	Eh	34.45S	138.39 E
Elizabeth [N.J.-U.S.]	184	Je	40.40N	74.13W
Elizabeth, Cape-	188	Cc	47.22N	124.22W
Elizabeth City	182	Ld	36.18N	76.14W
Elizabeth Reef	208	Gg	29.55S	159.05 E
Elizabethton	184	Fg	36.21N	82.13W
Elizabethtown [Ky.-U.S.]	184	Eg	37.42N	85.52W
Elizabethtown [N.C.-U.S.]	184	Hh	34.38N	78.37W
El Jadida	160	Ge	33.15N	8.30W
El Jadida [3]	162	Fc	32.54N	8.30W
El Jícaro	194	Dg	13.43N	86.08W
'Ēl Jilib	168	He	3.48N	47.07 E
Elk	120	Se	53.50N	22.22 E
Ełk	120	Sc	53.32N	22.47 E
El Kala	162	Ib	36.54N	8.27 E
El Kantara	162	Ib	35.13N	5.43 E
El Karimia	126	Nh	36.07N	1.33 E
Elk City [Id.-U.S.]	188	Hd	45.51N	115.29W
Elk City [Ok.-U.S.]	186	Gi	35.25N	99.25W
El Kelaa des Srarhna	162	Fc	32.03N	7.24W
El Kelaa des Srarhna [3]	162	Fc	32.03N	7.30W
El Kere	168	Gd	5.51N	42.06 E
Elkhart [In.-U.S.]	182	Jc	41.41N	85.58W
Elkhart [Ks.-U.S.]	186	Fh	37.00N	101.54W
El Khatt	162	Ef	19.00N	12.25W
Elkhead Mountains	186	Cf	40.50N	107.05W
El Khnâchîch	166	Ea	21.20N	3.45W
Elkhorn River	186	Hf	41.07N	96.19W
Elkins	184	Hf	38.56N	79.53W
Elk Lake	184	Gb	47.42N	80.11W
Elk Mountain	188	Lf	41.38N	106.32W
Elk Mountains	186	Cg	38.55N	106.50W
Elko	176	He	40.50N	115.46W
Elk Peak	188	Jc	46.27N	110.46W
Elk River	186	Jd	45.18N	93.35W
Elk River	184	Gf	38.21N	81.38W
Elku kalns	116	Kg	57.04N	25.23 E
Ell, Lake-	212	Fe	29.15S	127.45 E
Ellás=Greece (EN) [1]	112	Ih	39.00N	22.00 E
Ellé	122	Cg	47.52N	3.32W
Ellef Ringnes	174	Ib	78.30N	104.00W
Ellen, Mount-	182	Ed	38.07N	110.49W
Ellendale	182	Hb	46.06N	98.32W
Ellensburg	182	Cb	46.40N	120.32W
Ellenville	184	Je	41.43N	74.23W
Ellesmere	174	Kb	79.00N	82.00W
Ellesmere, Lake-	218	Ee	43.45S	172.30 E
Ellice	180	Hc	68.02N	103.25W
Ellice Islands → Tuvalu [1]	210	Ie	8.00S	178.00 E
Elliot [Austl.]	212	Gc	17.35S	133.35 E
Elliot [S.Afr.]	172	Df	31.18S	27.50 E
Elliot, Mount-	212	Jc	19.29S	146.58 E
Elliot Lake	180	Jg	46.23N	82.39W
Ellisras	172	Dd	23.40S	27.46 E
Elliston	212	Gf	33.39S	134.55 E
Ellisville	186	Lk	31.36N	89.12W
Ellmau	128	Gc	47.31N	12.18 E
Ellös	114	Cg	58.11N	11.27 E
Ellsworth [Ks.-U.S.]	186	Gg	38.44N	98.14W
Ellsworth [Me.-U.S.]	184	Mc	44.33N	68.26W
Ellsworth [Nb.-U.S.]	186	Ee	42.04N	102.15W
Ellsworth, Lake-	186	Gi	34.48N	98.20W
Ellsworth Land (EN)	222	Pf	75.30S	80.00W
Ellsworth Mountains	222	Pf	78.30S	85.00W
Ellwangen (Jagst)	120	Gh	48.57N	10.08 E
Elm	120	Gd	52.09N	10.53 E
El Macao	194	Md	18.46N	68.33W
Elmadağ	146	Ec	39.55N	33.15 E
Elma Dağı	130	Mk	38.46N	29.32 E
El Maestrat/El Maestrazgo	126	Ld	40.30N	0.10W
El Maestrazgo/El Maestrat	126	Ld	40.30N	0.10W
El Mahia	166	Ea	22.30N	2.30W
El Maitén	206	Ff	42.03S	71.10W
Elmaki	166	Gb	17.55N	8.20 E
El Malah	126	Ph	36.18N	3.14 E
Elmali	146	Cd	36.44N	29.56 E
Elmalı	146	Ic	39.25N	40.35 E
El Manteco	196	Ei	7.27N	62.32W
El Marfil	204	Bb	15.35S	60.19W
El Marsa	126	Mh	36.24N	0.55 E
El Medo	168	Gd	5.41N	41.46 E
El Meghaïer	162	Ic	33.57N	5.56 E
Elmhurst	186	Mf	41.53N	87.56W
El Milagro	206	Gd	31.01S	65.59W
Elmira	182	Lc	42.06N	76.50W
El Mrâyer	162	Fe	21.30N	8.10W
El Mreïti	162	Fe	23.29N	7.52W
El Mreyyé	158	Gg	19.30N	7.00W
Elmshorn	120	Fc	53.45N	9.39 E
Elmstein	124	Je	49.22N	7.56 E
Elne	122	Il	42.36N	2.58 E
El Nevado, Cerro-	206	Ge	35.35S	68.30W
El Niabo	168	Fe	4.33N	39.59 E
El Nihuil	206	Gd	34.58S	68.40W
El Novillo	192	Ec	28.40N	109.30W
El Novillo, Presa-	192	Ec	29.05N	109.45W
El Ochenta y Uno	192	Kg	21.35N	97.57W
Elorn	122	Bf	48.27N	4.16W
Elortondo	204	Bk	33.42S	61.37W
Elorza	202	Eb	7.03N	69.31W
Elota, Rio-	192	Ff	23.52N	106.56W
El Oued	162	Ic	33.20N	6.53 E
Eloy	188	Jj	32.45N	111.33W
El Palmar	196	Fh	8.01N	61.53W
El Palmito	192	Ge	25.40N	104.59W
El Panadés/El Penedès	126	Nc	41.25N	1.30 E
El Pao [Ven.]	196	Eh	8.06N	62.33W
El Pao [Ven.]	196	Bh	9.38N	68.08W
El Paraíso	194	Dg	13.51N	86.34W
El Paraíso [3]	194	Df	14.10N	86.30W
El Páramo	126	Gb	42.25N	5.45W
El Pardo, Madrid-	126	Id	40.32N	3.46W
El Paso [Il.-U.S.]	186	Lf	40.44N	89.01W
El Paso [Tx.-U.S.]	176	If	31.45N	106.29W
El Penedès/El Panadés	126	Nc	41.25N	1.30 E
El Perú	196	Fi	7.19N	61.49W
El Pico	202	Fg	15.57S	64.42W
El Pilar	196	Eg	10.32N	63.09W
El Pintado	206	Hb	24.38S	61.27W
El Port / Puerto de Sóller	126	Oe	39.48N	2.41 E
El Porvenir [Hond.]	194	Df	14.41N	87.11W
El Porvenir [Pan.]	194	Hi	9.12N	80.08W
El Porvenir [Ven.]	196	Bi	6.55N	68.42W
El Potosí	192	Ie	24.51N	100.19W
el Prat de Llobregat / Prat de Llobregat	126	Oc	41.20N	2.06 E
El Priorato/El Priorat	126	Mc	41.10N	1.00 E
El Priorat/El Priorato	126	Mc	41.10N	1.00 E
El Progreso [3]	194	Cf	14.50N	90.00W
El Progreso [Guat.]	194	Bf	14.51N	90.04W
El Progreso [Hond.]	190	Ge	15.21N	87.49W
El Puente del Arzobispo	126	Ge	39.48N	5.10W
El Puerto	192	Dc	28.45N	111.20W
El Puerto de Santa María	126	Fh	36.36N	6.13W
El Rastro	196	Ch	9.03N	67.27W
El Real de Santa María	194	Ii	8.08N	77.43W
El Reno	182	Hd	35.32N	97.57W
El Ribeiro	126	Db	42.25N	8.10W
Elrose	188	Ka	51.13N	108.01W
El Saler	126	Le	39.23N	0.20W
El Salto	190	Cd	23.47N	105.23W
El Salvador [1]	176	Kh	13.50N	88.55W
El Samán de Apure	196	Bi	7.55N	68.44W
El Sauce [Mex.]	192	De	24.34N	111.29W
El Sauce [Nic.]	194	Dg	12.53N	86.32W
El Sauz	192	Fc	29.03N	106.15W
Elsberry	186	Kg	39.10N	90.47W
Elsdorf	124	Id	50.56N	6.34 E
Else	124	Kb	52.12N	8.40 E
El Seibo	194	Md	18.46N	68.52W
Elsen, Paderborn-	124	Kc	51.44N	8.41 E
Elsen Nur	152	Fd	35.08N	92.20 E
'Ēl Shāma	168	Ge	2.46N	41.03 E
El Socorro	196	Dh	8.59N	65.44W
El Sombrero	202	Eb	9.23N	67.03W
Elst	124	Hc	51.55N	5.52 E
Elsterwerda	120	Je	51.27N	13.32 E
El Sueco	190	Cc	29.54N	106.24W
El Taht	126	Mi	35.27N	0.46 E
El Tala	206	Gc	26.07S	65.17W
Eltanin Bay	222	Pf	73.40S	82.00W
Eltham	218	Fc	39.26S	174.18 E
El Tigre	200	Je	8.55N	64.15W
El Tigre, Isla-	194	Dg	13.16N	87.38W
El Toboso	126	Je	39.31N	3.00W
El Tocuyo	202	Eb	9.47N	69.48W
Elton	132	Oe	49.08N	46.50 E
Elton, ozero-	136	Ef	49.10N	46.40 E
El Torcal	126	Hh	36.55N	4.35W
El Toro / Toro, Monte-	126	Qe	39.59N	4.07 E
El Trébol	204	Bk	32.12S	61.42W
El Trigo	204	Cl	35.52S	59.24W
El Triunfo [Hond.]	194	Dg	13.06N	87.00W
El Triunfo [Mex.]	192	Df	23.47N	110.08W
El Tuito	192	Gg	20.19N	105.22W
El Turbio	206	Fh	51.41S	72.05W
Eltville am Rhein	124	Kd	50.02N	8.07 E
Eltz	124	Jd	50.12N	7.18 E
Elūru	148	Ge	17.05N	81.15 E
Elva	114	Gg	58.13N	26.25 E
El Valle	194	Gi	8.31N	80.08W
El Vallés / El Vallès	126	Oc	41.35N	2.15 E
Elvas	126	Ef	38.53N	7.10W
El Vejo, Cerro-	202	Db	7.30N	73.05W
El Venado, Isla-	194	Fh	11.57N	83.44W
Elverum	114	Cf	60.53N	11.34 E
El Viejo	194	Dg	12.40N	87.10W
El Viejo, Volcán-	174	Kh	13.38N	87.11W
El Vigía	194	Li	8.38N	71.39W
El Vigía, Cerro-	192	Gg	21.25N	104.00W
El Wak	170	Hb	2.49N	40.56 E
Elwell, Lake-	188	Jb	48.22N	111.17W
Elwood	184	Ee	40.17N	85.50W
Elx / Elche	126	Lf	38.15N	0.42W
Ely [Eng.-U.K.]	118	Ni	52.24N	0.16 E
Ely [Mn.-U.S.]	182	Ib	47.54N	91.51W
Ely [Nv.-U.S.]	176	Hf	39.15N	114.53W
Elyria	184	Fe	41.22N	82.06W
El Yunque	197a	Cb	18.18N	65.47W
Elz	124	Kd	50.25N	8.02 E
Elzbach	124	Jd	50.12N	7.22 E
Emaé	219b	Dc	17.04S	168.22 E
Ema jõgi / Emajygi	116	Lf	58.20N	27.15 E
Emajygi / Ema jõgi	116	Lf	58.20N	27.15 E
Emali	170	Gc	2.05S	37.28 E
Emāmshahr [Iran]	144	Hb	36.50N	54.29 E
Emāmshahr [Iran]	144	Ib	36.25N	55.01 E
Emāmzādeh 'Abbās	146	Lf	32.25N	47.55 E
Emån	114	Dh	57.08N	16.30 E
Emba	136	Ff	48.50N	58.10 E
Emba	110	Lf	46.38N	53.04 E
Embaracai, Rio-	204	Ff	23.27S	53.58W
Embarcación	206	Hb	23.13S	64.06W
Embarras Portage	180	Ge	58.25N	111.27W
Embarras River	186	Mg	38.39N	87.37W
Embrun	122	Mj	44.34N	6.30 E
Embu	170	Gc	0.32S	37.27 E
Emden	120	Dc	53.22N	7.13 E
Emeldžak	138	He	58.27N	126.57 E
Emerald	210	Fg	23.32S	148.10 E
Emerald	188	Jj	76.50N	114.00W
Emerson	186	Hb	49.00N	97.12W
Emet	146	Cc	39.20N	29.15 E
Emi Koussi	158	Ig	19.55N	18.30 E
Emiliano Zapata	192	Ni	17.45N	91.46W
Emilia-Romagna [2]	128	Ef	44.45N	11.00 E
Emilio R. Coni	204	Cj	30.04S	58.16W
Emily Rocu	198	Hh	29.40S	87.25W
Emin/Dorbiljin	152	Db	46.32N	83.39 E
Emine, Nos-	130	Kg	42.42N	27.54 E
Emira Island	214	Dh	1.40S	150.00 E
Emirdağ	146	Dc	39.01N	31.10 E
Emisu, Tarso-	158	If	21.13N	18.32 E
Emlichheim	120	Cd	52.37N	6.51 E
Emmaboda	114	Dh	56.38N	15.32 E
Emmaste	114	Fg	58.43N	22.36 E
Emme	128	Bd	47.10N	7.35 E
Emmeloord, Noordoostpolder-	124	Hb	52.42N	5.44 E
Emmelshausen	124	Jd	50.09N	7.34 E
Emmen	122	Mb	52.47N	6.55 E
Emmendingen	120	Dh	48.08N	7.51 E
Emmen-Emmer-Compascuum	124	Jb	52.49N	7.03 E
Emmen-Klazienaveen	124	Jb	52.44N	7.01 E
Emmen-Nieuw-Weerdinge	124	Jb	52.52N	7.01 E
Emmental	128	Bd	46.55N	7.45 E
Emmen-Weerdinge	124	Ib	52.49N	6.57 E
Emmer	124	Lb	52.03N	9.23 E
Emmer-Compascuum, Emmen-	124	Jb	52.49N	7.03 E
Emmerich	120	Ce	51.50N	6.15 E
Emmet	212	Id	24.40S	144.28 E
Emmetsburg	186	Ie	43.07N	94.41W
Emmett	188	Ge	43.52N	116.30W
Emmonak	178	Gd	62.46N	164.30W
Emőd	120	Qi	47.56N	20.49 E
Emory	188	Jf	41.05N	111.16W
Emory Peak	182	Gf	29.13N	103.17W
Empalme	190	Bc	27.58N	110.51W
Empangeni	172	Ee	28.50S	31.48 E
Empedrado	206	Ii	27.57S	58.48W
Emperor Seamounts (EN)	106	Je	40.00N	171.00 E
Empoli	128	Eg	43.43N	10.57 E
Empordà / Ampurdán	126	Ob	42.12N	2.45 E
Emporia [Ks.-U.S.]	182	Hd	38.24N	96.11W
Emporia [Va.-U.S.]	184	Ig	36.42N	77.33W
Emporium	184	He	41.31N	78.14W
Empress Augusta Bay	219a	Bb	6.25S	155.05 E
Empress Mine	172	Dc	18.27S	29.27 E
Empúries / Ampurias	126	Pb	42.10N	3.05 E
Ems	122	Na	53.19N	7.03 E
Emsbach	124	Kd	50.24N	8.06 E
Emsdetten	120	Dd	52.11N	7.32 E
Ems-Jade-Kanal	120	Dc	53.30N	7.30 E
Emsland	120	Dd	52.50N	7.20 E
Emstek	124	Kb	52.50N	8.09 E
Emumägi/Emumjagi	116	Lf	58.54N	26.23 E
Emumjagi/Emumägi	116	Lf	58.54N	26.23 E
Ena	156	Ed	35.27N	137.24 E
Enånger	114	Df	61.32N	17.00 E
Enaratoli	150	Kg	3.55S	136.21 E
Enard Bay	118	Hc	58.06N	5.20W
Ena-San	156	Ed	35.26N	137.36 E
Enbetsu	154	Pb	44.44N	141.47 E
Encantada, Cerro de la-	174	Hf	31.00N	115.23W
Encantada, Sierra de la-	192	Hc	28.30N	102.20W
Encantadas, Serra das-	204	Fj	30.40S	53.00W
Encantado, Cerro-	190	Bc	27.03N	112.30W
Encarnación	200	Kh	27.20S	55.54W
Encarnación de Díaz	192	Hg	21.31N	102.14W
Enchi	166	Ed	5.49N	2.49W
Encinal	186	Gl	28.02N	99.21W
Encinasola	126	Ff	38.08N	6.52W
Encontrados	202	Db	8.46N	72.30W
Encounter Bay	212	Hg	35.35S	138.45 E
Encrucijada	194	Hb	22.37N	79.52W
Encruzilhada do Sul	204	Fj	30.32S	52.31W
Encs	120	Rh	48.20N	21.08 E
Ende	142	Oj	8.50S	121.39 E
Endeavour Strait	212	Ib	10.50S	142.15 E
Endelave	116	Di	55.45N	10.15 E
Enderbury Atoll	208	Je	3.08S	171.05W
Enderby	188	Fa	50.33N	119.08W
Enderby Land	222	Ee	67.30S	53.00 E
Endicott Mountains	178	Ic	67.50N	152.00W
Ené, Rio-	202	Df	11.09S	74.19W
Energetik	136	Fe	51.44N	58.48 E
Enewetak Atoll	208	Hc	11.30N	162.15 E
Enez	146	Bb	40.44N	26.04 E
Enez Körfezi	130	Ii	40.45N	26.00 E
Enfer, Pointe d'-	197b	Bc	14.24N	60.52W
Enfer, Portes d'-	170	Ed	5.05S	27.30 E
Enfield	184	Ig	36.11N	77.41W
Enfield, London-	124	Bc	51.40N	0.04W
Engadin/Engiadin'ota/Engadina	128	Dd	46.35N	10.00 E
Engadina/Engadin/Engiadin'ota	128	Dd	46.35N	10.00 E
Engaño, Cabo-	190	Ke	18.37N	68.20W
Engaru	154	Qb	44.03N	143.31 E
Engelberg	128	Cd	46.50N	8.24 E
Engelhard	184	Jh	35.31N	76.00W
Engels	112	Ke	51.30N	46.07 E
Engelskirchen	124	Jd	50.59N	7.24 E
Engenho	204	Db	15.10S	56.25W
Enger	124	Kb	52.08N	8.34 E
Engeren	116	Ec	61.35N	12.05 E
Engershatu	168	Fb	16.34N	38.15 E
Enggano, Pulau-	140	Mj	5.24S	102.16 E
Enghien/Edingen	124	Gd	50.42N	4.02 E
Engiadin'ota/Engadina/Engadin	128	Dd	46.35N	10.00 E
England [2]	118	Li	52.30N	1.30W
England [1]	110	Fe	52.30N	1.30W
Englehart	180	Jg	47.49N	79.52W
Englewood	186	Dg	39.39N	104.59W
English	184	Df	38.20N	86.28W
English Channel	110	Fe	50.20N	1.00W
English Channel (EN)=La Manche	110	Fe	50.20N	1.00W
English Coast	222	Qf	73.30S	73.00W
English River	186	Kb	49.13N	90.58W
English River	186	Ia	50.12N	95.00W
Engozero, ozero-	114	Hd	65.45N	33.30 E
Énguera	126	Lf	38.59N	0.41W
Engure/Engures	116	Jg	57.09N	23.06 E
Engures/Engure	116	Jg	57.09N	23.06 E
Engures, ozero- / Engures ezers	116	Jg	57.15N	23.10 E
Engures ezers / Engures, ozero-	116	Jg	57.15N	23.10 E
Enh-Gajvan	152	Gb	48.05N	97.35 E
Enid	176	Jf	36.19N	97.48W
Enid Lake	186	Li	34.10N	89.50W
Eniwa	154	Pc	42.53N	141.14 E
Eniwa-Dake	156a	Bb	42.47N	141.17 E
Enkenbach-Alsenborn	124	Je	49.29N	7.53 E
Enkhuizen	122	Lb	52.42N	5.17 E
Enklinge	116	Id	60.20N	20.45 E
Enköping	114	Dg	59.38N	17.04 E
Enna	128	Im	37.34N	14.16 E
Ennadai	180	Hd	61.10N	101.00W
Ennadai Lake	180	Hd	60.55N	101.20W
Enné	168	Bc	14.24N	18.45 E
Ennedi	158	Jg	17.15N	22.00 E
Ennell, Lough-/Loch Ainninn	118	Fh	53.28N	7.24W
Ennepetal	124	Jc	51.18N	7.21 E
Ennigerloh	124	Kc	51.50N	8.01 E
Enning	186	Ed	44.37N	102.31W
Ennis [Mt.-U.S.]	188	Jd	45.21N	111.44W
Ennis [Tx.-U.S.]	186	Hj	32.20N	96.38W
Ennis/Inis	118	Ei	52.50N	8.59W
Enniscorthy/Inis Córthaidh	118	Gi	52.30N	6.34W
Enniskillen/Inis Ceithleann	118	Fg	54.21N	7.38W
Ennistimon / Inis Díomáin	118	Di	52.57N	9.13W
Enns	128	Ib	48.12N	14.28 E
Enns	110	Hf	48.14N	14.30 E
Ennstaler Alpen	128	Ic	47.37N	14.35 E
Eno	114	He	62.48N	30.09 E
Enontekiö	114	Fb	68.23N	23.38 E
Enonvesi [Fin.]	116	Lc	61.20N	26.30 E
Enonvesi [Fin.]	116	Mb	62.10N	28.55 E
Enozero, ozero-	114	Jb	68.10N	38.00 E
Enrekang	150	Gg	3.34S	119.47 E
Enrique Carbó	204	Ck	33.08S	59.14W
Enriquillo	194	Le	17.54N	71.14W
Enriquillo, Lago-	190	Je	18.27N	71.39W
Enschede	122	Mb	52.12N	6.53 E
Ensenada [Arg.]	204	Dl	34.51S	57.55W
Ensenada [Mex.]	176	Hf	31.52N	116.37W
Enshi	152	Ie	30.16N	109.26 E
Enshū-Nada	156	Ed	34.30N	138.00 E
Entebbe	160	Kh	0.04N	32.28 E
Entenbühl	120	Ig	49.46N	12.24 E
Enterprise [Al.-U.S.]	184	Ej	31.19N	85.51W
Enterprise [N.W.T.-Can.]	180	Fd	60.39N	116.08W
Enterprise [Or.-U.S.]	188	Gd	45.25N	117.17W
Entinas, Punta-	126	Jh	36.41N	2.46W
Entrada, Punta-	190	Ab	30.22N	115.59W
Entraygues-sur-Truyère	122	Ij	44.39N	2.34 E
Entrecasteaux, Récifs d'- = D'Entrecasteaux Reefs (EN)	208	Hf	18.20S	163.00 E
Entrepeñas, Embalse de-	126	Jd	40.34N	2.42W
Entre Ríos	202	Fh	21.32S	64.12W
Entre Ríos [2]	206	Id	32.00S	59.00W
Entre Rios de Minas	204	Je	20.41S	44.04W
Entrevaux	122	Mk	43.57N	6.49 E
Entroncamento	126	De	39.28N	8.28W
Enugu	160	Hh	6.26N	7.29 E
Enugu Ezike	166	Gd	6.59N	7.27 E
Envermeu	124	De	49.54N	1.16 E
Envigado	202	Cb	6.08N	75.39W
Envira	202	De	7.18S	70.13W
Envira, Rio-	202	De	7.19S	70.15W
Enyamba	170	Dc	3.40S	24.58 E
Enyélé	170	Cb	2.49N	18.06 E
Enz	120	Fh	49.00N	9.10 E
Enza	128	Ef	44.54N	10.31 E
Enzan	154	Og	34.52N	138.44 E
Enzgau	124	Kf	48.48N	8.37 E
Eo	126	Ea	43.28N	7.03W
Eochaill/Youghal	118	Fj	51.57N	7.50W
Eolie o Lipari, Isole-=Lipari Islands (EN)	110	Hh	38.35N	14.55 E
Epanomi	130	Fi	40.26N	22.56 E
Epazote, Cerro-	190	Cd	24.35N	105.07W
Epe [Neth.]	124	Hb	52.21N	5.59 E
Epe [Nig.]	166	Fd	6.35N	3.59 E
Epéna	170	Cb	1.22N	17.29 E
Épernay	122	Je	49.03N	3.57 E
Epe-Vaassen	124	Hb	52.17N	5.58 E
Ephesus (EN)=Efes	130	Kl	37.55N	27.20 E
Ephraim	188	Jg	39.22N	111.35W
Ephrata	188	Fc	47.19N	119.33W
Epi, Ile-	208	Hf	16.43S	168.15 E
Epidamnus	130	Ch	41.19N	19.26 E
Epidaurus (EN) = Epidhavros	130	Gl	37.38N	23.09 E
Epidhavros = Epidaurus (EN)	130	Gl	37.38N	23.09 E
Épila	126	Kc	41.36N	1.17W
Épinal	122	Mf	48.11N	6.27 E
Epirus (EN)=Ipiros	110	Ih	39.30N	20.40 E
Epirus (EN)=Ipiros	130	Dj	39.30N	20.40 E
Episkopí	146	Ee	34.40N	32.54 E
Eppelheim	124	Ke	49.24N	8.38 E
Epping	124	Cc	51.42N	0.07 E
Eppingen	124	Ke	49.08N	8.54 E
Epsom	118	Mj	51.20N	0.16W
Epte	122	He	49.04N	1.31 E
Epukiro	172	Bd	21.41S	19.08 E
Epukiro	172	Bd	21.28S	19.59 E
Epulu	170	Eb	1.15N	28.21 E
Eqlīd	144	Hc	30.55N	52.39 E
Équateur = Equator (EN)	170	Eb	1.00N	20.00 E
Equator (EN)=Équateur [2]	170	Eb	1.00N	20.00 E
Equatorial Guinea (EN) = Guinea Ecuatorial [1]	160	Hh	2.00N	9.00 E
Equinox Mountain	184	Kd	43.15N	73.10W
Era [It.]	128	Eg	43.40N	10.38 E
Era [Sud.]	168	Dd	5.30N	29.50 E
Eraclea	128	Kj	40.15N	16.40 E
Eraclea Minoa	128	Hm	37.25N	13.18 E
Eradaka	219b	Dc	17.39S	168.08 E
Eräjärvi	116	Kc	61.35N	24.34 E
Eratini	130	Fk	38.22N	22.14 E
Erbaa	146	Kb	40.42N	36.36 E
Erbach	120	Eg	49.39N	9.00 E
Erbeskopf	120	Dg	49.44N	7.05 E
Erbīl	142	Gf	36.11N	44.01 E
Erbīl [3]	146	Je	36.10N	44.00 E
Ercek	146	Jc	38.39N	43.36 E
Erçek Gölü	146	Jc	38.39N	43.32 E
Erciş	146	Jc	39.00N	43.19 E
Erciyas Dağı	140	Ff	38.32N	35.28 E
Ercolano	128	Ij	40.48N	14.21 E
Ercsi	120	Oi	47.15N	18.54 E
Érd	120	Oi	47.22N	18.56 E
Erdaobaihe	152	Mc	42.28N	128.05 E
Erdao Jiang	154	Ic	42.35N	127.10 E
Erdek	146	Bb	40.24N	27.48 E
Erdek Körfezi	146	Bb	40.25N	27.45 E
Erdemli	146	Fd	36.37N	34.18 E
Erdene-Cagan	152	Kb	45.55N	115.30 E
Erdene-Dalaj	152	Hb	46.02N	104.55 E
Erdene-Mandal	152	Hb	48.30N	101.21 E
Erdi	158	Jg	19.05N	22.40 E
Erdi Ma	168	Cb	18.35N	23.30 E
Erding	120	Hh	48.18N	11.56 E
Erdinger Moos	120	Hh	48.20N	11.50 E
Erdre	122	Eg	47.13N	1.32W
Erebus, Mount-	222	Kf	77.32S	167.09 E
Erechim	206	Jc	27.38S	52.17W
Ereğli [Tur.]	144	Db	37.31N	34.04 E
Ereğli [Tur.]	144	Da	41.17N	31.25 E
Erei, Monti-	128	Im	37.35N	14.20 E
Ereke	150	Hg	4.45S	123.10 E
Eren	146	Dd	37.25N	30.05 E
Erenhot	142	Ne	43.35N	112.00 E
Erepecu, Lago do-	202	Gd	1.20S	56.35W
Eresma	126	Hc	41.26N	4.45W
Erétria	130	Gk	38.25N	23.48 E
Erfelek	146	Fb	41.55N	34.57 E
Erfengshan	154	Ag	35.50N	111.47 E
Erfoud	162	Gc	31.26N	4.14W
Erft	120	Ce	51.11N	6.44 E
Erftstadt	124	Id	50.48N	6.49 E
Erfurt	112	He	50.59N	11.02 E
Ergani	146	Hc	38.17N	39.46 E
Ergene	146	Bb	41.01N	26.22 E
Erges	126	Ee	39.40N	7.01W
Ergig, Bahr-	168	Bc	11.22N	15.24 E
Ergli/Ērgļi	114	Fh	56.55N	25.41 E
Ērgļi/Ergli	114	Fh	56.55N	25.41 E
Ergun He	140	Od	53.20N	121.28 E
Ergun Youqi (Labudalin)	152	La	50.16N	120.09 E
Ergun Zuoqi (Genhe)	142	Od	50.47N	121.32 E
Er Hai	152	Hf	25.45N	100.10 E
Eria	126	Gb	42.03N	5.44W
Eriba	168	Fb	16.37N	36.04 E
Eriboll, Loch-	118	Ic	58.30N	4.40W
Eric	180	Kf	51.52N	65.45W
Erice	128	Gl	38.02N	12.35 E
Ericeira	126	Cf	38.59N	9.25W
Erichsen Lake	180	Jb	70.38N	80.20W
Ericht, Loch-	118	Ie	56.50N	4.25W
Erick	186	Gi	35.13N	99.52W
Eridu	146	Lg	36.00N	44.00 E
Erie	176	Ke	42.08N	80.04W
Erie, Lake-	174	Ke	42.15N	81.00W
'Erigābo	168	Hc	10.37N	47.24 E
Erîgât	158	Gg	19.40N	4.50W
Erikoússa	130	Cj	39.53N	19.35 E
Eriksdale	186	Ga	50.52N	98.06W
Eriksenstretet	179	Oc	79.00N	26.00 E
Erikub Atoll	208	Id	9.08N	170.02 E
Erimanthos Óros	130	El	37.58N	21.48 E
Erimo-Misaki	152	Pc	41.55N	143.15 E
Eriskay	118	Fd	57.04N	7.13W
Eritrea [1]	160	Kg	16.30N	42.00 E
Eritrea [3]	158	Kg	15.00N	40.00 E
Erjas	126	Ee	39.40N	7.01W
Erkelenz	124	Ic	51.05N	6.19 E
Erken	116	He	59.50N	18.35 E
Erkowit	168	Fb	18.46N	37.07 E
Erlangdian → Dawu	154	Ci	31.33N	114.07 E
Erlangen	120	Hg	49.36N	11.01 E
Erlang Shan	152	Hf	29.58N	102.20 E
Erlauf	128	Jb	48.12N	15.11 E
Erldunda	212	Ge	25.14S	133.12 E
Erlenbach	124	Ke	49.07N	8.11 E
Erlong Shan	152	Mc	43.30N	128.44 E
Ermelo [Neth.]	124	Hb	52.19N	5.37 E
Ermelo [S.Afr.]	172	De	26.34S	29.58 E
Ermenek	146	Ed	36.38N	32.54 E
Ermenistan=Armenia (EN)	140	Gf	39.10N	43.00 E
Ermenistan=Armenia (EN)	144	Fb	39.10N	43.00 E
Ermenonville	124	Ee	49.08N	2.42 E
Ermesinde	126	Dc	41.13N	8.33W
Ermoúpolis	130	Hl	37.27N	24.56 E
Erndtebrück	124	Kd	50.59N	8.16 E
Erne/An Éirne	118	Eg	54.30N	8.15W
Ernée	122	Ff	48.18N	0.56W
Ernest Legouvé Reef	208	Lh	35.12S	150.35W

Ernici, Monti- ⛰	128	Hi	41.50N	13.20 E
Erode	148	Ff	11.21N	77.44 E
Eromanga	212	Ie	26.40S	143.16 E
Erongoberg ▲	172	Bd	21.40S	15.40 E
Erpengdianzi	154	Hd	41.12N	125.29 E
Errego	172	Fc	16.02S	37.10 E
Errigal/An Ea agail ▲	118	Ef	55.02N	8.07W
Erris Head/Ceann Iorrais ▶	110	Fe	54.19N	10.00W
Erromango, Ile- ◆	208	Hf	18.48S	169.05 E
Erseka	130	Di	40.20N	20.41 E
Erstein	122	Nf	48.26N	7.40 E
Ertai	152	Fb	46.02N	90.10 E
Ertil	136	Ee	51.50N	40.51 E
Ertix He ∿	140	Ke	47.52N	84.16 E
Erts	172	De	25.08S	29.55 E
Ertvågøy ◆	116	Ca	63.15N	8.25 E
Eruh	146	Jd	37.46N	42.15 E
Erval, Serra do- ⛰	204	Fk	30.25S	51.55W
Ervânia	204	Ee	21.43S	55.32W
Erve ∿	122	Fg	47.50N	0.20W
Ervy-le-Châtel	122	Jf	48.02N	3.55 E
Erwin	184	Fg	36.09N	82.25W
Erwitte	124	Kc	51.37N	8.21 E
Eryuan	152	Gf	26.09N	99.56 E
Erzeni ∿	130	Ch	41.26N	19.27 E
Erzgebirge=Ore Mountains (EN) ⛰	110	He	50.30N	13.15 E
Erzin	138	Ef	50.17N	95.10 E
Erzincan	144	Eb	39.44N	39.29 E
Erzurum	142	Gf	39.55N	41.17 E
Esan-Misaki ▶	154	Pd	41.48N	141.12 E
Esashi [Jap.]	154	Pd	41.52N	140.07 E
Esashi [Jap.]	154	Qb	44.56N	142.35 E
Esashi [Jap.]	154	Pe	39.12N	141.09 E
Esbjerg	112	Gd	55.28N	8.27 E
Esbo/Espoo	114	Ff	60.13N	24.40 E
Escalante	188	Jh	37.47N	111.36W
Escalante Desert ◢	188	Ih	37.50N	113.30W
Escalante River ∿	188	Jh	37.17N	110.53W
Escalaplano	128	Dk	39.37N	9.21 E
Escalón	190	Dc	26.45N	104.20W
Escalona	126	Hd	40.10N	4.24W
Escanaba	176	Ke	45.45N	87.04W
Escanaba River ∿	184	Dc	45.47N	87.04W
Escandón, Puerto de- ⌵	126	Ld	40.17N	1.00W
Escandorgue ▰	122	Jk	43.46N	3.14 E
Escarpada Point ▶	140	Oh	18.31N	122.13 E
Escarpé, Cap- ▶	219b	Ce	20.41S	167.13 E
Escatrón	126	Lc	41.17N	0.19W
Escaut=Schelde (EN) ∿	122	Kc	51.22N	4.15 E
Esch an der Alzette/Esch-sur-Alzette	122	Le	49.30N	5.59 E
Eschkopf ▲	124	Je	49.19N	7.51 E
Esch-sur-Alzette/Esch an der Alzette	122	Le	49.30N	5.59 E
Eschwege	120	Ge	51.11N	10.04 E
Eschweiler	120	Cf	50.49N	6.17 E
Escocesa, Bahía- ◧	194	Md	19.25N	69.45W
Escondida, Punta- ▶	192	Kj	15.49N	97.03W
Escondido	188	Gj	33.07N	117.05W
Escondido, Río- ∿	194	Fg	12.04N	83.45W
Escravos	166	Gd	5.36N	5.11 E
Escudo, Puerto del- ⌵	126	Ia	43.05N	3.50W
Escudo de Veraguas, Isla- ◆	194	Gi	9.06N	81.33W
Escuinapa de Hidalgo	190	Cd	22.51N	105.48W
Escuintla [3]	194	Bf	14.10N	91.00W
Escuintla [Guat.]	190	Ff	14.18N	90.47W
Escuintla [Mex.]	192	Mj	15.20N	92.38W
Escuro, Rio- [Braz.] ∿	204	Ha	12.50S	49.28W
Escuro, Rio- [Braz.] ∿	204	Ic	17.31S	46.39W
Ese	170	Eb	4.04N	26.40 E
Ese-Hajja	138	Ic	67.35N	134.55 E
Eséka	166	He	3.39N	10.46 E
Eşen	146	Cd	36.27N	29.16 E
Esendere	146	Kd	37.46N	44.40 E
Ésera / Éssera ∿	126	Mb	42.06N	0.15 E
Eşfahān [3]	144	Hc	32.50N	51.50 E
Eşfahān=Isfahan (EN)	142	Hf	32.40N	51.38 E
Esfandārān	146	Og	31.52N	52.32 E
Esfarāyen, Reshteh-ye- ⛰	146	Qd	36.46N	57.10 E
Esgueva ∿	126	Hc	41.40N	4.43W
Eshowe	172	Ee	28.58S	31.29 E
Eshtehārd	146	Ne	35.44N	50.23 E
Esigodini	172	Dd	20.18S	28.56 E
Esino ∿	128	Hg	43.39N	13.22 E
Esk ∿	118	Jg	54.58N	3.04W
Eskifjörður	114a	Cb	65.04N	14.01W
Eskilstuna	114	Dg	59.22N	16.30 E
Eskimo Point	176	Jc	61.07N	94.03W
Eskinşehir	142	Ff	39.46N	30.32 E
Esla ∿	126	Fc	41.29N	6.03W
Eslāmābād	144	Gc	34.11N	46.35 E
Eşler Dağı ▲	130	Ml	37.24N	29.43 E
Eslohe (Sauerland)	124	Kc	51.15N	8.10 E
Eslöv	114	Ci	55.50N	13.20 E
Eşme	146	Cc	38.24N	28.59 E
Esmeralda [Braz.]	204	Gi	28.03S	51.12W
Esmeralda [Cuba]	194	Hc	21.51N	78.07W
Esmeralda, Isla- ◆	206	Eg	48.57S	75.25W
Esmeralda Bank (EN) ▦	220b	Ab	14.57N	145.15 E
Esmeraldas	200	Ie	0.59N	79.42W
Es Mercadal / Mercadal	126	Qe	39.59N	4.05 E
Esnagami Lake ⬭	186	Ma	50.21N	86.48W
Esneux	124	Hd	50.32N	5.34 E
Espada, Punta- ▶	194	Lg	12.05N	71.07W
Espagnol Point ▶	197n	Ba	13.22N	61.09W
Espalion	122	Ij	44.31N	2.46 E
Espalmador, Isla- / s'Espalmador, Illa- ◆	126	Nf	38.47N	1.26 E
España=Spain (EN) [1]	112	Fg	40.00N	4.00W
Espanola [N.M.-U.S.]	186	Ch	36.06N	106.02W
Espanola [Ont.-Can.]	184	Gb	46.15N	81.46W
Española, Isla- ◆	202a	Bb	1.25S	89.42W
Espardell, Isla- / s'Espardell, Illa- ◆	126	Nf	38.47N	1.27 E
Esparta	194	Ei	9.59N	84.40W
Espeland	116	Ad	60.23N	5.28 E
Espelkamp	120	Ed	52.25N	8.37 E
Esperance	210	Dh	33.51S	121.53 E
Esperance, Cape- ▶	219a	Dc	9.15S	159.43 E
Esperance Bay ◧	212	Ef	33.50S	121.55 E
Esperance Harbour ◧	197k	Ba	14.04N	60.55W
Esperancita	204	Bc	16.55S	60.06W
Esperantina	202	Jd	3.54S	42.14W
Esperanza ⚗	222	Re	63.26S	57.00W
Esperanza [Arg.]	206	Hd	31.27S	60.56W
Esperanza [Mex.]	192	Ed	27.35N	109.56W
Esperanza [P.R.]	197a	Cb	18.06N	65.29W
Esperanza, Sierra la- ⛰	194	Ef	15.40N	85.45W
Espevær	114	Ag	59.36N	5.10 E
Espichel, Cabo- ▶	126	Cf	38.25N	9.13W
Espiel	126	Gf	38.12N	5.01W
Espigão, Serra do- ⛰	204	Gh	26.55S	50.25W
Espinal [Bol.]	204	Cc	17.13S	58.43W
Espinal [Col.]	202	Dc	4.10N	74.54W
Espinazo del Diablo, Sierra- ⛰	192	Ff	24.00N	106.00W
Espinhaço, Serra do- ⛰	198	Lg	17.30S	43.30W
Espinho	126	Dc	41.01N	8.38W
Espinilho, Serra do- ⛰	204	Ei	28.30S	55.06W
Espinillo	204	Cg	24.58S	58.34W
Espino	196	Dh	8.34N	66.01W
Espinosa	202	Jf	14.56S	42.50W
Espinouse, Monts de l'- ⛰	122	Ik	43.32N	2.46 E
Espírito Santo [2]	202	Jg	20.00S	40.30W
Espiritu Santo, Bahía del- ◧	192	Ph	19.20N	87.35W
Espíritu Santo, Isla- ◆	192	De	24.30N	110.22W
Espita	192	Og	21.01N	88.19W
Esplanada	202	Kf	11.47S	37.57W
Espoo/Esbo	114	Ff	60.13N	24.40 E
Espoo-Tapiola	116	Kd	60.11N	24.49 E
Esposende	126	Dc	41.32N	8.47W
Espumoso	204	Fi	28.44S	52.51W
Espuña, Sierra de- ⛰	126	Kg	37.52N	1.34W
Espungabera	172	Ed	20.28S	32.46 E
Esquel	200	Ij	42.55S	71.20W
Esquina	206	Id	30.01S	59.32W
Esquipular	194	Cf	14.34N	89.21W
Essandsjøen ⬭	116	Da	63.05N	12.00 E
Essaouira	160	Ge	31.31N	9.46W
Essaouira [3]	162	Fc	31.04N	9.03W
Essen [Bel.]	124	Gc	51.28N	4.28 E
Essen [Ger.]	112	Ge	51.27N	7.01 E
Essen (Oldenburg)	124	Jb	52.42N	7.55 E
Essendon, Mount- ▲	212	Ed	24.59S	120.28 E
Essequibo River ∿	198	Ke	6.50N	58.30W
Éssera / Ésera ∿	126	Mb	42.06N	0.15 E
Essex	188	Hi	34.42N	115.12W
Essex [3]	118	Nj	51.50N	0.35 E
Essex ▤	118	Nj	51.50N	0.30 E
Essex Mountain ▲	188	Ke	42.02N	109.13W
Esslingen am Neckar	120	Fh	48.45N	9.18 E
Esso	138	Ke	55.55N	158.40 E
Essonne [3]	122	If	48.36N	2.20 E
Essonne ∿	122	If	48.37N	2.29 E
Est [Burkina] [3]	166	Fc	12.00N	1.00 E
Est [Cam.] [3]	166	He	4.00N	14.00 E
Est, Canal de l'- ═	122	Lf	48.45N	5.35 E
Est, Cap- ▶	172	Ic	15.16S	50.29 E
Est, Ile de l'- ◆	222	Ec	46.15S	52.05 E
Est, Pointe de l' - ▶	180	Lg	49.08N	61.41W
Estaca de Bares, Punta de la- / Estaca de Vares, Punta de la- ▶	110	Fg	43.46N	7.42W
Estaca de Vares, Punta de la- / Estaca de Bares, Punta de la- ▶	110	Fg	43.46N	7.42W
Estados, Isla de los-=Staten Island (EN) ◆	198	Jk	54.47S	64.15W
Estados Unidos Mexicanos [1]	176	Ig	23.00N	102.00W
Estahbān	146	Ph	29.08N	54.04 E
Estaimpuis	124	Fd	50.42N	3.15 E
Estância	202	Kf	11.16S	37.26W
Estancias, Sierra de las- ⛰	126	Jg	37.35N	2.20W
Estanislao del Campo	204	Bg	25.03S	60.06W
Estarreja	126	Dd	40.45N	8.34W
Estats, Pica d'-/Estats, Pico d'- ▲	122	Hl	42.40N	1.24 E
Estats, Pic d'- ▲	122	Hl	42.40N	1.24 E
Estats, Pico d'-/Estats, Pica d'- ▲	122	Hl	42.40N	1.24 E
Estcourt	172	De	29.01S	29.52 E
Este	128	Fe	45.14N	11.39 E
Este, Punta- ▶	197a	Cb	18.08N	65.16W
Este, Punta del- ▶	206	Jd	34.59S	54.57W
Esteban Rams	204	Bi	29.47S	61.29W
Estelí	190	Gf	13.05N	86.23W
Estelí [3]	194	Dg	13.10N	86.20W
Estella	126	Jb	42.40N	2.02W
Estepa	126	Hg	37.18N	4.54W
Estepona	126	Gh	36.26N	5.08W
Esterel ⛰	122	Mk	43.30N	6.50 E
Esternay	124	Ff	48.44N	3.34 E
Esterri d'Àneu/Esterri de Aneu	126	Nb	42.38N	1.08 E
Esterri de Aneu / Esterri d'Àneu	126	Nb	42.38N	1.08 E
Esterwegen	124	Jb	52.59N	7.37 E
Estes Park	186	Df	40.23N	105.31W
Este Sudeste, Cayos del- ✱	190	Hf	12.26N	81.27W
Estevan	180	Hg	49.07N	103.05W
Estherville	186	Ie	43.24N	94.50W
Estissac	122	Jf	48.16N	3.49 E
Eston	188	Ka	51.10N	108.46W
Estonia (EN) ⌧	110	Id	59.00N	26.00 E
Estonia (EN) = Eesti	136	Cd	59.00N	26.00 E
Estonskaja Sovetskaja Socialističeskaja Respublika → Eesti	136	Cd	59.00N	26.00 E
Estonskaja SSR/Eesti Nõukogude Socialistlik Vabarijk → Eesti	136	Cd	59.00N	26.00 E
Estoril	126	Cf	38.42N	9.24W
Estrées-Saint-Denis	124	Ee	49.26N	2.39 E
Estreito	204	Gj	31.50S	51.44W
Estreito, Reprêsa do- ⊔	204	Ie	20.15S	47.09W
Estrêla [Braz.]	204	Gj	31.15S	51.45W
Estrêla [Braz.]	204	Gi	29.29S	51.58W
Estrela, Arroyo- ∿	204	Df	22.05S	56.25W
Estrela, Serra da- ⛰	204	Fc	16.27S	53.24W
Estrêla, Serra da- ⛰	110	Fg	40.20N	7.38W
Estrêla do Sul	204	Id	18.21S	47.49W
Estrella ▲	126	If	38.28N	3.35W
Estrella, Punta- ▶	192	Bb	30.55N	114.40W
Estrema, Serra da- ⛰	204	Jc	16.50S	45.07W
Estremadura ▤	126	Ce	39.15N	9.10W
Estremoz	126	Ef	38.51N	7.35W
Estrondo, Serra do- ⛰	202	Ie	9.00S	48.45W
Estry	124	Bf	48.54N	0.44W
Estuaire [3]	170	Ab	0.10N	10.00 E
Es Vedrà, Illa- / Vedrá, Isla- ◆	126	Nf	38.52N	1.12 E
Esztergom	120	Oi	47.48N	18.45 E
Etah	179	Ec	78.19N	72.38W
Étain	122	Le	49.13N	5.38 E
Etajima	156	Cd	34.15N	132.29 E
Etalle	124	He	49.41N	5.36 E
Étampes	122	If	48.26N	2.09 E
Étaples	122	Hd	50.31N	1.39 E
Etāwah	148	Fc	26.46N	79.02 E
Ethe, Virton-	124	He	49.35N	5.35 E
Ethel Reefs ✿	219d	Ab	16.56S	177.13 E
Ethiopia (EN)=Itiopya [1]	160	Kh	9.00N	39.00 E
Ethiopian Plateau (EN) ▰	158	Kg	10.00N	38.10 E
Etive, Loch- ⇌	118	He	56.35N	5.15W
Etna 🌋	110	Hh	37.50N	14.55 E
Etna ∿	116	Dd	60.50N	10.03 E
Etna (Mongibello) 🌋	110	Hh	37.50N	14.55 E
Etne	116	Ae	59.40N	5.56 E
Etoile Cay ✱	172b	Bb	5.53S	53.01 E
Etolin Island ◆	178	Me	56.08N	132.26W
Etolin Strait ⇌	178	Fd	60.20N	165.15W
Etomo-Misaki ▶	156a	Bb	42.20N	140.55 E
Etorofu Tō / Iturup, ostrov- ◆	140	Qe	44.54N	147.30 E
Etosha Pan ⬭	158	Ij	18.50S	16.20 E
Etoumbi	170	Bb	0.01N	14.57 E
Etrépagny	124	De	49.18N	1.37 E
Étretat	122	Ge	49.42N	0.12 E
Etropole	130	Gg	42.50N	24.00 E
Etruria	206	Hd	32.56S	63.15W
Etsch/Adige ∿	110	Hf	45.10N	12.20 E
Ettelbrüch/Ettelbruck	124	Ie	49.51N	6.07 E
Ettelbruck/Ettelbrüch	124	Ie	49.51N	6.07 E
Etten-Leur	124	Gc	51.35N	4.39 E
Ettersberg ▲	120	He	51.03N	11.15 E
Ettlingen	124	Kf	48.57N	8.24 E
Etzna Tixmucuy ⁖	192	Nh	19.35N	90.13W
Eu	122	Hd	50.03N	1.25 E
'Eua Iki ◆	221b	Bc	21.07S	174.59W
Eua Island ◆	216	Gd	21.22S	174.56W
Euboea (EN)=Évvoia ◆	110	Ih	38.30N	24.00 E
Eucla	210	Dh	31.43S	128.52 E
Euclid	184	Ge	41.34N	81.33W
Euclides da Cunha	202	Kf	10.31S	39.01W
Eucumbene, Lake- ⬭	212	Jg	36.05S	148.45 E
Eudora	186	Kj	33.07N	91.16W
Eufaula	184	Ej	31.54N	85.09W
Eufaula Lake ⬭	186	Ii	35.17N	95.31W
Euganei, Colli- ∩	128	Fe	45.19N	11.40 E
Eugene	176	Ge	44.02N	123.05W
Eugenia, Punta- ▶	174	Hg	27.50N	115.03W
Eugênio Penzo	204	Ef	22.13S	55.53W
Eugmo ◆	114	Fe	63.49N	22.45 E
Eume ∿	126	Da	43.25N	8.08W
Eunice [La.-U.S.]	186	Jk	30.30N	92.26W
Eunice [N.M.-U.S.]	186	Ej	32.26N	103.09W
Eupen	122	Md	50.38N	6.02 E
Euphrates (EN)=Al Furāt ∿	140	Gf	30.00N	47.25 E
Euphrates (EN)=Firat ∿	140	Gf	30.00N	47.25 E
Eupora	186	Lj	33.32N	89.16W
Eura	114	Ff	61.08N	22.08 E
Eurajoki	116	Ic	61.12N	21.44 E
Eurasia Basin (EN) ⊍	224	Ge	87.00N	80.00 E
Eure [3]	122	Ge	49.10N	1.00 E
Eure ∿	122	He	49.18N	1.12 E
Eure-et-Loir [3]	122	Hf	48.30N	1.30 E
Eureka [Ca.-U.S.]	176	Ge	40.47N	124.09W
Eureka [Ks.-U.S.]	186	Hh	37.49N	96.17W
Eureka [Mt.-U.S.]	188	Hb	48.53N	115.03W
Eureka [Nv.-U.S.]	182	Dd	39.31N	115.58W
Eureka [N.W.T.-Can.]	180	Ia	80.00N	85.59W
Eureka [S.D.-U.S.]	186	Gd	45.46N	99.38W
Eureka [Ut.-U.S.]	188	Ig	39.57N	112.07W
Eureka Sound ⇌	180	Ia	79.00N	87.00W
Europa, Ile de l'- ◆	158	Lk	22.20S	40.22 E
Europa, Picos de- ⛰	110	Fg	43.12N	4.48W
Europa, Punta de- ▶	126	Gh	36.10N	5.22W
Europe (EN) ■	106	Fd	50.00N	20.00 E
Europoort ⚓	122	Jc	51.58N	4.00 E
Euskal Mendiak / Vascos, Montes- ⛰	126	Jb	42.50N	2.10W
Euskirchen	120	Cf	50.40N	6.47 E
Eustis	184	Gk	28.51N	81.41W
Eutaw	184	Di	32.50N	87.53W
Eutin	120	Gb	54.08N	10.37 E
Euzkadi / Vascongadas = Basque Provinces (EN) ▤	126	Ja	43.00N	2.30W
Evale	170	Cf	16.33S	15.44 E
Evans, Lac- ⬭	180	Jf	50.50N	77.00W
Evans, Mount- ▲	188	Ic	46.05N	113.07W
Evans Strait ⇌	180	Jd	63.20N	82.00W
Evanston [Il.-U.S.]	186	Me	42.03N	87.42W
Evanston [Wy.-U.S.]	182	Ec	41.16N	110.58W
Evansville	176	Kf	37.58N	87.35W
Evant	186	Gk	31.29N	98.09W
Evart	184	Ed	43.54N	85.14W
Évaux-les-Bains	122	Ih	46.10N	2.29 E
Evaz	146	Oi	27.46N	53.59 E
Evciler [Tur.]	130	Mk	38.03N	29.54 E
Evciler [Tur.]	130	Jj	39.46N	26.46 E
Evelyn, Mount- ▲	212	Gb	13.36S	132.53 E
Evensk	142	Rc	61.57N	159.14 E
Everard, Lake- ⬭	212	Hf	31.25S	135.05 E
Everard Ranges ⛰	212	Ge	27.05S	132.30 E
Everest, Mount- (EN)= Qomolangma Feng ▲	140	Kg	27.59N	86.56 E
Everest, Mount- (EN)= Saragmatha ▲	140	Kg	27.59N	86.56 E
Everett	182	Cb	47.59N	122.13W
Everett Mountains ⛰	180	Kd	62.45N	67.10W
Evergem	124	Fc	51.07N	3.42 E
Evergem-Sleidinge	124	Fc	51.08N	3.41 E
Everglades City	184	Gm	25.52N	81.23W
Evergreen	184	Dj	31.26N	86.57W
Evertsberg	116	Ec	61.08N	13.57 E
Evesham	118	Li	52.05N	1.56W
Evesham, Vale of- ⋎	118	Li	52.05N	1.50W
Évian-les-Bains	122	Mh	46.23N	6.35 E
Evijärvi	114	Fe	63.22N	23.29 E
Evinayong	166	He	1.27N	10.34 E
Évinos ∿	130	Ek	38.19N	21.32 E
Evje	114	Bg	58.36N	7.51 E
Évora	112	Fh	38.34N	7.54W
Évora [2]	126	Ef	38.35N	7.50W
Evoron	138	If	51.23N	136.23 E
Evowghlī	146	Kc	38.43N	45.13 E
Evre ∿	122	Eg	47.22N	1.02W
Evrecy	124	Be	49.06N	0.30W
Evrejskaja avtonomnaja respublika	138	Ig	48.30N	132.00 E
Évreux	122	He	49.01N	1.09 E
Évron	122	Ff	48.10N	0.24W
Évros ∿	130	Ji	40.52N	26.12 E
Evrótas ∿	130	Fm	36.48N	22.41 E
Évry	122	If	48.38N	2.27 E
Évvoia=Euboea (EN) ◆	110	Ih	38.30N	24.00 E
Évvoia, Gulf of- (EN)= Vórios Evvoïkós Kólpos ◧	130	Gk	38.45N	23.10 E
Evzonoi	130	Fh	41.06N	22.33 E
Ewa Beach	221a	Cb	21.19N	158.00W
Ewing Seamount (EN) ⟑	158	Hk	23.20S	8.45 E
Ewo	170	Bc	0.55S	14.49 E
Excelsior Mountain ▲	188	Fg	38.02N	119.18W
Excelsior Mountains ⛰	188	Fg	38.10N	118.30W
Excelsior Springs	186	Ig	39.20N	94.13W
Exe ∿	118	Jk	50.37N	3.25W
Executive Committee Range ⛰	222	Nf	76.50S	126.00W
Exeter [Eng.-U.K.]	112	Fe	50.43N	3.31W
Exeter [N.H.-U.S.]	184	Ld	42.59N	70.56W
Exeter Sound ⇌	180	Lc	66.10N	62.00W
Exmoor ⛰	118	Jj	51.10N	3.45W
Exmouth [Austl.]	212	Cd	21.55S	114.07 E
Exmouth [Eng.-U.K.]	118	Jk	50.37N	3.25W
Exmouth Gulf ◧	208	Cg	22.00S	114.20 E
Exmouth Plateau (EN) ⊓	212	Cc	16.00S	114.00 E
Expedition Range ⛰	212	Jd	24.30S	149.05 E
Explorer Tablemount (EN) ⟑	190	He	16.55N	83.15W
Externsteine ★	124	Kc	51.52N	8.55 E
Extertal	124	Lb	52.04N	9.07 E
Extertal-Bösingfeld	124	Lb	52.04N	9.07 E
Extremadura [2]	126	Ge	39.00N	6.00W
Exuma Cays ❖	190	Id	24.00N	76.20W
Exuma Sound ⇌	190	Id	24.15N	76.00W
Eyasi, Lake- ⬭	158	Ki	3.40S	35.05 E
Eydehavn	116	Cf	58.31N	8.53 E
Eye	124	Db	52.19N	1.09 E
Eyemouth	118	Kf	55.52N	2.06W
Eye Peninsula ⊏	118	Gc	58.13N	6.05W
Eygurande	122	Ii	45.40N	2.28 E
Eyjafjallajökull ▲	114a	Bc	63.38N	19.36W
Ēyl	160	Lh	8.00N	49.51 E
Eymoutiers	122	Hi	45.44N	1.44 E
Eyneuil	146	Hb	41.03N	39.08 E
Eyrarbakki	114a	Bc	63.52N	21.09W
Eyre	212	Ff	32.15S	126.18 E
Eyre, Lake- ⬭	208	Eg	28.43S	137.11 E
Eyre Creek ∿	208	Eg	26.40S	139.00 E
Eyre Mountains ⛰	218	Cf	45.20S	168.20 E
Eyre North, Lake- ⬭	212	He	28.40S	137.10 E
Eyre Peninsula ⊏	208	Ef	34.00S	135.45 E
Eyre South, Lake- ⬭	212	He	29.30S	137.20 E
Eyrieux ∿	122	Kj	44.48N	4.48 E
Eystrup	124	Lb	52.47N	9.13 E
Eythorne	124	Dc	51.11N	1.17 E
Eyvānakī	146	Oe	35.24N	51.56 E
Eyzies-de-Tayac, Les-	122	Hj	44.56N	1.01 E
Ezequiel Ramos Mexía, Embalse- ⊔	206	Ge	39.30S	69.00W
Ezere	116	Jh	56.27N	22.17 E
Ežerelis	116	Jj	54.50N	23.38 E
Ezine	146	Bc	39.47N	26.20 E
Eznas/Jieznas	116	Kj	54.34N	24.17 E
Ežva	134	Ef	61.47N	50.40 E

F

Faaa	221e	Fc	17.33S	149.36W
Faaite Atoll ⊙	216	Lc	16.45S	145.14W
Fabens	186	Ck	31.30N	106.10W
Fåberg	116	Dc	61.10N	10.24 E
Faber Lake ⬭	180	Fd	63.55N	117.15W
Fåborg	114	Ci	55.06N	10.15 E
Fabriano	128	Gg	43.20N	12.54 E
Făcăeni	130	Ke	44.34N	27.54 E
Facatativá	202	Dc	4.49N	74.22W
Facha	164	Cd	29.30N	17.20 E
Fachi	160	Ig	18.06N	11.34 E
Facpi Point ▶	220c	Bb	13.20N	144.38 E
Fada	160	Jg	17.14N	21.33 E
Fada N'Gourma	160	Hg	12.04N	0.21 E
Faddeja, zaliv- ◧	138	Fa	76.30N	107.30 E
Faddejevski, ostrov- ◆	138	Ja	75.30N	144.00 E
Fadiffolu Atoll ⊙	148a	Ba	5.25N	73.30 E
Fāḑilī	146	Mi	26.58N	49.15 E
Faeara, Pointe- ▶	221e	Fc	17.52S	149.11W
Faenza	128	Ff	44.17N	11.53 E
Faeroe-Iceland Ridge (EN) ⋀	110	Fc	64.00N	10.00W
Faeroe Islands (EN)= Færøerne/Föroyar [5]	112	Fc	62.00N	7.00W
Faeroe Islands (EN)= Færøerne/Föroyar ❖	110	Fc	62.00N	7.00W
Faeroe Islands (EN) = Föroyar/Færøerne [5]	112	Fc	62.00N	7.00W
Faeroe Islands (EN)= Föroyar/Færøerne ❖	110	Fc	62.00N	7.00W
Færøerne/Föroyar=Faeroe Islands (EN) [5]	112	Fc	62.00N	7.00W
Færøerne/Föroyar=Faeroe Islands (EN) ❖	110	Fc	62.00N	7.00W
Fafa ∿	168	Bd	7.18N	18.16 E
Fafe	126	Dc	41.27N	8.10W
Fafen ∿	158	Lh	5.47N	44.11 E
Faga ∿	166	Fc	13.45N	0.58 E
Fagaloa Bay ◧	221c	Ba	13.54S	171.28W
Fagamalo	221c	Aa	13.25S	172.21W
Făgăraş	130	Hd	45.51N	24.58 E
Făgăraşului, Munţii- ⛰	130	Hd	45.35N	25.00 E
Fagataufa Atoll ⊙	208	Ng	22.14S	138.45W
Fågelmara	116	Fh	56.15N	15.57 E
Fagerhult	116	Fg	57.09N	15.40 E
Fagernes	114	Bf	60.59N	9.15 E
Fagersta	114	Df	60.00N	15.47 E
Făget	130	Fd	45.51N	22.11 E
Fagita	150	Jg	1.48S	130.25 E
Fagnano, Lago- ⬭	206	Gh	54.38S	68.00W
Fagne ⌧	122	Kd	50.10N	4.25 E
Faguibine, Lac- ⬭	158	Gg	16.45N	3.54W
Fahliān	146	Ng	30.12N	51.28 E
Fahner Höhe ▲	120	Ge	51.10N	10.45 E
Faial ◆	158	Ee	38.34N	28.42W
Fā'id	146	Eg	30.19N	32.19 E
Faïoa ◆	220h	Bc	13.23S	176.08W
Fairbairn Reservoir ⊔	212	Jd	23.40S	148.00 E
Fairbanks	176	Ec	64.51N	147.43W
Fairborn	184	Ef	39.48N	84.03W
Fairbury	182	Hc	40.08N	97.11W
Fairchild	186	Kd	44.36N	90.58W
Fairfield [Al.-U.S.]	184	Di	33.29N	86.55W
Fairfield [Ca.-U.S.]	188	Dg	38.15N	122.01W
Fairfield [Ia.-U.S.]	186	Kf	40.59N	91.57W
Fairfield [Id.-U.S.]	188	He	43.21N	114.48W
Fairfield [Il.-U.S.]	186	Lg	38.23N	88.22W
Fair Isle ◆	118	Lb	59.30N	1.40W
Fairlie	218	Df	44.06S	170.50 E
Fairmont [Mn.-U.S.]	182	Ic	43.39N	94.28W
Fairmont [W.V.-U.S.]	182	Ld	39.28N	80.08W
Fair Ness ▶	180	Kd	63.24N	72.05W
Fairview [Mt.-U.S.]	188	Mc	47.51N	104.03W
Fairview [Ok.-U.S.]	186	Gh	36.16N	98.29W
Fairview Peak ▲	188	De	43.35N	122.39W
Fairweather, Mount- ▲	174	Fd	58.54N	137.32W
Faisalabad (Lyallpur)	142	Jf	31.25N	73.05 E
Fais Island ◆	208	Fd	9.46N	140.31 E
Faistós = Phaistos (EN) ⁖	130	Hn	35.03N	24.48 E
Faith	182	Gb	45.02N	102.02W
Faizābād	148	Gc	26.47N	82.08 E
Fajardo	194	Od	18.20N	65.39W
Fajou, Ilet à- ◆	197e	Ab	16.21N	61.35W
Fakahina Atoll ⊙	208	Mf	15.59S	140.08W
Fakaofo Atoll ⊙	208	Je	9.22S	171.14W
Fakarava Atoll ⊙	208	Mf	16.20S	145.37W
Fakaura	156	Fa	40.38N	139.55 E
Fakel	114	Mh	57.40N	53.05 E
Fakenham	124	Cb	52.50N	0.50 E
Fakfak	150	Jg	2.55S	132.18 E
Fakhr	146	Pg	31.25N	54.01 E
Fakse Bugt ◧	116	Ei	55.10N	12.15 E
Faksefjell ▲	116	Ec	61.20N	12.52 E
Fakse Ladeplads	116	Ei	55.15N	12.08 E
Faku	154	Gc	42.30N	123.24 E
Falaba	166	Cd	9.51N	11.19W
Fala-Beguets ◆	220d	Bb	7.21N	151.40 E
Falaise	122	Ff	48.54N	0.12W
Falaise de Tiguidit ∩	166	Gb	16.22N	7.45 E
Falakrón Óros ⛰	130	Gh	41.19N	24.00 E
Falalu ◆	220d	Ba	7.38N	151.41 E
Falam	148	Id	22.55N	93.41 E
Falas ◆	220d	Ba	7.32N	151.46 E
Fălciu	130	Lc	46.18N	28.08 E
Falcón [2]	202	Ea	11.00N	69.50W
Falcon, Cap- ▶	126	Li	35.46N	0.48W
Falcon, Presa- ⊔	186	Gm	26.37N	99.11W
Falconara Marittima	128	Hg	43.37N	13.24 E
Falcone, Punta- ▶	128	Cj	40.58N	8.12 E
Falcon Reservoir ⊔	182	Hf	26.37N	99.11W
Faléa	166	Cc	12.16N	11.15W
Faleallej Pass ⇌	220d	Bb	7.26N	151.34 E
Falealupo	221c	Aa	13.30S	172.48W
Falelima	221c	Aa	13.32S	172.41W
Falémé ∿	158	Fg	14.46N	12.14W
Falenki	114	Mg	58.23N	51.36 E
Falerum	116	Gf	58.09N	16.13 E
Falešty	132	Ef	47.35N	27.44 E
Falevai	221c	Ba	13.55S	171.59W
Falfurrias	182	Hf	27.14N	98.09W
Falkenberg	114	Ch	56.54N	12.28 E
Falkensee	120	Jd	52.34N	13.05 E
Falkirk	118	Jf	56.00N	3.48W
Falkland Islands/Malvinas, Islas- [5]	200	Kk	51.45S	59.00W
Falkland Islands/Malvinas, Islas- ❖	198	Kk	51.45S	59.00W
Falkland Plateau (EN) ⊓	198	Lk	51.00S	50.00W
Falkland Sound ⇌	206	Ih	51.45S	59.25W
Falkonéra ◆	130	Gm	36.50N	23.53 E
Falköping	114	Cg	58.10N	13.31 E
Fallingbostel	120	Fd	52.52N	9.42 E
Fallon [Mt.-U.S.]	188	Mc	46.48N	105.00W
Fallon [Nv.-U.S.]	188	Fg	39.28N	118.47W

Index Symbols

- [1] Independent Nation
- [2] State, Region
- [3] District, County
- [4] Municipality
- [5] Colony, Dependency
- ■ Continent
- ⌧ Physical Region
- ▤ Historical or Cultural Region
- ▲ Mount, Mountain
- 🌋 Volcano
- ◠ Hill
- ⛰ Mountains, Mountain Range
- ∩ Hills, Escarpment
- ▰ Plateau, Upland
- ⌵ Pass, Gap
- ▁ Plain, Lowland
- ◣ Delta
- ⁘ Salt Flat
- ⋎ Valley, Canyon
- ◡ Crater, Cave
- ✲ Karst Features
- ⌣ Depression
- ▥ Polder
- ◢ Desert, Dunes
- ♣ Forest, Woods
- ☘ Heath, Steppe
- 🌴 Oasis
- ▶ Cape, Point
- ⛱ Coast, Beach
- ◨ Cliff
- ⊏ Peninsula
- ⧖ Isthmus
- ░ Sandbank
- ◆ Island
- ⊙ Atoll
- ✱ Rock, Reef
- ❖ Islands, Archipelago
- ⁂ Rocks, Reefs
- ✿ Coral Reef
- ◙ Well, Spring
- ⛲ Geyser
- ∿ River, Stream
- ⤵ Waterfall, Rapids
- ⩚ River Mouth, Estuary
- ⬭ Lake
- ⬬ Salt Lake
- ◌ Intermittent Lake
- ⊔ Reservoir
- ♒ Swamp, Pond
- ═ Canal
- ❄ Glacier
- ❅ Ice Shelf, Pack Ice
- 🌊 Ocean
- ≋ Sea
- ◧ Gulf, Bay
- ⇌ Strait, Fjord
- ⊖ Lagoon
- ▦ Bank
- ⟑ Seamount
- ⊓ Tablemount
- ⋀ Ridge
- ⊐ Shelf
- ⊍ Basin
- ⌐ Escarpment, Sea Scarp
- ⚡ Fracture
- ⊽ Trench, Abyss
- ⛉ National Park, Reserve
- ★ Point of Interest
- ⚑ Recreation Site
- ◓ Cave, Cavern
- 🏛 Historic Site
- ⁖ Ruins
- ⊞ Wall, Walls
- ✝ Church, Abbey
- ⛩ Temple
- ⚗ Scientific Station
- 🚉 Railway station
- ✈ Airport
- ⚓ Port
- ⚔ Military installation
- ⛯ Lighthouse
- ⚒ Mine
- ⋂ Tunnel
- ⌒ Dam, Bridge

Fall River	182	Mc	41.43N	71.08W
Falls City	182	Hc	40.03N	95.36W
Falmouth [Atg.]	197d	Bb	17.01N	61.46W
Falmouth [Eng.-U.K.]	118	Hk	50.08N	5.04W
Falmouth [Jam.]	194	Id	18.30N	77.39W
Falmouth [Ky.-U.S.]	184	Ef	38.40N	84.20W
Falmouth Bay	118	Hk	50.10N	5.05W
Falmouth Harbour	197d	Bb	17.01N	61.46W
Falo	220d	Bb	7.29N	151.53 E
False Bay	158	Il	34.15S	18.35 E
False Pass	178	Gf	54.52N	163.24W
Falset	126	Mc	41.08N	0.49 E
Falso, Cabo- [Dom.Rep.]	194	Le	17.47N	71.41W
Falso, Cabo- [Hond.]	194	Ff	15.12N	83.20W
Falso, Cabo- [Mex.]	190	Cd	22.52N	109.58W
Falso Cabo de Hornos	206	Gi	55.43S	68.05W
Falster	114	Ci	54.50N	12.00 E
Falsterbo	116	Ei	55.24N	12.50 E
Falterona	128	Fg	43.52N	11.42 E
Fălticeni	130	Jb	47.27N	26.18 E
Falun	112	Hc	60.36N	15.38 E
Fama	168	Cb	15.22N	20.34 E
Famagusta (EN)= Gazimağusa	144	Dc	35.07N	33.57 E
Famatina, Nevados de-	206	Gc	29.00S	67.51W
Famenne	122	Ld	50.15N	5.15 E
Fana	166	Dc	12.45N	6.57W
Fanan	220d	Bb	7.11N	151.59 E
Fanchang	152	Ke	31.00N	118.11 E
Fancy	197n	Ba	13.22N	61.12W
Fandriana	172	Hd	20.13S	47.20 E
Fangak	168	Ed	9.04N	30.53 E
Fangatau Atoll	208	Mf	15.50S	140.52W
Fangcheng	152	Je	33.09N	113.05 E
Fangliao	152	Lg	22.22N	120.25 E
Fangshan	154	Ce	39.43N	115.58 E
Fangxian	152	Je	32.03N	110.41 E
Fangzheng	152	Mb	45.50N	128.49 E
Fangzi	154	Ef	36.36N	119.08 E
Fanjiatun	154	Hc	43.42N	125.05 E
Fanjing Shan	152	If	27.57N	108.50 E
Fannaråken	116	Bc	61.31N	7.55 E
Fanning → Tabuaeran Atoll	208	Ld	3.52N	159.20W
Fano	128	Hg	43.50N	13.01 E
Fanø	116	Ci	55.25N	8.25 E
Fanø Bugt	116	Ci	55.25N	8.10 E
Fanshi	154	Be	39.11N	113.16 E
Fan Si Pan	140	Mg	22.15N	103.50 E
Fanuatapu	221c	Ba	13.59S	171.20W
Fanxian	154	Cg	35.53N	115.29 E
Fāqūs	146	Dg	30.44N	31.48 E
Farab	135	De	39.12N	63.38 E
Faraba	166	Cc	12.52N	11.23W
Faraday	222	Qe	65.15S	64.15W
Faraday Seamounts (EN)	110	Df	49.30N	28.30W
Faradje	170	Eb	3.44N	29.43 E
Faradofay	160	Lk	25.01S	46.59 E
Farafangana	172	Hd	22.48S	47.50 E
Farāfirah, Wāḥāt al- = Farafra Oasis (EN)	158	Jf	27.15N	28.10 E
Farafra Oasis (EN) = Farāfirah, Wāḥāt al-	158	Jf	27.15N	28.10 E
Farāh	142	If	32.22N	62.07 E
Farāh [3]	144	Jc	33.00N	62.30 E
Farāh	140	If	31.29N	61.24 E
Far'ah, Wādī al-	146	Hj	24.02N	38.09 E
Farahābād	146	Od	36.47N	53.06 E
Faranah	166	Cc	10.02N	10.44W
Farasān, Jazā'ir-	144	Ff	16.48N	41.54 E
Farasān al Kabīr	164	Hf	16.42N	42.00 E
Faraulep Atoll	208	Fd	8.36N	144.33 E
Farcău, Vîrful-	130	Hb	47.55N	24.27 E
Farciennes	124	Gd	50.26N	4.33 E
Fardes	126	Jg	37.35N	3.00W
Fare	221e	Db	16.42S	151.01W
Fareham	118	Lk	50.51N	1.10W
Farewell, Cape-	208	Ii	40.30S	172.43 E
Farewell Spit	218	Ed	40.30S	172.50 E
Färgelanda	116	Df	58.34N	11.59 E
Fargo	176	Je	46.52N	96.48W
Faribault	186	Jd	44.18N	93.16W
Faribault, Lac-	180	Ke	58.00N	72.00W
Farīd, Qarāt al-	146	Ch	28.43N	28.21 E
Faridpur	148	Hd	23.36N	89.50 E
Fārila	114	Df	61.48N	15.51 E
Farilhões, Ilhas-	126	Ce	39.28N	9.34W
Farim	166	Bc	12.29N	15.13W
Farini d'Olmo	128	Df	44.43N	9.34 E
Fariš	135	Fd	40.33N	66.52 E
Fāris	146	Ej	24.37N	32.54 E
Fāris	168	Ia	20.11N	50.56 E
Faris Seamount (EN)	178	Jf	54.30N	147.15W
Färjestaden	114	Dh	56.39N	16.27 E
Farkadhón	130	Fj	39.36N	22.04 E
Farmahīn	146	Me	34.30N	49.41 E
Farmakonisi	130	Kl	37.18N	27.08 E
Farmerville	186	Jj	32.47N	92.24W
Farmington [Me.-U.S.]	184	Lc	44.40N	70.09W
Farmington [Mo.-U.S.]	186	Kh	37.47N	90.25W
Farmington [N.M.-U.S.]	182	Fd	36.44N	108.12W
Farmville	184	Hg	37.17N	78.25W
Färnäs	116	Fc	61.00N	14.38 E
Farnborough	124	Bc	51.16N	0.44W
Farne Deep	118	Mf	55.30N	0.50W
Farne Islands	118	Lf	55.38N	1.38W
Farnham [Eng.-U.K.]	124	Bc	51.12N	0.48W
Farnham [Que.-Can.]	184	Kc	45.17N	72.59W
Farnham, Mount-	188	Ga	50.29N	116.30W
Faro	112	Fh	37.01N	7.56W
Faro [2]	126	Dg	37.12N	8.10W
Fårö	114	Eh	57.55N	19.10 E
Faro	166	Hd	9.21N	12.55 E
Faro, Punta-	194	Jh	11.07N	74.51W
Faro, Punta del- → Peloro, Capo-	128	Jl	38.16N	15.39 E
Faro, Sierra del-	126	Eb	42.37N	7.55W
Faro de Avión	126	Db	42.18N	8.16W
Faro de Chantada	126	Eb	42.37N	7.55W
Farofa, Serra da-	204	Gh	28.00S	50.10W
Fårösund	114	Eh	57.52N	19.03 E
Farosund	116	Hg	57.55N	19.05 E
Farquhar, Cape-	212	Cd	23.35S	113.35 E
Farquhar Group	158	Mj	10.10S	51.10 E
Farrar	118	Id	57.27N	4.35W
Farrāshband	146	Oh	28.53N	52.06 E
Farris	116	Ce	59.05N	10.00 E
Farruch, Cabo- / Ferrutx, Cap de-	126	Pe	39.47N	3.21 E
Farrukhābād	148	Fc	27.24N	79.34 E
Fārs [3]	144	Hd	29.00N	53.00 E
Fārs	140	Hg	29.00N	53.00 E
Fārs, Khalīj-e- = Persian Gulf (EN)	140	Hg	27.00N	51.00 E
Fārsābād	146	Mc	39.30N	48.05 E
Fársala	130	Fj	39.18N	22.23 E
Farshūţ	146	Ei	26.03N	32.09 E
Farsø	116	Ch	56.47N	9.21 E
Farsund	114	Bg	58.05N	6.48 E
Fartak, Ra's-	144	Hf	15.38N	52.15 E
Fartura, Rio-	204	Gc	16.29S	50.33W
Fartura, Serra da- [Braz.]	204	Hf	23.20S	49.25W
Fartura, Serra da- [Braz.]	204	Fh	26.21S	52.52W
Fārūj	146	Rd	37.14N	58.14 E
Farvel, Kap-/ Ũmánarssuaq	224	Nb	59.50N	43.50W
Farwell Island	222	Pf	72.49S	91.10W
Fāryāb [3]	144	Jb	36.00N	65.00 E
Fasā	146	Oh	28.56N	53.42 E
Fasano	128	Lj	40.50N	17.22 E
Fastnet Rock	118	Dj	51.24N	9.35W
Fastov	136	Ce	50.06N	30.01 E
Fataka Island	208	If	11.55S	170.12 E
Fatala	166	Cc	10.13N	14.00W
Fatehpur	148	Ec	28.01N	74.58 E
Fatež	132	Ic	52.06N	35.52 E
Father Lake	184	Ja	49.24N	75.18W
Fatick	166	Bc	14.20N	16.25W
Fátima	126	De	39.37N	8.39W
Faţīrah, Wādī-	146	Ei	26.39N	32.58 E
Fatsa	146	Gb	40.59N	37.24 E
Fatu Hiva, Ile-	208	Nf	10.28S	138.38W
Fatu Hutu, Ile-	208	Ne	9.00S	138.50W
Fatumanini, Passe-	220h	Ab	13.14S	176.13W
Fatunda	170	Cc	4.08S	17.13 E
Fauabu	219a	Ec	8.34S	160.43 E
Faucigny	122	Mh	46.05N	6.35 E
Faucille, Col de la-	122	Mh	46.22N	6.02 E
Faulkton	186	Gd	45.02N	99.08W
Faulquemont	124	Ie	49.03N	6.36 E
Fauquembergues	124	Ed	50.36N	2.05 E
Făurei	130	Kd	45.04N	27.14 E
Fauro	219a	Cb	6.55S	156.07 E
Fauske	114	Dc	67.15N	15.24 E
Fauville-en-Caux	124	Ce	49.39N	0.35 E
Faux-Lap	172	He	25.32S	45.30 E
Fåvang	116	Dc	61.26N	10.13 E
Favara	128	Hm	37.19N	13.39 E
Faversham	124	Cc	51.19N	0.54 E
Favignana	128	Gm	37.56N	12.20 E
Favignana	128	Gm	37.55N	12.19 E
Favorite	124	Kf	48.49N	8.16 E
Fawley	124	Ad	50.49N	1.21W
Fawn	180	Ie	55.22N	88.20W
Fa'w Qiblī	146	Ei	26.07N	32.24 E
Faxaflói	110	Dc	64.24N	23.00W
Faxinal	204	Gf	23.59S	51.22W
Faya-Largeau	160	Ig	17.55N	19.07 E
Fayaoué	219b	Ce	20.39S	166.32 E
Fayd	146	Ji	27.07N	42.31 E
Fayette [Al.-U.S.]	184	Di	33.42N	87.50W
Fayette [Oh.-U.S.]	184	Ee	41.41N	84.20W
Fayetteville [Ar.-U.S.]	182	Id	36.04N	94.10W
Fayetteville [N.C.-U.S.]	176	Lf	35.03N	78.54W
Fayetteville [Tn.-U.S.]	184	Dh	35.09N	86.35W
Faylakah, Jazīrat-	146	Mh	29.27N	48.20 E
Faysh Khābūr	146	Jd	37.04N	42.23 E
Fayu Island	208	Gd	8.35N	151.22 E
Fazenda de Cima	204	Db	15.56S	56.37W
Fazenda Nova	204	Gc	16.11S	50.48W
Fāzilka	148	Eb	30.24N	74.02 E
Fazrān	146	Mi	26.13N	49.12 E
Fazzān = Fezzan (E)	164	Bd	25.30N	14.00 E
Fazzān = Fezzan (EN)	158	If	26.00N	14.00 E
Fdérick	160	Ff	22.39N	12.43W
Feale/An Fhéil	118	Di	52.28N	9.40W
Fear, Cape-	182	Le	33.50N	77.58W
Featherston	218	Fd	41.07S	175.19 E
Feathertop, Mount-	212	Jg	36.54S	147.08 E
Fécamp	122	Ge	49.45N	0.22 E
Fecht	122	Nf	48.11N	7.26 E
Federación	206	Id	31.00S	57.54W
Federal	206	Id	30.55S	58.45W
Federovka [Kaz.]	136	Ge	53.38N	62.42 E
Federovka [Russia]	134	Gj	53.10N	55.10 E
Federsee	120	Fh	48.05N	9.38 E
Fedje	114	Af	60.47N	4.42 E
Fedorovka	132	Qd	51.16N	52.00 E
Fefan	220d	Bb	7.21N	151.51 E
Fegen	116	Eg	57.06N	13.02 E
Fegen	116	Eg	57.11N	13.09 E
Fehérgyarmat	120	Si	47.59N	22.31 E
Fehmarn	120	Hb	54.30N	11.10 E
Fehmarnbelt	120	Hb	54.35N	11.15 E
Fehrbellin	120	Id	52.48N	12.46 E
Feicheng	154	Df	36.15N	116.46 E
Feidong (Dianbu)	154	Di	31.53N	117.29 E
Fei Huang He	154	Fg	34.15N	120.17 E
Feijó	202	De	8.09S	70.21W
Feilding	216	Eh	40.12S	175.35 E
Feira	170	Ff	15.37S	30.25 E
Feira de Santana	200	Mg	12.15S	38.57W
Feiran Oasis	146	Eh	28.42N	33.38 E
Feistritz	128	Kc	47.01N	16.08 E
Feixi (Shangpaihe)	154	Di	31.42N	117.09 E
Feixian	154	Dg	35.16N	117.59 E
Feixiang	154	Cf	36.32N	114.47 E
Fejão Prêto ou Furtado, Rio-	204	Dc	17.33S	57.23W
Fejér [2]	120	Oi	47.10N	18.35 E
Fejø	116	Dj	54.55N	11.25 E
Feke	146	Fd	37.53N	35.58 E
Feuete-víz	120	Ok	45.47N	18.13 E
Felanitx	126	Pe	39.28N	3.08 E
Feldbach	128	Jd	46.57N	15.53 E
Feldberg	120	Di	47.52N	7.59 E
Feldioara	130	Id	45.49N	25.36 E
Feldkirch	128	Dc	47.14N	9.36 E
Feliciano, Arroyo-	204	Cj	31.06S	59.54W
Felidu Atoll	148a	Bb	3.30N	73.30 E
Felipe Carrillo Puerto	190	Ge	19.35N	88.03W
Felix, Cape -	180	Hc	69.55N	97.47W
Felixlândia	204	Jd	18.47S	44.55W
Felixstowe	118	Oj	51.58N	1.20 E
Felletin	122	Ii	45.53N	2.11 E
Feltre	128	Fd	46.01N	11.54 E
Femer Bælt	128	Dj	54.35N	11.15 E
Femø	116	Dj	54.55N	11.35 E
Femund	114	Ce	62.15N	11.50 E
Fena Valley Reservoir	220c	Bb	13.20N	144.45 E
Fener Burnu	146	Hb	41.07N	39.25 E
Fénérive	172	Hc	17.22S	49.25 E
Fenerwa	168	Fc	13.05N	39.01 E
Fénétrange	124	Jf	48.51N	7.01 E
Fengcheng [China]	152	Lc	40.28N	124.01 E
Fengcheng [China]	154	Cj	28.11N	115.47 E
Fengdu	152	If	29.58N	107.39 E
Fenghua	154	Fj	29.40N	121.24 E
Fengjie	152	Ie	31.06N	109.30 E
Fenglingdu	152	Je	34.40N	110.19 E
Fengnan (Xugezhuang)	154	Ee	39.34N	118.05 E
Fengning (Dagezhen)	154	Dd	41.12N	116.39 E
Fengqing	152	Gg	24.41N	99.53 E
Fengqiu	154	Cg	35.02N	114.24 E
Fengrun	154	Ee	39.50N	118.09 E
Fengshui Shan	152	La	52.15N	123.30 E
Fengtai [China]	154	De	39.51N	116.17 E
Fengtai [China]	154	Dh	32.43N	116.43 E
Fengweiba → Zhenkang	152	Gg	23.54N	99.00 E
Fengxian	154	Dg	34.42N	116.35 E
Fengxian (Nanqiao)	154	Fi	30.55N	121.27 E
Fengxiang	152	Ie	34.32N	107.34 E
Fengxiang → Luobei	152	Nb	47.36N	130.58 E
Fengxin	154	Cj	28.42N	115.23 E
Fengyang	154	Dh	32.53N	117.33 E
Fengzhen	152	Jc	40.28N	113.09 E
Fen He	154	Bf	35.36N	110.42 E
Feni Islands	208	Ge	4.05S	153.42 E
Fennimore	186	Ke	42.59N	90.39W
Fens, The-	118	Mi	52.40N	0.00
Fensfjorden	116	Ad	60.50N	4.50 E
Fenshui Guan	152	Kf	27.56N	117.50 E
Fenton	184	Fd	42.48N	83.42W
Fenua Fu	220h	Ac	13.23S	176.11W
Fenualoa	219c	Bb	10.16S	166.15 E
Fenyang	152	Jd	37.17N	111.45 E
Feodosija	136	Df	45.02N	35.23 E
Fer, Cap de-	162	Ib	37.05N	7.10 E
Fer, Point au-	186	Kl	29.20N	91.21W
Feragen	116	Db	62.30N	11.55 E
Férai	130	Ji	40.54N	26.10 E
Ferdows	144	Ic	34.00N	58.09 E
Fère-Champenoise	122	Jf	48.45N	3.59 E
Fère-en-Tardenois	124	Fe	49.12N	3.31 E
Ferentino	128	Hi	41.42N	13.15 E
Ferfer	168	Hd	5.06N	45.09 E
Fergana	142	Je	40.23N	71.46 E
Fergana	140	Je	40.30N	71.00 E
Ferganskaja oblast [3]	136	Hg	40.30N	71.20 E
Ferganski hrebet	136	Hg	41.00N	74.00 E
Fergus Falls	182	Hb	46.17N	96.04W
Ferguson Lake	180	Hc	69.00N	105.00W
Fergusson Island	214	Ei	9.30S	150.40 E
Ferkéssédougou	166	Dd	9.36N	5.12W
Ferkéssédougou [3]	166	Ed	9.20N	4.55W
Ferlo	158	Fg	15.00N	14.00W
Ferlo	158	Fg	15.42N	15.30W
Fermo	128	Hg	43.09N	13.43 E
Fermoselle	126	Fc	41.19N	6.23W
Fermoy/Mainistir Fhear Mai	118	Ei	52.08N	8.16W
Fernandina, Isla-	198	Gf	0.25S	91.30W
Fernandina Beach	184	Gj	30.40N	81.27W
Fernando de Noronha, Ilha-	198	Mf	3.51S	32.25W
Fernando de Noronha, Território de- [2]	202	Ld	3.50S	33.00W
Fernandópoliu	206	Kb	20.16S	50.00W
Fernán-Núñez	126	Hg	37.40N	4.43W
Fernelmont	124	Hd	50.35N	5.02 E
Fernie	188	Hb	49.30N	115.03W
Ferrandina	128	Kj	40.29N	16.27 E
Ferrara	128	Ff	44.50N	11.35 E
Ferrat, Cap-	126	Li	35.54N	0.23W
Ferrato, Capo-	128	Dk	39.18N	9.38 E
Ferré	204	Bl	34.08S	61.08W
Ferré, Cap-	197h	Bc	14.28N	60.49W
Ferreira do Alentejo	126	Df	38.03N	8.07W
Ferreñafe	202	Ce	6.38S	79.48W
Ferret, Cap-	122	Ej	44.37N	1.15W
Ferriday	186	Kk	31.38N	91.33W
Ferrières	124	Hd	50.24N	5.36 E
Ferro, Capo-	128	Di	41.09N	9.31 E
Ferro, Rio-	204	Ea	12.27S	54.31W
Ferro, Monte-	128	Cj	40.08N	8.36 E
Ferrutx, Cap de- / Farruch, Cabo-	126	Pe	39.47N	3.21 E
Ferry, Pointe-	197e	Ab	16.17N	61.49W
Ferté-Bernard, La-	122	Gf	48.11N	0.40 E
Ferté-Macé, La-	122	Ff	48.36N	0.22W
Ferté-Saint-Aubin, La-	122	Hg	47.43N	1.56 E
Ferté-sous-Jouarre, La-	122	Jf	48.57N	3.08 E
Fertilia	128	Cj	40.36N	8.17 E
Fertő	120	Mi	47.50N	16.45 E
Fès	160	Ge	34.02N	4.59W
Fès [3]	162	Gc	34.00N	5.00W
Feshi	170	Cd	6.07S	18.10 E
Fessenden	186	Gc	47.39N	99.38W
Festieux	124	Fe	49.31N	3.45 E
Festus	186	Kg	38.13N	90.24W
Feteşti	130	Ke	44.23N	27.50 E
Fethiye	144	Cb	36.37N	29.07 E
Fethiye Körfezi	146	Cd	36.40N	29.00 E
Fetlar	118	Ma	60.37N	0.52W
Fetsund	114	Cg	59.56N	11.10 E
Feuchtwangen	120	Gg	49.10N	10.20 E
Feuilles, Baie-aux-	180	Ke	58.55N	69.15W
Feuilles, Rivière-aux-	180	Ke	58.46N	70.05W
Feurs	122	Ki	45.45N	4.14 E
Fevik	116	Cf	58.23N	8.42 E
Feyzābād	142	Jf	37.06N	70.34 E
Fezzan (EN) = Fazzān	158	If	26.00N	14.00 E
Fezzan (EN) = Fazzān	164	Bd	25.30N	14.00 E
Fezzane, Emi-	166	Ha	21.42N	14.15 E
Ffestiniog	118	Ji	52.58N	3.55W
Fiambalá	206	Gc	27.41S	67.38W
Fianarantsoa	160	Lk	21.28S	47.05 E
Fianarantsoa [3]	172	Hd	21.30S	47.05 E
Fianga	168	Bd	9.55N	15.09 E
Fiche	168	Fd	9.48N	38.44 E
Fichtelgebirge	110	He	50.00N	12.00 E
Ficksburg	172	De	28.57S	27.50 E
Fidenza	128	Ef	44.52N	10.03 E
Fieni	130	Id	45.08N	25.25 E
Fier	122	Li	45.56N	5.50 E
Fieri	130	Ci	40.43N	19.34 E
Fife [3]	118	Je	56.05N	3.15W
Fife Ness	118	Ke	56.17N	2.36W
Fiffa	166	Dc	11.27N	9.52W
Fifth Cataract (EN) = Khāmis, Ash Shallāl al-	158	Kg	18.23N	33.47 E
Figalo, Cap-	126	Ki	35.35N	1.12W
Figeac	122	Ij	44.36N	2.02 E
Figeholm	116	Gg	57.22N	16.33 E
Figtree	172	Dd	20.22S	28.20 E
Figueira, Baia da-	204	Dc	16.33S	57.25W
Figueira da Foz	126	Dd	40.09N	8.52W
Figueira de Castelo Rodrigo	126	Fd	40.54N	6.58W
Figueras/Figueres	126	Ob	42.16N	2.58 E
Figueres/Figueras	126	Ob	42.16N	2.58 E
Figuig	160	Ge	32.06N	1.14W
Figuig [3]	162	Gc	33.00N	2.01W
Fiherenana	172	Gd	23.19S	43.37 E
Fījāj, Shaţţ al-	162	Ic	33.55N	9.10 E
Fiji	210	If	18.00S	178.00 E
Fiji Islands	208	If	18.00S	178.00 E
Fik	168	Gd	8.08N	42.18 E
Filabres, Sierra de los-	126	Jg	37.15N	2.20W
Filabusi	172	Dd	20.32S	29.16 E
Filadélfia	202	Ie	7.21S	47.30W
Filadelfia [C.R.]	194	Eh	10.26N	85.34W
Filadelfia [It.]	128	Kl	38.47N	16.17 E
Filakara	219b	Dc	16.49S	168.24 E
Fil'akovo	120	Ph	48.16N	19.50 E
Filamana	166	Dc	10.30N	7.57W
Filatova Gora	116	Mg	57.39N	28.21 E
Filchner Ice Shelf	222	Af	79.00S	40.00W
Filey	118	Mg	54.12N	0.17W
Filiaşi	130	Ge	44.33N	23.31 E
Filiátai	130	Dj	39.36N	20.49 E
Filiatrá	130	El	37.09N	21.35 E
Filicudi	128	Il	38.35N	14.35 E
Filingué	166	Fc	14.21N	3.19 E
Filiouri	130	Ii	40.57N	25.20 E
Filippiás	130	Dj	39.12N	20.53 E
Filippoi	130	Hh	41.02N	24.20 E
Filippoi = Philippi (EN)	130	Hh	41.02N	24.18 E
Filipstad	114	Dg	59.43N	14.10 E
Fillefjell	116	Cc	61.09N	8.15 E
Filliévres	124	Ed	50.19N	2.10 E
Fillmore	188	Ig	38.58N	112.20W
Fils	120	Fh	48.35N	9.20 E
Filtu	168	Gd	5.06N	40.40 E
Fimaina	130	Jl	37.35N	26.26 E
Fimi	158	Ii	3.01S	16.58 E
Fin [Iran]	146	Pi	27.38N	55.55 E
Fin [Iran]	146	Nf	33.57N	51.24 E
Finale Emilia	128	Ff	44.50N	11.17 E
Finale Ligure	128	Cf	44.10N	8.20 E
Findhorn	118	Jd	57.41N	3.32W
Fındık	146	Jd	37.31N	41.58 E
Fındıklı	146	Ib	41.17N	41.09 E
Findlay	184	Fe	41.02N	83.40W
Findlay, Mount-	188	Ga	50.04N	116.28W
Findlay Group	180	Ha	77.15N	104.00W
Fineveke	220h	Ab	13.19S	176.12W
Fingoé	172	Ec	15.10S	31.53 E
Finike	146	Dd	36.18N	30.09 E
Finistère [3]	122	Bf	48.20N	4.00W
Finisterre, Cabo de-	110	Fg	42.53N	9.16W
Finisterre Range	212	Ja	5.50S	146.05 E
Finke	210	Eg	25.34S	134.35 E
Finke, Mount-	212	Gf	30.55S	134.02 E
Finke River	208	Eg	27.00S	136.10 E
Finland/Suomi [1]	112	Ic	64.00N	26.00 E
Finland, Gulf of- (EN) = Finski zaliv	110	Ic	60.00N	27.00 E
Finland, Gulf of- (EN) = Soomenlaht	110	Ic	60.00N	27.00 E
Finland, Gulf of- (EN) = Suomenlahti	110	Ic	60.00N	27.00 E
Finlay	180	Fe	55.59N	123.50W
Finlay Mountains	186	Dk	31.30N	105.35W
Finne	120	He	51.13N	11.19 E
Finngrunden	116	Hc	61.00N	18.19 E
Finnigan, Mount-	212	Jc	15.50S	145.20 E
Finniss, Cape-	212	Gf	33.38S	134.51 E
Finnmark [3]	114	Fb	69.50N	24.10 E
Finnmark	116	Fc	61.40N	14.45 E
Finnmarksvidda	110	Ib	69.30N	24.20 E
Finnøy	116	Ae	59.10N	5.50 E
Finnskogen	116	Ed	60.40N	12.40 E
Finnsnes	114	Eb	69.14N	18.02 E
Finnveden	116	Eh	56.50N	13.40 E
Finote Selam	168	Fc	10.42N	37.12 E
Finschhafen	212	Ja	6.35S	147.50 E
Finse	116	Bd	60.36N	7.30 E
Finski zaliv = Finland, Gulf of- (EN)	110	Ic	60.00N	27.00 E
Finspång	114	Dg	58.43N	15.47 E
Finstadåa	116	Dc	61.47N	11.10 E
Finsteraarhorn	128	Cd	46.32N	8.08 E
Finsterwalde	120	Je	51.38N	13.43 E
Finström	116	Hd	60.16N	19.50 E
Fiora	128	Fh	42.20N	11.34 E
Fiorenzuola d'Arda	128	Df	44.56N	9.55 E
Firat=Euphrates (EN)	140	Gf	30.00N	47.25 E
Firenze = Florence (EN)	112	Hg	43.46N	11.15 E
Firenzuola	128	Ff	44.07N	11.23 E
Firmat	204	Bk	33.27S	61.29W
Firminópolis	204	Gc	16.40S	50.19W
Firminy	122	Ki	45.23N	4.18 E
Firozābād	148	Fc	27.09N	78.25 E
Firozpur	148	Eb	30.55N	74.36 E
Fīrūzābād	146	Oh	28.50N	52.36 E
Fīrūzābād [Iran]	146	Le	34.09N	46.25 E
Fīrūzābād [Iran]	146	Pg	31.59N	54.20 E
Fīrūz Kūh	146	Oe	35.45N	52.47 E
Fischbach	124	Je	49.44N	7.24 E
Fischbacher Alpen	128	Jc	47.25N	15.30 E
Fischland	120	Ib	54.22N	12.25 E
Fisher Glacier	222	Ef	73.15S	66.00 E
Fisher Peak	184	Gg	36.33N	80.50W
Fisher Strait	180	Jd	63.00N	84.00W
Fishguard	112	Fe	51.59N	4.59W
Fish River	172	Cf	31.14S	20.15 E
Fish River' Canyon	172	Be	27.35S	17.35 E
Fiskárdhon	130	Dk	38.28N	20.35 E
Fiskenæs Bank (EN)	179	Gf	63.18N	52.10W
Fiskenæsset	179	Gf	63.10N	50.45W
Fismes	122	Je	49.18N	3.41 E
Fišt, gora-	136	Dg	43.57N	39.55 E
Fitchburg	184	Ld	42.35N	71.48W
Fitjar	114	Ag	59.55N	5.20 E
Fito, Mount-	221c	Ba	13.55S	171.44W
Fitri, Lac-	168	Bc	12.50N	17.28 E
Fitzcarrald	202	Df	11.49S	71.48W
Fitzgerald [Alta.-Can.]	180	Ge	59.52N	111.40W
Fitzgerald [Ga.-U.S.]	184	Fj	31.43N	83.15W
Fitzroy Crossing	212	Fc	18.11S	125.35 E
Fitzroy River [Austl.]	208	Df	17.31S	123.35 E
Fitzroy River [Austl.]	212	Kd	23.32S	150.52 E
Fitzwilliam Island	184	Gc	45.30N	81.45W
Fiuggi	128	Hi	41.48N	13.13 E
Fiumicino	128	Gi	41.46N	12.14 E
Five Island Harbour	197d	Bb	17.06N	61.54W
Fivizzano	128	Ef	44.14N	10.08 E
Fizi	160	Ji	4.18S	28.57 E
Fizuli	136	Eh	39.35N	47.11 E
Fjærlandsfjorden	116	Bc	61.15N	6.40 E
Fjällbacka	116	Df	58.36N	11.17 E
Fjärås	114	Ch	57.26N	12.09 E
Fjerritslev	116	Cg	57.05N	9.16 E
Fjöllum, Jökulsá á-	114a	Ca	66.02N	16.27W
Fjugesta	116	Fe	59.10N	14.52 E
Flacq	172a	Bb	20.12S	57.43 E
Flade Isblink	179	Kb	81.25N	16.00W
Fladen	116	Dg	57.07N	11.35 E
Flagler	186	Eg	39.18N	103.04W
Flagstaff	176	Hf	35.12N	111.39W
Flåm	114	Bf	60.50N	7.07 E
Flamborough Head	118	Mg	54.07N	0.04W
Fläming	120	Ie	52.00N	13.00 E
Flaming Gorge Reservoir	188	Kf	41.15N	109.30W
Flamingo	184	Gm	25.09N	80.56W
Flamingo, Teluk-	150	Kh	5.33S	138.00 E
Flanders (EN)=Flandres/ Vlaanderen	110	Ge	51.00N	3.20 E
Flanders (EN)=Flandres/ Vlaanderen	122	Jc	51.00N	3.20 E
Flanderu (EN)=Vlaanderen/ Flandres	110	Ge	51.00N	3.20 E
Flanders (EN)=Vlaanderen/ Flandres	122	Jc	51.00N	3.20 E
Flanders, East- (EN) = Oost-Vlaanderen [3]	124	Fc	51.00N	3.40 E
Flanders, West- (EN) = West-Vlaanderen [3]	124	Ec	51.00N	3.00 E
Flanders Plain (EN) = Flandres, Plaine des-	122	Id	50.40N	2.50 E
Flanders Plain (EN) = Vlaamse Vlakte	122	Id	50.40N	2.50 E
Flandreau	186	Hd	44.03N	96.36W
Flandres/Vlaanderen = Flanders (EN)	110	Ge	51.00N	3.20 E
Flandres/Vlaanderen = Flanders (EN)	122	Jc	51.00N	3.20 E
Flandres, Plaine des- = Flanders Plain (EN)	122	Id	50.40N	2.50 E
Flannan Islands	118	Fc	58.20N	7.35W
Flåren	116	Fh	57.00N	14.05 E
Flasher	186	Fc	46.27N	101.14W
Fläsjön	114	Dd	64.06N	15.51 E
Flat	178	Hd	62.27N	158.01W
Flatey	114a	Ab	65.22N	22.56W
Flateyri	114a	Aa	66.03N	23.31W
Flathead Lake	182	Eb	47.52N	114.08W
Flathead Range	188	Ib	48.05N	113.28W
Flathead River	188	Hc	47.22N	114.47W
Flat Point	197b	Ab	18.15N	63.05W
Flat River	186	Kh	37.51N	90.31W
Flattery, Cape-	174	Ge	48.23N	124.43W
Flåvatnet	116	Ce	59.20N	8.50 E
Flaxton	186	Eb	48.54N	102.24W
Flaygreen Lake	180	Hf	53.50N	97.20W
Flèche, La-	122	Fg	47.42N	0.05W
Fleckenstein	124	Je	49.05N	7.48 E
Fleet	124	Bc	51.17N	0.50W
Fleetwood	118	Jh	53.56N	3.01W

Index Symbols

Freeport [N.Y.-U.S.] 184 Ke 40.40N 73.35W
Freeport [Tx.-U.S.] 182 Hf 28.55N 95.22W
Free State 172 De 29.00S 26.00 E
Freer 186 Gm 27.53N 98.37W
Freetown [Atg.] 197d Bb 17.03N 61.42W
Freetown [S.L.] 160 Fh 8.30N 13.15W
Fregenal de la Sierra 126 Ff 38.10N 6.39W
Fregene 128 Gi 41.51N 12.12 E
Fréhel, Cap- 122 Df 48.42N 2.19W
Frei 116 Ba 63.01N 7.48 E
Freiberg 120 Jf 50.55N 13.22 E
Freiberger Mulde 120 Ie 51.10N 12.48 E
Freiburg/Fribourg 128 Bd 46.50N 7.10 E
Freiburg/Fribourg [2] 128 Bd 46.40N 7.10 E
Freiburg im Breisgau 112 Gf 48.00N 7.51 E
Freilassing 120 Ii 47.51N 12.59 E
Freirina 206 Fc 28.30S 71.06W
Freisen 124 Je 49.33N 7.15 E
Freising 120 Hh 48.24N 11.44 E
Freistadt 128 Ib 48.30N 14.30 E
Freital 120 Je 51.01N 13.39 E
Fréjus 122 Mk 43.26N 6.44 E
Fréjus, Colle del- 122 Mi 45.07N 6.40 E
Fremantle, Perth- 212 Df 32.03S 115.45 E
Fremont [Ca.-U.S.] 182 Cd 37.34N 122.01W
Fremont [Nb.-U.S.] 182 Hc 41.26N 96.30W
Fremont [Oh.-U.S.] 184 Fe 41.21N 83.08W
Fremont River 188 Jg 38.24N 110.42W
French Frigate Shoals 208 Kb 23.45N 166.10W
French Guiana (EN) = Guyane Française [5] 200 Ke 4.00N 53.00W
French Lick 184 Df 38.33N 86.37W
Frenchman Creek 186 Ff 40.13N 100.50W
Frenchman River 182 Fb 48.24N 107.05W
French Pass 218 Ed 40.55S 173.50 E
French Plain (EN) 110 Gf 47.00N 1.00 E
French Polynesia (EN) = Polynésie Française [5] 210 Mf 16.00S 145.00W
French River 184 Gc 45.56N 80.54W
Frenda 162 Hb 35.04N 1.02 E
Frentani, Monti dei- 128 Ii 41.55N 14.30 E
Freren 124 Jb 52.29N 7.33 E
Fresco 166 Dd 5.05N 5.34W
Fresco, Rio- 202 He 6.39S 52.00W
Freshfield, Cape- 222 Je 68.22S 151.05 E
Fresnes-en-Woëvre 124 He 49.06N 5.37 E
Fresnillo de González Echevarría 190 Dd 23.10N 102.53W
Fresno 176 Hf 36.45N 119.45W
Fresno River 188 Eh 37.05N 120.33W
Fresquel 122 Ik 43.14N 2.24 E
Fresvikbreen 116 Bc 61.02N 6.45 E
Freu, Cabo- / Freu, Cap des- 126 Pe 39.45N 3.27 E
Freu, Cap des- / Freu, Cabo- 126 Pe 39.45N 3.27 E
Freudenberg 124 Jd 50.54N 7.52 E
Freudenstadt 120 Eh 48.26N 8.25 E
Frévent 122 Id 50.16N 2.17 E
Freycinet Estuary 212 Ce 26.25S 113.45 E
Freycinet Peninsula 212 Jh 42.15S 148.20 E
Freyming-Merlebach 124 Ie 49.09N 6.47 E
Freyre 204 Aj 31.10S 62.02W
Freyung 120 Jh 48.48N 13.33 E
Fri 130 Jn 35.25N 26.56 E
Fria 166 Cc 10.27N 13.32W
Fria, Cape- 158 Ij 18.27S 12.01 E
Frias 206 Gc 28.39S 65.09W
Fribourg/Freiburg 128 Bd 46.50N 7.10 E
Fribourg/Freiburg [2] 128 Bd 46.40N 7.10 E
Fridtjof Nansen, Mount- 222 Lg 85.21S 167.33W
Friedberg 128 Kc 47.26N 16.03 E
Friedberg (Hessen) 120 Ef 50.21N 8.46 E
Friedrichshafen 120 Fi 47.39N 9.29 E
Friedrichsthal 124 Je 49.19N 7.06 E
Friesach 128 Id 46.57N 14.24 E
Friese Gat 124 Ia 53.30N 6.05 E
Friese Wad 124 Ha 53.24N 5.45 E
Friesische Inseln/ Waddeneilanden = Frisian Islands (EN) 110 Hc 54.00N 6.00 E
Friesland [3] 124 Ha 53.03N 5.45 E
Friesland 110 Ge 53.05N 6.00 E
Friesland 122 La 53.05N 6.00 E
Friesoythe 120 Dc 53.01N 7.51 E
Frigate Island 197p Cb 12.25N 61.29W
Friggesund 116 Gc 61.54N 16.32 E
Frignano 128 Ef 44.20N 10.50 E
Frindsbury Reef 219a Da 5.00S 159.07 E
Frinnaryd 116 Fg 57.56N 14.49 E
Frinton-on-Sea 124 Dc 51.50N 1.15 E
Frio, Cabo- 198 Lh 22.53S 42.00W
Frio, Rio- 194 Eh 11.08N 84.46W
Frio Draw 186 Ei 34.50N 102.08W
Friona 186 Ei 34.38N 102.43W
Frio River 186 Gl 28.30N 98.10W
Frisco Peak 188 Ig 38.31N 113.14W
Frisian Islands (EN) = Friesische Inseln/ Waddeneilanden 110 Hc 54.00N 6.00 E
Frisian Islands (EN) = Waddeneilanden/ Friesische Inseln 110 Hc 54.00N 6.00 E
Fristad 116 Eg 57.50N 13.01 E
Fritsla 116 Eg 57.33N 12.47 E
Fritzlar 120 Fe 51.08N 9.17 E
Friuli 128 Ge 46.00N 13.00 E
Friuli-Venezia Giulia 128 Gd 46.00N 13.00 E
Frobisher Bay 174 Mc 62.30N 66.00W
Frobisher Lake 180 Ge 56.20N 108.20W
Froidchapelle 124 Gd 50.09N 4.20 E
Froissy 124 Ee 49.34N 2.13 E
Frolovo 136 Ef 49.45N 43.39 E
Fromberg 188 Kd 45.23N 108.54W
Frombork 120 Pb 54.22N 19.41 E
Frome 118 Kj 51.14N 2.20W
Frome, Lake- 208 Eh 30.50S 139.50 E
Fröndenberg 124 Jc 51.28N 7.46 E
Fronteira 126 Ee 39.03N 7.39W
Fronteiras 202 Je 7.05S 40.37W
Frontera 192 Mh 18.32N 92.38W
Frontera, Punta- 192 Mh 19.36N 92.42W
Fronteras 192 Eb 30.56N 109.31W
Frontignan 122 Jk 43.27N 3.45 E
Frontino, Páramo- 202 Cb 6.28N 76.04W
Front Range 174 If 39.45N 105.45W
Front Royal 184 Hf 38.56N 78.13W
Frosinone 128 Hi 41.38N 13.19 E
Frösö 116 Fa 63.11N 14.32 E
Frostburg 184 Hf 39.39N 78.56W
Frost Glacier 222 Ie 67.05S 129.00 E
Frövi 116 Fe 59.28N 15.22 E
Frøya 114 Be 63.43N 8.42 E
Frøysjøen 116 Ac 61.50N 5.05 E
Fruges 122 Id 50.31N 2.08 E
Frunze → Biškek [Kyrg.] 142 Je 42.54N 74.36 E
Frunze [Kyrg.] 135 Hd 40.06N 71.45 E
Frunzovka 130 Mb 47.20N 29.37 E
Fruška Gora 130 Cd 45.10N 19.35 E
Frutal 202 Ih 20.02S 48.55W
Frutigen 128 Bd 46.35N 7.40 E
Fry Canyon 188 Jh 37.38N 110.08W
Frýdek Místek 120 Og 49.41N 18.22 E
Frylinckspan 172 Ce 26.46S 22.28 E
Ftéri 130 Ej 39.09N 21.33 E
Fua'amotu 221b Ac 21.15S 175.08W
Fua Mulaku Island 148a Bc 0.15S 73.30 E
Fu'an 152 Kf 27.10N 119.44 E
Fu-chien Sheng → Fujian Sheng = Fukien (EN) [2] 152 Kf 26.00N 118.00 E
Fuchskauten 120 Ef 50.40N 8.05 E
Fuchū [Jap.] 156 Cd 34.34N 133.14 E
Fuchū [Jap.] 156 Fd 35.41N 139.28 E
Fuchun-Jiang 154 Fi 30.15N 120.15 E
Fuchunjiang-Shuiku 154 Ej 29.29N 119.31 E
Fucino, Conca del- 128 Hh 42.01N 13.31 E
Fudai 156 Ga 40.01N 141.52 E
Fuding 152 Lf 27.19N 120.08 E
Fuengirola 126 Hh 36.32N 4.37W
Fuente de Cantos 126 Ff 38.15N 6.18W
Fuente del Maestre 126 Ff 38.32N 6.27W
Fuente Obejuna 126 Gf 38.16N 5.25W
Fuentesaúco 126 Gc 41.14N 5.30W
Fuentes de Andalucía 126 Gg 37.28N 5.21W
Fuerte 190 Cc 25.54N 109.22W
Fuerte, Isla- 194 Ii 9.23N 76.11W
Fuerte, Sierra del- 192 Hd 27.30N 102.45W
Fuerte Olimpo 206 Ib 21.02S 57.54W
Fuerteventura 158 Ff 28.20N 14.00W
Fuga 150 Hc 18.52N 121.22 E
Fugong 152 Gf 27.03N 98.57 E
Fugou 154 Cg 34.04N 114.23 E
Fugu 152 Jd 39.02N 111.03 E
Fuguo → Zhanhua 154 Ef 37.42N 118.08 E
Fuhai/Burultokay 152 Eb 47.06N 87.23 E
Fuhayrī, Wādī- 144 Hf 16.04N 52.11 E
Fu He 154 Dj 28.36N 116.04 E
Fuji 154 Og 35.09N 138.38 E
Fujian Sheng (Fu-chien Sheng) = Fukien (EN) [2] 152 Kf 26.00N 118.00 E
Fujieda 156 Fd 34.51N 138.15 E
Fuji-Gawa 156 Fd 35.07N 138.38 E
Fujin 152 Nb 47.15N 132.01 E
Fujinomiya 156 Fd 35.12N 138.38 E
Fujioka 156 Fc 36.15N 139.03 E
Fuji-San 140 Pf 35.26N 138.43 E
Fujisawa 156 Fd 35.21N 139.27 E
Fujiyoshida 156 Fd 35.29N 138.47 E
Fukagawa 152 Pc 43.43N 142.03 E
Fūkah 146 Bg 31.04N 27.55 E
Fukang 152 Ec 44.10N 87.59 E
Fuka-Shima 156 Be 32.43N 131.56 E
Fukiage 156 Bf 31.30N 130.20 E
Fukien (EN) = Fu-chien Sheng → Fujian Sheng [2] 152 Kf 26.00N 118.00 E
Fukien (EN) = Fujian Sheng (Fu-chien Sheng) [2] 152 Kf 26.00N 118.00 E
Fukuchiyama 154 Mg 35.18N 135.07 E
Fukue 154 Jh 32.41N 128.50 E
Fukueichiao 152 Lf 25.19N 121.34 E
Fukue-Jima 154 Jh 32.41N 128.48 E
Fukui 152 Od 36.04N 136.13 E
Fukui Ken [2] 154 Ng 36.00N 136.20 E
Fukuma 156 Be 33.47N 130.28 E
Fukuoka 142 Pf 33.35N 130.24 E
Fukuoka Ken [2] 154 Kh 33.28N 130.45 E
Fukuroi 156 Ed 34.45N 137.54 E
Fukushima [Jap.] 152 Pd 37.45N 140.28 E
Fukushima [Jap.] 152 Pc 41.29N 140.15 E
Fukushima Ken [2] 154 Pf 37.25N 140.10 E
Fukuyama 152 Ne 34.29N 133.22 E
Fukuyama-Matsunaga 156 Cd 34.27N 133.16 E
Fūlādī, Kūh-e- 144 Kc 34.38N 67.32 E
Fūlād Mahalleh 146 Od 36.02N 53.44 E
Fulanga 219d Cc 19.08S 178.34W
Fulda 120 Ff 50.33N 9.40 E
Fulda 110 Ge 51.25N 9.39 E
Fuliji 154 Dh 33.47N 116.59 E
Fulin → Hanyuan 152 Hf 29.25N 102.12 E
Fuling 152 If 29.40N 107.21 E
Fullerton 186 Hf 41.22N 97.58W
Fulton [Arg.] 204 Cm 37.25S 58.48W
Fulton [Il.-U.S.] 186 Kf 41.52N 90.11W
Fulton [Ky.-U.S.] 186 Cg 36.30N 88.53W
Fulton [Mo.-U.S.] 186 Kg 38.52N 91.57W
Fulton [N.Y.-U.S.] 184 Id 43.20N 76.26W
Fulufjället 116 Ec 61.33N 12.43 E
Fumaiolo 128 Gg 43.47N 12.04 E
Fumay 122 Kd 50.00N 4.42 E
Fumel 122 Gj 44.30N 0.58 E
Funabashi 154 Og 35.42N 139.59 E
Funabiki 156 Gc 37.26N 140.35 E
Funafuti 210 Ie 8.01S 178.00 E
Funafuti Atoll 208 Ie 8.31S 179.08 E
Funagata 156 Gb 38.42N 140.18 E
Funagata-Yama 156 Gb 38.27N 140.37 E
Funakoshi-Wan 156 Hb 39.25N 142.00 E
Funan 154 Ch 32.38N 115.35 E
Funäsdalen 114 Ce 62.32N 12.33 E
Funchal 160 Fe 32.38N 16.54W
Fundación 202 Da 10.29N 74.12W
Fundão 126 Ed 40.08N 7.30W
Fundy, Bay of- 174 Me 45.00N 66.00W
Funeral Peak 188 Gh 36.08N 116.37W
Fungalei 220h Bb 13.17S 176.07W
Funhalouro 172 Ed 23.05S 34.24 E
Funing [China] 152 Ig 23.39N 105.33 E
Funing [China] 154 Eh 33.48N 119.47 E
Funing [China] 154 Ee 39.56N 119.15 E
Funiu Shan 152 Je 33.40N 112.10 E
Funtua 166 Gc 11.32N 7.19 E
Fuping 154 Ce 38.49N 114.15 E
Fuqing 152 Kf 25.47N 119.24 E
Furancungo 172 Eb 14.54S 33.37 E
Furano 154 Qc 43.21N 142.23 E
Füren 156a Ca 44.17N 142.25 E
Furenai 156a Cb 42.43N 142.15 E
Füren-Ko 156a Db 43.20N 145.20 E
Fürg 146 Ph 28.18N 55.13 E
Fur Jiang 154 Hc 42.37N 125.33 E
Furmanov 114 Jh 57.16N 41.07 E
Furnas, Represa de- 202 Ih 21.20S 45.50W
Furnas, Serra das- 204 Fb 15.45S 53.20W
Furneaux Group 208 Fi 40.10S 148.05 E
Furnes/Veurne 122 Ic 51.04N 2.40 E
Furqlus 146 Ge 34.36N 37.05 E
Furrīyānah 162 Ic 34.57N 8.34 E
Fürstenau 124 Jb 52.31N 7.43 E
Fürstenauer Berge 124 Jb 52.35N 7.45 E
Fürstenfeld 128 Kc 47.03N 16.05 E
Fürstenfeldbruck 120 Hh 48.11N 11.15 E
Fürstenlager 124 Ke 49.42N 8.38 E
Fürstenwalde 120 Kd 52.22N 14.04 E
Furtado, Rio- → Feijão Prêto, Rio- 204 Dc 17.33S 57.23W
Fürth [Ger.] 120 Gg 49.28N 11.00 E
Fürth [Hn.] 124 Ke 49.39N 8.47 E
Furth im Wald 120 Ig 49.18N 12.51 E
Furubira 156a Bb 43.16N 140.39 E
Furudal 114 Df 61.10N 15.08 E
Furukawa 152 Pd 38.34N 140.58 E
Furusund 116 He 59.40N 18.55 E
Fury and Hecla Strait 180 Jc 69.55N 84.00W
Fushan [China] 154 Ag 35.58N 111.51 E
Fushan [China] 154 Ff 37.30N 121.15 E
Fushë-Arëzi 130 Dg 42.04N 20.02 E
Fushë-Lura 130 Dh 41.48N 20.13 E
Fu Shui 154 Cj 29.52N 115.26 E
Fushun 142 Oe 41.46N 123.56 E
Fusong 152 Mc 42.20N 127.17 E
Füsselberg 124 Je 49.32N 7.14 E
Füssen 120 Gi 47.34N 10.42 E
Futa, Passo della- 128 Ff 44.05N 11.17 E
Futago-Yama 156 Be 33.35N 131.38 E
Futaoi-Jima 156 Bd 34.06N 130.47 E
Futog 130 Cd 45.15N 19.42 E
Futuna, Ile- 208 Jf 14.17S 178.09W
Fuwah 146 Dg 31.12N 30.33 E
Fuxian (Wafangdian) 152 Ld 39.38N 121.59 E
Fuxian Hu 152 Hg 24.30N 102.55 E
Fuxin 142 Oe 41.59N 121.38 E
Fuxin Monggolzu Zizhixian 154 Fc 42.06N 121.46 E
Fuyang 152 Ke 32.47N 115.46 E
Fuyang He 154 Dg 38.14N 116.05 E
Fuyang Zhan 154 Ch 32.56N 115.53 E
Fuyu [China] 152 Lb 45.10N 124.52 E
Fuyu [China] 152 Lb 47.48N 124.26 E
Fuyuan [China] 152 Nb 48.21N 134.18 E
Fuyuan [China] 152 Lc 42.44N 124.57 E
Fuyuan [China] 152 Hf 25.43N 104.20 E
Fuyun/Koktokay 142 Ke 47.13N 89.39 E
Füzesabony 120 Qi 47.45N 20.25 E
Fuzhou [China] 142 Ng 26.10N 119.20 E
Fuzhou [China] 152 Kf 27.58N 116.20 E
Fuzhou He 154 Fe 39.36N 121.35 E
Fyllas Bank (EN) 179 Gf 64.00N 53.00W
Fyn [2] 116 Di 55.20N 10.30 E
Fyn 110 Hd 55.20N 10.30 E
Fyne, Loch- 118 He 56.10N 5.20W
Fyresdal 114 Bg 59.11N 8.06 E
Fyresvatn 116 Ce 59.05N 8.10 E
Fzāra, Gara'et- 128 Bn 36.47N 7.30 E

G

Gaasbeek 124 Gd 50.48N 4.10 E
Gaasterland 124 Hb 52.54N 5.36 E
Gaasterland 124 Hb 52.53N 5.35 E
Gaasterland-Balk 124 Hb 52.54N 5.36 E
Gabaru Reef 220a Bb 7.53N 134.31 E
Gabba 168 Id 8.02N 50.08 E
Gabbs 188 Gg 38.52N 117.55W
Gabela 160 Ij 10.52S 14.23 E
Gabel a (Kutkašen) 132 Oi 40.58N 47.52 E
Gabès, Gulf of-(EN) = Qābis, Khalīj- 158 Ie 34.00N 10.25 E
Gabon [1] 160 Ii 1.00S 11.45 E
Gabon 170 Ab 0.25N 9.20 E
Gaborone 160 Jk 24.40S 25.55 E
Gabras 168 Dc 10.16N 26.14 E
Gabriel Strait 180 Kd 61.50N 65.40W
Gabriel y Galán, Embalse de- 126 Fd 40.15N 6.15W
Gabrovo 130 Ig 42.52N 25.19 E
Gabrovo [2] 130 Ig 42.52N 25.19 E
Gacé 122 Gf 48.48N 0.18 E
Gachsārān 146 Ng 30.12N 50.47 E
Gackle 186 Gc 46.38N 99.09W
Gacko 128 Mg 43.10N 18.32 E
Gadag 148 Fe 15.25N 75.37 E
Gäddede 114 Dd 64.30N 14.09 E
Gadê 152 Ge 34.13N 99.29 E
Gadjač 132 Id 50.22N 34.01 E
Gādor, Sierra de- 126 Jh 36.55N 2.45W
Gadsden 182 Je 34.02N 86.02W
Gadūk, Gardaneh-ye- 146 Oe 35.55N 52.55 E
Gadzi 168 Be 4.47N 16.42 E
Gael Hamkes Bugt 179 Jd 74.00N 22.00W
Găești 130 Ie 44.43N 25.19 E
Gaeta 128 Hi 41.12N 13.35 E
Gaeta, Golfo di- 128 Hi 41.05N 13.30 E
Gaferut Island 208 Fd 9.14N 145.23 E
Gaffney 184 Gh 35.05N 81.39W
Gag, Pulau- 150 Ig 0.25S 129.53 E
Gagan 219a Ba 5.14S 154.37 E
Gagarin [Russia] 136 Dd 55.35N 35.01 E
Gagarin [Uzb.] 135 Gd 40.40N 68.05 E
Gagévésouva, Pointe- 219b Ca 13.04S 166.32 E
Gaggenau 124 Kf 48.48N 8.20 E
Gagnef 114 Df 60.35N 15.04 E
Gagnoa 160 Gh 6.08N 5.56W
Gagnoa [3] 166 Dd 6.03N 6.00W
Gagnon 180 Kf 51.55N 68.10W
Gagra 136 Eg 43.17N 40.15 E
Gahkom 146 Ph 28.12N 55.50 E
Gahkom, Kūh-e- 146 Ph 28.10N 55.57 E
Gaiba, Laguna- 204 Dc 17.45S 57.43W
Gail 128 Hd 46.36N 13.53 E
Gaillac 122 Hk 43.54N 1.55 E
Gaillefontaine 124 De 49.39N 1.37 E
Gaillimh/Galway 112 Fe 53.16N 9.03W
Gaillimh/Galway [2] 118 Eh 53.20N 9.00W
Gaillon 124 De 49.10N 1.20 E
Gailtaler Alpen 128 Gd 46.40N 13.00 E
Gaiman 206 Gf 43.17S 65.29W
Gāinești 130 Ib 47.25N 25.55 E
Gainesville [Fl.-U.S.] 176 Kg 29.40N 82.20W
Gainesville [Ga.-U.S.] 182 Ke 34.18N 83.50W
Gainesville [Mo.-U.S.] 186 Jh 36.36N 92.26W
Gainesville [Tx.-U.S.] 182 He 33.37N 97.08W
Gainsborough 118 Mh 53.24N 0.46W
Gairdner, Lake- 208 Eh 31.35S 136.00 E
Gairloch 118 Hd 57.43N 5.40W
Gai Xian 152 Lc 40.24N 122.17 E
Gaiziņa kalns / Gajzinkalns 116 Kh 56.50N 25.59 E
Gaj 136 Fe 51.31N 58.30 E
Gajny 136 Fc 60.20N 54.15 E
Gajsin 136 Cf 48.50N 29.27 E
Gajvoron 132 Fe 48.22N 29.52 E
Gajzinkalns / Gaiziņa kalns 116 Kh 56.50N 25.59 E
Galaasija 135 Ee 39.52N 64.27 E
Galābovo 130 Ig 42.08N 25.51 E
Gala Gölü 130 Ji 40.45N 26.12 E
Galaico, Macizo- 126 Eb 42.30N 7.20W
Galán, Cerro- 206 Gc 25.55S 66.52W
Galana 158 Li 3.09S 40.08 E
Galanta 120 Nh 48.12N 17.44 E
Galap 220a Bb 7.38N 134.39 E
Galápagos, Islas-/Colón, Archipiélago de- = Galapagos Islands (EN) 198 Gf 0.30S 90.30W
Galapagos Fracture Zone (EN) 106 Mi 0.00 100.00W
Galapagos Islands (EN) = Colón, Archipiélago de-/ Galápagos, Islas- 198 Gf 0.30S 90.30W
Galapagos Islands (EN) = Galápagos, Islas-/Colón, Archipiélago de- 198 Gf 0.30S 90.30W
Galarza 204 Di 28.06S 56.41W
Galashiels 118 Kf 55.37N 2.49W
Galați 112 If 45.27N 28.03 E
Galați [2] 130 Kd 45.33N 27.56 E
Galatina 128 Mj 40.10N 18.10 E
Galatone 128 Mj 40.09N 18.04 E
Galatzó 126 Oe 39.38N 2.29 E
Galdar 162 Dd 28.09N 15.39W
Galdhøpiggen 114 Bf 61.37N 8.17 E
Galeana [Mex.] 192 Fb 30.07N 107.38W
Galeana [Mex.] 192 Ie 24.50N 100.04W
Galeh Dār 146 Oi 27.38N 52.42 E
Galela 150 If 1.50N 127.50 E
Galena [Ak.-U.S.] 178 Hd 64.44N 156.57W
Galena [Il.-U.S.] 186 Ke 42.25N 90.26W
Galeota Point 196 Fg 10.08N 60.59W
Galera, Punta- 206 Fe 39.59S 73.43W
Galera, Rio- 204 Bb 14.25S 60.07W
Galera Point 196 Fg 10.49N 60.55W
Galesburg 182 Ic 40.57N 90.22W
Galga 120 Pi 47.33N 19.43 E
Gal Gaduud [3] 168 Hd 5.00N 47.00 E
Galheirão, Rio- 204 Ja 12.23S 45.05W
Galheiros 204 Ia 13.18S 46.25W
Gali 132 Lh 42.36N 41.42 E
Galič [Russia] 136 Ed 58.23N 42.21 E
Galič [Ukr.] 132 De 49.06N 24.43 E
Galicea Mare 130 Ge 44.06N 23.18 E
Galicia 110 Fg 43.00N 8.00W
Galicia / Galiza [2] 126 Eb 43.00N 8.00W
Galicia (EN) = Galicija 110 If 49.50N 21.00 E
Galicia (EN) = Galicija [Eur.] 120 Qg 49.50N 21.00 E
Galicia (EN) = Galicja 110 If 49.50N 21.00 E
Galicia (EN) = Galicja 120 Qg 49.50N 21.00 E
Galicija [Eur.] = Galicia (EN) 120 Qg 49.50N 21.00 E
Galicija [Ukr.] 120 Tg 49.00N 24.00 E
Galicija = Galicia (EN) 110 If 49.50N 21.00 E
Galicja = Galicia 110 If 49.50N 21.00 E
Galicja = Galicia (EN) 120 Qg 49.50N 21.00 E
Galilee, Lake- 212 Jd 22.20S 145.55 E
Galimy 138 Kd 62.19N 156.00 E
Galina Point 194 Id 18.24N 76.53W
Galion 184 Fe 40.44N 82.46W
Galion, Baie du- 197h Bb 14.44N 60.57W
Galiton 128 Cm 37.30N 8.52 E
Galiuro Mountains 188 Jj 32.40N 110.20W
Galiza / Galicia [2] 126 Eb 43.00N 8.00W
Gālka'yo 160 Lh 6.49N 47.23 E
Galkino 134 Ki 55.00N 62.55 E
Gallarate 128 Ce 45.40N 8.47 E
Gallatin 184 Dg 36.24N 86.27W
Gallatin Range 188 Jd 45.15N 111.05W
Gallatin River 188 Jd 45.56N 111.29W
Galle 142 Ki 6.02N 80.13 E
Gállego 126 Lc 41.39N 0.51W
Gallegos, Rio- 198 Jk 51.36S 68.59W
Gallinas, Punta- 198 Id 12.25N 71.40W
Gallinas Peak 186 Di 34.15N 105.45W
Gallipoli 128 Lj 40.03N 17.58 E
Gallipoli Peninsula (EN) = Gelibolu Yarımadası 130 Ji 40.20N 26.30 E
Gallipolis 184 Ff 38.49N 82.14W
Gällivare 112 Ib 67.08N 20.42 E
Galljaaral 135 Fd 40.02N 67.35 E
Gällö 114 De 62.55N 15.14 E
Gallo 126 Jd 40.48N 2.09W
Gallo, Capo- 128 Hl 38.15N 13.19 E
Gallo Mountains 186 Bi 34.00N 108.15W
Galloway 118 If 55.00N 4.25W
Galloway, Mull of- 118 Ig 54.38N 4.50W
Gallup 176 If 35.32N 108.44W
Gallur 126 Kc 41.52N 1.19W
Gallura 128 Dj 41.00N 9.15 E
Galmaarden/Gammerages 124 Fd 50.45N 3.58 E
Galole 170 Hc 1.30S 40.02 E
Galt 184 Gd 43.22N 80.19W
Gal Tardo 168 He 3.37N 45.58 E
Galtasen 116 Eg 57.48N 13.30 E
Galty Mountains/Na Gaibhlte 118 Ei 52.23N 8.11W
Galut 152 Hb 46.43N 100.08 E
Galveston 176 Jg 29.18N 94.48W
Galveston Bay 174 Jg 29.36N 94.57W
Galveston Island 186 Il 29.13N 94.55W
Gálvez 206 Hd 32.02S 61.13W
Galway/Gaillimh 112 Fe 53.16N 9.03W
Galway/Gaillimh [2] 118 Eh 53.20N 9.00W
Galway Bay/Cuan na Gaillimhe 110 Fe 53.10N 9.15W
Gamaches 124 De 49.59N 1.33 E
Gamagōri 156 Ed 34.49N 137.13 E
Gamarra 202 Db 8.19N 73.44W
Gamba [China] 152 Ef 28.17N 88.31 E
Gamba [Gabon] 170 Ac 2.37S 10.00 E
Gambaga 166 Ec 10.32N 0.26W
Gambela 160 Kh 8.15N 34.36 E
Gambell 178 Ed 63.46N 171.46W
Gambia [1] 160 Fg 13.25N 16.00W
Gambia 158 Fg 13.28N 16.34W
Gambia (EN) = Gambie 166 Bc 13.28N 16.34W
Gambie = Gambia (EN) 166 Bc 13.28N 16.34W
Gambier, Iles- = Gambier Islands (EN) 208 Ng 23.09S 134.58W
Gambier Islands (EN) = Gambier, Iles- 208 Ng 23.09S 134.58W
Gambo 168 Ce 4.39N 22.16 E
Gamboma 170 Cc 1.53S 15.51 E
Gamboula 168 Be 4.08N 15.09 E
Gamda → Zamtang 152 He 32.23N 101.05 E
Gamelão 204 Db 15.29S 57.50W
Gamkonora, Gunung- 150 If 1.21N 127.31 E
Gamlakarleby/Kokkola 112 Ic 63.50N 23.07 E
Gamla Uppsala 116 Ge 59.54N 17.38 E
Gamleby 114 Dh 57.54N 16.24 E
Gammerages/Galmaarden 124 Fd 50.45N 3.58 E
Gamo Gofa [3] 168 Fd 5.45N 37.20 E
Gamua 220h Bb 13.15S 176.08W
Gamud 168 Fe 4.05N 38.06 E
Gamvik 114 Ga 71.03N 28.14 E
Ganāne, Webi- = Juba (EN) 158 Lh 0.15S 42.38 E
Gananoque 184 Ic 44.20N 76.10W
Ganāveh 146 Nh 29.32N 50.31 E
Gancedo 204 Bh 27.30S 61.42W
Gancevići 132 Ec 52.45N 26.29 E
Gand/Gent = Ghent (EN) 122 Jc 51.03N 3.43 E
Ganda 170 Be 12.59S 14.40 E
Gandadiwata, Bulu- 150 Gg 2.42S 119.27 E
Gandajika 170 Dd 6.45S 23.57 E
Gandak 148 Hc 25.39N 85.13 E
Gander 176 Ne 48.57N 54.34W
Ganderkesee 124 Ka 53.04N 8.33 E
Gandesa 126 Mi 41.03N 0.26 E
Gandhinagar 142 Jg 23.21N 72.40 E
Gāndhi Sāgar 148 Fd 24.30N 75.30 E
Gandia / Gandia 126 Lf 38.58N 0.11W
Gandia / Gandia 126 Lf 38.58N 0.11W
Gandia-El Grao de Gandia 126 Lf 38.59N 0.09W
Gandu 202 Kf 13.45S 39.30W
Ganetti 168 Eb 17.58N 31.13 E
Ganga = Ganges (EN) 140 Lg 23.20N 90.30 E
Gangaw 148 Id 22.10N 94.08 E
Gangca (Shaliuhe) 152 Hd 37.30N 100.14 E
Gangdisê Shan 140 Kf 31.00N 83.00 E
Ganges 122 Jk 43.56N 3.42 E
Ganges (EN) = Ganga 140 Lg 23.20N 90.30 E
Ganges, Mouths of the- (EN) 140 Lg 23.20N 90.30 E
Gangi 128 Im 37.48N 14.12 E
Gango 170 Cd 9.48S 15.40 E
Gangtok 142 Kg 27.20N 88.37 E
Gangu 152 Ie 34.45N 105.12 E
Gangziyao 154 Cf 36.17N 114.06 E
Ganhe 152 La 50.43N 123.00 E
Gan He 152 Mb 49.12N 125.14 E
Gani 150 Ig 0.47S 128.13 E
Ganjgah 146 Md 37.42N 48.16 E
Gan Jiang 152 Kf 29.12N 116.00 E
Ganjig → Horqin Zuoyi Houqi 152 Lc 42.57N 122.14 E
Gannan 152 Lb 47.53N 123.26 E
Gannat 122 Jh 46.06N 3.12 E
Gannett Peak 174 Ie 43.10N 109.40W
Gansbaai 172 Bf 34.35S 19.22 E

Index Symbols

[1] Independent Nation	Historical or Cultural Region	Pass, Gap	Depression	Coast, Beach	Rock, Reef	Waterfall, Rapids
[2] State, Region	Mount, Mountain	Plain, Lowland	Polder	Cliff	Islands, Archipelago	River Mouth, Estuary
[3] District, County	Volcano	Delta	Desert, Dunes	Peninsula	Rocks, Reefs	Lake
[4] Municipality	Hill	Salt Flat	Forest, Woods	Isthmus	Coral Reef	Salt Lake
[5] Colony, Dependency	Mountains, Mountain Range	Valley, Canyon	Heath, Steppe	Sandbank	Well, Spring	Intermittent Lake
Continent	Hills, Escarpment	Crater, Cave	Oasis	Island	Geyser	Reservoir
Physical Region	Plateau, I pland	Karst Features	Cape, Point	Atoll	River, Stream	Swamp, Pond

Canal	Lagoon	Escarpment, Sea Scarp	Historic Site	Airport
Glacier	Bank	Fracture	Ruins	Port
Ice Shelf, Pack Ice	Seamount	Trench, Abyss	Wall, Walls	Military installation
Ocean	Tablemount	National Park, Reserve	Church, Abbey	Lighthouse
Sea	Shelf	Point of Interest	Temple	Mine
Ridge	Basin	Recreation Site	Scientific Station	Tunnel
Strait, Fjord		Cave, Cavern	Railway station	Dam, Bridge

Ghurraḥ, Jabal al- 128 Cn 36.36N 8.23 E
Ghuzayyil, Sabkhat- 164 Dd 29.50N 19.45 E
Giaginskaja 132 Lg 44.47N 40.05 E
Giala, Jabal- 146 Ei 27.20N 32.57 E
Gialo Oasis (EN)=Jālū, Wāḥāt- 158 Jf 29.00N 21.20 E
Gia Nghia 148 Lf 11.59N 107.42 E
Giannutri 128 Fh 42.15N 11.05 E
Giant's Causeway/Clochán an Aifir 118 Gf 55.15N 6.35W
Giarre 128 Jm 37.43N 15.11 E
Gibara 194 Ic 21.07N 76.08W
Gibbon Point 197b Bb 18.14N 63.00W
Gibb River 212 Fc 16.25S 126.25 E
Gibbs Islands 222 Re 61.30S 55.31W
Gibellina 128 Gm 37.47N 12.58 E
Gibeon 172 Be 25.09S 17.43 E
Gibeon [3] 172 Bd 25.00S 18.30 E
Gibostad 114 Db 69.21N 18.00 E
Gibraleón 126 Fg 37.23N 6.58W
Gibraltar 112 Fh 36.11N 5.22W
Gibraltar [5] 112 Fh 36.11N 5.22W
Gibraltar, Estrecho de-= Gibraltar, Strait of- (EN) 110 Fh 35.57N 5.36W
Gibraltar, Strait of- (EN)= Djebel Ṭāriq, El Bōghāz- 110 Fh 35.57N 5.36W
Gibraltar, Strait of- (EN)= Gibraltar, Estrecho de- 110 Fh 35.57N 5.36W
Gibson Desert 208 Dg 24.30S 126.00 E
Gidami 168 Ed 8.58N 34.40 E
Giddings 186 Hk 30.11N 96.56W
Gidigič 130 Lb 47.04N 28.38 E
Gidole=Ghidole (EN) 168 Fd 5.37N 37.29 E
Gien 122 Ig 47.42N 2.38 E
Giens, Presqu'île de- 122 Mk 43.02N 6.08 E
Gier 122 Ki 45.35N 4.46 E
Gießen 120 Ef 50.35N 8.39 E
Gieten 124 Ia 53.01N 6.48 E
Giethoorn 124 Ib 52.43N 6.07 E
Gifford 180 Jh 70.21N 83.05W
Gifford Seamount (EN) 198 Ii 39.00S 82.00W
Gifhorn 120 Gd 52.29N 10.33 E
Gift Lake 180 Fe 55.49N 115.57W
Gifu 142 Pf 35.25N 136.45 E
Gifu Ken [2] 154 Ng 35.50N 137.00 E
Gigant 132 Lf 46.29N 41.20 E
Giganta, Cerro- 190 Bc 26.07N 111.36W
Giganta, Sierra de la- 190 Bc 26.18N 111.39W
Gigante 202 Cc 2.24N 75.34W
Gigen 130 Hf 43.42N 24.29 E
Gigha 118 Hf 55.41N 5.44W
Giglio 128 Eh 42.20N 10.55 E
Gijón 112 Fg 43.32N 5.40W
Gikongoro 170 Ec 2.30S 29.35 E
Gila Bend 188 Ij 32.57N 112.43W
Gila Bend Mountains 188 Ij 33.10N 113.10W
Gīlān [3] 144 Gb 37.00N 49.50 E
Gīlān-e-Gharb 146 Ke 34.08N 45.55 E
Gila River 182 Ee 32.43N 114.33W
Gilbert, Mount- 188 Ca 50.51N 124.20W
Gilbert River 212 Ic 16.35S 141.15 E
Gilbert Seamount (EN) 178 If 52.50N 150.10W
Gilbués 202 Ie 9.50S 45.21W
Gilé 172 Fc 16.09S 38.19 E
Giles Meterological Station 212 Fc 25.02S 128.18 E
Gilford Island 188 Ba 50.45N 126.25W
Gilgandra 212 Jf 31.42S 148.39 E
Gilgău 130 Gb 47.17N 23.43 E
Gilgil 170 Gc 0.30S 36.19 E
Gilgit 142 Jf 35.55N 74.18 E
Gilgit 128 Ea 35.44N 74.38 E
Giljuj 138 Hf 54.17N 127.05 E
Gillam 180 Ie 56.21N 94.43W
Gilleleje 116 Eh 56.07N 12.19 E
Gillen, Lake- 212 Ee 26.10S 124.40 E
Gillenfeld 124 Id 50.07N 6.54 E
Gillette 182 Fc 44.18N 105.30W
Gillian, Lake - 180 Jc 69.30N 75.30W
Gillingham 118 Nj 51.24N 0.33 E
Gilo 168 Ed 8.10N 33.15 E
Gilort 130 Ge 44.36N 23.27 E
Gilroy 188 Eh 37.00N 121.34W
Giluwe, Mount- 214 Ci 6.04S 143.53 E
Gilvān 146 Md 36.47N 49.08 E
Gimån 116 Gb 62.28N 16.20 E
Gimbi 168 Fd 9.10N 35.51 E
Gimie, Mount- 196 Ff 13.52N 61.01W
Gimli 180 Hf 50.39N 97.00W
Gimo 116 Hd 60.11N 18.11 E
Gimolskoje, ozero- 114 He 63.00N 32.15 E
Gimone 122 Hk 44.00N 1.06 E
Ginda 168 Fb 15.27N 39.06 E
Ginetu 219a Ac 9.30S 152.43 E
Gingin 212 Df 31.21S 115.42 E
Gin Gin 212 Kd 25.00S 151.58 E
Gingoog 150 Ie 8.50N 125.07 E
Ginir 168 Gd 7.08N 40.43 E
Ginosa 128 Kj 40.35N 16.45 E
Ginowan 156b Ab 26.17N 127.45 E
Giofra Oasis (EN)=Jufrah, Wāḥāt al- 158 If 29.10N 16.00 E
Gioia, Golfo di- 128 Jl 38.30N 15.45 E
Gioia del Colle 128 Kj 40.48N 16.55 E
Gioia Tauro 128 Jl 38.25N 15.54 E
Gion 168 Fd 8.24N 37.55 E
Gióna Óros 130 Fk 38.35N 22.15 E
Giovi, Passo dei- 128 Cf 44.33N 8.57 E
Giraltovce 120 Rg 49.07N 21.31 E
Girardot 202 Dc 4.18N 74.49W
Girdle Ness 118 Kd 57.08N 2.02W
Giresun 144 Ea 40.55N 38.24 E
Giresun Dağları 146 Hb 40.40N 38.10 E
Giri 170 Cb 0.28N 17.59 E
Giridih 148 Hd 24.11N 86.18 E
Girifṭu 170 Gb 2.00N 39.45 E
Girne 146 Ee 35.20N 33.19 E
Girón 202 Cd 3.10S 79.09W
Girona/Gerona 126 Oc 41.59N 2.49 E
Girona / Gerona [3] 126 Ob 42.10N 2.40 E
Gironde [3] 122 Fj 44.55N 0.30W
Gironde 110 Ff 45.35N 1.03W
Gironella 126 Nb 42.02N 1.53 E
Girou 122 Hk 43.46N 1.23 E
Girvan 118 If 55.15N 4.51W
Girvas 114 He 62.31N 33.44 E
Gisborne 210 Ih 38.39S 178.01 E
Gisenyi 170 Ec 1.42S 29.15 E
Gislaved 116 Eg 57.18N 13.32 E
Gisors 122 He 49.17N 1.47 E
Gissar 135 Ge 38.31N 68.36 E
Gissarski hrebet 135 Ge 39.00N 68.40 E
Gistad 116 Ff 58.27N 15.55 E
Gistel 124 Ec 51.10N 2.57 E
Gistral 126 Ea 43.28N 7.35W
Gitarama 170 Ec 2.05S 29.16 E
Gitega 170 Ec 3.26S 29.56 E
Gitu 146 Me 35.20N 48.05 E
Giudicarie, Valli- 128 Ed 46.00N 10.40 E
Giulianova 128 Hh 42.45N 13.57 E
Giumalău, Virful- 130 Ib 47.26N 25.29 E
Giurgeni 130 Ke 44.35N 27.48 E
Giurgiu 130 If 43.53N 25.58 E
Giurgiu [2] 130 Ie 44.13N 26.00 E
Give 116 Ci 55.51N 9.15 E
Givet 122 Kd 50.08N 4.50W
Givors 122 Ki 45.35N 4.46 E
Givry-en-Argonne 124 Gf 48.57N 4.53 E
Givry Island 220d Bb 7.07N 151.53 E
Giwa 166 Gc 11.18N 7.27 E
Giza (EN)=Al Jīzah 160 Ke 30.01N 31.13 E
Gižduvan 136 Gg 40.06N 64.40 E
Gižiga 138 Ld 62.03N 160.30 E
Gižiginskaja guba 138 Kd 61.10N 158.30 E
Gizo 214 Fi 8.06S 156.51 E
Gizo 219a Cc 8.07S 156.50 E
Giżycko 120 Rb 54.03N 21.47 E
Gjalicës, Mali i- 130 Dg 42.01N 20.28 E
Gjamyš, gora- 132 Oi 40.20N 46.25 E
Gjandža = Kirovabad 112 Kg 40.40N 46.22 E
Gjerstad 116 Cf 58.52N 9.00 E
Gjevilvatn 116 Cb 62.40N 9.25 E
Gjirokastra 130 Di 40.05N 20.10 E
Gjoa Haven 176 Jc 68.38N 95.57W
Gjøvik 112 Hc 60.48N 10.42 E
Gjuhës, Kep i- 130 Ci 40.25N 19.18 E
Glace Bay 180 Lg 46.12N 59.57W
Glacier Bay 178 Le 58.40N 136.00W
Glacier Peak 182 Cb 48.07N 121.07W
Glacier Strait 180 Ja 76.15N 79.00W
Gladbeck 124 Ic 51.34N 6.59 E
Gladenbach 124 Kd 50.46N 8.34 E
Gladewater 186 Ij 32.33N 94.56W
Gladstone [Austl.] 210 Gg 23.51S 151.16 E
Gladstone [Man.-Can.] 186 Ga 50.15N 98.50W
Gladstone [Mi.-U.S.] 184 Dc 45.51N 87.03W
Gladstone [Mo.-U.S.] 186 Ig 39.13N 94.34W
Glafsfjorden 116 Ee 59.35N 12.35 E
Gláma 114a Ab 65.48N 23.00W
Glåma 110 Hd 59.12N 10.57 E
Glamis Castle 118 Ke 56.37N 3.00W
Glamoč 128 Kf 44.03N 16.51 E
Glan 114 Dg 58.35N 15.55 E
Glan [Aus.] 128 Id 46.36N 14.25 E
Glan [Ger.] 120 Dg 49.47N 7.43 E
Glan-Münchweiler 124 Je 49.28N 7.26 E
Glarner Alpen 128 Cd 46.55N 9.00 E
Glärnisch 128 Cd 47.00N 9.00 E
Glarus 128 Dc 47.03N 9.04 E
Glarus [2] 128 Dd 46.55N 9.05 E
Glasgow [Ky.-U.S.] 184 Eg 37.00N 85.55W
Glasgow [Mt.-U.S.] 182 Fb 48.12N 106.38W
Glasgow [Scot.-U.K.] 112 Fd 55.53N 4.15W
Glashütte 120 Jf 50.51N 13.47 E
Glass 118 Id 57.25N 4.30W
Glassboro 184 Jf 39.42N 75.07W
Glass Mountains 186 Ek 30.25N 103.15W
Glastonbury 118 Kj 51.09N 2.43W
Glauchau 120 If 50.49N 12.32 E
Glava 116 Ee 59.33N 12.34 E
Glazov 112 Ld 58.09N 52.40 E
Gleann Dá Loch/ Glendalough 118 Gh 53.00N 6.20W
Gledićske Planine 130 Df 43.49N 20.55 E
Gleinalpe 128 Jc 47.10N 15.05 E
Gleisdorf 128 Jc 47.06N 15.43 E
Glen 124 Bb 52.50N 0.07W
Glénan, Iles de- 122 Cg 47.43N 4.00W
Glen Arbor 184 Ec 44.53N 85.58W
Glenavy 218 Df 44.55S 171.06 E
Glen Canyon 188 Jh 37.05N 111.41W
Glencoe [Mn.-U.S.] 186 Id 44.46N 94.09W
Glencoe [S.Afr.] 172 Ee 28.12S 30.07 E
Glendale [Az.-U.S.] 182 Ee 33.32N 112.11W
Glendale [Ca.-U.S.] 182 De 34.10N 118.17W
Glendalough/Gleann Dá Loch 118 Gh 53.00N 6.20W
Glendive 182 Gb 47.06N 104.43W
Glendo Reservoir 188 Me 42.31N 104.58W
Glenhope 216 Dh 41.39S 172.39 E
Glen Innes 210 Gg 29.44S 151.44 E
Glennallen 178 Jd 62.07N 145.33W
Glenner 128 Dd 46.46N 9.12 E
Glenns Ferry 188 He 42.57N 115.18W
Glenorchy 218 Cf 44.52S 168.24 E
Glenrock 188 Me 42.52N 105.52W
Glen Rose 186 Hj 32.14N 97.45W
Glenrothes 118 Je 56.12N 3.05W
Glens Falls 184 Kd 43.17N 73.41W
Glenville 184 Gf 38.57N 80.51W
Glenwood [Ia.-U.S.] 186 If 41.03N 95.45W
Glenwood [Mn.-U.S.] 186 Id 45.39N 95.23W
Glenwood Springs 182 Fd 39.32N 107.19W
Glibokaja 130 Ja 48.05N 26.00 E
Glina 128 Ke 45.20N 16.06 E
Glinjany 120 Ug 49.46N 24.33 E
Glittertinden 110 Gc 61.39N 8.33 E
Gliwice 120 Of 50.17N 18.40 E
Globe 182 Ee 33.24N 110.47W
Globino 132 He 49.24N 33.18 E
Głogów 120 Me 51.40N 16.05 E
Glomfjord 114 Cc 66.49N 13.58 E
Glommersträsk 114 Ed 65.16N 19.38 E
Glonn 120 Hh 48.11N 11.45 E
Glorieuses, Iles- 158 Lj 11.30S 47.20 E
Glottof, Mount- 178 Ie 57.30N 153.30W
Gloucester 118 Kj 51.55N 2.15W
Gloucester [Eng.-U.K.] 118 Kj 51.53N 2.14W
Gloucester [Ma.-U.S.] 184 Ld 42.41N 70.39W
Gloucester, Cape- 214 Di 5.27S 148.25 E
Gloucestershire [3] 118 Lj 51.50N 1.55W
Glover Island 197p Bb 11.59N 61.47W
Glover's Reef 194 De 16.49N 87.48W
Gloversville 184 Jd 43.03N 74.21W
Głowno 120 Pe 51.58N 19.44 E
Głubczyce 120 Nf 50.13N 17.49 E
Glubokoje [Bela.] 136 Cd 55.08N 27.41 E
Glubokoje [Kaz.] 136 Ie 50.06N 82.19 E
Glubokoje, ozero- 116 Md 60.30N 29.25 E
Głuchołazy 120 Nf 50.20N 17.22 E
Glücksburg 120 Fb 54.50N 9.33 E
Glückstadt 120 Fc 53.47N 9.25 E
Gluhov 136 De 51.43N 33.57 E
Gluša 132 Fc 53.06N 28.52 E
Glyngøre 116 Ch 56.46N 8.52 E
Gmünd [Aus.] 128 Ib 48.46N 14.59 E
Gmünd [Aus.] 128 Hd 46.54N 13.32 E
Gmunden 128 Hc 47.55N 13.48 E
Gnarp 114 De 62.03N 17.16 E
Gnesta 114 Dg 59.03N 17.18 E
Gniben 116 Dh 56.01N 11.18 E
Gniew 120 Oc 53.51N 18.49 E
Gniewkowo 120 Od 52.54N 18.25 E
Gniezno 120 Nd 52.31N 17.37 E
Gnjilane 130 Eg 42.28N 21.29 E
Gnosjö 114 Ch 57.22N 13.44 E
Gnowangerup 212 Df 33.56S 117.50 E
Goa, Damān and Diu [3] 148 Ee 15.35N 74.00 E
Goageb 172 Be 26.44S 17.15 E
Goālpāra 148 Ic 26.10N 90.37 E
Goat 219b Dd 18.42S 169.17 E
Goat Island 197d Ba 17.44N 61.51W
Goat Point 197d Ba 17.44N 61.51W
Goba 160 Kh 7.01N 39.59 E
Gobabis 160 Ik 22.30S 18.58 E
Gobabis [3] 172 Bd 22.00S 19.00 E
Göbel 130 Lj 40.00N 28.09 E
Gober 166 Gc 13.48N 6.51 E
Gobernador Gregores 206 Fg 48.46S 70.15W
Gobernador Ingeniero Valentín Virasoro 206 Ic 28.03S 56.02W
Gobernador Mansilla 204 Ck 32.33S 59.22W
Gobi Altai (EN) = Gov'altajn Nuruu 140 Me 44.00N 102.00 E
Gobi Desert (EN) = Gov' 140 Me 43.00N 106.00 E
Gobō 154 Mh 33.53N 135.10 E
Göçbeyli 130 Kj 39.13N 27.25 E
Goceano 128 Dj 40.30N 9.15 E
Goce Delčev 130 Gh 41.33N 23.42 E
Goch 120 Ce 51.40N 6.10 E
Gochas 172 Bd 24.55S 18.55 E
Goczałkowickie, Jezioro- 120 Og 49.53N 18.50 E
Göd 120 Pi 47.42N 19.08 E
Godafoss 114a Cb 65.41N 17.33W
Godalming 124 Bc 51.11N 0.36W
Godār 146 Qh 29.45N 57.30 E
Godār-e Shah 146 Me 34.45N 48.10 E
Godāvari 140 Kh 17.00N 81.45 E
Godbout, Rivière- 184 Na 49.21N 67.42W
Gode 168 Gd 5.55N 43.40 E
Godeč 130 Gf 43.01N 23.03 E
Godelbukta 222 Df 70.00S 20.58 E
Goderich 184 Gd 43.45N 81.43W
Goderville 124 Ce 49.39N 0.22 E
Godhavn/Qeqertarssuaq 224 Nc 69.20N 53.35W
Godhra 148 Ed 22.45N 73.38 E
Godinlabe 168 Hd 5.54N 46.40 E
Gödöllő 120 Pi 47.36N 19.22 E
Godoy Cruz 206 Gd 32.55S 68.50W
Gods Lake 180 If 54.40N 94.09W
Gods Lake 180 If 54.40N 94.20W
Gods Mercy, Bay of - 180 Id 63.30N 86.10W
Gods River 180 Ie 56.22N 92.52W
Godthåb/Nûk 179 Nc 64.15N 51.40W
Godthåbfjord 179 Gf 64.20N 51.30W
Godwin Austen (EN) = Qogir Feng 140 Jf 35.53N 76.30 E
Godwin Austen → K2 140 Jf 35.53N 76.30 E
Goedereede 124 Fc 51.49N 3.58 E
Goéland, Lac au- 180 Jg 49.45N 76.50W
Goélands, Lac aux- 180 Le 55.30N 64.30W
Goële 124 Ee 49.10N 2.40 E
Goelette Island 172b Bc 10.13S 51.08 E
Goeree 122 Jc 51.50N 3.55 E
Goes 122 Jc 51.30N 3.54 E
Gogama 180 Jg 47.40N 81.43W
Gō-Gawa 156 Cd 35.01N 132.13 E
Gogebic Range 184 Cb 46.45N 89.25W
Gogland, ostrov- 114 Gf 60.05N 27.00 E
Gog Magog Hills 124 Cb 52.09N 0.11 E
Gogounou 166 Fc 10.50N 2.50 E
Gogrial 168 Dd 8.32N 28.07 E
Gogu, Virful- 130 Fd 45.12N 22.30 E
Gogui 166 Db 15.39N 9.21W
Gohelle 124 Ed 50.28N 2.45 E
Goiandira 202 Ig 18.08S 48.06W
Goianésia 202 Ig 15.19S 49.04W
Goiânia 200 Lg 16.40S 49.16W
Goianinha 202 Ke 6.16S 35.12W
Goiás 202 Hg 15.56S 50.08W
Goiás [2] 202 If 12.00S 48.00W
Goiatuba 202 Ig 18.01S 49.22W
Goikul 220a Bc 7.22N 134.36 E
Göinge 116 Eh 56.20N 13.50 E
Goio-Erê 206 Jb 24.12S 53.01W
Goioxim 204 Gg 25.14S 52.01W
Goirle 124 Hc 51.34N 5.05 E
Góis 126 Dd 40.09N 8.07W
Goito 128 Ee 45.15N 10.40 E
Gojam [3] 168 Fc 10.33N 37.35 E
Gojō 156 Dd 34.21N 135.42 E
Gojōme 156 Gb 39.56N 140.07 E
Gojra 148 Eb 31.09N 72.41 E
Gojthski, pereval- 132 Kg 44.15N 39.18 E
Gokase-Gawa 156 Be 32.35N 131.42 E
Gokasho-Wan 156 Ed 34.20N 136.40 E
Gökbel Dağı 130 Kl 37.18N 28.00 E
Gökçay 146 Ed 36.36N 33.23 E
Gökçeada 144 Ca 40.10N 25.50 E
Gökçeören 130 Lk 38.35N 28.32 E
Gökçeyazi 130 Kj 39.38N 27.39 E
Gökdere 146 Ed 36.39N 33.35 E
Gökırmak 146 Fb 41.24N 35.08 E
Göksu [Tur.] 146 Fd 37.37N 35.35 E
Göksu [Tur.] 146 Fd 36.20N 34.05 E
Göksu [Tur.] 130 Mi 40.23N 29.58 E
Göksun 146 Gc 38.03N 36.30 E
Göktepe 130 Ll 37.16N 28.36 E
Gök Tepe 130 Mm 36.53N 29.17 E
Gokwe 172 Dc 18.13S 28.55 E
Gol 114 Bf 60.42N 8.57 E
Golāghāt 148 Ic 26.31N 93.58 E
Golaja Pristan 132 Hf 46.29N 32.31 E
Gołańcz 120 Nd 52.57N 17.18 E
Golconda [Il.-U.S.] 186 Lh 37.22N 88.29W
Golconda [Nv.-U.S.] 188 Gf 40.57N 117.30W
Gölcük 146 Cb 40.44N 29.44 E
Golčův Jeníkov 120 Lg 49.49N 15.30 E
Goldap 120 Sb 54.19N 22.19 E
Gold Beach 188 Ce 42.25N 124.25W
Gold Coast 210 Gg 27.58S 153.25 E
Gold Coast 158 Gh 5.20N 0.45W
Golden [B.C.-Can.] 180 Ff 51.18N 116.58W
Golden [Co.-U.S.] 186 Dg 39.46N 105.13W
Golden Bay 218 Ed 40.50S 172.50 E
Goldendale 188 Ed 45.49N 120.50W
Goldene Aue 120 Ge 51.25N 11.00 E
Golden Gate 188 Dh 37.49N 122.29W
Golden Hinde 180 Eg 49.39N 125.45W
Golden Meadow 186 Kl 29.23N 90.16W
Golden Vale/Machaire na Mumhan 118 Fi 52.30N 8.00W
Goldfield 188 Gh 37.42N 117.14W
Gold River 188 Bb 49.41N 126.08W
Goldsboro 182 Ld 35.23N 77.59W
Goldsworthy 212 Dd 20.20S 119.30 E
Göle 146 Jb 40.48N 42.36 E
Golegã 126 De 39.24N 8.29W
Goleniów 120 Kc 53.36N 14.50 E
Golešnica 130 Eh 41.42N 21.33 E
Goleta, Cerro- 192 Ih 18.38N 100.04W
Golfito 190 Hg 8.38N 83.11W
Golfo Aranci 128 Dj 41.00N 9.37 E
Gölgeli Dağları 130 Ml 37.15N 29.06 E
Gölhisar 130 Ml 37.08N 29.30 E
Goliad 186 Hl 28.40N 97.23W
Golija [Yugo.] 130 Df 43.19N 20.18 E
Golija [Yugo.] 130 Bf 43.02N 18.47 E
Goljak 130 Eg 42.44N 21.31 E
Goljama Kamčija 130 Kf 43.03N 27.29 E
Goljama Sjutkja 130 Hh 41.54N 24.01 E
Goljamo Konare 130 Hg 42.16N 24.33 E
Goljam Perelik 130 Hh 41.36N 24.34 E
Goljam Persenk 130 Hh 41.49N 24.33 E
Gölköy 146 Gb 40.15N 37.26 E
Gölkük 130 Kj 39.19N 27.59 E
Göllheim 124 Ke 49.35N 8.03 E
Gölmarmara 130 Kk 38.42N 27.56 E
Golmud 142 Lf 36.22N 94.55 E
Golmud He 152 Gd 36.54N 95.11 E
Golo 122a Ba 42.31N 9.32 E
Goloby 120 Ve 51.06N 25.06 E
Gologory 120 Ug 49.35N 24.30 E
Gololcha 168 Gd 8.12N 40.05 E
Golovin 178 Gd 64.33N 163.02W
Golovnin Seamount (EN) 138 Kg 46.50N 157.00 E
Golpāyegan 144 Hc 33.27N 50.18 E
Gölpazarı 146 Db 40.17N 30.19 E
Golšanka 120 Zb 54.00N 26.16 E
Golspie 118 Jd 57.58N 3.58W
Gol Tappeh 146 Kd 36.35N 45.45 E
Golubac 130 Ee 44.39N 21.38 E
Golub-Dobrzyń 120 Pc 53.08N 19.02 E
Golungo Alto 170 Bd 9.08S 14.47 E
Golyšmanovo 136 Gd 56.23N 68.23 E
Goma 160 Ji 1.37S 29.12 E
Gómara 126 Jc 41.37N 2.13W
Gombe 160 Ig 10.17N 11.10 E
Gombi 166 Hc 10.10N 12.44 E
Gomel 112 Je 52.25N 31.00 E
Gomelskaja oblast [3] 136 Ce 52.20N 29.40 E
Gomera 158 Ff 28.06N 17.08W
Gómez Farías 192 Ie 24.57N 101.02W
Gómez Palacio 190 Dc 25.34N 103.30W
Gomo 152 Ee 33.26N 85.21 E
Gomo Co 152 Ee 33.45N 85.35 E
Goms 128 Cd 46.25N 8.10 E
Gonābād 144 Ic 34.20N 58.42 E
Gonaïves 190 Je 19.27N 72.43W
Gonam 138 Ie 57.18N 131.20 E
Gonâve, Golfe de la- 190 Je 19.00N 73.30W
Gonâve, Ile de la- 190 Je 18.51N 73.03W
Gonbad-e Qābūs 144 Ib 37.15N 55.09 E
Gonda 148 Gc 27.08N 81.56 E
Gonder 160 Kg 12.38N 37.29 E
Gonder [3] 168 Fc 12.00N 38.00 E
Gondia 148 Gd 21.27N 80.12 E
Gondo 158 Gg 14.20N 3.10W
Gondomar 126 Dc 41.09N 8.32W
Gondwana 140 Kg 23.00N 81.00 E
Gönen 146 Bb 40.06N 27.39 E
Gönen 146 Bb 40.06N 27.36 E
Gonfreville-l'Orcher 124 Ce 49.30N 0.14 E
Gong'an (Doushi) 152 Je 30.05N 112.12 E
Gongbo'gyamda 152 Ff 29.59N 93.25 E
Gonggar 152 Ff 29.17N 90.50 E
Gongga Shan 140 Mg 29.34N 101.53 E
Gonghe 152 Hd 36.21N 100.47 E
Gongliu/Tokkuztara 152 Dc 43.30N 82.15 E
Gongola [2] 166 Hd 8.40N 11.20 E
Gongola 158 Ih 9.30N 12.04 E
Gongpoquan 152 Gc 41.50N 97.00 E
Gongshan 152 Gf 27.39N 98.35 E
Gongxian (Xiaoyi) 154 Bg 34.46N 112.57 E
Gongzhuling → Huaide 152 Lc 43.30N 124.52 E
Goñi 204 Dk 33.31S 56.24W
Goniądz 120 Sc 53.30N 22.45 E
Gonīshān 146 Pd 37.04N 54.06 E
Gonjo 152 Ge 30.52N 98.20 E
Gonohe 156 Ga 40.31N 141.19 E
Go-no-ura 156 Ae 33.45N 129.41 E
Gönük 146 Ic 39.00N 40.41 E
Gonzales 186 Hl 29.30N 97.27W
Gonzáles, Riacho- 204 Df 22.48S 57.54W
González 192 Jf 22.50N 98.27W
Goodenough, Cape- 222 Ie 66.16S 126.10 E
Goodenough Bay 212 Ja 9.55S 150.00 E
Goodenough Island 214 Ei 9.22S 150.16 E
Good Hope, Cape of- / Groeie Hoop, Kaap die- 158 Il 34.21S 18.28 E
Goodhouse 172 Be 28.57S 18.13 E
Gooding 188 He 42.56N 114.43W
Goodland 182 Gd 39.21N 101.43W
Goodnews Bay 178 Ge 59.07N 161.35W
Goodsir, Mount- 188 Ga 51.12N 116.20W
Good Spirit Lake 188 Na 51.34N 102.40W
Goodwin Sands 124 Dc 51.15N 1.35 E
Goodyear 188 Ij 33.26N 112.21W
Goole 118 Mh 53.42N 0.52W
Goomalling 212 Df 31.19S 116.49 E
Goondiwindi 210 Gg 28.32S 150.19 E
Goonyella 212 Jd 21.43S 147.58 E
Goor 124 Ib 52.14N 6.37 E
Goose Lake 182 Cc 41.57N 120.25W
Goose River 186 Hc 47.28N 96.52W
Gopło, Jezioro- 120 Od 52.35N 18.20 E
Göppingen 120 Fh 48.42N 9.40 E
Góra 120 Me 51.40N 16.33 E
Gora 130 Di 40.40N 20.30 E
Góra Kalwaria 120 Re 51.59N 21.12 E
Gorakhpur 148 Gc 26.45N 83.22 E
Goransko 130 Bf 43.07N 18.50 E
Gorata 130 Ih 41.45N 25.55 E
Goražde 128 Mg 43.40N 18.59 E
Gorda 188 Ei 35.55N 121.27W
Gorda, Cayo- 194 Ff 15.55N 82.15W
Gorda, Punta- [Ca.-U.S.] 188 Cf 40.16N 124.20W
Gorda, Punta- [Cuba] 194 Fb 22.24N 82.10W
Gorda, Punta- [Nic.] 194 Ff 14.21N 83.12W
Gördes 130 Lk 38.54N 28.18 E
Gördes 130 Kj 38.46N 27.58 E
Gordil 168 Cd 9.44N 21.35 E
Gordior 146 Ec 39.37N 32.00 E
Gordon [Nb.-U.S.] 186 Ee 42.48N 102.12W
Gordon [Wi.-U.S.] 186 Kc 46.15N 91.47W
Gordon, Lake- 212 Jh 43.05S 146.05 E
Gordon Horne Peak 188 Fa 51.46N 118.50W
Gordonvale 212 Jc 17.05S 145.47 E
Goré 168 Bd 7.55N 16.38 E
Gore 168 Fd 8.09N 35.34 E
Gore 218 Cg 46.06S 168.56 E
Görele 146 Hb 41.02N 39.00 E
Görenez Dağı 130 Lk 39.00N 28.01 E
Gorenjsko 128 Id 46.20N 14.10 E
Gorey/Guaire 118 Gi 52.40N 6.18W
Gorgān 142 Hf 36.50N 54.29 E
Gorgān 146 Pd 36.59N 54.05 E
Gorgān, Khalīj-e- 146 Od 36.40N 53.50 E
Gorgany 120 Uh 48.30N 24.15 E
Gorgin 146 Ld 36.15N 47.55 E
Gorgin 146 Ld 36.16N 47.52 E
Gorgol [3] 162 Ef 15.45N 13.00W
Gorgol el Abiod 162 Ef 16.14N 12.58W
Gorgona 128 Dg 43.25N 9.55 E
Gorgona, Isla- 202 Cc 2.59N 78.12W
Gorgora 168 Fc 12.14N 37.17 E
Gorham 184 Lc 44.23N 71.11W
Gori 136 Eg 42.00N 44.02 E
Gorinchem 122 Kc 51.50N 5.00 E
Goring 124 Ac 51.31N 1.08W
Goris 132 Oj 39.31N 46.22 E
Gorizia 128 He 45.57N 13.38 E
Gorj [2] 130 Gd 45.00N 23.20 E
Gorjačegorsk 138 De 55.24N 88.55 E
Gorjači Kljuc 132 Kg 44.36N 39.07 E
Gorjanci 128 Je 45.45N 15.20 E
Gorki [Bela.] 132 Gb 54.17N 31.00 E
Gorki [Russia] → Nižnij Novgorod 112 Kd 57.38N 45.05 E
Gorki [Russia] 138 Bc 65.05N 65.15 E
Gorkovskoje vodohranilišče = Gorky Reservoir (EN) 110 Kd 57.00N 43.10 E
Gorkum 120 Hf 50.10N 11.08 E
Gorky Reservoir (EN) = Gorkovskoje vodohranilišče 110 Kd 57.00N 43.10 E
Gørlev 116 Di 55.32N 11.14 E
Gorlice 120 Rg 49.40N 21.10 E
Görlitz 120 Ke 51.10N 15.00 E
Gorlovka 112 Jf 48.18N 38.03 E
Gornalunga 128 Jm 37.24N 15.03 E
Gorna Orjahovica 130 If 43.07N 25.41 E
Gornjak [Russia] 138 Df 51.00N 81.29 E
Gornjak [Ukr.] 120 Uf 50.16N 24.13 E
Gornji Milanovac 130 De 44.02N 20.27 E
Gornji Vakuf 128 Lg 43.56N 17.36 E

Gorno-Altajsk	142	Kd	51.58N	85.58 E
Gorno-Badahšanskaja avtonomnaja respublika	136	Hh	38.15N	73.00 E
Gorno-Čujski	138	Ge	57.40N	111.40 E
Gornozavodsk [Russia]	138	Jg	46.30N	141.55 E
Gornozavodsk [Russia]	134	Jg	58.25N	58.20 E
Gorny [Russia]	138	Ih	44.50N	133.56 E
Gorny [Russia]	132	Pd	51.45N	48.34 E
Gorny [Russia]	138	If	50.48N	136.26 E
Gornyj Altaj respublika	138	Df	51.00N	87.00 E
Gornyje Ključi	154	Lb	45.15N	133.30 E
Gorochan	168	Fd	9.26N	37.05 E
Gorodec [Russia]	114	Kh	56.40N	43.30 E
Gorodec [Russia]	116	Mf	58.30N	29.55 E
Gorodenka	132	De	48.42N	25.32 E
Gorodišče [Bela.]	120	Vc	53.16N	26.03 E
Gorodišče [Russia]	132	Nc	53.16N	45.42 E
Gorodišče [Ukr.]	132	Ge	49.17N	31.27 E
Gorodnica	132	Ed	50.49N	27.22 E
Gorodnja	132	Gd	51.55N	31.31 E
Gorodok [Bela.]	136	Cd	55.26N	29.59 E
Gorodok [Ukr.]	132	Ce	49.47N	23.39 E
Gorodok [Ukr.]	132	Ee	49.10N	26.31 E
Gorodovikovsm	136	Ef	46.05N	41.59 E
Gorohov	120	Uf	50.28N	24.47 E
Gorohovec	114	Kh	56.12N	42.42 E
Goroka	210	Fe	6.02S	145.22 E
Gorom Gorom	166	Ec	14.26N	0.14W
Gorong, Kepulauan-	150	Jg	4.05S	131.20 E
Gorongosa, Serra da-	172	Ec	18.24S	34.06 E
Gorontalo	142	Oi	0.33N	123.03 E
Goroual	166	Fc	14.42N	0.53 E
Goroubi	166	Fc	13.07N	2.18 E
Górowo Iławeckie	120	Qb	54.17N	20.30 E
Gorron	122	Ff	48.25N	0.49W
Goršečnoje	150	Ld	51.33N	38.09 E
Gorski Kotar	128	Ie	45.26N	14.40 E
Gorssel	124	Ib	52.12N	6.13 E
Gort	118	Eh	53.04N	8.50W
Goru, Vîrful-	130	Jd	45.48N	26.25 E
Görükle	130	Li	40.14N	28.50 E
Goryn	136	Ce	52.09N	27.17 E
Gorzów [2]	120	Ld	54.25N	15.15 E
Gorzów Wielkopolski	120	Ld	52.44N	15.15 E
Goschen Strait	212	Kb	10.09S	150.56 E
Gosen	154	Of	37.44N	139.11 E
Gosford	212	Kf	33.26S	151.21 E
Goshen	184	Ee	41.35N	85.50W
Goshogawara	154	Pd	40.48N	140.27 E
Gosier	197e	Bb	16.12N	61.30W
Goslar	120	Ge	51.54N	10.26 E
Gospić	128	Jf	44.33N	15.23 E
Gosport	118	Lk	50.48N	1.08W
Gossen	116	Bb	62.50N	6.55 E
Gossi	166	Eb	15.47N	1.15W
Gossinga	168	Dd	8.39N	25.59 E
Gostivar	130	Dh	41.48N	20.54 E
Gostyń	120	Me	51.53N	17.00 E
Gostynin	120	Pd	52.26N	19.29 E
Gota älv	110	Hd	57.42N	11.52 E
Göta Kanal	110	Hd	58.50N	13.58 E
Götaland	110	Hd	57.30N	14.30 E
Götaland	114	Dh	57.30N	14.30 E
Göteborg	112	Hd	57.43N	11.58 E
Göteborg och Bohus [2]	114	Cg	58.30N	11.30 E
Gotel Mountains	158	Ih	7.00N	11.40 E
Gotemba	156	Fd	35.18N	138.56 E
Götene	114	Cg	58.32N	13.29 E
Gotha	120	Gf	50.57N	10.43 E
Gothenburg	186	Ff	40.56N	100.09W
Gothèye	166	Fc	13.52N	1.34 E
Gotland [2]	114	Eh	57.30N	18.30 E
Gotland	110	Hd	57.30N	18.30 E
Gotō-Nada	156	Ae	32.45N	129.30 E
Gotō-Rettō	152	Me	32.50N	129.00 E
Gotowasi	150	If	0.38N	128.26 E
Gotska Sandön	114	Eg	58.25N	19.15 E
Gōtsu	154	Lg	35.00N	132.14 E
Gttingen	120	Fe	51.32N	9.56 E
Gottwaldov → Zlín	120	Ng	49.13N	17.39 E
Goubangzi	154	Fd	41.23N	121.48 E
Gouda	122	Kc	52.01N	4.43 E
Goudiri	166	Cc	14.11N	12.43W
Gouet	122	Df	48.32N	2.45W
Gough Island	158	Gm	40.20S	10.00W
Gough Lake	188	Ia	52.02N	112.28W
Gouin, Réservoir-	180	Kg	48.35N	74.50W
Goulbin Kaba	166	Gc	13.42N	6.19 E
Goulburn	210	Fh	34.45S	149.43 E
Goulburn Islands	212	Gb	11.50S	133.30 E
Gould Bay	222	Rf	78.10S	44.00W
Gould Coast	222	Mg	84.30S	150.00W
Goulia	166	Dc	10.01N	7.11W
Goulimine	162	Ed	28.59N	10.04W
Gouménissa	130	Fi	40.57N	22.27 E
Gouna	166	Hd	8.32N	13.34 E
Gounda	168	Cd	9.25N	20.57 E
Goundam	166	Eb	16.24N	3.38W
Goundi	168	Bd	9.22N	17.22 E
Goundoumaria	166	Hc	13.42N	11.10 E
Gounou Gaya	168	Bd	9.38N	15.31 E
Gourara	162	Hd	29.30N	0.40 E
Gouraya	126	Nh	36.34N	1.55 E
Gourcy	166	Ec	13.13N	2.21W
Gourdon	122	Hj	44.44N	1.23 E
Gouré	160	Ig	13.58N	10.18 E
Gourin	122	Cf	48.08N	3.36W
Gourma [Burkina]	158	Hg	12.20N	1.30 E
Gourma [Mali]	158	Gg	15.45N	2.00W
Gourma-Rharous	166	Eb	16.52N	1.55W
Gournay-en-Bray	122	He	49.29N	1.44 E
Gourniá	130	In	35.06N	25.48 E
Gouro	168	Bb	19.40N	19.28 E
Gourrama	162	Gc	32.20N	4.05W
Goussainville	124	Ee	49.01N	2.28 E
Gouyave	197p	Bb	12.10N	61.44W
Gouzeaucourt	124	Fd	50.03N	3.07 E
Gouzon	122	Ih	46.11N	2.14 E
Gov' = Gobi Desert (EN)	140	Me	43.00N	106.00 E
Gov'altajn Nuruu = Gobi Altai (EN)	140	Me	44.00N	102.00 E
Govena, mys-	138	Le	59.47N	166.02 E
Gove Peninsula	212	Hb	13.02S	136.50 E
Goverla, gora-	136	Cf	48.10N	24.32 E
Governador Valadares	200	Lg	18.51S	41.56W
Governor's Harbour	190	Ic	25.10N	76.14W
Gowanda	184	Hd	42.28N	78.57W
Gower	118	Ij	51.36N	4.10W
Gowganda	184	Gb	47.38N	80.46W
Goya	200	Kh	29.10S	59.20W
Goyave	197e	Ab	16.08N	61.34W
Goyaves, Ilets à-	197e	Ab	16.10N	61.48W
Goyder River	212	Hb	12.38S	135.05 E
Göynücek	146	Fb	40.24N	35.32 E
Göynük	146	Db	40.24N	30.47 E
Göynük	130	Ni	40.20N	30.29 E
Goyōmai-Kaikyō	156a	Db	43.24N	145.50 E
Goz Arian	168	Bc	14.35N	20.00 E
Goz Beïda	168	Cc	12.13N	21.25 E
Gozha Co	152	De	34.59N	81.06 E
Goz Kerki	168	Bb	15.30N	18.50 E
Gözlü Baba Dağı	130	Lk	38.15N	28.28 E
Gozo	110	Hh	36.05N	14.15 E
Graaff-Reinet	172	Cf	32.14S	24.32 E
Graafschap	122	Mb	52.05N	6.30 E
Graben Neudorf	124	Ke	49.10N	8.28 E
Grabia	120	Oe	51.26N	18.56 E
Grabière Point	197g	Bb	15.30N	61.29W
Grabo	166	De	4.55N	7.30W
Grabowa	120	Mb	54.26N	16.20 E
Gračac	128	Jf	44.18N	15.51 E
Gračanica	128	Mf	44.42N	18.18 E
Gračanica, Manastir-	130	Eg	42.36N	21.12 E
Gracias	194	Cf	14.35N	88.35W
Gracias a Dios [3]	194	Ef	15.20N	84.20W
Gracias a Dios, Cabo-	174	Kh	15.00N	83.08W
Graciosa [Azr.]	158	Ee	39.04N	28.00W
Graciosa [Can.Is.]	162	Ed	29.15N	13.30W
Gradačac	128	Mf	44.53N	18.26 E
Gradaús, Serra dos-	198	Kf	8.00S	50.45W
Grado [It.]	128	He	45.40N	13.23 E
Grado [Sp.]	126	Fa	43.23N	6.04W
Grænalon	114a	Cb	64.10N	17.24W
Grænlandshaf = Greenland Sea (EN)	224	Ld	77.00N	1.00W
Grafenau	120	Jh	48.51N	13.24 E
Grafham Water	124	Bb	52.19N	0.10W
Grafing bei München	120	Hh	48.03N	11.58 E
Grafschaft Bentheim	124	Jb	52.30N	7.05 E
Grafton [Austl.]	212	Ke	29.41S	152.56 E
Grafton [N.D.-U.S.]	182	Hb	48.25N	97.25W
Grafton [W.V.-U.S.]	184	Hf	39.21N	80.00W
Grafton, Mount-	188	Hg	38.40N	114.45W
Graham [Can.]	180	Ef	53.40N	132.30W
Graham [N.C.-U.S.]	184	Hg	36.05N	79.25W
Graham [N.W.T.-Can.]	180	Ia	77.17N	90.50W
Graham [Tx.-U.S.]	186	Gj	33.06N	98.35W
Graham, Mount-	182	Fe	32.42N	109.52W
Graham Land (EN)	222	Qe	66.00S	63.30W
Graham Moore, Cape-	180	Jb	72.51N	76.05W
Grahamstown	160	Jl	33.19S	26.31 E
Grain Coast	158	Gh	5.00N	9.00W
Graisivaudan	122	Li	45.15N	5.50 E
Grajaú	202	Ie	5.49S	46.08W
Grajaú, Rio-	202	Jd	3.41S	44.48W
Grajewo	120	Sc	53.39N	22.27 E
Gram	116	Ci	55.17N	9.04 E
Gramalote	194	Kj	7.54N	72.48W
Gramat	122	Hj	44.47N	1.43 E
Gramat, Causse de-	122	Hj	44.40N	1.50 E
Graminha, Représa da-	204	Ie	21.33S	46.38W
Grammichele	128	Im	37.13N	14.38 E
Grammont/Geraardsbergen	124	Fd	50.46N	3.52 E
Grámmos Óros	130	Di	40.20N	20.45 E
Grampian [3]	118	Kd	57.25N	2.35W
Grampian Mountains	110	Fd	56.45N	4.00W
Gramshi	130	Di	40.52N	20.11 E
Gran	116	Dd	60.22N	10.34 E
Granada [Col.]	202	Dc	3.33N	73.44W
Granada [Nic.]	190	Gf	11.56N	85.57W
Granada [Nic.] [3]	194	Eh	11.50N	86.00W
Granada [Sp.]	112	Fh	37.13N	3.41W
Granada [Sp.] [3]	126	Ig	37.15N	3.15W
Granada, Vega de-	126	Ig	37.15N	4.00W
Granard/Gránard	118	Fh	53.47N	7.30W
Gránard/Granard	118	Fh	53.47N	7.30W
Granby	180	Kg	45.24N	72.43W
Gran Canaria	158	Ff	28.00N	15.36W
Gran Chaco	198	Jh	23.00S	60.00W
Grand Anse Bay	197p	Bb	12.02N	61.45W
Grand Bahama	174	Lg	26.40N	78.20W
Grand Ballon	122	Ng	47.55N	7.08 E
Grand Bank	180	Lg	47.06N	55.47W
Grand Banks (EN)	174	Oe	45.00N	50.00W
Grand Bassa [3]	166	Dd	6.10N	9.40W
Grand-Bassam	160	Gh	5.12N	3.44W
Grand Bay	197p	Cb	12.29N	61.23W
Grand Bay	197g	Bb	15.14N	61.19W
Grand-Béréby	166	De	4.38N	6.55W
Grand-Bourg	196	Fe	15.53N	61.19W
Grand Caille Point	197k	Ab	13.52N	61.05W
Grandcamp-Maisy	124	Ae	49.23N	1.02W
Grand Canal	118	Gh	53.21N	6.14W
Grand Canal (EN) = Da Yunhe	140	Nf	39.54N	116.44 E
Grand Canyon	182	Ed	36.03N	112.09W
Grand Canyon	174	Hf	36.10N	112.45W
Grand' Case	197b	Ab	18.06N	63.03W
Grand Cayman	190	He	19.20N	81.15W
Grand Cess	166	De	4.24N	8.13W
Grand Colombier	122	Li	45.54N	5.46 E
Grand-Combe, La-	122	Kj	44.13N	4.02 E
Grand Coulee	188	Fc	47.56N	119.00W
Grand-Couronne	124	De	49.21N	1.01 E
Grandcourt	124	De	49.55N	1.30 E
Grand Cul de Sac Bay	197k	Ab	13.59N	61.02W
Grand Cul-de-Sac Marin	197e	Ab	16.20N	61.35W
Grande, Arroyo-	204	Dm	37.32S	57.34W
Grande, Bahía-	198	Jk	50.45S	68.45W
Grande, Boca-	202	Fb	8.45N	60.35W
Grande, Cachoeira-	204	Gb	15.37S	51.48W
Grande, Cerro-	192	If	23.40N	100.40W
Grande, Ciénaga-	194	Ji	9.13N	75.46W
Grande, Corixa-	204	Cc	17.10S	58.20W
Grande, Cuchilla- [Arg.]	204	Cj	31.45S	58.35W
Grande, Cuchilla- [Ur.]	198	Ki	33.15S	55.07W
Grande, Ile-	122	Cf	48.48N	3.35W
Grande, Ilha-	202	Jh	23.10S	44.10W
Grande, Rio-	202	Fb	8.39N	60.59W
Grande, Rio-	174	Jg	25.57N	97.09W
Grande, Rio-	174	Jg	25.57N	97.09W
Grande, Rio- [Braz.]	198	Kh	20.06S	51.04W
Grande, Rio- [Braz.]	198	Lg	11.05S	43.09W
Grande, Rio- (EN) = Bravo del Norte, Rio-	174	Jg	25.57N	97.09W
Grande, Rio- o Guapay, Rio-	198	Jg	15.51S	64.39W
Grande, Serra-	198	Lf	6.00S	40.52W
Grande, Sierra-	192	Gc	29.40N	104.55W
Grande Anse	197k	Ba	14.01N	60.54W
Grande-Anse	197e	Bb	16.18N	61.04W
Grande Brière	122	Dg	47.22N	2.15W
Grande Cache	180	Ff	53.14N	119.00W
Grande Casse, Pointe de la-	122	Mi	45.24N	6.50 E
Grande Cayemite	194	Kd	18.37N	73.45W
Grande Chartreuse	122	Li	45.22N	5.50 E
Grande Comore/Njazidja	158	Lj	11.35S	43.20 E
Grande de Santa Marta, Ciénaga-	194	Jh	10.50N	74.25W
Grande de Santiago, Rio-	174	Ig	21.36N	105.26W
Grande Inferior, Cuchilla-	204	Dk	33.50S	56.10W
Grande Kabylie	126	Ph	36.45N	4.00 E
Grande-Motte, La-	122	Kk	43.34N	4.07 E
Grande ou Sete Quedas, Ilha-	204	Ef	23.45S	54.03W
Grande Pointe [Guad.]	197a	Ac	15.59N	61.38W
Grande Pointe [Guad.]	197b	Bc	17.50N	62.50W
Grande Prairie	176	Hd	55.10N	118.48W
Grand Erg de Bilma	158	Ig	18.30N	13.50 E
Grand Erg Occidental	158	He	30.20N	0.01 E
Grand Erg Oriental	158	He	30.00N	7.00 E
Grande Rivière à Goyaves	197e	Ab	16.18N	61.37W
Grande Rivière de la Baleine	174	Ld	55.15N	77.45W
Grande Rivière du Nord	194	Kd	19.35N	72.11W
Grande Ronde River	188	Gc	46.05N	116.59W
Grandes, Salinas-	198	Ji	30.05S	65.05W
Grande Sebkha d'Oran	126	Li	35.32N	0.48W
Grandes Rousses, Les-	122	Mi	45.06N	6.07 E
Grande-Synthe	124	Ec	51.01N	2.17 E
Grand Etang	197p	Bb	12.06N	61.42W
Grande-Terre	196	Fd	16.20N	61.25W
Grande Vigie, Pointe de la-	197e	Ba	16.31N	61.28W
Grand Falls [N.B.-Can.]	180	Kg	47.03N	67.44W
Grand Falls [Newf.-Can.]	176	Ne	48.56N	55.40W
Grand Forks [B.C.-Can.]	188	Fb	49.02N	118.27W
Grand Forks [N.D.-U.S.]	176	Je	47.55N	97.03W
Grand Found, Anse du-	197b	Bc	17.53N	62.49W
Grand Gedeh [3]	166	Dd	5.45N	8.05W
Grand Haven	184	Dd	43.04N	86.10W
Grand Ilet	197e	Ac	15.50N	61.36W
Grand Island	176	Je	40.55N	98.21W
Grand Junction	176	If	39.05N	108.33W
Grand-Lahou	166	Dd	5.08N	5.01W
Grand Lake [La.-U.S.]	186	Kl	29.55N	91.35W
Grand Lake [La.-U.S.]	186	Jl	29.55N	92.47W
Grand Lake [N.B.-Can.]	184	Nc	45.42N	66.05W
Grand Lake [Newf.-Can.]	180	Lg	49.00N	57.20W
Grand Lake [Oh.-U.S.]	184	Ee	40.30N	84.32W
Grand Lake Victoria	184	Ib	47.35N	77.33W
Grand-Lieu, Lac de-	122	Eg	47.05N	1.40W
Grand Manan Channel	184	Nc	44.45N	66.52W
Grand Manan Island	180	Kh	44.40N	66.50W
Grand Marais [Mi.-U.S.]	184	Eb	46.40N	85.59W
Grand Marais [Mn.-U.S.]	186	Kc	47.45N	90.20W
Grand-Mère	184	Kb	46.37N	72.41W
Grand Morin	122	If	48.54N	2.50 E
Grândola	126	Df	38.10N	8.34W
Grândola, Serra de-	126	Df	38.06N	8.38W
Grand Passage	219b	Ad	18.45S	163.10 E
Grand-Popo	166	Fd	6.17N	1.50 E
Grand Portage	176	Lc	47.58N	89.41W
Grand Prairie	182	He	32.45N	96.59W
Grandpré	124	Ge	49.20N	4.52 E
Grand Rapids [Man.-Can.]	180	Hf	53.10N	99.17W
Grand Rapids [Mi.-U.S.]	176	Ke	42.58N	85.40W
Grand Rapids [Mn.-U.S.]	182	Ib	47.14N	93.31W
Grand Récif Sud	216	Cd	22.38S	167.00 E
Grand River [Mi.-U.S.]	184	Dd	43.04N	86.15W
Grand River [Mo.-U.S.]	186	Jg	39.23N	93.06W
Grand River [Ont.-Can.]	184	Hd	42.51N	79.34W
Grand River [S.D.-U.S.]	182	Fd	45.40N	100.32W
Grand'Rivière	197h	Ab	14.52N	61.11W
Grand Roy	197p	Bb	12.08N	61.45W
Grand Saint Bernard, Col du-	128	Be	45.50N	7.10 E
Grand-Sans-Toucher	197e	Ab	16.06N	61.41W
Grand Teton	182	Ec	43.44N	110.48W
Grand Traverse Bay	182	Jb	45.02N	85.30W
Grand Turk	190	Jd	21.28N	71.09W
Grand Turk	194	Lc	21.30N	71.10W
Grand Union Canal	124	Bc	51.30N	0.02W
Grand Valley	186	Bg	39.27N	108.03W
Grand Veymont, Le-	122	Lj	44.52N	5.32 E
Grandview [Man.-Can.]	186	Fa	51.10N	100.45W
Grandview [Mo.-U.S.]	186	Ig	38.53N	94.32W
Grandvilliers	124	De	49.40N	1.56 E
Grand Wash Cliffs	188	Ii	35.45N	113.45W
Granger	188	Ee	46.21N	120.11W
Grängesberg	116	Fd	60.05N	14.59 E
Grangeville	188	Gd	45.56N	116.07W
Gran Guardia	206	Ic	25.52S	58.53W
Granite City	186	Kg	38.42N	90.09W
Granite Falls	186	Id	44.49N	95.33W
Granite Pass	188	Ld	44.38N	107.30W
Granite Peak [Nv.-U.S.]	182	Dc	41.40N	117.35W
Granite Peak [U.S.]	182	Fb	45.10N	109.48W
Granite Range	188	Ff	41.00N	119.35W
Granitola, Punta-	128	Gm	37.34N	12.41 E
Grankulla/Kauniainen	116	Kd	60.13N	24.45 E
Granma [3]	194	Ic	20.30N	77.00W
Gran Malvina, Isla-/West Falkland	198	Kk	51.40S	60.00W
Gran Morelos [Mex.]	192	Fc	28.15N	106.30W
Gran Morelos [Mex.]	192	Eb	30.40N	108.35W
Gränna	116	Ff	58.01N	14.28 E
Granollers/Granollérs	126	Oc	41.37N	2.18 E
Granollérs/Granollers	126	Oc	41.37N	2.18 E
Gran Paradis/Gran Paradiso	128	Be	45.32N	7.16 E
Gran Paradiso/Gran Paradis	128	Be	45.32N	7.16 E
Gran Pilastro/Hochfeiler	128	Fd	46.58N	11.44 E
Gran San Bernardo, Colle del-	128	Be	45.50N	7.10 E
Gran Sasso d'Italia	110	Hg	42.25N	13.40 E
Grant	186	Ff	40.50N	101.56W
Grant, Mount-	188	Fg	38.34N	118.48W
Gran Tarajal	162	Ed	28.12N	14.01W
Grantham	118	Mi	52.55N	0.38W
Grant Island	222	Nf	74.24S	131.20W
Grantown-on-Spey	118	Jd	57.20N	3.38W
Grant Range	188	Hg	38.25N	115.30W
Grants	182	Fd	35.09N	107.52W
Grantsburg	186	Jd	45.47N	92.41W
Grants Pass	182	Cc	42.26N	123.19W
Granville	122	Ef	48.50N	1.36W
Granville Lake	180	He	56.00N	100.20W
Granvin	116	Bd	60.33N	6.43 E
Grao de Sagunto, Sagunto-	126	Le	39.40N	0.16W
Grappa, Monte-	128	Fe	45.52N	11.48 E
Grappler Bank (EN)	197a	Cc	17.48N	65.55W
Graskop	172	Ed	24.58S	30.49 E
Gräsmark	116	Ee	59.57N	12.55 E
Gräsö	114	Ef	60.25N	18.25 E
Grasse	122	Mk	43.40N	6.55 E
Grasset, Lac-	184	Ha	49.58N	78.10W
Grassrange	188	Kc	47.01N	108.48W
Gråsten	114	Bi	54.55N	9.36 E
Grästorp	116	Ef	58.20N	12.40 E
Graubünden / Grigioni / Grischun [2]	128	Dd	46.35N	9.35 E
Grau-du-Roi, Le-	122	Kk	43.32N	4.08 E
Graulhet	122	Hk	43.46N	2.00 E
Graus	126	Mb	42.11N	0.20 E
Grave	124	Hc	51.45N	5.45 E
Grave, Pointe de-	122	Ei	45.34N	1.04W
Gravedona	128	Dd	46.09N	9.18 E
Gravelbourg	180	Gg	49.53N	106.34W
Gravelines	122	Id	50.59N	2.07 E
Gravenhage, 's- /Den Haag = The Hague (EN)	112	Ge	52.06N	4.18 E
Gravenhage-Scheveningen, s-	122	Kb	52.06N	4.18 E
Gravenhurst	184	Hc	44.55N	79.22W
Gravenor Bay	197d	Ba	17.33N	61.45W
Graves	122	Fj	44.35N	0.30W
Gravesend	118	Nj	51.27N	0.24 E
Gravesend-Tilbury	118	Nj	51.28N	0.23 E
Gravina in Puglia	128	Kj	40.49N	16.25 E
Gravone	122a	Ab	41.55N	8.47 E
Gray	122	Lg	47.27N	5.35 E
Gray Feather Bank (EN)	214	Df	8.00N	148.40 E
Grayling	184	Ec	44.40N	84.43W
Grays	118	Nj	51.28N	0.20 E
Grays Harbor	188	Cc	46.56N	124.05W
Grayson	184	Ff	38.20N	82.57W
Grays Peak	182	Fd	39.37N	105.45W
Graz	112	Hf	47.04N	15.27 E
Grazalema	126	Gh	36.46N	5.22W
Grdelica	130	Fg	42.54N	22.04 E
Greåker	116	De	59.16N	11.02 E
Great	197p	Bb	12.10N	61.38W
Great Artesian Basin	208	Fg	25.00S	143.00 E
Great Astrolabe Reef	219d	Bc	18.52S	178.31 E
Great Australian Bight	208	Eh	35.00S	130.00 E
Great Bacolet Point	197p	Bb	12.05N	61.37W
Great Bahama Bank (EN)	174	Lg	23.15N	78.00W
Great Bardfield	124	Cc	51.56N	0.29 E
Great Barrier Island	208	Ih	36.10S	175.25 E
Great Barrier Reef	208	Ff	19.10S	149.00 E
Great Basin	174	Hf	40.00N	117.00W
Great Bay	184	Jf	39.30N	74.23W
Great Bear	180	Ed	64.54N	125.35W
Great Bear Lake	174	Hc	66.00N	120.00W
Great Belt (EN) = Store Bælt	110	Hd	55.30N	11.00 E
Great Bend	182	Hd	38.22N	98.46W
Great Blasket/An Blascaod Mór	118	Ci	52.05N	10.32W
Great Britain	110	Fd	54.00N	3.00W
Great Central Lake	188	Cb	49.27N	125.12W
Great Channel	140	Li	6.00N	94.00 E
Great Chesterford	124	Cb	52.04N	0.12 E
Great Dismal Swamp	184	Ig	36.30N	76.30W
Great Dividing Range	208	Fg	25.00S	147.00 E
Great Dunmow	124	Cc	51.53N	0.22 E
Greater Accra [3]	166	Fd	5.45N	0.10 E
Greater Antilles (EN) = Antillas Mayores	174	Lh	20.00N	74.00W
Greater Khingan Range (EN) = Da Hinggan Ling	140	Oe	49.00N	122.00 E
Greater London [3]	118	Mj	51.35N	0.05W
Greater Manchester [3]	118	Kh	53.35N	2.10W
Greater Sunda Islands (EN)	140	Nj	3.52S	111.20 E
Great Exhibition Bay	216	Df	34.40S	173.00 E
Great Exuma Island	190	Id	23.32N	75.50W
Great Falls	176	He	47.30N	111.17W
Great Fisher Bank (EN) = Storefiskbank	118	Qe	56.50N	4.00 E
Great Fish River	158	Ik	17.11S	28.08 E
Great Guana Cay	194	Ia	24.00N	76.20W
Great Harbour Cay	184	Im	25.45N	77.52W
Great Inagua	174	Lg	21.02N	73.20W
Great Indian Desert/Thar	140	Jg	27.00N	70.00 E
Great Karasberge (EN) = Groot-Karasberge	158	Ik	27.20S	18.45 E
Great Karroo (EN) = Groot Karoo	158	Jl	33.00S	22.00 E
Great Lake	212	Jh	41.52S	146.45 E
Great Lyakhov (EN) = Bolšoj Ljahovski, ostrov-	138	Jb	73.35N	142.00 E
Great Namaland/Groot Namaland	172	Be	26.00S	17.00 E
Great Nicobar	140	Li	7.00N	93.50 E
Great North East Channel	212	Ia	9.30S	143.25 E
Great Ormes Head	118	Jh	53.21N	3.52W
Great Ouse	118	Ni	52.44N	0.23 E
Great Plain of the Koukdjuak	180	Kc	66.25N	72.50W
Great Plains	174	Je	42.00N	100.00W
Great Reef	219c	Bb	16.15S	166.02 E
Great Ruaha	158	Ki	7.56S	37.52 E
Great Sacandaga Lake	184	Jd	43.08N	74.10W
Great Sale Cay	184	Hl	27.00N	78.12W
Great Salt Lake	174	He	41.10N	112.30W
Great Salt Lake Desert	182	Ec	40.40N	113.30W
Great Salt Plains Lake	186	Gh	36.44N	98.12W
Great Salt Pond	197c	Ab	17.15N	62.38W
Great Sandy Desert [Austl.]	208	Dg	21.30S	125.00 E
Great Sandy Desert [U.S.]	182	Cc	43.35N	120.15W
Great Sea Reef	219d	Bb	16.15S	178.33 E
Great Shelford	124	Cb	52.07N	0.08 E
Great Sitkin	178a	Cb	52.03N	176.07W
Great Slave Lake	174	Hc	61.30N	114.00W
Great Smoky Mountains	184	Fh	35.35N	83.30W
Great Stour	118	Oj	51.19N	1.15 E
Great Valley [U.S.]	184	Ie	40.15N	76.50W
Great Valley [U.S.]	182	Kd	36.30N	82.00W
Great Victoria Desert	208	Dg	28.30S	127.45 E
Great Yarmouth	118	Oi	52.37N	1.44 E
Grebbestad	114	Cg	58.42N	11.15 E
Grebenka	132	Hd	50.07N	32.25 E
Gréboun, Mont-	166	Gb	20.00N	8.35 E
Greci	130	Ld	45.11N	28.14 E
Gredos, Sierra de-	126	Gd	40.20N	5.05W
Greece (EN) = Ellás [1]	112	Ih	39.00N	22.00 E
Greeley [Co.-U.S.]	182	Gc	40.25N	104.42W
Greeley [Nb.-U.S.]	186	Gf	41.33N	98.32W
Greely Fiord	180	Ja	80.40N	85.00W
Greem-Bell, ostrov-	140	Ia	81.10N	64.00 E
Green	188	De	43.07N	123.28W
Green Bay	176	Ke	44.30N	88.01W
Green Bay	182	Jb	45.00N	87.30W
Greencastle	184	Df	39.38N	86.52W
Green Cay	194	Ia	24.02N	77.11W
Greeneville	184	Fg	36.10N	82.50W
Greenfield [In.-U.S.]	184	Ef	39.47N	85.46W
Greenfield [Ma.-U.S.]	184	Kd	42.36N	72.36W
Greenhorn Mountain	186	Dh	37.57N	105.00W
Green Island	218	Df	45.54S	170.26 E
Green Island [Atg.]	197d	Bb	17.03N	61.40W
Green Island [Gren.]	197p	Bb	12.14N	61.35W
Green Islands	208	Ge	4.30S	154.10 E
Greenland	197q	Ab	13.15N	59.34W
Greenland (EN) = Grønland/Kalaallit Nunaat [5]	224	Nd	70.00N	40.00W
Greenland (EN) = Grønland/Kalaallit Nunaat	174	Pb	70.00N	40.00W
Greenland (EN) = Kalaallit Nunaat/Grønland [5]	224	Nd	70.00N	40.00W
Greenland (EN) = Kalaallit Nunaat/Grønland	174	Pb	70.00N	40.00W
Greenland Basin (EN)	224	Ld	77.00N	0.00
Greenland Sea (EN) = Grænlandshaf	224	Ld	77.00N	1.00W
Greenland Sea (EN) = Grønlandshavet	224	Ld	77.00N	1.00W
Green Lookout Mountain	188	Dd	45.52N	122.08W
Green Mountains	174	Le	43.45N	72.45W
Greenock	118	If	55.57N	4.45W
Greenough River	212	Ce	28.51S	114.38 E
Green Peter Lake	188	Dd	44.28N	122.30W
Green River [U.S.]	184	Dg	37.55N	87.30W
Green River [U.S.]	174	If	38.11N	109.53W
Green River [Ut.-U.S.]	182	Ed	38.59N	110.10W
Green River [Wy.-U.S.]	182	Fc	41.32N	109.28W
Green River Lake	184	Eg	37.15N	85.15W
Greensboro	176	Lf	36.04N	79.47W
Greensburg [In.-U.S.]	184	Ef	39.20N	85.29W
Greensburg [Ks.-U.S.]	186	Gh	37.36N	99.18W
Greensburg [La.-U.S.]	186	Kk	30.51N	90.42W
Greenstone Point	118	Hd	57.55N	5.40W
Greenvale	212	Jc	18.55S	145.05 E
Greenville [Al.-U.S.]	184	Dj	31.50N	86.38W
Greenville [Il.-U.S.]	186	Lg	38.53N	89.25W
Greenville [Lbr.]	160	Gh	4.59N	9.02W
Greenville [Me.-U.S.]	184	Mc	45.28N	69.35W
Greenville [Ms.-U.S.]	182	Ie	33.25N	91.05W
Greenville [N.C.-U.S.]	182	Ld	35.37N	77.23W
Greenville [Oh.-U.S.]	184	Ee	40.06N	84.37W
Greenville [Pa.-U.S.]	184	Ge	41.24N	80.24W
Greenville [S.C.-U.S.]	176	Kf	34.51N	82.23W
Greenville [Tx.-U.S.]	182	He	33.08N	96.07W
Greenwich	184	Fe	41.02N	82.32W
Greenwich, London-	118	Mj	51.28N	0.00
Greenwood [Ms.-U.S.]	182	Ie	33.31N	90.11W
Greenwood [S.C.-U.S.]	184	Fh	34.12N	82.10W
Greenwood, Lake-	184	Gh	34.15N	82.00W
Greer	184	Fh	34.55N	82.14W
Greers Ferry Lake	186	Ji	35.30N	92.10W
Greeson, Lake-	186	Ji	34.10N	93.45W

Index Symbols

- [1] Independent Nation
- [2] State, Region
- [3] District, County
- [4] Municipality
- [5] Colony, Dependency
- Continent
- Physical Region
- Historical or Cultural Region
- Mount, Mountain
- Volcano
- Hill
- Mountains, Mountain Range
- Hills, Escarpment
- Plateau, Upland
- Pass, Gap
- Plain, Lowland
- Delta
- Salt Flat
- Valley, Canyon
- Crater, Cave
- Karst Features
- Depression
- Polder
- Desert, Dunes
- Forest, Woods
- Heath, Steppe
- Oasis
- Cape, Point
- Coast, Beach
- Cliff
- Peninsula
- Isthmus
- Sandbank
- Island
- Atoll
- Rock, Reef
- Islands, Archipelago
- Rocks, Reefs
- Coral Reef
- Well, Spring
- Geyser
- River, Stream
- Waterfall, Rapids
- River Mouth, Estuary
- Lake
- Salt Lake
- Intermittent Lake
- Reservoir
- Swamp, Pond
- Canal
- Glacier
- Ice Shelf, Pack Ice
- Ocean
- Sea
- Gulf, Bay
- Strait, Fjord
- Lagoon
- Bank
- Seamount
- Tablemount
- Ridge
- Shelf
- Basin
- Escarpment, Sea Scarp
- Fracture
- Trench, Abyss
- National Park, Reserve
- Point of Interest
- Recreation Site
- Cave, Cavern
- Historic Site
- Ruins
- Wall, Walls
- Church, Abbey
- Temple
- Scientific Station
- Railway station
- Airport
- Port
- Military installation
- Lighthouse
- Mine
- Tunnel
- Dam, Bridge

Grefrath 124 Ic 51.18N 6.19 E
Gregoria Pérez de Denis 204 Bi 28.14S 61.32W
Gregorio, Rio- 202 De 6.50S 70.46W
Gregório, Rio- 204 Ha 13.42S 49.58W
Gregory, Lake- 212 He 28.55S 139.00 E
Gregory Lake 212 Fd 20.10S 127.20 E
Gregory Range 208 Ff 19.00S 143.00 E
Gregory River 212 Hc 17.53S 139.17 E
Greifenburg 128 Hd 46.45N 13.11 E
Greifswald 120 Jb 54.06N 13.23 E
Greifswalder Bodden 120 Jb 54.15N 13.35 E
Greifswalder Oie 120 Jb 54.14N 13.55 E
Grein 128 Ib 48.13N 14.51 E
Greiz 120 If 50.39N 12.12 E
Grëko, Akra- 146 Fe 34.56N 34.05 E
Gremiha 112 Jb 68.03N 39.29 E
Gremjačinsk 134 Hg 58.34N 57.51 E
Grenå 114 Ch 56.25N 10.53 E
Grenada 186 Lj 33.47N 89.55W
Grenada [1] 176 Mh 12.07N 61.40W
Grenada 174 Mh 12.07N 61.40W
Grenada Basin (EN) 190 Lf 13.30N 62.00W
Grenada Lake 186 Lj 33.50N 89.40W
Grenadines 190 Lf 12.40N 61.15W
Grenchen 128 Bc 47.11N 7.25 E
Grenen 110 Hd 57.44N 10.40 E
Grenfell 186 Ea 50.25N 102.56W
Grenoble 112 Gf 45.10N 5.43 E
Grenora 186 Eb 48.37N 103.56W
Grense-Jakobselv 114 Hb 69.47N 30.50 E
Grenville 196 Ff 12.07N 61.37W
Grenville, Cape- 212 Ib 12.00S 143.15 E
Gréoux-les-Bains 122 Lk 43.45N 5.53 E
Gresham 188 Dd 45.30N 122.26W
Gresik 150 Fh 7.09S 112.38 E
Gressoney-la-Trinité 128 Be 45.50N 7.49 E
Gretas klackar 116 Gc 61.34N 17.50 E
Gretna 186 Kl 29.55N 90.03W
Grevelingen 124 Fc 51.45N 4.00 E
Greven 120 Dd 52.06N 7.37 E
Grevená 130 Ei 40.05N 21.25 E
Grevenbroich 120 Ce 51.05N 6.35 E
Grevenbroich, Lennestadt- 124 Kc 51.08N 8.01 E
Grevenmacher 124 Ie 49.41N 6.27 E
Grevesmühlen 120 Hc 53.52N 11.11 E
Grey 218 De 42.26S 171.11 E
Greybull 188 Kd 44.30N 108.03W
Greybull River 188 Kd 44.28N 108.03W
Grey Islands 180 Lf 50.50N 55.35W
Greymouth 216 Dh 42.27S 171.12 E
Grey Range 208 Fg 27.00S 143.35 E
Greystones/Ná Clocha Liatha 118 Gh 53.09N 6.04W
Greytow 172 Ee 29.07S 30.30 E
Greytown 218 Fd 41.05S 175.28 E
Gribanovski 132 Ld 51.29N 41.58 E
Gribb Bank (EN) 222 Ge 63.00S 90.30 E
Gribès, Mali i- 130 Ci 40.34N 19.34 E
Gribingui [3] 168 Bd 7.00N 19.30 E
Gribingui 168 Bd 8.33N 19.05 E
Griend 124 Ha 53.15N 5.20 E
Griesheim 124 Ke 49.52N 8.33 E
Grieskirchen 128 Hb 48.14N 13.50 E
Griffin 182 Ke 33.15N 84.16W
Griffith 212 Jf 34.17S 146.03 E
Grigioni / Grischun / Graubünden [2] 128 Dd 46.35N 9.35 E
Grigoriopol 130 Mb 47.09N 29.13 E
Grijalva 174 Jh 18.36N 92.39W
Grijalva, Rio- 192 Mh 18.36N 92.38W
Grim, Cape- 212 Ih 40.41S 144.41 E
Grimari 168 Cd 5.44N 20.03 E
Grimbergen 124 Gd 50.56N 4.23 E
Grimma 120 Ie 51.14N 12.43 E
Grimmen 120 Jb 54.06N 13.03 E
Grimsby 118 Mh 53.35N 0.05W
Grimsey 114a Ca 66.33N 18.00W
Grimsstadir 114a Cb 65.39N 16.07W
Grimstad 114 Bg 58.20N 8.36 E
Grimsvotn 114a Cb 64.24N 17.22W
Grindavik 114a Ac 63.50N 22.30W
Grindelwald 128 Cd 46.38N 8.03 E
Grindsted 114 Bi 55.45N 8.56 E
Grinnell 186 Jf 41.45N 92.43W
Grinnel Peninsula 180 Ia 76.40N 95.00W
Grintavec 128 Id 46.22N 14.32 E
Griquatown 172 Ce 28.49S 23.15 E
Grischun / Graubünden / Grigioni [2] 128 Dd 46.35N 9.35 E
Grise Fiord 176 Kb 76.10N 83.15W
Gris-Nez, Cap- 122 Hd 50.52N 1.35 E
Grisslehamn 116 Hd 60.06N 18.50 E
Grjazi 136 De 52.29N 39.57 E
Grjazovec 136 Ed 58.53N 40.15 E
Grmeč 128 Kf 44.43N 16.15 E
Grobiņa/Grobinja 114 Eh 56.33N 21.11 E
Grobinja/Grobiņa 114 Eh 56.33N 21.11 E
Groblersdal 172 De 25.15S 29.25 E
Grocka 130 De 44.41N 20.43 E
Grodk/Spremberg 120 Ke 51.33N 14.22 E
Grodków 120 Nf 50.43N 17.22 E
Grodnenskaja oblast [3] 136 Ce 53.45N 25.10 E
Grodno 112 Ie 53.42N 23.50 E
Grodzisk Mazowiecki 120 Qd 52.07N 20.37 E
Grodzjanka 132 Fc 53.34N 28.48 E
Groeie Hoop, Kaap die- / Good Hope, Cape of- 158 Il 34.21S 18.28 E
Groenlo 124 Ib 52.04N 6.39 E
Groesbeek 124 Hc 51.47N 5.56 E
Grofa, gora- 130 Ha 48.34N 24.03 E
Groix 122 Cg 47.38N 3.28W
Groix, Ile de- 122 Cg 47.38N 3.28W
Grójec 120 Qe 51.52N 20.52 E
Gröll Seamount (EN) 202 Lf 14.00S 32.00W
Gromnik 120 Nf 50.42N 17.07 E
Gronau (Westfalen) 120 Dd 52.12N 7.02 E
Grong 114 Cd 64.30N 12.27 E
Groningen [3] 124 Ia 53.13N 6.33 E
Groningen [Neth.] 112 Ge 53.13N 6.33 E
Groningen [Sur.] 202 Gb 5.48N 55.28W
Groningerwad 124 Ia 53.27N 6.25 E
Grønland/Kalaallit Nunaat = Greenland (EN) [5] 224 Nd 70.00N 40.00W
Grønland/Kalaallit Nunaat = Greenland (EN) 174 Pb 70.00N 40.00W
Grønlandshavet = Greenland Sea (EN) 224 Ld 77.00N 1.00W
Grønnedal 179 Hf 61.20N 47.45W
Grönskara 116 Fg 57.05N 15.44 E
Groot 158 Jl 33.45S 24.58 E
Groot Baai 197b Ab 18.01N 63.04W
Groote Eylandt 208 Ef 14.00S 136.40 E
Grootfontein 160 Ij 19.32S 18.05 E
Grootfontein [3] 172 Bc 19.00S 19.00 E
Groot-Karasberge = Great Karasberge (EN) 158 Ik 27.20S 18.45 E
Groot Karoo = Great Karroo (EN) 158 Jl 33.00S 22.00 E
Grootlaagte 172 Cd 20.55S 21.27 E
Groot Namaland/Great Namaland 172 Be 26.00S 17.00 E
Grootvloer 172 Ce 30.00S 20.40 E
Gropeni 130 Kd 45.05N 27.54 E
Gros Caps, Pointe des- 197e Bb 16.28N 61.25W
Gros Islet Bay 197k Ba 14.05N 60.58W
Gros Islets 197k Ba 14.05N 60.58W
Gros-Morne 197h Ab 14.43N 61.01W
Gros-Morne 180 Lg 49.00N 57.22W
Grosne 122 Kh 46.42N 4.56 E
Gros Piton 197k Ab 13.49N 61.04W
Große Aa 124 Jb 52.25N 7.23 E
Große Aue 124 Kb 52.30N 8.38 E
Großefehn 124 Ja 53.24N 7.33 E
Große Laaber 120 Ih 48.50N 12.30 E
Großenhain 120 Je 51.17N 13.33 E
Großenkneten 124 Kb 52.57N 8.16 E
Grosse Pointe 197e Bb 16.01N 61.17W
Großer Arber 120 Jg 49.07N 13.07 E
Großer Feldberg 124 Kd 50.13N 8.28 E
Großer Gleichberg 120 Gf 50.23N 10.35 E
Großer Inselsberg 120 Gf 50.52N 10.28 E
Grosseto 128 Fh 42.46N 11.08 E
Grosseto, Formiche di- 128 Eh 42.40N 10.55 E
Groß-Gerau 120 Eg 49.55N 8.29 E
Großglockner 110 Hf 47.04N 12.42 E
Großräschen 120 Je 51.35N 14.00 E
Groß-Umstadt 124 Ke 49.52N 8.56 E
Großvenediger 128 Gc 47.06N 12.21 E
Grostenquin 124 If 48.59N 6.44 E
Gros Ventre Range 188 Je 43.30N 110.15W
Groswater Bay 174 Nd 54.20N 57.30W
Grøtavær 114 Db 68.58N 16.16 E
Grote Nete 124 Gc 51.07N 4.34 E
Grotli 114 Be 62.01N 7.40 E
Grottaglie 128 Lj 40.32N 17.26 E
Grottammare 128 Hh 42.59N 13.52 E
Groumania 166 Ed 7.55N 4.00W
Groundhog River 184 Ga 49.43N 81.58W
Grouse Creek Mountains 188 If 41.55N 113.50W
Grove Mountains 222 Ff 72.53S 74.53 E
Groves 186 Jl 29.57N 93.55W
Grovfjord 114 Db 68.41N 17.09 E
Grow, Idaarderadeel- 124 Ha 53.06N 5.50 E
Grozny 112 Kg 43.20N 45.42 E
Grubišno Polje 128 Le 45.42N 17.10 E
Grudovo 130 Kg 42.21N 27.10 E
Grudziądz 120 Oc 53.29N 18.45 E
Grumento Nova 128 Jj 40.17N 15.53 E
Grumo Appula 128 Ki 41.01N 16.42 E
Grums 116 Ee 59.21N 13.06 E
Grünau 172 Be 27.47S 18.23 E
Grünberg 124 Kd 50.36N 8.57 E
Gründau 124 Ld 50.14N 9.05 E
Grundkallegrund 116 Hd 60.40N 18.45 E
Grundy 184 Fg 37.17N 82.06W
Gruñidera 192 Ie 24.15N 101.58W
Grünstadt 124 Ke 49.34N 8.10 E
Gruppo di Brenta 128 Ed 46.10N 10.55 E
Gruyère 128 Bd 46.40N 7.10 E
Gruža 130 Df 43.54N 20.47 E
Gruzinskaja Sovetskaja Socialističeskaja Respublika → Sakartvelo 136 Eg 42.00N 44.00 E
Gruzinskaja SSR/ Sakartvelos Sabčata Socialisturi Respublica → Sakartvelo 136 Eg 42.00N 44.00 E
Gruzinskaja SSR → Georgia (EN) 136 Eg 42.00N 44.00 E
Grybów 120 Qg 49.38N 20.56 E
Grycksbo 116 Fd 60.41N 15.28 E
Gryfice 120 Lc 53.56N 15.12 E
Gryfino 120 Kc 53.15N 14.30 E
Grythyttan 116 Fe 59.42N 14.32 E
Grytviken 222 Ad 54.17S 36.31W
Gstaad, Saanen- 128 Bd 46.28N 7.17 E
Guacanayabo, Golfo de- 190 Id 20.28N 77.30W
Guacara 196 Cg 10.14N 67.53W
Guaçu 204 Ef 22.11S 54.31W
Guadaira 126 Fg 37.20N 6.01W
Guadajoz 126 Hg 37.50N 4.51W
Guadalajara [3] 126 Jd 40.50N 2.30W
Guadalajara [Mex.] 176 Ig 20.40N 103.20W
Guadalajara [Sp.] 126 Id 40.38N 3.10W
Guadalaviar 126 Kd 40.21N 1.08W
Guadalbullón 126 Ig 37.59N 3.47W
Guadalcanal 126 Gf 38.06N 5.49W
Guadalcanal Island 208 He 9.32S 160.12 E
Guadalén 126 If 38.05N 3.32W
Guadalentín o Sangonera 126 Kg 37.59N 1.04W
Guadalete 126 Fh 36.35N 6.13W
Guadalfeo 126 Ih 36.43N 3.35W
Guadalimar 126 Ig 37.59N 3.44W
Guadalmanzor / Almanzora 126 Kg 37.14N 1.46W
Guadalmez 126 Gf 38.46N 5.04W
Guadalop / Guadalope 126 Lc 41.15N 0.03W
Guadalope / Guadalop 126 Lc 41.15N 0.03W
Guadalquivir 110 Fh 36.47N 6.22W
Guadalupe [Mex.] 190 Dc 25.41N 100.15W
Guadalupe [Mex.] 192 Hf 22.45N 102.31W
Guadalupe [Mex.] 192 Id 26.12N 101.23W
Guadalupe [Sp.] 126 Ge 39.27N 5.19W
Guadalupe, Isla de- 174 Hg 29.00N 118.16W
Guadalupe, Laguna de- → Setúbal 204 Bj 21.33S 60.35W
Guadalupe, Sierra de- 126 Ge 39.25N 5.25W
Guadalupe Bravos 192 Fb 31.23N 106.07W
Guadalupe Mountains 186 Dj 32.20N 105.00W
Guadalupe Peak 182 Ge 31.50N 104.52W
Guadalupe River 186 Hl 28.30N 96.53W
Guadalupe Victoria, Presa- 192 Gf 23.50N 104.55W
Guadalupe y Calvo 192 Fd 26.06N 106.58W
Guadarrama 126 He 39.53N 4.10W
Guadarrama, Puerto de- 126 Hd 40.43N 4.10W
Guadarrama, Sierra de- 126 Id 40.55N 4.00W
Guadazaón 126 Ke 39.42N 1.36W
Guadeloupe [5] 176 Mh 16.15N 61.35W
Guadeloupe 174 Mh 16.15N 61.35W
Guadeloupe, Canal de la- = Guadeloupe Passage (EN) 190 Le 16.40N 61.50W
Guadeloupe Passage 196 Fd 16.40N 61.50W
Guadeloupe Passage (EN) = Guadeloupe, Canal de la- 190 Le 16.40N 61.50W
Guadiana 110 Fh 37.14N 7.22W
Guadiana, Canal del- 126 Ie 39.20N 3.20W
Guadiana, Ojos del- 126 Ie 39.08N 3.31W
Guadiana Menor 126 Ig 37.56N 3.15W
Guadiaro 126 Gh 36.17N 5.17W
Guadiela 126 Jd 40.22N 2.49W
Guadix 126 Ig 37.18N 3.08W
Guafo, Boca del- 206 Ff 43.40S 74.15W
Guafo, Isla- 206 Ff 43.36S 74.43W
Guaiba 206 Jd 30.06S 51.19W
Guaíba, Rio- 204 Gj 30.15S 51.12W
Guaimaca 194 Df 14.52N 86.51W
Guaimorato, Laguna de- 194 Ef 15.58N 85.55W
Guainía [3] 202 Ec 2.30N 69.00W
Guainía, Rio- 198 Je 2.01N 67.07W
Guaiquinima, Cerro- 202 Fb 5.49N 63.40W
Guaira [3] 204 Dg 25.45S 56.30W
Guaira [Braz.] 206 Jb 24.04S 54.15W
Guaíra [Braz.] 204 He 20.19S 48.18W
Guaira Falls (EN) = Sete Quedas, Saltos das- 206 Jb 24.02S 54.16W
Guairas 204 Ja 12.39S 44.16W
Guaire/Gorey 118 Gi 52.40N 6.18W
Guaitecas, Islas- 206 Ff 43.57S 73.50W
Guajaba, Cayo- 194 Ic 21.50N 77.30W
Guajará Mirim 200 Jg 10.48S 65.22W
Guajira, Peninsula de la- 198 Id 12.00N 71.30W
Guajolotes, Sierra del- 192 Ge 26.00N 105.30W
Guakolak, Tanjung- 150 Eh 6.50S 105.14 E
Gualaco 194 Df 15.06N 86.07W
Gualán 194 Cf 15.08N 89.22W
Gualdo Tadino 128 Gg 43.14N 12.47 E
Gualeguay 204 Ck 33.09S 59.20W
Gualeguay, Rio- 204 Ck 33.19S 59.39W
Gualeguaychú 206 Id 33.01S 58.31W
Gualeguaychú, Rio- 204 Ck 33.05S 58.25W
Gualicho, Salina del- 206 Gf 40.24S 65.15W
Guam [5] 210 Fc 13.28N 144.47 E
Guam 208 Fc 13.28N 144.47 E
Guamini 206 He 37.02S 62.25W
Guampi, Sierra de- 202 Eb 6.00N 65.35W
Guamuchil 190 Cc 25.22N 108.22W
Gua Musang 150 Df 4.53N 101.58 E
Gu'an 154 De 39.24N 116.10 E
Guanabacoa 194 Fb 23.07N 82.18W
Guanabara, Baia de- 204 Kf 22.50S 43.10W
Guanacaste [3] 194 Eh 10.30N 85.15W
Guanacaste, Cordillera de- 194 Eh 10.45N 85.05W
Guanacevi 192 Ge 25.56N 105.57W
Guanahacabibes, Golfo de- 194 Eb 22.08N 84.35W
Guanahacabibes, Peninsula de- 194 Ec 21.57N 84.35W
Guana Island 197a Db 18.29N 64.34W
Guanaja 194 Ee 16.27N 85.54W
Guanaja, Isla de- 194 Ee 16.30N 85.55W
Guanajay 194 Fb 22.55N 82.42W
Guanajibo 197a Ab 18.10N 67.09W
Guanajibo, Punta- 197a Ab 18.12N 67.10W
Guanajuato 190 Dd 21.01N 101.15W
Guanajuato [2] 190 Dd 21.00N 101.00W
Guanambi 202 Jf 14.13S 42.47W
Guanare 202 Eb 9.03N 69.45W
Guanare, Rio- 196 Ch 8.13N 67.46W
Guanare Viejo, Rio- 194 Mi 8.19N 68.10W
Guanarito 196 Bh 8.42N 69.12W
Guandacol 206 Gc 29.31S 68.32W
Guandi Shan 152 Jd 38.09N 111.27 E
Guane 190 Hd 22.12N 84.05W
Guangde 152 Ke 30.51N 119.26 E
Guangdong Sheng (Kuang-tung Sheng) = Kwangtung (EN) [2] 152 Jg 23.00N 113.00 E
Guangfeng 154 Ej 28.27N 118.12 E
Guanghua 152 Je 32.18N 111.45 E
Guangji (Wuxue) 152 Kf 29.58N 115.32 E
Guangling 154 Ce 39.46N 114.16 E
Guangmao Shan 152 Hf 26.48N 100.56 E
Guangming Ding 154 Ei 30.09N 118.11 E
Guangnan 152 Ig 24.02N 105.04 E
Guangrao 154 Ef 37.03N 118.25 E
Guangshan 154 Ci 32.02N 114.53 E
Guangshui 154 Ci 31.37N 114.01 E
Guangxi Zhuangzu Zizhiqu (Kuang-hsi-chuang-tsu Tzu-chih-ch'ü) = Kwangsi Chuang (EN) [2] 152 Ig 24.00N 109.00 E
Guangyuan 142 Mf 32.27N 105.55 E
Guangzhou = Canton (EN) 142 Ng 23.07N 113.18 E
Guan He 154 Ch 32.18N 115.44 E
Guánica 197a Bc 17.59N 66.56W
Guanipa, Rio- 196 Eh 9.56N 62.26W
Guannan (Xin'anzhen) 154 Eg 34.04N 119.21 E
Guantánamo 176 Lg 20.08N 75.12W
Guantánamo [3] 194 Jc 20.10N 75.00W
Guantánamo, Bahía de- 194 Jd 20.00N 75.10W
Guantánamo Bay 190 Id 20.00N 75.10W
Guantánamo Bay Naval Station 194 Jd 20.00N 75.08W
Guantao (Nanguantao) 154 Cf 36.33N 115.18 E
Guanting Shuiku 154 Cd 40.13N 115.36 E
Guanxian 142 Mf 31.00N 103.38 E
Guanyun (Dayishan) 154 Eg 34.18N 119.14 E
Guapay, Rio- → Grande, Rio- 198 Jg 15.51S 64.39W
Guapé 204 Je 20.47S 45.55W
Guapi 202 Cc 2.35N 77.55W
Guápiles 194 Fh 10.13N 83.46W
Guapó 204 Hc 16.51S 49.33W
Guaporé 206 Jc 28.51S 51.54W
Guaporé 204 Gi 29.10S 51.54W
Guaporé, Rio- 198 Jg 11.55S 65.04W
Guaqui 202 Eg 16.35S 68.51W
Guará 204 Gg 25.23S 51.17W
Guara, Sierra de- 126 Lb 42.17N 0.10W
Guarabira 202 Ke 6.51S 35.29W
Guaranda 202 Cd 1.35S 78.59W
Guaraniaçu 206 Jc 25.06S 52.52W
Guarani de Goiás 204 Ia 13.57S 46.28W
Guarapiche, Rio- 196 Eh 9.57N 62.52W
Guarapuava 206 Jc 25.23S 51.27W
Guaraqueçaba 204 Hg 25.17S 48.21W
Guararapes 204 Ge 21.15S 50.38W
Guaratinguetá 204 Jf 22.49S 45.13W
Guaratuba 204 Hg 25.54S 48.34W
Guarayos, Rio- 204 Bb 14.38S 62.11W
Guarda 126 Ed 40.32N 7.16W
Guarda [2] 126 Ed 40.40N 7.10W
Guardafui, Cape- (EN) = 'Asäyr 158 Mg 11.49N 51.15 E
Guardal 126 Jg 37.36N 2.45W
Guarda-Mor 204 Ic 17.47S 47.06W
Guardiagrele 128 Ih 42.11N 14.13 E
Guardian Seamount (EN) 174 Ki 9.32N 87.40W
Guardo 126 Hb 42.47N 4.50W
Guardunha, Serra da- 126 Ed 40.05N 7.31W
Guarei, Rio- 204 Ff 22.40S 53.34W
Guareña 126 Gc 41.29N 5.23W
Guarenas 196 Cg 10.28N 66.37W
Guaribas, Rio- 204 Jc 16.22S 45.03W
Guaribe, Rio- 196 Dh 9.53N 65.11W
Guárico [2] 202 Eb 8.40N 66.35W
Guárico, Embalse del- 196 Ch 9.00N 67.20W
Guárico, Rio- 202 Eb 7.55N 67.23W
Guariquito, Rio- 196 Ci 7.40N 66.18W
Guarita, Rio- 204 Fh 27.11S 53.44W
Guaritico, Caño- 196 Bi 7.52N 68.53W
Guaritire, Rio- 204 Ba 13.43S 60.38W
Guarujá 204 If 24.00S 46.16W
Guarulhos 206 Kb 23.28S 46.32W
Guasave 190 Cc 25.34N 108.27W
Guasdualito 202 Db 7.15N 70.44W
Guasipati 202 Fb 7.28N 61.54W
Guasopa 219a Ac 9.14S 152.55 E
Guastalla 128 Ef 44.55N 10.39 E
Guatemala 176 Jh 14.38N 90.31W
Guatemala [1] 176 Jh 14.38N 90.31W
Guatemala [3] 194 Bf 14.40N 90.30W
Guatemala Basin (EN) 106 Mh 11.00N 95.00W
Guateque 202 Db 5.05N 73.30W
Guatimozin 204 Ak 33.27S 62.27W
Guatisimiña 202 Fc 4.33N 63.57W
Guatraché 206 He 37.40S 63.32W
Guaviare [2] 202 Dc 2.00N 72.00W
Guaviare, Rio- 198 Je 4.03N 67.44W
Guaviravi 204 Di 29.22S 56.50W
Guaxupé 204 Ie 21.18S 46.42W
Guayabal [Cuba] 194 Ic 20.42N 77.36W
Guayabal [Ven.] 196 Ci 8.00N 67.24W
Guayabero, Rio- 202 Ec 4.03N 67.44W
Guayalejo, Rio- 192 Kf 22.13N 97.52W
Guayama 194 Ne 17.59N 66.07W
Guayana, Macizo de la- = Guaiana Highlands (EN) 198 Ke 5.00N 60.00W
Guayana Basin (EN) 106 Ci 10.00N 52.00W
Guayaneco, Archipiélago- 206 Eg 47.45S 75.10W
Guayanés, Punta- 197a Cb 18.04N 65.48W
Guayanilla 197a Bb 18.02N 66.47W
Guayanilla, Bahía de- 197a Bc 17.58N 66.45W
Guayape, Rio- 194 Df 14.26N 86.02W
Guayaquil 200 If 2.10S 79.50W
Guayaquil, Golfo de- 198 Hf 3.00S 80.30W
Guaycurú, Rio- 204 Ch 27.19S 58.45W
Guaymas 176 Hg 27.56N 110.54W
Guayquiraró, Rio- 204 Cj 30.10S 58.34W
Guba [Eth.] 168 Fc 11.15N 35.20 E
Guba [Zaire] 170 Ee 10.38S 26.25 E
Guba Dolgaja 136 Fa 70.19N 58.45 E
Gubaha 136 Fd 58.52N 57.36 E
Guban 158 Lg 10.15N 44.26 E
Gubbio 128 Gg 43.21N 12.35 E
Gubdor 134 Hf 60.15N 56.35 E
Guben 120 Ke 51.57N 14.43 E
Gubin 120 Ke 51.56N 14.45 E
Gubio 166 Hc 12.30N 12.47 E
Gubkin 136 De 51.17N 37.33 E
Gúdar, Sierra de- 126 Ld 40.27N 0.42W
Gudara 136 Hh 38.23N 72.42 E
Gudauta 132 Lh 43.07N 40.37 E
Gudbrandsdalen 114 Bf 61.30N 10.00 E
Gudenå 116 Dh 56.29N 10.13 E
Gudermes 136 Eg 43.22N 46.08 E
Gudivāda 148 Ge 16.27N 80.59 E
Gudiyāttam 148 Ff 12.57N 78.52 E
Gudou Shan 152 Jg 22.12N 112.57 E
Güdül 146 Eb 40.13N 32.15 E
Güdür 148 Ff 14.08N 79.51 E
Gudvangen 116 Bd 60.52N 6.50 E
Guebwiller 122 Ng 47.55N 7.12 E
Guéckédou 166 Cd 8.33N 10.09W
Guelma 162 Ib 36.28N 7.26 E
Guelma [3] 162 Ib 36.15N 7.30 E
Guelph 180 Jh 43.33N 80.15W
Guelta Zemmur 162 Ed 25.08N 12.22W
Guemar 162 Ic 33.29N 6.48 E
Guémené-Penfao 122 Eg 47.38N 1.50W
Guénange 124 Ie 49.18N 6.11 E
Guéné 166 Fc 11.44N 3.13 E
Guer 122 Dg 47.54N 2.07W
Güera 162 De 20.52N 17.03W
Guéra [3] 168 Bc 11.30N 18.30 E
Guéra, Massif de- 158 Ig 11.55N 18.12 E
Guérande 122 Dg 47.20N 2.26W
Guerara 162 Hc 32.48N 4.30 E
Guerche-sur-l'Aubois, La- 122 Ih 46.57N 2.57 E
Guercif 162 Gc 34.14N 3.22W
Guerdjoumane, Djebel- 126 Oh 36.25N 2.51 E
Güere, Rio- 196 Dh 9.50N 65.08W
Guéréda 168 Cc 14.31N 22.05 E
Guéret 122 Hh 46.10N 1.52 E
Guérin-Kouka 166 Fd 9.41N 0.37 E
Guernica y Luno / Gernika-Lumo 126 Ja 43.19N 2.41W
Guernsey 118 Kl 49.27N 2.35W
Guerrero 192 Ic 28.20N 100.26W
Guerrero [2] 190 De 17.40N 100.00W
Guessou-Sud 166 Fc 10.03N 2.38 E
Guest Peninsula 222 Mf 76.18S 148.00W
Guge 168 Fd 6.12N 37.30 E
Gügerd, Kūh-e- 146 Oe 34.50N 53.00 E
Guglionesi 128 Ii 41.55N 14.55 E
Guguan Island 208 Fc 17.19N 145.51 E
Guia 204 Db 15.22S 56.14W
Guia Lopes da Laguna 204 De 21.26S 56.07W
Guiana (EN) = Guyana [1] 200 Ke 5.00N 59.00W
Guiana Highlands (EN) = Guayana, Macizo de la- 198 Ke 5.00N 60.00W
Guiana Island 197d Bb 17.06N 61.44W
Guichi (Chizhou) 152 Ke 30.38N 117.30 E
Guichón 204 Dk 32.21S 57.12W
Guide 152 Hd 36.00N 101.30 E
Guider 166 Hd 9.56N 13.57 E
Guidimaka [3] 162 Ef 15.30N 12.00W
Guidimouni 166 Gc 13.42N 9.30 E
Guiding 152 If 26.33N 107.16 E
Guidong 152 Jf 26.11N 113.58 E
Guiers 122 Li 45.37N 5.37 E
Guiglo 166 Dd 6.33N 7.29W
Guiglo [3] 166 Dd 6.30N 7.40W
Guijá 172 Ed 24.29S 33.00 E
Güija, Lago de- 194 Cf 14.13N 89.34W
Gui Jiang 140 Ng 23.28N 111.18 E
Guijk en Sint Agatha 124 Hc 51.44N 5.52 E
Guijuelo 126 Gd 40.33N 5.40W
Guil 122 Mj 44.40N 6.36 E
Guildford 118 Mj 51.14N 0.35W
Guiler Gol 154 Ga 46.03N 122.06 E
Guilin 142 Ng 25.21N 110.15 E
Guillaume Delisle, Lac- 180 Je 56.25N 76.00W
Guillestre 122 Mj 44.40N 6.39 E
Guilvinec 122 Bg 47.48N 4.17W
Guimarães [Braz.] 202 Jd 2.08S 44.36W
Guimarães [Port.] 126 Dc 41.27N 8.18W
Guimaras 150 Hd 10.35N 122.37 E
Guinchos Cay 194 Hb 22.45N 78.06W
Guinea (EN) = Guinée [1] 160 Fg 11.00N 10.00W
Guinea, Gulf of- 158 Hh 2.00N 2.30 E
Guinea, Gulf of- (EN) = Guinée, Golfe de- 158 Hh 2.00N 2.30 E
Guinea Basin (EN) 106 Di 0.00 5.00W
Guinea-Bissau (EN) = Guiné-Bissau [1] 160 Fg 12.00N 15.00W
Guinea Ecuatorial = Equatorial Guinea (EN) [1] 160 Hh 2.00N 9.00 E
Guinea Rise (EN) 106 Dj 4.00S 0.00
Guiné-Bissau = Guinea-Bissau (EN) [1] 160 Fg 12.00N 15.00W
Guinée = Guinea (EN) [1] 160 Fg 11.00N 10.00W
Guinée, Kolfe de- = Guinea, Gulf of- (EN) 158 Hh 2.00N 2.30 E
Guinée Forestière [3] 166 Dd 8.40N 9.50W
Guinée Maritime [3] 166 Cc 10.00N 14.00W
Güines 190 Hd 22.50N 82.02W
Guînes 124 Dd 50.52N 1.52 E
Guingamp 122 Cf 48.33N 3.09W
Guinguinéo 166 Bc 14.16N 15.57W
Guiones, Punta- 194 Ei 9.54N 85.41W
Guiping 152 Ig 23.23N 110.00 E
Guipúzcoa [3] 126 Ja 43.10N 2.10W
Guir 162 Gc 30.29N 2.18W
Guir, Hamada du- 158 Ge 31.00N 3.20W
Güira de Melena 194 Fb 22.48N 82.30W
Guiratinga 202 Hg 16.21S 53.45W
Güiria 202 Fa 10.34N 62.18W
Guiscard 124 Fe 49.39N 3.03 E
Guise 122 Je 49.54N 3.38 E
Guitiriz 126 Ea 43.11N 7.54W
Guiuan 150 Id 11.02N 125.43 E
Guixi 152 Kf 28.18N 117.15 E
Guixian 152 Ig 23.10N 109.35 E
Guiyang 142 Mg 26.38N 106.43 E
Guizhou Sheng (Kuei-chou Sheng) = Kweichow (EN) [2] 152 If 27.00N 107.00 E
Gujan-Mestras 122 Ej 44.38N 1.04W
Gujarāt [3] 148 Ed 22.51N 71.30 E
Gujarāt 148 Jg 22.51N 71.30 E
Gujranwala 142 Jf 32.09N 74.11 E

Gujrāt 148 Eb 32.34N 74.05 E
Gukovo 132 Ke 48.04N 39.58 E
Gulang 152 Hd 37.30N 102.54 E
Gulbarga 142 Jh 17.20N 76.50 E
Gulbene 136 Cd 57.12N 26.49 E
Gulča 136 Hg 40.19N 73.33 E
Gulf 204 Ad 19.08S 62.01W
Gulf Breeze 184 Dj 30.22N 87.07W
Gulf Coastal Plain (EN) 174 Jf 31.00N 92.00W
Gulfport 182 Je 30.22N 89.06W
Gulian 152 La 52.58N 122.09 E
Gulin 152 If 28.02N 105.47 E
Gulistan 136 Gg 40.30N 68.45 E
Guliya Shan 152 Lb 49.48N 122.25 E
Gulja 138 Hf 54.43N 121.03 E
Gulja/Yining 152 Dc 43.54N 81.21 E
Guljajpole 132 Jf 47.37N 36.18 E
Gulkana 178 Jd 62.16N 145.23W
Gulkeviči 132 Lg 45.19N 40.44 E
Gull Bay 186 Lb 49.47N 89.02W
Gulleråsen 116 Fc 61.04N 15.11 E
Gullfoss 114a Bb 64.20N 20.08W
Gullkronafjärd 116 Jd 60.05N 22.15 E
Gull Lake 180 Gf 50.08N 108.27W
Gullringen 116 Fg 57.48N 15.42 E
Gull River 186 Lb 49.50N 89.04W
Gullspång 116 Ff 58.59N 14.06 E
Güllü 130 Mk 38.16N 29.07 E
Güllük 146 Bd 37.14N 27.36 E
Gülpinar 130 Jj 39.32N 26.07 E
Gülşehir 146 Fc 38.45N 34.38 E
Gulstav 116 Dj 54.43N 10.41 E
Gulu 160 Kh 2.47N 32.18 E
Guma /Pishan 152 Cd 37.38N 78.19 E
Gumbiri, Jabal- 168 Ee 4.18N 30.57 E
Gumel 166 Gc 12.38N 9.23 E
Gummersbach 120 De 51.02N 7.33 E
Gummi 166 Gc 12.09N 5.07 E
Gümüşçey 130 Ki 40.17N 27.17 E
Gümüşhacıköy 146 Fb 40.53N 35.14 E
Gümüşhane 144 Ea 40.27N 39.29 E
Gümüşsu 130 Nk 38.14N 30.01 E
Guna 148 Fd 24.19N 77.19 E
Guna 168 Fc 11.44N 38.15 E
Gundagai 212 Jg 35.04S 148.07 E
Gundji 170 Db 2.05N 21.27 E
Gündoğdu 130 Ki 40.15N 27.07 E
Gündoğmuş 146 Ed 36.48N 32.01 E
Güney 130 Mk 38.09N 29.05 E
Güney Doğu Toroslar 140 Gf 38.30N 41.00 E
Gungu 170 Cd 5.44S 19.19 E
Gunma Ken [2] 154 Of 36.20N 139.05 E
Gunnar 180 Ge 59.23N 108.53W
Gunnbjørns Fjeld 224 Mc 68.55N 29.20W
Gunnedah 212 Kf 30.59S 150.15 E
Gunnison 182 Fd 38.33N 106.56W
Gunnison River 186 Bg 39.04N 108.33W
Gunt 135 Hf 37.30N 71.03 E
Guntakal 148 Fe 15.10N 77.23 E
Guntersville 184 Dh 34.21N 86.18W
Guntersville Lake 184 Dh 34.45N 86.03W
Guntūr 142 Kh 16.18N 80.27 E
Gunungapi, Pulau- 150 Ih 6.38S 126.40 E
Gunungsitoli 150 Cf 1.17N 97.37 E
Günz 120 Gh 48.27N 10.16 E
Günzburg 120 Gh 48.27N 10.16 E
Gunzenhausen 120 Gg 49.06N 10.45 E
Guo He 154 Dh 32.58N 117.13 E
Guojiadian 154 Hc 43.20N 124.37 E
Guoyang 154 Dh 33.31N 116.12 E
Guozhen 154 Bj 29.24N 113.09 E
Gurahonţ 130 Fc 46.16N 22.21 E
Gura Humorului 130 Ib 47.33N 25.54 E
Gurban Obo 152 Jc 43.06N 112.28 E
Gurbantünggüt Shamo 152 Eb 45.30N 87.30 E
Gurdžaani 132 Ni 41.43N 45.48 E
Güre 130 Mk 38.39N 29.10 E
Gurgei, Jabal- 168 Cc 13.50N 24.19 E
Gurghiului, Munţii- 130 Ic 46.41N 25.12 E
Gurgueia, Rio- 198 Lf 6.50S 43.24W
Guri → Raúl Leoni, Represa- 202 Fb 7.30N 63.00W
Gurjev → Atyrau 112 Lf 47.07N 51.56 E
Gurjevsk 138 Df 54.20N 86.00 E
Gurk 128 Id 46.52N 14.18 E
Gurk 128 Id 46.36N 14.31 E
Gurktaler Alpen 128 Hd 46.55N 14.00 E
Guro 172 Ec 17.26S 33.20 E
Gürpinar 146 Jc 38.18N 43.25 E
Gurskoje 138 If 50.20N 138.05 E
Gurskøy 114 Ae 62.15N 5.40 E
Gürsu 130 Mi 40.13N 29.12 E
Guruè 172 Fc 15.28S 36.59 E
Gurumeti 170 Fc 2.05S 33.57 E
Gürün 146 Gc 38.43N 37.17 E
Gurupá 202 Hd 1.25S 51.39W
Gurupá, Ilha Grande do- 202 Hd 1.00S 51.30W
Gurupi 200 Lg 11.43S 49.04W
Gurupi, Rio- 198 Lf 1.13S 46.06W
Gurupi, Serra do- 202 Id 5.00S 47.30W
Guru Sikhar 148 Ed 24.39N 72.46 E
Gus 114 Ji 55.00N 41.12 E
Gusau 160 Hg 12.10N 6.40 E
Gusev 128 Ce 54.37N 22.12 E
Gushan 154 Ge 39.54N 123.36 E
Gushi 152 Ke 32.02N 115.39 E
Gushikawa 156b Ab 26.21N 127.52 E
Güshk 146 Ph 28.13N 55.52 E
Gus-Hrustalny 114 Ji 55.38N 40.40 E
Gusinaja, guba- 138 Kb 72.00N 150.00 E
Gusinaja Zemlja, poluostrov- 136 Fa 71.50N 52.00 E
Gusinje 130 Cg 42.34N 19.50 E
Gusinoozersk 138 Ff 51.17N 106.30 E
Guspini 128 Ck 39.32N 8.37 E
Güssing 128 Kc 47.04N 16.20 E
Gustav Holm, Kap- 179 Ie 66.45N 34.00W
Gustavia 197b Bc 17.54N 62.52W
Gustavs/Kustavi 116 Id 60.33N 21.21 E
Gustavs/Kustavi 116 Id 60.30N 21.25 E
Gustavsfors 116 Ee 59.12N 12.06 E
Gustavus 178 Le 58.25N 135.44W
Güstrow 120 Ic 53.48N 12.10 E
Gusum 116 Gf 58.16N 16.29 E
Gütersloh 120 Ee 51.54N 8.23 E
Guthrie [Ok.-U.S.] 186 Hi 35.53N 97.25W
Guthrie [Tx.-U.S.] 186 Fj 33.37N 100.19W
Gutian 152 Kf 26.40N 118.42 E
Gutiérrez Zamora 192 Kg 20.27N 97.05W
Gutii, Vîrful- 130 Gb 47.42N 23.52 E
Guting → Yutai 154 Dg 35.00N 116.40 E
Gutu 172 Ec 19.39S 31.10 E
Guwāhāti 142 Lg 26.11N 91.44 E
Guyana = Guiana (EN) 200 Ke 5.00N 59.00W
Guyane Française = French Guiana (EN) [5] 200 Ke 4.00N 53.00W
Guyang 152 Jc 41.02N 110.04 E
Guyenne 122 Gj 44.35N 1.00 E
Guymon 182 Gd 36.41N 101.29W
Guyonneau, Anse- 197e Ab 16.14N 61.47W
Guyuan 152 Id 36.01N 106.17 E
Guyuan (Pingdingbu) 154 Cd 41.40N 115.41 E
Guzar 135 Fe 38.37N 66.18 E
Güzelyurt 146 Ee 35.12N 32.59 E
Güzelyurt Körfezi 146 Ee 35.15N 32.50 E
Gūzhān 146 Le 34.20N 46.57 E
Guzhen 154 Dh 33.20N 117.19 E
Guzhou → Rongjiang 152 If 25.58N 108.30 E
Guzmán, Laguna de- 192 Fb 31.20N 107.30W
Gvardejsk 114 Ei 54.40N 21.03 E
Gvardejskoje 132 Hg 45.06N 33.59 E
Gvary 116 Ce 59.23N 9.09 E
Gwa 148 Ie 17.36N 94.35 E
Gwadabawa 166 Gc 13.22N 5.14 E
Gwādar 142 Ig 25.07N 62.19 E
Gwai 172 Dc 19.17S 27.39 E
Gwai 158 Jj 17.59S 26.52 E
Gwalior 142 Jg 26.13N 78.10 E
Gwanda 172 Dd 20.56S 29.00 E
Gwane 170 Eb 4.43N 25.50 E
Gwda 120 Mc 53.04N 16.44 E
Gweebarra Bay/Béal an Bheara 118 Eg 54.52N 8.20W
Gwent [3] 118 Kj 51.45N 2.55W
Gweru 160 Jj 19.27S 29.49 E
Gweta 172 Dd 20.13S 25.14 E
Gwydir River 212 Je 29.27S 149.48 E
Gwynedd [3] 118 Ji 52.50N 3.50W
Gyaca 152 Ff 29.09N 92.38 E
Gya'gya → Saga 152 Ef 29.22N 85.15 E
Gyai Qu 152 Fe 31.30N 94.40 E
Gyaisi/Jiulong 152 Hf 28.58N 101.33 E
Gya La 152 Df 28.42N 84.35 E
Gyala Shankou 152 Df 28.42N 84.35 E
Gyangzê 152 Ef 29.00N 89.38 E
Gyaring Co 152 Ee 31.10N 88.15 E
Gyaring Hu 152 Ge 34.55N 98.00 E
Gyda 138 Cb 70.52N 78.30 E
Gydanskaja guba 138 Cb 71.20N 76.30 E
Gydanski poluostrov = Gyda Peninsula (EN) 140 Jb 70.50N 79.00 E
Gyda Peninsula (EN) = Gydanski poluostrov 140 Jb 70.50N 79.00 E
Gyigang → Zayü 152 Gf 28.43N 97.25 E
Gyirong (Zongga) 152 Ef 28.57N 85.12 E
Gyldenløves Fjord 179 Hf 64.10N 40.30W
Gyldenløves Høj 116 Di 55.33N 11.52 E
Gympie 210 Gg 26.11S 152.40 E
Gyoma 120 Qj 46.56N 20.50 E
Gyöngyös 120 Pi 47.47N 19.56 E
Győr 112 Hf 47.41N 17.38 E
Győr [2] 120 Ni 47.40N 17.39 E
Győr-Moson-Sopron 120 Ni 47.40N 17.15 E
Gypsumville 180 Hf 51.45N 98.35W
Gysinge 116 Gd 60.17N 16.53 E
Gyttorp 116 Fe 59.31N 14.58 E
Gyula 120 Rj 46.39N 21.17 E

H

Haacht 124 Gd 50.59N 4.38 E
Häädemeeste/Hjademeste 116 Kf 58.00N 24.28 E
Ha'afeva 221b Ba 19.57S 174.43W
Haafusia 220h Bb 13.18S 176.09W
Haag, Mount- 222 Qf 77.40S 79.00W
Haaksbergen 124 Ib 52.09N 6.45 E
Haamstede, Westerschouwen- 124 Fc 51.42N 3.45 E
Haanja Kõrgustik 116 Lg 57.30N 27.30 E
Ha'ano 221b Ba 19.40S 174.17W
Ha'apai Group 208 Jf 19.47S 174.27W
Haapajärvi 114 Fe 63.45N 25.20 E
Haapamäki 116 Kb 62.15N 24.28 E
Haapasaari 116 Ld 60.15N 27.10 E
Haapaselkä [Fin.] 116 Mb 62.10N 28.10 E
Haapaselkä [Fin.] 116 Mc 61.35N 28.15 E
Haapiti 221e Fc 17.34S 149.52W
Haapsalu 136 Cd 58.57N 23.32 E
Ha'arava 146 Fg 30.58N 32.24 E
Haardt 120 Dg 49.15N 8.00 E
Haardtkopf 124 Je 49.51N 7.04 E
Haaren, Wünnenberg- 124 Kc 51.34N 8.44 E
Haarlem 122 Kb 52.23N 4.38 E
Haarlemmermeer 124 Gb 52.20N 4.41 E
Haarlerberg 124 Ib 52.20N 6.25 E
Haarstrang 124 Kc 51.30N 8.20 E
Haast 210 Hi 43.52S 169.01 E
Haast Pass 218 Cf 44.06S 169.21 E
Habahe/Kaba 152 Eb 47.53N 86.12 E
Habarovsk 142 Pe 48.27N 135.06 E
Habarovski kraj [3] 138 If 53.00N 137.00 E
Habarūt 144 Hf 17.22N 52.42 E
Ḩabashīyah, Jabal- 168 Ib 16.45N 50.05 E
Habaswein 170 Gb 1.01N 39.29 E
Habay [Alta.-Can.] 180 Fe 58.52N 118.45W
Habay [Bel.] 124 He 49.45N 5.38 E
Habay [Som.] 168 Ge 1.08N 43.46 E
Ḩabbān 168 Hc 14.21N 47.05 E
Ḩābbānīyah 146 Jf 33.22N 43.35 E
Ḩabbānīyah, Hawr al- 146 Jf 33.17N 43.29 E
Habbārīyah, Bi'r al- 146 Jf 32.17N 42.12 E
Habibas, Iles- 126 Ki 35.44N 1.08W
Habichtswald 120 Fe 51.20N 9.25 E
Habo 116 Fg 57.55N 14.04 E
Haboro 152 Pc 44.22N 141.42 E
Ḩabshān 146 Ok 23.50N 53.37 E
Hache 120 Ec 53.05N 8.50 E
Hachenburg 124 Jd 50.39N 7.50 E
Hachijō 156 Fe 35.15N 139.45 E
Hachijō-Fuji 156 Fe 33.08N 139.46 E
Hachijō-Jima 152 Oe 33.05N 139.50 E
Hachiman 156 Ed 35.46N 136.57 E
Hachimori 156 Fa 40.22N 140.00 E
Hachinohe 142 Qe 40.30N 141.29 E
Hachiōji 156 Fd 35.39N 139.18 E
Hachiro-Gata 156 Fa 40.00N 140.00 E
Hacibey De 146 Kd 36.58N 44.18 E
Hackås 114 De 62.55N 14.31 E
Håckren 116 Ea 63.10N 13.35 E
Hačmas 136 Eg 41.25N 48.52 E
Hadagang 154 Kb 45.24N 131.12 E
Hadamar 124 Kd 50.27N 8.03 E
Ḩadan, Ḩarrat- 164 He 21.30N 41.23 E
Hadano 156 Fd 35.22N 139.14 E
Ḩadāribah, Ra's al- 168 Fa 22.04N 36.54 E
HaDarom [3] 146 Fg 30.40N 34.50 E
Hadd, Ra's al- 140 Hg 22.32N 59.59 E
Haddad 158 Ig 14.40N 18.46 E
Hadded 168 Hc 10.10N 48.28 E
Haddington 118 Kf 55.58N 2.47W
Haddummati Atoll 148a Bb 1.45N 73.30 E
Hadejia 166 Hc 12.27N 10.03 E
Hadejia 166 Hc 12.50N 10.51 E
Hadeland 116 Dd 60.25N 10.35 E
Hadeln 120 Ec 53.45N 8.45 E
Hadera 146 Ff 32.26N 34.55 E
Haderslev 114 Bi 55.15N 9.30 E
Hadīboh 144 Hg 12.39N 54.02 E
Hadim 146 Ed 36.59N 32.28 E
Hadimköy 146 Cb 41.09N 28.37 E
Ḩadīyah 144 Ed 25.34N 38.41 E
Hadjer el Hamis 168 Ac 12.51N 14.50 E
Hadjout 126 Oh 36.31N 2.25 E
Hadleigh 124 Cb 52.03N 0.56 E
Hadley Bay 180 Gb 72.30N 108.30W
Ha Dong 148 Ld 20.58N 105.46 E
Ḩadramawt 140 Gh 15.00N 50.00 E
Hadrian's Wall 118 Kg 54.59N 2.26W
Hadsten 116 Dh 56.20N 10.03 E
Hadsund 116 Dh 56.43N 10.07 E
Hadytajaha 134 Nc 66.57N 69.12 E
Hadyžensk 132 Kg 44.25N 39.31 E
Hadzibeisui liman 130 Nc 46.40N 30.30 E
Haedo, Cuchilla de- 204 Dj 31.40S 56.18W
Haeju 154 He 38.02N 125.42 E
Haena 214 Oc 22.13N 159.34W
Ḩafar al 'Atk 146 Lj 25.56N 46.47 E
Ḩafar al Bātin 144 Gd 28.27N 46.00 E
Haffner Bjerg 179 Fc 76.30N 63.00W
Ḩaffūz 128 Do 35.38N 9.40 E
Hafik 146 Gc 39.52N 37.24 E
Ḩafirat al 'Aydā 144 Ed 26.26N 39.12 E
Ḩafit 146 Pk 23.59N 55.49 E
Ḩafit, Jabal- 146 Pj 24.03N 55.46 E
Hafnarfjördur 114a Bb 64.04N 21.57W
Haft Gel 146 Mg 31.27N 49.27 E
Hāfūn 168 Ic 10.10N 51.05 E
Hāfūn, Rās-=Hafun, Ras-(EN) 158 Mg 10.27N 51.24 E
Hafun, Ras-(EN)=Hāfūn, Rās- 158 Mg 10.27N 51.24 E
Hāfūn Bay North 168 Ic 10.37N 51.15 E
Hāfūn Bay South 168 Ic 10.15N 51.05 E
Hagadera 170 Hb 0.02N 40.17 E
Hagby 116 Gh 56.33N 16.10 E
Hageland 124 Gd 50.55N 4.45 E
Hagemeister 178 Ge 58.40N 161.00W
Hagen 120 De 51.21N 7.28 E
Hagenow 120 Hc 53.26N 11.12 E
Hagere Hiywet 168 Fd 8.58N 37.53 E
Hagerman 188 He 42.49N 114.54W
Hagerstown 182 Ld 39.39N 77.43W
Hagetmau 122 Fk 43.40N 0.35W
Hagfors 114 Cf 60.02N 13.42 E
Häggenås 116 Fa 63.24N 14.55 E
Hagi 154 Kg 34.24N 131.25 E
Ha Giang 148 Kd 22.50N 104.59 E
Hagman, Puntan- 220b Ba 15.09N 145.48 E
Hagondange 122 Me 49.15N 6.10 E
Hags Head/Ceanna Cailligh 118 Di 52.57N 9.28W
Hague, Cap de la- 110 Ff 49.43N 1.57W
Haguenau 122 Nf 48.49N 7.47 E
Hagunia 162 Ed 27.26N 12.24W
Hahajima-Rettō 214 Cb 26.37N 142.10 E
Hahns Peak 186 Cf 40.56N 107.01W
Hahót 120 Mj 46.38N 16.56 E
Hai'an 154 Fh 32.33N 120.26 E
Haicheng 152 Lc 40.51N 122.43 E
Hai Duong 148 Ld 20.56N 106.19 E
Haifa (EN) = Ḩefa 142 Ff 32.50N 35.00 E
Haifeng 152 Kg 22.58N 115.21 E
Haiger 124 Kd 50.45N 8.13 E
Hai He 154 De 38.57N 117.43 E
Haikakan Sovetakan Socialistakan Respublika/Armjanskaja SSR → Hayastan 136 Eg 40.00N 45.00 E
Haikang(Leizhou) 152 Jg 20.56N 110.06 E
Haikou 142 Ng 20.05N 110.20 E
Hā'il 142 Gg 27.33N 41.42 E
Hailang He 154 Jb 44.33N 129.33 E
Hailar 142 Ne 49.14N 119.42 E
Hailar He 140 Ne 49.30N 117.50 E
Hailin 152 Mc 44.35N 129.22 E
Hailong (Meihekou) 152 Mc 42.32N 125.37 E
Hailsham 124 Cd 50.52N 0.16 E
Hailun 152 Mb 47.29N 126.55 E
Hailuoto/Karlö 110 Ib 65.02N 24.42 E
Haima Tan 150 Gd 10.52N 116.53 E
Haimen [China] 154 Fi 31.53N 121.10 E
Haimen [China] 154 Fj 28.40N 121.27 E
Haina 124 Kc 51.03N 8.56 E
Hainan Dao 140 Mh 19.00N 109.00 E
Hainaut 124 Fd 50.30N 4.00 E
Hainaut 122 Jd 50.20N 3.50 E
Hainburg an der Donau 128 Kb 48.09N 16.56 E
Haines 176 Fd 59.14N 135.27W
Haines Junction 180 Dd 60.45N 137.30W
Hainich 120 Ge 51.05N 10.27 E
Hainleite 120 Ge 51.20N 10.48 E
Hai Phong 142 Mg 20.52N 106.41 E
Haïti=Haiti (EN) [1] 176 Lh 19.00N 72.25W
Haiti (EN)=Haïti [1] 176 Lh 19.00N 72.25W
Haixing (Suji) 154 De 38.10N 117.29 E
Haixin Shan 152 Hd 37.00N 100.03 E
Haiyan (Sanjiaocheng) 152 Hd 36.58N 100.50 E
Haiyan (Wuyuanzhen) 154 Fi 30.31N 120.56 E
Haiyang (Dongcun) 154 Ff 36.46N 121.09 E
Haiyang Dao 154 Ge 39.03N 123.12 E
Haiyou → Sanmen 152 Lf 29.08N 121.22 E
Haiyuan 152 Id 36.35N 105.40 E
Haizhou 154 Eg 34.34N 119.08 E
Haizhou Wan 140 Nf 35.00N 119.30 E
Ḩajar Banga 168 Cc 11.30N 23.00 E
Hajdarken 136 Hh 39.55N 71.24 E
Hajdú-Bihar [2] 120 Ri 47.25N 21.30 E
Hajdúböszörmény 120 Ri 47.40N 21.31 E
Hajdúdorog 120 Ri 47.49N 21.30 E
Hajdúhadház 120 Ri 47.41N 21.40 E
Hajdúnánás 120 Ri 47.51N 21.26 E
Hajdúság 120 Ri 47.35N 21.30 E
Hajdúszoboszló 120 Ri 47.27N 21.24 E
Hajihi-Zaki 156 Fb 38.19N 138.31 E
Ḩājjīābād [Iran] 146 Ph 28.21N 54.27 E
Ḩājjīābād [Iran] 146 Ph 28.19N 55.55 E
Ḩājjīābād-e Māsīleh 146 Ne 34.49N 51.13 E
Hajla 130 Dg 42.43N 20.10 E
Hajnówka 120 Td 52.45N 23.36 E
Hajós 120 Pj 46.24N 19.07 E
Hajpudyrskaja guba 134 Ib 68.40N 59.30 E
Hakase-Yama 156 Fc 37.22N 139.43 E
Hakasija, respublika 138 Df 53.30N 90.00 E
Hakata-Wan 156 Be 33.40N 130.20 E
Hakefjord 116 Dg 57.41N 11.44 E
Hakha 148 Id 22.39N 93.37 E
Hakkâri 144 Fb 37.34N 43.45 E
Hakken-Zan 156 Dd 34.10N 135.54 E
Hakkōda San 156 Ga 40.40N 140.51 E
Hako-Dake 156a Ca 44.40N 142.25 E
Hakodate 142 Qe 41.45N 140.43 E
Hakone-Yama 156 Fd 35.13N 139.00 E
Hakui 154 Nf 36.53N 136.47 E
Hakupu 220k Bb 19.06S 169.50W
Haku-San 156 Ec 36.09N 136.45 E
Hal/Halle 122 Kd 50.44N 4.14 E
Halab 146 Md 36.17N 48.03 E
Ḩalab=Aleppo (EN) 142 Ff 36.12N 37.10 E
Ḩalabjah 146 Ke 35.10N 45.59 E
Halač 136 Gh 39.04N 64.53 E
Halachó 192 Ng 20.29N 90.05W
Halahei 154 Ga 46.11N 122.46 E
Ḩalā'ib 160 Kf 22.13N 36.38 E
Halalii Lake 221a Ab 21.52N 160.11W
Halangingie Point 220k Bb 19.03S 169.58W
Hålaveden 116 Ff 58.05N 14.45 E
Halawa 221a Eb 21.10N 156.44W
Halawa, Cape- 221a Eb 21.10N 156.43W
Ḩalbā 146 Ge 34.33N 36.05 E
Halberstadt 120 He 51.54N 11.03 E
Halcon, Mount- 150 Hd 13.16N 121.00 E
Haldean-Sogotyn-Daba 152 Gb 49.05N 97.55 E
Halden 114 Cg 59.09N 11.23 E
Haldensleben 120 Hd 52.18N 11.25 E
Haldia 148 Hd 22.08N 88.05 E
Haldwani 148 Fc 29.13N 79.31 E
Hale, Mount- 212 De 26.00S 117.10 E
Haleakala Crater 221a Ec 20.43N 156.12W
Haleiwa 221a Cb 21.36N 158.06W
Halemaumau 221a Fd 19.24N 155.17W
Hale River 212 Hd 24.56S 135.53 E
Halesworth 124 Db 52.21N 1.30 E
Haleyville 184 Dh 34.14N 87.37W
Ḩalfā al Gadida 160 Kg 15.19N 35.34 E
Half Assini 166 Ed 5.03N 2.53W
Halfeti 146 Gd 37.15N 37.52 E
Halfway 180 Fe 56.13N 121.26W
Halh-Gol 152 Kb 48.01N 118.10 E
Ḩalḩ 168 Gb 18.38N 41.22 E
Haliburton 184 Hc 45.03N 78.33W
Halifax 176 Me 44.39N 63.36W
Halifax, Mount- 212 Jc 19.05S 146.20 E
Halifax Bay 212 Jc 18.50S 146.30 E
Hālil 144 Id 27.28N 58.44 E
Hālīleh, Ra's-e- 146 Nh 28.46N 50.56 E
Halilovo 132 Ud 51.27N 58.10 E
Halin 168 Hd 9.08N 48.47 E
Haliut → Urad Zhonghou Lianheqi 152 Ic 41.34N 108.32 E
Haljala 116 Le 59.22N 26.09 E
Haljasavej 138 Cd 63.20N 78.30 E
Hall 178 Ed 60.40N 173.05W
Halladale 118 Jc 58.30N 3.50W
Hallam Peak 188 Fa 52.11N 118.46W
Halland [2] 114 Ch 56.45N 13.00 E
Halland 116 Eh 57.00N 12.45 E
Hallandsås 116 Eh 56.23N 13.00 E
Halla-san 154 Ih 33.22N 126.32 E
Ḩallat 'Ammār 146 Gh 29.08N 36.02 E
Hall Beach 180 Jc 68.10N 81.56W
Halle 120 He 51.30N 12.00 E
Halle/Hal 122 Kd 50.44N 4.14 E
Halle (Westfalen) 124 Kb 52.05N 8.22 E
Halleberg 116 Ef 58.23N 12.25 E
Hällefors 116 Fe 59.47N 14.30 E
Hälleforsnäs 116 Ge 59.10N 16.30 E
Hallein 128 Hc 47.41N 13.06 E
Hällekis 116 Ef 58.38N 13.25 E
Hallen 114 De 63.11N 14.05 E
Hallenberg 124 Kc 51.07N 8.38 E
Hallencourt 124 De 49.59N 1.53 E
Halle-Neustadt 120 He 51.31N 11.53 E
Hallertau 120 Hh 48.35N 11.50 E
Hallestad 116 Ff 58.44N 15.34 E
Hallettsville 186 Hl 29.27N 96.57W
Halley Bay 222 Af 75.31S 26.38W
Halli 116 Kc 61.52N 24.50 E
Hallie-Jackson Bank (EN) 219c Ba 9.45S 166.10 E
Halligen 120 Eb 54.35N 8.35 E
Hallingdal 114 Bf 60.40N 9.15 E
Hallingdalselva 116 Cd 60.23N 9.35 E
Hallingskarvet 110 Gc 60.37N 7.45 E
Hall in Tirol (Solbad Hall in Tirol) 128 Fc 47.17N 11.31 E
Hall Islands 208 Gd 8.37N 152.00 E
Halliste jõgi 116 Kf 58.23N 24.25 E
Hall Lake 180 Jc 68.40N 82.20W
Hall Land 179 Fb 81.12N 61.10W
Hallock 186 Hb 48.47N 96.57W
Hall Peninsula 174 Mc 63.30N 66.00W
Hallsberg 114 Dg 59.04N 15.07 E
Halls Creek 210 Df 18.13S 127.40 E
Hallstahammar 114 Dg 59.37N 16.13 E
Hallstatt 128 Hc 47.33N 13.39 E
Hallstavik 114 Ef 60.03N 18.36 E
Halluin 124 Fd 50.47N 3.08 E
Halmahera 208 Dd 1.00N 128.00 E
Halmahera, Laut-= Halmahera Sea (EN) 208 De 1.00S 129.00 E
Halmahera Sea (EN)= Halmahera, Laut- 208 De 1.00S 129.00 E
Halmer-Ju 136 Gb 67.58N 64.40 E
Halmeu 130 Gb 47.58N 23.01 E
Halmstad 112 Hd 56.39N 12.50 E
Haloze 128 Jd 46.20N 15.50 E
Ḩalq al Wādī 162 Jb 36.49N 10.18 E
Hals 114 Ch 57.00N 10.19 E
Hälsingland 116 Gc 61.30N 17.00 E
Halsön 116 Ib 62.50N 21.10 E
Halstead 124 Cc 51.57N 0.38 E
Halsteren 124 Gc 51.32N 4.16 E
Haltang He 152 Fd 39.00N 94.40 E
Halten Bank (EN) 114 Bd 64.45N 8.45 E
Haltern 124 Jc 51.44N 7.11 E
Haltiatunturi 114 Eb 69.18N 21.16 E
Haltom City 186 Hj 32.48N 97.16W
Halturin → Orlov 136 Ed 58.35N 48.55 E
Hālūl 146 Oj 25.40N 52.25 E
Halver 124 Jc 51.12N 7.29 E
Ham 122 Je 49.45N 3.04 E
Ham, Roches de- 124 Ae 49.02N 1.02W
Hamada 156 Cd 34.53N 132.03 E
Hamadān 142 Gf 34.48N 48.30 E
Hamadān [3] 144 Gb 35.00N 48.40 E
Hamadia 126 Ni 35.28N 1.52 E
Hamaguir 162 Gc 30.54N 3.02W
Ḩamāh 144 Eb 35.08N 36.45 E
Hamakita 156 Ed 34.49N 137.45 E
Hamamasu 156a Bb 43.36N 141.21 E
Hamamatsu 152 Oe 34.42N 137.44 E
Hamanaka 156a Db 43.05N 145.05 E
Hamanaka-Wan 156a Db 43.07N 145.10 E
Hamana-Ko 156 Ed 34.45N 137.34 E
Hamanen, Oued el- 162 Hd 25.52N 1.26 E
Hamaoka 156 Fd 34.39N 138.07 E
Hamar 112 Hc 60.48N 11.06 E
Hamar-Daban, hrebet- 138 Ff 51.10N 105.00 E
Hamasaka 156 Dd 35.38N 134.27 E
Ḩamāţah, Jabal- 164 Ge 24.12N 35.00 E
Hamatonbetsu 154 Qb 45.07N 142.23 E
Hambantota 148 Gg 6.10N 81.07 E
Hambre, Cayos del- 194 Fb 22.15N 82.47W
Hamburg [2] 120 Fc 53.35N 10.00 E
Hamburg [Ger.] 112 Ge 53.33N 10.00 E
Hamburg [S.Afr.] 172 Df 33.18S 27.28 E
Hamburg-Altona 120 Fc 53.33N 9.57 E
Hamburg-Harburg 120 Fc 53.28N 10.00 E
Hamburgsund 116 Df 58.33N 11.16 E
Ḩamd, Wādī al- 140 Fg 25.58N 36.42 E
Ḩamdah 164 Hf 19.02N 43.36 E
Häme [2] 114 Ff 61.30N 24.30 E
Häme 116 Kc 61.30N 25.30 E
Hämeenkangas 116 Jc 61.45N 22.40 E
Hämeenlinna/Tavastehus 114 Ff 61.00N 24.27 E
Hämeenselkä 116 Kb 62.30N 25.00 E
Hamelin Pool 212 Ce 26.15S 114.05 E
Hameln 120 Fd 52.06N 9.21 E
HaMerkaz [3] 146 Fg 32.05N 34.55 E
Hamero Hadad 168 Gd 7.28N 42.13 E
Hamersley Range 212 Dd 21.55S 116.45 E
Hamgyŏng-Namdo [2] 154 Id 40.00N 127.30 E
Hamgyŏng-Pukto [2] 154 Jd 41.45N 129.50 E
Hamgyŏng-Sanmaek 154 Jd 41.00N 128.45 E
Hamhŭng 142 Of 39.54N 127.32 E
Hami/Kumul 142 Le 42.48N 93.27 E
Ḩamīdīyeh 146 Mg 31.29N 48.26 E
Hamilton [Austl.] 212 Ig 37.45S 142.02 E
Hamilton [Ber.] 176 Mf 32.17N 64.46W
Hamilton [Mt.-U.S.] 182 Eb 46.15N 114.09W
Hamilton [N.Z.] 210 Ih 37.47S 175.17 E
Hamilton [Oh.-U.S.] 182 Kd 39.23N 84.33W
Hamilton [Ont.-Can.] 176 Le 43.15N 79.51W
Hamilton [Scot.-U.K.] 118 If 55.47N 4.03W
Hamilton [Tx.-U.S.] 186 Gk 31.42N 98.07W

Index Symbols

[1] Independent Nation
[2] State, Region
[3] District, County
[4] Municipality
[5] Colony, Dependency
Continent
Physical Region
Historical or Cultural Region
Mount, Mountain
Volcano
Hill
Mountains, Mountain Range
Hills, Escarpment
Plateau, Upland
Pass, Gap
Plain, Lowland
Delta
Salt Flat
Valley, Canyon
Crater, Cave
Karst Features
Depression
Polder
Desert, Dunes
Forest, Woods
Heath, Steppe
Oasis
Cape, Point
Coast, Beach
Cliff
Peninsula
Isthmus
Sandbank
Island
Atoll
Rock, Reef
Islands, Archipelago
Rocks, Reefs
Coral Reef
Well, Spring
Geyser
River, Stream
Waterfall, Rapids
River Mouth, Estuary
Lake
Salt Lake
Intermittent Lake
Reservoir
Swamp, Pond
Canal
Glacier
Ice Shelf, Pack Ice
Ocean
Sea
Gulf, Bay
Strait, Fjord
Lagoon
Bank
Seamount
Tablemount
Ridge
Shelf
Basin
Escarpment, Sea Scarp
Fracture
Trench, Abyss
National Park, Reserve
Point of Interest
Recreation Site
Cave, Cavern
Historic Site
Ruins
Wall, Walls
Church, Abbey
Temple
Scientific Station
Railway station
Airport
Port
Military installation
Lighthouse
Mine
Tunnel
Dam, Bridge

Hamilton, Lake-	186	Ji	34.30N	93.05W
Hamilton, Mount-	188	Hg	39.14N	115.32W
Hamilton River	212	Hd	23.30S	139.47 E
Ḩamin, Wādī al-	164	Dc	30.28N	22.00 E
Hamina/Fredrikshamn	114	Gf	60.34N	27.12 E
Hamm	120	De	51.41N	7.48 E
Ḩammām al 'Alīl	146	Jd	36.10N	43.16 E
Ḩammām al Anf	162	Jb	36.44N	10.20 E
Ḩammāmāt	162	Jb	36.24N	10.37 E
Ḩammāmāt, Khalīj-	162	Jb	36.05N	10.40 E
Hammam Bou Hadjar	126	Li	35.23N	0.58W
Hammami	158	Ff	23.03N	11.30W
Hammam Righa	126	Oh	36.23N	2.24 E
Ḩammār, Hawr al-	144	Gc	30.50N	47.10 E
Hammarstrand	116	Ga	63.06N	16.21 E
Hamme	124	Gc	51.06N	4.08 E
Hammelburg	120	Ff	50.07N	9.54 E
Hammerdal	114	De	63.36N	15.21 E
Hammeren	116	Fi	55.18N	14.47 E
Hammerfest	112	Ia	70.40N	23.45 E
Hamminkeln	124	Ic	51.44N	6.35 E
Hamminkeln-Dingden	124	Ic	51.46N	6.37 E
Hammond [In.-U.S.]	184	De	41.36N	87.30W
Hammond [La.-U.S.]	182	Ie	30.30N	90.28W
Hammonton	184	Jf	39.38N	74.48W
Hamont, Hamont-Achel-	124	Hc	51.15N	5.33 E
Hamont-Achel	124	Hc	51.15N	5.33 E
Hamont-Achel-Hamont	124	Hc	51.15N	5.33 E
Hamoyet, Jabal-	158	Kg	17.33N	38.02 E
Hampden	218	Df	45.20S	170.49 E
Hampshire [3]	118	Lk	51.00N	1.10W
Hampshire Downs	118	Lj	51.15N	1.15W
Hampton [Ia.-U.S.]	186	Je	42.45N	93.12W
Hampton [Va.-U.S.]	184	Ig	37.02N	76.23W
Hampton Butte	188	Ee	43.46N	120.17W
Hamp'yong	154	Ig	35.04N	126.31 E
Ḩamrā'	168	Dc	10.54N	29.54 E
Hamra [R.S.F.S.R.]	138	Gd	60.17N	114.10 E
Hamra [Swe.]	116	Fc	61.39N	15.00 E
Ḩamrā', Al Ḩamādah al-	158	If	29.30N	12.00 E
Hamra, Saguia el-	158	Ff	27.24N	13.43W
Hamrān	146	Kd	36.22N	45.44 E
Ḩamrat ash Shaykh	168	Dc	14.35N	27.58 E
Ḩamrīn, Jabal-	146	Ke	34.30N	44.30 E
Hāmūn-e Hirmand, Daryācheh-ye-	144	Jc	31.30N	61.20 E
Han	166	Ec	10.41N	2.27W
Hana	214	Oc	20.45N	155.59W
Hanahan	184	Hi	32.55N	80.00W
Hanaizumi	156	Gb	38.51N	141.12 E
Ḩanak	144	Ed	25.33N	36.56 E
Hanalei	221a	Ba	22.13N	159.30W
Hanamaki	154	Pe	39.23N	141.07 E
Hanang	158	Ki	4.26S	35.24 E
Hanaoka	156	Ga	40.21N	140.34 E
Hanapepe	221a	Bb	21.55N	159.35W
Hanau	120	Ef	50.08N	8.55 E
Han-Bogdo	152	Ic	43.12N	107.10 E
Hanceville	180	Ff	51.55N	123.02W
Hancheng	152	Jd	35.30N	110.25 E
Hanchuan	154	Bi	30.39N	113.46 E
Hancock	184	Cb	47.07N	88.35W
Handa	156	Ed	34.53N	136.56 E
Handan	142	Nf	36.35N	114.28 E
Handen	116	He	59.10N	18.08 E
Handeni	170	Gd	5.26S	38.01 E
Handlová	120	Oh	48.44N	18.46 E
Handöl	116	Ea	63.16N	12.26 E
Handyga	142	Pc	62.40N	135.36 E
Hānegev=Negev Desert (EN)	146	Fg	30.30N	34.55 E
Hanford	188	Fh	36.20N	119.39W
Han-gang	152	Md	37.45N	126.11 E
Hanga Roa	221d	Ab	27.09S	109.26W
Hang'bu He	154	Di	31.33N	117.05 E
Hanggin Houqi (Xamba)	152	Ic	40.59N	107.07 E
Hanggin Qi (Xin Zhen)	152	Id	39.54N	108.55 E
Hangö/Hanko	114	Fg	59.50N	22.57 E
Hangöudde/Hankoniemi	116	Je	59.50N	23.10 E
Hangu	154	De	39.16N	117.50 E
Hangzhou	142	Of	30.18N	120.11 E
Hangzhou Wan	154	Fi	30.25N	121.00 E
Ḩanīsh	164	Hg	13.45N	42.45 E
Ḩanīsh al Kabīr, Jazīrat al-	164	Hg	13.43N	42.45 E
Hanja, vozvyšennost-	116	Lg	57.30N	27.30 E
Ḩanjūrah, Ra's-	146	Pj	24.44N	54.39 E
Hanka, ozero- = Khanka, Lake- (EN)	140	Pe	45.00N	132.24 E
Hankasalmi	116	Lb	62.23N	26.26 E
Hankensbüttel	120	Gd	52.44N	10.36 E
Hanko/Hangö	114	Fg	59.50N	22.57 E
Hankoniemi/Hangöudde	116	Je	59.50N	23.10 E
Hankou, Wuhan-	154	Ci	30.35N	114.16 E
Hanksville	188	Jg	38.25N	110.10W
Hanlar	132	Oi	40.34N	46.20 E
Hanmej, gora-	134	Lc	67.08N	66.00 E
Hanmer Springs	218	Ee	42.31S	172.50 E
Hann, Mount-	212	Fc	15.50S	125.50 E
Hanna [Alta.-Can.]	180	Gf	51.38N	111.54W
Hanna [Wy.-U.S.]	188	Lf	41.52N	106.34W
Hannah Bay	180	Jf	51.15N	79.50W
Hannibal	182	Id	39.42N	91.22W
Hanningfield Reservoir	124	Cc	51.37N	0.28 E
Hannō	156	Fd	35.53N	139.17 E
Hannover	112	Ge	52.22N	9.43 E
Hann River	212	Fc	17.10S	126.10 E
Hannuit/Hannut	124	Hd	50.40N	5.05 E
Hannut/Hannuit	124	Hd	50.40N	5.05 E
Hano	116	Fi	56.00N	14.50 E
Hanöbukten	116	Fi	55.45N	14.30 E
Ha Noi	142	Mg	21.02N	105.51 E
Hanover [N.H.-U.S.]	184	Kd	43.42N	72.17W
Hanover [Ont.-Can.]	184	Gc	44.09N	81.02W
Hanover [Pa.-U.S.]	184	If	39.47N	76.59W
Hanover [S.Afr.]	172	Cf	31.04S	24.29 E
Hanover, Isla-	206	Fh	51.00S	74.40W
Hanpan, Cape-	212	Ka	5.01S	154.37 E
Han Pijesak	128	Mf	44.05N	18.57 E
Hansen Mountains	222	Ee	68.16S	58.47 E
Hanshan	154	Ei	31.43N	118.07 E
Hanshou	154	Aj	28.55N	111.58 E
Han Shui	140	Nf	30.34N	114.17 E
Hanstholm	116	Cg	57.07N	8.38 E
Han Sum	154	Eb	44.33N	119.58 E
Han-sur-Lesse, Rochefort-	124	Hd	50.08N	5.11 E
Han-sur-Nied	124	If	48.59N	6.26 E
Hantau	136	Hg	44.13N	73.48 E
Hantengri Feng	152	Dc	42.03N	80.11 E
Hants	118	Lj	51.10N	1.10W
Hanty-Mansijsk	142	Ic	61.00N	69.06 E
Hanty-Mansijski avtonomnyj okrug	136	Hc	62.00N	72.30 E
Hantzsch	180	Kc	67.32N	72.26W
Hanušovice	120	Mf	50.05N	16.55 E
Hanwang	152	He	31.25N	104.13 E
Hanyang	154	Ci	30.34N	114.01 E
Hanyang, Wuhan-	154	Ci	30.33N	114.16 E
Hanyū	156	Fc	36.11N	139.32 E
Hanyuan (Fulin)	152	Hf	29.25N	102.12 E
Hanzhong	142	Mf	32.59N	107.11 E
Hanzhuang	154	Dg	34.38N	117.23 E
Hao Atoll	208	Mf	18.15S	140.54W
Hāora	142	Kg	22.35N	88.20 E
Haoud el Hamra	162	Ic	31.58N	5.59 E
Hao Xi	154	Ej	28.28N	119.56 E
Haoxue	154	Bi	30.02N	112.25 E
Haparanda	114	Fd	65.50N	24.10 E
Hapčeranga	138	Kg	49.42N	112.20 E
Happy Valley-Goose Bay	176	Md	53.19N	60.24W
Hapsu	154	Jd	41.13N	128.51 E
Ḩaql	146	Fh	29.18N	34.57 E
Ḩaql al Burqān	146	Lh	28.55N	47.57 E
Ḩaql al Manāqīsh	146	Lh	29.02N	47.32 E
Ḩaql as Şābiriyah	146	Lh	29.48N	47.50 E
Hara, zaliv-/Hara laht	116	Ke	59.35N	25.30 E
Hara-Ajrag	152	Ib	45.50N	109.20 E
Harabali	136	Ef	47.25N	47.16 E
Ḩaraḑ	144	Ge	24.14N	49.11 E
Haraiki Atoll	208	Mf	17.28S	143.27W
Hara laht/Hara, zaliv-	116	Ke	59.35N	25.30 E
Haramachi	154	Pf	37.38N	140.58 E
Haram Dāgh	144	Gb	37.35N	46.43 E
Harami, pereval-	132	Oh	42.48N	46.12 E
Harand	146	Of	32.34N	52.26 E
Harani'ia Point	219a	Ed	10.21S	161.16 E
Hara Nur	152	Fb	48.05N	93.12 E
Hararḏēre	168	He	4.32N	47.53 E
Harare	160	Kj	17.50S	31.10 E
Harat	168	Fb	16.05N	39.28 E
Hara-Tas, krjaž-	138	Fb	72.00N	107.00 E
Haratini	220n	Bc	10.28S	160.58W
Ḩarat Zuwayyah	160	Jf	24.14N	21.59 E
Hara-Us-Nur	152	Fb	48.00N	92.10 E
Haraz	168	Bc	13.57N	19.26 E
Harāz	146	Od	36.40N	52.43 E
Harāzah, Jabal-	168	Eb	15.03N	30.27 E
Haraze	168	Cd	9.55N	20.48 E
Harbel	166	Cd	6.16N	10.21W
Harbin	142	Oe	45.45N	126.37 E
Harbor Beach	184	Fd	43.51N	82.39W
Harbour Breton	180	Lg	47.29N	55.50W
Harbour Grace	180	Mg	47.41N	53.15W
Harburg, Hamburg-	120	Fc	53.28N	10.00 E
Harcourt	184	Ob	46.30N	65.15W
Harcuvar Mountains	188	Ii	34.00N	113.30W
Harcyzsk	132	Kf	47.59N	38.11 E
Hardangen	116	Bd	60.20N	6.30 E
Hardangerfjorden	110	Gc	60.10N	6.00 E
Hardangerjøkulen	116	Bd	60.35N	7.25 E
Hardangervidda	114	Bf	60.20N	7.30 E
Hardelot Plage, Neufchâtel Hardelot-	124	Dd	50.38N	1.35 E
Hardenberg	124	Ib	52.34N	6.37 E
Harderwijk	122	Lb	52.21N	5.36 E
Hardin	182	Fb	45.44N	107.37W
Harding	172	Df	30.34S	29.58 E
Hardinsburg	184	Dg	37.47N	86.28W
Härdler	124	Kc	51.06N	8.14 E
Hardoi	148	Gc	27.25N	80.07 E
Hardwār	148	Fc	29.58N	78.10 E
Hardy, Peninsula-	206	Gi	55.25S	68.30W
Hareid	116	Bb	62.22N	6.02 E
Hareidlandet	114	Ae	62.20N	5.55 E
Hare Indian	180	Ec	66.18N	128.38W
Harelbeke	124	Fd	50.51N	3.18 E
Haren	124	Ia	53.11N	6.38 E
Haren (Ems)	124	Jb	52.47N	7.14 E
Harer	160	Lh	9.18N	42.08 E
Harerge [3]	168	Gd	9.00N	41.30 E
Harēri Mālinwarfā	168	He	4.34N	47.21 E
Harewa	168	Gd	9.54N	41.58 E
Harfleur	124	Ce	49.30N	0.12 E
Harg	116	Hd	60.11N	18.24 E
Hargeysa	160	Lh	9.30N	44.03 E
Harghita [2]	130	Ic	46.25N	25.45 E
Harghita, Munţii-	130	Ic	46.31N	25.33 E
Harghita, Vîrful-	130	Ic	46.27N	25.35 E
Hargla	116	Lg	57.31N	26.25 E
Harhorin	152	Hb	47.13N	102.50 E
Har Hu	152	Gd	38.15N	97.40 E
Ḩarīb	144	Gg	14.56N	45.30 E
Haridwār	148	Fc	29.58N	78.10 E
Harihari	218	De	43.09S	170.34 E
Hari kurk	116	Je	59.00N	22.50 E
Harim	146	Gd	36.12N	36.31 E
Harīm, Jabal al-	146	Qj	25.58N	56.14 E
Harima-Nada	156	Dd	34.30N	134.35 E
Haringey, London-	124	Bc	51.36N	0.06W
Haringvliet	124	Gc	51.49N	4.12 E
Harīrūd	140	If	37.24N	60.38 E
Härjångsfjället	116	Ea	63.01N	12.35 E
Harjavalta	114	Ff	61.19N	22.08 E
Härjedalen	116	Eb	62.20N	13.05 E
Härjehågna	116	Ec	61.44N	12.08 E
Hårkan	116	Fa	63.20N	14.55 E
Harkov	112	Je	50.00N	36.15 E
Harkovskaja oblast [3]	136	Df	49.40N	36.30 E
Harlan [Ia.-U.S.]	186	If	41.39N	95.19W
Harlan [Ky.-U.S.]	184	Fg	36.51N	83.19W
Harlan County Lake	186	Gf	40.04N	99.16W
Harlech Castle	118	Ii	52.52N	4.07W
Harlem	188	Kb	48.32N	108.47W
Harleston	124	Db	52.24N	1.18 E
Harlingen [Neth.]	122	La	53.10N	5.24 E
Harlingen [Tx.-U.S.]	182	Hf	26.11N	97.42W
Harlovka	114	Ib	68.47N	37.15 E
Harlovka	114	Ib	68.47N	37.20 E
Harlow	118	Nj	51.47N	0.08 E
Harlowton	188	Kc	46.26N	109.50W
Harlu	114	Hf	61.51N	30.54 E
Hārman	130	Id	45.43N	25.41 E
Harmancık	146	Cc	39.41N	29.10 E
Harmånger	114	Df	61.56N	17.13 E
Harmanli	130	Ih	41.56N	25.54 E
Harmil	168	Gb	16.30N	40.12 E
Harmony	186	Ke	43.33N	91.59W
Harnai	148	Ee	17.48N	73.06 E
Harney Basin	174	Ge	43.15N	120.40W
Harney Lake	182	Dc	43.14N	119.07W
Harney Peak	182	Gc	44.00N	103.30W
Härnön	116	Gb	62.35N	18.00 E
Härnösand	112	Hc	62.38N	17.56 E
Haro	126	Jb	42.35N	2.51W
Haro, Cabo-	192	Dd	27.50N	110.52W
Harovsk	136	Ed	59.59N	40.11 E
Harøya	116	Bb	62.45N	6.25 E
Harøyfjorden	116	Bb	62.45N	6.35 E
Harpenden	124	Bc	51.48N	0.21W
Harper [Ks.-U.S.]	186	Gh	37.17N	98.01W
Harper [Lbr.]	160	Gh	4.22N	7.43W
Harper, Mount-	178	Kd	64.14N	143.50W
Harper Pass	218	De	42.44S	171.53 E
Harplinge	116	Eh	56.45N	12.43 E
Harqin Qi (Jinshan)	154	Ed	41.57N	118.40 E
Harqin Zuoyi Monggolzu Zizhixian	154	Ed	41.05N	119.40 E
Ḩarrat al 'Uwayrid	144	Ed	27.00N	37.30 E
Harricana	180	Jf	51.10N	79.47W
Harricana, Rivière-	184	Ha	51.10N	79.45W
Harrington-Harbour	180	Lf	50.26N	59.30W
Harris	197c	Bc	16.28N	62.10W
Harris	118	Gd	57.53N	6.55W
Harris, Lake-	184	Gk	28.46N	81.49W
Harris, Sound of-	118	Fd	57.45N	7.08W
Harrisburg	176	Le	40.16N	76.52W
Harrismith	172	Ee	28.18S	29.03 E
Harrison [Ar.-U.S.]	186	Jh	36.14N	93.07W
Harrison [Mi.-U.S.]	184	Ec	44.01N	84.48W
Harrison [Nb.-U.S.]	186	Ee	42.41N	103.53W
Harrison, Cape-	180	Lf	54.56N	57.55W
Harrison Bay	178	Ib	70.30N	151.30W
Harrisonburg	184	Hf	38.27N	78.54W
Harrison Lake	188	Eb	49.31N	121.59W
Harrison Point	197q	Ab	13.18N	59.38W
Harrisonville	186	Ig	38.39N	94.21W
Harrisville [Mi.-U.S.]	184	Fc	44.39N	83.17W
Harrisville [W.V.-U.S.]	184	Gf	39.13N	81.04W
Harrodsburg	184	Eg	37.46N	84.51W
Harrogate	118	Lh	54.00N	1.33W
Harrow, London-	124	Bc	51.36N	0.20W
Harry S. Truman Reservoir	186	Jg	38.00N	93.45W
Har Sai Shan	152	Gd	35.26N	97.41 E
Harsewinkel	124	Kc	51.58N	8.14 E
Harshō	168	Hc	11.17N	47.30 E
Harsim	146	Lf	33.48N	46.50 E
Harsīn	146	Le	34.16N	47.35 E
Harstad	114	Db	68.47N	16.30 E
Harsvik	114	Cd	64.03N	10.02 E
Hart	184	Dd	43.42N	86.22W
Hart	180	Dc	65.51N	136.22W
Hartao	154	Gc	42.30N	122.08 E
Hartbees	158	Jk	28.45S	20.33 E
Hartberg	128	Jc	47.17N	15.58 E
Hårteigen	116	Bd	60.12N	7.04 E
Hartford [Ct.-U.S.]	176	Le	41.46N	72.41W
Hartford [Ky.-U.S.]	184	Dg	37.27N	86.55W
Hartford City	184	Ee	40.29N	85.23W
Hartington	186	He	42.37N	97.16W
Hartland	184	Nb	46.18N	67.32W
Hartland Point	118	Ij	51.02N	4.31W
Hartlepool	118	Lg	54.42N	1.11W
Hartmannberge	172	Ac	17.30S	12.23 E
Hartola	114	Gf	61.35N	26.01 E
Harts	158	Jk	28.24S	24.18 E
Hartselle	184	Dh	34.27N	86.56W
Harts Range	212	Gd	23.05S	134.55 E
Hartsville	184	Gh	34.23N	80.04W
Hartwell	184	Fh	34.21N	82.56W
Hartwell Lake	184	Fh	34.30N	82.55W
Harun, Bukit-	150	Gf	4.06N	115.46 E
Haruno	156	Ce	33.30N	133.30 E
Harves Bank (EN)	197c	Ac	16.52N	62.35W
Harvey [Austl.]	212	Df	33.05S	115.54 E
Harvey [N.D.-U.S.]	182	Hb	47.47N	99.56W
Harvey Bay	212	Kd	25.00S	153.00 E
Harwich	118	Oj	51.57N	1.17 E
Haryana [3]	148	Fc	29.30N	76.30 E
Harz	110	He	51.45N	10.30 E
Hasaki	156	Gd	35.44N	140.48 E
Hasama	156	Gb	38.42N	141.13 E
Hasan	138	Ih	42.26N	130.39 E
Ḩasanābād [Iran]	146	Ph	28.47N	54.19 E
Ḩasanābād [Iran]	146	Nd	36.28N	50.17 E
Hasan Dağı	146	Db	38.08N	34.12 E
Ḩasan Langī	146	Qi	27.22N	56.52 E
Hasavjurt	132	Oh	43.16N	46.35 E
Ḩasb, Sha'īb-	146	Kg	31.45N	44.17 E
Hāsbayyā	146	Ff	33.43N	35.52 E
Hasdo	148	Hd	21.44N	82.44 E
Hase	120	Dd	52.41N	7.18 E
Hasekijata	130	Kg	42.08N	27.30 E
Hasenkamp	204	Cj	31.31S	59.51W
Hashaf-Rūd	144	Jb	35.58N	61.07 E
Hashimoto	156	Dd	34.19N	135.37 E
Hashtpar	146	Md	37.48N	48.55 E
Hasi Hausert	162	Ee	22.35N	14.18W
Haskell	182	He	33.10N	99.44W
Haskerland	124	Hb	52.58N	5.47 E
Haskerland-Joure	124	Hb	52.58N	5.47 E
Haskovo	130	Ih	41.56N	25.33 E
Haskovo [2]	130	Ih	41.50N	25.55 E
Hasle	116	Fi	55.11N	14.43 E
Haslemere	118	Mj	51.06N	0.43W
Haslev	116	Di	55.20N	11.58 E
Hăşmaşu Mare, Vîrful-	130	Ic	46.30N	25.50 E
Haspengouws Plateau/Hesbaye	122	Ld	50.35N	5.10 E
Haspres	124	Fd	50.15N	3.25 E
Hassa	146	Gd	36.50N	36.29 E
Hassan	148	Ff	13.00N	76.05 E
Hassberge	120	Gf	50.12N	10.29 E
Hassela	114	De	62.07N	16.42 E
Hassel Sound	180	Ha	78.30N	99.00W
Hasselt	122	Ld	50.56N	5.20 E
Hassi Bel Guebbour	162	Id	28.30N	6.41 E
Hassi el Ghella	126	Ki	35.27N	1.03W
Hassi Mameche	126	Mi	35.51N	0.04 E
Hassi Messaoud	160	He	31.43N	6.03 E
Hassi R'mel	162	Hc	32.55N	3.16 E
Hassi Serouenout	162	Ie	24.00N	7.50 E
Hässleholm	114	Ch	56.09N	13.46 E
Hasslö	116	Fh	56.05N	15.25 E
Haßloch	124	Ke	49.23N	8.16 E
Hastière	124	Gd	50.13N	4.50 E
Hastière-Hastière par-delà	124	Gd	50.13N	4.50 E
Hastière-par-delà, Hastière	124	Gd	50.13N	4.50 E
Hastings [Bar.]	197q	Ab	13.04N	59.35W
Hastings [Eng.-U.K.]	118	Nk	50.51N	0.36 E
Hastings [Mi.-U.S.]	184	Ed	42.39N	85.17W
Hastings [Mn.-U.S.]	186	Jd	44.44N	92.51W
Hastings [Nb.-U.S.]	182	Hc	40.35N	98.23W
Hastings [N.Z.]	216	Eg	39.38S	176.50 E
Hästveda	116	Eh	56.16N	13.56 E
Hašuri	132	Mi	41.59N	43.33 E
Hasvik	114	Fa	70.29N	22.09 E
Ḩasy al Qaţţār	164	Ec	30.14N	27.11 E
Ḩasy Hague	164	Bd	26.17N	10.31 E
Hat'ae-Do	154	Hg	34.23N	125.17 E
Hatanga	142	Mb	71.58N	102.30 E
Hatanga	140	Mb	72.55N	106.00 E
Hatch	186	Cj	32.40N	107.09W
Hatches Creek	212	Hd	20.56S	135.12 E
Haţeg	130	Fd	45.37N	22.57 E
Hatgal	152	Ha	50.26N	100.09 E
Ḩaţībah, Ra's-	144	Ee	21.59N	38.55 E
Ha Tien	148	Kf	10.23N	104.29 E
Ha Tinh	148	Le	18.20N	105.54 E
Hato Mayor	194	Md	18.46N	69.15W
Ḩattā, Jabal-	146	Qj	24.45N	56.04 E
Hattem	124	Ib	52.28N	6.06 E
Hatten	124	Ka	53.03N	8.23 E
Hatteras, Cape-	174	Lf	35.13N	75.32W
Hatteras Inlet	184	Jh	35.00N	75.40W
Hatteras Island	182	Ld	35.25N	75.30W
Hattfjelldal	114	Cd	65.36N	14.00 E
Hattiesburg	182	Je	31.19N	89.16W
Hattingen	124	Jc	51.24N	7.10 E
Hatu Iti, Ile-	216	Ma	8.42S	140.43W
Hatutaa, Ile-	208	Me	7.30S	140.38W
Hatvan	120	Pi	47.40N	19.41 E
Hat Yai	148	Kg	7.01N	100.27 E
Hatyrka	138	Md	62.03N	175.05 E
Haubourdin	124	Ed	50.36N	2.59 E
Hauge	114	Bg	58.21N	6.17 E
Haugesund	112	Gd	59.25N	5.18 E
Hauho	116	Kc	61.10N	24.33 E
Hauhungaroa Range	218	Fc	38.40S	175.35 E
Haukeligrend	114	Bg	59.51N	7.11 E
Haukipudas	114	Fd	65.15N	25.28 E
Haukivesi	110	Ic	62.05N	28.30 E
Haukivuori	116	Lb	62.01N	27.13 E
Hauraha	219a	Ed	10.49S	161.57 E
Hauraki Gulf	216	Eg	36.35S	175.00 E
Hauroko, Lake-	218	Bf	45.55S	167.20 E
Hausa	162	Ed	27.06N	11.01W
Hausruck	128	Hb	48.07N	13.35 E
Haut, Isle au-	184	Mc	44.03N	68.38W
Haut Atlas=High Atlas (EN)	158	Ge	32.00N	6.00W
Haute-Champagne	124	Gf	49.18N	4.15 E
Haute-Corse [3]	122a	Aa	42.30N	9.00 E
Haute-Garonne [3]	122	Hk	43.25N	1.30 E
Haute-Guinée [3]	166	Dc	11.30N	10.00W
Haute-Kotto [3]	168	Cd	7.00N	23.00 E
Haute-Loire [3]	122	Ji	45.05N	3.50 E
Haute-Marne [3]	122	Lf	48.05N	5.10 E
Hauterive	184	Ma	49.11N	68.16W
Hautes-Alpes [3]	122	Mj	44.40N	6.30 E
Haute-Sangha [3]	168	Be	4.30N	16.00 E
Haute-Saône [3]	122	Mg	47.40N	6.10 E
Haute-Saône, Plateau de-	122	Lg	47.50N	6.00 E
Haute-Savoie [3]	122	Mi	46.00N	6.20 E
Hautes Fagnes/Hoge Venen	120	Bf	50.30N	6.00 E
Hautes-Pyrénées [3]	122	Gk	43.00N	0.10 E
Haute-Vienne [3]	122	Hi	45.50N	1.10 E
Haut-Mbomou [3]	168	Dd	6.00N	26.00 E
Hautmont	122	Jd	50.15N	3.56 E
Haut-Ogooué [3]	170	Bc	2.00S	14.00 E
Haut-Rhin [3]	122	Ng	48.00N	7.20 E
Hauts-Bassins [3]	166	Ec	12.30N	4.30W
Hauts-de-Seine [3]	122	If	48.50N	2.11 E
Hauts Plateaux	158	He	34.00N	0.01 E
Haut-Zaïre [2]	170	Eb	2.30N	25.30 E
Hauula	221a	Db	21.36N	157.54W
Hauz-Han	135	Cf	37.16N	61.15 E
Hauz-Hanskoje vodohranilišče	135	Cf	37.10N	61.20 E
Havana	186	Kf	40.18N	90.04W
Havana (EN)=La Habana	176	Kg	23.08N	82.22W
Havant and Waterloo	118	Mk	50.51N	0.59W
Havast	135	Gd	40.16N	68.51 E
Havasu, Lake-	188	Hi	34.30N	114.20W
Havel	120	Hd	52.53N	11.58 E
Havelange	124	Hd	50.23N	5.14 E
Havelange-Méan	124	Hd	50.22N	5.20 E
Havelberg	120	Id	52.49N	12.05 E
Havelland	120	Id	52.25N	12.45 E
Havelländisches Luch	120	Id	52.40N	12.40 E
Havelock [N.C.-U.S.]	184	Ih	34.53N	76.54W
Havelock [N.Z.]	218	Ed	41.17S	173.46 E
Havelock North	218	Gc	39.40S	176.53 E
Havelte	124	Ib	52.46N	6.16 E
Haverfordwest	118	Ij	51.49N	4.58W
Haverhill [Eng.-U.K.]	118	Ni	52.05N	0.26 E
Haverhill [Ma.-U.S.]	184	Ld	42.47N	71.05W
Havering, London-	124	Cc	51.36N	0.11 E
Havířov	120	Og	49.48N	18.27 E
Havlíčkův Brod	120	Lg	49.36N	15.34 E
Havøysund	114	Fa	71.03N	24.40 E
Havran	146	Bc	39.33N	27.06 E
Havre	176	Ie	48.33N	109.41W
Havre, Le-	112	Gf	49.30N	0.08 E
Havre-Saint-Pierre	176	Md	50.15N	63.36W
Havsa	130	Jh	41.33N	26.49 E
Havza	146	Fb	41.05N	35.45 E
Hawaii [2]	210	Kb	24.00N	167.00W
Hawaiian Islands	208	Kb	24.00N	167.00W
Hawaiian Ridge (EN)	106	Kg	24.00N	165.00W
Hawaii Island	208	Lc	19.30N	155.30W
Ḩawallī	144	Gd	29.19N	48.02 E
Ḩawār	146	Nj	25.40N	50.45 E
Hawarden	218	Ee	42.56S	172.39 E
Ḩawashīyah, Wādī-	146	Eh	28.31N	32.58 E
Hawaymī, Sha'īb al-	146	Kg	30.58N	44.15 E
Hawd	158	Lh	7.40N	47.43 E
Ḩawḑ Al Waqf	146	Ei	26.03N	32.22 E
Hawea, Lake-	218	Cf	44.30S	169.20 E
Hawera	216	Dg	39.35S	174.17 E
Hawi	210	Lb	20.14N	155.50W
Hawick	118	Kf	55.25N	2.47W
Ḩawīzah, Hawr al-	146	Lg	31.35N	47.38 E
Hawkdun Range	218	Cf	44.50S	170.00 E
Hawke Bay	216	Eg	39.25S	177.20 E
Hawke Harbour	180	Lf	53.01N	55.50W
Hawker	212	Hf	31.53S	138.25 E
Hawkes, Mount-	222	Rg	83.55S	56.05W
Hawke's Bay [2]	218	Gc	39.30S	176.40 E
Hawkesbury	184	Jc	45.36N	74.37W
Hawkhurst	124	Cc	51.02N	0.30 E
Hawkinsville	184	Fi	32.17N	83.28W
Hawksbill	184	Hf	38.33N	78.23W
Hawk Springs	188	Mf	41.48N	104.09W
Ḩawmat as Sūq	162	Jc	33.53N	10.51 E
Hawng Tuk	148	Jd	20.28N	99.56 E
Ḩawrā'	168	Hb	15.43N	48.18 E
Ḩawrān, Wādī-	144	Fc	33.58N	42.34 E
Ḩawsh 'Īsá	146	Dg	30.55N	30.17 E
Hawthorne	182	Dd	38.32N	118.38W
Hawthorne, Mount-	222	Pf	72.10S	98.39W
Haxtun	186	Ef	40.39N	102.38W
Hay	210	Fh	34.30S	144.51 E
Hay	174	Hc	60.51N	115.44W
Hayachine-San	156	Gb	39.34N	141.29 E
Hayakita	156a	Bb	42.45N	141.48 E
Hayange	122	Me	49.20N	6.03 E
Hayastan = Armenia (EN)	136	Eg	40.00N	45.00 E
Hayasui-no-Seto	154	Kh	33.20N	132.00 E
Hayato	156	Bf	31.45N	130.43 E
Haybān	168	Ec	11.13N	30.31 E
Haybān, Jabal-	168	Ec	11.15N	30.31 E
Hayden	188	Jj	33.00N	110.47W
Hayes [Man.-Can.]	180	Ie	57.00N	92.15W
Hayes [N.W.T.-Can.]	180	Hc	67.20N	95.02W
Hayes, Mount-	178	Jd	63.37N	146.43W
Hayes Halvø=Hayes Peninsula (EN)	224	Od	77.40N	64.30W
Hayes Peninsula (EN)=Hayes Halvø	224	Od	77.40N	64.30W
Ḩayl	146	Qj	24.33N	56.06 E
Hayl, Wādī al-	146	He	34.47N	39.18 E
Hayling Island	124	Bd	50.48N	0.58W
Haymana	146	Ec	39.27N	32.30 E
Haymana Platosu	146	Ec	39.25N	32.45 E
Hayrabolu	146	Bb	41.12N	27.06 E
Ḩayrān	164	Hf	16.02N	42.49 E
Hay River	176	Hc	60.51N	115.40W
Hay River	212	Hd	25.00S	138.00 E
Hayrūt	168	Ib	15.59N	52.09 E
Hays	182	Hd	38.53N	99.20W
Hay Springs	186	Ee	42.41N	102.41W
Haystack Peak	188	Ig	39.50N	113.55W
Hayward [Ca.-U.S.]	188	Dh	37.40N	122.05W
Hayward [Wi.-U.S.]	186	Kc	46.01N	91.29W
Haywards Heath	124	Bc	51.00N	0.06W
HaZafon [3]	146	Ff	32.50N	35.20 E
Hazar, Wādī-	168	Hb	17.50N	49.07 E
Hazarasp	135	Cd	41.19N	61.08 E
Hazard	184	Fg	37.15N	83.12W
Hazar Gölü	146	Hc	38.30N	39.25 E
Hazāribāgh	148	Hd	23.59N	85.21 E
Hazebrouck	122	Id	50.43N	2.32 E
Hazelton	180	Ee	55.15N	127.40W
Hazen	186	Fc	47.18N	101.38W
Hazen Strait	180	Ga	77.15N	110.00W
Ḩazeva	146	Fg	30.48N	35.15 E
Hazlehurst [Ga.-U.S.]	184	Fj	31.52N	82.36W
Hazlehurst [Ms.-U.S.]	186	Kk	31.52N	90.24W
Hazleton	184	Je	40.58N	76.00W
Hazlett, Lake-	212	Fd	21.30S	128.50 E
Hazrah, Ra's al-	146	Nj	24.22N	51.36 E
Hazro	146	Ic	38.15N	40.47 E
Heacham	124	Cb	52.55N	0.29 E
Headley	124	Bc	51.07N	0.49W
Healdsburg	188	Dg	38.37N	122.52W
Heanor	124	Aa	53.00N	1.18W
Heard Island	222	Fd	53.00S	73.35 E

Hearne 186 Hk 30.53N 96.36W
Hearst 180 Jg 49.41N 83.40W
Heart River 186 Fc 46.47N 100.51W
Heathrow Airport London 124 Bc 51.28N 0.30W
Hebbronville 186 Gm 27.18N 98.41W
Hebei Sheng (Ho-pei Sheng) =Hopeh (EN) [2] 152 Kd 39.00N 116.00 E
Heber City 188 Jf 40.30N 111.25W
Hebi 152 Jd 35.53N 114.09 E
Hebian 152 Jd 38.35N 113.06 E
Hebiji 154 Cf 36.00N 114.08 E
Hebrides 110 Fd 57.00N 6.30W
Hebrides, Sea of the- 118 Ge 57.00N 7.00W
Hebron [N.D.-U.S.] 186 Ec 46.54N 102.03W
Hebron [Newf.-Can.] 180 Le 58.15N 62.35W
Heby 116 Ge 59.56N 16.53 E
Hecate Strait 180 Ef 53.20N 131.00W
Hecelchakán 192 Ng 20.10N 90.08W
Hechi (Jnchengjiang) 152 Ig 24.44N 108.02 E
Hechingen 120 Eh 48.21N 8.59 E
Hechuan 152 Ie 30.07N 106.15 E
Hecla 186 Gd 45.43N 98.09W
Hecla and Griper Bay 180 Ga 76.00N 111.30W
Hecla Island 186 Ha 51.08N 96.45W
Heddalsvatnet 116 Ce 59.30N 9.15 E
Hede 114 Ce 62.25N 13.30 E
Hede → Sheyang 154 Fh 33.47N 120.15 E
Hedemarken 116 Dd 60.50N 11.20 E
Hedemora 114 Df 60.17N 15.59 E
Hedensted 116 Ci 55.46N 9.42 E
Hedesunda 114 Df 60.25N 17.00 E
Hedesunda fjärdarna 116 Gd 60.20N 17.00 E
Hedmark [2] 114 Cf 61.30N 11.45 E
Hedo-Misaki 156b Bb 26.52N 128.16 E
Heemskerk 124 Gb 52.30N 4.42 E
Heemstede 124 Gb 52.21N 4.37 E
Heerenberg, Bergh 's- 124 Ic 51.53N 6.16 E
Heerenveen 122 Lb 52.57N 5.55 E
Heerhugowaard 124 Gb 52.40N 4.50 E
Heerlen 122 Ld 50.54N 5.59 E
Ḥefa [3] 146 Ff 32.35N 35.00 E
Ḥefa = Haifa (EN) 142 Ff 32.50N 35.00 E
Hefei 142 Nf 31.47N 117.15 E
Hefeng 152 Jf 29.49N 110.01 E
Hegang 142 Pe 47.20N 130.12 E
Hegau 120 Ei 47.50N 8.45 E
Hegura Jima 152 Od 37.50N 136.55 E
Heide 120 Fb 54.12N 9.06 E
Heidelberg 120 Eg 49.25N 8.42 E
Heidenheim an der Brenz 120 Gh 48.41N 10.09 E
Heidenreichstein 128 Jb 48.52N 15.07 E
Hei-Gawa 156 Gb 39.38N 141.58 E
Heigun-Tō 156 Ce 33.47N 132.15 E
Hei He 152 Hd 38.15N 100.15 E
Heihe → Aihui 142 Od 50.13N 127.26 E
Heilbron 172 De 27.21S 27.58 E
Heilbronn 120 Fg 49.08N 9.13 E
Heiligenblut 128 Gd 47.02N 12.50 E
Heiligenhafen 120 Gb 54.22N 10.59 E
Heiligenhaus 124 Ic 51.19N 6.58 E
Heiligenstadt 120 Ge 51.23N 10.08 E
Heilinzi 154 Ib 44.33N 126.41 E
Heilong Jiang 140 Qd 52.56N 141.10 E
Heilongjiang Sheng (Hei-lung-chiang Sheng)= Heilungkiang (EN) [2] 152 Mb 48.00N 128.00 E
Heiloo 124 Gb 52.36N 4.43 E
Hei-lung-chiang Sheng→Heilongjiang Sheng=Heilungkiang (EN) [2] 152 Mb 48.00N 128.00 E
Heilungkiang (EN)= Heilongjiang Sheng (Hei-lung-chiang Sheng) [2] 152 Mb 48.00N 128.00 E
Heilungkiang (EN)=Hei-lung-chiang Sheng→Heilongjiang Sheng [2] 152 Mb 48.00N 128.00 E
Heimæy 114a Bc 63.26N 20.17W
Heimbach 124 Id 50.38N 6.29 E
Heimdal 114 Ce 63.21N 10.22 E
Heimsheim 124 Kf 48.48N 8.51 E
Heinävesi 114 Ge 62.26N 28.36 E
Heinola 114 Gf 61.13N 26.02 E
Heinsberg 124 Ic 51.04N 6.05 E
Heishan 154 Gd 41.42N 122.07 E
Heishan Xia 152 Hd 37.18N 104.39 E
Heishui [China] 154 Ec 42.06N 119.22 E
Heishui [China] 152 He 32.03N 103.05 E
Heist, Knokke- 122 Jc 51.21N 3.15 E
Heist-op-den-Berg 124 Gc 51.05N 4.43 E
Hei-Zaki 156 Hb 39.39N 142.00 E
Hejgijaha 134 Pd 65.27N 72.50 E
Hejian 154 De 38.27N 116.05 E
Hejing 152 Ec 42.18N 86.18 E
Hejjaha 134 Kb 68.18N 62.32 E
Hekimhan 146 Gc 38.49N 37.56 E
Hekinan 156 Ed 34.52N 136.58 E
Hekla 110 Ec 64.00N 19.40W
Hekou 154 Ci 31.20N 114.25 E
Hekou → Yanshan 154 Dj 28.18N 117.41 E
Hel 120 Ob 54.37N 18.48 E
Helagsfjället 114 Ce 62.55N 12.27 E
Helan 152 Id 38.35N 106.16 E
Helan Shan 152 Id 39.00N 106.00 E
Helden's Point 197c Ab 17.24N 62.50W
Helena [Ar.-U.S.] 182 Ie 34.32N 90.35W
Helena [Guy.] 202 Gb 6.41N 57.55W
Helena [Mt.-U.S.] 176 He 46.36N 112.01W
Helen Glacier 222 Ge 66.40S 93.55 E
Helen Reef 208 Ed 2.53N 131.47 E
Helensburgh 118 Ie 56.01N 4.44W
Helensville 218 Fb 36.40S 174.27 E
Helgaå 116 Fi 55.53N 14.08 E
Helgasjön 116 Fh 56.55N 14.45 E
Helgeland 114 Cd 66.15N 13.05 E
Helgoland 120 Db 54.12N 7.53 E
Helgoländer Bucht 120 Eb 54.10N 8.04 E
Helikón Óros 130 Fk 38.20N 22.50 E
Helixi 154 Ei 30.39N 119.01 E
Heljulja 116 Nc 61.37N 30.38 E
Hella 114a Bc 63.50N 20.24W
Hellberge 120 Hd 52.34N 11.17 E
Hèlleh 146 Nh 29.10N 50.40 E
Hellendoorn 122 Mb 52.24N 6.26 E
Hellendoorn-Nijverdal 124 Ib 52.22N 6.27 E
Hellenic Trough (EN) 110 Ii 35.00N 24.00 E
Hellental 124 Id 50.29N 6.26 E
Hellesylt 116 Be 62.05N 6.54 E
Hellín 126 Kf 38.31N 1.41W
Hells Canyon 182 Db 45.20N 116.45W
Hellweg 124 Kc 51.40N 8.00 E
Helmand [3] 144 Jc 31.00N 64.00 E
Helmand 140 If 31.12N 61.34 E
Helme 120 He 51.20N 11.20 E
Helmeringhausen 172 Be 25.54S 16.57 E
Helmond 122 Lc 51.29N 5.40 E
Helmsdale 118 Jc 58.07N 3.40W
Helmsdale 118 Jc 58.10N 3.40W
Helmstedt 120 Hd 52.14N 11.02 E
Helong 152 Mc 42.32N 129.00 E
Helpe Majeure 124 Fd 50.11N 3.47 E
Helpringham 124 Bb 52.56N 0.18W
Helpter Berge 120 Jc 53.30N 13.36 E
Helsingborg 112 Hd 56.03N 12.42 E
Helsinge 116 Eh 56.01N 12.12 E
Helsingfors/Helsinki 112 Ic 60.10N 24.58 E
Helsingør 114 Ch 56.02N 12.37 E
Helsinki/Helsingfors 112 Ic 60.10N 24.58 E
Helska, Mierzeja- 120 Ob 54.45N 18.39 E
Helston 118 Hk 50.05N 5.16W
Helvecia 204 Bj 31.06S 60.05W
Helwān (EN)=Ḩulwān 164 Fd 29.51N 31.20 E
Ḩemār 146 Qg 31.42N 57.31 E
Hemčik 138 Ef 51.40N 92.10 E
Hemel Hempstead 118 Mj 51.46N 0.28W
Hemer 124 Jc 51.23N 7.46 E
Hemnesberget 114 Cc 66.14N 13.38 E
Hemsby 124 Db 52.41N 1.42 E
Hemse 116 Hg 57.14N 18.22 E
Hemsedal 116 Cd 60.50N 8.40 E
Hemsö 114 Ee 62.45N 18.05 E
Hen 116 Dd 60.13N 10.14 E
Henan 152 He 34.33N 101.55 E
Hen and Chickens Islands 218 Fa 35.55S 174.45 E
Henan Sheng (Ho-nan Sheng)=Honan (EN) [2] 152 Je 34.00N 114.00 E
Henares 126 Id 40.24N 3.30W
Henashi-Zaki 156 Fa 40.37N 139.51 E
Henbury 212 Gd 24.35S 133.15 E
Hendaye 122 Ek 43.22N 1.47W
Hendek 146 Db 40.48N 30.45 E
Henderson [Arg.] 204 Bm 36.18S 61.43W
Henderson [Ky.-U.S.] 184 Dg 37.50N 87.35W
Henderson [N.C.-U.S.] 184 Hg 36.20N 78.25W
Henderson [Nv.-U.S.] 182 Dd 36.02N 115.01W
Henderson [Tx.-U.S.] 186 Ij 32.09N 94.48W
Henderson Island 208 Og 24.22S 128.19W
Henderson Seamount (EN) 182 Df 25.34N 119.33W
Hendersonville [N.C.-U.S.] 184 Fh 35.19N 82.28W
Hendersonville [Tn.-U.S.] 184 Dg 36.18N 86.37W
Hendījān 146 Mg 30.14N 49.43 E
Hendorābī, Jazīreh-ye- 146 Oi 26.40N 53.37 E
Hendrik Verwderddam 172 Df 30.45S 25.33 E
Hengām, Jazīreh-ye- 146 Pi 26.39N 55.53 E
Hengduan Shan 140 Lg 27.30N 99.00 E
Hengelo 122 Mb 52.15N 6.45 E
Hengshan [China] 152 Id 37.51N 109.20 E
Hengshan [China] 152 Jf 27.16N 112.51 E
Hengshan [China] 154 Kb 45.24N 131.01 E
Heng Shan [China] 152 Jf 27.18N 112.41 E
Heng Shan [China] 152 Jd 39.42N 113.45 E
Hengshui 152 Kd 37.39N 115.46 E
Hengxian 152 Ig 22.46N 109.15 E
Hengyang 142 Ng 26.56N 112.35 E
Henik Lakes 180 Hd 61.05N 97.20W
Hénin-Liétard 122 Id 50.25N 2.56 E
Henley-on-Thames 124 Bc 51.32N 0.54W
Hennan 114 De 62.02N 15.54 E
Hennan 116 Fb 62.05N 15.45 E
Hennebont 122 Cg 47.48N 3.17W
Hennef (Sieg) 124 Jd 50.47N 7.17 E
Hennigsdorf bei Berlin 120 Jd 52.38N 13.12 E
Henrietta Maria, Cape 180 Je 55.09N 82.19W
Henry, Mount- 188 Hb 48.53N 115.31W
Henry Bay 222 Ie 66.40S 120.40 E
Henryetta 186 Ii 35.27N 95.59W
Henry Kater Peninsula 180 Kc 69.15N 67.30W
Henry Mountains 188 Jh 37.55N 110.50W
Henrys Fork River 188 Je 43.45N 111.56W
Henslow, Cape- 219a Ec 9.56S 160.38 E
Hentej 140 Me 48.50N 109.00 E
Hentiesbaai 172 Ad 22.08S 14.18 E
Henzada 142 Lh 17.38N 95.28 E
Heping → Yanhe 152 If 28.31N 108.28 E
Heppenheim (Bergstraße) 124 Ke 49.38N 8.39 E
Heppner 188 Fd 45.21N 119.33W
Hepu (Lianzhou) 152 Ig 21.40N 109.12 E
Hequ 152 Jd 39.22N 111.15 E
Herakol Dağı 146 Id 37.45N 42.35 E
Heralds Cays 212 Jc 16.55S 149.10 E
Herāt 142 If 34.20N 62.12 E
Herāt [3] 144 Jc 34.30N 62.00 E
Hérault [3] 122 Jk 43.40N 3.30 E
Hérault 122 Jk 43.17N 3.26 E
Herbert [N.Z.] 218 Df 45.13S 170.46 E
Herbert [Sask.-Can.] 188 La 50.26N 107.12W
Herberton 212 Jc 17.23S 145.23 E
Herbert River 212 Jc 18.32S 146.17 E
Herbiers, Les- 122 Eh 46.52N 1.01W
Herborn 120 Ef 50.41N 8.19 E
Herby 120 Of 50.45N 18.40 E
Hercegnovi 130 Bg 42.27N 18.32 E
110 Hg 43.00N 17.50 E
Hercegovina 128 Lg 43.00N 17.50 E
Herdubreid 114a Cb 65.11N 16.21W
Heredia 190 Hf 10.00N 84.07W
Heredia [3] 194 Fh 10.30N 84.00W
Hereford 118 Ki 52.15N 2.50W
Hereford [Eng.-U.K.] 118 Ki 52.04N 2.43W
Hereford [Tx.-U.S.] 182 Ge 34.49N 102.24W
Hereford and Worcester [3] 118 Ki 52.10N 2.35W
Hereheretue Atoll 208 Mf 19.54S 144.58W
Hereke 130 Mi 40.48N 29.39 E
Herekino 218 Ea 35.16S 173.13 E
Herent 124 Gd 50.54N 4.40 E
Herentals 124 Gc 51.11N 4.50 E
Herfølge 116 Ei 55.25N 12.10 E
Herford 120 Ed 52.08N 8.41 E
Héricourt 122 Mg 47.35N 6.45 E
Herington 186 Hg 38.40N 96.57W
Heriot 216 Ci 45.51S 169.16 E
Herīs 146 Lc 38.14N 47.07 E
Herisau 128 Dc 47.24N 9.16 E
Herk 124 Hd 50.58N 5.07 E
Herk-de-Stad 124 Hd 50.56N 5.10 E
Herkimer 184 Jd 43.02N 74.59W
Herlen He 152 Kb 48.48N 117.00 E
Hermagor 128 Hd 46.37N 13.22 E
Hermanas 192 Id 27.14N 101.14W
Herma Ness 118 Ma 60.50N 0.54W
Hermano Peak 186 Bh 37.17N 108.48W
Hermansverk 116 Bc 61.11N 6.51 E
Hermanus 172 Bf 34.25S 19.16 E
Hermeskeil 124 Ie 49.39N 6.57 E
Hermiston 188 Fd 45.51N 119.17W
Hermitage 218 De 43.44S 170.05 E
Hermit Islands 208 Fe 1.32S 145.05 E
Hermosa de Santa Rosa, Sierra- 192 Id 28.00N 101.45W
Hermosillo 176 Hg 29.04N 110.58W
Hermoso Campo 204 Bh 27.36S 61.21W
Hernád 120 Qh 48.00N 20.58 E
Hernandarias 206 Jc 25.22S 54.45W
Hernández [Arg.] 204 Bk 32.21S 60.02W
Hernández [Mex.] 192 Hf 23.02N 102.02W
Hernani 126 Ka 43.16N 1.58W
Herne 120 De 51.33N 7.13 E
Herne Bay 118 Oj 51.23N 1.08 E
Herning 112 Gd 56.08N 8.59 E
Heroica Alvarado 192 Lh 18.46N 95.46W
Heroica Tlapacoyan 192 Kh 19.58N 97.13W
Heroica Zitácuaro 192 Ih 19.24N 100.22W
Hérouville-Saint-Clair 124 Be 49.12N 0.19W
Herowābād 146 Md 37.37N 48.32 E
Herradura 204 Ch 26.29S 58.18W
Herre 116 Ce 59.06N 9.34 E
Herrera 204 Ck 32.26S 58.38W
Herrera [3] 194 Gj 7.54N 80.38W
Herrera del Duque 126 Ge 39.10N 5.03W
Herrera de Pisuerga 126 Hb 42.36N 4.20W
Herrero, Punta- 192 Ph 19.10N 87.30W
Herrljunga 116 Ef 58.05N 13.02 E
Hers 122 Hk 43.18N 1.33 E
Herschel 180 Dc 69.35N 139.05W
Herselt 124 Gc 51.03N 4.53 E
Herserange 124 He 49.31N 5.47 E
Hershey 184 Ie 40.17N 76.39W
Hersilia 204 Bj 30.00S 61.51W
Herson 112 Jf 46.38N 32.35 E
Hersonesski, mys- 132 Hg 44.33N 33.25 E
Hersonskaja oblast [3] 136 Df 46.40N 33.30 E
Herstal 122 Ld 50.40N 5.38 E
Herten 124 Jc 51.36N 7.08 E
Hertford 118 Mj 51.48N 0.05W
Hertford 118 Mj 51.50N 0.05W
Hertfordshire [3] 118 Mj 51.45N 0.20W
Hertogenbosch, 's- /Den Bosch 122 Lc 51.41N 5.19 E
Hertugen Af Orleans Land 179 Jc 78.15N 21.12W
Hervás 126 Gd 40.16N 5.51W
Herve 124 Hd 50.38N 5.48 E
Herve, Plateau van-/Herveland 124 Hd 50.40N 5.50 E
Herveland/Herve, Plateau van- 124 Hd 50.40N 5.50 E
Hervey Bay 212 Ke 25.15S 152.50 E
Herzberg 120 Je 51.41N 13.14 E
Herzberg am Harz 120 Ge 51.39N 10.20 E
Herzebrock 124 Kc 51.53N 8.15 E
Herzegovina (EN) 110 Hg 43.00N 17.50 E
Herzele 124 Fd 50.53N 3.53 E
Herzliyya 146 Ff 32.10N 34.51 E
Herzogenrath 124 Id 50.52N 6.06 E
Herzog-Ernst-Bucht (Vahsel Bay) 222 Af 77.48S 34.39W
Hesāmābād 146 Me 35.52N 48.25 E
Hesbaye/Haspengouws Plateau 122 Ld 50.35N 5.10 E
Hesdin 122 Id 50.22N 2.02 E
Hesel 124 Ja 53.18N 7.36 E
Heshī 146 Md 37.30N 48.15 E
Heshun 152 Jd 37.18N 113.32 E
Hesse (EN)=Hessen [2] 120 Ff 50.30N 9.15 E
Hesselberg 120 Gg 49.05N 10.35 E
Hesselø 116 Dh 56.10N 11.45 E
Hessen=Hesse (EN) [2] 120 Ff 50.30N 9.15 E
Hess Tablemount (EN) 208 Jc 17.50N 174.15W
Heta 138 Eb 71.35N 99.45 E
Heta 140 Mb 71.54N 102.00 E
Hettange-Grande 124 Ie 49.24N 6.09 E
Hettinger 186 Ec 46.00N 102.39W
Heuberg 120 Eh 48.06N 8.55 E
Heuchin 124 Ed 50.28N 2.16 E
Heuru 219a Ed 10.12S 161.25 E
Hève, Cap de la- 122 Ge 49.31N 0.04 E
Heves 120 Qi 47.36N 20.17 E
Heves [2] 120 Qi 47.50N 20.15 E
Hexham 118 Kg 54.58N 2.06W
Hexi 152 Hf 27.44N 102.09 E
Hexian 154 Ei 31.43N 118.22 E
Hexian (Babu) 152 Jg 24.28N 111.34 E
Hexigten Qi (Jingfeng) 152 Kc 43.15N 117.31 E
Heydarābād 146 Kd 37.06N 45.27 E
Heysham 118 Kg 54.02N 2.54W
Heyuan 152 Jg 23.41N 114.43 E
Heywood 212 Ig 38.08S 141.38 E
Heze (Caozhou) 152 Kd 35.14N 115.28 E
Hezuo 152 Hd 35.02N 102.57 E
Hialeah 184 Gm 25.49N 80.17W
Hiawatha 186 Ig 39.51N 95.32W
Hibara-Ko 156 Gc 37.42N 140.03 E
Hibbing 182 Ib 47.25N 92.56W
Hibernia Reef 212 Eb 12.00S 123.25 E
Hibiki-Nada 156 Bd 34.15N 130.40 E
Hibiny 114 Hc 67.40N 33.35 E
Hiburi-Jima 156 Ce 33.10N 132.18 E
Hickman 184 Cg 36.34N 89.11W
Hickory 184 Gh 35.44N 81.21W
Hick's Cay 194 Ce 17.39N 88.08W
Hida-Gawa 156 Ed 35.25N 137.03 E
Hidaka [Jap.] 154 Qc 42.53N 142.28 E
Hidaka [Jap.] 156 Dd 35.28N 134.47 E
Hidaka-Gawa 156 De 33.53N 135.08 E
Hidaka Sanmyaku 154 Qc 42.25N 142.50 E
Hidalgo [2] 190 Ed 20.30N 99.00W
Hidalgo [Mex.] 190 Ed 24.15N 99.26W
Hidalgo [Mex.] 192 Jd 27.47N 99.52W
Hidalgo del Parral 176 Ig 26.56N 105.40W
Hida-Sanchi 156 Ec 36.20N 137.00 E
Hida-Sanmyaku 154 Nf 36.10N 137.30 E
Hiddensee 120 Jb 54.33N 13.07 E
Hidra 116 Bf 58.15N 6.35 E
Hidrolândia 204 Hc 16.58S 49.16W
Hidrolina 204 Hb 14.37S 49.25W
Hieflau 128 Ic 47.36N 14.44 E
Hiei-Zan 156 Dd 35.05N 135.50 E
Hienghène 216 Cd 20.35S 164.56 E
Hierro 158 Ff 27.45N 18.00W
Higashi 156b Bb 26.38N 128.08 E
Higashihiroshima 156 Cd 34.25N 132.43 E
Higashi-izu 156 Fd 34.48N 139.02 E
Higashi-matsuyama 156 Fc 36.02N 139.22 E
Higashimuroran 156a Bb 42.21N 141.02 E
Higashine 154 Pe 38.26N 140.24 E
Higashiōsaka 156 Dd 34.40N 135.37 E
Higashi Rishiri 156a Ba 45.16N 141.15 E
Higashi-Shina-Kai=East China Sea (EN) 140 Og 29.00N 125.00 E
Higgins 186 Fh 36.07N 100.02W
Higham Ferrers 124 Bb 52.18N 0.35W
High Atlas (EN)=Haut Atlas 158 Ge 32.00N 6.00W
Highland [3] 118 Id 57.30N 5.00W
Highland Park 186 Me 42.11N 87.48W
High Level 180 Fe 58.30N 117.05W
Highmore 186 Gd 44.31N 99.27W
High Plains 174 If 38.30N 103.00W
High Point 182 Ld 35.58N 79.59W
High Prairie 180 Fe 55.27N 116.30W
High River 180 Gf 50.35N 113.52W
Highrock Lake 180 He 55.49N 100.23W
High Springs 184 Fk 29.50N 82.36W
High Tatra (EN)=Vysoké Tatry 120 Pg 49.10N 20.00 E
High Willhays 118 Jk 50.41N 3.59W
Highwood Mountains 188 Jc 47.25N 110.30W
High Wycombe 118 Mj 51.38N 0.46W
Higuera de Zaragoza 192 Ee 25.59N 109.16W
Higüero, Punta- 194 Nd 18.22N 67.16W
Higuerote 196 Cg 10.29N 66.06W
Higüey 194 Md 18.37N 68.43W
Hiidenvesi 116 Kd 60.20N 24.10 E
Hii-Gawa 156 Cd 35.26N 132.52 E
Hiiraan [3] 168 He 4.00N 45.30 E
Hiitola 114 Gf 61.16N 29.42 E
Hiiumaa/Hiuma 110 Id 58.50N 22.40 E
Híjar 126 Lc 41.10N 0.27W
Hijāz, Jabal al- 164 Hf 19.45N 41.55 E
Hiji 156 Be 33.22N 131.32 E
Hiji-Gawa 156 Ce 33.36N 132.29 E
Hikami 156 Dd 35.11N 135.02 E
Hikari 154 Kh 33.58N 131.56 E
Hiketa 156 Dd 34.13N 134.24 E
Hikiä 116 Kd 60.45N 24.55 E
Hiki-Gawa 156 De 33.35N 135.26 E
Ḩikmah, Ra's al- 146 Bg 31.17N 27.44 E
Hikone 154 Ng 35.15N 136.15 E
Hiko-San 156 Be 33.29N 130.56 E
Hikueru Atoll 216 Mc 17.36S 142.37W
Hikurangi 218 Fa 35.36S 174.17 E
Hikurangi 218 Hb 37.55S 178.04 E
Hila 150 Ih 7.35S 127.24 E
Hilāl, Ra's al- 164 Dc 32.55N 22.11 E
Hiland 188 Le 43.08N 107.18W
Hilchenbach 124 Kc 51.00N 8.06 E
Hildburghausen 120 Gf 50.25N 10.45 E
Hilden 124 Ic 51.10N 6.56 E
Hildesheim 120 Fd 52.09N 9.58 E
Hillaby, Mount- 196 Gf 13.12N 59.35W
Hillared 116 Eg 57.38N 13.09 E
Hillary Coast 222 Kf 79.00S 161.00 E
Hill Bank 194 Ce 17.35N 88.42W
Hill City 186 Gg 39.22N 99.51W
Hillcrest Center 188 Fi 35.23N 118.57W
Hille 124 Kb 52.20N 8.45 E
Hillegom 124 Gb 52.18N 4.35 E
Hillekrog 116 Dj 54.36N 11.30 E
Hillerød 116 Ei 55.56N 12.19 E
Hillerstorp 116 Eg 57.19N 13.52 E
Hillesheim 124 Id 50.19N 6.41 E
Hillingdon, London- 124 Bc 51.31N 0.27W
Hillsboro [Il.-U.S.] 186 Lg 39.09N 89.29W
Hillsboro [N.D.-U.S.] 186 Hc 47.26N 97.03W
Hillsboro [Oh.-U.S.] 184 Ff 39.12N 83.37W
Hillsboro [Or.-U.S.] 188 Dd 45.31N 122.59W
Hillsboro [Tx.-U.S.] 186 Hj 32.01N 97.08W
Hillsborough 197p Cb 12.29N 61.26W
Hillsdale 184 Ee 41.55N 84.38W
Hillsville 184 Gg 36.46N 80.44W
Hillswich 118 La 60.28N 1.30W
Hilo 210 Lc 19.44N 155.05W
Hilo Bay 221a Fd 19.44N 155.05W
Hilok 138 Gf 51.22N 110.30 E
Hilok 140 Md 51.19N 106.59 E
Hilton Head Island 184 Gi 32.12N 80.45W
Hiltrup, Münster- 124 Jc 51.54N 7.38 E
Hilvan 146 Hd 37.30N 38.58 E
Hilvarenbeek 124 Hc 51.29N 5.08 E
Hilversum 122 Lb 52.14N 5.10 E
Himāchal Prādesh [3] 148 Fb 31.00N 78.00 E
Himalaya=Himalayas (EN) 140 Kg 29.00N 83.00 E
Himalayas (EN)=Himalaya 140 Kg 29.00N 83.00 E
Himara 130 Ci 40.07N 19.44 E
Himeji 152 Ne 34.49N 134.42 E
Hime-Jima 156 Be 33.43N 131.40 E
Hime-Kawa 156 Ec 37.02N 137.50 E
Hime-Shima 156 Ae 32.49N 128.41 E
Hime-Zaki 156 Fb 38.05N 138.34 E
Himi 154 Nf 36.51N 136.59 E
Himki 114 Ii 55.56N 37.28 E
Himmelbjerget 116 Ch 56.06N 9.42 E
Himmerfjärden 116 Ge 59.00N 17.43 E
Himmerland 116 Ch 56.50N 9.45 E
Himo 170 Gc 3.23S 37.33 E
Ḩimş=Homs (E) 142 Ff 34.44N 36.43 E
Hims, Bahrat- 146 Ge 34.39N 36.34 E
Hinai 156 Ga 40.13N 140.35 E
Ḩinākīyah, Wādī al- 146 Ij 24.30N 40.30 E
Hinca Renancó 206 Hd 34.50S 64.23W
Hinche 194 Kd 19.09N 72.01W
Hinchinbrook 178 Jd 60.22N 146.30W
Hinchinbrook Island 212 Jc 18.25S 146.15 E
Hinckley 124 Ab 52.32N 1.22W
Hindås 116 Eg 57.42N 12.27 E
Hindhead 124 Bc 51.06N 0.44W
Ḩindi, Badwēynta-=Indian Ocean (EN) 106 Gl 21.00S 82.00 E
Hindmarsh, Lake- 212 Ig 36.05S 141.55 E
Hinds 218 Df 44.00S 171.34 E
Hindsholm 116 Di 55.33N 10.40 E
Hindukush 140 Jf 35.00N 71.00 E
Hindustan 140 Jg 25.00N 79.00 E
Hinesville 184 Gj 31.51N 81.36W
Hinganghāt 148 Fd 20.34N 78.50 E
Hınıs 146 Ic 39.22N 41.44 E
Hınıs 146 Jc 39.18N 42.12 E
Hinlopenstretet 179 Oc 79.15N 21.00 E
Hinnøya 110 Hb 68.30N 16.00 E
Hino-Gawa 156 Cd 35.27N 133.22 E
Hinojosa del Duque 126 Gf 38.30N 5.09W
Hinokage 156 Be 32.39N 131.24 E
Hi-no-Misaki 156 Cd 35.26N 132.38 E
Hino-Misaki 156 De 33.53N 135.04 E
Hinterrhein 128 Dd 46.49N 9.25 E
Hinton 180 Ff 53.25N 117.34W
Hi-Numa 156 Gc 36.16N 140.30 E
Hınzır Burun 146 Fb 36.22N 35.45 E
Hiou 219b Ca 13.08S 166.33 E
Hipólito 192 Ie 25.41N 101.26W
Hippolytushoef, Wieringen- 124 Gb 52.54N 4.59 E
Hippone 128 Bn 36.52N 7.44 E
Hirado 154 Jh 33.22N 129.33 E
Hirado-Shima 154 Jh 33.19N 129.32 E
Hiraka 156 Gb 39.16N 140.29 E
Hirakata 156 Dd 34.48N 135.38 E
Hīrākud 148 Gd 21.15N 84.15 E
Hiraman 170 Gc 1.07S 39.55 E
Hiranai 156a Bc 40.54N 140.57 E
Hirara 152 Mg 24.48N 125.17 E
Hira-Shima 156 Ae 33.01N 129.15 E
Hirata 156 Cd 35.26N 132.49 E
Hiratsuka 156 Fd 35.19N 139.19 E
Hirfanlı barajı Gölü 146 Ec 39.10N 33.32 E
Hirgis 152 Fb 49.32N 93.48 E
Hirgis-Nur 140 Le 49.12N 93.24 E
Hirhafok 162 Ie 23.29N 5.45 E
Hîrlău 130 Jb 47.26N 26.54 E
Hiromi 156 Ce 33.15N 132.38 E
Hiroo 152 Pc 42.17N 143.19 E
Hirosaki 152 Pc 40.35N 140.28 E
Hiroshima 142 Pf 34.24N 132.27 E
Hiroshima Ken [2] 154 Lg 34.35N 132.50 E
Hiroshima-Wan 156 Cd 34.10N 132.20 E
Hirschhorn (Neckar) 124 Ke 49.27N 8.54 E
Hirson 122 Ke 49.55N 4.05 E
Hîrşova 130 Ke 44.41N 27.56 E
Hîrtibaciu 130 Hd 45.44N 24.14 E
Hirtshals 114 Bh 57.35N 9.58 E
Hirvensalmi 116 Lc 61.38N 26.48 E
Ḩīs 168 Hc 10.50N 46.54 E
Hisai 156 Ed 34.40N 136.28 E
Hisaka-Shima 156 Ae 32.48N 128.52 E
Hisar 148 Fc 29.10N 75.43 E
Hisar 130 Jg 42.35N 27.00 E
Hisarcik 130 Mj 39.15N 29.15 E
Hisarja 130 Hg 42.30N 24.42 E
Ḩismā 146 Fh 28.30N 35.50 E
Ḩişn al 'Abr 164 If 16.08N 47.14 E
Ḩişn aş Şaḩābī 164 Dc 30.01N 20.48 E
Hispaniola (EN)=La Española 174 Lh 19.00N 71.00W
Histon 124 Cb 52.15N 0.06 E
Histria 130 Le 44.30N 28.45 E
Hīt 146 Jf 33.38N 42.49 E
Hita 154 Kh 33.19N 130.56 E
Hitachi 154 Pf 36.36N 140.39 E
Hitachi-ōta 156 Gc 36.32N 140.31 E
Hitchin 124 Bc 51.57N 0.16W
Hitiaa 221e Fc 17.36S 149.18W
Hitotsuse-Gawa 156 Be 32.03N 131.31 E
Hitoyoshi 154 Kh 32.15N 130.45 E
Hitra 110 Gc 63.30N 8.45 E
Hiuchi-ga-Take 156 Fc 36.57N 139.17 E
Hiuchi-Nada 156 Cd 34.05N 133.15 E
Hiuma/Hiiumaa 110 Id 58.50N 22.40 E

Index Symbols

- [1] Independent Nation
- [2] State, Region
- [3] District, County
- [4] Municipality
- [5] Colony, Dependency
- Continent
- Physical Region
- Historical or Cultural Region
- Mount, Mountain
- Volcano
- Hill
- Mountains, Mountain Range
- Hills, Escarpment
- Plateau, Upland
- Pass, Gap
- Plain, Lowland
- Delta
- Salt Flat
- Valley, Canyon
- Crater, Cave
- Karst Features
- Depression
- Polder
- Desert, Dunes
- Forest, Woods
- Heath, Steppe
- Oasis
- Cape, Point
- Coast, Beach
- Cliff
- Peninsula
- Isthmus
- Sandbank
- Island
- Atoll
- Rock, Reef
- Islands, Archipelago
- Rocks, Reefs
- Coral Reef
- Well, Spring
- Geyser
- River, Stream
- Waterfall, Rapids
- River Mouth, Estuary
- Lake
- Salt Lake
- Intermittent Lake
- Reservoir
- Swamp, Pond
- Canal
- Glacier
- Ice Shelf, Pack Ice
- Ocean
- Sea
- Gulf, Bay
- Strait, Fjord
- Lagoon
- Bank
- Seamount
- Tablemount
- Ridge
- Shelf
- Basin
- Escarpment, Sea Scarp
- Fracture
- Trench, Abyss
- National Park, Reserve
- Point of Interest
- Recreation Site
- Cave, Cavern
- Historic Site
- Ruins
- Wall, Walls
- Church, Abbey
- Temple
- Scientific Station
- Railway station
- Airport
- Port
- Military installation
- Lighthouse
- Mine
- Tunnel
- Dam, Bridge

Hiv	132	Oi	41.46N	47.57 E
Hiva	136	Gg	41.25N	60.23 E
Hiva Oa, Ile-	208	Ne	9.45S	139.00W
Hiw	146	Ei	26.01N	32.16 E
Hjademeste/ Häädemeeste	116	Kf	58.00N	24.28 E
Hjallerup	116	Dg	57.10N	10.09 E
Hjälmare kanal	116	Fe	59.25N	15.55 E
Hjälmaren	110	Hd	59.15N	15.45 E
Hjelm	116	Dh	56.10N	10.50 E
Hjelmelandsvågen	114	Bg	59.15N	6.10 E
Hjelmsøya	114	Fa	71.05N	24.43 E
Hjeltefjorden	116	Ad	60.40N	4.55 E
Hjerkinn	116	Cb	62.13N	9.32 E
Hjo	114	Dg	58.18N	14.17 E
Hjørring	114	Bh	57.28N	9.59 E
Hlatikulu	172	Ee	26.58S	31.19 E
Hlavní město Praha [3]	120	Kf	50.05N	14.25 E
Hlavní město SSR Bratislava [3]	120	Nh	48.10N	17.10 E
Hlinsko	120	Lg	49.46N	15.54 E
Hlohovec	120	Nh	48.25N	17.48 E
Hluhluwe	172	Ee	28.02S	32.17 E
Hmelnickaja oblast [3]	136	Cf	49.30N	27.00 E
Hmelnicki	136	Cf	49.24N	26.57 E
Hmelnik	132	Ee	49.33N	27.59 E
Hnilec	120	Rh	48.53N	21.01 E
Ho	166	Fd	6.36N	0.28 E
Hoa Binh	148	Ld	20.50N	105.20 E
Hoanib	172	Ac	19.23S	13.06 E
Hoare Bay	180	Lc	65.30N	63.10W
Hoback Peak	188	Je	43.10N	110.33W
Hobart [Austl.]	210	Fi	42.53S	147.19 E
Hobart [Ok.-U.S.]	186	Gi	35.01N	99.06W
Hobbs	182	Ge	32.42N	103.08W
Hobbs Coast	222	Nf	74.50S	131.00W
Hobda	132	Sd	50.55N	54.38 E
Hoboken, Antwerpen-	124	Gc	51.10N	4.21 E
Hoboksar	152	Eb	46.47N	85.43 E
Hobq Shamo	152	Ic	40.30N	108.00 E
Hobro	114	Bh	56.38N	9.48 E
Hoburgen	114	Eh	56.55N	18.07 E
Hobyā	160	Lh	5.20N	48.38 E
Hocalar	130	Mk	38.37N	29.57 E
Hochalmspitze	128	Hc	47.01N	13.19 E
Hochfeiler/Gran Pilastro	128	Fd	46.58N	11.44 E
Hochgolling	128	Hc	47.16N	13.45 E
Hochschwab	128	Jc	47.36N	15.05 E
Höchstadt an der Aisch	128	Gg	49.42N	10.44 E
Höchstetters Forland	179	Kc	75.45N	20.00W
Höchst im Odenwald	124	Ke	49.48N	9.00 E
Hochtor	128	Gc	47.05N	12.48 E
Hockenheim	124	Ke	49.19N	8.33 E
Hodaka-Dake	156	Ec	36.17N	137.39 E
Hodda	168	Ic	11.30N	50.45 E
Hoddesdon	124	Cc	51.45N	0.00
Hodgenville	184	Eg	37.34N	85.44W
Hodh	158	Gg	16.10N	8.40W
Hodh ech Chargui [3]	162	Ff	17.00N	7.15W
Hodh el Gharbi [3]	162	Ff	16.30N	10.00W
Hódmezővásárhely	120	Qj	46.25N	20.20 E
Hodna, Chott el-	162	Hb	35.25N	4.45 E
Hodna, Monts du-	162	Hb	35.50N	4.50 E
Hodna, Plaine du-	126	Qi	35.35N	4.35 E
Hodonín	120	Nh	48.52N	17.08 E
Hodorov	132	De	49.25N	24.18 E
Hodžambas	135	Ee	38.06N	65.01 E
Hodža-Pirjah, gora-	135	Fe	38.47N	67.35 E
Hodžejli	136	Fg	42.23N	59.20 E
Hœdic, Ile de-	122	Dg	47.20N	2.52W
Hoegaarden	124	Gd	50.47N	4.53 E
Hoei/Huy	122	Ld	50.31N	5.14 E
Hoë Karoo	158	Jl	30.00S	21.30 E
Hoekse Waard	124	Gc	51.45N	4.25 E
Hoek van Holland	122	Kc	51.59N	4.09 E
Hoeselt	124	Hd	50.51N	5.29 E
Hof	120	Hf	50.19N	11.55 E
Höfdakaupstadur	114a	Bb	65.50N	20.19W
Hofgeismar	120	Fe	51.29N	9.24 E
Hofheim	124	Kd	50.05N	8.27 E
Hofmeyr	172	Df	31.39S	25.50 E
Höfn	114a	Cb	64.15N	15.13W
Hofors	114	Df	60.33N	16.17 E
Hofsjökull	110	Ec	64.49N	18.48W
Höfu	154	Kg	34.03N	131.34 E
Höganäs	116	Eh	56.12N	12.33 E
Hogarth, Mount-	212	Hd	21.48S	136.58 E
Hogback Mountain	188	Id	44.54N	112.07W
Hog Cliffs	197d	Ba	17.38N	61.44W
Hoge Venen/Hautes Fagnes	120	Bf	50.30N	6.00 E
Högfors/Karkkila	114	Ff	60.32N	24.11 E
Hog Island	197p	Bb	12.00N	61.44W
Hogne, Somme-Leuze-	124	Hd	50.15N	5.17 E
Hog Point	197d	Ba	17.43N	61.48W
Högsby	114	Dh	57.10N	16.02 E
Høgste Breakulen	116	Bc	61.41N	7.02 E
Høgstegia	116	Db	62.23N	10.08 E
Hogsty Reef	194	Kc	21.41N	73.49W
Hŏhang-nyŏng	154	Jd	41.48N	128.20 E
Hohe Acht	120	Cf	50.23N	7.03 E
Hohe Eifel	124	Id	50.16N	6.50 E
Hohenau	204	Eh	27.05S	55.45W
Hohenems	128	Dc	47.22N	9.41 E
Hohenloher Ebene	120	Fg	49.20N	9.40 E
Hohes Venn	120	Bf	50.30N	6.00 E
Hohe Tauern	128	Gc	47.10N	12.30 E
Hohhot	142	Ne	40.51N	111.38 E
Hohneck, Le-	122	Nf	48.02N	7.01 E
Hōhoku	156	Bd	34.17N	130.57 E
Höhr-Grenzhausen	124	Jd	50.26N	7.40 E
Höhtiäinen	116	Mb	62.50N	29.40 E
Hoh Xil Hu	152	Fd	35.35N	91.06 E
Hoh Xil Shan	140	Lf	35.20N	91.00 E
Hoi An	148	Le	15.52N	108.19 E
Hoima	170	Fb	1.26N	31.21 E
Hoisington	186	Gg	38.31N	98.47W
Hoj, vozvyšennost-	134	Ob	68.50N	71.30 E
Højer	116	Cj	54.58N	8.43 E
Hojniki	136	Ce	51.54N	29.56 E
Hōjō	154	Lh	33.58N	132.46 E
Hökensås	116	Ff	58.11N	14.08 E
Hokianga Harbour	218	Ea	35.30S	173.20 E
Hokitika	210	Ii	42.43S	170.58 E
Hok-Kai = Okhotsk, Sea of- (EN)	140	Qd	53.00N	150.00 E
Hokkaidō	140	Qe	43.00N	143.00 E
Hokkaidō Ken [2]	154	Qc	43.00N	143.00 E
Hokksund	116	Bg	59.47N	9.59 E
Hokmābād	146	Qd	36.37N	57.36 E
Hokota	156	Gc	36.10N	140.30 E
Hol	116	Cd	60.36N	8.22 E
Holap	220d	Ba	7.39N	151.54 E
Holbæk	116	Di	55.43N	11.43 E
Holbeach	124	Cb	52.48N	0.01 E
Holbeach Marsh	124	Cb	52.52N	0.02 E
Holbox, Isla-	192	Pg	21.33N	87.15W
Holbrook	182	Ee	34.54N	110.10W
Holdenville	186	Hi	35.05N	96.24W
Holderness	118	Mh	53.47N	0.10W
Holdrege	186	Gf	40.26N	99.22W
Hold With Hope	179	Jd	73.40N	21.45W
Hole in the Wall	184	Im	25.51N	77.12W
Hølen	116	De	59.32N	10.45 E
Holešov	120	Ng	49.20N	17.33 E
Holetown	197q	Ab	13.11N	59.39W
Holguín	176	Lg	20.53N	76.15W
Holguín [3]	194	Jc	20.40N	75.50W
Hol-Hol	168	Gc	11.20N	42.50 E
Holitna	178	Hd	61.40N	157.12W
Höljes	114	Cf	60.54N	12.36 E
Hollabrunn	128	Kb	48.33N	16.05 E
Holland	184	Dd	42.47N	86.07W
Holland [Eng.-U.K.]	124	Bb	52.52N	0.10W
Holland [Neth.]	110	Ge	52.20N	4.45 E
Hollandale	186	Kj	33.10N	90.58W
Hollandsbird Island	172	Ad	24.45S	14.34 E
Hollands Diep	124	Gc	51.40N	4.30 E
Hollesley Bay	124	Db	52.04N	1.33 E
Hollick-Kenyon Plateau	222	Pf	79.00S	97.00W
Hollis	186	Gi	34.41N	99.55W
Hollister [Ca.-U.S.]	188	Eh	36.51N	121.24W
Hollister [Id.-U.S.]	188	He	42.23N	114.35W
Hollola	116	Kc	61.03N	25.26 E
Höllviksnäs	116	Ei	55.25N	12.57 E
Holly Springs	186	Li	34.41N	89.26W
Hollywood	182	Kf	26.00N	80.09W
Holm	114	Hh	57.09N	31.12 E
Holma	166	Hd	9.54N	13.03 E
Holman Island	180	Fb	70.40N	117.35W
Hólmavík	114a	Bb	65.43N	21.41W
Holmes Reefs	208	Ff	16.30S	148.00 E
Holmestrand	116	De	59.29N	10.18 E
Holm Land	179	Kb	80.16N	18.20W
Holms	179	Gd	74.30N	57.00W
Holmsjö	116	Fh	56.25N	15.32 E
Holmsjön [Swe.]	114	De	62.25N	15.20 E
Holmsjön [Swe.]	116	Gb	62.40N	16.35 E
Holmsk	138	Jg	47.00N	142.03 E
Holmski	132	Kg	44.50N	38.24 E
Holmsland Klit	116	Ch	56.00N	8.10 E
Holmsund	114	Ee	63.42N	20.21 E
Holmsveden	116	Gc	61.07N	16.43 E
Holmudden	116	Hg	57.57N	19.21 E
Holod	130	Fc	46.47N	22.08 E
Holohit, Punta-	192	Og	21.37N	88.08W
Holothuria Banks (EN)	212	Fb	13.25S	126.00 E
Holsnøy	116	Ad	60.35N	5.05 E
Holstebro	114	Bh	56.21N	8.38 E
Holsted	116	Ci	55.30N	8.55 E
Holstein	186	Ie	42.29N	95.33W
Holsteinsborg/Sisimiut	224	Nc	67.05N	53.45W
Holt	124	Db	52.54N	1.05 E
Holten	124	Ib	52.17N	6.27 E
Holton	186	Ig	39.28N	95.44W
Holtoson	138	Ff	50.18N	103.20 E
Holtyn-Daba	152	Ib	47.40N	107.20 E
Holwerd, Westdongeradeel-	124	Ha	53.22N	5.54 E
Holy Cross	178	Hd	62.12N	159.47W
Holyhead	118	Ih	53.20N	4.38W
Holy Island [Eng.-U.K.]	118	Lf	55.41N	1.48W
Holy Island [Wales-U.K.]	118	Ih	53.18N	4.37W
Holyoke [Co.-U.S.]	186	Ef	40.35N	102.18W
Holyoke [Ma.-U.S.]	184	Kd	42.12N	72.37W
Holýšov	120	Jg	49.36N	13.07 E
Homa Bay	170	Fc	0.31S	34.27 E
Homalin	148	Id	24.52N	94.55 E
Homathko River	188	Ca	50.55N	124.50W
Homberg (Ohm)	124	Kd	50.44N	8.59 E
Hombori	166	Eb	15.17N	1.42W
Hombre Muerto, Salar del-	206	Gc	25.23S	67.06W
Homburg	120	Dg	49.19N	7.20 E
Home Bay	174	Mc	68.45N	67.10W
Homécourt	124	He	49.14N	5.59 E
Home Hill	212	Jc	19.40S	147.25 E
Homer [Ak.-U.S.]	176	Dd	59.39N	151.33W
Homer [La.-U.S.]	186	Jj	32.48N	93.04W
Homert	124	Kc	51.16N	8.06 E
Homerville	184	Fj	31.02N	82.45W
Homestead	184	Gm	25.29N	80.29W
Homewood	184	Di	33.29N	86.48W
Hommelstø	114	Cd	65.25N	12.30 E
Hommersåk	116	Af	58.55N	5.50 E
Homoine	172	Fd	23.52S	35.08 E
Homoljske Planina	130	Ee	44.20N	21.45 E
Homonhon	150	Id	10.44N	125.43 E
Homosassa	184	Fk	28.47N	82.37W
Homs (EN) = Ḥimṣ	142	Ff	34.44N	36.43 E
Honan (EN) = Henan Sheng (Ho-nan Sheng) [2]	152	Je	34.00N	114.00 E
Honan (EN) = Ho-nan Sheng → Henan Sheng [2]	152	Je	34.00N	114.00 E
Ho-nan Sheng → Henan Sheng = Honan (EN) [2]	152	Je	34.00N	114.00 E
Honaz	130	Ml	37.45N	29.17 E
Honaz Dağı	130	Ml	37.41N	29.18 E
Honbetsu	154	Qc	43.18N	143.33 E
Honda	202	Db	5.13N	74.45W
Honda, Bahia-	194	Lg	12.21N	71.47W
Hondeklipbaai	172	Bf	30.20S	17.18 E
Hòn Diên, Núi-	148	Lf	11.33N	108.38 E
Hondo	190	Ge	18.29N	88.19W
Hondo [Jap.]	154	Kh	32.27N	130.12 E
Hondo [N.M.-U.S.]	186	Dj	33.23N	105.16W
Hondo [Tx.-U.S.]	186	Gl	29.21N	99.09W
Hondo, Rio-	186	Dj	33.22N	104.24W
Hondschoote	124	Ed	50.59N	2.35 E
Hondsrug	122	Mb	52.50N	6.50 E
Honduras	176	Kh	15.00N	86.30W
Honduras, Cabo de-	194	De	16.01N	86.01W
Honduras, Golfo de- = Honduras, Gulf of- (EN)	174	Kh	16.10N	87.50W
Honduras, Gulf of-	174	Kh	16.10N	87.50W
Honduras, Gulf of- (EN) = Honduras, Golfo de-	174	Kh	16.10N	87.50W
Hønefoss	114	Cf	60.10N	10.18 E
Honey Lake	188	Ef	40.16N	120.19W
Honfleur	122	Ge	49.25N	0.14 E
Hông, Sông- [Asia] = Red River (EN)	140	Mg	20.17N	106.34 E
Hong'an (Huang'an)	154	Ci	31.17N	114.37 E
Hongch'ŏn	154	If	37.41N	127.52 E
Hong-Do	154	Hg	34.41N	125.13 E
Hong He	154	Ch	32.24N	115.32 E
Honghton Lake	184	Ec	44.22N	84.43W
Hong Hu	152	Je	30.00N	113.25 E
Honghu (Xindi)	154	Bj	29.50N	113.28 E
Honghui	152	Id	36.46N	105.03 E
Hong Kong/Xianggang [5]	142	Ng	22.15N	114.10 E
Hongliuyuan	152	Gc	41.02N	95.24 E
Hongluoxian	154	Fd	41.01N	120.52 E
Hongning → Wulian	154	Eg	35.45N	119.13 E
Hongor	154	Bb	45.48N	112.45 E
Hongqizhen	152	Ih	18.48N	109.30 E
Hongshui He	144	Mg	23.47N	109.33 E
Hongsŏng	154	If	36.36N	126.40 E
Hongtong	154	Af	36.15N	111.41 E
Hongū	156	De	33.50N	135.46 E
Honguedo, Détroit d'-	180	Lg	49.30N	65.00W
Hongwansi → Sunan	152	Gd	38.59N	99.25 E
Hongwŏn	154	Id	40.02N	127.58 E
Hongyuan (Hurama)	152	He	32.45N	102.38 E
Hongze (Gaoliangjian)	152	Ke	33.10N	119.58 E
Hongze Hu	152	Ke	33.20N	118.40 E
Honiara	210	Ge	9.27S	159.57 E
Honikulu, Passe-	220h	Ac	13.23S	176.11W
Honiton	118	Jk	50.48N	3.13W
Honjō	154	Pe	39.23N	140.03 E
Honkajoki	116	Jb	61.59N	22.16 E
Hon-kawane	156	Fd	35.07N	138.06 E
Honningsvåg	114	Ga	70.59N	26.01 E
Hōnō	116	Dg	57.42N	11.39 E
Honokaa	221a	Fc	20.05N	155.28W
Honokohau	221a	Eb	21.01N	156.37W
Honolulu	210	Lb	21.19N	157.52W
Honomu	221a	Fd	19.52N	155.07W
Honrubia	126	Je	39.37N	2.16W
Honshū	140	Pf	36.00N	136.00 E
Hontenisse	124	Gc	51.23N	4.00 E
Hontenisse-Kloosterzande	124	Gc	51.23N	4.00 E
Honuapo Bay	221a	Fd	19.05N	155.33W
Honuu	138	Jc	66.27N	143.06 E
Honyō	156	Fc	36.14N	139.10 E
Hood	180	Gc	67.25N	108.53W
Hood, Mount-	174	Ge	45.23N	121.41W
Hood Point	212	Df	34.23S	119.34 E
Hood River	188	Ed	45.43N	121.31W
Hoogeveen	122	Mb	52.43N	6.29 E
Hoogezand-Sappemeer	124	Ia	53.09N	6.48 E
Hooglede	124	Fd	50.59N	3.05 E
Hoogstraten	124	Gc	51.24N	4.46 E
Hooker	186	Fh	36.52N	101.13W
Hooker, Cape-	222	Kf	70.38S	166.45 E
Hook Head/Rinn Dúain	118	Gi	52.07N	6.55W
Hook Island	212	Jc	20.10S	148.55 E
Hoolehua	221a	Db	21.10N	157.05W
Hoonah	178	Le	58.07N	135.26W
Hooper, Cape-	180	Kc	68.24N	66.43W
Hooper Bay	178	Fd	61.31N	166.06W
Hoopeston	186	Mf	40.28N	87.40W
Höör	116	Ei	55.56N	13.32 E
Hoorn	122	Lb	52.38N	5.04 E
Hoornaar	124	Gc	51.53N	4.57 E
Hoover Dam	188	Hi	36.00N	114.27W
Hopa	146	Ib	41.25N	41.24 E
Hope [Ar.-U.S.]	186	Jj	33.40N	93.36W
Hope [Az.-U.S.]	188	Ij	33.44N	113.42W
Hope [B.C.-Can.]	188	Eb	49.23N	121.26W
Hope, Ben-	118	Ic	58.24N	4.36W
Hope, Lake-	212	Ef	32.50S	121.40 E
Hope, Point-	176	Cc	68.21N	166.50W
Hopedale	180	Le	55.50N	60.10W
Hopefield	172	Bf	33.04S	18.21 E
Hopeh (EN) = Hebei Sheng (Ho-pei Sheng) [2]	152	Kd	39.00N	116.00 E
Hopeh (EN) = Ho-pei Sheng → Hebei Sheng [2]	152	Kd	39.00N	116.00 E
Hopeh (EN) = Hu-pei Sheng → Hubei Sheng [2]	152	Je	31.00N	112.00 E
Ho-pei Sheng → Hebei Sheng = Hopeh (EN) [2]	152	Kd	39.00N	116.00 E
Hopelchén	192	Oh	19.46N	89.51W
Hopen	179	Oc	76.35N	25.10 E
Hopër	110	Kf	49.36N	42.19 E
Hopes Advance, Cap-	180	Kd	61.00N	69.35W
Hopetoun [Austl.]	212	Ig	35.44S	142.22 E
Hopetoun [Austl.]	210	Dh	33.57S	120.07 E
Hopetown	172	Ce	29.34S	24.03 E
Hopewell	184	Ig	37.17N	77.19W
Hopewell Islands	180	Je	58.20N	78.10W
Hopin	148	Jd	24.59N	96.31 E
Hopkins, Lake-	212	Fd	24.15S	128.50 E
Hopkinsville	182	Jd	36.52N	87.29W
Hopsten	124	Jb	52.23N	7.37 E
Hoptrup	116	Ci	55.11N	9.28 E
Hoquiam	182	Cb	46.59N	123.53W
Hor	138	Ig	47.55N	135.01 E
Hor	138	Ig	47.48N	134.43 E
Hōrai	156	Ed	34.55N	137.34 E
Hōrai-San	156	Dd	35.13N	135.53 E
Horasan	146	Jb	40.03N	42.11 E
Horaždovice	120	Jg	49.20N	13.42 E
Horb am Neckar	120	Eh	48.26N	8.41 E
Hörby	116	Ei	55.51N	13.39 E
Horconcitos	194	Fi	8.19N	82.10W
Hordaland [2]	114	Bf	60.15N	6.30 E
Hordogoj	138	Gd	62.32N	115.38 E
Horezmskaja oblast [3]	136	Gg	41.30N	60.40 E
Horezu	130	Hd	45.09N	24.01 E
Horgen	128	Cc	47.15N	8.36 E
Horgoš	130	Cc	46.09N	19.58 E
Horgos	136	Ig	44.10N	80.20 E
Hořice	120	Lf	50.22N	15.38 E
Horinger	154	Ad	40.24N	111.46 E
Horizon Tablemount (EN)	208	Kc	19.40N	168.30W
Horizontina	204	Eh	27.37S	54.19W
Horley	124	Bc	51.10N	0.10W
Horlick Mountains	222	Og	85.23S	121.00W
Hormigas	192	Gc	29.12N	105.45W
Hormoz	144	Id	27.06N	56.28 E
Hormoz, Kūh-e-	144	Id	27.27N	55.10 E
Hormoz, Tangeh-ye- = Hormuz, Strait of- (EN)	140	Hg	26.34N	56.15 E
Hormozgān [3]	144	Id	27.30N	56.00 E
Hormūd-e Bāgh	146	Pi	27.30N	54.18 E
Hormuz, Strait of- (EN) = Hormoz, Tangeh-ye-	140	Hg	26.34N	56.15 E
Horn	110	Db	66.28N	22.30W
Horn	180	Fd	61.30N	118.00W
Horn [Aus.]	128	Jb	48.39N	15.39 E
Horn [Swe.]	116	Fg	57.54N	15.50 E
Horn, Cape- (EN) = Hornos, Cabo de-	198	Jk	55.59S	67.16W
Hornád	120	Qh	48.00N	20.58 E
Hornaday	180	Fc	69.22N	123.56W
Hornavan	114	Dc	66.14N	17.30 E
Hornbach	124	Je	49.12N	7.22 E
Horn-Bad Meinberg	124	Kc	51.54N	8.57 E
Hornby Bay	180	Fc	66.35N	117.50W
Horncastle	118	Mh	53.13N	0.07W
Horndal	116	Gd	60.18N	16.25 E
Horndean	124	Bd	50.55N	0.59W
Horne, Iles de- = Horn Islands (EN)	208	Jf	14.19S	178.05W
Hörnefors	114	Ee	63.38N	19.54 E
Hornell	184	Id	42.19N	77.39W
Hornepayne	180	Jg	49.13N	84.47W
Hornindalsvatn	116	Bc	61.55N	6.25 E
Hornisgrinde	120	Eh	48.36N	8.12 E
Horn Islands (EN) = Horne, Iles de-	208	Jf	14.19S	178.05W
Hörnli	128	Cc	47.23N	8.56 E
Hornomoravský úval	120	Ng	49.25N	17.20 E
Hornos, Cabo de- = Horn, Cape- (EN)	198	Jk	55.59S	67.16W
Hornoy-le-Bourg	124	De	49.51N	1.54 E
Horn Plateau	180	Fd	62.10N	119.30W
Hornsea	118	Mh	53.55N	0.10W
Hornslandet	116	Gc	61.40N	17.30 E
Horns Rev	116	Bi	55.30N	7.45 E
Hornsund	179	Nc	76.58N	15.28 E
Hornsundtind	179	Nc	76.55N	16.10 E
Horog	142	Jf	37.31N	71.33 E
Horoizumi	156a	Cb	42.01N	143.07 E
Horokanai	156a	Ca	44.02N	142.09 E
Horol	132	He	49.29N	33.49 E
Horol [Russia]	154	Lb	44.30N	132.03 E
Horol [Ukr.]	132	He	49.47N	33.16 E
Horonobe	154	Pb	45.00N	141.51 E
Hořovice	120	Jg	49.50N	13.54 E
Horqin Youyi Qianqi (Ulan Hot)	142	Oe	46.04N	122.00 E
Horqin Youyi Zhongqi (Bayan Huxu)	152	Lb	45.04N	121.27 E
Horqin Zuoyi Houqi (Ganjig)	152	Lc	42.57N	122.14 E
Horqin Zuoyi Zhongqi (Baokang)	152	Lc	44.06N	123.19 E
Horqueta	206	Ib	23.24S	56.53W
Horred	116	Eg	57.21N	12.28 E
Horse Creek [Co.-U.S.]	186	Eg	38.05N	103.19W
Horse Creek [U.S.]	188	Nf	41.57N	103.58W
Horsehead Lake	186	Gc	47.02N	99.47W
Horsens	114	Bi	55.52N	9.52 E
Horsham [Austl.]	210	Fh	36.43S	142.13 E
Horsham [Eng.-U.K.]	118	Mj	51.04N	0.21W
Hørsholm	116	Ei	55.53N	12.30 E
Horšovský Týn	120	Ig	49.32N	12.57 E
Horst	124	Ic	51.28N	6.03 E
Horst	124	Gd	50.56N	4.47 E
Hörstel	124	Jb	52.19N	7.35 E
Horstmar	124	Jb	52.05N	7.19 E
Horsunlu	130	Ll	37.55N	28.36 E
Horta	162	Bb	38.32N	28.28W
Horta [3]	162	Bb	38.35N	28.40W
Horta, Cap de l'- / Huertas, Cabo de-	126	Lf	38.21N	0.24W
Horten	116	De	59.25N	10.30 E
Horton	180	Ec	70.01N	126.42W
Hörvik	116	Fh	56.03N	14.46 E
Ḥorvot 'Avedat	146	Fg	30.48N	34.46 E
Ḥorvot Meẓada	146	Fg	31.19N	35.21 E
Horwood Lake	184	Fa	48.03N	82.20W
Hosaina	168	Fd	7.33N	37.52 E
Hose Mountains	150	Ff	2.00N	114.10 E
Hosenofu	164	De	23.34N	21.15 E
Hoseynābād [Iran]	146	Ne	34.30N	50.59 E
Hoseynābād [Iran]	146	Le	35.33N	47.08 E
Hoseynīyeh	146	Mg	32.42N	48.14 E
Hoshāb	148	Cc	26.01N	63.56 E
Hosingen	124	Id	50.01N	6.05 E
Hoskins	214	Ei	5.30S	150.32 E
Hospet	148	Fe	15.16N	76.24 E
Hospital, Cuchilla del-	204	Ej	31.40S	54.53W
Hospitalet del Infante / l'Hospitalet de l'Infant	126	Md	40.59N	0.56 E
Hospitalet de Llobregat	126	Oc	41.22N	2.08 E
Hoste, Isla-	198	Jk	55.15S	69.00W
Hot	148	Je	18.06N	98.35 E
Hotagen	114	De	63.53N	14.29 E
Hotaka	156	Ec	36.20N	137.53 E
Hotan	142	Jf	37.07N	79.55 E
Hotan He	140	Ke	40.30N	80.48 E
Hotazel	172	Ce	27.15S	23.00 E
Hotin	132	Ee	48.29N	26.29 E
Hoting	114	Dd	64.07N	16.10 E
Hotont	152	Hb	47.23N	102.30 E
Hot Springs	182	Gc	43.26N	103.29W
Hot Springs → Truth or Consequences	182	Fe	33.08N	107.15W
Hot Springs National Park	176	Jf	34.30N	93.03W
Hot Springs Peak	188	Gf	41.22N	117.26W
Hotspur Seamount (EN)	202	Kg	18.00S	36.00W
Hottah Lake	180	Fc	65.05N	118.36W
Hottentot Bay	172	Ae	26.07S	14.57 E
Hotton	124	Hd	50.16N	5.27 E
Hottstedt	120	He	51.39N	11.30 E
Houaïlou	216	Cd	21.17S	165.38 E
Houat, Ile de-	122	Dg	47.24N	2.58W
Houdan	122	Hf	48.47N	1.36 E
Houeillès	122	Gj	44.12N	0.02 E
Houffalize	124	Hd	50.08N	5.47 E
Houghton	182	Jb	47.06N	88.34W
Houillères, Canal des-	124	If	48.42N	6.55 E
Houji → Liangshan	154	Dg	35.48N	116.07 E
Houlgate	124	Be	49.18N	0.04W
Houlton	182	Nb	46.08N	67.51W
Houma [China]	152	Jd	35.36N	111.23 E
Houma [La.-U.S.]	182	If	29.36N	90.43W
Houndé	166	Ec	11.30N	3.31W
Hourn, Loch-	118	Hd	57.10N	5.40W
Hourtin, Étang d'-	122	Ei	45.10N	1.06W
House Range	188	Ig	39.30N	113.15W
Houston [Mo.-U.S.]	186	Kh	37.22N	91.58W
Houston [Tx.-U.S.]	176	Jg	29.46N	95.22W
Houthalen-Helchteren	124	Hc	51.02N	5.22 E
Houthulst	124	Ed	50.59N	2.57 E
Houthulst-Merkem	124	Ed	50.57N	2.51 E
Houtman Abrolhos	212	Ce	28.40S	113.50 E
Houtskär/Houtskari	116	Id	60.15N	21.20 E
Houtskari/Houtskär	116	Id	60.15N	21.20 E
Houyet	124	Hd	50.11N	5.01 E
Houyet-Celles	124	Hd	50.19N	5.01 E
Hov	116	Di	55.55N	10.16 E
Hova	116	Ff	58.52N	14.13 E
Hovden	116	Be	59.32N	7.21 E
Hovden	116	Ac	61.40N	4.50 E
Hove	118	Mk	50.49N	0.10W
Hovgaard	179	Kc	80.00N	18.45W
Hovmantorp	116	Fh	56.47N	15.08 E
Hovu-Aksy	138	Ef	51.01N	93.43 E
Howa	168	Db	17.30N	27.08 E
Howar	158	Jg	17.30N	27.08 E
Howard	186	Hd	44.01N	97.32W
Howe, Cape-	208	Fh	37.31S	149.59 E
Howell	184	Fd	42.36N	83.55W
Howick [N.Z.]	218	Fb	36.54S	174.56 E
Howick [S.Afr.]	172	Ee	29.28S	30.14 E
Howland	184	Mc	45.14N	68.40W
Howland Island	208	Jd	0.48N	176.38W
Howrah → Hāora	142	Kg	22.35N	88.20 E
Howth	118	Gh	53.23N	6.04W
Howz Soltān	146	Ne	35.06N	51.06 E
Hoxie	186	Fg	39.21N	100.26W
Höxter	120	Fe	51.46N	9.23 E
Hoxud	152	Ec	42.16N	86.51 E
Hoy	118	Jc	58.52N	3.18W
Hoya	124	Lb	52.48N	9.09 E
Høyanger	114	Bf	61.13N	6.05 E
Hoyerswerda/Wojerecy	120	Ke	51.26N	14.15 E
Hoyos	126	Fd	40.10N	6.43W
Höyo-Shotō	156	Ce	33.50N	132.30 E
Hoytiäinen	114	Ge	62.48N	29.39 E
Hozat	146	Hc	39.07N	39.14 E
Hpunhpu	148	Jc	26.42N	97.17 E
Hradec Králové	120	Lf	50.13N	15.50 E
Hradiště	120	Jf	50.13N	13.08 E
Hrami	132	Ni	41.20N	45.07 E
Hrastnik	128	Jd	46.09N	15.06 E
Hřebeny	120	Kg	49.50N	14.10 E
Hristinovka	132	Fe	48.53N	29.56 E
Hroma	138	Jb	71.30N	144.49 E
Hromtau	136	Fe	50.18N	58.35 E
Hron	120	Oi	47.49N	18.45 E
Hrubieszów	120	Tf	50.49N	23.55 E
Hrubý-Jeseník	120	Nf	50.05N	17.10 E
Hrustalny	138	Ih	44.24N	135.06 E
Hrvatska = Croatia (EN)	128	Jf	45.00N	15.30 E
Hrvatska = Croatia (EN)	110	Hf	45.00N	15.30 E
Hrvatska = Croatia (EN)	128	Je	45.00N	15.30 E
Ḥrvot Shivta	146	Fg	30.53N	34.38 E
Hsin-chiang-wei-wu-erh -Tzu-chih-ch'ü → Xinjiang Uygur Zizhiqu [2]	152	Ec	42.00N	86.00 E
Hsinchu	152	Lg	24.48N	120.58 E
Hsinying	152	Lg	23.25N	120.20 E
Hsipaw	148	Jd	22.37N	97.18 E
Hsi-tsang Tzu-chih-ch'ü → Xizang Zizhiqu [2]	152	Ee	32.00N	90.00 E
Hsuphāng	148	Jd	20.18N	98.42 E
Huab	172	Ad	20.49S	13.24 E
Huabei Pingyuan	140	Nf	37.00N	117.00 E
Huachacalla	202	Eg	18.45S	68.17W
Huachinera	192	Eb	30.15N	108.50W
Huacho	202	Cf	11.07S	77.37W
Huaco	206	Gd	30.09S	68.31W
Huacrachuco	202	Ce	8.39S	77.05W
Huade	152	Jc	41.50N	114.00 E
Huadian	152	Mc	42.59N	126.38 E

Hua Hin 148 Jf 12.34N 99.58 E
Huahine, Iles- 208 Lf 16.45 S 151.00W
Huahine Iti 221e Eb 16.45 S 151.00W
Huahine Nui 221e Eb 16.43 S 151.00W
Huahuapán 192 Ge 24.31N 105.57W
Huai'an 154 Eh 33.30N 119.08 E
Huai'an (Chaigoubu) 154 Cd 40.40N 114.25 E
Huaibei 152 Ke 33.56N 116.48 E
Huaibin (Wulongji) 154 Ci 32.27N 115.23 E
Huaide (Gongzhuling) 152 Lc 43.30N 124.52 E
Huaidian → Shenqiu 152 Ke 33.27N 115.05 E
Huai He 140 Nf 33.12N 118.33 E
Huaiji 152 Jg 23.57N 112.12 E
Huailai (Shacheng) 152 Kc 40.29N 115.30 E
Huainan 142 Nf 32.32N 116.59 E
Huaining (Shipai) 154 Di 30.25N 116.39 E
Huairen 152 Jd 39.50N 113.07 E
Huairou 154 Dd 40.20N 116.37 E
Huaiyang 154 Ch 33.44N 114.52 E
Huaiyin (Wangying) 154 Eh 33.35N 119.02 E
Huaiyuan 154 Dh 32.58N 117.10 E
Huajuapán de León 190 Ee 17.48N 97.46W
Hualalai 221a Fd 19.41N 155.52W
Hualapai Mountains 188 Ii 34.40N 113.45W
Hualien 152 Lg 23.58N 121.36 E
Huallaga, Río- 198 If 5.07 S 75.30W
Huallanca 202 Ce 8.49 S 77.52W
Huamachuco 202 Ce 7.48 S 78.04W
Huamahuaca 206 Gb 23.13 S 65.23W
Huambo 160 Ij 12.47 S 15.43 E
Huambo 170 Ce 12.30 S 15.40 E
Huanan 152 Nb 46.14N 130.33 E
Huancabamba [Peru] 202 Ce 5.14 S 79.28W
Huancabamba [Peru] 202 Cf 10.21 S 75.32W
Huancané 202 Eg 15.12 S 69.46W
Huancapi 202 Df 13.41 S 74.04W
Huancavelica 200 Ig 12.46 S 75.02W
Huancavelica 202 Df 13.00 S 75.00W
Huancayo 200 Ig 12.04 S 75.14W
Huanchaca, Serranía- 204 Bb 14.30 S 60.39W
Huang'an → Hong'an 154 Ci 31.17N 114.37 E
Huangcaoba → Xingyi 152 Hf 25.03N 104.55 E
Huangchuan 152 Ke 32.00N 115.02 E
Huanggang 154 Ci 30.27N 114.53 E
Huanggangliang 152 Kc 43.33N 117.32 E
Huanggang Shan 152 Kf 27.50N 117.47 E
Huanggi Hai 154 Bd 40.51N 113.17 E
Huang Hai = Yellow Sea (EN) 140 Of 36.00N 124.00 E
Huang He = Yellow River (EN) 140 Nf 37.32N 118.19 E
Huanghe Kou 154 Ef 37.54N 118.48 E
Huangheyan → Madoi 142 Lf 35.00N 98.56 E
Huanghua 154 De 38.23N 117.21 E
Huanghuashi 154 Bj 28.14N 113.11 E
Huangliu 152 Ih 18.41N 108.46 E
Huangmao Jian 152 Kf 27.55N 119.11 E
Huangmei 154 Ci 30.05N 115.56 E
Huangnihe 154 Ic 43.33N 127.28 E
Huangpi 154 Ci 30.53N 114.22 E
Huangpu 152 Jg 23.05N 113.25 E
Huang Shan 152 Ke 30.10N 118.10 E
Huangshi 142 Nf 30.12N 115.00 E
Huang Shui 152 Hd 36.05N 103.20 E
Huangtu Gaoyuan 140 Mf 37.00N 108.00 E
Huanguelén 204 Bm 37.02 S 61.57W
Huangxian 152 Ld 37.32N 120.30 E
Huangyan 152 Lf 28.39N 121.17 E
Huangyan Dao 150 Gc 15.05N 117.45 E
Huangyuan 152 Hd 36.40N 101.12 E
Huangzhai → Yangqu 154 Be 38.05N 112.37 E
Huangzhong 152 Hd 36.30N 101.30 E
Huanren 152 Mc 41.16N 125.22 E
Huan Shui 154 Ci 30.40N 114.21 E
Huanta 202 Df 12.56 S 74.15W
Huantai (Suozhen) 154 Ef 36.57N 118.05 E
Huánuco 200 If 9.55 S 76.14W
Huánuco 202 Ce 9.30 S 75.50W
Huanxian 152 Id 36.36N 107.06 E
Huaraz 200 If 9.32 S 77.32W
Huarmey 202 Cf 10.04 S 78.10W
Huarong 154 Bj 29.31N 112.33 E
Huascarán, Nevado- 198 If 9.07 S 77.37W
Huasco 206 Fc 28.28 S 71.14W
Huatabampo 190 Cc 26.50N 109.38W
Huatong 154 Fd 40.03N 121.56 E
Huatulco 48 Kj 15.44N 96.15W
Huatusco de Chicuéllar 192 Kh 19.09N 96.57W
Hauchinango 192 Jg 20.11N 98.03W
Huautla de Jiménez 192 Kh 18.08N 96.51W
Huaxian (Daokou) 154 Cg 35.33N 114.30 E
Huayllay 202 Cf 11.01 S 76.21W
Huaynamota, Río- 192 Gg 21.51N 104.42W
Huaytará 202 Cf 13.36 S 75.22W
Hubbard Creek Lake 186 Gj 32.45N 99.00W
Hubbard Lake 184 Fc 44.49N 83.34W
Hubei Sheng (Hu-pei Sheng) = Hupeh (EN) 152 Je 31.00N 112.00 E
Hubli-Dhārwār 142 Jh 15.21N 75.10 E
Hubsugul Nur (Chövsgöl Nuur) 140 Md 51.00N 100.30 E
Hückelhoven 124 Ic 51.03N 6.13 E
Hückeswagen 124 Jc 51.09N 7.21 E
Hucknall 118 Lh 53.02N 1.11W
Hucqueliers 124 Dd 55.03N 1.54 E
Huczwa 120 Tf 50.49N 23.59 E
Hudat [Azer.] 132 Pi 41.34N 48.43 E
Hudat [Eth.] 168 Fe 4.45N 39.27 E
Huddersfield 118 Lh 53.39N 1.47W
Huddinge 116 Ge 59.14N 17.59 E
Ḩuddun 168 Hd 9.08N 47.32 E
Huddur Hadama 168 Ge 4.07N 43.55 E
Hude (Oldenburg) 124 Ka 53.07N 8.28 E
Huder 152 Lb 49.59N 121.30 E
Hudiksvall 112 Hc 61.44N 17.07 E
Hudson 174 Le 40.42N 74.02W
Hudson [Fl.-U.S.] 184 Fk 28.22N 82.42W
Hudson [N.Y.-U.S.] 184 Kd 42.15N 73.47W
Hudson, Lake- 186 Ih 36.20N 95.05W
Hudson Bay 180 Hf 52.52N 102.23W
Hudson Bay 174 Kd 60.00N 86.00W
Hudson Canyon (EN) 184 Kf 39.27N 72.12W
Hudson Hope 180 Fe 56.02N 121.55W
Hudson Land 179 Jd 73.45N 22.30W
Hudson Mountains 222 Pf 74.32 S 99.20W
Hudson Strait 174 Li 62.30N 72.00W
Hudžirt 152 Hb 47.05N 102.45 E
Hue 142 Mh 16.28N 107.36 E
Huebra 126 Fc 41.02N 6.48W
Huechucuicui, Punta- 206 Ff 41.47 S 74.02W
Hueco Montains 186 Dj 32.05N 105.55W
Huedin 130 Gc 46.52N 23.03 E
Huehuetenango 190 Fe 15.20N 91.28W
Huehuetenango 194 Bf 15.40N 91.35W
Huejutla de Reyes 192 Jg 21.08N 98.25W
Huelgoat 122 Cf 48.22N 3.45W
Huelma 126 Ig 37.39N 3.27W
Huelva 112 Fh 37.16N 6.57W
Huelva 126 Fg 37.40N 7.00W
Huelva, Ribera de- 126 Gg 37.27N 6.00W
Huércal-Overa 126 Kg 37.23N 1.57W
Huerfano Mountain 186 Bh 36.30N 108.10W
Huertas, Cabo de- / Horta, Cap de l'- 126 Lf 38.21N 0.24W
Huerva 126 Lc 41.39N 0.52W
Huesca 126 Lb 42.08N 0.05W
Huesca 126 Lb 42.10N 0.10W
Huéscar 126 Jg 37.49N 2.32W
Hueso, Sierra del- 192 Gb 30.15N 105.20W
Huesos, Arroyo de los- 204 Cm 36.30 S 59.09W
Huetamo de Núñez 192 Ih 18.35N 100.53W
Huete 126 Jd 40.08N 2.41W
Huez 122 Mi 45.06N 6.04 E
Ḩufrat an Naḩās 168 Cd 9.45N 24.19 E
Huftarøy 116 Ad 60.05N 5.15 E
Hugh Butler Lake 186 Ff 40.22N 100.42W
Hughenden 210 Fg 20.51 S 144.12 E
Hughes 178 Ic 66.03N 154.16W
Hughes Range 188 Hb 49.55N 115.28W
Hugo 186 Ii 34.01N 95.31W
Huguan 154 Bf 36.05N 113.12 E
Huhur He 154 Fc 43.55N 120.47 E
Hui'an 152 Kf 25.07N 118.47 E
Huiarau Range 218 Gc 38.35 S 177.10 E
Huib-Hochplato 172 Be 27.10 S 16.50 E
Huichang 152 Kf 25.33N 115.45 E
Huicheng → Shexian 154 Ej 29.53N 118.27 E
Huicholes, Sierra de los- 192 Gf 22.00N 104.00W
Huich'ŏn 152 Mc 40.10N 126.17 E
Huifa He 154 Ic 43.06N 126.53 E
Hui He [China] 154 Be 39.21N 112.37 E
Hui He [China] 152 Kb 48.51N 119.12 E
Huiji He 154 Ch 33.53N 115.37 E
Huila 202 Cc 2.30N 75.45W
Huila 170 Ce 15.00 S 15.00 E
Huila, Nevado del- 198 Ie 3.00N 76.00W
Huilai 152 Kg 23.05N 116.18 E
Huili 152 Hf 26.37N 102.19 E
Huimanguillo 192 Mi 17.51N 93.23W
Huimin 152 Kd 37.29N 117.30 E
Huinan (Chaoyang) 154 Ic 42.41N 126.03 E
Huisne 122 Gg 47.59N 0.11 E
Huissen 124 Hc 51.56N 5.55 E
Huiten Nur 152 Fd 35.30N 91.55 E
Huittinen 116 Jc 61.11N 22.42 E
Huivuilay, Isla de- 192 Dd 27.03N 110.01W
Huixian [China] 152 Ie 33.46N 106.06 E
Huixian [China] 154 Bg 35.27N 113.47 E
Huixtla 190 Fe 15.09N 92.28W
Huize 152 Hf 26.28N 103.18 E
Huizen 124 Hb 52.18N 5.16 E
Huizhou 152 Jg 23.02N 114.28 E
Hukou 154 Dj 29.44N 116.14 E
Hu Kou 152 Jd 36.09N 110.20 E
Hŭksan-Chedo 152 Me 34.30N 125.20 E
Hukuntsi 172 Cd 23.59 S 21.44 E
Hulah Lake 186 Hh 36.58N 96.10W
Hulan 152 Mb 46.03N 126.36 E
Hulan He 152 Mb 45.54N 126.42 E
Ḩulayfā' 144 Fd 26.00N 40.47 E
Hulett 188 Md 44.41N 104.36W
Hulga 134 Jd 64.15N 60.58 E
Hulin 152 Nb 45.52N 132.58 E
Hulin He 154 Hb 45.19N 124.06 E
Hull 180 Jg 45.26N 75.43W
Hull → Kingston upon Hull 112 Fe 53.45N 0.20W
Hull → Orona Atoll 208 Je 4.29 S 172.10W
Hull Bay 222 Nf 74.55 S 137.40W
Hull Glacier 222 Nf 75.05 S 137.15W
Hull Mountain 188 Dg 39.31N 122.59W
Hüls, Krefeld- 124 Ic 51.22N 6.31 E
Hulst 124 Gc 51.17N 4.04 E
Hultsfred 114 Dh 57.29N 15.50 E
Huludao 152 Lc 40.44N 120.59 E
Hulun Nur 140 Ne 49.00N 117.30 E
Ḩulwān = Helwān (EN) 164 Fd 29.51N 31.20 E
Hulwāt, Qūr al- 146 Hh 28.49N 38.50 E
Huma [China] 152 Ma 51.44N 126.36 E
Huma [Ton.] 221b Bc 21.19 S 174.56W
Humacao 194 Od 18.09N 65.50W
Huma He 152 Ma 51.42N 126.42 E
Humaitá [Braz.] 200 Jf 7.31 S 63.02W
Humaitá [Par.] 206 Ic 27.03 S 58.33W
Humansdorp 172 Cf 34.02 S 24.46 E
Humbe 170 Bf 16.42 S 14.54 E
Humber 110 Fe 53.40N 0.10W
Humberside 118 Mh 53.55N 0.30W
Humberto de Campos 202 Jd 2.37 S 43.27W
Humboldt 216 Cd 21.53 S 166.25 E
Humboldt [Ia.-U.S.] 186 Ie 42.43N 94.13W
Humboldt [Nb.-U.S.] 186 If 40.10N 95.57W
Humboldt [Sask.-Can.] 180 Gf 52.12N 105.07W
Humboldt [Tn.-U.S.] 184 Ch 35.49N 88.55W
Humboldt Gletscher 179 Fc 79.40N 63.45W
Humboldt Range 188 Ff 40.15N 118.10W
Humboldt River 174 He 40.02N 118.31W
Hume, Lake- 212 Jg 36.05 S 147.05 E
Humenné 120 Rh 48.56N 21.55 E
Hummelfjell 116 Db 62.27N 11.17 E
Hümmling, Der- 120 Dd 52.52N 7.31 E
Humphreys Peak 174 Hf 35.20N 111.40W
Humppila 114 Ff 60.56N 23.22 E
Humuya, Río- 194 Df 15.13N 87.57W
Hūn 160 If 29.07N 15.56 E
Húnaflói 110 Db 65.50N 20.50W
Hunan Sheng (Hu-nan Sheng) 152 Jf 28.00N 112.00 E
Hu-nan Sheng → Hunan Sheng 152 Jf 28.00N 112.00 E
Hunchun 154 Kc 42.52N 130.21 E
Hundested 116 Di 55.58N 11.52 E
Hunedoara 130 Fd 45.45N 22.54 E
Hunedoara 130 Fd 45.45N 22.52 E
Hünfeld 120 Ff 50.40N 9.46 E
Hünfelden 124 Kd 50.19N 8.11 E
Hunga Ha'apai 221b Ab 20.33 S 175.24W
Hungary (EN) = Magyarország 112 Hf 47.00N 20.00 E
Hunga Tonga 221b Ab 20.32 S 175.23W
Hungen 124 Kd 50.28N 8.54 E
Hŭngnam 152 Md 39.50N 127.38 E
Hungry Horse Reservoir 188 Ib 48.15N 113.50W
Hun He [China] 154 Gd 40.41N 122.12 E
Hun He [China] 154 Be 39.47N 113.15 E
Hunish, Rubha- 118 Gd 57.43N 6.20W
Hunjiang 152 Mc 41.55N 126.27 E
Hun Jiang 154 Hd 40.52N 125.42 E
Hunneberg 116 Ef 58.20N 12.27 E
Hunnebostrand 116 Df 58.27N 11.18 E
Hunsrück 120 Dg 49.50N 7.10 E
Hunstanton 118 Ni 52.57N 0.30 E
Hunte 120 Ec 53.14N 8.20 E
Hunter, Ile- 208 Ig 22.24 S 172.03 E
Hunter Island 212 Ih 40.30 S 144.45 E
Hunter Ridge (EN) 208 Ig 21.30 S 174.30 E
Hunter River 212 Kf 32.30 S 151.42 E
Hunterville 218 Fc 39.56 S 175.34 E
Huntingdon 118 Mi 52.30N 0.10W
Huntingdon [Eng.-U.K.] 118 Mi 52.20N 0.12W
Huntingdon [Pa.-U.S.] 184 He 40.31N 78.02W
Huntingdon [Que.-Can.] 184 Jc 45.05N 74.08W
Huntington [In.-U.S.] 184 Ee 40.53N 85.30W
Huntington [W.V.-U.S.] 182 Kd 38.24N 82.26W
Huntly [N.Z.] 218 Fb 37.33 S 175.10 E
Huntly [Scot.-U.K.] 118 Kd 57.27N 2.47W
Huntsville [Al.-U.S.] 176 Kf 34.44N 86.35W
Huntsville [Ont.-Can.] 180 Jg 45.20N 79.13W
Huntsville [Tx.-U.S.] 182 He 30.43N 95.33W
Hunucmá 192 Og 21.01N 89.52W
Hünxe 124 Ic 51.39N 6.47 E
Hunyani 172 Ec 15.37 S 30.39 E
Hunyuan 152 Jd 39.38N 113.44 E
Hunza → Baltit 148 Ea 36.20N 74.40 E
Hunze 122 Ma 53.13N 6.40 E
Huocheng (Shuiding) 152 Dc 44.03N 80.49 E
Huojia 154 Bg 35.16N 113.39 E
Huolongmen 152 Mb 49.49N 125.49 E
Huolu 154 Ce 38.05N 114.18 E
Huon, Ile- 208 Hf 18.01 S 162.57 E
Huon Gulf 212 Ja 7.10 S 147.25 E
Huon Peninsula 214 Di 6.25 S 147.30 E
Huonville 212 Jh 43.01 S 147.02 E
Huoqin 154 Dh 32.21N 116.17 E
Huoshan 152 Ke 31.19N 116.20 E
Huo Shan [China] 152 Ke 31.06N 116.12 E
Huo Shan [China] 152 Jd 37.00N 111.52 E
Huoxian 152 Jd 36.39N 111.47 E
Hupeh (EN) = Hubei Sheng (Hu-pei Sheng) 152 Je 31.00N 112.00 E
Hu-pei Sheng → Hubei Sheng = Hopeh (EN) 152 Je 31.00N 112.00 E
Hūr 146 Qg 30.50N 57.07 E
Hurama → Hongyuan 152 He 32.45N 102.38 E
Hurānd 146 Lc 38.40N 47.20 E
Hurd, Cape- 184 Gc 45.13N 81.44W
Hurdalssjøen 116 Dd 60.20N 11.05 E
Hurd Deep = La Grande Trench (EN) 118 Kl 49.40N 3.00W
Hurdiyo 168 Ic 10.32N 51.08 E
Hurepoix 122 If 48.30N 2.10 E
Hure Qi 154 Fc 42.44N 121.44 E
Hurkett 186 Lb 48.50N 88.29W
Hurmuli 138 If 51.01N 136.56 E
Huron 182 Hc 44.22N 98.13W
Huron, Lake- 174 Ke 44.30N 82.15W
Huron Mountains 184 Db 46.45N 87.45W
Hurricane 188 Ih 37.11N 113.17W
Hurricane Cliffs 188 Ih 37.00N 113.05W
Hurrungane 116 Bc 61.27N 7.51 E
Hursley 124 Ac 51.01N 1.24W
Hurst 186 Hj 32.49N 97.09W
Hurstpierpoint 124 Bd 50.55N 0.10W
Hürth 120 Cf 50.52N 6.52 E
Hurum 116 De 59.35N 10.35 E
Hurunui 218 Ee 42.54 S 173.18 E
Hurup 116 Ch 56.45N 8.25 E
Húsavík 114a Ca 66.03N 17.21W
Hushan → Cixi 154 Fi 30.10N 121.14 E
Huşi 130 Lc 46.41N 28.04 E
Huskvarna 116 Fg 57.48N 14.16 E
Huslia 178 Hc 65.42N 156.25W
Husnes 116 Ae 59.52N 5.46 E
Husnesfjorden 116 Ae 59.50N 5.35 E
Hussigny-Godbrange 124 He 49.29N 5.52 E
Hust 132 Ce 48.10N 23.27 E
Hustadvika 116 Ba 63.00N 7.05 E
Husum [Ger.] 120 Fb 54.28N 9.03 E
Husum [Swe.] 114 Ee 63.20N 19.10 E
Hutag 152 Hb 49.23N 102.43 E
Hutchinson [Ks.-U.S.] 182 Hd 38.05N 97.56W
Hutchinson [Mn.-U.S.] 186 Id 44.54N 94.22W
Hutch Mountain 188 Ji 34.47N 111.22W
Ḩūth 164 Hf 16.14N 43.58 E
Hutou 152 Nb 46.00N 133.36 E
Hutte Sauvage, Lac de la- 180 Ke 55.57N 65.45W
Hutton, Mount- 212 Je 25.51 S 148.20 E
Hutubi 152 Ec 44.07N 86.57 E
Hutuiti, Caleta- 221d Bb 27.07 S 109.17W
Hutuo He 154 De 38.14N 116.05 E
Huvhojtun, gora- 138 Le 57.44N 160.45 E
Huxley, Mount- 218 Cf 44.04 S 169.41 E
Huy 120 Ge 51.55N 10.55 E
Huy/Hoei 122 Ld 50.31N 5.14 E
Huzgan 146 Mg 31.27N 48.04 E
Huzhou → Wuxing 152 Le 30.47N 120.07 E
Hvaler 116 De 59.05N 11.00 E
Hvalynsk 136 Ee 52.30N 48.07 E
Hvammstangi 114a Bb 65.24N 20.57W
Hvannadalshnúkur 110 Ec 64.01N 16.41W
Hvar 128 Kg 43.11N 16.27 E
Hvar 128 Kg 43.07N 16.45 E
Hvarski kanal 128 Kg 43.15N 16.37 E
Hvatovka 132 Oc 52.21N 46.36 E
Hveragerdi 114a Bb 64.00N 21.12W
Hveravellir 114a Bb 64.54N 19.35W
Hvide Sande 116 Ci 55.59N 8.08 E
Hvítá [Ice.] 114a Bb 64.35N 21.46W
Hvítá [Ice.] 114a Bb 64.00N 20.58W
Hvittingfoss 116 De 59.29N 10.01 E
Hvojnaja 114 Ig 58.56N 34.31 E
Hwach'on-ni 154 Ie 38.58N 126.02 E
Hwange 160 Jj 18.21 S 26.30 E
Hwang-Hae = Yellow Sea (EN) 140 Of 36.00N 124.00 E
Hwanghae-Namdo 154 He 38.15N 125.30 E
Hwanghae-Pukto 154 Ie 38.30N 126.25 E
Hwangju 154 He 38.40N 125.45 E
Hyannis [Ma.-U.S.] 184 Le 41.39N 70.17W
Hyannis [Nb.-U.S.] 186 Ff 42.00N 101.44W
Hybo 116 Gc 61.48N 16.12 E
Hyde Park 196 Gi 6.30N 58.16W
Hyderābād [India] 142 Jh 17.23N 78.28 E
Hyderābād [Pak.] 142 Ig 25.22N 68.22 E
Hyères 122 Mk 43.07N 6.07 E
Hyères, Iles d'- 122 Ml 43.00N 6.20 E
Hyesan 152 Mc 41.24N 128.10 E
Hyltebruk 114 Ch 57.00N 13.14 E
Hyndman Peak 188 He 43.50N 114.10W
Hyōgo Ken 154 Mg 34.50N 134.48 E
Hyrov 120 Sg 49.32N 22.48 E
Hyrum 188 Jf 41.38N 111.51W
Hyrylä 116 Kd 60.24N 25.02 E
Hyrynsalmi 114 Gd 64.40N 28.32 E
Hysham 188 Lc 46.18N 107.14W
Hythe [Eng.-U.K.] 124 Ad 50.52N 1.24W
Hythe [Eng.-U.K.] 118 Oj 51.05N 1.05 E
Hyūga 154 Kh 32.25N 131.38 E
Hyūga-Nada 156 Be 32.25N 131.45 E
Hyvinge/Hyvinkää 114 Ff 60.38N 24.52 E
Hyvinkää/Hyvinge 114 Ff 60.38N 24.52 E

I

Iaco, Rio- 202 Ee 9.03 S 68.35W
Iacobeni 130 Ib 47.26N 25.19 E
Iakora 172 Hd 23.08 S 46.38 E
Ialomiţa 130 Ke 44.30N 27.30 E
Ialomiţa 130 Ke 44.42N 27.51 E
Ialomiţei, Balta- 130 Ke 44.30N 28.00 E
Iapó, Rio- 204 Gg 24.30 S 50.24W
Iaşi 112 If 47.10N 27.36 E
Iaşi 130 Kb 47.07N 27.39 E
Iba 150 Gc 15.20N 119.58 E
Ibadan 160 Hh 7.23N 3.54 E
Ibagué 200 Ie 4.27N 75.14W
Ibaiti 206 Jb 23.50 S 50.10W
Iballja 130 Cg 42.11N 20.00 E
Ibañeta, Puerto de- → Roncesvalles, Puerto de- 126 Ka 43.01N 1.19W
Ibans, Laguna de- 194 Ef 15.53N 84.52W
Ibar 130 Df 43.44N 20.45 E
Ibara 156 Cd 34.36N 133.28 E
Ibaraki 156 Dd 34.49N 135.34 E
Ibaraki Ken 154 Pf 36.25N 140.30 E
Ibaré 204 Ej 30.49 S 54.16W
Ibarra 200 Ie 0.21N 78.07W
Ibarreta 206 Ic 25.13 S 59.51W
Ibb 142 Gh 13.58N 44.12 E
Ibba 168 De 4.48N 29.06 E
Ibba 168 Dd 7.09N 28.41 E
Ibbenbüren 120 Dd 52.16N 7.44 E
Ibdekkene 166 Fb 18.28N 0.38 E
Ibembo 170 Db 2.38N 23.37 E
Ibenga 170 Cb 2.20N 18.08 E
Iberá, Esteros del- 204 Di 28.05 S 57.05W
Iberá, Laguna- 204 Di 28.30 S 57.09W
Iberian Basin (EN) 106 De 40.00N 16.00W
Iberian Mountains (EN) = Ibérica, Cordillera- 110 Fg 41.30N 2.30W
Iberian Peninsula (EN) = Península Ibérica 110 Fg 40.00N 4.00W
Ibérica, Cordillera- = Iberian Mountains (EN) 110 Fg 41.30N 2.30W
Iberville, Lac d' - 180 Ke 56.00N 73.10W
Ibestad 114 Db 68.48N 17.08 E
Ibi [Nig.] 166 Gd 8.11N 9.45 E
Ibi [Sp.] 126 Lf 38.38N 0.34W
Ibiá 202 Ig 19.29 S 46.32W
Ibiagui 204 Ja 13.03 S 44.12W
Ibiaí 204 Jc 16.51 S 44.55W
Ibibobo 202 Fh 21.35 S 62.58W
Ibicaraí 202 Kf 14.51 S 39.36W
Ibicuí, Rio- 198 Kh 29.25 S 56.47W
Ibicuí da Armada, Rio- 204 Ej 30.16 S 54.54W
Ibicuy 204 Ck 33.44 S 59.10W
Ibicuy, Río- 204 Ck 33.48 S 59.10W
Ibigawa 156 Ed 35.29N 136.34 E
Ibipetuba 202 Jf 11.00 S 44.32W
Ibiraiaras 204 Gi 28.22 S 51.39W
Ibirama 204 Hh 27.04 S 49.31W
Ibirapuitã, Rio- 204 Ei 29.22 S 55.57W
Ibirocai, Arroio- 204 Di 29.26 S 56.43W
Ibiruba 204 Fi 28.38 S 53.06W
Ibitinga 204 He 21.45 S 48.49W
Ibitinga, Represa- 204 He 21.41 S 49.05W
Ibity 172 Hd 20.10 S 46.58 E
Ibiza/Eivissa = Iviza (EN) 110 Gh 39.00N 1.25 E
Ibiza / La Vila d'Eivissa 126 Nf 38.54N 1.26 E
Iblei, Monti- 128 Im 37.10N 14.55 E
Ibn Hāni', Ra's- 146 Fe 35.35N 35.43 E
Ibn Qawrah 168 Ib 15.43N 50.32 E
Ibo 172 Gb 12.22 S 40.36 E
Ibo-Gawa 156 Dd 34.46N 134.35 E
Iboundji, Mont- 170 Bc 1.08 S 11.48 E
Ibrā' 144 Ie 22.38N 58.40 E
Ibrah 168 Dc 10.36N 25.20 E
Ibrāhīm, Jabal- 140 Gg 20.27N 41.09 E
Ibresi 114 Li 55.18N 47.05 E
'Ibrī 144 Ie 23.16N 56.32 E
Ibrīm 164 Fe 22.39N 32.05 E
Ibshawāy 146 Dh 29.22N 30.41 E
Ibuki-Sanchi 156 Ed 35.35N 136.25 E
Ibuki-Yama 156 Ed 35.25N 136.24 E
Ibusuki 154 Ki 31.16N 130.39 E
Ič̌a 138 Ke 55.28N 155.58 E
Ica 200 Ig 14.04 S 75.42W
Ica 202 Cf 14.20 S 75.30W
Içá, Rio- 198 Jf 3.07 S 67.58W
Icaiché 192 Oh 18.05N 89.10W
Icamaquã, Rio- 204 Ei 28.34 S 56.00W
Icana, Rio- 202 Ec 0.26N 67.19W
Icara 204 Hi 28.42 S 49.18W
Icaraíma 204 Ff 23.23S 53.41W
İçel 144 Db 36.48N 34.38 E
Iceland (EN) = Island 110 Eb 65.00N 18.00W
Iceland Basin (EN) 110 Dc 60.00N 20.00W
Ichalkaranji 148 Ee 16.42N 74.28 E
Ichibusa-Yama 156 Be 32.19N 131.06 E
Ichihara 154 Pg 35.31N 140.05 E
Ichikawa 156 Fd 35.44N 139.55 E
Ichi-Kawa 156 Dd 34.46N 134.43 E
Ichinohe 154 Pd 40.13N 141.17 E
Ichinomiya 154 Ng 35.18N 136.48 E
Ichinoseki 154 Pe 38.55N 141.08 E
Ich'ŏn [N.Kor.] 154 Ie 38.29N 126.53 E
Ich'ŏn [S.Kor.] 154 If 37.17N 127.27 E
Ichtegem 124 Fc 51.06N 3.00 E
Ičigemski hrebet 138 Ld 63.30N 164.00 E
Ičinskaja Sopka, vulkan- 140 Rd 55.39N 157.40 E
Ičnja 136 De 50.52N 32.25 E
Icó 202 Ke 6.24 S 38.51W
Icy Cape 178 Gb 70.20N 161.52W
Idaarderadeel 124 Ha 53.06N 5.50 E
Idaarderadeel-Grow 124 Ha 53.06N 5.50 E
Idabel 186 Ij 33.54N 94.50W
Idah 166 Gd 7.06N 6.44 E
Idaho 182 Ec 45.00N 115.00W
Idaho Falls 176 He 43.30N 112.02W
Idalia 186 Eg 39.43N 102.14W
Idān 168 Hd 6.03N 49.01 E
Idanha-a-Nova 126 Ee 39.55N 7.14W
Idar-Oberstein 120 Dg 49.42N 7.18 E
Idarwald 124 Je 49.50N 7.13 E
Idel 114 Id 64.08N 34.12 E
Ideles 162 Ie 23.49N 5.55 E
Ider 152 Hb 49.16N 100.41 E
Idfū 164 Fe 24.58N 32.52 E
Idhi Óros 110 Ih 35.15N 24.45 E
Idhra 130 Gl 37.21N 23.28 E
Idhra 130 Gl 37.20N 23.30 E
Idhras, Kólpos- 130 Gl 37.22N 23.22 E
Idice 128 Ff 44.35N 11.49 E
İdil 146 Id 37.21N 41.54 E
Idīni 162 Df 17.58N 15.40W
Idiofa 170 Cc 4.59 S 19.36 E
Idjil, Kédia d'- 162 Ee 22.38N 12.33W
Idkerberget 116 Fd 60.23N 15.14 E
Idle 118 Mh 53.27N 0.48W
Idlib 144 Eb 35.55N 36.38 E
Idokogo 170 Ab 0.35N 9.19 E
Idolo, Isla del- 192 Kg 21.25N 97.27W
Idre 116 Ec 61.52N 12.43 E
Idrica 116 Mh 56.18N 28.55 E
Idrija 128 Id 46.00N 14.02 E
Idro, Lago d'- 128 Ee 45.47N 10.30 E
Idstein 120 Ef 50.14N 8.16 E
Idževan 132 Ni 40.52N 45.04 E
Iecava 116 Kh 56.33N 24.11 E
Iecava 116 Jh 56.40N 23.40 E
Iepê 204 Gf 22.40 S 51.05W
Ieper/Ypres 122 Id 50.51N 2.53 E
Ierápetra 130 In 35.01N 25.45 E
Ierisós 130 Gi 40.24N 23.53 E
Ierisoú, Kólpos- 130 Gi 40.26N 23.55 E
Iernut 130 Hc 46.27N 24.15 E
Ie-Shima 156b Ab 26.43N 127.47 E
Ieshima-Shotō 156 Dd 34.40N 134.30 E
Iesolo 128 Ge 45.32N 12.38 E
Iezerul, Vîrful- 130 Hd 45.28N 24.57 E
Ifakara 170 Gd 8.08 S 36.41 E
Ifaki 166 Gd 7.48N 5.14 E
'Ifāl, Wādī al- 146 Fh 28.07N 35.02 E
Ifalik Atoll 208 Fd 7.15N 144.27 E
Ifanadiana 172 Hd 21.17 S 47.35 E
Ife 166 Fd 7.28N 4.34 E
Iferouâne 160 Hg 19.04N 8.24 E
Ifetesene 162 Hd 25.30N 4.33 E
Ifni 162 Ed 29.15N 10.08W
Ifon 166 Gd 6.58N 5.55 E
Iforas, Adrar des- 158 Hg 19.00N 2.00 E
Iga 156 Ed 34.49N 136.12 E
Igal 120 Nj 46.32N 17.57 E
Iganga 170 Fb 0.37N 33.29 E
Igara Paraná, Río- 202 Dd 2.09 S 71.47W

Index Symbols

- 1 Independent Nation
- 2 State, Region
- 3 District, County
- 4 Municipality
- 5 Colony, Dependency
- Continent
- Physical Region
- Historical or Cultural Region
- Mount, Mountain
- Volcano
- Hill
- Mountains, Mountain Range
- Hills, Escarpment
- Plateau, Upland
- Pass, Gap
- Plain, Lowland
- Delta
- Salt Flat
- Valley, Canyon
- Crater, Cave
- Karst Features
- Depression
- Polder
- Desert, Dunes
- Forest, Woods
- Heath, Steppe
- Oasis
- Cape, Point
- Coast, Beach
- Cliff
- Peninsula
- Isthmus
- Sandbank
- Island
- Atoll
- Rock, Reef
- Islands, Archipelago
- Rocks, Reefs
- Coral Reef
- Well, Spring
- Geyser
- River, Stream
- Waterfall, Rapids
- River Mouth, Estuary
- Lake
- Salt Lake
- Intermittent Lake
- Reservoir
- Swamp, Pond
- Canal
- Glacier
- Ice Shelf, Pack Ice
- Ocean
- Sea
- Gulf, Bay
- Strait, Fjord
- Lagoon
- Bank
- Seamount
- Tablemount
- Ridge
- Shelf
- Basin
- Escarpment, Sea Scarp
- Fracture
- Trench, Abyss
- National Park, Reserve
- Point of Interest
- Recreation Site
- Cave, Cavern
- Historic Site
- Ruins
- Wall, Walls
- Church, Abbey
- Temple
- Scientific Station
- Railway station
- Airport
- Port
- Military installation
- Lighthouse
- Mine
- Tunnel
- Dam, Bridge

Igarapava	204	Ie	20.03S	47.47W
Igarapé-Açu	202	Id	1.07S	47.37W
Igarapé-Miri	202	Id	1.59S	48.58W
Igarka	142	Kc	67.28N	86.35 E
Igatimí	206	Ib	24.05S	55.30W
Igawa	170	Fd	8.46S	34.23 E
Igbetti	166	Fd	8.45N	4.08 E
Iğdır	146	Kc	39.56N	44.02 E
Iggesund	114	Df	61.38N	17.04 E
Iglesias	128	Ck	39.19N	8.32 E
Iglesiente	128	Ck	39.20N	8.40 E
Igli	162	Gc	30.27N	2.18W
Iglino	134	Hi	54.50N	56.28 E
Igloolik	176	Kc	69.24N	81.49W
Ignace	180	Ig	49.26N	91.41W
Ignalina	114	Gi	55.22N	26.13 E
Ignatovo	114	If	60.49N	37.48 E
Iğneada	146	Bb	41.50N	27.58 E
Iğneada Burun	130	Lh	41.54N	28.03 E
Igombe	170	Fc	4.25S	31.58 E
Igoumenítsa	130	Dj	39.30N	20.16 E
Igra	136	Fd	57.33N	53.10 E
Igreja, Morro de-	204	Hi	28.08S	49.30W
Igren	132	Ie	48.29N	35.13 E
Igrim	136	Gc	63.12N	64.29 E
Iguaçu, Rio-	198	Kh	25.36S	54.36W
Igualada	126	Nc	41.35N	1.38 E
Iguala de la Independencia	190	Ee	18.21N	99.32W
Iguana, Sierra de la-	192	Id	26.30N	100.15W
Iguape	204	Ig	24.43S	47.33W
Iguariaça, Serra do-	204	Ei	29.03S	55.15W
Iguassu Falls (EN)=Iguazú, Cataratas del-	198	Kh	25.41S	54.26W
Iguatemi	202	Hh	23.35S	54.30W
Iguatemi, Rio-	204	Ef	23.55S	54.10W
Iguatu	200	Mf	6.22S	39.18W
Iguazú, Cataratas del- = Iguassu Falls (EN)	198	Kh	25.41S	54.26W
Iguéla	170	Ac	1.55S	9.19 E
Iguidi, 'Erg-	158	Gf	27.00N	6.00W
Iharagna	172	Ib	13.22S	50.00 E
Ihavandiffulu Atoll	148a	Ba	7.00N	72.55 E
Iheya-Jima	156b	Ab	27.03N	127.57 E
Ih-Hajrhan	152	Ib	46.56N	105.56 E
Ihiala	166	Gd	5.51N	6.51 E
Ihirene	162	He	20.28N	4.37 E
Ihnāsiyat al Madīnah	146	Dh	29.05N	30.56 E
Ih-Obo-Ula	152	Gc	44.55N	95.20 E
Ihosy	160	Lk	22.25S	46.07 E
Ihotry, Lac-	172	Gd	21.56S	43.41 E
Ihrhove, Westoverledingen-	124	Ja	53.10N	7.27 E
Ihsaniye	146	Dc	36.55N	34.46 E
Ihtiman	130	Gg	42.26N	23.49 E
Ih-Ula	152	Hb	49.27N	101.27 E
Ii	114	Fd	65.19N	25.27 E
Iida	154	Ng	35.31N	137.50 E
Iide-San	156	Fc	37.52N	139.41 E
Iijoki	114	Fd	65.20N	25.17 E
Iisaku/Isaku	116	Le	59.14N	27.41 E
Iisalmi	114	Ge	63.34N	27.11 E
Iisvesi	116	Lb	62.45N	26.50 E
Iittala	116	Kc	61.04N	24.10 E
Iivaara	114	Gd	65.47N	29.40 E
Iiyama	156	Fc	36.52N	138.20 E
Iizuka	156	Be	33.38N	130.41 E
Ija	138	Fe	55.02N	101.00 E
Ijebu Ode	166	Fd	6.49N	3.56 E
IJmuiden, Velsen-	124	Gb	52.28N	4.35 E
Ijoubbâne, 'Erg-	166	Da	22.30N	6.00W
IJssel	122	Lb	52.30N	5.50 E
IJsselmeer	122	Lb	52.45N	5.25 E
IJsselmuiden	124	Hb	52.34N	5.56 E
IJsselstein	124	Hb	52.01N	5.02 E
Ijuí	206	Jc	28.23S	53.55W
Ijuí, Rio-	204	Eh	27.58S	55.20W
Ijūin	156	Bf	31.37N	130.24 E
Ijuízinho, Rio-	204	Ei	28.20S	54.28W
Ijuw	220e	Bb	0.31S	166.57 E
Ijzendijke	124	Fc	51.20N	3.37 E
IJzer	122	Ic	51.09N	2.43 E
Ik	110	Ld	55.55N	52.36 E
Ikaalinen	114	Ff	61.46N	23.03 E
Ikalamavony	172	Hd	21.10S	46.32 E
Ikamatua	218	De	42.17S	171.42 E
Ikaria	130	Jl	37.35N	26.10 E
Ikarion Pélagos	130	Jl	37.30N	26.35 E
Ikast	116	Ch	56.08N	9.10 E
Ikatski hrebet	138	Gf	54.00N	111.15 E
Ikawa	156	Fd	35.13N	138.14 E
Ikeda [Jap.]	156	Cd	34.01N	133.48 E
Ikeda [Jap.]	152	Pc	42.55N	143.27 E
Ikeda-Ko	156	Bf	31.14N	130.34 E
Ikej	138	Ff	54.12N	100.04 E
Ikeja	166	Fd	6.36N	3.21 E
Ikela	160	Ji	1.11S	23.16 E
Ikelemba	170	Cb	0.07N	18.17 E
Ikerre	166	Gd	7.30N	5.14 E
Ikerssuaq	179	Ie	65.10N	39.45W
Iki	156	Ae	33.45N	129.45 E
Iki-Kàikyō	154	Jh	33.45N	129.50 E
Ikitsuki-Shima	156	Ae	33.25N	129.25 E
İkizdere	146	Ib	40.47N	40.33 E
Ikom	166	Gd	5.58N	8.42 E
Ikongo [Mad.]	172	Hd	21.53S	48.26 E
Ikongo [Tan.]	170	Gd	9.04S	36.51 E
Ikopa	172	Hc	16.50S	46.50 E
Ikot Ekpene	166	Gd	5.10N	7.43 E
Ikuno	156	Dd	35.10N	134.48 E
Ikurangi, Mount-	220p	Bb	21.12S	159.45W
Ila	166	Fd	7.40N	4.40 E
Ilaferh	162	He	21.50N	1.20 E
Ilagan	142	Oh	17.10N	121.54 E
Ilām [3]	144	Gc	33.00N	47.00 E
Ilām [Iran]	144	Gc	33.38N	46.26 E
Ilām [Nep.]	148	Hc	26.54N	87.56 E
Ilan	152	Lg	24.45N	121.44 E
Ilanski	138	Ee	56.10N	96.03 E
Ilaro	166	Fd	6.53N	3.01 E
Iława	120	Pc	53.37N	19.33 E
Ilbengja	138	Hd	62.55N	124.10 E
Ile-à-la-Crosse	180	Ge	55.27N	107.53W
Ilebo	160	Ji	4.44S	20.33 E
Ile-de-France	122	Ie	49.00N	2.20 E
Ile de France	179	Kc	77.45N	27.45W
Ile-de-France, Côte de l'-	122	Jf	48.55N	3.50 E
Ilek	136	Fe	51.32N	53.27 E
Ilek	110	Le	51.30N	53.20 E
Ileksa	114	Ie	62.30N	36.57 E
Ilerh	162	He	21.40N	2.22 E
Ile Rousse, L'-	122a	Aa	42.38N	8.56 E
Ileša	114	Le	62.37N	46.35 E
Ilesha [Nig.]	166	Fd	8.55N	3.25 E
Ilesha [Nig.]	166	Fd	7.37N	4.44 E
Ilet	114	Li	55.57N	48.14 E
Ilfracombe	118	Ij	51.13N	4.08W
Ilgaz	146	Eb	40.56N	33.38 E
Ilgaz Dağları	146	Eb	41.00N	33.35 E
Ilgın	146	Dc	38.17N	31.55 E
Ilha Grande	202	Ed	0.27S	65.02W
Ilha Grande, Baía da-	204	Jf	23.09S	44.30W
Ílhavo	126	Dd	40.36N	8.40W
Ilhéus	200	Mg	14.49S	39.02W
Ili	140	Je	45.24N	74.08 E
Ilia	130	Fd	45.56N	22.39 E
Iliamna	178	Ie	59.45N	154.54W
Iliamna Lake	178	He	59.30N	155.00W
Ilič	135	Gd	40.55N	68.29 E
İliç	146	Hc	39.28N	38.34 E
Ilica	130	Kj	39.52N	27.46 E
Iličevsk [Azer.]	132	Nj	39.33N	44.59 E
Iličevsk [Ukr.]	136	Df	46.18N	30.37 E
Ilidža	128	Mg	43.50N	18.19 E
Iligan	142	Oi	8.14N	124.14 E
Iligan Bay	150	He	8.25N	124.05 E
Ilim	138	Fe	56.50N	103.25 E
Ilimskoje vodohranilišče	138	Fe	57.20N	102.30 E
Ilinski [Russia]	138	Jg	47.59N	142.21 E
Ilinski [Russia]	114	Hf	61.02N	32.42 E
Ilinski [Russia]	134	Gg	58.35N	55.41 E
Ilion	184	Jd	43.01N	75.04W
Ilio Point	221a	Db	21.13N	157.16W
Ilir	138	Fe	55.13N	100.45 E
Ilirska Bistrica	128	Ie	45.34N	14.16 E
Iljaly	135	Bd	41.53N	59.40 E
Ilkal	148	Fe	15.58N	76.08 E
Ilkeston	124	Ab	52.58N	1.18W
Ill	122	Nf	48.40N	7.53 E
Illampu, Nevado del-	202	Eg	15.50S	68.34W
Illana Bay	150	He	7.25N	123.45 E
Illapel	206	Fd	31.38S	71.10W
Illa Sa Conillera / Isla Cunillera	126	Nf	38.59N	1.12 E
Illbillee, Mount-	212	Ge	27.02S	132.30 E
Ille	122	Ef	48.08N	1.40W
Ille-et-Vilaine [3]	122	Ef	48.10N	1.30W
Illéla	166	Gc	14.28N	5.15 E
Iller	120	Fh	48.23N	9.58 E
Illescas	126	Id	40.07N	3.50W
Ille-sur-Têt	122	Il	42.40N	2.37 E
Illi, Ba-	168	Bc	10.44N	16.21 E
Illimani, Nevado del-	198	Jg	16.39S	67.48W
Illingen	124	Je	49.22N	7.03 E
Illinois [2]	182	Jd	40.00N	89.00W
Illinois	174	Jf	38.58N	90.27W
Illinois Peak	188	Hc	47.02N	115.04W
Illizi	160	Hf	26.29N	8.28 E
Ilm	120	He	51.07N	11.40 E
Ilmajoki	116	Jb	62.44N	22.34 E
Ilmen, ozero-	110	Jd	58.20N	31.20 E
Ilmenau	120	Gf	50.41N	10.54 E
Ilmenau	120	Gc	53.23N	10.10 E
Il Montello	128	Ge	45.49N	12.07 E
Ilo	202	Dg	17.38S	71.20W
Iloilo	142	Oh	10.42N	122.34 E
Ilok	128	Ne	45.13N	19.23 E
Ilomantsi	114	He	62.40N	30.55 E
Ilorin	160	Hh	8.30N	4.33 E
Iloron, Cerro-	192	Gg	20.57N	104.22W
Ilova	128	Ke	45.25N	16.45 E
Ilovik	128	If	44.27N	14.33 E
Ilovlja	132	Ne	49.18N	44.01 E
Ilovlja	132	Me	49.14N	43.54 E
Ilpyrski	138	Le	59.52N	164.12 E
Ilski	132	Kg	44.51N	38.32 E
Iltin	138	Nc	67.52N	178.48W
Ilubabor [3]	168	Ed	7.50N	35.00 E
Ilukste/Ilūkste	116	Li	55.58N	26.26 E
Ilūkste/Iluuste	116	Li	55.58N	26.26 E
Ilulissat/Jakobshavn	224	Nc	69.20N	50.50W
Ilwaki	150	Ih	7.56S	126.26 E
Ilyč	134	He	62.32N	56.40 E
Ilz	120	Jh	48.35N	13.30 E
Iłżanka	120	Re	51.14N	21.47 E
Imabari	154	Lg	34.03N	133.00 E
Imagane	154	Pc	42.26N	140.01 E
Imaichi	154	Of	36.43N	139.41 E
Imán, Sierra del-	204	Eh	27.42S	55.28W
Imanburluk	134	Mj	53.40N	67.15 E
Imandra, ozero-	110	Jb	67.30N	33.00 E
Imano-Yama	156	Ce	32.51N	132.49 E
Imari	154	Jh	33.16N	129.53 E
Imarui	204	Hi	28.21S	48.49W
Imataca, Serranía de-	196	Fi	7.45N	61.00W
Imatra	114	Gf	61.10N	28.46 E
Imazu	156	Ed	35.24N	136.01 E
Imbabah, Al Qāhirah-	164	Fc	30.05N	31.13 E
Imbert	194	Ld	19.45N	70.50W
Imbituba	206	Kc	28.14S	48.40W
Imeni 26 Bakinskih Komissarov [Azer.]	136	Eh	39.19N	49.12 E
Imeni 26 Bakinskih Komissarov [Turk.]	136	Fh	39.21N	54.12 E
İmeni Gastello	138	Jd	61.35N	147.59 E
Imeni Karla Liebknechta	132	Id	51.38N	35.29 E
İmeni Mariny Raskovoj	138	Jd	62.05N	146.30 E
İmeni Poliny Osipenko	138	If	52.23N	136.25 E
Imi	160	Lh	6.28N	42.11 E
Imilili	162	De	22.50N	15.54W
Imi n'Tanout	162	Fc	31.03N	8.08W
Imišli	136	Eh	39.53N	48.03 E
Imjin-gang	154	If	37.47N	126.40 E
Imlay	188	Ff	40.42N	118.07W
Immenstadt im Allgäu	120	Gi	47.34N	10.13 E
Imo [2]	166	Gd	5.30N	7.20 E
Imola	128	Ff	44.21N	11.42 E
Imotski	128	Lg	43.27N	17.13 E
Imperatriz	200	Lf	5.32S	47.29W
Imperia	128	Cg	43.53N	8.03 E
Imperial	186	Ff	40.31N	101.39W
Imperial de Aragón, Canal-	126	Kb	42.02N	1.33W
Imperial Valley	188	Hj	32.50N	115.30W
Impfondo	160	Ih	1.37N	18.04 E
Imphāl	142	Lg	24.49N	93.57 E
Imphy	122	Jh	46.56N	3.15 E
Impilanti	114	Hf	61.41N	31.12 E
Imrali Adasi	130	Li	40.32N	28.32 E
İmroz	146	Ab	40.11N	25.55 E
Imst	128	Ec	47.14N	10.44 E
Imtan	146	Gf	32.24N	36.49 E
Imuris	192	Db	30.47N	110.52W
Im-Zouren	126	Ii	35.04N	3.50W
Ina	154	Ng	35.50N	137.57 E
Ina	120	Kc	53.32N	14.38 E
I-n-Abanrherit	166	Gb	17.58N	6.05 E
Inabu	156	Ed	35.13N	137.30 E
Inaccessible Island	158	Fl	37.17S	12.45W
Inaccessible Islands	222	Re	60.34S	46.44W
I-n-Afaleleh	162	Ie	23.34N	9.12 E
I Naftan, Puntan-	220b	Ba	15.05N	145.45 E
Ina-Gawa	156	Fc	37.23N	139.18 E
I-n-Amenas	160	Hf	28.03N	9.33 E
Inami	156	De	33.48N	135.12 E
Inanba-Jima	156	Fe	33.39N	139.18 E
Inangahua Junction	218	Dd	41.52S	171.56 E
Inanwatan	150	Jg	2.08S	132.10 E
Iñapari	202	Ef	10.57S	69.35W
Inarajan	220c	Bb	13.16N	144.45 E
I-n-Arhâta	166	Ea	21.09N	0.18W
Inari	112	Ib	68.54N	27.01 E
Inari, Lake- (EN)= Inarijärvi	110	Ib	69.00N	28.00 E
Inarijärvi=Inari, Lake- (EN)	110	Ib	69.00N	28.00 E
Inawashiro	156	Gc	37.34N	140.05 E
Inawashiro-Ko	154	Pf	37.30N	140.03 E
I-n-Azaoua	166	Ga	20.54N	7.28 E
I-n Azaoua	166	Ga	20.47N	7.31 E
Inazawa	156	Ed	35.15N	136.47 E
Inca	126	Oe	39.43N	2.54 E
Inca de Oro	206	Gc	26.45S	69.54W
Incaguasi	206	Fc	29.13S	71.03W
İnce Burun [Tur.]	130	Ki	40.28N	27.16 E
İnce Burun [Tur.]	140	Fe	42.07N	34.56 E
İncekum Burun	146	Ed	36.13N	33.58 E
Inceler	130	Ml	37.42N	29.35 E
I-n-Chaouâg	166	Fb	16.23N	0.10 E
Inchcape (Bell Rock)	118	Ke	56.26N	2.24W
Inchiri [3]	162	Df	20.00N	15.00W
Inch'ŏn	142	Of	37.28N	126.38 E
Incirliova	130	Kl	37.50N	27.43 E
Incudine, Monte-	122a	Bb	41.51N	9.12 E
Indaiá, Rio-	204	Jd	18.27S	45.22W
Indaia Grande, Ribeirão-	204	Fd	19.31S	52.29W
Indaiatuba	204	If	23.05S	47.14W
Indal	116	Gb	62.34N	17.06 E
Indalsälven	114	De	62.31N	17.27 E
Inda Selase	168	Fc	14.06N	38.17 E
Indawgyi	148	Jc	25.08N	96.20 E
Indefatigable Banks	118	Ph	53.35N	2.20 E
Independence [Ca.-U.S.]	188	Fh	36.48N	118.12W
Independence [Ia.-U.S.]	186	Ke	42.28N	91.54W
Independence [Ks.-U.S.]	182	Hd	37.13N	95.42W
Independence [Mo.-U.S.]	186	Ig	39.05N	94.04W
Independence [Va.-U.S.]	184	Gg	36.38N	81.11W
Independence Fjord	224	Me	82.00N	30.25W
Independence Mountains	188	Gf	41.15N	116.05W
Independência [Braz.]	204	Fa	13.34S	53.57W
Independência [Braz.]	202	Je	5.23S	40.19W
Independenta	130	Kd	45.29N	27.45 E
Inder → Jalaid Qi	152	Lb	46.41N	122.52 E
Inder, ozero-	132	Qe	48.25N	51.55 E
Inderborski	112	Lf	48.32N	51.47 E
India (EN)	140	Jh	20.00N	77.00 E
India (EN)=Bhārat Juktarashtra [1]	142	Jh	20.00N	77.00 E
India Muerta, Arroyo de la-	204	Fk	33.40S	54.04W
Indiana	184	He	40.39N	79.11W
Indiana [2]	182	Jc	40.00N	86.15W
Indianapolis	176	Kf	39.46N	86.09W
Indian Church	194	Ce	17.45N	88.40W
Indian Creek Point	197d	Bb	17.00N	61.43W
Indian Harbour	180	Lf	54.27N	57.13W
Indian Head	180	Hf	50.32N	103.40W
Indian Ocean	106	Gl	21.00S	82.00 E
Indian Ocean (EN)=Ḥindi, Badwēynta-	106	Gl	21.00S	82.00 E
Indian Ocean (EN)=Indico, Oceano-	106	Gl	21.00S	82.00 E
Indian Ocean (EN)= Indien,Océan-	106	Gl	21.00S	82.00 E
Indian Ocean (EN) = Indiese Oseaan	106	Gl	21.00S	82.00 E
Indian Ocean (EN)= Indonesia, Samudera-	106	Gl	21.00S	82.00 E
Indianola	186	Kj	33.27N	90.39W
Indianópolis	204	Id	19.02S	47.55W
Indian Peak	188	Ig	38.16N	113.53W
Indian Rock	188	Ec	46.01N	120.49W
Indian Springs	182	Dd	36.34N	115.40W
Indiantown	184	Gl	27.01N	80.28W
Indian Town Point	197d	Bb	17.06N	61.40W
Indiapora	204	Gd	19.57S	50.17W
Indias Occidentales=West Indies (EN)	190	Je	19.00N	70.00W
Indico, Oceano-=Indian Ocean (EN)	106	Gl	21.00S	82.00 E
Indiese Oseaan = Indian Ocean (EN)	106	Gl	21.00S	82.00 E
Indiga	136	Eb	67.41N	49.00 E
Indigirka	140	Qb	70.48N	148.54 E
Indigskaja guba	134	Dc	67.45N	48.20 E
Inđija	130	Dd	45.03N	20.05 E
Indio	182	De	33.43N	116.13W
Indio, Río-	194	Fh	10.57N	83.44W
Indio Rico	204	Bn	38.19S	60.53W
Indispensable Reefs	208	Hf	12.40S	160.25 E
Indispensable Strait	219a	Ec	9.00S	160.30 E
Indochina (EN)	140	Mh	16.00N	107.00 E
Indonesia [1]	142	Nj	5.00S	120.00 E
Indonesia, Samudera-= Indian Ocean (EN)	106	Gl	21.00S	82.00 E
Indore	142	Jg	22.43N	75.50 E
Indra	116	Li	55.53N	27.40 E
Indragiri	150	Dg	0.22S	103.26 E
Indramayu	150	Eh	6.20S	108.19 E
Indrāvati	148	Ge	18.44N	80.16 E
Indre [3]	122	Hh	46.50N	1.40 E
Indre	122	Gg	47.14N	0.11 E
Indre Arna	116	Ad	60.26N	5.30 E
Indre-et-Loire [3]	122	Gg	47.15N	0.45 E
Indus	140	Ig	24.20N	67.47 E
İnebolu	144	Da	41.58N	33.46 E
Inece	130	Kh	41.41N	27.04 E
Inecik	130	Ki	40.56N	27.16 E
İnegöl	144	Ca	40.05N	29.31 E
Inés Indart	204	Bl	34.24S	60.33W
Ineu	130	Ec	46.26N	21.51 E
Ineu, Vîrful-	130	Hb	47.32N	24.53 E
Inezgane	162	Fc	30.21N	9.32W
I-n-Ezzane	162	Je	23.29N	11.15 E
Inferior, Laguna-	192	Li	16.15N	94.45W
Infiernillo, Presa del-	190	De	18.35N	101.45W
Infiesto	126	Ga	43.21N	5.22W
Infreschi, Punta degli-	128	Jk	39.59N	15.25 E
Ingá	202	Ke	7.17S	35.36W
Inga	170	Bd	5.39S	13.39 E
Ingå/Inkoo	114	Ff	60.03N	24.01 E
Ingabu	148	Je	17.49N	95.16 E
Ingaí, Rio-	204	Je	21.10S	44.52W
I-n Gall	166	Gb	16.47N	6.56 E
Ingarö	116	He	59.15N	18.30 E
Ingavi	204	Bb	15.02S	60.29W
Ingelheim am Rhein	124	Ke	49.59N	8.02 E
Ingelmunster	124	Fd	50.55N	3.15 E
Ingelstad	116	Fh	56.45N	14.55 E
Ingende	170	Cc	0.15S	18.57 E
Ingeniero Guillermo N. Juárez	206	Hb	23.54S	61.51W
Ingeniero Jacobacci	206	Gf	41.18S	69.35W
Ingeniero Luiggi	206	He	35.25S	64.29W
Ingenio Santa Ana	206	Gc	27.28S	65.41W
Ingermanland (EN)	110	Id	59.00N	30.00 E
Ingham	210	Ff	18.39S	146.10 E
Ingička	135	Ee	39.47N	65.58 E
Inglefield Bredning	179	Fc	77.40N	65.00W
Inglefield Land	179	Fc	78.44N	68.20W
Inglewood [Austl.]	212	Ke	28.25S	151.05 E
Inglewood [Ca.-U.S.]	188	Fj	33.58N	118.21W
Inglewood [N.Z.]	218	Fc	39.09S	174.12 E
Ingoda	138	Gf	52.03N	113.30 E
Ingolf Fjord	179	Kb	80.35N	17.35W
Ingólfshödi	114a	Cc	63.48N	16.39W
Ingolsladt	120	Hh	48.46N	11.26 E
Ingrāj Bāzār	148	Hc	25.00N	88.09 E
I-n-Guezzâm	160	Hg	19.32N	5.42 E
Ingul	132	Gf	47.02N	31.59 E
Ingulec	136	Df	47.43N	33.10 E
Ingulec	132	Hf	46.41N	32.48 E
Inguri	132	Lh	42.24N	41.32 E
Ingušskaja respublika	136	Eg	43.15N	45.30 E
Inhaca, Ilha da-	158	Kk	26.02S	32.58 E
Inhambane	160	Kk	23.52S	35.23 E
Inhambane [3]	172	Ed	23.00S	34.30 E
Inhambane, Baía de-	172	Fd	23.50S	35.20 E
Inhaminga	172	Fc	18.25S	35.01 E
Inhanduí-Guaçu, Rio-	204	Fe	21.37S	52.59W
Inhanduízinho, Rio-	204	Fe	21.34S	53.36W
Inharrime	172	Fd	24.28S	35.01 E
Inhassoro	172	Fd	21.32S	35.12 E
Inhaúma	204	Ja	13.01S	44.39W
I-n-Hihaou	162	He	23.00N	2.00 E
Inhobi, Rio-	204	Ef	23.45S	54.40W
Inhumas	202	Ig	16.22S	49.30W
Iniö	116	Id	60.25N	21.25 E
Inírida, Río-	198	Je	3.55N	67.52W
Inis/Ennis	118	Ei	52.50N	8.59W
Inis Airc/Inishark	118	Ch	53.37N	10.16W
Inis Bó Finne/Inishbofin	118	Ch	53.38N	10.12W
Inis Ceithleann/Enniskillen	118	Fg	54.21N	7.38W
Inis Córthaidh/Enniscorthy	118	Gi	52.30N	6.34W
Inis Díomáin / Ennistimon	118	Di	52.57N	9.13W
Inis Eoghain/Inishowen Peninsula	118	Ff	55.15N	7.20W
Inishark/Inis Airc	118	Ch	53.37N	10.16W
Inishbofin/Iniu Bó Finne	118	Ch	53.38N	10.12W
Inisheer/Inis Oírr	118	Dh	53.03N	9.31W
Inishkea	118	Cg	54.08N	10.11W
Inishmaan/Inis Meáin	118	Dh	53.05N	9.35W
Inishmore/Árainn	118	Dh	53.07N	9.45W
Inishmurray/Inis Muirigh	118	Eg	54.26N	8.40W
Inishowen Peninsula/Inis Eoghain	118	Ff	55.15N	7.20W
Inishtranull	118	Ff	55.27N	7.14W
Inishturk/Inis Toirc	118	Ch	53.43N	10.05W
Inis Meáin/Inishmaan	118	Dh	53.05N	9.35W
Inis Muirigh/Inishmurray	118	Eg	54.26N	8.40W
Inis Oírr/Inisheer	118	Dh	53.03N	9.31W
Inis Toirc/Inishturk	118	Ch	53.43N	10.05W
Inja	138	Je	59.22N	144.50 E
Inja [Russia]	138	Df	50.27N	86.42 E
Inja [Russia]	138	Je	59.30N	144.48 E
Injeŭp	154	Je	38.04N	128.10 E
Injibara	168	Fc	10.55N	36.58 E
Injune	212	Je	25.51S	148.34 E
I-n-Kak	166	Fb	16.20N	0.17 E
Inkisi	170	Bc	4.46S	14.52 E
Inkoo/Ingå	114	Ff	60.03N	24.01 E
Inland Kaikoura Range	218	Ee	42.00S	173.35 E
Inland Sea (EN)= Setonaikai	140	Pf	34.10N	133.00 E
Inn	110	Hf	48.35N	13.28 E
Innamincka	212	Ie	27.45S	140.44 E
Inner Hebrides	118	Ge	57.00N	6.45W
Inner Mongolia (EN)=Nei Monggol Zizhiqu (Nei-meng-ku Tzu-chih-ch'ü) [2]	152	Jc	44.00N	112.00 E
Inner Silver Pit	118	Nh	53.30N	0.40 E
Inner Sound	118	Hd	57.30N	5.55W
Innerste	120	Fd	52.15N	9.50 E
Innisfail [Alta.-Can.]	188	Ia	52.02N	113.57W
Innisfail [Austl.]	212	Jc	17.32S	146.02 E
Innokentjevka	138	Ig	49.42N	136.55 E
Innokentjevski	138	Jg	48.38N	140.12 E
Innoko	178	Hd	62.14N	159.45W
In'noshima	156	Cd	34.19N	133.10 E
Innsbruck	112	Hf	47.16N	11.24 E
Innuksuac	180	Je	58.27N	78.08W
Innviertel	128	Hb	48.15N	13.15 E
Innvikfjorden	116	Bc	61.50N	6.35 E
Inny/An Eithne	118	Fh	53.35N	7.50W
Ino	156	Ce	33.33N	133.26 E
Inobonto	150	Hf	0.52N	123.57 E
Inongo	160	Ii	1.57S	18.16 E
Inoni	170	Cc	3.04S	15.39 E
Inönü	130	Nj	39.48N	30.09 E
I-n-Ouagar	166	Gb	16.12N	6.54 E
I-n-Ouzzal	162	He	21.34N	1.59 E
Inowrocław	120	Od	52.48N	18.15 E
I-n-Salah	160	Hf	27.13N	2.28 E
Insar	114	Kj	53.52N	44.23 E
Insar	114	Ki	54.42N	45.18 E
Inscription, Cape-	208	Cg	25.30S	112.59 E
Insjön	116	Fd	60.41N	15.05 E
Ińsko	120	Lc	53.27N	15.33 E
Instanbul Boğazi = Bosporus (EN)	110	Ig	41.00N	29.00 E
Instruč	116	Ij	54.39N	21.48 E
Insurăţei	130	Ke	44.55N	27.36 E
Inta	112	Mb	66.05N	60.08 E
I-n-Tabezas	166	Fb	17.54N	1.50 E
I-n-Tallak	166	Fb	16.19N	3.15 E
Intepe	130	Ji	40.00N	26.20 E
Interlaken	128	Bd	46.41N	7.52 E
International Falls	182	Ib	48.36N	93.25W
Interview	148	If	12.55N	92.43 E
Inthanon, Doi-	148	Je	18.35N	98.29 E
Intibucá [3]	194	Cf	14.20N	88.15W
Intiyaco	206	Hc	28.39S	60.05W
Intorsura Buzaului	130	Jd	45.41N	26.02 E
Intracoastal Waterway	186	Im	28.45N	95.40W
Inubō-Zaki	156	Gd	35.42N	140.52 E
Inukjuak	176	Ld	58.30N	78.15W
Inútil, Bahia-	206	Fh	52.45S	71.24W
Inuvik	176	Fc	68.25N	133.30W
Inuyama	156	Ed	35.23N	136.56 E
Inva	134	Gg	58.59N	55.40 E
Inveraray	118	He	56.13N	5.05W
Invercargill	210	Hi	46.25S	168.21 E
Inverell	212	Ke	29.47S	151.07 E
Inverness	112	Fd	57.27N	4.15W
Inverurie	118	Kd	57.17N	2.23W
Investigator Group	208	Eh	33.45S	134.30 E
Investigator Strait	212	Hg	35.25S	137.10 E
Inyangani	172	Ec	18.13S	32.46 E
Inyangani	158	Kj	18.18S	32.51 E
Inyati	172	Dc	19.40S	28.51 E
Inyazura	172	Ec	18.43S	32.10 E
Inyo Mountains	188	Gh	36.50N	117.45W
Inza	136	Ee	53.53N	46.28 E
Inzá	202	Cc	2.33N	76.04W
Inžavino	132	Mc	52.19N	42.31 E
Inzer	134	Hi	54.14N	57.34 E
Inzer	134	Hi	54.30N	56.28 E
Inzia	170	Cc	3.45S	17.57 E
Iō/Kazan-Rettō=Volcano Islands (EN)	140	Qg	25.00N	141.00 E
Ioánnina	112	Ih	39.40N	20.50 E
Ioannínon, Límni-	130	Dj	39.40N	20.53 E
Iokanga	114	Jb	68.03N	39.40 E
Iola	186	Ih	37.55N	95.24W
Iolotan	136	Gh	37.18N	62.21 E
Iona	170	Bf	16.52S	12.34 E
Iona	118	Ge	56.19N	6.25W
Ionava/Jonava	114	Fi	55.05N	24.17 E
Ion Corvin	130	Ke	44.07N	27.48 E
Ione	188	Eg	38.21N	120.56W
Ionia	184	Ed	42.59N	85.04W
Ionian Basin (EN)	110	Hh	36.00N	20.00 E
Ionian Islands (EN)=Iónioi Nísoi	110	Ih	38.30N	20.30 E
Ionian Sea (EN)=Ionio, Mar-	110	Hh	39.00N	19.00 E
Ionian Sea (EN)=Iónion Pélagos	110	Hh	39.00N	19.00 E
Ionio, Mar-=Ionian Sea (EN)	110	Hh	39.00N	19.00 E
Iónioi Nísoi [2]	130	Dk	38.40N	20.10 E
Iónioi Nísoi=Ionian Islands (EN)	110	Ih	38.30N	20.30 E
Iónion Pélagos=Ionian Sea (EN)	110	Hh	39.00N	19.00 E
Ioniškelis/Joniškėlis	116	Ki	56.00N	24.14 E
Ioniškis/Joniškis	114	Fh	56.16N	23.37 E
Iony, ostrov-	138	Je	56.15N	143.20 E
Iori	132	Oi	41.03N	46.27 E
Ios	130	Im	36.44N	25.18 E

Ios 130 Im 36.42N 25.20 E
Iō-Shima 154 Ki 31.51N 130.13 E
Iowa [2] 182 Ic 42.15N 93.15W
Iowa City 182 Ic 41.40N 91.32W
Iowa Falls 186 Je 42.31N 93.16W
Iowa Park 186 Gj 33.57N 98.40W
Iowa River 186 Kf 41.10N 91.02W
Iō-Yama 156a Da 44.10N 145.10 E
Ipa 132 Fc 52.07N 29.12 E
Ipameri 202 Ig 17.43S 48.09W
Ipatovo 136 Ef 45.43N 42.53 E
Ipaumirim 202 Ke 6.47S 38.43W
Ipel' 120 Oi 47.49N 18.52 E
Ipiales 202 Cc 0.50N 77.37W
Ipiaú 202 Kf 14.08S 39.44W
Ipiranga 204 Gg 25.01S 50.35W
Ipiros [2] 130 Dj 39.30N 20.40 E
Ipiros=Epirus (EN) 110 Ih 39.30N 20.40 E
Ipiros=Epirus (EN) 130 Dj 39.30N 20.40 E
Ipixuma, Rio- 202 Fe 5.50S 63.00W
Ipixuna 202 De 7.34S 72.36W
Ipoh 142 Mi 4.35N 101.05 E
Ipoly 120 Oi 47.49N 18.52 E
Iporá 202 Hg 16.28S 51.07W
Iporã 204 Ff 23.59S 53.37W
Ippy 168 Cd 6.15N 21.12 E
Ipsala 146 Bb 40.55N 26.23 E
Ipsizonos Óros 130 Gi 40.28N 23.34 E
Ipswich [Austl.] 210 Gg 27.36S 152.46 E
Ipswich [Eng.-U.K.] 112 Ge 52.04N 1.10 E
Ipswich [S.D.-U.S.] 186 Gd 45.27N 99.02W
Ipu 202 Jd 4.20S 40.42W
Iqaluit 176 Mc 63.44N 68.28W
Iqe 152 Fd 38.04N 94.24 E
Iquique 200 Ih 20.13S 70.10W
Iquitos 200 If 3.50S 73.15W
Iraan 186 Fk 30.54N 101.54W
Ira Banda 168 Cd 5.57N 22.06 E
Irabu-Jima 152 Mg 24.50N 125.10 E
Iracoubo 202 Hb 5.29N 53.13W
Iraél 134 Gd 64.27N 55.08 E
Irago-Suidō 156 Ed 34.35N 136.55 E
Irago-Zaki 156 Ed 34.35N 137.01 E
Iráklia 130 Gh 41.10N 23.16 E
Iráklia 130 Im 36.50N 25.26 E
Iráklion 112 Ih 35.20N 25.08 E
Irān=Iran (EN) [1] 142 Hf 32.00N 53.00 E
Iran (EN)=Irān [1] 142 Hf 32.00N 53.00 E
Iran, Pegunungan-=Iran Mountains (EN) 140 Ni 2.05N 114.55 E
Iran, Plateau of- (EN) 140 Hf 32.00N 56.00 E
Irani, Serra do- 204 Fh 27.00S 52.12W
Iran Mountains (EN)=Iran, Pegunungan- 140 Ni 2.05N 114.55 E
Irānshahr 142 Ig 27.13N 60.41 E
Irapa 196 Eg 10.34N 62.35W
Irapuá, Arroio- 204 Fj 30.15S 53.10W
Irapuato 176 Ig 20.41N 101.28W
Iraq (EN) = Al 'Irāq [1] 142 Gf 33.00N 44.00 E
'Irāq al 'Arabi 146 Kg 31.50N 45.50 E
Irati 206 Jc 25.27S 50.39W
Irati 126 Kb 42.35N 1.16W
Irazú, Volcán 174 Ki 9.59N 83.51W
Irbeni Väin 116 Ig 57.48N 22.05 E
Irbid 144 Ec 32.33N 35.51 E
Irbid [3] 146 Gf 32.27N 35.51 E
Irbiktepe 130 Jh 41.00N 26.30 E
Irbit 136 Gd 57.41N 63.03 E
Irbit 134 Kh 57.42N 63.07 E
Irebu 170 Cc 0.37S 17.45 E
Irecê 202 Jf 11.18S 41.52W
Iregua 126 Jb 42.27N 2.24W
Ireland 110 Fe 53.00N 8.00W
Ireland/Éire [1] 112 Fe 53.00N 8.00W
Ireland Trough (EN) 110 Ed 55.00N 12.40W
Iren 134 Hh 57.27N 56.59 E
Ireng River 202 Gc 3.33N 59.51W
Irês Corações 202 Ih 21.42S 45.16W
Iretama 204 Fg 24.27S 52.02W
Irgiz 136 Gf 48.36N 61.16 E
Irgiz 136 Gf 48.13N 62.08 E
Irharhar [Alg.] 162 Ie 21.01N 6.01 E
Irharhar [Alg.] 158 Hf 28.00N 6.15 E
Irherm 162 Fc 30.04N 8.26W
Iri 154 Ig 35.56N 126.57 E
Irian Jaya [3] 150 Kg 3.55S 138.00 E
Iriba 160 Jg 15.07N 22.15 E
Irîgui 158 Gg 16.43N 5.30W
Iriklinski 132 Ud 51.39N 58.38 E
Iriklinskoje vodohranilišče 132 Ud 51.45N 58.45 E
Iringa 160 Ki 7.46S 35.42 E
Iringa [3] 170 Gd 8.00S 35.30 E
Irinja, gora- 138 Fe 58.20N 104.30 E
Iriomote Jima 152 Lg 24.20N 123.50 E
Iriona 194 Ef 15.57N 85.11W
Iriri, Rio- 198 Kf 3.52S 52.37W
Irish Sea 110 Fe 53.30N 5.20W
Irish Sea (EN)=Muir Eireann 110 Fe 53.30N 5.20W
Irituia 202 Id 1.46S 47.26W
Irkeštam 135 Ie 39.38N 73.55 E
Irkutsk 142 Md 52.16N 104.20 E
Irkutskaja oblast [3] 138 Fe 56.00N 104.00 E
Irlir, gora- 135 Dc 42.40N 63.30 E
Irminio 128 In 36.46N 14.36 E
Irnijärvi 114 Gd 65.36N 29.05 E
Iro, Lac- 168 Bc 10.06N 19.25 E
Iroise, Mer d'- 122 Bf 48.15N 4.55W
Iron Gate (EN) = Portile de Fier 110 Ig 44.41N 22.31 E
Iron Knob 212 Hf 32.44S 137.08 E
Iron Mountain 182 Jb 45.49N 88.04W
Iron Mountains 118 Fg 54.15N 7.50W
Iron River [Mi.-U.S.] 182 Jb 46.05N 88.39W
Iron River [Wi.-U.S.] 186 Kc 46.34N 91.24W
Ironside Mountain 188 Fd 44.15N 118.08W
Ironton [Mo.-U.S.] 186 Kh 37.36N 90.38W
Ironton [Oh.-U.S.] 184 Ff 38.32N 82.40W
Ironwood 182 Ib 46.27N 90.10W
Iroquois Falls 180 Jg 48.46N 80.41W
Irō-Zaki 154 Og 34.35N 138.55 E
Irpen 136 De 50.31N 30.16 E
Irpinia 128 Ij 40.55N 15.00 E
Irrawaddy → Ayeyarwady 148 Ie 17.00N 95.00 E
Irrawaddy (EN) = Ayeyarwady 140 Lg 15.50N 95.06 E
Irrel 124 Ie 49.51N 6.28 E
Irsāva 120 Th 48.15N 23.05 E
Irsina 128 Kj 40.45N 16.14 E
Irtek 132 Rd 51.29N 52.42 E
Irthlingborough 124 Bb 52.19N 0.36W
Irtyš 140 Ic 61.04N 68.52 E
Irtyšsk 136 He 53.21N 75.27 E
Irumu 170 Eb 1.27N 29.52 E
Irún 126 Ka 43.21N 1.47W
Irurzun 126 Kb 42.55N 1.50W
Irves šaurums 116 Ig 57.48N 22.05 E
Irvine 118 If 55.37N 4.40W
Irving 186 Hj 32.49N 96.56W
Is, Jabal- 168 Fa 21.49N 35.39 E
Isa, Ra's- 164 Hf 15.11N 42.39 E
Isabel 186 Fd 45.24N 101.26W
Isabel, Bahía- 202a Ab 0.38S 91.25W
Isabela 197 Ab 18.31N 67.07W
Isabela → Basilan City 150 He 6.42N 121.58 E
Isabela, Cabo- 194 Ld 19.56N 71.01W
Isabela, Isla- [Ec.] 198 Gf 0.30S 91.06W
Isabela, Isla- [Mex.] 192 Gg 21.51N 105.55W
Isabella, Cordillera- 190 Gf 13.30N 85.30W
Isabel Segunda 194 Od 18.09N 65.27W
Isabey 130 Ml 38.00N 29.24 E
Isaccea 130 Ld 45.16N 28.28 E
Isachsen 176 Ib 78.50N 103.30W
Isafjörður 112 Db 66.03N 23.09W
Isahaya 154 Jh 32.50N 130.03 E
Isakov, Seamount (EN) 208 Ga 31.35N 151.07 E
Isana, Rio- 202 Ec 0.26N 67.19W
Isandja 170 Dc 2.59S 22.00 E
Isanga 170 Dc 1.26S 22.18 E
Isangi 170 Db 0.46N 24.15 E
Isanlu Makutu 166 Gd 8.16N 5.48 E
Isaouane-n-Irarraren 162 Id 27.15N 8.00 E
Isaouane-n-Tifernine 162 Id 27.00N 7.30 E
Isar 120 Ih 48.49N 12.58 E
Isarco/Eisack 128 Fd 46.27N 11.18 E
Isarco, Valle-/Eisacktal 128 Fd 46.45N 11.35 E
Isbergues 124 Ed 50.37N 2.27 E
Iscayachi 202 Eh 21.31S 65.03W
Ischgl 128 Ec 47.01N 10.17 E
Ischia 128 Hj 40.44N 13.57 E
Ischia 128 Hj 40.45N 13.55 E
Ise 152 Oe 34.29N 136.42 E
Isefjord 116 Di 55.50N 11.50 E
Iševjka 114 Li 54.28N 48.17 E
Isen 120 Ih 48.20N 12.45 E
Isenach 124 Ke 49.38N 8.28 E
Isen-Zaki 156b Bb 27.39N 128.55 E
Iseo, Lago d'- (Sebino) 128 Ee 45.45N 10.05 E
Iseran, Col de l'- 122 Ni 45.25N 7.02 E
Isère [3] 122 Li 45.10N 5.50 E
Isère 122 Kj 44.59N 4.51 E
Iśerit, gora- 134 If 61.08N 59.10 E
Iserlohn 120 De 51.22N 7.42 E
Isernia 128 Ii 41.36N 14.14 E
Isesaki 156 Fc 36.19N 139.12 E
Iset 140 Id 56.36N 66.24 E
Isetskoje 134 Lh 56.29N 65.21 E
Ise-Wan 154 Ng 34.40N 136.42 E
Iseyin 166 Fd 7.58N 3.36 E
Isfahan (EN) = Eşfahān 142 Hf 32.40N 51.38 E
Isfana 135 Ge 39.51N 69.32 E
Isfara 135 Hd 40.07N 70.38 E
Isfendiyar Dağları 144 Da 41.45N 34.10 E
Isfjorden 179 Nc 78.15N 15.00 E
Isha Baydabo = Baidoa (EN) 160 Lh 3.04N 43.48 E
Ishasha River 170 Ec 0.50S 29.40 E
Ishavet = Arctic Ocean (EN) 224 Be 85.00N 170.00 E
Isherton 202 Gc 2.19N 59.22W
Ishigaki 152 Lg 24.20N 124.09 E
Ishikari 156a Bb 43.13N 141.18 E
Ishikari-Dake 156a Cb 43.33N 143.00 E
Ishikari-Gawa 156a Bb 43.15N 141.20 E
Ishikari-Heiya 156a Bb 43.00N 141.40 E
Ishikari-Wan 152 Pc 43.25N 141.00 E
Ishikawa [Jap.] 152 Mf 26.27N 127.50 E
Ishikawa [Jap.] 156 Gc 37.09N 140.27 E
Ishikawa Ken [2] 154 Nf 36.35N 136.40 E
Ishim Steppe (EN) = Išimskaja step 140 Id 55.00N 67.30 E
Ishinomaki 152 Pd 38.25N 141.18 E
Ishinomaki-Wan 156 Gb 38.20N 141.15 E
Ishioka 154 Pf 36.11N 140.16 E
Ishitate-San 156 De 33.44N 134.03 E
Ishizuchi-Yama 156 Ce 33.45N 133.05 E
Ishodnaja, gora- 138 Nd 64.50N 173.26W
Ishpeming 184 Db 46.30N 87.40W
Isidro Alves 204 Ee 20.09S 55.12W
Isigny-sur-Mer 122 Ee 49.19N 1.06W
Isii 156 Dd 34.04N 134.26 E
Işıklar Dağı 146 Bb 40.50N 27.05 E
Işıklı 130 Mk 38.19N 29.51 E
Işıklı Göl 130 Mk 38.14N 29.55 E
Isili 128 Dk 39.44N 9.06 E
Isilkul 136 He 54.55N 71.16 E
Išim 142 Id 56.09N 69.27 E
Išim 140 Jd 57.45N 71.12 E
Išimbaj 136 Fe 53.28N 56.02 E
Išimskaja step = Ishim Steppe (EN) 140 Id 55.00N 67.30 E
Isinga 138 Gf 52.55N 112.00 E
Isiolo 170 Gb 0.21N 37.35 E
Isiro 160 Jh 2.48N 27.41 E
Isisford 212 Id 24.16S 144.26 E
Isjangulovo 134 Hj 52.12N 56.36 E
Iskandar 135 Gd 41.35N 69.43 E
Iskär 130 Hf 43.44N 24.27 E
Iskär, Jazovir- 130 Gg 42.25N 23.35 E
Iškašim 136 Hh 36.44N 71.39 E
Iskenderun=Alexandretta (EN) 142 Ff 36.37N 36.07 E
Iskenderun Körfezi=Alexandretta, Gulf of- (EN) 144 Eb 36.30N 35.40 E
İskilip 146 Fb 40.45N 34.29 E
Iski-Naukat 135 Id 40.14N 72.41 E
Iskininski 132 Rf 47.13N 52.36 E
Iskitim 138 Df 54.38N 83.18 E
Iskushuban 168 Ic 10.13N 50.14 E
Iskut 180 Ee 56.45N 131.48W
Isla Cristina 126 Eg 37.12N 7.19W
Islâhiye 146 Gd 37.26N 36.41 E
Islāmābād 142 Jf 33.42N 73.10 E
Islāmābād → Anantnāg 148 Fb 33.44N 75.09 E
Isla Mujeres 192 Pg 21.12N 86.43W
Island=Iceland (EN) [1] 112 Eb 65.00N 18.00W
Island=Iceland (EN) 110 Eb 65.00N 18.00W
Island Harbour 197b Ab 18.16N 63.02W
Island Lagoon 212 Hf 31.30S 136.40 E
Island Lake 180 If 53.58N 94.46W
Island Lake 180 If 53.45N 94.30W
Island Pond 184 Lc 44.50N 71.53W
Islands, Bay of- [Can.] 180 Lg 49.10N 58.15W
Islands, Bay of- [N.Z.] 218 Fa 35.10S 174.10 E
Islao, Massif de l'- 158 Lk 22.30S 45.20 E
Islas de la Bahía [3] 194 De 16.20N 86.30W
Islay 110 Fd 55.46N 6.10W
Islaz 130 Hf 43.44N 24.45 E
Isle 122 Fj 44.55N 0.15W
Isle-Jourdain, L'- 122 Hk 43.37N 1.05 E
Isle of Man [5] 118 Ig 54.15N 4.30W
Isle of Wight [3] 118 Lk 50.40N 1.15W
Isle-sur-la-Sorgue, L'- 122 Lk 43.55N 5.03 E
Isleta 186 Ci 34.55N 106.42W
Isle-Verte 184 Ma 48.01N 69.22W
Isloč 116 Lj 53.55N 26.13 E
Ismael Cortinas 204 Dk 33.56S 57.08W
Ismailia (EN)=Al Ismā'īlīyah 164 Fc 30.35N 32.16 E
Ismailly 132 Pi 40.47N 48.13 E
Ismantorps Borg 116 Gh 56.45N 16.40 E
Isnā 160 Kf 25.18N 32.33 E
Isny im Allgäu 120 Gi 47.42N 10.02 E
Isojärvi 116 Ic 61.45N 21.45 E
Isojoki/Storå 114 Ee 62.07N 21.58 E
Isoka 170 Fe 10.08S 32.38 E
Isola del Liri 128 Hi 41.41N 13.34 E
Isola di Capo Rizzuto 128 Ll 38.58N 17.05 E
Isonzo 128 He 45.43N 13.33 E
Isonzo (EN)=Soča 128 He 45.43N 13.33 E
Isosyöte 114 Gd 65.37N 27.35 E
Isparta 144 Db 37.46N 30.33 E
Isperih 130 Jf 43.43N 26.50 E
Ispica 128 In 36.47N 14.55 E
Ispir 146 Ib 40.29N 41.00 E
İspiriz Dağı 146 Jc 38.03N 43.55 E
Israel (EN)=Yisra'el [1] 142 Ff 31.30N 35.00 E
Isratu 168 Fb 16.20N 39.55 E
Issa 116 Mh 56.55N 28.50 E
Issano 202 Gb 5.49N 59.25W
Issaran, Ra's- 146 Eh 28.50N 32.56 E
Issel 120 Cd 52.00N 6.10 E
Isser 126 Ph 36.51N 3.40 E
Issia 166 Dd 6.29N 6.35W
Issia [3] 166 Dd 6.30N 6.35W
Issoire 122 Ji 45.33N 3.15 E
Issoudun 122 Hh 46.57N 2.00 E
Issyk 135 Kc 43.20N 77.28 E
Issyk-Kul' (Rybačje) 136 Hg 42.28N 76.11 E
Issyk-Kul, ozero- 140 Je 42.25N 77.15 E
Issyk-Kulskaja oblast [3] 136 Hg 42.10N 78.00 E
Ist 128 If 44.17N 14.47 E
İstanbul 142 Ee 41.01N 28.58 E
İstanbul-Bakırköy 130 Li 40.59N 28.52 E
İstanbul-Beyoğlu 130 Lh 41.02N 28.59 E
İstanbul-Kadıköy 130 Mi 40.59N 29.01 E
İstanbul-Üsküdar 146 Cb 41.01N 29.03 E
Isteren 116 Db 62.00N 11.50 E
Istgāh-e Eqbālīyeh 146 Ne 35.50N 50.45 E
Isthilart 204 Dj 31.11S 57.58W
Istiaia 130 Gk 38.57N 23.09 E
Istisu 132 Nj 39.57N 46.00 E
Istmina 202 Cb 5.09N 76.42W
Isto, Mount- 174 Ec 69.12N 143.48W
Istok 130 Dg 42.47N 20.29 E
Istokpoga, Lake- 184 Gl 27.22N 81.17W
Istra = Istria (EN) 110 Hf 45.00N 14.00 E
Istres 122 Kk 43.31N 4.59 E
Istria 130 Le 44.34N 28.43 E
Istria (EN) = Istra 110 Hf 45.00N 14.00 E
Isulan 150 He 7.02N 124.29 E
Itabaiana 202 Kf 10.41S 37.26W
Itabaianinha 202 Kf 11.16S 37.47W
Itaberá 204 Hf 23.51S 49.09W
Itaberaba 202 Jf 12.32S 40.18W
Itaberaí 202 Ig 16.02S 49.48W
Itabira 202 Jg 19.37S 43.13W
Itabirito 204 Ke 20.15S 43.48W
Itabuna 200 Mg 14.48S 39.16W
Itacaiúna, Rio- 202 Ie 5.21S 49.08W
Itacarambi 204 Jb 15.01S 44.03W
Itacoatiara 200 Kf 3.08S 58.25W
Itacolomi, Pico do- 204 Ke 20.26S 43.29W
Itacuai, Rio- 202 Dd 4.20S 70.12W
Itacumbi 204 Ei 28.44S 55.08W
Itacurubi del Rosario 204 Dg 24.29S 56.41W
Itaguari, Rio- 204 Jh 14.11S 44.40W
Itaguaru 204 Hb 15.44S 49.37W
Itagüí 202 Cb 6.12N 75.40W
Itaimbézinho 204 Gi 28.38S 50.34W
Itaituba 200 Kf 4.17S 55.59W
Itajaí 200 Lh 26.53S 48.39W
Itajubá 202 Ih 22.26S 45.27W
Itajuípe 202 Kf 14.41S 39.22W
Itaka 138 Gf 53.54N 118.42 E
Italia = Italy (EN) [1] 112 Hg 42.50N 12.50 E
Italiana, Penisola- 110 Hg 42.50N 12.50 E
Itálica 126 Fg 37.25N 6.05W
Italy (EN) = Italia [1] 112 Hg 42.50N 12.50 E
Itambacuri 202 Jg 18.01S 41.42W
Itambé, Pico de- 198 Lg 18.23S 43.21W
Itämeri = Baltic Sea (EN) 110 Hd 57.00N 19.00 E
Itampolo 172 Gd 24.41S 43.57 E
Itanagar 148 Ic 26.57N 93.15 E
Itanará, Rio- 204 Eg 24.00S 55.53W
Itanhaém 206 Kb 24.11S 46.47W
Itano 156 Dd 34.09N 134.28 E
Itapaci 204 Hb 14.57S 49.34W
Itapagé 202 Kd 3.41S 39.34W
Itapajipe 204 Hd 19.54S 49.22W
Itaparaná, Rio- 202 Fe 5.47S 63.03W
Itapebi 202 Kg 15.56S 39.32W
Itapecerica 204 Je 20.28S 45.07W
Itapecuru-Mirim 202 Jd 3.24S 44.20W
Itapemirim 202 Jh 21.01S 40.50W
Itaperina, Pointe- 158 Lk 24.59S 47.06 E
Itaperuna 202 Jh 21.12S 41.54W
Itapetinga 202 Jg 15.15S 40.15W
Itapetininga 206 Kb 23.36S 48.03W
Itapetininga, Rio- 204 Hf 23.35S 48.27W
Itapeva 204 Hf 23.58S 48.52W
Itapeva, Lagoa- 204 Hi 29.30S 49.55W
Itapicuru, Rio- [Braz.] 202 Kf 11.47S 37.32W
Itapicuru, Rio- [Braz.] 198 Lf 2.52S 44.12W
Itapipoca 202 Kd 3.31S 39.33W
Itapiranga [Braz.] 202 Gd 2.45S 58.01W
Itapiranga [Braz.] 204 Fh 27.08S 53.43W
Itapirapuã, Pico- 204 Hg 24.17S 49.12W
Itápolis 204 He 21.35S 48.46W
Itaporã 204 Ef 22.01S 54.54W
Itaporanga [Braz.] 204 Hf 23.42S 49.29W
Itaporanga [Braz.] 202 Ke 7.18S 38.10W
Itapuã 204 Gj 30.16S 51.01W
Itapúa [3] 204 Eh 26.50S 55.50W
Itapuranga 202 Ig 15.35S 49.59W
Itaqui 206 Ic 29.08S 56.33W
Itaquyry 204 Eg 24.56S 55.13W
Itararé 204 Hg 24.07S 49.20W
Itararé, Rio- 204 Hf 23.10S 49.42W
Itārsi 148 Fd 22.37N 77.45 E
Itarumã 204 Gd 18.42S 51.25W
Itati 204 Ch 27.16S 58.15W
Itatinga 204 Hf 23.07S 48.36W
Itatski 138 De 56.07N 89.20 E
Itaum 204 Ef 22.00S 55.20W
Itaúna 202 Jh 20.04S 44.34W
Itaya-Tōge 156 Gc 37.50N 140.13 E
Itbāy 158 Kf 22.00N 35.30 E
Itbayat 150 Hb 20.46N 121.50 E
Itchen 124 Ad 50.57N 1.22W
Ite 202 Dg 17.50S 70.58W
Itéa 130 Fk 38.26N 22.25 E
Ithaca 182 Lc 42.26N 76.30W
Ithaca (EN)=Itháki 130 Dk 38.24N 20.40 E
Itháki 130 Dk 38.22N 20.43 E
Itháki = Ithaca (EN) 130 Dk 38.24N 20.40 E
Ith Hils 120 Fd 52.05N 9.35 E
Ithnayn, Harrat- 146 Ii 26.40N 40.10 E
Itigi 170 Fd 5.42S 34.29 E
Itimbiri 158 Jh 2.02N 22.44 E
Itiopya=Ethiopia (EN) [1] 160 Kh 9.00N 39.00 E
Itiquira 202 Hg 17.05S 54.56W
Itiquira, Rio- 198 Kg 17.18S 56.44W
Itirapina 204 If 22.15S 47.49W
Itiúba 202 Kf 10.43S 39.51W
Itivdleq 179 Ge 66.38N 53.51W
Itō 154 Og 34.58N 139.05 E
Itoigawa 154 Nf 37.02N 137.51 E
Itoko 170 Dc 1.00S 21.45 E
Itoman 156b Ab 26.07N 127.40 E
Iton 122 Hf 49.09N 1.12 E
Itremo, Massif de l'- 172 Hd 20.45S 46.30 E
Itsā 146 Dh 29.15N 30.48 E
Itsukaichi 156 Cd 34.22N 132.22 E
Itsuki 156 Be 32.24N 130.50 E
Ittiri 128 Cj 40.36N 8.34 E
Itu [Braz.] 204 If 23.16S 47.19W
Itu [Nig.] 166 Gd 5.12N 7.59 E
Itu, Rio- 204 Ei 29.25S 55.51W
Itui, Rio- 202 Dd 4.38S 70.19W
Ituiutaba 202 Ig 18.58S 49.28W
Itula 170 Ec 3.29S 27.52 E
Itumbiara 202 Ig 18.25S 49.13W
Itumkale 132 Nh 42.43N 45.35 E
Ituna 188 Na 51.10N 103.30W
Itungi Port 170 Fd 9.35S 33.56 E
Itupiranga 202 Ie 5.09S 49.20W
Iturama 204 Gd 19.44S 50.11W
Itúrbide 192 Oh 19.40N 89.37W
Ituri 158 Jh 1.40N 27.01 E
Iturregui 204 Bm 36.50S 61.08W
Iturup, ostrov- / Etorofu Tō 140 Qe 44.54N 147.30 E
Itutinga 204 Je 21.18S 44.40W
Ituverava 206 Kb 20.20S 47.47W
Ituxi, Rio- 198 Jf 7.18S 64.51W
Ituzaingó 204 Dh 27.36S 56.41W
Itz 120 Gg 49.58N 10.52 E
Itzehoe 120 Fc 53.55N 9.31 E
Ivacevići 132 Dc 52.43N 25.21 E
Ivai 204 Gg 25.01S 50.52W
Ivai, Rio- [Braz.] 204 Fi 29.08S 53.16W
Ivai, Rio- [Braz.] 198 Kh 23.18S 53.42W
Ivaiporã 204 Gg 24.15S 51.45W
Ivajlovgrad 130 Jh 41.32N 26.08 E
Ivakoany, Massif de l'- 172 Hd 23.50S 46.25 E
Ivalojoki 114 Gc 68.43N 27.36 E
Ivančice 120 Mg 49.06N 16.22 E
Ivangorod 114 Gg 59.23N 28.20 E
Ivangrad 130 Cg 42.51N 19.52 E
Ivanhoe 210 Fh 32.54S 144.18 E
Ivanić-Grad 128 Ke 45.42N 16.24 E
Ivaniči 120 Uf 50.38N 24.24 E
Ivanjica 130 Df 43.35N 20.14 E
Ivanjska 128 Lf 44.55N 17.04 E
Ivankov 132 Fd 50.57N 29.58 E
Ivano-Frankovo 120 Tg 49.52N 23.46 E
Ivano-Frankovsk 112 If 48.55N 24.43 E
Ivano-Frankovskaja oblast [3] 136 Cf 48.40N 24.40 E
Ivanovka [Russia] 138 Hf 50.18N 127.59 E
Ivanovka [Ukr.] 132 Gf 46.57N 30.28 E
Ivanovo [Bela.] 132 Dc 52.10N 25.32 E
Ivanovo [Russia] 112 Kd 57.00N 40.59 E
Ivanovskaja oblast [3] 136 Ed 57.00N 41.50 E
Ivanovskoje 116 Me 59.12N 28.59 E
Ivanščica 128 Kd 46.11N 16.10 E
Ivdel 136 Gc 60.42N 60.28 E
Ivenec 116 Lk 53.55N 26.49 E
Ivigtut 179 Hf 61.15N 48.00W
Ivindo 158 Ii 0.09S 12.09 E
Ivinheima 204 Ff 22.10S 53.37W
Ivinheima, Rio- 202 Hh 23.14S 53.42W
Ivinski razliv 114 If 61.10N 35.00 E
Iviza (EN)=Eivissa/Ibiza 110 Gh 39.00N 1.25 E
Iviza (EN)=Ibiza/Eivissa 110 Gh 39.00N 1.25 E
Ivje 120 Vc 53.55N 25.51 E
Ivohibe 172 Hd 22.29S 46.52 E
Ivoire, Côte d'-=Ivory Coast (EN) 158 Gh 5.00N 5.00W
Ivolândia 204 Gc 16.34S 50.51W
Ivory Coast (EN) = Côte-d'Ivoire [1] 160 Gh 8.00N 5.00W
Ivory Coast (EN)=Ivoire, Côte d'- 158 Gh 5.00N 5.00W
Ivösjön 116 Fh 56.05N 14.25 E
Ivrea 128 Be 45.28N 7.52 E
Ivrindi 130 Kj 39.34N 27.29 E
Ivry-la-Bataille 124 Df 48.53N 1.28 E
Ivry-sur-Seine 124 Ef 48.49N 2.23 E
Ivujivik 176 Lc 62.25N 77.54W
Iwai-Jima 156 Be 33.47N 131.58 E
Iwaizumi 154 Pe 39.50N 141.48 E
Iwaki 142 Qf 36.55N 140.48 E
Iwaki-Gawa 156 Ga 41.01N 140.22 E
Iwaki-Hisanohama 156 Gc 37.09N 140.59 E
Iwaki-Jōban 156 Gc 37.02N 140.50 E
Iwaki-Kawamae 156 Gc 37.12N 140.45 E
Iwaki-Miwa 156 Gc 37.09N 140.42 E
Iwaki-Nakoso 156 Gc 36.56N 140.48 E
Iwaki-Onahama 156 Gc 36.57N 140.53 E
Iwaki-San 156 Ga 40.40N 140.20 E
Iwaki-Taira 156 Gc 37.05N 140.55 E
Iwaki-Uchigō 156 Gc 37.04N 140.50 E
Iwaki-Yoshima 156 Gc 37.05N 140.50 E
Iwaki-Yotsukura 156 Gc 37.07N 140.58 E
Iwakuni 152 Ne 34.09N 132.11 E
Iwami 156 Dd 35.35N 134.20 E
Iwami-Kōgen 156 Cd 35.00N 132.30 E
Iwamizawa 152 Pc 43.12N 141.46 E
Iwanai 154 Pc 42.58N 140.30 E
Iwanuma 156 Gb 38.07N 140.52 E
Iwase 156 Gc 36.21N 140.06 E
Iwasuge-Yama 156 Fc 36.44N 138.32 E
Iwata 156 Ed 34.42N 137.48 E
Iwate 154 Pe 39.30N 141.30 E
Iwate Ken [2] 154 Pe 39.30N 141.15 E
Iwate San 154 Pe 39.49N 141.26 E
Iwo 166 Fd 7.38N 4.11 E
Iwŏn 152 Mc 40.19N 128.37 E
Iwuy 124 Fd 50.14N 3.19 E
Ixiamas 202 Ef 13.45S 68.09W
Ixmiquilpan 192 Jg 20.29N 99.14W
Ixopo 172 Ef 30.08S 30.00 E
Ixtapa, Punta- 192 Ii 17.39N 101.40W
Ixtepec 190 Ee 16.34N 95.06W
Ixtlahuacán del Rio 192 Hg 20.52N 103.15W
Ixtlán del Rio 190 Dd 21.02N 104.22W
Iyah 168 Hd 9.00N 49.38 E
Iyo 154 Lh 33.46N 132.42 E
Iyo-mishima 156 Ce 33.58N 133.33 E
Iyo-Nada 156 Ce 33.40N 132.15 E
Iž 128 Jf 44.03N 15.06 E
Iž 114 Mh 56.00N 52.41 E
Izabal [3] 194 Cf 15.30N 89.00W
Izabal, Lago de- 190 Ge 15.30N 89.10W
Izad Khvāst 146 Og 31.31N 52.07 E
Izamal 192 Og 20.56N 89.01W
Izamal 190 Gd 20.56N 89.01W
Izapa 190 Ff 14.55N 92.10W
'Izbat al Jājah 146 Dj 24.48N 30.35 E
'Izbat Dush 146 Dj 24.34N 30.42 E
Izberbaš 136 Eg 42.33N 47.52 E
Izbiceni 130 Hf 43.50N 24.39 E
Izborsk 116 Mg 57.39N 28.01 E
Izegem 124 Fd 50.55N 3.12 E
Izeh 146 Mg 31.50N 49.50 E
Izena-Shima 156b Ab 26.56N 127.56 E
Iževsk 112 Ld 56.51N 53.14 E
Izjaslav 132 Ed 50.09N 26.51 E
Izjum 136 Df 49.12N 37.17 E
Izki 144 Ie 22.57N 57.49 E
Ižma 134 Fd 65.02N 53.55 E
Ižma 110 Lb 65.19N 52.54 E
Izmail 112 If 45.21N 28.50 E
İzmir (Smyrna) 142 Ef 38.25N 27.09 E
İzmir, Gulf of- (EN)=İzmir Körfezi 146 Bc 38.30N 26.50 E
İzmir-Bornova 146 Bc 38.27N 27.14 E
İzmir Körfezi=İzmir, Gulf of- (EN) 146 Bc 38.30N 26.50 E
İzmit 142 Ee 40.46N 29.55 E
İzmit Körfezi 146 Cb 40.45N 29.35 E
Iznajar, Embalse de- 126 Hg 37.15N 4.30W
Iznalloz 126 Ig 37.23N 3.31W
İznik 146 Cb 40.26N 29.43 E
İznik Gölü 146 Cb 40.26N 29.30 E

Index Symbols

[1] Independent Nation
[2] State, Region
[3] District, County
[4] Municipality
[5] Colony, Dependency
Continent
Physical Region
Historical or Cultural Region
Mount, Mountain
Volcano
Hill
Mountains, Mountain Range
Hills, Escarpment
Plateau, Upland
Pass, Gap
Plain, Lowland
Delta
Salt Flat
Valley, Canyon
Crater, Cave
Karst Features
Depression
Polder
Desert, Dunes
Forest, Woods
Heath, Steppe
Oasis
Cape, Point
Coast, Beach
Cliff
Peninsula
Isthmus
Sandbank
Island
Atoll
Rock, Reef
Islands, Archipelago
Rocks, Reefs
Coral Reef
Well, Spring
Geyser
River, Stream
Waterfall, Rapids
River Mouth, Estuary
Lake
Salt Lake
Intermittent Lake
Reservoir
Swamp, Pond
Canal
Glacier
Ice Shelf, Pack Ice
Ocean
Sea
Gulf, Bay
Strait, Fjord
Lagoon
Bank
Seamount
Tablemount
Ridge
Shelf
Basin
Escarpment, Sea Scarp
Fracture
Trench, Abyss
National Park, Reserve
Point of Interest
Recreation Site
Cave, Cavern
Historic Site
Ruins
Wall, Walls
Church, Abbey
Temple
Scientific Station
Railway station
Airport
Port
Military installation
Lighthouse
Mine
Tunnel
Dam, Bridge

Izobilny 132 Lg 45.19N 41.42 E
Izola 128 He 45.32N 13.40 E
Ižorskaja vozvyšennost 116 Me 59.35N 29.30 E
Izozog, Bañados del- 202 Fg 18.50S 62.10W
Izra' 146 Gf 32.51N 36.15 E
Izsák 120 Pj 46.48N 19.22 E
Iztočni Rodopi 130 Ih 41.44N 25.31 E
Izúcar de Matamoros 192 Jh 18.36N 98.28W
Izu-Hantō 154 Og 34.55N 138.55 E
Izuhara 154 Jg 34.12N 129.17 E
Izu Islands (EN) = Izu-Shotō 140 Pf 32.00N 140.00 E
Izumi [Jap.] 154 Kh 32.05N 130.22 E
Izumi [Jap.] 156 Gb 38.19N 140.51 E
Izumi [Jap.] 156 Dd 34.29N 135.26 E
Izumi-sano 156 Dd 34.24N 135.18 E
Izumo 154 Lg 35.22N 132.46 E
Izu-Shotō=Izu Islands (EN) 140 Pf 32.00N 140.00 E
Izvesti CIK, ostrova- = Izvestiya Tsik Islands (EN) 138 Da 75.55N 82.30 E
Izvestiya Tsik Iulands (EN) = Izvesti CIK, ostrova- 138 Da 75.55N 82.30 E

J

Jaala 116 Lc 61.03N 26.29 E
Jaama/Jama 116 Lf 58.59N 27.45 E
Jääsjärvi 116 Lc 61.35N 26.05 E
Jaba 146 Qe 35.55N 56.35 E
Jabal, Baḩr al-=Mountain Nile (EN) 158 Kh 9.30N 30.30 E
Jabal Abū Rujmayn 146 Ge 34.50N 37.56 E
Jabal al Awliyā' 168 Eb 15.14N 32.30 E
Jabal az Zannah 146 Oj 24.11N 52.38 E
Jabal Lubnān [3] 146 Ff 33.50N 35.40 E
Jabalón 126 Hf 38.53N 4.05W
Jabalpur 142 Jg 23.10N 79.57 E
Jabal Şabāyā 164 Hf 18.35N 41.03 E
Jabālyah 146 Fg 31.32N 34.29 E
Jabal Zuqar, Jazīrat- 164 Hg 14.00N 42.45 E
Jabbārah 164 Hf 19.27N 40.03 E
Jabbeke 124 Fc 51.11N 3.05 E
Jabjabah, Wādī- 168 Ea 22.37N 33.17 E
Jablah 146 Fe 35.21N 35.55 E
Jablanac 128 If 44.43N 14.53 E
Jablanica 130 Dh 41.15N 20.30 E
Jablanica [Bul.] 130 Hf 43.01N 24.06 E
Jablanica [Bos.] 128 Lg 43.39N 17.45 E
Jabločny 138 Jg 47.09N 142.03 E
Jablonec nad Nisou 120 Lf 50.44N 15.10 E
Jablonicki, pereval- 110 If 48.18N 24.28 E
Jablonovo 138 Gf 51.51N 112.50 E
Jablonovy hrebet = Yablonovy Range (EN) 140 Nd 53.30N 115.00 E
Jablunkovský průsmyk 120 Og 49.31N 18.45 E
Jaboatão 202 Ke 8.07S 35.01W
Jaboti 204 De 20.48S 56.23W
Jaboticabal 206 Kb 21.16S 48.19W
Jabrin 146 Ni 27.51N 51.26 E
Jabuka 128 Jg 43.05N 15.28 E
Jabung, Tanjung- 150 Dg 1.01S 104.22 E
Jabuticatubas 204 Kd 19.30S 43.45W
Jaca 126 Lb 42.34N 0.33W
Jacaltenango 194 Bf 15.40N 91.44W
Jacaré, Rio- 204 Je 21.03S 45.16W
Jacareí 204 Jf 23.19S 45.58W
Jacarezinho 206 Kb 23.09S 49.59W
Jáchal, Rio- 198 Ji 30.44S 68.08W
Jaciara [Braz.] 204 Ib 14.12S 46.41W
Jaciara [Braz.] 204 Eb 15.59S 54.57W
Jackman 184 Lc 45.38N 70.16W
Jack Mountain 188 Eb 48.47N 120.57W
Jackpot 188 Hf 41.59N 114.09W
Jacksboro 186 Gj 33.13N 98.10W
Jacks Mountain 184 Ie 40.45N 77.30W
Jackson [Al.-U.S.] 184 Dj 31.31N 87.53W
Jackson [Bar.] 197q Ab 13.10N 59.43W
Jackson [Ky.-U.S.] 184 Fg 37.33N 83.23W
Jackson [Mi.-U.S.] 182 Kc 42.15N 84.24W
Jackson [Mn.-U.S.] 186 Ie 43.37N 94.59W
Jackson [Mo.-U.S.] 186 Lh 37.23N 89.40W
Jackson [Ms.-U.S.] 176 Jf 32.18N 90.12W
Jackson [Oh.-U.S.] 184 Ff 39.03N 82.40W
Jackson [Tn.-U.S.] 182 Jd 35.37N 88.49W
Jackson [Wy.-U.S.] 188 Je 43.29N 110.38W
Jackson, Cape- 218 Fd 40.59S 174.19 E
Jackson, Mount- [Ant.] 222 Qf 71.23S 63.22W
Jackson, Mount- [Austl.] 212 Df 30.15S 119.16 E
Jackson Bay 218 Ce 43.55S 168.40 E
Jackson Head 218 Ce 43.58S 168.37 E
Jackson Lake 188 Je 43.55N 110.40W
Jacksonville [Ar.-U.S.] 186 Ji 34.52N 92.07W
Jacksonville [Fl.-U.S.] 176 Kf 30.20N 81.40W
Jacksonville [Il.-U.S.] 186 Kg 39.44N 90.14W
Jacksonville [N.C.-U.S.] 182 Le 34.45N 77.26W
Jacksonville [Tx.-U.S.] 182 He 31.58N 95.17W
Jacksonville Beach 182 Ke 30.18N 81.24W
Jacmel 190 Je 18.14N 72.32W
Jacobābād 148 Dc 28.17N 68.26 E
Jacobina 202 Jf 11.11S 40.31W
Jacob Lake 188 Ih 36.45N 112.13W
Jacobs 186 La 50.15N 89.46W
Jacona de Plancarte 192 Hh 19.57N 102.16W
Jacques-Cartier, Détroit de - 180 Lg 50.00N 63.30W
Jacques Cartier, Mont - 180 Kg 48.58N 65.57W
Jacuba, Rio- 204 Fd 18.25S 52.28W
Jacuí, Rio- 198 Ki 30.02S 51.15W
Jacuí-Mirim, Rio- 204 Fi 28.51S 53.07W
Jacundá 202 Id 4.33S 49.28W
Jacundá, Rio- 202 Hd 1.57S 50.26W
Jacupiranga 206 Kb 24.42S 48.00W
Jada 166 Hd 8.46N 12.09 E
Jadal 166 Fb 18.37N 5.00 E
Jadar 128 Nf 44.38N 19.16 E
Jaddi, Rās- 148 Cc 25.14N 63.31 E
Jade 120 Ec 53.25N 8.05 E
Jadebusen 120 Ec 53.30N 8.10 E
Jadīd Ra's al Fīl 168 Dc 12.40N 25.43 E
Jadito Wash 188 Ji 35.22N 110.50W
J.A.D. Jensens Nunatakker 179 Hf 62.45N 48.20W
Jädraås 116 Gd 60.51N 16.28 E
Jadransko More=Adriatic Sea (EN) 110 Hg 43.00N 16.00 E
Jadrin 114 Li 55.57N 46.11 E
Jādū 164 Bc 31.57N 12.01 E
Ja'ēl 168 Ic 10.56N 51.09 E
Jaén 126 Ig 37.46N 3.47W
Jaén [3] 126 If 38.00N 3.30W
Jæren 116 Af 58.45N 5.45 E
Jærens rev 116 Af 58.45N 5.29 E
Jaffa, Cape- 212 Hg 36.58S 139.40 E
Jaffna 142 Ji 9.40N 80.00 E
Jafr, Qā' al- 146 Gg 30.17N 36.20 E
Jägala jõgi 116 Ke 59.28N 25.04 E
Jagdalpur 142 Kh 19.04N 82.02 E
Jagdaqi 152 La 50.26N 124.02 E
Jagersfontein 172 De 29.44S 25.29 E
Jaghbūb, Wāḩāt al-= Jarabub Oasis (EN) 158 Jf 29.41N 24.43 E
Jagotin 132 Gd 50.17N 31.47 E
Jagst 120 Fg 49.14N 9.11 E
Jaguapitã 204 Gf 23.07S 51.33W
Jaguaquara 202 Kf 13.32S 39.58W
Jaguarão 206 Jd 32.34S 53.23W
Jaguarão, Rio- 204 Fk 32.39S 53.12W
Jaguarari 202 Jf 10.16S 40.12W
Jaguari 204 Ei 29.30S 54.41W
Jaguari, Rio- [Braz.] 204 Ei 29.42S 55.07W
Jaguari, Rio- [Braz.] 204 If 22.41S 47.17W
Jaguariaíva 206 Kb 24.15S 49.42W
Jaguaribe 202 Ke 5.53S 38.37W
Jaguaribe, Rio- 198 Mf 4.25S 37.45W
Jaguaruana 202 Kd 4.50S 37.47W
Jagüey Grande 194 Gb 22.32N 81.08W
Jahadyjaha 134 Pc 67.03N 72.01 E
Jahām, 'Irq- 146 Li 26.12N 47.00 E
Jahorina 128 Mg 43.42N 18.35 E
Jahrom 144 Hd 28.31N 53.33 E
Jaice 128 Lf 44.21N 17.17 E
Jaicoa, Cordillera- 197a Ab 18.25N 67.05W
Jaicós 202 Je 7.21S 41.08W
Jailolo 150 If 1.05N 127.30 E
Jailolo, Selat- 150 If 0.05N 129.05 E
Jaina, Isla de- 192 Ng 20.14N 90.40W
Jaipur 142 Jg 26.55N 75.49 E
Jaisalmer 148 Ec 26.55N 70.54 E
Jaja 138 De 56.12N 86.26 E
Jäjarm 146 Qd 36.58N 56.27 E
Jajere 166 Hc 11.59N 11.26 E
Jajpan 135 Hd 40.23N 70.50 E
Jajsan 132 Td 50.51N 56.14 E
Jajva 136 Fd 59.20N 57.16 E
Jajva 134 Hg 59.16N 56.42 E
Jakarta (Djakarta) 142 Mj 6.10S 106.46 E
Jakobshavn/Ilulissat 224 Nc 69.20N 50.50W
Jakobstad/Pietarsaari 114 Fe 63.40N 22.42 E
Jakoruda 130 Gg 42.02N 23.40 E
Jakupica 130 Eh 41.43N 21.26 E
Jakutsk 142 Oc 62.13N 129.49 E
Jakutskaja ASSR → Saha (Jakutija), respublika 138 Hc 67.00N 130.00 E
Jal 186 Ei 32.07N 103.12W
Jalaid Qi (Inder) 152 Lb 46.41N 122.52 E
Jalājil 146 Kj 25.41N 45.28 E
Jalālābād 144 Lc 34.26N 70.28 E
Jalālah al Baḩrīyah, Jabal al- 146 Eh 29.20N 32.20 E
Jalālah al Qiblīyah, Jabal al- 146 Eh 28.42N 32.22 E
Jalán, Río- 194 Df 15.43N 87.34W
Jalandhar 142 Jf 31.19N 75.34 E
Jalapa [3] 194 Cf 14.35N 89.55W
Jalapa [Guat.] 190 Gf 14.38N 89.59W
Jalapa [Mex.] 192 Mi 17.43N 92.49W
Jalapa [Nic.] 190 Gf 13.55N 86.08W
Jalapa Enriquez 176 Jh 19.32N 96.55W
Jalasjarvi 116 Fe 62.30N 22.45 E
Jales 204 Ge 20.16S 50.33W
Jälgaon 148 Fd 21.01N 75.34 E
Jalhay 124 Hd 50.34N 5.58 E
Jalībah 146 Lg 30.35N 46.32 E
Jalib Shahab 146 Lg 30.23N 46.09 E
Jalingo 166 Hd 8.53N 11.22 E
Jalisco [2] 190 Dd 20.20N 103.40W
Jāliţah=La Galite (EN) 158 He 37.32N 8.56 E
Jāliţah, Canal de- 128 Cm 37.20N 9.00 E
Jalkot 148 Ea 35.15N 73.17 E
Jallas 126 Cb 42.54N 9.08W
Jālna 148 Fe 19.50N 75.53 E
Jalón 126 Kc 41.47N 1.04W
Jalostotitlán 192 Hg 21.12N 102.28W
Jalpa 192 Hg 21.38N 102.58W
Jalpaiguri 148 Hc 26.31N 88.44 E
Jalpan 192 Jg 21.14N 99.29W
Jalpug, ozero- 132 Fg 45.25N 28.40 E
Jalta 136 Dg 44.30N 34.10 E
Jaltepec, Rio- 192 Li 17.26N 94.59W
Jālū 164 Dd 28.30N 21.05 E
Jālū, Wāḩāt-=Gialo Oasis (EN) 158 Jf 29.00N 21.20 E
Jaluit Atoll 208 Hd 6.00N 169.35 E
Jalūlā' 146 Ke 34.16N 45.10 E
Jalutorovsk 136 Gd 56.40N 66.18 E
Jam [Iran] 146 Pe 35.45N 55.02 E
Jam [Iran] 146 Oi 27.50N 52.22 E
Jama/Jaama 116 Lf 58.59N 27.45 E
Jamaari 166 Hc 11.40N 9.53 E
Jamaica 194 Jc 20.12N 75.09W
Jamaica [1] 176 Lh 18.15N 77.30W
Jamaica 174 Lh 18.15N 77.30W
Jamaica Channel 190 Ie 18.00N 75.30W
Jamaica Channel (EN)= Jamaïque, Canal de- 194 Jd 18.00N 75.30W
Jamaïque, Canal de-= Jamaica Channel (EN) 194 Jd 18.00N 75.30W
Jamal, poluostrov- = Yamal Peninsula (EN) 140 Ib 70.00N 70.00 E
Jamalo-Neneckij respublika 138 Cc 67.00N 75.00 E
Jamālpur 148 Hd 24.55N 89.56 E
Jamâme 160 Lh 0.04N 42.46 E
Jamantau, gora- 110 Le 54.15N 58.06 E
Jamanxim, Rio- 198 Kf 4.43S 56.18W
Jamari, Rio- 202 Fe 8.27S 63.30W
Jamarovka 138 Gf 50.38N 110.16 E
Jambi 142 Mj 1.38S 103.42 E
Jambi [3] 150 Dg 1.36S 103.37 E
Jambol 130 Jg 42.29N 26.30 E
Jambol [2] 130 Jg 42.15N 26.35 E
Jambongan, Pulau- 150 Ge 6.41N 117.25 E
Jambuair, Tanjung- 150 Ce 5.16N 97.30 E
Jambusar 148 Ed 22.03N 72.48 E
James Bay 174 Kd 51.00N 80.30W
Jameson Land 179 Jd 70.45N 23.45W
James River [U.S.] 174 Je 42.52N 97.18W
James River [U.S.] 184 Ig 36.56N 76.27W
James Ross 222 Re 64.15S 57.45W
James Ross Strait 180 Hc 69.50N 96.30W
Jamestown [Austl.] 212 Hf 33.12S 138.36 E
Jamestown [N.D.-U.S.] 182 Hb 46.54N 98.42W
Jamestown [N.Y.-U.S.] 182 Lc 42.05N 79.15W
Jamestown [St.Hel.] 160 Gj 15.56S 5.43W
Jamestown Reservoir 186 Gc 47.15N 98.40W
Jamm 116 Mf 58.24N 28.15 E
Jammer Bugt 114 Bh 57.20N 9.30 E
Jammu 142 Jf 32.44N 74.52 E
Jammu and Kashmir [3] 148 Fb 34.00N 76.00 E
Jāmnagar 142 Jg 22.28N 70.04 E
Jamno, Jezioro- 120 Mb 54.15N 16.10 E
Jampol 132 Fe 48.16N 28.17 E
Jämsä 114 Ff 61.52N 25.12 E
Jamsah 146 Ei 27.38N 33.35 E
Jämsänkoski 116 Kc 61.55N 25.11 E
Jamshedpur 142 Kg 22.48N 86.11 E
Jamsk 138 Ke 59.37N 154.10 E
Jämtland [2] 114 De 63.00N 14.40 E
Jämtland 114 Fe 63.25N 14.05 E
Janā 146 Mi 27.22N 49.54 E
Jana 140 Pb 71.31N 136.32 E
Janakpur 148 Hc 26.42N 85.55 E
Janaucu, Ilha- 202 Hc 0.30N 50.10W
Janaul 134 Gh 56.16N 54.59 E
Janda, Laguna de la- 126 Gh 36.15N 5.51W
Jandaia 204 Gc 17.06S 50.07W
Jandaq 146 Pe 34.02N 54.26 E
Jandiatuba, Rio- 202 Ed 3.28S 68.42W
Jandowae 212 Ke 26.47S 151.06 E
Jandula 126 Hf 38.03N 4.06W
Jane Peak 218 Cf 45.20S 168.19 E
Janesville 182 Jc 42.41N 89.01W
Jangada 204 Db 15.14S 56.29W
Jangada, Rio- 204 Db 15.12S 56.24W
Jangao Shan 152 Gf 25.31N 98.08 E
Jangijer 135 Gd 40.18N 68.50 E
Jangijul 135 Gd 41.07N 69.03 E
Jangirabad 135 Ed 40.03N 65.59 E
Jango 204 Ee 20.27S 55.29W
Jangy-Bazar 135 Hd 41.40N 70.52 E
Janikowo 120 Od 52.45N 18.07 E
Janin 146 Ff 32.28N 35.18 E
Janisjarvi, ozero- 114 He 62.00N 31.00 E
Janja 128 Nf 44.40N 19.19 E
Jan Mayen 110 Fa 71.00N 8.30W
Jan Mayen Ridge (EN) 110 Fb 69.00N 8.00W
Jano-Indigirskaja nizmennost 138 Ib 71.00N 139.30 E
Janos 190 Cb 30.56N 108.08W
Jánoshalma 120 Pj 46.18N 19.20 E
Jánosháza 120 Ni 47.07N 17.10 E
Janów Lubelski 120 Sf 50.43N 22.24 E
Janów Podlaski 120 Td 52.11N 23.11 E
Jansenville 172 Cf 32.56S 24.40 E
Janski zaliv 140 Pb 72.00N 136.00 E
Jantarny 116 Hj 54.53N 19.55 E
Jantra 130 If 43.38N 25.34 E
Januária 202 Jg 15.29S 44.22W
Janūbīyah, Aş Şahrā' al-= Southern Desert (EN) 158 Jf 24.00N 30.00 E
Janykurgan 136 Gg 43.55N 67.14 E
Janzhang Ansha 150 Ge 9.30N 116.59 E
Japan (EN) 140 Pf 35.00N 135.00 E
Japan (EN)=Nippon [1] 142 Pf 38.00N 137.00 E
Japan, Sea of- (EN) = Japonskoje more 140 Pf 40.00N 134.00 E
Japan, Sea of- (EN) = Nippon-Kai 140 Pf 40.00N 134.00 E
Japan, Sea of- (EN)=Tong-Hae 140 Pf 40.00N 134.00 E
Japan Basin (EN) 152 Nc 40.00N 135.00 E
Japan Trench (EN) 106 If 37.00N 143.00 E
Japiim 202 De 7.37S 72.54W
Japonskoje more = Japan, Sea of- (EN) 140 Pf 40.00N 134.00 E
Jäppilä 116 Lb 62.23N 27.26 E
Japtiksale 134 Pb 69.25N 72.29 E
Japurá 202 Ed 1.24S 69.25W
Japurá, Rio- 198 Jf 3.08S 64.46W
Jaqué 194 Hj 7.31N 78.10W
Jaquet, Point- 197g Ba 15.38N 61.26W
Jaquirana 204 Gi 28.54S 50.23W
Jar 114 Mg 58.17N 52.06 E
Jarabub Oasis (EN)= Jaghbūb, Wāḩāt al- 158 Jf 29.41N 24.43 E
Jarābulus 146 Hd 36.49N 38.01 E
Jaraguá [Braz.] 204 Hh 26.29S 49.04W
Jaraguá [Braz.] 204 Hb 15.45S 49.20W
Jaraguá, Serra do- 204 Hh 26.40S 49.15W
Jaraguari 204 Ee 20.09S 54.25W
Jaraiz de la Vera 126 Gd 40.04N 5.45W
Jarama 126 Id 40.02N 3.39W
Jaramillo 206 Gg 47.11S 67.09W
Jarandilla 126 Gd 40.08N 5.39W
Jaransk 136 Ed 57.18N 47.55 E
Jarash 146 Ff 32.17N 35.54 E
Jarau, Cêrro do- 204 Dj 30.18S 56.32W
Jarbah 158 Ie 33.48N 10.54 E
Järbo 114 Df 60.43N 16.36 E
Jarcevo [Russia] 132 Hb 55.05N 32.45 E
Jarcevo [Russia] 138 Ed 60.15N 90.10 E
Jardāwīyah 146 Jj 25.24N 42.42 E
Jardim 202 Gh 21.28S 56.09W
Jardine River 212 Ib 11.10S 142.30 E
Jardines de la Reina, Archipiélago de los- 190 Id 20.50N 78.55W
Jardinópolis 204 Ie 21.02S 47.46W
Jarega 134 Fe 63.27N 53.31 E
Jaremča 132 De 48.31N 24.33 E
Jarenga 114 Le 62.08N 49.03 E
Järfälla 116 Ge 59.24N 17.50 E
Jargava 130 Lc 46.27N 28.27 E
Jari, Rio- 198 Kf 1.09S 51.54W
Jarīd, Shaţţ al- 158 He 33.42N 8.26 E
Jarīr, Wādī- 146 Jj 25.38N 42.30 E
Jarjīs 162 Jc 33.30N 11.07 E
Jarkovo 134 Mh 57.26N 67.05 E
Jarmah 164 Bd 26.32N 13.04 E
Järna 116 Ge 59.06N 17.34 E
Jarnac 122 Fi 45.41N 0.10W
Järnlunden 116 Ff 58.10N 15.40 E
Jarny 122 Le 49.09N 5.53 E
Jarocin 120 Ne 51.59N 17.31 E
Jaroměř 120 Lf 50.21N 15.55 E
Jaroměřice nad Rokytnou 120 Lg 49.06N 15.54 E
Jaroslavl 112 Jd 57.37N 39.52 E
Jaroslavskaja oblast [3] 136 Dd 57.45N 39.15 E
Jaroslavski 154 Lb 44.10N 132.13 E
Jarosław 120 Sf 50.02N 22.42 E
Järpen 116 Ea 63.21N 13.29 E
Jarrāḩī 146 Mg 30.44N 48.46 E
Jarroto, ozero- 134 Oc 67.55N 71.40 E
Jar-Sale 138 Cc 66.50N 70.50 E
Jartai 152 Id 39.45N 105.46 E
Jartai Yanchi 152 Id 39.45N 105.40 E
Jarudej 134 Od 65.50N 71.50 E
Jarud Qi (Lubei) 152 Lc 44.30N 120.55 E
Järva-Jaani/Jarva-Jani 116 Ke 59.00N 25.49 E
Jarva-Jani/Järva-Jaani 116 Ke 59.00N 25.49 E
Järvakandi/Jarvakandi 116 Kf 58.45N 24.44 E
Jarvakandi/Järvakandi 116 Kf 58.45N 24.44 E
Järvenpää 114 Ff 60.28N 25.06 E
Jarvis Island 208 Ke 0.23S 160.01W
Järvsö 114 Df 61.43N 16.10 E
Jaščera 116 Ne 59.05N 30.00 E
Jaselda 132 Ec 52.07N 26.29 E
Jasień 120 Le 51.46N 15.01 E
Jasikan 166 Fd 7.24N 0.28 E
Jasinja 120 Uh 48.14N 24.31 E
Jasinovataja 132 Je 48.05N 37.57 E
Jasiołka 120 Rg 49.47N 21.30 E
Jasira 168 He 1.57N 45.16 E
Jasīred Mayd 168 Hc 11.12N 47.13 E
Jäsk 144 Id 25.38N 57.46 E
Jaškul 132 Nf 46.11N 45.17 E
Jaškul 132 Nf 46.17N 45.10 E
Jasło 120 Rg 49.45N 21.29 E
Jasmund 120 Jb 54.32N 13.35 E
Jasnogorsk 132 Jb 54.29N 37.42 E
Jasny [Russia] 136 Fe 51.01N 59.59 E
Jasny [Russia] 138 Hf 53.18N 128.03 E
Jason Islands 206 Hh 51.00S 61.00W
Jasper [Alta.-Can.] 176 Hd 52.53N 118.05W
Jasper [Al.-U.S.] 182 Je 33.50N 87.17W
Jasper [Fl.-U.S.] 184 Fj 30.31N 82.57W
Jasper [In.-U.S.] 184 Df 38.24N 86.56W
Jasper [Tn.-U.S.] 184 Eh 35.04N 85.38W
Jasper [Tx.-U.S.] 186 Jk 30.55N 93.59W
Jasper Seamount (EN) 174 Gf 30.32N 122.42W
Jaşşān 146 Kf 32.58N 45.53 E
Jastrowie 120 Mc 53.26N 16.49 E
Jastrzebie Zdrój 120 Og 49.58N 18.34 E
Jászapáti 120 Qi 47.31N 20.09 E
Jászárokszállás 120 Pi 47.38N 19.59 E
Jászberény 120 Pi 47.30N 19.55 E
Jász-Nagykun-Szolnok 120 Qi 47.15N 20.30 E
Jászság 120 Pi 47.25N 20.00 E
Jatai 200 Kg 17.53S 51.43W
Jatapu, Rio- 202 Gd 2.30S 58.17W
Játiva/Xàtiva 126 Lf 38.59N 0.31W
Jatobá, Rio- 204 Ea 12.23S 54.07W
Jaú 206 Kb 22.18S 48.33W
Jaú, Rio- 202 Fd 1.55S 61.25W
Jaua, Cerro- 202 Fc 4.48N 64.26W
Jauaperi, Rio- 198 Jf 1.26S 61.35W
Jauja 202 Cf 11.48S 75.30W
Jaumave 192 Jf 23.25N 99.23W
Jaunanna 116 Lg 57.13N 27.10 E
Jaunelgava/Jaunjelgava 114 Fh 56.37N 25.06 E
Jaunfeld 120 Id 46.36N 14.45 E
Jaungulbene 116 Lh 57.00N 26.42 E
Jaunjelgava/Jaunelgava 114 Fh 56.37N 25.06 E
Jaunpiebalga 116 Lg 57.05N 26.03 E
Jaunpur 148 Gc 25.44N 82.41 E
Jauru 204 Ed 18.35S 54.17W
Jauru, Rio- [Braz.] 204 Dc 16.22S 57.46W
Jauru, Rio- [Braz.] 202 Hg 18.40S 54.36W
Java (EN)=Jawa 140 Mj 7.20S 110.00 E
Javaes → Araguaia, Braço Menor do- 202 He 9.50S 50.12W
Javalambre 126 Ld 40.06N 1.00W
Javalambre, Sierra de- 126 Ld 40.05N 1.00W
Javan 135 Ge 38.19N 69.01 E
Javānrūd 146 Le 34.48N 46.30 E
Javari, Rio- 198 If 4.21S 70.02W
Java Sea (EN)=Jawa, Laut- 140 Mj 5.00S 110.00 E
Java Trench (EN) 106 Hk 10.30S 110.00 E
Jávea / Xàbia 126 Mf 38.47N 0.10 E
Javier / Xavier 126 Kb 42.36N 1.13W
Javor 128 Mf 44.07N 18.59 E
Javorie 120 Ph 48.27N 19.18 E
Javornik 120 Jg 49.08N 13.35 E
Javorníky 120 Og 49.20N 18.20 E
Javorov 132 Cd 50.00N 23.27 E
Javorová skála 120 Kg 49.31N 14.30 E
Jävre 114 Ed 65.09N 21.29 E
Jawa=Java (EN) 140 Mj 7.20S 110.00 E
Jawa, Laut-=Java Sea (EN) 140 Mj 5.00S 110.00 E
Jawa Barat [3] 150 Eh 7.00S 107.00 E
Jawa Tengah [3] 150 Eh 7.30S 110.00 E
Jawa Timur [3] 150 Fh 8.00S 113.00 E
Jawf, Wādī- 164 If 15.50N 45.30 E
Jawor 120 Me 51.03N 16.11 E
Jaworzno 120 Pf 50.13N 19.15 E
Jaya, Puncak- 208 Ee 4.10S 137.00 E
Jayapura 210 Fe 2.32S 140.42 E
Jayawijaya, Pegunungan- 150 Kg 4.30S 139.30 E
Jāyezān 146 Mg 30.50N 49.52 E
Jaypur 148 He 18.51N 82.35 E
Jazā'ir Siyāl 168 Fa 23.00N 36.02 E
Jaz Mūriān, Hāmūn-e- 144 Id 27.20N 58.55 E
Jazva 134 Hf 60.23N 56.50 E
Jazvān 146 Md 36.58N 48.40 E
Jazykovo 114 Li 54.20N 47.22 E
Jazzīn 146 Ff 33.32N 35.34 E
Jdiouia 126 Mi 35.56N 0.50 E
Jean-Rabel 194 Kd 19.52N 73.11W
Jebala 126 Gi 35.25N 5.30W
Jebal Bārez, Kūh-e- 144 Id 28.30N 58.20 E
Jebba 166 Fd 9.08N 4.50 E
Jebel 130 Ed 45.33N 21.14 E
Jebha 126 Hi 35.13N 4.40W
Jedincy 132 Ee 48.06N 27.19 E
Jedisa 132 Nh 42.32N 44.14 E
Jędrzejów 120 Qf 50.39N 20.18 E
Jeetze 120 Hc 53.09N 11.04 E
Jefferson 186 Ie 42.01N 94.23W
Jefferson, Mount- [Nv.-U.S.] 182 Dd 38.46N 116.55W
Jefferson, Mount- [Or.-U.S.] 188 Ed 44.40N 121.47W
Jefferson City 176 Jf 38.34N 92.10W
Jefferson River 188 Jd 45.56N 111.30W
Jeffersonville 184 Ef 38.17N 85.44W
Jef-Jef el Kebir 168 Ca 20.30N 21.25 E
Jefremov 136 De 53.11N 38.07 E
Jega 166 Fc 12.13N 4.23 E
Jegorjevsk 114 Ji 55.25N 39.07 E
Jegorlyk 132 Lf 46.32N 41.52 E
Jegorlykskaja 132 Lf 46.34N 40.44 E
Jehegnadzor 132 Nj 39.47N 45.18 E
Jeja 132 Kf 46.39N 38.36 E
Jejsk 136 Df 46.40N 38.15 E
Jejuí Guazú, Río- 204 Dg 24.13S 57.09W
Jēkabpils 136 Cd 56.30N 25.59 E
Jekaterinburg (Sverdlovsk) 142 Id 56.51N 60.36 E
Jekaterinburgskaja oblast 136 Gd 59.00N 62.00 E
Jekaterinovka 132 Nc 52.04N 44.30 E
Jelabuga 136 Fd 55.48N 52.05 E
Jelai 150 Fg 2.59S 110.45 E
Jelan 132 Md 50.57N 43.43 E
Jelancy 138 Ff 52.44N 106.27 E
Jelanec 132 Gf 47.42N 31.50 E
Jelcz 120 Ne 51.01N 17.18 E
Jelec 112 Je 52.37N 38.30 E
Jeleckj 134 Lc 67.03N 64.15 E
Jelenia Góra 120 Lf 50.55N 15.46 E
Jelenia Góra [2] 120 Lf 50.55N 15.45 E
Jelgava 136 Cd 56.39N 23.41 E
Jelica 130 Df 43.47N 20.20 E
Jelin vrh 130 Cf 43.02N 19.27 E
Jelizavety, mys- 140 Qd 54.30N 142.40 E
Jelizovo [Bela.] 132 Fc 53.24N 29.00 E
Jelizovo [Russia] 138 Kf 53.06N 158.20 E
Jelling 116 Ci 55.45N 9.26 E
Jelnja 132 Hb 54.35N 33.12 E
Jeloguj 138 Dd 63.10N 87.45 E
Jelow Gīr 146 Lf 32.58N 47.48 E
Jeløy 116 De 58.30N 10.40 E
Jelsk 132 Fd 51.49N 29.13 E
Jelva 134 Ee 63.05N 50.50 E
Jemaja, Pulau- 150 Ef 2.55N 105.45 E
Jemanželinsk 136 Ge 54.45N 61.20 E
Jember 150 Fh 8.10S 113.42 E
Jemca 114 Je 63.04N 40.18 E
Jemca 114 Je 63.32N 41.56 E
Jemeppe-sur-Sambre 124 Gd 50.28N 4.40 E
Jeminay 152 Eb 47.28N 85.48 E
Jemnice 120 Lg 49.01N 15.35 E
Jena 120 Hf 50.56N 11.35 E
Jenakijevo 132 Ke 48.12N 38.18 E
Jenašimski Polkan, gora- 138 Ee 59.50N 92.45 E
Jendyr 134 Mf 61.38N 67.20 E
Jeneponto 150 Gh 5.41S 119.42 E
Jenisej=Yenisey (EN) 140 Kb 71.50N 82.40 E
Jenisejsk 138 Ee 58.27N 92.10 E
Jenisejski krjaž = Yenisey Ridge (EN) 140 Ld 59.00N 92.30 E
Jenisejski zaliv = Yenisey Bay (EN) 138 Db 72.00N 81.00 E
Jennersdorf 128 Kd 46.56N 16.08 E
Jennings 186 Jk 30.13N 92.39W
Jenny Lind 180 Hc 68.50N 101.30W
Jenny Point 197g Bb 15.28N 61.15W
Jensen 188 Kf 40.22N 109.17W
Jens Munk 180 Jc 69.40N 79.40W
Jequié 200 Lg 13.51S 40.05W
Jequitai 204 Jc 17.15S 44.28W
Jequitai, Rio- 204 Jc 17.04S 44.50W
Jequitinhonha, Rio- 198 Mg 15.51S 38.53W
Jerada 162 Gc 34.19N 2.09W
Jeralijev 136 Fg 43.12N 51.43 E
Jerbogačen 138 Fd 61.15N 107.57 E
Jérémie 190 Je 18.39N 74.08W
Jeremoabo 202 Kf 10.04S 38.21W

Jerer 〰	168	Gd	7.40N	43.48 E
Jerevan	112	Kg	40.11N	44.30 E
Jerez, Punta- ▶	192	Kf	22.54N	97.46W
Jerez de García Salinas	190	Dd	22.39N	103.00W
Jerez de la Frontera	126	Fh	36.41N	6.08W
Jerez de los Caballeros	126	Ff	38.19N	6.46W
Jergeni ◭	110	Kf	47.00N	44.00 E
Jericho	212	Jd	23.36S	146.08 E
Jermak	136	He	52.02N	76.55 E
Jermakovskoje	138	Ef	53.16N	92.24 E
Jermentau	136	He	51.38N	73.10 E
Jermolajevo (Kumertau)	136	Fe	52.46N	55.47 E
Jeroaquara	204	Gb	15.23S	50.25W
Jerofej Pavlovič	138	Hf	53.58N	121.57 E
Jerome	188	He	42.43N	114.31W
Jersa 〰	134	Fc	66.19N	52.32 E
Jersey ◆	118	Kl	49.15N	2.10W
Jersey City	182	Mc	40.44N	74.04W
Jerseyville	186	Kg	39.07N	90.20W
Jeršov	136	Ee	51.20N	48.17 E
Jertarski	134	Lh	56.47N	64.25 E
Jerte 〰	126	Fe	39.58N	6.17W
Jerusalem (EN)= Yerushalayim	142	Ff	31.46N	35.14 E
Jeruslan 〰	132	Od	50.20N	46.25 E
Jervis Bay ◧	212	Kg	35.05S	150.44 E
Jerzu	128	Dk	39.47N	9.31 E
Jesberg	124	Lc	51.00N	9.09 E
Jesenice [Cro.]	128	Jf	44.14N	15.34 E
Jesenice [Slo.]	128	Id	46.27N	14.04 E
Jesenik	120	Nf	50.14N	17.12 E
Jesi	128	Hg	43.31N	13.14 E
Jesil	136	Ge	51.58N	66.24 E
Jeskianhor, kanal- ═	135	Fe	39.15N	66.00 E
Jessej	138	Fc	68.29N	102.10 E
Jessentuki	132	Mg	44.03N	42.51 E
Jessheim	114	Cf	60.09N	11.11 E
Jessore	148	Hd	23.10N	89.13 E
Ještěd ▲	120	Kf	50.42N	14.59 E
Jestro, Wabe- 〰	158	Lh	4.11N	42.09 E
Jesup	182	Ke	31.36N	81.53W
Jesús Carranza	192	Li	17.26N	95.02W
Jesús María	206	Hd	30.59S	64.06W
Jesús María, Boca de- ⇌	192	Ke	24.29N	97.40W
Jesús María, Río- 〰	192	Gg	21.55N	104.30W
Jetmore	186	Gg	38.03N	99.54W
Jeumont	124	Gd	50.18N	4.06 E
Jever	120	Dc	53.35N	7.54 E
Jevgenjevka	135	Kc	43.27N	77.40 E
Jevišovka 〰	120	Mh	48.52N	16.36 E
Jevlah	136	Eg	40.35N	47.10 E
Jevnaker	114	Cf	60.15N	10.28 E
Jevpatorija	136	Df	45.12N	33.18 E
Jeyḩūn	146	Pi	27.16N	55.12 E
Jeypore → Jaypur	148	He	18.51N	82.35 E
Jezercës ▲	110	Hg	42.26N	19.49 E
Jezero	128	Lf	44.21N	17.10 E
Jeziorak, Jezioro- ≈	120	Pc	53.50N	19.35 E
Jeziorany	120	Qc	53.58N	20.46 E
Jeziorka 〰	120	Rd	52.10N	21.06 E
Jhang Sadar	148	Eb	31.16N	72.19 E
Jhānsi	142	Jg	25.26N	78.35 E
Jhelum	148	Eb	32.56N	73.44 E
Jhelum 〰	140	Jf	31.12N	72.08 E
Jiaji → Qionghai	152	Jh	19.25N	110.28 E
Jialing Jiang 〰	140	Mg	29.34N	106.35 E
Jialu He 〰	154	Ch	33.40N	115.01 E
Jiamusi	142	Pe	46.49N	130.21 E
Ji'an [China]	152	Mc	41.08N	126.10 E
Ji'an [China]	142	Ng	27.12N	114.59 E
Jianchang	154	Ed	40.49N	119.46 E
Jianchuan	152	Gf	26.32N	99.53 E
Jiande (Baisha)	152	Kf	29.31N	119.17 E
Jiang'an	152	If	28.40N	105.07 E
Jiangbiancun	152	Kf	27.13N	115.57 E
Jiangcheng	152	Hg	22.37N	101.48 E
Jiangdu (Xiannümiao)	154	Eh	32.30N	119.33 E
Jiange	152	Ie	31.59N	105.28 E
Jianghua (Shuikou)	152	Jg	24.58N	111.56 E
Jiangjin	152	If	29.15N	106.18 E
Jiangle	152	Kf	26.48N	117.29 E
Jiangling (Jingzhou)	152	Je	30.21N	112.10 E
Jiangmen	152	Jg	22.35N	113.02 E
Jiangpu	154	Eh	32.03N	118.37 E
Jiangshan	154	Ej	28.45N	118.37 E
Jiangsu Sheng (Chiang-su Sheng)=Kiangsu (EN) [2]	152	Ke	33.00N	120.00 E
Jiangxi Sheng (Chiang-hsi Sheng) = Kiangsi (EN) [2]	152	Kf	28.00N	116.00 E
Jiangyou (Zhongba)	152	He	31.48N	104.39 E
Jianhu	154	Eh	33.28N	119.47 E
Jianli	152	Jf	29.50N	112.55 E
Jian'ou	152	Kf	27.08N	118.20 E
Jianping	154	Ed	41.27N	119.37 E
Jianping (Yebaishou)	152	Kc	41.55N	119.37 E
Jianshi	152	Ie	30.32N	109.43 E
Jianshui	152	Hg	23.39N	102.46 E
Jianyang	152	Kf	27.23N	118.03 E
Jiaocheng	152	Jd	37.32N	112.09 E
Jiaoding Shan ▲	152	Lc	41.11N	120.01 E
Jiaohe [China]	152	Mc	43.43N	127.20 E
Jiaohe [China]	154	De	38.01N	116.17 E
Jiaolai He [China] 〰	154	Ef	37.07N	119.35 E
Jiaolai He [China] 〰	154	Fc	43.02N	120.48 E
Jiaoliu He 〰	154	Gb	45.21N	122.48 E
Jiaonan (Wanggezhuang)	154	Eg	35.53N	119.58 E
Jiaoxian	152	Kd	36.20N	120.00 E
Jiaozhou-Wan ◧	154	Ff	36.10N	120.15 E
Jiaozuo	142	Nf	35.15N	113.18 E
Jiashan	154	Fi	30.51N	120.54 E
Jiashan (Mingguang)	154	Dh	32.47N	118.00 E
Jiashi/Payzawat	152	Cd	39.29N	76.39 E
Jiawang	154	Dg	34.27N	117.26 E
Jiaxian	154	Bh	33.58N	113.13 E
Jiaxing	152	Le	30.44N	120.46 E
Jiayin (Chaoyang)	152	Nb	48.52N	130.21 E
Jiayu	152	Jf	30.00N	113.57 E
Jiayuguan	152	Gd	39.49N	98.18 E
Jibalei	168	Ic	10.07N	50.47 E
Jibão, Serra do- ⛰	204	Jb	14.48S	45.15W
Jibiya	166	Gc	13.06N	7.14 E
Jibou	130	Gb	47.16N	23.15 E
Jicarón, Isla- ◆	194	Gj	7.16N	81.47W
Jičín	120	Lf	50.26N	15.22 E
Jiddah	142	Fg	21.29N	39.12 E
Jiddat al Ḩarāsīs ⧗	144	Ie	20.05N	56.00 E
Jiehu → Yinan	154	Eg	35.33N	118.27 E
Jieshou	154	Ch	33.17N	115.22 E
Jiesjjavrre ≈	114	Fb	69.40N	24.12 E
Jiexiu	152	Jd	37.00N	112.00 E
Jieyang	152	Kg	23.32N	116.25 E
Jieznas/Eznas	116	Kj	54.34N	24.17 E
Jifn, Wādī al- 〰	146	Jj	25.48N	42.15 E
Jiftūn, Jazā'ir- ❖	146	Ei	27.13N	33.56 E
Jīgley	168	He	4.25N	45.22 E
Jiguaní	194	Ic	20.22N	76.26W
Jigüey, Bahía de- ◧	194	Hb	22.08N	78.05W
Jigzhi	152	He	33.28N	101.29 E
Jihlava	120	Lg	49.24N	15.34 E
Jihlava 〰	120	Mh	48.55N	16.37 E
Jihlavské vrchy ⛰	120	Lg	49.15N	15.20 E
Jihočeský kraj [3]	120	Kg	49.05N	14.30 E
Jihomoravský kraj [3]	120	Mg	49.10N	16.40 E
Jijel	162	Ib	36.48N	5.46 E
Jijel [3]	162	Ib	36.45N	5.45 E
Jijia 〰	130	Lc	46.54N	28.05 E
Jijiga	168	Gd	9.21N	42.48 E
Jijona / Xixona	126	Lf	38.32N	0.30W
Jikharrah	164	Dd	29.17N	21.38 E
Jilava	130	Je	44.20N	26.05 E
Jilf al Kabīr, Haḑabat al- ▬	164	Ee	23.30N	26.00 E
Jilib	160	Lh	0.29N	42.47 E
Jilin	142	Oe	43.51N	126.33 E
Jilin Sheng (Chi-lin Sheng) =Kirin (EN) [2]	152	Mc	43.00N	126.00 E
Jiliu He 〰	152	La	52.02N	120.41 E
Jiloca 〰	126	Kc	41.21N	1.39W
Jima=Jimma (EN)	160	Kh	7.39N	36.49 E
Jimāl, Wādī- 〰	146	Fj	24.40N	35.06 E
Jimaní	194	Ld	18.28N	71.51W
Jimbe	170	De	11.05S	24.00 E
Jimbolia	130	Dd	45.48N	20.43 E
Jimena	126	Ig	37.50N	3.28W
Jimena de la Frontera	126	Gh	36.26N	5.27W
Jiménez	190	Dc	27.08N	104.55W
Jiménez de Teúl	192	Gf	23.10N	104.05W
Jimma (EN)=Jima	160	Kh	7.39N	36.49 E
Jimo	154	Ff	36.24N	120.27 E
Jimsar	152	Ec	43.59N	89.04 E
Jimulco ▲	192	He	25.20N	103.10W
Jināh	146	Dj	25.20N	30.31 E
Jinan (Tsinan)	142	Nf	36.35N	117.00 E
Jincheng [China]	152	Jd	35.32N	112.53 E
Jincheng [China]	154	Fd	41.12N	121.25 E
Jinchuan /Quqên	152	He	31.02N	102.02 E
Jind	148	Fc	29.19N	76.19 E
Jindřichův Hradec	120	Kg	49.09N	15.00 E
Jinfo Shan ▲	152	If	29.01N	107.14 E
Jing/Jinghe	152	Dc	44.39N	82.50 E
Jing'an	154	Cj	28.51N	115.21 E
Jingbian (Zhangjiapan)	152	Id	37.32N	108.45 E
Jingde	154	Ei	30.18N	118.30 E
Jingdezhen	142	Ng	29.18N	117.18 E
Jingfeng → Hexigten Qi	152	Kc	43.15N	117.31 E
Jinggang Shan ▲	152	Jf	26.42N	114.07 E
Jinggu	152	Hg	23.28N	100.39 E
Jinghai	154	De	38.57N	116.56 E
Jinghe/Jing	152	Dc	44.39N	82.50 E
Jinghong (Yunjinghong)	152	Hg	21.59N	100.48 E
Jinghong Dao ◆	150	Fe	9.45N	114.28 E
Jingjiang	154	Fh	32.01N	120.15 E
Jingle	154	Ae	38.22N	111.56 E
Jingmen	152	Je	31.00N	112.11 E
Jingning	152	Id	35.30N	105.45 E
Jingping → Pinglu	154	Be	39.32N	112.14 E
Jingpo Hu ≈	154	Jc	43.50N	128.53 E
Jingshan	154	Bi	31.04N	113.08 E
Jingtai	152	Hd	37.10N	104.08 E
Jingxian [China]	152	If	26.40N	109.37 E
Jingxian [China]	152	Ke	30.41N	118.29 E
Jingxing (Weishui)	154	Ce	38.03N	114.09 E
Jingyu	154	Ic	42.25N	126.48 E
Jingyuan	152	Hd	36.35N	104.40 E
Jingzhi	154	Ef	36.18N	119.22 E
Jingzhou → Jiangling	152	Je	30.21N	112.10 E
Jinhu (Licheng)	154	Eh	33.01N	119.01 E
Jinhua	152	Kf	29.09N	119.38 E
Jining [China]	142	Nf	35.26N	116.36 E
Jining [China]	142	Ne	41.02N	113.07 E
Jinja	160	Kh	0.26N	33.13 E
Jin Jiang 〰	154	Cj	28.23N	115.48 E
Jinkou	154	Ci	30.20N	114.07 E
Jinotega	190	Gf	13.06N	86.00W
Jinotega [3]	194	Eg	14.00N	85.25W
Jinotepe	190	Gf	11.51N	86.12W
Jinping	152	Hg	22.45N	103.15 E
Jinsha	152	If	27.18N	106.16 E
Jinsha → Nantong	154	Fh	32.06N	120.52 E
Jinsha Jiang 〰	140	Mg	28.46N	104.38 E
Jinshan	154	Fi	30.54N	121.09 E
Jinshan → Harqin Qi	154	Ed	41.57N	118.40 E
Jinshi	154	Aj	29.03N	111.52 E
Jinta	152	Gc	40.00N	99.00 E
Jintan	154	Ei	31.45N	119.34 E
Jinxi	152	Lc	40.46N	120.50 E
Jinxian [China]	152	Ld	39.06N	121.44 E
Jinxian [China]	154	Dj	28.21N	116.16 E
Jinxiang	154	Dg	35.04N	116.19 E
Jinyang	152	Hf	27.39N	103.12 E
Jinyun	154	Fj	28.39N	120.05 E
Jinzhai (Meishan)	154	Ci	31.40N	115.52 E
Jinzhou	142	Oe	41.09N	121.08 E
Jinzū-Gawa 〰	156	Ec	36.45N	137.13 E
Jiparaná, Rio- 〰	198	Jf	8.03S	62.52W
Jipijapa	202	Bd	1.22S	80.34W
Jiquilisco	194	Cg	13.19N	88.35W
Jiquilisco, Bahía de- ◧	194	Cg	13.10N	88.28W
Jirjā	164	Fd	26.20N	31.53 E
Jishou	152	If	28.18N	109.43 E
Jishu	154	Ib	44.16N	126.50 E
Jisr ash Shughur	146	Ge	35.48N	36.19 E
Jiu 〰	130	Gf	43.47N	23.48 E
Jiucai Ling ▲	152	Jf	25.33N	111.18 E
Jiucheng → Wucheng	154	Df	37.12N	116.04 E
Jiuding Shan ▲	152	He	31.30N	104.00 E
Jiujiang	142	Ng	29.39N	116.00 E
Jiuling Shan ⛰	152	Jf	28.55N	114.50 E
Jiulong/Gyaisi	152	Hf	28.58N	101.33 E
Jiuquan (Suzhou)	142	Lf	39.46N	98.34 E
Jiurongcheng	154	Gf	37.22N	122.33 E
Jiutai	152	Mc	44.10N	125.50 E
Jīwani, Rās- ▶	148	Cc	25.01N	61.44 E
Jixi [China]	142	Pe	45.15N	130.55 E
Jixi [China]	154	Ei	30.04N	118.36 E
Jixian [China]	154	Cg	35.23N	114.04 E
Jixian [China]	154	Dd	40.03N	117.24 E
Jixian [China]	154	Cf	37.34N	115.34 E
Jiyang	154	Df	36.59N	117.11 E
Jiyuan	154	Bg	35.06N	112.35 E
Jiyun He 〰	154	De	39.05N	117.45 E
Jiz, Wādī al- 〰	168	Ib	16.12N	52.14 E
Jīzān	142	Gh	16.54N	42.32 E
Jize	154	Cf	36.54N	114.52 E
Jizera 〰	120	Kf	50.10N	14.43 E
Jizerské Hory ⛰	120	Lf	50.50N	15.13 E
Jizl, Wādī al- 〰	146	Hj	25.39N	38.25 E
Jizō-Zaki ▶	154	Lg	35.33N	133.18 E
Jmbe	170	De	10.20S	16.40 E
Jnchengjiang → Hechi	152	Ig	24.44N	108.02 E
Joaçaba	204	Gh	27.10S	51.30W
Joal-Fadiout	166	Bc	14.10N	16.51W
João Câmara	202	Ke	5.32S	35.48W
João Monlevade	204	Kd	19.50S	43.08W
João Pessoa	200	Mf	7.07S	34.52W
João Pinheiro	202	Ig	17.45S	46.10W
Joaquín V. González	206	Hb	25.00S	64.11W
Jobado	194	Ic	20.54N	77.17W
Jódar	126	Ig	37.50N	3.21W
Jodhpur	142	Jg	26.17N	73.02 E
Jodoigne/Geldenaken	124	Gd	50.43N	4.52 E
Joensuu	112	Ic	62.36N	29.46 E
Joerg Plateau ▬	222	Qf	75.00S	69.30W
Joes Hill △	220g	Bb	1.48N	157.19W
Jōetsu	152	Od	37.06N	138.15 E
Joeuf	124	Ie	49.14N	6.01 E
Jôf di Montasio ▲	128	Hd	46.26N	13.26 E
Joffre, Mount- ▲	188	Ha	50.32N	115.13W
Jogbani	148	Hc	26.25N	87.15 E
Jõgeva/Jygeva	114	Gg	58.46N	26.26 E
Joghatāy	146	Qd	36.36N	57.01 E
Joghatāy, Kūh-e- ⛰	146	Qd	36.30N	57.00 E
Jōhana	156	Ec	36.31N	136.54 E
Johannesburg	160	Jk	26.15S	28.00 E
Jōhen	156	Ce	32.57N	132.35 E
John Day	188	Fd	44.25N	118.57W
John Day River 〰	182	Cb	45.44N	120.39W
John H. Kerr Reservoir ⊜	184	Hg	36.31N	78.18W
John Martin Reservoir ⊜	186	Eg	38.05N	103.02W
John o' Groat's	118	Jc	58.38N	3.05W
Johnson	186	Fh	37.34N	101.45W
Johnson, Pico de- ▲	192	Cc	29.13N	112.07W
Johnson City [Tn.-U.S.]	182	Kd	36.19N	82.21W
Johnson City [Tx.-U.S.]	186	Gk	30.17N	98.25W
Johnsons Crossing	180	Ed	60.29N	133.17W
Johnsons Point ▶	197d	Bb	17.02N	61.53W
Johnston Atoll [5]	210	Kc	17.00N	168.30W
Johnston Atoll ◆	208	Kc	17.00N	168.30W
Johnstone, Lake- ≈	212	Ef	32.20S	120.40 E
Johnstone Strait ⇌	188	Ca	50.25N	126.00W
Johnstown [N.Y.-U.S.]	184	Jd	43.01N	74.22W
Johnstown [Pa.-U.S.]	182	Lc	40.20N	78.56W
Johor [2]	150	Df	2.00N	103.30 E
Johor Baharu	142	Mi	1.28N	103.45 E
Joia	204	Ei	28.39S	54.08W
Joigny	122	Jg	47.59N	3.24 E
Joinvile	200	Lh	26.18S	48.50W
Joinville	122	Lf	48.27N	5.08 E
Joinville Island ◆	222	Re	63.15S	55.45W
Jokau	168	Ed	8.24N	33.49 E
Jokela	116	Kd	60.33N	24.59 E
Jokelbugten ◧	179	Kc	78.25N	19.00W
Jokioinen	116	Jd	60.49N	23.28 E
Jokkmokk	114	Ec	66.36N	19.51 E
Jøkuleggi ▲	116	Cc	61.03N	8.12 E
Jolfā	146	Kc	38.57N	45.38 E
Joliet	182	Jc	41.32N	88.05W
Joliette	180	Kg	46.01N	73.26W
Jolo	150	He	6.00N	121.00 E
Jolo Group ❖	140	Oi	6.00N	121.09 E
Jølstravatnet ≈	116	Bc	61.30N	6.15 E
Jomala	116	Hd	60.09N	19.58 E
Jombang	150	Fh	7.33S	112.14 E
Jomda	152	Ge	31.37N	98.20 E
Jönåker	116	Gf	58.44N	16.40 E
Jonava/Ionava	114	Fi	55.05N	24.17 E
Jonê	152	He	34.35N	103.32 E
Jones Bank ▦	118	Fl	49.50N	8.00W
Jonesboro [Ar.-U.S.]	182	Id	35.50N	90.42W
Jonesboro [La.-U.S.]	186	Jj	32.15N	92.43W
Jones Mountains ⛰	222	Pf	73.32S	94.00W
Jones Sound ⇌	174	Kb	76.00N	85.00W
Jonesville	184	Fg	36.41N	83.06W
Jonglei	168	Ed	6.50N	31.18 E
Jonglei [3]	168	Ed	7.20N	32.00 E
Jonglei, Tur'ah-=Jonglei Canal (EN) ═	168	Ed	9.22N	31.30 E
Jonglei Canal (EN)=Jonglei, Tur'ah- ═	168	Ed	9.22N	31.30 E
Joniškėlis/Ioniškelis	116	Ki	56.00N	24.14 E
Joniškis/Ioniškis	114	Fh	56.16N	23.37 E
Jönköping	112	Hd	57.47N	14.11 E
Jönköping [2]	114	Dh	57.30N	14.30 E
Jonquière	180	Kg	48.25N	71.15W
Jonuta	192	Mh	18.05N	92.08W
Jonzac	122	Fi	45.27N	0.26W
Joplin	176	Jf	37.06N	94.31W
Jordan	182	Fb	47.19N	106.55W
Jordan 〰	144	Ec	31.46N	35.33 E
Jordan (EN)=Al Urdun [1]	142	Ff	31.00N	36.00 E
Jordan Valley	188	Ge	42.58N	117.03W
Jordão, Rio- 〰	204	Fg	25.46S	52.07W
Jorhāt	142	Lg	26.45N	94.13 E
Jörn	114	Ed	65.04N	20.02 E
Joroinen	114	Ge	62.11N	27.50 E
Jørpeland	114	Bg	59.01N	6.03 E
Jos	160	Hh	9.55N	8.54 E
José A. Guisasola	204	Bn	38.40S	61.05W
José Battle y Ordóñez	204	Ek	33.28S	55.07W
José Bonifácio	204	He	21.03S	49.41W
José de San Martín	206	Ff	44.02S	70.29W
Joselandia	204	Dc	16.32S	56.12W
José Otávio	204	Ej	31.17S	54.07W
José Pedro Varela	204	Ek	33.27S	54.32W
Joseph, Lake- ≈	184	Hc	45.14N	79.45W
Joseph Bonaparte Gulf ◧	208	Df	14.55S	128.15 E
Josephine Seamount (EN) ⩚	110	Eh	36.52N	14.20W
Joseph Lake ≈	180	Kf	52.48N	65.17W
Joshimath	148	Fb	30.34N	79.34 E
Joškar-Ola	112	Kd	56.40N	47.55 E
Jos Plateau ▬	158	Hh	10.00N	9.30 E
Josselin	122	Dg	47.57N	2.33W
Jostedalen ⧗	116	Bc	61.35N	7.20 E
Jostedalsbreen ⛰	114	Bf	61.40N	7.00 E
Jostefonn ▲	116	Bc	61.26N	6.33 E
Jost Van Dyke ◆	197a	Db	18.28N	64.45W
Jotunheimen ⛰	110	Gc	61.40N	8.20 E
Joubertberge ⛰	172	Ac	18.45S	13.55 E
Joué-lès-Tours	122	Gg	47.21N	0.40 E
Jouquara, Rio- 〰	204	Db	15.06S	57.06W
Joure, Haskerland-	124	Hb	52.58N	5.47 E
Joutsa	114	Gf	61.44N	26.07 E
Joutseno	114	Gf	61.06N	28.30 E
Jovan, Deli- ⛰	130	Fe	44.15N	22.13 E
Jovellanos	194	Gb	22.48N	81.12W
Joviânia	204	Hc	17.49S	49.30W
Jowhar	160	Lh	2.46N	45.32 E
Jow Kār	146	Me	34.26N	48.42 E
Jowzjān [3]	144	Kb	36.30N	66.00 E
Joya, Laguna de la- ◎	192	Mj	15.55N	93.40W
Jreïda	162	Df	18.19N	16.03W
Juan Aldama	190	Dd	24.19N	103.21W
Juana Ramirez, Isla- ◆	192	Kg	21.50N	97.40W
Juan Blanquier	204	Cl	35.46S	59.18W
Juancheng	154	Cg	35.33N	115.30 E
Juan de Fuca, Strait of- ⇌	174	Ge	48.20N	124.00W
Juan de Nova, Ile- ◆	158	Lj	17.03S	42.45 E
Juan E. Barra	204	Bm	37.48S	60.29W
Juan Fernández,Archipiélago-= Juan Fernández Islands (EN) ❖	198	Ii	33.00S	80.00W
Juan Fernández Islands (EN) =Juan Fernández,Archipiélago- ❖	198	Ii	33.00S	80.00W
Juan G. Bazán	204	Bg	24.33S	60.50W
Juangriego	196	Eg	11.05N	63.57W
Juanjuí	202	Ce	7.11S	76.45W
Juan L. Lacaze	204	Dl	34.26S	57.27W
Juárez [Arg.]	206	Ie	37.40S	59.48W
Juárez [Mex.]	192	Id	27.37N	100.44W
Juárez, Sierra de- ⛰	192	Bb	32.00N	115.50W
Juarzohn	166	Dd	5.20N	8.58W
Juàzeirinho	202	Ke	7.04S	36.35W
Juàzeiro	200	Lf	9.25S	40.30W
Juàzeiro do Norte	200	Mf	7.12S	39.20W
Jūbā	160	Kh	4.51N	31.37 E
Juba (EN) = Ganāne, Webi- 〰	158	Lh	0.15S	42.38 E
Juba, Rio- 〰	204	Db	14.59S	57.44W
Jūbāl, Maḑīq- ⇌	146	Ei	27.40N	33.55 E
Jubaland (EN) ⧗	158	Lh	1.00N	42.00 E
Jubayl [Eg.]	146	Eh	28.12N	33.38 E
Jubayl [Leb.]	146	Fe	34.07N	35.39 E
Jubayt [Sud.]	168	Fb	18.57N	36.50 E
Jubayt [Sud.]	168	Fa	20.59N	36.18 E
Jubbada Dhexe [3]	168	Ge	1.15N	42.30 E
Jubbada Hoose [3]	168	Gf	0.30S	42.00 E
Jubbah	146	Ih	28.02N	40.56 E
Jubilee Lake ≈	212	Fe	29.10S	126.40 E
Juby, Cap- ▶	158	Ff	27.57N	12.55W
Júcar/Xúquer 〰	110	Fh	39.09N	0.14W
Juçara	204	Gb	15.53S	50.51W
Jucaro	194	Hc	21.37N	78.51W
Jüchen	124	Ic	51.06N	6.30 E
Juchipila	192	Hg	21.25N	103.07W
Juchipila, Rio- 〰	192	Hg	21.03N	103.25W
Juchitán de Zaragoza	176	Jh	16.26N	95.01W
Jučjugej	138	Jd	63.20N	142.15 E
Judas, Punta- ▶	194	Ei	9.31N	84.32W
Judayyidat 'Ar'ar	144	Fc	31.22N	41.26 E
Judenburg	128	Ic	47.10N	14.40 E
Judith Mountains ⛰	188	Kc	47.12N	109.15W
Judith River 〰	188	Kc	47.44N	109.38W
Judoma 〰	138	Ie	59.08N	135.03 E
Judomski hrebet ⛰	138	Jd	61.05N	141.30 E
Juegang → Rudong	154	Fh	32.19N	121.11 E
Juelsminde	116	Di	55.43N	10.01 E
Jufrah, Wāḩāt al- = Giofra Oasis (EN) 🌴	158	If	29.10N	16.00 E
Jug	134	Hh	57.43N	56.12 E
Jug	110	Kc	60.45N	46.20 E
Jugo Osetija	136	Eg	42.20N	44.05 E
Jugorski poluostrov	134	Kb	69.30N	62.30 E
Jugorski Šar, proliv- ⇌	136	Gb	69.45N	60.35 E
Jugoslavija = Yugoslavia (EN) [1]	112	Hg	44.00N	19.00 E
Jugo-Tala	138	Kc	66.03N	151.05 E
Jugydjan	134	Gf	61.42N	54.58 E
Juhaym	146	Kh	29.36N	45.24 E
Juhnov	132	Ib	54.43N	35.12 E
Juhor ⛰	130	Ef	43.50N	21.15 E
Juhoslovenská nížina ⧗	120	Ph	48.10N	19.40 E
Juhua Dao ◆	154	Fd	40.32N	120.48 E
Juigalpa	194	Eg	12.05N	85.24W
Juina, Rio- 〰	204	Ca	12.36S	58.57W
Juine 〰	122	If	48.32N	2.23 E
Juininha, Rio- 〰	204	Ca	12.55S	59.13W
Juist ◆	120	Cc	53.40N	7.00 E
Juiz de Fora	200	Lh	21.45S	43.20W
Jujuy [2]	206	Gb	23.00S	66.00W
Jukagirskoje ploskogorje ▬	138	Kc	66.00N	155.30 E
Jukonda 〰	134	Mg	59.38N	67.20 E
Juksejevo	134	Gg	59.52N	54.16 E
Jula 〰	114	Ke	63.48N	44.44 E
Juldybajevo	134	Hj	52.20N	57.52 E
Julesburg	186	Ef	40.59N	102.16W
Juli	202	Eg	16.13S	69.27W
Juliaca	202	Dg	15.30S	70.08W
Julia Creek	212	Id	20.39S	141.45 E
Julian Alps (EN)=Julijske Alpe ⛰	128	Hd	46.20N	13.45 E
Juliana Top ▲	202	Gc	3.41N	56.32W
Julianehåb/Qaqortoq	224	Nc	60.50N	46.10W
Jülich	120	Cf	50.56N	6.22 E
Jülicher Borde ⧗	124	Id	50.50N	6.30 E
Julijske Alpe=Julian Alps (EN) ⛰	128	Hd	46.20N	13.45 E
Julimes	192	Gc	28.25N	105.27W
Júlio de Castilhos	204	Fi	29.14S	53.41W
Jullundur → Jalandhar	142	Jf	31.19N	75.34 E
Julong/New Kowloon	142	Ng	22.20N	114.09 E
Julu	154	Cf	37.13N	115.02 E
Juma	114	Hd	65.05N	33.13 E
Juma He 〰	154	De	39.31N	116.08 E
Jumaymah, Birkat al- 🌴	146	Jh	29.36N	43.36 E
Jumentos Cays ❖	194	Jb	23.00N	75.50W
Jumet, Charleroi-	122	Kd	50.27N	4.26 E
Jumièges	124	Ce	49.26N	0.49 E
Jumilla	126	Kf	38.29N	1.17W
Jümme 〰	124	Ja	53.13N	7.31 E
Junāgadh	148	Ed	21.31N	70.28 E
Junan (Shizilu)	154	Eg	35.10N	118.50 E
Junaynah, Ra's al- ▲	146	Eh	29.01N	33.58 E
Juncal	192	De	24.50N	111.47W
Juncos	197a	Cb	18.13N	65.55W
Junction [Tx.-U.S.]	186	Gk	30.29N	99.46W
Junction [Ut.-U.S.]	188	Ig	38.14N	112.13W
Junction City	182	Hd	39.02N	96.50W
Jundiaí	206	Kb	23.11S	46.52W
Jundiaí do Sul	204	Gf	23.27S	50.17W
Jundūbah	162	Ib	36.30N	8.45 E
Jundūbah [3]	162	Ib	36.28N	8.41 E
Juneau	176	Fd	57.20N	134.27W
Junee	212	Jf	34.52S	147.35 E
Jungar Qi (Shagedu)	152	Jd	39.37N	110.58 E
Jungfrau ▲	128	Bd	46.32N	7.58 E
Junggar Pendi=Dzungarian Basin (EN) ⧗	140	Ke	45.00N	88.00 E
Junín [3]	202	Df	11.30S	75.00W
Junín [Arg.]	200	Ji	34.35S	60.57W
Junín [Peru]	202	Cf	11.10S	76.00W
Junín, Lago de- ≈	202	Cf	11.02S	76.05W
Junín de los Andes	206	Fe	39.56S	71.05W
Juniville	124	Ge	49.24N	4.23 E
Jūniyah	146	Ff	33.59N	35.38 E
Junjaha 〰	134	Jc	66.25N	62.00 E
Junlian	152	Hf	28.12N	104.34 E
Junsele	114	De	63.41N	16.54 E
Juntura	188	Fe	43.45N	118.05W
Junxian (Danjiang)	152	Je	32.31N	111.32 E
Juodupė	116	Kh	56.03N	25.44 E
Juojärvi ≈	116	Mb	62.45N	28.35 E
Juoksengi	114	Fc	66.34N	23.51 E
Jupiá, Represa de- ⊜	206	Jb	20.47S	51.39W
Juquiá	204	Ig	24.19S	47.38W
Juquiá, Rio- 〰	204	Ig	24.22S	47.49W
Juquiá, Serra do- ⛰	204	Gg	25.10S	52.00W
Jur	138	Ie	59.48N	137.29 E
Jur 〰	158	Jh	8.39N	29.18 E
Jura [2]	128	Ac	47.25N	6.15 E
Jura [3]	122	Lh	46.50N	5.50 E
Jura ⛰	110	Gf	46.45N	6.30 E
Jura ◆	118	Hf	56.00N	5.50W
Jūra/Jura 〰	114	Fi	55.03N	22.10 E
Jura/Jūra 〰	114	Fi	55.03N	22.10 E
Jura, Sound of- ⇌	118	Hf	55.55N	5.22W
Juradó	202	Cb	7.07N	77.46W
Juratiški	116	Kj	54.02N	26.00 E
Juraybȳ'āt	146	Kh	29.08N	45.30 E
Jurbarkas	114	Fi	55.08N	22.47 E
Jurdī, Wādī- 〰	146	Ei	26.33N	32.44 E
Jurga	138	De	55.42N	84.55 E
Jurgamyš	134	Li	55.25N	64.28 E
Juribej 〰	134	Nb	68.55N	69.05 E
Jurien Bay ◧	212	Cf	30.15S	115.00 E
Jurigue, Rio- 〰	204	Ec	16.29S	54.37W
Jurilovca	130	Le	44.46N	28.52 E
Jurja	114	Lg	59.03N	49.20 E
Jurjaha 〰	134	Gc	66.42N	56.00 E
Jurjevec	114	Kh	57.22N	43.06 E
Jurjev-Polski	114	Jh	56.31N	39.44 E
Jurjuzan	134	Ii	54.52N	58.28 E
Jurjuzan 〰	134	Hi	55.43N	56.57 E
Jurla	134	Gg	59.20N	54.16 E
Jūrmala/Jurmala	136	Cd	56.59N	23.38 E
Jurmala/Jūrmala	136	Cd	56.59N	23.38 E
Jurmo ◆	116	Ie	59.50N	21.35 E
Jurong	154	Ei	31.56N	119.10 E
Juruá	202	Ed	3.27S	66.03W
Juruá, Rio- 〰	198	Jf	2.37S	65.44W
Juruena, Rio- 〰	198	Kf	7.20S	58.03W
Jurumirim, Represa de- ⊜	206	Kb	23.20S	49.00W
Juruti	202	Gd	2.09S	56.04W
Jurva	116	Ib	62.41N	21.59 E
Jusan-Kō ◎	156a	Bc	41.00N	140.20 E
Jusayrah	146	Nj	25.53N	50.36 E

Index Symbols

[1] Independent Nation	▣ Historical or Cultural Region	⩀ Pass, Gap	⊔ Depression	⛱ Coast, Beach	✱ Rock, Reef	⇊ Waterfall, Rapids	═ Canal	◎ Lagoon	⌇ Escarpment, Sea Scarp	🏛 Historic Site	✈ Airport
[2] State, Region	▲ Mount, Mountain	▁ Plain, Lowland	⊏ Polder	◨ Cliff	❖ Islands, Archipelago	⋎ River Mouth, Estuary	❄ Glacier	▦ Bank	⚡ Fracture	⁘ Ruins	⚓ Port
[3] District, County	🌋 Volcano	◣ Delta	∴ Desert, Dunes	◩ Peninsula	✲ Rocks, Reefs	≈ Lake	❅ Ice Shelf, Pack Ice	⩚ Seamount	⩔ Trench, Abyss	▥ Wall, Walls	⚔ Military installation
[4] Municipality	△ Hill	⊟ Salt Flat	♣ Forest, Woods	⋈ Isthmus	✺ Coral Reef	≋ Salt Lake	🌊 Ocean	⏏ Tablemount	✿ National Park, Reserve	✝ Church, Abbey	⛯ Lighthouse
[5] Colony, Dependency	⛰ Mountains, Mountain Range	⋁ Valley, Canyon	⁂ Heath, Steppe	⋯ Sandbank	⦿ Well, Spring	⋰ Intermittent Lake	∿ Sea	⋀ Ridge	★ Point of Interest	⛩ Temple	⚒ Mine
■ Continent	◭ Hills, Escarpment	◡ Crater, Cave	🌴 Oasis	◆ Island	⇡ Geyser	⊜ Reservoir	◧ Gulf, Bay	⊐ Shelf	⛹ Recreation Site	⚗ Scientific Station	⌓ Tunnel
⧗ Physical Region	▬ Plateau, Upland	✣ Karst Features	▶ Cape, Point	⊙ Atoll	〰 River, Stream	⩰ Swamp, Pond	⇌ Strait, Fjord	⌣ Basin	◠ Cave, Cavern	🚉 Railway station	⌒ Dam, Bridge

Jusheng 152 Mb 48.44N 126.37 E
Ju Shui 154 Ci 31.09N 114.52 E
Juškozero 136 Dc 64.45N 32.08 E
Jussarö 116 Je 59.50N 23.35 E
Justo Daract 206 Gd 33.52S 65.11W
Jusva 134 Gg 58.59N 54.57 E
Jutai 202 Ee 5.11S 68.54W
Jutai, Rio- 198 Jf 2.43S 66.57W
Jüterbog 120 Je 51.59N 13.05 E
Juti 204 Ef 22.52S 54.37W
Jutiapa [3] 194 Bf 14.10N 89.50W
Jutiapa [Guat.] 190 Gf 14.17N 89.54W
Jutiapa [Hond.] 194 Df 15.46N 86.34W
Juticalpa 190 Gf 14.42N 86.15W
Jutland (EN)=Jylland 110 Gd 56.00N 9.15 E
Juuka 114 Ge 63.14N 29.15 E
Juva 114 Gf 61.54N 27.51 E
Juventud, Isla de la-=Pines, Isle of- (EN) 174 Kg 21.40N 82.50W
Juxian 152 Kd 35.33N 118.45 E
Jūybār 146 Od 36.38N 52.53 E
Juye 154 Dg 35.23N 116.05 E
Jūyom 146 Oh 28.10N 54.02 E
Juža 114 Kh 56.36N 42.01 E
Južnaja Keltma 134 Gf 60.30N 55.40 E
Južna Morava 130 Ef 43.41N 21.24 E
Južni Rodopi 130 Ih 41.15N 25.30 E
Južnoje 138 Jg 46.13N 143.27 E
Južno-Jenisejski 138 Ee 58.48N 94.45 E
Južno-Kurilsk 138 Jh 44.05N 145.52 E
Južno-Sahalinsk 142 Qe 46.58N 142.42 E
Južno-Uralsk 136 Ge 54.26N 61.15 E
Južny, mys- 138 Ke 57.42N 156.55 E
Južny Bug 110 Jf 46.59N 31.58 E
Južny Ural=Southern Urals (EN) 110 Le 54.00N 58.30 E
Jygeva/Jõgeva 114 Gg 58.46N 26.26 E
Jylland=Jutland (EN) 110 Gd 56.00N 9.15 E
Jylland Bank 116 Bh 56.55N 7.20 E
Jyske Ås 116 Dg 57.15N 10.14 E
Jyväskylä 112 Ic 62.14N 25.44 E

K

K2 (Godwin Austen) 140 Jf 35.53N 76.30 E
Ka 166 Fc 11.39N 4.11 E
Kaabong 170 Fb 3.31N 34.09 E
Kaahka 136 Fh 37.21N 59.38 E
Kaala 221a Cb 21.31N 158.09W
Kaala-Gomén 219b Be 20.40S 164.24 E
Kaalualu Bay 221a Fe 18.58N 155.37W
Kaamanen 114 Gb 69.06N 27.12 E
Kaap Kruis 172 Ad 21.46S 13.58 E
Kaap Plateau (EN)=Kaapplato 158 Jk 27.30S 23.45 E
Kaapplato=Kaap Plateau (EN) 158 Jk 27.30S 23.45 E
Kaapprovinsie/Cape Province [2] 172 Cf 32.00S 22.00 E
Kaapstad / Cape Town 160 Il 33.55S 18.22 E
Kaarst 124 Ic 51.15N 6.37 E
Kaarta 166 Cc 14.35N 10.00W
Kaba/Habahe 152 Eb 47.53N 86.12 E
Kabaena, Pulau- 150 Hh 5.15S 121.55 E
Kabah 192 Og 20.07N 89.29W
Kabala 166 Cd 9.35N 11.33W
Kabale 170 Ec 1.15S 29.59 E
Kabalega Falls (Murchison Falls) 170 Fb 2.17N 31.41 E
Kabalo 160 Ji 6.03S 26.55 E
Kabaman 219a Aa 4.38S 152.42 E
Kabambare 170 Ec 4.16S 27.07 E
Kabamet 170 Gb 0.30N 35.45 E
Kabanjahe 150 Cf 3.06N 98.30 E
Kabardino-Balkarskaja respublika 136 Eg 43.30N 43.30 E
Kabare 170 Ec 2.29S 28.48 E
Kabasalan 150 He 7.48N 122.45 E
Kaba-Shima [Jap.] 156 Ae 32.34N 129.47 E
Kaba-Shima [Jap.] 156 Ae 32.45N 129.00 E
Kabba 166 Gd 7.50N 6.04 E
Kåbdalis 114 Ec 66.09N 20.00 E
Kaberamaido 170 Fb 1.45N 33.10 E
Kabetogama Lake 186 Jb 48.28N 92.59W
Kabhegy 120 Ni 47.03N 17.39 E
Kabinakagami Lake 184 Ea 48.58N 84.25W
Kabinda 160 Ji 6.08S 24.29 E
Kabīr, Wādī al- 128 Dn 36.23N 9.52 E
Kabīr Kūh 146 Lf 33.25N 46.45 E
Kabkābīyah 168 Cc 13.39N 24.05 E
Kableškovo 130 Kg 42.39N 27.34 E
Kabna 168 Eb 19.10N 32.41 E
Kabo 168 Bd 7.35N 18.38 E
Kābol [3] 144 Kc 34.30N 69.00 E
Kābol (Kabūl) 142 If 34.31N 69.12 E
Kabompo 170 De 13.36S 24.12 E
Kabompo 158 Jj 14.11S 23.11 E
Kabondo Dianda 170 Ed 8.53S 25.40 E
Kabongo 170 Ed 7.19S 25.35 E
Kabou 166 Fd 9.27N 0.49 E
Kabūdiyāh, Ra's- 162 Jb 35.14N 11.10 E
Kabūd Rāhang 146 Me 35.12N 48.44 E
Kābul 140 Jf 33.55N 72.14 E
Kabūl → Kābol 142 If 34.31N 69.12 E
Kabunda 170 Ee 12.13S 29.23 E
Kabunga 170 Ec 1.42S 28.08 E
Kaburuang, Pulau- 150 If 3.48N 126.48 E
Kabwe 160 Jj 14.27S 28.27 E
Kača 132 Hg 44.44N 33.32 E
Kačanik 130 Eg 42.14N 21.15 E
Kačanovo 116 Lg 57.24N 27.53 E
Kačergine 116 Jj 54.53N 23.49 E
Kachchh, Gulf of 140 Ig 22.36N 69.30 E
Kachchh, Rann of 148 Dd 23.51N 70.30 E
Kachia 166 Gd 9.52E 7.57 E
Kachikau 172 Cc 18.09S 24.29 E
Kachin [2] 148 Jc 26.00N 97.30 E
Kachul (Kagul) 136 Cf 45.53N 28.14 E
Kačiry 136 He 53.04N 76.07 E
Kačkanar 136 Fd 58.42N 59.30 E
Kačug 138 Ff 54.00N 105.52 E
Kaczawa 120 Me 51.18N 16.27 E
Kadada 132 Oc 53.09N 46.01 E
Kadaň 120 Jf 50.23N 13.16 E
Kadan Kyun 148 Jf 12.30N 98.22 E
Kadei 158 Ih 3.31N 16.03 E
Kadijevka 136 Df 48.32N 38.40 E
Kadiköy 146 Bb 40.51N 26.50 E
Kadıköy, İstanbul- 130 Mi 40.59N 29.01 E
Kadina 212 Hf 33.58S 137.43 E
Kadınhanı 146 Ec 38.15N 32.14 E
Kadiolo 166 Dc 10.34N 5.45W
Kadiri 148 Ff 14.07N 78.10 E
Kadirli 144 Eb 37.23N 36.05 E
Kadja 168 Cc 12.02N 22.28 E
Kadmat Island 148 Ef 11.14N 72.47 E
Kadnikov 114 Jg 59.30N 40.24 E
Kadoka 186 Fe 43.50N 101.31W
Kadoma 160 Jj 18.21S 29.55 E
Kaduj 114 Ig 59.14N 37.09 E
Kaduna 160 Hg 10.31N 7.26 E
Kaduna [2] 166 Gc 11.00N 7.30 E
Kaduna 158 Hh 8.45N 5.48 E
Kāduqlī 160 Jg 11.01N 29.43 E
Kadykčan 138 Jd 63.05N 146.58 E
Kadžaran 132 Oj 39.11N 46.10 E
Kadžerom 134 Gd 64.41N 55.54 E
Kadži-Saj 135 Kc 42.08N 77.10 E
Kaech'ŏn 154 He 39.42N 125.53 E
Kaédi 160 Fg 16.08N 13.31W
Kaélé 166 Hc 10.07N 14.27 E
Kaena Point 221a Cb 21.35N 158.17W
Kaeo 218 Ea 35.06S 173.47 E
Kaesŏng 142 Of 37.58N 126.33 E
Kaesŏng Si [2] 154 Ie 38.05N 126.30 E
Kāf 136 Dg 31.24N 37.29 E
Kafakumba 170 Dd 9.41S 23.44 E
Kafan 136 Eh 39.12N 46.28 E
Kafanchan 166 Gd 9.35N 8.18 E
Kaffrine 166 Bc 14.06N 15.33W
Kafia Kingi 168 Cd 9.16N 24.25 E
Kafiréos, Dhiékplous- 130 Hl 38.00N 24.40 E
Kafirévs, Ákra- 130 Hk 38.10N 24.35 E
Kafr ad Dawwār 146 Dg 31.08N 30.07 E
Kafr ash Shaykh 164 Fc 31.07N 30.56 E
Kafta 168 Fc 13.54N 37.11 E
Kafu 170 Fb 1.39N 32.05 E
Kafue 160 Jj 15.47S 28.11 E
Kafue 158 Jj 15.56S 28.55 E
Kafue Dam 170 Ef 15.45S 28.28 E
Kafue Flats 170 Ef 15.40S 26.25 E
Kafufu 170 Fd 7.12S 31.31 E
Kaga 154 Nf 36.18N 136.18 E
Kaga Bandoro 168 Bd 7.02N 19.13 E
Kagalaska 178a Cb 51.47N 176.23W
Kagalnik 132 Kf 47.04N 39.18 E
Kagami 156 Be 32.34N 130.40 E
Kagan 136 Gh 39.43N 64.32 E
Kagarlyk 132 Ge 49.53N 30.56 E
Kagawa Ken [2] 154 Mg 34.15N 134.15 E
Kagera 158 Ki 0.57S 31.47 E
Kağızman 146 Jb 40.09N 43.07 E
Kagoshima 142 Pf 31.36N 130.33 E
Kagoshima Bay (EN)=Kagoshima-Wan 154 Ki 31.27N 130.40 E
Kagoshima Ken [2] 154 Ki 31.45N 130.40 E
Kagoshima-Taniyama 156 Bf 31.31N 130.31 E
Kagoshima-Wan = Kagoshima Bay (EN) 154 Ki 31.27N 130.40 E
Kagul → Kachul 136 Cf 45.53N 28.14 E
Kagul 130 Ld 45.32N 28.27 E
Kahal Tabelbala 162 Gd 28.45N 2.15W
Kahama 170 Fc 3.50S 32.36 E
Kahemba 160 Ii 7.17S 19.00 E
Kahi 132 Oi 41.23N 46.59 E
Kahiu Point 221a Eb 21.13N 156.58W
Kahler Asten 120 Ee 51.11N 8.29 E
Kahnūj 146 Qi 27.58N 57.47 E
Kahoku 156 Gb 38.30N 141.20 E
Kahoku-Gata 156 Ec 36.40N 136.40 E
Kahoolawe Island 208 Lb 20.33N 156.35W
Kahouanne, Ilet à- 197e Ab 16.22N 61.47W
Kahovka 136 Df 46.47N 33.32 E
Kahovskoje vodohranilišče = Kakhovua Reservoir (EN) 110 Jf 47.25N 34.10 E
Kahramanmaraş 144 Eb 37.36N 36.55 E
Kahrūyeh 146 Ng 31.43N 51.48 E
Kāhta 146 Hd 37.46N 38.36 E
Kahuku 221a Db 21.41N 157.57W
Kahuku Point 221a Db 21.43N 157.59W
Kahului 221a Ec 20.53N 156.27W
Kahului Bay 221a Ec 20.55N 156.30W
Kahurangi Point 218 Ed 40.46S 172.13 E
Kahurestan 144 Id 27.10N 55.45 E
Kai, Kepulauan- 208 Ee 5.35S 132.45 E
Kaiama 166 Fd 9.36N 3.57 E
Kaiapoi 218 Ee 43.23S 172.39 E
Kaibab Plateau 188 Ih 36.30N 112.15W
Kai Beuar 150 Jh 5.35S 133.00 E
Kaidu He/Karaxabar He 152 Ec 41.55N 86.38 E
Kaieteur Falls 202 Gc 5.10N 59.28W
Kaifeng 142 Nf 34.45N 114.25 E
Kaihua 154 Ej 29.10N 118.24 E
Kai Kecil 150 Jh 5.45S 132.40 E
Kaikohe 218 Ea 35.24S 173.48 E
Kaikoura 216 Dh 42.25S 173.41 E
Kaili 152 If 26.35N 107.59 E
Kailu 152 Lc 43.37N 121.19 E
Kailua [Hi.-U.S.] 221a Db 21.23N 157.44W
Kailua [Hi.-U.S.] 221a Fd 19.39N 155.59W
Kaimana 150 Jg 3.39S 133.45 E
Kaimanawa Mountains 218 Fc 39.15S 176.00 E
Kaimon-Dake 156 Bf 31.10N 130.32 E
Kain, Tournai- 124 Fd 50.38N 3.22 E
Kainach 128 Jd 46.54N 15.31 E
Kainan [Jap.] 156 De 33.36N 134.22 E
Kainan [Jap.] 156 Dd 34.09N 135.12 E
Kainantu 214 Di 6.15S 145.53 E
Kainji Dam 166 Fd 9.55N 4.40 E
Kainji Reservoir 166 Fc 10.30N 4.35 E
Kaipara Harbour 218 Fb 36.25S 174.15 E
Kaiparowits Plateau 188 Jh 37.20N 111.15W
Kaiser Franz Josephs Fjord 179 Jd 73.30N 24.00W
Kaisersesch 124 Jd 50.14N 7.09 E
Kaiserslautern 120 Dg 49.27N 7.45 E
Kaiserstuhl 120 Dh 48.06N 7.40 E
Kaishantun 152 Mc 42.43N 129.37 E
Kaišiadorys/Kajšjadoris 114 Fi 54.53N 24.31 E
Kaita 156 Cd 34.20N 132.32 E
Kaitaia 218 Ea 35.07S 173.14 E
Kaitangata 218 Cg 46.17S 169.51 E
Kaithal 148 Fc 29.48N 76.23 E
Kaitong → Tongyu 152 Lc 44.47N 123.05 E
Kaituma River 196 Gh 8.11N 59.41W
Kaiwaka 216 Dg 36.10S 174.26 E
Kaiwi Channel 214 Oc 21.13N 157.30W
Kaixian 152 Ie 31.10N 108.25 E
Kaiyuan [China] 152 Hg 23.47N 103.15 E
Kaiyuan [China] 152 Lc 42.33N 124.04 E
Kaiyuh Mountains 178 Hd 64.00N 158.00W
Kaja 158 Jg 12.02N 22.28 E
Kajaani 112 Ic 64.14N 27.41 E
Kajaapu 150 Dh 5.26S 102.24 E
Kajabbi 210 Fg 20.02S 140.02 E
Kajak 138 Fb 71.30N 103.15 E
Kajang 150 Df 2.59N 101.47 E
Kajdak, sor- 132 Rg 44.40N 53.30 E
Kajerkan 138 Dc 69.25N 87.30 E
Kajiado 170 Gc 1.51S 36.47 E
Kajiki 156 Bf 31.44N 130.40 E
Kajmakčalan 130 Ei 40.58N 21.48 E
Kajnar 130 Lb 47.50N 28.06 E
Kajo Kaji 168 Ee 3.53N 31.40 E
Kajrakkumskoje vodohranilišče 135 Hd 40.20N 70.05 E
Kajrakty 136 Hf 48.31N 73.14 E
Kajšjadoris/Kaišiadorys 114 Fi 54.53N 24.31 E
Kajuru 166 Gc 10.19N 7.41 E
Kākā 168 Ec 10.36N 32.11 E
Kaka 168 Fd 7.28N 39.06 E
Kakagi Lake 186 Jb 49.13N 93.52W
Kakamas 172 Ce 28.45S 20.33 E
Kakamega 170 Fb 0.17N 34.45 E
Kakamigahara 156 Ed 35.25N 136.50 E
Kakanj 128 Mf 44.08N 18.05 E
Kaka Point 221a Ec 20.32N 156.33W
Kakata 166 Cd 6.32N 10.21W
Kake 156 Cd 34.36N 132.19 E
Kakegawa 156 Ed 34.46N 138.00 E
Kakenge 170 Dc 4.51S 21.55 E
Kakeroma-Jima 156b Ba 28.08N 129.15 E
Kakhovka Reservoir (EN) = Kahovskoje vodohranilišče 110 Jf 47.25N 34.10 E
Kākī 146 Nh 28.19N 51.34 E
Kākināda 142 Kh 16.56N 82.13 E
Kakisa Lake 180 Fd 60.55N 117.40W
Kakizaki 156 Fc 37.16N 138.22 E
Kaklkan 146 Cd 36.15N 29.24 E
Kakogawa 156 Dd 34.46N 134.51 E
Kakpin 166 Ed 8.39N 3.48W
Kaktovik 178 Kb 70.08N 143.37W
Kakuda 156 Gc 37.58N 140.47 E
Kakuma 170 Fb 3.43N 34.52 E
Kakunodate 154 Pe 39.40N 140.32 E
Kakva 134 Jg 59.37N 60.50 E
Kakya 170 Gc 1.36S 39.02 E
Kalaa 126 Mi 35.35N 0.20 E
Kalaa Khasba 128 Co 35.38N 8.36 E
Kalaallit Nunaat/Grønland = Greenland (EN) [5] 224 Nd 70.00N 40.00W
Kalaallit Nunaat/Grønland = Kreenland (EN) 174 Pb 70.00N 40.00W
Kalabahi 150 Hh 8.13S 124.31 E
Kalabáka 130 Ej 39.42N 21.38 E
Kalabera 220b Ba 15.14N 145.48 E
Kalabo 170 De 14.58S 22.41 E
Kalâbsha 164 Fe 23.33N 32.50 E
Kalač 136 Ee 50.23N 41.01 E
Kalačinsk 136 Hd 55.03N 74.34 E
Kalač-na-Donu 136 Ef 48.43N 43.32 E
Kaladan 148 Id 20.09N 92.57 E
Ka Lae 214 Od 18.55N 155.41W
Kalahari Desert 158 Jk 23.00S 22.00 E
Kalaheo 221a Bb 21.56N 159.32W
Kalai-Mor 136 Gh 35.37N 62.31 E
Kalaj Humo 135 He 38.25N 70.47 E
Kalajoki 114 Fd 64.15N 23.57 E
Kalakan 138 Ge 55.10N 116.45 E
Kalaldi 166 Hd 6.30N 14.04 E
Kalāleh 146 Pd 37.25N 55.40 E
Kalámai 112 Ih 37.02N 22.07 E
Kalamákion 130 Gl 37.55N 23.43 E
Kalamazoo 182 Jc 42.17N 85.32W
Kalambo Falls 170 Fd 8.36S 31.14 E
Kalamitski zaliv 132 Hg 45.00N 33.25 E
Kálamos 130 Dk 38.37N 20.55 E
Kalamunda, Perth- 212 Df 31.57S 116.03 E
Kalan 144 Eb 39.07N 39.32 E
Kalanshiyū, Sarīr- 158 Jf 27.00N 21.30 E
Kalao, Pulau- 150 Hh 7.18S 120.58 E
Kalaotoa, Pulau- 150 Hh 7.22S 121.47 E
Kalapana 221a Gd 19.21N 154.59W
Kalaraš 132 Ff 47.16N 28.16 E
Kalärne 116 Gb 62.59N 16.05 E
Kalarski hrebet 138 Ge 56.30N 118.50 E
Kalasin [Indon.] 150 Ff 0.12N 114.16 E
Kalasin [Thai.] 148 Ke 16.29N 103.31 E
Kalāt 148 Dc 29.02N 66.35 E
Kalāteh 146 Pd 36.29N 54.10 E
Kalau 221b Bc 21.28S 174.57W
Kalaupapa 221a Eb 21.12N 156.59W
Kalaus 132 Ng 45.43N 44.07 E
Kalavárdha 130 Km 36.20N 27.57 E
Kálavrita 130 Fk 38.02N 22.07 E
Kalbā' 146 Qj 25.03N 56.21 E
Kalbīyah, Sabkhat al- 128 Eo 35.51N 10.17 E
Kaldbakur 114a Ab 65.49N 23.39W
Kaldygajty 132 Re 49.20N 52.38 E
Kale [Tur.] 146 Cd 36.14N 29.59 E
Kale [Tur.] 146 Cd 37.26N 28.51 E
Kalecik 146 Eb 40.06N 33.25 E
Kalehe 170 Ec 2.06S 28.55 E
Kalemie 160 Ji 5.56S 29.12 E
Käl-e Shur 144 Jb 35.05N 60.59 E
Kalevala 136 Db 65.12N 31.10 E
Kalewa 148 Id 23.12N 94.18 E
Kaleybar 146 Lc 38.47N 47.02 E
Kalgoorlie 210 Dh 30.45S 121.28 E
Kaliakoúdha 130 Ek 38.48N 21.46 E
Kaliakra, Nos- 130 Lf 43.18N 28.30 E
Kalibo 150 Hd 11.43N 122.22 E
Kali Limni 130 Kn 35.35N 27.08 E
Kalima 160 Ji 2.34S 26.37 E
Kalimantan/Borneo 140 Ni 1.00N 114.00 E
Kalimantan Barat [3] 150 Ff 0.01N 110.30 E
Kalimantan Selatan [3] 150 Gg 2.30S 115.30 E
Kalimantan Tengah [3] 150 Fg 2.00S 113.30 E
Kalimantan Timur [3] 150 Gf 1.30N 116.30 E
Kálimnos 130 Jm 36.57N 26.59 E
Kalinin [Russia] → Tver' 112 Jd 56.52N 35.55 E
Kalinin [Turk.] 136 Fg 42.07N 59.40 E
Kalininabad 135 Gf 37.53N 68.57 E
Kaliningrad [Russia] 112 Ie 54.43N 20.30 E
Kaliningrad [Russia] 114 Ii 55.55N 37.57 E
Kaliningradskaja oblast 136 Ce 54.45N 21.20 E
Kalinino → Tašir [Arm.] 132 Ni 41.08N 44.14 E
Kalinino [Russia] 132 Kg 45.05N 38.59 E
Kalininsk [Mol.] 130 Ka 48.07N 27.16 E
Kalininsk [Russia] 132 Nd 51.30N 44.30 E
Kalinkoviči 136 Ce 52.07N 29.23 E
Kalino 134 Hg 58.15N 57.35 E
Kalinovik 128 Mg 43.31N 18.26 E
Kalinovka 132 Fe 49.29N 28.32 E
Kaliro 170 Fb 0.54N 33.30 E
Kalispell 176 He 48.12N 114.19W
Kalisz 120 Oe 51.46N 18.06 E
Kalisz [2] 120 Of 51.45N 18.05 E
Kalisz Pomorski 120 Lc 53.19N 15.54 E
Kalitva 132 Le 48.10N 40.46 E
Kaliua 170 Fd 5.04S 31.48 E
Kalix 114 Fd 65.51N 23.08 E
Kalixälven 114 Fd 65.47N 23.13 E
Kalja 134 Jf 60.20N 60.01 E
Kaljazin 136 Dd 57.15N 37.55 E
Kalkandere 146 Ib 40.55N 40.28 E
Kalkar 124 Ic 51.44N 6.18 E
Kalkaska 184 Ec 44.44N 85.11W
Kalkfeld 172 Bd 20.53S 16.11 E
Kalkfontein 172 Cd 22.07S 20.54 E
Kalkim 130 Kj 39.48N 27.13 E
Kalkrand 172 Bd 24.03S 17.33 E
Kall 114 Ce 63.28N 13.15 E
Kållands Halvö 116 Ef 58.35N 13.05 E
Kållandsö 116 Ef 58.40N 13.10 E
Kallaste 114 Gg 58.41N 27.08 E
Kallavesi 110 Ic 62.50N 27.45 E
Kalletal 124 Kb 52.08N 8.57 E
Kallhäll 116 Ge 59.27N 17.48 E
Kallidhromon Óros 130 Fk 38.44N 22.34 E
Kallinge 114 Dh 56.14N 15.17 E
Kallonis, Kolpos- 130 Jj 39.07N 26.08 E
Kallsjön 114 Ce 63.35N 13.00 E
Kalmakkyrgan 135 Fa 46.58N 64.30 E
Kalmar 112 Hd 56.40N 16.22 E
Kalmar [2] 114 Dh 57.20N 16.00 E
Kalmarsund 114 Dh 56.40N 16.25 E
Kalmit 124 Ke 49.19N 8.05 E
Kalmius 132 Jf 47.03N 37.34 E
Kalmthout 124 Gc 51.23N 4.28 E
Kalmykija, respublika 136 Ef 46.30N 45.30 E
Kalmykovo 132 Qe 49.05N 51.47 E
Kalnciems 116 Jh 56.48N 23.34 E
Kalnik 128 Kd 46.10N 16.30 E
Kalocsa 120 Oj 46.32N 19.00 E
Kalofer 130 Hg 42.37N 24.59 E
Kalohi Channel 221a Ec 21.00N 156.56W
Kaloko 170 Ed 6.47S 25.47 E
Kalole 170 Ec 3.42S 27.22 E
Kaloli Point 221a Gd 19.37N 154.57W
Kalomo 170 Ef 17.02S 26.30 E
Kalpa 148 Fb 31.37N 78.10 E
Kalpákion 130 Dj 39.53N 20.35 E
Kalpeni Island 148 Ef 10.05N 73.38 E
Kalpin 152 Cc 40.31N 79.03 E
Kalsūbai 140 Jh 19.36N 73.43 E
Kaltern/Caldaro 128 Fd 46.25N 11.14 E
Kaltungo 166 Hd 9.49N 11.19 E
Kaluga 112 Je 54.31N 36.16 E
Kalulushi 170 Ee 12.50S 28.05 E
Kalumburu Mission 212 Fb 14.18S 126.39 E
Kalundborg 114 Ci 55.41N 11.06 E
Kaluš 136 Cf 49.03N 24.23 E
Kałuszyn 120 Rd 52.13N 21.49 E
Kalužskaja oblast [3] 136 De 54.20N 35.30 E
Kalvåg 114 Af 61.46N 4.53 E
Kalvarija 114 Fi 54.27N 23.14 E
Kalya 170 Fd 6.28S 30.03 E
Kalyān 148 Ee 19.15N 73.09 E
Kām 120 Mi 47.06N 16.53 E
Kama 170 Ec 3.32S 27.07 E
Kama [Russia] 134 Nf 60.27N 69.00 E
Kama [Eur.] 110 Ld 55.45N 52.00 E
Kamae 156 Be 32.48N 131.56 E
Kamaï 128 Bd 21.12N 17.30 E
Kamaing 148 Jc 25.31N 96.44 E
Kamaishi 154 Pe 39.16N 141.53 E
Kamakou 221a Eb 21.07N 156.52W
Kamakura 156 Fd 35.19N 139.32 E
Kamália 148 Eb 30.44N 72.39 E
Kamalo 221a Eb 21.03N 156.53W
Kaman 146 Ec 39.25N 33.45 E
Kamand, Āb-e- 146 Mf 33.28N 49.04 E
Kamanjab 172 Ac 19.35S 14.51 E
Kamanyola 170 Ec 2.46S 29.00 E
Kamarān 144 Ff 15.12N 42.35 E
Kamarang 202 Fb 5.53N 60.35W
Kama Reservoir (EN) = Kamskoje vodohranilišče 110 Ld 58.50N 56.15 E
Kamaši 136 Gh 38.48N 66.29 E
Kamativi 172 Dc 18.19S 27.03 E
Kambalda 212 Ef 31.10S 121.37 E
Kambalnaja Sopka, vulkan- 138 Kf 51.17N 156.57 E
Kambara 156 Fd 35.07N 138.36 E
Kambara 219d Cc 18.57S 178.57W
Kambarka 114 Nh 56.18N 54.14 E
Kambia 166 Cd 9.07N 12.55W
Kambja 116 Lf 58.11N 26.43 E
Kambove 170 Ee 10.52S 26.35 E
Kamčatka 138 Le 56.10N 162.30 E
Kamčatka, poluostrov- = Kamchatka Peninsula (EN) 140 Rd 56.00N 160.00 E
Kamčatskaja oblast [3] 138 Kf 54.50N 159.00 E
Kamčatski zaliv 138 Le 55.30N 163.00 E
Kamchatka Peninsula (EN) = Kamčatka, poluostrov- 140 Rd 56.00N 160.00 E
Kamčija 130 Kf 43.02N 27.53 E
Kamčijska Plato 130 Kg 42.56N 27.32 E
Kameda [Jap.] 156a Bc 41.49N 140.46 E
Kameda [Jap.] 156 Fc 37.52N 139.06 E
Kameda-Hantō 156a Bc 41.45N 141.00 E
Kámeiros 130 Km 36.18N 27.56 E
Kamelik 132 Pc 52.06N 49.30 E
Kamen 124 Jc 51.36N 7.40 E
Kaménai 130 Im 36.25N 25.25 E
Kamende 170 Dd 6.28S 24.33 E
Kamenec 120 Td 52.23N 23.49 E
Kamenec-Podolski 136 Cf 48.39N 26.33 E
Kamenjam, Rt- 128 Hf 44.46N 13.56 E
Kamenka [Kaz.] 132 Qd 51.07N 50.20 E
Kamenka [Mol.] 132 Fe 48.03N 28.45 E
Kamenka [Russia] 136 Ee 53.13N 44.03 E
Kamenka [Russia] 132 Kd 50.43N 39.25 E
Kamenka [Russia] 154 Nb 44.28N 136.01 E
Kamenka [Russia] 114 Kd 65.54N 44.04 E
Kamenka [Ukr.] 136 Df 49.03N 32.06 E
Kamenka-Bugskaja 120 Uf 50.01N 24.25 E
Kamenka-Dneprovskaja 132 If 47.29N 34.29 E
Kamen-Kaširski 132 Dd 51.36N 24.59 E
Kamen-na-Obi 138 Df 53.47N 81.20 E
Kamennogorsk 114 Gf 60.59N 29.12 E
Kamennoje, ozero- 114 Hd 64.30N 30.15 E
Kamennomostski 132 Lg 44.17N 40.12 E
Kamen-Rybolov 154 Kb 44.45N 132.04 E
Kamenskoje 138 Ld 62.30N 166.12 E
Kamensk-Šahtinski 132 Le 48.18N 40.16 E
Kamensk-Uralski 142 Id 56.28N 61.54 E
Kamenz/Kamjenc 120 Ke 51.16N 14.06 E
Kameoka 156 Dd 35.00N 135.35 E
Kameškovo 114 Jh 56.22N 41.01 E
Kamet 148 Fb 30.55N 79.35 E
Kameyama 156 Ed 34.51N 136.27 E
Kami-Agata 156 Ad 34.38N 129.25 E
Kamiah 188 Gc 46.14N 116.02W
Kamicharo 156a Cb 43.11N 143.52 E
Kamienna 120 Re 51.06N 21.47 E
Kamienna Góra 120 Mf 50.47N 16.01 E
Kamień Pomorski 120 Kc 53.58N 14.46 E
Kamiénsk 120 Pe 51.12N 19.30 E
Kamieskroon 172 Bf 30.09S 17.56 E
Kami-furano 156a Cb 43.29N 142.27 E
Kamiiso 154 Pd 41.49N 140.39 E
Kamiita 156 Dd 34.08N 134.24 E
Kamiji 170 Dd 6.39S 23.17 E
Kamikawa 156a Cb 43.50N 142.47 E
Kami-Koshiki-Jima 156 Af 31.50N 129.55 E
Kamina 160 Ji 8.44S 24.59 E
Kaminak Lake 180 Id 62.13N 95.00W
Kaminokuni 156a Bc 41.48N 140.05 E
Kamino-Shima 156 Ad 34.30N 129.25 E
Kaminoyama 154 Pe 38.09N 140.17 E
Kaminuriak Lake 180 Hd 63.00N 95.45W
Kamioka 154 Nf 36.16N 137.18 E
Kami-shihoro 156a Cb 43.13N 143.16 E
Kamisunagawa 156a Bb 43.28N 141.58 E
Kamitsushima 156 Ad 34.39N 129.28 E
Kamituga 170 Ec 3.04S 28.11 E
Kamiyama 156 De 33.58N 134.21 E
Kami-yūbetsu 156a Ca 44.11N 143.34 E
Kamjenc/Kamenz 120 Ke 51.16N 14.06 E
Kamloops 176 Gd 50.40N 120.20W
Kamloops Plateau 188 Ea 50.10N 120.35W
Kammersee → Attersee 128 Hc 47.55N 13.33 E
Kamnik 128 Id 46.14N 14.37 E
Kamo [Arm.] 132 Ni 40.22N 45.05 E
Kamo [Jap.] 156 Fc 37.39N 139.03 E
Kamo [N.Z.] 218 Fa 35.41S 174.17 E
Kamōda-Misaki 156 De 33.50N 134.45 E
Kamogawa 156 Gd 35.06N 140.05 E
Kamp 128 Jb 48.23N 15.48 E
Kampala 160 Kh 0.19N 32.35 E
Kampar 150 Df 4.18N 101.09 E
Kampar 150 Mi 0.32N 103.08 E
Kampen 122 Lb 52.33N 5.54 E
Kampene 170 Ec 3.36S 26.40 E
Kamphaeng Phet 148 Je 16.26N 99.33 E
Kamp-Lintorf 124 Ic 51.30N 6.32 E
Kamp'o 154 Jg 35.48N 129.30 E
Kâmpóng Cham 142 Mh 12.00N 105.27 E
Kâmpóng Chhnâng 148 Kf 12.15N 104.40 E

Kâmpóng Saôm	142	Mh	10.38N	103.30 E
Kâmpóng Saôm, Chhâk-	148	Kf	10.50N	103.32 E
Kâmpóng Thum	148	Kf	12.42N	104.54 E
Kâmpôt	148	Kf	10.37N	104.11 E
Kampti	166	Ec	10.08N	3.27W
Kampuchea → Cambodia	142	Mh	13.00N	105.00 E
Kamrau, Teluk-	150	Jg	3.32S	133.37 E
Kamsack	180	Hf	51.34N	101.54W
Kamsar	166	Cc	10.40N	14.36W
Kamskoje Ustje	114	Li	55.14N	49.16 E
Kamskoje vodohranilišče = Kama Reservoir (EN)	110	Ld	58.50N	56.15 E
Kam Summa	168	Ge	0.21N	42.44 E
Kamuenai	156a	Bb	43.08N	140.26 E
Kamui-Dake	156a	Cb	42.25N	142.52 E
Kamui-Misaki	152	Pc	43.20N	140.20 E
Kámuk, Cerro-	194	Fi	9.17N	83.04W
Kamvoúnia Óri	130	Ei	40.00N	21.52 E
Kāmyārān	146	Le	34.47N	46.56 E
Kamyšin	112	Ke	50.06N	45.24 E
Kamyšlov	136	Gd	56.52N	62.43 E
Kamyšovaja Buhta	132	Hg	44.31N	33.33 E
Kamysty-Ajat	134	Jj	53.01N	61.35 E
Kamyzjak	136	Ef	46.06N	48.05 E
Kan	146	Ne	35.45N	51.16 E
Kan	138	Ee	56.31N	93.47 E
Kana	172	Dc	18.32S	27.24 E
Kanaaupscow	180	Jf	54.01N	76.32W
Kanaaupscow	180	Jf	53.40N	77.08W
Kanab	182	Ed	37.03N	112.32W
Kanab Creek	188	Ih	36.24N	112.38W
Kanaga	178a	Cb	51.45N	177.10W
Kanagawa Ken [2]	154	Og	35.30N	139.10 E
Kanaliasem	150	Dg	1.44S	103.35 E
Kanami-Zaki	156b	Bb	27.53N	128.58 E
Kananga	160	Ji	5.54S	22.25 E
Kanariktok	180	Le	55.03N	60.10W
Kanaš	114	Li	55.31N	47.31 E
Kanathea	219d	Cb	17.16S	179.09W
Kanaya	156	Fd	34.48N	138.07 E
Kanayama	156	Ed	35.39N	137.09 E
Kanazawa	142	Pf	36.34N	136.39 E
Kanbalu	148	Jd	23.12N	95.31 E
Kanbe	148	Je	16.42N	96.01 E
Kanchanaburi	148	Jf	14.02N	99.33 E
Kānchenjunga	140	Kg	27.42N	88.08 E
Kānchipuram	148	Ff	12.50N	79.43 E
Kandalakša	112	Jb	67.09N	32.21 E
Kandalaksha, Gulf of- (EN) = Kandalakšski zaliv	110	Jb	66.35N	32.45 E
Kandalakšski zaliv = Kandalaksha, Gulf of- (EN)	110	Jb	66.35N	32.45 E
Kandangan	150	Gg	2.47S	115.16 E
Kándanos	130	Gn	35.20N	23.44 E
Kandava	114	Fh	57.03N	22.46 E
Kandavu Island	208	If	19.00S	178.13 E
Kandavu Passage	219d	Ac	18.45S	178.00 E
Kandel	124	Ke	49.05N	8.12 E
Kandel	120	Eh	48.04N	8.01 E
Kandhelioúsa	130	Jm	36.30N	26.58 E
Kandi	160	Hg	11.08N	2.56 E
Kandıra	146	Db	41.04N	30.09 E
Kandla	148	Ed	23.02N	70.14 E
Kandrian	214	Di	6.13S	149.33 E
Kandry	134	Gi	54.34N	54.10 E
Kandy	142	Ki	7.18N	80.38 E
Kane	184	He	41.40N	78.48W
Kane Basin	224	Od	79.35N	67.00W
Kaneh	146	Pi	27.04N	54.18 E
Kanem [3]	168	Bc	15.00N	16.00 E
Kanem	158	Ig	14.45N	15.30 E
Kaneohe	214	Oc	21.25N	157.48W
Kaneohe Bay	221a	Db	21.28N	157.48W
Kánestron, Ákra-	130	Gj	39.56N	23.45 E
Kanev	132	Ge	49.42N	31.29 E
Kanevskaja	136	Df	46.06N	38.58 E
Kaneyama	156	Fc	37.27N	139.30 E
Kang	172	Cd	23.44S	22.50 E
Kangaba	166	Dc	11.56N	8.25W
Kangal	146	Gc	39.15N	37.24 E
Kangalassy	138	Hd	62.17N	129.58 E
Kangâmiut	179	Ge	65.39N	53.55W
Kangān [Iran]	146	Oi	27.50N	52.03 E
Kangān [Iran]	146	Qj	25.48N	57.28 E
Kangar	150	De	6.26N	100.12 E
Kangaré	166	Dc	11.37N	8.08W
Kangaroo Island	208	Eh	35.50S	137.05 E
Kangasala	116	Kc	61.28N	24.05 E
Kangasniemi	114	Gf	61.59N	26.38 E
Kangâtsiaq	179	Ge	68.20N	53.18W
Kangāvar	146	Le	34.30N	47.58 E
Kangbao	154	Cd	41.51N	114.37 E
Kangding/Dardo	152	He	30.01N	101.58 E
Kangean, Kepulauan- = Kangean Islands (EN)	150	Gh	6.55S	115.30 E
Kangean, Pulau-	150	Gh	6.54S	115.20 E
Kangean Islands (EN) = Kangean, Kepulauan-	150	Gh	6.55S	115.30 E
Kangeeak Point	180	Lc	68.01N	64.45W
Kangen	158	Kh	6.47N	33.09 E
Kangerdlugssuaq	179	Ie	68.20N	31.40W
Kangetet	170	Gb	1.58N	36.06 E
Kanggup'o	154	Id	41.07N	127.31 E
Kanggye	152	Mc	40.58N	126.36 E
Kangi	168	Dd	8.10N	27.39 E
Kangjin	154	Ig	34.38N	126.46 E
Kangiqsujuaq	180	Kd	61.36N	71.57W
Kangirsuk	176	Lc	60.00N	70.01W
Kangmar	152	Ef	28.32N	89.43 E
Kangnŭng	152	Md	37.44N	128.54 E
Kango	170	Bb	0.09N	10.08 E
Kangondu	170	Gc	1.06S	37.42 E
Kangping	154	Gc	42.45N	123.20 E
Kangrinboqê Feng	152	De	31.04N	81.30 E
Kangto	148	Ic	27.52N	92.30 E
Kangwŏn-Do [N.Kor.] [2]	154	Ie	38.45N	127.35 E
Kangwŏn-Do [S.Kor.] [2]	154	Jf	37.45N	128.15 E
Kani	166	Dd	8.29N	6.36W
Kaniama	170	Dd	7.31S	24.11 E
Kanibadam	135	Hd	40.17N	70.25 E
Kaniet Islands	208	Fe	0.53S	145.30 E
Kanija	130	Lc	46.16N	28.13 E
Kanimeh	135	Ed	40.18N	65.09 E
Kanin, poluostrov- = Kanin Peninsula (EN)	110	Kb	68.00N	45.00 E
Kanina	130	Ci	40.26N	19.31 E
Kanin Kamen	134	Bb	68.15N	45.15 E
Kanin Nos	136	Eb	68.39N	43.14 E
Kanin Nos, mys-	110	Kb	68.39N	43.16 E
Kanin Peninsula (EN) = Kanin, poluostrov-	110	Kb	68.00N	45.00 E
Kanioumé	166	Eb	15.46N	3.09W
Kanita	156a	Bc	41.02N	140.38 E
Kanjiža	130	Dc	46.04N	20.03 E
Kankaanpää	114	Ff	61.48N	22.25 E
Kankakee	182	Jc	41.07N	87.52W
Kankakee River	186	Lf	41.23N	88.16W
Kankalabé	166	Cc	11.00N	12.00W
Kankan	160	Gg	10.23N	9.18W
Kanker	148	Gd	20.17N	81.29 E
Kankesanturai	148	Gg	9.49N	80.02 E
Kankossa	162	Ef	15.55N	11.31W
Kankunski	138	He	57.39N	126.25 E
Kanla	120	Hf	50.48N	11.35 E
Kanmav Kyun	148	Jf	11.40N	98.28 E
Kanmon-Kaikyō	156	Bd	33.56N	130.57 E
Kanmuri-Yama	156	Cd	34.28N	132.05 E
Kannapolis	182	Kd	35.30N	80.37W
Kannone-Jima	154	Jj	28.51N	128.58 E
Kannonkoski	116	Kb	62.58N	25.15 E
Kannus	114	Fe	63.54N	23.54 E
Kano	160	Hg	12.00N	8.31 E
Kano [2]	166	Gc	12.00N	9.00 E
Kanona	170	Fe	13.04S	30.38 E
Kan'onji	154	Lg	34.07N	133.39 E
Kanoya	154	Ki	31.23N	130.51 E
Kanozero, ozero-	114	Ic	67.00N	34.05 E
Kānpur	142	Kg	26.28N	80.21 E
Kansas [2]	182	Hd	38.45N	98.15W
Kansas	174	Jf	39.07N	94.36W
Kansas City [Ks.-U.S.]	176	Jf	39.07N	94.39W
Kansas City [Mo.-U.S.]	176	Jf	39.05N	94.35W
Kanshi	152	Kg	24.57N	116.52 E
Kansk	142	Ld	56.13N	95.41 E
Kansŏng	154	Je	38.22N	128.28 E
Kansu (EN) = Gansu Sheng (Kan-su Sheng) [2]	152	Hd	38.00N	102.00 E
Kansu (EN) = Kan-su Sheng → Gansu Sheng [2]	152	Hd	38.00N	102.00 E
Kan-su Sheng → Gansu Sheng = Kansu (EN) [2]	152	Hd	38.00N	102.00 E
Kansyat	150	Kg	2.15S	138.51 E
Kant	135	Jc	42.52N	74.50 E
Kantang	148	Jg	7.23N	99.32 E
Kantchari	166	Fc	12.29N	1.31 E
Kanté	166	Fd	9.57N	1.03 E
Kantemirovka	136	Df	49.45N	39.53 E
Kantō-Heiya	156	Fc	36.00N	139.30 E
Kantō-Sanchi	156	Fc	36.00N	138.45 E
Kantubek	135	Bb	45.06N	59.16 E
Kanturk/Ceann Toirc	118	Ei	52.10N	8.55W
Kanuma	156	Fc	36.34N	139.45 E
Kanye	160	Jk	24.58S	25.21 E
Kanyu	172	Cd	20.04S	24.36 E
Kanzenze	170	Ee	10.31S	25.12 E
Kao	221b	Aa	19.40S	175.01W
Kaohsiung	142	Og	22.38N	120.17 E
Kaôk Nhêk	148	Lf	13.05N	107.04 E
Kaoko Otavi	172	Ac	18.15S	13.37 E
Kaokoveld [3]	172	Ac	18.00S	13.00 E
Kaokoveld	158	Ij	19.30S	13.30 E
Kaolack	160	Fg	14.09N	16.04W
Kao Neua, Col de-	148	Le	18.23N	105.10 E
Kaouadja	168	Cd	8.00N	23.14 E
Kaouar	166	Hb	19.05N	12.52 E
Kapaa	221a	Ba	22.05N	159.19W
Kapanga	160	Ji	8.21S	22.35 E
Kapar	146	Ld	36.32N	47.30 E
Kapčagaj	136	Hg	43.52N	77.03 E
Kapčagajskoje vodohranilišče	136	Hg	43.45N	78.00 E
Kapchorwa	170	Fb	1.24N	34.27 E
Kap Dan	179	Ie	65.32N	37.30W
Kapelle	124	Fc	51.39N	3.57 E
Kapellskär	116	He	59.43N	19.04 E
Kapena	170	Ee	10.47S	28.20 E
Kapenguria	170	Gb	1.14N	35.07 E
Kapfenberg	128	Jc	47.26N	15.18 E
Kapıdağı Yarımadası	130	Ki	40.28N	27.50 E
Kapingamarangi Atoll	208	Gd	1.04N	154.46 E
Kapingamarangi Rise (EN)	208	Gd	1.00N	157.00 E
Kapiri Mposhi	170	Ee	13.58S	28.41 E
Kāpīsā [3]	144	Kc	34.45N	69.30 E
Kapiskau	180	Jf	52.45N	81.58W
Kapit	150	Ff	2.01N	112.56 E
~~Kapiti Island~~	218	Fd	40.50S	174.55 E
Kapka, Massif du-	168	Cb	15.07N	21.45 E
Kapoeta	160	Kh	4.47N	33.35 E
Kapona	170	Ed	7.11S	29.09 E
Kapos	120	Oj	46.44N	18.29 E
Kaposvár	120	Nj	46.22N	17.48 E
Kapp	116	Dd	60.42N	10.52 E
Kappeln	120	Fb	54.40N	9.56 E
Kapša	114	Hg	59.52N	33.45 E
Kapsan	154	Jd	41.05N	128.18 E
Kapuas [Indon.]	140	Mj	0.25S	109.40 E
Kapuas [Indon.]	150	Fg	3.01S	114.20 E
Kapuas Hulu, Pegunungan- = Kapuas Mountains (EN)	150	Ff	1.25N	113.15 E
Kapuas Mountains (EN) = Kapuas Hulu, Pegunungan	150	Ff	1.25N	113.15 E
Kapugargin	130	Lm	36.40N	28.50 E
Kapušany	120	Rg	49.03N	21.21 E
Kapuskasing	176	Ke	49.25N	82.26W
Kapustin Jar	132	Ne	48.35N	45.45 E
Kapustoje	114	Ic	67.17N	34.12 E
Kaputdžuh, gora-	132	Oj	39.12N	46.01 E
Kapuvár	120	Ni	47.36N	17.02 E
Kara	166	Fd	9.33N	1.12 E
Kara [3]	166	Fd	9.35N	1.05 E
Kara	134	Lb	69.10N	64.45 E
Kara Ada [Tur.]	130	Jk	38.25N	26.20 E
Kara Ada [Tur.]	130	Km	36.58N	27.28 E
Kara-Balta	136	Hg	42.49N	73.57 E
Karabas	136	Hf	49.30N	73.00 E
Karabaš	134	Ji	55.29N	60.13 E
Karabekaul	136	Gh	38.28N	64.10 E
Karabiga	130	Ki	40.24N	27.18 E
Karabil, vozvyšennost-	135	Df	36.20N	63.30 E
Kara-Bogaz-Gol	136	Fg	41.01N	52.59 E
Kara-Bogaz-Gol, proliv-	132	Ri	41.04N	52.59 E
Kara-Bogaz-Gol, zaliv-	110	Lg	41.00N	53.15 E
Karabuk	144	Da	41.12N	32.37 E
Karabulak [Kaz.]	135	Lb	44.54N	78.29 E
Karabulak [Kaz.]	136	Gg	42.31N	69.47 E
Kara Burun	130	Km	36.32N	27.58 E
Karaburun [Tur.]	146	Cb	41.21N	28.40 E
Karaburun [Tur.]	146	Bc	38.37N	26.31 E
Karabutak	136	Gf	49.57N	60.08 E
Karacabey	146	Cb	40.13N	28.21 E
Karaca Dağ	146	Hd	37.40N	39.50 E
Karačajevo-Čerkessakaja respublika	136	Eg	43.45N	41.45 E
Karačajevsk	132	Lh	43.44N	41.58 E
Karacaköy	146	Cb	41.22N	28.30 E
Karacaoğlan	130	Kh	41.32N	27.04 E
Karacasu	146	Cd	37.43N	28.37 E
Karačev	136	De	53.04N	34.59 E
Karāchi	142	Ig	24.52N	67.03 E
Kara Dağ [Tur.]	146	Ed	37.23N	33.10 E
Kara Dağ [Tur.]	146	Jd	37.40N	43.42 E
Karadah	132	Oh	42.29N	46.54 E
Karadeniz = Black Sea (EN)	110	Jg	43.00N	35.00 E
Kara Dong	152	Dd	38.26N	81.50 E
Karagajly	136	Hf	49.20N	75.48 E
Karaganda	142	Je	49.50N	73.10 E
Karagandinskaja oblast [3]	136	Hf	50.00N	74.00 E
Karaginski, ostrov-	140	Sd	58.48N	164.05 E
Karaginski zaliv	140	Sd	58.50N	164.00 E
Kara Gölü	130	Mm	36.42N	29.50 E
Karagoš, gora-	138	Df	51.44N	89.24 E
Karahalli	130	Mk	38.20N	29.32 E
Karaidelski	134	Hi	55.49N	57.05 E
Kara-Irtyš	140	Ke	47.52N	84.16 E
Karaisali	146	Fd	37.16N	35.03 E
Karaj	146	Ne	35.48N	50.59 E
Karaj	146	Ne	35.07N	51.35 E
Karak, gora-	136	Gg	44.59N	63.05 E
Kara-Kala	136	Fh	38.28N	56.18 E
Karakalpakstan respublika	136	Fg	43.30N	59.00 E
Karakax/Moyu	152	Cd	37.17N	79.42 E
Karakax He	152	Dd	38.06N	80.24 E
Karakaya Barajı	146	Hc	38.25N	38.45 E
Karakeçi	146	Hd	37.26N	39.26 E
Karakelong, Pulau-	150	If	4.15N	126.48 E
Karakoçan	146	Ic	38.02N	40.07 E
Karakoin, ozero-	135	Ga	46.10N	68.40 E
Karakojsu	132	Oh	42.30N	47.05 E
Karakolka	135	Kd	41.29N	77.24 E
Karakoram	140	Jf	34.00N	78.00 E
Karakoram Pass	140	Jf	35.30N	77.50 E
Karakore	168	Gc	10.25N	40.01 E
Karakoro	166	Cc	14.43N	12.03 E
Karakorum Shan	152	Cd	36.00N	76.00 E
Karakorum Shankou	135	Kg	35.30N	77.50 E
Karaköy	146	Ic	39.04N	41.42 E
Kara-Kul	135	Id	41.34N	72.47 E
Karakul, ozero-	136	Hh	39.05N	73.25 E
Karakumski kanal imeni V.I. Lenina	136	Gh	37.42N	64.20 E
Karakumy	140	Hf	39.00N	60.00 E
Karakuwisa	172	Bc	18.56S	19.40 E
Karam	138	Fe	55.09N	107.37 E
Karama	150	Gg	2.18S	119.06 E
Karaman	144	Db	37.11N	33.14 E
Karamanli	130	Ml	37.22N	29.49 E
Karamay	142	Ke	45.30N	84.55 E
Karamea	216	Dh	41.15S	172.06 E
Karamea Bight	218	Dd	41.25S	171.50 E
Karamet-Nijaz	136	Gh	37.43N	64.31 E
Karamiran He	152	Dd	37.50N	84.35 E
Karamiran Shankou	152	Ed	36.15N	87.05 E
Karamiševo	116	Mg	57.44N	28.50 E
Karamoja [3]	170	Fb	2.45N	34.15 E
Karamürsel	130	Mi	40.42N	29.36 E
Kara-myk	136	Hh	39.30N	71.51 E
Karamyš	132	Nd	51.18N	45.00 E
Karān	146	Mi	27.43N	49.49 E
Karaova	130	Kl	37.05N	27.40 E
Karapınar	146	Ed	37.43N	33.33 E
Kara-Saki	156	Ad	34.40N	129.29 E
Kara-Sal	132	Mf	47.18N	43.36 E
Karasay	152	Dd	36.48N	83.48 E
Karasburg	160	Ik	28.00S	18.43 E
Kara Sea (EN) = Karskoje more	224	Hd	76.00N	70.00 E
Karašica	128	Me	45.36N	18.36 E
Karasjok	114	Fb	69.27N	25.30 E
Kara Strait (EN) = Karskije Vorota, proliv-	140	Hb	70.30N	58.00 E
Karasu	146	Db	41.04N	30.47 E
Karasu [Tur.]	146	Jc	38.32N	43.10 E
Karasu [Tur.]	146	Ic	38.49N	41.28 E
Karasu [Tur.]	140	Ff	38.52N	38.48 E
Karasu Dağları	146	Ic	39.30N	40.45 E
Karasuk	138	Cf	53.44N	78.08 E
Karasuk	138	Cf	53.35N	77.30 E
Karasuyama	156	Gc	36.39N	140.08 E
Karatá, Laguna-	194	Fg	13.56N	83.30W
Karatal	136	Hf	46.26N	77.10 E
Karataş [Tur.]	146	Fd	36.36N	35.21 E
Karataş [Tur.]	130	Lk	38.34N	28.17 E
Karataş Burun	146	Fb	36.35N	35.22 E
Karatau	136	Hg	43.10N	70.29 E
Karatau, hrebet-	140	Ie	43.40N	69.00 E
Karatj	114	Ec	66.43N	18.33 E
Karatobe	132	Re	49.42N	53.33 E
Karaton	136	Ff	46.25N	53.34 E
Karatsu	154	Jh	33.26N	130.00 E
Karatsu-Wan	156	Be	33.30N	130.00 E
Kara-Turgaj	140	Ie	48.01N	62.45 E
Karaul [Kaz.]	136	Hf	49.00N	79.20 E
Karaul [Russia]	138	Db	70.10N	83.08 E
Karaulbazar	135	Ee	39.29N	64.47 E
Karaulkala	135	Bc	42.18N	58.41 E
Karáva	130	Ej	39.19N	21.36 E
Karavanke	128	Id	46.25N	14.25 E
Karavastase, Laguna e-	130	Ci	40.55N	19.30 E
Karávi	130	Gm	36.45N	23.35 E
Karavonisia	130	Jn	35.59N	26.26 E
Karawa	170	Db	3.20N	20.18 E
Karaxabar He/Kaidu He	152	Ec	41.55N	86.38 E
Karažal	136	Hf	47.59N	70.53 E
Karbalā'	142	Gf	32.36N	44.02 E
Karbalā [3]	146	Jf	32.30N	43.45 E
Kårbole	114	Df	61.59N	15.19 E
Karcag	120	Qi	47.19N	20.56 E
Kardeljevo (Ploče)	128	Lg	43.04N	17.26 E
Kardhámaina	130	Km	36.47N	27.09 E
Kardhámila	130	Jk	38.31N	26.06 E
Kardhiotissa	130	Im	36.38N	25.01 E
Kardhítsa	130	Ej	39.22N	21.55 E
Kärdla/Kjardla	114	Fg	59.01N	22.42 E
Kărdžali	130	Ih	41.39N	25.22 E
Kărdžali [2]	130	Ih	41.30N	25.30 E
Kareha, Jbel-	126	Gi	35.15N	5.30W
Karelia (EN)	110	Jc	64.00N	32.00 E
Karelija, respublika	136	Dc	63.30N	33.30 E
Karema	170	Fd	6.49S	30.26 E
Karen → Kayin	148	Je	17.30N	97.45 E
Karen	148	If	12.51E	92.53 E
Karesuando	114	Fb	68.27N	22.29 E
Karêt	158	Gf	24.00N	7.30W
Kärevere/Kjarevere	116	Lf	58.23N	26.30 E
Kargala	132	Sd	51.59N	55.10 E
Kargapazari Dağı	146	Ib	40.07N	41.35 E
Kargapolje	134	Li	55.57N	64.27 E
Kargasok	138	De	59.07N	81.01 E
Kargat	138	De	55.10N	80.17 E
Kargı	146	Fb	41.08N	34.30 E
Kargil	148	Fb	34.34N	76.06 E
Kargilik/Yecheng	142	Jf	37.54N	77.26 E
Kargopol	136	Dc	61.32N	38.58 E
Karhula	114	Gf	60.31N	26.57 E
Kari	166	Hc	11.14N	10.34 E
Kariaí	112	Ig	40.15N	24.15 E
Kariba	160	Jj	16.30S	28.45 E
Kariba, Lake-	158	Jj	17.00S	28.00 E
Kariba-Dake	156a	Ab	42.37N	139.56 E
Kariba Dam	172	Dc	16.30S	28.50 E
Karibib	160	Ik	21.58S	15.51 E
Karibib [3]	172	Bd	22.00S	16.00 E
Kariet-Arkmane	126	Ji	35.06N	2.45W
Karigasniemi	114	Fb	69.24N	25.50 E
Karijärvi	116	Jc	61.35N	22.30 E
Karikachi Tōge	156a	Cb	43.10N	142.40 E
Kārikāl	148	Ff	10.55N	79.50 E
Karikari, Cape-	218	Ea	34.47S	173.24 E
Karima (EN) = Kuraymah	160	Kg	18.33N	31.51 E
Karimama	166	Fc	12.04N	3.11 E
Karimata, Kepulauan- = Karimata Islands (EN)	150	Eg	1.25S	109.05 E
Karimata, Pulau-	150	Eg	1.36S	108.55 E
Karimata, Selat- = Karimata Strait (EN)	140	Mj	2.05S	108.40 E
Karimata Islands (EN) = Karimata, Kepulauan-	150	Eg	1.25S	109.05 E
Karimata Strait (EN) = Karimata, Selat-	140	Mj	2.05S	108.40 E
Karīmganj	148	Id	24.42N	92.33 E
Karīmnagar	148	Fe	18.26N	79.09 E
Karimunjawa, Kepulauan- = Karimunjawa Islands (EN)	150	Fh	5.50S	110.25 E
Karimunjawa Islands (EN) = Karimunjawa, Kepulauan-	150	Fh	5.50S	110.25 E
Karin [Som.]	168	Hc	10.51N	45.45 E
Karin [Som.]	168	Hc	10.59N	49.13 E
Karis/Karjaa	114	Ff	60.05N	23.40 E
Karisimbi	158	Ji	1.30S	29.27 E
Káristos	130	Hk	38.01N	24.25 E
Karjaa/Karis	114	Ff	60.05N	23.40 E
Karkār	168	Hd	9.57N	49.20 E
Karkaralinsk	136	Hf	49.23N	75.31 E
Karkar Island	208	Fe	4.40S	146.00 E
Karkas, Kūh-e	146	Nf	33.27N	51.48 E
Karkheh	144	Gc	31.31N	47.55 E
Karkinitski zaliv	110	Jf	45.55N	33.00 E
Karkkila/Högfors	114	Ff	60.32N	24.11 E
Karkku	116	Jc	61.25N	23.01 E
Kärkölä	116	Kd	60.55N	25.15 E
Kärla/Kjarla	116	Jf	58.16N	22.05 E
Karlholm	116	Gd	60.31N	17.37 E
Karlik Shan	140	Le	43.00N	94.30 E
Karlino	120	Lb	54.03N	15.51 E
Karliova	146	Ic	39.18N	41.01 E
Karl Marx, pik-	136	Hh	37.08N	72.29 E
Karl-Marx-Stadt → Chemnitz	112	He	50.50N	12.55 E
Karlobag	128	Jf	44.32N	15.05 E
Karlovac	128	Je	45.29N	15.33 E
Karlovka	132	Ie	49.28N	35.08 E
Karlovo	130	Hg	42.38N	24.48 E
Karlovy Vary	120	If	50.14N	12.52 E
Karlsbad	124	Kf	48.55N	8.35 E
Karlsborg	114	Df	58.32N	14.31 E
Karlshamn	114	Dh	56.10N	14.51 E
Karlskoga	114	Dg	59.20N	14.31 E
Karlskrona	112	Hd	56.10N	15.35 E
Karlsöarna	116	Gg	57.15N	18.00 E
Karlsruhe	120	Eg	49.01N	8.24 E
Karlstad [Mn.-U.S.]	186	Hb	48.35N	96.31W
Karlstad [Swe.]	112	Hd	59.22N	13.30 E
Karluk	178	Ie	57.34N	154.28W
Karmah = Kerma (EN)	168	Eb	19.38N	30.25 E
Karmana	135	Ed	40.09N	65.15 E
Karmøy	114	Ag	59.15N	5.15 E
Karnāli	148	Gc	28.45N	81.16 E
Karnataka (Mysore) [3]	148	Ff	13.30N	76.00 E
Karnobat	130	Jg	42.39N	26.59 E
Kärnten = Carinthia (EN) [2]	128	Hd	46.45N	14.00 E
Kärnten = Carinthia (EN)	128	Hd	46.45N	14.00 E
Karoi	172	Dc	16.50S	29.40 E
Karonga	160	Ki	9.56S	33.56 E
Karora	168	Fb	17.39N	38.22 E
Káros	130	Im	36.53N	25.39 E
Kárpathos	130	Kn	35.30N	27.14 E
Kárpathos = Karpathos (EN)	110	Ih	35.40N	27.10 E
Karpathos (EN) = Kárpathos	110	Ih	35.40N	27.10 E
Karpáthou, Stenón-	130	Kn	35.50N	27.30 E
Karpenision	130	Ek	38.55N	21.47 E
Karpinsk	134	Jg	59.45N	60.01 E
Karpuzlu	130	Kl	37.33N	27.50 E
Kars	144	Fa	40.37N	43.05 E
Karsakpaj	136	Gf	47.48N	66.45 E
Kärsämäki	114	Fe	64.00N	25.46 E
Karsava/Kārsava	114	Gh	56.47N	27.42 E
Kārsava/Karsava	114	Gh	56.47N	27.42 E
Karši	142	If	38.53N	65.48 E
Karşiyaka	130	Ki	40.26N	28.00 E
Karsiyaka	130	Kk	38.27N	27.07 E
Karskije Vorota, proliv- = Kara Strait (EN)	140	Hb	70.30N	58.00 E
Karskoje more = Kara Sea (EN)	224	Hd	76.00N	70.00 E
Kars Platosu	146	Jb	40.40N	43.07 E
Karst (EN) = Kras	110	Hf	45.48N	14.00 E
Kårsta	116	He	59.39N	18.14 E
Karstula	114	Fe	62.52N	24.47 E
Kartal	146	Cb	40.53N	29.10 E
Kartaly	136	Ge	53.03N	60.40 E
Kartaly-Ajat	134	Jj	53.01N	61.50 E
Karttula	116	Lb	62.53N	26.58 E
Kartuzy	120	Ob	54.20N	18.12 E
Karumai	156	Ga	40.20N	141.28 E
Karumba	212	Ic	17.29S	140.50 E
Kārūn	140	Gf	30.25N	48.12 E
Karungi	114	Fc	66.03N	23.57 E
Karungu	170	Fc	0.51S	34.09 E
Karunki	114	Fc	66.02N	24.01 E
Karūr	148	Ff	10.57N	78.05 E
Karvia	114	Fe	62.08N	22.34 E
Karviná	120	Og	49.51N	18.32 E
Kārwār	148	Ef	14.48N	74.08 E
Karwendelgebirge	128	Fc	47.28N	11.20 E
Karymskoje	138	Gf	51.37N	114.21 E
Kaş	146	Cd	36.12N	29.38 E
Kas	168	Cc	12.34N	24.14 E
Kas	136	Jd	59.58N	90.42 E
Kasaba [Tur.]	130	Mm	36.18N	29.44 E
Kasaba [Zam.]	170	Ee	10.44S	29.43 E
Kasado-Shima	156	Be	33.57N	131.50 E
Kasah	132	Mi	40.03N	43.52 E
Kasai	156	Dd	34.56N	134.49 E
Kasai	158	Ii	3.02S	16.57 E
Kasai Occidental [2]	170	Dc	5.00S	21.30 E
Kasai Oriental [2]	170	Dc	3.00S	23.00 E
Kasaji	170	De	10.22S	23.27 E
Kasaku	170	Ec	1.55S	25.50 E
Kasama [Jap.]	156	Gc	36.22N	140.16 E
Kasama [Zam.]	160	Kj	10.13S	31.12 E
Kasan	135	Ee	39.01N	65.35 E
Kasane	160	Jj	17.48S	25.09 E
Kasanga	170	Fd	8.28S	31.09 E
Kasangulu	170	Bc	4.36S	15.10 E
Kasansaj	135	Hd	41.10N	71.32 E
Kasaoka	156	Cd	34.30N	133.29 E
Kasaragod	148	Ef	12.30N	75.00 E
Kasari	156b	Ba	28.27N	129.41 E
Kasari-Zaki	156b	Ba	28.31N	129.42 E
Kašary	132	Le	49.02N	41.03 E
Kasatori-Yama	156	Ce	33.33N	132.55 E
Kasba Lake	180	Hd	60.20N	102.10W
Kasba Tatla	162	Fc	32.36N	6.16W
Kaseda	154	Ki	31.25N	130.19 E
Kasempa	170	Ee	13.27S	25.50 E
Kasenga	160	Jj	10.22S	28.37 E
Kasenye	170	Fb	1.24N	30.26 E
Kasese [Ug.]	170	Fb	0.10N	30.05 E
Kasese [Zaire]	170	Ec	1.38S	27.07 E
Kashaf-Rūd	144	Jb	35.58N	61.07 E
Kāshān	142	Hf	33.59N	51.29 E
Kashi	142	Jf	39.29N	75.58 E
Kashihara	156	Dd	34.31N	135.47 E
Kashima [Jap.]	156	Cd	35.31N	132.59 E
Kashima [Jap.]	156	Be	33.07N	130.07 E
Kashima [Jap.]	156	Gd	35.58N	140.38 E
Kashima-Nada	156	Gc	36.30N	140.45 E
Kashiobwe	170	Ed	9.39S	28.37 E
Kashiwazaki	154	Of	37.25N	138.30 E
Kashkū'īyeh	146	Qh	28.58N	56.37 E
Kāshmar	144	Ib	35.12N	58.27 E
Kashmīr	140	Jf	34.00N	76.00 E
Kashmor	148	Dc	28.26N	69.35 E
Kasimov	136	Ee	54.59N	41.28 E
Kašin	136	Dd	57.23N	37.37 E
Kasindi	170	Eb	0.02N	29.43 E

Index Symbols

- [1] Independent Nation
- [2] State, Region
- [3] District, County
- [4] Municipality
- [5] Colony, Dependency
- Continent
- Physical Region
- Historical or Cultural Region
- Mount, Mountain
- Volcano
- Hill
- Mountains, Mountain Range
- Hills, Escarpment
- Plateau, Upland
- Pass, Gap
- Plain, Lowland
- Delta
- Salt Flat
- Valley, Canyon
- Crater, Cave
- Karst Features
- Depression
- Polder
- Desert, Dunes
- Forest, Woods
- Heath, Steppe
- Oasis
- Cape, Point
- Coast, Beach
- Cliff
- Peninsula
- Isthmus
- Sandbank
- Island
- Atoll
- Rock, Reef
- Islands, Archipelago
- Rocks, Reefs
- Coral Reef
- Well, Spring
- Geyser
- River, Stream
- Waterfall, Rapids
- River Mouth, Estuary
- Lake
- Salt Lake
- Intermittent Lake
- Reservoir
- Swamp, Pond
- Canal
- Glacier
- Ice Shelf, Pack Ice
- Ocean
- Sea
- Gulf, Bay
- Strait, Fjord
- Lagoon
- Bank
- Seamount
- Tablemount
- Ridge
- Shelf
- Basin
- Escarpment, Sea Scarp
- Fracture
- Trench, Abyss
- National Park, Reserve
- Point of Interest
- Recreation Site
- Cave, Cavern
- Historic Site
- Ruins
- Wall, Walls
- Church, Abbey
- Temple
- Scientific Station
- Railway station
- Airport
- Port
- Military installation
- Lighthouse
- Mine
- Tunnel
- Dam, Bridge

Kas-Ket

Kaširа	114	Ji	54.52N	38.11 E
Kasiruta, Pulau-	150	Ig	0.25 S	127.12 E
Kasisty	138	Fb	73.40N	109.45 E
Kaškadarinskaja oblast [3]	136	Gh	38.50N	66.10 E
Kaškadarja	135	Ee	39.35N	64.38 E
Kaskaskia River	186	Lh	37.59N	89.56W
Kaskelen	136	Hg	43.09N	76.37 E
Kaskinen/Kaskö	114	Ee	62.23N	21.13 E
Kaskö/Kaskinen	114	Ee	62.23N	21.13 E
Kasli	134	Ji	55.53N	60.48 E
Kaslo	188	Gb	49.55N	116.55W
Kasongo	160	Ji	4.27 S	26.40 E
Kasongo-Lunda	170	Cd	6.28 S	16.49 E
Kásos	130	Jn	35.25N	26.55 E
Kásou, Stenón-	130	Jn	35.25N	26.35 E
Kaspi	132	Ni	41.58N	44.25 E
Kaspičan	130	Kf	43.18N	27.11 E
Kaspijsk	136	Eg	42.57N	47.35 E
Kaspijski	136	Ef	45.25N	47.22 E
Kaspijskoje more = Caspian Sea (EN)	110	Lg	42.00N	50.30 E
Kasplja	132	Gb	55.24N	30.43 E
Kasr, Ra's-	168	Fb	18.04N	38.33 E
Kassaar/Kassar	116	Jf	58.47N	22.40 E
Kassalā	160	Kg	15.28N	36.24 E
Kassalā [3]	168	Fc	14.40N	35.30 E
Kassándra	130	Gi	40.00N	23.30 E
Kassándras, Ákra-	130	Gj	39.57N	23.21 E
Kassándras, Kólpos- = Kassandra, Gulf of- (EN)	130	Gi	40.05N	23.30 E
Kassel	120	Fe	51.19N	9.30 E
Kassiópi	130	Cj	39.47N	19.55 E
Kastamonu	144	Da	41.22N	33.47 E
Kastanéai	130	Jh	41.39N	26.28 E
Kastellaun	124	Jd	50.04N	7.27 E
Kastéllion [Grc.]	130	Gn	35.30N	23.39 E
Kastéllion [Grc.]	130	In	35.12N	25.20 E
Kastéllos, Ákra-	130	Kn	35.23N	27.09 E
Kasterlee	124	Gc	51.15N	4.57 E
Kastlösa	116	Gh	56.28N	16.25 E
Kastoria	130	Ei	40.31N	21.16 E
Kastorias, Limni-	130	Ei	40.31N	21.18 E
Kastornoje	132	Kd	51.51N	38.07 E
Kastós	130	Dk	38.35N	20.55 E
Kasuga	156	Be	33.32N	130.27 E
Kasugai	156	Ed	35.14N	136.58 E
Kasulu	170	Fc	4.34 S	30.06 E
Kasumbalesa	170	Ee	12.13 S	27.48 E
Kasumi	156	Dd	35.38N	134.38 E
Kasumi-ga-Ura	154	Pf	36.00N	140.25 E
Kasumkent	132	Pi	41.42N	48.10 E
Kasungan	150	Fg	1.58 S	113.24 E
Kasungu	170	Fe	13.02 S	33.29 E
Kasupe	170	Gf	15.10 S	35.18 E
Kasūr	148	Eb	31.07N	74.27 E
Kaszuby	120	Ob	54.10N	18.15 E
Kataba	160	Jj	16.05 S	25.10 E
Katahdin, Mount-	182	Nb	45.55N	68.55W
Katajsk	134	Kh	56.18N	62.35 E
Katako-Kombe	170	Dc	3.24 S	24.25 E
Katanga	170	Ed	10.00 S	25.30 E
Katanga	138	Fd	60.10N	102.10 E
Katangli	138	Jf	51.43N	143.16 E
Katanning	212	Df	33.42 S	117.33 E
Katav-Ivanovsk	134	Ii	54.47N	58.15 E
Katchall	148	Ig	7.57N	93.22 E
Katchi	162	Ef	17.00N	13.55W
Katchiungo	170	Ce	12.33 S	16.14 E
Katende, Chutes de-	170	Dd	6.30 S	22.10 E
Katerini	130	Fi	40.16N	22.30 E
Katesh	170	Gc	4.31 S	35.23 E
Katete	170	Fe	14.06 S	32.05 E
Katha	148	Jd	24.11N	96.21 E
Katherine	210	Ef	14.28 S	132.16 E
Katherine River	212	Gb	14.39 S	131.42 E
Kāthiāwār	140	Jg	21.58N	70.30 E
Kāthmāṇḍāū = Kathmandu (EN)	142	Kg	27.43N	85.19 E
Kathmandu → Kāthmāṇḍāū	142	Kg	27.43N	85.19 E
Kathua	170	Gc	1.17 S	39.03 E
Kati	166	Dc	12.43N	8.05W
Katihār	148	Hc	25.32N	87.35 E
Katiki, Volcán-	221d	Bb	27.06 S	109.16W
Katima Mulilo	170	Df	17.28 S	24.14 E
Katiola	166	Dd	8.08N	5.06W
Katiola [3]	166	Dd	8.13N	5.02W
Katiu Atoll	216	Mc	16.26 S	144.22W
Katla	114a	Bc	63.36N	18.58W
Katlabuh, ozero-	130	Ld	45.25N	29.00 E
Katlanovo	130	Eh	41.54N	21.41 E
Katmai, Mount-	178	Ie	58.17N	154.56W
Káto Akhaia	130	Ek	38.09N	21.33 E
Katofio	170	Ee	11.02 S	28.01 E
Katompi	170	Ed	6.11 S	26.20 E
Katonga	170	Fb	0.10N	30.40 E
Katon-Karagaj	136	If	49.11N	85.37 E
Káto Ólimbos	130	Fj	39.55N	22.28 E
Katoomba	212	Kf	33.42 S	150.18 E
Katopasa, Gunung-	150	Hg	1.14 S	121.25 E
Katowice	112	He	50.16N	19.00 E
Katowice [2]	120	Of	50.15N	19.00 E
Katrancık Dağı	146	Dd	37.27N	30.25 E
Kātrīnā, Dayr- = Saint Catherine, Monastery of- (EN)	164	Fd	28.31N	33.57 E
Kātrīnā, Jabal-	158	Kf	28.31N	33.57 E
Katrineholm	114	Dg	59.00N	16.12 E
Katsina	160	Hg	13.00N	7.36 E
Katsina Ala	166	Gd	7.48N	8.52 E
Katsumoto	154	Jh	33.51N	129.42 E
Katsuta	154	Pf	36.24N	140.32 E
Katsuura	154	Pg	35.08N	140.18 E
Katsuyama [Jap.]	154	Nf	36.03N	136.30 E
Katsuyama [Jap.]	156	Cd	35.06N	133.41 E
Kattakurgan	136	Gh	39.55N	66.15 E
Kattavia	130	Kn	35.57N	27.46 E
Kattegat	110	Hd	57.00N	11.00 E
Katthammarsvik	116	Hg	57.26N	18.50 E
Katulo, Lagh-	170	Hb	2.08N	40.56 E
Katumbi	170	Fe	10.49 S	33.32 E
Katun	140	Kd	52.25N	85.05 E
Katwijk aan Zee	122	Kb	52.13N	4.24 E
Katwijk aan Zee, Katwijk-	124	Gb	52.12N	4.25 E
Katzenelnbogen	124	Jd	50.17N	7.57 E
Kau	150	If	1.11N	127.54 E
Kauai Channel	214	Oc	21.45N	158.50W
Kauai Island	208	Lb	22.03N	159.30W
Kaub	124	Jd	50.05N	7.46 E
Kauehi Atoll	216	Lc	15.51 S	145.09W
Kaufbeuren	120	Gi	47.53N	10.37 E
Kauhajoki	114	Fe	62.26N	22.11 E
Kauhava	114	Fe	63.06N	23.05 E
Kauiki Head	214	Oc	20.46N	155.59W
Kaukauna	186	Ld	44.17N	88.17W
Kaukauveld	158	Jk	20.00 S	21.50 E
Kaukonen	114	Fc	67.29N	24.54 E
Kaukura Atoll	208	Mf	15.45 S	146.42W
Kaula Island	208	Kb	21.40N	160.32W
Kaulakahi Channel	221a	Ba	22.02N	159.53W
Kaumalapau	221a	Ec	20.47N	156.59W
Kaunakakai	214	Oc	21.05N	157.02W
Kaunas	112	Ie	54.54N	23.54 E
Kaunasskoje vodohranilišče / Kauno marios	116	Kj	54.50N	24.15 E
Kauniainen/Grankulla	116	Kd	60.13N	24.45 E
Kauno marios / Kaunasskoje vodohranilišče	116	Kj	54.50N	24.15 E
Kaunos	130	Lm	36.50N	28.35 E
Kaupanger	114	Bf	61.11N	7.14 E
Kau Paulatmada, Gunung-	150	Ig	3.15 S	126.09 E
Kaura Namoda	166	Gc	12.36N	6.35 E
Kauriāla Ghāt	148	Gc	28.27N	80.59 E
Kaušany	132	Ff	46.39N	29.25 E
Kaustinen	114	Fe	63.32N	23.42 E
Kautokeino	114	Fb	68.59N	23.08 E
Kavacik	130	Lj	39.40N	28.30 E
Kavadarci	130	Fh	41.26N	22.01 E
Kavaja	130	Ch	41.11N	19.33 E
Kavak [Tur.]	130	Ji	40.36N	26.54 E
Kavak [Tur.]	146	Gb	41.05N	36.03 E
Kavaklidere	130	Ll	37.26N	28.22 E
Kavála	112	Ig	40.56N	24.25 E
Kaválas, Kólpos-	130	Hi	40.52N	24.25 E
Kavalerovo	138	Ih	44.19N	135.05 E
Kavali	148	Ff	14.55N	79.59 E
Kavār	146	Oh	29.11N	52.44 E
Kavaratti	142	Jh	10.33N	72.38 E
Kavaratti Island	148	Ef	10.33N	72.38 E
Kavarna	130	Lf	43.25N	28.20 E
Kavarskas/Kovarskas	116	Ki	55.24N	25.03 E
Kavendou, Mont-	158	Fg	10.41N	12.12W
Kavieng	214	Eh	2.34 S	150.48 E
Kavīr, Dasht-e-	140	Hf	34.40N	54.30 E
Kavkaz	132	Jg	45.21N	36.12 E
Kavkaz, Bolšoj- = Caucasus (EN)	110	Kg	42.30N	45.00 E
Kävlinge	116	Ei	55.48N	13.06 E
Kävlingeån	116	Ei	55.47N	13.06 E
Kawa	168	Eb	19.10N	30.39 E
Kawabe	156	Gb	39.39N	140.15 E
Kawachi-nagano	156	Dd	34.27N	135.34 E
Kawagoe	156	Fd	35.55N	139.28 E
Kawaguchi	156	Fd	35.48N	139.42 E
Kawaihae Bay	221a	Fc	20.02N	155.51W
Kawaihoa Point	221a	Ab	21.47N	160.12W
Kawakawa	218	Fa	35.23 S	174.04 E
Kawalusu, Pulau-	150	If	4.15N	125.19 E
Kawamata	156	Gc	37.40N	140.36 E
Kawambwa	170	Ed	9.47 S	29.05 E
Kawaminami	156	Be	32.12N	131.32 E
Kawamoto	156	Cd	34.59N	132.29 E
Kawanishi	156	Gc	37.59N	140.03 E
Kawanoe	156	Cd	34.01N	133.34 E
Kawartha Lakes	184	Hc	44.32N	78.30W
Kawasaki [Jap.]	156	Gb	38.10N	140.38 E
Kawasaki [Jap.]	154	Og	35.32N	139.43 E
Kawashiri-Misaki	156	Bd	34.26N	130.58 E
Kawauchi	156a	Bc	41.12N	141.00 E
Kawau Island	218	Fb	36.25 S	174.50 E
Kawaura	156	Be	32.21N	130.05 E
Kawerau	218	Gc	38.05 S	176.42 E
Kawhia	218	Fc	38.04 S	174.49 E
Kawich Range	188	Gh	37.40N	116.30W
Kawio, Kepulauan-	150	If	4.30N	125.30 E
Kawkareik	148	Je	16.33N	98.14 E
Kawm Umbū	164	Fe	24.28N	32.57 E
Kawthaung	148	Jg	9.59N	98.33 E
Kaxgar He	140	Jf	39.46N	78.15 E
Kax He	152	Dc	43.37N	81.48 E
Kaya	166	Ec	13.05N	1.05W
Kayah [2]	148	Je	19.15N	97.30 E
Kayak	178	Ke	59.52N	144.30W
Kayalı Dağı	130	Jj	39.58N	26.38 E
Kayan	140	Ni	2.55N	117.35 E
Kayanga	166	Cc	11.58N	15.00W
Kayangel Islands	208	Ed	8.04N	134.43 E
Kayangel Passage	220a	Ba	8.01N	134.42 E
Kaycee	188	Le	43.43N	106.38W
Kayenta	188	Jh	36.44N	110.17W
Kayes	160	Fg	14.26N	11.27W
Kayes [3]	166	Cc	14.00N	11.00W
Kayin	148	Je	17.30N	97.45 E
Kayoa, Pulau-	150	Ig	0.05S	127.25 E
Kayseri	142	Ff	38.43N	35.30 E
Kayuagung	150	Dg	3.24 S	104.50 E
Kayu Ara, Pulau-	150	Ef	1.31N	106.26 E
Kazačje	138	Ib	70.40N	136.13 E
Kazah	132	Ni	41.05N	45.22 E
Kazahskaja Sovetskaja Socialističeskaja Respublika → Kazakhstan	136	Gf	48.00N	68.00 E
Kazahskaja SSR/Kazak Sovettik Socialistik Respublikasy → Kazakhstan	136	Gf	48.00N	68.00 E
Kazahskaja SSR → Kazakhstan	136	Gf	48.00N	68.00 E
Kazahski melkosopočnik = Kazakh Hills (EN)	140	Je	49.00N	73.00 E
Kazahski zaliv	132	Rh	42.40N	52.25 E
Kazakh Hills (EN) = Kazahski melkosopočnik	140	Je	49.00N	73.00 E
Kazakhstan (EN) = Qazaqstan	136	Gf	48.00N	68.00 E
Kazakhstan (EN)	140	Ie	44.00N	65.00 E
Kazaklija	130	Lc	46.05N	28.38 E
Kazak Sovettik Socialistik Respublikasy → Qazaqstan	136	Gf	48.00N	68.00 E
Kazalinsk	136	Gf	45.46N	62.07 E
Kazan	112	Kd	55.45N	49.08 E
Kazan	174	Jc	64.02N	95.30W
Kazandžik	136	Fh	39.17N	55.34 E
Kazanka	132	Hf	47.50N	32.49 E
Kazanka	114	Li	55.48N	49.05 E
Kazanlăk	130	Ig	42.37N	25.24 E
Kazan-Rettō/Iō = Volcano Islands (EN)	140	Qg	25.00N	141.00 E
Kazanskoje	136	Gd	55.38N	69.14 E
Kazarman	136	Hg	41.20N	74.02 E
Kazatin	136	Cf	49.43N	28.50 E
Kazbegi	132	Nh	42.39N	44.39 E
Kazbek, gora-	110	Kg	42.42N	44.31 E
Kaz Dağı [Tur.]	130	Mk	38.35N	29.15 E
Kaz Dağı [Tur.]	144	Cb	39.42N	26.50 E
Kāzerūn	144	Hd	29.37N	51.38 E
Kažim	134	Ef	60.20N	51.32 E
Kazi-Magomed	132	Pi	40.02N	48.56 E
Kazimierza Wielka	120	Qf	50.16N	20.30 E
Kāzimkarabekir	146	Ed	37.14N	32.59 E
Kazıncbarcika	120	Qh	48.15N	20.38 E
Kazinga Channel	170	Ec	0.13 S	29.53 E
Kazlų-Rūda/Kazlu-Ruda	116	Jj	54.42N	23.32 E
Kazo	156	Fc	36.08N	139.36 E
Kaztalovka	132	Pe	49.46N	48.44 E
Kazumba	170	Dd	6.25 S	22.02 E
Kazuno	154	Pd	40.14N	140.48 E
Kazym	136	Gc	63.54N	65.50 E
Kazyr	138	Ef	53.50N	92.53 E
Kcynia	120	Nd	53.00N	17.30 E
Kdyně	120	Jg	49.24N	13.02 E
Ké	168	Bb	18.32N	17.55 E
Kéa	130	Hl	37.39N	24.20 E
Kéa	130	Hl	37.37N	24.20 E
Keaau	221a	Fd	19.37N	155.03W
Keahole Point	221a	Ed	19.44N	156.04W
Kealaikahiki Channel	221a	Ec	20.37N	156.50W
Kealaikahiki Point	221a	Ec	20.32N	156.42W
Kealakekua Bay	221a	Fd	19.28N	155.56W
Keams Canyon	188	Ji	35.49N	110.12W
Keanae	221a	Ec	20.52N	156.09W
Keanapapa Point	221a	Dc	20.54N	157.04W
Kearney	182	Hc	40.42N	99.05W
Kearns	188	Jf	40.39N	111.59W
Kéas, Stenón-	130	Hl	37.40N	24.12 E
Keats Bank (EN)	208	Id	5.23N	173.28 E
Keb	116	Mg	57.44N	28.38 E
Keban Barajı	146	Hc	38.53N	39.00 E
Kébémer	166	Bb	15.22N	16.27W
Kebir, Oued el-	128	Bn	36.51N	7.57 E
Kebnekaise	110	Hb	67.53N	18.33 E
Kebri Dehar	160	Lh	6.45N	44.17 E
Kebumen	150	Eh	7.40 S	109.39 E
Kecel	120	Pj	46.32N	19.16 E
Kechika	180	Ee	59.38N	127.09W
Kecskemét	120	Pj	46.54N	19.42 E
Kedah [2]	150	De	6.00N	100.40 E
Kédainiai/Kedajnjaj	114	Fi	55.18N	23.59 E
Kedajnjaj/Kédainiai	114	Fi	55.18N	23.59 E
Kedgwick	184	Nb	47.39N	67.21W
Kediri	142	Nj	7.49 S	112.01 E
Kédougou	166	Cc	12.33N	12.11W
Kedva	134	Fd	64.14N	53.30 E
Kędzierzyn-Koźle	120	Of	50.20N	18.10 E
Keele	180	Fd	64.24N	124.47W
Keele Peak	174	Fc	63.26N	130.19W
Keeling Islands → Cocos Islands [5]	142	Lk	12.10 S	96.55 E
Keeling Islands → Cocos Islands	140	Lk	12.10 S	96.55 E
Keelung	142	Og	25.08N	121.44 E
Keene	184	Kd	42.55N	72.17W
Keer-Weer, Cape-	212	Ib	13.58 S	141.30 E
Keetmanshoop	160	Ik	26.36 S	18.08 E
Keetmanshoop [3]	172	Be	26.30 S	18.30 E
Keewatin	180	Ig	49.46N	94.34W
Kefa [3]	168	Fd	7.00N	36.00 E
Kefallinia = Cephalonia (EN)	110	Ih	38.15N	20.35 E
Kefamenanu	150	Hh	9.27 S	124.29 E
Kefar Sava	146	Ff	32.10N	34.54 E
Keffi	166	Gd	8.51N	7.52 E
Keflavik	114a	Ab	64.01N	22.34W
Kegen	136	Hg	42.58N	79.12 E
Kegums	116	Kh	56.41N	24.44 E
Kehdingen	120	Fc	53.45N	9.20 E
Kehl	120	Dh	48.35N	7.49 E
Kehra	114	Fg	59.19N	25.18 E
Keighley	118	Lh	53.52N	1.54W
Keila/Kejla	114	Fg	59.19N	24.27 E
Keila jõgi / Kejla	116	Ke	59.25N	24.15 E
Keimoes	172	Ce	28.41 S	21.00 E
Keipel Bank (EN)	212	Le	25.15 S	159.30 E
Keita	166	Gc	14.46N	5.46 E
Kéita, Bahr-	168	Bd	9.14N	18.21 E
Keitele	110	Ic	62.55N	26.00 E
Keith [Austl.]	212	Ig	36.06 S	140.21 E
Keith [Scot.-U.K.]	118	Kd	57.32N	2.57W
Keith Arm	180	Fc	65.20N	122.00W
Keiyasi	219d	Ab	17.53 S	177.45 E
Kejla/Keila	114	Fg	59.19N	24.27 E
Kejla / Keila jõgi	116	Ke	59.25N	24.15 E
Kejvy	114	Ic	67.30N	37.45 E
Kekaha	221a	Bb	21.58N	159.43W
Kekerengu	218	Ee	42.00 S	174.00 E
Kékes	120	Qi	47.52N	20.01 E
Keklau	220a	Bb	7.35N	134.39 E
Kelafo	168	Gd	5.37N	44.13 E
Kelakam	166	Hc	13.35N	11.44 E
Kela Met	168	Fb	15.50N	38.23 E
Kelan	152	Jd	38.44N	111.34 E
Kelang	142	Mi	3.02N	101.27 E
Kelantan [2]	150	De	5.20N	102.00 E
Kelasa, Selat- = Gaspar Strait (EN)	150	Eg	2.40 S	107.15 E
Kelberg	124	Id	50.18N	6.55 E
Kelcyra	130	Di	40.19N	20.11 E
Kelefesia	221b	Bb	20.30 S	174.44W
Kelekçi	130	Ml	37.14N	29.28 E
Kelem	168	Fe	4.49N	35.59 E
Keles	130	Mj	39.55N	29.14 E
Keles	135	Gd	41.02N	68.37 E
Kelheim	120	Hh	48.55N	11.52 E
Kelifely, Causse du-	172	Hc	17.15 S	45.30 E
Kelifski uzboj	135	Ef	37.45N	64.40 E
Keli Hāji Ibrāhīm	146	Kd	36.42N	45.00 E
Kelkheim	124	Kd	50.08N	8.27 E
Kelkit	146	Hb	40.08N	39.27 E
Kelkit	144	Ea	36.32N	40.46 E
Kellé	170	Bc	0.06 S	14.33 E
Kellerberrin	212	Df	31.38 S	117.43 E
Kellerwald	120	Fe	51.03N	9.10 E
Kellett, Cape-	180	Eb	72.57N	125.27W
Kellett Strait	180	Fa	75.50N	117.40W
Kellog	138	Dd	62.27N	86.35 E
Kellogg	182	Db	47.32N	116.07W
Kelloselkä	114	Gc	66.56N	29.00 E
Kells/Ceanannas Mór	118	Gh	53.44N	6.53W
Kelmé/Kelme	114	Fi	55.39N	22.58 E
Kelme/Kelmé	114	Fi	55.39N	22.58 E
Kelmency	130	Ja	48.27N	26.47 E
Kelmis/La Calamine	124	Hd	50.43N	6.00 E
Kélo	168	Bd	9.19N	15.48 E
Kelowna	176	He	49.53N	119.29W
Kelsey	180	He	56.00N	97.00W
Kelsey Bay	180	Ef	50.24N	125.57W
Kelso	188	Dc	46.09N	122.54W
Kelso Bank (EN)	212	Ld	24.10 S	159.30 E
Kel Tepe [Tur.]	146	Eb	41.05N	32.27 E
Kel Tepe [Tur.]	130	Ni	40.39N	30.06 E
Keltie, Mount-	222	Jf	79.15 S	159.00 E
Keluang	150	Df	2.02N	103.19 E
Kelvin Seamount (EN)	182	Od	38.50N	64.00W
Kelyehēd	168	Hd	8.44N	49.10 E
Kem	136	Dc	64.57N	34.31 E
Kema	114	If	60.19N	37.15 E
Ké Macina	166	Dc	13.57N	5.23W
Kemah	146	Hc	39.36N	39.02 E
Kemaliye	146	Hc	39.16N	38.29 E
Kemalpaşa	130	Kk	38.25N	27.26 E
Kemalpaşa	146	Cc	40.00N	28.20 E
Kembé	168	Ce	4.36N	21.54 E
Kemer [Tur.]	146	Dd	36.36N	30.34 E
Kemer [Tur.]	130	Mm	36.28N	29.21 E
Kemer Baraji	130	Ll	37.30N	28.35 E
Kemeri/Ķemeri	116	Jh	56.56N	23.25 E
Ķemeri/Kemeri	116	Jh	56.56N	23.25 E
Kemerovo	142	Kd	55.20N	86.05 E
Kemerovskaja oblast [3]	138	De	55.00N	87.00 E
Kemi	112	Ib	65.44N	24.34 E
Kemi, Lake- (EN) = Kemijärvi	114	Gc	66.36N	27.24 E
Kemijärvi	114	Gc	66.40N	27.25 E
Kemijärvi = Kemi, Lake- (EN)	114	Gc	66.36N	27.24 E
Kemijoki	110	Ib	65.47N	24.30 E
Kemiö/Kimito	116	Jd	60.10N	22.40 E
Kemlja	114	Ki	54.43N	45.15 E
Kemmerer	188	Jf	41.48N	110.32W
Kémo-Gribingui [3]	168	Bd	6.00N	19.00 E
Kemp, Lake-	186	Gj	33.45N	99.13W
Kempaž	134	Jd	64.03N	61.02 E
Kempele	114	Fd	64.55N	25.30 E
Kempen	124	Ic	51.22N	6.25 E
Kempen/Campine	122	Lc	51.10N	5.20 E
Kempendjaj	138	Gd	62.02N	118.42 E
Kempenich	124	Jd	50.25N	7.08 E
Kemp Land	222	Ee	67.10 S	58.00 E
Kemps Bay	194	Ia	24.02N	77.33W
Kempsey	212	Kf	31.05 S	152.50 E
Kempston	124	Bb	52.06N	0.29W
Kempt, Lac-	180	Kg	47.25N	74.15W
Kempten/Allgäu	120	Gi	47.43N	10.19 E
Ken	148	Hc	25.46N	80.31 E
Ken, Loch-	118	If	55.02N	4.02W
Kena	114	Je	62.06N	39.05 E
Kenadsa	162	Gc	31.34N	2.26W
Kenai	176	Dc	60.33N	151.15W
Kenai Mountains	178	Ie	60.00N	150.00W
Kenai Peninsula	174	Ed	60.10N	150.00W
Kendal	118	Kg	54.20N	2.45W
Kendall	184	Gm	25.41N	80.19W
Kendall, Cape-	180	Id	63.36N	87.13W
Kendallville	184	Ee	41.27N	85.16W
Kendari	142	Oj	3.57 S	122.35 E
Kendawangan	150	Fg	2.32 S	110.12 E
Kenema	160	Fh	7.52N	11.12W
Kenge	160	Ii	4.52 S	16.59 E
Kengere	170	Ee	11.10 S	25.28 E
Keng Tung	148	Jd	21.17N	99.36 E
Kenhardt	172	Ce	29.19 S	21.12 E
Kéniéba	166	Cc	12.50N	11.14W
Keningau	150	Ge	5.20N	116.10 E
Kenitra	160	Ge	34.16N	6.36W
Kenitra [3]	162	Fc	34.00N	6.00W
Kenli (Xishuanghe)	154	Ef	37.35N	118.30 E
Kenmare	182	Gb	48.40N	102.05W
Kenmare/Neidín	118	Dj	51.53N	9.35W
Kenmare River/An Ribhéar	118	Dj	51.50N	9.50W
Kennebunk	184	Ld	43.23N	70.33W
Kennedy Peak	148	Id	23.19N	93.46 E
Kennedy Range	212	Cd	24.30 S	115.00 E
Kenner	186	Ki	29.59N	90.15W
Kennet	118	Mj	51.28N	0.57W
Kennett	186	Kh	36.14N	90.03W
Kennewick	188	Fc	46.12N	119.07W
Kennington	124	Cc	51.09N	0.53 E
Kenn Reef	208	Gg	21.10 S	155.50 E
Kénogami	184	La	48.26N	71.14W
Kénogami, Lac-	184	La	48.21N	71.28W
Kenogami River	180	Jf	51.06N	84.29W
Keno Hill	180	Dd	63.54N	135.18W
Kenora	176	Je	49.47N	94.29W
Kenosha	182	Jc	42.35N	87.49W
Kent [3]	118	Nj	51.20N	0.55 E
Kent	118	Nj	51.10N	0.55 E
Kent [S.L.]	166	Cd	8.10N	13.10W
Kent [Wa.-U.S.]	188	Dc	47.23N	122.14W
Kent, Vale of-	118	Nj	51.10N	0.30 E
Kentau	136	Gg	43.32N	68.33 E
Kent Group	212	Jg	39.30 S	147.20 E
Kenton	184	Fe	40.38N	83.38W
Kent Peninsula	180	Gc	68.30N	107.00W
Kentucky [2]	182	Jd	37.30N	85.15W
Kentucky Lake	182	Jd	36.25N	88.05W
Kentucky River	184	Ef	38.41N	85.11W
Kenya [1]	160	Kh	1.00N	38.00 E
Kenya, Mount-/Kirinyaga	158	Ki	0.10 S	37.20 E
Keokea	221a	Ec	20.42N	156.21W
Keokuk	182	Ic	40.24N	91.24W
Keonjhargarh	148	Hd	21.38N	85.35 E
Keowee, Lake-	184	Fh	34.55N	82.50W
Kepe	114	Hd	65.09N	32.08 E
Kepi	150	Kh	6.32 S	139.19 E
Kępno	120	Ne	51.17N	17.59 E
Kepsut	146	Cc	39.41N	28.09 E
Kerala [3]	148	Ff	11.00N	76.30 E
Kerama-Rettō	156b	Ab	26.10N	127.15 E
Kerang	212	Ig	35.44 S	143.55 E
Keratéa	130	Gl	37.48N	23.59 E
Kerava/Kervo	116	Kd	60.24N	25.07 E
Kerč	112	Jf	45.22N	36.27 E
Kerčenski poluostrov	132	Ig	45.15N	36.00 E
Kerdhilion Óros	130	Gi	40.47N	23.39 E
Kerema	214	Di	7.58 S	145.46 E
Keren	168	Fb	15.47N	38.27 E
Keret, ozero-	114	Hd	65.50N	32.50 E
Kerewan	166	Bc	13.29N	16.06W
Kerguelen	158	Nm	49.20 S	69.30 E
Kerguelen, Iles-	158	Nm	49.15 S	69.10 E
Kerguelen Plateau (EN)	106	Go	55.00 S	75.00 E
Kericho	170	Gc	0.22 S	35.17 E
Keri Kera	168	Ec	12.21N	32.46 E
Kerimäki	116	Mc	61.55N	29.17 E
Kerinci, Gunung-	140	Mj	1.42 S	101.16 E
Kerio	158	Kh	2.59N	36.07 E
Kerion	130	Dl	37.40N	20.49 E
Keriya/Yutian	142	Kf	36.52N	81.42 E
Keriya He	152	Dd	38.30N	82.10 E
Keriya Shankou	152	Dd	35.12N	81.44 E
Kerka	120	Mj	46.28N	16.36 E
Kerken	124	Ic	51.27N	6.26 E
Kerkennah Islands (EN) = Qarqannah, Juzur-	158	Ie	34.44N	11.12 E
Kerketevs Óros	130	Jl	37.44N	26.38 E
Kerki	136	Gh	37.50N	65.13 E
Kerkini Óros	130	Fh	41.21N	22.50 E
Kérkira	130	Cj	39.36N	19.55 E
Kérkira = Corfu (EN)	110	Hh	39.40N	19.45 E
Kerkiras, Stenón- = Corfu, Strait of- (EN)	130	Dj	39.35N	20.05 E
Kerkrade	124	Id	50.52N	6.04 E
Kerma (EN) = Karmah	168	Eb	19.38N	30.25 E
Kermadec Islands	208	Jh	30.00 S	178.30W
Kermadec Ridge (EN)	208	Jh	30.30 S	178.30W
Kermadec Trench (EN)	106	Km	30.00 S	177.00W
Kermajärvi	116	Mb	62.30N	28.40 E
Kermān	142	Hf	30.17N	57.05 E
Kermān [3]	144	Ic	30.50N	57.50 E
Kermānshāhān	146	Pg	31.17N	54.55 E
Kerme	130	Kl	37.02N	28.00 E
Kerme Körfezi	146	Bd	36.50N	28.00 E
Kermit	186	Ek	31.51N	103.06W
Kern River	188	Fi	35.13N	119.17W
Kérouané	166	Dd	9.16N	9.01W
Kerpen	124	Id	50.52N	6.41 E
Kerrobert	180	Gf	51.55N	109.08W
Kerrville	182	He	30.03N	99.08W
Kerry/Ciarraí [2]	118	Di	52.10N	9.30W
Kerry, Mountains of-	118	Dj	51.55N	9.50W
Kertamulya	150	Eg	0.23N	109.09 E
Kerteh	150	Df	4.31N	103.27 E
Kerteminde	116	Di	55.27N	10.40 E
Kerulen (Cherlen)	140	Ne	48.48N	117.00 E
Kervo/Kerava	116	Kd	60.24N	25.07 E
Kerzaz	162	Gd	29.27N	1.25W
Keržеnec	114	Kh	56.04N	45.01 E
Kesagami Lake	180	Jf	50.23N	80.10W
Kesälahti	116	Mc	61.54N	29.50 E
Keşan	144	Ca	40.51N	26.37 E
Keşap	146	Hb	40.55N	38.31 E
Kesen'numa	154	Pe	38.54N	141.35 E
Kesen'numa-Wan	156	Gb	38.50N	141.35 E
Keshan	152	Mb	48.04N	125.51 E
Keskastel	124	Jf	48.58N	7.02 E
Keskin	146	Ec	39.41N	33.37 E
Keski-Suomi [2]	114	Fe	62.30N	25.30 E
Kestenga	114	Hd	65.53N	31.45 E
Keswick	118	Jg	54.37N	3.08W
Keszthely	120	Nj	46.46N	17.15 E
Ket	140	Kd	58.55N	81.32 E
Kéta	166	Fd	5.55N	0.59 E

Ket-Kir

Ketanda	138	Jd	60.38N	141.30 E
Ketapang	142	Mj	1.52S	109.59 E
Ketčenery (Sovetskoje)	136	Ef	47.17N	44.30 E
Ketchikan	176	Fd	55.21N	131.35W
Ketchum	182	Ec	43.41N	114.22W
Ketchum Mountain	186	Fk	31.15N	101.00W
Kete Krachi	166	Ed	7.46N	0.03W
Ketelmeer	124	Hb	52.35N	5.45 E
Ketli, Jbel-	126	Gi	35.22N	5.17W
Ketmen, hrebet-	135	Lc	43.20N	80.00 E
Kétou	166	Fd	7.22N	2.36 E
Kętrzyn	120	Rb	54.06N	21.23 E
Kettering [Eng.-U.K.]	118	Mi	52.24N	0.44W
Kettering [Oh.-U.S.]	184	Ef	39.41N	84.10W
Kettle River	188	Fb	48.42N	118.07W
Kettle River Range	188	Fb	48.30N	118.40W
Keuka Lake	184	Id	42.27N	77.10W
Keur Massène	162	Df	16.33N	16.14W
Keuruu	114	Fe	62.16N	24.42 E
Keuruunselkä	116	Kb	62.10N	24.40 E
Kevelaer	124	Ic	51.35N	6.15 E
Kew	194	Kc	21.54N	72.02W
Kewanee	182	Jc	41.14N	89.56W
Keweenaw Bay	184	Cb	46.56N	88.23W
Keweenaw Peninsula	182	Jb	47.12N	88.25W
Key, Lough-/Loch Cè	118	Eg	54.00N	8.15W
Keya Paha River	186	Ge	42.54N	99.00W
Keyhole Reservoir	188	Md	44.21N	104.51W
Key Largo	184	Gm	25.04N	80.28W
Keystone Lake	186	Hh	36.15N	96.25W
Key West	176	Kg	24.33N	81.48W
Kez	114	Mh	57.56N	53.43 E
Kezi	172	Dd	20.55S	28.29 E
Kežma	138	Fe	59.02N	101.09 E
Kežmarok	120	Qg	49.08N	20.25 E
Kgalagadi [3]	172	Ce	25.00S	22.00 E
Kgatleng [3]	172	Dd	24.28S	26.05 E
Kghoti	172	Cd	24.55S	21.59 E
Khabr, Kūh-e-	144	Id	28.50N	56.26 E
Khābūr, Nahr al-	146	Ie	35.08N	40.26 E
Khadari, Wādī al-	168	Dc	10.29N	27.00 E
Khādim, Shūshat al-	146	Bh	28.35N	27.43 E
Khadki (Kirkee)	148	Ee	18.34N	73.52 E
Khadra	126	Mh	36.15N	0.35 E
Khafs Banbān	146	Lj	25.31N	46.27 E
Khairónia	130	Fk	38.30N	22.51 E
Khairpur	148	Dc	27.32N	68.46 E
Khāīz, Kūh-e-	146	Ng	30.27N	50.55 E
Khakhea	172	Cd	24.42S	23.30 E
Khalatse	148	Fb	34.20N	76.49 E
Khálki	130	Km	36.13N	27.37 E
Khálki	130	Km	36.14N	27.36 E
Khalkidhiki=Chalcidice (EN)	110	Ig	40.25N	23.25 E
Khalkis	130	Gk	38.28N	23.36 E
Khaluf	144	Ie	20.29N	57.59 E
Khambhāt	148	Ed	22.18N	72.37 E
Khambhāt, Gulf of-	140	Jg	21.00N	72.30 E
Khāmgaon	148	Fd	20.41N	76.34 E
Khamili	130	Jn	35.52N	26.14 E
Khamir	144	Ff	15.59N	43.57 E
Khāmis, Ash Shallāl al-=Fifth Cataract (EN)	158	Kg	18.23N	33.47 E
Khamis Mushayţ	144	Ff	18.18N	42.44 E
Khammam	148	Ge	17.15N	80.09 E
Khamseh	146	Md	36.40N	48.50 E
Khān	146	Qj	24.13N	56.20 E
Khan	172	Ad	22.42S	14.54 E
Khānābād	144	Kb	36.41N	69.07 E
Khān al Baghdādī	146	Jf	33.51N	42.33 E
Khān al Hammād	146	Kf	32.19N	44.17 E
Khānaqīn	144	Gc	34.21N	45.22 E
Khān az Zabīb	146	Gg	31.28N	36.06 E
Khandwa	148	Fd	21.50N	76.20 E
Khāneh Sorkh, Gardaneh-ye-	146	Qh	29.49N	56.06 E
Khānewāl	148	Eb	30.18N	71.56 E
Khangai Mountains (EN)=Changajn Nuruu	140	Le	47.30N	100.00 E
Khánia	112	Ih	35.31N	24.02 E
Khanion, Kólpos-	130	Gn	35.35N	23.50 E
Khanka, Lake- (EN)=Hanka, ozero-	140	Pe	45.00N	132.24 E
Khanka Lake (EN)=Xingkai Hu	140	Pe	45.00N	132.24 E
Khānpur	148	Ec	28.39N	70.39 E
Khān Shaykhūn	146	Ge	35.26N	36.38 E
Khan Takhtī	146	Kc	38.09N	44.55 E
Khān Yūnus	146	Fg	31.21N	34.19 E
Khānzīr, Rās-	168	Hc	10.50N	45.50 E
Khao Laem	148	Kf	14.19N	101.11 E
Khao Miang	148	Ke	17.42N	101.01 E
Khao Mokochu	148	Je	15.56N	99.06 E
Khao Saming	148	Kf	12.16N	102.26 E
Khar	146	Me	35.53N	48.55 E
Kharagpur	142	Kg	22.20N	87.20 E
Khárakas	130	In	35.01N	25.07 E
Khārān	146	Qh	28.55N	57.09 E
Kharānaq	146	Pf	32.20N	54.39 E
Kharānaq, Kūh-e-	146	Pf	32.10N	54.39 E
Kharga Oasis (EN)=Khārijah, Wāḩāt al-	158	Kf	25.20N	30.35 E
Khārijah, Wāḩāt al-=Kharga Oasis (EN)	158	Kf	25.20N	30.35 E
Kharīţ, Wādī al-	146	Ej	24.26N	33.03 E
Kharīţah, Shiqqat al-	164	If	17.10N	47.50 E
Khārk	146	Nh	29.15N	50.20 E
Khārk, Jazīreh-ye-	146	Nh	29.15N	50.20 E
Khār Kūh	146	Og	31.39N	53.46 E
Kharmān, Kūh-e-	144	Hd	29.13N	53.35 E
Kharshah, Qārat al-	146	Bg	30.35N	27.25 E
Khartoum (EN)=Al Kharţūm	160	Kg	15.36N	32.32 E
Khartoum (EN)=Al Kharţūm [3]	168	Eb	15.50N	33.00 E
Khartoum North (EN)=Al Kharţūm Bahrī	160	Kg	15.38N	32.33 E
Khāsh	144	Jc	31.31N	62.52 E
Khāsh	144	Jc	31.11N	62.05 E
Khashm al Qirbah	168	Fc	14.58N	35.55 E
Khāsi Jaintia	140	Lg	25.35N	91.38 E
Khatikhon, Yam-=Mediterranean Sea (EN)	110	Hh	35.00N	20.00 E
Khaţţ	164	Dd	28.40N	22.40 E
Khātūn, Kūh-e-	146	Og	30.25N	53.38 E
Khawr al Fakkān	146	Qk	25.21N	56.22 E
Khawr āl Juḩaysh	168	Ia	20.36N	50.59 E
Khawr al Mufattaḩ	146	Mh	28.40N	48.25 E
Khawr Umm Qaşr	146	Lg	30.02N	47.56 E
Khay'	164	Ff	18.45N	41.24 E
Khaybar	144	Ed	25.42N	39.31 E
Khaybar, Ḩarrat-	146	Hj	25.30N	39.45 E
Khazzī, Qārat-	158	Jf	21.26N	24.30 E
Khemis	126	Qh	36.10N	4.04 E
Khemis Anjra	126	Gi	35.41N	5.32W
Khémis Beni Arouss	126	Gi	35.19N	5.38W
Khemis Miliana	162	Hb	36.16N	2.13 E
Khemisset	162	Fc	33.49N	6.04W
Khemisset [3]	162	Fc	33.49N	6.00W
Khemmarat	148	Ke	16.03N	105.11 E
Khenchela	162	Ib	35.26N	7.08 E
Khenifra	162	Fc	32.56N	5.40W
Khenifra [3]	162	Fc	33.00N	5.08W
Kherāmeh	146	Oh	29.32N	53.21 E
Khersan	146	Ng	31.33N	50.22 E
Khersónisos Akrotiri	130	Hn	35.35N	24.10 E
Kheyrābād [Iran]	146	Ph	29.26N	55.19 E
Kheyrābād [Iran]	146	Mg	31.49N	48.23 E
Khionótripa	130	Hh	41.18N	24.05 E
Khios	130	Jk	38.22N	26.08 E
Khios=Chios (EN)	110	Ih	38.22N	26.00 E
Khirbat Isrīyah	146	Ge	35.21N	37.46 E
Khirr, Nahr al-	146	Kf	33.17N	44.21 E
Khlomón Óros	130	Fk	38.36N	23.00 E
Khlong Yai	148	Kf	11.46N	102.53 E
Khokhropār	148	Ec	25.42N	70.12 E
Khok Kloi	148	Jg	8.17N	98.19 E
Khok Samrong	148	Ke	15.03N	100.44 E
Kholm	144	Kb	36.42N	67.41 E
Khomām	146	Md	37.22N	49.40 E
Khomas Highland (EN)=Khomas Hochland	158	Ik	22.40S	16.20 E
Khomas Hochland=Khomas Highland (EN)	158	Ik	22.40S	16.20 E
Khomeyn	146	Nf	33.38N	50.04 E
Khomeynīshahr	144	Hc	32.42N	51.27 E
Khonj	146	Oi	27.52N	53.27 E
Khon Kaen	148	Ke	16.26N	102.50 E
Khonsār	146	Nf	33.21N	50.19 E
Khóra	130	El	37.03N	21.43 E
Khor Anghar	168	Gc	12.27N	43.18 E
Khorāsān [3]	144	Ic	35.00N	58.00 E
Khorāsān	144	Hf	34.00N	56.00 E
Khorāsānī, Godār-e	146	Qg	30.44N	57.03 E
Khóra Sfakion	130	Hn	35.12N	24.09 E
Khorat Plateau	140	Mh	15.30N	102.50 E
Khormūj, Kūh-e-	144	Hd	28.43N	51.22 E
Khorof Harar	170	Hb	2.14N	40.44 E
Khorramābād	144	Gc	33.30N	48.20 E
Khorramshahr	144	Gc	30.25N	48.11 E
Khorsābād	146	Jd	36.38N	43.17 E
Khoshyeylāq	146	Pd	36.53N	55.15 E
Khosrowābād	146	Mg	30.00N	48.25 E
Khosrowshah	146	Ld	37.57N	46.03 E
Khouribga	162	Fc	32.53N	6.54W
Khouribga [3]	162	Fc	32.56N	6.36W
Khowst	144	Kc	33.22N	69.57 E
Khrisí	130	Io	34.52N	25.42 E
Khrisoúpolis	130	Hi	40.59N	24.42 E
Khristianá	130	Im	36.14N	25.13 E
Khu Dağı	146	Jc	38.35N	43.40 E
Khuff [Lib.]	164	Cd	28.17N	18.20 E
Khuff [Sau.Ar.]	144	Ed	25.20N	37.20 E
Khulna	142	Kg	22.48N	89.33 E
Khūrān	146	Pi	26.50N	55.40 E
Khurays	144	Gd	25.05N	48.02 E
Khurayt	168	Dc	13.57N	26.02 E
Khurīyā Murīyā, Jazā'ir-=Kuria Muria Islands (EN)	140	Hh	17.30N	56.00 E
Khurr, Wādī al-	146	Jg	30.52N	42.10 E
Khursanīyah	146	Mi	27.18N	49.16 E
Khūshābar	146	Md	37.59N	48.54 E
Khutse	172	Cd	23.20S	24.34 E
Khuwayy	168	Dc	13.05N	29.14 E
Khuzdār	146	Dc	27.48N	66.37 E
Khūzestān [3]	144	Gc	32.00N	48.30 E
Khūzestān	140	Gf	30.33N	50.00 E
Khvojeh Lāk, Kūh-e-	146	Le	35.43N	46.29 E
Khvor	146	Pf	33.47N	55.03 E
Khvorāsgān	146	Nf	32.39N	51.45 E
Khvormūj	146	Nh	28.39N	51.23 E
Khvoshkūh	146	Qi	27.37N	56.41 E
Khvoy	146	Kc	38.33N	44.58 E
Khyber Pass	148	Eb	34.05N	71.10 E
Kia	219a	Db	7.32S	158.26 E
Kia	219d	Bb	16.14S	179.05 E
Kiamba	150	He	5.59N	124.37 E
Kiambi	170	Ed	7.20S	28.01 E
Kiamichi River	186	Ij	33.57N	95.14W
Kiangarow, Mount-	212	Ke	26.49S	151.33 E
Kiangsi (EN)=Jiangxi Sheng (Chiang-hsi Sheng) [2]	152	Kf	28.00N	116.00 E
Kiangsu (EN)=Chiang-su Sheng→Jiangsu Sheng [2]	152	Ke	33.00N	120.00 E
Kiangsu (EN)=Jiangsu Sheng (Chiang-su Sheng) [2]	152	Ke	33.00N	120.00 E
Kiantajärvi	114	Gd	65.03N	29.07 E
Kiáton	130	Fk	38.01N	22.45 E
Kibali	170	Eb	3.37N	28.34 E
Kibangou	170	Bc	3.27S	12.21 E
Kibartaj/Kybartai	116	Jj	54.38N	22.44 E
Kibasira Swamp	170	Gd	8.20S	36.18 E
Kibau	170	Gd	8.35S	35.17 E
Kibaya	170	Gd	5.18S	36.34 E
Kibbish	168	Fe	4.40N	35.53 E
Kiberg	114	Ha	70.17N	31.00 E
Kibikogen	156	Cd	34.45N	133.15 E
Kiboko	170	Gc	2.15S	37.42 E
Kibombo	170	Ec	3.54S	25.55 E
Kibondo	170	Fc	3.35S	30.42 E
Kibre Mengist	168	Fd	5.58N	39.00 E
Kıbrıs/Kypros=Cyprus (EN) [1]	142	Ff	35.00N	33.00 E
Kıbrıs/Kypros=Cyprus (EN)	140	Ff	35.00N	33.00 E
Kibungo	170	Fc	2.10S	30.32 E
Kibuye	170	Ec	2.03S	29.21 E
Kibwezi	170	Gc	2.25S	37.58 E
Kičevo	130	Dh	41.31N	20.58 E
Kichi Kichi	168	Bb	17.36N	17.19 E
Kicking Horse Pass	180	Ff	51.50N	116.30W
Kidal	160	Hg	18.26N	1.24 E
Kidapawan	150	Ie	7.01N	125.03 E
Kidatu	170	Gd	7.42S	36.57 E
Kidira	166	Cc	14.28N	12.13W
Kidnappers, Cape-	218	Gc	39.38S	177.06 E
Kiekie	221a	Ab	21.53N	160.13W
Kiel	112	He	54.20N	10.08 E
Kiel Canal (EN)=Nord-Ostsee-Kanal	110	Ge	53.53N	9.08 E
Kielce	112	Ie	50.52N	20.37 E
Kielce [2]	120	Qf	50.50N	20.35 E
Kieler Bucht	120	Gb	54.35N	10.35 E
Kienge	170	Ee	10.33S	27.33 E
Kierspe	124	Jc	51.08N	7.35 E
Kieta	210	Ge	6.15S	155.37 E
Kietrz	120	Of	50.05N	18.01 E
Kiev (EN)=Kijev	112	Je	50.26N	30.31 E
Kiev Reservoir (EN)=Kijevskoje vodohranilišče	110	Je	51.00N	30.25 E
Kiffa	160	Fg	16.36N	11.23W
Kifisiá	130	Gk	38.04N	23.49 E
Kifisós	130	Gk	38.26N	23.15 E
Kifrī	146	Ke	34.42N	44.58 E
Kigač	132	Pf	46.28N	49.08 E
Kigali	160	Ki	1.57S	30.04 E
Kiğı	146	Ic	39.19N	40.21 E
Kigille	168	Ed	8.40N	34.02 E
Kigoma	160	Ji	4.52S	29.38 E
Kigoma [3]	170	Fc	4.50S	30.05 E
Kigosi	170	Fc	4.40S	31.27 E
Kihelkonna	116	If	58.20N	21.54 E
Kihniö	116	Jb	62.12N	23.11 E
Kihnu	114	Fg	58.10N	24.00 E
Kiholo	221a	Fd	19.51N	155.55W
Kiholo Bay	221a	Fd	19.52N	155.56W
Kihti/Skiftet	116	Id	60.15N	21.05 E
Kii-Hantō	152	Oe	34.00N	135.45 E
Kiikka	116	Jc	61.20N	22.46 E
Kiil	132	Se	49.27N	54.50 E
Kiiminki	114	Fd	65.08N	25.44 E
Kii-Sanchi	156	Dd	34.15N	135.50 E
Kii-Suido	154	Mh	34.00N	134.55 E
Kija	138	De	56.52N	86.40 E
Kijev=Kiev (EN)	112	Je	50.26N	30.31 E
Kijevka	136	He	50.16N	71.34 E
Kijevskaja oblast [3]	136	De	50.20N	30.45 E
Kijevskoje vodohranilišče=Kiev Reservoir (EN)	110	Je	51.00N	30.25 E
Kijma	136	Ge	51.35N	67.34 E
Kikai-Jima	152	Mf	28.15N	130.00 E
Kikerino	116	Me	59.23N	29.38 E
Kikinda	130	Dd	45.50N	20.29 E
Kikládhes=Cyclades (EN)	110	Ih	37.00N	25.10 E
Kikonai	154	Pd	41.40N	140.26 E
Kikori	210	Fe	7.25S	144.13 E
Kikori River	208	Fe	7.23S	144.16 E
Kikuchi	156	Be	32.59N	130.49 E
Kikuma	156	Cd	34.03N	132.51 E
Kikvidze	132	Md	50.44N	43.03 E
Kikwit	160	Ii	5.02S	18.49 E
Kil [Nor.]	116	Cf	58.52N	9.19 E
Kil [Swe.]	114	Cg	59.30N	13.19 E
Kilafors	114	Df	61.15N	16.33 E
Kilambé, Cerro-	194	Eg	13.34N	85.42W
Kilauea	221a	Ba	22.13N	159.25W
Kilauea Crater	221a	Fd	19.24N	155.17W
Kilauea Point	221a	Ba	22.14N	159.24W
Kilbrannan Sound	118	Hf	55.40N	5.25W
Kilbuck Mountains	178	Hd	60.30N	159.45W
Kilchu	152	Mc	40.58N	129.20 E
Kilcoy	212	Ke	26.57S	152.33 E
Kildare/Cill Dara	118	Gh	53.10N	6.55W
Kildare/Cill Dara [2]	118	Gh	53.15N	6.45W
Kildin, ostrov-	114	Ib	69.20N	34.10 E
Kilembe	170	Cd	5.42S	19.55 E
Kilgore	186	Ij	32.23N	94.53W
Kilgoris	170	Fc	1.00S	34.53 E
Kiliç	130	Mi	40.40N	29.23 E
Kilifi	170	Gc	3.38S	39.51 E
Kili Island	208	Hd	5.39N	169.04 E
Kilija	136	Cf	45.27N	29.14 E
Kilijskoje girlo	130	Md	45.13N	29.43 E
Kilimanjaro [3]	170	Gc	4.00S	37.40 E
Kilimanjaro, Mount-	158	Ki	3.04S	37.22 E
Kilimli	146	Db	41.29N	31.50 E
Kilinailau Islands	214	Fh	4.45S	155.20 E
Kilindoni	160	Ki	7.55S	39.39 E
Kilingi-Nõmme/Kilingi-Nymme	114	Fg	58.08N	24.59 E
Kilingi-Nymme/Kilingi-Nõmme	114	Fg	58.08N	24.59 E
Kilis	146	Gd	36.44N	37.05 E
Kilitbahir	146	Bb	40.12N	26.20 E
Kilkee/Cill Chaoi	118	Di	52.41N	9.38W
Kilkenny/Cill Chainnigh	118	Fi	52.39N	7.15W
Kilkenny/Cill Chainnigh [2]	118	Fi	52.40N	7.20W
Kilkieran Bay	118	Dh	53.15N	9.45W
Kilkis	130	Fi	41.00N	22.52 E
Killala Bay/Cuan Chill Ala	118	Dg	54.15N	9.10W
Killarney/Cill Airne	118	Di	52.03N	9.30W
Killary Harbour/An Caoláire Rua	118	Dh	53.38N	9.55W
Killdeer	186	Ec	47.22N	102.45W
Killeen	182	He	31.08N	97.44W
Killinek	180	Ld	60.25N	64.40W
Killini	130	El	37.56N	21.09 E
Killini Óros	130	Fl	37.55N	22.26 E
Kilmallock/Cill Mocheallóg	118	Ei	52.25N	8.35W
Kilmarnock	118	If	55.37N	4.30W
Kilmez	114	Mh	57.03N	51.24 E
Kilmez	114	Mh	56.58N	50.29 E
Kilmore	212	Ig	37.18S	144.57 E
Kilombero	170	Gd	8.31S	37.22 E
Kilosa	160	Ki	6.50S	36.59 E
Kilpisjärvi	114	Eb	69.03N	20.48 E
Kilp-Javr	114	Hb	69.07N	32.28 E
Kilrush/Cill Rois	118	Di	52.39N	9.29W
Kilsbergen	116	Fe	59.20N	14.45 E
Kiltān Island	148	Ef	11.29N	73.00 E
Kilwa	170	Ed	9.17S	28.20 E
Kilwa Kisiwani	160	Ki	8.58S	39.30 E
Kilwa Kivinje	170	Gd	8.45S	39.24 E
Kilwa Masoko	170	Gd	8.56S	39.31 E
Kilyos→Kumköy	130	Mh	41.15N	29.02 E
Kim	186	Eh	37.15N	103.21W
Kimamba	170	Gd	6.47S	37.08 E
Kimba	212	Hf	33.09S	136.25 E
Kimball [Nb.-U.S.]	186	Ef	41.14N	103.40W
Kimball [S.D.-U.S.]	186	Ge	43.45N	98.57W
Kimball, Mount-	178	Kd	63.14N	144.39W
Kimbe	212	Ka	5.31S	150.12 E
Kimbe Bay	214	Ei	5.30S	150.30 E
Kimberley	208	Df	16.00S	126.00 E
Kimberley [B.C.-Can.]	180	Fg	49.41N	115.59W
Kimberley [S.Afr.]	160	Jk	28.43S	24.46 E
Kimberley Plateau	212	Fc	17.00S	127.00 E
Kimch'aek (Sŏngjin)	152	Mc	40.41N	129.12 E
Kimch'ŏn	152	Md	36.07N	128.07 E
Kimhandu	158	Ki	7.05S	37.35 E
Kimi	130	Hk	38.38N	24.06 E
Kimito/Kemiö	116	Jd	60.10N	22.40 E
Kimje	154	Ig	35.48N	126.53 E
Kimobetsu	156a	Bb	42.47N	140.56 E
Kimolos	130	Hm	36.48N	24.34 E
Kimongo	170	Bc	4.29S	12.58 E
Kimovsk	136	De	54.01N	38.36 E
Kimpu-San	156	Fd	35.52N	138.37 E
Kimry	136	Dd	56.52N	37.24 E
Kimvula	170	Cd	5.44S	15.58 E
Kinabalu, Gunong-	140	Ni	6.05N	116.33 E
Kinabatangan	150	Ge	5.42N	118.23 E
Kinango	170	Gc	4.08S	39.19 E
Kinaros	130	Jm	36.59N	26.17 E
Kincardine	180	Jh	44.11N	81.38W
Kind	116	Eg	57.35N	13.25 E
Kinda	170	Ed	9.18S	25.04 E
Kinda	116	Ff	58.05N	15.40 E
Kindamba	170	Bc	3.44S	14.31 E
Kinder	186	Jk	30.29N	92.51W
Kinder Scout	118	Lh	53.23N	1.52W
Kindersley	180	Gf	51.27N	109.10W
Kindi	166	Ec	12.26N	2.01W
Kindia	160	Fg	10.04N	12.51W
Kindu	160	Ji	2.57S	25.56 E
Kinel	114	Mj	53.14N	50.40 E
Kinesi	170	Fc	1.28S	33.52 E
Kinešma	136	Ed	57.28N	42.16 E
King	219a	Aa	4.24S	152.43 E
King, Cayos-	194	Fg	12.45N	83.20W
Kingaroy	212	Ke	26.33S	151.50 E
King Christian	180	Ha	77.45N	102.00W
King Christian IX Land (EN)=Kong Christian IX Land	224	Mc	68.00N	36.30W
King Christian X Land (EN)=Kong Christian X Land	224	Md	72.20N	32.30W
King City	182	Cd	36.13N	121.08W
King Edward River	212	Fb	14.14S	126.35 E
Kingfisher	186	Hi	35.52N	97.56W
King Frederik VI Coast (EN)=Kong Frederik VI Kyst	224	Nc	63.00N	43.30W
King Frederik VIII Land (EN)=Kong Frederik VIII Land	224	Md	78.30N	28.00W
King George Island	222	Re	62.00S	58.15W
King George Islands	180	Je	57.15N	78.30W
King George Sound	212	Dg	35.10S	118.10 E
Kingisepp	114	Gg	59.23N	28.37 E
King Island	208	Fh	39.50S	144.00 E
Kingissepp→Kuressaare	136	Cd	58.17N	22.29 E
King Lear Peak	188	Ff	41.12N	118.34W
King Leopold Ranges	212	Fc	17.30S	125.45 E
Kingman [Az.-U.S.]	182	Ed	35.12N	114.04W
Kingman [Ks.-U.S.]	186	Gh	37.39N	98.07W
Kingman Reef	208	Kd	6.19N	162.28W
Kingombe [Zaire]	170	Ec	3.52S	26.35 E
Kingombe [Zaire]	170	Ec	2.35S	26.37 E
Kingoome Inlet	188	Ba	50.49N	126.13W
Kingoonya	210	Eh	30.54S	135.18 E
King Peninsula	222	Of	73.12S	101.00W
Kingsclere	124	Ac	51.19N	1.15W
Kingscote	212	Hg	35.40S	137.38 E
King's Lynn	118	Ni	52.45N	0.24 E
King Sound	208	Df	17.00S	123.30 E
Kings Peak [Ca.-U.S.]	188	Cf	40.10N	124.08W
Kings Peak [U.S.]	174	He	40.46N	110.22W
Kingsport	182	Kd	36.32N	82.33W
Kings River	188	Fh	36.03N	119.49W
Kingston [Jam.]	176	Lh	18.00N	76.50W
Kingston [Nor.I.]	210	Hg	29.04S	167.58 E
Kingston [N.Y.-U.S.]	182	Mc	41.55N	74.00W
Kingston [N.Z.]	216	Ci	45.20S	168.43 E
Kingston [Ont.-Can.]	176	Le	44.14N	76.30W
Kingston Peak	188	Hi	35.42N	115.52W
Kingston South East	210	Eh	36.50S	139.51 E
Kingston upon Hull (Hull)	112	Fe	53.45N	0.20W
Kingston-upon-Thames, London-	118	Mj	51.28N	0.19W
Kingstown	176	Mh	13.09N	61.14W
Kingsville	182	Hf	27.31N	97.52W
Kings Worthy	124	Ac	51.05N	1.18W
Kingussie	118	Id	57.05N	4.04W
King William	174	Jc	69.00N	97.30W
King William's Town	160	Jl	32.51S	27.22 E
Kiniama	170	Ee	11.26S	28.19 E
Kınık	146	Bc	39.05N	27.23 E
Kinkala	170	Bc	4.22S	14.46 E
Kinlochleven	118	Ie	56.43N	4.58W
Kinna	116	Eg	57.30N	12.41 E
Kinnairds Head	118	Ld	57.42N	2.00W
Kinnared	116	Eg	57.02N	13.06 E
Kinnekulle	116	Ef	58.35N	13.23 E
Kinneret, Yam-	146	Ff	32.48N	35.35 E
Kino-Kawa	156	Dd	34.13N	135.08 E
Kinomoto	156	Ed	35.31N	136.13 E
Kinoosao	180	He	57.06N	102.01W
Kinós Kefalai	130	Fj	39.25N	22.34 E
Kinross	118	Je	56.13N	3.27W
Kinsale/Cionn tSáile	118	Ej	51.42N	8.32W
Kinsale, Old Head of-/An Seanchean	118	Ej	51.36N	8.32W
Kinsangire	170	Gd	7.26S	38.35 E
Kinsarvik	114	Bf	60.23N	6.43 E
Kinshasa [2]	170	Cc	4.00S	16.00 E
Kinshasa (Leopoldville)	160	Ii	4.18S	15.18 E
Kinsley	186	Gh	37.55N	99.25W
Kinston	182	Ld	35.16N	77.35W
Kintampo	166	Ed	8.03N	1.43W
Kintap	150	Gg	3.51S	115.13 E
Kintyre	118	Hf	55.32N	5.35W
Kin-Wan	156b	Ab	26.25N	127.54 E
Kinyan	166	Dc	11.51N	6.01W
Kinyeti	158	Kh	3.57N	32.54 E
Kinzig [Eur.]	120	Dh	48.37N	7.49 E
Kinzig [Ger.]	120	Ef	50.08N	8.54 E
Kioa	219d	Bb	16.39S	179.55 E
Kipaka	170	Ec	4.09S	26.30 E
Kiparissia	130	El	37.15N	21.40 E
Kiparissia, Gulf of- (EN)=Kiparissiakós Kólpos	130	El	37.30N	21.25 E
Kiparissiakós Kólpos=Kiparissia, Gulf of- (EN)	130	El	37.30N	21.25 E
Kipawa, Lac-	180	Jg	46.55N	79.00W
Kipembawe	170	Fd	7.39S	33.24 E
Kipengere Range	158	Ki	9.10S	34.15 E
Kiperčeny	130	Lb	47.32N	28.40 E
Kipili	170	Fd	7.26S	30.36 E
Kipini	170	Hc	2.32S	40.31 E
Kipling	186	Ea	50.10N	102.38W
Kippure	118	Gh	53.11N	6.20W
Kiprarenukk, mys- / Undva neem	116	If	58.25N	21.45 E
Kípros=Cyprus (EN)	144	Db	35.01N	33.00 E
Kipushi	170	Ee	11.46S	27.14 E
Kirakira	210	Hf	10.27S	161.56 E
Kiraz	146	Cc	39.21N	27.25 E
Kirazlı	116	Bb	40.01N	26.40 E
Kirbla	116	Jf	58.42N	23.49 E
Kircasalih	130	Jh	41.23N	26.48 E
Kirchberg (Hunsrück)	124	Je	49.57N	7.24 E
Kirchhain	124	Kd	50.49N	8.58 E
Kirchheimbolanden	124	Ke	49.40N	8.01 E
Kirchheim unter Teck	120	Fh	48.39N	9.27 E
Kirchhundem	124	Kc	51.06N	8.06 E
Kirchhundem-Rahrbach	124	Jc	51.02N	7.59 E
Kirchlengern	124	Kb	52.12N	8.38 E
Kirdimi	168	Bb	18.11N	18.38 E
Kireç	130	Lj	39.33N	28.22 E
Kirenga	140	Md	57.47N	107.59 E
Kirensk	142	Md	57.46N	108.08 E
Kirghizia (EN)=Kyrgyzstan	136	Hg	41.30N	75.00 E
Kirghiz Steppe (EN)	110	Lf	49.30N	50.30 E
Kirgizskaja Sovetskaja Socialističeskaja Respublika→Kyrgyzstan	136	Hg	41.30N	75.00 E
Kirgizskaja SSR/Kyrgyz Sovetik Socialistik Respublikasy→Kyrgyzstan	136	Hg	41.30N	75.00 E
Kirgizskaja SSR→Kyrgyzstan	136	Hg	41.30N	75.00 E
Kiri	170	Cc	1.27S	19.00 E
Kiribati [1]	210	Je	0.01S	174.00W
Kırıkhan	146	Gd	36.32N	36.19 E
Kırıkkale	144	Db	39.50N	33.31 E
Kirillov	114	Jg	59.54N	38.27 E
Kirillovskoje	116	Md	60.28N	29.28 E
Kirin (EN)=Chi-lin Sheng→Jilin Sheng [2]	152	Mc	43.00N	126.00 E
Kirin (EN)=Jilin Sheng (Chi-lin Sheng) [2]	152	Mc	43.00N	126.00 E
Kirinyaga/Kenya, Mount-	158	Ki	0.10S	37.20 E
Kirishima-Yama	156	Bf	31.56N	130.52 E
Kiriši	136	Dd	59.27N	32.02 E
Kiritimati Atoll (Christmas)	208	Ld	1.52N	157.20W
Kirja	114	Li	55.05N	46.52 E
Kirkağaç	146	Bc	39.06N	27.40 E
Kirkby Lonsdale	118	Kg	54.13N	2.36W
Kirkcaldy	118	Je	56.07N	3.10W
Kirkcudbright	118	Ig	54.50N	4.03W
Kirkee→Khadki	148	Ee	18.34N	73.52 E
Kirkenær	114	Cf	60.28N	12.03 E
Kirkenes	112	Jb	69.43N	30.03 E
Kirkjubæjarklaustur	114a	Bc	63.47N	18.04W
Kirkkonummi/Kyrkslätt	116	Kd	60.07N	24.26 E
Kirkland	188	Dc	47.41N	122.12W
Kirkland Lake	176	Ke	48.09N	80.02W

Index Symbols

- [1] Independent Nation
- [2] State, Region
- [3] District, County
- [4] Municipality
- [5] Colony, Dependency
- Continent
- Physical Region
- Historical or Cultural Region
- Mount, Mountain
- Volcano
- Hill
- Mountains, Mountain Range
- Hills, Escarpment
- Plateau, Upland
- Pass, Gap
- Plain, Lowland
- Delta
- Salt Flat
- Valley, Canyon
- Crater, Cave
- Karst Features
- Depression
- Polder
- Desert, Dunes
- Forest, Woods
- Heath, Steppe
- Oasis
- Cape, Point
- Coast, Beach
- Cliff
- Peninsula
- Isthmus
- Sandbank
- Island
- Atoll
- Rock, Reef
- Islands, Archipelago
- Rocks, Reefs
- Coral Reef
- Well, Spring
- Geyser
- River, Stream
- Waterfall, Rapids
- River Mouth, Estuary
- Lake
- Salt Lake
- Intermittent Lake
- Reservoir
- Swamp, Pond
- Canal
- Glacier
- Ice Shelf, Pack Ice
- Ocean
- Sea
- Gulf, Bay
- Strait, Fjord
- Lagoon
- Bank
- Seamount
- Tablemount
- Ridge
- Shelf
- Basin
- Escarpment, Sea Scarp
- Fracture
- Trench, Abyss
- National Park, Reserve
- Point of Interest
- Recreation Site
- Cave, Cavern
- Historic Site
- Ruins
- Wall, Walls
- Church, Abbey
- Temple
- Scientific Station
- Railway station
- Airport
- Port
- Military installation
- Lighthouse
- Mine
- Tunnel
- Dam, Bridge

Kırklareli	144	Ca	41.44N	27.12 E
Kirkpatrick, Mount- ▲	222	Kg	84.20S	166.19 E
Kırkpınar Dağı ▲	146	Fd	37.14N	34.15 E
Kirksville	182	Ic	40.12N	92.35W
Kirkūk	142	Gf	35.28N	44.23 E
Kirkwall	118	Kc	58.59N	2.58W
Kirkwood [Mo.-U.S.]	186	Kg	38.35N	90.24W
Kirkwood [S.Afr.]	172	Df	33.22S	25.15 E
Kırlangıç Burun ▶	146	Dd	36.13N	30.25 E
Kirn	120	Dg	49.47N	7.27 E
Kirobasi	146	Ed	36.43N	33.52 E
Kirov [Russia]	136	De	54.03N	34.21 E
Kirov [Russia]	112	Kd	58.33N	49.42 E
Kirova, zaliv- ◧	132	Pj	39.05N	49.05 E
Kirovabad → Gjandža	112	Kg	40.40N	46.22 E
Kirovaken	136	Eg	40.48N	44.28 E
Kirovgrad	134	Jh	57.26N	60.04 E
Kirovo	135	Hd	40.28N	70.34 E
Kirovo-Čepeck	136	Fd	58.35N	50.03 E
Kirovograd	112	Jf	48.30N	32.18 E
Kirovogradskaja oblast [3]	136	Df	48.20N	31.50 E
Kirovsk [Russia]	136	Db	67.37N	33.37 E
Kirovsk [Russia]	114	Hg	59.53N	31.01 E
Kirovsk [Turk.]	135	Cf	37.43N	60.24 E
Kirovskaja oblast	136	Ed	58.30N	50.00 E
Kirovski [Kaz.]	136	Hg	44.53N	78.12 E
Kirovski [Russia]	132	Pg	45.48N	48.08 E
Kirovski [Russia]	138	Kf	54.25N	155.37 E
Kirovski [Russia]	138	Hf	54.26N	127.00 E
Kirovski [Russia]	138	Ig	45.05N	133.27 E
Kirovskoje	135	Hc	42.39N	71.35 E
Kirpilski liman ◒	132	Kg	45.50N	38.05 E
Kirriemuir	118	Je	56.41N	3.01W
Kirs	136	Fd	59.21N	52.18 E
Kirsanov	132	Mc	52.41N	42.45 E
Kırşehir	144	Db	39.09N	34.10 E
Kīrthar Range ⛰	140	Ig	27.00N	67.20 E
Kirton	124	Bb	52.55N	0.03W
Kiruna	112	Ib	67.51N	20.13 E
Kirundu	170	Ec	0.44S	25.32 E
Kiryū	156	Fc	36.25N	139.20 E
Kiržač	114	Jh	56.11N	38.53 E
Kisa	114	Dh	57.59N	15.37 E
Kisabi	170	Ed	8.03S	29.11 E
Kisač	130	Cd	45.21N	19.44 E
Kisakata	156	Fb	39.14N	139.54 E
Kisaki	170	Gd	7.28S	37.36 E
Kisalföld ▬	120	Mi	47.30N	17.00 E
Kisangani	160	Jh	0.25N	25.12 E
Kisarazu	156	Fd	35.23N	139.55 E
Kisbér	120	Oi	47.30N	18.02 E
Kiselevsk	138	Df	54.03N	86.49 E
Kiserawe	170	Gd	6.54S	39.05 E
Kishangarh	148	Ec	26.34N	74.52 E
Kishb, Harrat al- ◠	164	He	22.47N	41.30 E
Kishi	166	Fd	9.05N	3.51 E
Kishiwada	154	Mg	34.28N	135.22 E
Kisii	170	Fc	0.41S	34.46 E
Kisiju	170	Gd	7.24S	39.20 E
Kišinev	112	If	46.59N	28.52 E
Kısır Dağı ▲	146	Jb	40.58N	43.04 E
Kiska ◆	178a	Bb	52.00N	177.30 E
Kiska Volcano 🌋	178a	Bb	52.07N	177.36 E
Kisko	116	Jd	60.14N	23.29 E
Kiskörei Víztároló ≈	120	Qi	47.44N	20.40 E
Kiskőrös	120	Pj	46.37N	19.18 E
Kiskunfélegyháza	120	Pj	46.33N	19.51 E
Kiskunhalas	120	Pj	46.26N	19.30 E
Kiskunmajsa	120	Pj	46.29N	19.45 E
Kiskunság ⊠	120	Pj	46.35N	19.15 E
Kislovodsk	136	Eg	43.54N	42.42 E
Kismanyo	160	Li	0.22S	42.32 E
Kisofukushima	156	Ed	35.51N	137.41 E
Kiso-Gawa ∿	154	Ng	35.05N	136.45 E
Kisoro	170	Ec	1.17S	29.41 E
Kiso-Sanmyaku ⛰	156	Ed	35.45N	137.45 E
Kisria, Daiet el- ≈	126	Oi	35.44N	2.47 E
Kissámou, Kólpos- ◧	130	Gn	35.35N	23.40 E
Kissidougou	166	Cd	9.11N	10.06W
Kissimmee	184	Gk	28.18N	81.24W
Kissimmee, Lake- ≈	184	Gl	27.55N	81.16W
Kissū, Jabal- ▲	168	Da	21.35N	25.09 E
Kistelek	120	Pj	46.28N	19.59 E
Kisterenye	120	Ph	48.01N	19.50 E
Kisújszállás	120	Qi	47.13N	20.46 E
Kisuki	156	Cd	35.17N	132.54 E
Kisumu	160	Ki	0.06S	34.45 E
Kisvárda	120	Sh	48.13N	22.05 E
Kita	160	Gg	13.03N	9.30W
Kitab	136	Gh	39.08N	66.54 E
Kita-Daitō-Jima ◆	152	Nf	25.55N	131.20 E
Kitaibaraki	154	Pf	36.48N	140.45 E
Kita-Iō-Jima ◆	214	Cb	25.26N	141.17 E
Kitaj, ozero- ≈	130	Md	45.35N	29.15 E
Kitakami	152	Pd	39.30N	141.10 E
Kitakami-Gawa ∿	156	Gb	38.25N	141.19 E
Kitakami-Sanchi ⛰	156	Gb	39.30N	141.30 E
Kitakata	154	Of	37.39N	139.52 E
Kitakyushū	142	Pf	33.53N	130.50 E
Kitale	160	Kh	1.01N	35.00 E
Kitami	152	Pc	43.48N	143.54 E
Kitamiaioi	156a	Cb	43.33N	143.57 E
Kitami-Fuji ▲	156a	Cb	43.42N	143.14 E
Kitami-Sanchi ⛰	154	Qb	44.30N	142.30 E
Kitami Tōge ⋁	156a	Cb	43.55N	142.55 E
Kitan-Kaikyō ═	156	Dd	34.15N	135.00 E
Kita-Taiheyō = Pacific Ocean (EN) ≋	214	Ch	22.00N	179.00 E
Kita-Ura ≈	156	Gc	36.00N	140.34 E
Kit Carson	186	Eg	38.46N	102.48W
Kitchener	180	Jh	43.27N	80.29W
Kitee	114	He	62.06N	30.09 E
Kitessa	168	Dd	5.22N	25.22 E
Kitgum	170	Fb	3.19N	32.53 E
Kíthira = Cythera (EN)	130	Fm	36.09N	23.00 E
Kíthira = Kythera (EN) ◆	110	Ih	36.15N	23.00 E
Kithira Channel (EN) = Kithíron, Dhiékplous- ═	130	Fm	36.00N	23.00 E
Kithíron, Dhiékplous- = Kithira Channel (EN) ═	130	Fm	36.00N	23.00 E
Kíthnos	130	Hl	37.25N	24.26 E
Kíthnos ◆	130	Hl	37.23N	24.25 E
Kithnou, Stenón- ═	130	Hl	37.25N	24.30 E
Kitimat	176	Gd	54.05N	128.38W
Kitimat Ranges ⛰	180	Ef	53.58N	128.39W
Kitoushi-Yama ▲	156a	Cb	43.27N	143.25 E
Kitriani ◆	130	Hm	36.54N	24.44 E
Kitridge Point ▶	197q	Bb	13.09N	59.25W
Kítros	130	Fi	40.22N	22.35 E
Kitsuki	156	Be	33.25N	131.37 E
Kittanning	184	He	40.49N	79.31W
Kittery	184	Ld	43.05N	70.45W
Kittilä	114	Fc	67.40N	24.54 E
Kitui	160	Ki	1.22S	38.01 E
Kitunda	170	Fd	6.48S	33.13 E
Kitutu	170	Ec	3.17S	28.05 E
Kitwe-Nkana	160	Jj	12.49S	28.13 E
Kitzbühel	128	Gc	47.27N	12.23 E
Kitzbüheler Alpen ⛰	128	Gc	47.20N	12.20 E
Kitzingen	120	Gg	49.44N	10.10 E
Kiunga [Kenya]	170	Hc	1.45S	41.29 E
Kiunga [Pap.N.Gui.]	214	Ci	6.07S	141.18 E
Kiuruvesi	114	Ge	63.39N	26.37 E
Kivalina	178	Gc	67.59N	164.33W
Kivercy	132	Dd	50.50N	25.31 E
Kivijärvi [Fin.] ≈	114	Fe	63.10N	25.09 E
Kivijärvi [Fin.] ≈	116	Ld	60.55N	27.40 E
Kivik	114	Di	55.41N	14.15 E
Kiviõli/Kiviyli	114	Gg	59.23N	26.59 E
Kiviyli/Kiviõli	114	Gg	59.23N	26.59 E
Kivu [2]	170	Ec	2.30S	27.30 E
Kivu, Lac- = Kivu, Lake- (EN) ≈	158	Ji	2.00S	29.10 E
Kivu, Lake- (EN) = Kivu, Lac- ≈	158	Ji	2.00S	29.10 E
Kiwai Island ◆	214	Ci	8.30S	143.25 E
Kīyāmakī Dāgh ▲	146	Kc	38.47N	45.51 E
Kıyıköy	146	Cb	41.25N	28.01 E
Kiyosato	156a	Db	43.51N	144.35 E
Kizel	136	Fd	59.03N	57.40 E
Kizema	114	Kf	61.09N	44.46 E
Kizilcabölük	130	Ml	37.37N	29.01 E
Kızılca Dağı ▲	146	Cd	36.55N	29.52 E
Kızılcahaman	146	Eb	40.28N	32.39 E
Kızıl Dağ ▲	146	Ed	36.25N	32.42 E
Kizilhisar	130	Ml	37.33N	29.18 E
Kızılırmak	146	Eb	40.22N	33.59 E
Kızılırmak ∿	140	Fe	41.45N	35.59 E
Kiziljurt	132	Oh	43.13N	46.55 E
Kizilskoje	134	Ij	52.44N	58.54 E
Kızıltepe	146	Id	37.12N	40.36 E
Kizimen, vulkan- 🌋	138	Le	55.03N	160.27 E
Kižinga	138	Ff	51.51N	109.55 E
Kizir ∿	138	Ef	54.10N	93.30 E
Kizljar	136	Eg	43.50N	46.42 E
Kizljarski zaliv ◧	132	Og	44.35N	46.55 E
Kizukuri	156a	Bc	40.48N	140.22 E
Kizyl-Arvat	136	Fh	39.01N	56.20 E
Kizyl-Atrek	136	Fh	37.38N	54.47 E
Kizyl-Su	136	Fh	39.46N	53.01 E
Kjahta	138	Ff	50.26N	106.25 E
Kjalvaz	132	Pj	38.38N	48.20 E
Kjardla/Kärdla	114	Fg	59.01N	22.42 E
Kjarevere/Kärevere	116	Lf	58.23N	26.30 E
Kjarla/Kärla	116	Jf	58.16N	22.05 E
Kjellerup	116	Ch	56.17N	9.26 E
Kjøllefjord	114	Ga	70.56N	27.27 E
Kjölur ⊠	114a	Bb	64.50N	19.25W
Kjøpsvik	114	Db	68.06N	16.21 E
Kjubjume	138	Jd	63.28N	140.30 E
Kjurdamir	136	Eg	40.20N	48.07 E
Kjusjur	138	Hb	70.35N	127.45 E
Kjustendil	130	Fg	42.17N	22.41 E
Kjustendil [2]	130	Fg	42.17N	22.41 E
Kjyosumi-Yama ▲	156	Gd	35.10N	140.09 E
Klabat, Gunung- ▲	150	If	1.28N	125.02 E
Kladanj	128	Mf	44.14N	18.42 E
Kladno	120	Kf	50.09N	14.07 E
Kladovo	130	Fe	44.37N	22.37 E
Klagenfurt	112	Hf	46.38N	14.18 E
Klaipėda/Klajpeda	112	Id	55.43N	21.07 E
Klajpeda/Klaipėda	112	Id	55.43N	21.07 E
Klamath	188	Cf	41.32N	124.02W
Klamath Falls	176	Ge	42.13N	121.46W
Klamath Mountains ⛰	182	Cc	41.40N	123.20W
Klamath River ∿	188	Cf	41.33N	124.04W
Klamono	150	Jg	1.08S	131.30 E
Klarälven ∿	110	Hd	59.23N	13.32 E
Klaten	150	Fh	7.42S	110.35 E
Klatovy	120	Jg	49.24N	13.19 E
Klavreström	116	Fg	57.08N	15.08 E
Klawer	172	Bf	31.44S	18.36 E
Klazienaveen, Emmen-	124	Jb	52.44N	7.01 E
Kleck	132	Ec	53.03N	26.40 E
Kłecko	120	Nd	52.38N	17.26 E
Kleinblittersdorf	124	Je	49.09N	7.02 E
Kleine Nete ∿	124	Gc	51.08N	4.34 E
Kleine Sluis, Anna Paulowna-	124	Gb	52.52N	4.52 E
Klein-Karoo = Little Karroo (EN) ⊠	172	Cf	33.42S	21.20 E
Kleinsee	172	Be	29.40S	17.05 E
Klekovača ⛰	128	Kf	44.26N	16.31 E
Kléla	166	Dc	11.40N	5.40W
Kleppe	116	Af	58.46N	5.40 E
Klerksdorp	172	De	26.58S	26.39 E
Kletnja	136	De	53.27N	33.17 E
Kletski	132	Me	49.19N	43.04 E
Kleve	120	Ce	51.47N	6.09 E
Klibreck, Ben- ▲	118	Ic	58.19N	4.30W
Klička	138	Gf	50.24N	118.01 E
Kljmoviči	136	De	53.37N	32.01 E
Klimovo	132	Hc	52.23N	32.16 E
Klin	136	Dd	56.20N	36.42 E
Klina	130	Dg	42.37N	20.35 E
Klincy	136	De	52.46N	32.17 E
Klingbach ∿	124	Ke	49.11N	8.24 E
Klingenthal	120	If	50.22N	12.28 E
Klínovec ▲	120	If	50.24N	12.58 E
Klintehamn	114	Eh	57.24N	18.12 E
Klippan	116	Eh	56.08N	13.06 E
Klipplaat	172	Cf	33.02S	24.21 E
Kliškovcy	130	Ja	48.23N	26.13 E
Klisura	130	Hg	42.42N	24.27 E
Klitmøller	116	Cg	57.02N	8.31 E
Kljazma ∿	110	Kd	56.10N	42.58 E
Ključevskaja Sopka, vulkan- 🌋	140	Sd	56.04N	160.38 E
Kljuci	138	Le	56.14N	160.58 E
Kłobuck	120	Of	50.55N	18.57 E
Kłodawa	120	Od	52.16N	18.55 E
Kłodzka, Kotlina- ⊠	120	Mf	50.30N	16.35 E
Kłodzko	120	Mf	50.28N	16.40 E
Kløfta	116	Dd	60.04N	11.09 E
Kłomnice	120	Pf	50.56N	19.21 E
Klondike Plateau ◠	180	Dd	63.10N	139.55W
Klondike River ∿	180	Dd	64.03N	139.26W
Klooga/Kloga	116	Ke	59.24N	24.10 E
Kloosteezande, Hontenisse-	124	Gc	51.23N	4.00 E
Klosi	130	Dh	41.29N	20.06 E
Klosterneuburg	128	Kb	48.18N	16.19 E
Klosters / Claustra	128	Dd	46.52N	9.52 E
Kloten	128	Cc	47.27N	8.35 E
Klotz, Lac - ≈	180	Kd	60.40N	73.00W
Kluane Lake ≈	180	Dd	61.15N	138.40W
Kluczbork	120	Of	50.59N	18.13 E
Knaben	116	Bf	58.39N	7.04 E
Knäred	116	Eh	56.32N	13.19 E
Kneža	130	Hf	43.30N	24.05 E
Knife River ∿	186	Fc	47.20N	101.23W
Knin	128	Kf	44.02N	16.12 E
Knislinge	116	Fh	56.11N	14.05 E
Knittelfeld	128	Ic	47.13N	14.49 E
Knivskjellodden ▶	114	Fa	71.11N	25.40 E
Knivsta	116	Ge	59.43N	17.48 E
Knjaževac	130	Ff	43.34N	22.15 E
Knobly Mountain ⛰	184	Hf	39.15N	79.05W
Knockmealdown Mountains/ Cnoc Mhaoldonn ⛰	118	Fi	52.15N	8.00W
Knokke-Heist	122	Jc	51.21N	3.15 E
Knokke-Westkapelle	124	Fc	51.19N	3.18 E
Knolls grund ▦	116	Gg	57.30N	17.30 E
Knøsen ▲	116	Dg	57.12N	10.18 E
Knosós = Cnossus (EN) ⊡	130	In	35.18N	25.10 E
Knox, Cape - ▶	180	Ef	54.11N	133.05W
Knox Coast ▦	222	He	66.30S	105.00 E
Knoxville [Ia.-U.S.]	186	Jf	41.19N	93.06W
Knoxville [Tn.-U.S.]	176	Kf	35.58N	83.56W
Knud Rasmussen Land ⊠	224	Nd	80.00N	55.00W
Knüllgebirge ▲	120	Ff	50.50N	9.30 E
Knutsholstind ▲	116	Cc	61.26N	8.34 E
Knysna	160	Jl	34.02S	23.02 E
Koartac	180	Kd	60.50N	69.30W
Koba	150	Eg	2.29S	106.24 E
Koba, Pulau- ◆	150	Jh	6.25S	134.28 E
Kobar Sink ⊠	168	Gc	14.00N	40.30 E
Kobayashi	154	Ki	31.59N	130.59 E
Kobdo	142	Le	48.01N	91.38 E
Kobdo (Chovd) ∿	152	Fb	48.06N	92.11 E
Kōbe	142	Pf	34.41N	135.10 E
Kobeljaki	132	Ie	49.08N	34.12 E
København [2]	116	Ei	55.40N	12.10 E
København = Copenhagen (EN)	112	Hi	55.40N	12.35 E
Kobenni	162	Ff	15.55N	9.05W
Kobern-Gondorf	124	Jd	50.19N	7.28 E
Kobjaj	138	Hd	63.30N	126.26 E
Koblenz	120	Df	50.21N	7.36 E
Kobo	168	Fc	12.09N	39.39 E
Koboldo	138	If	52.58N	132.42 E
Kobra ∿	114	Mg	59.19N	50.54 E
Kobrin	136	Ce	52.13N	24.23 E
Kobrinskoje	116	Ne	59.22N	30.14 E
Kobroor, Pulau- ◆	150	Jh	6.12S	134.32 E
Kobuk ∿	174	Cc	66.45N	161.00W
Kobuleti	132	Li	41.47N	41.45 E
Koca ∿	146	Eb	41.41N	32.15 E
Kocabaş ∿	146	Bb	40.22N	27.19 E
Koca Çay ∿	146	Bb	40.08N	27.57 E
Koca Çay [Tur.] ∿	146	Cd	36.17N	29.16 E
Koca Çay [Tur.] ∿	130	Lj	38.43N	28.30 E
Koca Çay/Orhaneli ∿	130	Lj	39.56N	28.32 E
Kočani	130	Fh	41.55N	22.25 E
Koçarlı	130	Kl	37.45N	27.42 E
Kocasu ∿	130	Mj	39.42N	29.31 E
Kočečum ∿	138	Fd	64.17N	100.10 E
Kočetovka	132	Lc	53.01N	40.31 E
Kočevje	128	Ie	45.39N	14.51 E
Kočevski Rog ▲	128	Ie	45.41N	15.00 E
Koch ◆	180	Jc	69.35N	78.20W
Kŏch'ang	154	Ig	35.41N	127.55 E
Ko Chang	148	Kf	12.00N	102.23 E
Koch Bihār	148	Hc	26.19N	89.26 E
Kochi	152	Ne	33.33N	133.33 E
Kōchi Ken [2]	154	Lh	33.20N	133.30 E
Kochisar Ovası ▬	146	Ec	38.50N	33.30 E
Kock	120	Se	51.39N	22.27 E
Kočkorka	135	Jc	42.11N	75.45 E
Kočmar	130	Kf	43.41N	27.28 E
Kočubej	136	Eg	44.23N	46.31 E
Kočubejevskoje	132	Lg	44.41N	41.50 E
Kodiak	176	Dd	57.48N	152.23W
Kodiak ◆	174	Dd	57.30N	153.30W
Kodino	114	Je	63.44N	39.40 E
Kodok	168	Ed	9.53N	32.07 E
Kodomari	156a	Bc	41.08N	140.18 E
Kodori ∿	132	Lh	42.49N	41.10 E
Kodry ⛰	130	Lb	47.15N	28.15 E
Kodyma ∿	132	Ge	48.01N	30.48 E
Kodža Balkan ⛰	130	Jg	42.50N	27.00 E
Koekenaap	172	Bf	31.29S	18.19 E
Koes	172	Be	25.59S	19.08 E
Kofa Mountains ⛰	188	Ij	33.20N	114.00W
Kofçaz	146	Bb	41.58N	27.12 E
Koffiefontein	172	Ce	29.30S	25.00 E
Kofiau, Pulau- ◆	150	Ig	1.11S	129.50 E
Köflach	128	Jc	47.04N	15.05 E
Koforidua	160	Gh	6.05N	0.15W
Kōfu [Jap.]	156	Cd	35.18N	133.29 E
Kōfu [Jap.]	152	Od	35.39N	138.35 E
Koga	156	Fc	36.12N	139.42 E
Kogaluc ∿	180	Je	59.38N	77.30W
Kōge	156	Dd	35.24N	134.15 E
Køge	114	Ci	55.27N	12.11 E
Køge Bugt ◧	116	Ei	55.30N	12.20 E
Kogel ∿	134	He	62.38N	57.07 E
Kogilnik (Kunduk) ∿	130	Md	45.51N	29.38 E
Kogon ∿	166	Cc	11.09N	14.42W
Kogota	156	Gb	38.32N	141.01 E
Kohala Mountains ⛰	221a	Fc	20.05N	155.43W
Kohāt	148	Eb	33.35N	71.26 E
Kohila	116	Ke	59.11N	24.40 E
Kohima	148	Ic	25.40N	94.07 E
Koh-i Mārān ▲	148	Dc	29.05N	66.50 E
Kohinggo ◆	219a	Cc	8.13S	157.10 E
Kohma	114	Jh	56.57N	41.07 E
Kohtla-Jarve/Kohtla-Järve	136	Cd	59.25N	27.14 E
Kohtla-Järve/Kohtla-Jarve	136	Cd	59.25N	27.14 E
Kohu Dağı ▲	130	Mm	36.30N	29.50 E
Kohunlich ⊡	192	Oh	18.30N	88.55W
Koide	156	Fc	37.14N	138.57 E
Koigi/Kojgi	116	Kf	58.49N	25.40 E
Koin ∿	134	Ee	63.10N	51.15 E
Koindu	166	Cd	8.28N	10.20W
Koitere ≈	114	He	62.58N	30.45 E
Kojā ∿	144	Jd	25.34N	61.13 E
Kojandytau ⛰	135	Lb	44.20N	78.45 E
Kojda	114	Kc	66.23N	42.31 E
Koje-Do ◆	154	Jg	34.52N	128.37 E
Kojetín	120	Ng	49.21N	17.20 E
Kojgi/Koigi	116	Kf	58.49N	25.40 E
Ko-Jima [Jap.] ◆	156	Fe	33.07N	139.40 E
Ko-Jima [Jap.] ◆	154	Od	41.22N	139.47 E
Kojŏ	152	Md	38.57N	127.52 E
Kojonup	212	Df	33.50S	117.09 E
Kojtaš	135	Fd	40.14N	67.22 E
Kojtezek, pereval- ⋁	135	If	37.29N	72.45 E
Kojur	146	Nd	36.23N	51.43 E
Kojva ∿	134	Ig	58.15N	58.14 E
Kokab	168	Cc	10.03N	22.04 E
Kokai-Gawa ∿	156	Gd	35.52N	140.08 E
Kokand	142	Je	40.33N	70.57 E
Kökar ◇	114	Eg	59.55N	20.55 E
Kökarsfjärden ≈	116	Ie	59.55N	20.45 E
Kokas	150	Jg	2.42S	132.26 E
Kokava nad Rimavicou	120	Ph	48.34N	19.50 E
Kokawa	156	Dd	34.17N	135.26 E
Kokčetav	142	Id	53.17N	69.25 E
Kokčetavskaja oblast [3]	136	He	53.30N	70.00 E
Kokemäenjoki ∿	116	Ic	61.33N	21.42 E
Kokemäki/Kumo	114	Ff	61.15N	22.21 E
Kok-Jangak	136	Hg	40.59N	73.15 E
Kokkina	146	Ee	35.10N	32.36 E
Kokkola/Gamlaklarleby	112	Ic	63.50N	23.07 E
Koko [Eth.]	168	Fc	10.20N	36.04 E
Koko [Nig.]	166	Fc	11.26N	4.30 E
Kokomo	182	Jc	40.29N	86.08W
Kokonau	150	Kg	4.43S	136.26 E
Kokong	172	Cd	24.27S	23.03 E
Koko Nor (EN) = Qinghai Hu ≈	140	Mf	37.00N	100.20 E
Kokpekty	136	If	48.45N	82.24 E
Kokšaal-Tau, hrebet- ⛰	136	Hg	41.00N	78.00 E
Kokšenga ∿	114	Kf	61.27N	42.38 E
Koksijde	124	Ec	51.06N	2.39 E
Koksoak ∿	180	Ke	58.31N	68.11W
Kokstad	160	Jl	30.32S	29.29 E
Koktal	135	Lb	44.05N	79.44 E
Koktokay/Fuyun	142	Ke	47.13N	89.39 E
Kokubu	154	Ki	31.44N	130.46 E
Kola	136	Db	68.53N	33.01 E
Kola, Pulau- ◆	150	Jh	5.30S	134.35 E
Kolahun	166	Cd	8.17N	10.05W
Kolaka	150	Hg	4.03S	121.36 E
Kolamadulu Atoll ◎	148a	Bb	2.25N	73.10 E
Kola Peninsula (EN) = Kolski poluostrov ▰	110	Jb	67.30N	37.00 E
Kolār Gold Fields	148	Ff	12.55N	78.17 E
Kolari	114	Fc	67.20N	23.48 E
Kólarovo	120	Ni	47.55N	18.00 E
Kolbäck	116	Ge	59.34N	16.15 E
Kolbäcksån ∿	116	Ge	59.32N	16.16 E
Kolbio	170	Hc	1.09S	41.12 E
Kolbuszowa	120	Rf	50.15N	21.47 E
Kolby	116	Di	55.48N	10.33 E
Kolčugino	114	Jh	56.16N	39.23 E
Kolda	166	Cc	12.53N	14.57W
Kolding	112	Gd	55.31N	9.29 E
Kole [Zaire]	170	Eb	2.07N	25.26 E
Kole [Zaire]	170	Dc	3.31S	22.27 E
Koléa	126	Oh	36.38N	2.46 E
Kolendo	138	Jf	53.43N	142.57 E
Kolente ∿	166	Cd	8.55N	13.08W
Kolesnoje	130	Mc	46.04N	29.45 E
Kolga	116	Ke	59.28N	25.29 E
Kolga, zaliv-/Kolga laht ◧	116	Ke	59.30N	25.15 E
Kolga laht/Kolga, zaliv- ◧	116	Ke	59.30N	25.15 E
Kolgompja, mys- ▶	116	Me	59.44N	28.35 E
Kolgujev, ostrov- ◆	110	Kb	69.05N	49.15 E
Kolhāpur	142	Jh	16.42N	74.13 E
Kolhozabad	135	Gf	37.35N	68.39 E
Kolhozbentskoje, vodohranilišče- ≈	135	Df	37.10N	62.30 E
Koli ◠	114	Ge	63.06N	29.53 E
Kolimbiné ∿	166	Cc	14.45N	11.00 E
Kolín	120	Lf	50.02N	15.13 E
Kolito	168	Fd	7.25N	38.07 E
Koljučinskaja guba ◧	138	Nc	66.50N	174.30W
Kolka	116	Jg	57.44N	22.27 E
Kolkasrags ▶	114	Fh	57.46N	22.37 E
Kolki	132	Dd	51.07N	25.42 E
Kollinai	130	Fl	37.17N	22.22 E
Kollumúli ▶	114a	Cb	65.47N	14.21W
Kolmården ▲	116	Gf	58.41N	16.35 E
Köln = Cologne (EN)	112	Ge	50.56N	6.57 E
Köln-Lövenich	124	Id	50.57N	6.50 E
Kolno	120	Rc	53.25N	21.56 E
Köln-Porz	120	Df	50.53N	7.03 E
Koło	120	Od	52.12N	18.38 E
Koloa	221a	Bb	21.54N	159.28W
Kołobrzeg	120	Lb	54.12N	15.33 E
Kolodnja	132	Hb	54.49N	32.11 E
Kologriv	114	Kg	58.51N	44.17 E
Kolokani	166	Dc	13.34N	8.03W
Koloko	166	Dc	11.05N	5.19W
Kolokolkova guba ◧	134	Fb	68.30N	52.30 E
Kololo	168	Gd	7.27N	41.59 E
Kolombangara Island ◆	214	Fi	8.00S	157.05 E
Kolomna	112	Jd	55.05N	38.49 E
Kolomyja	136	Cf	48.32N	25.01 E
Kolondiéba	166	Dc	11.06N	6.53W
Kolonga	221b	Ac	21.08S	175.04W
Kolonodale	150	Hg	2.00S	121.19 E
Kolosovka	136	Hd	56.28N	73.36 E
Kolossa ∿	166	Dc	13.52N	7.35W
Kolovai	221b	Ac	21.06S	175.20W
Kolozero, ozero- ≈	114	Hb	68.15N	33.15 E
Kolp ∿	114	Ig	59.20N	36.50 E
Kolpaševo	142	Kd	58.20N	82.50 E
Kolpino	114	Hg	59.45N	30.33 E
Kolpny	132	Jc	52.16N	37.00 E
Kolski poluostrov = Kola Peninsula (EN) ▰	110	Jb	67.30N	37.00 E
Koltubanovski	132	Rc	52.57N	52.02 E
Kolubara ∿	130	De	44.40N	20.15 E
Koluszki	120	Pe	51.44N	19.49 E
Koluton	136	Ge	51.42N	69.25 E
Kolva [Russia]	134	Hf	60.22N	56.33 E
Kolva [Russia]	136	Fb	65.55N	57.20 E
Kolvickoje, ozero- ≈	114	Hc	67.05N	33.30 E
Kölvrå	116	Ch	56.18N	9.08 E
Kolwezi	160	Jj	10.43S	25.28 E
Kolyma ∿	140	Sc	69.30N	161.00 E
Kolyma Plain (EN) = Kolymskaja nizmennost ▬	140	Rc	68.30N	154.00 E
Kolyma Range (EN) = Kolymskoje nagorje ◠	140	Rc	62.30N	155.00 E
Kolymskaja nizmennost = Kolyma Plain (EN) ▬	140	Rc	68.30N	154.00 E
Kolymskoje nagorje = Kolyma Range (EN) ◠	140	Rc	62.30N	155.00 E
Kolyšlej	132	Nc	52.40N	44.31 E
Kolžat	136	Ig	43.29N	80.37 E
Kom	170	Gb	1.05N	38.02 E
Kom ▲	130	Gf	43.10N	23.03 E
Komádi	120	Rj	47.00N	21.30 E
Komadugu Gana ∿	166	Hc	13.05N	12.24 E
Komadugu Yobe ∿	158	Ig	13.42N	13.24 E
Komagane	156	Ed	35.43N	137.54 E
Koma-ga-Take [Jap.] ▲	156	Fd	35.45N	138.13 E
Koma-ga-Take [Jap.] ▲	156	Gb	39.47N	140.50 E
Koma-ga-Take [Jap.] ▲	156a	Bb	42.04N	140.40 E
Komandorski Islands (EN) = Komandorskije ostrova ◆	140	Sd	55.00N	167.00 E
Komandorskije ostrova = Komandorski Islands (EN) ◆	140	Sd	55.00N	167.00 E
Komandorskiye Basin (EN) ∪	138	Le	57.00N	168.00 E
Komarin	132	Gd	51.27N	30.32 E
Komárno	120	Oi	47.46N	18.09 E
Komarno	120	Tg	49.34N	23.43 E
Komárom	120	Oi	47.44N	18.07 E
Komárom-Esztegom	120	Oi	47.40N	18.15 E
Komatipoort	172	Ee	25.25S	31.55 E
Komatsu	152	Od	36.24N	136.37 E
Komatsujima	156	Dd	34.01N	134.35 E
Komba, Pulau- ◆	150	Hh	7.47S	123.35 E
Kombissiri	166	Ec	12.04N	1.20W
Kombolcha	168	Fc	11.05N	39.45 E
Komebail Lagoon ◒	220a	Ac	7.24N	134.27 E
Komen/Comines	124	Ed	50.46N	2.59 E
Komi respublika	136	Fc	64.00N	55.00 E
Komi-Permijackij avtonomnyj okrug	136	Fd	60.00N	54.30 E
Komló	120	Oj	46.12N	18.16 E
Kommunarsk (Alčevsk)	132	Ke	48.27N	38.52 E
Kommunary	116	Nd	60.55N	30.10 E
Kommunizma, pik- = Communism Peak (EN) ▲	140	Jf	38.57N	72.08 E
Komodo, Pulau- ◆	150	Gh	8.36S	119.30 E
Komoé [3]	166	Ec	10.25N	4.20W
Komoé ∿	158	Gh	5.12N	3.44W
Komono	170	Bc	3.15S	13.14 E
Komoran, Pulau- ◆	150	Kh	8.18S	138.45 E
Komoro	156	Fc	36.19N	138.24 E
Komotini	130	Ih	41.07N	25.24 E
Komovi ⛰	130	Cg	42.41N	19.39 E
Kompasberg ▲	158	Jl	31.46S	24.32 E
Komrat	132	Ff	46.17N	28.38 E
Komsa	138	Dd	61.40N	89.25 E
Komsomolec	134	Kj	53.45N	62.02 E
Komsomolec, ostrov- ◆	140	La	80.30N	95.00 E
Komsomolec, zaliv- ◧	132	Rg	45.30N	52.45 E
Komsomolsk [Russia]	138	De	57.25N	86.02 E
Komsomolsk [Russia]	114	Jh	57.02N	40.22 E
Komsomolsk [Turk]	136	Gh	39.02N	63.36 E
Komsomolski [Kaz.]	136	Ff	47.20N	53.44 E
Komsomolski [Russia]	136	Gb	67.35N	63.47 E
Komsomolski [Russia]	132	Og	45.22N	46.01 E
Komsomolski [Russia]	114	Ki	54.27N	45.45 E
Komsomolski [Russia]	134	Kf	61.20N	63.15 E
Komsomolski [Russia]	138	Mc	69.12N	172.55 E
Komsomolsk-na-Amure	142	Pd	50.36N	137.02 E
Komsomolsk-na-Ustjurte	136	Fg	44.07N	58.17 E
Komsomoskoje [Ukr.]	132	Je	49.36N	36.33 E
Komsomolskje [Ukr.]	132	Kf	47.37N	38.05 E

Kom-Kre

Komsomolskoj Pravdy, ostrova- 138 Fa 77.15N 107.30 E
Kōmun-Do 154 Ig 34.02N 127.19 E
Kömür Burun 130 Jk 38.39N 26.25 E
Komusan 152 Mc 42.07N 129.42 E
Kona 166 Ec 14.57N 3.53W
Kona Coast 221a Fd 19.35N 155.56W
Konakovo 136 Dd 56.42N 36.46 E
Konar 144 Lc 34.25N 70.32 E
Konārak 148 Hh 19.54N 86.07 E
Konarha [3] 144 Lb 35.15N 71.00 E
Konda 136 Gc 60.40N 69.46 E
Kondagaon 148 Ge 19.36N 81.40 E
Kondinin 212 Df 32.30S 118.16 E
Kondinskoje 134 Mg 59.40N 67.25 E
Kondoa 160 Ki 4.54S 35.47 E
Kondopoga 112 Jc 62.13N 34.17 E
Kondratjevo 116 Md 60.36N 28.02 E
Kondrovo 136 De 54.49N 35.55 E
Kondurča 114 Mj 53.31N 50.24 E
Koné 216 Bd 21.04S 164.52 E
Konečnaja 136 He 50.45N 78.27 E
Konevic, ostrov- 116 Nd 60.50N 30.45 E
Kong 166 Ed 9.09N 4.37W
Kōng 148 Lf 13.32N 105.58 E
Kōng, Kaôh- 148 Kf 11.20N 103.00 E
Konga/Koonga 116 Jf 58.34N 24.00 E
Kongauru 220a Ac 7.04N 134.17 E
Kong Christian IX Land = King Christian IX Land (EN) 224 Mc 68.00N 36.30W
Kong Christian X Land = King Christian X Land (EN) 224 Md 72.20N 32.30W
Kongeå 116 Ci 55.23N 8.39 E
Kong Frederik VIII Land = King Frederik VIII Land (EN) 224 Md 78.30N 28.00W
Kong Frederik VI Kyst = King Frederik VI Coast (EN) 224 Nc 63.00N 43.30W
Konginkangas 116 Kb 62.46N 25.48 E
Kongju 154 If 36.27N 127.08 E
Kong Karls Land 179 Oc 78.50N 28.00 E
Kong Kong 168 Ed 7.26N 33.14 E
Kongolo 160 Ji 5.23S 27.00 E
Kongor 168 Ed 7.10N 31.21 E
Kong Oscars Fjord 224 Md 72.20N 23.00W
Kongoussi 166 Ec 13.19N 1.32W
Kongsberg 114 Bg 59.39N 9.39 E
Kongsøya 179 Oc 78.55N 28.40 E
Kongsvinger 114 Cf 60.12N 12.00 E
Kongur Shan 140 Jf 38.40N 75.21 E
Kongwa 170 Gd 6.12S 36.25 E
Kong Wilhelms Land 179 Jc 75.48N 23.15W
Koniecpol 120 Pf 50.48N 19.41 E
Königslutter am Elm 120 Gd 52.15N 10.49 E
Königswinter 124 Jd 50.41N 7.11 E
Königs Wusterhausen 120 Jd 52.17N 13.37 E
Konin 120 Od 52.13N 18.16 E
Konin [2] 120 Od 52.15N 18.15 E
Konispoli 130 Dj 39.39N 20.10 E
Kónitsa 130 Di 40.03N 20.45 E
Konj 128 Kg 43.43N 16.55 E
Konjed Jān 146 Nf 33.30N 50.27 E
Konjic 128 Lg 43.39N 17.58 E
Konjuh 128 Mf 44.18N 18.33 E
Konkan 148 Ee 18.05N 73.25 E
Konkiep 172 Be 28.00S 17.23 E
Konko 170 Ed 10.12S 27.27 E
Konkouré 166 Cd 9.58N 13.42W
Konnevesi 116 Lb 62.37N 26.19 E
Konnevesi 116 Lb 62.40N 26.35 E
Konnivesi 116 Lc 61.10N 26.10 E
Konoša 112 Kc 60.58N 40.15 E
Kōnosu 156 Fc 36.04N 139.30 E
Konotop 112 Je 51.14N 33.12 E
Konqi He 140 Ke 41.48N 86.47 E
Konrei 220a Bb 7.43N 134.37 E
Konsei-Tōge 156 Fc 36.52N 139.22 E
Konsen-Daichi 156a Db 43.20N 144.50 E
Końskie 120 Qe 51.12N 20.26 E
Konstantinovka 132 Je 48.29N 37.43 E
Konstantinovsk 132 Lf 47.35N 41.05 E
Konstanz 120 Fi 47.40N 9.11 E
Kontagora 160 Hg 10.24N 5.29 E
Kontcha 166 Hd 7.58N 12.14 E
Kontich 124 Gc 51.08N 4.27 E
Kontiolahti 114 Ge 62.46N 29.51 E
Kontiomäki 114 Gd 64.21N 28.09 E
Kontum 148 Lf 14.21N 108.00 E
Kontum, Plateau de- 148 Lf 13.55N 108.05 E
Konušin, mys- 114 Kc 67.10N 43.50 E
Konušinski bereg 134 Bc 66.45N 44.40 E
Konya 142 Ff 37.52N 32.31 E
Konya Ovası 146 Ed 37.30N 33.20 E
Konz 124 Ie 49.42N 6.35 E
Konza 170 Gc 1.45S 37.07 E
Konžakovski Kamen, gora- 110 Ld 59.38N 59.08 E
Koocanusa, Lake- 188 Hb 48.45N 115.15W
Kook, Punta- 221d Ab 27.08S 109.26W
Koolau Range 221a Db 21.21N 157.47W
Koonga/Konga 116 Jf 58.34N 24.00 E
Koorda 212 Df 30.50S 117.29 E
Koosa 116 Lf 58.31N 27.07 E
Kootenay Lake 188 Gb 49.35N 116.50W
Kootenay River 174 He 49.15N 117.39W
Kopa 135 Jc 43.31N 75.48 E
Kopaonik 130 Df 43.15N 20.50 E
Kópasker 114a Ca 66.18N 16.27W
Kópavogur 114a Bb 64.06N 21.55W
Kopejsk 136 Gd 55.08N 61.39 E
Koper 128 He 45.33N 13.44 E
Kopervik 114 Ag 59.17N 5.18 E
Kopetdag, hrebet- 140 Hf 37.45N 58.15 E
Kop Geçidi 146 Ib 40.01N 40.28 E
Ko Phangan 148 Jg 9.45N 100.00 E
Köping 114 Dg 59.31N 16.00 E
Köpingsvik 116 Gh 56.53N 16.43 E
Kopjevo 138 Df 54.59N 89.55 E
Kopliku 130 Cg 42.13N 19.26 E
Köpmanholmen 114 Ee 63.10N 18.34 E
Koporje 116 Me 59.40N 29.08 E
Koporski zaliv 116 Me 59.45N 28.45 E
Koppal 148 Fe 15.21N 76.09 E
Koppang 114 Cf 61.34N 11.04 E
Koppány 120 Oj 46.35N 18.26 E
Kopparberg 116 Fe 59.52N 14.59 E
Kopparberg [2] 114 Df 61.00N 14.30 E
Kopparstenarna 116 Hf 58.32N 19.20 E
Koppom 116 Ee 59.43N 12.09 E
Koprivnica 128 Kd 46.10N 16.50 E
Kopru 146 Dd 36.49N 31.10 E
Köprüören 130 Mj 39.30N 29.47 E
Kor 144 Hd 29.36N 53.18 E
Korab 110 Ig 41.44N 20.32 E
Korablino 114 Jj 53.57N 40.00 E
Korahe 168 Gd 6.36N 44.16 E
Korak 220a Bc 7.21N 134.34 E
Koralpe 128 Id 46.45N 15.00 E
Koramlik 152 Ed 37.32N 85.42 E
Korana 128 Je 45.30N 15.35 E
Korangi 148 Dd 24.47N 67.08 E
Koraput 148 Ge 18.49N 82.43 E
Korba 148 Gd 22.21N 82.41 E
Korbach 120 Ee 51.17N 8.52 E
Korça 130 Di 40.37N 20.46 E
Korčula 128 Lh 42.58N 17.08 E
Korčula 128 Kh 42.57N 16.55 E
Korčulanski kanal 128 Kg 43.03N 16.40 E
Kordān 146 Ne 35.56N 50.50 E
Kordel 124 Ie 49.50N 6.38 E
Kordestān [3] 144 Gb 35.30N 47.00 E
Kord Kūy 144 Hb 36.48N 54.07 E
Kordun 128 Je 45.10N 15.35 E
Korea Bay (EN) = Sŏjosŏn-man 140 Of 39.15N 125.00 E
Korean Peninsula (EN) 140 Of 35.30N 125.30 E
Korea Strait (EN) = Taehan-Haehyŏp 140 Of 34.40N 129.00 E
Korea Strait (EN) = Tsushima-Kaikyō 140 Of 34.40N 129.00 E
Korec 132 Ed 50.37N 27.10 E
Korem 168 Fc 12.30N 39.32 E
Korenovsk 136 Df 45.28N 39.28 E
Korf 138 Ld 60.18N 166.01 E
Korfovski 138 Ig 48.11N 135.04 E
Korgen 114 Cc 66.05N 13.50 E
Kõrgesaare/Kyrgesare 116 Jf 59.00N 22.25 E
Korhogo 160 Gh 9.27N 5.38W
Korhogo [3] 166 Dd 9.35N 5.55W
Koribundu 166 Cd 7.43N 11.42W
Korienzé 166 Eb 15.24N 3.47W
Korinthiakós Kólpos = Corinth, Gulf of- (EN) 110 Ih 38.12N 22.30 E
Kórinthos 130 Fl 37.55N 22.53 E
Kórinthos = Corinth (EN) 130 Fl 37.55N 22.53 E
Korinthou, Dhiórix- = Corinth Canal (EN) 130 Fl 37.57N 22.58 E
Koriolei 160 Lh 1.48N 44.30 E
Kőrishegy 120 Ni 47.12N 17.49 E
Koritnik 130 Dg 42.05N 20.34 E
Kōriyama 152 Pd 37.24N 140.23 E
Korjakskaja Sopka, vulkan- 140 Rd 53.20N 158.47 E
Korjakski avtonomnyj okrug 138 Le 60.00N 163.00 E
Korjakskoje nagorje = Koryak Range (EN) 140 Tc 62.30N 172.00 E
Korjažma 136 Ec 61.18N 47.07 E
Korjukovka 132 Hd 51.47N 32.17 E
Korkino 134 Ji 54.54N 61.25 E
Korkodon 138 Kd 64.43N 154.05 E
Korkuteli 146 Dd 37.04N 30.13 E
Korla 142 Ke 41.44N 86.09 E
Körmend 120 Mi 47.01N 16.36 E
Kormy, gora- 138 Fd 62.15N 106.08 E
Kornati 128 Jg 43.49N 15.20 E
Kornejevka 134 Ni 54.01N 68.27 E
Kornešty 130 Kb 47.23N 28.00 E
Korneuburg 128 Kb 48.21N 16.20 E
Kórnik 120 Nd 52.17N 17.04 E
Kornsjø 114 Cg 58.57N 11.39 E
Koro 166 Ec 14.05N 3.04W
Koroba 212 Ia 5.40S 142.45 E
Koroča 132 Jd 50.50N 37.13 E
Köroğlu Dağları 144 Da 40.40N 32.35 E
Köroğlu Tepe 146 Db 40.31N 31.53 E
Korogwe 170 Gd 5.09S 38.29 E
Koro Island 208 If 17.32S 179.42 E
Koroit 212 Ig 38.17S 142.22 E
Korolevo 120 Th 48.08N 23.07 E
Korolevu 219d Ac 18.12S 177.53 E
Korom, Bahr 168 Bc 10.35N 19.45 E
Koromiri 220p Cc 21.15S 159.43W
Koronadal 150 He 6.12N 125.01 E
Korónia, Límni- 130 Gi 40.40N 23.10 E
Koronowo 120 Nc 53.19N 17.57 E
Koronowskie, Jezioro- 120 Nc 53.22N 17.55 E
Koror 210 Ed 7.20N 134.29 E
Koror 208 Ed 7.20N 134.30 E
Körös 120 Qj 46.43N 20.12 E
Koro Sea 216 Ec 18.00S 180.00
Korosten 112 Ie 50.57N 28.39 E
Korostyšev 132 Fd 50.18N 29.05 E
Korotaiha 134 Jb 68.55N 60.55 E
Koro Toro 160 Ig 16.05N 18.30 E
Korovin Volcano 178a Db 52.22N 174.10W
Korpijärvi 116 Lc 61.15N 27.10 E
Korpilahti 114 Fe 62.01N 25.33 E
Korpo/Korppoo 116 Id 60.10N 21.35 E
Korppoo/Korpo 116 Id 60.10N 21.35 E
Korsakov 138 Jg 46.37N 142.51 E
Korshäs 114 Ee 62.47N 21.12 E
Korsholm/Mustasaari 116 Ia 63.05N 21.43 E
Korso 116 Kd 60.21N 25.06 E
Korsør 114 Ci 55.20N 11.09 E
Korsun-Ševčenkovski 132 Ge 49.26N 31.18 E
Korsze 120 Rb 54.10N 21.09 E
Kortemark 124 Fc 51.02N 3.02 E
Kortrijk/Courtrai 122 Jd 50.50N 3.16 E
Korucu 130 Kj 39.28N 27.22 E
Koru Dağ 130 Ji 40.42N 26.45 E
Koryak Range (EN) = Korjakskoje nagorje 140 Tc 62.30N 172.00 E
Korzybie 120 Mb 54.18N 16.50 E
Kos 130 Km 36.53N 27.18 E
Kos 130 Km 36.50N 27.10 E
Kosa 134 Gg 59.56N 55.01 E
Kosa 134 Gf 60.11N 55.10 E
Kosai 156 Ed 34.43N 137.30 E
Kosaja Gora 132 Jb 54.09N 37.31 E
Kosaka 156 Ga 40.20N 140.44 E
Kō-Saki 156 Ad 34.05N 129.13 E
Ko Samui 148 Jg 9.30N 99.58 E
Kosan-ŭp 152 Md 38.51N 127.25 E
Koščagyl 132 Rf 46.52N 53.47 E
Kościan 120 Md 52.06N 16.38 E
Kościerzyna 120 Nb 54.08N 18.00 E
Kosciusko 186 Lj 32.58N 89.35W
Kosciusko, Mount- 208 Fh 36.27S 148.16 E
Kose/Koze 116 Ke 59.11N 25.05 E
Köse Dağ 146 Gb 40.06N 37.58 E
Kosha 168 Ea 20.49N 30.32 E
Koshigaya 156 Fd 35.55N 139.45 E
Koshiji 156 Fc 37.24N 138.45 E
Koshiki-Kaikyō 156 Bf 31.45N 130.05 E
Koshiki Rettō 152 Me 31.45N 129.45 E
Koshimizu 156a Db 43.51N 144.25 E
Kōshoku 154 Of 36.38N 138.06 E
Kōshyū Seamount (EN) 156 Df 31.35N 135.50 E
Košice 112 If 48.43N 21.15 E
Kosjerić 130 Cf 44.00N 19.55 E
Kosju 134 Id 65.38N 58.59 E
Kosju 134 Ic 66.18N 59.53 E
Köşk 130 Ll 37.51N 28.03 E
Koski 116 Jd 60.39N 23.09 E
Koskolovo 116 Me 59.34N 28.30 E
Koslan 136 Ec 63.29N 48.52 E
Kosma 134 Dd 65.43N 49.50 E
Kosmaj 130 De 44.28N 20.33 E
Kosŏng 152 Md 38.40N 128.19 E
Kosov 130 Ia 48.15N 25.08 E
Kosovo [3] 130 Dg 42.35N 21.00 E
Kosovo 130 Eg 42.40N 21.05 E
Kosovska Mitrovica 130 Dg 42.53N 20.52 E
Kosrae (Kusaie) 208 Hd 5.19N 162.59 E
Kossol Passage 220a Bb 7.52N 134.36 E
Kossol Reef 220a Bb 7.57N 134.41 E
Kossou, Barrage de- 166 Dd 7.01N 5.29W
Kossovo 132 Dc 52.47N 25.10 E
Kostajnica 128 Ke 45.13N 16.33 E
Kostenec 130 Gg 42.16N 23.49 E
Koster 172 De 25.57S 26.42 E
Kosteröarna 116 Df 58.55N 11.05 E
Kostjukoviči 132 Hc 53.23N 32.06 E
Kostjukovka 132 Gc 52.32N 30.58 E
Kostolac 130 Ee 44.44N 21.12 E
Kostopol 132 Ed 50.53N 26.29 E
Kostriževka 130 Ia 48.31N 25.45 E
Kostroma 112 Kd 57.47N 40.59 E
Kostromskaja oblast [3] 136 Ed 58.30N 44.00 E
Kostrzyń 120 Nd 52.25N 17.14 E
Kostrzyn 120 Kd 52.37N 14.39 E
Kosva 134 Hg 58.50N 56.45 E
Koszalin 120 Mb 54.12N 16.09 E
Koszalin [2] 120 Mb 54.10N 16.10 E
Kőszeg 120 Mi 47.23N 16.33 E
Kota 142 Jg 25.16N 75.55 E
Kotaagung 150 Dh 5.30S 104.38 E
Kota Baharu 142 Mi 6.08N 102.15 E
Kotabaru 150 Gg 3.14S 116.13 E
Kotabumi 142 Mj 4.50S 104.54 E
Kotadabok 150 Dg 0.30S 104.33 E
Kota Kinabalu 142 Ni 5.59N 116.04 E
Kotamobagu 150 Hf 0.46N 124.19 E
Ko Tao 148 Jf 10.05N 99.52 E
Kotari 128 Jf 44.05N 15.30 E
Ko Tarutau 148 Jg 6.35N 99.40 E
Kota Tinggi 150 Df 1.44N 103.54 E
Kotel 130 Jg 42.53N 26.27 E
Kotelnič 136 Ed 58.20N 48.20 E
Kotelnikovo 132 Mf 47.38N 43.09 E
Kotelny, ostrov- 140 Pb 75.45N 138.44 E
Kotelva 132 Id 50.03N 34.45 E
Köthen 120 He 51.45N 11.58 E
Kotido 170 Fb 3.00N 34.09 E
Kotjužany 156 Gb 47.50N 28.27 E
Kotka 114 Gf 60.28N 26.55 E
Kot Kapūra 148 Eb 30.35N 74.54 E
Kotlas 112 Kc 61.16N 46.35 E
Kotlenik 130 Df 43.51N 20.42 E
Kotlenski prohod 130 Jg 42.53N 26.27 E
Kotlik 178 Gd 63.02N 163.33W
Kotlin, ostrov- 116 Md 60.00N 29.45 E
Kotly 116 Me 59.30N 28.48 E
Kotobi 166 Ed 6.42N 4.08W
Kotohira 156 Cd 34.11N 133.48 E
Koton Karifi 166 Gd 8.06N 6.48 E
Kotor 130 Bg 42.25N 18.46 E
Kotorosl 114 Jh 57.38N 39.57 E
Kotorska, Boka- 130 Bg 42.25N 18.40 E
Kotor Varoš 128 Lf 44.37N 17.22 E
Kotouba 166 Ed 8.41N 3.12W
Kotovo 136 Ee 50.18N 44.48 E
Kotovsk [Mol.] → Chynčešt' 132 Ff 46.49N 28.33 E
Kotovsk [Russia] 136 Ee 52.35N 41.32 E
Kotovsk [Ukr.] 136 Cf 47.43N 29.33 E
Kotra 120 Uc 53.32N 24.17 E
Kotri 148 Dc 25.22N 68.18 E
Kötschach 128 Gd 46.40N 13.00 E
Kottayam 148 Fg 9.35N 76.31 E
Kotto 158 Jh 4.14N 22.02 E
Kotton 168 Id 9.37N 50.32 E
Kotu 221b Ba 19.57S 174.48W
Kotu Group 208 Jg 20.00S 174.45W
Kotuj 140 Mb 71.55N 102.05 E
Kotujkan 138 Fb 70.40N 103.25 E
Koturdepe 132 Rj 39.26N 53.40 E
Kotzebue 176 Cc 66.53N 162.39W
Kotzebue Sound 174 Cc 66.20N 163.00W
Kouandé 166 Fc 10.20N 1.42 E
Kouango 168 Be 4.58N 19.59 E
Kouba Modounga 168 Bb 15.40N 18.15 E
Koudougou 160 Gg 11.44N 4.31W
Kouéré 166 Ec 10.27N 3.59W
Koufália 130 Fi 40.47N 22.35 E
Koufonísion [Grc.] 130 Jo 34.56N 26.10 E
Koufonísion [Grc.] 130 Im 36.55N 25.35 E
Koufonisiou, Stenón- 130 Jo 35.00N 26.10 E
Kouilou [3] 170 Bc 4.00S 12.00 E
Kouilou 158 Ii 4.28S 11.41 E
Koukdjuak 180 Kc 66.47N 73.10W
Kouki 168 Bd 7.10N 17.18 E
Koukourou 168 Cd 7.12N 20.02 E
Koulamoutou 170 Bc 1.08S 12.29 E
Koulikoro 166 Dc 12.51N 7.34W
Koulountou 166 Cc 13.15N 13.37W
Koumac 210 Hg 20.30S 164.12 E
Koumac, Grand Récif de- 219b Be 20.32S 164.04 E
Koumbi-Saleh 162 Ff 15.47N 7.58W
Koumi 156 Fc 36.05N 138.28 E
Koumpentoum 166 Cc 13.59N 14.34W
Koumra 168 Bd 8.55N 17.33 E
Koundara 160 Fg 12.29N 13.18W
Koundian 166 Cc 13.08N 10.42W
Kounoúpoi 130 Jm 36.32N 26.27 E
Kounradski 136 Hf 46.57N 75.01 E
Kounta 166 Eb 17.30N 0.40W
Koupéla 166 Ec 12.11N 0.21W
Kouqian → Yongji 154 Ic 43.40N 126.30 E
Kourou 202 Hb 5.09N 52.39W
Kouroussa 166 Dc 10.39N 9.53W
Koury 166 Ec 12.10N 4.48W
Koussané 166 Cc 14.52N 11.15W
Kousséri 166 Ic 12.05N 15.02 E
Koutiala 160 Gg 12.23N 5.27W
Koutoumo 219b Cf 22.40S 167.32 E
Koutous 166 Hc 14.30N 10.00 E
Kouvola 114 Gf 60.52N 26.42 E
Kouyou 170 Cc 0.45S 16.38 E
Kova 138 Fe 58.20N 100.20 E
Kovač 130 Cf 43.31N 19.07 E
Kovačica 130 Dd 45.06N 20.38 E
Koval 120 Pd 52.31N 19.10 E
Kovalevka 130 Nc 46.42N 30.31 E
Kovarskas/Kavarskas 116 Ki 55.24N 25.03 E
Kovdor 136 Db 67.33N 30.25 E
Kovdozero, ozero- 114 Hc 66.47N 32.00 E
Kovel 136 Ce 51.13N 24.43 E
Kovenskaja 134 Mf 61.24N 67.39 E
Kovinskaja grjada 138 Fe 57.15N 101.00 E
Kovozero, ozero- 114 Ic 67.50N 35.10 E
Kovrov 136 Ed 56.24N 41.20 E
Kovylkino 114 Ki 54.02N 43.58 E
Kowlī Kosh, Gardaneh-ye- 146 Og 30.47N 53.12 E
Kowŏn 152 Md 39.26N 127.15 E
Kowtal-e Doh Rāh 144 Lb 36.07N 71.15 E
Kowt-e 'Ashrow 144 Kc 34.27N 68.48 E
Kōyama 156 Bf 31.19N 130.57 E
Kōya-San 156 Dd 34.13N 135.35 E
Köyceğiz 146 Cd 36.55N 28.43 E
Köycegiz Gölü 130 Lm 36.55N 28.40 E
Koyoshi-Gawa 156 Gb 39.24N 140.01 E
Koyuk 178 Gd 64.56N 161.08W
Koyukuk 174 Dc 64.56N 157.30W
Kozaklı 146 Fc 39.13N 34.49 E
Kozan 146 Fd 37.27N 35.49 E
Kozáni 130 Ei 40.18N 21.47 E
Kozara 128 Ke 45.00N 16.55 E
Kozawa 156a Bb 42.58N 140.40 E
Koze/Kose 116 Ke 59.11N 25.05 E
Kozelsk 136 Dd 54.01N 35.46 E
Koževnikovo 138 De 56.18N 84.00 E
Kozhikode → Calicut 142 Jh 11.19N 75.46 E
Kozienice 120 Re 51.35N 21.33 E
Kožim 134 Id 65.43N 59.31 E
Kožim 134 Id 65.45N 59.15 E
Kozjak 130 Eh 41.06N 21.54 E
Kozloduj 130 Gf 43.47N 23.44 E
Kozlovka 114 Li 55.52N 48.13 E
Kozlovščina 120 Vc 53.14N 25.20 E
Kozlu 146 Db 41.25N 31.46 E
Kozluk 146 Ic 38.11N 41.29 E
Koźmin 120 Ne 51.50N 17.28 E
Kozmodemjansk 114 Lh 56.20N 46.36 E
Kožozero, ozero- 114 Je 63.05N 38.05 E
Kożuchów 120 Le 51.45N 15.35 E
Kožuf 130 Fh 41.09N 22.10 E
Kōzu-Shima 152 Oe 34.15N 139.10 E
Kožva 134 Hd 65.07N 56.57 E
Kožva 134 Hd 65.10N 57.00 E
Kozyrevsk 138 Ke 55.59N 159.59 E
Kpalimé 166 Fd 6.54N 0.38 E
Kpandu 166 Fd 7.00N 0.18 E
Kpessi 166 Fd 8.04N 1.16 E
Kra, Isthmus of- (EN) = Kra, Khokhok- 140 Lh 10.20N 99.00 E
Kra, Khokhok- = Kra, Isthmus of- (EN) 140 Lh 10.20N 99.00 E
Kraba 130 Ch 41.12N 19.59 E
Krabbfjärden 116 Gf 58.45N 17.40 E
Krabi 148 Jg 8.05N 98.53 E
Krabit, Mali i- 130 Cg 42.07N 19.59 E
Kra Buri 148 Jf 10.24N 98.47 E
Krâchéh 142 Mh 12.29N 106.01 E
Kragerø 114 Bg 58.52N 9.25 E
Kragujevac 130 De 44.01N 20.55 E
Kraichbach 124 Ke 49.22N 8.31 E
Kraichgau 120 Eg 49.10N 8.50 E
Kraichtal 124 Ke 49.07N 8.46 E
Krajina 130 Fe 44.10N 22.30 E
Krajište 130 Fg 42.35N 22.25 E
Krajnovka 132 Oh 43.57N 47.24 E
Krakatau, Gunung- 140 Mj 6.07S 105.24 E
Krak des Chevaliers 146 Ge 34.46N 36.19 E
Krakovec 120 Tg 49.56N 23.13 E
Kraków 112 He 50.03N 19.58 E
Kraków [2] 120 Pf 50.05N 20.00 E
Kraków-Nowa Huta 120 Qf 50.04N 20.05 E
Krakowsko-Częstochowska, Wyżyna- 120 Pf 50.50N 19.15 E
Kralendijk 196 Bf 12.10N 68.16W
Kraljevica 128 Ie 45.16N 14.34 E
Kraljevo 130 Df 43.44N 20.43 E
Kralupy nad Vltavou 120 Kf 50.14N 14.19 E
Kramatorsk 132 Je 48.43N 37.32 E
Kramfors 114 De 62.56N 17.47 E
Krammer 124 Gc 51.38N 4.15 E
Kranenburg 124 Ic 51.47N 6.01 E
Kranidhion 130 Gl 37.23N 23.09 E
Kranj 128 Id 46.14N 14.22 E
Krapina 128 Jd 46.10N 15.53 E
Krapkowice 120 Nf 50.29N 17.56 E
Kras = Karst (EN) 110 Hf 45.48N 14.00 E
Krasavino 136 Ec 60.59N 46.28 E
Krasiczyn 120 Sg 49.48N 22.39 E
Krasilov 132 Ee 49.37N 26.59 E
Kraskino 154 Kc 42.44N 130.48 E
Kraslava/Krāslava 114 Gi 55.54N 27.10 E
Krāslava/Kraslava 114 Gi 55.54N 27.10 E
Krasnaja Poljana 132 Lh 43.40N 40.12 E
Kraśnik 120 Sf 50.56N 22.13 E
Kraśnik Fabryczny, Kraśnik- 120 Sf 50.58N 22.12 E
Kraśnik-Kraśnik Fabryczny 120 Sf 50.58N 22.12 E
Krasnoarmejsk [Kaz.] 136 Ge 53.57N 69.43 E
Krasnoarmejsk [Russia] 136 Ee 51.02N 45.42 E
Krasnoarmejsk [Ukr.] 132 Je 48.11N 37.12 E
Krasnoarmejski 138 Mc 69.37N 172.02 E
Krasnodar 112 Jf 45.02N 39.00 E
Krasnodarski kraj [3] 136 Df 45.20N 39.30 E
Krasnodon 132 Ke 48.17N 39.44 E
Krasnogorodskoje 116 Mh 56.47N 28.18 E
Krasnogorsk [Russia] 138 Jg 48.26N 142.10 E
Krasnogorsk [Russia] 114 Ii 55.51N 37.20 E
Krasnogorski 134 Ji 54.36N 61.15 E
Krasnograd 136 Df 49.22N 35.27 E
Krasnogvardejsk 135 Fe 39.45N 67.16 E
Krasnogvardejskoje 132 Lg 45.49N 41.31 E
Krasnoholmski 134 Gh 56.02N 55.05 E
Krasnoilsk 130 Ia 48.02N 25.48 E
Krasnojarsk 142 Ld 56.01N 92.50 E
Krasnojarski 134 Ik 51.58N 59.57 E
Krasnojarski kraj [3] 138 Ee 57.30N 95.00 E
Krasnojarskoje vodohranilišče 138 Ee 55.05N 91.30 E
Krasnoje 120 Ug 49.49N 24.39 E
Krasnoje Selo 114 Hg 59.43N 30.03 E
Krasnoje Znamja 135 Df 36.50N 62.29 E
Krasnokamensk 138 Gf 50.00N 118.05 E
Krasnokamsk 136 Fd 58.04N 55.45 E
Krasnokutsk 136 He 52.59N 75.59 E
Krasnolesje 116 Jj 54.23N 22.25 E
Krasnolesny 132 Kd 51.52N 39.35 E
Krasnooktjabrski [Kyrg.] 135 Jc 42.45N 74.20 E
Krasnooktjabrski [Russia] 114 Lh 56.43N 47.37 E
Krasnooskolskoje vodohranilišče 132 Je 49.25N 37.35 E
Krasnoostrovski 116 Md 60.12N 28.39 E
Krasnoperekopsk 136 Df 45.57N 33.47 E
Krasnorečenski 154 Mb 44.38N 135.15 E
Krasnoščelje 114 Ic 67.23N 37.02 E
Krasnoselki 120 Uc 53.14N 24.30 E
Krasnoselkup 138 Dc 65.41N 82.28 E
Krasnoslobodsk [Russia] 114 Ki 54.27N 43.47 E
Krasnoslobodsk [Russia] 132 Ne 48.40N 44.31 E
Krasnoturinsk 136 Gd 59.46N 60.18 E
Krasnoufimsk 136 Fd 56.37N 57.46 E
Krasnouralsk 136 Gd 58.24N 60.03 E
Krasnousolski 136 Fe 53.54N 56.29 E
Krasnovišersk 136 Fc 60.23N 57.03 E
Krasnovodsk 142 He 40.00N 53.00 E
Krasnovodski poluostrov 110 Lg 40.30N 53.15 E
Krasnovodski zaliv 132 Rj 39.50N 53.15 E
Krasnozatonski 136 Fc 61.41N 51.01 E
Krasnozavodsk 114 Jh 56.29N 38.13 E
Krasnoznamensk [Kaz.] 136 Ge 51.03N 69.30 E
Krasnoznamensk [Russia] 116 Jj 54.52N 22.27 E
Krasny Čikoj 138 Ff 50.25N 108.45 E
Krasny Holm 114 Ig 58.04N 37.09 E
Krasny Jar [Russia] 138 De 57.07N 84.40 E
Krasny Jar [Russia] 136 Hd 55.14N 72.56 E
Krasnyje Barrikady 132 Of 46.13N 47.50 E
Krasnyje Okny 130 Mb 47.34N 29.23 E
Krasny Kut 136 Ee 50.58N 46.58 E
Krasny Liman 132 Je 48.59N 37.47 E
Krasny Luč 132 Ke 48.09N 38.57 E
Krasny Oktjabr 136 Gd 55.37N 64.48 E
Krasny Profintern 114 Jh 57.47N 40.29 E
Krasnystaw 120 Tf 50.59N 23.10 E
Krasny Sulin 132 Lf 47.53N 40.09 E
Kratovo 130 Fg 42.05N 22.12 E
Kraulshavn 179 Gd 74.10N 57.00W
Krawang 150 Eh 6.19S 107.17 E
Krefeld 120 Ce 51.20N 6.34 E
Krefeld-Hüls 124 Ic 51.22N 6.31 E
Kremastá, Límni- 130 Ek 38.50N 21.30 E

Index Symbols

[1] Independent Nation
[2] State, Region
[3] District, County
[4] Municipality
[5] Colony, Dependency
Continent
Physical Region
Historical or Cultural Region
Mount, Mountain
Volcano
Hill
Mountains, Mountain Range
Hills, Escarpment
Plateau, Upland
Pass, Gap
Plain, Lowland
Delta
Salt Flat
Valley, Canyon
Crater, Cave
Karst Features
Depression
Polder
Desert, Dunes
Forest, Woods
Heath, Steppe
Oasis
Cape, Point
Coast, Beach
Cliff
Peninsula
Isthmus
Sandbank
Island
Atoll
Rock, Reef
Islands, Archipelago
Rocks, Reefs
Coral Reef
Well, Spring
Geyser
River, Stream
Waterfall, Rapids
River Mouth, Estuary
Lake
Salt Lake
Intermittent Lake
Reservoir
Swamp, Pond
Canal
Glacier
Ice Shelf, Pack Ice
Ocean
Sea
Gulf, Bay
Strait, Fjord
Lagoon
Bank
Seamount
Tablemount
Ridge
Shelf
Basin
Escarpment, Sea Scarp
Fracture
Trench, Abyss
National Park, Reserve
Point of Interest
Recreation Site
Cave, Cavern
Historic Site
Ruins
Wall, Walls
Church, Abbey
Temple
Scientific Station
Railway station
Airport
Port
Military installation
Lighthouse
Mine
Tunnel
Dam, Bridge

Kremenchug Reservoir (EN) = Kremenčugskoje vodohranilišče ≈	110	Jf	49.20N	32.30 E
Kremenčug	112	Jf	49.04N	33.25 E
Kremenčugskoje vodohranilišče = Kremenchug Reservoir (EN) ≈	110	Jf	49.20N	32.30 E
Kremenec	132	Dd	50.06N	25.43 E
Kremennaja	132	Ke	49.03N	38.14 E
Kremmling	186	Cf	40.03N	106.24W
Krems ~	128	Jb	48.25N	15.36 E
Krems an der Donau	128	Jb	48.25N	15.36 E
Kremsmünster	128	Ib	48.03N	14.08 E
Krenitzin Islands ◈	178a	Eb	54.08N	166.00W
Kresta, zaliv- ◧	138	Nc	65.30N	179.00W
Krestcy	114	Hg	58.15N	32.31 E
Krestovy, pereval- ∪	132	Nh	42.32N	44.30 E
Kretek	150	Fh	7.59 S	110.19 E
Kretinga	114	Ei	55.55N	21.17 E
Kreuzau	124	Id	50.45N	6.29 E
Kreuzberg ▲	120	Ff	50.22N	9.58 E
Kreuzlingen	128	Dc	47.39N	9.10 E
Kreuztal	120	Df	50.58N	7.59 E
Kría Vrísi	130	Fi	40.41N	22.18 E
Kribi	160	Hh	2.57N	9.55 E
Kričev	136	De	53.43N	31.43 E
Kričim	130	Hg	42.08N	24.31 E
Krim ▲	128	Ie	45.56N	14.28 E
Krimml	128	Gc	47.13N	12.11 E
Krimpen aan den IJssel	124	Gc	51.55N	4.35 E
Kriós, Ákra- ▶	110	Ih	35.14N	23.35 E
Krishna ~	140	Kh	15.57N	80.59 E
Krishnanagar	148	Hd	23.24N	88.30 E
Kristdala	116	Gg	57.24N	16.11 E
Kristiansand	112	Gd	58.10N	8.00 E
Kristianstad	114	Dh	56.02N	14.08 E
Kristianstad [2]	114	Ch	56.15N	14.00 E
Kristiansund	112	Gc	63.07N	7.45 E
Kristiinankaupunki/ Kristinestad	114	Ee	62.17N	21.23 E
Kristineberg	114	Ed	65.04N	18.35 E
Kristinehamn	114	Dg	59.20N	14.07 E
Kristinestad/ Kristiinankaupunki	114	Ee	62.17N	21.23 E
Kríti = Crete (EN) [2]	130	Hn	35.35N	25.00 E
Kríti = Crete (EN) ◆	110	Ih	35.15N	24.45 E
Kritikón Pélagos = Crete, Sea of- (EN) ☰	130	Hn	36.00N	25.00 E
Krivaja ~	128	Mf	44.27N	18.10 E
Kriva Palanka	130	Fg	42.12N	22.21 E
Kriviči	116	Lj	54.44N	27.20 E
Krivodol	130	Gf	43.23N	23.29 E
Krivoje Ozero	132	Gf	47.57N	30.21 E
Krivoj Rog	112	Jf	47.54N	33.21 E
Križevci	128	Kd	46.02N	16.32 E
Krk	128	Ie	45.02N	14.35 E
Krk ◆	128	Ie	45.05N	14.35 E
Krka [Slo.]	128	Je	45.53N	15.36 E
Krka [Cro.]	128	Jg	43.43N	15.51 E
Krkonoše	120	Lf	50.46N	15.35 E
Krn ▲	128	Hd	46.16N	13.40 E
Krndija ⛰	128	Le	45.27N	17.55 E
Krnjača, Beograd-	130	De	44.52N	20.28 E
Krnov	120	Nf	50.05N	17.41 E
Krobia	120	Me	51.47N	16.58 E
Krøderen ≈	116	Cd	60.15N	9.40 E
Krokeaí	130	Fm	36.53N	22.33 E
Krokek	116	Gf	58.40N	16.24 E
Kroken	114	Dd	65.22N	14.16 E
Krokom	114	De	63.20N	14.28 E
Krolevec	132	Hd	51.32N	33.30 E
Kroměříž	120	Ng	49.18N	17.22 E
Krompachy	120	Qh	48.56N	20.52 E
Kronach	120	Hf	50.14N	11.19 E
Krŏng Kaôh Kŏng	148	Kf	11.37N	102.59 E
Kronoberg [2]	114	Dh	56.40N	14.40 E
Kronockaja Sopka, vulkan- ▲	138	Lf	54.47N	160.35 E
Kronocki, mys- ▶	138	Lf	54.43N	162.07 E
Kronocki zaliv ◧	138	Lf	54.00N	161.00 E
Kronoki	138	Lf	54.33N	161.14 E
Kronprins Christian Land ⊠	179	Jb	80.45N	22.00W
Kronprinsesse Mærtha Kyst ⊞	222	Bf	72.00 S	7.30W
Kronprins Frederiks Bjerge ⛰	179	Ie	67.20N	34.00W
Kronprins Olav Kyst ⊞	222	Ee	68.30 S	42.30 E
Kronštadt	136	Cc	60.01N	29.44 E
Kroonstad	160	Jk	27.46S	27.12 E
Kropotkin [Russia]	136	Ef	45.26N	40.34 E
Kropotkin [Russia]	138	Ge	58.36N	115.27 E
Kroppefjäll ▲	116	Ef	58.40N	12.13 E
Krośniewice	120	Pd	52.16N	19.10 E
Krosno	120	Rg	49.42N	21.46 E
Krosno [2]	120	Rg	49.40N	21.45 E
Krosno Odrzańskie	120	Ld	52.04N	15.05 E
Krossfjorden ≋	116	Ad	60.10N	5.05 E
Krotoszyn	120	Ne	51.42N	17.26 E
Kroviga, gora- ▲	138	Ed	60.40N	91.30 E
Krško	128	Je	45.58N	15.28 E
Krstača ▲	130	Dg	42.58N	20.08 E
Krugersdorp	160	Jk	26.05 S	27.35 E
Krui	150	Dh	5.11 S	103.56 E
Kruibeke	124	Gc	50.10N	4.19 E
Kruiningen	124	Gc	51.27N	4.02 E
Kruja	130	Ch	41.30N	19.48 E
Krulevščina	116	Li	55.03N	27.52 E
Krumbach	120	Gh	48.15N	10.22 E
Krumovgrad	130	Ih	41.28N	25.39 E
Krung Thep = Bangkok (EN)	142	Mh	13.45N	100.31 E
Krupanj	130	Ce	44.22N	19.22 E
Krupinica ~	120	Oh	48.05N	18.54 E
Krupinská vrchovina ◓	120	Ph	48.20N	19.15 E
Kruså	116	Cj	54.50N	9.25 E
Krušedol ✝	130	Cd	45.07N	19.57 E
Kruševac	130	Ef	43.35N	21.20 E
Kruševo	130	Eh	41.22N	21.15 E
Krušné Hory = Ore Mountains (EN) ⛰	110	He	50.30N	13.15 E
Krustpils	116	Lh	56.29N	26.00 E
Kruzof ◆	178	Le	57.10N	135.40W
Krym	132	Jg	45.23N	36.36 E
Krym, respublika	136	Dg	45.15N	34.20 E
Krymsk	136	Dg	44.54N	37.57 E
Krymskije gory = Crimean Mountains (EN) ⛰	110	Jg	44.45N	34.30 E
Krymski poluostrov = Crimea (EN) ▭	110	Jf	45.00N	34.00 E
Krynica	120	Qg	49.25N	20.56 E
Krzemieniucha ▲	120	Sb	54.12N	22.54 E
Krzepice	120	Of	50.58N	18.44 E
Krzna ~	120	Td	52.08N	23.31 E
Krzywiń	120	Me	51.58N	16.49 E
Krzyż	120	Md	52.53N	16.01 E
Ksar el Boukhari	162	Hb	35.53N	2.45 E
Ksar el Kebir	162	Fc	35.00N	5.59W
Ksar es Srhir	126	Gi	35.51N	5.34W
Ksenjevka	138	Gf	53.34N	118.44 E
Kšenski	132	Jd	51.52N	37.44 E
Ksour, Monts des- ⛰	162	Gc	32.45N	0.10W
Kū', Wādī al- ~	168	Dc	12.12N	25.43 E
Kuai He ~	154	Dh	33.09N	117.32 E
Kuala Belait	150	Ff	4.35N	114.11 E
Kuala Dungun	150	Df	4.47N	103.26 E
Kuala Kangsar	150	Df	4.46N	100.56 E
Kualakapuas	150	Fg	3.01 S	114.21 E
Kuala Kerai	150	De	5.32N	102.12 E
Kualakurun	150	Fg	1.07 S	113.53 E
Kualalangsa	150	Cf	4.32N	98.01 E
Kuala Lipis	150	Df	4.11N	102.03 E
Kuala Lumpur	142	Mi	3.10N	101.42 E
Kuala Lumpur [2]	150	Df	3.14N	101.40 E
Kuala Pilah	150	Df	2.44N	102.15 E
Kuala Rompin	150	Df	2.49N	103.29 E
Kuala Terengganu	142	Mi	5.20N	103.08 E
Kuancheng	154	Ed	40.37N	118.31 E
Kuandang	150	Hf	0.52N	122.55 E
Kuandian	152	Lc	40.45N	124.48 E
Kuang-hsi-chuang-tsu Tzu-chih-ch'ü → Guangxi Zhuangzu Zizhiqu [2]	152	Ig	24.00N	109.00 E
Kuang-tung Sheng → Guangdong Sheng [2]	152	Jg	23.00N	113.00 E
Kuantan	150	Df	3.48N	103.20 E
Kuba	136	Eg	41.20N	48.35 E
Kuban ~	110	Jf	45.20N	37.30 E
Kuba-Shima ◆	156b	Ab	26.10N	127.15 E
Kubaysah	146	Jf	33.35N	42.37 E
Kubbum	168	Cc	11.47N	23.47 E
Kubena ~	114	Jg	59.37N	39.48 E
Kubenskoje, ozero- ≈	114	Jg	59.40N	39.30 E
Kubnja ~	114	Li	55.32N	48.28 E
Kubokawa	154	Lh	33.12N	133.08 E
Kubolta ~	130	Lb	47.48N	28.03 E
Kubrat	130	Jf	43.48N	26.30 E
Kubumesaai	150	Gf	1.31N	115.06 E
Kučaj ⛰	130	Ef	43.53N	21.44 E
Kučevo	130	Ee	44.29N	21.41 E
Kuching	142	Ni	1.33N	110.20 E
Kuchinotsu	156	Be	32.36N	130.12 E
Kuçova (Qyteti Stalin)	130	Ci	40.48N	19.54 E
Kuçukçekmece	130	Li	40.59N	28.46 E
Küçükerenköy	146	Ee	35.22N	33.45 E
Küçükkuyu	130	Jj	39.32N	26.36 E
Küçuk Menderes ~	130	Kl	37.57N	27.16 E
Kučurgan ~	130	Mc	46.35N	29.55 E
Kudaka-Jima ◆	156b	Ab	26.10N	127.54 E
Kudamatsu	156	Bd	34.01N	131.53 E
Kudat	150	Ge	6.53N	116.50 E
Kudeb ~	116	Mg	57.30N	28.16 E
Kudirkos-Naumestis	116	Jj	54.43N	22.49 E
Kudowa Zdrój	120	Mf	50.27N	16.20 E
Kudremukh ▲	148	Ff	13.08N	75.16 E
Kudus	150	Fh	6.48 S	110.50 E
Kudymkar	136	Fd	59.01N	54.37 E
Kuee Ruins ⊡	221a	Fd	19.12N	155.23W
Kuei-chou Sheng → Guizhou Sheng = Kweichow (EN) [2]	152	If	27.00N	107.00 E
Kufi ~	146	Cc	38.10N	29.43 E
Kufrah, Wāḩāt al- = Kufra Oasis (EN) 🌴	158	Jf	24.10N	23.15 E
Kufra Oasis (EN) = Kufrah, Wāḩāt al- 🌴	158	Jf	24.10N	23.15 E
Kufstein	128	Gc	47.35N	12.10 E
Kuganavolok	114	Ie	62.16N	36.55 E
Kugmallit Bay ◧	180	Ec	69.30N	133.20W
Kugojeja ~	132	Kf	46.33N	39.38 E
Kūh, Ra's al- ▶	144	Id	25.48N	57.19 E
Kuḩaylī	168	Eb	19.29N	32.49 E
Kūhbonān	146	Qg	31.23N	56.19 E
Kūhdasht	146	Lf	33.32N	47.36 E
Kūh-e Būrh ▲	146	Pi	27.22N	54.40 E
Kūh-e Gāvbūs ⛰	146	Oi	27.10N	54.00 E
Kūh-e Karkas ▲	146	Nf	33.27N	51.48 E
Kūh-e Kārūn ▲	146	Ng	31.27N	50.18 E
Kūhestak	146	Qi	26.47N	57.02 E
Kūhīn, Gardaneh-ye- ∪	146	Md	36.23N	49.37 E
Kühlungsborn	120	Hb	54.09N	11.43 E
Kuhmo	114	Gd	64.08N	29.31 E
Kuhmoinen	116	Kc	61.34N	25.11 E
Kuhn ◆	179	Kd	74.45N	19.45W
Kūhpāyeh ▲	144	Ic	30.35N	57.15 E
Kūhpāyeh [Iran]	146	Qg	30.43N	57.30 E
Kūhpāyeh [Iran]	146	Of	32.43N	52.26 E
Kūhrān, Kūh-e- ▲	144	Id	26.46N	58.12 E
Kuhtuj ~	138	Je	59.23N	143.10 E
Kuhva ~	116	Mg	57.17N	28.17 E
Kuiseb ~	172	Ad	23.00 S	14.33 E
Kuishan Ding ▲	152	Ig	22.32N	109.52 E
Kuito	160	Ij	12.23 S	16.56 E
Kuiu ◆	178	Me	57.45N	134.10W
Kuivaniemi	114	Fd	65.35N	25.11 E
Kujang	152	Md	39.52N	126.01 E
Kujawy ⊟	120	Od	52.45N	18.30 E
Kujbyšev [Russia] → Samara	112	Le	53.12N	50.09 E
Kujbyšev [Russia] → Bulgar	114	Li	55.01N	49.06 E
Kujbyšev [Russia]	138	Ce	55.27N	78.29 E
Kujbyševskaja oblast	136	Fe	53.20N	50.30 E
Kujbyševski [Kaz.]	136	Ge	53.15N	65.51 E
Kujbyševski [Taj.]	135	Gf	37.53N	68.44 E
Kujbyševskoje vodohranilišče = Kuybyshev Reservoir (EN)	110	Ke	53.50N	49.00 E
Kujeda	134	Gh	56.26N	55.35 E
Kujgan	136	Hf	45.22N	74.10 E
Kuji	154	Pd	40.11N	141.46 E
Kuji-Gawa ~	156	Gi	36.30N	140.37 E
Kujtun	138	Ff	54.21N	101.35 E
Kujūkuri-Hama ⊞	156	Gd	35.40N	140.30 E
Kujū-San ▲	154	Kh	33.09N	131.15 E
Kūkalār, Kūh-e- ▲	146	Ng	31.50N	50.53 E
Kukalaya, Río- ~	194	Fg	13.39N	83.37W
Kukësi	130	Dg	42.05N	20.24 E
Kukkia ≈	116	Kc	61.20N	24.40 E
Kukmor	114	Mh	56.13N	50.52 E
Kükürt Tepe ▲	146	Ib	41.07N	41.27 E
Kūl ~	144	Id	27.15N	55.52 E
Kula [Bul.]	130	Ff	43.53N	22.31 E
Kula [Tur.]	146	Cc	38.30N	28.40 E
Kula [Yugo.]	130	Cd	45.37N	19.32 E
Kulai	150	Df	1.40N	103.36 E
Kulanak	135	Jd	41.18N	75.34 E
Kulandy	136	Ff	46.08N	59.31 E
Kular	138	Ib	70.32N	134.26 E
Kular, hrebet- ⛰	138	Ic	69.00N	133.30 E
Kulata	130	Gh	41.23N	23.22 E
Kulautuva	116	Jj	54.55N	23.43 E
Kulbus	168	Cc	14.24N	22.31 E
Kuldiga/Kuldīga	136	Cd	56.59N	21.59 E
Kuldīga/Kuldiga	136	Cd	56.59N	21.59 E
Kuldur	138	Ig	49.10N	131.40 E
Kulebaki	114	Ki	55.26N	42.32 E
Kulenjin	146	Me	35.40N	49.30 E
Kulen Vakuf	128	Kf	44.33N	16.06 E
Kulgera	210	Eg	25.50 S	133.18 E
Kulikov	120	Ug	49.55N	24.06 E
Kulim	150	De	5.22N	100.34 E
Kuljab	136	Gh	37.55N	69.47 E
Kuljabskaja oblast [3]	136	Gh	38.00N	69.40 E
Kullaa	116	Jc	61.28N	22.10 E
Kullen ▶	114	Ch	56.18N	12.26 E
Kulmasa	166	Ed	9.35N	2.27W
Kulmbach	120	Hf	50.06N	11.27 E
Kuloj [Russia]	114	Kf	61.03N	42.30 E
Kuloj [Russia]	114	Kf	61.01N	42.12 E
Kulp	146	Ic	38.30N	41.02 E
Kulsary	136	Ff	46.57N	54.02 E
Kultuk	138	Ff	51.44N	103.42 E
Kulu ~	138	Jd	62.15N	147.45 E
Kulu [India]	148	Fb	31.58N	77.06 E
Kulu [Tur.]	146	Ei	39.06N	33.05 E
Kulumadau	219a	Ac	9.03 S	152.43 E
Kulunda	138	Cf	52.35N	78.57 E
Kulundinskaja step ◓	138	Cf	52.45N	79.00 E
Kulundinskoje, ozero- ≈	138	Cf	53.00N	79.30 E
Kum ~	146	Bc	38.38N	27.32 E
Kum, Kūh-e- ▲	146	Oh	29.55N	53.45 E
Kuma	156	Ce	33.39N	132.54 E
Kuma [Russia]	134	Mg	59.33N	66.40 E
Kuma [Eur.]	110	Kg	44.56N	47.00 E
Kumagaya	154	Of	36.08N	139.23 E
Kumai [Indon.]	150	Fg	3.23S	112.33 E
Kumai [Indon.]	150	Fg	2.44S	111.43 E
Kumaishi	156a	Ab	42.08N	139.59 E
Kumajri (Leninakan)	112	Kg	40.47N	43.50 E
Kumak	132	Vd	51.13N	60.08 E
Kumamoto	142	Pf	32.48N	130.43 E
Kumamoto Ken [2]	154	Kh	32.30N	130.50 E
Kumano	154	Nh	33.54N	136.05 E
Kumano-Gawa ~	156	De	33.45N	135.59 E
Kumano-Nada ☰	156	Ee	34.00N	136.30 E
Kumanovo	130	Eg	42.08N	21.43 E
Kumara [N.Z.]	218	De	42.38S	171.11 E
Kumara [Russia]	138	Hf	51.35N	126.45 E
Kumasi	160	Gh	6.41N	1.37W
Kumba	166	Ge	4.38N	9.25 E
Kumbakonam	148	Ff	10.58N	79.23 E
Kumbe	150	Lh	8.21 S	140.13 E
Kumbo	166	Hd	6.12N	10.40 E
Kumboro Cape ▶	219a	Cb	7.18 S	157.32 E
Kūmch'ŏn	154	Ie	38.10N	126.30 E
Kum-Dag	136	Fh	39.13N	54.40 E
Kumdah	164	Ie	20.23N	45.05 E
Kume-Jima ◆	152	Mf	26.20N	126.45 E
Kumertau → Jermolajevo	136	Fe	52.46N	55.47 E
Kumhwa	154	Ie	38.17N	127.28 E
Kumihama	156	Dd	35.36N	134.54 E
Kuminski	136	Gd	58.40N	65.55 E
Kumköy (Kilyos)	130	Mh	41.15N	29.02 E
Kumkuduk	152	Fc	40.15N	91.55 E
Kumkurgan	135	Ff	37.50N	67.35 E
Kumla	114	Dg	59.08N	15.08 E
Kumlinge ◆	116	Id	60.15N	20.45 E
Kumluca	146	Dd	36.22N	30.18 E
Kummerower See ≈	120	Ic	53.49N	12.52 E
Kumo/Kokemäki	114	Ff	61.15N	22.21 E
Kumola ~	135	Fa	46.58N	64.30 E
Kumo-Manyčski kanal ═	132	Ng	45.27N	44.38 E
Kumon Taung ⛰	140	Lg	26.30N	96.50 E
Kumora	138	Ge	55.56N	111.13 E
Kumru	146	Gb	40.53N	37.17 E
Kumu	170	Eb	3.04N	25.09 E
Kumuh	132	Oh	42.11N	47.07 E
Kumukahi, Cape- ▶	214	Od	19.31N	154.49W
Kumul/Hami	142	Le	42.48N	93.27 E
Kümüx	152	Ec	42.15N	88.10 E
Kumzār	146	Qj	26.20N	56.25 E
Kunashiri-Tō / Kunašir, ostrov- ◆	140	Qe	44.05N	145.51 E
Kunašir, ostrov- / Kunashiri-Tō ◆	140	Qe	44.05N	145.51 E
Kunaširski proliv = Nemuro Strait (EN) ≋	138	Jh	43.50N	145.30 E
Kunchaung	148	Jd	23.50N	96.35 E
Kunda	114	Gg	59.30N	26.30 E
Kunda jōgi ~	116	Le	59.25N	26.27 E
Kundelungu, Monts- ⛰	170	Ed	9.30 S	28.00 E
Kundiawa	212	Ia	6.00 S	145.00 E
Kunduchi	170	Gd	6.40 S	39.13 E
Kunduk → Kogilnik ~	130	Md	45.51N	29.38 E
Kunduk → Sasyk, ozero- ≈	132	Fg	45.45N	29.40 E
Kunene ~	158	Ij	17.20 S	11.50 E
Kunene (EN) = Cunene ~	158	Ij	17.20 S	11.50 E
Künes/Xinyuan	152	Dc	43.24N	83.18 E
Künes He ~	152	Dc	43.32N	82.29 E
Kungälv	114	Ch	57.52N	11.58 E
Kungej-Alatau, hrebet- ⛰	136	Hg	42.50N	77.15 E
Kûngmiut	179	Ie	65.50N	36.45W
Kungrad	136	Fg	43.06N	58.54 E
Kungsbacka	114	Ch	57.29N	12.04 E
Kungsbackafjorden ◧	116	Eg	57.25N	12.04 E
Kungshamn	116	Df	58.21N	11.15 E
Kungsör	116	Ge	59.25N	16.05 E
Kungu	170	Cb	2.47N	19.12 E
Kungur	136	Fd	57.25N	56.57 E
Kunhegyes	120	Qi	47.22N	20.38 E
Kunhing	148	Jd	21.18N	98.26 E
Kunigami-Misaki ▶	156b	Bb	27.26N	128.43 E
Kunimi-Dake ▲	156	Be	32.33N	131.01 E
Kunisaki	156	Be	33.34N	131.45 E
Kunisaki-Hantō ▭	156	Be	33.30N	131.40 E
Kunja ~	114	Hh	57.09N	31.10 E
Kunja-Urgenč	136	Fg	42.20N	59.12 E
Kunlong	148	Jd	23.25N	98.39 E
Kunlun Guan ∪	152	Ig	23.06N	108.40 E
Kunlun Shan ⛰	140	Kf	36.00N	84.00 E
Kunlun Shankou ∪	152	Fd	35.40N	94.03 E
Kunming	142	Mg	25.08N	102.43 E
Kunnui	156a	Bb	42.26N	140.19 E
Kunovat ~	134	Ld	64.59N	65.35 E
Kunsan	152	Md	35.59N	126.43 E
Kunshan	154	Fi	31.22N	120.57 E
Kuntaur	166	Cc	13.40N	14.53W
Kununurra	212	Fc	15.47 S	128.44 E
Kunyao	170	Gb	1.47N	35.03 E
Kunyu Shan ▲	154	Ff	37.15N	121.46 E
Künzelsau	120	Fg	49.17N	9.41 E
Kuohijärvi ≈	116	Kc	61.15N	24.55 E
Kuolimo ≈	116	Lc	61.15N	27.35 E
Kuop Atoll ◎	208	Gd	7.03N	151.56 E
Kuopio	112	Ic	62.54N	27.41 E
Kuopio [2]	114	Ge	63.20N	27.35 E
Kuorboaivi ⌒	114	Gb	69.41N	27.45 E
Kuortane	116	Jb	62.48N	23.30 E
Kupa ~	128	Ke	45.28N	16.24 E
Kupang	142	Ok	10.10S	123.35 E
Kupiano	214	Dj	10.10S	148.02 E
Kupičev	120	Uf	50.58N	24.52 E
Kupino	138	Cf	54.22N	77.18 E
Kupiškis	114	Fi	55.49N	25.01 E
Kupjansk	136	Df	49.42N	37.37 E
Kupjansk-Uzlovoj	132	Je	49.39N	37.45 E
Küplü [Tur.]	130	Jh	41.07N	26.21 E
Küplü [Tur.]	130	Mi	40.06N	30.00 E
Kuppenheim	124	Kf	48.50N	8.15 E
Kupreanof ◆	178	Me	56.50N	133.30W
Kuqa	142	Ke	41.43N	82.57 E
Kura [Russia]	132	Mh	44.05B	44.45 E
Kura [Eur.]	110	Kh	39.20N	49.25 E
Kuragaty ~	135	Ic	43.55N	73.34 E
Kuragino	138	Ef	53.53N	92.40 E
Kurahashi-Jima ◆	156	Cd	34.08N	132.31 E
Kuraminski hrebet ⛰	135	Hd	40.50N	70.30 E
Kurashiki	154	Lg	34.35N	133.46 E
Kurashiki-Kojima	156	Cd	34.28N	133.48 E
Kurashiki-Tamashima	156	Cd	34.33N	133.40 E
Kura-Take ▲	156	Be	32.27N	130.20 E
Kuraymah = Karima (EN)	160	Kg	18.33N	31.51 E
Kurayoshi	154	Lg	35.28N	133.49 E
Kurbneshi	130	Dh	41.47N	20.05 E
Kurčatov	132	Id	51.41N	35.42 E
Kurdaj	135	Jc	43.18N	74.59 E
Kurdistan ⊠	140	Gf	37.00N	44.00 E
Kurdistan ⊟	144	Fb	37.00N	44.00 E
Kurdufān ⊠	158	Jg	13.00N	30.00 E
Kurdufān al Janūbīyah [3]	168	Dc	11.00N	29.30 E
Kurdufān ash Shamālīyah [3]	168	Dc	14.50N	29.40 E
Kure	154	Lg	34.14N	132.34 E
Küre	146	Eb	41.48N	33.43 E
Kure Island ◆	208	Jb	28.25N	178.25W
Kurejka ~	140	Kc	66.25N	87.12 E
Kuresaare (Kingissepp)	136	Cd	58.17N	22.29 E
Kurgaldžinski	136	He	50.30N	70.03 E
Kurgan	142	Id	55.26N	65.18 E
Kurganinsk	132	Lg	44.57N	40.35 E
Kurganskaja oblast [3]	136	Gd	55.00N	65.00 E
Kurgan-Tjube	136	Gh	37.51N	68.46 E
Kurgan-Tjubinskaja oblast [3]	136	Gh	37.30N	68.30 E
Kuria Island ◆	208	Id	0.14N	173.25 E
Kuria Muria Islands (EN) = Khurīyā Murīyā, Jazā'ir ◈	140	Hh	17.30N	56.00 E
Kuri Bay	212	Ec	15.35 S	124.50 E
Kurikka	114	Fe	62.37N	22.25 E
Kurikoma	156	Gb	38.50N	140.59 E
Kurikoma-Yama ▲	156	Gb	38.57N	140.47 E
Kuril Basin (EN) ∨	138	Jg	47.00N	150.00 E
Kuril Islands (EN) = Kurilskije ostrova ◈	140	Re	46.10N	152.00 E
Kurilo	130	Gg	42.49N	23.21 E
Kurilsk	138	Jg	45.16N	147.58 E
Kurilskije ostrova = Kuril Islands (EN) ◈	140	Re	46.10N	152.00 E
Kuril Trench (EN) ∨	106	Je	47.00N	155.00 E
Kuring Kuru	172	Bc	17.38 S	18.33 E
Kurino	156	Bf	31.57N	130.43 E
Kurinskaja kosa ⊞	132	Pj	39.05N	49.10 E
Kurinwás, Río- ~	194	Fg	12.49N	83.41W
Kuriyama	156a	Bb	43.03N	141.45 E
Kūrkhūd, Kūh-e- ▲	146	Qd	37.15N	56.30 E
Kurkosa	132	Pj	38.59N	49.08 E
Kurkūmā, Ra's- ▶	146	Gj	25.51N	36.39 E
Kurkur	146	Ek	23.54N	32.19 E
Kurlovski	114	Ji	55.29N	40.39 E
Kurmuk	168	Ec	10.33N	34.17 E
Kurnool	142	Jh	15.50N	78.03 E
Kurobe	154	Nf	36.51N	137.26 E
Kurobe-Gawa ~	156	Ec	36.55N	137.26 E
Kurogi	156	Be	33.14N	130.40 E
Kuroishi	154	Pd	40.38N	140.36 E
Kuroiso	154	Pf	36.58N	140.03 E
Kuromatsunai	154	Pc	42.43N	140.20 E
Kurono-Seto ≋	156	Be	32.05N	130.10 E
Kurort Družba	130	Kf	43.12N	28.00 E
Kurort Slănčev brjag	130	Kg	42.40N	27.42 E
Kurort Zlatni pjasăci	130	Lf	43.16N	28.02 E
Kuro-Shima ◆	154	Ji	31.52N	129.58 E
Kurovskoje	114	Ji	55.35N	38.59 E
Kurów	120	Se	51.25N	22.10 E
Kurow	216	Dh	44.44 S	170.28 E
Kurpiowska, Puszcza- ♣	120	Rc	53.20N	21.30 E
Kuršėnai/Kuršenaj	136	Cd	56.03N	22.58 E
Kuršenaj/Kuršėnai	136	Cd	56.03N	22.58 E
Kuršiu užūrekis ◧	116	Ii	55.05N	21.00 E
Kursk	112	Je	51.42N	36.12 E
Kurskaja kosa ⊞	114	Ei	55.18N	21.00 E
Kurskaja oblast [3]	136	De	51.45N	36.15 E
Kurski zaliv ◧	114	Ei	55.05N	21.00 E
Kuršumlija	130	Ef	43.09N	21.16 E
Kurtalan	146	Id	37.57N	41.42 E
Kurtamyš	136	Ge	54.55N	64.27 E
Kūrtī	160	Kg	18.07N	31.33 E
Kurtistown	221	Fd	19.36N	155.04W
Kurty ~	135	Kb	44.19N	76.42 E
Kuru ~	168	Dd	9.08N	26.57 E
Kurucaşile	146	Eb	41.51N	32.43 E
Kuruktag ⛰	152	Ec	41.30N	89.00 E
Kuruman	160	Jk	27.28 S	23.28 E
Kuruman ~	158	Jk	26.56 S	20.39 E
Kurume	154	Kh	33.19N	130.31 E
Kurunegala	148	Gg	7.29N	80.22 E
Kurur, Jabal- ▲	168	Ea	20.31N	31.32 E
Kurzeme = Courland (EN) ⊠	110	Id	56.50N	22.00 E
Kurzemes Augstiene / Kurzemskaja vozvyšennost ◓	116	Jh	56.45N	22.15 E
Kurzemskaja vozvyšennost / Kurzemes Augstiene ◓	116	Jh	56.45N	22.15 E
Kusa	134	Ii	55.20N	59.29 E
Kuşada Körfezi ◧	130	Kl	37.50N	27.08 E
Kuşadasi	146	Bd	37.51N	27.15 E
Kusagaki-Guntō ◈	152	Me	31.00N	129.00 E
Kusaie → Kosrae ◆	208	Hd	5.19N	162.59 E
Kusalu/Kuusalu	116	Ke	59.23N	25.25 E
Kusary	132	Pi	41.24N	48.29 E
Kusatsu [Jap.]	156	Fc	36.37N	138.35 E
Kusatsu [Jap.]	156	Dd	35.03N	135.59 E
Kuščevskaja	132	Kf	46.33N	39.37 E
Kuščinski	132	Oi	40.33N	46.06 E
Kusel	124	Je	49.33N	7.24 E
Kuş Gölü ≈	146	Bb	40.10N	27.59 E
Kushida-Gawa ~	156	Ed	34.36N	136.34 E
Kushikino	154	Ki	31.44N	130.16 E
Kushima	154	Ki	31.29N	131.14 E
Kushimoto	154	Mh	33.28N	135.47 E
Kushiro	142	Qe	42.58N	144.23 E
Kushiro-Gawa ~	156a	Db	42.59N	144.23 E
Kushtia	148	Hd	23.55N	89.07 E
Kuška	135	Dg	35.16N	62.18 E
Kuskokwim ~	174	Cc	60.17N	162.27W
Kuskokwim Bay ◧	174	Cd	59.45N	162.25W
Kuskokwim Mountains ⛰	174	Dc	62.30N	156.00W
Kušmurun	136	Ge	52.27N	64.40 E
Kušmurun, ozero- ≈	136	Ge	52.40N	64.45 E
Kušnarenkovo	134	Gi	55.06N	55.22 E
Kušnica	132	Ce	48.29N	23.20 E
Kusŏng	152	Md	39.59N	125.16 E
Kussharo Ko ≈	154	Rc	43.35N	144.15 E
Kustanaj	142	Id	53.10N	63.35 E
Kustanajskaja oblast [3]	136	Ge	53.00N	64.00 E
Kustavi/Gustavs	116	Id	60.33N	21.21 E
Kustavi/Gustavs ◆	116	Id	60.30N	21.25 E
Küstenkanal ═	120	Dc	53.08N	7.40 E
Kūstī	160	Kg	13.10N	32.40 E
Kustvlakte = Coast Plain (EN) ⊠	122	Ic	51.00N	2.30 E
Kusu	156	Be	33.16N	131.09 E
Kušum ~	132	Qd	51.06N	51.18 E
Kušva	136	Fd	58.18N	59.45 E
Kut, Ko- ◆	148	Kf	11.40N	102.35 E
Kut, Ko- ◆	148	Kf	11.40N	102.35 E
Kūt 'Abdollāh	146	Mg	31.13N	48.39 E
Kutacane	150	Cf	3.30N	97.48 E
Kutahya	144	Cb	39.25N	29.59 E
Kutaisi	112	Kg	42.15N	42.40 E
Kutch, Gulf of- → Kachchh, Gulf of	140	Ig	22.36N	60.30 E
Kutch, Rann of- ⊔	148	Ed	24.05N	70.10 E
Kutchan	154	Pc	42.54N	140.45 E
Kutcharo-Ko ≈	156a	Ca	45.10N	142.20 E
Kutina	128	Ke	45.29N	16.47 E
Kutkai	148	Jd	23.27N	97.56 E
Kutkašen → Gabel'a	132	Oi	40.58N	47.52 E
Kutná Hora	120	Lg	49.57N	15.16 E
Kutno	120	Pd	52.15N	19.23 E
Kutse, gora- / Kuutse Mägi ⌒	116	Lg	57.58N	26.24 E
Kuttara-Ko ≈	156a	Bb	42.30N	141.10 E
Kutu	160	Ii	2.44 S	18.09 E
Kutum	168	Cc	14.12N	24.40 E
Kúty	120	Nh	48.40N	17.01 E
Kuty	130	Ia	48.13N	25.15 E
Kuujjuaq	176	Md	58.10N	68.30W
Kuuli-Majak	136	Fg	40.16N	52.45 E

Kuurne 124 Fd 50.51N 3.17 E
Kuusalu/Kusalu 116 Ke 59.23N 25.25 E
Kuusamo 112 Ib 66.00N 29.11 E
Kuusankoski 116 Ld 60.54N 26.38 E
Kuutse Mägi / Kutse, gora- 116 Lg 57.58N 26.24 E
Kuvandyk 132 Td 51.29N 57.28 E
Kuvango 160 Ij 14.29S 16.18 E
Kuvdlorssuaq 179 Gd 74.38N 56.40W
Kuvšinovo 114 Ih 57.03N 34.13 E
Kuwait (EN) = Al Kuwayt 142 Gg 29.20N 47.59 E
Kuwait (EN) = Al Kuwayt [1] 142 Gg 29.30N 47.45 E
Kuwana 156 Ed 35.04N 136.39 E
Kuybychev Reservoir (EN) = Kujbyševskoje vodohranilišče 110 Ke 53.50N 49.00 E
Kuytun 152 Dc 44.25N 84.58 E
Kuyucak 130 Ll 37.55N 28.28 E
Kuzey Kibris = North Cyprus (EN) 144 Db 35.15N 33.40 E
Kuzneck 136 Ee 53.07N 46.36 E
Kuznecki Alatau 140 Kd 54.45N 88.00 E
Kuznečnoje 116 Mc 61.04N 29.58 E
Kuźnia Raciborska 120 Of 50.11N 18.15 E
Kuzomen 136 Db 66.18N 36.49 E
Kuzovatovo 114 Lj 53.33N 47.41 E
Kuzumaki 156 Ga 40.02N 141.26 E
Kuzuryū-Gawa 156 Ec 36.13N 136.08 E
Kvænangen 114 Ea 70.05N 21.13 E
Kvaløy 114 Eb 69.40N 18.30 E
Kvaløya 114 Fa 70.37N 23.52 E
Kvalsund 114 Fa 70.30N 24.00 E
Kvau 116 Cc 61.40N 9.42 E
Kvareli 132 Ni 41.57N 45.47 E
Kvarkeno 134 Ij 52.05N 59.40 E
Kvarnbergsvattnet 114 Dd 64.36N 14.03 E
Kvarner 128 If 44.45N 14.15 E
Kvarnerić 128 If 44.45N 14.35 E
Kvemo-Kedi 132 Oi 41.22N 46.31 E
Kvenna 116 Bd 60.01N 7.56 E
Kvichak 178 He 59.10N 156.40W
Kvichak Bay 178 He 58.48N 157.30W
Kvikkjokk 114 Dc 66.57N 17.47 E
Kvina 116 Bf 58.17N 6.56 E
Kvinesdal 114 Bg 58.19N 6.57 E
Kvissleby 116 Gb 62.17N 17.21 E
Kviteggia 116 Bb 62.05N 6.40 E
Kviteseid 116 Ce 59.24N 8.30 E
Kvitøya 224 Je 80.08N 32.35 E
Kwa 158 Ii 3.10S 16.11 E
Kwahu Plateau 166 Ed 6.30N 0.30W
Kwailibesi 219a Ec 8.20S 160.40 E
Kwajalein Atoll 208 Hd 9.05N 167.20 E
Kwakoegron 202 Gb 5.15N 55.20W
Kwale [Kenya] 170 Gc 4.11S 39.27 E
Kwale [Nig.] 166 Gd 5.45N 6.25 E
Kwamouth 170 Cc 3.10S 16.12 E
Kwa Mtoro 170 Gd 5.14S 35.26 E
Kwando 170 Df 18.27S 23.32 E
Kwangdae-ri 152 Mc 40.34N 127.33 E
Kwangju 142 Of 35.09N 126.55 E
Kwango 158 Ii 3.14S 17.22 E
Kwangsi Chuang (EN) = Guangxi Zhuangzu Zizhiqu (Kuang-hsi-chuang-tsu Tzu-chih-ch'ü) [2] 152 Ig 24.00N 109.00 E
Kwangtung (EN) = Guangdong Sheng 152 Jg 23.00N 113.00 E
Kwanmo-bong 154 Jd 41.42N 129.13 E
Kwara 166 Fd 8.30N 5.00 E
KwaZulu-Natal 172 Ee 29.00S 30.00 E
Kweichow (EN) = Guizhou Sheng (Kuei-chou Sheng) [2] 152 If 27.00N 107.00 E
Kweichow (EN) = Kuei-chou Sheng → Guizhou Sheng [2] 152 If 27.00N 107.00 E
Kwekwe 160 Jj 18.55S 29.49 E
Kweneng [3] 172 Cd 24.00S 24.00 E
Kwenge 158 Ii 4.50S 18.44 E
Kwethluk 178 Gd 60.49N 161.27W
Kwidzyn 120 Oc 53.45N 18.56 E
Kwigillingok 178 Ge 59.51N 163.08W
Kwilu 158 Ii 3.22S 17.22 E
Kwisa 120 Le 51.35N 15.25 E
Kwoka, Gunung- 150 Jg 0.31S 132.27 E
Kyabé 160 Ih 9.27N 18.57 E
Kyabram 212 Jg 36.19S 145.03 E
Kyaikkami 148 Je 16.04N 97.34 E
Kyaikto 148 Je 17.18N 97.01 E
Kyaka 170 Fc 1.16S 31.25 E
Kyancutta 210 Eh 33.08S 135.34 E
Kyan-Zaki 156b Ab 26.05N 127.40 E
Kyaukpyu 148 Id 20.51N 92.58 E
Kyaukse 148 Jd 21.36N 96.08 E
Kybartai/Kibartaj 116 Jj 54.38N 22.44 E
Kyeintali 148 Ie 18.00N 94.29 E
Kyelang 148 Fb 32.35N 77.02 E
Kyffhauser 120 He 51.25N 11.10 E
Kyjov 120 Ng 49.01N 17.08 E
Kyle, Lake- 172 Ed 20.12S 31.00 E
Kyle of Lochalsh 118 Hd 57.17N 5.43W
Kyll 120 Cg 49.48N 6.42 E
Kyllburg 124 Id 50.02N 6.35 E
Kyma 114 Ld 64.48N 47.31 E
Kymi [2] 114 Gf 61.00N 28.00 E
Kymijoki 116 Ld 60.30N 26.52 E
Kyn 134 Ih 57.52N 58.32 E
Kynnefjäll 116 Df 58.42N 11.41 E
Kynsivesi 116 Lb 62.25N 26.10 E
Kyoga, Lake- 158 Kh 1.30N 33.00 E
Kyōga-Dake 156 Be 33.00N 130.05 E
Kyōga-Misaki 154 Mg 35.45N 135.11 E
Kyonan 156 Fd 35.07N 139.49 E
Kyŏnggi-Do [2] 154 If 37.30N 127.15 E
Kyŏnggi-man 154 Hf 37.25N 126.00 E
Kyŏngju 152 Md 35.50N 129.13 E
Kyŏngsang-Namdo [2] 154 Jg 35.15N 128.30 E
Kyŏngsang-Pukto [2] 154 Jf 36.20N 128.40 E
Kyŏngsŏng 154 Jd 41.40N 129.40 E
Kyōto 142 Pf 35.00N 135.45 E
Kyōto Fu 154 Mg 35.25N 135.15 E
Kypros → Kípros = Cyprus (EN) 144 Db 35.01N 33.00 E
Kyra 138 Gg 49.36N 111.58 E
Kyren 138 Ff 51.41N 102.10 E
Kyrenia 146 Ee 35.20N 33.19 E
Kyrgesaare/Kõrgesaare 116 Je 59.00N 22.25 E
Kyrgyz Sovetik Socialistik Respublikasy/Kirgizskaja SSR → Kyrgyzstan 136 Hg 41.30N 75.00 E
Kyrgyzstan 136 Hg 41.30N 75.00 E
Kyritz 120 Id 52.57N 12.24 E
Kyrkheden 116 Ed 60.10N 13.29 E
Kyrksæterora 114 Be 63.17N 9.06 E
Kyrkslätt/Kirkkonummi 116 Kd 60.07N 24.26 E
Kyrö 116 Jd 60.42N 22.45 E
Kyrönjoki 116 Ia 63.14N 21.45 E
Kyrösjärvi 116 Jc 61.45N 23.10 E
Kyröskoski 116 Jc 61.40N 23.11 E
Kyštym 136 Gd 55.42N 60.34 E
Kysucké Nové Mesto 120 Og 49.18N 18.48 E
Kythera (EN) = Kíthira 110 Ih 36.15N 23.00 E
Kythraia 146 Ee 35.15N 33.29 E
Kyuquot Sound 188 Bb 49.55N 127.25W
Kyūshū 140 Pf 32.50N 131.00 E
Kyushu-Palau Ridge (EN) 106 Ih 20.00N 136.00 E
Kyūshū-Sanchi 156 Be 32.40N 131.10 E
Kyyjärvi 114 Fe 63.02N 24.34 E
Kyyvesi 116 Lc 61.55N 27.05 E
Kyzikos 146 Bb 40.28N 27.47 E
Kyzyl 142 Ld 51.42N 94.27 E
Kyzylart, pereval- 136 Hh 39.22N 73.20 E
Kyzyl-Kija 136 Hg 40.14N 72.12 E
Kyzylrabot 136 Hh 37.28N 74.45 E
Kyzylsu [Eur.] 135 Gf 37.22N 69.22 E
Kyzylsu [Eur.] 135 He 39.17N 71.25 E
Kyzylžar 136 Gf 48.17N 69.49 E
Kzyl-Orda 142 Ie 44.48N 65.28 E
Kzyl-Ordinskaja oblast [3] 136 Gf 45.00N 65.00 E
Kzyltu 136 He 53.41N 72.15 E

L

Laa an der Thaya 128 Kb 48.43N 16.23 E
Laakdal 124 Gc 51.05N 4.59 E
La Alberca 126 Fd 40.29N 6.06W
La Alcarria 126 Jd 40.31N 2.45W
La Almunia de Doña Godina 126 Kc 41.29N 1.22W
La Araucanía [2] 206 Fe 37.50S 73.15W
La Ardilla, Cerro- 192 Hf 22.15N 102.40W
La Armuña 126 Gc 41.05N 5.35W
Laasphe 124 Kd 50.56N 8.24 E
La Asunción 202 Fa 11.02N 63.53W
Laau Point 221a Db 21.06N 157.16W
Laayoune 126 Ni 35.42N 2.00 E
Lab 130 Eg 42.45N 21.01 E
Laba 132 Kg 45.10N 39.40 E
La Babia 192 Hc 28.34N 102.04W
Laba Dağı 130 Kl 37.22N 28.12 E
Labaddey 168 Ge 0.32N 42.45 E
Labadie Bank 118 Ek 50.30N 8.15W
La Banda 206 Hc 27.44S 64.15W
La Bañeza 126 Gb 42.18N 5.54W
La Barca 192 Hg 20.17N 102.34W
Labardén 204 Cm 36.57S 58.06W
La Barge 188 Je 42.16N 110.12W
La Barra, Punta- 194 Lh 11.30N 70.10W
La-Barre-en-Ouche 124 Cf 48.57N 0.40 E
Labbezanga 166 Fc 14.59N 0.43 E
Labé 160 Fg 11.19N 12.17W
Labe = Elbe (EN) 110 Ge 53.50N 9.00 E
Labelle 184 Jb 46.17N 74.45W
La Belle 184 Gl 26.46N 81.26W
La Berzosa 126 Fd 40.35N 6.40W
Labin 128 Ie 45.05N 14.08 E
Labinsk 136 Eg 44.35N 40.44 E
Labis 150 Df 2.23N 103.02 E
La Bisbal / la Bisbal d'Empordà 126 Pc 41.57N 3.03 E
la Bisbal d'Empordà/La Bisbal 126 Pc 41.57N 3.03 E
La Blanca, Laguna- 204 Bj 30.15S 60.38W
Laboe 120 Gb 54.24N 10.13 E
Laborec 120 Rh 48.31N 21.54 E
Laborie 197k Bb 13.45N 61.00W
Labota 150 Hg 2.52S 122.10 E
Labouheyre 122 Fj 44.13N 0.55W
Laboulaye 206 Hd 34.07S 63.24W
Labra, Peña- 126 Ha 43.03N 4.26W
Labrador 174 Md 55.00N 70.00W
Labrador Basin (EN) 174 Od 53.00N 48.00W
Labrador City 176 Md 52.57N 66.54W
Labrador Sea 174 Nd 57.00N 53.00W
Labrang → Xiahe 152 Hd 35.18N 102.30 E
Lábrea 200 Jf 7.16S 64.46W
Labrieville 184 Ma 49.19N 69.34W
Labrit 122 Fj 44.06N 0.33W
La Broye 128 Bd 46.55N 7.02 E
Labuan, Pulau- 150 Ge 5.19N 115.13 E
Labudalin → Ergun Youqi 152 La 50.16N 120.09 E
Labuha 150 Ig 0.37S 127.29 E
Labuhan 150 Eh 6.22S 105.50 E
Labuhanbajo 150 Gh 8.29S 119.54 E
Labuhanbilik 150 Df 2.31N 100.10 E
Labuk, Teluk- 150 Ge 6.10N 117.50 E
La Bureba 126 Ib 42.36N 3.24W
Labutta 148 Ie 16.09N 94.46 E
Labytnangi 142 Ic 66.39N 66.21 E
Lac [3] 168 Ac 13.30N 14.20 E
Lača, ozero- 114 Jf 61.20N 38.50 E
La Cadena 192 Ge 25.53N 104.12W
La Calamine/Kelmis 124 Hd 50.43N 6.00 E
La Calandria 204 Cj 30.48S 63.94W
Lac Allard 180 Lf 50.30N 63.30W
La Campiña 126 Hg 37.45N 4.45W
Lacanau 122 Ej 44.59N 1.05W
Lacanau, Étang de- 122 Ej 44.58N 1.07W
Lacanau-Lacanau-Océan 122 Ei 45.00N 1.12W
Lacanau-Océan, Lacanau- 122 Ei 45.00N 1.12W
Lacantún, Rio- 192 Ni 16.36N 90.39W
Laćarak 130 Ce 45.00N 19.34 E
La Carlota [Arg.] 206 Hd 33.26S 63.18W
La Carlota [Phil.] 150 Hd 10.25N 122.55 E
La Carlota [Sp.] 126 Hg 37.40N 4.56W
La Carolina 126 If 38.15N 3.37W
Lacaune 122 Ik 43.43N 2.42 E
Lacaune, Monts de- 122 Ik 43.40N 2.36 E
Lac du Bonnet 186 Ha 50.35N 96.05W
La Ceiba [Hond.] 176 Kh 15.47N 86.50W
La Ceiba [Ven.] 194 Li 9.28N 71.04W
Lacepede Bay 212 Hg 36.45S 139.45 E
Lacepede Islands 212 Ec 16.50S 122.10 E
La Cerdaña/La Cerdanya 126 Nb 42.24N 1.40 E
La Cerdanya/La Cerdaña 126 Nb 42.24N 1.40 E
Lacey 188 Dc 47.07N 122.49W
Lac Giao → Buon Me Thuot 148 Lf 12.40N 108.03 E
La Chaux-de-Fonds 128 Ac 47.06N 6.50 E
Lachay, Punta- 202 Cf 11.18S 77.39W
La China, Sierra- 204 Bm 36.47S 60.34W
Lachine 184 Kc 45.26N 73.40W
Lachlan River 208 Fh 34.21S 143.57 E
La Chorrera [Col.] 202 Dd 0.45S 73.00W
La Chorrera [Pan.] 190 Ig 8.53N 79.47W
Laçi 130 Ch 41.38N 19.43 E
Lačin 132 Oj 39.39N 46.33 E
La Ciutat de Mallorca / Palma 112 Gh 39.34N 2.39 E
Łąck 120 Pd 52.28N 19.40 E
Lackawanna 184 Hd 42.49N 78.49W
Lac La Biche 180 Gf 54.46N 111.58W
Lac la Martre 180 Fd 63.21N 117.00W
Lac Mégantic 180 Kg 45.35N 70.53W
La Colina 204 Bm 37.20S 61.32W
La Coloma 194 Fb 22.15N 83.34W
La Colorada 192 Dc 28.41N 110.25W
Lacombe 180 Gf 52.28N 113.44W
Lacon 186 Lf 41.02N 89.24W
La Concepción [Pan.] 194 Fi 8.31N 82.37W
La Concepción [Ven.] 194 Lh 10.48N 71.46W
La Concha 192 Gg 21.46N 105.29W
Laconi 128 Dk 39.51N 9.03 E
Laconia 182 Mc 43.32N 71.29W
Laconia, Gulf of- (EN) = Lakonikós Kólpos 130 Fm 36.35N 22.40 E
La Coronilla 204 Fk 33.44S 53.31W
La Coruña [3] 126 Da 43.10N 8.25W
La Coruña / A Cruña 112 Fg 43.22N 8.23W
La Côte-Saint-André 122 Li 45.23N 5.15 E
Lacq 122 Fk 43.25N 0.38W
Lacroix-sur-Meuse 124 Hf 48.58N 5.31 E
La Crosse [Ks.-U.S.] 186 Gg 38.32N 99.18W
La Crosse [Wi.-U.S.] 176 Je 43.49N 91.15W
La Cruz [Arg.] 206 Ic 29.10S 56.38W
La Cruz [C.R.] 194 Eh 11.04N 85.39W
La Cruz [Mex.] 190 Cd 23.55N 106.54W
La Cruz [Ur.] 206 Id 33.56S 56.15W
La Cruz de Rio Grande 194 Eg 13.06N 84.10W
La Cruz de Taratara 194 Mh 11.03N 69.44W
La Cuesta 192 Hc 28.45N 102.25W
La Cumbre 206 Hd 30.58S 64.30W
Lac Yora 168 Cb 19.08N 20.35 E
Ladário 204 Dd 19.01S 57.35W
Ladbergen 124 Jb 52.08N 7.45 E
Lądek-Zdrój 120 Mf 50.21N 16.50 E
Ladenburg 124 Ke 49.28N 8.37 E
La Désirade 196 Fd 16.19N 61.03W
La Digue Island 172b Ca 4.21S 55.50 E
Lâdik 146 Fb 40.36N 36.45 E
Ladismith 172 Cf 33.30S 21.16 E
Ladispoli 128 Gi 41.56N 12.05 E
Lado, Jabal- 168 Ed 5.06N 31.35 E
Ladoga, Lake- (EN) = Ladožskoje ozero 110 Jc 61.00N 31.00 E
Ladong 152 Ig 24.49N 109.34 E
La Dorada 202 Db 5.22N 74.42W
Ladožskoje ozero = Ladoga, Lake- (EN) 110 Jc 61.00N 31.00 E
Ladrones, Islas- 194 Fj 7.52N 82.26W
Laduškin 116 Ij 54.35N 20.10 E
Ladva-Vetka 114 If 61.20N 34.29 E
Lady Ann Strait 180 Ja 75.45N 80.00W
Ladybrand 172 De 29.19S 27.25 E
Lady Evelyn Lake 184 Gb 47.20N 80.10W
Lady Newnes Ice Shelf 222 Kf 73.40S 167.30 E
Ladysmith [B.C.-Can.] 188 Db 48.58N 123.49W
Ladysmith [S.Afr.] 160 Jk 28.34S 29.45 E
Ladysmith [Wi.-U.S.] 182 Ib 45.28N 91.07W
Ladyžin 132 Fe 48.40N 29.13 E
Lae 210 Fe 6.43S 147.01 E
Lae Atoll 208 Hd 8.56N 166.14 E
La Eduvigis 204 Ch 26.50S 59.05W
Laem, Khao- 148 Kf 14.19N 101.11 E
Laer [Ger.] 124 Jb 52.04N 7.21 E
Laer [Ger.] 124 Kb 52.06N 8.05 E
Lærdalsøyri 114 Bf 61.06N 7.29 E
La Escala / l'Escala 126 Pb 42.07N 3.08 E
La Esmeralda 202 Ec 3.10N 65.33W
Læsø 114 Bh 57.15N 10.00 E
Læsø Rende 116 Dg 57.15N 10.45 E
La Española = Hispaniola (EN) 174 Lh 19.00N 71.00W
La Esperanza [Bol.] 202 Ff 14.34S 62.10W
La Esperanza [Hond.] 194 Cf 14.20N 88.10W
La Estrada 126 Db 42.41N 8.29W
Lafayette [Al.-U.S.] 184 Ei 32.54N 85.24W
Lafayette [In.-U.S.] 182 Jc 40.25N 86.53W
Lafayette [La.-U.S.] 176 Jf 30.14N 92.01W
La Fère 124 Fe 49.40N 3.22 E
La Ferrière-sur-Risle 124 Cf 48.59N 0.48 E
La Ferté-Frênel 124 Cf 48.50N 0.30 E
La Ferté-Milon 124 Fe 49.10N 3.07 E
Laffān, Ra's- 146 Nj 25.54N 51.35 E
Lafia 166 Gd 8.29N 8.31 E
Lafiagi 166 Gd 8.52N 5.15 E
Lafnitz 128 Kd 46.57N 16.16 E
La Foa 219b Be 21.43S 165.49 E
La Follette 184 Eg 36.23N 84.07W
La Fria 194 Ki 8.13N 72.15W
Laft 146 Pi 26.54N 55.46 E
La Fuente de San Esteban 126 Fd 40.48N 6.15W
Laga, Monti della- 128 Hh 42.45N 13.35 E
La Galite (EN) = Jāliṭah 158 He 37.32N 8.56 E
La Gallareta 204 Bi 29.34S 60.23W
Lagamar 204 Id 18.13S 46.48W
Lagan 116 Eh 56.55N 13.59 E
Lagan 116 Eh 56.33N 12.56 E
Lagan/Abhainn an Lagáin 118 Hg 54.37N 5.53W
Lagarina, Val- 128 Fe 45.50N 11.10 E
La Garita Mountains 186 Ch 38.00N 106.40W
Lagarto 202 Kf 10.54S 37.41W
Lagash 146 Lg 31.27N 46.13 E
Lagawe 150 Hc 16.49N 121.06 E
Lage 124 Kc 51.59N 8.48 E
*Lågen [Nor.] 116 De 59.03N 10.05 E
Lågen [Nor.] 114 Cf 61.08N 10.25 E
Lagh Bogal 170 Gb 0.42N 40.55 E
Laghmān [3] 144 Lb 35.00N 70.15 E
Laghouat 160 He 33.48N 2.53 E
Laghouat [3] 162 Hc 33.30N 3.15 E
La Gloria 194 Ki 8.38N 73.48W
Lagny-sur-Marne 122 If 48.52N 2.43 E
Lagôa 204 Eb 14.08S 55.20W
Lagoa 126 Dg 37.08N 8.27W
Lagoa da Prata 204 Je 20.01S 45.33W
Lagoa Vermelha 206 Jc 28.13S 51.32W
Lagodehi 132 Oi 41.50N 46.14 E
La Gomera 194 Bf 14.05N 91.03W
Lagonegro 128 Jj 40.07N 15.46 E
Lagonoy Gulf 150 Hd 13.35N 123.45 E
Lágos 130 Ih 41.01N 25.07 E
Lagos [2] 166 Fd 6.30N 3.30 E
Lagos [Nig.] 160 Hh 6.27N 3.23 E
Lagos [Port.] 126 Dg 37.06N 8.40W
Lagos, Baia de- 126 Dg 37.06N 8.39W
Lagosa 170 Ed 5.57S 29.53 E
Lagos de Moreno 190 Dd 21.21N 101.55W
La Grande 182 Db 45.20N 118.05W
La Grande Fosse 118 Kl 49.40N 3.00W
La Grande Rivière 174 Ld 53.50N 79.00W
La Grande Trench (EN) = Hurd Deep 118 Kl 49.40N 3.00W
Lagrange 184 Ee 41.39N 85.25W
La Grange [Ky.-U.S.] 184 Ef 38.24N 85.23W
La Grange [Ga.-U.S.] 182 Je 33.02N 85.02W
La Grange [Tx.-U.S.] 186 Hl 29.54N 96.52W
La Granja → San Ildefonso 126 Id 40.54N 4.00W
La Gran Sabana 202 Fb 5.30N 61.30W
La Grita 202 Db 8.08N 71.59W
Lagskär 116 He 59.50N 20.00 E
La Guaira 200 Jd 10.36N 66.56W
La Guajira [3] 202 Da 11.30N 72.30W
Lagua Lichan, Puntan- 220b Ba 15.16N 145.50 E
Laguardia 126 Jb 42.33N 2.35W
La Guardia [Sp.] 126 Dc 41.54N 8.53W
La Guardia [Sp.] 126 Ie 39.47N 3.29W
La Guasima 192 Kg 21.06N 97.49W
Laguiole 122 Ij 44.41N 2.51 E
Laguna 206 Kc 28.29S 48.47W
Laguna Alsina 204 Am 36.49S 62.13W
Laguna Beach 188 Gj 33.33N 117.51W
Laguna Blanca 204 Cg 25.08S 58.15W
Laguna de Bay 150 Hd 14.23N 121.15 E
Laguna Limpia 204 Ch 26.29S 59.41W
Laguna Mountains 188 Gj 32.55N 116.25W
Laguna Paiva 206 Hd 31.19S 60.39W
Laguna Superior 190 Fe 16.20N 94.25W
Laguna Veneta 128 Ge 45.25N 12.20 E
Laguna Yema 204 Bg 24.15S 61.15W
Lagunillas [Bol.] 202 Fg 19.38S 63.43W
Lagunillas [Mex.] 192 Ii 17.50N 101.44W
Lagunillas [Ven.] 194 Lh 10.08N 71.16W
Lagunillas [Ven.] 194 Li 8.31N 71.24W
Laha 152 Lb 48.13N 124.36 E
La Habana [3] 194 Fb 22.45N 82.10W
La Habana = Havana (EN) 176 Kg 23.08N 82.22W
Lahad Datu 150 Ge 5.02N 118.19 E
Laham 166 Fc 14.54N 4.25 E
Lahat 150 Dg 3.48S 103.32 E
Lahdenpohja 114 Hf 61.33N 30.13 E
Lahewa 150 Cf 1.24N 97.11 E
Lahij 144 Fg 13.04N 44.53 E
Lāhījān 144 Hb 37.12N 50.01 E
Lahn 120 Df 50.18N 7.37 E
Lahnstein 124 Jd 50.20N 7.29 E
Laholm 114 Ch 56.31N 13.02 E
Laholmsbukten 116 Eh 56.35N 12.50 E
Lahore 142 Jf 31.35N 74.18 E
Lahr 120 Dh 48.20N 7.52 E
Lahti 112 Ic 60.58N 25.40 E
Laï 160 Ih 9.24N 16.18 E
Laiagam 214 Ci 5.31S 143.39 E
Lai'an 154 Eh 32.28N 118.26 E
Lai Chau 148 Kd 22.02N 103.10 E
Laich o'Moray 118 Jd 57.40N 3.30W
Laie 221a Db 21.39N 157.56W
Laifeng 152 If 29.31N 109.23 E
Laighean/Leinster 118 Gh 53.00N 7.00W
Laignes 122 Kg 47.50N 4.22 E
Laihia 114 Fe 62.58N 22.01 E
Lainioälven 114 Fc 67.22N 22.39 E
Lairg 118 Ic 58.01N 4.25W
Lairi 168 Bc 10.49N 17.06 E
Lairi, Batha de- 168 Bc 12.28N 16.45 E
Lais 150 Dg 3.32S 102.03 E
La Isabela 194 Gb 22.57N 80.01W
Laisamis 170 Gb 1.36N 37.48 E
Laiševo 114 Li 55.26N 49.32 E
Laishui 154 Ce 39.23N 115.42 E
Laisvall 114 Dc 66.08N 17.10 E
Laitila 114 Ef 60.53N 21.41 E
Laiwu 154 Df 36.12N 117.40 E
Laiwui 150 Ig 1.22S 127.40 E
Laixi (Shuiji) 154 Ff 36.52N 120.31 E
Laiyang 152 Ld 36.59N 120.39 E
Laiyuan 152 Jd 39.19N 114.43 E
Laizhou Wan 154 Ef 37.30N 119.30 E
Laja 206 Fe 37.16S 72.42W
Laja 134 Hc 66.20N 56.16 E
La Jara 126 He 39.40N 4.55W
Lajeado 204 Gi 29.27S 51.58W
Lajeado, Serra do- 204 Hd 19.08S 49.56W
Lajes [Braz.] 200 Kh 27.48S 50.19W
Lajes [Braz.] 202 Ke 5.41S 36.14W
Lajes do Pico 162 Bb 38.23N 28.16W
Lajosmizse 120 Pi 47.01N 19.33 E
Lajta 128 Lc 47.52N 17.18 E
La Junta [Co.-U.S.] 182 Gd 37.59N 103.33W
La Junta [Mex.] 192 Fc 28.28N 107.20W
Lak Bor 170 Hb 1.18N 40.40 E
Lake Cargelligo 212 Jf 33.18S 146.23 E
Lake Charles 176 Jf 30.12N 93.12W
Lake City 182 Ke 30.12N 82.38W
Lake District 118 Jg 54.30N 3.10W
Lake Fork Creek 188 Jf 40.13N 110.07W
Lake Geneva 186 Le 42.36N 88.26W
Lake George 184 Kd 43.25N 73.45W
Lake Grace 212 Df 33.06S 118.28 E
Lake Harbour 180 Kd 62.51N 69.53W
Lake Havasu City 188 Hi 34.27N 114.22W
Lake Itasca 186 Ic 46.51N 95.13W
Lake Jackson 186 Il 29.02N 95.27W
Lake King 212 Df 33.05S 119.40 E
Lakeland 182 Kf 28.03N 81.57W
Lake Louise 188 Ga 51.26N 116.11W
Lakemba 219d Cc 18.13S 178.47W
Lakemba Passage 219d Cb 17.53S 178.32W
Lake Mills 186 Je 43.25N 93.32W
Lake Minchumina 178 Id 63.53N 152.19W
Lake Murray 214 Ci 6.54S 141.28 E
Lake Oswego 188 Dd 45.26N 122.39W
Lake Placid 184 Kc 44.18N 73.59W
Lake Providence 186 Kj 32.48N 91.11W
Lake Pukaki 218 Df 44.11S 170.08 E
Lake Range 188 Ff 40.15N 119.25W
Lake River 180 Jf 54.28N 82.30W
Lakes Entrance 212 Jg 37.53S 147.59 E
Lakeside 188 If 41.13N 112.57W
Lake Tekapo 218 Df 44.00S 170.29 E
Lakeview 182 Cc 42.11N 120.21W
Lakeville 186 Jd 44.39N 93.14W
Lake Wales 184 Gl 27.55N 81.35W
Lakewood [Co.-U.S.] 186 Dg 39.44N 105.06W
Lakewood [Oh.-U.S.] 184 Ge 41.29N 81.50W
Lake Worth 184 Gl 26.37N 80.03W
Lakhdar, Chergui Kef- 126 Pi 35.57N 3.16 E
Lakhdaria 126 Ph 36.34N 3.35 E
Láki 130 Hh 41.50N 24.50 E
Lakin 186 Fh 37.58N 101.15W
Lakinsk 114 Jh 56.04N 39.58 E
Lákmos Óros 130 Ej 39.40N 21.07 E
Lakon, Ile- 208 Hf 14.17S 167.30 E
Lakonikós Kólpos = Laconia, Gulf of- (EN) 130 Fm 36.35N 22.40 E
Lakota [3] 166 Dd 5.53N 5.42W
Lakota [I.C.] 166 Dd 5.51N 5.41W
Lakota [N.D.-U.S.] 186 Gb 48.02N 98.21W
Laksefjorden 114 Ga 70.58N 27.00 E
Lakselv 114 Fa 70.03N 25.01 E
Lakshadweep [3] 148 Ef 11.00N 72.00 E
Lakshadweep 140 Jh 11.00N 72.00 E
La Laguna 204 Bb 14.30S 61.06W
Lalanna 172 Hd 23.28S 45.05 E
Lalapaşa 130 Jh 41.50N 26.44 E
Lāleh Zār, Kūh-e- 140 Hg 29.24N 56.46 E
La Leonesa 204 Ch 27.03S 58.43W
Lālī 146 Mf 32.21N 49.06 E
Lalibela 168 Fc 12.00N 39.04 E
La Libertad [3] 202 Ce 8.00S 78.30W
La Libertad [El Sal.] 190 Gf 13.29N 89.16W
La Libertad [Guat.] 194 Be 16.47N 90.07W
La Libertad [Guat.] 194 Bf 15.30N 91.50W
La Libertad [Hond.] 194 Df 14.43N 87.36W
La Ligua 206 Fd 32.27S 71.14W
Lalin 126 Db 42.39N 8.07W
La Linea 126 Gh 36.10N 5.19W
Lalin He 154 Hb 45.28N 125.43 E
Lalitpur 148 Fd 24.41N 78.25 E
Lalla Khedidja 126 Qh 36.27N 4.14 E
Lālmanir Hāt 148 Hc 25.54N 89.27 E
La Loche 180 Ge 56.29N 109.27W
La Louvière 122 Kd 50.29N 4.11 E
La Lucila 204 Bj 30.25S 61.01W
Lalzit, Gjiri i- 130 Ch 41.31N 19.29 E
La Maddalena 128 Di 41.13N 9.24 E
La Maiella 110 Hg 42.05N 14.07 E
La Maladeta/Malditos, Montes- 126 Mb 42.40N 0.50 E
La Malbaie 180 Kg 47.39N 70.10W
La Mancha 110 Fh 39.05N 3.00W
La Manche = English Channel (EN) 110 Fe 50.20N 1.00W
Lamap 216 Cc 16.26S 167.43 E
Lamar 182 Gd 38.05N 102.37W
La Maragateria 126 Fb 42.25N 6.10W
La Marina 126 Lf 38.35N 0.05W
La Marmora 128 Dk 39.59N 9.20 E
La Marque 186 Il 29.22N 94.58W
Lamas 202 Ce 6.25S 76.35W
Lamastre 122 Kj 44.59N 4.35 E
Lamawan 154 Ad 40.05N 111.25 E
Lambach 128 Hb 48.05N 13.53 E
Lamballe 122 Df 48.28N 2.31W
Lambar, Rio- 204 Jd 19.30S 45.00W
Lambaréné 160 Ii 0.42S 10.13 E

Index Symbols

[1] Independent Nation
[2] State, Region
[3] District, County
[4] Municipality
[5] Colony, Dependency
Continent
Physical Region
Historical or Cultural Region
Mount, Mountain
Volcano
Hill
Mountains, Mountain Range
Hills, Escarpment
Plateau, Upland
Pass, Gap
Plain, Lowland
Delta
Salt Flat
Valley, Canyon
Crater, Cave
Karst Features
Depression
Polder
Desert, Dunes
Forest, Woods
Heath, Steppe
Oasis
Cape, Point
Coast, Beach
Cliff
Peninsula
Isthmus
Sandbank
Island
Atoll
Rock, Reef
Islands, Archipelago
Rocks, Reefs
Coral Reef
Well, Spring
Geyser
River, Stream
Waterfall, Rapids
River Mouth, Estuary
Lake
Salt Lake
Intermittent Lake
Reservoir
Swamp, Pond
Canal
Glacier
Ice Shelf, Pack Ice
Ocean
Sea
Gulf, Bay
Strait, Fjord
Lagoon
Bank
Seamount
Tablemount
Ridge
Shelf
Basin
Escarpment, Sea Scarp
Fracture
Trench, Abyss
National Park, Reserve
Point of Interest
Recreation Site
Cave, Cavern
Historic Site
Ruins
Wall, Walls
Church, Abbey
Temple
Scientific Station
Railway station
Airport
Port
Military installation
Lighthouse
Mine
Tunnel
Dam, Bridge

Lam-Lav

Lambari 204 Je 21.58S 45.21W
Lambasa 216 Ec 16.26S 179.24 E
Lambay/Reachrainn 118 Gh 53.29N 6.01W
Lambayeque 202 Ce 6.42S 79.55W
Lambayeque [3] 202 Ce 6.20S 80.00W
Lambert Glacier 222 Ff 71.00S 70.00 E
Lambert Land 179 Jc 79.10N 21.00W
Lamberts Bay 160 Il 32.05S 18.17 E
Lambro 128 De 45.08N 9.32 E
Lambsheim 124 Ke 49.31N 8.17 E
Lambton, Cape - 180 Fb 71.04N 123.08W
Lamé 168 Ad 9.15N 14.32 E
Lame Deer 188 Ld 45.37N 106.40W
Lamego 126 Ec 41.06N 7.49W
Lamentin 197e Ab 16.16N 61.38W
La Mesa 188 Gj 32.46N 117.01W
Lamesa 182 Ge 32.44N 101.57W
La Meta 128 Hi 41.41N 13.56 E
Lamezia Terme 128 Kl 38.59N 16.17 E
Lamezia Terme - Nicastro 128 Kl 38.59N 16.19 E
Lamezia Terme - Sambiase 128 Kl 38.58N 16.17 E
Lamezia Terme - Sant'Eufemia Lamezia 128 Kl 38.55N 16.15 E
Lamía 130 Fk 38.54N 22.26 E
Lamina 204 De 20.34S 56.14W
Lamlam, Mount- 220c Bb 13.20N 144.40 E
Lammermuir Hills 118 Kf 55.52N 2.40W
Lammhult 116 Fg 57.10N 14.35 E
Lammi 114 Ff 61.05N 25.01 E
Lamoil 220d Ba 7.39N 151.41 E
Lamon Bay 140 Oh 14.25N 122.00 E
Lamone 128 Gf 44.29N 12.08 E
Lamoni 186 Jf 40.37N 93.56W
Lamont 184 Fj 30.21N 83.50W
La Montaña 198 If 10.00S 72.50W
La Moraña 126 Hd 40.45N 4.55W
La Mosquitia 194 Ef 15.00N 84.20W
Lamotrek Atoll 208 Fd 7.30N 146.20 E
Lamotte-Beuvron 122 Ig 47.36N 2.01 E
La Moure 186 Gc 46.21N 98.18W
Lampang 148 Je 18.16N 99.34 E
Lampasas 186 Gk 31.03N 98.12W
Lampazos de Naranjo 192 Id 27.01N 100.31W
Lampedusa 128 Go 35.30N 12.35 E
Lampertheim 120 Eg 49.36N 8.28 E
Lampeter 118 Ii 52.07N 4.05W
Lamphun 148 Je 18.35N 99.00 E
Lampione 128 Go 35.35N 12.20 E
Lampung [3] 150 Dg 5.00S 105.00 E
Lamu 160 Li 2.16S 40.54 E
Lamud 202 Ce 6.09S 77.55W
Lan 132 Ec 52.09N 27.18 E
Lana 128 Fd 46.37N 11.09 E
Lana, Río de la- 192 Li 17.49N 95.09W
Lanai City 221a Ec 20.50N 156.55W
Lanaihale 221a Ec 20.49N 156.52W
Lanai Island 208 Lb 20.50N 156.55W
Lanaken 124 Hd 50.53N 5.39 E
Lanao, Lake- 150 He 7.50N 124.15 E
Lanark 118 Jf 55.41N 3.48W
Lanbi Kyun 148 Jf 10.50N 98.15 E
Lancang (Menglangba) 152 Gg 22.37N 99.57 E
Lancang Jiang = Mekong (EN) 140 Mh 10.15N 105.55 E
Lancashire [3] 118 Kh 53.55N 2.40W
Lancashire Plain 118 Kh 53.40N 2.45W
Lancaster 118 Kh 53.45N 2.50W
Lancaster [Ca.-U.S.] 182 De 34.42N 118.08W
Lancaster [Eng.-U.K.] 118 Kg 54.03N 2.48W
Lancaster [Mo.-U.S.] 186 Jf 40.31N 92.32W
Lancaster [N.H.-U.S.] 184 Lc 44.29N 71.34W
Lancaster [Oh.-U.S.] 184 Ff 39.43N 82.37W
Lancaster [Ont.-Can.] 184 Jc 45.12N 74.30W
Lancaster [Pa.-U.S.] 182 Lc 40.01N 76.19W
Lancaster [S.C.-U.S.] 184 Gh 34.43N 80.47W
Lancaster Sound 174 Kb 74.13N 84.00W
Lançeiro 204 Fe 20.59S 53.43W
Lancelin 212 Df 31.01S 115.19 E
Lanciano 128 Ih 42.14N 14.23 E
Lančin 130 Ha 48.31N 24.49 E
Lancun 154 Ff 36.25N 120.11 E
Łańcut 120 Sf 50.05N 22.13 E
Land 116 Cd 60.45N 10.00 E
Låndana 160 Bd 5.15S 12.10 E
Landau an der Isar 120 Ih 48.41N 12.41 E
Landau in der Pfalz 120 Eg 49.12N 8.07 E
Land Bay 222 Mf 75.25S 141.45W
Landeck 128 Ec 47.08N 10.34 E
Landen 124 Hd 50.45N 5.05 E
Lander 182 Fc 42.50N 108.44W
Landerneau 122 Bf 48.27N 4.15W
Lander River 212 Gd 20.25S 132.00 E
Landeryd 116 Eg 57.05N 13.16 E
Landes [3] 122 Fj 44.00N 0.50W
Landes 122 Fj 44.15N 1.00W
Landesbergen 124 Lb 52.34N 9.08 E
Landeta 204 Ak 32.01S 62.04W
Landete 126 Ke 39.54N 1.22W
Landfallis 148 If 13.40N 93.02 E
Land Glacier 222 Mf 75.40S 141.45W
Landi Kotal 148 Eb 34.06N 71.09 E
Landless Corner 170 Ee 14.53S 28.04 E
Landrecies 124 Fd 50.08N 3.42 E
Landsberg am Lech 120 Gh 48.03N 10.52 E
Landsbro 116 Fg 57.22N 14.54 E
Land's End 110 Fe 50.03N 5.44W
Lands End 180 Fa 76.25N 122.45W
Landshut 120 Ih 48.32N 12.09 E
Landskrona 114 Ci 55.52N 12.50 E
Landsort 116 Gf 58.45N 17.50 E
Landsortsdjupet 116 Hf 58.40N 18.30 E
Landstuhl 124 Je 49.25N 7.34 E
Landusky 188 Kc 47.54N 108.37W
La Neuve-Lyre 124 Cf 48.54N 0.45 E
Lanfeng → Lankao 154 Cg 34.49N 114.48 E
Lang 188 Mb 49.56N 104.23W
La'nga Co 152 De 30.41N 81.17 E
Langadhás 130 Gi 40.45N 23.04 E
Langádhia 130 Fl 37.39N 22.03 E
Långan 114 De 63.19N 14.44 E
Langano, Lake- 168 Fd 7.36N 38.43 E
Langara 150 Hg 4.02S 123.00 E
Langarfoss 114a Cb 65.35N 14.15W
Langasian 150 Ie 8.16N 125.39 E
Langdon 186 Gb 48.46N 98.22W
Langeac 122 Ji 45.06N 3.29 E
Langeais 122 Gg 47.20N 0.24 E
Langeb 168 Fb 17.46N 36.41 E
Langebaan 172 Bf 33.06S 18.02 E
Langeberg 172 Cf 33.56S 20.45 E
Langedijk 124 Gb 52.42N 4.48 E
Langeland 114 Ci 55.00N 10.50 E
Langelands Bælt 116 Dj 54.50N 10.55 E
Längelmävesi 116 Kc 61.30N 24.20 E
Langen 124 Ke 49.59N 8.40 E
Langenberg 124 Kc 51.17N 8.34 E
Langenburg 186 Fa 50.50N 101.43W
Langenfeld (Rheinland) 124 Ic 51.06N 6.57 E
Langenhagen 120 Fd 52.27N 9.45 E
Langenselbold 124 Ld 50.11N 9.02 E
Langenthal 128 Bc 47.13N 7.49 E
Langeoog 120 Dc 53.46N 7.32 E
Langeri 138 Jf 50.08N 143.20 E
Langesund 116 Ce 59.00N 9.45 E
Langesundsfjorden 116 Cf 59.00N 9.48 E
Langevåg 116 Bb 62.27N 6.12 E
Langfang → Anci 152 Kd 39.29N 116.40 E
Långfjället 116 Eb 62.10N 12.20 E
Langfjorden 116 Bb 62.45N 7.30 E
Langhe 128 Bf 44.30N 8.00 E
Langholm 118 Kf 55.09N 3.00W
Langjökull 110 Ec 64.39N 20.00W
Langkawi, Pulau- 150 Ce 6.22N 99.48 E
Langkon 150 Ge 6.32N 116.42 E
Langlade 184 Ja 48.12N 75.57W
Langnau im Emmental 128 Bd 46.56N 7.46 E
Langogne 122 Jj 44.43N 3.51 E
Langon 122 Fj 44.33N 0.15W
Langorūd 146 Nd 37.11N 50.10 E
Langøya 114 Db 68.44N 14.50 E
Langreo 126 Ga 43.18N 5.41W
Langres 122 Lg 47.52N 5.20 E
Langres, Plateau de- 110 Gf 47.41N 5.03 E
Langrune-sur-Mer 124 Be 49.19N 0.22W
Langsa 142 Li 4.28N 97.58 E
Långsele 116 Ga 63.11N 17.04 E
Långshyttan 116 Gd 60.27N 16.01 E
Lang Son 148 Ld 21.50N 106.44 E
Lang Suan 148 Jg 9.55N 99.07 E
Languedoc 110 Gg 44.00N 4.00 E
Languedoc 122 Jj 44.00N 4.00 E
Langueyú, Arroyo- 204 Cm 36.39S 58.27W
Langwedel 124 Lb 52.58N 9.13 E
Langxi 152 Ei 31.08N 119.15 E
Langzhong 152 Ie 31.40N 106.04 E
Lan Hsu 152 Lg 22.00N 121.30 E
Laniel 184 Hb 47.06N 79.15W
Lanin, Volcán- 198 Ii 39.38S 71.30W
Lankao (Lanfeng) 154 Cg 34.49N 114.48 E
Länkipohja 116 Kc 61.44N 24.48 E
Lannemezan 122 Gk 43.08N 0.23 E
Lannemezan, Plateau de- 122 Gk 43.09N 0.27 E
Lannion 122 Cf 48.44N 3.28W
Lannion, Baie de- 122 Cf 48.43N 3.34W
La Noria 206 Gb 20.23S 69.53W
Lansdowne House 180 If 52.13N 87.53W
L'Anse 184 Cb 46.45N 88.27W
Lansing [Ia.-U.S.] 186 Ke 43.22N 91.13W
Lansing [Mi.-U.S.] 176 Ke 42.43N 84.34W
Lansjärv 114 Fc 66.39N 22.12 E
Łańskie, Jezioro- 120 Qc 53.33N 20.30 E
Lantar 138 Ie 56.05N 137.35 E
Lanta Yai, Ko- 148 Jg 7.35N 99.03 E
Lanteri 204 Ci 28.50S 59.39W
Lanterne 122 Mg 47.44N 6.03 E
Lanús 204 Cl 34.43S 58.24W
Lanusei 128 Dk 39.53N 9.32 E
Lanvaux, Landes de- 122 Dg 47.47N 2.36W
Lanxi [China] 154 Ej 29.13N 119.28 E
Lanxi [China] 154 Ha 46.15N 126.16 E
Lanxian (Dongcun) 154 Ae 38.17N 111.38 E
Lanyi He 154 Ae 38.40N 110.53 E
Lanzarote 158 Ff 29.00N 13.40W
Lanzhou 142 Mf 36.03N 103.41 E
Lanzo Torinese 128 Be 45.16N 7.28 E
Lao 128 Jk 39.47N 15.48 E
Laoag 142 Oh 18.12N 120.36 E
Laoang 150 Id 12.34N 125.00 E
Lao Cai 142 Mg 22.30N 103.57 E
Laocheng 154 Hc 42.37N 124.04 E
Laoha He 154 Ec 43.24N 120.39 E
Lao He 154 Cj 29.02N 115.47 E
Laohuanghe Kou 154 Ef 37.39N 119.02 E
Laois [2] 118 Fi 53.00N 7.30W
Laojunmiao → Yumen 142 Lf 39.50N 97.44 E
Laojun Shan 152 Je 33.45N 111.38 E
Lao Ling 154 Id 41.24N 126.10 E
Laon 122 Je 49.34N 3.37 E
Laona 186 Ld 45.34N 88.40W
Laonnois 124 Fe 49.35N 3.40 E
La Orchila, Isla- 202 Ea 11.48N 66.10W
La Oroya 200 Ig 11.32S 75.57W
Laos [1] 142 Mh 18.00N 105.00 E
Laoshan (Licun) 154 Ff 36.10N 120.25 E
Laotougou 154 Jc 42.54N 129.09 E
Laou 126 Gi 35.26N 5.05W
Laoye Ling 154 Kb 44.50N 130.10 E
Lapa 206 Kc 25.45S 49.42W
Lapai 166 Gd 9.03N 6.43 E
Lapalisse 122 Jh 46.15N 3.38 E
La Palma 194 Hi 8.24N 78.09W
La Palma [El Sal.] 194 Cf 14.19N 89.11W
La Palma [Pan.] 194 Hi 8.25N 78.09W
La Palma del Condado 126 Fg 37.23N 6.33W
La Paloma 204 El 34.40S 54.10W
La Pampa [2] 206 Ge 37.00S 66.00W
La Panne/De Panne 124 Ec 51.06N 2.35 E
La Paragua 202 Fb 6.50N 63.20W
La Partida, Isla- 192 De 24.30N 110.25W
La Paz [Arg.] 206 Gd 33.28S 67.33W
La Paz [Arg.] 206 Id 30.45S 59.39W
La Paz [Bol.] 200 Jg 16.30S 68.09W
La Paz [Bol.] [3] 202 Eg 15.00S 68.00W
La Paz [Col.] 194 Kh 10.23N 73.10W
La Paz [Hond.] 190 Gf 14.16N 87.40W
La Paz [Hond.] [3] 194 Df 14.15N 87.50W
La Paz [Mex.] 176 Hg 24.10N 110.18W
La Paz [Ur.] 204 Dl 34.46S 56.13W
La Paz [Ven.] 194 Lh 10.41N 72.00W
La Paz, Bahía de- 190 Bd 24.09N 110.25W
La Paz, Llano de- 192 De 24.00N 110.30W
La Paz Centro 194 Dg 12.20N 86.41W
La Pedrera 202 Ed 1.18S 69.40W
Lapeer 184 Fd 43.03N 83.19W
La Pelada 204 Bj 30.52S 60.59W
La Pérouse, Bahía- 221d Bb 27.04S 109.18W
La Perouse Strait (EN) = Laperuza, proliv- 140 Qe 45.30N 142.00 E
La Perouse Strait (EN) = Sōya-Kaikyō 140 Qe 45.30N 142.00 E
Laperuza, proliv- = La Perouse Strait (EN) 140 Qe 45.30N 142.00 E
La Pesca 190 Ed 23.47N 97.47W
La Petite-Pierre 124 Jf 48.52N 7.19 E
La Picasa, Laguna- 204 Al 34.20S 62.14W
La Piedad Cavadas 192 Hg 20.21N 102.00W
La Pine 188 Ee 43.40N 121.30W
Lapinjärvi/Lappträsk 116 Ld 60.36N 26.09 E
Lapinlahti 114 Ge 63.22N 27.30 E
La Plaine 197g Bb 15.20N 61.15W
La Plana 126 Ld 40.00N 0.05W
Lapland (EN) = Lappi 110 Ib 66.50N 22.00 E
Lapland (EN) = Lappland 110 Ib 66.50N 22.00 E
La Plant 186 Fd 45.10N 100.38W
La Plata 200 Ki 34.55S 57.57W
la Pobla de Lillet 126 Nb 42.15N 1.59 E
la Pobla de Segur / Pobla de Segur 126 Mb 42.15N 0.58 E
La Pocatière 184 Lb 47.21N 70.02W
La Porte 184 Dc 41.36N 86.43W
Lapovo 130 Ee 44.11N 21.06 E
Lappajärvi 114 Fe 63.08N 23.40 E
Lappeenranta/Villmanstrand 112 Ic 61.04N 28.11 E
Lappfjärd/Lapväärtti 116 Ib 62.15N 21.32 E
Lappi 116 Ic 61.06N 21.50 E
Lappi [2] 114 Gc 67.40N 26.30 E
Lappi = Lapland (EN) 110 Ib 66.50N 22.00 E
Lappo/Lapua 114 Fe 62.57N 23.00 E
Lappträsk/Lapinjärvi 116 Ld 60.36N 26.09 E
Lapri 138 He 55.45N 124.59 E
Laprida 206 He 37.33S 60.49W
Lâpseki 146 Bb 40.20N 26.31 E
Lapta 146 Ee 35.20N 33.10 E
Laptev Sea (EN) = Laptevyh, more- 224 Fd 76.00N 126.00 E
Laptevyh, more- = Laptev Sea (EN) 224 Fd 76.00N 126.00 E
Lapua/Lappo 114 Fe 62.57N 23.00 E
La Puebla / Sa Pobla 126 Pe 39.46N 3.01 E
La Puebla de Cazalla 126 Gg 37.14N 5.19W
Lapuna 204 Ba 15.13S 60.28W
La Puntilla 198 Hf 2.11S 81.01W
La Purísima 192 Cd 26.10N 112.04W
Lăpuş 130 Hb 47.30N 24.01 E
Lăpuş 130 Gb 47.39N 23.24 E
La Push 188 Cc 47.55N 124.38W
Lapväärtti/Lappfjärd 116 Ib 62.15N 21.32 E
Łapy 120 Sd 53.00N 22.53 E
Laqīyat al Arba'in 168 Da 20.03N 28.02 E
La Quemada 192 Hf 22.27N 102.45W
La Quiaca 206 Gb 22.06S 65.37W
L'Aquila 112 Hg 42.22N 13.22 E
Lar 144 Hd 27.41N 54.17 E
Lara [2] 202 Ea 10.10N 69.50W
La Rábida, Monasterio de- 126 Fg 37.12N 6.55W
Larache 162 Fb 35.12N 6.09W
Laragne-Montéglin 122 Lj 44.19N 5.49 E
Lārak 144 Id 26.52N 56.22 E
La Rambla 126 Hg 37.36N 4.44W
Laramie 176 Ie 41.19N 105.35W
Laramie Mountains 182 Fc 42.00N 105.40W
Laramie Peak 188 Me 42.17N 105.27W
Laramie River 188 Me 42.12N 104.32W
Laranjal, Rio- 204 Ff 23.12S 53.45W
Laranjeiras do Sul 206 Jc 25.25S 52.25W
Larantuka 150 Hh 8.21S 122.59 E
Larat 150 Jh 7.09S 131.45 E
Larat, Pulau- 150 Jh 7.10S 131.50 E
La Raya 194 Ji 8.20N 74.34W
L'Arba 126 Ph 36.34N 3.09 E
L'Arbaa Naït Irathen 126 Qh 36.38N 4.12 E
Lärbro 114 Eh 57.47N 18.47 E
Larche, Col de- 122 Mj 44.25N 6.53 E
Larde 172 Fc 16.28S 39.43 E
Larderello 128 Eg 43.14N 10.53 E
Laredo [Sp.] 126 Ia 43.24N 3.25W
Laredo [Tx.-U.S.] 176 Jg 27.31N 99.30W
Laren 124 Hb 52.16N 5.16 E
Lärestān 140 Hg 27.00N 55.30 E
Lārestān 144 Id 27.00N 55.30 E
Large Island 197p Cb 12.24N 61.30W
Largentière 122 Kj 44.32N 4.18 E
Largo, Cayo- 194 Gc 21.38N 81.28W
Largs 118 If 55.48N 4.52W
La Ribera 126 Kb 42.30N 2.00W
Larimore 186 Hc 47.54N 97.38W
Larino 128 Ii 41.48N 14.54 E
Lario → Como, Lago di- 128 Dd 46.00N 9.15 E
La Rioja 200 Jh 29.25S 66.50W
La Rioja 126 Jb 42.20N 2.20W
La Rioja [Arg.] [2] 206 Gc 30.00S 67.30W
La Rioja [Sp.] [2] 126 Jb 42.15N 2.30W
Lárisa 112 Ih 39.38N 22.25 E
La Rivière-Thibouville, Nassandres- 124 Ce 49.07N 0.44 E
Lārkāna 148 Dc 27.33N 68.13 E
Larmor-Plage 122 Cg 47.42N 3.23W
Larnaka/Lárnax 144 Dc 34.55N 33.38 E
Lárnax/Larnaka 144 Dc 34.55N 33.38 E
Larne/Latharna 118 Hg 54.51N 5.49W
Larned 186 Gg 38.11N 99.06W
La Robla 126 Gb 42.48N 5.37W
La Roche 219b De 21.28S 168.02 E
La Roche-en-Ardenne 122 Ld 50.11N 5.35 E
La Rochefoucauld 122 Gi 45.44N 0.23 E
La Roche-Guyon 124 De 49.05N 1.38 E
La Roda 126 Je 39.13N 2.09W
La Romana 190 Ke 18.25N 68.58W
La Ronge 180 Ge 55.06N 105.17W
La Ronge, Lac- 174 Id 55.05N 104.59W
Larose 186 Kl 29.35N 90.23W
La Rosita 192 Ic 28.24N 101.43W
Larouco 126 Ec 41.56N 7.40W
Larreynaga 194 Dg 12.40N 86.34W
Larrey Point 212 Dc 20.00S 119.10 E
Larrimah 210 Ef 15.35S 133.12 E
Larsa 146 Kg 31.16N 45.49 E
Lars Christensen Kyst 222 Fe 69.30S 68.00 E
Larsen, Mount- 222 Kf 74.51S 162.12 E
Larsen Ice Shelf 222 Qe 68.30S 62.30W
La Rumorosa 192 Aa 32.34N 116.06W
Laruns 122 Fk 43.00N 0.25W
Larvik 114 Bg 59.04N 10.00 E
Larzac, Causse du- 122 Jk 43.57N 3.11 E
La Sabana [Arg.] 204 Ch 27.52S 59.57W
La Sabana [Col.] 202 Ec 2.20N 68.32W
Las Adjuntas, Presa de- 192 Jf 23.55N 98.45W
La Sagra 126 Jg 37.57N 2.34W
La Sagra 126 Id 40.05N 4.00W
La Salle 186 Lf 41.20N 89.06W
La Salle, Pic- 190 Je 18.22N 71.59W
La Sal Mountains 188 Kg 38.30N 109.10W
Las Alpujarras 126 Ih 36.50N 3.25W
La Sanabria 126 Fb 42.08N 6.30W
Las Animas 186 Eg 38.04N 103.13W
Lās 'ānōd 168 Hd 8.26N 47.24 E
La Sarre 180 Jg 48.48N 79.12W
Las Aves, Islas- 202 Ea 11.58N 67.33W
Las Avispas 204 Bi 29.53S 61.18W
Las Bardenas 126 Kb 42.10N 1.25W
Las Bonitas 196 Di 7.52N 65.40W
Las Breñas 206 Hc 27.05S 61.05W
Las Cabezas de San Juan 126 Gh 36.59N 5.56W
Lascahobas 194 Ld 18.50N 71.56W
Lascano 204 Ek 33.40S 54.12W
Las Casitas, Cerro- 190 Cd 23.31N 109.53W
Lascaux, Grotte de- 122 Hi 45.03N 1.11 E
Las Cejas 206 He 26.53S 64.44W
Las Chilcas, Arroyo- 204 Cm 37.16S 58.26W
Las Choapas 190 Fe 17.55N 94.05W
Las Cinco Villas 126 Kb 42.05N 1.07W
Las Cruces 182 Fe 32.23N 106.29W
Läsdäred 168 Hc 10.10N 46.01 E
Läs Dawa'o 168 Hc 10.22N 49.03 E
La Segarra 126 Nc 41.30N 1.10 E
La Selva 126 Oc 41.40N 2.50 E
La Serena 200 Ih 29.54S 71.16W
La Serena 126 Gf 38.45N 5.30W
la Seu d'Urgell / Seo de Urgel 126 Nb 42.21N 1.28 E
Las Flores 206 Ie 36.03S 59.07W
Lāsh-e Joveyn 144 Jc 31.43N 61.37 E
Las Heras 206 Gd 32.51S 68.49W
Lashio 142 Lg 22.58N 97.48 E
Lashkar Gāh 142 If 31.35N 64.21 E
Las Hurdes 126 Fd 40.20N 6.20W
La Sila 110 Hh 39.15N 16.30 E
Łasin 120 Pc 53.32N 19.05 E
Läsjerd 146 Oe 35.24N 53.04 E
Łask 120 Pe 51.36N 19.07 E
Las Lajas 206 Fe 38.31S 70.22W
Las Lomitas 206 Hb 24.42S 60.36W
Las Margaritas 192 Ni 16.19N 91.59W
Las Mariñas 126 Da 43.20N 8.15W
Las Marismas 126 Fg 37.00N 6.15W
Las Mercedes 202 Eb 9.07N 66.24W
Las Mesteñas 192 Gc 28.13N 104.35W
Las Minas, Cerro- 190 Gf 14.33N 88.39W
Las Minas, Sierra de- 190 Ge 15.05N 90.00W
Las Mixtecas, Sierra de- 192 Ki 17.45N 97.15W
La Sola, Isla- 202 Fa 11.20N 63.34W
La Solana 126 If 38.56N 3.14W
Lasolo 150 Hg 3.29S 122.04 E
La Sorcière 197k Bb 13.59N 60.56W
Las Palmas [3] 162 Ed 28.20N 14.20W
Las Palmas de Gran Canaria 160 Ff 28.06N 15.24W
Las Palomas 192 Fb 33.03N 107.19W
Las Petas 204 Cc 16.23S 59.11W
La Spezia 112 Gg 44.07N 9.50 E
Las Piedras 206 Id 34.45S 56.13W
Las Plumas 200 Jj 43.40S 67.15W
Lās Qoray 168 Hc 11.15N 48.22 E
Las Rosas 204 Bk 32.28S 61.34W
Lassen Peak 182 Cc 40.29N 121.31W
Lassigny 124 Ee 49.35N 2.51 E
Laßnitz 128 Jd 46.46N 15.32 E
Lasso 220b Ba 15.02N 145.38 E
Las Tablas 194 Gj 7.46N 80.17W
Last Mountain Lake 180 Gf 51.10N 105.15W
Las Toscas 204 Ci 28.21S 59.17W
Lastovo 128 Kh 42.46N 16.55 E
Lastovo 128 Kh 42.45N 16.50 E
Lastovski kanal 128 Kh 42.50N 16.59 E
Las Tres Virgenes, Volcán- 190 Bc 27.27N 112.34W
Las Tunas [3] 194 Ic 21.00N 77.00W
Las Tunas, Punta- 197a Bb 18.30N 66.37W
Las Varillas 206 Hd 31.52S 62.43W
Las Vegas [N.M.-U.S.] 182 Fd 35.36N 105.13W
Las Vegas [Nv.-U.S.] 176 Hf 36.11N 115.08W
Las Villuercas 126 Ge 39.33N 5.27W
Łaszczów 120 Tf 50.32N 23.40 E
Lata 221c Db 14.14S 169.29W
Latacunga 202 Cd 0.55S 78.37W
La Tagua 202 Dd 0.03S 74.40W
Latakia (EN) = Al Lādhiqīyah 142 Ff 35.31N 35.07 E
Late Island 216 Gc 18.48S 174.39W
Laterza 128 Kj 40.37N 16.48 E
Latgale 116 Lh 56.45N 27.30 E
Latgales Augstiene / Latgalskaja vozvyšennost 116 Lh 56.10N 27.30 E
Latgalskaja vozvyšennost / Latgales Augstiene 116 Lh 56.10N 27.30 E
Latharna/Larne 118 Hg 54.51N 5.49W
Lathen 124 Jb 52.52N 7.19 E
La Tigra 204 Bh 27.06S 60.34W
Latina 128 Gi 41.28N 12.52 E
Latisana 128 Ge 45.47N 13.00 E
Latium (EN) = Lazio [2] 128 Gh 42.02N 12.23 E
La Toja 126 Db 42.27N 8.50W
La Toma 206 Gd 33.03S 65.37W
La Tontouta 219b Ce 22.00S 166.15 E
Latorica 120 Rh 48.28N 21.50 E
La Tortuga, Isla- 202 Ea 10.56N 65.20W
La Trinidad 194 Dg 12.58N 86.14W
La Trinidad de Orichuna 196 Bi 7.07N 69.45W
La Trinité 196 Fe 14.44N 60.58W
Latronico 128 Kj 40.05N 16.01 E
Lattari, Monti- 128 Ij 40.40N 14.30 E
La Tuque 180 Kg 47.27N 72.47W
Lātūr 148 Fe 18.24N 76.35 E
Latvia (EN) = Latvija 136 Cd 57.00N 25.00 E
Latvija = Latvia (EN) 136 Cd 57.00N 25.00 E
Latvijas Padomju Socialistiska Republika/ Latvijskaja SSR → Latvija 136 Cd 57.00N 25.00 E
Latvijas PSR → Latvija 136 Cd 57.00N 25.00 E
Latvijskaja Sovetskaja Socialističeskaja Respublika → Latvija 136 Cd 57.00N 25.00 E
Latvijskaja SSR/Latvijas Padomju Socialistiska Respublika → Latvija 136 Cd 57.00N 25.00 E
Lau 158 Kh 6.56N 30.16 E
Laubach 124 Kd 50.33N 8.59 E
Lauchert 120 Fh 48.05N 9.15 E
Lauchhammer 120 Je 51.30N 13.48 E
Lauenburg 120 Gc 53.22N 10.34 E
Lauf an der Pegnitz 120 Hg 49.31N 11.17 E
Laughlan Islands 219a Ac 9.15S 153.40 E
Laughlin Peak 186 Dh 36.38N 104.12W
Lau Group 208 Jf 18.20S 178.30W
Lauhanvuori 116 Jb 62.10N 22.10 E
Laujar de Andarax 126 Jh 36.59N 2.51W
Laukaa 114 Fe 62.25N 25.57 E
Laukuva 116 Ji 55.35N 22.08 E
Laulau, Bahía- 220b Ba 15.08N 145.46 E
Launceston [Austl.] 210 Fi 41.26S 147.08 E
Launceston [Eng.-U.K.] 118 Ik 50.38N 4.21W
La Unión [Bol.] 204 Bb 15.18S 61.05W
La Unión [Chile] 206 Ff 40.17S 73.05W
La Unión [Col.] 202 Cc 1.37N 77.08W
La Unión [El Sal.] 190 Gf 13.20N 87.51W
La Unión [Mex.] 192 Ii 17.58N 101.49W
La Unión [Peru] 202 Ce 9.46S 76.48W
La Unión [Sp.] 126 Lg 37.37N 0.52W
La Unión [Ven.] 194 Ni 8.13N 67.46W
Laura 212 Ic 15.34S 144.28 E
La Urbana 196 Cj 7.08N 66.56W
Laurel [Ms.-U.S.] 182 Je 31.42N 89.08W
Laurel [Mt.-U.S.] 182 Fb 45.40N 108.46W
Laureles 204 Ej 31.23S 55.52W
Laurel Hill 184 He 40.02N 79.17W
Laurel Mountain 184 Hf 39.20N 79.50W
Laurens 184 Fh 34.30N 82.01W
Laurentian Plateau (EN) = Laurentien, Plateau- 174 Md 50.00N 70.00W
Laurentian Scarp 184 Ic 45.50N 76.15W
Laurentide Scarp 184 Kb 46.38N 73.00W
Laurentien, Plateau- = Laurentian Plateau (EN) 174 Md 50.00N 70.00W
Lauria 128 Jj 40.02N 15.50 E
Lau Ridge (EN) 106 Kl 25.00S 179.00 E
Laurie River 180 He 56.00N 100.58W
Laurinburg 184 Hh 34.47N 79.27W
Laurium 184 Cb 47.14N 88.26W
Lauro Muller 204 Hi 28.24S 49.23W
Lausanne 112 Gf 46.30N 6.40 E
Lausitzer Gebirge 120 Kf 50.48N 14.40 E
Lausitzer Neiße 120 Kd 52.04N 14.46 E
Laut, Pulau- 150 Ef 4.43N 107.59 E
Laut, Pulau- 140 Nj 3.40S 116.10 E
Lautaret, Col du- 122 Mi 45.02N 6.24 E
Lautaro 206 Fe 38.31S 72.27W
Lautém 150 Ih 8.22S 126.54 E
Lauter 120 Eg 48.58N 8.11 E
Lauterbach 120 Ff 50.38N 9.24 E
Lauterbourg 124 Kf 48.59N 8.11 E
Lauterecken 124 Je 49.39N 7.36 E
Lauthala 219d Cb 16.45S 179.41W
Laut Kecil, Kepulauan- 150 Gg 4.50S 115.45 E
Lautoka 216 Ec 17.37S 177.27 E
Lauvergne Island 220d Cb 7.00N 152.00 E
Lauwersmeer 124 Ia 53.25N 6.15 E
Lauzerte 122 Hj 44.15N 1.08 E
Lauzon 184 Lb 46.50N 71.10W
Lava 120 Rb 54.37N 21.14 E
Lava, Nosy- [Mad.] 172 Hb 14.33S 47.36 E
Lava, Nosy- [Mad.] 172 Hb 12.49S 48.44 E
Lavaca River 186 Hl 28.50N 96.36W
Lava Flow 186 Bi 34.45N 108.20W
Laval 122 Ff 48.04N 0.46W
La Vall d'Uxó / Vall de Uxó 126 Le 39.49N 0.14W
Lavalle 204 Ci 29.01S 59.11W
Lavalleja [2] 204 El 34.00S 55.00W
Lāvān, Jazīreh-ye- 144 Hd 26.48N 53.00 E

Lavandou, Le- 122 Mk 43.08N 6.22 E
Lavanggu 219a Ed 11.37S 160.15 E
Lavant 128 Id 46.38N 14.56 E
Lavapié, Punta- 198 Ii 37.09S 73.35W
Lāvar Meydān 146 Pg 30.20N 54.30 E
Lavassaare 116 Kf 58.29N 24.16 E
Lavaur 122 Hk 43.42N 1.49 E
La Vecilla 126 Gb 42.51N 5.24W
La Vega 190 Je 19.13N 70.31W
La Vela de Coro 194 Mh 11.27N 69.34W
Lavelanet 122 Hl 42.56N 1.51 E
Lavello 128 Ji 41.03N 15.48 E
La Venta 190 Fe 18.08N 94.03W
Laventie 124 Ed 50.38N 2.46 E
La Ventura 192 Ie 24.37N 100.54W
La Vera 126 Gd 40.05N 5.30W
L'Averdy, Cape- 219a Ba 5.33S 155.04 E
Laverton 212 Ee 28.38S 122.25 E
Lavia 114 Ff 61.36N 22.36 E
La Victoria 202 Ea 10.14N 67.20W
La Vila d'Eivissa / Ibiza 126 Nf 38.54N 1.26 E
La Vila Joiosa / Villajoyosa 126 Lf 38.30N 0.14W
La Villita, Presa- 192 Hh 18.05N 102.05W
La Viña 202 Ce 6.54S 79.28W
Lavoisier Island 222 Qe 66.12S 66.44W
Lavougba 168 Cd 5.37N 23.19 E
Lavouras 204 Db 14.59S 56.47W
Lavras 202 Jh 21.14S 45.00W
Lavras do Sul 204 Fj 30.49S 53.55W
Lavrentija 138 Nc 65.33N 171.02W
Lávrion 130 Hl 37.43N 24.03 E
Lavumisa 172 Ee 27.15S 31.55 E
Lawas 150 Gf 4.51N 115.24 E
Lawdar 144 Gg 13.53N 45.52 E
Lawe 124 Ed 50.38N 2.42 E
Lawers, Ben- 118 Ie 56.33N 4.15W
Lawit, Gunong- 150 Ff 1.23N 112.55 E
Lawqah 146 Jh 29.49N 42.45 E
Lawra 166 Ec 10.39N 2.52W
Lawrence [Ks.-U.S.] 182 Hd 38.58N 95.14W
Lawrence [Ma.-U.S.] 182 Mc 42.42N 71.09W
Lawrence [N.Z.] 218 Cf 45.55S 169.42 E
Lawrenceburg [Ky.-U.S.] 184 Ef 38.02N 84.54W
Lawrenceburg [Tn.-U.S.] 184 Dh 35.15N 87.20W
Lawson, Mount- 212 Ja 7.44S 146.37 E
Lawton 176 Jf 34.37N 98.25W
Lawu, Gunung- 140 Nj 7.38S 111.11 E
Lawz, Jabal al- 146 Fh 28.41N 35.18 E
Laxå 114 Dg 58.59N 14.37 E
Lay 122 Eh 46.18N 1.17W
Laylā 142 Gg 22.17N 46.45 E
Layon 122 Fg 47.20N 0.45W
Layou 197n Ba 13.12N 61.17W
Layou 197g Bb 15.23N 61.26W
Laysan Island 208 Jb 25.50N 171.50W
Layton 188 Jf 41.04N 111.58W
La Zarca 192 Ge 25.50N 104.44W
Lazarev 138 Jf 52.13N 141.35 E
Lazarevac 130 De 44.23N 20.16 E
Lázaro Cárdenas, Presa- 192 Ge 25.35N 105.05W
Lazdijai/Lazdijaj 114 Fi 54.13N 23.33 E
Lazdijaj/Lazdijai 114 Fi 54.13N 23.33 E
Lāzeh 146 Oi 26.48N 53.22 E
Lazio = Latium (EN) [2] 128 Gh 42.02N 12.23 E
Lazo 154 Mc 43.25N 134.01 E
Lazovsk 132 Ff 47.38N 28.12 E
Łazy 120 Pf 50.27N 19.26 E
Lea 118 Nj 51.30N 0.01 E
Lead 182 Gc 44.21N 103.46W
Leader 188 Ka 50.53N 109.31W
Lead Hill 186 Jh 37.06N 92.38W
Leadville 182 Fd 39.15N 106.20W
Leaf River 186 Lk 31.00N 88.45W
League City 186 Il 29.31N 95.05W
Leamington 184 Fd 42.03N 82.36W
Leandro N. Alem 204 Bl 34.30S 61.24W
Leane, Lough-/Loch Léin 118 Di 52.05N 9.35W
Le'an Jiang 154 Dj 28.58N 116.41 E
Learmonth 212 Cd 22.13S 114.04 E
Leavenworth [Ks.-U.S.] 186 Ig 39.19N 94.55W
Leavenworth [Wa.-U.S.] 188 Ec 47.36N 120.40W
Łeba 120 Nb 54.47N 17.33 E
Łeba 120 Nb 54.43N 17.25 E
Lebach 124 Ie 49.24N 6.55 E
Lébamba 170 Bc 2.12S 11.30 E
Lebanon [In.-U.S.] 184 De 40.03N 86.28W
Lebanon [Ky.-U.S.] 184 Eg 37.34N 85.15W
Lebanon [Mo.-U.S.] 186 Jh 37.41N 92.40W
Lebanon [N.H.-U.S.] 184 Kd 43.38N 72.15W
Lebanon [Or.-U.S.] 188 Dd 44.32N 122.54W
Lebanon [Pa.-U.S.] 184 Ie 40.21N 76.25W
Lebanon [Tn.-U.S.] 184 Dg 36.12N 86.18W
Lebanon (EN)=Lubnān [1] 142 Ff 33.50N 35.50 E
Lebanon Mountains (EN)= Lubnān, Jabal- 144 Ec 34.00N 36.30 E
Lebap 135 Cd 41.02N 61.54 E
Le Bec-Hellouin 124 Ce 49.14N 0.43 E
Lebedin 136 De 50.36N 34.30 E
Lebediny 138 He 58.25N 125.58 E
Lebedjan 136 De 53.02N 39.07 E
Lebjažje [Kaz.] 136 He 51.28N 77.46 E
Lebjažje [Russia] 134 Mi 55.16N 66.29 E
Lebo 170 Db 4.29N 23.57 E
Lebomboberge 158 Kk 26.15S 32.00 E
Lebombo Mountains 158 Kk 26.15S 32.00 E
Lębork 120 Nb 54.33N 17.44 E
Le Bourget 124 Ef 48.56N 2.25 E
Lebrija 126 Fh 36.55N 6.04W
Łebsko, Jezioro- 120 Nb 54.44N 17.24 E
Lebu 206 Fe 37.37S 73.39W
Le Carbet 197h Ab 14.43N 61.11W
Le Cateau 124 Fd 50.06N 3.33 E
Le Catelet 124 Fd 50.01N 3.15 E
Lecce 112 Hg 40.23N 18.11 E
Lecco 128 De 45.51N 9.23 E
Lech 128 Ec 47.12N 10.09 E
Lech 120 Gh 48.44N 10.56 E
Lechang 152 Jf 25.15N 113.25 E
Lechfeld 120 Gh 48.10N 10.50 E
Lechiguiri, Cerro- 192 Li 16.43N 95.30W
Lechtaler Alpen 128 Ec 47.15N 10.30 E
Léconi 170 Bc 1.35S 14.14 E
Léconi 170 Bc 1.11S 13.16 E
Le Cornate 128 Eg 43.10N 10.58 E
Le Coudray-Saint-Germer 124 De 49.25N 1.50 E
Le Crotoy 124 Dd 50.13N 1.37 E
Łęczna 120 Se 51.19N 22.53 E
Łęczyca 120 Pd 52.04N 19.13 E
Led 114 Ke 62.20N 43.00 E
Lede 124 Fd 50.57N 3.59 E
Ledesma 126 Gc 41.05N 6.00W
Le Diamant 197h Ac 14.29N 61.02W
Ledjanaja, gora- 140 Tc 61.45N 171.15 E
Lednik Entuziastov 222 Cf 70.30S 16.00 E
Lednik Mušketova 222 Cf 72.00S 14.00 E
Ledo, Cabo- 170 Bd 9.41S 13.12 E
Ledolom Tajmyrski 222 Ge 66.00S 83.00 E
Lędyczek 120 Mc 53.33N 16.58 E
Lee/An Laoi 118 Ej 51.55N 8.30W
Leech Lake 182 Ib 47.09N 94.23W
Leeds [Al.-U.S.] 184 Di 33.33N 86.33W
Leeds [Eng.-U.K.] 112 Fe 53.50N 1.35W
Leeds [N.D.-U.S.] 186 Gb 48.17N 99.27W
Leek 124 Ia 53.10N 6.24 E
Leer (Ostfriesland) 120 Dc 53.14N 7.26 E
Leerdam 124 Hc 51.53N 5.06 E
Lées 122 Fk 43.38N 0.14W
Leesburg 182 Kf 29.49N 81.53W
Leeste, Weyhe- 124 Kb 52.59N 8.50 E
Leesville 186 Jk 31.08N 93.16W
Leeuwarden 122 La 53.12N 5.46 E
Leeuwarderadeel 124 Ha 53.16N 5.46 E
Leeuwarderadeel-Stiens 124 Ha 53.16N 5.46 E
Leeuwin, Cape- 212 Cf 34.25S 115.00 E
Leeward Islands 190 Le 17.00N 63.00W
Leeward Islands (EN)=Sous le Vent, Iles- 208 Lf 16.38S 151.30W
Léfini 170 Cc 2.57S 16.10 E
Lefka 130 Jh 41.52N 26.16 E
Lefke 146 Ee 35.07N 32.51 E
Lefkoşa/Levkosia = Nicosia (EN) 142 Ff 35.10N 33.22 E
Le François 197h Bb 14.37N 60.54W
Lefroy, Lake- 212 Ef 31.15S 121.40 E
Łęg 120 Rf 50.38N 21.49 E
Leganés 126 Id 40.19N 3.45W
Legazpi 142 Oh 13.09N 123.44 E
Legden 124 Jb 52.02N 7.06 E
Legé 122 Eh 46.53N 1.36W
Legges Tor 214 Jh 41.32S 147.40 E
Leggett 188 Dg 39.52N 123.43W
Leghorn (EN)=Livorno 112 Hg 43.33N 10.19 E
Legionowo 120 Qd 52.25N 20.56 E
Léglise 124 He 49.48N 5.32 E
Legnago 128 Fe 45.11N 11.18 E
Legnano 128 Ce 45.36N 8.54 E
Legnica 120 Me 51.13N 16.09 E
Legnica [2] 120 Me 51.15N 16.10 E
Le Grand-Quevilly 124 De 49.25N 1.02 E
Le Grand-Wintersberg 122 Ne 48.59N 7.37 E
Léguer 122 Cf 48.44N 3.32W
Leh 148 Fb 34.10N 77.35 E
Lehi 188 Jf 40.24N 111.51W
Lehmann 204 Bj 31.08S 61.27W
Le Houlme 124 De 49.31N 1.02 E
Lehrte 120 Fd 52.23N 9.58 E
Lehtimäki 116 Jb 62.47N 23.55 E
Lehua Island 221a Aa 22.01N 160.06W
Lehututu 172 Cd 23.53S 21.49 E
Leibnitz 128 Jd 46.46N 15.32 E
Leibo 152 Hf 28.13N 103.34 E
Leicester 112 Fe 52.38N 1.05W
Leicester 118 Mi 52.40N 1.00W
Leicestershire [3] 118 Mi 52.38N 1.00W
Leichhardt Range 212 Jd 20.40S 147.05 E
Leichhardt River 212 Hc 17.35S 139.48 E
Leiden 122 Kc 52.09N 4.30 E
Leidschendam 124 Gb 52.05N 4.26 E
Leie 122 Jc 51.03N 3.43 E
Leifear/Lifford 118 Fg 54.50N 7.29W
Leigh Creek 210 Eh 30.28S 138.25 E
Leighton Buzzard 124 Bc 51.55N 0.39W
Leigong Shan 152 If 26.23N 108.15 E
Leikanger 114 Ae 62.07N 5.20 E
Léim an Mhadaidh/ Limavady 118 Gf 55.03N 6.57W
Leimen 124 Ke 49.21N 8.41 E
Leimus 194 Ef 14.44N 84.07W
Leine 120 Fd 52.40N 9.40 E
Leinster/Laighean 118 Gh 53.00N 7.00W
Leipzig 112 He 51.18N 12.20 E
Leira 112 Cd 60.58N 9.18 E
Leiria 126 De 39.45N 8.48W
Leiria [2] 126 De 39.40N 8.50W
Leirvik 114 Ag 59.47N 5.30 E
Leisi/Lejsi 116 Jf 58.33N 22.30 E
Leisler, Mount- 212 Fd 23.30S 129.20 E
Leiston 124 Db 52.12N 1.34 E
Leitariegos, Puerto de- 126 Fa 43.00N 6.25W
Leitha 128 Lc 47.52N 17.18 E
Leithagebirge 128 Kc 47.58N 16.40 E
Leitir Ceanainn/Letterkenny 118 Fg 54.57N 7.44W
Leitrim/Liatroim [2] 118 Eg 54.20N 8.20W
Leiva, Cerro- 202 Dc 2.54N 74.48W
Leiyang 152 Jf 26.30N 112.57 E
Leizhou → Haikang 152 Jg 20.56N 110.06 E
Leizhou Bandao 140 Ng 20.40N 110.05 E
Lejasciems 116 Lg 57.08N 26.36 E
Lejsi/Leisi 116 Jf 58.33N 22.30 E
Lek 122 Lc 51.54N 4.36 E
Leka 114 Cd 65.05N 11.37 E
Lékana 170 Cc 2.19S 14.36 E
Leketi, Monts de la- 158 Ii 2.34S 14.17 E
Lekhainá 130 El 37.56N 21.16 E
Lekhal 126 Ph 36.20N 3.51 E
Lekitobi 150 Hg 1.58S 124.33 E
Lekki Lagoon 166 Fd 6.30N 4.07 E
Leknes 114 Cb 68.10N 13.42 E
Łęknica 120 Ke 51.32N 14.48 E
Lékoumou [3] 170 Bc 3.00S 13.50 E
Leksand 114 Df 60.44N 15.01 E
Leksozero, ozero- 114 He 63.45N 31.00 E
Leksula 150 Ig 3.46S 126.31 E
Leksvik 114 Ce 63.40N 10.37 E
Le Lamentin 196 Fe 14.37N 61.01W
Leland 186 Kj 33.24N 90.54W
Lelång 116 Ee 59.10N 12.10 E
Lelčicy 132 Fd 51.49N 28.21 E
Leleiwi Point 221a Gd 19.44N 155.00W
Lelepa 219b Dc 17.36S 168.13 E
Leleque 206 Ff 42.23S 71.03W
Leli 219a Ec 8.45S 161.02 E
Leli → Tianlin 152 Ig 24.22N 106.11 E
Lelija 128 Mg 43.26N 18.29 E
Leling 154 Df 37.44N 117.13 E
Léliogat 219b Ce 21.18S 167.35 E
Lelle 114 Fg 58.53N 25.00 E
Le Locle 128 Ac 47.05N 6.45 E
Le Lorrain 197h Ab 14.50N 61.04W
Lelystad 122 Lb 52.31N 5.27 E
Le Madonie 128 Hm 37.50N 14.00 E
Le Maire, Estrecho de- 206 Hh 54.50S 65.00W
Léman, Lac-=Geneva, Lake-(EN) 110 Gf 46.25N 6.30 E
Leman Bank 118 Oh 53.10N 1.58 E
Lemankoa 219a Ba 5.03S 154.34 E
Le Marin 197h Bc 14.28N 60.52W
Le Mars 186 He 42.47N 96.10W
Lembach 124 Je 49.00N 7.48 E
Lembeck 124 Ic 51.44N 6.59 E
Lemberg 124 Je 49.00N 7.23 E
Lembolovskaja vozvyšennost 116 Md 60.50N 30.15 E
Lembruch 124 Kb 52.32N 8.21 E
Leme 204 If 22.12S 47.24W
Lemelerberg 124 Ib 52.29N 6.23 E
Lemesós/Limassol 144 Dc 34.40N 33.02 E
Lemgo 120 Ed 52.02N 8.54 E
Lemhi Range 188 Id 44.30N 113.25W
Lemieux Islands 180 Ld 64.00N 64.20W
Lemju 134 He 63.50N 56.57 E
Lemland 116 Id 60.05N 20.10 E
Lemmer, Lemsterland- 124 Hb 52.51N 5.42 E
Lemmon 182 Gb 45.56N 102.10W
Lemmon, Mount- 188 Jj 32.26N 110.47W
Lemnos (EN)=Límnos 110 Ih 39.50N 25.15 E
Le Morne Rouge 197h Ab 14.46N 61.08W
Lemotol Bay 220d Bb 7.21N 151.35 E
Le Moyne, Lac- 180 Ke 57.00N 68.00W
Lempa, Río- 190 Gf 13.14N 88.49W
Lempäälä 116 Jc 61.19N 23.45 E
Lempira [3] 194 Cf 14.20N 88.40W
Lemro 148 Id 20.25N 93.20 E
Lemsid 162 Ed 26.33N 13.51W
Lemsterland 124 Hb 52.51N 5.42 E
Lemsterland-Lemmer 124 Hb 52.51N 5.42 E
Le Murge 110 Hg 40.50N 16.40 E
Lemvig 116 Ch 56.32N 8.18 E
Lemya 134 Jc 66.30N 62.00 E
Lena 140 Ob 72.25N 126.40 E
Lena, Mount- 188 Kf 40.50N 109.27W
Lénakel 219b Dd 19.32S 169.16 E
Lena Mountains (EN) = Prilenskoje plato 140 Oc 60.45N 125.00 E
Lena Tablemount (EN) 158 Ln 53.00S 45.00 E
Lençóis Paulista 204 Hf 22.36S 48.47W
Lendava 128 Kd 46.34N 16.27 E
Lendery 114 He 63.26N 31.12 E
Lendinara 128 Fe 45.05N 11.36 E
Le Neubourg 124 Ce 49.09N 0.55 E
Lenger 136 Gg 42.10N 69.55 E
Lengerich 120 Dd 52.11N 7.52 E
Lenghu 142 Lf 38.50N 93.30 E
Lengoué 170 Cb 0.49N 15.47 E
Lengshuijiang 152 Jf 27.41N 111.28 E
Lengua de Vaca, Punta- 206 Fd 30.14S 71.38W
Lengulu 170 Eb 3.15N 26.30 E
Lenhovda 114 Dh 57.00N 15.17 E
Lenina, pik- = Lenin Peak (EN) 140 Jf 39.19N 73.01 E
Leninabad → Chudžand 142 Ie 40.17N 69.37 E
Leninakan → Kumajri 112 Kg 40.47N 43.50 E
Lenin Canal (EN)=Volgo-Donskoj sudohodny kanal imeni V. I. Lenina 110 Kf 48.40N 43.37 E
Leningrad → Sankt-Peterburg 112 Jc 59.55N 30.15 E
Leningradskaja 132 Kf 46.17N 39.25 E
Leningradskaja 222 Je 69.30S 159.23 E
Leningradskaja oblast [3] 136 Dd 60.00N 31.40 E
Leningradskij [Russia] 138 Mc 69.17N 178.10 E
Leningradskij [Taj.] 136 Hh 38.09N 70.01 E
Lenino 132 Ig 45.17N 35.44 E
Leninogorsk [Kaz.] 142 Kd 50.27N 83.32 E
Leninogorsk [Russia] 136 Fe 54.38N 52.30 E
Lenin Peak (EN) = Lenina, pik- 140 Jf 39.19N 73.01 E
Leninsk [Russia] 132 Ne 48.42N 45.11 E
Leninsk [Turk.] 135 Bc 42.04N 59.24 E
Leninsk [Uzb.] 135 Id 40.40N 72.20 E
Leninski [Kaz.] 136 He 52.15N 76.50 E
Leninski [Mol.] 130 Lb 47.50N 28.16 E
Leninskij [Russia] 138 He 58.32N 128.58 E
Leninsk-Kuzneckij 142 Kd 54.38N 86.10 E
Leninskoje [Kaz.] 136 Ge 54.05N 65.23 E
Leninskoje [Russia] 138 Ig 47.59N 132.38 E
Leninskoje [Russia] 114 Lg 58.21N 47.07 E
Leninváros → Tiszaújváros 120 Ri 47.56N 21.05 E
Lenkoran 112 Kh 38.44N 48.50 E
Lenne 124 Jc 51.15N 7.50 E
Lennestadt 124 Kc 51.08N 8.01 E
Lennestadt-Grevenbrück 124 Kc 51.08N 8.01 E
Lennox 206 Gi 55.19S 67.00W
Lennox Hills 118 Ie 56.05N 4.10W
Leno-Angarskoje plato 138 Fe 55.00N 104.30 E
Lenoir 184 Gh 35.55N 81.32W
Le Nouvion-en-Thiérache 124 Fd 50.01N 3.47 E
Lens 122 Id 50.26N 2.50 E
Lensk 142 Nc 61.00N 114.50 E
Lenti 120 Mi 46.37N 16.33 E
Lentiira 114 Gd 64.21N 29.50 E
Lentini 128 Jm 37.17N 15.01 E
Lentua 114 Gd 64.14N 29.36 E
Lentvaris 116 Kj 54.38N 25.13 E
Léo 166 Ec 11.06N 2.06W
Leoben 128 Jc 47.23N 15.06 E
Léogâne 194 Kd 18.31N 72.38W
Leok 150 Hf 1.11N 121.26 E
Leola 186 Gd 45.43N 98.56W
Leominster 118 Ki 52.14N 2.45W
Léon 122 Ek 43.53N 1.18W
León 112 Fg 42.36N 5.34W
León 126 Gc 42.00N 6.00W
León [Mex.] 176 Ig 21.10N 101.42W
León [Nic.] 176 Kh 12.26N 86.54W
León [Nic.] [3] 194 Dg 12.35N 86.35W
León [Sp.] [3] 126 Gb 42.40N 6.00W
León, Montes de- 126 Fb 42.30N 6.20W
León, Puerto del- 126 Hh 36.50N 4.21W
Leonardville 172 Bd 23.29S 18.49 E
Leonberg 124 Kf 48.48N 9.01 E
Leone, Monte- 128 Cd 46.15N 8.10 E
Leones 204 Ak 32.39S 62.18W
Leonessa 128 Gh 42.34N 12.58 E
Leonforte 128 Im 37.38N 14.23 E
Leōnídhion 130 Fl 37.10N 22.52 E
Leonora 210 Dg 28.53S 121.20 E
Leon River 186 Hk 30.59N 97.24W
Leopold and Astrid Coast 222 Ge 67.10S 84.10 E
Leopoldina 202 Jh 21.32S 42.38W
Leopold McClintock, Cape- 180 Fa 77.38N 116.20W
Leopoldo de Bulhões 204 Hc 16.37S 48.46W
Leopoldsburg 124 Hc 51.07N 5.15 E
Leopoldville → Kinshasa 160 Ii 4.18S 15.18 E
Leovo 132 Ff 46.29N 28.15 E
Lepa 221c Bb 14.01S 171.28W
Lepar, Pulau- 150 Eg 2.57S 106.50 E
Le Parcq 124 Ed 50.23N 2.06 E
Lepaterique 194 Df 14.02N 87.27W
Lepe 126 Eg 37.15N 7.12W
Lepel 136 Ce 54.53N 28.46 E
Lepenica 130 Ee 44.10N 21.08 E
Le Petit Caux 124 De 49.55N 1.20 E
Le Petit-Couronne 124 De 49.23N 1.01 E
Le Petit-Quevilly 124 De 49.26N 1.02 E
Lephepe 172 Dd 23.22S 25.52 E
Leping 152 Kf 28.59N 117.07 E
Lepini, Monti- 128 Gi 41.35N 13.00 E
Le Plessis-Belleville 124 Ee 49.06N 2.46 E
Le Portel 124 Dd 50.42N 1.34 E
Leppävesi 116 Kb 62.15N 25.55 E
Leppävirta 116 Lb 62.29N 27.47 E
Le Prêcheur 197h Ab 14.48N 61.14W
Lepsøya 116 Bb 62.35N 6.10 E
Lepsy 136 Hf 46.12N 78.55 E
Lepsy 135 La 46.18N 78.20 E
Leptis Magna 164 Bc 32.38N 14.18 E
Leqemt (EN)=Nekemt 160 Kh 9.05N 36.33 E
Le Quesnoy 124 Fd 50.15N 3.38 E
Lercara Friddi 128 Hm 37.45N 13.36 E
Lerchenfeld Glacier 222 Af 77.50S 34.50W
Lere 166 Gc 10.23N 8.35 E
Léré 168 Ad 9.39N 14.13 E
Lérida 202 Dc 0.06N 70.43W
Lérida/Lleida 126 Mc 41.37N 0.37 E
Lérida / Lleida [3] 126 Nc 42.00N 1.10 E
Lérins, Iles de- 122 Nk 43.31N 7.03 E
Lerma 126 Ib 42.02N 3.45W
Lerma, Río- 192 Hg 20.13N 102.46W
Lermontov 132 Mg 44.06N 42.45 E
Le Robert 197h Bb 14.41N 60.57W
Léros 130 Jl 37.08N 26.50 E
Lerum 114 Ch 57.46N 12.16 E
Lerwick 118 La 60.09N 1.09W
Léry 124 De 49.17N 1.13 E
Le Saint-Esprit 197h Bb 14.34N 60.57W
Les Albères/Albères, Montes- 122 Il 42.28N 2.56 E
Les Allobroges 219b Dc 16.47S 168.09 E
Les Anses-d'Arlets 197h Ac 14.29N 61.05W
les Borges Blanques / Borjas Blancas 126 Mc 41.31N 0.52 E
Lesbos (EN)=Lésvos 110 Ih 39.10N 26.32 E
l'Escala / La Escala 126 Pb 42.07N 3.08 E
Les Cayes 190 Je 18.12N 73.46W
Le Serre 128 Kl 38.30N 16.30 E
Les Escoumins 184 Ma 48.25N 69.29W
Les Falaises 124 Ce 49.44N 0.21 E
Leshan 152 Hf 29.34N 103.45 E
Lesina, Lago di- 128 Ji 41.55N 15.25 E
Lesja 116 Cb 62.07N 8.52 E
Lesjöfors 114 Dg 59.59N 14.11 E
Leskino 138 Cb 72.25N 79.40 E
Lesko 120 Sg 49.29N 22.21 E
Leskov 222 Ad 56.40S 28.10W
Leskovac 130 Eg 42.59N 21.57 E
Leskoviku 130 Di 40.09N 20.35 E
Les Mangles 197e Ab 16.23N 61.27W
Lesnaja 120 Vd 52.55N 25.52 E
Lesnaja 132 Cc 52.11N 23.30 E
Lesneven 122 Bf 48.34N 4.19W
Lešnica 130 Ce 44.39N 19.19 E
Lesnoj [Russia] 136 Gd 57.01N 67.50 E
Lesnoj [Russia] 136 Fd 59.49N 52.10 E
Lesnoj, ostrov- 116 Md 60.02N 28.20 E
Lesný 120 If 50.02N 12.37 E
Lesogorski 116 Mc 61.01N 28.51 E
Lesosibirsk 142 Ld 58.15N 92.30 E
Lesotho [1] 160 Jk 29.30S 28.30 E
Lesozavodsk 138 Ig 45.26N 133.25 E
Lesozavodski 114 Hc 66.45N 32.50 E
Lesparre-Médoc 122 Fi 45.18N 0.56W
L'Espérance Rock 208 Jh 31.26S 178.54W
Les Ponts-de-Cé 122 Fg 47.25N 0.31W
Lessay 122 Ee 49.13N 1.32W
Lesse 122 Kd 50.14N 4.54 E
Lessebo 114 Dh 56.45N 15.16 E
Lessen/Lessines 124 Fd 50.43N 3.50 E
Lesser Antilles (EN) = Antillas Menores 174 Mh 15.00N 61.00W
Lesser Caucasus (EN)= Maly Kavkaz 110 Kg 41.00N 44.35 E
Lesser Khingan Range (EN) = Xiao Hinggan Ling 140 Oe 48.45N 127.00 E
Lesser Slave Lake 174 Hd 55.25N 115.30W
Lesser Sunda Islands (EN) 140 Oj 9.13S 121.12 E
Lessines/Lessen 124 Fd 50.43N 3.50 E
Lessini 128 Fe 45.41N 11.13 E
Les Tantes 197p Bb 12.19N 61.33W
Les Thilliers-en-Vexin 124 De 49.14N 1.36 E
Les Trois-Ilets 197h Ab 14.33N 61.03W
Lešukonskoje 114 Kd 64.52N 45.40 E
Lésvos=Lesbos (EN) 110 Ih 39.10N 26.32 E
Leszno 120 Me 51.51N 16.35 E
Leszno [2] 120 Me 51.50N 16.35 E
Letälven 116 Fe 59.05N 14.20 E
Letchworth 124 Bc 51.58N 0.13W
Letea, Ostrovul- 130 Md 45.20N 29.20 E
Letenye 120 Mj 46.26N 16.44 E
Lethbridge 176 He 49.42N 110.50W
Lethem 200 Ke 3.20N 59.50W
Leti, Kepulauan-=Leti Islands (EN) 150 Ih 8.13S 127.50 E
Letiahau 158 Jk 21.04S 24.25 E
Leticia 200 Jf 4.09S 69.57W
Leti Islands (EN)=Leti, Kepulauan- 150 Ih 8.13S 127.50 E
Leting 154 Ee 39.25N 118.55 E
Letka 114 Mg 58.59N 50.14 E
Letlhakane 172 Dd 21.25S 25.36 E
Letnerečenski 114 Id 64.19N 34.25 E
Letni bereg 114 Jd 64.50N 38.20 E
Letohrad 120 Mf 50.03N 16.31 E
Letovice 120 Mg 49.33N 16.36 E
Letpadan 148 Je 17.47N 95.45 E
Le Translay 124 De 49.58N 1.41 E
Letsôk-aw Kyun 148 Jf 11.37N 98.15 E
Letterkenny/Leitir Ceanainn 118 Fg 54.57N 7.44W
Leu 130 Ge 44.11N 24.00 E
Leucas (EN) = Levkás 130 Dk 38.43N 20.38 E
Leucate 122 Jl 42.55N 3.02 E
Leucate ou de Salses, Étang de- 122 Il 42.51N 3.00 E
Leuk 128 Bd 46.20N 7.38 E
Leukónoikon 146 Ee 35.15N 33.42 E
Leulumoega 221c Ba 13.49S 171.55W
Leuna 120 Ie 51.19N 12.01 E
Leušeny 130 Lc 46.51N 28.11 E
Leuser, Gunung- 140 Li 3.45N 97.11 E
Leutkirch im Allgäu 120 Gi 47.50N 10.02 E
Leuven/Louvain 122 Kd 50.53N 4.42 E
Leuze-en-Hainaut 124 Fd 50.36N 3.36 E
Levádhia 130 Fk 38.26N 22.53 E
Levaja Hetta 138 Cc 65.15N 73.20 E
Levanger 114 Ce 63.45N 11.18 E
Levante, Riviera di- 128 Df 44.15N 9.30 E
Levanzo 128 Gm 38.00N 12.20 E
Levaši 132 Oh 42.27N 47.20 E
Le Vauclin 197h Bb 14.33N 60.51W
Levelland 186 Ej 33.35N 102.23W
Lévêque, Cape- 212 Ec 16.25S 122.55 E
Leverkusen 120 Ce 51.01N 6.59 E
Leverkusen-Opladen 120 De 51.04N 7.01 E
Lévezou, Plateau du- 122 Ij 44.09N 2.53 E
Levice 120 Oh 48.13N 18.37 E
Levico Terme 128 Fd 46.01N 11.18 E
Levin 216 Eh 40.37S 175.17 E
Lévis 180 Kg 46.48N 71.10W
Levisa Fork 184 Ff 38.06N 82.37W
Levitha 130 Jm 37.00N 26.28 E
Levittown 184 Je 40.09N 74.50W
Levká Óri 130 Gn 35.20N 24.00 E
Levkás 130 Dk 38.50N 20.42 E
Levkás = Leucas (EN) 130 Dk 38.43N 20.38 E
Levkosia / Lefkoşa = Nicosia (EN) 142 Ff 35.10N 33.22 E
Levoča 120 Qg 49.02N 20.35 E
Levroux 122 Hh 46.59N 1.37 E
Levski 130 If 43.22N 25.08 E
Lev Tolstoj 132 Kc 53.12N 39.28 E
Levuka 219d Bb 17.41S 178.50 E
Levuo/Lėvuo 116 Kh 56.02N 24.28 E
Lėvuo/Levuo 116 Kh 56.02N 24.28 E
Lewes [De.-U.S.] 184 Jf 38.47N 75.08W
Lewes [Eng.-U.K.] 118 Nk 50.52N 0.01 E
Lewin Brzeski 120 Nf 50.46N 17.37 E
Lewis, Butt of- 118 Gc 58.31N 6.15W
Lewis, Isle of- 110 Fd 58.10N 6.40W
Lewis and Clark Lake 186 He 42.50N 97.45W
Lewisburg 184 Gg 37.49N 80.28W
Lewis Pass 218 Ee 42.24S 172.24 E
Lewis Range 174 He 48.30N 113.15W
Lewis River 188 Dd 45.51N 122.48W
Lewis Smith Lake 184 Dh 34.00N 87.07W
Lewiston [Id.-U.S.] 176 He 46.25N 117.01W
Lewiston [Me.-U.S.] 182 Mc 44.06N 70.13W
Lewistown [Mt.-U.S.] 182 Fb 47.04N 109.26W
Lewistown [Pa.-U.S.] 184 Ie 40.37N 77.36W
Lewisville 186 Jj 33.22N 93.35W
Lexington [Ky.-U.S.] 176 Kf 38.03N 84.30W
Lexington [Nb.-U.S.] 182 Hc 40.47N 99.45W
Lexington [N.C.-U.S.] 184 Gh 35.49N 80.15W
Lexington [Ok.-U.S.] 186 Hi 35.01N 97.20W
Lexington [Va.-U.S.] 184 Hg 37.47N 79.27W
Leygues, Iles- 222 Fc 48.45S 69.30 E

Index Symbols

[1] Independent Nation
[2] State, Region
[3] District, County
[4] Municipality
[5] Colony, Dependency
Continent
Physical Region
Historical or Cultural Region
Mount, Mountain
Volcano
Hill
Mountains, Mountain Range
Hills, Escarpment
Plateau, Upland
Pass, Gap
Plain, Lowland
Delta
Salt Flat
Valley, Canyon
Crater, Cave
Karst Features
Depression
Polder
Desert, Dunes
Forest, Woods
Heath, Steppe
Oasis
Cape, Point
Coast, Beach
Cliff
Peninsula
Isthmus
Sandbank
Island
Atoll
Rock, Reef
Islands, Archipelago
Rocks, Reefs
Coral Reef
Well, Spring
Geyser
River, Stream
Waterfall, Rapids
River Mouth, Estuary
Lake
Salt Lake
Intermittent Lake
Reservoir
Swamp, Pond
Canal
Glacier
Ice Shelf, Pack Ice
Ocean
Sea
Gulf, Bay
Strait, Fjord
Lagoon
Bank
Seamount
Tablemount
Ridge
Shelf
Basin
Escarpment, Sea Scarp
Fracture
Trench, Abyss
National Park, Reserve
Point of Interest
Recreation Site
Cave, Cavern
Historic Site
Ruins
Wall, Walls
Church, Abbey
Temple
Scientific Station
Railway station
Airport
Port
Military installation
Lighthouse
Mine
Tunnel
Dam, Bridge

Leyre 122 Ej 44.39N 1.01W
Leysdown-on-Sea 124 Cc 51.23N 0.55 E
Leyte 140 Oh 10.50N 124.50 E
Lez 122 Kj 44.13N 4.43 E
Leżajsk 120 Sf 50.16N 22.24 E
Lézard, Pointe à- 197e Ab 16.08N 61.47W
Lézarde, Rivière- 197h Ab 14.36N 61.01W
Lezha 130 Ch 41.47N 19.39 E
Lézignan-Corbières 122 Ik 43.12N 2.46 E
Lgov 136 De 51.41N 35.17 E
Lhari 152 Fe 30.48N 93.25 E
Lhaua 142 Lg 29.42N 91.07 E
Lhazê 152 Ef 29.13N 87.44 E
Lhazhong 152 Ee 31.28N 86.36 E
Lhokseumawe 150 Ce 5.10N 97.08 E
Lhoksukon 150 Ce 5.03N 97.19 E
L'Hôpital 124 Ie 49.10N 6.44 E
Lhorong 152 Ge 30.45N 95.48 E
l'Hospitalet de l'Infant / Hospitalet del Infante 126 Md 40.59N 0.56 E
Lhozhag 152 Ff 28.18N 90.51 E
Lhünzhub (Poindo) 152 Fe 30.17N 91.20 E
Liádhi 130 Jm 36.55N 26.10 E
Liákoura 130 Fk 38.32N 22.37 E
Liamone 122a Aa 42.04N 8.43 E
Liancheng 152 Kf 25.48N 116.48 E
Liancourt 124 Ee 49.20N 2.28 E
Liane 124 Dd 50.43N 1.36 E
Liangcheng 154 Bd 40.32N 112.28 E
Liangpran, Gunung- 150 Ff 1.04N 114.23 E
Liangshan (Houji) 154 Dg 35.48N 116.07 E
Liangzhou → Wuwei 142 Mf 37.58N 102.48 E
Liangzi Hu 152 Je 30.15N 114.32 E
Lianjiang 152 Jg 21.42N 110.14 E
Lianshui 154 Eh 33.47N 119.16 E
Lianxian 152 Jg 24.48N 112.26 E
Lianyin 152 La 53.26N 123.50 E
Lianyungang 152 Ke 34.38N 119.27 E
Lianyungang (Xinpu) 142 Nf 34.34N 119.15 E
Lianzhou → Hepu 152 Ig 21.40N 109.12 E
Lianzhushan 154 Kb 45.28N 131.45 E
Liaocheng 152 Kd 36.27N 115.58 E
Liaodong Bandao = Liaotung Peninsula (EN) 140 Of 40.00N 122.20 E
Liaodong Wan = Liaotung, Gulf of- (EN) 152 Lc 40.00N 121.30 E
Liao He 140 Oe 40.39N 122.12 E
Liaoning Sheng (Liao-ning Sheng) [2] 152 Lc 41.00N 123.00 E
Liao-ning Sheng → Liaoning Sheng [2] 152 Lc 41.00N 123.00 E
Liaotung, Gulf of- (EN) = Liaodong Wan 152 Lc 40.00N 121.30 E
Liaotung Peninsula (EN) = Liaodong Bandao 140 Of 40.00N 122.20 E
Liaoyang 152 Lc 41.16N 123.10 E
Liaoyuan 142 Oe 42.55N 125.09 E
Liaozhong 154 Gd 41.30N 122.42 E
Liard 174 Gc 61.52N 121.18W
Liard River 180 Ee 59.15N 126.09W
Liat, Pulau- 150 Eg 2.53 S 107.05 E
Liatorp 116 Fh 56.40N 14.16 E
Liatroim/Leitrim [2] 118 Eg 54.20N 8.20W
Liban 158 Lh 5.05N 40.05 E
Libano 204 Bm 37.32 S 61.18W
Libby 188 Hb 48.23N 115.33W
Libenge 160 Ih 3.39N 18.38 E
Liberal 182 Gd 37.02N 100.55W
Liberec 120 Lf 50.46N 15.03 E
Liberia 190 Gf 10.38N 85.27W
Liberia [1] 160 Fh 6.00N 10.00W
Libertad [Ur.] 204 Dl 34.38 S 56.39W
Libertad [Ven.] 202 Eb 8.20N 69.37W
Libertad [Ven.] 194 Li 8.08N 71.28W
Libertade, Rio- 202 He 9.35 S 52.17W
Libertador General Bernardo O'Higgins [2] 206 Fd 33.35 S 70.45W
Libertador General San Martin 206 Hb 23.48 S 64.48W
Libertador General San Martín, Cumbre del- 198 Jh 24.55 S 66.40W
Liberty [Mo.-U.S.] 186 Ig 39.15N 94.25W
Liberty [Tx.-U.S.] 186 Ik 30.03N 94.47W
Lībiyā = Libya (EN) [1] 160 If 27.00N 17.00 E
Lībīyah, Aş Şaḩrā' al- = Libyan Desert (EN) 158 Jf 24.00N 25.00 E
Libo 152 If 25.28N 107.52 E
Libobo, Tanjung- 150 Ig 0.54S 128.28 E
Liboi 170 Hb 0.24N 40.57 E
Libourne 122 Fj 44.55N 0.14W
Libramont-Chevigny 124 He 49.55N 5.23 E
Librazhdi 130 Dh 41.11N 20.19 E
Libreville 160 Hh 0.23N 9.27 E
Libro Point 150 Gd 11.26N 119.29 E
Libya (EN) = Lībiyā [1] 160 If 27.00N 17.00 E
Libyan Desert (EN) = Lībīyah, Aş Şaḩrā' al- 158 Jf 24.00N 25.00 E
Licantén 206 Fe 34.59S 72.00W
Licata 128 Hm 37.06N 13.56 E
Lice 146 Ic 38.28N 40.39 E
Licenciado Matienzo 204 Cm 37.55S 58.54W
Lich 124 Kd 50.31N 8.50 E
Licheng → Jinhu 154 Eh 33.01N 119.01 E
Lichfield 118 Li 52.42N 1.48W
Lichinga 160 Kj 13.20S 35.20 E
Lichtenau 124 Kc 51.37N 8.54 E
Lichtenburg 172 De 26.08S 26.08 E
Lichtenfels 120 Hf 50.09N 11.04 E
Lichtenvoorde 124 Ic 51.59N 6.34 E
Licking River 184 Ef 39.06N 84.30W
Licosa, Punta- 128 Ij 40.15N 14.54 E
Licuare 172 Fc 17.54S 36.49 E
Licun → Laoshan 154 Ff 36.10N 120.25 E
Licungo 172 Fc 17.40S 37.22 E
Lida 136 Ce 53.56N 25.18 E
Lidan 116 Ef 58.31N 13.09 E
Liddel 118 Kf 55.04N 2.57W
Liddon Gulf 180 Gb 75.00N 113.30W
Liden 114 De 62.42N 16.48 E
Lidhorikion 130 Fk 38.32N 22.12 E
Lidhult 116 Eh 56.50N 13.26 E
Lidingö 114 Eg 59.22N 18.08 E
Lidköping 114 Cg 58.30N 13.10 E
Lido 166 Fc 12.54N 3.44 E
Lido, Venezia- 128 Ge 45.25N 12.22 E
Lido di Ostia 128 Gi 41.44N 12.16 E
Lidzbark 120 Pc 53.17N 19.49 E
Lidzbark Warmiński 120 Qb 54.09N 20.35 E
Lié 122 Df 48.00N 2.40W
Liebenau 124 Lb 52.36N 9.06 E
Liebig, Mount- 212 Gd 23.15 S 131.20 E
Liechtenstein [1] 112 Gf 47.10N 9.30 E
Liège [3] 124 Hd 50.30N 5.40 E
Liège/Luik 112 Ge 50.38N 5.34 E
Lieksa 114 He 63.19N 30.01 E
Lielupe 114 Fh 57.03N 23.56 E
Lielvarde/Lielvärde 116 Kh 56.40N 24.49 E
Lielvärde/Lielvarde 116 Kh 56.40N 24.49 E
Lienen 124 Jb 52.09N 7.59 E
Lienz 128 Gd 46.50N 12.47 E
Liepāja/Liepaja 112 Id 56.35N 21.01 E
Liepaja/Liepāja 112 Id 56.35N 21.01 E
Liepajas, ozero- / Liepājas ezers 116 Ih 56.35N 20.35 E
Liepājas ezers / Liepajas, ozero- 116 Ih 56.35N 20.35 E
Liepna 116 Lg 57.16N 27.35 E
Liepupe 116 Kg 57.22N 24.22 E
Lier/Lierre 122 Kc 51.08N 4.34 E
Lierbyen 116 De 59.47N 10.14 E
Lierneux 124 Hd 50.17N 5.48 E
Lierre/Lier 122 Kc 51.08N 4.34 E
Liesborn, Wadersloh- 124 Kc 51.43N 8.16 E
Lieser 120 Dg 49.55N 7.01 E
Liesing 128 Jc 47.20N 15.02 E
Liestal 128 Bc 47.29N 7.44 E
Lieşti 130 Kd 45.37N 27.31 E
Lieto 116 Jd 60.30N 22.27 E
Lietuva = Lithuania (EN) 136 Cd 56.00N 24.00 E
Lietuvos Tarybu Socialistine Respublika/Litovskaja SSR → Lietuva 136 Cd 56.00N 24.00 E
Lietuvos TSR → Lietuva 136 Cd 56.00N 24.00 E
Lietvesi 116 Lc 61.30N 28.00 E
Lieurey 124 Ce 49.14N 0.29 E
Lieuvin 124 Ge 49.10N 0.30 E
Lievestuoreenjärvi 116 Lb 62.20N 26.10 E
Liévin 122 Id 50.25N 2.46 E
Lievre, Rivière du- 184 Jc 45.35N 75.25W
Liezen 128 Ic 47.34N 14.14 E
Lifford/Leifear 118 Fg 54.50N 7.29W
Li Fiord 180 Ia 80.17N 94.35W
Lifjell 116 Ce 59.30N 8.52 E
Lifou, Ile- 208 Hg 20.53S 167.13 E
Lifuka 221b Ba 19.48S 174.21W
Ligatne/Līgatne 116 Kg 57.07N 25.00 E
Līgatne/Ligatne 116 Kg 57.07N 25.00 E
Lighthouse Reef 194 De 17.20N 87.32W
Lignano Sabbiadoro 128 He 45.52N 13.09 E
Lignières 122 Ih 46.45N 2.10 E
Lignon 122 Ki 45.15N 4.08 E
Ligny-en-Barrois 122 Lf 48.41N 5.20 E
Ligonha 172 Fc 16.51S 39.09 E
Ligure, Mar- = Ligurian Sea (EN) 110 Gg 43.30N 9.00 E
Liguria [2] 128 Cf 44.30N 8.50 E
Ligurian Sea (EN) = Ligure, Mar- 110 Gg 43.30N 9.00 E
Lihir Group 208 Ge 3.05 S 152.40 E
Lihme 116 Ch 56.36N 8.44 E
Lihoslavl 114 Ih 57.09N 35.29 E
Lihou Reefs and Cays 208 Gf 17.25S 151.40 E
Lihue 214 Oc 21.59N 159.22W
Lihula 114 Fg 58.44N 23.49 E
Liinahamari 114 Hb 69.40N 31.22 E
Lijiang (Dayan) 142 Mg 26.56N 100.15 E
Lijin 154 Ef 37.29N 118.15 E
Lika 128 Jf 44.30N 15.30 E
Lika 128 Jf 44.46N 15.10 E
Likasi 160 Jj 10.59S 26.43 E
Likati 170 Db 3.21N 23.53 E
Likati 170 Db 2.53N 24.03 E
Likėnai/Likenaj 116 Kh 56.11N 24.42 E
Likenaj/Likėnai 116 Kh 56.11N 24.42 E
Likenäs 116 Ed 60.37N 13.02 E
Likhapani 148 Jc 27.19N 95.54 E
Likiep Atoll 208 Hc 9.53N 169.09 E
Likoma Islands 170 Fe 12.04S 34.44 E
Likoto 170 Dc 1.10S 24.45 E
Likouala [3] 170 Cb 2.00N 17.30 E
Likouala 170 Cc 1.13S 16.48 E
Likouala aux Herbes 170 Cc 0.50S 17.11 E
Liku 220k Bb 19.02S 169.47W
Lilibeo, Capo- → Boeo, Capo- 128 Gm 37.34N 12.41 E
Lilienfeld 128 Jb 48.01N 15.38 E
Lilienthal 124 Ka 53.08N 8.55 E
Lilla Edet 114 Cg 58.08N 12.08 E
Lille [Bel.] 124 Gc 51.14N 4.50 E
Lille [Fr.] 112 Ge 50.38N 3.04 E
Lille Bælt = Little Belt (EN) 110 Gd 55.20N 9.45 E
Lillebonne 122 Ge 49.31N 0.33 E
Lillehammer 114 Cf 61.08N 10.30 E
Lille Hellefiske Bank (EN) 179 Ge 65.05N 54.00W
Lillers 122 Id 50.34N 2.29 E
Lillesand 114 Bg 58.15N 8.24 E
Lillestrøm 116 De 59.57N 11.05 E
Lillhärdal 114 Df 61.51N 14.04 E
Lillie Glacier 222 Kf 70.45S 163.55 E
Lillo 126 Ie 39.43N 3.18W
Lillooet 180 Ff 50.42N 121.56W
Lillooet Range 188 Eb 50.00N 121.45W
Lillooet River 180 Fg 49.45N 122.10W
Lilongwe 160 Kj 13.59S 33.47 E
Liloy 150 He 8.08N 122.40 E
Lim [Afr.] 168 Bd 7.54N 15.46 E
Lim [Bos.] 128 Ng 43.45N 19.13 E
Lima 202 Cf 12.00S 76.35W
Lima 126 Dc 41.41N 8.50W
Lima [Mt.-U.S.] 188 Id 44.38N 112.36W
Lima [Oh.-U.S.] 182 Kc 40.43N 84.06W
Lima [Par.] 204 Df 23.54S 56.20W
Lima [Peru] 200 Ig 12.03S 77.03W
Lima [Swe.] 116 Ed 60.56N 13.21 E
Lima, Pulau-Pulau- 150 Gg 3.03S 107.24 E
Limagne 122 Jh 46.00N 3.20 E
Līmah 146 Qj 25.56N 56.25 E
Liman [Russia] 132 Og 45.45N 47.14 E
Liman [Ukr.] 130 Md 45.42N 29.46 E
Limanskoje 130 Mc 46.38N 29.54 E
Limari, Rio- 206 Fd 30.44S 71.43W
Limassol/Lemesós 144 Dc 34.40N 33.02 E
Limavady/Léim an Mhadaidh 118 Gf 55.03N 6.57W
Limay 124 Df 48.59N 1.44 E
Limay, Rio- 198 Ji 38.59S 68.00W
Limbara 128 Dj 40.51N 9.10 E
Limbaži 114 Fh 57.31N 24.47 E
Limbé 194 Kd 19.42N 72.24W
Limbe, Blantyre- 170 Gf 15.49S 35.03 E
Limbot 219b Cb 14.12S 167.34 E
Limboto 150 Hf 0.37N 122.57 E
Limbourg 124 Hd 50.37N 5.56 E
Limbourg/Limburg 122 Lc 51.05N 5.40 E
Limburg [Bel.] [3] 124 Hc 51.00N 5.30 E
Limburg [Neth.] [3] 124 Hc 51.14N 5.50 E
Limburg/Limbourg 122 Lc 51.05N 5.40 E
Limburg an der Lahn 120 Ef 50.23N 8.03 E
Limedsforsen 116 Ed 60.54N 13.23 E
Limeira 206 Kb 22.34S 47.24W
Limerick/Luimneach 112 Fe 52.40N 8.38W
Limerick/Luimneach [2] 118 Ei 52.30N 9.00W
Limestone, Haḑabat- 164 Fe 24.50N 32.00 E
Limfjorden 110 Gd 56.55N 9.10 E
Limia 126 Dc 41.41N 8.50W
Limingen 114 Cd 64.47N 13.36 E
Liminka 114 Fd 64.49N 25.29 E
Limmat 128 Cc 47.30N 8.15 E
Limmen Bight 212 Hb 14.45S 135.40 E
Limmen Bight River 212 Hc 15.15S 135.30 E
Limni 130 Gk 38.46N 23.19 E
Límnos = Lemnos (EN) 110 Ih 39.55N 25.15 E
Limoeiro 202 Ke 7.52S 35.27W
Limoges 112 Gf 45.51N 1.15 E
Limogne, Causse de- 122 Hj 44.20N 1.55 E
Limon 182 Gd 39.16N 103.41W
Limón [3] 194 Fi 10.00N 83.15W
Limón [C.R.] 176 Kh 10.00N 83.02W
Limón [Hond.] 194 Ef 15.52N 85.33W
Limone Piemonte 128 Bf 44.12N 7.34 E
Limousin [3] 122 Hi 45.30N 1.50 E
Limousin, Plateaux du- 122 Hi 45.50N 1.10 E
Limoux 122 Ik 43.04N 2.14 E
Limpopo 158 Jk 25.12S 33.32 E
Limu Ling 152 Ie 19.02N 109.43 E
Limuru 170 Gc 1.06S 36.39 E
Līnah 146 Jh 28.42N 43.48 E
Lin'an 152 Ke 30.14N 119.39 E
Linapacan 150 Gd 11.27N 119.49 E
Linares [Chile] 200 Ii 35.51S 71.36W
Linares [Mex.] 190 Ed 24.52N 99.34W
Linares [Sp.] 126 If 38.05N 3.38W
Linares Viejo 204 Bf 23.09S 61.46W
Linaro, Capo- 128 Fh 42.02N 11.50 E
Lincang 142 Mg 23.48N 100.04 E
Lincheng 154 Cf 37.26N 114.34 E
Lincheng → Xuecheng 154 Dg 34.48N 117.14 E
Lincoln 118 Mh 53.20N 0.30W
Lincoln [Arg.] 206 Hd 34.52S 61.32W
Lincoln [Eng.-U.K.] 118 Mh 53.14N 0.33W
Lincoln [Il.-U.S.] 186 Lf 40.09N 89.22W
Lincoln [Nb.-U.S.] 176 Je 40.48N 96.42W
Lincoln [N.Z.] 218 Ee 43.38S 172.29 E
Lincoln, Mount- 186 Cg 39.21N 106.07W
Lincoln City 188 Cd 44.59N 124.01W
Lincoln Sea 224 Ne 83.00N 56.00W
Lincolnshire [3] 118 Mh 53.00N 0.10W
Lincoln Wolds 118 Mh 53.20N 0.10W
Lindashalvøya 116 Ad 60.40N 5.15 E
Lindau 120 Fi 47.33N 9.41 E
Linde [Neth.] 124 Hb 52.49N 5.52 E
Linde [Russia] 138 Hd 64.59N 124.36 E
Linden [Guy.] 202 Gb 6.00N 58.18W
Linden [Tn.-U.S.] 184 Dh 35.37N 87.50W
Lindenows Fjord 179 Hf 60.25N 43.00W
Linderödsåsen 116 Ei 55.53N 13.56 E
Lindesberg 114 Dg 59.35N 15.15 E
Lindesnes 110 Gd 58.00N 7.02 E
Lindhorst 124 Lb 52.22N 9.17 E
Lindhos 130 Lm 36.06N 28.04 E
Lindi 160 Ki 10.00S 39.43 E
Lindi [3] 170 Gd 9.30S 38.20 E
Lindi 150 Jh 0.33N 25.05 E
Lindis Pass 218 Cf 44.35S 169.39 E
Lindlar 124 Jc 51.01N 7.23 E
Lindome 116 Eg 57.34N 12.05 E
Lindong → Bairin Zuoqi 152 Kc 43.59N 119.22 E
Lindsay [Ca.-U.S.] 188 Fh 36.12N 119.05W
Lindsay [Ont.-Can.] 184 Hc 44.21N 78.44W
Lindsdal 116 Gh 56.44N 16.18 E
Line Islands 208 Le 0.01S 157.00W
Linfen 152 Jd 36.03N 111.32 E
Lingayen 142 Oh 16.01N 120.14 E
Lingayen Gulf 150 Hc 16.15N 120.14 E
Lingbi 154 Dh 33.33N 117.33 E
Lingbo 114 Df 61.03N 16.41 E
Lingchuan 154 Bg 35.46N 113.16 E
Lingen (Ems) 120 Dd 52.31N 7.19 E
Lingfield 124 Bc 51.10N 0.01W
Lingga, Kepulauan- = Lingga Archipelago (EN) 140 Mj 0.02S 104.35 E
Lingga, Pulau- 150 Dg 0.12S 104.35 E
Lingga Archipelago (EN) = Lingga, Kepulauan- 140 Mj 0.02S 104.35 E
Linghed 116 Fd 60.47N 15.51 E
Lingling 152 Jf 26.24N 111.41 E
Lingomo 170 Db 0.38N 21.59 E
Lingqiu 154 Ce 39.26N 114.14 E
Lingshan 152 Ig 22.30N 109.17 E
Lingshan Dao 154 Fg 35.45N 120.10 E
Lingshi 154 Af 36.50N 111.46 E
Lingshou 154 Ce 38.18N 114.22 E
Linguère 160 Fg 15.24N 15.07W
Lingwu 152 Id 38.05N 106.20 E
Lingxian 154 Df 37.20N 116.35 E
Lingyuan 154 Ed 41.15N 119.23 E
Linh, Ngoc- 140 Mh 15.04N 107.59 E
Linhai 152 La 51.36N 124.22 E
Linhai (Taizhou) 152 Lf 28.52N 121.08 E
Linhares 202 Jg 19.25S 40.04W
Linhe 152 Ic 40.49N 107.28 E
Linhuaiguan 154 Dh 32.54N 117.39 E
Linjiang 154 Id 41.49N 126.55 E
Linköping 112 Hd 58.25N 15.37 E
Linkou 152 Nb 45.18N 130.18 E
Linkuva 116 Jh 56.02N 23.58 E
Linlü Shan 154 Bf 36.02N 113.42 E
Linmingguan → Yongnian 154 Cf 36.47N 114.30 E
Linn, Mount- 188 Df 40.03N 122.48W
Linneryd 116 Fh 56.40N 15.07 E
Linnhe, Loch- 118 He 56.37N 5.25W
Linnich 124 Id 50.59N 6.16 E
Linosa 128 Go 35.50N 12.50 E
Linovo 120 Ud 52.28N 24.35 E
Linqing 152 Kd 36.48N 115.49 E
Linqu 154 Ef 36.31N 118.32 E
Linquan 154' Ch 33.04N 115.16 E
Linru 154 Bg 34.10N 112.51 E
Lins 206 Kb 21.40S 49.45W
Linsell 116 Eb 62.09N 13.53 E
Linshu (Xiazhuang) 154 Eg 34.56N 118.38 E
Linslade 124 Bc 51.55N 0.40W
Linta 172 Ge 25.02S 44.05 E
Lintao 152 Hd 35.20N 104.00 E
Linthal 128 Cd 46.55N 9.00 E
Linton [Eng.-U.K.] 124 Cb 52.06N 0.16 E
Linton [N.D.-U.S.] 186 Fc 46.16N 100.14W
Linxi [China] 154 Ee 39.42N 118.26 E
Linxi [China] 142 Ne 43.36N 118.02 E
Linxia 142 Mf 35.28N 102.59 E
Linxian 152 Jd 37.57N 111.00 E
Linxiang 154 Bj 29.29N 113.28 E
Linyi [China] 154 Df 37.11N 116.51 E
Linyi [China] 152 Kd 35.09N 118.15 E
Linz 112 Hf 48.18N 14.18 E
Linze (Shahezhen) 152 Hd 39.10N 100.21 E
Lion, Golfe du- = Lion, Gulf of- (EN) 110 Gg 43.00N 4.00 E
Lion, Gulf of- (EN) = Lion, Golfe du- 110 Gg 43.00N 4.00 E
Lions Den 172 Ec 17.16S 30.02 E
Lion-sur-Mer 124 Be 49.18N 0.19W
Liopa 150 Ih 7.40S 126.00 E
Lios Mór/Lismore 118 Fi 52.08N 7.55W
Lios na gCearrbhach/Lisburn 118 Gg 54.31N 6.03W
Lios Tuathail/Listovel 118 Di 52.27N 9.29W
Liouesso 170 Cb 1.02N 15.43 E
Lipa 150 Hd 13.57N 121.10 E
Lipany 120 Qg 49.10N 20.58 E
Lipari 128 Il 38.28N 14.57 E
Lipari 128 Il 38.30N 14.55 E
Lipari, Isole → Eolie, Isole- 110 Hh 38.35N 14.55 E
Lipari Islands (EN) = Eolie o Lipari, I iole- 110 Hh 38.35N 14.55 E
Lipeck 112 Je 52.37N 39.35 E
Lipeckaja oblast [3] 136 De 52.45N 39.10 E
Lipenská přehradní nádrž 120 Kh 48.45N 14.05 E
Liperi 116 Ge 62.32N 29.22 E
Lipez, Cordillera de- 202 Eh 22.00S 66.45W
Liphook 124 Bc 51.04N 0.48W
Lipkani 130 Ja 48.13N 26.48 E
Lipljan 130 Eg 42.32N 21.08 E
Lipno 120 Pd 52.51N 19.10 E
Lipova 130 Ec 46.05N 21.42 E
Lipovcy 138 Ih 44.15N 131.45 E
Lippborg, Lippetal- 124 Kc 51.40N 8.02 E
Lippe 120 Ce 51.39N 6.38 E
Lipper Bergland 124 Kb 52.05N 8.57 E
Lippetal 124 Kc 51.40N 8.13 E
Lippetal-Eickelborn 124 Kc 51.39N 8.13 E
Lippetal-Lippborg 124 Kc 51.40N 8.02 E
Lippischer Wald 124 Kc 51.56N 8.45 E
Lippstadt 120 Ee 51.40N 8.21 E
Lipsko 120 Re 51.09N 21.39 E
Lipsoí 130 Jl 37.20N 26.45 E
Liptako 158 Hg 14.15N 0.02 E
Liptovský Mikuláš 120 Pg 49.05N 19.38 E
Lira 170 Fb 2.15N 32.54 E
Liranga 170 Cc 0.40S 17.36 E
Liri 128 Hi 41.25N 13.52 E
Liria / Llíria 126 Le 39.38N 0.36W
Lis 126 De 39.53N 8.58W
Lisa 130 Cf 43.08N 19.42 E
Lisac 130 Eg 42.45N 21.56 E
Lisakovsk 136 Ge 52.33N 62.28 E
Lisala 160 Jh 2.09N 21.31 E
Lisboa [2] 126 Ce 39.00N 9.08W
Lisboa = Lisbon (EN) 118 Fh 38.43N 9.08W
Lisbon 186 Hc 46.27N 97.41W
Lisbon (EN) = Lisboa 118 Fh 38.43N 9.08W
Lisbon Canyon (EN) 126 Cf 38.20N 9.20W
Lisburn/Lios na gCearrbhach 118 Gg 54.31N 6.03W
Lisburne, Cape- 178 Fc 68.52N 166.14W
Liscannor Bay/Bá Thuath Reanna 118 Di 52.55N 9.25W
Lisec 120 Uh 48.48N 24.45 E
Li Shan 154 Ag 35.25N 111.58 E
Lishi 152 Jd 37.29N 111.08 E
Lishu 154 Hc 43.19N 124.20 E
Lishui 152 Kf 28.30N 119.55 E
Lisianski Island 208 Jb 26.02N 174.00W
Lisičansk 136 Df 48.53N 38.28 E
Lisieux 122 Ge 49.09N 0.14 E
Liski (Gheorghiu-Dej) 136 De 51.00N 39.31 E
L'Isle-Adam 124 Ee 49.07N 2.14 E
Lismore 210 Gg 28.48S 153.17 E
Lismore/Lios Mór 118 Fi 52.08N 7.55W
Liss 124 Bc 51.02N 0.54W
Liss 146 Hg 31.14N 38.31 E
List 120 Ea 55.01N 8.26 E
Lista 116 Bf 58.10N 6.40 E
Listafjorden 116 Bf 58.10N 6.35 E
Lister, Mount- 222 Kf 78.04S 162.41 E
Lištica 128 Lg 43.23N 17.39 E
Listovel/Lios Tuathail 118 Di 52.27N 9.29W
Listowel 184 Gd 43.44N 80.57W
Liswarta 120 Pe 51.06N 19.01 E
Lit 116 Fa 63.19N 14.49 E
Litang [China] 152 Ig 23.12N 109.05 E
Litang [China] 152 He 30.02N 100.18 E
Litani Rivier 202 Hc 3.18N 54.06W
Litchfield 186 Id 45.08N 94.31W
Lithgow 210 Gh 33.29S 150.09 E
Líthinon, Ákra- 130 Ho 34.55N 24.44 E
Lithuania (EN) 110 Id 56.00N 24.00 E
Lithuania (EN) = Lietuva 136 Cd 56.00N 24.00 E
Litókhoron 130 Fi 40.06N 22.30 E
Litoměřice 120 Kf 50.32N 14.08 E
Litovel 120 Ng 49.43N 17.05 E
Litovko 138 Ig 49.17N 135.10 E
Litovskaja Sovetskaja Socialističeskaja Respublika → Lietuva 136 Cd 56.00N 24.00 E
Litovskaja SSR/Lietuvos Tarybu Socialistine Respublika → Lietuva 136 Cd 56.00N 24.00 E
Little Abaco Island 190 Ic 26.53N 77.43W
Little Abitibi River 184 Ha 49.29N 79.32W
Little Aden 144 Fg 12.45N 44.52 E
Little America 188 Kf 41.32N 109.47W
Little Andaman 140 Lh 10.45N 92.30 E
Little Bahama Bank (EN) 190 Ic 26.30N 78.00W
Little Barrier Island 218 Fb 36.10S 175.05 E
Little Beaver Creek 186 Ec 46.17N 103.56W
Little Belt (EN) = Lille Bælt 110 Gd 55.20N 9.45 E
Little Belt Mountains 188 Jc 46.51N 110.35W
Little Blue River 186 Hg 39.41N 96.40W
Little Bow River 188 Ib 49.53N 112.29W
Little Carpathians (EN) = Malé Karpaty 120 Nh 48.30N 17.20 E
Little Cayman 190 He 19.41N 80.03W
Little Colorado River 174 Hf 36.11N 111.48W
Little Current 180 Jg 45.58N 81.56W
Little Current 180 Jf 50.57N 84.36W
Little Dry Creek 188 Lc 47.21N 106.22W
Little Exuma Island 194 Jb 23.27N 75.37W
Little Falls 182 Ib 45.59N 94.21W
Littlefield 186 Ej 33.55N 102.20W
Little Fort 188 Ea 51.25N 120.12W
Little Grand Rapids 180 Hf 52.02N 95.25W
Little Halibut Bank 118 Lc 58.20N 1.15W
Littlehampton 124 Bd 50.48N 0.32W
Little Inagua Island 190 Jd 21.30N 73.00W
Little Karroo (EN) = Klein-Karoo 172 Cf 33.42S 21.20 E
Little Missouri 174 Ie 47.30N 102.25W
Little Namaland (EN) = Namakwaland 172 Be 29.00S 17.00 E
Little Nicobar 148 Ig 7.20N 93.40 E
Little Ouse 118 Ni 52.30N 0.22 E
Littleport 124 Cb 52.27N 0.18 E
Little Powder River 188 Md 45.28N 105.20W
Little Quill Lake 188 Ma 51.55N 104.05W
Little River 218 Ee 43.46S 172.47 E
Little Rock 176 Jf 34.44N 92.15W
Little Rocky Mountains 188 Kb 48.00N 108.45W
Little Scarcies 166 Cd 8.51N 13.09W
Little Sioux River 186 Hf 41.49N 96.04W
Little Sitkin 178a Bb 51.55N 178.30 E
Little Smoky 180 Fe 55.39N 117.37W
Little Snake River 186 Bf 40.27N 108.26W
Littleton [Co.-U.S.] 186 Dg 39.37N 105.01W
Littleton [N.H.-U.S.] 184 Lc 44.18N 71.46W
Little White River [Ont.-Can.] 184 Fb 46.15N 83.00W
Little White River [S.D.-U.S.] 186 Fe 43.44N 100.40W
Littoral [3] 166 He 4.30N 10.00 E
Litvínov 120 Jf 50.36N 13.36 E
Liuhe 152 Mc 42.16N 125.45 E
Liu He [China] 154 Ic 42.46N 126.13 E
Liu He [China] 154 Gd 41.48N 122.43 E
Liuheng Dao 154 Gj 29.43N 122.08 E
Liujia Xia 152 Hd 35.50N 103.00 E
Liukang Tenggaja, Kepulauan- 150 Gh 6.45S 118.50 E
Liupai → Tian'e 152 If 25.05N 107.12 E
Liupan Shan 152 Id 35.40N 106.15 E
Liuqu He 154 Fd 40.10N 120.15 E
Liuwa Plain 170 De 14.27S 22.25 E
Liuyang 154 Bj 28.09N 113.38 E
Liuzhangzhen → Yuanqu 152 Jd 35.19N 111.44 E
Liuzhou 142 Mg 24.22N 109.20 E
Līvāni/Livany 114 Gh 56.22N 26.12 E
Livanjsko Polje 128 Kg 43.51N 16.50 E
Livany/Līvāni 114 Gh 56.22N 26.12 E
Livarot 124 Ce 49.01N 0.09 E
Livengood 178 Jc 65.32N 148.33W
Livenza 128 Ge 45.35N 12.51 E
Live Oak 184 Fj 30.18N 82.59W
Livermore 186 Eh 37.41N 121.46W
Livermore, Mount- 186 Dk 30.37N 104.08W
Liverpool [Eng.-U.K.] 112 Fe 53.25N 2.55W

Liverpool [N.S.-Can.] 180 Lh 44.02N 64.43W
Liverpool, Cape - 180 Jb 73.38N 78.05W
Liverpool Bay [Can.] 180 Ec 70.00N 129.00W
Liverpool Bay [Eng.-U.K.] 118 Jh 53.30N 3.16W
Liverpool Range 212 Kf 31.40S 150.30 E
Liverpool River 212 Gb 12.00S 134.00 E
Livezi 130 Ge 44.14N 23.47 E
Livigno 128 Ed 46.32N 10.04 E
Livingston [Guat.] 194 Cf 15.50N 88.45W
Livingston [Mt.-U.S.] 182 Eb 45.40N 110.34W
Livingston [Newf.-Can.] 180 Kf 53.40N 66.10W
Livingston [Tn.-U.S.] 184 Eg 36.23N 85.19W
Livingston [Tx.-U.S.] 186 Ik 30.43N 94.56W
Livingston, Lake- 186 Ik 30.45N 95.15W
Livingstone, Chutes de-= Livingstone Falls (EN) 158 Ii 4.50S 14.30 E
Livingstone Falls (EN)= Livingstone, Chutes de- 158 Ii 4.50S 14.30 E
Livingstone Memorial 170 Fe 12.19S 30.18 E
Livingstone Mountains 170 Fd 9.45S 34.20 E
Livingstonia 170 Fe 10.36S 34.07 E
Livingston Island 222 Qe 62.36S 60.30W
Livno 128 Lg 43.50N 17.01 E
Livny 136 De 52.28N 37.37 E
Livonia 184 Fd 42.25N 83.23W
Livonia (EN)=Livonija 110 Id 57.30N 25.30 E
Livonija=Livonia (EN) 110 Id 57.30N 25.30 E
Livorno=Leghorn (EN) 112 Hg 43.33N 10.19 E
Livradois, Montu du- 122 Ji 45.30N 3.33 E
Livramento do Brumado 202 Jf 13.39S 41.50W
Livron-sur-Drôme 122 Kj 44.46N 4.51 E
Liwale 170 Gd 9.46S 37.56 E
Liwiec 120 Rd 52.35N 21.33 E
Liwonde 170 Gf 15.01S 35.13 E
Lixi 152 Hf 26.21N 102.03 E
Lixian [China] 152 Jf 29.40N 111.45 E
Lixian [China] 152 Ie 34.11N 105.02 E
Lixian [China] 154 Ce 38.29N 115.34 E
Lixin 154 Dh 33.09N 116.12 E
Lixoúrion 130 Dk 38.12N 20.26 E
Liyang 154 Ei 31.26N 119.29 E
Lizard 118 Hl 49.57N 5.13W
Lizard Point 110 Ff 49.56N 5.13W
Lizhu 154 Fj 29.58N 120.26 E
Lizy sur Ourcq 124 Fe 49.01N 3.02 E
Ljady 116 Mf 58.35N 28.55 E
Ljahoviči 132 Ec 53.04N 26.15 E
Ljahovskije ostrova = Lyakhov Islands (EN) 140 Qb 73.30N 141.00 E
Ljalja 134 Jg 59.10N 61.30 E
Ljamin 134 Of 61.18N 71.45 E
Ljangar 135 Ed 40.23N 65.59 E
Ljangasovo 114 Lg 58.33N 49.29 E
Ljapin 134 Je 63.38N 61.58 E
Ljaskelja 116 Nc 61.39N 31.03 E
Ljaskovec 130 If 43.06N 25.43 E
Ljig 130 De 44.14N 20.15 E
Ljuban [Bela.] 132 Ec 52.48N 27.59 E
Ljuban [Russia] 114 Hg 59.22N 31.13 E
Ljubar 132 Ee 49.55N 27.44 E
Ljubašcevka 130 Nb 47.50N 30.07 E
Ljubeli 128 Id 46.26N 14.16 E
Ljubercy 136 Dd 55.40N 37.55 E
Ljubesŏv 120 Ve 51.45N 25.37 E
Ljubim 114 Jg 58.22N 40.41 E
Ljubimec 130 Jh 41.50N 26.05 E
Ljubinje 128 Mh 42.57N 18.06 E
Ljubišnja 130 Cf 43.20N 19.07 E
Ljubljana 112 Hf 46.02N 14.30 E
Ljuboml 132 Cd 51.15N 23.59 E
Ljubotin 132 Ie 49.59N 35.55 E
Ljubovija 130 Ce 44.12N 19.22 E
Ljubuški 128 Lg 43.12N 17.33 E
Ljubytino 114 Hg 58.50N 33.25 E
Ljudinovo 136 De 53.51N 34.28 E
Ljugarn 114 Eh 57.19N 18.42 E
Ljungan 110 Hc 62.19N 17.23 E
Ljungaverk 116 Gb 62.29N 16.03 E
Ljungby 114 Ch 56.50N 13.56 E
Ljungbyholm 116 Gh 56.38N 16.10 E
Ljungdalen 114 Ce 62.51N 12.47 E
Ljungsbro 116 Ff 58.31N 15.30 E
Ljungskile 116 Df 58.14N 11.55 E
Ljusdal 114 Df 61.50N 16.05 E
Ljusnan 110 Hc 61.12N 17.08 E
Ljusne 114 Df 61.13N 17.08 E
Ljusterö 116 He 59.30N 18.35 E
Ljuta 116 Mf 58.33N 28.45 E
Llandilo 118 Jj 51.53N 3.59W
Llandovery 118 Jj 51.59N 3.48W
Llandrindod Wellu 118 Ji 52.15N 3.23W
Llandudno 118 Jh 53.19N 3.49W
Llanelli 118 Ij 51.42N 4.10W
Llanes 126 Ha 43.25N 4.45W
Llangefni 118 Ih 53.16N 4.18W
Llangollen 118 Ji 52.58N 3.10W
Llano 186 Gk 30.45N 98.41W
Llano Estacado 174 If 33.30N 102.40W
Llano River 186 Gk 30.35N 98.25W
Llanos 198 Je 5.00N 70.00W
Llanos de Sonora 190 Bc 28.20N 111.00W
Llanquihue, Lago- 206 Ff 41.08S 72.48W
Llata 202 Ce 9.25S 76.47W
Lleida/Lérida 126 Mc 41.37N 0.37 E
Lleida / Lérida 126 Nc 42.00N 1.10 E
Llerena 126 Ff 38.14N 6.01W
Lleyn 118 Ii 52.54N 4.30W
Llica 202 Eg 19.52S 68.16W
Llíria / Liria 126 Le 39.38N 0.36W
Llívia 126 Nb 42.28N 1.59 E
Llobregat 126 Oc 41.19N 2.09 E
Lloret de Mar 126 Oc 41.42N 2.51 E
Llorona, Punta- 194 Fi 8.37N 83.44W
Llorri / Orri, Pic de l'- 126 Nb 42.23N 1.12 E
Lloydminster 180 Gf 53.17N 110.00W
Llucena / Lucena del Cid 126 Ld 40.08N 0.17W
Lluchmayor/Llucmajor 126 Oe 39.29N 2.54 E
Llucmajor/Lluchmayor 126 Oe 39.29N 2.54 E
Llullaillaco, Volcán- 198 Jh 24.43S 68.33W
Lo 219b Ca 13.21S 166.38 E
Loa 188 Jg 38.24N 111.38W
Loa, Río- 206 Fb 21.26S 70.04W
Loanatit, Pointe- 219b Dd 19.21S 169.14 E
Loange 158 Ji 4.17S 20.02 E
Loango 170 Bc 4.39S 11.48 E
Loano 128 Cf 44.08N 8.15 E
Lobamba 172 Ee 26.27S 31.12 E
Lobatse 160 Jk 26.13S 25.41 E
Löbau/Lubij 120 Ke 51.06N 14.40 E
Lobaye 168 Be 4.00N 17.40 E
Lobaye 158 Ih 3.41N 18.35 E
Lobenstein 120 Hf 50.27N 11.39 E
Lobería 206 Ie 38.09S 58.47W
Łobez 120 Lc 53.39N 15.36 E
Lobito 160 Ij 12.22S 13.34 E
Lobo 150 Jg 3.45S 134.05 E
Lobo 166 Dd 6.02N 6.47W
Lobos 206 Ie 35.11S 59.06W
Lobos 162 Ed 28.45N 13.49W
Lobos, Cabo- 192 Cc 29.55N 112.45W
Lobos, Cay- 194 Ib 22.24N 77.32W
Lobos, Cayo- 192 Ph 18.22N 87.24W
Lobos, Isla- 192 Dd 27.20N 110.36W
Lobos, Islas de- 192 Kg 21.27N 97.15W
Lobos de Afuera, Islas- 202 Be 6.57S 80.42W
Lobos de Tierra, Isla- 202 Be 6.27S 80.52W
Lobva 136 Gd 59.12N 60.30 E
Łobżonka 120 Nc 53.07N 17.18 E
Locana 128 Be 45.25N 7.27 E
Locarno 128 Cd 46.10N 8.48 E
Loch Aillionn/Allen, Lough- 118 Eg 54.08N 8.08W
Loch Ainnínn 118 Fh 53.28N 7.24W
Loch Ainninn/Ennell, Lough- 118 Fh 53.28N 7.24W
Loch Arabhach/Arrow, Lough- 118 Eg 54.05N 8.20W
Lochboisdale 118 Fd 57.09N 7.19W
Loch Cairlinn/Carlingford Lough 118 Gg 54.05N 6.14W
Loch Ce/Key, Lough- 118 Eg 54.00N 8.15W
Loch Coirib/Corrib, Lough- 118 Dh 53.05N 9.10W
Loch Con/Conn, Lough- 118 Dg 54.04N 9.20W
Loch Cuan/Strangford Lough 118 Hg 54.26N 5.36W
Loch Deirgeirt/Derg, Lough- 118 Ei 53.00N 8.20W
Lochearnhead 118 Ie 56.23N 4.18W
Loch Éirne Íochtair/Lower Lough Erne 118 Fg 54.30N 7.50W
Loch Éirne Uachtair/Upper Lough Erne 118 Fg 54.20N 7.30W
Lochem 124 Ib 52.10N 6.25 E
Loches 122 Gg 47.08N 1.00 E
Loch Feabhail/Foyle, Lough- 118 Ff 55.05N 7.10W
Loch Garman/Wexford 112 Fe 52.20N 6.27W
Loch Garman/Wexford 118 Gi 52.20N 6.40W
Lochgilphead 118 He 56.03N 5.26W
Lochinver 118 Hc 58.09N 5.15W
Loch Katrine 118 Ie 56.18N 4.30W
Loch Lao/Belfast Lough 118 Hg 54.40N 5.50W
Loch Léin/Leane, Lough- 118 Di 52.05N 9.35W
Loch Leven 118 Je 56.13N 3.10W
Lochmaddy 118 Fd 57.36N 7.10W
Loch Measca/Mask, Lough- 118 Dh 53.35N 9.20W
Lochnagar 118 Je 56.55N 3.10W
Loch nEathach/Neagh, Lough- 110 Fe 54.38N 6.24W
Loch Ness 118 Id 57.15N 4.30W
Łochów 120 Rd 52.32N 21.48 E
Loch Pholl an Phúca / Poulaphouca Reservoir 118 Gh 53.10N 6.30W
Loch Ri/Ree, Lough- 118 Fh 53.35N 8.00W
Lochsa River 188 Hc 46.08N 115.36W
Loch Síleann/Sheelin, Lough- 118 Fh 53.48N 7.20W
Loch Suili/Swilly, Lough- 118 Ff 55.10N 7.38W
Loch Uí Ghadra/Gara, Lough- 118 Eh 53.55N 8.30W
Lochy 118 He 56.49N 5.06W
Lochy, Loch- 118 Ie 56.55N 4.55W
Lockerbie 118 Jf 55.07N 3.22W
Lockhart 186 Hl 29.53N 97.41W
Lock Haven 184 Ie 41.09N 77.28W
Löcknitz 120 Hc 53.07N 11.16 E
Lockport 184 Hd 43.11N 78.39W
Locminé 122 Dg 47.53N 2.50W
Locri 128 Kl 38.14N 16.16 E
Lod 146 Fg 31.58N 34.54 E
Lodalskåpa 114 Bf 61.47N 7.12 E
Loddon 124 Db 52.32N 1.29 E
Loddon River 212 Ig 36.41S 143.55 E
Lodejnoje Pole 136 Dc 60.44N 33.33 E
Lodève 122 Jk 43.43N 3.19 E
Lodi [Ca.-U.S.] 188 Eg 38.08N 121.16W
Lodi [It.] 128 De 45.19N 9.30 E
Lødingen 114 Db 68.25N 16.00 E
Lodja 160 Ji 3.29S 23.26 E
Lodosa 126 Jb 42.25N 2.05W
Lödöse 116 Ef 58.02N 12.08 E
Lodwar 160 Kh 3.07N 35.36 E
Łódź 112 He 51.46N 19.30 E
Łódź 120 Pe 51.45N 19.30 E
Loei 148 Ke 17.32N 101.34 E
Loeriesfontein 172 Bf 30.56S 19.26 E
Lofanga 221b Ba 19.50S 174.33W
Loffa 166 Dd 7.45N 10.00W
Loffa 158 Fh 6.36N 11.05W
Lofoten 110 Hb 68.30N 15.00 E
Lofoten Basin (EN) 110 Ga 70.00N 4.00 E
Lofsdalen 116 Eb 62.07N 13.16 E
Loftahammar 116 Gg 57.52N 16.40 E
Loga 166 Fc 13.37N 3.14 E
Logan [N.M.-U.S.] 186 Ei 35.22N 103.25W
Logan [Oh.-U.S.] 184 Ff 39.32N 82.24W
Logan [Ut.-U.S.] 182 Ec 41.44N 111.50W
Logan [W.V.-U.S.] 184 Gg 37.52N 81.58W
Logan, Mount- [Can.] 174 Ec 60.34N 140.24W
Logan, Mount- [Wa.-U.S.] 188 Eb 48.32N 120.57W
Logan Martin Lake 184 Di 33.40N 86.15W
Logan Mountains 180 Ed 61.00N 128.00W
Logansport 184 De 40.45N 86.21W
Loge 158 Ii 7.49S 13.06 E
Logojsk 116 Lj 54.12N 27.57 E
Logone 158 Ig 12.06N 15.02 E
Logone Birni 166 Ic 11.47N 15.06 E
Logone Occidental 168 Bd 8.40N 16.00 E
Logone Occidental 168 Bd 9.07N 16.26 E
Logone Oriental 168 Bd 8.20N 16.30 E
Logone Oriental 168 Bd 8.07N 16.26 E
Logroño [Arg.] 204 Bi 29.30S 61.42W
Logroño [Sp.] 126 Jb 42.28N 2.27W
Logrosán 126 Ge 39.20N 5.29W
Løgstør 114 Bh 56.58N 9.15 E
Logudoro 128 Cj 40.35N 8.40 E
Løgumkloster 116 Ci 55.03N 8.57 E
Lögurinn 114a Cb 65.15N 14.30W
Lohja/Lojo 114 Ff 60.15N 24.05 E
Lohjanjärvi 116 Jd 60.15N 23.55 E
Lohjanselkä/Lojo åsen 116 Kd 60.15N 24.10 E
Löhme 124 Kc 51.41N 8.42 E
Löhne 120 Ed 52.11N 8.41 E
Lohne (Oldenburg) 124 Kb 52.40N 8.14 E
Lohra 124 Kd 50.44N 8.38 E
Lohr am Main 120 Ff 49.59N 9.35 E
Lohusuu/Lokusu 116 Lf 58.53N 27.01 E
Lohvica 132 Hd 50.22N 33.15 E
Loi, Phou- 148 Kd 20.16N 103.12 E
Loiblpaß 128 Id 46.26N 14.16 E
Loi-Kaw 148 Je 19.41N 97.13 E
Loile 170 Dc 0.52S 20.12 E
Loimaa 114 Ff 60.51N 23.03 E
Loimijoki 116 Jc 61.13N 22.38 E
Loing 122 If 48.23N 2.48 E
Loir 122 Fg 47.33N 0.32W
Loire 122 Ji 45.30N 4.00 E
Loire 110 Ff 47.16N 2.11W
Loire, Canal latéral à la- 122 Jh 46.29N 3.59 E
Loire, Val de- 122 Hg 47.40N 1.35 E
Loire-Atlantique 122 Eg 47.15N 1.50W
Loiret 122 Ig 47.55N 2.20 E
Loir-et-Cher 122 Hg 47.30N 1.30 E
Loisach 120 Hi 47.56N 11.27 E
Loison 124 He 49.30N 5.17 E
Loja [Ec.] 200 If 4.00S 79.13W
Loja [Sp.] 126 Hg 37.10N 4.09W
Lojo/Lohja 114 Ff 60.15N 24.05 E
Lojo åsen/Lohjanselkä 116 Kd 60.15N 24.10 E
Loka 168 Ee 4.16N 31.01 E
Lokači 120 Uf 50.43N 24.44 E
Lokalahti 116 Id 60.41N 21.28 E
Lokandu 170 Ec 2.31S 25.47 E
Lokantekojärvi 114 Gc 68.56N 27.40 E
Lokbatan 132 Pi 40.21N 49.42 E
Lokčim 134 Ef 61.48N 51.45 E
Løken 116 De 59.48N 11.29 E
Lokeren 122 Jc 51.06N 4.00 E
Lokichar 170 Gb 2.23N 35.39 E
Lokichokio 170 Fb 4.12N 34.21 E
Lokitaung 170 Gb 4.16N 35.45 E
Løkken [Den.] 116 Cg 57.22N 9.43 E
Løkken [Nor.] 114 Be 63.05N 9.36 E
Loknja 114 Hh 56.49N 30.09 E
Loko 166 Gd 8.00N 7.50 E
Lokoja 166 Gd 7.48N 6.44 E
Lokolo 170 Cc 0.43S 19.40 E
Lokomo 166 Ie 2.41N 15.19 E
Lokoro 170 Cc 1.43S 18.23 E
Lokossa 166 Fd 6.38N 1.43 E
Lokot 132 Ic 52.33N 34.31 E
Lokoti 166 Hd 6.22N 14.20 E
Loksa 114 Fg 59.34N 25.44 E
Loks Land 180 Ld 62.27N 64.30W
Lokuru 219a Cc 8.35S 157.20 E
Lokusu/Lohusuu 116 Lf 58.53N 27.01 E
Lokwa Kangole 170 Gb 3.32N 35.54 E
Lol 158 Jh 9.13N 28.59 E
Lola 166 Dd 7.48N 8.32W
Lolimi 168 Ee 4.35N 33.59 E
Loliondo 170 Gc 2.03S 35.37 E
Lolland 110 He 54.45N 11.30 E
Lollar 124 Kd 50.38N 8.42 E
Lolo 170 Db 2.13N 23.00 E
Lolo 170 Bc 0.40S 12.28 E
Lolodorf 166 He 3.14N 10.44 E
Lolo Pass 188 Hc 46.40N 114.33W
Loloway 219b Cb 15.17S 167.58 E
Lom 130 Gf 43.49N 23.14 E
Lom [Afr.] 166 Hd 5.20N 13.24 E
Lom [Bul.] 130 Gf 43.50N 23.15 E
Loma Bonita 192 Lh 18.07N 95.53W
Lomaloma 219d Cb 17.17S 178.59W
Lomami 158 Jh 0.46N 24.16 E
Loma Mountains 158 Fh 9.10N 11.07W
Lomas de Vallejos 204 Dh 27.44S 57.56W
Loma Verde 204 Cl 35.16S 58.24W
Lomba 170 Df 15.36S 21.32 E
Lombarda, Serra- 202 Hc 2.50N 51.50W
Lombarde, Prealpi- 128 De 46.00N 9.30 E
Lombardia = Lombardy (EN) 128 De 45.40N 9.30 E
Lombardy (EN) = Lombardia 128 De 45.40N 9.30 E
Lomblen, Pulau- 140 Oj 8.25S 123.30 E
Lombok, Pulau- 140 Nj 8.45S 116.30 E
Lombok, Selat- 150 Gh 8.30S 115.50 E
Lomé 160 Hh 6.08N 1.13 E
Lomela 160 Ji 2.18S 23.17 E
Lomela 158 Ji 0.14S 20.42 E
Lomellina 128 Ce 45.15N 8.45 E
Loméméti 219b Dd 19.30S 169.27 E
Lomié 166 He 3.10N 13.37 E
Lomlom 219c Bb 10.19S 166.16 E
Lomma 116 Ei 55.41N 13.05 E
Lomme 124 Hd 50.08N 5.10 E
Lommel 122 Lc 51.14N 5.18 E
Lomnica 120 Ug 49.02N 24.47 E
Lomond, Loch- 118 Ie 56.08N 4.38W
Lomonosov 136 Cd 59.55N 29.40 E
Lomonosovki 136 Ge 52.50N 66.28 E
Lomonosov Ridge (EN) 224 De 88.00N 140.00 E
Lomont 122 Mg 47.21N 6.36 E
Lompobatang, Gunung- 150 Gh 5.20S 119.55 E
Lompoc 182 Ce 34.38N 120.27W
Lomsegga 116 Cc 61.49N 8.22 E
Łomża 120 Sc 53.11N 22.05 E
Łomża 120 Sc 53.10N 22.05 E
Lønahorg 116 Bd 60.42N 6.25 E
Loncoche 206 Fe 39.22S 72.38W
Londa 148 Ee 15.28N 74.31 E
Londerzeel 124 Gc 51.01N 4.18 E
Londiani 170 Gc 0.10S 35.36 E
Londinières 124 De 49.50N 1.24 E
London [Eng.-U.K.] 112 Fe 51.30N 0.10W
London [Kir.] 220g Bb 1.58N 157.29W
London [Ky.-U.S.] 184 Eg 37.08N 84.05W
London [Ont.-Can.] 176 Ke 42.59N 81.14W
London-Barnet 124 Bc 51.39N 0.12W
London-Bexley 124 Cc 51.26N 0.09 E
London Bridge 197p Bb 12.17N 61.35W
London-Bromley 124 Cc 51.25N 0.01 E
London-Croydon 118 Mj 51.23N 0.07W
Londonderry / Derry 112 Fd 55.00N 7.19W
Londonderry, Cape- 212 Fb 13.45S 126.55 E
London-Ealing 124 Bc 51.30N 0.19W
London-Enfield 124 Bc 51.40N 0.04W
London-Greenwich 118 Mj 51.28N 0.00
London-Haringey 124 Bc 51.36N 0.06W
London-Harrow 124 Bc 51.36N 0.20W
London-Havering 124 Cc 51.36N 0.11 E
London-Hillingdon 124 Bc 51.31N 0.27W
London-Kingston-upon-Thames 118 Mj 51.28N 0.19W
London-Redbridge 124 Cc 51.35N 0.08 E
London-Sutton 124 Bc 51.21N 0.12W
London-Wandsworth 124 Bc 51.27N 0.12W
London-Westminster 124 Bc 51.30N 0.07W
Londrina 200 Kh 23.18S 51.09W
Londuimbali 170 Ce 12.15S 15.19 E
Lone Pine 188 Fh 36.36N 118.04W
Long, Loch- 118 Ie 56.04N 4.50W
Longa 170 Ce 14.41S 18.29 E
Longa [Ang.] 170 Be 10.15S 13.30 E
Longa [Ang.] 170 Cf 16.25S 19.04 E
Longa, proliv- = De Long Strait (EN) 140 Tb 70.20N 178.00 E
Longá, Rio- 202 Jd 3.09S 41.56W
Long Akah 150 Ff 3.19N 114.47 E
Longarone 128 Gd 46.16N 12.18 E
Longbangun 150 Gf 0.36N 115.11 E
Long Bay [Bar.] 197q Bb 13.04N 59.29W
Long Bay [S.C.-U.S.] 182 Le 33.35N 78.45W
Long Beach [Ca.-U.S.] 176 Hf 33.46N 118.11W
Long Beach [N.Y.-U.S.] 184 Ke 40.35N 73.40W
Long Beach [Wa.-U.S.] 188 Cc 46.21N 124.03W
Long Branch 182 Mc 40.17N 73.59W
Long Buckby 124 Ab 52.18N 1.04W
Long Cay 194 Jb 22.37N 74.20W
Longchuan 152 Kg 24.10N 115.17 E
Long Creek 188 Nb 49.07N 103.00W
Long Eaton 124 Ab 52.54N 1.16W
Longfeng 154 Ha 46.31N 125.02 E
Longford / An Longfort 118 Fh 53.44N 7.47W
Longford / An Longfort 118 Fh 53.40N 7.40W
Long Forties 118 Nd 57.10N 0.05 E
Long Hu 154 Dj 29.37N 116.12 E
Longhua 154 Dd 41.18N 117.44 E
Longido 170 Gc 2.44S 36.41 E
Long Island [Atg.] 197d Bb 17.08N 61.45W
Long Island [Bah.] 174 Lg 23.10N 75.10W
Long Island [Can.] 180 Jf 54.50N 79.20W
Long Island [Can.] 184 Nc 44.20N 66.15W
Long Island [Pap.N.Gui.] 208 Fe 5.20S 147.05 E
Long Island [U.S.] 174 Le 40.50N 73.00W
Long Island Sound 184 Ke 41.05N 72.58W
Longjiang 152 Lb 47.20N 123.09 E
Longjuzhai → Danfeng 152 Je 33.44N 110.22 E
Longkou 152 Ld 37.39N 120.20 E
Longlac 180 Ig 49.50N 86.32W
Long Lake [N.D.-U.S.] 186 Fc 46.43N 100.07W
Long Lake [Ont.-Can.] 186 Mb 49.32N 86.45W
Longmalinau 150 Gf 3.30N 116.31 E
Long Men 152 Je 34.40N 110.30 E
Longmont 186 Df 40.10N 105.06W
Longnan 152 Jg 24.54N 114.48 E
Longobucco 128 Kk 39.27N 16.37 E
Longoz 130 Kf 43.02N 27.41 E
Longping → Luodian 152 If 25.26N 106.47 E
Long Point 184 Gd 42.34N 80.15W
Long Point Bay 184 Gd 42.40N 80.14W
Longpujungan 150 Gf 2.34N 115.40 E
Longquan 152 Kf 28.06N 119.05 E
Long Range Mountains 180 Lg 48.00N 58.30W
Longreach 210 Fg 23.26S 144.15 E
Long Sand 124 Dc 51.37N 1.10 E
Longs Peak 174 Ie 40.15N 105.37W
Long Sutton 124 Cb 52.47N 0.08 E
Longtan 154 Eh 32.10N 119.03 E
Longtown 118 Kf 55.01N 2.58W
Longueau 124 Ee 49.52N 2.21 E
Longué-Jumelles 122 Fg 47.23N 0.07W
Longueville-sur-Scie 124 De 49.48N 1.06 E
Longuyon 122 Le 49.26N 5.36 E
Long Valley 188 Ji 34.37N 111.16W
Longview [Tx.-U.S.] 182 Ie 32.30N 94.44W
Longview [Wa.-U.S.] 182 Cb 46.08N 122.57W
Longwu 152 Hg 24.07N 102.18 E
Longwy 122 Le 49.31N 5.46 E
Longxi 152 Hd 35.01N 104.38 E
Longxian 152 Id 35.00N 106.53 E
Longxian → Wengyuan 152 Jg 24.21N 114.13 E
Longxi Shan 152 Kf 26.35N 117.17 E
Long Xuyen 148 Lf 10.23N 105.25 E
Longyan 152 Kf 25.06N 117.01 E
Longyao 154 Cf 37.21N 114.46 E
Longyearbyen 224 Kd 78.13N 15.38 E
Longyou 154 Ej 29.01N 119.10 E
Longzhou 152 Ig 22.23N 106.49 E
Lonigo 128 Fe 45.23N 11.23 E
Löningen 120 Dd 52.44N 7.46 E
Lonja 128 Ke 45.27N 16.41 E
Lonjsko Polje 128 Ke 45.24N 16.42 E
Lönsboda 116 Fh 56.24N 14.19 E
Lons-le-Saunier 122 Lh 46.40N 5.33 E
Lontra, Ribeirão- 204 Fe 21.28S 53.37W
Lookout, Cape- [N.C.-U.S.] 182 Le 34.35N 76.32W
Lookout, Cape- [Or.-U.S.] 188 Dd 45.20N 124.00W
Lookout Mountain 184 Eh 34.40N 85.20W
Lookout Pass 182 Db 47.27N 115.42W
Loolmalasin 170 Gc 3.03S 35.49 E
Loop Head/Ceann Léime 118 Di 52.34N 9.56W
Loosdrechtse Plassen 124 Hb 52.10N 5.08 E
Lop 152 Dd 37.01N 80.16 E
Lopatina, gora- 140 Qd 50.52N 143.10 E
Lopatino 132 Nc 52.37N 45.47 E
Lopatka, mys- 140 Rd 50.52N 156.40 E
Lop Buri 148 Kf 14.48N 100.37 E
Lopča 138 He 55.44N 122.45 E
Lopévi 219b Dc 16.30S 168.21 E
Lopez, Cap-=Lopez, Cape-(EN) 158 Hi 0.37S 8.43 E
Lopez, Cape-(EN)=Lopez, Cap- 158 Hi 0.37S 8.43 E
Lop Nur 140 Le 40.30N 90.30 E
Lopnur/Yuli 152 Ec 41.22N 86.09 E
Lopori 158 Ih 1.14N 19.49 E
Loppersum 124 Ia 53.19N 6.45 E
Lopphavet 114 Ea 70.25N 22.00 E
Loppi 116 Kd 60.43N 24.27 E
Lopud 128 Lh 42.41N 17.57 E
Łopuszno 120 Qf 50.57N 20.15 E
Lora del Río 126 Gg 37.39N 5.32W
Lorain 182 Kc 41.28N 82.11W
Lorán, Boca- 196 Fh 9.00N 60.45W
Lorca 126 Kg 37.40N 1.42W
Lorch 124 Jd 50.03N 7.49 E
Lord Howe Island 208 Gh 31.35S 159.05 E
Lord Howe Rise (EN) 106 Jm 32.00S 162.00 E
Lord Mayor Bay 180 Ic 69.45N 92.00W
Lordsburg 186 Bj 32.21N 108.43W
Loreley 124 Jd 50.08N 7.43 E
Lorena 204 Jf 22.44S 45.08W
Lorengau 214 Dh 2.01S 147.17 E
Lorestān 144 Gc 33.30N 48.40 E
Loreto 202 Dd 5.00S 75.00W
Loreto [Arg.] 204 Dh 27.46S 57.17W
Loreto [Bol.] 202 Fg 15.13S 64.40W
Loreto [Braz.] 202 Ie 7.05S 45.09W
Loreto [It.] 128 Hg 43.26N 13.36 E
Loreto [Mex.] 192 If 22.16N 101.58W
Loreto [Mex.] 190 Bc 26.01N 111.21W
Loreto [Par.] 206 Ib 23.16S 57.11W
Loreto Aprutino 128 Hh 42.26N 13.59 E
Lorica 202 Cb 9.14N 75.49W
Lorient 112 Ff 47.45N 3.22W
Lőrinci 120 Pi 47.44N 19.41 E
Lorn, Firth of- 118 He 56.20N 5.40W
Lorne 212 Ig 38.33S 143.59 E
Lörrach 120 Di 47.37N 7.40 E
Lorrain, Plateau- 122 Me 49.00N 6.30 E
Lorrain, Rivière du- 197h Ab 14.50N 61.03W
Lorraine 122 Lf 49.00N 6.00 E
Lorraine, Plaine- 122 Lf 48.10N 5.50 E
Lorsch 124 Ke 49.39N 8.34 E
Los 114 Df 61.44N 15.10 E
Los, Iles de-=Los Islands (EN) 166 Cd 9.30N 13.48W
Los Alamos 176 If 35.53N 106.19W
Los Amates 194 Cf 15.16N 89.06W
Los Amores 204 Ci 28.06S 59.59W
Los Ángeles 200 Ii 37.28S 72.21W
Los Angeles 176 Hf 34.03N 118.15W
Los Angeles Aqueduct 188 Fi 35.22N 118.05W
Losap Atoll 208 Gd 6.54N 152.44 E
Los Banos 188 Eh 37.04N 120.51W
Los Blancos 206 Hb 23.36S 62.36W
Los Charrúas 204 Cj 31.10S 58.11W
Los Chiles 194 Eh 11.02N 84.43W
Los Conquistadores 204 Cj 30.36S 58.28W
Los Frailes, Islas- 196 Eg 11.12N 63.45W
Los Frentones 204 Bh 26.25S 61.25W
Los Gatos 188 Eh 37.14N 121.59W
Losheim 124 Ie 49.31N 6.45 E
Los Hermanos, Islas- 202 Fa 11.45N 64.25W
Łosice 120 Sd 52.14N 22.43 E
Lošinj 128 If 44.35N 14.28 E
Los Islands (EN)=Los, Iles de- 166 Cd 9.30N 13.48W
Los Juries 204 Ai 28.28S 62.06W
Los Lagos 206 Fe 39.51S 72.50W
Los Lagos 206 Ff 41.20S 73.00W
Los Llanos de Aridane 162 Dd 28.39N 17.54W
Los Médanos, Istmo de- 194 Mh 11.35N 69.45W
Los Mochis 176 Ig 25.45N 108.53W
Los Monegros 126 Lc 41.29N 0.03W
Los Monjes, Islas- 202 Da 12.25N 70.55W
Los Navalmorales 126 He 39.43N 4.38W
Loso 170 Ec 1.10S 27.10 E
Los Palacios 194 Fb 22.35N 83.12W
Los Palacios y Villafranca 126 Gg 37.10N 5.56W
Los Pedroches 126 Hf 38.27N 4.45W
Los Pirpintos 204 Ah 26.08S 62.05W
Los Remedios, Río de- 192 Fe 24.41N 106.28W
Los Reyes de Salgado 192 Hh 19.35N 102.29W
Los Roques, Islas- 202 Ea 11.50N 66.45W

Index Symbols

- 1 Independent Nation
- 2 State, Region
- 3 District, County
- 4 Municipality
- 5 Colony, Dependency
- Continent
- Physical Region
- Historical or Cultural Region
- Mount, Mountain
- Volcano
- Hill
- Mountains, Mountain Range
- Hills, Escarpment
- Plateau, Upland
- Pass, Gap
- Plain, Lowland
- Delta
- Salt Flat
- Valley, Canyon
- Crater, Cave
- Karst Features
- Depression
- Polder
- Desert, Dunes
- Forest, Woods
- Heath, Steppe
- Oasis
- Cape, Point
- Coast, Beach
- Cliff
- Peninsula
- Isthmus
- Sandbank
- Island
- Atoll
- Rock, Reef
- Islands, Archipelago
- Rocks, Reefs
- Coral Reef
- Well, Spring
- Geyser
- River, Stream
- Waterfall, Rapids
- River Mouth, Estuary
- Lake
- Salt Lake
- Intermittent Lake
- Reservoir
- Swamp, Pond
- Canal
- Glacier
- Ice Shelf, Pack Ice
- Ocean
- Sea
- Gulf, Bay
- Strait, Fjord
- Lagoon
- Bank
- Seamount
- Tablemount
- Ridge
- Shelf
- Basin
- Escarpment, Sea Scarp
- Fracture
- Trench, Abyss
- National Park, Reserve
- Point of Interest
- Recreation Site
- Cave, Cavern
- Historic Site
- Ruins
- Wall, Walls
- Church, Abbey
- Temple
- Scientific Station
- Railway station
- Airport
- Port
- Military installation
- Lighthouse
- Mine
- Tunnel
- Dam, Bridge

Los Roques Basin (EN)	196	Cf	12.20N	67.40W
Los Santos	194	Gj	7.56N	80.25W
Los Santos [3]	194	Gj	7.45N	80.30W
Losser	124	Jb	52.16N	7.01 E
Lossiemouth	118	Jd	57.43N	3.18W
Lossnen	116	Eb	62.30N	12.50 E
Los Taques	194	Lh	11.50N	70.16W
Los Telares	206	Hc	28.59S	63.26W
Los Teques	202	Ea	10.21N	67.02W
Los Testigos, Islas-	202	Fa	11.23N	63.06W
Lost River	188	Ef	41.56N	121.30W
Lost River Range	188	Id	44.10N	113.35W
Lost Trail Pass	182	Eb	45.41N	113.57W
Los Vilos	206	Fd	31.55S	71.31W
Lot [3]	122	Hj	44.30N	1.30 E
Lot	110	Gg	44.18N	0.20 E
Lota	206	Fe	37.05S	73.10W
Lotagipi Swamp	168	Ee	4.36N	34.55 E
Løten	116	Dd	60.49N	11.19 E
Lot-et-Garonne [3]	122	Gj	44.20N	0.30 E
Lothair	172	Ee	26.26S	30.27 E
Lothian [3]	118	Jf	55.55N	3.30W
Lothian	118	Jf	55.55N	3.05W
Loto	170	Dc	2.47S	22.30 E
Lotofaga	221c	Ba	13.59S	171.50W
Lotoi	170	Cc	1.35S	18.30 E
Lotru	130	Hd	45.20N	24.16 E
Lotrului, Munţii-	130	Gd	45.30N	23.52 E
Lotta	114	Hb	68.39N	30.20 E
Lottefors	116	Gc	61.25N	16.24 E
Löttorp	116	Gg	57.10N	16.59 E
Lotuke, Jabal-	168	Ee	4.07N	33.48 E
Louang Namtha	148	Kd	20.57N	101.25 E
Louangphrabang	142	Mh	19.52N	102.08 E
Loubomo	160	Ii	4.12S	12.41 E
Loučná	120	Lf	50.06N	15.48 E
Loudéac	122	Df	48.10N	2.45W
Loudima	170	Bc	4.07S	13.04 E
Loudon	184	Eh	35.44N	84.20W
Loudun	122	Gh	47.00N	0.04 E
Loué	122	Fg	48.00N	0.09W
Loue	122	Lg	47.01N	5.27 E
Loufan	154	Ae	38.04N	111.47 E
Louga	166	Bb	15.37N	16.13W
Louga [3]	166	Bb	15.00N	15.30W
Louge	122	Hk	43.27N	1.20 E
Loughborough	118	Li	52.47N	1.11W
Lougheed	180	Ha	77.30N	105.00W
Loughrea/Baile Locha Riach	118	Eh	53.12N	8.34W
Louhans	122	Lh	46.38N	5.13 E
Louhi	136	Db	66.04N	33.01 E
Louisa	184	Ff	38.07N	82.36W
Louiseville	184	Kb	46.16N	72.57W
Louisiade Archipelago	208	Kf	11.00S	153.00 E
Louisiana	186	Kg	39.27N	91.03W
Louisiana [2]	182	Ie	31.15N	92.15W
Louis Trichardt	172	Dd	23.01S	29.43 E
Louisville [Ky.-U.S.]	176	Kf	38.16N	85.45W
Louisville [Ms.-U.S.]	186	Lj	33.07N	89.03W
Louis-XIV, Pointe -	180	Jf	54.50N	79.30W
Loukoléla	170	Cc	1.02S	17.07 E
Loulan Yiji	152	Ec	40.32N	89.50 E
Loulé	126	Dg	37.08N	8.02W
Loum	166	Ge	4.43N	9.44 E
Lount Lake	186	Ia	50.10N	94.20W
Louny	120	Jf	50.22N	13.49 E
Loup City	186	Gf	41.17N	98.58W
Loupe, La-	122	Hf	48.28N	1.01 E
Loup River	182	Hc	41.24N	97.19W
Loups Marins, Lacs des -	180	Ke	56.40N	74.00W
Lourdes	122	Fk	43.06N	0.03W
Lourenço Marques → Maputo	160	Kk	25.58S	32.34 E
Lousa, Serra da-	126	Dd	40.04N	8.13W
Loushan Guan	152	If	28.02N	106.51 E
Louštín	120	Jf	50.12N	13.48 E
Louth [Austl.]	212	Jf	30.32S	145.07 E
Louth [Eng.-U.K.]	118	Mh	53.22N	0.01W
Louth/Lú [2]	118	Gh	53.55N	6.30W
Loutrá Aidhipsoú	130	Gk	38.51N	23.03 E
Loutrá Killínis	130	El	37.52N	21.07 E
Loutrákion	130	Fl	37.59N	23.00 E
Louvain/Leuven	122	Kd	50.53N	4.42 E
Louvet Point	197k	Bb	13.58N	60.53W
Louviers	122	He	49.13N	1.10 E
Lövånger	114	Ed	64.22N	21.18 E
Lovászi	120	Mj	46.33N	16.34 E
Lovat	110	Jd	58.14N	31.28 E
Lovćen	130	Bg	42.24N	18.49 E
Loveč	130	Hf	43.08N	24.43 E
Loveč [2]	130	Hf	43.08N	24.43 E
Loveland	186	Df	40.24N	105.05W
Lovell	182	Fc	44.50N	108.24W
Lovelock	182	Dc	40.11N	118.28W
Lövenich, Köln-	124	Id	50.57N	6.50 E
Lovere	128	Ee	45.49N	10.04 E
Loviisa/Lovisa	114	Gf	60.27N	26.14 E
Loving	186	Dj	32.17N	104.06W
Lovington	182	Ge	33.27N	103.21W
Lovisa/Loviisa	114	Gf	60.27N	26.14 E
Lovoi	170	Ed	8.05S	26.40 E
Lovosice	120	Kf	50.31N	14.03 E
Lovozero	114	Ib	68.01N	35.01 E
Lövstabruk	116	Gd	60.24N	17.53 E
Lövstabukten	116	Gd	60.35N	17.45 E
Lovua	170	De	11.31S	23.35 E
Lovua	170	Dd	6.07S	20.35 E
Low, Cape -	180	Id	63.06N	85.18W
Lowa	158	Ji	1.24S	25.52 E
Lowell	182	Mc	42.39N	71.18W
Löwemberg/Mark	120	Jd	52.53N	13.09 E
Lower Arrow Lake	188	Fb	49.40N	118.08W
Lower Austria (EN) = Niederösterreich [2]	128	Jb	48.30N	15.45 E
Lower California (EN) → Baja California	174	Hg	28.00N	112.00W
Lower Hutt	218	Fd	41.13S	174.55 E
Lower Lake	188	Dg	38.55N	122.36W
Lower Lake	188	Ef	41.15N	120.02W
Lower Lough Erne/Loch Éirne Íochtair	118	Fg	54.30N	7.50W
Lower Post	180	Ee	59.55N	128.30W
Lower Red Lake	186	Ic	48.00N	94.50W
Lower Rhine (EN) = Neder-Rijn	122	Mc	51.59N	6.20 E
Lower Saxony (EN) = Niedersachsen [2]	120	Fd	52.00N	10.00 E
Lower Trajan's Wall (EN) = Nižni Trajanov val	130	Ld	45.45N	28.30 E
Lower Tunguska (EN) = Nižnjaja Tunguska	140	Kc	65.48N	88.04 E
Lowestoft	118	Oi	52.29N	1.45 E
Lowestoft Ness	118	Oi	52.28N	1.44 E
Lowgar [3]	144	Kc	33.50N	69.00 E
Łowicz	120	Pd	52.07N	19.56 E
Lowlands	118	Jf	56.00N	4.00W
Lowrah	140	If	31.33N	66.33 E
Lowshān	146	Md	36.39N	49.32 E
Low Tatra (EN) = Nízke Tatry	120	Ph	48.54N	19.40 E
Lowther	180	Hb	74.35N	97.40W
Lowville	184	Jd	43.47N	75.30W
Loxton [Austl.]	212	If	34.27S	140.35 E
Loxton [S.Afr.]	172	Cf	31.30S	22.22 E
Loyalty Islands (EN) = Loyauté, Iles-	208	Hg	21.00S	167.00 E
Loyauté, Iles- = Loyalty Islands (EN)	208	Hg	21.00S	167.00 E
Loyoro	170	Fb	3.21N	34.17 E
Lozère [3]	122	Jj	44.30N	3.30 E
Lozère, Mont-	122	Jj	44.25N	3.46 E
Loznica	130	Ce	44.32N	19.13 E
Lozovaja	136	Df	48.53N	36.15 E
Lozva	136	Gd	59.36N	62.20 E
Lú/Louth [2]	118	Gh	53.55N	6.30W
Lua	170	Cb	2.46N	18.26 E
Luacano	170	De	11.16S	21.38 E
Luachimo	170	Dd	6.33S	20.59 E
Luaha-Sibuha	150	Cg	0.31S	98.28 E
Luahoko	221b	Ba	19.40S	174.24W
Luala	172	Fc	17.57S	36.30 E
Lualaba	158	Jh	0.26N	25.20 E
Luama	170	Ec	4.46S	26.53 E
Lua Makika	221a	Ec	20.35N	156.34W
Luampa	170	De	14.32S	24.10 E
Lu'an	152	Ke	31.44N	116.30 E
Luanda	160	Ii	8.48S	13.14 E
Luanda [3]	170	Bd	9.00S	13.15 E
Luando	158	Ij	10.19S	16.40 E
Luang, Khao-	148	Jg	8.31N	99.47 E
Luang, Thale-	148	Kg	7.30N	100.15 E
Luang Chiang Dao, Doi-	148	Je	19.23N	98.54 E
Luanginga	158	Jj	15.11S	22.55 E
Luang Prabang Range	148	Ke	18.30N	101.15 E
Luangue	170	Dc	4.17S	20.01 E
Luangwa	158	Kj	15.36S	30.25 E
Luan He	140	Nf	39.20N	119.10 E
Luaniva	220h	Bb	13.16S	176.07W
Luannan (Bencheng)	154	Ee	39.30N	118.42 E
Luanping (Anjiangying)	154	Dd	40.55N	117.19 E
Luanshya	160	Jj	13.08S	28.25 E
Luanxian	152	Kd	39.45N	118.44 E
Luanza	170	Ed	8.40S	28.40 E
Luapula [3]	170	Ee	10.40S	29.15 E
Luapula	158	Ji	9.26S	28.33 E
Luarca	126	Fa	43.32N	6.32W
Luashi	170	De	10.56S	23.37 E
Luau	170	De	10.42S	22.12 E
Luba	166	Ge	3.28N	8.40 E
Lubaantum	194	Ce	16.17N	88.58W
Lubaczów	120	Tf	50.10N	23.07 E
Lubaczówka	120	Sf	50.08N	22.35 E
Lubalo	170	Cd	9.07S	19.15 E
Lubalo	170	Cd	7.22S	19.20 E
Lubamba	170	Ed	5.14S	26.02 E
Lubań	120	Le	51.08N	15.18 E
Lubana/Lubāna	116	Lh	56.49N	26.49 E
Lubāna/Lubana	116	Lh	56.49N	26.49 E
Lubanas, ozero- / Lubānas ezers	116	Lh	56.40N	27.00 E
Lubānas ezers / Lubanas, ozero-	116	Lh	56.40N	27.00 E
Lubang Islands	150	Hd	13.45N	120.15 E
Lubango	160	Ij	14.55S	13.28 E
Lubao	160	Ji	5.22S	25.45 E
Lubartów	120	Se	51.28N	22.46 E
Lubawa	120	Pc	53.30N	19.45 E
Lübbecke	120	Ed	52.18N	8.37 E
Lubbeek	124	Gd	50.53N	4.50 E
Lübben (Spreewald)/Lubin	120	Je	51.57N	13.54 E
Lübbenau/Lubnjow	120	Je	51.52N	13.58 E
Lubbock	176	If	33.35N	101.51W
Lübeck	112	He	53.52N	10.42 E
Lübecker Bucht	120	Gb	54.00N	10.55 E
Lübeck-Travemünde	120	Gc	53.57N	10.52 E
Lubefu	170	Dc	4.43S	24.25 E
Lubefu	170	Dc	4.10S	23.00 E
Lubei → Jarud Qi	152	Lc	44.30N	120.55 E
Lubelska, Wyżyna-	120	Sf	51.00N	23.00 E
Lubenec	120	Jf	50.08N	13.20 E
Lubenka	132	Sd	50.28N	54.06 E
Lubero	170	Ec	0.06S	29.06 E
Lubéron, Montagne du-	122	Lk	43.48N	5.22 E
Lubi	170	Dc	4.59S	23.26 E
Lubie, Jezioro-	120	Lc	53.30N	15.50 E
Lubień Kujawski	120	Pd	52.25N	19.10 E
Lubij/Löbau	120	Ke	51.06N	14.40 E
Lubilash	158	Ji	6.02S	23.45 E
Lubin	120	Me	51.24N	16.13 E
Lubin/Lübben (Spreewald)	120	Je	51.57N	13.54 E
Lublin	112	Ie	51.15N	22.35 E
Lublin [2]	120	Se	51.15N	22.35 E
Lubliniec	120	Of	50.40N	18.41 E
Lubnān=Lebanon (EN) [1]	142	Ff	33.50N	35.50 E
Lubnān, Jabal- = Lebanon Mountains (EN)	144	Ec	34.00N	36.30 E
Lubnjow/Lübbenau	120	Je	51.52N	13.58 E
Lubny	136	De	50.01N	33.00 E
Luboń	120	Md	52.23N	16.54 E
Lubraniec	120	Od	52.33N	18.50 E
Lubsko	120	Ke	51.46N	14.59 E
Lubsza	120	Ke	51.55N	14.45 E
Lubudi	170	Ed	9.57S	25.58 E
Lubudi	158	Ji	9.13S	25.38 E
Lubue	170	Cc	4.10S	19.53 E
Lubukklinggau	150	Dg	3.10S	102.52 E
Lubuksikaping	150	Df	0.08N	100.10 E
Lubumba	170	Ec	3.58S	29.06 E
Lubumbashi	160	Jj	11.40S	27.30 E
Lubuskie, Pojezierze-	120	Ld	52.18N	15.20 E
Lubutu	160	Ji	0.44S	26.35 E
Lucala	170	Cd	9.16S	15.16 E
Lucala	170	Bd	6.38S	12.34 E
Lucania, Mount-	180	Dd	61.01N	140.29W
Lucas	204	Ea	13.05S	55.56W
Lucca	128	Eg	43.50N	10.29 E
Lucea	194	Hd	18.27N	78.10W
Luce Bay	118	Ig	54.47N	4.50W
Lucedale	186	Lk	30.55N	88.35W
Lučegorsk	138	Ig	46.25N	134.20 E
Lucélia	204	Ge	21.44S	51.01W
Lucena [Phil.]	150	Hd	13.56N	121.37 E
Lucena [Sp.]	126	Hg	37.24N	4.29W
Lucena del Cid / Llucena	126	Ld	40.08N	0.17W
Luc-en-Diois	122	Lj	44.37N	5.27 E
Lučenec	120	Ph	48.20N	19.41 E
Lucera	128	Ji	41.30N	15.20 E
Lucerne (EN) = Luzern	128	Cc	47.05N	8.20 E
Lucerne, Lake- (EN) = Vierwaldstätter See	128	Cc	47.00N	8.30 E
Lucero	192	Fb	30.49N	106.30W
Lucheng	154	Bf	36.18N	113.15 E
Lucheringo	172	Fb	11.43S	36.15 E
Lucheux	124	Ed	50.12N	2.25 E
Luchico	170	Cd	6.12S	19.42 E
Lüchow	120	Hd	52.58N	11.09 E
Lüchun	152	Hg	23.02N	102.19 E
Lucipara, Kepulauan-	150	Ih	5.30S	127.33 E
Lucira	170	Be	13.52S	12.32 E
Luck	136	Ce	50.47N	25.20 E
Luckau	120	Je	51.51N	13.43 E
Luckenwalde	120	Jd	52.05N	13.10 E
Lucknow	142	Kg	26.51N	80.55 E
Luçon	122	Eh	46.27N	1.10W
Lucrecia, Cabo-	194	Jc	21.04N	75.37W
Luc-sur-Mer	124	Be	49.18N	0.21W
Lucunga	170	Bd	6.49S	14.35 E
Lucusse	170	De	12.33S	20.51 E
Lüda → Dalian	142	Of	38.55N	121.39 E
Luda Kamčija	130	Kg	43.03N	27.29 E
Ludbreg	128	Kd	46.15N	16.37 E
Lüdenscheid	120	De	51.13N	7.37 E
Lüderitz	160	Ik	26.38S	15.10 E
Lüderitz [3]	172	Be	26.00S	15.00 E
Lüderitz Bay	172	Be	26.35S	15.10 E
Ludhiāna	142	Jf	30.54N	75.51 E
Lüdinghausen	120	De	51.46N	7.28 E
Ludington	182	Jc	43.57N	86.27W
Ludlow	118	Ki	52.22N	2.43W
Ludogorije	130	Jf	43.46N	26.56 E
Ludogorsko Plato	130	Kf	43.36N	27.03 E
Luduş	130	Hc	46.29N	24.06 E
Ludvika	114	Df	60.09N	15.11 E
Ludwigsburg	120	Fh	48.54N	9.11 E
Ludwigshafen am Rhein	120	Eg	49.29N	8.27 E
Ludwigslust	120	Hc	53.19N	11.30 E
Ludza	114	Gh	56.32N	27.45 E
Luebo	160	Ji	5.21S	21.25 E
Lueki	170	Ec	3.22S	25.51 E
Lueki	170	Ec	3.24S	25.57 E
Luele	170	Dd	7.55S	20.00 E
Luembe	170	Dd	6.37S	21.06 E
Luembé	170	Dd	6.37S	21.05 E
Luena [Ang.]	160	Ij	11.48S	19.55 E
Luena [Ang.]	170	De	12.31S	22.34 E
Luena [Zaire]	170	Ed	9.27S	25.47 E
Luena [Zam.]	170	Df	15.20S	23.30 E
Luengué	170	Df	16.54S	21.52 E
Luenha	172	Ec	16.24S	33.48 E
Luera Peak	186	Cj	33.47N	107.49W
Lueta	170	Dd	7.04S	21.40 E
Lueyang	152	Ie	33.25N	106.14 E
Lufeng	152	Kg	22.57N	115.41 E
Lufico	170	Bd	6.22S	13.30 E
Lufira	158	Ji	8.16S	26.27 E
Lufira, Chutes de la-	170	Ed	9.50S	27.30 E
Lufkin	182	Ie	31.20N	94.44W
Lug	136	De	44.23N	20.45 E
Luga	136	Cd	58.44N	29.50 E
Luga	136	Cd	59.43N	28.18 E
Lugano	128	Cd	46.00N	8.57 E
Lugano, Lago di- (Ceresio)	128	Cd	46.00N	9.00 E
Lugansk = Vorošilovgrad	112	Jf	48.34N	39.20 E
Luganville	210	Hf	15.32S	167.10 E
Lügde	122	Lc	51.57N	9.15 E
Lugela	172	Fc	16.26S	36.39 E
Lugenda	158	Kj	11.26S	38.33 E
Lugnaquillia	110	Fe	52.58N	6.27W
Lugo [3]	126	Eb	43.00N	7.30W
Lugo [It.]	128	Ff	44.25N	11.54 E
Lugo [Sp.]	126	Ea	43.00N	7.34W
Lugoj	130	Ed	45.41N	21.55 E
Lugovoj [Kaz.]	136	Hg	42.55N	72.47 E
Lugovoj [Russia]	136	Gd	59.44N	65.55 E
Lugovski	138	Ge	58.05N	112.55 E
Lugulu	170	Ec	2.17S	26.32 E
Luh	114	Kh	56.14N	42.28 E
Luhe	154	Eh	32.21N	118.50 E
Luhe	120	Gc	53.18N	10.11 E
Luhin Sum	152	Kb	46.41N	118.38 E
Luhit	148	Jc	27.48N	95.28 E
Luhovicy	114	Ji	54.59N	39.02 E
Luhuo	152	He	31.21N	100.40 E
Lui	170	Cd	8.41S	17.56 E
Luia	170	Dd	8.26S	21.45 E
Luiana	170	Df	17.22S	22.59 E
Luiana	158	Jj	17.27S	23.14 E
Luie	170	Cc	4.33S	17.41 E
Luik/Liège	112	Ge	50.38N	5.34 E
Luilaka	158	Ji	0.52S	20.12 E
Luilu	170	Dd	6.22S	23.50 E
Luimneach/Limerick	112	Fe	52.40N	8.38W
Luimneach/Limerick [2]	118	Ei	52.30N	9.00W
Luing	118	He	56.13N	5.39W
Luino	128	Cd	46.00N	8.44 E
Luio	170	De	13.15S	21.39 E
Lui Pătru, Vîrful-	130	Gd	45.30N	23.30 E
Luis Correia	202	Jd	2.53S	41.40W
Luishia	170	Ee	11.13S	27.07 E
Luitpold Coast	222	Af	78.30S	32.00W
Luiza	170	Dd	7.12S	22.25 E
Luján [Arg.]	206	Gd	32.22S	65.57W
Luján [Arg.]	206	Id	34.34S	59.07W
Lujiang	154	Di	31.15N	117.17 E
Lukafu	170	Ee	10.30S	27.33 E
Lukanga Swamp	170	Ee	14.25S	27.45 E
Lukavac	128	Mf	44.33N	18.32 E
Lukengo	170	Ed	5.46S	29.06 E
Lukenie	158	Ii	2.44S	18.09 E
Lukeville	188	Ik	31.57N	112.50W
Lukojanov	136	Ed	55.02N	44.30 E
Lukolela	170	Cc	1.03S	17.12 E
Lukonzolwa	170	Ed	8.47S	28.39 E
Lukov	120	Ue	51.14N	24.25 E
Lukovit	130	Hf	43.12N	24.10 E
Łuków	120	Se	51.56N	22.23 E
Lukuga	158	Ji	5.40S	26.55 E
Lukula	170	Bd	5.23S	12.57 E
Lukulu	170	De	14.23S	23.15 E
Lukusashi	170	Fe	14.38S	30.00 E
Luleå	112	Ib	65.34N	22.10 E
Luleälven	110	Ib	65.35N	22.03 E
Lüleburgaz	144	Ca	41.24N	27.21 E
Lüliang Shan	140	Nf	37.45N	111.25 E
Lulimba	170	Ec	4.42S	28.38 E
Luling	186	Hl	29.41N	97.39W
Lulong	154	Ee	39.53N	118.52 E
Lulonga	170	Cb	0.37N	18.23 E
Lulonga	158	Ih	0.43N	18.23 E
Lulua	158	Ji	5.02S	21.07 E
Lulu Fakahega, Mount-	220h	Bb	13.16S	176.10W
Luma	221c	Db	14.14S	169.32W
Lumajang	150	Fh	8.08S	113.13 E
Lumajangdong Co	152	De	34.00N	81.37 E
Lumbala Kaquengue	160	Jj	14.06S	21.25 E
Lumbala N'guimbo	170	De	12.39S	22.32 E
Lumberton	182	Le	34.37N	79.00W
Lumbo	172	Gc	15.00S	40.44 E
Lumbrales	126	Fd	40.56N	6.43W
Lumbres	124	Ed	50.42N	2.08 E
Lumby	188	Fa	50.15N	118.58W
Lumding	148	Ic	25.45N	93.10 E
Lumege	170	De	11.34S	20.48 E
Lumesule	170	Ge	11.14S	38.06 E
Lumi	214	Ch	3.29S	142.03 E
Lummen	124	Hd	50.59N	5.15 E
Lumparland	116	Id	60.10N	20.15 E
Lumphăt	148	Lf	13.30N	106.59 E
Lumsden [N.Z.]	218	Cf	45.44S	168.26 E
Lumsden [Sask.-Can.]	188	Ma	50.34N	104.53W
Lumuna	170	Ec	3.46S	26.24 E
Lumut	150	Df	4.14N	100.38 E
Luna	126	Gb	42.40N	5.49W
Luna, Laguna de-	204	Di	28.06S	56.46W
Lunan Shan	152	Hf	27.00N	102.30 E
Lunayyir, Harrat-	146	Gj	25.10N	37.50 E
Lunca Ilvei	130	Hb	47.22N	24.59 E
Lund	114	Ci	55.42N	13.11 E
Lunda [3]	170	Cd	9.30S	20.00 E
Lundazi	160	Kj	12.19S	33.13 E
Lunde	116	Gb	62.53N	17.51 E
Lundevatn	116	Bf	58.20N	6.35 E
Lundi	158	Kk	21.19S	32.24 E
Lundu	150	Ef	1.40N	109.51 E
Lundy Island	118	Ij	51.10N	4.40W
Lüneburg	120	Gc	53.15N	10.24 E
Lüneburger Heide	120	Gc	53.10N	10.20 E
Lunel	122	Kk	43.41N	4.08 E
Lünen	120	De	51.37N	7.31 E
Lunéville	122	Mf	48.36N	6.30 E
Lunga	158	Jj	14.34S	26.26 E
Lungué-Bungo	158	Jj	14.19S	23.14 E
Lungwebungu	170	De	14.19S	23.14 E
Lūni	148	Ec	26.00N	73.00 E
Lūni	148	Ed	24.41N	71.14 E
Lunigiana	128	Df	44.20N	9.55 E
Luninec	136	Ce	52.16N	26.50 E
Lunino	132	Nc	53.35N	45.14 E
Lunsemfwa	170	Fe	14.54S	30.12 E
Luntai/Būgūr	152	Dc	41.46N	84.10 E
Luobei (Fengxiang)	152	Nb	47.36N	130.58 E
Luobuzhuang	152	Ed	39.30N	88.15 E
Luocheng	152	Ig	24.51N	108.53 E
Luodian (Longping)	152	If	25.26N	106.47 E
Luoding	152	Jg	22.43N	111.33 E
Luohe	152	Je	33.30N	114.08 E
Luo He	152	Id	32.18N	109.12 E
Luoma Hu	154	Eg	34.10N	118.12 E
Luonteri	116	Lc	61.35N	27.45 E
Luoping	152	Hg	24.58N	104.19 E
Luopioinen	116	Kc	61.22N	24.40 E
Luoshan	154	Ch	32.13N	114.32 E
Luotian	154	Ci	30.48N	115.23 E
Luoxiao Shan	152	Jf	26.35N	114.00 E
Luoyang	142	Nf	34.41N	112.25 E
Luoyuan	152	Kf	26.31N	119.32 E
Luozi	170	Bc	4.57S	14.08 E
Lupa	170	Fd	8.39S	33.12 E
Lupane	172	Dc	18.56S	27.48 E
Łupawa	120	Nb	54.42N	17.07 E
Lupeni	130	Gd	45.21N	23.14 E
Luperón	194	Ld	19.54N	70.57W
Łupków	120	Sg	49.12N	22.06 E
Luputa	170	Dd	7.10S	23.42 E
Lūq	160	Lh	3.56N	42.32 E
Luqiao	154	Fj	28.39N	120.05 E
Luqu	152	He	34.36N	102.30 E
Luque	206	Ic	25.16S	57.34W
Luquillo	197a	Cb	18.22N	65.43W
Luray	184	Hf	38.40N	78.28W
Lure	122	Mg	47.41N	6.30 E
Lure, Montagne de-	122	Lj	44.07N	5.47 E
Luremo	170	Cd	8.30S	17.51 E
Lurgan/An Lorgain	118	Gg	54.28N	6.20W
Lurin	202	Cf	12.17S	76.52W
Lúrio	172	Gb	13.32S	40.30 E
Lúrio	158	Lj	13.31S	40.42 E
Lusaka	160	Jj	15.25S	28.17 E
Lusambo	160	Ji	4.58S	23.27 E
Lusanga	170	Cc	4.44S	18.58 E
Lusangi	170	Ec	4.37S	27.08 E
Lu Shan	152	Kf	29.30N	115.55 E
Lushan [China]	154	Cj	29.33N	115.58 E
Lushan [China]	154	Bh	33.44N	112.54 E
Lushi	152	Je	34.04N	111.02 E
Lushiko	170	Cd	6.12S	19.42 E
Lushnja	130	Ci	40.56N	19.42 E
Lushoto	170	Gc	4.47S	38.17 E
Lu Shui	154	Bj	29.54N	113.39 E
Lushui (Luzhangjie)	152	Gf	26.00N	98.50 E
Lüshun (Port Arthur) [China]	152	Ld	38.50N	121.13 E
Lusignan	122	Gh	46.26N	0.07 E
Lusk	182	Gc	42.46N	104.27W
Lussac-les-Châteaux	122	Gh	46.24N	0.43 E
Lustrafjorden	116	Bc	61.20N	7.20 E
Lūt, Dasht-e- = Lut, Dasht-i- (EN)	140	Hf	33.00N	57.00 E
Lut, Dasht-i- (EN) = Lūt, Dasht-e-	140	Hf	33.00N	57.00 E
Lu Tao	152	Lg	22.35N	121.30 E
Lutembo	170	De	13.28S	21.22 E
Luti	219a	Cb	7.14S	157.00 E
Lütjenburg	120	Gb	54.17N	10.35 E
Luton	118	Mj	51.53N	0.25W
Luton Airport	124	Bc	51.50N	0.22W
Lutong	150	Ff	4.28N	114.00 E
Lutshima	170	Cd	5.22S	18.59 E
Lutshima	170	Cd	5.22S	18.59 E
Lutterworth	124	Ab	52.27N	1.12W
Lutuai	170	De	12.40S	20.12 E
Lutugino	132	Ke	48.23N	39.13 E
Lützow-Holmbukta	222	De	69.10S	37.30 E
Lutzputs	172	Ce	28.22S	20.37 E
Luuk	150	He	5.58N	121.18 E
Luverne	186	He	43.39N	96.13W
Luvidjo	170	Ed	6.26S	26.59 E
Luvua	158	Ji	6.46S	26.58 E
Luvuei	170	De	13.06S	21.12 E
Luwegu	158	Ki	8.31S	37.23 E
Luwingu	170	Ee	10.16S	29.54 E
Luwuk	150	Hg	0.56S	122.47 E
Luxembourg [3]	124	He	50.00N	5.30 E
Luxembourg/Luxemburg	112	Gf	49.45N	6.05 E
Luxembourg/Luxemburg [1]	112	Gf	49.45N	6.05 E
Luxemburg/Luxembourg	112	Gf	49.45N	6.05 E
Luxemburg/Luxembourg [1]	112	Gf	49.45N	6.05 E
Luxeuil-les-Bains	122	Mg	47.49N	6.23 E
Luxi	152	Hg	24.34N	103.44 E
Luxi (Mangshi)	142	Lg	24.29N	98.40 E
Luxor (EN) = Al Uqşur	164	Fd	25.41N	32.39 E
Luy	122	Ek	43.39N	1.08W
Luy de Béarn	122	Fk	43.39N	0.47W
Luy de France	122	Fk	43.38N	0.47W
Luyi	154	Ch	33.51N	115.28 E
Luz	204	Jd	19.48S	45.41W
Luz, Costa de la-	126	Fh	36.40N	6.20W
Luza	136	Ec	60.39N	47.15 E
Luza	110	Kc	60.40N	46.25 E
Luzarches	124	Ee	49.07N	2.25 E
Luzern [2]	128	Cc	47.05N	8.10 E
Luzern = Lucerne (EN)	128	Cc	47.05N	8.20 E
Luzhai	152	Ig	24.31N	109.46 E
Luzhangjie → Lushui	152	Gf	26.00N	98.50 E
Luzhou	142	Mg	28.55N	105.20 E
Luziânia	202	Ig	16.15S	47.56W
Lužická Nisa	120	Kd	52.04N	14.46 E
Lužické Hory	120	Kf	50.48N	14.40 E
Luzilândia	202	Jd	3.28S	42.22W
Lužnice	120	Kg	49.16N	14.25 E
Luzon	140	Oh	16.00N	121.00 E
Luzon Strait (EN)	140	Og	21.00N	122.00 E
Luz-Saint-Sauveur	122	Gl	42.52N	0.01 E
Lužskaja guba	116	Me	59.35N	28.25 E
Lužskaja vozvyšennost	116	Mf	58.15N	28.45 E
Luzy	122	Jh	46.47N	3.58 E
Łużyca	120	Oe	51.33N	18.15 E
Lvov	112	If	49.50N	24.00 E
Lvovskaja oblast [3]	136	Cf	49.45N	24.00 E
Lwowa	214	Hj	10.44S	165.45 E
Lwówek	120	Md	52.28N	16.10 E
Lwówek Śląski	120	Le	51.07N	15.35 E
Lyakhov Islands (EN) = Ljahovskije ostrova	142	Qb	73.30N	141.00 E
Lyall, Mount-	218	Bf	45.17S	167.33 E
Lyallpur → Faisalabad	142	Jf	31.25N	73.05 E
Lychsele	114	Ed	64.36N	18.40 E
Lycia	130	Mm	36.30N	29.30 E
Lyckeby	116	Fh	56.12N	15.39 E
Lyckebyån	116	Fh	56.11N	15.40 E
Lyčkovo	114	Hh	57.57N	32.24 E
Lydd	118	Nk	50.57N	0.55 E
Lydd Airport	124	Cd	50.58N	0.56 E
Lydenburg	172	Ee	25.10S	30.29 E
Lydia	130	Lk	38.35N	28.30 E
Lygna	116	Bf	58.10N	7.02 E
Lygnern	116	Eg	57.29N	12.20 E

Lyme Bay 118 Kk 50.38N 3.00W
Lyminge 124 Dc 51.07N 1.05 E
Lymington 118 Lk 50.46N 1.33W
Łyna 120 Rb 54.37N 21.14 E
Lynchburg 182 Ld 37.24N 79.09W
Lynd 210 Ff 18.56S 144.30 E
Lynden 188 Db 48.57N 122.27W
Lyndon River 212 Cd 23.29S 114.06 E
Lyngdal 114 Bg 58.08N 7.05 E
Lyngen 114 Eb 69.58N 20.30 E
Lyngør 116 Cf 58.38N 9.10 E
Lyngseidet 114 Eb 69.35N 20.13 E
Lynn 184 Ld 42.28N 70.57W
Lynnaj, gora- 138 Ld 62.55N 163.58 E
Lynn Canal 178 Le 58.50N 135.15W
Lynn Deeps 124 Cb 52.58N 0.20 E
Lynn Lake 176 Id 56.51N 101.03W
Lyntupy 116 Li 55.02N 26.27 E
Lynx Lake 180 Gd 62.25N 106.20W
Lyon 112 Gf 45.45N 4.51 E
Lyon Inlet 180 Jc 66.20N 83.40W
Lyonnais, Monts du- 122 Ki 45.40N 4.30 E
Lyon River 212 De 25.00S 115.20 E
Lyons [Ga.-U.S.] 184 Fi 32.12N 82.19W
Lyons [Ks.-U.S.] 186 Gg 38.21N 98.12W
Lyons, Forêt de- 124 De 49.25N 1.30 E
Lyons-la-Forêt 124 De 49.24N 1.28 E
Lyra Reef 214 Eh 1.50S 153.35 E
Lys 122 Jc 51.03N 3.43 E
Łysa Góra 120 Nd 52.07N 17.33 E
Lysaja, gora- 116 Lj 54.12N 27.40 E
Lysá nad Labem 120 Kf 50.12N 14.50 E
Lysefjorden 116 Be 59.00N 6.14 E
Lysekil 114 Cf 58.16N 11.26 E
Lyskovo 136 Ed 56.03N 45.03 E
Lyss 128 Bc 47.04N 7.19 E
Lysva 136 Fd 58.07N 57.47 E
Lytham Saint Anne's 118 Jh 53.45N 3.01W
Lyttelton 218 Ee 43.36S 172.43 E
Lytton 188 Ea 50.14N 121.34W
Lyža 134 Hd 65.42N 56.40 E

M

Ma, Oued el- 162 Fe 24.03N 9.10W
Ma, Song 148 Le 19.45N 105.55 E
Maâdis, Djebel- 126 Qi 35.52N 4.44 E
Maalaea Bay 221a Ec 20.47N 156.29W
Ma'āmir 146 Mg 30.04N 48.20 E
Ma'ān 144 Ec 30.12N 35.44 E
Ma'Ān [3] 146 Gg 30.20N 35.35 E
Maanselka 114 Ge 63.54N 28.30 E
Maanselkä 110 Ib 68.07N 28.29 E
Ma'anshan 152 Ke 31.38N 118.30 E
Maardu 116 Ke 59.28N 24.56 E
Maarianhamina/Mariehamn 114 Ef 60.06N 19.57 E
Ma 'arrat an Nu 'mān 146 Ge 35.38N 36.40 E
Maarssen 124 Hb 52.08N 5.03 E
Maas=Meuse (EN) 110 Ge 51.49N 5.01 E
Maaseik 122 Lc 51.06N 5.48 E
Maaseik-Neeroeteren 124 Hc 51.05N 5.42 E
Maasin 150 Hd 10.08N 124.50 E
Maasmechelen/Mechelen 124 Hd 50.57N 5.40 E
Maassluis 124 Gc 51.55N 4.17 E
Maastricht 122 Ld 50.52N 5.43 E
Maasupa 219a Ec 9.18S 161.15 E
Ma'āzah, Al Haḍabat al- 164 Fd 27.44N 31.44 E
Mabalane 172 Ed 23.38S 32.31 E
Mabaruma 196 Gh 8.12N 59.47W
Mabechi-Gawa 156 Ga 40.31N 141.31 E
Mabella 186 Lb 48.37N 89.58W
Mabel Lake 188 Fa 50.35N 118.44W
Mablethorpe 118 Nh 53.21N 0.15 E
Mabote 172 Ed 22.03S 34.08 E
Ma'būs Yūsuf 160 Jf 25.45N 21.00 E
Maçaão 126 Ee 39.33N 8.00W
McAdam 180 Kg 45.36N 67.20W
Macaé 202 Jh 22.23S 41.47W
Macajai, Rio- 202 Fc 2.25N 60.50W
McAlester 182 He 34.56N 95.46W
McAllen 182 Hf 26.12N 98.15W
Macaloge 172 Fb 12.25S 35.25 E
Mac Alpine Lake 180 Hc 66.40N 102.50W
Macambará 204 Di 29.08S 56.03W
Macamic 184 Ha 48.48N 79.01W
Macamic, Lac- 184 Ha 48.46N 79.00W
Macao (EN)=Aomen/Macau 152 Jg 22.12N 113.33 E
Macao (EN)=Aomen/ Macau [5] 142 Ng 22.10N 113.33 E
Macao (EN)=Macau/Aomen 152 Jg 22.12N 113.33 E
Macao (EN)=Macau/ Aomen [5] 142 Ng 22.10N 113.33 E
Macapá 200 Ke 0.02N 51.03W
Macará 202 Cd 4.21S 79.56W
Macaracas 194 Gj 7.44N 80.33W
Macareo, Caño- 202 Fb 9.47N 61.36W
McArthur 184 Ff 39.14N 82.29W
Mc Arthur River 212 Hc 15.54S 136.40 E
Macas 202 Cd 2.18S 78.06W
Maçãs 126 Fc 41.29N 6.39W
Macatete, Sierra de- 192 Dd 28.00N 110.05W
Macau 200 Mf 5.07S 36.38W
Macau/Aomen=Macao (EN) 152 Jg 22.12N 113.33 E
Macau/Aomen=Macao (EN) [5] 142 Ng 22.10N 113.33 E
Macaúbas 202 Jf 13.02S 42.42W
Macauley Island 208 Ih 30.13S 178.33W
Macaya, Pic de- 190 Je 18.23N 74.02W
McBeth Fiord 180 Kc 69.43N 69.20W
McCamey 186 Ek 31.08N 102.13W
McCammon 188 Ie 42.39N 112.12W
Mc Carthy 178 Kd 61.26N 142.55W
McClellanville 184 Hi 33.06N 79.28W
MacClenny 184 Fj 30.18N 82.07W
Macclesfield 118 Kh 53.16N 2.07W
Macclesfield Bank (EN) 150 Fc 15.50N 114.20 E
McClintock 180 Ie 57.48N 94.12W
McClintock, Mount- 222 Jg 80.13S 157.26 E
McClintock Channel 174 Ib 71.00N 101.00W
McCluer Gulf (EN)=Berau, Teluk- 150 Jg 2.30S 132.30 E
McClure Strait 174 Hb 74.30N 116.00W
McClusky 186 Fc 47.29N 100.27W
McComb 182 Ie 31.14N 90.27W
McConaughy, Lake- 186 Ff 41.18N 101.46W
McConnelsville 184 Gf 39.39N 81.51W
McCook 182 Gc 40.12N 100.38W
McCormick 184 Fi 33.55N 82.19W
McDame 180 Ee 59.13N 129.14W
McDermitt 188 Gf 41.59N 117.36W
Macdhui, Ben- 118 Jd 57.04N 3.40W
Macdonald, Lake- 212 Fd 23.30S 129.00 E
Mc Donald Islands 222 Fd 52.59S 72.50 E
McDonald Peak [Ca.-U.S.] 188 Ef 40.58N 120.26W
McDonald Peak [Mt.-U.S.] 188 Ic 47.29N 113.46W
Macdonald Range 188 Hb 49.12N 114.46W
Macdonnell Ranges 208 Eg 23.45S 132.20 E
McDouglas Sound 180 Hd 75.15N 97.30W
Macduff 118 Kd 57.40N 2.29W
Macedo de Cavaleiros 126 Fc 41.32N 6.58W
Macedonia (EN)= Makedhonia 110 Ig 41.00N 23.00 E
Macedonia (EN)= Makedhonia 130 Fh 41.00N 23.00 E
Macedonia (EN) = Makedonija 130 Eh 41.50N 22.00 E
Macedonia (EN)= Makedonija 110 Ig 41.00N 23.00 E
Macedonia (EN)= Makedonija 130 Fh 41.00N 23.00 E
Maceió 200 Mf 9.40S 35.43W
Macenta 166 Dd 8.33N 9.28W
Macerata 128 Hg 43.18N 13.27 E
McGehee 186 Kj 33.38N 91.24W
McGill 188 Hg 39.23N 114.47W
Macgillycuddy's Reeks/Na Cruacha Dubha 118 Di 52.00N 9.50W
McGrath 178 Hd 62.58N 155.38W
MacGregor 186 Gb 49.57N 98.49W
McGregor 186 Jc 46.36N 93.19W
McGregor Lake 188 Ia 50.31N 112.53W
Mc Gregor Range 212 Ie 26.40S 142.45 E
McGuire, Mount- 188 Hd 45.10N 114.36W
Machachi 202 Cd 0.30S 78.34W
Machado 204 Je 21.41S 45.56W
Machagai 206 Hc 26.56S 60.03W
Machaila 172 Ed 22.15S 32.58 E
Machaire na Mumhan/ Golden Vale 118 Fi 52.30N 8.00W
Machaire Rátha/ Maghera 118 Gg 54.51N 6.40W
Machakos 170 Gc 1.31S 37.16 E
Machala 202 Cd 3.16S 79.58W
Machaneng 172 Dd 23.12S 27.30 E
Machareti 202 Fh 20.49S 63.24W
Machar Marshes 168 Ed 9.20N 33.10 E
Machattie, Lake- 212 Hd 24.50S 139.48 E
Machault 124 Ge 49.21N 4.30 E
Macheke 172 Ec 18.05S 31.51 E
Macheng 152 Je 31.10N 115.00 E
Machias 184 Nc 44.43N 67.28W
Machida 156 Fd 35.32N 139.27 E
Machilipatnam (Bandar) 148 Ge 16.10N 81.08 E
Machine, La- 122 Jh 46.53N 3.28 E
Machiques 202 Da 10.04N 72.34W
Machmi, Al- 146 Jg 31.32N 42.28 E
Machona, Laguna- 192 Mh 18.20N 93.40W
Machów 120 Rf 50.34N 21.40 E
Machupicchu 200 Ig 13.07S 72.34W
Macia 172 Ef 25.02S 33.06 E
Mc Ilwraith Range 212 Ib 13.45S 143.20 E
Măcin 130 Ld 45.15N 28.09 E
Macina 158 Gg 14.30N 5.00W
McIntosh 186 Fd 45.55N 101.21W
Macintyre River 212 Je 29.25S 148.45 E
Maçka 146 Hb 40.50N 39.38 E
Mackay [Austl.] 210 Fg 21.09S 149.11 E
Mackay [Id.-U.S.] 188 Ie 43.55N 113.37W
Mackay, Lake- 208 Dg 22.30S 129.00 E
McKay Lake 186 Mb 49.35N 86.22W
McKean Atoll 208 Je 3.36S 174.08W
McKeand 180 Kd 63.00N 65.05W
McKeesport 184 He 40.21N 79.52W
McKenzie 184 Cg 36.08N 88.31W
Mackenzie 174 Fc 69.15N 134.08W
Mackenzie Bay [Ant.] 222 Fe 68.20S 71.15 E
Mackenzie Bay [Can.] 174 Fc 69.00N 136.30W
McKenzie Island 180 If 51.05N 93.48W
Mackenzie King 174 Hb 77.45N 111.00W
Mackenzie Mountains 174 Gc 64.00N 130.00W
McKenzie River 188 Dd 44.07N 123.06W
Mackenzie River 212 Jd 24.00S 149.55 E
McKerrow, Lake- 218 Cf 44.30S 168.05 E
Mackinac, Straits of- 182 Kb 45.49N 82.45W
Mackinaw City 184 Ec 45.47N 84.44W
McKinley, Mount- 174 Dc 63.30N 151.00W
McKinley Park 178 Jd 63.44N 148.54W
McKinney 186 Hj 33.12N 96.37W
Mackinnon Road 170 Gc 3.44S 39.03 E
McLaughlin 186 Fd 45.49N 100.49W
McLean 186 Fi 35.14N 100.36W
McLeans Town 184 Il 26.39N 77.59W
Maclean Strait 180 Ha 77.30N 103.10W
Maclear 172 Df 31.02S 28.23 E
Macleay River 212 Kf 30.52S 153.01 E
Mc Leod, Lake- 208 Cg 24.10S 113.35 E
McLeod Bay 180 Gd 62.53N 110.15W
McLeod Lake 180 Ff 54.59N 123.02W
McLoughlin, Mount- 188 De 42.27N 122.19W
McLure 188 Ea 51.03N 120.14W
Macmillan 180 Dd 62.52N 135.55W
McMillan, Lake- 186 Dj 32.40N 104.20W
Macmillan Pass 180 Ed 63.00N 130.00W
McMinnville [Or.-U.S.] 188 Dd 45.13N 123.12W
McMinnville [Tn.-U.S.] 184 Eh 35.41N 85.46W
McMurdo 222 Kf 77.51S 166.37 E
McNaughton Lake 180 Ff 52.40N 117.50W
Macomb 186 Kf 40.27N 90.40W
Macomer 128 Cj 40.16N 8.47 E
Macomia 172 Gb 12.15S 40.08 E
Mâcon 122 Kh 46.18N 4.50 E
Macon 176 Kf 32.50N 83.38W
Macon [Mo.-U.S.] 186 Jg 39.44N 92.28W
Macon [Ms.-U.S.] 186 Lj 33.07N 88.34W
Macondo 170 De 12.36S 23.43 E
Mâconnais, Monts du- 122 Kh 46.18N 4.45 E
Macoris, Cabo- 194 Ld 19.47N 70.28W
Macouba 197h Ab 14.52N 61.09W
McPherson 182 Hd 38.22N 97.40W
Mc Pherson Range 212 Ke 28.20S 153.00 E
Macquarie 222 Jd 54.30S 158.30 E
Macquarie Harbour 212 Jh 42.20S 145.25 E
Macquarie Ridge (EN) 106 Jo 57.00S 159.00 E
Macquarie River 208 Fh 30.07S 147.24 E
Mac Robertson Land 222 Fe 70.00S 65.00 E
Macroom/Maigh Chromtha 118 Ej 51.54N 8.57W
Macugnaga 128 Be 45.58N 7.58 E
Macujer 202 Dc 0.24N 73.07W
Macuro 196 Fg 10.39N 61.56W
Macusani 202 Df 14.05S 70.26W
Macuspana 192 Mi 17.48N 92.36W
Mačva 130 Ce 44.49N 19.30 E
McVicar Arm 180 Fc 65.10N 120.30W
Ma'dabā 146 Fg 31.43N 35.48 E
Madagali 166 Hc 10.53N 13.38 E
Madagascar 158 Lj 20.00S 47.00 E
Madagascar (EN)= Madagasikara [1] 160 Lj 19.00S 46.00 E
Madagascar Basin (EN) 106 Fl 27.00S 53.00 E
Madagascar Plateau (EN) 106 Fm 30.00S 45.00 E
Madagasikara=Madagascar (EN) [1] 160 Lj 19.00S 46.00 E
Madā'in Şāliḩ 146 Gi 26.48N 37.53 E
Madalai 220a Ac 7.20N 134.28 E
Madama 166 Ha 21.58N 13.39 E
Madan 130 Hh 41.30N 24.57 E
Madang 210 Fe 5.13S 145.48 E
Madanīyīn 160 Ie 33.21N 10.30 E
Madanīyīn [3] 162 Jc 33.00N 10.45 E
Madaoua 166 Gc 14.05N 5.58 E
Madara 130 Kf 43.17N 27.06 E
Madara-Shima 156 Ae 33.35N 129.45 E
Madaroumfa 166 Gc 13.18N 7.09 E
Madau 219a Ac 9.00S 152.26 E
Madawaska Highlands 184 Hc 45.20N 78.15W
Maddalena 128 Di 41.15N 9.25 E
Maddalena, Colle della- 122 Mj 44.25N 6.53 E
Maddaloni 128 Ii 41.02N 14.23 E
Made, Made en Drimmelen- 124 Gc 51.41N 4.48 E
Made en Drimmelen 124 Gc 51.41N 4.48 E
Made en Drimmelen-Made 124 Gc 51.41N 4.48 E
Madeir 168 Dd 7.50N 29.12 E
Madeira [5] 160 Fe 32.40N 16.45W
Madeira 158 Fe 32.44N 17.00W
Madeira, Arquipélago da-= Madeira Islands (EN) 158 Fe 32.40N 16.45W
Madeira, Rio- 198 Kf 3.22S 58.45W
Madeira Islands (EN)= Madeira, Arquipélago da- 158 Fe 32.40N 16.45W
Madeleine, Ile de la - 180 Lg 47.26N 61.44W
Madeleine, Monts de la- 122 Jh 46.03N 3.50 E
Maden 146 Hc 38.23N 39.40 E
Madenassa Veld 158 Jj 19.00N 25.30 E
Madera [Ca.-U.S.] 188 Eh 36.57N 120.03W
Madera [Mex.] 190 Cc 29.12N 108.07W
Mader-Chih 126 Ri 35.26N 5.07 E
Madero, Puerto del- 126 Jc 41.48N 2.05W
Madesimo 128 Dd 46.26N 9.21 E
Madgaon 148 Ee 15.22N 73.49 E
Madhya Pradesh [3] 148 Fd 22.00N 79.00 E
Madimba 170 Cc 4.58S 15.08 E
Madina do Boé 166 Cc 11.45N 14.13W
Madinani 166 Dd 9.37N 6.57W
Madīnat al Abyār 164 Dc 32.11N 20.36 E
Madīnat ash Sha'b 142 Gh 12.50N 44.56 E
Madingo-Kayes 170 Bc 4.10S 12.18 E
Madingou 170 Bc 4.09S 13.34 E
Madirovalo 172 Hc 16.29S 46.30 E
Madison [Fl.-U.S.] 184 Fj 30.28N 83.25W
Madison [In.-U.S.] 184 Ef 38.44N 85.23W
Madison [Mn.-U.S.] 186 Hd 45.01N 96.11W
Madison [S.D.-U.S.] 186 He 44.00N 97.07W
Madison [Wi.-U.S.] 176 Ke 43.05N 89.22W
Madison [W.V.-U.S.] 184 Gf 38.03N 81.50W
Madison Range 188 Jd 45.15N 111.20W
Madison River 188 Jd 45.56N 111.30W
Madisonville 182 Jd 37.20N 87.30W
Madiun 150 Fh 7.37S 111.31 E
Mado Gashi 170 Gb 0.44N 39.10 E
Madoi (Huangheyan) 142 Lf 35.00N 98.56 E
Madon 122 Mf 48.36N 6.06 E
Madona 114 Gh 56.53N 26.20 E
Madra Dağı 130 Kj 39.23N 27.12 E
Madrakah, Ra's al- 144 If 18.59N 57.45 E
Madranbaba Dağı 130 Ll 37.38N 28.12 E
Madras [India] 142 Kh 13.05N 80.17 E
Madras [Or.-U.S.] 188 Ed 44.38N 121.08W
Madre, Laguna- [Mex.] 190 Ed 25.00N 97.40W
Madre, Laguna- [Tx.-U.S.] 182 Hf 27.00N 97.35W
Madre, Sierra- [N.Amer.] 174 Jh 15.20N 92.20W
Madre, Sierra- [Phil.] 140 Oh 16.20N 122.00 E
Madre de Dios 202 Df 12.36S 69.59W
Madre de Dios [3] 202 Df 12.00S 70.15W
Madre de Dios, Isla- 198 Ik 50.15S 75.05W
Madre de Dios, Rio- 198 Jg 10.59S 66.08W
Madre del Sur, Sierra-= Southern Sierra Madre (EN) 174 Jj 17.00N 100.00W
Madre de Oaxaca, Sierra- 192 Ki 17.30N 96.30W
Madre Occidental, Sierra-= Western Sierra Madre (EN) 174 Ig 25.00N 105.00W
Madre Oriental, Sierra-= Eastern Sierra Madre (EN) 174 Jg 22.00N 99.30W
Madrid 112 Fg 40.24N 3.41W
Madrid [2] 126 Id 40.30N 3.40W
Madrid-Aravaca 126 Id 40.27N 3.47W
Madridejos 126 Ie 39.28N 3.32W
Madrid-El Pardo 126 Id 40.32N 3.46W
Madrid-Vallecas 126 Id 40.23N 3.37W
Madrid-Villaverde 126 Id 40.21N 3.42W
Madrigal de las Altas Torres 126 Hc 41.05N 5.00W
Mad River 188 Cf 40.57N 124.07W
Madriz [3] 194 Dg 13.30N 86.30W
Madrona, Sierra- 126 Hf 38.25N 4.10W
Madula 170 Eb 0.28N 25.23 E
Madura, Palau- 140 Nj 7.00S 113.20 E
Madurai 142 Ji 9.56N 78.07 E
Madvār, Kūh-e- 144 Hc 30.36N 54.52 E
Madwīn 164 Cd 28.42N 17.31 E
Madyan 140 Fg 27.40N 35.35 E
Madžalis 132 Oh 42.08N 47.50 E
Maebara 156 Be 33.34N 130.13 E
Maebashi 152 Od 36.23N 139.04 E
Mae Hong Son 148 Je 19.16N 97.56 E
Mæl 116 Ce 59.56N 8.48 E
Mae Nam Khong=Mekong (EN) 140 Mh 10.15N 105.55 E
Maesawa 156 Gb 39.03N 141.07 E
Mae Sot 148 Je 16.40N 98.35 E
Maestra, Sierra- 174 Lh 20.00N 76.45W
Maevatanana 172 Hc 16.56S 46.49 E
Maéwo, Ile- 208 Hf 15.10S 168.10 E
Mafeteng 172 De 29.45S 27.18 E
Mafia Channel 170 Gd 7.50S 39.35 E
Mafia Island 158 Ki 7.50S 39.50 E
Mafikeng 160 Jk 25.53S 25.39 E
Mafra [Braz.] 206 Kc 26.07S 49.49W
Mafra [Port.] 126 Cf 38.56N 9.20W
Magadan 142 Rd 59.34N 150.48 E
Magadanskaja oblast [3] 138 Kd 62.30N 154.00 E
Magadi 170 Gc 1.54S 36.17 E
Magallanes, Estrecho de- = Magellan, Strait of- (EN) 198 Ik 54.00S 71.00W
Magallanes y Antártica Chilena [2] 206 Fh 51.30S 73.30W
Magangué 202 Db 9.14N 74.46W
Maganik 130 Cg 42.44N 19.16 E
Maganoy 150 He 6.51N 124.31 E
Magaria 166 Gc 12.59N 8.50 E
Magazine Mountain 186 Ji 35.10N 93.38W
Magdagači 138 Hf 53.29N 125.55 E
Magdala 204 Bm 36.06S 61.42W
Magdalena [3] 202 Db 10.00N 74.15W
Magdalena [Arg.] 204 Dl 35.04S 57.32W
Magdalena [Bol.] 202 Ff 13.20S 64.08W
Magdalena [Mex.] 190 Bb 30.38N 110.57W
Magdalena [N.M.-U.S.] 186 Ci 34.07N 107.14W
Magdalena, Bahía- 190 Cd 24.35N 112.00W
Magdalena, Isla- 190 Bd 24.55N 112.15W
Magdalena, Llano de la- 190 Bd 24.30N 111.40W
Magdalena, Río- [Col.] 198 Id 11.06N 74.51W
Magdalena, Río- [Mex.] 192 Cb 30.48N 112.32W
Magda Plateau 180 Jb 72.18N 82.55W
Magdeburg 112 He 52.10N 11.40 E
Magdeburger Börde 120 Hd 52.00N 11.30 E
Magdelaine Cays 208 Gf 16.35S 150.15 E
Magee 186 Lk 31.52N 89.44W
Magelang 150 Fh 7.28S 110.13 E
Magellan, Strait of- (EN) = Magallanes, Estrecho de- 198 Ik 54.00S 71.00W
Magellan Seamounts (EN) 208 Gc 17.30N 152.00 E
Magenta 128 Ce 45.28N 8.53 E
Magerøya 114 Fa 71.03N 25.45 E
Magetan 150 Fh 7.39S 111.20 E
Maggiorasca 128 Df 44.33N 9.29 E
Maggiore, Lago- (Verbano) 128 Ce 45.55N 8.40 E
Maghāghah 164 Fd 28.39N 30.50 E
Maghama 162 Ef 15.31N 12.50W
Maghera/Machaire Rátha 118 Gg 54.51N 6.40W
Maghnia 162 Gc 34.51N 1.44W
Magic Reservoir 188 He 43.20N 114.18W
Mágina, Sierra de- 126 Ig 37.45N 3.30W
Magistralny 138 Fe 56.03N 107.35 E
Maglaj 128 Mf 44.33N 18.06 E
Mäglenik 130 Ih 41.20N 25.45 E
Maglie 128 Mj 40.07N 18.18 E
Mäglíž 130 Ig 42.36N 25.33 E
Magnetawan River 184 Gc 45.46N 80.37W
Magnetic Island 212 Jc 19.10S 146.50 E
Magnitka 134 Ii 55.21N 59.43 E
Magnitnaja, gora- 134 Ij 53.10N 59.10 E
Magnitogorsk 112 Le 53.27N 59.04 E
Magnolia 186 Jj 33.16N 93.14W
Magnor 114 Cg 59.57N 12.12 E
Magny-en-Vexin 122 He 49.09N 1.47 E
Mago 138 Jf 53.18N 140.20 E
Magoé 172 Ec 15.48S 31.43 E
Magoebaskloof 172 Ed 23.51S 30.02 E
Magog 184 Kc 45.16N 72.09W
Magosa/Ammokhostos= Famagusta (EN) 144 Dc 35.07N 33.57 E
Magra [Alg.] 126 Qi 35.29N 4.58 E
Magra [It.] 128 Df 44.03N 9.58 E
Magtá Lahjar 162 Ef 17.50N 13.20W
Maguarinho, Cabo- 202 Id 0.20S 48.20W
Magude 172 Ee 25.02S 32.40 E
Magumeri 166 Hc 12.07N 12.49 E
Magura, gora- 120 Th 48.50N 23.44 E
Magway 148 Jd 20.00N 95.00 E
Magway 142 Lg 20.09N 94.55 E
Magyarország = Hungary (EN) [1] 112 Hf 47.00N 20.00 E
Mahābād 144 Gb 36.45N 45.53 E
Mahabalipuram 148 Gf 12.37N 80.12 E
Mahabe 172 Hc 17.05S 45.20 E
Mahabo 172 Gd 20.21S 44.39 E
Mahačkala 112 Kg 42.58N 47.30 E
Mahadday Wëyne 168 He 3.00N 45.32 E
Mahādeo Range 148 Ee 17.50N 74.15 E
Mahafaly, Plateau- 172 Gd 24.30S 44.00 E
Mahagi 170 Fb 2.18N 30.59 E
Mahajamba 172 Hc 15.33S 47.08 E
Mahājan 148 Ec 28.47N 73.50 E
Mahajanga 160 Lj 15.17S 46.43 E
Mahajanga [3] 172 Hc 16.30S 47.00 E
Mahajilo 172 Hc 19.42S 45.22 E
Mahakam 140 Nj 0.35S 117.17 E
Mahalapye 172 Dd 23.07S 26.46 E
Mahalevona 172 Hc 15.26S 49.55 E
Mahallāt 146 Nf 33.55N 50.27 E
Mahamid 168 Cb 15.09N 20.25 E
Māhān 146 Qg 30.05N 57.19 E
Mahānadi 140 Kg 20.19N 86.45 E
Mahanoro 172 Hc 19.53S 48.49 E
Mahārāshtra [3] 148 Ee 19.00N 75.00 E
Mahārlū, Daryācheh-ye- 146 Oh 29.25N 52.50 E
Mahās 168 He 4.24N 46.07 E
Maha Sarakham 148 Ke 16.12N 103.16 E
Mahavavy 158 Lj 15.57S 45.54 E
Mahbès 162 Fd 27.10N 9.50W
Mahḍah 146 Pj 24.24N 55.59 E
Mahdia 202 Gb 5.16N 59.09W
Mahe 148 Ff 11.42N 75.32 E
Mahébourg 172a Bb 20.24S 57.42 E
Mahé Island 158 Mi 4.40S 55.28 E
Mahendra Giri 148 Ge 18.58N 84.21 E
Mahenge 160 Ki 8.41S 36.43W
Maheno 218 Df 45.10S 170.50 E
Mahesāna 148 Ed 23.36N 72.24 E
Mahi 148 Ed 22.16N 72.58 E
Mahia Peninsula 216 Eg 39.10S 177.55 E
Mahmūdābād 146 Od 36.38N 52.15 E
Mahmudābād 146 Lc 39.25N 47.15 E
Mahmūd-e 'Erāqī 144 Kb 35.01N 69.20 E
Mahmudiye 146 Dc 39.30N 31.00 E
Mahmutşevketpaşa 130 Mh 41.09N 29.11 E
Māhneshān 146 Ld 36.45N 47.38 E
Mahnevo 134 Jg 58.27N 61.42 E
Mahnomen 186 Ic 47.19N 95.59W
Mahón / Maó 126 Qe 39.53N 4.15 E
Mahoré/Mayotte 158 Lj 12.50S 45.10 E
Mahrāt, Jabal- 168 Ib 17.00N 52.00 E
Mahuan Dao 150 Gd 10.50N 115.47 E
Mahua Point 219a Fd 10.28S 162.05 E
Maiana Atoll 208 Id 0.55N 173.00 E
Maiao, Ile- (Tubai-Manu) 208 Lf 17.34S 150.35W
Maicao 202 Da 11.23N 72.15W
Maicasagi, Lac- 184 Ia 49.52N 76.48W
Maîche 122 Mg 47.15N 6.48 E
Maicuru, Rio- 202 Hd 2.10S 54.17W
Maidenhead 124 Bc 51.31N 0.42W
Maidstone 118 Nj 51.17N 0.32 E
Maiduguri 160 Ig 11.51N 13.09 E
Măieruş 130 Id 45.54N 25.32 E
Maigh Chromtha/Macroom 118 Ej 51.54N 8.57W
Maigudo 168 Fd 7.26N 37.10 E
Maihara 156 Ed 35.20N 136.18 E
Maikala Range 148 Gd 22.30N 81.30 E
Maiko 170 Eb 0.14N 25.33 E
Maikona 170 Gb 2.56N 37.38 E
Maikoor, Pulau- 150 Jh 6.15S 134.15 E
Main 120 Ef 50.00N 8.18 E
Mainalon Óros 130 Fl 37.40N 22.15 E
Main Barrier Range 212 If 31.25S 141.25 E
Mainburg 120 Hh 48.39N 11.47 E
Main Camp 220g Ba 2.01N 157.25W
Main Channel 184 Gc 45.22N 81.50W
Mai-Ndombe, Lac- 158 Ii 2.10S 18.15 E
Main-Donau-Kanal 120 Gg 49.55N 10.50 E
Maindong → Coqên 152 Ee 31.15N 85.13 E
Maine [2] 182 Nb 45.15N 69.15W
Maine 122 Ff 48.15N 0.10W
Maine [Fr.] 122 Eg 47.09N 1.27W
Maine [Fr.] 122 Fg 47.25N 0.37W
Maine, Gulf of- 174 Me 43.00N 68.00W
Maine-et-Loire [3] 122 Fg 47.30N 0.20W
Mainé-Soroa 166 Hc 13.18N 12.02 E
Mainistir Fhear Mai/Fermoy 118 Ei 52.08N 8.16W
Mainistir na Búille/Boyle 118 Eh 53.58N 8.18W
Mainistir na Corann/ Midleton 118 Ej 51.55N 8.10W
Mainistir na Féile/ Abbeyfeale 118 Di 52.24N 9.18W
Mainit, Lake- 150 Ie 9.26N 125.32 E
Mainland [Scot.-U.K.] 110 Fd 59.00N 3.10W
Mainland [Scot.-U.K.] 110 Fc 60.20N 1.22W
Maintal 124 Kd 50.08N 8.51 E
Maintenon 122 Hf 48.35N 1.35 E
Maintirano 160 Lj 18.03S 44.03 E
Mainz 120 Eg 50.00N 8.15 E
Maio 162 Cf 23.10N 15.10W
Maio 158 Eg 15.15N 23.10W
Maipo, Volcán- 198 Ji 34.10S 69.50W
Maipú 206 Ie 36.52S 57.52W
Maiquetia 202 Ea 10.36N 66.57W
Maira 128 Bf 44.49N 7.38 E
Mairi 202 Jf 11.43S 40.08W
Mairipotaba 204 Hc 17.21S 49.31W
Maisān [3] 146 Lg 32.00N 47.00 E
Maisí, Punta- 190 Jd 20.15N 74.09W
Maišiagala/Maišjagala 116 Kj 54.51N 25.14 E
Maišjagala/Maišiagala 116 Kj 54.51N 25.14 E
Maiter 126 Qi 35.23N 4.17 E

Index Symbols

- [1] Independent Nation
- [2] State, Region
- [3] District, County
- [4] Municipality
- [5] Colony, Dependency
- Continent
- Physical Region
- Historical or Cultural Region
- Mount, Mountain
- Volcano
- Hill
- Mountains, Mountain Range
- Hills, Escarpment
- Plateau, Upland
- Pass, Gap
- Plain, Lowland
- Delta
- Salt Flat
- Valley, Canyon
- Crater, Cave
- Karst Features
- Depression
- Polder
- Desert, Dunes
- Forest, Woods
- Heath, Steppe
- Oasis
- Cape, Point
- Coast, Beach
- Cliff
- Peninsula
- Isthmus
- Sandbank
- Island
- Atoll
- Rock, Reef
- Islands, Archipelago
- Rocks, Reefs
- Coral Reef
- Well, Spring
- Geyser
- River, Stream
- Waterfall, Rapids
- River Mouth, Estuary
- Lake
- Salt Lake
- Intermittent Lake
- Reservoir
- Swamp, Pond
- Canal
- Glacier
- Ice Shelf, Pack Ice
- Ocean
- Sea
- Gulf, Bay
- Strait, Fjord
- Lagoon
- Bank
- Seamount
- Tablemount
- Ridge
- Shelf
- Basin
- Escarpment, Sea Scarp
- Fracture
- Trench, Abyss
- National Park, Reserve
- Point of Interest
- Recreation Site
- Cave, Cavern
- Historic Site
- Ruins
- Wall, Walls
- Church, Abbey
- Temple
- Scientific Station
- Railway station
- Airport
- Port
- Military installation
- Lighthouse
- Mine
- Tunnel
- Dam, Bridge

Maitland [Austl.] 212 Hf 34.22S 137.40 E
Maitland [Austl.] 210 Gh 32.44S 151.33 E
Maiz, Isla Grande del- 194 Fg 12.10N 83.03W
Maiz, Isla Pequeña del- 194 Fg 12.18N 82.59W
Maiz, Islas del- 190 Hf 12.15N 83.00W
Maizhokunggar 152 Ff 29.50N 91.40 E
Maizières-lès-Metz 124 Ie 49.13N 6.09 E
Maizuru 154 Mg 35.27N 135.20 E
Maizuru-Nishimaizuru 156 Dd 35.28N 135.19 E
Maizuru-Wan 156 Dd 35.30N 135.20 E
Maja [Russia] 140 Pd 60.17N 134.41 E
Maja [Russia] 138 If 54.37N 134.50 E
Majagual 194 Ji 8.35N 74.37W
Majakovski → Bagdati 132 Mh 42.02N 42.47 E
Majangat 152 Fb 48.20N 91.58 E
Majardah, Wādī- 128 Em 37.07N 10.13 E
Majāz al Bāb 128 Dn 36.39N 9.37 E
Majdanpek 130 Ee 44.25N 21.56 E
Majene 142 Nj 3.33S 118.57 E
Majërtën=Mijirtein (EN) 158 Lh 9.00N 50.00 E
Majevica 128 Mf 44.40N 18.40 E
Maji 168 Fd 6.10N 35.35 E
Majia He 152 Kd 38.09N 117.53 E
Majja 138 Id 61.38N 130.25 E
Majkain 136 He 51.27N 75.52 E
Majkamys 135 Ka 46.34N 77.37 E
Majkop 112 Kg 44.35N 40.07 E
Majli-Saj 135 Id 41.15N 72.30 E
Majma'ah 146 Kj 25.54N 45.20 E
Majmak 136 Hg 42.40N 71.14 E
Majmakan 138 Ie 57.30N 135.23 E
Majmeča 138 Fb 71.20N 104.15 E
Majn 138 Mc 65.03N 172.10 E
Majna [Russia] 114 Li 54.09N 47.37 E
Majna [Russia] 138 Ef 53.00N 91.28 E
Major,Puig-/Mayor,Puig- 126 Oe 39.48N 2.48 E
Majorca (EN)=Mallorca 110 Gh 39.30N 3.00 E
Majrur 168 Db 16.40N 26.53 E
Majski [Russia] 138 Hf 52.18N 129.38 E
Majski [Russia] 132 Nh 43.36N 44.03 E
Maju, Pulau- 150 If 1.20N 126.25 E
Majuro Atoll 208 Id 7.09N 171.12 E
Makabana 160 Ii 3.28S 12.36 E
Makaha 221a Cb 21.29N 158.13W
Makahuena Point 221a Bb 21.52N 159.27W
Makalamabedi 172 Cd 20.20S 23.53 E
Makale 150 Gg 3.06S 119.51 E
Makallé 206 Ic 27.13S 59.17W
Makalondi 166 Fc 12.50N 1.41 E
Makamby, Nosy- 172 Hc 15.42S 45.54 E
Makanči 136 If 46.51N 81.57 E
Makanza 170 Cb 1.36N 19.07 E
Makapala 221a Fc 20.13N 155.45W
Makapu Point 220k Ba 18.59S 169.55W
Makapuu Head 221a Db 21.18N 157.39W
Makara, prohod- 130 Ih 41.16N 25.26 E
Makarene, Irhazer- 166 Gb 18.07N 7.35 E
Makares 130 Il 37.05N 25.42 E
Makarfi 166 Gc 11.23N 7.53 E
Makari 166 Hc 12.35N 14.28 E
Makari Mountains 170 Ed 6.05S 29.50 E
Makarjev 114 Kh 57.57N 43.49 E
Makarov 138 Jg 48.39N 142.51 E
Makarov Basin (EN) 224 Ce 87.00N 170.00 E
Makarov Seamount (EN) 208 Gb 29.30N 153.30 E
Makarska 128 Lg 43.18N 17.02 E
Makā Rūd 146 Nd 36.21N 51.16 E
Makasar → Ujung Pandang 142 Nj 5.07S 119.24 E
Makasar, Selat-=Makassar Strait (EN) 140 Nj 2.00S 117.30 E
Makassar Strait (EN)=Makasar, Selat- 140 Nj 2.00S 117.30 E
Makat 112 Lf 47.40N 53.28 E
Makatea, Ile- 208 Mf 15.50S 148.15W
Makaw 148 Jc 26.27N 96.42 E
Makawao 221a Ec 20.51N 156.19W
Makay, Massif du- 172 Hd 21.15S 45.15 E
Makedhonia 130 Fi 40.40N 22.30 E
Makedhonia=Macedonia (EN) 110 Ig 41.00N 23.00 E
Makedhonia=Macedonia (EN) 130 Fh 41.00N 23.00 E
Makedonija = Macedonia (EN) 130 Eh 41.50N 22.00 E
Makedonija=Macedonia (EN) 110 Ig 41.00N 23.00 E
Makedonija=Macedonia (EN) 130 Fh 41.00N 23.00 E
Makejevka 132 Jf 48.00N 37.58 E
Makelulu, Mount- 220a Bb 7.34N 134.35 E
Makemo Atoll 208 Mf 16.35S 143.40W
Makeni 160 Fh 8.53N 12.03W
Makgadikgadi Pans 158 Jk 20.50S 25.30 E
Makhfar al Buşayyah 146 Lg 30.08N 46.07 E
Makhfar al Hammām 146 He 35.51N 38.45 E
Makhmūr 146 Je 35.46N 43.35 E
Makhyah, Wādī- 144 Gf 17.40N 49.01 E
Maki 156 Fc 37.45N 138.52 E
Makian, Pulau- 150 If 0.20N 127.25 E
Makikihi 218 Df 44.38S 171.09 E
Makinsk 136 He 52.40N 70.26 E
Makkah=Mecca (EN) 142 Fg 21.27N 39.49 E
Makkovik 180 Le 55.05N 59.11W
Maknassy 162 Ic 34.37N 9.36 E
Makó 120 Qj 46.13N 20.29 E
Makokou 160 Ih 0.34N 12.52 E
Makongai 219d Bb 17.27S 178.58 E
Makongolosi 170 Fd 8.24S 33.09 E
Makorako 218 Gi 39.09S 176.03 E
Makoua 160 Ih 0.01N 15.39 E
Makoura 219b Dc 17.08S 168.26 E
Makov 120 Og 49.22N 18.29 E
Maków Mazowiecki 120 Rd 52.52N 21.06 E
Makrá 130 Im 36.16N 25.53 E
Makrān 140 Hg 26.00N 60.00 E
Makrónisos 130 Hl 37.42N 24.07 E
Maksatiha 114 Ih 57.48N 35.55 E
Makteir 158 Ff 21.50N 11.40W
Makthar 162 Ib 35.51N 9.12 E
Makthar 128 Do 35.50N 9.13 E
Mākū 146 Kc 39.17N 44.31 E
Makū 144 Hd 27.52N 52.26 E
Makubetsu 156a Cb 42.54N 143.19 E
Makumbato 170 Fd 8.51S 34.50 E
Makumbi 170 Dd 5.51S 20.41 E
Makunduchi 170 Gd 6.25S 39.33 E
Makung 152 Kg 23.35N 119.35 E
Makurazaki 154 Ki 31.16N 139.19 E
Makurdi 160 Hh 7.44N 8.32 E
Makushin Volcano 178a Eb 53.53N 166.50W
Makušino 136 Gd 55.13N 67.13 E
Makuyuni 170 Gc 3.33S 36.06 E
Malå 114 Ed 65.11N 18.44 E
Mala/Mallow 118 Ei 52.08N 8.39W
Mala, Punta- 190 Ig 7.28N 80.00W
Malabang 150 He 7.38N 124.03 E
Malabar Coast 140 Jh 10.00N 76.15 E
Malabo 160 Hh 3.45N 8.47 E
Malabrigo 204 Ci 29.20S 59.58W
Malacca, Strait of- (EN)=Melaka, Selat- 140 Mi 2.30N 101.20 E
Malacky 120 Nh 48.27N 17.01 E
Malad City 188 Ie 42.12N 112.15W
Maladeta / Malditos, Montes- 126 Mb 42.40N 0.50 E
Malá Fatra 120 Og 49.08N 18.50 E
Málaga 126 Hh 36.48N 4.45W
Málaga [Col.] 202 Db 6.42N 72.44W
Málaga [Sp.] 110 Fh 36.43N 4.25W
Malagarasi 158 Ji 5.12S 29.47 E
Malagón 126 Ie 39.10N 3.51W
Malaimbandy 172 Hd 20.20S 45.36 E
Malaita Island 208 He 9.00S 161.00 E
Malaja Kuonamka 138 Gb 70.50N 113.20 E
Malaja Ob 138 Bc 66.08N 65.50 E
Malaja Sosva 136 Gc 63.10N 64.22 E
Malaja Višera 136 Dd 58.52N 32.14 E
Malaja Viska 132 Ge 48.39N 31.38 E
Malakāl 160 Kh 9.31N 31.39 E
Malakal Harbor 220a Ac 7.20N 134.26 E
Malakal Pass 220a Ac 7.17N 134.28 E
Mala Kapela 128 Jf 44.55N 15.28 E
Malakobi 219a Db 7.19S 158.07 E
Malang 142 Nj 7.59S 112.37 E
Malangen 114 Eb 69.30N 18.20 E
Malanje 160 Ii 9.33S 16.22 E
Malanje 170 Cd 9.30S 16.30 E
Malanville 166 Fc 11.52N 3.23 E
Malao 219b Cb 15.10S 166.51 E
Mała Panew 120 Nf 50.44N 17.52 E
Mälaren 110 Hd 59.30N 17.15 E
Malargüe 206 Ge 35.28S 69.35W
Malartic, Lac- 184 Ha 48.15N 78.05W
Malaspina Glacier 178 Ke 59.50N 140.30W
Malatya 142 Ff 38.21N 38.19 E
Malāvi 146 Lf 33.10N 47.50 E
Malawi 160 Kj 13.30S 34.00 E
Malawi, Lake- 158 Kj 12.00S 34.30 E
Malaya 150 Df 4.00N 102.00 E
Malaybalay 150 Ie 8.09N 125.05 E
Malāyer 144 Gc 34.17N 48.50 E
Malāyer 146 Me 34.16N 48.12 E
Malay Peninsula (EN) 140 Mi 6.00N 102.00 E
Malay Peninsula (EN)=Malaysia, Semenanjung- 150 Df 4.00N 102.00 E
Malaysia 142 Mi 4.00N 102.00 E
Malaysia, Semenanjung-=Malay Peninsula (EN) 150 Df 4.00N 102.00 E
Malazgirt 146 Jc 39.09N 42.31 E
Malberg 124 Id 50.03N 6.35 E
Malbor 146 Og 30.45N 52.05 E
Malbork 120 Pb 54.02N 19.01 E
Malbrán 206 Hc 29.21S 62.27W
Malchin 120 Ic 53.44N 12.47 E
Maldegem 124 Fc 51.13N 3.27 E
Malden 186 Lh 36.34N 89.57W
Malden Island 208 Le 4.03S 154.59W
Malditos, Montes- / Maladeta 126 Mb 42.40N 0.50 E
Maldive Islands 140 Ji 3.15N 73.00 E
Mal di Ventre 128 Ck 40.00N 8.20 E
Maldives 142 Ji 3.15N 73.00 E
Maldon 118 Nj 51.45N 0.40 E
Maldonado 206 Jd 34.54S 54.57W
Maldonado 204 El 34.40S 54.55W
Maldonado, Punta- 190 Hh 16.20N 98.35W
Malé 128 Ed 46.21N 10.55 E
Male 142 Ji 4.10N 73.30 E
Mâle, Lac du- 184 Ja 48.30N 75.30W
Malea, Cape- (EN) = Maléas, Ákra- 130 Gm 36.26N 23.12 E
Maléas, Ákra- = Malea, Cape- (EN) 130 Gm 36.26N 23.12 E
Male Atoll 140 Ji 4.29N 73.30 E
Malebo, Pool- 158 Ii 4.17S 15.20 E
Malegaon 148 Ed 20.33N 74.32 E
Maleha 166 Dc 11.48N 9.43W
Malek 168 Ed 6.04N 31.36 E
Malé Karpaty = Little Carpathians (EN) 120 Nh 48.30N 17.20 E
Malek Kandī 146 Ld 37.09N 46.06 E
Malékoula, Ile- 208 Hf 16.15S 167.30 E
Malema 172 Fb 14.57S 37.25 E
Malemba Nkulu 170 Ed 8.02S 26.48 E
Malenga 114 Ie 63.50N 36.25 E
Malesherbes 122 If 48.18N 2.25 E
Malgobek 132 Nh 43.32N 44.34 E
Malgomaj 114 Dd 64.47N 16.12 E
Malhada 204 Kb 14.21S 43.47W
Malhanski hrebet 138 Ff 50.30N 109.00 E
Malhão da Estrêla 126 Ed 40.19N 7.37W
Malha Wells 168 Db 15.08N 26.12 E
Malheur Lake 182 Dc 43.20N 118.45W
Malheur River 188 Gd 44.03N 116.59W
Mali 166 Cc 12.05N 12.18W
Mali 160 Gg 17.00N 4.00W
Mali 219d Bb 16.20S 179.21 E
Mali 148 Jc 25.42N 97.30 E
Mália 130 In 35.17N 25.28 E
Maliakós Kólpos 130 Fk 38.52N 22.38 E
Malik, Wādī al- 158 Kg 18.02N 30.58 E
Mali kanal 130 Cd 45.42N 19.19 E
Malik Siah, Kūh-i- 144 Jd 29.51N 60.52 E
Malili 150 Hg 2.38S 121.06 E
Målilla 116 Fg 57.23N 15.48 E
Mali Lošinj 128 If 44.32N 14.28 E
Malimba, Monts- 170 Ed 7.32S 29.30 E
Malin 132 Fd 50.46N 29.14 E
Malinalco 192 Jh 18.57N 99.30W
Malinaltepec 192 Ji 17.03N 98.40W
Malindi 160 Li 3.13S 40.07 E
Malines/Mechelen 122 Kc 51.02N 4.29 E
Malin Head/Cionn Mhálanna 110 Fd 55.23N 7.24W
Malino, Bukit- 150 Hf 0.45N 120.47 E
Malinovoje Ozero 138 Cf 51.40N 79.55 E
Malinyi 170 Gd 8.56S 36.08 E
Malipo 152 Hg 23.07N 104.42 E
Maliqi 130 Di 40.43N 20.41 E
Malita 150 Ie 6.25N 125.36 E
Maljen 130 De 44.07N 20.03 E
Maljovica 130 Gg 42.11N 23.22 E
Malka 132 Nh 43.44N 44.15 E
Malkara 146 Bb 40.53N 26.54 E
Malki Lom 130 Jf 43.39N 26.04 E
Malko Tărnovo 130 Kh 41.59N 27.32 E
Mallacoota 212 Jg 37.30S 149.50 E
Mallaig 118 Hd 57.00N 5.50W
Mallamalla Range 148 Fe 16.17N 79.29 E
Mallāq, Wādī- 128 Cn 36.32N 8.51 E
Mallawī 164 Fd 27.44N 30.50 E
Mallery Lake 180 Hd 64.00N 98.00W
Malles Venosta / Mals in Vinschgau 128 Ed 46.41N 10.32 E
Mallet 204 Gg 25.55S 50.50W
Mallnitz 128 Hd 46.59N 13.10 E
Mallorca=Majorca (EN) 110 Gh 39.30N 3.00 E
Mallow/Mala 118 Ei 52.08N 8.39W
Malm 114 Cd 64.04N 11.13 E
Malmbäck 116 Fg 57.35N 14.28 E
Malmberget 114 Ec 67.10N 20.40 E
Malmédy 122 Md 50.26N 6.02 E
Malmesbury 172 Bf 33.28S 18.44 E
Malmö 112 Hd 55.36N 13.00 E
Malmöhus 114 Ci 55.45N 13.30 E
Malmön 116 Df 58.21N 11.20 E
Malmslätt 116 Ff 58.25N 15.30 E
Malmyž 136 Fd 56.31N 50.41 E
Malo 219b Cb 15.41S 167.10 E
Maloarhangelsk 132 Jc 52.26N 36.29 E
Maloelap 208 Id 8.45N 171.03 E
Maloggia/Malojapaß 128 Dd 46.24N 9.41 E
Malojapaß/Maloggia 128 Dd 46.24N 9.41 E
Malojaroslavec 132 Jb 55.02N 36.28 E
Maloje Polesje 120 Uf 50.10N 24.30 E
Malolo 219d Ab 17.45S 177.10 E
Malolos 150 Hd 14.51N 120.49 E
Malombe, Lake- 170 Ge 14.38S 35.12 E
Malone 184 Jc 44.52N 74.19W
Malonga 170 De 10.24S 23.10 E
Małopolska 120 Pf 50.45N 20.00 E
Malorita 132 Dd 51.48N 24.05 E
Malošujka 114 Ie 63.47N 37.22 E
Måløy 114 Af 61.56N 5.07 E
Malozemelskaja tundra 134 Ec 68.00N 52.00 E
Malpaso 192 Mi 17.20N 93.30W
Malpelo, Isla de- 198 He 3.59N 81.35W
Malprabha 148 Fe 16.12N 76.03 E
Malsch 124 Kf 48.53N 8.20 E
Malše 120 Kh 48.59N 14.29 E
Mals in Vinschgau / Malles Venosta 128 Ed 46.41N 10.32 E
Malta 112 Hh 35.50N 14.30 E
Malta 110 Hh 35.54N 14.31 E
Malta [Lat.] 116 Lh 56.18N 27.15 E
Malta [Mt.-U.S.] 182 Fb 48.21N 107.52W
Malta, Canale di = Malta Channel (EN) 128 In 36.30N 14.30 E
Malta Channel (EN)=Malta, Canale di- 128 In 36.30N 14.30 E
Maltahöhe 160 Ik 24.50S 17.00 E
Maltahöhe 172 Bd 25.00S 16.30 E
Maltepe 130 Mi 40.55N 29.08 E
Malton 118 Mg 54.08N 0.48W
Maltsch 120 Kh 48.59N 14.29 E
Maluku 150 Ig 4.00S 128.00 E
Maluku, Kepulauan-= Moluccas (EN) 208 De 2.00S 128.00 E
Maluku, Laut-=Molucca Sea (EN) 140 Oj 0.05S 125.00 E
Malumfashi 166 Gc 11.48N 7.37 E
Malunda 150 Gg 3.00S 118.50 E
Malung 114 Cf 60.40N 13.44 E
Malungsfors 116 Ed 60.44N 13.33 E
Malūţ 168 Ec 10.26N 32.12 E
Maluu 219a Ec 8.21S 160.38 E
Malvern [Ar.-U.S.] 186 Ji 34.22N 92.49W
Malvern [Eng.-U.K.] 118 Ki 52.07N 2.19W
Malvinas 204 Ci 29.37S 58.59W
Malvinas, Islas-/Falkland Islands 200 Kk 51.45S 59.00W
Malvinas, Islas-/Falkland Islands 198 Kk 51.45S 59.00W
Maly, ostrov- 116 Ld 60.02N 27.58 E
Malya 170 Fc 2.59S 33.31 E
Maly Anjuj 138 Lc 68.35N 161.03 E
Maly Čeremšan 114 Mi 54.20N 50.01 E
Maly Dunaj 120 Nh 48.08N 17.09 E
Malygina, proliv- 138 Cb 73.00N 70.30 E
Maly Jenisej 138 Ef 51.40N 94.26 E
Maly Kavkaz=Lesser Caucasus (EN) 110 Kg 41.00N 44.35 E
Maly Ljahovski, ostrov- 138 Jb 74.07N 140.36 E
Maly Tajmyr, ostrov- 138 Fa 78.08N 107.08 E
Maly Tjuters, ostrov- 116 Le 59.45N 26.53 E
Maly Uzen 110 Kf 48.50N 49.38 E
Mama 138 Ge 58.20N 112.54 E
Mamadyš 114 Mi 55.45N 51.24 E
Mamagota 219a Bb 6.46S 155.24 E
Mamaia 130 Le 44.17N 28.37 E
Mamakan 138 Ge 57.48N 114.05 E
Mamantel 192 Nh 18.33N 91.05W
Mamanutha Group 219d Ab 17.34S 177.04 E
Mamaqān 146 Kd 37.51N 45.59 E
Mambaj 204 Ib 14.28S 46.07W
Mambajao 150 He 9.15N 124.43 E
Mambasa 170 Eb 1.21N 29.03 E
Mambéré 168 Be 3.31N 16.03 E
Mambili 170 Cb 0.07N 16.08 E
Mamborê 204 Fg 24.18S 52.32W
Mambova 170 Ef 17.44S 25.11 E
Mambrui 170 Hc 3.07S 40.09 E
Mamburao 150 Hd 13.14N 120.35 E
Mamedkala 132 Ph 42.12N 48.06 E
Mamer 124 Ie 49.38N 6.02 E
Mamers 122 Gf 48.21N 0.23 E
Mamfe 166 Gd 5.46N 9.17 E
Mamiá, Lago- 202 Fd 4.15S 63.05W
Mamisonski, pereval- 132 Mh 42.43N 43.45 E
Mamljutka 136 Ge 54.57N 68.35 E
Mammoth Cave 184 Dg 37.10N 86.08W
Mammoth Hot Springs 188 Jd 44.59N 110.43W
Mamonovo 120 Pb 54.28N 19.57 E
Mamoré, Rio- 198 Jg 10.23S 65.53W
Mamou 160 Fg 10.23N 12.05W
Mamoutzou 172 Hb 12.47S 45.14 E
Mampikony 172 Hc 16.05S 47.37 E
Mampodre, Picos de- 126 Ga 43.02N 5.12W
Mampong 166 Ed 7.04N 1.24W
Mamry, Jezioro- 120 Rb 54.08N 21.42 E
Mamuju 150 Gg 2.41S 118.54 E
Mamuno 172 Cd 22.17S 20.02 E
Ma'mūrah, Ra's al- 128 En 36.27N 10.49 E
Mamurokawa 156 Gb 38.54N 140.15 E
Man 160 Gh 7.24N 7.33W
Man 166 Dd 7.13N 7.41W
Man, Calf of- 118 Ig 54.03N 4.48W
Man, Isle of- 110 Fe 54.15N 4.30W
Mana 214 Oc 22.02N 159.46W
Mana 138 Ee 55.57N 92.28 E
Manacapuru 202 Fd 3.18S 60.37W
Manacor 126 Pe 39.34N 3.12 E
Manado 142 Oi 1.29N 124.51 E
Managua 176 Kh 12.09N 86.17W
Managua 194 Dg 12.05N 86.20W
Managua, Lago de- 190 Gf 12.20N 86.20W
Manakara 160 Lk 22.07S 48.00 E
Manama (EN)=Al Manāmah 142 Hg 26.13N 50.35 E
Manambolo 172 Gc 19.19S 44.17 E
Manam Island 208 Fe 4.05S 145.03 E
Manamo, Caño- 202 Fb 9.55N 62.16W
Mananara 172 Hc 16.10S 49.45 E
Mananara 172 Hd 23.21S 47.42 E
Mananjary 160 Lk 21.14S 48.17 E
Manankoro 166 Dc 10.28N 7.25W
Manantenina 172 Hd 24.17S 47.18 E
Manaoba 219a Ec 8.19S 160.47 E
Manapire, Rio- 196 Ci 7.42N 66.07W
Manapouri 210 Hi 45.34S 167.36 E
Manapouri, Lake- 218 Bf 45.30S 167.30 E
Manār, Jabal- 164 Hg 14.10N 44.17 E
Manas 142 Ke 44.18N 86.13 E
Manas, gora- 135 Hc 42.18N 71.06 E
Manas He 152 Eb 45.38N 85.12 E
Manas Hu 152 Eb 45.45N 85.55 E
Manasija, Manastir- 130 Ee 44.06N 21.28 E
Manati 194 Ic 21.19N 76.56W
Manati 194 Nd 18.26N 66.29W
Manatuto 150 Ih 8.30S 126.01 E
Manaure 194 Kh 11.46N 72.28W
Manaus 200 Jf 3.08S 60.01W
Manavgat 146 Dd 36.47N 31.26 E
Manbij [Syr.] 146 Gd 36.31N 37.57 E
Manbij [Syr.] 146 Gd 36.30N 37.50 E
Manbūbnagar 148 Fe 16.44N 77.59 E
Mancelona 184 Ec 44.54N 85.04W
Mancha Real 126 Ig 37.47N 3.37W
Manche 122 Ee 49.00N 1.10W
Mancheng 154 Ce 38.57N 115.19 E
Manchester [Ct.-U.S.] 184 Ke 41.47N 72.31W
Manchester [Eng.-U.K.] 112 Fe 53.30N 2.15W
Manchester [Ia.-U.S.] 186 Ke 42.29N 91.27W
Manchester [Ky.-U.S.] 184 Fg 37.09N 83.46W
Manchester [N.H.-U.S.] 182 Mc 42.59N 71.28W
Manchester [Tn.-U.S.] 184 Dh 35.29N 86.05W
Manchok 166 Gd 9.40N 8.31 E
Manchuria (EN) 142 Oe 47.00N 125.00 E
Manciano 128 Fh 42.35N 11.31 E
Mand 144 Hd 28.11N 51.17 E
Manda [Chad] 168 Bd 9.11N 18.13 E
Manda [Tan.] 170 Fe 10.28S 34.35 E
Manda, Jabal- 168 Cd 8.39N 24.27 E
Mandabe 172 Gd 21.02S 44.56 E
Mandaguari 206 Jb 23.32S 51.42W
Manda Island 170 Hc 2.17S 40.57 E
Mandal 114 Bg 58.02N 7.27 E
Mandalay 142 Lg 22.00N 96.05 E
Mandalay 148 Jd 21.00N 96.00 E
Mandal-Gobi 152 Ib 45.45N 106.12 E
Mandalī 146 Kf 33.45N 45.32 E
Mandalselva 116 Bf 58.02N 7.28 E
Mandalt → Sonid Zuoqi 152 Jc 43.50N 113.45 E
Mandalya körfezi 146 Bd 37.12N 27.20 E
Mandan 182 Gb 46.50N 100.54W
Mandaon 150 Hd 12.13N 123.17 E
Mandara, Monts-=Mandara Mountains (EN) 166 Hc 10.45N 13.40 E
Mandara Mountains (EN)=Mandara, Monts- 166 Hc 10.45N 13.40 E
Mandas 128 Dk 39.38N 9.07 E
Mandasor 148 Fd 24.04N 75.04 E
Mandera 160 Lh 3.56N 41.52 E
Manderscheid 124 Id 50.06N 6.49 E
Mandeville 194 Id 18.02N 77.30W
Mandi 148 Fb 31.43N 76.55 E
Mandiana 166 Dc 10.38N 8.41W
Mandimba 172 Fb 14.21S 35.39 E
Mandingues, Monts- 166 Cc 13.00N 11.00W
Mandioli, Pulau- 150 Ig 0.44S 127.14 E
Mandioré, Laguna- 204 Dd 18.08S 57.33W
Mandirituba 204 Hg 25.46S 49.19W
Mandji 170 Bc 1.42S 10.24 E
Mandla 148 Gd 22.36N 80.23 E
Mandø 116 Ci 55.15N 8.35 E
Mandoúdhion 130 Gk 38.48N 23.29 E
Mandrákion 130 Km 36.36N 27.08 E
Mandritsara 172 Hc 15.49S 48.48 E
Mandurah 212 Df 32.32S 115.43 E
Manduria 128 Lj 40.24N 17.38 E
Māndvi 148 Dd 22.50N 69.22 E
Mandya 148 Ff 12.33N 76.54 E
Måne 116 Ce 59.56N 8.48 E
Măneciu Ungureni 130 Id 45.19N 25.59 E
Manendragarh 148 Gd 23.10N 82.35 E
Maneromango 170 Gd 7.16S 38.46 E
Maneviči 132 Dd 51.19N 25.33 E
Manfalūţ 164 Fd 27.19N 30.58 E
Manfredonia 128 Ji 41.38N 15.55 E
Manfredonia, Golfo di- 128 Ki 41.35N 16.05 E
Manga [Afr.] 158 Ig 15.00N 14.00 E
Manga [Braz.] 202 Jf 14.46S 43.56W
Mangabeiras, Chapada das- 198 Lg 10.00S 46.30W
Mangai 170 Cc 4.03S 19.35 E
Mangaia Island 208 Lg 21.55S 157.55W
Mangakino 218 Fc 38.22S 175.46 E
Mangalia 130 Lf 43.48N 28.35 E
Mangalmé 168 Bc 12.21N 19.37 E
Mangalore 142 Jh 12.52N 74.53 E
Mangareva, Ile- 208 Ng 23.07S 134.57W
Mangfall 120 Ii 47.51N 12.08 E
Manggar 150 Eg 2.53S 108.16 E
Manggautu 219a Dd 11.30S 159.59 E
Mangin Yoma 148 Jd 24.20N 95.42 E
Mangistau 132 Qg 44.03N 51.57 E
Mangit 136 Gg 42.07N 60.01 E
Mangkalihat, Tanjung- 150 Gf 1.02N 118.59 E
Manglares, Cabo- 202 Cc 1.36N 79.02W
Mangnai 152 Fd 37.48N 91.55 E
Mangniu He 154 Ib 45.10N 126.58 E
Mango [Fiji] 219d Cb 17.27S 179.09W
Mango [Ton.] 221b Bb 20.20S 174.43W
Mangoche 170 Ge 14.28S 35.16 E
Mangoky [Mad.] 158 Lk 21.29S 43.41 E
Mangoky [Mad.] 172 Hd 23.27S 45.13 E
Mangole, Pulau- 150 Ig 1.53S 125.50 E
Mangonui 218 Ea 34.59S 173.32 E
Mangrove Cay 194 Ia 24.51N 76.14W
Mangrullo, Cuchilla- 204 Fk 32.27S 53.50W
Mangshi → Luxi 142 Lg 24.29N 98.40 E
Mangualde 126 Ed 40.36N 7.46W
Mangueira, Lagoa- 206 Jd 33.06S 52.48W
Mangueni, Plateau de- 158 If 22.35N 12.40 E
Mangui 152 La 52.03N 122.09 E
Mangula 172 Ec 16.52S 30.08 E
Mangum 186 Gi 34.53N 99.30W
Manguredjipa 170 Eb 0.21N 28.44 E
Mangyšlak 136 Fg 43.40N 51.15 E
Mangyšlak, plato- 136 Fg 43.25N 53.00 E
Mangyšlakskaja oblast 136 Fg 44.00N 53.30 E
Mangyšlakski zaliv 132 Qg 44.45N 51.00 E
Manhattan 182 Hd 39.11N 96.35W
Manhica 172 Ee 25.24S 32.48 E
Mani 170 Ed 6.27S 25.20 E
Mani 202 Dc 4.49N 72.17W
Mānī', Wādī al- 146 Ie 34.16N 41.02 E
Mania 172 Hc 19.42S 45.22 E
Maniago 128 Gd 46.10N 12.43 E
Manica 172 Ec 18.56S 32.53 E
Manica 172 Ec 19.00S 33.20 E
Manicaland 172 Ec 19.00S 32.30 E
Manicoré 200 Jf 5.49S 61.17W
Manicoré, Rio- 202 Fe 5.51S 61.19W
Manicouagan 180 Kf 51.00N 68.20W
Manicouagan 186 Kg 49.10N 68.15W
Manicouagan, Réservoir- 174 Md 51.30N 68.19W
Manigotagan 186 Ha 51.06N 96.18W
Manihi Atoll 208 Mf 14.24S 145.56W
Manihiki Anchorage 220n Ab 10.23S 161.03W
Manihiki Atoll 208 Kf 10.24S 161.01W
Manika, Plateau de la- 170 Ed 10.00S 26.00 E
Manila [Phil.] 142 Oh 14.35N 121.00 E
Manila [Ut.-U.S.] 188 Kf 40.59N 109.43W
Manila Bay 140 Oh 14.30N 120.45 E
Manilaid/Manilajd 116 Kf 58.08N 24.03 E
Manilajd/Manilaid 116 Kf 58.08N 24.03 E
Manily 138 Ld 62.30N 165.20 E
Maningrida Settlement 212 Gb 12.05S 134.10 E
Maniouro, Pointe- 219b Dc 17.41S 168.35 E
Manipa, Selat- 150 Ig 3.20S 127.23 E
Manipur 148 Id 25.00N 94.00 E
Manipur 148 Id 22.52N 94.05 E
Manisa 144 Cb 38.36N 27.26 E
Manisa Dağı 130 Kk 38.33N 27.28 E
Manises 126 Le 39.29N 0.27W
Manissau a-Missu, Rio- 202 Hf 10.58S 53.20W
Manistee 184 Dc 44.15N 86.18W
Manistee River 184 Dc 44.15N 86.21W
Manistique 182 Jb 45.57N 86.15W
Manistique Lake 184 Eb 46.15N 85.45W
Manitoba 180 Hf 55.00N 97.00W
Manitoba, Lake- 174 Jd 51.00N 98.45W
Manitou Islands 184 Ec 45.10N 86.00W
Manitou Lake 184 Gc 45.48N 82.00W
Manitoulin Island 180 Jg 45.45N 82.30W

Man-Mar

Manitou Springs	186	Dg	38.52N	104.55W
Manitouwadge	186	Nb	49.08N	85.47W
Manitowoc	186	Jc	44.06N	87.40W
Manitsoq/Sukkertoppen	186	Md	65.25N	53.00W
Maniwaki	180	Jg	46.23N	75.58W
Manizales	200	Ie	5.05N	75.32W
Manja	172	Gd	21.23S	44.20 E
Manja	134	Jd	64.23N	60.50 E
Manjača	128	Lf	44.35N	17.05 E
Manjacaze	172	Ed	24.42S	33.33 E
Manjakandriana	172	Hc	18.55S	47.47 E
Manji	156a	Bb	43.09N	141.59 E
Manjil	144	Gb	36.44N	49.24 E
Manjimup	212	Df	34.14S	116.09 E
Mānjra	148	Fe	18.49N	77.52 E
Mān Kāt	148	Jd	22.05N	98.01 E
Mankato [Ks.-U.S.]	186	Gg	39.47N	98.12W
Mankato [Mn.-U.S.]	182	Ic	44.10N	94.01W
Mankono	166	Dd	8.04N	6.12W
Mankono [3]	166	Dd	7.58N	6.02W
Mankoya	160	Jj	14.50S	25.00 E
Manley Hot Springs	178	Ic	65.00N	150.37W
Manlleu	126	Ob	42.00N	2.17 E
Manmād	148	Ed	20.15N	74.27 E
Manmanoc, Mount-	150	Hc	17.40N	121.06 E
Manna	150	Dh	4.27S	102.55 E
Mannahill	212	Hf	32.26S	139.59 E
Mannar	148	Fg	8.59N	79.54 E
Mannar, Gulf of-	140	Ji	8.30N	79.00 E
Mannheim	112	Gf	49.29N	8.28 E
Manning [Alta.-Can.]	180	Fe	56.55N	117.33W
Manning [S.C.-U.S.]	184	Gi	33.42N	80.12W
Manning, Cape-	220g	Ba	2.02N	157.26W
Manning Strait	219a	Db	7.24S	158.04 E
Manningtree	124	Dc	51.57N	1.04 E
Mann Ranges	212	Fe	26.00S	129.30 E
Mann River	212	Gb	12.20S	134.07 E
Mannu, Capo-	128	Cj	40.02N	8.22 E
Mannu, Rio- [It.]	128	Cj	40.50N	8.23 E
Mannu, Rio- [It.]	128	Cj	40.41N	8.59 E
Mano	166	Cd	6.56N	11.31W
Mano [Jap.]	156	Fc	37.58N	138.20 E
Mano [S.L.]	166	Cd	7.55N	12.00W
Manoa	202	Ee	9.40S	65.27W
Man of War, Cayos-	194	Fg	13.02N	83.22W
Manokwari	210	Ee	2.30S	134.36 E
Manombo	172	Gd	22.55S	43.28 E
Manompana	172	Hc	16.41S	49.45 E
Manonga	170	Fc	4.08S	34.12 E
Manono	160	Ji	7.18S	27.25 E
Manono	221c	Aa	13.50S	172.05W
Manosque	122	Lk	43.50N	5.47 E
Manouane, Lac-	180	Kf	50.40N	70.45W
Mano-Wan	156	Fc	37.55N	138.15 E
Manp'ojin	154	Id	41.09N	126.17 E
Manra Atoll (Sydney)	208	Je	4.27S	171.15W
Manresa	126	Nc	41.44N	1.50 E
Mans, Le-	112	Gf	48.00N	0.12 E
Mansa	160	Jj	11.12S	28.53 E
Mansa Konko	166	Bc	13.28N	15.33W
Mansel	174	Lc	62.00N	79.50W
Mansfield [Austl.]	212	Jg	37.03S	146.05 E
Mansfield [Eng.-U.K.]	118	Lh	53.09N	1.11W
Mansfield [La.-U.S.]	186	Jj	32.02N	93.43W
Mansfield [Oh.-U.S.]	182	Kc	40.46N	82.31W
Mansfield [Pa.-U.S.]	184	Ie	41.47N	77.05W
Mansfield, Mount-	184	Kc	44.33N	72.49W
Mansle	122	Gi	45.52N	0.11 E
Manso, Rio-	204	Db	14.42S	56.16W
Manso, Rio- ou Mortes, Rio das-	198	Kg	11.45S	50.44W
Mansôa	166	Bc	12.04N	15.19W
Mansourah	126	Qh	36.04N	4.28 E
Mansourah, Djebel-	126	Qh	36.02N	4.28 E
Manta	202	Bd	0.57S	80.42W
Manta, Bahia de-	202	Bd	0.50S	80.40W
Mantalingajan, Mount-	150	Ge	8.48N	117.40 E
Manteca	188	Eh	37.48N	121.13W
Mantecal [Ven.]	196	Bi	7.33N	69.09W
Mantecal [Ven.]	196	Di	6.52N	65.38W
Manteigas	126	Ed	40.24N	7.32W
Manteo	184	Jh	35.55N	75.40W
Mantes-la-Jolie	122	Hf	48.59N	1.43 E
Manti	188	Jg	39.16N	111.38W
Mantiqueira, Serra da-	198	Lh	22.00S	44.45W
Manto	194	Df	14.55N	86.23W
Manton	184	Ec	44.24N	85.24W
Mantova	128	Ee	45.09N	10.48 E
Mäntsälä	116	Kd	60.38N	25.20 E
Mänttä	114	Fe	62.02N	24.38 E
Mantua	194	Eb	22.17N	84.17W
Manturovo	136	Ed	58.22N	44.44 E
Mäntyharju	114	Gf	61.25N	26.53 E
Mäntyluoto	116	Ic	61.35N	21.29 E
Manu	202	Df	12.15S	70.50W
Manuae Atoll [Cook]	208	Lf	19.21S	158.56W
Manuae Atoll [Fr.Poly.]	208	Lf	16.32S	154.38W
Manua Islands	208	Kf	14.13S	169.35W
Manuangi Atoll	208	Mf	19.12S	141.16W
Manūbah	128	En	36.48N	10.06 E
Manuel	192	Jf	22.44N	98.19W
Manuel Alves, Rio-	202	If	11.19S	48.28W
Manuel Benavides	192	Hc	29.05N	103.55W
Manuel Derqui	204	Ch	27.50S	58.48W
Manuel J. Cobo	204	Dl	35.49S	57.54W
Manuel Ocampo	204	Bk	33.46S	60.39W
Manuga Reefs	219a	Ad	11.00S	153.21 E
Manui, Pulau-	150	Hg	3.35S	123.08 E
Manujān	146	Qi	27.24N	57.32 E
Mānūk, Tell-	146	Hf	33.10N	38.50 E
Manukau	210	Ih	36.56S	174.56 E
Manulu Lagoon	220g	Bb	1.56N	157.20W
Manus Island	208	Fe	2.05S	147.00 E
Many	186	Jk	31.34N	93.29W
Manyara, Lake-	170	Gc	3.35S	35.50 E
Manyas	146	Bb	40.02N	27.58 E
Manyč	110	Kf	47.15N	40.00 E
Manyč-Gudilo, ozero-	110	Kf	46.25N	42.35 E
Manyoni	170	Fd	5.45S	34.50 E
Manzanal, Puerto del-	126	Fb	42.32N	6.10W
Manzanares	126	Ie	39.00N	3.22W
Manzaneda, Cabeza de-	126	Ed	42.20N	7.15W
Manzanilla	126	Fg	37.23N	6.25W
Manzanillo [Cuba]	176	Lg	20.21N	77.07W
Manzanillo [Mex.]	176	Ih	19.03N	104.20W
Manzanillo, Bahia de- [Dom.Rep.]	194	Ld	19.45N	71.46W
Manzanillo, Bahia de- [Mex.]	192	Gh	19.04N	104.25W
Manzanillo, Punta-	194	Hi	9.38N	79.32W
Manzano Mountains	186	Ci	34.45N	106.20W
Manzhouli	142	Ne	49.33N	117.28 E
Manzilah, Buḩayrat al-	146	Eg	31.15N	32.00 E
Manzil Bū Ruqaybah	162	Ib	37.10N	9.48 E
Manzil bū Zalafah	128	En	36.41N	10.35 E
Manzil Tamīn	128	En	36.47N	10.59 E
Manzini	172	Ee	26.29S	31.22 E
Mao	219b	Dc	17.29S	168.29 E
Mao [Chad]	160	Ig	14.07N	15.19 E
Mao [Dom.Rep.]	190	Je	19.34N	71.05W
Maó / Mahón	126	Qe	39.53N	4.15 E
Maoke, Pegunungan-	150	Kg	4.00S	138.00 E
Maomao Shan	152	Hd	37.12N	103.10 E
Maoming	142	Ng	21.41N	110.52 E
Maoniu Shan	152	He	32.50N	104.12 E
Maotou Shan	152	Hg	24.31N	100.38 E
Maouri, Dallol-	166	Fc	12.05N	3.32 E
Mapai	172	Ed	22.51S	31.58 E
Mapanda	170	Dd	9.32S	24.16 E
Mapati	170	Bc	3.38S	13.21 E
Mapi	210	Ee	7.07S	139.23 E
Mapi	150	Kh	7.00S	139.16 E
Mapia, Kepulauan-	208	Ed	0.50N	134.20 E
Mapimi, Bolsón de-	174	Ig	27.30N	103.15W
Mapinhane	172	Fd	22.15S	35.07 E
Mapire	196	Di	7.45N	64.42W
Mapiri	202	Eg	15.15S	68.10W
Maple Creek	180	Gg	49.55N	109.27W
Maprik	214	Ch	3.38S	143.03 E
Mapuera, Rio-	202	Gd	1.05S	57.02W
Maputo [3]	172	Ee	26.00S	32.30 E
Maputo (Lourenço Marques)	160	Kk	25.58S	32.34 E
Maputo, Baia de-	158	Kk	26.05S	33.00 E
Maqên (Dawu)	152	He	34.29N	100.01 E
Maqran, Wādī al-	164	Ie	20.55N	47.12 E
Maqu	152	He	34.05N	101.45 E
Maquan He/Damqog Kanbab	152	Df	29.36N	84.09 E
Maquela do Zombo	160	Ii	6.03S	15.08 E
Maquinchao	206	Gf	41.15S	68.44W
Maquoketa	186	Ke	42.04N	90.40W
Mar, Serra do-	198	Lh	25.00S	48.00W
Mara [3]	170	Fc	2.30S	34.00 E
Mara	170	Fc	1.31S	33.56 E
Maraã	202	Ed	1.50S	65.22W
Marab	168	Fc	14.54N	37.55 E
Marabá	202	Ie	5.21S	49.07W
Marabahan	150	Fg	3.00S	114.45 E
Marabá Paulista	204	Gf	22.06S	51.56W
Maracá, Ilha de-	202	Hc	2.05N	50.25W
Maracaibo	200	Id	10.40N	71.37W
Maracaibo, Lago de- = Maracaibo, Lake- (EN)	198	Ie	9.50N	71.30W
Maracaibo, Lake- (EN) = Maracaibo, Lago de-	198	Ie	9.50N	71.30W
Maracaju	202	Gh	21.38S	55.09W
Maracaju, Serra de- [Braz.]	198	Kh	21.00S	55.00W
Maracaju, Serra de- [S.Amer.]	204	Ef	23.57S	55.01W
Maracanã	202	Id	0.46S	47.27W
Maracás	202	Jf	13.26S	40.27W
Maracay	200	Jd	10.15N	67.36W
Marādah	164	Cd	29.14N	19.13 E
Maradi	160	Hg	13.29N	7.06 E
Maradi [2]	166	Gc	14.15N	7.15 E
Marāgheh	144	Gb	37.23N	46.40 E
Marāh	144	Gd	25.04N	45.28 E
Maraho	168	Bb	18.21N	17.28 E
Marahuaca, Cerro-	198	Je	3.34N	65.27W
Marajó, Baia de-	198	Lf	1.00S	48.30W
Marajó, Ilha de-	198	Lf	1.00S	49.30W
Marakei Atoll	208	Id	1.58N	173.25 E
Maralal	170	Gb	1.06N	36.42 E
Maralinga	212	Gf	30.13S	131.35 E
Maralwexi/Bachu	152	Cd	39.46N	78.15 E
Maramag	150	He	7.46N	125.00 E
Maramasike Island	214	Gi	9.30S	161.25 E
Maramba	160	Jj	17.51S	25.52 E
Marampa	166	Cd	8.41N	12.28W
Maramureș [2]	130	Gb	47.40N	24.00 E
Maranchón	126	Jc	41.03N	2.12W
Marānd	144	Gb	38.26N	45.46 E
Marandellas	172	Ec	18.10S	31.36 E
Marang	150	De	5.12N	103.13 E
Maranhão [2]	202	Je	5.00S	45.00W
Maranhão, Rio-	202	If	14.34S	49.02W
Marano, Laguna di-	128	He	45.44N	13.10 E
Maranoa River	212	Je	27.50S	148.37 E
Marañón, Rio-	198	If	4.30S	73.35W
Marans	122	Fh	46.18N	1.00W
Marão	172	Ed	24.18S	34.07 E
Marão, Serra do-	126	Ec	41.15N	7.55W
Maraoué	166	Dd	6.54N	5.31W
Marapanim	202	Id	0.42S	47.42W
Marapi, Gunung-	150	Dg	0.23S	100.28 E
Marargiu, Capo-	128	Cj	40.20N	8.23 E
Marari, Serra do-	204	Gh	27.30S	51.00W
Mara Rosa	204	Ha	13.58S	49.09W
Mărășești	130	Kd	45.53N	27.14 E
Maratea	128	Jk	39.59N	15.43 E
Marathon	180	Ig	48.46N	86.26W
Marathon	186	Ek	30.12N	103.15W
Marathón	130	Gk	38.09N	23.58 E
Maratua, Pulau-	150	Gf	2.15N	118.36 E
Marau	204	Fi	28.27S	52.12W
Maravari	219a	Cb	7.54S	156.44 E
Marāveh Tappeh	146	Pd	37.55N	55.57 E
Maravilha	204	Fh	26.47S	53.09W
Maravillas Creek	186	El	29.34N	102.47W
Maravovo	219a	Dc	9.17S	159.38 E
Marāwah	164	Dc	32.29N	21.25 E
Marawi	150	He	8.13N	124.15 E
Marawī	168	Eb	18.29N	31.49 E
Marāwiḩ	146	Oj	24.18N	53.18 E
Marayes	206	Gd	31.29S	67.20W
Marbella	126	Hh	36.31N	4.53W
Marble Bar	212	Dd	21.11S	119.44 E
Marble Canyon	188	Jh	36.30N	111.50W
Marble Falls	186	Gk	30.34N	98.17W
Marble Hall	172	Dd	24.57S	29.13 E
Marburg	120	Ef	50.49N	8.46 E
Marca, Ponta da-	158	Ij	16.31S	11.42 E
Marcal	120	Ni	47.38N	17.32 E
Marcala	194	Df	14.07N	88.00W
Marçal Dağları	130	Kl	37.09N	28.00 E
Marcali	120	Nj	46.35N	17.25 E
March	118	Ni	52.33N	0.06 E
March	120	Mh	48.10N	16.59 E
Marche	122	Hh	46.10N	1.30 E
Marche = Marches (EN) [2]	128	Hh	43.30N	13.15 E
Marche, Plateau de la-	122	Hh	46.16N	1.30 E
Marche-en-Famenne	122	Ld	50.14N	5.20 E
Marchena	126	Gg	37.20N	5.24W
Marchena, Isla-	202a	Aa	0.20N	90.30W
Marches (EN) = Marche [2]	128	Hh	43.30N	13.15 E
Marchesato	128	Kk	39.05N	17.00 E
Marchfeld	128	Kb	48.15N	16.40 E
Mar Chiquita, Laguna-	204	Dm	37.37S	57.24W
Mar Chiquita, Laguna-	198	Ji	30.42S	62.36W
Marciana Marina	128	Eh	42.48N	10.12 E
Marcigny	122	Kh	46.16N	4.02 E
Marcilly-sur-Eure	124	Df	48.49N	1.21 E
Marcinelle, Charleroi-	124	Gd	50.25N	4.28 E
Marck	124	Dd	50.57N	1.57 E
Marcoing	124	Fd	50.07N	3.11 E
Marcos Juaréz	206	Fd	32.42S	62.06W
Marcus Baker, Mount-	178	Jd	61.26N	147.45W
Marcus Island (EN) = Minami-Tori-Shima	208	Gb	26.32N	142.09 E
Marcy, Mount-	182	Mc	44.07N	73.56W
Mardakert	132	Oi	40.12N	46.52 E
Mardakjan	132	Qi	40.29N	50.12 E
Mardān	148	Eb	34.09N	71.52 E
Mardarovka	130	Mb	47.30N	29.40 E
Mar del Plata	200	Ki	38.01S	57.35W
Marden	124	Cc	51.10N	0.30 E
Mardin	144	Fb	37.18N	40.44 E
Mardin Dağları	146	Id	37.20N	41.00 E
Maré, Ile-	208	Hg	21.30S	168.00 E
Mare, Muntele-	130	Gc	46.29N	23.14 E
Marechal Cândido Rondon	204	Eg	24.34S	54.04W
Maree, Loch-	118	Hd	57.40N	5.30W
Mareeba	212	Jc	17.00S	145.26 E
Marēg	168	He	3.47N	47.18 E
Maremma	128	Fh	42.30N	11.30 E
Marennes	122	Ei	45.49N	1.07W
Marettimo	128	Gm	37.56N	12.05 E
Mareuil-en-Brie	124	Ff	48.57N	3.45 E
Marfa	182	Ge	30.18N	104.01W
Marfil, Laguna-	204	Bb	15.30S	60.20W
Margai Caka	152	Ed	35.10N	86.55 E
Marganec	136	Df	47.38N	34.40 E
Margaret River	212	Df	33.57S	115.04 E
Margarida	204	De	21.41S	56.44W
Margarita, Isla-	202	Fa	11.00N	64.00W
Margarita Belén	204	Ch	27.16S	58.58W
Margaritión	130	Dj	39.21N	20.26 E
Margate [Eng.-U.K.]	118	Oj	51.24N	1.24 E
Margate [S.Afr.]	172	Ef	30.55S	30.15 E
Margeride, Monts de la-	122	Jj	44.50N	3.25 E
Marghera, Venezia-	128	Ge	45.28N	12.44 E
Margherita di Savoia	128	Ki	41.22N	16.09 E
Margherita Peak	158	Kh	0.22N	29.51 E
Marghine, Catena del-	128	Cj	40.20N	8.50 E
Marghita	130	Fb	47.21N	22.20 E
Marghūb, Kūh-e-	146	Qf	33.06N	57.30 E
Margilan	136	Hg	40.28N	71.46 E
Margina	130	Fd	45.51N	22.16 E
Marguerite Bay	222	Qe	68.30S	68.30W
Margut	124	He	49.35N	5.16 E
Marha	138	Hd	60.35N	123.10 E
Marha	140	Nc	63.20N	118.50 E
Mari	146	Ee	34.44N	33.18 E
Mari	146	Ie	34.39N	40.53 E
Maria Atoll [Fr.Poly.]	208	Ng	22.00S	136.10W
Maria Atoll [Fr.Poly.]	208	Lg	21.48S	154.41W
Maria Cleofas, Isla-	192	Fg	21.16N	106.14W
Maria Elena	206	Gb	22.21S	69.40W
Mariager	116	Ch	56.39N	10.00 E
Mariager Fjord	116	Dh	56.40N	10.20 E
Maria Grande, Arroyo-	204	Ci	29.21S	58.45W
Maria Ignacia	204	Cm	37.24S	59.30W
Maria Island [Austl.]	212	Jh	42.40S	148.05 E
Maria Island [Austl.]	212	Hb	14.55S	135.40 E
Maria Island [St.Luc.]	197k	Bb	13.44N	60.56W
Mariakani	170	Gc	3.52S	39.28 E
Maria Laach	124	Jd	50.25N	7.15 E
Maria Madre, Isla-	192	Fg	21.35N	106.33W
Maria Magdalena, Isla-	192	Fg	21.25N	106.25W
Mariana Islands	208	Fc	16.00N	145.30 E
Marianao	190	Hd	23.05N	82.26W
Mariana Trench (EN)	106	Ih	14.00N	147.30 E
Marianna [Ar.-U.S.]	186	Ki	34.46N	90.46W
Marianna [Fl.-U.S.]	184	Ej	30.47N	85.14W
Mariannelund	116	Fg	57.37N	15.34 E
Mariano I. Loza	204	Ci	29.22S	58.12W
Mariánské Lázně	120	Ig	49.58N	12.43 E
Marias, Islas-	174	Ig	21.25N	106.28W
Marias Pass	188	Ib	48.19N	113.21W
Marias River	182	Eb	47.56N	110.30W
Maria Theresa Reef	208	Lh	36.58S	151.23W
Mariato, Punta-	190	Hg	7.13N	80.53W
Maria van Diemen, Cape-	218	Ea	34.29S	172.39 E
Mariazell	128	Jc	47.46N	15.19 E
Ma'rib	144	Gf	15.30N	45.21 E
Maribo	116	Dj	54.46N	11.31 E
Maribor	128	Jd	46.33N	15.39 E
Marica	130	Ig	42.02N	25.50 E
Marica	110	Ig	40.52N	26.12 E
Maricao	197a	Bb	18.10N	66.58W
Maricopa	188	Ij	33.04N	112.03W
Maridī	168	De	4.55N	29.28 E
Maridī	168	Dd	6.05N	29.24 E
Marié, Rio-	202	Ed	0.25S	66.26W
Marie Byrd Land (EN)	222	Nf	80.00S	120.00W
Mariec	114	Lh	56.31N	49.51 E
Marie Galante	190	Le	15.56N	61.16W
Marie-Galante, Canal de-	197e	Bc	15.55N	61.25W
Mariehamn/Maarianhamina	114	Ef	60.06N	19.57 E
Marie Louise Island	172b	Bb	6.11S	53.09 E
Mariembourg, Couvin-	124	Gd	50.06N	4.31 E
Marienburg	124	Jd	50.04N	7.08 E
Marienmünster	124	Lc	51.50N	9.13 E
Marienstatt	124	Jd	50.40N	7.49 E
Mariental	160	Ik	24.36S	17.59 E
Mariestad	114	Cg	58.43N	13.51 E
Marietta [Ga.-U.S.]	182	Ke	33.57N	84.33W
Marietta [Oh.-U.S.]	184	Gf	39.26N	81.27W
Mariga	166	Gd	9.36N	5.57 E
Marignac	122	Gl	42.55N	0.39 E
Marignane	122	Lk	43.25N	5.13 E
Marigot [Dom.]	196	Fe	15.32N	61.18W
Marigot [Guad.]	196	Ec	18.04N	63.06W
Marigot [Haiti]	194	Kd	18.14N	72.19W
Marigot [Mart.]	197h	Ab	14.49N	61.02W
Marigot [St.Luc.]	197k	Ab	13.58N	61.02W
Mariinsk	138	De	56.13N	87.45 E
Mariinski Posad	114	Lh	56.08N	47.48 E
Mariinskoje	138	Jf	51.43N	140.19 E
Marijampole (Kapsukas)	114	Fi	54.33N	23.23 E
Marijskaja respublika	136	Ed	56.40N	48.00 E
Marília	206	Jb	22.13S	50.01W
Mariluz	204	Fg	24.02S	53.13W
Marimba	170	Cd	8.22S	17.02 E
Marimbondo, Cachoeira do-	204	He	20.18S	49.10W
Marin	126	Db	42.23N	8.42W
Marin, Cul-de-Sac du-	197h	Bc	14.27N	60.53W
Marina di Catanzaro, Catanzaro-	128	Kl	38.49N	16.36 E
Marina di Gioiosa Ionica	128	Kl	38.18N	16.20 E
Marina di Leuca, Castrignano del Capo-	128	Mk	39.48N	18.21 E
Marina di Pisa	128	Eg	43.40N	10.16 E
Marina di Ravenna	128	Gf	44.29N	12.17 E
Marina Gorka	136	Ce	53.31N	28.12 E
Marinduque	150	Hd	13.24N	121.58 E
Marineland	184	Gk	29.43N	81.12W
Marines	124	De	49.09N	1.59 E
Marinette	182	Jb	45.06N	87.38W
Maringá	200	Kh	23.25S	51.55W
Maringa	158	Ih	1.14N	19.48 E
Marinha Grande	126	De	39.45N	8.56W
Marino [It.]	128	Gi	41.46N	12.39 E
Marino [Van.]	219b	Db	14.59S	168.03 E
Marins, Pico dos-	204	Jf	22.27S	45.10W
Marinsko	116	Mf	58.46N	28.39 E
Marion	158	Km	46.36S	37.55 E
Marion [Al.-U.S.]	184	Di	32.32N	87.26W
Marion [Ia.-U.S.]	186	Ke	42.02N	91.36W
Marion [Il.-U.S.]	186	Lh	37.44N	88.56W
Marion [In.-U.S.]	184	Ee	40.33N	85.40W
Marion [Oh.-U.S.]	182	Kc	40.35N	83.08W
Marion [S.C.-U.S.]	184	Hh	34.11N	79.23W
Marion [Va.-U.S.]	184	Gg	36.51N	81.30W
Marion, Lake-	184	Gi	33.30N	80.25W
Marion Reefs	208	Gf	19.10S	152.20 E
Maripa	202	Eb	7.26N	65.09W
Mariposa	188	Fh	37.29N	119.58W
Mariquita, Cerro-	192	Jf	23.13N	98.22W
Marisa	150	Hf	0.28N	121.56 E
Mariscala	204	El	34.03S	54.47W
Mariscal Estigarribia	206	Hb	22.02S	60.38W
Marismas, Puerto de las-	126	Ff	38.02N	6.12W
Maritime	166	Fd	6.30N	1.20 E
Mariupol'	112	Jf	47.06N	37.33 E
Mariusa, Caño	196	Fh	9.43N	61.26W
Mariusa, Isla-	196	Fh	9.39N	61.19W
Marīvan	146	Le	35.31N	46.10 E
Marjamaa/Märjamaa	116	Kf	58.54N	24.21 E
Märjamaa/Marjamaa	116	Kf	58.54N	24.21 E
Marjanovka [Russia]	136	He	54.58N	72.38 E
Marjanovka [Ukr.]	120	Uf	50.23N	24.55 E
Mark	124	Gc	51.39N	4.39 E
Mark [Ger.]	124	Jc	51.13N	7.36 E
Mark [Swe.]	116	Eg	57.35N	12.35 E
Marka	160	Lh	1.43N	44.46 E
Markako, ozero-	136	If	48.45N	85.50 E
Markala	166	Dc	13.39N	6.05W
Markam (Gartog)	152	Gf	29.32N	98.33 E
Markaryd	114	Ch	56.26N	13.36 E
Markazi [3]	144	Hb	35.30N	51.30 E
Marken	124	Hb	52.27N	5.05 E
Markerwaard	124	Hb	52.31N	5.15 E
Market Deeping	124	Bb	52.40N	0.18W
Market Harborough	118	Mi	52.29N	0.55W
Markham, Mount-	222	Kg	82.51S	161.21 E
Markham Bay	180	Kd	63.30N	71.40W
Markham River	212	Ja	6.35S	146.25 E
Marki				
Märkische Schweiz				
Markit				
Markounda	168	Bd	7.37N	16.59 E
Markovac	130	Ee	44.14N	21.06 E
Markovka	132	Ke	49.31N	39.32 E
Markovo	142	Tc	64.40N	170.25 E
Markoye	166	Fc	14.39N	0.02 E
Marksburg	124	Jd	50.16N	7.40 E
Marksville	186	Jk	31.08N	92.04W
Marktoberdorf	120	Gi	47.47N	10.37 E
Marktredwitz	120	If	50.00N	12.05 E
Markulešty	130	Lb	47.51N	28.07 E
Marl	120	De	51.39N	7.05 E
Marlagne	124	Gd	50.25N	4.40 E
Marlborough [2]	218	Ed	41.50S	173.40 E
Marlborough [Austl.]	212	Jd	22.49S	149.53 E
Marlborough [Guy.]	196	Gi	7.29N	58.38W
Marle	122	Je	49.44N	3.46 E
Marlin	186	Hk	31.18N	96.53W
Marlinton	184	Gf	38.14N	80.06W
Marlow [Eng.-U.K.]	124	Bc	51.34N	0.46W
Marlow [Ok.-U.S.]	186	Hi	34.39N	97.57W
Marmande	122	Gj	44.30N	0.10 E
Marmara	146	Bb	40.35N	27.33 E
Marmara, Sea of- (EN) = Marmara Denizi	110	Ig	40.40N	28.15 E
Marmara Adası	146	Bb	40.38N	27.37 E
Marmara Denizi = Marmara, Sea of- (EN)	110	Ig	40.40N	28.15 E
Marmara Ereğlisi	130	Ki	40.58N	27.57 E
Marmara Gölü	130	Lk	38.37N	28.02 E
Marmarica (EN) = Barqah al Bahrīyah	158	Je	31.40N	24.30 E
Marmaris	144	Cb	36.51N	28.16 E
Marmelos, Rio dos-	202	Fe	6.08S	61.47W
Marmion Lake	186	Kb	48.54N	91.30W
Marmolada	128	Fd	46.26N	11.51 E
Marmora	184	Ic	44.29N	77.41W
Marmore, Cascata delle-	128	Gh	42.35N	12.45 E
Marne	120	Ec	53.57N	9.00 E
Marne [3]	122	Kf	48.55N	4.10 E
Marne	110	Gf	48.49N	2.24 E
Marne à la Saône, Canal de la-	122	Kf	48.44N	4.36 E
Marne au Rhin, Canal de la-	122	Nf	48.35N	7.47 E
Mårnes	114	Dc	67.09N	14.06 E
Marneuli	132	Ni	41.29N	44.45 E
Maro	168	Bd	8.25N	18.46 E
Maro	168	Bb	19.23N	16.38 E
Maroa	202	Ec	2.43N	67.33W
Maroantsetra	160	Lj	15.27S	49.44 E
Marokau Atoll	216	Mc	18.02S	142.17W
Marolambo	172	Hd	20.04S	48.08 E
Maromandia	172	Hb	14.11S	48.06 E
Maromme	122	He	49.28N	1.02 E
Maromokotro	172	Hb	14.01S	48.58 E
Maroni, Fleuve-	198	Ke	5.45N	53.58W
Marónia	130	Ii	40.55N	25.31 E
Maronne	122	Hi	45.04N	1.56 E
Maroochydore	212	Ke	26.39S	153.06 E
Maro Reef	208	Jb	25.25N	170.35W
Maros	150	Gg	5.00S	119.34 E
Maros	130	Dc	46.15N	20.12 E
Maroua	160	Ig	10.36N	14.20 E
Marovoay	172	Hc	16.06S	46.37 E
Marowijne River	202	Hb	5.45N	53.58W
Marqādah	146	Ie	35.44N	40.46 E
Mar Qu	152	He	31.58N	101.54 E
Marquard	172	De	28.54S	27.28 E
Marquenterre	124	Dd	50.20N	1.41 E
Marquesas Islands (EN) = Marquises, Iles-	208	Ne	9.00S	139.30W
Marquette	182	Jb	46.33N	87.24W
Marquion	124	Fd	50.13N	3.05 E
Marquis [Gren.]	197p	Bb	12.06N	61.37W
Marquis [St.Luc.]	197k	Ba	14.02N	60.55W
Marquis, Cape-	197k	Ba	14.03N	60.54W
Marquise	124	Dd	50.49N	1.42 E
Marquises, Iles- = Marquesas Islands (EN)	208	Ne	9.00S	139.30W
Marracuene	172	Ee	25.44S	32.41 E
Marradi	128	Ff	44.04N	11.37 E
Marrah, Jabal-	158	Jg	13.04N	24.21 E
Marrak	164	Hf	16.26N	41.54 E
Marrakech	160	Ge	31.38N	8.00W
Marrakech [3]	162	Fc	32.00N	8.00W
Marrawah	212	Ih	40.56S	144.41 E
Marree	210	Eg	29.39S	138.04 E
Marreh, Kūh-e-	146	Oh	29.15N	52.20 E
Marrero	186	Kl	29.54N	90.07W
Marresalja	134	Mb	69.44N	66.59 E
Marresal'skije Koški, ostrova-	134	Mb	69.30N	67.10 E
Marromeu	172	Fc	18.17S	35.56 E
Marrti	114	Gc	67.28N	28.22 E
Marrupa	172	Fb	13.12S	37.30 E
Marsá al 'Alam	164	Fd	25.05N	34.54 E
Marsá al Burayqah	164	Cc	30.25N	19.35 E
Marsá al Uwayjah	164	Cc	30.55N	17.52 E
Marsa Ben Mehidi	126	Ji	35.05N	2.11W
Marsabit	160	Kh	2.20N	37.59 E
Marsala	128	Gm	37.48N	12.26 E
Marsá Maṭrūḩ	160	Je	31.21N	27.14 E
Marsá Sha'b	168	Fa	22.52N	35.47 E
Marsá Umm Ghayj	146	Fj	25.38N	34.30 E
Marsberg	120	Ee	51.27N	8.51 E
Marsciano	128	Gh	42.54N	12.20 E
Marsdiep	124	Gb	52.58N	4.45 E
Marseille = Marseilles (EN)	112	Gg	43.18N	5.24 E
Marseille-en-Beauvaisis	122	He	49.35N	1.57 E
Marseilles (EN) = Marseille	112	Gg	43.18N	5.24 E
Marshall [Ak.-U.S.]	178	Gd	61.52N	162.04W
Marshall [Ar.-U.S.]	186	Ji	35.55N	92.38W
Marshall [Il.-U.S.]	186	Mg	39.23N	87.42W
Marshall [Lbr.]	166	Cd	6.09N	10.23W
Marshall [Mn.-U.S.]	182	Hc	44.27N	95.47W
Marshall [Mo.-U.S.]	186	Jg	39.07N	93.12W
Marshall [Tx.-U.S.]	182	Ie	32.33N	94.23W
Marshall Islands [1]	210	Hd	9.00N	168.00 E
Marshall Islands	208	Hd	9.00N	168.00 E
Marshall River	212	Hd	22.59S	136.59 E
Marshalltown	182	Ic	42.03N	92.54W
Marshfield	186	Kd	44.40N	90.10W
Marsh Harbour	190	Ic	26.33N	77.03W
Mārshinān, Kūh-e-	146	Of	32.53N	52.24 E
Marsh Island	186	Kl	29.35N	91.53W

Index Symbols

[1] Independent Nation
[2] State, Region
[3] District, County
[4] Municipality
[5] Colony, Dependency
Continent
Physical Region
Historical or Cultural Region
Mount, Mountain
Volcano
Hill
Mountains, Mountain Range
Hills, Escarpment
Plateau, Upland
Pass, Gap
Plain, Lowland
Delta
Salt Flat
Valley, Canyon
Crater, Cave
Karst Features
Depression
Polder
Desert, Dunes
Forest, Woods
Heath, Steppe
Oasis
Cape, Point
Coast, Beach
Cliff
Peninsula
Isthmus
Sandbank
Island
Atoll
Rock, Reef
Islands, Archipelago
Rocks, Reefs
Coral Reef
Well, Spring
Geyser
River, Stream
Waterfall, Rapids
River Mouth, Estuary
Lake
Salt Lake
Intermittent Lake
Reservoir
Swamp, Pond
Canal
Glacier
Ice Shelf, Pack Ice
Ocean
Sea
Gulf, Bay
Strait, Fjord
Lagoon
Bank
Seamount
Tablemount
Ridge
Shelf
Basin
Escarpment, Sea Scarp
Fracture
Trench, Abyss
National Park, Reserve
Point of Interest
Recreation Site
Cave, Cavern
Historic Site
Ruins
Wall, Walls
Church, Abbey
Temple
Scientific Station
Railway station
Airport
Port
Military installation
Lighthouse
Mine
Tunnel
Dam, Bridge

Marsica	128	Hi	41.55N	13.35 E
Marsico Nuovo	128	Jj	40.25N	15.44 E
Marsjaty	134	Jf	60.05N	60.29 E
Marsland	186	Ee	42.29N	103.16W
Mars-la-Tour	124	He	49.06N	5.54 E
Marson	124	Gf	48.55N	4.32 E
Märsta	116	Ge	59.37N	17.51 E
Marstal	116	Dj	54.51N	10.31 E
Marstrand	116	Dg	57.53N	11.35 E
Marta	128	Fh	42.14N	11.42 E
Martaban	148	Je	16.32N	97.37 E
Martaban, Gulf of- (EN)	140	Lh	16.30N	97.00 E
Martap	166	Hd	6.54N	13.03 E
Martapura [Indon.]	150	Dg	4.19S	104.22 E
Martapura [Indon.]	150	Fg	3.25S	114.51 E
Martelange/Martelingen	124	He	49.50N	5.44 E
Martelingen/Martelange	124	He	49.50N	5.44 E
Martés, Sierra de-	126	Le	39.20N	0.57W
Martha's Vineyard	182	Mc	41.25N	70.40W
Martigny	128	Bd	46.06N	7.05 E
Martigues	122	Lk	43.24N	5.03 E
Martil	126	Gi	35.37N	5.17W
Martim Vaz, Ilhas-	198	Nh	20.30S	28.51W
Martin	126	Lc	41.18N	0.19W
Martin [Slvk.]	120	Og	49.04N	18.55 E
Martin [S.D.-U.S.]	182	Gc	43.10N	101.44W
Martin [Tn.-U.S.]	184	Cg	36.21N	88.51W
Martina Franca	128	Lj	40.42N	17.20 E
Martinez de Hoz	204	Bl	35.19S	61.37W
Martinez de la Torre	192	Kg	20.04N	97.03W
Martin Garcia, Isla-	204	Cl	34.11S	58.15W
Martin Hills	222	Pg	82.04S	88.01W
Martinho Campos	204	Jd	19.20S	45.13W
Martinique [5]	176	Mh	14.40N	61.00W
Martinique	174	Mh	14.40N	61.00W
Martinique, Canal de la-= Martinique Passage (EN)	190	Le	15.10N	61.20W
Martinique Passage	196	Fe	15.10N	61.20W
Martinique Passage (EN)= Martinique, Canal de la-	190	Le	15.10N	61.20W
Martin Lake	184	Ei	32.50N	85.55W
Martin Peninsula	222	Of	74.25S	114.10W
Martinsburg	184	If	39.28N	77.59W
Martins Ferry	184	Ge	40.07N	80.45W
Martinsville [In.-U.S.]	184	Df	39.26N	86.25W
Martinsville [Va.-U.S.]	182	Ld	36.43N	79.53W
Marton	218	Fd	40.05S	175.23 E
Martos	126	Ig	37.43N	3.58W
Martre, Lac la-	180	Fd	63.20N	118.00W
Martuk	136	Fe	50.47N	56.31 E
Martuni	132	Ni	40.06N	45.18 E
Maru	166	Gc	12.21N	6.24 E
Marud	148	Ee	18.19N	72.58 E
Marudi	150	Ff	4.11N	114.19 E
Marudu, Teluk-	150	Ge	6.45N	116.55 E
Marugame	156	Cd	34.18N	133.47 E
Maruko	156	Fc	36.19N	138.15 E
Mārūn	146	Mg	31.02N	49.36 E
Marungu, Monts-	158	Ji	7.42S	30.00 E
Maruoka	156	Ec	36.09N	136.16 E
Maruseppu	156a	Ca	44.01N	143.19 E
Marutea Atoll [Fr.Poly.] [0]	208	Ng	21.30S	135.34W
Marutea Atoll [Fr.Poly.] [0]	208	Mf	17.00S	143.10W
Maruyama-Gawa	156	Dd	35.40N	134.50 E
Marvão	126	Ee	39.24N	7.23W
Marvast	146	Pg	30.30N	54.15 E
Marvast, Kavīr-e-	146	Pg	30.20N	54.25 E
Mårvatn	116	Cd	60.10N	8.15 E
Marv-Dasht	144	Hd	29.50N	52.40 E
Marvejols	122	Jj	44.33N	3.17 E
Marvine, Mount-	188	Jg	38.40N	111.39W
Marx	132	Od	51.42N	46.46 E
Mary	142	If	37.36N	61.50 E
Maryborough [Austl.]	210	Gg	25.32S	152.42 E
Maryborough [Austl.]	212	Ig	37.03S	143.45 E
Marydale	172	Ce	29.23S	22.05 E
Maryjskaja oblast [3]	136	Gh	37.15N	62.30 E
Maryland [2]	182	Ld	39.00N	76.45W
Maryland [3]	166	De	4.45N	8.00W
Maryport	118	Jg	54.43N	3.30W
Mary River	212	Gb	12.53S	131.38 E
Marysville [Ca.-U.S.]	188	Eg	39.09N	121.35W
Marysville [Ks.-U.S.]	186	Hg	39.51N	96.39W
Marysville [N.B.-Can.]	184	Nc	45.59N	66.35W
Marysville [Oh.-U.S.]	184	Fe	40.13N	83.22W
Marysville [Wa.-U.S.]	188	Db	48.03N	122.11W
Maryville [Mo.-U.S.]	182	Ic	40.21N	94.52W
Maryville [Tn.-U.S.]	184	Fh	35.46N	83.58W
Marzūq	160	If	25.55N	13.55 E
Marzūq, Ḥamādat-	164	Bd	26.00N	12.30 E
Marzūq, Ṣaḥrā'-	158	If	24.30N	13.00 E
Masachapa	194	Dh	11.47N	86.31W
Masāhim, Kūh-e-	146	Pg	30.21N	55.20 E
Masai Steppe	158	Ki	4.45S	37.00 E
Masaka	170	Fc	0.20S	31.44 E
Masākin	162	Jb	35.44N	10.35 E
Masalembo, Kepulauan-	150	Fh	5.30S	114.26 E
Masally	136	Eh	39.01N	48.40 E
Masalog, Puntan-	220b	Ba	15.01N	145.41 E
Masamba	150	Hg	2.33S	120.20 E
Masan	152	Md	35.11N	128.24 E
Masasi	160	Kj	10.43S	38.48 E
Masaya	190	Gf	11.58N	86.06W
Masaya [3]	194	Dh	12.00N	86.10W
Masbate	150	Hd	12.10N	123.35 E
Masbate	140	Oh	12.15N	123.30 E
Mascara	162	Hb	35.24N	0.08 E
Mascara [3]	162	Hb	35.30N	0.15 E
Mascareignes, Iles-/ Mascarene Islands	158	Mk	21.00S	57.00 E
Mascarene Basin (EN)	106	Fk	15.00S	56.00 E
Mascarene Islands/ Mascareignes, Iles-	158	Mk	21.00S	57.00 E
Mascarene Plateau (EN)	106	Gk	10.00S	60.00 E
Mascota	192	Gg	20.32N	104.49W
Mas-d'Azil, Le-	122	Hk	43.05N	1.22 E
Masee, Island-/Oiléan Mhic Aodha	118	Hg	54.50N	5.50W
Masela, Pulau-	150	Ih	8.09S	129.50 E
Maseru	160	Jk	29.28S	27.29 E
Maşfūţ	146	Qk	24.48N	56.06 E
Mashābih	146	Gj	25.37N	36.32 E
Mashan	154	Kb	45.12N	130.32 E
Mashava	172	Ed	20.02S	30.29 E
Mashhad	142	Hf	36.18N	59.36 E
Mashike	154	Pc	43.51N	141.31 E
Mashiki	156	Be	32.47N	130.50 E
Mashīz	146	Qh	29.56N	56.37 E
Mashkel	144	Jd	28.02N	63.25 E
Mashonaland North [3]	172	Ec	17.00S	31.00 E
Mashonaland South [3]	172	Ec	18.00S	31.00 E
Mashra' ar Raqq	168	Dd	8.25N	29.16 E
Mashū-Ko	156a	Db	43.35N	144.30 E
Masiaca	192	Ed	26.45N	109.18W
Masīlah, Wādī al-	140	Hh	15.10N	51.08 E
Masi-Manimba	170	Cc	4.46S	17.55 E
Masindi	170	Fb	1.42N	31.43 E
Maşīrah, Jazīrat-	140	Hg	20.29N	58.33 E
Maşīrah, Khalīj-	140	Hg	20.15N	57.40 E
Masisi	170	Ec	1.24S	28.49 E
Masjed-Soleymān	144	Gc	31.58N	49.18 E
Mask, Lough-/Loch Measca	118	Dh	53.35N	9.20W
Maskanah	146	Hd	36.01N	38.05 E
Maskelynes, Iles-	219b	Cc	16.32S	167.49 E
Maşloc	130	Ed	46.00N	21.27 E
Maslovare	128	Lf	44.34N	17.33 E
Masoala, Cap-	158	Mj	15.59S	50.13 E
Masoala, Presqu'île de-	172	Ic	15.40S	50.12 E
Mason	186	Gk	30.45N	99.14W
Mason Bay	218	Bg	46.55S	167.45 E
Mason City	176	Je	43.09N	93.12W
Masovia (EN)= Mazowsze	110	Ie	52.40N	20.20 E
Masparro, Rio-	194	Mi	8.04N	69.26W
Masqaţ=Muscat (EN)	142	Hg	23.29N	58.33 E
Massa	128	Ef	44.01N	10.09 E
Massachusetts [2]	182	Mc	42.15N	71.50W
Massachusetts Bay	184	Ld	42.20N	70.50W
Massaciuccoli, Lago di-	128	Eg	43.50N	10.20 E
Massafra	128	Lj	40.35N	17.07 E
Massaguet	168	Bc	12.28N	15.26 E
Massakori	168	Bc	13.00N	15.44 E
Massa Marittima	128	Eg	43.03N	10.53 E
Massangano	170	Bd	9.37S	14.17 E
Massangena	172	Ed	21.32S	32.57 E
Massapê	202	Jd	3.31S	40.19W
Massawa (EN)=Mitsiwa	160	Kg	15.37N	39.39 E
Massena	182	Mc	44.56N	74.57W
Massénya	168	Bc	11.24N	16.10 E
Masset	180	Ef	54.02N	132.09W
Masseube	122	Gk	43.26N	0.35 E
Massey Sound	180	Ia	78.00N	94.00W
Massiac	122	Ji	45.15N	3.13 E
Massiaru	116	Kg	57.52N	24.27 E
Massillon	184	Ge	40.48N	81.32W
Massinga	172	Fd	23.20S	35.22 E
Masson Island	222	Ge	66.08S	96.34 E
Massuma	170	De	14.05S	22.00 E
Mastābah	164	Ge	20.49N	39.26 E
Maştaga	132	Pi	40.32N	49.59 E
Masterton	216	Eh	40.57S	175.39 E
Mastūrah	164	Ge	23.06N	38.50 E
Masuda	152	Ne	34.40N	131.51 E
Māsūleh	146	Md	37.10N	48.59 E
Masurai, Gunung-	150	Dg	2.30S	101.51 E
Masuria (EN)	110	Ie	53.50N	21.30 E
Masurian Lakes (EN)	110	Ie	53.45N	21.45 E
Masvingo	160	Kk	20.05S	30.50 E
Masvingo [3]	172	Ed	21.00S	31.00 E
Maşyāf	146	Ge	35.03N	36.21 E
Maszewo	120	Lc	53.29N	15.02 E
Matabé, Cap-	219b	Cb	15.38S	166.46 E
Matabeleland North [3]	172	Dc	19.00S	27.30 E
Matabeleland South [3]	172	Dd	21.00S	29.30 E
Matachel	126	Ff	38.50N	6.17W
Matachewan	180	Jg	47.56N	80.39W
Matacu	204	Bc	17.21S	61.28W
Matadi	160	Ii	5.49S	13.27 E
Matador	186	Fi	34.01N	100.49W
Matagalpa	176	Kh	12.53N	85.57W
Matagalpa [3]	194	Eg	13.00N	85.30W
Matagami	180	Jg	49.45N	77.35W
Matagami, Lac-	184	Ia	49.54N	77.32W
Mata Gassile	168	Ge	2.30N	42.16 E
Matagorda Bay	186	Hl	28.35N	96.20W
Matagorda Island	182	Hf	28.15N	96.30W
Matagorda Peninsula	186	Hl	28.32N	96.07W
Mataiea	221e	Fc	17.46S	149.25W
Mataiva Atoll [0]	208	Mf	14.53S	148.40W
Mataj	136	Hf	45.51N	78.43 E
Matak, Pulau-	150	Ef	3.18N	106.16 E
Matakana Island	218	Kb	37.35S	176.05 E
Matala	170	Ce	14.43S	15.02 E
Matalaa, Pointe-	220h	Bc	13.20S	176.08W
Matale	148	Gg	7.28N	80.37 E
Mataliele	172	Df	30.24S	28.43 E
Matam	166	Cb	15.40N	13.15W
Matamey	166	Gc	13.26N	8.28 E
Matamoros [Mex.]	176	Jg	25.53N	97.30W
Matamoros [Mex.]	190	Dc	25.32N	103.15W
Matana, Danau-	150	Hg	2.28S	121.20 E
Ma'ṭan as Sarra	164	De	21.41N	21.52 E
Matancita	192	De	25.09N	111.59W
Matane	180	Kg	48.51N	67.32W
Matankari	166	Fc	13.46N	4.01 E
Matanza	204	Cl	34.33S	58.35W
Matanzas	176	Kg	23.03N	81.35W
Matanzas [3]	194	Gb	22.40N	81.10W
Matão	204	He	21.35S	48.22W
Matapalo, Cabo-	194	Fi	8.23N	83.19W
Matapan, Cape- (EN)= Tainaron, Akra-	110	Ih	36.23N	22.29 E
Matape, Rio-	192	Dc	28.17N	110.41W
Mata Point	220k	Bb	19.07S	169.50W
Matara	148	Gg	5.56N	80.33 E
Matara	168	Fc	14.35N	39.28 E
Mataram	142	Nj	8.35S	116.07 E
Mataranka	212	Gb	14.56S	133.07 E
Mataró	126	Oc	41.32N	2.27 E
Matarraña/Matarranya	126	Mc	41.14N	0.22 E
Matarranya/Matarraña	126	Mc	41.14N	0.22 E
Mataso	219b	Dc	17.15S	168.25 E
Matatula, Cape-	221c	Cb	14.15S	170.34W
Mataura	218	Cg	46.12S	168.52 E
Mataura	218	Cg	46.34S	168.44 E
Mata-Utu	210	Jf	13.17S	176.08W
Mata-Utu, Baie de-	220h	Bb	13.19S	176.07W
Matavai	216	Gb	13.28S	172.35W
Matavera	220p	Cb	21.13S	159.44W
Mataverj	221d	Ab	27.10S	109.27W
Matawai	218	Gc	38.21S	177.32 E
Matawin, Réservoir-	184	Kb	46.45N	73.50W
Matawin, Rivière-	184	Kb	46.55N	72.55W
Maţāy	146	Dh	28.25N	30.46 E
Maţbakhayn	164	Hf	17.29N	41.48 E
Matca	130	Kd	45.51N	27.32 E
Matehuala	190	Dd	23.39N	100.39W
Matemo, Ilha-	172	Gb	12.13S	40.36 E
Matera	128	Kj	40.40N	16.36 E
Matese	128	Ii	41.25N	14.20 E
Mátészalka	120	Si	47.57N	22.20 E
Matfors	114	De	62.21N	17.02 E
Matha	122	Fi	45.52N	0.19W
Mathematicians Seamounts (EN)	190	Be	15.30N	111.00W
Matheson	184	Ga	48.32N	80.28W
Mathis	186	Hl	28.06N	97.50W
Mathrákion	130	Cj	39.46N	19.31 E
Mathura	148	Fc	27.30N	77.41 E
Mati	150	Ie	6.57N	126.13 E
Mati	130	Ch	41.39N	19.34 E
Matias Cardoso	204	Kb	14.52S	43.56W
Matias Romero	190	Ee	16.53N	95.02W
Maticora, Rio-	194	Lh	11.01N	71.09W
Matina	194	Fh	10.05N	83.17W
Matinha	202	Id	3.06S	45.02W
Māţir	162	Ib	37.03N	9.40 E
Matiyure, Rio-	196	Ci	7.36N	67.39W
Matkaselkja	116	Nc	61.57N	30.33 E
Mātmāţah	162	Ic	33.33N	9.58 E
Matnog	150	Hd	12.35N	124.05 E
Mato, Cerro-	196	Di	7.15N	65.14W
Mato, Rio-	196	Di	7.09N	65.07W
Matočkin Šar, proliv-	136	Fa	73.30N	54.55 E
Mato Grosso [2]	202	Gf	14.00S	56.00W
Mato Grosso [Braz.]	204	Dd	18.18S	57.20W
Mato Grosso [Braz.]	200	Kg	15.00S	59.57W
Mato Grosso, Planalto do- = Mato Grosso, Plateau of- (EN)	198	Kg	15.30S	56.00W
Mato Grosso, Plateau of- (EN) = Mato Grosso, Planalto do-	198	Kg	15.30S	56.00W
Mato Grosso do Sul [2]	202	Hg	20.00S	55.00W
Matos Costa	204	Gh	26.27S	51.09W
Matosinhos	126	Dc	41.11N	8.42W
Matou	154	Cj	29.50N	115.32 E
Matou→Qiuxian	154	Cf	36.50N	115.10 E
Mátra	110	If	47.53N	19.57 E
Maţraḥ	144	Ie	23.29N	58.31 E
Matrei in Osttirol	128	Gc	47.00N	12.32 E
Matsiatra	172	Hd	21.25S	45.33 E
Matsudo	154	Og	35.48N	139.55 E
Matsue	152	Nd	35.28N	133.04 E
Matsukawa [Jap.]	156	Ed	35.36N	137.53 E
Matsukawa [Jap.]	156	Gc	37.40N	140.28 E
Matsu Liehtao	152	Kf	26.05N	119.56 E
Matsumae	156a	Bc	41.26N	140.07 E
Matsumae-Hantō	156a	Bc	41.40N	140.15 E
Matsumoto	152	Od	36.14N	137.58 E
Matsunaga, Fukuyama-	156	Cd	34.27N	133.16 E
Matsuo	156	Gb	39.58N	141.02 E
Matsu-Ōminato	156a	Bc	41.16N	141.09 E
Matsusaka	154	Ng	34.34N	136.32 E
Matsushima	156	Gb	38.22N	141.04 E
Matsutō	156	Ec	36.31N	136.33 E
Matsuura	156	Ae	33.22N	129.42 E
Matsuyama	142	Pf	33.50N	132.45 E
Matsuzaki	156	Fd	34.44N	138.45 E
Mattagami Lake	184	Gb	47.57N	81.35W
Mattagami River	180	Jf	50.43N	81.30W
Mattawa	184	Hb	46.19N	78.42W
Matterhorn [Eur.]	128	Be	45.58N	7.39 E
Matterhorn [Nv.-U.S.]	188	Hf	41.49N	115.23W
Matthew, Ile-	208	Ig	22.20S	171.20 E
Matthews Ridge	202	Fb	7.30N	60.10W
Matthew Town	190	Jd	20.57N	73.40W
Mattī, Sabhat-	168	Ia	23.30N	52.00 E
Mattighofen	128	Hb	48.06N	13.09 E
Mattoon	186	Lg	39.29N	88.22W
Matua, ostrov-	138	Kg	48.00N	153.10 E
Matucana	202	Cf	11.51S	76.24W
Matuku Island	216	Ec	19.10S	179.46 E
Matundu	170	Db	4.21N	23.40 E
Matundu	170	Gd	8.50S	39.30 E
Maturin	200	Je	9.45N	63.11W
Matvejev Kurgan	132	Kf	47.34N	38.55 E
Maúa	172	Fb	13.52S	37.09 E
Maubeuge	122	Jd	50.17N	3.58 E
Ma-ubin	148	Je	16.44N	95.39 E
Maudheimvidda	222	Bf	74.00S	8.00W
Maud Seamount (EN)	222	Ce	65.00S	2.35 E
Maués	202	Gd	3.24S	57.42W
Maués, Rio-	202	Gd	3.22S	57.44W
Mau Escarpment	170	Gc	0.40S	36.02 E
Mauges, Les-	122	Fg	47.10N	1.00W
Maug Islands	208	Fb	20.01N	145.13 E
Maui Island	208	Lb	20.45N	156.20W
Mauke Island	208	Lg	20.09S	157.23W
Mau Kyun	148	Jf	12.45N	98.20 E
Mauldre	124	Df	48.59N	1.49 E
Maule [2]	206	Fe	35.45S	72.15W
Mauléon	122	Fh	46.55N	0.45W
Mauléon-Licharre	122	Fk	43.14N	0.53W
Maullín	206	Ff	41.38S	73.37W
Maumee	184	Fe	41.34N	83.39W
Maumere	150	Hh	8.37S	122.14 E
Maun	160	Jj	19.58S	23.26 E
Maun	128	If	44.26N	14.55 E
Mauna Kea	208	Lc	19.50N	155.28W
Maunaloa	221a	Db	21.08N	157.13W
Mauna Loa	221a	Fd	19.28N	155.36W
Maunath	148	Gc	25.40N	82.38 E
Maunawili	221a	Db	21.21N	157.47W
Maunga Roa	220p	Bb	21.13S	159.48W
Maungdaw	148	Id	20.49N	92.22 E
Maunoir, Lac-	180	Fc	67.30N	125.00W
Maupihaa Atoll (Mopelia, Atoll-) [0]	208	Lf	16.50S	153.55W
Maupin	188	Ed	45.11N	121.05W
Maupiti, Ile-	208	Lf	16.27S	152.15W
Maurepas, Lake-	186	Kk	30.15N	90.30W
Maures, Massif des-	122	Mk	43.16N	6.23 E
Mauriac	122	Ii	45.13N	2.20 E
Maurice, Lake-	212	Ge	29.30S	131.00 E
Maurienne	122	Mi	45.13N	6.30 E
Mauritania (EN)= Mūrītāniyā [1]	160	Fg	20.00N	12.00W
Mauriti	202	Ke	7.23S	38.46W
Mauritius [1]	160	Mj	18.00S	57.40 E
Mauritius	158	Mk	20.17S	57.33 E
Mauron	122	Df	48.05N	2.18W
Maurs	122	Ij	44.43N	2.12 E
Mauston	186	Ke	43.48N	90.05W
Mauthausen	128	Ib	48.14N	14.31 E
Mauzé-sur-le-Mignon	122	Fh	46.12N	0.40W
Mavinga	170	Df	15.47S	20.24 E
Mavita	172	Ec	19.32S	33.09 E
Mavrovoúni [Grc.]	130	Fj	39.37N	22.47 E
Mavrovoúni [Grc.]	130	Gh	41.07N	23.08 E
Mawchi	148	Je	18.49N	97.09 E
Mawei	152	Kf	26.02N	119.30 E
Mawlaik	148	Id	23.38N	94.25 E
Mawlamyine	142	Le	16.30N	97.38 E
Mawqaq	146	Ii	27.25N	41.08 E
Mawson	222	Fe	67.36S	62.53 E
Mawson Coast	222	Fe	67.40S	63.30 E
Mawson Escarpment	222	Ff	73.05S	68.10 E
Maxcanú	190	Fd	20.35N	90.01W
Maxixe	172	Fd	23.51S	35.21 E
Maxwell Bay	180	Ib	74.32N	89.00W
May, Isle of-	118	Ke	56.10N	2.30W
Maya, Pulau-	150	Eg	1.10S	109.35 E
Mayaguana Island	190	Jd	22.23N	72.57W
Mayaguana Passage	194	Kb	22.32N	73.15W
Mayagüez	190	Ke	18.12N	67.09W
Mayahi	166	Gc	13.58N	7.40 E
Mayama	170	Bc	3.51S	14.54 E
Mayāmey	146	Pd	36.24N	55.42 E
Maya Mountains	190	Ge	16.40N	88.50W
Mayapán	190	Gd	20.38N	89.27W
Mayari	194	Jc	20.40N	75.41W
Maybell	186	Bf	40.31N	108.05W
Maychew	168	Fc	12.46N	39.34 E
Mayd	168	Hc	10.57N	47.06 E
Maydān	146	Ke	34.55N	45.37 E
Maydena	212	Jh	42.55S	146.30 E
Maydī	144	Ff	16.18N	42.48 E
Mayen	120	Df	50.20N	7.13 E
Mayenne	122	Ff	48.18N	0.37W
Mayenne [3]	122	Ff	48.05N	0.40W
Mayenne	122	Fg	47.30N	0.32W
Mayfa'ah	168	Hc	14.16N	47.35 E
Mayfield	184	Cg	36.44N	88.38W
May Glacier	222	Ie	67.00S	130.00 E
Mayi He	154	Jb	45.52N	128.46 E
Maymyo	148	Jd	22.02N	96.28 E
Maynas	202	Dd	3.00S	75.00W
Mayo	176	Fc	63.35N	135.54W
Mayo/Muigheo [2]	118	Dh	53.50N	9.30W
Mayo, Mountains of-	118	Dg	54.05N	9.30W
Mayo, Rio-	192	Ed	26.45N	109.47W
Mayo Darlé	166	Hd	6.30N	11.55 E
Mayo-Kébbi [3]	168	Bd	10.00N	15.30 E
Mayo-Kébbi	168	Ad	9.18N	13.33 E
Mayoko	170	Bc	2.18S	12.49 E
Mayon, Mount-	140	Oh	13.15N	123.41 E
Mayor, Puig-/Major, Puig-	126	Oe	39.48N	2.48 E
Mayor Island	218	Gb	37.15S	176.15 E
Mayor Pablo Lagerenza	206	Ha	19.58S	60.45W
Mayotte [5]	160	Lj	12.50S	45.10 E
Mayotte/Mahoré	158	Lj	12.50S	45.10 E
May Pen	190	Ie	17.58N	77.14W
Mayraira Point	150	Hc	18.39N	120.51 E
Mayran, Laguna de-	192	He	25.45N	102.45W
Mayreau Island	197n	Bb	12.39N	61.23W
May-sur-Orne	124	Be	49.06N	0.22W
Maysville	184	Ff	38.39N	83.46W
Mayumba [Gabon]	160	Ii	3.25S	10.39 E
Mayumba [Zaire]	170	Ed	7.16S	27.03 E
Mayum La	152	De	30.35N	82.27 E
Mayville	184	Hd	42.15N	79.32W
Mayyit, Al Baḥr al-=Dead Sea (EN)	140	Ff	31.30N	35.30 E
Mazabuka	170	Ef	15.51S	27.46 E
Mazagão	202	Hd	0.07S	51.17W
Mazamet	122	Ik	43.30N	2.24 E
Māzandarān [3]	144	Hb	36.00N	54.00 E
Māzandarān, Daryā-ye-= Caspian Sea (EN)	110	Lg	42.00N	50.30 E
Mazar	152	Cd	36.27N	77.03 E
Mazara del Vallo	128	Gm	37.39N	12.35 E
Mazār-e Sharīf	142	If	36.42N	67.06 E
Mazarrón, Golfo de-	126	Kg	37.30N	1.18W
Mazartag	152	Dd	38.29N	80.50 E
Mazaruni River	202	Gb	6.25N	58.38W
Mazatenango	190	Ff	14.32N	91.30W
Mazatlán	176	Ig	23.13N	106.25W
Mažeikiai/Mažejkjaj	114	Fh	56.20N	22.22 E
Mažejkjaj/Mažeikiai	114	Fh	56.20N	22.22 E
Mazhafah, Jabal-	146	Fh	28.48N	34.57 E
Mazhūr, 'Irq al-	146	Ji	27.25N	43.55 E
Mazinga	197c	Ab	17.29N	62.58W
Mazirbe	116	Jg	57.40N	22.10 E
Mazoe	172	Ec	17.30S	30.58 E
Mazoe	158	Kj	16.32S	33.25 E
Mazomeno	170	Ec	4.55S	27.13 E
Mazong Shan	152	Gc	41.33N	97.10 E
Mazowsze	120	Qd	52.40N	20.20 E
Mazowsze=Masovia (EN)	110	Ie	52.40N	20.20 E
Mazsalaca	116	Kg	57.45N	24.59 E
Mazunga	172	Dd	21.44S	29.52 E
Mazurskie, Pojezierze-	120	Qc	53.40N	21.00 E
Mazzarino	128	Im	37.18N	14.13 E
Mba	219d	Ab	17.32S	177.42 E
Mbabane	160	Kk	26.18S	31.07 E
Mbabo, Tchabal-	166	Hd	7.16N	12.09 E
Mbacké	166	Bc	14.48N	15.55W
Mbaéré	168	Be	3.47N	17.31 E
Mbaïki	160	Ih	3.53N	18.00 E
Mbakaou	166	Hd	6.19N	12.49 E
Mbakaou, Barrage de-	166	Hd	6.25N	13.00 E
Mbala	160	Ki	8.50S	31.22 E
Mbalam	166	He	2.13N	13.49 E
Mbale	160	Kh	1.05N	34.10 E
Mbali	168	Be	4.27N	18.20 E
Mbalmayo	166	He	3.31N	11.30 E
Mbam	158	Ih	4.24N	11.17 E
Mbamba Bay	170	Fe	11.17S	34.46 E
Mbandaka	160	Ih	0.04N	18.16 E
Mbanga	166	Ge	4.30N	9.34 E
Mbanika	219a	Dc	9.05S	159.12 E
M'banza Congo	170	Bd	6.16S	14.15 E
Mbanza-Ngungu	160	Ii	5.35S	14.47 E
Mbarangandu	170	Gd	8.57S	37.24 E
Mbarara	170	Fc	0.36S	30.38 E
Mbari	168	Ce	4.34N	22.43 E
Mbatiki	219d	Bb	17.46S	179.08 E
Mbava	219a	Cb	7.49S	156.37 E
Mbé	166	Hd	7.51N	13.36 E
Mbengga	219d	Bc	18.23S	178.08 E
Mbengwi	166	Hd	6.01N	10.00 E
Mbéré	168	Bd	9.07N	16.26 E
Mbeya	160	Ki	8.54S	33.27 E
Mbeya [3]	170	Fd	8.00S	33.30 E
Mbi	168	Be	4.28N	18.07 E
Mbigou	170	Bc	1.53S	11.56 E
Mbinda	160	Ii	2.07S	12.52 E
Mbinga	170	Ge	10.56S	35.01 E
Mbingué	166	Dc	10.00N	5.54W
Mbini	166	Ge	1.34N	9.37 E
Mbini [3]	166	He	1.30N	10.00 E
Mbini	158	Ih	1.30N	10.30 E
Mbini	166	He	1.40N	9.45 E
Mboki	168	Dd	5.19N	25.58 E
Mbokonimbeti	219a	Ec	8.57S	160.05 E
Mbomo	170	Bb	0.24N	14.44 E
Mbomou=Bomu (EN) [3]	168	Cd	5.30N	23.30 E
Mbomou=Bomu (EN)	158	Jh	4.08N	22.26 E
Mborokua	219a	Dc	9.02S	158.44 E
Mbour	166	Bc	14.24N	16.58W
Mbout	162	Ef	16.01N	12.35W
Mbozi	170	Fd	9.02S	32.56 E
Mbrés	168	Bd	6.40N	19.48 E
M'Bridge	170	Bd	7.14S	12.52 E
Mbua	219d	Bb	16.48S	178.37 E
Mbuji-Mayi	160	Ji	6.09S	23.33 E
Mbulo	219a	Dc	8.46S	158.21 E
Mbulu	170	Gc	3.51S	35.32 E
Mburucuyá	204	Ci	28.03S	58.14W
Mbutha	219d	Bb	16.39S	179.51 E
Mbuyuni	170	Gd	7.23S	36.32 E
Mbwemburu	170	Gd	9.29S	39.39 E
Mcensk	136	De	53.17N	36.32 E
M'Chedallah	126	Qh	36.22N	4.16 E
Mcherrah	162	Gd	27.00N	4.30W
Mchinga	170	Gd	9.44S	39.42 E
Mchinji	170	Fe	13.48S	32.54 E
Mdandu	170	Fd	9.09S	34.42 E
M'Daourouch	128	Bn	36.05N	7.49 E
Mdennah	162	Gd	25.00N	4.50W
Mdiq	126	Gi	35.41N	5.19W
Mead	184	Fa	49.29N	83.50W
Mead, Lake-	182	Ed	36.05N	114.25W
Meade	186	Fh	37.17N	100.20W
Meade	178	Hb	70.50N	156.25W
Meade Peak	188	Je	42.30N	111.15W
Meadow Lake	180	Gf	54.07N	108.20W
Meadville	184	Ge	41.38N	80.10W
Me-akan-Dake	156a	Cb	43.23N	143.59 E
Mealhada	126	Dd	40.22N	8.27W
Mealy Mountains	180	Lf	53.20N	59.30W
Meama	221b	Ba	19.45S	174.34W
Méan, Havelange-	124	Hd	50.22N	5.20 E
Meander Reef	150	Ge	8.09N	119.14 E
Meander River	180	Fe	59.02N	117.42W
Meanguera, Isla-	194	Dg	13.12N	87.43W
Mearim, Rio-	198	Lf	3.04S	44.35W
Meath/An Mhí [2]	118	Gh	53.35N	6.40W
Meaux	122	If	48.57N	2.52 E
Mecca (EN)=Makkah	142	Fg	21.27N	39.49 E
Mechara	168	Gd	8.34N	40.28 E
Mechelen/Maasmechelen	124	Hd	50.57N	5.40 E
Mechelen/Malines	122	Kc	51.02N	4.29 E
Mecheraa-Asfa	126	Ni	35.24N	1.03 E
Mecheria	162	Gc	33.33N	0.17W
Mechernich	124	Id	50.36N	6.39 E
Mechongué	204	Cn	38.09S	58.13W
Mecidiye	130	Ji	40.38N	26.32 E
Mecitözü	146	Fb	40.31N	35.19 E
Mecklenburgischer Höhenrücken	120	Ic	53.40N	12.10 E
Mecklenburg	120	Hc	53.30N	12.00 E
Mecklenburger Bucht	120	Hb	54.20N	11.40 E
Mecklenburger Schweiz	120	Ic	53.45N	12.35 E

Mecoacán, Laguna-	192	Mh	18.20N	93.10W
Meconta	172	Fb	14.59S	39.50 E
Mecsek	120	Oj	46.10N	18.18 E
Mecubúri	172	Gb	14.10S	40.31 E
Mecúfi	172	Gb	13.17S	40.33 E
Mecula	172	Fb	12.05S	37.39 E
Médala	162	Ff	15.30N	5.37W
Medan	142	Li	3.35N	98.40 E
Médanos [Arg.]	204	Ck	33.24S	59.05W
Médanos [Arg.]	206	He	38.50S	62.41W
Medanosa, Punta-	206	Gg	48.06S	65.55W
Mede	128	Ce	45.06N	8.44 E
Médéa	162	Hb	36.16N	2.45 E
Médéa [3]	162	Hb	36.20N	3.25 E
Medebach	124	Kc	51.12N	8.43 E
Medellin	150	Hd	11.08N	123.58 E
Medellin	200	Ie	6.15N	75.35W
Medelpad	116	Gb	62.35N	16.15 E
Medemblik	124	Hb	52.46N	5.06 E
Medenica	120	Tg	49.21N	23.45 E
Mederdra	162	Df	16.54N	15.40W
Medetzız	146	Fd	37.25N	34.40 E
Medford [Or.-U.S.]	176	Ge	42.19N	122.52W
Medford [Wi.-U.S.]	186	Kd	45.09N	90.20W
Medgidia	130	Le	44.15N	28.17 E
Medi	168	Ed	5.06N	30.44 E
Media Luna, Arrecife de la-	194	Ff	15.13N	82.36W
Medianeira	204	Eg	25.17S	54.05W
Mediaş	130	Hc	46.10N	24.21 E
Medical Lake	188	Gc	47.34N	117.41W
Medicine Bow	188	Lf	41.54N	106.12W
Medicine Bow Mountains	188	Lf	41.10N	106.25W
Medicine Butte	188	Jf	41.29N	110.48W
Medicine Hat	176	Hd	50.03N	110.40W
Medicine Lake	188	Mb	48.28N	104.24W
Medicine Lodge	186	Gh	37.17N	98.35W
Međimurje	128	Kd	46.25N	16.30 E
Medina (EN)=Al Madīnah [Sau.Ar.]	142	Fg	24.28N	39.36 E
Medina Az-Zahra	126	Hg	37.52N	4.50W
Medinaceli	126	Jc	41.10N	2.26W
Medina del Campo	126	Hc	41.18N	4.55W
Medina de Rioseco	126	Gc	41.53N	5.02W
Medina-Sidonia	126	Gh	36.27N	5.55W
Medinilla, Farallon de-	208	Fc	16.01N	146.04 E
Medininkai/Medininkaj	116	Kj	54.32N	25.46 E
Medinīpur	148	Hd	22.26N	87.20 E
Medio, Arroyo del-	204	Bk	33.16S	60.15W
Mediterranean Sea (EN)= Akdeniz	110	Hh	35.00N	20.00 E
Mediterranean Sea (EN)= Khaṭikhon, Yam-	110	Hh	35.00N	20.00 E
Mediterranean Sea (EN)= Méditerranée, Mer-	110	Hh	35.00N	20.00 E
Mediterranean Sea (EN)= Mediterráneo, Mar-	110	Hh	35.00N	20.00 E
Mediterranean Sea (EN)= Mediterraneo, Mar-	110	Hh	35.00N	20.00 E
Mediterranean Sea (EN)= Mesoyéios Thálassa	110	Hh	35.00N	20.00 E
Mediterranean Sea (EN)= Mutawassiṭ, Al Baḩr al-	110	Hh	35.00N	20.00 E
Méditerranée, Mer-= Mediterranean Sea (EN)	110	Hh	35.00N	20.00 E
Mediterráneo, Mar-= Mediterranean Sea (EN)	110	Hh	35.00N	20.00 E
Mediterraneo, Mar-= Mediterranean Sea (EN)	110	Hh	35.00N	20.00 E
Mediterrani Català, Sistema- / Costeras Catalanas, Cordilleras- = Catalan Coastal Range (EN)	110	Gg	41.35N	1.40 E
Medje	170	Eb	2.25N	27.18 E
Medjerda, Monts de la-	162	Ib	36.35N	8.15 E
Mednogorsk	136	Fe	51.26N	57.40 E
Medny, ostrov-	138	Lf	54.40N	167.50 E
Médoc	122	Fi	45.00N	1.00W
Mêdog	152	Gf	29.18N	95.27 E
Médouneu	170	Bb	1.01N	10.48 E
Medveđa	130	Eg	42.51N	21.36 E
Medvedica [Russia]	114	Ih	57.05N	37.31 E
Medvedica [Russia]	110	Kf	49.35N	42.41 E
Medvednica	128	Je	45.55N	15.58 E
Medvedok	114	Mh	57.24N	50.06 E
Medvenka	132	Jd	51.27N	36.08 E
Medveži, ostrova- = Bear Islands (EN)	140	Sb	70.52N	161.26 E
Medvežjegorsk	136	Dc	62.56N	34.29 E
Medway	124	Cc	51.23N	0.31 E
Medzilaborce	120	Rg	49.16N	21.55 E
Meekatharra	210	Cg	26.36S	118.29 E
Meeker	186	Cf	40.02N	107.55W
Meerane	120	If	50.51N	12.28 E
Meerbusch	124	Ic	51.16N	6.40 E
Meerut	148	Fc	28.59N	77.42 E
Meeteetse	188	Kd	44.09N	108.52W
Mefarlane, Lake-	212	Hf	32.00S	136.40 E
Mega [Eth.]	160	Kh	4.03N	38.20 E
Mega [Indon.]	150	Jg	0.41S	131.53 E
Mega, Pulau-	150	Dg	4.00S	101.02 E
Megalo	168	Gd	6.52N	40.47 E
Megálon Khorion	130	Km	36.27N	27.21 E
Megalópolis	130	Fl	37.24N	22.08 E
Megálo Sofráno	130	Jm	36.04N	26.25 E
Meganísion	130	Dk	38.38N	20.43 E
Meganom, mys-	132	Ig	44.48N	35.05 E
Mégara	130	Gk	38.00N	23.21 E
Megève	122	Mi	45.52N	6.37 E
Meghalaya [3]	148	Ic	26.00N	91.00 E
Megid	164	Dd	28.35N	22.10 E
Megion	136	Hc	61.00N	76.15 E
Megiscane, Lac-	184	Ia	48.30N	76.04W
Megri	132	Oj	38.55N	46.15 E
Mehadia	130	Fe	44.54N	22.22 E
Mehaigne	124	Hd	50.32N	5.13 E
Meharry, Mount-	212	Dd	23.00S	118.35 E
Mehdia	126	Ni	35.25N	1.45 E
Mehdīshahr	146	Oe	35.44N	53.22 E
Mehedinţi [2]	130	Fe	44.30N	23.00 E
Mehetia, Ile-	216	Lc	17.52S	148.03W
Mehrabān	146	Lc	38.05N	47.08 E
Mehrān	146	Lf	33.07N	46.10 E
Mehrān	146	Pi	26.52N	55.24 E
Mehrenga	114	Je	63.17N	41.20 E
Mehrīz	146	Pg	31.35N	54.28 E
Mehtar Lām	144	Lc	34.39N	70.10 E
Mehun-sur-Yèvre	122	Ig	47.09N	2.13 E
Meia Meia	170	Gd	5.49S	35.48 E
Meia Ponte, Rio-	202	Ig	18.32S	49.36W
Meiganga	166	Hd	6.31N	14.18 E
Meighen	180	Ha	79.55N	99.00W
Meihekou→Hailong	152	Mc	42.32N	125.37 E
Meiktila	148	Jd	20.52N	95.52 E
Meilü→Wuchuan	152	Jg	21.28N	110.44 E
Meinerzhagen	124	Jc	51.07N	7.39 E
Meiningen	120	Gf	50.33N	10.25 E
Meio, Rio do-	204	Ja	13.20S	44.34W
Meisenheim	124	Je	49.43N	7.40 E
Meishan [China]	152	He	30.05N	103.48 E
Meishan [China]	154	Ei	31.06N	119.43 E
Meishan → Jinzhai	154	Ci	31.40N	115.52 E
Meißen	120	Je	51.09N	13.29 E
Meißner	120	Fe	51.12N	9.50 E
Meitan (Yiquan)	152	If	27.48N	107.32 E
Meixian	152	Kg	24.21N	116.07 E
Meiyukou	154	Bd	40.01N	113.08 E
Méjean, Causse-	122	Jj	44.16N	3.22 E
Mejillones	206	Fb	23.06S	70.27W
Mékambo	170	Bb	1.01N	13.56 E
Mekdela	168	Fc	11.28N	39.20 E
Mekele=Meqele (EN)	160	Kg	13.30N	39.28 E
Mékhé	166	Bb	15.07N	16.38W
Mekherrhane, Sebkha-	158	Hf	26.22N	1.20 E
Meknès	160	Ge	33.54N	5.32W
Meknès [3]	162	Fc	33.00N	5.30W
Mekong (EN)=Lancang Jiang	140	Mh	10.15N	105.55 E
Mekong (EN)=Mae Nam Khong	140	Mh	10.15N	105.55 E
Mekong (EN)=Mékôngk	140	Mh	10.15N	105.55 E
Mekong (EN)=Mènam Khong	140	Mh	10.15N	105.55 E
Mekong Delta (EN)	140	Mi	10.20N	106.40 E
Mekongga, Gunung-	150	Hg	3.35S	121.15 E
Mékôngk=Mekong (EN)	140	Mh	10.15N	105.55 E
Mekoryuk	178	Fd	60.23N	166.12W
Mékrou	166	Fc	12.24N	2.49 E
Mel, Ilha do-	204	Hg	25.31S	48.20W
Melaab	126	Ni	35.43N	1.20 E
Mēladēn	168	Hc	10.25N	49.52 E
Melaka	142	Mi	2.12N	102.15 E
Melaka [2]	150	Df	2.15N	102.15 E
Melaka, Selat-=Malacca, Strait of- (EN)	140	Mi	2.30N	101.20 E
Melamo, Cabo-	158	Lj	14.24S	40.49 E
Melanesia	208	Hf	13.00S	164.00 E
Melanesian Basin (EN)	106	Jj	0.05S	160.35 E
Melawi	150	Ff	0.05N	111.29 E
Melbourne [Ar.-U.S.]	186	Kh	36.04N	91.54W
Melbourne [Austl.]	210	Fh	37.49S	144.58 E
Melbourne [Eng.-U.K.]	124	Ab	52.49N	1.26W
Melbourne [Fl.-U.S.]	182	Kf	28.05N	80.37W
Melbourne-Dandenong	212	Jg	37.59S	145.12 E
Melchor Múzquiz	190	Dc	27.53N	101.31W
Melchor Ocampo	192	Hi	17.59N	102.11W
Meldorf	120	Fb	54.05N	9.05 E
Mele, Capo-	128	Cg	43.57N	8.10 E
Melekeiok	220a	Bc	7.29N	134.38 E
Melela	172	Fc	17.04S	38.36 E
Melenci	130	Dd	45.31N	20.19 E
Melenki	136	Ed	55.23N	41.42 E
Meleto Dağı	146	Ic	38.35N	41.32 E
Meleuz	136	Fe	52.58N	55.59 E
Mélèzes, Rivière aux-	180	Ke	57.00N	69.00W
Melfa	128	Hi	41.30N	13.35 E
Melfi [Chad]	168	Bc	11.04N	17.56 E
Melfi [It.]	128	Jj	41.00N	15.39 E
Melfort	180	Hf	52.52N	104.36W
Melgaço	202	Hd	1.47S	50.44W
Melibocus	120	Eg	49.42N	8.40 E
Melilla [5]	160	Ge	35.19N	2.58W
Melincué, Laguna-	204	Bk	33.42S	61.28W
Melineşti	130	Ge	44.34N	23.43 E
Melipilla	206	Fd	33.42S	71.13W
Melita	186	Fb	49.16N	101.00W
Melíti	130	Ei	40.50N	21.35 E
Melito di Porto Salvo	128	Jm	37.55N	15.47 E
Melito di Porto Salvo, Punta di-	128	Jm	37.57N	15.45 E
Melitopol	112	Jf	46.50N	35.22 E
Melk	128	Jb	48.13N	15.19 E
Mella	128	Ee	45.13N	10.13 E
Mellakou	126	Ni	35.15N	1.14 E
Mellanfryken	116	Ee	59.40N	13.15 E
Melle [Fr.]	122	Fh	46.13N	0.08W
Melle [Ger.]	124	Kb	52.12N	8.21 E
Mellen	186	Kc	46.20N	90.40W
Mellerud	114	Cg	58.42N	12.28 E
Mellish Reef	212	Lc	17.25S	155.50 E
Mellish Seamount (EN)	208	Ia	34.00N	178.15 E
Mellit	168	Dc	14.08N	25.33 E
Melnik	130	Gh	41.31N	23.24 E
Mělník	120	Kf	50.21N	14.30 E
Melo	200	Ki	32.22S	54.11W
Melo, Río-	204	De	21.25S	57.55W
Melrhir, Chott-	158	He	34.20N	6.20 E
Melrose	188	Id	45.38N	112.40W
Melsungen	120	Fe	51.08N	9.33 E
Meltaus	114	Fc	66.54N	25.22 E
Melton Constable	124	Db	52.51N	1.02 E
Melton Mowbray	118	Mi	52.46N	0.53W
Meluco	172	Fb	12.33S	39.37 E
Meluli	172	Fc	16.28S	39.44 E
Melun	122	If	48.32N	2.40 E
Melville	188	Na	50.55N	102.48W
Melville	174	Ib	75.15N	110.00W
Melville, Cape-	212	Ib	14.10S	144.30 E
Melville, Lake-	180	Lf	53.42N	59.30W
Melville Bay	212	Hb	12.05S	136.45 E
Melville Bay (EN)=Melville Bugt	224	Od	75.35N	62.30W
Melville Bugt=Melville Bay (EN)	224	Od	75.35N	62.30W
Melville Hills	180	Fc	69.20N	123.00W
Melville Island	208	Ef	11.40S	131.00 E
Melville Peninsula	174	Kc	68.00N	84.00W
Melville Sound	180	Gc	68.05N	107.30W
Melvin, Lough-	118	Eg	54.25N	8.10W
Mélykút	120	Pj	46.13N	19.23 E
Memaliaj	130	Ci	40.20N	19.58 E
Memambetsu	156a	Db	43.55N	144.11 E
Memba	172	Gb	14.10S	40.30 E
Memba, Baía de-	172	Gb	14.11S	40.35 E
Memberamo	150	Kg	1.28S	137.52 E
Memboro	150	Gh	9.22S	119.32 E
Mēmele	116	Kh	56.24N	24.10 E
Memmert	120	Cc	53.39N	6.53 E
Memmingen	120	Gi	47.59N	10.10 E
Mempawan	150	Ef	0.22N	108.58 E
Memphis	164	Fd	29.52N	31.15 E
Memphis [Mo.-U.S.]	186	Jf	40.28N	92.10W
Memphis [Tn.-U.S.]	176	Jf	35.08N	90.03W
Memphis [Tx.-U.S.]	186	Fi	34.44N	100.32W
Memuro	154	Qc	42.55N	143.03 E
Memuro-Dake	156a	Cb	42.52N	142.45 E
Mena	168	Gd	5.30N	41.06 E
Mena [Ar.-U.S.]	186	Ii	34.35N	94.15W
Mena [Ukr.]	136	De	51.33N	32.14 E
Menabe	158	Lk	20.00S	44.40 E
Menai Strait	118	Ih	53.12N	4.12W
Ménaka	160	Hg	15.55N	2.26 E
Mènam Khong=Mekong (EN)	140	Mh	10.15N	105.55 E
Menangalaku	150	Gh	9.36S	119.01 E
Menard	186	Gk	30.55N	99.47W
Menawashei	168	Dc	12.40N	25.01 E
Menčul, gora-	120	Th	48.16N	23.49 E
Mendala, Puncak-	150	Lg	4.44S	140.20 E
Mendanau, Pulau-	150	Eg	2.51S	107.26 E
Mendanha	204	Kd	18.06S	43.30W
Mende	122	Jj	44.31N	3.30 E
Mendebo	158	Kh	6.50N	39.40 E
Mendelejevsk	114	Mi	55.57N	52.22 E
Menden (Sauerland)	120	De	51.26N	7.48 E
Mendes	126	Mi	35.39N	0.52 E
Méndez	192	Je	25.07N	98.34W
Mendi [Eth.]	168	Fd	9.48N	35.05 E
Mendi [Pap.N.Gui.]	214	Ci	6.10S	143.40 E
Mendig	124	Jd	50.22N	7.16 E
Mendip Hills	118	Kj	51.15N	2.40W
Mendocino	188	Dg	39.19N	123.48W
Mendocino, Cape-	174	Ge	40.25N	124.25W
Mendocino Fracture Zone (EN)	106	Lf	40.00N	145.00W
Mendota [Ca.-U.S.]	188	Eh	36.45N	120.23W
Mendota [Il.-U.S.]	186	Lf	41.33N	89.07W
Mendoza	200	Ji	32.54S	68.50W
Mendoza [2]	206	Gd	34.30S	68.30W
Mené, Landes du-	122	Df	48.15N	2.32W
Mene de Mauroa	194	Lh	10.43N	71.01W
Mene Grande	202	Db	9.49S	70.56W
Menemen	146	Bc	38.36N	27.04 E
Menen/Menin	122	Jd	50.48N	3.07 E
Meneng Point	220e	Bb	0.33S	166.57 E
Meneses	204	Dj	30.53S	56.30W
Ménez-Hom	122	Bf	48.13N	4.16W
Menfi	128	Gm	37.36N	12.58 E
Mengcheng	152	Ke	33.11N	116.30 E
Mengdingjie	152	Gg	23.31N	99.07 E
Menggala	150	Eg	4.28S	105.17 E
Mengíbar	126	Ig	37.58N	3.48W
Mengjin	154	Bg	34.50N	112.26 E
Mengla	152	Hg	21.30N	101.35 E
Menglangba→Lancang	152	Gg	22.37N	99.57 E
Menglian	152	Gg	22.20N	99.27 E
Mengoun Huizu Zizhixian	154	De	38.04N	117.06 E
Mengyin	154	Dg	35.42N	117.56 E
Mengzi	142	Mg	23.23N	103.34 E
Menihek Lakes	180	Kf	54.00N	66.30W
Menin/Menen	122	Jd	50.48N	3.07 E
Menindee	212	If	32.24S	142.26 E
Menindee Lake	212	If	22.00S	142.23 E
Meningie	212	Hg	35.42S	139.20 E
Menjapa, Gunung-	150	Gf	1.05N	116.05 E
Menno	186	He	43.14N	97.34W
Menoíkion Óros	130	Gh	41.11N	23.48 E
Menominee	184	Dc	45.07N	87.39W
Menongue	160	Ij	14.40S	17.39 E
Menor, Mar-	126	Lg	37.43N	0.48W
Menorca=Minorca (EN)	110	Gg	40.00N	4.00 E
Mentasta Lake	178	Kd	62.55N	143.45W
Mentawai, Kepulauan-= Mentawai Islands (EN)	140	Lj	2.00S	99.30 E
Mentawai, Selat-	140	Lj	2.00S	99.30 E
Mentawai Islands (EN)= Mentawai, Kepulauan-	140	Lj	2.00S	99.30 E
Menton	122	Nk	43.47N	7.30 E
Mentougou	154	De	39.56N	116.02 E
Menyuan	152	Hd	37.30N	101.35 E
Menzelinsk	114	Mi	55.45N	53.09 E
Menzies	212	Ee	29.41S	121.02 E
Menzies, Mount-	222	Ff	73.30S	61.50 E
Meon	124	Ad	50.49N	1.15W
Meoqui	190	Cc	28.17N	105.29W
Meponda	172	Eb	13.25S	34.52 E
Meppel	122	Mb	52.42N	6.11 E
Meppen	120	Dd	52.41N	7.19 E
Meqele(EN)=Mekele	160	Kg	13.30N	39.28 E
Mê Qu	152	He	33.58N	102.10 E
Mequinensa, Pantà de-/ Mequinenza, Embalse de-	126	Lc	41.15N	0.02W
Mequinenza, Embalse de-/ Mequinensa, Pantà de-	126	Lc	41.15N	0.02W
Mera	128	Dd	46.11N	9.25 E
Merabello, Gulf of- (EN) = Merabéllou, Kólpos-	130	In	35.14N	25.47 E
Merabéllou, Kólpos- = Merabello, Gulf of- (EN)	130	In	35.14N	25.47 E
Merak	150	Eh	5.56S	106.00 E
Meråker	114	Ce	63.26N	11.45 E
Méralab	219b	Db	14.27S	168.03 E
Meramangye, Lake-	212	Ge	28.25S	132.15 E
Meran / Merano	128	Fd	46.40N	11.09 E
Merano / Meran	128	Fd	46.40N	11.09 E
Meratus, Pegunungan-	150	Gg	2.45S	115.40 E
Merauke	210	Fe	8.28S	140.20 E
Mercadal / Es Mercadal	126	Qe	39.59N	4.05 E
Mercato Saraceno	128	Gg	43.57N	12.12 E
Merced	182	Cd	37.18N	120.29W
Mercedario, Cerro-	198	Ii	31.59S	70.14W
Mercedes [Arg.]	206	Id	34.39S	59.27W
Mercedes [Arg.]	206	Ic	29.12S	58.05W
Mercedes [Arg.]	200	Ji	33.40S	65.30W
Mercedes [Ur.]	200	Ki	33.16S	58.01W
Merchants Bay	180	Lc	67.10N	62.50W
Merchtem	124	Gd	50.58N	4.14 E
Mercury Islands	218	Fb	36.35S	175.50 E
Mercy, Cape -	180	Ld	64.56N	63.40W
Mercy Bay	180	Fb	74.15N	118.10W
Meredith, Cape-	206	Hh	52.12S	60.38W
Meredith, Lake-	186	Fi	35.36N	101.42W
Meredoua	162	Hd	25.20N	2.05 E
Merefa	136	Df	49.51N	36.00 E
Merelbeke	124	Fd	51.00N	3.45 E
Merenga	138	Kd	61.43N	156.05 E
Mergui	142	Lh	12.26N	98.36 E
Mergui Archipelago	140	Lh	12.00N	98.00 E
Méri	166	Hc	10.47N	14.06 E
Meriç	130	Jh	41.11N	26.25 E
Meriç	146	Bb	40.52N	26.12 E
Mérida [2]	202	Db	8.30N	71.10W
Mérida [Mex.]	176	Kg	20.58N	89.37W
Mérida [Sp.]	126	Ff	38.55N	6.20W
Mérida [Ven.]	200	Ie	8.36N	71.08W
Merida, Cordillera de-	198	Ie	8.40N	71.00W
Meridian	176	Kf	32.22N	88.42W
Mérig	219b	Cb	14.19S	167.48 E
Mérignac	122	Fj	44.50N	0.38W
Merikarvia	114	Ef	61.51N	21.30 E
Merín, Laguna-	206	Jd	32.45S	52.50W
Meringur	212	If	34.24S	141.29 E
Merir Island	208	Ed	4.19N	132.19 E
Merizo	220c	Bb	13.16N	144.40 E
Merke	135	Ic	42.52N	73.12 E
Merkem, Houthulst-	124	Ed	50.57N	2.51 E
Merkine/Merkinė	116	Kj	54.07N	24.20 E
Merkinė/Merkine	116	Kj	54.07N	24.20 E
Merkis/Merkys	114	Fi	54.10N	24.11 E
Merksem, Antwerpen-	124	Gc	51.15N	4.27 E
Merksplas	124	Gc	51.22N	4.52 E
Merkys/Merkis	114	Fi	54.10N	24.11 E
Meroe	168	Eb	16.05N	33.55 E
Meroe	168	Eb	16.56N	33.59 E
Merouane, Chott-	162	Ic	34.00N	6.02 E
Merredin	212	Df	31.29S	118.16 E
Merrick	118	If	55.08N	4.29W
Merrill	182	Jb	45.11N	89.41W
Merriman	186	Fe	42.55N	101.42W
Merritt	180	Ff	50.07N	120.47W
Merritt Island	182	Kf	28.21N	80.42W
Merritt Reservoir	186	Fe	42.35N	100.55W
Mersa Fatma	168	Gc	14.53N	40.19 E
Mersa Teklay	168	Fb	17.25N	38.45 E
Mersea Island	124	Cc	51.47N	0.57 E
Merseburg	120	He	51.22N	12.00 E
Mers el Kebir	126	Li	35.44N	0.43W
Mersey	118	Kh	53.25N	3.00W
Merseyside [3]	118	Kh	53.30N	3.00W
Mersin → İçel	144	Db	36.48N	34.38 E
Mersing	150	Df	2.26N	103.50 E
Mers-les-Bains	124	Dd	50.04N	1.23 E
Mersrags/Mērsrags	116	Jg	57.19N	23.01 E
Mērsrags/Mersrags	116	Jg	57.19N	23.01 E
Merta	148	Ec	26.39N	74.02 E
Merta Road	148	Ec	26.43N	73.55 E
Mertert	124	Ie	49.42N	6.29 E
Merthyr Tydfil	118	Jj	51.46N	3.23W
Merti	170	Gb	1.04N	38.40 E
Mértola	126	Eg	37.38N	7.40W
Mertule Maryam	168	Fc	10.50N	38.15 E
Mertvy Kultuk, sor-	132	Rg	45.30N	53.40 E
Mertz Glacier	222	Je	67.40S	144.45 E
Meru	170	Gb	0.03N	37.39 E
Méru	122	Ie	49.14N	2.08 E
Meru, Mount-	170	Gc	3.14S	36.45 E
Merure	204	Fb	15.33S	53.05W
Merville	124	Ed	50.38N	2.38 E
Merzifon	144	Ea	40.53N	35.29 E
Merzig	120	Cg	49.27N	6.38 E
Meša	114	Li	55.34N	49.24 E
Mesa [Az.-U.S.]	176	Hf	33.25N	111.50W
Mesa [Co.-U.S.]	186	Bg	39.14N	108.08W
Mesabi Range	186	Jc	47.30N	92.50W
Mesagne	128	Lj	40.34N	17.48 E
Mescalero	186	Dj	33.09N	105.46W
Meščera = Moscow Basin (EN)	110	Kd	55.00N	40.30 E
Meschede	120	Ee	51.21N	8.17 E
Mescit Dağı	146	Ib	40.22N	41.11 E
Meščovsk	132	Ib	54.19N	35.18 E
Mesegon	220d	Bb	7.09N	151.55 E
Meseta Meridional	110	Fh	39.30N	3.30W
Meseta Septentrional	110	Fg	42.20N	4.50W
Mesfinto	168	Fc	13.28N	37.23 E
Me-Shima	154	Jh	32.01N	128.25 E
Meshkān	146	Rd	36.39N	58.05 E
Meshkīnshahr	146	Lc	38.24N	47.40 E
Mesima	128	Jl	38.30N	15.55 E
Mesjagutovo	134	Ii	55.35N	58.20 E
Meskiana	128	Bo	35.38N	7.40 E
Meskiana, Oued-	128	Bo	35.48N	7.53 E
Meslo	168	Fd	6.22N	39.50 E
Mesnil-Val, Criel-sur-Mer-	124	Dd	50.03N	1.20 E
Mesola	128	Gf	44.55N	12.14 E
Mesolóngion	130	Ek	38.22N	21.26 E
Mesopotamia	144	Fc	34.00N	44.00 E
Mesopotamia [Arg.]	198	Kh	30.00S	58.00W
Mesopotamia [Asia]	140	Gf	34.00N	44.00 E
Mesoyéios Thálassa= Mediterranean Sea (EN)	110	Hh	35.00N	20.00 E
Mesquite [Nv.-U.S.]	188	Hh	36.48N	114.04W
Mesquite [Tx.-U.S.]	186	Hj	32.46N	96.36W
Mesra	126	Mi	35.50N	0.10 E
Messaad	162	Hc	34.10N	3.30 E
Messalo	158	Lj	11.40S	40.46 E
Messará, Órmos-	130	Ho	35.00N	24.40 E
Messina [It.]	112	Hh	38.11N	15.34 E
Messina [S.Afr.]	160	Kk	22.23S	30.00 E
Messina, Strait of- (EN) = Messina, Stretto di-	110	Hh	38.15N	15.35 E
Messina, Stretto di- = Messina, Strait of- (EN)	110	Hh	38.15N	15.35 E
Messini	130	Fl	37.03N	22.01 E
Messíni	130	El	37.15N	21.50 E
Messiniakós Kólpos	130	Fm	36.45N	22.10 E
Messojaha	138	Cc	67.52N	77.27 E
Mesta	130	Hi	40.51N	24.44 E
Mestecăniş, Pasul-	130	Ib	47.28N	25.20 E
Mesters Vig	179	Jd	72.15N	24.20W
Mestia	132	Mh	43.03N	42.43 E
Mestre, Espigão-	202	If	12.30S	46.00W
Mestre, Venezia-	128	Ge	45.29N	12.14 E
Mesuji	150	Eg	4.08S	105.52 E
Meta [3]	202	Dc	3.30N	73.00W
Meta, Río-	198	Je	6.12N	67.28W
Meta Incognita Peninsula	174	Mc	62.40N	68.00W
Metairie	186	Kl	29.59N	90.09W
Metaliferi, Munţii-	130	Fc	46.10N	22.50 E
Metallifere, Colline-	128	Eg	43.10N	10.55 E
Metán	206	Hc	25.29S	64.57W
Metangula	172	Eb	12.43S	34.49 E
Metaponto	128	Kj	40.20N	16.50 E
Metauro	128	Hg	43.50N	13.03 E
Metautu	221c	Ba	13.57S	171.54W
Meteghan	184	Nc	44.11N	66.10W
Metelen	124	Jb	52.09N	7.12 E
Metéora	130	Ej	39.43N	21.40 E
Meteor Seamount (EN)	158	Hm	48.00S	8.30 E
Meteor Trench (EN)	106	Do	56.30S	27.40W
Méthana	130	Gl	37.35N	23.23 E
Methánon, Khersónisos-	130	Gl	37.36N	23.22 E
Methven	218	De	43.38S	171.38 E
Methwold	124	Cb	52.31N	0.33 E
Metković	128	Lg	43.03N	17.39 E
Metlakatla	178	Me	55.08N	131.35W
Metlika	128	Je	45.39N	15.19 E
Metlili Chaamba	162	Hc	32.16N	3.38 E
Metmárfag	162	Ed	26.26N	13.26W
Metohija	130	Dg	42.40N	20.27 E
Metro	150	Eh	5.05S	105.20 E
Metropolis	186	Lh	37.09N	88.44W
Métsovon	130	Ej	39.46N	21.11 E
Métsovon, Zigós- = Métsovon Pass (EN)	130	Ej	39.47N	21.15 E
Métsovon Pass (EN) = Métsovon, Zigós-	130	Ej	39.47N	21.15 E
Mettet	124	Gd	50.19N	4.40 E
Mettingen	124	Jb	52.19N	7.47 E
Mettlach	124	Ie	49.30N	6.36 E
Mettmann	124	Ic	51.15N	6.58 E
Metu	160	Kh	8.20N	35.38 E
Metuje	120	Lf	50.20N	15.55 E
Metz	112	Gf	49.08N	6.10 E
Metzervisse	124	Ie	49.19N	6.17 E
Meu	122	Ef	48.02N	1.47W
Meulaboh	150	Cf	4.09N	96.08 E
Meulan	124	De	49.01N	1.54 E
Meulebeke	124	Fd	50.57N	3.17 E
Meureudu	150	Ce	5.16N	96.16 E
Meurthe	122	Mf	48.47N	6.09 E
Meurthe-et-Moselle [3]	122	Mf	48.35N	6.10 E
Meuse [3]	122	Lf	49.00N	5.30 E
Meuse	110	Ge	51.49N	5.01 E
Meuse (EN)=Maas	110	Ge	51.49N	5.01 E
Meuse, Côtes de-	122	Le	49.10N	5.30 E
Meuzenti	168	Bb	18.14N	17.06 E
Mexia	186	Hk	31.41N	96.29W
Mexiana, Ilha-	202	Ic	0.00	49.35W
Mexicali	176	Hf	32.40N	115.29W
Mexicana, Altiplanicie-= Mexico, Plateau of- (EN)	174	Ig	25.30N	104.00W
Mexican Hat	188	Kh	37.09N	109.52W
Mexicanos, Laguna de los-	192	Fc	28.09N	106.57W
Mexico	186	Kg	39.10N	91.53W
México [1]	176	Ig	23.00N	102.00W
México [2]	190	Ee	19.20N	99.30W
México, Golfo de-=Mexico, Gulf of- (EN)	174	Kg	25.00N	90.00W
Mexico, Gulf of-	174	Kg	25.00N	90.00W
Mexico, Gulf of- (EN)= México, Golfo de-	174	Kg	25.00N	90.00W
Mexico, Plateau of- (EN)= Mexicana, Altiplanicie-	174	Ig	25.30N	104.00W
Mexico Basin (EN)	106	Bg	25.00N	92.00W
Mexico City (EN)=Ciudad de México	176	Jh	19.24N	99.09W
Meybod	146	Of	32.16N	53.59 E
Meydān-e Gel	146	Ph	29.04N	54.50 E
Meyísti	130	Mm	36.09N	29.40 E
Meyísti	130	Mm	36.08N	29.34 E
Meymaneh	142	If	35.55N	64.47 E
Meymeh	146	Nf	33.27N	51.10 E
Meymeh	146	Lf	32.05N	47.16 E
Meža	114	Hi	55.43N	31.30 E
Mezcala	192	Ji	17.56N	99.37W

Index Symbols

- [1] Independent Nation
- [2] State, Region
- [3] District, County
- [4] Municipality
- [5] Colony, Dependency
- Continent
- Physical Region
- Historical or Cultural Region
- Mount, Mountain
- Volcano
- Hill
- Mountains, Mountain Range
- Hills, Escarpment
- Plateau, Upland
- Pass, Gap
- Plain, Lowland
- Delta
- Salt Flat
- Valley, Canyon
- Crater, Cave
- Karst Features
- Depression
- Polder
- Desert, Dunes
- Forest, Woods
- Heath, Steppe
- Oasis
- Cape, Point
- Coast, Beach
- Cliff
- Peninsula
- Isthmus
- Sandbank
- Island
- Atoll
- Rock, Reef
- Islands, Archipelago
- Rocks, Reefs
- Coral Reef
- Well, Spring
- Geyser
- River, Stream
- Waterfall, Rapids
- River Mouth, Estuary
- Lake
- Salt Lake
- Intermittent Lake
- Reservoir
- Swamp, Pond
- Canal
- Glacier
- Ice Shelf, Pack Ice
- Ocean
- Sea
- Gulf, Bay
- Strait, Fjord
- Lagoon
- Bank
- Seamount
- Tablemount
- Ridge
- Shelf
- Basin
- Escarpment, Sea Scarp
- Fracture
- Trench, Abyss
- National Park, Reserve
- Point of Interest
- Recreation Site
- Cave, Cavern
- Historic Site
- Ruins
- Wall, Walls
- Church, Abbey
- Temple
- Scientific Station
- Railway station
- Airport
- Port
- Military installation
- Lighthouse
- Mine
- Tunnel
- Dam, Bridge

Mezcalapa, Rio-	192	Mh	18.36N	92.39W
Mezdra	130	Gf	43.09N	23.42 E
Meždurečenskij	136	Gd	59.36N	65.53 E
Meždušarskij, ostrov-	136	Fa	71.20N	53.00 E
Mèze	122	Jk	43.25N	3.36 E
Mezen	112	Kb	65.50N	44.13 E
Mezen	110	Kb	66.00N	43.59 E
Mézenc, Mont-	122	Kj	44.55N	4.11 E
Mężenin	120	Sc	53.07N	22.29 E
Mezenskaja guba	110	Kb	66.40N	43.45 E
Mezenskaja Pižma	114	Ld	64.30N	48.32 E
Mežgorje	120	Th	48.30N	23.37 E
Mežica	128	Id	46.31N	14.52 E
Mézidon-Canon	124	Be	49.05N	0.04W
Mézin	122	Gj	44.03N	0.16 E
Mezőberény	120	Rj	46.49N	21.02 E
Mezőcsát	120	Qi	47.49N	20.55 E
Mezőföld	120	Oj	46.55N	18.35 E
Mezőkovácsháza	120	Qj	46.24N	20.55 E
Mezőkövesd	120	Qi	47.49N	20.35 E
Mezőtúr	120	Qi	47.00N	20.38 E
Mežozerny	134	Ii	54.10N	59.25 E
Mežpjanje	114	Ki	55.25N	45.00 E
Mezquital	192	Gf	23.29N	104.23W
Mezquital, Rio-	192	Ff	22.55N	104.54W
Mezquitic	192	Hf	22.23N	103.41W
Mgači	138	Jf	51.02N	142.18 E
Mglin	132	Hc	53.04N	32.53 E
Mhow	148	Fd	22.33N	75.46 E
Miahuatlán de Porfirio Diaz	192	Ki	16.20N	96.36W
Miajadas	126	Ge	39.09N	5.54W
Miaméré	168	Bd	9.02N	19.55 E
Miami [Az.-U.S.]	188	Jj	33.24N	110.52W
Miami [Fl.-U.S.]	176	Kg	25.46N	80.12W
Miami [Ok.-U.S.]	182	Id	36.53N	94.53W
Miami Beach	182	Kf	25.47N	80.08W
Miānābād	146	Qd	37.02N	57.27 E
Miāndowāb	144	Gb	36.58N	46.06 E
Miandrivazo	172	Hc	19.30S	45.28 E
Mianduhe	152	Lb	49.12N	121.09 E
Miāneh	144	Gb	37.26N	47.42 E
Miang, Khao-	148	He	17.42N	101.01 E
Miangas, Pulau-	150	Ie	5.35N	126.35 E
Mianning	152	Hf	28.31N	102.10 E
Miānwāli	148	Eb	32.35N	71.33 E
Mianyang	152	He	31.23N	104.49 E
Mianyang (Xiantaozhen)	154	Bi	30.22N	113.27 E
Miaodao Qundao	152	Ld	38.10N	120.45 E
Miao'er Shan	152	Jf	25.50N	110.22 E
Miao Ling	152	If	26.05N	108.00 E
Miarinarivo	172	Hc	18.56S	46.54 E
Miass	136	Gd	55.01N	60.06 E
Miass	136	Gd	56.06N	64.30 E
Miasskoje	134	Ji	55.15N	61.55 E
Miasteczko Krajeńskie	120	Nc	53.06N	17.01 E
Miastko	120	Mb	54.01N	17.00 E
Michael, Mount-	212	Ja	6.25S	145.20 E
Michajlova Island	222	Ge	66.30S	85.00 E
Michalovce	120	Rh	48.46N	21.55 E
Michelstadt	124	Le	49.41N	9.01 E
Miches	194	Md	18.59N	69.03W
Michigan (2)	182	Jc	44.00N	85.00W
Michigan, Lake-	174	Ke	44.00N	87.00W
Michigan City	182	Jc	41.43N	86.54W
Michipicoten Bay	184	Eb	47.55N	84.56W
Michipicoten Island	180	Ig	47.45N	85.45W
Michoacán (2)	190	De	19.10N	101.50W
Michów	120	Se	51.32N	22.19 E
Mico, Rio-	194	Eg	12.11N	84.16W
Micoud	197k	Bb	13.50N	60.54W
Micronesia	208	Gc	11.00N	159.00 E
Micronesia, Federated States of- (1)	210	Gd	6.30N	152.00 E
Mičurin	130	Kg	42.10N	27.51 E
Mičurinsk	112	Ke	52.54N	40.31 E
Midai, Pulau-	150	Ef	3.00N	107.47 E
Midar	162	Gc	34.57N	3.32W
Mid-Atlantic Ridge (EN)	106	Di	0.00	20.00W
Middelburg [Neth.]	122	Jc	51.30N	3.37 E
Middelburg [S.Afr.]	172	Cf	31.30S	25.00 E
Middelburg [S.Afr.]	172	De	25.47S	29.28 E
Middelfart	114	Bi	55.30N	9.45 E
Middelharnis	124	Gc	51.45N	4.12 E
Middelkerke	124	Ec	51.11N	2.49 E
Middelkerke-Westende	124	Ec	51.10N	2.46 E
Middle Alkali Lake	188	Ef	41.28N	120.04W
Middle America Trench (EN)	106	Mh	15.00N	95.00W
Middle Andaman	148	If	12.30N	92.50 E
Middle Atlas (EN)=Moyen Atlas	158	Ge	33.30N	4.30W
Middlebury	184	Kc	44.01N	73.10W
Middle Caicos	194	Lc	21.47N	71.43W
Middle Fork Feather River	188	Eg	38.47N	121.36W
Middle Island	172b	Ab	9.22S	46.21 E
Middle Loup River	186	Gf	41.?7N	98.23W
Middlemarch	218	Df	45.30S	170.07 E
Middle Reef	219a	Ee	12.35S	160.30 E
Middlesboro	182	Kd	36.36N	83.43W
Middlesbrough	112	Fe	54.35N	1.14W
Middlesex	194	Ce	17.02N	88.31W
Middlesex	124	Bc	51.35N	0.10W
Middlesex	118	Mj	51.30N	0.05W
Middleton	178	Je	59.25N	146.25W
Middleton Reef	208	Gg	29.30S	159.10 E
Middletown [Ct.-U.S.]	184	Ke	41.33N	72.39W
Middletown [N.Y.-U.S.]	184	Je	41.26N	74.26W
Middletown [Oh.-U.S.]	184	Ef	39.31N	84.25W
Midelt	162	Gc	32.41N	4.45W
Mid Glamorgan (3)	118	Jj	51.35N	3.35W
Midhordland	116	Ad	60.15N	5.55 E
Midhurst	124	Bd	50.59N	0.44W
Midi, Canal du-	110	Gg	43.36N	1.25 E
Midi de Bigorre, Pic du-	122	Gl	42.56N	0.08 E
Midi d'Ossau, Pic du-	122	Fl	42.51N	0.26W
Mid-Indian Basin (EN)	106	Gj	10.00S	80.00 E
Mid-Indian Ridge (EN)	106	Gj	3.00S	75.00 E
Midland [Mi.-U.S.]	184	Ed	43.37N	84.14W
Midland [Ont.-Can.]	180	Jh	44.45N	79.53W
Midland [S.D.-U.S.]	186	Fd	44.04N	101.10W
Midland [Tx.-U.S.]	182	Ge	32.00N	102.05W
Midlands (3)	172	Dc	19.00S	30.00 E
Midlands	118	Li	52.40N	1.50W
Midleton/Mainistir na Corann	118	Ej	51.55N	8.10W
Midnapore → Medinīpur	148	Hd	22.26N	87.20 E
Midongy du Sud	172	Hd	23.34S	47.01 E
Midou	122	Fk	43.54N	0.30W
Midouze	122	Fk	43.48N	0.51W
Mid-Pacific Mountains (EN)	106	Jg	20.00N	170.00 E
Midway Islands (5)	210	Jb	28.13N	177.22W
Midway Islands	208	Jb	28.13N	177.22W
Midwest	188	Le	43.25N	106.16W
Midwest City	186	Hi	35.27N	97.24W
Midyat	146	Id	37.25N	41.23 E
Midžor	110	Ig	43.24N	22.40 E
Miechów	120	Qf	50.23N	20.01 E
Miedwie, Jezioro-	120	Kc	53.15N	14.55 E
Międzychód	120	Ld	52.36N	15.53 E
Międzylesie	120	Mf	50.10N	16.40 E
Międzyrzec Podlaski	120	Se	52.00N	22.47 E
Międzyrzecz	120	Ld	52.27N	15.34 E
Międzyrzecze Łomżyńskie	120	Rd	52.45N	21.45 E
Miehikkälä	116	Ld	60.40N	27.42 E
Mie Ken (2)	154	Ng	34.35N	136.25 E
Miekojärvi	114	Fc	66.36N	24.23 E
Miélan	122	Gk	43.26N	0.19 E
Mielec	120	Rf	50.18N	21.25 E
Mielno	120	Mb	54.16N	16.01 E
Mien	116	Fh	56.25N	14.50 E
Mier	192	Jd	26.26N	99.09W
Miercurea Ciuc	130	Ic	46.21N	25.48 E
Mieres	126	Ga	43.15N	5.46W
Miersig	130	Ec	46.53N	21.51 E
Mier y Noriega	192	If	23.25N	100.07W
Miesbach	120	Hi	47.47N	11.50 E
Mieso	168	Gd	9.15N	40.45 E
Mifune	156	Be	32.43N	130.48 E
Migang Shan	152	Id	35.32N	106.13 E
Miguel Alamán, Presa-	192	Kh	18.13N	96.32W
Miguel Auza	192	He	24.18N	103.25W
Miguel Hidalgo, Presa-	192	Ed	26.40N	108.45W
Miha Chakaja → Senaki	136	Eg	42.17N	42.02 E
Mihăileşti	130	Ie	44.20N	25.54 E
Mihail Kogălniceanu	130	Le	44.22N	28.27 E
Mihajlov	136	De	54.16N	39.03 E
Mihajlovgrad	130	Gf	43.25N	23.13 E
Mihajlovgrad (2)	130	Gf	43.25N	23.13 E
Mihajlovka [Kaz.]	135	Hc	43.01N	71.31 E
Mihajlovka [Russia]	136	Ee	50.05N	43.15 E
Mihajlovsk	134	Ih	56.29N	59.07 E
Mihalıççık	146	Dc	39.52N	31.30 E
Mihara	156	Cd	34.24N	133.05 E
Mihara-Yama	156	Fd	34.43N	139.23 E
Mi He	154	Ef	37.12N	119.10 E
Mihonoseki	156	Cd	35.34N	133.18 E
Miho-Wan	156	Cd	35.30N	133.20 E
Miiraku	156	Ae	32.45N	128.40 E
Mijaly	132	Re	48.54N	53.50 E
Mijares/Millars	126	Le	39.55N	0.01W
Mijdaḥah	168	Hc	14.00N	48.26 E
Mijdrecht	124	Gb	52.12N	4.52 E
Mijirtein (EN)=Majērtēn	158	Lh	9.00N	50.00 E
Mikasa	154	Pc	43.20N	141.40 E
Mikata	156	Dd	35.34N	135.54 E
Miki	156	Dd	34.17N	134.07 E
Mikinai = Mycenae (EN)	130	Fl	37.43N	22.45 E
Mikindani	170	Ge	10.17S	40.07 E
Mikkeli (2)	114	Ge	62.00N	27.30 E
Mikkeli/Sankt Michel	112	Ic	61.41N	27.15 E
Mikomoto-Jima	156	Fd	34.34N	138.56 E
Mikonos	130	Il	37.27N	25.20 E
Mikonos	130	Il	37.27N	25.23 E
Mikonou, Stenón-	130	Il	37.30N	25.20 E
Mikrá Préspa, Límni-	130	Ei	40.45N	21.06 E
Mikre	130	Hf	43.02N	24.31 E
Mikró Sofráno	130	Jm	36.05N	26.24 E
Mikulkin, mys-	134	Cc	67.48N	46.40 E
Mikulov	120	Mh	48.49N	16.39 E
Mikumi	170	Gd	7.24S	36.59 E
Mikun	136	Fc	62.21N	50.05 E
Mikuni	156	Ec	36.13N	136.09 E
Mikuni-Sanmyaku	154	Of	36.15N	138.40 E
Mikuni-Tōge	156	Fc	36.46N	138.50 E
Mikuni-Yama	156	Dd	35.21N	134.01 E
Mikura-Jima	152	Oe	33.50N	139.35 E
Milaca	186	Jd	45.45N	93.39W
Miladummadulu Atoll	148a	Ba	6.15N	73.15 E
Milagro	202	Cd	2.07S	79.36W
Milājerd	146	Me	34.37N	49.12 E
Milan [Mo.-U.S.]	186	Jf	40.12N	93.07W
Milan [Tn.-U.S.]	184	Ch	35.55N	88.46W
Milan (EN) = Milano	112	Gf	45.28N	9.12 E
Milange	172	Fc	16.05S	35.47 E
Milano = Milan (EN)	112	Gf	45.28N	9.12 E
Milâs	146	Bd	37.19N	27.47 E
Milazzo	128	Jl	38.13N	15.14 E
Milazzo, Capo di-	128	Jl	38.16N	15.14 E
Milazzo, Golfo di-	128	Jl	38.15N	15.20 E
Milbank	182	Hb	45.13N	96.38W
Mildenhall	124	Cb	52.21N	0.31 E
Mildura	210	Fh	34.12S	142.09 E
Mile	152	Hg	24.28N	103.26 E
Mile	168	Gc	11.08N	40.55 E
Miléai	130	Gj	39.20N	23.09 E
Miles	210	Gg	26.40S	150.11 E
Miles City	182	Fb	46.25N	105.51W
Milet = Miletus (EN)	130	Kl	37.30N	27.16 E
Miletus (EN) = Milet	130	Kl	37.30N	27.16 E
Milevec	130	Fg	42.34N	22.27 E
Milevsko	120	Kg	49.27N	14.22 E
Milford	188	Ig	38.24N	113.01W
Milford Haven	118	Hj	51.44N	5.02W
Milford Lake	186	Hg	39.15N	97.00W
Milford Sound	216	Ch	44.40S	167.55 E
Milford Sound	218	Bf	44.35S	167.50 E
Milgis	170	Gb	1.48N	38.06 E
Milḥ, Baḥr al-	144	Fc	32.40N	43.35 E
Milḥ, Ra's al-	164	Ec	31.55N	25.02 E
Miliana	126	Oh	36.17N	2.14 E
Mili Atoll	208	Id	6.08N	171.55 E
Milicz	120	Ne	51.32N	17.17 E
Milkovo	138	Kf	54.43N	158.43 E
Milk River	188	Ib	49.09N	112.05W
Milk River	182	Eb	49.09N	112.05W
Milkūh	144	Jc	32.45N	61.55 E
Mill	180	Jd	63.57N	78.00W
Millars/Mijares	126	Le	39.55N	0.01W
Millau	122	Jj	44.06N	3.05 E
Milledgeville	184	Fi	33.04N	83.14W
Mille Lacs, Lac des -	180	Ig	48.50N	90.30W
Mille Lacs Lake	182	Ib	46.15N	93.40W
Millen	184	Gi	32.48N	81.57W
Miller [Nb.-U.S.]	186	Gf	40.57N	99.26W
Miller [S.D.-U.S.]	186	Gd	44.31N	98.59W
Millerovo	136	Ef	48.52N	40.25 E
Miller Seamount (EN)	178	Kf	53.30N	144.20W
Millerton	218	Dd	41.38S	171.52 E
Millevaches, Plateau de-	122	Ii	45.45N	2.11 E
Millicent	212	Ig	37.36S	140.22 E
Millington	184	Ch	35.20N	89.54W
Millinocket	184	Mc	45.39N	68.43W
Mill Island	222	He	65.30S	100.40 E
Millmerran	212	Ke	27.52S	151.16 E
Mills Lake	180	Fd	61.28N	118.15W
Millstatt	128	Hd	46.48N	13.35 E
Millville	184	Jf	39.24N	75.02W
Millwood Lake	186	Jj	33.45N	94.00W
Milne Land	179	Jd	71.20N	27.30W
Milo	158	Gg	11.04N	9.14W
Milolii	221a	Fd	19.11N	155.55W
Milos	130	Hm	36.45N	24.26 E
Milos = Milos (EN)	130	Hm	36.41N	24.25 E
Milos (EN) = Milos	130	Hm	36.41N	24.25 E
Milparinka	212	Ie	29.44S	141.53 E
Miltenberg	120	Fg	49.42N	9.15 E
Milton [Fl.-U.S.]	184	Dj	30.38N	87.03W
Milton [N.Z.]	218	Cg	46.07S	169.58 E
Milton-Freewater	188	Fd	45.56N	118.23W
Milton Keynes	118	Mi	52.03N	0.42W
Miltou	168	Bc	10.14N	17.26 E
Milumbe, Monts-	170	Ed	8.00S	27.30 E
Miluo	154	Bj	28.51N	113.05 E
Miluo Jiang	152	Jf	28.51N	112.59 E
Milwaukee	176	Ke	43.02N	87.55W
Milwaukee Depth (EN)	106	Bh	19.30N	67.45W
Milwaukee Seamounts (EN)	208	Ia	32.28N	171.55 E
Milwaukie	188	Dd	45.27N	122.38W
Mimi-Gawa	156	Be	32.20N	131.37 E
Mimizan	122	Ej	44.12N	1.14W
Mimoň	120	Kf	50.40N	14.44 E
Mimongo	170	Bc	1.38S	11.39 E
Mimoso	204	Hb	15.10S	48.05W
Min	152	Kf	26.05N	119.32 E
Mina	126	Mi	35.58N	0.31 E
Mina [Mex.]	192	Id	26.01N	100.32W
Mina [Nv.-U.S.]	188	Fg	38.24N	118.07W
Mina, Cerro-	194	Ki	8.21N	73.10W
Mīnā' Abd Allāh	146	Mh	29.01N	48.10 E
Mīnā' al Aḥmadī	146	Mh	29.04N	48.09 E
Mīnāb	146	Qi	27.09N	57.05 E
Mīnāb	146	Qi	27.01N	56.53 E
Mīnā' Barānīs	164	Ge	23.55N	35.28 E
Minahassa = Minahassa Peninsula (EN)	140	Oi	1.00N	124.35 E
Minahassa Peninsula (EN) = Minahassa	140	Oi	1.00N	124.35 E
Minakuchi	156	Ed	34.59N	136.11 E
Minamata	154	Kh	32.13N	130.24 E
Minami-Daitō-Jima	152	Nf	25.50N	131.15 E
Minami-furano	156a	Cb	43.10N	142.32 E
Minami-Iō-Jima	214	Cc	24.14N	141.28 E
Minami-kayabe	156a	Bc	41.53N	141.01 E
Minami-Tori-Shima = Marcus Island (EN)	208	Gb	26.32N	142.09 E
Minas [Cuba]	194	Ic	21.29N	77.37W
Minas [Indon.]	150	Df	0.50N	101.29 E
Minas [Ur.]	200	Ki	34.23S	55.14W
Minas de Riotinto	126	Fg	37.42N	6.35W
Minaș Gerais (2)	202	Jg	18.00S	44.30W
Mīnā' Su'ūd	146	Mh	28.44N	48.24 E
Minatitlán [Mex.]	190	Fe	17.59N	94.31W
Minatitlán [Mex.]	192	Gh	19.22N	104.04W
Minaya	126	Je	39.17N	2.19W
Minbu	148	Id	20.11N	94.53 E
Minbya	148	Id	20.22N	93.16 E
Minchinmávida, Volcán-	206	Ff	42.49S	72.28W
Mincio	128	Ee	45.04N	10.59 E
Mindanao	140	Oi	8.00N	125.00 E
Mindanao Sea	140	Oi	9.15N	123.40 E
Mindel	120	Gh	48.31N	10.23 E
Mindelheim	120	Gh	48.03N	10.29 E
Mindelo	160	Eg	16.53N	25.00W
Minden [Ger.]	120	Ed	52.17N	8.55 E
Minden [La.-U.S.]	186	Jj	32.37N	93.17W
Minden [Nb.-U.S.]	186	Gf	40.30N	98.57W
Mindif	166	Hc	10.24N	14.26 E
Mindoro	140	Oh	12.50N	121.05 E
Mindoro Strait	150	Hd	12.20N	120.40 E
Mindouli	170	Bc	4.17S	14.21 E
Mindszent	120	Qj	46.32N	20.12 E
Mine	156	Bd	34.12N	131.11 E
Minehead	118	Jj	51.13N	3.29W
Mine Head	118	Fj	52.00N	7.35W
Mineiros	202	Hg	17.34S	52.34W
Mineral del Monte	192	Jg	20.08N	98.40W
Mineralnyje Vody	136	Eg	44.12N	43.08 E
Mineral Wells	182	He	32.48N	98.07W
Minerva Reefs	208	Jg	23.50S	179.00W
Minervino Murge	128	Ki	41.05N	16.05 E
Minervois	122	Ik	43.25N	2.45 E
Minfeng/Niya	152	Dd	37.04N	82.46 E
Minga	170	Ee	11.08S	27.56 E
Mingala	168	Cd	5.06N	21.49 E
Mingan	180	Lf	50.18N	64.01W
Mingečaur	132	Oi	40.46N	47.02 E
Mingečaurskoje vodohranilišče	132	Oi	40.55N	46.45 E
Mingenew	212	De	29.11S	115.26 E
Minggang	154	Ch	32.27N	114.02 E
Mingguang → Jiashan	154	Dh	32.47N	118.00 E
Ming He	154	Cf	37.14N	114.47 E
Minglanilla	126	Ke	39.32N	1.36W
Mingoyo	170	Ge	10.06S	39.38 E
Mingshui	152	Mb	47.15N	125.53 E
Mingshui → Zhangqiu	154	Df	36.44N	117.33 E
Mingteke	152	Bd	37.09N	74.58 E
Mingteke Daban	152	Bd	37.00N	74.50 E
Minguez, Puerto-	126	Ld	40.50N	0.59W
Mingulay	118	Fe	56.50N	7.40W
Mingyuegou	154	Jc	43.08N	128.55 E
Minhe	154	Hd	36.20N	102.50 E
Minho	126	Dc	41.40N	8.30W
Minho	126	Dc	41.52N	8.51W
Minicoy Island	140	Ji	8.17N	73.02 E
Minigwal, Lake-	212	Ee	29.35S	123.10 E
Minija	116	Ii	55.20N	21.12 E
Minilya	212	Cd	23.51S	113.58 E
Minilya River	212	Cd	23.56S	113.51 E
Minipi Lake	180	Lf	52.28N	60.50W
Ministra, Sierra-	126	Jc	41.07N	2.30W
Minjar	134	Hi	55.04N	57.33 E
Min Jiang	140	Mg	28.46N	104.38 E
Minmaya	154	Pd	41.10N	140.28 E
Minna	160	Hh	9.37N	6.33 E
Minna Bluff	222	Kf	78.32S	166.30 E
Minneapolis [Ks.-U.S.]	186	Hg	39.08N	97.42W
Minneapolis [Mn.-U.S.]	176	Je	44.59N	93.13W
Minnedosa	180	Hf	50.14N	99.51W
Minnedosa River	186	Fb	49.53N	100.08W
Minnesota (2)	182	Ib	46.00N	94.15W
Minnesota River	182	Ic	44.54N	93.10W
Mino	156	Ed	35.32N	136.54 E
Miño	110	Fg	41.52N	8.51W
Minobu	156	Fd	35.22N	138.24 E
Minobu-Sanchi	156	Fd	35.15N	138.20 E
Minokamo	156	Ed	35.26N	137.00 E
Mino-Mikawa-Kōgen	156	Ed	35.10N	137.25 E
Minorca (EN) = Menorca	110	Gg	40.00N	4.00 E
Minot	176	Ie	48.14N	101.18W
Minqin	152	Hd	38.42N	103.11 E
Minqing	152	Kf	26.15N	118.52 E
Minquan	154	Cg	34.39N	115.08 E
Minquiers, les-	118	Km	48.58N	2.08W
Min Shan	152	He	33.35N	103.00 E
Minsk	112	Ie	53.54N	27.34 E
Minskaja oblast (3)	136	Ce	53.50N	27.40 E
Minskaja vozvyšennost	116	Lj	54.00N	27.10 E
Mińsk Mazowiecki	120	Rd	52.11N	21.34 E
Minta	166	He	4.35N	12.48 E
Minto, Lac -	180	Ke	57.15N	74.50W
Minto, Mount-	222	Kf	71.47S	168.45 E
Minto Inlet	180	Fb	71.19N	117.00W
Minto Reef	208	Gd	8.08N	154.17 E
Minturn	186	Cg	39.35N	106.26W
Mīnūdasht	146	Pd	37.10N	55.25 E
Minuf	146	Dg	30.28N	30.56 E
Minusinsk	138	Ef	53.43N	91.48 E
Minvoul	170	Bb	2.09N	12.08 E
Minwakh	168	Hb	16.48N	48.06 E
Minxian	152	He	34.26N	104.02 E
Miory	114	Gi	55.39N	27.41 E
Mios Num	150	Kg	1.30S	135.10 E
Miquan	152	Ec	44.05N	87.33 E
Miquelon	180	Jg	49.00N	76.00W
Miquelon	174	Ne	47.03N	56.20W
Mira	126	Dg	37.43N	8.47W
Mira [It.]	128	Ge	45.26N	12.08 E
Mira [Port.]	126	Dd	40.26N	8.44W
Mira, Peña-	126	Fc	41.55N	6.28W
Mīrābād	144	Jc	30.25N	61.50 E
Mirabela	204	Jc	16.15S	44.11W
Miracatu	204	Ig	24.17S	47.28W
Miracema	202	Jh	21.25S	42.11W
Miracema do Tocantins	202	Ie	9.33S	48.24W
Mirador, Serra do-	204	Hh	26.45S	49.50W
Miraflores [Col.]	202	Dc	1.30N	72.16W
Miraflores [Col.]	202	Db	5.12N	73.12W
Miraj	148	Ee	16.50N	74.38 E
Miramar	206	Ie	38.16S	57.51W
Miramar, Laguna-	192	Ni	16.20N	91.20W
Miramas	122	Lk	43.35N	5.00 E
Mirambeau	122	Fi	45.22N	0.34W
Miramichi Bay	180	Kg	47.07N	65.10W
Miramont-de-Guyenne	122	Gj	44.36N	0.22 E
Miran	152	Ed	39.15N	88.50 E
Miranda (2)	202	Ea	10.15N	66.25W
Miranda [Arg.]	204	Cm	36.32S	59.09W
Miranda [Braz.]	202	Gh	20.14S	56.22W
Miranda de Corvo	126	Dd	40.06N	8.20W
Miranda de Ebro	126	Jb	42.41N	2.57W
Miranda do Douro	126	Fc	41.30N	6.16W
Mirande	122	Gk	43.31N	0.25 E
Mirandela	126	Ec	41.29N	7.11W
Mirandola	128	Ff	44.53N	11.04 E
Mirandópolis	204	Ge	21.09S	51.06W
Mirante do Paranapanema	204	Gf	22.17S	51.54W
Mira Por Vos	194	Jb	22.04N	74.38W
Mirapuxi, Rio-	204	Ga	13.06S	51.10W
Mirassol	204	He	20.46S	49.28W
Miravalles	126	Fb	42.45N	6.53W
Miravalles, Volcán-	174	Kh	10.45N	85.10W
Miravete, Puerto de-	126	Ge	39.43N	5.43W
Mir-Bašir → Terter	132	Oi	40.19N	46.58 E
Mirbāṭ	144	Hf	16.58N	54.50 E
Mirdita	130	Ch	41.49N	19.56 E
Mirebalais	194	Kd	18.50N	72.06W
Mirebeau	122	Gh	46.47N	0.11 E
Mirecourt	122	Mf	48.18N	6.08 E
Mirepoix	122	Hk	43.05N	1.53 E
Mirgorod	136	Df	50.00N	33.40 E
Miri	142	Ni	4.23N	113.59 E
Miria	166	Gc	13.43N	9.07 E
Mirim, Lagoa-	198	Ki	32.45S	52.50W
Mirina	130	Ij	39.52N	25.04 E
Miriñay, Esteros del-	204	Di	28.49S	57.10W
Miriñay, Rio-	204	Dj	30.10S	57.39W
Mirny	142	Nc	62.33N	113.53 E
Mirny	222	Ge	66.33S	93.01 E
Mironovka	132	Ge	49.40N	31.01 E
Mirosławiec	120	Mc	53.21N	16.05 E
Mirpur	148	Eb	33.11N	73.46 E
Mirpur Khās	142	Ig	25.32N	69.00 E
Mirqah Sūr	146	Kd	36.50N	44.19 E
Mīrsāle	168	Hd	5.58N	47.54 E
Mirşani	130	He	44.01N	24.01 E
Mirtöön Pélagos	130	Gm	37.00N	24.00 E
Miryang	154	Jg	35.29N	128.45 E
Mirzāpur	148	Gc	25.09N	82.35 E
Misaki	156	Ce	33.23N	132.07 E
Misawa	154	Pd	40.41N	141.24 E
Misery, Mount-	197c	Ab	17.22N	62.48W
Mishan	152	Nb	45.34N	131.50 E
Mishawaka	184	De	41.40N	86.11W
Mishima	156	Fd	35.07N	138.54 E
Mi-Shima	154	Kg	34.47N	131.10 E
Mishraq, Khashm-	146	Lj	24.13N	46.18 E
Misilmeri	128	Hl	38.02N	13.27 E
Misima Island	214	Fj	10.40S	152.45 E
Misiones (2)	206	Jc	27.00S	55.00W
Misiones (3)	204	Dh	27.00S	57.00W
Misiones, Sierra de-	204	Eh	26.45S	54.20W
Miskah	146	Jj	24.53N	42.58 E
Miski, Enneri-	168	Bb	18.10N	17.45 E
Miškino	134	Ki	55.20N	63.55 E
Miskitos, Cayos-	190	Hf	14.23N	82.46W
Miskolc	112	If	48.06N	20.47 E
Miskolc (2)	120	Qh	48.06N	20.43 E
Mismār	168	Fb	18.13N	35.38 E
Misool, Pulau-	208	Ee	1.52S	130.10 E
Misquah Hills	182	Ib	47.17N	92.00W
Mişr = Egypt (EN) (1)	160	Jf	27.00N	30.00 E
Mişr al Jadīdah, Al Qāhirah-	164	Fc	30.06N	31.20 E
Mişrātah	160	Ie	32.23N	15.06 E
Mişrātah (3)	164	Cd	29.00N	16.00 E
Mişrātah, Ra's-	158	Ie	32.25N	15.05 E
Misserghin	126	Li	35.37N	0.44W
Missinaibi	180	Jf	50.44N	81.30W
Missinaibi Lake	184	Fa	48.23N	83.40W
Missinipe	180	He	55.36N	104.45W
Mission [S.D.-U.S.]	186	Fe	43.18N	100.40W
Mission [Tx.-U.S.]	186	Gm	26.13N	98.20W
Mission	188	Db	49.08N	122.18W
Mission Range	188	Ic	47.30N	113.55W
Mississippi (2)	182	Je	32.50N	89.30W
Mississippi	174	Kg	29.00N	89.15W
Mississippi Delta	174	Kg	29.10N	89.15W
Mississippi Fan (EN)	182	Jf	26.45N	88.30W
Mississippi River	184	Ic	45.26N	76.16W
Mississippi Sound	186	Lk	30.15N	89.00W
Misso	116	Lg	57.33N	27.23 E
Missoula	176	He	46.52N	114.01W
Missour	162	Gc	33.03N	3.59W
Missouri (2)	182	Id	38.30N	93.30W
Missouri	174	Jf	38.50N	90.08W
Missouri, Coteau du-	186	Gc	46.00N	99.30W
Missouri Valley	186	If	41.33N	95.53W
Mistassini	180	Kf	50.30N	74.00W
Mistassini	184	Ka	48.58N	72.40W
Mistassini, Lac-	174	Ld	51.00N	75.00W
Mistassini, Rivière-	180	Kg	48.42N	72.20W
Mistelbach an der Zaya	128	Kb	48.34N	16.34 E
Misterhult	116	Gg	57.28N	16.33 E
Mistrás	130	Fl	37.04N	22.22 E
Mistretta	128	Im	37.56N	14.22 E
Misugi	156	Ed	34.33N	136.15 E
Misumi [Jap.]	156	Bd	34.46N	131.58 E
Misumi [Jap.]	156	Be	32.37N	130.29 E
Mita, Punta-	192	Gg	32.04N	105.33W
Mitare, Rio-	194	Mh	11.28N	69.56W
Mitchell [Austl.]	212	Je	26.29S	147.58 E
Mitchell [Or.-U.S.]	188	Ed	44.34N	120.09W
Mitchell [S.D.-U.S.]	182	Hc	43.40N	98.01W
Mitchell, Mount-	174	Kf	35.46N	82.16W
Mitchell Range	212	Hb	12.50S	135.35 E
Mitchell River	208	Ff	15.12S	141.35 E
Mitchell River Mission	212	Ic	15.28S	141.44 E
Mitchelstown/Baile Mhistéala	118	Ei	52.16N	8.16W
Mithimna	130	Jj	39.22N	26.10 E
Mitiaro Island	208	Lf	19.49S	157.43W
Mitidja, Plaine de la-	126	Oh	36.36N	3.00 E
Mitilini	130	Jj	39.06N	26.33 E
Mitilinis, Stenón-	130	Jj	39.10N	26.35 E
Mitla	190	Ee	16.55N	96.17W
Mitla, Laguna-	192	Ii	17.03N	100.25W
Mito	152	Pd	36.22N	140.28 E
Mitomoni	170	Ge	11.32S	35.19 E
Mitsamiouli	172	Gb	11.23S	43.18 E
Mitsinjo	172	Hc	16.00S	45.52 E
Mitsio, Nosy-	172	Hb	12.54S	48.36 E
Mitsiwa = Massawa (EN)	160	Kg	15.37N	39.39 E
Mitsiwa Channel	168	Fb	15.30N	40.00 E
Mitsuishi	156a	Cb	42.15N	142.33 E
Mitsukaido	156	Fc	36.01N	139.59 E
Mitsuke	156	Fc	37.32N	138.56 E
Mitsushima	156	Ad	34.16N	129.20 E
Mittelfranken	120	Gg	49.20N	10.50 E
Mittelland	128	Bd	46.50N	7.05 E
Mittellandkanal	110	He	52.16N	11.41 E
Mittelmark	120	Jd	52.20N	13.20 E
Mittenwald	120	Hi	47.27N	11.15 E
Mittersheim	124	If	48.52N	6.56 E
Mittersill	128	Gc	47.16N	12.29 E
Mittweida	120	If	50.59N	12.59 E
Mitú	200	Ie	1.08N	70.03W

Mitumba, Monts-=Mitumba Range (EN)	158	Ji	6.00 S	29.00 E
Mitumba Range (EN)= Mitumba, Monts-	158	Ji	6.00 S	29.00 E
Mituva	116	Jj	55.00N	22.45 E
Mitwaba	170	Ed	8.38 S	27.20 E
Mitzic	170	Bb	0.47N	11.34 E
Miura	156	Fd	35.08N	139.37 E
Miura-Hantō	156	Fd	35.15N	139.40 E
Mixco Viejo	194	Bf	14.52N	90.40W
Mixian	154	Bg	34.31N	113.22 E
Mixteco, Rio-	192	Jh	18.11N	98.30W
Miya-Gawa	156	Ed	34.32N	136.42 E
Miyagi Ken [2]	154	Pe	38.30N	140.50 E
Miyagusuku-Jima	156b	Ab	26.22N	127.59 E
Miyāh, Wādī al-	146	Gi	26.06N	36.31 E
Miyāh, Wādī al- [Eg.]	146	Ej	25.00N	33.23 E
Miyāh, Wādī al- [Syr.]	146	He	34.44N	39.57 E
Miyake-Jima	152	Oe	34.05N	139.30 E
Miyako	152	Pd	39.38N	141.57 E
Miyako-Jima	152	Mg	24.45N	125.20 E
Miyakonojō	154	Ki	31.44N	131.04 E
Miyako-Rettō	152	Lg	24.25N	125.00 E
Miyako-Wan	156	Hb	39.40N	142.00 E
Miyama	156	Dd	35.17N	135.34 E
Miyanojō	156	Bf	31.54N	130.27 E
Miyanoura-Dake	154	Ki	30.20N	130.29 E
Miyata	156	Be	33.45N	130.45 E
Miyazaki	152	Ne	31.54N	131.26 E
Miyazaki Ken [2]	154	Kh	32.05N	131.20 E
Miyazu	154	Mg	35.32N	135.11 E
Miyazuka-Yama	156	Fd	34.24N	139.16 E
Miyazu-Wan	156	Dd	35.35N	135.13 E
Miyoshi	154	Lg	34.48N	132.51 E
Miyun	152	Kc	40.22N	116.53 E
Miyun Shuiku	154	Dd	40.31N	116.58 E
Mizan Teferi	168	Fd	6.53N	35.28 E
Mizdah	164	Bc	31.26N	12.59 E
Mizen Head/Carn Ui Néid	110	Fe	51.27N	9.49W
Mizhi	152	Jd	37.50N	110.03 E
Mizija	130	Gf	43.43N	23.51 E
Mizil	130	Je	45.01N	26.27 E
Mizorām [3]	148	Id	23.00N	93.00 E
Mizque	202	Eg	17.56 S	65.19W
Mizuho	156	Cd	34.50N	132.29 E
Mizuho	222	Ef	70.43 S	40.20 E
Mizunami	156	Ed	35.22N	137.15 E
Mizusawa	154	Pe	39.08N	141.08 E
Mjadel	116	Lj	54.54N	27.03 E
Mjakiševo	116	Mh	56.30N	28.54 E
Mjakit	138	Kd	61.23N	152.10 E
Mjällom	116	Ha	62.59N	18.26 E
Mjaundža	138	Jd	63.02N	147.13 E
Mjölby	114	Dg	58.19N	15.08 E
Mjøndalen	116	De	59.45N	10.01 E
Mjorn	116	Eg	57.54N	12.25 E
Mjøsa	110	Hc	60.40N	11.00 E
Mkoani	170	Gd	5.22 S	39.39 E
Mkokotoni	170	Gd	5.52 S	39.15 E
Mkushi Bona	170	Ee	13.37 S	29.23 E
Mkushi River	170	Fe	13.33 S	29.40 E
Mkuze	172	Ee	27.10 S	32.00 E
Mladá Boleslav	120	Kf	50.21N	14.54 E
Mladenovac	130	De	44.26N	20.42 E
Mlava	130	Ee	44.45N	21.14 E
Mława	120	Qc	53.06N	20.23 E
Mljet	128	Lh	42.45N	17.30 E
Mljetski kanal	128	Lh	42.48N	17.35 E
Mmadinare	172	Dd	21.53 S	27.45 E
Mnichovo Hradiště	120	Kf	50.32N	14.59 E
Mnogoveršinny	138	If	53.55N	139.50 E
Moa	194	Jc	20.40N	74.56W
Moa	166	Cd	6.59N	11.36W
Moa, Pulau-	150	Ih	8.10 S	127.56 E
Moab	182	Fd	38.35N	109.33W
Moabi	170	Bc	2.24 S	10.59 E
Moala	219d	Bc	18.36 S	179.53 E
Moamba	172	Ee	25.36 S	32.15 E
Moanda [Gabon]	170	Bc	1.34 S	13.11 E
Moanda [Zaire]	170	Bd	5.56 S	12.21 E
Moatize	172	Ec	16.10 S	33.46 E
Moba	160	Ji	7.03 S	29.47 E
Mobara	156	Gd	35.25N	140.17 E
Mobārakeh	146	Nf	32.20N	51.30 E
Mobaye	160	Jh	4.19N	21.11 E
Mobayi-Mbongo	170	Db	4.18N	21.11 E
Mobeka	170	Cb	1.53N	19.46 E
Moberly	182	Id	39.25N	92.26W
Mobile	176	Kf	30.42N	88.05W
Mobile Bay	182	Je	30.25N	88.00W
Mobridge	182	Gb	45.32N	100.26W
Mobuto Sese Seko, Lac-= Albert, Lake- (EN)	158	Kh	1.40N	31.00 E
Moca	194	Ld	19.24N	70.31W
Moçambique=Mozambique (EN)	160	Lj	15.03 S	40.45 E
Moçambique=Mozambique (EN) [1]	160	Kj	18.15 S	35.00 E
Moçambique, Canal de-= Mozambique Channel (EN)	158	Lk	20.00 S	43.00 E
Mocapra, Rio-	196	Ci	7.56N	66.46W
Mocha, Isla-	206	Fe	38.22 S	73.56W
Moc Hoa	148	Lf	10.46N	105.56 E
Mochudi	172	Dd	24.23 S	26.08 E
Mocimboa da Praia	160	Lj	11.20 S	40.21 E
Möckeln	116	Fh	56.40N	14.10 E
Mockfjärd	116	Fd	60.30N	14.58 E
Moco, Serra-	158	Ij	12.28 S	15.10 E
Mocoa	202	Cc	1.09N	76.38W
Mococa	204	Ie	21.28 S	47.01W
Mocovi	204	Ci	28.24 S	59.42W
Moctezuma [Mex.]	192	If	22.45N	101.05W
Moctezuma [Mex.]	192	Fb	30.12N	106.26W
Moctezuma [Mex.]	190	Cc	29.48N	109.42W
Moctezuma, Rio- [Mex.]	192	Jg	21.59N	98.34W
Moctezuma, Rio- [Mex.]	192	Ec	29.09N	109.40W
Mocuba	160	Kj	16.51 S	36.56 E
Mocubúri	172	Fb	14.39 S	38.54 E
Močurica	130	Jg	42.31N	26.32 E
Modane	122	Mi	45.12N	6.40 E
Modderrivier	172	Ce	29.02 S	24.37 E
Modena [It.]	128	Ef	44.40N	10.55 E
Modena [Ut.-U.S.]	188	Ih	37.49N	113.55W
Moder	122	Of	48.49N	8.06 E
Modesto	182	Cd	37.39N	120.59W
Modica	128	In	36.52N	14.46 E
Modjamboli	170	Db	2.28N	22.06 E
Modjigo	166	Hb	17.09N	13.12 E
Mödling	128	Kb	48.05N	16.28 E
Modriča	128	Mf	44.58N	18.18 E
Modum	116	Ce	59.55N	10.00 E
Moe	212	Jg	38.10 S	146.15 E
Moelv	114	Cf	60.56N	10.42 E
Moen	220d	Bb	7.26N	151.52 E
Moengo	202	Hb	5.37N	54.24W
Moen-jo-Daro	148	Dc	27.19N	68.07 E
Moenkopi Wash	188	Ji	35.54N	111.26W
Moerbeke	124	Fc	51.10N	3.56 E
Moers	120	Ce	51.27N	6.39 E
Moeskroen/Mouscron	122	Jd	50.44N	3.13 E
Moffat	118	Jf	55.20N	3.27W
Moga	170	Ec	2.21 S	26.49 E
Mogadishu (EN)=Muqdisho	160	Lh	2.03N	45.22 E
Mogadouro	126	Fc	41.20N	6.43W
Mogadouro, Serra do-	126	Fc	41.19N	6.40W
Mogāl	146	Nd	36.35N	50.35 E
Mogalakwena	172	Dd	22.27 S	28.55 E
Mogami	156	Gb	38.45N	140.30 E
Mogami-Gawa	154	Oe	38.54N	139.50 E
Mogami Trench (EN)	156	Fb	39.00N	139.00 E
Mogaung	148	Jc	25.18N	96.56 E
Mogho	168	Ge	4.49N	40.19 E
Mogielnica	120	Qe	51.42N	20.43 E
Mogilev	112	Je	53.56N	30.18 E
Mogilev-Podolskí	132	Ee	48.27N	27.48 E
Mogilevskaja oblast [3]	136	De	53.45N	30.30 E
Mogilno	120	Nd	52.40N	17.58 E
Mogincual	172	Gc	15.34 S	40.24 E
Mogoča	142	Nd	53.44N	119.44 E
Mogočin	138	De	57.43N	83.40 E
Mogogh	168	Ed	8.26N	31.19 E
Mogojto	138	Gf	54.25N	110.27 E
Mogojtuj	138	Gf	51.15N	114.58 E
Mogok	148	Jd	22.55N	96.30 E
Mogollon Rim	182	Ee	34.20N	111.00W
Mogotes, Punta-	204	Dn	38.06 S	57.33W
Mogotón, Pico-	194	Dg	13.45N	86.23W
Mogreïn	160	Ff	25.13N	11.34W
Mogroum	168	Bc	11.06N	15.25 E
Moguer	126	Fg	37.16N	6.50W
Mogzon	138	Gf	51.42N	111.59 E
Mohács	120	Ok	45.59N	18.42 E
Mohaka	218	Gc	39.07 S	177.12 E
Mohaka	218	Gc	39.07 S	177.12 E
Mohales Hoek	172	Df	30.15 S	27.25 E
Mohall	186	Fb	48.46N	101.31W
Moḥammadābād	146	Pg	31.47N	54.27 E
Mohammadia	126	Mi	35.35N	0.04 E
Mohammedia	162	Fc	33.42N	7.24W
Mohanganj	148	Id	24.54N	90.59 E
Mohang-ni	154	If	36.46N	126.08 E
Mohave, Lake-	182	Ed	35.25N	114.38W
Mohawk Mountains	188	Ij	32.25N	113.25W
Mohe	142	Od	53.27N	122.18 E
Moheda	116	Fh	57.00N	14.34 E
Mohéli/Mwali	158	Lj	12.15 S	43.45 E
Moher, Cliffs of-/Aillte an Mhothair	118	Di	52.58N	9.27W
Mohican, Cape-	178	Fd	60.12N	167.28W
Mohinora	174	Ig	26.06N	107.04W
Möhne	120	Ee	51.27N	8.00 E
Möhnesee	124	Kc	51.29N	8.05 E
Mohns Ridge (EN)	110	Ga	73.00N	5.00 E
Moholm	116	Ff	58.37N	14.02 E
Mohon, Charleville-Mézierès-	124	Ge	49.46N	4.43 E
Mohon Peak	188	Ii	34.57N	113.15W
Mohoro	170	Gd	8.08 S	39.10 E
Mohotani, Ile-	216	Na	9.59 S	138.49W
Mohovaja	138	Kf	53.01N	158.38 E
Moi	116	Bf	58.28N	6.32 E
Moikovac	130	Cg	42.58N	19.35 E
Moimenta da Beira	126	Ed	40.59N	7.37W
Moindou	219b	Be	21.42 S	165.41 E
Moinești	130	Jc	46.28N	26.29 E
Moirai	130	Hn	35.03N	24.52 E
Mo i Rana	112	Hb	66.18N	14.08 E
Mõisaküla/Myjzakjula	114	Fg	58.07N	25.10 E
Moisés Ville	204	Bj	30.43 S	61.29W
Moisie	180	Kf	50.11N	66.06W
Moisie	180	Kf	50.13N	66.06W
Moissac	122	Hj	44.06N	1.05 E
Moïssala	168	Bd	8.21N	17.46 E
Moitaco	196	Dh	8.01N	61.21W
Möja	116	He	59.25N	18.55 E
Mojácar	126	Kg	37.08N	1.51W
Mojada, Sierra-	192	Hd	27.15N	103.45W
Mojana, Caño-	194	Ji	9.02N	74.46W
Mojave	182	Dd	35.03N	118.10W
Mojave Desert	174	Hf	35.00N	117.00W
Mojiguaçu, Rio-	204	He	20.53 S	48.10W
Moji Mirim	204	If	22.26 S	46.57W
Mojjero	138	Fc	68.44N	103.30 E
Mojo	168	Fd	8.36N	39.09 E
Mojo	168	Gd	8.00N	41.50 E
Mojos, Llanos de-	198	Jg	15.00 S	65.00W
Moju, Rio-	202	Id	1.40 S	48.25W
Mojynty	136	Hf	47.10N	73.18 E
Mokambo	170	Ee	12.25 S	28.21 E
Mokapu Peninsula	221a	Db	21.26N	157.45W
Mokau	216	Dg	38.41 S	174.37 E
Mokau	218	Fc	38.42 S	174.35 E
Mokhotlong	172	De	29.17 S	29.05 E
Mokil Atoll	208	Gd	6.40N	159.47 E
Moklakan	138	Gf	54.48N	118.56 E
Möklinta	116	Gd	60.05N	16.32 E
Mokochu, Khao-	148	Je	15.56N	99.06 E
Mokohinau Islands	218	Fa	35.55 S	175.05 E
Mokolo	166	Hc	10.45N	13.48 E
Mokp'o	142	Of	34.47N	126.23 E
Mokra Gora	130	Dg	42.50N	20.25 E
Mokrany	120	Ue	51.48N	24.23 E
Mokrin	130	Dd	45.56N	20.25 E
Mokša	110	Ke	54.44N	41.53 E
Mokwa	166	Gd	9.17N	5.03 E
Mol	122	Lc	51.11N	5.07 E
Mola di Bari	128	Li	41.04N	17.05 E
Molango	192	Jg	20.47N	98.43W
Moláoi	130	Fm	36.48N	22.51 E
Molara	128	Dj	40.50N	9.45 E
Molas, Punta-	192	Pg	20.35N	86.44W
Molat	128	If	44.13N	14.50 E
Molatón	126	Kf	38.59N	1.24W
Molay-Littry, Le-	124	Be	49.15N	0.53W
Moldau (EN)=Vltava	110	He	50.21N	14.30 E
Moldava nad Bodvou	120	Qh	48.37N	21.00 E
Moldavia (EN)=Moldova	110	If	46.30N	27.00 E
Moldavia (EN) = Moldova	130	Jc	46.30N	27.00 E
Moldavia (EN) = Moldova	136	Cf	47.00N	29.00 E
Moldavskaja Sovetskaja Socialističeskaja Respublika → Moldova	136	Cf	47.00N	29.00 E
Moldavskaja SSR/ Respublika Sovetike Sočialiste Moldovenjaske → Moldova	136	Cf	47.00N	29.00 E
Moldavskaja SSR → Moldova	136	Cf	47.00N	29.00 E
Molde	112	Gc	62.44N	7.11 E
Moldefjorden	116	Bb	62.45N	7.05 E
Moldova	136	Cf	47.00N	29.00 E
Moldova	130	Jc	46.54N	26.58 E
Moldova = Moldavia (EN)	110	If	46.30N	27.00 E
Moldova = Moldavia (EN)	130	Jc	46.30N	27.00 E
Moldova Nouă	130	Ee	44.44N	21.41 E
Moldoveanu, Vîrful-	130	If	45.36N	24.44 E
Moldovița	130	Ib	47.41N	25.32 E
Mole	124	Bc	51.24N	0.20W
Molène, Ile de-	122	Bf	48.24N	4.58W
Molens van Kinderdijk	124	Gc	51.52N	4.40 E
Molepolole	160	Jk	24.25 S	25.30 E
Môle Saint-Nicolas	194	Kd	19.47N	73.22W
Molėtai / Moletaj	116	Ki	55.13N	25.36 E
Moletaj / Molėtai	116	Ki	55.13N	25.36 E
Molfetta	128	Ki	41.12N	16.36 E
Molihong Shan	154	Hc	42.11N	124.43 E
Molina, Parameras de-	126	Jd	40.55N	2.01W
Molina de Aragón	126	Kd	40.51N	1.53W
Molina de Segura	126	Kf	38.03N	1.12W
Moline	186	Kf	41.30N	90.31W
Moliniere Point	197p	Bb	12.05N	61.45W
Molise	128	Ii	41.40N	14.30 E
Molkābād	146	Oe	34.32N	52.35 E
Molkom	116	Ee	59.36N	13.43 E
Moll	204	Cl	35.04 S	59.39W
Möll	128	Hd	46.50N	13.26 E
Mollafeneri	130	Mi	40.54N	29.30 E
Mölle	116	Eh	56.17N	12.29 E
Mollendo	200	Ig	17.02 S	72.01W
Molliens-Dreuil	124	Ee	49.52N	2.01 E
Mölln	120	Gc	53.38N	10.41 E
Mollösund	116	Df	58.04N	11.28 E
Mölndal	114	Ch	57.39N	12.01 E
Mölnlycke	116	Eg	57.39N	12.09 E
Moločansk	132	If	47.10N	35.36 E
Moločny, liman-	132	If	46.30N	35.20 E
Molócuè	172	Fc	17.03 S	38.52 E
Molodečno	136	Ce	54.19N	26.53 E
Molodežnaja	222	Ee	67.40 S	45.51 E
Molodi	116	Mf	58.00N	28.52 E
Molodogvardejskoje	136	He	54.07N	70.50 E
Mologa	110	Jd	58.50N	37.11 E
Molokai Island	208	Lb	21.08N	157.00W
Moloma	114	Lg	58.20N	48.28 E
Molong	212	Jf	33.06 S	148.52 E
Molopo	158	Jk	28.31 S	20.13 E
Moloundou	166	Ie	2.02N	15.13 E
Molteno	172	Df	31.24 S	26.22 E
Molu, Pulau-	150	Jh	6.45 S	131.33 E
Moluccas (EN)=Maluku, Kepulauan-	208	De	2.00 S	128.00 E
Molucca Sea (EN)=Maluku, Laut-	140	Oj	0.05 S	125.00 E
Molygino	138	Ee	58.11N	94.45 E
Moma	172	Fc	16.44 S	39.14 E
Moma	138	Jc	66.20N	143.06 E
Mombaça	202	Ke	5.45 S	39.28W
Mombasa	160	Ki	4.03 S	39.40 E
Mombo	170	Gc	4.53 S	38.17 E
Momboyo	170	Cc	0.16 S	19.00 E
Mombuca, Serra da-	204	Fd	18.15 S	52.26W
Momčilgrad	130	Ih	41.32N	25.25 E
Momling	124	Le	49.50N	9.09 E
Momotombo, Volcán-	194	Dg	12.26N	86.33W
Mompono	170	Db	0.04N	21.48 E
Mompós	202	Db	9.14N	74.27W
Momski hrebet	138	Jc	66.00N	145.00 E
Mon [2]	148	Je	17.22N	97.20 E
Møn	114	Ci	55.00N	12.20 E
Mona, Canal de la-=Mona Passage (EN)	174	Mh	18.30N	67.45W
Mona, Isla-	190	Ke	18.05N	67.54W
Mona, Punta-	194	Fi	9.38N	82.37W
Monach Islands	118	Fd	57.32N	7.40W
Monaco [1]	112	Gg	43.42N	7.23 E
Monadhliath Mountains	118	Id	57.15N	4.10W
Monagas [2]	202	Fb	9.20N	63.00W
Monaghan/Muineachán	118	Gg	54.15N	6.58W
Monaghan/Muineachán [2]	118	Gg	54.10N	7.00W
Monahans	186	Ek	31.36N	102.54W
Mona Passage (EN)=Mona, Canal de la-	174	Mh	18.30N	67.45W
Monapo	172	Gb	14.55 S	40.18 E
Monarch Mountain	180	Ef	51.54N	125.54W
Monashee Mountains	180	Ff	51.00N	118.43W
Monastyrščina	132	Gb	54.19N	31.48 E
Monatélé	166	He	4.16N	11.12 E
Monbetsu [Jap.]	154	Qc	42.28N	142.07 E
Monbetsu [Jap.]	152	Pc	44.21N	143.22 E
Monbetsu-Shokotsu	156a	Ca	44.23N	143.16 E
Moncalieri	128	Be	45.00N	7.41 E
Moncalvo	128	Ce	45.03N	8.16 E
Monção [Braz.]	202	Id	3.30 S	45.15W
Monção [Port.]	126	Db	42.05N	8.29W
Moncayo	126	Kc	41.46N	1.50W
Moncayo, Sierra del-	126	Kc	41.45N	1.50W
Mončegorsk	136	Db	67.56N	32.58 E
Mönchengladbach	120	Ce	51.12N	6.26 E
Mönchengladbach-Rheydt	124	Ic	51.10N	6.27 E
Mönchengladbach-Wickrath	124	Ic	51.08N	6.25 E
Mönchgut	120	Jb	54.20N	13.40 E
Monchique	126	Dg	37.19N	8.33W
Monchique, Serra de-	126	Dg	37.19N	8.36W
Monclova	176	Ig	26.54N	101.25W
Moncton	176	Me	46.06N	64.07W
Mondai	204	Fh	27.05 S	53.25W
Mondego	126	Dd	40.09N	8.52W
Mondego, Cabo-	126	Dd	40.11N	8.55W
Mondeville	124	Be	49.10N	0.19W
Mondjoko	170	Dc	1.41 S	21.12 E
Mondo	168	Bc	13.43N	15.32 E
Mondoñedo	126	Ea	43.26N	7.22W
Mondorf-les-Bains/Bad Mondorf	124	Ie	49.30N	6.17 E
Mondoubleau	122	Gg	47.59N	0.54 E
Mondovi	128	Bf	44.23N	7.49 E
Mondragone	128	Hi	41.07N	13.53 E
Mondy	138	Ff	51.40N	100.59 E
Monédières, Les-	122	Hi	45.30N	1.52 E
Monemvasia	130	Gm	36.41N	23.03 E
Monessen	184	He	40.09N	79.53W
Monett	186	Jh	36.55N	93.55W
Monfalcone	128	He	45.49N	13.32 E
Monferrato	128	Cf	44.55N	8.05 E
Monforte	126	Ee	39.03N	7.26W
Monforte de Lemos	126	Eb	42.31N	7.30W
Monga	170	Db	4.12N	22.49 E
Mongala	170	Cb	1.53N	19.46 E
Mongalla	168	Ed	5.12N	31.46 E
Mongbwalu	170	Fb	1.57N	30.02 E
Mong Cai	148	Ld	21.32N	107.58 E
Monger, Lake-	212	De	29.15 S	117.05 E
Mongga	219a	Cb	7.57 S	156.59 E
Monggolküre/Zhaosu	152	Dc	43.10N	81.07 E
Monghyr → Munger	148	Hc	25.23N	86.28 E
Mongibello	110	Hh	37.50N	14.55 E
Mongibello → Etna	110	Hh	37.50N	14.55 E
Monginevro, Colle del-	122	Mj	44.56N	6.44 E
Mongo	160	Ig	12.11N	18.42 E
Mongo	166	Cd	9.34N	12.11W
Mongol Altajn Nuruu = Mongolian Altai (EN)	140	Le	46.30N	93.00 E
Mongol Ard Uls = Mongolia (EN) [1]	142	Me	47.00N	104.00 E
Mongolia (EN) = Mongol Ard Uls [1]	142	Me	47.00N	104.00 E
Mongolian Altai (EN) = Mongol Altajn Nuruu	140	Le	46.30N	93.00 E
Mongonu	166	Hc	12.41N	13.36 E
Mongororo	168	Cc	12.01N	22.28 E
Mongoumba	168	Be	3.38N	18.36 E
Mong Pan	148	Jd	20.19N	98.22 E
Mongrove, Punta-	192	Hi	17.56N	102.11W
Mongu	160	Jj	15.17 S	23.08 E
Monguel	162	Ef	16.25N	13.08W
Mong Yai	148	Jd	22.25N	98.02 E
Monheim	124	Ic	51.05N	6.53 E
Mönichkirchen	128	Kc	47.30N	16.02 E
Mon Idée, Auvillers-les-Forges-	124	Ge	49.52N	4.21 E
Monigotes	204	Bj	30.30 S	61.39W
Moni Hosiou Loukā	130	Fk	38.24N	22.49 E
Monistrol-sur-Loire	122	Ki	45.17N	4.10 E
Monito, Isla-	197a	Ab	18.09N	67.56W
Monitor Peak	188	Gg	38.50N	116.32W
Monitor Range	188	Gg	38.45N	116.40W
Monjolos	204	Jd	18.18 S	44.05W
Monkayo	150	Ie	7.50N	126.00 E
Monkey Bay	170	Fe	14.05 S	34.55 E
Monkey Point	194	Fg	11.36N	83.39W
Monkey River	194	Ce	16.22N	88.29W
Mońki	120	Sc	53.24N	22.49 E
Monkoto	170	Dc	1.38 S	20.39 E
Monmouth	118	Kj	51.45N	3.00W
Monmouth [Il.-U.S.]	186	Kf	40.55N	90.39W
Monmouth [Or.-U.S.]	188	Dd	44.51N	123.14W
Monmouth [Wales-U.K.]	118	Kj	51.50N	2.43W
Monmouth Mountain	188	Da	51.00N	123.47W
Mönne	120	De	51.28N	7.30 E
Monnikendam	124	Hb	52.27N	5.02 E
Monnow	118	Kj	51.48N	2.42W
Mono [3]	166	Fd	6.45N	1.50 E
Mono	219a	Bb	7.20 S	155.35 E
Monobe-Gawa	156	Ce	33.32N	133.42 E
Mono Lake	182	Dd	38.00N	119.00W
Monólithos	130	Km	36.07N	27.45 E
Monopoli	128	Lj	40.57N	17.18 E
Monor	120	Pi	47.21N	19.27 E
Monou	168	Cb	16.24N	22.11 E
Monóvar / Monòver	126	Lf	38.26N	0.50W
Monòver / Monóvar	126	Lf	38.26N	0.50W
Monowai, Lake-	218	Bf	45.55 S	167.25 E
Monreal del Campo	126	Kd	40.47N	1.21W
Monreale	128	Hl	38.05N	13.17 E
Monroe [Ga.-U.S.]	184	Fi	33.47N	83.43W
Monroe [La.-U.S.]	176	Jf	32.33N	92.07W
Monroe [Mi.-U.S.]	184	Fe	41.55N	83.24W
Monroe [N.C.-U.S.]	184	Gh	34.59N	80.33W
Monroe [Or.-U.S.]	188	Dd	44.19N	123.18W
Monroe [Wi.-U.S.]	186	Le	42.36N	89.38W
Monroe, Lake-	184	Df	39.05N	86.25W
Monroe City	186	Kg	39.39N	91.44W
Monroeville	184	Dj	31.31N	87.20W
Monrovia	160	Fh	6.19N	10.48W
Mons/Bergen	122	Jd	50.27N	3.56 E
Monsanto	126	Ed	40.02N	7.07W
Monschau	120	Cf	50.33N	6.15 E
Monselice	128	Fe	45.14N	11.45 E
Monserrate, Isla-	192	De	25.41N	111.05W
Monsheim	124	Ke	49.38N	8.12 E
Møns Klint	116	Ej	54.58N	12.33 E
Mönsterås	114	Dh	57.02N	16.26 E
Montabaur	120	Df	50.26N	7.50 E
Montagna Grande	128	Gm	37.56N	12.44 E
Montagne	122	Jh	46.10N	3.40 E
Montagu	222	Ad	58.25 S	26.20W
Montague	178	Je	60.00N	147.30W
Montague, Isla-	192	Bb	31.45N	114.48W
Montaigu	122	Eh	46.59N	1.19W
Montalbán	126	Ld	40.50N	0.48W
Montalbano Ionico	128	Kj	40.17N	16.34 E
Montalcino	128	Fg	43.03N	11.29 E
Montalegre	126	Ec	41.49N	7.48W
Montalto di Castro	128	Fh	42.21N	11.37 E
Montalto Uffugo	128	Kk	39.24N	16.09 E
Montalvânia	204	Jb	14.28 S	44.32W
Montana	128	Bd	46.18N	7.30 E
Montana [2]	182	Eb	47.00N	110.00W
Montana-Vermala	128	Bd	46.18N	7.30 E
Montánchez	126	Fe	39.13N	6.09W
Montánchez, Sierra de-	126	Ge	39.15N	5.55W
Montargis	122	Ig	48.00N	2.45 E
Montataire	124	Ee	49.16N	2.26 E
Montauban [Fr.]	122	Df	48.12N	2.03W
Montauban [Fr.]	122	Hj	44.01N	1.21 E
Montauk Point	184	Le	41.04N	71.52W
Montbard	122	Kg	47.37N	4.20 E
Montbéliard	122	Mg	47.31N	6.48 E
Montblanc	126	Nc	41.22N	1.10 E
Montbrison	122	Ki	45.36N	4.03 E
Montceau-les-Mines	122	Kh	46.40N	4.22 E
Mont Cenis, Col du-	110	Gf	45.15N	6.54 E
Montchanin	122	Kh	46.45N	4.27 E
Mont Darwin	172	Ec	16.46 S	31.35 E
Mont-de-Marsan	122	Fk	43.53N	0.30W
Montdidier	122	Ie	49.39N	2.34 E
Mont-Dore [Fr.]	122	Ii	45.34N	2.49 E
Mont-Dore [N.Cal.]	219b	Cf	22.17 S	166.35 E
Monte, Laguna del-	204	Am	37.00 S	62.28W
Monteagudo	202	Fg	19.49 S	63.59W
Monte Albán	176	Jh	17.02N	96.45W
Monte Alegre	202	Hd	2.01 S	54.04W
Monte Alegre, Rio-	204	Gc	17.16 S	50.41W
Monte Alegre de Goiás	204	Ia	13.14 S	47.10W
Montealegre del Castillo	126	Kf	38.47N	1.19W
Monte Alegre de Minas	204	Hd	18.52 S	48.52W
Monte Azul	202	Jg	15.09 S	42.53W
Montebello	184	Jc	45.39N	74.56W
Monte Bello Islands	212	Dd	20.25 S	115.30 E
Monte-Carlo	122	Nk	43.44N	7.25 E
Montecarlo	204	Eh	26.34 S	54.47W
Monte Carmelo	204	Id	18.43 S	47.29W
Monte Caseros	206	Id	30.15 S	57.39W
Montecatini Terme	128	Eg	43.53N	10.46 E
Montecchio Maggiore	128	Fe	45.30N	11.24 E
Monte Comán	206	Gd	34.36 S	67.54W
Montecristi	194	Ld	19.52N	71.39W
Monte Cristo	204	Bb	14.43 S	61.14W
Montecristo	128	Eh	42.20N	10.20 E
Monte Ermoso	204	Bn	38.55 S	61.33W
Monte Escobedo	192	Hf	22.18N	103.35W
Montefalco	128	Gh	42.52N	12.39 E
Montefeltro	128	Gg	43.55N	12.15 E
Montefiascone	128	Gh	42.32N	12.02 E
Montefrío	126	Hg	37.19N	4.01W
Montego Bay	176	Lh	18.30N	77.55W
Monteiro	202	Ke	7.53 S	37.07W
Montelíbano	194	Ji	8.02N	75.29W
Montélimar	122	Kj	44.34N	4.45 E
Monte Lindo, Arroyo-	204	Cg	25.28 S	59.25W
Monte Lindo, Rio-	206	Ib	23.56 S	57.12W
Monte Lindo Chico, Riacho-	204	Dg	25.53 S	57.53W
Monte Lindo Grande, Riacho-	204	Cg	25.45 S	58.06W
Montello [Nv.-U.S.]	188	Hf	41.16N	114.12W
Montello [Wi.-U.S.]	186	Le	43.48N	89.20W
Montemorelos	190	Ec	25.12N	99.49W
Montemor-o-Novo	126	Df	38.39N	8.13W
Montemor-o-Velho	126	Dd	40.10N	8.41W
Montemuro, Serra de-	126	Dc	40.58N	8.01W
Montenegro	206	Jc	29.42 S	51.28W
Montenegro (EN) = Crna Gora [2]	130	Cg	42.30N	19.18 E
Montenegro (EN)=Crna Gora	130	Cg	42.30N	19.18 E
Monte Plata	194	Md	18.48N	69.47W
Montepuez	172	Fb	13.07 S	39.00 E
Montepuez	172	Gb	12.32 S	40.27 E
Montepulciano	128	Fg	43.05N	11.47 E
Monte Quemado	206	Hc	25.48 S	62.52W
Monte Real	126	De	39.51N	8.52W
Montereale, Passo di-	128	Hh	42.31N	13.13 E
Montereau-faut-Yonne	122	If	48.23N	2.57 E
Monterey	182	Cd	36.37N	121.55W
Monterey Bay	182	Cd	36.45N	121.55W
Montería	200	Ie	8.46N	75.53W
Montero	202	Fg	17.20 S	63.15W
Monteros	206	Gc	27.10 S	65.30W
Monterotondo	128	Gh	42.03N	12.37 E
Monterrey	176	Ig	25.40N	100.19W
Montesano	188	Dc	46.59N	123.36W
Monte San Savino	128	Fg	43.20N	11.43 E
Monte Sant'Angelo	128	Ji	41.42N	15.57 E
Monte Santu, Capo di-	128	Dj	45.05N	9.44 E

Index Symbols

- [1] Independent Nation
- [2] State, Region
- [3] District, County
- [4] Municipality
- [5] Colony, Dependency
- Continent
- Physical Region
- Historical or Cultural Region
- Mount, Mountain
- Volcano
- Hill
- Mountains, Mountain Range
- Hills, Escarpment
- Plateau, Upland
- Pass, Gap
- Plain, Lowland
- Delta
- Salt Flat
- Valley, Canyon
- Crater, Cave
- Karst Features
- Depression
- Polder
- Desert, Dunes
- Forest, Woods
- Heath, Steppe
- Oasis
- Cape, Point
- Coast, Beach
- Cliff
- Peninsula
- Isthmus
- Sandbank
- Island
- Atoll
- Rock, Reef
- Islands, Archipelago
- Rocks, Reefs
- Coral Reef
- Well, Spring
- Geyser
- River, Stream
- Waterfall, Rapids
- River Mouth, Estuary
- Lake
- Salt Lake
- Intermittent Lake
- Reservoir
- Swamp, Pond
- Canal
- Glacier
- Ice Shelf, Pack Ice
- Ocean
- Sea
- Gulf, Bay
- Strait, Fjord
- Lagoon
- Bank
- Seamount
- Tablemount
- Ridge
- Shelf
- Basin
- Escarpment, Sea Scarp
- Fracture
- Trench, Abyss
- National Park, Reserve
- Point of Interest
- Recreation Site
- Cave, Cavern
- Historic Site
- Ruins
- Wall, Walls
- Church, Abbey
- Temple
- Scientific Station
- Railway station
- Airport
- Port
- Military installation
- Lighthouse
- Mine
- Tunnel
- Dam, Bridge

Montes Claros 200 Lg 16.43 S 43.52 W
Montes Claros de Goiás 204 Gb 15.54 S 51.13 W
Montesilvano 128 Ih 42.31 N 14.09 E
Montevarchi 128 Fg 43.31 N 11.34 E
Montevideo [2] 204 Dl 34.50 S 56.10 W
Montevideo [Mn.-U.S.] 186 Id 44.57 N 95.43 W
Montevideo [Ur.] 200 Ki 34.53 S 56.11 W
Monte Vista 186 Ch 37.35 N 106.09 W
Montfaucon 124 He 49.17 N 5.08 E
Montfort-l'Amaury 124 Df 48.47 N 1.49 E
Montfort-sur-Risle 124 Ce 49.18 N 0.40 E
Montgenèvre, Col de- 122 Mj 44.56 N 6.44 E
Montgomery 176 Kf 32.23 N 86.18 W
Montgomery Pass 188 Fh 38.00 N 118.20 W
Montguyon 122 Fi 45.13 N 0.11 W
Monthermé 124 Ge 49.53 N 4.44 E
Monthey 128 Ad 46.15 N 6.56 E
Monthois 124 Ge 49.19 N 4.43 E
Monticello [Ar.-U.S.] 186 Kj 33.38 N 91.47 W
Monticello [Fl.-U.S.] 184 Fj 30.33 N 83.52 W
Monticello [Ia.-U.S.] 186 Ke 42.15 N 91.12 W
Monticello [In.-U.S.] 184 De 40.45 N 86.46 W
Monticello [Ky.-U.S.] 184 Eg 36.50 N 84.51 W
Monticello [N.Y.-U.S.] 184 Je 41.39 N 74.41 W
Monticello [Ut.-U.S.] 184 Fd 37.52 N 109.21 W
Montiel 126 Jf 38.42 N 2.52 W
Montiel, Campo de- 126 Jf 38.46 N 2.44 W
Montiel, Cuchilla de- 204 Cj 31.05 S 59.10 W
Montignac 122 Hi 45.04 N 1.10 E
Montigny-le-Roi 122 Lf 48.00 N 5.30 E
Montigny-lès-Metz 122 Me 49.06 N 6.09 E
Montigny-le-Tilleul 124 Gd 50.23 N 4.22 E
Montijo [Pan.] 194 Gj 7.59 N 81.03 W
Montijo [Port.] 126 Df 38.42 N 8.58 W
Montijo [Sp.] 126 Ff 38.55 N 6.37 W
Montijo, Golfo de- 194 Gj 7.40 N 81.07 W
Montilla 126 Hg 37.35 N 4.38 W
Montividiu 204 Gc 17.24 S 51.14 W
Montivilliers 122 Ge 49.33 N 0.12 E
Mont Joli 180 Kg 48.35 N 68.11 W
Mont-Laurier 180 Jg 46.33 N 75.30 W
Mont-Louis 122 Il 42.31 N 2.07 E
Mont Louis 184 Oa 49.15 N 65.43 W
Montluçon 122 Ih 46.20 N 2.36 E
Montmagny 180 Kg 46.59 N 70.33 W
Montmarault 122 Ih 46.19 N 2.57 E
Montmédy 122 Le 49.31 N 5.22 E
Montmirail 122 Jf 48.52 N 3.32 E
Montmorency 124 Ef 49.00 N 2.20 E
Montmorillon 122 Gh 46.26 N 0.52 E
Montmort-Lucy 124 Ff 48.55 N 3.49 E
Monto 212 Kd 24.52 S 151.07 E
Montoire-sur-le-Loir 122 Gg 47.45 N 0.52 E
Montone 128 Gf 44.14 N 12.14 E
Montoro 126 Hf 38.01 N 4.23 W
Montpelier [Id.-U.S.] 182 Ec 42.19 N 111.18 W
Montpelier [Vt.-U.S.] 176 Le 44.16 N 72.35 W
Montpellier 112 Gg 43.36 N 3.53 E
Montpon-Ménestérol 122 Gi 45.01 N 0.10 E
Montréal 176 Le 45.31 N 73.34 W
Montreal Lake 180 Gf 54.20 N 105.40 W
Montreal River 184 Hb 47.08 N 79.27 W
Montréjeau 122 Gk 43.05 N 0.35 E
Montreuil [Fr.] 124 Ef 48.52 N 2.26 E
Montreuil [Fr.] 122 Hd 50.28 N 1.46 E
Montreuil-l'Argillé 124 Cf 48.56 N 0.29 E
Montreux 128 Ad 46.26 N 6.55 E
Montrose [Co.-U.S.] 182 Fd 38.29 N 107.53 W
Montrose [Scot.-U.K.] 118 Ke 56.43 N 2.29 W
Monts, Pointe des- 184 Na 49.19 N 67.23 W
Mont-Saint-Aignan 124 De 49.28 N 1.05 E
Mont-Saint-Michel, Baie du- 122 Ef 48.40 N 1.40 W
Mont-Saint-Michel, Le- 122 Ef 48.38 N 1.30 W
Montsalvy 122 Ij 44.42 N 2.30 E
Montsant, Serra del-/Montsant, Sierra de- 126 Mc 41.17 N 0.50 E
Montsant, Sierra de-/Montsant, Serra del- 126 Mc 41.17 N 0.50 E
Montsec, Serra del-/Montsech, Sierra del- 126 Mb 42.02 N 0.50 E
Montsech, Sierra del-/Montsec, Serra del- 126 Mb 42.02 N 0.50 E
Montsent de Pallars/Montseny 126 Nb 42.29 N 1.02 E
Montseny/Pallars, Montsent de- 126 Nb 42.29 N 1.02 E
Montseny, Macizo del- 126 Oc 41.48 N 2.24 E
Montserrado [3] 166 Cd 6.35 N 10.35 W
Montserrat [5] 176 Mh 16.45 N 62.12 W
Montserrat, Monasterio de-/Montserrat, Monestir de- 126 Nc 41.35 N 1.49 E
Montserrat, Monestir de-/Montserrat, Monasterio de- 126 Nc 41.35 N 1.49 E
Montuosa, Isla- 194 Fj 7.28 N 82.14 W
Montville 124 De 49.33 N 1.07 E
Monument Peak 188 He 42.07 N 114.14 W
Monument Valley 188 Jh 36.50 N 110.20 W
Monveda 170 Db 2.57 N 21.27 E
Monviso 110 Gg 44.40 N 7.07 E
Monywa 148 Jd 22.07 N 95.08 E
Monza 128 De 45.35 N 9.16 E
Monze 170 Ef 16.16 S 27.29 E
Monzen 156 Ec 37.17 N 136.46 E
Monzón 126 Mc 41.55 N 0.12 E
Mo'oka 156 Fc 36.27 N 139.59 E
Moonbeam 184 Fa 49.25 N 82.11 W
Moonie 212 Ke 27.40 S 150.19 E
Moonie River 212 Je 29.19 S 148.43 E
Moonta 212 Hf 34.04 S 137.35 E
Moora 210 Ch 30.39 S 116.00 E
Moorcroft 188 Md 44.16 N 104.57 W
Moore 186 Hi 35.20 N 97.29 W
Moore, Lake- 208 Cg 29.50 S 117.35 E
Moorea, Ile- 208 Mf 17.32 S 149.50 W
Moore's Island 184 Il 26.18 N 77.33 W
Moorhead 182 Hb 46.53 N 96.45 W
Moormerland 124 Ja 53.18 N 7.26 E
Moormerland-Neermoor 124 Ja 53.18 N 7.26 E
Moorreesburg 172 Bf 33.09 S 18.40 E
Moosburg an der Isar 120 Hh 48.28 N 11.56 E
Moose 174 Kd 50.48 N 81.18 W
Moosehead Lake 182 Nb 45.40 N 69.40 W
Moose Jaw 176 Id 50.23 N 105.32 W
Moose Jaw River 188 Ma 50.34 N 105.17 W
Moose Lake 186 Jc 46.25 N 92.45 W
Mooselookmeguntic Lake 184 Lc 44.53 N 70.48 W
Moose Mountain 186 Eb 49.45 N 102.37 W
Moose Mountain Creek 186 Eb 49.12 N 102.10 W
Moosomin 180 Hf 50.09 N 101.40 W
Moosonee 176 Kd 51.17 N 80.39 W
Mopeia 172 Fc 17.59 S 35.43 E
Mopelia, Atoll- → Maupihaa Atoll 208 Lf 16.50 S 153.55 W
Mopti 160 Gg 14.30 N 4.12 W
Mopti [3] 166 Ec 14.40 N 4.15 W
Moqokorei 168 He 4.04 N 46.08 E
Moquegua 202 Dg 17.12 S 70.56 W
Moquegua [3] 202 Dg 16.50 S 70.55 W
Mór 120 Oi 47.23 N 18.12 E
Mor, Glen- 118 Id 57.10 N 4.40 W
Mora [Cam.] 166 Hc 11.03 N 14.09 E
Mora [Port.] 126 Df 38.56 N 8.10 W
Mora [Sp.] 126 Ie 39.41 N 3.46 W
Mora [Swe.] 114 Df 61.00 N 14.33 E
Morača 130 Cg 42.16 N 19.09 E
Morača, Manastir- 130 Cg 42.46 N 19.24 E
Morādābād 142 Jg 28.50 N 78.47 E
Morada Nova de Minas 204 Jd 18.25 S 45.22 W
Móra d'Ebre/Mora de Ebro 126 Mc 41.05 N 0.38 E
Mora de Ebro/Móra d'Ebre 126 Mc 41.05 N 0.38 E
Mora de Rubielos 126 Ld 40.15 N 0.45 W
Morafenobe 172 Gc 17.49 S 44.55 E
Morąg 120 Pc 53.56 N 19.56 E
Mórahalom 120 Pj 46.13 N 19.53 E
Moraleda, Canal- 206 Ff 44.30 S 73.30 W
Moraleja 126 Fd 40.04 N 6.39 W
Morales [Col.] 194 Ki 8.17 N 73.52 W
Morales [Guat.] 194 Cf 15.29 N 88.49 W
Morales, Laguna- 192 Kf 23.35 N 97.45 W
Moramanga 172 Hc 18.57 S 48.11 E
Moran 188 Je 43.50 N 110.28 W
Morane Atoll 208 Ng 23.10 S 137.07 W
Morangas, Ribeirão- 204 Fd 19.39 S 52.19 W
Morant Bay 194 Ie 17.53 N 76.25 W
Morant Cays 190 Ie 17.24 N 75.59 W
Morant Point 194 Ie 17.55 N 76.10 W
Morar, Loch- 118 He 56.58 N 5.45 W
Morarano 172 Hc 17.46 S 48.10 E
Mora River 186 Di 35.44 N 104.23 W
Moraska, Góra- 120 Md 52.30 N 16.52 E
Morata, Puerto de- 126 Kc 41.29 N 1.31 W
Moratalla 126 Kf 38.12 N 1.53 W
Moratuwa 148 Fg 6.46 N 79.53 E
Morava 110 Hf 48.10 N 16.59 E
Morava = Moravia (EN) 110 Hf 49.30 N 17.00 E
Morava = Moravia (EN) 120 Mg 49.30 N 17.00 E
Moravia (EN) = Morava 110 Hf 49.30 N 17.00 E
Moravia (EN) = Morava 120 Mg 49.30 N 17.00 E
Moravian Gate (EN) = Moravská brána 110 Hf 49.33 N 17.42 E
Moravian Upland (EN) = Českomoravská Vrchovina 110 Hf 49.20 N 15.30 E
Moravica 130 Df 43.51 N 20.05 E
Moravská brána = Moravian Gate (EN) 110 Hf 49.33 N 17.42 E
Moravské Budějovice 120 Lg 49.03 N 15.49 E
Morawa 212 De 29.13 S 116.00 E
Morawhanna 202 Gb 8.16 N 59.45 W
Moray Firth 110 Fd 57.50 N 3.30 W
Morbach 124 Je 49.49 N 7.07 E
Morbihan [3] 122 Dg 47.55 N 2.50 W
Morbihan 122 Dg 47.35 N 2.48 W
Morbylånga 114 Dh 56.31 N 16.23 E
Morcenx 122 Fj 44.02 N 0.55 W
Mordāb 146 Md 37.26 N 49.25 E
Mordaga 152 La 51.14 N 120.43 E
Morden 180 Hg 49.11 N 98.05 W
Mordovo 132 Lc 52.05 N 40.46 E
Mordovskaja respublika 136 Ee 54.20 N 44.30 E
Möre 116 Fh 56.25 N 15.55 E
More, Ben- 118 Ie 56.23 N 4.31 W
Morea 172 Bd 22.41 S 15.54 E
More Assynt, Ben- 118 Ic 58.07 N 4.51 W
Moreau River 182 Gb 45.18 N 100.43 W
Morecambe 118 Kg 54.04 N 2.53 W
Morecambe Bay 118 Kg 54.07 N 3.00 W
Moree 210 Fg 29.28 S 149.51 E
Morehead [Ky.-U.S.] 184 Ff 38.11 N 83.25 W
Morehead [Pap.N.Gui.] 214 Ci 8.50 S 141.57 E
Morehead City 176 Lf 34.43 N 76.43 W
Moreiz, gora- 136 Gb 69.30 N 62.05 E
Moreju 134 Ib 68.20 N 59.45 E
Morelia 176 Ih 19.42 N 101.07 W
Morella 126 Ld 40.37 N 0.06 W
Morelos 192 Ic 28.25 N 100.53 W
Morelos [2] 190 Ee 18.45 N 99.00 W
Morena, Sierra- 110 Fh 38.00 N 5.00 W
Moreni 130 Ie 44.59 N 25.39 E
Møre og Romsdal [2] 114 Be 62.40 N 7.50 E
Moresby 180 Ef 52.45 N 131.50 W
Moreton Bay 212 Ke 27.20 S 153.15 E
Moreton Island 212 Ke 27.10 S 153.25 E
Moret-sur-Loing 122 If 48.22 N 2.49 E
Moreuil 122 Ie 49.46 N 2.29 E
Morez 122 Mh 46.31 N 6.02 E
Mörfelden 124 Ke 49.59 N 8.34 E
Morgan City 186 Kl 29.42 N 91.12 W
Morganfield 184 Dg 37.41 N 87.55 W
Morganton 184 Gh 35.45 N 81.41 W
Morgantown [Ky.-U.S.] 184 Dg 37.14 N 86.41 W
Morgantown [W.V.-U.S.] 184 Hf 39.38 N 79.57 W
Morges 128 Ad 46.31 N 6.30 E
Morghāb 144 Jb 38.18 N 61.12 E
Morhange 122 Mf 48.55 N 6.38 E
Mori [China] 152 Fc 43.49 N 90.11 E
Mori [Jap.] 154 Pc 42.06 N 140.35 E
Moriarty 186 Ci 34.59 N 106.03 W
Morichal Largo, Río- 196 Eh 9.27 N 62.25 W
Moriguchi 156 Dd 34.44 N 135.34 E
Morin Dawa (Nirji) 152 Lb 48.30 N 124.28 E
Morioka 142 Qf 39.42 N 141.09 E
Moriyoshi 156 Ga 40.07 N 140.22 E
Moriyoshi-Yama 156 Gb 39.59 N 140.33 E
Morjärv 114 Fc 66.04 N 22.43 E
Morki 114 Lh 56.28 N 49.00 E
Morko 116 Gf 59.00 N 17.40 E
Morkoka 138 Gc 65.03 N 115.40 E
Mørkøv 116 Di 55.40 N 11.32 E
Morlaix 122 Cf 48.35 N 3.50 W
Morlanwelz 124 Gd 50.27 N 4.14 E
Mörlunda 116 Fg 57.19 N 15.51 E
Mormanno 128 Jk 39.53 N 15.59 E
Morne-à-l'Eau 196 Fd 16.21 N 61.31 W
Morne Diablotin 190 Le 15.30 N 61.24 W
Mornington, Isla- 206 Eg 49.45 S 75.23 W
Mornington Island 212 Hc 16.35 S 139.24 E
Moro 188 Ed 45.29 N 120.44 W
Moro Almanzor, Plaza del- 126 Gd 40.15 N 5.18 W
Morobe 210 Fe 7.45 S 147.37 E
Morocco (EN) = Al Maghrib [1] 160 Ge 32.00 N 5.50 W
Morogoro 160 Ki 6.49 S 37.40 E
Morogoro [3] 170 Gd 8.20 S 37.00 E
Moro Gulf 150 He 6.51 N 123.00 E
Moroleón 192 Ig 20.08 N 101.12 W
Morombe 160 Lk 21.44 S 43.23 E
Morón [Arg.] 204 Cl 34.39 S 58.37 W
Morón [Cuba] 190 Id 22.06 N 78.38 W
Morón [Ven.] 202 Ea 10.29 N 68.11 W
Morona, Río- 202 Cd 4.45 S 77.04 W
Morondava 160 Lk 20.15 S 44.17 E
Morón de la Frontera 126 Gg 37.08 N 5.27 W
Morones, Sierra- 192 Hg 21.55 N 103.05 W
Moroni 160 Lj 11.41 S 43.16 E
Moron Us He 140 Lf 34.42 N 95.00 E
Morotai, Pulau- 208 Dd 2.20 N 128.25 E
Moroto 160 Kh 2.32 N 34.39 E
Morovița 130 Ed 45.16 N 21.16 E
Morozov 130 Ig 42.30 N 25.10 E
Morozovsk 136 Ef 48.20 N 41.50 E
Morpeth 118 Lf 55.10 N 1.41 W
Morphou → Güzelyurt 146 Ee 35.12 N 32.59 E
Morrilton 186 Ji 35.09 N 92.45 W
Morrinhos 202 Ig 17.44 S 49.07 W
Morrinsville 218 Fb 37.39 S 175.32 E
Morris [Il.-U.S.] 186 Lf 41.22 N 88.26 W
Morris [Man.-Can.] 180 Hg 49.21 N 97.22 W
Morris [Mn.-U.S.] 186 Id 45.35 N 95.55 W
Morris, Mount- 212 Ge 26.09 S 131.04 E
Morrisburg 184 Jc 44.54 N 75.11 W
Morris Jesup, Kap- 224 Me 83.45 N 35.50 W
Morrison Dennis Cays 194 Ff 14.28 N 82.53 W
Morristown 184 Fg 36.13 N 83.18 W
Morrito 194 Eh 11.37 N 85.05 W
Morro, Punta del- 192 Kh 19.51 N 96.27 W
Morro Bay 182 Cd 35.22 N 120.51 W
Morro do Chapéu 202 Jf 11.33 S 41.09 W
Morrosquillo, Golfo de- 194 Ji 9.35 N 75.40 W
Morro Vermelho, Serra do- 204 Jc 17.45 S 45.20 W
Mörrum 116 Fh 56.11 N 14.45 E
Morrumbala 172 Fc 17.20 S 35.35 E
Morrumbene 172 Fd 23.39 S 35.20 E
Mörrumsån 116 Fh 56.09 N 14.44 E
Mors 116 Ch 56.50 N 8.45 E
Moršansk 136 Ee 53.26 N 41.49 E
Morsbach 124 Jd 50.52 N 7.45 E
Morsberg 124 Ke 49.43 N 8.54 E
Mörsil 114 Ce 63.19 N 13.38 E
Mörskom/Myrskylä 116 Kd 60.40 N 25.51 E
Morsott 128 Co 35.40 N 8.01 E
Mortagne 122 Mf 48.33 N 6.27 E
Mortagne-au-Perche 122 Gf 48.31 N 0.33 E
Mortagne-sur-Sèvre 122 Fg 47.00 N 0.57 W
Mortain 122 Ff 48.39 N 0.56 W
Mortara 128 Ce 45.15 N 8.44 E
Mortcha 158 Jg 16.00 N 21.10 E
Morteau 122 Mg 47.04 N 6.37 E
Morteaux-Coulibœuf 124 Bf 48.56 N 0.04 W
Morteros 206 Hd 30.42 S 62.00 W
Mortes, Rio das- 204 Je 21.09 S 44.53 W
Mortes, Rio das- → Manso, Rio- 198 Kg 11.45 S 50.44 W
Mortesoro 168 Ec 10.12 N 34.09 E
Mortlock Islands 208 Gd 5.27 N 153.40 E
Morton 188 Dc 46.33 N 122.17 W
Mortsel 124 Gc 51.10 N 4.28 E
Morumbi 204 Ef 23.46 S 54.06 W
Morvan 122 Jg 47.05 N 4.00 E
Morven 212 Je 26.25 S 147.07 E
Morvern 118 He 56.35 N 5.50 W
Morvi 148 Ed 22.49 N 70.50 E
Morwell 210 Fh 38.14 S 146.24 E
Morzine 122 Mh 46.11 N 6.43 E
Moržovec, ostrov- 114 Kc 66.45 N 42.35 E
Moša 114 Je 62.25 N 39.48 E
Mosbach 120 Fg 49.21 N 9.09 E
Mosby 116 Bf 58.14 N 7.54 E
Mosčny, ostrov- 114 Gg 60.00 N 27.50 E
Mosconi 204 Bl 35.44 S 60.34 W
Moscos Islands 148 Jf 14.00 N 97.45 E
Moscow [Id.-U.S.] 182 Db 46.44 N 116.59 W
Moscow (EN) = Moskva 110 Jd 55.08 N 38.50 E
Moscow (EN) = Moskva [Russia] 112 Jd 55.45 N 37.35 E
Moscow Basin (EN) = Meščera 110 Kd 55.00 N 40.30 E
Moscow Canal (EN) = Moskvy, kanal imeni- 110 Jd 56.43 N 37.08 E
Moscow Upland (EN) = Moskovskaja vozvyšennost 110 Jd 56.30 N 37.30 E
Mosel = Moselle (EN) 110 Ge 50.22 N 7.36 E
Moselberge 124 Ie 49.57 N 6.56 E
Moselle [3] 122 Me 49.00 N 6.30 E
Moselle 110 Ge 50.22 N 7.36 E
Moselle (EN) = Mosel 110 Ge 50.22 N 7.36 E
Moses Lake 182 Db 47.08 N 119.17 W
Mosgiel 216 Di 45.53 S 170.22 E
Moshi 160 Ki 3.21 S 37.20 E
Mosina 120 Md 52.16 N 16.51 E
Mosjøen 114 Cd 65.50 N 13.12 E
Moskalvo 138 Jf 53.39 N 142.37 E
Moskenesøy 114 Cc 67.59 N 13.00 E
Moskovskaja oblast [3] 136 Dd 55.45 N 37.45 E
Moskovskaja vozvyšennost = Moscow Upland (EN) 110 Jd 56.30 N 37.30 E
Moskovski 135 Gf 37.40 N 69.39 E
Moskva [Russia] = Moscow (EN) 112 Jd 55.45 N 37.35 E
Moskva [Turk.] 135 Ee 38.27 N 64.24 E
Moskva = Moscow (EN) 110 Jd 55.08 N 38.50 E
Moskva, pik- 135 He 38.55 N 71.52 E
Moskvy, kanal imeni- = Moscow Canal (EN) 110 Jd 56.43 N 37.08 E
Moslavačka Gora 128 Ke 45.38 N 16.42 E
Moso 219b Dc 17.32 S 168.15 E
Mosomane 172 Dd 24.01 S 26.19 E
Mosoni-Duna 120 Ni 47.44 N 17.47 E
Mosonmagyaróvár 120 Ni 47.52 N 17.17 E
Mosquero 186 Ei 35.47 N 103.58 W
Mosquito, Baie - 180 Jd 60.40 N 78.00 W
Mosquito, Riacho- 204 Cf 22.12 S 57.57 W
Mosquito Coast (EN) = Mosquitos, Costa de los- 174 Kh 13.00 N 83.45 W
Mosquitos, Costa de los- = Mosquito Coast (E) 174 Kh 13.00 N 83.45 W
Mosquitos, Golfo de los- 174 Ki 9.00 N 81.20 W
Moss 112 Hd 59.26 N 10.42 E
Mossaka 170 Cc 1.13 S 16.48 E
Mossâmedes 204 Gc 16.07 S 50.11 W
Mossbank 188 Mb 49.55 N 105.59 W
Mossburn 216 Ci 45.41 S 168.15 E
Mosselbaai 160 Jl 34.11 S 22.08 E
Mossendjo 170 Bc 2.57 S 12.44 E
Mossman 210 Ff 16.28 S 145.22 E
Mossø 116 Ch 56.05 N 9.50 E
Mossoró 200 Mf 5.11 S 37.20 W
Moss Point 186 Lk 30.25 N 88.29 W
Mossuril 172 Gb 14.58 S 40.40 E
Most 120 Jf 50.32 N 13.39 E
Mostaganem 160 He 35.56 N 0.05 E
Mostaganem [3] 162 Hb 35.40 N 0.30 E
Mostar 128 Lg 43.21 N 17.49 E
Mostardas 204 Gj 31.06 S 50.57 W
Møsting, Kap- 179 Hf 63.45 N 41.00 W
Mostiska 132 Ce 49.48 N 23.09 E
Mostiștea 130 Je 44.15 N 26.54 E
Mostovskoj 132 Lg 44.22 N 40.48 E
Mosty 136 Ce 53.27 N 24.33 E
Mosul (EN) = Al Mawșil 142 Gf 36.20 N 43.08 E
Møsvatn 114 Bg 59.50 N 8.05 E
Mota 160 Fc 11.05 N 37.53 E
Mota 219b Ca 13.40 S 167.42 E
Motaba 170 Cb 2.03 N 18.03 E
Motacusito 204 Bc 17.35 S 61.31 W
Mota del Marqués 126 Gc 41.38 N 5.10 W
Motagua 174 Kh 15.44 N 88.14 W
Motajica 128 Le 45.04 N 17.40 E
Motala 114 Dg 58.33 N 15.03 E
Motala ström 116 Gf 58.38 N 16.10 E
Motatán 194 Li 9.24 N 70.36 W
Motatán, Río- 194 Li 9.32 N 71.02 W
Motegi 156 Gc 36.32 N 140.10 E
Mothe 219d Cc 18.40 S 178.30 W
Mothe-Achard, La- 122 Eh 46.37 N 1.40 W
Motherwell 118 Jf 55.48 N 4.00 W
Motīhāri 148 Gc 26.39 N 84.55 E
Motilla del Palancar 126 Ke 39.34 N 1.53 W
Motiti Island 218 Gb 37.40 S 176.25 E
Motlav 219b Ca 13.40 S 167.40 E
Motobu 156b Ab 26.40 N 127.55 E
Motol 120 Vd 52.17 N 25.40 E
Motovski zaliv 114 Hb 69.30 N 32.30 E
Motoyoshi 156 Gb 38.48 N 141.31 E
Motozintla de Mendoza 192 Mj 15.22 N 92.14 W
Motril 126 Ih 36.45 N 3.31 W
Motru 130 Fe 44.48 N 23.00 E
Motru 130 Ge 44.33 N 23.27 E
Motsuta-Misaki 156a Ab 42.36 N 139.49 E
Mott 186 Ec 46.22 N 102.20 W
Motteville 124 Ce 49.38 N 0.51 E
Motu 218 Gb 37.51 S 177.35 E
Motueka 218 Ed 41.07 S 173.01 E
Motuhora Island 218 Gb 37.50 S 177.00 E
Motu-Iti 221d Ac 27.11 S 109.27 W
Motu-Iti → Tupai Atoll 216 Kc 16.17 S 151.50 W
Motul 190 Gd 21.06 N 89.17 W
Motu-Nui 221d Ac 27.12 S 109.28 W
Motu One Atoll 208 Lf 15.48 S 154.33 W
Motupae 220n Ac 10.27 S 161.02 W
Motupena Point 219a Bb 6.32 S 155.09 E
Moturiki 219d Bb 17.46 S 178.45 E
Motutapu 220p Cb 21.14 S 159.43 W
Motu Tautara 221d Ab 27.05 S 109.26 W
Motutunga Atoll 208 Mf 17.06 S 144.22 W
Moubray Bay 222 Kf 72.11 S 170.15 E
Mouchard 122 Lh 46.58 N 5.48 E
Mouchoir Bank (EN) 190 Jd 20.57 N 70.42 W
Mouchoir Passage 194 Lc 21.10 N 71.00 W
Moudjéria 162 Ef 17.52 N 12.20 W
Mouila 160 Ii 1.52 S 11.01 E
Mouka 168 Cd 7.16 N 21.52 E
Moul 166 Hb 15.03 N 13.18 E
Mould Bay 176 Hb 76.15 N 119.30 W
Moule 196 Fd 16.20 N 61.21 W
Moule à Chique, Cap- 197k Bb 13.43 N 60.57 W
Moulins 122 Jh 46.34 N 3.20 E
Moulmein → Mawlamyine 142 Le 16.30 N 97.38 E
Moulouya 158 Ge 35.06 N 2.20 W
Moult 124 Be 49.07 N 0.10 W
Moultrie 184 Fj 31.11 N 83.47 W
Moultrie, Lake- 184 Gi 33.20 N 80.05 W
Mouly, Pointe de- 219b Ce 20.43 S 166.23 E
Moúnda, Ákra- 130 Dk 38.03 N 20.47 E
Moundou 160 Ih 8.34 N 16.05 E
Moundsville 184 Gf 39.54 N 80.44 W
Mo'unga'one 221b Ba 19.38 S 174.29 W
Moungoudou 170 Bc 2.40 S 12.41 E
Mountainair 186 Ci 34.31 N 106.15 W
Mountain Grove 186 Jh 37.08 N 92.16 W
Mountain Home [Ar.-U.S.] 186 Jh 36.21 N 92.23 W
Mountain Home [Id.-U.S.] 182 Dc 43.08 N 115.41 W
Mountain Nile (EN) = Jabal, Baḩr al- 158 Kh 9.30 N 30.30 E
Mountain Village 178 Gd 62.05 N 163.44 W
Mount Airy 184 Gg 36.31 N 80.37 W
Mount Barker 212 Df 34.38 S 117.40 E
Mount Carmel 186 Mg 38.25 N 87.46 W
Mount Desert Island 184 Mc 44.20 N 68.20 W
Mount Douglas 210 Fg 21.30 S 146.50 E
Mount Eba 212 Hf 30.12 S 135.40 E
Mount Forest 184 Gd 43.59 N 80.44 W
Mount Frere 172 Df 31.00 S 28.58 E
Mount Gambier 210 Fh 37.50 S 140.46 E
Mount Hagen 214 Ci 5.52 S 144.13 E
Mount Hope 212 Hf 34.07 S 135.23 E
Mount Isa 210 Eg 20.44 S 139.30 E
Mountlake Terrace 188 Dc 47.47 N 122.18 W
Mount Lebanon 184 Ge 40.23 N 80.03 W
Mount Lofty Ranges 212 Hg 35.15 S 138.50 E
Mount Magnet 210 Cg 28.04 S 117.49 E
Mount Maunganui 216 Eg 37.38 S 176.12 E
Mount Morgan 212 Kd 23.39 S 150.23 E
Mountnorris Bay 212 Gb 11.20 S 132.45 E
Mount Peck 188 Ha 50.10 N 115.02 W
Mount Pleasant [Ia.-U.S.] 186 Kf 40.58 N 91.33 W
Mount Pleasant [Mi.-U.S.] 184 Ed 43.35 N 84.47 W
Mount Pleasant [S.C.-U.S.] 184 Hi 32.47 N 79.52 W
Mount Pleasant [Tx.-U.S.] 186 Ij 33.09 N 94.58 W
Mount Pleasant [Ut.-U.S.] 188 Jg 39.33 N 111.27 W
Mount's Bay 118 Hk 50.03 N 5.25 W
Mount Somers 218 De 43.42 S 171.25 E
Mount Sterling [Il.-U.S.] 186 Kg 39.59 N 90.45 W
Mount Sterling [Ky.-U.S.] 184 Ff 38.04 N 83.56 W
Mount Vancouver 180 Dd 60.20 N 139.41 W
Mount Vernon [Al.-U.S.] 184 Cj 31.05 N 88.01 W
Mount Vernon [Austl.] 212 Dd 24.13 S 118.14 E
Mount Vernon [Il.-U.S.] 182 Jd 38.19 N 88.55 W
Mount Vernon [In.-U.S.] 184 Dg 37.56 N 87.54 W
Mount Vernon [Ky.-U.S.] 184 Eg 37.21 N 84.20 W
Mount Vernon [Oh.-U.S.] 184 Fe 40.23 N 82.30 W
Mount Vernon [Wa.-U.S.] 182 Cb 48.25 N 122.20 W
Moura [Austl.] 212 Jd 24.35 S 150.00 E
Moura [Port.] 126 Ef 38.08 N 7.27 W
Mourão 126 Ef 38.23 N 7.21 W
Mourdi 168 Cb 17.50 N 22.25 E
Mourdi, Dépression du- = Mourdi Depression (EN) 158 Jg 18.10 N 23.00 E
Mourdiah 166 Dc 14.26 N 7.31 W
Mourdi Depression (EN) = Mourdi, Dépression du- 158 Jg 18.10 N 23.00 E
Mourmelon-le-Grand 124 Ge 49.08 N 4.22 E
Mourne Mountains/Beanna Boirche 118 Gg 54.10 N 6.04 W
Mouscron/Moeskroen 122 Jd 50.44 N 3.13 E
Moussoro 160 Ig 13.39 N 16.29 E
Moustiers-Sainte-Marie 122 Mk 43.51 N 6.13 E
Moutier/Münster 128 Bc 47.16 N 7.22 E
Moutiers 122 Mi 45.29 N 6.32 E
Moutong 150 Hf 0.28 N 121.13 E
Mouy 124 Ee 49.19 N 2.19 E
Mouydir 158 Hf 25.00 N 4.10 E
Mouyondzi 170 Bc 3.58 S 13.57 E
Mouzaia 126 Oh 36.28 N 2.41 E
Mouzon 124 He 49.36 N 5.05 E
Movas 192 Ec 28.10 N 109.25 W
Moxico 170 De 11.51 S 20.01 E
Moxico [3] 170 De 12.00 S 20.00 E
Moy/An Mhuaidh 118 Dg 54.12 N 9.08 W
Moyahua 192 Hg 21.16 N 103.10 W
Moyale [Eth.] 160 Kh 3.32 N 39.04 E
Moyale [Kenya] 170 Gb 3.32 N 39.03 E
Moyamba 166 Cd 8.10 N 12.26 W
Moÿ-de-l'Aisne 124 Fe 49.45 N 3.22 E
Moyen Atlas = Middle Atlas (EN) 158 Ge 33.30 N 4.30 W
Moyen-Chari [3] 168 Bd 9.00 N 18.00 E
Moyenne Guinée [3] 166 Cc 11.15 N 12.30 W
Moyenneville 124 Dd 50.04 N 1.45 E
Moyen-Ogooué [3] 170 Bc 0.30 S 10.30 E
Moyeuvre-Grande 124 Ie 49.15 N 6.02 E
Moyo 170 Fb 3.40 N 31.43 E
Moyo, Pulau- 150 Gh 8.15 S 117.34 E
Moyobamba 200 If 6.02 S 76.58 W
Moyowosi 170 Fc 4.50 S 31.24 E
Moyto 168 Bc 12.35 N 16.33 E
Moyu/Karakax 152 Cd 37.17 N 79.42 E
Možajsk 114 Ii 55.32 N 36.02 E
Mozambique (EN) = Moçambique 160 Lj 15.03 S 40.45 E
Mozambique (EN) = Moçambique [1] 160 Kj 18.15 S 35.00 E
Mozambique, Canal de- = Mozambique Channel (EN) 158 Lk 20.00 S 43.00 E
Mozambique Channel (EN) = Moçambique, Canal de- 158 Lk 20.00 S 43.00 E

Mozambique Channel (EN) =Mozambique, Canal de- ⇌	158	Lk	20.00 S	43.00 E
Mozambique Plateau (EN) ⊓	158	Kl	32.00 S	35.00 E
Mozdok	136	Eg	43.44N	44.38 E
Možga	136	Fd	56.28N	52.13 E
Mozuli	116	Mh	56.32N	28.14 E
Mozyr	136	Ce	52.02N	29.16 E
Mpala	170	Ed	6.45 S	29.31 E
Mpanda	160	Ki	6.22 S	31.02 E
Mpigi	170	Fb	0.15N	32.20 E
Mpika	160	Kj	11.50 S	31.27 E
Mpoko ≈	168	Be	4.19N	18.33 E
Mporokoso	170	Fd	9.23 S	30.08 E
Mpouia	170	Cc	2.37 S	16.13 E
Mpui	170	Fd	8.21 S	31.50 E
Mpulungu	170	Fd	8.46 S	31.07 E
Mpwapwa	170	Gd	6.21 S	36.29 E
Mrągowo	120	Rc	53.52N	21.19 E
Mrakovo	134	Hj	52.43N	56.38 E
Mrkonjić Grad	128	Lf	44.25N	17.06 E
Mrocza	120	Nc	53.14N	17.36 E
Mroga ≈	120	Pd	52.09N	19.42 E
Msangesi ≈	170	Ge	11.40 S	36.45 E
Msid, Djebel- ▲	128	Cn	36.25N	8.04 E
Msif ≈	126	Qi	35.23N	4.45 E
M'Sila	162	Hb	35.42N	4.33 E
M'Sila [3]	162	Hb	35.00N	4.30 E
M'Sila ≈	126	Qi	35.31N	4.30 E
Mšinskaja	116	Nf	58.55N	30.03 E
Msta ≈	110	Jd	58.25N	31.20 E
Mstislavl	132	Gc	53.59N	31.45 E
Mszana Dolna	120	Qg	49.42N	20.05 E
Mtakuja	170	Fd	7.22 S	30.37 E
Mtama	170	Ge	10.18 S	39.22 E
Mtelo ▲	170	Gb	1.39N	35.23 E
Mtera Reservoir ⊜	170	Gd	7.01 S	35.55 E
Mtito Andei	170	Gc	2.41 S	38.10 E
Mtubatuba	172	Ee	28.30 S	32.08 E
Mtwara	160	Lj	10.16 S	40.11 E
Mtwara [3]	170	Ge	10.40 S	39.00 E
Mu, Cerro- ▲	194	Ki	9.29N	73.07W
Mua	220h	Ac	13.21 S	176.10W
Mu'a	221b	Ac	21.11 S	175.07W
Mua, Baie de- ◐	220h	Bc	13.23 S	176.09W
Muaná	202	Id	1.32 S	49.13W
Muang Huon	148	Kd	20.09N	101.27 E
Muang Khammouan	148	Ke	17.24N	104.48 E
Muang Không	148	Lf	14.07N	105.51 E
Muang Khôngxédôn	148	Le	15.34N	105.49 E
Muang Khoua	148	Kd	21.05N	102.31 E
Muang Pak Lay	148	Ke	18.12N	101.25 E
Muang Pakxan	148	Ke	18.22N	103.39 E
Muang Pakxong	148	Le	15.11N	106.14 E
Muang Sing	148	Kd	21.11N	101.09 E
Muang Tahoi	148	Le	16.10N	106.38 E
Muang Thai=Thailand (EN) [1]	142	Mh	15.00N	100.00 E
Muang Vangviang	148	Ke	18.56N	102.27 E
Muang Xaignabouri	148	Ke	19.15N	101.45 E
Muang Xay	148	Kd	20.42N	101.59 E
Muang Xépôn	148	Le	16.41N	106.14 E
Muanzanza	170	Dd	6.32 S	20.51 E
Muar	150	Df	2.02N	102.34 E
Muaraaman	150	Dg	3.07 S	102.12 E
Muarabungo	150	Dg	1.28 S	102.07 E
Muaraenim	150	Dg	3.39 S	103.48 E
Muaralasan	150	Gf	1.48N	117.12 E
Muarapajang	150	Gg	1.32 S	115.48 E
Muarasiberut	150	Cg	1.36 S	99.11 E
Muarasiram	150	Gg	0.46 S	116.11 E
Muaratebo	150	Dg	1.30 S	102.26 E
Muaratewe	150	Fg	0.57 S	114.53 E
Muarawahau	150	Gf	1.02N	116.52 E
Mubarek	135	Ee	39.16N	65.07 E
Mubende	170	Fb	0.35N	31.23 E
Mubi	160	Ig	10.16N	13.16 E
Much	124	Jd	50.55N	7.24 E
Muchinga Escarpment ◧	170	Fe	13.40 S	30.00 E
Muchinga Mountains ⛰	158	Kj	12.00 S	31.45 E
Muck ◆	118	Ge	56.50N	6.14W
Mücke	124	Ld	50.37N	9.02 E
Mucojo	172	Gb	12.04 S	40.28 E
Muconda	170	De	10.34 S	21.20 E
Mucua ≈	172	Ec	18.09 S	34.58 E
Mucubela	172	Fc	16.54 S	37.49 E
Mucuchies	194	Li	8.45N	70.55W
Mucumbura	172	Ec	16.10 S	31.42 E
Mucur	146	Fc	39.04N	34.23 E
Mucusso	170	Df	18.00 S	21.25 E
Mudanjiang	142	Oe	44.35N	129.34 E
Mudan Jiang ≈	140	Oe	46.18N	129.31 E
Mudanya	146	Cb	40.22N	28.52 E
Muddy Gap	188	Le	42.22N	107.27W
Mudgee	212	Jf	32.36 S	149.35 E
Mud Lake	188	Ie	43.53N	112.24W
Mud Lake ♒	188	Gh	37.55N	117.05W
Mudon	148	Je	16.15N	97.44 E
Mudug [3]	168	Hd	6.30N	48.00 E
Mudug ⊠	168	Hd	6.20N	47.00 E
Mudurnu	146	Db	40.28N	31.13 E
Muecate	172	Fb	14.53 S	39.38 E
Mueda	172	Fb	11.39 S	39.33 E
Muerto, Cayo- ◆	194	Ff	14.34N	82.44W
Muerto, Mar- ◉	192	Li	16.10N	94.10W
Mufulira	160	Jj	12.33 S	28.14 E
Mufu Shan △	152	Jf	29.00N	113.50 E
Mufu Shan ⛰	152	Jf	29.15N	114.20 E
Mugello ⊠	128	Fg	43.55N	11.25 E
Múggia	128	He	45.36N	13.46 E
Mughshin, Wādī- ≈	168	Ib	19.44N	55.00 E
Mugi	156	De	33.40N	134.25 E
Mu Gia, Deo- ⋂	148	Le	17.40N	105.47 E
Mugila, Monts- ⛰	170	Ed	6.49 S	29.08 E
Muğla	144	Cb	37.12N	28.22 E
Mugodžary ⛰	140	He	49.00N	58.40 E
Mugur an Na'ām	146	Ig	31.56N	40.30 E
Muhaiwir	146	If	33.28N	40.59 E
Muḩammad, Ra's- ►	164	Fd	27.42N	34.13 E
Muḩammad Oawl	168	Fa	20.54N	37.05 E
Muhen	138	Ig	48.10N	136.08 E
Muheza	170	Gd	5.10 S	38.47 E
Muhīt, Al Baḩr al-=Atlantic Ocean (EN) 🌊	106	Di	2.00N	25.00W
Mühlacher	120	Eh	48.57N	8.50 E
Mühldorf am Inn	120	Ih	48.15N	12.32 E
Mühlhausen in Thüringen	120	Ge	51.13N	10.27 E
Mühlig-Hofmann Gebirge ⛰	222	Cf	72.00 S	5.20 E
Mühlviertel ⊠	128	Ib	48.30N	14.10 E
Muhoršibir → Taksimo	138	Ff	51.01N	107.50 E
Muhos	114	Gd	64.50N	26.01 E
Muhu	116	Jf	58.37N	23.05 E
Muhu ◆	114	Fg	58.35N	23.15 E
Muhu, Proliv- / Muhu Väin ⇌	116	Jf	58.45N	23.15 E
Muhulu	170	Ec	1.03 S	27.17 E
Muhu Väin / Muhu, Proliv- ⇌	116	Jf	58.45N	23.15 E
Muhuwesi ≈	170	Ge	11.16 S	37.58 E
Muiderslot ⌇	124	Hb	52.20N	5.06 E
Muigheo/Mayo [2]	118	Dh	53.50N	9.30W
Muikamachi	154	Of	37.04N	138.53 E
Muineachán/Monaghan	118	Gg	54.15N	6.58W
Muineachán/Monaghan [2]	118	Gg	54.10N	7.00W
Muine Bheag	118	Gi	52.42N	6.57W
Muir Bhreatan=Saint George's Channel (EN) ⇌	110	Fe	52.00N	6.00W
Muir Eireann=Irish Sea (EN) ≋	110	Fe	53.30N	5.20W
Muiron Islands ⁂	212	Cd	21.35 S	114.20 E
Muir Seamount (EN) ⩚	174	Mf	33.41N	63.32W
Muite	172	Fb	14.02 S	39.02 E
Mujeres, Isla- ◆	192	Pg	21.13N	86.43W
Mujezerski	114	He	63.57N	32.01 E
Muji	152	Cd	37.27N	78.33 E
Mujnak	136	Fg	43.44N	59.02 E
Mujnakski zaliv ◐	135	Bc	43.50N	58.40 E
Mujunkum, peski- ∴	140	Je	44.00N	70.30 E
Mukačevo	136	Cf	48.26N	22.45 E
Mukah	150	Ff	2.54N	112.06 E
Mukawa	156a	Bb	42.35N	141.55 E
Mu-Kawa ≈	156a	Bb	42.33N	141.53 E
Mukawwar ◆	168	Fa	20.48N	37.13 E
Mukdahan	148	Ke	16.31N	104.42 E
Mukeru	220a	Bc	7.25N	134.30 E
Mukho	154	Jf	37.33N	129.07 E
Mukinbudin	212	Df	30.54 S	118.13 E
Mukojima-Rettō ⁂	214	Cb	27.37N	142.10 E
Mukomuko	150	Dg	2.35 S	101.07 E
Muksu ≈	135	He	39.17N	71.25 E
Mula	126	Kf	38.03N	1.30W
Mula ≈	148	Dc	27.57N	67.36 E
Mulainagiri ▲	148	Ff	13.24N	75.43 E
Mulaku Atoll ◎	148a	Bb	2.57N	73.34 E
Mulaly	136	Hf	45.27N	78.20 E
Mulan	152	Mb	46.00N	128.02 E
Mulanje	170	Gf	16.02 S	35.30 E
Mulanje ▲	158	Kj	16.03 S	35.31 E
Mulatre, Point- ►	197g	Bb	15.17N	61.15W
Mulatupo Sasardí	194	Ii	8.57N	77.45W
Mulchatna ≈	178	Hd	59.39N	157.08W
Mulchén	206	Fe	37.34 S	72.14W
Mulda	134	Kc	67.28N	63.34 E
Mulde ≈	120	Ie	51.48N	12.10 E
Mulebreen ❄	222	Ee	67.28 S	59.21 E
Mulegé	190	Bc	26.53N	112.01W
Mulegé, Sierra de- ⛰	190	Bc	37.30N	112.40W
Mulenda	170	Dc	4.18 S	24.58 E
Muleshoe	186	Ei	34.13N	102.43W
Mulgrave Island ◆	212	Ib	10.05 S	142.10 E
Mulhacén ▲	110	Fh	37.03N	3.19W
Mülheim an der Ruhr	124	Ic	51.26N	6.53 E
Mülheim-Kärlich	124	Jd	50.23N	7.30 E
Mulhouse	112	Gf	47.45N	7.20 E
Muli (Bowa)	152	Hf	27.55N	101.13 E
Mulifanua	221c	Aa	13.50 S	172.02W
Muling	154	Kb	44.34N	130.12 E
Muling (Bamiantong)	154	Kb	44.55N	130.32 E
Muling Guan ⋂	154	Ef	36.10N	118.46 E
Muling He ≈	154	Lb	45.53N	133.30 E
Mull, Island of- ◆	110	Fd	56.27N	6.00W
Mull, Sound of- ⇌	118	He	56.35N	5.50W
Mullen	186	Fe	42.03N	101.01W
Mullens	184	Gg	37.35N	81.25W
Muller, Pegunungan- ⛰	150	Ff	0.40N	113.50 E
Mullet Peninsula/An Muirthead ⊏	118	Cg	54.15N	10.04W
Mullett Lake ○	184	Ec	45.30N	84.30W
Mullewa	212	De	28.33 S	115.31 E
Müllheim	120	Di	47.48N	7.38 E
Mullingar/An Muileann gCearr	118	Fh	53.32N	7.20W
Mullsjö	116	Eg	57.55N	13.53 E
Mulobezi	170	Ef	16.47 S	25.10 E
Mulock Glacier ❄	222	Jf	79.03 S	159.10 E
Mulongo	170	Ed	7.50 S	26.57 E
Multān	142	Jf	30.11N	71.29 E
Multé	192	Ni	17.41N	91.24W
Multia	116	Kb	62.25N	24.47 E
Multien ⊠	124	Ee	49.05N	2.55 E
Mulu, Gunong- ▲	150	Ff	4.03N	114.56 E
Mulvane	186	Hh	37.29N	97.14W
Mulymja ≈	134	Lf	60.12N	64.32 E
Mumbué	170	Ce	13.53 S	17.19 E
Mumbwa	170	Ee	14.59 S	27.04 E
Mumhan/Munster ▣	118	Ei	52.30N	9.00W
Mumra	132	Og	45.43N	47.41 E
Mun ≈	140	Mh	15.19N	105.30 E
Muna	192	Og	20.29N	89.43W
Muna ≈	140	Oc	67.52N	123.10 E
Muna, Pulau- ◆	150	Hg	5.00 S	122.30 E
Munābāo	148	Ec	25.45N	70.17 E
Munamägi/Munamjagi △	116	Lg	57.38N	27.10 E
Munamjagi/Munamägi △	116	Lg	57.38N	27.10 E
Munaybarah, Sharm- ⇌	146	Gi	26.04N	36.38 E
Muncar	150	Fh	8.29 S	114.21 E
Münchberg	120	Hf	50.12N	11.47 E
München=Munich (EN)	112	Hf	48.09N	11.35 E
Münchhausen	124	Kd	50.57N	8.43 E
Muncho Lake	180	Ee	58.56N	125.46W
Munch'ŏn	154	Ie	39.14N	127.22 E
Muncie	182	Jc	40.11N	85.23W
Munda	219a	Cc	8.19 S	157.15 E
Mundaring, Perth-	212	Df	31.54 S	116.10 E
Munday	186	Gj	33.27N	99.38W
Mundemba	166	Ge	4.59N	8.40 E
Münden	120	Fe	51.25N	9.41 E
Mundesley	124	Db	52.52N	1.25 E
Mundford	124	Cb	52.30N	0.39 E
Mundiwindi	210	Dg	23.52 S	120.09 E
Mundo ≈	126	Kf	38.19N	1.40W
Mundo Novo	202	Jf	11.52 S	40.28W
Munellës, Mali i- ▲	130	Dh	41.58N	20.06 E
Munera	126	Je	39.02N	2.28W
Mungana	212	Ic	17.07 S	144.24 E
Mungbere	160	Jh	2.38N	28.30 E
Munger	148	Hc	25.23N	86.28 E
Mungindi	212	Je	28.58S	148.59 E
Munhango	170	Ce	12.10 S	18.34 E
Munh-Hajrhan-Ula ▲	140	Le	46.40N	91.30 E
Munich (EN)=München	112	Hf	48.09N	11.35 E
Muniesa	126	Lc	41.02N	0.48W
Munīfah	144	Gd	27.38N	49.00 E
Munising	184	Db	46.25N	86.40W
Munkedal	114	Cg	58.29N	11.41 E
Munkfors	114	Cg	59.50N	13.32 E
Munku-Sardyk, gora- ▲	140	Md	51.45N	100.20 E
Muñoz Gamero, Península- ⊏	206	Fh	52.30 S	73.10W
Munsan	154	If	37.55N	126.22 E
Münsingen	120	Fh	48.25N	9.30 E
Munster	122	Nf	48.03N	7.08 E
Münster [Ger.]	120	De	51.58N	7.38 E
Münster [Ger.]	124	Ke	49.55N	8.52 E
Münster/Moutier	128	Bc	47.16N	7.22 E
Munster/Mumhan	118	Ei	52.30N	9.00W
Münster-Hiltrup	124	Jc	51.54N	7.38 E
Münsterland [Ger.]	120	De	52.00N	7.30 E
Münsterland [Ger.]	124	Kb	52.45N	8.10 E
Münstermaifeld	124	Jd	50.15N	7.22 E
Muntenia ⊠	130	Ie	44.00N	26.00 E
Munteni Buzău	130	Je	44.38N	26.59 E
Muntok	150	Eg	2.04 S	105.11 E
Munzur Dağları ⛰	146	Hc	39.30N	39.10 E
Muong Sen	148	Ke	19.24N	104.08 E
Muonio	112	Ib	67.57N	23.42 E
Muonioälven ≈	110	Ib	67.11N	23.34 E
Muonionjoki ≈	110	Ib	67.11N	23.34 E
Muping	154	Ff	37.23N	121.36 E
Muqaddam ≈	168	Eb	18.04N	31.30 E
Muqayshiţ ⁂	146	Oj	24.10N	53.45 E
Muqdisho=Mogadishu (EN)	160	Lh	2.03N	45.22 E
Mur ≈	110	Hf	46.18N	16.55 E
Mura ≈	110	Hf	46.18N	16.55 E
Muradiye [Tur.]	146	Jc	39.00N	43.43 E
Muradiye [Tur.]	130	Kk	38.39N	27.24 E
Murafa ≈	132	Fe	48.13N	28.14 E
Murakami	154	Oe	38.14N	139.29 E
Murallón, Cerro- ▲	198	Ij	49.48 S	73.25W
Muráň	120	Qh	48.45N	20.02 E
Mur'aňyo	168	Ic	11.41N	50.27 E
Muraši	136	Ed	59.24N	48.59 E
Murat	122	Ii	45.07N	2.52 E
Murat ≈	140	Ff	38.52N	38.48 E
Murat Dağı ▲	144	Cb	38.55N	29.43 E
Muratlı [Tur.]	146	Ib	41.29N	41.41 E
Muratlı [Tur.]	130	Kh	41.10N	27.30 E
Murau	128	Ic	47.06N	14.10 E
Muravera	128	Dk	39.25N	9.34 E
Murayama	156	Gb	38.29N	140.23 E
Mūrchen Khvort	146	Nf	33.06N	51.30 E
Murchison	218	Ed	41.48 S	172.20 E
Murchison, Mount- [Austl.] ▲	212	De	26.46 S	116.25 E
Murchison, Mount- [N.Z.] ▲	218	De	43.01 S	171.17 E
Murchison Falls → Kabalega Falls ⤵	170	Fb	2.17N	31.41 E
Murchison River ≈	208	Cg	27.50 S	114.00 E
Murcia	112	Fh	37.59N	1.07W
Murcia [2]	126	Kg	38.00N	1.30W
Mur-de-Barrez	122	Ij	44.51N	2.39 E
Murdo	186	Fe	43.53N	100.43W
Mure, La-	122	Lj	44.54N	5.47 E
Mureaux, Les-	124	Df	49.00N	1.55 E
Mürefte	130	Ki	40.40N	27.14 E
Muren	142	Me	49.38N	100.10 E
Mureş [2]	130	Hc	46.30N	24.40 E
Mureş ≈	110	If	46.15N	20.12 E
Muret	122	Hk	43.28N	1.21 E
Murewa	172	Ec	17.39 S	31.47 E
Murfreesboro	182	Jd	35.51N	86.23W
Murg ≈	120	Eh	48.55N	8.10 E
Murgab	140	If	38.18N	61.12 E
Murgab [Taj.]	136	Hh	38.10N	73.59 E
Murgab [Turk.]	135	Df	37.32N	62.01 E
Murgaš ▲	130	Gg	42.50N	23.40 E
Murgeni	130	Lc	46.12N	28.01 E
Murgon	212	Ke	26.15 S	151.57 E
Muri	220p	Cc	21.15 S	159.43W
Muriaé	202	Jh	21.08 S	42.22W
Murici	202	Ke	9.19 S	35.56W
Muriege	170	Dd	9.53 S	21.13 E
Murihiti ◎	220n	Ab	10.23 S	161.02W
Murilo Atoll ◎	208	Gd	8.40N	152.11 E
Mūrītāniyā=Mauritania (EN) [1]	160	Fg	20.00N	12.00W
Müritz ○	120	Ic	53.25N	12.43 E
Murkong Selek	148	Jc	27.44N	95.18 E
Murmansk	112	Jb	68.58N	33.05 E
Murmanskaja oblast [3]	136	Db	68.00N	35.30 E
Murmaši	136	Db	68.49N	32.49 E
Murnau	120	Hi	47.41N	11.12 E
Muro / Muro de Mallorca	126	Pe	39.44N	3.03 E
Muro, Capo di- ►	122a	Ab	41.44N	8.40 E
Muro de Mallorca / Muro	126	Pe	39.44N	3.03 E
Muro Lucano	128	Jj	40.45N	15.29 E
Murom	112	Kd	55.34N	42.02 E
Muromcevo	136	Hd	56.23N	75.14 E
Muroran	142	Qe	42.18N	140.59 E
Muros	126	Cb	42.47N	9.02W
Muros y Noya, Ria de- ⋎	126	Db	42.45N	9.00W
Muroto	152	Ne	33.18N	134.09 E
Muroto Zaki ►	154	Mh	33.16N	134.10 E
Murowana Goślina	120	Nd	52.35N	17.01 E
Murphy [Id.-U.S.]	188	Ge	43.13N	116.33W
Murphy [N.C.-U.S.]	184	Eh	35.05N	84.01W
Murphysboro	186	Lh	37.46N	89.20W
Murrah al Kubrá, Al Buḩayrah al- ○	146	Eg	30.20N	32.23 E
Murray [Ky.-U.S.]	184	Cg	36.37N	88.19W
Murray [Ut.-U.S.]	188	Jf	40.40N	111.53W
Murray, Lake- [Pap.N.Gui.] ○	214	Ci	7.00 S	141.30 E
Murray, Lake- [S.C.-U.S.] ○	184	Gh	34.04N	81.23W
Murray Bridge	212	Hg	35.07 S	139.17 E
Murray Fracture zone (EN) ⚡	106	Lf	34.00N	135.00W
Murray Islands ⁂	212	Ia	9.55 S	144.05 E
Murray Ridge (EN) ⋀	106	Gg	21.00N	61.50 E
Murray River ≈	208	Eh	35.22 S	139.22 E
Murraysburg	172	Cf	31.58 S	23.47 E
Murro di Porco, Capo- ►	128	Jm	37.00N	15.20 E
Murrumbidgee River ≈	208	Fh	34.43 S	143.12 E
Murrupula	172	Fc	15.27 S	38.47 E
Murska Sobota	128	Kd	46.40N	16.10 E
Murten	128	Bd	46.56N	7.08 E
Murter ◆	128	Jg	43.47N	15.37 E
Murtle Lake ○	188	Fa	52.08N	119.38W
Murud, Gunong- ▲	150	Gf	3.52N	115.30 E
Murupara	218	Gc	38.27 S	176.42 E
Mururoa Atoll ◎	208	Ng	21.52 S	138.55W
Murwāra	148	Gd	23.51N	80.24 E
Murwillumbah	212	Ke	28.19 S	153.24 E
Mürz ≈	128	Jc	47.24N	15.17 E
Mürzzuschlag	128	Jc	47.36N	15.41 E
Muş	144	Fb	38.44N	41.30 E
Muša/Mūša ≈	114	Fh	56.24N	24.12 E
Mūša/Muša ≈	114	Fh	56.24N	24.12 E
Mūsa, Jabal-=Sinai, Mount- (EN) ▲	146	Eh	28.32N	33.59 E
Musa Ali ▲	168	Gc	12.30N	42.27 E
Musāfī	146	Qk	25.18N	56.10 E
Musā'id	164	Ed	31.36N	25.03 E
Musala ▲	110	Ig	42.11N	23.34 E
Musallam	146	Lg	31.53N	46.56 E
Musan	152	Mc	42.14N	129.13 E
Musandam Peninsula ⊏	146	Qi	26.18N	56.24 E
Musay'īd	146	Nj	25.00N	51.33 E
Musaymir	164	Hg	13.27N	44.37 E
Muscat (EN)=Masqaţ	142	Hg	23.29N	58.33 E
Muscat and Oman (EN) → Oman (EN) [1]	142	Hg	21.00N	57.00 E
Muscatine	186	Kf	41.25N	91.03W
Musgrave	210	Ff	14.47 S	143.30 E
Musgrave Ranges ⛰	208	Eg	26.10 S	131.50 E
Mūshā	146	Di	27.07N	31.14 E
Mus-Haja, gora- ▲	140	Qc	62.35N	140.50 E
Mushāsh al 'Ashawī	146	Mj	24.12N	48.50 E
Mushāsh Ramlān	146	Mj	24.25N	49.15 E
Mushayrib, Ra's- ►	146	Nj	24.18N	51.44 E
Mushie	170	Cc	3.01 S	16.54 E
Mūsi ≈	148	Ge	15.20N	80.06 E
Musi ≈	140	Mj	2.20 S	104.56 E
Mūsiān	146	Lf	32.28N	47.26 E
Musicians Seamounts (EN) ⩚	208	Kb	29.00N	162.00W
Muskegon	182	Jc	43.14N	86.16W
Muskegon Heights	184	Dd	43.12N	86.12W
Muskegon River ≈	184	Dd	43.14N	86.20W
Muskö ◆	116	He	59.00N	18.05 E
Muskogee	182	Hd	35.45N	95.22W
Muskoka, Lake- ○	184	Hc	45.00N	79.25W
Musoma	160	Ki	1.30 S	33.48 E
Musone ≈	128	Hg	43.28N	13.38 E
Mussaţţaḩah, Al Jazīrah al- ◆	128	Em	37.11N	10.20 E
Mussau Island ◆	214	Dh	1.25 S	149.38 E
Musselkanaal, Stadskanaal-	124	Jb	52.56N	7.02 E
Musselshell River ≈	182	Fb	47.21N	107.58W
Mussende	170	Ce	10.31 S	16.02 E
Mussidan	122	Gi	45.02N	0.22 E
Mussòmeli	128	Hm	37.35N	13.45 E
Must	152	Fb	46.40N	92.40 E
Muşţafá, Ra's- ►	128	Fn	36.50N	11.07 E
Mustafakemalpaşa	146	Cb	40.02N	28.24 E
Mustahil	168	Gd	5.15N	44.44 E
Mustāng	148	Gc	29.11N	83.58 E
Mustang Draw ≈	186	Fj	32.00N	101.40W
Mustang Island ◆	186	Hm	28.00N	96.55W
Mustasaari/Korsholm	116	Ia	63.05N	21.43 E
Musters, Lago- ○	206	Gg	45.27 S	69.13W
Mustique Island ◆	196	Ff	12.39N	61.15W
Mustjala	116	Jf	58.25N	22.04 E
Mustla	114	Fg	58.14N	25.52 E
Mustvee	114	Gg	58.52N	26.59 E
Musu-dan ►	154	Jd	40.50N	129.43 E
Muswellbrook	212	Kf	32.16 S	150.53 E
Muszyna	120	Qg	49.21N	20.54 E
Mūţ	164	Ed	25.29N	28.59 E
Mut	146	Ed	36.39N	33.27 E
Mūtaf, Ra's al- ►	144	Hd	27.41N	51.27 E
Mutalau	220k	Ba	18.56 S	169.50W
Mutarara	160	Kj	17.27 S	35.04 E
Mutare	160	Kj	18.58 S	32.40 E
Mutatá	202	Cb	7.16N	76.32W
Mutawassiţ, Al Baḩr al-=Mediterranean Sea (EN) ≋	110	Hh	35.00N	20.00 E
Mutha	170	Gc	1.48 S	38.26 E
Muting	150	Lh	7.23 S	140.20 E
Mutis, Gunung- ▲	150	Hh	9.34 S	124.14 E
Mutoko	172	Ec	17.24 S	32.13 E
Mutoraj	138	Fd	61.20N	100.20 E
Mutsamudu	160	Lj	12.09 S	44.25 E
Mutshatsha	170	De	10.39 S	24.27 E
Mutsu	152	Pc	41.05N	140.55 E
Mutsu-Wan ◐	154	Pd	41.10N	140.55 E
Muttaburra	212	Id	22.36 S	144.33 E
Mutterstadt	124	Ke	49.27N	8.21 E
Mutton/Oiléan Coarach ◆	118	Di	52.49N	9.31W
Mutton Bird Islands ⁂	218	Bg	47.15 S	167.25 E
Mutuali	172	Fb	14.53 S	37.00 E
Mutún	204	Dd	19.10 S	57.54W
Mutunópolis	204	Ha	13.40 S	49.15W
Mutusjärvi ○	114	Gb	69.31N	26.57 E
Muurame	116	Kb	62.08N	25.40 E
Mu Us Shamo=Ordos Desert (EN) ∴	140	Mf	38.45N	109.10 E
Muxima	170	Bd	9.32 S	13.57 E
Muy, Le-	122	Mk	43.28N	6.33 E
Muyinga	170	Fc	2.51 S	30.20 E
Muy Muy	194	Eg	12.46N	85.38W
Muzaffarābād	148	Eb	34.22N	73.28 E
Muzaffargarh	148	Eb	30.04N	71.12 E
Muzaffarnagar	148	Fc	29.28N	77.41 E
Muzaffarpur	148	Hc	26.07N	85.24 E
Muzambinho	204	Ie	21.22 S	46.32W
Muzat He ≈	152	Dc	41.15N	83.27 E
Muži	138	Bc	65.27N	64.40 E
Muzillac	122	Dg	47.33N	2.29W
Mužlja	130	Dd	45.21N	20.25 E
Muztag [China] ▲	140	Kf	36.25N	87.25 E
Muztag [China] ▲	140	Kf	35.55N	80.20 E
Muztagata ▲	152	Cd	38.17N	75.07 E
Mvolo	168	Dd	6.03N	29.56 E
Mvomero	170	Gd	6.20 S	37.25 E
Mvoung ≈	170	Bb	0.04N	12.18 E
Mwadingusha	170	Ee	10.45 S	27.15 E
Mwali/Mohéli ◆	158	Lj	12.15 S	43.45 E
Mwanza [3]	170	Fc	2.30 S	32.30 E
Mwanza [Mwi.]	170	Ff	15.37 S	34.31 E
Mwanza [Tan.]	160	Ki	2.31 S	32.54 E
Mwanza [Zaire]	170	Ed	7.54 S	26.45 E
Mwatate	170	Gc	3.30 S	38.23 E
Mweelrea ▲	118	Dh	53.38N	9.50W
Mweka	160	Ji	4.51 S	21.34 E
Mwene Ditu	160	Ji	7.03 S	23.27 E
Mwenezi	172	Ed	21.22 S	30.45 E
Mwenga	170	Ec	3.02 S	28.26 E
Mweru, Lake- ○	158	Ji	9.00 S	28.45 E
Mweru Wantipa, Lake- ○	170	Ed	8.42 S	29.46 E
Mwimbi	170	Fd	8.39 S	31.40 E
Mwinilunga	170	De	11.44 S	24.26 E
Mya ≈	158	He	31.40N	5.15 E
Myaing	148	Id	21.37N	94.51 E
Myanaung	148	Je	18.17N	95.19 E
Myanmar-Nainggan-Daw → Burma [1]	142	Lg	22.00N	98.00 E
Myaungmya	148	Ie	16.36N	94.56 E
Mycenae (EN) = Mikínai ⁘	130	Fl	37.43N	22.45 E
Myebon	148	Id	20.03N	93.22 E
Myingyan	142	Lg	21.28N	95.23 E
Myinmoletkat Taung ▲	148	Jf	13.28N	98.48 E
Myitta	148	Jf	14.10N	98.31 E
Myjava ≈	120	Mh	48.33N	16.58 E
Myjzakjula/Mõisaküla	114	Fg	58.07N	25.10 E
Mylius Erichsens Land ⊠	179	Jb	81.40N	24.00W
Myltkyinā	142	Lg	25.23N	97.24 E
Mymensingh	148	Id	24.45N	90.24 E
Mynämäki	114	Ef	60.40N	22.00 E
Mynaral	136	Hf	45.22N	73.39 E
Myōkō-Zan ▲	156	Fc	36.52N	138.06 E
Mýrdalsjökull ❄	114a	Bc	63.40N	19.06W
Myre	114	Db	68.51N	15.05 E
Myrskylä/Mörskom	116	Kd	60.40N	25.51 E
Myrtle Beach	182	Le	33.42N	78.54W
Myrtle Point	188	Ce	43.04N	124.08W
Mysen	114	Cg	59.33N	11.20 E
Mysia ▣	130	Kj	39.30N	28.00 E
Myśla ≈	120	Kd	52.40N	14.29 E
Myślenice	120	Pg	49.51N	19.56 E
Myślibórz	120	Kd	52.55N	14.52 E
Mysore	142	Jh	12.18N	76.39 E
Mysore → Karnataka [3]	148	Ff	13.30N	76.00 E
Mys Šmidta	138	Nc	68.45N	178.40W
Myszków	120	Pf	50.36N	19.20 E
Myszyniec	120	Rc	53.24N	21.21 E
My Tho	142	Mh	10.21N	106.21 E
Mytišči	114	Ii	55.56N	37.46 E
Mývatn ○	114a	Cb	65.36N	17.00W
Myzeqeja ♒	130	Ci	41.01N	19.36 E
M'Zab ⊠	162	Hc	32.35N	3.20 E
Mže ≈	120	Jg	49.46N	13.24 E
Mziha	170	Gd	5.54 S	37.47 E
Mzimba	170	Fe	11.54 S	33.36 E
Mzuzu	160	Kj	11.27 S	33.55 E

N

Naab ≈	120	Ig	49.01N	12.02 E
Naaldwijk	124	Gc	51.59N	4.12 E
Naalehu	214	Od	19.04N	155.35W
Naantali/Nådendal	114	Ff	60.27N	22.02 E
Naarden	124	Hb	52.18N	5.10 E
Naas/An Nás	118	Gh	53.13N	6.39W
Nabadid	168	Gd	9.38N	43.29 E
Nabão ≈	126	De	39.31N	8.21W
Nabari	156	Ed	34.37N	136.05 E
Naberera	170	Gc	4.12S	36.56 E
Naberežnyje Čelny	112	Ld	55.42N	52.19 E
Nābha	148	Fb	30.22N	76.09 E
Nabire	210	Ee	3.22 S	135.29 E
Nabī Shu'ayb, Jabal an- ▲	140	Gh	15.17N	43.59 E
Nabq	146	Fh	28.04N	34.25 E
Nābul	160	Ie	36.27N	10.44 E
Nābul [3]	162	Jb	36.45N	10.45 E
Nābulus	146	Ff	32.13N	35.16 E
Nābulus [3]	146	Ff	32.18N	35.17 E

Index Symbols

- [1] Independent Nation
- [2] State, Region
- [3] District, County
- [4] Municipality
- [5] Colony, Dependency
- ■ Continent
- ⊠ Physical Region
- ▣ Historical or Cultural Region
- ▲ Mount, Mountain
- 🌋 Volcano
- △ Hill
- ⛰ Mountains, Mountain Range
- ◭ Hills, Escarpment
- ⏏ Plateau, Upland
- ⋂ Pass, Gap
- ▭ Plain, Lowland
- ◣ Delta
- ⧈ Salt Flat
- ∨ Valley, Canyon
- ◡ Crater, Cave
- ✲ Karst Features
- ⌄ Depression
- ⊔ Polder
- ∴ Desert, Dunes
- 🌲 Forest, Woods
- ⋔ Heath, Steppe
- 🌴 Oasis
- ► Cape, Point
- ⌇ Coast, Beach
- ◧ Cliff
- ⊏ Peninsula
- ⋈ Isthmus
- ⋯ Sandbank
- ◆ Island
- ◎ Atoll
- ✳ Rock, Reef
- ⁂ Islands, Archipelago
- ❋ Rocks, Reefs
- ✻ Coral Reef
- ⊙ Well, Spring
- ⛲ Geyser
- ≈ River, Stream
- ⤵ Waterfall, Rapids
- ⋎ River Mouth, Estuary
- ○ Lake
- ◌ Salt Lake
- ◍ Intermittent Lake
- ⊜ Reservoir
- ♒ Swamp, Pond
- ═ Canal
- ❄ Glacier
- ❅ Ice Shelf, Pack Ice
- 🌊 Ocean
- ≋ Sea
- ◐ Gulf, Bay
- ⇌ Strait, Fjord
- ◉ Lagoon
- ▤ Bank
- ⩚ Seamount
- ⊓ Tablemount
- ⋀ Ridge
- ⊥ Shelf
- ∪ Basin
- ⟋ Escarpment, Sea Scarp
- ⚡ Fracture
- ∇ Trench, Abyss
- ♣ National Park, Reserve
- ★ Point of Interest
- ⚑ Recreation Site
- ⌒ Cave, Cavern
- 🏛 Historic Site
- ⁘ Ruins
- ⊞ Wall, Walls
- ⛪ Church, Abbey
- ⛩ Temple
- ⚗ Scientific Station
- 🚉 Railway station
- ✈ Airport
- ⚓ Port
- ⊛ Military installation
- ⛯ Lighthouse
- ⚒ Mine
- ◠ Tunnel
- ⌿ Dam, Bridge

Nabusanke 170 Fb 0.01N 32.03 E
Nacala 172 Gb 14.33S 40.40 E
Nacala-a-Velha 160 Lj 14.33S 40.36 E
Nacaome 194 Dg 13.31N 87.30W
Nacaroa 172 Fb 14.23S 39.55 E
Naceredine 126 Ph 36.08N 3.26 E
Nachikatsuura 156 De 33.39N 135.55 E
Nachingwea 170 Ge 10.23S 38.46 E
Nachi-San 156 De 33.42N 135.51 E
Náchod 120 Mf 50.26N 16.10 E
Nachuge 148 If 10.35N 92.28 E
Nachvak Fiord 180 Le 59.03N 63.45W
Nacimiento Reservoir 188 Ei 35.43N 121.00W
Nacka 114 Ee 59.18N 18.10 E
Nå Clocha Liatha/ Greystones 118 Gh 53.09N 6.04W
Nacogdoches 186 Ik 31.36N 94.39W
Na Comaraigh/Comeragh Mountains 118 Fi 52.13N 7.35W
Nacori, Sierra- 192 Ec 29.50N 108.50W
Nacozari, Rio- 192 Ec 29.48N 109.42W
Nacozari de Garcia 190 Cb 30.24N 109.39W
Na Cruacha/Blue Stack 118 Eg 54.45N 8.06W
Na Cruacha Dubha 118 Di 52.00N 9.50W
Na Cruacha Dubha/ Macgillycuddy's Reeks 118 Di 52.00N 9.50W
Nacunday, Rio- 204 Eh 26.03S 54.45W
Nada → Danxian 152 Ih 19.38N 109.32 E
Nådendal/Naantali 114 Ff 60.27N 22.02 E
Nadiād 148 Ed 22.42N 72.52 E
Nădlac 130 Dc 46.10N 20.45 E
Nador 162 Gb 35.11N 2.56W
Nador [3] 162 Gb 35.00N 3.00W
Nădusa 130 Fi 40.38N 22.04 E
Nadvoicy 136 Dc 63.52N 34.20 E
Nadvornaja 132 De 48.38N 24.34 E
Nadym 142 Jc 65.35N 72.42 E
Nadym 138 Cc 66.20N 72.30 E
Naeba-San 156 Fc 36.51N 138.41 E
Nærbø 116 Af 58.40N 5.39 E
Næstved 114 Ci 55.14N 11.46 E
Nafada 166 Hc 11.06N 11.20 E
Nafarroa / Navarra [2] 126 Kb 42.45N 1.40W
Näfels 128 Dc 47.06N 9.04 E
Nafṭah 128 Dn 36.57N 9.04 E
Naftan Rock 220b Bb 14.50N 145.32 E
Naft-e-Safid 146 Mg 31.40N 49.17 E
Naft-e-Shāh 146 Kf 33.59N 45.30 E
Naft Khāneh 146 Ke 34.02N 45.28 E
Nafūsah, Jabal- 158 Ie 31.50N 12.00 E
Nāg 148 Dc 27.24N 65.08 E
Naga 142 Oh 13.28N 123.39 E
Någa, Kreb en- 162 Fe 24.00N 6.00W
Nagagami Lake 184 Ea 49.28N 85.02W
Nagagami River 186 Na 50.25N 84.20W
Nagahama [Jap.] 156 Ed 35.23N 136.16 E
Nagahama [Jap.] 156 Ce 33.36N 132.29 E
Nagai 156 Gb 38.06N 140.02 E
Nagai 178 Ge 55.11N 159.55W
Na Gaibhlte/Galty Mountains 118 Ei 52.23N 8.11W
Nāgāland [3] 148 Ic 26.30N 94.00 E
Nagano 142 Pf 36.39N 138.11 E
Nagano Ken [2] 154 Nf 36.10N 138.00 E
Nagano-Matsushiro 156 Fc 36.34N 138.10 E
Nagano-Shinonoi 156 Fc 36.35N 138.06 E
Nagaoka 152 Od 37.27N 138.51 E
Nagappattinam 148 Ff 10.46N 79.50 E
Nagara-Gawa 156 Ed 35.02N 136.43 E
Nagarote 194 Dg 12.16N 86.34W
Nagarzê 152 Ff 28.59N 90.28 E
Nagasaki 142 Of 32.47N 129.56 E
Nagasaki-Hantō 156 Ae 32.40N 129.45 E
Nagasaki Ken [2] 154 Jh 33.00N 129.50 E
Nagashima 156 Ed 34.12N 136.19 E
Naga-Shima 156 Ce 33.50N 132.05 E
Nagashima 156 Be 32.10N 130.10 E
Naga-Shima-Kaikyō 156 Be 32.15N 130.10 E
Nagato 154 Kg 34.21N 131.10 E
Nagayo 156 Ae 32.50N 129.52 E
Nāgda 148 Fd 23.27N 75.25 E
Nāgercoil 148 Fg 8.10N 77.26 E
Naghora Point 214 Gj 10.50S 162.24 E
Nagichot 168 Ee 4.16N 33.34 E
Nagi-San 156 Dd 35.10N 134.10 E
Nagiso 156 Ed 35.36N 137.36 E
Nago 152 Mf 26.35N 128.01 E
Nagold 120 Eh 48.33N 8.43 E
Nagold 120 Eh 48.52N 8.42 E
Nagorno-Karabakh 136 Eh 39.55N 46.45 E
Nagorny [Russia] 138 Md 63.10N 179.05 E
Nagorny [Russia] 138 He 55.45N 124.58 E
Nagorsk 114 Mg 59.21N 50.48 E
Nago-Wan 156b Ab 26.35N 127.55 E
Nagoya 142 Pf 35.10N 136.55 E
Nāgpur 142 Jg 21.09N 79.06 E
Nagqu 142 Lf 31.30N 92.00 E
Nag's Head 197c Ab 17.13N 62.38W
Nagua 194 Md 19.23N 69.50W
Naguabo 197a Cb 18.13N 65.44W
Nagyatád 120 Nj 46.13N 17.22 E
Nagybajom 120 Mj 46.23N 16.31 E
Nagyecsed 120 Si 47.52N 22.24 E
Nagyhalász 120 Rh 48.08N 21.46 E
Nagykálló 120 Ri 47.53N 21.51 E
Nagykanizsa 120 Mj 46.27N 16.59 E
Nagykáta 120 Pi 47.25N 19.45 E
Nagykőrös 120 Pi 47.02N 19.47 E
Nagykunság 120 Qj 46.55N 20.15 E
Nagy-Milic 120 Rh 48.35N 21.28 E
Naha 142 Og 26.13N 127.40 E
Nahanni Butte 180 Fd 61.04N 123.24W
Nahari 156 De 33.25N 134.01 E
Nahariyya 146 Ff 33.00N 35.05 E
Nahāvand 144 Gc 34.12N 48.22 E
Nahe 120 Dg 49.58N 7.57 E
Nahičevan 112 Kh 39.13N 45.27 E
Nahičevanskaja respublika 136 Eh 39.15N 45.35 E
Na'hīmābād 146 Qg 30.51N 56.31 E
Nahodka 142 Pe 42.48N 132.52 E
Nahr al Qāsh 168 Fb 16.48N 35.51 E
Nahr Ar Rahad 168 Ec 12.43N 30.39 E
Nahr Ouassel 126 Oi 35.45N 2.46 E
Nahuala, Laguna- 192 Ji 16.50N 99.40W
Nahuel Huapí, Lago- 206 Ff 40.58S 71.30W
Nahunta 184 Gj 31.12N 81.59W
Naie 156a Bb 43.24N 141.52 E
Naiguatá, Pico- 202 Ea 10.33N 66.46W
Naila 120 Hf 50.19N 11.42 E
Na'īmābād 146 Pd 36.14N 54.39 E
Naiman Qi (Daqin Tal) 152 Lc 42.49N 120.38 E
Nā'īn 146 Of 32.52N 53.05 E
Nain 176 Md 57.00N 61.40W
Nairai 219d Bb 17.49S 179.24 E
Nairn 118 Jd 57.35N 3.53W
Nairobi 160 Ki 1.17S 36.49 E
Nairobi [3] 170 Gc 1.17S 36.50 E
Naissaar/Najssar 116 Ke 59.35N 24.25 E
Naitamba 219d Cb 17.01S 179.17W
Naizishan 154 Ic 43.41N 127.27 E
Najafābād 144 Hc 32.37N 51.21 E
Najd 140 Gg 25.00N 44.30 E
Najd 144 Fe 25.00N 44.30 E
Nájera 126 Jb 42.25N 2.44W
Najerilla 126 Jb 42.31N 2.42W
Naj' Ḩammādī 164 Fd 26.03N 32.15 E
Najibābād 148 Fc 29.38N 78.20 E
Najin 152 Nc 42.15N 130.18 E
Najō 156 Ec 35.47N 136.12 E
Najrān 164 Hf 17.30N 44.10 E
Najrān 164 Hf 17.30N 44.10 E
Najssar/Naissaar 116 Ke 59.35N 24.25 E
Najstenjarvi 114 He 62.18N 32.42 E
Naju 154 Ig 35.02N 126.43 E
Najzataš, pereval- 135 If 37.52N 73.46 E
Nakadōri-Jima 154 Jh 32.58N 129.05 E
Nakagawa 156a Ca 44.47N 142.05 E
Naka-Gawa [Jap.] 156 De 33.56N 134.42 E
Naka-Gawa [Jap.] 156 Gc 36.20N 140.36 E
Nakagusuku-Wan 156b Ab 26.15N 127.50 E
Nakahechi 156 De 33.47N 135.29 E
Naka-Iō-Jima 214 Cc 24.47N 141.20 E
Naka-Jima 156 Ce 33.58N 132.37 E
Nakajō 154 Oe 38.03N 139.24 E
Nakano-Koshiki-Jima 156 Af 31.48N 129.50 E
Nakalele Point 221a Eb 21.02N 156.35W
Nakama 156 Be 33.50N 130.43 E
Nakaminato 156 Gc 36.22N 140.36 E
Nakamura 154 Lh 32.59N 132.56 E
Nakanai Mountains 212 Ka 5.35S 151.10 E
Nakano 156 Fc 36.45N 138.22 E
Nakano-Dake 156 Fc 37.04N 139.06 E
Nakanojō 156 Fc 36.35N 138.51 E
Naka-no-Shima [Jap.] 154 Lf 36.05N 133.04 E
Naka-no-Shima [Jap.] 152 Mf 29.50N 129.50 E
Nakasato 156a Bc 40.58N 140.26 E
Naka-satsunai 156a Cb 42.42N 143.08 E
Nakashibetsu 156a Db 43.36N 145.00 E
Nakasongola 170 Fb 1.19N 32.28 E
Nakatonbetsu 156a Ca 44.58N 142.17 E
Nakatsu 154 Kh 33.34N 131.13 E
Nakatsugawa 154 Ng 35.29N 137.30 E
Nakfa 168 Fb 16.40N 38.30 E
Nakhon Pathom 148 Kf 13.49N 100.06 E
Nakhon Phanom 148 Ke 17.22N 104.46 E
Nakhon Ratchasima 142 Mh 14.57N 102.09 E
Nakhon Sawan 142 Mh 15.42N 100.06 E
Nakhon Si Thammarat 142 Li 8.26N 99.58 E
Nakijin 156b Ab 26.42N 127.59 E
Nakina 176 Kd 50.10N 86.42W
Nakkila 116 Ic 61.22N 22.00 E
Nakło nad Notecią 120 Nc 53.08N 17.35 E
Naknek 178 He 58.44N 157.02W
Nakonde 170 Fd 9.19S 32.46 E
Nakskov 114 Ci 54.50N 11.09 E
Näkten 116 Fb 62.50N 14.40 E
Naktong-gang 154 Jg 35.07N 128.57 E
Nakuru 160 Ki 0.20S 35.56 E
Nakusp 188 Ga 50.15N 117.48W
Näl 148 Dc 26.02N 65.29 E
Nalajch → Nalajha 152 Ib 47.45N 107.16 E
Nalajha (Nalajch) 152 Ib 47.45N 107.16 E
Nalčik 112 Kg 43.29N 43.37 E
Nallıhan 146 Db 40.11N 31.21 E
Nalón 126 Fa 43.32N 6.04W
Nälüt 160 Ie 31.52N 10.59 E
Nalwasha 170 Gc 0.43S 36.26 E
Na Machairi/Brandon Head 118 Ci 52.16N 10.15W
Namacurra 172 Fc 17.29S 37.01 E
Namai Bay 220a Bb 7.32N 134.39 E
Namak, Daryācheh-ye- = Namak Lake (EN) 140 Hf 34.45N 51.36 E
Namak, Kavīr-e- 144 Ic 34.30N 57.40 E
Namakan Lake 186 Jb 48.27N 92.35W
Namak-e Mīghān, Kavīr-e- 146 Me 34.13N 49.49 E
Namaki 146 Pg 31.16N 55.29 E
Namakia 172 Hc 15.56S 45.48 E
Namak Lake (EN) = Namak, Daryācheh-ye- 140 Hf 34.45N 51.36 E
Namakwaland = Little Namaland (EN) 172 Be 29.00S 17.00 E
Namanga 170 Gc 2.33S 36.47 E
Namangan 142 Je 41.00N 71.40 E
Namanganskaja oblast [3] 136 Hg 41.00N 71.20 E
Namanyere 170 Fd 7.31S 31.03 E
Namapa 172 Fb 13.43S 39.50 E
Namaqua Seamount (EN) 172 Af 31.30S 11.20 E
Namarroî 172 Fc 15.57S 36.51 E
Namasagali 170 Fb 1.01N 32.57 E
Namasale 170 Fb 1.30N 32.37 E
Namatanai 214 Eh 3.40S 152.27 E
Namathu 219d Bb 17.21S 179.26 E
Nambavatu 219d Bb 16.36S 178.55 E
Namber 150 Jg 1.04S 134.49 E
Nambour 212 Ke 26.38S 152.58 E
Nambouwalu 216 Ec 16.59S 178.42 E
Nam Can 148 Kg 8.46N 104.59 E
Namcha Barwa 140 Lg 29.38N 95.04 E
Namche Bazar 148 Hc 27.49N 86.43 E
Nam Co 140 Lf 30.45N 90.35 E
Namčy 138 Hd 62.35N 129.40 E
Namdalen 114 Cd 64.38N 12.35 E
Nam Dinh 142 Mg 20.25N 106.10 E
Nämdö 116 He 59.10N 18.40 E
Nam Du, Quan Dao- 148 Kg 9.42N 104.22 E
Namêche, Andenne- 124 Hd 50.28N 5.00 E
Namelaki Passage 220a Bc 7.24N 134.38 E
Namen/Namur 122 Kd 50.28N 4.52 E
Namerikawa 156 Ec 36.45N 137.20 E
Náměšt nad Oslavou 120 Mg 49.12N 16.09 E
Nametil 172 Fc 15.43S 39.21 E
Namib Desert/ Namibwoestyn 158 Ik 23.00S 15.00 E
Namibe 160 Ij 15.12S 12.10 E
Namibe [3] 170 Bf 15.20S 12.30 E
Namibia (South West Africa) [1] 160 Ik 22.00S 17.00 E
Namibwoestyn/Namib Desert 158 Ik 23.00S 15.00 E
Namie 154 Pf 37.29N 140.59 E
Namin 146 Mc 38.25N 48.30 E
Namioka 156 Ga 40.42N 140.35 E
Namiquipa 192 Fc 29.15N 107.40W
Namiranga 172 Gb 10.33S 40.30 E
Namja La 152 Df 29.58N 82.34 E
Namkham 148 Jd 23.50N 97.41 E
Namlea 150 Ig 3.18S 127.06 E
Namling 152 Ef 29.44N 89.05 E
Namnoi, Khao- 148 Jf 10.36N 98.38 E
Namoi River 212 Je 30.00S 148.07 E
Namoluk Island 208 Gd 5.55N 153.08 E
Namonuito Atoll 208 Gd 8.46N 150.02 E
Namorik Atoll 208 Hd 5.36N 168.07 E
Namous 162 Gc 30.28N 0.14W
Nampa 182 Dc 43.34N 116.34W
Nampala 166 Db 15.17N 5.33W
Nam Phan = Cochin China (EN) 140 Mg 11.00N 107.00 E
Nam Phong 148 Ke 16.45N 102.52 E
Nampi 154 De 38.02N 116.42 E
Namp'o 152 Md 38.44N 125.25 E
Nampula 160 Kj 15.07S 39.15 E
Nampula [3] 172 Fb 15.00S 39.30 E
Namsê Shankou 152 Df 29.58N 82.34 E
Namsos 112 Hc 64.30N 11.30 E
Namtu 148 Jd 23.05N 97.24 E
Namu 188 Ba 51.49N 127.52W
Namu Atoll 208 Hd 8.00N 168.10 E
Namuka-I-Lau 219d Cc 18.51S 178.38W
Namūli, Serra- 158 Kj 15.21S 37.00 E
Namuno 172 Fb 13.37S 38.48 E
Namur [3] 124 Gd 50.20N 4.50 E
Namur/Namen 122 Kd 50.28N 4.52 E
Namur-Saint Servais 124 Gd 50.28N 4.50 E
Namuruputh 170 Gb 4.34N 35.57 E
Namur-Wépion 124 Gd 50.25N 4.52 E
Namutoni 172 Bc 18.30S 17.55 E
Namwala 170 Ef 15.45S 26.26 E
Namwŏn 154 Ig 35.24N 127.23 E
Namysłów 120 Ne 51.05N 17.42 E
Nan 148 Ke 18.48N 100.46 E
Nan 140 Mh 15.42N 100.09 E
Nana 168 Bd 5.00N 15.50 E
Nana Barya 168 Bd 7.59N 17.43 E
Nanae 156a Bc 41.53N 140.41 E
Nanaimo 180 Fg 49.10N 123.56W
Nanakuli 221a Cb 21.23N 158.08W
Nanam 154 Jd 41.44N 129.40 E
Nana-Mambéré [3] 168 Bd 6.00N 16.00 E
Nanango 212 Ke 26.40S 152.00 E
Nanao 152 Od 37.03N 136.58 E
Nanao-Wan 156 Ec 37.10N 137.00 E
Nanatsu-Shima 156 Ec 37.35N 136.50 E
Nancha 152 Mb 47.08N 129.09 E
Nanchang 142 Ng 28.40N 115.58 E
Nancheng 152 Kf 27.32N 116.36 E
Nanchong 142 Mf 30.47N 106.03 E
Nancowry 148 Ig 7.59N 93.32 E
Nancy 112 Gf 48.41N 6.12 E
Nanda Devi 140 Jf 30.23N 79.59 E
Nandaime 194 Dh 11.46N 86.03W
Nandan [China] 152 Ig 24.59N 107.31 E
Nandan [Jap.] 154 Mg 34.15N 134.43 E
Nandaran → Qingyuan 154 Ce 38.46N 115.29 E
Nanded 142 Jh 19.09N 77.20 E
Nandewar Range 212 Kf 30.40S 151.10 E
Nandi 216 Ec 17.48S 177.25 E
Nandu Jiang 152 Jg 20.04N 110.22 E
Nanduri 219d Bb 16.27S 179.09 E
Nandyāl 148 Fe 15.29N 78.29 E
Nanfen 154 Gd 41.06N 123.45 E
Nanfeng 152 Kf 27.15N 116.30 E
Nanga-Eboko 166 He 4.41N 12.22 E
Nanga Parbat 140 Jf 35.15N 74.36 E
Nangapinoh 150 Fg 0.20S 111.44 E
Nangarhār [3] 144 Lc 34.15N 70.30 E
Nangatayap 150 Fg 1.32S 110.34 E
Nangis 122 If 48.33N 3.00 E
Nangnim-san 154 Id 40.21N 126.55 E
Nangnim-Sanmaek 154 Id 40.30N 127.00 E
Nangong 152 Kd 37.22N 115.23 E
Nangqên 152 Ge 32.15N 96.13 E
Nanguan 154 Af 36.42N 111.41 E
Nanguantao → Guantao 154 Cf 36.33N 115.18 E
Nangweshi 170 Df 16.26S 23.20 E
Nang Xian 152 Ff 29.02N 93.05 E
Nan Hai = South China Sea (EN) 140 Ni 10.00N 113.00 E
Nanhaoqian → Shangyi 154 Bd 41.06N 113.58 E
Nanhe 154 Cf 36.58N 114.41 E
Nanhua 152 Hf 25.16N 101.18 E
Nanhui 154 Fi 31.03N 121.46 E
Nan Hulsan Hu 152 Gd 36.45N 95.45 E
Nanjian 152 Hf 25.05N 100.32 E
Nanjiang 152 Ie 32.22N 106.45 E
Nanjing (Nanking) 142 Nf 31.59N 118.51 E
Nankai Trough (EN) 152 Ne 32.00N 135.00 E
Nanking → Nanjing 142 Nf 31.59N 118.51 E
Nankoku 154 Lh 33.39N 133.44 E
Nanle 154 Cf 36.06N 115.12 E
Nanling 154 Ei 30.55N 118.19 E
Nan Ling 140 Ng 25.00N 112.00 E
Nanlou Shan 154 Ic 43.24N 126.40 E
Nanma → Yiyuan 154 Ef 36.11N 118.10 E
Nanning 142 Mg 22.50N 108.18 E
Nannup 212 Df 33.59S 115.45 E
Nanortalik 179 Hf 60.32N 45.45W
Nanpan Jiang 152 Ig 24.56N 106.12 E
Nänpära 148 Gc 27.52N 81.30 E
Nanping [China] 142 Ng 26.42N 118.09 E
Nanping [China] 152 He 33.15N 104.13 E
Nanpu 154 Ee 39.16N 118.12 E
Nanqiao → Fengxian 154 Fi 30.55N 121.27 E
Nansei-Shotō = Ryukyu Islands (EN) 140 Og 26.30N 128.00 E
Nansen Cordillera (EN) 224 Ge 87.00N 90.00 E
Nansen Land 179 Hb 83.20N 46.00W
Nanshan Islands (EN) = Nansha Qundao 140 Ni 9.40N 113.30 E
Nansha Qundao = Nashan Islands (EN) 140 Ni 9.40N 113.30 E
Nansio 170 Fc 2.08S 33.03 E
Nant 122 Jj 44.01N 3.18 E
Nantais, Lac - 180 Kd 61.00N 73.50W
Nantai-San 156 Fc 36.46N 139.29 E
Nanterre 122 If 48.54N 2.12 E
Nantes 112 Ff 47.13N 1.33W
Nantes à Brest, Canal de- 122 Bf 48.12N 4.06W
Nanteuil-le-Haudouin 124 Ee 49.08N 2.48 E
Nanticoke 184 Je 41.13N 76.00W
Nantō 156 Ed 34.17N 136.29 E
Nantong 152 Le 32.00N 120.52 E
Nantong (Jinsha) 154 Fh 32.06N 120.52 E
Nantou 152 Lg 23.54N 120.51 E
Nantua 122 Lh 46.09N 5.37 E
Nantucket 184 Le 41.17N 70.06W
Nantucket Island 182 Mc 41.16N 70.03W
Nantucket Sound 184 Le 41.30N 70.15W
Nanuku Passage 219d Cb 16.45S 179.15W
Nanuku Reef 219d Cb 16.40S 179.26W
Nanumanga Island 208 Ie 6.18S 176.20 E
Nanumea Atoll 208 Ie 5.43S 176.00 E
Nanuque 202 Jg 17.50S 40.21W
Nanusa, Pulau-Pulau- 150 If 4.42N 127.06 E
Nanwan Shuiku 154 Bh 32.02N 113.57 E
Nanwei Dao = Spratly (EN) 150 Fe 8.42N 111.40 E
Nanwei Tan 152 Kg 21.00N 116.00 E
Nanweng He 152 Ma 51.10N 125.59 E
Nanxian 154 Bj 29.22N 112.25 E
Nanxiang 154 Fi 31.18N 121.17 E
Nanxiong 152 Jf 25.13N 114.18 E
Nanxun 154 Fi 30.53N 120.26 E
Nanyandang Shan 152 Lf 27.37N 120.06 E
Nanyang 142 Nf 32.56N 112.32 E
Nanyang Hu 154 Dg 35.15N 116.39 E
Nanyō 154 Pe 38.03N 140.10 E
Nanyuki 160 Kh 0.01N 37.04 E
Nanzhang 152 Je 31.45N 111.53 E
Nanzhao 152 Je 33.28N 112.29 E
Nao, Cabo de la-/Nau, Cap de la- 110 Gh 38.44N 0.14 E
Naococane, Lac- 180 Kf 52.50N 70.40W
Naoero / Nauru [1] 210 He 0.31S 166.56 E
Naoetsu 156 Fc 37.11N 138.14 E
Nāo-me-Toque 204 Fi 28.28S 52.49W
Naours, Souterrains de- 124 Ed 50.05N 2.17 E
Napa 188 Dg 38.18N 122.17W
Napanee 184 Ic 44.15N 76.57W
Napassoq 179 Ge 65.45N 52.38W
Napata 168 Eb 18.29N 31.51 E
Na-Peng 148 Jd 23.10N 98.26 E
Napf 128 Bc 47.01N 7.57 E
Napier 210 Ih 39.30S 176.54 E
Napier, Mount- 212 Fc 17.32S 129.10 E
Napier Mountains 222 Ee 66.30S 53.40 E
Naples [Fl.-U.S.] 184 Gl 26.08N 81.48W
Naples [Id.-U.S.] 188 Gb 48.34N 116.24W
Naples (EN) = Napoli 112 Hg 40.50N 14.15 E
Naples, Gulf of- (EN) = Napoli, Golfo di- 128 Ij 40.45N 14.10 E
Napo 152 Ig 23.25N 105.49 E
Napo, Rio- 198 If 3.20S 72.40W
Napoleon 186 Gc 46.30N 99.46W
Napoli = Naples (EN) 112 Hg 40.50N 14.15 E
Napoli, Golfo di- = Naples, Gulf of- (EN) 128 Ij 40.45N 14.10 E
Napostá 204 An 38.26S 62.15W
Napuka, Ile- 208 Mf 14.12S 141.15W
Naqa 168 Eb 16.16N 33.17 E
Naqadeh 144 Gb 36.57N 45.23 E
Naqsh-e-Rostam 146 Og 30.01N 52.50 E
Nar 118 Ni 52.45N 0.24 E
Nära 148 Dc 24.07N 69.07 E
Nara [Jap.] 152 Oe 34.41N 135.50 E
Nara [Mali] 166 Db 15.11N 7.15W
Naračenskibani 130 Hh 41.54N 24.45 E
Naracoorte 212 Ig 36.58S 140.44 E
Nara-Ken [2] 154 Mg 34.20N 135.55 E
Naran 154 Bb 45.20N 113.41 E
Naranjo 192 Ee 25.48N 108.31W
Naranjos [Bol.] 204 Cd 18.38S 59.09W
Naranjos [Mex.] 192 Kg 21.21N 97.41W
Narao 156 Ae 32.52N 129.04 E
Narathiwat 148 Kg 6.25N 101.48 E
Nārāyanganj 148 Id 23.37N 90.30 E
Narbonne 122 Ik 43.11N 3.00 E
Narca, Ponta da- 170 Bd 6.07S 12.16
Narcea 126 Fa 43.28N 6.06
Narcondam 148 If 13.15N 94.30
Nardò 128 Mj 40.11N 18.02
Naré 204 Bj 30.58S 60.28
Nares Land 179 Hb 82.25N 47.30
Nares Strait 174 Lb 78.50N 73.00
Narew 120 Td 52.55N 23.29
Narew 120 Qd 52.26N 20.42
Narian, Pointe- 219b Be 20.05S 164.00
Narin Gol 152 Fd 36.54N 92.51
Nariño [3] 202 Cc 1.30N 78.00
Narita 156 Gd 35.47N 140.18
Narjan-Mar 112 Lb 67.39N 53.00
Närke 116 Ff 59.05N 15.05
Narlı 146 Gd 37.27N 37.09
Narmada 140 Jg 21.38N 72.36
Narman 146 Ib 40.21N 41.52
Närnaul 148 Fc 28.03N 76.06
Narni 128 Gh 42.31N 12.31
Naroč 116 Lj 54.57N 26.49
Naroč 116 Lj 54.27N 26.45
Naroč, ozero- 132 Eb 54.50N 26.45
Naroda 134 Jd 64.15N 61.00
Narodnaja, gora- 110 Mb 65.04N 60.09
Naro-Fominsk 136 Dd 55.24N 36.43
Narok 170 Gc 1.05S 35.52
Narovlja 132 Fd 51.48N 29.31
Närpes/Närpio 116 Ib 62.28N 21.20
Närpio/Närpes 116 Ib 62.28N 21.20
Narrabri 212 Jf 30.19S 149.47
Narrandera 212 Jf 34.45S 146.33
Narrogin 212 Df 32.56S 117.10
Narromine 212 Jf 32.14S 148.15
Narrows, The- 197c Ab 17.12N 62.38W
Narryer, Mount- 212 De 26.30S 116.25
Narsimhapur 148 Fd 22.57N 79.12
Narssalik 179 Hf 61.42N 49.11W
Narssaq [Grld.] 179 Gf 64.00N 51.33W
Narssaq [Grld.] 179 Hf 61.00N 46.00W
Narssarssuaq 179 Hf 61.10N 45.15W
Narthákion 130 Fj 39.14N 22.22
Nartkala 132 Mh 43.32N 43.47
Narubis 172 Be 26.55S 18.35
Narugo 156 Gb 38.44N 140.43
Nāruja 130 Jd 45.50N 26.47
Naru-Shima 156 Ae 32.50N 128.56 E
Naruto 154 Mg 34.11N 134.37 E
Naruto-Kaikyō 156 Dd 34.15N 134.40 E
Narva 112 Id 59.23N 28.11
Narva 114 Gg 59.29N 28.02 E
Narva Jõesuu/Narva-Jyesuu 116 Me 59.21N 28.04 E
Narva-Jyesuu / Narva-Jõesuu 116 Me 59.21N 28.04 E
Narva laht 114 Gg 59.30N 27.40 E
Narvik 112 Hb 68.26N 17.25 E
Narvski zaliv 114 Gg 59.30N 27.40 E
Narvskoje vodohranilišče 116 Me 59.10N 28.30 E
Narym 138 De 58.58N 81.40 E
Naryn 142 Je 41.26N 75.59 E
Naryn 140 Je 40.54N 71.45 E
Naryncol 136 Ig 42.43N 80.08 E
Narynskaja oblast [3] 136 Hg 41.20N 75.40 E
Nås 114 Df 60.27N 14.29 E
Na Sailti/Saltee Islands 118 Gi 52.07N 6.36W
Näsåker 114 De 63.23N 16.54 E
Nasarawa 166 Gd 8.32N 7.43 E
Năsăud 130 Hb 47.17N 24.24 E
Nasawa 219b Db 15.12S 168.06 E
Nasbinals 122 Jj 44.40N 3.03 E
Na Sceiri/Skerries 118 Gh 53.35N 6.07W
Nāshik 142 Jg 20.05N 73.48 E
Nash Point 118 Jj 51.24N 3.27W
Nashtārud 146 Nd 36.45N 51.02 E
Nashua 184 Ld 42.44N 71.28W
Nashville [Ar.-U.S.] 186 Jj 33.57N 93.51W
Nashville [Ga.-U.S.] 184 Fj 31.12N 83.15W
Nashville [Il.-U.S.] 186 Lg 38.21N 89.23W
Nashville [In.-U.S.] 184 Df 39.12N 86.15W
Nashville [Tn.-U.S.] 176 Kf 36.09N 86.48W
Nashville Seamount (EN) 174 Nf 35.00N 57.20W
Našice 128 Me 45.30N 18.06 E
Nasielsk 120 Qd 52.36N 20.48 E
Näsijärvi 110 Ic 61.35N 23.40 E
Nāṣir 168 Ed 8.36N 33.04 E
Naskaupi 180 Lf 53.47N 60.51W
Nasorolevu 219d Bb 16.38S 179.24 E
Naṣr 164 Dd 28.59N 21.13 E
Naṣr 146 Dg 30.36N 30.23 E
Naṣrābād 146 Of 32.09N 52.08 E
Nass 180 Fe 55.00N 129.50W
Nassandres 124 Ce 49.07N 0.44 E
Nassandres-La Rivière Thibouville 124 Ce 49.07N 0.44 E
Nassau [Bah.] 176 Lg 25.05N 77.21W
Nassau [Ger.] 124 Jd 50.19N 7.48 E
Nassau, Bahia- 206 Gi 55.25S 67.40W
Nassau Island 208 Kf 11.33S 165.25W
Nassau River 212 Ic 15.58S 141.30 E
Nasser, Birkat- = Nasser, Lake-(EN) 158 Kf 22.40N 32.00 E
Nasser, Lake-(EN) = Nasser, Birkat- 158 Kf 22.40N 32.00 E
Nassian 166 Ed 9.24N 4.29W
Nässjö 114 Dh 57.39N 14.41 E
Nassogne 124 Hd 50.08N 5.21 E
Na Staighri Dubha/ Blackstairs Mountains 118 Gi 52.33N 6.49W
Nastapoka Islands 180 Je 56.50N 76.50W
Nastätten 124 Jd 50.12N 7.52 E
Nastola 116 Kd 60.57N 25.56 E
Nasu 156 Gc 37.02N 140.06 E
Nasu-Dake 156 Fc 37.07N 139.58 E
Näsviken 116 Gc 61.45N 16.52 E
Natá 194 Gi 8.20N 80.31W
Nata 172 Dd 20.13S 26.11 E
Nata 158 Jk 20.14S 26.10 E
Natal → KwaZulu-Natal 172 Ee 29.00S 30.00 E

Natal [B.C.-Can.]	188	Hb	49.44N	114.50W
Natal [Braz.]	200	Mf	5.47S	35.13W
Natal [Indon.]	150	Cf	0.33N	99.07 E
Natal Basin (EN)	106	Fm	30.00S	40.00 E
Natanz	146	Nf	33.31N	51.54 E
Natashquan	180	Lf	50.11N	61.49W
Natashquan	180	Lf	50.09N	61.37W
Natchez	182	Ie	31.34N	91.23W
Natchitoches	182	Ie	31.46N	93.05W
Natewa Bay	219d	Bb	16.35S	179.40 E
Nathorsts Land	179	Jd	72.20N	27.00W
Nathula	219d	Ab	16.53S	177.25 E
Natitingou	160	Hg	10.19N	1.22 E
Natityāy, Jabal-	164	Fe	23.01N	34.22 E
Natividad, Isla-	192	Bd	27.55N	115.10W
Natividade	202	If	11.43S	47.47W
Natori	154	Pe	38.11N	140.58 E
Natron, Lake-	158	Ki	2.25S	36.00 E
Naṭrūn, Wādī an-	146	Dg	30.25N	30.13 E
Natsudomari-Zaki	156a	Bc	41.00N	140.53 E
Nåttarö	116	Hf	58.50N	18.10 E
Nättraby	116	Fh	56.12N	15.31 E
Natuna, Kepulauan- = Natuna Islands (EN)	140	Mi	2.45N	109.00 E
Natuna Besar, Pulau-	150	Ef	4.00N	108.15 E
Natuna Islands (EN) = Natuna, Kepulauan-	140	Mi	2.45N	109.00 E
Naturaliste, Cape-	208	Ch	33.32S	115.01 E
Naturaliste Channel	212	Ce	25.25S	113.00 E
Naturita	186	Bg	38.14N	108.34W
Naturno / Naturns	128	Ed	46.39N	11.00 E
Naturns / Naturno	128	Ed	46.39N	11.00 E
Nau	135	Gd	40.09N	69.22 E
Nau, Cap de la-/Nao, Cabo de la-	110	Gh	38.44N	0.14 E
Naucelle	122	Ij	44.12N	2.21 E
Nauëji-Akmjane/Naujoji-Akmenė	114	Fh	56.21N	22.50 E
Naugo/Nauvo	116	Id	60.10N	21.50 E
Nauhcampatépetl → Cofre de Perote, Cerro-	192	Kh	19.29N	97.08W
Nauja Bay	180	Kc	68.58N	75.00W
Naujamestis/Naujamiestis	116	Ki	55.41N	24.09 E
Naujamiestis/Naujamestis	116	Ki	55.41N	24.09 E
Naujoji-Akmenė/Nauëji-Akmjane	114	Fh	56.21N	22.50 E
Naukluft	172	Bd	24.10S	16.10 E
Naumburg [Ger.]	124	Lc	51.15N	9.10 E
Naumburg [Ger.]	120	He	51.09N	11.49 E
Nā'ūr	146	Fg	31.53N	35.50 E
Nauru	208	He	0.31S	166.56 E
Nauru / Naoero [1]	210	He	0.31S	166.56 E
Nauški	138	Ff	50.28N	106.07 E
Nausori	216	Ec	18.02S	178.32 E
Nauta	202	Dd	4.32S	73.33W
Nautanwa	148	Gc	27.26N	83.25 E
Nautla	192	Kg	20.13N	96.47W
Nauvo/Naugo	116	Id	60.10N	21.50 E
Nava	192	Ic	28.25N	100.45W
Navacerrada, Puerto de-	126	Id	40.47N	4.00W
Nava del Rey	126	Gc	41.20N	5.05W
Navahermosa	126	He	39.38N	4.28W
Navajo Mountain	188	Jh	37.02N	110.52W
Navajo Reservoir	186	Ch	36.55N	107.30W
Navalmoral de la Mata	126	Ge	39.54N	5.32W
Navan → An Uaimh	118	Gh	53.39N	6.41W
Navarin, mys-	140	Tc	62.16N	179.10 E
Navarino, Isla-	198	Jk	55.05S	67.40W
Navarra / Nafarroa [2]	126	Kb	42.45N	1.40W
Navarro	204	Cl	35.01S	59.16W
Navarro Mills Lake	186	Hk	31.56N	96.45W
Navašino	114	Ki	55.33N	42.12 E
Navasota	186	Hk	30.23N	96.05W
Navasota River	186	Hk	30.20N	96.09W
Navassa	190	Ie	18.24N	75.01W
Navaste jõgi / Navesti	116	Kf	58.56N	24.58 E
Nävekvarn	116	Gf	58.38N	16.49 E
Naver	118	Ic	58.30N	4.15W
Navesti / Navaste jõgi	116	Kf	58.56N	24.58 E
Navia	126	Fa	43.32N	6.43W
Navia	126	Fa	43.33N	6.44W
Navidad, Bahía de-	192	Gh	19.10N	104.45W
Navidad Bank (EN)	194	Mc	20.00N	68.50W
Naviti	219d	Ab	17.07S	177.15 E
Navlja	136	De	52.50N	34.31 E
Navlja	132	Ic	52.42N	34.03 E
Năvodari	130	Le	44.19N	28.36 E
Navoi	136	Gg	40.10N	65.15 E
Navoja	190	Cc	27.06N	109.26W
Navolato	192	Fe	24.47N	107.42W
Navoloki	114	Jh	57.28N	41.59 E
Návpaktos	130	Ek	38.24N	21.50 E
Návplion	130	Fl	37.34N	22.48 E
Navrongo	166	Ec	10.54N	1.06W
Navsāri	148	Ed	20.55N	72.55 E
Navtílos	130	Gn	35.57N	23.13 E
Navua	219d	Bc	18.13S	178.10 E
Navy Board Inlet	180	Jb	73.30N	81.00W
Nawa	146	Gf	32.53N	36.03 E
Nawābshāh	148	Dc	26.15N	68.25 E
Nawāṣīf, Ḩarrat-	164	He	21.20N	42.10 E
Naws, Ra's-	144	If	17.18N	55.16 E
Náxos	130	Il	37.06N	25.23 E
Naxos	128	Jm	37.49N	15.15 E
Náxos = Naxos (EN)	110	Ih	37.02N	25.35 E
Naxos (EN) = Náxos	110	Ih	37.02N	25.35 E
Nayarit [2]	190	Cd	22.00N	105.00W
Nayarit, Sierra de-	190	Dd	22.00N	103.50W
Nayau	219d	Cb	17.58S	179.03W
Nāy Band [Iran]	146	Oi	27.23N	52.38 E
Nāy Band [Iran]	146	Qf	32.20N	57.34 E
Nāy Band, Kūh-e-	144	Ic	32.27N	57.23 E
Nāy Band, Ra's-e-	146	Oi	27.23N	52.34 E
Nayoro	152	Pc	44.21N	142.28 E
Nayyāl, Wādī-	146	Gh	28.58N	37.50 E
Nazaré [Braz.]	202	Kf	13.02S	39.00W
Nazaré [Port.]	126	Ce	39.36N	9.04W
Nazareth (EN) = Naẓerat	146	Ff	32.42N	35.18 E
Nazarovo	138	Ee	56.01N	90.36 E
Nazas	192	Ge	25.14N	104.08W
Nazas, Río-	174	Ig	25.35N	105.00W
Nazca	200	Ig	14.50S	74.55W
Nazca Ridge (EN)	106	Nl	22.00S	82.00W
Naze	152	Mf	28.23N	129.30 E
Naẓerat = Nazareth (EN)	146	Ff	32.42N	35.18 E
Nazik Gölü	146	Jc	38.48N	42.15 E
Nazilli	144	Cb	37.55N	28.21 E
Nazimiye	146	Hc	39.11N	39.50 E
Nazimovo	138	Ee	59.30N	90.58 E
Nazino	138	Cd	60.15N	78.58 E
Nazlū	146	Kd	37.42N	45.16 E
Nazran	132	Nh	43.15N	44.46 E
Nazret	168	Fd	8.34N	39.18 E
Nazw'a	144	Ie	22.54N	57.31 E
Nazym	134	Nf	61.12N	68.57 E
Nazyvajevsk	136	Hd	55.34N	71.21 E
Nbâk	162	Ef	17.15N	14.59W
Nchanga	170	Ee	12.31S	27.52 E
Ncheu	170	Fe	14.49S	34.38 E
Ndala	170	Fc	4.46S	33.16 E
N'dalatando	170	Bd	9.18S	14.54 E
Ndali	166	Fd	9.51N	2.43 E
Ndélé	160	Jh	8.24N	20.39 E
Ndélélé	166	He	4.02N	14.56 E
Ndendé	170	Bc	2.23S	11.23 E
Ndindi	170	Bc	3.46S	11.09 E
N'Djamena (Fort-Lamy)	160	Ig	12.07N	15.03 E
Ndola	160	Jj	12.58S	28.38 E
Ndouana, Pointe-	219b	Dc	16.35S	168.09 E
Ndrhamcha, Sebkha de-	162	Df	18.45N	15.48W
Ndui Ndui	219b	Cb	15.24S	167.46 E
Nduindui	214	Fi	9.48S	159.58 E
Né	122	Fi	45.40N	0.23W
Nea	219c	Ab	10.51S	165.47 E
Nea	114	Ce	63.13N	11.02 E
Néa Alikarnassós	130	In	35.20N	25.09 E
Néa Artáki	130	Gk	38.31N	23.38 E
Neagari	156	Ec	36.26N	136.26 E
Neagh, Lough-/Loch nEathach	110	Fe	54.38N	6.24W
Neagră, Marea- = Black Sea (EN)	110	Jg	43.00N	35.00 E
Neah Bay	188	Cb	48.22N	124.37W
Néa Ionía	130	Fj	39.23N	22.56 E
Neajlov	130	Je	44.11N	26.12 E
Neale, Lake-	212	Fd	24.20S	130.00 E
Neamţ [2]	130	Jb	47.00N	26.20 E
Neápolis [Grc.]	130	Gm	36.31N	23.04 E
Neápolis [Grc.]	130	Ei	40.19N	21.23 E
Neápolis [Grc.]	130	In	35.15N	25.37 E
Near Islands	174	Bd	52.40N	173.30W
Neath	118	Jj	51.40N	3.48W
Neath	118	Jj	51.37N	3.50W
Néa Zíkhni	130	Gh	41.02N	23.50 E
Néba	219b	Ae	20.09S	163.55 E
Nebaj	194	Bf	15.24N	91.08W
Nebbou	166	Ec	11.18N	1.53W
Nebit-Dag	142	Hf	39.30N	54.22 E
Neblina, Cerro de la-	198	Je	1.08N	66.10W
Nebo	212	Jd	21.40S	148.39 E
Nebo, Mount-	188	Jg	39.49N	111.46W
Nebolči	114	Hg	59.08N	33.21 E
Nebraska [2]	182	Gc	41.30N	100.00W
Nebraska City	182	Hc	40.41N	95.52W
Nebrodi (Caronie)	128	Im	37.55N	14.35 E
Necedah	186	Kd	44.02N	90.03W
Nechako	180	Ff	53.55N	122.44W
Nechako Reservoir	180	Ef	53.00N	126.10W
Nechar, Djebel-	126	Qi	35.52N	4.59 E
Neches River	186	Jl	29.55N	93.52W
Nechí	194	Ji	8.07N	74.46W
Nechí, Río-	194	Ji	8.08N	74.46W
Neckako Plateau	180	Ff	53.25N	124.40W
Neckar	120	Eg	49.31N	8.26 E
Neckargemünd	124	Ke	49.29N	8.50 E
Neckarsteinach	124	Ke	49.25N	8.50 E
Neckarsulm	120	Fg	49.11N	9.14 E
Necker Island	208	Kb	23.35N	164.42W
Necochea	200	Ki	38.34S	58.45W
Necy	124	Bf	48.50N	0.07W
Nedeley	168	Bb	15.34N	18.10 E
Nederland	186	Jl	29.58N	93.59W
Nederland = Netherlands (EN) [1]	112	Ge	52.15N	5.30 E
Nederlandse Antillen [Neth.Ant.] = Netherlands Antilles (EN) [5]	200	Jd	12.15N	69.00W
Nederlandse Antillen [Neth.Ant.] = Netherlands Antilles (EN) [5]	200	Jd	18.06N	63.10W
Neder-Rijn = Lower Rhine (EN)	122	Mc	51.59N	6.20 E
Nêdong	142	Lg	29.14N	91.46 E
Nedstrand	116	Ae	59.21N	5.51 E
Nedstrandefjorden	116	Ae	59.20N	5.50 E
Neede	124	Ib	52.08N	6.37 E
Needham Market	124	Db	52.09N	1.02 E
Needham's Point	197q	Ab	13.05N	59.36W
Needles	182	Ee	34.51N	114.37W
Neembucú [3]	204	Dh	27.00S	58.00W
Neenah	186	Ld	44.11N	88.28W
Neepawa	186	Ga	50.13N	99.29W
Neermoor, Moormerland-	124	Ja	53.18N	7.26 E
Neeroeteren, Maaseik-	124	Hc	51.05N	5.42 E
Neerpelt	124	Hc	51.13N	5.25 E
Nefasit	168	Fb	15.18N	39.04 E
Nefedova	136	Hd	58.48N	72.34 E
Nefṭah	162	Ic	33.52N	7.53 E
Neftečala	132	Pj	39.19N	49.13 E
Neftegorsk [Russia]	136	Fe	52.45N	51.13 E
Neftegorsk [Russia]	132	Kg	44.22N	39.42 E
Neftegorsk [Russia]	138	Jf	53.00N	143.00 E
Neftejugansk	136	Hc	61.05N	72.45 E
Neftekamsk → Nikolo-Berjozovka	136	Fd	56.06N	54.17 E
Neftekumsk	136	Eg	44.43N	44.59 E
Neftjanyje Kamin	132	Qi	40.15N	50.49 E
Negage	170	Cd	7.46S	15.18 E
Negara	150	Fh	8.22S	114.37 E
Negele = Neghelle (EN)	160	Kh	5.20N	39.37 E
Negeri Sembilan [2]	150	Df	2.45N	102.10 E
Negev Desert (EN) = Ḥānegev	146	Fg	30.30N	34.55 E
Neghelle (EN) = Negele	160	Kh	5.20N	39.37 E
Negla, Arroyo-	204	Df	22.52S	56.41W
Negola	170	Be	14.10S	14.30 E
Negomano	172	Fb	11.26S	38.33 E
Negombo	148	Fg	7.13N	79.50 E
Negonego Atoll	208	Mf	18.47S	141.48W
Negotin	130	Fe	44.13N	22.32 E
Negra, Cordillera-	202	Ce	9.25S	77.40W
Negra, Coxilha-	204	Ej	31.02S	55.45W
Negra, Peña-	126	Fb	42.11N	6.30W
Negra, Ponta-	204	Jf	23.21S	44.36W
Negra, Punta-	198	Hf	6.06S	81.10W
Negra, Serra-	204	Fc	16.30S	52.10W
Negra o de los Difuntos, Laguna-	204	Fl	34.03S	53.40W
Negreira	126	Db	42.54N	8.44W
Negreni	130	He	44.34N	24.36 E
Negreşti	130	Gb	47.52N	23.26 E
Negrine	162	Ic	34.29N	7.31 E
Negrinho, Rio-	204	Ed	19.20S	55.05W
Negro, Cabo-	126	Gi	35.41N	5.17W
Negro, Río- [Arg.]	198	Jj	41.02S	62.47W
Negro, Río- [Arg.]	204	Ch	27.27S	58.54W
Negro, Río- [Bol.]	202	Ff	14.11S	63.07W
Negro, Rio- [Braz.]	206	Jc	26.01S	50.30W
Negro, Rio- [Braz.]	202	Gg	19.13S	57.17W
Negro, Río- [Par.]	206	Ib	24.23S	57.11W
Negro, Río- [S.Amer.]	204	Ce	20.11S	58.10W
Negro, Río- [S.Amer.]	198	Kf	3.08S	59.55W
Negro, Río- [Ur.]	198	Ki	33.24S	58.22W
Negro, Río → Chixoy, Río-	194	Be	16.28N	90.33W
Negros	140	Oi	10.00N	123.00 E
Negru, Rîu-	130	Id	45.45N	25.46 E
Negru Vodă	130	Lf	43.49N	28.12 E
Nehajevski	132	Ld	50.27N	41.46 E
Nehalem River	188	Dd	45.40N	123.56W
Nehāvand	146	Me	35.56N	49.31 E
Nehe	152	Lb	48.28N	124.53 E
Nehoiu	130	Jd	45.26N	26.17 E
Néhoué, Baie de-	219b	Be	20.21S	164.09 E
Neiba	194	Ld	18.28N	71.25W
Neiba, Bahía de-	194	Ld	18.15N	71.02W
Neidín/Kenmare	118	Dj	51.53N	9.35W
Neige, Crêt de la-	122	Lh	46.16N	5.56 E
Neiges, Piton des-	158	Mk	21.05S	55.29 E
Neijiang	142	Mg	29.38N	104.58 E
Neilton	188	Dc	47.25N	123.52W
Nei-meng-ku Tzu-chih-ch'ü → Nei Monggol Zizhiqu [2]	152	Jc	44.00N	112.00 E
Nei Monggol Gaoyuan	140	Ne	42.00N	111.00 E
Nei Monggol Zizhiqu (Nei-meng-ku Tzu-chih-ch'ü) = Inner Mongolia (EN) [2]	152	Jc	44.00N	112.00 E
Neiqiu	154	Cf	37.17N	114.30 E
Neiva	200	Ie	2.56N	75.18W
Neja	136	Ed	58.19N	43.52 E
Nejanilini Lake	180	He	59.30N	97.50W
Nejdek	120	If	50.19N	12.44 E
Nejo	168	Fd	9.30N	35.32 E
Nejva	134	Kh	57.54N	62.18 E
Nekemt = Leqemt (EN)	160	Kh	9.05N	36.33 E
Neksø	116	Fi	55.04N	15.09 E
Nelemnoje	138	Kc	65.23N	151.08 E
Nelgese	138	Ic	66.40N	136.30 E
Nelichu	168	Ed	6.08N	34.25 E
Nelidovo	136	Dd	56.13N	32.50 E
Neligh	186	Ge	42.08N	98.02W
Neljaty	138	Ge	56.29N	115.50 E
Nelkan	138	Jd	64.15N	143.03 E
Nellore	142	Jh	12.56N	79.08 E
Nelma	138	Ig	47.40N	139.08 E
Nelson [2]	218	Ed	41.45S	172.30 E
Nelson	174	Jd	57.04N	92.30W
Nelson [B.C.-Can.]	180	Fg	49.29N	117.17W
Nelson [N.Z.]	210	Ii	41.16S	173.15 E
Nelson, Cape- [Austl.]	208	Fh	38.26S	141.33 E
Nelson, Cape- [Pap.N.Gui.]	212	Ja	9.00S	149.15 E
Nelson Island	178	Gd	60.35N	164.45W
Nelson's Dockyard	197d	Bb	17.00N	61.46W
Nelspruit	160	Kk	25.30S	30.58 E
Néma	160	Gg	16.36N	7.15W
Néma, Dahr-	162	Ff	16.14N	7.30W
Neman	114	Fi	55.03N	22.01 E
Neman	110	Id	55.18N	21.23 E
Nembrala	150	Hi	10.53S	122.50 E
Nemda	114	Kh	57.31N	43.15 E
Neméa	130	Fl	37.49N	22.39 E
Neméa	130	Fl	37.49N	22.40 E
Nemenčinė	116	Kj	54.50N	25.39 E
Nëmërçkes, Mali i-	130	Di	40.08N	20.24 E
Nemira, Vîrful-	130	Jc	46.15N	26.19 E
Nemirov [Ukr.]	132	Fe	48.59N	28.50 E
Nemirov [Ukr.]	120	Tf	50.08N	23.28 E
Némiscau	180	Jf	51.30N	77.00W
Nemjuga	114	Kd	65.29N	43.40 E
Nemours	122	If	48.16N	2.42 E
Nemrut Dağı	146	Jc	38.40N	42.12 E
Nemunas	110	Id	55.18N	21.23 E
Nemunėlis	116	Kh	56.24N	24.10 E
Nemuro	152	Qc	43.20N	145.35 E
Nemuro-Hantō	156a	Db	43.20N	145.35 E
Nemuro-Kaikyō = Nemuro Strait (EN)	138	Jh	43.50N	145.30 E
Nemuro Strait (EN) = Kunaširski proliv	138	Jh	43.50N	145.30 E
Nemuro Strait (EN) = Nemuro-Kaikyō	138	Jh	43.50N	145.30 E
Nemuro-Wan	156a	Db	43.25N	145.25 E
Nenagh/An tAonach	118	Ei	52.52N	8.12W
Nenana	178	Jd	64.34N	149.07W
Nenana	178	Jd	64.30N	149.00W
Nendo Island	208	Hf	10.40S	165.54 E
Nene	118	Ni	52.48N	0.13 E
Neneckij avtonomnaja respublika	136	Fb	67.30N	54.00 E
Nenjiang	142	Oe	49.10N	125.12 E
Nen Jiang	140	Oe	45.26N	124.39 E
Neo	156	Ed	35.38N	136.37 E
Neodesha	186	Ih	37.25N	95.41W
Néon Karlovásion	130	Jl	37.47N	26.42 E
Neosho	186	Ih	36.52N	94.22W
Neosho River	186	Ih	35.48N	95.18W
Néouvielle, Massif de-	122	Gl	42.51N	0.07 E
Nepal [1]	142	Kg	28.00N	84.00 E
Nepalganj	148	Gc	28.03N	81.37 E
Nephi	182	Ed	39.43N	111.50W
Nephin/Né Finn	118	Dg	54.01N	9.22W
Nepisiguit River	184	Ob	47.37N	65.38W
Nepoko	158	Jh	1.40N	27.01 E
Nepomuk	120	Jg	49.29N	13.34 E
Ner	120	Od	52.10N	18.40 E
Nera [It.]	128	Gh	42.26N	12.24 E
Nera [Rom.]	130	Ee	44.49N	21.22 E
Nérac	122	Gj	44.08N	0.21 E
Neratovice	120	Kf	50.16N	14.31 E
Nerău	130	Dd	45.58N	20.34 E
Nerbio / Nervión	126	Ja	43.14N	2.53W
Nerča	138	Gf	51.54N	116.30 E
Nerčinsk	138	Gf	51.58N	116.35 E
Nerčinski Zavod	138	Gf	51.17N	119.30 E
Nerehta	136	Ed	57.28N	40.34 E
Nereju	130	Jd	45.42N	26.43 E
Nereta	116	Kh	56.12N	25.24 E
Neretva	128	Lg	43.02N	17.27 E
Neretvanski kanal	128	Lg	43.03N	17.11 E
Nerica	134	Fd	65.20N	52.45 E
Neringa	114	Ei	55.24N	21.05 E
Neringa	114	Ei	55.18N	21.00 E
Neringa-Joudkrante/Neringa-Juodkrantė	116	Ii	55.35N	21.01 E
Neringa-Juodkrantė/Neringa-Juodkrante	116	Ii	55.35N	21.01 E
Neringa-Nida	116	Ii	55.18N	20.53 E
Neringa-Preila/Neringa-Prejla	116	Ii	55.20N	20.59 E
Neringa-Prejla/Neringa-Preila	116	Ii	55.20N	20.59 E
Neriquinha	170	Df	15.45S	21.33 E
Neris/Njaris	116	Kj	54.55N	25.45 E
Nerja	126	Ih	36.44N	3.52W
Nerjungri	138	He	56.40N	124.47 E
Nerl [Russia]	114	Ih	57.07N	37.39 E
Nerl [Russia]	114	Jh	56.11N	40.34 E
Nerpio	126	Jf	38.09N	2.18W
Nerussa	132	Hc	52.33N	33.47 E
Nerva	126	Fg	37.42N	6.32W
Nervi, Genova-	128	Df	44.23N	9.02 E
Nervión / Nerbio	126	Ja	43.14N	2.53W
Nes	116	Cd	60.34N	9.59 E
Nes, Ameland-	124	Ha	53.26N	5.48 E
Nesbyen	114	Bf	60.34N	9.06 E
Nesebăr	130	Kg	42.39N	27.44 E
Nesjøen	116	Db	63.00N	12.00 E
Neskaupstaður	114a	Db	65.09N	13.42W
Nesle	124	Ee	49.46N	2.45 E
Nesna	114	Cc	66.12N	13.02 E
Ness City	186	Gg	38.27N	99.54W
Nesterov [Russia]	114	Fi	54.42N	22.34 E
Nesterov [Ukr.]	132	Cd	50.03N	24.00 E
Néstos	130	Hi	40.51N	24.44 E
Nesttun	116	Ad	60.19N	5.20 E
Nesviž	132	Ec	53.13N	26.39 E
Netanya	146	Ff	32.20N	34.51 E
Netcong	184	Je	40.54N	74.43W
Nete	122	Kc	51.10N	4.15 E
Nethe	124	Lc	51.44N	9.23 E
Netherdale	212	Jd	21.08S	148.32 E
Netherlands (EN) = Nederland [1]	112	Ge	52.15N	5.30 E
Netherlands Antilles (EN) = Nederlandse Antillen [Neth.Ant.] [5]	200	Jd	12.15N	69.00W
Netherlands Antilles (EN) = Nederlandse Antillen [Neth.Ant.] [5]	200	Jd	18.06N	63.10W
Neto	128	Lk	39.12N	17.09 E
Netphen	124	Kd	50.55N	8.06 E
Nettebach	124	Jd	50.26N	7.28 E
Nettersheim	124	Id	50.30N	6.38 E
Nettetal	124	Ic	51.18N	6.12 E
Nettiling Lake	174	Lc	66.30N	70.40W
Nettuno	128	Gi	41.27N	12.39 E
Netzahualcóyotl, Presa-	192	Mi	17.00N	93.30W
Neubourg, Campagne du-	122	Ge	49.08N	1.00 E
Neubrandenburg	120	Jc	53.34N	13.16 E
Neuburg an der Donau	120	Hh	48.44N	11.11 E
Neuchâtel [2]	128	Ac	47.05N	6.50 E
Neuchâtel/Neuenburg	128	Ad	46.59N	6.56 E
Neuchâtel, Lac de-	128	Ad	46.55N	6.55 E
Neuenbürg	124	Kf	48.50N	8.35 E
Neuenburg/Neuchâtel	128	Ad	46.59N	6.56 E
Neuenhaus	124	Ib	52.30N	6.58 E
Neuenkirchen	124	Jb	52.15N	7.22 E
Neuerburg	124	Id	50.01N	6.18 E
Neufchâteau [Bel.]	122	Le	49.51N	5.26 E
Neufchâteau [Fr.]	122	Lf	48.21N	5.42 E
Neufchâtel-en-Bray	122	He	49.44N	1.27 E
Neufchâtel-Hardelot	124	Dd	50.37N	1.38 E
Neufchâtel Hardelot-Hardelot Plage	124	Dd	50.38N	1.35 E
Neufchâtel-sur-Aisne	124	Ge	49.26N	4.02 E
Neuffossé, Canal de-	124	Ed	50.45N	2.15 E
Neuhaus am Rennweg	120	Hf	50.31N	11.09 E
Neuilly-en-Thelle	124	Ee	49.13N	2.17 E
Neuilly-Saint-Front	124	Fe	49.10N	3.16 E
Neu-Isenburg	124	Kd	50.03N	8.42 E
Neukirchen-Vluyn	124	Ic	51.27N	6.35 E
Neum	128	Lh	42.55N	17.38 E
Neumagen-Dhron	124	Ie	49.51N	6.54 E
Neumarkter Sattel	128	Id	47.06N	14.22 E
Neumarkt in der Oberpfalz	120	Hg	49.17N	11.28 E
Neumünster	120	Fb	54.04N	9.59 E
Neunkirchen [Aus.]	128	Kc	47.43N	16.05 E
Neunkirchen [Ger.]	120	Dg	49.21N	7.11 E
Neunkirchen [Ger.]	124	Kd	50.48N	8.00 E
Neunkirchen [Ger.]	124	Jd	50.51N	7.20 E
Neuquén	200	Ji	39.00S	68.05W
Neuquén [2]	206	Ge	39.00S	70.00W
Neuquén, Río-	198	Ji	38.59S	68.00W
Neuruppin	120	Id	52.56N	12.48 E
Neuse River	184	Ih	35.06N	76.30W
Neusiedl am See	128	Kc	47.56N	16.50 E
Neusiedler See	120	Mi	47.50N	16.45 E
Neuss	120	Ce	51.12N	6.42 E
Neustadt (Hessen)	124	Ld	50.51N	9.07 E
Neustadt am Rübenberge	120	Fd	52.30N	9.28 E
Neustadt an der Aisch	120	Gg	49.35N	10.36 E
Neustadt an der Orla	120	Hf	50.44N	11.45 E
Neustadt an der Weinstraße	120	Eg	49.21N	8.09 E
Neustadt bei Coburg	120	Hf	50.19N	11.07 E
Neustadt in Holstein	120	Gb	54.06N	10.49 E
Neustrelitz	120	Jc	53.22N	13.05 E
Neu-Ulm	120	Gh	48.24N	10.01 E
Neuville-les-Dieppe	124	De	49.55N	1.06 E
Neuville-sur-Saône	122	Ki	45.52N	4.51 E
Neuwerk	120	Ec	53.55N	8.30 E
Neuwied	120	Df	50.26N	7.28 E
Neva	110	Jd	59.55N	30.15 E
Nevada [2]	182	Dd	39.00N	117.00W
Nevada [Ia.-U.S.]	186	Je	42.01N	93.27W
Nevada [Mo.-U.S.]	182	Id	37.51N	94.22W
Nevada, Sierra- [Sp.]	110	Fh	37.05N	3.10W
Nevada, Sierra- [U.S.]	174	Hf	38.00N	119.15W
Nevada del Cocuy, Sierra-	198	Ie	6.10N	72.15W
Nevada de Santa Marta, Sierra-	198	Id	10.50N	73.40W
Nevado, Cerro-	198	Ie	3.59N	74.04W
Neve, Serra da-	158	Ij	13.52S	13.26 E
Nevel	136	Cd	56.02N	29.55 E
Nevele	124	Fc	51.02N	3.33 E
Nevelsk	138	Jg	46.37N	141.57 E
Neverkino	132	Oc	52.47N	46.48 E
Nevers	122	Jg	46.59N	3.10 E
Nevesinje	128	Mg	43.16N	18.07 E
Nevinnomyssk	136	Eg	44.38N	41.58 E
Nevis	190	Le	17.10N	62.34W
Nevis, Ben-	110	Fd	56.48N	5.01W
Nevis Peak	197c	Ab	17.10N	62.34W
Nevjansk	136	Gd	57.32N	60.13 E
Nevşehir	144	Db	38.38N	34.43 E
Nevskoje	154	Lb	45.42N	133.40 E
Newala	170	Ge	10.56S	39.18 E
New Albany [In.-U.S.]	182	Jd	38.18N	85.49W
New Albany [Ms.-U.S.]	186	Li	34.29N	89.00W
New Alresford	124	Ac	51.05N	1.10W
New Amsterdam	200	Ke	6.17N	57.36W
Newark [De.-U.S.]	184	Jf	39.41N	75.45W
Newark [N.J.-U.S.]	182	Mc	40.44N	74.11W
Newark [N.Y.-U.S.]	184	Id	43.03N	77.06W
Newark [Oh.-U.S.]	182	Kc	40.03N	82.25W
Newark-on-Trent	118	Mh	53.05N	0.49W
New Bedford	182	Mc	41.38N	70.56W
New Bern	182	Ld	35.07N	77.03W
Newberry [Mi.-U.S.]	184	Eb	46.21N	85.30W
Newberry [S.C.-U.S.]	184	Gh	34.17N	81.37W
New Braunfels	182	Hf	29.42N	98.08W
New Britain	184	Ke	41.40N	72.47W
New Britain Island	208	Ge	5.40S	151.00 E
New Britain Trench (EN)	214	Ei	6.00S	153.00 E
New Brunswick	184	Je	40.29N	74.27W
New Brunswick [2]	180	Kg	46.30N	66.45W
New Buckenham	124	Db	52.28N	1.05 E
New Buffalo	184	De	41.47N	86.45W
Newburgh	182	Mc	41.30N	74.00W
Newbury	118	Lj	51.25N	1.20W
New Caledonia (EN) = Nouvelle-Calédonie [5]	210	Hg	21.30S	165.30 E
New Caledonia (EN) = Nouvelle-Calédonie	208	Hg	21.30S	165.30 E
New Caledonia Basin (EN)	208	Hg	30.00S	165.00 E
New Carlisle	184	Oa	48.01N	65.20W
New Castile (EN) = Castilla la Nueva	126	Id	40.00N	3.45W
Newcastle [Austl.]	210	Gh	32.56S	151.46 E
New Castle [In.-U.S.]	184	Ef	39.55N	85.22W
Newcastle [N.B.-Can.]	180	Kg	47.00N	65.34W
New Castle [Pa.-U.S.]	182	Kc	41.00N	80.22W
Newcastle [S.Afr.]	172	De	27.49S	29.55 E
Newcastle [St.C.N.]	197c	Ab	17.13N	62.34W
Newcastle [Wy.-U.S.]	182	Gc	43.50N	104.11W
Newcastle/An Caisleán Nua	118	Hg	54.12N	5.54W
Newcastle Creek	212	Gc	17.20S	133.23 E
Newcastle-under-Lyme	118	Kh	53.00N	2.14W
Newcastle-upon-Tyne	112	Fd	54.59N	1.35W
Newcastle Waters	210	Ef	17.24S	133.24 E
Newcastle West/An Caisleán Nua	118	Di	52.27N	9.03W
New Delhi	142	Jg	28.36N	77.12 E
New Denver	188	Ga	50.00N	117.22W
Newell	186	Ed	44.43N	103.25W
Newell, Lake-	188	Ja	50.25N	111.56W
New England	174	Le	44.00N	71.20W
New England Range	208	Gh	30.00S	151.50 E
New England Seamounts (EN)	174	Mf	38.00N	61.00W
Newenham, Cape-	178	Ge	58.37N	162.12W
New Forest	118	Lk	50.55N	1.35W

Index Symbols

- [1] Independent Nation
- [2] State, Region
- [3] District, County
- [4] Municipality
- [5] Colony, Dependency
- Continent
- Physical Region
- Historical or Cultural Region
- Mount, Mountain
- Volcano
- Hill
- Mountains, Mountain Range
- Hills, Escarpment
- Plateau, Upland
- Pass, Gap
- Plain, Lowland
- Delta
- Salt Flat
- Valley, Canyon
- Crater, Cave
- Karst Features
- Depression
- Polder
- Desert, Dunes
- Forest, Woods
- Heath, Steppe
- Oasis
- Cape, Point
- Coast, Beach
- Cliff
- Peninsula
- Isthmus
- Sandbank
- Island
- Atoll
- Rock, Reef
- Islands, Archipelago
- Rocks, Reefs
- Coral Reef
- Well, Spring
- Geyser
- River, Stream
- Waterfall, Rapids
- River Mouth, Estuary
- Lake
- Salt Lake
- Intermittent Lake
- Reservoir
- Swamp, Pond
- Canal
- Glacier
- Ice Shelf, Pack Ice
- Ocean
- Sea
- Gulf, Bay
- Strait, Fjord
- Lagoon
- Bank
- Seamount
- Tablemount
- Ridge
- Shelf
- Basin
- Escarpment, Sea Scarp
- Fracture
- Trench, Abyss
- National Park, Reserve
- Point of Interest
- Recreation Site
- Cave, Cavern
- Historic Site
- Ruins
- Wall, Walls
- Church, Abbey
- Temple
- Scientific Station
- Railway station
- Airport
- Port
- Military installation
- Lighthouse
- Mine
- Tunnel
- Dam, Bridge

Name	Page	Grid	Lat	Long
Newfoundland [2]	180	Lf	52.00N	56.00W
Newfoundland [+]	174	Ne	48.30N	56.00W
Newfoundland Basin (EN) [~]	106	De	45.00N	40.00W
New Galloway	118	If	55.05N	4.10W
New Georgia [#]	208	Ge	8.30S	157.20 E
New Georgia Island [+]	214	Fi	8.15S	157.30 E
New Georgia Sound (The Slot) [+]	214	Fi	8.00S	158.10 E
New Glasgow	180	Lg	45.35N	62.39W
New Guinea/Pulau Irian [+]	208	Fe	5.00S	140.00 E
New Guinea Trench (EN) [~]	208	Ee	0.05N	135.50 E
New Hampshire [2]	182	Mc	43.35N	71.40W
New Hampton	186	Je	43.03N	92.19W
New Hanover Island [+]	208	Ge	2.30S	150.15 E
New Harmony	184	Dr	38.08N	87.56W
New Haven	176	Le	41.18N	72.56W
Newhaven	118	Nk	50.47N	0.03 E
New Hebrides / Nouvelles-Hébrides [#]	208	Hf	16.01S	167.01 E
New Hebrides Trench (EN) [~]	106	Jl	20.00S	168.00 E
New Iberia	182	If	30.00N	91.49W
New Ireland Island [+]	208	Ge	3.20S	152.00 E
New Jersey [2]	182	Mc	40.15N	74.30W
New Kowloon/Julong	142	Ng	22.20N	114.09 E
New Liskeard	180	Jg	47.30N	79.40W
New London	182	Mc	41.21N	72.07W
New Madrid	186	Lh	36.36N	89.32W
Newman	212	Dd	23.15S	119.35 E
Newmarket [Eng.-U.K.]	118	Ni	52.15N	0.25 E
Newmarket [Ont.-Can.]	184	Hc	44.03N	79.28W
New Martinsville	184	Gf	39.39N	80.52W
New Meadows	188	Gd	44.58N	116.32W
New Mexico [2]	182	Fe	34.30N	106.00W
Newnan	184	Ei	33.23N	84.48W
New Norfolk	212	Jh	42.47S	147.03 E
New Orleans	176	Jg	29.58N	90.07W
New Philadelphia	184	Ge	40.30N	81.27W
New Pine Creek	188	Ee	42.01N	120.18W
New-Plymouth	210	Ih	39.04S	174.04 E
Newport [Ar.-U.S.]	186	Ki	35.37N	91.17W
Newport [Eng.-U.K.]	124	Cc	51.59N	0.15 E
Newport [Eng.-U.K.]	118	Lk	50.42N	1.18W
Newport [Fl.-U.S.]	184	Ej	30.14N	84.12W
Newport [Or.-U.S.]	182	Cc	44.38N	124.03W
Newport [R.I.-U.S.]	184	Le	41.30N	71.19W
Newport [Tn.-U.S.]	184	Fh	35.58N	83.11W
Newport [Vt.-U.S.]	184	Kc	44.56N	72.13W
Newport [Wales-U.K.]	118	Kj	51.35N	3.00W
Newport [Wa.-U.S.]	188	Gb	48.11N	117.03W
Newport Beach	182	De	33.37N	117.54W
Newport News	176	Lf	37.04N	76.28W
Newport Pagnell	124	Bb	52.05N	0.43W
New Providence Island [+]	190	Ic	25.02N	77.24W
Newquay	118	Hk	50.25N	5.05W
New Quebec Crater (EN) = Nouveau-Québec, Cratère du- [~]	180	Kd	61.30N	73.55W
New Richmond [Oh.-U.S.]	184	Ef	38.57N	84.16W
New Richmond [Que.-Can.]	184	Oa	48.10N	65.52W
New River [Blz.] [~]	194	Cd	18.22N	88.24W
New River [Guy.] [~]	202	Gc	3.23N	57.36W
New River [U.S.] [~]	184	Ff	38.50N	82.06W
New Rockford	186	Gc	47.41N	99.15W
New Romney	124	Cd	50.59N	0.56 E
New Ross / Ros Mhic Thriúin	118	Gi	52.24N	6.56W
Newry/an t-lúr	118	Gg	54.11N	6.20W
New Salem	186	Fc	46.51N	101.25W
New Sandy Bay	197n	Ba	13.20N	61.08W
New Schwabenland (EN) [#]	222	Cf	72.30S	1.00 E
New Siberia (EN) = Novaja Sibir, ostrov- [+]	140	Qb	75.00N	149.00 E
New Siberian Islands (EN) = Novosibirskije ostrova [#]	140	Qb	75.00N	142.00 E
New Smyrna Beach	184	Gk	29.02N	80.56W
New South Wales [2]	212	Jf	33.00S	146.00 E
Newton [Ia.-U.S.]	186	Jf	41.42N	93.03W
Newton [Il.-U.S.]	186	Lg	38.59N	88.10W
Newton [Ks.-U.S.]	182	Hd	38.03N	97.21W
Newton [Ma.-U.S.]	184	Ld	42.21N	71.13W
Newton [Ms.-U.S.]	186	Lj	32.19N	89.10W
Newton [N.J.-U.S.]	184	Je	41.03N	74.45W
Newton Abbot	118	Jk	50.32N	3.36W
Newton Stewart	118	Ig	54.57N	4.29W
Newtontoppen [#]	224	Fb	72.02N	17.30 E
Newtown	118	Ji	52.32N	3.19W
New Town	186	Ec	47.59N	102.30W
Newtownabbey/Baile na Mainistreach	118	Hg	54.42N	5.54W
Newtownards/Baile Nua na hArda	118	Hg	54.36N	5.41W
New Ulm	182	Ic	44.19N	94.28W
New Westminster	180	Fg	49.12N	122.55W
New York	176	Le	40.43N	74.01W
New York [2]	182	Lc	43.00N	75.00W
New York State Barge Canal	184	Hd	43.05N	78.43W
New Zealand [1]	210	Ii	41.00S	174.00 E
New Zealand [2]	208	Ii	41.00S	174.00 E
Nexpa, Rio- [~]	192	Hh	18.05N	102.46W
Neyagawa	156	Dd	34.46N	135.36 E
Neyriz	146	Ph	29.12N	54.19 E
Neyshabur	144	Mg	36.12N	58.50 E
Nežárka [~]	120	Kg	49.11N	14.43 E
Nežin	136	De	51.02N	31.57 E
Ngabé	170	Cc	3.12S	16.11 E
Ngahere	218	De	42.24S	171.26 E
Ngajangel [+]	220a	Ba	8.05N	134.43 E
Ngala	168	Hc	12.20N	14.11 E
Ngaliema, Chutes- [~]	158	Jh	0.30N	25.11 E
Ngamegei Passage	220a	Bb	7.44N	134.34 E
Ngami, Lake- [~]	172	Cd	20.37S	22.40 E
Ngamiland [3]	172	Cc	19.09S	22.47 E
Ngamring	152	Ef	29.14N	87.12 E
Ngangala	168	Ee	4.42N	31.55 E
Ngangerabeli Plain [~]	170	Hc	1.30S	40.15 E
Ngangla Ringco [~]	152	De	31.40N	83.00 E
Nganglong Kangri [#]	152	De	32.45N	81.12 E
Nganglong Kangri [#]	140	Kf	32.00N	83.00 E
Ngangzê Co [~]	152	Ee	31.00N	86.55 E
Ngao	148	Je	18.45N	99.59 E
Ngaoundéré	160	Ih	7.19N	13.35 E
Ngapara	218	Df	44.57S	170.45 E
Ngara	170	Fc	2.28S	30.39 E
Ngardmau	220a	Bb	7.37N	134.35 E
Ngardmau Bay [#]	220a	Bb	7.39N	134.35 E
Ngardololok	220a	Ac	7.00N	134.16 E
Ngaregur [#]	220a	Bb	7.45N	134.38 E
Ngarekeukl	220a	Ac	7.00N	134.14 E
Ngariungs [+]	220a	Ba	8.03N	134.43 E
Ngaruangl [+]	220a	Ba	8.10N	134.39 E
Ngaruangl Passage	220a	Ba	8.07N	134.40 E
Ngaruawahia	218	Fb	37.40S	175.09 E
Ngaruroro [~]	218	Gc	39.34S	176.55 E
Ngatangiia	220p	Cb	21.14S	159.43W
Ngatangiia Harbour [#]	220p	Cb	21.14S	159.43W
Ngateguil, Point- [#]	220a	Bc	7.26N	134.37 E
Ngatik Atoll [o]	208	Gd	5.51N	157.16 E
Ngatpang	220a	Bc	7.28N	134.32 E
Ngau Island [+]	219d	Bc	18.02S	179.18 E
Ngauruhoe [#]	218	Fc	39.09S	175.38 E
Ngawa/Aba	152	He	32.55N	101.45 E
Ngayu [~]	170	Eb	1.35N	27.13 E
Ngemelis Islands [#]	220a	Ac	7.07N	134.15 E
Ngeregong [+]	220a	Ac	7.07N	134.22 E
Ngergoi [+]	220a	Ac	7.05N	134.17 E
Ngesebus [+]	220a	Ac	7.03N	134.16 E
Nggamea [+]	219d	Cb	16.46S	179.46W
Nggatokae [+]	219a	Bc	8.46S	158.11 E
Nggela Pile [+]	219a	Ec	9.08S	160.20 E
Nggela Sule [+]	219a	Ec	9.05S	160.12 E
Nggidze [+]	219d	Cb	16.05S	179.09W
Ngidinga	170	Cd	5.37S	15.17 E
Ngiro, Ewaso- [~]	170	Gb	0.28N	39.55 E
Ngo	170	Cc	2.29S	15.45 E
Ngoangoa [~]	168	Dd	5.58N	25.10 E
Ngobasangel [~]	220a	Ac	7.16N	134.20 E
Ngoko [~]	170	Cb	1.40N	16.03 E
Ngola Shankou [~]	152	Gd	35.30N	99.36 E
Ngoma	170	Ef	15.58S	25.56 E
Ngoring Hu [~]	152	Gd	35.00N	97.30 E
Ngorongoro Crater [~]	158	Ki	3.10S	35.35 E
Ngoui	166	Cb	16.09N	13.56W
Ngouna [+]	219b	Dc	17.26S	168.21 E
Ngounié [3]	170	Bc	2.00S	11.00 E
Ngounié [~]	170	Bc	0.37S	10.18 E
Ngoura	168	Bc	12.52N	16.27 E
Ngouri	168	Bc	13.38N	15.22 E
Ngourti	166	Hb	15.19N	13.12 E
Ngousouboot, Pointe- [#]	219b	Ca	13.58S	167.27 E
Ngudu	170	Fc	2.58S	33.20 E
Nguigmi	160	Ig	14.15N	13.07 E
Ngulu Atoll [o]	208	Ed	8.18N	137.29 E
Nguni	170	Gc	0.50S	38.20 E
Nguru	160	Ig	12.53N	10.28 E
Nhachengue	172	Fd	22.51S	35.11 E
Nhamundá	202	Gd	2.14S	56.43W
Nhamundá, Rio- [~]	202	Gd	2.12S	56.41W
Nhandeara	204	Ge	20.40S	50.02W
Nhandutiba	204	Jb	14.37S	44.12W
Nharea	170	Cd	11.28S	16.53 E
Nha Trang	142	Mh	12.15N	109.11 E
Nhecolândia	204	Db	19.16S	57.04W
Nhia [~]	170	Be	10.15S	14.12 E
Nhulunbuy	210	Ef	12.05S	136.50 E
Niafounké	166	Eb	15.56N	4.00W
Niagara Escarpment [#]	184	Gc	44.30N	80.35W
Niagara Falls [~]	174	La	43.05N	79.04W
Niagara Falls [N.Y.-U.S.]	182	Lc	43.06N	79.02W
Niagara Falls [Ont.-Can.]	184	Hd	43.06N	79.04W
Niagara River [~]	184	Hd	43.15N	79.04W
Niagassola	166	Dc	12.19N	9.07W
Niah	150	Ff	3.52N	113.44 E
Niakaramandougou	166	Dd	8.40N	5.17W
Niamey	160	Gg	13.31N	2.07 E
Niamey [2]	166	Fc	14.00N	2.00 E
Niandan [~]	166	Dc	10.35N	9.45W
Niangara	160	Jh	3.42N	27.52 E
Niangoloko	166	Eb	15.50N	3.00W
Nia-Nia	170	Eb	1.24N	27.36 E
Nianzishan	152	Lb	47.31N	122.50 E
Niao Dao [#]	152	Gd	37.20N	99.50 E
Niaoshu Shan [#]	152	He	34.54N	104.04 E
Niari [3]	170	Bc	3.30S	13.00 E
Niari [~]	170	Bc	3.56S	12.12 E
Nias, Palau- [+]	140	Li	1.05N	97.35 E
Niassa [3]	172	Fb	13.00S	36.00 E
Niassa, Lago-=Nyasa, Lake- (EN) [~]	158	Kj	12.00S	34.30 E
Nias, Ile- [+]	208	Mf	16.09S	146.21W
Nibâk	146	Nj	24.24N	50.50 E
Nibe	116	Ch	56.59N	9.38 E
Nica/Nica	134	Lh	57.29N	64.33 E
Nica/Nica	116	Hs	56.25N	20.56 E
Nicanor Olivera	204	Cn	38.17S	59.12W
Nicaragua [1]	176	Kh	13.00N	85.00W
Nicaragua, Lago de-= Nicaragua, Lake- (EN) = [~]	174	Kh	11.35N	85.25W
Nicastro, Lamezia Terme-	128	Kl	38.59N	16.19 E
Nice	112	Gg	43.42N	7.15 E
Niceville	184	Dj	30.31N	86.29W
Nichicun, Lac- [~]	180	Kf	53.08N	70.55W
Nichinan [Jap.]	156	Dd	31.30N	133.16 E
Nichinan [Jap.]	154	Ki	31.36N	131.23 E
Nicholas Channel	194	Gb	23.25N	80.05W
Nicholas, Canal- (EN)= Nicolás, Canal- [~]	190	Hd	23.25N	80.05W
Nicholasville	184	Ef	37.53N	84.34W
Nicholls Town	194	Ia	25.08N	78.00W
Nicholson Range [#]	212	De	27.15S	116.45 E
Nicholson River [~]	208	Ef	17.31S	139.36 E
Nickerson Ice Shelf [~]	222	Mf	75.45S	145.00W
Nickol Bay [#]	212	Dd	20.40S	116.50 E
Nicobar Islands [#]	140	Li	8.00N	93.30 E
Nicocli	194	Ii	8.26N	76.48W
Nicolajevka	130	Nb	47.33N	30.41 E
Nicola River [~]	188	Ea	50.25N	121.18W
Nicolás, Canal-=Nicholas Channel (EN) [~]	190	Hd	23.25N	80.05W
Nicolet	184	Kb	46.14N	72.37W
Nicopolis (EN)= Nikópolis [~]	130	Dj	39.00N	20.45 E
Nicosia	128	Im	37.45N	14.24 E
Nicosia (EN)=Lefkosa / Levkosia	142	Ff	35.10N	33.22 E
Nicosia (EN)=Levkosia / Lefkosa	142	Ff	35.10N	33.22 E
Nicotera	128	Jl	38.33N	15.56 E
Nicoya	190	Gf	10.09N	85.27W
Nicoya, Golfo de- [#]	190	Hg	9.47N	84.48W
Nicoya, Peninsula de-= Nicoya Peninsula (EN) [#]	174	Ki	10.00N	85.25W
Nicoya Peninsula (EN)= Nicoya, Peninsula de- [#]	174	Ki	10.00N	85.25W
Nicuadala	172	Fc	17.37S	36.50 E
Niculiţel	130	Ld	45.11N	28.29 E
Nida	124	Ld	50.25N	9.00 E
Nidda	120	Id	50.06N	8.34 E
Nidda [~]	120	Id	50.20N	8.47 E
Nidder [~]	124	Id	50.42N	6.29 E
Nideggen	124	Id	50.42N	6.29 E
Nidelva [Nor.] [~]	116	Da	63.26N	10.25 E
Nidelva [Nor.] [~]	116	Cf	58.24N	8.48 E
Nido, Sierra del- [#]	192	Fc	29.30N	106.45W
Nidže [#]	130	Ei	41.00N	21.50 E
Nidzica	120	Qc	53.22N	20.26 E
Nidzica [~]	120	Qf	50.12N	20.40 E
Nidzkie, Jezioro- [~]	120	Rc	53.37N	21.30 E
Niebüll	120	Eb	54.48N	8.50 E
Niel	124	Ie	49.23N	6.40 E
Nieddu [#]	128	Dj	40.44N	9.34 E
Niederbayern [#]	120	Ih	48.35N	12.30 E
Niederbronn-les-Bains	122	Nf	48.58N	7.38 E
Niedere Tauern [#]	128	Hc	47.20N	14.00 E
Niederlausitz [#]	120	Ke	51.40N	14.15 E
Nieder-Olm	124	Ke	49.54N	8.13 E
Niederösterreich = Lower Austria (EN) [2]	128	Jb	48.30N	15.45 E
Niedersachsen=Lower Saxony (EN) [2]	120	Fd	52.00N	10.00 E
Niederwald [#]	120	Df	50.10N	8.00 E
Niederzier	124	Id	50.53N	6.28 E
Niefang	166	Hd	1.50N	10.14 E
Niegocin, Jezioro- [~]	120	Rb	54.00N	21.50 E
Niel	124	Ie	49.23N	4.20 E
Nielfa, Puerto de- [#]	126	Hf	38.32N	4.23W
Niéllé	166	Dc	10.12N	5.38W
Niellim	168	Bd	9.42N	17.49 E
Niemba	170	Ed	5.57S	28.26 E
Niemba [~]	170	Ed	5.57S	28.26 E
Niemodlin	120	Nf	50.39N	17.37 E
Niéna	166	Dc	11.25N	6.20W
Nienburg (Weser)	120	Fd	52.38N	9.13 E
Niepołomice	120	Qf	50.03N	20.13 E
Niermalak, Pointe- [#]	219b	Cb	14.21S	167.24 E
Niers [~]	120	Be	51.43N	5.57 E
Nierstein	124	Ke	49.53N	8.20 E
Niesky/Niska	120	Le	51.18N	14.49 E
Nieszawa	120	Od	52.50N	18.55 E
Nieuport/Nieuwpoort	122	Ic	51.08N	2.45 E
Nieuw Amsterdam	202	Gb	5.53N	55.05W
Nieuwe Pekela	124	Ia	53.04N	6.59 E
Nieuweschans	124	Ia	53.11N	7.15 E
Nieuw Milligen, Apeldoorn-	124	Hb	52.14N	5.45 E
Nieuw Nickerie	200	Ke	5.57N	56.59W
Nieuwolda	124	Ia	53.14N	6.59 E
Nieuwoudtville	172	Dc	31.22S	19.06 E
Nieuwpoort/Nieuport	122	Ic	51.08N	2.45 E
Nieuw-Weerdinge, Emmen-	124	Jb	52.52N	7.01 E
Nièvre [3]	122	Jg	47.05N	3.30 E
Nièvre [~]	123	Jh	46.59N	3.10 E
Niğde	144	Db	37.59N	34.42 E
Nigel	172	De	26.25S	28.28 E
Nigenán [~]	192	Fd	34.13N	57.19 E
Niger [1]	160	Gd	16.00N	8.00 E
Niger [~]	160	Gd	9.40N	6.00 E
Niger [3]	158	Hh	5.33N	6.33 E
Niger Basin (EN) [#]	158	Gg	15.00N	2.00 E
Niger Delta [#]	160	Hh	4.50N	6.00 E
Nigeria [1]	160	Hh	10.00N	8.00 E
Night Hawk Lake [~]	184	Fa	48.28N	81.00W
Nightingale Island [+]	158	Fi	37.24S	12.28W
Nigrita	130	Ei	40.54N	23.30 E
Nihiru Atoll [o]	208	Mf	16.42S	142.50W
Nihoa Island [+]	208	Kb	23.06N	161.58W
Nihonmatsu	156	Pf	37.35N	140.26 E
Nihuil, Embalse del- [~]	206	Ge	35.05S	68.45W
Niigata	156	Oe	37.55N	139.03 E
Niigata Ken [2]	156	Of	37.30N	139.00 E
Nihama	154	Lh	33.58N	133.16 E
Niihau Island [+]	208	Kb	21.55N	160.10W
Nii-Jima [+]	156	Oe	34.20N	139.15 E
Niikappu-Gawa [~]	156a	Cb	42.22N	142.16 E
Niimi	156	Dd	34.59N	133.28 E
Niitsu	156	Oe	37.48N	139.07 E
Niitsu	156	Gb	39.36N	141.49 E
Nijar	126	Hg	36.58N	2.12W
Nijkerk	124	Hb	52.13N	5.29 E
Nijlen	124	Hc	51.10N	4.39 E
Nijmegen	112	Lc	51.50N	5.52 E
Nijverdal, Hellendoorn-Nikel	124	Ib	52.22N	6.27 E
Niki	130	Ei	40.55N	21.25 E
Nikitin Seamount (EN) [~]	140	Kj	3.00S	83.00 E
Nikki	166	Fd	9.56N	3.12 E
Nikkō	156	Fc	36.44N	139.35 E
Nikolajev [Ukr.]	112	Jf	46.58N	32.00 E
Nikolajev [Ukr.]	132	Ce	49.32N	23.58 E
Nikolajevka	135	Kc	43.37N	77.01 E
Nikolajevka	116	Mf	58.14N	29.32 E
Nikolajevo	136	Ee	50.02N	45.31 E
Nikolajevski	136	Df	47.20N	30.08 E
Nikolajevska oblast [3]	138	Hf	54.50N	129.25 E
Nikolajevsk-na-Amure	142	Qd	53.08N	140.44 E
Nikolo-Berjozovka (Neftekamsk)	136	Fd	56.06N	54.17 E
Nikolsk [Russia]	136	Ed	53.42N	46.03 E
Nikolsk [Russia]	136	Ed	59.33N	45.31 E
Nikolski [Ak.-U.S.]	178a	Bb	53.15N	168.22W
Nikolski [Kaz.] → Satpajev	136	Gf	47.55N	67.33 E
Nikopol [Bul.]	130	Hf	43.42N	24.54 E
Nikopol [Ukr.]	136	Df	47.35N	34.25 E
Nikpôlis = Nicopolis (EN) [~]	130	Dj	39.00N	20.45 E
Nikpey	146	Md	36.50N	48.10 E
Niksar	146	Gb	40.36N	36.58 E
Nikšić	130	Bg	42.46N	18.58 E
Nikumaroro Atoll (Gardner) [o]	208	Je	4.40S	174.32W
Nikunau Island [+]	208	Ie	1.23S	176.26 E
Nîl, Kûh-e- [#]	146	Ng	30.52N	50.49 E
Nîl, Nahr an-=Nile (EN) [~]	158	Ke	30.10N	31.06 E
Nila, Pulau- [+]	150	Ih	6.44S	129.31 E
Nilakka [~]	114	Ge	63.07N	26.33 E
Niland	188	Hj	33.14N	115.31W
Nilandu Atoll [o]	148a	Bb	3.00N	72.55 E
Nile [3]	170	Fb	3.00N	31.30 E
Nile (EN)=Nîl, Nahr an- [~]	158	Ke	30.10N	31.06 E
Nile Delta (EN) [#]	158	Ke	31.20N	31.00 E
Nîleh, Kûh-e- [#]	146	Nf	32.59N	50.32 E
Niles	184	De	41.50N	86.15W
Nilka	152	Dc	43.47N	82.20 E
Nîl Kowtal [#]	144	Kc	34.48N	67.22 E
Nilsiä	114	Ge	63.12N	28.05 E
Nilüfer [~]	130	Li	40.18N	28.27 E
Nimba [3]	166	Dd	6.45N	8.45W
Nimba, Monts-=Nimba Mountains (EN) [#]	158	Gh	7.35N	8.28W
Nimba Mountains (EN)= Nimba, Monts- [#]	158	Gh	7.35N	8.28W
Nîmes	112	Gg	43.50N	4.21 E
Nimjad	162	Df	17.25N	15.41W
Nimmitabel	212	Jg	36.31S	149.16 E
Nimpkish River [~]	188	Sa	50.32N	126.59W
Nimrod Glacier [~]	222	Kg	82.27S	161.00 E
Nimrud [~]	146	Jd	36.06N	43.20 E
Nimrûz [3]	144	Jc	30.30N	62.00 E
Nims [~]	124	Id	50.00N	6.28 E
Nimule	160	Kh	3.36N	32.03 E
Nimún, Punta- [#]	192	Od	20.46N	90.25W
Nin	128	Jf	44.14N	15.11 E
Nina	172	Bd	22.57S	18.16 E
Ninawá [3]	146	Jc	35.45N	42.45 E
Ninawá=Nineveh (EN) [~]	146	Fh	36.22N	43.09 E
Nine Degree Channel [#]	140	Ji	9.00N	73.00 E
Ninetyeast Ridge (EN) [~]	106	Gj	10.00S	90.00 E
Ninety Mile Beach [Austl.] [#]	212	Jg	38.15S	147.25 E
Ninety Mile Beach [N.Z.] [#]	218	Ea	34.45S	173.00 E
Nineveh (EN)=Ninawá [~]	146	Fb	36.22N	43.09 E
Ning'an	152	Mc	44.22N	129.23 E
Ningbo	142	Md	29.53N	121.33 E
Ningcheng (Tianyi)	152	Kc	41.34N	119.25 E
Ningde	152	Kf	26.41N	119.31 E
Ningdu	152	Kf	26.31N	115.59 E
Ningguo	154	Ei	30.39N	119.00 E
Ninghai	154	Fj	29.19N	121.26 E
Ning-hsia-hui-tu Tzu-chih-ch'ü → Ningxia Huizu Zizhiqu [2]	152	Id	37.00N	106.00 E
Ningjin [China]	154	Cf	37.37N	114.55 E
Ningjin [China]	154	Df	37.39N	116.48 E
Ningjing Shan [#]	152	Ge	31.45N	97.15 E
Ninglang	152	Hf	27.17N	100.52 E
Ningling	154	Cg	34.27N	115.18 E
Ningnan	152	Hf	27.05N	102.44 E
Ningqiang	152	Ie	32.48N	106.15 E
Ningsia Hui (EN) = Ningxia Huizu Zizhiqu (Ning-hsia-hui-tsu Tzu-chih-ch'ü) [2]	152	Id	37.00N	106.00 E
Ningxian	152	Id	35.27N	107.50 E
Ningxiang	154	Bj	28.16N	112.33 E
Ningxia Huizu Zizhiqu (Ning-hsia-hui-tsu Tzu-chih-ch'ü) = Ningsia Hui (EN) [2]	152	Id	37.00N	106.00 E
Ningyang	154	Dg	35.45N	116.48 E
Ningyō-Tōge [#]	156	Cd	35.19N	133.56 E
Ninh Binh	148	Ld	20.15N	105.59 E
Ninh Hoa	148	Lf	12.29N	109.08 E
Ninigo Group [#]	208	Fe	1.15S	144.15 E
Niniva [+]	221b	Ba	19.46S	174.38W
Ninocminda (Bogdanovka)	132	Mi	41.15N	43.36 E
Ninohe	156	Pc	40.16N	141.18 E
Ninove	124	Gd	50.50N	4.00 E
Nioaque	202	Gh	21.08S	55.48W
Niobrara	186	He	42.45N	98.00W
Niobrara [~]	174	Fa	42.45N	98.00W
Nioghalvfjerdsfjorden [~]	170	Kc	2.43S	17.41 E
Nioki	166	Dc	14.15N	6.00W
Niono	166	Dc	14.15N	6.00W
Nioro du Rip	160	Eg	13.45N	15.48W
Nioro du Sahel	160	Fg	15.14N	9.37W
Niort	112	Ff	46.19N	0.27W
Nipawin	180	Hf	53.22N	104.00W
Nipe, Bahia de- [#]	194	Jc	20.47N	75.42W
Nipesotu-Yama [#]	156a	Cb	42.23N	143.02 E
Nipigon	176	Ke	49.01N	88.16W
Nipigon Bay [#]	184	Db	48.53N	87.50W
Nipigon, Lake- [~]	184	Cb	49.50N	88.30W
Nipissing, Lake- [~]	174	Le	46.17N	80.00W
Nippon=Japan (EN) [1]	142	Pf	38.00N	137.00 E
Nippon-Kai=Japan, Sea of- (EN) [~]	140	Pf	40.00N	134.00 E
Nippur [~]	146	Kf	32.10N	45.10 E
Niquelândia	202	If	14.27S	48.27W
Niquero	194	Ic	20.03N	77.35W
Niquitao, Teta de- [#]	194	Li	9.07N	70.30W
Niquivil	206	Gd	30.25S	68.42W
Nir	146	Lc	38.02N	47.59 E
Niraj [~]	130	Hc	46.29N	24.28 E
Nirasaki	156	Fc	35.43N	138.27 E
Nirji → Morin Dawa	152	Lb	48.30N	124.28 E
Nirmal	148	Fe	19.06N	78.21 E
Niš	112	Mg	43.19N	21.54 E
Nisa	126	Ce	39.31N	7.39W
Nişāb	144	Gg	14.24N	46.38 E
Nişāva [~]	130	Lj	43.22N	21.46 E
Niscemi	128	Im	37.09N	14.23 E
Nishibetsu-Gawa [~]	156a	Db	43.23N	145.17 E
Nishikawa	156	Gb	38.26N	140.08 E
Nishiki	156	Bd	34.16N	131.57 E
Nishino'omote	152	Ne	30.44N	131.00 E
Nishi-No-Shima [+]	154	Lf	36.06N	133.00 E
Nishino-Shima [+]	214	Cb	27.30N	140.53 E
Nishiokoppe	156a	Ca	44.20N	142.57 E
Nishi-Sonogi-Hantō [#]	156	Ae	32.55N	129.45 E
Nishiwaki	156	Dd	34.59N	134.58 E
Nisiros	130	Km	36.35N	27.10 E
Niska/Niesky	120	Ke	51.18N	14.49 E
Niška Banja	130	Ff	43.18N	22.01 E
Nisko	120	Sf	50.31N	22.09 E
Nismes, Viroinval-	124	Gd	50.05N	4.33 E
Nisoi Aiyaiou [2]	130	Il	37.40N	25.40 E
Nisporeny	132	Ff	47.06N	28.10 E
Nissan [~]	219a	Ba	4.30S	154.14 E
Nissan [~]	116	Eh	56.40N	12.51 E
Nisser [~]	116	Ce	59.10N	8.30 E
Nissum Bredning [~]	116	Ch	56.40N	8.20 E
Nissum Fjord [~]	116	Ch	56.20N	8.15 E
Nita	156	Cd	35.12N	133.00 E
Nitchequon	180	Kf	53.15N	70.44W
Niterói	200	Lh	22.53S	43.07W
Nith [~]	118	Jf	55.00N	3.35W
Nitra	120	Oh	48.19N	18.05 E
Nitra [~]	120	Oi	47.46N	18.10 E
Niuafo'ou Island [+]	208	Jf	15.35S	175.38W
Niuato Putapu Island [+]	208	Jf	15.57S	173.45W
Niue [1]	210	Kf	19.02S	169.55W
Niue Island [+]	208	Jf	19.02S	169.55W
Niu'erhe	152	La	51.30N	121.40 E
Niufu	156a	Ca	44.35N	142.35 E
Niulakita Island [+]	208	If	10.45S	179.30 E
Niutao Island [+]	208	Ie	6.06S	177.16 E
Niutg, Gunung- [#]	150	If	1.00N	109.55 E
Niutoushan	152	Ke	31.00N	119.35 E
Nivala	114	Fe	63.58N	25.01 E
Nive [~]	122	Ek	43.30N	1.29W
Nivelles/Nijvel	122	Jd	50.36N	4.20 E
Nivernais [~]	122	Jg	47.00N	3.30 E
Nivernais, Canal du- [#]	122	Jg	47.40N	3.40 E
Nivernais, Collines du- [#]	122	Jg	47.10N	3.30 E
Nivillers	122	Ie	49.28N	2.10 E
Nixon	186	Hl	29.16N	97.46W
Niya/Minfeng	152	Dd	37.04N	82.46 E
Niza	146	Fh	35.12N	42.20 E
Nizāmābad	148	Fe	18.40N	78.07 E
Nižankoviči	120	Sg	49.40N	22.48 E
Nižegorodskaja oblast	136	Ed	56.15N	44.45 E
Nizip	144	Fc	37.01N	37.46 E
Nizke Tatry = Low Tatra (EN) [#]	120	Ph	48.54N	19.40 E
Nizký-Jeseník [#]	120	Ng	49.50N	17.30 E
Nižná	120	Pg	49.15N	19.34 E
Nižneangarsk	142	Md	55.47N	109.33 E
Nižnegorski	132	Jg	45.27N	34.44 E
Nižnejansk	138	Ib	71.24N	136.00 E
Nižnekamsk	136	Fd	55.38N	51.49 E
Nižnekolymsk	138	Lc	68.38N	160.56 E
Nižnetroicki	134	Fi	54.20N	53.41 E
Nižneudinsk	142	Ld	54.54N	99.03 E
Nižnevartovsk	142	Jc	61.00N	77.00 E
Nižni Baskunčak	136	Ef	48.13N	46.50 E
Nižni Bestjah	138	Hd	61.48N	129.55 E
Nižni Casučej	138	Gf	50.27N	115.08 E
Nižni Lomov	136	Ee	53.32N	43.41 E
Nižni Odes	134	Gd	63.40N	54.52 E
Nižni Oseredok, ostrov-	132	Pg	45.45N	48.35 E
Nižni Tagil	112	Qd	57.55N	59.57 E
Nižni Trajanov val = Lower Trajan's Wall (EN) [~]	130	Ld	45.45N	28.30 E
Nižnjaja Peša	136	Eb	66.43N	47.36 E
Nižnjaja Pojma	138	Db	56.08N	97.18 E
Nižnjaja Salda	134	Jg	58.05N	60.42 E
Nižnjaja Tavda	136	Jd	57.40N	66.12 E
Nižnjaja Tojma	114	Ke	62.22N	44.15 E
Nižnjaja Tunguska=Lower Tunguska (EN) [~]	140	Kc	65.48N	88.04 E
Nižnjaja Tura	134	Jf	58.38N	59.51 E
Nižnjaja Zolotica	114	Jd	65.41N	40.13 E
Njamunas [~]	110	Id	55.18N	21.23 E
Njandoma	136	Ec	61.43N	40.12 E
Njaris/Neris [~]	134	Ih	56.03N	59.38 E
Njazepetrovsk	134	Ih	56.03N	59.38 E
Njazidja/Grande Comore [+]	158	Lj	11.35S	43.20 E
Njegoš [#]	130	Bg	42.48N	18.45 E
Njinjo	170	Gd	8.48S	38.54 E
Njombe	160	Ki	9.20S	34.46 E

Index Symbols

[1] Independent Nation	[2] State, Region	[3] District, County
[4] Municipality	[5] Colony, Dependency	[6] Continent
[7] Physical Region		

Historical or Cultural Region · Mount, Mountain · Volcano · Hill · Mountains, Mountain Range · Hills, Escarpment · Plateau, Upland · Pass, Gap · Plain, Lowland · Delta · Salt Flat · Valley, Canyon · Crater, Cave · Karst Features · Depression · Polder · Desert, Dunes · Forest, Woods · Heath, Steppe · Oasis · Cape, Point · Coast, Beach · Cliff · Peninsula · Isthmus · Sandbank · Island · Atoll · Rock, Reef · Islands, Archipelago · Rocks, Reefs · Coral Reef · Well, Spring · Geyser · River, Stream · Waterfall, Rapids · River Mouth, Estuary · Lake · Salt Lake · Intermittent Lake · Reservoir · Swamp, Pond · Canal · Glacier · Ice Shelf, Pack Ice · Ocean · Sea · Gulf, Bay · Strait, Fjord · Lagoon · Bank · Seamount · Tablemount · Ridge · Shelf · Basin · Escarpment, Sea Scarp · Fracture · Trench, Abyss · National Park, Reserve · Point of Interest · Recreation Site · Cave, Cavern · Historic Site · Ruins · Wall, Walls · Church, Abbey · Temple · Scientific Station · Railway station · Airport · Port · Military installation · Lighthouse · Mine · Tunnel · Dam, Bridge

Nova Gaia 170 Ce 10.05S 17.32 E
Nova Gorica 128 He 45.57N 13.39 E
Nova Gradiška 128 Le 45.16N 17.23 E
Nova Granada 204 He 20.29S 49.19W
Nova Iguaçu 200 Lh 22.45S 43.27W
Novaja Igirma 138 Fe 57.10N 103.55 E
Novaja-Ivanovka 130 Md 45.59N 29.04 E
Novaja Kahovka 132 Hf 46.43N 33.23 E
Novaja Kazanka 132 Pe 48.58N 49.37 E
Novaja Ladoga 114 Hf 60.05N 32.16 E
Novaja Ljalja 136 Gd 59.03N 60.36 E
Novaja Odessa 132 Gf 47.18N 31.47 E
Novaja Sibir, ostrov- = New Siberia (EN) 140 Qb 75.00N 149.00 E
Novaja Vodolaga 132 Ie 49.45N 35.52 E
Novaja Zemlja = Novaya Zemlya (EN) 140 Hb 74.00N 57.00 E
Nova Lamego 166 Cc 12.17N 14.13W
Nova Lima 202 Jh 19.59S 43.51W
Nova Londrina 204 Ff 22.45S 53.00W
Nova Mambone 172 Fd 20.58S 35.00 E
Nova Olinda do Norte 202 Gd 3.45S 59.03W
Nová Paka 120 Lf 50.29N 15.31 E
Nova Prata 204 Gi 28.47S 51.36W
Novara 128 Ce 45.28N 8.38 E
Nova Roma 204 Ia 13.51S 46.57W
Nova Russas 202 Jd 4.42S 40.34W
Nova Scotia [2] 180 Lh 45.00N 63.00W
Nova Scotia 174 Me 45.00N 63.00W
Nova Sintra 162 Cf 14.54N 24.40W
Nova Sofala 172 Ed 20.10S 34.44 E
Novato 188 Dg 38.06N 122.34W
Nova Varoš 130 Cf 43.28N 19.49 E
Nova Venécia 202 Jg 18.43S 40.24W
Novaya Zemlya (EN) = Novaja Zemlja 140 Hb 74.00N 57.00 E
Nova Zagora 130 Jg 42.29N 26.01 E
Novelda 126 Lf 38.23N 0.46W
Novellara 128 Ef 44.51N 10.44 E
Nové Mesto nad Váhom 120 Nh 48.46N 17.50 E
Nové Zámky 120 Oi 47.59N 18.11 E
Novgorod 112 Jd 58.31N 31.17 E
Novgorodka 116 Mg 57.00N 28.37 E
Novgorod-Severski 136 De 52.01N 33.16 E
Novgorodskaja oblast [3] 136 Dd 58.20N 32.40 E
Novi Bečej 130 Dd 45.36N 20.08 E
Novigrad [Cro.] 128 He 45.19N 13.34 E
Novigrad [Cro.] 128 Jf 44.11N 15.33 E
Novi Kričim 130 Hg 42.03N 24.28 E
Novi Ligure 128 Cf 44.46N 8.47 E
Novillero 192 Gf 22.21N 105.39W
Novion-Porcien 124 Ge 49.36N 4.25 E
Novi Pazar [Bul.] 130 Kf 43.21N 27.12 E
Novi Pazar [Yugo.] 130 Df 43.08N 20.31 E
Novi Sad 112 Hf 45.15N 19.50 E
Novi Travnik 128 Lf 44.10N 17.39 E
Novi Vinodolski 128 Ie 45.08N 14.47 E
Novoaleksandrovsk 132 Lg 45.24N 41.14 E
Novoaleksejevka [Kaz.] 132 Sd 50.08N 55.42 E
Novoaleksejevka [Ukr.] 132 If 46.16N 34.39 E
Novoaltajsk 138 Df 53.24N 83.58 E
Novoanninski 136 Ee 50.31N 42.45 E
Novoarhangelsk 132 Ge 48.39N 30.50 E
Novo Aripuanã 202 Fe 5.08S 60.22W
Novoazovsk 132 Kf 47.05N 38.05 E
Novobirjusinski 138 Ee 56.58N 97.55 E
Novobogdanovka 132 If 47.05N 35.18 E
Novočeboksarsk 114 Lh 56.08N 47.29 E
Novočeremšansk 114 Mi 54.23N 50.10 E
Novočerkassk 136 Ef 47.25N 40.03 E
Novodevičje 114 Lj 53.35N 48.51 E
Novograd-Volynski 136 Ce 50.36N 27.36 E
Novogrudok 132 Dc 53.37N 25.50 E
Nôvo Hamburgo 206 Jc 29.41S 51.08W
Novohopërsk 132 Ld 51.06N 41.37 E
Novo Horizonte 204 He 21.28S 49.13W
Novoizborsk 116 Mg 57.43N 28.05 E
Novojenisejsk 138 Ee 58.19N 92.27 E
Novojerudinski 138 Ee 59.47N 93.30 E
Novokačalinsk 138 Ig 45.05N 131.59 E
Novokazalinsk 142 Ie 45.50N 62.10 E
Novokubansk 132 Lg 45.06N 41.01 E
Novokujbyševsk 136 Ee 53.08N 49.58 E
Novokuzneck 142 Kd 53.45N 87.06 E
Novolazarevskaja 222 Cf 70.46S 11.50 E
Novolukoml 114 Gi 54.38N 29.07 E
Novo Mesto 128 Je 45.48N 15.10 E
Novomičurinsk 114 Ji 54.02N 39.48 E
Novomihajlovka 138 Ih 44.17N 133.50 E
Novo Miloševo 130 Dd 45.43N 20.18 E
Novomirgorod 132 Ge 48.45N 31.39 E
Novomoskovsk [Ukr.] 136 Df 48.37N 35.16 E
Novomoskovsk [Russia] 112 Je 54.05N 38.13 E
Novonikolajevski 132 Md 50.55N 42.24 E
Novoorsk 136 Fe 51.24N 58.59 E
Novopokrovskaja 132 Lg 45.56N 40.42 E
Novopolock 136 Cd 55.31N 28.40 E
Novorossijsk 112 Jg 44.45N 37.45 E
Novorybnaja 138 Fb 72.50N 105.45 E
Novoržev 136 Cd 57.02N 29.20 E
Novošahtinsk 136 Df 47.47N 39.54 E
Novoselica 130 Ja 48.13N 26.17 E
Novoselje 116 Mf 58.05N 29.00 E
Novoselki 120 Ud 52.04N 24.25 E
Novoselovo 138 Ef 54.55N 91.00 E
Novosergijevka 136 Fe 52.03N 53.39 E
Novosibirsk 142 Kd 55.02N 82.55 E
Novosibirskaja oblast [3] 138 Ce 55.30N 80.00 E
Novosibirskije ostrova = New Siberian Islands (EN) 140 Qb 75.00N 142.00 E
Novosibirskoje vodohranilišče = Novosibirsk Reservoir (EN) 138 Df 54.40N 82.35 E
Novosibirsk Reservoir (EN) = Novosibirskoje vodohranilišče 138 Df 54.40N 82.35 E
Novosil 132 Jc 52.59N 37.01 E
Novosineglazovski 134 Ji 55.05N 61.25 E
Novosokolniki 136 Dd 56.19N 30.12 E
Novospasskoje 114 Lj 53.09N 47.44 E
Novotroick 136 Fe 51.12N 58.35 E
Novotroickoje 136 Hg 43.39N 73.45 E
Novoukrainka 132 Ge 48.19N 31.32 E
Novouljanovsk 114 Li 54.10N 48.23 E
Novouzensk 136 Ee 50.29N 48.08 E
Novovjatsk 114 Lg 58.31N 49.43 E
Novovolynsk 136 Ce 50.46N 24.09 E
Novovoronežski 132 Kd 51.17N 39.16 E
Novozybkov 136 De 52.32N 32.00 E
Novska 128 Ke 45.20N 16.59 E
Novy Bug 132 Hf 47.43N 32.29 E
Nový Bydžov 120 Lf 50.15N 15.29 E
Novy Jaričev 120 Ug 49.50N 24.21 E
Novyje Aneny 130 Mc 46.53N 29.13 E
Novyje Burasy 132 Oc 52.06N 46.06 E
Nový Jičín 120 Og 49.36N 18.01 E
Novy Oskol 136 De 50.43N 37.54 E
Novy Pogost 116 Li 55.30N 27.32 E
Novy Port 142 Jc 67.40N 72.52 E
Novy Tap 134 Mh 56.55N 67.15 E
Novy Terek 132 Oh 43.37N 47.25 E
Novy Uzen 136 Fg 43.19N 52.55 E
Novy Vasjugan 138 Ce 58.34N 76.29 E
Novy Zaj 114 Mi 55.17N 52.02 E
Nowa Dęba 120 Rf 50.26N 21.46 E
Nowa Huta, Kraków- 120 Qf 50.04N 20.05 E
Nowa Ruda 120 Mf 50.35N 16.31 E
Nowa Sarzyna 120 Sf 50.23N 22.22 E
Nowa Sól 120 Le 51.48N 15.44 E
Now Bandegān 146 Oh 28.52N 53.53 E
Nowbarān 146 Me 35.08N 49.42 E
Nowdesheh 146 Le 35.11N 46.15 E
Nowe 120 Oc 53.40N 18.43 E
Nowe Miasto Lubawskie 120 Pc 53.27N 19.35 E
Nowe Miasto-nad-Pilicą 120 Qe 51.38N 20.35 E
Nowe Warpno 120 Kc 53.44N 14.20 E
Nowfel low Shātow 146 Ne 34.27N 50.55 E
Nowgong 148 Ic 26.21N 92.40 E
Nowogard 120 Lc 53.40N 15.08 E
Nowogród 120 Rc 53.15N 21.53 E
Nowood River 188 Ld 44.17N 107.58W
Nowra 172 Kf 34.53S 150.36 E
Now Shahr 146 Nd 36.39N 51.31 E
Nowy Dwór Gdański 120 Pb 54.13N 19.06 E
Nowy Dwór Mazowiecki 120 Qd 52.26N 20.43 E
Nowy Korczyn 120 Qf 50.20N 20.50 E
Nowy Sącz 120 Qg 49.38N 20.42 E
Nowy Sącz [2] 120 Qg 49.40N 20.40 E
Nowy Targ 120 Qg 49.29N 20.02 E
Nowy Tomyśl 120 Md 52.20N 16.07 E
Noya/Anoia 126 Nc 41.28N 1.56 E
Noya / Noia 126 Db 42.47N 8.53W
Noyant 122 Gg 47.31N 0.08 E
Noyon 122 Ie 49.35N 3.00 E
Nozaki-Jima 156 Ae 33.11N 129.08 E
Nozay 122 Eg 47.34N 1.38W
Nsanje 170 Gf 16.55S 35.16 E
Nsawan 166 Ed 5.48N 0.21W
Nsefu 170 Fe 13.03S 32.07 E
Nsukka 166 Gd 6.52N 7.23 E
Ntadembele 170 Cc 2.11S 17.08 E
Ntchisi 170 Fe 13.22S 34.00 E
Ntem 158 Hh 2.10N 9.57 E
Ntoum 170 Ab 0.22N 9.47 E
Ntui 166 He 4.27N 11.38 E
Ntusi 170 Fb 0.03N 31.13 E
Nuageuses, Iles- 222 Fc 48.40S 68.58 E
Nuanetsi 158 Kk 22.40S 31.49 E
Nūbah, Jibāl an- 158 Kg 12.00N 30.45 E
Nubian Desert (EN) = Nūbiyah, Aş Şahrā' an- 158 Kf 20.30N 33.00 E
Nūbiyah, Aş Şahrā' an- = Nubian Desert (EN) 158 Kf 20.30N 33.00 E
Nucet 130 Fc 46.28N 22.35 E
Nudha 219a Ec 9.32S 160.48 E
Nueces Plain 182 Hf 28.30N 99.15W
Nueces River 182 Hf 27.50N 97.30W
Nueltin Lake 174 Jc 60.50N 99.30W
Nü'er He 154 Fd 41.06N 121.09 E
Nueva 206 Ei 55.15S 66.32W
Nueva Asunción [3] 204 Be 21.00S 60.20W
Nueva Ciudad Guerrero 192 Jd 26.35N 99.15W
Nueva Esparta [2] 202 Fa 11.00N 64.00W
Nueva Germania 204 Df 23.54S 56.34W
Nueva Gerona 190 Hd 21.53N 82.48W
Nueva Imperial 206 Fe 38.44S 72.57W
Nueva Italia de Ruiz 192 Hh 19.01N 102.06W
Nueva Ocotepeque 194 Cf 14.24N 89.13W
Nueva Palmira 204 Ck 33.53S 58.25W
Nueva Rosita 176 Ig 27.57N 101.13W
Nueva San Salvador 190 Gf 13.41N 89.17W
Nueva Segovia [3] 194 Dg 13.40N 86.10W
Nueve de Julio 206 He 35.27S 60.52W
Nuevitas 190 Id 21.33N 77.16W
Nuevitas, Bahia de- 194 Ic 21.30N 77.12W
Nuevo, Cayo- 192 Mg 21.51N 92.05W
Nuevo, Golfo- 198 Jj 42.42S 64.36W
Nuevo Berlin 204 Ck 32.59S 58.03W
Nuevo Casas Grandes 176 If 30.25N 107.55W
Nuevo Laredo 176 Jg 27.30N 99.31W
Nuevo León [2] 190 Ec 25.40N 100.00W
Nuevo Mundo, Cerro- 202 Eh 21.55S 66.53W
Nuevo Rocafuerte 202 Cd 0.56S 75.25W
Nugaal [3] 168 Hd 8.30N 48.00 E
Nugāl 168 Hd 9.30N 46.30 E
Nugālēd, Dēh- 158 Lh 7.58N 49.51 E
Nugālēd, Dōho- 168 Hd 8.35N 48.35 E
Nūgātsiaq 179 Gd 71.39N 53.45W
Nugget Point 218 Cg 46.27S 169.49 E
Nûgssuaq 179 Gd 70.30N 51.30W
Nuguria Islands 208 Ge 3.20S 154.45 E
Nuguš 134 Gj 53.05N 56.00 E
Nuhaka 218 Gc 39.02S 177.45 E
Nui Atoll 208 Ie 7.15S 177.10 E
Nuijama 116 Md 60.58N 28.32 E
Nuiqsut 178 Ib 70.20N 151.00W
Nu Jiang 140 Lh 16.31N 97.37 E
Nûk/Godthåb 224 Nc 64.15N 51.40W
Nukapu 219c Ab 10.07S 165.59 E
Nukey Bluff 212 Hf 32.35S 135.40 E
Nukhayb 144 Fc 32.02N 42.15 E
Nukhaylak 160 Jg 19.08N 26.20 E
Nukiki 219a Cb 6.45S 156.29 E
Nukuaéta 220h Ac 13.22S 176.11W
Nuku'alofa 210 Jg 21.08S 175.12W
Nukufetau Atoll 208 Ie 8.00S 178.22 E
Nukufotu 220h Bb 13.11S 176.10W
Nukuhifala 220h Bb 13.17S 176.05W
Nukuhione 220h Bb 13.16S 176.06W
Nuku Hiva, Ile- 208 Me 8.54S 140.06W
Nukulaelae Atoll 208 Ie 9.23S 179.52 E
Nukuloa 220h Bb 13.11S 176.09W
Nukumanu Islands 208 Ge 4.30S 159.30 E
Nukumbasanga 219d Cb 16.18S 179.15W
Nukunonu Atoll 208 Je 9.10S 171.53W
Nukuoro Atoll 208 Gd 3.51N 154.58 E
Nukus 142 He 42.50N 59.29 E
Nukutapu 220h Bb 13.13S 176.08W
Nukuteatea 220h Bb 13.12S 176.08W
Nulato 178 Hd 64.43N 158.06W
Nules 126 Le 39.51N 0.09W
Nullagine 210 Dg 21.53S 120.06 E
Nullagine River 212 Ed 20.43S 120.33 E
Nullarbor 212 Gf 31.26S 130.55 E
Nullarbor Plain 208 Dh 31.00S 129.00 E
Nulu'erhu Shan 152 Kc 41.40N 119.50 E
Numakawa 156a Ba 45.15N 141.51 E
Numan 166 Hd 9.28N 12.02 E
Numancia 150 Ie 9.52N 125.58 E
Numancia 126 Jc 41.47N 2.30W
Numanohata 156a Bb 42.40N 141.41 E
Numata [Jap.] 156a Bb 43.49N 141.55 E
Numata [Jap.] 154 Of 36.38N 139.03 E
Numatinna 168 Dd 7.14N 27.37 E
Numazu 154 Og 35.06N 138.52 E
Nümbrecht 124 Jd 50.54N 7.33 E
Numedal 114 Bf 60.05N 9.05 E
Numena 170 Ee 11.46S 26.31 E
Número Cinco, Canal- 204 Cm 37.14S 58.06W
Número Doce, Canal- 204 Cn 36.30S 59.08W
Número Dos, Canal- 204 Cm 36.51S 58.03W
Número Nueve, Canal- 204 Cm 36.08S 58.36W
Número Once, Canal- 204 Bm 36.28S 60.01W
Número Quince, Canal- 204 Dl 35.55S 57.45W
Número Uno, Canal- 204 Cm 36.40S 58.35W
Numfoor, Pulau- 150 Jg 1.03S 134.54 E
Nuneaton 118 Li 52.32N 1.28W
Nungarin 212 Df 31.11S 118.06 E
Nungnain Sum 152 Kb 45.45N 118.56 E
Nungo 172 Fb 13.25S 37.46 E
Nunivak 174 Cd 60.00N 166.30W
Nunkirchen, Wadern- 124 Ie 49.32N 6.53 E
Nunn 186 Df 40.45N 104.46W
Nunspeet 124 Hb 52.22N 5.46 E
Nunukan Timur, Pulau- 150 Gf 4.05N 117.40 E
Nuomin He 152 Lb 48.21N 124.32 E
Nuorgam 114 Ga 70.05N 27.51 E
Nuoro 112 Gg 40.19N 9.20 E
Nupani 219c Ab 10.04S 165.40 E
Nūq 146 Pg 30.55N 55.35 E
Nuqayr 146 Mi 27.48N 48.21 E
Nuqrah 146 Ij 25.34N 41.24 E
Nuquş, Jabal- 164 Fe 24.49N 34.36 E
Nuqui 202 Cb 5.43N 77.16W
Nūr 146 Pg 31.25N 54.20 E
Nūr 146 Od 36.15N 52.20 E
Nura 136 Gf 48.57N 62.20 E
Nura 140 Id 50.30N 69.59 E
Nūrābād 146 Ng 30.48N 51.27 E
Nuraghe Santu Antine 128 Cj 40.29N 8.45 E
Nurata 136 Gg 40.34N 65.35 E
Nur Dağları 146 Gd 36.45N 36.20 E
Nure 128 De 45.03N 9.49 E
Nurek 136 Gh 38.25N 69.20 E
Nurhak Dağı 144 Eb 38.04N 37.29 E
Nūrī 168 Eb 18.30N 32.02 E
Nurki 138 Ie 56.42N 138.28 E
Nurlat 136 Fe 54.28N 50.48 E
Nurlati 114 Li 55.38N 48.17 E
Nurmes 114 Ge 63.33N 29.07 E
Nurmijärvi 116 Kd 60.28N 24.48 E
Nurmo 116 Jb 62.50N 22.54 E
Nürnberg 112 Hf 49.27N 11.05 E
Nurra 128 Cj 40.45N 8.15 E
Nurri, Mount- 212 Jf 31.42S 146.02 E
Nurugas 172 Bc 19.11S 18.54 E
Nurzec 120 Sd 52.33N 22.28 E
Nusa Tenggara Barat [3] 150 Gh 8.50S 117.30 E
Nusa Tenggara Timur [3] 150 Hh 9.30S 122.00 E
Nusaybin 146 Id 37.03N 41.13 E
Nushagak 178 He 58.57N 158.29W
Nushan 152 Gf 25.00N 99.00 E
Nu-Shima 156 Dd 34.10N 134.50 E
Nutak 180 Le 57.31N 62.00W
Nuttal 148 Dc 28.45N 68.08 E
Nuutele 221c Bb 14.02S 171.22W
Nuwākot 148 Gc 28.08N 83.53 E
Nuwara 148 Gg 6.58N 80.46 E
Nuwaybi 'al Muzayyinah 164 Fd 28.58N 34.39 E
Nyabing 212 Df 33.32S 118.09 E
Nyagquka/Yajiang 152 He 30.07N 100.58 E
Nyagrong/Xinlong 152 He 30.57N 100.12 E
Nyahanga 170 Fc 2.23S 33.33 E
Nyahua 170 Fc 4.58S 33.34 E
Nyainqêntanglha Feng 152 Fe 30.12N 90.33 E
Nyainqêntanglha Shan 140 Kf 30.10N 90.00 E
Nyakanazi 170 Fc 3.00S 31.15 E
Nyala 160 Jg 12.03N 24.53 E
Nyalam 152 Ef 28.15N 85.55 E
Ny-Ålesund 179 Nc 78.56N 11.57 E
Nyalikungu 170 Fc 3.11S 33.47 E
Nyamandhlovu 172 Dc 19.51S 28.16 E
Nyamapanda 172 Ec 16.55S 32.52 E
Nyamlell 168 Dd 9.07N 26.58 E
Nyamtumbo 170 Ge 10.30S 36.06 E
Nyanding 168 Ed 8.40N 32.41 E
Nyanga [3] 170 Bc 3.00S 11.00 E
Nyanga 158 Ii 2.58S 10.15 E
Nyanza [3] 170 Fc 0.30S 34.30 E
Nyanza-Lac 170 Ec 4.21S 29.36 E
Nyasa, Lake- (EN) = Niassa, Lago- 158 Kj 12.00S 34.30 E
Nyaunglebin 148 Je 17.57N 96.44 E
Nyborg 114 Ci 55.19N 10.48 E
Nybro 114 Dh 56.45N 15.54 E
Nyda 138 Cc 66.36N 72.54 E
Nyda 134 Pc 66.40N 72.50 E
Nyeboe Land 179 Gb 81.45N 56.40W
Nyêmo 152 Ff 29.30N 90.07 E
Nyeri 170 Gc 0.25S 36.57 E
Nyerol 168 Ed 8.41N 32.02 E
Ny Friesland 179 Nc 79.30N 17.00 E
Nyhammar 116 Fd 60.17N 14.58 E
Nyhem 116 Fb 62.54N 15.40 E
Nyika 158 Ki 2.37S 38.44 E
Nyika Plateau 158 Kj 10.40S 33.50 E
Nyikog Qu 152 He 30.24N 100.40 E
Nyimba 170 Fe 14.33S 30.48 E
Nyingchi 152 Ff 29.38N 94.23 E
Nyirbátor 120 Si 47.50N 22.08 E
Nyíregyháza 120 Ri 47.57N 21.43 E
Nyiri Desert 170 Gc 2.20S 37.20 E
Nyiro, Mount- 170 Gb 2.08N 36.51 E
Nyírség 120 Ri 47.50N 21.55 E
Nykøbing [Den.] 114 Ci 55.55N 11.41 E
Nykøbing [Den.] 116 Ch 56.48N 8.52 E
Nykøbing [Den.] 114 Ci 54.46N 11.53 E
Nyköping 114 Dg 58.45N 17.00 E
Nyköpingsån 116 Gf 58.45N 17.01 E
Nykroppa 116 Fe 59.38N 14.18 E
Nyland 116 Ga 63.00N 17.46 E
Nylstroom 172 Dd 24.42S 28.20 E
Nymburk 120 Lf 50.11N 15.03 E
Nymphe Bank (EN) 118 Fj 51.30N 7.05W
Nynäshamn 114 Dg 58.54N 17.57 E
Nyngan 210 Fh 31.34S 147.11 E
Nyon 128 Ad 46.23N 6.15 E
Nyong 158 Hh 3.17N 9.54 E
Nyonga 170 Fd 6.43S 32.04 E
Nyons 122 Lj 44.22N 5.08 E
Nyřany 120 Jg 49.43N 13.13 E
Nyrob 134 Hf 60.42N 56.45 E
Nyš 138 Jf 51.30N 142.49 E
Nysa 120 Nf 50.29N 17.20 E
Nysa Kłodzka 120 Nf 50.49N 17.50 E
Nysa Łużycka 120 Kd 52.04N 14.46 E
Nyslott/Savonlinna 114 Gf 61.52N 28.53 E
Nyssa 188 Ge 43.53N 117.00W
Nystad/Uusikaupunki 114 Ef 60.48N 21.25 E
Nysted 116 Dj 54.40N 11.45 E
Nytva 136 Fd 57.56N 55.20 E
Nyūdō-Zaki 154 Od 40.00N 139.35 E
Nyunzu 170 Ed 5.57S 28.01 E
Nyūzen 156 Ec 36.56N 137.30 E
Nzambi 170 Bc 3.58S 11.16 E
Nzara 168 De 4.40N 28.14 E
Nzega 170 Fc 4.13S 33.11 E
Nzérékoré 160 Gh 7.45N 8.49W
N'zeto 170 Bd 7.05S 12.50 E
Nzi 158 Gh 5.57N 4.50W
Nzilo, Barrage de- 170 Ee 10.35S 25.30 E
Nzo 166 Dd 6.16N 7.03W
Nzoro 170 Eb 3.18N 29.26 E
Nzwani/Anjouan 158 Lj 12.15S 44.25 E

O

Oa, Mull of- 118 Gf 55.35N 6.20W
Oahe, Lake- 174 Ie 45.30N 100.25W
Oahu Island 208 Lb 21.30N 158.00W
O-akan-Dake 156a Db 43.27N 144.10 E
Oakdale [Ca.-U.S.] 188 Eh 37.46N 120.51W
Oakdale [La.-U.S.] 186 Jk 30.49N 92.40W
Oakham 118 Mi 52.40N 0.44W
Oak Harbor 188 Db 48.18N 122.39W
Oak Lake 186 Fb 49.40N 100.45W
Oakland [Ca.-U.S.] 176 Gf 37.47N 122.13W
Oakland [Md.-U.S.] 184 Hf 39.25N 79.24W
Oakley [Id.-U.S.] 188 Ie 42.15N 113.53W
Oakley [Ks.-U.S.] 186 Gd 39.08N 100.51W
Oak Park 186 Mf 41.53N 87.48W
Oak Ridge 182 Kd 36.01N 84.16W
Oakridge 188 De 43.45N 122.28W
Oakville 184 Hd 43.27N 79.41W
Oamaru 216 Di 45.05S 170.59 E
Oancea 130 Ld 45.55N 28.06 E
Oani-Gawa 156 Ga 40.12N 140.16 E
Oarai 156 Gc 36.18N 140.33 E
Oaro 218 Ee 42.31S 173.30 E
Oasis 188 Hf 41.01N 114.37W
Oasis 162 Hd 26.00N 5.00 E
Oates Coast 222 Jf 70.00S 160.00 E
Oaxaca [2] 190 Ee 17.00N 96.30W
Oaxaca de Juárez 176 Jh 17.03N 96.43W
Ob 140 Ic 66.45N 69.30 E
Oba 180 Jg 48.55N 84.17W
Obala 166 He 4.10N 11.32 E
Obama [Jap.] 156 Be 32.43N 130.13 E
Obama [Jap.] 154 Mg 35.30N 135.45 E
Obama-Wan 156 Dd 35.30N 135.40 E
Oban [N.Z.] 216 Ci 46.52S 168.10 E
Oban [Scot.-U.K.] 118 He 56.25N 5.29W
Obanazawa 154 Pe 38.36N 140.24 E
Obando 200 Je 4.07N 67.45W
Oban Hills 166 Gd 5.30N 8.35 E
Obeliai/Obeljaj 116 Ki 55.58N 25.59 E
Obeljaj/Obeliai 116 Ki 55.58N 25.59 E
Oberá 206 Ic 27.29S 55.08W
Oberbayern 120 Hi 47.50N 11.50 E
Oberderdingen 124 Ke 49.04N 8.48 E
Oberfranken 120 Hf 50.10N 11.30 E
Oberhausen 120 Ce 51.28N 6.51 E
Oberkirchen, Schmallenberg- 124 Kc 51.09N 8.18 E
Oberland [Switz.] 128 Bd 46.35N 7.30 E
Oberland [Switz.] 128 Dd 46.45N 9.05 E
Oberlausitz 120 Ke 51.15N 14.30 E
Oberlin 186 Fg 39.49N 100.32W
Obermoschel 124 Je 49.44N 7.46 E
Obernkirchen 124 Lb 52.16N 9.08 E
Oberösterreich = Upper Austria (EN) [2] 128 Hb 48.15N 14.00 E
Oberpfalz 120 Ig 49.30N 12.10 E
Oberpfälzer Wald = North Bohemian Forest (EN) 120 Ig 49.50N 12.30 E
Oberpullendorf 128 Kc 47.30N 16.31 E
Ober-Ramstadt 124 Ke 49.50N 8.45 E
Oberstdorf 120 Gi 47.24N 10.16 E
Oberursel (Taunus) 124 Kd 50.12N 8.35 E
Obervellach 128 Hd 46.56N 13.12 E
Oberwesel 124 Jd 50.06N 7.44 E
Ob Gulf (EN) = Obskaja guba 140 Jc 69.00N 73.00 E
Obi, Kepulauan- 150 Ig 1.30S 127.45 E
Obi, Pulau- 208 De 1.30S 127.45 E
Obi, Selat- 150 Ig 0.52S 127.33 E
Óbidos [Braz.] 200 Kf 1.55S 55.31W
Óbidos [Port.] 126 Ce 39.22N 9.09W
Obihiro 152 Pc 42.55N 143.12 E
Obilić 130 Eg 42.41N 21.05 E
Obira 156a Ba 44.01N 141.38 E
Obispos 194 Li 8.36N 70.05W
Obispo Trejo 206 Hd 30.46S 63.25W
Obitočnaja kosa 132 Jf 46.35N 36.15 E
Oblučje 138 Ig 48.59N 131.05 E
Obninsk 136 Dd 55.05N 36.37 E
Obo 160 Jh 5.24N 26.30 E
Obock 168 Gc 11.57N 43.17 E
Obojan 136 De 51.13N 36.16 E
Obokote 170 Ec 0.52S 26.19 E
Obol 114 Gi 55.24N 29.01 E
Oborniki 120 Md 52.39N 16.51 E
Obouya 170 Cc 0.56S 15.43 E
Obozerski 136 Ec 63.28N 40.20 E
Obra 120 Ld 52.36N 15.28 E
Obrenovac 130 De 44.39N 20.12 E
Obrovac 128 Jf 44.12N 15.41 E
Obrovo 120 Vd 52.27N 25.43 E
Obruchev Rise (EN) 138 Lf 52.30N 166.00 E
Obruk Platosu 146 Ec 38.02N 33.30 E
Obšči Syrt 110 Le 51.50N 51.00 E
Obskaja guba = Ob Gulf (EN) 140 Jc 69.00N 73.00 E
Ob' Tablemount (EN) 158 Ln 52.30S 42.00 E
Ōbu 156 Ed 35.01N 136.58 E
Obuasi 166 Ed 6.12N 1.40W
Obudu 166 Gd 6.40N 9.10 E
Obuhov 132 Gd 50.07N 30.37 E
Obva 134 Gg 58.35N 55.25 E
Obzor 130 Kg 42.49N 27.53 E
Oca 126 Ib 42.46N 3.26W
Oca, Montes de- 126 Ib 42.20N 3.15W
Očakov 136 Df 46.38N 31.33 E
Ocala 182 Kf 29.11N 82.07W
Očamčira 132 Lh 42.46N 41.27 E
Ocampo [Mex.] 192 Ec 28.11N 108.23W
Ocampo [Mex.] 192 Hd 27.20N 102.21W
Ocaña [Col.] 202 Db 8.15N 73.20W
Ocaña [Sp.] 126 Ie 39.56N 3.31W
Occhito, Lago di- 128 Ii 41.35N 14.55 E
Occidental, Cordillera- [Col.] 198 Ie 5.00N 76.00W
Ocean Bight 194 Kc 21.15N 73.15W
Ocean City [Md.-U.S.] 182 Ld 38.20N 75.05W
Ocean City [N.J.-U.S.] 184 Jf 39.16N 74.35W
Ocean Falls 180 Ef 52.21N 127.40W
Oceania (EN) 208 Ie 5.00S 175.00 E
Ocean Point 184 Il 26.16N 77.03W
Oceanside 182 De 33.12N 117.23W
Ocean Springs 186 Lk 30.25N 88.50W
Očejón, Pico- 126 Ic 41.07N 3.15W
Očenyrd, gora- 134 Mb 68.05N 66.20 E
Očer 136 Fd 57.53N 54.45 E
Ochagabia / Ochagavia 126 Kb 42.55N 1.05W
Ochagavia / Ochagabia 126 Kb 42.55N 1.05W
Ochiai 156 Cd 35.02N 133.45 E
Ochiishi-Misaki 156a Db 43.10N 145.28 E
Ochil Hills 118 Je 56.23N 3.35W
Och'onjang 154 Jd 40.55N 128.50 E
Ocho Rios 194 Id 18.25N 77.07W
Ochsenfurt 120 Gg 49.39N 10.05 E
Ochtrup 124 Jb 52.13N 7.11 E
Ockelbo 114 Dd 60.53N 16.43 E
Öckerö 116 Dg 57.43N 11.39 E
Ocmulgee River 184 Fj 31.58N 82.32W
Ocna Mureş 130 Gc 46.23N 23.51 E
Ocna Sibiului 130 Hd 45.53N 24.03 E
Ocoa, Bahia de- 194 Ld 18.22N 70.39W
Oconee River 184 Fj 31.58N 82.32W
Oconto 186 Md 44.55N 87.52W
Ocosingo 192 Mi 17.04N 92.15W
Ocotal 194 Dg 13.38N 86.29W
Ocotepeque [3] 194 Cf 14.30N 89.00W
Ocotlán 190 Dd 20.21N 102.46W
Ocotlán de Morelos 192 Ki 16.48N 96.43W
Ocracoke Inlet 184 Ih 35.10N 76.05W
Ocracoke Island 184 Jh 35.09N 75.53W
Ocreza 126 Ee 39.32N 7.50W
Octeville-sur-Mer 124 Ce 49.33N 0.07 E
October Revolution Island (EN) = Oktjabrskoj Revoljuci, ostrov- 140 Lb 79.30N 97.00 E
Ocú 194 Gj 7.57N 80.47W

Index Symbols

Symbol											
[1] Independent Nation	Historical or Cultural Region	Pass, Gap	Depression	Coast, Beach	Rock, Reef	Waterfall, Rapids	Canal	Lagoon	Escarpment, Sea Scarp	Historic Site	Airport
[2] State, Region	Mount, Mountain	Plain, Lowland	Polder	Cliff	Islands, Archipelago	River Mouth, Estuary	Bank	Glacier	Fracture	Ruins	Port
[3] District, County	Volcano	Delta	Desert, Dunes	Peninsula	Rocks, Reefs	Lake	Seamount	Ice Shelf, Pack Ice	Trench, Abyss	Wall, Walls	Military installation
[4] Municipality	Hill	Salt Flat	Forest, Woods	Isthmus	Coral Reef	Salt Lake	Ridge	Ocean	Point of Interest	Church, Abbey	Lighthouse
[5] Colony, Dependency	Mountains, Mountain Range	Valley, Canyon	Heath, Steppe	Sandbank	Well, Spring	Intermittent Lake	Shelf	Tablemount	National Park, Reserve	Temple	Mine
Continent	Hills, Escarpment	Crater, Cave	Oasis	Island	Geyser	Sea	Basin	Recreation Site	Scientific Station	Railway station	Tunnel
Physical Region	Plateau, Upland	Karst Features	Cape, Point	Atoll	River, Stream	Swamp, Pond	Gulf, Bay	Strait, Fjord	Cave, Cavern	Scientific Station	Dam, Bridge

Name	Page	Grid	Lat.	Long.
Ono-i-Lau Islands	208	Jg	20.39S	178.42W
Onojō	156	Be	33.34N	130.29 E
Onomichi	154	Lg	34.25N	133.12 E
Onon	140	Nd	51.42N	115.50 E
Onoto	196	Dh	9.36N	65.12W
Onotoa Atoll	208	Ie	1.52S	175.34 E
Ons, Isla de-	126	Db	42.23N	8.56W
Onsala	114	Ch	57.25N	12.01 E
Onseepkans	172	Be	28.45S	19.17 E
Onslow	210	Cg	21.39S	115.06 E
Onslow Bay	182	Le	34.20N	77.20W
On-Take	156	Bf	31.35N	130.39 E
Ontake-San	156	Ed	35.53N	137.29 E
Ontario [2]	180	If	50.00N	86.00W
Ontario [Ca.-U.S.]	188	Gi	34.04N	117.39W
Ontario [Or.-U.S.]	182	Dc	44.02N	116.58W
Ontario, Lake-	174	Le	43.40N	78.00W
Ontario Peninsula	174	Ke	43.50N	81.00W
Onteniente/Ontinyent	126	Lf	38.49N	0.37W
Ontinyent/Onteniente	126	Lf	38.49N	0.37W
Ontojärvi	114	Gd	64.08N	29.09 E
Ontonagon	184	Cb	46.52N	89.19W
Ontong Java Atoll	208	Ge	5.20S	159.30 E
Ō-Numa	156a	Bc	41.59N	140.41 E
Oodnadatta	210	Eg	27.33S	135.28 E
Ooidonk	124	Fc	51.01N	3.35 E
Ookala	221a	Fc	20.01N	155.17W
Ooldea	210	Eh	30.27S	131.50 E
Oologah Lake	186	Ih	36.39N	95.36W
Ooltgensplaat, Oostflakkee-	124	Gc	51.41N	4.21 E
Oostburg	124	Fc	51.20N	3.30 E
Oostelijk Flevoland	124	Hb	52.30N	5.40 E
Oostende/Ostende	122	Ic	51.14N	2.55 E
Oosterhout	122	Kc	51.38N	4.51 E
Oosterschelde=East Schelde (EN)	122	Jc	51.30N	4.00 E
Oosterwolde, Ooststellingwerf-	124	Ha	53.00N	6.18 E
Oosterzele	124	Fd	50.57N	3.48 E
Oostflakkee	124	Gc	51.41N	4.21 E
Oostflakkee-Ooltgensplaat	124	Gc	51.41N	4.21 E
Oostkamp	124	Fc	51.09N	3.14 E
Oost-Souburg, Vlissingen-	124	Fc	51.28N	3.36 E
Ooststellingwerf	124	Ib	53.00N	6.18 E
Ooststellingwerf-Oosterwolde	124	Ha	53.00N	6.18 E
Oost Vieland, Vieland-	124	Ha	53.17N	5.06 E
Oost-Vlaanderen = Flanders, East- (EN) [3]	124	Fc	51.00N	3.40 E
Ootmarsum	124	Ib	52.25N	6.54 E
Opala	170	Dc	0.37S	24.21 E
Opalenica	120	Md	52.19N	16.23 E
Opanake	148	Gg	6.36N	80.37 E
Opari	168	Ee	3.56N	32.03 E
Oparino	114	Lg	59.53N	48.25 E
Opasatika	184	Fa	49.31N	82.58W
Opasatika Lake	184	Fa	49.06N	83.08W
Opasatika River	184	Fa	50.15N	82.25W
Opatija	128	Ie	45.20N	14.19 E
Opatów	120	Rf	50.49N	21.26 E
Opatówka	120	Rf	50.42N	21.50 E
Opava	120	Ng	49.57N	17.54 E
Opava	120	Og	49.51N	18.17 E
Opelika	182	Je	32.39N	85.23W
Opelousas	186	Jk	30.32N	92.05W
Opémisca, Lac-	184	Ja	49.58N	74.57W
Opheim	188	Lb	48.51N	106.24W
Ophir	178	Hd	63.10N	156.31W
Ophthalmia Range	212	Dd	23.15S	119.30 E
Opienge	170	Eb	0.12N	27.30 E
Opihikao	221a	Gd	19.26N	154.53W
Opinaca	180	Jf	52.14N	78.02W
Opiscotéo, Lac-	180	Kf	53.09N	68.10W
Opladen, Leverkusen-	120	De	51.04N	7.01 E
Opobo	166	Ge	4.34N	7.27 E
Opočka	136	Cd	56.42N	28.41 E
Opoczno	120	Qe	51.23N	20.17 E
Opole	120	Nf	50.41N	17.55 E
Opole [2]	120	Nf	50.40N	17.55 E
Opole Lubelskie	120	Re	51.09N	21.58 E
Oporny	136	Ff	46.13N	54.29 E
Opotiki	218	Gc	38.01S	177.17 E
Opp	184	Dj	31.17N	86.22W
Oppa-Wan	156	Gb	38.35N	141.30 E
Oppdal	114	Be	62.36N	9.40 E
Oppenheim	120	Eg	49.51N	8.21 E
Oppland [2]	114	Bf	61.10N	9.40 E
Opportunity	188	Gc	47.39N	117.15W
Opsa	116	Li	55.31N	26.54 E
Opsterland	124	Ia	53.03N	6.04 E
Opsterland-Beetsterzwaag	124	Ia	53.03N	6.04 E
Opua	216	Dg	35.18S	174.07 E
Opunake	218	Ec	39.27S	173.51 E
Oputo	192	Eb	30.03N	109.20W
Oquossoc	184	Lc	45.04N	70.44W
Or	132	Ud	51.12N	58.33 E
Ora	164	Cd	28.20N	19.35 E
Oradea	112	If	47.04N	21.56 E
Orahovac	130	Dg	42.24N	20.40 E
Orahovica	128	Le	45.32N	17.53 E
Orai	148	Fc	25.59N	79.28 E
Oraibi Wash	188	Ji	35.26N	110.49W
Oran	160	Ge	35.42N	0.38W
Oran [3]	162	Gb	36.00N	0.35W
Orange [Austl.]	210	Fh	33.17S	149.06 E
Orange [Fr.]	122	Kj	44.08N	4.48 E
Orange [Tx.-U.S.]	182	Ie	30.01N	93.44W
Orange [Va.-U.S.]	184	Hf	38.14N	78.07W
Orange/Oranje	158	Ik	28.38N	16.27 E
Orange, Cabo-	198	Ke	4.24N	51.33W
Orangeburg	182	Ke	33.30N	80.52W
Orange Free State → Free State	172	De	29.00S	26.00 E
Orange Lake	184	Fk	29.25N	82.13W
Orange Park	184	Gj	30.10N	81.42W
Orangeville	184	Gd	43.55N	80.06W
Orange Walk	190	Ge	18.06N	88.33W
Orange Walk [3]	194	Ce	17.44N	88.40W
Oranienburg	120	Jd	52.45N	13.14 E
Oranje/Orange	158	Ik	28.38S	16.27 E
Oranje Gebergte	202	Hc	3.00N	55.00W
Oranjemund	172	Be	28.38S	16.24 E
Oranjestad	202	Da	12.33N	70.06W
Oranžerei	132	Og	45.50N	47.36 E
Orapa	172	Dd	21.16S	25.22 E
Orăştie	130	Gd	45.50N	23.12 E
Orava	120	Pg	49.08N	19.10 E
Oraviţa	130	Ed	45.02N	21.42 E
Orayská Priehradní Nádrž	120	Pg	49.20N	19.35 E
Orb	122	Jk	43.15N	3.18 E
Orba	128	Cf	44.53N	8.37 E
Orba Co	152	De	34.33N	81.06 E
Ørbæk	116	Di	55.16N	10.41 E
Orbec	124	Ce	49.01N	0.25 E
Orbetello	128	Fh	42.27N	11.13 E
Orbetello, Laguna di-	128	Fh	42.25N	11.15 E
Órbigo	126	Gc	41.58N	5.40W
Orbiquet	124	Ce	49.09N	0.14 E
Orbost	212	Jg	37.42S	148.27 E
Örbyhus	116	Gd	60.14N	17.42 E
Orcas Island	188	Db	48.39N	122.55W
Orchej (Orgejev)	136	Cf	47.23N	28.50 E
Orchies	124	Fd	50.28N	3.14 E
Orchon → Orhon	140	Md	50.21N	106.05 E
Orcia	128	Fh	42.58N	11.21 E
Orco	128	Be	45.10N	7.52 E
Ord, Mount-	212	Fc	17.20S	125.35 E
Ordenes / Ordes	126	Da	43.04N	8.24W
Ordes / Órdenes	126	Da	43.04N	8.24W
Ordos Desert (EN)=Mu Us Shamo	140	Mf	38.45N	109.10 E
Ord River	208	Df	15.30S	128.21 E
Ordu	144	Ea	41.00N	37.53 E
Ordubad	132	Oj	38.55N	46.01 E
Ordynskoje	138	Df	54.22N	81.58 E
Ordžonikidze [Kaz.]	134	Jj	52.25N	61.45 E
Ordžonikidze [Russia] → Vladikavkaz	112	Kg	43.03N	44.40 E
Ordžonikidze [Ukr.]	132	If	47.40N	34.04 E
Ordžonikidzeabad	136	Gh	38.34N	69.02 E
Ore älv	116	Fc	61.08N	14.35 E
Orebić	128	Lh	42.58N	17.11 E
Örebro	112	Hd	59.17N	15.13 E
Örebro [2]	114	Dg	59.30N	15.00 E
Oredež	116	Nf	58.50N	30.13 E
Oregon	184	Fe	41.38N	83.28W
Oregon [2]	182	Cc	44.00N	121.00W
Oregon City	188	Cb	45.21N	122.36W
Oregon Inlet	184	Jh	35.50N	75.35W
Öregrund	116	Hd	60.20N	18.26 E
Orehov	132	If	47.34N	35.47 E
Orehovo-Zujevo	112	Jd	55.49N	38.59 E
Orel	112	Je	52.59N	36.05 E
Orel	132	Ie	48.31N	34.55 E
Orel, gora-	138	Jf	53.55N	140.01 E
Orellana [Peru]	202	Cd	4.40S	78.10W
Orellana [Peru]	202	Ce	6.54S	75.04W
Orem	182	Ec	40.19N	111.42W
Ore Mountains (EN)= Erzgebirge	110	He	50.30N	13.15 E
Ore Mountains (EN)= Krušné Hory	110	He	50.30N	13.15 E
Ören	146	Bd	37.18N	29.17 E
Orenbel	146	Hb	40.00N	39.10 E
Orenburg	112	Le	51.54N	55.06 E
Orenburgskaja oblast [3]	136	Fe	52.00N	55.00 E
Örencik	146	Cc	39.16N	29.34 E
Orense	206	Ie	38.40S	59.47W
Orense / Ourense	126	Eb	42.20N	7.51W
Orense / Ourense [3]	126	Eb	42.10N	7.30W
Oreón, Dhiavlos-	130	Fk	38.54N	22.55 E
Orepuki	218	Bg	46.17S	167.44 E
Orestiás	130	Jh	41.30N	26.31 E
Øresund	110	Hd	55.50N	12.40 E
Oreti	218	Cg	46.28S	168.17 E
Orewa	218	Fb	36.35S	174.42 E
Orford	124	Db	52.05N	1.32 E
Orford Ness	118	Oi	52.05N	1.34 E
Orgaña	126	Nb	42.13N	1.20 E
Organ Needle	186	Cj	32.21N	106.33W
Orgaz	126	Ie	39.39N	3.54W
Orgejev → Orchej	136	Cf	47.23N	28.50 E
Orgelet	122	Lh	46.31N	5.37 E
Orgon Tal	154	Bc	43.20N	112.40 E
Orgosolo	128	Dj	40.12N	9.21 E
Orgūn	144	Kc	32.57N	69.11 E
Orhaneli	130	Lj	39.54N	29.00 E
Orhaneli/Koca Çay	130	Lj	39.56N	28.32 E
Orhangazi	130	Mi	40.30N	29.18 E
Orhomenós	130	Fk	38.35N	22.54 E
Orhon (Orchon)	140	Md	50.21N	106.05 E
Orhy, Pico de-	126	La	43.00N	1.00W
Orichuna, Río-	196	Bi	7.30N	68.13W
Orick	188	Cf	41.17N	124.04W
Oriental	192	Kh	19.22N	97.37W
Oriental, Cordillera- [Col.]	198	Ie	6.00N	73.00W
Oriental, Cordillera- [Dom.Rep.]	194	Md	18.55N	69.15W
Oriente	206	He	38.44S	60.37W
Orihuela	126	Lf	38.05N	0.57W
Oriku	130	Ci	40.17N	19.25 E
Ori Lekánis	130	Hh	41.08N	24.33 E
Orillia	180	Jh	44.37N	79.25W
Orimattila	114	Ff	60.48N	25.45 E
Orinoco, Delta del-	202	Fb	9.15N	61.30W
Orinoco, Río-	198	Je	8.37N	62.15W
Oripää	116	Jd	60.51N	22.41 E
Orissa [3]	148	Gd	21.00N	84.00 E
Orissaare/Orissare	114	Fg	58.34N	23.05 E
Orissare/Orissaare	114	Fg	58.34N	23.05 E
Oristano	128	Ck	39.54N	8.36 E
Oristano, Golfo di-	128	Ck	39.50N	8.30 E
Orituco, Río-	196	Ch	8.45N	67.27W
Orivesi	114	Ff	61.41N	24.21 E
Orivesi	110	Ic	62.15N	29.25 E
Oriximiná	202	Gd	1.45S	55.52W
Orizaba	176	Jh	18.51N	97.06W
Orizaba, Pico de- (Citlaltépetl, Volcán-)	174	Jh	19.01N	97.16W
Orizona	204	Hc	17.03S	48.18W
Orjahovo	130	Gf	43.44N	23.58 E
Ørje	116	De	59.29N	11.39 E
Orjen	130	Bg	42.34N	18.33 E
Orjiva	126	Ih	36.54N	3.25W
Orkanger	114	Be	63.19N	9.52 E
Orkdalen	116	Ca	63.15N	9.50 E
Örkelljunga	116	Eh	56.17N	13.17 E
Orkla	116	Ca	63.18N	9.50 E
Orkney	172	De	27.00S	26.39 E
Orkney [3]	118	Kb	59.00N	3.00W
Orkney Islands	110	Fd	59.00N	3.00W
Orla	120	Me	51.35N	16.40 E
Orlândia	204	Ie	20.43S	47.53W
Orlando	176	Kg	28.32N	81.23W
Orlando, Capo d'-	128	Il	38.10N	14.45 E
Orlanka	120	Td	52.52N	23.12 E
Orléanais	122	Hf	48.40N	1.20 E
Orléans	112	Gf	47.55N	1.54 E
Orlice	120	Lf	50.12N	15.49 E
Orlické Hory	120	Mf	50.10N	16.30 E
Orlik	138	Ef	52.30N	99.55 E
Orlov (Halturin)	136	Ed	58.35N	48.55 E
Orlovskaja oblast	136	De	52.45N	36.30 E
Orlovski	132	Mf	46.52N	42.06 E
Orlovski, mys-	114	Jc	67.16N	41.18 E
Orly	122	If	48.45N	2.24 E
Ormāra	148	Cc	25.12N	64.38 E
Ormes	124	Ce	49.03N	0.59 E
Ormoc	150	Hd	11.00N	124.37 E
Ormond	218	Gc	38.33S	177.55 E
Ormond Beach	184	Gk	29.17N	81.02W
Ornain	122	Kf	48.46N	4.47 E
Ornans	122	Mg	47.06N	6.09 E
Ornäs	116	Fd	60.31N	15.32 E
Orne [3]	122	Gf	48.40N	0.05 E
Orne [Fr.]	122	Me	49.17N	6.11 E
Orne [Fr.]	122	Fe	49.19N	0.14W
Orne Seamount (EN)	216	Je	27.30S	157.30W
Orneta	120	Qb	54.08N	20.08 E
Ornö	116	He	59.05N	18.25 E
Örnsköldsvik	114	Ee	63.18N	18.43 E
Oro	154	Id	40.01N	127.27 E
Oro, Río de-	204	Ch	27.04S	58.34W
Oro, Río del-	192	Ge	25.35N	105.03W
Orocué	202	Dc	4.48N	71.20W
Orodara	166	Ec	10.59N	4.55W
Orofino	188	Gc	46.29N	116.15W
Orogrande	186	Cj	32.23N	106.08W
Orohena, Mont-	221e	Fc	17.31S	149.28W
Oroluk Atoll	208	Gd	7.32N	155.18 E
Orom	170	Fb	3.20N	33.40 E
Oromocto	180	Kg	45.51N	66.29W
Oron	166	Ge	4.50N	8.14 E
Orona Atoll (Hull)	208	Je	4.29S	172.10W
Orongo	221d	Ac	27.10S	109.26W
Oronsay	118	Ge	56.01N	6.14W
Orontes (EN) = 'Āṣī, Nahr al-	144	Eb	36.02N	35.58 E
Oropesa	126	Ge	39.55N	5.10W
Oropesa / Orpesa	126	Md	40.06N	0.09 E
Oroqen Zizhiqi (Alihe)	152	La	50.35N	123.42 E
Oroquieta	150	He	8.29N	123.48 E
Orós	202	Ke	6.15S	38.55W
Orós, Açude-	202	Ke	6.15S	39.05W
Orosei	128	Dj	40.23N	9.42 E
Orosei, Golfo di-	128	Dj	40.15N	9.45 E
Orosháza	120	Qj	46.34N	20.40 E
Oro-Shima	156	Be	33.52N	130.02 E
Oroszlány	120	Oi	47.29N	18.19 E
Orote Peninsula	220c	Bb	13.26N	144.38 E
Orote Point	220c	Bb	13.27N	144.37 E
Orotukan	138	Kd	62.17N	151.50 E
Oroville [Ca.-U.S.]	188	Eg	39.31N	121.33W
Oroville [Wa.-U.S.]	188	Fb	48.56N	119.26W
Orpesa / Oropesa	126	Md	40.06N	0.09 E
Orp-Jauche	124	Gd	50.40N	4.57 E
Orqohan	152	Lb	49.36N	121.23 E
Orr	186	Jb	48.03N	92.50W
Orrefors	116	Fh	56.50N	15.45 E
Orri, Pic de l'- / Llorri	126	Nb	42.23N	1.12 E
Orsa	114	Df	61.07N	14.37 E
Orša	112	Je	54.30N	30.24 E
Orsasjön	116	Fc	61.05N	14.35 E
Orsay	124	Ef	48.42N	2.11 E
Orsjön	116	Gc	61.35N	16.20 E
Orsk	112	Le	51.12N	58.34 E
Orşova	130	Fe	44.42N	22.25 E
Ørsta	114	Be	62.12N	6.09 E
Örsundsbro	116	Ge	59.44N	17.18 E
Orta, Lago d'- (Cusio)	128	Ce	45.50N	8.25 E
Ortaca	146	Cd	36.49N	28.47 E
Ortakent	130	Kl	37.02N	27.21 E
Ortaklar	130	Kl	37.53N	27.30 E
Orta Nova	128	Ji	41.19N	15.42 E
Orte	128	Gh	42.27N	12.23 E
Ortegal, Cabo-	126	Ea	43.45N	7.53W
Ortenberg	124	Ld	50.21N	9.03 E
Orthez	122	Fk	43.29N	0.46W
Orthon, Río-	202	Ef	10.50S	66.04W
Ortigueira [Braz.]	206	Jb	24.12S	50.55W
Ortigueira [Sp.]	126	Ea	43.34N	7.44W
Ortisei / Sankt Ulrich in Gröden	128	Fd	46.34N	11.40 E
Ortiz [Mex.]	192	Dc	28.15N	110.43W
Ortiz [Ven.]	196	Ch	9.37N	67.17W
Ortles/Ortlergruppe	128	Ed	46.30N	10.40 E
Ortolo	122a	Ab	41.30N	8.55 E
Ortona	128	Ih	42.21N	14.24 E
Ortonville	186	Hd	45.19N	96.27W
Orto-Tokoj	135	Kc	42.20N	76.02 E
Örtze	120	Fd	52.40N	9.57 E
Orukuizu	220a	Ac	7.10N	134.17 E
Orūmīyeh	142	Gf	37.33N	45.04 E
Orūmīyeh, Daryācheh-ye-= Urmia, Lake- (EN)	140	Gf	37.40N	45.30 E
Oruro	200	Jg	17.59S	67.09W
Oruro [3]	202	Eg	18.40S	67.30W
Orust	116	Df	58.10N	11.38 E
Orūzgān	144	Kc	32.56N	66.38 E
Orūzgān [3]	144	Kc	33.15N	66.00 E
Orval, Abbaye d'-	124	He	49.38N	5.22 E
Orvault	122	Eg	47.16N	1.37W
Orvieto	128	Gh	42.43N	12.07 E
Orville Escarpment	222	Qf	75.45S	65.30W
Orvilos, Óros-	130	Gh	41.23N	23.36 E
Orwell	124	Dc	51.58N	1.18 E
Orxois	124	Fe	49.08N	3.12 E
Orz	120	Rd	52.50N	21.30 E
Orzinuovi	128	De	45.24N	9.55 E
Orzyc	120	Rd	52.47N	21.13 E
Orzysz	120	Rc	53.49N	21.56 E
Oš	136	Hg	40.32N	72.50 E
Os	114	Ce	62.30N	11.12 E
Osa	136	Fd	57.17N	55.26 E
Oša	116	Lh	56.21N	26.29 E
Osa	120	Oc	53.33N	18.45 E
Osa, Península de-	190	Hg	8.35N	83.33W
Osage	186	Je	43.17N	92.49W
Osage River	182	Id	38.35N	91.57W
Ōsaka	142	Pf	34.40N	135.30 E
Osaka	156	Ed	35.57N	137.14 E
Osaka Bay (EN)=Ōsaka-Wan	154	Mg	34.36N	135.27 E
Ōsaka-Fu [2]	154	Mg	34.45N	135.35 E
Osakarovka	136	He	50.32N	72.39 E
Ōsaka-Wan=Osaka Bay (EN)	154	Mg	34.36N	135.27 E
Osām	130	Hf	43.42N	24.51 E
Osan	154	If	37.09N	127.04 E
Osasco	204	If	23.32S	46.46W
Osat	128	Nf	44.02N	19.20 E
Osawatomie	186	Ig	38.31N	94.57W
Osborne	186	Gg	39.26N	98.42W
Osburger Hochwald	124	Je	49.40N	6.50 E
Osby	114	Ch	56.22N	13.59 E
Osceola [Ar.-U.S.]	186	Li	35.42N	89.58W
Osceola [Ia.-U.S.]	182	Ic	41.02N	93.46W
Osceola [Mo.-U.S.]	186	Jh	38.03N	93.42W
Oschatz	120	Je	51.18N	13.07 E
Oschersleben	120	Hd	52.02N	11.15 E
Oschiri	128	Dj	40.43N	9.06 E
Osen	114	Cd	64.18N	10.31 E
Osered	132	Ld	50.01N	40.48 E
Osetr	132	Kb	55.00N	38.45 E
Ōse-Zaki	154	Jh	32.38N	128.42 E
Oshamanbe	154	Pc	42.30N	140.22 E
Oshawa	180	Jh	43.54N	78.51W
Oshekehia Lake	172	Bc	18.08S	15.45 E
Oshika	156	Gb	38.17N	141.31 E
Oshika-Hantō	154	Pe	38.22N	141.27 E
Oshikango	172	Bc	17.22S	15.55 E
Ōshima	156	Fd	34.44N	139.20 E
Ōshima	156	Ce	33.55N	132.11 E
Ōshima	156	Ae	33.04N	129.36 E
Ō-Shima [Jap.]	156	De	33.28N	135.50 E
Ō-Shima [Jap.]	154	Od	41.30N	139.15 E
Ō-Shima [Jap.]	154	Jh	32.04N	128.26 E
Ō-Shima [Jap.]	156	De	33.38N	134.30 E
Ō-Shima [Jap.]	156	Be	33.54N	130.27 E
Ō-Shima [Jap.]	156	Ae	32.34N	128.54 E
Ō-Shima [Jap.]	156	Ae	33.30N	129.33 E
Ō-Shima [Jap.]	156	Cd	34.10N	133.05 E
Ō-Shima [Jap.]	156	Bf	31.32N	131.25 E
Ō-Shima [Jap.]	152	Oe	34.54N	139.30 E
Oshima-Hantō	154	Pd	41.40N	140.30 E
Ōshima-Kaikyō	156b	Ba	28.10N	129.15 E
Oshkosh [Nb.-U.S.]	186	Ef	41.24N	102.21W
Oshkosh [Wi.-U.S.]	182	Jc	44.01N	88.33W
Oshnavīyeh	146	Kd	37.02N	45.06 E
Oshogbo	160	Hh	7.46N	4.34 E
Oshtorān Kūh	144	Gc	33.20N	49.16 E
Oshtorīnān	146	Me	34.01N	48.38 E
Oshwe	170	Cc	3.24S	19.30 E
Osich'ŏn-ni	154	Jd	41.25N	128.16 E
Osijek	112	Hf	45.33N	18.42 E
Osilo	128	Cj	40.45N	8.40 E
Osimo	128	Hg	43.28N	13.29 E
Osinki	114	Lj	52.52N	49.31 E
Osinniki	138	Df	53.37N	87.31 E
Osipaonica	130	Ee	44.33N	21.04 E
Osipoviči	132	Fc	53.19N	28.40 E
Osječenica	128	Kf	44.29N	16.17 E
Oskaloosa	186	Jf	41.18N	92.39W
Oskarshamn	114	Dh	57.16N	16.26 E
Oskarström	116	Eh	56.48N	12.58 E
Oskélanéo	184	Ja	48.08N	75.05W
Oskino	138	Fd	60.48N	107.58 E
Öskjuvatn	114a	Cb	65.02N	16.45W
Oskol	132	Je	49.06N	37.25 E
Oskū	146	Ld	37.55N	46.06 E
Oslava	120	Mg	49.05N	16.22 E
Ösling	122	Le	49.55N	6.00 E
Osljanka, gora-	134	Ig	59.10N	58.33 E
Oslo	112	Hd	59.55N	10.45 E
Oslo [2]	114	Cg	59.55N	10.45 E
Oslofjorden	110	Hd	59.20N	10.35 E
Osmānābād	148	Fe	18.10N	76.03 E
Osmancık	146	Fb	40.59N	34.49 E
Osmaneli	130	Ni	40.22N	30.01 E
Osmaniye	144	Eb	37.05N	36.14 E
Osmino	116	Mf	58.54N	29.15 E
Osmjanskaja vozvyšennost	116	Kj	54.30N	26.00 E
Osmjany	132	Db	54.27N	25.57 E
Ösmo	116	Gf	58.59N	17.54 E
Osmussaar/Osmussar	116	Je	59.20N	23.15 E
Osmussar/Osmussaar	116	Je	59.20N	23.15 E
Osnabrück	112	Ge	52.16N	8.03 E
Osning	124	Kb	52.10N	8.05 E
Oso, Sierra del-	192	Gd	26.00N	105.25W
Osobloga	120	Nf	50.27N	17.58 E
Osogovske Planine	130	Fg	42.10N	22.30 E
Osor	128	If	44.42N	14.24 E
Osório	206	Jc	29.54S	50.16W
Osorno	200	Ij	40.34S	73.09W
Osoyoos	180	Fg	49.02N	119.28W
Osøyra	114	Af	60.11N	5.28 E
Ospino	196	Bh	9.18N	69.27W
Osprey Reef	208	Ff	13.55S	146.40 E
Oss	122	Lc	51.46N	5.31 E
Ossa, Mount-	208	Fi	41.54S	146.01 E
Ossa, Óros-	130	Fj	39.49N	22.40 E
Ossabaw Island	184	Gj	31.47N	81.06W
Ossa de Montiel	126	Jf	38.58N	2.45W
Osse	122	Gj	44.07N	0.17 E
Ossining	184	Ke	41.10N	73.52W
Ossjøen	116	Dc	61.15N	11.55 E
Osškaja oblast [3]	136	Hg	40.45N	73.20 E
Ossora	138	Le	59.15N	163.02 E
Ostanvik	116	Fc	61.10N	15.13 E
Ostaškov	136	Dd	57.09N	33.07 E
Ostbevern	124	Jb	52.03N	7.51 E
Oste	120	Fc	53.50N	9.05 E
Ostende/Oostende	122	Ic	51.14N	2.55 E
Oster [Ukr.]	132	Gd	50.55N	30.57 E
Oster [Ukr.]	132	Gd	50.53N	30.55 E
Oster [Eur.]	132	Gc	53.47N	31.45 E
Osterburg in der Altmark	120	Hd	52.47N	11.44 E
Österbybruk	116	Gd	60.12N	17.54 E
Österdalälven	114	Df	60.33N	15.08 E
Østerdalen	114	Cf	62.00N	10.40 E
Osterfjorden	116	Ad	60.30N	5.20 E
Osterforse	116	Ga	63.09N	17.01 E
Östergarnsholm	116	Hg	57.25N	19.00 E
Östergötland [2]	114	Dg	58.25N	15.45 E
Östergötland	116	Ff	58.25N	15.35 E
Osterholz Scharmbeck	120	Ec	53.14N	8.48 E
Österlen	116	Fi	55.30N	14.10 E
Östermark/Teuva	114	Ee	62.29N	21.44 E
Osterode am Harz	120	Ge	51.44N	10.11 E
Osterøya	114	Af	60.35N	5.35 E
Österreich = Austria (EN) [1]	112	Hf	47.30N	14.00 E
Östersjön=Baltic Sea (EN)	110	Hd	57.00N	19.00 E
Østersøen=Baltic Sea (EN)	110	Hd	57.00N	19.00 E
Östersund	112	Hc	63.11N	14.39 E
Osterwick, Rosendahl-	124	Jb	52.01N	7.12 E
Østfold [2]	114	Cg	59.20N	11.30 E
Ostfriesische Inseln=East Frisian Islands (EN)	120	Dc	53.45N	7.25 E
Ostfriesland=East Friesland (EN)	120	Dc	53.20N	7.40 E
Østgrønland=East Greenland (EN) [2]	179	Id	72.00N	35.00W
Östhammar	114	Ed	60.16N	18.22 E
Osthofen	124	Ke	49.42N	8.20 E
Östmark	116	Ed	60.17N	12.45 E
Ostrach	120	Fh	48.05N	9.25 E
Östra Silen	116	Ee	59.15N	12.20 E
Ostrava	112	Hf	49.50N	18.17 E
Ostrhauderfehn	124	Ja	53.08N	7.37 E
Ostróda	120	Pc	53.43N	19.59 E
Ostrog	132	Ed	50.19N	26.32 E
Ostrogožsk	136	De	50.52N	39.05 E
Ostrołęka	120	Rc	53.06N	21.34 E
Ostrołęka [2]	120	Rc	53.05N	21.35 E
Ostrošicki Gorodok	116	Lj	54.03N	27.46 E
Ostrov [Bela.]	120	Vd	52.48N	26.01 E
Ostrov [Czech.]	120	If	50.18N	12.57 E
Ostrov [Rom.]	130	Ke	44.07N	27.22 E
Ostrov [Russia]	136	Cd	57.23N	28.22 E
Ostrov [Russia]	116	Mf	58.28N	28.44 E
Ostrovec	116	Lj	54.38N	26.06 E
Ostrovicës, Mali i-	130	Di	40.34N	20.27 E
Ostrovskoje	114	Kh	57.50N	42.13 E
Ostrowiec Świętokrzyski	120	Rf	50.57N	21.23 E
Ostrów Lubelski	120	Se	51.30N	22.52 E
Ostrów Mazowiecka	120	Rd	52.49N	21.54 E
Ostrów Wielkopolski	120	Ne	51.39N	17.49 E
Ostryna	120	Uc	53.41N	24.37 E
Ostrzeszów	120	Ne	51.25N	17.57 E
Ostsee=Baltic Sea (EN)	110	Hd	57.00N	19.00 E
Oststeirisches Hügelland	128	Jd	47.00N	15.45 E
Osttirol	128	Gd	46.55N	12.30 E
Ostuni	128	Lj	40.44N	17.35 E
Ōsumi	156	Bf	31.36N	130.59 E
Osumi	130	Ci	40.48N	19.52 E
Ōsumi-Hantō	156	Bf	31.15N	130.50 E
Ōsumi Islands (EN)=Ōsumi-Shotō	140	Pf	30.35N	130.59 E
Ōsumi-Shotō=Osumi Islands (EN)	140	Pf	30.35N	130.59 E
Osuna	126	Gg	37.14N	5.07W
Osveja	116	Mi	55.59N	28.10 E
Osvejskoje, ozero-	116	Mh	56.00N	28.15 E
Oswego	182	Lc	43.27N	76.31W
Oswestry	118	Ji	52.52N	3.04W
Oświęcim	120	Pf	50.03N	19.12 E
Osyka	186	Kk	31.00N	90.28W
Ōta	156	Fc	36.18N	139.22 E
Ota	156	Ed	35.56N	136.03 E
Otago [2]	218	Cf	45.00S	169.10 E
Otago Peninsula	218	Df	45.50S	170.45 E
Ōtake	154	Lg	34.12N	132.13 E
Otakeho	218	Fc	39.33S	174.03 E
Otaki	218	Fd	40.45S	175.08 E
Ōtakime-Yama	156	Gc	37.22N	140.42 E
Otanoshike	156a	Db	43.01N	144.16 E
Otar	136	Hg	43.31N	75.12 E
Otaru	152	Pc	43.13N	141.00 E
Otautau	218	Bg	46.09S	168.00 E
Otava	116	Lc	61.39N	27.04 E
Otava	120	Kg	49.26N	14.12 E
Otavi	172	Bc	19.39S	17.20 E
Otawara	154	Pf	36.52N	140.02 E

Ote-Pal

Index Symbols

Independent Nation	Historical or Cultural Region	Pass, Gap	Depression
State, Region	Mount, Mountain	Plain, Lowland	Polder
District, County	Volcano	Delta	Desert, Dunes
Municipality	Hill	Salt Flat	Forest, Woods
Colony, Dependency	Mountains, Mountain Range	Valley, Canyon	Heath, Steppe
Continent	Hills, Escarpment	Crater, Cave	Oasis
Physical Region	Plateau, Upland	Karst Features	Cape, Point

Coast, Beach	Rock, Reef	Waterfall, Rapids	Canal
Cliff	Islands, Archipelago	River Mouth, Estuary	Glacier
Peninsula	Rocks, Reefs	Lake	Ice Shelf, Pack Ice
Isthmus	Coral Reef	Salt Lake	Ocean
Sandbank	Well, Spring	Intermittent Lake	Sea
Island	Geyser	Reservoir	Gulf, Bay
Atoll	River, Stream	Swamp, Pond	Strait, Fjord

Lagoon	Escarpment, Sea Scarp	Historic Site	Airport
Bank	Fracture	Ruins	Port
Seamount	Trench, Abyss	Wall, Walls	Military installation
Tablemount	National Park, Reserve	Church, Abbey	Lighthouse
Ridge	Point of Interest	Temple	Mine
Shelf	Recreation Site	Scientific Station	Tunnel
Basin	Cave, Cavern	Railway station	Dam, Bridge

Pal-Pat

Paldiski 136 Cd 59.20N 24.06 E
Pale di San Martino 128 Fd 46.14N 11.53 E
Paleleh 150 Hf 1.04N 121.57 E
Palembang 142 Mj 2.55S 104.45 E
Palena 128 Ii 41.59N 14.08 E
Palencia 126 Hb 42.01N 4.32W
Palencia [3] 126 Hb 42.25N 4.30W
Palen Lake 188 Hj 33.46N 115.12W
Palenque 176 Jh 17.30N 92.00W
Palenque [Mex.] 192 Ni 17.31N 91.58W
Palenque [Pan.] 194 Hi 9.13N 79.41W
Palenque, Punta- 194 Ld 18.14N 70.09W
Palermo 112 Hh 38.07N 13.22 E
Palermo, Golfo di- 128 Hl 38.10N 13.25 E
Palestina = Palestine (EN) 144 Dc 32.15N 34.47 E
Palestina = Palestine (EN) 146 Ff 32.15N 34.47 E
Palestine 182 He 31.46N 95.38W
Palestine (EN) = Palestina 144 Dc 32.15N 34.47 E
Palestine (EN) = Palestina 146 Ff 32.15N 34.47 E
Palestrina 128 Gi 41.50N 12.53 E
Pālghāt 148 Ff 10.47N 76.39 E
Palgrave Point 172 Ad 20.28S 13.16 E
Palhoça 204 Hh 27.38S 48.40W
Pāli 148 Ec 25.46N 73.20 E
Palinuro, Capo- 128 Jj 40.02N 15.16 E
Palinuro, Centola- 128 Jj 40.02N 15.17 E
Palisades Reservoir 188 Je 43.04N 111.26W
Paliseul 124 He 49.54N 5.08 E
Palivere 116 Jf 59.00N 23.45 E
Palizada 192 Mh 18.15N 92.05W
Paljakka 114 Gd 64.45N 28.07 E
Paljavaam 138 Mc 68.50N 170.50 E
Paljenik 110 Hg 44.15N 17.36 E
Pälkäne 116 Kc 61.20N 24.16 E
Palkino 116 Mg 57.29N 28.10 E
Palk Strait 140 Ji 10.00N 79.45 E
Palla Bianca/Weißkugel 128 Ed 46.48N 10.44 E
Pallars 126 Mb 42.25N 0.55 E
Pallasovka 136 Ee 50.03N 46.55 E
Pallastunturi 114 Fb 68.06N 24.02 E
Palliser, Cape- 216 Eh 41.37S 175.16 E
Palliser, Iles- 208 Mf 15.30S 146.30W
Palma 172 Gb 10.46S 40.28 E
Palma / La Ciutat de Mallorca 112 Gh 39.34N 2.39 E
Palma, Badia de-/Palma, Bahia de- 126 Oe 39.27N 2.35 E
Palma, Bahia de-/Palma, Badia de- 126 Oe 39.27N 2.35 E
Palma, Rio- 202 If 12.33S 47.52W
Palma, Sierra de la- 192 Id 26.00N 101.35W
Palma del Rio 126 Gg 37.42N 5.17W
Palma di Montechiaro 128 Hm 37.11N 13.46 E
Palmar, Laguna del- 204 Bi 29.35S 60.42W
Palmar, Rio- 194 Lh 10.11N 71.52W
Palmar, Salto- 204 Cg 24.18S 59.18W
Palmares 202 Ke 8.41S 35.36W
Palmares do Sul 204 Gj 30.16S 50.31W
Palmarito 202 Db 7.37N 70.10W
Palmar Sur 190 Hg 8.58S 83.29W
Palmas [Braz.] 202 If 10.08S 48.18W
Palmas [Braz.] 206 Jc 26.30S 52.00W
Palmas, Cape- 158 Gh 4.22N 7.44W
Palmas, Golfo di- 128 Cl 39.00N 8.30 E
Palmas Bellas 194 Gi 9.14N 80.05W
Palma Soriano 190 Id 20.13N 76.00W
Palm Bay 184 Gk 28.01N 80.35W
Palm Beach 182 Kf 26.42N 80.02W
Palmdale 188 Fi 34.35N 118.07W
Palmeira 204 Gg 25.25S 50.00W
Palmeira das Missões 206 Jc 27.55S 53.17W
Palmeira dos Indios 202 Ke 9.25S 36.37W
Palmeirais 202 Je 5.58S 43.04W
Palmeiras, Rio- 204 Gb 15.25S 51.10W
Palmeiras de Goiás 204 Hc 16.47S 49.53W
Palmeirinhas, Ponta das- 158 Ii 9.05S 13.00 E
Palmela 126 Df 38.34N 8.54W
Palmer 178 Jd 61.36N 149.07W
Palmer Archipelago 222 Qe 64.10S 62.00W
Palmer Land (EN) 222 Qf 71.30S 65.00W
Palmer Station 222 Qe 64.46S 64.05W
Palmerston 218 Df 45.29S 170.43 E
Palmerston Atoll 208 Kf 18.04S 163.10W
Palmerston North 210 Ii 40.28S 175.17 E
Palmetto Point 197d Ba 17.35N 61.52W
Palmi 128 Jl 38.21N 15.51 E
Palmira [Col.] 200 Ie 3.32N 76.16W
Palmira [Cuba] 194 Gb 22.14N 80.23W
Palm Islands 212 Jc 18.40S 146.30 E
Palmital 204 Fg 24.39S 52.16W
Palmitas 204 Dk 33.27S 57.48W
Palmito 204 Cd 18.53S 58.22W
Palmitos 204 Fh 27.05S 53.08W
Palm Springs 182 De 33.50N 116.33W
Palmyra 144 Ec 34.33N 38.17 E
Palmyra Atoll 208 Kd 5.52N 162.06W
Palo Alto 182 Cd 37.27N 122.09W
Paloh 150 Ef 1.43N 109.18 E
Paloich 168 Ec 10.28N 32.32 E
Palomani, Nevado- 198 Jg 14.38S 69.14W
Palomar Mountain 182 De 33.22N 116.50W
Palomera, Sierra- 126 Kd 40.40N 1.12W
Palopo 142 Oj 3.00S 120.12 E
Palos, Cabo de- 110 Fh 37.38N 0.41W
Palo Santo 204 Cg 25.34S 59.21W
Palotina 204 Fg 24.17S 53.50W
Palouse River 188 Fc 46.35N 118.13W
Palpa 202 Cf 14.32S 75.11W
Palsa 116 Lg 57.23N 26.24 E
Pålsboda 116 Fe 59.04N 15.20 E
Paltamo 114 Gd 64.25N 27.50 E
Palu [Indon.] 142 Nj 0.53S 119.53 E
Palu [Tur.] 146 Hc 38.42N 39.57 E
Palu, Pulau- 150 Hh 8.20S 121.43 E
Pam 219b Be 20.15S 164.17 E
Pama 166 Fc 11.15N 0.42 E
Påmark/Pomarkku 116 Ic 61.42N 22.00 E
Pambarra 172 Fd 21.56S 35.06 E
Pambeguwa 166 Gc 10.40N 8.17 E
Pamekasan 150 Fh 7.10S 113.28 E
Pamiers 122 Hk 43.07N 1.36 E
Pamir 140 Jf 38.00N 73.00 E
Pamir 136 Hh 37.01N 72.41 E
Pâmiut/Frederikshåb 179 Hf 62.00N 49.45W
Pamlico Sound 182 Ld 35.20N 75.55W
Pampa 182 Gd 35.32N 100.58W
Pampa del Indio 204 Ch 26.02S 59.55W
Pampa del Infierno 204 Bh 26.31S 61.10W
Pampa de los Guanacos 206 Hc 26.14S 61.51W
Pampas 202 Df 12.24S 74.54W
Pampas 198 Ji 35.00S 63.00W
Pampeiro 204 Ej 30.38S 55.16W
Pamplona [Col.] 202 Db 7.23N 72.38W
Pamplona [Sp.] 112 Fg 42.49N 1.38W
Pamukkale 130 Ml 37.47N 29.04 E
Pamukova 130 Ni 40.31N 30.09 E
Pamunkey River 184 Ig 37.32N 76.48W
Pan, Tierra del- 126 Gc 41.50N 6.00W
Pana 186 Bc 1.41S 12.39 E
Panagjurište 130 Hg 42.30N 24.11 E
Panaitan, Pulau- 150 Eh 6.36S 105.12 E
Panaitolikón Óros 130 Ek 38.43N 21.39 E
Panaji (Panjim) 142 Jh 15.29N 73.50 E
Panakhaïkón Óros 130 Ek 38.12N 21.54 E
Panamá 176 Li 9.00N 80.00W
Panamá [Pan.] = Panama City (EN) 176 Li 8.58N 79.31W
Panamá = Panama (EN) [3] 194 Hi 9.00N 79.00W
Panama (EN) = Panamá [3] 194 Hi 9.00N 79.00W
Panamá, Bahia de- 194 Hi 8.50N 79.15W
Panamá, Canal de- = Panama Canal (EN) 190 Ig 9.20N 79.55W
Panamá, Golfo de- = Panama, Gulf of- (EN) 174 Li 8.00N 79.10W
Panama, Gulf of- (EN) = Panamá, Golfo de- 174 Li 8.00N 79.10W
Panama, Isthmus of- (EN) = Panamá, Istmo de- 174 Li 9.20N 79.30W
Panamá, Istmo de- = Panama, Isthmus of- (EN) 174 Li 9.20N 79.30W
Panama Canal (EN) = Panamá, Canal de- 190 Ig 9.20N 79.55W
Panama City 176 Kf 30.10N 85.41W
Panama City (EN) = Panamá [Pan.] 176 Li 8.58N 79.31W
Panamá La Vieja 194 Hi 9.00N 79.29W
Panambi 204 Fi 28.18S 53.30W
Panamint Range 188 Gh 36.30N 117.20W
Panao 202 Ce 9.49S 76.00W
Panarea 128 Jl 38.40N 15.05 E
Panaro 128 Ff 44.55N 11.25 E
Pana Tinai 219a Ad 11.14S 153.10 E
Pana-Wina 219a Ad 11.11S 153.01 E
Panay 140 Oh 11.15N 122.30 E
Pancake Range 188 Hg 39.00N 115.45W
Pančevo 130 De 44.52N 20.39 E
Pančičev vrh 130 Df 43.15N 20.45 E
Panciu 130 Kd 45.54N 27.05 E
Pancros 219b Db 15.58S 168.12 E
Panda 172 Ed 24.03S 34.43 E
Panda ma Tenga 172 Dc 18.32S 25.38 E
Pandan 150 Hd 11.43N 122.06 E
Pan de Azúcar 204 El 34.48S 55.14W
Pandeiros, Ribeirão- 204 Jb 15.42S 44.36W
Pandelis/Pandėlys 116 Kh 56.01N 25.21 E
Pandėlys/Pandelis 116 Kh 56.01N 25.21 E
Pandharpur 148 Fe 17.40N 75.20 E
Pándheon 130 Fi 40.05N 22.20 E
Pāndhurna 148 Fd 21.36N 78.31 E
Pandivere Kõrgustik / Pandivere vozvyšennost 116 Le 59.00N 26.15 E
Pandivere vozvyšennost / Pandivere Kõrgustik 116 Le 59.00N 26.15 E
Pando 206 Id 34.43S 55.57W
Pando [3] 202 Ef 11.20S 67.40W
Pandokrátor 130 Cj 39.45N 19.52 E
Pandora 194 Fi 9.45N 82.57W
Pandrup 116 Cg 57.14N 9.41 E
Pandu 170 Cb 4.59N 19.16 E
Panevežis/Panevėžys 136 Cd 55.44N 24.22 E
Panevėžys/Panevežis 136 Cd 55.44N 24.22 E
Panfilov 136 Ig 44.08N 80.01 E
Panga 170 Eb 1.51N 26.25 E
Pangai 221b Ba 19.48S 174.21W
Pangaion Óros 130 Hi 40.50N 24.05 E
Pangalanes, Canal de- 158 Lk 22.48S 47.50 E
Pangani 170 Gd 5.26S 38.58 E
Pangani or Ruvu 170 Gc 5.26S 38.58 E
Pange 124 Ie 49.05N 6.22 E
Panggoe 210 Ge 7.01S 157.05 E
Pangi 170 Ec 3.11S 26.38 E
Pangkajene 150 Gg 4.50S 119.32 E
Pangkalanberandan 150 Cf 4.01N 98.17 E
Pangkalanbuun 150 Fg 2.41S 111.37 E
Pangkalaseang, Tanjung- 150 Hg 0.42S 123.26 E
Pangkalpinang 150 Eg 2.08S 106.08 E
Pangnirtung 176 Mc 66.08N 65.44W
Pang-Pang 219b Dc 17.41S 168.32 E
Panguitch 182 Ed 37.49N 112.26W
Panguma 166 Cd 8.24N 11.13W
Pangutaran Group 150 He 6.15N 120.30 E
Panhandle 186 Fi 35.21N 101.23W
Pania Mutombo 170 Dd 5.11S 23.51 E
Paniau 221a Ab 21.57N 160.05W
Panié, Mont- 216 Bd 20.36S 164.46 E
Pānīpat 148 Fc 29.23N 76.58 E
Paniza, Puerto de- 126 Kc 41.15N 1.20W
Panjang 150 Eh 5.29S 105.18 E
Panjang, Pulau- 150 Ef 2.44N 108.55 E
Panjgūr 148 Cc 26.58N 64.06 E
Panjim → Panaji 142 Jh 15.29N 73.50 E
Panjwīn 146 Ke 35.36N 45.58 E
Pankow, Berlin- 120 Jd 52.34N 13.24 E
Pankshin 166 Gd 9.20N 9.27 E
P'anmunjŏm 154 If 37.57N 126.40 E
Panopah 150 Fg 1.56S 111.11 E
Panorama 206 Jb 21.21S 51.51W
Panshan 154 Gd 41.12N 122.03 E
Panshi 152 Mc 42.56N 126.02 E
Pant 124 Cc 51.53N 0.39 E
Pantanal 198 Kg 18.00S 56.00W
Pantar, Pulau- 150 Hh 8.25S 124.07 E
Pantego 184 Ih 35.34N 76.36W
Pantelleria 128 Fn 36.50N 11.57 E
Pantelleria 110 Hh 36.47N 12.00 E
Pantelleria, Canale di- 128 Fn 36.40N 11.45 E
Pante Makassar 150 Hh 9.12S 124.23 E
Pantoja 202 Cd 0.58S 75.10W
Pánuco 192 Jf 22.03N 98.10W
Pánuco 174 Jg 22.16N 97.47W
Panxian 152 Hf 25.45N 104.39 E
Panyam 166 Gd 9.25N 9.13 E
Panzi 170 Cd 7.13S 17.58 E
Panzós 194 Cf 15.24N 89.40W
Pao, Río- [Ven.] 196 Dh 8.06N 64.17W
Pao, Río- [Ven.] 196 Bh 8.33N 68.01W
Paola [It.] 128 Kk 39.21N 16.03 E
Paola [Ks.-U.S.] 186 Ig 38.35N 94.53W
Paoli 184 Df 38.33N 86.28W
Paopao 221e Fc 17.30S 149.49W
Paoua 168 Bd 7.15N 16.26 E
Pápa 120 Ni 47.20N 17.28 E
Papa 221a Fd 19.13N 155.52W
Papaaloa 221a Fd 19.59N 155.13W
Papagaio, Rio- → Saturninā, Rio- 204 Ca 13.55S 58.18W
Papagaios 204 Jd 19.32S 44.45W
Papagayo, Golfo del- 190 Gf 10.45N 85.45W
Papaikou 221a Fd 19.47N 155.06W
Papakura 218 Fb 37.03S 174.57 E
Papaloapan, Rio- 192 Lh 18.42N 95.38W
Papanduva 204 Gh 26.25S 50.09W
Papanin Seamount (EN) 224 Ca 46.00N 170.00 E
Papantla de Olarte 190 Ed 20.27N 97.19W
Papar 150 Ge 5.44N 115.56 E
Paparoa Range 218 De 42.05S 171.35 E
Papa Stour 118 La 60.30N 1.40W
Papa Westray 118 Kb 59.22N 2.54W
Papeete 210 Mf 17.32S 149.34W
Papenburg 120 Dc 53.04N 7.24 E
Papenburg-Aschendorf (Ems) 124 Ja 53.04N 7.22 E
Papenoo 221e Fc 17.30S 149.25W
Papes ezers / Papes ozero 116 Ih 56.15N 20.55 E
Papes ozero / Papes ezers 116 Ih 56.15N 20.55 E
Papetoai 221e Fc 17.30S 149.52W
Papey 114a Cb 64.36N 14.11W
Paphos/Baf 146 Ee 34.50N 32.35 E
Papija 130 Kg 42.07N 27.51 E
Papikion Óros 130 Ih 41.15N 25.18 E
Papile/Papilė 116 Jh 56.09N 22.45 E
Papilė/Papile 116 Jh 56.09N 22.45 E
Papillion 186 Hf 41.09N 96.03W
Papua, Gulf of- 208 Fe 8.32S 145.00 E
Papua New Guinea 210 Fe 6.00S 150.00 E
Papua Passage 220p Bc 21.15S 159.47W
Papuk 128 Le 45.31N 17.39 E
Papun 148 Je 18.04N 97.27 E
Pará [2] 202 Hd 4.00S 53.00W
Pará 114 Ji 54.23N 40.53 E
Pará, Rio- 198 Lf 1.30S 48.55W
Pará, Rio- 204 Jd 19.13S 45.07W
Parabel 138 De 58.43N 81.31 E
Parabel 138 De 58.40N 81.30 E
Paraburdoo 212 Dd 23.15S 117.45 E
Paracas 202 Cf 13.49S 76.16W
Paracatu 202 Ig 17.13S 46.52W
Paracatu, Rio- [Braz.] 204 Ic 17.30S 46.32W
Paracatu, Rio- [Braz.] 204 Jc 16.30S 45.04W
Paracel Islands (EN) = Xisha Qundao 140 Nh 16.30N 112.15 E
Pārachinār 148 Eb 33.54N 70.06 E
Paraćin 130 Ef 43.52N 21.25 E
Paracuru 202 Kd 3.24S 39.04W
Parada Km 329 204 Ek 32.30S 55.25W
Paradip 148 Hd 20.19N 86.42 E
Paradise [Ca.-U.S.] 188 Eg 39.46N 121.37W
Paradise [Mi.-U.S.] 184 Eb 46.38N 85.03W
Paragould 186 Kh 36.03N 90.29W
Paragua, Rio- 202 Fb 6.55N 62.55W
Paraguá, Rio- 202 Ff 13.34S 61.53W
Paraguaçu, Rio- 198 Mg 12.45S 38.54W
Paraguaçu Paulista 204 Gf 22.25S 50.34W
Paraguai, Rio- 198 Kh 27.18S 58.38W
Paraguaipoa 194 Lh 11.21N 71.57W
Paraguaná, Península de- 202 Da 11.55N 70.00W
Paraguari 206 Ic 25.38S 57.09W
Paraguari [3] 204 Dg 26.00S 57.10W
Paraguay 200 Kh 23.00S 58.00W
Paraguay, Rio- 198 Kh 27.18S 58.38W
Paraíba [2] 202 Ke 7.10S 36.30W
Paraiba do Sul, Rio- 198 Lh 21.37S 41.03W
Paraibuna, Represa do- 204 Jf 23.25S 45.35W
Paraibuna, Rio- 204 Jf 23.22S 45.40W
Parainen/Pargas 114 Ff 60.18N 22.18 E
Paraiso [Braz.] 204 Fd 19.03S 52.59W
Paraiso [Mex.] 192 Mh 18.24N 93.14W
Paraiso, Rio- 204 Bb 15.08S 61.52W
Parakou 160 Hh 9.21N 2.37 E
Param 220d Bb 7.22N 151.48 E
Paramaribo 200 Ke 5.50N 55.10W
Paramera, Sierra de la- 126 Hd 40.30N 4.46W
Paramithiá 130 Dj 39.28N 20.31 E
Páramo de Masa, Puerto de- 126 Ib 42.38N 3.44W
Paramušir, ostrov- 140 Rd 50.25N 155.50 E
Paraná 200 Ji 31.45S 60.30W
Paraná [2] 206 Jb 24.00S 51.00W
Paraná, Pico- 204 Hg 25.14S 48.48W
Paraná, Rio- 198 Ki 33.43S 59.15W
Paranã, Rio- 198 Lg 12.30S 48.14W
Paraná de las Palmas, Rio- 204 Cl 34.18S 58.33W
Paranaguá 200 Lh 25.31S 48.30W
Paraná-Guazú, Rio- 204 Ck 34.00S 58.25W
Paranaiba 202 Hg 19.40S 51.11W
Paranaíba, Rio- 198 Kh 20.07S 51.05W
Paranaiguara 204 Gd 18.53S 50.28W
Paranapanema, Rio- 198 Kh 22.40S 53.09W
Paranapiacaba, Serra do- 198 Lh 24.20S 49.00W
Paranapuã-Guaçu, Ponta do- 204 Ig 24.24S 47.00W
Paranavai 206 Jb 23.04S 52.28W
Parandak 146 Ne 35.21N 50.42 E
Paranéstion 130 Hh 41.16N 24.30 E
Paranhos 204 Ef 23.55S 55.25W
Paraoa Atoll 208 Mf 19.09S 140.43W
Paraopeba 204 Jd 19.18S 44.25W
Paraopeba, Rio- 204 Jd 18.50S 45.11W
Parapara 219b Ca 13.32S 167.20 E
Paraparaumu 218 Fd 40.55S 175.00 E
Paraspóri 130 Kn 35.54N 27.14 E
Parati 204 Jf 23.13S 44.43W
Paratodos, Serra- 204 Jb 14.40S 44.50W
Paratunka 138 Kf 52.52N 158.12 E
Pārāu, Kūh-e- 146 Le 34.37N 47.05 E
Paraúna 204 Gc 17.02S 50.26W
Paravae 220n Bc 10.27S 160.58W
Paray-le-Monial 122 Kh 46.27N 4.07 E
Parbati 148 Fc 25.51N 76.36 E
Parbhani 148 Fe 19.16N 76.47 E
Parchim 120 Hc 53.26N 11.51 E
Parczew 120 Se 51.39N 22.54 E
Pardo 204 Cm 36.15S 59.22W
Pardo, Rio- [Braz.] 204 Jb 15.48S 44.48W
Pardo, Rio- [Braz.] 204 He 20.10S 48.38W
Pardo, Rio- [Braz.] 204 Hf 22.55S 49.58W
Pardo, Rio- [Braz.] 204 Fi 29.59S 52.23W
Pardo, Rio- [Braz.] 202 Hh 21.46S 52.09W
Pardo, Rio- [Braz.] 202 Kg 15.39S 38.57W
Pardubice 120 Lf 50.02N 15.45 E
Parea 221e Eb 16.49S 150.58W
Parecis, Chapada dos- 198 Kg 13.00S 60.00W
Parecis, Rio- 204 Da 12.56S 56.43W
Paredes de Nava 126 Hb 42.09N 4.41W
Parelhas 202 Ke 6.41S 36.39W
Paren 138 Ld 62.28N 163.05 E
Parent 180 Kg 47.55N 74.37W
Parentis-en-Born 122 Ej 44.21N 1.04W
Pareora 218 Df 44.29S 171.13 E
Parepare 142 Nj 4.01S 119.38 E
Pârga 130 Dj 39.17N 20.24 E
Pargas/Parainen 114 Ff 60.18N 22.18 E
Pargolovo 116 Nd 60.03N 30.30 E
Parham 197d Bb 17.05N 61.46W
Parhar 136 Gh 37.31N 69.23 E
Pari, Rio- 204 Db 15.36S 56.08W
Paria, Golfo de-/Paria, Gulf of- 202 Fa 10.20N 62.00W
Paria, Gulf of-/Paria, Golfo de- 202 Fa 10.20N 62.00W
Paria, Peninsula de- 196 Eg 10.40N 62.30W
Pariaguán 202 Fb 8.51N 64.43W
Pariaman 150 Dg 0.38S 100.08 E
Paria River 188 Jh 36.52N 111.36W
Paricutin, Volcan- 192 Hh 19.28N 102.15W
Parida, Isla- 194 Fi 8.07N 82.20W
Pari das Pedras 204 Ja 12.45S 44.47W
Parigi 150 Hg 0.48S 120.10 E
Parika 202 Gb 6.52N 58.25W
Parikkala 114 Gf 61.33N 29.30 E
Parima, Serra- 198 Je 3.00N 64.20W
Parinacota 206 Ga 18.12S 69.16W
Pariñas, Punta- 198 Hf 4.40S 81.20W
Paringul Mare, Virful- 130 Gd 45.20N 23.30 E
Parintins 200 Kf 2.36S 56.44W
Paris [Fr.] 112 Gf 48.52N 2.20 E
Paris [Il.-U.S.] 186 Mg 39.36N 87.42W
Paris [Kir.] 220g Ab 1.56N 157.31W
Paris [Ky.-U.S.] 184 Ef 38.13N 84.14W
Paris [Tn.-U.S.] 184 Cg 36.19N 88.20W
Paris [Tx.-U.S.] 182 He 33.40N 95.33W
Paris Basin (EN) = Parisien, Bassin- 110 Gf 49.00N 2.00 E
Parisien, Bassin- = Paris Basin (EN) 110 Gf 49.00N 2.00 E
Parita 194 Gi 8.00N 80.31W
Parita, Bahia de- 194 Gi 8.08N 80.24W
Parit Buntar 150 De 5.07N 100.30 E
Parkano 114 Fe 62.01N 23.01 E
Parkent 135 Gd 41.18N 69.40 E
Parker 188 Hi 34.09N 114.17W
Parker, Mount- 212 Fc 17.10S 128.20 E
Parkersburg 182 Kd 39.17N 81.33W
Parker Seamount (EN) 178 If 52.35N 151.15W
Parkes 210 Fh 33.08S 148.11 E
Park Falls 186 Kd 45.56N 90.27W
Parkland 188 Dc 47.09N 122.26W
Park Range 182 Fc 40.00N 106.30W
Park Rapids 186 Ic 46.55N 95.04W
Park River 186 Hb 48.24N 97.45W
Park Valley 188 If 41.50N 113.21W
Parma 128 Ef 44.56N 10.26 E
Parma [It.] 128 Eg 44.48N 10.20 E
Parma [Oh.-U.S.] 184 Ge 41.24N 81.44W
Parnaguá 202 Jf 10.13S 44.38W
Parnaiba 200 Lf 2.54S 41.47W
Parnaiba, Rio- 198 Lf 3.00S 41.50W
Parnamirim [Braz.] 202 Ke 8.05S 39.34W
Parnamirim [Braz.] 202 Ke 5.55S 35.15W
Parnarama 202 Je 5.41S 43.06W
Parnassós Óros = Parnassus (EN) 110 Ih 38.30N 22.37 E
Parnassus 218 Ee 42.43S 173.17 E
Parnassus (EN) = Parnassós Óros 110 Ih 38.30N 22.37 E
Párnis Óros 130 Gk 38.10N 23.40 E
Párnon Óros 130 Fl 37.12N 22.38 E
Pärnu/Pjarnu 112 Id 58.24N 24.32 E
Pärnu-Jaagupi/Pjarnu-Jagupi 116 Kf 58.36N 24.25 E
Pärnu jõgi / Pjarnu 114 Fg 58.23N 24.34 E
Pärnu laht / Pjarnu, zaliv- 114 Fg 58.15N 24.25 E
Parola 116 Kc 61.03N 24.22 E
Paroo River 208 Fh 31.28S 143.32 E
Paropamisus/Salseleh-ye Safid Kūh 140 If 34.30N 63.30 E
Páros 130 Il 37.06N 25.09 E
Páros 130 Il 37.06N 25.12 E
Parowan 188 Ih 37.51N 112.57W
Parpaillon 122 Mj 44.35N 6.40 E
Parque Industrial 204 Jd 19.57S 44.01W
Parral 206 Fe 36.09S 71.50W
Parral, Rio- 192 Gd 27.35N 105.25W
Parras, Sierra de- 192 He 25.25N 102.00W
Parras de la Fuente 190 Dc 25.25N 102.11W
Parravicini 204 Dm 36.27S 57.46W
Parrett 118 Jj 51.13N 3.01W
Parrita 194 Ei 9.30N 84.19W
Parry, Cape - 180 Fb 70.12N 124.35W
Parry, Kap- [Grld.] 179 Jd 72.28N 22.00W
Parry, Kap- [Grld.] 179 Ec 77.00N 71.00W
Parry Bay 180 Jc 68.00N 82.00W
Parry Islands 174 Ib 76.00N 110.00W
Parry Peninsula 180 Fc 69.45N 124.35W
Parry Sound 180 Jg 45.21N 80.02W
Parseta 120 Lb 54.12N 15.33 E
Parsons [Ks.-U.S.] 182 Hd 37.20N 95.16W
Parsons [W.V.-U.S.] 184 Hf 39.06N 79.43W
Parsons Range 212 Hb 13.30S 135.15 E
Partanna 128 Gm 37.43N 12.53 E
Parthenay 122 Fh 46.39N 0.15W
Partille 116 Eg 57.44N 12.07 E
Partinico 128 Hl 38.03N 13.07 E
Partizansk 138 Ih 43.13N 133.05 E
Partizánske 120 Oh 48.38N 18.23 E
Partizanskoje 138 Ee 55.30N 94.30 E
Paru, Rio- 198 Kf 1.33S 52.38W
Paru de Este, Rio- 202 Hc 1.10N 54.40W
Paru de Oeste, Rio- 198 Kf 1.30S 56.00W
Paruru 219a Ec 9.51S 160.49 E
Parvān [3] 144 Kb 35.15N 69.30 E
Pārvomaj 130 Ig 42.06N 25.13 E
Parys 172 De 27.04S 27.16 E
Paša 114 Hf 60.28N 32.55 E
Pasadena [Ca.-U.S.] 176 Hf 34.09N 118.09W
Pasadena [Tx.-U.S.] 186 Il 29.42N 95.13W
Paşaeli Yarımadası 130 Lh 41.20N 28.25 E
Paşalimanı Adası 130 Ki 40.28N 27.37 E
Pasangkaju 150 Gg 1.10S 119.20 E
Pāsārgād 146 Og 30.17N 52.55 E
Pasarwajo 150 Hh 5.29S 122.50 E
Pascagoula 182 Je 30.23N 88.31W
Paşcani 130 Jb 47.15N 26.44 E
Pasco 182 Db 46.14N 119.06W
Pasco [3] 202 Cf 10.30S 75.15W
Pascoal 204 Ba 13.38S 61.06W
Pascoal, Monte- 202 Kg 16.54S 39.24W
Pascua, Isla de- / Rapa Nui = Easter Island (EN) 208 Qg 27.07S 109.22W
Pas-de-Calais [3] 122 Id 50.30N 2.20 E
Pas-en-Artois 124 Ed 50.09N 2.30 E
Pasewalk 120 Jc 53.31N 13.59 E
Pasinler 146 Ib 40.00N 41.41 E
Pašino 138 De 55.11N 83.02 E
Pasión, Rio de la- 194 Be 16.28N 90.33W
Pasir Mas 150 De 6.02N 102.08 E
Pasirpengarayan 150 Df 0.51N 100.16 E
Pasir Puteh 150 De 5.50N 102.24 E
Påskallavik 116 Gg 57.10N 16.27 E
Paškovski 132 Kg 45.01N 39.05 E
Pasłęk 120 Pb 54.05N 19.39 E
Pasłęka 120 Pb 54.25N 19.50 E
Pasman 128 Jg 43.57N 15.21 E
Pasni 142 Ig 25.16N 63.28 E
Paso de Indios 206 Gf 43.52S 69.06W
Paso de Cerro 204 Ej 31.31S 55.46W
Paso de los Libres 206 Ic 29.43S 57.05W
Paso de los Toros 206 Id 32.49S 56.31W
Paso Tranqueras 204 Ej 31.12S 55.45W
Passamaquoddy Bay 184 Nc 45.06N 66.59W
Passa Três, Serra- 204 Hb 14.40S 49.30W
Passau 120 Jh 48.35N 13.29 E
Passero, Capo- 128 Jn 36.40N 15.10 E
Passo Fundo 200 Kh 28.15S 52.24W
Passo Fundo, Rio- 204 Fh 27.16S 52.42W
Passos 202 Ig 20.43S 46.37W
Pastaza, Rio- 198 If 4.50S 76.25W
Pasteur 206 He 35.08S 62.14W
Pasto 200 Ie 1.13N 77.17W
Pastora Peak 188 Kh 36.47N 109.10W
Pastoria, Laguna de- 192 Ki 16.00N 97.40W
Pastos Bons 202 Je 6.36S 44.05W
Pastrana 126 Jd 40.25N 2.55W
Paštrik 130 Dg 42.14N 20.32 E
Pasubio 128 Fe 45.47N 11.10 E
Pasvalis/Pasvalys 114 Fh 56.02N 24.28 E
Pasvalys/Pasvalis 114 Fh 56.02N 24.28 E
Pásztó 120 Pi 47.55N 19.42 E
Patagonia 198 Jj 44.00S 68.00W
Patagónica, Cordillera- 198 Ij 46.00S 71.30W
Patan 148 Hc 27.40N 85.20 E
Pātan 148 Ed 23.50N 72.07 E
Patani 150 If 0.18N 128.48 E
Pata Peninsula 220d Bb 7.23N 151.35 E
Patchogue 184 Ke 40.46N 73.01W
Pate 170 Hc 2.08S 41.00 E
Patea 218 Fc 39.46S 174.29 E
Patea 218 Fc 39.46S 174.30 E
Pategi 166 Gd 8.44N 5.45 E
Patensie 172 Cf 33.46S 24.49 E

Index Symbols

[1] Independent Nation	Historical or Cultural Region	Pass, Gap	Depression	Coast, Beach
[2] State, Region	Mount, Mountain	Plain, Lowland	Polder	Cliff
[3] District, County	Volcano	Delta	Desert, Dunes	Peninsula
[4] Municipality	Hill	Salt Flat	Forest, Woods	Isthmus
[5] Colony, Dependency	Mountains, Mountain Range	Valley, Canyon	Heath, Steppe	Sandbank
[6] Continent	Hills, Escarpment	Crater, Cave	Oasis	Island
Physical Region	Plateau, Upland	Karst Features	Cape, Point	Atoll

Rock, Reef	Waterfall, Rapids	Canal	Lagoon	Escarpment, Sea Scarp	Historic Site	Airport
Islands, Archipelago	River Mouth, Estuary	Bank	Seamount	Fracture	Ruins	Port
Rocks, Reefs	Glacier	Ice Shelf, Pack Ice	Trench, Abyss	Wall, Walls	Military installation
Coral Reef	Lake	Ocean	Tablemount	National Park, Reserve	Church, Abbey	Lighthouse
Well, Spring	Salt Lake	Sea	Ridge	Point of Interest	Temple	Mine
Geyser	Intermittent Lake	Gulf, Bay	Shelf	Recreation Site	Scientific Station	Tunnel
River, Stream	Reservoir	Strait, Fjord	Basin	Cave, Cavern	Railway station	Dam, Bridge
	Swamp, Pond					

Pesčany, mys- 132 Qh 43.10N 51.18 E
Pesčany, ostrov- 138 Gb 74.20N 115.55 E
Pescara 112 Hg 42.28N 14.13 E
Pescara 128 Ih 42.28N 14.13 E
Pescasseroli 128 Hi 41.48N 13.47 E
Peschici 128 Ki 41.57N 16.01 E
Pescia 128 Eg 43.54N 10.41 E
Pescocostanzo 128 Ii 41.53N 14.04 E
Peshāwar 142 Jf 34.01N 71.33 E
Peshkopia 130 Dh 41.41N 20.26 E
Pesio 128 Bf 44.28N 7.53 E
Peskovka 114 Mg 59.03N 52.22 E
Pesmes 122 Lg 47.17N 5.34 E
Pesočny 116 Nd 60.05N 30.20 E
Peso da Régua 126 Ec 41.10N 7.47W
Pesqueira 202 Ke 8.22S 36.42W
Pesqueria, Rio- 192 Je 25.54N 99.11W
Pessac 122 Fj 44.48N 0.37W
Pest [2] 120 Pi 47.25N 19.20 E
Pešter 130 Df 43.05N 20.02 E
Peštera 130 Hg 42.02N 24.18 E
Pestovo 136 Dd 58.36N 35.47 E
Petacalco, Bahía de- 190 De 17.57N 102.05W
Petah Tiqwa 146 Ff 32.05N 34.53 E
Petäjävesi 116 Kb 62.15N 25.12 E
Petal 186 Lk 31.21N 89.17W
Petalioi 130 Hl 38.01N 24.17 E
Petalioi, Gulf of- (EN) = Petaliōn, Kólpos- 130 Hk 38.00N 24.05 E
Petaliōn, Kólpos- = Petalioi, Gulf of- (EN) 130 Hk 38.00N 24.05 E
Petaluma 188 Dg 38.14N 122.39W
Pétange/Petingen 124 He 49.33N 5.53 E
Petare 202 Ea 10.29N 66.49W
Petatlán 192 Ii 17.31N 101.16W
Petatlán, Rio- 192 Fd 26.09N 107.45W
Petauke 170 Fe 14.15S 31.20 E
Petén [3] 194 Be 16.50N 90.00W
Petén 190 Fe 16.15N 89.50W
Petén Itzá, Lago- 194 Ce 16.59N 89.50W
Petenwell Lake 186 Ld 44.05N 89.45W
Peterborough [Austl.] 212 Hf 32.58S 138.50 E
Peterborough [Eng.-U.K.] 118 Mi 52.35N 0.15W
Peterborough [Ont.-Can.] 180 Jh 44.18N 78.19W
Peterhead 118 Ld 57.30N 1.46W
Peter I, Øy- 222 Pe 68.47S 90.35W
Peter Island 197a Db 18.22N 64.35W
Peterlee 118 Lg 54.46N 1.19W
Petermann Gletscher 179 Fb 80.45N 61.00W
Petermann Ranges 212 Fd 25.00S 129.45 E
Petermanns Bjerg 224 Md 73.10N 28.00W
Peter Pond Lake 180 Ge 55.55N 108.40W
Petersberg 120 He 51.35N 11.57 E
Petersburg [Ak.-U.S.] 178 Me 56.49N 132.57W
Petersburg [In.-U.S.] 184 Df 38.30N 87.16W
Petersburg [Va.-U.S.] 182 Ld 37.14N 77.24W
Petersburg [W.V.-U.S.] 184 Hf 39.01N 79.09W
Petersfield 118 Mk 51.00N 0.56W
Petershagen 124 Kb 52.23N 8.58 E
Peter the Great Bay (EN) = Petra Velikogo, zaliv- 140 Pe 42.40N 132.00 E
Petilia Policastro 128 Kk 39.07N 16.47 E
Petingen/Pétange 124 He 49.33N 5.53 E
Petit-Bourg 197e Ab 16.12N 61.36W
Petit-Canal 197e Bb 16.23N 61.29W
Petit Canouan 197n Bb 12.47N 61.17W
Petit Cul-de-Sac Marin 197e Ab 16.12N 61.33W
Petite Kabylie 126 Rh 36.35N 5.25 E
Petite Rivière de l'Artibonite 194 Kd 19.08N 72.29W
Petites Pyrénées 122 Hk 43.05N 1.10 E
Petite-Terre, Iles de la- 197e Bb 16.10N 61.07W
Petit-Goâve 194 Kd 18.26N 72.52W
Petit Martinique Island 197p Ca 12.32N 61.22W
Petit-Mécatina, Rivière du- 180 Lf 50.39N 59.25W
Petit Morin 122 Jf 48.56N 3.07 E
Petit Mustique Island 197n Bb 12.51N 61.13W
Petit Nevis Island 197n Bb 12.58N 61.15W
Petitot 180 Fd 60.14N 123.29W
Petit Saint-Bernard, Col du- 128 Ae 45.40N 6.55 E
Petit Saint Vincent Island 197n Bb 12.33N 61.23W
Petit Savanne 197g Bb 15.15N 61.17W
Petitsikapau Lake 180 Kf 54.40N 66.25W
Petkula 114 Gc 67.40N 26.41 E
Petlalcingo 192 Kh 18.05N 97.54W
Peto 190 Gd 20.08N 88.55W
Petorca 206 Fd 32.15S 71.00W
Petoskey 184 Ec 45.22N 84.57W
Petra 146 Fg 30.19N 35.29 E
Petralia Soprana 128 Im 37.47N 14.06 E
Petra Pervogo, hrebet- 135 He 39.00N 71.10 E
Petra Velikogo, zaliv- = Peter the Great Bay 140 Pe 42.40N 132.00 E
Petre, Point- 184 Id 43.50N 77.09W
Petre Bay 218 Je 43.55S 176.40W
Petrel 222 Re 63.28S 56.17W
Petrela 130 Ch 41.15N 19.51 E
Petrella Tifernina 128 Ii 41.41N 14.42 E
Petrič 130 Gh 41.24N 23.13 E
Pétrie, Récif- 216 Bc 18.30S 164.20 E
Petrikov 132 Fc 52.08N 28.31 E
Petrila 130 Gd 45.27N 23.25 E
Petrinja 128 Ke 45.27N 16.17 E
Petrodvorec 114 Gg 59.53N 29.50 E
Petrólea 202 Db 8.30N 72.35W
Petrolia 184 Fd 42.52N 82.09W
Petrolina 202 Je 9.24S 40.30W
Petrolina de Goiás 204 Hc 16.06S 49.20W
Petronanski prohod 130 Gf 43.08N 23.08 E
Petronell 128 Kb 48.07N 16.51 E
Petropavlovka 138 Ff 50.38N 105.19 E
Petropavlovsk 142 Id 54.54N 69.06 E
Petropavlovsk-Kamčatski 138 Rd 53.01N 158.39 E
Petrópolis 200 Lh 22.31S 43.10W
Petroşani 130 Gd 45.25N 23.22 E
Petrovac [Yugo.] 130 Bg 42.12N 18.57 E
Petrovac [Yugo.] 130 Ee 44.22N 21.25 E
Petrova Gora 128 Je 45.17N 15.47 E
Petrovaradin 130 Cd 45.15N 19.53 E
Petrovka 130 Nc 46.55N 30.40 E
Petrovsk 136 Ee 52.18N 45.23 E
Petrovski Jam 114 Ie 63.18N 35.15 E
Petrovsk-Zabajkalski 142 Md 51.17N 108.50 E
Petrov Val 132 Nd 50.10N 45.12 E
Petrozavodsk 112 Jc 61.47N 34.20 E
Petuhovo 136 Gd 55.06N 67.58 E
Petuški 114 Ji 55.59N 39.28 E
Petworth 124 Bd 50.59N 0.36W
Peuetsagoe, Gunung- 150 Cf 4.55N 96.20 E
Peumo 206 Fd 34.24S 71.10W
Peureulak 150 Cf 4.48N 97.53 E
Pevek 142 Tc 69.42N 170.17 E
Pevensey 124 Cd 50.48N 0.21 E
Pevensey Bay 124 Cd 50.48N 0.22 E
Peyia 146 Ee 34.53N 32.23 E
Peza 114 Kd 65.34N 44.33 E
Pézenas 122 Jk 43.27N 3.25 E
Pezinok 120 Nh 48.18N 17.16 E
Pfaffenhofen an der Ilm 120 Hh 48.32N 11.31 E
Pfaffenhoffen 124 Jf 48.51N 7.37 E
Pfalz 124 Je 49.20N 7.57 E
Pfalzel, Trier- 124 Ie 49.46N 6.41 E
Pfälzer Bergland 124 Je 49.35N 7.30 E
Pfälzer Wald 120 Dg 49.15N 7.50 E
Pfarrkirchen 120 Ih 48.26N 12.52 E
Pfinz 124 Ke 49.11N 8.25 E
Pfinztal 124 Ke 49.02N 8.30 E
Pforzheim an der Enz 120 Eh 48.53N 8.42 E
Pfrimm 124 Ke 49.39N 8.22 E
Pfullendorf 120 Fi 47.55N 9.15 E
Pfunds 128 Ed 46.58N 10.33 E
Pfungstadt 124 Ke 49.48N 8.36 E
Pha-an 148 Je 16.53N 97.38 E
Phalaborwa 172 Ed 23.55S 31.13 E
Phalodi 148 Ec 27.08N 72.22 E
Phangan, Ko- 148 Jg 9.45N 100.00 E
Phangnga 148 Jg 8.28N 98.32 E
Phan Ly Cham 148 Lf 11.13N 108.31 E
Phanom 148 Jg 8.49N 98.50 E
Phan Rang 148 Lf 11.34N 108.59 E
Phan Thiet 148 Lf 10.56N 108.06 E
Pharr 186 Gm 26.12N 98.11W
Phatthalung 148 Kg 7.38N 100.04 E
Phayao 148 Ke 18.07N 100.11 E
Phenix City 182 Je 32.29N 85.01W
Phet Buri 148 Jf 13.06N 99.56 E
Phetchabun, Thiu Khao- 148 Ke 16.20N 100.55 E
Phichit 148 Ke 16.24N 100.21 E
Philadelphia [Ms.-U.S.] 186 Lj 32.46N 89.07W
Philadelphia [Pa.-U.S.] 176 Lf 39.57N 75.07W
Philae 164 Fe 23.35N 32.52 E
Philip 186 Fd 44.02N 101.40W
Philippeville 122 Kd 50.12N 4.33 E
Philippi 184 Gf 39.08N 80.03W
Philippi (EN) = Filippoi 130 Fi 40.12N 22.07 E
Philippi, Lake- 212 Hd 24.20S 139.00 E
Philippi Glacier 222 Ge 66.45S 88.20 E
Philippine Basin (EN) 106 Ih 17.00N 132.00 E
Philippine Islands (EN) = Pilipinas 140 Oh 13.00N 122.00 E
Philippines (EN) = Pilipinas [1] 142 Oh 13.00N 122.00 E
Philippine Sea (EN) 140 Oh 20.00N 130.00 E
Philippine Trench (EN) 106 Ii 9.00N 127.00 E
Philippsburg 124 Ke 49.14N 8.27 E
Philipsburg [Mt.-U.S.] 188 Ic 46.20N 113.08W
Philipsburg [Neth.Ant.] 196 Ec 18.01N 63.04W
Philip Smith Mountains 178 Jc 68.30N 148.00W
Philipstown 172 Cf 30.26S 24.29 E
Phillipsburg 186 Gg 39.45N 99.19W
Philpots 180 Jb 74.55N 80.00W
Phitsanulok 142 Mh 16.49N 100.15 E
Phnom Penh (EN) = Phnum Pénh 142 Mh 11.33N 104.55 E
Phnum Pénh = Phnom Penh (EN) 142 Mh 11.33N 104.55 E
Phoenix 176 Hf 33.27N 112.05W
Phoenix → Rawaki Atoll 208 Je 3.43S 170.43W
Phoenix Islands 208 Je 4.00S 172.00W
Phôngsali 148 Kd 21.41N 102.06 E
Phrae 148 Ke 18.07N 100.11 E
Phra Nakhon Si Ayutthaya 142 Mh 14.21N 100.33 E
Phrygia 130 Mk 38.30N 29.50 E
Phuket 142 Li 7.54N 98.24 E
Phuket, Ko- 140 Li 8.00N 98.20 E
Phulbani 148 Gd 20.28N 84.14 E
Phumĭ Mlu Prey 148 Lf 13.48N 105.16 E
Phumĭ Sâmraông 148 Kf 14.11N 103.31 E
Phu My 148 Lf 14.10N 109.03 E
Phuoc Binh 148 Lf 11.50N 106.58 E
Phu Quoc 148 Kf 10.13N 103.58 E
Phu Quoc, Dao- 148 Kf 10.12N 104.00 E
Phu Tho 148 Ld 21.24N 105.13 E
Piaanu Pass 220d Ab 7.20N 151.26 E
Piacenza 128 De 45.01N 9.40 E
Piana degli Albanesi 128 Hm 37.59N 13.17 E
Piana Mwanga 170 Ed 7.40S 28.10 E
Piancó 202 Ke 7.12S 37.57W
Pianguan 152 Jd 39.28N 111.32 E
Pianosa [It.] 128 Eh 42.35N 10.05 E
Pianosa [It.] 128 Jh 42.15N 15.45 E
Piaseczno 120 Rd 52.05N 21.01 E
Piaski 120 Se 51.08N 22.51 E
Piątek 120 Pd 52.05N 19.28 E
Piatra 130 If 43.49N 25.10 E
Piatra Neamţ 130 Jc 46.55N 26.20 E
Piatra Olt 130 He 44.22N 24.16 E
Piauí [2] 202 Je 7.00S 43.00W
Piauí, Rio- 198 Lf 6.38S 42.42W
Piave 110 Hf 45.32N 12.44 E
Piaxtla, Punta- 192 Ff 23.38N 106.50W
Piaxtla, Rio- 192 Ff 23.42N 106.49W
Piazza Armerina 128 Im 37.23N 14.22 E
Pibor 168 Ed 8.26N 33.13 E
Pibor Post 168 Ed 6.48N 33.08 E
Pica 206 Gb 20.30S 69.21W
Picardie = Picardy (EN) 122 Je 50.00N 3.30 E
Picardy (EN) = Picardie 122 Je 50.00N 3.30 E
Picayune 186 Lk 30.26N 89.41W
Piccolo San Bernardo, Colle del- 128 Ae 45.40N 6.55 E
Picentini, Monti- 128 Jj 40.45N 15.10 E
Pichanal 200 Jh 23.20S 64.15W
Pichilemu 206 Fd 34.23S 72.00W
Pichilingue 192 De 24.20N 110.20W
Pichna 120 Oe 51.50N 18.40 E
Pichones, Cayos- 194 Ff 15.45N 82.55W
Pichucalco 192 Mi 17.31N 93.04W
Pickering 118 Mg 54.14N 0.46W
Pickering, Vale of- 118 Mg 54.10N 0.45W
Pickle Lake 180 If 51.29N 90.10W
Pickwick Lake 184 Ch 34.55N 88.10W
Pico 158 Ee 38.28N 28.20W
Picos 200 Lf 7.05S 41.28W
Pico Truncado 206 Gg 46.48S 67.58W
Picquigny 122 Ie 49.57N 2.09 E
Picton 216 Dh 41.18S 174.00 E
Picton 206 Gi 55.04S 67.00W
Pictou 180 Lg 45.41N 62.43W
Picunda 132 Lh 43.12N 40.21 E
Pidurutalagala 140 Ki 7.00N 80.46 E
Piedecuesta 202 Db 6.59N 73.03W
Piedimonte Matese 128 Ii 41.20N 14.22 E
Piedmont 174 Kf 35.00N 81.00W
Piedmont [Al.-U.S.] 184 Ei 33.55N 85.37W
Piedmont [Mo.-U.S.] 186 Kh 37.09N 90.42W
Piedmont (EN) = Piemonte [2] 128 Be 45.00N 8.00 E
Piedra 126 Kc 41.19N 1.48W
Piedra, Monasterio de- 126 Kc 41.10N 1.50W
Piedrabuena 126 He 39.02N 4.10W
Piedrafita, Puerto de- 126 Fb 42.36N 6.57W
Piedrahita 126 Gd 40.28N 5.19W
Piedras 202 Cd 3.38S 79.54W
Piedras, Punta- 206 Ie 35.25S 57.08W
Piedras, Rio de las- 202 Ef 12.30S 69.14W
Piedras Negras 176 Ig 28.42N 100.31W
Piedras Negras 194 Be 17.12N 91.15W
Piedra Sola 206 Id 32.04S 56.21W
Piekary Śląskie 120 Of 50.24N 18.58 E
Pieksämäki 114 Ge 62.18N 27.08 E
Pielach 128 Jb 48.15N 15.22 E
Pielavesi 114 Ge 63.14N 26.45 E
Pielinen 112 Ic 63.15N 29.40 E
Piemonte = Piedmont (EN) [2] 128 Be 45.00N 8.00 E
Pieniężno 120 Qb 54.15N 20.08 E
Pieni Salpausselkä 116 Lc 61.10N 27.20 E
Piennes 124 He 49.19N 5.47 E
Pienza 128 Fg 43.04N 11.41 E
Pierce 188 Hc 46.29N 115.48W
Piéria Óri 130 Fi 40.12N 22.07 E
Pierre 176 Ie 44.22N 100.21W
Pierrefitte-sur-Aire 124 Hf 48.54N 5.20 E
Pierrefonds 124 Ee 49.21N 2.59 E
Pierrelatte 122 Kj 44.23N 4.42 E
Pieskehaure 114 Dc 66.57N 16.30 E
Piešťany 120 Nh 48.36N 17.50 E
Pietarsaari/Jakobstad 114 Fe 63.40N 22.42 E
Pietermaritzburg 160 Kk 29.37S 30.16 E
Pietersburg 160 Jk 23.54S 29.25 E
Pietraperzia 128 Im 37.25N 14.08 E
Pietrasanta 128 Eg 43.57N 10.14 E
Piet Retief 172 Ee 27.01S 30.50 E
Pietrii, Virful- 130 Fd 45.23N 22.40 E
Pietroşani 130 If 43.43N 25.38 E
Pietrosu, Virful- [Rom.] 130 Ib 47.08N 25.11 E
Pietrosu, Virful- [Rom.] 110 If 47.23N 25.33 E
Pieve di Cadore 128 Gd 46.26N 12.22 E
Pigeon Island 197k Ba 14.06N 60.58W
Pigeon River 186 Lb 48.02N 89.41W
Piggott 186 Kh 36.23N 90.11W
Pigg's Peak 172 Ee 25.58S 31.15 E
Pigs, Bay of- (EN) = Cochinos, Bahía de- 194 Gb 22.07N 81.10W
Pigüé 204 Am 37.37S 62.25W
Pi He 154 Dh 32.26N 116.34 E
Pihkva järv = Pskov, Lake- (EN) 110 Id 58.00N 28.00 E
Pihlajavesi 114 Gf 61.45N 28.45 E
Pihlava 116 Ic 61.33N 21.36 E
Pihtipudas 114 Fe 63.23N 25.34 E
Piikkiö 116 Jd 60.26N 22.31 E
Piirisaar/Pirissar 116 Lf 58.23N 27.40 E
Pijijiapan 192 Mj 15.42N 93.14W
Pijol, Pico- 194 Df 15.06N 87.35W
Pikalevo 114 Ig 59.32N 34.03 E
Pikangikum 180 If 51.49N 94.00W
Pikelot Island 208 Fd 8.05N 147.38 E
Pikes Peak 182 Fd 38.51N 105.03W
Piketberg 172 Bf 32.54S 18.46 E
Pikiutdleq 179 Hf 64.45N 40.10W
Pikou 154 Ge 39.24N 122.21 E
Pikounda 170 Cb 0.33N 16.42 E
Pila 204 Cm 36.01S 58.08W
Piła 120 Mc 53.10N 16.44 E
Piła [2] 120 Mc 53.10N 16.45 E
Pila, Sierra de la- 126 Kf 38.16N 1.11W
Pilar [Arg.] 204 Bj 31.27S 61.15W
Pilar [Braz.] 202 Ke 9.36S 35.56W
Pilar [Par.] 206 Ic 26.52S 58.23W
Pilas Group 150 He 6.45N 121.35 E
Pilat, Mont- 122 Ki 45.23N 4.35 E
Pilatus 128 Cd 46.59N 8.20 E
Pilaya, Río- 202 Fh 20.55S 64.04W
Pilcaniyeu 206 Ff 41.08S 70.40W
Pilcomayo, Río- 198 Kh 25.21S 57.42W
Pile, Jezioro- 120 Mc 53.35N 16.30 E
Pili 130 Ej 39.28N 21.37 E
Pili 150 Hd 13.37N 123.17 E
Pilībhīt 148 Fc 28.38N 79.48 E
Pilica 120 Re 51.52N 21.17 E
Pilion Óros 130 Gj 39.24N 23.05 E
Pilipinas = Philippine Islands (EN) 140 Oh 13.00N 122.00 E
Pilipinas = Philippines (EN) [1] 142 Oh 13.00N 122.00 E
Pilis 120 Oi 47.41N 18.53 E
Pillahuincó, Sierra de- 204 Bn 38.18S 60.45W
Pillar, Cape- 212 Jh 43.15S 148.00 E
Pilna 114 Ki 55.33N 45.55 E
Pilões, Rio- 204 Gc 16.14S 50.54W
Pilões, Serra dos- 204 Ic 17.50S 47.13W
Pilón, Río- 192 Je 25.32N 99.32W
Pilos 130 Em 36.55N 21.42 E
Pilos = Pylos (EN) 130 Em 36.56N 21.40 E
Pilot Peak 188 Hf 41.02N 114.06W
Pilot Rock 188 Fd 45.29N 118.50W
Pilsen (EN) = Plzeň 112 Hf 49.45N 13.24 E
Piltene 114 Eh 57.15N 21.42 E
Pilzno 120 Rg 49.59N 21.17 E
Pim 136 Hc 61.18N 71.57 E
Pimba 212 Hf 31.15S 136.47 E
Pimenteiras 202 Je 6.14S 41.25W
Pimža jõgi 116 Lg 57.57N 27.59 E
Pina 126 Lc 41.29N 0.32W
Pinacate, Cerro- 192 Cb 31.45N 113.31W
Pinaki Atoll 208 Nf 19.22S 138.44W
Pinamar 204 Dm 37.07S 56.50W
Piñami, Arroyo- 192 Cd 27.44N 113.47W
Pinang → George Town 142 Mi 5.25N 100.20 E
Pinar 126 Gh 36.46N 5.26W
Pinarbaşi 146 Gc 38.50N 36.30 E
Pinar del Río 176 Kg 22.25N 83.42W
Pinar del Río [3] 194 Eb 22.35N 83.40W
Pinarhisar 130 Kh 41.37N 27.30 E
Pinchbeck 124 Bb 52.48N 0.09W
Pincher Creek 180 Gg 49.30N 113.48W
Pinçon, Mont- 122 Ff 48.58N 0.37W
Pîncota 130 Ec 46.20N 21.42 E
Pindaíba, Ribeirão 204 Gb 14.48S 52.00W
Pindaré, Rio- 202 Jd 3.17S 44.47W
Pindaré-Mirim 202 Id 3.37S 45.21W
Pindaval 204 Dc 17.08S 56.09W
Pindhos Óros = Pindus Mountains (EN) 110 Ih 39.45N 21.30 E
Pindus Mountains (EN) = Pindhos Óros 110 Ih 39.45N 21.30 E
Pine Bluff 182 Ie 34.13N 92.01W
Pine Bluffs 188 Mf 41.11N 104.04W
Pine Creek 212 Gb 13.49S 131.49 E
Pine Falls 180 Hf 50.35N 96.15W
Pinega 136 Ec 64.42N 43.22 E
Pinega 110 Kc 64.08N 41.54 E
Pine Island Glacier 222 Of 75.00S 101.00W
Pineland 186 Jk 31.15N 93.58W
Pine Mountain [Ga.-U.S.] 184 Ei 32.51N 84.47W
Pine Mountain [U.S.] 184 Fg 36.55N 83.20W
Pine Pass 180 Fe 55.50N 122.30W
Pine Point 176 Hc 61.01N 114.15W
Pine Ridge 186 Ee 43.02N 102.33W
Pinerolo 128 Bf 44.53N 7.21 E
Pines, Isle of- (EN) = Juventud, Isla de la- 174 Kg 21.40N 82.50W
Pines, Isle of- (EN) = Pins, Ile des- 208 Hg 22.37S 167.30 E
Pines, Lake O' The- 186 Ij 32.46N 94.35W
Pinetown 172 Ee 29.46S 30.46 E
Ping 140 Mh 15.42N 100.09 E
Pingbian 152 Hg 22.56N 103.46 E
Pingchang 152 Ie 31.38N 107.06 E
Pingding 154 Bf 37.48N 113.37 E
Pingdingbu → Guyuan 154 Cd 41.40N 115.41 E
Pingdingshan 152 Je 33.41N 113.27 E
Pingding Shan 152 Mb 46.39N 128.30 E
Pingdu 154 Ef 36.47N 119.57 E
Pingelap Atoll 208 Hd 6.13N 160.42 E
Pingelly 212 Df 32.32S 117.05 E
Pinggu 154 Dd 40.08N 117.07 E
Pingguo 152 Ig 23.21N 107.34 E
Pinghu 154 Fi 30.42N 121.02 E
Pingjiang 154 Bj 28.45N 113.37 E
Pingle 152 Jg 24.43N 110.42 E
Pingli 152 Ie 32.27N 109.21 E
Pingliang 142 Mf 35.32N 106.41 E
Pinglu (Jingping) 154 Be 39.32N 112.14 E
Pingluo 142 Mf 38.56N 106.34 E
Pingma → Tiandong 152 Ig 23.40N 107.09 E
Pingnan 152 Jg 23.38N 110.23 E
Pingouins, Ile des- 222 Ec 46.25S 50.19 E
Pingquan 152 Kc 41.00N 118.36 E
Pingshan 154 Ce 38.21N 114.01 E
Pingshun 154 Bf 36.12N 113.26 E
Pingtan 152 Kf 25.31N 119.48 E
Pingtung 152 Lg 22.40N 120.29 E
Pingüicas, Cerro- 192 Jg 21.10N 99.42W
Pingvallavatn 114a Bb 64.15N 21.09W
Pingvellir 114a Bb 64.17N 21.03W
Pingwu 152 He 32.27N 104.35 E
Pingxiang [China] 152 Ig 22.11N 106.46 E
Pingxiang [China] 152 Jf 27.43N 113.48 E
Pingyang 152 Lf 27.40N 120.30 E
Pingyao 152 Jd 37.12N 112.13 E
Pingyi 154 Dg 35.30N 117.38 E
Pingyin 154 Df 36.17N 116.26 E
Pingyu 154 Ch 32.58N 114.36 E
Pingyuan 154 Df 37.10N 116.25 E
Pinhal 204 If 22.12S 46.45W
Pinhão 204 Gg 25.43S 51.38W
Pinheiro Machado 204 Fj 31.34S 53.23W
Pinhel 126 Ed 40.46N 7.04W
Pini, Pulau- 150 Cf 0.08N 98.40 E
Piniós [Grc.] 130 Fj 39.53N 22.44 E
Piniós [Grc.] 130 El 37.48N 21.14 E
Pinipel 219a Ba 4.24S 154.08 E
Pinjug 114 Lf 60.16N 47.54 E
Pinka 128 Kc 47.00N 16.35 E
Pink Mountain 180 Fe 56.06N 122.35W
Pinnaroo 212 Ig 35.16S 140.55 E
Pinneberg 120 Fc 53.39N 9.48 E
Pinnes, Ákra- 130 Hi 40.07N 24.18 E
Pinolosean 150 Hf 0.23N 124.07 E
Pinos 192 If 22.18N 101.34W
Pinos, Mount- 174 Hf 34.50N 119.09W
Pinos-Puente 126 Ig 37.15N 3.45W
Pinrang 150 Gg 3.48S 119.38 E
Pins, Cap des- 219b Ce 21.04S 167.28 E
Pins, Ile des- = Pines, Isle of- (EN) 208 Hg 22.37S 167.30 E
Pins, Pointe aux- 184 Gd 42.15N 81.51W
Pinsk 136 Ce 52.08N 26.06 E
Pinta, Isla- 202a Aa 0.35N 90.44W
Pintas, Sierra de las- 192 Bb 31.40N 115.10W
Pinto [Arg.] 206 Hc 29.09S 62.39W
Pinto [Sp.] 126 Id 40.14N 3.41W
Pintwater Range 188 Hh 36.55N 115.30W
Pio 219a Ed 10.12S 161.42 E
Pioche 188 Hh 37.56N 114.27W
Piombino 128 Eh 42.55N 10.32 E
Piombino, Canale di- 128 Eh 42.55N 10.30 E
Pioneer Mountains 188 Id 45.40N 113.00W
Pioner, ostrov- 140 Lb 79.50N 92.30 E
Pionerski [Russia] 136 Gc 61.12N 62.57 E
Pionerski [Russia] 114 Ei 54.57N 20.13 E
Pionki 120 Re 51.30N 21.27 E
Piorini, Lago- 202 Fd 3.35S 63.15W
Piorini, Rio- 202 Fd 3.23S 63.30W
Piotrków [2] 120 Pe 51.25N 19.40 E
Piotrków Trybunalski 120 Pe 51.25N 19.42 E
Piove di Sacco 128 Ge 45.18N 12.02 E
Pipa Dingzi 152 Mc 43.57N 128.14 E
Pipéri 130 Hj 39.19N 24.21 E
Pipestone 186 Hd 44.01N 96.19W
Pipestone Creek 186 Fb 49.42N 100.45W
Pipi 168 Cd 7.27N 22.48 E
Pipinas 204 Dl 35.32S 57.20W
Pipmouacan, Réservoir- 180 Kg 49.40N 70.20W
Piqan → Shanshan 152 Fc 42.52N 90.10 E
Piqua 184 Ee 40.08N 84.14W
Piqueras, Puerto de- 126 Jb 42.03N 2.32W
Piquiri, Rio- 206 Jb 24.03S 54.14W
Piquiri, Serra do- 204 Fg 24.53S 52.25W
Piracanjuba 204 Hc 17.18S 49.01W
Piracanjuba, Rio- [Braz.] 204 Hc 17.18S 48.13W
Piracanjuba, Rio- [Braz.] 204 Hd 18.14S 48.48W
Piracema 204 Je 20.31S 44.29W
Piracicaba 206 Kb 22.43S 47.38W
Piracicaba, Rio- 204 Hf 22.36S 48.19W
Piraçununga 204 Ie 21.59S 47.25W
Piracuruca 202 Jd 3.56S 41.42W
Piraeus (EN) = Piraiévs 112 Ih 37.57N 23.38 E
Pirai do Sul 204 Hg 24.31S 49.56W
Piraiévs = Piraeus (EN) 112 Ih 37.57N 23.38 E
Piraju 204 Hf 23.12S 49.23W
Pirajuí 204 He 21.59S 49.29W
Pirámide, Cerro- 198 Ij 49.01S 73.32W
Piran 128 He 45.32N 13.34 E
Piranè 206 Ic 25.43S 59.06W
Piranhas 204 Gc 16.31S 51.51W
Piranhas, Rio- 204 Gc 16.01S 51.52W
Pīrān Shahr 146 Kd 36.40N 45.05 E
Pirapora 200 Lg 17.21S 44.56W
Pirarajá 206 Jd 33.44S 54.45W
Pirate Well 194 Kb 22.26N 73.04W
Piratini 204 Fj 31.27S 53.06W
Piratini, Rio- 204 Fk 32.01S 52.25W
Piratinim, Rio- 204 Ei 28.06S 55.27W
Pirdop 130 Hg 42.42N 24.11 E
Pirenópolis 204 Hb 15.51S 48.57W
Pires do Rio 202 Ig 17.18S 48.17W
Pirgós 130 Fi 40.38N 22.44 E
Pirgos 130 El 37.41N 21.27 E
Piriápolis 204 Ei 34.54S 55.17W
Pirin 130 Gh 41.40N 23.30 E
Pirineos = Pyrenees (EN) 110 Gg 42.40N 1.00 E
Pirineus, Serra dos- 204 Hc 16.15S 49.10W
Piripiri 202 Jd 4.16S 41.47W
Pirissar/Piirisaar 116 Lf 58.23N 27.40 E
Piritu 196 Bh 9.23N 69.12W
Piritu, Islas- 196 Dg 10.10N 64.56W
Pirizal 204 Dc 16.16S 56.23W
Pirjatin 132 Hd 50.14N 32.30 E
Pirmasens 120 Dg 49.12N 7.36 E
Pirna 120 Jf 50.58N 13.56 E
Piron 219a Ad 11.20S 153.27 E
Pirón 126 Hc 41.23N 4.31W
Pirot 130 Ff 43.09N 22.36 E
Pirre, Cerro- 194 Ij 7.49N 77.43W
Pirrit Hills 222 Pg 81.17S 85.21W
Pirsagat 132 Pj 39.53N 49.19 E
Pīr Tāj 146 Me 35.45N 48.07 E
Pirttikylä/Pörtom 116 Ib 62.42N 21.37 E
Piru 150 Ig 3.04S 128.12 E
Pis 220d Ba 7.41N 151.46 E
Pisa 128 Eg 43.43N 10.23 E
Pisa 120 Rc 53.15N 21.52 E
Pisagua 206 Fa 19.36S 70.13W
Pisano 128 Eg 43.46N 10.33 E
Pisar 220d Cb 7.19N 152.01 E
Pisciotta 128 Jj 40.06N 15.14 E
Pisco 200 Ig 13.42S 76.13W
Pişcolt 130 Fb 47.35N 22.18 E
Pisek 128 Kg 49.19N 14.10 E
Pishan/Guma 152 Cd 37.38N 78.19 E
Pīsh Qal'eh 146 Qd 37.35N 57.05 E
Pishvā 146 Ne 35.18N 51.44 E
Piso Firme 204 Ba 13.41S 61.52W
Pišpek = Frunze 142 Je 42.54N 74.36 E
Pisshiri-Dake 156a Ba 44.20N 141.55 E
Pista 114 Hd 65.28N 30.45 E
Pisticci 128 Kj 40.23N 16.33 E
Pistoia 128 Eg 43.55N 10.54 E
Pisuerga 126 Hc 41.33N 4.52W
Pisz 120 Rc 53.38N 21.49 E
Pita 166 Cc 11.05N 12.24W
Pitalito 202 Cc 1.53N 76.02W
Pitanga 206 Jb 24.46S 51.44W
Pitanga, Serra da- 204 Gg 24.52S 51.48W

Pitangui 204 Jd 19.40S 44.54W
Pitcairn [5] 210 Og 24.00S 129.00W
Pitcairn Island 208 Ng 25.04S 130.05W
Piteå 114 Ed 65.20N 21.30 E
Piteälven 110 Ib 65.14N 21.32 E
Pitești 112 Ig 44.51N 24.52 E
Pithiviers 122 If 48.10N 2.15 E
Pithorāgarh 148 Gc 29.35N 80.13 E
Piti 220c Bb 13.28N 144.41 E
Piti 170 Fd 7.00S 32.44 E
Pitiquito 192 Cb 30.42N 112.02W
Pitkjaranta 136 Dc 61.35N 31.31 E
Pitkkala 116 Jc 61.28N 23.34 E
Pitljar 138 Bc 65.52N 65.55 E
Pitlochry 118 Je 56.43N 3.45W
Pitomača 128 Le 45.57N 17.14 E
Piton, Pointe du- 197e Ba 16.30N 61.27W
Pit River 182 Cc 40.45N 122.22W
Pitrufquén 206 Fe 38.59S 72.39W
Pitt 180 Ef 53.40N 129.50W
Pitt Island 208 Ji 44.20S 176.10W
Pittsburg 182 Id 37.25N 94.42W
Pittsburgh 176 Le 40.26N 80.00W
Pittsfield [Il.-U.S.] 186 Kg 39.36N 90.48W
Pittsfield [Ma.-U.S.] 184 Kd 42.27N 73.15W
Pittsfield [Me.-U.S.] 184 Mc 44.47N 69.23W
Pitt Strait 218 Jf 44.15S 176.20W
Pitu 150 If 1.41N 128.01 E
Piúí 204 Je 20.28S 45.58W
Piura 200 Hf 5.12S 80.38W
Piura [3] 202 Be 5.00S 80.20W
Piuthān 148 Gc 28.06N 82.52 E
Piva 130 Bf 43.21N 18.51 E
Pivan 138 If 50.27N 137.05 E
Pivijay 194 Jh 10.28N 74.38W
Pižma [Russia] 114 Lh 57.36N 48.58 E
Pižma [Russia] 134 Fd 65.24N 52.05 E
Pizzo 128 Kl 38.44N 16.40 E
Pjakupur 138 Cd 65.00N 77.48 E
Pjalica 114 Jc 66.12N 39.32 E
Pjalma 136 Dc 62.27N 35.53 E
Pjana 114 Ki 55.37N 45.58 E
Pjandž 136 Gh 37.15N 69.07 E
Pjandž 140 If 37.06N 68.20 E
Pjaozero, ozero- 110 Jb 66.05N 30.55 E
Pjarnu/Pärnu 112 Id 58.24N 24.32 E
Pjarnu / Pärnu jõgi 114 Fg 58.23N 24.34 E
Pjarnu, zaliv- / Pärnu laht 114 Fg 58.15N 24.25 E
Pjarnu-Jagupi/Pärnu-Jaagupi 116 Kf 58.36N 24.25 E
Pjasina 140 Kb 73.47N 87.01 E
Pjasino, ozero- 138 Dc 69.45N 87.30 E
Pjasinski zaliv 138 Db 74.00N 85.00 E
Pjatigorsk 112 Kg 44.03N 43.04 E
Pjatihatki 132 He 48.27N 33.40 E
Pjórsá 110 Dc 63.45N 20.50W
Pjuhjarjavi, ozero- 116 Nc 61.50N 30.00 E
Pjussi/Püssi 116 Le 59.17N 26.57 E
Pkulagalid 220a Bb 7.36N 134.33 E
Pkulagasemieg 220a Ac 7.08N 134.23 E
Pkurengel 220a Ac 7.27N 134.28 E
Plá 204 Bl 35.07S 60.13W
Placentia 180 Mg 47.14N 53.58W
Placentia Bay 174 Ne 47.15N 54.30W
Placer 150 Hd 11.52N 123.55 E
Placerville 188 Eg 38.43N 120.48W
Placetas 190 Id 22.19N 79.40W
Plácido Rosas 204 Fk 32.45S 53.44W
Plačkovci 130 Ig 42.49N 25.28 E
Plačkovica 130 Fh 41.46N 22.32 E
Plainfield 184 Je 40.37N 74.25W
Plains [Mt.-U.S.] 188 Hc 47.27N 114.53W
Plains [Tx.-U.S.] 186 Ej 33.11N 102.50W
Plainview [Nb.-U.S.] 186 He 42.21N 97.47W
Plainview [Tx.-U.S.] 182 Ge 34.11N 101.43W
Plainville 186 Gg 39.14N 99.18W
Pláka, Ákra- 130 Ii 40.02N 25.25 E
Plake 130 Eh 41.14N 21.02 E
Plampang 150 Gh 8.48S 117.48 E
Planá 120 Ig 49.52N 12.44 E
Plana, Illa- / Plana o Nueva Tabarca, Isla- 126 Lf 38.10N 0.28 E
Plana Cays 194 Kb 22.37N 73.33W
Plana o Nueva Tabarca, Isla- / Plana, Illa- 126 Lf 38.10N 0.28 E
Planco, Peñón- 192 Ge 24.35N 104.15W
Plane, Île- 126 Li 35.46N 0.54W
Planeta Rica 202 Cb 8.25N 75.35W
Planet Depth (EN) 106 Hj 10.20S 110.30 E
Planézes 122 Ij 45.00N 2.50 E
Plankinton 186 Ge 43.43N 98.29W
Plantation 184 Gl 26.05N 80.14W
Plantaurel 122 Hk 43.04N 1.30 E
Plant City 184 Fk 28.01N 82.08W
Plasencia 126 Fd 40.02N 6.05W
Plast 136 Ge 54.22N 60.55 E
Plaster Rock 184 Nb 46.54N 67.24W
Plastun 138 Ih 44.48N 136.17 E
Plasy 120 Jg 49.56N 13.24 E
Plata, Rio de la- [P.R.] 197a Bb 18.30N 66.14W
Plata, Rio de la- [S.Amer.] 198 Ki 35.00S 57.00W
Plataiai 130 Gk 38.13N 23.16 E
Platani 128 Hm 37.24N 13.16 E
Plateau [2] 166 Gd 8.50N 9.00 E
Plateau [3] 170 Cc 2.10S 15.00 E
Plateaux [3] 170 Fd 7.30N 1.10 E
Platen, Kapp- 179 Ob 80.31N 22.48 E
Plati 130 Fi 40.39N 22.32 E
Plato 202 Db 9.47N 74.47W
Platte 186 Ge 43.23N 98.51W
Platte 174 Je 41.00N 95.52W
Platte Island 158 Mi 5.52S 55.23 E
Platte River 186 Ig 39.16N 94.50W
Platteville 186 Ke 42.44N 90.29W
Plattsburgh 182 Mc 44.42N 73.29W
Plattsmouth 186 If 41.01N 95.53W
Plau 120 Ic 53.27N 12.16 E
Plauen 120 If 50.30N 12.08 E
Plauer See 120 Ic 53.30N 12.20 E
Plav 130 Cg 42.36N 19.57 E
Plavecký Mikuláš 120 Nh 48.30N 17.18 E
Pļaviņas/Pljavinjas 114 Fh 56.38N 25.46 E
Plavsk 132 Jc 53.43N 37.18 E
Playa Azul 190 De 17.59N 102.24W
Playa Noriega, Laguna- 192 Dc 29.10N 111.50W
Playa Vicente 192 Li 17.50N 95.49W
Playón Chico 194 Hi 9.18N 78.14W
Pleasanton [Ks.-U.S.] 186 Ig 38.11N 94.43W
Pleasanton [Tx.-U.S.] 186 Gl 28.58N 98.29W
Pleasant Point 218 Df 44.16S 171.08 E
Pleasant Valley 186 Fi 35.15N 101.48W
Plechý 120 Jh 48.49N 13.53 E
Pleiku 148 Lf 13.59N 108.00 E
Pleiße 120 Ie 51.20N 12.22 E
Plenița 130 Ge 44.13N 23.11 E
Plenty, Bay of- 208 Ih 37.45S 177.10 E
Plentywood 182 Gb 48.47N 104.34W
Pleščenicy 132 Eb 54.29N 27.55 E
Pleseck 136 Ec 62.44N 40.18 E
Plešivec 120 Qh 48.33N 20.25 E
Pleșu, Vîrful- 130 Fc 46.32N 22.11 E
Pleszew 120 Ne 51.54N 17.48 E
Plétipi, Lac- 180 Kf 51.42N 70.08W
Plettenberg 124 Jc 51.13N 7.53 E
Plettenbergbaai 172 Cf 34.03S 23.22 E
Pleven 112 Ig 43.25N 24.37 E
Pleven [2] 130 Hf 43.25N 24.37 E
Plibo 166 De 4.35N 7.40W
Pliska 130 Kf 43.22N 27.07 E
Pliszka 120 Kd 52.15N 14.40 E
Plitvice 128 Jf 44.54N 15.36 E
Pljavinjas/Pļaviņas 114 Fh 56.38N 25.46 E
Plješevica 128 Jf 44.45N 15.45 E
Pljevlja 130 Cf 43.21N 19.21 E
Pljusa 114 Gg 58.25N 29.20 E
Pljusa 114 Gg 59.13N 28.11 E
Ploča, Rt- 128 Jg 43.30N 15.58 E
Ploče → Kardeljevo 128 Lg 43.04N 17.26 E
Płock 120 Pd 52.35N 19.45 E
Płock 120 Pd 52.33N 19.43 E
Plöckenstein 120 Jh 48.49N 13.53 E
Ploërmel 122 Dg 47.56N 2.24W
Ploiești 112 Ig 44.57N 26.01 E
Plomárion 130 Jk 38.59N 26.22 E
Plomb du Cantal 122 Ii 45.03N 2.46 E
Plön 120 Gb 54.10N 10.26 E
Płonia 120 Kc 53.25N 14.36 E
Płonka 120 Qd 52.37N 20.30 E
Płońsk 120 Qd 52.38N 20.23 E
Plopana 130 Kc 46.41N 27.13 E
Płoty 120 Lc 53.50N 15.16 E
Plouguerneau 122 Bf 48.36N 4.30W
Plovdiv 112 Ig 42.09N 24.45 E
Plovdiv [2] 130 Hg 42.09N 24.45 E
Plummer 188 Gc 47.20N 116.53W
Plumridge Lakes 212 Fe 29.30S 125.25 E
Plumtree 172 Dd 20.31S 27.48 E
Plungé/Plunge 114 Ei 55.56N 21.48 E
Plunge/Plungė 114 Ei 55.56N 21.48 E
Plymouth [Eng.-U.K.] 112 Fe 50.23N 4.10W
Plymouth [In.-U.S.] 184 De 41.21N 86.19W
Plymouth [Ma.-U.S.] 184 Le 41.58N 70.41W
Plymouth [Mont.] 190 Le 16.42N 62.13W
Plymouth Sound 118 Ik 50.25N 4.05W
Plzeň=Pilsen (EN) 112 Hf 49.45N 13.24 E
Plzeňská pahorkatina 120 Jg 49.50N 13.15 E
Pniewy 120 Md 52.31N 16.15 E
Pô 166 Ec 11.10N 1.09W
Po 110 Hg 44.57N 12.05 E
Po, Foci del-=Po, Mouths of the- (EN) 128 Gf 44.52N 12.30 E
Po, Mouths of the- (EN)= Po, Foci del- 128 Gf 44.52N 12.30 E
Poarta de Fier a Transilvaniei, Pasul- 130 Fd 45.25N 22.40 E
Poarta Orientală, Pasul- 130 Fd 45.08N 22.20 E
Poás, Volcán- 194 Eh 10.11N 84.13W
Pobé 166 Fd 6.58N 2.41 E
Pobeda, gora- 140 Qc 65.12N 146.12 E
Pobeda Ice Island 222 Ge 64.30S 97.00 E
Pobedy, pik- 140 Ke 42.02N 80.05 E
Pobla de Segur / la Pobla de Segur 126 Mb 42.15N 0.58 E
Pobla de Trives / Puebla de Trives 126 Eb 42.20N 7.15W
Poblet, Monasterio de- / Poblet, Monestir de- 126 Nc 41.20N 1.05 E
Poblet, Monestir de- / Poblet, Monasterio de- 126 Nc 41.20N 1.05 E
Pobrežije 130 Jf 43.56N 26.21 E
Pocahontas 186 Kh 36.16N 90.58W
Pocatello 176 He 42.52N 112.27W
Počep 132 Hc 52.57N 33.28 E
Pocerina 130 Ce 44.38N 19.35 E
Počinok 136 De 54.23N 32.29 E
Počitelj 128 Lg 43.08N 17.44 E
Pocito, Sierra del- 126 He 39.20N 4.05W
Pocito Casas 192 Dc 28.32N 111.06W
Pocklington Reef 214 Fj 11.00S 155.00 E
Poções 202 Jf 14.31S 40.21W
Poço Fundo, Cachoeira- 204 Jc 16.10S 45.51W
Poconé 202 Gg 16.15S 56.37W
Pocono Mountains 184 Je 41.10N 75.20W
Poços de Caldas 202 Ih 21.48S 46.34W
Pocri 194 Gj 7.40N 80.07W
Podborovje [Russia] 114 Ig 59.32N 35.01 E
Podborovje [Russia] 116 Mg 57.51N 28.46 E
Podbrezová 120 Ph 48.49N 19.31 E
Podčerje 134 He 63.55N 57.30 E
Poděbrady 120 Lf 50.09N 15.07 E
Podgajcy 120 Vg 49.12N 25.12 E
Podgorica (Titograd) 112 Hg 42.26N 19.16 E
Po di Volano 128 Gf 44.49N 12.15 E
Podjuga 114 Jf 61.07N 40.54 E
Podkamennaja Tunguska=Stony Tunguska (EN) 140 Lc 61.36N 90.18 E
Podlasie 120 Sd 52.30N 23.00 E
Podlaska, Nizina- 120 Sc 53.00N 22.45 E
Podlužje 130 Ce 44.45N 19.55 E
Podolia (EN) = Podolskaja vozvyšennost 110 If 49.00N 28.00 E
Podolsk 136 Dd 55.27N 37.33 E
Podolskaja vozvyšennost = Podolia (EN) 110 If 49.00N 28.00 E
Podor 166 Cb 16.40N 14.57W
Podporožje 136 Dc 60.54N 34.09 E
Podravina 128 Le 45.40N 17.40 E
Podravska Slatina 128 Le 45.42N 17.42 E
Podrima 130 Dg 42.24N 20.33 E
Podromanija 128 Mg 43.54N 18.46 E
Podsvilje 116 Mi 55.09N 28.01 E
Podujevo 130 Eg 42.55N 21.12 E
Podunajská nížina 120 Nh 48.00N 17.40 E
Podvološino 138 Fe 58.15N 108.25 E
Poel 120 Hb 54.00N 11.26 E
Poenița, Vîrful- 130 Gc 46.15N 23.20 E
Pofadder 172 Be 29.10S 19.22 E
Pogăniș 130 Ed 45.41N 21.21 E
Pogar 132 Hc 52.33N 33.16 E
Poggibonsi 128 Fg 43.28N 11.09 E
Pöggstall 128 Jb 48.19N 15.11 E
Pogibi 138 Jf 52.15N 141.45 E
Pogny 124 Gf 48.52N 4.29 E
Pogoanele 130 Je 44.55N 27.00 E
Pogórze Karpackie 120 Qg 49.52N 21.00 E
Pogradeci 130 Di 40.54N 20.39 E
Pograničny 138 Ih 44.26N 131.20 E
Pogrebišče 132 Fe 49.29N 29.14 E
Poguba Xoréu, Rio- 204 Ec 16.29S 54.58W
P'ohang 152 Md 36.02N 129.22 E
Pohja/Pojo 116 Jd 60.06N 23.31 E
Pohjankangas 116 Jc 62.00N 22.30 E
Pohjanlahti=Bothnia, Gulf of- (EN) 110 Hc 63.00N 20.00 E
Pohjanmaa 116 Jb 63.00N 22.30 E
Pohjois-Karjala [2] 114 Ge 63.00N 30.00 E
Pohlheim 124 Kd 50.32N 8.42 E
Pohorje 128 Jd 46.32N 15.28 E
Po Hu 154 Di 30.15N 116.32 E
Pohue Bay 221a Fd 19.01N 155.48W
Pohvistnevo 136 Fe 53.40N 52.08 E
Poiana Mare 130 Gf 43.55N 23.04 E
Poiana Ruscă, Munții 130 Fd 45.41N 22.30 E
Pöide/Pejde 116 Jf 58.30N 22.50 E
Poie 170 Dc 2.55S 23.10 E
Poindimié 216 Cd 20.56S 165.20 E
Poindo → Lhünzhub 152 Fe 30.17N 91.20 E
Poinsett, Cape- 222 He 65.42S 113.18 E
Poinsett, Lake- 186 Hd 44.34N 97.05W
Point Arena 188 Dg 38.55N 123.41W
Point au Fer Island 186 Kl 29.15N 91.15W
Pointe-à-Pitre 190 Le 16.14N 61.32W
Pointe Duble 197e Bb 16.20N 61.00W
Pointe-Noire 197e Ab 16.14N 61.47W
Pointe Noire 160 Ii 4.48S 11.51 E
Point Hope 178 Fc 68.21N 166.41W
Point Lake 180 Gc 65.15N 113.00W
Point Lay 178 Gc 69.45N 163.03W
Point Pleasant [N.J.-U.S.] 184 Je 40.06N 74.02W
Point Pleasant [W.V.-U.S.] 184 Ff 38.53N 82.07W
Poisson-Blanc, Lac- 184 Jc 46.00N 75.44W
Poissonnier Point 212 Dc 20.00S 119.10 E
Poissy 122 If 48.56N 2.03 E
Poitevin, Marais- 122 Eh 46.22N 1.06W
Poitiers 112 Gf 46.35N 0.20 E
Poitou 122 Fh 46.40N 0.30W
Poitou, Plaine et Seuil du- 122 Gh 46.26N 0.17 E
Poivre Islands 172b Bb 5.46S 53.19 E
Poix-de-Picardie 122 He 49.47N 1.59 E
Poix-Terron 124 Ge 49.39N 4.39 E
Pojarkovo 138 Hg 49.42N 128.50 E
Pojkovski 136 Hc 60.59N 72.00 E
Pojo/Pohja 116 Jd 60.06N 23.31 E
Pojuba, Rio- 204 Ec 16.30S 54.59W
Pokhara 148 Gc 28.14N 83.59 E
Poko 170 Eb 3.09N 26.53 E
Pokoinu 220p Bb 21.12S 159.49W
Pokój 120 Nf 50.56N 17.50 E
Pokrovka 135 Lc 42.19N 78.01 E
Pokrovsk 138 Hd 61.29N 129.10 E
Pokrovskoje [Russia] 132 Jc 52.38N 36.51 E
Pokrovskoje [Ukr.] 132 Jf 47.59N 36.13 E
Pokšenga 114 Kd 64.01N 44.15 E
Pokutje 130 Ia 48.20N 25.05 E
Pola 114 Hg 58.05N 31.40 E
Polabí 120 Lf 50.10N 15.10 E
Polacca 188 Ji 35.50N 110.23W
Pola de Laviana 126 Ga 43.15N 5.34W
Pola de Lena 126 Ga 43.10N 5.49W
Pola de Siero 126 Ga 43.23N 5.40W
Polanco 204 Ek 33.54S 55.09W
Poland 220g Ab 1.52N 157.33W
Poland (EN)=Polska [1] 112 He 52.00N 19.00 E
Polanów 120 Mb 54.08N 16.39 E
Polar Plateau 222 Cg 90.00S 0.00
Polar Urals (EN)=Poljarny Ural 110 Mb 66.55N 64.30 E
Polatli 144 Db 39.36N 32.09 E
Polch 124 Jd 50.18N 7.19 E
Połczyn Zdrój 120 Mc 53.46N 16.06 E
Pol-e Khomrī 144 Kb 35.56N 68.43 E
Pole of Inaccessibility (EN) 222 Eg 82.06S 54.58 E
Pol-e-Safid 146 Od 36.06N 53.01 E
Polesella 128 Ff 44.58N 11.45 E
Polesie Lubelskie 120 Te 51.30N 23.20 E
Polesine 128 Fe 45.00N 11.45 E
Polesje=Polesye (EN) 110 Ie 52.00N 27.00 E
Polessk 116 Ij 54.51N 21.02 E
Polesskoje 132 Fd 51.16N 29.27 E
Polesye (EN)=Polesje 110 Ie 52.00N 27.00 E
Polevskoj 136 Gd 56.28N 60.11 E
Polewali 150 Gg 3.25S 119.20 E
Poležan 130 Gh 41.43N 23.30 E
Polgár 120 Ri 47.52N 21.07 E
Pölgyo 154 Ig 34.51N 127.21 E
Poli 166 Hd 8.29N 13.15 E
Poliaigos 130 Hm 36.46N 24.38 E
Poliçani 130 Di 40.08N 20.21 E
Policastro, Golfo di- 128 Jk 40.00N 15.35 E
Police 120 Kc 53.33N 14.35 E
Police - Trzebież 120 Kc 53.39N 14.32 E
Policoro 128 Kj 40.13N 16.41 E
Poligny 122 Lh 46.50N 5.43 E
Poligus 138 Ed 61.58N 94.40 E
Polikastron 130 Fh 41.00N 22.34 E
Polikhnitos 130 Jj 39.05N 26.11 E
Polillo Islands 140 Oh 14.50N 122.05 E
Pólis 146 Ee 35.02N 32.25 E
Polist 114 Hg 58.07N 31.32 E
Polistena 128 Kl 38.24N 16.04 E
Políyros 130 Gi 40.23N 23.27 E
Poljarny [Russia] 138 Mc 69.01N 178.45 E
Poljarny [Russia] 136 Db 69.13N 33.28 E
Poljarny Ural=Polar Urals (EN) 110 Mb 66.55N 64.30 E
Polkowice 120 Me 51.32N 16.06 E
Pöllau 128 Jc 47.18N 15.50 E
Polle 220d Bb 7.20N 151.15 E
Pollença/Pollensa 126 Pe 39.53N 3.01 E
Pollensa/Pollença 126 Pe 39.53N 3.01 E
Pollino 110 Hh 39.55N 16.10 E
Polochic, Rio- 194 Cf 15.28N 89.22W
Polock 136 Cd 55.29N 28.52 E
Polog 130 Dh 42.00N 21.00 E
Pologi 136 Df 47.28N 36.15 E
Polonina 120 Jh 48.30N 23.30 E
Polonnaruwa 148 Gg 7.56N 81.00 E
Polonnoje 132 Ed 50.06N 27.29 E
Polousny krjaž 138 Jc 69.30N 144.00 E
Polska=Poland (EN) [1] 112 He 52.00N 19.00 E
Polski Gradec 130 Jg 42.11N 26.06 E
Polski Trămbeš 130 If 43.22N 25.38 E
Polson 188 Hc 47.41N 114.09W
Poltár 120 Ph 48.27N 19.48 E
Poltava 112 Jf 49.35N 34.34 E
Poltavka 136 He 54.22N 71.45 E
Poltavskaja oblast [3] 136 Df 49.45N 33.50 E
Põltsamaa/Pyltsamaa 114 Fg 58.39N 25.59 E
Põltsamaa/Pyltsamaa 116 Lf 58.23N 26.08 E
Poluj 138 Bc 66.30N 66.31 E
Polunočnoje 136 Gc 60.52N 60.25 E
Polür 146 Oe 32.52N 52.03 E
Põlva/Pylva 114 Gg 58.04N 27.06 E
Polvijärvi 114 Ge 62.51N 29.22 E
Polynesia 208 Le 4.00S 156.00W
Polynésie Française=French Polynesia (EN) [5] 210 Mf 16.00S 145.00W
Pom, Laguna de- 192 Mh 18.35N 92.15W
Pomarance 128 Eg 43.18N 10.52 E
Pomarkku/Påmark 116 Ic 61.42N 22.00 E
Pombal [Braz.] 202 Ke 6.46S 37.47W
Pombal [Port.] 126 De 39.55N 8.38W
Pombo, Rio- 204 Fe 20.53S 52.23W
Pomerania (EN)= Pommern 110 He 54.00N 16.00 E
Pomerania (EN)= Pommern 120 Lc 54.00N 16.00 E
Pomeranian Bay (EN)= Pommersche Bucht 120 Kb 54.20N 14.20 E
Pomeranian Bay (EN)= Pomorska, Zatoka- 120 Kb 54.20N 14.20 E
Pomeroy 184 Ff 39.03N 82.03W
Pomio 210 Ge 5.32S 151.30 E
Pomme de Terre Reservoir 186 Jh 37.51N 93.19W
Pommern=Pomerania (EN) 110 He 54.00N 16.00 E
Pommern=Pomerania (EN) 120 Lc 54.00N 16.00 E
Pommersche Bucht= Pomeranian Bay (EN) 120 Kb 54.20N 14.20 E
Pommersfelden 128 Gg 49.46N 10.49 E
Pomona 188 Gi 34.04N 117.45W
Pomona Lake 186 Ig 38.40N 95.35W
Pomorije 130 Kg 42.33N 27.39 E
Pomorska, Zatoka-= Pomeranian Bay (EN) 120 Kb 54.20N 14.20 E
Pomorski bereg 114 Id 64.00N 36.15 E
Pomorskie, Pojezierze- 120 Mc 53.30N 16.30 E
Pomorski proliv 136 Eb 68.40N 50.00 E
Pomošnaja 132 Ge 48.14N 31.29 E
Pompano Beach 184 Gl 26.15N 80.07W
Pompei 128 Ij 40.45N 14.30 E
Pompeu 204 Jd 19.12S 44.59W
Ponape 210 Gd 6.52N 158.15 E
Ponape Island 208 Gd 6.55N 158.15 E
Ponca City 182 Hd 36.42N 97.05W
Ponce 176 Mh 18.01N 66.37W
Poncheville, Lac- 184 Ia 50.12N 76.55W
Pondcreek 186 Hh 36.40N 97.48W
Pondicherry 148 Ff 11.56N 79.53 E
Pondicherry [3] 148 Ff 11.55N 79.45 E
Pond Inlet 176 Lb 72.41N 78.00W
Pond Inlet 180 Jb 72.48N 77.00W
Ponea 220n Ac 10.28S 161.01W
Ponente, Riviera di- 128 Cf 44.10N 8.20 E
Ponérihouen 219b Be 21.05S 165.24 E
Pones 220d Bb 7.12N 151.59 E
Ponferrada 126 Fb 42.33N 6.35W
Pongaroa 218 Gd 40.33S 176.11 E
Pongo 158 Jh 8.42N 27.40 E
Pongola 172 Ee 26.52S 32.20 E
Pong Qu 152 Ef 26.49N 87.09 E
Poniatowa 120 Se 51.11N 22.05 E
Ponoj 112 Kb 67.05N 41.07 E
Ponoj 110 Kb 66.59N 41.10 E
Ponomarevka 132 Sc 53.09N 54.12 E
Ponorogo 150 Fh 7.52S 111.27 E
Pons 122 Fi 45.35N 0.33W
Pons/Ponts 126 Nc 41.55N 1.12 E
Ponsul 126 Ee 39.40N 7.31W
Pont-à-Celles 124 Gd 50.30N 4.21 E
Ponta Delgada 160 Ee 37.44N 25.40W
Ponta Delgada [3] 162 Bb 37.48N 25.30W
Ponta Grossa 200 Kh 25.05S 50.09W
Pont-à-Mousson 122 Mf 48.54N 6.04 E
Ponta Porã 200 Kh 22.32S 55.43W
Pontarlier 122 Mh 46.54N 6.22 E
Pontassieve 128 Fg 43.46N 11.26 E
Pont-Audemer 122 Ge 49.21N 0.31 E
Pontaut 204 Bm 37.44S 61.20W
Pontávert 124 Fe 49.25N 3.49 E
Pontchartrain, Lake- 182 Ie 30.10N 90.10W
Pontchâteau 122 Dg 47.26N 2.05W
Pont-de-Claix, Le- 122 Li 45.07N 5.42 E
Pont-de-l'Arche 124 De 49.18N 1.10 E
Pont de Suert 126 Mb 42.24N 0.45 E
Pont-de-Vaux 122 Kh 46.26N 4.56 E
Ponte Alta 204 Gh 27.29S 50.23W
Ponte Alta, Serra da- 204 Id 19.42S 47.40W
Ponteareas / Puenteareas 126 Db 42.11N 8.30W
Ponte Branca 204 Fc 16.27S 52.40W
Pontecorvo 128 Hi 42.27N 13.40 E
Ponte de Lima 126 Dc 41.46N 8.35W
Ponte de Pedrā 204 Da 13.35S 57.21W
Ponte de Pedra 204 Ec 17.06S 54.23W
Ponte de Pedra, Rio- → Sacuriuiná, Rio- 204 Da 13.58S 57.18W
Pontedera 128 Eg 43.40N 10.38 E
Ponte de Sor 126 De 39.15N 8.01W
Pontedeume / Puentedeume 126 Da 43.24N 8.10W
Ponte Firme, Chapada da- 204 Id 18.05S 46.25W
Ponteix 188 Lb 49.49N 107.30W
Ponte Nova 202 Jh 20.24S 42.54W
Pontés e Lacerda 204 Cb 15.11S 59.21W
Pontevedra 126 Db 42.26N 8.38W
Pontevedra [3] 126 Db 42.30N 8.30W
Pontevedra, Ria de- 126 Db 42.22N 8.45W
Ponte Vermelha 204 Ed 19.29S 54.25W
Pont-Farcy 124 Af 48.56N 1.02W
Pontfaverger-Moronvilliers 124 Ge 49.18N 4.19 E
Ponthieu 122 Hd 50.10N 1.55 E
Pontiac [Il.-U.S.] 186 Lf 40.53N 88.38W
Pontiac [Mi.-U.S.] 184 Fd 42.37N 83.18W
Pontianak 142 Mj 0.02S 109.20 E
Pontian Kechil 150 Df 1.29N 103.23 E
Pontine Islands (EN) = Ponziane, Isole- 128 Gj 40.55N 13.00 E
Pontivy 122 Df 48.04N 2.59W
Pontivy, Pays de- 122 Dg 48.00N 3.00W
Pont-l'Abbé 122 Bg 47.52N 4.13W
Pont-l'Evêque 124 Ce 49.18N 0.11 E
Pontoise 122 Ie 49.03N 2.06 E
Pontorson 122 Ef 48.33N 1.31W
Pontremoli 128 Df 44.22N 9.53 E
Pontresina 128 Dd 46.28N 9.53 E
Ponts/Pons 126 Nc 41.55N 1.12 E
Pont-Sainte-Maxence 124 Ee 49.18N 2.36 E
Pont-Saint-Esprit 122 Kj 44.15N 4.39 E
Pontypool 118 Jj 51.43N 3.02W
Ponza 128 Gj 40.54N 12.58 E
Ponza 128 Gj 40.55N 12.55 E
Ponziane, Isole- = Pontine Islands (EN) 128 Gj 40.55N 13.00 E
Pool [3] 170 Bc 3.30S 15.00 E
Poole 118 Lk 50.43N 1.59W
Pool Malebo 158 Ii 4.02S 16.03 E
Poona→Pune 142 Jh 18.32N 73.52 E
Poopó 202 Eg 18.23S 66.59W
Poopó, Lago de- = Poopó, Lake- (EN) 198 Jg 18.45S 67.07W
Poopó, Lake- (EN) = Poopó, Lago de- 198 Jg 18.45S 67.07W
Poor Knights Islands 218 Fa 35.30S 174.45 E
Pōōsaspea neem / Pyzaspea 116 Je 59.15N 23.25 E
Popa Taung 148 Jd 21.08N 95.12 E
Popayán 200 Ie 2.27N 76.36W
Poperinge 122 Id 50.51N 2.43 E
Poperinge-Watou 124 Ed 50.51N 2.37 E
Popigaj 138 Gb 71.55N 110.47 E
Popigaj 138 Fb 72.55N 106.00 E
Poplar 188 Mb 48.07N 105.12W
Poplar 180 Hf 53.00N 97.18W
Poplar Bluff 182 Id 36.45N 90.24W
Poplar River 188 Mb 48.05N 105.11W
Popocatépetl, Volcán- 174 Jh 19.02N 98.38W
Popokabaka 170 Cd 5.42S 16.35 E
Popoli 128 Hh 42.10N 13.50 E
Popomanaseu, Mount- 219a Ec 9.42S 160.03 E
Popondetta 214 Di 8.46S 148.14 E
Popovo 130 Jf 43.21N 26.14 E
Poppberg 120 Hg 49.20N 11.45 E
Poppel, Ravels- 124 Hc 51.27N 5.02 E
Poprad 112 If 49.03N 20.19 E
Poprad 120 Qg 49.38N 20.42 E
Poptún 194 Ce 16.21N 89.26W
Por 120 Tf 50.48N 23.01 E
Porangahau 218 Gd 40.18S 176.38 E
Porangatu 204 Ha 13.26S 49.10W
Porbandar 148 Dd 21.38N 69.36 E
Porcien 124 Ge 49.40N 4.20 E
Porcos, Rio dos- 204 Ja 12.42S 45.07W
Porcuna 126 Hg 37.52N 4.11W
Porcupine 184 Ga 48.32N 81.10W
Porcupine 174 Ec 66.35N 145.15W
Porcupine Bank (EN) 110 Ee 53.20N 13.30W
Porcupine Creek 188 Lb 48.09N 106.22W
Porcupine Hills 188 Ha 50.05N 114.10W
Porcupine Plain 180 Dc 67.30N 137.30W
Pordenone 128 Ge 45.57N 12.39 E
Poreč 128 He 45.13N 13.37 E
Poreč 130 Fe 44.20N 22.05 E
Porecatú 204 Gf 22.43S 51.24W

Index Symbols

[1] Independent Nation
[2] State, Region
[3] District, County
[4] Municipality
[5] Colony, Dependency
Continent
Physical Region
Historical or Cultural Region
Mount, Mountain
Volcano
Hill
Mountains, Mountain Range
Hills, Escarpment
Plateau, Upland
Pass, Gap
Plain, Lowland
Delta
Salt Flat
Valley, Canyon
Crater, Cave
Karst Features
Depression
Polder
Desert, Dunes
Forest, Woods
Heath, Steppe
Oasis
Cape, Point
Coast, Beach
Cliff
Peninsula
Isthmus
Sandbank
Island
Atoll
Rock, Reef
Islands, Archipelago
Rocks, Reefs
Coral Reef
Well, Spring
Geyser
River, Stream
Waterfall, Rapids
River Mouth, Estuary
Lake
Salt Lake
Intermittent Lake
Reservoir
Swamp, Pond
Canal
Glacier
Ice Shelf, Pack Ice
Ocean
Sea
Gulf, Bay
Strait, Fjord
Lagoon
Bank
Seamount
Tablemount
Ridge
Shelf
Basin
Escarpment, Sea Scarp
Fracture
Trench, Abyss
National Park, Reserve
Point of Interest
Recreation Site
Cave, Cavern
Historic Site
Ruins
Wall, Walls
Church, Abbey
Temple
Scientific Station
Railway station
Airport
Port
Military installation
Lighthouse
Mine
Tunnel
Dam, Bridge

Porećje	116	Kk	53.53N	24.08 E
Poreckoje	114	Li	55.13N	46.19 E
Porhov	136	Cd	57.45N	29.32 E
Pori/Björneborg	112	Ic	61.29N	21.47 E
Poríon ◆	130	Gn	35.58N	23.16 E
Porirua	216	Dh	41.08 S	174.50 E
Pórisvatn ≈	114a	Bb	64.20N	18.55W
Porjus	114	Ec	66.57N	19.49 E
Porkkala ◆	116	Ke	59.55N	24.25 E
Porlamar	202	Fa	10.57N	63.51W
Porma ∿	126	Gb	42.29N	5.28W
Pornic	122	Dg	47.07N	2.06W
Poronajsk	142	Qe	49.14N	143.04 E
Poronin	120	Qg	49.20N	20.04 E
Póros	130	Gl	37.30N	23.27 E
Póros ◆	130	Gl	37.30N	23.31 E
Poroshiri-Dake ▲	154	Qc	42.42N	142.35 E
Porosozero	114	He	62.44N	32.42 E
Porozovo	120	Ud	52.54N	24.27 E
Porpoise Bay ◧	222	Ie	66.30 S	128.30 E
Porquis Junction	184	Ga	48.43N	80.52W
Porrentruy / Pruntrut	128	Bc	47.25N	7.10 E
Porreras / Porreres	126	Oe	39.31N	3.00 E
Porreres / Porreras	126	Oe	39.31N	3.00 E
Porretta, Passo della- ⊔	128	Ef	44.02N	10.56 E
Porretta Terme	128	Ef	44.09N	10.59 E
Porsangen ▃	110	Ia	70.50N	26.00 E
Porsangerhalvøya ⊟	114	Fa	70.50N	25.00 E
Porsgrunn	114	Bg	59.09N	9.40 E
Porsuk ∿	146	Dc	39.42N	31.59 E
Portachuelo	202	Fg	17.21 S	63.24W
Portadown/ Port an Dúnáin	118	Gg	54.26N	6.27W
Portage	186	Le	43.33N	89.28W
Portage la Prairie	180	Hg	49.57N	98.18W
Port Alberni	180	Fg	49.14N	124.48W
Portalegre	126	Ee	39.17N	7.26W
Portalegre [2]	126	Ee	39.15N	7.35W
Portales	182	Ge	34.11N	103.20W
Port Alfred	172	Df	33.36 S	26.55 E
Port Alice	180	Ef	50.23N	127.27W
Port Allegany	184	He	41.48N	78.18W
Port an Dúnáin/Portadown	118	Gg	54.26N	6.27W
Port Angeles	182	Cb	48.07N	123.27W
Port Antonio	190	Ie	18.11N	76.28W
Port Arthur [Austl.]	212	Jh	43.09 S	147.51 E
Port Arthur [Tx.-U.S.]	176	Jg	29.55N	93.55W
Port Arthur → Lüshun	152	Ld	38.50N	121.13 E
Port Augusta	210	Eh	32.30 S	137.46 E
Port-au-Prince	176	Lh	18.32N	72.20W
Port-au-Prince, Baie de- ◧	194	Kd	18.40N	72.30W
Port Austin	184	Fc	44.03N	83.01W
Port aux Français	222	Fc	49.25 S	70.10 E
Porta Westfalica	124	Kb	52.15N	8.56 E
Port-Bergé-Vaovao	172	Hc	15.33 S	47.38 E
Port-Bergé-Vao Vao	172	Hc	15.33 S	47.38 E
Port Blair	142	Lh	11.36N	92.45 E
Portbou/Port-Bou	126	Pb	42.25N	3.10 E
Port-Bou/Portbou	126	Pb	42.25N	3.10 E
Port Burwell [Newf.-Can.]	176	Mc	60.25N	64.49W
Port Burwell [Ont.-Can.]	184	Gd	42.39N	80.49W
Port-Cartier	180	Kf	50.01N	66.53W
Port Chalmers	218	Df	45.49 S	170.37 E
Port Charlotte	182	Kf	26.59N	82.06W
Port Clinton	184	Fe	41.30N	82.58W
Port Coquitlam	188	Db	49.16N	122.46W
Port-de-Bouc	122	Kk	43.24N	4.59 E
Port-de-Paix	194	Kd	19.57N	72.50W
Port Dickson	150	Df	2.31N	101.48 E
Port Edward	172	Ef	31.03 S	30.13 E
Portel [Braz.]	202	Hd	1.57 S	50.49W
Portel [Port.]	126	Ef	38.18N	7.42W
Port Elgin	184	Gc	44.26N	81.24W
Port Elizabeth [S.Afr.]	160	Jl	33.58 S	25.40 E
Port Elizabeth [St.Vin.]	197n	Ba	13.00N	61.16W
Port Ellen	118	Gf	55.39N	6.12W
Port-en-Bessin-Huppain	122	Fe	49.21N	0.45W
Port Erin	118	Ig	54.05N	4.43W
Porter Point ▶	197n	Ba	13.23N	61.11W
Porterville [Ca.-U.S.]	182	Dd	36.04N	119.01W
Porterville [S.Afr.]	172	Bf	33.00 S	19.00 E
Portete, Bahía de- ◧	194	Lg	12.13N	71.55W
Port Fairy	212	Ig	38.23 S	142.14 E
Port Fitzroy	218	Fb	36.10 S	175.21 E
Port-Gentil	160	Hi	0.43 S	8.47 E
Port Gibson	186	Kk	31.58N	90.58W
Port Harcourt	160	Hh	4.46N	7.01 E
Port Hardy	180	Ef	50.43N	127.29W
Port Hawkesbury	180	Lg	45.37N	61.21W
Porthcawl	118	Jj	51.29N	3.43W
Port Hedland	210	Cg	20.19 S	118.34 E
Port Heiden	178	He	56.55N	158.41W
Porthmadog	118	Ii	52.55N	4.08W
Port Hope Simpson	180	Lf	52.30N	56.17W
Port Huron	182	Kc	42.58N	82.27W
Portile de Fier = Iron Gate (EN) ⊔	110	Ig	44.41N	22.31 E
Port-Ilič	132	Pj	38.53N	48.51 E
Portimão	126	Dg	37.08N	8.32W
Port Isabel	186	Hm	26.04N	97.13W
Portiţa ∿	130	Me	44.41N	29.00 E
Port Láirge/Waterford	112	Fe	52.15N	7.06W
Port Láirge/Waterford [2]	118	Fi	52.10N	7.40W
Portland [Austl.]	212	Ig	38.21 S	141.36 E
Portland [In.-U.S.]	184	Ee	40.26N	84.59W
Portland [Me.-U.S.]	176	Le	43.39N	70.17W
Portland [N.D.-U.S.]	186	Hc	47.30N	97.22W
Portland [N.Z.]	218	Fa	35.48 S	174.20 E
Portland [Or.-U.S.]	176	Ge	45.33N	122.36W
Portland [Tx.-U.S.]	186	Hm	27.53N	97.20W
Portland, Bill of- ▶	118	Kk	50.31N	2.28W
Portland, Promontoire - ▶	180	Je	58.41N	78.33W
Portland Bight ◧	194	Ie	17.57N	77.08W
Portland Island ◆	218	Gc	39.20 S	177.50 E
Portland Point ▶	194	Ie	17.42N	77.11W
Port-la-Nouvelle	122	Jk	43.01N	3.03 E
Port Laoise/Portlaoise	118	Fh	53.02N	7.17W
Portlaoise/Port Laoise	118	Fh	53.02N	7.17W
Port Lavaca	182	Hf	28.37N	96.38W
Port Lincoln	210	Eh	34.44 S	135.52 E
Port Loko	166	Cd	8.46N	12.47W
Port Louis	196	Fd	16.25N	61.32W
Port-Louis	160	Mk	20.10 S	U.30 E
Port Macquarie	212	Kf	31.26 S	152.44 E
Port Maria	194	Id	18.22N	76.54W
Port-Menier	180	Lg	49.49N	64.20W
Port Moller	178	Ge	55.59N	160.34W
Port Moody	188	Db	49.17N	122.51W
Port Moresby	210	Fe	9.30 S	147.07 E
Port Nelson ⊜	180	Ie	57.04N	92.30W
Portneuf, Rivière- ∿	184	Ma	48.37N	69.05W
Port Nolloth	160	Ik	29.17 S	16.51 E
Port Nouveau-Québec	176	Md	58.35N	65.59W
Porto [2]	126	Dc	41.15N	8.20W
Porto [Fr.]	122a	Aa	42.16N	8.42 E
Porto [Port.]	112	Fg	41.09N	8.37W
Porto, Golfe de- ◧	122a	Aa	42.16N	8.37 E
Porto Acre	202	Ee	9.34 S	67.31W
Porto Alegre [Braz.]	200	Ki	30.04 S	51.11W
Porto Alegre [Sao T.P.]	166	Ge	0.02N	6.32 E
Porto Amboim	160	Ij	10.44 S	13.45 E
Porto Azzurro	128	Eh	42.46N	10.24 E
Portobelo	194	Hi	9.33N	79.39W
Porto Cedro	204	Ed	18.17 S	55.02W
Porto Cervo	128	Di	41.08N	9.35 E
Porto Curupai	204	Ff	22.50 S	53.53W
Porto de Moz	200	Kf	1.45 S	52.14W
Porto Empedocle	128	Hm	37.17N	13.32 E
Porto Esperança [Braz.]	204	Db	14.02 S	56.06W
Porto Esperança [Braz.]	204	Dd	19.37 S	57.27W
Porto Esperança [Braz.]	204	Dc	17.47 S	57.07W
Porto Esperidião	204	Cb	15.51 S	58.28W
Porto Estrêla	204	Db	15.20 S	57.14W
Portoferraio	128	Eh	42.49N	10.19 E
Port of Ness	118	Gc	58.30N	6.15W
Porto Franco	202	Ie	6.20 S	47.24W
Port of Spain	200	Jd	10.39N	61.31W
Porto Fundação	204	Ea	13.39 S	55.18W
Portogruaro	128	Ge	45.47N	12.50 E
Porto Lucena	204	Eh	27.51 S	55.01W
Pörtom/Pirttikyla	116	Ib	62.42N	21.37 E
Portomaggiore	128	Ff	44.42N	11.48 E
Porto Mendes	204	Eg	24.30 S	54.20W
Porto Moniz	162	Dc	32.51N	17.10W
Porto Moroco	204	Ea	13.24 S	55.35W
Porto Morrinho	204	Dc	16.38 S	57.49W
Porto Murtinho	200	Kh	21.42 S	57.52W
Porto Novo [Ben.]	160	Hh	6.29N	2.37 E
Porto Novo [C.V.]	162	Bf	17.07N	25.04W
Port Orford	188	Ce	42.45N	124.30W
Porto San Giorgio	128	Hg	43.11N	13.48 E
Porto Santana	202	Hd	0.03 S	51.11W
Porto Sant'Elpidio	128	Hg	43.15N	13.45 E
Porto Santo ◆	158	Fe	33.04N	16.20W
Porto Santo Stefano	128	Fh	42.26N	11.07 E
Portoscuso	128	Ck	39.12N	8.23 E
Porto Seguro	202	Kg	16.26 S	39.05W
Porto Tolle	128	Gf	44.56N	12.22 E
Porto Torres	128	Cj	40.50N	8.24 E
Porto União	204	Gh	26.15 S	51.05W
Porto Válter	202	De	8.15 S	72.45W
Porto Vecchio	122a	Bb	41.35N	9.17 E
Porto Velho	200	Jf	8.46 S	63.54W
Portoviejo	200	Hf	1.03 S	80.27W
Porto Xavier	204	Eh	27.54 S	55.08W
Port Phillip Bay ◧	212	Ig	38.05 S	144.50 E
Port Pirie	210	Eh	33.11 S	138.01 E
Portree	118	Gd	57.24N	6.12W
Port Renfrew	188	Cb	48.33N	124.25W
Port Rois/Portrush	118	Gf	55.12N	6.40W
Port Royal	184	If	38.10N	77.12W
Portrush/Port Rois	118	Gf	55.12N	6.40W
Port Said (EN) = Būr Sa'īd	160	Ke	31.16N	32.18 E
Port Saint Joe	182	Jf	29.49N	85.18W
Port Saint Johns	172	Df	31.38 S	29.33 E
Port-Saint-Louis-du-Rhône	122	Kk	43.23N	4.48 È
Port-Salut	194	Kd	18.05N	73.55W
Port Saunders	180	Lf	50.39N	57.18W
Port Shepstone	160	Kl	30.46 S	30.22 E
Portsmouth [Dom.]	196	Fe	15.35N	61.28W
Portsmouth [Eng.-U.K.]	118	Lk	50.48N	1.05W
Portsmouth [N.H.-U.S.]	182	Mc	43.03N	70.47W
Portsmouth [Oh.-U.S.]	182	Kd	38.45N	82.59W
Portsmouth [Va.-U.S.]	182	Ld	36.50N	76.26W
Portsmouth City Airport ✈	124	Ad	50.46N	1.04W
Port Sudan (EN)=Būr Sūdān	160	Kg	19.37N	37.14 E
Port Sulphur	186	Ll	29.29N	89.42W
Port Talbot	118	Jj	51.36N	3.47W
Porttipahdantekojärvi ≈	114	Gb	68.06N	26.33 E
Port Townsend	188	Db	48.07N	122.46W
Portugal [1]	112	Fh	39.30N	8.00W
Portugalete	126	Ia	43.19N	3.01W
Portuguesa [2]	202	Eb	9.10N	69.15W
Portuguesa, Río- ∿	202	Eb	7.57N	67.32W
Portuguesa, Sierra de- ⛰	196	Bh	9.35N	69.45W
Portuguese Guinea (EN) → Guinea-Bissau (EN) [1]	160	Fg	12.00N	15.00W
Portús, Coll del-/Perthus, Col de- ⊔	126	Ob	42.28N	2.51 E
Port-Vendres	122	Jl	42.31N	3.07 E
Port-Vila	210	Hf	17.44 S	168.19 E
Port Wakefield	212	Hf	34.11 S	138.09 E
Port Washington	186	Me	43.23N	87.53W
Porvenir [Bol.]	204	Ba	13.59 S	61.39W
Porvenir [Bol.]	202	Ef	11.15 S	68.41W
Porvenir [Chile]	206	Fh	53.18 S	70.22W
Porvenir [Ur.]	204	Dk	32.23 S	57.59W
Porvoo/Borgå	114	Ff	60.24N	25.40 E
Porvoonjoki ∿	116	Kd	60.23N	25.40 E
Porz, Köln-	120	Df	50.53N	7.03 E
Posada, Fiume di- ∿	128	Dj	40.39N	9.45 E
Posadas [Arg.]	200	Kh	27.25 S	55.50W
Posadas [Sp.]	126	Gg	37.48N	5.06W
Posavina ⊠	128	Le	45.00N	17.30 E
Poschiavo / Puschlav	128	Ed	46.20N	10.04 E
Pošehonje	114	Jg	58.30N	39.08 E
Posets	126	Mb	42.39N	0.25 E
Posht-e Bādām	146	Pf	33.02N	55.23 E
Posio	114	Gc	66.06N	28.09 E
Posjet	154	Kc	42.39N	130.48 E
Poskam/Zepu	152	Cd	38.12N	77.18 E
Poso	142	Oj	1.23 S	120.44 E
Poso, Danau- ≈	150	Hg	1.52 S	120.35 E
Posof	146	Jb	41.31N	42.42 E
Posŏng	154	Ig	34.46N	127.05 E
Pospeliha	138	Df	52.02N	81.56 E
Posse	202	If	14.05 S	46.22W
Possession, Ile de la- ◆	222	Ec	46.14 S	49.55 E
Possession Island ◆	172	Be	27.01 S	15.30 E
Pößneck	120	Hf	50.42N	11.36 E
Post	186	Fj	33.12N	101.23W
Posta de San Martín	204	Bk	33.09 S	60.31W
Postavy	136	Cd	55.07N	26.50 E
Poste-de-la-Baleine	180	Je	55.20N	76.50W
Poste Maurice Cortier/Bidon V	162	He	22.18N	1.05 E
Poste Weygand	162	He	24.29N	0.40 E
Postmasburg	172	Ce	28.18 S	23.05 E
Postojna	128	Ie	45.47N	14.14 E
Posto Simões Lopes	204	Eb	14.14 S	54.41W
Postville [Ia.-U.S.]	186	Ke	43.05N	91.34W
Postville [Newf.-Can.]	180	Lf	54.55N	59.58W
Potchefstroom	172	De	26.46 S	27.01 E
Poteau	186	Ii	35.03N	94.37W
Potenza	128	Jj	40.38N	15.48 E
Potenza ∿	128	Hg	43.25N	13.40 E
Poteriteri, Lake- ≈	218	Bg	46.05 S	167.05 E
Potes	126	Ha	43.09N	4.37W
Potgietersrus	172	Dd	24.15 S	28.55 E
Potholes Reservoir ⊜	188	Fc	47.01N	119.19W
Poti	112	Kg	42.08N	41.39 E
Poti, Rio- ∿	202	Je	5.02 S	42.50W
Potigny	124	Bf	48.58N	0.14W
Potiskum	160	Ig	11.43N	11.04 E
Potnarhvin	219b	Dd	18.45 S	169.12 E
Potomac ∿	174	Lf	38.00N	76.18W
Potosí [3]	202	Eh	20.40 S	67.00W
Potosí [Bol.]	200	Jg	19.35 S	65.45W
Potosí [Mex.]	190	Dd	24.51N	100.19W
Potosí, Bahía- ◧	192	Ii	17.35N	101.30W
Potosí, Cerro- ▲	192	Ie	24.52N	100.13W
Pototan	150	Hd	10.55N	122.40 E
Potrerillos	206	Gc	26.26S	69.29W
Potrero, Río-	204	Bc	17.32S	61.35W
Potsdam [Ger.]	120	Jd	52.24N	13.04 E
Potsdam [N.Y.-U.S.]	184	Jc	44.40N	75.01W
Pott ◆	219b	Ad	19.35 S	163.36 E
Potters Bar	124	Bc	51.41N	0.10W
Pottstown	184	Je	40.15N	75.38W
Pottsville	184	Ie	40.42N	76.13W
Pouancé	122	Eg	47.45N	1.10W
Pouébo	219b	Be	20.24 S	164.34 E
Pouembout	219b	Be	21.08 S	164.54 E
Poughkeepsie	184	Ke	41.43N	73.56W
Poulaphouca Reservoir / Loch Pholl an Phúca ⊜	118	Gh	53.10N	6.30W
Poum	219b	Be	20.14 S	164.01 E
Pourtalé	204	Bm	37.02 S	60.36W
Pouso Alegre	202	Ih	22.13 S	45.56W
Pouss	166	Ic	10.51N	15.03 E
Poutasi	221c	Bb	14.01 S	171.41W
Poŭthĭsăt	148	Kf	12.32N	103.55 E
Poutrincourt, Lac- ≈	184	Ja	49.13N	74.04W
Po Valley (EN)=Padana, Pianura- ⌣	110	Gf	45.20N	10.00 E
Považská Bystrica	120	Og	49.07N	18.28 E
Považský Inovec ⛰	120	Nh	48.35N	18.00 E
Povenec	114	Ie	62.51N	34.45 E
Poverty Bay ◧	218	Gc	38.45 S	178.00 E
Povlen ⛰	130	Ce	44.09N	19.44 E
Póvoa de Varzim	126	Dc	41.23N	8.46W
Povorino	132	Md	51.12N	42.17 E
Povungnituk	176	Lc	60.02N	77.10W
Povungnituk ∿	180	Jd	60.03N	77.16W
Powassan	184	Hb	46.05N	79.22W
Powder River [Or.-U.S.] ∿	188	Gd	44.45N	117.03W
Powder River [U.S.] ∿	182	Fb	46.44N	105.26W
Powell	188	Kd	44.45N	108.46W
Powell, Lake- ⊜	182	Ed	37.25N	110.45W
Powell Lake ≈	188	Ca	50.11N	124.24W
Powell River	180	Fg	49.52N	124.33W
Powers	184	Dc	45.39N	87.32W
Powers Lake	186	Eb	48.34N	102.39W
Powidzkie, Jezioro- ≈	120	Nd	52.24N	17.57 E
Powys [3]	118	Ji	52.25N	3.20W
Poxoréu	202	Hg	15.50 S	54.23W
Poxoréu, Rio- [Braz.] ∿	204	Ec	16.32 S	54.46W
Poxoréu, Rio- [Braz.] ∿	204	Ec	16.08 S	54.14W
Poya	219b	Be	21.21 S	165.09 E
Poyang Hu ≈	140	Ng	29.00N	116.25 E
Poza de la Sal	126	Ib	42.40N	3.30W
Pozanti	146	Fd	37.25N	34.52 E
Požarevac	130	Ee	44.37N	21.12 E
Poza Rica de Hidalgo	176	Jg	20.33N	97.27W
Požarskoje	154	Ma	46.16N	134.04 E
Požega	130	Df	43.51N	20.02 E
Poznań	112	He	52.25N	16.55 E
Poznań [2]	120	Md	52.25N	16.30 E
Pozoblanco	126	Hf	38.22N	4.51W
Pozo Borrado	204	Bi	28.56 S	61.41W
Pozo Colorado	204	Cf	23.22 S	58.55W
Pozo del Mortero	204	Bg	24.24 S	61.02W
Pozo del Tigre	204	Bc	17.34 S	61.59W
Pozo Dulce	204	Ai	29.04 S	62.02W
Pozos, Punta- ▶	206	Gg	47.57 S	65.47W
Pozuelos	202	Fa	10.11N	64.39W
Pozzallo	128	In	36.43N	14.51 E
Pozzuoli	128	Ij	40.49N	14.07 E
Pra [Ghana] ∿	166	Ed	6.27N	1.47W
Pra [Russia]	114	Ji	54.45N	41.01 E
Prabuty	120	Pc	53.46N	19.10 E
Prachatice	120	Jg	49.01N	14.00 E
Prachin Buri	148	Kf	14.02N	101.22 E
Prachuap Khiri Khan	148	Jf	11.48N	99.47 E
Praděd ▲	120	Nf	50.06N	17.14 E
Prades	122	Il	42.37N	2.26 E
Prado	202	Kg	17.21 S	39.13W
Præstø	116	Ei	55.07N	12.03 E
Prague (EN)=Praha	112	He	50.05N	14.26 E
Praha=Prague (EN)	112	He	50.05N	14.26 E
Prahova [2]	130	Id	45.10N	26.00 E
Prahova ∿	130	Je	44.43N	26.27 E
Praia	160	Eg	14.55N	23.31W
Praia a Mare	128	Jk	39.54N	15.47 E
Praia da Rocha	126	Dg	37.07N	8.32W
Praia Rica	204	Eb	14.51 S	55.33W
Praid	130	Ic	46.33N	25.08 E
Prainha	202	Hd	1.48 S	53.29W
Prairie Dog Town Fork ∿	186	Gi	34.26N	99.21W
Prairie du Chien	186	Ke	43.03N	91.09W
Prangli ◆	116	Ke	59.38N	24.50 E
Prānhita ∿	148	Fe	18.49N	79.55 E
Prapat	150	Cf	2.40N	98.56 E
Prasat	148	Kf	14.38N	103.24 E
Praslin	197k	Bb	13.53N	60.54W
Praslin, Port- ◧	197k	Bb	13.53N	60.54W
Praslin Island ◆	172b	Ca	4.19 S	55.44 E
Prasonísion ◆	130	Kn	35.52N	27.46 E
Prat, Isla- ◆	206	Fg	48.15 S	75.00W
Prata	202	Ig	19.18 S	48.55W
Prata, Rio da- ∿	204	Hd	18.49 S	49.54W
Pratapgarh	148	Ed	24.02N	74.47 E
Prat de Llobregat / el Prat de Llobregat	126	Oc	41.20N	2.06 E
Prato	128	Fg	43.53N	11.06 E
Pratomagno ⛰	128	Fg	43.40N	11.40 E
Pratt	182	Hd	37.39N	98.44W
Prättigau ⊠	128	Dd	46.55N	9.40 E
Pratt Seamount (EN) ⊻	178	Ke	56.10N	142.30W
Prattville	184	Di	32.28N	86.29W
Pratudinho, Rio- ∿	204	Ja	13.58 S	45.10W
Pravda	135	Cf	36.50N	60.33 E
Pravda Coast ≋	222	Ge	67.00 S	94.00 E
Pravdinsk [Russia]	114	Kh	56.33N	43.33 E
Pravdinsk [Russia]	116	Ij	54.28N	21.00 E
Pravia	126	Fa	43.29N	6.07W
Praxedis G. Guerrero	192	Gb	31.22N	106.00W
Praya	150	Gh	8.42 S	116.17 E
Prealpi Venete ⛰	128	Fd	46.25N	11.50 E
Predazzo	128	Fd	46.19N	11.36 E
Predeal	130	Id	45.30N	25.34 E
Predeal, Pasul- ⊔	130	Id	45.28N	25.36 E
Predel ⊔	128	Hd	46.25N	13.35 E
Predil, Passo del- ⊔	128	Hd	46.25N	13.35 E
Predivinsk	138	Ee	57.04N	93.37 E
Predporožny	138	Jd	65.00N	143.20 E
Pré-en-Pail	122	Ff	48.27N	0.12W
Preetz	120	Gb	54.14N	10.17 E
Pregolia ∿	114	Ei	54.42N	20.24 E
Pregradnaja	132	Lh	43.58N	41.12 E
Preilj/Prejli	114	Gh	56.19N	26.48 E
Preissac, Lac- ≈	184	Ha	48.25N	78.28W
Prejli/Preilj	114	Gh	56.19N	26.48 E
Prekmurje ⊠	128	Kd	46.45N	16.15 E
Prekornica ▲	130	Cg	42.40N	19.12 E
Prekule/Priekulė	116	Ii	55.36N	21.12 E
Přelouč	120	Lf	50.02N	15.33 E
Premià de Mar/Premiá de Mar	126	Oc	41.29N	2.22 E
Premiá de Mar/Premià de Mar	126	Oc	41.29N	2.22 E
Premnitz	120	Id	52.32N	12.20 E
Premuda ◆	128	If	44.21N	14.37 E
Prenaj/Prienai	114	Fi	54.39N	23.59 E
Prenj ⛰	128	Lg	43.32N	17.52 E
Prenjasi	130	Dh	41.04N	20.32 E
Prentice	186	Kd	45.33N	90.17W
Prentiss	186	Lk	31.36N	89.52W
Prenzlau	120	Jc	53.19N	13.52 E
Preobraženije	138	Ih	42.58N	133.55 E
Preobraženka	138	Fd	60.04N	107.58 E
Preparis Island ◆	148	If	14.52N	93.41 E
Preparis North Channel ▃	148	Ie	15.27N	94.05 E
Preparis South Channel ▃	150	Bd	14.45N	94.05 E
Přerov	120	Ng	49.27N	17.27 E
Prescott [Ar.-U.S.]	186	Jj	33.48N	93.23W
Prescott [Az.-U.S.]	182	Ee	34.33N	112.28W
Preseli, Mynydd- ▲	118	Ij	51.58N	4.42W
Preševo	130	Eg	42.19N	21.39 E
Presho	186	Fe	43.53N	100.04W
Presicce	128	Mk	39.54N	18.16 E
Presidencia Roque Sáenz Peña	200	Jh	26.50 S	60.30W
Presidente Epitácio	206	Jb	21.46 S	52.06W
Presidente Frei ⊞	222	Re	62.12 S	58.55W
Presidente Hayes [3]	204	Cf	24.00 S	59.00W
Presidente Juscelino	204	Jd	18.39 S	44.05W
Presidente Murtinho	204	Fb	15.39 S	53.54W
Presidente Olegário	204	Id	18.25 S	46.25W
Presidente Prudente	206	Jb	22.07 S	51.22W
Presidente Venceslau	204	Ge	21.52 S	51.50W
President Thiers Seamount (EN) ⊻	208	Mg	24.39 S	145.51W
Presidio	182	Gf	29.33N	104.23W
Presidio, Río del- ∿	192	Ff	23.06N	106.17W
Preslav	130	Jf	43.10N	26.49 E
Presnovka	134	Mi	54.40N	67.09 E
Prešov	120	Rh	49.00N	21.14 E
Prespa ⛰	130	Hh	41.43N	24.53 E
Prespa, Lake- (EN)= Prespansko jezero ≈	110	Ig	40.55N	21.00 E
Prespansko jezero=Prespa, Lake- (EN) ≈	110	Ig	40.55N	21.00 E
Presque Isle	182	Nb	46.41N	68.01W
Prestea	166	Ed	5.26N	2.09W
Přeštice	120	Jg	49.35N	13.21 E
Preston [Eng.-U.K.]	118	Kh	53.46N	2.42W
Preston [Id.-U.S.]	182	Ec	42.06N	111.53W
Preston [Ont.-Can.]	184	Gd	43.23N	80.21W
Prestonsburg	184	Fg	37.40N	82.46W
Preststranda	116	Ce	59.06N	9.04 E
Prestwick	118	If	55.30N	4.37W
Prêto, Rio- [Braz.] ∿	202	Jf	11.21 S	43.52W
Prêto, Rio- [Braz.] ∿	204	Ha	13.37 S	48.06W
Prêto, Rio- [Braz.] ∿	204	Ic	17.00 S	46.12W
Prêto, Rio- [Braz.] ∿	204	Gd	18.44 S	50.23W
Preto do Igapó Açu, Rio- ∿	202	Gd	4.26 S	59.48W
Pretoria	160	Jk	25.45 S	28.10 E
Pretty Rock Butte ▲	186	Fc	46.10N	101.42W
Preußisch-Oldendorf	124	Kb	52.18N	8.30 E
Préveza	130	Dk	38.57N	20.45 E
Prey	124	Df	48.58N	1.13 E
Prey Vêng	148	Lf	11.29N	105.19 E
Priangarskoje plato ⏢	138	Ee	57.30N	97.00 E
Priargunsk	138	Gf	50.27N	119.00 E
Pribelski	134	Hi	54.24N	56.29 E
Pribilof Islands ❖	174	Cd	57.00N	170.00W
Priboj	130	Cf	43.35N	19.32 E
Příbram	120	Kg	49.42N	14.01 E
Price [Que.-Can.]	184	Ma	48.39N	68.12W
Price [Ut.-U.S.]	188	Jg	39.36N	110.48W
Price River ∿	188	Jg	39.10N	110.06W
Prichard	184	Cj	30.44N	88.05W
Prickly Pear Cays ❖	197b	Ab	18.16N	63.11W
Prickly Point ▶	197p	Bc	11.59N	61.45W
Pridneprovskaja vozvyšennost = Dnepr Upland (EN) ⏢	110	Jf	49.00N	32.00 E
Priego	126	Jd	40.27N	2.18W
Priego de Córdoba	126	Hg	37.26N	4.11W
Priei, Măgura- ▲	130	Fc	46.58N	22.50 E
Priekule	114	Eh	56.29N	21.37 E
Priekulė/Prekule	116	Ii	55.36N	21.12 E
Prienai/Prenaj	114	Fi	54.39N	23.59 E
Priene ∴	146	Bd	37.40N	27.13 E
Prieska	160	Jk	29.40 S	22.42 E
Priest Lake ≈	188	Gb	48.34N	116.52W
Prieta, Peña- ▲	126	Ha	43.01N	4.44W
Prieta, Sierra- ⛰	192	Cb	31.15N	112.55W
Prievidza	120	Oh	48.46N	18.39 E
Prignitz ⊠	120	Hc	53.00N	12.00 E
Prijedor	128	Kf	44.59N	16.42 E
Prijepolje	130	Cf	43.24N	19.39 E
Prijutovo	136	Fe	53.58N	53.58 E
Prikaspijskaja nizmennost = Caspian Depression (EN) ⌣	110	Lf	48.00N	52.00 E
Prilenskoje plato = Lena Mountains (EN) ⏢	140	Oc	60.45N	125.00 E
Prilep	130	Eh	41.21N	21.34 E
Priluki	136	De	50.36N	32.24 E
Primavera ⊞	222	Qe	64.09 S	60.57W
Primeira Cruz	202	Jd	2.30 S	43.26W
Primorje	116	Hj	54.56N	20.00 E
Primorsk [Russia]	114	Gf	60.22N	28.36 E
Primorsk [Russia]	120	Pb	54.44N	19.59 E
Primorsk [Ukr.]	132	Jf	46.43N	36.22 E
Primorski hrebet ⛰	138	Ff	52.30N	106.00 E
Primorski kraj [3]	138	Ig	45.30N	135.30 E
Primorsko	130	Kg	42.16N	27.46 E
Primorsko-Ahtarsk	136	Df	46.03N	38.11 E
Primorskoje [Russia]	116	Ld	60.32N	27.56 E
Primorskoje [Ukr.]	130	Nd	45.59N	30.15 E
Primošten	128	Jg	43.36N	15.55 E
Primrose Lake ≈	180	Gf	54.55N	109.45W
Prims ∿	120	Cg	49.20N	6.44 E
Prince Albert	176	Id	53.12N	104.46W
Prince Albert Mountains ⛰	222	Jf	76.00 S	161.30 E
Prince Albert Peninsula ⊟	180	Fb	72.30N	116.00W
Prince Albert Road	172	Cf	33.13 S	22.02 E
Prince Albert Sound ▃	180	Gb	70.25N	115.00W
Prince Alfred, Cape - ▶	180	Fb	74.05N	124.29W
Prince Charles ◆	174	Lc	67.50N	76.00W
Prince Charles Mountains ⛰	222	Ff	72.00 S	67.00 E
Prince-de-Galles, Cap - ▶	180	Kd	61.36N	71.30W
Prince Edward ◆	158	Km	46.33 S	37.57 E
Prince Edward Island [2]	180	Lg	46.30N	63.00W
Prince EdKard Island ◆	174	Me	46.30N	63.00W
Prince Edward Islands ❖	158	Km	46.35 S	37.56 E
Prince George	176	Gd	53.55N	122.49W
Prince Gustaf Adolf Sea ▤	174	Ib	78.30N	107.00W
Prince of Wales [Ak.-U.S.] ◆	178	Me	55.47N	132.50W
Prince of Wales [Can.] ◆	174	Jb	72.40N	99.00W
Prince of Wales, Cape- ▶	174	Cc	65.40N	168.05W
Prince of Wales Island ◆	212	Ib	10.40 S	142.10 E
Prince of Wales Mountains ⛰	180	Ja	77.45N	78.00W
Prince of Wales Strait ▃	180	Fb	72.45N	118.00W
Prince Patrick ◆	174	Hb	76.45N	119.30W
Prince Regent Inlet ▃	180	Ib	72.45N	90.30W
Prince Rupert	176	Fd	54.19N	130.19W
Prince Rupert Bay ◧	197g	Ba	15.34N	61.29W
Prince Rupert Bluff ▶	197g	Ba	15.35N	61.29W
Princes Risborough	124	Bc	51.43N	0.49W
Princess Anne	184	Jf	38.12N	75.41W
Princess Charlotte Bay ◧	212	Ib	14.25 S	144.00 E
Princess Elizabeth Land ⊠	222	Ff	70.00 S	80.00 E
Princess Margaret Range ⛰	180	Ia	79.00N	88.30W
Princess Royal ◆	180	Ef	52.55N	128.50W
Princeton [B.C.-Can.]	180	Fg	49.27N	120.31W
Princeton [Il.-U.S.]	186	Lf	41.23N	89.28W
Princeton [In.-U.S.]	184	Df	38.21N	87.34W
Princeton [Ky.-U.S.]	184	Dg	37.07N	87.53W
Princeton [Mo.-U.S.]	186	Jf	40.24N	93.35W
Prince William Sound ▃	174	Ec	60.40N	147.00W
Principe ◆	158	Hh	1.37N	7.25 E
Prineville	188	Ed	44.18N	120.51W
Prineville Reservoir ⊜	188	Ed	44.08N	120.42W
Prins Christians Sund ▃	179	Hf	60.00N	43.10W
Prinsesse Astrid Kyst ≋	222	Cf	70.45 S	12.30 E
Prinsesse Ragnhild Kyst ≋	222	Df	70.15 S	27.30 E
Prins Harald Kyst ≋	222	De	69.30 S	36.00 E
Prins Karls Forland ◆	179	Nc	78.32N	11.10 E
Prinzapolka	190	Hf	13.24N	83.34W
Prinzapolka, Río- ∿	194	Fg	13.24N	83.34W
Priora, Mount- ▲	212	Ja	6.51 S	145.58 E

Index Symbols

Qalīb ash Shuyūkh 144 Gd 29.12N 47.55 E
Qallābāt 168 Fc 12.58N 36.09 E
Qalmarz, Godār-e- 146 Qf 33.26N 56.14 E
Qalyūb 146 Dg 30.11N 31.13 E
Qamata 172 Df 31.58S 27.24 E
Qamdo 142 Lf 31.15N 97.12 E
Qamīnis 164 Dc 31.40N 20.01 E
Qamsar 146 Nf 33.45N 51.26 E
Qamūdah 162 Ic 35.00N 9.21 E
Qamūdah [3] 162 Ic 34.50N 9.20 E
Qânâq/Thule 224 Od 77.35N 69.40W
Qandahār 142 If 31.35N 65.45 E
Qandahār [3] 144 Kc 31.00N 65.45 E
Qandala 168 Hc 11.23N 49.53 E
Qangdin Gol 154 Cc 43.27N 115.03 E
Qanţarat al Faḩş 128 Dn 36.23N 9.54 E
Qapqal 152 Dc 43.48N 80.47 E
Qaqortoq/Julianehåb 224 Nc 60.50N 46.10W
Qarā Dāgh 146 Lc 38.48N 47.13 E
Qārah 164 Ed 29.37N 26.30 E
Qarah Būlāq 146 Ke 34.32N 45.12 E
Qarah Dagh 146 Jd 37.00N 43.30 E
Qarah Tappah 146 Ke 34.25N 44.56 E
Qarānqū 146 Ld 37.23N 47.43 E
Qardo 160 Lh 9.30N 49.03 E
Qareh Āghāj 146 Ld 36.46N 48.46 E
Qareh Sū [Asia] 144 Gb 39.27N 47.30 E
Qareh Sū [Iran] 144 Hc 34.52N 51.25 E
Qareh Sū [Iran] 144 Ib 37.00N 56.50 E
Qareh Ẕīā'Od Dīn 146 Kc 38.53N 45.02 E
Qarkilik/Ruoqiang 142 Kf 39.02N 88.00 E
Qarnayn, Jazīrat al- 146 Oj 24.56N 52.52 E
Qarqan/Qiemo 142 Kf 38.08N 85.32 E
Qarqan He 140 Kf 39.30N 88.15 E
Qarqannah, Juzur- = Kerkennah Islands (EN) 158 Ie 34.44N 11.12 E
Qartājannah 128 En 36.51N 10.20 E
Qārūn, Birkat- 164 Fd 29.28N 30.40 E
Qaryat Abū Nujaym 164 Cc 30.35N 15.24 E
Qaryat al Gharab 146 Kg 31.27N 44.48 E
Qaryat al Qaddāḩīyah 164 Cc 31.22N 15.14 E
Qaryat al 'Ulyā 144 Gd 27.33N 47.42 E
Qaryat az Zarrūq 164 Cc 32.22N 15.09 E
Qaryat az Zuwaytīnah 164 Dc 30.58N 20.07 E
Qaryat Hubayn al Gharbīyah 146 Je 34.21N 42.05 E
Qaşabah, Ra's al- 146 Fh 28.02N 34.38 E
Qaşabāt, Hanshīr al- 128 Dn 36.24N 9.54 E
Qasigiánguit/Christianshåb 179 Ge 68.45N 51.30W
Qaşr al Azraq 146 Gg 31.53N 36.49 E
Qasr Al Hayr 146 Ge 34.23N 37.36 E
Qaşr al Qarahbullī 164 Bc 32.45N 13.43 E
Qaşr 'Amij 146 If 33.30N 41.45 E
Qaşr Bū Hādī 164 Cc 31.03N 16.40 E
Qaşr Burqu' 146 Gf 32.37N 37.58 E
Qasr-e Shīrīn 144 Gc 34.31N 45.35 E
Qaşr Farāfirah 160 Jf 27.15N 28.10 E
Qaşr Ḩamān 144 Ge 20.50N 45.50 E
Qaşr Qārūn 146 Dh 29.25N 30.25 E
Qaşş Abū Sa'īd 146 Bi 27.00N 27.35 E
Qatana 146 Gf 33.26N 36.05 E
Qaţar [1] 142 Hg 25.30N 51.15 E
Qaţar 140 Hg 25.30N 51.15 E
Qatlīsh 146 Qd 37.50N 57.19 E
Qaţrānī, Jabal- 146 Dh 29.41N 30.35 E
Qatrūyeh 146 Ph 29.09N 54.43 E
Qattara Depression (EN) = Qaţţārah, Munkhafaḑ al- 158 Je 30.00N 27.30 E
Qawām al Hamzah 146 Kg 31.43N 44.58 E
Qawz Abu Ḑulū' 168 Eb 16.55N 32.30 E
Qawz Rajab 168 Fb 16.04N 35.34 E
Qaysān 168 Ec 10.45N 34.48 E
Qayyārah 146 Je 35.48N 43.17 E
Qazaqstan = Kazakhstan (EN) 136 Gf 48.00N 68.00 E
Qazvīn 142 Gf 36.16N 50.00 E
Qeqertarssuaq/Godhavn 224 Nc 69.20N 53.35W
Qeshm 146 Qi 26.58N 56.16 E
Qeshm 144 Id 26.45N 55.45 E
Qeydār 146 Md 36.07N 48.35 E
Qeys, Jazīreh-ye- 144 Hd 26.32N 53.58 E
Qezel 144 Gb 36.45N 49.22 E
Qian'an [China] 154 Ed 40.01N 118.42 E
Qian'an [China] 154 Hb 44.58N 124.01 E
Qianfangzi 154 Ad 40.01N 111.23 E
Qian Gorlos (Quianguozhen) 152 Lb 45.05N 124.52 E
Qian He 154 Dh 32.55N 117.10 E
Qianjiang [China] 154 Bi 30.25N 112.54 E
Qianjiang [China] 152 Ig 23.37N 108.58 E
Qianjiang [China] 152 If 29.30N 108.45 E
Qianning/Gartar 152 He 30.27N 101.29 E
Qianshan 154 Di 30.38N 116.35 E
Qian Shan 152 Lc 40.35N 123.00 E
Qiansuo 152 Hf 25.27N 100.41 E
Qianwei 152 Hf 29.08N 103.56 E
Qianxi [China] 152 If 27.03N 106.04 E
Qianxi [China] 154 Ed 40.08N 118.19 E
Qianyang (Anjiang) 152 Jf 27.19N 110.13 E
Qiaojia 152 Hf 27.00N 103.00 E
Qiaowan 152 Gc 40.36N 96.42 E
Qibilī 162 Ic 33.42N 8.58 E
Qichun (Caojiahe) 154 Ci 30.15N 115.26 E
Qidaogou 154 Id 41.31N 126.18 E
Qidong 154 Fi 31.48N 121.39 E
Qiemo/Qarqan 142 Kf 38.08N 85.32 E
Qift 146 Ei 26.00N 32.49 E
Qijiang 152 If 29.00N 106.39 E
Qijiaojing 152 Fc 43.28N 91.36 E
Qike → Xunke 152 Mb 49.34N 128.28 E
Qili → Shitai 154 Di 30.12N 117.28 E
Qilian (Babao) 152 Hd 38.14N 100.15 E
Qilian Shan 152 Gd 39.12N 98.35 E
Qilian Shan 140 Lf 38.30N 100.00 E
Qimantag 152 Fd 37.00N 91.00 E
Qimen 152 Kf 29.57N 117.39 E
Qinā 160 Kf 26.10N 32.43 E
Qinā, Wādī- 146 Ei 26.12N 32.44 E
Qin'an 152 Ie 34.50N 105.35 E
Qingchengzi 154 Gd 40.44N 123.36 E
Qingchuan 152 Ie 32.32N 105.11 E
Qingdao (Tsingtao) 142 Of 36.05N 120.21 E
Qingduizi 154 Fd 41.27N 121.52 E
Qingfeng 154 Cg 35.54N 115.07 E
Qinggang 152 Mb 46.41N 126.03 E
Qinggil/Qinghe 152 Fb 46.43N 90.24 E
Qinghai Hu = Koko Nor (EN) 140 Mf 37.00N 100.20 E
Qinghai Sheng (Ch'ing-hai Sheng) = Tsinghai (EN) [2] 152 Gd 36.00N 96.00 E
Qing He 154 Hc 42.16N 124.10 E
Qinghe/Qinggil 152 Fb 46.43N 90.24 E
Qinghe (Gexianzhuang) 154 Cf 37.03N 115.39 E
Qinghemen 154 Fd 41.45N 121.25 E
Qingjian 152 Jd 37.10N 110.09 E
Qingjiang 142 Nf 33.31N 119.03 E
Qing Jiang 152 Je 30.24N 111.30 E
Qingjiang (Zhangshuzhen) 152 Kf 28.02N 115.31 E
Qingkou → Ganyu 154 Eg 34.50N 119.07 E
Qinglong 154 Ed 40.26N 118.58 E
Qinglong He 154 Ee 39.51N 118.51 E
Qingshan 154 Ci 30.39N 114.27 E
Qingshuihe 152 Jd 39.56N 111.41 E
Qingshui Jiang 152 If 27.11N 109.48 E
Qingtian 152 Lf 28.12N 120.17 E
Qingxian 154 De 38.35N 116.48 E
Qingxu 154 Bf 37.36N 112.21 E
Qingyang [China] 154 Di 30.38N 117.50 E
Qingyang [China] 152 Id 36.01N 107.48 E
Qingyuan 152 Lc 42.06N 124.56 E
Qingyuan (Nandaran) 154 Ce 38.46N 115.29 E
Qingyun (Xiejiaji) 154 Df 37.46N 117.22 E
Qing Zang Gaoyuan = Tibet, Plateau of- (EN) 140 Kf 32.30N 87.00 E
Qin He 154 Bg 35.01N 113.25 E
Qinhuangdao 152 Kg 40.00N 119.32 E
Qin Ling 140 Mf 34.00N 108.00 E
Qinshui 154 Bg 35.41N 112.10 E
Qintong 154 Fh 32.39N 120.06 E
Qinxian 154 Bf 36.46N 112.42 E
Qinyang 154 Bg 35.05N 112.56 E
Qinyuan 154 Bf 36.29N 112.20 E
Qinzhou 152 Ig 22.02N 108.30 E
Qionghai (Jiaji) 152 Jh 19.25N 110.28 E
Qionglai 152 He 30.24N 103.28 E
Qiongzhou Haixia 140 Ng 20.10N 110.15 E
Qipan Guan 152 Ie 32.45N 106.11 E
Qiqihar 142 Oe 47.21N 123.58 E
Qīr 146 Oh 28.29N 53.04 E
Qira 152 Dd 37.02N 80.53 E
Qiryat Gat 146 Fg 31.36N 34.46 E
Qiryat Shemona 146 Ff 33.13N 35.34 E
Qiryat Yam 146 Ff 32.51N 35.04 E
Qishn 144 Hf 15.26N 51.40 E
Qi Shui 154 Ci 30.09N 115.22 E
Qishuyan 154 Fi 31.41N 120.04 E
Qitai 142 Ke 44.01N 89.28 E
Qitaihe 152 Nb 45.49N 130.51 E
Qiuxian (Matou) 154 Cf 36.50N 115.10 E
Qixia 154 Ff 37.18N 120.50 E
Qixian [China] 154 Cg 34.33N 114.46 E
Qixian [China] 154 Bf 37.23N 112.21 E
Qixian (Zhaoge) 154 Cg 35.35N 114.12 E
Qiyang 152 Jf 26.44N 111.50 E
Qizhou 154 Ci 30.04N 115.20 E
Qogir Feng = Godwin Austen (EN) 140 Jf 35.53N 76.30 E
Qog Qi 152 Ic 41.31N 107.00 E
Qog Ul 152 Kc 44.50N 116.19 E
Qohrūd, Kūhhā-ye- 140 Hf 32.40N 53.00 E
Qoltag 152 Ec 42.20N 88.45 E
Qom 142 Hf 34.39N 50.54 E
Qom 146 Ne 34.48N 51.02 E
Qomolangma Feng = Everest, Mount- (EN) 140 Kg 27.59N 86.56 E
Qomrud 146 Ne 34.43N 51.04 E
Qomsheh 144 Hc 32.00N 51.50 E
Qondūz 142 If 36.45N 68.51 E
Qondūz [3] 144 Kb 36.45N 68.30 E
Qondūz 144 Kb 37.00N 68.16 E
Qoqek/Tacheng 142 Ke 46.45N 82.57 E
Qôrnoq 179 Gf 64.30N 51.19W
Qorveh 146 Le 35.10N 47.48 E
Qoşbeh-ye Naşşār 144 Gc 30.02N 48.27 E
Qoţbābād [Iran] 146 Qi 27.46N 56.06 E
Qoţbābād [Iran] 146 Oh 28.39N 53.37 E
Qoţūr 146 Kc 38.28N 44.25 E
Qotūr 146 Kc 38.46N 45.16 E
Quadros, Lagoa dos- 204 Gi 29.42S 50.05W
Quairading 212 Df 32.01S 117.25 E
Quakenbrück 120 Dd 52.41N 7.57 E
Quanah 186 Gi 34.18N 99.44W
Quanbao Shan 152 Je 34.08N 111.26 E
Quang Ngai 148 Le 15.07N 108.48 E
Quang Tri 148 Le 21.02N 106.29 E
Quan He 154 Ch 32.55N 115.52 E
Quanjiao 154 Eh 32.09N 118.16 E
Quang Trach 148 Le 17.45N 106.27 E
Quanzhou [China] 152 Jf 26.01N 110.4 E
Quanzhou [China] 142 Ng 24.57N 118.35 E
Qu'Appelle River 180 Hf 50.27N 101.19W
Quaraí 206 Id 30.23S 56.27W
Quaraí, Rio- 204 Dj 30.12S 57.36W
Quaregnon 124 Fd 50.26N 3.51 E
Quartu Sant'Elena 128 Dk 39.14N 9.11 E
Quartz Lake 180 Jb 70.57N 80.40W
Quartz Mountain 188 De 43.10N 122.40W
Quartzsite 188 Hj 33.40N 114.13W
Quatre, Isle- 197n Bb 12.57N 61.15W
Quatsino Sound 188 Aa 50.25N 128.10W
Qūchān 142 Hf 37.06N 58.30 E
Qué 170 Ce 14.43S 15.06 E
Queanbeyan 212 Jg 35.21S 149.14 E
Québec 176 Le 46.49N 71.13W
Québec [2] 180 Kf 54.00N 72.00W
Quebó 204 Db 14.36S 56.04W
Quebra Anzol, Rio- 204 Id 19.09S 47.38W
Quebracho 204 Dj 31.57S 57.57W
Quebradillas 197a Bb 18.28N 66.56W
Quedas do Iguaçu 204 Fg 25.31S 52.54W
Quedlinburg 120 He 51.47N 11.09 E
Queen, Cape - 180 Jd 64.43N 78.18W
Queen Alexandra Range 222 Jg 84.00S 168.00 E
Queen Bess, Mount - 180 Ff 51.18N 124.33W
Queenborough 124 Cc 51.25N 0.46 E
Queen Charlotte Islands 174 Fd 51.30N 129.00W
Queen Charlotte Sound 180 Ef 51.30N 129.30W
Queen Charlotte Strait 174 Gd 50.40N 127.25W
Queen Elizabeth Islands 174 Ib 79.00N 105.00W
Queen Elizabeth Range 222 Kg 83.20S 162.00 E
Queen Mary Land 222 Ge 69.00S 96.00 E
Queen Maud Gulf 174 Ic 68.25N 102.30W
Queen Maud Land (EN) 222 Cf 72.30S 12.00 E
Queen Maud Range 222 Lg 86.00S 160.00W
Queens Channel [Austl.] 212 Fb 14.45S 129.25 E
Queens Channel [N.W.T.-Can.] 180 Ha 76.11N 96.00W
Queensland [2] 212 Id 22.00S 145.00 E
Queenstown [Austl.] 212 Jh 42.05S 145.33 E
Queenstown [Guy.] 196 Gi 7.12N 58.29W
Queenstown [N.Z.] 218 Cf 45.02S 168.40 E
Queenstown [S.Afr.] 160 Jl 31.52S 26.52 E
Queguay, Cuchilla del- 204 Dj 31.50S 57.30W
Queguay Grande, Río- 204 Ck 32.09S 58.09W
Queich 124 Ke 49.14N 8.23 E
Queimadas 202 Kf 10.58S 39.38W
Queiros 204 Ge 21.49S 50.13W
Quela 170 Cd 9.15S 17.05 E
Quelimane 160 Kj 17.51S 36.52 E
Quemado 186 Bi 34.20N 108.30W
Quemado de Güines 194 Gb 22.48N 80.15W
Quembo 170 De 14.57S 20.22 E
Quemoy (EN) = Chinmen 152 Kg 24.25N 118.25 E
Quemú-Quemú 206 He 36.03S 63.33W
Quepos 194 Ei 9.25N 84.09W
Quequén 206 Ie 38.32S 58.42W
Quequén Grande, Río- 204 Cn 38.34S 58.43W
Quequén Salado, Río- 204 Bn 38.56S 60.31W
Quercy 122 Hj 44.15N 1.15 E
Querétaro 176 Ig 20.36N 100.23W
Querétaro [2] 190 Ed 21.00N 99.55W
Querobabi 192 Db 30.03N 111.01W
Quesada [C.R.] 194 Eh 10.19N 84.26W
Quesada [Sp.] 126 Ig 37.51N 3.04W
Queshan 152 Je 32.42N 114.04 E
Quesnel 180 Ff 52.59N 122.30W
Quesnel Lake 180 Ff 52.32N 121.05W
Questa 186 Dh 36.42N 105.36W
Quetena 202 Eh 22.10S 67.25W
Quetico Lake 186 Kb 48.37N 91.52W
Quetta 142 If 30.12N 67.00 E
Quevas, Cerro- 192 Dc 29.15N 111.20W
Quevedo 202 Cd 1.02S 79.27W
Queyras 122 Mj 44.44N 6.49 E
Quezaltenango 176 Jh 14.50N 91.31W
Quezaltenango [3] 194 Bf 14.45N 91.40W
Quezon 150 Ge 9.14N 117.56 E
Quezon City 142 Oh 14.38N 121.00 E
Qufu 154 Dg 35.35N 116.59 E
Quianguozhen → Qian Gorlos 152 Lb 45.05N 124.52 E
Quibala 170 Be 10.44S 14.59 E
Quibaxe 170 Bd 8.30S 14.36 E
Quibdó 202 Cb 5.42N 76.39W
Quiberon 122 Cg 47.29N 3.07 E
Quiberon, Baie de- 122 Dg 47.32N 3.00W
Quiberon, Presqu'île de- 122 Cg 47.30N 3.08W
Quíbor 194 Mi 9.56N 69.37W
Quiché [3] 194 Bf 15.30N 90.55W
Quierschied 124 Je 49.19N 7.03 E
Quiha 168 Fc 13.28N 39.33 E
Quiindy 204 Dh 25.58S 57.16W
Quijarro 204 Cd 19.26S 58.08W
Quilá 192 Fe 24.23N 107.13W
Quillabamba 202 Df 12.49S 72.43W
Quillacollo 202 Eg 17.26S 66.17W
Quillagua 206 Gb 21.39S 69.33W
Quillan 122 Il 42.52N 2.11 E
Quillebeuf-sur-Seine 124 Ce 49.28N 0.31 E
Quillota 206 Fd 32.53S 71.16W
Quilmes 206 Id 34.44S 58.16W
Quilon 148 Fg 8.53N 76.36 E
Quilpie 212 Ie 26.37S 144.15 E
Quilqué 206 Fd 33.03S 71.27W
Quimarí, Alto de- 194 Ii 8.07N 76.23W
Quimbele 170 Cd 6.30S 16.14 E
Quimilí 206 Hc 27.38S 62.25W
Quimome 204 Bc 17.42S 61.16W
Quimome, Río- 204 Bc 17.36S 61.09W
Quimper 122 Bf 48.00N 4.06W
Quimperlé 122 Cg 47.52N 3.33W
Quinault River 188 Cc 47.23N 124.18W
Quincy [Ca.-U.S.] 188 Eg 39.56N 120.57W
Quincy [Fl.-U.S.] 184 Ej 30.37N 84.32W
Quincy [Il.-U.S.] 182 Id 39.56N 91.23W
Quincy [Ma.-U.S.] 184 Ld 42.15N 71.01W
Quincy [Wa.-U.S.] 188 Fc 47.14N 119.51W
Quindío [3] 202 Cc 4.30N 75.40W
Quingey 122 Lg 47.06N 5.53 E
Quinhagak 178 Ge 59.45N 161.43W
Qui Nhon 142 Mh 13.46N 109.14 E
Quiñihual 204 Bm 37.47S 61.36W
Quiniluban Group 150 Hd 11.27N 120.48 E
Quinn River 188 Ff 40.25N 119.00W
Quiñones 192 De 24.22N 111.25W
Quintanar de la Orden 126 Ie 39.34N 3.03W
Quintana Roo [2] 190 Ge 19.40N 88.30W
Quinze, Lac des- 184 Hb 47.30N 79.00W
Quionga 172 Gb 10.35S 40.33 E
Quipungo 170 Be 14.45S 14.05 E
Quirigua 194 Cf 15.18N 89.07W
Quirihue 206 Fe 36.17S 72.32W
Quirima 170 Ce 10.48S 18.09 E
Quirinópolis 202 Hg 18.32S 50.30W
Quiroga 126 Eb 42.29N 7.16W
Quiros, Cap- 219b Cb 14.56S 167.01 E
Quisiro 194 Lh 10.53N 71.17W
Quissanga 172 Gb 12.25S 40.29 E
Quissico 172 Ed 24.43S 34.45 E
Quitasueño, Banco- 190 Hf 14.20N 81.15W
Quitengues 170 Be 14.06S 14.05 E
Quiterage 172 Gb 11.45S 40.27 E
Quitéria, Rio- 204 Ge 20.16S 51.08W
Quitilipi 204 Bh 26.52S 60.13W
Quitman [Ga.-U.S.] 184 Fj 30.47N 83.33W
Quitman [Ms.-U.S.] 186 Lj 32.03N 88.43W
Quito 200 If 0.13S 78.30W
Quitovac 192 Cb 31.32N 112.42W
Quixadá 202 Kd 4.58S 39.01W
Quixeramobim 202 Ke 5.12S 39.17W
Qujiang 154 Cj 28.14N 115.46 E
Qu Jiang [China] 152 Ie 30.01N 106.24 E
Qu Jiang [China] 152 Kf 29.32N 119.31 E
Qujing 152 Hf 25.31N 103.45 E
Qul'ān, Jazā'ir- 146 Fj 24.22N 35.23 E
Qulansiyah 144 Hg 12.41N 53.29 E
Qulaybīah 162 Jb 36.51N 11.06 E
Qulbān al 'Isāwīyah 146 Gg 30.38N 37.53 E
Qulbān an Nabk al Gharbī 146 Gg 31.15N 37.26 E
Qulbān Layyah 146 Lh 29.50N 46.03 E
Qumar He 140 Lf 34 42N 95.00 E
Qumarlêb 152 Ge 34.35N 95.18 E
Qunayfidhah, Nafūd- 146 Kj 24.45N 45.30 E
Quoi 220d Ba 7.32N 151.59 E
Quoich 180 Id 63.56N 93.25W
Quorn 212 Hf 32.21S 138.03 E
Quqên/Jinchuan 152 He 31.02N 102.02 E
Quraitu 146 Ke 34.36N 45.30 E
Qurayyāt, Juzur- 162 Jb 35.48N 11.02 E
Qurbah 128 En 36.35N 10.52 E
Qurdūd 168 Dc 10.17N 29.56 E
Qūr Laban 146 Cg 30.23N 28.59 E
Qurunbāliyah 128 En 36.36N 10.30 E
Qūş 164 Fd 25.55N 32.45 E
Qusaybah 146 Ie 34.24N 40.59 E
Quşay'ir 168 Ic 14.55N 50.20 E
Qutdligssat 179 Gd 70.12N 53.00W
Quthing 172 Df 30.24S 27.42 E
Quţū 164 Hf 18.30N 41.04 E
Quwaiz 164 He 20.27N 44.53 E
Quxian 152 Kf 28.54N 118.53 E
Qüxü 152 Ff 29.23N 90.45 E
Quyang 154 Ce 38.37N 114.41 E
Quy Chau 148 Le 19.33N 105.06 E
Quzhou 154 Cf 36.47N 114.56 E
Qyteti Stalin → Kuçova 130 Ci 40.48N 19.54 E

R

Ra'a as Saffānīyah 144 Gd 27.59N 48.37 E
Raab 120 Ni 47.41N 17.38 E
Raahe/Brahestad 114 Fd 64.41N 24.29 E
Rääkkylä 116 Mb 62.19N 29.37 E
Raalte 124 Ib 52.23N 6.17 E
Raamsdonk 124 Gc 51.41N 4.54 E
Raanes Peninsula 180 Ia 78.20N 86.20W
Raasay, Island of- 118 Gd 57.25N 6.04W
Raasay, Sound of- 118 Gd 57.25N 6.05W
Raasiku/Raziku 116 Ke 59.22N 25.11
Rab 128 If 44.45N 14.46
Rab 128 If 44.46N 14.46 E
Raba 142 Nj 8.27S 118.46 E
Rába 120 Ni 47.41N 17.38 E
Raba 120 Qf 50.09N 20.30 E
Rabāble 168 Hd 8.14N 48.18 E
Rabaçal 126 Ec 41.30N 7.12W
Rabat [Malta] 128 Io 35.50N 14.29 E
Rabat [Mor.] 160 Ge 34.02N 6.50W
Rabat-Salé [2] 162 Fc 34.02N 6.50W
Rabaul 210 Ge 4.12S 152.12 E
Rábca 120 Ni 47.41N 17.37 E
Rabenau 124 Kd 50.40N 8.52 E
Rabī', Ash Shallāl ar- = Fourth Cataract (EN) 158 Kg 18.47N 32.03 E
Rabiah 146 Jd 36.47N 42.07 E
Rābigh 144 Ee 22.48N 39.02 E
Rabinal 194 Bf 15.06N 90.27W
Rabka 120 Pg 49.36N 19.56 E
Rabočeostrovsk 114 Id 64.59N 34.44 E
Rabyānah, Şaḩrā'- 158 Jf 24.30N 21.00 E
Rabyānah, Wāḩāt al- = Rebiana Oasis (EN) 164 De 24.14N 21.59 E
Răcăciuni 130 Jc 46.20N 26.59 E
Racalmuto 128 Hm 37.24N 13.44 E
Răcăşdia 130 Ee 44.59N 21.38 E
Racconigi 128 Bf 44.46N 7.46 E
Race, Cape- 174 Ne 46.40N 53.10W
Race Point 184 Ld 42.04N 70.14W
Rach Gia 142 Mh 10.01N 105.05 E
Rachid 162 Ef 18.48N 11.41W
Raciąż 120 Qd 52.47N 20.06 E
Racibórz 120 Of 50.06N 18.13 E
Racine 182 Jc 42.43N 87.48W
Ráckeve 120 Oi 47.10N 18.57 E
Racos 130 Ic 46.03N 25.30 E
Råda 116 Ed 60.00N 13.36 E
Radama, Iles- 172 Hb 14.00S 47.47 E
Radan 130 Eg 43.02N 21.30 E
Rădăuţi 130 Ib 47.51N 25.55 E
Radbuza 120 Jg 49.46N 13.24 E
Radeberg 120 Je 51.07N 13.55 E
Radebeul 120 Je 51.06N 13.39 E
Radeče 128 Jd 46.04N 15.11 E
Radehov 120 Uf 50.13N 24.43 E
Radenthein 128 Hd 46.48N 13.43 E
Radevormwald 124 Jc 51.12N 7.22 E
Radew 120 Lb 54.07N 15.50 E
Radford 184 Gg 37.07N 80.34W
Radnevo 130 Ig 42.18N 25.56 E
Radolfzell 120 Ei 47.44N 8.58 E
Radom 112 Ie 51.25N 21.10 E
Radom [2] 120 Re 51.25N 21.10 E
Radomir 130 Fg 42.33N 22.58 E
Radomka 120 Re 51.43N 21.26 E
Radomsko 120 Pe 51.05N 19.25 E
Radomyšl 132 Fd 50.29N 29.14 E
Radomyśl Wielki 120 Rf 50.12N 21.16 E
Radoškoviči 116 Lj 54.12N 27.17 E
Radotín 120 Kg 49.59N 14.22 E
Radovanu 130 Je 44.12N 26.31 E
Radoviš 130 Fh 41.38N 22.28 E
Radøy 116 Ad 60.40N 5.00 E
Radstadt 128 Hc 47.23N 13.27 E
Radun 120 Vb 54.02N 25.07 E
Radunia 120 Ob 54.25N 18.45 E
Raduša 128 Lg 43.52N 17.29 E
Radvaniči 120 Ue 51.59N 24.09 E
Radviliškis 114 Fi 55.50N 23.33 E
Radwā, Jabal- 144 Ee 24.36N 38.18 E
Radymno 120 Sg 49.57N 22.48 E
Radziejów 120 Od 52.38N 18.32 E
Radzyń Podlaski 120 Se 51.48N 22.38 E
Rae 180 Fd 62.50N 116.00W
Rāe Bareli 148 Gc 26.13N 81.14 E
Rae Isthmus 180 Ic 66.55N 86.10W
Raesfeld 124 Ic 51.46N 6.51 E
Raeside, Lake- 212 Ee 29.30S 121.50 E
Raetihi 218 Fc 39.26S 175.17 E
Raevavae, Ile- 208 Mg 23.52S 147.40W
Raevski, Groupe- 216 Mc 16.45S 144.14W
Rāf, Jabal- 146 Hh 29.12N 39.48 E
Rafaela 200 Ji 31.17S 61.30W
Rafaï 168 Ce 4.58N 23.56 E
Rafḩā' 144 Fd 29.42N 43.30 E
Rafi 166 Fc 13.28N 4.10 E
Rāfkā 146 Qe 35.55N 57.36 E
Rafsanjān 144 Ic 30.24N 56.01 E
Räfsö/Reposaarı 116 Ic 61.37N 21.27 E
Raga 160 Jh 8.28N 25.41 E
Ragay Gulf 150 Hd 13.30N 122.45 E
Ragged Island 194 Jb 22.12N 75.44W
Ragged Island Range 190 Id 22.42N 75.55W
Ragged Point 197q Bb 13.10N 59.25W
Raglan 218 Fb 37.48S 174.52 E
Raguencau 184 Ma 49.04N 68.32W
Ragunda 114 De 63.04N 16.24 E
Ragusa 128 In 36.55N 14.44 E
Raguva 116 Ki 55.30N 24.45 E
Raha 150 Hg 4.51S 122.43 E
Raḩá, Ḩarrat ar- 146 Gi 27.40N 36.40 E
Rahad al Bardī 168 Cc 11.18N 23.53 E
Rahama 166 Gc 10.25N 8.41 E
Rahaţ, Ḩarrat- 164 He 23.00N 40.05 E
Rahat Dağı 130 Ml 37.08N 29.49 E
Rahden 124 Kb 52.26N 8.37 E
Rāhgāmāti 148 Id 22.38N 92.12 E
Rahīmyār Khan 148 Ec 28.25N 70.18 E
Rahmanovskije Ključi 136 If 49.35N 86.35 E
Rahmet 136 Gf 49.19N 65.16 E
Råholt 116 Dd 60.16N 11.11 E
Rahouia 126 Ni 35.32N 1.01 E
Rahov 132 De 48.02N 24.18 E
Rahrbach, Kirchhundem- 124 Jc 51.02N 7.59 E
Raia 126 Df 39.00N 8.17W
Raiatea, Ile- 208 Lf 16.50S 151.25W
Raices 204 Cj 31.54S 59.16W
Rāichūr 142 Jh 16.12N 77.22 E
Raiganj 148 Hc 25.37N 88.07 E
Raigarh 148 Gd 21.54N 83.24 E
Raijua, Pulau- 150 Hi 10.37S 121.36 E
Rainbow Peak 188 Hd 44.55N 115.17W
Rainier, Mount- 174 Ge 46.52N 121.46W
Rainy Lake 182 Ib 48.42N 93.10W
Rainy River 186 Ib 48.43N 94.29W
Rainy River 186 Ib 48.50N 94.41W
Raipur 142 Kg 21.14N 81.38 E
Raisi, Punta- 128 Hl 38.11N 13.06 E
Raisio/Reso 114 Ff 60.29N 22.11 E
Raita Bank (EN) 214 Mb 25.25N 169.30W
Raja Ampat, Kepulauan- 150 Jg 0.50S 130.25 E
Rājahmundry 142 Kh 16.59N 81.47 E
Rajakoski 114 Gb 68.59N 29.07 E
Rajang 140 Ni 2.07N 111.12 E
Rājapālaiyam 148 Fg 9.27N 77.34 E
Rājasthān [3] 148 Ec 26.00N 74.00 E
Rājasthān Canal 148 Eb 31.10N 75.00 E
Rajbiraj 148 Hc 26.30N 86.50 E
Rajčihinsk 138 Hg 49.43N 129.27 E
Rajevski 134 Gi 54.04N 54.56 E
Rājgarh 148 Fc 28.38N 75.23 E
Rajgródzkie, Jezioro- 120 Sc 53.45N 22.38 E
Rajka 120 Ni 48.00N 17.12 E
Rajkot 142 Jg 22.18N 70.47 E
Raj Nāndgaon 148 Gd 21.06N 81.02 E
Rajony respublikanskogo podčinenija → Čujskaja oblast 136 Hg 42.30N 73.50 E
Rājshāhi 148 Hd 24.22N 88.36 E
Rakahanga Atoll 208 Ke 10.02S 161.05W
Rakaia 218 Ee 43.45S 172.01 E
Rakaia 218 Ee 43.54S 172.13 E
Rakan, Ra's- 146 Ni 26.10N 51.13 E
Rakata, Pulau- 150 Eh 6.10S 105.26 E
Raka Zangbo 152 Ef 29.24N 87.58 E
Rakhawt, Wādī- 168 Ib 18.16N 51.50 E
Rakht-e Shāh 146 Mf 33.17N 49.23 E
Rakitnoje 154 Mb 45.36N 134.17 E
Rakitovo 130 Hh 41.59N 24.05 E
Rakkestad 116 De 59.26N 11.21 E
Rakoniewice 120 Md 52.10N 16.16 E
Rakops 172 Cd 21.01S 24.20 E
Rakovnicka panev 120 Jf 50.10N 13.30 E
Rakovník 120 Jf 50.06N 13.43 E
Rakovski 130 Hg 42.18N 24.58 E
Raków 120 Rf 50.42N 21.03 E

Index Symbols

- [1] Independent Nation
- [2] State, Region
- [3] District, County
- [4] Municipality
- [5] Colony, Dependency
- ■ Continent
- ○ Physical Region
- Historical or Cultural Region
- Mount, Mountain
- Volcano
- Hill
- Mountains, Mountain Range
- Hills, Escarpment
- Plateau, Upland
- Pass, Gap
- Plain, Lowland
- Delta
- Salt Flat
- Valley, Canyon
- Crater, Cave
- Karst Features
- Depression
- Polder
- Desert, Dunes
- Forest, Woods
- Heath, Steppe
- Oasis
- Cape, Point
- Coast, Beach
- Cliff
- Peninsula
- Isthmus
- Sandbank
- Island
- Islands, Archipelago
- Rock, Reef
- Rocks, Reefs
- Coral Reef
- Well, Spring
- Geyser
- River, Stream
- Waterfall, Rapids
- River Mouth, Estuary
- Lake
- Salt Lake
- Intermittent Lake
- Sea
- Gulf, Bay
- Strait, Fjord
- Canal
- Glacier
- Ice Shelf, Pack Ice
- Ocean
- Ridge
- Shelf
- Basin
- Lagoon
- Bank
- Seamount
- Tablemount
- Fracture
- Point of Interest
- Recreation Site
- Cave, Cavern
- Escarpment, Sea Scarp
- Trench, Abyss
- National Park, Reserve
- Church, Abbey
- Temple
- Scientific Station
- Railway station
- Historic Site
- Ruins
- Wall, Walls
- Military installation
- Lighthouse
- Mine
- Tunnel
- Dam, Bridge
- Airport
- Port

Rewa	148	Gd	24.32N	81.18 E
Rewa	219d	Bc	18.08S	178.33 E
Rewāri	148	Fc	28.11N	76.37 E
Rex, Mount-	222	Qf	74.54S	75.57W
Rexburg	188	Je	43.49N	111.47W
Rexpoëde	124	Ed	50.56N	2.32 E
Rey	144	Hb	35.35N	51.25 E
Rey, Arroyo del-	204	Ci	29.12S	59.36W
Rey, Isla del-	190	Ig	8.22N	78.55W
Rey, Laguna del-	192	Hd	27.00N	103.25W
Rey Bouba	166	Hd	8.40N	14.11 E
Reyes, Point-	188	Dg	38.00N	123.01W
Reyhanli	146	Gd	36.18N	36.32 E
Reykjalid	114a	Cb	65.39N	16.55W
Reykjanes	110	Dc	63.49N	22.43W
Reykjanes Ridge (EN)	110	Dc	62.00N	27.00W
Reykjavík	112	Dc	64.09N	21.57W
Reynolds Range	212	Gd	22.20S	132.50 E
Reynosa	176	Jg	26.07N	98.18W
Reyssouze	122	Kh	46.27N	4.54 E
Rež	134	Jh	57.23N	61.24 E
Rež	134	Kh	57.54N	62.20 E
Rezé	122	Eg	47.12N	1.34W
Rezekne/Rēzekne	112	Id	56.30N	27.19 E
Rēzekne/Rezekne	112	Id	56.30N	27.19 E
Rezelm, Lacul-	130	Le	44.54N	28.57 E
Rezina	132	Ff	47.43N	28.58 E
Reznas, ozero- / Rēznas ezers	116	Lh	56.20N	27.30 E
Rēznas ezers / Reznas, ozero-	116	Lh	56.20N	27.30 E
Rezovo	130	Lh	41.59N	28.02 E
Rezvān	146	Qi	27.34N	56.06 E
Rezve	130	Lh	41.59N	28.01 E
Rgotina	130	Fe	44.01N	22.17 E
Rhaetian Alps (EN)=Alpi Retiche	128	Dd	46.30N	10.00 E
Rhaetian Alps (EN)= Rätische Alpen	128	Dd	46.30N	10.00 E
Rhallamane	158	Ff	23.15N	10.00W
Rhauderfehn	124	Ja	53.08N	7.34 E
Rhaunen	124	Je	49.51N	7.21 E
Rheda-Wiedenbrück	120	Ee	51.51N	8.18 E
Rheden	124	Ib	52.01N	6.01 E
Rheden-Dieren	124	Ib	52.03N	6.08 E
Rheider Land	124	Ja	53.13N	7.18 E
Rhein=Rhine (EN)	110	Ge	51.52N	6.02 E
Rheinberg	124	Ic	51.33N	6.36 E
Rheine	120	Dd	52.17N	7.27 E
Rheinfall	128	Cc	47.41N	8.38 E
Rheinfelden (Baden)	120	Di	47.34N	7.48 E
Rheingaugebirge	120	Ef	50.05N	8.00 E
Rheinhessen	124	Ke	49.52N	8.07 E
Rheinisches Schiefergebirge =Rhenish Slate Mountains (EN)	110	Ge	50.25N	7.10 E
Rheinland-Pfalz=Rhineland-Palatinate (EN) [2]	120	Cf	50.00N	7.00 E
Rheinsberg / Mark	120	Ic	53.06N	12.53 E
Rheinstetten	124	Kf	48.58N	8.18 E
Rhenen	124	Hc	51.58N	5.35 E
Rhenish Slate Mountains (EN)=Rheinisches Schiefergebirge	110	Ge	50.25N	7.10 E
Rheris	162	Gc	30.41N	4.57W
Rheydt, Mönchengladbach-	124	Ic	51.10N	6.27 E
Rhin=Rhine (EN)	110	Ge	51.52N	6.02 E
Rhine (EN)=Rein	110	Ge	51.52N	6.02 E
Rhine (EN)=Rhein	110	Ge	51.52N	6.02 E
Rhine (EN)=Rhin	110	Ge	51.52N	6.02 E
Rhine (EN)=Rijn	110	Ge	51.52N	6.02 E
Rhine Bank (EN)	206	Ji	50.30S	53.30W
Rhinelander	182	Jb	45.38N	89.25W
Rhineland-Palatinate (EN)= Rheinland-Pfalz [2]	120	Cf	50.00N	7.00 E
Rhinluch	120	Id	52.50N	12.50 E
Rhino Camp	170	Fb	2.58N	31.24 E
Rhiou	126	Mi	35.59N	0.53 E
Rhir, Cap-	162	Fc	30.38N	9.54W
Rho	128	De	45.32N	9.02 E
Rhode Island [2]	182	Mc	41.40N	71.30W
Rhode Island Sound	184	Le	41.25N	71.15W
Rhodes (EN) = Ródhos	112	Ih	36.26N	28.13 E
Rhodes (EN) = Ródhos	110	Ih	36.10N	28.00 E
Rhodesia → Zimbabwe [1]	160	Jj	20.00S	30.00 E
Rhodes Peak	188	Hc	46.41N	114.47W
Rhodope Mountains (EN) = Rodopi	110	Ig	41.30N	24.30 E
Rhomara	126	Hi	35.10N	4.57W
Rhön	120	Gf	50.25N	10.05 E
Rhondda	118	Jj	51.40N	3.30W
Rhône [3]	122	Ki	46.00N	4.30 E
Rhône	110	Gg	43.20N	4.50 E
Rhône au Rhin, Canal du-	122	Lg	47.06N	5.19 E
Rhourd el Baguel	162	Ic	31.24N	6.57 E
Rhue	122	Ii	45.23N	2.29 E
Rhum	118	Ge	57.00N	6.20W
Rhyl	118	Jh	53.19N	3.29W
Riaba	166	Ge	3.24N	8.42 E
Riacho de Santana	202	Jf	13.37S	42.57W
Riangnom	168	Ed	9.55N	30.01 E
Riaño	126	Gb	42.58N	5.01W
Riánsares	126	Ie	39.32N	3.18W
Rías Altas	126	Da	43.30N	8.30W
Rías Bajas	126	Db	42.30N	9.00W
Riau [3]	150	Df	1.00N	102.00 E
Riau, Kepulauan-=Riau Archipelago (EN)	140	Mi	1.00N	104.30 E
Riau Archipelago (EN)= Riau, Kepulauan-	140	Mi	1.00N	104.30 E
Riaza	126	Ic	41.17N	3.28W
Riaza	126	Ic	41.42N	3.55W
Ribadavia	126	Db	42.17N	8.08W
Ribadeo	126	Ea	43.32N	7.02W
Ribadesella	126	Ga	43.28N	5.04W
Ribagorça / Ribagorza	126	Mb	42.15N	0.30 E
Ribagorza / Ribagorça	126	Mb	42.15N	0.30 E
Ribamar	202	Jd	2.33S	44.03W
Ribas do Rio Pardo	204	Fe	20.27S	53.46W
Ribatejo	126	De	39.15N	8.30W
Ribáuè	172	Fb	14.57S	38.17 E
Ribble	118	Kh	53.44N	2.50W
Ribe	114	Bi	55.21N	8.46 E
Ribe [2]	116	Ci	55.35N	8.45 E
Ribécourt-Dreslincourt	124	Ee	49.31N	2.55 E
Ribeira	204	Hg	24.39S	49.00W
Ribeira → Santa Eugenia	126	Db	42.33N	9.00W
Ribeira, Rio-	204	Ig	24.40S	47.24W
Ribeira Brava	162	Cf	16.37N	24.18W
Ribeira Grande	162	Bf	17.11N	25.04W
Ribeirão Prêto	200	Lh	21.10S	47.48W
Ribeirãozinho	204	Fc	16.22S	52.36W
Ribeiro Gonçalves	202	Ie	7.32S	45.14W
Ribemont	124	Fe	49.48N	3.28 E
Ribera	128	Hm	37.30N	13.16 E
Ribérac	122	Gi	45.15N	0.20 E
Riberalta	200	Jg	10.59S	66.06W
Ribnica	128	Ie	45.44N	14.44 E
Ribnitz-Damgarten	120	Ib	54.15N	12.28 E
Ricardo Flores Magón	192	Fc	29.58N	106.58W
Riccia	128	Ii	41.29N	14.50 E
Riccione	128	Gg	43.59N	12.39 E
Rice Lake	184	Hc	44.08N	78.13W
Rich	162	Gc	32.15N	4.30W
Richan	186	Jb	49.59N	92.49W
Richard Collinson Inlet	180	Gb	72.45N	113.00W
Richards	180	Ec	69.20N	134.35W
Richard's Bay	160	Kk	28.47S	32.06 E
Richardson	186	Hj	32.57N	96.44W
Richardson Mountains	174	Fc	66.00N	135.20W
Richardson Seamount (EN)	222	Cc	40.45S	14.10 E
Richard Toll	166	Bb	16.28N	15.41W
Rîchât, Guel er-	162	Ee	21.07N	11.24W
Richel	124	Ha	53.18N	5.10 E
Richel Griend	124	Ha	53.18N	5.15 E
Richelieu	122	Gg	47.01N	0.19 E
Richer	186	Hb	49.39N	96.28W
Richey	188	Mc	47.39N	105.04W
Richfield	182	Ed	38.46N	112.05W
Richibucto	184	Ob	46.41N	64.52W
Richland	182	Db	46.17N	119.18W
Richland Center	186	Ke	43.22N	90.21W
Richmond [Austl.]	212	Id	20.44S	143.08 E
Richmond [Ca.-U.S.]	182	Cd	37.57N	122.22W
Richmond [Eng.-U.K.]	118	Lg	54.24N	1.44W
Richmond [In.-U.S.]	182	Kd	39.50N	84.54W
Richmond [Ky.-U.S.]	182	Kd	37.45N	84.18W
Richmond [N.Z.]	218	Ed	41.21S	173.11 E
Richmond [S.Afr.]	172	Cf	31.23S	23.56 E
Richmond [Tx.-U.S.]	186	Il	29.35N	95.46W
Richmond [Va.-U.S.]	176	Lf	37.30N	77.28W
Richmond, Mount-	218	Ed	41.28S	173.24 E
Richmond Hill	184	Hd	43.52N	79.27W
Richmond Peak	197n	Ba	13.17N	61.13W
Richthofen, Mount-	186	Df	40.29N	105.57W
Rickmansworth	124	Bc	51.38N	0.28W
Ricobayo, Embalse de-	126	Gc	41.35N	5.50W
Ridā'	164	Hg	14.25N	44.50 E
Ridderkerk	124	Gc	51.52N	4.36 E
Ridgecrest	188	Gi	35.38N	117.36W
Ridgway	184	He	41.25N	78.45W
Riding Mountain	186	Fa	50.55N	100.25W
Riecito, Río-	196	Bi	6.50N	68.51W
Ried	124	Ke	49.50N	8.25 E
Ried im Innkreis	128	Hb	48.13N	13.30 E
Riedlingen	120	Fh	48.09N	9.28 E
Riemst	124	Hd	50.48N	5.36 E
Ries	120	Gh	48.55N	10.40 E
Riesa	120	Je	51.18N	13.18 E
Riesco, Isla-	206	Fh	53.00S	72.30W
Riesi	128	Im	37.17N	14.05 E
Riet	158	Jk	29.00S	23.53 E
Rietavas/Retavas	116	Ii	55.43N	21.49 E
Rietberg	124	Kc	51.48N	8.26 E
Rietbron	172	Cf	32.54S	23.09 E
Rietfontein [Nam.]	172	Cd	21.58S	20.58 E
Rietfontein [S.Afr.]	172	Ce	26.44S	20.01 E
Rieti	128	Gh	42.24N	12.51 E
Rif	158	Ge	35.00N	4.00W
Rifle	186	Cg	39.32N	107.47W
Rifstangi	110	Eb	66.32N	16.12W
Rift Valley [3]	170	Gb	0.30N	36.00 E
Rift Valley	158	Kh	0.30N	36.00 E
Rīga/Riga	112	Id	56.57N	24.06 E
Riga/Rīga	112	Id	56.57N	24.06 E
Riga, Gulf of- (EN) = Rīgas jūŗas līcis	110	Id	57.30N	23.35 E
Riga, Gulf of- (EN) = Riia laht	110	Id	57.30N	23.35 E
Riga, Gulf of- (EN) = Rižski zaliv	110	Id	57.30N	23.35 E
Rigachikum	166	Gc	10.38N	7.28 E
Rīgas jūŗas līcis = Riga, Gulf of- (EN)	110	Id	57.30N	23.35 E
Rīgestān=Registan (EN)	140	If	31.00N	65.00 E
Riggins	188	Gd	45.25N	116.19W
Rigolet	180	Lf	54.10N	58.26W
Rig-Rig	168	Ac	14.16N	14.21 E
Rihand Sagar	148	Hd	24.05N	83.05 E
Riia laht = Riga, Gulf of- (EN)	110	Id	57.30N	23.35 E
Riihimäki	114	Ff	60.45N	24.46 E
Riiser-Larsen-Halvøya	222	De	68.55S	34.00 E
Riito	192	Ba	32.10N	114.45W
Riječki zaljev = Rijeka, Gulf of- (EN)	128	Ie	45.15N	14.25 E
Rijeka	112	Hf	45.21N	14.24 E
Rijeka, Gulf of- (EN)= Riječki zaljev	128	Ie	45.15N	14.25 E
Rijksmuseum Kröller-Müller	124	Hb	52.06N	5.47 E
Rijn=Rhine (EN)	110	Ge	51.52N	6.02 E
Rijssen	124	Ib	52.18N	6.37 E
Rijswijk	124	Gb	52.03N	4.21 E
Rika	120	Th	48.08N	23.22 E
Rikā, Wādī ar-	164	He	22.25N	44.50 E
Rikubetsu	156a	Cb	43.28N	143.43 E
Rikuzentakada	154	Pe	39.01N	141.38 E
Rila	130	Gg	42.08N	23.08 E
Rila	130	Gg	42.08N	23.33 E
Riley	188	Fe	43.32N	119.29W
Riley, Mount-	186	Ck	31.58N	107.05W
Rilski Manastir	130	Gg	42.08N	23.20 E
Rima	158	Hg	13.04N	5.10 E
Rimatara, Ile-	208	Lg	22.38S	152.51W
Rimava	120	Qh	48.15N	20.21 E
Rimavská Şobota	120	Qh	48.23N	20.01 E
Rimbo	114	Eg	59.45N	18.22 E
Rimé	168	Bc	14.02N	18.03 E
Rimforsa	116	Ff	58.08N	15.40 E
Rimini	128	Gf	44.04N	12.34 E
Rimito/Rymättylä	116	Jd	60.25N	21.55 E
Rîmnic	130	Kd	45.32N	27.31 E
Rîmnicu Sărat	130	Kd	45.23N	27.03 E
Rîmnicu Vîlcea	130	Hd	45.06N	24.22 E
Rimouski	176	Me	48.27N	68.32W
Rimše/Rimšė	116	Li	55.30N	26.33 E
Rimšė/Rimše	116	Li	55.30N	26.33 E
Rinbung	152	Ef	29.15N	89.52 E
Rincón	197a	Ab	18.21N	67.16W
Rincon	196	Bf	12.14N	68.20W
Rincón, Bahía de-	197a	Bc	17.57N	66.19W
Rincón del Bonete, Lago Artificial de-	206	Id	32.45S	56.00W
Rincón de Romos	192	Hf	22.14N	102.18W
Rindal	114	Be	63.03N	9.13 E
Ringe	116	Di	55.14N	10.29 E
Ringebu	116	Dc	61.31N	10.10 E
Ringerike	116	Dd	60.05N	10.15 E
Ringgold Isles	208	Jf	16.15S	179.25W
Ringim	166	Gc	12.09N	9.10 E
Ringkøbing	114	Bh	56.05N	8.15 E
Ringkøbing [2]	116	Ch	56.10N	8.45 E
Ringkøbing Fjord	114	Bi	56.00N	8.15 E
Ringlades	130	Dj	39.25N	20.04 E
Ringsjön	116	Ei	55.50N	13.30 E
Ringsted	114	Ci	55.27N	11.49 E
Ringvassøy	114	Eb	69.55N	19.15 E
Rínia	130	Il	37.25N	25.13 E
Rinjani, Gunung-	150	Gh	8.24S	116.28 E
Rinn Chathóir/Cahore Point	118	Gi	52.34N	6.11W
Rinn Dúain/Hook Head	118	Gi	52.07N	6.55W
Rinteln	120	Fd	52.11N	9.05 E
Rinya	120	Nk	45.57N	17.27 E
Rio Azul	204	Gg	25.43S	50.47W
Riobamba	200	If	1.40S	78.38W
Río Branco	204	Fk	32.34S	53.25W
Rio Branco	200	Jf	9.58S	67.48W
Rio Branco do Sul	204	Hg	25.10S	49.18W
Rio Brilhante	202	Hh	21.48S	54.33W
Río Bueno	206	Ff	40.19S	72.58W
Río Caribe	202	Fa	10.42N	63.07W
Río Chico	196	Dg	10.19N	65.59W
Rio Claro [Braz.]	204	If	22.24S	47.33W
Rio Claro [Trin.]	196	Fg	10.18N	61.11W
Rio Colorado	206	He	39.01S	64.05W
Río Cuarto	200	Ji	33.08S	64.20W
Rio de Janeiro	200	Lh	22.54S	43.15W
Rio de Janeiro [2]	202	Jh	22.30S	42.30W
Río de Jesús	194	Gj	7.59N	81.10W
Río de Oro	194	Ki	8.57N	73.23W
Río de Oro	162	Ee	24.00N	14.00W
Río de Oro, Bahía de-	162	De	23.45N	15.50W
Rio do Sul	206	Kc	27.13S	49.39W
Rio Fortuna	204	Hi	28.06S	49.07W
Río Gallegos	200	Jk	51.37S	69.10W
Rio Grande	200	Ki	32.02S	52.05W
Río Grande [Arg.]	206	Gh	53.47S	67.42W
Río Grande [Nic.]	194	Dg	12.59N	86.34W
Río Grande [P.R.]	197a	Cb	18.23N	65.50W
Rio Grande City	186	Gm	26.23N	98.49W
Río Grande de Añasco	197a	Ab	18.17N	67.10W
Río Grande de Manati	197a	Bb	18.29N	66.32W
Río Grande de Matagalpa	190	Hf	12.54N	83.32W
Rio Grande do Norte [2]	202	Ke	5.40S	36.00W
Rio Grande do Sul [2]	206	Jc	30.00S	54.00W
Rio Grande Rise (EN)	106	Cm	31.00S	35.00W
Riohacha	202	Da	11.32N	72.54W
Río Hato	194	Gi	8.23N	80.10W
Río Lagartos	192	Og	21.36N	88.10W
Rio Largo	202	Ke	9.29S	35.51W
Riom	122	Ji	45.54N	3.07 E
Rio Maior	126	De	39.20N	8.56W
Río Mayo	206	Fg	45.41S	70.16W
Riom-és-Montagnes	122	Ii	45.17N	2.40 E
Rio Miranda	202	Gg	19.25S	57.20W
Río Mulatos	202	Eg	19.42S	66.47W
Ríon	130	Ek	38.18N	21.47 E
Río Negro	206	Ff	40.47S	73.14W
Río Negro [Arg.] [2]	206	Gf	40.00S	67.00W
Rio Negro [Braz.]	204	Dd	19.33S	56.12W
Rio Negro [Braz.]	206	Kc	26.06S	49.48W
Río Negro [Ur.] [2]	204	Dk	32.45S	57.20W
Rio Negro, Pantanal do-	202	Gg	18.50S	56.00W
Rionero in Vulture	128	Jj	40.56N	15.40 E
Rioni	132	Lh	42.10N	41.38 E
Rio Novo	204	Dc	16.28S	56.30W
Rio Pardo	206	Jc	29.59S	52.22W
Rio Prêto, Serra do-	204	Gd	18.18S	50.42W
Río San Juan [3]	194	Eh	11.10N	84.30W
Río Segundo	206	Hd	31.40S	63.55W
Riosucio	202	Cb	7.27N	77.07W
Río Tercero	206	Hd	32.11S	64.06W
Rio Tinto	202	Ke	6.48S	35.05W
Rioverde	190	Dd	21.56N	100.01W
Rio Verde	202	Hg	17.43S	50.56W
Rio Verde, Serra do-	204	Fc	17.32S	52.25W
Rio Verde de Mato Grosso	202	Hg	18.56S	54.52W
Rio Verde do Sul	204	Ef	22.54S	55.27W
Rioz	122	Mg	47.25N	6.04 E
Řip	120	Kf	50.24N	14.18 E
Ripanj	130	De	44.38N	20.32 E
Ripley [Eng.-U.K.]	124	Aa	53.02N	1.24W
Ripley [Tn.-U.S.]	184	Ch	35.44N	89.33W
Ripley [W.V.-U.S.]	184	Gf	38.49N	81.44W
Ripoll	126	Ob	42.12N	2.12 E
Ripon	118	Lg	54.08N	1.31W
Riposto	128	Jm	37.44N	15.12 E
Ripple Mountain	188	Gb	49.02N	117.05W
Risan	130	Bg	42.31N	18.42 E
Risaralda [3]	202	Cb	5.00N	75.45W
Risbäck	114	Dd	64.42N	15.32 E
Rīshah, Wādī-	146	Kj	25.33N	44.05 E
Rī Shahr	146	Nh	28.55N	50.50 E
Rishiri	154	Pb	45.11N	141.15 E
Rishiri-Suidō	156a	Ba	45.10N	141.30 E
Rishiri-Tō	152	Pb	45.11N	141.15 E
Rishiri-Yama	156a	Ba	45.11N	141.15 E
Rīshmūk	146	Ng	31.15N	50.20 E
Rishon Leẕiyyo	146	Fg	31.58N	34.48 E
Rising Star	186	Gj	32.06N	98.58W
Risle	122	Ge	49.26N	0.23 E
Risnjak	128	Ie	45.26N	14.37 E
Rîşnov	130	Id	45.35N	25.27 E
Risør	114	Bg	58.43N	9.14 E
Risoux, Mont-	122	Mh	46.36N	6.10 E
Risøyhamn	114	Db	69.00N	15.45 E
Riß	120	Fh	48.17N	9.49 E
Risti	114	Fg	59.03N	24.01 E
Ristiina	116	Lc	61.30N	27.16 E
Ristijarvi	114	Gd	64.30N	28.13 E
Ristna, mys- / Ristna neem	116	If	58.55N	21.55 E
Ristna neem / Ristna, mys-	116	If	58.55N	21.55 E
Rīsū	146	Qf	33.52N	57.28 E
Ritchie's Archipelago	148	If	12.14N	93.10 E
Ritidian Point	220c	Ba	13.39N	144.51 E
Ritscher-Hochland	222	Bf	73.20S	9.30W
Ritter, Mount-	182	Dd	37.42N	119.20W
Ritterhude	124	Ka	53.11N	8.45 E
Rituerto	126	Jc	41.36N	2.22W
Ritzville	188	Fc	47.08N	118.23W
Riva-Bella, Ouistreham-	124	Be	49.17N	0.16W
Rivadavia [Arg.]	206	Gd	33.11S	68.28W
Rivadavia [Arg.]	206	Hb	24.11S	62.53W
Riva del Garda	128	Ee	45.53N	10.50 E
Rivas	176	Kh	11.26N	85.51W
Rivas [3]	194	Eh	11.25N	85.50W
Rive-de-Gier	122	Ki	45.22N	4.37 E
Rivera [2]	204	Ej	31.30S	55.15W
Rivera [Arg.]	206	He	37.12S	63.14W
Rivera [Ur.]	200	Ki	30.54S	55.31W
River Cess	166	Dd	5.27N	9.35W
Riverdale	186	Fc	47.30N	101.22W
Riverhead	184	Ke	40.55N	72.40W
Riverina	212	Jg	35.25S	145.30 E
River Inlet	180	Ef	51.41N	127.15W
Rivers [2]	166	Ge	4.50N	6.30 E
Rivers, Lake of the-	188	Mb	49.45N	105.45W
Riversdale [N.Z.]	218	Cf	45.54S	168.44 E
Riversdale [S.Afr.]	172	Cf	34.07S	21.15 E
Riverside	182	De	33.59N	117.22W
Riverton [N.Z.]	218	Bg	46.21S	168.00 E
Riverton [Wy.-U.S.]	182	Fc	43.02N	108.23W
Rivesaltes	122	Il	42.46N	2.52 E
Riviera Beach	184	Gl	26.47N	80.04W
Rivière-à-Pierre	184	Kb	46.58N	72.11W
Rivière-du-Loup	180	Kg	47.50N	69.32W
Rivière-Pilote	197h	Bc	14.29N	60.54W
Rivière-Salée	197h	Bb	14.32N	60.59W
Rivoli	128	Be	45.04N	7.31 E
Rivungo	170	Df	16.15S	22.00 E
Riwaka	218	Ed	41.05S	173.00 E
Riwoqê	152	Ge	31.13N	96.29 E
Rixensart	124	Gd	50.43N	4.35 E
Riyadh (EN)=Ar Riyāḑ	142	Gg	24.38N	46.43 E
Rize	144	Fa	41.02N	40.31 E
Rize, gora-	135	Bf	37.48N	58.13 E
Rıze Dağları	146	Ib	40.30N	40.50 E
Rizhao	152	Kd	35.27N	119.28 E
Rizokarpásso → Dipkarpas	146	Fe	35.36N	34.23 E
Rižski zaliv = Riga, Gulf of- (EN)	110	Id	57.30N	23.35 E
Rizzuto, Capo-	128	Ll	38.53N	17.05 E
Rjabovo	116	Md	60.17N	29.01 E
Rjapina/Räpina	116	Lf	58.03N	27.35 E
Rjazan	112	Je	54.38N	39.44 E
Rjazanovski	114	Ji	55.08N	39.35 E
Rjazanskaja oblast [3]	136	Ee	54.30N	40.40 E
Rjažsk	112	Ke	53.43N	40.04 E
Rjukan	114	Bg	59.52N	8.34 E
Rjuven	116	Be	59.13N	7.10 E
Rkiz	162	Df	16.50N	15.20W
Roa [Nor.]	116	Dd	60.17N	10.37 E
Roa [Sp.]	126	Ic	41.42N	3.55W
Road Town	190	Le	18.27N	64.37W
Roag, Loch-	118	Gc	58.16N	6.50W
Roan Antelope	170	Ee	13.08S	28.24 E
Roannais	122	Kh	46.05N	4.10 E
Roanne	122	Kh	46.02N	4.04 E
Roanoke	174	Lf	35.56N	76.43W
Roanoke [Al.-U.S.]	184	Ei	33.09N	85.22W
Roanoke [Va.-U.S.]	176	Lf	37.16N	79.57W
Roanoke Rapids	184	Ig	36.28N	77.40W
Roan Plateau	188	Kg	39.35N	108.55W
Roaringwater Bay	118	Dj	51.25N	9.30W
Roatán	194	De	16.18N	86.35W
Roatán, Isla de-	194	De	16.23N	86.30W
Robāţ	146	Qd	37.55N	57.42 E
Robāţ	146	Pg	30.04N	54.49 E
Robāt-e-Khān	144	Ic	33.21N	56.02 E
Robāt-e-Kord	146	Qf	33.45N	56.37 E
Robāt Karīm	146	Ne	35.28N	51.05 E
Robbie Bank (EN)	208	Jf	11.03S	176.53W
Robe, Mount-	212	If	31.40S	141.20 E
Röbel	120	Ic	53.23N	12.36 E
Robert Lee	186	Fk	31.54N	100.29W
Roberts	204	Bl	35.09S	61.57W
Roberts, Mount-	212	Ke	28.13S	152.28 E
Roberts Creek Mountain	188	Gg	39.52N	116.18W
Robertsfors	114	Ed	64.11N	20.51 E
Robert S. Kerr Lake	186	Ii	35.25N	95.00W
Robertson	172	Bf	33.46S	19.50 E
Robertson Bay	222	Kf	71.25S	170.00 E
Robertson Range	212	Ed	23.10S	121.00 E
Robertsport	166	Cd	6.45N	11.22W
Roberval	180	Kg	48.31N	72.13W
Robi	168	Fd	7.38N	39.52 E
Robinson Crusoe (EN) = Robinson Crusoe, Isla-	198	Ii	33.38S	78.52W
Robinson Crusoe, Isla- = Robinson Crusoe (EN)	198	Ii	33.38S	78.52W
Robinson Range	212	De	25.45S	119.00 E
Robinson River	212	Hc	16.03S	137.16 E
Roboré	200	Kg	18.20S	59.45W
Rob Roy	219a	Cb	7.23S	157.36 E
Robson, Mount-	174	Hd	53.07N	119.09W
Robstown	186	Hm	27.27N	97.40W
Roby	186	Fj	32.45N	100.23W
Roca, Cabo da-	110	Fh	38.47N	9.30W
Rocamadour	122	Hj	44.48N	1.38 E
Roca Partida, Isla-	190	Be	19.01N	112.02W
Roca Partida, Punta-	192	Lh	18.42N	95.10W
Rocas, Atol das-	198	Mf	3.52S	33.49W
Roccaraso	128	Ii	41.51N	14.05 E
Ročegda	136	Ec	62.42N	43.23 E
Rocha	206	Jd	34.29S	54.20W
Rocha [2]	204	Fk	34.00S	54.00W
Rochdale	118	Kh	53.38N	2.09W
Rochechouart	122	Gi	45.49N	0.49 E
Rochedo	204	Ed	19.57S	54.52W
Rochefort [Bel.]	122	Ld	50.10N	5.13 E
Rochefort [Fr.]	122	Fi	45.56N	0.59W
Rochefort-Han-sur-Lesse	124	Hd	50.08N	5.11 E
Rochelle	186	Lf	41.56N	89.04W
Rochelle, La-	112	Ff	46.10N	1.09W
Rocher River	180	Gd	61.23N	112.45W
Roche's Bluff	197c	Bc	16.42N	62.09W
Rochester [Eng.-U.K.]	118	Nj	51.24N	0.30 E
Rochester [In.-U.S.]	184	De	41.04N	86.13W
Rochester [Mn.-U.S.]	182	Ic	44.02N	92.29W
Rochester [N.H.-U.S.]	184	Ld	43.18N	70.59W
Rochester [N.Y.-U.S.]	176	Le	43.10N	77.36W
Roche-sur-Yon, La-	122	Eh	46.40N	1.26W
Rochlitzer Berg	120	Ie	51.05N	12.48 E
Rocigalgo	126	He	39.35N	4.35W
Rockall	110	Ed	57.35N	13.48W
Rockall Rise (EN)	110	Ed	57.00N	14.00W
Rock Creek Butte	188	Fd	44.49N	118.07W
Rockefeller Plateau	222	Ng	80.00S	135.00W
Rockenhausen	124	Je	49.38N	7.50 E
Rockford	182	Jc	42.17N	89.06W
Rockglen	188	Mb	49.10N	105.57W
Rockhampton	210	Gg	23.23S	150.31 E
Rock Hill	182	Ke	34.55N	81.01W
Rockingham [Austl.]	212	Df	32.17S	115.44 E
Rockingham [N.C.-U.S.]	184	Hh	34.56N	79.46W
Rock Islands	182	Ic	41.30N	90.34W
Rockland	182	Nc	44.06N	69.06W
Rocklands Reservoir	212	Ig	37.15S	142.00 E
Rockledge	184	Gk	28.20N	80.43W
Rockneby	116	Gh	56.49N	16.20 E
Rockport	186	Hl	28.01N	97.04W
Rock River	186	Kf	41.29N	90.37W
Rock Sound	184	Im	24.53N	76.09W
Rocksprings	186	Fk	30.01N	100.13W
Rock Springs	182	Fc	41.35N	109.13W
Rockville [In.-U.S.]	184	Df	39.45N	87.15W
Rockville [Md.-U.S.]	184	If	39.05N	77.09W
Rockwood	184	Eh	35.52N	84.41W
Rocky Ford	186	Eg	38.03N	103.43W
Rocky Island Lake	184	Fb	46.56N	83.04W
Rocky Mount	182	Ld	35.56N	77.48W
Rocky Mountain	182	Eb	47.49N	112.49W
Rocky Mountain House	180	Gf	52.22N	114.55W
Rocky Mountains	174	He	48.00N	116.00W
Rocky Point [Blz.]	194	Cd	18.22N	88.06W
Rocky Point [Nam.]	172	Ac	19.01S	12.29 E
Rocroi	124	Ge	49.55N	4.31 E
Rodach	120	Gf	50.08N	10.52 E
Rodalben	124	Je	49.14N	7.38 E
Roda Velha, Rio-	204	Ja	12.27S	45.33W
Rødberg	116	Cd	60.16N	8.58 E
Rødby	116	Dj	54.42N	11.24 E
Rødby Havn, Rødby-	114	Ci	54.39N	11.21 E
Rødby-Rødby Havn	114	Ci	54.39N	11.21 E
Roddickton	180	Lf	50.51N	56.07W
Rødding	116	Ci	55.22N	9.04 E
Rödeby	116	Fh	56.15N	15.36 E
Rodeio Bonito	204	Fh	27.28S	53.10W
Roden	124	Ia	53.09N	6.26 E
Rodeo [Arg.]	206	Gd	30.12S	69.06W
Rodeo [Mex.]	192	Ge	25.11N	104.34W
Rodeo [N.M.-U.S.]	186	Bk	31.50N	109.02W
Röder	120	Je	51.30N	13.25 E
Rodez	122	Ij	44.20N	2.34 E
Rodgau	124	Kd	50.01N	8.53 E
Rodholívos	130	Gi	40.56N	23.59 E
Ródhos = Rhodes (EN)	112	Ih	36.26N	28.13 E
Ródhos = Rhodes (EN)	110	Ih	36.10N	28.00 E
Rodi Garganico	128	Ji	41.55N	15.53 E
Roding	118	Nj	51.31N	0.06 E
Rodna	130	Hb	47.25N	24.49 E
Rodnei, Munţii-	130	Hb	47.35N	24.40 E
Rodney, Cape-	178	Fd	64.39N	166.24W
Rodniki	114	Jh	57.07N	41.48 E
Rodonit, Gjiri i-	130	Ch	41.35N	19.30 E
Rodonit, Kep i-	130	Ch	41.35N	19.27 E
Rodopi=Rhodope Mountains (EN)	110	Ig	41.30N	24.30 E
Rodrigues Island	158	Nj	19.42S	63.25 E
Roebourne	212	Dd	20.47S	117.09 E
Roebuck Bay	212	Ec	18.04S	122.15 E
Roer	124	Hc	51.12N	5.59 E
Roermond	122	Lc	51.12N	6.00 E
Roeselare/Roulers	122	Jd	50.57N	3.08 E
Roes Welcome Sound	180	Id	64.30N	86.45W

Roetgen	124	Id	50.39N	6.12 E
Rogačev	132	Gc	53.09N	30.06 E
Rogačevka	132	Kd	51.31N	39.34 E
Rogagua, Laguna-	202	Ef	13.45 S	66.55W
Rogaguado, Laguna-	202	Ef	12.55 S	65.45W
Rogaland [2]	114	Bg	59.00N	6.15 E
Rogaška Slatina	128	Jd	46.15N	15.38 E
Rogatica	128	Ng	43.48N	19.01 E
Rogatin	120	Ug	49.19N	24.40 E
Rogers	186	Ih	36.20N	94.07W
Rogers, Mount-	184	Gg	36.39N	81.33W
Rogers City	184	Fc	45.25N	83.49W
Rogers Lake	188	Gi	34.52N	117.51W
Rogers Peak	188	Jg	38.04N	111.32W
Rogersville	184	Fg	36.25N	82.59W
Roggan	180	Jf	54.24N	79.30W
Roggeveldberge	172	Bf	31.50 S	19.50 E
Roggewein, Cabo-	221d	Bb	27.07 S	109.15W
Rognan	114	Dc	67.06N	15.23 E
Rogozhina	130	Ch	41.05N	19.40 E
Rogozna	130	Df	43.04N	20.40 E
Rogoźno	120	Md	52.46N	17.00 E
Rogue River	188	Ce	42.26N	124.25W
Rohan, Plateau de-	122	Df	48.10N	2.50W
Rohl	168	Dd	7.05N	29.46 E
Rohrbach in Oberösterreich	128	Hb	48.34N	13.59 E
Rohrbach-lès-Bitche	124	Je	49.03N	7.16 E
Rohri	148	Dc	27.41N	68.54 E
Rohtak	148	Fc	28.54N	76.34 E
Roi, Le Bois du-	122	Kh	46.59N	4.02 E
Roi Et	148	Ke	16.05N	103.42 E
Roi Georges, Iles du-	208	Mf	14.32 S	145.08W
Roine	116	Kc	61.25N	24.05 E
Roisel	124	Fe	49.57N	3.06 E
Roja	114	Fh	57.30N	22.51 E
Roja, Punta- / Rotja, Punta-	126	Nf	38.38N	1.34 E
Rojas	206	Hd	34.12 S	60.44W
Rojo, Cabo- [Mex.]	190	Ed	21.33N	97.20W
Rojo, Cabo- [P.R.]	194	Nd	18.01N	67.15W
Rokan	150	Df	2.00N	100.52 E
Rokiškis	114	Fi	55.59N	25.37 E
Rokitnoje	132	Ed	51.21N	27.14 E
Rokkasho	156a	Bc	40.58N	141.21 E
Rokycany	120	Jg	49.45N	13.36 E
Rokytná	120	Mg	49.05N	16.21 E
Rola Co	152	Ed	35.25N	88.25 E
Rolândia	204	Gf	23.18 S	51.22W
Røldal	116	Be	59.49N	6.48 E
Rolla [Mo.-U.S.]	182	Id	37.57N	91.46W
Rolla [N.D.-U.S.]	186	Gb	48.52N	99.37W
Rolleston	218	Ee	43.35 S	172.23 E
Rolvsøya	114	Fa	71.00N	24.00 E
Roma [Austl.]	210	Fg	26.35 S	148.47 E
Roma [It.] = Rome (EN)	112	Hg	41.54N	12.29 E
Roma [Swe.]	114	Eh	57.32N	18.26 E
Romagna	128	Gf	44.30N	12.15 E
Romaine	180	Lf	50.18N	63.48W
Roman	130	Jc	46.55N	26.55 E
Romanche	122	Li	45.05N	5.43 E
Romanche Gap (EN)	106	Dj	0.10 S	18.15W
Romang	204	Ci	29.30 S	59.46W
Romang, Pulau-	150	Ih	7.35 S	127.26 E
România=Romania (EN) [1]	112	If	46.00N	25.30 E
Romania (EN)=România [1]	112	If	46.00N	25.30 E
Romanija	128	Mg	43.51N	18.43 E
Roman-Koš, gora-	136	Dg	44.36N	34.16 E
Romano, Cayo-	194	Ib	22.04N	77.50W
Romanovka	138	Gf	53.14N	112.46 E
Romans-sur-Isère	122	Li	45.03N	5.03 E
Romanzof, Cape-	174	Cc	61.49N	166.09W
Romanzof Mountains	178	Kc	69.00N	144.00W
Rombas	124	Ie	49.15N	6.05 E
Romblon	150	Hd	12.35N	122.15 E
Rome [Ga.-U.S.]	182	Je	34.16N	85.11W
Rome [N.Y.-U.S.]	182	Lc	43.13N	75.28W
Rome [Or.-U.S.]	188	Ge	42.50N	117.37W
Rome (EN) = Roma [It.]	112	Hg	41.54N	12.29 E
Romeleåsen	116	Ei	55.34N	13.33 E
Romerike	116	Dd	60.05N	11.10 E
Romilly-sur-Seine	122	Jf	48.31N	3.43 E
Rommani	162	Fc	33.32N	6.36W
Romme	116	Fd	60.26N	15.30 E
Rommerskirchen	124	Ic	51.02N	6.41 E
Romney Marsh	124	Cc	51.02N	0.55 E
Romny	136	De	50.45N	33.29 E
Rømø	114	Bi	55.10N	8.30 E
Romodanovo	114	Ki	54.28N	45.18 E
Romont	128	Ad	46.42N	6.55 E
Romorantin-Lanthenay	122	Hg	47.22N	1.45 E
Romsdal	116	Bb	62.35N	7.50 E
Romsdalen	116	Bb	62.30N	7.55 E
Romsdalsfjorden	116	Bb	62.40N	7.15 E
Romsdalshorn	116	Bd	62.29N	7.50 E
Romsey	118	Lk	50.59N	1.30W
Ronas Hill	118	La	60.38N	1.20W
Ronave	220e	Ba	0.29 S	166.56 E
Roncador, Cayos de-	190	Hf	13.32N	80.03W
Roncador, Serra do-	198	Kg	13.00 S	51.50W
Roncador Reef	208	Ge	6.13 S	159.22 E
Roncesvalles	126	Ka	43.01N	1.19W
Roncesvalles o de Ibañeta, Puerto de-	126	Ka	43.01N	1.19W
Ronciglione	128	Gh	42.17N	12.13 E
Ronco	128	Gf	44.24N	12.12 E
Ronda	126	Gh	36.44N	5.10W
Ronda, Serrania de-	126	Gh	36.45N	5.05W
Ronda do Sul	204	Cb	15.57 S	59.42W
Rondane	114	Bf	61.55N	9.45 E
Rønde	114	Ch	56.18N	10.29 E
Ronde, Point-	197g	Ba	15.33N	61.29W
Ronde Island	196	Ff	12.18N	61.31W
Rondeslottet	116	Cc	61.55N	9.46 E
Rondon	204	Ff	23.23 S	52.48W
Rondón, Pico-	202	Fc	1.36N	63.08W
Rondônia	200	Jg	10.52 S	61.57W
Rondônia [2]	202	Ff	11.00 S	63.00W
Rondonópolis	200	Kg	16.28 S	54.38W
Rong'an (Chang'an)	152	If	25.16N	109.23 E
Rongcheng	154	Ce	39.03N	115.52 E
Rongcheng (Yatou)	154	Gf	37.10N	122.25 E
Rongelap Atoll	208	Hc	11.09N	166.50 E
Rongerik Atoll	208	Hc	11.21N	167.26 E
Rongjiang (Guzhou)	152	If	25.58N	108.30 E
Rongxian	152	Jg	22.48N	110.30 E
Rongzhag/Danba	152	He	30.48N	101.54 E
Rønne	114	Di	55.06N	14.42 E
Ronne Bay	222	Qf	72.30 S	74.00W
Ronneby	114	Dh	56.12N	15.18 E
Ronnebyån	116	Fh	56.10N	15.18 E
Ronne Ice Shelf	222	Qf	78.30 S	61.00W
Ronse/Renaix	122	Jd	50.45N	3.36 E
Ronuro, Rio-	198	Kg	11.56 S	53.33W
Roodepoort	172	De	26.11 S	27.54 E
Roof Butte	182	Fd	36.28N	109.05W
Rooiboklaagte	172	Cd	20.20 S	21.15 E
Roon, Pulau-	150	Jg	2.23 S	134.33 E
Rooniu, Mont-	221e	Fc	17.49 S	149.12W
Roorkee	148	Fc	29.52N	77.53 E
Roosendaal	122	Kc	51.32N	4.28 E
Roosevelt [Az.-U.S.]	188	Jj	33.40N	111.09W
Roosevelt [Ut.-U.S.]	188	Kf	40.18N	109.59W
Roosevelt, Mount-	180	Ee	58.23N	125.04W
Roosevelt, Rio-	198	Jf	7.35 S	60.20W
Roosevelt Island	222	Lf	79.30 S	162.00W
Root Portage	186	Ka	50.53N	91.18W
Ropa	120	Rg	49.46N	21.29 E
Ropar	148	Fb	30.58N	76.20 E
Ropaži	116	Kh	56.58N	24.26 E
Ropczyce	120	Rf	50.03N	21.37 E
Rope, The-	220q	Ab	25.04 S	130.05W
Roper River	208	Ef	14.43 S	135.27 E
Roquefort	122	Fj	44.02N	0.19W
Roque Pérez	204	Cl	35.25 S	59.20W
Roquetas de Mar	126	Jh	36.46N	2.36W
Roraima, Monte-	198	Je	5.12N	60.44W
Roraima	202	Fc	1.30N	61.00W
Røros	114	Ce	62.35N	11.24 E
Rorschach	128	Dc	47.30N	9.30 E
Rørvik	114	Cd	64.51N	11.14 E
Ros	132	Ge	49.39N	31.35 E
Rosa, Cap-	128	Cn	36.57N	8.14 E
Rosa, Lake-	194	Kc	20.55N	73.20W
Rosa, Monte-	110	Gf	45.55N	7.53 E
Rošal	114	Ji	55.41N	39.55 E
Rosala	116	Je	59.50N	22.25 E
Rosalia	188	Gc	47.14N	117.22W
Rosalia, Punta-	221d	Bb	27.03 S	109.19W
Rosalie	197g	Bb	15.22N	61.16W
Rosalind Bank (EN)	194	Ge	16.30N	80.30W
Rosamond Lake	188	Fi	34.50N	118.04W
Rosamorada	192	Gf	22.08N	105.12W
Rosana	204	Ff	22.36 S	53.01W
Rosário	202	Jd	2.57 S	44.14W
Rosario	200	Ji	32.57 S	60.40W
Rosario [Mex.]	192	Dd	26.27N	111.38W
Rosario [Mex.]	190	Cd	23.00N	105.52W
Rosario [Par.]	206	Ib	24.27 S	57.03W
Rosario [Ven.]	194	Kh	10.19N	72.19W
Rosario, Arroyo-	192	Bb	30.03N	115.45W
Rosario, Bahia-	192	Bc	29.50N	115.45W
Rosario, Cayo del-	194	Gc	21.38N	81.53W
Rosario, Islas del-	194	Jh	10.10N	75.46W
Rosario, Sierra del-	192	He	25.35N	103.50W
Rosario de Arriba	190	Ab	30.01N	115.40W
Rosario de la Frontera	206	Hc	25.48 S	64.58W
Rosario de Lerma	206	Gb	24.59 S	65.35W
Rosario del Tala	204	Ck	32.18 S	59.09W
Rosário do Sul	206	Jd	30.15 S	54.55W
Rosário Oeste	202	Gf	14.50 S	56.25W
Rosarito	192	Bc	28.38N	114.04W
Rosarno	128	Jl	38.29N	15.58 E
Rosas/Roses	126	Pb	42.16N	3.11 E
Rosa Seamount (EN)	190	Bc	26.12N	114.58W
Rosa Zarate	202	Cc	0.18N	79.27W
Roščino	116	Md	60.13N	29.43 E
Roscoe Glacier	222	Ge	66.30 S	95.20 E
Ros Comáin/Roscommon	118	Eh	53.38N	8.11W
Ros Comáin/Roscommon [2]	118	Eh	53.40N	8.30W
Roscommon	184	Ec	44.30N	84.35W
Roscommon/Ros Comáin	118	Eh	53.38N	8.11W
Roscommon/Ros Comáin [2]	118	Eh	53.40N	8.30W
Ros Cré/Roscrea	118	Fi	52.57N	7.47W
Roscrea/Ros Cré	118	Fi	52.57N	7.47W
Rose, Pointe de la-	197h	Bb	14.33N	61.03W
Roseau [Dom.]	176	Mh	15.18N	61.24W
Roseau [Dom.]	197g	Bb	15.18N	61.24W
Roseau [Mn.-U.S.]	186	Ib	48.51N	95.46W
Roseau [St.Luc.]	197k	Ab	13.58N	61.02W
Roseau River	186	Hb	49.08N	97.14W
Rosebery	212	Jh	41.46 S	145.32 E
Rosebud	188	Lc	46.16N	106.27W
Rosebud Creek	188	Lc	46.16N	106.28W
Rosebud River	188	Ia	51.25N	112.37W
Roseburg	182	Cc	43.13N	123.20W
Rosemary Bank (EN)	118	Cb	59.15N	10.10W
Rosenberg	182	Hf	29.33N	95.48W
Rosendahl	124	Jb	52.01N	7.12 E
Rosendahl-Osterwick	124	Jb	52.01N	7.12 E
Rosendal	114	Bf	59.59N	6.01 E
Rosenheim	120	Ii	47.51N	12.08 E
Rosental	128	Id	46.33N	14.15 E
Roses/Rosas	126	Pb	42.16N	3.11 E
Roses, Golf de- / Roses, Golfo de-	126	Pb	42.10N	3.15 E
Roses, Golfo de- / Roses, Golf de-	126	Pb	42.10N	3.15 E
Roseţi	130	Ke	44.13N	27.26 E
Roseto degli Abruzzi	128	Ih	42.41N	14.01 E
Rosetown	180	Gf	51.33N	108.00W
Rosetta (EN)=Rashīd	164	Fc	31.24N	30.25 E
Roseville	188	Eg	38.45N	121.17W
Roshage	114	Bh	57.07N	8.38 E
Rosica	130	If	43.15N	25.42 E
Rosières-en-Santerre	124	Ee	49.49N	2.43 E
Rosignano Solvay	128	Eg	43.23N	10.26 E
Rosignol	202	Gb	6.17N	57.32W
Roşiori de Vede	130	He	44.07N	24.59 E
Roskilde	114	Ci	55.39N	12.05 E
Roskilde [2]	116	Ei	55.35N	12.10 E
Roslagen	116	He	59.30N	18.40 E
Ros Láir/Rosslare	118	Gi	52.17N	6.23W
Roslavl	136	Ce	53.58N	32.53 E
Roslyn	188	Ec	47.13N	120.59W
Ros Mhic Thriúin/New Ross	118	Gi	52.24N	6.56W
Røsnæs	116	Di	55.45N	10.55 E
Rosny-sur-Seine	124	Df	49.00N	1.38 E
Rösrath	124	Jd	50.54N	7.12 E
Ross [Austl.]	212	Jh	42.02 S	147.29 E
Ross [Bela.]	120	Uc	53.16N	24.29 E
Ross [N.Z.]	218	De	42.54 S	170.49 E
Ross, Cape-	150	Gd	10.56N	119.13 E
Ross, Mount-	222	Fc	49.25 S	69.08 E
Rossano	128	Kk	39.34N	16.38 E
Rossan Point/Ceann Ros Eoghain	118	Eg	54.42N	8.48W
Ross Barnett Reservoir	186	Lj	32.30N	90.00W
Rosseau Lake	184	Hc	45.10N	79.35W
Rossel Island	208	Gf	11.26 S	154.07 E
Ross Ice Shelf	222	Lg	81.30 S	175.00W
Rossija = Russia (EN)	136	Jc	60.00N	100.00 E
Rossijskaja Sovetskaja Federativnaja Socialističeskaja Respublika (RSFSR) → Rossija	136	Jc	60.00N	100.00 E
Ross Island	222	Kf	77.30 S	168.00 E
Ross Lake	188	Eb	48.53N	121.04W
Rossland	188	Gb	49.05N	117.48W
Rosslare/Ros Láir	118	Gi	52.17N	6.23W
Roßlau	120	Ie	51.53N	12.15 E
Rosso	160	Fg	16.31N	15.49W
Ross-on-Wye	118	Kj	51.55N	2.35W
Rossoš	136	De	50.11N	39.39 E
Ross River	180	Ed	61.59N	132.27W
Ross Sea (EN)	222	Lf	76.00 S	175.00W
Røssvatn	114	Cd	65.45N	14.00 E
Røst	114	Cc	67.31N	12.07 E
Rosta	114	Eb	69.02N	18.40 E
Rostamī	146	Nh	28.52N	51.02 E
Rostam Kalā	146	Od	36.42N	53.27 E
Rostāq	144	Hd	26.53N	53.52 E
Rösterkopf	124	Ie	49.40N	6.50 E
Rosthern	180	Gf	52.40N	106.20W
Rostock	112	He	54.05N	12.08 E
Rostock-Warnemünde	120	Ib	54.10N	12.05 E
Rostov	136	Dd	57.13N	39.25 E
Rostov-na-Donu	112	Jf	47.14N	39.42 E
Rostovskaja oblast [3]	136	Ef	47.45N	41.15 E
Roswell [Ga.-U.S.]	184	Eh	34.03N	84.22W
Roswell [N.M.-U.S.]	176	If	33.24N	104.32W
Rot	116	Fc	61.15N	14.02 E
Rota	126	Fh	36.37N	6.21W
Rota Island	208	Fc	14.10N	145.12 E
Rotenburg (Wümme)	120	Fc	53.07N	9.24 E
Rotenburg an der Fulda	120	Ff	50.59N	9.43 E
Roter Main	120	Hf	50.03N	11.27 E
Roth	120	Hg	49.15N	11.06 E
Rothaargebirge	120	Ee	51.05N	8.15 E
Rothenburg ob der Tauber	120	Gg	49.23N	10.11 E
Rother [Eng.-U.K.]	124	Bd	50.57N	0.22W
Rother [Eng.-U.K.]	118	Nk	50.57N	0.45 E
Rothera	222	Qe	67.46 S	68.54W
Rotherham	118	Lh	53.26N	1.20W
Rothesay	118	Hf	55.51N	5.03W
Rothorn	128	Cd	46.47N	8.03 E
Rothschild Island	222	Qe	69.25 S	72.30W
Rothwell	124	Bb	52.25N	0.48W
Roti, Pulau-	140	Ok	10.45 S	123.10 E
Roti, Selat-	150	Hi	10.25 S	123.25 E
Rotja, Punta- / Roja, Punta-	126	Nf	38.38N	1.34 E
Rotnes	116	Dd	60.04N	10.53 E
Roto	212	Jf	33.03 S	145.29 E
Rotoiti, Lake-	218	Ed	41.50 S	172.50 E
Rotondella	128	Kj	40.10N	16.31 E
Rotondo, Monte-	122a	Ba	42.13N	9.03 E
Rotoroa, Lake-	218	Ed	41.50 S	172.40 E
Rotorua	216	Eg	38.09 S	176.15 E
Rotorua, Lake-	218	Gc	38.05 S	176.15 E
Rotselaar	124	Gd	50.57N	4.43 E
Rott	120	Jh	48.25N	13.20 E
Rottenburg am Neckar	120	Eh	48.28N	8.56 E
Rotterdam	112	Ge	51.55N	4.28 E
Rottnaälven	116	Ed	59.48N	13.07 E
Rottnen	116	Fh	56.45N	15.05 E
Rottneros	116	Ee	59.48N	13.07 E
Rottnest Island	212	Df	32.00 S	115.30 E
Rottumerplaat	122	Ma	53.35N	6.30 E
Rottweil	120	Eh	48.10N	8.37 E
Rotuma Island	208	If	12.30 S	177.05 E
Roubaix	122	Jd	50.42N	3.10 E
Roubion	122	Kj	44.31N	4.42 E
Roudnice nad Labem	120	Kf	50.26N	14.16 E
Rouen	112	Gf	49.26N	1.05 E
Rouergue	122	Ij	44.30N	2.30 E
Rouge, Rivière-	184	Jc	45.38N	74.42W
Rouillac	122	Fi	45.47N	0.04W
Roulers/Roeselare	122	Jd	50.57N	3.08 E
Roumois	122	Ge	49.30N	0.30 E
Roundup	182	Fb	46.27N	108.33W
Rousay	118	Jb	59.01N	3.02W
Roussillon	122	Ki	45.22N	4.49 E
Roussillon	122	Il	42.30N	2.30 E
Roussin, Cap-	219b	Ce	21.21 S	167.59 E
Routot	124	Ce	49.23N	0.44 E
Rouyn	176	Le	48.14N	79.01W
Rovaniemi	112	Ib	66.30N	25.43 E
Rovenskaja oblast [3]	136	Ce	51.00N	26.30 E
Rovereto	128	Fe	45.53N	11.02 E
Rovigo	128	Fe	45.04N	11.47 E
Rovinari	130	Ge	44.55N	23.11 E
Rovinj	128	He	45.05N	13.38 E
Rovkulskoje, ozero-	114	Hd	64.00N	31.00 E
Rovno	112	Ie	50.37N	26.15 E
Rovnoje	132	Od	50.47N	46.05 E
Rovuma=Ruvuma (EN)	158	Lj	10.29 S	40.28 E
Rowa, Iles-	219b	Ca	13.37 S	167.32 E
Rowley	180	Jc	69.05N	78.55W
Rowley Shoals	208	Cf	17.30 S	119.00 E
Roxas [Phil.]	150	Gd	10.28N	119.30 E
Roxas [Phil.]	150	Hd	11.35N	122.45 E
Roxboro	184	Hg	36.24N	78.59W
Roxburgh	218	Cf	45.33 S	169.19 E
Roxen	116	Ff	58.30N	15.40 E
Roxo, Cap-	158	Fg	12.20N	16.43W
Roy [N.M.-U.S.]	186	Di	35.57N	104.12W
Roy [Ut.-U.S.]	188	If	41.10N	112.02W
Roya	122	Nk	43.48N	7.35 E
Royal Canal	118	Gh	53.21N	6.15W
Royale, Isle-	182	Jb	48.00N	89.00W
Royal Leamington Spa	118	Li	52.18N	1.31W
Royal Society Range	222	Jf	78.10 S	162.36 E
Royal Tunbridge Wells	118	Nj	51.08N	0.16 E
Royan	122	Ei	45.38N	1.02W
Royat	122	Ji	45.46N	3.03 E
Roye	122	Ie	49.42N	2.48 E
Roy Hill	212	Dd	22.38 S	119.57 E
Røyken	116	De	59.45N	10.23 E
Royston	118	Mi	52.03N	0.01W
Rožaj	130	Dg	42.51N	20.10 E
Różan	120	Rd	52.53N	21.25 E
Rozdol	120	Ug	49.24N	24.08 E
Rozewie, Przylądek-	120	Ob	54.51N	18.21 E
Rožišče	132	Dd	50.54N	25.19 E
Rožňava	120	Qh	48.40N	20.32 E
Rožniatov	120	Uh	48.51N	24.14 E
Roznov	130	Jc	46.50N	26.31 E
Rožnov pod Radhoštěm	120	Og	49.28N	18.09 E
Rožnów	120	Qg	49.46N	20.42 E
Rożnowskie, Jezioro-	120	Qg	49.48N	20.45 E
Rozoy-sur-Serre	124	Ge	49.43N	4.08 E
Roztocze	110	Ie	50.30N	23.20 E
Rrësheni	130	Ch	41.47N	19.54 E
RSFSR → Russia (EN)	136	Jc	60.00N	100.00 E
RSFSR → Rossija	136	Jc	60.00N	100.00 E
Rtanj	130	Ef	43.47N	21.54 E
Rtiščevo	136	Ee	52.16N	43.52 E
Ruacana, Quedas-	158	Ij	17.23 S	14.15 E
Ruahine Range	218	Gc	39.50 S	176.05 E
Ruapehu	208	Ih	39.17 S	175.34 E
Ruapuke Island	216	Ci	46.45 S	168.30 E
Rua Sura	219a	Ec	9.30 S	160.36 E
Ruatahuna	218	Gc	38.38 S	176.58 E
Rubbestadneset	116	Ae	59.49N	5.17 E
Rubcovsk	142	Kd	51.33N	81.10 E
Rubeho Mountains	170	Gd	6.55 S	36.30 E
Rubeshibe	154	Qc	43.47N	143.38 E
Rubežnoje	132	Ke	48.59N	38.26 E
Rubi	170	Db	2.48N	23.54 E
Rubiataba	204	Hb	15.08 S	49.48W
Rubiku	130	Ch	41.46N	19.45 E
Rubio	202	Db	7.43N	72.22W
Rubio	126	Ic	41.26N	3.47W
Ruby	178	Hd	64.44N	155.30W
Ruby Lake	188	Hf	40.15N	115.30W
Ruby Mountains	188	Hf	40.25N	115.35W
Ruby Range	188	Id	45.15N	112.15W
Rucăr	130	Id	45.24N	25.10 E
Rucava	116	Ih	56.10N	21.00 E
Ruciane Nida	120	Rc	53.39N	21.35 E
Ruda	120	Of	50.10N	18.18 E
Rudabánya	120	Qh	48.23N	20.38 E
Rūdak	146	Nh	35.51N	51.33 E
Rūdān	146	Qi	27.17N	57.13 E
Ruda Śląska	120	Of	50.18N	18.51 E
Rūdbār [Afg.]	144	Jc	30.09N	62.36 E
Rūdbār [Iran]	146	Md	36.48N	49.24 E
Rüdersdorf bei Berlin	120	Jd	52.27N	13.47 E
Rüdesheim am Rhein	124	Je	49.59N	7.55 E
Rudiškes/Rūdiškės	116	Kj	54.30N	24.58 E
Rūdiškės/Rudiškes	116	Kj	54.30N	24.58 E
Rudki	120	Tg	49.34N	23.30 E
Rudkøbing	114	Ci	54.56N	10.43 E
Rudnaja-Pristan	138	Ih	44.25N	135.49 E
Rudničny	114	Mg	59.38N	52.29 E
Rudnik	130	De	44.08N	20.30 E
Rudnik [Bul.]	130	Kg	42.57N	27.46 E
Rudnik [Pol.]	120	Sf	50.28N	22.15 E
Rudnik [Yugo.]	130	De	44.08N	20.31 E
Rudnja [Russia]	132	Nd	50.49N	44.36 E
Rudnja [Russia]	136	De	54.57N	31.07 E
Rudno	120	Tg	49.44N	23.57 E
Rudny [Kaz.]	136	Ge	52.57N	63.07 E
Rudny [Russia]	154	Mb	44.28N	135.00 E
Rudolf, Lake-/Turkana, Lake-	158	Kh	3.30N	36.00 E
Rudolstadt	120	Hf	50.43N	11.20 E
Rudong (Juegang)	154	Fh	32.19N	121.11 E
Rudozem	130	Hh	41.29N	24.51 E
Rūd Sar	146	Nd	37.08N	50.18 E
Rudyard	188	Jb	48.34N	110.33W
Rue	122	Hd	50.16N	1.40 E
Ruecas	126	Ge	39.00N	5.55W
Ruelle	122	Gi	45.41N	0.14 E
Rufā'ah	168	Ec	14.46N	33.22 E
Ruffec	122	Gh	46.01N	0.12 E
Ruffing Point	197a	Db	18.45N	64.25W
Rufiji	158	Ki	8.00 S	39.20 E
Rufino	206	Hd	34.16 S	62.42W
Rufisque	166	Bc	14.43N	17.17W
Rufunsa	170	Ef	15.05 S	29.40 E
Rugao	154	Fh	32.24N	120.34 E
Rugby [Eng.-U.K.]	118	Li	52.23N	1.15W
Rugby [N.D.-U.S.]	182	Gb	48.22N	99.59W
Rügen	110	He	54.25N	13.24 E
Rugles	124	Cf	48.49N	0.42 E
Ru He	154	Ch	32.55N	114.24 E
Ruhea	148	Hc	26.10N	88.25 E
Ruhengeri	170	Ec	1.30 S	29.38 E
Rühlertwist	124	Jb	52.39N	7.06 E
Ruhner Berge	120	Hc	53.17N	11.55 E
Ruhnu, ostrov-	114	Fh	57.50N	23.15 E
Ruhnu, ostrov- / Ruhnu saar	114	Fh	57.50N	23.15 E
Ruhnu saar / Ruhnu, ostrov-	114	Fh	57.50N	23.15 E
Ruhr	120	Ce	51.27N	6.44 E
Rui'an	152	Lf	27.48N	120.38 E
Ruichang	154	Cj	29.41N	115.38 E
Ruiena/Rūjiena	114	Fh	57.54N	25.17 E
Ruijin	152	Kf	25.59N	116.03 E
Ruili	152	Gg	24.03N	97.46 E
Ruiselede	124	Fc	51.03N	3.24 E
Ruiz	192	Gg	21.57N	105.09W
Ruiz, Nevado del-	202	Cc	4.54N	75.18W
Ruj	130	Fg	42.51N	22.35 E
Rūja/Ruja	116	Kg	57.38N	25.10 E
Ruja/Rūja	116	Kg	57.38N	25.10 E
Rujan	130	Eg	42.23N	21.49 E
Rujen	130	Fg	42.10N	22.31 E
Rūjiena/Ruiena	114	Fh	57.54N	25.17 E
Ruki	158	Ih	0.05N	18.17 E
Rukwa [3]	170	Fd	7.00 S	31.20 E
Rukwa, Lake-	158	Ki	8.00 S	32.15 E
Rūl Ḑadnah	146	Qk	25.33N	56.21 E
Rülzheim	124	Ke	49.10N	8.18 E
Ruma	130	Cd	45.01N	19.49 E
Rumaylah	168	Fc	12.57N	35.02 E
Rumbek	160	Jh	6.48N	29.41 E
Rumberpon, Pulau-	150	Jg	1.50 S	134.15 E
Rum Cay	190	Jd	23.40N	74.53W
Rumes	124	Fd	50.33N	3.18 E
Rumford	184	Lc	44.33N	70.33W
Rumia	120	Ob	54.35N	18.25 E
Rumigny	124	Ge	49.48N	4.16 E
Rumija	130	Cg	42.06N	19.12 E
Rumilly	122	Li	45.52N	5.57 E
Rum Jungle	212	Gb	13.01 S	131.00 E
Rummah, Wādī ar-	146	Ki	26.38N	44.18 E
Rumoi	152	Pc	43.56N	141.39 E
Rumphi	170	Fe	11.01 S	33.52 E
Run	124	Hc	51.40N	5.20 E
Runan	154	Ci	33.00N	114.21 E
Runanga	218	De	42.24 S	171.15 E
Runaway, Cape-	218	Gb	37.32 S	177.59 E
Rundēni/Rundeni	116	Lh	56.14N	27.52 E
Rundeni/Rundēni	116	Lh	56.14N	27.52 E
Rundu	160	Ij	17.55 S	19.45 E
Rungu	170	Eb	3.11N	27.52 E
Rungwa	160	Ki	6.57 S	33.31 E
Rungwa	170	Fd	7.36 S	31.50 E
Runmarö	116	He	59.15N	18.45 E
Runn	116	Fd	60.35N	15.40 E
Ruokolahti	114	Gf	61.17N	28.50 E
Ruoqiang/Qarkilik	142	Kf	39.02N	88.00 E
Ruo Shui	140	Le	40.20N	99.40 E
Ruotsalainen	116	Kc	61.15N	25.55 E
Ruotsinpyhtää/Strömfors	116	Ld	60.32N	26.27 E
Ruovesi	114	Ff	61.59N	24.05 E
Ruovesi	116	Kc	61.55N	24.10 E
Rupanco	206	Ff	40.46 S	72.42W
Rupea	130	Ic	46.02N	25.13 E
Rupel	124	Gc	51.07N	4.19 E
Rupert	188	Ie	42.37N	113.41W
Rupert	180	Jf	51.30N	78.48W
Rupert, Baie de-	180	Jf	51.35N	79.00W
Ruppert Coast	222	Mf	75.45 S	141.00W
Rur	120	Be	51.12N	5.59 E
Rurrenabaque	200	Jg	14.28 S	67.34W
Rurstausee	124	Id	50.38N	6.24 E
Rurutu, Ile-	208	Lg	22.26 S	151.20W
Rušan	136	Hh	37.57N	71.31 E
Rusape	172	Ec	18.32 S	32.07 E
Ruşayris, Khazzān ar- = Rusayris, Lake- (EN)	168	Ec	11.40N	34.20 E
Rusayris, Lake- (EN) = Ruşayris, Khazzān ar-	168	Ec	11.40N	34.20 E
Ruse	112	Ig	43.50N	25.57 E
Ruse [2]	130	If	43.50N	25.57 E
Ruşeţu	130	Ke	44.57N	27.13 E
Rushan (Xiacun)	154	Ff	36.55N	121.30 E
Rushden	124	Bb	52.17N	0.35W
Rushville	186	Kf	40.07N	90.34W
Rusk	186	Ik	31.48N	95.09W
Rusken	116	Fg	57.17N	14.20 E
Rusne/Rusnė	116	Ii	55.19N	21.16 E
Rusnė/Rusne	116	Ii	55.19N	21.16 E
Russel	180	Hb	73.55N	98.35W
Russell [Ks.-U.S.]	186	Gg	38.54N	98.52W
Russell [Man.-Can.]	186	Hf	50.47N	101.15W
Russell [N.Z.]	218	Fa	35.16 S	174.08 E
Russell Islands	214	Fi	9.04 S	159.12 E
Russellville [Al.-U.S.]	184	Dh	34.30N	87.44W
Russellville [Ar.-U.S.]	186	Ji	35.17N	93.08W
Russellville [Ky.-U.S.]	184	Dg	36.51N	86.53W
Russel Range	212	Ef	33.25 S	123.30 E
Rüsselsheim	120	Eg	50.00N	8.25 E
Russia (EN) = Rossija	136	Jc	60.00N	100.00 E
Russian River	188	Dg	38.27N	123.08W
Rust	128	Kc	47.48N	16.40 E
Rustavi	136	Eg	41.33N	45.02 E
Rustenburg	172	De	25.37 S	27.08 E
Ruston	182	Ie	32.32N	92.38W
Rutaki Passage	220p	Bc	21.15 S	159.48W
Rutana	170	Fc	3.55 S	30.00 E
Rutanzige, Lac-=Edward, Lake- (EN)	158	Ji	0.25 S	29.30 E
Rute	126	Hg	37.19N	4.22W
Ruteng	150	Hh	8.36 S	120.27 E
Rutenga	172	Ed	21.15 S	30.44 E
Rüthen	124	Ke	51.29N	8.27 E
Ruthenia (EN)	130	Ga	48.20N	23.30 E

Index Symbols

- [1] Independent Nation
- [2] State, Region
- [3] District, County
- [4] Municipality
- [5] Colony, Dependency
- Continent
- Physical Region
- Historical or Cultural Region
- Mount, Mountain
- Volcano
- Hill
- Mountains, Mountain Range
- Hills, Escarpment
- Plateau, Upland
- Pass, Gap
- Plain, Lowland
- Delta
- Salt Flat
- Valley, Canyon
- Crater, Cave
- Karst Features
- Depression
- Polder
- Desert, Dunes
- Forest, Woods
- Heath, Steppe
- Oasis
- Cape, Point
- Coast, Beach
- Cliff
- Peninsula
- Isthmus
- Sandbank
- Island
- Atoll
- Rock, Reef
- Islands, Archipelago
- Rocks, Reefs
- Coral Reef
- Well, Spring
- Geyser
- River, Stream
- Waterfall, Rapids
- River Mouth, Estuary
- Lake
- Salt Lake
- Intermittent Lake
- Reservoir
- Swamp, Pond
- Canal
- Glacier
- Ice Shelf, Pack Ice
- Ocean
- Sea
- Gulf, Bay
- Strait, Fjord
- Lagoon
- Bank
- Seamount
- Tablemount
- Ridge
- Shelf
- Basin
- Escarpment, Sea Scarp
- Fracture
- Trench, Abyss
- National Park, Reserve
- Point of Interest
- Recreation Site
- Cave, Cavern
- Historic Site
- Ruins
- Wall, Walls
- Church, Abbey
- Temple
- Scientific Station
- Railway station
- Airport
- Port
- Military installation
- Lighthouse
- Mine
- Tunnel
- Dam, Bridge

Rutherfordton	184	Gh	35.22N	81.57W
Ruthin	118	Jh	53.07N	3.18W
Rutland	184	Kd	43.37N	72.59W
Rutland	118	Mi	52.40N	0.40W
Rutland	148	If	11.25N	92.10 E
Rutog	142	Jf	33.29N	79.42 E
Rutshuru	170	Ec	1.11 S	29.27 E
Rutter	184	Gb	46.06N	80.40W
Rutul	132	Oi	41.33N	47.29 E
Ruutana	116	Kc	61.31N	24.02 E
Ruvo di Puglia	128	Ki	41.09N	16.29 E
Ruvu	170	Gd	6.48 S	38.39 E
Ruvu → Pangani	170	Gc	5.26 S	38.58 E
Ruvuma [3]	170	Ge	10.30 S	35.50 E
Ruvuma	158	Lj	10.29 S	40.28 E
Ruvuma (EN) = Rovuma	158	Lj	10.29 S	40.28 E
Ruwayshid, Wādī-	146	Hf	32.41N	38.04 E
Ruwer	124	Ie	49.47N	6.42 E
Ruya	172	Ec	16.34 S	33.12 E
Ruyang	154	Bg	34.10N	112.28 E
Ru'yas, Wādī ar-	164	Cd	27.06N	19.24 E
Ruyigi	170	Fc	3.29 S	30.15 E
Ruza	114	Ii	55.39N	36.18 E
Ruzajevka [Kaz.]	134	Mj	52.49N	67.01 E
Ruzajevka [Russia]	136	Ee	54.05N	44.54 E
Ružany	120	Ud	52.48N	24.58 E
Ružomberok	120	Pg	49.05N	19.18 E
Rwanda [1]	160	Ji	2.30 S	30.00 E
Ry	116	Ch	56.05N	9.46 E
Ryan	186	Hi	34.01N	97.57W
Rybachi Peninsula (EN) = Rybači, poluostrov-	110	Jb	69.45N	32.35 E
Rybači	116	Ii	55.09N	20.45 E
Rybači, poluostrov- = Rybachi Peninsula (EN)	110	Jb	69.45N	32.35 E
Rybačje → Issyk-Kul'	136	Hg	42.28N	76.11 E
Rybinsk	112	Jd	58.03N	38.52 E
Rybinskoje vodohranilišče = = Rybinsk Reservoir (EN)	110	Jd	58.30N	38.25 E
Rybinsk Reservoir (EN) = Rybinskoje vodohranilišče	110	Jd	58.30N	38.25 E
Rybnica	132	Ff	47.45N	29.01 E
Rybnik	120	Of	50.06N	18.32 E
Rybnoje	136	De	54.46N	39.33 E
Rybnovsk	138	Jf	53.15N	141.55 E
Rychnov nad Kněžnou	120	Mf	50.10N	16.17 E
Rychwał	120	Od	52.05N	18.09 E
Ryd	116	Fh	56.28N	14.41 E
Rydaholm	116	Fh	56.59N	14.16 E
Ryde	124	Ad	50.43N	1.10W
Rye	118	Nk	50.57N	0.44 E
Rye	118	Mg	54.10N	0.45W
Rye Bay	124	Cd	50.55N	0.48 E
Ryegate	188	Kc	46.18N	109.15W
Rye Patch Reservoir	188	Ff	40.38N	118.18W
Ryes	124	Be	49.19N	0.37W
Ryfylke	116	Be	59.30N	6.30 E
Ryki	120	Re	51.38N	21.56 E
Rylsk	136	De	51.36N	34.43 E
Rymanów	120	Rg	49.34N	21.53 E
Rymättylä/Rimito	116	Jd	60.25N	21.55 E
Ryn	120	Rc	53.56N	21.33 E
Ryńskie, Jezioro-	120	Rc	53.53N	21.30 E
Ryōhaku-Sanchi	156	Ec	36.05N	136.45 E
Ryōsō-Yosui	156	Gd	35.22N	140.25 E
Ryōtsu	154	Oe	38.05N	138.26 E
Ryōtsu-Wan	156	Fb	38.10N	138.30 E
Ryō-Zen	156	Gc	37.46N	140.41 E
Rypin	120	Pc	53.05N	19.25 E
Ryškany	132	Ef	47.57N	27.32 E
Ryssby	116	Fh	56.52N	14.10 E
Rytterknægten	116	Fi	55.06N	14.54 E
Ryūgasaki	156	Gd	35.54N	140.10 E
Ryukyu Islands (EN) = Nansei-Shotō	140	Og	26.30N	128.00 E
Ryūkyū-Shotō	152	Mf	25.30N	126.30 E
Ryukyu Trench (EN)	106	Ig	25.45N	128.00 E
Rzepin	120	Kd	52.22N	14.50 E
Rzeszów	112	Ie	50.03N	22.00 E
Rzeszów [2]	120	Rf	50.05N	22.00 E
Ržev	112	Jd	56.16N	34.20 E

S

Šaa, gora-	132	Nh	42.39N	44.43 E
Sa'ādatābād [Iran]	146	Og	30.08N	52.38 E
Sa'ādatābād [Iran]	146	Og	30.06N	53.08 E
Sa'ādatābād [Iran]	146	Ph	28.02N	55.50 E
Sääksjarvi	116	Jc	61.24N	22.24 E
Saalbach	124	Ke	49.15N	8.27 E
Saale	120	He	51.57N	11.55 E
Saaler Bodden	120	Ib	54.20N	12.28 E
Saalfeld	120	Hf	50.39N	11.22 E
Saalfelden am Steinernen Meer	128	Gc	47.25N	12.51 E
Saaminki	116	Mc	61.52N	28.50 E
Saane	128	Bd	46.59N	7.16 E
Saâne	124	Ce	49.54N	0.56 E
Saanen	128	Bd	46.30N	7.15 E
Saanen-Gstaad	128	Bd	46.28N	7.17 E
Saar	120	Cg	49.42N	6.34 E
Saar-Bergland	124	Ie	49.27N	6.45 E
Saarbrücken	112	Gf	49.14N	7.00 E
Saarbrücken-Dudweiler	124	Je	49.17N	7.02 E
Saarburg	120	Cg	49.36N	6.33 E
Sääre/Sjare	116	Ig	57.57N	21.53 E
Saaremaa/Sarema	110	Id	58.25N	22.30 E
Saarijärvi	114	Fe	62.43N	25.16 E
Saaristomeri	116	Id	60.20N	21.10 E
Saarland [2]	120	Cg	49.20N	7.00 E
Saarlouis	120	Cg	49.19N	6.45 E
Šaartuz	136	Gh	37.16N	68.06 E
Saarwellingen	124	Ie	49.21N	6.49 E
Saas Fee	128	Bd	46.07N	7.55 E
Saatly	132	Pj	39.57N	48.26 E
Saavedra	204	Am	37.45 S	62.22W
Sab, Tônlé-	150	Dd	11.34N	104.57 E
Saba	190	Le	17.38N	63.10W
Saba	116	Me	59.05N	29.10 E
Saba Bank (EN)	196	Ed	17.30N	63.30W
Šabac	130	Ce	44.45N	19.43 E
Sabadell	126	Oc	41.33N	2.06 E
Sabae	154	Ng	35.57N	136.11 E
Sabah [2]	150	Ge	5.30N	117.00 E
Sab'ah, Qārat as-	164	Cd	27.20N	17.10 E
Sabak Bernam	150	Df	3.46N	100.59 E
Sabalān, Kūhhā-ye-	140	Gf	38.15N	47.49 E
Sab'ān	146	Ii	27.04N	41.58 E
Sabana, Archipiélago de-	194	Hb	22.30N	79.00W
Sabana de la Mar	194	Md	19.04N	69.23W
Sabanagrande	194	Dg	13.50N	87.15W
Sabanalarga	202	Da	10.38N	74.56W
Sabancuy	192	Nh	18.58N	91.11W
Sabaneta	194	Ld	19.12N	70.58W
Sabaneta, Puntan-	220b	Ba	15.17N	145.49 E
Sabang [Indon.]	150	Ce	5.55N	95.19 E
Sabang [Indon.]	150	Gf	0.11N	119.51 E
Şabanözü	146	Eb	40.29N	33.18 E
Săbăoani	130	Jb	47.01N	26.51 E
Sabarei	170	Gb	4.20N	36.55 E
Sab'Atayn, Ramlat as-	164	If	15.30N	46.10 E
Sabatini, Monti-	128	Gh	42.10N	12.15 E
Sabaudia	128	Hi	41.18N	13.01 E
Sabaudia, Lago di-	128	Hi	41.15N	13.05 E
Şabbāgh, Jabal-	146	Fh	28.12N	34.04 E
Sab 'Bi 'Ār	146	Gf	33.46N	37.41 E
Sa Bec	148	Lf	10.18N	105.46 E
Şabḥā	146	Gf	32.20N	36.30 E
Sabhā	160	If	27.02N	14.26 E
Sabhā [3]	164	Bd	26.00N	14.00 E
Sabhā, Wāḥāt- = Sebha Oasis (EN)	158	If	27.00N	14.25 E
Sabi	158	Kk	21.00 S	35.02 E
Sabidana, Jabal-	168	Fb	18.04N	36.50 E
Sabile	116	Jg	57.05N	22.29 E
Sabina	128	Gh	42.20N	12.45 E
Sabinal	192	Fb	30.57N	107.30W
Sabinal, Peninsula de-	194	Ic	21.40N	77.18W
Sabiñánigo	126	Lb	42.31N	0.22W
Sabinas	190	Dc	27.51N	101.07W
Sabinas, Rio-	192	Id	27.37N	100.42W
Sabinas Hidalgo	190	Dc	26.30N	100.10W
Sabine Lake	186	Jl	29.50N	93.50W
Sabine Pass	186	Jl	29.44N	93.52W
Sabine Peninsula	180	Ga	76.25N	109.50W
Sabine River	182	Ie	30.00N	93.45W
Sabini, Monti-	128	Gh	42.15N	12.50 E
Şabir, Jabal-	144	Fg	13.30N	44.03 E
Sabirabad	132	Pj	39.59N	48.29 E
Šabla	130	Lf	43.32N	28.32 E
Sable, Anse de-	197e	Ab	16.07N	61.34W
Sable, Cape- [Can.]	174	Me	43.25N	65.35W
Sable, Cape- [U.S.]	174	Kg	25.12N	81.05W
Sable, Ile de-	208	Gf	19.15 S	159.56 E
Sable Island	174	Ne	43.55N	59.55W
Sables-d'Olonne, Les-	122	Eh	46.30N	1.47W
Sablé-sur-Sarthe	122	Fg	47.50N	0.20W
Sablūkah, Ash Shallāl as- = Sixth Cataract (EN)	158	Kg	16.20N	32.42 E
Sabonetau, Serra do-	204	Kb	15.20 S	43.50W
Sabonkafi	166	Gc	14.38N	8.45 E
Sabór	126	Ec	41.10N	7.07W
Şabrātah	164	Bc	32.47N	12.29 E
Sabres	122	Fj	44.09N	0.44W
Sabrina Coast	222	He	67.00 S	119.30 E
Sabtang	150	Hb	20.19N	121.52 E
Sabugal	126	Ed	40.21N	7.05W
Sabunči	132	Pi	40.27N	49.57 E
Şabyā	144	Ff	17.09N	42.37 E
Sabzevār	142	Hf	36.13N	57.42 E
Saca, Virful-	130	Ic	46.30N	25.15 E
Sacajawea Peak	182	Db	45.15N	117.17W
Sacalin, Insulă-	130	Me	44.50N	29.39 E
Sacandica	170	Cd	5.58 S	15.56 E
Sacatepéquez [3]	194	Bf	14.35N	90.45W
Sacavém	126	Cf	38.46N	9.05W
Sac City	186	Ie	42.25N	95.00W
Sacco	128	Hi	41.31N	13.32 E
Sacedón	126	Jd	40.29N	2.43W
Săcel	130	Hb	47.38N	24.26 E
Săcele	130	Id	45.37N	25.41 E
Sachayoj	204	Bh	26.41 S	61.50W
Sačhere	132	Mh	42.20N	43.22 E
Sachigo	180	Ie	55.05N	89.00W
Sachsen = Saxony (EN)	120	Ie	51.20N	13.30 E
Sachsenhagen	124	Lb	52.24N	9.16 E
Sachs Harbour	180	Eb	72.00N	125.08W
Šack [Russia]	114	Ji	54.04N	41.42 E
Šack [Ukr.]	120	Te	51.30N	24.00 E
Sackets Harbor	184	Id	43.57N	76.07W
Saco [Me.-U.S.]	184	Ld	43.29N	70.28W
Saco [Mt.-U.S.]	188	Lb	48.28N	107.21W
Sacramento	174	Gf	38.03N	121.56W
Sacramento [Braz.]	202	Ig	19.53 S	47.27W
Sacramento [Ca.-U.S.]	176	Gf	38.35N	121.30W
Sacramento, Pampa del-	202	Ce	8.00 S	75.50W
Sacramento Mountains	174	If	33.10N	105.50W
Sacramento Valley	182	Cd	39.15N	122.00W
Sacre ou Timalacia, Rio-	204	Ca	13.55 S	58.02W
Săcueni	130	Fb	47.21N	22.06 E
Sacuriuiná ou Ponte de Pedra, Rio-	204	Da	13.58 S	57.18W
Sádaba	126	Kb	42.17N	1.16W
Sa'dābād	146	Nh	29.23N	51.07 E
Şa'dah	142	Gh	16.57N	43.44 E
Sada-Misaki	156b	Ce	33.22N	132.01 E
Sada-Misaki-Hantō	156	Ce	33.25N	132.15 E
Sadani	170	Gd	6.03 S	38.47 E
Sadao	148	Kg	6.39N	100.31 E
Saddle Mountains	188	Fc	46.50N	119.55W
Saddle Peak [India]	148	If	13.09N	93.01 E
Saddle Peak [Mt.-U.S.]	188	Jd	45.57N	110.58W
Sad-e Eskandar	146	Pd	37.10N	55.00 E
Sadiya	148	Jc	27.50N	95.40 E
Sa'dīyah, Hawr as-	146	Lf	32.00N	46.45 E
Sad Kharv	146	Qd	36.19N	57.05 E
Sado	126	Df	38.29N	8.55W
Sado-Kaikyō	156	Fc	37.55N	138.40 E
Sado-Shima	140	Pf	38.00N	138.25 E
Sadowara	156	Be	32.04N	131.26 E
Sa Dragonera, Illa- / Dragonera, Isla-	126	Oe	39.35N	2.19 E
Šadrinsk	136	Gd	56.05N	63.38 E
Saeby	114	Ch	57.20N	10.32 E
Saeh, Teluk-	150	Gh	8.00 S	117.30 E
Saengcheon	154	Ie	39.55N	126.34 E
Saerbeck	124	Jb	52.11N	7.38 E
Şafā, Wādī aş-	146	Pk	23.26N	55.41 E
Şafājah	146	Hi	26.30N	39.30 E
Safājah, Jazīrat-	146	Ei	26.45N	33.59 E
Safané	166	Ec	12.08N	3.13W
Şafāqis = Sfax (EN)	160	Ie	34.44N	10.46 E
Şafāqis = Sfax (EN) [3]	162	Jc	34.30N	10.30 E
Safata Harbour	221c	Bb	14.00 S	171.50W
Säffle	114	Cg	59.08N	12.56 E
Safford	182	Fe	32.50N	109.43W
Saffron Walden	118	Ni	52.01N	0.15 E
Safi	160	Ge	32.18N	9.14W
Safi [3]	162	Fc	31.55N	9.00W
Safia, Hamāda-	166	Ea	23.10N	4.15W
Şafīābād	146	Od	36.45N	57.58 E
Safid	144	Hb	37.23N	50.11 E
Safid, Kūh-e	146	Lf	33.55N	47.30 E
Safonovo [Russia]	114	Ld	65.41N	47.43 E
Safonovo [Russia]	136	Dd	55.06N	33.14 E
Şafrā' al Asyāḥ	146	Ji	26.50N	43.57 E
Şafrā' as Sark	146	Kj	25.25N	44.20 E
Safranbolu	146	Eb	41.15N	32.42 E
Şafwān	146	Lg	30.07N	47.43 E
Saga [Jap.]	152	Ne	33.15N	130.18 E
Saga [Jap.]	156	Ce	33.05N	133.06 E
Saga [Kaz.]	136	Ge	50.30N	64.14 E
Saga (Gya'gya)	152	Ef	29.22N	85.15 E
Sagae	156	Gb	38.22N	140.17 E
Sagaing	148	Jd	21.52N	95.59 E
Sagaing [3]	148	Jd	23.30N	95.30 E
Saga Ken [2]	154	Kh	33.15N	130.15 E
Sagamihara	156	Fd	35.34N	139.22 E
Sagami-Nada	156	Fd	35.00N	139.30 E
Sagami-Wan	156	Fd	35.15N	139.20 E
Sagan	168	Fd	5.17N	36.57 E
Şagan	136	He	50.37N	79.15 E
Saganaga Lake	186	Kb	48.14N	90.52W
Saganoseki	156	Be	33.15N	131.53 E
Şagany, ozero-	130	Md	45.45N	29.55 E
Sāgar [India]	148	Ff	14.10N	75.02 E
Sāgar [India]	142	Jg	23.50N	78.42 E
Sagara	156	Fd	34.40N	138.12 E
Sagaredžo	132	Ni	41.43N	45.16 E
Sagavanirktok	178	Jb	70.20N	148.00W
Sagawa	156	Ce	33.29N	133.16 E
Sage	188	Jf	41.50N	110.56W
Saghād	146	Og	31.12N	52.30 E
Saginaw	182	Kc	43.25N	83.58W
Saginaw Bay	182	Kc	43.50N	83.40W
Sagiz	136	Ff	47.32N	53.45 E
Sagiz [Kaz.]	136	Ff	48.12N	54.56 E
Sagiz [Kaz.]	132	Rf	47.32N	53.27 E
Saglek Bay	180	Le	58.30N	63.00W
Saglouc	176	Lc	62.12N	75.38W
Şagonar	132	Ef	51.32N	92.51 E
Sagone, Golfe de-	122a	Aa	42.06N	8.41 E
Sagres	126	Dg	37.01N	8.56W
Şagu	130	Ec	46.03N	21.17 E
Sagu/Sauvo	116	Jd	60.21N	22.42 E
Saguache	186	Cg	38.05N	106.08W
Sagua de Tánamo	194	Jc	20.35N	75.14W
Sagua la Grande	190	Hd	22.49N	80.05W
Saguenay	174	Me	48.10N	69.45W
Saguia el-Hamra	162	Ed	26.50N	12.00W
Sagunto / Sagunt o Morvedre	126	Le	39.41N	0.16W
Sagunto-Grao de Sagunto	126	Le	39.40N	0.16W
Sagunt o Morvedre / Sagunto	126	Le	39.41N	0.16W
Sa'gya	152	Ef	28.53N	88.10 E
Saha (Jakutija), respublika	138	Hc	67.00N	130.00 E
Sahagún [Col.]	202	Cb	8.57N	75.27W
Sahagún [Sp.]	126	Gb	42.22N	5.02W
Sahalin, ostrov- = Sakhalin (EN)	140	Qd	51.00N	143.00 E
Sahalinskaja oblast [3]	138	Jf	50.00N	143.30 E
Sahalinski zaliv	138	Jf	53.45N	141.30 E
Sahara	158	Hf	21.00N	6.00 E
Saharan Atlas (EN) = Atlas Saharien	158	He	34.00N	2.00 E
Sahāranpur	142	Jg	29.58N	77.23 E
Sahel [3]	166	Ec	14.10N	0.50W
Sahel	166	Gg	15.40N	8.30W
Şahin	130	Jh	41.01N	26.50 E
Sāhīwāl [Pak.]	148	Eb	30.41N	72.57 E
Sāhīwāl [Pak.]	148	Eb	31.58N	72.20 E
Sahlābād	144	Ic	32.10N	59.51 E
Sahneh	146	Le	34.29N	47.41 E
Sahnovščina	132	Ie	49.09N	35.57 E
Sahova Kosa, mys-	132	Qi	40.13N	50.22 E
Sahrihan	135	Id	40.40N	72.03 E
Šahrisabz	136	Gh	39.03N	66.41 E
Šahristan, pereval-	136	Ge	39.35N	68.38 E
Šahtersk [Russia]	138	Jg	49.13N	142.09 E
Šahtersk [Ukr.]	132	Ke	48.01N	38.32 E
Šahterski	138	Md	64.46N	177.47 E
Šahtinsk	136	Hf	49.40N	72.37 E
Šahty	136	Ef	47.42N	40.13 E
Sahuaripa	190	Cc	29.03N	109.14W
Sahuayo de Diaz	190	Dd	20.04N	102.43W
Šahunja	136	Ed	57.43N	46.35 E
Sahūq, Wādī-	146	Jj	25.40N	42.30 E
Šahy	120	Oh	48.05N	18.58 E
Sahyadri/Western Ghats	140	Jh	14.00N	75.00 E
Sai Buri	148	Kg	6.42N	101.37 E
Saïda	160	He	34.50N	0.09 E
Saïda [3]	162	Hc	33.35N	0.30 E
Saïda, Monts de-	126	Mi	35.10N	0.30 E
Sa'īdābād	144	Id	29.28N	55.42 E
Saidaiji	156	Dd	34.39N	134.02 E
Said Bundas	168	Cd	8.35N	24.30 E
Saïdia	126	Ji	35.04N	2.13W
Saidor	214	Di	5.37 S	146.28 E
Saidu	148	Eb	34.45N	72.21 E
Saigō	156	Cc	36.13N	133.20 E
Saigon → Thanh-pho Ho Chi Minh	142	Mh	10.45N	106.40 E
Saihan Tal → Sonid Youqi	152	Jc	42.45N	112.36 E
Saihan Toroi	152	Hc	41.54N	100.24 E
Saijō	156	Ce	33.55N	133.10 E
Saikai	156	Ae	33.03N	129.44 E
Sai-Kawa	156	Fc	36.37N	138.14 E
Saiki	154	Kh	32.57N	131.54 E
Saiki-Wan	156	Be	33.00N	131.55 E
Sail Rock	197n	Bb	12.37N	61.16W
Saimaa	110	Ic	61.15N	28.15 E
Saimaa Canal (EN) = Sajmenski kanal	116	Mc	61.05N	28.18 E
Sain Alto	192	Hf	23.35N	103.15W
Sā in Dezh	146	Ld	36.40N	46.33 E
Sains-Richaumont	124	Fe	49.49N	3.42 E
Saint Abb's Head	118	Kf	55.54N	2.09W
Saint-Affrique	122	Ik	43.57N	2.53 E
Saint Agnes Head	118	Hk	50.23N	5.07W
Saint-Agrève	122	Ki	45.01N	4.24 E
Saint Albans [Eng.-U.K.]	118	Mj	51.46N	0.21W
Saint Albans [Vt.-U.S.]	184	Kc	44.49N	73.05W
Saint Albans [W.V.-U.S.]	184	Gf	38.24N	81.53W
Saint Alban's Head → Saint Albhelm's Head	118	Kk	50.34N	2.04W
Saint Albert	180	Gf	53.38N	113.38W
Saint Albhelm's or Saint Alban's Head	118	Kk	50.34N	2.04W
Saint-Amand-les-Eaux	122	Jd	50.26N	3.26 E
Saint-Amand-Montrond	122	Ih	46.43N	2.31 E
Saint-André, Cap-	158	Lj	16.11 S	44.27 E
Saint-André, Plaine de-	122	Hf	48.55N	1.10 E
Saint-André-de-Cubzac	122	Fi	45.00N	0.27W
Saint-André-de-l'Eure	124	Df	48.54N	1.17 E
Saint-André-sur-Cailly	124	De	49.33N	1.13 E
Saint Andrews [N.B.-Can.]	184	Nc	45.06N	67.02W
Saint Andrews [Scot.-U.K.]	118	Ke	56.20N	2.48W
Saint Anne	118	Kl	49.40N	2.10W
Saint Ann's Bay	194	Id	18.26N	77.16W
Saint Ann's Head	118	Hj	51.41N	5.10W
Saint Anthony [Id.-U.S.]	188	Je	43.58N	111.41W
Saint Anthony [Newf.-Can.]	180	Lf	51.22N	55.35W
Saint Arnaud	212	Ig	36.37 S	143.15 E
Saint-Aubert	184	Lb	47.14N	70.15W
Saint-Aubin-sur-Mer	124	Be	49.20N	0.24W
Saint Augustine	182	Kf	29.51N	81.25W
Saint-Augustin-Saguenay	180	Lf	51.14N	58.39W
Saint Austell	118	Ik	50.20N	4.48W
Saint-Avold	122	Me	49.06N	6.42 E
Saint Barthélemy	190	Le	17.55N	62.50W
Saint Barthélemy, Canal de-	197b	Bb	18.00N	63.00W
Saint Barthélemy, Kanaal Van-	197b	Bb	18.00N	63.00W
Saint-Barthélemy, Pic de-	122	Hl	42.49N	1.45 E
Saint Bees Head	118	Jg	54.32N	3.38W
Saint-Benoit	172a	Bb	21.02 S	55.43 E
Saint-Benoît-sur-Loire	122	Ig	47.49N	2.18 E
Saint-Bonnet	122	Mj	44.41N	6.05 E
Saint-Brévin-les-Pins	122	Dg	47.15N	2.10W
Saint Brides Bay	118	Hj	51.48N	5.15W
Saint-Brieuc	122	Df	48.31N	2.47W
Saint-Brieuc, Baie de-	122	Df	48.38N	2.40W
Saint-Calais	122	Gg	47.55N	0.45 E
Saint-Camille	184	Lb	46.29N	70.12W
Saint Catharines	180	Jh	43.10N	79.15W
Saint Catherine, Monastery of- (EN) = Kātrīnā, Dayr-	164	Fd	28.31N	33.57 E
Saint Catherine, Mount-	197p	Bb	12.10N	61.40W
Saint Catherines Island	184	Gj	31.38N	81.10W
Saint Catherine's Point	118	Lk	50.34N	1.15W
Saint-Céré	122	Hj	44.52N	1.54 E
Saint-Chamond	122	Ki	45.28N	4.30 E
Saint Charles	182	Id	38.47N	90.29W
Saint-Chély-d'Apcher	122	Jj	44.48N	3.17 E
Saint-Christol, Plateau de-	122	Lj	44.00N	5.50 E
Saint Christopher/Saint Kitts	174	Mh	17.21N	62.48W
Saint Christopher-Nevis [1]	176	Mh	17.21N	62.48W
Saint-Cirq-Lapopie	122	Hj	44.28N	1.40 E
Saint Clair, Lake-	174	Ke	42.25N	82.41W
Saint Clair River	184	Fd	42.37N	82.31W
Saint Clair Shores	184	Fd	42.30N	82.54W
Saint-Clair-sur-l'Elle	124	Ae	49.12N	1.02W
Saint-Claud	122	Gi	45.54N	0.28 E
Saint-Claude	122	Lh	46.23N	5.52 E
Saint-Claude	197e	Ab	16.02N	61.42W
Saint Claude	186	Gb	49.40N	98.22W
Saint Cloud	176	Je	45.33N	94.10W
Saint Croix	190	Le	17.45N	64.45W
Saint Croix Falls	186	Jd	45.24N	92.38W
Saint Croix River	182	Ic	44.45N	92.49W
Saint-Cyr-l'École	124	Ef	48.48N	2.04 E
Saint David Bay	197g	Bb	15.26N	61.15W
Saint David's [Gren.]	197p	Bb	12.04N	61.39W
Saint David's [Wales-U.K.]	118	Hj	51.54N	5.16W
Saint David's Head	118	Hj	51.55N	5.19W
Saint David's Point	197p	Bb	12.01N	61.40W
Saint-Denis [Fr.]	122	If	48.56N	2.22 E
Saint-Denis [Reu.]	160	Mk	20.52 S	55.28 E
Saint-Dié	122	Mf	48.17N	6.57 E
Saint-Dizier	122	Kf	48.38N	4.57 E
Sainte-Adresse	124	Ce	49.30N	0.05 E
Sainte-Anne [Guad.]	197e	Bb	16.14N	61.23W
Sainte-Anne [Mart.]	197h	Bc	14.26N	60.53W
Sainte-Anne-des-Monts	184	Na	49.07N	66.29W
Sainte-Baume, Chaîne de la-	122	Lk	43.20N	5.45 E
Sainte-Énimie	122	Jj	44.22N	3.25 E
Sainte Genevieve	186	Kh	37.59N	90.03W
Sainte-Geneviève	124	Ee	49.17N	2.12 E
Saint Elias, Mount-	174	Ec	60.18N	140.55W
Saint Elias Mountains	174	Fc	60.30N	139.30W
Saint-Élie	202	Hc	4.50N	53.17W
Sainte-Livrade-sur-Lot	122	Gj	44.24N	0.36 E
Saint-Éloy-les-Mines	122	Ih	46.09N	2.50 E
Sainte-Luce	197h	Bc	14.28N	60.56W
Sainte Luce	172	Hd	24.46 S	47.12 E
Sainte-Lucie, Canal de- = Saint Lucia Channel (EN)	196	Fe	14.09N	60.57W
Sainte-Marie [Guad.]	197e	Ab	16.06N	61.34W
Sainte-Marie [Mart.]	197h	Ab	14.47N	61.00W
Sainte-Marie, Cap- = Sainte-Marie, Cape- (EN)	158	Lk	25.36 S	45.08 E
Sainte-Marie, Cape- (EN) = Sainte-Marie, Cap-	158	Lk	25.36 S	45.08 E
Sainte-Marie, Ile-	158	Lj	16.50 S	49.55 E
Sainte-Marie-aux-Mines	122	Nf	48.15N	7.11 E
Sainte-Maure-de-Touraine	122	Gg	47.06N	0.37 E
Sainte-Maxime	122	Mk	43.18N	6.38 E
Sainte-Menehould	122	Ke	49.05N	4.54 E
Sainte-Rose	197e	Ab	16.20N	61.42W
Sainte-Rose-du-Dégelé	184	Mb	47.33N	68.39W
Sainte Rose du Lac	186	Ga	51.03N	99.32W
Saintes	122	Fi	45.45N	0.38W
Saintes, Canal des-	197e	Ac	15.55N	61.40W
Saintes, Iles des-	196	Fe	15.52N	61.37W
Sainte-Savine	122	Kf	48.18N	4.03 E
Saintes-Maries-de-la-Mer	122	Kk	43.27N	4.26 E
Sainte-Thérèse	184	Kc	45.22N	73.15W
Saint-Étienne	112	Gf	45.26N	4.24 E
Saint-Étienne-du-Rouvray	122	He	49.23N	1.06 E
Sainte-Victoire, Montagne-	122	Lk	43.32N	5.39 E
Saint-Félicien	184	Ka	48.39N	72.28W
Saint-Florent	122a	Ba	42.41N	9.18 E
Saint-Florent, Golfe de-	122a	Ba	42.45N	9.16 E
Saint-Florentin	122	Jf	48.00N	3.44 E
Saint-Florent-sur-Cher	122	Ih	46.59N	2.15 E
Saint-Flour	122	Ji	45.02N	3.05 E
Saint Francis	186	Fg	39.46N	101.48W
Saint Francis River	186	Ki	34.38N	90.35W
Saint Francisville	186	Kk	30.47N	91.23W
Saint-François	197e	Bb	16.15N	61.17W
Saint François Island	172b	Bb	7.10 S	52.44 E
Saint Francois Mountains	186	Kh	37.30N	90.35W
Saint-Gaudens	122	Gk	43.07N	0.44 E
Saint George	178	Fe	56.35N	169.35W
Saint George [Austl.]	212	Je	28.02 S	148.35 E
Saint George [N.B.-Can.]	184	Nc	45.10N	66.48W
Saint George [Ut.-U.S.]	182	Ed	37.06N	113.35W
Saint George, Cape - [Newf.-Can.]	180	Lg	48.28N	59.16W
Saint George, Cape- [Pap.N.Gui.]	214	Eh	4.52 S	152.52 E
Saint George, Point-	188	Cf	41.47N	124.15W
Saint George Harbour	184	Nd	43.15N	66.10W
Saint George Island	184	Ek	29.39N	84.55W
Saint-Georges	184	Lb	46.10N	70.38W
Saint George's	176	Mh	12.03N	61.45W
Saint-George's Bay	180	Lg	48.20N	59.00W
Saint George's Channel	110	Fe	52.00N	6.00W
Saint George's Channel (EN) = Muir Bhreatan	110	Fe	52.00N	6.00W
Saint-Georges-du-Vièvre	124	Ce	49.15N	0.35 E
Saint-Germain-en-Laye	122	If	48.54N	2.05 E
Saint-Gervais-d'Auvergne	122	Ih	46.02N	2.49 E
Saint-Gervais-les-Bains	122	Mi	45.54N	6.43 E
Saint-Ghislain	124	Fd	50.27N	3.49 E
Saint-Ghislain-Baudour	124	Fd	50.29N	3.49 E
Saint-Gildas, Pointe de-	122	Dg	47.08N	2.15W
Saint-Gilles	122	Kk	43.41N	4.26 E
Saint-Gilles-Croix-de-Vie	122	Eh	46.41N	1.55W
Saint-Girons	122	Hl	42.59N	1.09 E
Saint-Gobain	124	Fe	49.36N	3.23 E
Saint Gotthard Pass (EN) = San Gottardo, Passo del-	110	Gf	46.30N	8.30 E
Saint Govan's Head	118	Ij	51.36N	4.55W
Saint Helena [5]	160	Gj	15.57 S	5.42W
Saint Helena	158	Gj	15.57 S	5.42W
Saint Helena Bay	158	Il	32.45 S	18.05 E
Saint Helena Island	184	Gi	32.30N	80.30W
Saint Helena Sound	184	Gi	32.27N	80.25W
Saint Helens [Austl.]	212	Jh	41.20 S	148.15 E
Saint Helens [Eng.-U.K.]	118	Kh	53.28N	2.44W
Saint Helens [Or.-U.S.]	188	Dd	45.52N	122.48W
Saint Helens, Mount-	188	Dc	46.12N	122.11W
Saint Helier	118	Kl	49.12N	2.07W
Saint-Hubert	124	Hd	50.03N	5.23 E
Saint-Hyacinthe	184	Kc	45.38N	72.57W
Saint Ignace	186	Kc	45.52N	84.43W
Saint Ignace Island	186	Mb	48.48N	87.55W
Saint Ignatius	188	Hc	47.19N	114.06W
Saint Ives [Eng.-U.K.]	124	Bb	52.18N	0.04W
Saint Ives [Eng.-U.K.]	118	Hk	50.12N	5.29W
Saint James	186	Ie	43.59N	94.38W
Saint James, Cape -	180	Ef	51.57N	131.01W
Saint-Jean	180	Kg	45.13N	73.15W
Saint-Jean, Baie de-	197b	Bc	17.55N	62.51W
Saint-Jean, Lac-	174	Le	48.35N	72.00W
Saint-Jean-d'Angély	122	Fi	45.57N	0.31W
Saint-Jean-de-Luz	122	Ek	43.23N	1.40W
Saint-Jean-de-Maurienne	122	Mi	45.17N	6.21 E
Saint-Jean-de-Monts	122	Dh	46.47N	2.04W
Saint-Jean-du-Gard	122	Jj	44.06N	3.53 E
Saint-Jean-Pied-de-Port	122	Ek	43.10N	1.14W
Saint-Jérôme [Que.-Can.]	184	La	48.26N	71.52W
Saint-Jérôme [Que.-Can.]	180	Kg	45.46N	74.00W

Saint Joe River 188 Gc 47.21N 116.42W
Saint John 196 Dc 18.20N 64.42W
Saint John [Can.] 174 Me 45.15N 66.04W
Saint John [Ks.-U.S.] 186 Gh 38.00N 98.46W
Saint John [Lbr.] 166 Cd 5.55N 10.05W
Saint John [N.B.-Can.] 176 Me 45.16N 66.03W
Saint John's [Atg.] 190 Le 17.06N 61.51W
Saint Johns [Az.-U.S.] 188 Ki 34.30N 109.22W
Saint Johns [Mi.-U.S.] 184 Ed 43.00N 84.33W
Saint John's [Mont.] 197c Bc 16.48N 62.11W
Saint John's [Newf.-Can.] 176 Ne 47.34N 52.43W
Saint Johnsbury 184 Kc 44.25N 72.01W
Saint Johns River 184 Gj 30.24N 81.24W
Saint Joseph [Dom.] 197g Bb 15.24N 61.26W
Saint Joseph [La.-U.S.] 186 Kk 31.55N 91.14W
Saint-Joseph [Mart.] 197h Ab 14.40N 61.03W
Saint Joseph [Mi.-U.S.] 184 Dd 42.06N 86.29W
Saint Joseph [Mo.-U.S.] 182 Id 39.46N 94.51W
Saint-Joseph [N.Cal.] 219b Ce 20.27S 166.36 E
Saint-Joseph [Reu.] 172a Bb 21.22S 55.37 E
Saint Joseph, Lake- 180 If 51.06N 90.36W
Saint Joseph Island 184 Fb 46.13N 83.57W
Saint Joseph River 184 Dd 42.06N 86.29W
Saint-Junien 122 Gi 45.53N 0.54 E
Saint-Just-en-Chaussée 124 Ee 49.30N 2.26 E
Saint Kilda 118 Ed 57.49N 8.36W
Saint Kitts/Saint Christopher 174 Mh 17.21N 62.48W
Saint-Lary-Soulan 122 Gl 42.49N 0.19 E
Saint Laurent 200 Ke 5.30N 54.02W
Saint-Laurent=Saint Lawrence (EN) 174 Me 49.15N 67.00W
Saint Lawrence 174 Bc 63.30N 170.30W
Saint Lawrence 174 Me 49.15N 67.00W
Saint Lawrence (EN)= Saint-Laurent 174 Me 49.15N 67.00W
Saint Lawrence, Gulf of- 174 Me 48.00N 62.00W
Saint-Léger-en-Yvelines 124 Df 48.43N 1.46 E
Saint-Léonard 184 Nb 47.10N 67.56W
Saint-Léonard-de-Noblat 122 Hi 45.50N 1.29 E
Saint-Lewis 180 Lf 52.22N 55.58W
Saint-Lô 122 Ee 49.07N 1.05W
Saint-Louis [Guad.] 197e Bc 15.57N 61.20W
Saint Louis [Mo.-U.S.] 176 Jf 38.38N 90.11W
Saint-Louis [Sen.] 160 Fg 16.02N 16.30W
Saint-Loup-sur-Semouse 122 Mg 47.53N 6.16 E
Saint Lucia 172 Ee 28.23S 32.25 E
Saint Lucia 176 Mh 13.53N 60.58W
Saint Lucia 174 Mh 13.53N 60.58W
Saint Lucia, Cape- 158 Kk 28.32S 32.24 E
Saint Lucia, Lake- 172 Ee 28.00S 32.30 E
Saint Lucia Channel 196 Fe 14.09N 60.57W
Saint Lucia Channel (EN)= Sainte-Lucie, Canal de- 196 Fe 14.09N 60.57W
Saint Magnus Bay 118 La 60.25N 1.35W
Saint-Maixent-l'Ecole 122 Fh 46.25N 0.12W
Saint-Malo 112 Ff 48.39N 2.01W
Saint-Malo, Golfe de- 110 Ff 48.45N 2.00W
Saint-Marc 190 Je 19.06N 72.43W
Saint-Marc, Canal de- 194 Kd 18.50N 72.45W
Saint-Marcellin 122 Li 45.09N 5.19 E
Saint Margaret's at Cliffe 124 Dc 51.09N 1.19 E
Saint Margaret's Hope 118 Kc 58.49N 2.57W
Saint Maries 188 Gc 47.19N 116.35W
Saint Martin 190 Le 18.04N 63.04W
Saint Martin, Cap- 197h Ab 14.52N 61.13W
Saint-Martin-Boulogne 124 Dd 50.43N 1.40 E
Saint-Martin-de-Ré 122 Eh 46.12N 1.22W
Saint-Martin-des-Besaces 124 Be 49.01N 0.51W
Saint Martins 184 Oc 45.21N 65.32W
Saint-Martin-Vésubie 122 Nj 44.04N 7.15 E
Saint Mary, Cape- 184 Nc 44.05N 66.13W
Saint Mary Peak [Austl.] 212 Hf 31.30S 138.35 E
Saint Mary Peak [U.S.] 188 Hc 46.40N 114.20W
Saint Mary's 118 Gl 49.55N 6.20W
Saint Marys [Austl.] 212 Jh 41.35S 148.10 E
Saint Marys [Oh.-U.S.] 184 Ee 40.32N 84.22W
Saint Marys [W.V.-U.S.] 184 Gf 39.24N 81.13W
Saint Mary's, Cape- 180 Mg 46.49N 54.12W
Saint Mary's Bay [N.S.-Can.] 184 Nc 44.25N 66.10W
Saint Mary's Bay [N.W.T.-Can.] 180 Mg 46.50N 53.47W
Saint Marys River 184 Gj 30.45N 81.30W
Saint Matthew 174 Bb 60.30N 172.45W
Saint Matthias Group 208 Fe 1.30S 149.48 E
Saint-Maur-des-Fossés 122 If 48.48N 2.30 E
Saint-Maurice, Rivière- 180 Kg 46.21N 72.31W
Saint Michael 178 Gd 63.29N 162.02W
Saint Michaels 188 Ki 35.46N 109.04W
Saint-Michel 124 Ge 49.55N 4.08 E
Saint-Mihiel 122 Lf 48.54N 5.33 E
Saint-Nazaire 122 Dg 47.17N 2.12W
Saint Neots 124 Bb 52.13N 0.16W
Saint-Nicolas/Sint Niklaas 122 Kc 51.10N 4.08 E
Saint-Nicolas-d'Aliermont 124 De 49.53N 1.13 E
Saint-Nicolas-de-Port 122 Mf 48.38N 6.18 E
Saint-Omer 122 Id 50.45N 2.15 E
Saintonge 122 Fi 45.50N 0.30W
Saint Patrick's 197c Bc 16.41N 62.12W
Saint Paul 176 Je 44.58N 93.07W
Saint-Paul 158 Ol 38.55S 77.41 E
Saint Paul 178 Ee 57.07N 170.17W
Saint Paul 166 Cd 6.23N 10.48W
Saint Paul [Alta.-Can.] 180 Gf 53.59N 111.17W
Saint Paul [Nb.-U.S.] 186 Gf 41.13N 98.27W
Saint-Paul [Reu.] 172a Bb 21.00S 55.16 E
Saint Paul, Cape- 166 Fd 5.49N 0.57 E
Saint-Paul-lès-Dax 122 Ek 43.44N 1.03W
Saint Paul's 197c Ab 17.24N 62.49W
Saint Paul's Point 220q Ab 25.04S 130.05W
Saint-Péray 122 Kj 44.57N 4.50 E
Saint Peter 186 Jd 44.17N 93.57W
Saint Peter Port 118 Kl 49.27N 2.32W
Saint Peter's 197c Bc 16.46N 62.12W
Saint Petersburg → Sankt-Peterburg 112 Jc 59.55N 30.15 E
Saint Petersburg 176 Kg 27.46N 82.38W
Saint Petersburg Beach 184 Fl 27.45N 82.45W
Saint-Pierre [Mart.] 196 Fe 14.45N 61.11W
Saint-Pierre [Reu.] 160 Mk 21.19S 55.29 E
Saint-Pierre [St.P.M.] 180 Lg 46.46N 56.12W
Saint-Pierre, Lac- 184 Kb 46.10N 72.50W
Saint Pierre and Miquelon (EN) = Saint-Pierre et Miquelon 176 Ne 46.55N 56.10W
Saint-Pierre-en-Port 124 Ce 49.48N 0.29 E
Saint-Pierre et Miquelon = Saint Pierre and Miquelon (EN) 176 Ne 46.55N 56.10W
Saint Pierre Island 172b Bb 9.19S 50.43 E
Saint-Pierre-sur-Dives 124 Be 49.01N 0.02W
Saint-Pol-de-Léon 122 Cf 48.41N 3.59W
Saint-Pol-sur-Mer 124 Ec 51.02N 2.21 E
Saint-Pol-sur-Ternoise 122 Id 50.23N 2.20 E
Saint-Pons 122 Ik 43.29N 2.46 E
Saint-Pourçain-sur-Sioule 122 Jh 46.18N 3.17 E
Saint-Quentin 122 Je 49.51N 3.17 E
Saint-Quentin, Canal de- 124 Fe 49.36N 3.11 E
Saint-Raphaël 122 Mk 43.25N 6.46 E
Saint-Rémy-de-Provence 122 Kk 43.47N 4.50 E
Saint-Rigaux, Mont- 122 Kh 46.12N 4.29 E
Saint-Riquier 124 Dd 50.08N 1.57 E
Saint Roch Basin 180 Ic 68.50N 95.00W
Saint-Romain-de-Colbosc 124 Ce 49.32N 0.22 E
Saint-Saëns 124 De 49.40N 1.17 E
Saint Sauflieu 124 Ee 49.47N 2.15 E
Saint-Savin 122 Gh 46.34N 0.52 E
Saint-Sébastien, Cap- 172 Hb 12.26S 48.44 E
Saint-Seine-l'Abbaye 122 Kg 47.26N 4.47 E
Saint-Servais, Namur- 124 Gd 50.28N 4.50 E
Saint Simon 124 Fe 49.45N 3.10 E
Saint Simons Island 184 Gj 31.14N 81.21W
Saint Stanislas Bay 220g Bb 1.53N 157.30W
Saint Stephen 180 Kg 45.12N 67.17W
Saint-Sylvain 124 Be 49.03N 0.13W
Saint Teresa Beach 184 Ek 29.58N 84.28W
Saint Thomas 184 Gd 42.47N 81.12W
Saint Thomas 190 Le 18.21N 64.55W
Saint-Trond/Sint-Truiden 122 Ld 50.49N 5.12 E
Saint-Tropez 122 Mk 43.16N 6.38 E
Saint-Tropez, Golfe de- 122 Mk 43.17N 6.38 E
Saint-Valéry-en-Caux 122 Ge 49.52N 0.44 E
Saint-Valéry-sur-Somme 122 Hd 50.11N 1.38 E
Saint-Vallier 122 Ki 45.10N 4.49 E
Saint-Venant 124 Ed 50.37N 2.33 E
Saint-Vincent 128 Be 45.45N 7.39 E
Saint Vincent 174 Mh 13.15N 61.12W
Saint-Vincent, Baie de- 219b Cf 22.00S 166.05 E
Saint-Vincent, Cap- 158 Lk 21.57S 43.16 E
Saint Vincent, Gulf- 212 Hf 35.00S 138.05 E
Saint Vincent and the Grenadines 176 Mh 13.15N 61.12W
Saint-Vincent-de-Tyrosse 122 Ek 43.40N 1.18W
Saint Vincent Island 184 Ek 29.40N 85.07W
Saint Vincent Passage 196 Ff 13.30N 61.00W
Saint-Vith / Sankt-Vith 122 Md 50.17N 6.08 E
Saint-Wandrille-Rançon 124 Ce 49.32N 0.46 E
Saint-Yrieix-la-Perche 122 Hi 45.31N 1.12 E
Saipan 220a Ad 6.54N 134.08 E
Saipan Channel 220b Ba 15.05N 145.41 E
Saipan Island 208 Fc 15.12N 145.45 E
Saira 204 Ak 32.24S 62.06W
Sairecábur, Cerro- 202 Eh 22.43S 67.54W
Saitama Ken 154 Of 36.00N 139.50 E
Saito 154 Kh 32.06N 131.24 E
Sajak 136 Hf 46.55N 77.22 E
Sajama 202 Eg 18.07S 69.00W
Sajama, Nevado de- 198 Jg 18.06S 68.54W
Sajānan 128 Dm 37.03N 9.14 E
Sajat 135 De 38.49N 63.51 E
Sajid 164 Hf 16.52N 41.55 E
Sajir, Ra's- 168 Ib 16.45N 53.35 E
Sajmenski kanal = Saimaa Canal (EN) 116 Mc 61.05N 28.18 E
Sajn-Šand 142 Ne 44.55N 110.11 E
Sajó 120 Ri 47.56N 21.08 E
Sajószentpéter 120 Qh 48.13N 20.43 E
Sajram 135 Gc 42.18N 69.45 E
Sajzī 146 Of 32.41N 52.07 E
Saka 170 Gc 0.09S 39.20 E
Sakai 154 Mg 34.35N 135.28 E
Sakaide 156 Cd 34.19N 133.51 E
Sakaiminato 156 Cd 35.33N 133.15 E
Sakākah 144 Fd 29.59N 40.06 E
Sakakawea, Lake- 182 Gb 47.50N 102.20W
Sakala, vozvyšennost- / Sakala Kõrgustik 116 Kf 58.00N 25.30 E
Sakala Kõrgustik / Sakala, vozvyšennost- 116 Kf 58.00N 25.30 E
Sakami 180 Jf 53.18N 76.45W
Sakami, lac- 180 Jf 53.15N 76.45W
Sâkâne, 'Erg i-n- 166 Ea 20.40N 0.51W
Sakania 170 Ee 12.43S 28.33 E
Sakao 219b Cb 14.58S 167.07 E
Sakar 135 De 38.59N 63.45 E
Sakar 130 Jh 41.59N 26.16 E
Sakaraha 172 Gd 22.54S 44.32 E
Sakar-Čaga 135 Cf 37.39N 61.40 E
Sakartvelo = Georgia (EN) 136 Eg 42.00N 44.00 E
Sakartvelos Sabčata Socialisturi Respublica/ Gruzinskaja SSR → Sakartvelo 136 Eg 42.00N 44.00 E
Sakata 152 Od 38.55N 139.50 E
Sakchu 154 Hd 40.23N 125.02 E
Sakhalin (EN) = Sahalin, ostrov- 140 Qd 51.00N 143.00 E
Sakht Sar 146 Nd 36.53N 50.41 E
Saki 132 Hg 45.07N 33.37 E
Šakiai/Šakjaj 114 Fi 54.57N 23.01 E
Sakishima Islands (EN)= Sakishima-Shotō 140 Og 24.30N 125.00 E
Sakishima-Shotō= Sakishima Islands (EN) 140 Og 24.30N 125.00 E
Sakito 156 Ae 33.02N 129.34 E
Sakiz Boğazı 130 Jk 38.20N 26.12 E
Šakjaj/Šakiai 114 Fi 54.57N 23.01 E
Sakmara 110 Le 51.46N 55.01 E
Sakon Nakhon 148 Ke 17.10N 104.01 E
Sakrivier 172 Cf 30.54S 20.28 E
Šakša 134 Hi 54.47N 56.15 E
Saksaulski 136 Gf 47.05N 61.13 E
Sakskøbing 116 Dj 54.48N 11.39 E
Saku 154 Of 36.09N 138.26 E
Sakuma 156 Ed 35.05N 137.47 E
Sakura 156 Gd 35.43N 140.13 E
Sakurai 156 Dd 34.31N 135.50 E
Sakura-Jima 156 Bf 31.35N 130.40 E
Säkylä 116 Jc 61.02N 22.20 E
Sal 158 Eg 16.45N 22.55W
Sal 136 Ef 47.31N 40.45 E
Sal, Cay- 194 Gb 23.42N 80.24W
Sal, Punta- 194 Df 15.53N 87.37W
Sala 114 Dg 59.55N 16.36 E
Šalá 120 Nh 48.09N 17.53 E
Sala 168 Cb 17.00N 20.53 E
Salabangka, Kepulauan- 150 Hg 3.02S 122.25 E
Salaca 116 Kg 57.39N 24.15 E
Salacgriva/Salacgrīva 114 Fh 57.46N 24.27 E
Salacgrīva/Salacgriva 114 Fh 57.46N 24.27 E
Sala Consilina 128 Jj 40.23N 15.36 E
Salada 192 Hc 28.36N 103.28W
Salada, Laguna- 192 Ba 32.20N 115.40W
Saladas 206 Ic 28.15S 58.38W
Saladillo 206 Ie 35.38S 59.46W
Saladillo, Arroyo- 204 Bj 31.22S 60.30W
Saladillo Amargo, Arroyo- 204 Bj 31.01S 60.19W
Saladillo Dulce, Arroyo- 204 Bj 31.01S 60.19W
Salado, Arroyo- [Arg.] 204 Bm 36.27S 61.06W
Salado, Arroyo- [Mex.] 192 De 24.25N 111.30W
Salado, Riacho- 204 Ch 26.30S 58.18W
Salado, Rio- 186 Ci 34.16N 106.52W
Salado, Rio- 190 Ec 26.52N 99.19W
Salado, Rio- [Arg.] 198 Ki 35.44S 57.21W
Salado, Rio- [Arg.] 198 Ji 31.42S 60.44W
Salado, Rio- [Arg.] 206 Gh 38.49S 64.57W
Salado, Valle- 192 He 24.47N 102.50W
Salaga 166 Ed 8.33N 0.31W
Salagle 168 Ge 1.50N 42.18 E
Salāhuddīn 146 Je 34.40N 44.00 E
Salailua 221c Aa 13.41S 172.34W
Salairski krjaž 138 Df 54.00N 85.00 E
Sălaj 130 Fb 47.10N 23.00 E
Šalakuša 114 Je 62.15N 40.18 E
Salal 168 Bc 14.51N 17.13 E
Şalālah [Oman] 142 Hh 17.05N 54.10 E
Salālah [Sud.] 164 Ge 21.19N 36.13 E
Salamá 194 Bf 15.06N 90.16W
Salamanca 126 Gd 40.50N 6.00W
Salamanca [Chile] 206 Fd 31.47S 70.58W
Salamanca [Mex.] 190 Dd 20.34N 101.12W
Salamanca [N.Y.-U.S.] 184 Hd 42.11N 78.43W
Salamanca [Sp.] 112 Fg 40.58N 5.39W
Salamat 168 Cc 11.00N 20.30 E
Salamat, Bahr- 168 Bd 9.27N 18.06 E
Salamina 194 Jh 10.30N 74.48W
Salamis 130 Gl 37.58N 23.29 E
Salamis 130 Gl 37.55N 23.30 E
Salamis 146 Ee 35.10N 33.54 E
Salamīyah, Sabkhat as- 146 Pj 24.00N 53.45 E
Salang, Tūnel-e- 144 Kb 35.19N 69.02 E
Salani 221c Bb 14.00S 171.34W
Salantai/Salantaj 116 Ih 56.05N 21.30 E
Salantaj/Salantai 116 Ih 56.05N 21.30 E
Salas 126 Fa 43.24N 6.16W
Salas de los Infantes 126 Ib 42.01N 3.17W
Salat 220d Cb 7.14N 152.01 E
Salat 122 Gk 43.10N 0.58 E
Salatiga 150 Fh 7.19S 110.30 E
Salavat 112 Le 53.25N 55.58 E
Salawati, Pulau- 208 Ee 1.07S 130.52 E
Sala y Gómez 208 Qg 26.28S 105.28W
Sala y Gómez Ridge (EN) 106 Mi 25.00S 98.00W
Salazar 204 Am 36.18S 62.12W
Salbris 122 Ig 47.26N 2.03 E
Salcantay, Nevado de- 198 Ig 13.22S 72.34W
Šalčininkai/Šal'čininkaj 116 Kj 54.18N 25.30 E
Šal'čininkaj/Šalčininkai 116 Kj 54.18N 25.30 E
Salda Gölü 130 Ml 37.33N 29.42 E
Saldaña 126 Hb 42.31N 4.44W
Saldanha 160 Il 33.00S 17.56 E
Saldungaray 204 Bn 38.12S 61.47W
Saldus 136 Cd 56.40N 22.31 E
Salé 162 Fc 34.04N 6.48W
Sale 212 Jg 38.06S 147.04 E
Salebabu, Pulau- 150 If 3.55N 126.40 E
Şāleḩābād 146 Me 34.56N 48.20 E
Salehard 142 Ic 66.33N 66.40 E
Saleimoa 221c Ba 13.48S 171.52W
Salelologa 221c Aa 13.44S 172.10W
Salem [Fl.-U.S.] 184 Fk 29.58N 83.28W
Salem [Il.-U.S.] 184 Cf 38.38N 88.57W
Salem [India] 142 Jh 11.39N 78.10 E
Salem [In.-U.S.] 184 Df 38.36N 86.06W
Salem [Ma.-U.S.] 184 Ld 42.31N 70.55W
Salem [Mont.] 197c Bc 16.45N 62.13W
Salem [Mo.-U.S.] 186 Kh 37.39N 91.32W
Salem [N.J.-U.S.] 184 Jf 39.35N 75.28W
Salem [Oh.-U.S.] 184 Ge 40.54N 80.52W
Salem [Or.-U.S.] 176 Ge 44.57N 123.01W
Salem [S.D.-U.S.] 186 He 43.44N 97.23W
Salem [Va.-U.S.] 184 Gg 37.17N 80.03W
Salemi 128 Gm 37.49N 12.48 E
Sälen 116 Ec 61.10N 13.16 E
Salentina, Penisola- = Salentine Peninsula (EN) 110 Hg 40.30N 18.00 E
Salentine Peninsula (EN) = Salentina, Penisola- 110 Hg 40.30N 18.00 E
Salerno 112 Hg 40.41N 14.47 E
Salerno, Golfo di- 128 Ij 40.30N 14.40 E
Salers 122 Ii 45.08N 2.30 E
Salève, Mont- 122 Mh 46.07N 6.10 E
Salgir 132 Ig 45.38N 35.01 E
Salgótarján 120 Ph 48.07N 19.49 E
Salgueiro 202 Ke 8.04S 39.06W
Salher 148 Ed 20.41N 73.52 E
Salhus 114 Af 60.30N 5.16 E
Šali 132 Nh 43.06N 45.56 E
Sali 128 Jg 43.56N 15.10 E
Salice Terme 128 Df 44.55N 9.01 E
Salida 182 Fd 38.32N 106.00W
Salies-de-Béarn 122 Fk 43.29N 0.55W
Salihli 144 Cb 38.29N 28.09 E
Salima 170 Fe 13.47S 34.26 E
Salīma, Wāḩāt- = Salimah Oasis (EN) 160 Jf 21.22N 29.19 E
Salimah Oasis (EN) = Salīma, Wāḩāt- 160 Jf 21.22N 29.19 E
Salina 128 Il 38.35N 14.50 E
Salina [Ks.-U.S.] 176 Jf 38.50N 97.37W
Salina [Ut.-U.S.] 188 Jg 38.58N 111.51W
Salina Cruz 190 Ee 16.10N 95.12W
Salinas [Ca.-U.S.] 176 Gf 36.40N 121.38W
Salinas [Ec.] 202 Bd 2.13S 80.58W
Salinas [P.R.] 197a Bc 17.59N 66.17W
Salinas, Bahía de- 194 Eh 11.03N 85.43W
Salinas, Cabo de-/Ses Salines, Cap de- 126 Pe 39.16N 3.03 E
Salinas, Punta- [Dom.Rep.] 194 Ld 18.12N 70.34W
Salinas, Punta- [P.R.] 197a Bb 18.29N 66.10W
Salinas, Rio- 194 Be 16.28N 90.33W
Salinas de Hidalgo 192 If 22.38N 101.43W
Salinas Peak 186 Cj 33.18N 106.31W
Saline, Point- 196 Fg 12.00N 61.48W
Saline Island 197p Cb 12.26N 61.29W
Saline River [Ks.-U.S.] 186 Hg 38.51N 97.30W
Saline River [U.S.] 186 Jj 33.10N 92.08W
Salines, Pointe des- 197h Bc 14.24N 60.53W
Salinópolis 202 Id 0.37S 47.20W
Salins-les-Bains 122 Lh 46.57N 5.53 E
Salisbury 180 Jd 63.35N 77.00W
Salisbury [Dom.] 197g Bb 15.26N 61.27W
Salisbury [Eng.-U.K.] 118 Lj 51.05N 1.48W
Salisbury [Md.-U.S.] 182 Ld 38.22N 75.36W
Salisbury [N.C.-U.S.] 184 Gh 35.40N 80.29W
Salisbury Plain 118 Lj 51.15N 1.55W
Săliște 130 Gd 45.47N 23.53 E
Šalja 136 Fd 57.15N 58.43 E
Saljany 136 Eh 39.35N 48.59 E
Šalkar, ozero- 132 Qd 50.35N 51.40 E
Šalkar-Jega-Kara, ozero- 132 Vd 50.45N 60.55 E
Salkhad 146 Gf 32.29N 36.43 E
Salla 114 Gc 66.50N 28.40 E
Sallent de Gállego 126 Lb 42.46N 0.20W
Salling 116 Ch 56.40N 9.00 E
Salliqueló 206 He 36.45S 62.56W
Sallisaw 186 Ii 35.28N 94.47W
Sallūm 168 Fb 19.23N 37.06 E
Sallūm, Khalīj as- = Salum, Gulf of- (EN) 164 Ec 31.40N 25.20 E
Sallyana 148 Gc 28.22N 82.10 E
Salm 124 Ie 49.51N 6.51 E
Salmās 144 Fb 38.11N 44.47 E
Salmi 114 Hf 61.24N 31.54 E
Salmo 188 Gb 49.12N 117.17W
Salmon 182 Eb 45.11N 113.54W
Salmon Arm 180 Ff 50.42N 119.16W
Salmon Bank (EN) 214 Kb 26.56N 176.28W
Salmon Falls Creek Reservoir 188 He 42.05N 114.45W
Salmon Mountain 188 Hd 45.38N 114.50W
Salmon Mountains 188 Df 41.00N 123.00W
Salmon River 174 He 45.51N 116.46W
Salmon River Mountains 182 Dc 44.45N 115.30W
Salmtal 124 Ie 49.56N 6.48 E
Salmyš 132 Sc 52.01N 55.21 E
Salo 168 Be 3.12N 16.07 E
Salò 128 Ee 45.36N 10.31 E
Salo 114 Ff 60.23N 23.08 E
Salobra, Rio- 204 De 20.12S 56.29W
Salobreña 126 Ih 36.44N 3.35W
Salomon, Cap- 197h Ab 14.30N 61.06W
Salon-de-Provence 122 Lk 43.38N 5.06 E
Salonga 158 Ii 0.10S 19.50 E
Salonika (EN) = Thessaloníki 112 Ig 40.38N 22.56 E
Salonika, Gulf of- (EN) = Thermaïkós Kólpos 110 Ig 40.20N 22.45 E
Salonta 130 Ec 46.48N 21.39 E
Salop 118 Ki 52.40N 2.50W
Salor 126 Ee 39.39N 7.03W
Salou 126 Nc 41.04N 1.08 E
Salouël 124 Ee 49.52N 2.15 E
Saloum 166 Bc 13.50N 16.45W
Salpausselkä 110 Ic 61.00N 26.30 E
Sal-Rei 162 Cf 16.11N 22.55W
Salsbruket 114 Cd 64.48N 11.52 E
Salseleh-ye Safīd Kūh/ Paropamisus 140 If 34.30N 63.30 E
Salses, Étang de- → Leucate, Étang de- 122 Il 42.51N 3.00 E
Salsipuedes, Canal de- 192 Cc 28.40N 113.00W
Salsipuedes, Punta- 194 Fi 8.28N 83.37W
Salsk 136 Ef 46.28N 41.29 E
Salski 114 If 61.48N 36.03 E
Salso [It.] 128 Im 37.39N 14.49 E
Salso [It.] 128 Hm 37.06N 13.57 E
Salsola 128 Ji 41.37N 15.40 E
Salsomaggiore Terme 128 Df 44.49N 9.59 E
Salt 126 Oc 41.59N 2.47 E
Salta 200 Jh 24.47S 65.24W
Salta 206 Hb 25.00S 64.30W
Saltash 118 Ik 50.24N 4.12W
Salt Basin 186 Dk 31.50N 105.00W
Saltburn-by-the-Sea 118 Mg 54.35N 0.58W
Salt Cay 194 Lc 21.20N 71.11W
Salt Creek 188 Gh 36.15N 116.49W
Salt Draw 186 Ek 31.19N 103.28W
Saltee Islands/Na Sailtí 118 Gi 52.07N 6.36W
Salten 114 Dc 67.45N 15.31 E
Salt Fork Brazos 186 Gj 33.15N 100.00W
Salt Fork of Arkansas River 186 Hh 36.36N 97.03W
Salt Fork Red 186 Gi 34.30N 99.22W
Saltholm 116 Ei 55.40N 12.45 E
Saltillo 176 Ig 25.25N 101.01W
Salt Lake City 176 He 40.46N 111.53W
Salto 204 Dj 31.25S 57.00W
Salto 128 Gh 42.23N 12.54 E
Salto [Arg.] 206 Hd 34.17S 60.15W
Salto [Ur.] 200 Ki 31.23S 57.58W
Salto da Divisa 202 Kg 16.00S 39.57W
Salto del Guairá 206 Jb 24.05S 54.15W
Salto Grande 204 Hf 22.54S 49.59W
Salton Sea 174 Hf 33.20N 115.50W
Salt River [Az.-U.S.] 182 Ee 33.23N 112.18W
Salt River [U.S.] 188 Je 43.07N 111.02W
Saltsjöbaden 116 He 59.17N 18.18 E
Saltvik 114 Ef 60.17N 20.03 E
Saluafata Harbour 221c Ba 13.55S 171.38W
Saluda 184 Ig 37.36N 76.36W
Salum, Gulf of- (EN) = Sallūm, Khalīj as- 164 Ec 31.40N 25.20 E
Saluzzo 128 Bf 44.39N 7.29 E
Salvación, Bahía- 206 Eh 50.55S 75.05W
Salvador [Braz.] 200 Mg 12.59S 38.31W
Salvador [Niger] 166 Ha 23.14N 12.05 E
Salvador, Lake- 186 Kl 29.45N 90.15W
Salvador Mazza 206 Hb 22.10S 63.43W
Salvaterra de Magos 126 De 39.01N 8.48W
Salvatierra [Mex.] 192 Ig 20.13N 100.53W
Salvatierra [Sp.] 126 Jb 42.51N 2.23W
Salwa, Dawḩat as- 146 Nj 25.30N 50.40 E
Salwá Baḩrī 164 Fe 24.44N 32.56 E
Salween (EN) = Thanlwin 140 Lg 16.31N 97.37 E
Salyersville 184 Fg 37.45N 83.04W
Salza 128 Ic 47.40N 14.43 E
Salzach 120 Ih 48.12N 12.56 E
Salzburg 112 Hf 47.48N 13.02 E
Salzburg 128 Gc 47.20N 13.00 E
Salzburger Kalkalpen 128 Gc 47.35N 12.55 E
Salzgitter 120 Gd 52.05N 10.20 E
Salzkammergut 128 Hc 47.45N 13.30 E
Salzkotten 124 Kc 51.40N 8.36 E
Salzwedel 120 Hd 52.51N 11.09 E
Samadāy, Ra's- 146 Fj 25.00N 34.56 E
Samagaltaj 138 Ef 50.36N 95.03 E
Samaḩ [Lib.] 164 Cd 28.10N 19.10 E
Samaḩ [Sau.Ar.] 146 Kh 28.52N 45.30 E
Samaipata 202 Fg 18.09S 63.52W
Samalayuca 192 Fb 31.21N 106.28W
Samales Group 150 He 6.00N 121.45 E
Samalga Pass 178a Eb 52.48N 169.25W
Samālūt 164 Fd 28.18N 30.42 E
Samambaia, Rio- 204 Ff 22.45S 53.21W
Samaná 194 Md 19.13N 69.19W
Samaná, Bahía de- 190 Ke 19.10N 69.25W
Samaná, Cabo- 194 Md 19.18N 69.09W
Samana Cay 194 Kb 23.06N 73.42W
Samandağı 146 Fd 36.07N 35.56 E
Samangān 144 Kb 36.15N 67.40 E
Samani 152 Pc 42.07N 142.56 E
Samanlı Dağları 130 Mi 40.32N 29.10 E
Samar 140 Oh 12.00N 125.00 E
Samara (Kujbyšev) [Russia] 112 Le 53.12N 50.09 E
Samarai 210 Gf 10.36S 150.39 E
Samarinda 142 Nj 0.30S 117.09 E
Samarkand 142 If 39.40N 66.58 E
Samarkandskaja oblast 136 Gg 40.10N 66.20 E
Sāmarrā' 144 Fc 34.12N 43.52 E
Samar Sea 150 Hd 11.50N 124.32 E
Samaru 166 Gc 11.10N 7.38 E
Samatan 122 Gk 43.30N 0.56 E
Samate 150 Jg 0.58S 131.04 E
Samba [Zaire] 170 Ec 4.38S 26.22 E
Samba [Zaire] 170 Db 0.14N 21.19 E
Samba Caju 170 Cd 8.45S 15.25 E
Sambalpur 148 Gd 21.27N 83.58 E
Sambar, Tanjung- 150 Fg 2.59S 110.19 E
Sambas 150 Ef 1.20N 109.15 E
Sambava 172 Ib 14.15S 50.10 E
Samber 122 Kd 50.28N 4.52 E
Sāmbhar 148 Fc 26.55N 75.12 E
Sambiase, Lamezia Terme- 128 Kl 38.58N 16.17 E
Samboja 150 Gg 1.02S 117.02 E
Sambor 136 Cf 49.32N 23.11 E
Samborombón, Bahía- 206 Ie 36.00S 57.12W
Samborombón, Rio- 204 Dl 35.43S 57.20W
Sambre 122 Kd 50.28N 4.52 E
Sambre à l'Oise, Canal de la- 122 Je 49.39N 3.20 E
Samburg 138 Cc 67.00N 78.25 E
Samch'ŏnp'o 152 Me 34.55N 128.04 E
Samdi Dağı 146 Kd 37.19N 44.15 E
Samdŏng-ni 154 Ie 39.21N 126.14 E
Samdŭng 154 Ie 38.59N 126.11 E
Same [Indon.] 150 Ih 8.59S 125.40 E
Same [Tan.] 170 Gc 4.04S 37.44 E
Samer 124 Dd 50.38N 1.45 E
Sam Ford Fiord 180 Kb 70.40N 70.35W
Samfya 170 Ee 11.20S 29.32 E
Sāmi 130 Dk 38.15N 20.39 E
Sāmī Ghar 144 Kc 31.43N 67.01 E
Samīrah 146 Ji 26.18N 42.05 E
Šamkir (Šamhor) 132 Oi 40.48N 46.01 E
Şamli 130 Kj 39.48N 27.51 E
Samnah, Jabal- 146 Ei 26.26N 33.34 E
Samoa I Sisifo=Western Samoa (EN) 217 Jf 13.40S 172.30W
Samoa Islands 208 Jf 14.00S 171.00W
Samobor 128 Je 45.48N 15.43 E
Samojlovka 132 Md 51.10N 43.43 E
Samokov 130 Gg 42.20N 23.33 E
Samolva 116 Lf 58.16N 27.45 E
Sámos 130 Jl 37.45N 26.58 E

Index Symbols

1 Independent Nation
2 State, Region
3 District, County
4 Municipality
5 Colony, Dependency
Continent
Physical Region
Historical or Cultural Region
Mount, Mountain
Volcano
Hill
Mountains, Mountain Range
Hills, Escarpment
Plateau, Upland
Pass, Gap
Plain, Lowland
Delta
Salt Flat
Valley, Canyon
Crater, Cave
Karst Features
Depression
Polder
Desert, Dunes
Forest, Woods
Heath, Steppe
Oasis
Cape, Point
Coast, Beach
Cliff
Peninsula
Isthmus
Sandbank
Island
Atoll
Rock, Reef
Islands, Archipelago
Rocks, Reefs
Coral Reef
Well, Spring
Geyser
River, Stream
Waterfall, Rapids
River Mouth, Estuary
Lake
Salt Lake
Intermittent Lake
Reservoir
Swamp, Pond
Canal
Glacier
Ice Shelf, Pack Ice
Ocean
Sea
Gulf, Bay
Strait, Fjord
Lagoon
Bank
Seamount
Tablemount
Ridge
Shelf
Basin
Escarpment, Sea Scarp
Fracture
Trench, Abyss
National Park, Reserve
Point of Interest
Recreation Site
Cave, Cavern
Historic Site
Ruins
Wall, Walls
Church, Abbey
Temple
Scientific Station
Railway station
Airport
Port
Military installation
Lighthouse
Mine
Tunnel
Dam, Bridge

Sámos 110 Ih 37.45N 26.48 E
Samosir, Pulau- 150 Cf 2.35N 98.50 E
Samothrace (EN) = Samothráki 130 Ii 40.27N 25.35 E
Samothráki 130 Ii 40.29N 25.31 E
Samothráki = Samothrace (EN) 130 Ii 40.27N 25.35 E
Sampacho 206 Hd 33.23S 64.43W
Sampaga 150 Gg 2.19S 119.07 E
Sampit 142 Nj 2.32S 112.57 E
Sampit 150 Fg 3.00S 113.03 E
Sampoku 156 Fb 38.30N 139.30 E
Sampwe 170 Ed 9.20S 27.23 E
Sam Rayburn Reservoir 186 Ik 31.27N 94.37W
Samro, ozero- 116 Mf 58.55N 28.50 E
Samsjøen 116 Da 63.05N 10.40 E
Samsø 114 Ci 55.50N 10.35 E
Samsø Bælt 116 Di 55.50N 10.45 E
Sam Son 148 Ld 19.44N 105.54 E
Samsun 142 Fe 41.17N 36.20 E
Samsun Daği 130 Kl 37.40N 27.15 E
Samtredia 132 Mh 42.11N 42.17 E
Samuel, Mount- 212 Gc 19.41S 134.09 E
Samuhú 204 Bh 27.31S 60.24W
Samui, Ko- 140 Li 9.30N 100.00 E
Samur 132 Pi 41.53N 48.32 E
Samur-Apšeronski kanal 132 Pi 40.35N 49.35 E
Samus 138 De 56.46N 84.44 E
Samut Prakan 148 Kf 13.36N 100.36 E
Samut Sakhon 148 Kf 13.31N 100.15 E
San 160 Gg 13.08N 4.53W
San [Asia] 148 Lf 13.32N 105.57 E
San [Pol.] 120 Rf 50.45N 21.51 E
Şan'ā' 142 Gh 15.23N 44.12 E
Sana 128 Ke 45.03N 16.23 E
Sanaag [3] 168 Hc 10.10N 47.50 E
Şanabū 164 Di 27.30N 30.47 E
Sanae 222 Bf 70.18S 2.22W
Sanâfir 146 Fi 27.55N 34.42 E
Sanāg 168 Hd 7.45N 48.00 E
Sanaga 158 Hh 3.35N 9.38 E
San Agustín 200 Ie 1.53N 76.16W
San Agustín 204 Cn 38.01S 58.21W
San Agustín, Cabo- 192 Bc 28.05N 115.20W
San Agustin, Cape- 150 Ie 6.16N 126.11 E
Sanak Islands 178 Gf 54.25N 162.35W
Sanalona, Presa- 192 Fe 24.53N 107.00W
San Ambrosio, Isla- 206 Ec 26.21S 79.52W
Sanana 150 Ig 2.04S 125.08 E
Sanana, Pulau- 150 Ig 2.12S 125.55 E
Sanandaj 144 Gb 35.19N 47.00 E
San Andreas 188 Eg 38.12N 120.41W
San Andrés [3] 190 Hf 12.35N 81.42W
San Andres, Cerro- 192 Ih 19.48N 100.36W
San Andrés, Isla de- 198 Hd 12.32N 81.42W
San Andrés, Laguna de- 192 Kf 22.40N 97.50W
San Andrés de Giles 204 Cl 34.27S 59.27W
San Andrés del Rabanedo 126 Gb 42.37N 5.36W
San Andres Mountains 182 Fe 32.55N 106.45W
San Andres Peak 186 Cj 32.43N 106.30W
San Andrés Tuxtla 190 Ee 18.27N 95.13W
San Andrés y Providencia [3] 202 Ba 12.30N 81.45W
Sananduva 204 Gh 27.57S 51.48W
San Angelo 182 Ge 31.28N 100.26W
San Antonio [Blz.] 194 Ce 16.30N 89.02W
San Antonio [Chile] 206 Fd 33.35S 71.38W
San Antonio [Tx.-U.S.] 176 Jg 29.28N 98.31W
San Antonio [Ur.] 204 Dj 31.20S 57.45W
San Antonio, Cabo- [Arg.] 198 Ki 36.40S 56.42W
San Antonio, Cabo- [Cuba] 174 Kg 21.52N 84.57W
San Antonio, Cabo de- / Sant Antoni, Cap de- 126 Mf 38.48N 0.12 E
San Antonio, Canal- 204 Aj 31.42S 62.15W
San Antonio, Punta- 192 Bc 29.45N 115.45W
San Antonio, Sierra de- 192 Db 30.00N 110.20W
San Antonio Abad / Sant Antoni de Portmany 126 Nf 38.58N 1.18 E
San Antonio Bay 186 Hl 28.20N 96.45W
San Antonio de Caparo 194 Lj 7.35N 71.27W
San Antonio de Cortés 194 Cf 15.05N 88.04W
San Antonio de los Baños 194 Fb 22.53N 82.30W
San Antonio de los Cobres 206 Gb 24.11S 66.21W
San Antonio del Táchira 202 Db 7.50N 72.27W
San Antonio de Tamanaco 196 Ch 9.14N 66.03W
San Antonio Oeste 200 Jj 40.44S 64.57W
San Antonio River 182 Hf 28.30N 96.50W
Sanare 194 Mi 9.45N 69.39W
Sanary-sur-Mer 122 Lk 43.07N 5.48 E
San Augustine 186 Ik 31.32N 94.07W
Sanāw 168 Ib 17.50N 51.05 E
San Bartolomeo in Galdo 128 Ji 41.24N 15.01 E
San Baudilio de Llobregat / Sant Boi de Llobregat 126 Oc 41.21N 2.03 E
San Benedetto del Tronto 128 Hh 42.57N 13.53 E
San Benedetto Po 128 Ee 45.02N 10.55 E
San Benedicto, Isla- 190 Be 19.18N 110.49W
San Benito [Guat.] 194 Ce 16.55N 89.54W
San Benito [Tx.-U.S.] 186 Hm 26.08N 97.38W
San Benito, Islas- 192 Bc 28.20N 115.35W
San Benito Abad 194 Ji 8.56N 75.02W
San Benito Mountain 188 Eh 36.22N 120.38W
San Bernardino 176 Hf 34.06N 117.17W
San Bernardino, Passo del- 128 Dd 46.30N 9.10 E
San Bernardino Mountains 188 Gi 34.10N 117.00W
San Bernardino Strait 150 Hd 12.32N 124.10 E
San Bernardo [Arg.] 204 Bh 27.17S 60.42W
San Bernardo [Chile] 206 Fd 33.36S 70.43W
San Bernardo [Mex.] 192 De 25.32N 111.45W
San Bernardo, Islas de- 194 Ji 9.45N 75.50W
San Bernardo, Punta de- 194 Ji 9.42N 75.42W
San Bernardo del Viento 202 Cb 9.22N 75.57W
San Blas [3] 194 Hi 7.50N 81.10W
San Blas [Mex.] 190 Cd 21.31N 105.16W
San Blas [Mex.] 190 Cc 26.05N 108.46W
San Blas [Mex.] 192 Id 27.25N 101.40W
San Blas, Archipiélago de- 194 Hi 9.30N 78.30W
San Blas, Cape- 182 Jf 29.40N 85.22W
San Blas, Cordillera de- 194 Hi 9.18N 79.00W
San Blas, Golfo de- 194 Hi 9.30N 79.00W
San Blas, Punta- 194 Hi 9.34N 78.58W
San Borja 202 Ef 14.49S 66.51W
San Borjas, Sierra de- 192 Cc 28.40N 113.45W
San Buenaventura 192 Id 27.05N 101.32W
Sancai 168 Fc 10.43N 35.40 E
San Carlos [Arg.] 204 Eh 27.45S 55.54W
San Carlos [Chile] 206 Fe 36.25S 71.58W
San Carlos [Mex.] 192 Ic 29.01N 100.51W
San Carlos [Mex.] 192 Je 24.35N 98.56W
San Carlos [Nic.] 194 Eh 11.07N 84.47W
San Carlos [Pan.] 194 Hi 8.29N 79.57W
San Carlos [Par.] 204 Df 22.16S 57.18W
San Carlos [Phil.] 150 Hd 10.30N 123.25 E
San Carlos [Phil.] 150 Hc 15.55N 120.20 E
San Carlos [Ur.] 206 Jd 34.48S 54.55W
San Carlos [Ven.] 202 Eb 9.40N 68.39W
San Carlos, Bahía- 192 Cd 27.55N 112.45W
San Carlos, Mesa de- 192 Bc 29.40N 115.25W
San Carlos, Punta- 192 Cc 28.00N 112.45W
San Carlos, Riacho- 204 Df 22.49S 57.53W
San Carlos, Río- [C.R.] 194 Eh 10.47N 84.12W
San Carlos, Río- [Ven.] 196 Bh 9.07N 68.25W
San Carlos de Bariloche 200 Ij 41.08S 71.15W
San Carlos de Bolívar 206 He 36.15S 61.06W
San Carlos de la Rápita / Sant Carles de la Ràpita 126 Md 40.37N 0.36 E
San Carlos del Zulia 202 Db 9.01N 71.55W
San Carlos de Río Negro 202 Ec 1.55N 67.04W
San Carlos Reservoir 188 Jj 33.13N 110.24W
San Cataldo 128 Hm 37.29N 13.59 E
San Cayetano 204 Cn 38.20S 59.37W
Sancerre 122 Ig 47.20N 2.50 E
Sancerrois, Collines du- 122 Ig 47.20N 2.30 E
Sanchahe 154 Ib 44.59N 126.03 E
Sánchez 194 Md 19.14N 69.36W
Sánchez Magallanes 192 Mh 18.17N 93.59W
San Clemente [Ca.-U.S.] 182 De 33.26N 117.37W
San Clemente [Sp.] 126 Je 39.24N 2.26W
San Clemente del Tuyú 204 Dm 36.22S 56.43W
San Clemente Island 188 Fj 32.55N 118.30W
Sancois 122 Ih 46.50N 2.55 E
San Cosme 204 Ch 27.22S 58.31W
San Cristóbal [Arg.] 206 Hd 30.19S 61.14W
San Cristóbal [Bol.] 204 Ba 13.56S 61.50W
San Cristóbal [Cuba] 194 Fb 22.43N 83.03W
San Cristóbal [Dom.Rep.] 194 Ld 18.25N 70.06W
San Cristóbal [Mex.] 192 Li 17.49N 94.32W
San Cristóbal [Ven.] 200 Ie 7.46N 72.14W
San Cristóbal, Bahía de- 192 Bd 27.25N 114.40W
San Cristóbal, Isla- 198 Hf 0.50S 89.26W
San Cristóbal de las Casas 190 Fe 16.45N 92.38W
San Cristóbal Island 208 Hf 10.36S 161.45 E
San Cristóbal Verapaz 194 Bf 15.23N 90.24W
Sancti Spiritus 190 Id 21.56N 79.27W
Sancti Spiritus [3] 194 Hb 22.00N 79.30W
Sancy, Puy de- 122 Ii 45.32N 2.50 E
Sand 114 Bg 59.29N 6.15 E
Sand 172 Ed 22.25S 30.05 E
Sanda 156 Dd 34.53N 135.14 E
Sandai 150 Fg 1.15S 110.31 E
Sandakan 142 Ni 5.50N 118.07 E
Sandal, Baie de- 219b Ce 20.49S 167.10 E
Sandal, ozero- 114 Ie 62.25N 34.10 E
Sandane 114 Bf 61.46N 6.13 E
Sandanski 130 Gh 41.34N 23.17 E
Sandaré 166 Cc 14.42N 10.18W
Sandared 116 Eg 57.43N 12.47 E
Sandarne 116 Gc 61.16N 17.10 E
Sanday 118 Kb 59.15N 2.30W
Sande 116 De 59.36N 10.12 E
Sandefjord 114 Cg 59.08N 10.14 E
Sandégué 166 Ed 7.59N 3.33W
Sandeid 114 Ag 59.33N 5.50 E
Sanders 188 Ki 35.13N 109.20W
Sanderson 182 Ge 30.09N 102.24W
Sandersville 184 Fi 32.59N 82.48W
Sandfontein 172 Bd 22.11S 19.58 E
Sandgate 124 Dc 51.04N 1.09 E
Sandhammaren 116 Fi 55.23N 14.12 E
Sandhamn 116 He 59.17N 18.55 E
Sand Hills 182 Gc 41.45N 102.00W
Sandia 202 Ef 14.17S 69.26W
Sandia Crest 186 Ci 35.13N 106.27W
San Diego [Bol.] 204 Bc 16.04S 60.28W
San Diego [Ca.-U.S.] 176 Hf 32.43N 117.09W
San Diego, Cabo- 198 Jk 54.38S 65.07W
Sandıklı 146 Dc 38.28N 30.17 E
San Dimitri Point 128 In 36.05N 14.05 E
Sand in Taufers / Campo Tures 128 Fd 46.55N 11.57 E
Sand Lake 186 Ia 50.05N 94.39W
Sand Mountain 184 Dh 34.20N 86.02W
Sandnes 114 Ag 58.51N 5.44 E
Sandnessjøen 114 Cc 66.01N 12.38 E
Sandoa 160 Ji 9.41S 22.52 E
Sandō bank 116 Hf 58.10N 19.15 E
Sandomierska, Kotlina- 120 Rf 50.30N 22.00 E
Sandomierz 120 Rf 50.41N 21.45 E
San Domino 128 Jh 42.05N 15.30 E
Sandoná 202 Cc 1.18N 77.28W
San Donà di Piave 128 Ge 45.38N 12.34 E
Sandoval, Boca de- 192 Ke 24.58N 97.32W
Sandover River 212 Hd 21.43S 136.32 E
Sandoway 148 Ie 18.28N 94.22 E
Sandown 118 Lk 50.39N 1.09W
Sandpoint 182 Db 48.16N 116.33W
Sand Point 178 Ge 55.20N 160.30W
Sandras Daği 130 Ll 37.04N 28.51 E
Sandray 118 Fe 56.54N 7.25W
Sandspit 180 Ef 53.15N 131.50W
Sand Springs [Mt.-U.S.] 188 Lc 47.09N 107.27W
Sand Springs [Ok.-U.S.] 186 Hh 36.09N 96.07W
Sandstone [Austl.] 212 De 27.59S 119.17 E
Sandstone [Mn.-U.S.] 186 Jc 46.08N 92.52W
Sandu 152 Jf 26.08N 113.16 E
Sandusky [Mi.-U.S.] 184 Fd 43.25N 82.50W
Sandusky [Oh.-U.S.] 182 Kc 41.27N 82.42W
Sandveld 172 Cd 21.20S 20.10 E
Sandvig-Allinge 114 Di 55.15N 14.49 E
Sandvika 116 De 59.54N 10.31 E
Sandviken 114 Df 60.37N 16.46 E
Sandwich 118 Oj 51.17N 1.20 E
Sandwich Bay 180 Lf 53.35N 57.15W
Sandy 124 Bb 52.07N 0.17W
Sandy Cape [Austl.] 208 Gg 24.40S 153.15 E
Sandy Cape [Austl.] 212 Ih 41.25S 144.45 E
Sandy Desert 148 Cc 28.46N 62.30 E
Sandykači 136 Gh 36.32N 62.35 E
Sandy Lake 180 If 53.02N 93.14W
Sandy Lake 180 If 53.02N 92.55W
Sandy Point 184 Il 26.01N 77.24W
Sandy Point Town 196 Ed 17.22N 62.50W
Sandžak 130 Cf 43.10N 20.00 E
Sanem 124 He 49.33N 5.56 E
San Estanislao 206 Ib 24.39S 56.26W
San Esteban 194 Ef 15.17N 85.52W
San Esteban, Bahía de- 192 Ee 25.40N 109.15W
San Esteban, Isla- 192 Cc 28.42N 112.36W
San Esteban de Gormaz 126 Ic 41.35N 3.12W
San Felice Circeo 128 Hi 41.14N 13.05 E
San Felipe [Chile] 206 Fd 32.45S 70.44W
San Felipe [Col.] 202 Ec 1.55N 67.06W
San Felipe [Mex.] 190 Bb 31.00N 114.52W
San Felipe [Mex.] 192 Ig 21.29N 101.13W
San Felipe [Ven.] 202 Ea 10.20N 68.44W
San Felipe, Cayos de- 194 Fc 21.58N 83.30W
San Felipe, Cerro de- 126 Kd 40.24N 1.51W
San Felipe Creek 188 Hj 33.09N 115.46W
San Feliu de Llobregat / Sant Feliu de Llobregat 126 Oc 41.23N 2.03 E
San Felix, Isla- 206 Dc 26.17S 80.05W
San Fermín, Punta- 192 Bb 30.25N 114.40W
San Fernando [Chile] 206 Fd 34.35S 71.00W
San Fernando [Mex.] 190 Ed 24.51N 98.10W
San Fernando [Mex.] 192 Bb 29.59N 115.17W
San Fernando [Phil.] 150 Hc 15.01N 120.41 E
San Fernando [Phil.] 150 Hc 16.37N 120.19 E
San Fernando [Sp.] 126 Fh 36.28N 6.12W
San Fernando [Trin.] 202 Fa 10.17N 61.28W
San Fernando, Río- [Bol.] 204 Cc 17.13S 58.23W
San Fernando, Río- [Mex.] 192 Ke 24.55N 97.40W
San Fernando de Apure 200 Je 7.54N 67.28W
San Fernando de Atabapo 202 Ec 4.03N 67.42W
San Fernando del Valle de Catamarca 200 Jh 28.30S 65.45W
Sanford [Fl.-U.S.] 182 Kf 28.48N 81.16W
Sanford [Me.-U.S.] 184 Ld 43.26N 70.46W
Sanford [N.C.-U.S.] 184 Hh 35.29N 79.10W
Sanford, Mount- 178 Kd 62.13N 144.09W
San Francisco [Arg.] 206 Hd 31.26S 62.05W
San Francisco [Bol.] 204 Cc 17.42S 59.38W
San Francisco [Ca.-U.S.] 176 Gf 37.48N 122.24W
San Francisco [Pan.] 194 Gi 8.15N 80.58W
San Francisco, Isla- 192 De 24.50N 110.35W
San Francisco Bay 174 Gf 37.43N 122.17W
San Francisco Creek 186 El 29.53N 102.19W
San Francisco de Arriba 192 Gd 26.15N 102.50W
San Francisco de Bellocq 204 Bn 38.42S 60.01W
San Francisco de la Paz 194 Df 14.55N 86.14W
San Francisco del Laishi 204 Ch 26.14S 58.38W
San Francisco del Oro 190 Cc 26.52N 105.51W
San Francisco del Rincón 192 Ig 21.01N 101.51W
San Francisco de Macorís 190 Je 19.18N 70.15W
San Francisco Gotera 194 Cg 13.42N 88.06W
San Francisco Javier / Sant Francesc de Formentera 126 Nf 38.42N 1.25 E
San Francisco Mountains 188 Kj 33.45N 109.00W
San Francisco River 188 Kj 32.59N 109.22W
San Fratello 128 Il 38.01N 14.36 E
San Gabriel 204 Di 28.58S 57.12W
San Gabriel, Punta- 192 Cc 28.25N 112.50W
San Gabriel Mountains 188 Gi 34.20N 117.45W
San Gallán, Isla- 202 Cf 13.50S 76.28W
Sangamon River 186 Kf 40.07N 90.20W
Sangar [Iran] 146 Md 37.08N 49.02 E
Sangar [Russia] 142 Oc 63.55N 127.31 E
Sangatte 124 Dd 50.56N 1.45 E
San Gavino Monreale 128 Ck 39.33N 8.47 E
Sangay, Volcán- 198 If 2.00S 78.20W
Sange 170 Ed 7.02S 28.21 E
Sangeang, Pulau- 150 Gh 8.12S 119.04 E
San Gemini 128 Gh 42.37N 12.33 E
Sanger 188 Fh 36.42N 119.27W
Sangerhausen 120 He 51.28N 11.18 E
San Germán [Cuba] 194 Ic 20.36N 76.08W
San Germán [P.R.] 194 Nd 18.05N 67.03W
Sanggan He 154 Cd 40.24N 115.18 E
Sanggau 150 Ff 0.08N 110.36 E
Sangha 150 Ii 1.13S 16.49 E
Sangha [C.A.R.] [3] 158 Be 3.30N 16.00 E
Sangha [Con.] [3] 170 Cb 2.00N 15.00 E
Sangihe, Kepulauan- = Sangihe Islands (EN) 140 Oi 3.00N 125.30 E
Sangihe, Pulau- 150 If 3.35N 125.32 E
Sangihe Islands (EN) = Sangihe, Kepulauan- 140 Oi 3.00N 125.30 E
San Gil 202 Db 6.32N 73.08W
San Gimignano 128 Fg 43.28N 11.02 E
San Giovanni in Fiore 128 Kk 39.15N 16.42 E
San Giovanni in Persiceto 128 Ff 44.38N 11.11 E
San Giovanni Rotondo 128 Ji 41.42N 15.44 E
San Giovanni Valdarno 128 Fg 43.34N 11.32 E
Sangju 154 Jf 36.25N 128.10 E
Sāngli 142 Jh 16.52N 74.34 E
Sangmélima 166 He 2.56N 11.59 E
Sangoli 146 Pd 37.25N 54.35 E
San Gorgonio 174 Hf 34.05N 116.50W
San Gottardo, Passo del- = Saint Gotthard Pass (EN) 110 Gf 46.30N 8.30 E
Sangradouro Grande, Rio- 204 Dc 16.24S 57.10W
Sangre de Cristo Mountains 174 If 37.30N 105.15W
San Gregorio 204 Al 34.19S 62.02W
Sangre Grande 196 Fg 10.35N 61.07W
Sangri 152 Ff 29.20N 92.15 E
Sangro 128 Ih 42.14N 14.32 E
Sangue, Rio do- 202 Gf 11.00S 58.40W
Sangüesa 126 Kb 42.35N 1.17W
Sanguinaires, Iles- 122a Ab 41.53N 8.35 E
San Gustavo 204 Cj 30.41S 59.23W
Sangyuan → Wuqiao 154 Df 37.38N 116.23 E
Sangzhi 152 Jf 29.23N 110.11 E
San He 154 Eh 33.00N 118.34 E
Sanhe [China] 154 Dd 40.00N 117.01 E
Sanhe [China] 152 La 50.30N 120.04 E
Sanhe-San 156 Cd 35.08N 132.37 E
Sanhezhen 154 Di 31.30N 117.15 E
San Hilario [Arg.] 204 Ch 26.02S 58.39W
San Hilario [Mex.] 192 De 24.22N 110.59W
San Hipólito, Bahía- 192 Cd 26.55N 113.55W
San Ignacio [Arg.] 204 Eh 27.16S 55.32W
San Ignacio [Blz.] 190 Ge 17.10N 89.04W
San Ignacio [Bol.] 202 Fg 16.23S 60.59W
San Ignacio [Bol.] 202 Ef 14.53S 65.36W
San Ignacio [Mex.] 190 Bc 27.27N 112.51W
San Ignacio [Mex.] 192 Ff 25.55N 106.25W
San Ignacio [Par.] 206 Ic 26.52S 57.03W
San Ignacio, Isla de- 192 Ee 25.25N 108.55W
San Ignacio, Laguna- 192 Cd 26.55N 113.15W
San Ildefonso (La Granja) 126 Id 40.54N 4.00W
San Ildefonso, Cape- 150 Hc 16.02N 121.59 E
San Ildefonso, Cerro- 194 Cf 15.31N 88.17W
Saniquellie 166 Dd 7.22N 8.43W
San Isidro [Arg.] 206 Id 34.27S 58.30W
San Isidro [Phil.] 150 Hd 11.24N 124.21 E
San Isidro de El General 190 Hg 9.22N 83.42W
Saniyah 146 If 33.49N 42.43 E
San Jacinto 194 Ji 9.50N 75.07W
San Jacinto Peak 188 Gj 33.49N 116.41W
San Jaime 204 Cj 30.20S 58.19W
San Javier [Arg.] 206 Id 30.35S 59.57W
San Javier [Sp.] 126 Lg 37.48N 0.51W
San Javier [Ur.] 204 Ck 32.41S 58.08W
San Javier, Río- 204 Bj 31.30S 60.20W
San Javier de Loncomilla 206 Fe 35.36S 71.45W
San Jerónimo Taviche 192 Ki 16.44N 96.35W
Sanjiachang 152 Hg 24.45N 101.53 E
Sanjiaocheng → Haiyan 152 Hd 36.58N 100.50 E
Sanjō 154 Of 37.37N 138.57 E
San Joan de Labritja / San Juan Bautista 126 Ne 39.05N 1.30 E
San Joaquín 202 Ff 13.04S 64.49W
San Joaquín, Río- 202 Ff 13.08S 63.41W
San Joaquin, Sierra de- 204 Eg 24.48S 56.00W
San Joaquin River 188 Eh 36.43N 121.50W
San Joaquin Valley 174 Gf 36.50N 120.10W
San Jon 186 Ei 35.06N 103.20W
San Jorge 206 Hd 31.54S 61.52W
San Jorge, Bahía de- 192 Cb 31.10N 113.15W
San Jorge, Golfo- 198 Jj 46.00S 67.00W
San Jorge, Golfo de- / Sant Jordi, Golf de- 126 Md 40.53N 1.00 E
San Jorge, Río- 194 Ji 9.07N 74.44W
San Jorge, Serranía- 204 Be 20.21S 60.59W
San Jorge Island 219a Dc 8.27S 159.35 E
San José [2] 204 Dl 34.15S 56.45W
San José [3] 194 Ei 9.40N 84.00W
San José [Arg.] 204 Eh 27.46S 55.47W
San José [Ca.-U.S.] 176 Gf 37.20N 121.53W
San José [C.R.] 176 Ki 9.56N 84.05W
San José [Mex.] 192 Dd 27.32N 110.09W
San José [Par.] 204 Dg 25.33S 56.45W
San Jose [Phil.] 150 Hd 12.21N 121.04 E
San Jose [Phil.] 150 Hc 15.48N 121.00 E
San José, Isla- [Mex.] 190 Bc 25.00N 110.38W
San José, Isla- [Pan.] 194 Hi 8.15N 79.07W
San José, Salinas de- 204 Bd 19.07S 60.54W
San José, Serranía de- 204 Bc 17.52S 60.49W
San Jose de Buenavista 150 Hd 10.46N 122.30 E
San José de Chiquitos 202 Fg 17.51S 60.47W
San José de Feliciano 204 Cj 30.23S 58.45W
San José de Gracia 192 Fd 26.08N 107.58W
San José de Guanipa 202 Fb 8.54N 64.09W
San José de Jachal 206 Gd 30.14S 68.45W
San José de las Lajas 194 Fb 22.58N 82.09W
San José del Cabo 190 Cd 23.03N 109.41W
San José del Guaviare 200 Ie 2.35N 72.38W
San José del Rosario 206 Dg 24.12S 56.48W
San José de Mayo 206 Id 34.20S 56.42W
San José de Ocuné 202 Dc 4.15N 70.20W
San José de Tiznados 196 Ch 9.23N 67.33W
San Juan [2] 206 Gd 31.00S 69.00W
San Juan [Arg.] 200 Ji 31.30S 68.30W
San Juan [Bol.] 204 Cc 17.52S 59.59W
San Juan [Bol.] 204 Bd 18.08S 60.08W
San Juan [C.Amer.] 174 Kh 10.56N 83.42W
San Juan [Dom.Rep.] 190 Je 18.48N 71.14W
San Juan [P.R.] 176 Mh 18.28N 66.07W
San Juan [U.S.] 174 Hf 37.18N 110.28W
San Juan, Cabezas de- 197a Cb 18.23N 65.36W
San Juan, Cabo- 158 Hh 1.10N 9.21 E
San Juan, Muela de- 126 Kd 40.26N 1.44W
San Juan, Pico- 190 Hd 21.59N 80.09W
San Juan, Punta- 221d Ab 27.03S 109.22W
San Juan, Río- [Arg.] 206 Gd 32.17S 67.22W
San Juan, Río- [Mex.] 192 Jd 26.10N 99.00W
San Juan, Río- [Mex.] 192 Lh 18.36N 95.40W
San Juan, Río- [Ven.] 196 Eg 10.14N 62.39W
San Juan, Volcán- 192 Gg 21.30N 104.57W
San Juan Bautista / Sant Joan de Labritja 126 Ne 39.05N 1.30 E
San Juan Bautista de las Misiones 206 Ic 26.38S 57.10W
San Juan Bautista Tuxtepec 192 Kh 18.06N 96.07W
San Juan de Colón 194 Ki 8.02N 72.16W
San Juan de Guadalupe 192 He 24.38N 102.44W
San Juan del Cesar 194 Kh 10.46N 72.59W
San Juan del Norte 190 Hf 10.55N 83.42W
San Juan de los Cayos 202 Ea 11.10N 68.25W
San Juan de los Lagos 192 Hg 21.15N 102.14W
San Juan de los Morros 202 Ea 9.55N 67.21W
San Juan del Río [Mex.] 192 Ge 24.47N 104.27W
San Juan del Río [Mex.] 192 Jg 20.29N 100.00W
San Juan del Sur 190 Gf 11.15N 85.52W
San Juan de Payara 196 Ci 7.39N 67.36W
San Juanico, Isla- 192 Fg 21.55N 106.40W
San Juanico, Punta- 192 Cd 26.05N 112.15W
San Juan Island 188 Db 48.32N 123.05W
San Juan Mountains 182 Fd 37.35N 107.10W
San Juan Neembucú 204 Dh 26.39S 57.56W
San Juan Nepomuceno [Col.] 202 Cb 9.57N 75.05W
San Juan Nepomuceno [Par.] 204 Eh 26.06S 55.58W
San Juan y Martínez 194 Fb 22.16N 83.50W
San Julián 200 Jj 49.19S 67.40W
San Just, Sierra de- 126 Ld 40.46N 0.48W
San Justo 206 Hd 30.47S 60.35W
Sankarani 158 Gg 12.01N 8.19W
Sankt Anton am Arlberg 128 Ec 47.08N 10.16 E
Sankt Augustin 124 Jd 50.47N 7.11 E
Sankt Gallen 128 Dc 47.25N 9.25 E
Sankt Gallen [2] 128 Dc 47.20N 9.10 E
Sankt Goar 120 Df 50.09N 7.43 E
Sankt Goarshausen 124 Jd 50.09N 7.44 E
Sankt Ingbert 120 Dg 49.17N 7.07 E
Sankt Johann im Pongau 128 Hc 47.21N 13.12 E
Sankt Michael im Lungau 128 Hc 47.06N 13.38 E
Sankt Michel/Mikkeli 112 Ic 61.41N 27.15 E
Sankt Moritz 128 Dd 46.30N 9.52 E
Sankt-Peterburg (Leningrad) 112 Jc 59.55N 30.15 E
Sankt Peter-Ording 120 Eb 54.18N 8.38 E
Sankt Pölten 128 Jb 48.12N 15.38 E
Sankt Ulrich in Gröden / Ortisei 128 Fd 46.34N 11.40 E
Sankt Veit an der Glan 128 Id 46.46N 14.22 E
Sankt-Vith / Saint-Vith 122 Md 50.17N 6.08 E
Sankt Wendel 120 Dg 49.28N 7.10 E
Sankt Wolfang im Salzkammergut 128 Hc 47.44N 13.27 E
Sankuru 158 Ji 4.17S 20.25 E
San Lázaro 206 Ib 22.10S 57.55W
San Lázaro, Cabo- 190 Bd 24.48N 112.19W
San Lázaro, Sierra de- 192 Df 23.25N 110.00W
San Leandro 188 Dh 37.43N 122.09W
Şanlıurfa (Urfa) 144 Eb 37.08N 38.46 E
San Lorenzo 190 Fe 17.44N 94.45W
San Lorenzo [Arg.] 204 Bk 32.45S 60.44W
San Lorenzo [Ec.] 200 Ie 1.17N 78.50W
San Lorenzo [Hond.] 194 Dg 13.25N 87.27W
San Lorenzo, Isla- [Mex.] 192 Cc 28.38N 112.51W
San Lorenzo, Isla- [Peru] 202 Cf 12.05S 77.15W
San Lorenzo, Río- [Mex.] 192 Je 25.07N 98.32W
San Lorenzo, Río- [Mex.] 192 Fe 24.15N 107.24W
San Lorenzo de El Escorial 126 Hd 40.35N 4.09W
Sanlúcar de Barrameda 126 Fh 36.47N 6.21W
Sanlúcar la Mayor 126 Fg 37.23N 6.12W
San Lucas [Mex.] 190 Cd 22.53N 109.54W
San Lucas [Mex.] 192 Gf 22.33N 104.24W
San Lucas, Cabo- 174 Ig 22.50N 109.55W
San Lucas, Serranía de- 202 Db 8.00N 74.20W
San Lucido 128 Kk 39.18N 16.03 E
San Luis [2] 206 Gd 34.00S 66.00W
San Luis [Arg.] 200 Ji 33.20S 66.20W
San Luis [Bol.] 204 Cc 17.39S 58.42W
San Luis [Cuba] 194 Jc 20.12N 75.51W
San Luis [Guat.] 194 Ce 16.14N 89.27W
San Luis [Mex.] 192 Dc 29.33N 111.05W
San Luis, Isla- 192 Bb 29.58N 114.26W
San Luis, Sierra de- 194 Mh 11.11N 69.42W
San Luis de la Paz 192 Ig 21.18N 100.31W
San Luis del Palmar 204 Ch 27.31S 58.34W
San Luis de Palenque 202 Db 5.25N 71.40W
San Luis Gonzaga, Bahía- 192 Bc 30.00N 114.25W
San Luis Obispo 176 Gf 35.17N 120.40W
San Luis Pass 186 Il 29.05N 95.08W
San Luis Peak 186 Ch 37.59N 106.56W
San Luis Potosí 176 Ig 22.09N 100.59W
San Luis Potosí [2] 190 Dd 22.30N 100.30W
San Luis Río Colorado 190 Bb 32.29N 114.48W
San Luis Valley 182 Fd 37.25N 106.00W
Sanluri 128 Ck 39.34N 8.54 E
San Manuel [Arg.] 204 Cm 37.47S 58.50W
San Manuel [Az.-U.S.] 188 Jj 32.36N 110.38W
San Marcial, Punta- 192 De 25.30N 111.00W
San Marco, Capo- 128 Hm 37.30N 13.01 E
San Marcos [3] 194 Bf 15.00N 91.55W
San Marcos [Col.] 202 Cb 8.39N 75.08W
San Marcos [Guat.] 194 Bf 14.58N 91.48W
San Marcos [Hond.] 194 Cf 14.24N 88.56W
San Marcos [Mex.] 192 Gg 20.47N 104.11W
San Marcos [Mex.] 192 Ji 16.48N 99.21W
San Marcos [Nic.] 194 Dh 11.55N 86.12W
San Marcos [Tx.-U.S.] 182 Hf 29.53N 97.57W
San Marcos, Isla- 192 Cd 27.13N 112.06W
San Marcos, Sierra de- 192 Hd 26.30N 101.55W
San Marino 128 Gg 43.55N 12.28 E
San Marino [1] 112 Hg 43.55N 12.28 E
San Martín 206 Gd 33.04S 68.28W
San Martin [3] 202 Ce 7.00S 76.50W
San Martín 192 Ab 30.30N 116.05W
San Martín 222 Qe 68.11S 67.00W
San Martín, Cerro- 192 Ih 18.19N 94.48W
San Martín, Lago- 206 Fg 48.52S 72.40W
San Martín, Río- 202 Ff 13.08S 63.43W
San Martín de los Andes 206 Ff 40.10S 71.21W
San Martín de Valdeiglesias 126 Hd 40.21N 4.24W
San Martino di Castrozza 128 Fd 46.16N 11.48 E
San Mateo [Ca.-U.S.] 188 Dh 37.35N 122.19W
San Mateo [Ven.] 196 Dh 9.45N 64.33W

San-Sao

Index Symbols

⬚1 Independent Nation	⬚ Historical or Cultural Region	◁ Pass, Gap	◇ Depression	◈ Coast, Beach
⬚2 State, Region	▲ Mount, Mountain	▨ Plain, Lowland	◔ Polder	◵ Cliff
⬚3 District, County	▲ Volcano	◣ Delta	▨ Desert, Dunes	◷ Peninsula
⬚4 Municipality	▨ Hill	◻ Salt Flat	◼ Forest, Woods	◽ Isthmus
⬚5 Colony, Dependency	▨ Mountains, Mountain Range	◵ Valley, Canyon	◷ Heath, Steppe	◸ Sandbank
◇ Continent	◿ Hills, Escarpment	◹ Crater, Cave	◺ Oasis	◻ Island
◈ Physical Region	◼ Plateau, Upland	◽ Karst Features	◾ Cape, Point	◿ Atoll

▨ Rock, Reef	▨ Waterfall, Rapids	▨ Canal	▨ Lagoon	▨ Escarpment, Sea Scarp
◨ Islands, Archipelago	◧ River Mouth, Estuary	◧ Glacier	◧ Bank	◧ Fracture
▨ Rocks, Reefs	◧ Ice Shelf, Pack Ice	◧ Lake	◧ Seamount	◧ Trench, Abyss
◧ Coral Reef	◧ Salt Lake	◧ Ocean	◧ Tablemount	◧ National Park, Reserve
◧ Well, Spring	◧ Intermittent Lake	◧ Sea	◧ Ridge	◧ Point of Interest
◧ Geyser	◧ Reservoir	◧ Gulf, Bay	◧ Shelf	◧ Recreation Site
◧ River, Stream	◧ Swamp, Pond	◧ Strait, Fjord	◧ Basin	◧ Cave, Cavern

▨ Historic Site	◈ Airport
◈ Ruins	◈ Port
◈ Wall, Walls	◈ Military installation
◈ Church, Abbey	◈ Lighthouse
◈ Temple	◈ Mine
◈ Scientific Station	◈ Tunnel
◈ Railway station	◈ Dam, Bridge

Saona, Isla- 194 Md 18.09N 68.40W
Saône 110 Gf 45.44N 4.50 E
Saône-et-Loire [3] 122 Kh 46.40N 4.30 E
Saonek 150 Jg 0.28S 130.47 E
São Nicolau 204 Ei 28.11S 55.16W
São Nicolau 158 Eg 16.35N 24.15W
São Patricio, Rio- 204 Hb 15.02S 49.15W
São Paulo 200 Lh 23.32S 46.37W
São Paulo [2] 206 Kb 22.00S 49.00W
São Paulo de Olivença 202 Ed 3.27S 68.48W
São Pedro, Ribeirão- 204 Ic 16.54S 46.32W
São Pedro do Sul [Braz.] 204 Ei 29.37S 54.10W
São Pedro do Sul [Port.] 126 Dd 40.45N 8.04W
São Pedro e São Paulo, Penedos de- 198 Ne 0.56N 29.22W
São Raimundo Nonato 202 Je 9.01S 42.42W
São Romão [Braz.] 202 Ig 16.22S 45.04W
São Romão [Braz.] 204 Ed 18.33S 54.27W
São Roque 204 De 21.43S 57.46W
São Roque, Cabo de- 198 Mf 5.29S 35.16W
São Roque, Serra de- 204 Ib 14.40S 46.50W
São Sebastião 204 Jf 23.48S 45.25W
São Sebastião, Ilha de- 198 Lh 23.50S 45.18W
São Sebastião, Ponta- 158 Kk 22.05S 35.24 E
São Sebastião da Boa Vista 202 Id 1.42S 49.31W
São Sebastião do Paraiso 202 Ih 20.55S 47.00W
São Sepé 204 Fj 30.10S 53.34W
São Simão 202 Hg 18.56S 50.30W
São Tiago 158 Eg 15.05N 23.40W
São Tomé 160 Hh 0.20N 6.44 E
São Tomé 158 Hh 0.12N 6.39 E
São Tomé, Cabo de- 202 Jh 22.00S 40.59W
Sao Tome and Principe (EN) = São Tomé e Principe [1] 160 Hh 1.00N 7.00 E
São Tomé e Principe = Sao Tome and Principe (EN) [1] 160 Hh 1.00N 7.00 E
Saoura 162 Gd 27.50N 2.50W
Saoura 158 Gf 28.48N 0.50W
São Vicente 158 Eg 16.50N 25.00W
São Vicente [Braz.] 206 Kb 23.58S 46.23W
São Vicente [Braz.] 204 Ia 13.38S 46.31W
São Vicente, Cabo de- 110 Fh 37.01N 9.00W
São Xavier, Serra de- 204 Ei 29.15S 54.15W
Sápai 130 Ih 41.02N 25.42 E
Sapanca 130 Ni 40.41N 30.16 E
Sapanca Gölü 130 Ni 40.43N 30.15 E
Sape [Braz.] 202 Ke 7.06S 35.13W
Sape [Indon.] 150 Gh 8.34S 118.59 E
Sape, Selat- 150 Gh 8.39S 119.18 E
Sapele 166 Gd 5.55N 5.42 E
Sapelo Island 184 Gj 31.28N 81.15W
Şaphane 130 Mj 39.01N 29.14 E
Şaphane Daği 130 Mj 39.03N 29.16 E
Sapiéntza 130 Em 36.45N 21.42 E
Šapkina 134 Fc 66.44N 52.25 E
Sapo, Serrania del- 194 Hi 7.50N 78.17W
Sa Pobla / La Puebla 126 Pe 39.46N 3.01 E
Saponé 166 Ec 12.03N 1.36W
Sapopema 204 Gf 23.55S 50.35W
Saposoa 202 Ce 6.56S 76.48W
Sapphire Mountains 188 Ic 46.20N 113.45W
Sapporo 142 Qe 43.03N 141.21 E
Sapri 128 Jj 40.04N 15.38 E
Saptajev (Nikolski) 136 Gf 47.55N 67.33 E
Sapulpa 182 Hd 36.00N 96.06W
Sapulut 150 Gf 4.42N 116.29 E
Sāqand 144 Pf 32.33N 55.12 E
Sāqiyat Sīdī Yūsuf 128 Cn 36.13N 8.21 E
Saqqez 144 Gb 36.14N 46.16 E
Sarāb 144 Gb 37.56N 47.32 E
Saraburi 148 Kf 14.30N 100.55 E
Saraf Doungous 168 Bc 12.33N 19.42 E
Sarafjagān 146 Ne 34.28N 50.28 E
Saragmatha = Everest, Mount- (EN) 140 Kg 27.59N 86.56 E
Saragossa (EN) = Zaragoza [Sp.] 112 Fg 41.38N 0.53W
Sarai 114 Jj 53.44N 41.03 E
Sarajevo 112 Hg 43.50N 18.25 E
Saraji Mine 212 Jd 22.30S 148.20 E
Sarakhs 144 Jb 36.32N 61.11 E
Sarakiná 130 Hk 38.40N 24.37 E
Šarakol 134 Kj 52.03N 62.47 E
Saraktaš 134 Fe 51.47N 56.18 E
Saraland 184 Cj 30.49N 88.02W
Saramati 148 Jc 25.44N 95.02 E
Saran 136 Hf 49.46N 72.52 E
Saran, Gunung- 150 Fg 0.25S 111.18 E
Saranac Lake 184 Jc 44.20N 74.08W
Saranci 130 Gg 42.43N 23.46 E
Saranda 130 Dj 39.52N 20.00 E
Sarandi 204 Fh 27.56S 52.55W
Sarandi, Arroyo- 204 Cj 30.13S 59.19W
Sarandi del Yi 204 Ek 33.21S 55.38W
Sarandi Grande 204 Dk 33.44S 56.20W
Šaranga 114 Lh 57.12N 46.34 E
Sarangani Bay 150 Ie 5.57N 125.11 E
Sarangani Islands 150 Ie 5.25N 125.26 E
Saranley 168 Ge 2.23N 42.16 E
Saransk 112 Ke 54.11N 45.11 E
Sarapul 112 Ld 56.28N 53.48 E
Sarapulskoje 138 Ig 48.50N 135.58 E
Sarare 194 Mi 9.47N 69.10W
Sararé, Rio- 204 Cb 14.51S 59.58W
Sarasota 182 Kf 27.20N 82.34W
Sarata 132 Ff 46.01N 29.41 E
Sărățel 130 Hb 47.03N 24.25 E
Saratoga 188 Lf 41.27N 106.48W
Saratoga Springs 182 Mc 43.04N 73.47W
Saratok 150 Ff 1.24N 111.31 E
Saratov 112 Ke 51.34N 46.02 E
Saratov Reservoir (EN) = Saratovskoje vodohranilišče 110 Ke 52.50N 47.50 E
Saratovskaja oblast [3] 136 Ee 51.30N 47.00 E
Saratovskoje vodohranilišče = Saratov Reservoir (EN) 110 Ke 52.50N 47.50 E
Saravan 148 Le 15.43N 106.25 E
Sarawak [2] 150 Ff 2.30N 113.30 E
Saray 146 Bb 41.26N 27.55 E
Sarāyā 146 Fe 35.47N 35.58 E
Saraya 166 Cc 12.50N 11.45W
Saraykōy 146 Cd 37.55N 28.56 E
Sarbāz 144 Jd 26.39N 61.15 E
Sárbogárd 120 Oj 46.53N 18.38 E
Sarca 128 Ee 45.52N 10.52 E
Sarcelle, Passe de la- 219b Cf 22.28S 167.13 E
Sarcelles 124 Ef 49.00N 2.23 E
Sarcidano 128 Dk 39.40N 9.15 E
Sardara 128 Ck 39.37N 8.49 E
Sar Dasht [Iran] 146 Kd 36.09N 45.28 E
Sar Dasht [Iran] 146 Mf 32.32N 48.52 E
Sardegna [2] 128 Cj 40.00N 9.00 E
Sardegna = Sardinia (EN) 110 Gh 40.00N 9.00 E
Sardegna, Mar di- 128 Bk 40.00N 7.30 E
Sardes 130 Lk 38.29N 28.03 E
Sardinal 194 Eh 10.31N 85.39W
Sardinata 202 Db 8.07N 72.48W
Sardinia (EN) = Sardegna 110 Gh 40.00N 9.00 E
Sardis Lake 186 Li 34.27N 89.43W
Sarektjåkkå 114 Dc 67.25N 17.46 E
Sarema/Saaremaa 110 Id 58.25N 22.30 E
Sar-e Pol 144 Kb 36.14N 65.55 E
Sar Eskand Khān 146 Ld 37.29N 47.04 E
Sar-e Yazd 146 Pg 31.36N 54.35 E
Sargasso Sea 174 Mg 29.00N 65.00W
Sargatskoje 136 Hd 55.37N 73.30 E
Sargodha 148 Eb 32.05N 72.40 E
Šargun 135 Fe 38.31N 67.59 E
Sarh 160 Ih 9.09N 18.23 E
Sarhro, Jebel- 162 Fc 31.00N 6.00W
Sāri 142 Hf 36.34N 53.04 E
Saria 130 Kn 35.50N 27.15 E
Sariçakaya 146 Db 40.02N 30.31 E
Sarigan Island 208 Fc 16.42N 145.47 E
Sarigöl 146 Cc 38.14N 28.43 E
Sarıkamış 146 Jb 40.15N 42.35 E
Sarıkaya 146 Fc 39.48N 35.24 E
Sarikei 150 Ff 2.07N 111.31 E
Sariköy 130 Ki 40.12N 27.36 E
Sarina 212 Jd 21.26S 149.13 E
Sarine 128 Bd 46.59N 7.16 E
Sariñena 126 Lc 41.48N 0.10W
Sarıoğlan 146 Fc 39.05N 35.59 E
Sarir 164 Dd 27.30N 22.30 E
Sariwŏn 152 Md 38.30N 125.45 E
Sarıyer 146 Cb 41.10N 29.03 E
Sarj, Jabal as- 128 Do 35.56N 9.32 E
Šarja 112 Kd 58.24N 45.30 E
Sark 118 Kl 49.26N 2.21W
Sarkad 120 Rj 46.45N 21.23 E
Sarkand 136 Hf 45.25N 79.54 E
Şarkikaraağaç 146 Dc 38.04N 31.23 E
Şarkışla 146 Gc 39.21N 36.26 E
Šarkovščina 116 Li 55.22N 27.32 E
Şarköy 130 Ki 40.37N 27.06 E
Sarlat-la-Canéda 122 Hj 44.53N 1.13 E
Šarlyk 132 Sc 52.54N 54.42 E
Sarmi 210 Ee 1.51S 138.44 E
Sarmiento 200 Jj 45.35S 69.05W
Sarmizegetuza 130 Fd 45.31N 22.47 E
Särna 116 Ec 61.41N 13.08 E
Sarnen 128 Cd 46.54N 8.15 E
Sărnena Gora 130 Ig 42.35N 25.30 E
Sarnia 180 Jh 42.58N 82.23W
Sarny 136 Ce 51.21N 26.36 E
Saroako 150 Hg 2.31S 121.22 E
Sarolangun 150 Dg 2.18S 102.42 E
Saroma 156a Ca 44.02N 143.45 E
Saroma-Ko 154 Qb 44.10N 143.40 E
Šaromy 138 Kf 54.23N 158.14 E
Saronic Gulf (EN) = Saronikós Kólpos 130 Gl 37.45N 23.30 E
Saronikós Kólpos = Saronic Gulf (EN) 130 Gl 37.45N 23.30 E
Saronno 128 De 45.38N 9.02 E
Saros, Gulf of- (EN) = Saros Körfezi 146 Bb 40.30N 26.20 E
Saros Körfezi = Saros, Gulf of- (EN) 146 Bb 40.30N 26.20 E
Sárospatak 120 Rh 48.19N 21.35 E
Sar Passage 220a Ac 7.12N 134.23 E
Sarpinskije ozera 132 Nf 47.45N 45.00 E
Šar Planina 130 Dg 42.05N 20.50 E
Sarpsborg 116 De 59.17N 11.07 E
Sarqaq 179 Gd 70.00N 51.39W
Sarrabus 128 Dk 39.20N 9.30 E
Sarralbe 122 Ne 49.00N 7.01 E
Sarrāt, Wādī- 128 Co 35.59N 8.23 E
Sarre 120 Cg 49.42N 6.34 E
Sarrebourg 122 Nf 48.44N 7.03 E
Sarreguemines 122 Ne 49.06N 7.03 E
Sarre-Union 122 Nf 48.56N 7.05 E
Sarria 126 Eb 42.47N 7.24W
Sarstún, Rio- 194 Cf 15.54N 88.54W
Sartang 138 Ic 67.30N 133.20 E
Sartène 122a Ab 41.37N 8.59 E
Sarthe [3] 122 Gf 48.00N 0.05 E
Sarthe 122 Fg 47.32N 0.31W
Sartu → Anda 154 Ha 46.35N 125.00 E
Sarufutsu 156a Ca 45.18N 142.13 E
Saru-Gawa 156a Cb 42.30N 142.00 E
Saruhanlı 146 Bc 38.44N 27.34 E
Sarukaishi-Gawa 156 Gb 39.25N 141.08 E
Sārūq 146 Me 34.25N 49.30 E
Saruyama-Misaki 156 Ec 37.18N 136.43 E
Sárvár 120 Mi 47.15N 16.56 E
Sarvestān 146 Oh 29.16N 53.13 E
Sárviz 120 Oj 46.22N 18.48 E
Saryagač 135 Gd 41.28N 69.11 E
Sarybarak 135 Hc 43.24N 71.29 E
Sary-Bulak 135 Jd 41.54N 75.47 E
Saryč, mys- 110 Jg 44.23N 33.45 E
Saryg-Sep 138 Ef 51.30N 95.40 E
Sary-Išikotrau 135 Kb 45.15N 76.25 E
Sarykamys 136 Ff 46.00N 53.41 E
Sarykamyšskoje, ozero- 136 Fg 41.53N 57.58 E
Sarykolski hrebet 135 Je 38.30N 74.15 E
Šaryn-Gol 152 Ib 49.20N 106.30 E
Saryozek 136 Hg 44.22N 77.54 E
Saryšagan 136 Hf 46.05N 73.38 E
Saryšiganak, zaliv- 135 Ca 46.35N 61.25 E
Sarysu 140 Ie 45.12N 66.36 E
Sary-Taš 136 Hh 39.44N 73.16 E
Saryžaz 135 Lc 42.54N 79.31 E
Sarzana 128 Df 44.07N 9.58 E
Sasabe 192 Db 31.27N 111.31W
Sasabeneh 168 Gd 8.00N 43.44 E
Sasa-ga-Mine 156 Ce 33.49N 133.17 E
Sasago-Tōge 156 Fd 35.37N 138.45 E
Sasamungga 219a Cb 7.02S 156.47 E
Sasarām 148 Gd 24.57N 84.02 E
Sasari, Mount- 219a Dc 8.11S 159.33 E
Sascut 130 Kc 46.11N 27.04 E
Sásd 120 Oj 46.15N 18.07 E
Sasebo 152 Me 33.12N 129.44 E
Saseginaga, Lac- 184 Hb 47.05N 78.34W
Saskatchewan [2] 180 Gf 54.00N 106.00W
Saskatchewan 174 Jd 53.12N 99.16W
Saskatoon 176 Id 52.07N 106.38W
Saskylah 138 Gb 72.00N 114.00 E
Sasluya, Cerro- 194 Eg 13.45N 85.03W
Sasovo 136 Ee 54.22N 41.54 E
Sassafras Mountain 184 Fh 35.03N 82.48W
Sassandra 160 Gh 4.57N 6.05W
Sassandra [3] 166 Dd 5.20N 6.10W
Sassandra 158 Gh 4.58N 6.05W
Sassari 162 Gg 40.43N 8.34 E
Sassenberg 124 Kc 51.59N 8.03 E
Sassenheim 124 Gb 52.14N 4.33 E
Sassetot-le-Mauconduit 124 Ce 49.48N 0.32 E
Saßnitz 120 Jb 54.31N 13.39 E
Sasso Marconi 128 Ff 44.24N 11.15 E
Sassuolo 128 Ef 44.33N 10.47 E
Sastobe 135 Hc 42.34N 70.03 E
Sastre 204 Bj 31.45S 61.50W
Sasyk, ozero- (Kunduk) 132 Fg 45.45N 29.40 E
Sasykkol, ozero- 136 If 46.40N 81.00 E
Sata 156 Bf 31.04N 130.42 E
Sata Cape- (EN) = Sata-Misaki 140 Pf 30.59N 130.37 E
Satakunta 116 Jc 61.30N 23.00 E
sa Talaiassa / Atalayasa 126 Nf 38.55N 1.15 E
Sata-Misaki = Sata, Cape- (EN) 140 Pf 30.59N 130.37 E
Satan, Pointe de- 219b Dd 19.00S 169.17 E
Sātāra 148 Ee 17.41N 73.59 E
Sataua 221c Aa 13.28S 172.40W
Satawal Island 208 Fd 7.21N 147.02 E
Satawan Atoll 208 Gd 5.25N 153.35 E
Satellite Bay 180 Fa 77.25N 117.15W
Säter 114 Df 60.21N 15.45 E
Satihaure 114 Ec 67.30N 18.45 E
Satipo 202 Df 11.16S 74.37W
Satīt 168 Fc 14.20N 35.50 E
Satka 136 Fd 55.03N 59.01 E
Šatki 114 Ki 55.11N 44.08 E
Sātmāla Range 148 Fe 19.30N 78.45 E
Satna 148 Gd 24.35N 80.50 E
Šator 128 Kf 44.09N 16.37 E
Sátoraljaújhely 120 Rh 48.24N 21.40 E
Sātpura Range 140 Jg 21.25N 76.10 E
Satsuma-Hantō 156 Bf 31.25N 130.25 E
Satsunai-Gawa 156a Cb 42.55N 143.15 E
Satsunan-Shotō 152 Mf 29.00N 130.00 E
Sattahip 148 Kf 12.39N 100.54 E
Satulung 130 Gb 47.34N 23.26 E
Satu Mare 130 Fb 47.48N 22.53 E
Satu Mare [2] 130 Fb 47.46N 22.56 E
Satun 148 Kg 6.39N 100.03 E
Saturninā ou Papagaio, Rio- 204 Ca 13.55S 58.18W
Saualpe 128 Id 46.50N 14.40 E
Sauce 206 Ic 30.00S 58.46W
Sauce Corto, Arroyo- 204 Bm 36.55S 61.48W
Sauceda Mountains 188 Ij 32.30N 112.30W
Sauce Grande, Rio- 204 Bn 38.59S 61.07W
Saucillo 190 Cc 28.01N 105.17W
Sauda 116 Be 59.39N 6.20 E
Saudade, Serra da- [Braz.] 204 Jd 19.20S 45.50W
Saudade, Serra da- [Braz.] 204 Fc 16.20S 53.53W
Sauðárkrókur 114a Bb 65.45N 19.39W
Saudi Arabia (EN) = Al 'Arabīyah As-Su'ūdīyah [1] 142 Gg 25.00N 45.00 E
Sauer [Eur.] 120 Cg 49.44N 6.31 E
Sauer [Eur.] 124 Kf 48.55N 8.10 E
Sauerland 120 De 51.10N 8.00 E
Sauêruiná, Rio- 202 Gf 12.00S 58.40W
Sauga jõgi 116 Kf 58.19N 24.25 E
Saugatuck 184 Dd 42.40N 86.12W
Saugues 122 Jj 44.58N 3.33 E
Sauk Centre 186 Id 45.44N 94.57W
Sauk Rapids 186 Id 45.34N 94.09W
Saül 202 Hc 3.37N 53.12W
Šaulder 135 Gc 42.47N 68.24 E
Sauldre 122 Hg 47.16N 1.30 E
Saulieu 122 Kg 47.16N 4.14 E
Saulkrasti/Saulkrasty 114 Fh 57.17N 24.29 E
Saulkrasty/Saulkrasti 114 Fh 57.17N 24.29 E
Saulnois 124 If 48.52N 6.30 E
Sault 122 Lj 44.05N 5.25 E
Sault Sainte-Marie [Mi.-U.S.] 182 Kb 46.30N 84.21W
Sault Sainte-Marie [Ont.-Can.] 176 Ke 46.31N 84.20W
Saulx 122 Kf 48.45N 4.35 E
Saumarez Reefs 208 Gg 21.50S 153.40 E
Saumâtre, Étang- 194 Kd 18.35N 72.00W
Saumlaki 150 Jh 7.57S 131.19 E
Saumur 122 Fg 47.16N 0.05W
Saunders 222 Ad 57.47S 26.27W
Saunders Coast 222 Mf 77.45S 150.00W
Saurimo 160 Ji 9.38S 20.24 E
Sauro 128 Kj 40.18N 16.21 E
Sautar 170 Ce 11.09S 18.25 E
Sauteurs 197p Bb 12.14N 61.38W
Sauveterre, Causse de- 122 Jj 44.22N 3.17 E
Sauveterre-de-Guyenne 122 Fj 44.42N 0.05W
Sauvo/Sagu 116 Jd 60.21N 22.42 E
Sauwald 128 Hb 48.28N 13.40 E
Sava 110 Ig 44.50N 20.28 E
Savage River 212 Jh 41.33S 145.09 E
Savai'i Island 208 Jf 13.35S 172.25W
Savala 132 Ld 51.06N 41.29 E
Savalou 166 Fd 7.56N 1.58 E
Savanes [3] 166 Fc 10.30N 0.30 E
Savan Island 197n Bb 12.48N 61.12W
Savanna 186 Ke 42.05N 90.08W
Savannah 174 Kf 32.02N 80.53W
Savannah [Ga.-U.S.] 176 Kf 32.04N 81.05W
Savannah [Tn.-U.S.] 184 Ch 35.14N 88.14W
Savannah Beach 184 Gi 32.01N 80.51W
Savannakhét 142 Mh 16.33N 104.45 E
Savanna-la-Mar 190 Ie 18.13N 78.08W
Savanne 186 Kb 48.59N 90.12W
Savannes Bay 197k Bb 13.45N 60.56W
Savant Lake 180 If 50.15N 90.42W
Savant Lake 186 Ka 50.30N 90.20W
Savaştepe 146 Bc 39.22N 27.40 E
Savdirī 168 Dc 14.25N 29.05 E
Savè 160 Hh 8.02N 2.29 E
Save [Afr.] 158 Kk 21.00S 35.02 E
Save [Fr.] 122 Hk 43.47N 1.17 E
Saveån 116 Dg 57.43N 11.59 E
Sāveh 144 Hb 35.01N 50.20 E
Săveni 130 Jb 47.57N 26.52 E
Saverdun 122 Hk 43.14N 1.35 E
Saverne 122 Nf 48.44N 7.22 E
Savigliano 128 Bf 44.38N 7.40 E
Savigsivik 179 Fc 76.00N 64.45W
Săvineşti 130 Jc 46.51N 26.28 E
Savinjske Alpe 128 Id 46.20N 14.30 E
Savinski 136 Ec 62.57N 40.13 E
Savio 128 Gf 44.19N 12.20 E
Săvîrşin 130 Fc 46.01N 22.14 E
Savitaipale 114 Gf 61.12N 27.42 E
Šavnik 130 Cg 42.57N 19.06 E
Savo 116 Lb 62.30N 27.30 E
Savo 219a Dc 9.08S 159.48 E
Savoie [3] 122 Mi 45.30N 6.25 E
Savoie = Savoy (EN) 122 Mi 45.24N 6.30 E
Savona 128 Cf 44.17N 8.30 E
Savonlinna/Nyslott 114 Gf 61.52N 28.53 E
Savonranta 114 Ge 62.11N 29.12 E
Savonselkä 116 Lb 62.05N 27.20 E
Savoonga 178 Ed 63.42N 170.27W
Savoy (EN) = Savoie 122 Mi 45.24N 6.30 E
Şavşat 146 Jb 41.15N 42.20 E
Savsjö 114 Dh 57.25N 14.40 E
Savudrija, Rt- 128 He 45.30N 13.31 E
Savukoski 114 Gc 67.17N 28.10 E
Savur 146 Id 37.33N 40.53 E
Savusavu 216 Ec 17.34S 178.15 E
Savusavu Bay 219d Bb 16.45S 179.15 E
Savu Sea (EN) = Sawu, Laut- 140 Oj 9.40S 122.00 E
Savuto 128 Kk 39.02N 16.06 E
Sawahlunto 150 Dg 0.40S 100.47 E
Sawai Mādhopur 148 Fc 25.59N 76.22 E
Sawākin 160 Kg 19.07N 37.20 E
Sawākin, Jazā'ir- = Suakin Archipelago (EN) 158 Kg 19.07N 37.20 E
Sawankhalok 148 Je 17.19N 99.54 E
Sawara 156 Gd 35.53N 140.29 E
Sawasaki-Hana 154 Of 37.47N 138.12 E
Sawatch Range 186 Cg 39.10N 106.25W
Sawbā = Sobat (EN) 158 Kh 9.45N 31.45 E
Sawbridgeworth 124 Cc 51.49N 0.09 E
Sawdā', Jabal as- 164 Cd 28.40N 15.30 E
Sawfajjīn 164 Cc 31.54N 15.07 E
Sawhāj = Sohag (EN) 160 Kf 26.33N 31.42 E
Sawkanah 164 Cd 29.04N 15.47 E
Sawla 166 Ed 9.17N 2.25W
Sawqirah 144 If 18.10N 56.30 E
Şawqirah, Ghubbat- 144 If 18.35N 56.45 E
Sawtooth Mountains 188 He 44.00N 115.00W
Sawu, Kepulauan- 150 Hi 10.30S 121.50 E
Sawu, Laut- = Savu Sea (EN) 140 Oj 9.40S 122.00 E
Sawu, Pulau- 140 Ok 10.30S 121.54 E
Şawwān, Ard aş- 146 Gg 31.00N 37.00 E
Sax 126 Lf 38.32N 0.49W
Saxby River 212 Ic 18.25S 140.53 E
Saxmundham 124 Db 52.13N 1.30 E
Saxony (EN) = Sachsen 120 Ie 51.20N 13.30 E
Say 166 Fc 13.07N 2.21 E
Sayabec 184 Na 48.36N 67.37W
Saya de Malha Bank (EN) 158 Nj 11.00S 61.00 E
Sayago 126 Fc 41.20N 6.10W
Sayan 202 Cf 11.08S 77.12W
Sayang, Pulau- 150 If 0.18N 129.54 E
Sayaxché 194 Be 16.31N 90.10W
Saydā 144 Ec 33.33N 35.22 E
Sayhūt 142 Hh 15.12N 51.14 E
Saylorville Lake 186 Jf 41.48N 93.46W
Säynätsalo 116 Kb 62.08N 25.46 E
Sayō 156 Dd 35.01N 134.22 E
Sayram Hu 152 Dc 44.35N 81.10 E
Sayula 192 Hh 19.52N 103.37W
Saywūn 168 Hb 15.56N 48.47 E
Sazanit, Ishull i- 130 Ci 40.30N 19.16 E
Sázava 120 Kg 49.53N 14.54 E
Sázava 120 Kg 49.53N 14.24 E
Sbaa 162 Gd 28.13N 0.10W
Sbisseb 126 Pi 35.42N 3.51 E
Sbruč 132 Ee 48.32N 26.25 E
Scaër 122 Cf 48.02N 3.42W
Scafell Pike 118 Jg 54.27N 3.12W
Scalea 128 Jk 39.49N 15.47 E
Scalone, Passo dello- 128 Jk 39.38N 15.57 E
Scammon, Laguna- 192 Bd 27.45N 114.15W
Scammon Bay 178 Fd 61.53N 165.38W
Scandinavia (EN) 110 Hc 65.00N 16.00 E
Scandinavian Highland (EN) 110 Hc 64.00N 13.00 E
Scanno 128 Hi 41.54N 13.53 E
Scansano 128 Fh 42.41N 11.20 E
Scapa Flow 118 Jc 58.54N 3.05W
Scapegoat Mountain 188 Ic 47.19N 112.50W
Ščapino 138 Ke 55.15N 159.25 E
Ščara 132 Dc 53.27N 24.44 E
Scaramia, Capo- 128 In 36.47N 14.29 E
Scarba 118 He 56.11N 5.42W
Scarborough [Eng.-U.K.] 118 Mg 54.17N 0.24W
Scarborough [Trin.] 202 Fa 11.11N 60.44W
Scarp 118 Fc 58.05N 7.05W
Scarpe 122 Jd 50.30N 3.27 E
Sčastje 132 Ke 48.44N 39.14 E
Sceaux 124 Ef 48.47N 2.17 E
Ščedro 128 Kg 43.05N 16.42 E
Ščekino 132 Jb 54.01N 37.29 E
Ščekurja 134 Jd 64.15N 60.52 E
Ščeljajur 136 Fb 65.21N 53.25 E
Scenic 186 Ee 43.47N 102.30W
Ščerbakty 136 He 52.29N 78.14 E
Schaalsee 120 Gc 53.35N 10.57 E
Schaarbeek/Schaerbeek 124 Gd 50.51N 4.23 E
Schaerbeek/Schaarbeek 124 Gd 50.51N 4.23 E
Schaffhausen 128 Cc 47.40N 8.40 E
Schaffhausen [2] 128 Cc 47.45N 8.40 E
Schagen 124 Gb 52.48N 4.48 E
Schärding 128 Hb 48.27N 13.26 E
Scharmützelsee 120 Kd 52.15N 14.03 E
Scharnhörn 120 Ec 53.57N 8.25 E
Scheeßel 124 La 53.10N 9.29 E
Schefferville 176 Md 54.47N 64.49W
Scheibbs 128 Jb 48.00N 15.10 E
Schelde 122 Kc 51.22N 4.15 E
Schelde (EN) = Escaut 122 Kc 51.22N 4.15 E
Schell Creek Range 182 Ed 39.10N 114.40W
Schenectady 182 Mc 42.48N 73.57W
Scheno 168 Fd 9.35N 39.25 E
Scherfede, Warburg- 124 Lc 51.32N 9.02 E
Scherpenheuvel-Zichem 124 Gd 50.59N 4.59 E
Scheveningen, 's-Gravenhage- 122 Kb 52.06N 4.18 E
Schiedam 122 Kc 51.55N 4.24 E
Schiermonnikoog 122 Ma 53.28N 6.15 E
Schifferstadt 124 Ke 49.23N 8.22 E
Schiffgraben 120 Hd 52.02N 11.10 E
Schifflange 124 Ie 49.30N 6.01 E
Schijndel 124 Hc 51.37N 5.28 E
Schiltigheim 122 Nf 48.36N 7.45 E
Schio 128 Fe 45.43N 11.21 E
Schipbeek 124 Ib 52.15N 6.14 E
Schladming 128 Hc 47.23N 13.41 E
Schlei 120 Fb 54.35N 9.50 E
Schleiden 120 Cf 50.32N 6.28 E
Schleiz 120 Hf 50.35N 11.49 E
Schleswig 120 Fb 54.31N 9.33 E
Schleswig-Holstein [2] 120 Gb 54.00N 10.30 E
Schlitz 120 Ff 50.40N 9.34 E
Schloß Holte-Stukenbrock 124 Kc 51.55N 8.38 E
Schloß Neuhaus, Paderborn- 124 Kc 51.44N 8.42 E
Schluchsee 120 Ei 47.49N 8.10 E
Schlüchtern 120 Ff 50.21N 9.31 E
Schmallenberg 124 Kc 51.09N 8.18 E
Schmallenberg-Bödefeld-Freiheit 124 Kc 51.15N 8.24 E
Schmallenberg-Oberkirchen 124 Kc 51.09N 8.18 E
Schmelz 124 Ie 49.26N 6.51 E
Schmida 128 Kb 48.20N 16.14 E
Schneeberg 120 Il 50.36N 12.38 E
Schneeberg [Aus.] 128 Jc 47.46N 15.52 E
Schneeberg [Ger.] 120 Hf 50.00N 11.51 E
Schneifel 124 Id 50.16N 6.23 E
Schoberpaß 128 Ic 47.27N 14.40 E
Schoberspitze 128 Ic 47.17N 14.09 E
Schœlcher 197h Ab 14.37N 61.06W
Schönebeck 120 Hd 52.01N 11.45 E
Schönecken 124 Id 50.10N 6.28 E
Schongau 120 Gi 47.49N 10.54 E
Schöningen 120 Gd 52.08N 10.57 E
Schoondijke 124 Fc 51.21N 3.33 E
Schoonebeek 124 Ib 52.40N 6.53 E
Schoonhoven 124 Gc 51.55N 4.51 E
Schorfheide 120 Jd 52.55N 13.35 E
Schoten 124 Gc 51.15N 4.30 E
Schotten 124 Ld 50.30N 9.08 E
Schouten Islands 208 Fe 3.30S 144.30 E
Schouwen 122 Jc 51.43N 3.50 E
Schramberg 120 Eh 48.14N 8.23 E
Schreiber 180 Ig 48.48N 87.15W
Schriesheim 124 Ke 49.29N 8.40 E
Schrobenhausen 120 Hh 48.33N 11.16 E
Schruns 128 Dc 47.04N 9.55 E
Schuls / Scuol 128 Ed 46.48N 10.17 E
Schultz Lake 180 Hd 64.45N 97.30W
Schurz 188 Fg 38.58N 118.46W
Schussen 120 Fi 47.37N 9.32 E
Schüttorf 124 Jb 52.19N 7.14 E
Schwabach 120 Hg 49.20N 11.02 E
Schwaben = Swabia (EN) 120 Gh 48.20N 10.30 E
Schwäbisch-Bayerisches Alpenvorland = Swabian-Bavarian Plateau (EN) 110 Hf 48.15N 10.30 E
Schwäbische Alb = Swabian Jura (EN) 110 Gf 48.25N 9.30 E
Schwäbisch Gmünd 120 Fh 48.48N 9.47 E
Schwäbisch Hall 120 Fg 49.06N 9.44 E
Schwalbach (Saar) 124 Ie 49.18N 6.49 E
Schwalm 120 Ff 50.45N 9.25 E
Schwalm 124 Lc 51.07N 9.24 E
Schwalmstadt 120 Ff 50.55N 9.12 E

Schwalmtal 124 Ic 51.15N 6.15 E
Schwandorf 120 Ig 49.20N 12.07 E
Schwaner, Pegunungan- 150 Fg 0.40S 112.40 E
Schwanewede 124 Ka 53.14N 8.36 E
Schwarzach 120 Ig 49.24N 12.09 E
Schwarzbach 124 Je 49.17N 7.40 E
Schwarze Elster 120 Ie 51.49N 12.51 E
Schwarzer Mann 124 Id 50.15N 6.22 E
Schwarzrand 172 Be 26.00S 17.10 E
Schwarzwald=Black Forest (EN) 110 Gf 48.05N 8.15 E
Schwarzwalder Hochwald 124 Ie 49.39N 6.55 E
Schwatka Mountains 178 Hc 67.25N 157.00W
Schwaz 128 Fc 47.20N 11.42 E
Schwechat 128 Kb 48.08N 16.28 E
Schwechat 128 Kb 48.08N 16.28 E
Schwedt / Oder 120 Kc 53.04N 14.18 E
Schweich 124 Ie 49.49N 6.45 E
Schweinfurt 120 Gf 50.03N 10.14 E
Schweiz / Suisse / Svizra / Svizzera = Switzerland (EN) [1] 112 Gf 46.00N 8.30 E
Schweizer-Reneke 172 De 27.11S 25.18 E
Schwelm 124 Jc 51.17N 7.17 E
Schwerin 120 Hc 53.38N 11.23 E
Schweriner See 120 Hc 53.45N 11.28 E
Schwerte 124 Jc 51.27N 7.34 E
Schwetzingen 124 Ke 49.23N 8.34 E
Schwielochsee 120 Kd 52.03N 14.12 E
Schwyz 128 Cc 47.03N 8.40 E
Schwyz [2] 128 Cc 47.10N 8.50 E
Sciacca 128 Hm 37.31N 13.03 E
Scicli 128 In 36.47N 14.42 E
Ščigry 136 De 51.53N 36.55 E
Scilly, Isles of- 110 Ff 49.57N 6.15W
Scioto River 184 Ff 38.44N 83.01W
Ščirec 120 Tg 49.34N 23.54 E
Scobey 188 Mb 48.47N 105.25W
Scordia 128 Im 37.18N 14.51 E
Scoresby Land 179 Jd 71.45N 26.30W
Scoresbysund 224 Md 70.35N 21.40W
Scoresby Sund 224 Md 70.20N 23.30W
Scorff 122 Cg 47.46N 3.21W
Ščors 136 De 51.48N 31.59 E
Scotia Ridge (EN) 106 Co 57.00S 45.00W
Scotia Sea (EN) 198 Lk 57.00S 40.00W
Scotland [2] 118 Ie 56.30N 4.30W
Scotland 110 Fd 56.30N 4.30W
Scotlandville 186 Kk 30.31N 91.11W
Scotstown 184 Lc 45.31N 71.17W
Scott 180 Gf 52.27N 108.23W
Scott, Cape- [Austl.] 212 Fb 13.30S 129.50 E
Scott, Cape- [B.C.-Can.] 180 Ef 50.47N 128.25W
Scott, Mount- 188 De 42.56N 122.01W
Scott Base 222 Kf 77.51S 166.46 E
Scottburgh 172 Ef 30.19S 30.40 E
Scott Channel 188 Aa 50.45N 128.30W
Scott City 186 Fg 38.29N 100.54W
Scott Coast 222 Kf 76.30S 162.30 E
Scott Glacier [Ant.] 222 Mg 85.45S 153.00W
Scott Glacier [Ant.] 222 He 66.15S 100.05 E
Scott Inlet 180 Kb 71.05N 71.05W
Scott Island 222 Le 67.24S 179.55W
Scott Islands 188 Aa 50.48N 128.40W
Scott Peak 188 Id 44.21N 112.50W
Scott Reef 212 Eb 14.00S 121.50 E
Scottsbluff 176 Ie 41.52N 103.40W
Scottsboro 184 Dh 34.40N 86.01W
Scottsburg 184 Ef 38.41N 85.46W
Scottsdale [Austl.] 212 Jh 41.10S 147.31 E
Scottsdale [Az.-U.S.] 182 Ee 33.30N 111.56W
Scotts Head 197g Bb 15.13N 61.23W
Scottsville 184 Dg 36.45N 86.11W
Scottville 184 Dd 43.59N 86.17W
Scranton 176 Le 41.24N 75.40W
Scrivia 128 Ce 45.03N 8.54 E
Scrub Cays 194 Ia 24.07N 76.55W
Scrub Island 197b Bb 18.17N 62.57W
Ščučin 132 Dc 53.39N 24.48 E
Ščučinsk 136 He 53.00N 70.11 E
Ščučja 134 Nc 66.45N 68.20 E
Ščučje 136 Gd 55.15N 62.43 E
Scugog, Lake- 184 Hc 44.10N 78.51W
Ščugor 134 Hd 64.12N 57.32 E
Scunthorpe 118 Mh 53.36N 0.38W
Scuol / Schuls 128 Ed 46.48N 10.17 E
Scutari (EN) = Shkodra 112 Hg 42.05N 19.30 E
Scutari, Lake- (EN) = Shkodrës, Liqen i- 110 Hg 42.10N 19.20 E
Scutari, Lake- (EN) = Skadarsko jezero 110 Hg 42.10N 19.20 E
Seaford 118 Nk 50.46N 0.06 E
Seahorse Point 180 Jd 63.47N 80.10W
Sea Islands 182 Ke 31.20N 81.20W
Seal 180 Ie 59.04N 94.47W
Seal Island 184 Nd 43.30N 66.01W
Sealpunt 158 Jl 34.06S 23.24 E
Searcy 186 Ki 35.15N 91.44W
Searles Lake 188 Gi 35.43N 117.20W
Seaside [Ca.-U.S.] 188 Eh 36.37N 121.50W
Seaside [Or.-U.S.] 188 Dc 46.01N 123.55W
Seattle 176 Ge 47.36N 122.20W
Seaward Kaikoura Range 218 Ee 42.15S 173.35 E
Seba 150 Hi 10.29S 121.50 E
Sébaco 194 Dg 12.51N 86.06W
Sebago Lake 184 Ld 43.50N 70.35W
Sebaiera 162 Ee 24.51N 13.02W
Sebaou 126 Ph 36.55N 3.51 E
Sebastian, Cape- 188 Ce 42.19N 124.26W
Sebastián Vizcaino, Bahía- 174 Hg 28.00N 114.30W
Sebastopol 188 Dg 38.24N 122.49W
Sebastopol (EN) = Sevastopol 112 Jg 44.36N 33.32 E
Sebatik, Pulau- 150 Gf 4.10N 117.45 E
Sebba 166 Fc 13.26N 0.32 E
Sebderat 168 Fb 15.27N 36.39 E
Sébé 170 Bc 1.02S 13.06 E
Šebekino 136 De 50.27N 37.00 E
Sébékoro 166 Dc 12.49N 8.50W
Seberi 204 Fh 27.29S 53.24W
Sebeş 130 Gd 45.58N 23.34 E
Sebeş 130 Gd 46.00N 23.34 E
Sebes-Körös 130 Dc 46.55N 20.59 E
Sebeşului, Munţii- 130 Gd 45.38N 23.27 E
Sebewaing 184 Fd 43.44N 83.27W
Sebež 136 Cd 56.19N 28.31 E
Sebha Oasis (EN) = Sabhā, Wāḥāt- 158 If 27.00N 14.25 E
Şebınkarahisar 146 Hb 40.18N 38.26 E
Sebino → Iseo, Lago d'- 128 Ee 45.45N 10.05 E
Sebiş 130 Fc 46.22N 22.07 E
Sebou 158 Ge 34.16N 6.41W
Sebring 184 Gl 27.30N 81.26W
Sebuku, Pulau- 150 Gg 3.30S 116.22 E
Šebunino 138 Jg 46.24N 141.56 E
Secas, Islas- 194 Gi 7.58N 82.02W
Secchia 128 Ee 45.04N 11.00 E
Sechura 202 Be 5.33S 80.51W
Sechura, Bahia de- 202 Be 5.40S 81.00W
Sechura, Desierto de- 202 Be 6.00S 80.30W
Seckau 128 Ic 47.16N 14.47 E
Seclin 124 Fd 50.33N 3.02 E
Secondigny 122 Fh 46.37N 0.25W
Secos, Ilhéus- 162 Cf 14.58N 24.40W
Secretary Island 218 Bf 45.15S 166.55 E
Sécure, Rio- 202 Fg 15.10S 64.52W
Šėda 126 Df 38.56N 8.03W
Seda 116 Kg 57.38N 25.12 E
Seda [Lat.] 116 Kg 57.32N 25.43 E
Seda [Lith.] 116 Jh 56.10N 22.00 E
Sedalia 182 Id 38.42N 93.14W
Sedan 122 Ke 49.42N 4.57 E
Sedanka 178a Eb 53.50N 166.10W
Sedano 126 Ib 42.43N 3.45W
Sedbergh 118 Kg 54.20N 2.31W
Seddenga 168 Ea 20.33N 30.18 E
Seddon 218 Fd 41.40S 174.04 E
Seddon, Kap- 179 Gc 75.20N 58.45W
Seddonville 218 Dd 41.33S 171.59 E
Seddülbahir 130 Ji 40.03N 26.10 E
Sedelnikovo 136 Hd 56.57N 75.18 E
Séderon 122 Lj 44.12N 5.32 E
Sédhiou 166 Bc 12.44N 15.33W
Sedini 128 Cj 40.51N 8.49 E
Šedok 132 Lg 44.13N 40.52 E
Sedom 146 Fg 31.04N 35.24 E
Sedona 188 Ji 34.52N 111.46W
Sedrata 128 Bn 36.08N 7.32 E
Sedro Woolley 188 Db 48.30N 122.14W
Šeduva 114 Fi 55.48N 23.45 E
Sée 122 Ef 48.39N 1.26W
Seeheim [Ger.] 124 Ke 49.46N 8.40 E
Seeheim [Nam.] 172 Be 26.50S 17.45 E
Seeis 172 Bd 22.29S 17.39 E
Seeland 128 Bc 47.05N 7.05 E
Seeling, Mount- 222 Og 82.28S 103.00W
Seelow 120 Kd 52.31N 14.23 E
Sées 122 Gf 48.36N 0.10 E
Seesen 120 Ge 51.54N 10.11 E
Seewarte Seamounts (EN) 158 Ee 33.00N 28.30W
Şefaatli 146 Fc 39.31N 34.46 E
Sefadu 166 Cd 8.39N 10.59W
Seferihisar 146 Bc 38.11N 26.51 E
Séféto 166 Dc 14.08N 9.51W
Sefid Dasht 146 Nf 32.09N 51.10 E
Sefrou 162 Gc 33.50N 4.50W
Sefuri-San 156 Be 33.26N 130.22 E
Segaf, Kepulauan- 150 Jg 2.10S 130.28 E
Ségalas 122 Ij 44.12N 2.26 E
Segamat 150 Df 2.30N 102.49 E
Segangane 126 Ii 35.10N 3.01W
Şegarcea 130 Ge 44.06N 23.45 E
Šegarka 136 De 57.16N 84.02 E
Segbana 166 Fc 10.56N 3.42 E
Segeg 168 Gd 7.40N 42.50 E
Segesta 128 Gm 37.55N 12.50 E
Segeža 112 Jc 63.44N 34.19 E
Seghe 219a Cc 8.25S 157.51 E
Seglinge 116 Id 60.15N 20.40 E
Segmon 116 Ee 59.17N 13.01 E
Segorbe 126 Le 39.51N 0.29W
Ségou 160 Gg 13.27N 6.15W
Ségou [3] 166 Dc 14.00N 6.20W
Segovia 126 Hd 40.57N 4.07W
Segovia [3] 126 Ic 41.10N 4.00W
Segovia, Rio- → Coco, Rio- 190 Hf 15.00N 83.08W
Segozero, ozero- 110 Jc 63.18N 33.45 E
Segré 122 Fg 47.41N 0.52W
Segre 126 Mc 41.40N 0.43 E
Seguam 178a Db 52.17N 172.30W
Séguédine 166 Ha 20.12N 12.59 E
Séguéla 166 Dd 7.57N 6.40W
Séguéla [3] 166 Dd 8.05N 6.32W
Seguin 182 Hf 29.34N 97.58W
Segula 178a Bb 52.01N 178.07 E
Segura 126 Lf 38.06N 0.38W
Segura, Sierra de- 126 Jf 38.00N 2.45W
Segura de la Sierra 126 Jf 38.18N 2.39W
Sehithwa 172 Cd 20.27S 22.42 E
Seia 126 Ed 40.25N 7.42W
Seibal 194 Be 16.27N 90.05W
Seiche 122 Eg 48.00N 1.46W
Seiland 114 Fa 70.25N 23.15 E
Seiling 186 Gh 36.09N 98.56W
Seille [Fr.] 122 Me 49.07N 6.11 E
Seille [Fr.] 122 Kh 46.31N 4.56 E
Sein, Ile de- 122 Bf 48.02N 4.51W
Seinäjoki 114 Fe 62.47N 22.50 E
Seine 110 Gf 49.26N 0.26 E
Seine, Baie de la-=Seine, Bay of the- (EN) 110 Ff 49.30N 0.30W
Seine, Bay of the- (EN) = Seine, Baie de la- 110 Ff 49.30N 0.30W
Seine, Val de- 122 Jf 48.30N 3.20 E
Seine-et-Marne [3] 122 If 48.30N 3.00 E
Seine-Maritime [3] 122 Ge 49.45N 1.00 E
Seine-Saint-Denis [3] 122 If 48.55N 2.30 E
Seine Seamount (EN) 110 Ei 33.45N 14.25W
Seini 130 Gb 47.45N 23.17 E
Seistan (EN) = Sīstān 140 If 30.30N 62.00 E
Seixal 126 Cf 38.38N 9.06W
Sejaha 138 Cb 70.10N 72.30 E
Sejerø 116 Di 55.55N 11.10 E
Sejerø Bugt 116 Di 55.50N 11.15 E
Sejm 110 Je 51.27N 32.34 E
Sejmčan 138 Kd 62.52N 152.27 E
Sejny 120 Tb 54.07N 23.20 E
Sekakes 172 Df 30.04S 28.21 E
Sekayu 150 Dg 2.50S 103.54 E
Sekenke 170 Fc 4.16S 34.10 E
Seki 156 Ed 35.28N 136.54 E
Šeki 136 Eg 41.10N 47.11 E
Seki 146 Cd 36.44N 29.33 E
Sekincau, Gunung- 150 Dh 5.05S 104.18 E
Seki-Zaki 156b Be 33.16N 131.54 E
Sekoma 172 Cd 24.36S 23.58 E
Sekondi-Takoradi 160 Gh 4.53N 1.45W
Sekota 168 Fc 12.37N 39.03 E
Šeksna 136 Dd 59.13N 38.32 E
Šelagski, mys- 138 Mb 70.10N 170.45 E
Selah 188 Ec 46.39N 120.32W
Selajar, Pulau- 150 Hh 6.05S 120.30 E
Selajar, Selat- 150 Hh 5.42S 120.28 E
Selangor [2] 150 Df 3.10N 101.30 E
Selaön 116 Ge 59.25N 17.10 E
Selaru, Pulau- 150 Jh 8.09S 131.00 E
Selatan, Cape- (EN) = Selatan, Tanjung- 140 Nj 4.10S 113.48 E
Selatan, Tanjung-=Selatan, Cape- (EN) 140 Nj 4.10S 113.48 E
Selawik 178 Gc 66.37N 160.03W
Selawik Lake 178 Hc 66.30N 160.40W
Selb 120 If 50.10N 12.08 E
Selbjørn 116 Ae 60.00N 5.10 E
Selbjørnsfjorden 116 Ae 59.55N 5.10 E
Selbu 116 Da 63.13N 11.02 E
Selbukta 222 Bf 71.40S 12.25W
Selbusjøen 116 Da 63.15N 10.55 E
Selby [Eng.-U.K.] 118 Lh 53.48N 1.04W
Selby [S.D.-U.S.] 186 Fd 45.31N 100.02W
Selco 132 Ic 53.23N 34.05 E
Selçuk 146 Bd 37.56N 27.22 E
Seldovia 178 Ie 59.27N 151.43W
Sele 128 Ij 40.29N 14.56 E
Sele, Piana del- 128 Ij 40.30N 14.55 E
Selebi-Pikwe 160 Jk 22.13S 27.58 E
Selečka Planina 130 Eh 41.05N 21.35 E
Šelehov 138 Ff 52.10N 104.01 E
Selemdža 140 Od 51.49N 128.53 E
Selencia 146 Kf 33.04N 44.33 E
Selendi 130 Lk 38.45N 28.53 E
Selendi 130 Lk 38.40N 28.41 E
Selenduma 138 Ff 50.55N 106.10 E
Selenga (Selenge) 140 Md 52.16N 106.16 E
Selenge [Mong.] 152 Hb 49.25N 103.59 E
Selenge [Zaire] 170 Cc 1.58S 18.11 E
Selenge→Selenga 140 Md 52.16N 106.16 E
Selenginsk 138 Ff 51.59N 106.57 E
Selenica 130 Ci 40.32N 19.38 E
Selennjah 138 Jc 67.55N 145.00 E
Sélestat 122 Nf 48.16N 7.27 E
Selety 136 He 53.06N 73.00 E
Seletyteniz, ozero- 136 He 53.15N 73.15 E
Seleucia 146 Kf 33.05N 44.35 E
Selevac 130 De 44.30N 20.53 E
Seleznevo 116 Md 60.44N 28.37 E
Selfoss 114a Bc 63.56N 21.00W
Seli 166 Cd 8.33N 12.48W
Sélibabi 162 Ef 15.10N 12.11W
Seliger, ozero- 136 Dd 57.20N 33.05 E
Seligman 188 Ii 35.20N 112.53W
Šelihova, zaliv- = Shelikhov Gulf (EN) 140 Rc 60.00N 158.00 E
Selimağa 130 Lj 39.35N 28.33 E
Selimiye 146 Bd 37.24N 27.40 E
Selingenstadt 124 Kd 50.03N 8.59 E
Selinunte 128 Gm 37.35N 12.48 E
Seližarovo 114 Hh 56.51N 33.29 E
Seljatin 130 Ib 47.52N 25.14 E
Selje 116 Ab 62.03N 5.22 E
Seljord 116 Bg 59.29N 8.37 E
Selkirk [Man.-Can.] 186 Ha 50.09N 96.52W
Selkirk [Scot.-U.K.] 118 Kf 55.33N 2.50W
Selkirk Mountains 180 Ff 50.00N 117.00W
Sella 126 Ga 43.28N 5.04W
Sellasia 130 Fl 37.10N 22.25 E
Selle 124 Fd 50.19N 3.23 E
Selles-sur-Cher 122 Hg 47.16N 1.33 E
Sells 188 Jk 31.55N 111.53W
Selm 124 Jc 51.42N 7.28 E
Selma [Al.-U.S.] 182 Je 32.25N 87.01W
Selma [Ca.-U.S.] 188 Fh 36.34N 119.37W
Selmer 184 Ch 35.11N 88.36W
Selmęt Wielki, Jezioro- 120 Sc 53.50N 22.30 E
Selon 114 Hg 58.14N 30.50 E
Selong 150 Gh 8.39S 116.32 E
Selsey 124 Bd 50.44N 0.47W
Selsey Bill 118 Mk 50.43N 0.48W
Seltz 124 Kf 48.53N 8.06 E
Selu, Pulau- 150 Jh 7.32S 130.54 E
Sélune 122 Ef 48.39N 1.26W
Selva 204 Ai 29.46S 62.03W
Selvagens, Ilhas- 158 Fe 30.05N 15.55W
Selvānā 146 Kd 37.25N 44.51 E
Selvas 198 Jf 5.00S 68.00W
Selway River 188 Hc 46.08N 115.36W
Selwyn, Détroit de- 219b Dc 16.04S 168.11 E
Selwyn Lake 180 He 60.00N 104.30W
Selwyn Mountains 174 Fc 63.10N 130.20W
Selwyn Range 208 Fg 21.35S 140.35 E
Selz 124 Ke 49.00N 8.02 E
Šemaha 132 Pi 40.39N 48.38 E
Semani 130 Ci 40.54N 19.26 E
Semara 160 Ff 26.44N 11.41W
Semarang 142 Nj 6.58S 110.25 E
Sematan 150 Ef 1.48N 109.46 E
Semau, Pulau- 150 Hi 10.13S 123.22 E
Sembakung 150 Gf 3.47N 117.30 E
Sembé 170 Bb 1.39N 14.36 E
Semberija 128 Nf 44.45N 19.10 E
Sembuan 150 Gg 0.19S 115.30 E
Semenicului, Munţii- 130 Fd 45.05N 22.05 E
Semenov 114 Kh 56.49N 44.29 E
Semenovka 132 Hc 52.11N 32.40 E
Semeru, Gunung- 140 Nj 7.58S 113.35 E
Semichi Islands 178a Db 52.42N 174.00 E
Semidi Islands 178 He 56.07N 156.44W
Semiluki 136 De 51.43N 39.02 E
Semily 120 Lf 50.36N 15.20 E
Seminoe Reservoir 188 Le 42.00N 106.50W
Seminole [Ok.-U.S.] 186 Hi 35.14N 96.14W
Seminole [Tx.-U.S.] 186 Ej 32.43N 102.39W
Seminole, Lake- 182 Ke 30.46N 84.50W
Semipalatinsk 142 Kd 50.28N 80.13 E
Semipalatinskaja oblast [3] 136 If 48.30N 80.10 E
Semirara Islands 150 .Hd 11.57N 121.27 E
Semīrom 146 Ng 31.22N 51.47 E
Semisopochnoi 178a Bb 52.00N 179.35 E
Semitau 150 Ff 0.33N 111.58 E
Semiun, Pulau- 150 Ef 4.31N 107.44 E
Semizbugy 136 He 50.12N 74.48 E
Semliki 158 Kh 1.14N 30.28 E
Semmering 128 Jc 47.38N 15.49 E
Semnān [3] 144 Hb 35.00N 53.30 E
Semnān 142 Hf 35.33N 53.24 E
Semnon 122 Eg 47.54N 1.45W
Semois 122 Ke 49.53N 4.45 E
Šemonaiha 136 Ie 50.39N 81.54 E
Semporna 150 Gf 4.28N 118.36 E
Semuda 150 Fg 2.51S 112.58 E
Semur-en-Auxois 122 Kg 47.29N 4.20 E
Senador Mourão 204 Kc 17.51S 43.22W
Senador Pompeu 202 Ke 5.35S 39.22W
Senaja 150 Ge 6.45N 117.03 E
Senaki (Miha Chakaja) 136 Eg 42.17N 42.02 E
Sena Madureira 202 Ee 9.04S 68.40W
Senanga 170 Df 16.07S 23.16 E
Senarpont 124 De 49.53N 1.43 E
Senatobia 186 Li 34.39N 89.58W
Sendai [Jap.] 142 Qf 38.15N 140.53 E
Sendai [Jap.] 154 Ki 31.49N 130.18 E
Sendai-Gawa [Jap.] 156 Bf 31.51N 130.12 E
Sendai-Gawa [Jap.] 156 Dd 35.34N 134.11 E
Sendai-Wan 154 Pe 38.10N 141.15 E
Senden 124 Jc 51.51N 7.30 E
Sendenhorst 124 Jc 51.50N 7.50 E
Senderg 146 Qi 26.52N 57.37 E
Seneca 186 Hg 39.50N 96.04W
Seneca Lake 184 Id 42.40N 76.57W
Sénégal=Senegal (EN) [1] 160 Fg 14.00N 14.00W
Sénégal=Senegal (EN) 158 Fg 15.48N 16.32W
Senegal (EN)=Sénégal [1] 160 Fg 14.00N 14.00W
Senegal (EN)=Sénégal 158 Fg 15.48N 16.32W
Sénégal Oriental [3] 166 Cc 13.30N 13.00W
Senekal 172 De 28.30S 27.32 E
Senetosa, Punta di- 122a Ab 41.33N 8.47 E
Seney 184 Eb 46.21N 85.56W
Senftenberg/Zły Komorow 120 Ke 51.31N 14.01 E
Sengata 142 Ni 0.28N 117.33 E
Sengilej 114 Lj 53.58N 48.46 E
Senguerr, Rio- 206 Gg 45.32S 68.54W
Sengwa 172 Dc 17.05S 28.03 E
Senhor do Bonfim 200 Lg 10.27S 40.11W
Senica 120 Nh 48.41N 17.23 E
Senigallia 128 Hg 43.43N 13.13 E
Senirkent 146 Dc 38.07N 30.33 E
Senj 128 If 45.00N 14.54 E
Senja 110 Hb 69.20N 17.30 E
Senjsko Bilo 128 Jf 44.55N 15.03 E
Senkaku-Shotō 152 Lf 25.45N 124.00 E
Şenkaya 146 Jb 40.35N 42.21 E
Senkevičevka 120 Vf 50.29N 25.05 E
Şenkursk 136 Ec 62.08N 42.53 E
Senlin Shan 154 Kc 43.12N 130.38 E
Senlis 122 Ie 49.12N 2.35 E
Senmonorom 148 Lf 12.27N 107.12 E
Senn, Dahr Ou- 162 Ef 17.55N 11.00W
Sennestadt, Bielefeld- 124 Kc 51.57N 8.35 E
Senneterre 180 Jg 48.24N 77.14W
Senno 114 Gi 54.47N 29.41 E
Sennoj 132 Oc 52.07N 46.59 E
Senorbi 128 Dk 39.32N 9.08 E
Senqu 172 Be 28.38S 16.27 E
Sens 122 Jf 48.12N 3.17 E
Sensée 124 Fd 50.16N 3.06 E
Sensuntepeque 194 Cg 13.52N 88.38W
Senta 130 Dd 45.56N 20.05 E
Sentinel Peak 180 Ff 54.58N 122.00W
Sentinel Range 222 Pf 78.10S 85.30W
Senyavin Islands 208 Gd 6.55N 158.00 E
Şenyurt 146 Id 37.06N 40.40 E
Senzaki-Wan 156 Bd 34.25N 131.20 E
Senžarka 134 Mi 54.45N 67.50 E
Seo de Urgel / la Seu d'Urgell 126 Nb 42.21N 1.28 E
Seoni 148 Fd 22.05N 79.32 E
Seoul (EN)=Sŏul 142 Of 37.34N 127.00 E
Séoune 122 Gj 44.10N 0.41 E
Sepanjang, Pulau- 150 Gh 7.10S 115.50 E
Separation Point 218 Ed 40.47S 173.00 E
Sepetovka 136 Ce 50.12N 27.04 E
Sepik River 208 Fe 3.51S 144.34 E
Sępólno Krajeńskie 120 Nc 53.28N 17.32 E
Sępopol 120 Qb 54.15N 21.00 E
Sępopolska, Nizina- 120 Rb 54.15N 21.10 E
Septemvri 130 Hg 42.13N 24.06 E
Septentrional, Cordillera- 194 Ld 19.35N 70.45W
Septeuil 124 Df 48.54N 1.41 E
Sept-Iles 176 Md 50.12N 66.23W
Sept Iles, Les- 122 Cf 48.53N 3.28W
Sepúlveda 126 Ic 41.18N 3.45W
Sequeros 126 Fd 40.31N 6.01W
Sequillo 126 Gc 41.45N 5.30W
Sera 156 Cd 34.36N 133.01 E
Sera, Pulau- 150 Jh 7.40S 131.05 E
Šerabad 136 Gh 37.43N 66.59 E
Šerabad 135 Ff 37.22N 67.03 E
Serafettin Dağları 146 Ic 39.05N 41.10 E
Serafimovič 132 Me 49.36N 42.47 E
Serahs 136 Gh 36.30N 61.13 E
Seraidi 128 Bn 36.55N 7.40 E
Seraing 122 Ld 50.36N 5.31 E
Seram 208 De 3.00S 129.00 E
Seram, Laut-=Ceram Sea (EN) 208 De 2.30S 128.00 E
Serang 150 Eh 6.07S 106.09 E
Serasan, Pulau- 150 Ef 2.30N 109.03 E
Serasan, Selat- 150 Ef 2.20S 109.00 E
Serbia (EN) = Srbija [2] 130 Df 44.00N 21.00 E
Serbia (EN) = Srbija 110 Ig 43.00N 21.00 E
Serbia (EN)=Srbija 130 Df 44.00N 21.00 E
Şercaia 130 Id 45.50N 25.08 E
Serchio 128 Eg 43.47N 10.16 E
Serdo 168 Gc 11.58N 41.18 E
Serdoba 132 Nc 52.34N 44.01 E
Serdobsk 136 Ee 52.29N 44.16 E
Sereba 168 Gc 13.12N 40.32 E
Serebrjansk 136 If 49.43N 83.20 E
Serebrjanski 114 Ib 68.52N 35.32 E
Sered' 120 Nh 48.17N 17.45 E
Seredka 116 Mf 58.10N 28.25 E
Şereflikoçhisar 146 Ec 38.56N 33.33 E
Serein 122 Jg 47.55N 3.31 E
Seremban 150 Df 2.43N 101.56 E
Serengeti Plain 170 Fc 2.50S 35.00 E
Serenje 170 Fe 13.14S 30.14 E
Šereševo 120 Ud 52.31N 24.19 E
Seret 132 De 48.38N 25.52 E
Serfopoúla 130 Hl 37.15N 24.36 E
Sergač 136 Ed 55.33N 45.28 E
Sergeievka 154 Lc 43.23N 133.22 E
Sergeja Kirova, ostrova- 138 Da 77.10N 90.00 E
Sergejevka [Russia] 154 Kb 44.20N 131.40 E
Sergejevka [Kaz.] 136 Ge 53.51N 67.28 E
Sergijev Posad (Zagorsk) 112 Jd 56.18N 38.08 E
Sergino 142 Ic 62.30N 65.40 E
Sergipe [2] 202 Kf 10.30S 37.10W
Sergokala 132 Oh 42.30N 47.40 E
Sergozero, ozero- 114 Ic 66.45N 36.50 E
Seria 150 Ff 4.37N 114.19 E
Serian 150 Ff 1.10N 110.34 E
Seriana, Val- 128 De 45.50N 9.50 E
Seribu, Kepulauan- 150 Fh 5.36S 106.33 E
Sérifontaine 124 De 49.21N 1.46 E
Sérifos 130 Hl 37.09N 24.30 E
Sérifos 130 Hl 37.10N 24.30 E
Serifou, Stenón- 130 Hl 37.15N 24.30 E
Serik 146 Dd 36.55N 31.06 E
Seringapatam Reef 212 Eb 13.40S 122.05 E
Serio 128 De 45.16N 9.45 E
Šerlovaja Gora 136 Gf 50.34N 116.18 E
Sermata, Kepulauan- 150 Ih 8.10S 128.40 E
Sermilik 179 Ie 66.00N 38.45W
Sernovodsk 114 Mj 53.54N 51.09 E
Sernur 114 Lh 56.57N 49.11 E
Sernyje Vody 114 Mj 53.53N 50.59 E
Sero 146 Kd 37.33N 44.40 E
Serock 120 Rd 52.31N 21.03 E
Serodino 204 Bk 32.37S 60.57W
Serov 142 Id 59.29N 60.31 E
Serowe 160 Jk 22.23S 26.43 E
Serpa 126 Eg 37.56N 7.36W
Serpent, Vallée du- 166 Dc 14.50N 8.00W
Serpentine Lakes 212 Fe 28.30S 129.10 E
Serpent's Mouth/Serpiente, Boca de la- 202 Fa 10.10N 61.58W
Serpiente, Boca de la-/Serpent's Mouth 202 Fa 10.10N 61.58W
Serpnevoje 130 Lc 46.23N 28.59 E
Serpuhov 112 Je 54.55N 37.25 E
Serra, Aparados da- 204 Hi 28.45S 49.45W
Serra Bonita 204 Ib 15.13S 46.49W
Serra das Araras 204 Jb 15.30S 45.21W
Serra do Navio 200 Ke 0.59N 52.03W
Serra do Salitre 204 Id 19.06S 46.41W
Serra Dourada 204 Ka 12.50S 43.56W
Sérrai 130 Gh 41.05N 23.33 E
Serralada Pirinenca=Pyrenees (EN) 110 Gg 42.40N 1.00 E
Serrana, Banco de- 190 Hf 14.23N 80.12W
Serranilla, Banco- 190 Ie 15.50N 79.50W
Serranópolis 204 Fd 18.16S 52.00W
Serra San Bruno 128 Kl 38.35N 16.20 E
Serrat, Cap- 162 Ib 37.14N 9.13 E
Serra Talhada 202 Ke 7.59S 38.18W
Serre 122 Je 49.41N 3.23 E
Serre, Massif de la- 122 Lg 47.10N 5.35 E
Serre-Ponçon, Lac de- 122 Mj 44.27N 6.16 E
Serres 122 Lj 44.26N 5.43 E
Serrezuela 206 Gd 30.38S 65.23W
Serrinha [Braz.] 202 Kg 16.23S 39.35W
Serrinha [Braz.] 202 Kf 11.39S 39.00W
Serriola, Bocca- 128 Gg 43.31N 12.21 E
Serro 204 Kd 18.37S 43.23W
Serrota 126 Gd 40.30N 5.04W
Serrote, Rio- 204 Ee 21.27S 54.40W
Sersou, Plateau du- 126 Ni 35.30N 2.00 E
Sertã 126 De 39.48N 8.06W
Sertão 198 Lg 10.00S 41.00W
Sertãozinho 204 Ie 21.08S 47.59W
Sértar 152 He 32.20N 100.20 E
Serti 166 Hd 7.30N 11.22 E
Serua, Pulau- 150 Jh 6.18S 130.01 E
Serui 150 Kg 1.53S 136.14 E
Serule 172 Dd 21.55S 27.19 E

Index Symbols

[1] Independent Nation
[2] State, Region
[3] District, County
[4] Municipality
[5] Colony, Dependency
Continent
Physical Region
Historical or Cultural Region
Mount, Mountain
Volcano
Hill
Mountains, Mountain Range
Hills, Escarpment
Plateau, Upland
Pass, Gap
Plain, Lowland
Delta
Salt Flat
Valley, Canyon
Crater, Cave
Karst Features
Depression
Polder
Desert, Dunes
Forest, Woods
Heath, Steppe
Oasis
Cape, Point
Coast, Beach
Cliff
Peninsula
Isthmus
Sandbank
Island
Atoll
Rock, Reef
Islands, Archipelago
Rocks, Reefs
Coral Reef
Well, Spring
Geyser
River, Stream
Waterfall, Rapids
River Mouth, Estuary
Lake
Salt Lake
Intermittent Lake
Reservoir
Swamp, Pond
Canal
Glacier
Ice Shelf, Pack Ice
Ocean
Sea
Gulf, Bay
Strait, Fjord
Lagoon
Bank
Seamount
Tablemount
Ridge
Shelf
Basin
Escarpment, Sea Scarp
Fracture
Trench, Abyss
National Park, Reserve
Point of Interest
Recreation Site
Cave, Cavern
Historic Site
Ruins
Wall, Walls
Church, Abbey
Temple
Scientific Station
Railway station
Airport
Port
Military installation
Lighthouse
Mine
Tunnel
Dam, Bridge

Sérvia 130 Ei 40.11N 22.00 E
Sêrxü 152 Ge 32.56N 98.02 E
Seryitsi 130 Ii 40.00N 25.10 E
Seryševo 138 Hf 51.02N 128.25 E
Sesayap 150 Gf 3.36N 117.15 E
Sesayap 150 Gf 3.36N 117.15 E
Sese 170 Eb 2.11N 25.47 E
Seseganaga Lake 186 Ka 50.10N 90.15W
Sese Islands 170 Fc 0.20S 32.20 E
Sesfontein 172 Ac 19.07S 13.39 E
Sesheke 170 Df 17.29S 24.18 E
Sesia 128 Ce 45.05N 8.37 E
Sesibi 168 Ea 20.05N 30.31 E
Sesimbra 126 Cf 38.26N 9.06W
Šešma 114 Mi 55.20N 51.12 E
Sesnut 116 Be 59.42N 7.21 E
s'Espalmador, Illa- / Espalmador, Isla- 126 Nf 38.47N 1.26 E
s'Espardell, Illa- / Espardell, Isla- 126 Nf 38.47N 1.27 E
Sessa Aurunca 128 Hi 41.14N 13.56 E
Ses Salines, Cap de-/ Salinas, Cabo de- 126 Pe 39.16N 3.03 E
Sestao 126 Ja 43.18N 3.00W
Sesto Fiorentino 128 Fg 43.50N 11.12 E
Sesto San Giovanni 128 De 45.32N 9.14 E
Sestriere 128 Af 44.57N 6.53 E
Sestri Levante 128 Df 44.16N 9.24 E
Sestroreck 114 Gf 60.06N 29.59 E
Šešupė 114 Fi 55.00N 22.10 E
Šešuvis 116 Ji 55.12N 22.31 E
Sesvenna, Piz- 128 Ed 46.42N 10.25 E
Sesvete 128 Ke 45.50N 16.07 E
Šeta/Šėta 116 Ki 55.14N 24.18 E
Šėta/Šeta 116 Ki 55.14N 24.18 E
Setaka 156 Be 33.09N 130.28 E
Setana 154 Oc 42.26N 139.51 E
Sète 122 Jk 43.24N 3.41 E
Sete de Setembro, Rio- 204 Fa 12.56S 52.51W
Sete Lagoas 202 Jg 19.27S 44.14W
Setenil 126 Gh 36.51N 5.11W
Sete Quedas, Ilha- → Grande, Ilha- 204 Ef 23.45S 54.03W
Sete Quedas, Saltos das- = Guaíra Falls (EN) 206 Jb 24.02S 54.16W
Setermoen 114 Eb 68.52N 18.28 E
Setesdal 114 Bg 59.05N 7.35 E
Setesdalsheiane 116 Be 59.30N 7.10 E
Seti 148 Gc 28.58N 81.06 E
Sétif 160 He 36.12N 5.24 E
Sétif [3] 162 Ib 36.05N 5.00 E
Seto 156 Ed 35.13N 137.05 E
Setonaikai=Inland Sea (EN) 140 Pf 34.10N 133.00 E
Setouchi 156b Ba 28.08N 129.20 E
Šetpe 136 Fg 44.06N 52.02 E
Settat 162 Fc 33.00N 7.37W
Settat [3] 162 Fc 33.00N 7.30W
Setté Cama 170 Ac 2.32S 9.45 E
Sette-Daban, hrebet- 138 Id 62.00N 138.00 E
Settle 118 Kg 54.04N 2.16W
Setúbal 112 Fh 38.32N 8.54W
Setúbal [2] 126 Df 38.20N 8.30W
Setúbal, Baía de- 126 Df 38.27N 8.53W
Setúbal o de Guadalupe, Laguna- 204 Bj 31.33S 60.35W
Seudre 122 Ei 45.48N 1.09W
Seugne 122 Fi 45.42N 0.32W
Seui 128 Dk 39.50N 9.19 E
Seuil-d'Argonne 124 Hf 48.58N 5.03 E
Seul, Lac- 174 Jd 50.20N 92.30W
Seulles 124 Be 49.20N 0.27W
Seurre 122 Lg 47.00N 5.09 E
Sevan 136 Eg 40.32N 44.57 E
Sevan, Lake- (EN) = Sevan, ozero- 110 Kg 40.20N 45.20 E
Sevan, ozero- = Sevan, Lake- (EN) 110 Kg 40.20N 45.20 E
Sévaré 166 Ec 14.32N 4.06W
Sevastopol = Sebastopol (EN) 112 Jg 44.36N 33.32 E
Ševčenko → Aktau 142 He 43.35N 51.05 E
Ševčenko, zaliv- 135 Ca 46.30N 60.15 E
Sevenoaks 118 Nj 51.16N 0.12 E
Sever 126 Ee 39.40N 7.32W
Sévérac-le-Château 122 Jj 44.19N 3.04 E
Severn 118 Kj 51.20N 3.10W
Severn [Can.] 174 Kd 56.02N 87.36W
Severn [U.K.] 118 Kj 51.35N 2.40W
Severnaja Dvina=Northern Dvina (EN) 110 Kc 64.32N 40.30 E
Severnaja Keltma 134 Ff 61.30N 54.00 E
Severnaja Pseašho, gora- 132 Lh 43.47N 40.30 E
Severnaja Sosva 136 Gc 64.10N 65.28 E
Severnaja Zemlja= Severnaya Zemlya (EN) 140 Lb 79.30N 98.00 E
Severnaya Zemlya (EN)= Severnaja Zemlja 140 Lb 79.30N 98.00 E
Severn Lake 180 If 53.52N 90.58W
Severnoje [Russia] 132 Rb 54.05N 52.32 E
Severnoje [Russia] 138 Ce 56.21N 78.23 E
Severny 136 Gb 67.38N 64.06 E
Severnyje Uvaly = Northern Uvales (EN) 110 Kd 59.30N 49.00 E
Severny Kommunar 134 Gg 58.23N 54.02 E
Severny Ledovity okean = Arctic Ocean (EN) 224 Be 85.00N 170.00 E
Severny Ural=Northern Urals (EN) 110 Lc 62.00N 59.00 E
Severobajkalsk 138 Fe 55.40N 109.25 E
Severočeský kraj [3] 120 Kf 50.35N 14.15 E
Severodoneck 132 Ke 48.57N 38.31 E
Severodvinsk 112 Jc 64.34N 39.50 E
Severo-Jenisejski 138 Ed 60.28N 93.01 E
Severo-Kazahstanskaja oblast [3] 136 Ge 54.30N 68.00 E
Severo-Krymski kanal 132 Ig 45.30N 34.35 E
Severo-Kurilsk 142 Rd 50.40N 156.08 E
Severomoravský kraj 120 Ng 49.45N 17.50 E
Severomorsk 136 Db 69.04N 33.24 E
Severo-Osetinskaja respublika 136 Eg 43.00N 44.10 E
Severo-Sibirskaja nizmennost = North Siberian Plain (EN) 140 Mb 72.00N 104.00 E
Severouralsk 136 Gc 60.09N 60.01 E
Sevier 188 Ig 38.35N 112.14W
Sevier Bridge Reservoir 188 Jg 39.21N 111.57W
Sevier Desert 188 Ig 39.25N 112.50W
Sevier Lake 182 Ed 38.55N 113.09W
Sevier River 182 Ed 39.04N 113.06W
Sevilla [3] 126 Gg 37.30N 5.30W
Sevilla [Col.] 202 Cc 4.16N 75.53W
Sevilla [Sp.] =Seville (EN) 112 Fh 37.23N 5.59W
Sevilla, Isla- 194 Fi 8.14N 82.24W
Seville (EN)=Sevilla [Sp.] 112 Fh 37.23N 5.59W
Sevlijevo 130 If 43.01N 25.06 E
Sèvre Nantaise 122 Eg 47.12N 1.33W
Sèvre Niortaise 122 Eh 46.18N 1.08W
Sevron 122 Lh 46.32N 5.16 E
Sevsk 132 Ic 52.08N 34.30 E
Sewa 166 Cd 7.18N 12.08W
Seward [Ak.-U.S.] 176 Ec 60.06N 149.26W
Seward [Nb.-U.S.] 186 Hf 40.55N 97.06W
Seward Peninsula 174 Cc 65.00N 164.00W
Sewell 206 Fd 34.05S 70.21W
Seyäkhal 146 Md 37.09N 49.52 E
Seybaplaya 192 Nh 19.39N 90.40W
Seybaplaya, Punta- 192 Nh 19.45N 90.42W
Seybouse, Oued- 128 Bn 36.53N 7.46 E
Seychelles [1] 160 Mi 8.00S 55.00 E
Seychelles Islands 158 Mi 4.35S 55.40 E
Seydān 146 Og 30.01N 53.01 E
Seydişehir 146 Dd 37.25N 31.51 E
Seyðisfjörður 112 Eb 65.16N 14.00W
Seyfe Gölü 146 Fc 39.13N 34.23 E
Seyf Tāleh 146 Le 35.57N 46.19 E
Seyhan 144 Db 36.43N 34.53 E
Seyitgazi 146 Dc 39.27N 30.43 E
Seyitömer 130 Mj 39.34N 29.52 E
Seyla' 168 Gc 11.21N 43.30 E
Seymour [Austl.] 212 Jg 37.02S 145.08 E
Seymour [In.-U.S.] 184 Ef 38.58N 85.53W
Seymour [Mo.-U.S.] 186 Jh 37.09N 92.46W
Seymour [S.Afr.] 172 Df 32.33S 26.46 E
Seymour [Tx.-U.S.] 182 He 33.35N 99.16W
Seyne-sur-Mer, La- 122 Lk 43.06N 5.53 E
Sezana 128 He 45.42N 13.52 E
Sézanne 122 Jf 48.43N 3.43 E
Sfaktiria 130 Em 36.56N 21.40 E
Sfax (EN)=Şafāqis 160 Ie 34.44N 10.46 E
Sfax (EN)=Şafāqis [3] 162 Jc 34.30N 10.30 E
Sferracavallo, Capo- 128 Dk 39.43N 9.40 E
Sfîntu Gheorghe [Rom.] 130 Id 45.52N 25.47 E
Sfîntu Gheorghe [Rom.] 130 Me 44.53N 29.26 E
Sfîntu Gheorghe, Braţul- 130 Me 44.53N 29.36 E
Sfîntu Gheorghe, Ostrovul- 130 Md 45.07N 29.22 E
Sfizef 126 Li 35.14N 0.15W
Shaanxi Sheng (Shaan-hsi Sheng)=Shensi (EN) [2] 152 Id 36.00N 109.00 E
Shaba [2] 170 Ed 8.30S 25.00 E
Sha'bah, Wādī ash- 146 Ij 25.59N 41.55 E
Shabeellaha Dhexe [3] 168 He 3.00N 46.00 E
Shabeellaha Hoose [3] 168 Ge 2.00N 44.40 E
Shabēlle, Webi-=Shebeli Webi (EN) 158 Lh 0.12S 42.45 E
Shabestar 146 Kc 38.11N 45.42 E
Shabunda 170 Ec 2.42S 27.20 E
Shache/Yarkant 142 Jf 38.24N 77.15 E
Shacheng → Huailai 152 Kc 40.29N 115.30 E
Shackleton Coast 222 Kg 82.00S 162.00 E
Shackleton Glacier 222 Lg 84.35S 176.15W
Shackleton Ice Shelf 222 He 66.00S 101.00 E
Shackleton Range 222 Ag 80.40S 26.00W
Shaddādī 146 Id 36.02N 40.45 E
Shādegān 146 Mg 30.40N 48.38 E
Shadwān, Jazīrat- 164 Fd 27.30N 33.55 E
Shaftesbury 118 Kk 51.01N 2.12W
Shagedu→Jungar Qi 152 Jd 39.37N 110.58 E
Shāghir Bazar 146 Id 36.52N 40.53 E
Shag Rocks 222 Rd 54.26S 36.33W
Shāh'Abbās 146 Oe 34.44N 52.10 E
Shah Alam 150 Df 3.05N 101.29 E
Shahdol 148 Gd 23.13N 81.18 E
Sha He [China] 154 Cf 37.09N 114.46 E
Sha He [China] 154 Ch 33.39N 114.38 E
Shahezhen → Linze 152 Hd 39.10N 100.21 E
Shah Jahān, Kūh-e- 146 Qd 37.02N 57.54 E
Shāhjahānpur 148 Fc 27.53N 79.55 E
Shah Kūh 144 Hb 36.35N 54.31 E
Shahmīrzād 146 Oe 35.47N 53.20 E
Shāhpūr 146 Nh 29.39N 51.03 E
Shāhpūr 146 Nh 32.50N 51.45 E
Shahrak 146 Nd 36.14N 50.40 E
Shahr-e-Bābak 146 Pg 30.10N 55.09 E
Shahr-e Khafr 146 Oh 28.56N 53.14 E
Shahr Kord 144 Hc 32.19N 50.50 E
Shāhrūd 146 Md 37.17N 48.43 E
Shahu, Kūh-e- 146 Le 34.45N 46.30 E
Shāh Zeyd 146 Od 36.13N 52.22 E
Shā'ib al Banāt, Jabal- 158 Kf 26.59N 33.29 E
Shā'īt, Wādī- 146 Ej 24.33N 33.01 E
Shakaga-Dake 156 Be 33.11N 130.53 E
Shakawe 160 Ji 18.23S 21.51 E
Shaker Heights 184 Ge 41.29N 81.36W
Shaki 166 Fd 8.40N 3.23 E
Shakotan-Dake 156a Bb 43.16N 140.26 E
Shakotan-Hantō 156a Bb 43.15N 140.30 E
Shakotan-Misaki 156a Bb 43.23N 140.28 E
Shaktoolik 178 Gd 64.20N 161.09W
Shāl 146 Me 35.54N 49.46 E
Shala, Lake- 168 Fd 7.29N 38.32 E
Shalamzār 146 Nf 32.02N 50.49 E
Shalānbōd 168 Ge 1.40N 44.42 E
Shalar, Nahr- 146 Ke 35.44N 45.45 E
Shaler Mountains 180 Gb 71.45N 111.00W
Shaliuhe → Gangca 152 Hd 37.30N 100.14 E
Shaluli Shan 140 Lf 30.45N 99.45 E
Shām, Bādiyat ash-=Syrian Desert (EN) 140 Ff 32.00N 40.00 E
Shām, Jabal ash- 140 Hg 23.10N 57.20 E
Shamattawa 180 Ie 55.52N 92.05W
Shambe 168 Ed 7.07N 30.46 E
Shambu 168 Fd 9.33N 37.07 E
Shamīl 146 Qi 27.30N 56.53 E
Shāmīyah 140 Ff 34.00N 39.59 E
Shammar, Jabal- 140 Gg 27.20N 41.45 E
Shamo, Lake- 168 Fd 5.50N 37.40 E
Shamokin 184 Ie 40.47N 76.34W
Shamrock 186 Fi 35.13N 100.15W
Shams 146 Pg 31.04N 55.02 E
Shamsī 168 Db 19.03N 29.54 E
Shamwa 172 Ec 17.18S 31.34 E
Shan [2] 148 Jd 22.00N 98.00 E
Shandan 142 Mf 38.50N 101.08 E
Shandī 160 Kg 16.42N 33.26 E
Shandian He 154 Dc 42.20N 116.20 E
Shandong Bandao= Shantung Peninsula (EN) 140 Of 37.00N 121.00 E
Shandong Sheng (Shan-tung Sheng) = Shantung (EN) [2] 152 Kd 36.00N 119.00 E
Shandūr Pass 148 Ea 36.04N 72.31 E
Shangani 172 Dc 19.42S 29.22 E
Shangani 172 Dc 18.30S 27.11 E
Shangbahe 154 Ci 30.39N 115.06 E
Shangcai 154 Ch 33.16N 114.15 E
Shangcheng 154 Ci 31.49N 115.24 E
Shangdu 152 Jc 41.31N 113.32 E
Shanggao 154 Cj 28.15N 114.55 E
Shanghai 142 Of 31.14N 121.28 E
Shanghai Shi (Shang-hai Shih) [5] 152 Le 31.14N 121.28 E
Shang-hai Shih→Shanghai Shi [5] 152 Le 31.14N 121.28 E
Shanghang 152 Kf 25.04N 116.21 E
Shanghe 154 Df 37.19N 117.09 E
Shanghekou 152 Lc 40.26N 124.51 E
Shangnan 152 Je 33.31N 110.50 E
Shangpaihe → Feixi 154 Di 31.42N 117.09 E
Shangqiu (Zhuji) 152 Ke 34.24N 115.37 E
Shangrao 152 Kf 28.29N 117.59 E
Shan Guan 152 Kf 27.28N 117.05 E
Shangxian 152 Ie 33.55N 109.57 E
Shangyi (Nanhaoqian) 154 Bd 41.06N 113.58 E
Shangyu (Baiguan) 154 Fi 30.01N 120.53 E
Shangzhi 152 Mb 45.13N 127.55 E
Shanhaiguan 154 Ed 40.01N 119.45 E
Shanhetun 154 Ib 44.43N 127.14 E
Shan-hsi Sheng → Shanxi Sheng = Shansi (EN) [2] 152 Jd 37.00N 112.00 E
Shanmatang Ding 152 Jg 24.45N 111.50 E
Shannon 218 Fd 40.33S 175.25 E
Shannon 179 Kc 75.20N 18.10W
Shannon/Aerfort na Sionainne 118 Ei 52.42N 8.57W
Shannon/An tSionainn 110 Fe 52.36N 9.41W
Shannon, Mount- 212 Ie 29.58S 141.30 E
Shannon, Mouth of the- 118 Di 52.30N 9.53W
Shanshan (Piqan) 152 Fc 42.52N 90.10 E
Shansi (EN)=Shan-hsi Sheng → Shanxi Sheng [2] 152 Jd 37.00N 112.00 E
Shansi (EN)=Shanxi Sheng (Shan-hsi Sheng) [2] 152 Jd 37.00N 112.00 E
Shansonggang 154 Ic 42.30N 126.13 E
Shanṭah, Ra's- 146 Qi 26.22N 56.26 E
Shantar Islands (EN) = Šantarskije ostrova 140 Pd 55.00N 137.36 E
Shantou 142 Ng 23.26N 116.42 E
Shantung (EN) = Shandong Sheng (Shan-tung Sheng) [2] 152 Kd 36.00N 119.00 E
Shantung Peninsula (EN)= Shandong Bandao 140 Of 37.00N 121.00 E
Shan-tung Sheng→Shandong Sheng [2] 152 Kd 36.00N 119.00 E
Shanxian 154 Dg 34.47N 116.05 E
Shanxi Sheng (Shan-hsi Sheng)=Shansi (EN) [2] 152 Jd 37.00N 112.00 E
Shanyin (Daiyue) 154 Be 39.30N 112.48 E
Shanyincheng 154 Be 39.27N 112.56 E
Shaoguan 142 Ng 24.57N 113.34 E
Shaoshan 152 Jf 27.55N 112.32 E
Shaowu 152 Kf 27.21N 117.29 E
Shaoxing 142 Og 30.00N 120.30 E
Shaoyang 142 Ng 27.13N 111.31 E
Shapinsay 118 Kb 59.03N 2.51W
Shaqlāwah 146 Kd 36.23N 44.18 E
Shaqq al Ju'ayfir 168 Db 15.16N 26.00 E
Shaqrā' 144 Gg 13.21N 45.42 E
Shaqū 146 Qi 27.14N 56.22 E
Sharāf 146 Jg 30.37N 43.45 E
Sharafah 168 Dc 12.04N 27.07 E
Sharafkhāneh 146 Kc 38.11N 45.29 E
Sharāh, Jibāl ash- 146 Fg 30.10N 35.30 E
Sharā 'Iwah 146 Oj 25.02N 52.14 E
Shareh 146 Kd 37.38N 44.50 E
Shari 152 Pc 43.55N 144.40 E
Shārī, Buḩayrat- 146 Ke 34.23N 44.07 E
Shari-Dake 156a Db 43.46N 144.43 E
Sharifābād [Iran] 146 Ne 35.25N 51.47 E
Sharifābād [Iran] 146 Nd 36.12N 50.08 E
Shark Bay 208 Cg 25.30S 113.30 E
Shark Bay (Denham) 212 Ce 25.55S 113.32 E
Sharm ash Shaykh 164 Fd 27.50N 34.16 E
Sharon 184 Ge 41.16N 80.30W
Sharon Springs 186 Fg 38.54N 101.45W
Sharqīyah, Aş Şaḥrā' ash- = Arabian Desert (EN) 158 Kf 28.00N 32.00 E
Sharshar, Jabal- 146 Dk 23.52N 30.20 E
Shary 144 Fd 27.15N 43.27 E
Shashe 172 Dd 21.24S 27.27 E
Shashemene 168 Fd 7.13N 38.36 E
Shashi 142 Nf 30.22N 112.11 E
Shashi 158 Jk 22.12S 29.21 E
Shasta, Mount- 174 Ge 41.20N 122.20W
Shasta Lake 182 Cc 40.50N 122.25W
Shāṭi', Wādī ash- 164 Bd 27.10N 13.25 E
Shattuck 186 Gh 36.16N 99.53W
Shaunavon 180 Gg 49.40N 108.25W
Shawan 152 Ec 44.21N 85.37 E
Shawano 186 Ld 44.47N 88.36W
Shawinigan 180 Kg 46.33N 72.45W
Shawnee 182 Hd 35.20N 96.55W
Shawneetown 186 Lh 37.42N 88.08W
Shaw River 212 Dd 20.20S 119.17 E
Shāwshāw, Jabal- 146 Ci 26.03N 28.56 E
Shayang 154 Bi 30.42N 112.34 E
Shaybārā 146 Gj 25.25N 36.51 E
Shaykh Ahmad 146 Lf 32.53N 46.26 E
Shaykh Fāris 146 Lf 32.05N 47.36 E
Shaykh Sa'd 146 Lf 32.34N 46.17 E
Shaykh 'Uthmān 144 Fg 12.52N 44.59 E
Shebar, Kowtal-e- 144 Kc 34.54N 68.14 E
Shebele, Wabē-=Shebeli Webi (EN) 158 Lh 0.12S 42.45 E
Shebeli Webi (EN)= Shabēlle, Webi- 158 Lh 0.12S 42.45 E
Shebeli Webi (EN)= Shebele, Wabē- 158 Lh 0.12S 42.45 E
Sheberghān 142 If 36.41N 65.45 E
Sheboygan 186 Me 43.46N 87.44W
Shebshi Mountains 158 Ih 8.30N 11.45 E
Shedin Peak 180 Ee 55.50N 127.00W
Sheelin, Lough-/Loch Sileann 118 Fh 53.48N 7.20W
Sheenjek 178 Kc 66.45N 144.33W
Sheep Haven/Cuan na gCaorach 118 Ff 55.10N 7.52W
Sheep Mountain 188 Hj 32.32N 114.14W
Sheep Range 188 Hh 36.45N 115.05W
Sheerness 118 Nj 51.27N 0.45 E
Sheffield [Al.-U.S.] 184 Dh 34.46N 87.40W
Sheffield [Eng.-U.K.] 112 Fe 53.23N 1.30W
Sheffield [Tx.-U.S.] 186 Fk 30.41N 101.50W
Shefford 124 Bb 52.02N 0.20W
Shek Hasan 168 Fc 12.04N 35.53 E
Shek Husen 168 Gd 7.45N 40.42 E
Shelburne [N.S.-Can.] 180 Kh 43.46N 65.19W
Shelburne [Ont.-Can.] 184 Gc 44.04N 80.12W
Shelby [Mt.-U.S.] 182 Eb 48.30N 111.51W
Shelby [N.C.-U.S.] 184 Gh 35.17N 81.32W
Shelbyville [Il.-U.S.] 186 Lg 39.24N 88.48W
Shelbyville [In.-U.S.] 184 Ef 39.31N 85.47W
Shelbyville [Tn.-U.S.] 184 Dh 35.29N 86.27W
Shelbyville, Lake- 186 Lg 39.30N 88.40W
Sheldon 186 Ie 43.11N 95.51W
Sheldon Point 178 Gd 63.32N 164.52W
Shelikhov Gulf (EN) = Šelihova, zaliv- 140 Rc 60.00N 158.00 E
Shelikof Strait 178 Ie 57.30N 155.00W
Shell 188 Ld 44.33N 107.44W
Shellbrook 180 Gf 53.13N 106.24W
Shellharbour 210 Gh 34.35S 150.52 E
Shelter Point 218 Cg 47.06S 168.13 E
Shelton 188 Dc 47.13N 123.06W
Shenandoah 186 If 40.46N 95.22W
Shenandoah Mountain 184 Hf 38.58N 79.00W
Shenandoah Valley 184 Hf 38.45N 78.45W
Shenchi 154 Be 39.05N 112.11 E
Shendam 166 Gd 8.53N 9.32 E
Shending Shan 152 Nb 46.34N 133.27 E
Shenge 166 Cd 7.55N 12.57W
Shëngjini 130 Ch 41.49N 19.35 E
Shengsi (Caiyuanzhen) 154 Gi 30.42N 122.29 E
Shengsi Liedao 152 Le 30.45N 122.40 E
Shengxian 152 Lf 29.35N 120.45 E
Shengze 154 Fi 30.55N 120.39 E
Shenjiamen → Putuo 154 Gj 29.57N 122.18 E
Shenmu 152 Jd 38.52N 110.35 E
Shenqiu (Huaidian) 152 Ke 33.27N 115.05 E
Shensi (EN)=Shaan-hsi Sheng→Shaanxi Sheng [2] 152 Id 36.00N 109.00 E
Shensi (EN)=Shaanxi Sheng (Shaan-hsi Sheng) [2] 152 Id 36.00N 109.00 E
Shenton, Mount- 212 Ee 28.00S 123.22 E
Shenxian 154 Ce 38.01N 115.33 E
Shenyang 142 Oe 41.48N 123.24 E
Shenze 154 Ce 38.11N 115.11 E
Shepherd, Iles-=Shepherd Islands (EN) 219b Dc 16.55S 168.35 E
Shepherd Islands (EN)= Shepherd, Iles- 219b Dc 16.55S 168.35 E
Shepparton 210 Fh 36.23S 145.25 E
Sheppey 118 Nj 51.24N 0.50 E
Shepshed 124 Ab 52.45N 1.17W
Sheqi 154 Bh 33.04N 112.56 E
Sherard, Cape- 180 Jb 74.36N 80.10W
Sherard Osborn Fjord 179 Gb 82.10N 51.30W
Sherborne 118 Kk 50.57N 2.31W
Sherbro Island 158 Fh 7.33N 12.42W
Sherbrooke 176 Le 45.24N 71.54W
Sherda 168 Ba 20.08N 16.45 E
Shere Hill 166 Gd 9.57N 9.03 E
Sheridan [Mt.-U.S.] 188 Id 45.27N 112.12W
Sheridan [Wy.-U.S.] 176 Ie 44.48N 106.58W
Sheridan Lake 186 Eg 38.30N 102.15W
Sheringham 118 Oi 52.57N 1.12 E
Sherman 182 He 33.38N 96.36W
Sherman Station 184 Mc 45.54N 68.26W
Sherridon 180 He 55.07N 101.05W
Sherwood Forest 118 Lh 53.10N 1.10W
She Shui 154 Ci 30.52N 114.22 E
Shetland [3] 118 La 60.30N 1.30W
Shetland Islands (Zetland) 110 Fc 60.30N 1.30W
Shewa [3] 168 Fd 9.20N 38.55 E
Shewa Gimira 168 Fd 7.00N 35.50 E
Shexian 154 Bf 36.33N 113.40 E
Shexian (Huicheng) 154 Ej 29.53N 118.27 E
Sheyang (Hede) 154 Fh 33.47N 120.15 E
Sheyenne River 182 Hb 47.05N 96.50W
Shiant Islands 118 Gd 57.54N 6.30W
Shibām 168 Hb 15.56N 48.38 E
Shibamīnah, Wādī- 144 Ie 22.12N 55.30 E
Shibata [Jap.] 154 Of 37.57N 139.20 E
Shibata [Jap.] 156 Gb 38.05N 140.50 E
Shibayama-Gata 156 Ec 36.21N 136.23 E
Shibazhan 152 Ma 42.28N 125.20 E
Shibecha 154 Rc 43.17N 144.36 E
Shibetsu [Jap.] 154 Rc 43.40N 145.08 E
Shibetsu [Jap.] 152 Pc 44.10N 142.23 E
Shibetsu-Gawa 156a Db 43.40N 145.06 E
Shibin al Kawm 164 Fc 30.33N 31.01 E
Shibiutan 156a Ca 44.47N 142.35 E
Shibi-Zan 156 Bf 31.59N 130.22 E
Shīb Kūh 144 Hd 27.20N 52.40 E
Shibukawa 154 Of 36.29N 139.00 E
Shibushi 156 Bf 31.28N 131.07 E
Shibushi-Wan 156 Ki 31.25N 131.12 E
Shichinohe 156 Ga 40.41N 141.10 E
Shichiyo Islands 220d Bb 7.23N 151.40 E
Shidao 152 Ld 36.51N 122.18 E
Shido 156 Dd 34.19N 134.10 E
Shidongsi → Gaolan 152 Hd 36.23N 103.55 E
Shiel, Loch- 118 He 56.50N 5.50W
Shiga Ken [2] 154 Ng 35.15N 136.10 E
Shi He 154 Ch 32.32N 115.52 E
Shihezi 152 Ec 44.18N 86.02 E
Shiiba 156 Be 32.28N 131.09 E
Shijaku 130 Ch 41.20N 19.34 E
Shijiazhuang 142 Nf 38.00N 114.30 E
Shijiusuo 154 Eg 35.24N 119.32 E
Shika 156 Ec 37.01N 136.46 E
Shikabe 156a Bb 42.02N 140.47 E
Shikārpur 148 Dc 27.57N 68.38 E
Shiki Islands 220d Bb 7.24N 151.53 E
Shikine-Jima 156 Fd 34.19N 139.13 E
Shikoku 140 Pf 33.30N 133.30 E
Shikoku Basin (EN) 152 Oe 30.00N 135.30 E
Shikoku-Sanchi 156 Ce 33.45N 133.35 E
Shikotan-Tō / Šikotan, ostrov- 138 Jh 43.47N 146.45 E
Shilabo 168 Gd 6.05N 44.45 E
Shiliguri 142 Kg 26.42N 88.26 E
Shiliu → Changjiang 152 Ih 19.20N 109.03 E
Shilla 148 Fb 32.24N 78.12 E
Shillong 142 Lg 25.34N 91.53 E
Shimabara 154 Kh 32.47N 130.22 E
Shimabara-Hantō 156 Be 32.45N 130.15 E
Shimabara-Wan 156 Be 32.50N 130.30 E
Shimada 156 Fd 34.49N 138.09 E
Shima-Hantō 156 Ed 34.25N 136.45 E
Shimane-Hantō 156 Cd 35.30N 133.00 E
Shimane Ken [2] 154 Lg 35.00N 132.20 E
Shimanto-Gawa 156 Ce 32.56N 133.00 E
Shimaura-Tō 156 Bd 34.50N 131.50 E
Shimian 152 Hf 29.10N 102.26 E
Shimizu [Jap.] 154 Og 35.01N 138.29 E
Shimizu [Jap.] 154 Og 35.01N 138.29 E
Shimla 142 Jf 31.06N 77.10 E
Shimoda 154 Og 34.40N 138.57 E
Shimodate 156 Fc 36.19N 139.58 E
Shimoga 142 Jh 13.55N 75.34 E
Shimo-Jima 156 Be 32.25N 130.05 E
Shimokawa 156a Ca 44.18N 142.38 E
Shimokita-Hantō 156a Bc 41.15N 141.05 E
Shimo-Koshiki-Jima 156 Af 31.40N 129.40 E
Shimo la Tewa 170 Gc 3.57S 39.44 E
Shimoni 170 Gc 4.39S 39.23 E
Shimonoseki 152 Ne 33.57N 130.57 E
Shimono-Shima 156 Ad 34.15N 129.15 E
Shimotsu 156 Dd 34.07N 135.08 E
Shimotsuma 156 Fc 36.11N 139.58 E
Shin, Loch- 118 Ic 58.07N 4.32W
Shinano 156 Fc 36.47N 138.10 E
Shinano-Gawa 156 Fc 37.57N 139.04 E
Shināş 146 Qj 24.43N 56.27 E
Shindand 144 Jc 33.18N 62.08 E
Shinga 170 Dc 3.16S 24.38 E
Shingbwiyang 148 Jc 26.41N 96.13 E
Shingū 152 Oe 33.44N 135.59 E
Shingwidzi 172 Ed 23.01S 30.43 E
Shinji 156 Cd 35.24N 132.54 E
Shinji-Ko 156 Cd 35.27N 133.02 E
Shinjō 152 Pd 38.46N 140.18 E
Shinkafe 166 Gc 13.05N 6.31 E
Shinminato 156 Ec 36.47N 137.04 E
Shinnanyō 156 Bd 34.05N 131.45 E
Shinshiro 156 Ed 34.53N 137.30 E
Shintoku 154 Qc 43.12N 142.55 E
Shin-tone-Gawa 156 Gd 35.57N 140.27 E
Shintotsugawa 156a Bb 43.32N 141.40 E
Shinyanga 160 Ki 3.40S 33.26 E
Shinyanga [3] 170 Fc 3.30S 33.00 E
Shiogama 156 Gb 38.19N 141.01 E
Shiojiri 154 Nf 36.06N 137.58 E
Shiokubi-Misaki 156a Bc 41.43N 140.57 E
Shio-no-Misaki 152 Oe 33.25N 135.45 E
Shipai → Huaining 154 Di 30.25N 116.39 E
Shiping 152 Hg 23.44N 102.28 E
Shipki La 152 Ce 31.49N 78.45 E
Shippegan 180 Lg 47.45N 64.42W
Shiprock 186 Bh 36.47N 108.41W
Shipshaw, Rivière- 184 La 48.30N 71.15W
Shipu 154 Fj 29.17N 121.57 E
Shipugi Shankou 152 Ce 31.49N 78.45 E
Shiquan 152 Ie 33.05N 108.15 E
Shiquanhe 142 Jf 32.29N 79.52 E
Shiquan He 152 Ce 32.28N 79.44 E
Shiragami Dake 156 Ga 40.30N 140.01 E
Shiragami-Misaki 154 Pd 41.25N 140.12 E
Shirahama 156 De 33.40N 135.20 E
Shirakawa [Jap.] 154 Pf 37.07N 140.13 E
Shirakawa [Jap.] 156 Ed 35.36N 137.12 E

Shirakawa [Jap.] 156 Ec 36.17N 136.53 E
Shirane-San [Jap.] 156 Fd 35.40N 138.13 E
Shirane-San [Jap.] 152 Od 36.48N 139.22 E
Shirane-San [Jap.] 156 Fc 36.38N 138.32 E
Shiranuka 154 Rc 42.57N 144.05 E
Shiraoi 154 Pc 42.31N 141.16 E
Shirase Coast 222 Mf 78.30S 156.00W
Shirataka 156 Gb 38.11N 140.06 E
Shirataki 156a Cb 43.53N 143.09 E
Shīrāz 142 Hg 29.36N 52.32 E
Shirbīn 146 Dg 31.11N 31.32 E
Shire 158 Kj 17.42S 35.19 E
Shiren 154 Id 41.54N 126.34 E
Shiretoko-Dake 156a Da 44.15N 145.14 E
Shiretoko-Hantō 156a Da 44.00N 145.00 E
Shiretoko-Misaki 152 Qc 44.21N 145.20 E
Shīrgāh 146 Od 36.17N 52.54 E
Shiribetsu-Gawa 156a Bb 42.52N 140.21 E
Shiriha-Misaki 156a Db 42.56N 144.45 E
Shirikishinai 156a Bc 41.48N 141.05 E
Shīrīn 146 Qi 27.10N 56.41 E
Shīrīn sū 146 Me 35.29N 48.27 E
Shiriya-Zaki 152 Pc 41.26N 141.28 E
Shīr Kūh 140 Hf 31.37N 54.04 E
Shirley Mountains 188 Le 42.15N 106.30W
Shiroishi 154 Pe 38.00N 140.37 E
Shirone 156 Fc 37.46N 139.00 E
Shirotori 156 Ed 35.53N 136.52 E
Shirouma-Dake 156 Fc 36.45N 137.46 E
Shirshov Ridge (EN) 138 Me 57.30N 171.00 E
Shīrvān 144 Ib 37.24N 57.55 E
Shīrvān 146 Lf 33.33N 46.49 E
Shirwan Mazīn 146 Kd 37.03N 44.10 E
Shishaldin Volcano 174 Cd 54.45N 163.57W
Shishi-Jima 156 Be 32.17N 130.15 E
Shishmaref 178 Fc 66.14N 166.09W
Shishou 152 Jf 29.42N 112.23 E
Shitai (Qili) 154 Di 30.12N 117.28 E
Shitara 156 Ed 35.05N 137.34 E
Shithāthah 146 Jf 32.33N 43.29 E
Shitou Shan 152 Ma 51.02N 125.12 E
Shivwits Plateau 188 Ih 36.10N 113.40W
Shiwa 154 Pe 39.33N 141.35 E
Shiwan Dashan 152 Ig 21.45N 107.35 E
Shiwa Ngandu 170 Fe 11.12S 31.43 E
Shiwpuri 148 Fc 25.26N 77.39 E
Shixian 154 Jc 43.05N 129.46 E
Shiyan 152 Je 32.34N 110.48 E
Shiyang He 152 Hd 39.00N 103.25 E
Shizilu → Jūnan 154 Eg 35.10N 118.50 E
Shizugawa 156 Gb 38.40N 141.28 E
Shizui 154 Ic 43.03N 126.09 E
Shizuishan (Dawukou) 152 Id 39.03N 106.24 E
Shizukuishi 156 Gb 39.42N 140.59 E
Shizunai 154 Qc 42.20N 142.22 E
Shizunai-Gawa 156a Cb 42.20N 142.22 E
Shizuoka 142 Pf 34.58N 138.23 E
Shizuoka Ken [2] 154 Og 35.00N 138.25 E
Shkodra = Scutari (EN) 112 Hg 42.05N 19.30 E
Shkodrës, Liqen i- = Scutari, Lake- (EN) 110 Hg 42.10N 19.20 E
Shkumbini 130 Ch 41.01N 19.26 E
Shoal Lake 186 Fa 50.26N 100.34W
Shoal Lake 186 Ib 49.32N 95.00W
Shoal Lakes 186 Ha 50.20N 97.40W
Shōbara 154 Lg 34.51N 133.01 E
Shodo-Shima 156 Dd 34.30N 134.15 E
Shō-Gawa 156 Ec 36.47N 137.04 E
Shokanbetsu-Dake 156a Bb 43.43N 141.31 E
Shokotsu-Gawa 156a Ca 44.23N 143.17 E
Sholāpur → Solāpur 142 Jh 17.41N 75.55 E
Shoqān 146 Qd 37.20N 56.58 E
Shoranūr 148 Ff 10.46N 76.17 E
Shoreham-by-Sea 118 Mk 50.49N 0.16W
Shortland Islands 214 Fi 6.55S 155.53 E
Shosambetsu 156a Ba 44.32N 141.46 E
Shoshone 188 He 42.56N 114.24W
Shoshone Mountains 182 Dd 39.15N 117.25W
Shoshone Peak 188 Gh 36.56N 116.16W
Shoshone River 188 Kd 44.52N 108.11W
Shoshong 172 Dd 23.02S 26.31 E
Shoshoni 188 Ke 43.14N 108.07W
Shotor Khūn 144 Jc 34.20N 64.55 E
Shouchang 154 Ej 29.23N 119.12 E
Shouguang 154 Ef 36.53N 118.44 E
Shouxian (Shouyang) 154 Dh 32.35N 116.47 E
Shouyang → Shouxian 154 Dh 32.35N 116.47 E
Shōwa 156 Gb 39.51N 140.03 E
Show Low 188 Ji 34.15N 110.02W
Shqiperia = Albania (EN) [1] 112 Hg 41.00N 20.00 E
Shreveport 176 Jf 32.30N 93.45W
Shrewsbury 118 Ki 52.43N 2.45W
Shropshire [3] 118 Ki 52.40N 2.50W
Shuangcheng 152 Mb 45.21N 126.17 E
Shuangjiang → Tongdao 152 If 26.14N 109.45 E
Shuangliao 152 Lc 43.30N 123.30 E
Shuangyang 152 Mc 43.31N 125.28 E
Shuangyashan 142 Pe 46.37N 131.10 E
Shucheng 154 Di 31.28N 116.57 E
Shufu 152 Cd 39.27N 75.52 E
Shuguri Falls 170 Gd 8.31S 37.23 E
Shu He 154 Eg 34.07N 118.30 E
Shuicheng 152 Hf 26.34N 104.52 E
Shuiding → Huocheng 152 Dc 44.03N 80.49 E
Shuiji → Laixi 154 Ff 36.52N 120.31 E
Shuijiahu → Changfeng 154 Dh 32.29N 117.10 E
Shuikou → Jianghua 152 Jg 24.58N 111.56 E
Shuiye 154 Cf 36.08N 114.06 E
Shuizhai → Xiangcheng 154 Ch 33.27N 114.53 E
Shūl 146 Ng 30.10N 51.38 E
Shulan 152 Mc 44.26N 126.55 E
Shule 152 Cd 39.25N 76.06 E
Shule He 140 Le 40.20N 92.50 E
Shulu (Xinji) 154 Cf 37.56N 115.14 E
Shumagin Islands 178 He 55.07N 159.45W
Shumarinai-Ko 156a Ca 44.20N 142.13 E
Shunayn, Sabkhat- 164 Dc 30.10N 21.00 E
Shungnak 178 Hc 66.53N 157.02W
Shunyi 154 Dd 40.09N 116.38 E
Shuolong 152 Ig 22.51N 106.55 E
Shuoxian 152 Jd 39.18N 112.25 E
Shūr [Iran] 146 Oh 28.12N 52.09 E
Shūr [Iran] 146 Oh 28.33N 53.12 E
Shūr [Iran] 146 Ne 35.09N 51.30 E
Shūr [Iran] 146 Pi 26.59N 55.47 E
Shurāb 146 Ic 33.07N 55.18 E
Shūr Āb 146 Pg 31.45N 55.15 E
Shurugwi 172 Dc 19.40S 30.00 E
Shūsf 144 Jc 31.48N 60.01 E
Shūsh 146 Mf 32.12N 48.17 E
Shūsh = Susa (EN) 146 Mf 32.12N 48.17 E
Shushica 130 Ci 40.34N 19.34 E
Shūshtar 144 Gc 32.03N 48.51 E
Shuswap Lake 188 Fa 50.57N 119.15W
Shūt 146 Oe 34.44N 52.53 E
Shuwak 168 Fc 14.23N 35.52 E
Shuyang 152 Ke 34.01N 118.52 E
Shuzenji 156 Fd 34.58N 138.55 E
Shwebo 148 Jd 22.34N 95.42 E
Shwell 148 Jd 23.56N 96.17 E
Shyok 148 Fa 35.13N 75.53 E
Sia 150 Jh 6.49S 134.19 E
Siagne 122 Mk 43.32N 6.57 E
Siāh Band 144 Jc 32.25N 62.35 E
Siāh-Chashmeh 146 Kc 39.04N 44.23 E
Siāh-Kūh 146 Oe 34.38N 52.16 E
Siak 150 Df 1.13N 102.09 E
Sialkot 142 Jf 32.30N 74.31 E
Sianów 120 Mb 54.15N 16.16 E
Siantan, Pulau- 150 Ef 3.10N 106.15 E
Siargao 150 Ie 9.53N 126.02 E
Šiaškotan, ostrov- 140 Re 48.49N 154.06 E
Siátista 130 Ei 40.16N 21.33 E
Siau, Pulau- 150 If 2.42N 125.24 E
Šiauliai 112 Id 55.53N 23.19 E
Šiauliai/Šjauljaj 112 Id 55.53N 23.19 E
Siavonga 170 Ef 16.32S 28.43 E
Siazan 136 Eg 41.04N 49.06 E
Sibā'i, Jabal as- 164 Fd 25.43N 34.09 E
Sibaj 136 Fe 52.42N 58.39 E
Sibari, Cassano allo Ionio- 128 Kk 39.45N 16.27 E
Sibasa 172 Ed 22.56S 30.29 E
Šibenik 128 Jg 43.44N 15.53 E
Siberimanua 150 Cg 2.09S 99.34 E
Siberut, Pulau- 140 Lj 1.20S 98.55 E
Siberut, Selat- 150 Cg 0.42S 98.35 E
Sibi 148 Dc 29.33N 67.53 E
Sibigo 150 Cf 2.51N 95.55 E
Sibillini, Monti- 128 Hh 42.55N 13.15 E
Sibircatajaha 134 Lb 69.05N 64.43 E
Sibircevo 138 Ih 44.16N 132.20 E
Sibirjakova, ostrov- 138 Cb 72.50N 79.00 E
Sibiti 170 Bc 3.41S 13.21 E
Sibiu 112 If 45.48N 24.09 E
Sibiu [2] 130 Hd 45.46N 24.12 E
Sibolga 142 Li 1.45N 98.48 E
Sibsāgar 148 Ic 26.59N 94.38 E
Sibu 142 Ni 2.18N 111.49 E
Sibuguey Bay 150 He 7.30N 122.40 E
Sibut 160 Ih 5.44N 19.05 E
Sibutu Islands 150 Gf 4.45N 119.20 E
Sibutu Passage 150 Gf 4.56N 119.36 E
Sibuyan 150 Hd 12.25N 122.34 E
Sibuyan Sea 150 Hd 12.50N 122.40 E
Siby 166 Dc 12.22N 8.22W
Sibyllenstein 120 Ke 51.12N 14.05 E
Sicani, Monti- 128 Hm 37.40N 13.15 E
Sicasica 202 Eg 17.22S 67.45W
Si Chon 148 Jg 9.00N 99.56 E
Sichuan Pendi 140 Mf 30.01N 105.00 E
Sichuan Sheng (Ssu-ch'uan Sheng) = Szechwan (EN) [2] 152 He 30.00N 103.00 E
Sicilia [2] 128 Im 37.45N 14.15 E
Sicilia = Sicily (EN) 110 Hh 37.30N 14.00 E
Sicilia, Canale di- = Sicily, Strait of- (EN) 110 Hh 37.20N 11.20 E
Sicilia, Mar di- 128 Gn 36.30N 13.00 E
Sicily (EN) = Sicilia 110 Hh 37.30N 14.00 E
Sicily, Strait of- (EN) = Sicilia, Canale di- 110 Hh 37.20N 11.20 E
Sicily, Strait of- (EN) = Tūnis, Canal de- 110 Hh 37.20N 11.20 E
Sico Tinto, Rio- 194 Ef 15.58N 84.58W
Sicuani 200 Ig 14.15S 71.15W
Šid 130 Cd 45.08N 19.14 E
Sidamo [3] 168 Fd 5.48N 38.50 E
Siddipet 148 Fe 18.06N 78.51 E
Side 146 Dd 36.46N 31.22 E
Sidéradougou 166 Ec 10.40N 4.15W
Siderno 128 Kl 38.16N 16.18 E
Siders/Sierre 128 Bd 46.17N 7.32 E
Šiderty 136 He 51.40N 74.50 E
Šiderty 136 He 52.32N 74.50 E
Sidheros, Ákra- 130 Jn 35.19N 26.19 E
Sidhirókastron 130 Gh 41.14N 23.23 E
Sīdī 'Abd ar Raḥmān 146 Cg 30.58N 28.44 E
Sidi Aïch 126 Qh 36.37N 4.41 E
Sidi Akacha 126 Nh 36.28N 1.18 E
Sidi Ali 126 Mh 36.06N 0.25 E
Sīdī 'Alī al Makkī, Ra's- 128 Em 37.11N 10.17 E
Sīdī Barrānī 164 Ec 31.36N 25.55 E
Sidi Bel Abbes 162 Gb 35.12N 0.38W
Sidi Bel Abbes [3] 162 Gc 34.45N 0.35W
Sidi Bennour 162 Fc 32.39N 8.26W
Sidi di Daoud 126 Ph 36.51N 3.52 E
Sidi Ifni 160 Ff 29.33N 10.10W
Sidi Kacem 162 Fc 34.13N 5.42W
Sidikalang 150 Cf 2.45N 98.19 E
Sidi Lakhdar 126 Mh 36.10N 0.27 E
Sīdī Zayd, Jabal- 128 En 36.29N 10.20 E
Sidlaw Hills 118 Ke 56.30N 3.00W
Sidmouth 118 Jk 50.41N 3.15W
Sidney [B.C.-Can.] 180 Fg 48.39N 123.24W
Sidney [Mt.-U.S.] 182 Gb 47.43N 104.09W
Sidney [Nb.-U.S.] 182 Gc 41.09N 102.59W
Sidney [Oh.-U.S.] 184 Ee 40.16N 84.10W
Sidney Lanier, Lake- 184 Fh 34.15N 83.57W
Sidobre 122 Ik 43.40N 2.30 E
Sidorovsk 138 Dc 66.35N 82.30 E
Sidra 120 Tc 53.33N 23.30 E
Sidra, Gulf of- (EN) = Surt, Khalīj- 158 Ie 31.30N 18.00 E
Sidrolândia 204 Ee 20.55S 54.58W
Siedlce 120 Sd 52.11N 22.16 E
Siedlce [2] 120 Sd 52.10N 22.15 E
Siedlecka, Wysoczyzna- 120 Sd 52.10N 22.15 E
Sieg [Ger.] 120 Df 50.45N 7.05 E
Sieg [Ger.] 124 Kd 50.55N 8.01 E
Siegburg 120 Df 50.48N 7.12 E
Siegen 120 Ef 50.52N 8.02 E
Siemiatycze 120 Sd 52.26N 22.53 E
Siĕmréab 148 Kf 13.22N 103.51 E
Siena 128 Fg 43.19N 11.21 E
Sieniawa 120 Sf 50.11N 22.36 E
Sienne 122 Ee 49.00N 1.34W
Sieradz 120 Oe 51.36N 18.45 E
Sieradz [2] 120 Oe 51.35N 18.45 E
Sieradzka, Niecka- 120 Oe 51.35N 18.50 E
Sierck-les-Bains 124 Ie 49.26N 6.21 E
Sierpc 120 Pd 52.52N 19.41 E
Sierra Blanca 186 Dk 31.11N 105.21W
Sierra Blanca Peak 182 Fe 33.23N 105.48W
Sierra Colorada 206 Gf 40.35S 67.48W
Sierra Leone [1] 160 Fh 8.30N 11.30W
Sierra Leone Basin (EN) 106 Di 5.00N 17.00W
Sierra Leone Rise (EN) 106 Di 5.30N 21.00W
Sierra Mojada 190 Dc 27.17N 103.42W
Sierre/Siders 128 Bd 46.17N 7.32 E
Siete Palmas 204 Cg 25.13S 58.20W
Siete Puntas, Rio- 204 Df 23.34S 57.20W
Şieu 130 Hb 47.11N 24.13 E
Sifié 166 Dd 7.59N 6.55W
Sífnos 130 Hm 37.00N 24.40 E
Sig 162 Gb 35.32N 0.11W
Siğacik Körfezi 130 Jk 38.12N 26.45 E
Sigean 122 Ik 43.02N 2.59 E
Sighetu Marmaţiei 130 Gb 47.56N 23.53 E
Sighişoara 130 Hc 46.13N 24.48 E
Sigli 150 Ce 5.23N 95.57 E
Siglufjörður 114a Ba 66.09N 18.55W
Sigmaringen 120 Fh 48.05N 9.13 E
Signal Peak 188 Hj 33.22N 114.03W
Signy Island 222 Re 60.43S 45.38W
Signy-l'Abbaye 124 Ge 49.42N 4.25 E
Signy-le-Petit 124 Ge 49.54N 4.17 E
Sigtuna 114 Dg 59.37N 17.43 E
Siguanea, Ensenada de la- 194 Fc 21.38N 83.05W
Siguatepeque 194 Df 14.32N 87.49W
Sigüenza 126 Jc 41.04N 2.38W
Siguiri 160 Gg 11.25N 9.10W
Sigulda 114 Fh 57.09N 24.53 E
Si He 154 Dg 35.11N 116.42 E
Sihong 154 Eh 33.28N 118.13 E
Sihote-Alin 140 Pe 48.00N 138.00 E
Sihou → Changdao 154 Ff 37.56N 120.42 E
Sihuas 202 Ce 8.34S 77.37W
Siikainen 116 Ic 61.52N 21.50 E
Siilinjärvi 114 Ge 63.02N 27.40 E
Siirt 144 Fb 37.56N 41.57 E
Sijunjung 150 Dg 0.42S 100.58 E
Sikaiana 219a Fc 8.22S 162.45 E
Sikakap 150 Dg 2.46S 100.13 E
Sīkān 146 Lf 33.10N 47.39 E
Sikanni Chief 180 Fe 58.17N 121.46W
Sīkar 148 Fc 27.37N 75.09 E
Sikasso 160 Gg 11.20N 5.40W
Sikasso [3] 166 Dc 10.55N 7.00W
Sikéa [Grc.] 130 Gi 40.03N 23.58 E
Sikéa [Grc.] 130 Fm 36.46N 22.56 E
Sikeston 182 Jd 36.53N 89.35W
Sikinos 130 Im 36.50N 25.05 E
Sikkim [3] 148 Hc 27.50N 88.30 E
Siklós 120 Ok 45.51N 18.18 E
Sikonge 170 Fd 5.38S 32.46 E
Šikotan, ostrov- / Shikotan-Tō 138 Jh 43.47N 146.45 E
Siktjah 138 Hc 69.55N 125.10 E
Sil 126 Eb 42.27N 7.43W
Sila Grande 128 Kk 39.20N 16.30 E
Sila Greca 128 Kk 39.30N 16.30 E
Šilalė/Šilalė 114 Fi 55.29N 22.12 E
Šilalė/Šilalė 114 Fi 55.29N 22.12 E
Silao 192 Ig 20.56N 101.26W
Silaogou 154 Be 39.59N 113.03 E
Sila Piccola 128 Kk 39.05N 16.35 E
Silba 128 If 44.23N 14.42 E
Silchar 148 Id 24.49N 92.48 E
Šilda 132 Ud 51.47N 59.50 E
Silgadapet 116 Ab 62.05N 5.10 E
Şile 146 Cb 41.05N 29.35 E
Sile 128 Ge 45.28N 12.35 E
Silega 136 Ec 64.03N 44.02 E
Silesia (EN) = Śląsk 110 He 51.00N 16.45 E
Silesia (EN) = Śląsk 120 Me 51.00N 16.45 E
Silet 162 He 22.39N 4.35 E
Silhouette Island 172b Ca 4.29S 55.14 E
Silifke 144 Db 36.22N 33.56 E
Siligir 138 Gc 68.27N 114.50 E
Siling Co 140 Kf 31.50N 89.00 E
Siling Jiao 150 Ge 8.20N 115.27 E
Silisili, Mauga- 221c Aa 13.35S 172.27W
Silistra 130 Ke 44.07N 27.16 E
Silistra [2] 130 Kf 44.07N 27.16 E
Silivri 146 Cb 41.04N 28.15 E
Siljan 114 Df 60.50N 14.45 E
Šilka 138 Gf 51.51N 116.02 E
Šilka 140 Od 53.22N 121.32 E
Silkeborg 114 Bh 56.10N 9.34 E
Sillamäe/Sillamjae 114 Gg 59.24N 27.43 E
Sillamjae/Sillamäe 114 Gg 59.24N 27.43 E
Sillaro 128 Ff 44.34N 11.51 E
Silleiro, Cabo- 126 Db 42.07N 8.54W
Sillé-le-Guillaume 122 Ff 48.12N 0.08W
Sillian 128 Gd 46.45N 12.25 E
Sillil 168 Gc 11.00N 43.26 E
Siloam Springs 186 Ih 36.11N 94.32W
Siloana Plains 170 Df 17.15S 23.10 E
Šilovo 136 Ee 54.24N 40.52 E
Silsbee 186 Ik 30.21N 94.11W
Siltou 168 Bb 16.52N 15.43 E
Šilutė/Šilute 136 Cd 55.21N 21.30 E
Šilute/Šilutė 136 Cd 55.21N 21.30 E
Silvan 146 Ic 38.08N 41.01 E
Silvassa 148 Ed 20.20N 73.05 E
Silver Bank (EN) 194 Mc 20.30N 69.45W
Silver Bank Passage 194 Lc 21.00N 70.15W
Silver Bay 182 Ib 47.17N 91.16W
Silver City 182 Fe 32.46N 108.17W
Silverdalen 116 Fg 57.32N 15.44 E
Silver Lake 188 Ee 43.06N 120.53W
Silver Spring 184 If 39.02N 77.03W
Silver Springs 188 Fg 39.25N 119.13W
Silverthrone Mountain 188 Ba 51.31N 126.06W
Silverton [Co.-U.S.] 186 Ch 37.49N 107.40W
Silverton [Tx.-U.S.] 186 Fi 34.28N 101.19W
Silves [Braz.] 202 Gd 2.54S 58.27W
Silves [Port.] 126 Dg 37.11N 8.26W
Silvi 128 Ih 42.34N 14.06 E
Silvia 202 Cc 2.37N 76.24W
Silvies River 188 Fe 43.22N 118.48W
Silvretta 128 Ed 46.50N 10.15 E
Silyānah 162 Ib 36.05N 9.22 E
Silyānah [3] 162 Ib 36.00N 9.30 E
Silyānah, Wādī- 128 Dn 36.33N 9.25 E
Sim 134 Hi 54.59N 57.41 E
Sim 134 Hi 54.32N 56.30 E
Sim, Cap- 162 Fc 31.23N 9.51W
Simanggang 150 Ff 1.15N 111.26 E
Šimanovsk 138 Hf 52.01N 127.36 E
Simao 152 Hg 22.40N 101.02 E
Simard, Lac- 184 Hb 47.38N 78.40W
Simareh 146 Mf 32.08N 48.03 E
Simav 146 Cc 39.05N 28.59 E
Simav 144 Ca 40.23N 28.31 E
Simav Dağ 130 Lj 39.04N 28.54 E
Simav Gölü 130 Lj 39.09N 28.55 E
Simayama-Jima 156 Ae 32.40N 128.38 E
Simba 170 Db 0.36N 22.55 E
Simbo 170 Fc 4.53S 29.44 E
Simbo 219a Cc 8.18S 156.34 E
Simbruini, Monti- 128 Hj 41.55N 13.15 E
Simcoe 184 Gd 42.50N 80.18W
Simcoe, Lake- 180 Jh 44.27N 79.20W
Simen 168 Fc 13.25N 38.00 E
Simenti 166 Cc 13.00N 13.25W
Simeto 128 Jm 37.24N 15.06 E
Simeulue, Pulau- 140 Li 2.35N 96.05 E
Simferopol 112 Jf 44.57N 34.06 E
Simi 130 Km 36.36N 27.50 E
Simi 130 Km 36.35N 27.50 E
Simiti 194 Kj 7.58N 73.58W
Simitli 130 Gh 41.53N 23.06 E
Simla → Shimla 142 Jf 31.06N 77.10 E
Şimleu Silvaniei 130 Fb 47.14N 22.48 E
Simmental 128 Bd 46.35N 7.25 E
Simmerath 124 Id 50.36N 6.18 E
Simmerbach 124 Je 49.48N 7.31 E
Simmern (Hunsrück) 120 Dg 49.59N 7.31 E
Simmertal 124 Je 49.48N 7.33 E
Simnas 116 Jj 54.20N 23.45 E
Simo 114 Fd 65.39N 24.55 E
Simojärvi 114 Gc 66.06N 27.03 E
Simojoki 114 Fd 65.37N 25.03 E
Simojovel de Allende 192 Mi 17.12N 92.38W
Simonstown 172 Bf 34.14S 18.26 E
Simpele 114 Gf 61.26N 29.22 E
Simpelejärvi 116 Mc 61.30N 29.25 E
Simplon Pass 128 Bd 46.15N 8.00 E
Simpson Desert 208 Eg 25.00S 137.00 E
Simpson Hill 212 Fe 26.30S 126.30 E
Simpson Peninsula 180 Ic 68.45N 89.10W
Simrishamn 114 Di 55.33N 14.20 E
Simsonbaai 197b Ab 18.02N 63.08W
Simušir, ostrov- 140 Re 46.58N 152.02 E
Sina 148 Fe 17.22N 75.54 E
Sīnā' = Sinai Peninsula (EN) 158 Kf 29.30N 34.00 E
Sinabang 150 Cf 2.29N 96.23 E
Sinadogo 168 Hd 5.22N 46.22 E
Sinai, Mount- (EN) = Mūsa, Jabal- 146 Eh 28.32N 33.59 E
Sinaia 130 Id 45.21N 25.33 E
Sinai Peninsula (EN) = Sīnā' 158 Kf 29.30N 34.00 E
Sinajana 220c Bb 13.28N 144.45W
Sinaloa [2] 190 Cc 25.00N 107.30W
Sinaloa, Llanos de- 190 Cc 25.00N 107.30W
Sinaloa, Rio- 192 Ee 25.18N 108.30W
Sinaloa de Leyva 192 Ee 25.50N 108.14W
Sinalunga 128 Fg 43.12N 11.44 E
Sinamaica 202 Da 11.05N 71.51W
Sinan 152 If 27.56N 108.11 E
Sinara 134 Kh 56.17N 62.23 E
Sināwin 164 Bc 31.02N 10.36 E
Sinazongwe 170 Ef 17.15S 27.28 E
Şincai 130 Hc 46.39N 24.23 E
Sincanli 146 Dc 38.45N 30.15 E
Sincé 194 Ji 9.14N 75.06W
Sincelejo 200 Ie 9.18N 75.24W
Sinch'am 154 Jc 42.07N 129.25 E
Sinch'ang 154 Jd 40.07N 128.28 E
Sinch'on 154 He 38.28N 125.27 E
Sinclair, Lake- 184 Fi 33.11N 83.16W
Sind 148 Dc 25.30N 69.00 E
Sind [3] 140 Ig 25.30N 69.00 E
Sindal 116 Dg 57.28N 10.13 E
Sindangbarang 150 Eh 7.27S 107.08 E
Sindara 170 Bc 1.02S 10.40 E
Sindfeld 124 Kc 51.32N 8.48 E
Sindi 114 Fg 58.24N 24.42 E
Sındırgı 146 Cc 39.14N 28.10 E
Sındırgı Geçidi 130 Lj 39.10N 28.04 E
Sindominic 130 Ic 46.35N 25.47 E
Sindri 148 Hd 23.42N 86.29 E
Sinegorje 138 Kd 62.03N 150.25 E
Šine-Ider 152 Gb 48.56N 99.33 E
Sinekli 130 Lh 41.14N 28.12 E
Sinelnikovo 132 Ie 48.18N 35.31 E
Sines 126 Dg 37.57N 8.52W
Sines, Cabo de- 126 Dg 37.57N 8.53W
Sine-Saloum [3] 166 Bc 14.00N 15.50W
Singako 168 Bd 9.50N 19.29 E
Singapore / Singapura [1] 142 Mi 1.17N 103.51 E
Singapore Strait (EN) = Singapura, Selat- 150 Df 1.15N 104.00 E
Singapura / Singapore [1] 142 Mi 1.17N 103.51 E
Singapura, Selat- = Singapore Strait (EN) 150 Df 1.15N 104.00 E
Singaraja 150 Gh 8.07S 115.06 E
Singatoka 219d Ac 18.08S 177.30 E
Sing Buri 148 Kf 14.53N 100.25 E
Singen 120 Ei 47.46N 8.50 E
Singeroz Băi 130 Hb 47.22N 24.41 E
Singida 160 Ki 4.49S 34.45 E
Singida [3] 170 Fd 5.30S 34.30 E
Singitic Gulf (EN) = Singitikós Kólpos 130 Gi 40.10N 23.55 E
Singitikós Kólpos = Singitic Gulf (EN) 130 Gi 40.10N 23.55 E
Singkaling Hkamti 148 Jc 26.00N 95.42 E
Singkang 150 Hg 4.08S 120.01 E
Singkawang 150 Ef 0.54N 109.00 E
Singkep, Pulau- 150 Dg 0.30S 104.25 E
Singkil 150 Cf 2.17N 97.49 E
Singleton [Austl.] 212 Kf 32.34S 151.10 E
Singleton [Eng.-U.K.] 124 Bd 50.55N 0.44W
Singleton, Mount- 212 De 29.28S 117.18 E
Singö 116 Hd 60.10N 18.45 E
Siniscola 128 Dj 40.34N 9.41 E
Sini vrăh 130 Ih 41.51N 25.01 E
Sinj 128 Kg 43.42N 16.38 E
Sinjah 168 Ec 13.09N 33.56 E
Sinjai 150 Hh 5.07S 120.15 E
Sinjaja 116 Mg 57.05N 28.33 E
Sinjajevina 130 Cf 43.00N 19.18 E
Sinjār 146 Id 36.19N 41.52 E
Sinjār, Jabal- 146 Id 36.23N 41.52 E
Sinjuža 132 Ge 48.03N 30.50 E
Sinkiang Uighur (EN) = Xinjiang Uygur Zizhiqu (Hsin-chiang-wei-wu-erh Tzu-chih-ch'ü) [2] 152 Ec 42.00N 86.00 E
Sin-le-Noble 124 Fd 50.22N 3.07 E
Sinmi-Do 154 He 39.33N 124.53 E
Sinn 124 Kd 50.39N 8.20 E
Sinn al Kadhdhāb 164 Fe 23.30N 32.05 E
Sinnamary 202 Hb 5.23N 53.00W
Sinni 128 Kj 40.08N 16.41 E
Sînnicolau Mare 130 Dc 46.05N 20.38 E
Sinnūris 146 Dh 29.25N 30.52 E
Sinnyŏng 154 Jf 36.02N 128.47 E
Sinoe [3] 166 Dd 5.20N 8.40W
Sinoe, Lacul- 130 Le 44.38N 28.53 E
Sinop 144 Ea 41.59N 35.09 E
Sinop Burun 146 Fa 42.02N 35.12 E
Sinp'o 154 Jd 40.02N 128.12 E
Sinsang 154 Ie 39.39N 127.25 E
Sinsheim 120 Eg 49.15N 8.53 E
Sint-Amandsberg, Gent- 124 Fc 51.04N 3.45 E
Sîntana 130 Ec 46.21N 21.30 E
Sint-Andries, Brugge- 124 Fc 51.12N 3.10 E
Sintang 150 Ff 0.04N 111.30 E
Sint Eustatius 190 Le 17.30N 62.59W
Sint-Gillis-Waas 124 Gc 51.13N 4.08 E
Sint Kruis 196 Bf 12.18N 69.08W
Sint Laureins 124 Fc 51.15N 3.31 E
Sint Maarten 190 Le 18.04N 63.04W
Sint Nicolaas 196 Bf 12.26N 69.55W
Sint Niklaas/Saint-Nicolas 122 Kc 51.10N 4.08 E
Sint-Oedenrode 124 Hc 51.34N 5.28 E
Sinton 186 Hl 28.02N 97.33W
Sint-Pieters-Leeuw 124 Gd 50.47N 4.14 E
Sintra 126 Cf 38.48N 9.23W
Sint-Truiden/Saint-Trond 122 Ld 50.49N 5.12 E
Sintu 168 Fd 8.12N 36.56 E
Sinú, Rio- 194 Ji 9.24N 75.49W
Sinŭiju 142 Oe 40.06N 124.24 E
Sinujif 168 Hd 8.30N 48.59 E
Sinzig 124 Jd 50.33N 7.15 E
Sió 120 Oj 46.23N 18.40 E
Siocon 150 He 7.42N 122.08 E
Siófok 120 Oj 46.54N 18.03 E
Sioma 170 Df 16.40S 23.35 E
Sion/Sitten 128 Bd 46.15N 7.20 E
Siorapaluk 178 Ec 77.39N 71.00W
Sioule 122 Jh 46.22N 3.19 E
Sioux City 176 Je 42.30N 96.23W
Sioux Falls 176 Je 43.32N 96.44W
Sioux Lookout 180 If 50.06N 91.55W
Sipalay 150 He 9.45N 122.24 E
Šipan 128 Lh 42.43N 17.54 E
Siparia 196 Fg 10.08N 61.30W
Šipčenski prohod 130 Ig 42.46N 25.19 E
Siping 142 Oe 43.11N 124.24 E
Sipiwesk 180 He 55.27N 97.24W
Sipiwesk Lake 180 He 55.05N 97.35W
Siple, Mount- 222 Nf 73.15S 126.06W
Siple Coast 222 Mg 82.00S 153.00W
Siple Island 222 Nf 73.39S 125.00W
Siple Station 222 Pf 75.55S 83.55W
Sipolilo 172 Ec 16.39S 30.42 E
Sipora, Pulau- 150 Cg 2.12S 99.40 E
Sippola 116 Ld 60.44N 27.00 E
Siqueira Campos 204 Hf 23.42S 49.50W
Siquia, Rio- 194 Eg 12.09N 84.13W
Siquijor 150 He 9.13N 123.31 E
Siquisique 202 Ea 10.34N 69.42W

Index Symbols

[1] Independent Nation
[2] State, Region
[3] District, County
[4] Municipality
[5] Colony, Dependency
Continent
Physical Region
Historical or Cultural Region
Mount, Mountain
Volcano
Hill
Mountains, Mountain Range
Hills, Escarpment
Plateau, Upland
Pass, Gap
Plain, Lowland
Delta
Salt Flat
Valley, Canyon
Crater, Cave
Karst Features
Depression
Polder
Desert, Dunes
Forest, Woods
Heath, Steppe
Oasis
Cape, Point
Coast, Beach
Cliff
Peninsula
Isthmus
Sandbank
Island
Atoll
Rock, Reef
Islands, Archipelago
Rocks, Reefs
Coral Reef
Well, Spring
Geyser
River, Stream
Waterfall, Rapids
River Mouth, Estuary
Lake
Salt Lake
Intermittent Lake
Reservoir
Swamp, Pond
Canal
Glacier
Ice Shelf, Pack Ice
Ocean
Sea
Gulf, Bay
Strait, Fjord
Lagoon
Bank
Seamount
Tablemount
Ridge
Shelf
Basin
Escarpment, Sea Scarp
Fracture
Trench, Abyss
National Park, Reserve
Point of Interest
Recreation Site
Cave, Cavern
Historic Site
Ruins
Wall, Walls
Church, Abbey
Temple
Scientific Station
Railway station
Airport
Port
Military installation
Lighthouse
Mine
Tunnel
Dam, Bridge

Šira	138	Ef	54.29N	90.02 E
Sira	114	Bg	58.25N	6.38 E
Sira ∿	116	Bf	58.17N	6.24 E
Şīr Abū Nu'Ayr ◆	146	Pj	25.13N	54.13 E
Si Racha	148	Kf	13.10N	100.57 E
Siracusa=Syracuse (EN)	112	Hh	37.04N	15.18 E
Sir Alexander, Mount - ▲	180	Ff	53.56N	120.23W
Sirasso	166	Dd	9.16N	6.06W
Şirāţ, Jabal- ⛰	164	Hf	17.00N	43.50 E
Sirba ∿	166	Fc	13.46N	1.40 E
Şīr Banī Yās ◆	146	Oj	24.19N	52.37 E
Sirdalen ⧗	116	Bf	58.50N	6.40 E
Sirdalsvatn ≈	116	Bf	58.35N	6.40 E
Sire [Eth.]	168	Fd	8.58N	37.00 E
Sire [Eth.]	168	Fd	8.16N	39.30 E
Sir Edward Pellew Group ▣	212	Hc	15.40 S	136.50 E
Siret	130	Jb	47.57N	26.04 E
Siret ∿	110	If	45.24N	28.01 E
Sirevåg	114	Ag	58.30N	5.47 E
Şirhān, Wādī as- ∿	144	Ec	30.30N	38.00 E
Şiria	130	Ec	46.16N	21.38 E
Sīrīk	144	Id	26.29N	57.09 E
Sirik, Tanjong- ►	150	Ff	2.46N	111.19 E
Sirina ◆	130	Jm	36.21N	26.41 E
Sirino ▲	128	Jj	40.07N	15.50 E
Sirius Seamount (EN) ⊻	178	Gf	52.00N	160.50W
Širjajevo	132	Gf	47.24N	30.13 E
Sir James Mac Brian, Mount- ▲	180	Ed	62.08N	127.40W
Sirjān, Kavīr-e- ◢	146	Ph	29.30N	55.30 E
Sirmione	128	Ee	45.29N	10.36 E
Şirnak	146	Jd	37.32N	42.28 E
Širokaja Pad	138	Jf	50.15N	142.11 E
Široki	138	Jd	63.04N	148.01 E
Širokoje	132	Hf	47.38N	33.14 E
Sironcha	148	Fe	18.50N	79.58 E
Síros ◆	130	Hl	37.26N	24.55 E
Sirpsindiği	130	Jh	41.50N	26.29 E
Sirr, Nafūd as- ◢	146	Kj	25.15N	44.45 E
Sirrayn ◆	164	Hf	19.38N	40.36 E
Sirretta Peak ▲	188	Fi	35.59N	118.20W
Sirrī, Jazīreh-ye- ◆	146	Pj	25.55N	54.32 E
Sirsa	148	Fc	29.32N	75.01 E
Sir Sandford, Mount- ▲	188	Ga	51.40N	117.52W
Sirte Desert (EN)=As Sidrah ⧗	158	Ie	30.30N	17.30 E
Sir Thomas, Mount- ▲	212	Fe	27.11 S	129.46 E
Širvintos	114	Fi	55.03N	25.01 E
Sir Wilfrid Laurier, Mount - ▲	180	Ff	52.48N	119.45W
Sisak	128	Ke	45.29N	16.22 E
Si Sa Ket	148	Ke	15.07N	104.19 E
Sīsakht	146	Ng	30.47N	51.33 E
Sisal	192	Ng	21.10N	90.02W
Sisante	126	Je	39.25N	2.13W
Sisargas, Islas- ▣	126	Da	43.22N	8.50W
Šišchid-Gol ∿	152	Ga	51.30N	97.10 E
Sishen	172	Ce	27.55 S	22.59 E
Sishui	154	Dg	35.40N	117.17 E
Sisian	132	Oj	39.31N	46.03 E
Sisili ∿	166	Ec	10.16N	1.15W
Sisimiut/Holsteinsborg	224	Nc	67.05N	53.45W
Siskiyou Mountains ⛰	188	Df	41.55N	123.15W
Sisŏphŏn	148	Kf	13.35N	102.59 E
Sissano	214	Ch	3.00 S	142.03 E
Sisseton	186	Hd	45.40N	97.03W
Sissonne	124	Fe	49.34N	3.54 E
Sīstān=Seistan (EN) ⧗	140	If	30.30N	62.00 E
Sīstān-e Balūchestān [3]	144	Jd	28.30N	60.30 E
Sisteron	122	Lj	44.12N	5.56 E
Sisters	188	Ed	44.17N	121.33W
Sistranda	114	Be	63.43N	8.50 E
Sitāpur	148	Gc	27.34N	80.41 E
Sitasjaure ≈	114	Dc	68.00N	17.25 E
Siteki	172	Ee	26.27 S	31.57 E
Sitges	126	Nc	41.14N	1.49 E
Sithonia ⊐	130	Gi	40.05N	23.55 E
Sitia	130	Jn	35.12N	26.07 E
Sitio d'Abadia	204	Ib	14.48 S	46.16W
Sitio Nuevo	194	Jh	10.46N	74.43W
Sitka	176	Fd	57.03N	135.14W
Sitkalidak ◆	178	Ie	57.10N	153.14W
Sitna ∿	130	Kb	47.30N	27.10 E
Sitnica ∿	130	Dg	42.53N	20.52 E
Sitona	168	Fc	14.23N	37.22 E
Sitrah [Bhr.]	146	Ni	26.10N	50.40 E
Sitrah [Eg.]	146	Bh	28.42N	26.54 E
Sittard	122	Ld	51.00N	5.53 E
Sittee Point ►	194	Ce	16.48N	88.15W
Sitten/Sion	128	Bd	46.15N	7.20 E
Sittingbourne	124	Cc	51.20N	0.45 E
Sittoung	148	Je	17.10N	96.58 E
Sittwe (Akyab)	142	Lg	20.09N	92.54 E
Siuna	194	Eg	13.44N	84.46W
Siuslaw River ∿	188	Cd	44.01N	124.08W
Siva ∿	114	Mh	56.49N	53.55 E
Sivac	130	Cd	45.42N	19.23 E
Sivaki	138	Hf	52.38N	126.45 E
Sīvan ∿	144	Hd	29.51N	52.46 E
Sivas	142	Ff	39.50N	37.03 E
Sivaš, ozero- ≈	132	Ig	45.50N	34.40 E
Sivasli	130	Mk	38.30N	29.42 E
Šiveluč, vulkan- 🌋	138	Le	56.33N	161.25 E
Sivera, ozero- / Sivera ezers ≈	116	Li	55.58N	27.25 E
Sivera ezers / Sivera, ozero- ≈	116	Li	55.58N	27.25 E
Siverek	144	Eb	37.45N	39.19 E
Siverski	114	Hg	59.22N	30.02 E
Sivomaskinski	134	Kc	66.40N	62.31 E
Sivrice	146	Hc	38.27N	39.19 E
Sivrihisar	146	Dc	39.27N	31.34 E
Sivry-Rance	124	Gd	50.10N	4.16 E
Sivry Rance-Rance	124	Gd	50.09N	4.16 E
Sivry-sur-Meuse	124	He	49.19N	5.16 E
Sīwah	160	Jf	29.12N	25.31 E
Sīwah, Wāḩāt-=Siwa Oasis (EN) 🌴	158	Jf	29.10N	25.40 E
Siwalik Range ⛰	140	Jg	29.00N	80.00 E
Siwān	148	Gc	26.13N	84.22 E
Siwa Oasis (EN)=Sīwah, Wāḩāt- 🌴	158	Jf	29.10N	25.40 E
Sixaola, Río- ∿	194	Fi	9.35N	82.34W
Six Cross Road	197q	Bb	13.07N	59.28W
Six-Fours-la-Plage	122	Lk	43.06N	5.51 E
Sixian	154	Dh	33.29N	117.53 E
Six Men's Bay ◧	197q	Ab	13.16N	59.38W
Sixth Cataract (EN)= Sablūkah, Ash Shallāl as- ⤵	158	Kg	16.20N	32.42 E
Siyah-Chaman	146	Ld	37.35N	47.10 E
Siyang (Zhongxing)	154	Eh	33.43N	118.40 E
Siziwang Qi (Ulan Hua)	154	Ad	41.31N	111.41 E
Sjælland=Zealand (EN) ◆	110	Hd	55.30N	11.45 E
Sjamozero, ozero- ≈	114	Hf	61.55N	33.15 E
Sjare/Sääre	116	Ig	57.57N	21.53 E
Sjas ∿	114	Hf	60.10N	32.31 E
Sjasstroj	114	Hf	60.09N	32.36 E
Šjašupe ∿	114	Fi	55.00N	22.10 E
Šjauljaj	112	Id	55.53N	23.19 E
Šjauljaj/Šiauliai	112	Id	55.53N	23.19 E
Sjenica	130	Df	43.16N	20.00 E
Sjnjaja ∿	138	Hd	61.00N	126.57 E
Sjoa ∿	116	Cc	61.41N	9.33 E
Sjöbo	116	Ei	55.38N	13.42 E
Sjøholt	114	Be	62.29N	6.50 E
Sjujutlijka ∿	130	Ig	42.17N	25.55 E
Sjun ∿	134	Gi	55.43N	54.17 E
Sjuøyane ▣	179	Ob	80.43N	20.45 E
Skadarsko jezero = Scutari, Lake- (EN) ≈	110	Hg	42.10N	19.20 E
Skadovsk	136	Df	46.07N	32.56 E
Skælskør	116	Di	55.15N	11.19 E
Skærbæk	116	Ci	55.09N	8.46 E
Skagatá ►	114a	Ba	66.07N	20.06W
Skagen	114	Ch	57.44N	10.36 E
Skagern ≈	116	Ff	59.00N	14.15 E
Skagerrak ≋	110	Gd	57.45N	9.00 E
Skaget ▲	116	Cc	61.17N	9.12 E
Skagit River ∿	188	Db	48.20N	122.25W
Skagway	176	Fd	59.28N	135.19W
Skaidi	114	Fa	70.26N	24.30 E
Skaland	114	Db	69.27N	17.18 E
Skälderviken ◧	116	Eh	56.20N	12.40 E
Skålevik	116	Bf	58.04N	8.00 E
Skalisty Golec, gora- [Russia]	138	Ie	55.55N	130.30 E
Skalisty Golec, gora- [Russia]	138	Ge	56.20N	119.10 E
Skanderborg	114	Bh	56.02N	9.56 E
Skåne ⧗	110	Hd	56.00N	13.30 E
Skånevik	116	Ae	59.44N	5.59 E
Skänninge	116	Ff	58.24N	15.05 E
Skanör	116	Ei	55.25N	12.52 E
Skántzoura ◆	130	Hj	39.05N	24.07 E
Skara	114	Cg	58.22N	13.25 E
Skaraborg [2]	114	Cg	58.20N	13.30 E
Skärblacka	116	Ff	58.34N	15.54 E
Skärdu	148	Fa	35.18N	75.37 E
Skärhamn	116	Dg	57.59N	11.33 E
Skarnes	116	Dd	60.15N	11.41 E
Skärplinge	114	Df	60.28N	17.46 E
Skarsstind ▲	116	Cb	62.03N	8.35 E
Skarsvåg	114	Fa	71.06N	25.56 E
Skarszewy	120	Ob	54.05N	18.27 E
Skarvdalsegga ▲	116	Cb	62.09N	8.03 E
Skaryszew	120	Re	51.19N	21.15 E
Skarżysko-Kamienna	120	Qe	51.08N	20.53 E
Skasøy ◆	116	Ca	63.20N	8.35 E
Skät ∿	130	Gf	43.44N	23.51 E
Skattkärr	116	Ee	59.25N	13.41 E
Skattungbyn	116	Fc	61.12N	14.52 E
Skaudvilė/Skaudvile	114	Fi	55.27N	22.33 E
Skaudvile/Skaudvilė	114	Fi	55.27N	22.33 E
Skaulen ▲	116	Be	59.38N	6.35 E
Skawa ∿	120	Pf	50.02N	19.26 E
Skawina	120	Pg	49.59N	19.49 E
Skee	116	Df	58.56N	11.19 E
Skeena ∿	174	Fd	54.09N	130.02W
Skeena Mountains ⛰	180	Ee	56.45N	128.40W
Skegness	118	Nh	53.10N	0.21 E
Skeidarársandur ▤	114a	Cc	63.54N	17.14W
Skeldon	202	Gb	5.53N	57.08W
Skeleton Coast ▤	172	Ac	17.50 S	12.45 E
Skellefteå	112	Ic	64.46N	20.57 E
Skellefteälven ∿	110	Ic	64.42N	21.06 E
Skelleftehamn	114	Ed	64.41N	21.14 E
Skëndërbeut, Mali i- ▲	130	Ch	41.35N	19.50 E
Skene	116	Eg	57.29N	12.38 E
Skerki Bank (EN) ▤	162	Jb	37.45N	10.50 E
Skerries/Na Sceirí	118	Gh	53.35N	6.07W
Skerryvore ✳	118	Fe	56.20N	7.05W
Skhiza ◆	130	Em	36.44N	21.46 E
Skhoinoúsa ◆	130	Im	36.50N	25.30 E
Ski	114	Cg	59.43N	10.50 E
Skiathos	130	Gj	39.10N	23.29 E
Skiathos ◆	130	Gj	39.10N	23.28 E
Skibbereen/An Sciobairín	118	Dj	51.33N	9.15W
Skibotn	114	Eb	69.24N	20.16 E
Skidel	132	Dc	53.38N	24.17 E
Skien	112	Gd	59.12N	9.36 E
Skierniewice	120	Qe	51.58N	20.08 E
Skierniewice [2]	120	Qe	52.00N	20.10 E
Skiftet/Kihti ≋	116	Id	60.15N	21.05 E
Skikda	160	He	36.52N	6.54 E
Skikda [3]	162	Ib	36.45N	6.50 E
Skillet Fork ∿	186	Lg	38.08N	88.07W
Skillingaryd	116	Fg	57.26N	14.05 E
Skinári, Ákra- ►	130	Dl	37.56N	20.42 E
Skinnskatteberg	116	Fe	59.50N	15.41 E
Skipton	118	Kh	53.58N	2.01W
Skiptvet	116	De	59.28N	11.11 E
Skiropoúla ◆	130	Hk	38.50N	24.21 E
Skiros	130	Hk	38.54N	24.34 E
Skiros ◆	130	Hk	38.53N	24.32 E
Skive	114	Bh	56.34N	9.02 E
Skive Å ∿	116	Ch	56.34N	9.04 E
Skjærhalden	116	De	59.02N	11.02 E
Skjåk	116	Cc	61.52N	8.22 E
Skjálfandafljót ∿	114a	Cb	65.59N	17.38W
Skjeberg	116	De	59.14N	11.12 E
Skjern	114	Bi	55.57N	8.30 E
Skjern Å ∿	114	Bi	55.55N	8.24 E
Skjervøy	114	Ea	70.02N	20.59 E
Skjoldungen	179	Hf	63.20N	41.20W
Sklad	138	Hb	71.52N	123.35 E
Šklov	132	Gb	54.14N	30.18 E
Skobeleva, pik- ▲	135	Ie	39.51N	72.47 E
Skœrfjorden ≋	179	Kc	77.30N	19.10W
Škofja Loka	128	Id	46.10N	14.18 E
Skog	116	Gc	61.10N	16.55 E
Skógafoss ⤵	114a	Bc	63.32N	19.31W
Skoghall	116	Ee	59.19N	13.26 E
Skogshorn ▲	116	Cd	60.53N	8.42 E
Skokie	186	Me	42.02N	87.46W
Skole	120	Th	48.58N	23.32 E
Skópelos	130	Gj	39.07N	23.44 E
Skópelos ◆	130	Gj	39.10N	23.40 E
Skopí	130	Jn	35.11N	26.02 E
Skopin	114	Jj	53.52N	39.37 E
Skopje	112	Ig	42.00N	21.29 E
Skórcz	120	Oc	53.48N	18.32 E
Skorovatn	114	Cd	64.39N	13.07 E
Skorpa ◆	116	Ac	61.35N	4.50 E
Skørping	116	Ch	56.50N	9.53 E
Skorpiós ◆	130	Dk	38.42N	20.45 E
Škotovo	154	Lc	43.20N	132.21 E
Skotselv	116	Ce	59.51N	9.53 E
Skoura	162	Fc	31.04N	6.43W
Skövde	114	Cg	58.24N	13.50 E
Skovorodino	142	Od	53.59N	123.55 E
Skowhegan	184	Mc	44.46N	69.43W
Skradin	128	Jg	43.49N	15.56 E
Skreia	116	Dd	60.39N	10.56 E
Skreia ▲	116	Dd	60.34N	11.04 E
Skrekken ▲	116	Bd	60.13N	7.49 E
Skridulaupen ▲	116	Bc	61.55N	7.35 E
Skrimkolla ▲	116	Cb	62.23N	9.04 E
Skriveri/Skrīveri	116	Kh	56.37N	25.10 E
Skrīveri/Skriveri	116	Kh	56.37N	25.10 E
Skrunda	114	Eh	56.41N	22.00 E
Skrwa ∿	120	Pd	52.33N	19.32 E
Skudenesfjorden ≋	116	Ae	59.05N	5.20 E
Skudeneshavn	114	Ag	59.09N	5.17 E
Skuodas	114	Eh	56.17N	21.31 E
Skurup	116	Ei	55.28N	13.30 E
Skutskär	116	Gd	60.38N	17.25 E
Skvira	132	Fe	49.44N	29.42 E
Skwierzyna	120	Ld	52.35N	15.30 E
Skye, Island of- ◆	110	Fd	57.15N	6.10W
Slagelse	114	Ci	55.24N	11.22 E
Slagnäs	114	Ed	65.36N	18.10 E
Slamet, Gunung- ▲	140	Mj	7.14 S	109.12 E
Slaná ∿	120	Ri	47.56N	21.08 E
Slancy	136	Cd	59.08N	28.02 E
Slaney/An tSláine ∿	118	Gi	52.21N	6.30W
Slănic	130	Id	45.15N	25.56 E
Slănic Moldova	130	Jc	46.12N	26.26 E
Slannik ⧗	130	Jf	43.06N	26.13 E
Slano	128	Lh	42.47N	17.54 E
Slaný	120	Kf	50.14N	14.06 E
Śląsk=Silesia (EN) ⧗	110	He	51.00N	16.45 E
Śląsk=Silesia (EN) ◙	120	Me	51.00N	16.45 E
Śląska, Wyżyna- ▃	120	Of	50.28N	18.40 E
Slate Islands ▣	186	Mb	48.34N	86.45W
Slatina	130	He	44.26N	24.22 E
Slatina ∿	120	Ph	48.32N	19.10 E
Slaton	186	Fj	33.26N	101.39W
Slave Coast ▤	158	Hh	6.00N	3.30 E
Slave Lake	180	Ge	55.17N	114.46W
Slave River ∿	174	Hc	61.18N	113.39W
Slavgorod [Bela]	132	Gc	53.27N	31.01 E
Slavgorod [Russia]	138	Cf	53.03N	78.48 E
Slavičin	120	Ng	49.06N	17.53 E
Slavjanka	138	Ih	42.55N	131.20 E
Slavjanka ▲	130	Gh	41.23N	23.36 E
Slavjansk	112	Jf	48.52N	37.37 E
Slavjansk-na-Kubani	136	Df	45.15N	38.08 E
Slavkoje	120	Th	48.45N	23.31 E
Slavkoviči	116	Mg	57.37N	29.10 E
Slavonia (EN) = Slavonija ⧗	110	Hf	45.00N	18.00 E
Slavonia (EN)=Slavonija ◙	128	Le	45.00N	18.00 E
Slavonija =' Slavonia (EN) ⧗	110	Hf	45.00N	18.00 E
Slavonija=Slavonia (EN) ◙	128	Le	45.00N	18.00 E
Slavonska Požega	128	Le	45.20N	17.41 E
Slavonski Brod	128	Me	45.09N	18.02 E
Slavsk	116	Ii	55.01N	21.37 E
Slavuta	136	Ce	50.18N	26.52 E
Sława	120	Me	51.53N	16.04 E
Sławatycze	120	Te	51.43N	23.30 E
Sławno	120	Mb	54.22N	16.40 E
Slayton	186	Id	44.01N	95.45W
Sleaford	118	Mh	53.00N	0.24W
Slea Head/Ceann Sléibhe ►	118	Ci	52.06N	10.27W
Sleat, Sound of- ≋	118	Hd	57.10N	5.50W
Sleen	124	Ib	52.47N	6.49 E
Sleeper Islands ▣	180	Je	57.25N	79.50W
Sléibhte Chill Mhantáin/ Wicklow Mountains ⛰	118	Gh	53.02N	6.24W
Sleidinge, Evergem-	124	Fc	51.08N	3.41 E
Slesin	120	Od	52.23N	18.19 E
Slessor Glacier ❄	222	Af	79.50 S	28.30W
Slessor Peak ▲	222	Qe	66.31 S	64.58W
Slettefjell ▲	116	Cc	61.13N	8.44 E
Sletterhage ►	116	Dh	56.06N	10.31 E
Ślęża ▲	120	Mf	50.52N	16.45 E
Ślęża ∿	120	Me	51.10N	16.58 E
Sliabh Bearnach/Slieve Bernagh ▲	118	Ei	52.50N	8.35W
Sliabh Bladhma/Slieve Bloom ▲	118	Fh	53.10N	7.35W
Sliabh Eachtai/Slieve Aughty ▲	118	Eh	53.10N	8.30W
Sliabh Gamh ▲	118	Eg	54.10N	8.50W
Sliabh Gamh/Ox or Slieve Gamph Mountains ▲	118	Eg	54.10N	8.50W
Sliabh Mis/Slieve Mish ▲	118	Di	52.10N	9.50W
Sliabh Speirín/Sperrin Mountains ⛰	118	Fg	54.50N	7.05W
Slidell	186	Lk	30.17N	89.47W
Slide Mountain ▲	184	Jd	42.00N	74.23W
Slidre ⧗	116	Cc	61.10N	9.00 E
Sliedrecht	124	Gc	51.50N	4.46 E
Slieve Aughty/Sliabh Eachtai ▲	118	Eh	53.10N	8.30W
Slieve Bernagh/Sliabh Bearnach ▲	118	Ei	52.50N	8.35W
Slieve Bloom/Sliabh Bladhma ▲	118	Fh	53.10N	7.35W
Slievekimalta ▲	118	Ei	52.45N	8.15W
Slieve Mish/Sliabh Mis ▲	118	Di	52.10N	9.50W
Sligeach/Sligo	112	Fe	54.17N	8.28W
Sligeach/Sligo [2]	118	Eg	54.10N	8.40W
Sligo/Sligeach	112	Fe	54.17N	8.28W
Sligo/Sligeach [2]	118	Eg	54.10N	8.40W
Sligo Bay/Cuan Shligigh ◧	118	Eg	54.20N	8.40W
Slinge ∿	124	Ib	52.08N	6.31 E
Slingebeek ∿	124	Ic	51.59N	6.18 E
Slite	116	Hg	57.43N	18.48 E
Sliven	130	Jg	42.40N	26.19 E
Sliven [2]	130	Jg	42.40N	26.19 E
Slivnica	130	Gg	42.51N	23.02 E
Sljudjanka	138	Ff	51.38N	103.40 E
Slobodka	130	Mb	47.54N	29.12 E
Slobodskoj	136	Fd	58.47N	50.12 E
Slobodzeja	132	Ff	46.43N	29.43 E
Slobozia [Rom.]	130	Ke	44.34N	27.22 E
Slobozia [Rom.]	130	Ie	44.30N	25.11 E
Slochteren	124	Ia	53.12N	6.50 E
Slocum Mountain ▲	188	Gi	35.18N	117.13W
Slonim	136	Ce	53.05N	25.18 E
Sloten	124	Hb	52.54N	5.40 E
Slotermeer ≈	124	Hb	52.55N	5.40 E
Slough	118	Mj	51.31N	0.36W
Slovakia (EN)= Slovensko ⧗	110	Hf	48.45N	19.30 E
Slovakia (EN) = Slovenská Republika	112	Hf	48.00N	17.00 E
Slovečna	132	Fd	51.41N	29.42 E
Slovenia (EN) = Slovenija	128	Id	46.00N	15.00 E
Slovenia (EN) = Slovenija ⧗	110	Hf	46.00N	15.00 E
Slovenia (EN) = Slovenija ◙	128	Id	46.00N	15.00 E
Slovenija=Slovenia (EN)	128	Id	46.00N	15.00 E
Slovenija = Slovenia (EN) ⧗	110	Hf	46.00N	15.00 E
Slovenija = Slovenia (EN) ◙	128	Id	46.00N	15.00 E
Slovenska Bistrica	128	Jd	46.24N	15.34 E
Slovenská Republika = Slovakia (EN)	112	Hf	48.00N	17.00 E
Slovenske Gorice	128	Jd	46.35N	15.55 E
Slovenské rudohorie	120	Ph	48.45N	20.00 E
Slovenský kras ⛰	120	Qh	48.35N	20.40 E
Słubice	120	Kd	52.20N	14.35 E
Sluč [Bela.]	132	Ec	52.08N	27.32 E
Sluč [Ukr.]	132	Ed	51.37N	26.38 E
Sluck	136	Ce	53.02N	27.31 E
Slunj	128	Je	45.07N	15.35 E
Słupca	120	Nd	52.19N	17.52 E
Słupia ∿	120	Mb	54.35N	16.50 E
Słupsk	120	Nb	54.28N	17.01 E
Słupsk [2]	120	Mb	54.30N	17.00 E
Sly ∿	126	Nh	36.06N	1.08 E
Småland ◙	114	Dh	57.20N	15.05 E
Smålandsfarvandet ◧	116	Di	55.06N	11.20 E
Smålandsstenar	116	Eg	57.10N	13.24 E
Smalininkai/Smalininkaj	116	Ji	55.01N	22.32 E
Smalininkaj/Smalininkai	116	Ji	55.01N	22.32 E
Smallingerland-Drachten	122	Ma	53.06N	6.05 E
Smallwood Reservoir ≈	174	Md	54.00N	64.30W
Smederevo	130	De	44.39N	20.56 E
Smederevska Palanka	130	De	44.22N	20.58 E
Smedjebacken	114	Df	60.08N	15.25 E
Smela	136	Df	49.13N	31.53 E
Smidovič	138	Ig	48.36N	133.50 E
Šmidta, ostrov- ◆	140	La	81.08N	90.48 E
Šmidta, poluostrov- ⊐	138	Jf	54.15N	142.40 E
Śmigiel	120	Md	52.01N	16.32 E
Smilde	124	Ib	52.56N	6.28 E
Smiltene	114	Fh	57.28N	25.56 E
Smirnovo	134	Ni	54.31N	69.28 E
Smirnyh	138	Jg	49.45N	142.53 E
Smith	204	Bl	35.30 S	61.36W
Smith Arm ◧	180	Fc	66.15N	124.00W
Smith Bay [Ak.-U.S.] ◧	178	Ib	70.51N	154.25W
Smith Bay [Can.] ◧	180	Ja	77.15N	79.00W
Smith Center	186	Gg	39.47N	98.47W
Smithers	180	Ef	54.47N	127.10W
Smithfield [S.Afr.]	172	Df	30.09 S	26.30 E
Smithfield [Ut.-U.S.]	188	Jf	41.50N	111.50W
Smith Mountain Lake ≈	184	Hg	37.10N	79.40W
Smith Peak ▲	188	Gb	48.50N	116.39W
Smith River ∿	188	Jc	47.25N	111.29W
Smiths Falls	180	Jh	44.54N	76.01W
Smith's Knoll ▤	118	Pi	52.50N	2.10 E
Smith Sound ◧	188	Ba	51.18N	127.48W
Smithton	210	Fi	40.51 S	145.07 E
Smjadovo	130	Kf	43.04N	27.01 E
Smjörfjoll ▲	114a	Cb	65.35N	14.46W
Smögen	116	Df	58.21N	11.13 E
Smoke Creek Desert ◢	188	Ff	40.30N	119.40W
Smokey Dome ▲	188	He	43.29N	114.56W
Smoky Bay ◧	212	Gf	32.20 S	133.45 E
Smoky Cape ►	212	Kf	30.56 S	153.05 E
Smoky Falls	180	Jf	50.03N	82.10W
Smoky Hill ∿	174	Jf	39.03N	96.48W
Smoky Hills ⛰	186	Gg	39.15N	99.00W
Smoky River ∿	180	Fe	56.11N	117.19W
Smøla ◆	114	Be	63.25N	8.00 E
Smolensk	112	Je	54.47N	32.03 E
Smolenskaja oblast [3]	136	De	55.00N	33.00 E
Smolenskaja vozvyšennost = Smolensk Upland (EN) ▃	110	Je	54.40N	33.00 E
Smolensko, oblast de- (E) [3]	136	De	55.00N	33.00 E
Smolensk Upland (EN) = Smolenskaja vozvyšennost ▃	110	Je	54.40N	33.00 E
Smolevići	132	Fb	54.03N	28.02 E
Smolianica	120	Ud	52.40N	24.40 E
Smólikas Óros ▲	110	Ig	40.06N	20.55 E
Smoljan	130	Hh	41.35N	24.41 E
Smoljan [2]	130	Hh	41.40N	24.40 E
Smooth Rock Falls	184	Ga	49.20N	81.39W
Smorgon	136	Ce	54.31N	26.23 E
Smørstabbren ▲	116	Cc	61.32N	8.06 E
Smrdeš ⛰	130	Fh	41.34N	22.28 E
Smygehamn	116	Ei	55.21N	13.22 E
Smygehuk ►	116	Ei	55.21N	13.23 E
Smyley, Cape- ►	222	Qf	72.00 S	78.50W
Smyrna	184	Ei	33.53N	84.31W
Smyrna → İzmir	142	Ef	38.25N	27.09 E
Smyšljajevka	114	Mj	53.17N	50.24 E
Smythe, Mount- ▲	174	Gd	57.50N	124.59W
Snacke Point ►	197b	Bb	18.17N	62.58W
Snæfell ▲	114a	Cb	64.48N	15.34W
Snaefell ▲	118	Ig	54.16N	4.27W
Snæfellsjökull ▲	114a	Ab	64.49N	23.46W
Snag	180	Dd	62.23N	140.22W
Snake Bay Settlement	212	Gb	11.25 S	130.40 E
Snake Range ⛰	188	Hg	39.00N	114.15W
Snake River [Can.] ∿	180	Ec	65.57N	134.13W
Snake River [U.S.] ∿	174	He	46.12N	119.02W
Snake River Plain ▁	182	Ec	42.45N	114.30W
Snare ∿	180	Fd	63.15N	116.08W
Snares Islands ▣	216	Ci	48.00 S	166.35 E
Snarumselva ∿	116	Cd	59.57N	9.58 E
Snåsa	114	Cd	64.15N	12.22 E
Sneek	122	La	53.02N	5.40 E
Snekermeer ≈	122	La	53.04N	5.40 E
Snežnaja, gora- ▲	138	Lc	65.18N	165.30 E
Snežnik ▲	128	Ie	45.26N	14.36 E
Snežnogorsk	138	Dc	68.15N	87.35 E
Šnežnoje	132	Kf	47.59N	38.50 E
Śniardwy, Jezioro- ≈	120	Rc	53.46N	21.44 E
Śnieżka ▲	110	He	50.45N	15.43 E
Śnieżnik ▲	120	Mf	50.12N	16.50 E
Snigirevka	132	Hf	47.04N	32.45 E
Snillfjord	116	Ca	63.24N	9.30 E
Snina	120	Sh	48.59N	22.08 E
Snizort, Loch- ≋	118	Gd	57.30N	6.25W
Snjatyn	132	De	48.29N	25.34 E
Snøhetta ▲	110	Gc	62.20N	9.17 E
Snohomish	188	Dc	47.55N	122.06W
Snønuten ▲	116	Be	59.31N	6.54 E
Snøonipa ▲	116	Bc	61.42N	6.41 E
Snota ∿	116	Cb	62.51N	9.06 E
Snov ∿	132	Gd	51.32N	31.33 E
Snowbird Lake ≈	180	Hd	60.40N	102.50W
Snowdon ▲	110	Fe	53.04N	4.05W
Snowdonia ⧗	118	Jh	53.05N	3.55W
Snowdrift	180	Gd	62.23N	110.47W
Snowflake	188	Ji	34.30N	110.05W
Snow Hill	184	Jf	38.11N	75.24W
Snow Lake	180	Hf	54.53N	100.02W
Snow Mountain ▲	182	Cd	39.23N	122.46W
Snowshoe Peak ▲	188	Hb	48.13N	115.41W
Snowville	188	If	41.58N	112.43W
Snowy Mountain [N.Amer.] ▲	188	Fb	49.02N	119.57W
Snowy Mountain [N.Y.-U.S.] ▲	184	Jd	43.42N	74.23W
Snowy Mountains ⛰	212	Jg	36.30 S	148.20 E
Snowy River ∿	212	Jg	37.48 S	148.32 E
Snudy, ozero- ≈	116	Li	55.40N	27.15 E
Snug Corner	194	Kb	22.32N	73.53W
Snuŏl	148	Lf	12.04N	106.26 E
Snyder	182	Ge	32.44N	100.55W
Soalala	172	Hc	16.07 S	45.21 E
Soalara	172	Gd	23.35 S	43.44 E
Soanierana-Ivongo	172	Hc	16.54 S	49.34 E
Soar ∿	124	Ab	52.52N	1.17W
Şoarş	130	Hd	45.56N	24.55 E
Soavinandriana	172	Hc	19.10 S	46.43 E
Sob [Russia]	134	Mc	66.20N	66.02 E
Sob [Ukr.]	132	Fe	48.41N	29.17 E
Soba	166	Gc	10.59N	8.04 E
Sobaek-Sanmaek ⛰	154	Jf	36.00N	128.00 E
Sobat (EN)=Sawbā ∿	158	Kh	9.45N	31.45 E
Sobernheim	124	Je	49.48N	7.39 E
Soběslav	120	Kg	49.16N	14.44 E
Sōbetsu	156a	Bb	42.33N	140.51 E
Sobinka	114	Jh	56.01N	40.07 E
Sobolevo [Russia]	132	Qd	51.59N	51.48 E
Sobolevo [Russia]	138	Kf	54.17N	156.00 E
Sobolew	120	Re	51.41N	21.40 E
Sobo-San ▲	156	Be	32.47N	131.21 E
Sobradinho	204	Fi	29.24 S	53.03W
Sobral	200	Lf	3.42 S	40.21W
Sobrarbe ⧗	126	Mb	42.20N	0.05 E
Soca	204	El	34.41 S	55.41W
Soča=Isonzo (EN) ∿	128	He	45.43N	13.33 E
Sochaczew	120	Qd	52.14N	20.14 E
Soči	112	Jg	43.35N	39.45 E
Société, Iles de la-=Society Islands (EN) ▣	208	Lf	17.00 S	150.00W
Society Islands (EN)= Société, Iles de la- ▣	208	Lf	17.00 S	150.00W
Socompa, Paso- ⌣	198	Jh	24.27 S	68.18W
Socorro [Col.]	202	Db	6.27N	73.16W

Socorro [N.M.-U.S.] 182 Fe 34.04N 106.54W
Socorro, Isla- 190 Be 18.45N 110.58W
Socotra (EN) = Suquṭrá 140 Hh 12.30N 54.00 E
Soc Trang 148 Lg 9.36N 105.58 E
Socuéllamos 126 Je 39.17N 2.48W
Sodankylä 114 Gc 67.25N 26.36 E
Soda Springs 188 Je 42.39N 111.36W
Söderåsen 116 Eh 56.04N 13.05 E
Söderfors 114 Df 60.23N 17.14 E
Söderhamn 114 Df 61.18N 17.03 E
Söderköping 116 Gf 58.29N 16.18 E
Södermanland [2] 114 Dg 59.15N 16.40 E
Södermanland 116 Ge 59.10N 16.50 E
Söderslätt 116 Ei 55.30N 13.15 E
Södertälje 114 Dg 59.12N 17.37 E
Södertörn 116 Ge 59.05N 18.00 E
Sodo 168 Fd 6.51N 37.45 E
Södra Dellen 116 Gc 61.50N 16.45 E
Södra Gloppet 116 Ia 63.05N 21.00 E
Södra Kvarken 116 Hd 60.20N 19.08 E
Södra-Midsjöbanken 116 Gi 55.40N 17.20 E
Södra Vi 116 Fg 57.45N 15.48 E
Soe 150 Hh 9.52S 124.17 E
Soekmekaar 172 Dd 23.28S 29.58 E
Soela, Proliv- / Soela Väin 116 Jf 58.40N 22.30 E
Soela Väin / Soela, Proliv- 116 Jf 58.40N 22.30 E
Soest [Ger.] 120 Ee 51.35N 8.07 E
Soest [Neth.] 124 Hb 52.10N 5.20 E
Soeste 124 Ja 53.10N 7.44 E
Soester Borde 124 Kc 51.38N 8.03 E
Soestwetering 124 Ib 51.30N 6.09 E
Sofádhes 130 Fj 39.20N 22.06 E
Sofala [3] 172 Ec 19.30S 34.40 E
Sofala, Baia de- 158 Kk 20.11S 34.45 E
Sofia [2] 130 Gg 42.43N 23.25 E
Sofia 172 Hc 15.27S 47.23 E
Sofia (EN)=Sofija 112 Ig 42.41N 23.19 E
Sofija=Sofia (EN) 112 Ig 42.41N 23.19 E
Sofijsk 138 If 52.20N 134.01 E
Sofporog 136 Db 65.48N 31.28 E
Sofrâna, Nisídhes- 130 Jm 36.04N 26.24 E
Sōfu-Gan 152 Pf 29.50N 140.20 E
Sogamoso 202 Db 5.43N 72.56W
Soganlı 146 Eb 41.11N 32.38 E
Sogara, Lake- 170 Fd 5.15S 31.00 E
Sogda 138 If 50.24N 132.18 E
Sögel 120 Dd 52.51N 7.31 E
Sogeri 214 Di 9.10S 147.32 E
Sogn 116 Ac 61.05N 5.55 E
Sogndalsfjøra 116 Bc 61.14N 7.06 E
Søgne 116 Bf 58.05N 7.49 E
Sognefjell 116 Bc 61.35N 7.55 E
Sognefjorden 116 Gc 61.05N 5.10 E
Sognesjøen 116 Ac 61.05N 5.00 E
Sogn og Fjordane [2] 114 Bf 61.30N 6.50 E
Sogod 150 Hd 10.23N 124.59 E
Sogo Nur 152 Hc 42.20N 101.20 E
Sogoža 114 Jg 58.30N 39.06 E
Söğüt 130 Nj 40.00N 30.11 E
Söğütalan 130 Li 40.03N 28.34 E
Söğüt Gölü 146 Cd 37.03N 29.53 E
Sog Xian 152 Fe 31.51N 93.42 E
Soh 135 He 39.57N 71.08 E
Sohag (EN)=Sawhāj 160 Kf 26.33N 31.42 E
Sohano 214 Ei 5.29S 154.41 E
Sohŭksan-Do 154 Hg 34.04N 125.07 E
Soignies/Zinnik 122 Kd 50.35N 4.04 E
Soini 116 Kb 62.52N 24.13 E
Soisalo 116 Mb 62.40N 28.10 E
Soissonnais, Plateau du- 122 Je 49.20N 3.10 E
Soissons 122 Je 49.22N 3.20 E
Sōja 156 Cd 34.40N 133.44 E
Sojana 114 Kd 65.53N 43.30 E
Sojma 134 Ec 67.00N 51.00 E
Šojna 134 Bc 67.52N 44.08 E
Sŏjosŏn-man=Korea Bay (EN) 140 Of 39.15N 125.00 E
Sojuznoje 132 Vd 50.50N 60.10 E
Sok 136 Fe 53.25N 50.10 E
Sokal 132 Dd 50.29N 24.17 E
Šokalskogo, proliv- 138 Ea 79.00N 100.00 E
Sokch'o 152 Md 38.12N 128.36 E
Söke 144 Cb 37.45N 27.24 E
Sokele 170 Dd 9.55S 24.36 E
Sokirjany 132 Ee 48.28N 27.25 E
Sokna 114 Bf 60.14N 9.54 E
Soko Banja 130 Ef 43.39N 21.53 E
Sokodé 160 Hh 8.59N 1.08 E
Sokol 136 Ed 59.29N 40.13 E
Sokol 130 Ce 44.18N 19.25 E
Sokółka 120 Tc 53.25N 23.31 E
Sokolo 166 Dc 14.44N 6.07W
Sokolov 120 If 50.11N 12.38 E
Sokołów Podlaski 120 Sd 52.25N 22.15 E
Sokone 166 Bc 13.53N 16.22W
Sokosti 114 Gb 68.20N 28.01 E
Sokoto 160 Hg 13.04N 5.15 E
Sokoto [2] 166 Gc 12.20N 5.20 E
Sokoto 158 Hg 11.24N 4.07 E
Sokourala 166 Dd 9.13N 8.05W
Sōl 168 Hd 9.20N 49.25 E
Sol 168 Hd 9.40N 48.30 E
Sol, Costa del- 126 Ih 36.46N 3.55W
Sol, Pico do- 204 Ke 20.07S 43.28W
Sola 219b Ca 13.53S 167.33 E
Sola 120 Pf 50.04N 19.13 E
Solai 170 Gb 0.02N 36.09 E
Solakrossen 116 Af 58.53N 5.36 E
Solanet 204 Cm 36.51S 58.31W
Solāpur 142 Jh 17.41N 75.55 E
Solbad Hall in Tirol → Hall in Tirol 128 Fc 47.17N 11.31 E
Solcy 136 Dd 58.09N 30.20 E
Sölden 128 Ed 46.58N 11.00 E
Soldier Point 197d Bb 17.02N 61.41W
Soldotna 178 Id 60.29N 151.04W
Solec Kujawski 120 Oc 53.06N 18.14 E
Soledad [Arg.] 204 Bj 30.37S 60.55W
Soledad [Ca.-U.S.] 188 Eh 36.26N 121.19W
Soledad [Col.] 202 Da 10.55N 74.46W
Soledad [Ven.] 202 Fb 8.10N 63.34W
Soledad, Boca de- 192 Ce 25.17N 112.09W
Soledad, Isla-/East Falkland 198 Kk 51.45S 58.50W
Soledade 206 Jc 28.50S 52.30W
Sølen 116 Dc 61.55N 11.30 E
Sølensjøen 116 Dc 61.55N 11.35 E
Solentiname, Archipiélago de- 194 Fh 11.10N 85.00W
Solenzara 122a Bb 42.16N 9.24 E
Sole Pit 118 Oh 53.40N 1.30 E
Solesmes 124 Fd 50.11N 3.30 E
Solferino 128 Ee 45.23N 10.34 E
Solgen 116 Fg 57.33N 15.07 E
Solgne 124 Ie 48.58N 6.18 E
Soligalič 114 Kg 59.07N 42.13 E
Soligorsk 136 Ce 52.49N 27.31 E
Solihull 118 Li 52.25N 1.45W
Solikamsk 136 Fd 59.39N 56.47 E
Sol-Ileck 112 Le 51.12N 55.03 E
Solimán, Punta- 192 Ph 19.50N 87.27W
Solimoes → Amazonas, Rio-=Amazon (EN) 198 Lf 0.10S 49.00W
Solingen 120 De 51.11N 7.05 E
Solińskie, Jezioro- 120 Sg 49.22N 22.30 E
Solis, Presa- 192 Ig 20.05N 100.36W
Sollebrunn 116 Ef 58.07N 12.32 E
Sollefteå 114 De 63.10N 17.16 E
Sollentuna 116 Ge 59.28N 17.54 E
Sóller 126 Oe 39.46N 2.42 E
Sollerön 116 Fd 60.55N 14.37 E
Solling 120 Fe 51.45N 9.35 E
Solms 124 Kd 50.46N 9.36 E
Solna 116 He 59.22N 18.01 E
Solnečnogorsk 114 Ih 56.10N 37.00 E
Solnečny 138 Id 60.10N 137.35 E
Sologne 122 Hg 47.50N 2.00 E
Sologne Bourbonnaise 122 Jh 46.40N 3.30 E
Solok 150 Dg 0.48S 100.39 E
Sololá 194 Bf 14.46N 91.11W
Sololá [3] 194 Bf 14.40N 91.15W
Solomon Basin (EN) 214 Ei 7.00S 152.00 E
Solomon Islands 208 Ge 8.00S 159.00 E
Solomon Islands (British Solomon Islands) [1] 210 Ge 8.00S 159.00 E
Solomon River 182 Hd 38.54N 97.22W
Solomon Sea 208 Ge 8.00S 155.00 E
Solon Springs 186 Kc 46.22N 91.48W
Sølør 116 Dd 60.30N 11.55 E
Solor, Kepulauan- 150 Hh 8.25S 123.30 E
Solothurn 128 Bc 47.15N 7.30 E
Solothurn [2] 128 Bc 47.20N 7.40 E
Solotvin 120 Uh 48.38N 24.31 E
Soloveckije ostrova 114 Id 65.05N 35.45 E
Solovjevka 116 Nd 60.44N 30.20 E
Solovjevsk [Russia] 138 Gg 49.54N 115.43 E
Solovjevsk [Russia] 138 Hf 54.15N 124.30 E
Sölöz 130 Mi 40.23N 29.25 E
Solre-le-Château 124 Gd 50.10N 4.05 E
Solsona 126 Nc 41.59N 1.31 E
Solt 120 Oj 46.48N 19.00 E
Solta 128 Kg 43.23N 16.17 E
Soltānābād [Iran] 146 Rd 36.23N 58.02 E
Soltānābād [Iran] 146 Mg 31.03N 49.42 E
Soltānī, Khowr-e- 146 Nh 29.00N 50.50 E
Soltānīyeh 146 Md 36.26N 48.48 E
Soltau 120 Fd 52.59N 9.50 E
Soltvadkert 120 Pj 46.35N 19.23 E
Solvang 188 Ei 34.36N 120.08W
Sölvesborg 114 Dh 56.03N 14.33 E
Solvyčegodsk 114 Lf 61.21N 46.52 E
Solway Firth 118 Jg 54.50N 3.35W
Solwezi 160 Jj 12.11S 26.24 E
Soma 146 Bc 39.10N 27.36 E
Sōma 154 Pf 37.48N 140.57 E
Somain 124 Fd 50.22N 3.17 E
Somalia (EN)=Soomaaliya [1] 160 Lh 10.00N 49.00 E
Somali Basin (EN) 106 Fi 0.00 52.00 E
Sombo 170 Dd 8.42S 20.57 E
Sombor 130 Cd 45.46N 19.07 E
Sombrerete 190 Dd 23.38N 103.39W
Sombrero 190 Le 18.36N 63.26W
Sombrero Channel 148 Ig 7.41N 93.35 E
Sombrio 204 Hi 29.07S 49.40W
Sombrio, Lagoa do- 204 Hi 29.12S 49.42W
Somcuța Mare 130 Gb 47.31N 23.28 E
Someren 124 Hc 51.23N 5.43 E
Somero 116 Jd 60.37N 23.32 E
Somerset [3] 118 Jk 51.10N 3.10W
Somerset 118 Kj 51.00N 3.00W
Somerset 174 Jb 73.30N 93.30W
Somerset [Austl.] 212 Ib 10.35S 142.15 E
Somerset [Ky.-U.S.] 182 Kd 37.05N 84.36W
Somerset [Pa.-U.S.] 184 He 40.02N 79.05W
Somerset East 172 Df 32.42S 25.35 E
Somerton 188 Hj 32.36N 114.43W
Somerville Lake 186 Hk 30.18N 96.40W
Someș 130 Fa 48.07N 22.20 E
Someșu Mare 130 Gb 47.09N 23.55 E
Someșu Mic 130 Gb 47.09N 23.55 E
Somme [3] 122 Ie 49.55N 2.30 E
Somme 122 Hd 50.11N 1.39 E
Somme, Baie de- 124 Dd 50.14N 1.33 E
Somme, Bassurelle de la- 124 Dd 50.15N 1.10 E
Somme, Canal de la- 122 Hd 50.11N 1.39 E
Somme-Leuze 124 Hd 50.20N 5.22 E
Somme-Leuze-Hogne 124 Hd 50.15N 5.17 E
Sommen 116 Ff 58.08N 14.58 E
Sommen 114 Dh 58.00N 15.15 E
Sommepy-Tahure 124 Ge 49.15N 4.33 E
Sömmerda 120 He 51.09N 11.06 E
Somogy [2] 120 Nj 46.25N 17.35 E
Somontano Pirenaico 126 Lc 42.02N 0.20W
Somosierra, Puerto de- 126 Ic 41.09N 3.35W
Somosomo Strait 219d Bb 16.47S 179.58 E
Somotillo 194 Dg 13.02N 86.53W
Somoto 190 Gf 13.28N 86.35W
Somovo 132 Kd 51.45N 39.25 E
Sompolno 120 Od 52.24N 18.31 E
Somport, Puerto de- 126 Lb 42.48N 0.31W
Son 140 Kg 25.50N 84.55 E
Soná 194 Gi 8.01N 81.19W
Sona 120 Qd 52.33N 20.35 E
Sonaguera 194 Df 15.38N 86.20W
Sonāri, Ákra 130 Lm 36.27N 28.13 E
Sŏnch'on 154 He 39.48N 124.55 E
Søndeled 114 Bg 58.46N 9.05 E
Sønderborg 114 Bi 54.55N 9.47 E
Sønder-Jylland [2] 116 Ci 55.00N 9.00 E
Sønder-Omme 116 Ci 55.50N 8.54 E
Sondershausen 120 Ge 51.22N 10.52 E
Søndre Strømfjord 224 Nc 66.59N 50.40W
Søndre Strømfjord 179 Ge 66.10N 53.10W
Søndre Upernavik 179 Gd 72.10N 55.38W
Sondrio 128 Dd 46.10N 9.52 E
Sonepat 148 Fc 28.59N 77.01 E
Song 166 Hd 9.50N 12.37 E
Songa 116 Be 59.47N 7.43 E
Songavatn 116 Be 59.50N 7.35 E
Song Cau 148 Lf 13.27N 109.13 E
Songe 116 Cf 58.41N 9.01 E
Songea 160 Kj 10.41S 35.39 E
Songeons 124 De 49.33N 1.52 E
Songhua Hu 154 Ic 43.30N 126.51 E
Songhua Jiang=Sungari (EN) 140 Pe 47.42N 132.30 E
Songjiang 152 Le 31.01N 121.14 E
Songjiang → Antu 154 Jc 42.33N 128.20 E
Songjianghe 154 Ic 42.10N 127.30 E
Sŏngjin → Kimch'aek 152 Mc 40.41N 129.12 E
Songjŏng 154 Ig 35.08N 126.48 E
Songkhla 142 Mi 7.13N 100.34 E
Songling 152 Lb 48.02N 121.08 E
Songnim 154 He 38.44N 125.38 E
Songo [Ang.] 170 Bd 7.21S 14.50 E
Songo [Moz.] 172 Ec 15.33S 32.48 E
Songololo 170 Bd 5.42S 14.02 E
Songpan (Sungqu) 152 He 32.37N 103.34 E
Songsa-dong 154 Hd 39.49N 124.49 E
Song Shan 152 Je 34.31N 113.00 E
Songshuzhen 154 Ic 42.01N 127.09 E
Songueur 126 Ni 35.11N 1.30 E
Songxian 154 Bg 34.12N 112.09 E
Songzi (Xinjiangkou) 154 Ai 30.10N 111.46 E
Sonid Youqi (Saihan Tal) 152 Jc 42.45N 112.36 E
Sonid Zuoqi (Mandalt) 152 Jc 43.50N 113.45 E
Sonkari 116 Lb 62.50N 26.35 E
Sonkël, ozero- 135 Jd 41.50N 75.10 E
Sonkovo 114 Ih 57.47N 37.09 E
Son La 142 Mg 21.19N 103.54 E
Sonmiāni Bay 148 Dc 25.15N 66.30 E
Sonneberg 120 Hf 50.21N 11.10 E
Sono, Rio do- [Braz.] 202 Ie 9.00S 48.11W
Sono, Rio do- [Braz.] 204 Jc 17.02S 45.32W
Sonobe 156 Dd 35.07N 135.28 E
Sonoita 190 Bb 31.51N 112.50W
Sonoma Peak 188 Gf 40.52N 117.36W
Sonora [2] 190 Bc 29.20N 110.40W
Sonora 190 Bc 28.48N 111.49W
Sonora [Ca.-U.S.] 188 Eh 37.59N 120.23W
Sonora [Tx.-U.S.] 186 Fk 30.34N 100.39W
Sonqor 146 Le 34.47N 47.36 E
Sonsbeck 124 Ic 51.37N 6.22 E
Sonsonate 190 Gf 13.43N 89.44W
Sonsorol Islands 208 Ed 5.20N 132.13 E
Sonthofen 120 Gi 47.31N 10.17 E
Sontra 120 Fe 51.04N 9.56 E
Soomaaliya=Somalia (EN) [1] 160 Lh 10.00N 49.00 E
Soomenlaht=Finland, Gulf of- (EN) 110 Ic 60.00N 27.00 E
Soonwald 124 Je 49.56N 7.35 E
Sørværøy 114 Cc 67.38N 12.40 E
Sopi, Tanjung- 150 If 2.39N 128.34 E
Sopo 168 Dd 8.51N 26.11 E
Sopockin 120 Tc 53.50N 23.42 E
Sopot [Bul.] 130 Hg 42.39N 24.45 E
Sopot [Pol.] 120 Ob 54.28N 18.34 E
Sopron 120 Mi 47.41N 16.36 E
Sopur 148 Eb 34.18N 74.28 E
Sor 126 De 39.00N 8.17W
Sora 128 Hi 41.43N 13.37 E
Sorachi-Gawa 156a Bb 43.32N 141.52 E
Soråker 116 Gb 62.31N 17.30 E
Sorak-san 152 Md 38.07N 128.28 E
Sorano 128 Fh 42.41N 11.43 E
Soratfeld 124 Kc 51.40N 8.55 E
Sorbas 126 Jg 37.07N 2.07W
Sorbe 126 Id 40.51N 3.08W
Sörberget 116 Gb 62.31N 17.22 E
Sore 122 Fj 44.19N 0.35W
Sorel 180 Kg 46.03N 73.07W
Sorell, Cape- 212 Jh 42.10S 145.10 E
Soresina 128 De 45.17N 9.51 E
Sorezaru Point 219a Cb 7.37S 156.38 E
Sørfjorden 116 Bd 60.25N 6.40 E
Sørfold 116 Dc 67.28N 15.28 E
Sorgues 122 Kj 44.00N 4.52 E
Sorgun 146 Fc 39.50N 35.19 E
Soria 126 Jc 41.46N 2.28W
Soria [3] 126 Jc 41.40N 2.40W
Soriano [2] 204 Dk 33.30S 57.45W
Sørkapp 224 Kd 76.28N 16.36 E
Sorkh, Godār-e- 146 Pf 33.05N 55.05 E
Sorkh, Kūh-e- 146 Pf 33.05N 55.05 E
Sorkheh 146 Oe 35.28N 53.13 E
Sorø 116 Di 55.26N 11.34 E
Sorocaba 200 Lh 23.29S 47.27W
Soroči Gory 114 Li 55.24N 49.55 E
Soročinsk 136 Fe 52.26N 53.10 E
Soroka 132 Fe 48.07N 28.16 E
Sorol Atoll 208 Fd 8.08N 140.23 E
Sorong 210 Ee 0.53S 131.15 E
Sorot 116 Mg 57.04N 28.50 E
Soroti 160 Kh 1.43N 33.37 E
Sørøya 110 Ia 70.36N 22.46 E
Sørøyane 116 Ab 62.20N 5.45 E
Sorraia 126 Df 38.56N 8.53W
Sørreisa 114 Eb 69.09N 18.10 E
Sorrentina, Penisola- 128 Ij 40.35N 14.30 E
Sorrento 128 Ij 40.37N 14.22 E
Sør Rondane 222 Df 72.00S 25.00 E
Sorsatunturi 114 Gc 67.24N 29.38 E
Sorsavesi 116 Lb 62.30N 27.35 E
Sorsele 114 Dd 65.32N 17.30 E
Sorsk 138 Ef 54.00N 90.20 E
Sorso 128 Cj 40.48N 8.34 E
Sorsogon 150 Hd 12.58N 124.00 E
Sort 126 Nb 42.24N 1.08 E
Šortandi 136 He 51.42N 71.05 E
Sortavala 136 Dc 61.44N 30.41 E
Sortland 114 Db 68.42N 15.24 E
Sør-Trøndelag [2] 114 Ce 63.00N 10.40 E
Sorum 134 Ne 63.50N 68.05 E
Sørumsand 116 De 59.58N 11.15 E
Šoša 114 Ih 56.33N 36.09 E
Sŏsan 154 If 36.47N 126.27 E
Sösdala 116 Eh 56.02N 13.40 E
Sos del Rey Católico 126 Kb 42.30N 1.13W
Sosna 132 Kc 52.42N 38.55 E
Sosnogorsk 112 Lc 63.37N 53.51 E
Sosnovka [Russia] 132 Lc 53.14N 41.22 E
Sosnovka [Russia] 114 Mh 56.18N 51.17 E
Sosnovka [Russia] 114 Jc 66.31N 40.33 E
Sosnovka [Ukr.] 132 Dd 50.15N 24.13 E
Sosnovo 116 Nd 60.31N 30.29 E
Sosnovo-Ozerskoje 138 Gf 52.31N 111.35 E
Sosnovy Bor 116 Me 59.48N 29.10 E
Sosnowiec 120 Pf 50.18N 19.08 E
Sospel 122 Nk 43.53N 7.27 E
Šostka 136 De 51.52N 33.31 E
Sosumav 172 Hb 13.03S 48.54 E
Sosva 136 Gd 59.32N 62.20 E
Sosva [Russia] 136 Gc 63.40N 62.02 E
Sosva [Russia] 136 Gd 59.10N 61.50 E
Sotavento [3] 162 Cf 14.40N 23.25W
Sotavento, Islas de-=Windward Islands (EN) 198 Jd 11.10N 67.00W
Sotik 170 Gc 0.41S 35.07 E
Sotkamo 114 Gd 64.08N 28.25 E
Soto la Marina 192 Jf 23.48N 98.13W
Soto la Marina, Rio- 192 Kf 23.45N 97.45W
Sotonera, Embalse de la- 126 Lb 42.05N 0.48W
Sotouboua 166 Fd 8.34N 0.59 E
Sotra 116 Ad 60.20N 5.05 E
Sotsudaka-Zaki 156b Ba 28.15N 129.10 E
Sottern 116 Fe 59.05N 15.30 E
Sotteville-lès-Rouen 122 He 49.25N 1.06 E
Sottrum 124 La 53.07N 9.14 E
Sottunga 116 Id 60.10N 20.40 E
Sotuf, Adrar- 162 De 21.42N 15.36W
Sotuta 192 Og 20.36N 89.01W
Souanké 170 Bb 2.05N 14.03 E
Soubré 166 Dd 5.47N 6.36W
Soubré [3] 166 Dd 5.47N 6.38W
Soúdha 130 Hn 35.29N 24.04 E
Souf 158 He 33.25N 6.50 E
Soufflenheim 124 Jf 48.50N 7.58 E
Souflion 130 Jh 41.12N 26.18 E
Soufrière 196 Ff 13.52N 61.04W
Soufrière [Guad.] 190 Le 16.03N 61.40W
Soufrière [St.Vin.] 190 Lf 13.21N 61.11W
Soufrière Bay 197g Bb 15.13N 61.22W
Soufrière Hills 197c Bc 16.43N 62.10W
Souillac 122 Hj 44.54N 1.29 E
Souilly 122 Le 49.01N 5.17 E
Souk Ahras 162 Ib 36.17N 7.57 E
Souk el Arba du Rharb 162 Fc 34.41N 5.59W
Sŏul=Seoul (EN) 142 Of 37.34N 127.00 E
Soulac-sur-Mer 122 Ei 45.31N 1.06W
Sŏul Si [2] 154 If 37.35N 127.00 E
Soultz-sous-Forêts 124 Jf 48.56N 7.53 E
Soumagne 124 Hd 50.37N 5.45 E
Soummam 126 Rh 36.44N 5.04 E
Sounding Creek 188 Ja 52.06N 110.28W
Soúnion 130 Hl 37.39N 24.02 E
Soúnion, Ákra- 130 Hl 37.39N 24.01 E
Sources, Mont aux- 158 Jk 28.46S 28.52 E
Soure [Braz.] 202 Id 0.44S 48.31W
Soure [Port.] 126 Dd 40.03N 8.38W
Sour el Ghozlane 162 Hb 36.09N 3.41 E
Souris 180 Hg 49.38N 100.15W
Souris 174 Je 49.39N 99.34W
Sous 162 Fc 30.25N 9.30W
Sous 162 Fc 30.22N 9.37W
Sousa 200 Mf 6.45S 38.14W
Sousel 126 Ef 38.57N 7.40W
Sous le Vent, Iles-=Leeward Islands (EN) 208 Lf 16.38S 151.30W
Sousse (EN)=Sūsah [3] 162 Jb 35.45N 10.30 E
Sousse (EN)=Sūsah [Tun.] 160 Ie 35.49N 10.38 E
Sout 172 Cf 33.03S 23.29 E
Souterraine, La- 122 Hh 46.14N 1.29 E
South Africa/Suid-Afrika [1] 160 Jl 30.00S 26.00 E
South Alligator River 212 Gb 12.15S 132.24 E
Southam 124 Ab 52.15N 1.23W
South America (EN) 106 Ck 15.00S 60.00W
Southampton 174 Kc 64.20N 84.40W
Southampton [Eng.-U.K.] 112 Fe 50.55N 1.25W
Southampton [N.Y.-U.S.] 184 Ke 40.54N 72.23W
Southampton, Cape- 180 Jd 62.08N 83.44W
Southampton Airport 124 Ad 50.55N 1.23W
Southampton Water 124 Ad 50.52N 1.20W
South Andaman 148 If 11.45N 92.45 E
Southard, Cape- 222 Ie 66.33S 122.04 E
South Auckland-Bay of Plenty [2] 218 Fb 38.00S 176.00 E
South Aulatsivik 180 Le 56.47N 61.30W
South Australia [2] 212 Ge 30.00S 135.00 E
South Australian Basin (EN) 106 Im 40.00S 128.00 E
Southaven 186 Li 35.00N 90.00W
South Baldy 186 Cj 33.59N 107.11W
South Bay 180 Jd 64.00N 83.25W
South Bend 182 Jc 41.41N 86.15W
South Benfleet 124 Cc 51.32N 0.33 E
Southborough 124 Cc 51.09N 0.15 E
South Boston 184 Hg 36.42N 78.58W
Southbridge 218 Ee 43.48S 172.15 E
South Buganda [3] 170 Fc 0.30S 32.00 E
South Caicos 194 Lc 21.31N 71.30W
South Carolina [2] 182 Ke 34.00N 81.00W
South China Basin (EN) 106 Hh 15.00N 115.00 E
South China Sea (EN)=Bien Dong 140 Ni 10.00N 113.00 E
South China Sea (EN)=Cina Selatan, Laut- 140 Ni 10.00N 113.00 E
South China Sea (EN)=Nan Hai 140 Ni 10.00N 113.00 E
South Dakota [2] 182 Gc 44.15N 100.00W
South Downs 118 Mk 50.55N 0.25W
South-East [3] 172 De 25.00S 25.45 E
South East Cape 208 Fi 43.39S 146.50 E
Southeast Indian Ridge (EN) 106 Ho 50.00S 110.00 E
Southeast Pacific Basin (EN) 106 Mp 60.00S 115.00W
South East Point [Austl.] 208 Fh 39.00S 146.20 E
South East Point [Kir.] 220g Bb 1.40N 157.10W
Southend 180 He 56.20N 103.14W
Southend-on-Sea 118 Nj 51.33N 0.43 E
Southern [Bots.] [3] 172 Cd 24.45S 24.00 E
Southern [Mwi.] [3] 170 Gf 15.30S 35.00 E
Southern [S.L.] [3] 166 Cd 7.40N 12.15W
Southern [Ug.] [3] 170 Fc 0.30S 30.30 E
Southern [Zam.] [3] 170 Ef 16.00S 27.00 E
Southern Alps 208 Ii 43.30S 170.35 E
Southern Cook Islands 208 Lg 20.00S 159.00W
Southern Cross 210 Ch 31.13S 119.19 E
Southern Desert (EN)=Janūbīyah, Aş Şaḩrā' al- 158 Jf 24.00N 30.00 E
Southern Ghats 148 Ff 10.00N 76.50 E
Southern Gilbert Islands 214 Jh 1.30S 175.30 E
Southern Guinea (EN) 158 Ii 8.00S 14.00 E
Southern Indian Lake 174 Jd 57.10N 98.40W
Southern Pines 184 Hh 35.11N 79.24W
Southern Region (EN)=Al Iglīm al Janūbīyah [2] 168 Dd 6.00N 30.00 E
Southern Sierra Madre (EN)=Madre del Sur, Sierra- 174 Jj 17.00N 100.00W
Southern Uplands 110 Fd 55.30N 3.30W
Southern Urals (EN)=Južny Ural 110 Le 54.00N 58.30 E
Southern Yemen (EN) → Yemen, People's Democratic Republic of- (EN) [1] 142 Gh 14.00N 46.00 E
South Esk 118 Ke 56.43N 2.28W
South Fiji Basin (EN) 106 Jl 26.00S 175.00 E
South Foreland 118 Oj 51.09N 1.23 E
South Fork 188 Ge 42.26N 116.53W
South Fork Flathead River 188 Ib 48.07N 113.45W
South Fork Grand River 186 Ed 45.43N 102.17W
South Fork Kern River 186 Fi 35.40N 118.27W
South Fork Moreau River 186 Ed 45.09N 102.50W
South Fork Powder River 186 Le 43.40N 106.30W
South Fork Republican River 186 Ff 40.03N 101.31W
South Georgia/Georgia del Sur 222 Ad 54.15S 36.45W
South Glamorgan [3] 118 Jj 51.30N 3.15W
South Haven 184 Dd 42.24N 86.16W
South Honshu Ridge (EN) 106 Ig 24.00N 142.00 E
South Horr 170 Gb 2.06N 36.55 E
South Indian Basin (EN) 222 Hd 60.00S 120.00 E
South Island [F.S.M.] 220d Bc 6.59N 151.59 E
South Island [Kenya] 170 Gb 2.38N 36.36 E
South Island [N.Z.] 208 Ii 44.00S 171.00 E
South Island [Sey.] 172b Ab 9.26S 46.23 E
South Island [Sey.] 172b Bc 10.10S 51.10 E
South Korea (EN)=Taehan-Min'guk [1] 142 Of 38.00N 127.30 E
South Lake Tahoe 188 Eg 38.57N 120.01W
Southland [2] 218 Bf 45.45S 168.00 E
South Loup River 186 Gf 41.04N 98.40W
South Lueti 170 Df 16.14S 23.12 E
South Magnetic Pole (1980) (EN) 222 Ie 65.08S 139.03 E
South Malosmadulu Atoll 148a Ba 5.10N 72.58 E
South Mountain 188 Ge 42.44N 116.54W
South Nahanni 180 Fd 61.03N 123.22W
South Negril Point 190 Ie 18.16N 78.22W
South Orkney Islands (EN) 222 Re 60.35S 45.30W
South Pass 174 Ie 42.22N 108.55W
South Pass [F.S.M.] 220d Bb 7.14N 151.48 E
South Pass [U.S.] 186 Ll 28.55N 89.20W
South Platte 174 Ie 41.15N 100.45W
South Point 197q Ab 13.02N 59.31W
South Pole (EN) 222 Bg 90.00S 0.00
South Porcupine 184 Ga 48.28N 81.13W
Southport [Eng.-U.K.] 118 Jh 53.39N 3.01W
Southport [N.C.-U.S.] 184 Hi 33.55N 78.01W
South Reef 219a Ee 13.00S 160.32 E
South Ronaldsay 118 Kc 58.46N 2.50W
South Rukuru 170 Fe 10.44S 34.14 E
South Saint Paul 186 Jd 44.52N 93.02W

Index Symbols

[1] Independent Nation
[2] State, Region
[3] District, County
[4] Municipality
[5] Colony, Dependency
Continent
Physical Region
Historical or Cultural Region
Mount, Mountain
Volcano
Hill
Mountains, Mountain Range
Hills, Escarpment
Plateau, Upland
Pass, Gap
Plain, Lowland
Delta
Salt Flat
Valley, Canyon
Crater, Cave
Karst Features
Depression
Polder
Desert, Dunes
Forest, Woods
Heath, Steppe
Oasis
Cape, Point
Coast, Beach
Cliff
Peninsula
Isthmus
Sandbank
Island
Atoll
Rock, Reef
Islands, Archipelago
Rocks, Reefs
Coral Reef
Well, Spring
Geyser
River, Stream
Waterfall, Rapids
River Mouth, Estuary
Lake
Salt Lake
Intermittent Lake
Reservoir
Swamp, Pond
Canal
Glacier
Ice Shelf, Pack Ice
Ocean
Sea
Gulf, Bay
Strait, Fjord
Lagoon
Bank
Seamount
Tablemount
Ridge
Shelf
Basin
Escarpment, Sea Scarp
Fracture
Trench, Abyss
National Park, Reserve
Point of Interest
Recreation Site
Cave, Cavern
Historic Site
Ruins
Wall, Walls
Church, Abbey
Temple
Scientific Station
Railway station
Airport
Port
Military installation
Lighthouse
Mine
Tunnel
Dam, Bridge

Name	Page	Grid	Lat.	Long.
South Sandwich Islands (EN)	222	Ad	56.00 S	26.30W
South Sandwich Trench (EN)	106	Do	56.30 S	25.00W
South Saskatchewan River	174	Id	53.15N	105.05W
South Shetland Islands (EN)	222	Re	62.00 S	58.00W
South Shields	118	Lg	55.00N	1.25W
South Sioux City	186	He	42.28N	96.24W
South Sister	188	Ed	44.12N	121.45W
South Taranaki Bight	218	Fc	39.40 S	174.15 E
South Trap	218	Bg	47.30 S	167.55 E
South Tyne	118	Kg	54.59N	2.08W
South Uist	118	Fd	57.15N	7.24W
South Umpqua River	188	De	43.20N	123.25W
Southwell	124	Ba	53.04N	0.57W
South Wellesley Islands	212	Hc	17.05 S	139.25 E
South West Africa → Namibia [1]	160	Ik	22.00 S	17.00 E
South West Cape	212	Jh	43.34 S	146.02 E
Southwest Cape [N.Z.]	208	Hi	47.17 S	167.27 E
Southwest Cape [V.I.U.S.]	197a	Dc	17.42N	64.53W
Southwest Indian Ridge (EN)	106	Fm	32.00 S	55.00 E
Southwest Miramichi River	184	Ob	46.50N	65.45W
Southwest Pacific Basin (EN)	106	Km	40.00 S	150.00W
Southwest Pass	186	Ll	29.00N	89.20W
South West Point	197p	Cb	12.27N	61.30W
South West Point	220g	Ab	1.52N	157.33W
Southwest Point	194	Jb	22.10N	74.10W
Southwold	118	Oi	52.20N	1.40 E
South Yorkshire [3]	118	Lh	53.30N	1.25W
Soutpansberg	172	Dd	22.58 S	29.50 E
Soverato	128	Kl	38.41N	16.33 E
Sovetabad	135	Gd	40.14N	69.42 E
Sovetsk [Russia]	136	Cd	55.05N	21.52 E
Sovetsk [Russia]	136	Ed	57.36N	48.58 E
Sovetskaj Gavan	142	Qe	48.58N	140.18 E
Sovetski [Russia]	136	Gc	61.20N	63.29 E
Sovetski [Russia]	114	Lh	56.47N	48.30 E
Sovetski [Russia]	116	Md	60.29N	28.40 E
Sovetski, proliv-	156a	Db	43.24N	145.50 E
Sovetskoje → Ketčenery	136	Ef	47.17N	44.30 E
Şowghān	146	Qh	28.20N	56.54 E
Sowie, Góry-	120	Mf	50.38N	16.30 E
Sōya	156a	Ba	45.28N	141.53 E
Sōya-Kaikyō = La Perouse Strait (EN)	140	Qe	45.30N	142.00 E
Sōya-Misaki	152	Pb	45.31N	141.56 E
Soyatita	192	Fe	25.45N	107.22W
Soyo	170	Bd	6.05 S	12.20 E
Sož	110	Je	51.57N	30.48 E
Sozopol	130	Kg	42.25N	27.42 E
Spa	122	Ld	50.29N	5.52 E
Spain (EN) = España [1]	112	Fg	40.00N	4.00W
Špakovskoje	132	Mg	45.06N	42.00 E
Spalding	118	Mi	52.47N	0.10W
Spanish Fork	188	Jf	40.07N	111.39W
Spanish Peak	188	Fd	44.24N	119.46W
Spanish Point	197d	Ba	17.33N	61.44W
Spanish Sahara (EN) → Western Sahara (EN) [5]	160	Ff	24.30N	13.00W
Spanish Town [B.V.I.]	197a	Db	18.27N	64.26W
Spanish Town [Jam.]	190	Ie	17.59N	76.57W
Sparbu	114	Ce	63.55N	11.28 E
Spargi, Isola-	128	Di	41.15N	9.20 E
Sparks	182	Dd	39.32N	119.45W
Sparreholm	116	Ge	59.04N	16.49 E
Sparta [Il.-U.S.]	186	Lg	38.07N	89.42W
Sparta [N.C.-U.S.]	184	Gg	36.30N	81.07W
Sparta [Tn.-U.S.]	184	Eh	35.56N	85.29W
Sparta [Wi.-U.S.]	186	Ke	43.57N	90.47W
Sparta (EN) = Spárti	130	Fl	37.05N	22.26 E
Spartanburg	182	Ke	34.57N	81.55W
Spartel, Cap-	158	Ge	35.48N	5.56W
Spárti = Sparta (EN)	130	Fl	37.05N	22.26 E
Spartivento, Capo- [It.]	110	Hh	37.55N	16.04 E
Spartivento, Capo- [It.]	128	Cl	38.53N	8.50 E
Spas-Demensk	132	Ib	54.24N	34.01 E
Spas-Klepiki	114	Ji	55.10N	40.13 E
Spassk-Dalni	138	Ih	44.37N	132.48 E
Spassk-Rjazanski	114	Ji	54.27N	40.22 E
Spátha, Ákra- = Spatha, Cape- (EN)	130	Gn	35.42N	23.44 E
Spatha, Cape- (EN) = Spátha, Ákra-	130	Gn	35.42N	23.44 E
Spearfish	182	Gc	44.30N	103.52W
Spearman	186	Fh	36.12N	101.12W
Speedway	184	Df	39.47N	86.15W
Speicher	124	Ie	49.56N	6.38 E
Speightstown	196	Gf	13.15N	59.39W
Speke Gulf	170	Fc	2.20 S	33.15 E
Spello	128	Gh	42.59N	12.40 E
Spenard	178	Jd	61.11N	149.55W
Spence Bay	176	Jc	69.32N	93.31W
Spencer [Ia.-U.S.]	182	Hc	43.09N	95.09W
Spencer [In.-U.S.]	184	Df	39.17N	86.46W
Spencer [Nb.-U.S.]	186	Ge	42.53N	98.42W
Spencer [W.V.-U.S.]	184	Gf	38.48N	81.22W
Spencer, Cape-	212	Hg	35.18 S	136.53 E
Spencer Gulf	208	Eh	34.00 S	137.00 E
Spenge	124	Kb	52.08N	8.29 E
Spenser Mountains	218	Ee	42.10 S	172.35 E
Sperillen	116	Dd	60.30N	10.05 E
Sperkhiós	130	Fk	38.52N	22.34 E
Sperlonga	128	Hi	41.15N	13.26 E
Sperone, Capo-	128	Cl	38.55N	8.25 E
Sperrin Mountains/Sliabh Speirin	118	Fg	54.50N	7.05W
Spessart	120	Fg	49.55N	9.30 E
Spétsai	130	Gl	37.16N	23.09 E
Spétsai	130	Gl	37.16N	23.08 E
Spey	118	Jd	57.40N	3.06W
Spey Bay	118	Jd	57.40N	3.05W
Speyer	120	Eg	49.19N	8.26 E
Speyer-bach	124	Ke	49.19N	8.27 E
Speyside	196	Fg	11.18N	60.32W
Spezzano Albanese	128	Kk	39.40N	16.19 E
Spicer Islands	180	Jc	68.10N	79.00W
Spiekeroog	120	Dc	53.46N	7.42 E
Spiess Seamount (EN)	222	Cd	54.40 S	0.15 E
Spiez	128	Bd	46.41N	7.42 E
Spijkenisse	124	Gc	51.51N	4.21 E
Spilimbergo	128	Gd	46.07N	12.54 E
Spilion	130	Hn	35.13N	24.32 E
Spilsby	124	Ca	53.11N	0.06 E
Spina	128	Gf	44.42N	12.08 E
Spinazzola	128	Kj	40.58N	16.05 E
Spincourt	124	He	49.20N	5.40 E
Spirit River	180	Fe	55.47N	118.50W
Spirovo	114	Ih	57.27N	35.01 E
Spiš	120	Qg	49.05N	20.30 E
Spišská Nová Ves	120	Qh	48.57N	20.34 E
Spitak	132	Ni	40.49N	44.14 E
Spitsbergen	224	Kd	78.45N	16.00 E
Spitsbergen	224	Kd	78.00N	19.00 E
Spittal an der Drau	128	Hd	46.48N	13.30 E
Spitzbergen Bank (EN)	179	Oc	76.00N	23.00 E
Spjelkavik	114	Be	62.28N	6.23 E
Split	112	Hg	43.31N	16.26 E
Split Lake	180	He	56.10N	96.10W
Spluga, Passo dello-	128	Dd	46.29N	9.20 E
Splügenpaß	128	Dd	46.29N	9.20 E
Spógi/Špogi	116	Lh	56.02N	26.52 E
Špogi/Spógi	116	Lh	56.02N	26.52 E
Spokane	176	He	47.40N	117.23W
Spokane, Mount-	188	Gc	47.55N	117.07W
Spokane River	188	Fc	47.44N	118.20W
Špola	136	Df	49.01N	31.24 E
Spoleto	128	Gh	42.44N	12.44 E
Spooner	186	Kd	45.50N	91.53W
Spoon River	186	Kf	40.18N	90.04W
Sporovo	120	Vd	52.25N	25.27 E
Spotsylvania	184	If	38.12N	77.35W
Sprague	188	Gc	47.18N	117.59W
Sprague River	188	Ee	42.34N	121.51W
Spratly (EN) → Nanwei Dao	150	Fe	8.42N	111.40 E
Spray	188	Fd	44.50N	119.48W
Spreča	128	Mf	44.44N	18.06 E
Spree	120	Jd	52.32N	13.13 E
Spreewald	120	Je	51.55N	14.00 E
Spremberg/Grodk	120	Ke	51.33N	14.22 E
Sprengisandur	114a	Bb	64.40N	18.07W
Springbok	160	Ik	29.43 S	17.15 E
Spring Creek	186	Fd	45.45N	100.18W
Springdale	186	Ih	36.11N	94.08W
Springe	120	Fd	52.13N	9.33 E
Springer	186	Dh	36.22N	104.36W
Springer, Mount-	184	Ja	49.48N	74.51W
Springerville	186	Ki	34.08N	109.17W
Springfield [Co.-U.S.]	186	Eh	37.24N	102.37W
Springfield [Il.-U.S.]	176	Kf	39.47N	89.40W
Springfield [Ma.-U.S.]	182	Mc	42.07N	72.36W
Springfield [Mn.-U.S.]	186	Id	44.14N	94.59W
Springfield [Mo.-U.S.]	176	Jf	37.14N	93.17W
Springfield [N.Z.]	218	De	43.20 S	171.56 E
Springfield [Oh.-U.S.]	182	Kd	39.55N	83.48W
Springfield [Or.-U.S.]	182	Cc	44.03N	123.01W
Springfield [S.D.-U.S.]	186	He	42.49N	97.54W
Springfield [Tn.-U.S.]	184	Dg	36.31N	86.52W
Springfontein	172	Df	30.19 S	25.36 E
Spring Garden	202	Gb	6.59N	58.31W
Spring Hall	197q	Ab	13.19N	59.36W
Springhill [La.-U.S.]	186	Jj	33.00N	93.28W
Springhill [N.S.-Can.]	180	Lg	45.39N	64.03W
Spring Mountains	188	Hh	36.10N	115.40W
Springs	172	De	26.13 S	28.25 E
Springsure	212	Jd	24.07 S	148.05 E
Spring Valley	186	Je	43.41N	92.23W
Spring Valley	188	Hg	39.10N	114.30W
Springville	188	Jf	40.10N	111.37W
Spruce Knob	174	Lf	38.42N	79.32W
Spruce Mountain [Az.-U.S.]	188	Ii	34.28N	112.24W
Spruce Mountain [Nv.-U.S.]	188	Hf	40.33N	114.49W
Spulico, Capo-	128	Kk	39.58N	16.38 E
Spurn Head	118	Nh	53.34N	0.07 E
Squamish	180	Fg	49.42N	123.09W
Squillace	128	Kl	38.47N	16.31 E
Squillace, Golfo di-	128	Kl	38.45N	16.50 E
Squinzano	128	Mj	40.26N	18.02 E
Srbica	130	Dg	42.45N	20.47 E
Srbija = Serbia (EN) [2]	130	Df	44.00N	21.00 E
Srbija = Serbia (EN)	110	Ig	43.00N	21.00 E
Srbija = Serbia (EN)	130	Df	44.00N	21.00 E
Srbobran	130	Cd	45.33N	19.48 E
Srê Âmbêl	148	Kf	11.07N	103.46 E
Sredinny hrebet	140	Rd	56.00N	158.00 E
Sredna Gora	130	Hg	42.30N	25.00 E
Srednekolymsk	138	Kc	67.27N	153.41 E
Srednerusskaja vozvyšennost = Central Russian Uplands (EN)	110	Je	52.00N	38.00 E
Srednesatyginski Tuman, ozero-	134	Lg	59.45N	65.25 E
Srednesibirskoje ploskogorje = Central Siberian Uplands (EN)	140	Mc	65.00N	105.00 E
Sredni Kujto, ozero-	114	Hd	65.05N	31.30 E
Sredni Ural = Central Urals (EN)	110	Ld	58.00N	59.00 E
Sredni Urgal	138	If	51.13N	132.58 E
Sredni Verecki, pereval-	132	Ce	48.49N	23.07 E
Srednjaja Ahtuba	132	Ne	48.43N	44.52 E
Srednjaja Olëkma	138	He	55.28N	120.40 E
Śrem	120	Nd	52.08N	17.01 E
Sremska Mitrovica	130	Ce	44.58N	19.37 E
Sremski Karlovci	130	Cd	45.12N	19.56 E
Sretensk	142	Nd	52.15N	117.43 E
Sri Gangānagar	148	Ec	29.55N	73.53 E
Sri Jayawardenepura	148	Gg	6.54N	80.02 E
Srijem	130	Cd	45.00N	19.40 E
Srīkākulam	148	Ge	18.18N	83.54 E
Sri Lanka	140	Ki	7.30N	80.30 E
Sri Lanka (Ceylon) [1]	142	Ki	7.40N	80.50 E
Srīnagar	142	Jf	34.05N	74.49 E
Srivardhan	148	Ee	18.02N	73.01 E
Środa Śląska	120	Me	51.10N	16.36 E
Środa Wielkopolska	120	Nd	52.14N	17.17 E
Srpska Crnja	130	Dd	45.43N	20.42 E
Sruth na Maoile/North Channel	110	Fd	55.10N	5.40W
Ssu-ch'uan Sheng → Sichuan Sheng = Szechwan (EN) [2]	152	He	30.00N	103.00 E
Staaten River	212	Ic	16.24 S	141.17 E
Stabroek	124	Gc	51.20N	4.22 E
Stack Skerry	118	Ib	59.02N	4.30W
Stade	120	Fc	53.36N	9.29 E
Staden	124	Fd	50.59N	3.01 E
Stadhavet	116	Ab	62.15N	5.05 E
Städjan	116	Ec	61.58N	12.52 E
Stadlandet	116	Ab	62.05N	5.20 E
Stadskanaal	122	Ma	53.00N	6.55 E
Stadskanaal-Musselkanaal	124	Jb	52.56N	7.02 E
Stadtallendorf	124	Ld	50.50N	9.00 E
Stadthagen	124	Lb	52.19N	9.12 E
Stadtkyll	124	Id	50.21N	6.32 E
Stadtlohn	124	Ic	51.59N	6.56 E
Stadtoldendorf	120	Fe	51.54N	9.39 E
Staffa	118	Ge	56.25N	6.10W
Staffanstorp	116	Ei	55.38N	13.13 E
Staffelsee	120	Hi	47.42N	11.10 E
Staffora	128	De	45.04N	9.01 E
Stafford	118	Ki	52.48N	2.07W
Stafford	118	Li	52.50N	2.00W
Staffordshire [3]	118	Li	52.55N	2.00W
Staicele/Stajcele	116	Kg	57.44N	24.39 E
Stainach	128	Ic	47.32N	14.06 E
Staines	124	Bc	51.26N	0.31W
Stakčín	120	Sg	49.00N	22.13 E
Stalać	130	Ef	43.40N	21.25 E
Stalham	124	Db	52.46N	1.31 E
Stalingrad → Volgograd	112	Kf	48.44N	44.25 E
Ställdalen	116	Fe	59.56N	14.56 E
Stalowa Wola	120	Sf	50.35N	22.02 E
Stamford [Ct.-U.S.]	184	Ke	41.03N	73.32W
Stamford [Eng.-U.K.]	118	Mi	52.39N	0.29W
Stamford [Tx.-U.S.]	186	Gj	32.57N	99.48W
Stamford, Lake-	186	Gj	33.05N	99.35W
Stampriet	172	Bd	24.20 S	18.28 E
Stamsund	114	Cb	68.08N	13.51 E
Stanberry	186	If	40.13N	94.35W
Stancija Jakkabag	136	Ff	38.59N	66.42 E
Stancija-Karakul	136	Gh	39.30N	63.50 E
Standerton	172	De	26.58 S	29.07 E
Standish	184	Fd	44.00N	83.57W
Stanford	188	Jc	47.09N	110.13W
Stånga	116	Hg	57.17N	18.28 E
Stångån	116	Ff	58.27N	15.37 E
Stange	116	Dd	60.43N	11.11 E
Stanger	172	Ee	29.27 S	31.14 E
Stanke Dimitrov	130	Gg	42.16N	23.07 E
Stanley [Austl.]	212	Jh	40.46 S	145.18 E
Stanley [Falk.Is.]	200	Kk	51.42 S	57.51W
Stanley [N.D.-U.S.]	186	Eb	48.19N	102.23W
Stann Creek	190	Ge	16.59N	88.13W
Stann Creek [3]	194	Ce	16.50N	88.30W
Stanovoje nagorje = Stanovoy Upland (EN)	140	Nd	56.00N	114.00 E
Stanovoj hrebet = Stanovoy Range (EN)	140	Od	56.20N	126.00 E
Stanovoy Range (EN) = Stanovoj hrebet	140	Od	56.20N	126.00 E
Stanovoy Upland (EN) = Stanovoje nagorje	140	Nd	56.00N	114.00 E
Stans	128	Cd	46.58N	8.22 E
Stansted Airport	124	Cc	51.54N	0.13 E
Stansted Mountfitchet	124	Cc	51.54N	0.12 E
Stanthorpe	212	Ke	28.39 S	151.57 E
Stanton Banks	118	Fe	56.15N	7.50W
Staphorst	124	Ib	52.38N	6.14 E
Staples	186	Ic	46.21N	94.48W
Stapleton	186	Ff	41.29N	100.31W
Stąporków	120	Qe	51.09N	20.34 E
Starachowice	120	Re	51.03N	21.04 E
Staraja Majna	114	Li	54.36N	48.59 E
Staraja Russa	136	Dd	57.59N	31.23 E
Staraja-Vyževka	120	Ue	51.27N	24.34 E
Stará L'ubovňa	120	Qg	49.18N	20.42 E
Stara Moravica	130	Cd	45.52N	19.28 E
Stara Pazova	130	De	44.59N	20.10 E
Stara Planina = Balkan Mountains (EN)	110	Ig	43.15N	25.00 E
Stara Zagora	112	Ig	42.25N	25.38 E
Stara Zagora [2]	130	Ig	42.25N	25.38 E
Starbuck Island	208	Le	5.37 S	155.53W
Staretina	128	Kf	44.02N	16.43 E
Stargard Szczeciński	120	Lc	53.20N	15.02 E
Stari Begejski kanal	130	Dd	45.29N	20.25 E
Starica	114	Ih	56.30N	34.56 E
Starigrad	128	Kg	43.11N	16.36 E
Stari Vlah	130	Df	43.23N	20.10 E
Starke	184	Fk	29.57N	82.07W
Starkville	186	Lj	33.28N	88.48W
Starnberg	120	Hh	48.00N	11.21 E
Starnberger See (Würmsee)	120	Hi	47.55N	11.20 E
Starobelsk	136	Df	49.15N	38.58 E
Starodub	136	De	52.35N	32.46 E
Starogard Gdański	120	Oc	53.59N	18.33 E
Starokonstantinov	132	Ee	49.43N	27.13 E
Starominskaja	136	Df	46.31N	39.06 E
Staroščerbinovskaja	132	Kf	46.37N	38.42 E
Starosubhangulovo	134	Hj	53.06N	57.20 E
Starotimoškino	114	Lj	53.43N	47.32 E
Start Point	118	Jk	50.13N	3.38W
Staryje Dorogi	132	Fc	53.02N	28.17 E
Stary Krym	132	Ig	45.02N	35.05 E
Stary Oskol	136	De	51.18N	37.51 E
Stary Sambor	132	Ce	49.29N	23.01 E
Stary Terek	132	Og	44.01N	47.24 E
Staßfurt	120	He	51.52N	11.35 E
Staszów	120	Rf	50.34N	21.10 E
State College	184	Ie	40.48N	77.52W
Staten Island (EN) = Estados, Isla de los-	198	Jk	54.47 S	64.15W
Statesboro	184	Gi	32.27N	81.47W
Statesville	184	Gh	35.47N	80.53W
Stathelle	116	Ce	59.03N	9.41 E
Stathmós Krioneriou	130	Ek	38.20N	21.35 E
Statland	114	Cd	64.30N	11.08 E
Staunton	182	Ld	38.10N	79.05W
Stavanger	112	Gd	58.58N	5.45 E
Stavelot	124	Hd	50.23N	5.56 E
Staveren	122	Lb	52.53N	5.22 E
Stavern	116	Df	59.00N	10.02 E
Stavnoje	120	Sh	48.59N	22.45 E
Stavropol	112	Kf	45.02N	41.59 E
Stavropolskaja vozvyšennost	132	Mg	45.10N	43.00 E
Stavropolski kraj [3]	136	Eg	45.00N	43.15 E
Stavrós [Grc.]	130	Fj	39.19N	22.14 E
Stavrós [Grc.]	130	Gi	40.40N	23.42 E
Stavroúpolis	130	Hh	41.12N	24.42 E
Stawell	212	Ig	37.04 S	142.46 E
Stawiski	120	Sc	53.23N	22.09 E
Stawiszyn	120	Oe	51.55N	18.07 E
Stayton	188	Dd	44.48N	122.48W
Steamboat Springs	182	Fc	40.29N	106.50W
Stębark	120	Qc	53.30N	20.05 E
Stebnik	120	Tg	49.14N	23.34 E
Stedingen	124	Ka	53.10N	8.30 E
Steele	186	Gc	46.51N	99.55W
Steelpoort	172	Ed	24.48 S	30.12 E
Steenbergen	124	Gc	51.35N	4.19 E
Steen River	180	Fe	59.38N	117.06W
Steensby Inlet	180	Jb	70.10N	78.25W
Steenstrups Gletscher	179	Gc	75.15N	57.30W
Steenvoorde	124	Ed	50.48N	2.35 E
Steenwijk	122	Mb	52.47N	6.08 E
Ştefăneşti	130	Kb	47.48N	27.12 E
Stefanie, Lake- (EN) = Chew Bahir	158	Kh	4.38N	36.50 E
Stefansson	180	Gb	73.20N	105.30W
Ştefleşti, Vîrful-	130	Gd	45.32N	23.48 E
Stege	116	Ej	54.59N	12.18 E
Steiermark = Styria (EN) [2]	128	Ic	47.15N	15.00 E
Steiermark = Styria (EN)	128	Ic	47.15N	15.00 E
Steigerwald	120	Gg	49.40N	10.20 E
Steilrandberge	172	Ac	17.53 S	13.20 E
Steinach	128	Fc	47.05N	11.28 E
Steinbach	180	Hg	49.32N	96.41W
Steinen, Rio-	202	Hf	12.05 S	53.46W
Steinfeld (Oldenburg)	124	Kb	52.36N	8.13 E
Steinfort/Steinfurt	124	He	49.40N	5.55 E
Steinfurt	120	Dd	52.09N	7.20 E
Steinfurt/Steinfort	124	He	49.40N	5.55 E
Steinfurt-Borghorst	124	Jb	52.08N	7.25 E
Steinhagen	124	Kb	52.01N	8.24 E
Steinhausen	172	Bd	21.49 S	18.20 E
Steinheim	124	Lc	51.51N	9.06 E
Steinhuder Meer	120	Fd	52.28N	9.19 E
Steinkjer	114	Cd	64.01N	11.30 E
Steinkopf	172	Be	29.18 S	17.43 E
Steinshamn	116	Bb	62.47N	6.29 E
Steinsøy	114	Af	61.00N	4.30 E
Steirisch-Niederösterreichische Kalkalpen	128	Jc	47.45N	15.30 E
Stekene	124	Gc	51.12N	4.02 E
Stekolny	138	Ke	60.00N	150.50 E
Stella	172	Ce	26.33 S	24.53 E
Stellenbosch	172	Bf	33.58 S	18.50 E
Stello	122a	Ba	42.47N	9.25 E
Stelvio, Passo dello- / Stilfser Joch	128	Ed	46.32N	10.27 E
Stemwede	124	Kb	52.26N	8.26 E
Stenay	122	Le	49.29N	5.11 E
Stendal	120	Hd	52.36N	11.51 E
Stende	116	Jg	57.10N	22.28 E
Stende	116	Ig	57.40N	21.42 E
Stenhouse Bay	212	Hg	35.17 S	136.56 E
Stenstorp	116	Ef	58.16N	13.43 E
Stenungsund	114	Cg	58.05N	11.49 E
Stepanakert	112	Kh	39.49N	46.44 E
Stepanavan	132	Ni	40.59N	44.20 E
Stephens, Cape-	218	Ed	40.42 S	173.57 E
Stephens, Mount-	222	Rg	83.23 S	51.27W
Stephens Passage	178	Me	57.50N	133.50W
Stephenville [Newf.-Can.]	180	Lg	48.33N	58.35W
Stephenville [Tx.-U.S.]	186	Gj	32.13N	98.12W
Steps Point	221c	Cb	14.22 S	170.45W
Sterea Ellás kai Évvoia [2]	130	Hk	38.20N	24.30 E
Sterkstroom	172	Df	31.32 S	26.32 E
Sterlibaševo	134	Gj	53.28N	55.15 E
Sterling [Co.-U.S.]	182	Gc	40.37N	103.13W
Sterling [Il.-U.S.]	186	Lf	41.48N	89.42W
Sterling City	186	Fk	31.50N	100.59W
Sterlitamak	112	Le	53.37N	55.58 E
Šternberk	120	Ng	49.44N	17.19 E
Sterzing / Vipiteno	128	Fd	46.54N	11.26 E
Stettin → Szczecin	112	He	53.24N	14.32 E
Stettiner Haff	120	Kc	53.46N	14.14 E
Stettler	180	Gf	52.19N	112.43W
Steubenville	182	Kc	40.22N	80.39W
Stevenage	118	Mj	51.54N	0.11W
Stevenson Entrance	178	Ie	57.45N	152.20W
Stevens Point	182	Jc	44.31N	89.34W
Stewart	180	Ee	55.56N	129.59W
Stewart	180	Dd	63.18N	139.24W
Stewart Crossing	180	Dd	63.19N	136.33W
Stewart Island	208	Hi	47.00 S	167.50 E
Stewart Islands	208	He	8.20 S	162.40 E
Steyerberg	124	Lb	52.34N	9.02 E
Steyning	124	Bd	50.53N	0.20W
Steynsburg	172	Df	31.15 S	25.49 E
Steyr	128	Ib	48.03N	14.25 E
Steyr	128	Ib	48.02N	14.25 E
Štiavnické vrchy	120	Oh	48.15N	18.50 E
Stidia	126	Li	35.50N	0.05W
Stiene	116	Kg	57.19N	24.28 E
Stiens, Leeuwarderadeel-	124	Ha	53.16N	5.46 E
Stigliano	128	Kj	40.24N	16.14 E
Stigtomta	116	Gf	58.48N	16.47 E
Stikine	174	Fd	56.40N	132.30W
Stikine Ranges	180	Ee	57.35N	131.00W
Stilfontein	172	De	26.50 S	26.50 E
Stilfser Joch / Stelvio, Passo dello-	128	Ed	46.32N	10.27 E
Stilis	130	Fk	38.55N	22.37 E
Stillwater [Mn.-U.S.]	186	Jd	45.04N	92.49W
Stillwater [Ok.-U.S.]	182	Hd	36.07N	97.04W
Stillwater Range	188	Fg	39.50N	118.15W
Stilo	128	Kl	38.29N	16.28 E
Stilo, Punta-	128	Kl	38.27N	16.35 E
Štimlje	130	Eg	42.26N	21.03 E
Stînişoarei, Munţii-	130	Ib	47.20N	26.00 E
Stinnett	186	Fi	35.50N	101.27W
Štip	130	Fh	41.44N	22.12 E
Stirling	118	Je	56.07N	3.57W
Stirling Range	212	Df	34.25 S	117.50 E
Stjernøya	114	Fa	70.18N	22.45 E
Stjørdalshalsen	116	Ca	63.28N	10.44 E
Stobi	130	Eh	41.33N	21.59 E
Stobrawa	120	Nf	50.50N	17.32 E
Stocka	116	Gc	61.54N	17.20 E
Stockach	120	Fi	47.51N	9.01 E
Stockbridge	124	Ac	51.06N	1.29W
Stockerau	128	Kb	48.23N	16.13 E
Stockholm	112	Hd	59.20N	18.03 E
Stockholm [2]	114	Dg	59.20N	18.00 E
Stockport	118	Kh	53.25N	2.10W
Stocks Seamount (EN)	198	Mg	12.15 S	32.00W
Stockton [Ca.-U.S.]	176	Gf	37.57N	121.17W
Stockton [Mo.-U.S.]	186	Jh	37.42N	93.48W
Stockton Lake	186	Jh	37.40N	93.45W
Stockton-on-Tees	118	Lg	54.34N	1.19W
Stockton Plateau	182	Ge	30.30N	102.30W
Stoczek Łukowski	120	Re	51.58N	21.58 E
Stöde	114	De	62.25N	16.35 E
Stoēng Trēng	148	Lf	13.31N	105.58 E
Stoer, Point of-	118	Hc	58.20N	5.25W
Stogovo	130	Dh	41.29N	20.39 E
Stohod	120	Ve	51.52N	25.44 E
Stoholm	116	Ch	56.29N	9.10 E
Stoj, gora-	132	Ce	48.39N	23.15 E
Stojba	142	Pd	52.49N	131.43 E
Stoke-on-Trent	118	Kh	53.00N	2.10W
Stokksnes	114a	Cb	64.14N	14.58W
Stokmarknes	114	Db	68.34N	14.55 E
Stol	130	Fe	44.11N	22.09 E
Stolac	128	Lg	43.05N	17.58 E
Stolbcy	132	Ec	53.31N	26.43 E
Stolberg (Rheinland)	120	Cf	50.46N	6.14 E
Stolbovoj, ostrov-	138	Ib	74.05N	136.00 E
Stolin	132	Ed	51.57N	26.52 E
Stolzenau	124	Lb	52.31N	9.04 E
Ston	128	Lh	42.50N	17.42 E
Stone	118	Ke	52.54N	2.10W
Stonehaven	118	Ke	56.58N	2.13W
Stonehenge	212	Id	24.22 S	143.17 E
Stonehenge	118	Lj	51.11N	1.49W
Stoner	186	Bh	37.37N	108.18W
Stonewall	186	Ha	50.09N	97.21W
Stony	178	Hd	61.45N	156.35W
Stony Rapids	180	Ge	59.16N	105.50W
Stony River	178	Hd	61.47N	156.41W
Stony Stratford	124	Bb	52.03N	0.51W
Stony Tunguska (EN) = Podkamennaja Tunguska	140	Lc	61.36N	90.18 E
Stör	120	Fc	53.50N	9.25 E
Storå	116	Fe	59.43N	15.08 E
Storå	116	Ch	56.19N	8.19 E
Storå/Isojoki	114	Ee	62.07N	21.58 E
Stora Gla	116	Ee	59.30N	12.30 E
Stora Le	116	De	59.05N	11.55 E
Stora Lulevatten	114	Ec	67.08N	19.20 E
Storavan	114	Ed	65.42N	18.12 E
Storby	116	Hd	60.13N	19.34 E
Stord	114	Ag	59.55N	5.25 E
Stordal	116	Bb	62.23N	7.01 E
Store Bælt = Great Belt (EN)	116	Hd	55.30N	11.00 E
Storebro	116	Fg	57.35N	15.51 E
Storefiskbank = Great Fisher Bank (EN)	118	Qe	56.50N	4.00 E
Store Heddinge	116	Ei	55.19N	12.25 E
Store Hellefiske Bank (EN)	179	Ge	67.30N	55.00W
Store Koldewey	179	Kc	76.20N	18.30W
Store Kvien	116	Dc	61.34N	10.33 E
Støren	114	Ce	63.02N	10.18 E
Store Nupsfonn	116	Be	59.54N	7.08 E
Store Sølnkletten	116	Dc	61.59N	10.18 E
Storfjorden [Nor.]	116	Bb	62.25N	6.30 E
Storfjorden [Sval.]	179	Nc	77.30N	20.00 E

Storfors 116 Fe 59.32N 14.16 E
Storis Passage 180 Hc 67.40N 98.30W
Storkerson Bay 180 Fb 73.00N 124.00W
Storkerson Peninsula 180 Gb 73.00N 106.30W
Storlien 114 Ce 63.19N 12.06 E
Stormarn 120 Gc 53.45N 10.20 E
Storm Bay 212 Jh 43.10S 147.30 E
Storm Lake 182 Hc 42.39N 95.13W
Stornoway 118 Gc 58.12N 6.23W
Storøya 179 Ob 80.08N 27.50 E
Storožinec 132 De 48.10N 25.46 E
Storsjøen [Nor.] 116 Dd 61.35N 11.15 E
Storsjøen [Nor.] 116 Dd 60.25N 11.40 E
Storsjön [Swe.] 116 Gd 60.35N 16.45 E
Storsjön [Swe.] 110 Hc 63.15N 14.20 E
Storsteinfjellet 114 Db 68.14N 17.52 E
Storstrøm [2] 116 Dj 55.00N 11.50 E
Storstrømmen 179 Jc 77.20N 23.00W
Storsudret 116 Hh 57.00N 18.15 E
Storuman 112 Hb 65.06N 17.06 E
Storuman 114 Dd 65.14N 16.54 E
Storvätteshågna 116 Eb 62.07N 12.27 E
Storvigelen 116 Eb 62.32N 12.04 E
Storvik 116 Gd 60.35N 16.32 E
Storvreta 116 Ge 59.58N 17.42 E
Stöttingfjället 114 Dd 64.38N 17.44 E
Stoughton 188 Nb 49.41N 103.03W
Stour [Eng.-U.K.] 124 Dc 51.18N 1.22 E
Stour [Eng.-U.K.] 118 Lk 50.43N 1.47W
Stour [Eng.-U.K.] 118 Oj 51.52N 1.16 E
Stourbridge 118 Ki 52.27N 2.09W
Støvring 116 Ch 56.53N 9.51 E
Stowmarket 124 Cb 52.11N 0.59 E
Strabane/An Srath Bán 118 Fg 54.49N 7.27W
Stradella 128 De 45.05N 9.18 E
Straelen 124 Ic 51.27N 6.16 E
Strakonice 120 Jg 49.16N 13.55 E
Straldža 130 Jg 42.36N 26.41 E
Stralsund 112 He 54.18N 13.06 E
Strand 172 Bf 34.06S 18.50 E
Stranda 114 Be 62.19N 6.54 E
Strand Bay 180 Ia 79.00N 94.00W
Strangford Lough/Loch Cuan 118 Hg 54.26N 5.36W
Strängnäs 116 Ge 59.23N 17.02 E
Stranraer 118 Hg 54.54N 5.02W
Strasbourg [Fr.] 112 Gf 48.35N 7.45 E
Strasbourg [Sask.-Can.] 188 Ma 51.04N 104.57W
Strašeny 132 Ff 47.06N 28.34 E
Straßwalchen 128 Hc 47.59N 13.15 E
Stratford [N.Z.] 218 Fc 39.21S 174.17 E
Stratford [Ont.-Can.] 184 Gd 43.22N 80.57W
Stratford [Tx.-U.S.] 186 Eh 36.20N 102.04W
Stratford-upon-Avon 118 Li 52.12N 1.41W
Strathclyde [3] 118 If 55.50N 4.50W
Strathgordon 212 Jh 42.54S 146.10 E
Strathmore 188 Ia 51.03N 113.23W
Strathmore 118 Je 56.40N 3.05W
Strathroy 184 Gd 42.57N 81.38W
Strathy Point 118 Ic 58.35N 4.01W
Straubenhardt 124 Kf 48.50N 8.30 E
Straubing 120 Ih 48.53N 12.34 E
Straumnes 114a Aa 66.26N 23.08W
Straumsjøen 114 Db 68.41N 14.30 E
Strausberg 120 Jd 52.35N 13.53 E
Strawberry Mountain 188 Fd 44.19N 118.43W
Strawberry River 188 Jf 40.10N 110.24W
Straža 130 Fg 42.15N 22.14 E
Stražica 130 If 43.14N 25.58 E
Strážiště 120 Kg 49.32N 14.58 E
Stražovské vrchy 120 Oh 48.55N 18.30 E
Streaky Bay 212 Gf 32.48S 134.13 E
Streaky Bay 212 Gf 32.35S 134.10 E
Streator 186 Lf 41.07N 88.50W
Středočeská pahorkatina 120 Kg 49.30N 14.15 E
Středočeský kraj [3] 120 Kg 49.55N 14.30 E
Středoslovenský kraj [3] 120 Ph 48.50N 19.10 E
Strehaia 130 Ge 44.37N 23.12 E
Strei 130 Gd 45.51N 23.03 E
Střela 120 Jg 49.54N 13.32 E
Strelasund 120 Jb 54.20N 13.05 E
Strelka 138 Ee 58.03N 93.05 E
Strelna 114 Jc 66.04N 38.39 E
Strenči 114 Fh 57.39N 25.38 E
Stresa 128 Ce 45.53N 8.32 E
Streževoj 138 Cd 60.42N 77.35 E
Stříbro 120 Ig 49.46N 13.00 E
Strickland River 212 Ia 6.00S 142.05 E
Strîmbeni 130 He 44.28N 24.58 E
Strimón 130 Gi 40.47N 23.51 E
Strimonikós Kólpos 130 Gi 40.40N 23.50 E
Strjama 130 Hg 42.10N 24.56 E
Strofádhes, Nisoi- 130 Dl 37.15N 21.00 E
Ströhen, Wagenfeld- 124 Kb 52.32N 8.39 E
Strohgäu 124 Kf 48.50N 9.00 E
Stromberg 124 Je 49.57N 7.46 E
Stromboli 128 Jl 38.47N 15.14 E
Strömfors/Ruotsinpyhtää 116 Ld 60.32N 26.27 E
Stromness 118 Jc 58.57N 3.18W
Strömsbro 116 Gd 60.42N 17.10 E
Strömsbruk 114 Dc 61.53N 17.19 E
Strömsnäsbruk 116 Eh 56.33N 13.43 E
Strömstad 114 Cg 58.56N 11.10 E
Strömsund 114 De 63.51N 15.35 E
Strongili 130 Hm 36.58N 24.55 E
Stròngoli 128 Lk 39.16N 17.03 E
Stronsay 118 Kb 59.08N 2.38W
Stropkov 120 Rg 49.12N 21.40 E
Stroud 118 Kj 51.45N 2.12W
Struer 114 Bh 56.29N 8.37 E
Struga 130 Dh 41.11N 20.41 E
Strugi-Krasnyje 114 Gg 58.17N 29.08 E
Strule 118 Fg 54.40N 7.24W
Struma 110 Ig 40.47N 23.51 E
Strumble Head 118 Hi 52.02N 5.04W
Strumica 130 Fh 41.26N 22.39 E
Stry 136 Cf 49.14N 23.49 E
Stry 132 De 49.24N 24.13 E
Strydenburg 172 Ce 29.58S 23.40 E
Stryn 114 Bf 61.55N 6.47 E
Strynsvatn 116 Bc 61.55N 7.05 E
Strzegom 120 Mf 50.57N 16.21 E
Strzegomka 120 Me 51.08N 16.50 E
Strzelce Krajeńskie 120 Ld 52.53N 15.32 E
Strzelce Opolskie 120 Of 50.31N 18.19 E
Strzelin 120 Nf 50.47N 17.03 E
Strzelno 120 Od 52.38N 18.11 E
Strzyżów 120 Rg 49.52N 21.47 E
Stuart 184 Gi 27.12N 80.16W
Stuart 178 Gd 63.35N 162.30W
Stuart, Mount- 188 Ec 47.29N 120.54W
Stuart Bluff Range 212 Gd 22.45S 132.15 E
Stuart Lake 180 Ff 54.33N 124.35W
Stuart Range 212 Ge 29.10S 134.55 E
Stubaier Alpen 128 Fc 47.10N 11.05 E
Stubbekøbing 116 Ej 54.53N 12.03 E
Stubbenkammer 120 Jb 54.35N 13.40 E
Stubbs Bay 197n Ba 13.08N 61.10W
Štubik 130 Fe 44.18N 22.21 E
Studenica, Manastir- 130 Df 43.28N 20.37 E
Studholme Junction 218 Df 44.44S 171.08 E
Stugun 114 De 63.10N 15.36 E
Stuhr 124 Ka 53.02N 8.45 E
Stupino 114 Ji 54.57N 38.03 E
Stura di Demonte 128 Bf 44.40N 7.53 E
Stura di Lanzo 128 Be 45.06N 7.44 E
Sturge Island 222 Ke 67.27S 164.18 E
Sturgeon Bay 186 Md 44.50N 87.23W
Sturgeon Falls 180 Jg 46.22N 79.55W
Sturgeon Lake 186 Kb 50.00N 90.45W
Sturgis [Mi.-U.S.] 184 Ee 41.48N 85.25W
Sturgis [S.D.-U.S.] 186 Ed 44.25N 103.31W
Sturkö 116 Fh 56.05N 15.40 E
Sturt Creek 212 Fd 20.08S 127.24 E
Sturt Desert 212 Ie 28.30S 141.00 E
Stutterheim 172 Df 32.33S 27.28 E
Stuttgart [Ar.-U.S.] 186 Ki 34.30N 91.33W
Stuttgart [Ger.] 112 Gf 48.46N 9.11 E
Stviga 132 Ec 52.04N 27.55 E
Stykkishólmur 114a Ab 65.04N 22.44W
Styr 136 Ce 52.07N 26.35 E
Styria (EN) = Steiermark [2] 128 Ic 47.15N 15.00 E
Styria (EN) = Steiermark 128 Ic 47.15N 15.00 E
Styrsö 116 Dg 57.37N 11.46 E
Suafa Point 219a Ec 8.19S 160.41 E
Suai 150 Ih 9.21S 125.17 E
Suakin Archipelago (EN) = Sawākin, Jazā'ir- 158 Kg 19.07N 37.20 E
Suao 152 Lg 24.36N 121.51 E
Suardi 204 Bj 30.32S 61.58W
Suata 214 Fi 7.34S 158.44 E
Subačius/Subačjus 116 Ki 55.44N 24.53 E
Subačjus/Subačius 116 Ki 55.44N 24.53 E
Subang 150 Eh 6.34S 107.45 E
Subansiri 148 Jc 26.48N 93.49 E
Subao Ding 152 Jf 27.10N 110.18 E
Šubarkuduk 136 Ff 49.09N 56.31 E
Šubarši 132 Te 48.38N 57.12 E
Subate 116 Lh 56.01N 26.04 E
Subay', 'Urūq- 164 He 22.15N 43.05 E
Subaytilah 162 Ib 35.14N 9.08 E
Subbéticas, Cordillera- 126 Jf 38.30N 2.30W
Subei (Dangchengwan) 152 Fd 39.36N 94.58 E
Subi, Pulau- 150 Ef 2.55N 108.50 E
Subiaco 128 Hi 41.55N 13.06 E
Sublette 186 Fh 37.29N 100.50W
Subotica 130 Cc 46.06N 19.40 E
Subpolar Urals (EN) = Pripoljarny Ural 110 Lb 65.00N 60.00 E
Subugo 170 Gc 1.40S 35.49 E
Suceava 130 Jb 47.38N 26.15 E
Suceava [2] 130 Ib 47.40N 25.45 E
Suceava 130 Jb 47.32N 26.32 E
Sucha Beskidzka 120 Pg 49.44N 19.36 E
Süchbaatar → Suhe-Bator 142 Md 50.15N 106.12 E
Suchedniów 120 Qe 51.03N 20.51 E
Suchiapa, Rio- 192 Mi 16.36N 93.01W
Suchitepéquez [3] 194 Bf 14.25N 91.20W
Sucia, Bahia- 197a Ac 17.57N 67.10W
Sucio, Rio- 194 Ij 7.27N 77.07W
Suck/An tSuca 118 Eh 53.16N 8.03W
Suckling, Mount- 212 Ja 9.45S 148.55 E
Sucre [2] 202 Fa 10.25N 63.30W
Sucre [3] 202 Db 9.00N 75.00W
Sucre [Bol.] 200 Jg 19.02S 65.17W
Sucre [Col.] 202 Db 8.50N 74.43W
Suçuarana, Serra da- 204 Jb 14.25S 45.00W
Sucunduri, Rio- 202 Ge 5.30S 59.40W
Sućuraj 128 Lg 43.08N 17.12 E
Sucuriú, Rio- 202 Hh 20.47S 51.38W
Sud, Canal du- 194 Kd 18.40N 73.05W
Sud, Massif du- 194 Kd 18.25N 73.55W
Suda 114 Ig 59.11N 37.33 E
Suda 114 Ig 59.12N 37.30 E
Sudak 136 Dg 44.50N 34.59 E
Sudan 158 Ig 11.30N 15.00 E
Sudan (EN) = As Sūdān [1] 160 Jg 15.00N 30.00 E
Sudbury [Eng.-U.K.] 118 Ni 52.02N 0.44 E
Sudbury [Ont.-Can.] 176 Ke 46.30N 81.00W
Suddie 196 Gi 7.07N 58.29W
Sude 120 Gc 53.22N 10.45 E
Sudeten (EN) = Sudety 110 He 50.30N 16.00 E
Sudety = Sudeten (EN) 110 He 50.30N 16.00 E
Sudirman, Pegunungan- 150 Kg 4.12S 137.00 E
Sudočje, ozero- 135 Bc 43.25N 58.30 E
Sudogda 114 Ji 55.59N 40.50 E
Sudost 132 Hc 52.19N 33.24 E
Sud-Ouest [Burkina] [3] 166 Ec 10.30N 3.15W
Sud-Ouest [Cam.] [3] 166 Gd 5.20N 9.20 E
Sudovaja Višnja 120 Tg 49.43N 23.26 E
Südradde 124 Jb 52.41N 7.34 E
Südtirol / Trentino-Alto Adige [2] 128 Fd 46.30N 11.20 E
Sudža 132 Id 51.13N 35.16 E
Sue 158 Jh 7.41N 28.03 E
Sueca 126 Le 39.12N 0.19W
Suess Land 179 Jd 72.45N 26.00W
Suez (EN) = As Suways 160 Kf 29.58N 32.33 E
Suez, Gulf of-(EN) = Suways, Khalīj as- 158 Kf 28.10N 33.27 E
Suez Canal (EN) = Suways, Qanāt as- 158 Ke 29.55N 32.33 E
Suffolk 182 Ld 36.44N 76.37W
Suffolk [3] 118 Li 52.10N 1.05W
Suffolk 118 Ni 52.25N 1.00 E
Sufiān 146 Kc 38.17N 45.59 E
Sugana, Val- 128 Fd 46.00N 11.40 E
Suga-no-Sen 156 Dd 35.22N 134.31 E
Sugar Island 184 Eb 46.25N 84.12W
Sugarloaf Mountain 184 Lc 45.01N 70.22W
Suğla Gölü 146 Ed 37.20N 32.02 E
Sugoj 138 Kd 64.15N 154.29 E
Suguta 170 Gb 2.03N 36.33 E
Suha 130 Ke 44.08N 27.36 E
Suhai Hu 152 Fd 38.55N 94.05 E
Şuḩār 144 Ie 24.22N 56.45 E
Suhe-Bator (Süchbaatar) 142 Md 50.15N 106.12 E
Suhiniči 132 Ib 54.06N 35.20 E
Suhl 120 Gf 50.36N 10.42 E
Suhodolskoje, ozero- 116 Nd 60.35N 30.30 E
Suhoj Log 134 Kh 56.55N 62.01 E
Suhona 110 Kc 60.46N 46.24 E
Suhr 128 Cc 47.25N 8.04 E
Suhumi 112 Kg 43.01N 41.02 E
Suhurlui 130 Kd 45.25N 27.35 E
Suiá-Missu, Rio- 202 Hf 11.13S 53.15W
Suibara 156 Fc 37.50N 139.12 E
Suichang 152 Kf 28.34N 119.15 E
Suid-Afrika/South Africa [1] 160 Jl 30.00S 26.00 E
Suide 152 Jd 37.28N 110.15 E
Suifenhe 152 Nc 44.25N 131.09 E
Suifen He 154 Kc 43.20N 131.49 E
Sui He 154 Eh 33.29N 118.06 E
Suihua 152 Mb 46.38N 126.57 E
Suijiang 152 Hf 28.37N 104.00 E
Suileng 152 Mb 47.17N 127.08 E
Suining [China] 152 Ie 30.30N 105.34 E
Suining [China] 154 Dh 33.54N 117.56 E
Suipacha 204 Cl 34.45S 59.41W
Suiping 154 Bh 33.09N 113.59 E
Suippe 122 Je 49.25N 3.57 E
Suippes 122 Ke 49.08N 4.32 E
Suir/An tSiúir 118 Gi 52.15N 7.00W
Suisse / Svizra / Svizzera / Schweiz = Switzerland (EN) [1] 112 Gf 46.00N 8.30 E
Suisse Normande 124 Bf 48.53N 0.50W
Suita 156 Dd 34.45N 135.32 E
Suixi 154 Dh 33.55N 116.47 E
Suixian 154 Cg 34.25N 115.04 E
Suiyang 154 Kb 44.26N 130.53 E
Suizhong 152 Lc 40.21N 120.20 E
Suj 152 Ic 42.12N 108.01 E
Šuja 114 Ff 61.54N 34.15 E
Šuja [Russia] 136 Ed 56.52N 41.23 E
Šuja [Russia] 114 Ff 61.59N 34.15 E
Sujer 134 Li 55.59N 65.47 E
Suji → Haixing 154 De 38.10N 117.29 E
Sujko Seamount (EN) 224 Cs 44.30N 170.20 E
Sujstamo 116 Nc 61.49N 31.05 E
Sukabumi 150 Eh 6.55S 106.56 E
Sukadana 150 Eg 1.15S 109.57 E
Sukagawa 154 Pf 37.17N 140.23 E
Sukaraja 150 Fg 2.23S 110.35 E
Sukeva 114 Ge 63.54N 27.26 E
Sukhothai 148 Je 17.01N 99.49 E
Suki 168 Ec 13.23N 33.58 E
Sukkertoppen/Manitsoq 179 Ge 65.25N 53.00W
Sukkozero 136 Dc 63.09N 32.23 E
Sukkur 142 Ig 27.42N 68.52 E
Sukon 150 Hg 0.56S 123.10 E
Sukses 172 Bd 21.01S 16.52 E
Suksun 134 Hh 57.07N 57.24 E
Sukumo 152 Ne 32.56N 132.44 E
Sukumo-Wan 156 Ce 32.55N 132.40 E
Sul, Baía- 204 Hh 27.40S 48.35W
Sul, Canal do- 202 Id 0.10S 49.30W
Sula [Nor.] 116 Bb 62.25N 6.10 E
Sula [Nor.] 114 Af 61.10N 4.55 E
Sula [Russia] 134 Fc 67.16N 52.07 E
Sula [Russia] 114 Ld 64.41N 47.46 E
Sula [Ukr.] 132 He 49.40N 32.43 E
Sula, Kepulauan = Sulu Archipelago, (EN) 208 De 1.52S 125.22 E
Sulaimāniya 144 Gb 35.33N 45.26 E
Sulaimāniya [3] 146 Ke 35.40N 45.30 E
Sulaimān Range 140 Jf 30.30N 70.10 E
Sulak 132 Oh 43.17N 47.31 E
Sulak 136 Eg 43.17N 47.34 E
Sula Sgeir 118 Gb 59.05N 6.10W
Sulawesi/Celebes 140 Oj 2.00S 121.10 E
Sulawesi, Laut- = Celebes Sea (EN) 140 Oi 3.00N 122.00 E
Sulawesi Selatan [3] 150 Gg 4.00S 120.00 E
Sulawesi Tengah [3] 150 Hg 1.00S 121.00 E
Sulawesi Tenggara [3] 150 Hg 4.00S 122.30 E
Sulawesi Utara [3] 150 Hf 1.00N 123.00 E
Sulaymān 128 En 36.42N 10.30 E
Sulb 168 Ea 20.26N 30.20 E
Sulcis 128 Ck 39.05N 8.40 E
Suldalsvatn 116 Be 59.35N 6.45 E
Süldeh 146 Od 36.34N 52.01 E
Sulechów 120 Ld 52.06N 15.37 E
Sulęcin 120 Ld 52.26N 15.08 E
Suleja 134 Ii 55.11N 58.50 E
Sulejów 120 Pe 51.22N 19.53 E
Süleoğlu 130 Jh 41.46N 26.55 E
Sule Skerry 118 Ib 59.10N 4.10W
Sulima 166 Cd 6.58N 11.35W
Sulina 130 Md 45.09N 29.40 E
Sulina, Braţul- 130 Md 45.09N 29.41 E
Sulingen 120 Ed 52.41N 8.48 E
Sulitjelma 114 Dc 67.09N 16.03 E
Sulitjelma 114 Dc 67.08N 16.24 E
Suljukta 136 Gh 39.56N 69.37 E
Sulkava 114 Gf 61.47N 28.23 E
Sullana 200 Hf 4.53S 80.42W
Süller 130 Mk 38.09N 29.29 E
Sullivan [In.-U.S.] 184 Df 39.06N 87.24W
Sullivan [Mo.-U.S.] 186 Kg 38.13N 91.10W
Sullivan Lake 188 Ja 52.00N 112.00W
Sully-sur-Loire 122 Ig 47.46N 2.22 E
Sulmona 128 Hh 42.03N 13.55 E
Sulphur [La.-U.S.] 186 Jk 30.14N 93.23W
Sulphur [Ok.-U.S.] 186 Hi 34.31N 96.58W
Sulphur Creek 186 Ed 44.46N 102.25W
Sulphur River 186 Jj 33.07N 93.52W
Sulphur Springs 186 Ij 33.08N 95.36W
Sulphur Springs Draw 186 Fj 32.12N 101.36W
Sultandağı 146 Dc 38.32N 31.14 E
Sultan Dağları 146 Dc 38.20N 31.20 E
Sultanhanı 146 Ec 38.15N 33.33 E
Sultanhisar 130 Ll 37.53N 28.10 E
Sultānpur 148 Gc 26.16N 82.04 E
Sulu Archipelago 140 Oi 6.00N 121.00 E
Sulu Archipelago (EN) = Sula Kepulauan 208 De 1.52S 125.22 E
Sulu Basin (EN) 150 Ge 8.00N 121.30 E
Suluova 146 Fb 40.47N 35.42 E
Sulūq 164 Dc 31.40N 20.15 E
Sulu Sea 140 Ni 9.00N 120.00 E
Sulz am Neckar 120 Eh 48.21N 8.37 E
Sulzbach/Saar 124 Je 49.18N 7.04 E
Sulzbach-Rosenberg 120 Hg 49.30N 11.45 E
Sulzberger Bay 222 Mf 77.00S 152.00W
Šumadija 130 De 44.20N 20.40 E
Sumalata 150 Hf 0.59N 122.30 E
Sumāmus 146 Nd 36.50N 50.30 E
Šumanaj 135 Bc 42.37N 58.55 E
Sumatera = Sumatra (EN) 140 Mj 0.01N 102.00 E
Sumatera Barat [3] 150 Dg 1.00S 100.30 E
Sumatera Selatan [3] 150 Dg 3.30S 104.00 E
Sumatera Utara [3] 150 Cf 2.00N 99.00 E
Sumatra (EN) = Sumatera 140 Mj 0.01N 102.00 E
Šumava = Bohemian Forest (EN) 110 Hf 49.00N 13.30 E
Sumayr 164 Hf 17.47N 41.26 E
Sumba, Pulau- 140 Nj 10.00S 120.00 E
Sumba, Selat- = Sumba Strait (EN) 150 Hh 9.05S 120.00 E
Sumbar 132 Sj 38.00N 55.15 E
Sumba Strait (EN) = Sumba, Selat- 150 Hh 9.05S 120.00 E
Sumbawa, Pulau- 140 Nj 8.40S 118.00 E
Sumbawa Besar 150 Gh 8.30S 117.26 E
Sumbawanga 170 Fd 7.58S 31.37 E
Sumbe 160 Ij 11.12S 13.51 E
Sumber 152 Ib 46.21N 108.20 E
Sumbi Point 219a Cb 7.19S 157.04 E
Sumbu 170 Fd 8.31S 30.29 E
Sumburgh Head 118 Lb 59.51N 1.16W
Sumedang 150 Eh 6.52S 107.55 E
Sūme'eh Sarā 146 Md 37.18N 49.19 E
Sümeg 120 Nj 46.59N 17.17 E
Šumen 130 Jf 43.16N 26.55 E
Šumen [2] 130 Jf 43.20N 27.00 E
Sumenep 150 Fh 7.01S 113.52 E
Šumerlja 112 Kd 55.30N 46.26 E
Sumgait 112 Kg 40.33N 49.40 E
Sumgait 132 Pi 40.37N 49.37 E
Sumidouro, Rio- 204 Da 13.28S 56.39W
Šumiha 136 Gd 55.14N 63.19 E
Sumisu-Jima 152 Oe 31.40N 140.00 E
Sumkino 136 Gd 58.09N 68.21 E
Summer, Lake- [N.M.-U.S.] 186 Di 34.38N 104.26W
Summer, Lake- [N.Z.] 218 Ee 42.40S 172.15 E
Summer Lake 188 Ee 42.50N 120.45W
Summerland 188 Fb 49.39N 119.33W
Summerside 180 Lg 46.24N 63.47W
Summersville 184 Gf 38.17N 80.52W
Summerville 184 Eh 34.29N 85.21W
Summit Lake 180 Fe 54.17N 122.38W
Summit Mountain 188 Gg 39.23N 116.28W
Summit Peak 186 Ch 37.21N 106.42W
Sumoto 156 Dd 34.20N 134.54 E
Šumperk 120 Mg 49.58N 16.59 E
Sumprabum 148 Jc 26.33N 97.34 E
Sumsar 135 Hd 41.13N 71.23 E
Šumskaja oblast [3] 136 De 51.00N 34.15 E
Šumšu, ostrov- 138 Kf 50.45N 156.20 E
Sumter 182 Ke 33.55N 80.20W
Sumuştā al Waqf 146 Dh 28.55N 30.51 E
Sumy 112 Je 50.54N 34.48 E
Suna 114 Mh 57.53N 50.07 E
Suna 114 Ie 62.08N 34.12 E
Sunagawa 154 Pc 43.29N 145.55 E
Šunak, gora- 136 Hf 47.05N 72.35 E
Sunan 154 He 39.15N 125.40 E
Sunan (Hongwansi) 152 Gd 38.59N 99.25 E
Sunart, Loch- 118 He 56.45N 5.45W
Sunaysilah 146 Ie 35.35N 41.53 E
Sunburst 188 Jb 48.53N 111.55W
Sunbury 184 Ie 40.52N 76.47W
Sunchales 206 Hd 30.56S 61.34W
Suncho Corral 206 Hc 27.56S 63.27W
Sunch'ŏn [N.Kor.] 152 Md 39.25N 125.56 E
Sunch'ŏn [S.Kor.] 152 Me 34.57N 127.29 E
Sun City 188 Ij 33.36N 112.17W
Suncun → Xinwen 152 Kd 35.49N 117.38 E
Sunda, Selat- = Sunda Strait (EN) 140 Mj 6.00S 105.45 E
Sundance 188 Md 44.24N 104.23W
Sundarbans 148 Hd 22.00N 89.00 E
Sundargarh 148 Gd 22.07N 84.02 E
Sunda Strait (EN) = Sunda, Selat- 140 Mj 6.00S 105.45 E
Sunday Strait 212 Ec 16.20S 123.15 E
Sundborn 116 Fd 60.39N 15.46 E
Sundbron 116 Ha 63.01N 18.11 E
Sundbyberg 116 Ge 59.22N 17.58 E
Sunde 114 Ag 59.50N 5.43 E
Sunderland 118 Lg 54.55N 1.23W
Sundern (Sauerland) 124 Kc 51.20N 8.00 E
Sundgau 122 Ng 47.40N 7.15 E
Sündiken Dağları 146 Dc 39.55N 31.00 E
Sundridge 184 Hc 45.46N 79.24W
Sundsvall 112 Hc 62.23N 17.18 E
Sundsvallsbukten 116 Gb 62.20N 17.35 E
Sunflower, Mount- 186 Eg 39.04N 102.01W
Sungaidareh 150 Dg 0.58S 101.30 E
Sungaigerong 150 Dg 2.59S 104.52 E
Sungaiguntung 150 Df 0.18N 103.37 E
Sungai Kolok 148 Kg 6.02N 101.58 E
Sungai Lembing 150 Df 3.55N 103.02 E
Sungailiat 150 Eg 1.51S 106.08 E
Sungaipenuh 150 Dg 2.05S 101.23 E
Sungai Petani 150 De 5.39N 100.30 E
Sungai Siput 150 Df 4.49N 101.04 E
Sungari (EN) = Songhua Jiang 140 Pe 47.42N 132.30 E
Sungqu → Songpan 152 He 32.37N 103.34 E
Sungurlu 146 Fb 40.10N 34.23 E
Sunharon Roads 220b Bb 14.57N 145.36 E
Suning 154 Ce 38.25N 115.50 E
Sunja 128 Ke 45.21N 16.33 E
Sunjiapuzi 154 Ic 42.02N 126.34 E
Sunkar, gora- 135 Ib 44.12N 73.55 E
Sun Kosi 148 Hc 26.55N 87.09 E
Sunnadalsøra 114 Be 62.40N 8.33 E
Sunnan 114 Cd 64.04N 11.38 E
Sunndalen 116 Cb 62.40N 8.45 E
Sunndalsfjorden 116 Cb 62.45N 8.25 E
Sunne 114 Cg 59.50N 13.09 E
Sunnerbo 116 Eh 56.45N 13.50 E
Sunnersta 116 Ge 59.48N 17.39 E
Sunnfjord 116 Ac 61.25N 5.20 E
Sunnhordland 116 Ae 59.55N 6.00 E
Sunnmøre 116 Bb 62.20N 6.40 E
Sunnyside 188 Fc 46.20N 120.00W
Sunnyvale 188 Dh 37.23N 122.01W
Su-no-Saki 156 Fd 34.58N 139.45 E
Sun River 188 Jc 47.30N 111.25W
Sunsas, Serrania de- 204 Cc 17.57S 59.35W
Suntar 138 Gd 62.04N 117.40 E
Suntar-Hajata, hrebet- = Suntar-Khayata Range (EN) 140 Qc 62.00N 143.00 E
Suntar-Khayata Range (EN) = Suntar-Hajata, hrebet- 140 Qc 62.00N 143.00 E
Suntaži 116 Kh 56.49N 24.57 E
Sun Valley 182 Ec 43.42N 114.21W
Sunwu 152 Mb 49.27N 127.19 E
Sunyani 160 Gh 7.20N 2.20W
Sunža 132 Oh 43.26N 46.08 E
Suojarvi 136 Dc 62.04N 32.21 E
Suokonmäki 116 Kb 62.47N 24.30 E
Suolahti 114 Fe 62.34N 25.52 E
Suomenlahti = Finland, Gulf of- (EN) 110 Ic 60.00N 27.00 E
Suomenniemi 116 Lc 61.19N 27.27 E
Suomenselkä 110 Ic 62.55N 24.00 E
Suomi/Finland [1] 112 Ic 64.00N 26.00 E
Suomussalmi 114 Gd 64.54N 29.00 E
Suō-Nada 156 Be 33.50N 131.30 E
Suonenjoki 114 Ge 62.37N 27.08 E
Suontee 116 Lc 61.40N 26.35 E
Suordah 138 Ic 66.43N 132.04 E
Suozhen → Huantai 154 Ef 36.57N 118.05 E
Supamo, Rio- 196 Fi 6.48N 61.50W
Superior [Az.-U.S.] 188 Jj 33.18N 110.06W
Superior [Mt.-U.S.] 188 Hc 47.12N 114.53W
Superior [Nb.-U.S.] 186 Gf 40.01N 98.04W
Superior [Wi.-U.S.] 176 Je 46.44N 92.05W
Superior, Lake- 174 Ke 48.00N 88.00W
Supetar 128 Kg 43.23N 16.33 E
Suphan Buri 148 Kf 14.29N 100.10 E
Süphan Dağı 144 Fb 38.54N 42.48 E
Supiori, Pulau- 150 Kg 0.45S 135.30 E
Supoj 132 Ge 49.38N 31.50 E
Support Force Glacier 222 Rg 83.05S 47.30W
Suprasl 120 Tc 53.13N 23.20 E
Suprasl 120 Sc 53.12N 22.55 E
Sup'ung 152 Lc 40.27N 124.57 E
Sup'ung-chosuji 154 Hd 40.30N 125.05 E
Suq ash Shuyūkh 146 Lg 30.53N 46.28 E
Suqian 152 Ke 33.55N 118.13 E
Sūq Suwayq 146 Hj 24.23N 38.27 E
Suquṭrá = Socotra (EN) 140 Hh 12.30N 54.00 E
Sūr 142 He 22.31N 59.30 E
Şūr 144 Ec 33.16N 35.11 E
Sur, Cabo- 221d Ac 27.12S 109.26W
Sur, Point- 188 Eh 36.18N 121.54W
Sura 132 Nc 53.53N 45.44 E
Sura 110 Kd 56.06N 46.00 E
Surab 135 Hd 40.03N 70.33 E
Surabaya 142 Nj 7.15S 112.45 E
Surahammar 116 Ge 59.43N 16.13 E
Sürak 144 Id 25.43N 58.48 E
Surakarta 142 Nj 7.35S 110.50 E
Şūrān 146 Ge 35.17N 36.45 E
Šurany 120 Oh 48.06N 18.11 E
Surar 168 Gd 7.29N 40.54 E
Surat 142 Jg 21.10N 72.50 E
Surat Thani 142 Li 9.06N 99.20 E
Suraž [Bela.] 114 Hi 55.26N 30.43 E
Suraž [Russia] 136 De 53.02N 32.29 E
Surčin 130 De 44.47N 20.17 E
Sur del Cabo San Antonio, Punta- 206 Ie 36.52S 56.40W
Surduc 130 Gb 47.15N 23.21 E
Sûre 120 Cg 49.44N 6.31 E

Index Symbols

[1] Independent Nation
[2] State, Region
[3] District, County
[4] Municipality
[5] Colony, Dependency
Continent
Physical Region
Historical or Cultural Region
Mount, Mountain
Volcano
Hill
Mountains, Mountain Range
Hills, Escarpment
Plateau, Upland
Pass, Gap
Plain, Lowland
Delta
Salt Flat
Valley, Canyon
Crater, Cave
Karst Features
Depression
Polder
Desert, Dunes
Forest, Woods
Heath, Steppe
Oasis
Cape, Point
Coast, Beach
Cliff
Peninsula
Isthmus
Sandbank
Island
Atoll
Rock, Reef
Islands, Archipelago
Rocks, Reefs
Coral Reef
Well, Spring
Geyser
River, Stream
Waterfall, Rapids
River Mouth, Estuary
Lake
Salt Lake
Intermittent Lake
Reservoir
Swamp, Pond
Canal
Glacier
Ice Shelf, Pack Ice
Ocean
Sea
Gulf, Bay
Strait, Fjord
Lagoon
Bank
Seamount
Tablemount
Ridge
Shelf
Basin
Escarpment, Sea Scarp
Fracture
Trench, Abyss
National Park, Reserve
Point of Interest
Recreation Site
Cave, Cavern
Historic Site
Ruins
Wall, Walls
Church, Abbey
Temple
Scientific Station
Railway station
Airport
Port
Military installation
Lighthouse
Mine
Tunnel
Dam, Bridge

Surendranagar 148 Ed 22.42N 71.41 E
Surgères 122 Fh 46.06N 0.45W
Surgut 142 Jc 61.14N 73.20 E
Surgutiha 138 Dd 63.47N 87.20 E
Surhandarinskaja oblast (3) 136 Gh 38.00N 67.30 E
Surhandarja 135 Ff 37.14N 67.20 E
Surhob 136 Hh 38.54N 70.04 E
Surigao 150 Ie 9.45N 125.30 E
Surin 148 Kf 14.53N 103.30 E
Suriname = Surinam (EN) (1) 200 Ke 4.00N 56.00W
Suripá, Rio- 194 Mj 7.47N 69.53W
Sūrīyah=Syria (EN) (1) 142 Ff 35.00N 38.00 E
Sūrmaq 146 Og 31.03N 52.48 E
Surmelin 124 Fe 49.04N 3.31 E
Sürmene 146 Ib 40.55N 40.07 E
Surna 116 Cb 62.59N 8.40 E
Surnadalsøra 116 Cb 62.59N 8.39 E
Surovikino 136 Ef 48.36N 42.54 E
Surovo 138 Fe 55.39N 105.36 E
Sur-Pakri/Suur-Pakri 116 Je 59.50N 23.45 E
Surprise, Ile- 219b Ad 18.32S 163.02 E
Surprise, Lac- 184 Ja 49.20N 74.57W
Surrey (3) 118 Mj 51.25N 0.30W
Surrey 118 Mj 51.20N 0.05W
Sursee 128 Cc 47.10N 8.07 E
Sursk 132 Nc 53.04N 45.42 E
Surskoje 114 Li 54.31N 46.44 E
Surt 160 Ie 31.13N 16.35 E
Surt, Khalīj-=Sidra, Gulf of-(EN) 158 Ie 31.30N 18.00 E
Surte 116 Eg 57.49N 12.01 E
Surtsey 114a Bc 63.20N 20.38W
Süriç 146 Hd 36.58N 38.24 E
Surud Ad 158 Lg 10.42N 47.09 E
Suruga-Wan 154 Og 34.55N 138.35 E
Surulangun 150 Dg 2.37S 102.45 E
Survey Pass 178 Ic 67.52N 154.10W
Sur Vjajn / Suur Väin 116 Jf 58.30N 23.20 E
Surwold 124 Jb 52.57N 7.31 E
Šuša 132 Oj 39.43N 46.44 E
Susā 116 Di 55.11N 11.46 E
Susa [It.] 128 Be 45.08N 7.03 E
Susa [Jap.] 156 Bd 34.37N 131.36 E
Susa (EN) = Shūsh 146 Mf 32.12N 48.17 E
Susa, Val di- 128 Be 45.10N 7.10 E
Sušac 128 Kh 42.46N 16.30 E
Sūsah [Lib.] 164 Dc 32.54N 21.58 E
Sūsah [Tun.] = Sousse (EN) 160 Ie 35.49N 10.38 E
Sūsah=Sousse (EN) (3) 162 Jb 35.45N 10.30 E
Susak 128 If 44.31N 14.18 E
Susaki 152 Ne 33.22N 133.17 E
Susami 156 De 33.33N 135.29 E
Susamyr 135 Ic 42.09N 73.59 E
Susanville 182 Cc 40.25N 120.39W
Suşehri 146 Hb 40.11N 38.06 E
Suseja 116 Kh 56.23N 25.00 E
Šušenskoje 138 Ef 53.19N 92.01 E
Sušice 120 Jg 49.14N 13.30 E
Susitna 178 Id 61.16N 150.30W
Suslonger 114 Lh 56.18N 48.12 E
Susoh 150 Cf 3.43N 96.50 E
Susong 154 Di 30.10N 116.06 E
Suspiro 204 Ej 30.38S 54.22W
Suspiro del Moro, Puerto del- 126 Ig 37.08N 3.40W
Susquehanna River 182 Ld 39.33N 76.05W
Susques 206 Gb 23.25S 66.29W
Sussex 184 Oc 45.43N 65.31W
Sussex 118 Mk 50.55N 0.30W
Sussex, Vale of- 118 Mk 51.00N 0.15W
Susubona 219a Dc 8.19S 159.27 E
Susuman 142 Qc 62.47N 148.10 E
Susurluk 146 Cc 39.54N 28.10 E
Susuzmüsellim 130 •Kh 41.06N 27.03 E
Šušvė 116 Ji 55.08N 23.53 E
Susz 120 Pc 53.44N 19.20 E
Sütçüler 146 Dd 37.30N 30.59 E
Suteşti 130 Kd 45.13N 27.26 E
Sutherland 172 Cf 32.24S 20.40 E
Sutherland Falls 218 Bf 44.48S 167.44 E
Sutherlin 188 De 43.25N 123.19W
Sutla 128 Je 45.51N 15.41 E
Sutlej 140 Jg 29.23N 71.02 E
Sutton 184 Gf 38.41N 80.43W
Sutton, London- 124 Bc 51.21N 0.12W
Sutton Bridge 124 Cb 52.46N 0.11 E
Sutton in Ashfield 124 Aa 53.07N 1.16W
Sutton Scotney 124 Ac 51.09N 1.20W
Suttor River 212 Jd 21.25S 147.45 E
Suttsu 154 Pc 42.48N 140.14 E
Sutwik 178 He 56.34N 157.05W
Su'uholo 219a Ec 9.46S 161.58 E
Suunduk 132 Ud 51.46N 58.46 E
Suure-Jaani 114 Fg 58.31N 25.29 E
Suur-Pakri/Sur-Pakri 116 Je 59.50N 23.45 E
Suur Väin / Sur-Vjajn 116 Jf 58.30N 23.20 E
Suva 210 If 18.08S 178.25 E
Suvadiva Atoll 140 Ji 0.30N 73.13 E
Suva Gora 130 Eh 41.51N 21.03 E
Suva Planina 130 Ff 43.08N 22.13 E
Suvasvesi 114 Ge 62.40N 28.10 E
Suvorov 132 Jb 54.08N 36.32 E
Suvorovo [Mol.] 130 Mc 46.33N 29.35 E
Suvorovo [Ukr.] 130 Ld 45.35N 29.00 E
Suvorovskaja 132 Mg 44.10N 42.38 E
Suwa 154 Of 36.02N 138.08 E
Suwa-Ko 156 Fc 36.03N 138.05 E
Suwałki 120 Sb 54.07N 22.56 E
Suwałki (2) 120 Sb 54.05N 22.55 E
Suwalskie, Pojezierze- 120 Sb 54.15N 23.00 E
Suwannee River 184 Fk 29.18N 83.09W
Suwanose-Jima 152 Mf 29.40N 129.45 E
Suwarrow Atoll 208 Kf 13.15S 163.05W
Suwayqīyah, Hawr as- 146 Lf 32.40N 46.03 E
Suways, Khalīj as-=Suez, Gulf of-(EN) 158 Kf 28.10N 33.27 E
Suways, Qanāt as-=Suez Canal (EN) 158 Ke 29.55N 32.33 E
Suwŏn 152 Md 37.16N 127.01 E
Suxian [China] 152 Ke 33.36N 116.58 E
Suxian [China] 152 Je 31.44N 113.25 E
Suzaka 156 Fc 36.39N 138.18 E
Suzdal 114 Jh 56.28N 40.27 E
Suzhou 142 Of 31.16N 120.37 E
Suzhou/Jiuquan 142 Lf 39.46N 98.34 E
Suzi He 154 Hd 41.56N 124.20 E
Suzu 152 Od 37.25N 137.17 E
Suzuka 156 Ed 34.51N 136.35 E
Suzuka-Sanmyaku 156 Ed 35.10N 136.20 E
Suzu-Misaki 154 Nf 37.28N 137.20 E
Suzun 138 Df 53.47N 82.19 E
Suzzara 128 Ef 45.00N 10.45 E
Sværholthalvøya 114 Ga 70.30N 26.05 E
Svågan 116 Gc 61.54N 16.33 E
Svalbard (5) 224 Kd 78.00N 20.00 E
Svaljava 132 Ce 48.32N 22.59 E
Svalöv 116 Ei 55.55N 13.06 E
Svaneholm 116 Ee 59.11N 12.33 E
Svaneke 114 Di 55.08N 15.09 E
Svängsta 116 Fh 56.16N 14.46 E
Svanøy 116 Ac 61.30N 5.05 E
Svapa 132 Id 51.44N 34.59 E
Svappavaara 114 Ec 67.39N 21.04 E
Svärdsjö 116 Fd 60.45N 15.55 E
Svartå 116 Fe 59.08N 14.31 E
Svartälven 116 Fe 59.20N 14.35 E
Svartån [Swe.] 116 Fe 59.17N 15.15 E
Svartån [Swe.] 116 Ge 59.37N 16.33 E
Svartån [Swe.] 116 Ff 58.28N 15.33 E
Svartenhuk Halvø=Svartenhuk Peninsula (EN) 179 Gd 71.30N 55.20W
Svartenhuk Peninsula (EN) =Svartenhuk, Halvø 179 Gd 71.30N 55.20W
Svartisen 114 Cc 66.38N 13.58 E
Svatovo 136 Df 49.24N 38.13 E
Svay Riĕng 148 Lf 11.05N 105.48 E
Sveabreen 222 Cf 72.08S 1.53 E
Sveagruva 179 Nc 78.39N 16.25 E
Svealand 116 Hc 60.30N 15.30 E
Svealand 114 Dg 59.55N 15.30 E
Svedala 116 Ei 55.30N 13.14 E
Sveg 114 De 62.02N 14.21 E
Švėkšna 116 Ii 55.32N 21.30 E
Svelgen 114 Af 61.45N 5.18 E
Svelvik 116 De 59.37N 10.24 E
Švenčėneljaj/Švenčioneliai 114 Gi 55.09N 26.02 E
Švenčėnis/Švenčionys 114 Gi 55.07N 26.12 E
Švenčioneliai/Švenčėneljaj 114 Gi 55.09N 26.02 E
Švenčionys/Švenčėnis 114 Gi 55.07N 26.12 E
Svendborg 114 Ci 55.03N 10.37 E
Svendsen Peninsula 180 Ja 77.50N 84.00W
Svenljunga 114 Ch 57.30N 13.07 E
Svenska högarna 116 He 59.35N 19.35 E
Svenskøya 179 Oc 78.43N 26.30 E
Svenstavik 114 De 62.46N 14.27 E
Šventoj/Šventoji 116 Ih 56.04N 20.59 E
Šventoji/Šventoj 116 Ih 56.04N 20.59 E
Sverdlovsk → Jekaterinburg 142 Id 56.51N 60.36 E
Sverdrup, ostrov- 138 Cb 74.30N 79.35 E
Sverdrup Channel 138 Ha 80.00N 96.30W
Sverdrup Islands 174 Jb 79.00N 98.00W
Sverige=Sweden (EN) (1) 112 Hc 62.00N 15.00 E
Svetac 128 Jg 43.02N 15.45 E
Svete/Svēte 116 Jh 56.40N 23.38 E
Svēte/Svete 116 Jh 56.40N 23.38 E
Sveti Naum 130 Di 40.55N 20.45 E
Sveti Nikola, prohod- 130 Ff 43.27N 22.36 E
Sveti Nikole 130 Eh 41.52N 21.57 E
Sveti Stefan 130 Bg 42.16N 18.54 E
Svetlaja 138 Ig 46.31N 138.18 E
Svetli 138 Ge 58.34N 116.00 E
Svetlogorsk [Bela.] 136 Ce 52.38N 29.42 E
Svetlogorsk [Russia] 116 Ij 54.55N 20.08 E
Svetlograd 136 Ef 45.19N 42.40 E
Svetlovodsk 132 He 49.02N 33.15 E
Svetly [Russia] 136 Ge 50.51N 60.53 E
Svetly [Russia] 114 Ei 54.41N 20.08 E
Svetly Jar 132 Ne 48.29N 44.46 E
Svetogorsk 114 Gf 61.07N 28.58 E
Svetozarevo 130 Ef 43.59N 21.15 E
Sviča 120 Ug 49.04N 24.06 E
Svid 114 Jf 61.13N 38.45 E
Svidnik 120 Rg 49.18N 21.35 E
Svidník 120 Kg 49.23N 14.58 E
Svijaga 136 Ed 55.39N 48.28 E
Svilaja 128 Kg 43.50N 16.26 E
Svilengrad 130 Jh 41.46N 26.12 E
Svincovy Rudnik 135 Ff 37.52N 66.28 E
Svinecea Mare, Vîrful- 130 Fe 44.48N 22.09 E
Svir 116 Lj 54.50N 26.34 E
Svir 110 Jc 60.30N 32.48 E
Svirica 114 Hf 60.30N 32.54 E
Svirsk 138 Ff 53.04N 103.18 E
Svisloč 132 Dc 53.03N 24.07 E
Svisloč 132 Fc 53.27N 28.59 E
Svištov 130 If 43.37N 25.20 E
Svit 120 Qg 49.03N 20.12 E
Svitava 120 Mg 49.11N 16.38 E
Svitavy 120 Mg 49.46N 16.27 E
Svizra / Svizzera / Schweiz / Suisse = Switzerland (EN) (1) 112 Gf 46.00N 8.30 E
Svizzera / Schweiz / Suisse / Svizra = Switzerland (EN) (1) 112 Gf 46.00N 8.30 E
Svjatoj Nos, mys- [Russia] 110 Jb 68.10N 39.43 E
Svjatoj Nos, mys- [Russia] 138 Jb 72.45N 140.45 E
Svobodny 142 Od 51.24N 128.07 E
Svoge 130 Gg 42.58N 23.21 E
Svolvær 114 Db 68.14N 14.34 E
Svratka 120 Mh 48.52N 16.38 E
Svrljig 130 Ff 43.25N 22.08 E
Svulrya 116 Ed 60.25N 12.24 E
Svytaya Anna Trough (EN) 224 He 80.00N 70.00 E
Swabia (EN)=Schwaben 120 Gh 48.20N 10.30 E
Swabian-Bavarian Plateau (EN)=Schwäbisch-Bayerisches Alpenvorland 110 Hf 48.15N 10.30 E
Swabian Jura (EN)= Schwäbische Alb 110 Gf 48.25N 9.30 E
Swaffham 124 Cb 52.39N 0.41 E
Swain Reefs 208 Gg 21.40S 152.15 E
Swains Atoll 208 Jf 11.03S 171.05W
Swainsboro 184 Fi 32.36N 82.20W
Swakop 172 Ad 22.41S 14.31 E
Swakopmund 160 Ik 22.41S 14.34 E
Swakopmund (3) 172 Ad 22.30S 15.00 E
Swale 118 Lg 54.06N 1.20W
Swalmen 124 Ic 51.14N 6.02 E
Swanage 118 Lk 50.37N 1.58W
Swan Hill 212 Ig 35.21S 143.34 E
Swan Range 188 Ic 47.50N 113.40W
Swan River 180 Hf 52.06N 101.16W
Swansboro 184 Ih 34.36N 77.07W
Swansea [Austl.] 212 Jh 42.08S 148.04 E
Swansea [Wales-U.K.] 112 Fe 51.38N 3.57W
Swansea Bay 118 Jj 51.35N 3.52W
Swans Island 184 Mc 44.10N 68.25W
Swanson Lake 186 Ff 40.09N 101.06W
Swan Valley 188 Je 43.28N 111.20W
Swartberge 158 Jl 33.23S 21.48 E
Swarzędz 120 Nd 52.26N 17.05 E
Swastika 184 Ga 48.07N 80.12W
Swaziland (1) 160 Kk 26.30S 31.10 E
Sweden (EN)=Sverige (1) 112 Hc 62.00N 15.00 E
Swedru 166 Ed 5.32N 0.42W
Sweet Grass Hills 188 Jb 48.55N 111.30W
Sweet Home 188 Dd 44.24N 122.44W
Sweetwater 182 Ge 32.28N 100.25W
Sweetwater River 182 Fc 42.31N 107.02W
Swellendam 172 Cf 34.02S 20.26 E
Świder 120 Rd 52.08N 21.12 E
Świdnica 120 Mf 50.51N 16.29 E
Świdnik 120 Se 51.14N 22.41 E
Świdwin 120 Lc 53.47N 15.47 E
Świebodzin 120 Ld 52.15N 15.32 E
Świecie 120 Oc 53.25N 18.28 E
Świętej Anny, Góra- 120 Of 50.28N 18.13 E
Świętokrzyskie, Góry- 120 Qf 50.55N 21.00 E
Swift Current 180 Gf 50.17N 107.50W
Swift Current Creek 188 La 50.40N 107.44W
Swift River 180 Ed 60.05N 131.11W
Swilly, Lough-/Loch Suili 118 Ff 55.10N 7.38W
Swinburne, Cape - 180 Hb 71.14N 98.33W
Swindon 118 Lj 51.34N 1.47W
Swinford/Béal Átha na Muice 118 Eh 53.57N 8.57W
Świnoujście 120 Kc 53.53N 14.14 E
Swisttal 124 Id 50.44N 6.54 E
Switzerland (EN) = Schweiz / Suisse / Svizra / Svizzera (1) 112 Gf 46.00N 8.30 E
Switzerland (EN) = Suisse / Svizra / Svizzera / Schweiz (1) 112 Gf 46.00N 8.30 E
Switzerland (EN) = Svizra / Svizzera / Schweiz / Suisse (1) 112 Gf 46.00N 8.30 E
Switzerland (EN) = Svizzera / Schweiz / Suisse / Svizra (1) 112 Gf 46.00N 8.30 E
Syčevka 132 Ib 55.51N 34.15 E
Syców 120 Ne 51.19N 17.43 E
Sydfalster-Gedser 114 Ci 54.35N 11.57 E
Sydkap Ice Cap 180 Ja 76.30N 85.00W
Sydney [Austl.] 210 Gh 33.52S 151.13 E
Sydney [N.S.-Can.] 176 Me 46.09N 60.11W
Sydney→ Manra Atoll 208 Je 4.27S 171.15W
Sydney-Campbelltown 212 Kf 34.04S 150.49 E
Sydney Lake 186 Ia 50.40N 94.24W
Sydney Mines 180 Lg 46.14N 60.12W
Sydney-Penrith 212 Kf 33.45S 150.42 E
Syktyvkar 112 Lc 61.40N 50.46 E
Sylacauga 184 Di 33.10N 86.15W
Sylane 114 Ce 63.02N 12.13 E
Sylarna 114 Ce 63.02N 12.13 E
Sylhet 148 Id 24.54N 91.52 E
Sylling 116 De 59.54N 10.17 E
Sylt 120 Eb 54.55N 8.20 E
Sylva 134 Hh 57.40N 56.57 E
Sylvania 184 Gi 32.45N 81.38W
Sylvania Tablemount (EN) 214 Ge 11.58N 165.00 E
Sylvan Pass 182 Ec 44.28N 110.08W
Sylvester 184 Fj 31.32N 83.49W
Sylvester, Lake- 212 Hc 18.50S 135.50 E
Sym 138 Ed 60.15N 90.02 E
Syndassko 138 Fb 73.14N 108.05 E
Synja 134 Ld 65.12N 64.45 E
Synnfjell 116 Cc 61.05N 9.45 E
Syowa 222 De 69.00S 39.35 E
Syracuse [Ks.-U.S.] 186 Fh 37.59N 101.45W
Syracuse [N.Y.-U.S.] 176 Le 43.03N 76.09W
Syracuse (EN)=Siracusa 112 Hh 37.04N 15.18 E
Syrdarinskaja oblast (3) 136 Gg 40.30N 68.40 E
Syrdarja 136 Gg 40.52N 68.38 E
Syrdarja=Syr Darya (EN) 140 Ie 46.03N 61.00 E
Syr Darya (EN)= Syrdarja 140 Ie 46.03N 61.00 E
Syria (EN) 140 Ff 35.00N 38.00 E
Syria (EN)=Sūrīyah (1) 142 Ff 35.00N 38.00 E
Syriam 148 Je 16.46N 96.15 E
Syrian Desert (EN) = Shām, Bādiyat ash- 140 Ff 32.00N 40.00 E
Syrkovoje, ozero- 134 Lf 60.40N 65.00 E
Syrski 132 Kc 52.36N 39.28 E
Sysert 134 Jh 56.31N 60.49 E
Sysmä 114 Ff 61.30N 25.41 E
Sysola 136 Fc 61.42N 50.58 E
Syssleback 116 Ed 60.44N 12.52 E
Sysulp, gora- 130 Ha 48.29N 24.17 E
Syverma, plato- 140 Lc 67.00N 99.00 E
Syzran 112 Ke 53.09N 48.27 E
Szabolcs-Szatmár-Bereg 120 Sh 48.00N 22.10 E
Szamocin 120 Nc 53.02N 17.08 E
Szamos 130 Fa 48.07N 22.20 E
Szamotuły 120 Md 52.37N 16.35 E
Szarvas 120 Qj 46.52N 20.33 E
Szczawnica Krościenko 120 Qg 49.26N 20.30 E
Szczebrzeszyn 120 Sf 50.42N 22.59 E
Szczecin (2) 120 Kc 52.35N 14.30 E
Szczecin (Stettin) 112 He 53.24N 14.32 E
Szczecinek 120 Mc 53.43N 16.42 E
Szczeciński, Zalew- 120 Kc 53.46N 14.14 E
Szczekociny 120 Pf 50.38N 19.50 E
Szczerców 120 Pe 51.18N 19.09 E
Szczucin 120 Rf 50.18N 21.04 E
Szczuczyn 120 Sc 53.34N 22.18 E
Szczytno 120 Qc 53.34N 21.00 E
Szechwan (EN)=Sichuan Sheng (Ssu-ch'uan Sheng) (2) 152 He 30.00N 103.00 E
Szechwan (EN)=Ssu-ch'uan Sheng→Sichuan Sheng (2) 152 He 30.00N 103.00 E
Szécsény 120 Ph 48.05N 19.31 E
Szeged 112 If 46.15N 20.10 E
Szeged (2) 120 Qj 46.16N 20.08 E
Szeghalom 120 Ri 47.02N 21.10 E
Székesfehérvár 112 Hf 47.12N 18.25 E
Szekszárd 120 Oj 46.21N 18.43 E
Szendrő 120 Qh 48.24N 20.44 E
Szentendre 120 Pi 47.40N 19.05 E
Szentes 120 Qj 46.39N 20.16 E
Szentgotthárd 120 Mj 46.57N 16.17 E
Szerencs 120 Rh 48.10N 21.12 E
Szeskie Wzgórza 120 Sb 54.14N 22.22 E
Szigetvár 120 Nj 46.03N 17.48 E
Szkwa 120 Rc 53.10N 21.45 E
Szlichtyngowa 120 Me 51.43N 16.15 E
Szob 120 Oi 47.49N 18.52 E
Szolnok 120 Qi 47.11N 20.12 E
Szolnok → Jász-Nagykun-Szolnok 120 Qi 47.15N 20.30 E
Szombathely 120 Mi 47.14N 16.37 E
Szprotawa 120 Le 51.34N 15.33 E
Sztum 120 Pc 53.56N 19.01 E
Szubin 120 Nc 53.00N 17.44 E
Szydłów 120 Rf 50.35N 21.01 E
Szydłowiec 120 Qe 51.14N 20.51 E

T

Taakoka 220p Cc 21.15S 159.43W
Taalintendas/Dalsbruk 116 Jd 60.02N 22.31 E
Taavetti 116 Ld 60.55N 27.34 E
Tab 120 Oj 46.44N 18.02 E
Tabacal 206 Hb 23.16S 64.15W
Ţabāh 146 Ji 27.02N 42.08 E
Tabaqah 146 He 35.52N 38.34 E
Tabar Islands 208 Ge 2.50S 152.00 E
Ţabarqah 162 Ib 36.57N 8.45 E
Ţabas 146 Qf 33.36N 56.54 E
Tabasará, Serrania de- 194 Gi 8.33N 81.40W
Tabasco (2) 190 Fe 18.00N 92.40W
Tabasco y Campeche, Llanos de- 190 Fe 18.15N 91.00W
Tabašino 114 Lh 56.59N 47.43 E
Tābask, Kūh-e- 146 Nh 29.52N 51.49 E
Tabay 204 Ci 28.18S 58.17W
Tabelbala 162 Gd 29.24N 3.15W
Taber 180 Gg 49.47N 112.08W
Taberg 116 Fg 57.41N 14.05 E
Taberg 116 Fg 57.41N 14.05 E
Tabernacle 217c Ab 17.23N 62.46W
Tabernas 126 Jg 37.03N 2.23W
Tabernes de Valldigna / Tavernes de Valldigna 126 Le 39.04N 0.16W
Tabiteuea Atoll 208 Ie 1.20S 174.50 E
Tabla 166 Fc 13.46N 3.01 E
Tablas 150 Hd 12.24N 122.02 E
Tablas Strait 150 Hd 12.40N 121.48 E
Tablat 126 Ph 36.25N 3.19 E
Tablazo, Bahia del- 194 Lh 10.52N 71.35W
Table Cape 218 Gc 39.06S 178.00 E
Table Rock Lake 186 Jh 36.35N 93.30W
Tabocas 204 Jb 14.39S 45.28W
Taboco, Rio- 204 Ed 19.53S 55.58W
Tabola 132 Pg 45.53N 48.20 E
Tábor 120 Kg 49.25N 14.41 E
Tabora 160 Ki 5.01S 32.48 E
Tabora (3) 170 Fd 5.20S 32.30 E
Tabory 134 Lg 58.31N 64.33 E
Tabou 160 Gh 4.25N 7.21W
Tabrīz 142 Gf 38.05N 46.18 E
Tábua 126 Dd 40.21N 8.02W
Tabuaeran Atoll (Fanning) 208 Ld 3.52N 159.20W
Tabuk 150 Hc 17.24N 121.25 E
Tabūk 146 Fg 28.23N 36.35 E
Ţaburbah 128 Dn 36.50N 9.50 E
Tabursuq 128 Dn 36.28N 9.15 E
Taburşuq, Monts de- 128 Dn 36.25N 9.05 E
Tabusintac 184 Ob 47.24N 65.02W
Tabwemasana 219b Cb 15.22S 166.45 E
Täby 114 Eg 59.30N 18.03 E
Tacámbaro de Codallos 192 Ih 19.14N 101.28W
Tacarcuna, Cerro- 194 Ij 8.05N 77.17W
Tacarigua, Laguna de- 196 Dg 10.15N 65.50W
Tacheng/Qoqek 142 Ke 46.45N 82.57 E
Tachibana-Wan 156 Be 32.45N 130.05 E
Tachichilte, Isla de- 192 Ee 24.59N 108.04W
Tachikawa [Jap.] 156 Fb 38.48N 139.58 E
Tachikawa [Jap.] 156 Fd 35.42N 139.23 E
Táchira (2) 202 Db 7.50N 72.05W
Tachiumet 164 Bd 26.19N 10.03 E
Tachov 120 Ig 49.48N 12.40 E
Tachungnya 220b Bb 14.58N 145.36 E
Tacinski 132 Le 48.13N 41.17 E
Tacir 130 Mi 40.32N 29.44 E
Tacloban 142 Oh 11.15N 125.00 E
Tacna 200 Ig 18.01S 70.15W
Tacna (3) 202 Dg 17.40S 70.20W
Tacoma 176 Ge 47.15N 122.27W
Tacotalpa, Rio- 192 Mi 17.50N 92.52W
Tacuaral 204 Cd 18.59S 58.07W
Tacuarembó 206 Id 31.44S 55.59W
Tacuarembó (2) 204 Ek 32.10S 55.30W
Tacuarembó, Rio- 204 Ek 32.25S 55.29W
Tacuari, Rio- 204 Fk 32.46S 53.18W
Tacuati 204 Df 23.27S 56.35W
Tadami 156 Fc 37.21N 139.17 E
Tadarimana, Rio- 204 Ec 16.29S 54.31W
Tademait, Plateau du- 158 Hf 28.30N 2.15 E
Tadine 219b Ce 21.33S 167.53 E
Tadjeraout 162 He 21.17N 1.20 E
Tadjetaret 162 Ie 22.00N 7.30 E
Tadjourah 168 Gc 11.45N 42.54 E
Tadjourah, Golfe de- 168 Gc 11.45N 43.00 E
Tadoule Lake 180 He 58.35N 98.20W
Tadoussac 184 Ma 48.09N 69.43W
Tadžikskaja Sovetskaja Socialističeskaja Respublika → Tajikistan 136 Hh 39.00N 71.00 E
Tadžikskaja SSR/ Respublikai Soveth Socialisti Todžikiston → Tajikistan 136 Hh 39.00N 71.00 E
Tadžikskaya SSR → Tajikistan 136 Hh 39.00N 71.00 E
T'aebaek-Sanmaek 140 Of 37.40N 128.50 E
Taechon 154 If 36.21N 126.36 E
T'aech'on 154 He 39.55N 125.30 E
Taedong-gang 154 He 38.42N 125.15 E
Taegu 142 Of 35.52N 128.36 E
Taeha-dong 154 Kf 37.31N 130.48 E
Taehan-Haehyŏp=Korea Strait (EN) 140 Of 34.40N 129.00 E
Taehan-Min' guk=South Korea (EN) (1) 142 Of 38.00N 127.30 E
Taehuksan-Do 154 Hg 34.40N 125.25 E
Taejŏn 142 Of 36.20N 127.26 E
Tafahi Island 208 Jf 15.52S 173.55W
Tafalla 126 Kb 42.31N 1.40W
Tafassasset 158 If 21.56N 10.12 E
Tafassasset, Ténéré du- 166 Ha 21.20N 11.00 E
Taff 118 Jj 51.27N 3.09W
Tafilalt 162 Gc 31.18N 4.18W
Tafiré 166 Dd 9.04N 5.10W
Tafi Viejo 206 Gc 26.44S 65.16W
Taflan 146 Gb 41.25N 36.09 E
Tafna 126 Ki 35.18N 1.28W
Tafraout 162 Fd 29.43N 9.00W
Tafresh 146 Ne 34.41N 50.01 E
Taft 146 Pg 31.45N 54.14 E
Taftān, Kuh-e- 140 Ig 28.36N 61.06 E
Taftanāz 146 Ge 35.59N 36.47 E
Taga 221c Aa 13.46S 172.28W
Taga Dzong 148 Hc 27.04N 89.53 E
Tagajō 156 Gb 38.18N 140.58 E
Tagama 158 Hg 15.50N 8.12 E
Taganrog 112 Jf 47.12N 38.56 E
Taganrogski zaliv 132 Kf 46.50N 38.25 E
Tagant (3) 162 Ef 18.30N 10.30W
Tagant 158 Fg 17.31N 12.07W
Tagarev, gora- 135 Ae 38.19N 57.18 E
Tagawa 156 Be 33.39N 130.48 E
Tagbilaran 150 He 9.39N 123.51 E
Tageru, Jabal- 168 Db 16.25N 27.10 E
Taggia 128 Bg 43.52N 7.51 E
Taghit 162 Gc 30.55N 2.02W
Tagil 134 Kg 58.33N 62.30 E
Tagish Lake 180 Ed 60.00N 134.00W
Tagliamento 128 He 45.38N 13.06 E
Taglio di Po 128 Ge 45.00N 12.12 E
Tagomago, Illa- / Tagomago, Isla de- 126 Ne 39.02N 1.39 E
Tagomago, Isla de- / Tagomago, Illa- 126 Ne 39.02N 1.39 E
Tagounit 162 Fd 29.58N 5.35W
Tagpochau, Ogso- 220b Ba 15.11N 145.45 E
Tāgrīfat 164 Cd 29.12N 17.21 E
Taguatinga 202 If 12.25S 46.26W
Taguersimet 162 De 24.09N 15.07W
Tagula 219a Ad 11.20S 153.00 E
Tagula Island 208 Gf 11.30S 153.20 E
Tagum 150 Ie 7.21N 125.50 E
Tagus (EN)=Tajo 110 Fh 38.40N 9.24W
Tagus (EN)=Tejo 110 Fh 38.40N 9.24W
Tah 162 Ed 27.37N 12.50W
Tahaa, Ile- 216 Kc 16.38S 151.30W
Tahakopa 218 Cg 46.31S 169.23 E
Tahan, Gunong- 140 Mi 4.39N 102.14 E
Tahanea Atoll 208 Mf 16.52S 144.45W
Tahat 158 Hf 23.18N 5.32 E
Tahe 152 La 52.22N 124.48 E
Tāherī 146 Oi 27.42N 52.21 E
Tahgong, Puntan- 220b Ba 15.06N 145.39 E
Tahiataš 135 Bc 42.20N 59.33 E
Tahifet 162 Ie 22.56N 9.15 E
Tahir Geçidi 146 Jc 39.52N 42.20 E
Tahiti, Ile- 208 Mf 17.37S 149.27W
Tahkuna neem / Takuna, mys- 116 Je 59.05N 22.30 E
Tahlequah 186 Ii 35.55N 94.58W
Tahoe, Lake- 188 Fg 38.54N 120.00W
Tahoua 160 Hg 14.54N 5.16 E
Tahoua (2) 166 Gb 16.00N 5.30 E

Tah-Tar

Ṭahṭā	164	Fd	26.46N	31.28 E
Tahta-Bazar	135	Dg	35.55N	62.55 E
Tahtabrod	136	Ge	52.40N	67.35 E
Tahtakarača pereval	135	Fe	39.17N	66.55 E
Tahtaköprü	130	Mj	39.57N	29.39 E
Tahtakupyr	136	Gg	43.01N	60.22 E
Tahtali Dağları	146	Gc	38.46N	36.47 E
Tahtamygda	138	Hf	54.09N	123.38 E
Tahuata, Ile-	208	Ne	9.57S	139.05W
Tahulandang, Pulau-	150	If	2.20N	125.25 E
Tahuna	150	If	3.37N	125.29 E
Taï	166	Dd	5.52N	7.27W
Tai'an [China]	152	Kd	36.09N	117.05 E
Tai'an [China]	154	Gd	41.24N	122.27 E
Taiarapu, Presqu'île de-	221e	Fc	17.47S	149.14W
Taibai Shan	152	Ie	33.57N	107.40 E
Taibilla, Canal del-	126	Kg	37.43N	1.22W
Taibilla, Sierra de-	126	Jf	38.10N	2.10W
Taibus Qi (Baochang)	152	Kc	41.55N	115.22 E
Taicang	154	Fi	31.26N	121.06 E
Taichung	142	Og	24.09N	120.41 E
Taieri	218	Dg	46.03S	170.12 E
Taiga	138	De	56.04N	85.37 E
Taigonos Peninsula (EN) = Tajgonos, poluostrov-	138	Ld	61.35N	161.00 E
Taigu	154	Bf	37.26N	112.33 E
Taihang Shan	140	Nf	37.00N	114.00 E
Taihape	218	Fc	39.41S	175.48 E
Taihe [China]	154	Ch	33.11N	115.38 E
Taihe [China]	152	Jf	26.50N	114.52 E
Taiheiyō = Pacific Ocean (EN)	106	Ki	5.00N	155.00W
Taihu	152	Ke	30.26N	116.10 E
Tai Hu	140	Of	31.15N	120.10 E
Taikang	152	Je	34.00N	114.56 E
Taiki	156a	Cb	42.30N	143.16 E
Tailai	152	Lb	46.24N	123.26 E
Tailles, Plateau des-	124	Hd	50.15N	5.45 E
Taim	204	Fk	32.30S	52.35W
Tain	118	Id	57.48N	4.04W
Tainan	142	Og	23.00N	120.11 E
Tainaron, Ákra- = Matapan, Cape- (EN)	110	Ih	36.23N	22.29 E
Tain-l'Hermitage	122	Ki	45.04N	4.51 E
Taiof	219a	Ba	5.31S	154.39 E
Taipei	142	Og	25.03N	121.30 E
Taiping	150	Df	4.51N	100.44 E
Taiping (Gantang)	154	Ei	30.18N	118.07 E
Taipingchuan	154	Gb	44.24N	123.11 E
Taiping Dao	150	Fd	10.15N	113.42 E
Taiping Ling	152	Lb	47.36N	120.12 E
Tairadate	156a	Bc	41.09N	140.38 E
Tairadate-Kaikyō	156a	Bc	41.10N	140.40 E
Taisei	156a	Ab	42.14N	139.49 E
Taisetsu-Zan	140	Qe	43.40N	142.48 E
Taisha	156	Cd	35.24N	132.40 E
Taishaku-San	156	Fc	36.58N	139.28 E
Tai Shan	140	Nf	36.30N	117.20 E
Taishō	156	Ce	33.12N	132.57 E
Taitao, Peninsula de- = Taitao Peninsula (EN)	198	Ij	46.30S	74.25W
Taitao Peninsula (EN) = Taitao, Peninsula de-	198	Ij	46.30S	74.25W
Taitung	152	Lg	22.45N	121.09 E
Taiwa	156	Gb	38.26N	140.52 E
Taiwan	140	Og	23.30N	121.00 E
Taiwan (Formosa) [1]	142	Og	23.30N	121.00 E
Taiwan Haixia = Taiwan Strait (EN)	140	Ng	24.00N	119.00 E
Taiwan Strait (EN) = Taiwan Haixia	140	Ng	24.00N	119.00 E
Taixian	154	Fh	32.31N	120.08 E
Taixing	154	Fh	32.10N	120.00 E
Taiyang Shan	152	Ie	33.37N	106.26 E
Taiyetos Óros-	130	Fl	37.06N	22.18 E
Taiyuan	142	Nf	37.50N	112.37 E
Taiyue Shan	154	Bf	36.48N	112.00 E
Taizhou	154	Eh	32.29N	119.55 E
Taizhou → Linhai	152	Lf	28.52N	121.08 E
Taizhou Wan	154	Fj	28.40N	121.37 E
Taizi He	154	Gd	41.00N	122.23 E
Ta'izz	142	Gh	13.38N	44.02 E
Tājābād	146	Pg	30.02N	54.24 E
Tajarḩī	164	Be	24.21N	14.28 E
Tajgonos, mys-	138	Ld	60.35N	160.10 E
Tajgonos, poluostrov- = Taigonos Peninsula (EN)	138	Ld	61.35N	161.00 E
Tajikistan (EN) = Tojikiston	136	Hh	39.00N	71.00 E
Tajima	154	Of	37.12N	139.46 E
Tajimi	156	Ed	35.19N	137.08 E
Tajin	190	Ed	20.27N	97.23W
Tājirwīn	128	Co	35.54N	8.33 E
Tajito	192	Cb	30.58N	112.18W
Tajmba	138	Ed	60.22N	98.50 E
Tajmyr	138	Ea	76.05N	98.55 E
Tajmyr, ozero-	140	Mb	74.30N	102.30 E
Tajmyr, poluostrov- = Taymyr Peninsula (EN)	140	Mb	76.00N	104.00 E
Tajmyra	140	Lb	76.00N	99.40 E
Tajmyrlyr	138	Hb	72.30N	121.39 E
Tajo = Tagus (EN)	110	Fh	38.40N	9.24W
Tajo-Segura, Canal de Trasvase-	126	Je	39.30N	2.05W
Tajrīsh	144	Hb	38.48N	51.25 E
Tajšet	142	Ld	55.57N	98.00 E
Tajumulco, Volcán-	174	Jh	15.02N	91.54W
Tajuña	126	Id	40.07N	3.35W
Tak	148	Je	16.52N	99.08 E
Taka Atoll	214	He	11.07N	169.40 E
Takāb	146	Ld	36.24N	47.07 E
Takaba	170	Hb	3.27N	40.14 E
Takahagi	154	Pf	36.42N	140.41 E
Takahama	156	Dd	35.29N	135.33 E
Takahara-Gawa	156	Ec	36.27N	137.15 E
Takaharu	156	Bf	31.55N	130.59 E
Takahashi	154	Lg	34.47N	133.37 E
Takahashi-Gawa	156	Cd	34.32N	133.42 E
Takahata	156	Gc	38.00N	140.12 E
Takahe, Mount-	222	Of	76.17S	112.05W
Takaka	218	Ed	40.51S	172.48 E
Takakuma-Yama	156	Bf	31.28N	130.49 E
Takalar	150	Gh	5.28S	119.24 E
Takalous	162	Ie	23.25N	7.02 E
Takamatsu	152	Ne	34.21N	134.03 E
Takamori	156	Be	32.48N	131.08 E
Takanabe	156	Be	32.08N	131.31 E
Takanawa-Hantō	156	Ce	34.00N	132.55 E
Takanawa-San	156	Ce	33.57N	132.50 E
Takanosu	156	Ga	40.14N	140.22 E
Takaoka [Jap.]	156	Bf	31.57N	131.17 E
Takaoka [Jap.]	154	Nf	36.45N	137.01 E
Takapoto Atoll	216	Lb	15.00S	148.10W
Takapuna	218	Fb	36.48S	174.47 E
Takara-Jima	152	Mf	29.10N	129.05 E
Takarazuka	156	Dd	34.49N	135.21 E
Takaroa Atoll	216	Mb	14.28S	144.58W
Takasaki	154	Of	36.20N	139.01 E
Taka-Shima [Jap.]	156	Af	31.26N	129.45 E
Taka-Shima [Jap.]	156	Be	32.40N	131.50 E
Takatshwane	172	Cd	22.36S	21.55 E
Takatsu-Gawa	156	Bd	34.42N	131.49 E
Takatsuki	154	Mg	34.51N	135.37 E
Takayama	154	Nf	36.08N	137.15 E
Takebe	156	Cd	34.53N	133.54 E
Takefu	154	Ng	35.54N	136.10 E
Takehara	156	Cd	34.21N	132.54 E
Takeo	156	Ae	33.12N	130.00 E
Tåkern	116	Ff	58.20N	14.50 E
Take-Shima	154	Kf	37.22N	131.58 E
Tākestān	144	Gb	36.05N	49.14 E
Taketa	156	Be	32.58N	131.24 E
Takêv	148	Kf	10.59N	104.47 E
Takhādīd	146	Kh	29.59N	44.30 E
Takhār [3]	144	Kb	36.30N	69.30 E
Takhmaret	126	Mi	35.06N	0.41 E
Takht-e Soleimān	146	Nd	36.20N	51.00 E
Taki [Jap.]	156	Cd	35.16N	132.38 E
Taki [Pap.N.Gui.]	219a	Bb	6.29S	155.50 E
Takijuq Lake	180	Gc	66.05N	113.00W
Takikawa	154	Pc	43.33N	141.54 E
Takingeun	150	Cf	4.38N	96.50 E
Takinoue	156a	Ca	44.13N	143.03 E
Takko	156	Ga	40.20N	141.09 E
Takla Lake	180	Ee	55.30N	126.00W
Takla Landing	180	Ee	55.29N	125.58W
Takla Makan (EN) = Taklimakan Shamo	140	Kf	39.00N	83.00 E
Takob	135	Ge	38.51N	69.00 E
Tako-Bana	156	Cd	35.35N	133.05 E
Takolokouzet, Massif de-	166	Gb	18.40N	9.30 E
Taksimo (Muhoršibir)	138	Ff	51.01N	107.50 E
Taku	156	Be	33.19N	130.06 E
Takua Pa	148	Jg	8.52N	98.21 E
Takum	166	Gd	7.16N	9.59 E
Takuma	156	Cd	34.14N	133.40 E
Takume Atoll	208	Mf	15.49S	142.12W
Takuna, mys- / Tahkuna neem	116	Je	59.05N	22.30 E
Takutea Island	208	Lf	19.49S	158.18W
Tala	192	Hg	20.40N	103.42W
Tālah	162	Ib	35.35N	8.40 E
Talaimmannar	148	Fg	9.05N	79.44 E
Talāīyeh	146	Kd	37.50N	45.00 E
Talaja	138	Kd	61.03N	152.30 E
Talak	158	Hg	18.20N	6.00 E
Talamanca, Cordillera de-	194	Fi	9.30N	83.40W
Talara	200	Hf	4.35S	81.25W
Talas	136	Hg	42.29N	72.14 E
Talas	135	Ic	44.05N	70.20 E
Talasea	212	Ka	5.20S	150.05 E
Talasskaja oblast	135	Ic	42.25N	72.15 E
Talasski Alatau, hrebet-	135	Hc	42.10N	72.00 E
Talata Mafara	166	Gc	12.34N	6.04 E
Talaud, Kepulauan- = Talaud Islands (EN)	140	Oi	4.20N	126.50 E
Talaud Islands (EN) = Talaud, Kepulauan-	140	Oi	4.20N	126.50 E
Talavera, Isla-	204	Dh	27.32S	56.26W
Talavera de la Reina	126	He	39.57N	4.50W
Talawdī	168	Ec	10.38N	30.23 E
Talbot Inlet	180	Ja	77.55N	77.35W
Talca	200	Ii	35.26S	71.40W
Talcahuano	200	Ii	36.43S	73.07W
Tālcher	148	Hd	20.57N	85.13 E
Taldom	114	Ih	56.45N	37.32 E
Taldy-Kurgan	142	Je	44.59N	78.23 E
Taldy-Kurganskaja oblast [3]	136	Hf	44.00N	78.00 E
Talēḩ	168	Hd	9.09N	48.26 E
Tal-e Khosravī	146	Ng	30.47N	51.29 E
Talence	122	Fj	44.49N	0.36W
Ṭalesh, Kūhhā-Ye-	146	Md	37.35N	48.38 E
Talgar	136	Hg	43.18N	77.13 E
Taliabu, Pulau-	150	Hg	1.48S	124.48 E
Talica	136	Gd	57.01N	63.43 E
Talimardžan	136	Gh	38.21N	65.31 E
Tali Post	168	Ed	5.54N	30.47 E
Talisajan	142	Ni	1.37N	118.11 E
Taliwang	150	Gh	8.44S	116.52 E
Talkeetna	178	Id	62.20N	150.07W
Talkeetna Mountains	178	Jd	62.10N	148.15W
Talkheh	146	Kd	37.40N	45.46 E
Talladega	184	Di	33.26N	86.06W
Tall 'Afar	146	Jd	36.22N	42.27 E
Tallah	146	Dh	28.05N	30.44 E
Tallahassee	176	Kf	30.25N	84.16W
Tallahatchie River	186	Kj	33.33N	90.10W
Tall al Abyaḑ	146	Hd	36.41N	38.57 E
Tallapoosa River	184	Di	32.30N	86.16W
Tallard	122	Mj	44.28N	6.03 E
Tällberg	116	Fd	60.49N	15.00 E
Tall Birāk at Taḩtānī	146	Id	36.38N	41.05 E
Tallinn	112	Id	59.25N	24.45 E
Tall Kayf	146	Jd	36.29N	43.08 E
Tall Kūshik	146	Jd	36.48N	42.04 E
Tallulah	186	Kj	32.25N	91.11W
Tălmaciu	130	Hd	45.39N	24.16 E
Talmenka	138	Df	53.51N	83.45 E
Talmest	162	Fc	31.09N	9.00W
Talnah	138	Dc	69.30N	88.15 E
Talnoje	132	Ge	48.53N	30.42 E
Talo	158	Kg	10.44N	37.55 E
Talofofo	220c	Bb	13.20N	144.46 E
Talon	138	Je	59.48N	148.50 E
Tāloqān	144	Kb	36.44N	69.33 E
Talovaja	132	Ld	51.06N	40.48 E
Talpa de Allende	192	Gg	20.23N	104.51W
Talsi	114	Fh	57.17N	22.37 E
Taltal	200	Ih	25.24S	70.29W
Taltson	180	Gd	61.24N	112.45W
Taluk	150	Dg	0.32S	101.35 E
Talvik	114	Fa	70.03N	22.58 E
Talwār	146	Md	36.00N	48.00 E
Tama	168	Cc	14.45N	22.25 E
Tamaghzah	162	Ic	34.23N	7.57 E
Tamala	132	Mc	52.33N	43.18 E
Tamalameque	194	Ki	8.52N	73.38W
Tamale	160	Gh	9.24N	0.50W
Tamames	126	Fd	40.39N	6.06W
Tamana	156	Be	32.55N	130.33 E
Tamanaco, Río-	196	Dh	9.25N	65.23W
Tamana Island	208	Ie	2.29S	175.59 E
Tamano	154	Lg	34.30N	133.56 E
Tamanoura	156	Ae	32.38N	128.37 E
Tamanrasset	160	Hf	22.47N	5.31 E
Tamanrasset [3]	162	Ie	23.00N	5.30 E
Tamanrasset	158	Hf	22.03N	0.10 E
Tamar	118	Ik	50.22N	4.10W
Támara	202	Db	5.50N	72.10W
Tamara	130	Cg	42.27N	19.33 E
Tamarit de Llitera/Tamarite de Litera	126	Mc	41.52N	0.26 E
Tamarite de Litera/Tamarit de Llitera	126	Mc	41.52N	0.26 E
Tamarugal, Pampa del-	206	Gb	21.00S	69.25W
Tamási	120	Oj	46.38N	18.17 E
Tamassoumit	162	Ef	18.35N	12.39W
Tamaulipas [2]	190	Ed	24.00N	98.45W
Tamaulipas, Llanos de-	190	Ed	25.00N	98.25W
Tamaulipas, Sierra de-	192	Jf	23.30N	98.30W
Tamayama	156	Gb	39.50N	141.11 E
Tamazula de Gordiano	192	Hh	19.38N	103.15W
Tamazunchale	190	Ed	21.16N	98.47W
Tambach	170	Gb	0.36N	35.31 E
Tambacounda	160	Fg	13.12N	15.48W
Tambara	172	Ec	16.44S	34.15 E
Tambelan, Kepulauan- = Tambelan Islands (EN)	150	Ef	1.00N	107.30 E
Tambelan, Pulau-	150	Ef	0.58N	107.34 E
Tambelan Islands (EN) = Tambelan, Kepulauan-	150	Ef	1.00N	107.30 E
Tambo	212	Jd	24.53S	146.15 E
Tambohorano	172	Gc	17.29S	43.58 E
Tambora, Gunung-	150	Gh	8.14S	117.55 E
Tambores	204	Dj	31.52S	56.16W
Tambov	112	Ke	52.43N	41.27 E
Tambovskaja oblast [3]	136	Ee	52.45N	41.40 E
Tambre	126	Db	42.49N	8.53W
Tambunan	150	Ge	5.40N	116.22 E
Tambura	160	Jh	5.36N	27.28 E
Tamchaket	162	Ef	17.20N	10.40W
Tame	202	Db	6.27N	71.45W
Tâmega	126	Dc	41.05N	8.21W
Tâmega	126	Dc	41.05N	8.21W
Tamel Aike	206	Fg	48.19S	70.58W
Tamesi	190	Ed	22.13N	97.52W
Tamesnar	158	Hg	18.25N	3.33 E
Tamgak, Monts-	158	Hg	19.11N	8.42 E
Tamgue, Massif du-	158	Fg	12.00N	12.18W
Tamiahua	192	Kg	21.16N	97.27W
Tamiahua, Laguna de-	190	Ed	21.35N	97.35W
Tamianglajang	150	Gg	2.07S	115.10 E
Tamil Nādu [3]	148	Ff	11.00N	78.00 E
Tamiš	130	De	44.51N	20.39 E
Tamise/Temse	124	Gc	51.08N	4.13 E
Tamitatoala, Rio-	202	Hf	11.56S	53.36W
Ṭāmiyah	146	Dh	29.29N	30.58 E
Tam Ky	148	Le	15.34N	108.29 E
Tammaro	128	Ii	41.09N	14.50 E
Tammela	116	Jd	60.48N	23.46 E
Tammerfors/Tampere	112	Ic	61.30N	23.45 E
Tammisaari/Ekenäs	114	Fg	59.58N	23.26 E
Tämnaren	116	Gd	60.10N	17.20 E
Tamnava	130	De	44.25N	20.05 E
Tamou	166	Fc	12.45N	2.11 E
Tampa	176	Kg	27.57N	82.27W
Tampa Bay	182	Kf	27.45N	82.35W
Tampake-Misaki	156a	Bb	43.43N	141.20 E
Tampere/Tammerfors	112	Ic	61.30N	23.45 E
Tampico	176	Jg	22.13N	97.51W
Tampin	150	Df	2.28N	102.14 E
Tamri	162	Fc	30.43N	9.50 E
Tamsag-Bulak	152	Kb	47.14N	117.21 E
Tamsalu	114	Gg	59.10N	26.07 E
Tamsweg	128	Hc	47.08N	13.48 E
Tamu	148	Id	24.13N	94.19 E
Tamuín	192	Jg	21.59N	98.45W
Tamuín	190	Ed	22.00N	98.44W
Tamuín, Río-	192	Jg	21.47N	98.28W
Tamworth [Austl.]	210	Gh	31.05S	150.55 E
Tamworth [Eng.-U.K.]	118	Li	52.39N	1.40W
Tamyang	154	Ig	35.19N	126.59 E
Tana [Eur.]	110	Ia	70.28N	28.18 E
Tana [Kenya]	158	Li	2.32S	40.31 E
Tana, Lake-	158	Kg	12.00N	37.20 E
Tanabe	154	Mh	33.42N	135.44 E
Tana bru	114	Ga	70.16N	28.10 E
Tanacross	178	Kd	63.23N	143.21W
Tanafjorden	114	Ga	70.54N	28.40 E
Tanaga	178a	Cb	51.50N	178.00W
Tanagro	128	Jj	40.38N	15.14 E
Tanagura	156	Gc	37.02N	140.23 E
Tanahbala, Pulau-	150	Cg	0.25S	98.25 E
Tanahgrogot	150	Gg	1.55S	116.12 E
Tanahjampea, Pulau-	150	Hh	7.05S	120.42 E
Tanahmasa, Pulau-	150	Cg	0.12S	98.27 E
Tanahmerah	150	Lh	6.05S	140.17 E
Tanah Merah	150	De	5.48N	102.09 E
Tanakpur	148	Gc	29.05N	80.07 E
Tanalyk	134	Ij	51.46N	58.45 E
Tanami	212	Fc	19.59S	129.43 E
Tanami Desert	208	Eg	20.00S	132.00 E
Tan An	148	Lf	10.32N	106.25 E
Tanana	178	Ic	65.10N	152.05W
Tanana	174	Dc	65.09N	151.55W
Tanapag	220b	Ba	15.14N	145.45 E
Tanapag, Puetton-	220b	Ba	15.14N	145.44 E
Tanāqīb, Ra's at-	146	Mi	27.50N	48.53 E
Tanargue, Le-	122	Kj	44.37N	4.09 E
Tanaro	128	Ce	45.01N	8.47 E
Tanba-Sanchi	156	Dd	35.15N	135.35 E
Tancheng	154	Eg	34.37N	118.20 E
Tanch'ŏn	152	Mc	40.25N	128.57 E
Tancítaro, Pico de-	190	De	19.26N	102.18W
Tanda	166	Ed	7.48N	3.10W
Tanda, Lac-	166	Eb	15.45N	4.42W
Tandag	150	Ie	9.04N	126.12 E
Tandaltī	168	Ec	13.01N	31.52 E
Tăndărei	130	Ke	44.39N	27.40 E
Tandil	200	Ki	37.20S	59.05W
Tandil, Sierras del-	204	Cm	37.24S	59.06W
Tandjilé [3]	168	Bd	9.30N	16.30 E
Tando Ādam	148	Dc	25.46N	68.40 E
Tandsjöborg	114	Df	61.42N	14.43 E
Tanḑubāyah	168	Db	18.40N	28.37 E
Taneatua	218	Gc	38.04S	177.00 E
Tane-Ga-Shima	152	Ne	30.40N	131.00 E
Taneichi	156	Ga	40.24N	141.43 E
Tan Emellel	162	Id	27.28N	9.45 E
Tanew	120	Sf	50.27N	22.16 E
Tanezrouft	158	Gf	24.00N	0.45W
Tanezzuft	164	Bd	25.51N	10.19 E
Tanf, Jabal at-	146	Hf	33.30N	38.42 E
Tanga	160	Ki	5.04S	39.06 E
Tanga [3]	170	Gd	5.30S	38.00 E
Tangail	148	Hd	24.15N	89.55 E
Tanga Islands	208	Ge	3.30S	153.15 E
Tangalla	148	Gg	6.01N	80.48 E
Tanganyika [2]	170	Fd	6.00S	35.00 E
Tanganyika, Lac- = Tanganyika, Lake- (EN)	158	Ji	6.00S	29.30 E
Tanganyika, Lake-	158	Ji	6.00S	29.30 E
Tanganyika, Lake- (EN) = Tanganyika, Lac-	158	Ji	6.00S	29.30 E
Tangará	202	Ke	6.11S	35.49W
Tangarare	219a	Dc	9.35S	159.39 E
Tangdan → Dongchuan	152	Hf	26.07N	103.05 E
Tāngehgol	146	Pd	37.25N	55.50 E
Tanger = Tangier (EN)	160	Ge	35.48N	5.48W
Tanger = Tangier (EN) [3]	162	Fb	35.45N	5.45W
Tangerang	150	Eh	6.11S	106.37 E
Tangermünde	120	Hd	52.33N	11.57 E
Tanggu	152	Kd	39.00N	117.36 E
Tanggula Shan	152	Fe	33.05N	91.00 E
Tanggula Shan (Dangla Shan)	140	Lf	33.00N	92.00 E
Tanggula Shankou	152	Fe	32.42N	92.27 E
Tanggulashanqu / Tuotuoheyan	142	Lf	34.15N	92.29 E
Tanghe	152	Je	32.37N	112.57 E
Tang He	154	Bh	32.10N	112.20 E
Tangier (EN) = Tanger	160	Ge	35.48N	5.48W
Tangier (EN) = Tanger [3]	162	Fb	35.45N	5.45W
Tang La	140	Kg	28.00N	89.15 E
Tango	156	Dd	35.44N	135.05 E
Tangra Yumco	140	Kf	31.00N	86.25 E
Tangshan	142	Nf	39.35N	118.09 E
Tanguiéta	166	Fc	10.37N	1.16 E
Tangxian	154	Ce	38.46N	114.58 E
Tangyin	154	Cg	35.54N	114.21 E
Tangyuan	152	Mb	46.45N	129.53 E
Tanhoj	138	Ff	51.33N	105.07 E
Tanhuijo, Arrecife-	192	Kg	21.07N	97.17W
Taniantaweng Shan	152	Ge	30.00N	98.00 E
Tanimbar, Kepulauan- = Tanimbar Islands (EN)	208	Ee	7.30S	131.30 E
Tanimbar Islands (EN) = Tanimbar, Kepulauan-	208	Ee	7.30S	131.30 E
Tanintharyi	148	Jf	13.00N	99.00 E
Tanjung [Indon.]	150	Gg	2.11S	115.23 E
Tanjung [Indon.]	150	Dg	1.23S	103.58 E
Tanjungbalai	150	Cf	2.58N	99.48 E
Tanjungpandan	150	Eg	2.45S	107.39 E
Tanjungpinang	150	Df	0.55N	104.27 E
Tanjungredep	150	Gf	2.09N	117.29 E
Tanjungselor	150	Gf	2.51N	117.22 E
Tankenberg	124	Ib	52.21N	6.58 E
Tanna, Ile-	208	Hf	19.30S	169.20 E
Tännäs	114	Ce	62.27N	12.40 E
Tanner, Mount-	188	Fb	49.40N	118.34W
Tannis Bugt	116	Dg	57.40N	10.15 E
Tannu-Ola	140	Ld	51.00N	94.00 E
Tano	166	Ed	5.07N	2.56W
Tanout	160	Hg	14.58N	8.53 E
Ṭanṭā	160	Ke	30.47N	31.00 E
Tan Tan	162	Ed	28.30N	11.02W
Tan-Tan [3]	162	Ed	28.30N	11.00W
Tan Tan Plage	162	Ed	28.26N	11.15W
Tantoyuca	192	Jg	21.21N	98.14W
Tanum	114	Cg	58.43N	11.20 E
Tanzania [1]	160	Ki	6.00S	35.00 E
Tao, Ko-	148	Jf	10.05N	99.52 E
Tao'an (Taonan)	152	Lb	45.20N	122.46 E
Tao'er He	140	Oe	45.42N	124.05 E
Taoghe	172	Cd	20.37S	22.35 E
Tao He	152	Hd	35.50N	103.20 E
Taojiang	154	Bj	28.33N	112.05 E
Taolagnaro	160	Lk	25.01S	46.59 E
Taonan → Tao'an	152	Lb	45.20N	122.46 E
Taongi Atoll	208	Hc	14.37N	168.58 E
Taormina	128	Jm	37.51N	15.17 E
Taos	182	Fd	36.24N	105.24W
Taoudenni	160	Gf	22.42N	3.56W
Taougrite	126	Mh	36.15N	0.55 E
Taounate	162	Gc	34.33N	4.39W
Taounate [3]	162	Gc	34.04N	4.06W
Taoura	128	Cn	36.10N	8.02 E
Taourirt	162	Gc	34.25N	2.54W
Taouz	162	Gc	31.00N	4.00W
Taoyuan	152	Lg	25.00N	121.18 E
Tapa	136	Cd	59.15N	25.59 E
Tapachula	176	Jh	14.54N	92.17W
Tapaga, Cape-	221c	Bb	14.01S	171.23W
Tapah	150	Df	4.11N	101.16 E
Tapajera	204	Fi	28.09S	52.01W
Tapajós, Rio-	198	Kf	2.24S	54.41W
Tapaktuan	150	Cf	3.16N	97.11 E
Tapalqué	204	Bm	36.21S	60.01W
Tapan	150	Dg	2.10S	101.04 E
Tapanahoni Rivier	202	Hc	4.22N	54.27W
Tapanlieh	152	Lg	21.58N	120.47 E
Tapanui	218	Cf	45.57S	169.16 E
Tapauá	202	Fe	5.45S	64.23W
Tapauá, Rio-	198	Jf	5.40S	64.21W
Tapenagá, Río-	204	Ci	28.04S	59.10W
Taperas	204	Bc	17.54S	60.23W
Tapes	206	Jd	30.40S	51.23W
Tapes, Serra do-	204	Gj	30.25S	51.55W
Tapeta	166	Dd	6.29N	8.51W
Taphan Hin	148	Ke	16.12N	100.26 E
Tapili	170	Eb	3.25N	27.40 E
Tapini	214	Di	8.19S	146.59 E
Tapiola, Espoo-	116	Kd	60.11N	24.49 E
Tapiraí	204	Id	19.52S	46.01W
Tapirapuã	204	Db	14.51S	57.45W
Tapolca	120	Nj	46.53N	17.26 E
Tappahannock	184	Ig	37.55N	76.54W
Tappi-Zaki	154	Pd	41.18N	140.22 E
Tappu	156a	Ba	44.04N	141.52 E
Tapsuj	134	Je	62.20N	61.30 E
Tāpti	140	Jg	21.06N	72.41 E
Tapul Group	150	He	5.30N	121.00 E
Tapurucuara	202	Ed	0.24S	65.02W
Taputapu, Cape-	221c	Cb	14.19S	170.50W
Tāqbostān	146	Le	34.30N	46.58 E
Ṭaqṭaq	146	Ke	35.53N	44.35 E
Taquara	206	Jc	29.39S	50.47W
Taquaral, Serra do-	204	Fb	15.42S	52.30W
Taquari	204	Fc	17.50S	53.17W
Taquari, Pantal do-	202	Gg	18.10S	56.30W
Taquari, Rio- [Braz.]	204	Hf	23.16S	49.12W
Taquari, Rio- [Braz.]	204	Gi	29.56S	51.44W
Taquari, Rio- [Braz.]	198	Kg	19.15S	57.17W
Taquari, Serra do-	204	Fd	18.18S	53.49W
Taquaritinga	204	He	21.24S	48.30W
Taquarituba	204	Hf	23.31S	49.15W
Taquaruçu, Rio-	204	Fe	21.35S	52.08W
Tar	135	Id	40.38N	73.26 E
Tara	130	Cf	43.55N	19.25 E
Tara	118	Gh	53.34N	6.35W
Tara [Austl.]	212	Ke	27.17S	150.28 E
Tara [Jap.]	156	Be	33.02N	130.11 E
Tara [Russia]	136	Hd	56.54N	74.22 E
Tara [Russia]	138	Ce	56.40N	74.50 E
Tara [Eur.]	130	Bf	43.21N	18.51 E
Taraba	166	Hd	8.34N	10.15 E
Tarabuco	202	Fg	19.10S	64.57W
Ṭarābulus = Tripoli (EN)	144	Ec	34.26N	35.51 E
Ṭarābulus = Tripoli (EN)	160	Ie	32.54N	13.11 E
Ṭarābulus = Tripoli (EN) [3]	164	Bc	32.40N	13.15 E
Ṭarābulus = Tripolitania (EN)	158	Ie	31.00N	14.00 E
Ṭarābulus = Tripolitania (EN)	164	Bc	30.00N	15.00 E
Taradale	218	Gc	39.32S	176.51 E
Tarāghin	164	Bd	25.59N	14.26 E
Tarahumara, Sierra-	190	Cc	28.26N	106.50W
Tarakan	142	Ni	3.18N	117.38 E
Tarakan, Pulau-	150	Gf	3.21N	117.36 E
Taraklija	132	Fg	45.57N	28.41 E
Tarama Jima	152	Lg	24.40N	124.40 E
Taran, mys-	114	Ei	54.57N	19.59 E
Taranaki [2]	218	Fc	39.10S	174.40 E
Tarancón	126	Id	40.01N	3.00W
Taranga Island	218	Fa	36.00S	174.45 E
Taransay	118	Fd	57.55N	7.10W
Taranto	112	Hg	40.28N	17.14 E
Taranto, Golfo di- = Taranto, Gulf of- (EN)	110	Hg	40.10N	17.20 E
Taranto, Gulf of- (EN) = Taranto, Golfo di-	110	Hg	40.10N	17.20 E
Tarapacá	206	Ga	19.55S	69.31W
Tarapacá [2]	206	Ga	20.00S	69.20W
Tarapaina	219a	Ec	9.23S	161.24 E
Tarapoto	202	Ce	6.30S	76.25W
Taraquá	202	Ec	0.06N	68.28W
Tarara	219a	Bb	6.02S	155.24 E
Tarare	122	Ki	45.54N	4.26 E
Tararua Range	218	Fd	40.40S	175.25 E
Tarašča	132	Ge	49.34N	30.31 E
Tarascon	122	Kk	43.48N	4.40 E
Tarascon-sur-Ariège	122	Hl	42.51N	1.36 E
Tarat	162	Id	26.08N	9.21 E
Tarata	202	Dg	17.27S	70.02W
Tarauacá	202	De	8.10S	70.46W
Tarauacá, Rio-	198	Jf	6.42S	69.48W
Taravao	221e	Fc	17.44S	149.19W
Taravao, Baie de-	221e	Fc	17.43S	149.17W
Taravo	122a	Ab	41.42N	8.48 E
Tarawa Atoll	208	Id	1.25N	173.00 E
Tarawera	218	Gc	39.02S	176.35 E
Tarazi	146	Mg	31.05N	48.18 E
Tarazona	126	Kc	41.54N	1.44W
Tarazona de la Mancha	126	Ke	39.15N	1.55W

Index Symbols

[1] Independent Nation
[2] State, Region
[3] District, County
[4] Municipality
[5] Colony, Dependency
Continent
Physical Region
Historical or Cultural Region
Mount, Mountain
Volcano
Hill
Mountains, Mountain Range
Hills, Escarpment
Plateau, Upland
Pass, Gap
Plain, Lowland
Delta
Salt Flat
Valley, Canyon
Crater, Cave
Karst Features
Depression
Polder
Desert, Dunes
Forest, Woods
Heath, Steppe
Oasis
Cape, Point
Coast, Beach
Cliff
Peninsula
Isthmus
Sandbank
Island
Atoll
Rock, Reef
Islands, Archipelago
Rocks, Reefs
Coral Reef
Well, Spring
Geyser
River, Stream
Waterfall, Rapids
River Mouth, Estuary
Lake
Salt Lake
Intermittent Lake
Reservoir
Swamp, Pond
Canal
Glacier
Ice Shelf, Pack Ice
Ocean
Sea
Gulf, Bay
Strait, Fjord
Lagoon
Bank
Seamount
Tablemount
Ridge
Shelf
Basin
Escarpment, Sea Scarp
Fracture
Trench, Abyss
National Park, Reserve
Point of Interest
Recreation Site
Cave, Cavern
Historic Site
Ruins
Wall, Walls
Church, Abbey
Temple
Scientific Station
Railway station
Airport
Port
Military installation
Lighthouse
Mine
Tunnel
Dam, Bridge

Tarbagataj, hrebet- 140 Ke 47.10N 83.00 E
Tarbagatay Shan 152 Db 47.10N 83.00 E
Tarbat Ness 118 Jd 57.50N 3.40W
Tarbert [Scot.-U.K.] 118 Gd 57.54N 6.49W
Tarbert [Scot.-U.K.] 118 Hf 55.52N 5.26W
Tarbes 122 Gk 43.14N 0.05 E
Tarboro 184 Ih 35.54N 77.32W
Tarcăului, Munţii- 130 Jc 46.45N 26.20 E
Tarcoola 212 Gf 30.41S 134.33 E
Tardenois 124 Fe 49.12N 3.40 E
Tardienta 126 Lc 41.59N 0.32W
Tardoire 122 Gi 45.52N 0.14 E
Tardoki-Jani, gora- 138 Ig 48.50N 137.55 E
Taree 210 Gh 31.54S 152.28 E
Taremert-n-Akli 162 Id 25.53N 5.18 E
Tarentaise 122 Mi 45.30N 6.30 E
Tarfā', Ra's at- 164 Hf 17.02N 42.22 E
Ţarfā', Wādī aţ- 146 Dh 28.38N 30.43 E
Ţarfah, Jazīrat aţ- 164 Hg 14.37N 42.55 E
Tarfaya 160 Ff 27.57N 12.55W
Targa 126 Qi 35.41N 4.09 E
Tărgoviški prohod 130 Jf 43.12N 26.30 E
Tărgovište 130 Jf 43.15N 26.34 E
Tărgovište [2] 130 Jf 43.15N 26.34 E
Tarhankut, mys- 132 Hg 45.21N 32.30 E
Tarhăus, Vîrful- 130 Jc 46.38N 26.10 E
Tarhūnah 164 Bc 32.26N 13.38 E
Tarhūnī, Jabal at- 164 De 22.12N 22.25 E
Tariba 194 Kj 7.49N 72.13W
Ţarīf 144 He 24.01N 53.45 E
Tarifa 126 Gh 36.01N 5.36W
Tarifa, Punta de- 126 Gh 36.00N 5.37W
Tarija 200 Jh 21.31S 64.45W
Tarija [3] 202 Fh 21.30S 64.00W
Tarik 220d Bb 7.21N 151.47 E
Tariku 150 Kg 2.55S 138.26 E
Tariku-Taritatu 150 Kg 2.50S 138.25 E
Tarīm [Yem.] 144 Gf 16.03N 49.00 E
Tarīm [Sau.Ar.] 146 Fi 27.54N 35.24 E
Tarim Basin (EN) = Tarim Pendi 140 Ke 41.00N 84.00 E
Tarime 170 Fc 1.21S 34.22 E
Tarim He 140 Ke 41.05N 86.40 E
Tarim Pendi=Tarim Basin (EN) 140 Ke 41.00N 84.00 E
Tarin Kowt 144 Kc 32.52N 65.38 E
Taritatu 150 Kg 2.54S 138.27 E
Tarjalan 152 Hb 49.38N 101.59 E
Tarjannevesi 116 Kb 62.10N 24.05 E
Tarjat 152 Gb 48.10N 99.40 E
Tarka, Vallée de- 166 Gc 14.30N 6.30 E
Tarkastad 172 Df 32.00S 26.16 E
Tarkio 186 If 40.27N 95.23W
Tarko-Sale 138 Cd 64.55N 78.05 E
Tarkwa 166 Ed 5.18N 1.59W
Tarlac 142 Oh 15.29N 120.35 E
Tarm 116 Ci 55.55N 8.32 E
Tarma 202 Cf 11.25S 75.42W
Tarn [3] 122 Hk 43.50N 2.00 E
Tarn 122 Hj 44.06N 1.02 E
Tarna 120 Pi 47.31N 19.59 E
Tärnaby 114 Dd 65.43N 15.16 E
Tarn-et-Garonne [3] 122 Hj 44.00N 1.10 E
Tarnica 120 Sg 49.06N 22.47 E
Tarnobrzeg 120 Rf 50.35N 21.41 E
Tarnobrzeg [2] 120 Rf 50.35N 21.40 E
Tarnogród 120 Sf 50.23N 22.45 E
Tarnos 122 Ek 43.32N 1.28W
Tarnów 112 Ie 50.01N 21.00 E
Tarnów [2] 120 Qf 50.00N 21.00 E
Tarnowskie Góry 120 Of 50.27N 18.52 E
Tärnsjö 116 Gd 60.09N 16.56 E
Taro 128 Ef 45.00N 10.15 E
Taron 219a Aa 4.28S 153.04 E
Tarongers, Costa dels- / Azahar, Costa del- 126 Me 39.58N 0.01 E
Taroom 210 Fg 25.39S 149.49 E
Taroudant 162 Fc 30.29N 8.52W
Tarpon Springs 184 Fk 28.09N 82.45W
Tarquinia 128 Fh 42.15N 11.45 E
Tarra, Rio- 194 Ki 9.04N 72.27W
Tarrafal 162 Cf 15.17N 23.46W
Tarragona 112 Gg 41.07N 1.15 E
Tarragona [3] 126 Mc 41.10N 1.00 E
Tarraleah 212 Jh 42.10S 146.30 E
Tarrant 184 Di 33.38N 86.46W
Tàrrega 126 Nc 41.39N 1.09 E
Tarsus 144 Db 36.55N 34.53 E
Tart 152 Fd 37.07N 92.57 E
Tartagal 206 Hb 22.32S 63.49W
Tartaro 128 Fe 45.02N 11.30 E
Tartas 122 Fk 43.50N 0.48W
Tartas 138 Ce 55.37N 76.44 E
Tartu 112 Id 58.23N 26.45 E
Tartūs 144 Ec 34.53N 35.53 E
Tarumae-Yama 156a Bb 42.41N 141.23 E
Tarumizu 154 Ki 31.29N 130.42 E
Tarusa 132 Jb 54.43N 37.11 E
Tārūt 146 Ni 26.34N 50.04 E
Tarutau, Ko- 148 Jg 6.35N 99.40 E
Tarutino 132 Ff 46.12N 29.09 E
Tarutung 150 Cf 2.01N 98.58 E
Tarvisio 128 Hd 46.30N 13.35 E
Tarvo 204 Bb 15.06S 60.34W
Tarvo, Rio- 204 Bb 14.57S 61.03W
Tasajera, Sierra- 192 Gc 29.35N 105.35W
Tašanta 138 Dg 49.43N 89.11 E
Tasaral, ostrov- 135 Ja 46.15N 74.05 E
Tašauz 136 Fg 41.52N 59.59 E
Tašauzskaja oblast [3] 136 Fg 41.00N 58.40 E
Tasāwah 164 Bd 25.59N 13.29 E
Tasbuget 136 Gg 44.48N 65.38 E
Tasejeva 138 Ee 58.06N 94.01 E
Taseko Lake 188 Da 51.15N 123.35W
Tasendjanet 162 Hd 25.40N 0.59 E
Tashk, Daryācheh-ye- 144 Hd 29.45N 53.35 E
Tasikmalaya 142 Mj 7.20S 108.12 E
Tåsinge 116 Di 55.00N 10.36 E
Tašir (Kalinino) 132 Ni 41.08N 44.14 E
Tasiussaq 179 Gd 73.18N 56.00W
Taskan 138 Kd 62.58N 150.20 E
Taškent 142 Ie 41.20N 69.18 E
Taškentskaja oblast [3] 136 Gg 41.20N 69.40 E
Taškepri 136 Gh 36.17N 62.38 E
Taškeprinskoje, vodohranilišče- 135 Df 36.15N 62.40 E
Tasker 166 Hb 15.04N 10.42 E
Taşköprü 146 Fb 41.30N 34.14 E
Taš-Kumyr 136 Hg 41.20N 72.14 E
Taşlıçay 146 Jc 39.38N 43.23 E
Tasman, Mount- 218 De 43.34S 170.09 E
Tasman Basin (EN) 106 Jn 43.00S 158.00 E
Tasman Bay 216 Dh 41.10S 173.15 E
Tasmania [2] 212 Jh 43.00S 147.00 E
Tasmania 208 Fi 43.00S 147.00 E
Tasman Peninsula 212 Jh 43.05S 147.50 E
Tasman Plateau (EN) 106 In 48.00S 148.00 E
Tasman Sea 208 Hh 40.00S 163.00 E
Tăşnad 130 Fb 47.29N 22.35 E
Taşova 146 Gb 40.46N 36.20 E
Tassah, Wādī- 128 Cn 36.35N 8.54 E
Tassara 166 Gb 16.01N 5.39 E
Taštagol 138 Df 52.47N 88.00 E
Tåstrup 116 Ei 55.39N 12.19 E
Tastūr 128 Dn 36.33N 9.27 E
Tasty-Taldy 136 Ge 50.47N 66.31 E
Taşucu 146 Ed 36.19N 33.53 E
Ţasūj 146 Kc 38.19N 45.21 E
Tata [3] 162 Fd 29.40N 8.00W
Tata [Hun.] 120 Oi 47.39N 18.19 E
Tata [Mor.] 162 Fd 29.45N 7.59W
Tataba 150 Hg 1.18S 122.49 E
Tatabánya 120 Oi 47.34N 18.25 E
Tatakoto Atoll 208 Nf 17.20S 138.23W
Tata Mailau 150 Ih 8.55S 125.30 E
Tatarbunary 132 Fg 45.49N 29.35 E
Tatarsk 142 Jd 55.13N 75.58 E
Tatarstan, respublika 136 Fd 55.20N 50.50 E
Tatar Strait (EN) = Tatarski proliv 140 Qd 50.00N 141.15 E
Tatau 150 Ff 2.53N 112.51 E
Taţāwīn 162 Jc 32.56N 10.27 E
Tateyama 154 Og 34.59N 139.52 E
Tathlina Lake 180 Fd 60.30N 117.30W
Tathlīth 144 Ff 19.32N 43.30 E
Tatiščevo 132 Nd 51.40N 45.35 E
Tatla Lake 188 Ca 51.55N 124.36W
Tatla Lake 188 Ca 51.58N 124.25W
Tatlow, Mount- 188 Ca 51.23N 123.52W
Tatnam, Cape - 180 Ie 57.16N 91.00W
Tatra Mountains (EN) 110 Hf 49.15N 20.00 E
Tatsuno [Jap.] 156 Dd 34.52N 134.33 E
Tatsuno [Jap.] 156 Ed 35.58N 137.58 E
Tatsuruhama 156 Ec 37.04N 136.53 E
Tatta 148 Dd 24.45N 67.55 E
Tatui 204 If 23.21S 47.51W
Tatum 186 Ej 33.16N 103.19W
Tatvan 144 Fb 38.30N 42.16 E
Tau 116 Ae 59.04N 5.54 E
Tau [Am.Sam.] 221c Db 14.15S 169.30W
Tau [Ton.] 221b Bc 21.01S 175.00W
Tauá 202 Je 6.01S 40.26W
Taubaté 200 Lh 23.02S 45.33W
Tauberbischofsheim 120 Fg 49.37N 9.40 E
Taučik 136 Fg 44.15N 51.20 E
Tauere Atoll 208 Mf 17.22S 141.30W
Tauern 110 Hf 47.15N 13.15 E
Taufstein 120 Ff 50.31N 9.14 E
Tauhunu 220n Ac 10.25S 161.03W
Tauhunu 220n Ac 10.25S 161.03W
Taujsk 138 Je 59.46N 149.20 E
Taujskaja guba 138 Je 59.15N 150.00 E
Taukum 135 Jb 44.50N 75.30 E
Taumako 219c Ba 9.57S 167.13 E
Taumarunui 218 Fc 38.52S 175.15 E
Taum Sauk Mountain 186 Kh 37.34N 90.44W
Taunay 204 De 20.18S 56.05W
Taung 172 Ce 27.33S 24.47 E
Taungdwingyi 148 Jd 20.01N 95.33 E
Taunggyi 148 Jd 20.47N 97.02 E
Taungthonlon 148 Jd 24.58N 95.48 E
Taungup 148 Ie 18.51N 94.14 E
Taunton [Eng.-U.K.] 118 Jj 51.01N 3.06W
Taunton [Ma.-U.S.] 184 Le 41.54N 71.06W
Taunus 120 Ef 50.10N 8.15 E
Taunusstein 124 Kd 50.08N 8.10 E
Taupo 216 Eg 38.41S 176.05 E
Taupo, Lake- 216 Eg 38.50S 175.55 E
Tauragé/Taurage 114 Fi 55.16N 22.19 E
Taurage/Tauragé 114 Fi 55.16N 22.19 E
Tauranga 210 Ih 37.42S 176.10 E
Taurianova 128 Kl 38.21N 16.01 E
Taurion 122 Hi 45.53N 1.24 E
Taurisano 128 Mk 39.57N 18.13 E
Tauroa Point 218 Ea 35.10S 173.04 E
Taurus Mountains (EN)= Toros Dağları 140 Ff 37.00N 33.00 E
Tauste 126 Kc 41.55N 1.15W
Tauu Islands 208 Ge 4.45S 157.00 E
Tauz 136 Eg 41.01N 45.35 E
Ţavālesh, Kūhhā-Ye- 146 Mc 38.42N 48.18 E
Tavas 146 Cd 37.34N 29.04 E
Tavas Ovasi 146 Cd 37.30N 28.55 E
Tavastehus/Hämeenlinna 114 Ff 61.00N 24.27 E
Tavau/Davos 128 Dd 46.47N 9.50 E
Tavda 136 Gd 58.03N 65.15 E
Tavda 140 Id 57.47N 67.16 E
Tavendroua 219b Cc 16.21S 167.22 E
Tavernes de Valldigna / Tabernes de Valldigna 126 Le 39.04N 0.16W
Taveta 170 Gc 3.24S 37.41 E
Taveuni Island 216 Fc 16.51S 179.58W
Taviano 128 Mk 39.59N 18.05 E
Tavignano 122a Bb 42.06N 9.33 E
Tavira 126 Eg 37.07N 7.39W
Tavistock 118 Ik 50.33N 4.08W
Tavolara 128 Dj 40.55N 9.40 E
Tavoliere 128 Ji 41.35N 15.25 E
Tavolžan 136 He 52.44N 77.30 E
Tavoy → Dawei 142 Lh 14.05N 98.12 E
Tavričanka 154 Kc 43.20N 131.52 E
Tavropoúu, Tekhnití Limni- 130 Ej 39.15N 21.40 E
Tavşan Adalari 130 Jj 39.55N 26.05 E
Tavşanlı 146 Cc 39.35N 29.30 E
Tavua 216 Ec 17.27S 177.51 E
Taw 118 Ij 51.04N 4.11W
Tawakoni, Lake- 186 Ij 32.55N 96.00W
Tawas City 182 Kc 44.16N 83.31W
Tawau 142 Ni 4.15N 117.54 E
Tawfīqīyah 168 Ed 9.26N 31.37 E
Ţawīlah, Juzur- 146 Ei 27.35N 33.46 E
Tawitawi Group 150 He 5.10N 120.15 E
Ţawkar 160 Kg 18.26N 37.44 E
Ţawūq 146 Ke 35.08N 44.27 E
Tawūq Chāy 146 Ke 34.35N 44.31 E
Tawurghā', Sabkhat- 164 Cc 31.10N 15.15 E
Tawzar 162 Ic 33.55N 8.08 E
Taxco de Alarcón 192 Jh 18.33N 99.36W
Taxkorgan 152 Cd 37.47N 75.14 E
Tay 118 Je 56.30N 3.30W
Tay, Firth of- 118 Ke 56.28N 3.00W
Tay, Loch- 118 Ie 56.30N 4.10W
Tayandu, Kepulauan- 150 Jh 5.30S 132.15 E
Tayēgle 168 Ge 4.02N 44.36 E
Taylor [Nb.-U.S.] 186 Gf 41.46N 99.23W
Taylor [Tx.-U.S.] 182 He 30.34N 97.25W
Taylor, Mount- 182 Fd 35.14N 107.37W
Taylorville 186 Lg 39.33N 89.18W
Taymā' 144 Ed 27.38N 38.29 E
Taymyr Peninsula (EN) = Tajmyr, poluostrov- 140 Mb 76.00N 104.00 E
Tay Ninh 148 Lf 11.18N 106.06 E
Tayside [3] 118 Je 56.30N 3.40W
Taytay 150 Gd 10.49N 119.31 E
Taz 140 Jc 67.29N 78.41 E
Taza [3] 162 Gc 34.00N 4.00W
Taza [Mor.] 160 Ge 34.13N 4.01W
Taza [Russia] 138 Gf 54.55N 111.05 E
Tāzah Khurmātū 146 Ke 35.18N 44.20 E
Tazawako 156 Gb 39.42N 140.44 E
Tazawa-Ko 156 Gb 39.43N 140.40 E
Tazenakht 162 Fc 30.35N 7.12W
Tazerbo Oasis (EN)= Tāzirbū, Wāḩāt al- 158 Jf 25.45N 21.00 E
Tazewell [Tn.-U.S.] 184 Fg 36.27N 83.34W
Tazewell [Va.-U.S.] 184 Gg 37.07N 81.34W
Tāzīāzet 162 De 20.55N 15.40W
Tazin Lake 180 Ge 59.48N 109.05W
Tāzirbū, Wāḩāt al-=Tazerbo Oauis (EN) 158 Jf 25.45N 21.00 E
Tazlău 130 Jc 46.50N 26.47 E
Tazmalt 126 Qh 36.43N 4.08 E
Tazouikert 166 Ea 21.46N 1.13W
Tazovskaja guba 134 Qb 69.05N 76.00 E
Tazovski 138 Cc 67.28N 78.42 E
Tazrouk 162 Ie 23.27N 6.14 E
Tazumal 194 Cg 14.00N 89.40W
Tbilisi 112 Kg 41.43N 44.49 E
Tchad=Chad (EN) [1] 160 Ig 15.00N 19.00 E
Tchad, Lac- = Chad, Lake- (EN) 158 Ig 13.20N 14.00 E
Tchamba [Cam.] 166 Hd 8.37N 12.48 E
Tchamba [Togo] 166 Fd 9.02N 1.25 E
Tchibanga 170 Bc 2.51S 11.02 E
Tchien 166 Dd 6.04N 8.08W
Tchigaï, Plateau du- 158 If 21.30N 14.50 E
Tchikala-Tcholohanga 170 Ce 12.38S 16.04 E
Tchin Tabaraden 166 Gb 15.58N 5.50 E
Tcholliré 166 Hd 8.24N 14.10 E
Tczew 120 Ob 54.06N 18.47 E
Tea, Rio- 202 Ed 0.30S 65.09W
Teaca 130 Hc 46.55N 24.31 E
Teacapán 192 Gf 22.33N 105.45W
Teaiti Point 220p Bb 21.11S 159.47W
Te Anau 218 Bf 45.25S 167.43 E
Te Anau, Lake- 216 Ci 45.15S 167.45 E
Teano 128 Ii 41.15N 14.04 E
Teapa 192 Mi 17.33N 92.57W
Te Araroa 216 Eg 37.38S 178.22 E
Te Aroha 218 Fb 37.32S 175.42 E
Tea Tree 212 Gd 22.11S 133.17 E
Te Atu Kura 220p Bb 21.14S 159.45W
Te Awamutu 218 Fc 38.00S 175.19 E
Teberda 132 Lh 43.28N 41.43 E
Tébessa 160 He 35.24N 8.07 E
Tébessa [3] 162 Ic 35.00N 7.45 E
Tébessa, Oued- 128 Bo 35.48N 7.53 E
Tebicuary, Rio- [Par.] 204 Dh 26.26S 56.51W
Tebicuary, Rio- [Par.] 204 Ch 26.36S 58.16W
Tebingtinggi [Indon.] 150 Dg 3.36S 103.05 E
Tebingtinggi [Indon.] 150 Cf 3.20N 99.09 E
Tebulosmta, gora- 132 Nh 42.33N 45.16 E
Teča 134 Kh 56.17N 62.59 E
Tecate 190 Ab 32.34N 116.38W
Tecer Dağları 146 Gc 39.27N 37.11 E
Techirghiol 130 Le 44.03N 28.36 E
Tecka 206 Ff 43.29S 70.48W
Tecklenburg 124 Jb 52.13N 7.50 E
Tecomán 190 De 18.55N 103.53W
Tecomate, Laguna- 192 Ji 16.45N 99.25W
Tecoripa 192 Ec 28.37N 109.57W
Tecpan de Galeana 190 De 17.15N 100.41W
Tecuala 190 Cd 22.23N 105.27W
Tecuci 130 Kd 45.52N 27.25 E
Tedegra 168 Ba 20.46N 19.34 E
Tedori-Gawa 156 Ec 36.29N 136.28 E
Tedžen 136 Gh 37.23N 60.31 E
Tedžen 140 If 37.24N 60.38 E
Tedženstroj 136 Gh 36.54N 60.53 E
Teeli 138 Ef 50.57N 90.18 E
Teenuse jõgi / Tenuze 114 Fg 58.44N 23.58 E
Tees 118 Lg 54.33N 1.16W
Tees Bay 118 Lg 54.35N 1.05W
Tefé 200 Jf 3.22S 64.42W
Tefé, Rio- 202 Fd 3.35S 64.47W
Tefedest 162 Ie 24.40N 5.30 E
Tefenni 146 Cd 37.18N 29.47 E
Tegal 142 Mj 6.52S 109.08 E
Tegea (EN) = Teyéa 130 Fl 37.27N 22.25 E
Tegelen 124 Ic 51.20N 6.08 E
Tegernsee 120 Hi 47.43N 11.46 E
Tegina 166 Gc 10.04N 6.11 E
Tégoua 219b Ca 13.15S 166.37 E
Tegucigalpa 176 Kh 14.06N 87.13W
Teguidda I-n-Tessoum 166 Gb 17.26N 6.39 E
Teguldet 138 De 57.20N 88.20 E
Tehachapi 188 Fi 35.08N 118.27W
Tehachapi Mountains 188 Fi 34.56N 118.40W
Tehamiyam 168 Fb 18.20N 36.32 E
Te Hapua 216 Df 34.30S 172.55 E
Tehaupoo 221e Fc 17.49S 149.18W
Tehek Lake 180 Hd 64.55N 95.30W
Téhini 166 Ed 9.36N 3.40W
Tehi-n-Isser 162 Ie 24.48N 8.08 E
Tehoru 150 Ig 3.23S 129.30 E
Tehrān 142 Hf 35.40N 51.26 E
Tehuacán 190 Ee 18.27N 97.23W
Tehuantepec 190 Ee 16.20N 95.14W
Tehuantepec, Golfo de- = Tehuantepec, Gulf of- (EN) 174 Jh 16.00N 94.50W
Tehuantepec, Gulf of- (EN) =Tehuantepec, Golfo de- 174 Jh 16.00N 94.50W
Tehuantepec, Isthmus of- (EN)=Tehuantepec, Istmo de- 174 Jh 17.00N 94.30W
Tehuantepec, Istmo de-= Tehuantepec, Isthmus of- (EN) 174 Jh 17.00N 94.30W
Tehuantepec Ridge (EN) 190 Ef 13.30N 98.00W
Tehuata Atoll 208 Mf 16.50S 141.55W
Teiga Plateau 168 Db 15.38N 25.40 E
Teignmouth 118 Jk 50.33N 3.30W
Teil, Le- 122 Kj 44.33N 4.41 E
Teili/Delet 116 Id 60.15N 20.35 E
Teith 118 Ie 56.14N 4.20W
Teiuş 130 Gc 46.12N 23.41 E
Teixeira Pinto 166 Bc 12.04N 16.02W
Teja 138 Ed 60.27N 92.38 E
Tejkovo 136 Ed 56.50N 40.34 E
Tejo=Tagus (EN) 110 Fh 38.40N 9.24W
Teju 148 Jc 27.55N 96.10 E
Te Kaha 218 Gb 37.44S 177.41 E
Te Kao 218 Ea 34.39S 172.58 E
Tekapo, Lake- 218 De 43.50S 170.30 E
Te Karaka 218 Gc 38.28S 177.52 E
Tekax 192 Og 20.12N 89.17W
Teke 130 Mh 41.04N 29.39 E
Teke 130 Jh 41.21N 26.57 E
Teke Burun [Tur.] 130 Ji 40.02N 26.10 E
Teke Burun [Tur.] 130 Jk 38.05N 26.36 E
Tekeli 136 Hg 44.48N 78.57 E
Tekes 152 Dc 43.10N 81.43 E
Tekes He 152 Dc 43.35N 82.30 E
Tekeze 158 Kg 14.20N 35.50 E
Tekija 130 Fe 44.41N 22.25 E
Tekiliktag 152 Dd 36.35N 80.20 E
Tekirdağ 144 Ca 40.59N 27.31 E
Tekman 146 Ic 39.38N 41.31 E
Te Kopuru 218 Eb 36.02S 173.55 E
Te Kou 220p Bb 21.14S 159.46W
Tekouiat 162 He 22.20N 2.30 E
Tekro 168 Cb 19.34N 20.57 E
Te Kuiti 218 Fc 38.20S 175.10 E
Tela 190 Ge 15.44N 87.27W
Telagh 162 Gc 34.47N 0.34W
Telataï 166 Fb 16.31N 1.30 E
Telavåg 114 Af 60.16N 4.49 E
Telavi 136 Eg 41.55N 45.29 E
Tel Aviv [3] 146 Ff 32.05N 34.48 E
Tel Aviv-Yafo 142 Ff 32.04N 34.46 E
Telč 120 Lg 49.11N 15.27 E
Telchac Puerto 192 Og 21.21N 89.16W
Telciu 130 Hb 47.26N 24.24 E
Tele 170 Db 2.48N 23.54 E
Teleac 130 Hc 46.41N 24.48 E
Telečkoje ozero 138 Df 51.30N 87.45 E
Telefomin 214 Ci 5.08S 141.31 E
Telegraph Creek 180 Ee 57.54N 131.09W
Telekitonga 221b Bb 20.24S 174.32W
Telekivavu'u 221b Bb 20.19S 174.32W
Telêmaco Borba 204 Gg 24.23S 50.28W
Telemark [2] 114 Bg 59.30N 8.40 E
Telemark 116 Ce 59.30N 8.45 E
Telén 206 Ge 36.16S 65.30W
Telen 150 Gf 0.26N 116.42 E
Teleneşty 130 Lb 47.30N 28.16 E
Teleno 126 Fb 42.21N 6.23W
Teleorman [2] 130 Ie 44.10N 25.15 E
Teleorman 130 If 43.52N 25.26 E
Telerhteba, Djebel- 162 Ie 24.10N 6.51 E
Telescope Peak 188 Gh 36.10N 117.05W
Telescope Point 197p Bb 12.08N 61.36W
Telese 128 Ii 41.13N 14.32 E
Telfān, Hadjer- 168 Bc 12.05N 18.57 E
Telford 118 Ki 52.40N 2.30W
Telgte 124 Jc 51.59N 7.47 E
Télimélé 166 Cc 10.54N 13.02W
Teljo, Jabal- 168 Dc 14.42N 25.56 E
Tell al Ubaid 146 Lg 30.59N 46.01 E
Tellaro 128 Jn 36.50N 15.06 E
Tell Atlas (EN)=Atlas Tellien 158 He 36.00N 2.00 E
Tell City 184 Dg 37.57N 86.46W
Teller 178 Fc 65.16N 166.22W
Telok Anson 150 Df 4.02N 101.01 E
Teloloapan 192 Jh 18.21N 99.51W
Telposiz, gora- 110 Lc 63.54N 59.10 E
Telsen 206 Gf 42.24S 66.57W
Telšiai/Telšjaj 136 Cd 55.59N 22.17 E
Telšjaj/Telšiai 136 Cd 55.59N 22.17 E
Teltow 120 Jd 52.24N 13.16 E
Telukbetung 142 Mj 5.27S 105.16 E
Telukbutun 150 Ef 4.13N 108.12 E
Telukdalem 150 Cf 0.34N 97.49 E
Téma 160 Gh 5.37N 0.01W
Temacine 162 Ic 33.01N 6.01 E
Te Manga 220p Bb 21.13S 159.45W
Tematangi Atoll 208 Mg 21.41S 140.40W
Tembenči 138 Ed 64.36N 99.58 E
Tembi 130 Fj 39.53N 22.35 E
Tembilahan 150 Dg 0.19S 103.09 E
Temblador 196 Eh 8.59N 62.44W
Tembleque 126 Ie 39.42N 3.30W
Temblor Range 188 Fi 35.30N 119.55W
Tembo 170 Cd 7.42S 17.17 E
Tembo, Chutes- 158 Ii 8.50S 15.20 E
Tembo, Mont- 170 Bb 1.50N 12.00 E
Tembué 172 Eb 14.51S 32.50 E
Teme 118 Ki 52.09N 2.18W
Temerin 130 Cd 45.25N 19.53 E
Temerloh 150 Df 3.27N 102.25 E
Teminabuan 150 Jg 1.26S 132.01 E
Temir 136 Ff 49.08N 57.09 E
Temir 132 Te 48.31N 57.29 E
Temirlanovka 135 Gc 42.36N 69.17 E
Temirtau 142 Jd 50.05N 72.56 E
Témiscaming 184 Hb 46.44N 79.06W
Témiscouata, Lac- 184 Mb 47.40N 68.50W
Temki 168 Bc 11.29N 18.13 E
Temnikov 114 Ki 54.40N 43.13 E
Temo 128 Cj 40.17N 8.28 E
Temoe, Ile- 208 Ng 23.20S 134.29W
Temores 192 Ed 27.16N 108.15W
Tempe 188 Jj 33.25N 111.56W
Tempio Pausania 128 Dj 40.54N 9.06 E
Temple 182 He 31.06N 97.21W
Templeman, Mount- 188 Ga 50.43N 117.14W
Templemore/An Teampall Mór 118 Fi 52.48N 7.50W
Templin 120 Jc 53.07N 13.30 E
Tempoal, Rio- 192 Jg 21.47N 98.27W
Tempué 170 Ce 13.27S 18.53 E
Temrjuk 132 Jg 45.15N 37.23 E
Temse/Tamise 124 Gc 51.08N 4.13 E
Temuco 200 Ii 38.44S 72.36W
Temuka 218 Df 44.15S 171.16 E
Tena 202 Cd 0.59S 77.48W
Tenacatita, Bahia de- 192 Gh 19.10N 104.50W
Tenala/Tenhola 116 Jd 60.04N 23.18 E
Tenāli 148 Ge 16.15N 80.35 E
Tenancingo de Degollado 192 Jh 18.58N 99.36W
Tenasserim [3] 148 Jf 13.00N 99.00 E
Tenasserim 140 Lh 12.35N 97.52 E
Tenasserim 148 Jf 12.24N 98.37 E
Tenby 118 Ij 51.41N 4.43W
Tence 122 Ki 45.07N 4.17 E
Tench Island 214 Eh 1.38S 150.42 E
Tende, Col di- 128 Bf 44.09N 7.34 E
Tendaho 168 Gc 11.38N 41.00 E
Tende 122 Nj 44.05N 7.36 E
Tende, Col de- 128 Bf 44.09N 7.34 E
Ten Degree Channel 140 Lh 10.00N 92.30 E
Tendō 156 Gb 38.22N 140.22 E
Tendrara 162 Gc 33.03N 2.00W
Tendre, Mont- 128 Ad 46.36N 6.19 E
Tendrovskaja kosa 132 Gf 46.15N 31.45 E
Ténenkou 166 Ec 14.28N 4.55W
Tenente Lira, Rio- 204 Db 15.56S 57.39W
Ténéré 158 Ig 17.36N 10.55 E
Ténéré, 'Erg du- 166 Hb 17.35N 10.55 E
Tenerife 158 Ff 28.19N 16.34W
Ténès 162 Hb 36.31N 1.18 E
Ténès, Cap- 126 Nh 36.33N 1.21 E
Teng 148 Je 19.52N 97.45 E
Tengah, Kepulauan- 150 Gh 7.30S 117.30 E
Tengchong 152 Gg 24.59N 98.32 E
Te Nggano, Lake- 214 Gj 11.45S 160.25 E
Tenggarong 150 Gg 0.24S 116.58 E
Tengger Shamo 140 Mf 38.00N 104.10 E
Tengiz, ozero- 140 Id 50.25N 69.00 E
Tengréla 166 Dc 10.29N 6.24W
Tengréla [3] 166 Dc 10.27N 6.25W
Tengxian [China] 152 Jg 23.18N 110.49 E
Tengxian [China] 154 Dg 35.07N 117.10 E
Tenhola/Tenala 116 Jd 60.04N 23.18 E
Teniente General Rosendo M. Fraga 204 Af 23.45S 62.09W
Tenkāsi 148 Fg 8.58N 77.18 E
Tenke 170 Ee 10.33S 26.08 E
Tenkeli 138 Jb 70.01N 140.55 E
Tenkodogo 166 Ec 11.47N 0.22W
Tenna 128 Hg 43.14N 13.47 E
Tennant Creek 210 Ef 19.40S 134.10 E
Tennessee [2] 182 Jd 35.50N 85.30W
Tennessee 174 Kf 37.04N 88.33W
Tenneville 124 Hd 50.06N 5.32 E
Tenojoki 114 Ga 70.28N 28.18 E
Tenom 150 Ge 5.08N 115.57 E
Tenosique de Pino Suárez 192 Ni 17.29N 91.26W
Tenri 156 Dd 34.36N 135.49 E
Tenryū 156 Ed 34.52N 137.47 E
Tenryū-Gawa 154 Ng 34.35N 137.48 E
Tensift 162 Fc 32.02N 9.21W
Ten Sleep 188 Ld 44.02N 107.27W
Tenterden 124 Cc 51.03N 0.42 E
Tenterfield 212 Ke 29.03S 152.01 E
Tenuku 136 Ge 81.40N 16.45 E
Tenuze / Teenuse jõgi 114 Fg 58.44N 23.58 E
Ten-Zan 156 Be 33.20N 130.08 E
Teocaltiche 192 Hg 21.26N 102.35W
Teodelina 204 Bl 34.11S 61.32W
Teodoro Sampaio 204 Ff 22.31S 52.10W
Teófilo Otoni 200 Lg 17.51S 41.30W
Teotepec, Cerro- 174 Ih 16.50N 100.50W
Teotihuacán 192 Jh 19.44N 98.50W
Teotilán del Camino 192 Kh 18.08N 97.05W

Tepa [Indon.] 150 Ih 7.52S 129.31 E
Tepa [W.F.] 220h Bb 13.19S 176.09W
Te Pae Roa Ngake o Tuko 220n Bb 10.23S 161.00W
Tepako, Pointe- 220h Bb 13.16S 176.08W
Tepalcatepec, Rio- 192 Ih 18.35N 101.59W
Tepa Point 220k Bb 19.07S 169.56W
Tepatitlán de Morelos 192 Hg 20.49N 102.44W
Tepehuanes 190 Cc 25.21N 105.44W
Tepehuanes, Rio- 192 Ge 25.11N 105.26W
Tepehuanes, Sierra de- 190 Cc 25.00N 105.40W
Tepelena 130 Di 40.18N 20.01 E
Tepi 168 Fd 7.03N 35.30 E
Tepic 176 Ig 21.30N 104.54W
Teplá 120 Ig 49.59N 12.52 E
Teplá 120 If 50.14N 12.52 E
Teplice 120 Jf 50.39N 13.50 E
Tepoca, Bahia de- 192 Cb 30.15N 112.50W
Tepopa, Cabo- 192 Cc 29.20N 112.25W
Te Puka 220n Ac 10.26S 161.02W
Te Puke 218 Gb 37.47S 176.20 E
Tequepa, Bahía de- 192 Ii 17.17N 101.05W
Tequila 192 Hg 20.54N 103.47W
Tequisquiapan 192 Jg 20.31N 99.52W
Ter 126 Pb 42.01N 3.12 E
Téra 160 Hg 14.01N 0.45 E
Tera [Port.] 126 Df 38.56N 8.03W
Tera [Sp.] 126 Gc 41.54N 5.44W
Teradomari 156 Fc 37.38N 138.45 E
Terai 140 Kg 26.30N 85.15 E
Teraina Island (Washington) 208 Kd 4.43N 160.24W
Terakeka 168 Ed 5.26N 31.45 E
Teramo 128 Hh 42.39N 13.42 E
Terampa 150 Ef 3.14N 106.14 E
Ter Apel, Vlagtwedde- 124 Jb 52.52N 7.06 E
Terborg, Wisch- 124 Ic 51.55N 6.22 E
Tercan 146 Ic 39.47N 40.24 E
Terceira 158 Ee 38.43N 27.13W
Tercero, Río- 206 Hd 32.55S 62.19W
Terebovlja 132 De 49.18N 25.42 E
Terehovka 154 Kc 43.38N 131.55 E
Terek 132 Nh 43.29N 44.08 E
Terek 110 Kg 43.44N 47.30 E
Térékolé 166 Cb 15.07N 10.53W
Terek-Saj 135 Hd 41.29N 71.13 E
Terengganu [2] 150 De 5.00N 103.00 E
Terenos 204 Ee 20.26S 54.50W
Teresa Cristina 204 Gg 24.48S 51.07W
Teresina 200 Lf 5.05S 42.49W
Teresinha 202 Hc 0.58N 52.02W
Tereška 132 Od 51.50N 46.45 E
Terespol 120 Td 52.05N 23.36 E
Teressa 148 Ig 8.15N 93.10 E
Teresva 132 Cf 47.59N 23.15 E
Terevaka, Cerro- 221d Ab 27.05S 109.23W
Tergnier 122 Je 49.39N 3.18 E
Terhazza 166 Ea 23.36N 4.56W
Teriberka 114 Ib 69.10N 35.10 E
Teriberka 114 Ib 69.09N 35.08 E
Terlingua Creek 186 El 29.10N 103.36W
Termas de Rio Hondo 206 Hc 27.29S 64.52W
Terme 146 Gb 41.12N 36.59 E
Termez 142 If 37.14N 67.16 E
Termini Imerese 128 Hm 37.59N 13.42 E
Termini Imerese, Golfo di- 128 Hl 38.00N 13.45 E
Terminillo 128 Hh 42.28N 13.01 E
Términos, Laguna de- 190 Fe 18.37N 91.33W
Termit, Massif de- 166 Hb 16.15N 11.17 E
Termit-Kaoboul 166 Hb 15.43N 11.37 E
Termoli 128 Ji 42.00N 15.00 E
Termonde/Dendermonde 124 Gc 51.02N 4.07 E
Termunten 124 Ja 53.18N 7.03 E
Ternaard, Westdongeradeel- 124 Ha 53.23N 5.58 E
Ternate 150 If 0.48N 127.24 E
Ternej 138 Ig 45.05N 136.35 E
Terneuzen 122 Jc 51.20N 3.50 E
Terni 128 Gh 42.34N 12.37 E
Ternitz 128 Kc 47.43N 16.02 E
Ternois 124 Ed 50.25N 2.19 E
Ternopol 112 If 49.34N 25.38 E
Ternopolskaja oblast [3] 136 Cf 49.20N 25.35 E
Terpenija, mys- 138 Jg 48.38N 144.40 E
Terpenija, zaliv- 140 Qe 49.00N 143.30 E
Terrace 180 Ef 54.31N 128.35W
Terrace Bay 186 Mb 48.47N 87.09W
Terracina 128 Hi 41.17N 13.15 E
Terra de Basto 126 Ec 41.25N 8.00W
Terra Firma 172 Ce 25.36S 23.24 E
Terråk 114 Cd 65.05N 12.25 E
Terralba 128 Ck 39.43N 8.39 E
Terra Rica 204 Ff 22.43S 52.38W
Terrassa 126 Oc 41.34N 2.01 E
Terrebonne Bay 186 Kl 29.09N 90.35W
Terre-de-Bas 197e Ac 15.51N 61.39W
Terre-de-Haut 197e Ac 15.58N 61.35W
Terre Haute 182 Jd 39.28N 87.24W
Terrell 186 Hj 32.44N 96.17W
Terre Plaine 122 Jg 47.25N 4.00 E
Terres Froides 122 Li 45.30N 5.30 E
Terril 126 Gh 37.00N 5.11W
Territoire de Belfort [3] 122 Mg 47.45N 6.55 E
Terry 188 Mc 46.47N 105.19W
Tersa 132 Nd 50.46N 44.42 E
Terschelling 124 Ha 53.21N 5.13 E
Terschelling 122 La 53.24N 5.20 E
Terschelling-West-Terschelling 124 Ha 53.21N 5.13 E
Tersef 168 Bc 12.55N 16.49 E
Terskej-Alatau, hrebet- 136 Hg 42.10N 78.45 E
Terski bereg 114 Jc 66.10N 39.30 E
Tersko-Kumski kanal 132 Ng 44.47N 44.37 E
Terter (Mir-Bašir) 132 Oi 40.19N 46.58 E
Teruel 126 Kd 40.21N 1.06W
Teruel [3] 126 Ld 40.40N 0.40W
Tervakoski 116 Kd 60.48N 24.37 E
Tervel 130 Kf 43.45N 27.24 E
Tervo 116 Lb 62.57N 26.45 E
Tervola 114 Fc 66.05N 24.48 E
Tes 152 Fa 50.27N 93.30 E
Teša 114 Ki 55.38N 42.10 E
Tesalia 202 Cc 2.29N 75.44W
Tesaret 162 Hd 25.40N 2.43 E
Tesdrero, Cerro- 162 Hf 22.47N 103.04W
Teseney 168 Fb 15.07N 36.40 E
Teshekpuk Lake 178 Ib 70.35N 153.30W
Teshikaga 154 Rc 43.29N 144.28 E
Teshio 154 Pb 44.53N 141.44 E
Teshio-Dake 154 Qc 43.58N 142.50 E
Teshio-Gawa 154 Pb 44.53N 141.44 E
Teshio-Sanchi 156a Ba 44.20N 142.00 E
Tesijn → Tesijn Gol 140 Ld 50.28N 93.04 E
Tesijn Gol (Tesijn) 140 Ld 50.28N 93.04 E
Teslić 128 Lf 44.37N 17.52 E
Teslin 180 Ed 60.09N 132.45W
Teslin 180 Ed 61.34N 134.50W
Teslin Lake 180 Ed 60.00N 132.30W
Teslui 130 He 44.09N 24.29 E
Tesocoma 192 Ed 27.41N 109.16W
Tesouras, Rio- 204 Gb 14.36S 50.51W
Tesouro 204 Fc 16.04S 53.34W
Tessala, Monts du- 126 Li 35.15N 0.45W
Tessalit 160 Hf 20.14N 0.59 E
Tessaoua 166 Gc 13.45N 7.59 E
Tessenderlo 124 Hc 51.04N 5.05 E
Test 118 Lk 50.55N 1.29W
Test, Tizi n'- 162 Fc 30.50N 8.20W
Testa, Capo- 128 Di 41.14N 9.08 E
Teste, La- 122 Ej 44.38N 1.09W
Têt 122 Jl 42.44N 3.02 E
Tetari, Cerro- 194 Ki 9.59N 72.55W
Tetas, Punta- 206 Fc 23.31S 70.38W
Tete 160 Kj 16.10S 33.36 E
Tete [3] 172 Ec 15.30S 33.00 E
Te Teko 218 Gc 38.02S 176.48 E
Tetepare I iland 219a Cc 8.45S 157.35 E
Téterchen 124 Ie 49.14N 6.34 E
Tetere 219a Ec 9.25S 160.15 E
Teterev 132 Gd 51.01N 30.08 E
Teterow 120 Ic 53.47N 12.34 E
Teteven 130 Hg 42.55N 24.16 E
Tetiaroa Atoll 208 Mf 17.05S 149.32W
Tetijev 132 Fe 49.23N 29.41 E
Tetjuši 114 Li 54.57N 48.49 E
Teton Peak 188 Ic 47.55N 112.48W
Teton Range 188 Je 43.50N 110.55W
Teton River 188 Jc 47.56N 110.31W
Tétouan 160 Ge 35.34N 5.22W
Tétouan [3] 162 Fb 35.35N 5.38W
Tetovo 130 Dg 42.01N 20.59 E
Tetri-Ckaro 132 Ni 41.33N 44.27 E
Teuco, Río- 204 Bg 25.38S 60.12W
Teufelskopf 124 Ie 49.36N 6.49 E
Teulada 128 Cl 38.58N 8.46 E
Teulada, Capo- 110 Gh 38.52N 8.38 E
Teul de Gonzáles Ortega 192 Hg 21.28N 103.29W
Teun, Pulau- 150 Ih 6.59S 129.08 E
Teupasenti 194 Df 14.13N 86.42W
Teuquito, Río- 204 Bg 24.22S 61.09W
Teuri-Tō 156a Ba 44.25N 141.20 E
Teutoburger Wald 120 Ee 52.10N 8.15 E
Teuva/Östermark 114 Ee 62.29N 21.44 E
Teuz 130 Ec 46.39N 21.33 E
Tevai 219c Bb 11.37S 166.55 E
Tevaitoa 221e Db 16.46S 151.28W
Tevere = Tiber (EN) 110 Hg 41.44N 12.14 E
Teverya 146 Ff 32.47N 35.32 E
Teviot 118 Kf 55.36N 2.26W
Tevli 120 Ud 52.19N 24.23 E
Tevriz 136 Hd 57.34N 72.24 E
Tevšruleh 152 Hb 47.25N 101.55 E
Te Waewae Bay 218 Bg 46.15S 167.30 E
Tewkesbury 118 Kj 51.59N 2.09W
Têwo (Dêngkagoin) 152 He 34.03N 103.21 E
Texada Island 188 Cb 49.40N 124.24W
Texarkana [Ar.-U.S.] 182 Ie 33.26N 94.02W
Texarkana [Tx.-U.S.] 176 Jf 33.26N 94.03W
Texas 212 Ke 28.51S 151.11 E
Texas [2] 182 He 31.30N 99.00W
Texas City 182 If 29.23N 94.54W
Texcoco 192 Jh 19.31N 98.53W
Texel 124 Ga 53.03N 4.47 E
Texel 122 Ka 53.05N 4.45 E
Texel-De Koog 124 Ga 53.07N 4.46 E
Texel-Den Burg 124 Ga 53.03N 4.47 E
Texoma, Lake- 182 He 33.55N 96.37W
Teyéa = Tegea (EN) 130 Fl 37.27N 22.25 E
Teza 114 Jh 56.32N 41.57 E
Teze-Jel 136 Gh 37.55N 60.22 E
Teziutlán 190 Ee 19.49N 97.21W
Tezpur 148 Ic 26.38N 92.48 E
Tha-anne 180 Id 60.31N 94.37W
Thabana Ntlenyana 158 Jk 29.30S 29.15 E
Thabazimbi 172 Dd 24.41S 27.21 E
Thai, Ao-=Thailand, Gulf of- (EN) 140 Mh 10.00N 102.00 E
Thai Binh 148 Ld 20.27N 106.20 E
Thailand (EN)=Muang Thai [1] 142 Mh 15.00N 100.00 E
Thailand, Gulf of- (EN)= Thai, Ao- 140 Mh 10.00N 102.00 E
Thai Nguyen 148 Ld 21.36N 105.50 E
Thal 148 Eb 31.30N 71.40 E
Thālith, Ash Shallāl ath-= Third Cataract (EN) 158 Kg 19.49N 30.19 E
Thamad Bū Ḥashīshah 164 Cd 25.50N 18.05 E
Thamarīd 168 Ib 17.39N 54.02 E
Thame 124 Bc 51.45N 0.59W
Thames 216 Eg 37.08S 175.33 E
Thames 110 Ge 51.28N 0.43 E
Thames River 184 Fd 42.19N 82.28W
Thamūd 144 Gf 17.15N 49.54 E
Thāna 142 Jh 19.12N 72.58 E
Thandaung 148 Je 19.04N 96.41 E
Thanh Hoa 142 Mh 19.48N 105.46 E
Thanh-pho Ho Chi Minh (Saigon) 142 Mh 10.45N 106.40 E
Thanjāvūr 148 Ff 10.48N 79.09 E
Thanlwin = Salween (EN) 140 Lg 16.31N 97.37 E
Thann 122 Ng 47.49N 7.05 E
Thaon-les-Vosges 122 Mf 48.15N 6.25 E
Thap Sakae 148 Jf 11.14N 99.31 E
Thar/Great Indian Desert 140 Jg 27.00N 70.00 E
Thargomindah 212 Ie 28.00S 143.49 E
Tharrawaddy 148 Je 17.39N 95.48 E
Tharros 128 Ck 39.54N 8.28 E
Tharthār, Baḥrath- 144 Fc 33.59N 43.12 E
Tharthār, Wādī ath- 146 Je 33.59N 43.12 E
Thasi Gang Dzong 148 Ic 27.19N 91.34 E
Thásou 130 Hi 40.47N 24.43 E
Thásos 110 Ig 40.49N 24.42 E
Thásou, Dhíavlos- 130 Hi 40.49N 24.42 E
Thathlīth, Wādī- 164 He 20.25N 44.55 E
Thaton 148 Je 16.56N 97.20 E
Thau, Bassin de- 122 Jk 43.23N 3.36 E
Thaxted 124 Cc 51.57N 0.22 E
Thaya 120 Mh 48.37N 16.56 E
Thayawthadangyi Kyun 148 Jf 12.20N 98.00 E
Thayetchaung 148 Jf 13.52N 98.16 E
Thayetmyo 148 Je 19.19N 95.11 E
The Alberga River 212 He 27.06S 135.33 E
The Aldermen Islands 218 Gb 37.00S 176.05 E
Thebai=Thebes (EN) 164 Fd 25.43N 32.35 E
Thebes (EN)=Thebai 164 Fd 25.43N 32.35 E
Thebes → Thivai 130 Gk 38.19N 23.19 E
The Black Sugarloaf 212 Kf 31.20S 151.33 E
The Borders 118 Kf 55.35N 2.50W
The Bottom 196 Ed 17.38N 63.15W
The Broads 118 Oi 52.40N 1.30 E
The Cheviot 118 Kf 55.28N 2.09W
The Cheviot Hills 118 Kf 55.30N 2.10W
The Crane 197q Bb 13.06N 59.26W
The Dalles 182 Cb 45.36N 121.10W
Thedford 182 Gc 41.59N 100.35W
The Entrance 212 Kf 33.21S 151.30 E
The Everglades 182 Kf 26.00N 81.00W
The Gap 188 Jh 36.25N 111.30W
The Granites 212 Gd 20.35S 130.21 E
The Hague (EN)=Den Haag/'s-Gravenhage 112 Ge 52.06N 4.18 E
The Knob 184 He 41.14N 78.22W
The Little Minch 118 Gd 57.35N 6.55W
Thelle 124 De 49.23N 1.51 E
Thelon 174 Jc 64.16N 96.05W
The Macumba River 208 Eg 27.45S 136.50 E
The Merse 118 Kf 55.50N 2.10W
The Naze 124 Di 51.42N 1.47 E
The Neales River 212 He 28.08S 136.47 E
The Needles 118 Lk 50.39N 1.34W
Theniet el Had 126 Oi 35.32N 2.01 E
Theodore 212 Kd 24.57S 150.05 E
Theológos 130 Hi 40.40N 24.42 E
The Pas 176 Id 53.50N 101.15W
The Pillories 197n Bb 12.54N 61.12W
Thérain 122 Ie 49.15N 2.27 E
Thermaïkós Kólpos = Salonika, Gulf of- (EN) 110 Ig 40.20N 22.45 E
Thermopilai = Thermopylae (EN) 130 Fk 38.48N 22.32 E
Thermopolis 182 Fc 43.39N 108.13W
Thermopylae (EN) = Thermopilai 130 Fk 38.48N 22.32 E
Thérouanne 124 Ed 50.38N 2.15 E
The Round Mountain 212 Kf 30.27S 152.16 E
The Sandlings 118 Oi 52.10N 1.30 E
Thesiger Bay 180 Fb 71.30N 124.00W
The Slot → New Georgia Sound 214 Fi 8.00S 158.10 E
The Solent Spithead 118 Lk 50.46N 1.20W
Thessalia [2] 130 Fj 39.30N 22.10 E
Thessalia=Thessaly (EN) 110 Ih 39.30N 22.10 E
Thessalia = Thessaly (EN) 130 Fj 39.30N 22.10 E
Thessalon 184 Fb 46.15N 83.34W
Thessaloniki = Salonika (EN) 112 Ig 40.38N 22.56 E
Thessaly (EN)= Thessalia 110 Ih 39.30N 22.10 E
Thessaly (EN) = Thessalia 130 Fj 39.30N 22.10 E
The Stevenson River 212 He 27.06S 135.33 E
Thet 124 Cb 52.24N 0.45 E
Thetford 118 Ni 52.25N 0.45 E
Thetford Mines 184 Lb 46.05N 71.18W
The Twins 218 Ed 41.14S 172.40 E
Theux 124 Hd 50.33N 5.49 E
The Valley 190 Le 18.03N 63.04W
The Warburton River 212 He 27.55S 137.28 E
The Wash 110 Ge 52.55N 0.15 E
The Weald 118 Nj 51.05N 0.05 E
The Witties 194 Ff 14.10N 82.45W
Thiaucourt-Regniéville 124 Hf 48.57N 5.52 E
Thiberville 124 Ce 49.08N 0.27 E
Thibodaux 186 Kl 29.48N 90.49W
Thief River Falls 182 Hb 48.07N 96.10W
Thiel Mountains 222 Pg 85.15S 91.00W
Thiene 128 Fe 45.42N 11.29 E
Thiérache, Collines de la- 122 Je 49.48N 3.55 E
Thiers 122 Ji 45.51N 3.34 E
Thiès 160 Fg 14.48N 16.56W
Thiès [3] 166 Bc 14.55N 16.50W
Thiesi 128 Cj 40.31N 8.43 E
Thika 170 Gc 1.03S 37.05 E
Thikombia 216 Fc 15.44S 179.55W
Thillot, Le- 122 Mg 47.53N 6.46 E
Thimerais 122 Hf 48.40N 1.20 E
Thimphu 142 Kg 27.28N 89.39 E
Thio 216 Cd 21.37S 166.14 E
Thionville 122 Me 49.22N 6.10 E
Thiou 166 Ec 13.48N 2.40W
Thira 130 Im 36.25N 25.26 E
Thira → Thira (EN) 130 Im 36.24N 25.26 E
Thira (EN) = Thira 130 Im 36.24N 25.26 E
Thirasia 130 Im 36.25N 25.20 E
Third Cataract (EN)= Thālith, Ash Shallāl ath- 158 Kg 19.49N 30.19 E
Thirsk 118 Lg 54.14N 1.20W
Thisted 114 Bh 56.57N 8.42 E
Thithia 219d Cb 17.45S 179.18W
Thiu Khao Phetchabun 148 Ke 16.20N 100.55 E
Thivai (Thebes) 130 Gk 38.19N 23.19 E
Thiviers 122 Gi 45.25N 0.55 E
Thlewiaza 180 Id 60.28N 94.42W
Thoa 180 Gd 60.31N 109.45W
Tho Chu, Dao- 148 Kg 9.00N 103.50 E
Thoen 148 Je 17.41N 99.14 E
Tholen 124 Gc 51.32N 4.13 E
Tholen 122 Kc 51.35N 4.05 E
Tholey 124 Je 49.29N 7.04 E
Thomasset, Rocher- 208 Nf 10.21S 138.25W
Thomaston 184 Ei 32.54N 84.20W
Thomasville [Al.-U.S.] 184 Dj 32.18N 87.47W
Thomasville [Ga.-U.S.] 182 Ke 30.50N 83.59W
Thomasville [N.C.-U.S.] 184 Gh 35.53N 80.05W
Thompson 180 He 55.45N 97.45W
Thompson Falls 188 Hc 47.36N 115.21W
Thompson River [B.C.-Can.] 188 Ea 50.12N 121.34W
Thompson River [U.S.] 186 Jg 39.45N 93.36W
Thompson Sound 218 Bf 45.10S 167.00 E
Thomsen 180 Fb 73.40N 119.30W
Thomson 184 Fi 33.28N 82.30W
Thomson River 212 Ie 25.11S 142.53 E
Thomson's Falls 170 Gb 0.02N 36.22 E
Thon 124 Fe 49.53N 3.55 E
Thon Buri 142 Mh 13.43N 100.24 E
Thong Pha Phum 148 Jf 14.44N 98.38 E
Thongwa 148 Je 16.46N 96.32 E
Thonon-les-Bains 122 Mh 46.22N 6.29 E
Thoreau 186 Bi 35.24N 108.13W
Thornaby-on-Tees 118 Lg 54.34N 1.18W
Thornbury 216 Ci 46.17S 168.06 E
Thorney 124 Bb 52.37N 0.06W
Thornhill 118 Jf 55.18N 3.40W
Thorshavn 112 Fc 62.01N 6.46W
Thouars 122 Fh 46.58N 0.13W
Thouet 122 Fg 47.17N 0.06W
Thouquet-Paris-Plage, Le- 122 Hd 50.31N 1.35 E
Thrace (EN) = Thráki 110 Ig 41.20N 26.45 E
Thrace (EN) = Thráki 130 Jh 41.20N 26.45 E
Thrace (EN) = Trakya 110 Ig 41.20N 26.45 E
Thrace (EN) = Trakya 130 Jh 41.20N 26.45 E
Thráki [2] 130 Jh 41.10N 25.30 E
Thráki = Thrace (EN) 110 Ig 41.20N 26.45 E
Thráki=Thrace (EN) 130 Jh 41.20N 26.45 E
Thrakikón Pélagos 130 Hi 40.30N 25.00 E
Thrapston 124 Bb 52.24N 0.32W
Three Forks 182 Eb 45.54N 111.33W
Three Kings Islands 208 Ih 34.10S 172.10 E
Three Kings Trough (EN) 106 Jm 32.00S 170.30 E
Three Pagodas Pass 148 Je 15.18N 98.23 E
Three Points, Cape- 158 Gh 4.45N 2.06W
Three Rivers 184 Ee 41.57N 85.38W
Three Sisters Islands 219a Ed 10.10S 161.57 E
Throckmorton 186 Gj 33.11N 99.11W
Throssel, Lake- 212 Ee 27.25S 124.15 E
Thu Dau Mot 148 Lf 10.58N 106.39 E
Thuin 122 Kd 50.20N 4.17 E
Thule 222 Ad 59.27S 27.19W
Thule/Qânâq 224 Od 77.35N 69.40W
Thule, Mount - 180 Jb 73.00N 78.27W
Thun 128 Bd 46.45N 7.40 E
Thunder Bay 176 Ke 48.23N 89.15W
Thunder Bay [Ont.-Can.] 186 Lb 48.24N 89.00W
Thunder Bay [Ont.-Can.] 184 Fc 45.04N 83.25W
Thunder Butte 186 Fd 45.19N 101.53W
Thuner See 128 Bd 46.40N 7.45 E
Thung Song 148 Jg 8.11N 99.41 E
Thur 128 Cc 47.36N 8.35 E
Thurgau [2] 128 Dc 47.40N 9.10 E
Thüringen 120 Gf 50.40N 11.00 E
Thüringer Wald=Thuringian Forest (EN) 110 He 50.30N 11.00 E
Thuringian Forest (EN)= Thüringer Wald 110 He 50.30N 11.00 E
Thurles/Durlas 118 Fi 52.41N 7.49W
Thursday Island 212 Ib 10.35S 142.13 E
Thurso 118 Fd 58.35N 3.32W
Thurso 118 Jc 58.35N 3.30W
Thurston Island 222 Pf 72.06S 99.00W
Thury-Harcourt 124 Bf 48.59N 0.29W
Thusis/Tusaun 128 Dd 46.42N 9.26 E
Thuwayrāt, Nafūd ath- 146 Kj 26.00N 44.50 E
Thuy Phong 148 Lf 11.14N 108.43 E
Thwaites Iceberg Tongue 222 Of 74.00S 108.30W
Thy 116 Ch 57.00N 8.30 E
Thyborøn 116 Ch 56.42N 8.13 E
Tianbaoshan 154 Jc 42.57N 128.57 E
Tianchang 152 Ke 32.37N 119.00 E
Tiandong (Pingma) 152 Ig 23.40N 107.09 E
Tian'e (Liupai) 152 If 25.05N 107.12 E
Tianguá 202 Jd 3.44S 40.59W
Tianjin (Tientsin) 142 Nf 39.08N 117.12 E
Tianjin Shi (T'ien-chin Shih) [4] 152 Kd 39.08N 117.12 E
Tianjun (Xinyuan) 142 Lf 37.18N 99.15 E
Tianlin (Leli) 152 Ig 24.22N 106.11 E
Tian Ling 154 Kb 44.24N 130.10 E
Tianmen 152 Je 30.40N 113.10 E
Tianmu Shan 154 Ei 30.31N 119.36 E
Tianmu Xi 154 Ej 29.59N 119.24 E
Tianqiaoling 154 Jc 43.35N 129.35 E
Tian Shan 140 Ke 42.00N 80.01 E
Tianshan → Ar Horqin Qi 152 Lc 43.55N 120.05 E
Tianshifu 152 Lc 41.15N 124.20 E
Tianshui 142 Mf 34.35N 105.43 E
Tiantai 154 Fj 29.08N 121.00 E
Tianwangsi 154 Ei 31.45N 119.12 E
Tianyi → Ningcheng 152 Kc 41.34N 119.25 E
Tianzhen 154 Cd 40.24N 114.05 E
Tianzhen → Gaoqing 154 Df 37.10N 117.50 E
Tianzhuangtai 154 Gd 40.49N 122.06 E
Tiaraju 204 Ej 30.15S 54.23W
Tiarei 221e Fc 17.32S 149.20W
Tiaret 160 He 35.20N 1.14 E
Tiaret [3] 162 Hc 34.50N 1.30 E
Tiaret, Monts de- 126 Ni 35.26N 1.15 E
Tiassalé 166 Ed 5.54N 4.50W
Tiavea 221c Ba 13.57S 171.24W
Tib, Ra's aṭ- = Bon, Cape- (EN) 158 Ie 37.05N 11.03 E
Tibaji 204 Gg 24.30S 50.24W
Tibaji, Rio- 204 Kf 22.47S 51.01W
Tibasti, Sarīr- 158 If 24.00N 17.00 E
Tibati 160 Ih 6.28N 12.38 E
Tiber (EN) = Tevere 110 Hg 41.44N 12.14 E
Tiberina, Vai- 128 Gg 43.30N 12.10 E
Tibesti 158 If 21.30N 17.30 E
Tibet (EN)=Xizang Zizhiqu (Hsi-tsang Tzu-chih-ch'ü) [2] 152 Ee 32.00N 90.00 E
Tibet, Plateau of- (EN)= Qing Zang Gaoyuan 140 Kf 32.30N 87.00 E
Tibidabo 126 Oc 41.25N 2.07 E
Tibni 146 He 35.35N 30.49 E
Tibro 116 Ff 58.26N 14.10 E
Tibú 194 Ki 8.40N 72.42W
Tibugá, Golfo de- 202 Cb 5.45N 77.20W
Tiburón, Cabo- 194 Ii 8.42N 77.21W
Tiburón, Isla- 190 Bc 29.00N 112.25W
Ticao 150 Hd 12.31N 123.42 E
Tice 184 Gl 26.41N 81.49W
Tichá Orlice 120 Mf 50.09N 16.05 E
Tichit 160 Gg 18.26N 9.31W
Tichit, Dahr- 162 Ff 18.30N 9.25W
Tichka, Tizi n'- 162 Fc 31.17N 7.21W
Tichla 162 Ee 21.36N 14.58W
Ticinesi, Alpi- 128 Cd 46.20N 8.45 E
Ticino [2] 128 Cd 46.20N 9.00 E
Ticino 128 De 45.09N 9.14 E
Ticul 190 Gd 20.24N 89.32W
Tidaholm 114 Cg 58.11N 13.57 E
Tidan 116 Ef 58.42N 13.48 E
Tiddim 148 Id 23.22N 93.40 E
Tidikelt, Plaine du- 158 Hf 27.00N 1.30 E
Tidirhine 162 Gc 34.51N 4.31W
Tidjikja 160 Fg 18.32N 11.27W
Tidore 150 If 0.40N 127.26 E
Tidra, Ile- 158 Fg 19.44N 16.24W
Tiebissou 166 Dd 7.10N 5.13W
Tiechang 154 Id 41.40N 126.12 E
Tiel 122 Lc 51.54N 5.25 E
Tieli 152 Mb 47.04N 128.02 E
Tieling 154 Gc 42.18N 123.51 E
Tielongtan 152 Cd 35.10N 79.32 E
Tielt 122 Jc 51.00N 3.20 E
Tienba 166 Dd 8.30N 7.10W
T'ien-chin Shih → Tianjin Shi [4] 152 Kd 39.08N 117.12 E
Tienen/Tirlemont 124 Gd 50.48N 4.57 E
Tiengemeten 124 Gc 51.45N 5.20 E
Tientsin → Tianjin 142 Nf 39.08N 117.12 E
Tieroko, Tarso- 168 Ba 20.45N 17.52 E
Tierp 114 Df 60.20N 17.30 E
Tierra Amarilla [Chile] 206 Fc 27.29S 70.17W
Tierra Amarilla [N.M.-U.S.] 186 Ch 36.42N 106.33W
Tierra Blanca 190 Ee 18.27N 96.21W
Tierra Colorada 192 Ji 17.10N 99.35W
Tierra del Fuego [2] 206 Gh 54.00S 67.00W
Tierra del Fuego 198 Jk 54.00S 69.00W
Tierralta 202 Cb 8.10N 76.04W
Tiétar 126 Fe 39.50N 6.01W
Tietê, Rio- 198 Kh 20.40S 51.35W
Tietjerksteradeel 124 Ia 53.12N 6.00 E
Tietjerksteradeel-Bergum 124 Hb 52.17N 5.58 E
Tifariti 162 Ed 26.09N 10.33W
Tiffany Mountain 188 Fb 48.40N 119.56W
Tiffin 184 Fe 41.07N 83.11W
Tifton 182 Ke 31.27N 83.31W
Tiga 219b Ce 21.08S 167.49 E
Tigalda 178a Fb 54.05N 165.05W
Tigănești 130 If 43.54N 25.22 E
Tighennif 126 Mi 35.25N 0.15 E
Tigil 138 Ke 57.48N 158.40 E
Tigil 138 Ke 57.20N 158.20 E
Tignère 166 Hd 7.22N 12.39 E
Tigray [3] 168 Fc 14.00N 39.00 E
Tigre 192 Hh 19.53N 102.59W
Tigre, Cerro del- 192 Jf 23.03N 99.16W
Tigre, Rio- [S.Amer.] 198 If 4.30S 74.10W
Tigre, Rio- [Ven.] 196 Eh 9.20N 62.30W
Tigris (EN)=Dicle 140 Gf 31.00N 47.25 E
Tigris (EN)=Dijlah 140 Gf 31.00N 47.25 E
Tigrovy Hvost, mys- 135 Bc 43.57N 58.45 E
Tiguent 162 Df 17.15N 16.00W
Tiguentourine 162 Id 27.43N 9.33 E
Tigui 168 Bb 18.38N 18.47 E
Tigzirt 126 Qh 36.54N 4.07 E
Tih, Jabal at- 164 Fd 29.35N 34.00 E
Tih, Ṣaḥrā' at- = At Tih Desert (EN) 164 Fc 30.05N 34.00 E
Tihāmat 144 Ff 18.30N 41.30 E
Tihāmat Ash Shām 164 Hf 19.15N 41.10 E
Tihāmat 'Asīr 164 Hf 17.30N 42.20 E
Tihi okean = Pacific Ocean (EN) 106 Ki 5.00N 155.00W
Tihoreck 112 Kf 45.51N 40.09 E
Tihuṭa, Pasul- 130 Ib 47.15N 25.00 E
Tihvin 136 Dd 59.38N 33.31 E
Tiirismaa 116 Kc 61.01N 25.31 E
Tiji 164 Bc 32.01N 11.22 E
Tijirît 162 Ee 20.30N 15.00W
Tijuana 176 Hf 32.32N 117.01W
Tijucas 204 Hh 27.14S 48.38W
Tijucas, Baía do- 204 Hh 27.15S 48.31W
Tijucas, Rio- 204 Hh 27.15S 48.38W

Index Symbols

[1] Independent Nation
[2] State, Region
[3] District, County
[4] Municipality
[5] Colony, Dependency
Continent
Physical Region
Historical or Cultural Region
Mount, Mountain
Volcano
Hill
Mountains, Mountain Range
Hills, Escarpment
Plateau, Upland
Pass, Gap
Plain, Lowland
Delta
Salt Flat
Valley, Canyon
Crater, Cave
Karst Features
Depression
Polder
Desert, Dunes
Forest, Woods
Heath, Steppe
Oasis
Cape, Point
Coast, Beach
Cliff
Peninsula
Isthmus
Sandbank
Island
Atoll
Rock, Reef
Islands, Archipelago
Rocks, Reefs
Coral Reef
Well, Spring
Geyser
River, Stream
Waterfall, Rapids
River Mouth, Estuary
Lake
Salt Lake
Intermittent Lake
Reservoir
Swamp, Pond
Canal
Glacier
Ice Shelf, Pack Ice
Ocean
Sea
Gulf, Bay
Strait, Fjord
Lagoon
Bank
Seamount
Tablemount
Ridge
Shelf
Basin
Escarpment, Sea Scarp
Fracture
Trench, Abyss
National Park, Reserve
Point of Interest
Recreation Site
Cave, Cavern
Historic Site
Ruins
Wall, Walls
Church, Abbey
Temple
Scientific Station
Railway station
Airport
Port
Military installation
Lighthouse
Mine
Tunnel
Dam, Bridge

Tijucas, Serra do- ⛰	204	Hh	27.16S	49.10W
Tijucas do Sul	204	Hg	25.56S	49.10W
Tijuco, Rio- ≈	204	Gd	18.40S	50.05W
Tikal ⊡	176	Kh	17.20N	89.39W
Tikanlik	152	Ec	40.42N	87.38 E
Tikchik Lakes ≋	178	Hd	60.07N	158.35W
Tikehau Atoll ◎	216	Lb	15.00S	148.10W
Tikei, Ile- ◆	216	Mb	14.58S	144.32W
Tikitiki	218	Hb	37.47S	178.25 E
Tikkakoski	116	Kb	62.24N	25.38 E
Tikkurila	116	Kd	60.18N	25.03 E
Tiko	166	Ge	4.05N	9.22 E
Tikopia Island ◆	208	Hf	12.19S	168.49 E
Tikrīt	144	Fc	34.36N	43.42 E
Tikšeozero, ozero- ≋	114	Hc	66.15N	31.45 E
Tiksi	142	Ob	71.36N	128.48 E
Tiladummati Atoll ◎	148a	Ba	6.50N	73.05 E
Tilamuta	150	Hf	0.30N	122.20 E
Tilburg	122	Lc	51.34N	5.05 E
Tilbury	118	Nj	51.28N	0.23 E
Tilcara	206	Gb	23.34S	65.22W
Til-Châtel	122	Lg	47.31N	5.10 E
Tileagd	130	Fb	47.04N	22.12 E
Tilemsès	166	Fb	15.37N	4.44 E
Tilemsi, Vallée du- ⧗	158	Hg	19.00N	0.02 E
Tilia ≈	162	Gd	27.22N	0.02W
Tiličiki	138	Ld	60.20N	166.03 E
Tiligul ≈	132	Gf	47.07N	30.57 E
Tiligulski liman ◙	132	Gf	46.50N	31.10 E
Till ≈	118	Kf	55.41N	2.12W
Tillabéry	166	Fc	14.13N	1.27 E
Tillamook	188	Dd	45.27N	123.51W
Tillamook Bay ◧	188	Dd	45.30N	123.53W
Tillanchong ◆	148	Ig	8.30N	93.37 E
Tillberga	116	Ge	59.41N	16.37 E
Tille ≈	122	Lg	47.07N	5.21 E
Tillia	166	Fb	16.08N	4.47 E
Tillières-sur-Avre	124	Df	48.46N	1.04 E
Tillingham ≈	124	Cd	50.58N	0.44 E
Tillsonburg	184	Gd	42.51N	80.44W
Tilly-sur-Seulles	124	Be	49.11N	0.37W
Tiloa	166	Fb	15.04N	2.03 E
Tílos ◆	130	Km	36.25N	27.25 E
Tilpa	212	If	30.57S	144.24 E
Tim	132	Jd	51.37N	37.11 E
Tim ≈	132	Jc	52.15N	37.22 E
Ţimā	164	Fd	26.54N	31.26 E
Timagami	184	Gb	47.00N	80.05W
Timagami, Lake - ≋	180	Jg	46.57N	80.05W
Timalacia, Rio- → Sacre, Rio- ≈	204	Ca	13.55S	58.02W
Timane, Rio- ≈	204	Be	20.16S	60.08W
Timan Ridge (EN) = Timanski krjaž ⛰	110	Lc	65.00N	51.00 E
Timanski bereg ⊜	134	Eb	68.20N	51.45 E
Timanski krjaž = Timan Ridge (EN) ⛰	110	Lc	65.00N	51.00 E
Timaru	210	Ii	44.24S	171.15 E
Timaševsk	136	Df	45.35N	38.58 E
Timbalier Bay ◧	186	Kl	29.10N	90.20W
Timbalier Island ◆	186	Kl	29.04N	90.28W
Timbaúba	202	Ke	7.31S	35.19W
Timbédra	162	Ff	16.14N	8.10W
Timbó	204	Hh	26.50S	49.18W
Timbuktu (EN)= Tombouctou	160	Gg	16.46N	2.59W
Timedouine, Ras- ▲	126	Qh	36.28N	4.09 E
Timétrine	166	Eb	19.27N	0.26W
Timétrine ⧗	166	Eb	19.20N	0.42W
Timfi Óros ▲	130	Dj	39.57N	20.50 E
Timfristós ▲	130	Ek	38.57N	21.49 E
Tîmia	166	Gb	18.04N	8.40 E
Timimoun	160	Hf	29.15N	0.15 E
Timimoun, Sebkha de- ⊞	162	Hd	29.00N	0.05 E
Timiris, Cap— ►	162	Df	19.23N	16.32W
Timirjazevo	136	Ge	53.45N	66.33 E
Timiş [2]	130	Ed	45.38N	21.13 E
Timiş ≈	130	De	44.51N	20.39 E
Timiskaming, Lake- ≋	184	Hb	47.35N	79.35W
Timişoara	112	If	45.45N	21.13 E
Ti-m-Merhsoï ⊻	166	Gb	18.00N	5.40 E
Timmins	176	Ke	48.28N	81.20W
Timmoudi	162	Gd	29.19N	1.08W
Timms Hill ▲	186	Kd	45.27N	90.11W
Timok ≈	130	Fe	44.13N	22.40 E
Timon	202	Je	5.06S	42.49W
Timor, Laut-=Timor Sea (EN) ▤	208	Df	11.00S	128.00 E
Timor, Pulau- ◆	140	Oj	8.50S	126.00 E
Timor Sea (EN)=Timor, Laut- ▤	208	Df	11.00S	128.00 E
Timor Timur [3]	150	Ih	8.35S	126.00 E
Timor Trough (EN) ⊽	106	Ij	9.50S	126.00 E
Timote	206	He	35.21S	62.14W
Timotes	202	Db	8.59N	70.44W
Timpton ≈	138	He	58.43N	127.12 E
Timrå	114	De	62.29N	17.18 E
Tims Ford Lake ≋	184	Dh	35.15N	86.10W
Tin, Ra's at- ►	164	Dc	32.37N	23.08 E
Tinaca Point ►	140	Oi	5.33N	125.20 E
Tinaco	196	Bh	9.42N	68.26W
Tinakula ◆	219c	Ab	10.24S	165.47 E
Ti-n-Alkoum	162	Je	24.34N	10.11 E
Ti-n-Amzi [Alg.] ≈	162	He	20.32N	4.37 E
Ti-n-Amzi [Niger] ≈	166	Fb	17.54N	4.32 E
Tinaquillo	196	Bh	9.55N	68.18W
Tinchebray	124	Bf	48.46N	0.44W
Tindalo	168	Ed	5.39N	31.03 E
Tindari ⊡	128	Jl	38.10N	15.04 E
Tindila	166	Dc	10.16N	8.15W
Tindouf	160	Gf	27.42N	8.09W
Tindouf, Hamada de- ◢	162	Fd	27.45N	8.25W
Tindouf, Sebkha de- ⊞	162	Fd	27.45N	7.35W
Tinée ≈	122	Nk	43.55N	7.11 E
Tineo	126	Fa	43.20N	6.25W
Ti-n-Essako	166	Fb	18.27N	2.29 E
Tin Fouye	162	Id	28.15N	7.45 E
Tinghert, Ḥamādat- ◢	158	If	28.50N	10.00 E
Tinglev	116	Cj	54.56N	9.15 E
Tingmiarmiut	179	Hf	62.25N	42.15W
Tingo Maria	202	Ce	9.10S	76.00W
Tingri (Xêgar)	152	Ef	28.41N	87.00 E
Tingsryd	114	Dh	56.32N	14.59 E
Tingstäde	116	Hg	57.44N	18.36 E
Tingvoll	114	Be	62.54N	8.12 E
Tinian Channel ▬	220b	Bb	14.54N	145.37 E
Tinian Island ◆	208	Fc	15.00N	145.38 E
Tini Wells	168	Cb	15.02N	22.48 E
Tinkisso ≈	166	Dc	11.21N	9.10W
Tinnelva ≈	116	Ce	59.34N	9.15 E
Tinniswood, Mount- ▲	188	Da	50.19N	123.50W
Tinnoset	116	Ce	59.43N	9.02 E
Tinnsjo ≋	116	Ce	59.54N	8.55 E
Tinogasta	206	Gc	28.04S	67.34W
Tínos	130	Il	37.32N	25.10 E
Tínos ◆	130	Il	37.35N	25.10 E
Tínou, Stenón- ▬	130	Il	37.38N	25.10 E
Tinrhert, Hamada de- ◢	158	Hf	28.50N	10.00 E
Tinrhir	162	Fc	31.31N	5.32W
Tinsukia	148	Jc	27.30N	95.22 E
Tintagel Head ►	118	Ik	50.41N	4.46W
Tintamarre, Ile- ◆	197b	Bb	18.07N	63.00W
Ti-n-Tarabine ≈	162	Ie	21.16N	7.24 E
Tîntăreni	130	Ge	44.36N	23.29 E
Tintina	206	Hc	27.02S	62.43W
Tinto ≈	126	Fg	37.12N	6.55W
Ti-n-toumma ⧗	158	Ig	16.04N	12.40 E
Tinwald	218	De	43.55S	171.43 E
Ti-n-Zaouâtene	160	Hg	19.56N	2.55 E
Tiobraid Árann/Tipperary	118	Ei	52.29N	8.10W
Tiobraid Árann/Tipperary [2]	118	Ei	52.40N	8.20W
Tioga	186	Eb	48.24N	102.56W
Tioman, Pulau- ◆	150	Df	2.48N	104.11 E
Tione di Trento	128	Ed	46.02N	10.43 E
Tioro, Selat-=Tioro, Strait (EN) ▬	150	Hg	4.40S	122.20 E
Tioro Strait (EN)=Tioro, Selat- ▬	150	Hg	4.40S	122.20 E
Tiøtta	114	Cd	65.50N	12.24 E
Tiouilit	162	Df	18.52N	16.10W
Tipasa	126	Oh	36.35N	2.27 E
Tipitapa	190	Gf	12.12N	86.06W
Tipperary/Tiobraid Árann	118	Ei	52.29N	8.10W
Tipperary/Tiobraid Árann [2]	118	Ei	52.40N	8.20W
Tipton, Mount- ▲	188	Hi	35.32N	114.12W
Tip Top Mountain ▲	186	Nb	48.16N	85.59W
Tiptree	124	Cc	51.49N	0.45 E
Tiracambu, Serra do- ⛰	202	Id	3.15S	46.30W
Tirahart ≈	162	He	23.45N	2.30 E
Tīrān	146	Nf	32.42N	51.09 E
Tīrān, Maḍīq- ▬	146	Fi	27.55N	34.28 E
Tirana	112	Hg	41.20N	19.50 E
Tirania ≈	162	Ie	23.08N	9.01 E
Tirano	128	Ed	46.13N	10.10 E
Tiraspol	136	Cf	46.50N	29.37 E
Tirat Karmel	146	Ff	32.46N	34.58 E
Tire	144	Cb	38.04N	27.45 E
Tirebolu	146	Hb	41.00N	38.50 E
Tiree ◆	118	Ge	56.31N	6.49W
Tiree, Passage of- ▬	118	Ge	56.30N	6.30W
Tîrgovişte	130	Ie	44.56N	25.27 E
Tîrgu Bujor	130	Kd	45.52N	27.54 E
Tîrgu Cărbuneşti	130	Ge	44.57N	23.31 E
Tîrgu Frumos	130	Jb	47.12N	27.00 E
Tîrgu Jiu	130	Gd	45.03N	23.17 E
Tîrgu Lăpuş	130	Gb	47.27N	23.52 E
Tîrgu Mureş	112	If	46.33N	24.34 E
Tîrgu Neamţ	130	Jb	47.12N	26.22 E
Tîrgu Ocna	130	Jc	46.17N	26.37 E
Tîrgu Secuiesc	130	Jd	46.00N	26.08 E
Tîrguşor	130	Le	44.27N	28.25 E
Tirich Mir ▲	140	Jf	36.15N	71.50 E
Tiryns ⊡	130	Fl	37.36N	22.48 E
Tiririca, Serra da- ⛰	204	Ic	17.06S	47.06W
Tiris ⧗	158	Ff	23.10N	13.30W
Tiris Zemmour [3]	162	Fe	24.00N	10.00W
Tirlemont/Tienen	124	Gd	50.48N	4.57 E
Tirljanski	134	Ii	54.12N	58.33 E
Tîrnava Mare ≈	130	Gc	46.09N	23.42 E
Tîrnava Mică ≈	130	Gc	46.11N	23.55 E
Tîrnăveni	130	Hc	46.20N	24.17 E
Tirnavos	130	Fj	39.45N	22.17 E
Tiro	166	Cd	9.45N	10.39W
Tirol/Tirolo=Tyrol (EN) ▣	128	Fd	47.00N	11.20 E
Tirol=Tyrol (EN) [2]	128	Fc	47.10N	11.25 E
Tirolo/Tirol=Tyrol (EN) ▣	128	Fd	47.00N	11.20 E
Tiros	204	Jd	19.00S	45.58W
Tirreno, Mar-=Tyrrhenian Sea (EN) ▤	110	Hh	40.00N	12.00 E
Tirschenreuth	120	Ig	49.53N	12.21 E
Tirso ≈	128	Ck	39.53N	8.32 E
Tirstrup	116	Dh	56.18N	10.42 E
Tirua Point ►	218	Fc	38.23S	174.38 E
Tiruchchirappalli	142	Jh	10.49N	78.41 E
Tiruliai/Tiruliaj	116	Ji	55.44N	23.18 E
Tirunelveli	142	Ji	8.44N	77.42 E
Tirupati	148	Ff	13.39N	79.25 E
Tirza ≈	116	Lg	57.09N	26.37 E
Tisa=Tisza (EN) ≈	110	If	45.15N	20.17 E
Tis Abay ⤵	168	Fc	11.20N	37.40 E
Tisdale	180	Hf	52.51N	104.04W
Tisnaren ≋	116	Ff	58.55N	15.55 E
Tisovec	120	Ph	48.42N	19.57 E
Tissemsilt	162	Hb	35.36N	1.49 E
Tissø ≋	116	Di	55.35N	11.20 E
Tisza ≈	110	If	45.15N	20.17 E
Tisza (EN)=Tisa ≈	110	If	45.15N	20.17 E
Tiszaföldvár	120	Qj	46.59N	20.15 E
Tiszafüred	120	Qi	47.37N	20.46 E
Tiszakécske	120	Qj	46.56N	20.06 E
Tiszántúl ⧗	120	Qj	47.00N	21.00 E
Tiszaújváros (Leninváros)	120	Ri	47.56N	21.05 E
Tiszavasvári	120	Ri	47.58N	21.21 E
Titao	166	Ec	13.46N	2.04W
Tit-Ary	138	Hb	71.55N	127.01 E
Titicaca, Lago- ≋	198	Jg	15.50S	69.20W
Titikaveka	220p	Bc	21.15S	159.45W
Titlagarh	148	Gd	20.18N	83.09 E
Titlis ▲	128	Cd	46.47N	8.26 E
Titograd → Podgorica	112	Hg	42.26N	19.16 E
Titova Korenica	128	Jf	44.45N	15.42 E
Titovo Užice → Užice	130	Cf	43.52N	19.51 E
Titov Veles	130	Eh	41.42N	21.48 E
Titov vrh ▲	130	Dh	41.58N	20.50 E
Titran	114	Be	63.40N	8.18 E
Titteri ⛰	126	Pi	35.59N	3.15 E
Titu	130	Ie	44.39N	25.32 E
Titule	170	Eb	3.17N	25.32 E
Titusville [Fl.-U.S.]	182	Kf	28.37N	80.49W
Titusville [Pa.-U.S.]	184	He	41.37N	79.42W
Tituvenaj/Tytuvėnai	116	Ji	55.33N	23.09 E
Tiva ≈	170	Gc	2.20S	39.55 E
Tivaouane	166	Bc	14.57N	16.49W
Tiveden ⧗	116	Ff	58.45N	14.40 E
Tiverton	118	Jk	50.55N	3.29W
Tivoli [Gren.]	197p	Bb	12.10N	61.37W
Tivoli [It.]	128	Gi	41.58N	12.48 E
Ţiwāl ≈	168	Cc	10.22N	22.43 E
Tiwi	170	Gc	4.14S	39.35 E
Tiyo	168	Gc	14.41N	40.57 E
Tizatlán ⊡	192	Jh	19.21N	98.15W
Tizimín	190	Gd	21.09N	88.09W
Tizi Ouzou	162	Hb	36.42N	4.03 E
Tizi Ouzou [3]	162	Hb	36.35N	4.05 E
Tiznados, Río- ≈	196	Ch	8.16N	67.47W
Tiznit	162	Fd	29.43N	9.43W
Tiznit [3]	162	Fd	29.07N	9.04W
Tjačev	120	Th	48.02N	23.36 E
Tjanšan ⛰	152	Dc	42.00N	80.01 E
Tjasmin ≈	132	He	49.03N	32.50 E
Tjeggelvas ≋	114	Dc	66.35N	17.40 E
Tjeuuemeer ≋	122	Lb	52.54N	5.50 E
Tjøme ◆	116	De	59.10N	10.25 E
Tjorn ◆	116	Df	58.00N	11.38 E
Tjub-Karagan, mys- ►	132	Qg	44.38N	50.20 E
Tjubuk	134	Jh	56.03N	60.58 E
Tjuhtet	138	De	56.32N	89.29 E
Tjukalinsk	136	Hd	55.52N	72.12 E
Tjuleni, ostrov- ◆	132	Og	44.30N	47.30 E
Tjuleni, ostrova- ⁂	132	Qg	44.55N	50.10 E
Tjulgan	136	Fe	52.22N	56.12 E
Tjumen	142	Id	57.09N	65.32 E
Tjumenskaja oblast [3]	136	Gd	57.00N	69.00 E
Tjung ≈	138	Hd	63.42N	121.30 E
Tjup	135	Lc	42.44N	78.20 E
Tjuri/Türi	114	Fg	58.50N	25.27 E
Tjust ⧗	116	Gg	57.50N	16.15 E
Tjuzašu, pereval- ⌓	135	Ic	42.19N	73.50 E
Tkibuli	132	Mh	42.19N	42.59 E
Tkvarčeli	136	Eg	42.52N	41.40 E
Tlacolula	192	Ki	16.57N	96.29W
Tlacotalpan	192	Lh	18.37N	95.40W
Tlahualilo, Sierra del- ⛰	192	Hd	26.30N	103.20W
Tlalnepantla	192	Jh	19.33N	99.12W
Tlapa de Comonfort	192	Ji	17.33N	98.33W
Tlapaneco, Río- ≈	192	Jh	18.00N	98.48W
Tlaquepaque	192	Hg	20.39N	103.19W
Tlaxcala	190	Ee	19.19N	98.14W
Tlaxcala [2]	190	Ee	19.25N	98.10W
Tlemcen	162	Gc	34.52N	1.19W
Tlemcen [3]	162	Gc	34.45N	1.30W
Tleń	120	Oc	53.38N	18.20 E
Tleta Rissana	126	Gi	35.14N	5.59W
Tletat ed Douaïr	126	Oi	35.59N	2.55 E
Tljarata	132	Oh	42.06N	46.22 E
Tlumač	120	Vh	48.46N	25.06 E
Tłuszcz	120	Rd	52.26N	21.26 E
Tmassah	164	Cd	26.22N	15.48 E
Toaca, Vîrful- ▲	130	Ic	46.55N	25.59 E
Toagel Mlungui ▬	220a	Ab	7.32N	134.28 E
Toamasina	160	Lj	18.10S	49.24 E
Toamasina [3]	172	Hc	18.00S	48.40 E
Toau Atoll ◎	216	Lc	15.55S	146.00W
Toay	206	He	36.40S	64.21W
Toba	154	Ng	34.29N	136.51 E
Toba, Danau-=Toba, Lake- (EN) ≋	140	Li	2.35N	98.50 E
Toba, Lake- (EN)=Toba, Danau- ≋	140	Li	2.35N	98.50 E
Tobago ◆	198	Jd	11.15N	60.40W
Tobago Basin (EN) ⊽	196	Ff	12.30N	60.30W
Tobago Cays ⁂	197n	Bb	12.39N	61.22W
Toba Kākar Range ⛰	148	Db	31.15N	68.00 E
Tobarra	126	Kf	38.35N	1.41W
Tobejuba, Isla- ◆	196	Fh	9.20N	60.52W
Tobelo	150	If	1.25N	127.31 E
Tobermory [Ont.-Can.]	184	Gc	45.15N	81.40W
Tobermory [Scot.-U.K.]	118	Ge	56.37N	6.05W
Tōbetsu	156a	Bb	43.14N	141.29 E
Tobi Island ◆	208	Ed	3.00N	131.10 E
Tobin, Kap- ►	179	Jd	70.30N	21.30W
Tobin, Mount- ▲	188	Gf	40.22N	117.32W
Tobin Lake [Austl.] ≋	212	Fd	21.45S	125.50 E
Tobin Lake [Sask.-Can.] ≋	180	Hf	53.40N	103.20W
Tobi-Shima ◆	156	Fb	39.12N	139.32 E
Toblach / Dobbiaco	128	Gd	46.44N	12.14 E
Toboali	150	Eg	3.00S	106.30 E
Tobol	136	Ge	52.40N	62.39 E
Tobol ≈	140	Id	58.10N	68.12 E
Tobolsk	142	Id	58.12N	68.16 E
Tobruk (EN)=Ţubruq	160	Je	32.05N	23.59 E
Tobseda	136	Fb	68.36N	52.20 E
Tocantinópolis	200	Lf	6.20S	47.25W
Tocantins	202	If	10.30S	48.00W
Tocantins, Rio- ≈	198	Lf	1.45S	49.10W
Tocantinzinho, Rio- ≈	204	Ha	13.57S	48.20W
Toccoa	184	Fh	34.35N	83.19W
Toce ≈	128	Ce	45.56N	8.29 E
Tochigi	156	Fc	36.23N	139.44 E
Tochigi Ken [2]	154	Of	36.50N	139.50 E
Tochio	156	Fc	37.29N	138.58 E
Töcksfors	116	De	59.31N	11.50 E
Toco	196	Fg	10.50N	60.57W
Tocoa	194	Df	15.41N	86.03W
Toconao	206	Gb	23.11S	68.01W
Tocopilla	200	Ih	22.05S	70.12W
Tocumen	194	Hi	9.05N	79.23W
Tocuyo, Río- ≈	194	Mh	11.03N	68.20W
Todd Mountain ▲	184	Nb	46.32N	66.43W
Todi	128	Gh	42.47N	12.24 E
Tödi ▲	128	Cd	46.49N	8.55 E
Todo-ga-Saki ►	152	Pd	39.33N	142.05 E
Todos os Santos, Baía de- ◧	198	Mg	12.48S	38.38W
Todos Santos	190	Bd	23.27N	110.13W
Todos Santos, Bahía- ◧	192	Ab	31.48N	116.42W
Tofino	180	Eg	49.09N	125.54W
Tofte	116	De	59.33N	10.34 E
Toftlund	116	Ci	55.11N	9.04 E
Tofua Island ◆	216	Fc	19.45S	175.05W
Toga ◆	219b	Ca	13.26S	166.41 E
Tōgane	156	Gd	35.33N	140.21 E
Tog Ḍarōr ⧗	168	Hc	10.25N	50.00 E
Togdere ≈	168	Hd	9.01N	47.07 E
Tog-Dheer [3]	168	Hd	9.50N	45.50 E
Togi	156	Ec	37.08N	136.43 E
Togiak	178	Ge	59.04N	160.24W
Togian Islands (EN)= Togian, Kepulauan- ⁂	150	Hg	0.20S	122.00 E
Togliatti	112	Ke	53.31N	49.26 E
Togni	168	Fb	18.05N	35.10 E
Togo [1]	160	Hh	8.00N	1.10 E
Togrog Ul → Qahar Youyi Qianqi	154	Bd	40.46N	113.13 E
Togtoh	152	Jc	40.17N	111.15 E
Togučin	138	De	55.16N	84.33 E
Toguzak ≈	134	Ki	54.05N	62.48 E
Togwotee Pass ⌓	182	Ec	43.45N	110.04W
Tohen	168	Ic	11.44N	51.15 E
Tohma ≈	146	Hc	38.31N	38.25 E
Tohmajärvi	114	He	62.11N	30.23 E
Tohopekaliga, Lake- ≋	184	Gk	28.12N	81.23W
Toi	156	Fd	34.54N	138.47 E
Toijala	114	Ff	61.10N	23.52 E
Toi-Misaki ►	154	Ki	31.26N	131.19 E
Toisvesi	116	Jb	62.20N	23.45 E
Tojikiston = Tajikistan (EN)	136	Hh	39.00N	71.00 E
Tōjō	156	Cd	34.53N	133.16 E
Tojtepa	135	Gd	41.03N	69.22 E
Tok	178	Kd	63.20N	142.59W
Tok ▲	120	Jg	49.43N	13.50 E
Tok ≈	132	Rc	52.46N	52.22 E
Tokachi-Dake ▲	156a	Cb	43.25N	142.41 E
Tokachi-Gawa ≈	156a	Cb	42.41N	143.37 E
Tokachi-Heiya ▭	156a	Cb	43.00N	143.20 E
Tokachimitsumata	156a	Cb	43.31N	143.07 E
Tōkai [Jap.]	156	Gc	36.27N	140.34 E
Tōkai [Jap.]	156	Ed	35.01N	136.51 E
Tokaj	120	Rh	48.07N	21.25 E
Tokaj ≈	132	Ld	51.18N	41.04 E
Tōkamachi	154	Of	37.08N	138.46 E
Tokanui	218	Cg	46.34S	168.57 E
Tokara Islands (EN)= Tokara-Rettō ⁂	140	Og	29.35N	129.45 E
Tokara-Kaikyō ▬	154	Ki	30.10N	130.15 E
Tokara-Rettō=Tokara Islands (EN) ⁂	140	Og	29.35N	129.45 E
Tokashiki-Jima ◆	156b	Ab	26.13N	127.21 E
Tokat	144	Ea	40.19N	36.34 E
Tŏkch'ŏn	154	Ie	39.45N	126.15 E
Tok-Do ◆	154	Kf	37.22N	131.58 E
Tokelau [5]	210	Je	9.00S	171.46W
Tokelau/Union Islands ⁂	208	Je	9.00S	171.45W
Toki	156	Ed	35.22N	137.11 E
Tokke ≋	116	Ce	59.00N	9.15 E
Tokke ≈	116	Be	59.27N	7.58 E
Tokkuztara/Gongliu	152	Dc	43.30N	82.15 E
Tokmak [Kyrg.]	135	Hg	42.49N	75.19 E
Tokmak [Ukr.]	136	Df	47.13N	35.43 E
Tokomaru Bay	216	Eg	38.08S	178.20 E
Tokoname	156	Ed	34.53N	136.49 E
Tokoro	156a	Da	44.08N	144.03 E
Tokoroa	216	Eg	38.13S	175.52 E
Tokoro-Gawa ≈	156a	Da	44.08N	144.04 E
Toksovo	116	Nd	60.10N	30.42 E
Toksu/Xinhe	152	Dc	41.34N	82.38 E
Toksun	152	Ec	42.47N	88.38 E
Toktogul	136	Hg	41.50N	73.01 E
Toktogulskoje vodohranilišče ⊏	135	Id	41.45N	73.00 E
Tokuji	156	Bd	34.11N	131.39 E
Tokulu ◆	221b	Bb	20.06S	174.48W
Tokunoshima	156b	Bb	27.45N	129.00 E
Toku-no-Shima ◆	152	Mf	27.45N	128.50 E
Tokur	138	If	53.09N	132.50 E
Tokushima	152	Ne	34.04N	134.34 E
Tokushima Ken [2]	154	Mh	33.50N	134.10 E
Tokuyama [Jap.]	154	Kg	34.03N	131.49 E
Tokuyama [Jap.]	156	Ed	35.43N	136.27 E
Tokwe ≈	172	Ed	20.09S	31.54 E
Tōkyō	142	Pf	35.40N	139.46 E
Tokyo Bay (EN)=Tōkyō-Wan ◧	154	Og	35.38N	139.57 E
Tōkyō To [2]	154	Og	35.40N	139.20 E
Tōkyō-Wan=Tokyo Bay (EN) ◧	154	Og	35.38N	139.57 E
Tola ≈	140	Me	48.57N	104.48 E
Tolaga Bay	218	Hc	38.22S	178.18 E
Tolbazy	134	Gi	54.02N	55.59 E
Tolbuhin → Dobrič	130	Kf	43.34N	27.50 E
Tolbuhin [2]	130	Kf	43.34N	27.50 E
Toledo [Blz.]	194	Ce	16.25N	88.55W
Toledo [Blz.] [3]	194	Ce	16.15N	88.58W
Toledo [Braz.]	206	Jb	24.44S	53.45W
Toledo [Oh.-U.S.]	176	Ke	41.39N	83.32W
Toledo [Phil.]	150	Hd	10.23N	123.38 E
Toledo [Sp.]	112	Fh	39.52N	4.01W
Toledo [Sp.] [3]	126	Ie	39.50N	4.00W
Toledo, Montes de- ⛰	126	He	39.35N	4.20W
Toledo Bend Reservoir ⊏	182	Ie	31.30N	93.45W
Tolentino	128	Hg	43.12N	13.17 E
Tolfa	128	Fh	42.09N	11.56 E
Tolfa, Monti della- ⛰	128	Fh	42.10N	11.55 E
Tolga	114	Ce	62.25N	11.00 E
Toli	152	Db	45.57N	83.37 E
Toliara	160	Lk	23.21S	43.39 E
Toliara [3]	172	Gd	22.00S	44.00 E
Tolima [3]	202	Cc	3.45N	75.15W
Tolima, Nevado del- ▲	198	Ie	4.40N	75.19W
Toling → Zanda	152	Ce	31.28N	79.50 E
Tolitoli	150	Hf	1.02N	120.49 E
Toll ◆	220d	Bb	7.22N	151.37 E
Tollarp	116	Ei	55.56N	13.59 E
Tollja, zaliv- ◧	138	Ea	76.40N	100.00 E
Tolmacëvo	116	Nf	58.48N	30.01 E
Tolmezzo	128	Hd	46.24N	13.01 E
Tolmin	128	Hd	46.11N	13.44 E
Tolna	120	Oj	46.26N	18.47 E
Tolna [2]	120	Oj	46.30N	18.35 E
Tolo	170	Cc	2.56S	18.34 E
Tolo, Gulf of- (EN)=Tolo, Teluk- ◧	140	Oj	2.00S	122.30 E
Tolo, Teluk-=Tolo, Gulf of- (EN) ◧	140	Oj	2.00S	122.30 E
Toločin	114	Gi	54.25N	29.41 E
Tolosa	126	Ja	43.08N	2.04W
Tolstoj, mys- ►	140	Rd	59.10N	155.05 E
Toltén	206	Fe	39.13S	73.14W
Tolú	202	Cb	9.32N	75.34W
Toluca, Nevado de- ▲	174	Jh	19.08N	99.44W
Toluca de Lerdo	176	Jh	19.17N	99.40W
Tom ≈	140	Kd	56.50N	84.27 E
Toma	166	Ec	12.46N	2.53W
Tomah	186	Ke	43.59N	90.30W
Tomakomai	152	Pc	42.38N	141.36 E
Tomamae	156a	Ba	44.18N	141.39 E
Tomanivi ▲	219d	Bb	17.37S	178.01 E
Tomar	126	De	39.36N	8.25W
Tómaros ▲	130	Dj	39.32N	20.45 E
Tomaševka	132	Cd	51.33N	23.40 E
Tomás Young	204	Ai	28.36S	62.11W
Tomaszów Lubelski	120	Tf	50.28N	23.25 E
Tomaszów Mazowiecki	120	Qe	51.32N	20.01 E
Tomatlán	192	Gh	19.56N	105.15W
Tombador, Serra do- ⛰	202	Gf	12.00S	57.40W
Tombigbee River ≈	182	Je	31.04N	87.58W
Tomboco	170	Bd	6.45S	13.18 E
Tombouctou=Timbuktu (EN)	160	Gg	16.46N	2.59W
Tombstone	188	Jk	31.43N	110.04W
Tombua	160	Ij	15.48S	11.52 E
Tomé	206	Fe	36.37S	72.57W
Tomé-Açu	202	Id	2.25S	48.09W
Tomelilla	114	Ci	55.33N	13.57 E
Tomelloso	126	Ie	39.10N	3.01W
Tomichi Creek ≈	186	Cg	38.31N	106.58W
Tomie	156	Ae	32.37N	128.46 E
Tominé ≈	166	Cc	10.53N	13.18W
Tomini, Gulf of- (EN)= Tomini, Teluk- ◧	140	Oj	0.20S	121.00 E
Tomini, Teluk-=Tomini, Gulf of- (EN) ◧	140	Oj	0.20S	121.00 E
Tominian	166	Ec	13.17N	4.35W
Tomioka [Jap.]	156	Fc	36.15N	138.52 E
Tomioka [Jap.]	156	Gc	37.20N	140.59 E
Tomkinson Ranges ⛰	212	Fe	26.10S	129.05 E
Tomma ◆	114	Cc	66.15N	12.48 E
Tommot	138	He	58.58N	126.19 E
Tomo, Río- ≈	202	Eb	5.20N	67.48W
Tomochic	192	Fc	28.20N	107.51W
Tomorit, Mali i- ▲	130	Di	40.40N	20.09 E
Tomotu Neo ◆	219c	Ab	10.41S	165.47 E
Tomotu Noi ◆	219c	Bb	10.50S	166.02 E
Tompa	120	Pj	46.12N	19.33 E
Tompe	150	Gg	0.12S	119.48 E
Tompo	138	Id	64.00N	136.00 E
Tompo ≈	138	Id	62.50N	134.47 E
Tom Price	212	Dd	22.40S	117.55 E
Tomsk	142	Kd	56.30N	84.58 E
Tomskaja oblast [3]	138	De	58.20N	81.30 E
Tomtabacken ▲	116	Fg	57.30N	14.28 E
Tomur Feng ▲	140	Ke	42.02N	80.05 E
Tom White, Mount- ▲	178	Kd	60.40N	143.40W
Tonaki-Shima ◆	156b	Ab	26.21N	127.09 E
Tonalá	190	Fe	16.04N	93.45W
Tonale, Passo del- ⌓	128	Ed	46.16N	10.35 E
Tonami	156	Ec	36.38N	136.57 E
Tonara	128	Dj	40.02N	9.10 E
Tonasket	188	Fb	48.42N	119.26W
Tonb-e Bozorg ◆	146	Pi	26.15N	55.03 E
Tonbetsu-Gawa ≈	156a	Ca	45.08N	142.23 E
Tonbridge	118	Nj	51.12N	0.16 E
Tondano	150	Hf	1.19N	124.54 E
Tondela	126	Dd	40.31N	8.05W
Tønder	114	Bi	54.56N	8.54 E
Tone-Gawa ≈	156	Gd	35.44N	140.51 E
Tonekābon	144	Hb	36.53N	50.56 E
Toney ▲	222	Of	75.48S	115.48W
Tonga	168	Ed	9.28N	31.03 E
Tonga [1]	210	Jf	20.00S	175.00W
Tongaat	172	Ee	29.37S	31.03 E
Tonga Islands ⁂	208	Jf	20.00S	175.00W
Tonga Ridge (EN) ⊽	208	Jg	21.00S	175.00W
Tongariki ◆	219b	Dc	17.01S	168.37 E
Tongatapu Group ⁂	208	Jg	21.10S	175.10W
Tongatapu Island ◆	216	Fd	21.10S	175.10W
Tonga Trench (EN) ⊽	106	Kl	20.00S	173.00W
Tongbai	154	Bh	32.21N	113.24 E
Tongbai Shan ▲	152	Je	32.20N	113.14 E
Tongcheng [China]	154	Di	31.04N	116.56 E
Tongcheng [China]	154	Bj	29.15N	113.49 E
Tongcheng → Dong'e	154	Df	36.19N	116.14 E
Tongchuan	152	Id	35.10N	109.03 E
Tongdao (Shuangjiang)	152	If	26.14N	109.45 E
Tongde	152	Hd	35.29N	100.32 E
Tongeren/Tongres	122	Ld	50.47N	5.28 E
Tonggu	154	Cj	28.33N	114.21 E
Tongguzbasti	152	Dd	38.23N	82.00 E

Tonggu Zhang	152	Kg	24.12N	116.22 E
Tong-Hae=Japan, Sea of- (EN)	140	Pf	40.00N	134.00 E
Tonghai	142	Mg	24.15N	102.45 E
Tonghe	152	Mb	46.01N	128.42 E
Tonghua	142	Oe	41.43N	125.55 E
Tongjiang	152	Nb	47.39N	132.30 E
Tongjosŏn-man	140	Of	39.30N	128.00 E
Tongliao	142	Oe	43.37N	122.15 E
Tongling	152	Ke	30.49N	117.47 E
Tonglu	154	Ej	29.48N	119.39 E
Tongmun'gŏ-ri	152	Mc	40.58N	127.08 E
Tongoa	219b	Dc	16.54S	168.33 E
Tongoy	206	Fd	30.15S	71.30W
Tongren [China]	152	Hd	35.40N	102.07 E
Tongren [China]	152	If	27.45N	109.09 E
Tongres/Tongeren	122	Ld	50.47N	5.28 E
Tongsa Dzong	148	Ic	27.31N	90.30 E
Tongshan	154	Cj	29.36N	114.30 E
Tongta	148	Jd	21.20N	99.16 E
Tongtian He/Zhi Qu	140	Lf	33.26N	96.36 E
Tongue	118	Ic	58.28N	4.25W
Tongue of the Ocean	194	Ia	24.12N	77.10W
Tongue River	182	Fb	46.24N	105.52W
Tongxian	152	Kd	39.52N	116.38 E
Tongxin	152	Id	36.59N	105.50 E
Tongxu	154	Cg	34.29N	114.27 E
Tongyu (Kaitong)	152	Lc	44.47N	123.05 E
Tongyu Yunhe	154	Fh	34.46N	119.51 E
Tongzi	152	If	28.09N	106.50 E
Tonichi	192	Ec	28.35N	109.34W
Tönisvorst	124	Ic	51.19N	6.28 E
Tonj	168	Dd	7.17N	28.45 E
Tonj	158	Jh	7.31N	29.25 E
Tonk	148	Fc	26.10N	75.47 E
Tonkin (EN)=Bac-Phan	140	Mg	22.00N	105.00 E
Tonkin, Gulf of- (EN)= Beibu Wan	140	Mh	20.00N	108.00 E
Tonkin, Gulf of- (EN)=Vinh Bac Phan	140	Mh	20.00N	108.00 E
Tônlé Sab, Bœng-=Tonle Sap (EN)	140	Mh	13.00N	104.00 E
Tonle Sap (EN)=Tônlé Sab, Bœng-	140	Mh	13.00N	104.00 E
Tonnay-Charente	122	Fi	45.57N	0.54W
Tonneins	122	Gj	44.23N	0.19 E
Tönning	120	Eb	54.19N	8.57 E
Tōno	154	Pe	39.19N	141.32 E
Tonopah	182	Dd	38.04N	117.14W
Tonoshō	156	Dd	34.29N	134.11 E
Tonosí	194	Gj	7.24N	80.27W
Tønsberg	114	Cg	59.17N	10.25 E
Tonstad	114	Bg	58.40N	6.43 E
Tonumeia	221b	Bb	20.28S	174.46W
Tonya	146	Hb	40.53N	39.16 E
Tooele	182	Ec	40.32N	112.18W
Toora-Hem	138	Ef	52.28N	96.22 E
Tootsi	116	Kf	58.34N	24.43 E
Toowoomba	210	Gg	27.33S	151.57 E
Topalu	130	Le	44.33N	28.03 E
Topeka	176	Jf	39.03N	95.41W
Topki	138	De	55.18N	85.40 E
Topko, gora-	138	Ie	57.00N	137.23 E
Topl'a	120	Rh	48.45N	21.45 E
Topleţ	130	Fe	44.48N	22.24 E
Toplica	130	Ef	43.13N	21.51 E
Topliţa	130	Ic	46.55N	25.20 E
Topola	130	De	44.16N	20.42 E
Topol'čany	120	Oh	48.34N	18.10 E
Topolnica	130	Hg	42.11N	24.18 E
Topolobampo	190	Cc	25.36N	109.03W
Topolobampo, Bahía de-	192	Ee	25.30N	109.05W
Topolog	130	Hd	44.56N	24.16 E
Topolovgrad	130	Jg	42.05N	26.20 E
Topozero, ozero-	110	Jb	65.40N	32.00 E
Toppenish	188	Ec	46.23N	120.19W
Toprakkale	146	Gd	37.06N	36.07 E
Top Springs	212	Gc	16.38S	131.50 E
Toquepala	202	Eg	17.38S	69.56W
Tor	168	Ed	7.51N	33.36 E
Tora	220d	Ba	7.39N	151.53 E
Toraigh/Tory Island	118	Ef	55.16N	8.13W
Tora Island Pass	220d	Ba	7.39N	151.53 E
Toråker	116	Gd	60.31N	16.29 E
Torbalı	146	Bc	38.10N	27.21 E
Torbat-e Heydarīyeh	142	Hf	35.16N	59.13 E
Torbat-e Jam	144	Jb	35.14N	60.36 E
Torbay	118	Jk	50.28N	3.30W
Torbay-Brixham	118	Jk	50.24N	3.30W
Torbay-Paignton	118	Jk	50.28N	3.30W
Torbay-Torquay	118	Jk	50.29N	3.29W
Torbert, Mount-	178	Id	61.25N	152.24W
Torch Lake	184	Ec	45.00N	85.19W
Torčin	120	Vf	50.44N	25.05 E
Tordesillas	126	Hc	41.30N	5.00W
Tordino	128	Hh	42.44N	13.59 E
Töre	114	Fd	65.54N	22.39 E
Töreboda	114	Dg	58.43N	14.08 E
Torekov	116	Eh	56.26N	12.37 E
Torenberg	122	Lb	52.15N	5.55 E
Torez	132	Kf	47.59N	38.41 E
Torgau	120	Ie	51.34N	13.00 E
Torgelow	120	Kc	53.38N	14.01 E
Torgun	132	Od	50.10N	46.20 E
Torhamn	116	Fh	56.05N	15.50 E
Torhout	122	Jc	51.04N	3.06 E
Toribulu	150	Hg	0.19S	120.01 E
Torigni-sur-Vire	124	Be	49.05N	0.59W
Torii-Tōge	156	Ed	35.59N	137.49 E
Torino = Turin (EN)	112	Gf	45.03N	7.40 E
Toriparu	204	Fc	16.20S	53.55W
Tori-Shima [Jap.]	156b	Bb	27.52N	128.14 E
Tori-Shima [Jap.]	156b	Ab	26.35N	126.50 E
Tori-Shima [Jap.]	152	Pe	30.25N	140.15 E
Torit	168	Ee	4.24N	32.34 E
Torixoreu	202	Hg	16.15S	52.26W
Torkoviči	114	Hg	58.53N	30.20 E
Törmänen	114	Gb	68.36N	27.29 E
Tormes	126	Fc	41.18N	6.29W
Tornado Mountain	188	Hb	49.58N	114.39W
Tornavacas, Puerto de-	126	Gd	40.16N	5.37W
Torneå/Tornio	114	Fd	65.51N	24.08 E
Torneälven	110	Ib	65.48N	24.08 E
Torneträsk	114	Eb	68.22N	19.06 E
Torngat Mountains	174	Md	59.00N	64.00W
Tornio/Torneå	114	Fd	65.51N	24.08 E
Tornionjoki	110	Ib	65.48N	24.08 E
Tornquist	204	An	38.06S	62.14W
Toro	126	Gc	41.31N	5.24W
Toro	116	Gf	58.50N	17.50 E
Toro, Cerro del-	198	Jh	29.08S	69.48W
Toro, Isla del-	192	Kg	21.35N	97.32W
Toro, Monte- / El Toro	126	Qe	39.59N	4.07 E
Toroiaga, Vîrful-	130	Hb	47.44N	24.43 E
Torokina	219a	Bb	6.14S	155.03 E
Tōro-Ko	156a	Db	43.08N	144.30 E
Törökszentmiklős	120	Qi	47.11N	20.25 E
Torola, Río-	194	Cg	13.52N	88.30W
Toronto	176	Le	43.39N	79.23W
Toropec	136	Dd	56.31N	31.39 E
Tororo	170	Fb	0.41N	34.11 E
Toros Dağları=Taurus Mountains (EN)	140	Ff	37.00N	33.00 E
Torquato Severo	204	Ej	31.02S	54.11W
Torquay, Torbay-	118	Jk	50.29N	3.29W
Torrá, Cerro-	198	Ie	4.38N	76.15W
Torrance	188	Fj	33.50N	118.19W
Torre Annunziata	128	Ij	40.45N	14.27 E
Torreblanca	126	Md	40.13N	0.12 E
Torrecilla	126	Hh	36.41N	5.00W
Torrecilla en Cameros	126	Jb	42.16N	2.37W
Torre del Greco	128	Ij	40.47N	14.22 E
Torre del Mar	126	Hh	36.44N	4.06W
Torredembarra	126	Nc	41.09N	1.24 E
Torre de Moncorvo	126	Ec	41.10N	7.03W
Torre de' Passeri	128	Hh	42.14N	13.56 E
Torredonjimeno	126	Ig	37.46N	3.57W
Torrejón de Ardoz	126	Id	40.27N	3.29W
Torrelaguna	126	Id	40.50N	3.32W
Torrelavega	126	Ha	43.21N	4.03W
Torre Miró, Port de- / Torre Miró, Puerto de-	126	Ld	40.42N	0.05W
Torre Miró, Puerto de- / Torre Miró, Port de-	126	Ld	40.42N	0.05W
Torremolinos	126	Hh	36.37N	4.30W
Torrens, Lake-	208	Eh	31.00S	137.50 E
Torrens Creek	212	Jd	20.46S	145.02 E
Torrent de l'Horta/Torrente	126	Le	39.26N	0.28W
Torrente/Torrent de l'Horta	126	Le	39.26N	0.28W
Torrenueva	126	If	38.38N	3.22W
Torreón	176	Ig	25.33N	103.26W
Torre-Pacheco	126	Lg	37.44N	0.57W
Torre Pellice	128	Bf	44.49N	7.13 E
Tôrres	206	Kc	29.21S	49.44W
Torres	220d	Ab	7.19N	151.27 E
Torrès, Iles-=Torres Islands (EN)	208	Hf	13.15S	166.37 E
Torres Islands (EN)=Torrès, Iles-	208	Hf	13.15S	166.37 E
Torres Novas	126	De	39.29N	8.32W
Torres Strait	208	Ff	10.25S	142.10 E
Torres Vedras	126	Ce	39.06N	9.16W
Torrevieja	126	Lg	37.59N	0.41W
Torridon, Loch-	118	Hd	57.35N	5.50W
Torriglia	128	Df	44.31N	9.10 E
Torrijos	126	He	39.59N	4.17W
Torrington [Ct.-U.S.]	184	Ke	41.48N	73.08W
Torrington [Wy.-U.S.]	182	Gc	42.04N	104.11W
Torroella de Montgrí	126	Pb	42.02N	3.08 E
Torröjen	114	Ce	63.55N	12.56 E
Torrox	126	Ih	36.46N	3.58W
Torsås	114	Dh	56.24N	16.00 E
Torsby	114	Cf	60.08N	13.00 E
Torshälla	116	Ge	59.25N	16.28 E
Torsken	114	Db	69.20N	17.06 E
Torsö	114	Cg	58.50N	13.50 E
Torto	128	Hm	37.58N	13.46 E
Tortola	190	Le	18.27N	64.36W
Tortolì	128	Dk	39.55N	9.39 E
Tortona	128	Cf	44.54N	8.52 E
Tortorici	128	Il	38.02N	14.49 E
Tortosa	126	Md	40.48N	0.31 E
Tortosa, Cabo de-/Tortosa, Cap de-	126	Md	40.43N	0.55 E
Tortosa, Cap de-/Tortosa, Cabo de-	126	Md	40.43N	0.55 E
Tortue, Ile de la-	190	Jd	20.04N	72.49W
Tortuga, Isla-	192	Dd	27.26N	111.55W
Tortum	146	Ib	40.19N	41.35 E
Torud	146	Pe	35.26N	55.07 E
Torugart, pereval-	140	Je	40.32N	75.24 E
Torul	146	Hb	40.35N	39.18 E
Toruń	120	Oc	53.02N	18.35 E
Toruń [2]	120	Oc	53.00N	18.35 E
Torunos	194	Li	8.30N	70.04W
Toruńska, Kotlina-	120	Oc	53.00N	18.30 E
Torup	114	Ch	56.58N	13.05 E
Tõrva/Tyrva	114	Fg	58.01N	25.59 E
Tory Island/Toraigh	118	Ef	55.16N	8.13W
Torysa	120	Rh	48.39N	21.21 E
Toržok	136	Dd	57.03N	35.01 E
Tosa	154	Lh	33.29N	133.25 E
Tosas, Puerto de- / Toses, Collada de-	126	Ob	42.20N	2.01 E
Tosashimizu	154	Lh	32.46N	132.57 E
Tosa-Wan	154	Lh	33.25N	133.35 E
Tosa-yamada	156	Ce	33.36N	133.40 E
Toscana = Tuscany (EN) [2]	128	Eg	43.25N	11.00 E
Toscano, Arcipelago- = Tuscan Archipelago (EN)	110	Hg	42.45N	10.20 E
Toses, Collada de- / Tosas, Puerto de-	126	Ob	42.20N	2.01 E
Toshibetsu-Gawa [Jap.]	156a	Cb	42.54N	143.25 E
Toshibetsu-Gawa [Jap.]	156a	Ab	42.25N	139.48 E
Tōshi-Jima	156	Ed	34.31N	136.52 E
To-Shima	156	Fd	34.31N	139.17 E
Tosno	114	Hg	59.34N	30.50 E
Toson-Cengel	152	Gb	48.47N	98.15 E
Toson Hu	152	Gd	37.08N	96.52 E
Töss	128	Cc	47.33N	8.33 E
Tossa	126	Oc	41.43N	2.56 E
Tostado	206	Hc	29.14S	61.46W
Tõstamaa/Tystama	116	Jf	58.17N	23.52 E
Tosu	156	Be	33.22N	130.30 E
Tosya	146	Fb	41.01N	34.02 E
Totak	116	Be	59.40N	7.55 E
Totana	126	Kg	37.46N	1.30W
Toten	116	Dd	60.40N	10.50 E
Toteng	172	Cd	20.23S	22.59 E
Tôtes	122	He	49.41N	1.03 E
Totes Gebirge	128	Hc	47.42N	13.55 E
Tōtias	168	Ge	3.57N	43.58 E
Totland	124	Ad	50.40N	1.32W
Totma	136	Ed	60.00N	42.45 E
Totness	202	Gb	5.53N	56.19W
Toto	170	Bd	7.10S	14.25 E
Totonicapán	190	Ff	14.55N	91.22W
Totonicapán [3]	194	Bf	15.00N	91.20W
Totora	202	Eg	17.42S	65.09W
Totoras	204	Bk	32.35S	61.11W
Totota	166	Dd	6.49N	9.56W
Totoya	219d	Cc	18.57S	179.50W
Totten Glacier	222	He	66.45S	116.10 E
Totton	124	Ad	50.55N	1.29W
Tottori	152	Nd	35.30N	134.14 E
Tottori Ken [2]	154	Lg	35.25N	133.50 E
Tou, Motu-	220p	Bb	21.11S	159.48W
Touâjil	162	Ee	21.45N	12.35W
Touat	158	Gf	27.40N	0.01W
Touba	166	Dd	8.17N	7.41W
Touba [3]	166	Dd	8.15N	7.45W
Toubkal, Jebel-	158	Ge	31.03N	7.55W
Touch	122	Hk	43.38N	1.24 E
Toucy	122	Jg	47.44N	3.18 E
Tougan	166	Ec	13.04N	3.04W
Touggourt	160	He	33.06N	6.04 E
Tougué	166	Cc	11.27N	11.41W
Touho	219b	Be	20.47S	165.14 E
Toûîl	162	Hb	35.33N	2.36 E
Toukoto	166	Dc	13.28N	9.52W
Toul	122	Lf	48.41N	5.54 E
Toulépleu	166	Dd	6.35N	8.25W
Toulon	112	Gg	43.07N	5.56 E
Toulouse	112	Gg	43.36N	1.26 E
Toulumne River	188	Eh	37.36N	121.10W
Toumodi	166	Dd	6.33N	5.01W
Tounassine, Hamada-	162	Fd	28.36N	5.10W
Toungo	166	Hd	8.07N	12.03 E
Toungoo	142	Lh	18.56N	96.26 E
Touques	122	Ge	49.22N	0.06 E
Toura	168	Bc	10.30N	15.19 E
Touraine	122	Gg	47.12N	0.30 E
Touraine, Val de-	122	Hg	47.20N	1.30 E
Tourcoing	122	Jd	50.43N	3.09 E
Tour-du-Pin, La-	122	Li	45.34N	5.27 E
Touriñán, Cabo-	126	Ca	43.03N	9.18W
Tourine	162	Ee	22.00N	12.15W
Tournai/Doornik	122	Jd	50.36N	3.23 E
Tournai-Kain	124	Fd	50.38N	3.22 E
Tournon	122	Ki	45.04N	4.50 E
Tournus	122	Kh	46.34N	4.54 E
Touros	202	Ke	5.12S	35.28W
Tours	112	Gf	47.23N	0.41 E
Tourteron	124	Ge	49.32N	4.39 E
Toury	122	Hf	48.12N	1.56 E
Touside, Pic-	168	Ba	21.02N	16.25 E
Toussoro	168	Cd	9.02N	23.55 E
Toutouba	219b	Cb	15.34S	167.16 E
Touwsrivier	172	Cf	33.20S	20.00 E
Toužim	120	If	50.04N	12.59 E
Tovar	194	Li	8.20N	71.46W
Tovarkovski	132	Kc	53.43N	38.13 E
Tovdalselva	116	Cf	58.12N	8.06 E
Tove	124	Bb	52.04N	0.50W
Tōwa	156	Gb	39.23N	141.15 E
Towada	154	Pd	40.35N	141.13 E
Towada-Kō	156	Ga	40.28N	140.55 E
Towanda	184	Ie	41.46N	76.27W
Tower	186	Jc	47.48N	92.17W
Towner	186	Fb	48.21N	100.25W
Townsend	188	Jc	46.19N	111.31W
Townshend, Cape-	212	Kd	22.15S	150.30 E
Townsville	210	Ff	19.16S	146.48 E
Towot	168	Ed	6.12N	34.25 E
Towson	184	If	39.24N	76.36W
Towuti, Danau-	150	Hg	2.45S	121.32 E
Toxkan He	152	Dc	41.08N	80.11 E
Tōya	156a	Bb	42.39N	140.48 E
Toyah Creek	186	Ek	31.18N	103.27W
Tōya-Ko	154	Pc	42.33N	140.50 E
Toyama	142	Pf	36.41N	137.13 E
Toyama Ken [2]	154	Nf	30.40N	137.10 E
Toyama Trench (EN)	156	Ec	38.00N	138.00 E
Toyama-Wan	154	Nf	37.00N	137.15 E
Tōyō	154	Mh	33.22N	134.18 E
Toyohashi	152	Oe	34.46N	137.23 E
Toyokoro	156a	Cb	42.48N	143.28 E
Toyonaka	156	Dd	34.47N	135.28 E
Toyo'oka	152	Od	35.33N	137.54 E
Toyosaka	156	Fc	37.55N	139.12 E
Toyota	154	Ng	35.05N	137.09 E
Toyotama	156	Ad	34.27N	129.19 E
Toyotomi	156a	Ba	45.08N	141.47 E
Toyoura	156	Bd	34.10N	130.55 E
Trabancos	126	Gc	41.27N	5.11W
Traben Trabach	124	Je	49.57N	7.07 E
Trabzon	142	Fe	40.59N	39.43 E
Traer	186	Je	42.12N	92.28W
Trafalgar, Cabo-	126	Fh	36.11N	6.02W
Tragacete	126	Kd	40.21N	1.51W
Traiguén	206	Fe	38.15S	72.41W
Trail	176	He	49.06N	117.43W
Traill	179	Jd	72.45N	24.00W
Trairas, Rio-	204	Hb	14.07S	48.31W
Trairi	202	Kd	3.17S	39.15W
Traisen	128	Jb	48.22N	15.46 E
Trakai/Trakaj	114	Fi	54.38N	24.57 E
Trakaj/Trakai	114	Fi	54.38N	24.57 E
Trakt	134	Ee	62.44N	51.11 E
Trakya = Thrace (EN)	110	Ig	41.20N	26.45 E
Trakya = Thrace (EN)	130	Jh	41.20N	26.45 E
Tralee/Trá Lí	118	Di	52.16N	9.42W
Tralee Bay/Bá Thrá Lí	118	Di	52.15N	9.59W
Trá Lí/Tralee	118	Di	52.16N	9.42W
Trá Mhór/Tramore	118	Fi	52.10N	7.10W
Tramore/Trá Mhór	118	Fi	52.10N	7.10W
Tramping Lake	188	Ka	52.10N	108.48W
Trăn	130	Fg	42.50N	22.39 E
Tranås	114	Dg	58.03N	14.59 E
Trancoso	126	Ed	40.47N	7.21W
Tranebjerg	116	Di	55.50N	10.36 E
Tranemo	116	Eg	57.29N	13.21 E
Trang	142	Li	7.33N	99.36 E
Trangan, Pulau-	150	Jh	6.35S	134.20 E
Trani	128	Ki	41.17N	16.25 E
Transantarctic Mountains (EN)	222	Lg	85.00S	175.00W
Transcaucasia (EN)	110	Kg	41.00N	45.00 E
Transilvania = Transylvania (EN)	110	If	46.30N	25.00 E
Transilvania = Transylvania (EN)	130	Hc	46.30N	25.00 E
Transkei	158	Jl	31.30S	29.00 E
Transkei	172	Df	32.45S	28.30 E
Transtrand	116	Ec	61.05N	13.19 E
Transtrandsfjällen	116	Ec	61.15N	12.58 E
Transylvania (EN) = Transilvania	110	If	46.30N	25.00 E
Transylvania (EN) = Transilvania	130	Hc	46.30N	25.00 E
Transylvanian Alps (EN)= Carpáţii Meridionali	110	If	45.30N	24.15 E
Trants Bay	197c	Bc	16.46N	62.09W
Trapani	112	Hh	38.01N	12.29 E
Trapper Peak	188	Hd	45.54N	114.18W
Trappes	124	Ef	48.47N	2.01 E
Traralgon	212	Jg	38.12S	146.32 E
Trarza [3]	162	Ef	18.00N	15.00W
Trarza	158	Fg	17.20N	14.40W
Traşcăului, Munţii-	130	Gc	46.23N	23.33 E
Trasimeno, Lago-	128	Gg	43.10N	12.05 E
Träslövsläge	116	Eg	57.04N	12.16 E
Trás os Montes e Alto Douro	126	Ec	41.30N	7.15W
Trat	148	Kf	12.13N	102.16 E
Traun	128	Ib	48.13N	14.14 E
Traun	128	Ib	48.16N	14.22 E
Traunsee	128	Hc	47.52N	13.48 E
Traunstein	120	Ii	47.53N	12.39 E
Trave	120	Gc	53.54N	10.50 E
Travemünde, Lübeck-	120	Gc	53.57N	10.52 E
Travers, Mount-	216	Dh	42.01S	172.44 E
Traverse, Lake-	186	Hd	45.43N	96.40W
Traverse City	182	Jc	44.46N	85.37W
Traverse Islands	222	Ad	56.36S	27.43W
Travers Reservoir	188	Ia	50.14N	112.51W
Travesía	194	Df	15.20N	87.53W
Tra Vinh	148	Lg	9.56N	106.20 E
Travnik	128	Lf	44.14N	17.40 E
Travo	122a	Bb	41.54N	9.24 E
Trbovlje	128	Jd	46.10N	15.03 E
Treasurers	219c	Ba	9.53S	167.09 E
Treasury Islands	219a	Bb	7.22S	155.37 E
Trebbia	128	De	45.04N	9.41 E
Třebíč	120	Lg	49.13N	15.53 E
Trebinje	128	Mh	42.43N	18.21 E
Trebisacce	128	Kk	39.52N	16.32 E
Trebišnjica	128	Lg	43.01N	17.47 E
Trebišov	120	Rh	48.40N	21.43 E
Treblinka	120	Sd	52.40N	22.03 E
Trebnje	128	Je	45.54N	15.01 E
Třeboň	120	Kg	49.01N	14.48 E
Třebońska pánev	120	Kg	49.00N	14.50 E
Trégorrois	122	Cf	48.45N	3.15W
Tregrosse Islets	208	Gf	17.40S	150.45 E
Tréguier	122	Cf	48.47N	3.14W
Treherne	186	Gb	49.38N	98.41W
Treignac	122	Hi	45.32N	1.48 E
Treinta y Tres	206	Jd	33.14S	54.23W
Treinta y Tres [2]	204	Ek	33.00S	54.15W
Treis-Karden	124	Jd	50.11N	7.17 E
Trélazé	122	Fg	47.27N	0.28W
Trelew	206	Gf	43.15S	65.18W
Trelleborg	112	Hd	55.22N	13.10 E
Trélon	124	Gd	50.04N	4.06 E
Tremadog Bay	118	Ii	52.40N	4.10W
Tremblant, Mount-	174	Le	46.15N	74.34W
Tremiti, Isole-=Tremiti Islands (EN)	110	Hg	42.10N	15.30 E
Tremiti Islands (EN)= Tremiti, Isole-	110	Hg	42.10N	15.30 E
Tremonton	188	If	41.43N	112.10W
Tremp	126	Mb	42.10N	0.54 E
Třemšín	120	Jg	49.33N	13.48 E
Trenche, Rivière-	184	Kb	47.35N	72.58W
Trenčín	120	Oh	48.54N	18.04 E
Trenque Lauquen	206	He	35.58S	62.42W
Trent	118	Mh	53.42N	0.40W
Trent, Vale of-	118	Li	52.45N	1.50W
Trentino-Alto Adige / Südtirol [2]	128	Fd	46.30N	11.20 E
Trento	128	Fd	46.04N	11.08 E
Trenton [Mo.-U.S.]	186	Jf	40.05N	93.37W
Trenton [N.J.-U.S.]	176	Le	40.13N	74.45W
Trenton [Ont.-Can.]	184	Ic	44.06N	77.35W
Tréon	124	Df	48.41N	1.20 E
Trepassey	180	Mg	46.44N	53.22W
Tréport, Le-	122	Hd	50.04N	1.22 E
Tres Árboles	206	Id	32.24S	56.43W
Tres Arroyos	200	Ji	38.22S	60.15W
Tres Bocas	204	Ck	32.44S	59.45W
Tres Carações	202	Ih	21.42S	45.16W
Tres Cruces, Cerro-	192	Mj	15.28N	92.24W
Três de Maio	204	Eh	27.47S	54.14W
Tres Esquinas	202	Cc	0.43N	75.15W
Tres Isletas	204	Bh	26.21S	60.26W
Treska	130	Eh	41.59N	21.19 E
Treskavica	128	Mg	43.35N	18.24 E
Três Lagoas	200	Kh	20.48S	51.43W
Três Marias, Reprêsa-	202	Ig	18.15S	45.15W
Tres Montes, Peninsula-	206	Eg	46.50S	75.30W
Três Passos	206	Jc	27.27S	53.56W
Tres Picos, Cerro-	198	Ji	38.09S	61.57W
Tres Picos, Cerro-	192	Li	16.36N	94.13W
Três Pontas	204	Je	21.22S	45.31W
Tres Puntas, Cabo- [Arg.]	198	Jj	47.06S	65.53W
Tres Puntas, Cabo- [Guat.]	194	Cf	15.58N	88.37W
Três Ranchos	204	Id	18.22S	47.47W
Três Rios	204	Kf	22.07S	43.12W
Třešt'	120	Lg	49.18N	15.28 E
Tres Valles	192	Kh	18.15N	96.08W
Tres Zapotes	190	Ee	18.28N	95.24W
Tretten	114	Cf	61.19N	10.19 E
Treuchtlingen	120	Gh	48.57N	10.55 E
Treuer Range	212	Gd	22.15S	130.50 E
Treungen	116	Ce	59.02N	8.33 E
Trêve, Lac la-	184	Ja	49.58N	75.31W
Trevi	128	Gh	42.52N	12.45 E
Trévières	124	Be	49.19N	0.54W
Treviglio	128	De	45.31N	9.35 E
Trevinca, Peña-	126	Fb	42.15N	6.46W
Treviño	126	Jb	42.44N	2.45W
Treviso	128	Ge	45.40N	12.15 E
Trevose Head	118	Hk	50.33N	5.01W
Trgovište	130	Fg	42.21N	22.06 E
Triagoz, Les-	122	Cf	48.53N	3.40W
Triánda	130	Lm	36.24N	28.10 E
Triangle	172	Ed	21.02S	31.28 E
Triángulos, Arrecifes-	192	Mg	20.57N	92.16W
Trianísia	130	Jm	36.18N	26.45 E
Tribeč	120	Oh	48.27N	18.15 E
Tribune	186	Fg	38.28N	101.45W
Tricarico	128	Kj	40.37N	16.09 E
Tricase	128	Mk	39.56N	18.22 E
Trichūr	148	Ff	10.31N	76.13 E
Tri City	188	De	43.02N	123.15W
Trie-Château	124	De	49.17N	1.50 E
Triel-sur-Seine	124	Ef	48.59N	2.01 E
Trier	120	Cg	49.45N	6.38 E
Trier-Ehrang	124	Ie	49.49N	6.41 E
Trier-Pfalzel	124	Ie	49.46N	6.41 E
Trieste	112	Hf	45.40N	13.46 E
Trieste, Golfo di-	128	He	45.40N	13.30 E
Trieux	122	Cf	48.50N	3.03W
Trifels	124	Je	49.11N	7.59 E
Triglav	110	Hf	46.23N	13.50 E
Trigno	128	Ih	42.04N	14.48 E
Tríkala	130	Ej	39.33N	21.46 E
Trikhonís, Límni-	130	Ek	38.34N	21.30 E
Trikomo → Yeniboğaziçi	146	Ee	35.17N	33.52 E
Trikomon → Yeniboğaziçi	146	Ee	35.17N	33.52 E
Trikora, Puncak-	150	Kg	4.15S	138.45 E
Trilport	124	Ef	48.57N	2.57 E
Trim/Baile Átha Troim	118	Gh	53.34N	6.47W
Trimouille, La-	122	Hh	46.28N	1.03 E
Trincheras	192	Gc	28.55N	104.18W
Trincomalee	142	Ki	8.34N	81.14 E
Trindade	202	Ig	16.40S	49.30W
Trindade, Ilha da-	198	Nh	20.31S	29.19W
Třinec	120	Og	49.41N	18.42 E
Tring	124	Bc	51.47N	0.39W
Tringia	130	Ej	39.38N	21.25 E
Trinidad	198	Jd	10.30N	61.15W
Trinidad [Bol.]	200	Jg	14.47S	64.47W
Trinidad [Ca.-U.S.]	188	Cf	41.07N	124.07W
Trinidad [Co.-U.S.]	176	If	37.10N	104.31W
Trinidad [Cuba]	190	Id	21.48N	79.59W
Trinidad [Mex.]	192	Ec	28.25N	109.06W
Trinidad [Ur.]	206	Id	33.32S	56.54W
Trinidad, Golfo-	206	Eg	49.55S	75.25W
Trinidad, Isla-	204	Bn	39.08S	61.58W
Trinidad, Laguna-	204	Be	20.21S	61.35W
Trinidad and Tobago [1]	200	Jd	11.00N	61.00W
Trinidade Spur (EN)	106	Cl	21.00S	35.00W
Trinitapoli	128	Ki	41.21N	16.05 E
Trinity	186	Ik	30.57N	95.22W
Trinity	174	Jg	29.47N	94.42W
Trinity Bay [Austl.]	212	Jc	16.25S	145.35 E
Trinity Bay [Can.]	180	Mg	48.15N	53.10W
Trinity Islands	178	Ie	56.33N	154.25W
Trinity Range	188	Ff	40.20N	118.45W
Trinity River	188	Df	41.11N	123.42W
Trinkitat	168	Fb	18.41N	37.43 E
Trino	128	Ce	45.12N	8.18 E
Trionto	128	Kk	39.37N	16.45 E
Trionto, Capo-	128	Kk	39.37N	16.45 E
Triora	128	Bf	43.59N	7.46 E
Tripoli (EN)=Ţarābulus	160	Ie	32.54N	13.11 E
Tripoli (EN)=Ţarābulus	144	Ec	34.26N	35.51 E
Tripoli (EN)=Ţarābulus [3]	164	Bc	32.40N	13.15 E
Tripolis	130	Fl	37.31N	22.22 E
Tripolitania (EN) = Ţarābulus	158	Ie	31.00N	14.00 E
Tripolitania (EN)= Ţarābulus	164	Bc	30.00N	15.00 E
Tripura [3]	148	Id	24.00N	92.00 E
Trisanna	128	Ec	47.07N	10.30 E
Tristan da Cunha	158	Fi	37.05S	12.17W
Tristan da Cunha Group	158	Fi	37.15S	12.30W
Triste, Golfo-	196	Bg	10.40N	68.10W
Triunfo	204	Ee	20.46S	55.47W
Trivandrum	142	Ji	8.29N	76.55 E
Trivento	128	Ii	41.47N	14.33 E
Trjavna	130	Ig	42.52N	25.30 E
Trnava	120	Nh	48.22N	17.35 E
Troarn	124	Be	49.11N	0.11W

Index Symbols

[1] Independent Nation
[2] State, Region
[3] District, County
[4] Municipality
[5] Colony, Dependency
Continent
Physical Region
Historical or Cultural Region
Mount, Mountain
Volcano
Hill
Mountains, Mountain Range
Hills, Escarpment
Plateau, Upland
Pass, Gap
Plain, Lowland
Delta
Salt Flat
Valley, Canyon
Crater, Cave
Karst Features
Depression
Polder
Desert, Dunes
Forest, Woods
Heath, Steppe
Oasis
Cape, Point
Coast, Beach
Cliff
Peninsula
Isthmus
Sandbank
Island
Atoll
Rock, Reef
Islands, Archipelago
Rocks, Reefs
Coral Reef
Well, Spring
Geyser
River, Stream
Waterfall, Rapids
River Mouth, Estuary
Lake
Salt Lake
Intermittent Lake
Reservoir
Swamp, Pond
Canal
Glacier
Ice Shelf, Pack Ice
Ocean
Sea
Gulf, Bay
Strait, Fjord
Lagoon
Bank
Seamount
Tablemount
Ridge
Shelf
Basin
Escarpment, Sea Scarp
Fracture
Trench, Abyss
National Park, Reserve
Point of Interest
Recreation Site
Cave, Cavern
Historic Site
Ruins
Wall, Walls
Church, Abbey
Temple
Scientific Station
Railway station
Airport
Port
Military installation
Lighthouse
Mine
Tunnel
Dam, Bridge

Tro-Tuz

Trobriand Islands 208 Ge 8.30S 151.05 E
Trödje 116 Gd 60.49N 17.12 E
Trofors 114 Cd 65.34N 13.25 E
Trögd 116 Ge 59.30N 17.15 E
Trogir 128 Kg 43.32N 16.15 E
Troglav [Bos.] 128 Mg 43.02N 18.33 E
Troglav [Eur.] 128 Kg 43.58N 16.36 E
Trøgstad 116 De 59.38N 11.18 E
Troia 128 Ji 41.22N 15.18 E
Troick [Russia] 138 Ee 57.23N 94.55 E
Troick [Russia] 142 Id 54.06N 61.35 E
Troickoje [Russia] 138 Df 52.28N 84.45 E
Troickoje [Russia] 138 Ig 49.30N 136.32 E
Troickoje [Ukr.] 130 Nb 47.38N 30.12 E
Troicko Pečorsk 136 Fc 62.44N 56.06 E
Troina 128 Im 37.47N 14.36 E
Troisdorf 124 Jd 50.49N 7.10 E
Trois Fourches, Cap des- 162 Gb 35.26N 2.58W
Trois-Pistoles 184 Ma 48.07N 69.10W
Trois Pitons, Morne- 197g Bb 15.22N 61.20W
Trois-Ponts 124 Hd 50.22N 5.52 E
Trois-Rivières [Guad.] 197e Ac 15.59N 61.39W
Trois-Rivières [Que.-Can.] 176 Le 46.21N 72.33W
Troissereux 124 Ee 49.29N 2.03 E
Troisvierges/Ulflingen 124 Hd 50.07N 6.00 E
Trojan 130 Hg 42.53N 24.43 E
Trojanovka 120 Ve 51.21N 25.25 E
Trojanski Manastir 130 Hg 42.53N 24.48 E
Trojanski prohod 130 Hg 42.48N 24.40 E
Trojebratski 136 Ge 54.25N 66.03 E
Trollhättan 114 Cg 58.16N 12.18 E
Trollheimen 114 Be 62.50N 9.05 E
Trollhetta 116 Cb 62.51N 9.19 E
Trolltindane 116 Bd 62.29N 7.43 E
Tromba 204 Ha 13.28S 48.45W
Trombetas, Rio- 198 Kf 1.55S 55.35W
Tromelin 158 Mj 15.52S 54.25 E
Tromøya 116 Cf 58.30N 8.50 E
Troms [3] 114 Eb 69.07N 19.15 E
Tromsø 112 Hb 69.40N 19.00 E
Tron 116 Db 62.10N 10.43 E
Trona 188 Gi 35.46N 117.24W
Tronador, Monte- 198 Ij 41.10S 71.54W
Trondheim 112 Hc 63.25N 10.25 E
Trondheimsfjorden 110 Hc 63.40N 10.50 E
Tronto 128 Hh 42.54N 13.55 E
Troodos 144 Dc 34.55N 32.53 E
Tropea 128 Jl 38.41N 15.54 E
Tropeiros, Serra dos- 204 Jb 14.43S 44.33W
Tropoja 130 Dg 42.24N 20.10 E
Trosa 114 Dg 58.54N 17.33 E
Troškūnai/Troškunaj 116 Ki 55.32N 24.59 E
Troškunaj/Troškūnai 116 Ki 55.32N 24.59 E
Trostberg 120 Ih 48.02N 12.33 E
Trostjanec 132 Id 50.29N 34.59 E
Trotuş 130 Kc 46.03N 27.14 E
Trou Gras Point 197k Bb 13.52N 60.53W
Troumasse 197k Bb 13.49N 60.54W
Trout Lake [Mi.-U.S.] 184 Eb 46.12N 85.01W
Trout Lake [N.W.T.-Can.] 180 Fd 60.35N 121.10W
Trout Lake [Ont.-Can.] 180 If 53.54N 89.56W
Trout Lake [Ont.-Can.] 180 If 51.12N 93.19W
Trout Peak 188 Kd 44.36N 109.32W
Trout River 180 Lg 49.29N 58.08W
Trouville-sur-Mer 122 Ge 49.22N 0.05 E
Trowbridge 118 Kj 51.20N 2.13W
Troy [Al.-U.S.] 182 Je 31.48N 85.58W
Troy [Mo.-U.S.] 186 Kg 38.59N 90.59W
Troy [Mt.-U.S.] 188 Hb 48.28N 115.53W
Troy [N.Y.-U.S.] 182 Mc 42.43N 73.40W
Troy [Oh.-U.S.] 184 Ee 40.02N 84.12W
Troy (EN)=Truva [Tur.] 146 Bc 39.57N 26.15 E
Troyes 112 Gf 48.18N 4.05 E
Troy Peak 182 Dd 38.19N 115.30W
Trstenik 130 Df 43.37N 21.00 E
Trubčevsk 136 De 52.36N 33.46 E
Truchas Peak 186 Di 35.58N 105.39W
Trucial Coast (EN) 140 Hg 24.00N 53.00 E
Trucial States (EN) → United Arab Emirates (EN) [1] 142 Hg 24.00N 54.00 E
Truckee 188 Eg 39.20N 120.11W
Trudfront 132 Og 45.56N 47.41 E
Trudovoje 138 Ih 43.18N 132.05 E
Trufanova 114 Kd 64.29N 44.05 E
Trujillo [2] 202 Db 9.25N 70.30W
Trujillo [Hond.] 190 Ge 15.55N 86.00W
Trujillo [Peru] 200 If 8.10S 79.02W
Trujillo [Sp.] 126 Ge 39.28N 5.53W
Trujillo [Ven.] 202 Db 9.22N 70.26W
Trujillo, Rio- 192 Hf 23.39N 103.08W
Truk Islands 208 Gd 7.25N 151.47 E
Trumann 186 Ki 35.41N 90.31W
Trumbull, Mount- 182 Ed 36.25N 113.10W
Trun 124 Gf 48.51N 0.02 E
Trung Phan=Annam (EN) 140 Mh 15.00N 108.00 E
Truro [Eng.-U.K.] 118 Hk 50.16N 5.03W
Truro [N.S.-Can.] 176 Me 45.22N 63.16W
Truskavec 132 Ce 49.17N 23.34 E
Truth or Consequences (Hot Springs) 182 Fe 33.08N 107.15W
Trutnov 120 Lf 50.34N 15.54 E
Truva [Tur.]=Troy (EN) 146 Bc 39.57N 26.15 E
Truyère 122 Ij 44.38N 2.34 E
Trysil 114 Cf 61.18N 12.16 E
Trysil 116 Ec 61.25N 12.25 E
Trysilelva 116 Ee 59.23N 13.32 E
Trysilfjellet 116 Ec 61.18N 12.11 E
Trzcianka 120 Mc 53.03N 16.28 E
Trzcińsko Zdrój 120 Kd 52.58N 14.35 E
Trzebiatów 120 Lb 54.04N 15.14 E
Trzebiez, Police- 120 Kc 53.39N 14.32 E
Trzebinia-Siersza 120 Pf 50.11N 19.25 E
Trzebnica 120 Ne 51.19N 17.03 E
Trzebnicki, Wał- 120 Me 51.30N 16.20 E
Trzebnickie, Wzgórza- 120 Me 51.15N 17.00 E
Trzemeszno 120 Nd 52.35N 17.50 E
Tsaidam Basin (EN)= Qaidam Pendi 152 Fd 37.00N 95.00 E
Tsamandá, Óri- 130 Dj 39.48N 20.21 E
Tsarap 148 Fb 33.31N 76.56 E
Tsaratanana 172 Hc 16.46S 47.38 E
Tsaratanana (EN)= Tsaratanana, Massif du- 158 Lj 14.00S 49.00 E
Tsaratanana, Massif du-= Tsaratanana (EN) 158 Lj 14.00S 49.00 E
Tsau 172 Cd 20.10S 22.27 E
Tsavo 170 Gc 2.59S 38.28 E
Tses 172 Be 25.58S 18.08 E
Tsévié 166 Fd 6.25N 1.13 E
Tshabong 160 Jk 26.02S 22.06 E
Tshane 160 Jk 24.01S 21.43 E
Tshangalele, Lac- 170 Ee 10.55S 27.03 E
Tshela 160 Ii 4.59S 12.56 E
Tshesebe 172 Dd 20.43S 27.37 E
Tshibala 170 Dd 6.56S 21.28 E
Tshibamba 170 Dd 9.06S 22.34 E
Tshikapa 160 Ji 6.25S 20.48 E
Tshilenge 170 Dd 6.15S 23.46 E
Tshimbalanga 170 Dd 9.43S 23.06 E
Tshimbulu 170 Dd 6.29S 22.51 E
Tshinsenda 170 Ee 12.16S 27.55 E
Tshofa 170 Ed 5.14S 25.15 E
Tsholotsho 172 Dc 19.46S 27.45 E
Tshopo 170 Eb 0.33N 25.07 E
Tshuapa 158 Ji 0.14S 20.42 E
Tshwaane 172 Cd 22.38S 22.05 E
Tsiafajavona 172 Hc 19.21S 47.15 E
Tsihombe 172 He 25.17S 45.30 E
Tsimlyansk Reservoir (EN) = Cimljanskoje vodohranilišče 110 Kf 48.00N 43.00 E
Tsinan → Jinan 142 Nf 36.35N 117.00 E
Tsinghai (EN)=Ch'ing-hai Sheng → Qinghai Sheng [2] 152 Gd 36.00N 96.00 E
Tsinghai (EN)=Qinghai Sheng (Ch'ing-hai Sheng) [2] 152 Gd 36.00N 96.00 E
Tsingtao → Qingdao 142 Of 36.05N 120.21 E
Tsiribihina 172 Gc 19.42S 44.31 E
Tsiroanomandidy 172 Hc 18.50S 46.00 E
Tsis 220d Bb 7.18N 151.50 E
Tsjokkarassa 114 Fb 69.59N 24.32 E
Tsodilo Hill 172 Cc 18.50S 21.45 E
Tsu 152 Oe 34.43N 136.31 E
Tsubame 156 Fc 37.39N 138.56 E
Tsubata 154 Nf 36.40N 136.44 E
Tsubetsu 156a Db 43.43N 144.01 E
Tsuchiura 154 Pf 36.05N 140.12 E
Tsugaru-Hantō 156a Bc 41.00N 140.30 E
Tsugaru-Kaikyō=Tsugaru Strait (EN) 140 Qe 41.40N 140.55 E
Tsugaru Strait (EN)= Tsugaru-Kaikyō 140 Qe 41.40N 140.55 E
Tsuken-Jima 156b Ab 26.15N 127.57 E
Tsukidate 156 Gb 38.44N 141.01 E
Tsukigata 156a Ab 43.20N 141.39 E
Tsukumi 156 Be 33.04N 131.52 E
Tsukura-Se 156 Af 31.18N 129.47 E
Tsukushi-Sanchi 156 Be 33.25N 130.30 E
Tsumeb 160 Ij 19.13S 17.42 E
Tsumeb [3] 172 Bc 19.00S 17.30 E
Tsumkwe 172 Cc 19.32S 20.30 E
Tsuna 156 Dd 34.26N 134.54 E
Tsuno-Shima 156 Bd 34.22N 130.52 E
Tsuru 156 Fd 35.35N 138.50 E
Tsuruga 152 Od 35.39N 136.04 E
Tsuruga-Wan 156 Ed 35.45N 136.05 E
Tsurugi 156 Ec 36.26N 136.37 E
Tsurugi-San 156 De 33.51N 134.03 E
Tsurui 156a Db 43.14N 144.21 E
Tsurumi-Dake 156 Be 33.18N 131.27 E
Tsurumi-Saki 156 Ce 32.56N 132.05 E
Tsuruoka 154 Oe 38.44N 139.50 E
Tsuruta 156 Ga 40.44N 140.26 E
Tsushima 140 Of 34.30N 129.20 E
Tsushima [Jap.] 156 Ed 35.10N 136.43 E
Tsushima [Jap.] 156 Ce 33.07N 132.30 E
Tsushima-Kaikyō=Korea, Strait (EN) 140 Of 34.40N 129.00 E
Tsuwano 156 Bd 34.28N 131.46 E
Tsuyama 154 Lg 35.03N 134.00 E
TTPI → Pacific Islands, Trust Territory of the- [5] 210 Gc 10.00N 155.00 E
Tua 126 Ec 41.13N 7.26W
Tuai 218 Gc 38.49S 177.08 E
Tuaim/Tuam 118 Eh 53.31N 8.50W
Tuakau 218 Fb 37.15S 174.57 E
Tual 150 Jh 5.40S 132.45 E
Tuam/Tuaim 118 Eh 53.31N 8.50W
Tuamotu, Iles-=Tuamotu Archipelago (EN) 208 Mf 19.00S 142.00W
Tuamotu Archipelago (EN) =Tuamotu, Iles- 208 Mf 19.00S 142.00W
Tuamotu Ridge (EN) 106 Ll 20.00S 145.00W
Tuapa 220k Ba 18.57S 169.54W
Tuapse 112 Jg 44.07N 39.05 E
Tuaran 150 Ge 6.11N 116.14 E
Tuasivi 221c Aa 13.40S 172.07W
Tuasivi, Cape- 221c Aa 13.40S 172.07W
Tuatapere 216 Ci 46.08S 167.41 E
Tuba 138 Ef 54.00N 91.40 E
Tuba City 188 Jh 36.08N 111.14W
Tubaï, Ile- 208 Mg 23.18S 149.30W
Tubai-Manu → Maiao, Ile- 208 Lf 17.34S 150.35W
Tubal, Wādī at- 146 Jf 32.19N 42.13 E
Tuban 150 Fh 6.54S 112.03 E
Tubarão 206 Kc 28.30S 49.01W
Ṭubayq, Jabal at- 146 Gh 29.32N 37.30 E
Tubbataha Reefs 150 Ge 8.51N 119.56 E
Tubeke/Tubize 124 Gd 50.41N 4.12 E
Tübingen 120 Fh 48.32N 9.03 E
Tubize/Tubeke 124 Gd 50.41N 4.12 E
Ṭubruq=Tobruk (EN) 160 Je 32.05N 23.59 E
Tubuai Islands (EN) = Tubuaï ou Australes, Iles- 208 Lg 23.00S 150.00W
Tubuaï ou Australes, Iles- = Tubuai Islands (EN) 208 Lg 23.00S 150.00W
Tubutama 192 Db 30.53N 111.29W
Tucacas 202 Ea 10.48N 68.19W
Tucacas, Punta- 194 Mh 10.52N 68.13W
Tucavaca 204 Cd 18.36S 58.55W
Tucavaca, Rio- 204 Cd 18.37S 58.59W
Tuchola 120 Nc 53.35N 17.50 E
Tucholska, Równina- 120 Oc 53.40N 18.30 E
Tuchów 120 Rg 49.54N 21.03 E
Tucker Glacier 222 Kf 72.35S 169.20 E
Tucson 176 Hf 32.13N 110.58W
Tucumán [2] 206 Gc 27.00S 65.30W
Tucumcari 182 Gd 35.10N 103.44W
Tucunuí 202 Id 3.42S 49.27W
Tucupido 202 Eb 9.17N 65.47W
Tucupita 202 Fb 9.04N 62.03W
Tudela 126 Kb 42.05N 1.36W
Tudia, Sierra de- 126 Ff 38.05N 6.20W
Tudmur 144 Ec 34.33N 38.17 E
Tudora 130 Jb 47.31N 26.38 E
Tuela 126 Ec 41.30N 7.12W
Tuensang 148 Ic 26.17N 94.40 E
Tuerto 126 Gb 42.18N 5.53W
Tufanbeyli 146 Gc 38.18N 36.11 E
Tufi 210 Fe 9.08S 149.20 E
Tugela 158 Kk 29.14S 31.30 E
Tug Fork 184 Ff 38.25N 82.35W
Tuguegarao 142 Oh 17.37N 121.44 E
Tugulym 134 Lh 57.04N 64.39 E
Tugur 138 If 53.51N 136.52 E
Tuhai He 154 Ee 38.05N 118.13 E
Tujiabu → Yongxiu 152 Kf 29.05N 115.49 E
Tujmazy 136 Fe 54.36N 53.42 E
Tukan 134 Hj 53.50N 57.31 E
Tukangbesi, Kepulauan-= Tukangbesi Islands (EN) 150 Hh 5.40S 123.50 E
Tukangbesi Islands (EN)= Tukangbesi, Kepulauan- 150 Hh 5.40S 123.50 E
Tukayel 168 Hd 8.05N 45.20 E
Tukayyid 146 Kh 29.47N 45.36 E
Tukituki 218 Gc 39.36S 176.56 E
Tuko Village 220n Ab 10.22S 161.02W
Tūkrah 164 Dc 32.32N 20.34 E
Tuktoyaktuk 176 Fc 69.27N 133.02W
Tukums 116 Fh 56.59N 23.10 E
Tukuringra, hrebet- 138 Hf 54.30N 126.00 E
Tukuyu 170 Fd 9.15S 33.39 E
Tula 170 Gc 0.50S 39.51 E
Tula 190 Ed 20.06N 99.19W
Tula [Mex.] 192 Jf 23.00N 99.43W
Tula [Russia] 112 Je 54.12N 37.37 E
Tula de Allende 192 Jg 20.03N 99.21W
Tula Mountains 222 Ee 66.54S 51.06 E
Tulancingo 190 Ed 20.05N 98.22W
Tulare 188 Fh 36.13N 119.21W
Tulare Lake Bed 188 Fh 36.03N 119.49W
Tularosa 186 Cj 33.04N 106.01W
Tularosa Valley 186 Cj 32.45N 106.10W
Tulcán 202 Cc 0.48N 77.43W
Tulcea 130 Ld 45.10N 28.48 E
Tulcea [2] 130 Md 45.12N 29.10 E
Tulčin 132 Fe 48.39N 28.52 E
Tulelake 188 Ef 41.57N 121.29W
Tulemalu Lake 180 Hd 62.55N 99.25W
Tulgheş 130 Ic 46.57N 25.46 E
Tuli 172 Dd 21.55S 29.12 E
Tuli 172 Dd 21.48S 29.04 E
Tulia 186 Fi 34.32N 101.46W
Tulihe 152 La 50.30N 121.51 E
Tullahoma 184 Dh 35.22N 86.11W
Tullamore/An Tulach Mhór 118 Fh 53.16N 7.30W
Tulle 122 Hi 45.16N 1.46 E
Tulln 128 Kb 48.20N 16.03 E
Tulln 128 Kb 48.22N 16.03 E
Tullner Becken 128 Jb 48.25N 15.55 E
Tullow/An Tulach 118 Gi 52.48N 6.44W
Tullus 168 Cc 11.03N 24.33 E
Tully 212 Jc 17.56S 145.56 E
Ṭulmaythah 164 Dc 32.43N 20.57 E
Tuloma 110 Jb 68.52N 32.49 E
Tulos, ozero- 114 He 63.35N 30.35 E
Tulsa 176 Jf 36.09N 95.58W
Tulskaja oblast [3] 136 De 54.00N 37.30 E
Tuluá 202 Cc 4.05N 76.12W
Tuluksak 178 Gd 61.06N 160.58W
Tulum 192 Pg 20.13N 87.28W
Tulum 190 Gd 20.15N 87.27W
Tulun 142 Md 54.35N 100.33 E
Tulungagung 150 Fh 8.04S 111.54 E
Tuma 114 Ji 55.10N 40.36 E
Tuma, Rio- 194 Eg 13.03N 84.44W
Tumaco 200 Ie 1.49N 78.46W
Tumaco, Rada de- 202 Cc 1.50N 78.40W
Tumacuari, Pico- 202 Fc 1.15N 64.40W
Tuman-gang 154 Kc 42.18N 130.41 E
Tumba 116 Ge 59.12N 17.49 E
Tumbarumba 212 Jg 35.47S 148.01 E
Tumbes 200 Hf 4.05S 80.35W
Tumbes [3] 202 Bd 3.50S 80.30W
Tumča 114 Hc 66.35N 31.45 E
Tumd Youqi 152 Jc 40.33N 110.32 E
Tumd Zuoqi 152 Jc 40.43N 111.06 E
Tumen 142 Oe 42.58N 129.49 E
Tumen Jiang 154 Kc 42.18N 130.41 E
Tumeremo 202 Fb 7.18N 61.30W
Tumkur 148 Ff 13.21N 77.05 E
Tummel 118 Je 56.43N 3.44W
Tummo 164 Be 23.00N 14.10 E
Tumon Bay 220c Ba 13.31N 144.48 E
Tumpat 150 De 6.12N 102.10 E
Tumu 166 Ec 10.52N 1.59W
Tumucumaque, Serra- 198 Ke 2.20N 55.00W
Tumwater 188 Dc 47.01N 122.54W
Tuna, Punta- 197a Cc 18.00N 65.52W
Tunapuna 196 Fg 10.38N 61.23W
Tunas 204 Hg 24.58S 49.06W
Tunas, Sierra de las- 192 Fc 29.40N 107.15W
Tunas Chicas, Laguna- 204 Am 36.01S 62.20W
Tunaydah 146 Cj 25.31N 29.21 E
Tunçbilek 130 Mj 39.37N 29.29 E
Tunduma 170 Fd 9.18S 32.46 E
Tunduru 170 Ge 11.07S 37.21 E
Tundža 130 Jh 41.40N 26.34 E
Tunga 166 Gd 8.07N 9.12 E
Tungabhadra 148 Fe 15.57N 78.15 E
Tungaru 168 Ec 10.14N 30.42 E
Tungnaá 114a Bb 64.10N 19.34W
Tungokočen 138 Gf 53.33N 115.34 E
Tungsten 180 Ed 62.05N 127.42W
Tungua 221b Bb 20.01S 174.46W
Tuni 148 Ge 17.21N 82.33 E
Tūnis=Tunis (EN) 160 Ie 36.48N 10.11 E
Tūnis=Tunis (EN) [3] 162 Jb 36.30N 10.00 E
Tūnis=Tunisia (EN) [1] 160 Ie 34.00N 9.00 E
Tunis (EN)=Tūnis 160 Ie 36.48N 10.11 E
Tunis (EN)=Tūnis [3] 162 Jb 36.30N 10.00 E
Tūnis, Canal de-=Sicily, Strait of- (EN) 110 Hh 37.20N 11.20 E
Tūnis, Khalīj- 162 Jb 37.00N 10.30 E
Tunisia (EN)=Tūnis [1] 160 Ie 34.00N 9.00 E
Tunja 200 Ie 5.31N 73.22W
Tunkhannock 184 Je 41.32N 75.57W
Tunliu 154 Bf 36.18N 112.53 E
Tunnhovdfjorden 116 Cd 60.25N 8.55 E
Tunø 116 Di 55.55N 10.25 E
Tunumuk 180 Ec 69.00N 134.57W
Tununak 178 Fd 60.35N 165.16W
Tunungayualok 180 Le 56.05N 61.05W
Tunxi 152 Kf 29.45N 118.15 E
Tuo He 154 Dh 33.16N 117.45 E
Tuo Jang 152 If 28.55N 105.26 E
Tuostah 138 Ic 67.50N 135.40 E
Tuotuo He 152 Fe 34.03N 92.46 E
Tuotuoheyan / Tanggulashanqu 142 Lf 34.15N 92.29 E
Tupã 206 Jb 21.56S 50.30W
Tupaciguara 204 Hd 18.35S 48.42W
Tupai Atoll (Motu-Iti) 216 Kc 16.17S 151.50W
Tupanciretã 206 Jc 29.05S 53.51W
Tupelo 182 Je 34.16N 88.43W
Tupik 138 Gf 54.28N 119.57 E
Tupinambaranas, Ilha- 202 Gd 3.00S 58.00W
Tupiraçaba 204 Hb 14.29S 48.34W
Tupiza 202 Eh 21.27S 65.43W
Tupper Lake 184 Jc 44.13N 74.29W
Tupungato, Cerro- 206 Gd 33.22S 69.47W
Tuquan 152 Lb 45.22N 121.33 E
Túquerres 202 Cc 1.06N 77.37W
Tur 130 Fa 48.04N 22.33 E
Tura 136 Gd 57.12N 66.56 E
Tura [India] 148 Ic 25.31N 90.13 E
Tura [Russia] 142 Mc 64.17N 100.15 E
Turabah [Sau.Ar.] 144 Fe 21.13N 41.39 E
Turabah [Sau.Ar.] 144 Fd 28.13N 42.59 E
Turagua, Serranías- 196 Di 7.20N 64.35W
Turakina 218 Fd 40.02S 175.13 E
Turān 146 Qe 35.40N 56.50 E
Turan 138 Ef 52.08N 93.55 E
Turana, hrebet- 138 If 51.30N 132.00 E
Turangi 218 Fc 38.59S 175.48 E
Turano 128 Gh 42.26N 12.47 E
Turanskaja nizmennost 140 Ie 44.30N 63.00 E
Turawa 120 Of 50.45N 18.05 E
Turawskie, Jezioro- 120 Of 50.43N 18.10 E
Turbaco 194 Jh 10.19N 75.25W
Turbat 148 Cc 25.59N 63.04 E
Turbo 200 Ie 8.06N 76.43W
Turcoaia 130 Ld 45.07N 28.11 E
Turda 130 Gc 46.34N 23.47 E
Tūreh 146 Me 34.02N 49.17 E
Tureia Atoll 208 Ng 20.50S 138.32W
Turek 120 Od 52.02N 18.30 E
Turenki 116 Kd 60.55N 24.38 E
Turfan Depression (EN)= Turpan Pendi 140 Ke 42.30N 89.30 E
Turgai Gates (EN) = Turgajskaja ložbina 140 Id 51.00N 64.30 E
Turgai Upland (EN) = Turgajskoje plato 140 Id 51.00N 64.00 E
Turgaj 136 Gf 49.38N 63.28 E
Turgaj 140 Ie 48.01N 62.45 E
Turgajskaja ložbina = Turgai Gates (EN) 140 Id 51.00N 64.30 E
Turgajskaja oblast [3] 136 Ge 50.30N 66.00 E
Turgajskoje plato = Turgai Upland (EN) 140 Id 51.00N 64.00 E
Turgeon, Rivière- 184 Ha 50.00N 78.55W
Turgutlu 146 Bc 38.30N 27.50 E
Turhal 146 Gb 40.24N 36.06 E
Türi/Tjuri 114 Fg 58.50N 25.27 E
Turia / Túria 126 Le 39.27N 0.19W
Túria / Turia 126 Le 39.27N 0.19W
Turiaçu, Baía de- 202 Id 1.30S 45.15W
Turiec 120 Og 49.06N 18.52 E
Turijsk 120 Ue 51.10N 24.37 E
Turimiquire, Cerro- 202 Fa 10.03N 64.00W
Turin (EN) = Torino 112 Gf 45.03N 7.40 E
Turinsk 136 Gd 58.03N 63.42 E
Turja 132 Dd 51.48N 24.52 E
Turka [Russia] 138 Ff 52.57N 108.13 E
Turka [Ukr.] 120 Tg 49.07N 23.01 E
Turkana 170 Gb 4.00N 35.30 E
Turkana, Lake-/Rudolf, Lake- 158 Kh 3.30N 36.00 E
Türkeli 146 Fb 41.57N 34.21 E
Turkestan 142 Ie 43.18N 68.15 E
Turkestanski hrebet 136 Gh 39.35N 69.00 E
Túrkeve 120 Qi 47.06N 20.45 E
Turkey (EN)=Türkiye [1] 142 Ff 39.00N 35.00 E
Turkey Creek 212 Fc 17.02S 128.12 E
Turki 132 Mc 52.01N 43.16 E
Türkiye=Turkey (EN) [1] 142 Ff 39.00N 35.00 E
Türkmenistan 136 Fh 40.00N 60.00 E
Turkmenistan Sovet Socialistik Respublikasy/ Turkmenskaja SSR → Türkmenistan 136 Fh 40.00N 60.00 E
Turkmen-Kala 135 Df 37.26N 62.19 E
Turkmenskaja Sovetskaja Socialističeskaja Respublika → Türkmenistan 136 Fh 40.00N 60.00 E
Turkmenskaja SSR/ Turkmenistan Sovet Socialistik Respublikasy → Türkmenistan 136 Fh 40.00N 60.00 E
Turkmenski zaliv 132 Rj 39.00N 53.30 E
Türkoğlu 146 Gd 37.31N 36.49 E
Turks and Caicos Islands [5] 176 Lg 21.45N 71.35W
Turks Island Passage 194 Lc 21.25N 71.19W
Turks Islands 190 Jd 21.24N 71.07W
Turku/Åbo 112 Ic 60.27N 22.17 E
Turku-Pori [2] 114 Ff 61.00N 22.30 E
Turkwel 170 Gb 3.06N 36.06 E
Turlock 188 Eh 37.30N 120.51W
Turmantas 116 Li 55.42N 26.34 E
Turnagain, Cape- 218 Gd 40.30S 176.37 E
Turneffe Islands 190 Ge 17.22N 87.51W
Turnhout 122 Kc 51.19N 4.57 E
Turnov 120 Lf 50.35N 15.09 E
Turnu Măgurele 130 Hf 43.45N 24.52 E
Turnu Roşu, Pasul- 130 Hd 45.33N 24.16 E
Turočak 138 Df 52.16N 87.05 E
Turó de L'Home 126 Oc 41.45N 2.25 E
Turopolje 128 Ke 45.38N 16.07 E
Turpan 142 Ke 42.56N 89.10 E
Turpan Pendi=Turfan Depression (EN) 140 Ke 42.30N 89.30 E
Turquino, Pico- 190 Ie 19.59N 76.51W
Turrialba 194 Fi 9.54N 83.41W
Tursuntski Tuman, ozero- 134 Kf 60.35N 63.55 E
Turtas 134 Ng 58.57N 69.10 E
Turtas 134 Ng 59.06N 68.50 E
Turtkul 136 Gg 41.35N 61.00 E
Turtle Mountain 186 Fb 49.05N 100.15W
Turugart Shankou 140 Je 40.32N 75.24 E
Turuhan 138 Dc 65.56N 87.42 E
Turuhansk 138 Dc 65.49N 87.59 E
Turvânia 204 Gc 16.39S 50.09W
Turvo 204 Hi 28.56S 49.41W
Turvo, Rio- [Braz.] 204 Hd 19.56S 49.55W
Turvo, Rio- [Braz.] 204 Gc 17.46S 50.12W
Tusaun/Thusis 128 Dd 46.42N 9.26 E
Tuscaloosa 182 Je 33.13N 87.33W
Tuscan Archipelago (EN) = Toscano, Arcipelago- 110 Hg 42.45N 10.20 E
Tuscania 128 Fh 42.25N 11.52 E
Tuscany (EN) = Toscana [2] 128 Eg 43.25N 11.00 E
Tuscarora Mountain 184 Ie 40.10N 77.45W
Tuscarora Mountains 188 Gf 41.00N 116.20W
Tuščibas, zaliv- 135 Ba 46.10N 59.45 E
Tuscola 186 Lg 39.48N 88.17W
Tusenøyane 179 Oc 77.05N 22.00 E
Tuskar 132 Jd 51.40N 36.15 E
Tuskegee 184 Ei 32.26N 85.42W
Tuşnad Băi 130 Ic 46.09N 25.51 E
Tustna 116 Ca 63.10N 8.05 E
Tuszyma 120 Rf 50.09N 21.30 E
Tuszyn 120 Pe 51.37N 19.34 E
Tutajev 136 Dd 57.52N 39.32 E
Tutak 146 Jc 39.32N 42.46 E
Tuticorin 148 Fg 8.47N 78.08 E
Tutira 218 Gc 39.12S 176.53 E
Tutóia 202 Jd 2.45S 42.16W
Tutoko Peak 218 Bf 44.36S 167.58 E
Tutončana 138 Ed 64.05N 93.50 E
Tutova 130 Kc 46.06N 27.32 E
Tutrakan 130 Je 44.03N 26.37 E
Tuttle Creek Lake 186 Hg 39.22N 96.40W
Tuttlingen 120 Ei 47.59N 8.49 E
Tutuala 150 Ih 8.24S 127.15 E
Tutuila Island 208 Jf 14.18S 170.42W
Tutupaca, Volcán- 202 Do 17.01S 70.22W
Tuupovaara 116 Nb 62.29N 30.36 E
Tuusniemi 114 Ge 62.49N 28.30 E
Tuva, respublika 138 Ef 51.30N 94.00 E
Tuvalu (Ellice Islands) [1] 210 Ie 8.00S 178.00 E
Tuvalu Islands 208 Ie 8.00S 178.00 E
Tuvana-i-Ra Island 216 Fd 21.00S 178.43W
Tuvana-i-Tholo Island 208 Iq 21.02S 178.49W
Tuxford 124 Ba 53.13N 0.53W
Tuxpan [Mex.] 190 Cd 21.57N 105.18W
Tuxpan [Mex.] 192 Hh 19.33N 103.24W
Tuxpan, Arrecife- 192 Kg 21.02N 97.13W
Tuxpan, Rio- 192 Kg 20.53N 97.18W
Tuxpan de Rodriguez Cano 190 Ed 20.57N 97.24W
Tuxtla Gutiérrez 176 Jh 16.45N 93.07W
Tuy 126 Db 42.03N 8.38W
Tuy, Rio- 196 Dg 10.24N 65.59W
Tuy An 148 Lf 13.17N 109.16 E
Tuy Hoa 148 Lf 13.05N 109.18 E
Tüyserkān 146 Me 34.33N 48.27 E
Tuz, Lake- (EN)=Tuz Gölü 140 Ff 38.45N 33.25 E
Tuz Gölü=Tuz, Lake- (EN) 140 Ff 38.45N 33.25 E
Tuzkan, ozero- 135 Fd 40.35N 67.30 E
Tūz Khurmātū 144 Fc 34.53N 44.38 E
Tuzla 128 Mf 44.33N 18.41 E
Tuzla Gölü 146 Fc 39.01N 35.50 E
Tuzlov 132 Lf 47.23N 40.08 E
Tuzluca 146 Jb 40.03N 43.39 E
Tuzly 130 Nd 45.56N 30.05 E

Tva-Urf

Tvååker 116 Eg 57.03N 12.24 E
Tvărdica 130 Ig 42.42N 25.54 E
Tvedestrand 114 Bg 58.37N 8.55 E
Tver' (Kalinin) 112 Jd 56.52N 35.55 E
Tver'skaja oblast 136 Dd 57.20N 34.40 E
Tweed 118 Lf 55.46N 2.00W
Tweedsmuir Hills 118 Jf 55.30N 3.22W
Tweerivier 172 Be 25.35 S 19.37 E
Twello, Voorst- 124 Ib 52.14N 6.07 E
Twente 122 Mb 52.17N 6.40 E
Twentekanaal 124 Ib 52.13N 6.53 E
Twilight Cove 212 Ff 32.20 S 126.00 E
Twin Buttes Reservoir 186 Fk 31.20N 100.35W
Twin Falls 176 He 42.34N 114.28W
Twin Islands 180 Jf 53.50N 80.00W
Twin Peaks 188 Hd 44.35N 114.29W
Twisp 188 Eb 48.22N 120.07W
Twiste 124 Lc 51.29N 9.09 E
Twistringen 120 Ed 52.48N 8.39 E
Two Butte Creek 186 Eg 38.02N 102.08W
Two Harbors 186 Kc 47.01N 91.40W
Two Rivers 186 Md 44.09N 87.34W
Two Thumb Range 218 De 43.45 S 170.40 E
Tychy 120 Of 50.09N 18.59 E
Tyczyn 120 Sg 49.58N 22.02 E
Tydal 114 Ce 63.04N 11.34 E
Tygda 138 Hf 53.07N 126.20 E
Tyin 116 Cc 61.14N 8.14 E
Tyin 116 Cc 61.15N 8.15 E
Tyler 182 He 32.21N 95.18W
Tylertown 186 Kk 31.07N 90.09W
Tylösand 116 Eh 56.39N 12.44 E
Tylöskog 116 Ff 58.40N 15.10 E
Tym 138 De 59.30N 80.07 E
Tymovskoje 138 Jf 50.50N 142.41 E
Tympákion 130 Hn 35.06N 24.45 E
Tynda 142 Od 55.10N 124.43 E
Tyne 118 Lf 55.01N 1.26W
Tyne and Wear [3] 118 Lg 55.00N 1.35W
Tynemouth 118 Lf 55.01N 1.24W
Týn nad Vltavou 120 Kg 49.14N 14.26 E
Tynset 114 Ce 62.17N 10.47 E
Tyra, Cayos- 194 Fg 12.50N 83.20W
Tyrifjorden 116 Dd 60.05N 10.10 E
Tyringe 116 Eh 56.10N 13.35 E
Tyrma 138 If 50.01N 132.10 E
Tyrnyauz 132 Mh 43.23N 42.56 E
Tyrol (EN)=Tirol [2] 128 Fc 47.10N 11.25 E
Tyrol (EN)=Tirol/Tirolo 128 Fd 47.00N 11.20 E
Tyrone 184 He 40.41N 78.15W
Tyrrell, Lake- 212 Ig 35.20 S 142.50 E
Tyrrel Lake 180 Gd 63.05N 105.30W
Tyrrhenian Basin (EN) 110 Hh 40.00N 13.00 E
Tyrrhenian Sea (EN)= Tirreno, Mar- 110 Hh 40.00N 12.00 E
Tyrva/Tõrva 114 Fg 58.01N 25.59 E
Tyrvää 116 Jc 61.21N 22.53 E
Tysmenica 120 Uh 48.49N 24.56 E
Tyśmienica 120 Se 51.33N 22.30 E
Tysnesøy 114 Af 60.00N 5.35 E
Tysse 116 Ad 60.22N 5.45 E
Tyssedal 116 Bd 60.07N 6.34 E
Tystama/Tõstamaa 116 Jf 58.17N 23.52 E
Tystberga 116 Gf 58.52N 17.15 E
Tyszowce 120 Tf 50.36N 23.41 E
Tytuvénai/Tituvenaj 116 Ji 55.33N 23.09 E
Tywyn 118 Ii 52.35N 4.05W
Tzanconeja, Rio- 192 Ni 16.51N 91.47W
Tzaneen 172 Ed 23.50 S 30.09 E
Tzintzuntzan 192 Ih 19.38N 101.34W
Tzucacab 192 Og 20.04N 89.05W

U

Uaboe 220e Ab 0.31 S 166.54 E
Uacurizal, Ilha do- 204 Dc 16.25 S 56.05W
Ua Huka, Ile- 208 Ne 8.54 S 139.33W
Uanukuhahaki 221b Ba 19.58 S 174.29W
Ua Pou, Ile- 208 Me 9.23 S 140.03W
Uaroo 212 Dd 23.00 S 115.10 E
Uatumã, Rio- 198 Kf 2.26 S 57.37W
Uaupés 200 Jf 0.08 S 67.05W
Uaupés, Rio- 198 Je 0.02N 67.16W
Uaxactún 190 Ge 17.25N 89.29W
Ub 130 De 44.27N 20.05 E
Ubá 202 Jh 21.07 S 42.56W
Übach-Palenberg 120 Cf 50.56N 6.05 E
Ubagan 136 Ge 54.23N 64.40 E
Ubaila 146 If 33.06N 40.15 E
Ubaitaba 202 Kf 14.18 S 39.20W
Ubajay 204 Cj 31.47 S 58.18W
Ubangi 158 Ii 0.30 S 17.42 E
Ubatuba 204 Jf 23.26 S 45.04W
Ubay 150 Hd 10.03N 124.28 E
Ubaye 122 Mj 44.28N 6.18 E
Ubayyiḑ, Wādī al- 144 Fc 32.34N 43.48 E
Ube 154 Kh 33.56N 131.15 E
Úbeda 126 If 38.01N 3.22W
Ubekendt Ejland 179 Gd 71.10N 53.45W
Uberaba 200 Lg 19.45 S 47.55W
Uberaba, Lagoa- 204 Dc 17.30 S 57.45W
Uberlândia 200 Lg 18.56 S 48.18W
Überlingen 120 Fi 47.46N 9.10 E
Ubiaja 166 Gd 6.39N 6.23 E
Ubiña, Peña- 126 Ga 43.01N 5.57W
Ubiratã 204 Fg 24.32 S 52.56W
Ubon Ratchathani 142 Mh 15.15N 104.54 E
Ubort 132 Fc 52.06N 28.30 E
Ubrique 126 Gh 36.41N 5.27W
Ubsu-Nur (Uvs Nuur) 140 Ld 50.20N 92.45 E
Ubundu 160 Ji 0.21 S 25.29 E
Učaly 136 Fe 54.20N 59.31 E
Učami 138 Ed 63.50N 96.39 E
Učaral 136 If 46.08N 80.52 E
Ucayali [3] 202 De 7.10 S 75.15W
Ucayali, Rio- 198 If 4.30 S 73.30W
Uccle/Ukkel 124 Gd 50.48N 4.19 E
Üçdoruk Tepe 146 Ib 40.45N 41.05 E
Ucero 126 Ic 41.31N 3.04W
Uchiko 156 Ce 33.34N 132.38 E
Uchi Lake 186 Ja 51.05N 92.35W
Uchinomi 156 Dd 34.30N 134.19 E
Uchinoura 156 Bf 31.16N 131.05 E
Uchiura-Wan 154 Pc 42.18N 140.35 E
Uchte 120 Ed 52.30N 8.55 E
Učka 128 Ie 45.17N 14.12 E
Uckange 124 Ie 49.18N 6.09 E
Uckermark 120 Jc 53.10N 13.35 E
Uckfield 124 Cd 50.58N 0.06 E
Učkuduk 136 Gg 42.10N 63.30 E
Učkurgan 135 Id 41.01N 72.04 E
Ucrainskaja Sovetskaja Socialističeskaja Respublika → Ukrayina 136 Df 49.00N 32.00 E
Ucross 188 Ld 44.33N 106.31W
Ucua 170 Bd 8.40 S 14.12 E
Učur 140 Pd 58.48N 130.35 E
Uda [Russia] 138 Ff 51.45N 107.25 E
Uda [Russia] 140 Pd 54.42N 135.14 E
Uda [Russia] 138 Ee 56.05N 99.34 E
Udačny 138 Gc 66.25N 112.20 E
Udaipur 142 Jg 24.35N 73.41 E
Udaj 132 Hd 50.05N 33.07 E
Udaquiola 204 Cm 36.34 S 58.31W
Udbina 128 Jf 44.32N 15.46 E
Uddevalla 114 Cg 58.21N 11.55 E
Uddjaure 110 Hb 65.58N 17.50 E
Uden 124 Hc 51.40N 5.37 E
Udgir 148 Fe 18.23N 77.07 E
Udhampur 148 Fb 32.56N 75.08 E
Udimskí 114 Kf 61.09N 45.52 E
Udine 128 Hd 46.03N 13.14 E
Udipi 148 Ef 13.21N 74.45 E
Udmurtskaja respublika 136 Fd 57.20N 52.50 E
Udoha 116 Mg 57.58N 29.50 E
Udomlja 114 Ih 57.56N 35.02 E
Udone-Jima 156 Fd 34.28N 139.17 E
Udon Thani 148 Ke 17.25N 102.48 E
Udot 220d Bb 7.23N 151.43 E
Udskaja guba 140 Pd 55.00N 136.00 E
Udskoje 138 If 54.36N 134.30 E
Udy 132 Je 49.47N 36.35 E
Udžary 132 Oi 40.31N 47.40 E
Udzungwa Range 170 Gd 8.05 S 35.50 E
Uebonti 150 Hg 0.55 S 121.38 E
Uecker 120 Kc 53.45N 14.04 E
Ueckermünde 120 Kc 53.44N 14.03 E
Ueda 152 Od 36.24N 138.16 E
Uele 158 Jh 4.09N 22.26 E
Uelen 138 Oc 66.13N 169.48W
Uelzen 120 Gd 52.58N 10.34 E
Ueno 156 Ed 34.46N 136.06 E
Uere 158 Jh 3.42N 25.24 E
Ufa 112 Le 54.44N 55.56 E
Ufa 110 Le 54.40N 56.00 E
Uftjuga 114 Lf 61.28N 46.12 E
Ugab 158 Ik 21.12 S 13.38 E
Ugāle/Ugale 116 Ig 57.19N 21.52 E
Ugale/Ugāle 116 Ig 57.19N 21.52 E
Ugalla 170 Fd 5.08 S 30.42 E
Uganda [1] 160 Kh 1.00N 32.00 E
Ugărčin 130 Hf 43.06N 24.25 E
Ugashik 178 He 57.32N 157.25W
Ughelli 166 Gd 5.30N 5.59 E
Ugijar 126 Ih 36.57N 3.03W
Uglegorsk 138 Jg 49.05N 142.06 E
Uglekamensk 138 Ih 43.18N 133.08 E
Ugleuralski 134 Hg 58.59N 57.38 E
Uglič 136 Dd 57.33N 38.23 E
Ugljan 128 Jf 44.05N 15.10 E
Uglovoje 154 Lc 43.20N 132.06 E
Ugnev 120 Tf 50.20N 23.45 E
Ugo 156 Gb 39.13N 140.23 E
Ugolnyje Kopi 138 Md 64.42N 177.50 E
Ugoma 170 Ec 4.55 S 26.50 E
Ugra 136 De 54.30N 36.07 E
Ugtal-Cajdam 152 Ib 48.25N 105.30 E
Uh 120 Rh 48.33N 22.00 E
Uherske Hradiště 120 Ng 49.04N 17.27 E
Uhlava 120 Jg 49.45N 13.23 E
Uhlenhorst 172 Bd 23.45 S 17.55 E
Uhta 112 Lc 63.33N 53.40 E
Uibh Fhaili/Offaly [2] 118 Fh 53.20N 7.30W
Uig 118 Gd 57.30N 6.20W
Uige 160 Ii 7.35 S 15.04 E
Uige [3] 170 Cd 7.00 S 15.30 E
'Uiha 221b Ba 19.54 S 174.25W
Uijec 220d Bb 7.10N 151.57 E
Üijöngbu 154 If 37.44N 127.02 E
Uiju 154 Hd 40.12N 124.32 E
Uil 136 Ff 49.04N 54.42 E
Uil 136 Ff 48.36N 52.30 E
Uilpata, gora- 132 Mh 42.47N 43.44 E
Uinta Mountains 182 Ec 40.45N 110.05W
Uinta River 188 Kf 40.14N 109.51W
Uis 172 Ad 21.08 S 14.49 E
Uišong 154 Jf 36.21N 128.42 E
Uitenhage 160 Jl 33.40 S 25.28 E
Uithoorn 124 Gb 52.14N 4.52 E
Uithuizen 124 Ia 53.25N 6.42 E
Uithuizerwad 124 Ia 53.30N 6.40 E
Uj 136 Ge 54.20N 63.58 E
Ujae Atoll 208 Hd 9.05N 165.40 E
Ujan 146 Og 30.45N 52.05 E
Ujandina 138 Jc 68.23N 145.50 E
Ujar 138 Ee 55.48N 94.20 E
Ujarrás 194 Fi 9.50N 83.40W
Ujedinenija, ostrov- 138 Da 77.30N 82.30 E
Ujelang Atoll 208 Hd 9.49N 160.55 E
Újfehértó 120 Ri 47.48N 21.41 E
Uji 156 Dd 34.53N 135.47 E
Uji-Guntō 154 Ji 31.10N 129.28 E
Ujiie 156 Fc 36.41N 139.57 E
Ujiji 160 Ji 4.55 S 29.41 E
Ujjain 142 Jg 23.11N 75.46 E
Ujungpandang 150 Gg 4.40 S 119.58 E
Ujung Pandang=Makasar (EN) 142 Nj 5.07 S 119.24 E
Uk 138 Ee 55.04N 98.52 E
Ukata 166 Gc 10.50N 5.50 E
Ukeng, Bukit- 150 Gf 1.45N 115.08 E
Ukerewe Island 170 Fc 2.03 S 33.00 E
Uke-Shima 156b Ba 28.02N 129.15 E
Ukhaydir 146 Jf 32.26N 43.36 E
Ukiah [Ca.-U.S.] 182 Cd 39.09N 123.13W
Ukiah [Or.-U.S.] 188 Fd 45.08N 118.56W
Uki Ni Masi 219a Ed 10.15 S 161.44 E
Ukkel/Uccle 124 Gd 50.48N 4.19 E
Ukmergé/Ukmerge 114 Fi 55.14N 24.47 E
Ukmerge/Ukmergé 114 Fi 55.14N 24.47 E
Ukraine (EN) 110 Jf 49.00N 35.00 E
Ukraine (EN) = Ukrayina 136 Df 49.00N 32.00 E
Ukrainskaja SSR/Ukrainska Radyanska Socialistična Respublika → Ukrayina 136 Df 49.00N 32.00 E
Ukrainska Radyanska Socialistična Respublika/Ukrainskaja SSR → Ukrayina 136 Df 49.00N 32.00 E
Ukrayina = Ukraine (EN) 136 Df 49.00N 32.00 E
Ukrina 128 Le 45.05N 17.56 E
Uku 170 Be 11.25 S 14.18 E
Uku-Jima 156 Ae 33.16N 129.07 E
Ula 146 Cd 37.05N 28.26 E
Ula 120 Ub 54.06N 24.20 E
Ulaidh/Ulster 118 Gg 54.30N 7.00W
Ulalu 220d Bb 7.25N 151.40 E
Ulan (Xiligou) 152 Gd 36.55N 98.16 E
Ulan → Otog Qi 152 Id 39.07N 108.00 E
Ulanbaatar → Ulan-Bator 142 Me 47.55N 106.53 E
Ulan-Badrah 154 Ac 43.58N 110.37 E
Ulan-Bator (Ulaanbaatar) 142 Me 47.55N 106.53 E
Ulanbel 136 Hg 44.49N 71.10 E
Ulan-Burgasy, hrebet- 138 Ff 52.30N 108.30 E
Ulangom 142 Le 49.58N 92.02 E
Ulanhad/Chifeng 152 Kc 42.16N 118.57 E
Ulan Hol 136 Ef 45.27N 46.46 E
Ulan Hot/Horqin Youyi Qianqi 142 Oe 46.04N 122.00 E
Ulan Hua → Siziwang Qi 154 Ad 41.31N 111.41 E
Ulan-Hus 152 Eb 49.02N 89.23 E
Ulanów 120 Sf 50.30N 22.16 E
Ulansuhai Nur 152 Ic 40.56N 108.49 E
Ulan-Tajga 152 Ga 50.45N 98.30 E
Ulan-Ude 142 Md 51.50N 107.37 E
Ulan Ul Hu 152 Fe 34.45N 90.25 E
Ulas 146 Gc 39.27N 37.03 E
Ulawa Island 214 Gi 9.46 S 161.57 E
Ulbeja 138 Je 59.20N 144.25 E
Ulchin 154 Jf 36.59N 129.24 E
Ulcinj 130 Ch 41.56N 19.13 E
Uleåborg/Oulu 112 Ib 65.01N 25.30 E
Ulefoss 114 Bg 59.17N 9.16 E
Ulegej 142 Ke 48.56N 89.57 E
Ulety 138 Gf 51.22N 112.30 E
Uleza 130 Ch 41.40N 19.53 E
Ulfborg 116 Ch 56.16N 8.20 E
Ulflingen/Troisvierges 124 Hd 50.07N 6.00 E
Ulft, Gendringen- 124 Ic 51.54N 6.24 E
Ulgain Gol 152 Kb 45.31N 117.50 E
Ulhāsnagar 148 Ee 19.10N 73.07 E
Uliastaj → Dong Ujimqin Qi 152 Kc 45.31N 116.58 E
Uliga 210 Id 7.09N 171.13 E
Ulindi 158 Ji 1.40 S 25.52 E
Ulithi Atoll 208 Ed 9.58N 139.40 E
Ulja 138 Je 58.48N 141.40 E
Uljanovka [Russia] 116 Ne 59.37N 30.55 E
Uljanovka [Ukr.] 132 Ge 48.20N 30.13 E
Uljanovsk 112 Ke 54.20N 48.24 E
Uljanovskaja oblast [3] 136 Ee 54.00N 48.00 E
Uljanovski 136 He 50.05N 73.45 E
Uljasutaj 142 Le 47.45N 96.49 E
Ulkan 138 Fe 55.55N 107.55 E
Ulla 126 Db 42.39N 8.44W
Ullapool 118 Hd 57.54N 5.10W
Ullared 114 Ch 57.08N 12.43 E
Ulldecona 126 Md 40.36N 0.27 E
Ullsfjorden 114 Eb 69.58N 20.00 E
Ullswater 118 Kg 54.34N 2.54W
Ullŭng-Do 154 Kf 37.29N 130.52 E
Ullvettern 116 Fe 59.25N 14.15 E
Ulm 120 Fh 48.25N 10.00 E
Ulmen 124 Id 50.13N 6.59 E
Ulmeni 130 Jd 45.04N 26.39 E
Ulmu 130 Je 44.16N 26.55 E
Ulongwé 172 Eb 14.43 S 34.21 E
Ulricehamn 116 Ch 57.47N 13.25 E
Ulrichstein 124 Ld 50.35N 9.12 E
Ulrum 124 Ia 53.22N 6.20 E
Ulrum-Zoutkamp 124 Ia 53.20N 6.18 E
Ulsan 152 Md 35.33N 129.19 E
Ulsteinvik 114 Ae 62.20N 5.53 E
Ulster 120 Ff 50.51N 9.59 E
Ulster/Ulaidh 118 Gg 54.30N 7.00W
Ulster Canal 118 Gg 54.27N 6.40W
Ulu 168 Ec 10.43N 33.29 E
Ulu/Uulu 116 Kf 58.13N 24.29 E
Ulua, Rio- 190 Ge 15.56N 87.43W
Ulubat Gölü 146 Cb 40.10N 28.35 E
Ulubey 146 Cc 38.09N 29.33 E
Uludağ 144 Ca 40.04N 29.13 E
Uludere 146 Jd 37.27N 42.51 E
Uluggat/Wuqia 152 Cd 39.40N 75.07 E
Ulukışla 146 Fd 37.33N 34.30 E
Ulungur He 140 Ke 46.58N 87.28 E
Ulungur Hu 152 Eb 47.20N 87.10 E
Ulus 146 Eb 41.35N 32.39 E
Ulus Dağ 130 Lj 39.18N 28.24 E
Ulva 118 Ge 56.28N 6.12W
Ulverston 118 Jg 54.12N 3.06W
Ulverstone 212 Jh 41.09 S 146.10 E
Ulvik 116 Bd 60.34N 6.54 E
Ulvön 116 Ha 63.05N 18.40 E
Ulysses 186 Fh 37.35N 101.22W
Ulytau 136 Gf 48.35N 67.05 E
Ulytau, gora- 136 Gf 48.45N 67.00 E
Uly-Žilanšik 136 Gf 48.51N 63.47 E
Uma 152 La 52.36N 120.38 E
Umag 128 He 45.25N 13.32 E
Umala 202 Eg 17.24 S 67.58W
Umán 192 Og 20.53N 89.45W
Uman 136 Df 48.47N 30.09 E
Uman 220d Bb 7.18N 151.53 E
'Umān=Oman (EN) [1] 142 Hg 21.00N 57.00 E
'Umān = Oman (EN) 140 Hg 22.10N 58.00 E
'Umān, Khalīj-=Oman, Gulf of- (EN) 140 Hg 25.00N 58.00 E
Umanak 179 Gd 70.36N 52.15W
Ùmánarssuaq/Farvel, Kap- 224 Nb 59.50N 43.50W
Umatac 220c Bb 13.18N 144.40 E
Umba 136 Db 66.41N 34.17 E
Umbelasha 168 Cd 9.51N 24.50 E
Umbertide 128 Gg 43.18N 12.20 E
Umboi Island 208 Fe 5.36 S 148.00 E
Umbozero, ozero- 114 Ic 67.45N 34.20 E
Umbria [2] 128 Gh 43.00N 12.30 E
Ume 172 Dc 17.15 S 28.20 E
Umeå 112 Ic 63.50N 20.15 E
Umeälven 110 Ic 63.47N 20.16 E
Umm al Arānib 164 Bd 26.08N 14.45 E
Umm al Hayf, Wādī- 144 Hf 18.37N 53.59 E
Umm al Jamaājim 146 Ki 26.59N 45.19 E
Umm al Qaywayn 144 Id 25.35N 55.34 E
Ummanz 120 Jb 54.30N 13.10 E
Umm ar Rizam 164 Dc 32.32N 23.00 E
Umm as Samīm 144 Ie 21.30N 56.45 E
Umm aṯ Ṭūz 146 Je 34.47N 42.42 E
Umm Bāb 146 Nj 25.12N 50.48 E
Umm Bel 168 Dc 13.32N 28.04 E
Umm Buru 168 Cb 15.01N 23.36 E
Umm Dhibbān 168 Dc 14.14N 29.37 E
Umm Durmān=Omdurman (EN) 160 Kg 15.38N 32.30 E
Umm Inderaba 168 Eb 15.12N 31.54 E
Umm Kaddādah 168 Dc 13.36N 26.42 E
Umm Lajj 144 Ed 25.04N 37.13 E
Umm Naqqāṭ, Jabal- 146 Fj 25.30N 34.14 E
Umm Qam'ul 146 Pj 24.47N 54.42 E
Umm Ruwābah 160 Kg 12.54N 31.13 E
Umm Sayyālah 168 Ec 14.25N 31.00 E
Umm Urūmah 146 Gj 25.46N 36.33 E
Umnak 174 Cd 58.25N 168.10W
Umne-Gobi 152 Fb 49.06N 91.43 E
Umpqua River 188 Ce 43.42N 124.03W
Umpulu 170 Ce 12.42 S 17.40 E
Umsini, Gunung- 150 Jg 1.35 S 133.30 E
Umtata 160 Jl 31.35 S 28.47 E
Umuarama 206 Jb 23.45 S 53.20W
Umurbey 130 Ji 40.14N 26.36 E
Umvukwes 172 Ec 17.01 S 30.52 E
Umvuma 172 Ec 19.19 S 30.35 E
Umzingwani 172 Dd 22.12 S 29.56 E
Una 128 Ke 45.16N 16.55 E
Unabetsu-Dake 156a Db 43.52N 144.51 E
Unac 128 Kf 44.29N 16.08 E
Unai 202 Ig 16.23 S 46.53W
Unalakleet 178 Gd 63.53N 160.47W
Unalaska 174 Cd 53.45N 166.45W
Unare, Rio- 196 Dg 10.06N 65.12W
Unauna, Pulau- 150 Hg 0.10 S 121.35 E
'Unayzah 146 Fg 30.29N 35.48 E
'Unayzah 142 Gg 26.06N 43.56 E
Uncia 202 Eg 18.27 S 66.37W
Uncompahgre Peak 182 Fd 38.04N 107.28W
Uncompahgre Plateau 186 Bg 38.30N 108.25W
Unden 116 Ff 58.45N 14.25 E
Underberg 172 De 29.50 S 29.22 E
Under-Han 142 Ne 47.19N 110.39 E
Undjuljung 138 Hc 66.20N 124.40 E
Undu Point 219d Cb 16.08 S 179.57W
Undva neem 116 If 58.25N 21.45 E
Undva neem / Kiprarenukk, mys- 116 If 58.25N 21.45 E
Uneča 132 Hc 52.50N 32.44 E
'Ung, Jabal al- 128 Dn 36.45N 9.35 E
Unga 178 Ge 55.15N 160.45W
Ungava, Péninsule d'-= Ungava Peninsula (EN) 174 Lc 60.00N 74.00W
Ungava Bay 174 Md 59.30N 67.30W
Ungava Peninsula (EN)= Ungava, Péninsule d'- 174 Lc 60.00N 74.00W
Ungen' 132 Ef 47.13N 27.50 E
Unggi 154 Kc 42.21N 130.23 E
Ungureni 130 Jb 47.53N 26.47 E
Ungwatiri 168 Fb 16.55N 36.05 E
União 202 Jd 4.35 S 42.52W
União da Vitória 206 Jc 26.13 S 51.05W
União dos Palmares 202 Ke 9.10 S 36.02W
Uničov 120 Ng 49.49N 17.07 E
Uniejów 120 Oe 51.58N 18.49 E
Unije 128 If 44.38N 14.15 E
Unimak 174 Cd 54.50N 164.00W
Unimak Pass 178 Gf 54.35N 164.43W
Unini, Rio- 202 Fd 1.41 S 61.30W
Union [Mo.-U.S.] 186 Kg 38.27N 91.00W
Union [S.C.-U.S.] 184 Gh 34.42N 81.37W
Union City 184 Cg 36.26N 89.03W
Unionale 172 Cf 33.40 S 23.08 E
Unión de Reyes 194 Gb 22.48N 81.32W
Unión de Tula 192 Gh 19.58N 104.16W
Union Island 196 Ff 12.36N 61.26W
Union Islands/Tokelau 208 Je 9.00 S 171.45W
Union Seamount (EN) 180 Eg 49.35N 132.45W
Union Springs 184 Ei 32.09N 85.49W
Uniontown 184 Hf 39.54N 79.44W
Unionville 186 Jf 40.29N 93.01W
United Arab Emirates (EN) = Al Imārāt al 'Arabīyah al Muttaḩidah [1] 142 Hg 24.00N 54.00 E
United Arab Republic (EN) → Egypt (EN) [1] 160 Jf 27.00N 30.00 E
United Kingdom [1] 112 Fe 54.00N 2.00W
United Kingdom of Great Britain and Northern Ireland [1] 112 Fe 54.00N 2.00W
United States [1] 176 Jf 38.00N 97.00W
United States of America [1] 176 Jf 38.00N 97.00W
Unity [Or.-U.S.] 188 Fd 44.29N 118.13W
Unity [Sask.-Can.] 180 Gf 52.27N 109.10W
University City 186 Kg 38.39N 90.19W
Unna 120 De 51.32N 7.41 E
Unnāb, Wādī al- 146 Gg 30.11N 36.39 E
Unnukka 116 Lb 62.25N 27.55 E
Unst 110 Fc 60.45N 0.55W
Unstrut 120 He 51.10N 11.48 E
Unterfranken 120 Fg 50.00N 10.00 E
Unterwalden nid dem Wald [2] 128 Cd 46.55N 8.30 E
Unterwalden ob dem Wald [2] 128 Cd 46.50N 8.20 E
Unuli Horog 152 Fd 35.12N 91.58 E
Ünye 144 Ea 41.08N 37.17 E
Unža 110 Kd 57.20N 43.08 E
Unzen-Dake 156 Be 32.45N 130.17 E
Uoleva 221b Ba 19.51 S 174.24W
Uozu 154 Nf 36.48N 137.24 E
Upa 120 Lf 50.22N 15.54 E
Upata 202 Fb 8.01N 62.24W
Upemba, Lac- 170 Ed 8.36 S 26.26 E
Upernavik 179 Gd 72.20N 56.00W
Upin 150 Ig 2.56 S 129.11 E
Upington 160 Jk 28.25 S 21.15 E
Upland 124 Kc 51.18N 8.42 E
Upolu Island 208 Jf 13.55 S 171.45W
Upolu Point 214 Oc 20.16N 155.52W
Upper [3] 166 Ec 10.30N 1.30W
Upper Arlington 184 Fe 40.01N 83.03W
Upper Arrow Lake 188 Ga 50.30N 117.55W
Upper Austria (EN) = Oberösterreich [2] 128 Hb 48.15N 14.00 E
Upper Hutt 218 Fd 41.07 S 175.04 E
Upper Klamath Lake 182 Cc 42.23N 122.00W
Upper Lake 188 Ef 41.44N 120.08W
Upper Lough Erne/Loch Eirne Uachtair 118 Fg 54.20N 7.30W
Upper Red Lake 186 Ib 48.10N 94.40W
Upper Sandusky 184 Fe 40.48N 83.17W
Upper Sheik 168 Hd 9.57N 45.09 E
Upper Thames Valley 118 Lj 51.40N 1.40W
Upper Trajan's Wall (EN) = Verhni Trajanov val 130 Lc 46.40N 29.00 E
Upper Volta (EN) → Burkina Faso [1] 160 Gg 13.00N 2.00W
Uppingham 124 Bb 52.35N 0.43W
Uppland 116 Gd 60.00N 17.50 E
Upplands Väsby 116 Ge 59.31N 17.54 E
Uppsala 112 Hd 59.52N 17.38 E
Uppsala [2] 114 Df 60.00N 17.45 E
Upsala 186 Kb 49.02N 90.29W
Upshi 148 Fb 33.50N 77.49 E
Upton 188 Md 44.06N 104.38W
Uqbān 164 Hf 15.30N 42.23 E
'Uqlat aş Şuqūr 146 Jj 25.53N 42.15 E
Uqturpan/Wushi 152 Cc 41.10N 79.16 E
Ur 144 Gc 30.58N 46.06 E
Urabá, Golfo de- 202 Cb 8.25N 77.00W
Uracoa 196 Eh 9.00N 62.21W
Uracoa, Rio- 196 Eh 9.08N 62.20W
Uradarja 135 Fe 38.51N 66.02 E
Urad Qianqi 152 Ic 40.49N 108.37 E
Urad Zhonghou Lianheqi (Haliut) 152 Ic 41.34N 108.32 E
Uraga-Suido 156 Fd 35.15N 139.45 E
Ura-Guba 114 Hb 69.18N 32.48 E
Urahoro 156a Cb 42.48N 143.38 E
Urahoro-Gawa 156a Cb 42.44N 143.40 E
Uraj 136 Gc 60.08N 64.40 E
Urakawa 154 Qc 42.09N 142.47 E
Ural 110 Lf 47.00N 51.48 E
Ural Mountains (EN) = Uralskije gory 110 Ld 57.00N 60.00 E
Uralsk 112 Le 51.14N 51.22 E
Uralskaja oblast [3] 136 Ff 49.45N 51.00 E
Uralskije gory = Ural Mountains (EN) 110 Ld 57.00N 60.00 E
Urambo 170 Fd 5.04 S 32.03 E
Uranium City 176 Id 59.34N 108.36W
Uraricoera 202 Fc 3.27N 60.59W
Uraricoera, Rio- 198 Je 3.02N 60.30W
Ura-Tjube 136 Gh 39.53N 69.01 E
Urawa 154 Og 35.51N 139.39 E
'Uray'irah 146 Mj 25.57N 48.53 E
Urayq, Nafūd al- 146 Jj 25.17N 42.25 E
Urbana [Il.-U.S.] 186 Lf 40.07N 88.12W
Urbana [Oh.-U.S.] 184 Fe 40.06N 83.45W
Urbandale 186 Jf 41.38N 93.48W
Urbania 128 Gg 43.40N 12.31 E
Urbano Santos 202 Jd 3.12 S 43.23W
Urbino 128 Gg 43.43N 12.38 E
Urbino, Étang d'- 122a Ba 42.02N 9.28 E
Urbión, Picos de- 126 Jb 42.01N 2.52W
Urcel 124 Fe 49.30N 3.33 E
Urcos 202 Df 13.42 S 71.38W
Urdinarrain 204 Ck 32.41 S 58.53W
Urdoma 114 Lf 61.47N 48.29 E
Urdžar 136 If 47.05N 81.37 E
Uré 194 Ji 7.46N 75.31W
Ure 118 Lg 54.01N 1.12W
Uren 136 Ed 57.29N 45.48 E
Urenui 218 Fc 39.00 S 174.23 E
Ures 190 Bc 29.26N 110.24W
Ureshino 156 Ab 33.06N 129.59 E
'Urf, Jabal al- 146 Ei 27.49N 32.55 E

Index Symbols

[1] Independent Nation
[2] State, Region
[3] District, County
[4] Municipality
[5] Colony, Dependency
Continent
Physical Region
Historical or Cultural Region
Mount, Mountain
Volcano
Hill
Mountains, Mountain Range
Hills, Escarpment
Plateau, Upland
Pass, Gap
Plain, Lowland
Delta
Salt Flat
Valley, Canyon
Crater, Cave
Karst Features
Depression
Polder
Desert, Dunes
Forest, Woods
Heath, Steppe
Oasis
Cape, Point
Coast, Beach
Cliff
Peninsula
Isthmus
Sandbank
Island
Atoll
Rock, Reef
Islands, Archipelago
Rocks, Reefs
Coral Reef
Well, Spring
Geyser
River, Stream
Waterfall, Rapids
River Mouth, Estuary
Lake
Salt Lake
Intermittent Lake
Reservoir
Swamp, Pond
Canal
Glacier
Ice Shelf, Pack Ice
Ocean
Sea
Gulf, Bay
Strait, Fjord
Lagoon
Bank
Seamount
Tablemount
Ridge
Shelf
Basin
Escarpment, Sea Scarp
Fracture
Trench, Abyss
National Park, Reserve
Point of Interest
Recreation Site
Cave, Cavern
Historic Site
Ruins
Wall, Walls
Church, Abbey
Temple
Scientific Station
Railway station
Airport
Port
Military installation
Lighthouse
Mine
Tunnel
Dam, Bridge

Urfa → Şanlıurfa 144 Eb 37.08N 38.46 E
Urfa Platosu 146 Hd 37.10N 38.50 E
Urgal 138 If 51.00N 132.50 E
Urgel, Llanos de-/Urgell, Pla d'- 126 Mc 41.25N 0.36 E
Urgell, Pla d'-/Urgel, Llanos de- 126 Mc 41.25N 0.36 E
Urgen 154 Ab 44.45N 110.40 E
Urgenč 142 Ie 41.33N 60.38 E
Ürgüp 146 Fc 38.38N 35.56 E
Urgut 136 Gh 39.23N 67.14 E
Uri 148 Eb 34.05N 74.02 E
Uri [2] 128 Cd 46.40N 8.30 E
Uribiá 202 Da 11.42N 72.17W
Uricki 136 Ge 53.19N 65.34 E
Urique, Rio- 192 Fd 26.29N 107.58W
Urjala 116 Jc 61.05N 23.32 E
Urjupinsk 136 Ee 50.48N 42.02 E
Urk 122 Lb 52.39N 5.36 E
Urkan 138 Hf 53.27N 126.56 E
Urla 146 Bc 38.18N 26.46 E
Urlaţi 130 Je 44.59N 26.14 E
Urluk 138 Ff 50.03N 107.55 E
Urmi 138 Ig 48.43N 134.16 E
Urmia, Lake- (EN) = Orūmīyeh, Daryācheh-ye- 140 Gf 37.40N 45.30 E
Uromi 166 Gd 6.42N 6.20 E
Uroševac 130 Eg 42.22N 21.10 E
Urshult 116 Fh 56.32N 14.47 E
Ursus 120 Qd 52.12N 20.53 E
Urtazym 134 Ij 52.15N 58.50 E
Urtigueira, Serra da- 204 Gg 24.15S 51.00W
Uru, Rio- 204 Hb 15.24S 49.36W
Uruaçu 202 If 14.30S 49.10W
Uruana 204 Hb 15.30S 49.41W
Uruapan del Progreso 190 De 19.25N 101.58W
Uruará, Rio- 202 Hd 2.00S 53.38W
Urubamba, Rio- 198 Ig 10.43S 73.48W
Urubici 204 Hi 28.02S 49.37W
Urubú, Cachoeira do- 204 Ha 12.52S 48.13W
Urucará 202 Gd 2.32S 57.45W
Uruçuí 202 Je 7.14S 44.33W
Urucuia, Rio- [Braz.] 204 Jc 16.08S 45.05W
Urucuia, Rio- [Braz.] 204 Ib 15.38S 46.10W
Urucum, Serra do- 204 Dd 19.13S 57.33W
Urucurituba 202 Gd 2.41S 57.40W
Uruguai, Rio- 198 Ki 34.12S 58.18W
Uruguaiana 200 Kh 29.45S 57.05W
Uruguay [1] 200 Ki 33.00S 56.00W
Uruguay, Rio- 198 Ki 34.12S 58.18W
Urukthapel 220a Ac 7.15N 134.24 E
Urumbaba Dağı 130 Lj 38.25N 28.49 E
Ürümqi 142 Ke 43.48N 87.35 E
Urup 132 Lg 44.59N 41.10 E
Urup, ostrov- 140 Qe 46.00N 150.00 E
Uruša 138 Hf 54.03N 122.55 E
Urussu 114 Mi 54.38N 53.24 E
Uruwira 170 Fd 6.27S 31.21 E
Urville, Cape d'- (EN) = Perkam, Tanjung- 150 Kg 1.28S 137.54 E
Uryū 156a Bb 43.39N 141.51 E
Uryū-Gawa 156a Bb 43.40N 141.54 E
Urziceni 130 Je 44.43N 26.38 E
Uržum 136 Fd 57.10N 50.01 E
Usa 156 Be 33.31N 131.22 E
Usa [Russia] 110 Lb 65.57N 56.55 E
Usa [Russia] 132 Nc 53.02N 45.18 E
Uşak 144 Cb 38.41N 29.25 E
Usakos 172 Bd 22.01S 15.32 E
Ušakovo 138 Hf 51.54N 126.35 E
Ušakovskoje 138 Nb 71.00N 178.35W
Usambara Mountains 158 Ki 4.45S 38.30 E
Usarp Mountains 222 Jf 71.10S 160.00 E
Usas Escarpment 222 Nf 76.00S 125.00W
Ušba, gora- 132 Mh 43.06N 42.40 E
Usborne, Mount- 206 Ih 51.42S 58.50W
Ušće 130 Df 43.29N 20.38 E
Usedom 120 Jb 54.00N 14.00 E
Useldange 124 He 49.46N 5.59 E
'Ushayrah 146 Kj 25.35N 45.46 E
'Ushayrah 164 He 21.46N 40.38 E
Ushibuka 156 Be 32.13N 130.01 E
Ushikubi-Misaki 156a Bc 41.08N 140.48 E
Ushimado 156 Dd 34.37N 134.09 E
'Ushsh, Wādī al- 146 Fd 27.18N 42.15 E
Ushuaia 200 Jk 54.47S 68.20W
Usingen 124 Kd 50.20N 8.32 E
Usinsk 136 Fb 65.57N 57.29 E
Üsküdar, İstanbul- 146 Cb 41.01N 29.03 E
Üsküp 130 Kh 41.44N 27.24 E
Uslar 120 Fe 51.40N 9.39 E
Úslava 120 Jg 49.54N 13.32 E
Usman 136 De 52.00N 39.43 E
Usman 132 Kd 51.54N 39.20 E
Usmas, ozero- / Usmas ezers 116 Ig 57.13N 22.00 E
Usmas ezers / Usmas, ozero- 116 Ig 57.13N 22.00 E
Usogorsk 136 Ec 63.28N 48.35 E
Usoke 170 Fd 5.06S 32.20 E
Usolje 136 Fd 59.25N 56.41 E
Usolje-Sibirskoje 138 Ff 52.47N 103.38 E
Usora 128 Mf 44.43N 18.04 E
Ussel 122 Ii 45.33N 2.19 E
Ussuri 140 Pe 48.28N 135.02 E
Ussurijsk 142 Pe 43.48N 131.59 E
Usta 114 Kh 56.53N 45.28 E
Ust-Barguzin 138 Ff 53.27N 108.59 E
Ust-Bolšereck 138 Kf 52.40N 156.18 E
Ust-Cilma 136 Fb 65.27N 52.06 E
Ust-Čorna 120 Uh 48.17N 24.02 E
Ust-Donecki 132 Lf 47.39N 40.55 E
Ust-Džeguta 132 Mg 44.05N 42.01 E
Uster 128 Cc 47.20N 8.43 E
Ustevatn 116 Bd 60.30N 8.00 E
Ust-Hajrjuzovo 138 Ke 57.04N 156.50 E
Ustica 128 Hl 38.42N 13.11 E
Ustica 110 Hh 38.42N 13.10 E
Ust-Ilimsk 142 Md 58.03N 102.43 E
Ustilug 120 Uf 50.50N 24.09 E
Ústí nad Labem 120 Kf 50.40N 14.02 E
Ústí nad Orlicí 120 Mg 49.58N 16.24 E
Ustinov → Iževsk 112 Ld 56.51N 53.14 E
Ust-Išim 136 Hd 57.44N 71.10 E
Ustja 136 Ec 61.33N 42.36 E
Ust-Judoma 138 Ie 59.10N 135.02 E
Ustjurt, plato- 140 He 43.00N 56.00 E
Ustjužna 114 Ig 58.53N 36.28 E
Ustka 120 Mb 54.35N 16.50 E
Ust-Kamčatsk 142 Sd 56.15N 162.30 E
Ust-Kamenogorsk 142 Ke 49.58N 82.38 E
Ust-Kan 138 Df 50.57N 84.55 E
Ust-Kara 136 Gb 69.15N 64.59 E
Ust-Karsk 138 Gf 52.41N 118.45 E
Ust-Katav 134 Ii 54.56N 58.10 E
Ust-Kujga 142 Pc 70.00N 135.36 E
Ust-Kut 142 Md 56.46N 105.40 E
Ust-Labinsk 136 Df 45.13N 39.40 E
Ust-Luga 114 Gg 59.39N 28.15 E
Ust-Maya 142 Pc 60.25N 134.32 E
Ust-Muja 138 Ge 56.28N 115.30 E
Ust-Nera 142 Qc 64.34N 143.12 E
Ust-Njukža 138 He 56.30N 121.48 E
Uštobe 136 Hf 45.13N 77.59 E
Ust-Olenëk 138 Gb 72.58N 119.42 E
Ust-Omčug 138 Jd 61.05N 149.30 E
Ust-Ordynski 138 Ff 52.48N 104.45 E
Ust-Ordynski Burjatski avtonomnyj okrug 138 Ff 53.30N 104.00 E
Ustovo 130 Hh 41.34N 24.47 E
Ust-Pinega 114 Jd 64.10N 41.58 E
Ust-Pit 138 Ee 58.59N 92.00 E
Ust-Port 138 Dc 69.45N 84.25 E
Ust-Požva 134 Hg 59.05N 56.05 E
Ustrzyki Dolne 120 Sg 49.26N 22.37 E
Ust-Sobolevka 138 Ig 46.10N 137.59 E
Ust-Šonoša 114 Jf 61.11N 41.20 E
Ust-Uda 138 Ff 54.10N 103.03 E
Ust-Ujskoje 134 Ki 54.15N 63.57 E
Ust-Umalta 138 If 51.42N 133.18 E
Ustupo 194 Ii 9.08N 77.56W
Usú 142 Ke 44.27N 84.37 E
Usui-Tōge 156 Fc 36.22N 138.38 E
Usuki 154 Kh 33.08N 131.49 E
Usuki-Wan 156 Be 33.10N 131.50 E
Usulután 194 Cg 13.21N 88.27W
Usumacinta 174 Jh 18.22N 92.40W
Ušumun 138 Hf 52.46N 126.37 E
Usu-San 156a Bb 42.32N 140.49 E
Usva 134 Hg 58.40N 57.35 E
Usva 134 Hg 58.17N 57.47 E
Utah [2] 182 Ed 39.30N 111.30W
Utah Lake 182 Ec 40.13N 111.49W
Utajärvi 114 Gd 64.45N 26.23 E
Utashinai 156a Cb 43.31N 142.03 E
Utata 138 Ff 50.51N 102.45 E
Ute Creek 186 Ei 35.21N 103.50W
Utembo 158 Jj 17.06S 22.01 E
Utena 114 Fi 55.29N 25.40 E
Ute Reservoir 186 Ei 35.21N 103.31W
Utete 170 Gd 7.59S 38.47 E
Uthai Thani 148 Ke 15.20N 100.02 E
Utiariti 204 Ca 13.02S 58.17W
Utica 182 Lc 43.06N 75.15W
Utiel 126 Ke 39.34N 1.12W
Utiel, Sierra de- 126 Ke 39.36N 1.08W
Utila 194 De 16.06N 86.54W
Utila, Isla de- 194 De 16.06N 86.56W
Utique 128 Em 37.04N 10.04 E
Utirik Atoll 208 Hc 11.15N 169.48 E
Utlängan 116 Fh 56.00N 15.45 E
Utljukski liman 132 If 46.20N 35.15 E
Uto 154 Kh 32.40N 130.41 E
Utö [Fin.] 116 Ie 59.45N 21.25 E
Utö [Swe.] 114 Eg 58.55N 18.15 E
Utorgoš 116 Nf 58.17N 30.15 E
Utoro 156a Da 44.06N 144.58 E
Utrata 120 Qd 52.13N 20.15 E
Utrecht [3] 124 Hb 52.05N 5.08 E
Utrecht [Neth.] 112 Ge 52.05N 5.08 E
Utrecht [S.Afr.] 172 Ee 27.28S 30.20 E
Utrera 126 Gg 37.11N 5.47W
Utsira 116 Ae 59.20N 4.55 E
Utsjoki 114 Gb 69.53N 27.00 E
Utsunomiya 142 Pf 36.33N 139.52 E
Uttaradit 148 Ke 17.38N 100.06 E
Uttarkāshi 148 Fb 30.45N 78.19 E
Uttar Pradesh [3] 148 Fc 28.00N 80.00 E
Utuado 194 Nd 18.16N 66.42W
Utukok 178 Gb 70.04N 162.18W
Utuloa 220h Ab 13.16S 176.11W
Utupua Island 208 Hf 11.20S 166.36 E
Uturoa 221e Db 16.44S 151.26W
Utva 132 Rd 51.29N 52.40 E
Uudenmaa [2] 114 Ff 60.30N 25.00 E
Uukuniemi 116 Nc 61.47N 30.01 E
Uulu/Ulu 116 Kf 58.13N 24.29 E
Uusikaupunki/Nystad 114 Ef 60.48N 21.25 E
Uusimaa 116 Kd 60.30N 25.00 E
Uva 136 Fd 56.58N 52.14 E
Uvac 130 Cf 43.36N 19.30 E
Uvalde 182 Hf 29.13N 99.47W
Uvarovo 136 Ee 52.00N 42.15 E
Uvdal 116 Cd 60.20N 8.30 E
Uvéa, Ile- 208 Jf 13.18S 176.10W
Uvelka 134 Ji 54.05N 61.35 E
Uvelski 134 Ji 54.26N 61.27 E
Uvildy, ozero- 134 Ji 55.35N 60.30 E
Uvinza 170 Fd 5.06S 30.22 E
Uvira 160 Ji 3.24S 29.08 E
Uvs Nuur → Ubsu-Nur 140 Ld 50.20N 92.45 E
Uwa 156 Ce 33.21N 132.30 E
Uwajima 152 Ne 33.13N 132.34 E
Uwajima-Wan 156 Ce 33.15N 132.30 E
Uwa-Kai 156 Ce 33.20N 132.15 E
Uwayl 168 Dd 8.46N 27.24 E
'Uwaynāt, Jabal al- = Uweinat, Gebel- (EN) 158 Jf 21.54N 24.58 E
'Uwaynat Wannīn 164 Bd 28.05N 12.59 E
Uweinat, Gebel- (EN) = 'Uwaynāt, Jabal al- 158 Jf 21.54N 24.58 E
Uwekuli 150 Hg 1.25S 121.06 E
Uwi, Pulau- 150 Ef 1.05N 107.24 E
Uxin Qi (Dabqig) 152 Id 38.27N 109.08 E
Uxmal 176 Kg 20.20N 89.46W
Uyo 166 Gd 5.07N 7.57 E
Uyuni 200 Jh 20.28S 66.50W
Uyuni, Salar de- 198 Jh 20.20S 67.42W
Už [Eur.] 120 Rh 48.33N 22.00 E
Už [Ukr.] 132 Gd 51.15N 30.12 E
Uzbekistan (EN) = Ŭzbekiston 136 Gg 41.00N 64.00 E
Uzbekiston Sovet Socialistik Respublikasy/Uzbekskaja SSR → Ŭzbekiston 136 Gg 41.00N 64.00 E
Uzbekskaja Sovetskaja Socialističeskaja Respublika → Ŭzbekiston 136 Gg 41.00N 64.00 E
Uzbekskaja SSR/Uzbekiston Sovet Socialistik Respublikasy → Ŭzbekiston 136 Gg 41.00N 64.00 E
Ŭzbekiston = Uzbekistan (EN) 136 Gg 41.00N 64.00 E
Uzbel Shankou 152 Bd 38.42N 73.48 E
Uzen 136 Fg 43.22N 52.50 E
Uzerche 122 Hi 45.25N 1.34 E
Uzès 122 Kj 44.01N 4.25 E
Uzgen 135 Id 40.44N 73.21 E
Užgorod 136 Cf 48.37N 22.22 E
Užice (Titovo Užice) 130 Cf 43.52N 19.51 E
Uzin 132 Ge 49.52N 30.27 E
Uzlovaja 132 Kb 54.01N 38.12 E
Uzlovoje 120 Sh 48.23N 22.27 E
Užokski, pereval- 132 Ce 49.02N 22.58 E
Uzümlü 130 Mm 36.44N 29.14 E
Uzun Ada 130 Jk 38.28N 26.42 E
Uzunagač [Kaz.] 135 Kc 43.36N 76.19 E
Uzunagač [Kaz.] 135 Kc 43.08N 76.20 E
Uzunköprü 146 Bb 41.16N 26.41 E
Užur 138 De 55.20N 90.00 E
Užventis 116 Ji 55.44N 22.37 E
Uzynkair, mys- 135 Bb 45.47N 59.20 E

V

Vääksy 116 Kc 61.11N 25.33 E
Vaal 158 Jk 29.24S 23.38 E
Vaala 114 Gd 64.34N 26.50 E
Vaals 124 Id 50.46N 6.01 E
Vaalwater 172 Dd 24.20S 28.03 E
Vaasa [2] 114 Fe 63.12N 23.00 E
Vaasa/Vasa 112 Ic 63.06N 21.36 E
Vaassen, Epe- 124 Hb 52.17N 5.58 E
Vabalninkas 116 Ki 55.58N 24.49 E
Vác 120 Pi 47.47N 19.08 E
Vacacai, Rio- 204 Fi 29.55S 53.06W
Vacaria 206 Jc 28.30S 50.56W
Vacaria, Rio- 204 Fe 21.55S 53.59W
Vacaville 188 Eg 38.21N 121.59W
Vaccarès, Étang de- 122 Kk 43.32N 4.34 E
Vache, Ile à- 194 Kd 18.04N 73.38W
Väddö 116 Hd 60.00N 18.50 E
Vadehavet 116 Ci 55.15N 8.40 E
Vădeni 130 Kd 45.22N 27.56 E
Vadheim 116 Ac 61.13N 5.49 E
Vadodara 142 Jg 22.18N 73.12 E
Vado Ligure 128 Cf 44.17N 8.27 E
Vadsø 112 Ia 70.05N 29.46 E
Vadstena 114 Dg 58.27N 14.54 E
Vaduz 112 Gf 47.08N 9.30 E
Værlandet 116 Ac 61.20N 4.45 E
Vaga 110 Kc 62.48N 42.56 E
Vagaj 134 Mh 56.28N 67.18 E
Vagaj 134 Nh 57.55N 69.01 E
Vågåmo 114 Bf 61.53N 9.06 E
Vaganski vrh 128 Jf 44.21N 15.30 E
Vågåvatn 116 Cc 61.50N 8.50 E
Vaggeryd 114 Dh 57.30N 14.07 E
Vaghena 219a Cb 7.25S 157.43 E
Vagil 134 Kg 59.45N 62.40 E
Vagis, gora- 138 Jf 52.20N 142.15 E
Vagnhärad 116 Gf 58.57N 17.31 E
Vågsøy 116 Ac 62.00N 5.05 E
Váh 120 Ni 47.55N 18.00 E
Vah 140 Jc 60.45N 76.45 E
Vahitahi Atoll 208 Nf 18.44S 138.52W
Vahruši 114 Mg 58.43N 50.02 E
Vahš 135 Gf 37.43N 68.49 E
Vahsel Bay → Herzog-Ernst-Bucht 222 Af 77.48S 34.39W
Vahtan 114 Lh 57.59N 46.42 E
Vaiaau 221e Db 16.52S 151.28W
Vaigat 179 Gd 70.30N 54.00W
Vaihingen an der Enz 124 Kf 48.56N 8.58 E
Vaihu 221d Ab 27.10S 109.23W
Väike-Maarja/Vjaike-Maarja 116 Le 59.04N 26.12 E
Väike-Pakri/Vjajke-Pakri 116 Je 59.50N 23.50 E
Väike Väin / Vjajke-Vjajn 116 Jf 58.30N 23.10 E
Vailala 220h Bb 13.13S 176.09W
Vailala, Pointe- 220h Ab 13.13S 176.10W
Vaileka 219d Bb 17.23S 178.09 E
Vailheu, Récif- 172 Gb 11.48S 43.04 E
Vailly-sur-Aisne 124 Fe 49.25N 3.31 E
Vainikkala 116 Md 60.52N 28.18 E
Vainode/Vajnëde 116 Ih 56.26N 21.45 E
Vairaatea Atoll 208 Nf 19.19S 139.20W
Vaison-la-Romaine 122 Lj 44.14N 5.04 E
Vaitape 221e Db 16.31S 151.45W
Vaitoare 221e Db 16.41S 151.28W
Vaitupu Island 208 Ie 7.28S 178.41 E
Vajgač, ostrov- 110 La 70.00N 59.30 E
Vajnëde/Vainode 116 Ih 56.26N 21.45 E
Vakaga [3] 168 Cd 10.00N 23.30 E
Vakfıkebir 146 Hb 41.03N 39.20 E
Vaksdal 116 Ad 60.29N 5.44 E
Val 138 Jf 52.19N 143.09 E
Vala 114 Mh 56.59N 51.16 E
Valaam 114 Hf 61.24N 30.59 E
Valaam, ostrov- 116 Nc 61.20N 31.05 E
Valahia = Walachia (EN) 110 Ig 44.00N 25.00 E
Valahia = Walachia (EN) 130 He 44.00N 25.00 E
Valais / Wallis [2] 128 Bd 46.15N 7.30 E
Valamarës, Mali i- 130 Di 40.47N 20.28 E
Valamaz 114 Mh 57.36N 52.14 E
Valandovo 130 Fh 41.19N 22.34 E
Valašské Meziříčí 120 Ng 49.29N 17.58 E
Valáxa 130 Hk 38.49N 24.29 E
Vålberg 116 Ee 59.24N 13.12 E
Valburg 124 Hc 51.55N 5.49 E
Valcabra 126 Jg 37.30N 2.43W
Vâlčedrâm 130 Gf 43.42N 23.27 E
Valcheta 206 Gf 40.42S 66.09W
Valdagno 128 Fe 45.39N 11.18 E
Valdahon 122 Mg 47.09N 6.21 E
Valdai Hills (EN) = Valdajskaja vozvyšennost 110 Jd 57.00N 33.30 E
Valdaj 136 Dd 57.59N 33.14 E
Valdajskaja vozvyšennost = Valdai Hills (EN) 110 Jd 57.00N 33.30 E
Valdarno 128 Fg 43.45N 11.15 E
Valdavia 126 Hb 42.24N 4.16W
Valdecañas, Embalse de- 126 Ge 39.45N 5.30W
Valdeganga 126 Ke 39.09N 1.40W
Val-de-Marne [3] 122 If 48.47N 2.29 E
Valdemārpils/Valdemarpils 114 Fh 57.24N 22.39 E
Valdemarpils/Valdemārpils 114 Fh 57.24N 22.39 E
Valdemarsvik 114 Dg 58.12N 16.32 E
Valdepeñas 126 If 38.46N 3.23W
Valderaduey 126 Gc 41.31N 5.42W
Valderas 126 Gb 42.05N 5.27W
Valderrama, Cienaga de- 194 Ki 8.56N 72.10W
Valderrobres/Vall-de-roures 126 Md 40.53N 0.09 E
Valdés, Peninsula- 198 Jj 42.30S 64.00W
Valdez 176 Ec 61.07N 146.16W
Val d'Isère 122 Mi 45.27N 6.59 E
Valdivia 200 Ii 39.48S 73.14W
Valdivia Seamount (EN) 158 Hk 25.20S 6.15 E
Valdobbiadene 128 Fe 45.54N 12.00 E
Val-d'Oise [3] 122 Ie 49.10N 2.10 E
Val-d'Or 176 Le 48.07N 77.47W
Valdosta 176 Kf 30.50N 83.17W
Valdres 116 Cc 60.55N 9.10 E
Vale [Geor.] 132 Mi 41.36N 42.51 E
Vale [Or.-U.S.] 188 Gd 44.01N 117.15W
Valea lerii 130 Gc 46.39N 23.21 E
Valea lui Mihai 130 Fb 47.31N 22.09 E
Valea Vişeului 130 Hb 47.54N 24.10 E
Valença [Braz.] 204 Kf 22.15S 43.43W
Valença [Braz.] 202 Kf 13.22S 39.05W
Valença do Minho 126 Db 42.02N 8.38W
Valença do Piauí 202 Je 6.24S 41.45W
Valençay 122 Hg 47.09N 1.34 E
Valence [Fr.] 122 Gj 44.06N 0.55 E
Valence [Fr.] 122 Kj 44.56N 4.54 E
Valencia 200 Jd 10.11N 68.00W
Valencia 126 Le 39.30N 0.40W
València/Valencia 112 Fh 39.28N 0.22W
Valencia/València 112 Fh 39.28N 0.22W
Valencia / València [3] 126 Le 39.20N 0.50W
València / Valencia [3] 126 Le 39.20N 0.50W
València, Golf de-/Valencia, Golfo de- 110 Fh 39.30N 0.00
Valencia, Golfo de-/València, Golf de- 110 Fh 39.30N 0.00
Valencia, Lago de- 196 Cg 10.11N 67.45W
Valencia de Alcántara 126 Ee 39.25N 7.14W
Valencia de Don Juan 126 Gb 42.18N 5.31W
Valencia-El Grao 126 Le 39.27N 0.20W
Valenciennes 122 Jd 50.21N 3.32 E
Vălenii de Munte 130 Jd 45.11N 26.02 E
Valentia/Dairbhre 118 Cj 51.55N 10.20W
Valentin 154 Mc 43.07N 134.19 E
Valentine 182 Gc 42.52N 100.33W
Valenza 128 Ce 45.01N 8.38 E
Våler 114 Cf 60.40N 11.50 E
Valera 202 Db 9.19N 70.37W
Valga 136 Cd 57.49N 26.05 E
Valge jõgi 116 Ke 59.32N 25.36 E
Valhalla Mountains 188 Gb 49.45N 117.48W
Valiente, Peninsula- 194 Gi 9.05N 81.51W
Valier 188 Ib 48.18N 112.15W
Valinco, Golfe de- 122a Ab 41.40N 8.49 E
Valjevo 130 Ce 44.16N 19.53 E
Valka 114 Gh 57.47N 26.01 E
Valkeakoski 114 Ff 61.16N 24.02 E
Valkeala 116 Ld 60.57N 26.48 E
Valkenswaard 124 Hc 51.21N 5.28 E
Valkininkai/Valkininkaj 116 Kj 54.18N 25.55 E
Valkininkaj/Valkininkai 116 Kj 54.18N 25.55 E
Valko/Valkom 116 Ld 60.25N 26.15 E
Valkom/Valko 116 Ld 60.25N 26.15 E
Valkumej 138 Mc 69.41N 170.30 E
Valladolid [3] 126 Hc 41.35N 4.40W
Valladolid [Mex.] 190 Gd 20.41N 88.12W
Valladolid [Sp.] 112 Fg 41.39N 4.43W
Valldal 116 Bb 62.20N 7.21 E
Vall-de-Roures/Valderrobres 126 Md 40.53N 0.09 E
Vall de Uxó / La Vall d'Uxó 126 Le 39.49N 0.14W
Valle 114 Bg 59.12N 7.32 E
Valle [Col.] [3] 202 Cc 3.40N 76.30W
Valle [Hond.] [3] 194 Dg 13.30N 87.35W
Vallecas, Madrid- 126 Id 40.23N 3.37W
Valle d'Aosta / Vallée d'Aoste [2] 128 Be 45.45N 7.15 E
Valle de Cabuérniga 126 Ha 43.14N 4.18W
Valle de Guanape 196 Dh 9.54N 65.41W
Valle dei Templi 128 Hm 37.18N 13.35 E
Valle de la Pascua 202 Eb 9.13N 66.00W
Valle de los Caidos 126 Hd 40.39N 4.09W
Valle de Santiago 192 Ig 20.23N 101.12W
Valle de Topia 192 Fe 25.13N 106.25W
Valle de Zaragoza 192 Gd 27.28N 105.49W
Valledupar 202 Da 10.28N 73.15W
Vallée d'Aoste / Valle d'Aosta [2] 128 Be 45.45N 7.15 E
Vallée Jonction 184 Lb 46.23N 70.55W
Valle Hermoso 192 Ke 25.39N 97.52W
Vallejera, Puerto de- 126 Gd 40.30N 5.42W
Vallejo 182 Cd 38.07N 122.14W
Vallejo, Sierra de- 192 Gg 20.55N 105.20W
Valle Nacional 192 Ki 17.47N 96.19W
Vallenar 200 Ih 28.35S 70.46W
Vallentuna 116 He 59.32N 18.05 E
Vallès / Vallés 126 Oc 41.35N 2.15 E
Valletta 112 Hh 35.54N 14.31 E
Valley City 182 Hb 46.55N 97.59W
Valley Falls 188 Ee 42.31N 120.15W
Valleyfield 180 Kg 45.15N 74.08W
Valley Station 184 Ef 38.06N 85.52W
Valleyview 180 Fe 55.02N 117.08W
Vallgrund 114 Ee 63.12N 21.14 E
Vallhagar 116 Hg 57.20N 18.10 E
Vallimanca 204 Bm 36.21S 61.02W
Vallimanca, Arroyo- 204 Bl 35.40S 60.02W
Vallo della Lucania 128 Jj 40.14N 15.16 E
Valloires, Abbaye de- 124 Dd 50.20N 1.47 E
Vallorbe 128 Ad 46.43N 6.23 E
Valls 126 Nc 41.17N 1.15 E
Valls d'Andorra → Andorra [1] 112 Gg 42.30N 1.30 E
Vallsta 116 Gc 61.32N 16.22 E
Vallvik 116 Gc 61.11N 17.11 E
Valmaseda / Balmaseda 126 Ia 43.12N 3.12W
Valmiera 136 Cd 57.32N 25.29 E
Valmont 124 Ce 49.44N 0.31 E
Valnera 126 Ia 43.10N 3.45W
Valognes 122 Ee 49.31N 1.28W
Valois, Plaine du- 122 Ie 49.10N 2.45 E
Valoria la Buena 126 Hc 41.48N 4.32W
Valpaços 126 Ec 41.36N 7.19W
Valparaiso 184 De 41.28N 87.03W
Valparaíso 200 Ii 33.02S 71.38W
Valparaiso [Braz.] 204 Ge 21.13S 50.51W
Valparaiso [Mex.] 192 Hf 22.46N 103.34W
Valpovo 128 Me 45.39N 18.25 E
Valréas 122 Kj 44.23N 4.59 E
Vals 158 Jk 27.23S 26.31 E
Vals, Tanjung- 150 Kh 8.26S 137.38 E
Valsjöbyn 114 Dd 64.04N 14.08 E
Valtellina 128 Dd 46.10N 9.55 E
Valtimo 114 Ge 63.40N 28.48 E
Váltou, Óri- 130 Ej 39.10N 21.20 E
Valujki 136 De 50.12N 38.08 E
Valul-Lui Traian 130 Le 44.15N 28.30 E
Valverde 162 Dd 27.48N 17.55W
Valverde de Júcar 126 Je 39.43N 2.12W
Valverde del Camino 126 Fg 37.34N 6.45W
Valverde del Fresno 126 Fd 40.13N 6.52W
Vamdrup 116 Ci 55.25N 9.17 E
Våmhus 114 Df 61.08N 14.28 E
Vamizi, Ilha- 172 Gb 11.02S 40.40 E
Vammala 114 Ff 61.20N 22.54 E
Vámos 130 Hn 35.25N 24.12 E
Van 144 Fb 38.28N 43.20 E
Van, Lake- (EN) = Van Gölü 140 Gf 38.33N 42.46 E
Vanajanselkä 114 Ff 61.09N 24.15 E
Vanak 146 Ng 31.32N 51.19 E
Vanak 146 Ng 31.41N 50.52 E
Vanån 116 Fd 60.31N 14.14 E
Vanault-les-Dames 124 Gf 48.51N 4.46 E
Vanavana Atoll 208 Ng 20.47S 139.09W
Vanavara 138 Fd 60.22N 102.16 E
Van Buren [Ar.-U.S.] 186 Ii 35.26N 94.21W
Van Buren [Me.-U.S.] 184 Nb 47.09N 67.56W
Vanč 135 He 38.23N 71.29 E
Vanceburg 184 Ff 38.36N 83.19W
Vancouver [B.C.-Can.] 176 Ge 49.16N 123.07W
Vancouver [Wa.-U.S.] 182 Cb 45.39N 122.40W
Vancouver Island 174 Ge 49.45N 126.00W
Vandalia [Il.-U.S.] 186 Lg 38.58N 89.06W
Vandalia [Oh.-U.S.] 184 Ef 39.53N 84.12W
Vanderbijl Park 172 De 26.42S 27.54 E
Vanderhoof 180 Ff 54.01N 124.01W
Vanderlin Island 212 Hc 15.45S 137.00 E
Van Diemen, Cape- 212 Gb 11.10S 130.25 E
Van Diemen Gulf 212 Gb 11.50S 132.00 E
Vandmtor, ozero- 134 Le 62.15N 65.45 E
Vändra/Vjandra 114 Fg 58.40N 25.01 E
Vänern 110 Hd 58.55N 13.30 E
Vänersborg 114 Cg 58.22N 12.19 E
Vang 116 Cc 61.08N 8.35 E
Vangaindrano 172 Hd 23.23S 47.33 E
Van Gölü = Van, Lake- (EN) 140 Gf 38.33N 42.46 E
Vangunu Island 208 Ge 8.40S 158.05 E
Van Horn 182 Ge 31.03N 104.50W
Vanick, Rio- 204 Fa 13.06S 52.52W
Vanier 180 Hb 76.00N 103.50W
Vanikolo 219c Bb 11.37S 166.58 E
Vanikolo Islands 208 Hf 11.37S 167.03 E
Vanimo 214 Ch 2.40S 141.18 E
Vanino 138 Jg 49.11N 140.19 E
Vankavesi 116 Jc 61.50N 23.50 E
Vanna 114 Ea 70.09N 19.51 E
Vännäs 114 Ee 63.55N 19.45 E
Vanne 124 Jf 48.12N 3.16 E
Vannes 122 Dg 47.40N 2.45W
Van Ninh 148 Lf 12.42N 109.14 E
Vannsjø 116 De 59.25N 10.50 E

Index Symbols

- ① Independent Nation
- ② State, Region
- ③ District, County
- ④ Municipality
- ⑤ Colony, Dependency
- ■ Continent
- ✖ Physical Region

- Historical or Cultural Region
- Mount, Mountain
- Volcano
- Hill
- Mountains, Mountain Range
- Hills, Escarpment
- Plateau, Upland

- Pass, Gap
- Plain, Lowland
- Delta
- Salt Flat
- Valley, Canyon
- Crater, Cave
- Karst Features

- Depression
- Polder
- Desert, Dunes
- Forest, Woods
- Heath, Steppe
- Oasis
- Cape, Point

- Coast, Beach
- Cliff
- Peninsula
- Isthmus
- Sandbank
- Island
- Atoll

- Rock, Reef
- Islands, Archipelago
- Rocks, Reefs
- Coral Reef
- Well, Spring
- Geyser
- River, Stream

- Waterfall, Rapids
- River Mouth, Estuary
- Lake
- Salt Lake
- Ocean
- Sea
- Gulf, Bay
- Strait, Fjord

- Canal
- Glacier
- Ice Shelf, Pack Ice
- Intermittent Lake
- Reservoir
- Shelf
- Basin

- Lagoon
- Bank
- Fracture
- Seamount
- Tablemount
- Ridge
- Point of Interest

- Escarpment, Sea Scarp
- Trench, Abyss
- National Park, Reserve
- Recreation Site
- Cave, Cavern

- Historic Site
- Ruins
- Wall, Walls
- Church, Abbey
- Temple
- Scientific Station
- Railway station

- Airport
- Port
- Military installation
- Lighthouse
- Mine
- Tunnel
- Dam, Bridge

Viana do Castelo 126 Dc 41.42N 8.50W
Viana do Castelo [2] 126 Dc 41.55N 8.25W
Vianden 124 Ie 49.55N 6.16 E
Vianen 124 Hb 52.00N 5.05 E
Viangchan (Vientiane) 142 Mh 17.58N 102.36 E
Vianópolis 204 Hc 16.45S 48.32W
Viar 126 Gg 37.36N 5.50W
Viareggio 128 Eg 43.52N 10.14 E
Viarmes 124 Ee 49.08N 2.22 E
Viaur 122 Hj 44.08N 1.58 E
Viborg 114 Bh 56.26N 9.24 E
Viborg [2] 116 Ch 56.30N 9.30 E
Vibo Valentia 128 Kl 38.40N 16.06 E
Vic 126 Oc 41.56N 2.15 E
Vicari 128 Hm 37.49N 13.34 E
Vicecomodoro Marambio 222 Re 64.16S 56.44W
Vicente Guerrero 190 Dd 23.45N 103.59W
Vicenza 128 Fe 45.33N 11.33 E
Vichada [3] 202 Ec 5.00N 69.30W
Vichada, Río- 198 Je 4.55N 67.50W
Vichadero 204 Ej 31.48S 54.43W
Vichy 122 Jh 46.07N 3.25 E
Vicksburg 182 Ie 32.14N 90.56W
Vico, Lago di- 128 Gh 42.19N 12.10 E
Vic-sur-Aisne 124 Fe 49.24N 3.07 E
Vic-sur-Cère 122 Ij 44.59N 2.37 E
Victor Bay 222 Ie 66.20S 136.30 E
Victor Harbour 212 Hg 35.34S 138.37 E
Victoria [2] 212 Ig 38.00S 145.00 E
Victoria 174 Hb 71.00N 114.00W
Victoria [Arg.] 206 Hd 32.37S 60.10W
Victoria [B.C.-Can.] 176 Ge 48.25N 123.22W
Victoria [Cam.] 166 Ge 4.01N 9.12 E
Victoria [Chile] 206 Fe 38.13S 72.20W
Victoria [Gren.] 196 Ff 12.12N 61.42W
Victoria [Mala.] 150 Ge 5.17N 115.15 E
Victoria [Malta] 128 In 36.02N 14.14 E
Victoria [Rom.] 130 Hd 45.44N 24.41 E
Victoria [Sey.] 160 Mi 4.38S 55.27 E
Victoria [Tx.-U.S.] 176 Jg 28.48N 97.00W
Victoria/Ying zhan 142 Ng 22.17N 114.09 E
Victoria, Lake- [Afr.] 158 Ki 1.00S 33.00 E
Victoria, Lake- [Austl.] 212 If 34.00S 141.15 E
Victoria, Mount- [Bur.] 140 Lg 21.14N 93.55 E
Victoria, Mount- [Pap.N.Gui.] 208 Fe 8.53S 147.33 E
Victoria, Sierra de la- 204 Fg 25.55S 54.00W
Victoria and Albert Mountains 180 Ka 79.00N 75.00W
Victoria de Durango 176 Ig 24.02N 104.40W
Victoria de las Tunas 190 Id 20.58N 76.57W
Victoria Falls 160 Jj 17.56S 25.50 E
Victoria Falls 158 Jj 17.55S 25.21 E
Victoria Fjord 179 Hb 82.20N 48.00W
Victoria Land (EN) 222 Jf 75.00S 159.00 E
Victoria Nile 158 Kh 2.14N 31.26 E
Victoria Peak [B.C.-Can.] 188 Ba 50.03N 126.06W
Victoria Peak [Blz.] 194 Ce 16.48N 88.37W
Victoria River 208 Df 15.12S 129.43 E
Victoria River Downs 212 Gc 16.24S 131.00 E
Victoria Strait 180 Hc 69.30N 100.00W
Victoriaville 180 Kg 46.03N 71.58W
Victoria West 172 Cf 31.25S 23.04 E
Victorville 188 Gi 34.32N 117.18W
Victory, Mount- 212 Ja 9.10S 149.05 E
Vičuga 136 Ed 57.15N 42.00 E
Vicuña 206 Fc 29.59S 70.44W
Vicuña Mackenna 206 Hd 33.54S 64.23W
Vidå 116 Cj 54.58N 8.41 E
Vidal 188 Hi 34.11N 114.34W
Vidalia 186 Kk 31.34N 91.26W
Videbæk 116 Ch 56.05N 8.38 E
Videira 206 Jc 27.00S 51.08W
Videla 204 Bj 30.56S 60.39W
Videle 130 Ie 44.17N 25.31 E
Vidigueira 126 Ef 38.13N 7.48W
Vidin 130 Ff 43.59N 22.52 E
Vidin [2] 130 Ff 43.59N 22.52 E
Vidisha 148 Fd 23.42N 77.47 E
Vidlič 130 Ff 43.08N 22.47 E
Vidojevica 130 Ef 43.10N 21.32 E
Vidöstern 116 Fg 57.04N 14.01 E
Vidourle 122 Kk 43.32N 4.08 E
Vidra [Rom.] 130 Jd 45.55N 26.54 E
Vidra [Rom.] 130 Je 44.16N 26.09 E
Vidsel 114 Ed 65.49N 20.31 E
Viduša 128 Mh 42.54N 18.18 E
Vidzeme 116 Kg 57.10N 26.00 E
Vidzemes Augstiene / Vidzemskaja vozvyšennost 116 Kh 56.45N 26.00 E
Vidzemskaja vozvyšennost / Vidzemes Augstiene 116 Kh 56.45N 26.00 E
Vidzy 116 Li 55.23N 26.47 E
Vie 124 Be 49.09N 0.04W
Viechtach 120 Ig 49.05N 12.53 E
Viedma 200 Jj 40.50S 63.00W
Viedma, Lago- 198 Ij 49.35S 72.35W
Vieille Case 197g Ba 15.36N 61.24W
Vieja, Sierra- 186 Dk 30.30N 104.40W
Viejo, Cerro- 190 Bb 30.20N 112.15W
Viekšniai/Viekšnjai 116 Jh 56.14N 22.28 E
Viekšnjai/Viekšniai 116 Jh 56.14N 22.28 E
Vielha / Viella 126 Mb 42.42N 0.48 E
Viella / Vielha 126 Mb 42.42N 0.48 E
Vielsalm 124 Hd 50.17N 5.55 E
Viels-Maisons 124 Ff 48.54N 3.24 E
Vienna [Mo.-U.S.] 186 Kg 38.11N 91.57W
Vienna [W.V.-U.S.] 184 Gf 39.20N 81.33W
Vienna (EN) = Wien 112 Hf 48.12N 16.22 E
Vienna Woods (EN) = Wienerwald 128 Jb 48.10N 16.00 E
Vienne 122 Ki 45.31N 4.52 E
Vienne [3] 122 Gh 46.30N 0.30 E
Vienne 110 Gf 47.13N 0.05 E
Vientiane → Viangchan 142 Mh 17.58N 102.36 E
Vientos, Paso de los- = Windward Passage (EN) 174 Lh 20.00N 73.50W
Vieques, Isla de- 190 Ke 18.08N 65.25W
Vieques, Pasaje de- 197a Cb 18.08N 65.40W
Vieques, Sonda de- 197a Cb 18.17N 65.25W
Vierge Point 197b Kb 13.49N 60.53W
Viernheim 124 Ke 49.32N 8.35 E
Viersen 120 Ce 51.15N 6.23 E
Vierville-sur-Mer 124 Be 49.22N 0.54W
Vierwaldstätter See = Lucerne, Lake- (EN) 128 Cc 47.00N 8.30 E
Vierzon 122 Ig 47.13N 2.05 E
Viesca 192 He 25.21N 102.48W
Viesite/Viesīte 116 Kh 56.20N 25.38 E
Viesīte/Viesite 116 Kh 56.20N 25.38 E
Vieste 128 Ki 41.53N 16.10 E
Viet Nam = Vietnam (EN) [1] 142 Mh 13.00N 108.00 E
Vietnam (EN) = Viet Nam [1] 142 Mh 13.00N 108.00 E
Viet Tri 148 Ld 21.18N 105.26 E
Vieux Fort 196 Ff 13.44N 60.57W
Vieux-Fort, Pointe du- 197e Ac 15.57N 61.43W
Vieux Fort Bay 197k Bb 13.44N 60.58W
Vieux-Habitants 197e Ab 16.04N 61.46W
Vievis/Vevis 116 Kj 54.45N 24.58 E
Viga 114 Kg 59.15N 43.42 E
Vigala 116 Kf 58.43N 24.22 E
Vigan 150 Hc 17.34N 120.23 E
Vigan, Le- 122 Jk 43.59N 3.36 E
Vigeland 116 Bf 58.05N 7.18 E
Vigevano 128 Ce 45.19N 8.51 E
Vigia 202 Id 0.48S 48.08W
Vigia Chico 192 Ph 19.46N 87.35W
Vignacourt 124 Ed 50.01N 2.12 E
Vignemale 126 Lb 42.46N 0.08W
Vigneulles-lès-Hattonchâtel 124 Hf 48.59N 5.43 E
Vignoble 122 Lh 46.50N 5.30 E
Vignola 128 Ef 44.29N 11.00 E
Vigny 124 De 49.05N 1.56 E
Vigo 112 Fg 42.14N 8.43W
Vigo, Ría de- 126 Db 42.15N 8.45W
Vigra 116 Bb 62.30N 6.05 E
Vigrestad 116 Af 58.34N 5.42 E
Vihanti 114 Fd 64.30N 25.00 E
Vihiers 122 Fg 47.09N 0.32W
Vihorevka 138 Fe 56.12N 101.09 E
Vihorlat 120 Sh 48.55N 22.10 E
Vihren 130 Gh 41.46N 23.24 E
Vihti 114 Ff 60.25N 24.20 E
Viiala 116 Jc 61.13N 23.47 E
Viinijärvi 116 Mb 62.39N 29.14 E
Viinijärvi 116 Mb 62.45N 29.15 E
Viitasaari 114 Fe 63.04N 25.52 E
Viivikonna/Vijvikonna 116 Le 59.14N 27.41 E
Vijayawāda 142 Kh 16.31N 80.37 E
Vijvikonna/Viivikonna 116 Le 59.14N 27.41 E
Vik 114a Bc 63.25N 19.01W
Vika 116 Fd 60.57N 14.27 E
Vikarbyn 116 Fd 60.55N 15.01 E
Vikbolandet 116 Gf 58.30N 16.40 E
Viken 116 Eh 56.09N 12.34 E
Viken 116 Ff 58.40N 14.20 E
Vikenara Point 219a Dc 8.34S 159.53 E
Vikersund 116 De 59.59N 10.02 E
Vikingbanken 118 Pa 60.20N 2.30 E
Vikmanshyttan 116 Fd 60.17N 15.49 E
Vikna 114 Cd 64.53N 10.58 E
Vikna 114 Cd 64.54N 11.00 E
Viksoyri 116 Bc 61.05N 6.34 E
Viktorija 179 Pb 80.10N 36.45 E
Vila da Maganja 172 Fc 17.18S 37.31 E
Vila de Rei 126 De 39.40N 8.09W
Vila do Bispo 126 Dg 37.05N 8.55W
Vila do Conde 126 Dc 41.21N 8.45W
Vila do Porto 162 Bb 36.56N 25.09W
Vila Flor 126 Ec 41.18N 7.09W
Vilafranca del Maestrat / Villafranca del Cid 126 Ld 40.25N 0.15W
Vilafranca del Penedès / Villafranca del Panadés 126 Nc 41.21N 1.42 E
Vila Franca de Xira 126 Df 38.57N 8.59W
Vila Franca do Campo 162 Bb 37.43N 25.26W
Vila Franca do Save 172 Ed 21.09S 34.32 E
Vila Gamito 172 Eb 14.10S 32.59 E
Vilagarcia de Arousa / Villagarcia de Arosa 126 Db 42.36N 8.45W
Vila Gouveia 172 Ec 18.03S 33.11 E
Vilaine 122 Dg 47.23N 2.27W
Viļaka/Viljaka 114 Gh 57.14N 27.46 E
Vila Machado 172 Ec 19.17S 34.12 E
Vilanculos 160 Kk 22.00S 35.19 E
Viļani/Viljani 114 Gh 56.33N 26.59 E
Vila Nova da Cerveira 126 Dc 41.56N 8.45W
Vila Nova de Famalicão 126 Dc 41.25N 8.32W
Vila Nova de Foz Côa 126 Ec 41.05N 7.12W
Vila Nova de Gaia 126 Dc 41.08N 8.37W
Vilanova i la Geltrú / Villanueva y Geltrú 126 Nc 41.14N 1.44 E
Vila Paiva de Andrada 172 Ec 18.41S 34.04 E
Vila Pouca de Aguiar 126 Ec 41.30N 7.39W
Vila Real 126 Ec 41.18N 7.45W
Vila Real [2] 126 Ec 41.35N 7.35W
Vila-Real / Villarreal de los Infantes 126 Le 39.56N 0.06W
Vila Real de Santo António 126 Eg 37.12N 7.25W
Vilar Formoso 126 Fd 40.37N 6.50W
Vila Velha 202 Jh 20.20S 40.17W
Vila Velha de Ródão 126 Ee 39.40N 7.42W
Vila Viçosa 126 Ef 38.47N 7.25W
Vilcabamba 202 Df 13.05S 73.01W
Vilcabamba, Cordillera- 202 Df 13.00S 73.00W
Vîlcea [2] 130 He 45.10N 24.10 E
Vilches 126 If 38.12N 3.30W
Vildbjerg 116 Ch 56.12N 8.46 E
Viled 114 Lf 61.22N 47.15 E
Vilejka 136 Ce 54.30N 26.53 E
Vilhelmina 114 Dd 64.37N 16.39 E
Vilhena 200 Jg 12.43S 60.07W
Vilija 132 Db 54.55N 25.40 E
Viljaka/Viļaka 114 Gh 57.14N 27.46 E
Viljandi 136 Cd 58.22N 25.35 E
Viljany/Viļani 114 Gh 56.33N 26.59 E
Viljuj 140 Oc 64.24N 126.26 E
Viljujsk 138 Hd 63.40N 121.33 E
Viljujskoje plato = Vilyui Range (EN) 140 Mc 66.00N 108.00 E
Viljujskoje vodohranilišče 138 Gd 62.30N 111.00 E
Vilkaviškis 114 Fi 54.43N 23.02 E
Vilkickogo, ostrov- [Russia] 138 Cb 73.30N 76.00 E
Vilkickogo, ostrov- [Russia] 138 Ka 75.40N 152.30 E
Vilkickogo, proliv- = Vilkitski Strait (EN) 140 Mb 77.55N 103.00 E
Vilkija 114 Fi 55.03N 23.35 E
Vilkitski Strait (EN) = Vilkickogo, proliv- 140 Mb 77.55N 103.00 E
Vilkovo 132 Fg 45.23N 29.35 E
Villa Aberastain 206 Gd 31.39S 68.35W
Villa Ahumada 190 Cb 30.37N 106.31W
Villa Altagracia 194 Ld 18.40N 70.10W
Villa Ana 204 Ci 28.29S 59.37W
Villa Ángela 206 Hc 27.35S 60.43W
Villa Atuel 206 Gd 34.50S 67.54W
Villa Berthet 204 Bh 27.17S 60.25W
Villablino 126 Fb 42.56N 6.19W
Villa Bruzual 202 Eb 9.20N 69.06W
Villa Cañas 204 Bk 34.00S 61.36W
Villacañas 126 Ie 39.38N 3.20W
Villacarrillo 126 If 38.07N 3.05W
Villacastin 126 Hd 40.47N 4.25W
Villach 128 Hd 46.36N 13.50 E
Villacidro 128 Ck 39.27N 8.44 E
Villa Clara 204 Cj 31.50S 58.49W
Villaclara [3] 194 Hb 22.30N 80.00W
Villa Constitución [Arg.] 206 Hd 33.14S 60.20W
Villa Constitución [Mex.] 190 Bc 25.09N 111.43W
Villa Coronado 192 Gd 26.45N 105.10W
Villada 126 Hb 42.15N 4.58W
Villa de Arriaga 192 Ig 21.54N 101.23W
Villa de Cos 192 Hf 23.17N 102.21W
Villa de Cura 196 Cg 10.02N 67.29W
Villa de Maria 206 Hc 29.54S 63.43W
Villa de Reyes 192 Ig 21.48N 100.56W
Villa de San Antonio 194 Df 14.16N 87.36W
Villadiego 126 Ib 42.31N 4.00W
Villa Dolores 206 Gd 31.56S 65.12W
Villa Elisa 204 Ck 32.10S 58.24W
Villa Flores 192 Mi 16.14N 93.14W
Villa Florida 204 Dh 26.23S 57.09W
Villafranca del Bierzo 126 Fb 42.36N 6.48W
Villafranca del Cid / Vilafranca del Maestrat 126 Ld 40.25N 0.15W
Villafranca de los Barros 126 Ff 38.34N 6.20W
Villafranca del Panadés / Vilafranca del Penedès 126 Nc 41.21N 1.42 E
Villafranca di Verona 128 Ee 45.21N 10.50 E
Villa Frontera 190 Dc 26.56N 101.27W
Villagarcia de Arosa / Vilagarcia de Arousa 126 Db 42.36N 8.45W
Villa General Roca 206 Gd 32.39S 66.28W
Villa Gesell 204 Dm 37.15S 56.55W
Villagrán 192 Je 24.29N 99.29W
Villaguay 206 Id 31.51S 59.01W
Villa Guillermina 204 Ci 28.14S 59.28W
Villa Hayes 206 Ic 25.06S 57.34W
Villa Hermandarias 204 Cj 31.13S 59.59W
Villahermosa 176 Jh 17.59N 92.55W
Villa Hidalgo 192 Gd 26.16N 104.54W
Villa Huidobro 206 Hd 34.50S 64.35W
Villajoyosa / La Vila Joiosa 126 Lf 38.30N 0.14W
Villalba 126 Ea 43.18N 7.41W
Villaldama 192 Id 26.30N 100.26W
Villalón de Campos 126 Gb 42.06N 5.02W
Villalpando 126 Gc 41.52N 5.24W
Villamalea 126 Ke 39.22N 1.35W
Villamanrique 126 Jf 38.33N 3.00W
Villa Maria 200 Ji 32.25S 63.15W
Villamartín 126 Gh 36.52N 5.38W
Villa Matamoros 192 Gd 26.50N 105.35W
Villa Media Agua 206 Gd 31.59S 68.25W
Villamil 202a Ab 0.56S 91.01W
Villa Minetti 204 Bi 28.37S 61.39W
Villa Montes 200 Jh 21.15S 63.30W
Villandraut 122 Fj 44.28N 0.22W
Villa Nueva 206 Gd 32.54S 68.47W
Villanueva 192 Hf 22.21N 102.53W
Villanueva [Col.] 194 Kh 10.37N 72.59W
Villanueva [N.M.-U.S.] 186 Di 35.17N 105.23W
Villanueva de Córdoba 126 Hf 38.20N 4.37W
Villanueva del Arzobispo 126 Jf 38.10N 3.00W
Villanueva de la Serena 126 Gf 38.58N 5.48W
Villanueva del Fresno 126 Ef 38.23N 7.10W
Villanueva de los Infantes 126 If 38.44N 3.01W
Villanueva del Rio y Minas 126 Gg 37.39N 5.42W
Villanueva y Geltrú/Vilanova i la Geltrú 126 Nc 41.14N 1.44 E
Villa Ocampo [Arg.] 206 Ic 28.28S 59.22W
Villa Ocampo [Mex.] 190 Cc 26.27N 105.31W
Villa Ojo de Agua 206 Hc 29.31S 63.42W
Villa Oliva 204 Dh 26.01S 57.53W
Villa Pesqueira 192 Ec 29.08N 109.58W
Villaputzu 128 Dk 39.26N 9.34 E
Villa Ramirez 204 Bk 32.11S 60.12W
Villarcayo 126 Ib 42.56N 3.34W
Villar del Arzobispo 126 Le 39.44N 0.49W
Villa Regina 206 Ge 39.06S 67.04W
Villa Rosario 202 Db 7.50N 72.29W
Villarreal de los Infantes / Vila-Real 126 Le 39.56N 0.06W
Villarrica [Chile] 206 Fe 39.16S 72.16W
Villarrica [Par.] 206 Ic 25.45S 56.26W
Villarrobledo 126 Je 39.16N 2.36W
Villasalto 128 Dk 39.29N 9.23 E
Villa San Giovanni 128 Jl 38.13N 15.38 E
Villa San Martín 206 Hc 28.18S 64.12W
Villasimius 128 Dk 39.08N 9.31 E
Villatoro, Puerto de- 126 Gd 40.33N 5.10W
Villa Unión [Mex.] 192 Ic 28.15N 100.43W
Villa Unión [Mex.] 190 Cd 23.12N 106.16W
Villaverde, Madrid- 126 Id 40.21N 3.42W
Villavicencio 200 Ie 4.09N 73.37W
Villaviciosa 126 Ga 43.29N 5.26W
Villazón 202 Eh 22.06S 65.36W
Ville-de-Laval 184 Kc 45.33N 73.44W
Ville de Paris [3] 122 If 48.52N 2.20 E
Ville de Toulouse Bank (EN) 174 Hh 11.30N 117.00W
Villedieu-les-Poêles 122 Ef 48.50N 1.13W
Ville-en-Tardenois 124 Fe 49.11N 3.48 E
Villefranche-de-Lauragais 122 Hk 43.24N 1.44 E
Villefranche-de-Rouergue 122 Ij 44.21N 2.03 E
Villefranche-sur-Saône 122 Ki 45.59N 4.43 E
Ville-Marie 184 Hb 47.20N 79.26W
Villemur-sur-Tarn 122 Hk 43.52N 1.31 E
Villena 126 Lf 38.38N 0.51W
Villeneuve d'Ascq 124 Fd 50.38N 3.09 E
Villeneuve-Saint-Georges 124 Ef 48.44N 2.27 E
Villeneuve-sur-Lot 122 Gj 44.24N 0.43 E
Villeneuve-sur-Yonne 122 Jf 48.05N 3.18 E
Ville Platte 186 Jk 30.42N 92.16W
Villers-Bocage [Fr.] 124 Ee 50.00N 2.20 E
Villers-Bocage [Fr.] 124 Be 49.05N 0.39W
Villers-Bretonneux 124 Ee 49.52N 2.31 E
Villers-Carbonnel 124 Ee 49.52N 2.54 E
Villers-Cotterêts 124 Fe 49.15N 3.05 E
Villers-la-Ville 124 Gd 50.35N 4.32 E
Villers-sur-Mer 124 Be 49.19N 0.01W
Villerupt 122 Le 49.28N 5.56 E
Villerville 124 Ce 49.24N 0.08 E
Ville-sur-Tourbe 124 Ge 49.11N 4.47 E
Villeurbanne 122 Ki 45.46N 4.53 E
Villiersdorp 172 Bf 33.59S 19.17 E
Villingen-Schwenningen 120 Eh 48.04N 8.28 E
Villmanstrand/Lappeenranta 112 Ic 61.04N 28.11 E
Villmar 124 Kd 50.23N 8.12 E
Vilnius/Vilnjus 112 Ie 54.41N 25.19 E
Vilnjus/Vilnius 112 Ie 54.41N 25.19 E
Vilok 120 Sh 48.08N 22.50 E
Vilppula 116 Kb 62.01N 24.31 E
Vils [Ger.] 120 Hg 49.10N 11.59 E
Vils [Ger.] 120 Jh 48.35N 13.10 E
Vilsandi 116 If 58.20N 21.45 E
Vilsbiburg 120 Ih 48.27N 12.21 E
Vilshofen 120 Jh 48.38N 13.11 E
Vilusi 130 Bg 42.44N 18.36 E
Vilvoorde/Vilvorde 122 Kd 50.56N 4.26 E
Vilvorde/Vilvoorde 122 Kd 50.56N 4.26 E
Vilyui Range (EN) = Viljujskoje plato 140 Mc 66.00N 108.00 E
Vimeu 124 Dd 50.05N 1.35 E
Vimianzo 126 Ca 43.07N 9.02W
Vimmerby 114 Dh 57.40N 15.51 E
Vimoutiers 122 Gf 48.55N 0.12 E
Vimperk 120 Jg 49.03N 13.47 E
Vimy 124 Ed 50.22N 2.49 E
Vina 166 Id 7.45N 15.36 E
Viña del Mar 200 Ii 33.02S 71.34W
Vinalhaven Island 184 Mc 44.05N 68.52W
Vinalopó 126 Lf 38.11N 0.36W
Vinaròs / Vinaroz 126 Md 40.28N 0.29 E
Vinaroz / Vinaròs 126 Md 40.28N 0.29 E
Vînători 130 Hc 46.14N 24.56 E
Vincennes 182 Jd 38.41N 87.32W
Vincennes Bay 222 He 66.30S 109.30 E
Vincente, Puntan- 220b Bb 14.56N 145.40 E
Vinci 128 Eg 43.47N 10.55 E
Vindafjorden 116 Ae 59.20N 5.55 E
Vindelälven 116 Ee 63.54N 19.52 E
Vindeln 114 Ed 64.12N 19.44 E
Vinderup 116 Ch 56.29N 8.47 E
Vindhya Range 140 Jg 24.37N 77.00 E
Vindö 116 He 59.20N 18.40 E
Vineland 184 Jf 39.29N 75.02W
Vingåker 114 Dg 59.02N 15.52 E
Vingeanne 122 Lg 47.21N 5.29 E
Vinh 142 Mh 18.40N 105.40 E
Vinhais 126 Fc 41.50N 7.00W
Vinh Bac Phan = Tonkin, Gulf of- (EN) 140 Mh 20.00N 108.00 E
Vinh Linh 148 Le 17.04N 107.02 E
Vinica [Mace.] 130 Fh 41.53N 22.30 E
Vinica [Slo.] 128 Je 45.28N 15.15 E
Vinita 186 Ih 36.39N 95.09W
Vinju Mare 130 Fe 44.25N 22.52 E
Vinkovci 128 Me 45.17N 18.49 E
Vinnica 112 If 49.14N 28.29 E
Vinnickaja oblast [3] 136 Cf 49.00N 28.50 E
Vinniki 132 De 49.48N 24.11 E
Vino, Tierra del- 126 Gc 41.30N 5.30W
Vinogradov 132 Ce 48.09N 23.02 E
Vinslöv 116 Eh 56.06N 13.55 E
Vinson Massif 222 Pf 78.35S 85.25W
Vinstervåtn 116 Cc 61.20N 9.00 E
Vinstra 114 Bf 61.36N 9.45 E
Vinstra 116 Cc 61.36N 9.45 E
Vintilă Vodă 130 Jd 45.28N 26.43 E
Vintjärn 116 Gd 60.50N 16.03 E
Vinton 186 Ke 42.10N 92.00W
Vintschgau/Venosta, Val- 128 Ed 46.40N 10.35 E
Vipiteno / Sterzing 128 Fd 46.54N 11.26 E
Vipya Plateau 170 Fe 11.09S 34.00 E
Viqueque 150 Ih 8.52S 126.22 E
Vir 128 Jf 44.18N 15.03 E
Virac 150 Hd 13.35N 124.15 E
Viramgām 148 Ed 23.07N 72.02 E
Virandozero 114 Id 64.01N 36.03 E
Viranşehir 146 Hd 37.13N 39.45 E
Virbalis 116 Jj 54.37N 22.49 E
Vircava 116 Jh 56.35N 23.43 E
Virden 180 Hg 49.51N 100.55W
Virdois/Virrat 114 Fe 62.14N 23.47 E
Vire 122 Ff 48.50N 0.53W
Vire 122 Ee 49.20N 1.07W
Virei 170 Bf 15.43S 12.54 E
Vireux-Wallerand 124 Gd 50.05N 4.44 E
Vîrful, Curcubăta- 130 Fc 46.25N 22.35 E
Virgin Gorda 196 Dc 18.30N 64.25W
Virginia [2] 182 Ld 37.30N 78.45W
Virginia [Mn.-U.S.] 182 Ib 47.31N 92.32W
Virginia [S.Afr.] 172 De 28.12S 26.49 E
Virginia Beach 182 Ld 36.51N 75.59W
Virginia City 188 Fg 39.19N 119.39W
Virgin Islands 174 Mh 18.20N 66.45W
Virgin Islands of the United States [5] 176 Mh 18.20N 64.52W
Virgin Mountains 188 Ih 36.40N 113.50W
Virgin Passage 197a Cb 18.20N 65.10W
Virgin River 188 Hh 36.35N 114.18W
Virihaure 114 Dc 67.22N 16.33 E
Virkby/Virkkala 116 Kd 60.13N 24.01 E
Virkkala/Virkby 116 Kd 60.13N 24.01 E
Virmasvesi 116 Lb 62.50N 26.55 E
Virôchey 148 Lf 13.59N 106.49 E
Viroin 122 Kd 50.05N 4.43 E
Viroinval 124 Gd 50.05N 4.33 E
Viroinval-Nismes 124 Gd 50.05N 4.33 E
Virojoki 114 Gf 60.35N 27.42 E
Viroqua 186 Ke 43.34N 90.53W
Virovitica 128 Le 45.50N 17.23 E
Virpazar 130 Cg 42.15N 19.06 E
Virrat/Virdois 114 Fe 62.14N 23.47 E
Virserum 114 Dh 57.19N 15.35 E
Virsko More 128 If 44.20N 15.00 E
Virton 122 Le 49.34N 5.32 E
Virton-Ethe 124 He 49.35N 5.35 E
Virtsu 114 Fg 58.37N 23.31 E
Virudanagar 148 Fg 9.36N 77.58 E
Virvičja/Virvyčia 116 Jh 56.14N 22.30 E
Virvyčia/Virvičja 116 Jh 56.14N 22.30 E
Vis 128 Kg 43.03N 16.12 E
Vis 128 Kg 43.02N 16.10 E
Visalia 182 Dd 36.20N 119.18W
Visayan Sea 150 Hd 11.35N 123.51 E
Visby 114 Eh 57.38N 18.18 E
Viscount Melville Sound 174 Hb 74.10N 113.00W
Visé/Wezet 124 Hd 50.44N 5.42 E
Višegrad 128 Ng 43.48N 19.17 E
Višegrad 130 Jh 41.59N 26.20 E
Višera [Russia] 110 Lc 59.55N 56.50 E
Višera [Russia] 136 Fc 61.57N 52.25 E
Viseu [2] 126 Ed 40.45N 7.50W
Viseu [Braz.] 202 Id 1.12S 46.07W
Viseu [Port.] 126 Ed 40.39N 7.55W
Vişeu de Sus 130 Hb 47.43N 24.26 E
Vishākhapatnam 142 Kh 17.42N 83.18 E
Visingsö 116 Ff 58.03N 14.20 E
Viskafors 116 Eg 57.38N 12.50 E
Viskan 114 Ch 57.14N 12.12 E
Viski kanal 128 Kg 43.07N 16.17 E
Vislanda 116 Fh 56.47N 14.27 E
Vislinski zaliv 120 Pb 54.27N 19.40 E
Visnes 116 Ae 59.21N 5.14 E
Višnevka 130 Lc 46.22N 28.27 E
Visoki Dečani 130 Dg 42.33N 20.16 E
Visoko 128 Mg 43.59N 18.11 E
Visokoi 222 Ad 56.42S 27.12W
Visonggo 219d Bb 16.13S 179.40 E
Visp 128 Bd 46.17N 7.53 E
Vissefjärda 116 Fh 56.32N 15.35 E
Vista 188 Gj 33.12N 117.15W
Visten 116 Ee 59.40N 13.20 E
Vistonias, Órmos- 130 Ii 40.58N 25.05 E
Vistonis, Limni- 130 Ih 41.03N 25.07 E
Vistula (EN) = Wisła 110 He 54.22N 18.55 E
Vištytis 116 Jj 54.27N 22.44 E
Visuvisu Point 219a Cb 7.57S 157.31 E
Vit 130 Hf 43.41N 24.45 E
Vitebsk 112 Jd 55.12N 30.11 E
Vitebskaja oblast [3] 136 Cd 55.20N 29.00 E
Viterbo 128 Gh 42.25N 12.06 E
Vithkuqi 130 Di 40.31N 20.35 E
Vitichi 202 Eh 20.13S 65.29W
Vitigudino 126 Fc 41.01N 6.26W
Viti Levu 208 If 18.00S 178.00 E
Vitim 138 Ge 59.33N 112.28 E
Vitim 140 Nd 59.26N 112.34 E
Vitimski 138 Ge 58.18N 113.18 E
Vitimskoje ploskogorje 138 Gf 54.00N 114.00 E
Vitinja → Cureski prohod 130 Gg 42.47N 23.45 E
Vitjaz Strait 214 Di 5.35S 147.00 E
Vitolište 130 Eh 41.11N 21.50 E
Vitória 200 Lh 20.19S 40.21W
Vitoria / Vitoria-Gasteiz 126 Jb 42.51N 2.40W
Vitória da Conquista 200 Lg 14.51S 40.51W
Vitória de Santo Antão 202 Ke 8.07S 35.18W
Vitoria-Gasteiz / Vitoria 126 Jb 42.51N 2.40W
Vitorog 128 Lf 44.08N 17.03 E
Vitosa 130 Gg 42.33N 23.15 E
Vitré 122 Ef 48.08N 1.12W
Vitry-en-Artois 124 Ed 50.20N 2.59 E
Vitry-le-François 122 Kf 48.44N 4.35 E
Vitsi 130 Ei 40.39N 21.23 E
Vittangi 114 Ec 67.41N 21.39 E
Vitteaux 122 Kg 47.24N 4.32 E
Vittel 122 Lf 48.12N 5.57 E
Vittinge 116 Ge 59.54N 17.04 E
Vittoria 128 In 36.57N 14.32 E
Vittorio Veneto 128 Ge 45.59N 12.18 E
Vityaz Depth (EN) 106 Je 44.00N 151.00 E
Vityaz I Depth (EN) 106 Ih 11.20N 141.30 E
Vityaz II Depth (EN) 106 Kl 23.27S 175.00W
Vityaz III Depth (EN) 106 Km 32.00S 178.00W
Vityaz Seamount (EN) 208 Jc 13.30N 173.15W
Vityaz Trench (EN) 106 Jj 10.00S 170.00 E
Vivarais, Monts du- 122 Ki 44.55N 4.15 E
Vivarais, Plateaux du- 122 Kj 44.50N 4.45 E
Viver 126 Le 39.55N 0.36W

Vivero 126 Ea 43.40N 7.35W
Viverone, Lago di- 128 Ce 45.25N 8.05 E
Vivi 138 Ed 63.52N 97.50 E
Vivian 186 Jj 32.53N 93.59W
Viviers 122 Kj 44.29N 4.41 E
Vivo 172 Dd 23.03S 29.17 E
Vivoratá 204 Dm 37.40S 57.39W
Vivorillo, Cayos- 194 Ff 15.50N 83.18W
Viwa 219d Ab 17.08S 176.56 E
Vizcaino, Desierto de- 190 Bc 27.40N 114.40W
Vizcaino, Sierra- 192 Bd 27.20N 114.00W
Vizcaya / Bizkaia [3] 126 Ja 43.15N 2.55W
Vizcaya, Golfo de- 110 Fg 44.00N 4.00W
Vizcaya, Golfo de- = Biscay, Bay of- (EN) 110 Fg 43.50N 2.30W
Vize 130 Kh 41.34N 27.45 E
Vize, ostrov- 140 Jb 79.30N 77.00 E
Vizianagaram 148 Ge 18.07N 83.25 E
Vizille 122 Li 45.05N 5.46 E
Vizinga 136 Fc 61.05N 50.10 E
Viziru 130 Kd 45.00N 27.42 E
Vižnica 132 De 48.14N 25.12 E
Vizzini 128 Im 37.10N 14.45 E
Vjajke-Maarja/Väike-Maarja 116 Le 59.04N 26.12 E
Vjajke-Pakri/Väike-Pakri 116 Je 59.50N 23.50 E
Vjajke-Vjajn / Väike Väin 116 Jf 58.30N 23.10 E
Vjalje, ozero- 116 Ne 59.00N 30.20 E
Vjalozero, ozero- 116 Ic 66.50N 35.10 E
Vjandra/Vändra 114 Fg 58.40N 25.01 E
Vjartsilja 114 He 62.10N 30.48 E
Vjatka 110 Ld 55.36N 51.30 E
Vjatskije Poljany 136 Fd 56.14N 51.04 E
Vjatski uval 114 Lg 58.00N 49.45 E
Vjazemski 138 Ig 47.31N 134.45 E
Vjazma 112 Jd 55.13N 34.18 E
Vjazniki 114 Kh 56.15N 42.12 E
Vjeio, Rio- 194 Dg 12.17N 86.54W
Vjosa 130 Ci 40.37N 19.20 E
Vlaamse Banken 124 Ec 51.15N 2.30 E
Vlaamse Vlakte = Flanders Plain (EN) 122 Id 50.40N 2.50 E
Vlaanderen/Flandres= Flanders (EN) 122 Jc 51.00N 3.20 E
Vlaardingen 122 Kc 51.54N 4.21 E
Vlădeasa, Virful- 130 Fc 46.45N 22.48 E
Vlădeni 130 Kb 47.25N 27.20 E
Vladičin Han 130 Fg 42.43N 22.04 E
Vladikavkaz (Ordžonikidze) [Russia] 112 Kg 43.03N 44.40 E
Vladimir 112 Kd 56.10N 40.25 E
Vladimirskaja oblast [3] 136 Ed 56.00N 40.40 E
Vladimirski Tupik 132 Hb 55.42N 33.18 E
Vladimir-Volynski 136 Ce 50.51N 24.22 E
Vladivostok 142 Pe 43.10N 131.56 E
Vlad Ţepeş 130 Ke 44.21N 27.05 E
Vlagtwedde 124 Ja 53.02N 7.08 E
Vlagtwedde-Ter Apel 124 Jb 52.52N 7.06 E
Vlahina 130 Fh 41.54N 22.52 E
Vlăhiţa 130 Ic 46.21N 25.31 E
Vlasenika 128 Mf 44.11N 18.57 E
Vlašić 128 Lf 44.19N 17.40 E
Vlašic 130 Ce 44.27N 19.35 E
Vlašim 120 Kg 49.42N 14.54 E
Vlasotince 130 Fg 42.58N 22.08 E
Vlasovo 138 Ib 70.40N 134.35 E
Vlieland 124 Ha 53.17N 5.06 E
Vlieland 122 Ka 53.15N 5.00 E
Vlieland-Oost Vlieland 124 Ha 53.17N 5.06 E
Vliestroom 124 Ha 53.17N 5.10 E
Vlissingen 122 Jc 51.26N 3.35 E
Vlissingen-Oost-Souburg 124 Fc 51.28N 3.36 E
Vloesberg/Flobecq 124 Fd 50.44N 3.44 E
Vlorë 112 Hg 40.27N 19.30 E
Vlorës, Gjiri i- 130 Ci 40.25N 19.25 E
Vlotho 124 Kb 52.10N 8.51 E
Vltava=Moldau (EN) 110 He 50.21N 14.30 E
Vöcklabruck 128 Hb 48.01N 13.39 E
Vodice 128 Jg 43.46N 15.47 E
Vodla 114 If 61.49N 36.00 E
Vodlozero, ozero- 114 Ie 62.20N 37.00 E
Vodňany 120 Kg 49.09N 14.11 E
Vodnjan 128 Hf 44.57N 13.51 E
Vodny 134 Fe 63.32N 53.20 E
Voerde (Niederrhein) 120 Ce 51.35N 6.41 E
Voeren/Fouron 124 Hd 50.45N 5.48 E
Vôge, La- 122 Mf 48.05N 6.05 E
Vogel Peak 166 Hd 8.24N 11.47 E
Vogelsberg 120 Ff 50.30N 9.15 E
Voghera 128 Df 44.59N 9.01 E
Vogtland 120 If 50.30N 12.05 E
Voh 219b Be 20.58S 164.42 E
Võhandu jõgi / Vyhandu 116 Lf 58.03N 27.40 E
Vohémar 172 Ib 13.22S 50.00 E
Vohipeno 172 Hd 22.20S 47.52 E
Vöhl 124 Kc 51.12N 8.56 E
Vohma 136 Ed 58.58N 46.45 E
Vohma 114 Lg 58.45N 46.36 E
Voi 160 Ki 3.23S 38.34 E
Voikoski 116 Lc 61.16N 26.48 E
Voinjama 160 Gh 8.25N 9.45W
Vóïon Óros 130 Ei 40.15N 21.03 E
Voire 122 Kf 48.27N 4.25 E
Voiron 122 Li 45.22N 5.35 E
Voitsberg 128 Jc 47.02N 15.09 E
Voiviis, Limni- 130 Fj 39.32N 22.45 E
Vojens 116 Ci 55.15N 9.19 E
Vojkar 134 Ld 65.38N 64.40 E
Vojmsjön 114 Dd 65.00N 16.24 E
Vojnić 128 Je 45.19N 15.42 E
Vojnilov 120 Ug 49.04N 24.33 E
Vojvodina [3] 130 Cd 45.00N 20.00 E
Voj-Vož 136 Fc 62.56N 54.59 E
Voknavolok 114 Hd 64.57N 30.31 E
Vokré, Hoséré- 158 Ih 8.21N 13.15 E
Volary 120 Jh 48.55N 13.54 E
Volcán 194 Fi 8.46N 82.38W
Volcánica, Cordillera- 174 Ih 18.00N 101.00W
Volcano 221a Fd 19.26N 155.20W
Volcano Islands (EN)=lō/Kazan-Rettō 140 Qg 25.00N 141.00 E
Volcano Islands (EN)= Kazan-Rettō/lō 140 Qg 25.00N 141.00 E
Volčansk [Russia] 134 Jg 59.59N 60.04 E
Volčansk [Ukr.] 132 Jd 50.16N 37.01 E
Volčiha 138 Df 52.02N 80.23 E
Volda 114 Be 62.09N 6.06 E
Voldafjorden 116 Ab 62.10N 6.00 E
Volga 114 Jh 57.57N 38.25 E
Volga 110 Kf 45.55N 47.52 E
Volga-Baltic Canal (EN)= Volgo-Baltijski vodny put imeni V. I. Lenina 110 Jd 59.58N 37.10 E
Volga Delta (EN) 110 Kf 46.30N 47.00 E
Volga Hills (EN) = Privolžkaja vozvyšennost 110 Ke 52.00N 46.00 E
Volgo-Baltijski vodny put imeni V.I. Lenina=Volga-Baltic Canal (EN) 110 Jd 59.58N 37.10 E
Volgodonsk 136 Ef 47.33N 42.08 E
Volgo-Donskoj sudohodny kanal imeni V. I. Lenina= Lenin Canal (EN) 110 Kf 48.40N 43.37 E
Volgograd (Stalingrad) 112 Kf 48.44N 44.25 E
Volgograd Reservoir (EN) = Volgogradskoje vodohranilišče 110 Kf 49.20N 45.00 E
Volgogradskaja oblast [3] 136 Ef 49.30N 44.30 E
Volgogradskoje vodohranilišče = Volgograd Reservoir (EN) 110 Kf 49.20N 45.00 E
Volhov 112 Jd 59.55N 32.20 E
Volhov 110 Jc 60.08N 32.20 E
Volhynia 110 Ie 51.00N 25.00 E
Volhynia (EN) [3] 120 Uf 51.00N 25.00 E
Volissós 130 Ik 38.29N 25.55 E
Volja 134 Je 63.11N 61.16 E
Volka 120 Vd 52.43N 25.43 E
Völkermarkt 128 Id 46.39N 14.38 E
Völklingen 120 Cg 49.15N 6.51 E
Volkmarsen 124 Lc 51.24N 9.07 E
Volkovysk 132 Dc 53.10N 24.31 E
Volkovysskaja vozvyšennost 120 Uc 53.10N 24.30 E
Volksrust 172 De 27.24S 29.53 E
Vollenhove 124 Hb 52.40N 5.57 E
Vollsjö 116 Ei 55.42N 13.46 E
Volme 124 Jc 51.24N 7.27 E
Volmunster 124 Je 49.07N 7.21 E
Volna, gora- 138 Kd 63.30N 154.57 E
Volnjansk 132 If 47.54N 35.29 E
Volnovaha 132 Jf 47.37N 37.36 E
Voločajevka 2-ja 138 Ig 48.36N 134.36 E
Voločisk 132 Ee 49.31N 26.13 E
Volodarsk 114 Kh 56.14N 43.13 E
Volodarski 132 Pf 46.26N 48.31 E
Volodarskoje 136 Ge 53.18N 68.08 E
Vologda 112 Jd 59.12N 39.55 E
Vologodskaja oblast [3] 136 Ed 60.00N 41.00 E
Volokolamsk 114 Ih 56.03N 35.58 E
Volokonovka 132 Jd 50.29N 37.52 E
Vólos 112 Ih 39.22N 22.57 E
Vološka 114 Jf 61.21N 40.03 E
Vološka 114 Jf 61.42N 39.15 E
Volosovo 114 Gg 59.28N 29.31 E
Volovec 120 Th 48.42N 23.17 E
Volovo 132 Kc 53.35N 38.01 E
Voložin 132 Eb 54.06N 26.32 E
Volquart Boons Kyst 179 Jd 70.20N 24.20W
Volsini, Monti- 128 Fh 42.40N 11.55 E
Volsk 136 Ee 52.02N 47.23 E
Volta [3] 166 Fd 7.00N 0.30 E
Volta 158 Hh 5.46N 0.41 E
Volta, Lake- 158 Hh 7.30N 0.15 E
Volta Blanche=White Volta (EN) 158 Gh 8.38N 0.59W
Volta Noire=Black Volta (EN) [3] 166 Ec 12.30N 4.00W
Volta Noire=Black Volta (EN) 158 Gh 8.38N 1.30W
Volta Redonda 200 Lh 22.32S 44.07W
Volta Rouge=Red Volta (EN) 158 Gh 10.34N 0.30W
Volterra 128 Eg 43.24N 10.51 E
Voltoya 126 Hd 41.13N 4.31W
Voltri, Genova- 128 Cf 44.26N 8.45 E
Volturino 128 Jj 40.25N 15.48 E
Volturno 128 Hi 41.01N 13.55 E
Volubilis 162 Fc 34.04N 5.33W
Vólvi, Limni- 130 Gi 40.41N 23.28 E
Volynskaja grjada 120 Ue 51.05N 25.00 E
Volynskaja oblast [3] 136 Ce 51.10N 25.00 E
Volynskaja vozvyšennost 132 Dd 50.30N 25.00 E
Volžsk 136 Ed 55.55N 48.19 E
Volžski [Russia] 112 Kf 48.48N 44.44 E
Volžski [Russia] 114 Mj 53.28N 50.08 E
Voma 219d Bc 18.00S 178.08 E
Vomano 128 Ih 42.39N 14.02 E
Vonavona 219a Cc 8.12S 157.05 E
Vondrozo 172 Hd 22.47S 47.17 E
Von Frank Mountain 178 Id 63.33N 154.20W
Vónitsa 130 Dk 38.55N 20.53 E
Vonne 122 Gh 46.25N 0.15 E
Võnnu/Vynnu 116 Lf 58.15N 27.10 E
Voorne 124 Gc 51.52N 4.05 E
Voorschoten 124 Gb 52.08N 4.28 E
Voorst 124 Ib 52.10N 6.09 E
Voorst-Twello 124 Ib 52.14N 6.07 E
Vop 132 Hb 54.56N 32.44 E
Vopnafjördur 114a Cb 65.45N 14.50W
Vora 130 Ch 41.23N 19.40 E
Vórā/Vöyri 116 Ja 63.09N 22.15 E
Vorarlberg [2] 128 Dc 47.15N 9.50 E
Vóras Óros 130 Ei 41.00N 21.50 E
Vorau 128 Jc 47.24N 15.53 E
Vorden 124 Ib 52.06N 6.20 E
Vorderrhein 128 Dd 46.49N 9.26 E
Vordingborg 114 Ci 55.01N 11.55 E
Voreifel 124 Jd 50.10N 7.00 E
Vorga Šor 134 Kc 67.35N 63.40 E
Voria Pindhos 130 Dj 40.20N 20.55 E
Vórioi Sporádhes, Nisoi-= Northern Sporades (EN) 110 Ih 39.15N 23.55 E
Vórios Evvoïkós Kólpos= Evvoia, Gulf of- (EN) 130 Gk 38.45N 23.10 E
Vorkuta 112 Mb 67.27N 63.58 E
Vorma 114 Cf 60.09N 11.27 E
Vormsi 116 Je 59.02N 23.05 E
Vormsi 114 Fg 59.00N 23.15 E
Vorniceni 130 Jb 47.59N 26.40 E
Vorogovo 138 Dd 60.58N 89.28 E
Vorona 132 Md 51.22N 42.03 E
Voroncovo [Russia] 138 Db 71.40N 83.40 E
Voroncovo [Russia] 116 Mg 57.15N 28.49 E
Voronež 112 Je 51.40N 39.10 E
Voronež 132 Kd 51.31N 39.05 E
Voronežskaja oblast [3] 136 Ee 51.00N 40.15 E
Voronin Trough (EN) 224 Ge 80.00N 85.00 E
Vorona 114 Ib 69.09N 35.47 E
Voronovo 116 Kj 54.09N 25.19 E
Voropajevo 116 Li 55.07N 27.19 E
Vorošilovgrad → Lugansk 112 Jf 48.34N 39.20 E
Vorošilovgradskaja oblast [3] 136 Df 49.00N 39.10 E
Vorotan 132 Oj 39.15N 46.43 E
Vorotynec 114 Kh 56.02N 45.52 E
Vorožba 132 Id 51.10N 34.11 E
Vorskla 132 Ie 48.52N 34.05 E
Vorsma 114 Ki 55.58N 43.17 E
Vörts järv / Vyrtsjarv, ozero- 114 Gg 58.15N 26.05 E
Võru/Vyru 136 Cd 57.52N 27.05 E
Voruh 135 He 39.52N 70.35 E
Vosges [3] 122 Mf 48.10N 6.20 E
Vosges 110 Gf 48.30N 7.10 E
Voskresensk 114 Ji 55.22N 38.42 E
Voskresenskoje 114 Kh 56.51N 45.27 E
Voss 116 Bd 60.40N 6.30 E
Vossa 116 Ad 60.39N 5.42 E
Vossevangen 114 Bf 60.39N 6.26 E
Vostočno-Kazahstanskaja oblast [3] 136 If 49.00N 84.00 E
Vostočno-Kounradski 136 Hf 46.58N 75.07 E
Vostočno Sibirskoje more = East Siberian Sea (EN) 224 Cd 74.00N 166.00 E
Vostočny [Russia] 134 Jg 58.48N 61.52 E
Vostočny [Russia] 138 Jg 48.19N 142.40 E
Vostočny, hrebet- 138 Lf 55.00N 160.30 E
Vostočny Sajan=Eastern Sayans (EN) 140 Ld 53.00N 97.00 E
Vostok 222 Hf 78.28S 106.48 E
Vostok Island 208 Lf 10.06S 152.23W
Vostrecovo 138 Ig 45.56N 134.59 E
Võsu/Vyzu 116 Ke 59.30N 25.50 E
Votkinsk 136 Fd 57.05N 53.59 E
Votkinskoje vodohranilišče = Votkinsk Reservoir (EN) 110 Ld 57.30N 55.10 E
Votkinsk Reservoir (EN) = Votkinskoje vodohranilišče 110 Ld 57.30N 55.10 E
Votuporanga 204 He 20.24S 49.59W
Vouga 126 Dd 40.41N 8.40W
Vouillé 122 Gh 46.38N 0.10 E
Voulgára 130 Ej 39.06N 21.54 E
Vouliagméni 130 Gl 37.49N 23.47 E
Voulte-sur-Rhône, La- 122 Kj 44.48N 4.47 E
Voúrinos Óros 130 Ei 40.11N 21.40 E
Voúxa, Ákra- 130 Gn 35.38N 23.36 E
Vouziers 122 Ke 49.24N 4.42 E
Voves 122 Hf 48.16N 1.38 E
Vovodo 168 Cd 5.40N 24.21 E
Voxna 116 Fc 61.21N 15.34 E
Voxnan 116 Gc 61.17N 16.26 E
Voyeykov Ice Shelf 222 Ie 66.20S 124.38 E
Vöyri/Vörå 116 Ja 63.09N 22.15 E
Vože, ozero- 114 Jf 60.35N 39.05 E
Vožega 114 Jf 60.30N 40.12 E
Vožega 114 Jf 60.33N 39.13 E
Voznesenje 114 If 61.01N 35.27 E
Voznesensk 136 Df 47.35N 31.20 E
Vozroždenija, ostrov- 135 Bb 45.05N 59.15 E
Vraca 130 Gf 43.12N 23.33 E
Vraca [2] 130 Gf 43.12N 23.33 E
Vraca 130 Dh 41.54N 20.45 E
Vradijevka 132 Gf 47.51N 30.34 E
Vrakhiónas 130 Dl 37.48N 20.45 E
Vran 128 Lg 43.39N 17.27 E
Vrancea [2] 130 Jd 45.50N 26.42 E
Vranica 128 Lg 43.57N 17.44 E
Vranje 130 Eg 42.33N 21.54 E
Vranov nad Topl'ou 120 Rh 48.54N 21.41 E
Vrăška čuka, prohod- 130 Ff 43.50N 22.23 E
Vratnica 130 Eg 42.08N 21.07 E
Vratnik, prohod- 130 Jg 42.49N 26.10 E
Vrbas 130 Cd 45.34N 19.39 E
Vrbas 128 Le 45.07N 17.31 E
Vrbno pod Pradědem 120 Nf 50.08N 17.23 E
Vrbovsko 128 Je 45.22N 15.05 E
Vrchlabí 120 Lf 50.38N 15.37 E
Vrede 172 De 27.30S 29.06 E
Vreden 124 Ib 52.02N 6.50 E
Vredenburg 172 Bf 32.54S 17.59 E
Vredendal 172 Bf 31.41S 18.35 E
Vresse, Vresse-sur-Semois- 124 Ge 49.52N 4.56 E
Vresse-sur-Semois 124 Ge 49.52N 4.56 E
Vresse-sur-Semois-Vresse 124 Ge 49.52N 4.56 E
Vretstorp 116 Fe 59.02N 14.52 E
Vrhnika 128 Ie 45.58N 14.18 E
Vries 124 Ia 53.05N 6.36 E
Vriezenveen 124 Ib 52.26N 6.36 E
Vrigstad 116 Fg 57.21N 14.28 E
Vron 124 Dd 50.19N 1.45 E
Vršac 130 Ed 45.07N 21.18 E
Vryburg 160 Jk 26.55S 24.45 E
Vryheid 172 Ee 27.52S 30.38 E
Vsetín 120 Ng 49.21N 18.00 E
Vsevidof, Mount- 178a Eb 53.07N 168.43W
Vsevoložsk 114 Hf 60.04N 30.41 E
Vstrečny 138 Lc 68.00N 165.58 E
Vtačnik 120 Oh 48.42N 18.37 E
Vuanggava 219d Cc 18.52S 178.54W
Vučitrn 130 Dg 42.49N 20.58 E
Vučjak 130 Fh 41.28N 22.20 E
Vuka 128 Me 45.21N 19.00 E
Vukovar 128 Me 45.21N 19.00 E
Vuktyl 136 Fc 63.50N 57.25 E
Vulavu 219a Dc 8.31S 159.48 E
Vulcan 130 Gd 45.23N 23.16 E
Vulcan, Vírful- 130 Fc 46.14N 22.58 E
Vulcano 128 Il 38.25N 15.00 E
Vulkanešty 132 Fg 45.38N 28.27 E
Vulture 128 Jj 40.57N 15.38 E
Vung Tau 148 Lf 10.21N 107.04 E
Vunindawa 219d Bb 17.49S 178.19 E
Vunisea Station 216 Ec 19.03S 178.09 E
Vuohijarvi 116 Lc 61.10N 26.40 E
Vuoksa 116 Nd 60.35N 30.42 E
Vuoksa, ozero- [Russia] 116 Mc 61.00N 30.00 E
Vuoksa, ozero- Russia 116 Md 60.38N 29.55 E
Vuollerim 114 Ec 66.25N 20.36 E
Vuosjärvi 116 Ka 63.00N 25.30 E
Vuotso 114 Gb 68.06N 27.08 E
Vuranimala 219a Ec 9.05S 160.51 E
Vyborg 112 Ic 60.42N 28.45 E
Vyčegda 110 Kc 61.18N 46.36 E
Vyčegodski 114 Lf 61.17N 46.48 E
Východočeský kraj [3] 120 Lf 50.10N 16.00 E
Východoslovenska nižina 120 Rh 48.35N 21.50 E
Východoslovenský kraj [3] 120 Rg 49.00N 21.15 E
Vyg 114 Ie 63.17N 35.17 E
Vygoda [Ukr.] 130 Nc 46.38N 30.24 E
Vygoda [Ukr.] 120 Uh 48.52N 24.01 E
Vygozero, ozero 110 Jc 63.35N 34.45 E
Vyhandu / Võhandu jõgi 116 Lf 58.03N 27.40 E
Vyja 114 Le 62.57N 46.42 E
Vyksa 136 Ed 55.20N 42.12 E
Vym 136 Fc 62.13N 50.25 E
Vynnu/Võnnu 116 Lf 58.15N 27.10 E
Vyrica 136 Dd 59.24N 30.19 E
Vyrnwy 118 Ki 52.45N 2.50W
Vyrtsjarv, ozero- / Vörts järv 114 Gg 58.15N 26.05 E
Vyru/Võru 136 Cd 57.52N 27.05 E
Vyša 132 Mb 54.03N 42.06 E
Vyšgorod 132 Gd 50.38N 30.29 E
Vyšgorodok 116 Mh 56.55N 28.05 E
Vyškov 120 Mg 49.17N 17.00 E
Vyškovski, pereval- 120 Th 48.38N 23.45 E
Vyšni Voloček 136 Dd 57.37N 34.32 E
Vysock 114 Gf 60.36N 28.36 E
Vysoké Tatry = Hight Tatra (EN) 120 Pg 49.10N 20.00 E
Vysokogorny 138 If 50.07N 139.10 E
Vysokogorsk 154 Mb 44.23N 135.23 E
Vysokoje 132 Cc 52.22N 23.26 E
Vysokovsk 114 Ih 56.21N 36.29 E
Vyšši Brod 120 Kh 48.37N 14.18 E
Vytebet 132 Ic 53.53N 35.38 E
Vytegra 136 Dc 61.01N 36.28 E
Vyvenka 138 Ld 60.10N 165.20 E
Vyzu/Võsu 116 Ke 59.30N 25.50 E
Vzmorje 138 Jg 47.45N 142.30 E

W

Wa 166 Ec 10.03N 2.29W
Waal 122 Kc 51.55N 4.30 E
Waalre 124 Hc 51.23N 5.27 E
Waalwijk 124 Hc 51.41N 5.04 E
Waar, Meos- 150 Jg 2.05S 134.23 E
Waardgronden 124 Ha 53.12N 5.05 E
Waarschoot 124 Fc 51.09N 3.36 E
Wabana 180 Mg 47.38N 52.57W
Wabao, Cap- 219b Ce 21.36S 167.51 E
Wabasca 180 Ge 56.00N 113.53W
Wabasca 180 Fe 58.21N 115.20W
Wabash 184 Ee 40.48N 85.49W
Wabash 174 Kf 37.46N 88.02W
Wabasha 186 Jd 44.23N 92.02W
Wabash River 186 Lh 37.46N 88.02W
Wabowden 180 Hf 54.55N 98.38W
Wąbrzeźno 120 Oc 53.17N 18.57 E
Wabu Hu 152 Ke 32.20N 116.55 E
Wachau 128 Jb 48.20N 15.25 E
Wachile 168 Fe 4.33N 39.03 E
Wachusett Seamount (EN) 208 Lh 32.00S 151.20W
Waco 176 Jf 31.55N 97.08W
Waconda Lake 186 Gg 39.30N 98.30W
Wadayama 156 Dd 35.20N 134.51 E
Wad Bandah 168 Dc 13.06N 27.57 E
Waddān 164 Cd 29.10N 16.08 E
Waddān, Jabal- 164 Cd 29.20N 16.20 E
Waddeneilanden/Friesische Inseln = Frisian Islands (EN) 110 Hc 54.00N 6.00 E
Waddeneilanden = West Frisian Islands (EN) 122 Ka 53.30N 5.00 E
Waddenzee 124 Ha 53.20N 5.30 E
Waddington, Mount- 174 Gd 51.23N 125.15W
Wadena 186 Ic 46.26N 95.08W
Wadern 124 Ie 49.32N 6.53 E
Wadern-Nunkirchen 124 Ie 49.32N 6.53 E
Wadersloh 124 Kc 51.44N 8.15 E
Wadersloh-Liesborn 124 Kc 51.43N 8.16 E
Wadesboro 184 Gh 34.58N 80.04W
Wadhams 188 Ba 51.30N 127.31W
Wādī Bīshah 144 Fe 21.24N 43.26 E
Wādī Fajr 144 Ec 30.17N 38.18 E
Wādī Ḥalfā' 160 Kf 21.56N 31.20 E
Wādī Jimāl, Jazīrat- 146 Fj 24.40N 35.10 E
Wādī Mūsá 146 Fg 30.19N 35.29 E
Wādī Shīḥan 168 Ib 18.10N 52.57 E
Wad Madanī 160 Kg 14.24N 33.32 E
Wad Nimr 168 Ec 14.32N 32.08 E
Wadowice 120 Pg 49.53N 19.30 E
Wadsworth 188 Fg 39.38N 119.17W
Wafangdian → Fuxian 152 Ld 39.38N 121.59 E
Wafrah 144 Gd 28.25N 47.56 E
Waga-Gawa 156 Gb 39.18N 141.07 E
Wagenfeld 124 Kb 52.33N 8.35 E
Wagenfeld-Ströhen 124 Kb 52.32N 8.39 E
Wageningen 124 Hc 51.57N 5.41 E
Wagêr, Qar- 168 Hc 10.01N 45.30 E
Wager Bay 174 Kc 65.26N 88.40W
Wagga Wagga 210 Fh 35.07S 147.22 E
Waghäusel 124 Ke 49.15N 8.30 E
Wagin 210 Ch 33.18S 117.21 E
Waginger See 128 Ib 47.58N 12.50 E
Wagoner 186 Ii 35.58N 95.22W
Wagon Mound 186 Dh 36.01N 104.42W
Wagontire Mountain 188 Fe 43.21N 119.53W
Wagrien 120 Gb 54.15N 10.45 E
Wągrowiec 120 Nd 52.49N 17.11 E
Wah 148 Eb 33.48N 72.42 E
Waha 160 If 28.10N 19.57 E
Wahai 150 Ig 2.48S 129.30 E
Wahiawa 214 Oc 21.30N 158.02W
Wahoo 186 Hf 41.13N 96.37W
Wahpeton 182 Hb 46.16N 96.36W
Waialeale, Mount- 221a Ba 22.04N 159.30W
Waialua 221a Cb 21.35N 158.08W
Waianae 221a Cb 21.27N 158.12W
Waiau 216 Dh 42.39S 173.03 E
Waiau 218 Ee 42.47S 173.22 E
Waiblingen 120 Fh 48.50N 9.18 E
Waibstadt 124 Ke 49.18N 8.56 E
Waidhofen/Ybbs 128 Ic 47.58N 14.46 E
Waidhofen an der Thaya 128 Jb 48.49N 15.17 E
Waigame 150 Ig 1.50S 129.49 E
Waigeo, Pulau- 208 Ee 0.14S 130.45 E
Waihi 218 Fb 37.24S 175.50 E
Waihou 218 Fb 37.10S 175.33 E
Waikabubak 150 Gh 9.38S 119.25 E
Waikare, Lake- 218 Fb 37.25S 175.10 E
Waikaremoana, Lake- 216 Eg 38.45S 177.05 E
Waikato 218 Fb 37.23S 174.43 E
Waikawa 218 Cg 46.38S 169.08 E
Waikouaiti 218 Df 45.36S 170.41 E
Wailangilala 219d Cb 16.45S 179.06W
Wailua 221a Ba 22.03N 159.20W
Wailuku 214 Oc 20.53N 156.30W
Waimamaku 218 Ea 35.34S 173.29 E
Waimanalo Beach 221a Db 21.20N 157.42W
Waimangaroa 218 Dd 41.43S 171.46 E
Waimate 218 Df 44.45S 171.03 E
Waimea [Hi.-U.S.] 221a Fc 20.02N 155.40W
Waimea [Hi.-U.S.] 221a Bb 21.57N 159.40W
Waimes 124 Id 50.25N 6.07 E
Wainfleet All Saints 124 Ca 53.06N 0.15 E
Wainganga 140 Jh 19.36N 79.48 E
Waingapu 150 Hh 9.39S 120.16 E
Waini Point 196 Gh 8.24N 59.49W
Waini River 196 Gh 8.24N 59.51W
Wainwright [Ak.-U.S.] 178 Gb 70.38N 160.01W
Wainwright [Alta.-Can.] 180 Gf 52.49N 110.52W
Waiouru 218 Eg 39.29S 175.40 E
Waipahu 221a Cb 21.23N 158.01W
Waipara 218 Ee 43.03S 172.45 E
Waipawa 218 Gc 39.56S 176.35 E
Waipiro 218 Hc 38.02S 178.20 E
Waipu 218 Fa 35.59S 174.26 E
Waipukurau 218 Gd 40.00S 176.33 E
Wairakei 218 Gc 38.37S 176.05 E
Wairarapa, Lake- 218 Fd 41.15S 175.15 E
Wairau 218 Fd 41.31S 174.03 E
Wairoa 216 Eg 39.03S 177.26 E
Wairoa 218 Fb 36.11S 174.02 E
Waitaki 218 Df 44.56S 171.09 E
Waitangi 216 Fh 43.56S 176.34W
Waitara 216 Dg 39.00S 174.14 E
Waitati 218 Df 45.45S 170.34 E
Waitemata 218 Fb 36.50S 174.40 E
Waitotara 218 Fc 39.48S 174.44 E
Waiuku 218 Fb 37.15S 174.44 E
Waiwerang 150 Hh 8.23S 123.09 E
Waiyevo 216 Fc 16.48S 179.59W
Wājid 168 Ge 3.50N 43.14 E
Wajima 154 Nf 37.24N 136.54 E
Wajir 160 Lh 1.42N 40.04 E
Waka [Eth.] 168 Fd 7.09N 37.19 E
Waka [Zaire] 170 Db 1.01N 20.13 E
Wakamatsu-Shima 156 Ae 32.54N 129.00 E
Wakasa-Wan 152 Od 35.45N 135.40 E
Wakatipu, Lake- 216 Ci 45.05S 168.35 E
Wakaya 219d Bb 17.37S 179.00 E
Wakayama 142 Pf 34.13N 135.11 E
Wakayama Ken [2] 154 Mh 33.55N 135.20 E
Wake 156 Dd 34.48N 134.08 E
Wa Keeney 186 Gg 39.01N 99.53W
Wakefield [Eng.-U.K.] 118 Lh 53.42N 1.29W
Wakefield [N.Z.] 218 Ed 41.24S 173.03 E
Wake Island [5] 210 Hc 19.18N 166.36 E
Wake Island 208 Hc 19.18N 166.36 E
Wakkanai 142 Qe 45.25N 141.40 E
Waku Kungo 170 Ce 11.25S 15.07 E
Wakunai 219a Ba 5.52S 155.13 E
Wakuya 156 Gb 38.33N 141.05 E
Wala 170 Fd 5.46S 32.04 E
Walachia (EN) = Valahia 110 Ig 44.00N 25.00 E
Walachia (EN) = Valahia 130 He 44.00N 25.00 E

Index Symbols

[1] Independent Nation
[2] State, Region
[3] District, County
[4] Municipality
[5] Colony, Dependency
Continent
Physical Region
Historical or Cultural Region
Mount, Mountain
Volcano
Hill
Mountains, Mountain Range
Hills, Escarpment
Plateau, Upland
Pass, Gap
Plain, Lowland
Delta
Salt Flat
Valley, Canyon
Crater, Cave
Karst Features
Depression
Polder
Desert, Dunes
Forest, Woods
Heath, Steppe
Oasis
Cape, Point
Coast, Beach
Cliff
Peninsula
Isthmus
Sandbank
Island
Atoll
Rock, Reef
Islands, Archipelago
Rocks, Reefs
Coral Reef
Well, Spring
Geyser
River, Stream
Waterfall, Rapids
River Mouth, Estuary
Lake
Salt Lake
Intermittent Lake
Reservoir
Swamp, Pond
Canal
Glacier
Ice Shelf, Pack Ice
Ocean
Sea
Gulf, Bay
Strait, Fjord
Lagoon
Bank
Seamount
Tablemount
Ridge
Shelf
Basin
Escarpment, Sea Scarp
Fracture
Trench, Abyss
National Park, Reserve
Point of Interest
Recreation Site
Cave, Cavern
Historic Site
Ruins
Wall, Walls
Church, Abbey
Temple
Scientific Station
Railway station
Airport
Port
Military installation
Lighthouse
Mine
Tunnel
Dam, Bridge

Wałbrzych 112 He 50.46N 16.17 E
Wałbrzych [2] 120 Mf 50.45N 16.15 E
Walchensee 120 Hi 47.35N 11.20 E
Walcheren 122 Jc 51.33N 3.35 E
Walcott, Lake- 188 Ie 42.40N 113.23W
Walcourt 124 Gd 50.15N 4.25 E
Walcourt-Fraire 124 Gd 50.16N 4.30 E
Wałcz 120 Mc 53.17N 16.28 E
Waldböckelheim 124 Je 49.49N 7.43 E
Waldbröl 120 Df 50.53N 7.37 E
Waldeck 124 Lc 51.12N 9.05 E
Waldeck 124 Kc 51.17N 8.50 E
Waldems 124 Kd 50.15N 8.18 E
Walden 186 Cf 40.44N 106.17W
Waldfischbach-Burgalben 124 Je 49.17N 7.40 E
Waldkirchen 120 Jh 48.44N 13.36 E
Waldkraiburg 124 Ke 49.34N 8.49 E
Wald-Michelbach 120 Ig 49.35N 12.07 E
Waldnaab 184 If 38.37N 76.54W
Waldorf 124 Ie 49.45N 6.45 E
Waldrach 186 Ii 34.54N 94.05W
Waldron 186 Ii 34.54N 94.05W
Waldshut-Tiengen 120 Ei 47.37N 8.13 E
Waldviertel 146 Hf 33.30N 39.15 E
Waleabahi, Pulau- 178 Fc 65.36N 168.05W
Walej, Sha'ib al- 118 Ji 52.30N 3.30W
Wales 110 Fe 52.30N 3.30W
Wales [2] 180 Ic 67.50N 86.40W
Wales 166 Ec 10.21N 0.48W
Wales 124 Ie 49.39N 6.08 E
Walewale 210 Fh 30.01S 148.07 E
Walferdange 222 Of 75.15S 105.00W
Walgett 186 Hb 48.55N 97.55W
Walgreen Coast 170 Ec 1.25S 28.03 E
Walhalla 186 Ic 47.06N 94.35W
Walikale 182 Dd 38.40N 118.43W
Walker 212 Jd 21.10S 149.10 E
Walker Lake 186 Ed 44.01N 102.14W
Walkerston 188 Hc 47.28N 115.56W
Wall 184 Fd 42.36N 82.23W
Wallace 212 Ke 28.56S 151.56 E
Wallaceburg 212 Hf 33.56S 137.38 E
Wallangarra 212 Ic 15.05S 141.50 E
Wallaroo 118 Jh 53.26N 3.03W
Wallary Island 182 Db 46.08N 118.20W
Wallasey 124 Ke 49.20N 8.39 E
Walla Walla 124 Kb 52.21N 8.01 E
Walldorf 197n Ba 13.19N 61.15W
Wallenhorst 124 Ac 51.36N 1.08W
Wallibu 128 Bd 46.15N 7.30 E
Wallingford
Wallis / Valais [2] 208 Jf 13.18S 176.10W
Wallis, Iles-=Wallis Islands (EN) 210 Jf 14.00S 177.00W
Wallis and Futuna (EN)= Wallis-et-Futuna [5] 210 Jf 14.00S 177.00W
Wallis-et-Futuna=Wallis and Futuna (EN) [5] 208 Jf 13.18S 176.10W
Wallis Islands (EN)=Wallis, 188 Gd 45.43N 117.32W
Iles- 188 Gd 45.10N 117.30W
Wallowa 124 Dc 51.12N 1.24 E
Wallowa Mountains 118 Jg 54.07N 3.15W
Walmer 182 Id 36.04N 90.57W
Walney, Isle of- 208 Hg 22.37S 168.57 E
Walnut Ridge 178 Ge 58.45N 160.20W
Walpole, Ile- 118 Li 52.35N 1.58W
Walrus Islands 182 Gd 37.37N 104.47W
Walsall 120 Fd 52.52N 9.35 E
Walsenburg 184 Gi 32.54N 80.39W
Walsrode 184 Ej 31.49N 85.08W
Walterboro 186 Gi 34.22N 98.19W
Walter F. George Lake 120 Gf 50.54N 10.34 E
Walters 184 Ic 45.58N 76.57W
Waltershausen 124 Dc 51.51N 1.17 E
Waltham 124 Jc 51.38N 7.24 E
Walton-on-the-Naze 172 Ad 23.00S 14.30 E
Waltrop
Walvisbaai/Walvis Bay [3] 160 Ik 22.59S 14.31 E
Walvisbaai=Walvis Bay (EN) 160 Ik 22.59S 14.31 E
Walvisbaai=Walvis Bay (EN) 158 Ik 22.57S 14.30 E
Walvis Bay/Walvisbaai [3] 172 Ad 23.00S 14.30 E
Walvis Bay (EN)= Walvisbaai 160 Ik 22.59S 14.31 E
Walvis Bay (EN)= Walvisbaai 158 Ik 22.57S 14.30 E
Walvis Ridge (EN) 106 El 28.00S 3.00 E
Wama 170 Ce 12.14S 15.34 E
Wamba 158 Ii 3.56S 17.12 E
Wamba [Kenya] 170 Gb 0.59N 37.19 E
Wamba [Nig.] 166 Gd 8.56N 8.36 E
Wamba [Zaire] 170 Eb 2.09N 28.00 E
Wamena 150 Kg 4.00S 138.57 E
Wami 158 Ki 6.08S 38.49 E
Wampusirpi 194 Ef 15.15N 84.37W
Wamsutter 188 Lf 41.40N 107.58W
Wan 150 Kh 8.23S 137.56 E
Wana 148 Db 32.17N 69.35 E
Wanaka 210 Hi 44.42S 169.08 E
Wanaka, Lake- 218 Cf 44.30S 169.10 E
Wan'an 152 Jf 26.32N 114.48 E
Wanapiri 150 Kg 4.33S 135.59 E
Wanapitei Lake 184 Gb 46.45N 80.45W
Wandel Hav=Wandel Sea (EN) 179 Kb 83.00N 15.00W
Wandel Sea (EN)=Wandel Hav 179 Kb 83.00N 15.00W
Wandsworth, London- 124 Bc 51.27N 0.12W
Wanganui 216 Eg 39.56S 175.02 E
Wanganui 218 Fc 39.58S 175.00 E
Wangaratta 212 Jg 36.22S 146.20 E
Wangcun [China] 152 Jd 39.58N 112.53 E
Wangcun [China] 154 Df 36.41N 117.42 E
Wangda/Zogang 152 Gf 29.37N 97.58 E
Wangdu 154 Ce 38.43N 115.09 E
Wangen im Allagäu 120 Fi 47.41N 9.50 E
Wangerooge 120 Dc 53.46N 7.55 E
Wanggameti, Gunung- 150 Hi 10.07S 120.14 E
Wanggezhuang → Jiaonan 154 Eg 35.53N 119.58 E
Wangiwangi, Pulau- 150 Hh 5.20S 123.35 E
Wangjiang 154 Di 30.08N 116.41 E
Wangkui 152 Mb 46.50N 126.29 E
Wangpan Yang 140 Of 30.33N 121.26 E
Wangping 152 Mc 43.18N 129.46 E
Wangying → Huaiyin 154 Eh 33.35N 119.02 E
Wani, Laguna- 194 Ff 14.50N 83.25W
Wanie-Rukula 170 Eb 0.14N 25.34 E
Wanitsuka-Yama 156 Bf 31.45N 131.17 E
Wanlewêyn 168 Ge 2.35N 44.55 E
Wān Namton 148 Jd 22.03N 99.33 E
Wannian (Chenying) 154 Dj 28.42N 117.04 E
Wanning 152 Jh 18.59N 110.24 E
Wanquan 154 Cd 40.52N 114.44 E
Wansbeck 118 Lf 55.10N 1.34W
Wan Shui 154 Di 30.30N 117.01 E
Wanxian 142 Mf 30.48N 108.21 E
Wanyuan 152 Ie 32.03N 108.04 E
Wanzai 154 Cj 28.06N 114.27 E
Wanzhi → Wuhu 154 Ei 31.21N 118.23 E
Wapato 188 Ec 46.27N 120.25W
Wapiti 188 Kd 44.28N 109.28W
Wapiti 188 Fe 55.08N 118.19W
Wapsipinicon River 186 Kf 41.44N 90.20W
Waqooyi Galbeed [3] 168 Gc 10.00N 44.00 E
Warangal 142 Jh 18.18N 79.35 E
Waratah Bay 212 Jg 38.50S 146.05 E
Warburg 120 Fe 51.30N 9.10 E
Warburger Borde 124 Lc 51.35N 9.12 E
Warburg-Scherfede 124 Lc 51.32N 9.02 E
Warburton Bay 180 Gd 63.50N 111.30W
Warburton Mission 212 Fe 26.10S 126.35 E
Warburton Range 212 Fe 26.10S 126.40 E
Ward 218 Fd 41.50S 174.08 E
Warden 172 De 27.56S 29.00 E
Wardenburg 124 Ka 53.04N 8.12 E
Wardha 148 Fd 20.45N 78.37 E
Ward Hunt Strait 212 Ja 9.25S 149.55 E
Ware [B.C.-Can.] 180 Ee 57.27N 125.38W
Ware [Eng.-U.K.] 124 Bc 51.49N 0.01W
Waregem 124 Fd 50.53N 3.25 E
Waremme/Borgworm 122 Ld 50.42N 5.15 E
Waren [Ger.] 120 Ic 53.31N 12.41 E
Waren [Indon.] 210 Ee 2.16S 136.20 E
Warendorf 120 De 51.57N 7.59 E
Warin Chamrap 148 Ke 15.14N 104.52 E
Warka 120 Re 51.47N 21.10 E
Warkworth 218 Fb 36.24S 174.40 E
Warmbad [3] 172 Be 28.00S 18.30 E
Warmbad [Nam.] 172 Be 28.29S 18.41 E
Warmbad [S.Afr.] 172 Dd 24.53S 28.17 E
Warming Land 179 Gb 81.50N 52.45W
Warmington 124 Ab 52.08N 1.24W
Warminster 118 Kj 51.13N 2.12W
Warm Springs [Nv.-U.S.] 188 Gg 38.13N 116.20W
Warm Springs [Or.-U.S.] 188 Ed 44.46N 121.16W
Warnemünde, Rostock- 120 Ib 54.10N 12.05 E
Warner, Mount- 188 Da 51.03N 123.12W
Warner Mountains 182 Cc 41.40N 120.20W
Warner Peak 188 Fe 42.27N 119.44W
Warner Robins 182 Ke 32.37N 83.36W
Warner Valley 188 Fe 42.30N 119.55W
Warnes 202 Fg 17.30S 63.10W
Warnow 120 Ib 54.06N 12.09 E
Waroona 212 Df 32.50S 115.55 E
Warragul 212 Jg 38.10S 145.56 E
Warrego Range 212 Je 25.00S 145.45 E
Warrego River 208 Fh 30.24S 145.21 E
Warren [Ar.-U.S.] 186 Jj 33.38N 92.05W
Warren [Mi.-U.S.] 184 Fd 42.28N 83.01W
Warren [Mn.-U.S.] 186 Hb 48.12N 96.46W
Warren [Oh.-U.S.] 182 Kc 41.15N 80.49W
Warren [Pa.-U.S.] 184 He 41.52N 79.09W
Warrenpoint/An Pointe 118 Gg 54.06N 6.15W
Warrensburg 186 Jg 38.46N 93.44W
Warrenton 172 Ce 28.09S 24.47 E
Warri 166 Gd 5.31N 5.45 E
Warrington [Eng.-U.K.] 118 Kh 53.24N 2.37W
Warrington [Fl.-U.S.] 184 Dj 30.23N 87.16W
Warrior Reefs 212 Ia 9.35S 143.10 E
Warrnambool 210 Fh 38.23S 142.29 E
Warroad 182 Hb 48.54N 95.19W
Warrumbungle Range 212 Jf 31.30S 149.40 E
Warsaw [In.-U.S.] 184 Ee 41.14N 85.51W
Warsaw [Mo.-U.S.] 186 Jg 38.15N 93.23W
Warsaw [N.Y.-U.S.] 184 Hd 42.45N 78.07W
Warsaw (EN)=Warszawa [Pol.] 112 Ie 52.15N 21.00 E
Warshīkh 168 He 2.18N 45.48 E
Warstein 124 Kc 51.27N 8.22 E
Warstein-Belecke 124 Kc 51.29N 8.20 E
Warszawa [2] 120 Qd 52.15N 21.00 E
Warszawa [Pol.] =Warsaw (EN) 112 Ie 52.15N 21.00 E
Warta 110 He 52.35N 14.39 E
Waru 150 Jg 3.24S 130.40 E
Warwich 212 Ke 28.13S 152.02 E
Warwick 118 Li 52.25N 1.30W
Warwick [Eng.-U.K.] 118 Li 52.17N 1.34W
Warwick [R.I.-U.S.] 184 Le 41.42N 71.23W
Warwickshire [3] 118 Li 52.10N 1.35W
Wasagu 166 Gc 11.22N 5.48 E
Wasatch Range 174 He 41.15N 111.30W
Wascana Creek 188 Ma 50.40N 104.55W
Wasco 188 Fi 35.36N 119.20W
Waseca 186 Jd 44.05N 93.30W
Washburn 186 Fc 47.17N 101.02W
Washess Bay 220g Ab 1.49N 157.31W
Wāshim 148 Fd 20.10N 76.58 E
Washington [2] 182 Cb 47.30N 120.30W
Washington [D.C.-U.S.] 176 Lf 38.54N 77.01W
Washington [Eng.-U.K.] 118 Lg 54.54N 1.31W
Washington [Ga.-U.S.] 184 Fi 33.44N 82.44W
Washington [Ia.-U.S.] 186 Kf 41.18N 91.42W
Washington [In.-U.S.] 184 Df 38.40N 87.10W
Washington [N.C.-U.S.] 184 Ih 35.33N 77.03W
Washington [Pa.-U.S.] 184 Ge 40.11N 80.16W
Washington → Teraina Island 208 Kd 4.43N 160.24W
Washington, Mount- 174 Le 44.15N 71.15W
Washington Court House 184 Ff 39.32N 83.29W
Washington Island 186 Md 45.23N 86.55W
Washington Land 179 Fb 80.15N 65.00W
Washita River 186 Hi 34.12N 96.50W
Washtucna 188 Fc 46.45N 118.19W
Wasile 150 If 1.04N 127.59 E
Wasilków 120 Tc 53.12N 23.12 E
Wasior 150 Jg 2.43S 134.30 E
Wāsiţ [3] 146 Lf 32.35N 46.00 E
Waskaganish 176 Ld 51.25N 78.45W
Wąsosz 120 Me 51.34N 16.42 E
Waspán 190 Hf 14.44N 83.58W
Wassamu 156a Ca 44.02N 142.24 E
Wassenaar 124 Gb 52.09N 4.24 E
Wassenberg 124 Ic 51.06N 6.09 E
Wasserburg am Inn 120 Ih 48.04N 12.14 E
Wasserkuppe 120 Ff 50.30N 9.56 E
Wassigny 124 Fd 50.01N 3.36 E
Wassuk Range 188 Fg 38.40N 118.50W
Wassy 122 Kf 48.30N 4.57 E
Waswanipi, Lac- 184 Ia 49.32N 76.29W
Watampone 142 Oj 4.32S 120.20 E
Watansoppeng 150 Gg 4.21S 119.53 E
Watari 156 Gb 38.02N 140.51 E
Waterbeach 124 Cb 52.16N 0.12 E
Waterberg 172 Bd 20.25S 17.15 E
Waterbury 182 Mc 41.33N 73.02W
Water Cays 194 Ib 23.40N 77.45W
Wateree Pond 184 Gh 34.25N 80.50W
Waterford/Port Láirge 112 Fe 52.15N 7.06W
Waterford/Port Láirge [2] 118 Fi 52.10N 7.40W
Waterford Harbour/Cuan Phort Láirge 118 Gi 52.10N 6.57W
Wateringues 122 Id 50.55N 2.15 E
Waterloo [Bel.] 122 Kd 50.43N 4.24 E
Waterloo [Ia.-U.S.] 182 Ic 42.30N 92.20W
Waterloo [Il.-U.S.] 186 Kg 38.20N 90.09W
Waterlooville 124 Ad 50.52N 1.01W
Watersmeet 184 Cb 46.18N 89.11W
Watertown [N.Y.-U.S.] 182 Lc 43.57N 75.56W
Watertown [S.D.-U.S.] 182 Hc 44.54N 97.07W
Watertown [Wi.-U.S.] 186 Le 43.12N 88.43W
Waterville 182 Nc 44.33N 69.38W
Watford 118 Mj 51.40N 0.25W
Watford City 186 Ec 47.48N 103.17W
Wa'th 168 Ed 8.10N 32.07 E
Watheroo 212 Df 30.17S 116.04 E
Watīr, Wādī- 146 Fh 29.01N 34.40 E
Watkins Glen 184 Id 42.23N 76.53W
Watling → San Salvador 190 Jd 24.02N 74.28W
Watlington 124 Ac 51.38N 1.00W
Watonga 186 Gi 35.51N 98.25W
Watou, Poperinge- 124 Ed 50.51N 2.37 E
Watrous 188 Gf 51.40N 105.28W
Watsa 160 Jh 3.03N 29.32 E
Watseka 186 Mf 40.47N 87.44W
Watsi [C.R.] 194 Ff 9.37N 82.52W
Watsi [Zaire] 170 Dc 0.19S 21.04 E
Watsi Kengo 170 Dc 0.48S 20.33 E
Watson Lake 176 Gc 60.07N 128.48W
Watsonville 188 Eh 36.55N 121.45W
Watt, Morne- 197g Bb 15.19N 61.19W
Watton 124 Cb 52.34N 0.50 E
Watts Bar Lake 184 Eh 35.48N 84.39W
Wattwil 128 Dc 47.18N 9.05 E
Watubela, Kepulauan- 150 Jg 4.35S 131.40 E
Wau 212 Ja 7.20S 146.45 E
Waubay Lake 186 Hd 45.25N 97.25W
Wauchope 212 Kf 31.27S 152.44 E
Wauchula 184 Gl 27.33N 81.49W
Waucoba Mountain 188 Fh 37.00N 118.01W
Waukara, Gunung- 150 Gg 1.15S 119.42 E
Waukarlycarly, Lake- 212 Ed 21.25S 121.50 E
Waukegan 182 Jc 42.22N 87.50W
Waukesha 186 Le 43.01N 88.14W
Waupaca 186 Ld 44.21N 89.05W
Wausau 182 Jc 44.59N 89.39W
Wauseon 184 Ee 41.33N 84.09W
Wauwatosa 186 Me 43.03N 88.00W
Wave Hill 212 Gc 17.29S 130.57 E
Waveney 118 Oi 52.28N 1.45 E
Waver/Wavre 122 Kd 50.43N 4.37 E
Waverly [Ia.-U.S.] 186 Je 42.44N 92.29W
Waverly [Oh.-U.S.] 184 Ff 39.07N 82.59W
Waverly [Tn.-U.S.] 184 Dg 36.05N 87.48W
Waves 184 Jh 35.37N 75.29W
Wavre/Waver 122 Kd 50.43N 4.37 E
Wāw 160 Jh 7.42N 28.00 E
Wawa [Nig.] 166 Fd 9.55N 4.27 E
Wawa [Ont.-Can.] 180 Jg 47.59N 84.47W
Wawa, Rio- 194 Fg 13.53N 83.28W
Wāw al Kabīr 160 If 25.20N 16.43 E
Wāw an Nāmūs 164 Ce 24.55N 19.45 E
Wāw Nahr 168 Dd 7.03N 27.13 E
Wawo 150 Hg 3.41S 121.02 E
Wawotobi 150 Hg 3.51S 122.06 E
Waxahachie 186 Hj 32.24N 96.51W
Waxweiler 124 Id 50.06N 6.22 E
Waxxari 152 Ed 38.37N 87.22 E
Way, Lake- 212 Ee 26.50S 120.20 E
Waya 219d Ab 17.18S 177.08 E
Wayabula 150 If 2.17N 128.12 E
Wayan 188 Je 43.00N 111.22W
Waycross 182 Ke 31.13N 82.21W
Wayne [Nb.-U.S.] 186 He 42.14N 97.01W
Wayne [W.V.-U.S.] 184 Ff 38.14N 82.27W
Waynesboro [Ga.-U.S.] 184 Fi 33.06N 82.01W
Waynesboro [Ms.-U.S.] 186 Lk 31.40N 88.39W
Waynesboro [Pa.-U.S.] 184 If 39.45N 77.36W
Waynesboro [Va.-U.S.] 184 Hf 38.04N 78.54W
Waynesville [Mo.-U.S.] 186 Jh 37.50N 92.12W
Waynesville [N.C.-U.S.] 184 Fh 35.29N 83.00W
Waynoka 186 Gh 36.35N 98.53W
Waziers 124 Fd 50.23N 3.07 E
Wda 120 Oc 53.25N 18.29 E
Wdzydze, Jezioro- 120 Nc 54.00N 17.50 E
Wé 216 Cd 20.55S 167.16 E
We, Pulau- 150 Ce 5.51N 95.18 E
Wear 118 Lg 54.55N 1.22W
Weatherford [Ok.-U.S.] 186 Gi 35.32N 98.42W
Weatherford [Tx.-U.S.] 182 He 32.46N 97.48W
Weaverville 188 Df 40.44N 122.56W
Weber 218 Gd 40.24S 176.20 E
Webster 186 Hd 45.20N 97.31W
Webster City 186 Je 42.28N 93.49W
Webster Springs 184 Gf 38.29N 80.25W
Weda 150 If 0.21N 127.52 E
Weda, Teluk- 150 If 0.20N 128.00 E
Weddell Island 206 Hh 51.50S 61.00W
Weddell Sea (EN) 222 Rf 72.00S 45.00W
Wedel 120 Fc 53.35N 9.41 E
Wedgeport 184 Od 43.44N 65.59W
Wedza 172 Ec 18.35S 31.35 E
Weed 188 Df 41.25N 122.27W
Weener 120 Dc 53.10N 7.21 E
Weerdinge, Emmen- 124 Ib 52.49N 6.57 E
Weert 122 Lc 51.15N 5.43 E
Weesp 124 Hb 52.18N 5.02 E
Wegberg 124 Ic 51.09N 6.16 E
Węgliniec 120 Le 51.17N 15.13 E
Węgorzewo 120 Rb 54.14N 21.44 E
Węgrów 120 Sd 52.25N 22.01 E
Wehni 168 Fc 12.40N 36.42 E
Weichang (Zhuizishan) 152 Kc 41.55N 117.39 E
Weida 120 If 50.46N 12.04 E
Weiden in der Oberpfalz 120 Ig 49.41N 12.10 E
Weifang 142 Nf 36.43N 119.06 E
Weihai 152 Ld 37.27N 122.02 E
Weihe 154 Jb 44.55N 128.23 E
Wei He 140 Nf 34.36N 110.10 E
Weil 124 Kd 50.28N 8.16 E
Weilburg 120 Ef 50.29N 8.15 E
Weilerbach 124 Je 49.29N 7.38 E
Weilerswist 124 Id 50.46N 6.50 E
Weilheim in Oberbayern 120 Hi 47.50N 11.09 E
Weilmünster 124 Kd 50.26N 8.21 E
Weimar [Ger.] 124 Kd 50.46N 8.43 E
Weimar [Ger.] 120 Hf 50.59N 11.19 E
Weinan 152 Ie 34.30N 109.34 E
Weingarten 120 Fi 47.48N 9.38 E
Weinheim 120 Eg 49.33N 8.40 E
Weining 152 Hf 26.46N 104.18 E
Weinsberger Wald 128 Ib 48.25N 15.00 E
Weinstraße 124 Ke 49.20N 8.05 E
Weinviertel 128 Kb 48.35N 16.30 E
Weipa 210 Ff 12.41S 141.52 E
Weirton 184 Ge 40.24N 80.37W
Weiser 188 Gd 44.15N 116.58W
Weiser River 188 Gd 44.15N 116.59W
Weishan Hu 152 Ke 34.35N 117.15 E
Weishi 154 Cg 34.25N 114.10 E
Weishui → Jingxing 154 Ce 38.03N 114.09 E
Weiße Elster 120 He 51.26N 11.57 E
Weißenberg 124 Je 49.15N 7.49 E
Weißenburg in Bayern 120 Gg 49.02N 10.59 E
Weißenfels 120 He 51.12N 11.58 E
Weißer Main 120 Hf 50.05N 11.24 E
Weißerstein 124 Id 50.24N 6.22 E
Weißkugel/Palla Bianca 128 Ed 46.48N 10.44 E
Weiss Lake 184 Eh 34.15N 85.35W
Weißwasser/Běla Woda 120 Ke 51.31N 14.38 E
Weitra 128 Ib 48.42N 14.53 E
Weixi 152 Gf 27.13N 99.19 E
Weixian 154 Cf 36.59N 115.15 E
Weixin (Zhaxi) 152 If 27.46N 105.04 E
Weiz 128 Jc 47.13N 15.37 E
Wejherowo 120 Ob 54.37N 18.15 E
Welbourn Hill 210 Eg 27.21S 134.06 E
Welch 184 Gg 37.26N 81.36W
Weldiya 168 Fc 11.48N 39.35 E
Weld Range 212 De 26.55S 117.25 E
Welega [3] 168 Fd 8.38N 35.40 E
Welel 168 Ed 8.56N 34.52 E
Weligama 148 Gg 5.58N 80.25 E
Welkenraedt 124 Hd 50.39N 5.58 E
Welker Seamount (EN) 178 Ke 55.07N 140.20W
Welkite 168 Fd 8.17N 37.49 E
Welkom 160 Jk 27.59S 26.45 E
Welland 180 Jh 42.59N 79.15W
Welland 118 Ni 52.53N 0.02 E
Welland Canal 184 Hd 43.14N 79.13W
Wellesley Islands 208 Ef 16.45S 139.30 E
Wellin 124 Hd 50.05N 5.07 E
Wellingborough 118 Mi 52.19N 0.42W
Wellington [2] 218 Fd 40.10S 175.30 E
Wellington [Austl.] 212 Jf 32.33S 148.57 E
Wellington [Eng.-U.K.] 118 Jk 50.59N 3.14W
Wellington [Ks.-U.S.] 186 Hh 37.16N 97.24W
Wellington [Nv.-U.S.] 188 Fg 38.45N 119.22W
Wellington [N.Z.] 210 Ii 41.17S 174.46 E
Wellington, Isla- 198 Ij 49.20S 74.40W
Wellington, Lake- 212 Jg 38.10S 147.15 E
Wellington Channel 180 Ia 75.10N 93.00W
Wells [Eng.-U.K.] 118 Kj 51.13N 2.39W
Wells [Eng.-U.K.] 118 Ni 52.58N 0.51 E
Wells [Nv.-U.S.] 182 Dc 41.07N 115.01W
Wells, Lake- 212 Ee 26.45S 123.15 E
Wells, Mount- 212 Fc 17.26S 127.14 E
Wellsboro 184 Ie 41.45N 77.18W
Wellsford 218 Fb 36.18S 174.31 E
Wellton 188 Hj 32.40N 114.08W
Welmel 168 Gd 5.35N 40.55 E
Wełna 120 Md 52.36N 16.50 E
Welo [3] 168 Fc 12.00N 40.00 E
Wels 128 Ib 48.10N 14.02 E
Welshpool 118 Ji 52.40N 3.09W
Welver 124 Jc 51.37N 7.58 E
Welwitschia 172 Ad 20.21S 14.57 E
Welwyn Garden City 118 Mj 51.48N 0.13W
Wema 170 Dc 0.26S 21.38 E
Wemding 120 Gh 48.52N 10.43 E
Wen'an 154 De 38.52N 116.30 E
Wenatchee 182 Cb 47.25N 120.19W
Wenatchee Mountains 188 Ec 47.20N 120.45W
Wenchang 152 Jh 19.43N 110.44 E
Wenchi 166 Ed 7.44N 2.06W
Wenchit 168 Fc 10.03N 38.35 E
Wenden 124 Jd 50.58N 7.52 E
Wendeng 152 Ld 37.10N 122.01 E
Wendland 120 Gc 53.10N 11.00 E
Wendo 168 Fd 6.37N 38.25 E
Wendover 188 Hf 40.45N 114.02W
Wengyuan (Longxian) 152 Jg 24.21N 114.13 E
Wen He 154 Ef 37.06N 119.29 E
Wenling 152 Lf 28.23N 121.22 E
Wenquan 152 Fe 33.15N 91.55 E
Wenquan/Arixang 152 Dc 44.59N 81.04 E
Wenshan 152 Hg 23.22N 104.23 E
Wenshui 154 Bf 37.26N 112.01 E
Wensu 152 Dc 41.15N 80.14 E
Wensum 124 Db 52.37N 1.22 E
Wentworth 212 If 34.07S 141.55 E
Wenxian 152 He 32.52N 104.40 E
Wenzhou 142 Og 27.57N 120.38 E
Wenzhu 152 Jf 27.00N 114.00 E
Wepener 172 De 29.46S 27.00 E
Wépion, Namur- 124 Gd 50.25N 4.52 E
Werda 172 Ce 25.16S 23.17 E
Werder 160 Lh 7.00N 45.21 E
Werder 120 Jc 53.40N 13.25 E
Werdohl 124 Jc 51.16N 7.46 E
Were Ilu 168 Fc 10.38N 39.23 E
Werkendam 124 Gc 51.49N 4.55 E
Werl 124 Jc 51.33N 7.55 E
Werlte 124 Jb 52.51N 7.41 E
Wermelskirchen 124 Jc 51.09N 7.13 E
Werne 124 Jc 51.40N 7.38 E
Wernigerode 120 Ge 51.50N 10.47 E
Werra 110 Ge 51.26N 9.39 E
Werribee 212 Ig 37.54S 144.40 E
Werris Creek 212 Kf 31.21S 150.39 E
Werse 124 Jb 52.02N 7.41 E
Wertach 120 Gh 48.24N 10.53 E
Wertheim 120 Fg 49.45N 9.31 E
Wesel 120 Ce 51.40N 6.37 E
Weser 110 Ge 53.32N 8.34 E
Weserbergland 120 Fe 51.55N 9.30 E
Wesergebirge 120 Fd 52.15N 9.10 E
Weslaco 186 Gm 26.09N 98.01W
Wesley 197g Ba 15.34N 61.19W
Wesleyville 180 Mg 49.09N 53.34W
Wessel, Cape- 212 Hb 11.00S 136.45 E
Wesseling 124 Id 50.50N 6.59 E
Wessel Islands 208 Ef 12.00S 136.45 E
Wessington Springs 186 Gd 44.05N 98.34W
West Allis 186 Le 43.01N 88.00W
West Baines River 212 Gc 15.26S 130.08 E
West Bay 186 Ll 29.00N 89.30W
West Bend 186 Le 43.25N 88.11W
West Bengal [3] 148 Hd 24.00N 88.00 E
West Berlin = Berlin 112 He 52.31N 13.24 E
West Branch 184 Ec 44.17N 84.14W
West Bridgford 124 Ab 52.55N 1.07W
West Bromwich 118 Li 52.31N 1.59W
Westbrook 184 Ld 43.41N 70.21W
West Burra 118 La 60.05N 1.10W
West Caicos 194 Kc 21.47N 72.17W
West Cape 208 Hi 45.55S 166.26 E
West Caroline Basin (EN) 106 Ii 4.00N 138.00 E
West Carpathians (EN)= Západné Karpaty 120 Og 49.30N 19.00 E
West Des Moines 186 Jf 41.35N 93.43W
Westdongeradeel 124 Ha 53.23N 5.58 E
Westdongeradeel-Holwerd 124 Ha 53.22N 5.54 E
Westdongeradeel-Ternaard 124 Ha 53.23N 5.58 E
Westeinderplassen 124 Gb 52.15N 4.30 E
West Elk Mountains 186 Cg 38.40N 107.15W
West End 184 Hl 26.41N 78.58W
Westende, Middelkerke- 124 Ec 51.10N 2.46 E
West End Village 197b Ab 18.11N 63.09W
West Entrance 220a Bb 7.57N 134.30 E
Westerbork 124 Ib 52.51N 6.36 E
Westerburg 124 Jd 50.34N 7.59 E
Westerland 120 Eb 54.54N 8.18 E
Westerlo 124 Gc 51.05N 4.55 E
Western [Ghana] [3] 166 Ed 5.30N 2.30W
Western [Kenya] [3] 170 Fb 0.30N 34.35 E
Western [S.L.] [3] 166 Cd 8.20N 13.00W
Western [Ug.] [3] 170 Fb 1.00N 31.00 E
Western [Zam.] [3] 170 Df 15.00S 24.00 E
Western Australia [2] 212 Ed 25.00S 122.00 E
Western Desert (EN) = Gharbīyah, Aş Şaḩrā' al- 158 Jf 27.30N 28.00 E
Western Dvina (EN) = Daugava 136 Cd 57.04N 24.03 E
Western Dvina (EN)= Zapadnaja Dvina 110 Id 57.04N 24.03 E
Western Entrance 219a Bb 6.55S 155.40 E
Western Ghats/Sahyadri 140 Jh 14.00N 75.00 E
Western Isles [3] 118 Fd 57.40N 7.10W
Western Port 212 Jg 38.25S 145.10 E
Western River 180 Gc 66.22N 107.15W
Western Sahara (EN) [5] 160 Ff 24.30N 13.00W
Western Samoa (EN)= Samoa I Sisifo [1] 210 Jf 13.40S 172.30W
Western Sayans (EN)= Zapadny Sajan 140 Ld 53.00N 94.00 E
Western Sierra Madre (EN) =Madre Occidental, Sierra- 174 Ig 25.00N 105.00W
Western Turkistan (EN) 140 He 41.00N 60.00 E
Westerschelde=West Schelde (EN) 122 Jc 51.25N 3.45 E
Westerschouwen 124 Fc 51.41N 3.43 E

Westerschouwen-Haamstede 124 Fc 51.42N 3.45 E
Westerstede 120 Dc 53.15N 7.56 E
Westerwald 120 Df 50.40N 7.55 E
Westerwoldse A 124 Ja 53.10N 7.10 E
West European Basin (EN) 106 Dh 47.00N 15.00W
West Falkland/Gran Malvina, Isla- 198 Kk 51.40S 60.00W
West Fayu Island 208 Fd 8.05N 146.44 E
West Fork Big Blue River 186 Hf 40.42N 96.59W
Westfriesland = West Friesland (EN) 122 Kb 52.45N 4.50 E
West Friesland (EN) = Westfriesland 122 Kb 52.45N 4.50 E
West Frisian Islands (EN) = Waddeneilanden 122 Ka 53.30N 5.00 E
Westgate-on-Sea 124 Dc 51.22N 1.21 E
West Glacier 188 Ib 48.30N 113.59W
West Glamorgan [3] 118 Jj 51.40N 3.55W
West Grand Lake 184 Nc 45.15N 67.52W
West Greenland (EN) = Vestgrønland [2] 179 He 69.00N 49.30W
West Helena 186 Ki 34.33N 90.39W
West Hollywood 184 Gm 25.59N 80.11W
Westhope 186 Fb 48.55N 101.01W
West Ice Shelf 222 Ge 67.00S 85.00 E
West Indies 190 Je 19.00N 70.00W
West Indies (EN) = Indias Occidentales 190 Je 19.00N 70.00W
West Island 172b Ab 9.22S 46.13 E
Westkapelle 124 Fc 51.31N 3.26 E
Westkapelle, Knokke- 124 Fc 51.19N 3.18 E
West Lafayette 184 De 40.27N 86.55W
Westland [2] 218 De 43.10S 170.30 E
West Liberty 184 Fg 37.55N 83.16W
Westlock 180 Gf 54.09N 113.52W
West Lunga 170 De 13.06S 24.39 E
Westmalle 124 Gc 51.18N 4.41 E
West Mariana Basin (EN) 106 Ih 15.00N 137.00 E
Westmeath/An Iarmhí [2] 118 Fh 53.30N 7.30W
West Melanesian Trench (EN) 214 Dh 1.00S 150.00 E
West Memphis 182 Id 35.08N 90.11W
West Mersea 124 Cc 51.46N 0.54 E
West Midlands [3] 118 Li 52.30N 2.00W
Westminster 184 If 39.35N 76.59W
Westminster, London- 124 Bc 51.30N 0.07W
West Monroe 186 Jj 32.31N 92.09W
Westmorland 118 Kg 54.30N 2.40W
West Nicholson 160 Jk 21.03S 29.22 E
West Nueces River 186 Gl 29.16N 99.56W
Weston [Mala.] 150 Ge 5.13N 115.36 E
Weston [W.V.-U.S.] 184 Gf 39.03N 80.28W
Weston [Wy.-U.S.] 188 Md 44.42N 105.18W
Weston-super-Mare 118 Kj 51.21N 2.59W
Westoverledingen 124 Ja 53.10N 7.27 E
Westoverledingen - Ihrhove 124 Ja 53.10N 7.27 E
West Palm Beach 176 Kg 26.43N 80.04W
West Pensacola 184 Dj 30.27N 87.15W
West Plains 182 Id 36.44N 91.51W
West Point [Ms.-U.S.] 186 Lj 33.36N 88.39W
West Point [Nb.-U.S.] 186 Hf 41.51N 96.43W
Westport 210 Ii 41.45S 171.36 E
Westport/Cathair na Mart 118 Dh 53.48N 9.32W
Westray 118 Kb 59.20N 3.00W
Westree 184 Gb 47.27N 81.32W
Westrich 124 Je 49.20N 7.25 E
West Road 124 Cd 50.52N 0.50 E
West Schelde (EN) = Westerschelde 122 Jc 51.25N 3.45 E
West Scotia Basin (EN) 198 Kk 57.00S 53.00W
West Siberian Plain (EN) = Zapadno-Sibirskaja ravnina 140 Jc 60.00N 75.00 E
Weststellingwerf 124 Ib 52.53N 6.00 E
Weststellingwerf-Wolvega 124 Ib 52.53N 6.00 E
West Sussex [3] 118 Mk 51.00N 0.40W
West Tavaputs Plateau 188 Jf 40.00N 110.25W
West-Terschelling, Terschelling- 124 Ha 53.21N 5.13 E
West Union [Ia.-U.S.] 186 Ke 42.57N 91.49W
West Union [Oh.-U.S.] 184 Ff 38.48N 83.33W
West Virginia [2] 182 Kd 38.45N 80.30W
West-Vlaanderen = Flanders, West- (EN) [3] 124 Ec 51.00N 3.00 E
Westwood 188 Ef 40.18N 121.00W
West Wyalong 212 Jf 33.55S 147.13 E
West Yellowstone 182 Ec 44.30N 111.05W
West Yorkshire [3] 118 Lh 53.40N 1.30W
Wetar, Pulau- 208 De 7.48S 126.18 E
Wetaskiwin 180 Gf 52.58N 113.22W
Wete 170 Gd 5.04S 39.43 E
Wětošow/Vetschau 120 Ke 51.47N 14.04 E
Wetter 124 Kd 50.18N 8.49 E
Wetter (Hessen) 124 Kd 50.54N 8.43 E
Wetter (Ruhr) 124 Jc 51.23N 7.24 E
Wetterau 120 Ef 50.15N 8.50 E
Wetteren 122 Jc 51.00N 3.53 E
Wetzlar 120 Ef 50.33N 8.30 E
Wetzstein 120 Hf 50.27N 11.27 E
Wevelgem 124 Fd 50.48N 3.10 E
Wewahitchka 184 Ej 30.07N 85.12W
Wewak 210 Fe 3.34S 143.38 E
Wexford/Loch Garman 112 Fe 52.20N 6.27W
Wexford/Loch Garman [2] 118 Gi 52.20N 6.40W
Wexford Harbour/Cuan Loch Garman 118 Gi 52.20N 6.25W
Wey 118 Mj 51.23N 0.28W
Weyburn 180 Hg 49.41N 103.52W
Weyhe 124 Kb 52.59N 8.52 E
Weyhe-Leeste 124 Kb 52.59N 8.50 E
Weymouth and Melcombe Regis 118 Kk 50.36N 2.28W
Wezet/Visé 124 Hd 50.44N 5.42 E
Whakatane 216 Eg 37.58S 177.00 E
Whale Cove 180 Id 62.14N 92.10W
Whalsay 118 Ma 60.22N 0.59W
Whangarei 210 Ih 35.43S 174.19 E
Wharfe 118 Lh 53.51N 1.07W
Wharton 186 Hl 29.19N 96.06W
Wharton Basin (EN) 106 Hk 19.00S 100.00 E
Wharton Lake 180 Hd 64.00N 99.55W
Whataroa 218 De 43.16S 170.22 E
Wheatland 188 Me 42.03N 104.57W
Wheat Ridge 186 Dg 39.46N 105.07W
Wheeler 188 Dd 45.42N 123.52W
Wheeler 180 Ke 57.02N 67.14W
Wheeler Lake 184 Dh 34.40N 87.05W
Wheeler Peak [N.M.-U.S.] 182 Fd 36.34N 105.25W
Wheeler Peak [U.S.] 174 Hf 38.59N 114.19W
Wheeling 182 Kc 40.05N 80.43W
Whidbey Island 188 Db 48.15N 122.40W
Whitby 118 Mg 54.29N 0.37W
Whitchurch [Eng.-U.K.] 118 Ki 52.58N 2.41W
Whitchurch [Eng.-U.K.] 124 Bc 51.53N 0.50W
Whitchurch [Eng.-U.K.] 124 Ac 51.13N 1.20W
White 180 Jc 65.50N 85.00W
White, Lake- 212 Fd 21.05S 129.00 E
White Bay 174 Nd 50.00N 56.30W
White Bear Lake 186 Jd 45.04N 93.01W
White Butte 186 Ec 46.23N 103.19W
White Carpathians (EN) = Bilé Karpaty 120 Nh 48.55N 17.50 E
White Cliffs 212 If 30.51S 143.05 E
White Cloud 184 Ed 43.33N 85.46W
Whitecourt 180 Ff 54.09N 115.41W
Whitefish 182 Eb 48.25N 114.20W
Whitefish Bay 182 Kb 46.40N 84.50W
Whitefish Point 184 Eb 46.45N 85.00W
Whitefish Range 188 Hb 48.40N 114.26W
Whitehall [Mi.-U.S.] 184 Dd 43.24N 86.21W
Whitehall [Mt.-U.S.] 188 Id 45.52N 112.06W
Whitehall [Oh.-U.S.] 184 Ff 39.58N 82.54W
Whitehall [Wi.-U.S.] 186 Kd 44.22N 91.19W
Whitehaven 118 Jg 54.33N 3.35W
Whitehorse 176 Fc 60.43N 135.03W
White Island [Ant.] 222 Ee 66.44S 48.35 E
White Island [N.Z.] 218 Gb 37.30S 177.10 E
White Lake 186 Jl 29.45N 92.30W
White Lake (EN) = Beloje ozero 110 Jc 60.11N 37.35 E
Whiteman Range 212 Ja 5.50S 149.55 E
Whitemark 212 Jh 40.07S 148.01 E
White Mountain 178 Gd 64.35N 163.04W
White Mountain Peak 182 Dd 37.38N 118.15W
White Mountains [Ak.-U.S.] 178 Jc 65.30N 147.00W
White Mountains [U.S.] 182 Mc 44.10N 71.35W
White Mountains [U.S.] 188 Fh 37.30N 118.15W
Whitemouth Lake 186 Ib 49.14N 95.40W
Whitemouth River 186 Ha 50.07N 96.02W
White Nile (EN) = Abyaḍ, Al Baḥr al- [3] 168 Ec 12.40N 32.30 E
White Nile (EN) = Abyaḍ, Al Baḥr al- 158 Kg 15.38N 32.31 E
White Pass [N.Amer.] 178 Le 59.37N 135.08W
White Pass [Wa.-U.S.] 188 Ec 46.38N 121.24W
White River 180 Ig 48.35N 85.17W
White River 186 Fe 43.34N 100.45W
Whiteriver 188 Kj 33.50N 109.58W
White River [In.-U.S.] 184 Df 38.25N 87.44W
White River [Nv.-U.S.] 188 Hh 37.18N 115.08W
White River [Tx.-U.S.] 186 Fj 33.14N 100.56W
White River [U.S.] 188 Kf 40.04N 109.41W
White River [U.S.] 182 Hc 43.45N 99.30W
White River [U.S.] 174 Jf 33.53N 91.03W
White River [Yuk.-Can.] 180 Dd 63.10N 139.32W
White Salmon 188 Ed 45.44N 121.29W
Whitesand Bay 118 Ik 50.20N 4.35W
White Sea (EN) = Beloje more 110 Kb 66.00N 44.00 E
White Sea-Baltic Canal (EN) = Belomorsko-Baltijski kanal 110 Jc 63.30N 34.48 E
White Settlement 186 Hj 32.45N 97.27W
White Sulphur Springs 188 Jc 46.33N 110.54W
Whiteville 184 Hh 34.20N 78.42W
White Volta 158 Gh 8.38N 0.59W
White Volta (EN) = Volta Blanche 158 Gh 8.38N 0.59W
Whitewater 186 Bg 38.59N 108.27W
Whitewater Baldy 188 Bj 33.20N 108.39W
Whitewater Bay 184 Gm 25.16N 81.00W
Whitewater Lake 186 Ea 50.50N 89.10W
Whitewood 186 Ea 50.20N 102.15W
Whitianga 218 Fb 36.50S 175.42 E
Whitmore Mountains 222 Og 82.35S 104.30W
Whitney 184 Hc 45.30N 78.14W
Whitney, Lake- 186 Hk 31.55N 97.23W
Whitney, Mount- 174 Hf 36.35N 118.18W
Whitstable 124 Dc 51.21N 1.06 E
Whitsunday Island 212 Jd 20.15S 149.00 E
Whittier 178 Jd 60.46N 148.41W
Whittlesea 212 Jg 37.31S 145.07 E
Whittlesey 124 Bb 52.33N 0.08W
Wholdaia Lake 180 Hd 60.45N 104.10W
Whyalla 212 Hf 33.02S 137.35 E
Wiarton 184 Gc 44.45N 81.09W
Wiawso 166 Ed 6.12N 2.29W
Wibaux 188 Mc 46.59N 104.11W
Wichita 176 Jf 37.41N 97.20W
Wichita Falls 176 Jf 33.54N 98.30W
Wichita Mountains 186 Gi 34.45N 98.40W
Wichita River 186 Gi 34.07N 98.10W
Wick 118 Jc 58.26N 3.06W
Wick 118 Jc 58.25N 3.05W
Wickenburg 188 Ij 33.58N 112.44W
Wickepin 212 Df 32.46S 117.30 E
Wickham 124 Ad 50.54N 1.10W
Wickham Market 124 Db 52.09N 1.22 E
Wickiup Reservoir 188 Ee 43.40N 121.43W
Wickliffe 184 Cg 36.58N 89.05W
Wicklow/Cill Mhantáin 118 Gi 52.59N 6.03W
Wicklow/Cill Mhantáin [2] 118 Gi 53.00N 6.30W
Wicklow Head/Ceann Chill Mhantáin 118 Hi 52.58N 6.00W
Wicklow Mountains/Sléibhte Chill Mhantáin 118 Gh 53.02N 6.24W
Wicko, Jezioro- 120 Mb 54.33N 16.35 E
Wickrath, Mönchengladbach- 124 Ic 51.08N 6.25 E
Widawa 120 Me 51.13N 16.55 E
Wide Bay 212 Ka 5.05S 152.05 E
Widefield 186 Dg 38.42N 104.40W
Widgiemooltha 212 Ef 31.30S 121.34 E
Wi-Do 154 Ig 35.38N 126.17 E
Więcbork 120 Nc 53.22N 17.30 E
Wied 124 Jd 50.27N 7.28 E
Wiehengebirge 120 Ed 52.20N 8.40 E
Wiehl 124 Jd 50.57N 7.32 E
Wieliczka 120 Qg 49.59N 20.04 E
Wielimie, Jezioro- 120 Mc 53.47N 16.50 E
Wielki Dział 120 Tf 50.18N 23.25 E
Wielkopolska 120 Ne 51.50N 17.20 E
Wielkopolskie-Kujawskie, Pojezierze- 120 Md 52.25N 16.30 E
Wieluń 120 Oe 51.14N 18.34 E
Wien [2] 128 Kb 48.15N 16.25 E
Wien = Vienna (EN) 112 Hf 48.12N 16.22 E
Wiener Becken 128 Kc 48.00N 16.28 E
Wiener Neustadt 128 Kc 47.48N 16.15 E
Wienerwald = Vienna Woods (EN) 128 Jb 48.10N 16.00 E
Wieprz 120 Re 51.32N 21.49 E
Wieprza 120 Mb 54.26N 16.22 E
Wieprz-Krzna, Kanał- 120 Se 51.56N 22.56 E
Wierden 124 Ib 52.22N 6.36 E
Wieringen 124 Hb 52.56N 5.02 E
Wieringen-Den Oever 124 Hb 52.56N 5.02 E
Wieringen-Hippolytushoef 124 Gb 52.54N 4.59 E
Wieringermeer 124 Hb 52.51N 5.01 E
Wieringermeer Polder 124 Gb 52.50N 5.00 E
Wieringermeer-Wieringerwerf 124 Hb 52.51N 5.01 E
Wieringerwerf, Wieringermeer- 124 Hb 52.51N 5.01 E
Wieruszów 120 Oe 51.18N 18.08 E
Wierzchowo, Jezioro- 120 Mc 53.50N 16.45 E
Wierzyca 120 Oc 53.51N 18.50 E
Wiesbaden 112 Ge 50.05N 8.15 E
Wiese 120 Di 47.35N 7.35 E
Wieslautern 124 Je 49.05N 7.49 E
Wiesloch 120 Eg 49.18N 8.42 E
Wietingsmoor 124 Kb 52.39N 8.39 E
Wietmarschen 124 Jb 52.32N 7.08 E
Wieżyca 120 Ob 54.17N 18.10 E
Wigan 118 Kh 53.32N 2.35W
Wigger 128 Bc 47.15N 7.55 E
Wiggins 186 Lk 30.51N 89.08W
Wight, Isle of- 110 Fe 50.40N 1.20W
Wigry, Jezioro- 120 Tb 54.05N 23.07 E
Wigston 124 Ab 52.35N 1.06W
Wigtown 118 Ig 54.52N 4.26W
Wigtown Bay 118 Ig 54.46N 4.15W
Wijchen 124 Hc 51.48N 5.44 E
Wijdefjorden 179 Nc 79.50N 15.30 E
Wijk bij Duurstede 124 Hc 51.59N 5.22 E
Wil 128 Dc 47.27N 9.05 E
Wilbur 188 Fc 47.46N 118.42W
Wilburton 186 Ii 34.55N 95.19W
Wilcannia 210 Fh 31.34S 143.23 E
Wild Coast 158 Jl 32.00S 29.50 E
Wildeshausen 120 Ed 52.54N 8.26 E
Wild Horse 188 Jb 49.01N 110.12W
Wildspitze 128 Ed 46.53N 10.52 E
Wilga 120 Re 51.50N 21.20 E
Wilhelm-II-Land 222 Ge 69.00S 90.00 E
Wilhelminakanaal 124 Gc 51.43N 4.53 E
Wilhelmshaven 120 Ec 53.31N 8.08 E
Wilhelmstal 172 Bd 21.54S 16.20 E
Wilkes-Barre 182 Lc 41.15N 75.50W
Wilkesboro 184 Gg 36.09N 81.09W
Wilkes Land (EN) 222 Hf 71.00S 120.00 E
Wilkins Coast 222 Qe 69.40S 63.00W
Wilkins Sound 222 Qf 70.15S 73.00W
Willamette River 188 Dd 45.39N 122.46W
Willandra Billabong Creek 212 If 33.08S 144.06 E
Willapa Bay 188 Cc 46.37N 124.00W
Willard 186 Ci 34.36N 106.02W
Willards, Punta- 192 Cc 28.50N 112.35W
Willcox 188 Kj 32.15N 109.50W
Willebadessen 124 Lc 51.38N 9.02 E
Willebadessen-Peckelsheim 124 Lc 51.36N 9.08 E
Willebroek 124 Gc 51.04N 4.22 E
Willemstad [Neth.] 124 Gc 51.41N 4.26 E
Willemstad [Neth.Ant.] 200 Jd 12.06N 68.56W
Willeroo 212 Gc 15.17S 131.35 E
William Bill Dannelly Reservoir 184 Di 32.15N 86.45W
Williams 182 Ed 35.15N 112.11W
Williamsburg [Ky.-U.S.] 184 Eg 36.44N 84.10W
Williamsburg [Va.-U.S.] 184 Ig 37.17N 76.43W
Williams Lake 180 Ff 52.08N 122.09W
Williamson Glacier 222 He 66.30S 114.30 E
Williamsport 182 Lc 41.16N 77.03W
Williamston 184 Ih 35.50N 77.06W
Williamstown 184 Ef 38.38N 84.34W
Willich 124 Ic 51.16N 6.33 E
Willikie's 197d Bb 17.03N 61.42W
Willingdon, Mount- 188 Ga 51.48N 116.17W
Willis Groüp 208 Gf 16.20S 150.00 E
Willis Islands 222 Ad 54.00S 38.11W
Williston [N.D.-U.S.] 182 Gb 48.09N 103.37W
Williston [S.Afr.] 172 Cf 31.20S 20.53 E
Williston Lake 176 Gd 56.00N 124.00W
Willits 188 Dg 39.25N 123.21W
Willmar 182 Hb 45.07N 95.03W
Willoughby Bay 197d Bb 17.02N 61.44W
Willow Bunch Lake 188 Mb 49.27N 105.28W
Willowlake 180 Fd 62.42N 123.08W
Willowmore 172 Cf 33.17S 23.29 E
Willows 188 Dg 39.31N 122.12W
Willow Springs 186 Kh 36.59N 91.58W
Wills, Lake- 212 Fd 21.20S 128.40 E
Wills Point 186 Ij 32.43N 95.57W
Wilma Glacier 222 Ee 67.12S 56.00 E
Wilmington [De.-U.S.] 182 Ld 39.44N 75.33W
Wilmington [N.C.-U.S.] 176 Lf 34.13N 77.55W
Wilmington [Oh.-U.S.] 184 Ff 39.28N 83.50W
Wilnsdorf 124 Kd 50.49N 8.06 E
Wilseder Berg 120 Fc 53.10N 9.56 E
Wilson 182 Ld 35.44N 77.55W
Wilson, Cape- 180 Jc 66.59N 81.27W
Wilson, Mount- 186 Ch 37.51N 107.59W
Wilson Bluff 222 Ff 74.20S 66.47 E
Wilson Lake [Al.-U.S.] 184 Dh 34.49N 87.30W
Wilson Lake [Ks.-U.S.] 186 Gg 38.57N 98.40W
Wilsons Promontory 212 Jg 38.55S 146.20 E
Wilton River 212 Gb 14.45S 134.33 E
Wilts 118 Lj 51.20N 2.00W
Wiltshire [3] 118 Lj 51.30N 2.00W
Wiltz 122 Le 49.58N 5.55 E
Wiluna 212 Ee 26.36S 120.13 E
Wimereux 124 Dd 50.46N 1.37 E
Winamac 184 De 41.03N 86.36W
Winburg 172 De 28.37S 27.00 E
Winchelsea 124 Cd 50.55N 0.43 E
Winchester [Eng.-U.K.] 118 Lj 51.04N 1.19W
Winchester [In.-U.S.] 184 Ee 40.10N 84.59W
Winchester [Ky.-U.S.] 184 Ef 38.01N 84.11W
Winchester [Va.-U.S.] 184 Hf 39.11N 78.12W
Windeck 124 Jd 50.49N 7.34 E
Windemin, Pointe- 219b Cc 16.34S 167.27 E
Winder 184 Fi 34.00N 83.47W
Windermere 118 Kg 54.22N 2.56W
Windermere [B.C.-Can.] 188 Ha 50.30N 115.58W
Windermere [Eng.-U.K.] 118 Kg 54.23N 2.54W
Windhoek 160 Ik 22.34S 17.06 E
Windhoek [3] 172 Bd 22.30S 17.00 E
Windischgarsten 128 Ic 47.43N 14.20 E
Wind Mountain 186 Dj 32.02N 105.34W
Windom 186 Ie 43.52N 95.07W
Windom Mountain 186 Ch 37.37N 107.35W
Windorah 212 Ie 25.26S 142.39 E
Window Rock 188 Ki 35.41N 109.03W
Wind River 188 Ke 43.08N 108.12W
Wind River Peak 188 Ke 42.42N 109.07W
Wind River Range 182 Fc 43.05N 109.25W
Windrush 118 Lj 51.42N 1.25W
Windsor [Eng.-U.K.] 118 Mj 51.29N 0.38W
Windsor [N.S.-Can.] 180 Lh 44.59N 64.09W
Windsor [Ont.-Can.] 180 Jh 42.18N 83.01W
Windsor Forest 184 Gj 31.58N 81.10W
Windward Islands 190 Lf 13.00N 61.00W
Windward Islands (EN) = Barlovento, Islas de- 174 Mh 15.00N 61.00W
Windward Islands (EN) = Sotavento, Islas de- 198 Jd 11.10N 67.00W
Windward Islands (EN) = Vent, Iles du- 208 Mf 17.30S 149.30W
Windward Passage (EN) = Vent, Canal du- 194 Lh 20.00N 73.50W
Windward Passage (EN) = Vientos, Paso de los- 174 Lh 20.00N 73.50W
Winfield [Al.-U.S.] 184 Di 33.56N 87.49W
Winfield [Ks.-U.S.] 182 Hd 37.15N 96.59W
Wingene 124 Fc 51.04N 3.16 E
Wingen-sur-Moder 124 Jf 48.55N 7.22 E
Winisk 176 Kd 55.15N 85.12W
Winisk 174 Kd 55.17N 85.05W
Winisk Lake 180 If 52.55N 87.20W
Winkler 186 Hb 49.11N 97.56W
Winklern 128 Gd 46.52N 12.52 E
Winneba 166 Ed 5.20N 0.37W
Winnebago, Lake- 182 Jc 44.00N 88.25W
Winnemucca 182 Dc 40.58N 117.44W
Winnemucca Lake 188 Ff 40.10N 119.20W
Winner 182 Hc 43.22N 99.51W
Winnett 188 Kc 47.00N 108.21W
Winnfield 186 Jk 31.55N 92.38W
Winnibigoshish, Lake- 186 Ic 47.27N 94.12W
Winnipeg 176 Je 49.53N 97.09W
Winnipeg 174 Jd 50.38N 96.19W
Winnipeg, Lake- 174 Jd 52.00N 97.00W
Winnipeg Beach 186 Ha 50.31N 96.58W
Winnipegosis 180 Hf 51.39N 99.56W
Winnipegosis, Lake- 174 Jd 52.30N 100.00W
Winnipesaukee, Lake- 184 Ld 43.35N 71.20W
Winnsboro 186 Kj 32.10N 91.43W
Winnweiler 124 Je 49.34N 7.51 E
Winona [Mn.-U.S.] 182 Ic 44.03N 91.39W
Winona [Mo.-U.S.] 186 Kh 37.06N 91.19W
Winona [Ms.-U.S.] 186 Lj 33.29N 89.44W
Winschoten 122 Na 53.08N 7.02 E
Winsen (Luhe) 120 Gc 53.22N 10.13 E
Winslow [Az.-U.S.] 182 Ed 35.01N 110.42W
Winslow [Eng.-U.K.] 124 Bc 51.57N 0.52W
Winslow Reef 208 Je 1.36S 174.57W
Winston-Salem 182 Kd 36.06N 80.15W
Winterberg 120 Ee 51.12N 8.32 E
Winter Harbour 180 Gb 75.00N 111.00W
Winter Harbour 180 Gb 74.46N 110.40W
Winter Haven 182 Kf 28.01N 81.44W
Winter Park [Co.-U.S.] 186 Dg 39.47N 105.45W
Winter Park [Fl.-U.S.] 184 Gk 28.36N 81.20W
Winters 186 Gk 31.57N 99.58W
Winterset 186 If 41.20N 94.01W
Winterswijk 122 Mc 51.58N 6.44 E
Winterthur 128 Cc 47.30N 8.45 E
Winton [Austl.] 210 Fg 22.23S 143.02 E
Winton [N.C.-U.S.] 184 Ig 36.24N 76.56W
Winton [N.Z.] 218 Cg 46.09S 168.20 E
Wipper [Ger.] 120 He 51.20N 11.10 E
Wipper [Ger.] 120 He 51.47N 11.42 E
Wisbech 118 Ni 52.40N 0.10 E
Wiscasset 184 Mc 44.00N 69.40W
Wisch 124 Ic 51.55N 6.22 E
Wisch-Terborg 124 Ic 51.55N 6.22 E
Wisconsin [2] 182 Jc 44.45N 89.30W
Wisconsin 174 Je 43.00N 91.15W
Wisconsin Range 222 Ng 85.45S 125.00W
Wisconsin Rapids 182 Jc 44.23N 89.49W
Wiseman 178 Ic 67.25N 150.06W
Wisła 120 Og 49.39N 18.50 E
Wisła = Vistula (EN) 110 He 54.22N 18.55 E
Wiślana, Mierzeja- 120 Pb 54.25N 19.30 E
Wiślane, Żuławy- 120 Ob 54.10N 19.00 E
Wiślany, Zalew- 120 Pb 54.27N 19.40 E
Wisłok 120 Sf 50.13N 22.32 E
Wisłoka 120 Rf 50.27N 21.23 E
Wismar 120 Hc 53.54N 11.28 E
Wismarbucht 120 Hc 53.57N 11.25 E
Wissant 124 Dd 50.53N 1.40 E
Wissembourg 122 Ne 49.02N 7.57 E
Wissen 120 Df 50.47N 7.45 E
Wissenkerke 124 Fc 51.35N 3.45 E
Wissey 124 Cb 52.34N 0.21 E
Witbank 160 Jk 25.56S 29.07 E
Witchekar Lake 186 Fb 49.15N 100.16W
Witdraai 172 Ce 26.58S 20.41 E
Witham 124 Cc 51.47N 0.38 E
Witham 118 Ni 52.56N 0.04 E
Withernsea 118 Nh 53.44N 0.02 E
Witkowo 120 Nd 52.27N 17.47 E
Witmarsum, Wonseradeel- 124 Ha 53.06N 5.28 E
Witney 118 Lj 51.48N 1.29W
Witnica 120 Kd 52.40N 14.55 E
Witputz 172 Be 27.37S 16.42 E
Witten 120 De 51.26N 7.20 E
Wittenberg [Ger.] 120 Ie 51.52N 12.39 E
Wittenberg [Wi.-U.S.] 186 Ld 44.49N 89.10W
Wittenberge 120 Hc 53.00N 11.45 E
Wittenoom 212 Dd 22.17S 118.19 E
Wittingen 120 Gd 52.44N 10.43 E
Wittlich 120 Cg 49.59N 6.53 E
Wittmund 120 Dc 53.34N 7.47 E
Wittow 120 Jb 54.38N 13.19 E
Wittstock 120 Ic 53.09N 12.30 E
Witu 170 Hc 2.23S 40.26 E
Witu Islands 214 Dh 4.40S 149.18 E
Witvlei 172 Bd 22.23S 18.32 E
Witzenhausen 120 Fe 51.20N 9.52 E
Wivenhoe 124 Cc 51.51N 0.58 E
Wizard Reef 158 Mi 8.57S 51.01 E
Wizna 120 Sc 53.13N 22.26 E
Wjelsk 120 Oe 51.32N 18.52 E
W. J. Van Blommestein Meer 202 Hc 4.45N 55.00W
Wkra 120 Qd 52.27N 20.44 E
Władysławowo 120 Ob 54.49N 18.25 E
Włocławek 120 Pd 52.39N 19.02 E
Włocławek [2] 120 Od 52.40N 19.00 E
Włodawa 120 Te 51.34N 23.32 E
Włoszczowa 120 Pf 50.25N 19.59 E
Wodonga 212 Jg 36.17S 146.54 E
Wodzisław Śląski 120 Of 50.00N 18.28 E
Woensdrecht 124 Gc 51.25N 4.18 E
Woerden 124 Gb 52.05N 4.52 E
Woerth 124 Jf 48.56N 7.45 E
Woëvre, Plaine de la- 122 Le 49.15N 5.45 E
Wohlthat-Massif 222 Cf 71.35S 12.20 E
Woippy 124 Ie 49.09N 6.09 E
Wojerecy/Hoyerswerda 120 Ke 51.26N 14.15 E
Wokam, Pulau- 150 Jh 5.37S 134.30 E
Woken He 154 Ja 46.19N 129.34 E
Woking 118 Mj 51.20N 0.34W
Wokingham 124 Bc 51.25N 0.50W
Wolbrom 120 Pf 50.24N 19.46 E
Wolcott 184 Id 43.13N 76.42W
Wołczyn 120 Oe 51.01N 18.03 E
Woldberg 124 Hb 52.25N 5.55 E
Woleai Atoll 208 Fd 7.21N 143.52 E
Woleu-Ntem [3] 170 Bb 2.00N 12.00 E
Wolf, Isla- 202a Aa 1.23N 91.49W
Wolf, Volcán- 202a Ab 0.01S 91.20W
Wolfach 120 Eh 48.18N 8.13 E
Wolf Creek 188 Ic 47.00N 112.04W
Wolf Creek 186 Gh 36.35N 99.30W
Wolfen 120 Ie 51.40N 12.17 E
Wolfenbüttel 120 Gd 52.10N 10.33 E
Wolfhagen 120 Fe 51.19N 9.10 E
Wolf Point 182 Fb 48.05N 105.39W
Wolfratshausen 120 Hi 47.54N 11.25 E
Wolf River 186 Ld 44.11N 88.48W
Wolfsberg 128 Id 46.50N 14.50 E
Wolfsburg 120 Gd 52.26N 10.48 E
Wolfstein 124 Je 49.35N 7.36 E
Wolgast 120 Jb 54.03N 13.46 E
Wolica 120 Tf 50.54N 23.12 E
Wolin 120 Kc 53.50N 14.35 E
Wolin 120 Kc 53.51N 14.38 E
Wollaston 124 Bb 52.15N 0.40W
Wollaston, Islas- 206 Gi 55.40S 67.30W
Wollaston Forland 179 Jd 74.35N 20.15W
Wollaston Lake 180 He 58.05N 103.38W
Wollaston Lake 174 Id 58.15N 103.20W
Wollaston Peninsula 174 Hc 70.00N 115.00W
Wollongong 210 Gh 34.25S 150.54 E
Wöllstein 124 Je 49.49N 7.58 E
Wolmaransstad 172 De 27.12S 26.13 E
Wołomin 120 Rd 52.21N 21.14 E
Wołów 120 Me 51.29N 16.55 E
Wolseley 180 Hf 50.25N 103.19W
Wolstenholme, Cap- 180 Jd 62.34N 77.30W
Wolstenholme Fjord 179 Ec 76.40N 69.45W
Wolsztyn 120 Md 52.08N 16.06 E
Wolvega, Weststellingwerf- 124 Ib 52.53N 6.00 E
Wolverhampton 118 Ki 52.36N 2.08W
Wolverton 118 Mi 52.04N 0.50W
Wŏnju 152 Md 37.21N 127.58 E
Wŏnsan 142 Of 39.10N 127.26 E
Wonseradeel 124 Ha 53.06N 5.28 E
Wonseradeel-Witmarsum 124 Ha 53.06N 5.28 E
Wonthaggi 212 Jg 38.36S 145.35 E
Woodall Mountain 186 Li 34.45N 88.11W
Woodbridge 118 Oi 52.06N 1.19 E

Index Symbols

[1] Independent Nation
[2] State, Region
[3] District, County
[4] Municipality
[5] Colony, Dependency
Continent
Physical Region
Historical or Cultural Region
Mount, Mountain
Volcano
Hill
Mountains, Mountain Range
Hills, Escarpment
Plateau, Upland
Pass, Gap
Plain, Lowland
Delta
Salt Flat
Valley, Canyon
Crater, Cave
Karst Features
Depression
Polder
Desert, Dunes
Forest, Woods
Heath, Steppe
Oasis
Cape, Point
Coast, Beach
Cliff
Peninsula
Isthmus
Sandbank
Island
Atoll
Rock, Reef
Islands, Archipelago
Rocks, Reefs
Coral Reef
Well, Spring
Geyser
River, Stream
Waterfall, Rapids
River Mouth, Estuary
Lake
Salt Lake
Intermittent Lake
Reservoir
Swamp, Pond
Canal
Glacier
Ice Shelf, Pack Ice
Ocean
Sea
Gulf, Bay
Strait, Fjord
Lagoon
Bank
Seamount
Tablemount
Ridge
Shelf
Basin
Escarpment, Sea Scarp
Fracture
Trench, Abyss
National Park, Reserve
Point of Interest
Recreation Site
Cave, Cavern
Historic Site
Ruins
Wall, Walls
Church, Abbey
Temple
Scientific Station
Railway station
Airport
Port
Military installation
Lighthouse
Mine
Tunnel
Dam, Bridge

Woodbridge Bay ◧	197g	Bb	15.19N	61.25W
Woodhall Spa	124	Ba	53.09N	0.13W
Woodland [Ca.-U.S.]	188	Eg	38.41N	121.46W
Woodland [Wa.-U.S.]	188	Dd	45.54N	122.45W
Woodlark Island ◆	208	Ge	9.05S	152.50 E
Wood Mountain ⛰	188	Lb	49.14N	106.20W
Woodridge	186	Hb	49.17N	96.09W
Wood River 〜	188	Lb	50.08N	106.10W
Wood River Lakes ≈	178	He	59.30N	158.45W
Woodroffe, Mount- ▲	212	Ge	26.20S	131.45 E
Woods, Lake- ≈	212	Gc	17.50S	133.30 E
Woods, Lake of the- ≈	174	Je	49.15N	94.45W
Woods Hole	184	Le	41.31N	70.40W
Woodside	188	Jg	39.21N	110.18W
Woodstock [Eng.-U.K.]	118	Lj	51.52N	1.21W
Woodstock [N.B.-Can.]	180	Kg	46.09N	67.34W
Woodstock [Ont.-Can.]	184	Gd	43.08N	80.45W
Woodstock [Vt.-U.S.]	184	Kd	43.37N	72.31W
Woodville [Ms.-U.S.]	186	Kk	31.01N	91.18W
Woodville [N.Z.]	218	Fd	40.20S	175.52 E
Woodville [Tx.-U.S.]	186	Ik	30.46N	94.25W
Woodward	182	Hd	36.26N	99.24W
Wooler	118	Kf	55.33N	2.01W
Woomera	212	Hf	31.11S	137.10 E
Wooramel River 〜	212	Ce	25.47S	114.10 E
Wooster	184	Ge	40.46N	81.57W
Worcester ▣	118	Ki	52.15N	2.10W
Worcester [Eng.-U.K.]	118	Ki	52.11N	2.13W
Worcester [Ma.-U.S.]	182	Mc	42.16N	71.48W
Worcester [S.Afr.]	160	Il	33.39S	19.27 E
Worcester Range ⛰	222	Jf	78.50S	161.00 E
Wörgl	128	Gc	47.29N	12.04 E
Workai, Pulau- ◆	150	Jh	6.40S	134.40 E
Workington	118	Jg	54.39N	3.33W
Worksop	118	Lh	53.18N	1.07W
Workum	124	Hb	52.59N	5.27 E
Worland	182	Fc	44.01N	107.57W
Wormer	124	Gb	52.30N	4.52 E
Wormhout	124	Ed	50.53N	2.28 E
Worms	120	Eg	49.38N	8.21 E
Worms Head ▶	118	Ij	51.34N	4.20W
Wörrstadt	124	Ke	49.50N	8.06 E
Wörth am Rhein	124	Ke	49.03N	8.16 E
Wörther-See ≈	128	Id	46.37N	14.10 E
Worthing	118	Mk	50.48N	0.23W
Worthington	182	Hc	43.37N	95.36W
Wosi	150	Ig	0.11S	127.58 E
Wotho Atoll ◎	208	Hc	10.06N	165.59 E
Wotje Atoll ◎	208	Id	9.27N	170.02 E
Woudenberg	124	Hb	52.05N	5.25 E
Wounnioné, Pointe- ▶	219b	Db	14.54S	168.02 E
Wounta, Laguna de- ⊜	194	Fg	13.38N	83.34W
Wour	168	Ba	21.21N	15.57 E
Wousi	219b	Cb	15.22S	166.39 E
Wowoni, Pulau- ◆	150	Hg	4.08S	123.06 E
Woy Woy	212	Kf	33.30S	151.20 E
Wrangel, ostrov- = Wrangel Island (EN) ◆	140	Tb	71.00N	179.30 E
Wrangel Island (EN) = Wrangel, ostrov- ◆	140	Tb	71.00N	179.30 E
Wrangell	176	Fd	56.28N	132.23W
Wrangell, Cape- ▶	178a	Ab	52.50N	172.26 E
Wrangell Mountains ⛰	174	Ec	62.00N	143.00W
Wrath, Cape- ▶	110	Fd	58.37N	5.01W
Wray	182	Gc	40.05N	102.13W
Wreake 〜	124	Ab	52.41N	1.05W
Wreck Reef ✱	208	Gg	22.15S	155.10 E
Wrecks, Bay of- ◧	220g	Bb	1.52N	157.17W
Wrexham	118	Kh	53.03N	3.00W
Wright Island ◆	222	Of	74.03S	116.45W
Wright Patman Lake ≈	186	Ij	33.16N	94.14W
Wrightson, Mount- ▲	188	Jk	31.42N	110.50W
Wrigley	180	Fd	63.19N	123.38W
Wrigley Gulf ◧	222	Nf	74.00S	129.00W
Wrocław [2]	120	Me	51.05N	17.00 E
Wrocław = Breslau (EN)	112	He	51.06N	17.00 E
Wronki	120	Md	52.43N	16.23 E
Wrotham	124	Cc	51.18N	0.19 E
Wroxham	124	Db	52.42N	1.24 E
Września	120	Nd	52.20N	17.34 E
Wschodnia 〜	120	Rf	50.30N	21.18 E
Wschowa	120	Me	51.48N	16.19 E
Wu'an	154	Cf	36.42N	114.12 E
Wuchale	168	Fc	11.31N	39.37 E
Wuchang	154	Ib	44.55N	127.11 E
Wuchang, Wuhan-	154	Ci	30.32N	114.18 E
Wucheng (Jiucheng)	154	Df	37.12N	116.04 E
Wuchiu Hsu ◆	152	Kg	25.00N	119.27 E
Wuchuan	154	Ad	41.08N	111.25 E
Wuchuan (Duru)	152	If	28.28N	107.57 E
Wuchuan (Meilü)	152	Jg	21.28N	110.44 E
Wuda	152	Id	39.30N	106.33 E
Wudan → Ongniud Qi	152	Kc	42.58N	119.01 E
Wudao	152	Ld	39.28N	121.30 E
Wudaoliang	152	Fd	35.15N	93.14 E
Wudi	154	Df	37.44N	117.36 E
Wudil	166	Gc	11.49N	8.51 E
Wuding	152	Hf	25.36N	102.27 E
Wudu	152	He	33.24N	105.00 E
Wugang	152	Jf	26.48N	110.32 E
Wugong (Puji)	152	Ie	34.15N	108.14 E
Wuhai	152	Id	39.32N	106.55 E
Wuhan	142	Nf	30.30N	114.20 E
Wuhan-Hankou	154	Ci	30.35N	114.16 E
Wuhan-Hanyang	154	Ci	30.33N	114.16 E
Wuhan- Wuchang	154	Ci	30.32N	114.18 E
Wuhe	152	Ke	33.08N	117.51 E
Wuhu	142	Nf	31.18N	118.27 E
Wuhu (Wanzhi)	154	Ei	31.21N	118.23 E
Wujia He 〜	152	Ic	40.56N	108.52 E
Wujiang	154	Fi	31.09N	120.38 E
Wu Jiang 〜	140	Mg	29.43N	107.24 E
Wukari	160	Hh	7.51N	9.47 E
Wukro	168	Fc	13.48N	39.37 E
Wular ≈	148	Eb	34.30N	74.30 E
Wulff Land ⊠	179	Hb	82.19N	50.00W
Wulian (Hongning)	154	Eg	35.45N	119.13 E
Wuliang Shan ⛰	152	Hg	24.00N	101.00 E
Wuliaru, Pulau- ◆	150	Jh	7.27S	131.04 E
Wuling Shan ⛰	140	Mg	28.20N	110.00 E
Wulongbei	154	Hd	40.15N	124.16 E
Wulongji → Huaibin	154	Ci	32.27N	115.23 E
Wulur	150	Ih	7.09S	128.39 E
Wum	166	Hd	6.23N	10.04 E
Wumei Shan ▲	154	Cj	28.47N	114.50 E
Wümme 〜	124	Ka	53.10N	8.40 E
Wuning	154	Cj	29.17N	115.05 E
Wünnenberg	124	Kc	51.31N	8.42 E
Wünnenberg-Haaren	124	Kc	51.34N	8.44 E
Wunnummin Lake ≈	180	If	52.55N	89.10W
Wun Rog	168	Dd	9.00N	28.21 E
Wunstorf	120	Fd	52.26N	9.25 E
Wuntho	148	Jd	23.54N	95.41 E
Wupper 〜	120	Ce	51.05N	7.00 E
Wuppertal	120	De	51.16N	7.11 E
Wuqi	152	Id	36.57N	108.15 E
Wuqia/Ulugqat	152	Cd	39.40N	75.07 E
Wuqiao (Sangyuan)	154	Df	37.38N	116.23 E
Wuqing	154	De	39.23N	117.04 E
Wuqing (Yangcun)	154	De	39.23N	117.04 E
Würm 〜	124	Kf	48.53N	8.42 E
Würmsee → Starnberger See ≈	120	Hi	47.55N	11.20 E
Wurno	166	Gc	13.18N	5.26 E
Würselen	124	Id	50.49N	6.08 E
Würzburg	112	Gf	49.48N	9.56 E
Wurzen	120	Ie	51.22N	12.44 E
Wu Shan ⛰	152	Ie	31.00N	110.00 E
Wushaoling ⋎	152	Hd	37.15N	102.50 E
Wusheng Guan ⋎	152	Je	31.45N	114.04 E
Wuski/Uqturpan	152	Cc	41.10N	79.16 E
Wusong	154	Fi	31.23N	121.29 E
Wüst Seamount (EN) ⌓	158	Gl	34.00S	3.40W
Wusuli Jiang 〜	152	Ob	48.28N	135.02 E
Wutach 〜	120	Ei	47.37N	8.15 E
Wutai [China]	154	Be	38.43N	113.14 E
Wutai [China]	152	Dc	44.38N	82.06 E
Wutai Shan ▲	152	Jd	39.04N	113.28 E
Wuustwezel	124	Gc	51.23N	4.36 E
Wuvulu Island ◆	208	Fe	1.43S	142.50 E
Wuwei	154	Di	31.17N	117.54 E
Wuwei (Liangzhou)	142	Mf	37.58N	102.48 E
Wuxi [China]	142	Of	31.32N	120.18 E
Wuxi [China]	152	Ie	31.27N	109.34 E
Wu Xia ⋎	152	Je	31.02N	110.10 E
Wuxiang (Duancun)	154	Bf	36.50N	112.51 E
Wuxing (Huzhou)	152	Le	30.47N	120.07 E
Wuxue → Guangji	152	Kf	29.58N	115.32 E
Wuyang [China]	152	Jd	36.29N	113.07 E
Wuyang [China]	154	Bh	33.26N	113.35 E
Wuyang → Zhenyuan	152	If	27.05N	108.26 E
Wuyi [China]	154	Ej	28.54N	119.50 E
Wuyi [China]	154	Cf	37.49N	115.54 E
Wuyiling	152	Mb	48.37N	129.20 E
Wuyi Shan ⛰	140	Ng	27.00N	117.00 E
Wuyuan [China]	142	Me	41.08N	108.17 E
Wuyuan [China]	154	Dj	29.15N	117.52 E
Wuyuanzhen → Haiyan	154	Fi	30.31N	120.56 E
Wuzhai	154	Ae	38.54N	111.49 E
Wuzhen	154	Ai	31.42N	112.00 E
Wuzhi Shan [China] ▲	154	Ed	40.31N	118.02 E
Wuzhi Shan [China] ▲	152	Ih	18.54N	109.40 E
Wuzhong	152	Id	38.00N	106.10 E
Wuzhou	142	Ng	23.32N	111.21 E
Wyalkatchem	212	Df	31.10S	117.22 E
Wyandotte	184	Fd	42.12N	83.10W
Wyandra	212	Je	27.15S	145.59 E
Wye	124	Cc	51.11N	0.56 E
Wye 〜	118	Kj	51.37N	2.39W
Wyemandoo, Mount- ▲	212	De	28.31S	118.32 E
Wyk auf Föhr	120	Eb	54.42N	8.34 E
Wylie, Lake- ≈	184	Gh	35.07N	81.02W
Wymondham	118	Oi	52.34N	1.07 E
Wyndham [Austl.]	210	Df	15.28S	128.06 E
Wyndham [N.Z.]	218	Cg	46.20S	168.51 E
Wyndmere	186	Hc	46.16N	97.08W
Wynne	186	Ki	35.14N	90.47W
Wynniatt Bay ◧	180	Gb	72.50N	111.00W
Wynyard [Austl.]	212	Jh	40.59S	145.41 E
Wynyard [Sask.-Can.]	180	Hf	51.47N	104.10W
Wyoming	184	Ed	42.54N	85.42W
Wyoming [2]	182	Fc	43.00N	107.30W
Wyoming Peak ▲	182	Ec	42.36N	110.37W
Wyśmierzyce	120	Qe	51.38N	20.49 E
Wysoka	120	Nc	53.11N	17.05 E
Wysokie Mazowieckie	120	Sd	52.56N	22.32 E
Wyszków	120	Rd	52.36N	21.28 E
Wyszogród	120	Qd	52.23N	20.11 E
Wytheville	184	Gg	36.57N	81.07W
Wyvjlle Thomson Ridge (EN) ⌓	118	Fa	60.10N	8.00W
Wyvis, Ben- ▲	118	Id	57.42N	4.30W

X

Xābia / Jávea	126	Mf	38.47N	0.10 E
Xaintrie ⊠	122	Ii	45.00N	2.10 E
Xainza	152	Ee	30.50N	88.37 E
Xaitongmoin	152	Ef	29.26N	88.08 E
Xai-Xai	160	Kk	25.04S	33.39 E
Xamba → Hanggin Houqi	152	Ic	40.59N	107.07 E
Xam Nua	148	Kd	20.25N	104.02 E
Xá-Muteba	170	Cd	9.34S	17.50 E
Xangongo	160	Ij	16.46S	14.59 E
Xang Qu 〜	152	Ef	29.22N	89.09 E
Xanten	120	Ce	51.40N	6.27 E
Xánthi	130	Hh	41.08N	24.53 E
Xanthos ⛬	146	Cd	36.20N	29.20 E
Xanxerê	206	Jc	26.53S	52.23W
Xapuri	202	Ef	10.39S	68.31W
Xar Hudag	152	Jb	45.06N	114.30 E
Xar Moron 〜	154	Ac	42.37N	111.02 E
Xar Moron He 〜	152	Lc	43.24N	120.39 E
Xarrama 〜	126	Df	38.14N	8.20W
Xàtiva/Játiva	126	Lf	38.59N	0.31W
Xau, Lake- ≈	172	Cd	21.15S	24.44 E
Xavantes, Represa de- ◫	204	Hf	23.20S	49.35W
Xavantina	204	Fe	21.15S	52.48W
Xavier / Javier	126	Kb	42.36N	1.13W
Xayar	152	Dc	41.15N	82.50 E
Xebert	154	Fc	44.00N	122.00 E
Xêgar → Tingri	152	Ef	28.41N	87.00 E
Xenia	184	Ff	39.41N	83.56W
Xiachengzi	154	Kb	44.41N	130.26 E
Xiacun → Rushan	154	Ff	36.55N	121.30 E
Xiaguan	152	Hf	25.32N	100.12 E
Xiahe (Labrang)	152	Hd	35.18N	102.30 E
Xiajin	154	Cf	36.57N	116.00 E
Xiamen = Amoy (EN)	142	Ng	24.32N	118.06 E
Xi'an	142	Mf	34.15N	108.50 E
Xianbin Ansha ∴	150	Ge	9.48N	116.38 E
Xianfeng	152	If	29.41N	109.09 E
Xiangcheng	154	Bh	33.51N	113.29 E
Xiangcheng/Qagchêng	152	Gf	28.56N	99.46 E
Xiangcheng (Shuizhai)	154	Ch	33.27N	114.53 E
Xiangfan	142	Nf	32.03N	112.05 E
Xianggang/Hong Kong [5]	142	Ng	22.15N	114.10 E
Xianghua Ling ▲	152	Jf	25.26N	112.32 E
Xianghuang Qi (Xin Bulag)	152	Jc	42.12N	113.59 E
Xiang Jiang 〜	140	Ng	29.26N	113.08 E
Xiangkhoang	148	Ke	19.20N	103.22 E
Xiangkhoang, Plateau de- ⏜	148	Ke	19.30N	103.10 E
Xiangquan He 〜	152	Ce	32.05N	79.20 E
Xiangshan (Dancheng)	152	Lf	29.29N	121.52 E
Xiangshan Gang ◧	154	Fj	29.35N	121.38 E
Xiangtan	142	Ng	27.54N	112.55 E
Xiangtang	154	Cj	28.26N	115.59 E
Xiangyin	154	Bj	28.41N	112.53 E
Xiangyuan	154	Bf	36.32N	113.02 E
Xianju	152	Lf	28.50N	120.42 E
Xianning	154	Cj	29.52N	114.17 E
Xiannümiao → Jiangdu	154	Eh	32.30N	119.33 E
Xiantaozhen → Mianyang	154	Bi	30.22N	113.27 E
Xianxia Ling ▲	152	Kf	28.24N	118.40 E
Xianxian	154	De	38.12N	116.07 E
Xianyang	152	Ie	34.26N	108.40 E
Xiaobole Shan ▲	152	La	51.46N	124.09 E
Xiao'ergou	152	Lb	49.10N	123.43 E
Xiaogan	152	Je	30.52N	113.58 E
Xiao He 〜	154	Bf	37.38N	112.24 E
Xiao Hinggan Ling = Lesser Khingan Range (EN) ⛰	140	Oe	48.45N	127.00 E
Xiaoling He 〜	154	Fd	40.55N	121.12 E
Xiaoluan He 〜	154	Dd	41.36N	117.05 E
Xiaoqing He 〜	154	Ef	37.19N	118.59 E
Xiaoshan	154	Fi	30.10N	120.16 E
Xiaowutai Shan ▲	154	Ce	39.57N	114.59 E
Xiaoxian	154	Dg	34.11N	116.56 E
Xiaoyi	154	Af	37.07N	111.48 E
Xiaoyi → Gongxian	154	Bg	34.46N	112.57 E
Xiapu	152	Kf	26.57N	119.59 E
Xiawa	154	Fc	42.36N	120.33 E
Xiayi	154	Dg	34.14N	116.07 E
Xiazhuang → Linshu	154	Eg	34.56N	118.38 E
Xicalango, Punta- ▶	192	Nh	19.41N	92.00W
Xichang	142	Mg	27.52N	102.15 E
Xicheng → Yangyuan	154	Cd	40.08N	114.10 E
Xicoténcatl	192	Jf	23.00N	98.56W
Xicotepec de Juárez	192	Kg	20.17N	97.57W
Xiejiaji → Qingyun	154	Df	37.46N	117.22 E
Xifei He 〜	154	Dh	32.38N	116.39 E
Xifeng	154	Hc	42.45N	124.44 E
Xifengzhen	152	Id	35.40N	107.42 E
Xigazê	142	Kg	29.15N	88.52 E
Xi He [China] 〜	154	Dj	29.38N	116.53 E
Xi He [China] 〜	152	Hc	42.23N	101.03 E
Xiheying	154	Ce	39.53N	114.42 E
Xihua	154	Ch	33.48N	114.31 E
Xi Jang 〜	140	Ng	23.05N	114.23 E
Xiji [China]	154	Ia	46.09N	127.08 E
Xiji [China]	152	Id	35.52N	105.35 E
Xi Jiang 〜	152	Jg	23.05N	114.23 E
Xijir Ulan Hu ≈	152	Fd	35.12N	90.18 E
Xikouzi	152	La	42.58N	120.29 E
Xiliao He 〜	140	Oe	43.24N	123.42 E
Xiligou → Ulan	152	Gd	36.55N	98.16 E
Xilin	152	Ig	24.30N	105.05 E
Xilin Gol 〜	154	Dc	43.55N	116.05 E
Xilin Hot → Abagnar Qi	142	Ne	43.58N	116.08 E
Xilitla	192	Jg	21.20N	98.58W
Xilókastron	130	Fk	38.05N	22.38 E
Ximiao	152	Hc	41.04N	100.14 E
Xin'an	154	Bg	34.43N	112.09 E
Xin'anjiang	154	Ei	29.27N	119.15 E
Xin'anjiang Shuiku ◫	152	Kf	29.25N	119.05 E
Xin'anzhen → Guannan	154	Eg	34.04N	119.21 E
Xin'anzhen → Xinyi	152	Ke	34.17N	118.14 E
Xin Barag Youqi (Altan-Emel)	152	Kb	48.41N	116.47 E
Xin Barag Zuoqi (Amgalang)	152	Kb	48.13N	118.14 E
Xinbin	154	Hd	41.44N	125.02 E
Xin Bulag → Xianghuang Qi	152	Jc	42.12N	113.59 E
Xincai	152	Je	32.40N	114.57 E
Xinchang	154	Fj	29.30N	120.54 E
Xincheng [China]	152	Ig	24.04N	108.39 E
Xincheng [China]	154	Bf	37.57N	112.33 E
Xincheng [China]	152	Id	38.33N	106.10 E
Xincheng (Gaobeidian)	154	Ce	39.20N	115.50 E
Xindi → Honghu	154	Bj	29.50N	113.28 E
Xing'an → Ankang	142	Mf	32.37N	109.03 E
Xingcheng	154	Fd	40.38N	120.43 E
Xingguo	152	Kf	26.22N	115.21 E
Xinghai	152	Gd	35.45N	99.59 E
Xinghe	152	Jc	40.52N	113.56 E
Xinghua	154	Eh	32.56N	119.49 E
Xingkai Hu = Khanka Lake (EN) ≈	140	Pe	45.00N	132.24 E
Xinglong	154	Dd	40.25N	117.31 E
Xinglongzhen	154	Ia	46.26N	127.03 E
Xingren	152	If	25.26N	105.08 E
Xingtai	142	Nf	37.00N	114.30 E
Xingtang	154	Ce	38.26N	114.33 E
Xingu, Rio- 〜	198	Kf	1.30S	51.53W
Xingxingxia	152	Gc	41.47N	95.07 E
Xingyang	154	Bg	34.47N	113.21 E
Xingyi (Huangcaoba)	152	Hf	25.03N	104.55 E
Xingzi	154	Dj	29.28N	116.03 E
Xinhe	154	Cf	37.32N	115.14 E
Xinhe/Toksu	152	Dc	41.34N	82.38 E
Xin Hot → Abag Qi	152	Jc	44.01N	114.59 E
Xinhuai He 〜	154	Fg	34.23N	120.05 E
Xinhui → Aohan Qi	154	Ec	42.18N	119.53 E
Xining	142	Mf	36.37N	101.46 E
Xinji → Shulu	154	Cf	37.56N	115.14 E
Xinjian	154	Cj	28.41N	115.50 E
Xin Jiang 〜	154	Dj	28.37N	116.40 E
Xinjiangkou → Songzi	154	Ai	30.10N	111.46 E
Xinjiang Uygur Zizhiqu (Hsin-chiang-wei-wu-erh Tzu-chih-ch'ü) = Sinkiang Uighur (EN) [2]	152	Ec	42.00N	86.00 E
Xinjin	152	He	30.25N	103.46 E
Xinjin (Pulandian)	152	Ld	39.24N	121.59 E
Xinkai He 〜	154	Gc	43.36N	122.31 E
Xinle	154	Ce	38.15N	114.40 E
Xinlin	154	Ec	43.58N	118.03 E
Xinlitun [China]	154	Gc	42.01N	122.11 E
Xinlitun [China]	152	Ma	50.58N	126.39 E
Xinlong/Nyagrong	152	He	30.57N	100.12 E
Xinmin	154	Gc	42.00N	122.50 E
Xinpu → Lianyungang	142	Nf	34.34N	119.15 E
Xinqing	152	Mb	48.15N	129.31 E
Xintai	154	Dg	35.54N	117.44 E
Xinwen (Suncun)	152	Kd	35.49N	117.38 E
Xinxian [China]	152	Jd	38.24N	112.43 E
Xinxian [China]	154	Ci	31.42N	114.50 E
Xinxiang	142	Nf	35.17N	113.50 E
Xinyang	152	Je	32.05N	114.07 E
Xinye	154	Bh	32.30N	112.22 E
Xinyi (Xin'anzhen)	152	Ke	34.17N	118.14 E
Xinyi He 〜	154	Eg	34.29N	119.49 E
Xinyuan/Künes	152	Dc	43.24N	83.18 E
Xinyuan → Tianjun	142	Lf	37.18N	99.15 E
Xinzhan	154	Ic	43.52N	127.20 E
Xin Zhen → Hanggin Qi	152	Id	39.54N	108.55 E
Xinzheng	154	Bg	34.25N	113.46 E
Xinzhou	154	Ci	30.51N	114.49 E
Xinzo de Limia	126	Eb	42.03N	7.43W
Xiong Xian	154	De	38.59N	116.06 E
Xionyuecheng	154	Gd	40.12N	122.08 E
Xiping [China]	154	Bh	33.22N	114.00 E
Xiping [China]	154	Ej	28.27N	119.29 E
Xisha Qundao = Paracel Islands (EN) ⁙	140	Nh	16.30N	112.15 E
Xishuangbanna ⛰	152	Gg	22.15N	100.00 E
Xishuanghe → Kenli	154	Ef	37.35N	118.30 E
Xishui	154	Ci	30.28N	115.15 E
Xi Taijnar Hu ≈	152	Fd	37.15N	93.30 E
Xitianmu Shan ▲	152	Ke	30.21N	119.25 E
Xi Ujimqin Qi (Bayan Ul Hot)	152	Kc	44.31N	117.33 E
Xiuning	154	Ej	29.47N	118.11 E
Xiushui	152	Jf	29.02N	114.33 E
Xiu Shui 〜	154	Cj	29.13N	116.00 E
Xiuwu	154	Bg	35.13N	113.27 E
Xiuyan	152	Lc	40.18N	123.10 E
Xiwanzi → Chongli	154	Cd	40.57N	115.12 E
Xixabangma Feng ▲	152	Ef	28.21N	85.47 E
Xixian	154	Ch	32.21N	114.43 E
Xixiang	152	Ie	32.58N	107.45 E
Xixona / Jijona	126	Lf	38.32N	0.30W
Xiyang	154	Bf	37.38N	113.41 E
Xizang Zizhiqu (Hsi-tsang Tzu-chih-ch'ü) = Tibet (EN) [2]	152	Ee	32.00N	90.00 E
Xizhong Dao ◆	154	Fe	39.25N	121.18 E
Xochicalco ⛬	192	Jh	18.45N	99.20W
Xochimilco	192	Jh	19.16N	99.06W
Xorkol	152	Fd	39.04N	91.05 E
Xpujil ⛬	192	Oh	18.35N	89.25W
Xuancheng	154	Ei	30.56N	118.44 E
Xuande Qundao ⁙	150	Fc	17.08N	111.30 E
Xuan'en	152	Ie	30.02N	109.30 E
Xuanhan	152	Ie	31.23N	107.39 E
Xuanhua	152	Kc	40.39N	115.05 E
Xuanwei	152	Hf	26.19N	104.05 E
Xuchang	142	Nf	34.00N	113.58 E
Xuecheng (Lincheng)	154	Dg	34.38N	117.14 E
Xuefeng Shan ⛰	152	Jf	27.35N	110.50 E
Xue Shan ⛰	152	Gf	27.30N	99.55 E
Xugezhuang → Fengnan	154	Ee	39.34N	118.05 E
Xugou	154	Eg	34.37N	119.08 E
Xugui	152	Gd	35.45N	96.08 E
Xuguit Qi (Yakeshi)	152	Lb	49.16N	120.41 E
Xümatang	152	Ge	33.57N	97.00 E
Xun Jiang 〜	152	Jg	23.28N	111.18 E
Xunke (Qike)	152	Mb	49.34N	128.28 E
Xunwu	152	Kg	24.59N	115.33 E
Xunxian	154	Cg	35.40N	114.33 E
Xupu	152	Jf	27.54N	110.35 E
Xúquer/Júcar 〜	110	Fh	39.09N	0.14W
Xushui	154	Ce	39.02N	115.40 E
Xuwen	152	Jg	20.22N	110.10 E
Xuyi	152	Ke	32.58N	118.33 E
Xuyong (Yongning)	152	If	28.13N	105.26 E
Xuzhou	142	Nf	34.12N	117.13 E

Y

Ya'an	142	Mg	30.00N	102.57 E
Yabassi	166	Ge	4.28N	9.58 E
Yabe	156	Be	32.42N	130.59 E
Yabebyry	204	Dh	27.24S	57.11W
Yabelo	168	Fe	4.53N	38.07 E
Yablonovy Range (EN) = Jablonovy hrebet ⛰	140	Nd	53.30N	115.00 E
Yabrai Shan ⛰	152	Hc	40.00N	103.10 E
Yabrīn 🌴	168	Ha	23.15N	48.59 E
Yabrūd	146	Gf	33.58N	36.40 E
Yabucoa	197a	Cb	18.03N	65.53W
Yabuli	152	Mc	44.56N	128.37 E
Yabulu	212	Jc	19.00S	146.40 E
Yacaré Cururú, Cuchilla- ⛰	204	Dj	30.30S	56.33W
Yacaré Norte, Riacho- 〜	204	Cf	22.43S	58.14W
Yacaré Sur, Riacho- 〜	204	Cf	22.43S	58.14W
Yachats	188	Cd	44.20N	124.03W
Yacuma, Río- 〜	202	Ef	13.38S	65.23W
Yacyretá, Isla- ◆	204	Dh	27.25S	56.30W
Yadé, Massif du- ⛰	168	Bd	7.00N	15.30 E
Yādgīr	148	Fe	16.46N	77.08 E
Yadong/Chomo	152	Ef	27.38N	89.03 E
Yae-Dake ▲	156b	Ab	26.38N	127.56 E
Yaeyama-Rettō ⁙	152	Lg	24.20N	124.00 E
Yafran	164	Bc	32.04N	12.31 E
Yağcilar	130	Lj	39.25N	28.23 E
Yagishiri-Tō ◆	156a	Ba	44.26N	141.25 E
Yagoua	166	Ic	10.20N	15.14 E
Yagradagzê Shan ▲	152	Gd	35.09N	95.39 E
Yaguajay	194	Hb	22.19N	79.14W
Yaguari	204	Ej	31.31S	54.58W
Yaguari, Arroyo- 〜	204	Di	29.44S	57.37W
Yahualı	146	Fc	38.05N	35.25 E
Yahualica de Gonzáles Gallo	192	Hg	21.08N	102.51W
Yahuma	170	Db	1.06N	23.10 E
Yaita	156	Fc	36.50N	139.55 E
Yaizu	156	Fd	34.51N	138.19 E
Yajiang/Nyagquka	152	He	30.07N	100.58 E
Yakacik	146	Ed	36.05N	32.45 E
Yake-Dake ▲	156	Ec	36.14N	137.35 E
Yakeishi-Dake ▲	156	Gb	39.10N	140.50 E
Yakeshi → Xuguit Qi	152	Lb	49.16N	120.41 E
Yake-Yama ▲	156	Gb	39.58N	140.48 E
Yakima	176	Ge	46.36N	120.31W
Yakima River 〜	188	Fc	46.15N	119.02W
Yako	166	Ec	12.58N	2.16W
Yakumo	152	Pc	42.15N	140.16 E
Yaku-Shima ◆	152	Ne	30.20N	130.30 E
Yakutat	178	Le	59.33N	139.44W
Yakutat Bay ◧	178	Ke	59.45N	140.45W
Yala	148	Kg	6.32N	101.19 E
Yalahán, Laguna de- ⊜	192	Pg	21.30N	87.15W
Yalcubul, Punta- ▶	192	Og	21.35N	88.35W
Yale Point ▲	188	Kh	36.25N	109.48W
Yalewa Kalou ◆	219d	Ab	16.40S	177.46 E
Yalgoo	212	De	28.20S	116.41 E
Yalikavak	130	Kl	37.06N	27.18 E
Yaliköy	130	Lh	41.29N	28.17 E
Yalinga	168	Cd	6.31N	23.13 E
Yaloké	168	Bd	5.19N	17.05 E
Yalong Jiang 〜	140	Mg	26.37N	101.48 E
Yalova	146	Cb	40.39N	29.15 E
Yalu Jiang 〜	140	Of	39.55N	124.20 E
Yalvaç	146	Dc	38.17N	31.11 E
Yām, Ramlat- ⁖	164	If	17.42N	45.09 E
Yamada [Jap.]	156	Be	33.33N	130.45 E
Yamada [Jap.]	154	Pe	39.28N	141.57 E
Yamada-Wan ◧	156	Hb	39.30N	142.00 E
Yamaga	156	Be	33.01N	130.41 E
Yamagata	152	Pd	38.15N	140.15 E
Yamagata Ken [2]	154	Pe	38.30N	140.00 E
Yamagawa	156	Bf	31.12N	130.39 E
Yamaguchi	152	Ne	34.10N	131.29 E
Yamaguchi Ken [2]	154	Kh	34.10N	131.30 E
Yamakuni	156	Be	33.24N	131.02 E
Yamal Peninsula (EN) = Jamal, poluostrov- ⊏	140	Ib	70.00N	70.00 E
Yamamoto	156	Ga	40.06N	140.03 E
Yamanaka	156	Ec	36.15N	136.22 E
Yamanashi Ken [2]	154	Og	35.30N	138.45 E
Yamashiro	156	Ce	33.57N	133.43 E
Yamato Rise (EN) ⌓	154	Me	39.30N	134.30 E
Yamatsuri	156	Gc	36.53N	140.25 E
Yamazaki	156	Dd	35.00N	134.33 E
Yambi, Mesa de- ⊠	202	Dc	1.30N	71.20W
Yambio	160	Jh	4.34N	28.23 E
Yambo	168	Fd	8.25N	36.00 E
Yambu Head ▶	197n	Ba	13.09N	61.09W
Yambuya	170	Db	1.16N	24.33 E
Yame	156	Be	33.13N	130.34 E
Yamethin	148	Jd	20.26N	96.09 E
Yamma Yamma, Lake- ≈	212	Ie	26.20S	141.25 E
Yamoto	156	Gb	38.25N	141.13 E
Yamoussoukro	166	Dd	6.49N	5.17W
Yampa River 〜	182	Fc	40.32N	108.59W
Yampi Sound	212	Ec	16.11S	123.40 E
Yamuna 〜	140	Kg	25.30N	81.53 E
Yamunanagar	148	Fb	30.08N	76.59 E
Yamzho Yumco ≈	152	Ff	29.00N	90.40 E
Yanagawa	156	Be	33.10N	130.24 E
Yanahara	156	Dd	34.57N	134.05 E
Yanahuanca	202	Cf	10.30S	76.30W
Yanai	156	Ce	33.58N	132.07 E
Yanam	148	Ge	16.51N	82.15 E
Yan'an	142	Mf	36.36N	109.30 E
Yanaoca	202	Df	14.13S	71.26W
Yanbian	152	Hf	26.51N	101.32 E
Yanbu'	144	Ee	24.05N	38.03 E
Yanchang	152	Jd	36.39N	110.03 E
Yancheng [China]	152	Le	33.16N	120.10 E
Yancheng [China]	154	Bh	33.35N	114.00 E
Yanchi	152	Id	37.47N	107.24 E
Yandé ◆	219b	Ae	20.03S	163.48 E
Yandina	219a	Dc	9.07S	159.13 E
Yandja	170	Cc	1.41S	17.43 E
Yandua ◆	219d	Bb	16.49S	178.18 E
Yanfolila	166	Dc	11.11N	8.08W
Yangalia	168	Cd	6.58N	21.01 E
Yangambi	160	Jh	0.47N	24.28 E
Yangcheng	154	Bg	35.32N	112.36 E
Yangchun	152	Jg	22.11N	111.48 E
Yangcun	154	De	39.23N	117.04 E
Yangcun → Wuqing	154	De	39.23N	117.04 E
Yangdŏg-ŭp	154	Ie	39.13N	126.39 E
Yangganga ◆	219d	Bb	16.35S	178.35 E
Yanggang-Do [2]	154	Jd	41.15N	128.00 E

Yanggao	152	Jc	40.21N	113.47 E
Yanggeta	219d	Ab	17.01S	177.20 E
Yanggu	154	Cf	36.08N	115.48 E
Yang He	154	Cd	40.24N	115.18 E
Yangi	130	Mm	36.55N	29.01 E
Yangjiang	152	Jg	21.59N	111.59 E
Yangjiazhangzi	154	Fd	40.48N	120.30 E
Yangon = Rangoon (EN)	142	Lh	16.47N	96.10 E
Yangor	220e	Ab	0.32S	166.54 E
Yangqu (Huangzhai)	154	Be	38.05N	112.37 E
Yangquan	152	Jd	37.49N	113.34 E
Yangquanqu	152	Jd	37.04N	111.30 E
Yangshuo	152	Jg	24.46N	110.28 E
Yang Sin, Chu-	148	Lf	12.24N	108.26 E
Yangtze Kiang → Chang Jiang	140	Of	31.48N	121.10 E
Yangxian	152	Ie	33.20N	107.35 E
Yangxin [China]	152	Kf	29.50N	115.11 E
Yangxin [China]	154	Df	37.39N	117.34 E
Yangyuan (Xicheng)	154	Cd	40.08N	114.10 E
Yangzhou	152	Ke	32.20N	119.25 E
Yanhe (Heping)	152	If	28.31N	108.28 E
Yanji	152	Mc	42.56N	129.30 E
Yanjin	154	Cg	35.09N	114.11 E
Yankton	182	Hc	42.53N	97.23W
Yanling	154	Cg	34.07N	114.11 E
Yanqi	152	Ke	42.04N	86.34 E
Yanqing	154	Cd	40.28N	115.57 E
Yan Shan	140	Ne	40.18N	117.36 E
Yanshan [China]	154	De	38.03N	117.12 E
Yanshan [China]	152	Hg	23.38N	104.24 E
Yanshan (Hekou)	154	Dj	28.18N	117.41 E
Yanshi	154	Bg	34.44N	112.47 E
Yanshou	154	Jb	45.28N	128.19 E
Yantai	142	Of	37.28N	121.24 E
Yanutha	219d	Ac	16.14S	178.00 E
Yanweigang	154	Eg	34.28N	119.46 E
Yanyuan	152	Hf	27.26N	101.32 E
Yanzhou	152	Kd	35.33N	116.49 E
Yao [Chad]	168	Bc	12.51N	17.34 E
Yao [Jap.]	156	Dd	34.38N	135.36 E
Yaodu → Dongzhi	154	Di	30.06N	117.01 E
Yaoundé	160	Ih	3.52N	11.31 E
Yapacani	202	Fg	16.36S	64.18W
Yapei	166	Ed	9.10N	1.10W
Yapen, Pulau-	208	Ee	1.45S	136.15 E
Yapen, Selat-	150	Kg	1.30S	136.10 E
Yapeyú	204	Di	29.28S	56.49W
Yap Islands	208	Ed	9.32N	138.08 E
Yapraklı	146	Eb	40.46N	33.47 E
Yapu	148	Jf	14.51N	98.03 E
Yaqian → Yuexi	154	Di	30.51N	116.22 E
Yaque del Norte, Río-	194	Ld	19.51N	71.41W
Yaque del Sur, Río-	194	Ld	18.17N	71.06W
Yaqueling	154	Ai	30.40N	111.36 E
Yaqui	174	Hg	27.37N	110.39W
Yaracuy [2]	202	Ea	10.20N	68.45W
Yaraka	210	Fg	24.53S	144.04 E
Yaralıgöz	146	Fb	41.45N	34.10 E
Yare	118	Oi	52.35N	1.44 E
Yaren	220e	Ab	0.33S	166.54 E
Yari, Río-	198	If	0.23S	72.16W
Yariga-Take	156	Ec	36.20N	137.39 E
Yarim	144	Fg	14.21N	44.22 E
Yaritagua	202	Ea	10.05N	69.08W
Yarkant/Shache	142	Jf	38.24N	77.15 E
Yarkant He	140	Ke	40.28N	80.52 E
Yarlung Zangbo Jiang	140	Lg	24.02N	90.59 E
Yarmouth [Eng.-U.K.]	124	Ad	50.41N	1.30W
Yarmouth [N.S.-Can.]	176	Me	43.50N	66.07W
Yarram	214	Jg	38.33S	146.41 E
Yarumal	202	Cb	6.58N	75.25W
Yasawa	219d	Ab	16.47S	177.31 E
Yasawa Group	208	If	17.00S	177.23 E
Yashi	166	Gc	12.22N	7.55 E
Yashima	156	Gb	39.09N	140.10 E
Ya-Shima	156	Ce	33.45N	132.10 E
Yashiro-Jima	156	Ce	33.55N	132.15 E
Yasothon	148	Ke	15.46N	104.12 E
Yass	212	Jf	34.50S	148.55 E
Yassiören	130	Lh	41.18N	28.35 E
Yasugi	156	Cd	35.26N	133.15 E
Yāsūj	144	Hc	30.45N	51.33 E
Yasun Burnu	146	Gb	41.09N	37.41 E
Yatağan	146	Cd	37.20N	28.09 E
Yatate Tōge	156	Gb	40.26N	140.37 E
Yatate-Yama	156	Ad	34.12N	129.14 E
Yatenga [3]	166	Ec	13.48N	2.10W
Yaté-Village	216	Cd	22.09S	166.57 E
Yathata	219d	Cb	17.15S	179.32W
Yathkyed Lake	180	Hd	62.40N	98.00W
Yatolema	170	Db	0.21N	24.33 E
Yatou → Rongcheng	154	Gf	37.10N	122.25 E
Yatsu-ga-Take	156	Fd	35.59N	138.23 E
Yatsushiro	152	Ne	32.30N	130.36 E
Yatsushiro-Kai	156	Be	32.20N	130.25 E
Yatta Plateau	170	Gc	2.00S	38.00 E
Yauco	194	Nd	18.02N	66.51W
Yauri	202	Df	14.47S	71.29W
Yauyos	202	Cf	12.24S	75.57W
Yavari, Río-	202	Dd	4.21S	70.02W
Yavi, Cerro-	202	Eb	5.32N	65.59W
Yaviza	194	Ii	8.11N	77.41W
Yawatahama	154	Lh	33.27N	132.24 E
Yaxchilán	190	Fe	16.54N	90.58W
Yaxian (Sanya)	142	Mh	18.27N	109.28 E
Yayladağı	146	Ge	35.56N	36.01 E
Yazd	142	Hf	31.53N	54.25 E
Yazd [3]	144	Hc	31.30N	54.30 E
Yazılıkaya	146	Dc	39.13N	30.45 E
Yazoo City	186	Kj	32.51N	90.28W
Yazoo River	186	Kj	32.22N	91.00W
Ybbs	128	Jb	48.10N	15.06 E
Ybbs an der Donau	128	Jc	48.10N	15.05 E
Yding Skovhøj	116	Ch	56.01N	9.48 E
Ydre	116	Fg	57.52N	15.15 E
Ydstebøhamn	116	Ae	59.03N	5.25 E
Ye	142	Lh	15.15N	97.51 E
Yebaishou → Jianping	152	Kc	41.55N	119.37 E
Yebbi Bou	168	Ba	20.58N	18.04 E
Yébigé	168	Ba	22.04N	17.49 E
Yecheng/Kargilik	142	Jf	37.54N	77.26 E
Yech'ŏn	154	Jf	36.39N	128.27 E
Yecla	126	Kf	38.37N	1.07W
Yécora	190	Cc	28.20N	108.58W
Yëd	168	Ge	4.48N	43.02 E
Yedi Burun	130	Mm	36.23N	29.05 E
Yedseram	166	Hc	12.16N	14.09 E
Yefira	130	Fi	40.44N	22.42 E
Yegros	204	Dh	26.24S	56.25W
Yeguas	126	Hf	38.02N	4.15W
Yeha	168	Fc	14.21N	39.05 E
Yei	168	Ee	4.05N	30.40 E
Yei	168	Ee	4.40N	30.30 E
Yeji [China]	154	Ci	31.51N	115.55 E
Yeji [Ghana]	166	Ed	8.13N	0.39W
Yekepa	166	Dd	7.35N	8.32W
Yelgu	168	Ec	10.01N	32.31 E
Yélimané	166	Cb	15.07N	10.36W
Yell	110	Fc	60.35N	1.05W
Yellice Dağı	130	Mj	39.23N	29.57 E
Yellowhead Pass	180	Ff	52.50N	117.55W
Yellowknife	176	Hc	62.27N	114.21W
Yellowknife	180	Gd	62.23N	114.20W
Yellow River (EN) = Huang He	140	Nf	37.32N	118.19 E
Yellow Sea (EN) = Huang Hai	140	Of	36.00N	124.00 E
Yellow Sea (EN) = Hwang-Hae	140	Of	36.00N	124.00 E
Yellowstone	174	Ie	47.58N	103.59W
Yellowstone Lake	174	He	44.25N	110.22W
Yellowstone National Park	188	Jd	44.58N	110.42W
Yell Sound	118	La	60.33N	1.15W
Yeltes	126	Fd	40.56N	6.31W
Yelwa [Nig.]	166	Gd	8.51N	9.37 E
Yelwa [Nig.]	166	Fc	10.50N	4.44 E
Yemen (EN) = Al Yaman	142	Gh	15.00N	44.00 E
Yemen, People's Democratic Republic of- (EN) → Al Yaman	142	Gh.	15.00N	44.00 E
Yenagoa	166	Ge	4.55N	6.16 E
Yenangyaung	148	Id	20.28N	94.53 E
Yen Bay	148	Kd	21.42N	104.52 E
Yendi	166	Ed	9.26N	0.01W
Yenge	170	Dc	0.55S	20.40 E
Yengisar	152	Cd	38.56N	76.09 E
Yengo	170	Cb	0.22N	15.29 E
Yeniboğaziçi	146	Ee	35.17N	33.52 E
Yenice [Tur.]	130	Kj	39.55N	27.18 E
Yenice [Tur.]	146	Fd	36.59N	35.03 E
Yeni Erenkoy	146	Fe	35.35N	34.15 E
Yenice [Tur.]	146	Eb	41.18N	32.08 E
Yenifoça	130	Jk	38.44N	26.51 E
Yenihisar	130	Kl	37.22N	27.15 E
Yenimahalle, Ankara-	146	Ec	39.56N	32.52 E
Yenipazar	130	Ll	37.48N	28.12 E
Yenişehir	146	Cb	40.16N	29.39 E
Yenisey (EN) = Jenisej	140	Kb	71.50N	82.40 E
Yenisey Bay (EN) = Jenisejski zaliv	138	Db	72.00N	81.00 E
Yenisey Ridge (EN) = Jenisejski krjaž	140	Ld	59.00N	92.30 E
Yennádhion	130	Km	36.01N	27.56 E
Yeo, Lake-	212	Ee	28.05S	124.25 E
Yeovil	118	Kk	50.57N	2.39W
Yepes	126	Ie	39.54N	3.38W
Yeppoon	212	Kd	23.08S	150.45 E
Yeràkion	130	Fm	37.00N	22.42 E
Yerbabuena	192	Hf	23.00N	103.30W
Yerer	168	Gd	7.32N	42.05 E
Yerington	188	Fg	38.59N	119.10W
Yerkesik	130	Ll	37.07N	28.17 E
Yerköy	146	Fc	39.38N	34.29 E
Yerlisu	130	Ji	40.46N	26.39 E
Yermak Plateau (EN)	179	Mb	82.00N	6.00 E
Yeroḥam	146	Fg	31.00N	34.55 E
Yerres	122	If	48.43N	2.27 E
Yerupajá, Nevado-	198	Ig	10.16S	76.54W
Yerushalayim [3]	146	Fg	31.45N	35.00 E
Yerushalayim = Jerusalem (EN)	142	Ff	31.46N	35.14 E
Yerville	124	Ce	49.40N	0.54 E
Yerwa	166	Hc	11.13N	12.53 E
Yesa, Embalse de-	126	Kb	42.36N	1.09W
Yeşan	154	If	36.41N	126.51 E
Yeşilhisar	146	Fc	38.21N	35.06 E
Yeşilırmak	144	Ea	41.24N	36.35 E
Yeşilköy	146	Cb	40.57N	29.49 E
Yeşilova	130	Ml	37.30N	29.46 E
Yeşilyurt	130	Ll	37.11N	28.17 E
Yeso	204	Cj	30.56S	59.28W
Yeste	126	Jf	38.22N	2.18W
Yetti	158	Gf	26.10N	7.50W
Ye-u	148	Jd	22.46N	95.26 E
Yeu, Ile d'-	122	Dh	46.43N	2.20W
Yèvre	122	Ig	47.13N	2.04 E
Yexian [China]	154	Ef	37.11N	119.58 E
Yexian [China]	154	Bh	33.38N	113.21 E
Yguazú, Río-	204	Eg	25.20S	55.00W
Yhú	204	Eg	24.59S	55.59W
Yí, Río-	204	Dk	33.07S	57.08W
Yiali	130	Km	36.40N	27.05 E
Yi'an	152	Mb	47.53N	125.17 E
Yiannitsá	130	Fi	40.48N	22.25 E
Yiaros	130	Hl	37.37N	24.43 E
Yibin	142	Mg	28.47N	104.35 E
Yibug Caka	152	Ee	33.55N	87.05 E
Yichang	142	Nf	30.42N	111.22 E
Yicheng [China]	154	Ag	35.44N	111.43 E
Yicheng [China]	154	Bi	31.42N	112.16 E
Yichuan	152	Jd	36.00N	110.06 E
Yichun [China]	152	Jf	27.47N	114.25 E
Yichun [China]	152	Mb	47.41N	128.55 E
Yidilzeli	146	Gc	39.52N	36.38 E
Yidu [China]	152	Je	30.23N	111.28 E
Yidu [China]	152	Kd	36.41N	118.29 E
Yidun (Dagxoi)	152	Ge	30.25N	99.28 E
Yifag	168	Fc	12.02N	37.41 E
Yifeng	154	Cj	28.25N	114.47 E
Yığılca	146	Db	40.58N	31.27 E
Yigo	220c	Ba	13.32N	144.53W
Yi He [China]	154	Bg	34.41N	112.33 E
Yi He [China]	154	Eg	34.07N	118.15 E
Yilan	152	Mb	46.18N	129.33 E
Yıldız Dağı	144	Ea	40.08N	36.56 E
Yıldız Dağları	146	Bb	41.50N	27.10 E
Yiliang	152	Hg	24.59N	103.08 E
Yimianpo	154	Jb	45.04N	128.03 E
Yimin He	152	Kb	49.15N	119.42 E
Yinan (Jiehu)	154	Eg	35.33N	118.27 E
Yinchuan	142	Mf	38.28N	106.19 E
Yindarlgooda, Lake-	212	Ef	30.45S	121.55 E
Yingcheng [China]	154	Bi	30.57N	113.33 E
Yingcheng [China]	154	Hb	44.08N	125.54 E
Yingde	152	Jg	24.13N	113.24 E
Ying He	152	Ke	32.30N	116.31 E
Yingjiang	152	Gg	24.45N	97.58 E
Yingjin He	154	Ec	42.20N	119.19 E
Yingkou	142	Oe	40.40N	122.12 E
Yingkou (Dashiqiao)	154	Gd	40.39N	122.31 E
Yingshan	154	Ci	30.45N	115.40 E
Yingshang	154	Dh	32.38N	116.16 E
Yingshouyingzi	154	Dd	40.33N	117.37 E
Yingtan	154	Dj	28.13N	117.00 E
Yingxian	154	Be	39.33N	113.10 E
Ying zhan/Victoria	142	Ng	22.17N	114.09 E
Yining/Gulja	152	Dc	43.54N	81.21 E
Yinma He	154	Hb	44.50N	125.45 E
Yinqing Qunjiao	150	Fe	8.55N	112.35 E
Yin Shan	140	Me	41.30N	109.00 E
Yi'ong Zangbo	152	Gf	29.56N	95.10 E
Yioúra	130	Hj	39.24N	24.10 E
Yipinglang	152	Hf	25.13N	101.55 E
Yiquan → Meitan	152	If	27.48N	107.32 E
Yirga Alem	168	Fd	6.44N	38.24 E
Yirol	168	Ed	6.33N	30.30 E
Yirshi	152	Kb	47.17N	119.55 E
Yishui	152	Eg	35.47N	118.38 E
Yisra'el = Israel (EN) [1]	142	Ff	31.30N	35.00 E
Yithion	130	Fm	36.45N	22.34 E
Yitong	154	Hc	43.20N	125.17 E
Yitong He	154	Hb	44.45N	125.40 E
Yitulihe	152	La	50.41N	121.33 E
Yiwu	152	Fj	29.19N	120.04 E
Yiwu/Aratürük	152	Fc	43.15N	94.35 E
Yixian [China]	154	Dj	29.56N	117.56 E
Yixian [China]	154	Fd	41.33N	121.14 E
Yixian [China]	154	Ce	39.21N	115.30 E
Yixing	154	Ei	31.21N	119.48 E
Yixun He	154	Dd	41.00N	117.41 E
Yiyang [China]	154	Dj	28.24N	117.24 E
Yiyang [China]	154	Bg	34.30N	112.10 E
Yiyang [China]	152	Jf	28.41N	112.28 E
Yiyuan (Nanma)	154	Ef	36.11N	118.10 E
Yizheng	154	Eh	32.16N	119.10 E
Yläne	116	Jd	60.53N	22.25 E
Ylikitka	114	Gc	66.08N	28.30 E
Yli-Li	114	Fd	65.22N	25.50 E
Ylimarkku/Övermark	116	Ib	62.37N	21.28 E
Ylistaro	114	Fe	62.57N	22.31 E
Ylitornio	114	Fc	66.18N	23.40 E
Ylivieska	114	Fd	64.05N	24.33 E
Ylöjärvi	116	Jc	61.33N	23.36 E
Ymers	179	Jd	73.20N	25.00W
Yngaren	116	Gf	58.50N	16.35 E
Yngen	116	Fe	59.45N	14.20 E
Ynykčanski	138	Id	60.08N	137.47 E
Yoboki	168	Gc	11.28N	42.06 E
Yobuko	156	Ae	33.33N	129.54 E
Yodo-Gawa	156	Dd	34.41N	135.25 E
Yogoum	168	Bb	17.27N	19.31 E
Yoğuntaş	130	Kh	41.50N	27.04 E
Yogyakarta	142	Nj	7.48S	110.22 E
Yoichi	154	Pc	43.12N	140.41 E
Yojoa, Lago de-	194	Df	14.50N	88.00W
Yōju	154	If	37.18N	127.38 E
Yokadouma	160	Ih	3.31N	15.03 E
Yōkaichi	156	Ed	35.07N	136.11 E
Yōkaichiba	156	Gd	35.40N	140.28 E
Yokkaichi	154	Ng	34.58N	136.37 E
Yoko	166	Hd	5.32N	12.19 E
Yokoate-Jima	152	Mf	28.50N	129.00 E
Yokohama	142	Pf	35.27N	139.39 E
Yokosuka	154	Og	35.18N	139.40 E
Yokote	152	Pd	39.18N	140.34 E
Yola	160	Ih	9.12N	12.29 E
Yolaina, Serranías de-	194	Fh	11.40N	84.20W
Yolombo	170	Dc	1.32S	23.15 E
Yom	148	Ke	15.52N	100.16 E
Yom	148	Ke	15.52N	100.16 E
Yŏmju	154	He	39.50N	124.33 E
Yomou	166	Dd	7.34N	9.16W
Yomra	146	Hb	40.58N	39.54 E
Yon	122	Eh	46.30N	1.18W
Yona	220c	Bb	13.25N	144.47 E
Yonago	154	Lg	35.26N	133.20 E
Yonaguni-Jima	154	Lg	24.25N	123.00 E
Yonaha-Dake	156b	Ab	26.43N	128.13 E
Yonan	154	If	37.55N	126.05 E
Yoneshiro-Gawa	156	Ga	40.13N	140.00 E
Yonezawa	152	Pd	37.55N	140.07 E
Yong	166	He	4.54N	13.12 E
Yong'an	152	Kf	25.58N	117.29 E
Yŏngan	152	Mc	41.15N	129.30 E
Yongchang	152	Hd	38.17N	102.07 E
Yongcheng	154	Dh	33.56N	116.21 E
Yongch'on	154	Jg	35.59N	127.59 E
Yongchuan	152	If	29.22N	105.59 E
Yongch'u-gap	154	Jf	37.03N	129.26 E
Yongdeng	152	Hd	36.44N	103.24 E
Yongding He	152	Kd	39.20N	117.04 E
Yŏngdŏk	154	Jf	36.24N	129.22 E
Yŏngdong	154	If	36.10N	127.47 E
Yonghung	154	Ie	39.33N	127.14 E
Yongji (Kouqian)	154	Ic	43.40N	126.30 E
Yongjing	152	Hd	36.00N	103.17 E
Yŏngju	152	Md	36.49N	128.37 E
Yongkang	152	Lf	28.51N	120.05 E
Yongle Qundao	150	Fc	16.35N	111.40 E
Yongnian (Linmingguan)	154	Cf	36.47N	114.30 E
Yongning → Xuyong	152	If	28.13N	105.26 E
Yongqing	154	De	39.19N	116.29 E
Yŏngsanp'o	154	Ig	35.00N	126.43 E
Yongsheng	152	Hf	26.41N	100.45 E
Yongshu Jiao	150	Fe	9.35N	112.50 E
Yŏngwŏl	154	Jf	37.11N	128.28 E
Yongxiu (Tujiabu)	152	Kf	29.05N	115.49 E
Yonibana	166	Cd	8.26N	12.14W
Yonkers	184	Ke	40.56N	73.54W
Yonne [3]	122	Jg	47.55N	3.45 E
Yonne	122	If	48.23N	2.58 E
Yopal	202	Db	5.21N	72.23W
Yopurga	152	Cd	39.15N	76.45 E
York	118	Lg	54.10N	1.30W
York [Al.-U.S.]	184	Ci	32.29N	88.18W
York [Austl.]	212	Df	31.53S	116.46 E
York [Eng.-U.K.]	118	Lh	53.58N	1.05W
York [Nb.-U.S.]	186	Hf	40.52N	97.36W
York [Pa.-U.S.]	182	Ld	39.57N	76.44W
York, Cape-	208	Ff	10.40S	142.30 E
York, Kap-	224	Od	76.05N	67.05W
York, Vale of-	118	Lg	54.10N	1.20W
Yorke Peninsula	212	Hf	35.00S	137.30 E
Yorkshire Dales	118	Kg	54.15N	2.10W
Yorkshire Wolds	118	Mh	54.00N	0.40W
York Sound	212	Fb	14.50S	125.05 E
Yorkton	176	Id	51.13N	102.28W
Yorktown	184	Ig	37.14N	76.32W
Yoro	194	Df	15.09N	87.07W
Yoro [3]	194	Df	15.15N	87.15W
Yoron-Jima	156b	Bb	27.03N	128.26 E
Yoro-Shima	156b	Ba	28.02N	129.10 E
Yorosso	166	Ec	12.21N	4.47W
Yorubaland Plateau	166	Fd	8.00N	4.30 E
Yörük	130	Ki	40.56N	27.04 E
Yosemite National Park	182	Dd	35.28N	119.33W
Yosemite Rock	198	Hi	31.58S	83.15W
Yoshida [Jap.]	156	Ce	33.16N	132.32 E
Yoshida [Jap.]	156	Cd	34.40N	132.42 E
Yoshii	156	Ae	33.18N	129.40 E
Yoshii-Gawa	156	Dd	34.36N	134.02 E
Yoshino-Gawa	156	Dd	34.05N	134.36 E
Yŏsu	152	Me	34.44N	127.44 E
Yotaú	202	Fg	16.03S	63.03W
Yōtei-Zan	156a	Bb	42.49N	140.47 E
Yotvata	146	Fh	29.53N	35.03 E
Youghal/Eochaill	118	Fj	51.57N	7.50W
Youghal Harbour/Cuan Eochaille	118	Fj	51.52N	7.50W
You Jiang	140	Mg	22.50N	108.06 E
Youllemmedene	158	Hg	16.00N	1.00 E
Young [Austl.]	212	Jf	34.19S	148.18 E
Young [Ur.]	204	Dk	32.41S	57.38W
Young, Cape-	218	Je	43.42S	176.37W
Younghusband Peninsula	212	Hg	36.00S	139.30 E
Young Island	222	Ke	66.25S	162.30 E
Young's Island	197n	Ba	13.08N	61.13W
Youngs Rock	220q	Ab	25.03S	130.06W
Youngstown	182	Kc	41.05N	80.40W
Youshashan	152	Fd	38.04N	90.53 E
Youssoufia	162	Fc	32.15N	8.32W
Youyang	152	If	28.49N	108.45 E
Yozgat	144	Db	39.50N	34.48 E
Ypacaraí	206	Ic	25.23S	57.16W
Ypacaraí, Laguna-	204	Dg	25.17S	57.20W
Ypané, Río-	204	Df	23.29S	57.19W
Ypé Jhú	204	Ef	23.54S	55.20W
Ypoá, Lago-	204	Dg	25.48S	57.28W
Yport	124	Ce	49.44N	0.19 E
Ypres/Ieper	122	Id	50.51N	2.53 E
Yreka	182	Cc	41.44N	122.43W
Yser	122	Ic	51.09N	2.43 E
Yssingeaux	122	Ki	45.08N	4.07 E
Ystad	114	Ci	55.25N	13.49 E
Ytambey, Río-	204	Eg	24.46S	54.24W
Ythan	118	Ld	57.25N	2.00W
Ytre Arna	116	Ad	60.28N	5.26 E
Ytre Sula	116	Ac	61.05N	4.40 E
Ytterhogdal	116	Fb	62.11N	14.56 E
Ytterlännäs	114	De	63.01N	17.41 E
Yttermalung	116	Ed	60.35N	13.50 E
Ytyk-Kjuël	138	Id	62.28N	133.25 E
Yu 'Alliq, Jabal-	146	Eg	30.22N	33.31 E
Yuan'an	154	Ai	31.04N	111.39 E
Yuanbaoshan	154	Ec	42.19N	119.19 E
Yuanbao Shan	152	If	25.24N	109.11 E
Yuan Jiang [Asia] = Red River (EN)	140	Mg	20.17N	106.34 E
Yuanjiang [China]	154	Bj	28.50N	112.23 E
Yuanjiang [China]	152	Hg	23.22N	102.26 E
Yuan Jiang [China]	140	Ng	28.58N	111.49 E
Yuanling	152	Jf	28.30N	110.25 E
Yuanmou	152	Hf	25.45N	101.52 E
Yuanping	152	Jd	38.43N	112.42 E
Yuanqu (Liuzhangzhen))	152	Jd	35.19N	111.44 E
Yuanshi	154	Cf	37.45N	114.30 E
Yuba City	182	Cd	39.08N	121.37W
Yūbari	152	Pc	43.04N	141.59 E
Yūbari-Dake	156a	Cb	43.06N	142.15 E
Yūbari-Gawa	156a	Bb	43.08N	141.35 E
Yūbari-Sanchi	156a	Cb	43.10N	142.15 E
Yuba River	188	Eg	39.07N	121.36W
Yubdo	168	Fd	8.58N	35.27 E
Yūbetsu	154	Qb	43.13N	144.05 E
Yūbetsu-Gawa	156a	Ca	44.14N	143.37 E
Yucatán [2]	190	Gd	20.50N	89.00W
Yucatán, Canal de- = Yucatan Channel (EN)	174	Kg	21.45N	85.45W
Yucatán, Peninsula de- = Yucatan Peninsula (EN)	174	Kh	19.30N	89.00W
Yucatan Basin (EN)	190	Ge	20.00N	84.00W
Yucatan Channel (EN) = Yucatán, Canal de-	174	Kg	21.45N	85.45W
Yucatan Peninsula (EN) = Yucatán, Peninsula de-	174	Kh	19.30N	89.00W
Yucheng	154	Df	36.56N	116.39 E
Yuci	152	Jd	37.41N	112.49 E
Yucuyácua, Cerro-	190	Ee	17.07N	97.40W
Yuda	156	Gb	39.19N	140.48 E
Yudi Shan	152	Lb	52.17N	121.52 E
Yueliang Pao	154	Gb	45.44N	123.55 E
Yueqing	152	Lf	28.08N	120.58 E
Yuexi	152	Hf	28.37N	102.36 E
Yuexi (Yaqian)	154	Di	30.51N	116.22 E
Yueyang	152	Jf	29.18N	113.12 E
Yufu-Dake	156	Be	33.17N	131.23 E
Yugan	152	Kf	28.42N	116.39 E
Yugoslavia (EN) = Jugoslavija [1]	112	Hg	44.00N	19.00 E
Yu He	154	Be	39.51N	113.26 E
Yuhuang Ding	154	Df	36.20N	117.01 E
Yuki	170	Cc	3.55S	19.25 E
Yukon	180	Hi	35.31N	97.44W
Yukon	174	Cc	62.33N	163.59W
Yukon Flats	178	Jc	66.35N	146.00W
Yukon Plateau	174	Fc	61.30N	135.40W
Yukon Territory [3]	180	Dd	63.00N	136.00W
Yüksekova	146	Kd	37.19N	44.10 E
Yukuhashi	156	Be	33.44N	130.58 E
Yule River	212	Dd	20.41S	118.17 E
Yuli/lopnur	152	Ec	41.22N	86.09 E
Yulin [China]	142	Ng	22.39N	110.08 E
Yulin [China]	142	Mf	38.14N	109.48 E
Yuling Guan	152	Ke	30.04N	118.53 E
Yulin Jiao	140	Mh	17.50N	109.30 E
Yulongxue Shan	152	Hf	27.09N	100.12 E
Yuma [Az.-U.S.]	176	Hf	32.43N	114.37W
Yuma [Co.-U.S.]	186	Ef	40.08N	102.43W
Yuma, Bahia de-	194	Md	18.21N	68.35W
Yumare	196	Bg	10.37N	68.41W
Yumari, Cerro-	202	Ec	4.27N	66.50W
Yumbe	170	Fb	3.28N	31.15 E
Yumbi [Zaire]	170	Cc	1.53S	16.32 E
Yumbi [Zaire]	170	Ec	1.14S	26.14 E
Yumen (Laojunmiao)	142	Lf	39.50N	97.44 E
Yumenkou	152	Jd	35.42N	110.37 E
Yumenzhen	152	Gc	40.17N	97.12 E
Yumin	152	Db	45.59N	82.28 E
Yumurtalık	146	Fd	36.49N	35.45 E
Yuna, Río-	194	Md	19.12N	69.37W
Yunak	146	Dc	38.49N	31.45 E
Yunaska	178a	Db	52.40N	170.50W
Yuncheng [China]	152	Jd	35.02N	111.00 E
Yuncheng [China]	154	Cg	35.35N	115.56 E
Yungas	198	Jg	16.20S	66.45W
Yungay	206	Fe	37.07S	72.01W
Yungui Gaoyuan	140	Mg	26.00N	105.00 E
Yunhe → Peixian	154	Dg	34.44N	116.56 E
Yuni	156a	Bb	42.59N	141.46 E
Yunjinghong → Jinghong	152	Hg	21.59N	100.48 E
Yunkai Dashan	152	Jg	22.30N	111.00 E
Yunlin	152	Lg	23.43N	120.33 E
Yun Ling	152	Gf	27.00N	99.30 E
Yunmeng	154	Bi	31.01N	113.45 E
Yunnan Sheng (Yün-nan Sheng) [2]	152	Hg	25.00N	102.00 E
Yün-nan Sheng → Yunnan Sheng [2]	152	Hg	25.00N	102.00 E
Yunomae	156	Be	32.15N	130.57 E
Yunotsu	156	Cd	35.05N	132.21 E
Yun Shui	154	Bi	30.43N	113.57 E
Yunxian	152	Je	32.50N	110.50 E
Yunxiao	152	Kg	24.05N	117.18 E
Yunyang	152	Ie	31.00N	108.55 E
Yunzhong Shan	152	Jd	38.50N	112.27 E
Yuquan	154	Ib	45.27N	127.08 E
Yuqueri	204	Ci	28.53S	58.02W
Yura	202	Dg	16.12S	71.42W
Yura-Gawa	156	Dd	35.31N	135.17 E
Yurimaguas	200	If	5.54S	76.05W
Yuriria	192	Ig	20.12N	101.09W
Yuruari, Río-	196	Fi	6.44N	61.40W
Yurungkax He	152	Dd	38.05N	80.20 E
Yuscarán	194	Dg	13.55N	86.51W
Yushan	154	Ej	28.41N	118.15 E
Yushan	140	Og	23.30N	121.00 E
Yu Shan	152	Kf	27.00N	116.00 E
Yushe	154	Bf	37.04N	112.58 E
Yushu [China]	154	Ib	44.50N	126.33 E
Yushu [China]	142	Lf	33.06N	96.48 E
Yushutun	152	Lb	47.06N	123.41 E
Yūsuf, Baḥr-	146	Dh	29.19N	30.50 E
Yusufeli	146	Ib	40.50N	41.33 E
Yutai (Guting)	154	Dg	35.00N	116.40 E
Yutian	154	De	39.53N	117.45 E
Yutian/Keriya	142	Kf	36.52N	81.42 E
Yuty	206	Ic	26.32S	56.18W
Yutz	124	Ie	49.21N	6.11 E
Yuwan-Dake	156b	Ba	28.18N	129.19 E
Yuxi	152	Hg	24.27N	102.34 E
Yuxian [China]	152	Jd	39.49N	114.35 E
Yuxian [China]	152	Jd	38.03N	113.28 E
Yuxian [China]	154	Bg	34.09N	113.29 E
Yuxikou	154	Ei	31.26N	118.18 E
Yuyao	154	Fi	30.04N	121.10 E
Yuya-Wan	156	Bd	34.20N	130.55 E
Yuza	156	Fb	39.01N	139.53 E
Yuzawa [Jap.]	156	Fc	36.56N	138.47 E
Yuzawa [Jap.]	154	Pe	39.10N	140.30 E
Yvel	122	Dg	47.59N	2.23W
Yvelines [3]	122	Hf	48.50N	1.50 E
Yverdon	128	Ad	46.46N	6.40 E
Yvetot	122	Ge	49.37N	0.46 E
Yvette	124	Ef	48.40N	2.20 E
Yxlan	116	He	59.40N	18.50 E
Yxningen	116	Gf	58.15N	16.20 E

Index Symbols

[1] Independent Nation
[2] State, Region
[3] District, County
[4] Municipality
[5] Colony, Dependency
Continent
Physical Region
Historical or Cultural Region
Mount, Mountain
Volcano
Hill
Mountains, Mountain Range
Hills, Escarpment
Plateau, Upland
Pass, Gap
Plain, Lowland
Delta
Salt Flat
Valley, Canyon
Crater, Cave
Karst Features
Depression
Polder
Desert, Dunes
Forest, Woods
Heath, Steppe
Oasis
Cape, Point
Coast, Beach
Cliff
Peninsula
Isthmus
Sandbank
Island
Atoll
Rock, Reef
Islands, Archipelago
Rocks, Reefs
Coral Reef
Well, Spring
Geyser
River, Stream
Waterfall, Rapids
River Mouth, Estuary
Lake
Salt Lake
Intermittent Lake
Reservoir
Swamp, Pond
Canal
Glacier
Ice Shelf, Pack Ice
Ocean
Sea
Gulf, Bay
Strait, Fjord
Lagoon
Bank
Seamount
Tablemount
Ridge
Shelf
Basin
Escarpment, Sea Scarp
Fracture
Trench, Abyss
National Park, Reserve
Point of Interest
Recreation Site
Cave, Cavern
Historic Site
Ruins
Wall, Walls
Church, Abbey
Temple
Scientific Station
Railway station
Airport
Port
Military installation
Lighthouse
Mine
Tunnel
Dam, Bridge

Z

Zaajatskaja 134 Jj 52.53N 61.35 E
Zaalajski hrebet [img] 135 Ie 39.25N 72.50 E
Zaanstad 122 Kb 52.26N 4.49 E
Žabaj 134 Nj 51.42N 68.22 E
Zabajkalsk 138 Gg 49.40N 117.21 E
Zabarjad [img] 164 Ge 23.37N 36.12 E
Zāb-e Kūchek 146 Ke 36.00N 45.15 E
Zabīb, Ra's az- 128 Em 37.16N 10.04 E
Zabid 144 Fg 14.12N 43.18 E
Zabīd, Wādī- 144 Fg 14.07N 43.06 E
Żabinka 132 Dc 52.13N 24.01 E
Ząbkowice Śląskie 120 Mf 50.36N 16.53 E
Žabljak 130 Cf 43.09N 19.08 E
Żabłudów 120 Tc 53.01N 23.20 E
Zabok 128 Jd 46.02N 15.55 E
Zābol 144 Jc 31.02N 61.30 E
Zābol [3] 144 Kc 32.00N 67.15 E
Zabolot 116 Kb 53.56N 24.46 E
Zabolotje 120 Ue 51.37N 24.26 E
Zabolotov 130 Ia 48.25N 25.23 E
Zabré 166 Ec 11.10N 0.38W
Zábřeh 120 Mg 49.53N 16.52 E
Zabrze 120 Of 50.18N 18.46 E
Zacapa 190 Gf 14.58N 89.32W
Zacapa [3] 194 Cf 15.00N 89.30W
Zacapu 192 Ih 19.50N 101.43W
Zacatecas 176 Ig 22.47N 102.35W
Zacatecas [2] 190 Dd 23.00N 103.00W
Zacatecoluca 194 Cg 13.30N 88.52W
Zacatepec 192 Jh 18.39N 99.12W
Zacatlán 192 Kh 19.56N 97.58W
Zaccar, Djebel- [img] 126 Oh 36.20N 2.13 E
Zacoalco de Torres 192 Hg 20.14N 103.35W
Zacualtipán 192 Jg 20.39N 98.36W
Zaculeu [img] 194 Bf 15.21N 91.29W
Zadar 112 Hg 44.07N 15.15 E
Zadarski kanal [img] 128 Jf 44.10N 15.10 E
Zadetkyi Kyun [img] 148 Jg 9.58N 98.13 E
Zadi 170 Bc 4.46 S 14.52 E
Zadoi 152 Fe 33.10N 94.58 E
Zadonsk 132 Kc 52.23N 38.58 E
Za'farānah 164 Pd 29.07N 32.33 E
Zafferano, Capo- 128 Hl 38.07N 13.32 E
Žafir 144 He 23.07N 53.46 E
Zafra 126 Ff 38.25N 6.25W
Żagań 120 Le 51.37N 15.19 E
Žagarė/Zagare 116 Jh 56.19N 23.14 E
Zagare/Žagarė 116 Jh 56.19N 23.14 E
Zāgheh 146 Mf 33.30N 48.42 E
Zāgh Marz 146 Od 36.47N 53.17 E
Zaghrah, Wādī- 146 Fh 28.40N 34.20 E
Zaghwān 162 Jb 36.24N 10.09 E
Zaghwān [3] 162 Jb 36.25N 10.10 E
Zaghwān, Jabal- [img] 128 En 36.21N 10.07 E
Zagora 160 Ge 30.19N 5.50W
Zagóra [img] 128 Kg 43.40N 16.15 E
Zagória [img] 130 Dj 39.45N 20.50 E
Zagorje [img] 128 Jd 46.05N 16.00 E
Zagórów 120 Nd 52.11N 17.55 E
Zagorsk → Sergijev Posad 112 Jd 56.18N 38.08 E
Zagórz, Sanok- 120 Sg 49.31N 22.17 E
Zagreb 112 Hf 45.48N 16.00 E
Zāgros, Kūhhā-ye- = Zagros Mountains (EN) 140 Gf 33.40N 47.00 E
Zagros Mountains (EN) = Zāgros, Kūhhā-ye- 140 Gf 33.40N 47.00 E
Zagubica 130 Ee 44.12N 21.48 E
Za'gya Zangbo 152 Ee 31.55N 88.58 E
Zagyva 120 Qi 47.00N 20.12 E
Zāhedān 142 Ig 29.30N 60.52 E
Zahlah 146 Ff 33.51N 35.53 E
Zahmet 136 Gh 37.48N 62.29 E
Zahrān 164 Hf 17.40N 43.30 E
Zahrez Chergúi [img] 126 Pi 35.14N 3.32 E
Zailijski Alatau, hrebet- [img] 135 Kc 43.00N 77.00 E
Žailma 136 Ge 51.32N 61.40 E
Zaire [3] 170 Bd 6.30 S 13.30 E
Zaïre 158 Ii 6.04 S 12.24 E
Zaïre 158 Ii 6.04 S 12.24 E
Zaire (Congo, Democratic Republic of the-) [1] 160 Ji 1.00 S 25.00 E
Zaisan, Lake- (EN) = Zaisan, ozero- 140 Ke 48.10N 83.50 E
Žaj 114 Mi 55.36N 51.40 E
Zaječar 130 Ff 43.54N 22.17 E
Zajsan 142 Ke 47.30N 84.55 E
Zajsan, ozero- = Zaisan, Lake- (EN) 140 Ke 48.10N 83.50 E
Zak 158 Jk 29.35N 21.11 E
Zaka 172 Gd 20.20 S 31.29 E
Zakamensk 138 Ff 50.23N 103.20 E
Zakarpatska oblast [3] 136 Cf 48.20N 23.20 E
Zakataly 136 Eg 41.38N 46.37 E
Zakháro 130 Ei 37.29N 21.39 E
Zākhū 144 Fb 37.08N 42.41 E
Zákinthos 130 Dl 37.47N 20.54 E
Zákinthos=Zante (EN) 110 Ih 37.47N 20.47 E
Zakinthou Dhiavlos- [img] 130 Dl 37.50N 21.00 E
Zakopane 120 Pg 49.19N 19.57 E
Zakouma 168 Bc 10.54N 19.49 E
Žaksy 136 Ge 51.53N 67.20 E
Zala [2] 120 Mj 46.40N 16.50 E
Zalaegerszeg 120 Mj 46.50N 16.51 E
Zalalövö 120 Mj 46.51N 16.36 E
Zalamea de la Serena 126 Gf 38.39N 5.39W
Zalamea la Real 126 Fg 37.41N 6.39W
Zalantum → Butha Qi 152 Lb 48.02N 122.42 E
Zalari 138 Ff 53.36N 102.32 E
Zalaszentgrót 120 Mj 46.57N 17.05 E
Žalau 130 Gb 47.12N 23.03 E
Zaleščiki 132 De 48.39N 25.44 E

Žalim 144 Fe 22.43N 42.10 E
Zalingei 168 Cc 12.54N 23.29 E
Zaltan 164 Cd 28.55N 19.50 E
Zaltbommel 124 Hc 51.49N 5.17 E
Žaltidjal [img] 130 Ih 41.30N 25.05 E
Žaltyr 136 Ge 51.35N 69.58 E
Žaltyr, ozero- [img] 132 Qf 47.25N 51.05 E
Zamakh 144 Gf 16.28N 47.35 E
Zamami-Shima [img] 156b Ab 26.15N 127.18 E
Zambeze = Zambezi (EN) 158 Kj 18.50S 36.17 E
Zambezi 158 Kj 18.50S 36.17 E
Zambezi (EN) = Zambeze 158 Kj 18.50S 36.17 E
Zambézia [3] 172 Fc 17.00S 37.00 E
Zambezi Escarpment [img] 172 Ec 16.15S 30.10 E
Zambia [1] 160 Jj 15.00S 30.00 E
Zamboanga 142 Oi 6.54N 122.04 E
Zamboanga Peninsula [img] 156 Hc 7.32N 122.16 E
Zambrah, Jazirat- [img] 128 Jb 37.08N 10.48 E
Zambrano 194 Ji 9.45N 74.49W
Zambrów 120 Sd 53.00N 22.15 E
Zambué 172 Ec 15.07S 30.49 E
Zamfara [3] 166 Fc 12.02N 4.03 E
Zamkova, gora- 120 Vc 53.34N 25.53 E
Zamkowa, Góra- [img] 120 Qb 54.25N 20.25 E
Zammar 146 Jd 36.47N 42.40 E
Zamora [3] 126 Gc 41.45N 6.00W
Zamora [Ec.] 202 Cd 4.04 S 78.52W
Zamora [Sp.] 126 Gc 41.30N 5.45W
Zamora, Rio- 202 Cd 2.59 S 78.15W
Zamora de Hidalgo 190 De 19.59N 102.16W
Zamość 120 Tf 50.44N 23.15 E
Zamość [2] 120 Tf 50.44N 23.15 E
Zampa-Misaki [img] 156b Ab 26.26N 127.43 E
Zamtang (Gamda) 152 Jd 32.23N 101.05 E
Zamuro, Punta- [img] 194 Mh 11.26N 68.50W
Zamzam 164 Cc 31.24N 15.17 E
Zanaga 170 Bc 2.51 S 13.50 E
Žanatas 136 Gg 43.36N 69.43 E
Zancara 126 Ie 39.18N 3.18W
Zanda (Toling) 152 Ce 31.28N 79.50 E
Zandvoort 122 Kb 52.22N 4.32 E
Zanesville 182 Kd 39.55N 82.02W
Zangelan 132 Oj 39.05N 46.38 E
Zanhuang 154 Cf 37.38N 114.26 E
Zanjān 144 Gb 36.40N 48.29 E
Zanjān [3] 144 Gb 36.35N 48.15 E
Zanjānrūd 146 Ld 37.08N 47.47 E
Žannetty, ostrov- [img] 138 Ka 76.45N 158.25 E
Zannone [img] 128 Hj 40.55N 13.05 E
Zante (EN) = Zákinthos [img] 110 Ih 37.47N 20.47 E
Zanthus 212 Ef 31.02S 123.34 E
Zanzibar 160 Ki 6.10S 39.11 E
Zanzibar [2] 170 Gd 6.10S 39.20 E
Zanzibar [3] 170 Gd 6.00S 39.50 E
Zanzibar Channel 170 Gd 6.00S 39.00 E
Zanzibar Island [img] 158 Ki 6.10S 39.20 E
Zaolin 152 Jd 39.09N 113.03 E
Zaó-San [img] 156 Gb 38.08N 140.28 E
Zaouatallaz 162 Ie 24.52N 8.26 E
Zaoyang 152 Je 32.08N 112.45 E
Zaozerny 138 Ee 55.57N 94.42 E
Zaozhuang 152 Ke 34.58N 117.34 E
Zap 146 Jd 36.00N 43.21 E
Zapacos Norte, Rio- 204 Ac 17.03S 62.23W
Zapacos Sur, Rio- 204 Ac 17.03S 62.23W
Zapadnaja Dvina 114 Hh 56.17N 32.03 E
Zapadnaja Dvina=Western Dvina (EN) 110 Id 57.04N 24.03 E
Zapadna Morava 130 Ef 43.41N 21.24 E
Západné Karpaty=West Carpathians (EN) 120 Og 49.30N 19.00 E
Zapadni Rodopi [img] 130 Hh 41.45N 24.05 E
Zapadno-Karelskaja vozvyšennost 114 He 63.40N 31.40 E
Zapadno-Sibirskaja ravnina = West Siberian Plain (EN) [img] 140 Jc 60.00N 75.00 E
Zapadny Sajan = Western Sayans (EN) 140 Ld 53.00N 94.00 E
Západočeský kraj [3] 120 Lg 49.45N 13.00 E
Západoslovenský kraj [3] 120 Nh 48.20N 18.00 E
Zapala 200 Ih 38.55S 70.05W
Zapardiel 126 Gc 41.29N 5.02W
Zapata 186 Gm 26.52N 99.19W
Zapata, Peninsula de- [img] 194 Eb 22.20N 81.35W
Zapatera, Isla- [img] 194 Eh 11.45N 85.50W
Zapatosa, Cienaga de- [img] 194 Ki 9.05N 73.50W
Zapljusje 116 Mf 58.24N 29.56 E
Zapoljarny 136 Db 69.26N 30.48 E
Zapopan 192 Hg 20.43N 103.24W
Zaporožje 112 Jf 47.50N 35.10 E
Zaporožskaja oblast [3] 136 Df 47.15N 35.50 E
Zapotitlán, Punta- 192 Lh 18.35N 94.49W
Za Qu 152 Ge 32.00N 96.55 E
Zara 146 Gc 39.55N 37.48 E
Zaraf, Bahr az- 168 Ed 9.25N 31.10 E
Zarafšan 136 Gg 41.39N 64.10 E
Zaragoza [3] 126 Lc 41.35N 1.00W
Zaragoza [Col.] 202 Db 7.30N 74.52W
Zaragoza [Mex.] 192 Jf 23.58N 99.46W
Zaragoza [Mex.] 192 If 22.02N 100.44W
Zaragoza [Mex.] 192 Ic 28.29N 100.55W
Zaragoza [Sp.]=Saragossa (EN) 112 Fg 41.38N 0.53W
Zarajsk 114 Jh 54.47N 38.53 E
Zarand [Iran] 146 Me 35.08N 49.00 E
Zarand [Iran] 142 Hf 30.48N 56.53 E
Zarand-e-Kohneh 146 Ne 35.17N 50.30 E
Zaranj 142 Ig 31.06N 61.53 E
Zarasai/Zarasaj 114 Gi 55.43N 26.19 E
Zarasaj/Zarasai 114 Gi 55.43N 26.19 E
Zárate 200 Ki 34.05S 59.02W
Zarautz / Zarauz 126 Ja 43.17N 2.10W
Zarauz / Zarautz 126 Ja 43.17N 2.10W
Zaraza 202 Eb 9.21N 65.19W
Zarcovski 114 Hi 55.53N 32.16 E
Zard Kūh 140 Hf 32.22N 50.04 E

Zardob 132 Oi 40.14N 47.42 E
Zarečensk 114 Hc 66.40N 31.23 E
Zarghat 146 Ii 26.32N 40.29 E
Zarghun 148 Db 30.31N 68.50 E
Zarghūn Shahr 144 Kc 32.51N 68.25 E
Zaria 160 Hg 11.04N 7.42 E
Žarkamys 136 Ff 47.59N 56.29 E
Žarma 136 If 48.48N 80.55 E
Zārnešti 130 Id 45.33N 25.18 E
Zarqān 146 Oh 29.46N 52.43 E
Zarrineh 146 Kd 37.05N 45.40 E
Zarrīnshahr 146 Nf 32.30N 51.25 E
Zaruma 202 Cd 3.42 S 79.38W
Zarumilla 202 Bd 3.30 S 80.16W
Žary 120 Le 51.38N 15.09 E
Žaryk 136 Hf 48.52N 72.54 E
Zarzaitine 162 Id 28.05N 9.45 E
Zasa 116 Lh 56.15N 26.01 E
Žaškov 132 Ge 49.15N 30.09 E
Zaslavl 116 Lj 54.00N 27.22 E
Zaslavskoje vodohranilišče [img] 116 Lj 54.00N 27.30 E
Zastava 130 Ia 48.25N 25.49 E
Zastron 172 Df 30.18S 27.07 E
Zätäb 120 Jf 50.20N 13.33 E
Zatišje 130 Mb 47.47N 29.48 E
Zatobolsk 134 Kj 53.12N 63.43 E
Zatoka 130 Nc 46.07N 30.25 E
Zauche [img] 120 Id 52.15N 12.35 E
Zavadovskogo Island [img] 222 Ge 66.30S 86.00 E
Zavāreh 146 Of 33.30N 52.29 E
Zaventem 124 Gd 50.53N 4.28 E
Zavety Iliča 138 Jg 49.02N 140.19 E
Zavidovići 128 Mf 44.27N 18.09 E
Zavitinsk 138 Hf 50.01N 129.26 E
Zavodoukovsk 136 Ge 56.33N 66.32 E
Zavodovski [img] 222 Ad 56.20S 27.35W
Zavolžje 114 Mh 56.38N 43.21 E
Zavolžsk 114 Kh 57.32N 42.10 E
Zawidów 120 Le 51.01N 15.02 E
Zawiercie 120 Pf 50.30N 19.25 E
Zāwiat al Mukhaylá 164 Dc 32.10N 22.17 E
Zāwiat Masūs 164 Dc 31.35N 21.01 E
Zāwiyat Qirzah 164 Bc 30.10N 14.20 E
Zāwiyat Shaminās 146 Bg 31.31N 26.24 E
Zawr, Ra's az- 146 Mi 27.26N 49.19 E
Zaya 128 Kb 48.31N 16.55 E
Zāyandeh 146 Of 32.20N 52.50 E
Zaydūn, Wādī- 146 Ej 25.53N 33.04 E
Zayü (Gyigang) 152 Gf 28.43N 97.25 E
Zaza, Rio- 194 Hc 21.37N 79.32W
Zazir 162 If 19.50N 5.13 E
Zbaraž 132 De 49.42N 25.47 E
Zbąszyń 120 Ld 52.16N 15.55 E
Zborov 120 Vg 49.37N 25.09 E
Ždanicky les 112 Jf 47.00N 37.33 E
Ždanov → Mariupol' 112 Jf 47.00N 37.33 E
Ždanovsk 132 Oj 39.45N 47.33 E
Žd'árské vrchy 120 Mg 49.35N 16.03 E
Ždiar 120 Qg 49.16N 20.15 E
Zdolbunov 132 Ed 50.33N 26.15 E
Zduńska Wola 120 Oe 51.36N 18.57 E
Zealand (EN) = Sjælland [img] 110 Hd 55.30N 11.45 E
Zebediela 172 Dd 24.19S 29.16 E
Zebës, Mali i- [img] 130 Dh 41.55N 20.14 E
Zebil 130 Le 44.57N 28.46 E
Zečća [img] 128 If 44.46N 14.19 E
Zeddine 126 Mh 36.12N 1.50 E
Zedelgem 124 Fc 51.09N 3.08 E
Zeeland [3] 124 Fc 51.27N 3.45 E
Zeeland [img] 124 Jc 51.27N 3.45 E
Zeerust 172 Ec 25.33N 26.06 E
Zefat 146 Ff 32.58N 35.30 E
Zegrzyńskie, Jezioro- [img] 120 Rd 52.30N 21.05 E
Zehdenick 120 Jd 52.59N 13.20 E
Zeil, Mount- [img] 212 Gd 23.25S 132.25 E
Žeimelis/Zeimjalis 116 Jh 56.14N 23.58 E
Žeimena/Žejmena 114 Hi 54.54N 23.53 E
Žeimjalis/Žeimelis 116 Jh 56.14N 23.58 E
Zeist 124 Hb 52.05N 5.15 E
Zeitz 120 Ie 51.03N 12.09 E
Žeja 140 Od 53.45N 127.15 E
Žeja 140 Od 53.45N 127.35 E
Žejmena/Žeimena 114 Hi 54.54N 23.53 E
Zejskoje vodohranilišče [img] 138 Hf 54.00N 127.30 E
Zékog 152 Hd 35.00N 101.35 E
Želanija, mys- [img] 140 Ib 76.57N 68.35 E
Zelaya [3] 194 If 13.00N 84.00W
Želča [img] 116 Lf 58.18N 27.50 E
Zele 124 Gc 51.04N 4.02 E
Želechów 120 Re 51.49N 21.54 E
Zelee, Cape- [img] 219a Ec 9.44S 161.34 E
Zelenaja Rošča 116 Md 60.08N 29.14 E
Zelenčukskaja 132 Lh 43.51N 41.34 E
Zelengora [img] 128 Mg 43.20N 18.35 E
Zelenoborsk 136 Gc 61.29N 63.59 E
Zelenoborskij 136 Db 66.50N 32.18 E
Zelenodolsk 136 Ee 55.53N 48.31 E
Zelenogorsk 136 Cc 60.12N 29.42 E
Zelenograd 114 Mh 56.01N 37.12 E
Zelenogradsk 116 Ij 54.57N 20.27 E
Zelenokumsk 132 Mh 44.23N 43.53 E
Zeletin 130 Kc 46.03N 27.23 E
Zeležné hory 120 Mg 49.50N 15.45 E
Železnik 130 Df 44.43N 20.23 E
Železnodorožny [Russia] 138 Fe 57.55N 102.50 E
Železnodorožny [Russia] 114 Ei 54.22N 21.19 E
Železnogorsk 136 Fc 62.37N 50.55 E
Železnogorsk 136 De 52.21N 35.23 E
Železnogorsk-Ilimski 138 Fe 56.40N 104.05 E
Železnovodsk 132 Mg 44.08N 43.00 E
Zelfana 162 Hc 32.24N 4.14 E
Želiezovce 120 Ph 48.03N 18.40 E
Želiva 120 Lg 49.43N 15.06 E
Želin [img] 130 Df 43.29N 20.48 E

Zell am See 128 Gc 47.19N 12.47 E
Zell am Ziller 128 Fc 47.14N 11.53 E
Zelów 120 Pe 51.28N 19.13 E
Želtau Ajtau [img] 135 Ib 44.30N 74.00 E
Želtye Vody 132 He 48.23N 33.31 E
Želudok 120 Vc 53.33N 25.07 E
Zelva 120 Uc 53.04N 24.54 E
Želva 116 Ki 55.13N 25.13 E
Zelzate 122 Jc 51.12N 3.49 E
Žemaičiu Aukštuma / Zemajtskaja vozvyšennost [img] 116 Ji 55.45N 22.30 E
Žemaiciy-Naumiestis/Žemaičju-Naumiestis 116 Ii 55.21N 21.37 E
Žemaitija [img] 116 Ii 55.55N 22.30 E
Žemaiciy-Naumiestis 116 Ii 55.21N 21.37 E
Zemaitskaja vozvyšennost / Žemaičiu Aukštuma [img] 116 Ji 55.45N 22.30 E
Zembin 116 Mj 54.24N 28.19 E
Zembretta, Ile- [img] 128 Em 37.10N 10.53 E
Zemetčino 132 Mc 53.31N 42.38 E
Zemgale [img] 116 Kh 56.30N 25.00 E
Zemio 168 Dd 5.19N 25.08 E
Zemmora 126 Mi 35.43N 0.45 E
Zemmour [img] 158 Ff 25.30N 12.00W
Zempoala [img] 192 Sh 48.50N 22.02 E
Zempoaltepec [img] 174 Jh 17.00N 96.50W
Zemra, Djebel- [img] 126 Pi 35.14N 3.54 E
Zemst 124 Gd 50.59N 4.28 E
Zemun, Beograd- 130 De 44.53N 20.25 E
Zengfeng Shan [img] 154 Jc 42.25N 128.44 E
Zenica 128 Lf 44.13N 17.55 E
Zenker Seamount (EN) [img] 222 Bc 41.00S 6.00W
Zenkov 132 Id 50.13N 34.22 E
Zenne 124 Gc 51.04N 4.26 E
Zenobia Peak [img] 186 Bf 40.40N 108.48W
Zentsúji 156 Cd 34.14N 133.47 E
Zenzach 126 Pi 35.21N 3.22 E
Zenza do Itombe 170 Bd 9.16S 14.13 E
Žepce 128 Mf 44.26N 18.03 E
Zepu/Poskam 152 Cd 38.12N 77.18 E
Zéralda 126 Oh 36.43N 2.50 E
Zeravšan 135 Ge 39.10N 68.40 E
Zeravšan [img] 140 If 39.22N 63.45 E
Zeravšanski hrebet [img] 136 Gh 39.15N 68.30 E
Zerbst 120 Ie 51.58N 12.05 E
Žerdevka 132 Mh 51.53N 41.28 E
Zerind 130 Ec 46.37N 21.31 E
Zermatt 128 Bd 46.02N 7.44 E
Zernez 128 Ed 46.42N 10.07 E
Zernograd 136 Ef 46.48N 40.19 E
Zeroua 126 Ph 36.22N 3.21 E
Žešart 134 De 62.05N 49.09 E
Zestafoni 132 Mh 42.07N 43.02 E
Zeta 130 Cg 42.28N 19.16 E
Zetland → Shetland Islands [img] 110 Fc 60.30N 1.30W
Žetybaj 136 Fg 43.34N 52.04 E
Žetykol, ozero- [img] 132 Vd 51.05N 60.55 E
Zeune Islands [img] 219a Bb 6.18S 155.50 E
Zeven 120 Fc 53.18N 9.17 E
Zevenaar 124 Ic 51.55N 6.05 E
Zevenbergen 124 Gc 51.38N 4.36 E
Zeydābād 146 Ph 29.37N 55.33 E
Zeydar 146 Pd 36.20N 55.53 E
Zeytinbağı 130 Li 40.23N 28.47 E
Zeytindağ 130 Kk 38.58N 27.04 E
Zézere 126 Fc 39.28N 8.20W
Zghartā 146 Fe 34.24N 35.54 E
Zgierz 120 Pe 51.52N 19.25 E
Zgorzelec 120 Le 51.10N 15.00 E
Zhabdun → Zhongba 142 Kg 29.41N 84.10 E
Zhag'yab 152 Ge 30.40N 97.40 E
Zhangbei 152 Jc 41.13N 114.43 E
Zhangde → Anyang 142 Nf 36.01N 114.25 E
Zhangdian → Zibo 154 Gd 36.48N 118.04 E
Zhangguangcai Ling [img] 154 Jb 45.00N 129.00 E
Zhang He [img] 154 Cf 36.27N 114.42 E
Zhangjiakou 152 Jc 40.49N 114.53 E
Zhangjiapan → Jingbian 152 Id 37.32N 108.45 E
Zhangling 152 La 52.58N 123.31 E
Zhanglou 154 Dh 32.40N 116.47 E
Zhangping 152 Kf 25.25N 117.27 E
Zhangshuzhen → Qingjiang 152 Kf 28.02N 115.31 E
Zhangwei Xinhe 154 Ge 38.13N 117.48 E
Zhangwu 152 Lc 42.23N 122.33 E
Zhangye 152 Id 38.57N 100.28 E
Zhangzi 152 Jd 36.04N 112.53 E
Zhan He 152 Kb 48.38N 126.52 E
Zhanhua (Fuguo) 154 Ge 37.42N 118.08 E
Zhanjiang 142 Ng 21.13N 110.23 E
Zhanyi 152 He 25.35N 103.46 E
Zhao'an 152 Kg 23.49N 117.10 E
Zhaodong 152 Lb 46.04N 125.56 E
Zhaoge → Qixian 154 Cg 35.35N 114.12 E
Zhaojue 152 He 28.02N 102.56 E
Zhaoqing 152 Jg 23.04N 112.28 E
Zhaosu/Monggolküre 152 Dc 43.10N 81.07 E
Zhaosutai He [img] 154 Kc 42.56N 123.38 E
Zhaotong 142 Mg 27.20N 103.46 E
Zhaoxian 154 Df 37.45N 114.48 E
Zhaoyang Hu [img] 154 Ee 35.00N 116.48 E
Zhaoyuan 152 Lb 45.30N 125.05 E
Zhari Namco [img] 152 Ef 30.53N 85.35 E
Zhaxi → Weixin 152 If 27.46N 105.04 E
Zhaxi Co [img] 152 Ee 32.12N 85.10 E
Zhecheng 154 Dg 34.05N 115.18 E
Zheduo Shankou [img] 152 He 30.06N 101.48 E
Zhejiang Sheng (Che-Chiang Sheng) [2] 152 Kf 29.00N 120.00 E

Zhen'an 152 Ie 33.27N 109.10 E
Zhenba 152 Ie 32.37N 107.50 E
Zhenghe 152 Kf 27.20N 118.58 E
Zhenghe Qunjiao [img] 150 Fd 10.20N 114.20 E
Zhengxiangbai Qi (Qagan Nur) 154 Cc 42.14N 115.59 E
Zhengyang 154 Ci 32.36N 114.23 E
Zhengzhou 142 Nf 34.42N 113.41 E
Zhenhai 154 Fj 29.57N 121.43 E
Zhenjiang 152 Ke 32.03N 119.26 E
Zhenkang (Fengweiba) 152 Gg 23.54N 99.00 E
Zhenlai 152 Lb 45.50N 123.14 E
Zhenning 152 If 26.05N 105.46 E
Zhenping 154 Bh 33.02N 112.14 E
Zhenxiong 152 Hf 27.28N 104.52 E
Zhenyuan 152 Id 23.52N 100.53 E
Zhicheng 152 Jf 30.17N 111.29 E
Zhidan (Bao'an) 152 Id 36.48N 108.46 E
Zhidoi 152 Ge 34.46N 95.46 E
Zhijiang 152 If 27.32N 109.42 E
Zhi Qu/Tongtian He [img] 140 Lf 33.26N 96.36 E
Zhiziluo → Bijiang 152 Gf 26.39N 99.00 E
Zhob 148 Db 32.04N 69.50 E
Zhongba (Zhabdun) 142 Kg 29.41N 84.10 E
Zhongba → Jiangyou 152 He 31.48N 104.39 E
Zhongdian 152 Gf 27.42N 99.41 E
Zhōngguó = China (EN) [img] 140 Mg 35.00N 105.00 E
Zhonghua Renmin Gongheguo = China (EN) 142 Mf 35.00N 105.00 E
Zhongning 152 Id 37.28N 105.41 E
Zhongshan 152 Jg 22.31N 113.23 E
Zhongwei 142 Mf 37.30N 105.09 E
Zhongxiang 152 Je 31.10N 108.02 E
Zhongxing → Siyang 154 Eh 33.43N 118.40 E
Zhoukou 150 Fd 11.20N 114.30 E
Zhoukoudianzhen 154 Jb 33.33N 114.40 E
Zhoushan Dao [img] 154 Gi 30.00N 122.00 E
Zhoushan Qundao [img] 140 Of 30.00N 122.00 E
Zhuanghe 152 Ld 39.42N 122.58 E
Zhucheng 154 Ff 35.58N 119.28 E
Zhu Dao [img] 154 Fe 39.05N 121.10 E
Zhugqu 152 He 33.46N 104.18 E
Zhuhe 152 Bj 29.44N 113.07 E
Zhuizishan → Weichang 152 Kc 41.55N 117.39 E
Zhuji 152 Fj 29.43N 120.13 E
Zhujiang → Shangqiu 152 Ke 34.24N 115.37 E
Zhujiang Kou [img] 152 Jg 22.20N 113.45 E
Zhumadian 152 Je 32.54N 114.03 E
Zhuoxian 152 Jd 39.26N 116.00 E
Zhuozhang He [img] 154 Bf 36.36N 113.10 E
Zhuozi 152 Id 40.52N 112.33 E
Zhuozi Shan [img] 152 Id 39.36N 107.00 E
Zhushan 152 Je 32.16N 110.12 E
Zhuzhou 142 Ng 27.52N 113.12 E
Ziama Mansouria 162 Ip 36.40N 5.29 E
Ziar nad Hronom 120 Oh 48.36N 18.52 E
Žibá' 144 Ed 27.21N 35.40 E
Zibo (Zhangdian) 142 Ng 36.48N 118.04 E
Zicavo 122a Bb 41.54N 9.08 E
Židáčov 120 Ug 49.17N 24.12 E
Zielona Góra 112 Le 51.56N 15.31 E
Zielona Góra [2] 120 Le 51.55N 15.30 E
Zierikzee 122 Jc 51.38N 3.55 E
Žiežmariai/Žežmarjaj 116 Kj 54.47N 24.36 E
Ziftá 146 Dg 30.43N 31.15 E
Žigalovo 138 Fe 54.48N 105.08 E
Zigana Geçidi [img] 146 Hb 40.38N 39.25 E
Zigansk 146 Hc 66.45N 123.30 E
Zigey 168 Bc 14.43N 15.47 E
Zigong 142 Mg 29.20N 104.48 E
Zigui 152 Je 31.01N 110.42 E
Ziguinchor 160 Fg 12.35N 16.16W
Žigulevsk 136 Ee 53.27N 49.29 E
Zihuatanejo 190 De 17.38N 101.33W
Zijng Shan [img] 152 Id 37.12N 112.50 E
Zijpenberg [img] 124 Hb 52.04N 6.00 E
Zilair 134 Gj 52.04N 6.00 E
Žilálet [img] 126 Gb 18.28N 7.48 E
Zile 144 Ea 40.18N 35.54 E
Žilina 112 Hf 49.14N 18.45 E
Zillah 160 If 28.33N 17.35 E
Ziller [img] 120 Hi 47.24N 11.50 E
Zillertaler Alpen [img] 120 Hi 47.00N 11.55 E
Žiloj 132 Qi 40.20N 50.33 E
Zilupe 116 Mh 56.25N 28.07 E
Zima 142 Md 53.55N 102.04 E
Zimapán 192 Jg 20.45N 99.21W
Zimatlán de Álvarez 192 Ki 16.52N 96.47W
Zimba 172 Eb 17.02S 26.30 E
Zimbabwe [1] 160 Jj 20.00S 30.00 E
Zimbabwe (Rhodesia) [1] 160 Jj 20.00S 30.00 E
Zimbor 130 Gb 47.00N 23.16 E
Zimi 166 Cd 7.19N 11.18W
Zimmi 168 Cd 46.00N 40.45 E
Zimnicea 130 If 43.40N 25.22 E
Zimovniki 132 Mf 47.08N 42.29 E
Zina 166 Ib 11.16N 14.58 E
Zincirli 146 Gd 37.00N 36.41 E
Zinder 160 Hg 13.48N 8.59 E
Zinder [2] 166 Hb 15.00N 10.00 E
Zingst 120 Ib 54.25N 12.50 E
Zinjibar 164 Ig 13.08N 45.23 E
Zinkov 132 Id 49.46N 34.21 E
Zinnik/Soignies 124 Jf 48.49N 7.44 E
Zinsel du Nord 124 Jf 48.49N 7.44 E
Zion [U.S.] 182 He 42.27N 87.50W
Zion [St.C.N.] 197c Me 17.09N 62.32W
Zipaquirá 202 Db 5.02N 74.01W
Zirc 120 Ni 47.16N 17.52 E

Zir-Zyw

Index Symbols

[1] Independent Nation	Pass, Gap	Depression	Coast, Beach
[2] State, Region	Mount, Mountain	Polder	Cliff
[3] District, County	Volcano	Desert, Dunes	Peninsula
[4] Municipality	Hill	Forest, Woods	Isthmus
[5] Colony, Dependency	Mountains, Mountain Range	Heath, Steppe	Sandbank
Continent	Hills, Escarpment	Oasis	Island
Physical Region	Plateau, Upland	Cape, Point	Atoll

Historical or Cultural Region	Rock, Reef	Waterfall, Rapids	Canal
Islands, Archipelago	River Mouth, Estuary	Glacier	
Rocks, Reefs	Lake	Ice Shelf, Pack Ice	
Coral Reef	Salt Lake	Ocean	
Well, Spring	Sea	Reservoir	
Geyser	Intermittent Lake	Gulf, Bay	
River, Stream	Swamp, Pond	Strait, Fjord	

Lagoon	Escarpment, Sea Scarp	Historic Site	Airport
Bank	Fracture	Ruins	Port
Seamount	Trench, Abyss	Wall, Walls	Military installation
Tablemount	National Park, Reserve	Church, Abbey	Lighthouse
Ridge	Point of Interest	Temple	Mine
Shelf	Recreation Site	Scientific Station	Tunnel
Basin	Cave, Cavern	Railway station	Dam, Bridge